The Encyclopedia of Indianapolis

The Encyclopedia of Indianapolis

EDITED BY

DAVID J. BODENHAMER

AND

ROBERT G. BARROWS

with the assistance of
David G. Vanderstel

A PROJECT OF THE POLIS RESEARCH CENTER OF
INDIANA UNIVERSITY–PURDUE UNIVERSITY, INDIANAPOLIS

Indiana University Press   Bloomington & Indianapolis

*Indiana University Press wishes to
thank and publicly acknowledge*
ALLEN W. CLOWES
*for a major personal gift that made
publication of this encyclopedia
possible at an affordable price.*

The paper used in this publication meets the minimum requirements of American National Standard
for Informational Sciences—Permanence of Paper for Printed Library Materials. ANSI Z39.48-1984.

Manufactured in the United States of America

Library of Congress Cataloging-in-publication Data

The Encyclopedia of Indianapolis / edited by David J. Bodenhamer and Robert G. Barrows,
with the assistance of David G. Vanderstel.

p.   cm.

Includes index.

ISBN 0-253-31222-1

1. Indianapolis (Ind.)—History—Encyclopedias. 2. Indianapolis (Ind.)—Encyclopedias.
I. Bodenhamer, David J. II. Barrows, Robert G. (Robert Graham), 1994.
III. Vanderstel, David Gordon.

F534.I357E63 1994

977.2'52'003 dc20

94-16665

1 2 3 4 5 99 98 97 96 95 94

CONTENTS

EDITORIAL STAFF

PREFACE

Indianapolis is an important midwestern city with a rich heritage and increasing national prominence. A transportation hub since the 1850s—in a real sense the "Crossroads of America"—by the late 19th and early 20th centuries Indianapolis ranked among the nation's largest and most prosperous cities. It also was a city of consequence. Local attorney Benjamin Harrison captured the presidency in 1888, a former mayor headed the national Democratic party, four residents were nominated for vice-president on national tickets, the Socialist Party of America was formed and held its first convention in Indianapolis—all events that symbolized the city's significance in national politics. Equally well known was its cultural heritage. National literary figures such as poet James Whitcomb Riley and novelists Meredith Nicholson and Booth Tarkington claimed Indianapolis as home, as did one of America's largest publishers, Bobbs-Merrill. And so many labor unions established headquarters in the city—including the United Mine Workers and the Teamsters—that Indianapolis was recognized for several decades as the nation's labor capital.

During the first half of the 20th century the city was a center for automobile manufacturing and the automotive parts industry. Early on, numerous local shops produced cars still prized for their classic character—Stutz, National, Marmon. This activity spurred the creation of the Indianapolis Motor Speedway to test new cars and led later to the first 500–Mile Race, now the largest single-day sporting event in the world. Automobile manufacturing ultimately disappeared from the city, but other industries flourished, especially during World War II when Indianapolis claimed the title "Toolmaker to the Nation."

Although Indianapolis exhibited prosperity and stability during the early to mid 20th century—95 percent of its dwellings in 1930 were single-family residences, highest among the nation's largest cities—there was also a darker side to these decades. Nowhere was "Americanization" stronger or the Ku Klux Klan more active than in Indianapolis. And into the 1960s the city had a reputation as one of the most segregated of northern cities.

Following a decline in its economic base and the flight of more affluent residents to the suburbs, Indianapolis and Marion County created Unigov in 1969, one of the nation's earliest and more successful consolidations of city-county gover ents. The city's population jumped from 485,000 to 745,000, and the area from 82 to 369 square miles. With a new governmental structure came an effective public-private partnership to revitalize the city, stimulated in part by the Lilly Endowment, the nation's fourth largest charitable trust. This activity led to the creation of a new urban landscape and a sense of civic purpose so pronounced that the national media in the 1980s touted Indianapolis as a model for the revitalization of the so-called Rust Belt.

This rich history often goes unclaimed, even by long-time residents. The reason is not hard to discover: Indianapolis has no adequate record of its past, especially for the 20th century. Astonishingly, the last comprehensive work on the city appeared in 1910. The works that have appeared since then, largely journalistic in tone, pay scant attention to developments since World

War II. Currently three generations of city residents exist without a common memory, lacking an acknowledged heritage on which to build their community's future.

The *Encyclopedia of Indianapolis* aims to remedy this deficit of knowledge in part by providing a comprehensive reference work on the city, concentrating on the 20th century and especially its recent past. The volume's general entries capture vital information about people, organizations, and events; its overview essays, which introduce the volume, create an interpretive context that provides meaning and significance. Included are the good and the bad, praiseworthy developments as well as notorious ones. Numerous entries offer a much-needed synthesis of important local issues such as the man-made or built environment or philanthropy or neighborhoods. Other entries explain in some detail the structure and workings of local government or politics or education, including topics such as special taxing districts, political participation, and special education. Entries trace the historical development of their subjects but make them as current as possible. Thus the entries on religion, for example, carry their story to the 1990s, as do the ones on business and the economy, labor, sports, fine and performing arts, cultural institutions, ethnic groups, and so forth.

To acquaint readers with the city's chronology, this volume includes an abbreviated timeline. This list of events, although by no means inclusive, orients readers to Indianapolis in a way different from entries that focus on single topics or events. Also useful is the statistical section that presents data in tabular and graphic form. Other tables and charts accompany the articles they help to explain or illustrate. Providing yet another perspective on the city across time are the photographs that appear throughout the volume.

An initial index lists entries by subject, thus permitting access to all articles relating to a topic such as women or visual arts. Cross references within the general entries—identified by SMALL CAPITALS—direct readers to entries of the same title, and a comprehensive name and subject index is a detailed guide to all persons, institutions, and events mentioned in the individual articles. Finally, a bibliography at the end of an entry steers readers to other published work on the subject.

This *Encyclopedia of Indianapolis* represents the efforts of over 500 individuals, including the 485 authors who wrote the entries. A dedicated staff verified as much information as possible within the constraints of time and budget, but even the greatest care in an enterprise so large cannot prevent all errors. But if this work can be viewed not as the conclusion of a study of the city but rather as its beginning, then the mistakes and omissions of the present should spur future efforts to correct and amplify the record. In this vein the editors echo the sentiments of the city's first narrator, Ignatius Brown, in his "Historical Sketch of Indianapolis" (1857):

> Mistakes have doubtless been made, but if the attempt causes them to be rectified, and fuller information given on the facts herein alluded to, the writer's object will be attained, and the future historian will be gratified.

ACKNOWLEDGMENTS

The *Encyclopedia of Indianapolis* project was born in the mid–1980s when a new cityscape renewed pride in the Hoosier capital and stimulated an interest in its history. It was John Gallman, director of Indiana University Press, who first suggested the idea of an encyclopedia, based on the success of a similar project in Cleveland which the Press had published. Under the auspices of the Center for American Studies at Indiana University–Purdue University at Indianapolis (IUPUI), a small group met regularly during the summer of 1987 to discuss ways to link the city's past and present. Although an editorial staff did not arrive until 1989, these specialists in Indiana and Indianapolis history—Jan Shipps, Ralph D. Gray, James H. Madison, Robert M. Taylor, Jr., and Robert G. Barrows—effectively launched the *Encyclopedia* project. The IUPUI School of Liberal Arts and its dean, first William M. Plater and then John D. Barlow, provided valuable support and encouragement, as did Chancellor Gerald L. Bepko. At no time during the project's history did this support waver or lessen.

This project incurred many debts during its five-year life. A local advisory committee met with the editorial staff as work began in earnest in mid–1989 and continued to be available as needed. Thomas W. Binford, the committee's chair, remained a strong advocate and advisor throughout the *Encyclopedia*'s development and made numerous corporate and personal contacts on its behalf. Others on the advisory committee also shared their enthusiasm and support for the project. The Indiana Historical Society early committed staff to identify and reproduce photographs and other illustrations from its collections for use in the volume. Susan S. Sutton, the Society's coordinator of visual reference services, was especially helpful in this task.

Funding for the *Encyclopedia* came from a variety of sources. The Indianapolis Foundation and the City of Indianapolis early demonstrated faith in the project with key grants that allowed the editors to attract additional support from the National Endowment for the Humanities. Over the years a number of families, foundations, and corporations donated money at critical junctures to keep the work on schedule. Allen W. Clowes made a major grant to subsidize publication costs. The project also received a sizable number of small gifts from individuals who, though too numerous to list separately, lifted the staff's spirits by these expressions of confidence. A list of donors appears elsewhere in this volume.

The *Encyclopedia* represents a community partnership in ways that many university-based projects aspire to but never reach. This partnership is readily apparent in the roster of over 500 experts from the broader Indianapolis community who participated actively as researchers, writers, or consultants. Among this number were 485 authors, more than 400 of whom work outside traditional academic settings. Many authors also declined payment for their entries, an act of generosity that lessened the cost of the project.

The following individuals assisted the editors of the *Encyclopedia* in compiling and refining entry lists for the topics indicated: *African-Americans*: Wilma Gibbs, Emma Lou Thornbrough; *Built Environment*: J. Marsh Davis, Paul C. Diebold, Mary Ellen Gadski, Glory-June Greiff, H. Roll

McLaughlin, Elizabeth B. Monroe, Todd Mozingo, Jane R. Nolan, Suzanne T. Rollins, Philip V. Scarpino, Andrew Seager, William L. Selm, Linda Weintraut; *Cultural Institutions*: Peter T. Harstad, Richard Hurst, Paul Richard, Carol Norris Vincent; *Demography and Ethnicity*: James J. Divita; *Economy*: James H. Madison; *Education*: William J. Reese; *Government*: William A. Blomquist; *Labor*: James Wallihan; *Literature*: J. Kent Calder, Cathy Gibson, James Powell; *Medicine and Health Care*: Katherine Mandusic McDonell; *Military and Veterans Affairs*: Alan T. Nolan, Wayne Sanford, Raymond L. Shoemaker; *Neighborhoods and Communities*: Lamont J. Hulse; *Performing Arts*: Ralph Adams, Norman R. Brandenstein, Anita Heppner Plotinsky, Richard J Roberts, Deborah Sargent Shaver, Charles Staff; *Philanthropy and Social Service*: Patricia Dean, Robert L. Payton; *Politics*: George Geib; *Public Safety and Crime*: William Doherty; *Radio and Television*: Howard Caldwell, Jack Morrow, James Philippe, Jim Shelton (d. 1993); *Religion*: L. C. Rudolph, Jan Shipps, Robert M. Taylor, Jr.; *Sports*: R. Dale Ogden; *Transportation*: Victor Bogle, Ralph D. Gray, Glory-June Greiff, John L. Larson, Jerry Marlette; *Visual Arts*: John J. Cooney, Claudia Kheel, JoAnn Kuebler, Mary Jane Meeker, Julia Muney Moore, Joyce Sommers, Harriet Warkel; *Women and Women's Issues*: Leigh Darbee, Emma Lou Thornbrough, Barbara Zimmer. Several of these individuals—William A. Blomquist, Patricia Dean, James J. Divita, George Geib, Ralph D. Gray, Katherine Mandusic McDonell, Elizabeth B. Monroe, William J. Reese, L. C. Rudolph, Jan Shipps, and Robert M. Taylor, Jr.—also served as contributing editors who read and commented on submissions for their sections.

No project of this complexity can succeed without a dedicated and capable staff. The support staff of Barb Waldsmith, Emma Hall, Shannon Justus, and Julie McNeely performed heroically, especially in the intense final six months; Marcia Pilon skillfully orchestrated their work and provided essential quality control. Several research assistants—Connie Zeigler, Michelle Hale, Jeff Duvall, and Bill Dalton—deserve separate recognition for producing excellent work under tight deadlines. Deb Markisohn demonstrated persistence and creativity in locating and identifying the illustrations for the volume. Brad Clay and Tom Cooke were equally resourceful in compiling the statistical abstract. Monty Hulse, assistant director of the POLIS Research Center, masterfully coordinated the project's development and public relations efforts. David Vanderstel joined the project as assistant editor in 1991 and made so many valuable contributions that a list of them would inevitably be incomplete.

Indiana University Press also played a vital role in developing this volume. John Gallman offered encouragement, assistance, and sound advice that kept the editors from making egregious mistakes. The Press's thoroughly professional editorial, design, and production staff, particularly Sharon L. Sklar, eased the project's way through its final months. Especially noteworthy is the contribution of Bobbi Diehl, whose editorial pen improved the entries in every respect.

Special thanks are due Shirley S. McCord, former editor at the Indiana Historical Bureau and now part-time editor at the Indiana Historical Society, who read virtually the entire manuscript as an unpaid volunteer. Her eye for detail and knowledge of Indiana history saved us from many errors (and her stylistic preferences substantially reduced the number of commas in the volume).

To the vast number of people who have encouraged the editorial staff—and to the patient and supportive families of overworked researchers, support staff, and editors—we offer heartfelt appreciation and a sigh of relief. We trust that our collective efforts have produced a work worthy of the city it chronicles.

David J. Bodenhamer
Robert G. Barrows

Encyclopedia of Indianapolis

Major Donors
As of July 31, 1994

Partners ($50,000+)

City of Indianapolis, Indiana
The Indianapolis Foundation
National Endowment for the Humanities

Sponsors ($10,000–$24,999)

The Associated Group
Allen W. Clowes
Indiana Historical Society
Indianapolis Newspapers, Inc.
Eli Lilly and Company
Marsh Supermarkets, Inc.
Mrs. Frank E. (Marianne) McKinney
NBD Indiana, Inc.
W.C. Griffith Foundation

Benefactors ($5,000–$9,999)

American States Insurance Companies
Indianapolis Chamber of Commerce Foundation
Cornelius and Anna Cook O'Brien Foundation
Historic Landmarks Foundation of Indiana, Inc.

Contributors ($2,500–$4,999)

Indianapolis Business Journal

Investors ($1,000–$2,499)

American United Life Insurance Companies
Barnes & Thornburg
Benicorp Insurance Company
Thomas W. Binford
David and Penny Bodenhamer
Boehringer Mannheim Corporation
Ice Miller Donadio & Ryan
Inland Container Corporation Foundation, Inc.
John O. LaFollette
William McConnell, Jr.
The New England
Riley Bennett & Egloff
Ruddell Trust Fund
Dr. and Mrs. Gene E. Sease
Service Supply Co., Inc.
Jan and Tony Shipps
Mr. and Mrs. Richard M. Small
Frank C. Springer Jr.
State Life Insurance Co.
Walker Family Foundation
Hal and Clara Woodard
Dr. and Mrs. Don B. Ziperman

Subscribers ($500–$999)

Cornelius M. Alig
Leigh Darbee and Robert G. Barrows
John H. Darlington, Jr.
Mr. and Mrs. Jack Dustman
William L. Elder
Faris Mailing, Inc.
Lamont Hulse and Cathleen Donnelly
Jungclaus-Campbell Company, Inc.
Mr. and Mrs. James L. Kennedy
Lilly Industries, Inc.
Rhett McDaniel
Eugene S. Pulliam
Mr. and Mrs. John G. Rauch, Jr.
RCI
Alice Marie Roggie
Sheridan and Associates, Inc.
Mr. and Mrs. J. Richard Sparks
Christopher and Ann M. Stack
E. Andrew Steffen
Barbara E. Stokely
Greg Norman True
Dr. Donald J. Wolfram Memorial
WRTV-6
WTHR-TV

Friends ($100–$499)   Alexander & Alexander, Inc.; John D. and Pat Barlow; John J. Barton; Mr. and Mrs. Hermann L. Beem; Len and Katie Betley; Jim and Martha Ann Bettis; Bingham Summers Welsh & Spilman; Borshoff Johnson & Co. Inc.; Diamond Chain Company; Caroline Dunn; Jean S. Duwe; Harrison Eiteljorg; Murvin and Linda Enders; Daniel F. Evans; Dr. and Mrs. James P. Fadely; Fifth Third Bank of Central Indiana; Margaret F. Flack; William L. Fortune; David and Mary Jane Frisby; Phyllis and Ed Gabovitch; Ralph Gerdes; Dr. David M. Gibson; Ralph D. Gray; John and Marilyn Hoffman; Mark M. Holeman; Byron P. Hollett; Virginia L. Hood; Elsa M. Hubert; Mr. and Mrs. Harry V. Huffman; Mr. and Mrs. Robert A. Hulse; Inland Mortgage Corporation; Glenn W. Irwin, Jr.; J. Yanan & Associates, Inc.; Mrs. John H. Jefferson; Daniel and Carlyn Johnson; S. Carroll Kahn; Drs. Patricia and Gerald Keener; Hugh and Louise Kirtland; Mrs. Earl W. Knapp; Krieg DeVault Alexander & Capehart Attorneys; Mr. and Mrs. Halbert W. Kunz; Charles Latham, Jr.; Donald L. Lindemann; M & J Management Corp.; Edward P. Madinger; Mr. and Mrs. Stanley Malless; Marketrends, Inc.; Jerry and Marie Marlette; Mays Chemical Co., Inc.; Mr. and Mrs. E. Kirk McKinney, Jr.; Medical Billing & Accounting, Inc.; Ronald V. Morris; Mortgage Credit Services; Nancy and John Myrland; Mr. and Mrs. Robert Payton; Peoples Bank and Trust Company; The Petticrew Foundation; Mr. and Mrs. Ralph M. Reahard; Robert H. Reynolds; Rollins Construction Company, Inc.; Josephine Rothrock; Robert and Alice Schloss; Pauline K. Selby; Percy Simmons; Slippery Noodle Inn; George P. Smith, II; Bill and Jo Ann Spencer; Mrs. Samuel Reid Sutphin; Trust Investment Advisors; David G. and Sheryl D. Vanderstel; VASA North America, Inc.; Ted and Carolyn Vest; William A. and Carol N. Vincent; Richard C. Vonnegut, Sr.; Lucille W. Wade; Mr. and Mrs. Harry A. Weaver, Jr.; George M. and Joyce D. Wilson; Dr. and Mrs. Kenneth R. Woolling.

READER'S GUIDE

To gain the greatest benefit from this volume, readers should understand its scope, types of entries, and indexing and cross-referencing schemes.

Scope. This work encompasses subjects, organizations, and events that, in the opinion of the editors, have been central to the development of Indianapolis and Marion County. Its geographical coverage extends to the eight counties that form the Indianapolis Metropolitan Area, although readers will not find detailed information on locales outside of Marion County. Chronologically, the volume covers the county's entire history from 1820 to the present, but the editors have given proportionately greater weight to entries on the 20th century because of the paucity of published work for this period. (The last comprehensive history of the city, Jacob Piatt Dunn's two-volume *Greater Indianapolis*, appeared in 1910.)

In each case the subject of an entry—whether individual, entity, or event—must have had a significant impact upon the development of Greater Indianapolis to warrant inclusion in the volume. Longevity in the city by itself had no bearing upon the selection process, nor did the ultimate fame or notoriety of individuals who lived here but achieved recognition elsewhere.

The work limits biographical entries to individuals who died prior to March, 1994. Persons alive at that date may be mentioned in other entries, however, and such individuals are noted in the index. With few exceptions, institutional sketches are limited to entities that are or were located in Indianapolis or Marion County. Some of these organizations no longer exist, having ceased operations or moved from the area, but are included because of their significance. Readers will find corporate or organizational entries under their official name as of March, 1994. Occasionally the editors have created an entry under the more commonly known name and referred readers to the current title by a "See" reference.

Types of Entries. The encyclopedia contains three types of narrative entries, a timeline, and a statistical abstract. Most numerous are the brief factual sketches about people, organizations, and events. These *general entries,* listed alphabetically after the overview essays discussed below, contain basic information and typically range from 250 to 750 words. Also listed alphabetically are longer entries, essentially *mini-essays,* that convey information about subjects that go beyond the particular institution or event. These entries discuss specific items within a somewhat broader context or group. For example, the entry on "Theaters" traces the development of these institutions and carries information about individual theaters, some of which may have a separate entry but most of which do not. Similarly, the mini-essay on "Children's Literature" discusses individual authors and titles for which no separate entries exist. In a section preceding the general entries and mini-essays are the *overview essays,* which average about 5,000 words. These pieces are intended as interpretive introductions to the broad topics and themes that explain the city's history; most also provide a chronological narrative that should prove helpful to readers. All entries identify the authors.

The *timeline,* which follows the overview essays, provides a capsule chronology of key events in the city's history. Readers may refer to the index for more detailed information, although some items find mention only in the timeline. Specific dates are included when known. Preceding the index is a *statistical abstract* that includes historical and contemporary data about Greater Indianapolis. This information comes from the various sources identified at the bottom of the tables and graphs and much of it appears as given for the first time.

Bibliographic Citations. Many of the entries in this volume are followed by bibliographic citations. These sources are guides for further reading and do not necessarily reflect the materials used by the author. The citation of any work does not constitute an endorsement of its accuracy or scholarship.

Indices and Cross-Referencing. This volume employs three methods of cross-referencing and indexing information. Within each general entry SMALL CAPITALS indicate the names of individuals, organizations, events, and topics that have separate, related entries in the encyclopedia. At the end of the overview essays, which do not employ the small capitalizations, we have placed "See also" references to the longer general entries that relate to the essay. Finally, two indices are provided. The first is a subject guide to the entries; the second lists names of individuals, organizations, and places that appear in the main text.

The Encyclopedia of Indianapolis

INTRODUCTION

In 1993 ABC News selected Indianapolis to gauge public response to the new national administration because its analysts believed the city most nearly approximated the nation-at-large. Over 50 years earlier *American Magazine* reached a similar judgment when it declared Indianapolis "the typical city in which to find the typical American family." Such characterizations did not surprise residents, who doubtless received them with mixed pride. Boosters long had proclaimed Indianapolis as the most American of places, but they also had promoted it as a leading city, not merely a representative one. This desire to rank above average was so pronounced in 1909, for example, that civic fathers inscribed "I am myself the citizen of no mean city," from the Apostle Paul's protest in Acts 21:39, on the cornerstone of a new city hall (now the Indiana State Museum). Yet the words seem at odds with the imposing building, so obviously designed to signify importance. Instead of touting Indianapolis, the inscription's defensive tone hints at the ambivalence with which residents and others viewed the city.

In truth Indianapolis is representative, as the following essays and entries make clear. This trait is often its strength. Throughout its past the city has mirrored American society, paradoxes and all, in ways too numerous to list. It was and is predominately white, even though it has a large African-American community. It was and is prosperous and middle-class with a high degree of home ownership, conditions that describe whites and blacks alike. It reflects the religious diversity of modern America but remains primarily Protestant. Oriented toward economic progress, the city repeatedly has turned to businessmen to set a public agenda and act with government to address civic concerns. It was and remains a conservative, male-dominated community, yet it has also been one in which women made substantial contributions even when they did not exercise formal power. It has been—and still is—politically moderate-to-conservative, a testament to its competitive two-party system. But it has also provided a home base for political groups as ideologically diverse as the Ku Klux Klan and John Birch Society and the Socialist Party of America.

Proud of its status as an American "Everytown," Indianapolis nonetheless has attempted to distinguish itself from rival cities, especially those in the Midwest, by fashioning and promoting new identities. (Ironically, this competitive boosterism is a quintessential American trait.) The city continually has redefined what it is and what it wants to be. So it has been, by turns, the Railroad City, the Crossroads of America, the 100 Percent American City, Toolmaker to the Nation, the Amateur Sports Capital. These slogans all contained some truth—but not enough to take permanent hold or to ward off competing claims.

In seeking to reinvent itself (another American habit), Indianapolis has not been an innovative city as much as an adaptive one. The pattern was established early when Alexander Ralston modified Pierre L'Enfant's scheme for Washington, D.C., for his plan of Indiana's new capital, using a circle and diagonal avenues to break the monotonous midwestern street grid. More recent adaptations include city-county consolidation, public-private partnerships, and privatization of governmental services. There are areas—Unigov, for example—in which Indianapolis claims

1

leadership, yet rarely has it been first. Even in combining local governments, the city borrowed ideas and learned lessons from others. But if not in first place, Indianapolis has often been in the first rank of cities to embrace innovation—and in the process to improve upon it—whenever change promised to advance public or private interests. Such a pragmatic approach has made progress less visible to outsiders and residents alike; it has made Indianapolis appear average, thus spurring new efforts to forge a new civic identity.

The city continually seeks a new identity—a niche, in modern terms—in part because it does not know well its own rich history. Treating the past as a foreign country, Americans visit it infrequently and then primarily for purposes of celebration. Residents of Indiana's capital are no different. Yet the city's dynamic and complex culture is best revealed, and perhaps only understood, through the experiences that led to its creation and influenced its development. The true identity of Indianapolis comes as much, if not more, from its past than its present.

What themes explain Indianapolis and its culture? Homogeneous, middle-class, conservative, provincial: these terms by default have become interpretive categories that frame the city. Too many observers have voiced these characterizations to dismiss them casually, but in fact the terms oversimplify instead of enlighten, obscure rather than inform. Consider homogeneity. Even though immigrant numbers were slight compared to other northern cities, Indianapolis has a distinctive ethnic heritage. From the 1850s on a large and influential German community existed—until the Americanization campaigns of the World War I era forced its assimilation. The city housed numerous other national groups that contributed to the urban culture. Perhaps because they were relatively few in number foreign immigrants quickly became culturally American, a circumstance that lessened their visibility and ultimately erased most signs of their presence. Eastern European immigrants, for example, lived in Haughville in the early 20th century; today few traces remain to identify the area as a former ethnic enclave. Indeed, the absence of long-standing immigrant communities made neighborhoods less identifiable (and less important) in Indianapolis than elsewhere; this, in turn, may have made race more prominent because the ethnic configuration of the city was otherwise so simple. Even focusing on foreign immigration is misleading because it ignores altogether the large numbers of native-born upland southerners who moved to Indianapolis during the 20th century. This internal migration also shaped the community and arguably created a southside subculture.

Other themes have equally complex histories. For instance, the absence of navigable waterways made transportation an early and continuing focus. Crisscrossing roads and railroads soon anchored Indianapolis in the region's (and the nation's) rapidly expanding economy and eased the city's cultural and political isolation. In the 20th century the automobile reinforced transportation's signal contribution to the civic identity. It also made possible the growth of ever more distant suburbs that redefined the Hoosier capital as Greater Indianapolis and threatened its image as a cohesive community.

Indianapolis is a midwestern city and as such embodies (perhaps exaggerates) the region's middle-class values. Stability, orderly change, cooperation, compromise, conciliation, self-reliance, patriotism, faith: these watchwords find constant expression in the city's past and present. They explain the emphasis on planning that runs from Ralston's 1821 plat through Kessler's boulevard and park system to the regional center schemes of the 1980s and 1990s, all plans that promoted purposeful change—and reinforced the social order. They reveal the reasons underlying the rich tradition of voluntarism and philanthropy that extends from the Indianapolis Benevolent Society and Charity Organization Society of the 19th century to the current-day

Indianapolis Foundation, Lilly Endowment, and United Way. They help us understand the city's fusion of sacred and secular, seen most dramatically today in the civil religion of the War Memorial Plaza and earlier in the presence of four churches on the Circle, the heart (or soul) of the Mile Square.

The overview essays that follow serve as windows into these themes and others. They also provide an interpretive guide to Indianapolis' heritage and culture on topics ranging from fine and performing arts to sports, from government to business and economy, from religion to the urban environment. The essays—and their extension into the general entries—point to what the city has been, what it is today, and, by implication, what it can become. Both authors and editors offer them to promote understanding of Indianapolis and to invite reflection on its future.

The Editors

AFRICAN-AMERICANS

Emma Lou Thornbrough

On the eve of the Civil War there were only 468 African-Americans in Indianapolis, slightly less than 3 percent of the population. In 1860 there were only 11,428 blacks in the entire state out of a total population of 1,338,710—most of them concentrated in the counties along the Ohio River and the eastern part of the state where there were white Quaker communities. But, wherever their residence, African-Americans were not citizens in the eyes of the law and were regarded by most whites as basically an inferior and degraded people. They could not vote or serve in the state militia; their children were barred from public schools; they could not testify in court in a case against a white person; and intermarriage between a white person and one with as little as one-eighth Negro ancestry was prohibited under severe penalties. Under Article XIII of the 1851 state constitution blacks were even barred from coming into the state to reside.

In spite of discrimination and humiliation African-Americans in Indianapolis had a sense of identity and community. In 1836 Bethel African Methodist Episcopal Church (A.M.E.) was founded, and in 1846 Second (Colored) Baptist Church, two institutions that have survived until the present. In 1848 the first branch of the Prince Hall (Negro) Masonic Lodge was organized in the city. Early black residents thought of themselves as Americans, entitled to the rights of other citizens. The principal reason for the calling of the first black state conventions was to oppose efforts of the Indiana Colonization Society to persuade blacks to move to Liberia in Africa. In 1851, while white delegates were meeting to frame a constitution that barred them from the state, a convention of African-Americans that met in Indianapolis passed resolutions declaring that as Americans they were entitled to the same rights as other citizens "according to the letter and spirit" of the United States Constitution and Declaration of Independence.

As soon as the Civil War began, in spite of Article XIII, more and more blacks, most of them fugitive slaves from Kentucky and Tennessee, moved into the state. In the following years the number of immigrants from the South increased. The largest number came to Indianapolis, and many blacks from small towns and rural areas in Indiana also moved to the state capital. By 1900

Emma Lou Thornbrough is Professor Emeritus of History at Butler University in Indianapolis.

Members of the Tyree family gathered on their front porch, ca. 1895, in an area now occupied by IUPUI. [Indiana Historical Society, #C4715]

there were 15,931 blacks in the city, almost 10 percent of the population. By 1910 the number had grown to 21,816.

After the Civil War most legal disabilities were removed. The 14th and 15th Amendments to the U.S. Constitution, framed for the benefit of the emancipated slaves in the South, gave citizenship and political rights to Indiana blacks. Article XIII was voided by the state Supreme Court. In 1869 the state legislature provided for separate public schools for blacks, and in 1877 amended the law to give school authorities the option of segregated schools or admitting blacks to the same schools as whites. Indianapolis remained a segregated city despite changes in the law. A state civil right law (1885) that prohibited racial discrimination in places of public accommodation was a dead letter. Barred by white prejudice, which was reinforced by policies of white realtors, blacks were confined to clearly recognizable "colored neighborhoods" in which they developed their own businesses and institutions.

Most African-Americans lived in an area slightly north and west of the center of the city. Newcomers who arrived after the Civil War also settled in neighborhoods on the near east side. On Indiana Avenue and adjacent streets were located businesses, restaurants, and places of entertainment to serve the needs of a growing black community. In this area were also offices of black physicians and lawyers. Excluded from "white" organizations, these professionals formed their own local societies, which in turn were affiliated with the black National Medical Association and the National Bar Association. Segregated elementary schools taught by black teachers were also located in the "colored neighborhoods." These teachers were never permitted to teach in "white" schools regardless of their education and qualifications. Most black residents appeared to accept discrimination and segregation as inevitable and spent more of their energies on building the black community than on challenging the existing social order.

Churches were the most powerful and influential institutions in the black community. They were not only centers of religion but also of cultural and charitable activities. Congregations of churches founded before the Civil War grew and many new churches were established. The largest number of new settlers were Baptists, and Baptist churches were most numerous, but new A.M.E. churches were also founded. Jones Tabernacle of the A.M.E. Zion denomination was one of the largest congregations in the city. Membership in other denominations was small. Black clergymen were recognized leaders in secular as well as religious life, and many of them were active in politics. Moses Broyles of Second Baptist Church was prominent in the movement to win political rights and in forging ties between blacks and the Republican party.

Next to the church, fraternal organizations were probably the most influential institutions. Many new orders were founded. Some, like the Knights and Daughters of Tabor, were all black. Others, like the Knights of Pythias and Elks, were the counterparts of white orders. Much social life centered in these lodges and the women's auxiliaries. Non-members shared in the pageantry of their parades and their elaborate funeral rituals. All orders had benevolent programs, including care of sick and elderly members and widows and orphans. Leadership in a fraternal order was often a stepping-stone to civic and political leadership. James S. Hinton, the first African-American elected to the state legislature, was a prominent Mason.

In addition to church related organizations and secret fraternal orders there were dozens of musical, cultural, and purely social clubs. Women's clubs affiliated with the Indiana State Federation of Colored Women's Clubs carried on cultural and benevolent activities and helped develop leadership and a sense of sisterhood among members. Flanner House, for many years the only social service center in the city for blacks, was founded in 1898, followed in 1902 by the Senate Avenue YMCA, which became the largest "Colored Y" in the United States. The African-American press strengthened a sense of community, reflecting and also shaping racial attitudes. The first was the short-lived *Leader*. More enduring were the *World* and the *Freeman* and longest lived of all, the *Recorder*, which continues publication today.

The "Great Migration," the movement of blacks from the rural South to cities in the North that began during World War I, brought another influx of new settlers that reshaped the black community. By 1920 the African-American population of Indianapolis had reached 34,678; by 1930 it was 43,967, or 12 percent of the whole. The increase put a strain on existing housing, schools, and public services and led to an increase in prejudice and demands for legalized segregation. As middle class blacks, seeking better housing, began to move into white neighborhoods they encountered opposition, sometimes intimidation and violence. In 1926, under pressure from white civic organizations, the city council, which was dominated by the Ku Klux Klan, passed a residential zoning ordinance intended to prevent blacks from moving into a city block without the consent of the white residents. The ordinance was promptly declared unconstitutional, but efforts to restrict movement of African-Americans into white neighborhoods continued.

In the 1920s there were also moves to tighten segregation in the public schools. Elementary schools had been largely segregated from the beginning, but there was no separate high school for blacks. The first black pupil had graduated from Indianapolis (later Shortridge) High School in 1876 and blacks had continued to be freely admitted since then. In 1922 the Indianapolis

Fraternal organizations, such as the Persian Oriental Band shown here in 1952,
have been important in the African-American community since the
19th century. [Indiana Historical Society, #C2193]

school board, under pressure from a variety of white organizations, voted to begin construction
of a separate black high school. Blacks in the city countered these actions by founding the Indianapolis branch of the National Association for the Advancement of Colored People (NAACP) in
1913, an organization that was to play the leading role in later years against legalized segregation.
The Indianapolis branch successfully brought suit against the residential zoning ordinance and
strongly opposed a separate high school, as did other black organizations and the black press. A
suit brought by NAACP lawyers for an injunction against construction of the school was denied
on appeal to the state Supreme Court. However, after the school, Crispus Attucks, opened in
1927, it soon became a cultural center for the black community and an institution of pride even
among groups that had opposed it.

Tightening of segregation also acted as a stimulus to the development of a distinctive black
culture. In Indianapolis this was most notable in the field of music and entertainment. The 1920s
and 1930s were the heyday of jazz on Indiana Avenue, where local musicians, some of whom
later won national fame, played in bands in the Walker Ballroom and nearby nightclubs.

The Great Depression that began in 1929 and the unemployment which accompanied it
were probably more devastating to African-Americans, already a marginal group, than to any
other segment of the population. Consequently the New Deal, with its programs of public works
and relief, not only brought new hope but also resulted in a political revolution among black voters who, with few exceptions, had always been loyal Republicans. In 1932, for the first time, two
black Democrats (including Henry J. Richardson, Jr. from Marion County) were elected to the
state legislature. Since 1936, although some black leaders have remained Republicans, African-
Americans have voted for Democratic candidates by wide margins in local, state, and national
elections.

World War II and the prospect of employment in defense industries brightened economic prospects among both white and black residents. Because of labor shortages black workers were given opportunities for jobs in industry and other fields previously closed to them. The official policy of the recently organized CIO prohibited racial discrimination in member unions. Although some locals opposed the policy, blacks joined labor unions in large numbers for the first time and a few black men and women were advanced from janitorial positions to the assembly line.

Prospects of employment also brought increased numbers of African-Americans to the city. Their numbers were even greater than those who had come during the "Great Migration" of the World War I years. By 1950 the black population of Indianapolis was 63,567, or 15 percent of the whole. Migration continued during the prosperous postwar years. By 1960 the number of blacks in the city was 98,049, nearly 21 percent. The incorporation of the whole of Marion County, including the predominantly white suburbs, by the Unigov Act in 1969 reduced the percentage of blacks in the city although their numbers continued to increase at a greater rate than that of whites.

The civil rights movement, which began following the war, brought the most important changes in the status of blacks since Reconstruction. The Indianapolis branch of the NAACP and the state conference of that organization took the lead in demanding the end of segregation and discrimination. Willard Ransom, graduate of Harvard Law School and a veteran of World War II, who was elected as state president five times, was the recognized leader of the movement. Also important was realtor William T. Ray, president of the Indianapolis NAACP. Other stalwarts were Jessie Jacobs and Andrew Ramsey. They had strong support from other black organizations: the Federation of Associated Clubs, fraternal orders, ministers and church groups, and many others. A coalition of white organizations, which included the Federation of Churches, Jewish organizations, PTAs, the CIO, the League of Women Voters, and others, played an important part in lobbying in the state legislature. The result was a series of effective civil rights laws.

The first law, passed in 1949, abolished segregation in public education from the kindergarten level to the state universities. Other measures, adopted in the 1960s, created an Indiana Civil Rights Commission with authority to enforce laws outlawing discrimination in places of public accommodation, employment, and housing. Creation of an Indianapolis Human Rights Commission with authority to hear complaints of denial of civil rights supplemented the work of the state commission. The Indianapolis Urban League, founded in 1965, also supplemented the work of government agencies in the fields of employment and housing.

A prolonged struggle over the desegregation of public schools mandated by the 1949 law was complicated by changing residential patterns which resulted in *de facto* segregation. Nevertheless the NAACP, other African-American organizations, white organizations that favored integration, and even the director of the Civil Rights Commission accused the Indianapolis school board of policies that perpetuated segregation. In 1968 the U.S. Department of Justice, acting under authority of the 1964 federal Civil Rights Law, brought suit against Indianapolis Public Schools (IPS), charging it with *de jure* segregation. The prolonged litigation finally ended in 1981 when about 6,000 black students from the city schools were sent to the largely white schools in the outlying townships of Marion County under a one-way busing plan ordered by the federal district court. Meanwhile, schools within the borders of IPS had begun a system of two-way busing of both white and black students as a means of desegregation. However, as the school population declined to slightly less than 50,000 from more than 100,000 in the 1960s, genuine desegregation became less attainable.

Beginning in the 1950s African-Americans also became more visible and influential in shaping school policies, and the number of black teachers and administrators increased. Under court orders faculties were desegregated and more black principals were appointed. In 1955 Grant Hawkins became the first black member of the school board, and Jessie Jacobs was also elected before the desegregation suit began. In 1976 Mary Busch, who has been reelected repeatedly, was chosen as a member of a pro-integration board. By 1988 a majority of the seven-member school board were African-Americans, and in 1991 Shirl E. Gilbert II became the first black superintendent of IPS. Meanwhile the number of black teachers and administrators in the township schools increased. Dr. Percy Clark, who was named superintendent of Lawrence Township schools in 1982, was regarded as particularly able and successful.

African-Americans have also become more active and visible in city politics and government. In the 19th century three blacks, all Republicans, were elected to the city council—Robert Bruce Bagby, John A. Puryear, and Henry Sweetland. Sumner Furniss, a Republican, elected in 1918, was the only black to serve between 1900 and 1934 when Theodore Cable, the first black Democrat, was elected. Thereafter several African-Americans, both Republicans and Democrats, were elected until the adoption of the Unigov law in 1969 created a county-wide council dominated by white Republicans. Black Democrats, however, have had continuous control of certain inner city districts. Two who have had long tenure are Rozelle Boyd and Glenn Howard. Republican Paula Parker-Sawyers was elected a council member-at-large and was also appointed as deputy mayor, a post that other African-Americans have also held.

Dr. Benjamin Osborne, a Democratic stalwart, was repeatedly elected trustee of Center Township, and all of his successors have been black Democrats. Mercer M. Mance, elected judge in Marion County Superior Court in 1958, was the first of several African-American judges in Indianapolis–Marion County.

Among black Republican members of the state legislature from Indianapolis since World War II have been Robert Lee Brokenburr, the first black senator, and representatives Harriette Bailey Conn and Ray Crowe. Among Democrats, Henry J. Richardson, elected in 1932, was one of the first two black Democrats to serve in the lower chamber. Daisy Lloyd, another Democrat, elected in 1964, was the first black woman representative. Since reapportionment in 1972 black Democrats have had continuous control of some districts in the central city and have gained seniority and influence. William A. Crawford has served in the House of Representatives since his election in 1972. Julia Carson, after two terms as representative, was a member of the Senate from 1977 to 1990 when she resigned to become trustee of Center Township. In state government, Republican William T. Ray served as administrative assistant to Governor Otis Bowen, the highest position held by a black to that time.

In the decades after World War II, when the civil rights movement was at its height, a period of unprecedented economic growth and a breakdown of restrictive hiring practices, due in part to fair employment legislation, opened new employment opportunities to educated African-Americans. Corporations like banks and insurance companies actively recruited them. The finance center at Fort Benjamin Harrison employed large numbers, and government offices began hiring more blacks for supervisory as well as routine jobs. School systems sought teachers and administrators, and there were growing numbers of African-American lawyers, physicians, and other professionals.

Members of this expanding middle class moved from older "colored" neighborhoods to formerly all-white areas on the north side of the city. Some of these neighborhoods became predominantly black, but whites remained a majority in others. Neighborhood associations—Butler-Tarkington, Meridian-Kessler, Mapleton-Fall Creek—worked to maintain a racial balance. Other middle class families moved to suburban areas in outlying townships. The Grandview development in Washington Township became the first predominantly black neighborhood outside the city limits. Increased incomes and fair housing laws enabled more and more black families to move outside Center Township, where blacks had always been concentrated. The 1990 census showed a total of 169,654 African-Americans (21 percent) within the Unigov boundaries. Of these, 56 percent lived outside of Center Township. The largest number resided in Washington Township, where they were about one-fourth of the total population, but there were also increasing numbers of blacks in Lawrence, Pike, and Wayne townships.

Meanwhile, older black neighborhoods in the inner city deteriorated and many of the residents faced unemployment as opportunities for workers without skills and education declined. The percentage of persons classified as below the poverty line increased, and social problems became more severe. Many households were headed by single women who were dependent on welfare to care for their children. Unemployment among young black males, many of them school dropouts, was widespread, and crime among them a growing problem.

As inner city neighborhoods deteriorated, businesses that had served the needs of their residents disappeared. Supermarkets owned by chains moved out of the area, and small black owned businesses failed. Indiana Avenue, which had been the center of black business and entertainment, shared in the decay and decline. But in the 1970s the Indiana Avenue Association, which was headed by Willard Ransom, began a rejuvenation of the area. One result was the restoration of the Walker Theatre and the founding of the Madame Walker Urban Life Center. Part of Lockefield Gardens, a housing project built during the New Deal era, was restored and construction of new apartments and offices replaced some of the abandoned buildings.

Today churches remain, as they always have been, a powerful influence in the black community. Black clergymen continue to be active in shaping racial attitudes on such matters as school desegregation, politics, and other public policies. Although some churches have followed their congregations as they have moved outside the inner city, some of the oldest, most prestigious remain in their old locations. All the established churches have expanded and institutionalized their community services and welfare activities. These include day care centers, nursery schools, clinics, geriatric centers, and housing for the elderly and homeless. Some pastors carry their message to a wider audience by means of radio and television.

In addition to the older churches there are scores of small churches, some of them "store front," others in modest little frame church buildings. Their forms of worship, reminiscent of small churches in the rural South, attract large numbers of recent migrants.

Baptists of various kinds remain the largest denomination, followed by Methodists, but membership in other Protestant churches—Presbyterians, Christians, and Episcopalians—has grown. Many influential members of the black community are members of Witherspoon Presbyterian Church. Light of the World Christian Church (formerly Second Christian) under the leadership of Rev. T. Garrott Benjamin, with one of the largest congregations in the city, attracts whites as well as blacks.

Churches affiliated with the Pentecostal Assemblies of the World, a denomination founded in Indianapolis in the early years of this century by Bishop Garfield T. Haywood, have attracted a large following. Christ Temple Church, founded by Haywood, has continued to grow. More recently Grace Apostolic Church has moved into an impressive structure designed by architect Walter Blackburn.

The number of black Roman Catholics has grown to an estimated 10,000. Most blacks attend two churches, St. Bridget (scheduled to be closed in 1994) and Holy Angels. Martin Center, founded by Father Boniface Hardin in 1969 to deal with a variety of racial problems, serves members of all denominations. A non-denominational college opened in connection with the center in 1977 was accredited in 1987 and given university status in 1990.

Fraternal orders continue to have large memberships and to exert influence, and, as the number of college educated African-Americans has grown, Greek letter fraternities and sororities have become influential in civic affairs as well as social life. Clubs affiliated with the Indiana State Federation of Colored Women's Clubs have declined in number and membership. The Indianapolis branch of the National Council of Negro Women has attracted younger educated women, some of whom are in business, others in the professions, who are leaders in community affairs.

The civil rights movement, which had as its goals the breaking down of racial barriers and the integration of blacks into the mainstream of American society, also led to an upsurge of racial pride and interest in the history of African-Americans. This in turn led to increased interest in Africa and African culture and their survival in the United States. These developments manifested themselves in many forms, from slogans like "Black Pride" and "Black Is Beautiful" to changes in curriculum in universities to include courses in African-American history and related subjects and the publication of scholarly books and fiction about Africa and African-Americans. Material on African-American history has been integrated into the curriculum of classes at all levels in the Indianapolis Public Schools. Freetown Village, a living history museum, intends to build a replica of the black community in Indianapolis in the 1870s. The Children's Museum has had a number of exhibits about African-American artists. Whites as well as blacks enjoy these exhibits and listen to music that shows African and African-American influences. Indiana Black Expo, begun in 1971, has been an annual event to celebrate the achievements of African-Americans and to instill self-esteem and pride among black citizens. Blacks eat "soul food" and celebrate Kwanzaa, the African harvest festival. More recently there has been increasing interest in introducing an "Afro-centric" curriculum into the schools.

All Americans of African descent share an awareness of race and racism, but the African-American community in Indianapolis is by no means monolithic on some questions. For example, many members do not like the currently popular designation "African-American" and prefer to be called simply "black." There are obviously increasing differences in economic and social status as well as differences on racial issues. Some black youths, faced with the apparent hopelessness of their situation, appear to be completely alienated. Nevertheless, it appears that most African-Americans in Indianapolis retain the ideal of a racially integrated society and believe that on the whole the city has a better record on race relations and is a better place for blacks to live than most other large cities. They cite as one piece of evidence that there has never been a large scale race riot or racial disorder like the ones that have erupted in other cities.

Proponents of the view that Indianapolis has a good record and is a good place to live suggest a number of reasons. The period since World War II has for many African-Americans been one of increased economic opportunities and rising expectations. The growing black community has been able to expand peaceably into better housing in neighborhoods formerly closed to it. Certainly the absence of high population density found in the huge multi-storied housing projects and the generally crowded conditions in the ghettos of some cities has been a factor in reducing racial tensions in Indianapolis. Moreover, black political leaders, ministers, business-men, leaders of the Indianapolis Urban League, the NAACP, the SCLC, and other influential African-Americans have been moderates. Radical young blacks who made headlines in the 1960s and the 1970s have been co-opted by the moderates or have gone elsewhere. Many white religious organizations and civic organizations, including the Chamber of Commerce and the Lilly Endowment, have joined efforts of the black community to make Indianapolis a better place for members of all races. The state legislature enacted civil rights laws before Congress passed the Civil Rights Act of 1964. The Indiana Civil Rights Commission, the state Office of Equal Opportunity, and the Indianapolis Human Rights Commission (renamed Equal Oppor-tunity Division) have worked to resolve cases of racial discrimination in employment and hous-ing. Most blacks have seen Unigov as intended to reduce their political power and influence, but Republican mayors elected since its adoption have appointed African-Americans to city offices and advisory boards and have shown awareness of problems of the black community. Never-theless, there is a widespread feeling that recent city administrations have concentrated their efforts and the resources of the city on projects favored by the white power structure and have neglected social problems in the black community such as housing and high rates of infant mortality.

In recent years the number of African-Americans in the Indianapolis Police Department has increased and more officers have been promoted to higher ranks. Recently the first black chief of police has been appointed. Still, there is a widespread feeling that police are not as vigilant in black neighborhoods as in white and that they harass young blacks and use unnecessary force and brutality in arresting blacks suspected of crime. Killing by police of several black suspects and other acts of violence against them have aroused bitter criticism. African-American members of the City-County Council and the Black Ministerial Alliance have protested, and the national office of the NAACP has conducted hearings on police conduct in Indianapolis. Relations with the police are probably the most ominous sign of racial tensions in the city.

While economic recession, growing unemployment, and signs of a revival of white racism in recent years have aroused apprehension of possible racial troubles, data from the United States census of 1990 and other recent research indicate that Indianapolis is a better place for African-Americans than other cities in the Midwest. Nearly two thirds of black households live in single family or two family unattached houses. More than 40 percent of black residents own their own homes, a figure exceeded by only six other cities in the United States. While a majority of African-Americans (57 percent) live in predominantly black neighborhoods, about one third live in neighborhoods with a white majority. A majority (56 percent) have moved outside the inner city (Center Township) where 90 percent lived in 1960.

There was a decline in the traditional black family nationally during the 1980s, but the de-cline in Indianapolis was the smallest in the Midwest. Indianapolis has a higher percentage of married couples with children living together than other cities in the region. Although 53 percent of black households with children are headed by a single woman, the figure is the lowest in the Midwest. In spite of adverse economic conditions and increasing unemployment in recent years the 1990 census shows that income for blacks in Indianapolis compares favorably with that in other cities. About one fourth of black families reported annual income of less than $10,000, but this number was less than the national average. In every other income bracket up to $50,000 a year Indianapolis blacks ranked above the national average for black wage earners, although the city was below the national average for the few who earned more than $50,000.

In the years since World War II African-Americans in Indianapolis along with African-Americans nationally have won long sought victories in the courts and legislative halls. Many enjoy a better standard of living, better housing, and better educational opportunities than their parents and grandparents. But while members of this group have prospered beyond their own hopes and expectations, there is increasing poverty and hopelessness in the inner city. The ideals of a truly racially integrated and racially just society have not been achieved, and some long time integrationists see little hope that they will ever be reached. Some of them feel that the desegregation that has occurred has weakened the feeling of community and identity which formerly existed among African-Americans. For example, some miss the old restaurants and places of entertainment where blacks congregated but which closed as racial bars to formerly "white" establishments were lifted. Some African-Americans also feel that desegregation, which resulted in closing of neighborhood "colored schools," lessened the importance of black teachers as role models and community leaders. Moreover, increasing signs of racism and white prejudice in the 1990s make even the most fortunate African-Americans apprehensive about the future of race relations in the city.

See also: AFRICAN-AMERICAN BUSINESSES; AFRICAN-AMERICAN CHURCHES; AFRICAN-AMERICAN PRESS; AFRICAN-AMERICAN WOMEN'S ORGANIZATIONS; AFRICAN-AMERICANS IN POLITICS; BLUES; CIVIL RIGHTS; INDIANA AVENUE; JAZZ; RELIGION AND RACE; SCHOOL DESEGREGATION; and individual names, institutions, and organizations.

BROADCASTING

Howard Caldwell

Commercial broadcasting came to Indianapolis in the 1920s, as early as it appeared in most American cities. Purdue University engineering graduate Francis F. Hamilton signed on the air on New Year's Eve in 1921 with 9JK, the city's first station, later to become WLK. Hatfield Electric's WOH was heard a year later. Neither of these ventures survived more than a year. Despite favorable reaction by the *Indianapolis News*, the *Indianapolis Star*, and L. S. Ayres and Company, all of whom saw the medium's advertising potential, and despite an effort to cover the Indianapolis 500–Mile Race, these early stations lacked sponsors and listeners.

On election night, 1924, Merchants Heat and Light Company signed on with WFBM (now WNDE), and permanent radio had arrived in Indianapolis. Two years later, former WOH radio engineer Noble B. Watson was back on the air with WKBF, and the city had its second permanent radio outlet.

Amateurs provided most of the limited programming during those first few years. The stations had a large pool of singers and instrumentalists from which to choose. Schedules were casual; if nothing much was available, the stations would sign off for a while. Within a few years, however, coverage of public events like the Indianapolis 500, the state high school basketball finals, the opening of the state's biggest theater (the Indiana Theatre in downtown Indianapolis), and a destructive tornado began to attract listeners. By the end of the 1920s, radio was definitely part of the Indianapolis scene.

Network radio came to WFBM (CBS) in 1929 and WKBF (NBC) in 1933, opening up a new venue in programming. Entertainers from the stage and screen added radio to their careers on programs that were heard from coast to coast. A number of them were still on stage in the early 1930s and when visiting Indianapolis, usually at downtown theaters, they originated programs from the local stations. Some performers had established identity on radio first and enlarged their audience by making stage appearances. For example, the Indiana Theatre booked a weekend appearance of Freeman Gosden and Charles Correll, who created the popular radio program "Amos 'n Andy."

Howard Caldwell served as news anchor at WRTV (Channel 6) in Indianapolis from 1959 to 1994.

Local entertainers also sought radio exposure. Nearly every night radio carried remote broadcasts of orchestras from various hotels and clubs. The house band at the Indiana Theatre, the Charlie Davis group featuring young vocalist Dick Powell, could be heard during the late 1920s. During the decade when big band music became the rage, orchestras performed their weekly network programs from local stages. Indiana's own Hoagy Carmichael Orchestra broadcast from the Columbia Club in 1928 where the composer was both pianist and conductor. During consecutive weeks in 1939 Tommy Dorsey and his orchestra, then Benny Goodman and his group, broadcast from the stage of the Lyric Theater.

With network radio came soap operas, which engaged listeners with their daily 15–minute dramas about the trials and tribulations of women. Radio announcers were in heavy demand to handle not only musical segments but to read commercials, news, and sports (now available from the news wire services). The Great Depression encouraged people to stay home more and listen, but when people traveled they could still listen if they owned one of the new car radios.

Radio did not change much in Indianapolis in the late 1930s and 1940s. Growth in numbers of radio stations was slower than in many cities, especially before World War II. Only two more stations—WIBC (1938) and WISH (1941)—appeared during this era. Within a 200–mile radius of Indianapolis there were numerous cities with signals that penetrated the local area. Many listeners in Indianapolis actually tuned their sets to WLW in Cincinnati. WLW's local connection was reciprocal. It broadcast Indianapolis radio evangelist Howard Cadle's "Nation's Family Prayer Period" across the country from his pulpit at the Cadle Tabernacle. During the pre–World War II era, WLW also became a source of programs that were fed to the NBC Blue and Red networks. As late as 1950 the "nation's station," as WLW called itself, was still listed in the Sunday program logs of the *Indianapolis Star.*

In the 1940s local radio turned increasingly to playing records introduced by announcers whose melodic voices picked up a following of their own. The decade could be divided into two parts. War news and the popular morale-building music dominated wartime programming. The postwar period featured local radio personalities like WIBC's Easy Gwynn and WFBM's Paul "The Happy Monster" Roberts, who by now were known as disc jockeys. Before the decade ended the city had become a five-station AM market with the addition of WXLW in 1948. But by the end of the 1940s something else was brewing: local groups began to vie for the first local television channel.

The Radio Corporation of America (RCA) had introduced television at the 1939 World's Fair in New York City. TV had a positive economic effect on Indianapolis and the state many months before local service was launched. During the summer of 1947 the *Indianapolis Star* noted that the city was "now becoming the center of the vast RCA Corporation's television production." An RCA executive revealed that 3,300 workers were employed in Indianapolis alone and that another 500 would be needed within the next 60 days. The demand for television receivers caused the plant to double its production. Six years later RCA was involved in a multimillion-dollar plant expansion, adding hundreds of jobs. The Indianapolis plant was then one of the company's largest.

By June, 1948, the *Indianapolis Star Magazine* estimated there were 150 TV sets in Indianapolis picking up out-of-state signals. Although P. R. Mallory, a local radio components dealer, had set up the city's first operating TV station in 1945, the first commercial television came to Indianapolis on Memorial Day, 1949, with complete coverage of the 500–Mile Race. That year the FCC awarded Channel 6 to Harry Bitner, who headed a corporation that had owned WFBM Ra-

Control room of an early city television station in the late 1940s. [Indiana Historical Society, Bretzman Collection, #20873]

Jim Shelton hosted the "Pick-A-Pocket" show on WIBC from 1947 to 1968. [Indiana State Museum]

dio since 1939. It became WFBM-TV, originally as a CBS affiliate with access to the NBC, ABC, and Dumont networks. Within eight years the city would have three more stations: WTTV, Channel 10 (later Channel 4), signed on in November, 1949, as an affiliate of NBC, and later, ABC. WISH, Channel 8, in 1954, was an NBC affiliate originally although it switched to CBS the next year; and WLW-I, Channel 13, affiliated with ABC in 1957. (Channel 4 became an independent station when it gave up ABC to Channel 13. In 1979 Channel 6 switched to the ABC network and Channel 13 to NBC.)

Although television had a significant effect on the city's economy, TV broadcasting did not ensure immediate profits for the state's first station. The *Indianapolis News* reported that WFBM-TV lost $57,000 during its first four months, although station officials predicted that profits would come once network TV became available. In 1949 an estimated 7,200 TV sets were in use in Indianapolis.

Network service for local TV began in the fall of 1950 and apparently it did make a difference. A study released by the Federal Communications Commission (FCC) in 1953 determined that only 14 of 108 stations operating nationally throughout 1952 lost money. None was in Indianapolis. A rapid decline in the price of television sets increased viewership dramatically. By 1953 there were over 137,000 sets in the Indianapolis area.

TV's first decade in Indianapolis was similar to the first decade of radio in that stations offered mostly local programs. There were children's shows, women's shows, variety shows, local contest shows, news, and sports. Program titles included Channel 6's quiz show "Test the Press" (1949–1955), Channel 8's "Chuckles Open House" (1954–1956), and Channel 13's "Kindergarten College" (1957–1973). Announcers were in demand because most local commercials were live in the studio. Movies were prevalent at all four local stations, usually with a movie host or hostess. One-time film actress Frances Farmer became one of the most popular personalities in the city as host of "Frances Farmer Presents" (1958–1964, Channel 6). Local exercise girl Debbie Drake was a ratings winner for Channel 8. WTTV became the local play-by-play station for Indiana University and Purdue University basketball, and WFBM-TV carried the state high school basketball tourney before it too switched to WTTV in the 1970s.

Radio in the 1950s added one AM station, as well as the city's first permanent FM stations. The new AM was WGEE, which replaced WXLW at 1590 in 1956. WXLW had moved to 950 the year before. The new FMs included two noncommercial stations—WAJC (1950), operated by the Arthur Jordan Conservatory of Music (later part of Butler University), and WIAN (1954), located at Shortridge High School. WFMS became the city's first permanent commercial FM in 1957, while WFBM created the first AM-FM-TV combination in the city when WFBM-FM signed on in 1959.

The decade also found radio moving aggressively into news, adding mobile units and establishing news departments to cover local events. It became extremely competitive, and for the first time local broadcasters began to purchase newspaper advertising to promote their stations.

Radio clung to traditional formats into the 1960s for its entertainment programming. The city's newest AM stations, WIGO (1963) and WNDY (1964), signed on during this transitional decade. Things changed in 1963, however, when Star Stations headed by Don Burden purchased the WISH radio properties, both AM and FM. Burden adopted the call letters WIFE and changed the AM format to Top 40 music geared to attract a young listening audience. He also launched a promotion campaign unlike any done before in Indianapolis. On-air personalities were featured as the "WIFE Good Guys" in large newspaper ads and billboards, and the stations staged a contest offering $113,000 to lure listeners. An audience survey company, Hooper, showed the operation dominating the market in early 1964.

Reaction by the competition was swift. Many stations started prize money contests of their own and moved into more contemporary music. Broadcast advertising revenue picked up at all three daily newspapers, which now featured radio-television columnists. But when FCC investigators found the Hooper ratings had been based on only a few days of sampling, they questioned Burden's responsibility as a station owner; the commission renewed WIFE's licenses for only one year. Over the next two years the stations were accused of rigging contests and falsifying billing. Burden also was accused of making improper political contributions and slanting station newscasts toward a certain candidate. More FCC investigations and hearings dragged on until 1975, when the commission decided that Burden and Star Stations were unqualified to own any radio stations and took away all his licenses.

WIFE's ratings success, however, changed Indianapolis radio. The market became more contemporary and highly competitive, with formats aimed at particular demographic groups. Stations adopted country, rock, middle-of-the-road, nostalgia, and beautiful music formulas. FM stations also started to grow in the late 1960s, as more radios were able to receive the signals. WNAP and WTLC both began operations in 1968; WNAP competed directly with WIFE, while WTLC was the city's first station to cater to African-American listeners.

The 1960s was also the last decade for much locally produced entertainment programming on television. By the 1970s most of the shows were gone. One exception was the Jim Gerard Show on WTTV-4, which continued well into the 1980s. Contributing to the demise of local programming in Indianapolis was the availability through syndication of popular network programs of previous years and talk shows featuring nationally known personalities. Syndicated programming continued to be a staple of Indianapolis TV into the 1990s. Local TV also began to expand the length of news broadcasts. WRTV-6 and WISH-8 went to hour-long early evening news in 1966 and 1968, respectively. WLW-I (now WTHR-13) would not make the same move until 1976.

Public television came to Indianapolis in 1970 with WFYI. The commercial stations assisted this effort, but 9,000 local women volunteers raised most of the $300,000 needed to clear the way for sign on. Ardath Burkhart organized what became known as "Ardath's March," a door-to-door effort in March, 1970, that raised $280,000. Channel 20 signed on the following October.

A development of great significance to local TV was the use of videotape for news programs by the late 1970s. Tape did not have to be put through a processor or a film splicer and could be reused. It became standard equipment along with the TelePrompTer and microwave equipment that provided stations the opportunity to report directly from the scene of local happenings.

In the 1980s satellite capability further expanded local TV remote capabilities. Stations could do live or taped interviews with their representatives or senators directly from Washington. It was also possible to receive reports of special interest from local stations elsewhere. It was a step away from dependency on network service. In 1984 WPDS-59 signed on and added the city's fourth TV news operation, although it lasted less than a year.

News continued to dominate local TV programming in the 1990s. Two of the four network affiliates expanded the length of early evening news broadcasts, this time to 90 minutes, WRTV-6 in 1987 and WISH-8 two years later. All offered local weekday newscasts early in the morning, at noon, and in late evening, with early and late evening broadcasts on weekends. In the early 1990s WXIN-59 began a half hour late night newscast and WRTV-6 produced a separate nightly broadcast for WTTV-4.

In radio, FM stations began to dominate the market in the late 1970s and early 1980s. Suburban stations in Greenfield (WSMJ) and Shelbyville (WSVL) were purchased by new owners and began to compete for listeners and advertising dollars as WIKS and WENS, respectively. WFMS rose to the top of the Indianapolis ratings after adopting a modern country format, and ratings at WFBQ began to increase with the addition of morning personalities Bob Kevoian and Tom Griswold. "Bob and Tom" came from Michigan with a show featuring irreverent humor that pushed the bounds of good taste for some listeners. Local attorney John Price formed an organization, Decency in Broadcasting, and complained to the FCC about material aired by WFBQ's morning personalities. In 1990 the FCC fined WFBQ $10,000 for airing four comedy routines it ruled indecent. Still, the controversial duo has been number one or two in morning radio ratings almost without exception since the mid–1980s, and readers of *Rolling Stone* magazine chose WFBQ as its station of the year in 1990.

In 1993 WFBQ became the first Indianapolis station to buy one of its competitors when it purchased WRZX from WIN Communications. FCC regulations now permit the ownership of more than one AM or FM in a market. WFMS also used the new rule to buy a second station, Butler's WAJC, which it changed to WGRL, a commercial operation playing a new hit country format.

Like stations throughout the country, each Indianapolis radio outlet tries to serve a particular audience. Ratings indicate the most popular programming includes country music, mainstream rock, or news and talk, a format to which traditional AM power WIBC moved more aggressively in 1993. Noncommercial station audience figures for the city rank among the lowest in the country at about 6 percent. This compares to Cincinnati or Columbus, Ohio, where listeners to noncommercial stations make up 15 percent of the audience. Missing from commercial radio in this market are major stations specializing in jazz or classical music. WSYW offers classical music, but its low power limits its coverage area.

Audience ratings tend to reflect the strength of a station's signal. 1993 Arbitron surveys for Indianapolis (the 37th largest radio market) show the top stations among the most powerful in the city. WFMS placed first in the Spring, 1993, survey, followed by WFBQ and WIBC, the only AM station listed among the top ten. The dominance of FM is typical of most large cities. Since 1975 the percentage of FM listeners in Indianapolis has grown from 35 to more than 75 percent. Yet Indianapolis always has had fewer stations than other cities of similar size. Duncan's American Radio, Inc., providers of broadcast statistics for clients in 200 American markets, lists five peer cities similar in size to Indianapolis. All had more radio stations in 1993, ranging from 24 in Kansas City to 31 in San Antonio. Indianapolis had 21 stations, prompting Duncan to label this market "under radioed."

The market had almost as many television stations. Eleven full-power stations serve Indianapolis viewers (Bloomington is also considered part of the Indianapolis TV market, which A. C. Nielsen Co. ranks as the nation's 26th largest), with five low-power TV stations reaching smaller coverage areas. The four major commercial networks (ABC, CBS, NBC, Fox) have affiliates in the city; those stations (Channels 6, 8, 13, and 59) together with independent Channel 4 generate two and one-half times the advertising revenue of the market's radio stations, and more than 40 percent of the city's total media-related revenue. In addition, there are two noncommercial stations, local PBS affiliate Channel 20, and Butler University's Channel 69. Increased competition for viewers also has come from cable television. Indianapolis has two cable franchises—American Cablevision serves the pre-Unigov city limits, while Comcast operates in the outer areas of Marion County.

The local television market is centered on Indianapolis but it also serves 35 other counties in central Indiana. Included in this sizable area are a number of persons living in rural areas and small communities who have different interests and standards than their urban peers. Figures from the A. C. Nielsen Co. show that the viewing area comprises 2.25 million people over two years of age. TV households are figured at just under 900,000. In television, the main battles for the local viewing audience have been between Channels 6 and 8, although at times Channel 13 has challenged.

In addition to television viewing, television production changes have occurred in Indianapolis in the 1990s. In 1992 French-owned Thomson Consumer Electronics (owners of the RCA and GE television trademarks) began constructing its headquarters for the Americas on the north side of the city. The company, which manufacturers televisions, VCRs, and other visual and audio electronic products in three Indiana plants, including one in Indianapolis, is the successor company to RCA.

No network affiliates were in financial difficulties in the early 1990s, but independent WTTV Channel 4 changed ownership four times between 1977 and 1991. Attempting to cut costs, in 1990 it eliminated the news department that it had maintained, though modestly, since sign on in 1949. Part of the problem came from the appearance of another independent station in Indianapolis in 1984. WPDS (WXIN), Channel 59, offered movies and old syndicated entertainment programming that vied for an audience similar to that of Channel 4. However, WPDS's journey was bumpy too. Originally owned locally, by 1992 it had made three out-of-state ownership changes. Affiliating with the Fox Network in 1986, the current WXIN has strengthened its role and in the process resurrected a nightly local newscast seven days a week. WTTV has settled back into a routine of its traditional Indiana and Purdue basketball along with IHSAA boys and girls tournament play plus movies. Studies show that the Indianapolis market is filled with basketball fans with loyal viewing habits, possibly more than anywhere else in the country.

Radio has also had its moments of regrouping to meet the changing economic times. In the early 1990s black oriented WTLC-FM reduced its award-winning news department to two people and within a year dismantled it entirely. Management stated African-American issues would continue to be addressed through talk show formats, with music geared to younger blacks. The station also dropped its nostalgia format on WTUX, its AM outlet (now WTLC-AM), and targeted older black listeners.

Criticism of the small presence of African-Americans in broadcasting has surfaced periodically and never more than in the 1990s. A 1993 IUPUI survey on race relations in Indianapolis revealed dissatisfaction among African-Americans with their representation in media positions. In television much of that criticism focuses on the absence of black anchors on prime time news broadcasts. Until 1993 no local TV station had a regularly assigned black anchor on any week night newscast, although Janet Langhart, the first African-American regular on any local TV program, hosted "Indy Today," a morning show in 1972–1973. In September, 1991, WXIN-59 was the first station to hire an African-American member of a regularly scheduled news team, meteorologist Chris Wright. In May, 1993, WISH named Tina Cosby the first black weekday evening news anchor on any local station. The next year WRTV hired James Adams to co-anchor the late weekday newscast it produced for WTTV. African-Americans regularly anchored news and sports on weekend broadcasts, and substituted occasionally on prime time news. However, this change did not occur until the 1980s. Prior to that decade most stations employed blacks as photographers, photo editors, and reporters, but not in featured on-camera roles.

Issues of interest to the black community have fared better. In the 1960s Channel 6 was honored for a series of editorials on civil rights and received the prestigious DuPont Award for a documentary, "The Negro in Indianapolis," carried on both TV and radio. In the 1980s Channel 13 became the first station in the city to receive a national Emmy Award with a documentary on the Ku Klux Klan and its past Indiana connections. Still, the fact remains that blacks are more prominent in other nearby television markets. In Cincinnati there are six black weekday news anchors; in Columbus, Ohio, there are five.

Women have moved into the once male-dominated broadcast industry far more rapidly than blacks in Indianapolis. The change began after World War II when women were added to the sales staffs for both radio and TV. A few became voices on local radio. Gwendolyn Schort joined the announcing staff at WFBM on October 24, 1937. Ann Wagner Harper became the first female DJ in Indianapolis, if not in the Midwest, when she appeared on afternoon radio programs on WFBM and WIBC in the 1940s and 1950s. That same decade, Kay Field was doing weather on WISH-TV. Other early female broadcast personalities included Paula Carr, Faith Levitt, and Carolyn Churchman. Women also began appearing on locally produced commercials in the 1950s.

Making inroads into TV newsrooms was more difficult. Two women who were hired early in reportorial roles are Linda Lupear and Barbara Boyd, the latter also one of the first African-American women hired in an on-camera role. Lupear joined Channel 8 in the mid–1960s, and later became a reporter for Channel 6. Boyd (who retired in 1994) became a consumer reporter for Channel 6 in the late 1960s and co-anchored the noon news for four years during the mid–1980s. The city's most successful female broadcaster, however, is Jane Pauley. Pauley was anchoring the noon news at Channel 8 when NBC's Chicago TV station hired her in 1975. By 1977 she was a co-host on NBC's "Today" show.

Female anchors on weekends became quite common by the 1970s, but it was the 1980s before they appeared in prime time anchor slots. The transition was made a little easier because most local newscasts by then had two anchors. In the 1970s that meant two males. By the 1990s all major newscasts had male-female anchor combinations. In addition, women have moved into another vital newsroom slot, that of news producers who make day-to-day judgments on news content.

While broadcasting has a reputation as a career where people frequently change jobs, those who come to central Indiana to work in the industry tend to stay. Employment rosters at the local stations are filled with examples, including many who are on the air. Howard Caldwell, who retired in 1994, had been with Channel 6 news since 1959. Mike Ahern has anchored Channel 8's news since 1967 and was in radio in the city before that. Retired Channel 8 weather reporter Stan Wood worked in the market more than 30 years. Channel 13 sports director Don Hein and weather reporter Bob Gregory each have been with that station more than 20 years. Channel 13 news anchor Tom Cochrun also has worked in the city more than 20 years, in both radio and television. Fred Heckman headed WIBC Radio's news department for more than 30 years before his retirement in 1993.

Radio and television have informed and entertained the people of Indianapolis for almost 75 years, and as the industry has grown it also has changed. Radio no longer features programs and network series. That format has moved to television. Today radio uses specialized music formulas to appeal to particular segments of listeners, though news and talk programming has become common on the AM band. Television continues to serve large audiences with programs provided primarily by the broadcast networks, while the independent stations still rely on syndicated fare and movies. However, the television audience also has become more splintered in recent years as cable has offered viewers additional choices.

The real growth period of Indianapolis broadcasting has been very short. In just the last 45 years radio has expanded from four AM stations to more than 20 outlets on both the AM and FM bands. Television has developed from one fledgling facility to more than ten stations and two cable systems. Yet, ownership of the city's electronic media remains mostly outside the state. None of the five major commercial TV stations in the city is owned by an Indiana company, and both cable systems have headquarters out of state. Only three of the top ten radio stations are owned locally.

Future developments in radio, television, and cable will center around changes in technology and regulation. Fiber optics, high definition television, and digital radio are just three terms likely to become more familiar in years to come. What began in this city as an unsuccessful venture for Francis Hamilton continues to grow as an integral part of people's daily lives.

See also: BROADCASTING CONTROVERSIES; BROADCASTING, EDUCATIONAL AND PUBLIC; NEWS BROADCASTING; SPORTS BROADCASTING; and individual names and stations.

BUILT ENVIRONMENT

Elizabeth Brand Monroe

In 1888 a supplement to *Harper's Weekly* featured Indianapolis as "a solid, pushing city" and the home of presidential candidate Benjamin Harrison. The author of the article enthused over the new State House, civic auditorium, and Union Terminal and commended the city's residents for their "wide, well-shaded streets" whose "restful, home-like appearance" made Indianapolis more pleasant than larger cities. Adjacent to "practically inexhaustible" natural gas fields and with the second largest railroad center in the country, Indianapolis, according to the author, could become a large manufacturing city—"there is no question about the growth of the Hoosier capital."

Evidence of future greatness had not always been apparent. Settler John Nowland described his family's first home as a log cabin, 18 by 20 feet, with a dirt floor and a large fireplace at one end capable of taking ten-foot logs. Cabins served as both residences and places of business. John McCormick kept the first Indianapolis tavern at his cabin, while John Shunk manufactured hats at his and George Pogue, the first blacksmith, made ironwork. Isaac Wilson built the first gristmill at Fall Creek and located his family in a cabin nearby.

Changes came quickly. In 1821 surveyors Elias P. Fordham and Alexander Ralston laid out streets and lots for the new capital city. This Mile Square plan provided 100 12–lot blocks bounded by broad streets in a grid pattern. A central circular block and four diagonal streets overlay the grid and created a formal focus for the small knoll on which the governor's house was to be built. Balanced statehouse and courthouse squares, marketplaces, and blocks "reserved for religious purposes" completed the design. As streets were cleared and lots sold new construction transformed "a boundless contiguity of shade" into the makings of a tidy village.

Of course it was a village of the 1820s, without paved streets, sidewalks, or other public amenities. But by late 1825 its 500 citizens could boast a post office, several churches, a school, gristmill, brickyard, two sawmills, several shops, seven taverns, and a new courthouse in which the state legislature would meet until the completion of the new State House in 1835. Substantial frame and brick buildings rose in the area between the courthouse and State House squares. New

---

Elizabeth Brand Monroe is Assistant Professor of History at Indiana University–Purdue University, Indianapolis.

roads—the Michigan Road, connecting settlements along Lake Michigan through Indianapolis to Madison on the Ohio River, and the National Road, running east-west to connect the capitals of midwestern states to Washington, D.C.—brought stage and freight lines and new commerce. In 1836 the legislature authorized a Central Canal which would pass along the town's western edge.

With these new transportation routes parts of the town began to differentiate based on use. By the late 1830s travelers along Washington Street passed mercantile establishments and hotels. Near White River and the new canal visitors could see lumber, grist, and textile mills. Artisans continued to work in their homes, which were scattered about town, but some townsfolk began to move to new residential areas in the eastern half of Indianapolis. The center of town had become sufficiently congested that governors' families refused to live in the official residence on the Circle.

By 1850 state pride and responsibility had brought a city charter and three grand buildings to this community of 8,000. In the 1840s the legislature appropriated funds for asylums for the deaf and dumb (opened 1850) and blind (opened 1853) and a hospital for the insane (opened 1848). The original town plat had provided space for the State House, but the new state institutions had to be located outside the perimeter of the original Mile Square. The Asylum for the Blind was just to the north. This imposing four-story classical building on a raised basement loomed over all other Indianapolis structures, and its south lantern served as the vantage point of J. T. Palmatary's 1854 bird's-eye view of the city. That illustration also confirmed the size and scale of the Asylum for the Deaf and Dumb, located east of the city just south of Washington Street, and the Hospital for the Insane, two miles west of White River. These monumental, three-and-a-half-story classical buildings on raised basements with domes, extended wings, galleries, and pavilions dwarfed other Indianapolis buildings. They also maintained the prominence of state government in the city's growth.

In the foreground of Palmatary's view Indianapolis appeared to be a city of scattered one- and two-story detached brick and frame residences shaded by trees set in large fenced yards with appropriate outbuildings to the rear. In the background spires of the city's churches, the lanterns of Bates' and Little's hotels, and the dome of the new Odd Fellows Hall defined the area soon to be called "downtown." On the southern horizon and to the west brick chimneys of the city's industries and the cupola of the new 400–foot Union Terminal marked the industrial fringe.

Palmatary also provided vignettes of Washington Street between Illinois and Delaware streets and individual illustrations of churches and industrial buildings, as well as the courthouse and State House. Washington Street had narrow two- and three-story brick commercial buildings, many with canopies overhanging the street. Trade signs in front of these buildings and studies of Indianapolis in the 1850s indicated that many merchants had begun to specialize in dry goods, groceries, or hardware. Only three larger buildings (two hotels and the Odd Fellows Hall) broke this panorama on the north side of the street. The south side contained several one-story frame shops as well as the imposing, classical Indianapolis branch of the State Bank of Indiana. Palmatary also showed individual drawings of the recently built Little's and Bates' hotels, large three-story structures which occupied important corners at Washington and Alabama and Washington and Illinois streets.

Views of Indianapolis churches showed relatively small-scale auditoria in brick or frame built above raised basements with central entrances at the head of broad stairs. To this basic form the members of First Presbyterian Church, Second Presbyterian Church, Roberts Chapel, the Methodist Church, the German Lutheran Church, and the Baptist Church applied a classical temple design usually with spire, modeled more or less on the popular 18th-century St. Martin-in-the-Fields in London. But at St. John Catholic Church, Fourth Presbyterian Church, and the Christian Church in Indianapolis the outer garb of the buildings was in the new Gothic style with pinnacles, crockets, and towers associated with New York architects Richard Upjohn and Ithiel Town. The Episcopal Church combined elements of both styles with a classical temple design and Gothic windows.

Palmatary's illustrations and Christian Schrader's sketches showed industries still scattered about the city, but many had located near the new rail lines on the south and the canal and river on the west. For example Robert Underhill built his Steam Foundry in 1835 on Pennsylvania Street near Vermont. Its long, one-story brick building with large square stack and outlying frame buildings were replaced in the 1860s by the new Second Presbyterian Church. Underhill had relocated to larger quarters on South Pennsylvania Street in the early 1850s. William Sheets opened his two-story frame paper mill near the intersection of Market and West streets at the lock of the new canal. During the 1840s it was the largest manufacturer of print paper in Indiana. Just across the waterway stood a large brick flour mill. Farther west between the canal and the river was the four-and-one-half story Geisendorff Woolen Mill.

But the most impressive building in the Palmatary and Schrader illustrations was the Union Terminal of 1853. This enormous train shed and passenger depot was 420 feet long by 200 feet wide and could service five trains and their passengers at once. A monitor ran the entire length of the roof, furnishing light to the interior and ventilating the space. Built along Louisiana Street three blocks south of Washington Street, the station became the magnet for industrial development in Indianapolis. Soon rail lines approaching the city from every direction swept around the outer limits of the built-up area to stop at the new building. While the earliest railroads had already built their individual terminals near the southern edge of the city, these were soon demoted to freight depots; all passenger trains departed from the Union Terminal. During the early 1850s Indianapolis gained a "railroad car factory, several saw and grist mills, three planing mills, two woolen factories and carding machines, a large foundry, four chair and cabinet factories, three carriage and wagon factories, a bell and brass foundry, two large slaughter houses, and other establishments."

The city also doubled its population; the 1860 census reported 18,611 residents in the Hoosier capital. The following two decades saw the population quadruple. The 1860s and 1870s found the city trying to house its new citizens as well as improve their quality of life. New subdivisions expanded the geographical area of the city, public and private utilities provided "modern" conveniences, parks offered recreation, and new industries associated with the military buildup of the Civil War remained after the conflict ended.

An 1876 map of Marion County revealed that additions had doubled the platted area around the Mile Square and had sprinkled Center Township with new subdivisions. While the outlying townships remained rural, small villages like New Augusta, Oaklandon, Cumberland, Southport, and Bridgeport had developed at stations along the rail lines about eight to ten miles from the Union Terminal. Residential areas of the city had expanded north and east. To the east Irvington offered prosperous citizens meandering streets in a sylvan park, and Woodruff Place provided landscaped boulevards, fountains, and statuary. What is now the near north side, then the outer fringes of northern settlement, had developed as far as 14th Street. High-style Second Empire houses such as the Morris-Butler House on Park Avenue represented the tastes of affluent

Nineteenth-century homes on New York Street between West Street and the Central Canal. [Indiana Historical Society, #C5899]

residents. On the east and southeast edges of the downtown the areas now known as Lockerbie Square and Fletcher Place contained both small cottages and more substantial dwellings. To the south of the Mile Square small cottages clustered near factories. No settlements were shown west of White River.

City improvements made life in Indianapolis safer and more pleasant. By 1860 many downtown streets were illuminated by gas lamps; gaslights then moved indoors, and by the 1870s new houses were equipped with gaslines for lighting. In 1871 the Water Works Company began supplying piped water to some areas of the city. About the same time a rudimentary sewer system began to replace the at-grade wooden gutters and culverts laid in the early 19th century that spilled their malodorous contents into the river. By the end of the decade the first telephone exchange had been established. Electric service did not come to the city until the 1890s, but small generators powered individual plants earlier. Other public services that had more obvious effects on the growth of Indianapolis included the introduction of a street railway system in the 1860s. A fire tower on the roof of the Glenn Block served as an observation post as well as the location of the city's fire bell.

But even the diligence of fire companies, horse-drawn steam-powered pumpers, and the advent of the city water works could not prevent the devastation of fires. The most extensive ones occurred in the downtown business and industrial areas. Fires destroyed whole blocks of Pennsylvania and Meridian streets in the late 19th century. As these areas were rebuilt new guidelines required "fireproof" construction techniques, and later standpipes and watertowers.

While fires forced the replacement of some buildings, others in the downtown area fell before pressure to make better use of valuable property near the railroads. Washington Street and its immediate neighborhood remained commercial, but during the 1860s and 1870s in the blocks between the retail district and Union Terminal wholesalers built new fireproof warehouses. Three- and four-story brick buildings had cast iron interior structural members and cast iron storefronts in a wide variety of decorative styles. The Morrison Block at 47–49 South Meridian Street and the Holland and Ostermeyer Building at 29 Maryland Street were typical of this era.

Indianapolis industries started during the Civil War era also changed the face of the city. Herman Sturm, a German immigrant, helped create a munitions plant that operated for a time on the grounds of the State House before moving to a site one and a half miles east of the city. Production at the new plant became so important to the war effort that the War Department opened a U.S. Arsenal on an adjacent 76–acre tract. Now the site of Arsenal Technical High School, the parklike Arsenal with its seven handsome buildings and drives became a leisure destination during the summer months.

Kingan and Company opened in 1863, burned in 1865, and was immediately rebuilt. Located next to the White River with buildings on both sides of the Indianapolis and St. Louis Railroad connected by tunnels under the tracks, Kingan's was one of the largest meat-packing plants in the world. Its extensive multi-story brick buildings housed the first refrigerating units in the meat-packing industry: fans and grates blew cold air over meat stored in the plant's basements. By the late 1870s railroad congestion and the need for larger stockyards brought a city bond issue to help private investors cover costs for the Belt Line Railroad providing a common right-of-way and track around Indianapolis and an enlarged stockyards southwest of the city.

This expansion of railyards and industry near the White River south of the city threatened one of Indianapolis' oldest landmarks—the city cemetery. Beginning as a convenient unclaimed site in the early 1820s, over the years purchases and donations of land had turned the area between the Vandalia Railroad, Kentucky Avenue, and the river into a public cemetery. Attempts had been made over the years to beautify the site by planting evergreens, but by the 1860s erosion of some of the grounds by the river and crowding caused by Civil War interments spurred calls for a new location. In 1863 a group of prominent citizens formed the Association of Crown Hill and purchased the Williams farm and adjacent tracts northwest of the city. "Crown Hill" was the highest point near the city. The association hired landscape architect John Chislett to design a picturesque park in the manner of Mount Auburn Cemetery in Boston. Many of the burials at the city cemetery were reinterred at Crown Hill, which soon became a pastoral retreat for young couples, families, and tourists. Within a decade streetcar lines ran to the popular Crown Hill stop.

Extension of the street railways helped determine where new residential areas would develop. By 1890 Indianapolis had a population of over 100,000, almost six times the 1860 figure. Many new residents lived in the Mile Square where housing became denser. Lots from the 1820s were subdivided and working class people, with the help of Indianapolis' 94 building associations, built cottages in areas like Cottage Home and Ransom Place. More prosperous citizens built in newly created subdivisions along the streetcar lines.

Houses both small and large exhibited the late 19th century penchant for diversity in style, material, and color. Gone was the "goods-box" architecture of white, square houses with no ornament or variety. In their place houses of the 1880s had porches, pillars, bay windows, colorful paint, and ornamental woodwork. In adopting new color schemes and materials Indianapolis homebuilders followed design trends of the East Coast, but in siting their homes Hoosier residents maintained the older pattern of a single-family residence surrounded by its own fenced yard, a tradition lost in many densely populated eastern cities. According to the author of the 1888 *Harper's Weekly* article, "a fair specimen of the most comfortable houses in the city" was Benjamin Harrison's home on North Delaware Street.

Limestone became the signature building material of the late 19th century in Indianapolis. Cast iron had served both structural and decorative purposes during the Civil War era, but a building faced in limestone created a much grander impression. The Bals-Wocher House (951 North Delaware), Charles Kuhn House (340 West Michigan), and Propylaeum (1410 North Delaware) featured limestone details like window lintels and sills, beltcourses, and porch columns. Limestone also accented First Lutheran Church, St. John Catholic Church, New York Street United Methodist Church, and Central Avenue United Methodist Church, and completely sheathed the Roberts Park Church.

New housing developments north of the Mile Square led to new neighborhood churches (for example the Central Avenue United Methodist Church). In addition, older congregations built new, larger buildings several of which clustered in the two or three blocks north of New York Street. While the pull of the northern suburbs had begun to draw churches in that direction, the commercial district had not yet overrun the center of the city. The financial panic of the early 1870s slowed commercial growth, and when established businesses grew they were as likely to expand upward as outward. By the late 19th century businesses on Washington Street and surrounding blocks had risen to five and six stories.

Public buildings expanded horizontally as well as vertically. The new State House of 1888 covered both the original city block dedicated to state government and the block to the north that had formerly contained the western market. The dome and entrance to this enormous limestone seat of government were now centered on Market Street to the east. A new brick meat market and Tomlinson Hall, a combination civic auditorium and produce market built of brick and trimmed in limestone, rose on the eastern market block. Just to the south the cupola atop the dome of the 1876 limestone Marion County Courthouse stopped 40 feet short of the State House's 234 feet. What the courthouse lacked in height it made up for in its grand Second Empire design.

Civic buildings were not the only "public" palaces of Indianapolis in the late 19th century. The original Union Terminal was replaced in 1888 by the brick and granite Romanesque revival Union Station. Its three-story barrel vault waiting area became a favorite meeting place, and its ten-story clock tower was visible to anyone in the warehouse district. Another frequent rendezvous was the new English's Opera House and Hotel on the northwest quadrant of the Circle. Built in 1880 and 1884 and extended in 1896, this four-story curved complex had short towers above its rounded corners. Its first story glass storefronts were shaded from the summer sun by the new retractable canvas awnings that appeared at the end of the century. The Bates House modernized to keep pace with English's, and the Spencer House on Illinois Street near Union Station advertised that it was "the only hotel in the city thoroughly equipped with fire escapes."

One block west of English's Hotel Indianapolis residents could visit the Cyclorama, a large windowless drum-shaped building lit by a circular skylight. Inside, a 400–foot painting of the battle of Atlanta (followed in later years by "Gettysburg" and "Jerusalem") surrounded visitors. But views of battles and biblical cities could not hold Hoosiers' attention for long. By 1904 the Cyclo-

English's Hotel and Opera House and the Traction Terminal are visible on the right
in this 1910 view of West Market Street, taken from Monument Circle
looking toward the State House. [Indiana Historical Society,
Bass Collection, #20055]

rama building had been replaced by the new train shed of the Indianapolis Traction and Terminal
Company. The nine-track shed could handle 400 cars daily and serviced an electric interurban
rail system that radiated from the capital city. An adjacent nine-story building housed the headquarters of the traction line as well as other businesses.

The interurban lines and suburban streetcar lines changed the shape of the city. In 1910 the
census reported over 233,000 residents, many of whom lived outside the Mile Square, although
still largely in Center Township. Interurbans and streetcars allowed commuters to move beyond
the comfortable two-mile radius of pedestrian travel. Streetcar routes extended five miles north
and south of the terminal while the interurbans stretched into neighboring counties and beyond.

New housing spread similar tentacles. At streetcar stops the apartment building appeared.
Well into the 1890s Indianapolis was still a city of single-family residences. But population pressures demanded more efficient use of space for housing individuals of moderate means. Apartments of the early 20th century were the height of style and located in prestigious areas alongside
large homes and prosperous businesses. (The poor usually lived in older buildings converted to
boarding houses or in small cottages adjacent to the factories where they worked.) Early apartments in the immediate downtown area could rise many stories (Blacherne Apartments, 1895,
7 stories; Savoy Apartments, 1898, 6 stories); further removed from the downtown, low-rise

apartments predominated (St. Clair Apartments, 1899, 3 stories; Coulter Flats, 1907, 3 stories; Buckingham Apartments, 1910, 3 stories), particularly where Maple Road (now 38th Street) crossed the streetcar lines.

Skeletal metal construction, efficient elevators, widespread use of telephones, electric light, and central heating systems allowed professional men, financial and insurance businesses, and retailers to consolidate their offices and stores in high-rise buildings. In the late 19th and early 20th centuries Indianapolis designers took advantage of the new technologies in the Majestic Building (1896, 10 stories), Indianapolis News Building (1897, 10 stories), L. S. Ayres Department Store (1905, 8 stories), William H. Block Department Store (1910, 8 stories), Hume-Mansur Building (1911, 10 stories), Merchants Bank Building (1913, 17 stories), and Fletcher Trust Building (1915, 15 stories).

The scale of the new buildings raised new demands for decoration. Designers and owners wanted inexpensive, maintenance free, and lightweight materials. Terra cotta, a ceramic material that could be molded in intricate patterns, met these needs. Initially terra cotta blocks of cartouches and medallions provided relief in brick walls (for example, the Diener Building); later it sheathed whole facades (William H. Block and Company, Hume-Mansur Building). Terra cotta also played an important role in several of the new entertainment facilities in Indianapolis. The Athenaeum (1898) had cartouches of this material. The Murat Temple (1909) also featured terra cotta decoration, and the facade of the Circle Theatre (1916), the first movie house in Indianapolis, was completely sheathed in it.

Early 20th century skyscrapers soon eclipsed the new centerpiece of Indianapolis. The Indiana State Soldiers and Sailors Monument was dedicated in 1902 to Indiana men who had served their nation during the Civil War. The monument, centered in the old Circle Park, consisted of a 248–foot limestone obelisk crowned by a bronze "Victory" and surrounded by statuary, pools, fountains, and steps. While the monument was no longer the highest building in the city after 1913, it reoriented business and professional development away from the Washington Street corridor northward toward the center of the old Mile Square.

Other civic improvements of the early 20th century reflected the city's increasing size and its new ability, granted by the 1891 charter, to invest in infrastructure. The city purchased what were to become Riverside and Brookside parks and made $20 million in street improvements. A new $1 million levee controlled the White River after the 1913 flood, and Pogue's Run was enclosed. George Kessler created landscaped drives along White River, Fall Creek, and Pleasant Run. Garfield Park was improved with a pagoda, greenhouse, bridges, and sunken gardens. The monumental Indianapolis Public Library (1916) on St. Clair Street demonstrated the city's interest in its reading public. Six branch libraries (for example Riverside Branch No. 1) funded by Andrew Carnegie brought services to scattered neighborhoods.

The new charter increased the powers of local government and raised the issue of adequate facilities for conducting the city's business. Since its earliest charter in the 1840s Indianapolis had no permanent seat but had operated from temporary quarters in a variety of buildings. In 1909 this condition ended with the opening of the new monumental City Hall one block north of the city market and civic auditorium.

At the same time the state began to take an increased interest in the health of Indianapolis residents. The old city hospital had been rebuilt along "modern" lines in the 1870s, but was located in a swampy area near where Indiana Avenue crossed Fall Creek. The swamps were drained in the early 20th century and the state allocated funds for Long Hospital, located about four blocks south and dedicated in 1914 as the teaching center for Indiana University's medical school. In 1919 Emerson Hall, a lecture hall and classroom building, opened.

Federal activity in Indianapolis would also change the shape of the city. In 1903 Congress authorized the establishment of Fort Benjamin Harrison. Initial construction on the installation, about seven miles from downtown, was completed in 1908 when the Tenth Infantry Regiment moved to the site. Brick headquarters, barracks, officers' quarters, hospital, stables, and other support buildings clustered near the intersection of Post Road and the extension of what would become 56th Street.

At the same time the Army built Fort Benjamin Harrison, the U.S. Court House and Post Office at Meridian and Ohio streets was under construction. This limestone Beaux-Arts building inspired public architecture in Indianapolis for the next four decades. Its grand scale and classical details set the tone for what was to become the Indiana World War Memorial Plaza, a five-block area to the immediate north. In 1920 these blocks were dedicated to veterans of World War I after the city successfully lobbied the American Legion to locate its national headquarters in Indianapolis. The plan called for removing most buildings from the designated area, leaving only the classical buildings—the public library and federal building—at each end. New buildings would include a large memorial hall, two auxiliary buildings, a cenotaph, obelisk, and mall. Work began in 1925 on the west auxiliary building and in 1926 on the memorial building, but the latter was not completed until 1965. Complementing the scale and materials of the War Memorial, the 330–foot-long, 212–foot-high Indianapolis Scottish Rite Cathedral (1929) lined the western edge of the plaza.

The War Memorial Plaza reshaped the city, for by the 1920s the other potential grand space around the Soldiers and Sailors Monument was lost in the canyon created by new buildings on Monument Circle. The first of these, the Guaranty Building of 1923, conformed to the recently passed city ordinance controlling height around the Circle. The Test Building, an interesting combination of offices and parking structure, also rose to nine stories. But the last downtown highrise of the 1920s, the Circle Tower, took advantage of the setback provisions of the ordinance, and above the ninth story climbed an additional five stories, each stepped back from the one beneath. A two-story tower topped the limestone design.

The only other additions to the pre–World War II Indianapolis skyline developed 25 blocks to the north along Meridian Street. At Fall Creek Parkway the ten-story Marott Hotel opened in 1927, and two years later the ten-story Admiral Apartments opened four blocks beyond. Both buildings made use of new brick colors and textures.

The Admiral and the Circle Tower Building shared the Art Deco massing and details of the "machine age." Another contemporary Art Deco design, the Coca-Cola Building on Massachusetts Avenue, demonstrated how the sleek new styling (this time executed in white terra cotta) enhanced the hygienic image of the spotless bottling plant. A mile and a half north of the Admiral, Jordan Hall, a very large limestone classroom building of the recently relocated Butler University, represented an unusual combination of Art Deco and Gothic form and details. A year later in 1928 the new brick Butler Fieldhouse provided seats for 15,000 avid basketball fans. It, too, bore Art Deco details. However, the smaller brick Coliseum at the State Fairgrounds, completed in 1939 as a Public Works Administration project, had more lavish deco designs in its limestone accents.

While the classical reigned at the War Memorial Plaza and Art Deco in some high-rise buildings and sports facilities, the new industries of Indianapolis of the first four decades of the 20th century occupied more utilitarian structures that took advantage of the properties of concrete.

The early structures of the Big Four railyards in Beech Grove, built about 1902, were brick, but the neighboring multi-story grain elevators were reinforced poured concrete. Some of the concrete grain elevators between West Street and the White River in downtown Indianapolis dated from soon after the merger of the Evans Milling Company and the Acme Milling Company in 1909. Eight years later the Diamond Chain Manufacturing Company, just south of Acme-Evans, built a four-story plant using reinforced concrete posts and beams and the recently developed concrete floor slab. A similar system formed the new tire and rubber plant on South East Street. Several blocks west, Eli Lilly and Company's administration, research, and manufacturing buildings of the early 20th century also used the new systems, as did the International Harvester plant of the late 1930s.

The industry to make the greatest impact on the city was automobile manufacture. The four-story Cole Motor Car Company and Stutz Motor Car Company plants spread over entire in-town blocks of the city. Of typical concrete frame construction with large industrial windows and brick spandrels, the Stutz building in addition sported terra cotta medallions with the letter "S". Related industries in Indianapolis included the Wheeler-Schebler Carburetor Company, Prest-O-Lite (headlights) Company, Allison Engine Company, and plants for Marmon, Duesenberg, and over 50 other automobiles.

In addition to factories for parts and assembly, the industry also spawned a new building type—the automobile showroom. Usually one story, with large show windows facing the street and offices and garage bays to the rear, showroom buildings soon lined the 800 to 1400 blocks of Meridian Street, Illinois Street, and Capitol Avenue. Indianapolis' auto magnates also created for the city "the greatest spectacle in racing" whose oval track soon spread over more than a half-mile-square area and led to the development of a new town, Speedway.

But the greatest effect of the automobile on Indianapolis was the same as that felt elsewhere—the impact of widespread car ownership. A luxury in the 1900s and 1910s, by the 1920s many middle class families had a car. Traffic led to the widening and paving of city streets, creation of designated parking areas and structures, and development of new building types for fuel, service, food, and lodging. Gasoline stations, restaurants, and auto courts soon lined the new U.S. highway system, luring customers by distinctive lighted signage. Even the downtown skyscrapers that had formerly identified themselves with painted signs on secondary walls (the ghosts of some remain today) resorted to new, bright roof-top lights.

Storage of automobiles led to detached garages at home and multi-level parking structures near downtown businesses. By the 1930s newer neighborhood shops built farther out in developing suburbs placed adjoining stores along the edge of small nose-in parking lots, thereby doubling the number of conveniently located parking spaces. And of course the car extended the distance of the reasonable commute and allowed the suburban resident to move away from the interurban and streetcar lines.

The automobile ultimately destroyed other forms of transportation, but not before independent towns had developed near streetcar stops and interurban stations. Clusters of shops, schools, churches, and movie theaters formed the cores of Broad Ripple, Fountain Square, Beech Grove, Haughville, and University Heights with housing radiating from these services. During the first half of the century Indianapolis annexed many of these communities, but their distinctive street patterns made their mark on the landscape.

The world wars also had an effect on the city's built environment. Health care for veterans brought Indianapolis a new hospital facility along Cold Spring Road in 1932. Developed from stock Veterans Administration plans, the colonial revival hospital "campus" gave permanently disabled veterans a parklike home and allowed as well for rehabilitation and temporary treatment.

Other hospitals also enlarged and expanded. The city constructed the yellow brick Bryce and Ott buildings at 10th Street and Indiana Avenue in the mid–1920s to serve as the main buildings of the new municipal hospital. A decade later the Flower Mission Memorial Hospital was built one block west. The William H. Coleman Hospital, adjacent to Long Hospital four blocks to the south of the City Hospital, provided medical services for women in Indianapolis; one block west the Ball Residence for Nurses opened; to the south the new Dental School began classes; Riley Hospital for Children rose to the north; and farther to the west the Indiana Rotary Convalescent Home offered long-term care.

The redevelopment of this 20–block area as a large public health care facility destroyed many small houses built in the late 19th century and completely changed the scale of this end of the downtown. Just to the east, slum housing was torn down to make way for Lockefield Gardens (1937), one of the nation's earliest attempts at public housing. Again changing scale (and eliminating much of the historic street pattern), the Public Works Administration built a complex of 23 three- and four-story tan and brown brick apartment buildings around a landscaped mall.

Almost 30 years later the next attempt at residential urban renewal removed low-income housing and businesses and replaced them with the 30–story Riley Towers, intended as a large complex of apartments and stores, although the stores were never built. To appeal to the middle class rental market the developers resorted to large expanses of glass and cantilevered balconies, popular features of new apartments in Chicago and major East Coast cities. Five years later in 1968 the first section of the John J. Barton Apartments opened as new housing for the elderly. The high-rise Barton building of concrete shear-wall construction had blind north and south end walls that expanded at the upper six stories. Raised above East Street by means of pylons, the long four-story building, at right angles to its partner, shares similar concrete details.

Two other contemporary high-rise apartments were built near the intersection of 38th and Meridian streets. Both featured the popular glass walls with contrasting concrete columns and balconies. They also represented the farthest extent of high-rise housing units in Indianapolis. Extending north beyond them the prime residential areas contained the two-story houses of the interwar years.

In post–World War II Indianapolis, most families wanted their own one-story "modern" house. Ranch house subdivisions developed north and west of White River, along Allisonville Road and east to Fort Benjamin Harrison, along east and west Washington Street about four miles from the city center, and along the major southern arteries. The typical development subdivided farmland bounded by through streets that continued the downtown grid. Subdivision streets, however, did not continue the grid but interrupted it with meandering "ways," "drives," and "crescents." These patterns limited access, allowed for cohesive design, and eliminated through traffic.

The typical ranch house of the 1950s had three bedrooms, open-plan living room, dining room, and entrance hall, eat-in kitchen, and one bath. More expensive versions, as well as those built in the 1960s and 1970s, had more bedrooms, more baths, walk-in closets, and recreation or family rooms. Later models also had attached garages of one and later two bays. While the plans of all ranch houses were similar, exterior materials varied from asbestos and masonite siding on the least expensive to brick and limestone veneer on the most expensive. Other variations included shutters, porches, and reversed plans that created mirror-image houses. And of course the easiest means of making personal statements in areas of identical housing were with paint colors and landscaping.

Another popular postwar housing choice was the two- or three-story garden apartment. Aimed at the single members and young couples of the middle class, it offered suburban-like greenspace and ease of parking. At The Meadows at 38th Street and Keystone Avenue, 600 garden apartments were built beside a shopping center and office park. Other garden units went up near Fort Benjamin Harrison as the Army expanded its finance center in 1954, greatly increasing nearby housing needs.

The greatest postwar change in the built environment of Indianapolis was the construction of the interstate highway system. Four-lane, limited-access, elevated highways snaking through the city destroyed blocks of buildings (and displaced their residents), truncated neighborhoods, and interrupted surface traffic flow. At their interchanges they created new "towns" just as the railroads had done a century before. A hamlet into the postwar era, Castleton burgeoned as a shopping metropolis. Park 100 extended between two interchanges in the northwest quadrant of I-465. And at the Keystone Avenue interchange both shopping and offices developed at "the crossing."

Earlier postwar commercial developments within the city included the strip shopping center of anchor grocery and drug stores and intervening hardware stores, beauty salons, and dry cleaners, usually sited on large corner lots of major through streets. Stores formed an L-shape on the rear perimeter of the lot or paralleled the street, and parking spaces filled the space between.

In 1958 the mall arrived in Indianapolis when Glendale opened to shoppers. Unlike the strip shopping center that lined the street, the mall centered itself in a vast parking area and faced inward to an enclosed plaza. Anchored by two or more department stores and lined with specialty shops and restaurants the mall attracted the suburban dweller who declined to make the long trip downtown to the stores on Washington Street. Within a few years new malls appeared—Lafayette Square, Castleton, Washington Square, and Greenwood. The downtown stores suffered the consequences. While Penney's built on the Circle in 1950, H. P. Wasson and Company remodeled in 1948, and L. S. Ayres and Company added space, by the 1970s the downtown stores were lucky to hold their own against sizable sales in their mall branches.

Downtown offices faced similar competition. Companies built their own mid-rise office buildings north along Meridian Street in the 1950s and 1960s. Offices lined Meridian from 16th Street to 22nd; between 30th and 40th streets insurance companies clustered. Downtown construction slowed and almost halted. Then in 1959 American Fletcher National Bank opened a new, glass curtain-wall office tower on the Circle. In 1964 Indianapolis Power and Light remodeled an existing building in the southeast quadrant of the Circle with new concrete aggregate panels. In the late 1960s Indiana National Bank began a 37–story headquarters that soon displaced the 1913 Merchants National Bank as the state's tallest building.

Local, state, and federal government also built new facilities downtown. In 1960 the State Office Building rose 13 stories to the west of the State House. A glass-wall skyscraper provided city and county offices and courtrooms. The main Post Office building spread over an entire block south of Union Station, and a new federal office building on pylons covered a block along the east side of War Memorial Plaza. Other facilities attempted to bring the public to downtown events. The Indiana Convention Center opened in 1972, Market Square Arena two years later.

Cultural institutions in Indianapolis launched their own construction programs. In the early 1970s the Indianapolis Museum of Art built much of its campus at 38th Street and Michigan

The Pyramids on the city's far north side have been nationally recognized as an outstanding example of modern architecture. [Indiana Historical Society. Photo by Kim Charles Ferrill]

Road. Pavilions named for generous benefactors were connected by a raised terrace in front of the limestone and glass Krannert Pavilion. The Children's Museum at 30th and Meridian streets opened its new multi-story brick building in 1976. Defying local tradition it turned its back on Indianapolis' premier street by placing the entry adjacent to the Illinois Street parking lot. The concrete panel Indianapolis Motor Speedway Museum opened in the track infield in 1975.

Educational facilities expanded to serve the waves of postwar baby boomers who sought college and professional degrees. IUPUI began to consolidate its facilities near the medical and dental schools along Michigan Street west of the downtown. To provide land for the new campus, another 16 blocks of slum housing were cleared. Butler University also expanded. In 1963 the enormous concrete and limestone Clowes Memorial Hall, seating 2,200 in its main auditorium, became the performing arts center of both the university and the city. Just the year before Irwin Library, a glass box with three levels of concrete arcade, created a light counterpoint across the entrance boulevard from the massive theater building. Twelve years later Gallahue Hall, at the 46th Street entrance, again returned to the signature limestone of Jordan and Clowes halls.But for the most part the materials of choice for large buildings in the postwar era were concrete and glass. The effect of either or both materials could become so distinctive as to serve as a company logo. An excellent example was the Pyramids built by the College Life Insurance Company of America in 1972. Three 11–story glass and concrete office buildings, located near the intersection of I-465 and Michigan Road, gave the area a nickname and provided a landmark to highway travelers.

By the early 1980s "interstate architecture" was also visible at the new interchanges where national fast-food and lodging chains built restaurants and motels. Styles and themes also identified another interchange cluster, the garden apartment complex. The northern edge of Marion County, both inside and outside the interstate loop, was soon lined with apartment complexes. A new variant was the condominium complex. The less expensive condos were hard to distinguish from apartments, but the more exclusive ones tended to resemble tightly packed housing enclaves behind landscaped walls.

Single-family housing developments continued the postwar tradition of meandering street patterns and adopted the enclave approach, but replaced the condominium wall with a landscaped earth berm. The berm provided privacy to lots on the grid-street perimeter and allowed builders to turn houses on these lots to face the subdivision drives and courts. But the houses of the 1980s and 1990s were no longer the one-story ranch; they rose to one and one-half stories. Rising land prices and the buying public's desire for less yard reduced lot size. At the same time higher construction costs required conversion of attics to livable floor space. The use and number of rooms remained the same from the postwar era, but smaller lots and the demand for two-car garages pushed at least two bedrooms and a bathroom to the second story. The most expensive new houses rose to two stories, included more bedroom and bathroom suites, added libraries and great rooms, and expanded to three- and four-car garages.

As the suburbs passed the county line, service areas and office parks expanded. While the Pyramid buildings made an architectural statement to all who passed by, other, less remarkable office buildings nestled in the College Park area. At the Keystone interchange, the original simple square building of 1975 was eclipsed in the mid–1980s by large curved silver mirror-glass and precast concrete skyscrapers.

The ideal location of Park 100 on a 300–acre site near the Chicago (I-65) exit from the I-465 loop led in the 1980s to the 1,000–acre expansion of the business park. Now stretching from the 73rd to the 86th Street exits, this enormous complex of low-rise multi-use buildings of independent design offered a progression of corporate building images. Other business and industrial centers that have expanded greatly since the 1970s include DowElanco, Park Fletcher, the Meridian Street corridor at I-465, and the first three interchanges of I-69.

In the late 1970s municipal authorities decided to refocus attention on the downtown, especially by using amateur sports as a magnet for its redevelopment. Market Square Arena was by then five years old and the Convention Center seven years old. A new, 61,000–seat inflated dome built adjacent to the Convention Center added to the latter's versatility and ultimately provided a home to the Indianapolis Colts. The Hoosier Dome helped spark a nearby civic building renaissance. Within a decade new improvements in the area included the Canal Walk, the Pan American Building and Plaza (which house two ice rinks and a 1,100–car underground parking structure), the tan dolomite and red sandstone Eiteljorg Museum of American Indian and Western Art, and a Convention Center expansion with second story ballroom and skywalks to the neighboring Hyatt Regency and Westin hotels.

These hotels as well as the nearby Embassy Suites in Claypool Court capitalized on the new sports and convention centers. Both the Hyatt (located in Merchants Plaza) and Embassy Suites include shopping malls with central courts that rise unobstructed for 19 stories and 12 stories respectively. The Hyatt also shares its block with an office tower. All three hotels return to the premise of recent architecture around the Indianapolis interstate system that shape and color should identify buildings for the public.

In the late 1970s, 1980s, and early 1990s Indianapolis also saw a rebirth of the downtown office tower. Indiana National Bank's tallest building record lasted only 12 years, being superseded in 1982 by the 38–story American United Life Insurance Company Building (AUL), itself superseded by the 51–story Bank One Tower in 1990. Although the AUL Building is no longer the highest in the city nor is its exterior material (limestone) unique, its architects chose to seek distinctiveness by means of shape. The tower with its severely clipped corners rises diagonally on its block to a flat limestone band which extends around the building until it is abruptly sliced off on the southeast elevation by a steep single-slope roof.

Soon after, in the late 1980s, architects for First Indiana Plaza (in three contrasting shades of granite), 300 North Meridian (dark brown granite), and Market Tower (gray and brown granite) resorted to rich color choice and alluded to the roof form of the War Memorial. But the most spectacular essay in form was the new Bank One Tower. Location also played a part since the building stands directly south of the War Memorial Plaza. From the vantage of any high point on North Meridian Street as far out as 131st Street, the stepped pyramidal roof of the gray granite tower with its twin antennas serves as a beacon for the new skyline.

Form, color, and visibility also determined the designs of the enlarged and reclad Lilly campus and the Farm Bureau Insurance building in the southeast quadrant of downtown Indianapolis. The latter opened its national headquarters in 1992 in a large five-story red brick office building with connected two story polygonal penthouses. The eye-catching color and form deserve close inspection as an excellent example of both environmental clean-up of an abandoned industrial site and as a clever (and economical) renovation of an existing structure.

The end served in the Farm Bureau design—reuse and adaptation of the existing built environment for contemporary needs—has been fundamental to many recent projects. For the past 25 years Indianapolis residents, civic leaders, and developers have actively promoted the city's architectural heritage. Beginning with individual efforts to preserve residences in Lockerbie Square, the Old Northside, and along North Meridian Street, local preservationists have encouraged the establishment of historic districts with architectural review guidelines. By the late 1970s what had once been a trickle of single-family residence and house museum restorations had become a steady stream of tax-incentive renovations of apartments, stores, and offices. Buildings in the wholesale district such as Union Station, apartment blocks such as Lockefield Gardens and Real Silk Lofts, and stores along Massachusetts Avenue and in Lockerbie Market Place were rehabilitated to federal standards.

Public restoration projects encouraged these private efforts by enhancing the downtown in general. At the City Market combined restoration of the landmark building with sensitive additions showed developers that not every project had to create a museum. During the 1980s the Circle Theatre, Indiana Theatre, and Walker Theatre restorations provided needed space for the symphony, repertory theater, and other performing arts organizations in auditoria that had fallen into disuse. A similar effort is now underway at the Athenaeum.

Restoration of the State House and the decision to build a new government center to the west emphasized Hoosiers' respect for their civic heritage. As executed, the new limestone State Office Building and the reclad old one spread over parts of four former city blocks and create grand colonnades receding from the State House toward White River. A more sentimental public project has restored the Soldiers and Sailors Monument to its former glory after years of neglect.

The built environment of Indianapolis in early 1994 offers three images—readily identifiable mega-buildings of distinctive color and form; smaller, human-scale buildings of the city's first

150 years; and the prospect that a monumental urban concourse will revitalize downtown shopping. If the Circle Centre Mall developers achieve their goal, the prospect will link the architecture of the past to the future of the city.

See also: CITY PLANNING; COMMERCE AND INDUSTRY, ARCHITECTURAL AND SPATIAL CHARACTERISTICS OF; INFRASTRUCTURE (PUBLIC UTILITIES); LANDSCAPE DESIGN; LOST INDIANAPOLIS; MULTI-FAMILY RESIDENTIAL ARCHITECTURE; RELIGIOUS ARCHITECTURE; SINGLE-FAMILY RESIDENTIAL ARCHITECTURE; and individual names, buildings, and organizations.

CULTURAL INSTITUTIONS

David G. Vanderstel

When it was established in 1821 to become the seat of state government in 1825, Indianapolis was little more than an isolated frontier village. There were occasional festivities, such as Fourth of July celebrations, but most of the settlement's civic energy was tied to the economy. Even the earliest signs of progress, the first newspapers—the *Indianapolis Gazette* (1822) and the *Western Censor & Emigrants Guide* (1823)—were given over primarily to government business and economic promotion. Yet the town's founders anticipated greater things to come from the "city of Indiana," believing that it would attract all manner of enterprising people.

Growing to approximately 1,900 inhabitants by 1830 and 2,700 by 1840, Indianapolis became a crossroads for peoples and cultures from most parts of the young republic, especially the Upland South and the Old Northwest. That intermingling produced a conflict of cultures that continued for many decades. While individuals of a southern rural background were more numerous in the capital, settlers from the East and New England (a distinct minority) controlled the reins of civic and cultural leadership. Encouraged to "mingle freely and unsuspiciously with [their] neighbors [and] bring up their habits, by successful example, to the New England standard," they were influenced by a sense of regional superiority and by New England Protestantism, which preached civilization and Christianity to save the West—and ultimately the nation—from barbarism and license.

Many Easterners perceived their roles as critical to the building of the new community. Consequently, they worked to ensure that Indiana's capital possessed a certain moral and cultural character supported by appropriate institutions. Men such as James Blake, Isaac Coe, Calvin Fletcher, and Samuel Merrill became involved in all forms of civic and reform activities, constituting an informal network that shaped much of the capital's character and affected its daily life.

Cultural tensions, evident from the town's founding, produced undercurrents in society that affected popular attitudes toward established institutions. Easterners generally believed Hoosiers to be from "among the lower class of people in the South." Sarah Fletcher, the Kentucky-born wife of Calvin Fletcher who had recently moved to Indianapolis, attended a quilting party in January,

David G. Vanderstel is Assistant Editor of the *Encyclopedia of Indianapolis* and Adjunct Assistant Professor of History at Indiana University–Purdue University, Indianapolis.

1822, where she encountered "several ladys who were forrmaly from Kentucky & I think in their descorse a mong the Females they use a gradeal of vulgarity." Easterners also judged those of southern ancestry to possess a strong antiintellectualism and a suspicion of "book learning," which produced a lesser emphasis on schooling in the southern-dominated society.

The earliest institutions reflected the diversity and ambitions of Indianapolis' small but growing population. Seeking to nurture their faith and to shape the capital's moral character, settlers organized churches and Sunday schools in their homes or shops. Baptist, Methodist, and Presbyterian congregations eventually became institutionalized when sufficient numbers of people joined and subscribed to a building fund. Private or subscription schools provided educational opportunities for boys whose parents were willing to pay the quarterly fees. Female academies, offering somewhat comparable instruction for girls, were founded by the 1830s. A county seminary opened on University Square in 1834, and specialized instruction was available in architectural drawing, penmanship, and other areas of study. By the 1840s several local masters taught dancing and manners.

Much of the town's early culture stemmed from the New England drive for elevation and moral improvement. In the fall of 1824 a group of young men organized the "Indianapolis Legislature," a debating society and forerunner to late 19th century literary societies; the group met Saturday evenings in the county courthouse for 10 years to debate public issues. Women also attended these sessions. Literature was important to advocates of civic betterment. Books were available through personal libraries (Harvey Gregg reputedly had over 2,700 volumes), at "book auctions," or through the "Indianapolis Library," founded in 1828 to provide books for patrons who purchased $5 shares. The General Assembly established a state library in 1825 and appropriated $50 the first year for book acquisitions. In 1833, however, the legislature instructed the secretary of state not to use state funds for the "purchases of novels or romances." The capital's first bookstore (opened 1833) was a branch of a Cincinnati firm, further demonstrating the extent of cultural traffic originating in the Queen City. By 1851 the *Indianapolis Journal* listed four bookstores in the city "that will compare favorably with those of any town in the west" and serve as an "index to the intelligence of the people."

The formative years witnessed many efforts to establish institutions typically associated with more settled and culturally advanced areas. A local singing school, the Society for the Cultivation of Church Music (1824), was undoubtedly the first voluntary organization to promote the arts locally. Another early gathering, the loftily named Indianapolis Handelian Society, performed such popular instrumental songs as "Hail Columbia" and "Yankee Doodle" at the 1828 Fourth of July celebration. A group of men founded the Indiana Historical Society in December, 1830, to preserve the historical past and to promote knowledge among the citizens. Yet this somewhat elitist and filiopietistic society languished until the late 19th century when it became a cornerstone for the preservation of state and local history. Most of these early institutions survived only briefly, which testified to the difficulty of supporting and maintaining them in an isolated town.

Another indicator of local culture was architecture. Simple log and frame buildings dominated the early townscape. As Indianapolis grew, structures arose that represented a taste for aesthetics and high culture in a frontier setting. Noteworthy among these buildings was the 1835 State House, a Greek Revival–style building designed by Town and Davis of New York, one of the nation's leading architectural firms. By 1851 well-known Maryland architect Francis Costigan had moved to Indianapolis, thus symbolizing an advance in local aspirations.

Until it was capable of supporting more permanent institutions, Indianapolis depended upon traveling exhibitions, "cabinets of curiosities," and performing troupes to provide culture and entertainment. Taverns such as Thomas Carter's welcomed such actors as "Mr. and Mrs. Smith," reputedly of the New York theater, to stage plays of a mixed character. The Smiths gave dramatic recitations and portrayals; Mrs. Smith in addition was noted for singing the "Star Spangled Banner" while dancing a "hornpipe, blindfolded, amongst eggs." By 1840 Indianapolis had its first homegrown amateur theatrical group, the Thespian Corps, which performed Robert Dale Owen's *Pocahontas* as its inaugural production. The corps faded after a few years, as did most local cultural enterprises of the 19th century.

Indianapolis' geographical isolation produced an insular view of the world that effectively arrested local cultural development. A latter-day puritanism among local Protestants, inspired by frontier revivalism, also proved to be an obstacle. Approaching the arts with suspicion and hostility, religious enthusiasts criticized the arts for gratifying the senses, stirring the imagination in secular ways, and representing the decadence of the Old World aristocracy. One subscriber to the *Indiana Journal*, seeking to maintain a degree of decorum and social order in the city, wrote in 1840 that the theater was "the most fruitful source of crime, profligacy, and misery to be found in our great cities." Another correspondent argued in 1851 that "there is no greater exhibition of human depravity than for children to be educated in dancing." The Rev. Henry Ward Beecher of Second Presbyterian Church, in a series of essays entitled *Lectures to Young Men* (1844), denounced the theater, condemned promiscuous balls, and equated card playing with gambling. This spiritual-cultural conflict presented a dilemma for some local residents who regarded the arts as a measure of civilized society. Nevertheless, a religious conservatism continued to affect the development of Indianapolis culture in subsequent decades.

Two events in the 1840s altered the face of local culture. In October, 1847, the Madison and Indianapolis Railroad became the first of many railroads to enter the capital, ending Indianapolis' isolation and breaking through the provincialism that had prevailed earlier. The railroad stimulated the growth of new businesses and industries which, though remaining small and locally oriented, expanded Indianapolis' influence in central Indiana while leaving Cincinnati's status as the economic center of the West largely unaffected. The railroad also placed the city on the entertainment circuit and regularly brought musicians and actors to perform. A growing complement of hotels and local newspapers demonstrated the spirit of commerce and culture that permeated the city.

The other significant event was the arrival of German immigrants who ultimately had a greater influence on Indianapolis than any other foreign group. Within a decade of their arrival the Germans had successfully transplanted a rich and complex network of cultural institutions. They founded the German language newspaper *Volksblatt* (1848) to provide news from home and abroad. They established "Vereins" or clubs like the Indianapolis Turngemeinde (1851) to emphasize gymnastics and German culture, music and singing societies like the Liederkranz and Maennerchor, and instrumental bands. They also founded the German-English School (1859) to teach classes in German and to preserve their native culture.

By midcentury Indianapolis had begun to offer its citizens more cultural opportunities. In October, 1852, the city hosted the first Indiana State Fair, which showcased the latest in agricultural methods and technology, promoted local commerce, and attracted one of the largest public gatherings annually. The decade also saw the construction of Indianapolis' first true theaters, including the 1,500 seat Metropolitan, built in 1858 at a cost of $60,000; this event also marked the shift from amateur theater staged in taverns to professional companies marketed by agents. (Ten years later in 1868 the Metropolitan was outclassed by the opening of the Academy of Music, a 2,500–seat auditorium with dress boxes, dress circle, and two galleries.) The Handel and Haydn Society organized, and in the spring of 1859 Indianapolis had its first full opera performance, although its attraction for Indianapolitans was questionable. Historian Jacob Piatt Dunn noted that "the performances were kindly noticed, but do not appear to have been as well patronized as either Christy's Minstrels or the Peake Family of Swiss Bell Ringers which followed in the same week."

The Civil War was a watershed for Indianapolis. During the decade the city's population rose dramatically, from 18,611 to 48,244, including larger numbers of Germans, Irish, African-Americans, and Jews, all of whom established separate ethnic enclaves and introduced new institutions. Business expansion and population growth produced an increased civic optimism and greater prosperity. This activity made Indianapolis a more attractive location in which to live and work and increased the market for cultural wares desired by the rising middle and upper classes, but it also widened class distinctions. The war drew out the city's inherent cultural and regional tensions as citizens debated the critical issues of slavery and secession. But the war also undercut opposition to popular entertainment such as minstrel shows, circuses, and especially the theater, which allowed people of every class to escape temporarily the concerns of war.

The immediate postwar years brought renewed vitality to the capital city. One of its first signs was the crusade to establish a free public library. On Thanksgiving Day, 1868, the Rev. Hanford Edson of Second Presbyterian Church delivered a sermon in which he claimed "the deficiency that is really fatal to [the city's] character—is the want of a public library." Acknowledging that libraries helped the scholar and the student and also shaped the moral character of cities, he concluded: "No community can be respectable without books. The people, the whole body of citizens, gain more than indirect benefit from the proximity of a public library." Joining the effort were public school superintendent Abram Shortridge, Henry Lieber, and Volney T. Malott, all proponents of free public education who considered the library a spur to public morality and civic improvement. Five years later, in 1873, the 12,790–volume library opened at Pennsylvania and Michigan streets as part of the city's school system.

The 1870s, although marred by an economic panic, began a half century of significant change for Indianapolis. During that time the Hoosier capital passed from frontier town to modern city. This emergence brought new cultural institutions as the city now claimed the critical mass needed to support a cultural infrastructure. The appearance of wealthy entrepreneurs for whom the cultivation of the arts was an essential part of life finally brought so-called high culture to the city. This cultural elite, consisting of those of new wealth, founding families, progressive businessmen, and civic-minded women, established institutions that marked their aspirations for themselves and their city.

Indianapolis' cultural leadership became highly visible during the 1880s and 1890s, a period generally recognized as the city's "golden age." Benefiting from economic prosperity, the middle and upper classes traveled abroad or summered along the Atlantic seaboard and brought a new cosmopolitan spirit back to the city. They built homes on the fashionable north side and in newly established suburbs like Irvington, which now boasted a university. Many helped to establish artistic institutions and joined philanthropic causes or instigated social reform. While these new leaders believed that exposure to the heritage of Western civilization would improve

A bequest by John Herron allowed for an early art museum in the city.
Free admission to the museum must have attracted many patrons as depicted
in Harry A. Davis's *Free Day at Herron*. [Harry A. Davis, American, b. 1914.
Free Day at Herron, 1938. Lithograph, 8 3/4 x 11 3/8 inches, gift of the artist,
82.105, from the exhibition: *Views of Indianapolis: Artistic Perspectives*,
collection of the Indianapolis Museum of Art.]

the community, the institutions they established had little appeal for the urban working class and
the newly arrived immigrants.

The period witnessed a rising interest in the fine arts. While local artist Jacob Cox was still
revered as the "old master," a new generation of European-trained painters sought to make Indianapolis a center of art training. In the late 1870s James F. Gookins and John W. Love, fresh from
the Ecole des Beaux-Arts in Paris, organized the Indiana School of Art, which ultimately failed
due to insufficient patronage. But not until 1883 with the founding of the Indianapolis Art Association, a "society for the study and promotion of art," did the city move to join the ranks of
America's cultural centers. Seeking to establish a permanent art museum and to sponsor art training schools and annual exhibitions, the association brought recognition to Indianapolis by exhibiting works of the New York- and German-trained "Hoosier Group." With Englishman John
Herron's bequest in 1895 the Art Association established an art institute (1902) and museum
(1906), which finally brought the great art of Europe and America to the capital. During those
same years the Cyclorama, a large circular building at Market and Illinois streets, attracted thousands to view a life-size painting depicting the Battle of Atlanta.

Indianapolis also began to blossom as a literary center in the late 19th century. Contemporary authors visited the capital to lecture and local residents met to discuss literary topics. Gradually a close circle of writers arose, influencing the state's literature and gaining national prominence. Authors including James Whitcomb Riley, Lew Wallace, Booth Tarkington, and Meredith Nicholson produced an often sentimental literature that portrayed a simpler past. Their popularity helped turn local publisher Bowen-Merrill (later Bobbs-Merrill) into one of the country's leading firms.

Although the performing arts lagged behind the artistic and literary interests in the city, both theatrical and musical organizations made substantial progress during the 1880s. Dubbed "the first theatre in the West," English's Opera House opened on the Circle in September, 1880. It attracted leading stars in opera, ballet, drama, and music productions whose casts were supplemented with local talent. The English's success encouraged the development of other theaters—notably, Dickson's Grand Opera House and the Park—despite continued opposition from religious elements who considered theater "irredeemably depraved." Less expensive theaters provided "clean wholesome attractions," including vaudeville, minstrels, and circuses for a wider audience.

While other cities had established symphony orchestras by this time, Indianapolis was unsuccessful in securing local support. Musical entertainment depended upon imported talent, including noted national and international performers and other cities' symphonies. Local voluntary concert associations and the German community's musical activities kept musical tastes alive despite failed attempts to organize an orchestra. The city, however, clearly demonstrated its love of music. At the dedication of Tomlinson Hall (1886), a music festival to raise funds for the Soldiers and Sailors Monument was a resounding success. It led to an annual May Music Festival (1889–1898) that drew thousands from around the state and the nation. Still, it was not until 1930 when Ferdinand Schaefer organized the Indianapolis Symphony Orchestra that the city finally claimed a professional musical organization.

Desiring affiliations with individuals of similar class and status, late 19th century Indianapolis residents developed a passion for clubs and associations. An interest in refined culture led to the founding of the Indianapolis Woman's Club (1875) and the male-only Indianapolis Literary Club (1877), both of which offered literary, social, and aesthetic programs. By 1880 the city boasted some 50 different literary clubs. Numerous special-interest clubs also formed: Republicans established the Columbia Club; business leaders joined the Commercial Club (later the Chamber of Commerce); women joined the Propylaeum, the Contemporary Club, the Dramatic Club, or one of several other artistic associations. Fraternal organizations and labor unions attracted increased membership. Churches too benefited from this associational movement as many new programs appealed to various social groups.

The construction of prominent structures in the downtown area symbolized the emerging public consciousness of the new urban culture. Public architecture captured the city's spirit of progress, optimism, and pride; it also portrayed the city as a vibrant community and served notice of local economic prosperity. The Marion County Courthouse (1876), Tomlinson Hall (1886), the second Union Station (1887–1888), the new State House (1888), the Chamber of Commerce building and Das Deutsche Haus (later the Athenaeum, 1893), the Soldiers and Sailors Monument (1888–1902), and numerous bank and retail buildings gave Indianapolis a monumental and modern image. The accompanying emergence of exclusive neighborhoods likewise showcased the influence of the city's elite, a development noted by Berry R. Sulgrove, who wrote in 1884 that "in nothing, except music, is the improvement of taste more noticeable than in the houses now built for residences."

While Indianapolis experienced a flowering of high culture, it also witnessed new expressions of popular culture. Spectator sports, especially baseball, boxing, and gymnastics, attracted large crowds. As bicycling became a popular form of recreation, local manufacturers produced various models for consumers who organized bicycling clubs and lobbied for the development of public parks. Such excessive leisure time concerned religious leaders, however, who cautioned about its impact on Sunday observance.

The 1890s witnessed collateral developments that influenced the city's cultural institutions. Indianapolis' population reached 105,436—more than double the size of the 1870 city—and included large numbers of eastern and southern European immigrants and African-Americans who established distinct neighborhoods and institutions. The discovery of natural gas in the region created an economic boom and channeled additional monies into the city's institutions. Indianapolis adopted a more progressive image, accomplished in part by the founding of the Commercial Club (1890), that promoted civic improvements and elevated local businessmen to positions of civic and cultural leadership. Noting this new urban enthusiasm, Booth Tarkington wrote: "It was idealistic, and its ideals were expressed in the new kind of young men in business downtown. . . . They loved their city and worked for it with a plutonic energy" because they knew a more prosperous city meant more prosperous individuals and a better life.

One of the decade's most significant developments—the public park movement—symbolized that idealism. Although many cities had provided public spaces since the mid–1800s, Indianapolis traditionally had refused free donations of land for public use. With the success of New York City's Central Park, however, citizens criticized local government for failing to appropriate park funds. A June 15, 1873, editorial in *People*, a pro-labor newspaper, expressed strong class animosities in explaining why Indianapolis lacked parks: "[Civic and business leaders] are rich, have horses and vehicles for drives, and don't need parks because they live in big fine yards; . . . parks are to be for the working classes who live where houses are crowded in tight together."

The successes of other major cities in providing public recreational and leisure spaces coupled with the concerns of social reformers about the effects of urbanization encouraged the creation of playgrounds, ball fields, gardens, and foot and bicycle paths. Urban planning, inspired by the City Beautiful movement and the idealized designs of the 1893 World's Columbian Exposition in Chicago, provided other incentives. But it was the combined leadership of business and government through the Commercial Club that spurred Indianapolis to establish a Department of Public Parks and begin acquiring park lands. By the late 1890s park acreage exceeded 1,100 acres, 953 of which comprised Riverside Park, making it larger than New York's Central Park. Countering earlier criticism, the city reported in 1899, "it is not for the special benefit of the rich that large parks are built, as some . . . would have us believe, but observation will show that their quietness is more often sought by the workmen and their families to whom a day in the park means more than it is possible to estimate." Although largely untouched by the slums and congestion found elsewhere, Indianapolis established one of the nation's largest park systems. By the 1910s it included public school playgrounds and public golf courses. At the same time the growing popularity of golf and tennis led to the creation of country clubs for the city's elite.

By the dawn of the 20th century Indianapolis possessed most of the ingredients to provide diverse cultural opportunities for most residents. Despite existing class distinctions, a growing civic consciousness stimulated pride in the city's rich heritage. Increasingly the Circle became the civic center of Indianapolis. Beginning in 1876 with a celebration of the nation's centennial—an event marked by a parade and other festivities—Indianapolis residents established the Circle as *the* public gathering spot. To mark the new century local businessmen sponsored a week-long carnival in October, 1900, erecting ceremonial arches over Meridian Street near the Circle. They created a midway with performers, staged historical pageants and parades, and strung the site with electric lights. In May, 1902, thousands of citizens gathered on the Circle to dedicate the Soldiers and Sailors Monument. Three years later the Indianapolis Turnverein staged a celebration on the Circle as part of the 29th National Gymnastics Festival. Over the ensuing decades the city marked special occasions—GAR encampments, victory celebrations, holidays— with massive parades, public festivities and musical concerts, all centered on the Circle.

The early 20th century brought improved public transportation that effectively changed the size and appearance of the city. Electric interurbans connected the capital with points throughout the state and marketed recreational excursions from the hinterlands to the state capital. Electric streetcars, which had replaced mule-drawn trolleys in the mid–1890s, extended the city and provided transportation to and from work, access to the downtown business and shopping district, and passage to various recreational spots.

The streetcar also contributed to a new form of public entertainment. Amusement parks, located at the city's outskirts, capitalized on the successes of New York's Coney Island and the wonders of the 1893 Columbian Exposition by dazzling the public with electrically powered rides and unusual attractions. Intended as inexpensive and easily accessible entertainment, Fairview Park, White City at Broad Ripple, Wonderland, and Riverside amusement parks broke down class barriers—but not racial barriers—by providing a pastoral though commercialized escape from urban life.

Perhaps more than anything else, the automobile significantly altered life and culture in 20th century Indianapolis. Cars early became a part of the urban economy and popular culture. Around 1910 Indianapolis was considered the nation's fourth most important automobile manufacturing city, behind Detroit, Toledo, and Cleveland. By the 1920s many local manufacturers specialized in producing high-powered luxury automobiles such as the Duesenberg, Marmon, and Stutz, all of which became symbols of affluence for the nation's and city's elite. Consumer infatuation with motor vehicles produced a recreational industry of road rallies, motor clubs, auto shows, and races, highlighted by the Indianapolis 500–Mile Race, "the greatest spectacle in racing." As Booth Tarkington noted in *The Magnificent Ambersons*: "Automobiles have come, and they bring a greater change in our life than most of us suspect. . . . I think men's minds are going to be changed in subtle ways because of automobiles."

Almost as important as automobiles were motion picture theaters, which replaced nickelodeons as a form of popular entertainment. Between 1900 and 1930 nearly 200 theaters opened in Indianapolis. Many downtown "movie palaces" provided opulent settings reminiscent of the great opera houses. The Circle Theatre (1916) was the first theater in the city and reputedly the second oldest in the nation specially designed to show films. Within a few years other theaters—Loews, Apollo, Lyric, the Indiana—opened; by 1920 there were 13 movie theaters operating within a few blocks of the Circle.

The city's musical culture became more diverse and inclusive during these years. A People's Concert Association (1905) provided inexpensive concerts for large audiences, including children. Ragtime became extremely popular and in the process became one of the first commercial outlets for women in the arts. It also generated huge sales of pianos and sheet music and made

The Children's Museum, ca. 1993. [The Children's Museum]

Indianapolis a center of music publishing. Jazz and blues, inspired by the large migration of southern African-Americans, bolstered Indianapolis' reputation as a musical center. The jazz and blues culture broke down economic and racial barriers and spawned clubs throughout the city, especially along Indiana Avenue. Dancing too emerged as a popular pastime with dance halls such as the Casino Gardens, the Lyric Ballroom, Tomlinson Hall, and the Indiana Roof opening. Another popular venue was the 10,000–seat Cadle Tabernacle (1921), used primarily for religious gatherings but also for dances, concerts, prizefights, and Ku Klux Klan rallies.

The diversification and popularization of local culture continued as commercial radio broadcasting debuted in 1921. By the time WFBM, the first permanent station in Indianapolis, aired in November, 1924, residents had been introduced to the electronic medium through local demonstrations and the "Radio Room" in the L. S. Ayres department store. The next year the Broadcast Listeners' Association sponsored a radio exposition at Cadle Tabernacle to showcase the latest equipment; Indianapolis at that time had an estimated 20,000 radio receivers. Network radio came to WFBM in 1929 and WKBF in 1933 and provided listeners with greater variety in programming. As radio gained popularity more broadcasts originated "live" from local theaters, showcasing new talent and giving performers celebrity status.

Although cautiously conservative in its economic and political leadership, Indianapolis in the 1920s saw the founding of other institutions dedicated to the general improvement of contemporary urban life. Inspired by the Brooklyn (New York) Children's Museum, Mary Stewart Carey established a children's museum in her Meridian Street mansion. The Children's Museum, which would later receive national and international acclaim, proved that museums were for the masses—including children—not just for the cultural elite. Seeking to alter the notion that the study of history was for gentlemen scholars, Christopher Coleman, director of the Indiana Historical Bureau and executive secretary of the Indiana Historical Society, worked to popularize the past through expanded public programs, publications, and a new genealogy section at the society.

The city's key cultural institutions experienced a temporary setback in the early 1930s and 1940s. The Great Depression forced most people to resort to inexpensive forms of entertainment found in public parks, movie theaters, and on the radio. Local amusement parks and the Indiana State Fair offered special incentives to help citizens have fun during hard times. Meanwhile, much of the city's social leadership, dubbed "The Fashionable Four Hundred," retreated into their society- and club-filled world and abandoned older central neighborhoods in favor of newer residential developments to the north, thereby contributing to the further separation of classes within the city.

While the Great Depression may have signaled the end of the "golden age" and emphasized the city's inherent class and ethnic divisions, World War II reunited the community. Wartime production triggered economic growth. Public rallies and parades, war bond drives, recycling efforts, and servicemen's clubs sparked local patriotism. Attendance at local parks, the movies, and Riverside Amusement Park increased, bolstered by the large number of troops stationed at Fort Benjamin Harrison. And with the end of the war Indianapolis returned to the Circle to celebrate.

The postwar years welcomed another period of sustained growth, but one that ultimately had a detrimental effect on Indianapolis. Restrained since the Depression and restricted by war, demand for consumer goods exploded, and wartime industries quickly converted to peacetime production. Wages rose rapidly, allowing people to buy the automobiles, homes, furnishings, and clothing postponed by the war. Increased car ownership coupled with the new consumerism stimulated a housing boom at the city's periphery, construction of new roads and highways, and the building of shopping centers away from the city center. A revived and expanded "automobile culture"—characterized by drive-in restaurants and theaters (the Pendleton Pike Drive-In theater with its 50–foot screen opened in June, 1940, and others followed)—altered the face of the city.

Television soon became the consumer item most in demand. In 1947 Indianapolis became a principal center for the production of RCA televisions. Broadcast television premiered in the city appropriately on Memorial Day, 1949, when WFBM-TV provided "live" coverage of the 500–Mile Race. Within a year there were an estimated 8,000 television sets in the city; by 1952 that number had risen to over 137,000. Yet amidst this popularization of culture the Dramatic Club, a bastion of the city's upper class since the late 19th century, introduced its Christmas cotillion (1950) to present local debutantes, thereby revealing the cultural extremes that continued to exist.

The postwar years brought increased popularity to the Indianapolis 500–Mile Race. In 1956 the raceway opened its Hall of Fame Museum, which highlighted the race's history and its impact on local and national culture. The next year the race was preceded by the 500 Festival, a popular celebration of the city and the race that now embraces concerts, a half-marathon, and special events throughout the month of May, including the nation's second largest parade.

With the dispersion of population made possible by the automobile, Indianapolis' downtown—traditionally the heart of the city's cultural life—began to suffer. Retail sales declined and businesses closed. Movie theaters shut down, replaced by suburban theaters and television. The city's industrial base shrank, which contributed to general urban decay and stimulated rapid suburban flight. The nicknames "Naptown" and "India-no-place" became more salient as the downtown resembled a ghost town and the vibrancy of previous years slipped away.

Civic leaders soon realized that the future of Indianapolis depended upon broad-based urban revitalization, a concept that included the strengthening of the city's cultural institutions. The 1960s saw a spurt in institutional development, spurred in part by reaction to demolition or threatened loss of historical structures. A renewed interest in the city's past fostered the establishment of Historic Landmarks Foundation of Indiana (1960) and the Marion County-Indianapolis Historical Society (1961). William Conner's house passed from Eli Lilly's hands to Earlham College; the college established Conner Prairie (1964), a museum dedicated to interpreting life in pioneer Indiana. The Indiana State Museum, long confined to the basement of the State House, moved to the former city hall (1967). Continued patronage of the arts led to the 1966 donation of Oldfields, J. K. Lilly, Jr.'s estate, to the Indianapolis Art Association for use in developing a new Indianapolis Museum of Art (1970). Local supporters of the arts founded the Penrod Society (1966) and the Fine Arts Society of Indianapolis (1968).

In addition to the institutional resurgence, popular culture took new forms, especially as television expanded its influence. Affected in part by local coverage of the Coliseum explosion (October 31, 1963), the assassination and funeral of President John F. Kennedy three weeks later, and the ongoing war in Vietnam, TV became a regular and necessary part of daily life. Also after decades of a fairly isolated existence, Indianapolis made the regular circuit of major popular entertainers. The city had seen some of the best dance bands, instrumentalists, and vocalists of the mid–20th century. But not until the arrival of the Beatles, who performed at the Indiana State Fairgrounds in 1964, did the city finally reach the "big time," at least as a popular music venue. In subsequent years most top-drawer musicians played the city, drawing yet another segment of the population—youth—into the cultural mix.

The adoption of Unigov seemed to breathe new life into the capital city in the 1970s and 1980s. Its skyline underwent transformation; so too did its public and cultural life. Skyscrapers, a convention center, and interstate highways soon dominated the urban landscape, and the city witnessed the flowering of new or expanded cultural institutions. An urban state university took shape just west of downtown along White River, and farther north Butler University became a key site for the city's cultural programming. The Indianapolis Repertory Theatre sparked a local theater movement, and public television debuted. Market Square Arena attracted more sports and special events, including Elvis Presley's last public concert (June 26, 1977). A new generation of enclosed shopping malls opened. And the city's acquisition of Eagle Creek Park created one of the nation's largest municipal parks.

Local enthusiasm continued into the 1980s and 1990s. As civic leaders targeted downtown development as the key to a rejuvenated city, there was a proliferation of commercial art galleries, suggesting a resurgent patronage of artists. The Indianapolis Symphony Orchestra moved to the restored Circle Theatre, reinvigorating downtown nightlife and bringing new musical and cultural acclaim for the city. The Eiteljorg Museum of American Indian and Western Art and a new wing of the Indianapolis Museum of Art scheduled special events and exhibitions to attract broader, nontraditional audiences. The Arts Council of Indianapolis organized to promote the arts and to strengthen the relationship of the arts and economic development and the local business community.

The same years witnessed a broadening of cultural events that were more inclusive of the city's population. Both Indiana Black Expo and the International Festival showcased the cultural diversity of Indianapolis. The Indianapolis Hebrew Congregation and the Indianapolis–Marion County Public Library sponsored popular lecture programs that recalled the lyceums of the

1880s. As entertainment and leisure time activities became more important, urban planners began development of White River State Park, which included a new Indianapolis Zoo. The completion of the Hoosier Dome and the opening of Deer Creek Music Center in adjacent Hamilton County provided two new venues for concerts, sporting events, and festivals. Indianapolis also made its mark nationally by hosting the National Sports Festival and Pan American Games, serving as a filming site for the movies *Hoosiers* and *Eight Men Out*, and contributing comedian David Letterman and news correspondent Jane Pauley to national television.

As impressive as the transformation of the 1970s and 1980s was, it was not new to Indianapolis. It had occurred once before in the civic boosterism of the late 19th century. Then a new civic leadership used its influence to encourage support for cultural institutions. Today Indianapolis residents hear leaders uttering words similar to those of a century ago, proclaiming that cultural institutions are necessary for a prosperous community.

Contemporary Indianapolis enjoys a reputation as an emerging cultural center. In 1994 the city possessed a major symphony orchestra, several chamber ensembles, choirs, dance companies, theater companies, a first-class art museum and a children's museum reputed to be the largest in the world, state and public libraries, and several historical organizations. It had six institutions of higher learning, a zoo, and numerous world-class sports facilities. It boasted annual ethnic and music festivals that celebrated the community's cultural diversity. None of the cultural institutions that Indianapolis residents take for granted, however, with the exception of the public library system, existed prior to the 20th century. Most are products of the post–World War II decades.

Having lost its momentum—and possibly its identity—at midcentury, Indianapolis in the 1990s is experiencing a renaissance similar to that of the 1890s. The key question for the future, however, will be whether Indianapolis can extend its cultural traditions into the 21st century, or whether it will look back on the late 20th century as a golden age from which the city of the future retreated.

See also: HISTORICAL ORGANIZATIONS AND EVENTS; LIBRARIES AND ARCHIVES; LITERARY ORGANIZATIONS AND EVENTS; MUSEUMS; PARKS; THEATERS; and individual names, institutions, and organizations.

DEMOGRAPHY AND ETHNICITY

James J. Divita

The first residents of the land we call Indiana in their memory were the Indians in the Woodland and Mississippian periods (1000 B.C.–1500 A.D.). They mastered the process of fire-hardening pottery, domesticated many plants, and built two notable reminders of their presence—the earthworks in Mounds State Park near Anderson and Angel Mounds near Evansville. By the time of Christopher Columbus' arrival in the Americas, however, they had abandoned their traditional sites, probably the result of climatic change.

In the late 17th century French missionaries, trappers, and explorers began to traverse the waterways of Indiana. The legendary Jesuit Father Jacques Marquette traveled eastward along the southern shore of Lake Michigan shortly before his death (1675). Four years later Robert Cavelier de la Salle and companions camped near the site of present South Bend on their way west to trace the course of the "Father of Waters." Within a half century forts or trading posts were erected at present Fort Wayne, Lafayette, and Vincennes.

The Indians with whom the French, and then the British, dealt were themselves newcomers. The Potawatomi and the Miami moved southeast of Lake Michigan from present Wisconsin and Illinois by 1680. The Lenni Lenape (or Delawares) arrived from present Ohio, forced by English settlement to withdraw from the Atlantic seaboard and cross the Appalachians. As early as the 1760s the Miami invited the Delawares to settle along the White River; by 1794, however, Delaware families resided on the west fork of White River in central Indiana where they hunted the abundant game and tapped the sugar maple trees of present Marion County. Shunning forested, poorly drained terrain for drier camp sites, the Delawares selected higher ground north of present Waverly in Morgan County and near Castleton just south of the Marion-Hamilton county line.

To the Europeans, White River was but one of the several tributaries of the much more important Wabash River. Undoubtedly French traders continued to buy and sell in central Indiana even after King Louis XV of France ceded this territory to his rival King George III of Britain in 1763. Then in 1783 King George transferred central Indiana to his former subjects, the rebellious Americans.

James J. Divita is Professor of History at Marian College in Indianapolis.

Following the adoption of the Northwest Ordinance of 1787 white American settlers began crossing the Ohio River into present Clark County, becoming "Hoosiers" and marking the beginning of the end to Indian occupation of the territory. Between 1799 and 1806 Moravian missionaries ministered unsuccessfully to the Delawares along White River north of Marion County. The Battle of Tippecanoe (1811) and the subsequent war between Britain and the United States showed how both sides were willing to use the Indians as pawns in their military conflict. Throughout the territorial period as well as in the years following Indiana's admission into the Union (1816) many more thousands of settlers arrived from Kentucky, Tennessee, and the Atlantic coastal states. To accommodate the growing white population the Delawares and other tribes had to be removed from central (and eventually northern) Indiana. By the 1818 Treaty of St. Mary's (Ohio) the Delawares agreed to move west within three years to lands reserved beyond the Mississippi River.

Even before the Indians vacated the "New Purchase," as the ceded territory was called, the state legislature in Corydon appointed a commission to select a centrally located site for a state capital. Commissioner John Tipton, accompanied by his black manservant (reputedly the first African-American in the area), and the other commissioners in June, 1820, recommended locating the capital on the east bank of White River at the mouth of Fall Creek. The legislature approved the site in January, 1821, and named the new capital "Indianapolis." Upon accepting the federal government's donation of four sections of land, legislators authorized Alexander Ralston and Elias Pym Fordham to plat the town. The next year the legislature organized Marion County.

Indianapolis' first residents were squatters along the banks of White River, Fall Creek, Pogue's Run, and Pleasant Run. Among them were John McCormick, whose cabin the commissioners utilized for their deliberations, and George Pogue, reputedly killed by Indians while trying to retrieve stolen horses. These and other early settlers were followed by the so-called Whitewater and Kentucky factions, rival political groups divided by place of origin. The Whitewater faction, former residents of southeastern Indiana's Whitewater River valley, originated in Ohio and Pennsylvania and opposed slavery; the Kentucky faction included recent residents of that state, many of whom favored slavery. Other early arrivals included Cheney Lively Britton, Ralston's housekeeper and probably the first permanent African-American resident, and easterners like Calvin Fletcher, the Vermont-born lawyer, businessman, and diarist (1821), and Nicholas McCarty, a Virginia-born merchant and landholder (1823). From the very beginning Indianapolis clearly had a diverse population.

Inaccessibility and disease hindered the initial growth of Indianapolis. The nearest organized towns were distant Connersville and Brookville, and few passable roads connected the capital with the outside world. Many newcomers died from malaria during the summer heat and humidity of 1821 and 1822. Although state government transferred from Corydon to Indianapolis in late 1824, the new capital did not grow quickly. Its population in 1840 was only about 2,700 and all lots in the Mile Square had not been sold until 1850. Samuel Henderson, the town's first mayor, eventually abandoned Indianapolis for the West in 1849 because he saw no future for the Hoosier capital.

Henderson obviously was wrong; Indianapolis did have a future despite relatively slow growth. The town became more accessible, not by river (which frequently was too shallow for navigation in the summer), but with the construction of the Central Canal (1836), the completion of the National Road to Indianapolis (1838), and the arrival of the first railroad (1847). The population also grew with the addition of Irish immigrants who came to work on internal improvements projects and German immigrants who came to escape the revolutions in their homeland.

By 1850 Indianapolis' population had grown to 8,100, comparable to the cities of Madison and New Albany. Roughly 65 percent were native-born, including about 15 percent each from Kentucky, Ohio, and Pennsylvania; natives of North Carolina and Virginia each comprised about 6 percent. African-Americans constituted 6.5 percent of the population and European immigrants 35 percent, although neither group was particularly welcome among the predominantly white Anglo population. Scattered incidents clearly revealed the racism and nativism inherent among local residents. On July 4, 1845, a rowdy mob fatally beat a black man on a downtown street without provocation. African-American residents were denied ordinary rights of citizenship and required to register in the county courthouse. After 1851 African-Americans were prohibited by Article 13 of the new state constitution from entering Indiana. Puritanical neighbors disliked Germans who drank and danced, especially on the Sabbath. In 1855 police precipitated a riot when they attempted to arrest a beer dealer in an eastside German neighborhood. Likewise many native-born citizens voiced their disapproval of naturalized Irish and German voters who rallied in opposition to temperance legislation. By midcentury ethnic and racial tensions were clearly evident in Indianapolis, thus setting the stage for future relations between resident racial and ethnic groups.

The Civil War, however, energized and united the Hoosier capital. The movement of troops and supplies to support the Union effort called attention to Indianapolis as a transportation hub and as an attractive manufacturing center offering jobs in diverse industries. In 1863 Kingan meat packers of Belfast, Ireland, located a plant on the banks of White River to purvey meat for the Union army. The company recruited laborers in Ireland and provided them with steady, year-round employment packing pork in its refrigerated slaughterhouse. Railroads entered Indianapolis from every direction and employed large numbers of unskilled laborers to repair right-of-way and equipment. This quickened economic tempo stimulated a rapid growth in population—from 18,600 in 1860 to 48,200 in 1870 and 75,000 by 1880, making Indianapolis the 24th largest city in the nation.

According to the 1880 census 86 percent of Indianapolis' residents were natives of the United States. Of those over 61 percent were native Hoosiers, 11 percent from Ohio, 8 percent from Kentucky, and about 6 percent from Pennsylvania and New York. The foreign-born population, mostly immigrants from Germany and Ireland, comprised 14 percent of the total. The number of Germans was smaller than that of Ohio-born residents but exceeded that of Kentuckians. Many of the Germans were intellectuals who had fled their homeland after the 1848 revolts. Dedicated to establishing and maintaining a German community in the Hoosier capital, some Germans established banks, savings and loan associations, and insurance corporations; others engaged in the brewing and construction industries and settled with Alsatians and Danes in the district south of Union Station. German Jews, who initially settled south and east of the Circle, later moved to more fashionable neighborhoods north of the Circle and were soon joined by affluent German businessmen and professionals. The presence of German freethinkers was symbolized by the Athenaeum turner hall and social center. Germans also sought to preserve their language and culture by establishing their own newspaper (1848), school (1859), and churches (both Protestant and Catholic), as well as successfully demanding that Indianapolis public schools offer German language instruction (1869). They enriched the city's culture by forming singing societies, sponsoring musical performances, and operating theaters.

The Yorger Meat Company, 1004 Virginia Avenue, ca. 1890, catered to the city's large German community. [Indiana Historical Society, Bass Collection]

Yugoslavian immigrants in a 1923 wedding ceremony at Haughville's Holy Trinity Catholic Church. [Indiana Historical Society, #C1785]

The Irish originally settled along the Central Canal northwest and southwest of the Circle. With the introduction of the streetcar, however, Irishmen and their families could reside on the east side and still hold jobs at Kingan and Company. The Irish were also accustomed to hard physical labor as railroad and factory workers in Brightwood and elsewhere. Although not maintaining as extensive a network as the Germans, the Irish sought to preserve their cultural identity and community through various institutions including the Ancient Order of Hibernians, the St. Patrick's Total Abstinence (Temperance) Society, and the first Catholic church north of Washington Street, all organized in the 1870s. They even established the Indianapolis Circle of the Fenian Brotherhood, which participated in the 1866 attack on British Canada to support Irish independence.

Construction of the Belt Line Railroad during the 1870s contributed to urban growth and expansion. Built to enable freight to bypass the Mile Square and to reduce noise, soot, and traffic congestion in the central business district, the railroad opened outlying districts to industrial and residential development. The rail line facilitated the construction of the Union Stockyards in West Indianapolis (1877) and provided factories with easier access to raw materials, fuel, and markets. By 1880 Indianapolis had become the third largest pork packing center in the world, behind Chicago and Cincinnati.

By the early 20th century many other immigrant groups had joined the Germans and Irish. Jews from Russia, Poland, and the Ottoman Empire settled around Morris and Meridian streets. Italians, many of whom sold fruits and vegetables, lived southeast of the Circle. Serbs, Macedonians, and Romanians worked for railroads, foundries, and meat packers and, like the Greeks, opened small businesses on the city's near west side. Slovenes, Poles, and Hungarians moved into Haughville where they worked in foundries and factories. Besides these Europeans a small but growing number of Middle Easterners and Asians lived in Indianapolis. Syrians congregated on one southwestside street; the Chinese opened laundries along Fort Wayne, Massachusetts, and Indiana avenues. All of these groups established distinct ethnic neighborhoods that formed a great arc around three sides of the Mile Square. Only the north side remained the city's affluent, white, native-dominated district, a location that was attractive to the upwardly mobile immigrant descendants.

The 1910 federal census indicated that 42,000, or 18 percent, of Indianapolis' residents were African-Americans or immigrants. African-Americans numbered 22,000, or 9.3 percent of the total population, the highest percentage of any city north of the Ohio River. At that time New York City was 1.9 percent black, Chicago 2 percent, and Detroit 1.2 percent. Blacks migrated primarily from Kentucky, Tennessee, Georgia, and rural Indiana, and occupied housing north of the Kingan plant and around the Atlas Engine Works along Indiana and Martindale avenues. The rising African-American population meant increased competition with foreign laborers for the unskilled jobs of the day. The immigrant population, however, numbering approximately 20,000, or 8.5 percent of the total, was low in comparison to other northern urban areas—New York, 40.4 percent; Chicago, 35.7 percent; and Detroit, 33.6 percent.

The Indianapolis establishment tended to deny the presence and local contributions of immigrants and African-Americans. The leadership preferred to advertise Indianapolis as the "Crossroads of America," "this 100 percent American town," and "the Capital of the Land of Opportunity." In 1910 the Commercial Club (later Chamber of Commerce) declared, "There is almost a total absence of the foreign floating element," concluding that problems with tenements and violence were virtually unknown in the capital. The Indianapolis Board of Trade boasted that the city "is drawing its population from surrounding counties and states rather than from the immigrant tide." These groups touted homogeneity as the city's strength and noted "more than 91 percent of the population of the city and its suburbs are native-born Americans." The statistic, while true, was misleading, since 27 of every 100 native-born residents were part of a subculture—they were either black or had an immigrant parent.

Unmentioned was the participation of foreigners and African-Americans in the economy and political process. It was clear, however, that no Republican could be elected without black support, and no Democrat could be elected without immigrant votes. Minority residents like Leon Kahn, a Jew, and John Puryear, a black, were elected to the City Council, and three immigrants served as mayors before 1910—Charles G. Coulon, William J. Wallace, and Thomas Taggart. Although they were American-born mayors, Republican Caleb S. Denny and Democrat Thomas L. Sullivan were viewed as representing Irish interests. Still, the Board of Trade declared, "This is without question the most American section in the country."

Even though Indianapolis did not possess the large immigrant population of other urban areas, it did welcome the settlement house movement as a means of assimilating minorities into the American mainstream. Community leaders established Flanner House (1898) to teach African-Americans domestic and self-help skills. In 1908 John H. Holliday, newspaper publisher and an organizer of Foreign House (1911), declared that immigrants "crowd together in the most densely populated districts of the cities and complicate the problems of municipal government." Methodist deaconesses worked with Italians, and Presbyterians operated the Cosmopolitan Community Center to teach English and domestic skills to eastern Europeans. In 1923 Foreign House and Cosmopolitan merged into the American Settlement. Since settlement workers treated African-Americans and immigrants as unique people requiring special programs, they helped to shape American society in a way that they did not foresee. Strengthened were the African-Americans' desires to share in the nation's economic rewards and the immigrants' wishes to retain their ethnic identities while becoming loyal Americans.

Between 1890 and 1920 Indianapolis' population tripled from 105,000 to 314,000. The emerging automotive industry and wartime manufacturing provided increased employment opportunities and drew new residents primarily from rural and small town Indiana. The proportion of foreign born, meanwhile, declined from 13.6 percent to 5.4 percent, attributable in part to immigrants returning home and to an overall reduction of emigration caused by stricter immigration restriction laws and World War I.

Throughout the war Indianapolis residents, possessing strong roots in the least cosmopolitan sections of Indiana and the South, experienced a steady flow of unpleasant overseas war news and anti-German propaganda, which fired extreme xenophobia locally. As a result city officials banned the study of the German language in city schools (1918), thereby strengthening the "100 Percent American" traditions of Indianapolis. Capitalizing on this environment, the Ku Klux Klan became very popular in many neighborhoods, especially Brightwood, West Indianapolis, and the area south of Crown Hill Cemetery. Of Indianapolis residents eligible for membership at least 25 percent joined the Klan. Some affiliated because it upheld strict American values; others joined because it provided a social outlet. Regardless of the reasons given for joining, the Klan's anti-Catholic, anti-black, and anti-Jewish propaganda revealed the organization's true purpose and proved its general popularity locally.

Representing one segment of the city's residents Klanners intimidated others through torchlit parades of white-hooded members and by gathering to burn oil-soaked crosses in the night. Klan opponents responded with public speeches, petty violence, and economic boycotts. When the Klan supported Republican candidates for governor and mayor (1924–1925) Republican-oriented immigrant and black voters—the latter Republican since Lincoln's Emancipation Proclamation—began to vote Democratic. Ultimately the Klan declined, not because of its opponents' acts, but because of the criminality of its leadership and the corruption of its political allies.

The onset of the Great Depression greatly slowed the growth of the city. After decennial increases ranging from 34 percent to 60 percent between 1880 and 1920, the 1940 population of 387,000 was only 23.2 percent larger than the 1920 population. The foreign-born portion declined to 2.7 percent while the African-American population rose to 13.2 percent. The old black core neighborhoods—situated around Crispus Attucks High School between Missouri Street and White River, to the northeast along Martindale Avenue, and to the southeast around New Crown Cemetery—were the least racially mixed districts of the city. Those census tracts reporting no African-Americans were often ones with heavy foreign-born concentrations, such as Haughville and the district south of Union Station to the city limits. Ethnic settlement patterns of 1920 remained essentially the same through 1940, except that central and eastern Europeans exchanged addresses around Military Park for better ones along West 16th Street.

World War II and the subsequent years brought major changes to the capital city. The population increased 10.4 percent between 1940 and 1950, and another 11.5 percent to over 476,000 by 1960. Some of this growth could be attributed to employment opportunities offered by wartime defense industries and expanded production lines in electronics and automotive parts. At the same time the City of Indianapolis encompassed all of Center Township and spread into adjoining Perry, Warren, Washington, and Wayne townships.

During the postwar years the African-American population increased twice as rapidly as the general population between 1940–1950 and five times faster than the city between 1950–1960. These new residents found housing south of Crown Hill Cemetery and between the Crispus Attucks and Martindale areas on the north side. By 1960 African-Americans accounted for one in five city residents and had expanded their residential areas as far north as 34th Street.

Natives of the Upper South comprised a sizable portion of the city's new residents—Kentuckians accounted for 16.2 percent, Tennesseeans for 8.1 percent. Many took up residence in neighborhoods previously occupied by immigrant families on the south, east, and west sides of Indianapolis. By 1970, 16 percent of the city's population had been born in the South, a proportion which exceeded the combined contributions from the northeastern, north central (excluding Indiana), and western portions of the country.

Reflecting a decreased movement of immigrants to central Indiana, the foreign born comprised slightly more than 2 percent of the city's 1950 population. Concomitantly, descendants of immigrants vacated their traditional neighborhoods for more affluent, outlying districts. They were joined in the 1950s by displaced Latvians who took up residence on the east and far north sides. Likewise, the Jewish community, which had relocated from the south and near north sides to the northern boundaries of Marion County, began sponsoring Jewish families who were finally permitted to leave the Soviet Union. By 1970 an estimated 3,000 residents were from Latvia, Lithuania, and other parts of the Soviet Union. Most importantly, however, ethnically based neighborhoods, except for African-Americans, faded from the local scene as former residents dispersed throughout the city.

Facing an eroding industrial base and a declining population in the districts surrounding the Circle, Mayor Richard G. Lugar and the local Republican leadership proposed legislation to broaden the tax base through a merger of Indianapolis and Marion County governments. With the passage of the Unigov legislation in 1969 the General Assembly created an Indianapolis with 744,000 residents. The African-American segment of the population declined for the first time—from 20.6 percent to 18 percent —which also symbolized the reduction of black political power in the new city-county government. At the same time the African-American population, which averaged an annual increase of 3,600 newcomers, spread north beyond 38th Street and west into Haughville. The housing problem for blacks worsened when the city closed the Lockefield Gardens housing project and the state began acquiring land for the new IUPUI campus and as right-of-way for new interstate highways.

Between 1970 and 1980 Indianapolis lost population for the first time in its history—a 5.9–percent decline to an estimated 700,000. While the construction of Interstates 65 and 70 destroyed neighborhoods and businesses in the central city, the building of Interstates 69, 74, and the 465 beltway made Indianapolis more accessible to whites who wished to live in the suburbs and adjoining counties but continue to work in the capital. Industries and businesses also began to relocate along the interstate highways. This "white flight" increased the black portion of the city's population to 21.8 percent, higher than the pre-Unigov percentage. The three most populous African-American census tracts were south of 38th Street and Sherman Drive, northeast of 38th Street and Emerson Avenue, and around 25th Street and College Avenue. The old Attucks and Martindale core areas became more depopulated. By 1990 the city had regained population, but its total of 731,000 was still smaller than its population at the introduction of Unigov 20 years earlier.

Since 1970 Hispanics have become a significant element in the Indianapolis population. At that time natives of Mexico, Puerto Rico, and Cuba numbered 1,200. In 1990 first- and second-generation Hispanics numbered 8,450, or 1.1 percent of Marion County's residents. They did not predominate in any one neighborhood, but were clustered around Fort Benjamin Harrison, west of Lafayette Square shopping center, around Woodruff Place, near St. Vincent and Community hospitals, east of Indianapolis International Airport, and in West Indianapolis. Although some held menial jobs, many were businessmen and professionals.

The Asian contingent of Indianapolis also has grown during recent decades. In 1970 the city was home to nearly 2,500 people of Asian origin; by 1980 they exceeded 4,200. Asian Indians became the single largest group, followed by Filipinos, Chinese, Koreans, and Japanese. Some were medical students who remained to practice medicine here, while others became involved in businesses or professions. A small number of Vietnamese arrived following the end of the Vietnam war. No clear pattern of settlement according to country of origin developed, but Asians resided near Fort Harrison and occupied inexpensive housing and apartment complexes around West 38th Street and Moller Road. By 1990 residents of Asian origin numbered over 7,500. Asian Indians still accounted for the largest single group, but the Chinese surpassed the number of Filipinos located here.

During the 1980s the African-American population increased by 6.6 percent, a rate that exceeded the city's total population increase of 4.4 percent; blacks numbered 166,000, or 22 percent of the 1990 total population. Several sections of the city lost residents, including the old core areas, and census tracts around Grandview School, west of the State Fairgrounds, and along the west bank of Fall Creek below 34th Street. However, areas with African-American residents extended north to 46th Street, with heavier concentrations around Arlington High School to the northeast, between Haughville and Marian College west of White River, and immediately east of

Crown Hill Cemetery. While four Marion County census tracts reported no black residents in 1980, all contained some black residents by 1990; 16 tracts, however, reported fewer than 10 black residents.

The city's "foreign stock" in 1970 was drawn from several dozen nationalities; 76 percent were from Europe and the Soviet Union, 12 percent from Central and South America, 6 percent from Asia, and 6 percent from other areas. The largest European representations were (in descending order) German, British, Irish, Italian, Soviet, Polish, Yugoslav, Austrian, Hungarian, and Latvian. Canadians were the third largest group (after the British) while Mexicans ranked 17th.

Ten years later Marion County residents were asked to identify their ancestry, no matter how long ago their ancestors emigrated. Nearly one half cited a single ancestry group, including English, 12.5 percent; German, 9 percent; and Irish, 4.4 percent. Another 28.3 percent claimed ancestors from more than one country. Combining single and multiple ancestry responses, approximately three fourths of the county's residents had an ancestral tie to only six European states—Germany, England, Ireland, France, Italy, and Poland. By 1990 over 77 percent of Marion County residents reported at least one ancestor of European origin, with German (26 percent), Irish (14 percent), and English (12 percent) descendants comprising over one half of the respondents.

Within contemporary Indianapolis and Marion County there are three principal regions of habitation. The inner region is centered on Monument Circle, the city's traditional heart, and is bounded by White River and Interstates 65 and 70. Here are located the seats of state and local government, a state university, the Hoosier Dome and other sports arenas, railroad and bus terminals, and the skyscraper-monuments of business, banking, and insurance.

The second region extends from the inner region's boundaries to 46th Street on the north, Raymond Street on the south, Emerson Avenue on the east, and Holt Road on the west. Principal inhabitants include low-middle and low income blacks, Appalachian whites, and some foreign born, many of whom are struggling against poverty, unemployment, crime, and political impotence. Vestiges of the old industrial belt and immigrant neighborhoods are found here.

The third and outermost region contains neighborhoods of white and black upper middle classes involved primarily in businesses, the professions, and skilled trades. Included in this region are the city's airport, industrial and office parks, and many of the county's newly developed residential areas. In Pike and Washington townships those developments are located north of 38th Street along Eagle Creek and north of 79th Street eastward along the Hamilton County line to Geist Reservoir. In northwest Wayne Township housing subdivisions rise rapidly from 10th to 38th streets west of I-465. In Warren Township development comes east of 30th Street and Mitthoefer Road, while in Perry Township new housing appears south of Stop 11 Road between Shelby Street and Emerson Avenue.

Can Indianapolis, the nation's twelfth largest city, truly be considered a cosmopolitan metropolis? Many residents as well as outsiders believe that the city has no diversity in its population. Like the urban elite of a century ago, they view homogeneity as a major attribute. Likewise, the city's name has been parodied as "Naptown," implying a degree of blandness and lack of excitement. Through its national promotions, the Hoosier capital is portrayed as a city of homeowners and park settings, proud of its "small city" atmosphere, an urban area with a human face. Redevelopment means finally accepting federal aid for minimal public housing, and erecting tall buildings and sports complexes downtown to demonstrate progress. This public image suits the conservative political nature of the place. For 12 years from 1956 to 1968 the city's mayors were all Democratic. In the subsequent two decades, however, the mayors have all been Republican, with one serving for 16 years, the longest mayoral tenure in the city's history. And despite a sizable minority population the capital city has yet to have a mayor representing a racial minority.

The demographic profile of Indianapolis truly reveals a city with a diverse population. Except for the large proportion of African-Americans, however, the city is not as ethnically diverse as other northern industrial and commercial centers. Nevertheless, native Hoosiers live here, together with upland southerners, European immigrants and their descendants, African-Americans, Hispanics, and Asians. Each group has affected, and continues to affect, the city's life in a unique way. Consider the successes of Indiana Black Expo and the Circle City Classic, or the many ethnic festivals held throughout the year—Octoberfest in German Park, the Italian Street Festival at Holy Rosary Church, the Grape Arbor dance at the Slovenian National Home, the Greek Festival at the Greek Orthodox Church, the downtown Hispanic "Fiesta," and the west side's Balkan Festival. Even though country-western and rock music may abound on the radio dial, the city's population does support a black station and German, Spanish, and Asian Indian language programs. Ethnic clubs sponsor fund raisers and social events. The International Center, and subsequently the Nationalities Council, have sponsored the annual International Festival of foods and culture. Indianapolis Public Schools are incorporating multicultural themes into the curriculum. Humor about Kentuckians, pickup trucks, and abandoned cars without wheels acknowledges the Appalachian origin of many Indianapolis residents. Among the city's mayors since 1948 are eight Indianapolis natives—Feeney, Bayt, Clark, Boswell, Losche, Barton, Lugar, and Goldsmith—and a native of Cincinnati—Hudnut. Of the natives three were Catholics (including one Slovene- and two Irish-Americans), one was accused of a Klan background, and one was a Jew.

Upon close examination, cultural diversity has existed in Indianapolis from the city's inception, but local residents have only recently been willing to acknowledge and encourage it. Unfortunately, some seek to balance the myth of the homogeneity of the American people by insisting on a "multiculturalism" tinged with racial superiority. Resistance to this approach comes not only from residents and outside observers who see the city in its entirety, but also from those who view the city as comprised of different peoples and cultures, each of which contributes something valuable and unique to the character of the capital. That, in fact, is the true strength of a great city—to unite peoples and draw upon their cultures and traditions to create an exciting and vibrant urban environment.

When, in October, 1993, the Ku Klux Klan received permission to hold a rally on the grounds of the Indiana State House and the Black Panthers decided to hold a counter rally on the Circle, Indianapolis and the nation were reminded of their respective heritages of cultural diversity and deeply rooted bigotry and racism. The public, though protective of the First Amendment right to freedom of speech, was generally perturbed by those who sought to encourage discord within the city. Mayor Stephen Goldsmith pointed out that Indianapolis welcomed cultural diversity but disliked racism and racists. These rallies served to unite the city, if only briefly, in its opposition against anyone who attempted to undermine racial and ethnic harmony. Ironically, the rallies were held the same weekend as the International Festival, which celebrates the city's cultural diversity. These unfortunate incidents helped to make lethargic Indianapolis residents aware of the need to accept all individuals on an equal footing and recognize that in a city which is part of a nation "one out of many," peaceful coexistence is a necessity.

See also: AMERICANIZATION AND NATIVISM; DEMOGRAPHIC PROFILE; MIGRATION PATTERNS; and individual ethnic groups and topics.

ECONOMY

James H. Madison

Three features are particularly important in understanding the history of the Indianapolis economy. First, Indianapolis has been shaped by a pattern of growth that has been relatively steady and moderate. Rather than growth by great leaps forward or radical twists and turns, the city's economy has moved at a pace that has enabled its people to adjust and accommodate to change. Related to the relatively steady speed of growth and change is the diversified nature of the Indianapolis economy, which has always consisted of a mixture of manufacturing, retail, and service industries and which has never had to depend on a dominant specialty, company, or industry. From the beginning there was a mixture, too, of public and private contributions to growth. Finally, transportation has always been of primary importance in shaping the city's history, from the flatboat to the railroad to the interstate truck and automobile. In these three areas—the moderate speed of growth, the mixture of activity, and the development of transportation—are to be found much of the city's particular economic history. Even in the late 20th century, when Indianapolis began to take on new outward forms, these three characteristics remained basic for understanding the city's past, present, and future.

The Indianapolis economy did not thrive prior to 1847. The place in these years, banker Hugh McCulloch recalled, was "an almost inaccessible village." Lack of a good navigable river or other means of adequate transportation constituted a severe handicap to economic development. Indeed, except for the very important function of serving as the state's capital—a source of considerable economic benefit from 1825 to the present—the business prospects for Indianapolis in these early years were not at all exceptional.

The high cost of transportation to and from Indianapolis meant that business activity was locally oriented and simple in form. Most important were the general stores that offered all manner of merchandise. Located on Washington Street, these retailers served town residents and, especially on Saturdays, farmers from Marion County. Retail trade remained simple and slight because of the challenges merchants faced in obtaining goods to sell and customers to buy them.

James H. Madison is Professor of History at Indiana University, Bloomington.

Commerce was slow to develop also because the town had no banks until 1834, when the Indianapolis Branch of the State Bank of Indiana opened its doors.

Manufacturing, like retailing, was simple in form and local in scope. Most manufacturing was of the household variety, whereby men and women produced goods at home for their own use. By the 1830s there were a few small artisans and craftsmen who made boots and shoes, clothing, furniture, and simple wood and iron tools for sale in the local market. And there were a few gristmills and sawmills that used the water power of Fall Creek, White River, and the Central Canal, though none of these sources was sufficient to power large-scale manufacturing.

A major attempt to stimulate an economic takeoff in Indianapolis began in 1828. Several leading citizens, including Nicholas McCarty, James M. Ray, James Blake, and Noah Noble, joined to form the Indianapolis Steam Mill Company. Using their close ties to the government, they obtained land from the state at a nominal price and permission to cut timber on state-owned property—one of the first in a long line of joint private-public endeavors for economic development in Indianapolis. By 1831 the Steam Mill Company had erected a three-story mill, with impressive capability to saw wood, grind grain, and card wool. This ambitious, multipurpose company was by far the biggest business in the town. It proved, in fact, to be too big, capable of producing more goods than the local market could consume. And because access to markets outside Indianapolis was so limited by poor transportation the mill seldom operated at full capacity. In 1835 the enterprise closed, becoming in relative terms one of the largest business failures in the city's history.

Rather than the great leap forward envisioned by the Indianapolis Steam Mill Company, industrial development before 1847 occurred in small steps. An important advance came in 1835 with Robert Underhill's iron foundry, which manufactured skillets, andirons, and plows. Five years later John Carlisle opened a large merchant flour mill, shipping flour by flatboat and wagon to the Ohio River. Another developing industry in the 1830s and 1840s was pork packing. Like flour milling it was dependent on growth in agriculture, sparked by newly arrived pioneers to the fertile soil of central Indiana. John H. Wright began one of the first profitable, large-scale pork packing operations in 1841. Wright's marriage into the Jeremiah Mansur family led to expanded operations by the mid–1840s, as the growing firm slaughtered thousands of hogs and packed the pork for shipment via flatboat down White River to the Mississippi River system.

With completion of the Madison and Indianapolis Railroad in 1847 the village became accessible at last. This first railroad to the capital city led to construction of other lines and stimulated an economic boom. New and fancier stores, some with display windows, appeared on Washington Street. On South Meridian Street, near the railroad depot, wholesale merchants began business. Soon warehouses and offices covered several blocks south of Washington Street. Gradually the hinterland that Indianapolis wholesale and retail merchants served expanded through Marion County and into contiguous counties. Indianapolis became the place to shop for much of the growing population of central Indiana. New banks appeared in the 1850s also, led by the brothers Stoughton A. and Calvin Fletcher and providing the financial base for economic growth.

Manufacturing attracted even more attention than commerce or banking. From businessmen, boosters, and newspapers came calls for attracting industry. "If Indianapolis ever arrives to anything more than a respectable inland town," the *Indianapolis Journal* editorialized on March 19, 1849, "it must be by becoming a manufacturing city." Such arguments led in 1853 to the formation of the Indianapolis Board of Trade, composed of 36 of the city's leading businessmen and boosters. In the next year they published their first circular, dedicated to proclaiming the advantages of the city to distant manufacturers and investors. Indianapolis, the Board of Trade asserted, possessed advantages of excellent railroad transportation, central location, mild and healthy climate, a low cost of living, broad tree-lined streets, many churches, and free public schools. Investment in "all classes of manufactures will yield large and certain returns," the circular promised. A larger pamphlet, published in 1857 and titled *Indianapolis: Its Manufacturing Interests, Wants, and Facilities*, repeated earlier lists of advantages accruing to businesses locating in the city. This promotional effort also listed 61 industries most likely to prove profitable for newcomers, ranging from agricultural implements to woolen goods.

The industry that boosters identified as most necessary was a rolling mill that would shape iron produced elsewhere into railroad rails. Not only would such a mill supply the booming market for rails in Indiana and other western states, but it also would attract heavy industry to the city, perhaps even a locomotive factory. The Board of Trade joined newspapers and the city council to entice investors from the East for the rolling mill. City banks and local businessmen, led by James Blake, invested large sums. The rolling mill began production just as the Panic of 1857 hit. The next years were difficult, but because the enterprise was so closely identified with the economic reputation and welfare of the city as to be, in banker Calvin Fletcher's words, "a public improvement," the community kept it going. The city council contributed support in 1860 by reducing the company's tax assessment by one half "on account of the mill being an institution of public benefit." As the economy recovered the rolling mill revived and during the Civil War it functioned as the leading industry of the city, just as its boosters had promised.

More prosaic industries also flourished in the 1850s. Businesses that processed agricultural products grew rapidly during the mid–19th century and had a collective impact on the city far larger than that of the rolling mill. The city boasted a dozen flour mills by the eve of the Civil War. Pork packing continued to expand, making Indianapolis one of the major centers of the industry. The construction of a five-story pork packing house in 1862 by Kingan Brothers brought the city one of the most modern facilities in the world. Blacksmith shops and machine shops began to specialize in agricultural implements, with Hasslemen and Vinton's machine shop producing 100 threshing machines in 1860. The Civil War only added to the demand for Indianapolis products, creating a manufacturing boom that brought life to dozens of new businesses.

The great push forward that began in the 1850s came largely as a result of the railroads. Businessmen and boosters proclaimed Indianapolis as the "railroad city" and well into the 20th century advertised its superior rail connections that earned for the city the title "Crossroads of America." Such claims received added validity when city leaders, with Mayor John Caven in the forefront, constructed a Belt Railroad that in 1877 efficiently linked major lines entering the city. Just before its completion Caven predicted that with the new facility "our city will be girt about with a cordon of industries like the pillar of cloud by day and the pillar of fire by night, telling us the angel of prosperity is going before us and leading us on." Caven's biblical imagery was exaggerated, but industry did indeed locate along the belt line south and west of the city. With new factories came workers' homes and industrial suburbs, including Haughville, Brightwood, and West Indianapolis, the latter located near the new stockyards built in conjunction with the Belt Railroad.

Aided by this superior transportation system, industrialization became the driving force in the city's economic development in the late 19th and early 20th centuries. Jobs attracted newcomers, mostly young men and women from the farms of southern Indiana, the hills of Tennessee and Kentucky, and the cities and countrysides of Europe. By 1880 nearly 10,000 industrial workers produced over $27 million worth of goods, making the city the leading industrial center in Indiana. By 1900 the city's manufacturing output had more than doubled and then doubled again by the eve of World War I, by which time the city ranked 20th in the nation in value of manufactured product, ahead of Louisville and Columbus, Ohio, but lagging behind St. Louis, Cleveland, Detroit, and Chicago. A special boost to manufacturing near the end of the century came from the opening of the natural gas fields in east-central Indiana. The promise made in 1894 by the Indianapolis Board of Trade—that "beyond all doubt the gas supply is inexhaustible"—was dashed within a decade, but the energy of natural gas gave an important boost to manufacturing.

Historians often refer to the economic changes of the late 19th and early 20th centuries as an industrial revolution, emphasizing the jarring and painful transition from a rural, agricultural to an urban, industrial economy. There is evidence of such change in Indianapolis and of the challenges and sufferings that accompanied industrialization. Many men and women and some children in the city labored long hours, for low wages, and under unsafe conditions, as they did elsewhere in the industrializing world. During the periodic depressions, as in the mid–1870s and early 1890s, workers suffered unemployment with no more than slight assistance from public and private sources. In response, workers and their allies attempted to form unions and to seek government regulation of the economy. Sometimes they went on strike, as in the great railroad strikes of 1877. In one nationally known experiment in Indianapolis, workers actually owned and managed a factory, the Columbia Conserve Company. Indianapolis businessmen resisted such efforts, particularly union campaigns for a closed shop. Under the leadership of David M. Parry and the Employers' Association of Indianapolis, organized in 1904, businesses successfully countered the growing power of unions. Industrialization also brought pollution of air and water. One of the city's best known residents, Booth Tarkington, complained in many of his novels of the coal smoke that hung heavy and dirty over the city. The Indianapolis Commercial Club, founded in 1890 by Col. Eli Lilly and William Fortune, addressed some of the problems of growth and change, including road and sewer improvements, unemployment relief, and the need for a city university.

The costs of industrialization in Indianapolis were severe, but likely not as harsh as in many other cities. Particularly important in smoothing some of the rough edges of industrialization was the diversified nature of the city's economy. No single firm and no single industry dominated, with the result that downswings in one industry or company did not wreak havoc on the entire city. Moreover, most industries evolved over decades, changing gradually rather than radically or abruptly.

The continuing importance of agriculture and natural resource based industries best illustrates the diversified and evolutionary quality of the city's manufacturing. The capital's leading industries by value of product in 1900 were not greatly different from those of 1850, including, in order, slaughtering and meat packing, foundry and machine shop products, flour and gristmill products, printing and publishing, carriages and wagons, and liquors and malts. Most of these industries depended on the agricultural production of midwestern farms and the timber of nearby forests. Among the many companies based on agriculture were Acme-Evans Company, a major flour miller, National Starch, begun in 1867 by William F. Piel to convert corn to starch and other products, and Van Camp Company, a cannery that became one of the nation's leading producers of pork and beans.

The foundry and machine production begun before the Civil War expanded in the late 19th century, with a large number of companies making products ranging from stoves and saws to steam engines. Boosters argued the need also for iron and steel manufacturing, but several attempts to begin production resulted in failure, due in part to the distance from adequate coal and iron deposits.

One new industry that did have a successful beginning in turn-of-the-century Indianapolis, aided by the large number of machine shops, was automobile manufacturing. In the 1890s buggy manufacturer Charles H. Black built a gasoline engine vehicle. The transition from buggies, wagons, bicycles, and carriages to automobiles was one made by several Indianapolis entrepreneurs and craftsmen, including David M. Parry and Joseph J. Cole. Nordyke and Marmon, a manufacturer of flour mill machinery, began making cars in 1903, while a bicycle maker, the Waverly Company, experimented with electric power automobiles. With automobiles came also auto parts manufacturers, such as James A. Allison and Carl G. Fisher. Their Prest-O-Lite Company began in the first decade of the new century to provide lamps for night driving. These two men were leaders in building the Indianapolis Motor Speedway, intended in part to test and promote automobiles. Auto parts manufacturing rather than finished cars became the city's contribution to the industry, however, as Cole, Marmon, and other car builders found they could not compete with Detroit.

The pattern of diversified manufacturing that prevailed in 1900 persisted through the first half of the 20th century, with the leading industries in 1950 including machinery, automobile parts and accessories, foods (especially meats), and durable household goods. The major addition to the industrial mix was pharmaceuticals, due largely to the rapid growth in the early 20th century of Eli Lilly and Company. Indianapolis boosters continued to emphasize the city's central location, transportation facilities, livestock and grain markets, diversified industries, and peaceful industrial relations. In common with counterparts across the nation, the city's industries struggled through the Great Depression of the 1930s, marked by long unemployment lines, failed businesses, and shortened work weeks. And then they faced the boom times of World War II, with companies straining to produce the huge volumes of pharmaceuticals, aviation parts, and other war goods that made major contributions to defeating the Axis powers.

The postwar economy seemed at first to be a continuation of patterns now a century old, with the city thriving on a diversified manufacturing base and a strong downtown retail and wholesale trade. Especially encouraging was the location during the 1950s of new factories for Ford, Chrysler, and Western Electric. The national prosperity of the late 1940s and 1950s gave additional encouragement to those who were content to continue in traditional channels. Yet change was in the making during the 1950s and 1960s even though the effects were not clearly perceived until during and after the recession of 1979–1982. Fundamental shifts were under way across America and in Indianapolis that would have major consequences. These changes would bring difficult, sometimes unhappy transitions, but by the 1990s it appeared that Indianapolis had weathered them with more success than many other metropolitan areas.

One shift was the decline in the relative importance of the manufacturing sector, particularly the durable goods industry. Indianapolis remained more heavily dependent on durable goods, particularly motor vehicle parts, than did the metropolitan areas of the United States generally, so that cyclical slowdowns in these areas hit the city's economy especially hard. This dependence was particularly evident in the recession of 1979–1982, which caused an estimated loss of 28,500 manufacturing jobs. The city's auto and machine tool industries took the brunt of the blow. But more than cyclical change was at work. Long term trends pointed with growing clarity to a fundamental shift away from manufacturing. By the late 1960s there were more jobs in the

Eli Lilly and Company's first building at 15 West Pearl Street, ca. 1876.
[Eli Lilly and Company Archives]

city's service sector than in manufacturing; in 1980 manufacturing accounted for fewer than a quarter of the jobs in the city. The 1980s brought sometimes shocking illustrations of these long-term changes, most notably in the closing of the Chrysler plant, even after a major government loan, and the loss of Western Electric, which once employed 8,000 workers. Both factories were located on the Shadeland Avenue industrial corridor, once the pride of the manufacturing city but looking more like a ghost corridor by 1990.

These changes brought home to Indianapolis the facts of national and international economic forces that were often beyond the control of local business leaders. Oil shortages, international competition, changing patterns of taste—all provided new arenas for business competition. Especially noticeable were the many Indianapolis companies, like their counterparts elsewhere, that were becoming parts or branches of larger corporations based outside the city. The phenomenon was not unknown in the city's earlier history: Kingan and Company's meat packing plant opened in the city during the Civil War as part of a far-flung business based in Belfast, Ireland; in the 1920s General Motors acquired David Parry's automobile company and also the Allison Engineering Company. But the late 20th century brought waves of mergers, acquisitions, and reorganizations. A list compiled by the Indianapolis Chamber of Commerce in

1966 of nearly 200 of the city's largest manufacturing firms included only 66 based in the city. The acquisition of the food processing firm of Stokely–Van Camp by Chicago-based Quaker Oats in 1983 not only eliminated 870 jobs but left the city with only one Fortune 500 member, Eli Lilly and Company. Increasingly, it seemed, decisions made outside Indianapolis had larger impact on the local economy. Some observers worried that such mergers and acquisitions reflected local management that was too conservative and city banks that were too small. There was concern also that substitution of branch plants for home-owned companies deprived the community of committed leadership and service.

Although the city's manufacturing sector by the 1980s was no longer as dominant as it had once been, it was far from dead. There were still thriving machine shops, for example, as there had been more than a century earlier. And the motor vehicle parts factories continued to employ large numbers of workers at relatively high wages. But the most important manufacturing growth was in newer industries that often depended on higher levels of research and technology—electronic, pharmaceutical, and medical instrument firms—rather than more traditional industries. The city's economic development efforts focused increasingly on these kinds of high technology and environmentally clean businesses, which citizens hoped would bring benefits of stable employment, high pay, and an educated work force.

Just as manufacturing changed in the last half of the 20th century so too did commerce. By 1950 Indianapolis had enjoyed a century of expanding retail and wholesale trade, nearly all of it located in the central business district. Trains and interurbans once brought thousands of shoppers to the downtown; now automobiles served that purpose, bringing increasing traffic congestion and problems in parking. New highways, particularly the interstate highways that began to enter Indianapolis, promised even more customers to the city that could justly continue to proclaim itself the "Crossroads of America." At the same time, however, new suburbs and shopping centers sprang up miles from the Circle. Glendale and Eastgate malls opened in the 1950s, followed by numerous others on the periphery. Downtown shopping declined drastically, nearly 33 percent in the years from 1948 to 1966. The construction of Interstate 465, the beltway completed around the city in 1970, enabled retailers and all kinds of other businesses to locate even farther from the central business district.

Increasingly the action was at the mall. Stores, including branches of big department chains, restaurants, branch banks, groceries, movie theaters, doctors' offices—all located in or near the malls, the shopping strips, and the interstate highways that surrounded and penetrated the city. Indianapolis, like other American cities, was turning inside out, becoming a doughnut with a hole in the center, a downtown that attracted office workers during the day but was dark and vacant at night. One of the many blows to downtown retailing came in 1982 when Brooks Brothers, a traditional clothing store that always located near the heart of a city's business district, announced that it had changed plans and would not open its new Indianapolis store near the Circle but rather far north at Keystone at the Crossing. Downtown retail renewal efforts, such as Claypool Court and Union Station, did not alter the fundamental shift, a fact underscored by the 1992 closure of L. S. Ayres department store on Washington Street. Talk of building a large mall on Washington Street began in the 1960s and took planning form in the 1980s as Circle Centre Mall, which boosters hoped would bring major department stores and smaller mall-type retailers to downtown.

Retailing flourished, but on the periphery, not in the core of the city. It was part of the booming service sector of the late 20th century Indianapolis economy. In the Mile Square and in the

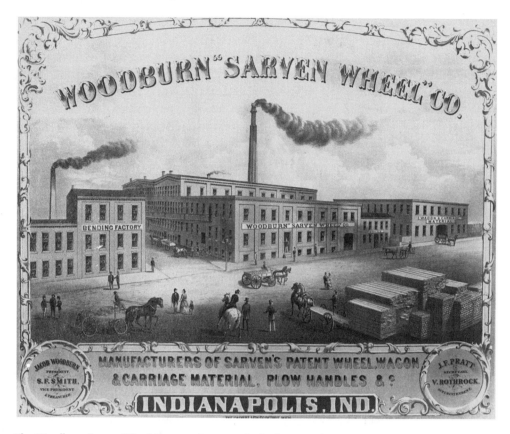

The Woodburn Sarven Wheel Company's patented wheel was used by carriage makers across the country during the late 19th century. [Indiana Historical Society, #C5775]

suburbs business services such as data processing, advertising, insurance, public relations, and temporary employment agencies became increasingly important and provided much of the job expansion by the 1980s. So too did legal and medical services. Indianapolis hospitals, like many other service industries, benefited from new highways bringing people from as far south as Bloomington and Bedford and as far north as Kokomo. New entertainment attractions also enticed paying visitors, whether to the Indianapolis Colts football games, The Children's Museum, or the Indianapolis Zoo. In such ways the city was beginning to cast a larger shadow in Indiana and the Midwest, seeming to many to be less a small town with a large number of people and more like the big city it really was.

Indianapolis banks also extended their reach. A turning point came with state legislation in 1985 that allowed Indiana banks to cross county lines and to acquire or to be acquired by out-of-state banks. The new law brought major changes to the three banks—Indiana National, American Fletcher, and Merchants National —that had long dominated the Indianapolis market. Mergers and acquisitions enabled bank expansion far beyond Marion County and included the acquisition in the late 1980s and early 1990s of these "Big Three" banks by out-of-state corporations. Proponents hoped that these changes would provide more sophisticated and powerful banking and financial services to the city's businesses, but others expressed concern about the loss of local control.

These changes in late 20th century Indianapolis—in banking and retailing, in manufacturing, and in the geographic spread and reshaping of the city—were common to most of urban America. But in Indianapolis there were additional elements that gave unusual direction and force and doubtless enabled the city to make transitions with more success than many of its counterparts.

Led by the Indianapolis Chamber of Commerce and its aggressively conservative head, William H. Book, the city's business elite in the 1940s and 1950s attempted to keep taxes low, avoid the snares of federal aid, and maintain Indianapolis as a pleasant city with a small-town feeling. It was during these decades that the derogatory label "India-no-place" had its greatest salience. The 1960s brought winds of change, however, and by 1969 an economic development study suggested that Indianapolis was on the verge of a takeoff. The recession of 1979–1982 slowed some projects, but by 1986 Mayor William H. Hudnut III could with some validity label Indianapolis "the entrepreneurial city." Hudnut and others pointed with pride to an active, risk-taking leadership that had effected major changes in the city, particularly its downtown. They gloried in such outside judgments as the proclamation by *Time* magazine in 1984 that "India-no-place is no more" and the inclusion by business guru John Naisbitt a year later of Indianapolis on his list of the ten best places in which to start a business. Perhaps signaling the new economic vitality as clearly as any outside judgment was the appearance in 1980 of the *Indianapolis Business Journal*, reporting and assessing the rapid changes occurring in the city.

This entrepreneurial city and its new leadership devoted both public and private resources to a variety of citywide initiatives but ultimately came to focus on downtown revitalization. Beginning with John J. Barton and Richard G. Lugar in the 1960s and continuing with Hudnut through the 1980s, stronger city mayors began to seek federal aid and to combine it with local property tax abatements and low-interest city loans for downtown urban renewal. The implementation in 1970 of Unigov, which combined many city and county government functions, gave activist mayors a large base of money and power. Lugar and Hudnut were especially successful in gaining the respect and confidence of the city's business community. Private investment added millions of dollars to downtown construction. Local philanthropy played a major role also, including the Krannert Charitable Trust and especially the Lilly Endowment. Once local leaders had begun revitalization efforts, the Lilly Endowment jumped in to contribute many millions of dollars to downtown projects. All this diversity of growth and development was orchestrated by shifting partnerships of private and public leadership. Perhaps most important was the Greater Indianapolis Progress Committee (GIPC), an advisory group of city leaders who played a major role in planning and building support for downtown revitalization.

The most visible features of the entrepreneurial city of the 1970s and 1980s were the buildings that rose from the downtown core, including office structures like the American United Life Building and the Bank One Tower and public places like the Indianapolis Zoo, the renewed Union Station, and the new structures on the new campus of Indiana University–Purdue University, Indianapolis. Aggressive and imaginative leadership also developed sports facilities and events that led to proclaiming Indianapolis as "Sportsville, USA" and lured large numbers of visitors and their money to the city.

The successes visible by the 1980s did not hide challenges that appeared increasingly troublesome by the 1990s. Some of the building projects in which the city was a partner were losing

Women assembling chain at the Diamond Chain Company in 1918.
[Diamond Chain Company]

money, and the Circle Centre Mall faced frustrating delays. Some observers also suggested that the city had concentrated too heavily on the downtown, allowing the periphery to develop without sufficient attention. Less obvious, but increasingly recognized as fundamental in importance, were the problems facing the city's woefully inadequate public schools. As early as 1982 an analysis of the Indianapolis economy concluded that the mediocre local education levels were hindering the growth of knowledge-intensive, high-tech business in the city. Black residents bore special burdens of inadequate schools, of an outrageously high infant mortality rate, of low per capita incomes, and of joblessness, especially among young black men, that was exacerbated by the decline of manufacturing employment that had attracted many of their grandparents to the city. There was sentiment also that Indianapolis lagged behind other midwestern cities in providing attractive job possibilities for women, particularly in executive positions. One problem that hit without regard to race or gender was air pollution, both from industry and from the growing number of automobiles. Not only did poor air quality affect residents' health but leaders believed that it also kept some businesses from locating in the city. And as the city expanded outward there was growing concern about the need to develop a multicounty framework for dealing with automobile congestion, inadequate public transportation, and other problems facing the larger metropolitan area.

Even as they identified new challenges the people of Indianapolis could look back with pride on the accomplishments of recent decades. Despite ups and downs, the economy appeared to be relatively stable and prosperous, still diversified in thriving manufacturing, retail, and service industries. The construction of a United Airlines maintenance facility in the early 1990s promised to bring several thousand well-paying jobs to the metropolitan area. Although the decades of the 1970s and 1980s had provided special enthusiasms for economic development and for pride of place, this was not the first generation in Indianapolis able to look back with some sense of accomplishment. The generation of the 1850s, for example, had worked hard and successfully to attract railroads and build a manufacturing base. The political leadership of Mayor Caven in the 1870s had engaged city government in economic development a century before the administrations of Lugar and Hudnut. And the leadership of private citizens such as Col. Eli Lilly in the 1890s had revitalized the city long before GIPC. There was continuity in the city's economic development, mixed, as always, with change. The city's economic future was likely to be of a similar blend, with its residents and leaders deciding the relative proportions. As in the past they would need to pay special attention to maintaining the moderate speed of growth and change, to balancing the mixture of manufacturing, retail, and service industries, and to ensuring continued transportation access that connected the people of Indianapolis to each other and to the world beyond.

See also: AGRICULTURE AND AGRICULTURAL INDUSTRIES; AUTOMOBILE INDUSTRY; BANKING INDUSTRY; INSURANCE INDUSTRY; METAL PROCESSING AND FABRICATION; RETAILING; and individual names, companies, and organizations.

EDUCATION

William J. Reese

As the prosperity of a city depends, in a large measure, upon the facilities for education afforded its children, any step tending to develop that source of wealth and greatness, should be made known to those who receive its benefits." So wrote Thomas B. Elliott, president of the board of visitors of the Indianapolis public schools, in 1867. Like some civic leaders today, Elliott and his contemporaries believed that many citizens failed to support public schools adequately and that many pupils disliked the discipline of the classroom. But the city still had a responsibility to build schools to help improve and control the rising generation.

Free, tax-supported public education was one of the great social experiments of the 19th century. Schools have remained a barometer of civic life, sensitively registering changing climates of opinion and the highest aspirations and harshest civic realities. Indianapolis is a very different place in the 1990s than when its first public schools opened in the early 1850s. Yet thoughtful citizens still believe that a good society requires effective public schools.

Historians often describe the history of urban schools as a familiar tale of rise and fall. The metaphor helps contrast the high hopes of the 19th century with today's sober realities. But it wrongly implies that city systems once enjoyed some golden age when schools effectively met everyone's social, moral, and intellectual needs. Every generation of children, teachers, and school officials encounters unique problems. But city schools have perennially faced the consequences of serving neighborhoods stratified by race, ethnicity, and income. Society has constantly expected schools to solve intractable problems, asking teachers to perform miracles and then becoming disillusioned with their failures. In the 1990s some influential citizens want to dismantle urban school systems, enabling markets and private schools to revitalize them.

The men and women who built the Indianapolis schools dreamed different dreams. They were less enamored by private schools. They envisioned a city system that embraced children and youth from all social classes, one in which the poor had a fair chance to rise, based on hard work and talent. "The free schools are the people's schools," wrote William A. Bell, president of

William J. Reese is Professor of Education, History, and American Studies at Indiana University, Bloomington, and editor of the *History of Education Quarterly.*

the school commissioners, in 1879. "What a people wishes to become it must put into its schools. . . . A Republican form of government can only rest on general intelligence, and general intelligence can be secured only through free public schools." With access to a complete system of education including high schools, "the child of the humblest citizen can acquire an education that will enable him to compete even-handed in the battle of life with the child of a millionaire."

Modern advocates of private schools have in a sense rediscovered earlier educational arrangements, those made before Indianapolis opened its first public schools in 1853. Before the 1850s, children and youth largely learned to read and write at home, and their education was supplemented by academic and moral instruction in a host of institutions. Sunday schools, an 18th century British invention, were popular with many of the city's Protestant denominations. Some Indianapolis neighborhoods also had partially tax-supported district schools that taught elementary subjects, similar to one-room schools in the countryside. Students whose parents could afford the tuition or boarding fees attended various private schools, often called seminaries or academies. These schools, which taught elementary and sometimes advanced subjects for the older pupils, added to the rich mix of institutions that educated children in the growing city. In addition to the handful of prestigious academies, countless short-lived private schools opened and closed in antebellum Indianapolis, leaving little trace of their influence.

The idea that in theory all children should attend school together in free public schools soon gained support. By the 1850s many prominent Whigs and civic leaders feared evident social class divisions and believed government could ameliorate these and other public ills. Such reformers led the way in the creation of a unified system of free, tax-supported schools within the city limits. These reformers continued to praise the salutary role of Sunday schools and moral instruction generally, but they grew suspicious of private education, seeing it as a divisive element in urban life, certain to deepen antagonisms between rich and poor.

Prominent businessmen, professionals, and leading Protestant ministers increasingly endorsed the public schools. Town notables were appointed to the board of visitors, which was replaced by an elected board of school commissioners. Middle and upper middle class Protestants took public schools seriously, often withdrawing their children from private academies and complimenting the work of the common schools.

After the Civil War the system grew impressively, with the school term increasing from 110 to 180 days. Unfavorable rulings by the state Supreme Court regarding tax-supported education had previously thwarted progress, but the removal of legal obstacles enabled public education to expand rapidly in the coming decades. Between 1869 and 1879 the number of schools increased from 13 to 25, the teaching staff grew from 78 to 212, and daily pupil attendance jumped from 5,160 to 13,336. Even so, schools remained small. None had more than 7 teachers, and whoever taught the highest grades was the "principal teacher," later a full-time administrator. Indianapolis High School, opened permanently in 1863, was the pinnacle of the system.

Lay school visitors or commissioners delegated considerable authority to the superintendent, who usually supervised or taught in the high school. His staff grew as enrollments increased. Board members formally hired the teachers, but uniting all the schools into a coherent system was the mission of central administration.

Superintendents, working with local principals, implemented a host of important reforms: they created more age-graded classes, hired women as elementary teachers, purchased uniform textbooks, standardized procedures for class promotion, and emphasized expert supervision. The curriculum was modest, emphasizing moral education and basic subjects. Few families could afford to send their children, whose labor was essential to family survival, to high school; those enrolled had passed a tough entrance test.

Hence most teachers and school officials worried more about the morals and minds of the masses than the favored few. In 1879 H. S. Tarbell, superintendent of schools, complained that those who especially needed moral education and intellectual training never enrolled. Most at risk were "the children from the lower walks of life," but the schools reached only "the great middle classes. The greater part of the children of parents in the highest intellectual, social and financial circles are in our schools, but the children of the lowest ranks do not reach the schools, or remain in them but a short time." Many of the poor never attended school; those who did were frequently late or absent; and even the most conscientious pupils usually left the system by the sixth grade.

The deleterious effects of poverty upon children were constant concerns, and so were the actions of certain teenagers. According to Superintendent Tarbell, many adolescents employed in marginal jobs loitered on Indianapolis street corners, young hooligans all. Their ill-begotten "homes" could hardly curb vice and immorality. When they did attend school these youth "come enough to annoy, enough to throw a web of evil influences about some other youth, enough to take time and energy of teachers from more hopeful pupils, but not enough to get more from the schools than the beginning of an intellectual furnishing, with the moral influences thrown away." Because of these "vicious" adolescents, sound child rearing was "well nigh impossible" in certain neighborhoods.

Tarbell was referring to white, working class, teenage boys who worked as bootblacks, messengers for shopkeepers, factory hands, or apprentices in shady businesses. Schools stood for law and order. Administrators regularly published statistics on attendance, punctuality, and other indices of progress. Like his predecessors, Superintendent Tarbell remained fearful of class conflict but now wondered whether the schools could really help the poor. Sounding quite Darwinian, he concluded that each generation saw some progress, "but it is Utopian to anticipate that the mass of children will rise in any great degree beyond the status of their parents."

Ironically, educational aspirations seemed highest among the most aggrieved workers: black citizens. In 1867 board president Elliott highlighted the plight of the "colored" population. Blacks were currently barred from the schools, an outrage. "If general education is for the protection of the community, and adds to its wealth and greatness, is not that prosperity lessened by so much as any class are permitted to grow up in ignorance? Is an ignorant black man a less evil than an ignorant white? Is a black savage a milder type of heathen than a white one?" An injury to one, Elliott affirmed, "affects all injuriously, with no compensating advantage to any."

The last census had counted 1,653 African-Americans in Indianapolis, of whom about 300 attended "private colored pay schools," largely "conducted and supported by themselves. . . . " The high attendance rate revealed the African-American zeal for learning and aspirations to full citizenship. "The ratio of school attendance to the total school population is almost without precedent," claimed Elliott, despite their ungraded classrooms and poorly trained teachers. Writing on behalf of the school visitors, he thus concluded: "In our judgement humanity, justice, and sound public policy, demand that this class of our citizens shall receive the benefit of our common school system."

Such compassion still existed in Indianapolis after the Civil War, but it was hardly widespread. In 1869 blacks were admitted to the public schools, but into segregated classes; within a decade they comprised 9 percent of the total enrollment. In the 1870s Superintendent Abram C.

A typical classroom for students of the Indianapolis Free Kindergarten Society,
ca. 1914. [Butler University Archives]

Shortridge heroically integrated Indianapolis High School despite white protest, and blacks attended integrated high schools until the 1920s. While condemning unruly white teenagers, educational leaders consistently praised African-Americans for their faith in the ameliorating effects of education. Black adults flocked to evening schools in the 1870s. "In the colored [night] schools," wrote the superintendent, "so great was the anxiety of the pupils (mostly adults, and gray-headed) to learn that all that was necessary was to provide the opportunity." However, the white male toughs at school preferred to annoy their teachers than to study; their schools "were not worth their cost."

A few citizens continued to dream of a socially and racially integrated school system, but the ideal was unrealized. How to retain the support of the native white middle and upper classes while appealing to more groups remained a challenge. Although Indianapolis had only a small percentage of foreign-born residents, it did have a sizable number of Germans who successfully petitioned under state law for German language instruction for their children. Schools emphatically aimed to Americanize everyone; German instruction, however, ensured that an important minority group did not form its own schools but pledged allegiance to the public schools. German language instruction was also offered to non-German children, and nearly 2,500 students took the subject in 16 different schools by 1883. Special language programs for English language students also helped train future teachers, and German remained a popular subject until it was banned during World War I.

Attracting poorer working class children to the schools proved more difficult. Some observers in the 1870s and 1880s resigned themselves to the idea that poverty made full attendance impossible. Other educators said the schools shared the blame, since their arid curriculum repelled many students. Perhaps the idea of a common curriculum was harmful to the poor, who might benefit from a different, more practical education. Although everyone in school ultimately was affected by what these reformers had in mind, the working classes seemed especially fit for a new type of education.

As early as the 1860s the superintendent sought to improve the quality of mass education for everyone. The curriculum was still oriented around the three R's in the lowest grades, plus the addition of English grammar, geography, and history in the grammar grades. One teacher, Nebraska Cropsey, later a renowned primary school supervisor, traveled widely to study the Oswego system, which stressed that young children learn best from contact with objects, not just books. Handling and manipulating physical materials, for example, taught children about space, texture, form, color, and dimension. Local educators also debated the theories of famous European writers such as Johann Pestalozzi and Friedrich Froebel, who stressed the importance of play, group work, and affection in education.

By the 1890s Cropsey and the city superintendent called for the creation of public kindergartens. Across the nation, however, urban systems embraced manual training as the best hope for the curriculum, turning education into a more active process for students. That schools should train the hand as well as the mind was the common refrain, and pupils needed to learn eye and hand coordination, craft skills, and familiarity with tools. As cities grew larger and more complex and as industrialism undermined crafts, many educators thought that manual training could teach important values and skills otherwise lost to the young.

Reformers proclaimed that there was more to school than spelling, multiplication, or memorization. Historically, every classroom in Indianapolis had emphasized rote memorization: pupils sat in bolted-down double desks or individual seats arranged by rows and mastered textbook material to recite aloud to their teachers. Though it would later become transformed into vocational education for the working classes, manual training promised to enliven the curriculum, to awaken those deadened by traditional pedagogy, and to make schools more interesting.

By the 1880s children in the elementary grades received a broadened curriculum. Though the traditional subjects remained dominant, students now had classes in drawing, penmanship, music, painting, and clay modeling. Critics called these innovations "fads" and "frills," but the schools now recognized the capacity of the young to create and learn by doing. Similarly, mechanical drawing and other manual training courses entered the high school.

A second high school to serve the south side opened in 1888 in temporary quarters south of Union Station; the permanent building, named Manual High School, opened in 1895. This high school was academically oriented, offering regular courses of study found in the older high school, which was soon renamed Shortridge. But the idea circulated that manual training might be especially useful for certain social classes. In 1888 the superintendent of schools said that the "great masses" of pupils, who were not destined for college and found academics tough, especially needed a more utilitarian education.

The seeds of differentiated learning had been planted, as Indianapolis shared the national mania for manual training and then vocational education. School enrollments swelled in the final decades of the century, which educators attributed to curriculum changes and the overall attractiveness of the system, overlooking other demographic changes. For decades to come school leaders faced more demands for new buildings, courses of study, and social services to meet the changing needs of society.

Despite the common use of the phrase school "system," individual schools varied enormously. Educators in the mid–19th century emphasized the importance of a common curriculum, which all students could presumably master. Within a generation this faith had slowly eroded. Shortridge High School became the city's most prominent public school, serving a small percentage of mostly middle and upper class youth. Many educators were already convinced that working class children were, to use a popular phrase, hand-minded. Blacks were integrated in the high schools but segregated in the lower grades, further undermining the idea of commonality.

The 20th century brought further changes to the schools. Like those in other cities, the Indianapolis schools adopted numerous innovations between the turn of the century and World War I. Reformers transformed the social functions of manual training and sponsored other new programs. As before, educators tried to enroll more working class children in the system, even in the city's expanding high schools, and they struggled with the old questions of race and social class, with uneven results.

Indianapolis had entered a great age of reform. Educators and various civic leaders again turned to the public schools to improve and control youth, especially teenagers newly displaced from the workplace due to child labor reforms and more effective compulsory education laws. Whereas educators in the 1880s worried about 12–year-olds who dropped out, school people now worried about 14–year-olds. And the perennial question of what knowledge was of the most worth again preoccupied concerned citizens and educators.

By 1909 the Indianapolis schools had an average daily attendance of over 25,000 pupils. Most were in elementary schools, but this figure marked a doubling of enrollments since the 1880s. That many politicians, social reformers, and civic leaders supported the expanding system gave educators a renewed sense of importance. In an age deeply divided between labor and capital, a division which frightened schoolmen as well as business leaders, the schools promised social amelioration and the proper socialization of the young. Although many reformers felt compassion for the poor, educators and social activists embraced business models of efficiency and tried to apply them to schooling. How to fit pupils into their proper niche became an overriding concern.

Didactic teaching methods and self-contained classrooms—with a teacher in the front of a room listening to recitations of basic subject material from his or her charges—still remained common. But the innovative ideas of the late 19th century had changed the schools. How to make schools more practical, how to tap children's interests, how to connect classroom learning with the real world of work dominated educational discussion. The language of what is loosely called progressive education had antiintellectual overtones. Advocates contrasted the great benefits of basket weaving with the exaggerated benefits of reading books. But the attempt to build a cohesive city system continued.

Superintendent C. N. Kendall wrote in 1909 that educators had to respond more effectively to the many working class children then entering the schools. Educators questioned the capacity of these pupils to master an academic curriculum, though they believed manual training and especially vocational education would serve them well. "Critics of the . . . public schools overlook the fact that in the old-time schools the children were more largely from educated families than now," wrote Kendall. "The children of the uneducated did not attend school, or, if they did, they attended irregularly. . . . The high school or academy pupils were almost exclusively from cultivated homes. Large numbers of our present high school [students] come from homes of a different sort."

For too long schools had remained too bookish, said modern educators, even though children learned best by working with their hands. This seemed universally true but especially for the poor, whose parents rarely appreciated books or the life of the mind. Progressive thinkers knew that children were active creatures often bored by books. Superintendent Kendall said that schools should draw upon "the natural interest of the child." "Shall we keep the child poring over books until he becomes more than wearied with the whole idea of school?"

Manual training challenged the reign of books, and the new educational gospel emphasized that many pupils preferred shop class to algebra. Indianapolis thus expanded manual training programs in most elementary grades and created shop classes for boys and cooking classes for girls in the upper grammar grades. Everyone now pursued some type of manual training, but school officials increasingly emphasized the importance of vocationalism. The poor especially needed job training; they were the ones reportedly unhappy at school, finding academic study too difficult and discouraging as they faced a future of dead-end jobs.

The Manual Training High School on the south side quickly weakened academic requirements in its manual training programs. In 1902 principal Charles E. Emmerich said this would contribute to "the greatest good to the greatest number." In fact, many of Manual's students continued to elect academic courses. Other educators in the city directed manual training at the black working classes, and the skills taught seemed to confirm their lowly status. The manual training supervisor wrote in 1909 that African-American children needed better job training: "In the colored schools even more attention is given to the industrial work. The girls have sewing from the third grade through the eighth. In the eighth year they draft, cut and make their graduation dresses. In addition to cooking they have laundry work and some housekeeping, sweeping, dusting, and the like." Young African-American boys learned how to repair old shoes.

The social functions of the Indianapolis schools expanded remarkably in the 20th century. While the schools never abandoned their commitment to academics, especially in the more middle class schools, the system now offered an array of new courses and programs. Schools not only trained hands as well as minds, but they also extended their reach in other directions. This was reflected by the hiring of more administrators, beyond the superintendent and his immediate staff, by 1910. There were directors or supervisors for the primary schools, grammar schools, German instruction, physical education and school hygiene, civics, school gardening, art, manual training, domestic arts, special education, evening schools, truancy, and full-time principals at the high schools.

The idea that schools should provide social services as well as vocational subjects also proved irresistible. Civic groups successfully lobbied for more school playgrounds: to promote health, to teach team spirit, and to counter vice. School gardens became enormously popular, teaching interesting knowledge without recourse to books and helping the poor beautify their homes and neighborhoods. Vacation schools emphasized manual training and some remedial academic work; and medical inspectors probed into the medical histories of underachieving students.

Indianapolis also established ungraded classes for those who misbehaved or were chronically truant as well as special classes for "backward" or mentally deficient pupils. This movement toward special education reflected the growing complexity of the system. Since social promotion was uncommon in the 19th century, children with chronic learning problems often became permanent residents in the same classroom. Superintendent Kendall, however, in 1909 reported the establishment of two classes for "retarded" pupils, those too old for their grade. Other special education teachers traveled from school to school working with those with other learning problems.

These pupils were mostly poor. Educators characterized them both as children in need and a drag upon regular classrooms. Not surprisingly, they received a heavy dose of manual training. Katrina Meyers, who taught the special class at the Washington School, complained that her pupils, so accustomed to failure at school, "have learned chronic habits of idleness, and many are mischievous and troublesome."

Meyers later served as director of sewing both in the "colored schools" and the "schools for defective children," the catch-all phrase for special students. That she worked with black female students and the mentally handicapped was not unusual; many believed African-Americans were mentally inferior. Truant officers and social workers, however, graphically described the dire effects of racism and poverty upon black families. Family separations, divorce, and one-parent households were becoming depressingly common as job discrimination denied African-Americans access to the American dream. Black attendance rates, once the pride of schoolmen, sank as disillusioned young people learned that education did not guarantee social mobility. Meyers typically reported that sewing taught black girls a trade and "habits of industry, accuracy, economy, skill, and neatness and . . . strengthen[ed] the intellectual, industrial, and moral character of the child."

Vocationalism reached every part of the system, with different results. High school enrollments boomed, fostering the creation of Arsenal Technical High School in 1912. Like Manual, Tech offered both academic and strictly vocational subjects. Shortridge, too, offered some manual and vocational classes, but it aimed its courses higher, providing classes in the decorative arts like jewelry making and in white collar pursuits like sales and advertising. Manual and Tech offered an array of vocational courses for industrial jobs, and their students often had a watered-down academic curriculum. A state vocational education law in 1913 fostered additional courses of study, strengthening the utilitarian aims of the schools.

Indianapolis high schools were transformed not only by the vocational education movement but also by the rise of a student culture that reshaped the high school experience. Though every city school had physical education classes, organized athletics—men's baseball, football, and basketball—became common, providing the essence of "school spirit." An intense football rivalry deteriorated in 1907 into a riot, prompting the elimination of competitive games between Shortridge and Manual.

Besides athletics, numerous student activities, usually sponsored but not fully controlled by teachers, became prominent in all high schools after the turn of the century. Various clubs, societies, sororities and fraternities (even after they were banned), student newspapers, yearbooks, and activities helped fill the school day. Students were supposed to know (and glory in) their class colors, class yell, and place in the crowd.

By World War I, as enrollments continued to climb, school administrators realized that these new programs, services, and innovations had redefined the social purposes of education. The booming enrollments at Manual and Tech seemed proof enough that Indianapolis offered a practical education, though the elimination of jobs for teenagers may have accounted for rising enrollments more than the appeal of particular courses of study. Compared with the spartan curriculum of an earlier era, the schools had nevertheless undergone a revolution. School employees taught children how to grow flowers and vegetables, examined their teeth and adenoids, instructed them in civics, taught them how to play, provided manual training in different doses, taught a wider variety of courses, and occasionally questioned the value of books. Once interscholastic athletics resumed, rival communities of students and adults again cheered for their

Shortridge High School students, ca. 1920. [Indiana Historical Society, Bass Collection, #287788F]

team and booed the opposition. In the jargon of the day, everyone would use his or her leisure time well.

The schools continued to embrace these ideas in the coming decades. Between the 1920s and World War II Indianapolis retained most of these curricular innovations and quite a few social services despite the ravages of economic depression. New programs on testing, evaluation, and course placement also became prominent. The idea that schools had a place for everyone, though not the same place, had triumphed, and urban leaders remained convinced that schools were vital social institutions.

Even though the Great Depression led to budget cuts, the Indianapolis system effectively weathered most challenges. Children from privileged social groups still benefited most from the system, but enrollments continued to climb. Enrollments jumped from over 33,000 pupils in 1910 to over 46,000 in 1940 and mushroomed as hard times displaced many teenagers from the workplace. High school enrollments skyrocketed. Special education classes also spread, as new groups of children with learning problems attracted considerable interest, leading to more segregated classes.

The Indianapolis schools had become an essential part of community life, offering a range of services and courses of study to a larger population of students. Despite the scarcity of jobs, the commitment to vocational training, particularly for the poor, and to a high quality academic training, especially for the white middle and upper classes, was reinforced by the Depression.

Since the early 1900s elementary schools utilized homogeneous ability grouping, clustering the brightest pupils together in each grade. By the 1930s psychological and intelligence tests became common, providing teachers and administrators with information used to place children in ability groups and formal tracks. Working class children fared worst on these standardized tests, which measured academic competence and familiarity with middle class norms. School officials, however, said these tests measured individual achievement and potential; the consequence was that pupils in the slowest reading groups in elementary schools generally had difficulty enrolling in a high school college preparatory track.

The sheer growth of the system led to more bureaucracy and a more impersonal working environment for teachers. Hiring more specialists as teachers and administrators took its toll. "The present tendency toward specialization in all lines of work shows its result in a certain segregation in large organizations," wrote a member of the central office in 1920. "Each person is so occupied with his own line of work that he loses touch with the work of others who are engaged with him in a common effort." Teacher activists emphasized that the consolidation of power at the top required the formation of a strong union of pedagogues to protect their interests.

One example of greater specialization occurred when the school board concurred with white supremacy groups and opened the all-black Crispus Attucks High School in 1927. Blacks strongly opposed its creation. Although the elementary schools had always been segregated, the high schools had been integrated since the 1870s. As the number of African-Americans attending high school increased, racists had periodically petitioned for a separate high school. They had finally succeeded.

Native white chauvinism found additional outlets in the 1920s. Indianapolis established special civics programs in all the schools in the early 1900s, and citizenship training was often tinged with xenophobia. Patriotic activities proliferated during the war and 100 Percent Americanism was an easy next step. Despite the relatively small percentage of immigrants in Indianapolis, the elementary schools in the 1920s held plays warning every newcomer to obey the laws, to respect the truant officer, and to pledge loyalty to America. Americanization programs were even prominent in the "colored" schools, implying that native blacks needed tutelage in the ABC's of citizenship.

The Indianapolis schools revealed their staying power despite the hard times. They grew in size and complexity. In 1939 over 43,000 students were enrolled in the city's 85 elementary schools, and an amazing 20,000 were in the city's high schools, which now numbered seven. Unemployment forced many teenagers to stay in school who would have preferred finding a job. Broad Ripple was annexed to Indianapolis in the 1920s, and the high school located there was thus added to the city system. But the suburban townships remained educationally autonomous.

High schools remained multipurpose institutions. They were called "comprehensive" high schools, offering a variety of academic and vocational courses and an assortment of student activities from clubs to organized sports. Shortridge was the premier academic institution, though Tech and Manual also offered some strong academic programs. As African-American critics predicted, some academic programs weakened at Crispus Attucks in the 1930s, though its sports teams, barred from competing with the white high schools, attracted considerable acclaim. Many black residents became proud of their high school and its dedicated corps of teachers, some of whom had advanced graduate degrees.

Vocationalism and national service gained additional support during World War II. School gardens again became popular, and teachers and pupils ran scrap drives, sold savings bonds, and otherwise contributed to the war effort. In one month alone the schools sold nearly $100,000 worth of war stamps. Some youth were indifferent, of course, and student leaders criticized classmates for not doing more. In 1944 a contributor to a school newspaper emphasized that the local schools were part of the home front. "Committed to the policy of making the schools a source of security and service to all age levels," he wrote, "the schools are giving special attention to a program of counseling and classes for returning service men, to special evening vocational, academic, apprenticeship and citizenship courses."

The fight against fascism rekindled concerns about the role of schools in a democracy. Blacks, who helped defeat fascism abroad, knew only segregation at home. The state banned segregated schools in 1949, allowing students at Crispus Attucks to apply for admission elsewhere. Most African-Americans still attended largely segregated elementary schools, and the problems of racial segregation defined city politics for decades to come.

The dominant ideals of the Indianapolis schools in 1948 were outlined in a policy document entitled *To Form a More Perfect Union*. Men were living in propitious times, wrote Clarence L. Farrington, president of the board of school commissioners, in a preface to the report. He emphasized "the strategic role of the public schools and public libraries as guardians of our free institutions." Schools helped define and preserve the "American Way of Life."

The report emphasized that the schools had to teach all children to become law-abiding citizens. In language common in previous decades, the author underscored the "interdependence" of society, requiring people to learn their place in society and mutual obligations. "Loyalties and 'school spirit,' cultivated by participation in larger school group activities, the emotional appeal of music, art, and literature, and the common participation in such exercises as the pledge of allegiance to the flag and to the republic are convincing evidence of the unifying influence of the public schools." Whether children served as crossing guards, attended assembly, joined a club, or listened to the guidance counselor, they were learning their civic duties.

The author adamantly argued that schools respected each individual, that everyone had different talents and interests. Guidance began in the first grade, and standardized tests in grades 1, 4, and 7 helped sort each pupil into the proper ability group and track. "To establish justice, equality of opportunity, in the educational sense, does not mean that all children should take identical courses of study," the writer emphasized. Rather, "each child should be given the training most suitable for his needs."

Guidance programs and vocational education remained influential. Children were taught the "American Way of Life," pledging allegiance not only to the nation but to the idea that a differentiated curriculum reflected democratic principles. Schools taught children to get along and to defer to authority and innumerable rules and regulations. This would lead to domestic tranquility and a smoothly functioning society.

After the war the Indianapolis city schools seemed well positioned to prosper. The baby boom, economic growth, and continued emphasis on the value of education seemed propitious. School enrollments again climbed. By the mid–1960s Indianapolis had a little over a half million residents; over 105,000 of them were enrolled in its regular day schools and over 7,000 in adult classes. In 1965 Indianapolis had 109 elementary schools, 10 high schools, and a School for Practical Nursing. Head Start classes and other Great Society programs soon appeared, and the capacity of the system to grow seemed almost limitless.

In the 1950s and 1960s, the Indianapolis Public Schools (IPS) nevertheless held fast to earlier curricular reforms. The use of standardized tests and the creation of more special education programs were prime examples. An unquestioned faith in vocationalism led to the opening of Harry E. Wood High School in 1953. High school graduates across the city soon also received specialized diplomas that specified their track, helping employers sort out job applications more easily. Still supportive of the school system's role in training workers and citizens, commercial and industrial leaders strongly endorsed vocationalism. They published detailed guides on local businesses and industries to help familiarize students with future job opportunities.

The Indianapolis schools therefore grew in size but pursued familiar objectives. H. L. Shibler, superintendent of schools in the 1950s, cooperated with business and civic leaders and emphasized the moral and vocational goals of education. Shibler proudly noted that the local schools were nationally recognized for their commitment to free enterprise. Local high schools annually received a lion's share of awards from the conservative Valley Forge Freedoms Foundation, an anti-Communist organization. Shibler also waged war against juvenile delinquency, another contemporary fear.

Shibler applauded the expansion of the system and its vocational character. Educators had long discredited the idea that all children should or could master the same subjects. Like most school administrators, Shibler supported standardized tests, the results of which revealed each child's achievement, intelligence, and potential. Reflecting the tenor of the times, he also said that schools resembled business corporations. Unlike factories, however, schools could not discard unwanted products. "Each pupil," he wrote in 1955, "needs a custom-job of training; but we deal in such large numbers that we cannot hand-craft each pupil's training job; we have to use mass production methods." Like a Ford, children could be customized, but mostly they rolled off the assembly line.

Virulently anti-Communist, Shibler emphasized the material benefits of graduating from high school. He applauded the "American Way of Life," meaning support for free enterprise, anti-Communism, and consumerism. He was ecstatic when a former Soviet teacher and government official fled to freedom and then lectured at the Murat Temple on a national tour. The speaker reportedly smuggled hot-water heaters, radios, and televisions—all poorly made —from behind the Iron Curtain in order to demonstrate the superiority of American capitalism. Teachers and students were told that Americans enjoyed better working conditions and consumed better products than the Communists. Soviets were industrial slaves whose lives were darkened by bad toasters and other shoddy goods.

Emphasizing the material benefits of education seemed to undermine older moral concerns, leading some critics to call the schools godless. Shibler responded that most teachers were in fact practicing Christians, who led their classes in morning prayer and Bible reading. As the schools garnered additional awards from the Freedoms Foundation their patriotic colors never waved more brightly, and their nonsectarian Christian character presumably softened their heady vocationalism. The U.S. Supreme Court would not rule school prayer and Bible reading unconstitutional until the early 1960s.

The increasingly massive size of the Indianapolis system would have amazed its founding fathers. High schools now enrolled the vast majority of teenagers, and the dropout rate of 47 percent in 1959 was slightly lower than the national average. School sports and other student activities continued to compete with time for homework, and the academic quality of rival high schools differed considerably. In 1957 both *Time* and *Newsweek* magazines named Shortridge one of America's best high schools.

Shortridge and Broad Ripple sent the highest percentage of graduates to college. A survey in 1959 revealed that 57 percent of Broad Ripple's ninth graders aspired to attend college, compared with 2 percent at Harry Wood and 7 percent at Crispus Attucks. The sorting process seemed complete, confirming the local school superintendent's belief in the late 19th century that mobility for the poor would be negligible.

By the 1960s IPS began to face major challenges. School leaders confronted one crisis after another. Demographic changes spawned serious problems. As in other cities, blacks had long been segregated and the movement of whites to suburban townships accelerated. The percentage of African-American and poor students in Center Township, the core of IPS, increased in the coming decades. The city schools again confronted the familiar problems of social class and race but even more acutely as economic opportunities for the inner city poor deteriorated.

By the late 1960s, when enrollments neared their peak, Republican Mayor Richard Lugar and his party successfully merged city and county governments, except for the public schools. The nearby township school districts remained autonomous. Lugar had graduated first in his class at Shortridge and was a former school commissioner; he thus understood the nature of local politics. He hardly wanted to undermine support for Unigov, which fostered extensive suburban development, by proposing the consolidation of the white suburbs with increasingly black and poor city schools.

Unigov was approved in 1969, a year after a black parent sued the Indianapolis school board for deliberately segregating its schools. Voluntary busing within IPS began in 1970, and in the following year U.S. District Judge S. Hugh Dillin ruled that the system had engaged in *de jure* segregation. By 1973 Dillin ordered busing for desegregation within IPS and some surrounding townships; Wayne, Warren, and Lawrence townships annexed segments of IPS in 1978 with court approval; and 7,000 black students were bused from IPS to other townships beginning in 1981.

Between the 1970s and the present, the Indianapolis schools faced steady decline. Student enrollment in IPS dropped from over 100,000 in the mid–1960s to 47,000 by 1992. Busing was largely peaceful but it did not produce substantially higher levels of academic achievement for black pupils. Some of the IPS schools remained very racially segregated, since whites continued to move to the suburbs. City school officials had the unenviable task of managing decline, something for which urban educators had little experience.

By the 1990s IPS had a majority black school board and a black superintendent but worsening budgets and the problems typical of inner cities. While the city had a graduation rate slightly higher than the nation in the 1950s, it now had the worst dropout rates in the state. Test scores declined precipitously. Citizens' task forces studied how to combat school violence, low academic achievement, and persistent racial segregation. In 1992 superintendent Shirl Gilbert II persuaded Judge Dillin to approve a Select Schools plan, promoting school choice, ostensibly to improve school achievement and help further desegregate IPS. Whether any of these goals will be met remains unclear, however well intentioned the plan and worthy the aims.

"We're . . . Building a World Class School System," read one of the brochures promoting the Select Schools plan. The hyperbole contrasted sharply with everyday realities. The avowed goals for schools were academic excellence, the establishment of mutual trust and respect within the schools, participatory decision making, diversity, and responsible citizenship. It was very difficult to disagree with these goals, which nevertheless seem so disparate from everyday realities.

Since the 19th century the Indianapolis schools have never squarely addressed the problems produced by poverty and racial discrimination. The schools did not create these problems, but the system quickly abandoned the idea that all children could master an intellectually challenging, or even common, curriculum. A variety of social services, from lunches to playgrounds, benefited many children, but the commitment to helping children weakened by hard times seemed a low priority among citizens who opposed paying for often costly services.

When reformers built the public schools in the 1850s they had high expectations for the emerging system. Some idealists hoped for a high-quality academic curriculum that everyone could master, and they dreamed of a system that would provide opportunity for everyone. A few Radical Republicans even believed in racial integration. These reformers condemned private schools as class-biased, harmful to the common good. Successive generations of reformers carried the banner of public education quite high, as schools added new social services, courses of study, and vocational curricula.

This faith in the power of public schools to serve as effective educators of the young has diminished in recent decades, part of the general malaise accompanying the decline of American cities. As a new wave of reformers in the 1990s touts the advantages of markets and condemns the public schools, the continuing question is whether either the public or private sector will seriously address the enduring problems of social class and racial discrimination. They remain the unfulfilled promise of the common school.

See also: EDUCATION, EARLY CHILDHOOD; EDUCATION, FEMALE; EDUCATION, SPECIAL; EDUCATION, VOCATIONAL; HIGH SCHOOLS; HIGHER EDUCATION; PHILANTHROPY AND EDUCATION; PUBLIC SCHOOLS, RELIGION IN; SCHOOL DESEGREGATION; SCHOOL FINANCE; SCHOOLS, CURRICULA OF; SCHOOLS, PRIVATE; SCHOOLS, RELIGIOUS; SCHOOLS, SOCIAL SERVICES IN; and individual names, institutions, and organizations.

GOVERNMENT

William A. Blomquist

Over 160 years, municipal government in Indianapolis has evolved from the adoption of the first town charter in 1832 to the distinctive Unigov structure in place today. That evolution has been shaped by the need to organize and perform local government functions and the desire of residents for the most economical local government possible. Accordingly, municipal government in Indianapolis primarily facilitates residents' pursuit of their economic livelihoods with minimal other interference in their lives or demands for their participation. Another shaping feature has been the city's status as the capital of a state without a strong tradition of home rule. Indianapolis' governmental structure and functions have been influenced strongly by the actions of Indiana state government officials, who created the city for their own purposes and then severely constrained its ability to grow and adapt.

Indianapolis did not emerge as a city after a long period of settlement. It was instead created rather abruptly by officials of the state of Indiana to be its capital. In 1821, the Indiana General Assembly approved a site near the center of the state, on the White River at the mouth of Fall Creek, and gave it the name Indianapolis. The General Assembly officially moved the state capital to Indianapolis in 1824, and met here for the first time in 1825, even though no municipal government yet existed. Indianapolis was the state capital for 23 years before it became an incorporated city. Alexander Ralston's plan for the new capital did not even include a site for a city hall.

The local government structure that greeted the arriving state legislators was county government. Marion County was established in 1821, with the first county judge and sheriff appointed by the state. The first elected county officers—the clerk, recorder, associate judges, and three county commissioners—met for the first time on April 15, 1822.

Concerns about vice and crime prompted local citizens to form the first town government for Indianapolis on September 7, 1832. Voters elected a town board of five trustees, with Samuel Henderson chosen as board president by his peers. In a rare act of municipal "home rule," the town board adopted a general ordinance that served as Indianapolis' first charter, laying out the

William A. Blomquist is Associate Professor of Political Science at Indiana University–Purdue University, Indianapolis.

five wards to be represented by the trustees and defining their terms and duties. The board's action constituted the first and last example of municipal "home rule" in Indianapolis.

Indianapolis' first town government operated on a minimal scale. Total receipts of the town government in 1835 were $1,610, and remained below $3,000 per year into the 1840s. It provided law enforcement through the town marshal and what volunteers he could gather and fire protection through the town's provision of a hand-drawn pumper for the use of the Marion Fire, Hose and Protective Association, a volunteer unit organized in 1835. The second floor of the firehouse provided the meeting room for the town board of trustees.

Local government officials were, however, forced by events and the dismal quality of life in Indianapolis to extend their activities beyond police and fire protection. In the aftermath of a cholera epidemic in 1832–1833, the board of trustees established a board of health composed of five physicians and five citizens, appointed a sanitary commissioner for each of the town's five wards, and appropriated $1,000 for health and sanitation, including the conversion of a section of the "Governor's House" on the Circle into a hospital. Indiana's 1830s financial distress, compounded by the nationwide Panic of 1837, spurred local action to care for the growing number of impoverished residents. A benevolent society, organized in 1835, gathered food and clothing for the poor, and the Marion County commissioners approved the construction of county's first poorhouse, in Wayne Township. The poorhouse also became the destination for the local mentally ill, as neither the state nor local governments had yet created an institution for their care.

Indianapolis' first town charter was supplanted by a reincorporation act and special charter adopted on February 17, 1838. The new charter expanded the governing board to six members (renamed the "board of councilmen"), increased the town's police powers, and expanded its jurisdiction to the entire four-square-mile congressional donation while limiting the town board's taxing authority to the Mile Square. The president of the board of councilmen also had the authority of a justice of the peace and the town marshal that of a constable. An 1839 amendment to the town's special charter lengthened the terms of councilmen from one year to two.

This second town government lasted until 1847, when Indianapolis became an incorporated city under a special act of the Indiana General Assembly. The legislature passed the Indianapolis charter bill on February 13, 1847, subject to a local referendum to be held on March 27. By an overwhelming 449 to 19 count, voters endorsed the new charter and it became effective on March 30.

The first city charter for Indianapolis provided for the election of councilmen from each of seven city wards and a separately elected mayor with the authority of a justice of the peace and power to veto actions of the board of councilmen. Samuel Henderson, who had been Indianapolis' first postmaster and first town board president, was elected the new city's first mayor. The new charter also authorized the city government to tax real property at a rate not to exceed 15 cents per $100 valuation. Still, there was no city hall, nor would there be one for another half century; most city government functions were conducted in borrowed space in the county courthouse.

With the ratification of the new state constitution in 1851, the Indiana General Assembly enacted a general charter for cities within the state. The city of Indianapolis adopted the charter in 1853. It increased the number of councilmen to two from each ward and made the mayor president of the board of councilmen, but limited these elective offices to one-year terms. The charter also provided for an elected office of city treasurer, paid with a percentage of tax revenues collected, and quadrupled the ceiling on city property tax rates to 60 cents per $100 valuation.

The recently constructed City-County Building (rear) rises above the Marion County Courthouse (front) in 1961. [Indiana Historical Society, Bass Collection, #307507-2]

An 1890s view of a Marion County courtroom. [Indiana Historical Society]

Amendments to the general charter in 1857 and 1859 increased the length of terms of elected municipal officials to two and then to four years.

The 1850s and 1860s were a period of rapid growth in Indianapolis' population and in the demands upon the city government. The city needed new streets as well as maintenance on the few original ones, a reliable water and sanitation system, and more extensive police and fire protection. Fulfilling these needs was costly. The city's budget in 1847 had been $4,000. In 1860 it was 20 times larger, about $87,000. By 1870 it was nearly another five times larger, at $405,000. In 1870 Indianapolis had nine miles of paved streets, 18 miles of paved sidewalks, and three miles of streets illuminated by gas lights.

One of the more controversial public issues of the 1850s was whether to establish a regular, uniformed, and paid police department to replace the constable-and-volunteer system. Many Indianapolis residents resisted this proposition. In 1854 the board of councilmen passed an ordinance establishing a regular, paid police department of 14 officers, two from each of the city's wards. The next year, in December, 1855, the councilmen succumbed to local political pressure, abolished the police department, and even eliminated the deputy assigned to the city marshal's office. However, the absence of a police department proved even more unacceptable, and a month later, in January, 1856, the board of councilmen reinstated a police force of ten men. Uniformed for the first time in 1862, the police department in 1863 was increased to 25 officers—seven day patrolmen and 18 at night. In the meantime, in August, 1859, the board of councilmen also voted to establish Indianapolis' first regular, paid fire department.

Indianapolis city government continued to try to keep up with the needs of a city that was rapidly emerging as a regional center. In the 1880s, Indianapolis had grown to an area of approximately 20 square miles, with 35,000 homes, businesses, and factories. The city government budget was approaching $1 million per year. In 1890, although Indianapolis was less than 70 years old, its population passed the 100,000 mark, a pace of growth exceeding even that of Los Angeles' first 70 years.

Also in 1890, local businessmen established the Commercial Club, soon to be the Indianapolis Chamber of Commerce, with Col. Eli Lilly as its first president. One of the chamber's initial activities was to assist the city, still woefully behind in getting streets paved, by holding a street paving exposition at Tomlinson Hall next to City Market. In the course of demonstrating their equipment and crews, the exhibitors paved several blocks of downtown streets.

The street paving exposition began a century of close connection between the Chamber of Commerce and city government. The relationship that started under Col. Lilly's leadership grew stronger during the 20th century. William H. Book, the chamber's executive vice-president from 1934 to 1964, and his successor, Carl Dortch, were two of the most knowledgeable and influential persons in governing the city. They reinforced and strengthened the pattern of city reliance on the chamber for leadership in agenda-setting and for expertise and advice in addressing municipal problems, a pattern that continues today.

Largely through the Indianapolis Chamber of Commerce, local businessmen at the turn of the century took an active interest in the functions and structure of city government. Municipal reform movements throughout the United States during the last decade of the 19th century and first decade of the 20th focused on separating politics from administration to make city governments operate in a more "business-like" fashion. In Indianapolis, local businessmen and other reformers of the period promoted separate departments governed by public boards. Board members would be appointed rather than elected, insulating decision-making about local government services from the pressure of local politics.

Indianapolis adopted with abandon the organizational model of separate departments governed by appointed boards. Separate departments and boards were created for most existing city government functions, and virtually all new ones. From the 1920s through the 1960s, the business model was taken a step farther, as separate municipal "corporations" were created to perform local government functions. Each independent municipal corporation had its own powers and responsibilities, its own territorial jurisdiction, and its own appointed governing board. The creation of these independent municipal corporations was a response to the urbanization of the remainder of Marion County, to severe state-imposed limitations on Indianapolis city government, and to the structure and powers of Marion County government.

Urbanization extended beyond the boundaries of the city of Indianapolis, and the development of suburban communities within Marion County accelerated through the 1960s. By the 1940s the city was exporting residents to the suburban ring. While annexation of these outlying urbanizing areas in the county was legally possible, it was extremely difficult practically. In Indiana, annexation requires approval in a referendum of the voters in the area to be annexed. In all but a few cases, residents of areas within Marion County outside Indianapolis chose to incorporate their own city or town or to remain unincorporated. Suburban Marion County residents in unincorporated areas received police protection from the Marion County Sheriff's Department, while those in separate incorporated areas had the option of creating their own patrol force. Fire protection was available from township volunteer fire departments. Public education was available through township school districts or by creating separate school districts, as did residents of the incorporated municipalities of Beech Grove and Speedway. Annexation did not offer suburban Marion County residents sufficiently attractive benefits to offset the costs of higher tax rates and less political independence, so very few annexation efforts met with approval.

The city could not offer outlying residents more capital-intensive services, such as water and sewer systems or road construction and maintenance, largely because of state-imposed limitations on municipal indebtedness. The 1851 Indiana Constitution, written and ratified after the state's canal fiasco of the 1830s and 1840s, restricted the indebtedness of municipal corporations to 2 percent of the assessed valuation of property within the corporation's territory. This limit inhibited the city's ability to generate local government services such as water and sewers, street construction and maintenance, solid waste collection and disposal at a pace equivalent to the city's growth, much less to extend such services to newly urbanizing areas outside the territorial limits. Even the construction and maintenance of adequate buildings to house municipal operations for a city whose population grew from around 100,000 in 1890 to nearly 400,000 by 1950 was difficult to finance under those circumstances.

Marion County government was, if anything, even less equipped to function as a municipal government than the city of Indianapolis. Jacksonian-era ideas about government strongly influenced the structure of county, as well as state, government in Indiana. There was no chief executive officer within the county government structure, and no fewer than nine county officers were separately and directly elected (assessor, auditor, clerk, coroner, prosecutor, recorder, sheriff, surveyor, and treasurer). A county board of commissioners composed of three members elected from districts exercised residual county policy-making authority. A separately elected legislative body, a county council of seven members (reduced to five in 1967), concerned itself primarily with the county budget. This structure was generally not regarded as conducive to the efficient performance of a wide array of municipal government functions.

Other reform ideas surfaced during the first half of the 20th century. A 1925 study conducted by the New York Bureau of Municipal Research recommended the consolidation of city, township, and county governments in Marion County. In the late 1920s proposals for municipal home rule and for a city manager charter for Indianapolis stimulated public debate. The General Assembly even approved a city manager charter for Indianapolis, but it was declared unconstitutional by the Indiana Supreme Court. The Indianapolis Committee on Post-War Planning, created in 1943, discussed the problems of local government in Marion County, and a metropolitan survey conducted in 1952 called for the inclusion of most of the urbanized portion of Marion County into a single municipal unit known as Greater Indianapolis.

However, the "business model" of creating separate municipal corporations governed by boards of directors provided simpler, less comprehensive means around the problems of local government in Marion County. Because each municipal corporation had its own territorial jurisdiction, government functions provided by these special-purpose governments could be extended to areas outside the city of Indianpolis—in some cases, even to the county boundaries. Each municipal corporation could borrow up to its own 2 percent debt limit, which facilitated the production of more capital-intensive services.

From the mid–1940s to the mid–1960s, a parade of special legislation to create special-purpose governments in Marion County proceeded through the Indiana General Assembly. In 1943, the General Assembly passed a bill to place the Indianapolis City Hospital under the supervision of a five-member bipartisan board. The city's old sewer and sanitation department was turned into a separate government unit, the Indianapolis Sanitary District, in 1945, and authorized to exercise territorial jurisdiction beyond the city limits. Legislation adopted in 1947 established the Indianapolis Public Library District—now the Indianapolis–Marion County Public Library—and extended its service and taxing area beyond the city limits. In 1951, legislation created a separate municipal corporation encompassing all of Marion County responsible for public health and hospital activities—now the Health and Hospital Corporation of Marion County. In 1953, the City-County Building Authority was organized as a municipal corporation to finance, construct, and operate a new office building for the joint use of the city and county governments. In 1955, the Indianapolis Housing Authority was formed, and a Metropolitan Planning Commission was created to assume the authority from the city and county over land use planning and zoning. In 1961, an Indianapolis Airport Authority and an Indianapolis–Marion County Parks and Recreation District were created, each with a county-wide base. In 1963, legislation established a Metropolitan Thoroughfare Authority (later named the Mass Transportation Authority) with county-wide authority for construction and maintenance of major roads and streets. In 1965, the Capital Improvement Board was created to finance, construct, and operate an Indianapolis convention and exhibition center. Not all proposals for county-wide special-purpose governments were adopted: a 1957 plan to consolidate the school districts within the county, and a 1967 proposal for a county-wide police force, were defeated by strong local opposition. Nevertheless, the 1967 Census of Governments recorded 60 government units within Marion County: the county itself, 23 cities and towns, nine townships, 11 school districts, and 16 special-purpose governments.

The creation of the special-purpose municipal corporations had extended the service and taxing areas for several local government functions from the city boundaries to the county boundaries. However, each municipal corporation performing each function was governed by a different appointed board that determined policy, levied taxes, and issued bonds. Since their jurisdictions exceeded the city limits, most of the governing boards had some positions appointed by the mayor, some by the city council (formally the Common Council), and some by the county council and/or the county commissioners. Voters did not elect these board members, and no elected government official or body could appoint a majority of them. Board members served staggered terms with vague or no provision for removal, so local voters could replace their city council members, mayor, county council members, and county commissioners without necessarily changing the governance of several important local government services. On paper, Indianapolis had a strong mayor-council form of municipal government; in practice, neither the mayor nor the council controlled the administration of several key local government services. The Indianapolis League of Women Voters expressed the frustration felt by some residents in the title of its 1959 publication, *Who's in Charge Here?*

Partisan politics exacerbated the dispersion of authority over municipal services. The city of Indianapolis frequently elected Democrats to the mayor's office and common council. The Republican party fared better in the elections for county and state offices. In 1960, while Democrats controlled the city government, a city-county merger proposal introduced by Democratic State Senator Nelson G. Grills could not gain the support of Republican legislators. Democrats gained control of state government in 1964 for the first time in several elections. In the 1965 session of the Indiana General Assembly, Indianapolis Mayor John J. Barton, a Democrat, and Marion County Democratic Party Chairman James W. Beatty urged the legislature to adopt proposals reconstituting the special-district boards so the mayor could appoint a majority of the board members. Marion County Republicans vigorously opposed the changes, the Pulliam newspapers denounced them as a "power grab," and Barton and Governor Roger Branigin soon disassociated themselves from the proposed reforms.

In the 1967 municipal elections, Barton was defeated by Republican Richard G. Lugar, a school board member and a member of the Greater Indianapolis Progress Committee (GIPC), created by Barton. Republicans also carried a majority of the common council seats. In 1968, the Republicans won a majority of the county government offices, the Marion County delegation to the Indiana General Assembly, majorities in both chambers of the General Assembly, and the governor's office. In the 1969 state legislative session, the Republicans pressed for municipal government reorganization, this time successfully.

The 1969 Indiana General Assembly passed a bill consolidating some of the elective offices of the city and county, bringing a few more of the municipal government functions under the control of those consolidated offices, and absorbing several of the separately incorporated towns in Marion County. The new municipal government structure was known as Unigov, short for "unified government," even though it did not really unify local government within Marion County.

Unigov was considerably more effective in consolidating political leadership in Marion County than in consolidating service delivery or eliminating multiple taxing districts. Political leadership is centered in a mayor who is elected county-wide and in a 29–member City-County Council that replaced the county council and the city's common council. The Unigov reorganization created six principal departments of city-county government that absorbed the functions of some of the earlier independent municipal corporations, although six of these remain as well. Four incorporated municipalities—Beech Grove, Lawrence, Southport, and Speedway—were left out of the Unigov structure, as were the local school districts, township fire departments, township property assessment and poor relief functions, the Marion County court system, and the separately elected Marion County offices (these last are specified in the state constitution and could not be eliminated by statute).

Assessments of Unigov's effect on the effectiveness of municipal government in Indianapolis have been difficult to make. In the years since the Unigov reorganization, Indianapolis has had three mayors, one City-County Council president, and the mayors and the majorities on the City-County Council have been of the same political party. This stability of political leadership has contributed to such indicators of success as the city's favorable bond rating. Furthermore, the first two post-Unigov mayors—Richard G. Lugar and William H. Hudnut III—were regarded by many residents (as well as by many of their peers) as having provided extraordinary leadership during their tenure. It has been difficult to separate Unigov's effect on the perceived effectiveness of city government from the effects of leadership stability and exceptionally capable mayors. Undoubtedly, the effects are intertwined: Unigov has contributed to the stability of political leadership and the visibility of mayors Lugar and Hudnut through its effect on Indianapolis politics.

Unigov's consolidation of political leadership has benefited Marion County Republicans. Republicans have retained the mayor's office and the majority of City-County Council seats each year since Unigov's implementation in 1970, sometimes by rather lopsided margins. Although replacement of the pre-Unigov structure with the more visible and potentially more accountable mayor and council was promoted in part as a means of restoring public participation in local government (since voters presumably would know "who's in charge here"), there is little evidence that it has done so. Instead, a lawsuit was initiated to stop Republican members of the City-County Council from making city budget decisions in closed party caucuses, and research performed for Lilly Endowment, Inc. in the early 1990s reportedly was sharply critical of the domination of decision-making by a business elite and the exclusion of individual citizens and groups. Perhaps underscoring the research findings, Endowment officials refused to make them public.

Indianapolis' third Unigov mayor, Stephen Goldsmith, took office in January, 1992, and initiated several projects that may rearrange certain aspects of city government and service delivery. The efforts include privatizing the delivery of some services, decentralizing the delivery of others, and increasing the involvement of neighborhoods in making decisions about and setting priorities among still others. Halfway through his first term, however, no actions were taken or announced to alter the basic organization of municipal government in Indianapolis by amending the Unigov law.

See also: CHARTERS, CITY; UNIGOV, CREATION OF (1967–1971); UNIGOV, STRUCTURE OF; UNIGOV AND POLITICAL PARTICIPATION; UNIGOV AND PUBLIC FINANCE; UNIGOV AND SERVICE DELIVERY; and individual mayors, government departments, townships, and counties.

JOURNALISM

Ann Mauger Colbert
David G. Vanderstel

Settlers on the American frontier generally experienced an initial period of isolation and separation from the outside world. To learn about current events they often gathered at the general store to hear the news read aloud from letters and newspapers delivered by infrequent postal deliveries. Occasional travelers who passed through the area or merchants who did business in other cities also were key sources of news and information. A settlement could claim that it had attained a "civilized" state when it ended its dependence upon outside sources and provided residents with a locally produced newspaper.

As the state's capital Indianapolis immediately possessed an advantage over other Hoosier communities in its ability to provide news. In January, 1822, six months after its founding, the city claimed its first newspaper, the *Indianapolis Gazette*, published by Pennsylvanian George Smith. Issued at irregular intervals because of poor communications with other cities, this modest, politically neutral paper was the first local advertising outlet and source of news. More important, it expressed an optimism for the future improvement of the town and laid a foundation for later journalistic enterprises. One year later, on March 7, 1823, Kentuckians Harvey Gregg and Douglass Maguire began the *Western Censor & Emigrants Guide*. Unlike its competitor, the *Western Censor* took a political stance by opposing presidential candidate Andrew Jackson and his Democratic supporters.

These two newspapers characterized the basic trends in Indianapolis journalism over the ensuing decades. They promoted the capital city to potential settlers in hopes of expanding the population and the local economy. Given the proximity of state government, political events and topics dominated the papers' contents; indeed, most 19th–century newspapers began and operated as party organs. As the community grew newspapers also prodded civic leaders on key issues affecting local growth and development. Later the increased availability of printing technology, coupled with the growing diversity of community interests, spawned numerous specialty newspapers that provided public forums and political tools to address important contemporary issues.

Ann Mauger Colbert is Journalism Coordinator at Indiana University–Purdue University, Fort Wayne.
David G. Vanderstel is Assistant Editor of the *Encyclopedia of Indianapolis*.

The success of these early newspapers depended upon publishers' abilities to obtain suffi-cient advertising and subscribers as well as to secure additional printing contracts or job-work. The *Gazette*'s Smith, who attended the first land sale in Indianapolis in October, 1821, obviously foresaw the settlement's potential and opened a small printing and bookbinding office. His prim-itive equipment consisted of a few type cases, stands, and a two-pull Ramage handpress. After writing his editorials, Smith and stepson Nathaniel Bolton set them in type, made up the forms, and inked them with buckskin balls stuffed with wool and greased with coon oil. This slow, hard work limited production to no more than 75 impressions an hour.

Early Indianapolis newspapers did not meet the modern definitions of a newspaper. While each had its own particular character, a typical publication consisted of four pages (as small as 9 inches by 12 inches) printed on rag paper. Set in very small type, the paper's dense copy con-tained no illustrations and few typographical breaks or headlines. The front page was usually de-voted to national news and often included political addresses and legislation. Most news items were "dispatches" or excerpts taken from other newspapers. State and local news, editorials (of-ten containing personal invective), and literary contributions (including morality tales) could be found on the inside pages. The back page consisted almost exclusively of advertisements and le-gal notices. Even as papers became larger, this textual density remained. Only after the midcen-tury advent of new printing presses and the rising popularity of "illustrated" magazines did newspapers begin to alter their appearance.

Besides the labor-intensive production, Indianapolis publishers initially had to contend with a fairly limited circulation, estimated by the 1830s at 10 percent of the local population. Only those possessing an interest or investment in the political and economic affairs of the community were willing or able to subscribe to a newspaper. Local deliveries were handled by carriers; out-of-town subscribers received papers through the mail or by stagecoach lines. Regular non-local subscribers included other editors from around the nation who relied on local papers to obtain regional news.

Every publisher took a risk in printing a regularly issued newspaper. The number of sub-scribers, the amount of advertising revenue, and the paper's political or ideological stance affected its survival; as a result, many Indianapolis papers ran for just one or two years with some existing for only a few months. Papers were also subject to mergers and acquisitions, name changes, and altered formats which changed with the philosophies of their owner-publishers. The *Western Censor* , for example, became the *Indiana Journal* in 1825 and remained a local fixture until ab-sorbed by the *Indianapolis Star* in 1904. The *Indiana Democrat*, begun in 1830 by Alexander Mor-rison to support the Jacksonian Democrats, merged with the *Indiana State Gazette* and became the *Indiana Democrat and State Gazette*. The paper subsequently dropped "State Gazette" from its title and merged in 1840 with the *Constitution* to become the *Indiana Democrat and the Spirit of the Constitution*. This unwieldy name lasted for one year until new owners George A. and Jacob P. Chapman renamed it the *Indiana State Sentinel*, which served as the only consistent voice of the Democratic party in the city until the *Indianapolis News* acquired it in 1906. Not until the 20th century did the local press attain a greater degree of stability.

During the mid–19th century the first of Indiana's daily newspapers appeared in Madison and New Albany. Soon thereafter the anti-Democratic *Indiana Journal*, edited by John Douglass and later John D. Defrees, became the first Indianapolis paper to publish a daily edition, although only during the legislative sessions after 1842. Both the *Journal* and the *Sentinel* began publishing regular daily editions in April, 1851, thereby indicating the increased importance of communicating non-legislative news. Daily papers made next-day coverage more important to the reader—and increasingly placed non-daily publications at a competitive disadvantage. (The first reputed instance of next-day coverage in Indianapolis occurred in 1852 when J. H. McNeely, city editor of the *Journal*, witnessed an evening fire at the Eagle Machine Works, returned to the print shop to stop the presses, and inserted a brief notice of the incident for the morning paper.) But some weeklies were able to attract and hold an audience. *The Locomotive*, begun in 1845, was a weekly nonpolitical paper containing gossip, stories, poetry by local authors, and coverage of society events; it was said to be the first paper that Indianapolis women read regularly.

While early 19th century newspapers experienced changes in ownership, names, and printing technology, one element of publishing remained fairly constant—the political ideologies espoused by the papers. Political factionalism became increasingly apparent in Indiana and Indianapolis during the Jacksonian era, and local newspapers, through their editorials and politically biased reporting, emerged as the principal tools to rally the electorate. The Chapman brothers turned the *Sentinel* into the leading Democratic journal of its day and adopted the rooster as the local party's official symbol.

Samuel V. B. Noel and John Douglass led the pro-Whig *Journal*, which issued a special campaign paper, *The Spirit of '76*, to support William Henry Harrison's presidential candidacy in 1840. Four years later the Whigs issued *The Whig Rifle* while the Democrats countered with *Chapman's Coon Skinner*. These newspapers promoted an active democracy by encouraging voter participation. They also monitored the activities of politicians and parties in an effort to hold them accountable.

Although political partisanship dominated the local press, other interests sparked a remarkably diverse group of specialty newspapers for the capital city. Religious conflict and denominational politics, for example, were often as fierce as that of government. Seeking to convert—and control—sinners, churches and denominations created religious periodicals to communicate with their members, inspire missionary work, encourage benevolence and charity, and promote Sunday school studies among children and adults. Early examples of Indianapolis' religious press included the *Christian Record*, begun in Bloomington in 1843 and published in Indianapolis from 1850 to 1866; the *Gospel Herald*, relocated from Madison, Indiana, in 1853; *The Witness*, a Baptist publication, 1857–1864; and *The Little Sower*, a Sunday school paper published by the Christian church, 1869–1884, which led to the founding of several other papers aimed at Christian youth.

Related to religious newspapers were publications affiliated with particular reforms. The temperance movement, active in Marion County since 1828, saw its cause promoted in the *Family Visitor* (1848–1850) and the *Temperance Chart* (1850–1856). Opponents of slavery supported several abolitionist journals: the *Indiana Freeman* (1844–1845) edited by Henry Depuy; the *Free Soil Banner*, published by William Greer and Lew Wallace (1848–1854); and the *Indiana American*, an antislavery-antiliquor weekly previously published in Brookville and edited by Rev. T. A. Goodwin in Indianapolis from 1857 to 1862. Advocates of free public education supported the *Common School Advocate* (1846–1852), a semimonthly published by Henry F. West. The State Teachers' Association began the *Indiana School Journal* (1856–early 1900s) to address contemporary educational issues.

Located at the heart of an agricultural state, Indianapolis was home to several short-lived agricultural newspapers. Bound by tradition and generally unreceptive to progressive ideas, Hoosier farmers showed great reluctance in adopting scientific farming. Nevertheless, many individuals published agricultural papers in hopes of improving farming practices. The *Indiana*

Farmer, also known as the *Indiana Farmer and Stock Register* and *Indiana Farmer and Advocate of Western Productive Industry*, began in 1836; the *Western Cultivator* lasted only one year (1844). The most successful paper was the *Indiana Farmer and Gardener*, begun in 1845 by the *Journal* and edited by Rev. Henry Ward Beecher of Indianapolis' Second Presbyterian Church. Devoted to "agriculture, horticulture, rural affairs, and domestic economy," the paper merged with the Cincinnati-based *Western Farmer and Gardener* in January, 1846, and counted 1,200 subscribers by year's end. It folded, however, when Beecher left Indianapolis in 1847.

Another specialized audience was the growing German community. In 1848 Julius Boetticher established the pro-Democratic party *Volksblatt*, the first German language newspaper in the city. Five years later Theodore Hielscher, a participant in the 1848 German revolution, started the *Freie Presse* to support the free soil and abolition movements and later the Republican party. The first German daily was the *Telegraph*, which began in 1865 by absorbing the *Volksblatt*. An opposition paper, the *Tribuene*, began in 1877 by acquiring the *Freie Presse*. Among the many immigrant groups that settled in Indianapolis the Germans maintained the only foreign language press.

Until the 1860s coverage of news was limited; speeches, stories, and legislation consumed most of the non-advertising space. The Civil War, however, made news a necessity for an ever-expanding readership. After the first Battle of Bull Run, the *Journal* began publishing telegraphic dispatches, reports on battles and military movements, and casualty lists. The immediacy of these reports changed the face of newspapers and led to significant developments in local journalism in the postwar years.

New technology made it possible to serve the increased demand for news. Indianapolis' newspapers were printed by handpresses until the 1840s when *Journal* editor John Defrees installed the city's first steam-driven press. The *Journal* saw its circulation grow dramatically during the Civil War, leading its owners to buy larger presses twice in three years. Beginning in 1869 the *Indianapolis News* became the city's first evening paper; it reported a circulation of 4,000 by the time owner-editor John H. Holliday purchased a four-cylinder Hoe press in 1871. Within four years circulation had risen so much that Holliday had to buy a six-cylinder Hoe press capable of 15,000 impressions an hour.

Historian Jacob Piatt Dunn singled out the year 1870 as the beginning of a new era in Indianapolis journalism. It marked the first year that the capital city had a permanent afternoon paper—the *News*—which had first appeared on December 7, 1869. Holliday announced that the paper would be "conducted sincerely, truthfully, independently, being the organ of neither individual, sect or (political) party and will always endeavor to promote the common good and improvement." Not only was the *News* known for its well-edited content and reasonable price—2 cents per issue—but over time it developed a strong reputation for employing the best journalists, including Hilton U. Brown, Meredith Nicholson, and Louis Howland. The *News* ultimately demonstrated that local readers would support a less biased publication, and it stimulated a flurry of competitor and specialty newspapers to address the needs of the increasingly urban community.

During the 1870s African-Americans exceeded 8 percent of the city's total population, a proportion that grew steadily into the 20th century. Believing that newspapers were essential to the survival of their community, many black entrepreneurs established newspapers that offered black readers a distinctive perspective on current events. The Bagby brothers—Benjamin, James, and Robert, all of whom were educators—founded the *Indianapolis Leader* in mid–1879, purported to be the first African-American paper in the city. This strongly Republican weekly lasted until

1890, and it inspired the creation of several other papers. The *Indianapolis Colored World* (1883–1932) began as a Republican paper but in 1896 switched to support the presidential candidacy of Democrat William Jennings Bryan and to take a more militant stand on race matters. One paper from that era, the *Indianapolis Recorder*, established by George P. Stewart and William H. Porter in 1896, continues to serve Indianapolis' African-American community. Circulation in the early 1990s revealed a stable readership of more than 11,000.

The latter third of the 19th century witnessed the rise of numerous, though sometimes short-lived, newspapers which, apart from the *News* and the *Journal*, represented the rapidly changing face of the expanding capital city. The first *Indianapolis Sun* began in 1870 as a Republican paper and survived less than one year. Another *Sun* began in 1873 and became an organ of the Greenback party in 1874 and the National (Grange) party in 1882 before being discontinued in 1884. The *People* made its debut on November 6, 1870, as a Sunday weekly devoted to local news, literature, and politics. Among the first Indianapolis papers to use illustrations, *People* degenerated into a tabloid that chronicled crimes and scandals. On July 14, 1881, the *Indianapolis Times*, a morning daily published by William R. Holloway, began a five-year run before being acquired by the *Journal*. A third *Sun* newspaper appeared in March, 1888. The emerging business community led to the founding of the short-lived *Journal of Commerce* (1876), which became a local model for future business publications. Labor interests spawned several general labor newspapers including radical labor leader Calvin Light's *Workingmen's Map* (1876–1877) and Thomas Gruelle's *The Labor Signal* (1881), the organ of the Central Trades and Labor Union. In addition, several national and international unions headquartered in Indianapolis published newspapers or magazines for their members. Music activities were covered in *Benham's Musical Review* (1866) and *Willard's Musical Visitor* (1870). The religious press saw the birth of the *Central Catholic* (1875), the *Indiana Baptist*, and the *American Christian Review*, the latter two begun in the mid–1880s. The German language papers *Telegraph*, its Sunday edition *Spottvogel*, and the *Tribuene*, edited by Philip Rappaport, continued to serve the vibrant German community. In 1907 the papers merged to become the *Telegraph und Tribuene*; it published in German until anti-German sentiments of World War I forced its closure in 1918.

The so-called Gilded Age of the late 19th century witnessed the emergence of Indianapolis as a great literary center, assisted in part by the efforts of newspaperman George C. Harding. As editor at various times of the *Saturday Herald*, the *Saturday Review*, the *Journal*, and the *Sentinel*, Harding personally contributed to the journalistic and literary traditions of the city through his writings and encouragement of local writers. Many of Indianapolis' more famous authors—including James Whitcomb Riley, who worked at the *Journal* from 1877 to 1885—began their careers with the help of this editor. Humorist Frank McKinney "Kin" Hubbard built his reputation from the columns of the *Indianapolis News*. John Barton "Johnny" Gruelle, the creator of Raggedy Ann, got his start initially with *People* and then with the newly established *Indianapolis Star*. Although author Booth Tarkington was not a journalist, his first book, *The Gentleman from Indiana* (1899), provided a vivid description of newspaper life in the Hoosier state.

Indianapolis experienced a 60–percent growth in population between 1890 and 1900 to 169,164; within 30 years the population rose to 364,161. But in the course of that expansion the city witnessed a decline in the number of local newspapers, in part because of numerous mergers and acquisitions. One paper active in that process was the *Indianapolis Star*, a new daily owned by Muncie industrialist George F. McCulloch and edited by Merle Sidener. Its first edition (June 6, 1903) proclaimed that the *Star* was to be "an independent paper for the people—a newspaper, not an organ." The *Star*'s greatest emphasis was state and local news, which helped to raise its circulation from 27,000 to 70,000 within its first six months. Over the next few years the *Star* absorbed the *Journal* (1904) and the *Sentinel* (1906), leaving the *Star* as the city's only morning newspaper.

By the early 1910s Indianapolis had three principal newspapers—the *Star*, the *News*, and the *Indiana Daily Times*, successor to the third *Sun* newspaper and later known as the *Indianapolis Times*. The African-American community supported four small newspapers—the *World*, the *Ledger*, the *Freeman*, and the *Recorder* . As the city grew several publishers, such as the Home-News Publishing Company, began printing weekly neighborhood and community newspapers that included "local civic affairs, society news, church news, personal items, club and business news, and anything of interest to local people."

The early decades of the 20th century also saw the emergence of journalists whose influence shaped the character of Indianapolis and national newspapers. Roy W. Howard, a teenage reporter for the *News* and a graduate of Manual High School, served as general news manager (1907) and later president (1912–1920) of United Press news service before becoming chairman of Scripps Howard newspapers (1920–1952). Around 1906 Kent Cooper, a native of Columbus, Indiana, and writer for the *Times*, arranged with the Scripps-McRae Press Association to transmit brief Indiana news reports by voice over the telephone; he later introduced the method to the United Press and Associated Press news services. Louis Howland, who edited the *News* from 1911 to 1934, became known for his weekly "Case and Comment" editorials. Eugene Jepson Cadou, Sr., quickly earned a reputation as a crack reporter for the *Times* by covering the 1920s investigation and trial of David Curtis (D. C.) Stephenson and the Ku Klux Klan; he later joined the International News Service and became its Indiana manager.

Women journalists also made significant contributions. For several decades in the late 19th and early 20th centuries, Grace Julian Clarke wrote a column and edited a woman's page for the *Indianapolis Star*. Mary Elizabeth Bostwick was one of the first female reporters in Indianapolis. She covered the 1913 flood for the *Sun* and later wrote for the *Star* from 1914 to 1958. Margaret Moore Post worked for over fifty years with Indianapolis Newspapers, Inc. and founded the journalism program at Franklin College.

Although early 20th century Indianapolis had fewer newspapers than in previous decades, they were of better quality. Improved technologies allowed faster printing, the incorporation of photographs, and the inclusion of up-to-date stories received from wire services. Newspapers were larger in format and contained a wide variety of special sections designed to appeal to various segments of the population. On the whole, these were good times for Indianapolis journalism. But times were tougher for publishers. Competition from radio and economic problems associated with the Great Depression hurt local newspapers, contributing to increased failures and mergers in the 1930s and afterward.

Indianapolis newspapers have had a long history of advocacy for the community's well-being. After the appearance and relative success of the gossip and local news-oriented *Locomotive* in August, 1845, other city papers began to offer more in-depth stories about local events. Fires proved to be a particular problem in the city during the latter decades of the 19th century, and the local papers campaigned vigorously for stricter building codes and a better equipped fire department. When a fire at the National Surgical Institute killed 19 people in 1892, accusations by local newspapers regarding carelessness of public officials brought about rapid improvements in the city's enforcement of safety codes. Journalists, inspired by Progressive Era muckraking,

Kin Hubbard, whose "Abe Martin"
cartoon character appeared in the
Indianapolis News for more than 25 years.
[Indiana Historical Society,
Bass Collection]

Eugene C. Pulliam
[Indianapolis Star/News Library]

soon began to address social problems, expose corruption, and focus on needed civic improvements.

Investigative journalism came into its own as a result of a startling series of reports on the Ku Klux Klan by the *Indianapolis Times*. Reporter Frank J. Prince exposed bribes that linked top Republican city and state officials to Grand Dragon D. C. Stephenson and the Indiana Klan. The series effectively broke the organization's strength in the state and won the *Times* a Pulitzer Prize in 1928. The *News* won a Pulitzer in 1932 for its investigation and disclosure of wasteful spending by city and state governments. During his 30–year tenure *Star* managing editor Robert P. Early adopted a crusading approach, which laid the foundation for future investigative reports. By the 1970s newspapers had teams of reporters who devoted their time to uncovering business and government corruption and addressing problems of society. The *Star* won its first Pulitzer Prize in 1975 for its six-month investigation and expose of police corruption in Indianapolis. Its second Pulitzer came in 1991 for an examination of Indiana malpractice and medical licensing procedures.

One Depression-era success story has affected the history and development of Indianapolis journalism since the 1940s. After serving one year as a reporter for a Kansas City, Kansas, paper, Eugene C. Pulliam moved to Lebanon, Indiana, and began buying and selling small newspapers around the country. He purchased the *Star* (1944) and the *News* (1948), improved their content with new and expanded sections, and hired skilled writers such as editorialist Jameson G. Campaigne and *Times* columnist Lowell Nussbaum. Pulliam's political conservatism and Republican leanings were evident on the editorial pages (and sometimes the front pages) of both papers, causing many readers to complain that Indianapolis newspapers presented only a narrow, conservative perspective of the world. In reality, however, the two papers generally maintained a strict separation between editorial page writers and members of the news staff.

The 1960s and 1970s brought significant changes to local journalism. On October 11, 1965, the *Indianapolis Times*, an important afternoon paper edited by popular columnist Irving Leibowitz, ceased publication after 76 years. Competition from television led to a decline in the appeal of an afternoon newspaper. The demise of the *Times*, which had provided contrasting views to the *Star* and *News* for years, essentially made Indianapolis a "one newspaper town," given the same ownership and similar editorial stance of the *Star* and the *News*. An alternative or "underground" press, which tended to be more liberal and socially conscious than the mainline papers, attempted to fill the void but most of these poorly financed efforts soon disappeared.

In recent decades the expansion of the city, the increasing visibility and importance of the local business community, and a diverse population all have contributed to the reemergence of the specialty press that was reminiscent of other periods of Indianapolis' past. The *Commercial*, in existence since the early 1900s, remains active in providing legal, financial, and business news. The *Indianapolis Business Journal* entered the market in 1980 and has become the principal source of information—and promotion—of local businesses. Suburban and neighborhood newspapers, especially those published by the Topics Suburban Newspapers, focused their coverage on events in specific communities. *Indianapolis Monthly*, founded in 1977 at a time when many such "city magazines" appeared, emphasized local personalities, home and garden projects, fashion, dining, and specialty businesses. *Indianapolis Woman/IW* began in 1984, capitalizing on the growing interest in women's issues; it ceased publication in 1989. *Indy's Child*, a monthly paper devoted to parenting and child-oriented issues, emerged in 1984. The *Indianapolis Recorder* and the *Herald* (1957) continued to serve the city's African-American community.

Despite the longevity of several local publications, Indianapolis' newspapers have never possessed the kind of regional reputation of some of their urban neighbors such as the *Chicago Tribune* and the *Louisville Courier-Journal*. The capital city's location placed it on the margins of the tri-state area that regional leaders Chicago, Cincinnati, and Louisville have served. The *Star*, however, has managed to win a fairly strong statewide audience—due in part to its coverage of state governmental activities centered in Indianapolis—even though it must compete with major out-of-state media at its northern and southern borders.

Certain themes that have dominated many Indianapolis newspapers throughout the city's history continue to be present in the *Star* and the *News*. Politics remain a major focus of local journalism, although it is questionable whether the papers' partisan editorials wield as much clout as they once did. The local press still has a significant voice in civic matters and often highlights issues or questions that affect the city's interests. The tradition of investigative journalism begun in the 1920s is still alive in the 1990s, although with mixed success.

The future challenge for Indianapolis publishers will be to incorporate the rapidly developing information services and technologies in order to keep their papers and magazines both current and appealing. Also facing them will be the challenge voiced by the *Indianapolis Times* in its inaugural issue of July 15, 1881; "to keep the public informed as to the growth of business, to encourage new enterprises, and by every means in its power to contribute to the growth and development of the city…[and] never to lose the good will nor forfeit the confidence of the public."

See also: AFRICAN-AMERICAN PRESS; LABOR NEWSPAPERS; NEWSPAPERS, ALTERNATIVE; POLITICAL JOURNALISM; RELIGIOUS PRESS; and individual names and publications.

LABOR

James Wallihan

The lives of working people in Indianapolis and the institutions they built have paralleled, in large measure, those in comparable American cities, especially in the Midwest. Yet labor in Indianapolis achieved certain distinctions. By virtue of its size, its central location, and its status as the state capital, the city for years was home to many national and international unions, labor gatherings, and events. It was the site of the noted Columbia Conserve experiment in worker ownership. And it was widely considered the primary battlefield between labor and the employer-backed open shop movement during the first half of the 20th century.

An 1822 report noted the establishment of the first manufacturing facility in Indianapolis—a grain mill on Fall Creek near North Street—and listed some 60 people by occupation: 13 carpenters, four cabinet makers, eight blacksmiths, tailors, tanners, bricklayers, a hatter, a cooper, a saddler, five merchants and storekeepers, four physicians, three lawyers, two printers and editors, a minister, and a school teacher. No mention is made of the broader work force, which presumably included various helpers, employees of "houses of entertainment," team drivers, and general laborers.

In 1836 the town's carpenters formed an association, though little is known of its activities. Local typographical workers were among the founders of the National Typographical Union in 1852, the oldest continuing union in the nation. In 1850 several groups of artisans paraded in Indianapolis and formed the Mechanics Mutual Protections, a trades organization similar to ones found in other northern cities. The group set forth such objectives as "remunerative wages," "protections" against illness and "pecuniary distress," and cultivation of "a proper understanding between the employer and the employed." But apparently the local base was not yet sufficient to sustain permanent citywide organization and little subsequent reference was made to the "Protections."

The impact of the Civil War on the Indianapolis economy spurred the transformation from town to small city. The war years saw the addition of a substantial number of African-Americans to the city's work force, most of whom were employed in domestic and other forms of service, as

James Wallihan is Professor of Labor Studies at Indiana University–Purdue University, Indianapolis.

The Columbia Conserve Company was governed by a workers' council. All
employees were eligible to participate in the council's weekly Friday meetings.
[Columbia Conserve Company Collection, Lilly Library, Indiana University,
Bloomington.]

well as general labor. Women found wartime employment in many factories. Irish, Germans, and
other immigrants supplemented the predominantly U.S. born work force, some bringing skills
and political and union traditions from their homelands. The city became a center for various
metal-working industries, meat packing, grain milling, and railroading. While the typical establishment remained small, one business, the Kingan and Company meat packing plant (later Hygrade), employed as many as 600 workers, most of them Irish.

The organization of labor reflected this growth. In 1863–1864 alone the number of local
unions grew from 3 to 17. The additions included the Journeymen Shoemakers, the Machinists
and Blacksmiths, and the Brotherhood of Locomotive Engineers. The Shoemakers published a
list of "society shops," employers who agreed to union wage scales, and "non-society shops,"
whose employees were considered scabs. In 1863 the Typographical Union struck the *Daily Sentinel*. The newspaper fired the strikers and advertised for replacements, noting that no union
members need apply. An editorial railed over the "foolishness of strikes" and declared that workers would achieve fairness by allowing employers to establish wages, following the laws of supply
and demand.

The postwar years were a time of labor ferment nationally. While money wages rose, hours
remained long and conditions difficult, especially for many nonskilled workers. Factory hands,
store employees, and domestic workers alike typically labored at least six nine-hour days or 54
hours a week, and many exceeded 70 hours. Worker gatherings in Indianapolis, as elsewhere, demanded improved education, disability relief, wage increases, job control, and an eight-hour day.

In 1865 a "Workingmen's Convention" met in the city and a Grand Eight Hour League of the State of Indiana was organized, largely under the leadership of John Fehrenbatch of the local Machinists and Blacksmiths. City employees gained an eight-hour day and 48–hour week by decade's end but long hours continued for others. Five years later Fehrenbatch went on to become president of the national Machinists and Blacksmiths Union and moved to its Cleveland headquarters.

Indianapolis labor leaders participated in a variety of national worker conventions and congresses from which issued pronouncements, platforms, and sometimes organizations, most of them short-lived. These postwar stirrings represented an attempt to establish a nationwide program to advance the interests of labor through both economic and political means. These national and regional gatherings both reflected and spurred local organization. Gradually citywide organizations took root; by 1873, for example, several Indianapolis unions had formed a city trades assembly.

The nationwide depression that began in late 1873 visited desperation upon thousands of Indianapolis workers and ushered in a period of heightened class conflict. Wages had doubled since the beginning of the Civil War, to the point where by 1873 some skilled workers earned $2.50 per day. Two years later pay for skilled labor had declined by half, much more for unskilled workers. Most workers had to accept wage cuts. Given the pervasiveness of hard times, most strikes proved futile. In December, 1873, employees at the city's rolling mills protested a 20 percent cut and payment in notes rather than cash. But they returned to work rather than face unemployment. As the depression deepened, labor turned increasingly to political action. At several conventions in the city, including an 1877 effort to form a branch of the national Workingmen's party, representatives supported monetary reform and either independent political action by labor or the election of labor candidates on Republican and Democratic tickets. Many labor groups also worked closely with the Greenback party.

In response to the depression, Indianapolis mayor John Caven advocated a variety of relief efforts, including construction of the Belt Line Railroad, that provided a number of benefits to the city. At one point Caven averted a full-scale riot when he addressed over 1,000 people gathered to demand bread and led them to the city's bakeries, where bread was provided. Caven, along with Governor James Williams, also supported leniency for local strikers during the nationwide Railroad Strike of 1877, a position for which the two were roundly criticized in some quarters.

The depression especially affected the position of the city's black workers. Before the crash, the city trades assembly had supported the admission of African-American workers to trades unions. With jobs scarce, labor was torn by hostility against blacks. Politicians fueled racial conflicts, especially between Irish and blacks, which sometimes culminated in election violence. African-American workers were used as strikebreakers in a number of disputes elsewhere in Indiana during this period, with the result that they often became embroiled in labor hostilities.

By the end of the decade the city was edging out of the depression, but low wages and long hours continued to make life difficult for most workers. In its first report on factory wages, the Indiana Department of Statistics reported in 1881 that the prevailing rate for common labor ranged from $1.00 to $1.50 for a 10– to 12–hour day, although certain skilled workmen earned up to $4.50 per day. Still, Indianapolis ranked above all midwestern cities except Chicago and St. Louis.

At least two philosophical strains commingled through the labor movement of the 1870s and 1880s. One was practical and in many respects conservative, preferring organization along narrow craft lines and focusing on improvements in working conditions and pay. This strain was embodied by the emerging American Federation of Labor (AFL). The other strain, represented by the Knights of Labor, advocated the inclusion of all manner of workers in broad and more loosely knit umbrella bodies and favored more radical social and political transformation. Because of severe repression by employers and government, the Knights of Labor operated as a secret society through most of the 1870s. When it emerged toward the end of the decade growth was phenomenal, with all manner of local assemblies arising in communities around the East and Midwest, including Indianapolis. It is likely that a majority of the local unions in the city at some time had an affiliation or other organizational relationship with the Knights. While there were some leaders who clearly opposed the Knights' philosophy, many unions that later affiliated exclusively with the AFL maintained attachments to the Knights during much of the 1880s.

The 1880s saw the establishment of a number of organizations that survive to the present. In 1880 representatives of the printers, the cigar makers, and the iron molders created the Indianapolis Trades Assembly, renamed the Central Labor Union (CLU) in 1883, predecessor of today's Central Indiana Labor Council. In 1881 Samuel L. Leffingwell of Typographical Union No. 1 called for and participated in a Pittsburgh conference that created the Federation of Organized Trades and Labor Unions (FOTLU), which became the AFL five years later. Following its creation in 1885, Leffingwell became president of the Indiana FOTLU, which later became the Indiana Federation of Labor and is now the Indiana AFL-CIO. The 31 delegates represented both craft unionist and Knights of Labor tendencies.

Leadership in the post–Civil War labor movement of Indianapolis was assumed disproportionately by men from International Typographical Union Local 1. In addition to Leffingwell, prominent spokesmen included Calvin Light, Thomas Gruelle, Lycurgus McCormick, and, toward the end of the century, Edgar Perkins, all from Local 1. These printers were to some extent occupationally selected for such tasks. The craft required literacy and communications skills and bred familiarity with public affairs. Printers were also likely to have a broad knowledge of labor conditions elsewhere. Furthermore, hours and working conditions in the trade were relatively less demanding, leaving time and energy for outside pursuits. Printing unionists assumed direction of the lively labor press in Indianapolis. Labor newspapers flourished during this era. Bearing names such as the *Union*, the *Labor Signal*, *Our Organette* (the ITU Local 1 paper), and the *Workingmen's Map*, they were a source of news and opinion not found in the general press.

Indianapolis witnessed other developments during the period. While not a mining center itself, the city became a center of coal miners' union activity. The first unions in the Indiana coal fields were local assemblies of the Knights of Labor, but a rival association, the National Federation of Miners and Mine Laborers, which later became the National Progressive Union, was organized in Indianapolis in 1885 and soon became a dominant force in the state. Beginning in 1886 a tradition of labor day celebrations began with a parade and speeches. But not all workers celebrated. Women and African-Americans were less successful in promoting their interests. Even though women made up fully one fourth of the non-farm work force in the U.S. by 1874, an effort that year to form an organization of Indianapolis women workers failed. The women were divided between those who wanted to focus on wages, striking if necessary, and those who preferred to limit their efforts to caring for sick members and providing death benefits. Mutual aid of this sort was the primary function of many early unions.

By the 1890s the Knights of Labor, never tightly organized nationally, consisted mostly of a few remaining local assemblies, while the AFL-affiliated craft unions, with the building trades at their core, consolidated. The Indianapolis building trades were among the first in the nation to achieve the eight-hour day, beginning in 1891. Seven years later local carpenters, bricklayers, masons, painters, and plasterers had the eight-hour day and overtime pay. By 1892, two thirds of the 83 local unions in the city were affiliated with the Central Labor Union, with the railway brotherhoods accounting for most of the non-affiliates. Total union membership stood at 11,000. In 1894 the CLU affiliated with the AFL, which established its national headquarters in the city. It remained until 1896 when President Samuel Gompers moved the federation to Washington, D.C.

The list of unions in the 1890s included two locals—Hod Carriers and Teamsters—made up primarily of African-Americans. The use of blacks brought in from out of state as strikebreakers, or threats to do so, had occurred repeatedly since the 1870s, fostering hostility on the part of white unions, which often denied them membership. In 1898 the African-American newspaper the *Freeman* denounced mine operators for this practice and suggested that if they were so concerned, "let them employ negro workmen in times of peace." The *Indianapolis Recorder* urged the unions to drop their barriers and allow admission to African-American labor. Earlier, in 1893, Indiana adopted legislation making it illegal to discharge or threaten to discharge an employee for union activity or to require an employee to pledge to remain non-union as a condition of employment. The state thus led the way in banning the "yellow dog contract."

Yet progress did not always come easily, and for some it came not at all. On New Year's Day, 1892, the Citizens Street Railway told employees to turn in the badges that allowed them free streetcar transportation while off duty. Added to grievances over general hours, pay, and working conditions, this demand precipitated a street rail strike that idled city transit for nine days. This strike, resumed the following month with even greater militancy, failed to resolve the issues. The following year brought a Teamsters strike. In 1894 workers struck the Pullman Sleeping Car Company near Chicago, affecting rail service to Indianapolis and inspiring other laborers to protest. In 1895 local iron molders struck.

After the turn of the century Indianapolis became home to many national unions. In 1905 nine unions were headquartered in the city, including the Typographical Union, Bricklayers, Carpenters, Barbers, the United Mine Workers, and the Teamsters. At one time or another at least a dozen unions had national headquarters in Indianapolis, largely because of its central location and ease of access by rail. By World War II most had left the city, typically for Washington, D.C.

During the same period the city also became known as the center of employer opposition to labor—the open shop movement—led by the virulently anti-worker businessman David M. Parry. In 1902 Parry became president of the National Association of Manufacturers and a year later founded and was elected president of the Citizens' Industrial Association, which spearheaded the open shop campaign. In 1904 the Employers' Association of Indianapolis was founded to support the open shop effort. Over the next dozen years these organizations propagandized against labor, absorbed the Commercial Vehicle Protective Association that had formed to oppose a Teamster strike in 1913, and claimed credit for defeating labor candidates in the 1914 municipal elections and for securing the passage of an anti-boycott ordinance in 1916. Thus Indianapolis became the open shop, as well as the union, capital of the nation.

The city attracted notoriety when several members of the Ironworkers Union, headed by the McNamara brothers, were indicted in connection with the dynamiting of the *Los Angeles Times* building. The McNamaras were tried in Los Angeles and 40 others in Indianapolis, with 38 of them convicted of transporting dynamite. The Street Railway Strike of 1913 also attracted national attention. Violence ensued when 800 operators stopped work, seeking union recognition and improved wages and working conditions, with large property loss, three deaths, and many injuries. When the employer refused mediation the governor called out 1,800 Indiana National Guardsmen; eventually the Public Service Commission negotiated a settlement. A citywide Teamster strike followed shortly. Ironically, while the open shop forces railed at the McNamaras, the streetcar operators, and labor goals in general, other employers contributed to efforts to attract more union headquarters to the city.

World War I, with its attendant labor shortages and increased federal role in the economy, brought temporary improvement to the labor climate of the city. But in the national hysteria that followed the war, the anti-labor forces resumed their attacks on labor. In 1919 the Indianapolis city council, with the support of the *Star* and the *News*, but over the objections of the *Times*, passed an ordinance banning all forms of picketing. The Anti-Picketing Ordinance of 1919, although a restriction of the rights of free speech and association, was upheld by the Indiana Supreme Court in 1924 and remained in force until the mid–1930s.

Anti-labor forces held sway through the 1920s. In 1920 the Associated Employers of Indianapolis (previously the Employers' Association of Indianapolis) boasted that 85 percent of the city's businesses were open shop operations. And labor itself divided over issues unrelated to conditions in the work place. With the Ku Klux Klan in ascendancy, the Central Labor Union passed a resolution condemning the Klan as "UnAmerican and unconstitutional." Three local unions withdrew, objecting that the resolution did not address a labor issue.

Yet in this climate William Hapgood, son of a Chicago plow manufacturer, developed the remarkable Columbia Conserve experiment. In 1917 Hapgood assumed control of the small Indianapolis canning plant and began to turn operations, management, and ownership over to the employees. For this he was roundly denounced in the business community, where he was labeled a "Socialist" and a "sentimentalist" and his plan "destructive to the moral fiber of workmen." Under the plan the business was run by an elected committee of ten employees. Hours were reduced from 55 to 50, time clocks were abolished, pension, sickness, and accident plans were installed, and employees were placed on annual salaries—all actions virtually unheard of in a seasonal industry. Salaries were based on need. Single employees got the equivalent of $22 per week and married employees $33 plus $2 per child. Net profits were distributed to employees for the purchase of common stock. By 1930 the employees, through trustees, controlled 61 percent of the stock.

The onset of the Great Depression brought difficulties to the worker-controlled company. Wages in 1933 were half those of three years earlier. William's son, Powers Hapgood, a United Mine Workers organizer and supporter of John Brophy against John L. Lewis, brought Brophy and two other unionists to Columbia. A falling-out ensued in which the three newcomers labeled William Hapgood "autocratic" and a "capitalist," with Powers supporting his father. William fired the three labor men and Powers left with them.

In 1942 the workers at Columbia Conserve conducted a weeklong strike. Afterward, the workers sued the trustees, who exercised their stockholder rights, in a back-wage dispute. A judge broke up the cooperative and distributed the stock to current and former workers. The new enterprise then signed a labor agreement with the Congress of Industrial Organizations (CIO).

Although it created new problems for working men and women, the Depression did not quash all vestiges of labor militancy. The widely noted Real Silk Hosiery Mills Strike, beginning in June, 1933, arose out of a union recognition dispute between the AFL-affiliated Full-Fashioned Hosiery Workers and a company union. Some 800 workers struck for recognition, higher wages, and abolition of the bonus and penalty systems. Several violent incidents occurred. A new federal board resolved the issue by allowing the company union to represent the main plant and the Hosiery Workers the two smaller facilities.

One change brought by the Depression was the formation of the Congress of Industrial Organizations, an AFL rival that represented all workers in entire industries rather than skilled labor only. The 1935 National Labor Relations Act made this new form of representation easier to achieve, and CIO unionism spread rapidly in cities throughout the nation. In Indianapolis men like Jim Robb, a Scottish-born miner and organizer with the Steel Workers Organizing Committee, which in 1942 became the United Steelworkers of America (USWA), helped workers organize in several local plants. In 1942 USWA Local 1150 was established at the Link-Belt plant on the west side, succeeding a local of the Amalgamated Association of Iron, Steel, and Tin Workers. The following year the Steelworkers won an election at Diamond Chain and chartered Local 1697. The Machinists and the International Brotherhood of Electrical Workers, both AFL unions, and the CIO Electrical Workers, Auto Workers, Rubber Workers, and others organized actively in manufacturing during and after the war. Wartime labor shortages, a subject addressed by the War Manpower Commission, and the emphasis on industrial peace eased the organizing task.

Other patterns changed during World War II. By 1943, 74 percent of African-American men still worked as unskilled laborers and 83 percent of the women in domestic service, with median wages for black families near the prewar level of $17 per week. But increasing wartime labor shortages permitted women and African-American workers to gain jobs previously denied them, not always with the approval of whites. Allison, the city's largest defense plant, placed a few African-Americans on machines in 1943, which led to a strike by several hundred white workers. But whites in other departments were unsympathetic with the strikers and management remained firm, although it failed to advance more black workers to machine operator positions. A similar situation occurred at the Indianapolis Chevrolet plant. At other firms, Bridgeport Brass and Curtiss-Wright among them, efforts to upgrade African-Americans to operator positions met with opposition but advanced slowly. Progress at RCA was more substantial. Union reaction varied. While the CIO was generally supportive and aggressively pursued many complaints, some local unions remained officially neutral.

Union growth continued after the war, especially in the city's new manufacturing facilities, building trades, retail sales, transportation, and utilities. Union membership as a percentage of the work force probably peaked in Indianapolis at some point in the 1950s, as it did nationally. The national merger of the AFL and the CIO in 1955 was followed shortly by mergers at the state federation and local central labor council levels. Leading figures in the local labor movement of the time included Dallas Sells, president of the Indiana AFL-CIO, Jim Robb, director of District 30 of the Steelworkers, Gene San Soucie of the Teamsters, and Max Bridenthal, president of the Central Labor Council.

In 1968 the UAW separated from the AFL-CIO at all levels. Sells resigned as state president, and the UAW disaffiliated from the Central Labor Council, establishing a counterpart Community Action Program (CAP) Council. Despite the 1981 national reaffiliation of the UAW with the AFL, the CAP Council continues as a parallel body to the Central Labor Council.

During the late 1960s and early 1970s the national trend toward unionization by government employees caught on in Indianapolis. Federal employees at Fort Benjamin Harrison, Naval Avionics, and other facilities formed locals of the American Federation of Government Employees; Veterans Hospital employees affiliated with the Service Employees; the Postal Workers, Letter

Carriers, and Mailhandlers developed new strength following a 1969–1970 national strike and the passage of the Postal Reorganization Act; and service and maintenance employees of the city, school corporations, and Indiana University–Purdue University at Indianapolis (IUPUI) formed locals of the American Federation of State, County, and Municipal Employees (AFSCME). Teachers in area school systems transformed their local associations of the National Education Association (NEA) into strong union organizations that represented both the professional and employment interests of teachers through collective bargaining. Police and fire fighter unions bargained separately with the city.

Some militant labor actions occurred during the late 1970s. Despite the lack of enabling legislation, the locals of the Fraternal Order of Police (FOP), representing city police, staged a "park-in" in 1977 when the Hudnut administration sought to limit the availability of patrol cars for personal use. Labor actions during the period also included a wildcat strike by members of UAW 1226 at the Chrysler Electrical Plant at 30th Street and Shadeland Avenue, called in sympathy with the employees of the plant's cafeteria contractor, and bitter contract disputes between Steelworkers Local 1150 and FMC Link-Belt.

In the late 1970s the UAW-CAP Council, the Central Labor Council, and the Teamsters revived the Labor Day parade, which continued for some dozen years before it was replaced with a festival. Attendance typically ranged from 5,000 to 10,000, with more paraders than bystanders.

In the late 1970s the city lost its last national union when the Barbers, Beauticians, and Allied Industries International Association, which had moved its headquarters from Cleveland to Indianapolis in 1902, merged with the Washington, D.C.–based United Food and Commercial Workers. The increased presence of government in union affairs and the desire for a common site to ease communications among unions had led to Indianapolis' demise as the nation's labor capital.

The years following 1979–1980 were a period of long-term decline for workers and unions across the country, with plant shutdowns, unilateral wage cuts, and concessionary contracts reported weekly. Hardest hit were the established industrial areas of the East and Midwest, including Indianapolis. The manufacturing corridor along Shadeland Avenue near 30th Street virtually disappeared. The Chrysler electrical plant, which had employed over 3,000 UAW members, underwent permanent layoffs before it closed later in the 1980s. The Western Electric plant across the street shut its doors, taking almost 7,000 jobs. RCA too suffered severe cuts.

The new Reagan administration took a strong anti-labor stance in 1981 by firing some 10,000 striking air traffic controllers, including many in Indianapolis. Soon employers in other industries pressed for concessions from unions. As non-union discount stores entered the Indianapolis market, grocery chains forced concessions, with wages in some slashed to near federal minimum. Kroger remained the only chain locally whose stores remained fully unionized, albeit at greatly reduced wage and benefit levels. Following the court-ordered breakup of AT&T, locals of the Communications Workers of America, which had played leadership roles in the local labor movement, endured severe cutbacks at Indiana Bell and AT&T.

The effect of the 1980s turmoil on workers and unions was immeasurable. Real incomes declined for thousands of Indianapolis workers, but perhaps more stressful was the fear of plant closings, permanent layoffs, and dislocation. When displaced workers found new jobs, most earned substantially lower pay. Relatively well-paid manufacturing workers moved to lower paying service sector jobs. In many local unions workers who had served as local officers found themselves among the junior workers in their bargaining units when younger workers' jobs were eliminated. As such, they were thrust back into the leadership but with a more senior constituency and a more limited set of objectives. The reduction of union membership in the 1980s also cut severely into the financial base of the state and local central bodies.

As Indianapolis labor moved into the mid–1990s, its struggle continued. Federal employees, union-represented in many agencies, faced closure of the largest area facility, Fort Benjamin Harrison, a move that will cost thousands of civilian jobs. Municipal employees and their unions (locals of AFSCME) confronted a city administration that wanted to privatize many services. Meanwhile, state employees advanced. A 1990 contest between the Unity Team (a UAW, Teachers, and State Employee Association coalition) and AFSCME featured extensive broadcast advertising and resulted in state-recognized representation for most of the city's 24,000 state workers and for thousands more around the state. Both unions continued to press for legislation to enable full collective bargaining for state employees.

As of 1994 the three largest employers in the city—the three levels of government—were significantly, though not entirely, unionized. With Allison broken into smaller units, Kroger was the city's next largest unionized employer. Missing from previous decades are the large auto and electric companies that dominated the city's union labor force as late as 1979. The list reflects what has occurred to labor since the 1960s. Government employees have organized while union jobs have been lost in manufacturing. But non-union employers have also been cut back, with Eli Lilly Company and others trimming payrolls in the early 1990s.

Labor unions in Indianapolis in the mid–1990s remain diverse. They include manufacturing, service, and government unions; the full complement of building and construction trades, from Sheet Metal Workers, Electrical Workers, Pipefitters, Carpenters and Elevator Constructors, to Iron Workers, Teamsters, Operating Engineers, Roofers, Insulators, Cement Masons, Glaziers, Plasterers, and Painters; retail and food locals like the Bakery Workers, the Food and Commercial Workers, the Retail, Wholesale and Department Store Workers, and the Oil, Chemical, and Atomic Workers; the communications and transportation sector, with the Teamsters, the Amalgamated Transit Union, the Machinists and other airline unions, and the railroad brotherhoods; the utilities with the Brotherhood of Electrical Workers and the Firemen and Oilers; and the printing trades, principally the Graphic Communications International Union, a consolidation of many once-separate crafts. A number of white collar and office worker locals exist, including Office and Professional Employees (OPEIU Local 1), locals of the CWA, various government employee units, and the independent Electric Utility Workers Union at Indianapolis Power and Light Company. Several unions operate exclusively in the entertainment sector, including the Musicians and locals of the International Alliance of Theatrical Stage Employees, as well as the football and basketball players' unions.

The city's union base, though impaired in recent years, remains in place, adapting unevenly, as it has over the past century and a half, to changes in the employment landscape. Labor's future, in Indianapolis as elsewhere, will be determined by how aggressively and in what forms it addresses the needs of working people.

See also: LABOR MILITANCY; LABOR NEWSPAPERS; WORK FORCE; and individual names and unions.

LITERATURE

J. Kent Calder

The literary history of Indianapolis, like the city's history in general, is the story of the determined fulfillment of grand expectations. The same men who so rationally planned the new state capital, choosing the site primarily for its central location and providing it a Hellenistic name that suited their neoclassical visions, also saw to it that the means for realizing their ideals were available. When they came to the capital they brought books and an appreciation of their value in a frontier town. While the actual number of books in early Indianapolis may not have been large, according to historian Jacob Piatt Dunn "they were within reach of the earnest seeker." Though Indianapolis was similar to other frontier communities in the degree of illiteracy among its inhabitants, from the start it attracted a number of individuals who were intellectually curious and who read widely beyond their immediate business or professional interests. These men and women and their descendants laid the foundation for the blossoming that a little more than a half century later would make Indianapolis a literary center as well as a geographic one.

Calvin Fletcher was one of these residents. The Vermont native arrived with his new bride in October, 1821, and along with his extraordinary ambition he brought a love of books and learning. His diary, published in nine volumes by the Indiana Historical Society (1972–1983), covers his personal life and business dealings as a teacher, lawyer, politician, land speculator, and banker from the years 1817 to 1866. It stands as perhaps the most important historical and literary document of the city's early history. Among its many historical uses is its valuable record of what Fletcher read and what was being read in Indianapolis at this time. Not only did this list include numerous law books, but also newspapers, journals, novels, lectures, sermons, history, and travel books. The Bible, of course, was a staple, as was Plutarch.

Samuel Merrill was another New Englander who played a significant role in establishing a literary tenor for the new city. In fact, a number of writers suggest that Indianapolis' literary history properly begins when Merrill, in his role as state treasurer, oversaw the transfer of state property from Corydon to Indianapolis in the fall of 1824. That property included the Indiana State Library. One of a number of professional men in the town who had personal book collections

J. Kent Calder is Managing Editor, *Traces of Indiana and Midwestern History*, Indiana Historical Society, Indianapolis.

that included literature as well as law books, Merrill loaned his books to interested readers. He established one of the city's earliest bookstores, and the business evolved after his death in 1855 into one of the nation's most important trade publishers, the Bobbs-Merrill Company. Developed by three generations of Merrills, the company was an essential element in the creation of a literary atmosphere that reached its peak in the 1880s and 1890s.

Merrill also made another significant contribution to the city's literary future: his daughter, Catharine. Educated by her father at a school in the rear of the State Treasury on Maryland Street, Catharine acquired his love of literature. Encouraged by her mother to keep a journal, she developed literary skills at an early age. Catharine's writings in *Catharine Merrill: Life and Letters* (1934), edited by niece Katharine Merrill Graydon, reflect a life dominated by books: "My first recollection of perfect felicity," she recalled, "was when creeping softly through the darkness of Christmas morning I 'caught' Pa and Ma, and standing by the bedside received in my trembling hands the package of books (always books till the last Christmas of his life) wrapped in brown paper and tied with a knotted string."

Diary entries indicate that the young Catharine longed to write, perhaps in the vein of her beloved Sir Walter Scott. But it was as a teacher that Catharine Merrill made her greatest contribution to the literary culture of Indianapolis. She began her first school in 1843. It met in the back parlor of her home, and in it children from the city's most prominent families—Cathcart, Davidson, Fletcher, Morris, Vance—learned "not only to read and write, but also to love literature and knowledge of various kinds, and most of all to revere goodness." In 1869 Ovid Butler, president of the North Western Christian University board of trustees, appointed her to the Demia Butler Chair as professor of literature, making her the second woman in the nation to attain a college professorship. Even after she retired in 1883 from what was by then Butler University, she continued conducting literature classes in her home. Her influence on the cultural life of the city was profound, and before her death in 1900 a literary club was established in her name.

Many others contributed to the burgeoning literary culture of Indianapolis during its first half century. Some collected books and established bookstores. Some set up newspapers that promoted books and had bookmaking capability. Some taught; some wrote; and many read. At the same time, the cultures of the northern and southern sections of the country began to mix, forming a distinctive style and voice for the city.

Newspapers were perhaps the most important means of fostering the book atmosphere of Indianapolis and melding its disparate cultures. When Merrill arrived in 1824, two newspapers were already publishing. George Smith and Nathaniel Bolton, previously of Madison, Indiana, had published the first issue of the *Indianapolis Gazette* on January 28, 1822, and the *Western Censor and Emigrants Guide* appeared a little over a year later on March 7, 1823. (In 1825 the latter became the *Indiana Journal*.) The first issue of the *Gazette* contained an announcement for a proposed book on the legal duties of county officers, *The Indiana Justice and Farmers' Scrivener*, and by February it was announcing that *Almanacs for 1822* were on sale at its office. The *Western Censor* promoted the first book of national importance with its notice in 1823 of James Fenimore Cooper's *The Pilot*.

These early newspapers also provided outlets for poetry. Sarah T. Bolton was by far the most important of Indianapolis' pioneer poets. Born in Kentucky in 1814 to a family with Virginia roots, she moved to the capital after her marriage to publisher and editor Nathaniel Bolton in 1831. Having published her first poem in a Madison, Indiana, newspaper at the age of 13, Bolton continued to write and publish during her years in Indianapolis despite the need to manage a large farm and keep a tavern. By the time the collection *The Life and Poems of Sarah T. Bolton* was published in Indianapolis in 1880, she was considered the city's poet laureate.

An Indianapolis newspaper was also responsible for publishing the poem that popularized the word *Hoosier* far beyond the boundaries of Indiana. On January 1, 1833, the *Indiana Journal* ran "The Hoosier's Nest," John Finley's ten-stanza poem about the satisfactions of life on the Indiana frontier. Though the poem was not the Richmond, Indiana, poet's best work, it was picked up by newspapers around the country and even appeared in the English press as an example of American backwoods verse. It was the first poem of the genre to become internationally famous. The word *Hoosier* had appeared in print before 1833, but the publication of Finley's poem made it part of the American vocabulary.

The newly popularized term quickly acquired two divergent connotations. Westerners tended to consider Hoosiers in the context of Finley's poem, as representatives of the pioneer virtues of independence, hard work, and democracy, while those in the more settled parts of the country took the term to typify what Indianapolis-born author Joseph Chamberlain Furnas has called "adenoidal uncouthness." It would be a while yet before the Hoosier hayseed would make his native intelligence apparent to the rest of the country.

By the 1850s Indianapolis boasted four bookstores, one of which was owned by Samuel Merrill. On June 22, 1851, the *Journal* praised "the intelligence and literary taste" of the city's citizens, concluding that "the condition of the bookstores in a place is a sure index to the intelligence of the people." While the city had a right to be proud of its literary attainments, it was still a frontier town. Furnas described it aptly in his biography of Robert Louis Stevenson, *Voyage to Windward* (1951), as the home of Stevenson's future wife, Fanny Van de Grift:

> The place was as flat as your hand and only twenty years old. . . . It had plenty of iron-weed, stumps, whisky, loose women, and shoddy shacks, and floods of tobacco juice as brown as the spring floods of Fall Creek and Pogue's Run. Also present were energy, sapped by "fever 'n' ager"; enterprise braked by an elementary economy just turning from cattle-running to farming; ambition slowed down by the National Road, which, bisecting the town, too often tempted intending residents farther westward; and refinement, imported as books and furniture from southward and eastward, but diluted by the dense ignorance of the bulk of the population.

A neighbor of the Van de Grifts, Eunice Bullard Beecher, penned a similar description of her time in Indianapolis. As the wife of Presbyterian minister Henry Ward Beecher, Eunice, a native of Massachusetts, lived in the city from 1839 to 1847. She considered the culture primitive, suffered numerous bouts of illness, and lost two of her five children in Indiana. Her autobiographical novel, *From Dawn to Daylight: or The Simple Story of a Western Home* (1859), presented a harsh portrait of Indianapolis and her treatment by her congregation. The novel, published anonymously, was derided in the city's papers as "a dreary affair" reflecting the "acid bite of a disappointed woman" and having "no literary merit." Not surprisingly it mysteriously disappeared from the shelves of the Indianapolis Public Library. The literary pill of critical self-appraisal would never be easy for the city to swallow.

The years immediately following the Civil War saw the publication of a number of practical and important books in the city, as well as the formation of a variety of clubs that fostered literary study. Persuaded by Governor Oliver P. Morton, Catharine Merrill compiled and wrote *The Indiana Soldier in the War for the Union*. The two volumes, published by Merrill and Company, appeared anonymously in 1866 and 1869. Publications by men rarely exhibited such humility. William R. Holloway's *Indianapolis* was published in the city in 1870, and later in the decade two other Indianapolis imprints appeared: Charles Manning Walker's *Sketch of the Life, Character, and Public Service of Oliver P. Morton* (1878) and William Wesley Woollen's *Madison from 1844 to 1852* (1879). By the end of the seventies the city had as many as 50 literary clubs, the most prominent of which were the Indianapolis Woman's Club (1875) and the Indianapolis Literary Club (1877).

The capital city's carefully tended literary garden came to flower in the 1880s. Lecture series brought important writers and thinkers to the city, and local residents presented well-attended courses on such topics as temperance, science, philosophy, literature, and music. Well-known writers and orators who came to town in this decade included George Washington Cable, A. Bronson Alcott, Robert Ingersoll, Oscar Wilde, and Matthew Arnold. Though Arnold was not favorably received in many cities during his 1884 lecture tour, he wrote to his daughter that in Indianapolis he "had a capital audience, and found some zealous disciples."

These years also saw the rise to popularity of poet James Whitcomb Riley, who moved to the city in 1879 to work for the *Journal*, and the beginnings of the transition of the Merrill publishing firm from legal to general trade publishing. In just a few years Riley would be the country's most popular poet, and the firm would lead the nation in producing bestsellers. The turning point was the publication in 1883 of a second edition of Riley's book, *"The Old Swimmin'-Hole" and 'Leven More Poems*. The success of this book set a standard for accomplishment in trade publishing. Thereafter, the firm and the poet worked hand in hand to increase Riley's popularity and the publisher's profits. It was one of the 19th century's most successful publishing collaborations.

Riley's success marks the beginning of what is generally described as the Golden Age of Indiana literature. It was a period when urbanization and industrialization brought about great change and great prosperity. The urban middle class grew in numbers and became more affluent, and mechanization altered the traditional patterns of even those who stayed on the farm. The passing of the pioneer generation made their experiences and values seem much more worthy of being kept alive. Something that seemed particularly Hoosier was being lost, and Riley's sentimental and nostalgic verses about lazy childhood days in the Indiana countryside provided a tonic to growing anxieties. The poet's images of rustic simplicity and wholesomeness found an audience in the rest of the country as well, for the Golden Age was characterized by the general belief that the Indiana experience typified that of the nation.

The writing of state and local history was another response to these rapidly changing social conditions. A number of Indianapolis' most prominent men focused their energies on researching and writing Indiana history. Longtime journalist Berry R. Sulgrove's important work *A History of Indianapolis and Marion County, Indiana* appeared in 1884. Banker and businessman William H. English turned his attention to historical research after an unsuccessful run for the vice-presidency on the Democratic ticket in 1880. English not only amassed a large collection of materials related to early Indiana history, but he also became aware of the inadequate care and resources that had been devoted to the historical collections in the State Library. Judge Daniel Wait Howe and political journalist Jacob Piatt Dunn made similar discoveries in the course of their researches. These men formed a core of leadership for improving the State Library and for reinvigorating the Indiana Historical Society. Organized in 1830, the society had been virtually inactive for years until this group reorganized it and inaugurated a publishing program. Today, the organization remains one of the city's most active publishers.

Indianapolis children helped Hoosier poet James Whitcomb Riley celebrate his birthday in 1911. The celebration continued annually thereafter and was known as Riley Day. [Indiana Historical Society, Bass Collection, #207580F. Photo by Lester Negley.]

Novelist Booth Tarkington had several formal portraits taken with his pet poodles. [Indiana Historical Society, #C5073]

Indiana's Golden Age, which encompassed the last two decades of the 19th century and the first two decades of the 20th, was a time when the Hoosier state and its capital, Indianapolis, were at the center of national attention. In politics the state supplied vice-presidential and presidential candidates for both parties, and its vote often determined the outcome of presidential elections. The state and city were manufacturing and transportation centers, yet the common perception was that Hoosiers had managed to retain something of their pioneer roots. In this period the word *Hoosier* even acquired new meaning, as journalist John Bartlow Martin aptly explained in his classic 1947 study, *Indiana: An Interpretation*:

> The golden age meant a way of life, a cast of mind. It meant a Hoosier who was proud of his own success and his neighbor's success and his town's success, a man who was confident of the future, a man who sometimes shrewdly wore the cloak of rusticity the better to conceal his schemes. The rude backwoodsman had come to greatness, just as he had known he would; he had confounded those who jibed at him. And all this is the Indiana idea, the idea that people elsewhere hold of the Indiana character; it arose during these golden years.

The most important promoters of the "Indiana idea" were the Indianapolis publisher Bowen-Merrill, which changed its name to Bobbs-Merrill in 1903, and the authors who lived in the capital city or close by. These included, among others, Charles Major, Shelbyville; Maurice Thompson and Lew Wallace, Crawfordsville; George Ade, Kentland; George Barr McCutcheon, Lafayette; Gene Stratton-Porter, Geneva; and Riley, Frank McKinney "Kin" Hubbard, Meredith Nicholson, and Booth Tarkington, Indianapolis. From humor to nature stories to mystery and romance to gentle realism, these authors espoused the conservative and traditional values of a pre-industrial Midwest: individualism, hard work, simplicity, modesty, and optimism. In so doing, they found a broad national audience and sold many books.

After its success with Riley's poems, Bowen-Merrill began an active search for manuscripts. In 1897 it found, almost by accident, Charles Major's manuscript "Charles Brandon, Duke of Suffolk." Salesman Lee Burns had called on the Shelbyville lawyer's office in hopes of selling some law books and ended up coming back to Indianapolis with the manuscript. Director of Publications John J. Curtis read it and liked it but had a problem with the title. He changed it to *When Knighthood Was in Flower*, from a line in a Leigh Hunt poem, and launched the book in 1898 with what is considered to be the first national advertising campaign for a single book. Its overwhelming success, 200,000 copies sold in two years, set the stage for the firm's future as the country's best-known publisher of popular literature. After a second success with Maurice Thompson's *Alice of Old Vincennes* in 1900, the firm had its pick of authors and manuscripts. Throughout the years it continued to encourage and publish Hoosier authors, and in so doing it did as much as the writers to create the impression of a Golden Age.

Indianapolis authors Meredith Nicholson and Booth Tarkington did much to add to that image. Nicholson was a longtime resident of Indianapolis and did most of his publishing with Bobbs-Merrill. Much of his fiction, like *The House of a Thousand Candles* (1905), deftly combined mystery, romance, happy endings, and Indiana settings for the delight of a national audience. His essays, especially *The Hoosiers* (1900), are still important for their interpretation of the Indiana idea. Tarkington is considered the dean of Indiana letters for his numerous novels, plays, and short stories. He lived in Indianapolis throughout his life and utilized Hoosier settings in most of his work. He won Pulitzer prizes for two Indianapolis novels, *The Magnificent Ambersons* (1918) and

Alice Adams (1921). His numerous novels chronicled in a realistic vein the changing circumstances of middle and upper class families as they came to terms with a world of industrial complexity.

One of the city's best-known politicians also contributed to the state's literary reputation. Albert J. Beveridge practiced law in Indianapolis for 12 years before serving two consecutive terms in the U.S. Senate from 1900 to 1912 as a Progressive Republican. Beveridge joined Theodore Roosevelt's Progressive party in 1912 and ran on that ticket for governor in 1912 and senator in 1914. Both times he lost. With Roosevelt he rejoined the Republican party in 1916 and was defeated in his final run for the Senate in 1922. Throughout his political career he produced books that exhibited a desire for first-hand information and a talent for effective writing. Beveridge's most important literary work was the four-volume biography, *The Life of John Marshall* (1916, 1918). Acclaimed by scholars and critics, this work remains an outstanding example of historical biography. At the time of his death in 1927, Beveridge was working on a similar definitive treatment of Abraham Lincoln, published a year later. His legacy as politician and writer represents the best aspects of the Indiana idea.

Journalist, diplomat, and historian Claude G. Bowers was another Indianapolis author who reached a national audience in the twenties and thirties with popular historical works. An ardent Democrat, Bowers provided partisan interpretations of American politics in the 1790s and 1860s in his best-known works, *Jefferson and Hamilton* (1925) and *The Tragic Era* (1929). Though criticized by recent historians, his work continues to be read today.

Indianapolis had achieved literary prominence in the years before and just after World War I by producing popular literature that satisfied a national yearning for nostalgia, escape, simplicity, and humor. After the war, as tastes changed, the Indiana idea lost its currency. The 1920s had little use for Riley's dreamy evocations of a bucolic world or stories that looked backward with fondness to a preindustrial era. Technology, mass production, and advertising created a new popular conception of the good life. Accumulation of wealth and consumption of new material goods seized the American imagination. Farm and village life was seen as narrow and intolerant, and young midwesterners moved in droves to cities. America's best writers still came from the Midwest, but it was Chicago that attracted them, not Indianapolis. In the second and third decades of the 20th century, writers like Theodore Dreiser, Sherwood Anderson, and Sinclair Lewis, who captured with harsh realism the forces at work in American society, were at the center of American literature.

A couple of writers from Indianapolis, Janet Flanner and Margaret Anderson, found places in this larger literary world. Indianapolis-born Anderson arrived in Chicago in 1908 during a renaissance of the arts; she went to the Windy City because, in her words, "there was no creative opinion in Indianapolis." After writing for various magazines, including the *Dial*, she launched the *Little Review* in March, 1914. The monthly became an important outlet for the new voices in American literature. Its purpose was to promote a new attitude in American writing that was uncompromising in its search for truth, experimental in its language, less concerned with regionalism, and more occupied with private experience. Anderson moved the magazine to New York in 1917 and later to Paris, where she would become famous for publishing installments of James Joyce's *Ulysses* and Ernest Hemingway's early work. In Paris, Anderson met and became friends with another expatriate Hoosier writer, Janet Flanner. One of three daughters of a well-known Indianapolis family, Flanner moved to Paris in 1922 and wrote an autobiographical novel, *The Cubical City*, that was published in 1924. The next year she began publishing letters from Paris as "Genet" in the *New Yorker*, which had just begun publication. She would write for the magazine for the rest of her life. In 1966 a collection of her writings, *Paris Journal*, won the National Book Award.

The early work of midwesterners like Hemingway, F. Scott Fitzgerald, and Hart Crane signaled the beginning of the end of what literary critic Ronald Weber has termed the "midwestern ascendancy in American writing." These writers exhibited a modernist spirit in their preoccupations with the dislocations and disillusionment of the postwar world. The 1930s also saw the rise of a literary movement that combined elements of modernism and regionalism. The southern literary renaissance began with the publication in 1929 of William Faulkner's *The Sound and the Fury* and Thomas Wolfe's *Look Homeward, Angel*. New York City became America's undisputed publishing center.

Though Indianapolis ceased to be a literary center in the years following the Golden Age, it continued to produce important writers who drew inspiration from the city's literary traditions. Shortridge High School became an important training ground for the city's aspiring writers, and Kurt Vonnegut, Jr., class of 1940, is perhaps the school's best-known literary graduate. Born in Indianapolis to a prominent German-American family, Vonnegut emerged in the 1960s as the most trenchant commentator on human folly since Mark Twain. In short stories, plays, and especially novels such as *Player Piano* (1952), *The Sirens of Titan* (1959), *Cat's Cradle* (1963), *God Bless You, Mr. Rosewater* (1965), and *Slaughterhouse-Five* (1969), this self-described "total pessimist" blended fantasy, black humor, and a keen sense of the absurd in protest of 20th-century horrors, especially the dehumanization of the individual in a technological society. He expressed the fears of a generation just coming of age and in doing so found a large audience. Though Vonnegut has not lived in Indianapolis since leaving high school, he told a group at Butler University in 1983: "Every joke I've ever told, every attitude I've ever struck, came from School 43 and Shortridge. I never needed any new material from any other place."

Dan Wakefield is another Shortridge graduate who left the city for a writing career. Encouraged by the example of Vonnegut and inspired by Indiana's literary tradition, Wakefield went to New York in 1952 to fulfill his ambition. In his book *New York in the Fifties* (1992), he describes the stimulating intellectual communities that existed in New York at that time and attracted artistically inclined young people from throughout the country. Quoting from an interview with Kansas City native Calvin Trillin, Wakefield writes, "The immigrant saga of the fifties was . . . people coming in from the Midwest instead of from Europe." Wakefield established himself as a journalist by contributing to magazines like the *Nation*, *Esquire*, and *Atlantic Monthly* and by writing nonfiction books that include *Island in the City: The World of Spanish Harlem* (1959) and *Supernation at Peace and War* (1968). His first novel, *Going All the Way* (1970), reflected the restlessness of two young men who return to Indianapolis from military service in 1954 and look forward to beginning a "real life" but are thwarted by the narrowness, intolerance, and lack of opportunity that surrounds them. Vonnegut helped Wakefield find a publisher and wrote favorable reviews of the book that secured its success. Wakefield's subsequent novels include *Starting Over* (1973), which was made into a feature film, and *Selling Out* (1985). His autobiographal *Returning: A Spiritual Journey* (1988) included some discussion of his youth in the Indiana capital.

Like Hoosier authors of the past, Vonnegut and Wakefield have written about Indianapolis as a typical American city, but in books like *Going All the Way* and Vonnegut's *Breakfast of Champions* (1973), which takes place in the fictional Midland City, the characteristics represented are much different than those that concerned Tarkington and Nicholson. The middle class that the earlier authors praised for its civility and culture has become fearful, shallow, bigoted, and crassly ambitious by the time of Vonnegut and Wakefield. Of course, these attitudes reflect the spirit of the times, and both authors appear to have revised these opinions in recent years. Vonnegut appeared in the city in the wake of the publication of *Fates Worse Than Death: An Autobiographical Collage of the 1980s* (1991), a book that the *New York Times Book Review* said offered "a rare insight into an author who has customarily hidden his heart," to keynote the first Wordstruck literary festival. He spoke warmly of growing up in Indianapolis and of the inspiration he received from the city's literary traditions. Wakefield, likewise, has addressed interested Indianapolis audiences since the publication of *New York in the Fifties* about the necessary ingredients that go into making a literary community, and he acknowledges being impressed by the vitality of Indianapolis' current literary scene. In 1992 he told a group gathered at the Indiana Humanities Council (IHC) Achievement Awards dinner that the future literary life of the country will depend on the regional publishing and that with its tradition, its organizations, its publications, its events, and its active writing community, Indianapolis has the makings of an important regional center for writing and publishing.

Organizations that provide literary programming for the city include the IHC, the Writers' Center of Indianapolis, the Indianapolis–Marion County Public Library, and Butler University. These organizations not only bring to town some of the country's most prominent writers, but they also offer opportunities for local writers to meet the public with readings and programs devoted to regional literature. The lively journals *Nuvo*, which reminds Dan Wakefield of the early *Village Voice*, and *Arts Indiana* are thoughtful outlets for the city's best cultural journalism, and publications like the annual *Hopewell Review* from Arts Indiana Press present high-quality fiction and poetry. The Indiana Historical Society's illustrated magazine, *Traces*, publishes creative nonfiction and essays on the region's rich heritage. These journals and the organizations that sponsor them provide the foundation for Indianapolis' literary community.

Among the city's most prominent contemporary writers are poets Jared Carter, Alice Friman, Mari Evans, and Richard Pflum. Vesle Fenstermaker writes poetry and fiction, as does L. E. McCullough. The stories of Jerome Donahue, Barbara Shoup, Alison Jester, and David Hoppe appear regularly in regional publications. *Indianapolis Star* columnist (now editor) Dan Carpenter wrote provocative essays about Indiana for more than a decade, and his best work is now available in the collection *Hard Pieces* (1993). Susan Neville of Butler University has received national recognition for her stories and essays; her book of stories *The Invention of Flight* (1984) received the Flannery O'Connor Award for Short Fiction. Alan T. Nolan, a classmate of Vonnegut's at Shortridge and an Indianapolis lawyer, has published novels and history books. Nolan's *The Iron Brigade* (1961) has been listed among the "100 best books ever written on the Civil War," and his *Lee Considered* (1991) received much critical attention and acclaim. Butler University professor Emma Lou Thornbrough's *The Negro in Indiana before 1900* (1957) and *Indiana in the Civil War Era* (1965) are still in print and still the most important sources on their respective topics. Nancy N. Baxter writes historical novels that are compelling recreations of Indiana experience, and her Guild Press of Indiana is building an important list of regional history titles. Michael Z. Lewin has put Indianapolis on the map in the growing field of regional mystery writing, and Joseph J. Andrew, another Indianapolis lawyer, has written a potential bestseller with his spy-thriller, *The Disciples* (1993). The Hoosier capital serves as the setting for much of *High Cotton* (1992), a favorably received autobiographical novel by Darryl Pinckney.

In March, 1991, Indianapolis lost one of the most vibrant members of its literary community with the passing of poet Etheridge Knight. Knight, who began writing poems while in the Indiana State Prison at Michigan City, is a testament to the healing power of poetry. His first book, *Poems from Prison*, appeared in 1968. His *Belly Song and Other Poems* was nominated for the National Book Award and the Pulitzer Prize in 1973. In 1985 the Poetry Society of America awarded him the Shelley Memorial Award, and the *Essential Etheridge Knight* appeared in 1986. The January, 1991, tribute to Knight, which attracted poets of the stature of Donald Hall, Robert Bly, and Galway Kinnell, may have been the most important literary event to take place in the city in this century.

Though Knight is gone, his work, like that of Sarah T. Bolton, Catharine Merrill, James Whitcomb Riley, Booth Tarkington, and Meredith Nicholson, continues to encourage a new generation of authors. "Creativity sparks others' creativity," writes Dan Wakefield, "and tradition begets inspiration." Indianapolis today provides a "capital audience" for literary programming, to use Matthew Arnold's phrase from the 1880s, and a nurturing environment for aspiring writers. Perhaps the city is only a generation away from a new Golden Age as a center for regional writing and publishing.

See also: BOOK TRADE; HISTORIES OF INDIANAPOLIS; LITERARY ORGANIZATIONS AND EVENTS; LITERATURE, CHILDREN'S; PRINTING AND PUBLISHING INDUSTRIES; and individual authors, titles, and organizations.

MEDICINE

Katherine Mandusic McDonell

Disease was prevalent among residents of early Indianapolis. The city's low-lying swampy land, combined with a lack of knowledge about disease-causing mechanisms and proper sanitation methods, led to much sickness. Outbreaks of diseases such as malaria (popularly known as "ager" or "ague"), dysentery, whooping cough, scarlet fever, measles, pneumonia, erysipelas (black tongue), pleurisy, and milk sickness frequently occurred among the early residents. The latter disease was caused by eating the meat or drinking the milk of animals that had grazed on the white snakeroot plant (which contained the poison tremotol). Epidemics of typhoid fever, smallpox, yellow fever, and cholera were also common, killing large numbers of people. Cholera, one of the most dreaded diseases of the early 19th century, first struck Indianapolis in 1833 and again in 1849, 1854, and 1866.

Physicians could offer little assistance to the sick and suffering during much of the 19th century. They lacked knowledge of germs and infection and thus had few effective treatments. Prior to the Civil War, bloodletting and purging with harsh drugs such as calomel (a compound of mercury) and jalap were the most common remedies. Surgery was limited because of the absence of anesthesia and asepsis. Most patients were treated in their own homes rather than in hospitals.

Very few doctors had a formal education. Many studied under a practicing physician through an apprenticeship. Some had a few courses at a medical school. But standards at these early schools were lax, and almost anyone who wanted to become a physician in the early 19th century could do so. By midcentury most cities, including Indianapolis, had an abundance of doctors.

In 1821 Samuel Mitchell (d. 1837) came to Indianapolis from Kentucky to become the city's first physician. He was followed by Isaac Coe, a New Jersey native who later left Indianapolis; Livingston Dunlap (1799–1862), a graduate of Transylvania University; Kenneth Scudder (d. 1829), a New Jersey native; and Jonathan Cool, also a New Jersey native. From 1821 to 1825 Indianapolis had only five physicians to care for the sick and suffering. The scarcity of physicians in Indianapolis, however, was short-lived. By 1836 the city had 14 regular, or orthodox, physicians and a number of other sectarian doctors.

Katherine Mandusic McDonell is former Executive Director, Indiana Medical History Museum.

Because of the harsh treatments employed by these doctors, many persons avoided physicians altogether and relied on home remedies. For some, distance or cost made medical care inaccessible. Also, beginning in the 1830s, Indianapolis residents had a variety of forms of alternative health care available to them. Although licensing legislation had existed in the state since 1816, most of this legislation was ineffective.

The most popular alternative medical sects in 19th-century Indianapolis were the Thomsonians and the homeopaths. The former sect, founded by a New Hampshire farmer and self-proclaimed doctor, Samuel Thomson, advocated the use of a variety of botanical remedies as a substitute for bloodletting and the harsh regimens of the regular physicians. Thomson's explanation of disease and his directions for medical cures were written in lay language. During one year, two of the fifteen doctors advertising in the two Indianapolis newspapers were botanics, or Thomsonians. This sect remained popular throughout the 1830s and 1840s, but by the 1850s its popularity waned. Schisms occurred within the sect, with some of its prominent members founding other sects.

Homeopathy, another form of alternative medicine, was founded by Samuel Christian Hahnemann in the late 18th century. Hahnemann believed that "like cures like." Accordingly, administering very small doses of drugs that in large doses reproduced symptoms of the disease would cure the patient. Homeopathy, however, did not gain acceptance in Indianapolis until after the Civil War; then it became very popular, especially among Indianapolis' German population, and remained so until the early 20th century.

By the 1830s and 1840s important changes were occurring in medicine. In Europe hospitals became important to medical education, and doctors abandoned bloodletting and purging as ineffective therapies. They also learned that many diseases ran their course with or without medical interference. Doctors still had few effective remedies, but they relied on milder tonics rather than the harsh treatments of the previous era. Professional associations and university training also became important.

These ideas filtered back to the United States and were accepted by a number of physicians on the East Coast. Change came slowly to Indiana and Indianapolis, although physicians in the city played the leading role in restricting entry into the profession by establishing professional medical societies. Indianapolis doctors also took the lead in establishing hospitals and improving public health. Not until the end of the century was the reform of medicine complete.

Indianapolis established its first medical society in 1823. Known as the Central Medical Society, its major purpose was to license physicians. This association was short-lived. Not until 1848, with the formation of the Indianapolis Medical Society, was there a permanent group. The organization remained small and relatively inactive throughout much of the century. The Indiana State Medical Society (now the Indiana State Medical Association), which was formed the next year, was more active in educating physicians, monitoring the profession, and providing a means for sharing scientific knowledge. Indianapolis physicians played a major role in establishing this society; its president was Livingston Dunlap and 18 of 28 charter members were from Indianapolis–Marion County. The society included the leading physicians of Indianapolis: Dunlap, Patrick H. Jameson, John L. Mothershead, John M. Kitchen, George W. Mears, and John S. Bobbs. These men spearheaded efforts to establish medical institutions that still exist in the city today.

The idea of building a municipal hospital originated with Livingston Dunlap in the 1830s. For much of the 19th century hospitals were places of last resort for society's destitute. The only institution caring for the sick poor was the Marion County Poor Farm (established 1832), which provided minimal medical care (although hospital facilities were added in 1869). Dunlap, along with several other physicians, saw the need for a permanent place to care for the city's sick poor. Interest in such a hospital waxed and waned but peaked during epidemics. The city council approved the hospital plan in 1854, and the next year the city began construction of the facility. Financial problems plagued the institution. Building costs exceeded budget, and the structure was left vacant for years until it was used during the Civil War to house sick soldiers. After the war the federal government returned the facility to the city and it opened as a charity hospital.

Indianapolis physicians also played a major role in establishing a state mental hospital. In 1845 a committee purchased land for such an institution, and the following year the state legislature passed an act establishing the facility. The Indiana Hospital for the Insane (later Central State Hospital) admitted its first patients in 1848.

The city established its first permanent board of health in 1859. That body established municipal sanitary and food inspection standards. Prior to this, the city council appointed temporary boards of health during epidemics. During the cholera epidemic of 1833, for example, a board of health studied ways to prevent the spread of the disease. Subsequent ad hoc boards investigated the possibility of erecting a pesthouse and establishing a new sanitary system within the city.

Although Indianapolis played a prominent role in establishing medical societies, hospitals, and a board of health, it trailed other cities in the state in establishing a medical school. The first school in Indianapolis was short-lived; begun in 1848, it went out of business in 1852.

The Civil War interrupted Indianapolis doctors' efforts to reform health care. Governor Oliver P. Morton appointed Indianapolis physicians John M. Kitchen and Patrick H. Jameson to take care of all military camps in the Indianapolis area. The sick and wounded were cared for at Camp Morton, Indianapolis City Hospital, and other temporary hospitals in the city.

Contagious diseases were quite common during the war, with more men dying from sickness than wounds. Caring for the wounded on the battlefield presented special problems. In March, 1862, the state created the Indiana Sanitary Commission. Headquartered in Indianapolis and headed by Indianapolis businessman William Hanneman, this organization carried supplies for soldiers, surgeons, and nurses to the battlefield.

The last half of the 19th century saw continued medical reform and progress. With the discoveries of Joseph Lister, Louis Pasteur, and Robert Koch and the subsequent advent of the germ theory and bacteriology at the end of the century, medicine became more of a science with a body of specialized knowledge. Medical schools, medical societies, hospitals, and medical journals thrived. Bacteriology and the germ theory led to an increased interest in public health.

Advances in medical science led to the decline in popularity of sectarian medicine. Homeopathic medicine and eclectic medicine, however, remained popular and by the early 20th century had gained acceptance by the orthodox medical profession. Eclectic physicians used primarily botanic remedies, but claimed to borrow the best cures from all forms of medicine. New alternative forms of medicine—osteopathy, Christian Science, and chiropractic medicine—loomed on the horizon. Osteopathy, founded by Missouri doctor Andrew Still in the 1890s, was based on the principle that when the human body was sick it could be repaired by placing its parts in proper relationship. Christian Science, founded by Mary Baker Eddy, looked at disease as a function of mind and spirit. Chiropractic medicine stressed that disease results from a lack of normal nerve functions and employs manipulation and adjustment of the spinal column.

Top left: Col. Eli Lilly, founder of Eli Lilly and Company. [Eli Lilly and Company Archives]

Top right: Medical students in the Pathology Building at Central State Hospital ca. 1900 observing an operation. [Indiana Historical Society, #C5618]

Bottom: Sunnyside Sanitarium provided medical treatment for tuberculosis patients such as the children shown in this 1925 photograph. [Indiana Historical Society, Bass Collection, #91948-F]

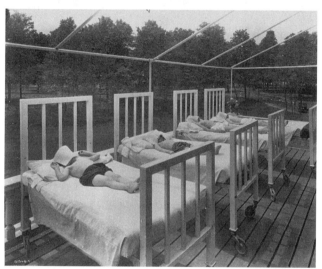

Several medical schools opened in Indianapolis after the Civil War. The first was the Indiana Medical College (1869). That school affiliated with Indiana University in 1871, but the affiliation lasted only until 1876. In 1873 some of the faculty left the school to form a rival medical college, the College of Physicians and Surgeons (1874–1878). In 1879, yet another school emerged, the Central College of Physicians and Surgeons. During the last half of the 19th century Indianapolis also had a number of other schools that represented the various alternative forms of medicine. All of these schools were proprietary in nature and relied on income from tuition for operating support. Standards were low and financial problems abounded. Yet the establishment of medical schools within the city gave prospective medical students the opportunity to obtain formal education, rather than merely apprenticeship training.

Although the Indianapolis Medical Society remained small, it met monthly to share medical cases and exchange ideas. The Indiana State Medical Association, in which Indianapolis doctors played an important role, likewise gave physicians an opportunity to control the direction of the profession. Local physicians were also active in the American Medical Association (formed in 1847), and in 1879 Indianapolis physician Theophilus T. Parvin became its president. All three medical societies—local, state, and national—lobbied to limit entrance into the profession. In 1885 doctors had to obtain a license in the county in which they practiced. In 1897 the General Assembly created the State Board of Medical Registration and Examination to regulate the practice of medicine and to issue licenses.

The profession of medicine was enhanced by the creation of medical journals that allowed doctors to disseminate knowledge, share cases and treatments, and critically evaluate new therapies. The Indiana State Medical Association published its *Transactions* from 1849 to 1907 (which then became the *Journal* and is now *Indiana Medicine*). It is the oldest continuous medical publication in the state. A number of other journals were published within the city, including the *Indianapolis Medical Journal*.

With the growth of medical schools came the need for clinical facilities at hospitals and other institutions where students could observe patients. These institutions continued to serve primarily the poor. By the end of the century, however, hospitals offered advanced medical care for the middle class. This transformation was aided by the introduction of professional nursing and aseptic operating techniques.

At the end of the Civil War the federal government turned City Hospital over to the city, which opened the facility as a 75–bed charity hospital. During its early years the institution resembled an almshouse more than a hospital. The physical building was in disrepair, and the hospital lacked a trained nursing staff. In 1879 superintendent William Niles Wishard introduced important changes at the institution. Among his achievements were new and expanded facilities, a nurse training school, and aseptic hospital procedures. By 1885 City Hospital had been transformed into a modern hospital facility.

As poverty in the city increased so did the hospital population. Once-modern facilities rapidly became outdated. Overcrowding and underfunding characterized the hospital well into the 20th century. To meet the need for hospital bed space, two other institutions opened—St. Vincent Hospital (1881) and Protestant Deaconess (1899). Both were financed through private philanthropy and provided a higher quality of care than that available at City Hospital.

The city also opened a dispensary for outpatient care of the poor. Like City Hospital and other local hospitals, medical students used the facility for clinical training. Originally established in 1870 as a public-private venture, it was reorganized in 1879 and operated exclusively as a governmental agency. The dispensary experienced a tremendous increase in business during economic recessions and depressions. The City Dispensary merged with Indiana University's Bobbs' Free Dispensary in 1909 and moved to the medical school. It eventually became part of the social services division of Indiana University. Later in the 20th century outpatient clinics were established throughout the city and outpatient departments of hospitals fulfilled the need for outpatient care.

The Flower Mission also provided care for the sick poor. Funded through private donations, it originated in 1876 when a group of women decided to take flowers to the sick poor. The women instituted a training program for nurses at City Hospital, visited the sick poor in their homes, investigated cases and determined the proper course of action, and provided district or public health nursing to the poor. In 1895 the Flower Mission, with Lilly family money, established Eleanor Hospital, a hospital for poor sick children under the age of 15. The hospital closed its doors in 1909. Flower Mission also established a hospital in 1936 to care for incurable cases, particularly patients suffering from tuberculosis.

The key to good hospital care and improved public health was a well-trained nursing staff. City Hospital superintendent Wishard was instrumental in opening the Flower Mission Training School for Nurses (which later became the Wishard Hospital School of Nursing). In 1895 St. Vincent Hospital established the second nurse training school within the city; in 1899 Protestant Deaconess Hospital opened its school. By the early 20th century the city also had established a system of public health, or district, nursing to provide care for patients in their homes.

Indianapolis likewise took a lead in the public health movement. In 1880, according to an account cited by Indiana medical historian Thurman Rice, only three cities in the country had a death rate higher than Indianapolis. The common killers included typhoid fever, infantile diarrhea (also known as cholera infantum or "summer complaint"), tuberculosis, smallpox, diphtheria, pneumonia, and venereal disease. The local board of health, assisted by the newly created State Board of Health, undertook measures to improve the public health and reduce the city's death rate.

Indianapolis physician Thaddeus Stevens in 1881 secured legislation establishing a board of health within the state and a method of collecting vital statistics. In 1896 another Indianapolis resident, pharmacist and chemist John Hurty, became secretary of the board of health and turned the organization into a major force within Indiana. Although Hurty technically lacked jurisdiction over Indianapolis, he worked closely with city health officials to reduce the incidence of typhoid fever by providing Indianapolis with a safe water supply.

Cholera infantum, or infantile diarrhea, was the leading cause of death among children under the age of one. Doctors believed that the unhealthy living conditions of the poor contributed to the high incidence of cholera infantum. In 1890 a group of citizens established the privately funded Summer Mission for Sick Children to provide day outings to Fairview Park. These outings were designed to relieve the misery of poor, sick children. They did little to lessen the incidence of the disease. By the late 1890s doctors pointed to the lack of a pure milk supply within the city as a major contributing factor, and the city appointed a milk inspector to ensure its safety. In 1903 the *Indianapolis News* established a fund to provide pasteurized milk to the residents of Indianapolis. These efforts helped reduce the infant mortality rate.

The care of the mentally ill improved slightly during this period. During the second half of the 19th century the organic and physiological causes of mental illness had been identified. Leaders in the field began looking at mental asylums as hospitals and mental illness as a disease. In 1896 Central State Hospital dedicated its Pathological Department, a state-of-the-art research facility for the study of mental illness. All the scientific advances and research, however, produced no immediate cures and little improvement in living conditions at the hospital. In 1898 Norways Sanitorium opened as a private treatment facility for patients with nervous and mental disorders.

Up until 1899 the state had assumed the primary responsibility for the care of the mentally ill. Patients rejected by the state hospital were cared for in the Marion County Poor Asylum. With growing numbers of the mentally ill at the institution, and increasing numbers being rejected by the state, the city and county funded a mental institution for the "incurably insane" at Julietta. This facility remained open until 1938. Whether at state or municipal facilities, the care of the mentally ill was far from perfect, and the institutions were constantly under public scrutiny. This scrutiny and criticism have continued to the present day.

Deinstitutionalization of mental patients began in the 1950s with the introduction of various tranquilizers that helped control certain forms of mental illness. The result was the opening of community mental health centers such as Midtown Community Mental Health Center and Tri-County Mental Health Center. This deinstitutionalization was completed in 1994 when Central State Hospital closed its doors and the Indianapolis community assumed responsibility for the care of these patients in community mental health centers and group homes.

The late 19th century and first decade of the 20th century also saw the growth of professional dentistry, optometry, and pharmacy. Indianapolis dentists played a key role in establishing the Indiana State Dental Association (1858) and were important in the establishment of both the Indiana State Dental College (later the Indiana University School of Dentistry) and the Indiana State Board of Dental Examiners in 1879. In 1907 a State Board of Examination and Registration was formed in Indianapolis to examine optometrists.

The Indiana Pharmaceutical Association had been established in 1882, but pharmacy was not regulated until 1899 when the General Assembly created a State Board of Pharmacy. Until the late 19th century most pharmacists compounded drugs in their own laboratories. The rise of large pharmaceutical companies, however, eventually made drugstore laboratories obsolete. These companies also began conducting medical research on various drug therapies, and thus medical research moved out of the physician's office and the drugstore into the laboratories and medical schools.

In Indianapolis the founding of Eli Lilly and Company in 1876 by Col. Eli Lilly transformed pharmaceutical and medical research within the city. The company, incorporated in 1881, hired its first full-time pharmacist in 1886. As the 20th century opened, Lilly enlarged its research efforts, eventually building separate facilities and a test clinic. In the 1920s the company began the first commercial production of insulin. It became a pharmaceutical giant and one of the leaders in research on cardiovascular disease, pernicious anemia, and cancer, and the production of sulfa drugs and antibiotics. Lilly, like the Indiana University Medical Center, has become a major recruiter of the world's best medical scientists. The firm employs thousands of individuals locally and invests millions of dollars in drug research and development.

Twentieth century developments revolutionized medicine. To assist in the diagnosis of disease, for example, doctors had available a number of bacteriological and chemical tests and a variety of diagnostic instruments such as the stethoscope, ophthomaloscope, X-ray, and electrocardiograph. By the 1970s accuracy in diagnosis improved further with the use of computerized axial tomography (CAT scans) and magnetic resonance imaging. Twentieth century medical discoveries included Salvarsan for syphilis (1909), insulin for diabetes (1922), sulfa drugs (1935), penicillin (1943), vitamin B12 for pernicious anemia (1955), vaccines for polio (1954 and 1956), and cobalt treatments for cancer (1960s). Surgery likewise improved throughout the century. By the late 1960s and 1970s doctors were performing major organ transplants. Most recently, physicians have looked to genetic engineering to better understand disease.

The 20th century also witnessed a major reform of medical education. At the turn of the century all the medical schools in Indianapolis were private or proprietary. In 1910 a Carnegie Foundation report by Abraham Flexner criticized proprietary medical education and urged that state government assume this responsibility. Prior to the release of this report, Indiana schools had changed the way they operated. In 1905 one of these schools, the Central College of Physicians and Surgeons, joined with the Fort Wayne Medical College to form the Indiana Medical College (which was a part of Purdue University). Indiana University in 1903 began offering its first courses in medicine in Bloomington, with two years of clinical training in Indianapolis. In 1908 all Indiana medical schools merged with Indiana University to form the Indiana University School of Medicine.

The medical school used City Hospital and other area hospitals for teaching and research purposes. The Robert Long Hospital, built in 1914 with private money, was the first hospital devoted to the medical school, and the medical school complex expanded rapidly around this facility. Even so, the legislature was frugal with money. The school had few full-time faculty, and many professors divided their time between Bloomington and Indianapolis. As a result Indiana University ranked very low in a survey done in the mid–1930s by the American Medical Association of the nation's 77 acceptable medical schools. A special committee formed by the Indiana State Medical Association recommended that the first two years of the medical school move to Indianapolis and that the legislature allocate more money for the school.

After World War II the legislature did grant more money to the school, but not until 1958, with the opening of a medical sciences building, was the first year of medical school available in Indianapolis. The quality of medical education improved rapidly. By 1970 the Indiana University School of Medicine had become one of the nation's leading medical schools and Indiana University Medical Center (consisting of the school and its affiliated hospitals) had become a leader in medical research and hospital care.

With the advent of bacteriology, the 20th century witnessed a rapid expansion of public health services. Public health included concerns about communicable diseases, infant and child hygiene, sanitation, food and milk control, and school health supervision. Public health officials emphasized preventive medicine through public education.

In 1905 the Indianapolis Board of Health became part of the Board of Health and Charities. This government agency operated as a separate entity until 1951 when the General Assembly created the Health and Hospital Corporation of Marion County. This body provided health and hospital services to all of Marion County and oversaw the work of Wishard Hospital, as well as the public health efforts of the Board of Health. Today, the Public Health Division of the Corporation provides preventive and diagnostic health programs, health education, immunization and epidemiological programs, environmental health regulation, and code enforcement. It has several clinics and district health offices throughout the county.

Tuberculosis, venereal disease, pneumonia, influenza, infant mortality, and industrial accidents and related occupational diseases were common during the early decades of the 20th century. By midcentury cancer, heart disease, polio, and traffic accidents were major concerns of public health officials. Public health concerns in the 1990s include AIDS, infant mortality, drug abuse, environmental hazards, heart disease, and the resurgence of tuberculosis.

During the early 20th century tuberculosis (also known as consumption and the white plague) occupied much attention of public health officials. The Marion County Society for the Study and Prevention of Tuberculosis (founded in 1912 and later known as the Marion County Tuberculosis Association) and the Indianapolis Public Health Nursing Association (also founded in 1912) actively educated the public about the disease. In 1903 the Flower Mission opened a small hospital on the grounds of Wishard Hospital to care for tuberculosis patients. Five years later the city opened its first tuberculosis clinic. In 1917 Sunnyside Sanitarium opened near Oaklandon as an outgrowth of the pulmonary department of Wishard Hospital. Sunnyside provided state-of-the-art care and treatment for tuberculosis patients. It continued in operation until 1969, when new treatments for tuberculosis made the facility obsolete.

These facilities primarily served the white population of Indianapolis. The death rate for blacks from tuberculosis was particularly high. In 1919, 134 African-Americans out of a population of 30,000 died during the first seven months of the year. The movement to provide care for black tuberculosis patients began with the black-run Woman's Improvement Club. With their guidance and support, a black tuberculosis camp opened at Oak Hill in 1905. In 1919 Flanner House opened its Free Tuberculosis Clinic. The Woman's Improvement Club also convinced the Flower Mission to maintain a ward for African-American patients at its 100–bed tuberculosis hospital that opened in 1936. The death rate for blacks, however, remained high primarily because of poor living conditions and inadequate funding. In 1940, 188 blacks per thousand in Indiana died from tuberculosis compared to 34 per thousand for whites. The introduction in 1945 of streptomycin helped reduce the number of deaths from tuberculosis. By the 1960s tuberculosis no longer posed a serious threat, although boards of health elsewhere have reported a resurgence of a virulent strain of the disease among the homeless in the 1990s.

Early in the century influenza epidemics, especially the Spanish flu, claimed many lives. The worst epidemic struck in 1918 when 548,000 individuals died from the disease. In Indianapolis alone, 969 individuals died (out of a population of 289,577). The board of health undertook a number of measures such as cleaning and fumigating streetcars, restricting admission to theaters, and banning public gatherings to help prevent the spread of the disease.

Polio epidemics occurred in 1949 and 1951. Hospitals around the city purchased iron lungs, which were large chambers to force normal breathing in polio victims. With the development of polio vaccines in 1954 and 1956, the threat of the disease subsided.

Venereal disease was another concern of 20th-century health officials. Many viewed syphilis, gonorrhea, and other sexually transmitted diseases as a problem of morality rather than as illnesses. In 1914 Indianapolis appointed a venereal disease investigator to monitor cases, and four years later the state required reporting of venereal cases. Until the discovery of penicillin in 1943, the only available treatment for the disease was Salvarsan, a mercurial compound discovered in 1909. In 1943 the Indianapolis Social Hygiene Association (later the Social Health Association of Central Indiana) was formed to educate the public about venereal disease. That same year Indianapolis opened the nation's first isolation hospital for the treatment of those suffering from venereal disease. Although cases of syphilis dramatically declined after the introduction of antibiotics, the State Board of Health has recently reported an increase of venereal diseases, now termed sexually transmitted diseases (STDs). The most recent threat has been the increased number of AIDS cases. The first AIDS case in Marion County was reported in 1982. By 1990, 307 AIDS cases had been reported and the number continues to rise.

At the turn of the century infant mortality was particularly high, especially among black children. In an effort to reduce the infant mortality rate, public health officials focused on child and maternal health. They began healthy baby and pure milk campaigns. Well-baby clinics, which offered health screening, were opened throughout the city. With the passage of the Sheppard-Towner Act in 1921 and Title V of the Social Security Act in 1935, many of these programs received federal funding.

Today, infant mortality among blacks remains prominent on the local public health agenda. A 1987 National Children's Defense Fund report revealed that Indianapolis had the highest black infant mortality rate in the United States. To reduce infant mortality, the City-County Council allocated $1.5 million in 1990 to launch the Indianapolis Campaign for Healthy Babies. Although the Campaign for Healthy Babies initially resulted in a decline in infant mortality, a recent study has revealed that the mortality rate among black infants is higher now than it was in 1987.

The early interest in maternal health led to the birth control and family planning movement. Public health nurses realized that the many health problems of poor women could be traced to frequent pregnancies. An organized birth control movement began in the early 1900s and operated illegally until the late 1930s. The local chapter of Planned Parenthood started in 1932 as part of the larger birth control movement.

Hospitals became an important part of the health care system during the 20th century. Before the outbreak of World War II a number of new hospitals opened in Indianapolis, including Methodist, St. Francis, William Coleman Hospital for Women, the James Whitcomb Riley Hospital for Children, and the Robert Long Hospital. Even with these hospitals, Indianapolis could not keep pace with the need for hospital beds. Particularly acute was the lack of adequate space for African-Americans. Until the 1940s only City Hospital accepted black patients, even though an Indianapolis Foundation-funded study in the 1920s revealed the need for more bed space for African-American patients. In the 1940s St. Vincent Hospital opened its wards to black patients.

The Great Depression had an adverse effect on the city's hospitals since charity care increased dramatically. Hospital care was expensive, and increasing numbers of individuals were unable to pay for this care. One hospital, Protestant Deaconess, closed its doors. Others contemplated accepting health insurance, although the state and local medical societies viewed insurance as a form of socialized medicine and staunchly opposed any third-party intrusion into the field. In 1944 Methodist Hospital became the city's first hospital to sign an agreement with Blue Cross Hospital Services, and others soon followed its lead.

The world wars strained the financial and human resources of the city's hospitals. Many of Indianapolis' health care professionals were called to active duty. In 1918 the Indianapolis chapter of the American Red Cross outfitted a base hospital in honor of Col. Eli Lilly. Officially known as U.S. Army Base Hospital No. 32, the unit originally was stationed at Fort Benjamin Harrison and then deployed to Contrexeville, France. During World War II Indianapolis physicians again served on active duty. The Indiana University School of Medicine funded another base hospital, which functioned in England and Germany.

With public resources going toward the war efforts, private philanthropy became important to meet the growing needs for equipment and services at hospitals. Hospitals (including publicly funded ones) established guilds to serve as fund-raising arms. After the war the shortage of bed space became even more acute. The Indianapolis Hospital Development Association, formed in 1951 by local businessmen, assessed Indianapolis' hospital needs and undertook a $12 million campaign to add 825 beds by 1975. To participate in this campaign all hospitals had to admit African-American patients. The campaign resulted in the expansion of existing hospital bed space and the opening of Community Hospital.

By the 1960s hospitals were affected by the spiraling cost of health care. With the advent of Medicare and Medicaid, the federal government heavily subsidized health care for the elderly and the indigent. The result was increased hospital admissions, increased physicians' fees, and increased insurance premiums. In 1983 the government acted to control costs, resulting in the loss of millions of dollars by hospitals. Inflation, expensive new technology, and declining hospital admissions led to lean years in 1983 and 1984. Some local hospitals downsized, cut staff, and relied more heavily on outpatient services. Health maintenance organizations emerged in the city, formed by hospitals, insurance companies, and physicians to trim expenses, and hospitals began to offer wellness programs to reduce health care costs.

As medical science improved, interest in alternative health care declined but by no means disappeared. Homeopathy, osteopathy, chiropractic medicine, and Christian Science remained popular at the turn of the century. Homeopathy declined by the mid–1920s but has recently enjoyed a resurgence of popularity. Chiropractic medicine and osteopathy remain popular, with many practitioners in the city. In 1975 the city opened its first osteopathic hospital—Westview Hospital. It is estimated that one third of all Americans use therapies and treatments outside mainstream medicine. Included among the alternative forms of medicine are chiropractic, spiritual healing, herbal medicine, acupuncture, homeopathy, and folk remedies.

Indianapolis in the 1990s is the center of the state's health care industry. Especially through the presence of both the Indiana University Medical Center and Eli Lilly and Company, the city also has gained regional, national, and even international recognition. Health care contributes significantly to the city's economy, employing thousands of workers in health-related concerns. Changes in health care, most notably national health care reform, will affect the city in profound if yet unknown ways. What is not likely to change is the city's continuing emergence as a leader in medical and dental research and treatment, a development that rests upon the vast intellectual and fiscal investments of the past 175 years.

See also: DENTISTRY; HOSPITALS; MEDICAL SCHOOLS; MEDICINE, ALTERNATIVE; NURSING; PHILANTHROPY AND HEALTH CARE; PUBLIC HEALTH; and individual names and institutions.

NEIGHBORHOODS AND COMMUNITIES

Lamont J. Hulse

Metropolitan Indianapolis encompasses eight counties, scores of cities and towns, and hundreds of suburban and urban communities. Recognizing individual communities within this region often proves a challenge for newcomers and natives alike because traditional boundaries, always uncertain even in the most stable periods, have changed as the city has grown. In Marion County alone more than 200 neighborhood organizations existed in the early 1990s, but many areas lacked an association to register a claim to neighborhood status. It is also difficult to recognize where neighborhoods begin and end because the city lacks the ethnic divisions seen in Chicago or the physical boundaries important in Pittsburgh or Cincinnati. Instead, more subtle distinctions of urban geography, both natural and man-made, differentiate Indianapolis neighborhoods.

How has Indianapolis defined its neighborhoods? Here, the concept of neighborhoods stems from historic patterns of settlement and growth, the development of speculative housing, and the incorporation of previously independent communities into the expanding city. The region's natural geography, so prominent in defining the character of many cities, has not much influenced the growth of Indianapolis, with only the White River, its tributaries, floodplains, and swamps posing any barriers to development.

When the Indiana legislature sent a commission into the wilderness of central Indiana to locate a new capital city in 1820, the commissioners chose a site on what they thought would be a navigable river. The very earliest settlers built homes on the banks of White River, though floods and malaria quickly forced their relocation. By the following year, when Alexander Ralston arrived to plat Indianapolis, it was apparent that White River was neither navigable nor hospitable to settlement. Ralston's plan moved the new state capital a safe distance from the river and imposed a rectilinear street pattern that shaped the city's development. The slow growth of Indianapolis during its earliest years seemed to confirm Ralston's assumption that growth could be accommodated in an area of one square mile. At first, development centered on Washington Street between New Jersey and Illinois streets. But after 1825 when the legislature moved to the

Lamont J. Hulse is Assistant Director of the POLIS Research Center, Indiana University–Purdue University, Indianapolis.

new capital, the town slowly expanded north and south of Washington Street. Thirty years would pass before it would move beyond the Mile Square.

During its pioneer period settlers in outlying areas of Marion County traveled infrequently to the young town. Instead they visited the agricultural villages of Millersville, West Newton, Southport, and others to mill grain, purchase basic supplies at country stores, or repair tools at blacksmith shops. Clusters of farmhouses and outbuildings marked rural settlements such as Allisonville and Mt. Jackson as early as the 1830s, yet contemporary maps did not register villages at these locations until after the Civil War. Even as late as the 1880s the development of commercial farming spurred the establishment of agricultural crossroads villages at Five Points and Flackville.

Transportation improvements provided the stimulus for the growth of Indianapolis. After 1825, when legislators attempted travel to the new town, they realized the need for improved overland transportation and approved funding for a network of new roads in central Indiana. New roads attracted new settlements. Augusta and New Bethel (now Wanamaker) began as way stations on the Michigan Road. Even prior to its completion through central Indiana in 1838, the National Road contributed to the development of Marion County. When the survey route was announced in 1830 entrepreneurs established a number of towns and villages along the right of way, including Cumberland in Warren Township, Bridgeport in Wayne Township, and Stringtown on the west bank of the White River.

More ambitious transportation projects in the 1830s and the 1840s promoted new settlements in rural Marion County and spurred new connections with Indianapolis. Construction on the Central Canal, abandoned after 1839, led to the establishment of Broad Ripple at the canal's northern terminus and the development of an industrial district on the near west side that was home for many immigrants and African-American citizens. The growth of railroads after 1847 prompted the establishment of new depot towns in rural Marion County. Acton, Castleton, Lawrence, Oaklandon, and New Augusta appeared even as the tracks were extended through the county in the 1850s. Other railroad towns, among them Nora and Malott Park, developed later in the 19th century.

Railroads also promoted the establishment of new neighborhoods in the capital city and encouraged growth beyond Ralston's original plat. The economic boom brought by the railroads in the 1850s and 1860s created both industrial and residential development, often within the same neighborhood. In the years immediately following the railroads' arrival, the coexistence of homes, factories, and locomotives was not seen as a problem by residents of new neighborhoods like Fletcher Place. The concentration of railroad tracks on the near south side attracted shops, factories, and immigrant workers in the neighborhoods of Irish Hill. The arrival of German immigrants accelerated after 1849 and many of them moved to the new neighborhoods built directly east of the city. One area now partially preserved in the Lockerbie Square Historic District earned the name "Germantown," but it was only one of many eastside neighborhoods with a heavy concentration of German-born residents.

Indianapolis never developed the commuter railway network that promoted suburban development in many cities in the eastern United States. However, by the mid–19th century the combination of smoke, noise, and traffic from railroads and adjacent industries drove middle and upper middle class residents to new neighborhoods away from the railroad tracks on the south and east sides. Floodplains and the canal blocked residential development to the west so affluent

Plat of Irvington, showing the
suburb's distinctive curving
streets from the 1889 *Atlas of
Indianapolis and Marion County.*
[Indiana Historical Society]

citizens moved north of the Circle, establishing the north side of Indianapolis as the most desirable location in the city.

Initially, residents of northside suburbs could walk a few blocks south to offices and shops. But the introduction of mule-drawn streetcars after 1864 launched the suburban ideal in Indianapolis by providing transportation to neighborhoods physically separated from downtown. The streetcar suburbs of Irvington and Woodruff Place featured curvilinear streets or shaded esplanades, green lawns, and parkways, all designed to contrast the rurality of suburban life with the industrializing city. Although Mapleton was platted more conventionally, landscaped meadows and hills in the adjacent Crown Hill Cemetery provided an agrarian setting for this suburb.

Most upper middle class citizens reconciled the suburban ideal with a rectilinear street pattern. The spacious Victorian homes of the area now known as the Old Northside were placed evenly and squarely along streets that intersected at right angles. In the decades following the Civil War, many of the city's established families moved into houses on the streets between College and Senate avenues, including attorney Benjamin Harrison. Harrison's election to the presidency in 1888 brought additional prominence to the neighborhood. This prestige extended into the Herron-Morton neighborhood, developed after 1890 on the former site of a Civil War prison camp and, later, state fairgrounds.

The consolidation in 1870s of all railroads serving Indianapolis in a belt line to the south and east of the Mile Square confirmed those areas as industrial districts. Soon factories, shops, and foundries also extended west of White River. Developers created a number of industrial suburbs along the new tracks, including Brightwood, North Indianapolis, West Indianapolis, and Haughville. Railroads continued to influence the development of industrial suburbs into the 20th century with the establishment of Beech Grove in 1906, Speedway in 1912, and, less successfully, Mars Hill in 1911.

Late 19th century Indianapolis attracted neither the number nor variety of immigrants who came to other midwestern cities. However, the industry that followed the completion of the Belt Line Railroad did attract some immigrants who clustered in neighborhoods adjacent to the tracks. Haughville assumed a distinctly eastern European character when immigrants from Slovenia sought employment in the neighborhood's foundries and factories. Small communities of Serbians, Rumanians, Bulgarians, and Macedonians established themselves east of White River and north of Washington Street. In addition to German neighborhoods on the near east side, German-American merchants established thriving commercial districts along Virginia Avenue as far south as the streetcar turnaround at Fountain Square. New arrivals from Ireland joined second- and third-generation residents of Irish Hill. By the turn of the 20th century new immigrants from Denmark, Greece, and Italy, as well as Jewish immigrants from eastern Europe, formed small but distinct ethnic enclaves on the near south side.

Between 1880 and 1900 the population of Indianapolis more than doubled. Economic growth linked first to the completion of the belt railroad and later to the prosperity brought by nearby natural gas discoveries attracted more than 100,000 new residents to Marion County. Population growth was concentrated in the city itself; several rural townships in Marion County actually lost residents during the same period. New construction provided visible evidence of the era's affluence as developers reshaped the downtown into a commercial center. The completion of Union Station in 1888 initiated a commercial building boom on the near south side as wholesale firms located warehouses and salesrooms near the station. North of the wholesale district lay new retail establishments, banks, and professional offices, as well as a new State House. The expansion

Platted in 1872, Woodruff Place was not annexed by Indianapolis for another 90 years. [Indiana Historical Society, #C5802]

of industry and commerce boosted the demand for land in and near the city. Increased land values brought more intensive land use practices. Developers erected multi-story commercial and apartment buildings that, compared to the structures they replaced, towered over downtown streets.

Indianapolis also grew in area through a series of annexations that encompassed most of Center Township and beyond, including the former suburbs of North and West Indianapolis, Brightwood, Haughville, Mt. Jackson, and Irvington. Much of the remaining vacant land between the city and the newly annexed suburbs became residential districts. By 1900 the city had grown to 27.21 square miles.

The conversion of streetcars to electric power in 1894 extended the public transit network beyond Center Township. And a new type of passenger transportation came to Indianapolis in 1900 when an interurban electric railroad line connected the city south to Greenwood and Franklin. By the turn of the century electric streetcars and interurbans carried commuters farther away from the Mile Square to semirural outposts such as Warfleigh, Ravenswood, Fairview, and Broad Ripple in Washington Township. Stop 7 and Stop 11 roads marked the extension of the interurbans south of Indianapolis, where the electric cars promoted the development of University Heights and Edgewood and facilitated the growth of Southport.

The automobile also influenced the emergence of new neighborhoods. First introduced at the turn of the century as an expensive novelty, cars quickly gained acceptance among the wealthier citizens of Indianapolis. In 1904 the city contracted with George E. Kessler, a leader in the City Beautiful movement, to design a boulevard and park system. The new boulevards allowed affluent citizens to motor to Brendonwood, Golden Hill, Crows Nest, and Woodstock, exclusive areas on the highlands overlooking White River or Fall Creek. The growth of the automobile industry, centered locally in the town of Speedway (platted in 1912), increased the affordability of vehicles. By the 1920s many middle class residents regularly commuted by car to Forest Manor, Warren Park, Emerson Heights, and Tuxedo Heights or to northern suburbs now known as the Meridian-Kessler and Butler-Tarkington neighborhoods. This period also saw the construction of grand mansions along U.S. Highway 31 on the north side, an area preserved since 1986 as the North Meridian Street Historic District.

The very scale of residential development, as well as the commercial and industrial redevelopment that replaced older Center Township neighborhoods in the 1920s, prompted a desire to control urban and suburban growth. A comprehensive zoning ordinance in 1922 provided the city a tool to regulate future development. The ordinance divided the city into industrial, commercial, and residential districts and restricted the construction of inappropriate buildings in any district. For instance, the construction of apartment houses was barred in most single-family residential districts, which themselves fell into three classes according to lot size. The zoning ordinance also regulated house size and the placement of the house on the lot. By recognizing the existing functional arrangements of the city and the socioeconomic structure of existing neighborhoods, zoning in Indianapolis ensured that growth would continue along paths set earlier.

Other efforts sought to restrict the expansion of African-American neighborhoods, traditionally concentrated on the near west side. The residential segregation of the city's black population, suggested as early as the 1830s, became firmly established by the early 1900s. The "Great Migration" from the South to northern cities after World War I brought thousands of new African-Americans to the neighborhood around Indiana Avenue. The black population of Indianapolis more than doubled between 1910 and 1930, increasing from nearly 22,000 to nearly 44,000. Most of these new arrivals squeezed into the thriving westside area centered on Indiana Avenue.

During the 1920s, when the Ku Klux Klan exercised significant power in the city, many white residents of surrounding neighborhoods formed associations—the Mapleton Civic Organization the first and largest—to preserve residential segregation. African-American citizens mounted a successful court challenge against a 1926 zoning ordinance that sought approval of a majority of the homeowners before a black could move into a white neighborhood. Legislation proved unnecessary, however, as custom inhibited movement of black citizens beyond the "white supremacy dead line." The resulting concentration of African-Americans within the Indiana Avenue neighborhood placed further demands on the existing housing supply. The shortage of housing became especially acute during the Great Depression, although it was partially alleviated by the construction of Lockefield Gardens, a New Deal public housing project that opened in 1938.

With the exception of a few public projects and affluent suburbs, economic depression impeded growth during the 1930s. When Indianapolis industries geared up production to meet wartime demands, housing construction and neighborhood development resumed. The General Motors Allison plant in Speedway and the Naval Avionics facility in Warren Township, among other wartime industries, attracted thousands of new workers to Marion County. In response, the Indianapolis Chamber of Commerce promoted a major housing drive that resulted in construction of 9,000 new houses between 1940 and 1942.

The end of World War II brought mortgage support for veterans and funds for highway construction, legislation that led to a new suburban boom along roads and highways radiating away from the city. During the 1950s nearly 52,000 new housing units were built in the city, an increase of 30 percent. From 1960 to 1970 another 45,000 new units were constructed. As in earlier eras, most home buyers looked north of the city. In Lawrence and Washington townships the completion of State Road 37 promoted the construction of the housing developments of Devington, Brockton, Eastwood, and Ivy Hills. Suburbanization moved north along Keystone and College avenues, preserving the village of Broad Ripple but overtaking the depot town at Nora. Washington Township farms along Spring Mill and Ditch roads became the subdivisions of Greenbriar, Delaware Trails, and Westlane.

Although Washington Township recorded the most dramatic growth rates, postwar suburban development encompassed all areas of Marion County. South of Indianapolis, Madison Avenue was rebuilt as an expressway to carry southbound commuters past industrial congestion to new subdivisions such as Southdale and Perry Manor. The older Perry Township neighborhoods of University Heights, Homecroft, and Edgewood also attracted new residents. Although the west and east sides had their share of custom-built homes, postwar industrial development in Wayne and Warren townships created a market for more affordable housing. Mass-produced housing allowed industrial workers to participate in the suburban boom. The largest of these 1950s subdivisions, Eagledale, attracted employees from Speedway's factories to its 3,400 new homes. Industrialization on the east side promoted similar, if smaller, developments near the city of Lawrence and in Warren Township.

African-Americans who attempted to participate in the suburban boom initially met opposition from white neighborhoods. Homeowners in the area around Crown Hill Cemetery organized the Fairmap Realty Company in an unsuccessful attempt to purchase homes and prevent their sale to black families. But not everyone resisted change. Residents north of 38th Street responded more positively by forming the Butler-Tarkington Neighborhood Association in 1953 to ease the integration of that northside neighborhood.

In the 1960s several African-American professionals and business people built new suburban homes in the vicinity of Kessler Boulevard and Grandview Avenue, houses financed by a Louisville insurance company when local institutions rejected their applications. The Grandview development marked a new era of housing opportunity for African-Americans in Indianapolis. The suburban migration of black citizens increased after the 1960s when courts struck down the city's restrictive housing practices. In several instances white residents of suburban neighborhoods cooperated with African-American newcomers to stabilize their neighborhoods during integration through the efforts of organizations such as the Highland-Kessler Civic League, the Devington Communities Association, and SHARP (Spring Mill Hoover Association for Residential Participation).

These developments aided the integration of Indianapolis housing. In 1960, 90 percent of all black citizens lived in Center Township and more than 75 percent of blacks lived in neighborhoods where more than seven of ten residents were also black. By 1990 a majority (56 percent) of Marion County's black population lived in suburban areas outside of Center Township. More than 34 percent of all African-Americans in Indianapolis lived in neighborhoods where the majority of their neighbors were white, with another 9 percent living in neighborhoods with a relatively stable mix of black and white residents.

The suburbanization of Indianapolis has included the outmigration of industry and commerce. After World War II construction of Shadeland Avenue provided Lawrence and Warren townships with an industrial bypass or "belt" highway that functioned much like the belt railway established in the 19th century. Major new factories located along this artery, including Western Electric in 1950 and Chrysler in 1952. Beginning with Park Fletcher in 1962 entrepreneurs built office and industrial parks on the fringes of the county, a trend that accelerated in the 1970s and 1980s with such developments as College Park and Keystone at the Crossing.

As late as the 1950s most suburbanites regularly patronized downtown stores and many visited the City Market for weekly grocery shopping. But the farther they moved from the central city the more these suburban residents found downtown shopping inconvenient. They drove instead to the new nearby shopping malls of Glendale at 62nd Street and Keystone Avenue and Eastgate near Shadeland Avenue and Washington Street. Strip malls, anchored by chain grocery stores, also became fixtures on the major thoroughfares out of the city. By the 1970s enclosed shopping malls marked the major compass points at the edges of Marion County. Commercial development attracted new residential subdivisions, especially at Castleton and Greenwood.

The construction of the I-465 "outer loop" drew suburban development toward the edges of Marion County and beyond. In 1962 the first section of I-465 opened in the northwest corner of the county. Other portions of the outer loop were added throughout the decade and by 1970 Indianapolis was completely encircled by a multi-lane expressway linked to the federal interstate system. During the 1970s highways I-70, I-65, and I-69 provided additional transportation links between the central city and the suburbs.

I-465 encouraged residential development around the entire perimeter of the county. Garden apartment complexes adjacent to the interstates became particularly popular with baby boomers entering the housing market in the 1960s and 1970s. Between 1960 and 1970 the percentage of multi-family housing units in Marion County increased significantly, from about 20 percent to nearly 32 percent. But the single-family detached house remained the suburban ideal for Indianapolis residents, and construction of houses outpaced apartments in the years following the construction of I-465. The city added more than 80,000 new housing units between 1970 and 1990.

While all sides of the city grew during the 1970s and 1980s, growth was notable in Pike and Lawrence townships where recreational facilities at Eagle Creek and Geist reservoirs proved especially attractive to home buyers. Yet the most dramatic growth in metropolitan Indianapolis took place to the north in Hamilton County, where the interstate allowed comparatively easy access to the town of Carmel. Population in Carmel and Clay Township grew 120 percent between 1970 and 1990. In the 1980s residential development expanded to include the Fishers area along the I-69 corridor and began to extend toward Noblesville and Westfield. Because I-465 passed far to the north of the Johnson County line, this southern county lagged behind its northern counterpart. However, the growth of the Greenwood area in the 1980s showed respectable comparisons, as did Hancock County to the east. Economic development efforts centered at the Indianapolis International Airport in the late 1980s and early 1990s promised a similar residential boom in Hendricks County. In 1993 the U.S. Census Bureau announced the inclusion of Anderson in Madison County into the area known as the Indianapolis Metropolitan Statistical Area, an announcement that emphasized the extension of Greater Indianapolis even farther north.

The outward growth of Indianapolis since World War II marked the deterioration of the old city. Between 1950 and 1990 over 155,000 people moved out of Center Township. Remaining were low-income residents who had few resources to maintain the old city's houses and neighborhoods. During the 1950s city leaders refused to accept federal funding for urban renewal projects, a policy that limited the availability of better housing in the central city. There were some private efforts to build new houses. The Chamber of Commerce, working in cooperation with Flanner House, promoted a major redevelopment project north of Crispus Attucks High School. Although some in the city declared that the Flanner House redevelopment proved the wisdom of shunning federal funds, increasing problems in the inner city forced acceptance of these monies in the 1960s. But the result was not favorable to existing neighborhoods. Public developments—the Barton Apartments, Blackburn Terrace, and Concord Village—provided housing for some citizens, but these projects replaced existing single-family houses and concentrated low-income residents within Center Township. Urban renewal projects begun after 1970, especially the construction of the IUPUI campus and the I-65/I-70 inner loop, displaced other large residential neighborhoods. And court-imposed school busing to achieve racial balance after 1971 not only encouraged the outmigration of white residents but also deprived many neighborhoods of the schools that provided institutional anchors.

When first presented in the late 1960s the need for a consolidated city-county government was rationalized in part by the inequities between a declining urban center and a booming suburban periphery. The passage of Unigov expanded the borders of Indianapolis to Marion County, encompassing many previously independent towns. But large areas remained separate from the old city. Beech Grove, Lawrence, Southport, and Speedway were excluded from city-county consolidation and remained self-governing municipalities. Local school districts, excluded from the consolidation, also preserved a distinction between the central city, defined generally by the Indianapolis Public Schools district, and the suburbs served by township schools.

The consolidation of power under Unigov did permit city leaders to address the redevelopment of downtown Indianapolis, however. Comprehensive planning efforts in 1980 and 1990 produced Regional Center Plans I and II. Guided by these plans and aided by a strategy that created public-private partnerships, leaders promoted the physical development of the urban center, added tourism and sports to the economic base, and attempted to ensure that the downtown could compete with suburban office parks in attracting employers. The merit and success of these initiatives continues to be debated in the 1990s. Yet few people disagree that long-term development of downtown Indianapolis depends on attracting a larger and more diverse population to live in the urban center.

Beginning with Lockerbie Square in the 1960s, historic preservation efforts successfully revitalized several downtown neighborhoods. Organized as the Historic Urban Neighborhoods of Indianapolis (HUNI), the historic preservation movement has been an important factor in the redevelopment of downtown Indianapolis. The restoration of older houses in areas such as the Old Northside, Chatham Arch, Cottage Home, Fletcher Place, and Ransom Place has attracted new residents into Center Township. Even so, some citizens criticized historic preservation for replacing lower income, largely minority residents with middle class, usually white "gentrifiers."

Since the 1960s neighborhood organizations have played an increasingly important role in the city. Citizens Forum, founded in 1964, organized block clubs among African-Americans in the inner city. Federal funding through Community Action of Greater Indianapolis and the Model Cities programs also fostered neighborhood organizations. Community development corporations (CDCs) such as Eastside Community Investments (organized in 1976) have played important roles in addressing issues involving housing and economic development. In addition, downtown and midtown churches have supported the organization of development corporations and neighborhood associations. Large, consolidated neighborhood organizations, especially United Northwest Area and Meridian-Kessler, provided effective representation for smaller neighborhoods like Riverside, Sugar Grove Addition, Johnson Woods, and Forest Hills.

Most neighborhood organizations languished in the wake of downtown development that dominated the 1980s. Despite claims by the Hudnut administration to have directed significant funding from the federal Community Development Block Grant program to the neighborhoods, many neighborhood leaders complained of the unequal allocation of resources between the regional center and the periphery. This discontent surfaced during the 1991 mayoral election when candidates Louis Mahern, Jr., and Stephen Goldsmith both emphasized neighborhood development rather than downtown renewal in their platforms.

The 1991 mayoral election highlighted the importance of neighborhoods as both a political and cultural issue. Some of the new interest in neighborhoods in the 1990s relates to policy initiatives from the Goldsmith administration that created a deputy mayor for neighborhoods and widely advertised its interest in "Building Better Neighborhoods." Political leaders began to confront historically derived definitions of neighborhoods in Indianapolis as they considered new methods of neighborhood governance. Other citizens explored the heritage and culture of their neighborhoods as tools for creating a sense of community in smaller, more comprehensible units within the metropolis. A "Vision Statement" published in June, 1993, by Vision Indianapolis Tomorrow placed neighborhoods as one of the four priorities to be addressed by the city, calling for a "community with neighborhoods which affirm their history and civic pride."

Neighborhood represents one kind of community, but there are many others available in Indianapolis. Communities of association, based on friendship, kinship, professional affiliation, or common interests and lifestyles, provide the sense of belonging sought by many citizens of the modern city. Undoubtedly numerous residents, desiring minimal interaction with their neighbors, expect little more from their local communities than a secure housing investment and safety from crime. However, the discussion about neighborhoods that pervaded the city in the early 1990s suggests that other residents are attempting to tie their definition of community to specific places. If they succeed, Indianapolis, which in the 19th century called itself a city of homes, may yet become a city of neighborhoods.

See also: DOWNTOWN DEVELOPMENT; HISTORIC PRESERVATION; PUBLIC HOUSING; REAL ESTATE DEVELOPMENT AND DEVELOPERS; and individual townships, neighborhoods, towns, and suburbs.

PERFORMING ARTS

Marianne W. McKinney

The 1993 *Indianapolis Arts Directory* listed 5 dance companies, 43 performing music organizations, and 29 theater groups. Each category reveals a wide range in the size and mission of the various organizations. Such diversity reflects the many audiences for performing arts in Indianapolis during the last decade of the 20th century. It also reflects the emergence of a mature cultural consciousness in modern Indianapolis, a development that the city's founders could not have predicted.

Music. Music is the oldest, largest, and most visible of the performing arts in Indianapolis, with its roots extending into the early years of the 19th century. While it emerged before the large and highly musical German immigration that followed the revolutions of 1848 in Europe, Indianapolis' musical culture benefited greatly from this influx. By 1850, 13 percent of the Indianapolis population had German origins; by 1890, they comprised 25 percent of the city's population. The Germans brought a love of music, a desire to perform, and traditional continental musical training which previously had been a rarity in the Indiana capital.

Indianapolis had some musical activity before the German tide arrived, but it was scattered and unschooled by comparison. For years after its founding Indianapolis was known as a capital in the wilderness; its citizens did not have a cultural bent. An early singing school for the "cultivation of church music" began in 1824, and in 1828 a singing organization, the Handelian Society, joined a local band on July 4 to present the city's first public concert. The program included "Hail Columbia," "Auld Lang Syne," "Yankee Doodle," and other "suitable odes."

But these secular events started no trend. Most musical performances remained confined to Indianapolis churches. The First Baptist Church, Meridian Methodist Church, and Second Presbyterian Church were the most active in music, featuring large choirs. Under the pastorate of Henry Ward Beecher (1839–1847) Second Presbyterian established a music school and sponsored a small flute and string orchestra. This hardy band of 15 players was the first "orchestra" in the city, although its purpose was to accompany the choir, not to give independent concerts. Some

---

Marianne W. McKinney is program annotator and pre-concert lecturer for the Indianapolis Symphony Orchestra.

The Indianapolis Opera's 1992-93 season performance of *The Merry Widow*
[Indianapolis Opera. Photo by Denis Ryan Kelly, Jr.]

church members, in fact, would not attend worship until the music was over, considering such an addition to the service as pagan.

By the late 1830s traveling musicians began to visit Indianapolis. Perhaps inspired by these musicians, 30 instrumentalists formed the Indianapolis Band in 1840, the first regular performing group to be free of any church affiliation. Significantly, its leader was a German immigrant, Abraham Protzmann. The Indianapolis Band had a life of only five years when it was replaced by the German Military Band. The defining German influence was beginning. But the German Military Band also lasted only a few years. On June 9, 1849, the newspaper *Locomotive* asked: "Why is it that Indianapolis cannot establish and support a Band, to play for the numerous public celebrations that take place in this city? Is it because we have no persons capable of being instructed or because we are too indolent to undertake it?"

By the 1850s and 1860s, however, Indianapolis had a large contingent of music instructors. Boosted by the perspectives and talents of German immigrants, Indianapolis residents keenly sought instruction and incorporated music into their lives. In July, 1851, Professor P. R. Pearsall established one of the city's first secular music schools; other small independent schools soon followed.

Although music instruction was scarce earlier, pianos were featured possessions in private homes. The first piano arrived in 1831, a gift from James Blake to his wife, who gave small concerts in her home. Others shared her enthusiasm and an important feature of music in Indianapolis began: performances in the home. Home concerts or salon-type events continue to typify Indianapolis music; indeed, such performance has consistently found acceptance in the city.

German professors of music shaped the growth of home concerts and the quality of early performances by circulating with their own repertoire. By the late 1860s and 1870s these instructors produced cozy musical soirees in their own homes as well. A certain Professor Bahr was a popular home entertainer; his performances in the 1880s featured poems by his neighbor, James Whitcomb Riley. Most of these home concerts were not free: Bahr's programs, for example, cost 80 cents for reserved seats, 25 cents for unreserved.

After the Civil War interest in music increased. By 1866 music was part of the curriculum of the public schools, using the text *Loomis' Progressive Music Lessons*. This course of study involved both theory and applied music. Professor Carl Weegman, the first professional director of the Maennerchor, a German male singing society, established a popular music school called the Central School of Music in 1871 and operated it until his death in 1900. The Indianapolis Matinee Musicale, the oldest continuously performing organization in the city, opened in 1876. The abundant number of capable teachers, mostly German, guaranteed that pupils who sought advanced study elsewhere left with a sound musical foundation.

Effective music training resulted in a flourishing musical culture. From the mid–19th century, musical performance in Indianapolis was vibrant. From the 1850s through the 1870s the Germans established grand singing societies and choruses outside of the churches; instrumental performances became more frequent, and halls specifically designed for musical performances emerged. Indianapolis had four significant performing halls by midcentury: the Germania Theatre, the Maennerchor Hall, the Grand Opera House, and the Park Theatre. Music "societies" composed of singers and instrumentalists popped up everywhere. In 1851 the 100–member Haydn and Handel Society was formed. In 1854 Edouard Langerich established the Maennerchor, one of the largest and earliest singing societies in the United States. Its repertoire was extensive, featuring the finest of German lieder and works of Beethoven, Mendelssohn, Schubert, and Schumann.

By the 1860s and 1870s eight or nine separate singing groups gave regular concerts, most prominently the Saengerchor, Concordia, Lyra, Liederkranz, Harmonie, and Choral Union. The groups not only performed in Indianapolis, but also participated in large regional Sangerfests, or singing conventions of German societies. Both the *Locomotive* and the *Indiana Journal* reviewed the concerts. By this time Indianapolis also had a significant resident music critic, Berry R. Sulgrove, whose reviews remain treasures for those interested in the concerts.

Although choral concerts were dominant, the 1860s and 1870s also witnessed the beginning of orchestral groups. In 1862 the orchestral Philharmonic Society was established under Max Leckner. Another notable figure, Professor H. D. Beissenherz, former director of the city theater in Ebersfield, Prussia, created and conducted a small competing orchestra at the Metropolitan Theatre on the corner of Washington and Tennessee streets. Like the singing societies, local amateurs and theater musicians trained by local instructors comprised these small orchestras.

Along with the German influence, the railroads stimulated musical performance in the mid–19th century. By the 1850s Indianapolis was becoming the center of a rail system that brought all kinds of musical entertainment and artists to the city, including such performers as Jenny Lind and Ole Bull. Madame Anna Bishop, the celebrated English soprano, performed at the Masonic Hall in 1851. Five years later, in May, 1856, a large musical group led by Professor George Root arrived by train from New York; Root organized Indianapolis' first musical convention, a four-day affair devoted both to instruction and performance. And in 1859 the New York Metropolitan Opera arrived for its first visit, bringing a production of Bellini's *La Sonnambula*.

The Indianapolis Symphony Orchestra has performed in the restored
Circle Theatre since 1984. [Indianapolis Symphony Orchestra]

The success of the musical convention made music festivals a feature of late 19th-century
Indianapolis cultural life. Perhaps the most significant event of this type was the music festival of
1886. Under the leadership of Professor Carl Barus, 650 voices and an orchestra of 50 players
joined soloist Lilli Lehmann for a mammoth benefit concert to raise money for the proposed Soldiers and Sailors Monument. The concert netted $5,000 and ensured the erection of the monu-
ment that today symbolizes the city.

By the last quarter of the 19th century Indianapolis citizens had a choice of singing concerts,
instrumental concerts, and opera on a fairly regular basis. Orchestras continued to be popular,
with Karl Schneider in 1895 establishing the first group to call itself the Indianapolis Symphony
Orchestra. (It performed for ten years but was not the predecessor of the current ISO.) Building
on this enthusiasm for music, Ona B. Talbot functioned as the city's first native impresario during
the 1890s and early 20th century. Through her efforts, symphony orchestras from New York,
Pittsburgh, and Boston, famous chamber quartets, and noted international soloists visited Indianapolis. Such exposure broadened the tastes and the musical sophistication of the populace and
prepared the city to develop significant professionalism in music as the new century dawned.

The 20th century witnessed two major directions in Indianapolis music. One was the continuing development of traditional music from the 19th century both in public and salon performances; the other was the emergence of different types of popular music, notably jazz, blues, big

band, and rock activity. The classically oriented Maennerchor expanded into a presenting organization. Under its aegis, Indianapolis heard the talents of great musicians such as Szigeti, Myra
Hess, and Artur Schnable, among hundreds of other major guest artists. In 1915 (and continuing
to the present) the Indianapolis Park Department's free summer concerts at Garfield Park, Holliday Park, and Broad Ripple Park brought quality performances to the public, while private citizens hosted salons featuring classically trained singers and musicians.

In 1930 a portentous event occurred for classical music in the city: Ferdinand Schaefer organized the orchestra that became the Indianapolis Symphony Orchestra. Four years later radio
station WKBF (WCKN) broadcast the ISO nationally in a program dedicated to Admiral Byrd at
his South Pole base. By 1937 this group was fully professional and offered a long season of excellent music.

The ISO truly arrived as a major orchestra when in 1953 critics listed it among the nation's
top ten major symphony orchestras, a position it has held ever since. The ISO had fine conductors
who followed Maestro Schaefer: Fabien Sevitsky, Izler Solomon, John Nelson, and currently Raymond Leppard. All these music directors developed the repertoire, guided the musicians, and
wove the ISO deeply into the fabric of Indianapolis culture. The orchestra reached new prominence under the leadership of Maestro Leppard, who became music director in 1986. It now tours
the United States and Europe regularly, produces recordings, broadcasts locally and nationally,
and operates on an annual budget of $14 million. The Indianapolis Symphony became one of
the few orchestras in the United States to own its own concert hall when it acquired the restored
Circle Theatre. By 1993 its audiences numbered over 300,000 annually.

Classical musical forms and traditions continued to dominate Indianapolis performing arts
in the late 20th century. In 1975 the Indianapolis Opera Company debuted and although it
struggled early, even disbanding briefly in 1981, by the 1990s it offered several performances
each year, often featuring nationally prominent talent. Chamber groups also emerged in the
1980s and 1990s, with Suzuki and Friends, Ronen Ensemble, Faulkner Chamber Players, and
Tarkington Trio, among others, attracting local and regional audiences.

While 19th-century German immigration shaped the Indianapolis classical tradition, another demographic development influenced the city's popular music of the 20th century. Around
1915 southern blacks began to arrive in large numbers and with them came blues and jazz,
which flourished in the city from the 1920s to the 1960s. The heart of this music was a four-block
stretch of Indiana Avenue between North and Ohio streets known sometimes as "The Yellow
Brick Road" and "Funky Broadway." At one point in the 1920s, 25 successful clubs such as the
Sunset Terrace, the Cotton Club, the Mitchellynne, and the Paradise operated on the Avenue. By
far the largest and most prestigious performing center was Madam C. J. Walker's building,
opened in 1927. At the Walker Theatre the best of the best performed: it was the most important
place on the Avenue.

In the 1920s and 1930s, with the great talents of Leroy Carr and Francis "Scrapper" Blackwell on piano and guitar respectively, Indianapolis developed a unique sound known as "Indianapolis Blues." Another early star was James "Yank" Rachell, a blues mandolin player who
continued to perform in the early 1990s. These key figures created a musical world and atmosphere that rivaled the great jazz centers of New Orleans and Chicago. The fertile Indianapolis
African-American culture gave birth to and attracted jazz greats such as the Montgomery brothers, J. J. Johnson, Noble Sissle, Jimmie Coe, Dizzy Gillespie, Charlie Parker, the original Ink Spots,
the Hampton family, Duke Ellington, Count Basie, Willis Dyar, B. B. King, Cab Calloway, Terry

The Wisdom Brothers Band appeared at Indianapolis' Cotton Club in the mid-1930s. [Indiana Historical Society, Duncan Schiedt Collection, #C5912]

Vinegar, Bob Womack, Fats Waller, and Louis Armstrong. Erroll Grandy, sometimes known as the "godfather of Indianapolis jazz," was a magnificent pianist who performed with distinction and drew national greats to visit. Indianapolis residents also formed many jazz bands. Two early groups of note were the Patent Leather Kids and the Brown Buddies. Many local bands not only played for Indianapolis but went on the road, taking the Indianapolis style and talents to neighboring states. The Avenue was more than a local jazz community; it was a national jazz-blues mecca.

For many years Indiana Avenue was almost exclusively a black phenomenon. Whites came downtown primarily to dance to the big bands that performed at the Indiana Roof Ballroom, built in 1927 above the Indiana Theatre. It was a marvelous venue, boasting a recreation of a Spanish village complete with a moonlit sky that produced dramatic thunderstorms. The Roof booked bands of national stature such as Stan Kenton, Paul Whiteman, and Guy Lombardo. After their own gig, big band leaders and musicians often would walk over to the Avenue for all-night jamming.

White citizens had other options besides the Indiana Roof. Major hotels such as the Claypool, Antlers, and the Marott featured name bands for dancing. The Indianapolis Athletic Club and the Columbia Club offered members a place to listen to dance bands and jazz. The Casino Gardens on Lafayette Road, Lyric Theatre, and Circle Theatre were also important venues, as were Broad Ripple and Riverside amusement parks. Pit orchestras such as those at the Indiana Theatre, Lyric Theater, Washington Theater, and Colonial Theater were other significant spots playing jazz and popular music.

Early in the 20th century another current of music was quite popular in Indianapolis. Ragtime, made popular by the success of Scott Joplin in nearby Missouri, attracted two local women, May Aufderheide and Julia Niebergall, as active composers. J. Russel Robinson and Russell Smith were perhaps the most famous native performers in the ragtime field: both became nationally known. Ragtimers and vaudeville performers were very successful in Indianapolis throughout the 1910s and 1920s, often led by Frank Clay, known as the "Black Sousa." His military band was the training ground of future jazz greats such as trumpeter Raymond Valentine. These bands played hotels (such as the Severin) and also appeared on the popular showboat, *The Sunbeam*, docked at Broad Ripple Park. Ragtime and vaudeville performances drew racially mixed audiences, unlike early blues and jazz. The "Indy Sound" created by Indianapolis blacks was soon taken up by local white musicians; by 1940 it had gained a diverse following throughout the city and the nation.

By the 1960s and 1970s Indianapolis jazz faced a downturn. The big bands were no longer economically viable. Audiences disappeared, drawn to competing mediums, especially television. But by the 1980s a renaissance occurred in local jazz and blues. New clubs sprang up, such as the Slippery Noodle, the Chatterbox, Donnelly's Pub, Mugwumps, and the Jazz Cooker. The growth of black identity and pride stimulated the total restoration and reconstruction of the Walker Building (now the Madame Walker Urban Life Center), reviving a significant jazz and performing arts venue on Indiana Avenue. In 1986 the *Indianapolis News* reported 26 jazz clubs successfully functioning throughout the city. Also important in the revival were the Blues Society, founded in 1986, to promote Indianapolis blues and jazz, and WFYI-FM, which until the early 1990s devoted numerous programming hours each week to the genre.

In the 1960s as rock music swept the country, Indianapolis teens welcomed popular groups such as the Beatles and the Rolling Stones. In the 1970s new venues opened for rock musicians, including Middle Earth (later renamed The Ritz) and The Vogue, a former Broad Ripple movie theater. These sites not only enabled Indianapolis residents to see national "rock stars" in smaller, more intimate locations but also gave their stages over to local singers and groups, propelling a few such as Henry Lee Summer into national recording contracts.

Late in the century another significant locale for musical performances emerged with the 1989 construction of Deer Creek Music Center near Noblesville, ten miles north of Indianapolis. Deer Creek offered a 6,000–seat amphitheater with adjacent seating for another 8,000 patrons on the surrounding land. This site attracted all kinds of concerts during the summer months and became extremely popular, booking 50 or 60 concerts a season. By the 1990s, then, Indianapolis could offer a music menu to serve any taste throughout the year.

Theater. In 1993 Indianapolis was home to approximately 800 paid actors, most of them part-time, and 29 professional and community theaters. But unlike music, commitment to theater evolved slowly in the city. Throughout the 19th century theater met strong resistance from disapproving church groups and reformers. Many citizens viewed actors as frivolous and unstable and believed that the theater did not fit comfortably with the local culture or prevailing moral attitudes.

Indianapolis' first theatrical event, as chronicled by the *Indianapolis Gazette*, occurred on December 31, 1823, when Carter's Tavern hosted two popular plays, *The Doctor's Courtship* and *Jealous Lover*, with an "orchestra" of one fiddler who played "only solemn music." The price of admission was 37 cents. The audience of 40 sat on two-inch planks stretched across supports. Candles were the only illumination. This theatrical experiment closed after a few performances and nothing was tried again until 1837 when William Lindsay and Company arrived from Cincinnati with scenery, wagons loaded with props, and actors to present three plays at Merr Olleman's wagon shop opposite the courthouse on Washington Street. These performances were received with greater enthusiasm than the Carter Tavern event, and in 1838 the troupe returned to introduce the city to Shakespeare.

A theatrical evening at that time was quite a long affair, with two or three plays usually presented in succession. Fiddlers helped the audience endure the multiple presentations by performing between acts and at intermissions. Sometimes magic acts—or "necromantic interludes" as the playbills called them—filled the time it took to unroll the background scenery from large scrolls. Fire was a constant hazard in these candlelit tents and halls.

In 1840 a few citizens formed the first home-based amateur dramatic group—the male-only Indianapolis Thespian Society—in a warehouse at Market and Mississippi streets. Its first performance was a historical drama, *Pocahontas*, by Robert Dale Owen; admission was 25 cents or an item of equal value. After the demise of the Thespian Society, other amateur groups emerged briefly throughout the 19th century. The Dramatic Club, founded in 1872, presented numerous plays at the Propylaeum; it is the oldest continuous theater company in the city. Amateur theater, like amateur music, has been a constant feature of Indianapolis performing arts and has been key to keeping theater alive in the community.

By midcentury Indianapolis was host to several touring companies. In 1851 the touring Toledo Company arrived to perform in the newly constructed Masonic Hall, which concurrently hosted the state's Constitutional Convention. To accommodate the performances constitutional deliberations were limited to daytime only, with the theater taking over the same rooms at night. Soon other theatrical venues opened. In 1852 the first tent theater opened during the State Fair; the third floor of the Athenaeum Building also included a small theater; and Washington Hall and Union Hall offered new sites. But these latter buildings were multipurpose facilities in which theaters occupied only a small section.

On September 28, 1859, a landmark event occurred when the Metropolitan Theatre opened as the first building in Indianapolis dedicated solely to theatrical activities. Built by local entrepreneur Valentine Butsch at a cost of $60,000, the Metropolitan stood at the corner of Tennessee and Washington streets. This theater featured three stories, measured 82 by 125 feet, seated 1,200 patrons, and included a balcony from which the orchestra played "alluring airs." The Metropolitan was a profitable enterprise despite the protests of local churches against the "immoral character" of theater.

During the Civil War drama attracted large audiences in Indianapolis. Soldiers from 24 local army camps packed the theaters. Indianapolis was host to major touring companies, including such stars as J. H. Hackett, William Crane, Joe Jefferson, Tommaso Salvini, Henry Irving, and Edwin Booth. John Wilkes Booth also performed in the city.

The growth of theater throughout the 1860s laid the foundation for important new developments. In 1868 Valentine Butsch built another theater, called the Academy of Music, that seated 2,500, with a "freedman's bureau" for African-Americans on the upper level. When it was destroyed by fire in 1877, Dillard Ricketts resurrected the old Metropolitan, which had become a "variety" house, and renamed it the Park Theatre (1879). Perhaps its highest theatrical moment was the 1883 appearance of Lillie Langtry in *As You Like It*. Shortly thereafter the Park Theatre became more a home for vaudeville, old-time melodrama, and minstrel shows as two new structures, the Grand and the English, built in the 1880s by local businessman and politician William H. English, became the focal points for Indianapolis theater.

The larger of the two buildings was English's Opera House, sometimes called "the finest theater in the West." It seated 2,000 in an elaborate Egyptian-style setting of crimson drapes and festoons, using gas jets as footlights. Later in 1889 the theater acquired its first electric lights which, curiously, were left on during performances. Although sometimes called "English's folly," it became a success as English imported the likes of Sarah Bernhardt, Mesdames Gerster and Campariori, Adelina Patti, Oscar Wilde, Ethel Barrymore, and Otis Skinner. The English Theatre finally closed on April 30, 1948, still in its original location on the Circle.

English's other theater, the Grand Opera House, was also lavish, featuring satin and velvet draperies, cherry red walls, and blue silk wainscoting. During the opera season a stock company offered weekly productions. The overall scope of the fare at both theaters consisted of comedy, tragedy, light and grand opera, and a few variety shows.

Observers in the 1880s and 1890s estimated that the local theater-going public numbered about 10,000. Indianapolis had by then earned a reputation of being "a good theater town." Touring companies regularly gave three night performances and one matinee during visits to the city. Impresarios William H. Leake and James Dickson served the local audiences by booking a wide variety of productions from Shakespeare to burlesque, with a few animal acts thrown in on occasion. And a tribe of Native Americans annually presented *Hiawatha* along the banks of the Central Canal at Fairview Park.

Vaudeville was well represented in Indianapolis. The Park Theatre hosted minstrel and vaudeville shows and was known locally as a "variety house." Tickets for these events were 15, 25, and 35 cents. Later, the Majestic Theatre (1907) sponsored vaudeville, but after a few years it evolved into a center for burlesque. Minstrel shows were also popular, with one of the favorite companies being Thatcher, Primrose, and West.

By the end of the 19th century theater as an institution and drama as a fine art had arrived socially and culturally in the Hoosier capital, as evidenced by the emergence in 1907 of the beautiful Murat Theatre at 502 North New Jersey, seating 2,000 and built at a cost of $365,000. For years thereafter the Murat was the major site of theater in Indianapolis.

In the 1910s a new form of theater developed: film. Indianapolis responded with enthusiasm to "the movies." In 1916 the Circle Theatre was built. By the 1930s Indianapolis had several major movie houses: the Loews, Apollo, Lyric, and Indiana theaters. None showed films exclusively, and all featured stage productions as well; some (like the Apollo and Indiana) had their own bands. But with *The Jazz Singer* in 1927—the first film to incorporate sound—legitimate theater took a predictable downturn. Indianapolis wanted movies, not live theater. Soon the Great Depression made professional theater too expensive. Movie houses, which had also presented legitimate stage productions, now embraced motion pictures exclusively.

But if large professional productions declined in number, local theater groups of more modest nature thrived. The community theater known as Indianapolis Civic Theatre (later Booth Tarkington Civic Theatre) was founded in 1925. The nation's oldest continuously operating community theater, it has a permanent home at the Indianapolis Museum of Art. Starlight Musicals, a summer stock effort, arrived in 1945, beginning in Garfield Park, moving on to the Fairground, and finally to Butler University. It closed in 1993. Avondale Playhouse, in the Meadows Shopping Center, was a popular venue in the 1960s.

In the 1950s and 1960s touring groups were well received (usually performing at the Murat) and local amateur groups were increasingly active. Clowes Memorial Hall on the Butler University campus hosted many Broadway traveling productions. Churches, dinner theaters, and other independent groups added events to the theatrical calendar in the 1970s and 1980s, with such groups as the Catholic Theatre Guild, Indianapolis Episcopal Theatre Guild, Seminary Players, and Beef & Boards. Corporate sponsorships sustained new amateur and limited equity companies, among them the Phoenix Theatre, Theatre on the Square, and Edyvean Repertory Theatre at Christian Theological Seminary. And the Indiana Repertory Theatre emerged as a major regional professional company.

Theaters with specific missions also appeared. The Soul People Repertory Company provided theater with an African-American slant; the Junior Civic, Indianapolis Children's Theatre Workshop, the Kid Connection, and Afro-American Children's Theatre provided training grounds for children; the Indiana Puppetry Guild emerged; the Epilogue Players (founded for men and women over 50) offered three or four plays annually. The list is long and varied. By the end of the 20th century Indianapolis theater offered a year-round array to suit widely varying tastes.

Dance. Dance is the smallest component of the performing arts in Indianapolis and the last to emerge. In the 19th century, significant dance performance was almost nonexistent. In 1843 a wandering dance master opened a small school that offered not only dance but also the "Science of Manners." At this time dance was equated with correct deportment and personal grace of movement. This original dancing school faded, but by 1848 a Mr. Taylor and a Monsieur de Granville founded another school specializing in the slow waltz and polka.

In 1860 Beniville Gresh and Edward Heines each started dance academies that had much longer lifespans. Once again the curriculum featured the waltz, two-step, and polka. From time to time students gave public performances and recitals. In 1895 the Metropolitan School of Music, located at North and Walnut streets, included a small dance school in its quarters. This small school in 1928 became part of the Jordan School of Fine Arts when philanthropist Arthur Jordan purchased and merged the Metropolitan School of Music and the Fine Arts College founded by Oliver Pierce in 1907. Dance finally had a reputable home for instruction and performance.

Not everyone welcomed even these small efforts. The *Indianapolis Star* in 1908 reported that the Indianapolis Association of Protestant Ministers took a dim view of dance. Influential clergy considered it at odds with proper moral development of young people, warning, "We must not teach anything which can only find satisfaction in the ballroom."

Professional dance came to Indianapolis rather late but grew rapidly once established. In 1957 Turner and Hale organized the first Ballet Society of Indianapolis. Its purpose was to help the Jordan School and to import dance companies from around the United States. Two years later the Civic Ballet Society was formed; by 1973 it had grown into Indianapolis Ballet Theatre. Artistic director George Verdak led the company, building on his experience with the Ballet Russe de Monte Carlo. In 1988 Dace Dindonis, another ballet star, succeeded him. Under these two dancers-turned-artistic directors, the company grew prodigiously. By 1993 it had toured over 55 cities in 17 states, playing to annual audiences of 65,000, with eight performances in Indianapolis. The company regularly attracts international ballet stars as guest artists.

In 1972 a second important dance company emerged: Dance Kaleidoscope. This company found many audiences in school performances and annually presented substantial dance performances of difficult repertoire. Like IBT, Dance Kaleidoscope attracted an important dance figure, David Hochoy (1991), to lead its efforts. His work with the Martha Graham Company and experiences with Lincoln Center in New York brought professional expertise to this small company of eight dancers which, despite its size, has attracted national attention. In 1993 international ballet star Mikhail Baryshnikov agreed to be on its board of advisors. Dance Kaleidoscope performs 130 concerts annually throughout the Midwest, in the Indianapolis schools, and of course in its own seasonal offering.

Indianapolis experienced a renaissance in performing arts during the last quarter of the 20th century, with music, dance, and theater reflecting much activity and wide diversity. The single most decisive factor in this revival was the financial support of the Lilly Endowment. From 1937 to 1993 the Endowment gave 283 grants totaling $46,224,630 for the establishment and support of performing arts organizations in Indianapolis. Its first grant to the performing arts was $6,400 given to the Indiana State Symphony Society in 1937.

Endowment grants to the performing arts grew rapidly especially in the 1970s and 1980s, as seen in the following table:

Years	Number of Grants	Amount
1937–1949	23	$143,700
1950–1959	25	$1,383,000
1960–1969	25	$2,695,000
1970–1979	75	$8,174,847
1980–1989	94	$21,606,100
1990–1993	41	$12,221,633

Without this financial support the history of the performing arts in Indianapolis would obviously be much different.

The Lilly Endowment has not been the sole source of support for the performing arts in Indianapolis. Since 1924, the year it first generated income, the Indianapolis Foundation has granted over $6.2 million in support of the performing arts. Created in 1969, the Indiana Arts Commission offers grants and assistance programs to music, theater, and dance, as well as to the visual arts. Cathedral Arts, Inc. sponsors the International Violin Competition, and since 1989 the Arts Council of Indianapolis has offered organizational grants and artist fellowships for the performing arts. Other local sponsors have included the Clowes Fund and corporations such as PSI Energy and American Cablevision. The result has been a blossoming and vibrant performing arts climate which is a model for other mid-sized cities.

Indianapolis in the last decade of the 20th century boasts a world class symphony orchestra under the direction of an internationally known conductor, excellent professional and community theater, active chamber ensembles, a successful opera company, professional dance companies, and several outstanding presenting organizations. The city also hosts major music competitions including the quadrennial International Violin Competition and the American Pianists Competition, and music festivals including the Indiana Avenue Jazz Festival and the ISO's Midwinter Festival. These events and organizations build upon a rich heritage, especially in music. Together they create a vibrant performing arts culture in the Hoosier capital.

See also: BLUES; CLASSICAL MUSIC; JAZZ; MUSIC, NINETEENTH-CENTURY; PHILANTHROPY AND THE ARTS; THEATER, CHILDREN'S; THEATER, PROFESSIONAL; and individual names, institutions, and organizations.

PHILANTHROPY

Robert L. Payton
Patricia A. Dean

P hilanthropy permeates our lives. One cannot live through a day in Indianapolis without benefiting directly or indirectly from past and present voluntary actions for the public good. It is not necessary to go into The Children's Museum or to listen to public radio or to support a church financially or to help the Girl Scouts plant trees. Each of us, directly or indirectly, benefits from The Children's Museum's influence on children, conversations enriched by National Public Radio reports, the community outreach programs of churches, and improvement in our environment.

"Philanthropy" is increasingly used as the umbrella term for a wide variety of nonprofit, voluntary activities, much as the word "charity" was used until this century. In its narrower, current usage, the word charity is equated with almsgiving, relief, and other forms of service to the poor and afflicted. In this sense, charity is the oldest and probably the most fundamental philanthropic value, deeply entwined with religion and society.

There are two philanthropic approaches to human suffering and vulnerability: the first is the act of mercy; the second is the work of prevention. Debates about strategy and the relative effectiveness of the different approaches have raged throughout the history of Indianapolis and continue today. The recent Campaign for Healthy Babies, for example, won support from some individuals because they embraced its immediate goal of reducing the suffering caused by high infant mortality in Indianapolis; it gained support from others because they were concerned with the long-term fiscal cost of unhealthy, uneducated children and adults.

Philanthropy also brings into sharp relief the underlying issues of the political agenda: the extent to which individuals should be expected to be responsible for themselves and their own welfare (self-help); the extent to which families especially, but also neighbors and friends, should be responsible for one another (mutual aid); the extent to which basic human needs should be underwritten or directly met by government through taxation (poor relief); and the extent to which human needs might be met by the voluntary contributions of individuals and groups with no direct and tangible benefit to themselves (what we are calling here philanthropy).

Robert L. Payton is Professor of Philanthropic Studies and former director of the Indiana University Center on Philanthropy at Indiana University–Purdue University, Indianapolis.
Patricia A. Dean is former Assistant Director of Academic Programs and Research for the Indiana University Center on Philanthropy.

Unlike many, if not most, of the important areas of the life and history of Indianapolis, the records of philanthropy are scattered, ill-kept, and unsystematic. We can only estimate the numbers of volunteers, the numbers of hours they contributed, the numbers of donors and the amounts they contributed, even the names and number of organizations that brought together volunteers and received contributions. Although organized philanthropy is evident in every civilized culture and is evident in history long before democracy, Christianity, and universities, knowledge of the scope and scale of philanthropy remains uncertain and incomplete.

Organized community philanthropy began in Indianapolis with the Indianapolis Benevolent Society in 1835. The purpose of the society was to provide financial, material, and personal assistance to people in difficulty, regardless of their origins or background: "to give temporary aid . . . to meet the needs of individuals on a community basis without regard to race or creed." Some citizens of the new community responded voluntarily to the distress of others, who were often strangers "down on their luck." Rather than simply respond as individuals, they organized a voluntary association that gathered resources (money and gifts-in-kind), saw to their distribution, and sent volunteers as "friendly visitors" into homes to offer advice on household management. The tradition of organized philanthropy in this fashion was an accepted part of the inherited values and practices brought by settlers to Indianapolis.

Later, assistance became specialized and certain needs were given priority. The special claims of widows, orphans, strangers, and the poor received precedence in Indianapolis, as they did in the most ancient human documents about charity and philanthropy. One of the early establishments serving strangers in Indianapolis was the Young Men's Christian Association, founded in 1854; it combined a place to eat and sleep with assistance in coping with everyday problems and religious instruction and moral guidance. The Home for Friendless Women opened in 1867 as a shelter for the widows and orphans of soldiers who had died in the Civil War. Assistance was assumed to be temporary; young widows often remarried, learned a trade, or became domestics—that is, in one way or another acquired the capacity for self-help and left the rolls of the destitute. The Home for Friendless Women illustrates another common practice, if not principle, of philanthropic organizations: change over time. In 1936 the facility changed its function and name, becoming the Indianapolis Home for the Aged (and later the Indianapolis Retirement Home).

Also in 1867 German immigrants founded the General Protestant Orphan Home, reflecting both mutual aid and philanthropy. Ethnicity was the backbone of mutual aid in American society; religion, language, and culture—all reflecting place of origin—provided the organizing mechanisms for much mutual aid and philanthropy. (However, the earliest known instance of mutual assistance in Indianapolis—a volunteer fire company organized in 1826—was unrelated to ethnicity.) Lutheran Child and Family Services, another example of mutual aid, originated in an asylum for orphans and the elderly founded in 1883 by a Bible society of St. Paul and Trinity Lutheran churches. Mutual aid also included services no longer associated with philanthropy, such as marital matchmaking, savings clubs, and burial services.

The late 19th century—from about 1870 on—was a period of great innovation and activity in American philanthropy. It saw the emergence of what was called "scientific philanthropy," based on the new human science of psychology and the new social science of sociology. Scientific philanthropy sought to be more efficient in the use of resources and more effective in achieving self-sufficiency for the poor. In addition to helping the deserving poor, those committed to scientific philanthropy were fiercely determined to weed out the unworthy, especially the able-bodied unemployed, who were thought to be either lazy or vicious—or both.

It was, in fact, concern over the harm allegedly done by almsgiving that was most often used in the 19th century as an argument against philanthropy, public or private. Almsgiving alone had come to be considered harmful, even destructive of the incentive to help oneself. In 1886 the Indianapolis Benevolent Society issued a statement asserting that "The curse of unearned bread and ill-advised or careless almsgiving is almost as great, and often far greater than the [curse] of want that it is intended to relieve." Rather than give alms to the able-bodied poor, Andrew Carnegie argued in "The Gospel of Wealth" (1889) that it would be better to throw one's money into the ocean. Help was considered to be more than a matter of distributing alms. What was needed was advice, instruction, training, motivation to learn the coping skills necessary for successful survival in the new society. Friendly visitor volunteers, followed by paid social workers, helped mothers become better housekeepers, helped them keep their children in school or find them employment, and brought pressure on fathers and husbands to seek work and, especially, to avoid wasting the family's income on alcohol.

Much charitable assistance was organized and provided by and through churches, and religious education was part of what they offered. Salvation was thought by many to be the highest form of philanthropy. Presumably as popular in Indianapolis as it was elsewhere in the United States, Charles Shelton's *In His Steps* advocated the strong identification of good works with religious conversion.

The idea of "charity organization" was first institutionalized in Great Britain in 1869 with the founding of the Charity Organization Society. Charity organization owed much of its conceptual framework to the extraordinary genius of the Scottish pastor and theologian Thomas Chalmers, who, a generation earlier, had developed a system of charitable service and neighborhood social reform in Glasgow.

Historians disagree about the first charity organization in the United States; one view asserts that it began in Buffalo, New York, in 1880, a year before the founding of a comparable organization in Cleveland. Indianapolis, however, records the establishment of its Charity Organization Society in 1879, in the offices of Benjamin Harrison, at the instigation of the Reverend Oscar C. McCulloch.

McCulloch (1843–1891), pastor of Plymouth Congregational Church, was one of the most prominent and effective religious leaders in Indianapolis. His was a modified version of the Social Gospel; his religion and theology were permeated by a sense of the social dimension of Christianity. His sermons reflected the unavoidable intellectual struggle with Darwin and Darwin's interpreters, who argued for the survival of the fittest. Beyond Darwin, McCulloch found in the writings of Peter Kropotkin what he called the Law of Mutual Aid. "This is the great bank of sympathy," said McCulloch, "from which we draw God's inexhaustible fund; older than selfishness, the most ancient thing there is next to the pulsation of life is the fact of human sympathy."

Lost in the national shadow of the great Social Gospel personalities of Walter Rauschenbusch and Washington Gladden (although he did receive national attention as president of the National Conference of Charities and Correction in the early 1890s), McCulloch practiced what he preached and preached what he practiced. His imprint is everywhere on the philanthropic culture of the Indianapolis of his time.

However sensitive McCulloch was to human suffering and need, he was also a man of his time in his embrace of scientific philanthropy and charity organization. He shared in the stern condemnation of the undeserving poor and called for individual reform (a long-term goal focus-

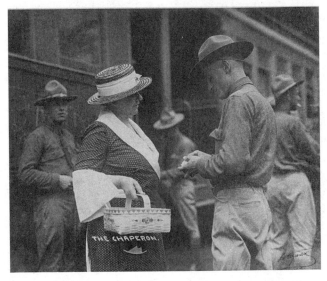

Top left: Oscar Carleton McCulloch was active in a variety of charitable organizations in the city during the late 19th century. [Indiana Historical Society, Personal—M]

Top right: The Indianapolis Public Library provided a bookmobile for Long Hospital patients, ca. 1924. [IUPUI Archives]

Bottom: Red Cross volunteers provided encouragement to the many World War I soldiers who passed through the city. [Indiana Historical Society, Bretzman Collection]

ing on prevention of need) at a time when society was increasingly responsive to the immediate needs of the vulnerable.

Let Oscar McCulloch—some of whose ideas are preserved for us in *The Open Door*, a collection of his sermons published posthumously by his widow in 1892—stand as surrogate for an anonymous group of leaders determined to shape a new and more civil society in Indianapolis. Their work is evident in all of the organizations mentioned in this essay, and in hundreds more.

McCulloch not only put his stamp on charity organization, he may also have sent through a friend the idea for federated fund raising and giving that launched the first effort at a United Way in Denver in 1888. The evidence is currently too thin, but it may be possible one day to make a more solid case that both charity organization and federated fund raising in the United States began in Indianapolis. Regardless of the ideas' origins, what is called the United Way began in the city as the Community Chest in 1920—and then became the Community Fund in 1923, the Indianapolis Community Chest in 1950, the United Fund of Greater Indianapolis in 1962, the United Way of Greater Indianapolis in 1970, and finally emerged in its present form as the United Way of Central Indiana in 1986.

Wherever philanthropic ideas originated, Indianapolis has proved to be an active borrower and adapter, an active planter and gardener of philanthropic ideas and practices. Few cities owe more to their philanthropic tradition.

The profusion of assistance in human services appeared on all sides. A Flower Mission was organized in 1876, enlisting young women to visit the sick and brighten their day with gifts of flowers. It later became the parent of the Newsboys' Home, a tuberculosis sanitarium, and a children's hospital. The Free Kindergarten Society, organized in 1881, illustrates again the interaction of philanthropy and government. Its work was privately supported (that is, its income was derived from charitable contributions) until 1902 when it became state supported (that is, its income was derived from government, tax-based appropriations). Ultimately it became a part of the system of public education. There is an analogous history with parks and playgrounds.

Indianapolis borrowed the innovations of neighborhood settlement houses from Chicago's Jane Addams (whose Hull-House was established in 1889) and other settlement house pioneers. Flanner House was founded in 1898 to provide social services for African-Americans—more precisely, "for the industrial and moral uplift of colored girls and boys." Founded in 1905, Christamore House was a settlement house where young women and Butler College students donated their services to the poor.

Borrowing another idea, the Charity Organization Society formed the Dime Savings and Loan Association in 1887. Boston philanthropist Joseph Lee (a leader in the parks movement) and others were instrumental in bringing financial institutions into the reach of the poor. The poor were never thought to be wholly without resources: they always had something to give (the parable of the widow's mite was a powerful lesson), and something to save for a rainy day. What the poor lacked was access to the established financial institutions, which had scant interest in those whose wealth was measured in coins rather than bills, in IOUs rather than stock certificates.

Charity organization as a political and economic philosophy assumed that helping the poor to help themselves would prevent the need for public charity and dissipate the appeals of socialism. In this sense, McCulloch sided with the individualism of Herbert Spencer and Andrew Carnegie, rather than with the anticapitalism of Frederick Maurice or Washington Gladden. This passing reference reminds us that issues of social welfare—who should receive it, how it should be provided—bring philanthropy to the center of the American political stage, often to the top of the political agenda. To what extent should individuals be responsible for their own welfare; to what extent should they rely on the assistance provided by family and friends; to what extent should they be able to call on assistance from government as a right; and to what extent should they rely on philanthropy as a privilege?

Wheeler Mission, founded by William V. Wheeler in 1893, the Salvation Army (1889), the Jewish Welfare Federation (1904), the Indianapolis Church Federation (1912), and the Catholic Community Center (1919) suggest the continuing prominence and diversity of religiously sponsored charitable institutions and organizations. In time, reliance on the clergy, supported by volunteers, gave way to the trained professional and the field of social work. It had become increasingly evident that untrained volunteers had little understanding of the circumstances of the poor, still less, formal knowledge of human psychology and behavior. Social work required training in exactly the same way that medicine and law and engineering required it.

In Indianapolis social work education began in 1890 with a series of lectures, as it began at about the same time in New York as a summer lecture series called the School of Philanthropy. As a professional field, social work began to emerge in the last decade of the 19th century and was born officially in Indiana in 1911 as the Indiana University Department of Social Services (known as the School of Social Work since 1966). Modern social work is more sensitive to the dignity and rights of the person in need than was 19th-century charity; it is also more diffident about matters of character and personal development.

Philanthropy involves interventions in the lives of others, that is, philanthropy engages in the public's business with no public mandate. Philanthropy originates with individuals who have ideas, exercise their moral imagination, see problems, and conceive of ways to address the problems. These individuals then enlist others who share their values. People with shared values and a shared vision or mission come together in organizations. Although lacking a public mandate, philanthropy is restrained by governmental legislation. For instance, whatever money may be gained through a philanthropic enterprise is not to be shared privately but must be used for the public purposes of the organization. (In legal terminology, surplus income must result in no "private inurement.")

One such philanthropic organization is the general purpose, endowed philanthropic foundation, one of America's most distinctive and original contributions to philanthropy. Philanthropic foundations have played a significant role in the formation of public policy in the United States. Foundations were especially strategic in their approach, seeking out the root causes of social problems and formulating policies for their solution.

No philanthropic foundation is better known or has played a more pervasive role in Indiana and in Indianapolis than the Lilly Endowment (founded in 1937 by J. K. Lilly, Sr., and his sons J. K., Jr., and Eli). Cooperation with public agencies and for-profit corporations has enabled the Endowment to leverage other funds for broad community purposes (and sometimes, as with the Hoosier Dome, to sharp criticism). There is little information about earlier private foundations (that is, those foundations endowed by a single individual donor or family), or much evidence of their role in the philanthropic history of Indianapolis. The Indianapolis Foundation, begun in 1916, was an early example of the community foundation idea that had originated in Cleveland two years earlier.

As the third sector of a three-sector model of American society, philanthropy functions alongside government and the private economic marketplace. The interaction of the three sectors is evident in the career of Indianapolis resident Albert J. Beveridge, who became one of the most important voices in the third-sector initiative to enact child labor legislation.

The special role of the third sector was transformed by reform movements in the late 19th and 20th centuries. Philanthropic organizations affirmed values of compassion and community, supporting efforts to alleviate the suffering of the poor and to enhance the quality of life of the community. Political leaders in Indianapolis, beginning with mayors Richard Lugar and William H. Hudnut III, have developed political strategies that assume the full participation of the private philanthropic community in public life. The causes of philanthropic organizations were often taken up by political leaders, leading to legislation, or they were the background for humanitarian and civil rights legal decisions and constitutional interpretation in the courts.

Indianapolis' well-known decline in the middle of this century, along with other important midwestern industrial cities, was reversed only by dint of the combined efforts of community leaders drawn from all three sectors to identify targets for common action. The Greater Indianapolis Progress Committee, formed in 1965, brought corporations, labor unions, foundations, the media, churches, nonprofit organizations, and others together to affirm a community-wide effort of renewal and reform.

The national leadership role of two Indiana business leaders affected Indianapolis' new philosophy. Frank Sparks, one of the founders of what is now Arvin Industries, played an important role in the funding of colleges and universities by business corporations; J. Irwin Miller, of Cummins Engine Corporation, became one of the best known and most widely respected business leaders for his support of the architectural development of his home community of Columbus, Indiana, but also for his introduction of ethics training for Cummins employees and for ethical policy development for his company. In Indianapolis, colleagues and admirers of Sparks and Miller have long been influenced by their model.

Indianapolis businesses followed the leadership of their peers in Cleveland and Minneapolis and organized local 2 percent and 5 percent clubs as standards for corporate contributions. Business and philanthropy cooperated with local government in the stupendously successful Tenth Pan American Games in 1987. Business leaders have also played a leading role in reforming and strengthening public education in Indiana.

The Indianapolis Public Schools (IPS) reflect a recent national trend toward replacing public funds with philanthropic dollars. The IPS system has its own fund-raising foundation, as do other public school districts and publicly supported colleges and universities. We may perhaps observe a new cycle: from philanthropic initiative to publicly funded service—and unexpectedly back to philanthropic initiative. Once again the issue of self-help and mutual aid is weighed against government assistance, with philanthropy often playing the role of advocate of diverse positions. Private advocacy advanced by voluntary associations is used in infinite variety to influence public policy, leading to the reform of public institutions or to the establishment of new agencies or services.

Long established is the working relationship between government and philanthropy in the field of welfare. The notion of a poor law—a local tax for the support of the local poor—became established in British law in the late 16th century and was best known in its formulation under the Statute of Charitable Uses of 1601. In his day, the ubiquitous Oscar McCulloch served as a poor law commissioner; Indiana's poor law continues to this day. Public agencies succeed private ones in many cases. In other cases, government works through private charitable organizations, finding that they often provide more efficient service than can public bureaucracies. In another link between government and philanthropy, the City of Indianapolis contracts with the Better Business Bureau to provide oversight of charitable solicitation in the community. Fund-raising abuses have from time to time encouraged official militancy, but for the most part fund raising in all its forms flourishes in Indianapolis as it does elsewhere, with a high level of public trust and a low level of governmental control.

Indianapolis also has its own version of "the hidden third sector." There exists among the poor and marginalized of the city a framework of mutual aid and philanthropy that is far more pervasive and effective than the philanthropic and political establishments recognize. In many poor neighborhoods government is perceived as an enemy, or at best as an unwelcome intruder. As other observers have discovered, "leaders" in the hidden third sector never label themselves as such and would not recognize themselves if described in the language of organizational leadership as studied and taught. Hidden third sector leadership is natural and unaffected, based on the trust that gravitates toward the trustworthy—often women whose lives revolve around the multivalent work of neighborhood churches. The emphasis here is on congregations as the core community; in many neighborhoods, the only surviving "mediating institution" is the local church.

Churches continue to play a major role in the larger life of the community. Research conducted by Independent Sector, a national center for philanthropic data, suggests that the 23 percent of people who attend church frequently provide a disproportionate measure of community leadership in all areas—in the arts, environment, international relief and development, education, hospitals. Indeed, significant amounts (no one knows how much) of religious giving flow through churches to a wide variety of mostly social and human service purposes.

How the city works in its charitable and philanthropic activities, then, is a study of the interaction of formal and informal institutions, organizations, and individuals. Both charity, as good works to relieve suffering and misery, and philanthropy, as strategies to prevent further occurrences of suffering and deprivation, are at work in the alliances of government, marketplace, and voluntary action. Self-help, mutual aid, government assistance, and philanthropy; ideas, values, organization, and resources—all interact freely in an open society to provide, among other things, human services that touch the most ancient, elemental, powerful, and redeeming forces of human nature.

See also: FOUNDATIONS AND TRUSTS; FRATERNAL ORGANIZATIONS; PHILANTHROPY AND BUSINESS; PHILANTHROPY AND COMMUNITY DEVELOPMENT; PHILANTHROPY AND EDUCATION; PHILANTHROPY AND HEALTH CARE; PHILANTHROPY AND RELIGION; PHILANTHROPY AND SOCIAL SERVICES; PHILANTHROPY AND THE ARTS; VOLUNTARISM; and individual names, institutions, and organizations.

POLITICS

George W. Geib

Highly competitive political activity has always characterized the quest for power in Indianapolis. In contrast to the one-party dominance found in many American localities, vigorous two-party races have consistently marked both city and county elections. Three features have usually caused local voter turnout to exceed national averages: Indianapolis has possessed active, well-developed political organizations, including both parties and interest groups; the city has enjoyed varied, and often highly partisan, mass media; and the mix of local population has led to serious differences of both issues and personalities that encourage political competition. Political interest is so widespread that local humorists suggest the first words of many area infants are "Although I am not currently a candidate. . . . "

The political struggles of the 1820s and 1830s reflected the differing origins of the city's first residents. Indianapolis lay astride a number of overland transportation routes that brought settlers from neighboring Ohio, the upper South, the Middle Atlantic states, and, in much smaller numbers, New England and Europe. The earliest competitors were called the Whitewater and Kentucky factions, reflecting their origins respectively in the Whitewater River valley northwest of Cincinnati and in the neighboring state of Kentucky.

Biographies of early local political activists suggest that they came to Indianapolis, at least in part, to win public offices in the community. These early offices, mostly county positions such as recorder, clerk, judge, and commissioner, paid cash salaries on a frontier characterized by barter and subsistence farming. The related quest for patronage (the ability to award jobs or contracts to one's supporters) has remained an important motive for many local candidates.

In addition, early candidates strove to encourage community growth, often through attempts to attract transportation routes such as the National Road and the early railroads to the city. Congressman Oliver H. Smith was typical when he tied a career in banking to political efforts to promote the Indianapolis and Bellefontaine Railroad. This linkage of politics and promotional boosterism helped to define the relationship of the media to politics. The theme of job creation, an obvious part of such boosterism, has remained a distinguishing feature of many local campaigns.

George W. Geib is Professor of History at Butler University in Indianapolis.

A strong personal orientation has always been present in Indianapolis politics. Candidates, political workers, and officeholders have sought informal gathering places that permit interaction outside the formal offices and assemblies of government. Churches, clubs, and public spaces such as the City Market have functioned in this way. So have the city's hotels and taverns. The latter connection also helps explain why many reform groups opposed to local leaders have treated temperance, prohibition, and liquor licensing as key local issues.

Reform issues first became prominent in the city in the 1830s and 1840s, and have continued to exercise a periodic interest for voters since. Many of the reforms proposed in that Jacksonian era reflected broader national trends for personal, moral improvement. Improvement of prisons, which found expression in the 1851 state constitution's commitment to reformation over punishment of criminals, is typical. Abolition, women's rights, public education, and public health also enjoyed support, frequently through separate societies formed around the cause. Reformers who emphasized social changes were often at variance with other political leaders who concentrated upon economic or patronage issues. Reform became particularly disruptive when it attracted a voter following that cut across party lines or made demands that were not subject to political compromise. This became most apparent in the political dislocations, local as well as national, that surrounded the slavery issue in the 1850s.

Many political analysts have sought to identify the roots of this reform interest. Some have seen it as a reaction to social change and dislocation, arguing that many reformers were searching for an orderly society in a disorderly world. However, the close ties between reform and civic boosterism, with its aggressive quest for physical growth, render this theory questionable in Indianapolis. Other analysts offer an explanation that identifies many reformers with a tradition of religious piety which emphasizes ethical public behavior by the individual as a mark of personal salvation.

Some interpreters see religion and reform as facets of a rough congruence between political behavior and regional and ethnic origins. Reform was particularly popular among individuals of Protestant New England background, whose strong "town meeting" sense of community values carried over into a search for civic improvement, both economic and moral. Reform often had an antiethnic, or nativist, dimension that identified local problems with foreign immigrants. This nativism reinforced the Protestant dimensions of reform in a city whose 19th-century foreign-born population included many Irish and German Catholics. Most local studies stress the focusing effect of the liquor issue. Irish and German voters were generally drinkers, and their votes were instrumental in striking down the most serious of the temperance laws late in the 1850s. Yet German voters, in their turn, became early supporters of antislavery candidates.

The local focus of the earliest city politicians partly stemmed from the fact that the city and county were established during the "era of good feelings," a brief period when organized two-party competition did not exist at the national level. Once such competition returned with the creation of the Whig and Democratic parties in the 1830s, many area candidates and voters adopted their national labels and platforms, but with varying degrees of conviction. Indiana Whigs, like their national counterparts, became advocates of such issues as banks and internal improvements and of such candidates as William Henry Harrison. Indianapolis was one of many cities that saw a log cabin erected as a Whig political symbol in the 1840 "hard cider" election, the first captured locally by that party. Democrats articulated issues of executive authority and Manifest Destiny. Federal taxes, especially the tariff, became a staple of local discourse. Torchlight

With the slogan "Keep the ball rolling for Harrison," this metal framed campaign ball was rolled along the National Road all the way from Maryland to the Harrison house on North Delaware Street in Indianapolis in an 1888 campaign publicity stunt. [Benjamin Harrison Home]

As Indianapolis mayor during the 1910s and early 1920s, Lew Shank was a colorful figure on the local political scene. [Indiana Historical Society, #C5797]

parades and other public assemblies helped to encourage record high voter participation levels among the white, male electorate.

Each subsequent realignment of the American electorate has been reflected in Indianapolis politics. These realignments, rapid and enduring shifts in electoral behavior, have occurred in the United States about once each generation. One shift took place in the 1850s when the Whig party collapsed and Democrats divided over slavery and other sectional issues. As a replacement, leaders and voters experimented with a number of alternatives, including a separate Free Soil party in 1848 and 1852, a short-lived nativist American party in 1856, and an equally temporary People's party formed by Jacob P. Chapman in the mid–1850s as an early attempt to link, or fuse, former Whigs with antislavery Democrats. More successful fusionist efforts eventually led to the creation of a local Republican party that by 1860 united free-soil supporters from both of the former major parties, in opposition to a much altered Democratic party.

Abraham Lincoln carried Marion County in the 1860 election, and spoke in the city as he journeyed to Washington and to a presidency whose central event was the Civil War. As residents of a northern free state, most Marion County residents favored union and opposed secession. But the parties and their supporters divided angrily over many specific issues related to the support of the war. Predictably, Republican leaders such as Governor Oliver P. Morton and Brigadier General Benjamin Harrison gave strong support to recruitment, war taxes, and other measures designed to secure military victory. Democratic leaders including Thomas A. Hendricks objected to the often high-handed methods of Morton's administration, arguing that local autonomy and civil rights were being sacrificed to excessive or illegal wartime demands. Political passions ran high, especially in the disturbances, later called the Battle of Pogue's Run, which occurred during and after the May, 1863, Democratic state convention.

Public occasions, such as the passage through the city of the Lincoln funeral cortege in 1865, offered an opportunity to keep these passions alive as the war ended. Many Republicans characterized their Democratic opponents with the derogatory label "copperheads," alleging that they were like snakes waiting to strike at the Union if given the opportunity. The Civil War treason trials, especially the notable 1866 U.S. Supreme Court case of *Ex parte Milligan* that involved several local political leaders, played a similar role in public debate. For a generation after the war a good dinner-table conversation could always be started by asking if the shadowy pro-southern group, the Knights of the Golden Circle, had really been a threat. Veterans groups, notably the Grand Army of the Republic, held both state and national reunions ("encampments") in Indianapolis that helped rekindle patriotic partisanship.

The new Republican and Democratic parties also entered a long era of debate over economic issues. Strong "boom or bust" business cycles characterized the 19th century. Notable panics, or depressions, occurred in 1857, 1873, and 1893. Each panic and its aftermath offered new opportunity to debate the economic future of the city as well as the nation. Economic discourse normally started with proposals to promote economic development and job creation in a community heavily dependent upon railroads. Republican Mayor John Caven's proposal for the Indianapolis Belt Line Railroad is the best remembered of these proposals. By enacting a package of development activities in the 1880s, including a new Union Station, a stockyards complex, and new rail construction, Caven presented a program that he and his fellow Republicans could offer as proof of their commitment to prosperity.

Local politicians also needed to wrestle with the emergence of organized labor. Indianapolis was a center of labor activity, often tied to railroads and allied manufacturing industries. In hard times the city experienced strikes and other labor actions related to job security, wages, and workplace safety. Railroad-related stoppages, such as the nationwide strike of 1877 and later street railway strikes, made themselves keenly felt. Workers often sought to express concerns or seek legislative relief by means of political activities. Perhaps the best remembered of these efforts was the Workingmen's party of the mid–1880s. The Socialist party, which held its national convention in 1900 in Indianapolis to select Eugene Debs of Terre Haute as its presidential candidate, would also tap some of this discontent.

Late 19th century Indiana saw each of the two major parties enjoying almost exactly 50 percent of the popular vote, making it one of the half dozen swing states that could decide presidential elections. Aware of this fact, both parties frequently looked to Indiana for either vice-presidential or presidential candidates. Indianapolis provided such candidates several times. Benjamin Harrison, grandson of William Henry Harrison, was the Republican presidential nominee in 1888 and 1892. The Columbia Club, formed as the Harrison Marching Society to support his 1888 bid, became the city's most influential political club. Later the Indianapolis Athletic Club, originally formed in 1920 to promote amateur sport, would provide a similar focus for the Democrats. Vice-presidential nominees with Indianapolis connections included George Julian (Free Soil, 1852), William English (Democrat, 1880), Thomas Hendricks (Democrat, 1884), Charles Fairbanks (Republican, 1904, 1916), and Thomas Marshall (Democrat, 1912, 1916).

The importance of Indianapolis and surrounding Marion County to statewide political success caused both parties to institute or participate in innovative organizational activities as part of the search for partisan electoral advantage. Democrats copied the example of such urban organizations as New York's Tammany Hall by creating manageable voting districts, or wards, to promote partisan voter turnout. Commonly called "machines" by their opponents, these ward organizations often operated from taverns or other convenient clubhouses and frequently relied upon patronage as a motivational tool. Such a situation blurred the line between politics (the search for office) and government (the exercise of that office). Often the most successful politician was a person who moved easily between the two activities. Thomas Taggert, whose remarkable career extended from the 1880s to the 1930s, was a prime example of this type of politician, serving as both mayor of Indianapolis and Democratic national chairman.

The search for advantage also led both parties to continue to seek support from the community's ethnic groups. Catholic Irish, especially in such westside areas such as Pat Ward's Bottom, were sought by Democrats; Ulster Protestants, of whom John Caven was perhaps the best known, were often found in Republican ranks. The city's Germans displayed an eclecticism that reflected the regions and political divisions of their homeland. Some Germans sought to express themselves through third-party movements, often under Socialist labels. The first successful Jewish candidate, Leon Kahn, won election to the common council in 1869.

The even balance and strong election-day discipline of the parties did not prevent intensive factional divisions within their ranks. Such divisions arose from many causes. Neighborhood loyalty and particularism was often a source of rivalry. The Irvington struggles of the 1870s and the longtime attempt by Woodruff Place residents to retain their town's autonomy are good examples. Other struggles could be national. When William Jennings Bryan captured the 1896 Democrat presidential nomination with a "silver" platform, his "gold" opponents held the National Democratic party convention in Indianapolis to nominate a rival.

With elections usually closely contested, election days were boisterous affairs. Party symbols, especially the Republican eagle and the Democratic rooster, were promoted to the illiterate. Charges of voter irregularities, whether directed against stiffs (persons voting in the name of the deceased) and mummy-dummies (persons voting in another's name) were common. Ballot counting at Tomlinson Hall was often more frantic than voting itself, especially after the so-called Tally Sheet Forgeries of 1886 and the indictments of the mayor and police chief for election fraud in 1915. Such complaints helped justify several important election reforms of the era, including voter registration laws, precinct organizations, and the use of the secret (or Australian) ballot in place of ballots prepared by the parties themselves.

These ballot reforms were indicative of a larger demand for political change at the turn of the century that is often described as part of the Progressive movement. Progressivism in Indianapolis had several key features. Its rhetoric showed a concern for participatory democracy, an aversion to ward politics, and an interest in efficient administration of public services. It also had a strong tendency to factionalism. It owed much to the emerging role of women in politics, both as advocates of social reforms and later as champions of women's suffrage. State laws of the 1920s, which required half of all political party posts to be held by women, provided an important entry-level opportunity for these individuals newly enfranchised under the 19th Amendment.

Progressives worked through existing party structures to achieve their ends in such areas as public health and municipal services. They often sought to improve municipal services through commissions, usually nonpartisan in selection, that would encourage professionalism. Local school boards were—and remain—a visible example. More often Republicans than Democrats, Progressives contributed to intraparty struggles such as the rivalry of GOP senators Charles Fairbanks and Albert J. Beveridge. In 1912 many reformers supported the national third-party Progressive ticket, when the Bull Moose insurgency of former President Theodore Roosevelt split the Republican vote and ushered in a period of Democratic dominance.

Both state and national concerns have influenced 20th-century local politics in Indianapolis and Marion County. The political arena has often seen issues arise, emotions develop, and electoral behavior shift in response to events that involve these larger constituencies. At the state level, Marion County has been affected by the so-called "long waves" of Indiana electoral behavior—a pattern of relatively long (20- to 30–year) periods of Republican ascendency alternating with shorter (5- to 15–year) periods of Democratic advantage. National electoral patterns have also made themselves felt. Thus, the era from 1896 to 1928 was one nationally of Republican advantage, the years from 1930 to 1965 ones of Democrat advantage, and the years since 1966 ones in which the Democrats have often gained support for Congress and the Republicans for president. In all three periods, of course, an active two-party system and factional divisions in the stronger party assured occasional victories by the weaker side.

An example of the effect of national politics is World War I. Like the Civil War before it, the start of the conflict in 1914 and the entry of the United States into that war in 1917 did much to affect local political attitudes and activities. Most local residents favored the Allied cause and participated in recruiting rallies, bond drives, and other expressions deemed patriotic. In Indianapolis, as in much of America, the German-American community found itself at odds with widespread popular support for the Allied cause. Many German-American voters uneasily sought to support candidates who favored peace, or at least U.S. neutrality. After the declaration of war in 1917, some local residents allowed their patriotism and hostility to the Kaiser's government to carry over into local affairs. A variety of repressive activities largely eliminated separate German-American political expression and left harsh memories that influenced attitudes on both civil liberties and peace issues.

Some of these attitudes continued in new forms after the 1918 armistice. Veterans groups, including the American Legion that established its national headquarters in Indianapolis, promoted local observances and memorials and encouraged both parties to nominate veterans for office. Business groups, often exploiting fears of radical ideas associated with the revolutionary movements that swept postwar Europe, moved to identify their programs with American ideals in such campaigns as the movement for the open shop, where union membership would not be a consideration in employment.

The most visible and divisive new movement in the 1920s was the Ku Klux Klan. It enjoyed special success in Indiana thanks in part to an antiestablishment political rhetoric that exploited the failure of local leaders to promote new school construction and other public works, in part to membership recruitment by skilled organizers such as D. C. Stephenson, and in part to the use of such new communication techniques as radio. Control of the public schools was of particular interest in Indianapolis. The Klan's greatest success came in the mid–1920s when it supported the successful candidacy of Republican John Duvall for mayor and helped elect a United Protestant school board ticket. Vigorous opposition by local newspapers and a highly publicized criminal conviction of Stephenson ended the group's serious influence by 1930. The Klan left a heritage of factionalism, especially in the Republican party, as well as much suspicion in the African-American and Catholic communities that the Klan had so often criticized.

The onset of the Great Depression in 1930 produced a marked shift in voting behavior that favored the Democratic party. It benefited from a substantial increase in voter participation levels, especially among working class and second-generation immigrant Americans, and from the defection of most African-American voters from the Republicans to the Democrats. The rapid growth and increased political involvement of organized labor also played a major role. Unions became a significant factor in local affairs. Democratic candidates, including long-time Congressman Louis Ludlow, campaigned effectively to help forge and maintain this coalition. So too did party leaders such as Frank E. McKinney, Sr., whose talents eventually led to his selection as Democratic national chairman during the Truman presidency.

If social issues often captured public attention in the 1920s, economic concerns dominated during the 1930s and 1940s. Public relief efforts, business and utility regulation, labor-management relations, and the underlying philosophy of such government intervention became the issues most often debated. Democratic leaders—Frank McHale and Philip L. Bayt, most prominently—gained power as they lobbied for legislation and administered government initiatives. Such men also extended the already significant role of patronage in politics. Patronage became more important in the 1930s as the result of the decision to finance most party activity by regular contributions from public employees. The "two percent club" required each government worker to contribute that percentage of his wages to the party appointing him. First developed by Democrat Governor Paul McNutt, the practice was eventually used by both parties at the city and county level. It remained a prominent feature of local politics until the 1980s when a combination of federal court rulings and media criticism caused it to be abandoned.

Despite local participation in many relief and regulatory activities, Indianapolis gained a reputation for political conservatism between 1930 and 1960. In part this can be traced to such local power brokers as publisher Eugene C. Pulliam and Chamber of Commerce executive William Book, Sr., who became vocal spokesmen for free enterprise and patriotic causes and who sought to influence the nomination of candidates whose views mirrored their own. The image of conservatism also can be traced to the outpouring of patriotism and civic endeavor produced during World War II. This carried over into the "Red Scare" of the Cold War years of the late 1940s and early 1950s. Best known through such national events as the Army-McCarthy hearings, this fear of domestic radicalism prompted the Indianapolis Chamber of Commerce and other local groups to encourage both parties to focus much of their attention upon programs in education and law designed to promote economic and political ideas identified with an American system.

During the 1950s new considerations began to alter local politics, contributing eventually to a major power shift that occurred in the middle 1960s. One new consideration was the rapid suburbanization of the county. The movement of local residents to suburban areas had, of course, begun long before. But now the pace of change, and the extent of the county devoted to residential housing, grew as never before. Rural voters, often Democratic and once dominant in many of the outlying townships, were quickly submerged by middle class suburbanites, disproportionately Republican and often insistent upon the extension of city services to their areas.

As middle class voters moved out of older neighborhoods in Center Township they were replaced by other groups who often showed Democratic leanings. Some new immigrants arrived, mainly from eastern Europe and Latin America. A large white community from the upland South emerged on the near east and south sides. Simultaneously, the city's African-American community grew rapidly on the near north and west sides. That community's leaders participated actively in the new civil rights movement, including the legal process which resulted in court orders for desegregation by the early 1970s and the implementation of one-way school busing a decade later.

Political leaders offered varied institutional responses to these demographic changes. Some local leaders in the 1950s sought a step-by-step approach, through annexations and joint city-county commissions such as the library board, that would slowly expand the city's authority.

Some Democrats, led by Mayor John J. Barton in the early 1960s, envisioned public-private partnerships including the Greater Indianapolis Progress Committee and the Indianapolis Housing Authority. Yet these proposed changes took shape in a state where rural elements often resisted urban growth, sometimes aided by the unusual nature of the Indiana General Assembly. From 1921 until 1962 the state legislature failed to redistrict, eventually giving very disproportionate power to rural interests. Because Indiana's constitution did not provide home rule, instead requiring state legislation to empower local government, this proved a major hurdle to urban political reformers until the 1960s.

In the middle 1960s many of the pressures and desires for institutional change were exploited by a reorganized Republican party. Since the 1930s the GOP had seen regular competition at its county conventions for its chairmanship. These contests were partly factional, partly a battle over patronage, partly differences between self-styled moderates and conservatives, and partly a matter of strong personalities. The chairmanship had been held by such colorful figures as James L. Bradford and Henry Ostrum. In the 1950s effective control had passed to H. Dale Brown, an early Eisenhower supporter who had been rewarded with a major voice in federal patronage in Indianapolis. Brown's power, however, had slipped after the Kennedy victory of 1960, and in 1966 he was replaced by a candidate of the Republican Action Committee.

The Action Committee was a coalition of political leaders, among them Beurt SerVaas, L. Keith Bulen, and Thomas Hasbrook. It elevated Bulen to county chairman, and then went on in 1967 to capture the mayor's office with the youthful Richard Lugar. Lugar in turn used his popularity, along with new Republican strength in the recently reapportioned Indiana General Assembly, to create a partially consolidated city-county government commonly styled Unigov. In addition to consolidating many government functions, the Unigov act united the city and county for the purposes of electing mayor and council. This addition of Republican suburban voters to the older city electorate assured at least a quarter century of GOP control of key local government offices, and permitted Republicans to take credit for achievements by the new city-county government. Under the Unigov banner, for example, Lugar actively began to seek federal funds, to institute visible improvements in the city-county infrastructure, and to assume control over many quasi-independent boards and commissions.

In 1975 the mayor's office passed to William H. Hudnut III in the closest election of the period, with his victory made possible only by the suburban votes added by the Unigov consolidation. Hudnut brought a booster's enthusiasm to the office. He actively continued Lugar's emphasis upon downtown revitalization and construction. He sought cooperation with neighborhood associations, voluntary groups that were emerging as important vehicles for community expression. He brought civilian control to the scandal-tinged Indianapolis Police Department. And he showed great political skill when under the public eye. His political support, for example, was greatly enhanced when he took highly visible personal leadership of the city's responses to the freak Blizzard of 1978.

The period after 1966 saw rapid changes in styles of campaigning. Lugar and Hudnut both benefited from a strong grassroots precinct organization managed first by Bulen and then by long-time county chairman John W. Sweezy, a skilled planner and organizer who commenced a long tenure as county chairman in 1972. This organization was also important as a training structure for many of the individuals who would staff city and county boards and commissions.

Over time this volunteer organization would be supplemented by new technological approaches emphasizing use of television to help set the public agenda and a host of computer-assisted mechanisms to raise funds and contact voters by telephone and direct mail. Polls and focus groups would bid to replace the press as the primary indicator of public opinion in the community. Television also reduced the influence of the print media by offering alternative sources of news and views. The costs of campaigns, particularly those associated with television advertising, rose rapidly. Races for mayor, which had cost under $200,000 in the 1970s, cost $1 million or more by the 1990s. This elevated fund raising into a central feature of all high visibility campaigns, and reduced the traditional reliance upon Lincoln Day and Jefferson-Jackson Day dinners. It also placed a premium upon candidates who could perform well in the spotlight of television.

The period of Republican advantage after 1966 was never without active challenge. The Democratic party enjoyed a secure base in central Indianapolis, and from this base could control Center Township offices, normally win the seat in Congress held by long-term Representative Andrew Jacobs, Jr., and occasionally, as in 1974 and 1990, win important county offices such as prosecutor. The Indianapolis African-American community, although lacking one clear leadership voice, was often critical of Republican activities, particularly those which involved the city's troubled police force and police action shootings. Small but persistent Republican-sponsored tax increases also spawned a number of taxpayer protest campaigns, the most important of which was the revival in 1982 of the Indianapolis Taxpayers Association led by Carl Moldthan. Several of the preexisting, or "excluded," local town and city jurisdictions which survived the Unigov reorganization also created bases of local loyalty critical of many central government activities. Indianapolis remained a diverse community that involved substantial numbers of local residents in the competitive search for public office.

After three easy reelection victories, Hudnut was succeeded as mayor in 1991 by former Republican prosecutor Stephen Goldsmith. Goldsmith's campaign reflected much of the new political emphasis upon technology and television, and hinted at an independence from traditional party structures—characteristics of many high-visibility local candidates throughout the country. His campaign spoke to social issues of concern to an increasingly active body of evangelical Christian groups. Goldsmith was also keenly aware of a growing antitaxation sentiment in the electorate, and campaigned on a platform that emphasized cost-cutting initiatives using such labels as privatization and downsizing. Some commentators predicted his administration might represent as important a break with political precedent as Lugar's had in the 1960s.

By the 1990s Indianapolis was obviously very different from the small country town where its first political candidates had campaigned almost two centuries before. Yet in the strongly competitive nature of its electoral process, the extensive use of mass media to reach the electorate, and the varied attempts to deal with the interests of a diverse population, it continued to show remarkable continuity along with its fascinating changes. Politics remains, as it had always been, a significant feature of local life.

See also: AFRICAN-AMERICANS IN POLITICS; DEMOCRATIC PARTY; GERMANS IN POLITICS; IRISH IN POLITICS; KU KLUX KLAN; POLITICS, ANTEBELLUM; REPUBLICAN PARTY; and individual names, organizations, and elections.

RELIGION

Jan Shipps

In the first three or four decades after the passage of the Bill of Rights with its prohibition of an establishment of religion and its provision for the free exercise thereof, American religion assumed a form and shape that differed significantly from the official or state-supported churches of the colonial era. In many areas of the new nation this traditional establishment pattern persisted long after 1820, the year commissioners selected a mile-square tract in central Indiana for a new state capital. Although many who settled in the area during its first 20 years were former residents of states with religious establishments, Indianapolis came into existence during the period of the early republic when American religion had begun to change. Perhaps this explains why the contours of religion in the Hoosier capital became so distinctly representative, even prototypical, of the shape that religion would assume in the United States in the 19th and first half of the 20th centuries.

As was the pattern in other recently inhabited regions of the young republic, the town's first religious meetings were held in such places as a schoolhouse built in 1821 at Kentucky Avenue and Illinois Street, a much-frequented open air site on a wooded knoll in the center of town (known as the Circle), or in the larger homes, barns, and shops of the struggling settlement. Conducted by traveling preachers of every stripe, these early meetings attracted residents of the town without regard to denomination. Sometimes they became occasions for doctrinal debates and heated discussions about ritual and the requirements for redemption. Camp meetings and revivals were not uncommon, sometimes achieving spectacular success. Yet a sizable proportion of the newly arrived populace declined invitations to enlist in one of the several Hoosier armies marching toward Zion.

But if religious and ecclesiastical fluidity characterized early Indianapolis, the Hoosier capital was by no means irreligious. Quite the reverse. A multidenominational Sunday school was first organized in 1823 and three years later the Indianapolis Sabbath School Union (which followed the general plan of the American Sunday School Union) was founded. Among its pupils were non–church members as well as students from many different denominations. Other trans-

Jan Shipps is Professor of History and Religious Studies at Indiana University–Purdue University, Indianapolis.

denominational units were organized in the mid–1820s, including the Indianapolis Bible Society and the Indianapolis Tract Society in 1825 and the Marion County Temperance Union a year later.

Before its second decade was over, however, religion in this fledgling urban district started settling into what would become the standard United States configuration. A Protestant mainstream started to develop in Indianapolis before 1840, even though some congregations lacked permanently stationed preachers, church buildings, or full organizational form. By that time, too, there were enough Irish and German Catholics in Indianapolis to form a parish and build a small frame church, thereby posing both a foreign and a Catholic challenge to the native Protestant order. Also present were clusters of immigrant Lutherans and representatives of the European Reformed churches, African-American Baptists and Methodists, native-born Unitarians, Universalists, Quakers, and Mormons, all of whom stood outside the Protestant mainstream. In addition, the largest number of Indianapolis residents were unchurched. By a ratio of roughly four to one during the antebellum decades, religiously unaffiliated residents greatly outnumbered citizens who were connected to one or another religious organization.

Even so, early journals, diaries, and newspaper accounts indicate that the decisive element in the young town's religious environment was mainstream Protestantism. The first Protestant groups to organize were the Methodists, Baptists, and Presbyterians (both New and Old School varieties). All three created churches or chapels, classes, "meetings," and "societies" that would become churches in the 1820s. As elsewhere in the nation, other organized congregations—Episcopalians, Disciples of Christ (Christians), Congregationalists, and Lutherans (at least the ones whose services were conducted in English)—also filled the mainstream Protestant camp.

Appropriately, since they would become the city's preeminent Protestant body with the greatest number of churches and members for almost a century, the Methodists were first on the scene. They organized a class in 1821 and for the next seven years Methodist circuit riders regularly visited members of this group. From 1825 to 1829 they held worship services in a hewn log sanctuary located on Maryland Street between Meridian and Illinois streets. After 1828, when a full-time preacher was assigned, the congregation erected a brick building at the southwest corner of the Circle and Meridian Street.

Baptists established a church rather than a class in 1822, allowing this denomination to claim the first bona fide ecclesiastical institution in the state's capital city. They built a one-story brick church at the southwest corner of Meridian and Maryland streets virtually at the same time the Methodists abandoned their primitive Maryland Street building. This pattern of Baptists following and competing with Methodists continued in the city for many generations. Except in selected census years when the city had more Black Baptists than Methodists, Indianapolis would not have more Baptists than Methodists until after World War II, even though Baptists nationally outnumbered Methodists by early in the 20th century.

While Indianapolis Presbyterians started sharing a preacher with Presbyterians in Bloomington in 1822, they did not formally constitute themselves as a church until a year after that. A little more than a dozen years later, a general denominational disagreement over revivalism and voluntary associations led to a division that separated American Presbyterians into a traditional or Old School camp and an evangelical or New School camp. In 1838 this disagreement was manifested locally when 15 members of the First Presbyterian Church withdrew to organize a Second Presbyterian Church. The new church's pastor was Henry Ward Beecher, who, after leaving Indianapolis, became one of the nation's most eminent clergymen. A Congregational church was also founded in the city in 1857, appearing so late mainly because a Plan of Union adopted by the nation's Congregationalists and Presbyterians prevented the organization of rival congregations in newly settled areas. This plan worked to the advantage of the Presbyterians not only in Indianapolis but throughout the nation.

Despite its status as a new denomination, one which officially came into existence in 1830, a local Disciples of Christ (Campbellite) congregation was organized in 1833 and quickly became a part of the Protestant mainstream. Building a house of worship on Kentucky Avenue in 1836, the Disciples in 1855 started North Western Christian University, a coeducational denominational college that became Butler University in 1877.

The remaining constituent bodies in the Protestant mainstream, the Lutherans and the Episcopalians, organized congregations in 1837. Bringing together 20 members including several heads of households, the First English Lutheran Church built its house of worship near the center of the city, where Meridian and Ohio streets cross. The Episcopalian congregation, initially composed of 30 leading citizens of Indianapolis, selected a site on the northeast quadrant of the Circle. There they erected a plain, solid edifice that they used for 20 years before removing it and selling it to the African Methodist congregation. This done, they embarked on the construction of a substantial stone structure that would become Christ Church Cathedral, an architectural monument that continues to this day to represent Protestant Christianity in the heart of the city.

Although the level of church membership increased very slowly in Indianapolis, as elsewhere, most of the city's cultural and civic leaders were members (and often leading laypersons) of mainline Protestant denominations. The result was the emergence of a virtual religious establishment in Indianapolis, one that would maintain its position for another 100 years or more. Not only were civic leaders squarely within the Protestant mainstream, the city's various congregations were tied into the national denominational structures that functioned as a virtual U.S. religious establishment by the middle of the 19th century.

If such a religious establishment was palpable but not actual at both the national and the local levels, and if the conception of a religious mainstream is, finally, simply a metaphorical concept, in 19th century Indianapolis the notion of a Protestant center was not merely metaphor. For a century or more, the religious center was real in a very literal sense. The Circle, the center of the Mile Square, was home for many years to five of the city's notable and long-standing Protestant congregations. Nearly all the others located their church buildings only a block or two from the Circle.

As was true in other metropolitan areas across the nation, however, the religious contours of Indianapolis started to change around midcentury. Ethnic parishes of Catholics and Lutherans and a German Reformed Church, as well as a Hebrew congregation, were all established in Indianapolis in the 1850s. In the same decade, smaller sectarian groups such as German Evangelicals and United Brethren also organized.

Many of these congregations rapidly attained the same kind of stability and assumed the same sort of growth potential as the mainstream congregations. While this made them equally significant as urban institutional expressions of religion, it did not confer mainstream status on them. Consequently, the members of these ethnic congregations and smaller groups were by no means as influential in the cultural and civic affairs of Indianapolis as were Methodists, Presbyterians, Episcopalians, and Baptists in the 19th century.

The same cannot be said of the Quakers who organized in the city in 1854. Many influential Indianapolis citizens were Quakers, including one who became a leader of the Indianapolis Min-

During the 19th century, the Circle was home to five major Protestant
congregations. [Indiana Historical Society, Bass Collection, #298598]

Communal events such as this near southeastside baptism in the 1920s, probably
in Pleasant Run, were important events in the city's African-American churches.
[Indiana Historical Society, #C575]

isterial Association and who, in the early 20th century, would become the executive secretary of
the city's Church Federation. Nor can it be said about the Unitarians and Universalists, national
religious societies which, like the Quakers, were never a part of the Protestant center but were still
attractive to persons of consequence. While neither of these societies formed strong units in the
city, both had influential members such as a judge of the federal court, a state librarian, and a secretary of state.

Also on the margins of the Protestant mainstream, but only because of their color, were the city's African-Americans. In 1836 Bethel Chapel organized as the first separate African-American Methodist institution. Not until the 1850s, however, was this society able to worship in a building of its own. Sited on the near west side, close to the present IUPUI campus, the Bethel African Methodist Episcopal congregation obtained its first church building from the Episcopalians when the Christ Church congregation started the building that became Christ Church Cathedral. During this same decade another African-American congregation, Second Baptist Church, likewise started to worship in its own building located in the African-American neighborhood between North and Blackford streets. These were the only two African-American churches in the city until the mid–1860s, but between the Civil War and the end of the century more than two dozen African-American congregations formed, most within the framework of the African Methodist Episcopal, AME Zion, and Black Baptist traditions. After the substantial migration of African-Americans to the city in the 1920s and 1930s, the number of such congregations increased so dramatically that by 1936 the denomination with the largest number of Indianapolis congregations was the so-called Negro Baptists. Together with the various ethnic and sectarian groups, these institutions formed flood walls and levees—to take the mainstream metaphor seriously—that kept the Protestant current in the center of Indianapolis society and culture.

Large numbers of religiously unaffiliated individuals and families were situated neither in the Protestant mainstream nor in the ethnic congregations and assorted sectarian groups that functioned as the mainstream's boundaries, its perimeter. All sorts of religious messages were (and still are) directed to this unchurched population, so much so that, despite its established congregations, the city became something of a spiritual and ecclesiastical emporium. From the 1820s forward a virtual religious marketplace has existed where evangelists of every variety—missionaries, exhorters, preachers—have held meetings, conducted revivals, and made appeals to potential consumers of religion.

From the outset this religious perimeter has been regarded as a field "white to the harvest" by practically all of the city's organized religious bodies as well as by many potential faith communities. Although the response has varied across time, the unchurched surely swelled the ranks at revival meetings and joined with the city's churched population in numerous religio-political events. They also made use of area clergy and religious structures for weddings and funerals and almost certainly swelled the size of the congregations in the churches, especially at Christmas and Easter time. The existence of a substantial body of unchurched people in the region helps to explain the 20th century success of Cadle Tabernacle, which for more than 40 years was the world's largest permanent structure specifically designed for revival meetings. And perhaps this population is a reason why the contemporary city is able to support local religious radio and television stations.

Despite its participation in Indianapolis religion outside its institutional framework, scholars have rarely, if ever, considered the area's unchurched population as a part of the story of religion in the city. Yet if religion in Indianapolis is viewed in all its fullness and complexity, it is important to consider these unaffiliated residents. The urban religious configuration is incomplete without them.

Although it is difficult to estimate the relative size of the city's religious population and its constituent elements, records exist for selected years. William Holloway, an early historian of Indianapolis, provided data about membership in the city's churches in 1830 and 1850, and his totals for 1870 represent the results of a systematic survey. Census records supply membership

Religious Affiliation in Indianapolis: Selected Years, 1830 to 1990

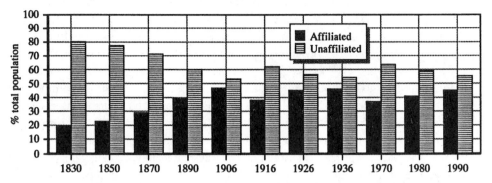

Sources: William R. Holloway, *Indianapolis* (Indianapolis, 1870); Jacob Piatt
Dunn, *Greater Indianapolis* (Chicago, 1910); U.S. Census; data published by
the Glenmary Research Center, Atlanta, Georgia. The Glenmary data are self-
reported and thus omit a substantial number of denominations and
independent congregations that did not provide information.

statistics for the churches in Marion County for 1890, 1906, 1916, 1926, and 1936, and Glenmary Research Center publications provide estimated membership numbers for 1970, 1980, and
1990. The task of counting members among these religious bodies is everywhere made infinitely
complicated because available statistics reflect institutional self-reporting. Some groups count (or
once counted) family units, while others provide totals of adults in full standing, all communicants, or all communicants plus unbaptized or unconfirmed youngsters in the congregations.
Still, these records allow for rough comparison of denominational sizes. It is also possible to calculate the number of religiously unaffiliated persons in the city. Subtracting the total numbers of
church members from the city's total population and turning both into percentages provides a
crude approximation of the comparable proportions of church members and religiously unaffiliated persons in the city across Indianapolis' history (see chart). Although imprecise, such a measure nevertheless provides enough evidence to suggest that at many points in the city's history
the number of residents unconnected to religious organizations has exceeded the number of
church members.

The records for Indianapolis suggest that the total membership of churches in the Protestant
mainstream was considerably larger in the antebellum period than membership of the city's racial and ethnic congregations, sectarian associations, and unconventional societies. Comparable
totals for the later decades of the 19th and the early decades of the 20th centuries show much
closer total memberships. Significantly, the mainstream has lost ground consistently since the
1960s.

The relative numbers of churched and unchurched persons across the city's history point to
the presence of potential religious "consumers." But what sort of religious marketplace existed to
serve them? Here the early decades established a pattern of rich variety that continued throughout the city's history. Several examples will illustrate: (1) An often reprinted report tells the story
of an 1822 meeting held at the James Givens farm on the outskirts of Indianapolis where Methodist circuit rider James Scott preached and "people got religion in droves." A total of 265 unchurched persons were brought into membership in the old Wesley Chapel. (2) The recently

discovered missionary journals of one William E. McLellin, an 1831 convert to Mormonism, make it clear that willing audiences were generally found in Indianapolis to listen to the Latter-day Saints' gospel message. (3) The history of the Disciples of Christ in Indianapolis recounts the astonishing success of these religious innovators. Disciples were followers of Alexander Campbell and Barton W. Stone who joined forces to organize a new "church to end all churches" in 1830. Only two years after this new "New Testament" movement began, Elder John O'Kane visited the city and appealed to enough residents to start a Campbellite movement. In the years immediately following, Elders Joel Lee Jones, Michael Combs, Love H. Jameson, and Andrew Prather all came to the city to conduct "protracted meetings." Sufficient numbers joined to give the Indianapolis Christian Church enough stature to carry it and future congregations directly into the Protestant mainstream. A partial explanation for this may be that Christian Chapel, organized in early 1833, kept a resident evangelist on its staff for 20 years.

These examples demonstrate the variety of the early religious offerings. Methodists used revival techniques to convict listeners of sinfulness and offered protection from eternal punishment through a personal encounter with the Savior. Mormons used the coming forth of the Book of Mormon as evidence of a new dispensation that would be the "winding up scene" just prior to the second coming. The Disciples used rational argument more than revival in an attempt to unite all Christians in the "true and apostolic" church.

Efforts to reach the religiously unaffiliated in the mid to late 20th century continued some of these approaches. A Billy Graham rally held at the Indiana State Fairgrounds in 1959 attracted as many as 35,000 people to one of its services, for instance. Revival and healing services are regularly broadcast from Indianapolis on religious television and radio. Pairs of young Latter-day Saint missionaries still canvass the city's residential areas with regularity. And while protracted meetings may be a remnant of a bygone era, independent Holiness and Pentecostal churches still attract roving evangelists. Moreover, since the 1960s new offerings have extended and complicated the Indianapolis religious marketplace: among them Zen Buddhism, the Way, the Eckanar Satsang Society, the Unification Church (whose members follow the Rev. Sun Myung Moon), the Psychic Science Spiritualists, and perhaps most important, both traditional and nontraditional forms of Islam.

Conversion or persuasion has not always led to affiliation with an existing denominational unit or even to identification with a particular faith tradition. Indeed, antiinstitutional Freethinkers once stood on the periphery of Indianapolis religion in the 19th century, and supporters of the skeptic Robert Ingersoll and atheist Madalyn Murray O'Hair located themselves along the perimeter in the 20th century. Yet religious unbelief has never characterized this fringe area. Instead, it is abundantly clear, to use religious historian Jon Butler's powerful image, that in Indianapolis, as elsewhere in the nation, people outside the mainstream were "awash in a sea of faith." In addition to their willingness to listen and sometimes respond to the solicitations among others of Unitarians and Universalists, Millerites, and, later, Seventh-Day Adventists, so many have swelled local evangelistic audiences across the years that it is possible to read cultural significance into this response.

Scholars have shown that immigrants' membership in churches familiar to them, churches whose worship services were conducted in their native languages, often was critical in the process of acculturation. A similar situation undoubtedly operated for the number of native-born citizens who moved to Indianapolis from agrarian and mountainous regions of the U.S., especially in the 20th century. Strangers to the urban environment, they found reminders of their rural backgrounds in revivalism and the experientially oriented Christianity of the Holiness and Pentecostal traditions, two large movements that started on the religious margins. They likewise found a home in innumerable center city storefront churches and informal spiritual gatherings. These forms of religion helped newcomers to become incorporated into this midwestern urban culture just as Jewish, Catholic, Lutheran, and Reformed worship and parish life assisted European immigrants. Also important were the large number of fraternal organizations which, although not religious in the traditional sense, were oriented toward ritual. For the very large proportion of the male population of the city participating in such activities from 1850 to 1950 and even beyond, these organizations might well be significant in a quasi-religious sense.

As important as is (and was) the religious perimeter to the history of religion in this very typical American city, however, the perception that Indianapolis is (and always has been) home to many churches is widespread. Historians nearly all agree with Jacob Piatt Dunn that "Indianapolis was unquestionably more moral and religious than the average frontier town." There is general agreement, too, that the Indiana capital became and has remained a "city of churches."

The large proportion of the city's residents who existed outside the religious mainstream was crucial to the success of organized revivalism, one of the standard strategies used to generate membership in Protestant churches. But the histories of the city's churches, ethnic congregations, and sectarian groups reveal another strategy of church growth: the planting of mission churches. What made Indianapolis a city of churches is the manner in which existing congregations established mission or daughter congregations in new areas as the city expanded.

One of the most obvious, interesting, and consistent denominational examples is what happened to the Presbyterians in Indianapolis. An 1838 secession from the First Presbyterian Church led to the organization of the Second Presbyterian Church. In 1851 Third Presbyterian Church (later Tabernacle) was organized as a mission from the First Presbyterian Church. In 1867 a colony went out from Third Presbyterian, daughter congregation to First Presbyterian, to organize Fifth Presbyterian. First Presbyterian also established Seventh Presbyterian as a mission enterprise. Meantime, also in 1851, Second Presbyterian organized Fourth Presbyterian, and, in 1867, Olivet Church (later Sixth Presbyterian).

Such symmetry was rarely duplicated, but a similar motif is found in the history of most of Indianapolis Protestantism. More often, however, the initial separation was made on the basis of geographical jurisdiction. Within area Methodism the pioneer congregation of the Methodist Episcopal Church (Wesley Chapel) was divided in 1842 to create a western and an eastern charge and these became the bases of the Meridian Street and Roberts Park churches. While the latter was still called Wesley Chapel, its members facilitated the organization of Ames Methodist. Strange Chapel—so named in honor of the Rev. John Strange, an eminent early Indiana Methodist—was also organized under the western charge. Then doctrinal issues entered the picture and, like the Presbyterians, this congregation subsequently divided along conservative-liberal lines: the liberal wing changed the name of Strange Chapel to St. John's Methodist in 1871; a local missionary enterprise of the more conservative members became Third Street Methodist (organized 1866). Meantime, colonies from the Roberts Park congregation established Asbury, Trinity, and Grace Methodist.

Local mission efforts of the city's first Baptist congregation (First Baptist) led to the founding of the South Street Baptist, Garden Baptist, North Baptist, and River Avenue Baptist churches in the 19th century. In the same period Second Baptist, a black congregation, planted the White Lick, Olivet, Mount Zion, Georgetown, New Bethel, and Tabernacle Baptist churches. This pat-

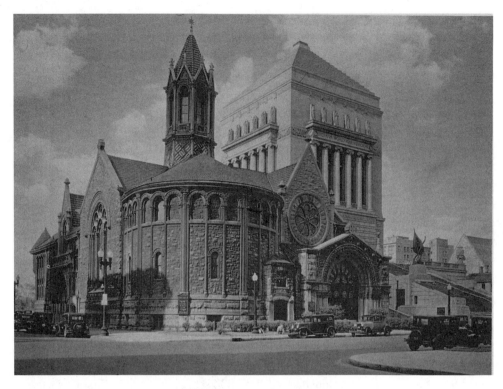

The juxtaposition of civil and sacred religion: the Indiana War Memorial looms behind First Baptist Church on the northeast corner of Meridian and Vermont streets, shown here in 1932. The church moved to its present location on the far north side in 1960. [Indiana Historical Society, Bass Collection, #224259F]

tern extended beyond the mainstream to smaller denominations and ethnic congregations as they multiplied the number and variety of Christians in Indianapolis.

Thus it is obvious from an examination of religion across the city's history that preaching revivals and establishing mission churches were and still are two complementary forms of church growth. From the outset they were religion's warp and woof in Indianapolis. But if these threads formed its fabric, there remained the question of design. The conceptions that governed its creation are as important to the story of religion in the city as is the description of its configuration and how that changed across time.

Although several Protestant denominations held to the parish concept, however much it was ignored in actuality, an important feature of historical Catholicism was the practice of making geographical divisions in an area and establishing churches to serve its residents in each one. With its accompanying tradition of a centralized hierarchy having dominion over local parishes, the history of the Catholic church in Indianapolis is marked by a reasonable degree of system and order. In the early years the systematic subdivision of parishes reflected the arrival of a substantial population of Irish, German, and Italian immigrants. In the 20th century the progression of parish formation, which sometimes involved building and staffing a parochial school as well as a church, occurred as Catholics started moving outward from the metropolitan center.

The formation of new parishes ordinarily reflected an increase in the number of Catholics in particular areas of the city, but after World War II parish formation sometimes occurred prior to the settlement of the new suburbs. Yet whether parish organization reflected or anticipated the appearance of new Catholic residents, this pattern of planting left no areas without churches to serve their inhabitants. It also avoided confusion and competition between several churches in contiguous or overlapping areas.

A certain degree of system and order was also present within the various forms of Protestantism, especially those overseen by supervisory judicatories. So many different versions of Protestantism with so many different judicatories were present in the city, however, that some areas had more local churches than were needed while others had none. By the time of World War I the need for some form of transdenominational coordination became obvious; otherwise even a modicum of order would be hard to achieve. Long established churches already were starting to move away from the very center of the city as they followed their members to outlying neighborhoods, and ministers and laity from several denominations contended for place in every newly established subdivision.

By no means unique to Indianapolis, the matter of planning church locations was one of several incentives that moved mainstream Protestants beyond the level of cooperation or informal accord achieved by active ministerial associations. The nationwide Federal Council of Churches of Christ, organized in 1908, recognized this problem and promoted the organization of local federations. Only four years later Indianapolis responded by forming the Indianapolis Church Federation. This brought together in a single cooperative venture American Baptists, Disciples of Christ, Quakers, Episcopalians, Lutherans, Presbyterians, Methodists, and Congregationalists. One of the first urban interchurch bodies in the U.S., the Indianapolis organization set a pattern for interchurch associations throughout the nation. On this specific front religion in the Hoosier capital was more than simply representative; it stood in the vanguard.

In part the local Church Federation sought to encourage evangelism through the sort of "church extension" represented by midweek services in center city areas and Sunday evening meetings in individual churches. Likewise concerned with the moral environment, its member churches and staff both worked diligently to generate consensus on moral and ethical issues. At many points the Federation exerted pressure on the political and business community alike as it sought to uphold justice and enhance public morality. In its early years, for example, the Federation's executive committee joined the public morals committee of the ministerial association to conduct a monthly "vice survey." Results were brought directly to the attention of so-called violators of public morality as well as to reporters for the city's newspapers.

The Federation's contribution to the shape of Indianapolis Protestantism came through a "comity committee" charged with the responsibility of regulating the location of new churches so that they would not be too near other churches but yet people in every area would be served by a Protestant congregation. In its second year this committee appealed to all Protestant groups to approve the Federation's plans for the location of every sort of religious enterprise so that "no new churches [would be] established or old ones relocated without careful investigation." While compliance was voluntary, this work of the comity committee was generally effective, with this part of the Federation's agenda carried forward from 1913 well into the 1960s.

The Federation was initially composed of mainstream Protestant congregations that supported its work financially, albeit sometimes sparsely. Its member organizations were equally committed to evangelical Christianity and the social gospel in the beginning. But over the years, especially after World War II, emphasis on social issues surpassed in importance such activities as holiday worship services in downtown theaters and visitation evangelism. Religious education, various kinds of social service, a chaplaincy initiative, and race relations at times appeared to overwhelm other dimensions of the Federation's work.

This shift reflects the fact that the Church Federation became the locale for a merging of the Protestant mainstream with the institutions and organizations that once had existed on its periphery. Quite early on the Federation extended formal membership to many congregations whose denominations had once been regarded as standing far outside the mainstream, including African-American churches. The Federation in Indianapolis foreshadowed what would happen across the U.S. in the 1950s when prevailing attitudes made no distinction between mainstream denominations and the many varieties of Protestantism that traditionally had been positioned outside the center—or for that matter between Protestantism, Catholicism, and Judaism.

A local chapter of the National Conference of Christians and Jews was organized and became active during the 1950s, when being Protestant, Catholic, or Jewish were equally legitimate ways to be American. Yet the cooperative approach to working with both Catholics and Jews on the part of the overwhelmingly Protestant Church Federation came to signify the full integration of these two forms of the Judeo-Christian tradition into the city's religious life. Not until the 1960s, however, would Catholic parishes become official members.

As was true of the nation generally, Indianapolis diversified in the 20th century, becoming slightly more pluralistic after World War I and much more pluralistic after World War II. But the change was not so much in the presence of different ethnicities and types of people as it was in sheer numbers. The population increased to nearly a half million in 1960, a growth accompanied by movement to the edges of the city. The subsequent creation of concentric circles of Indianapolis suburbs undercut the focus on the central city, mandating construction of religious edifices at a rapid rate. While the 1950s saw an expansion in church membership in nearly all denominational families, the social dislocation of the following decade contributed to a gradual decrease in numbers of members of mainline Protestant churches. This decline in turn diminished the power and even the very presence of the 19th and early 20th century Protestant establishment.

In the years following the 1960s the once-settled religious constellation started to come apart. The traditional liberal Christianity of the mainstream denominations was challenged by the growth and increasing visibility of what might be called an evangelical-fundamentalist-pentecostal-holiness coalition, by a Catholicism more obviously integrated into the life of the city after Vatican II, by the appearance of organized stakes and wards of the Church of Jesus Christ of Latter-day Saints, and by the arrival in the city of a surprising number of citizens entirely unconnected to the Judeo-Christian tradition: Buddhists, Hindus, and especially Muslims.

Such changes are reflected in an altered configuration in the religion of the modern city. Where once the mainstream held the center, surrounded by less culturally influential forms of Christianity as well as Judaism, now Protestantism in particular and the Judeo-Christian alliance generally showed signs of a liberal-conservative breach. The more conservative tide—represented by the Indianapolis Baptist Temple (which is currently as close as the city gets to having a "megachurch") and the huge numbers of adherents reported by Pentecostal, Holiness, and independent evangelical congregations—may very well surpass the traditional Protestant current in membership numbers and may be mounting a challenge in terms of cultural influence as well.

Examination of the list of some 1,100 congregations and religious enterprises in the 1993 Yellow Pages reveals a much enlarged Judeo-Christian center. Split into liberal and conservative branches, the center is now bounded by a wide variety of such unconventional congregations as the Cathedral of Praise Bibleway Church Worldwide, Psychic Science Spiritualist Church, Unity associations, and the Metropolitan Community Church which brings gays and lesbians into the Christian fold, as well as by a new set of ethnic Christian congregations (Korean, Latino, Vietnamese) and churches that represent worldwide faiths other than Christian or Jewish—Bahai, Muslim, Zen Buddhist, and so on. But what has not changed is the broad band of religiously unaffiliated individuals that encircles the whole. If the nature of the city's religious marketplace has changed, the marketplace itself is still a going concern.

One additional form of religion that has been present virtually from the beginning and remains in place as the city nears the end of the 20th century are a variety of cultural expressions that have religious overtones. These are a critical feature of this city's civic spirit, part of its vitality and essence. Symbolized by the Soldiers and Sailors Monument that filled the religious vacuum left on the Circle when four of its five churches gave way to commercial and business enterprises, this form of religion remains intact. Its civil religion component is manifest in the Indiana World War Memorial Plaza north of the Circle in which is located the War Memorial and the national and state headquarters of the American Legion. It is expressed as well in the religiously inclusive invocations and benedictions that mark public occasions of all kinds.

Not universally recognized as religion but present in the city's corporate life from time to time, these cultural expressions—a recognition of that remarkable elixir that transcends individual and corporate existence—remain at the heart of Indianapolis. Periodically bursting forth at holiday time and in times of great celebration, as at the end of World Wars I and II, it has also been present in times of crisis, as in the days following the assassinations of Abraham Lincoln, John F. Kennedy, and Martin Luther King, Jr. It surfaces as well in celebrations of the city's history, and materializes in gatherings such as the one each Thanksgiving when thousands gather on the Circle to join the mayor when he lights the "world's tallest (now largest) Christmas tree."

This overarching form of religion functions as what might be called cultural glue. It is a phenomenon that ties residents of the city's many neighborhoods together. This civic faith gives to the city and its residents, both churched and unchurched, not so much a glimpse of the shape of religion in the Indiana capital as a sort of subliminal perception of religion as one of the critical factors that shaped Indianapolis and made it what it is today.

————

See also: AFRICAN-AMERICAN CHURCHES; PHILANTHROPY AND RELIGION; PUBLIC SCHOOLS, RELIGION IN; RELIGION AND RACE; RELIGION AND SOCIAL SERVICES; RELIGIOUS ARCHITECTURE; RELIGIOUS BROADCASTING; RELIGIOUS PRESS; SCHOOLS, RELIGIOUS; WOMEN IN RELIGION; and individual names, denominations, congregations, and institutions.

SPORTS

Randy Roberts

I t was a defining moment for two cities, both hovering on the fringes of "major city" status. Very late one stormy March night in 1984, professional movers in Baltimore, Maryland, loaded their vans with the records and equipment of the National Football League's Baltimore Colts and headed west on I-70 toward Indianapolis. As the sun rose the news spread quickly through Baltimore. The Colts were gone—for good. The pride of Baltimore, the team that had defeated the New York Giants for the 1958 NFL championship in what was generally known as the greatest game ever, had moved to another town. For residents of Baltimore it seemed impossible. The Colts had departed, noted one sportswriter, "with all the grace of a snake-oil salesman backing out of a prairie tank town." Baltimore, however, had lost more than the Colts, the team's NFL and Super Bowl trophies, and Johnny Unitas' uniform. The city had lost a step in its quest for major city status. In late 20th century America, major cities came to be defined by what they offered their residents. Major cities sponsored a wide range of entertainments—ballet, opera, theater, museums, and, of course, NFL football. Baltimore was suddenly and desperately lacking in the "of course" category.

As Baltimore took a step backward, Indianapolis leaped forward. Mayor William H. Hudnut III, Indianapolis' chief negotiator for the Colts, denied that his city had robbed Baltimore of anything. "We didn't steal the Colts—Baltimore lost them," he told one reporter. "Cities don't automatically grow and prosper. You've got to work at it." And Hudnut had. In the high stakes game of professional football franchise movement and urban redevelopment, Hudnut had laid down a winning hand. He had promised Colts owner Robert Irsay free rent in the recently constructed Hoosier Dome and, to sweeten the pot, "a ten-year, $12.5 million loan at eight percent, a $2.5 million line of credit, a brand new $4 million training facility, the first $500,000 of luxury box income for the first twelve years, fifty percent of the suite income thereafter, exclusive right to sell programs and novelties, and a guarantee of $7 million in ticket income for the first twelve years." Finding no better offer, Irsay accepted. Justifying the move, he commented, "This is my team. I own it, and I'll do whatever I want with it."

Randy Roberts is Associate Professor of History at Purdue University, West Lafayette.

The acquisition of the Colts was one part of an attempt by Indianapolis leaders to use sports as the primary instrument for rebuilding the image and revitalizing the economy of the city. In many ways the sports strategy made sense; the city's leaders were simply drawing on a rich sporting heritage. From the late 19th century through the 20th century sports reflected the aspirations of the residents of Indianapolis and mirrored the economic and social change in the city.

Gilded Age Indianapolis bustled with sporting activities. As in other American cities of the period, most sporting behavior followed class lines. For the elite sports served a social as well as a recreational function. Following the practice in the East, leading Indianapolis residents formed exclusive clubs that promoted their social, political, and economic concerns. Union Clubs and Union Leagues advanced Republican political causes. The Commercial Club served an economic function. For social interaction, occasionally with a thin veneer of culture, the elite turned to a wide range of clubs and societies, including the fashionable Indianapolis Literary Club, the Fortnightly Club, the Dramatic Club, and the Art Association of Indianapolis.

Sports clubs added to this complex web of elite associations. An early historian of the Brookline Country Club in Boston, America's first such club, noted, "Everyone [in Boston's society] was either in it or out of it; and those who were in it were proud of the fact and guarded its boundaries jealously. They played with each other, not with others; they competed with each other, not with others; above all, they married each other only, and so their children carried on the good (?) tradition." Similar notions, though seldom officially pronounced, were common in many athletic clubs and country clubs. Indianapolis society was no exception. The Indianapolis Country Club underscored these sporting and social functions, combining sports with a full program of dances, dinners, and other social activities. Like many elite eastern country clubs, in the 1890s the Indianapolis Country Club added golf to the sports activities. Its golf course, built in 1897, was the first in Indiana.

Working class and immigrant residents of Indianapolis also had their athletic outlets. German immigrants organized a Turnverein; Irish immigrants formed a Gaelic Athletic Club. Although illegal, bare-knuckle prizefights were held in the city's levee region, and in legal exhibition in 1883 John L. Sullivan, the heavyweight champion of the world, entertained a large crowd of spectators at the Park Theater.

Several sports transcended class concerns. Baseball, for example, attracted participants and spectators from every economic station. Baseball was played in the city at least as early as the mid–1860s, and it enjoyed great popularity in the late 19th century on both the amateur and professional levels. Indianapolis professional teams played in the International League, the American Association, the National League, the Western League, and the American League.

In the late 19th century the National League dominated professional baseball. Two years after the organization of the league, Indianapolis joined the circuit in 1878, but the team folded—an "utter failure financially"—after one year. In 1887 John T. Brush moved a St. Louis team to Indianapolis, but after three seasons the team was forced out of the National League. Despite its baseball tradition Indianapolis did not find a permanent place in the major leagues, remaining instead "a minor league town." A charter member of the American Association, Indianapolis spent most of the 20th century as home to one of minor league baseball's most successful organizations.

The bicycle craze of the 1890s also attracted enthusiasts from all classes. Early cyclists came primarily from the upper middle class. Equipment was expensive, and such organizations as the League of American Wheelmen catered to wealthier participants. But in the early 1890s bicycle

Marshall W. "Major" Taylor at his first European race in Berlin, 1901. [Indiana State Museum]

Wilbur Shaw won the Indianapolis 500 in 1937, 1939, and 1940. [Indianapolis Motor Speedway]

National Basketball Association Hall-of-Famer Oscar Robertson (the "Big O") played for the Crispus Attucks Tigers when they won the state high school championship in 1955. Attucks repeated in 1956 and won the state title again in 1959. [Indiana Historical Society, *Indianapolis Recorder* Collection, #C4492]

costs dropped sharply with the invention of the relatively inexpensive "safety" bicycle. Suddenly the sport was opened to rich and poor alike.

The greatest cyclist of the period came from Indianapolis. Marshall W. "Major" Taylor began his racing career in the mid–1890s, and by the turn of the century he was hailed as the "Fastest Bicycle Rider in the World," winning national sprint championships in 1898, 1899, and 1900 and setting national and world records. During the first decade of the 20th century Taylor toured Europe and Australia, earning many thousands of dollars as a professional cyclist before retiring in 1910.

Taylor's successes are all the more remarkable given the fact that he was an African-American and faced open discrimination and hostility throughout the United States. Bicycle racing, like almost every other form of athletic competition, fell victim to Jim Crow laws during the late 19th century. By 1890 the managers of organized professional baseball had segregated their sport. In boxing, heavyweight champion John L. Sullivan proposed in 1892 to fight all contenders: "In this challenge I include all fighters—first come, first served—who are white. I will not fight a Negro. I never have and I never shall." And true to his word he never did, even though several of the leading challengers were black.

Such prejudices haunted Taylor throughout his career. In 1894 the League of American Wheelmen adopted a "whites only" membership policy. On the racing track Taylor confronted vile racial insults, physical attacks, and rough, unsportsmanlike tactics. He was banned from racing in the South and in several northern states. His white competitors tried, but failed, to force him out of the sport. Only his reputation and the commercial uses of his name guaranteed a place for him in the almost exclusively white organization.

The new century saw interest in another form of wheeled racing eclipse bicycle racing in popularity. Automobiles dominated the 20th century just as horse-drawn carriages had dominated the 19th. Indianapolis became the home of many of the early automobile manufacturers. Before the mass production of automobiles and the shift in the industry to Detroit, Indianapolis mechanics produced vehicles of unusual craftsmanship and quality. The Duesenberg, in particular, has been singled out as one of the most finely crafted automobiles in the history of the industry, and the Stutz Bearcat, which was often pictured in John Held, Jr., drawings, became a symbol of the "flaming youth" of the 1920s.

To test and showcase the automobiles, entrepreneur Carl Graham Fisher formed the Indianapolis Motor Speedway Company and arranged for the construction of the Indianapolis Motor Speedway. Completed in 1909, the 2.5-mile track began to host automobile and motorcycle races. On May 30, 1911, the Speedway hosted the first Indianapolis 500–Mile Race. The month of the race conformed to the still rural tempo of Indiana; practice runs, time trials, and the race itself were confined to the month of May, following spring corn planting, to allow local farmers to attend the activities.

The first Indianapolis 500 was won by Ray Harroun in an Indianapolis-built black and yellow Marmon Wasp in 6 hours and 42 minutes at an average speed of 74.59 miles per hour. The race and the resulting publicity stimulated Marmon sales, thus guaranteeing future races. The 500 was good for business, especially in Indianapolis. In 1912 Joe Dawson drove a National, another locally built automobile, to victory.

The 500 put Indianapolis on the sporting map. Cars from across the United States and Europe were entered in the race. In 1913 a French-built Peugeot won the contest, and European drivers in European automobiles were victorious in the 1914, 1915, and 1916 races. It was not until the 1920s that Americans and American automobiles once again asserted their dominance. But by then the race itself was more important than the cars or the drivers. By the 1920s it had become an American institution, linking Indianapolis in the minds of people throughout the world with speed and daring.

In an age of athletic boosterism, the Indianapolis 500 was the benchmark. The 1920s was the Golden Age of sports in America. After a long struggle with Victorian notions of respectability, which was anchored to the Protestant work ethic, evangelical religious denominations, and popular concepts of republicanism, sports gained wide popular acceptance. By the 1920s America was tied together as never before by transportation and communication infrastructures. Railroads and highways crisscrossed the country; newspapers, magazines, and the radio covered the events of the day; consumption of sports reached new levels. Throughout the decade sports heroes dominated the headlines—Babe Ruth and Lou Gehrig in baseball, Jack Dempsey and Gene Tunney in boxing, Red Grange in football, Big Bill Tilden in tennis, and Bobby Jones in golf.

Sports were so popular during the 1920s that entrepreneurs and boosters attempted to use athletics and sports heroes to advance the reputations of their towns. In 1923, for instance, citizens of Shelby, Montana, a small town on the edge of a rich oil field, paid heavyweight champion Jack Dempsey $300,000 to defend his title in their community. Other towns staged golf exhibitions with Bobby Jones or Walter Hagen or tennis events with Big Bill Tilden. But no city had a single event like the Indianapolis 500. Year after year it attracted national and international attention.

If the Indianapolis 500 was the major sporting event held in the city each year, there were other less important activities that filled out the sporting calendar. High school and college sports attracted considerable attention. The Butler University football and basketball teams, coached by the legendary Paul D. "Tony" Hinkle, provided decades of solid entertainment. Although Purdue University to the northwest and Indiana University to the south provided more nationally prominent teams, Butler was always capable of defeating one of the bigger universities on its schedule. In addition, the final games of the state high school basketball tournament held in Butler Fieldhouse became the focus of the state's winter sports activities. All schools, large and small, played in the tournament, and they all played for the same title. This arrangement, though patently unfair to small schools, did produce a series of David and Goliath matches, and occasionally an underdog champion. Probably the most famous basketball game ever played in Indiana was the 1954 championship contest between Muncie Central and tiny Milan, which had only 73 boys in the entire school. It has been estimated that when Milan's Bobby Plump hit a 15–foot jump shot to win the game in the final second, 90 percent of all Indiana families were watching the game on television or listening to it on the radio.

The high school tournament did not allow African-American high schools to compete until 1942, when the Indiana High School Athletic Association responded to wartime pressures and integrated high school sports to conform to the American ideal of democracy. Indeed, en route to the 1954 championship, Milan defeated Indianapolis Crispus Attucks, an all-black high school which boasted a talented 6´3´´ sophomore forward named Oscar Robertson. (Robertson went on to lead Crispus Attucks to the 1955 and 1956 state titles and became one of the greatest players in the history of the game.) But even then an integrated state championship did not mean that sports—or life—in Indianapolis was color-blind.

Segregation in professional sports extended beyond World War II, both nationally and in Indianapolis. Organized baseball was not integrated until 1946 when Jackie Roosevelt Robinson broke the "color line" by signing a contract with the Brooklyn Dodgers. Before then Robinson played with the Kansas City Monarchs in the segregated Negro American League. Several Indianapolis teams played in the Negro Leagues. The Indianapolis ABCs—named for their sponsor, the American Brewing Company—was one of the leading barnstorming teams and members of the Negro National League between 1914 and 1924.

The all-black Indianapolis Clowns of the Negro American League gained even greater fame than the ABCs. Although the Clowns played a serious brand of baseball, the team was best known for its showmanship and flamboyant style. The Clowns were baseball's equivalent to basketball's Harlem Globetrotters. Barnstorming the country during the 1930s and first half of the 1940s, they occasionally played in grass skirts and painted bodies, and used such names as Selassie, Mofike, Wahoo, and Tarzan. Like the Harlem Globtrotters, the Indianapolis Clowns survived the integration of professional sports, but they did so at the price of racial stereotyping. They were popular precisely because they conformed to white stereotypes of blacks as naturally talented, undisciplined, even amusing athletes, players more intent on providing a good laugh than winning the game.

The integration of professional sports meant less for Indianapolis than many other large cities. The reason was simple enough: Indianapolis was not a major sports town. During the mid–1950s and mid–1970s it did not have a franchise in the National Football League, the National Basketball Association, or baseball's National or American Leagues. It was, in the argot of professional sports, a bush league town, and that image plagued the city's civic leaders, particularly when the city began a slow economic decline in the 1960s. Called Naptown and India-no-place, it lived in the shadow of Chicago, St. Louis, and Cincinnati, cities with richer major league sporting traditions and histories.

Indianapolis turned to sports to upgrade its image. The process began in the administration of Mayor Richard Lugar (1968 –1976). In 1973 developers approached Lugar with plans to build a new basketball arena for the American Basketball Association's Indiana Pacers on Indianapolis' north side, close to the city's wealthiest suburbs. Lugar liked the idea of a modern basketball arena—it was, after all, demeaning to have a professional franchise play at the State Fairgrounds—but not the location. He envisioned a revived, not diminished, downtown. His solution was to build Market Square Arena (MSA) in the heart of the downtown and use it as the anchor for a planned urban revival. The arena was completed in 1974 at a cost of $16.4 million. The Pacers moved into MSA that same year, and at the time it was one of the finest basketball arenas in the country. In 1975 the Pacers became one of the ABA franchises to be successfully merged into the National Basketball Association, a move that probably would not have occurred had the team still been playing at the Fairgrounds. Indianapolis was no longer a minor league town.

Sports and urban revival became even more closely intertwined during the administration of Mayor William H. Hudnut III (1976–1992). During Hudnut's first two years in office a policy group that included leading government officials, real estate developers, business leaders, Chamber of Commerce members, and representatives of local foundations and trusts made and studied proposals for the economic development of Indianapolis. As Hudnut later wrote, the group wanted Indianapolis to become "a destination city rather than a pass through city." The members realized that the American economy had fundamentally changed, and that service, entertainment, and high tech industries were replacing the country's traditional heavy industries. In line with these developments, the policy group targeted amateur sports, conventions and tourism, culture and arts, educational research, and health and medical technology as areas for development. And rather than pour money into the suburbs, they decided to redevelop the downtown to achieve their goals.

During the 1980s Hudnut guided Indianapolis toward the realization of the master plan. Several older structures were restored to give the city a cleaner look: Monument Circle was bricked; the city market was refurbished; Union Station was rid of drunks and dope addicts, given a face-lift, and transformed into a "festival marketplace"; and two old movie palaces were renovated to house the Indianapolis Symphony Orchestra and the Indiana Repertory Theatre.

New hotels and restaurants were built in anticipation of increased downtown traffic. In addition, ground was broken for Circle Centre, a mammoth downtown mall.

Sports development, however, was the engine that drove all the other activities. Between 1979 and 1989 the city, supported by large contributions from the Lilly Endowment and several other foundations, spent $126.4 million dollars to build a sports infrastructure. Most of the money ($121.9 million) was used in athletic facilities in the downtown area, where the city built the Indianapolis Sports Center (1979, $7 million), the Indiana University Natatorium (1982, $21.5 million), the Indiana University Track and Field Stadium (1982, $5.9 million), the Hoosier Dome (1984, $77.5 million), the Indiana/World Skating Academy (1987, $7 million), and renovated the Indianapolis Sports Center (1988, $3 million). Outside of the downtown the city constructed the Major Taylor Velodrome (1982, $2.5 million), the William Kuntz Soccer Complex (1987, $1.3 million), and the Rowing Course at Eagle Creek Park (1987, $0.7 million).

The investment paid handsome dividends. The facilities attracted numerous amateur sports events to Indianapolis. The Indiana Sports Corporation, a not-for-profit organization that has coordinated efforts to bring amateur sports events to the city, has hosted the National Sports Festival (1982), the National Collegiate Athletic Association basketball finals (1980, 1986, 1991), and the Pan American Games (1987), as well as other regional, national, and international competitions. It also succeeded in convincing several amateur sports organizations to establish headquarters in Indianapolis.

In the process "India-no-place" became the "amateur sports capital of the world." Sports gave Indianapolis a new, improved national image. National magazines and newspapers dubbed Indianapolis the "Cinderella of the Rustbelt," the "Star of the Snowbelt," and "Cornbelt city with Sunbelt sizzle." The infrastructure developments also helped Indianapolis become a major league professional sports town. The construction of the Hoosier Dome was essential to the city's acquiring the Colts of the National Football League in 1984. "We are becoming major league, growing, I hope, to greatness," Hudnut announced after the Colts' decision became public. In the minds of Hudnut and the developers of modern Indianapolis, being a major league sports city was a prerequisite to emerging out of the shadow of Chicago, St. Louis, and Cincinnati and becoming an important American city.

Only in the 1990s did the cost of the focused development become apparent. Dollars spent to develop a sports infrastructure in Indianapolis' downtown were dollars not spent to upgrade the city's poorer neighborhoods, social services, and public health programs. In particular, African-American residents complained that the sports first strategy gave millions of dollars to already wealthy developers and left them with only a handful of custodial jobs, jobs which did not pay enough to buy high-priced Pacers or Colts tickets.

Those issues will undoubted be debated well into the next century, particularly as some boosters and developers clamor for the city to build a new baseball park to attract a major league baseball team. But the debate should not obscure Indianapolis' sporting heritage and achievements. Sports has influenced the city's development for over a century. It undoubtedly will help shape the future.

See also: AMATEUR SPORTS GOVERNING BODIES; BASEBALL; BASKETBALL; FOOTBALL; INDIANAPOLIS 500–MILE RACE; and individual names, sports, and organizations.

TRANSPORTATION

Ralph D. Gray

An efficient transportation network is essential to a city's economic well-being and the safety and comfort of its citizens. Indianapolis in the 1990s can point with justifiable pride to its basic transportation infrastructure—an extensive system of road, rail, and air transport facilities that links the city to all parts of the country and the world and continues to give reality to the state's motto, "Crossroads of America." A remarkably complete network of interstate and state highways, expressways and boulevards, roads and streets gives even the remotest corner easy access to all other destinations within Marion County. As an automobile city, however, Indianapolis has limited public mass transit facilities and few plans to develop more. Of more immediate concern in the 1990s were ways to improve upon the existing system by accommodating the ever-increasing number of cars and trucks through resurfaced roadways and additional parking and terminal facilities, by expanding air transport services and facilities, and by rescuing the railroads from total abandonment.

Indianapolis exemplifies the transportation changes that have occurred in America since 1820, beginning with river and road improvements. The prospects of extensive river navigation, coupled with a site near the center of the state, were largely responsible for the location of the new state capital at a point near where Fall Creek empties into the west fork of White River. But the river proved not to be navigable over extended periods for vessels more sophisticated than rafts and flatboats. In 1831, planning to haul stone for the National Road, Captain Robert Hanna brought the steamboat named for him up the river to Indianapolis, but when he attempted to descend the river the vessel grounded. It remained stuck for several weeks. Not until 1865, when the *Governor Morton* was launched at Indianapolis, did steamboating reappear on White River, and then only briefly. This vessel sank at its moorings in 1866 and was scuttled. Although Indianapolis historian Jacob Piatt Dunn, writing in 1910, insisted that the river was a "navigable stream," given minor improvements at obstructed points, and could point to much early legislation based on the same assumption, the state instead expended its money for water improve-

Ralph D. Gray is Professor of History at Indiana University–Purdue University, Indianapolis.

ments on canal projects. Consequently, no two-way traffic developed on the river, and the attempt to provide this by means of a canal through Indianapolis proved equally futile.

Indiana participated fully in the internal improvements movement that swept through the Old Northwest in the 1830s. In 1836, after more than a year of intense discussion, the Indiana General Assembly adopted a "Mammoth Internal Improvement" program that called for the construction of eight road, river, canal, and railroad projects expected to cost in excess of $10,000,000. Among the projects authorized, and by far the most expensive one, was the Central Canal designed to connect the Wabash and Erie Canal (running between Toledo, Ohio, and Lafayette, Indiana) with the Ohio River at Evansville via Indianapolis. Although the state expended more than $800,000 in construction costs on this huge undertaking before a financial collapse in 1839 halted all such work, only nine miles of canal between Broad Ripple and Indianapolis were completed, watered, and put into local operation for a few years. Subsequently millers and recreational boaters used the canal, and in the 20th century the towpath has been frequented by hikers, bikers, and joggers. Today the canal offers a scenic, park-like vista to onlookers while also serving to bring water from the river to the Indianapolis Water Company's filtration plant near West 16th Street, but as a long-distance transportation artery it was a total failure.

Given its misfortunes in waterway endeavors, the city necessarily devoted much attention to overland travel and traffic. Its status as state capital required roads from outlying regions into the political center, and in 1821, shortly after a commission had located the city, the legislature authorized the construction of ten new "state roads" converging in Indianapolis. The majority of these roads approached the city from the south and southeast, where the state's early population had concentrated, but additional roads leading to the city from all directions soon appeared. Most important for Indianapolis's early recognition as the transportation hub of the state was the location of the National Road and the Michigan Road. The former road, authorized by Congress in 1806 but constructed primarily between 1815 and 1852, stretched westward from Cumberland, Maryland, toward the Mississippi River at St. Louis. Passing through Indiana and Indianapolis in the 1830s, it became the major east-west highway in America during the pre–Civil War period and brought thousands of settlers to the state and to its capital. Similarly, the Michigan Road, connecting Madison on the Ohio River with Michigan City on Lake Michigan, was the main north-south route through the state and crossed the National Road near the center of Indianapolis. Essentially complete by 1839, this road brought travelers and considerable trade to the city from the prosperous Ohio Valley and contributed to the growth of the northern sector of the state. These and other roads in central Indiana at this time, however, were little more than marked trails through the countryside, unpaved and often unimproved beyond the removal of trees and only the taller stumps. Effective overland travel to and through Indianapolis awaited further improvements by way of new technology.

That technology was the railroad, introduced into the United States in the early 1830s and into Indianapolis in 1847. Railroads had been discussed in Indiana since the 1820s and several companies were chartered by the state legislature in 1832 and afterwards. But no lines were completed until the Madison and Indianapolis Railroad reached its destination on October 1, 1847. On that day two trains puffed majestically into the city, greeted by the governor and a wildly enthusiastic crowd. The successful completion of this long-awaited railroad touched off a railroad-building boom within the state, and within five years Indianapolis was the hub of a rail as well as a road system, with seven separate lines entering the city from all directions. These included the Indianapolis and Bellefontaine, the Terre Haute and Richmond, the Peru and Indianapolis, the Indianapolis and Cincinnati, and the Indianapolis and Lafayette railroad companies. By the end of the decade, when more than 2,000 miles of track crisscrossed the state, each of the major cities within the state was linked to the capital city.

The proprietors of the railroads entering the city cooperated in building a single line—a union railway—that connected the lines with each other for greater ease and safety in freight interchange. (This concept was expanded upon in the 1870s, when a U-shaped "belt railroad" on the west, south, and east sides of the city connected all the lines serving Indianapolis.) The early companies also cooperated in building—in 1853, for the first time anywhere—a union station. Located on South Illinois Street, where the second (and current) Union Station now stands, the original structure spanned the tracks of five lines and facilitated passenger interchange. Most significantly, however, the nation's fifth largest railroad network in 1860 had a powerful impact upon the state's economy.

Indianapolis in particular benefited from its new status as a railroad center, soon earning the sobriquet, "The Railroad City." Not only did the population of Indianapolis jump from 8,091 in 1850 (not yet first in the state) to 18,611 in 1860 (and first place by a large margin), but its economic transformation was equally broad and dramatic. Stockyards, agricultural processing plants, manufacturing establishments, and countless wholesale and retail businesses appeared in the capital city, clustered in areas adjacent to rail lines, and they all aided in developing Indianapolis into a major urban center. By 1880 at least a dozen rail lines radiated from the city, and in 1888, when the new Union Station was ready for use, 80 passenger trains a day from 16 different railroads arrived at the station, and that number increased to 150 trains daily by 1900. The late 19th century also witnessed various unsavory tactics by the railroads as they increasingly dominated the economic and political life of the nation, but their role as the primary carrier of goods and people in the interior region of the state was unchallenged until the early 20th century.

Given the railroad's virtual monopoly on intercity travel, it is understandable that little was done to improve the roads and streets within the state. Such improvements were the province of local governments, yet they commanded few resources for the task. Some county road improvements, inadequate at best, resulted from the obligation of all males between the ages of 21 and 50 to work on the roads from two to four days a year, but more was done by private companies given the right to charge a toll upon roads they had improved, usually by simple grading and graveling procedures. At the same time, a few city streets were paved with stone, wooden block, or brick. In Indianapolis, in addition to Washington Street (which had been "macadamized" to carry the National Road through the city), a few downtown city streets were paved shortly after the Civil War. By 1874, however, only 12 miles of streets had been hard-surfaced, either "bowlderized" (cobblestoned) or paved with pine blocks; the remaining 140 miles were either graveltopped or dirt streets. Both types were disagreeably muddy in wet and dusty in dry weather.

During the administration of Mayor Thomas A. Taggart, who had pointed out that in 1891 the city had only a "trivial quantity of improved streets" and few of the "many other characteristics that make a substantial city," a start was made in developing a boulevard system. Broad, scenic routes, mainly along natural waterways, were laid out by the new city parks department, and this work was expanded upon later during the City Beautiful movement that swept the nation in the early 20th century.

An important change in the central city also occurred between 1905 and 1920, involving elevation of all the railroad tracks entering Union Station. This reconstruction effort, costing in excess of $10 million, eliminated both the 43-year-old tunnel that had carried Illinois Street under the tracks and the Virginia Avenue viaduct, a landmark repeatedly condemned as unsafe, that had carried traffic over the tracks for 27 years. Newspaperman William Herschell, writing in 1912, believed that trains had "menaced life" in the southern part of the city since 1847, but the elevation project, by eliminating a series of dangerous grade crossings, would permit the people of Indianapolis once again to take pride in its appellation, "The Railroad City."

Even if the street surfaces left much to be desired, the beginnings of regularly scheduled public mass transit had come as early as 1864. In that year, on October 3 (just in time for the Indiana State Fair in Military Park), mule-drawn, 12–seat streetcars were placed into service on a one-mile line between Union Station and the park. Mayor John Caven handled the reins on the first trip up Illinois Street, as officials of the Citizens Street Railway Company filled the car. Soon other lines opened along Virginia, Massachusetts, and Fort Wayne avenues, and the Illinois line reached all the way north to Crown Hill Cemetery by 1867.

A major improvement in the streetcar system came in 1890, when the first electric streetcars were put into operation shortly after their use had been pioneered elsewhere. Again introduced along the Illinois Street line, amid even larger crowds than had welcomed the first steam locomotive into the city four decades earlier, the electric cars replaced their mule-drawn predecessors almost instantly. By 1894, electrification of the city system was complete and the mules had been turned out to pasture.

By this time, of course, many more remarkable transportation changes were in the offing. The 1890s witnessed not only the advent of the electric interurban (streetcars running between as well as within cities), but also the heyday of the bicycle and the birth of the automobile. All of these developments had, and continue to have, an enormous impact upon urban transportation, economic development, and residential housing patterns.

The great popularity of bicycles in the 1890s, following the dual development of the "safety" bicycle and pneumatic tires, awakened the American people to the possibilities of independent travel over long distances. This in turn led to a greatly increased demand for improved roads, something farmers had long been seeking without success. The cyclists' campaign dovetailed nicely with the arrival of rural free delivery, for rural mail carriers also required improved roads in order to make their deliveries at all times of the year, but even the added voices of motorists, after the automobile appeared on the scene in significant numbers following 1900, led to little in the way of smooth-paved, reliable intercity roads until after World War I.

In the meantime, the adaptation of electric streetcar technology to intercity travel brought a rapidly increasing number of interurbans into Indianapolis. Introduced elsewhere in the state during the 1890s, the initial interurban car entered downtown Indianapolis from Greenwood on January 1, 1900. Other early lines came in from Terre Haute, Lafayette, Kokomo, Fort Wayne, Richmond, Shelbyville, and Mooresville. The large number of interurban lines converging at the capital soon led to construction of the celebrated Traction Terminal Building (1904), its open-ended train shed covering nine sets of tracks. All but one of the 13 interurban lines serving Indianapolis converged at the terminal, located on Market Street near the State House. At one time more than 600 trains a day used the terminal, carrying as many as 7 million passengers a year as well as considerable amounts of freight. Boasting of a 2,400–mile network of interurban lines, Indiana in general and Indianapolis in particular was known as the "Interurban Capital of the World." Every major city in the state, excepting only Evansville to the southwest, was connected to Indianapolis via this outstanding rail system; the "cars" also tied the first suburbs of Indianapolis closely to the central business district and promoted the growth of both.

In the 1920s, however, the interurbans confronted a rival system of transportation for individual passengers that eventually doomed the former system. Not only did the automobile become enormously popular, with widespread ownership and use, but troubled economic conditions within the industry and, later, the entire country forced the interurbans to their knees. Only the South Shore line, more of a heavy-duty electric railroad than a true interurban, in northwest Indiana has survived to this time. The last interurban train operating from Indianapolis belonged to the Indiana, Columbus and Southern Traction Company, the successor company to the first interurban line into the city, and its operations came to an abrupt halt following an accident in September, 1941.

One of the most powerful influences on the way Americans lived during the 20th century was the automobile. A late 19th century development, resulting from a series of technological discoveries in both Europe and the United States, the automobile appeared in Indiana and then in Indianapolis during the middle years of the 1890s. Its impact as a determining factor in the way cities function was not felt until the early years of the new century. Ultimately the burgeoning industry spread to more than 50 cities throughout the state. Among the automobiles manufactured in Indianapolis were the superbly engineered Marmon (1902); the Waverly (1903), an electric; the Premier (1903); the Overland (1903), moved from Terre Haute to Indianapolis in 1907; the National (1904), after earlier producing the National Electric in 1900; the Cole (1909); the Pathfinder (1911); the Stutz (1913), particularly its famed "Bearcat"; and the Duesenberg (1920), perhaps the finest automobile ever crafted, the production of which the Duesenberg brothers had moved to Indianapolis from Elizabeth, New Jersey, in order to be near the Indianapolis Motor Speedway.

According to a listing of Indiana-built automobiles compiled in 1967, more than 250 different makes of cars and trucks originated in Indiana, including 50 in Indianapolis. As late as 1920, nearly 100,000 motor vehicles a year rolled out of the Indianapolis factories. By that time, however, Henry Ford had revolutionized the production of automobiles, his assembly-line techniques bringing the cost of a new car (as little as $295 at one time) down to within the limits of the general population and driving most of his competition out of business. Gradually the Indianapolis manufacturers dropped by the wayside, but the Indianapolis Motor Speedway, built in 1909 and home to its famed 500–mile race since 1911, is a vivid reminder of the days when Indianapolis rivaled Detroit as a motor capital. Indianapolis-built cars (a Marmon and a National) won the first two 500–mile races, and Indianapolis has remained a major supplier of parts and accessories for the motor vehicle industry.

For city administrators, however, the most salient fact about the automobile revolution in America was the insatiable demand it unleashed for better and safer roads and streets on which to operate, and for places to park at their destination. Automobiles also required fuel and frequent maintenance; by 1940, 33 service stations offered both within the downtown Mile Square. There was also the problem of traffic safety and control. As early as 1922, Mayor Lew Shank mounted a strong attack on speeding motorists within the city. The speed limits at that time were 10 miles per hour in business sections, 20 in residential sections, and 30 in outlying areas, but enforcement was lax. In December, 1922, however, following the deaths of two young women struck by a speeding motorist, the mayor ordered arrests and jail terms for all speeders. He was forced to abandon such extralegal procedures, but his point had been made. That it needed to be reasserted periodically is clear from the poor safety record of the city in subsequent decades.

The Virginia Avenue viaduct, built to carry traffic over rail lines,
became unnecessary after the tracks were elevated in the early 20th century.
[Indiana Historical Society, Bass Collection #91483]

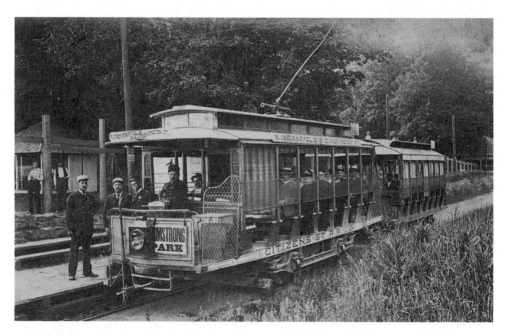

A North Indianapolis and East Washington Street summer streetcar, ca. 1910.
[Indiana Historical Society]

During World War II, with its resultant restrictions on consumer goods, including of course gasoline and tires, there were sharp drops in automobile travel and, therefore, accidents. At the same time, mass transit systems responded well to the demand for increased services. The *India-*

napolis Star reported in 1943 that the "transportation battle on the local front" had been won, although war demands had strained the capacities of the city's streetcars, buses, trackless trolleys, and taxicabs. Ridership on the streetcars, the most heavily used system, reached 10.1 million in December, 1941, up 49 percent over that of December, 1940, and an average of 15,000 persons a day (21,000 on Sundays) used the 900 to 1,000 buses operating in and out of the Traction Terminal Building.

Even so, following the conclusion of war, Americans returned to their private automobiles as rapidly as possible and all of the trends so disturbing to city planners resumed. Their attention focused on the congested city streets and the lack of adequate downtown parking, with such expedients as parking meters (an innovation first used in Oklahoma City in 1935) and the institution of one-way streets being undertaken. Paradoxically, perhaps, the planners also called for additional expressways and thoroughfares. Of particular concern, however, was the failure of the city to have conducted a survey of its traffic patterns and the growing demands for parking. Civic leaders recognized that parking facilities for the future should be planned, not randomly placed in vacant building lots. But the practice continued; in 1960, 24 of 78 city blocks in the downtown area were used for parking, with another third of the area used for streets and alleys.

This planning-needs theme was expanded upon by businessman Robert S. Norwood, who commented in 1945 that solving its traffic and parking problems was vital to the city's continued economic growth. Norwood also suggested a positive side to what many considered a detriment—the absence of mountains or large bodies of water near the city—when he pointed out that "no major obstacles hinder its well-ordered . . . four-way directional growth." Other voices spoke out regarding the city's transportation problems, but no comprehensive analysis was made until 1957 when the Barton Transportation Study, initiated by future mayor John J. Barton, was issued. It called for additional one-way streets, widened intersections, and the removal of dangerous "jogs" in various main thoroughfares, ideas that when carried out did reduce impediments to an orderly traffic flow within the city. A more comprehensive study followed in 1968, which laid the basis for additional thoroughfare construction and reductions in traffic flow congestion, but its recommendations for a revitalized mass transit system did not materialize. Indianapolis has remained a driving city, with automobiles, usually with only one occupant, bringing nine of every ten workers to the central city daily, and parking has remained in the hands of private businesses or as adjuncts to various governmental institutions. In the 1980s, however, a few low-rise garages and underground parking facilities under city and state government auspices were built.

The last electric streetcar on rails was taken out of service in January, 1953, after which time a combination of trackless trolleys and motor buses provided basic intracity transportation. The city's 440 public transit vehicles in 1952, traveling 43,000 miles daily, carried 72 million passengers. As commuters turned to personal automobiles, however, a slow but steady decline in passengers and mileage set in, so that 30 years later the city bus line carried 15 million riders along 50 routes while traveling approximately 20,000 miles a day. Since 1975 bus service has been provided by the Indianapolis Public Transportation Corporation, also known as the Metro system, a public corporation heavily subsidized by federal, state, and city taxes. In recent years federal assistance has declined (from $4.9 million in 1981 to $2.9 million in 1990), state support has remained stable at approximately $3 million a year, while local funding has doubled since 1981 to approximately $4.2 million in 1990. At the same time, income from users of the service has remained steady or declined somewhat, because fare increases—from a basic rate of 20 cents in

1960 to 75 cents (but $1 during rush hours) in 1990—have been followed by decreases in the number of passengers.

Metro has made many improvements and modifications in its equipment, routes, and promotional activities, including the inauguration of such new services as circular routes downtown and bus stop shelters in residential areas. More, however, in the way of an integrated program to keep automobiles out of the center city while expanding the frequency and duration of city bus operations will be necessary in order for Indianapolis to have an efficient and effective public mass transit system. The alternatives are increased air pollution and traffic congestion, both of which can threaten continued growth of the downtown area and the mobility and employment opportunities of its citizens. In addition to the bus system, public transportation services include more than a dozen taxicab companies, the largest of which are Yellow Cab and Metro Taxi, and an assortment of limousine, van, and charter bus services.

Of inestimable significance to the city of Indianapolis are the interstate highways that converge there. Seven interstate "spokes," more than radiate from any other city in the nation, reach out in all directions (except southwest); moreover, these seven routes are connected to each other by means of I-465, a "circumurban" or belt highway some 55 miles long (53.6 miles in the inner lane, 55.6 miles in the outer lane) that was completed in 1970. The seven interstates—I-65 north to Chicago, I-65 south to Louisville, I-74 northwest to Crawfordsville and Peoria, I-74 southeast to Cincinnati, I-70 west to Terre Haute and St. Louis, I-70 east to Columbus and Pittsburgh, and I-69 (the Industrial Highway) northeast to Fort Wayne and connections in Michigan via I-94 to Detroit—are, of course, part of the 41,000–mile interstate and national defense highway system authorized by Congress in 1956 (and later expanded). Completed in the 1970s, they have helped Indianapolis continue its claim to be located at the true crossroads in the "Crossroads of America" state; they have also transformed the industrial locations of the city, stimulated the development of business clusters and a variety of industrial parks at highway interchanges, and given a powerful boost to the trucking industry centered in Indianapolis.

I-465 now carries more than 100,000 vehicles a day, second in the state only to I-80/94 in northwest Indiana. Its good safety record overall improved markedly in 1974, when the interstate speed limit was lowered from 70 to 55 miles per hour. There are 31 interchanges on the beltway, providing access to the six national highways and other major thoroughfares that also converge on the state capital. In 1966, only four years after the first four-lane section of I-465 (on the northwest side) was opened and long before all sections were complete, it was decided to widen the entire route from 4 to 6 lanes. The entire beltway was originally built at a cost of $115 million. A four-year reconstruction project undertaken in 1990 to repair the northeast quadrant will cost an estimated $75 million.

The interstates, of course, divert most long-distance travel and freight from clogged city streets that previously served as national roads, and have spawned suburban growth along the new travel corridors. Although suburban shopping centers antedate the interstate highway system, gigantic new shopping malls such as Castleton Square, easily accessible from the interstates and offering virtually unlimited parking, joined with older malls such as Glendale in siphoning retail business from downtown Indianapolis. It remains to be seen whether the downtown development of the 1990s, including the Circle Centre Mall, can reverse this trend significantly.

Moreover, and perhaps unwittingly, by routing I-465 some 11.5 miles north of the city center, but only 4.5 miles south of it, the highway planners spurred growth on the north side, particularly in southern Hamilton and Boone counties, both of which are touched by the interstate, but delayed growth on the south side. By running, however, two interstates through the heart of the city, the so-called "inner loop" with a dangerous "spaghetti bowl" configuration at the point where the two routes join and then diverge, the planners have also seen to it that interstates serve much of the suburban population as convenient (except in rush hours) routes into and away from the heart of the city. This latter feature, along with the development of new downtown attractions, has given renewed confidence to downtown business owners and developers regarding a viable economic future for the heart of the city.

Trucking in America began almost as soon as the automobile appeared, but the primitiveness of the early trucks, built on automobile frames and using solid rubber tires (which vibrated violently at speeds above 15 miles per hour), as well as the absence of decent intercity roads (of the nation's 2,000,000 miles of roads in 1904, 1,846,336 miles were unimproved), prevented a significant industry from developing until the 1920s. The performance of these rudimentary trucks during General Pershing's expedition into Mexico in 1916–1917, followed by outstanding accomplishments by the Motor Freight Corps during World War I, demonstrated the reliability and versatility of the truck. When the good roads movement of the early 20th century finally bore fruit—helped, ironically, by railroad companies expecting additional farm commodity traffic because of improved farm-to-railhead roads—the modern trucking industry was born. In 1916 Congress imposed a federal gasoline tax designed to raise money for building hard-surfaced roads throughout the nation. This was made available to states with highway departments and an acceptable road-building plan that would connect county seats and all other large cities and towns. Consequently Indiana, like many other states, established a state highway department in 1917. Although it had to be reconstituted in 1919, the new department directed the construction of an extensive highway network that centered on Indianapolis.

Meanwhile, basic improvements in truck technology, especially tires, braking systems, and overall durability, laid the foundations for the movement of local and long-distance commercial freight on rubber and concrete. Although the earliest Indianapolis trucking companies started their operations prior to 1920, most of the area's largest firms date from the 1920s and 1930s. By 1950 the trucking industry was among the largest in the city and the state, with more than 3,000 companies and 167,000 employees statewide. Ten years later, 242,000 Hoosiers, including 42,000 in Marion County, earned livelihoods directly from trucking. This latter figure included nearly 3,400 workers at the International Harvester Company's truck engine plant, the largest in the world. By that time, too, more than 100 common carrier lines had Interstate Commerce Commission authority to serve Indianapolis. Most of them also had terminal facilities in the city and some of them had licenses to serve cities nationwide. Truckers delivered more than 50 percent of the products manufactured within Marion County, more than 80 percent of the wholesale goods received there. Among specialized trucking operations also centered in Indianapolis were long-distance household goods moving companies, with three of the industry giants— Mayflower, American Red Ball (the oldest in the state if not the nation, dating from 1921), and Wheaton Van Lines—headquartered in Indianapolis. Its centralized location, geographically and demographically, and the number of highways concentrated there made the city a natural choice for these operations.

The airline industry is also an important part of the transportation services available in Indianapolis. Commercial air transport came to the city in 1931, following completion of the Indianapolis Municipal Airport on the southwest outskirts of Marion County. World War I ace Weir Cook, for whom the airport was named in 1944, had helped select the site and design its facilities in 1928. Planned with an eye on future expansion as well as safety considerations, it has served the community and the entire central Indiana–eastern Illinois area well for more than 60 years. As early as 1934 four major carriers provided service to Indianapolis, and this number rose to six passenger lines (four trunk line carriers—American, Delta, Eastern, and TWA; two local service carriers—Lake Central and Ozark) and four freight carriers by 1967. By then, too, jet travel had been inaugurated (1964), the main runway having been extended to the required 10,000 feet. In 1967 the total number of passengers in and out of Weir Cook each year exceeded 1.3 million, having doubled during the decade. For that same period, airmail and air freight poundage had both tripled, to 9 million and 69 million pounds respectively. Of course, the growth of airline passenger service, among other factors, has had a devastating impact upon railroad passenger service; in 1990, only one or two Amtrak passenger trains a day operated out of Indianapolis's once teeming Union Station.

In 1976, over the opposition of traditionalists and those who had known Captain Weir Cook, the name of the airport was changed to Indianapolis International Airport. This better reflected the expanded role of the facility, including the award of Foreign Trade Zone status, and its future expectations. Additional new construction, including major renovations to the terminal building and the erection of new automobile parking and airplane maintenance facilities, occurred in the 1980s, and additional expansion will be required in the 1990s. Despite the bankruptcy of several carriers following airline deregulation and major restructuring among those remaining, the Indianapolis airport was served by 17 airlines in the early 1990s and remains in a strong competitive position. Although not the hub of any carrier, it has excellent connections with the major hubs in the nation, something that offers a choice of carriers and competitive rates to many travelers from Indianapolis, and it is the "mini-hub" for USAir, the largest carrier in Indianapolis in 1990 with 40 percent of the passengers on its 49 daily flights. In all, by the early 1990s some five million passengers a year passed through Indianapolis International. The airport is also home to American Trans Air, the largest charter airline in the nation. Moreover, in 1991 the U.S. Postal Service selected Indianapolis as the hub for its increasingly voluminous airmail package express service, and United Airlines announced its decision to place a $1 billion aircraft maintenance hub in the city.

Indianapolis has the basis for an outstanding transportation system. Successively the center of the state's pioneer roads and railroads, its interurbans and its automobile industry, in more recent times it is a major hub in the nation's interstate highway system, boasts of one of the largest concentrations of medium- and long-distance trucking companies, enjoys good rail connections for freight if not for passenger service, and has a spacious and modern international airport. Strategically located within a day's drive of 50 percent of the nation's population and several of its largest markets, the city is well equipped from a transportation standpoint for the challenges of the 21st century. It has neither navigable waterways nor an effective public mass transit system, but as an automobile city and as one of the nation's major transportation hubs, its integrated network of road, rail, and air transport facilities is among the best in the nation.

See also: AUTOMOBILE CULTURE; AUTOMOBILE INDUSTRY; AVIATION; INTERURBANS; PUBLIC TRANSPORTATION; RAILROADS; ROADS AND HIGHWAYS; STREETCARS; and individual names and companies.

URBAN ENVIRONMENT

Philip V. Scarpino

A trip by automobile from Monument Circle in the heart of Indianapolis to the far reaches of Marion County and on to adjoining counties is a journey past the material signposts of the city's environmental history. A drive north begins in canyons between downtown high rises, home to an experimental introduction of peregrine falcons. It continues into aging streetcar suburbs, some of which have been restored; over Fall Creek, in places channelized between concrete retaining walls; past increasingly recent automobile suburbs; under the I-465 beltway and beyond, where industrial campuses and subdivisions sprout up amid cornfields and crumbling barns. Over 25 miles to the north in Hamilton County, streets in Westfield numbered 165th and higher testify to Indianapolis' past and projected growth. The automobile, the energy it burns, and the roads it travels upon have played central roles in shaping city and country and in contributing to the evolution of their intertwined and symbiotic histories.

It is not necessary to drive out of Indianapolis to find the environment; it surrounds us. The environmental history of Indianapolis and Marion County is a study of the journey we have taken to arrive at the present, an examination of the interaction between people and this place over time. Although there are many things that we did not create and cannot control, the environment that we inhabit from downtown to suburbs to farm fields is largely a human artifact. It is an artifact that blends varying proportions of natural and artificial elements and that reflects the changing and often conflicting values of those who imposed their own visions of order on city and country.

Most Americans currently live in cities or in suburbs, and in that sense Indianapolis has been typical of the American environmental experience. Since the mid–19th century cities like Indianapolis have evolved in a way that has limited routine contact with nature, created the illusion that people have controlled nature, and masked the vital connections between urbanites and the ecosystems that sustain them. From the beginning of settlement there have been people who had a vision of the city as a place of beauty. Over the course of the city's history many have worked to make their visions come true, from Alexander Ralston's plat for the Mile Square in

Philip V. Scarpino is Associate Professor of History at Indiana University–Purdue University, Indianapolis.

1821, to the movement for city parks and boulevards in late 19th and early 20th centuries, to a series of land-use and development plans drafted by the city from the mid–1960s to the present. At the same time, as Indianapolis expanded and developed, residents and their officials have had to confront the often unintended and unanticipated environmental consequences of mostly unplanned and unregulated growth.

On the near north side of Indianapolis, the Morris-Butler House Museum, built in 1864, sits in the shadow of I-65 and close by the high rises of downtown—two powerful symbols of the environment of the late 20th century juxtaposed against one that represents the 19th century. If Indianapolis is a city of homes, then perhaps the home that these two families occupied from 1864 to 1959 offers a useful device for introducing the environmental history of the city. In many ways the histories of the Morris and Butler families paralleled the environmental history of Indianapolis and Marion County.

Morris Morris was one of the first settlers in the Indianapolis area. He purchased a large piece of property southeast of present-day Washington and Meridian streets. There he set about removing the trees, establishing a farm, and opening one of the community's first gristmills. By 1840, when Indianapolis had grown to a small town of 2,692, there were 26 gristmills and 2 flour mills in Marion County, most of which were powered by water. Mills, and the developing market system of which they were a part, accelerated environmental transformation by encouraging deforestation to expand agricultural production, by damming free-flowing streams, and by discarding their refuse in the water. Jacob Cox's landscape painting *Morris Morris Farm*, done about 1840, shows "Morris hole" on Pogue's Run in the foreground, a place where cattle drank and boys swam. By late in the 19th century Morris Morris' farm had itself been incorporated into the expanding city. Pogue's Run had become an open sewer, the symbol and substance of the environmental impact of rapid, unregulated, and largely unplanned urban, industrial growth.

Settlers like Morris migrated to an area that had been occupied by Native Americans for thousands of years; from the settlers' perspective, however, this was new land, a wilderness inhabited by wild animals and wild people. In the 1820s Marion County was covered with the beech-maple forest typical of most of central Indiana, which in turn was populated with an abundance of forest-dwelling insects, birds, and animals. White River, Fall Creek, Pogue's Run, and other streams and wetlands, like Bacon's Swamp, abounded with aquatic life and seasonally hosted flocks of migratory waterfowl. Morris and other pioneers initiated profound changes in the environment by removing the forest for agriculture, an act that they believed improved the land, enhanced its productivity, and promoted progress.

Destruction of the forest habitat, along with unregulated hunting and fishing for personal use and for market, brought an accompanying reduction in numbers and diversity of fish and wildlife. Especially hard hit were those species with economic value, such as furbearers, or those deemed dangerous or destructive, such as bears, wolves, snakes, and gars. At the same time, other species of plants and animals found favorable niches in the newly humanized environment. "Weeds" and "pests" prospered as land in Marion County underwent the conversion from forest to farms. As Indianapolis expanded and enveloped farmland during the 19th and 20th centuries, other species of native and exotic plants and animals adapted and flourished in the city.

This significant alteration in the visual landscape and in the biological composition resulted from acting on an important cluster of values and attitudes toward nature. Settlers thought of land as property, to be bought and sold and used as the owner wished. Indeed, Indianapolis and Marion County had already been subject to the rectangular survey, which facilitated sale to private individuals by superimposing an orderly grid on a diverse landscape. Settlers also considered nature and the products of nature (trees, furs, minerals, crops) as commodities that had a cash value in a market. Other important and related attitudes included the belief that God created nature to serve people; that progress was measured by improving nature; that improvement required that nature be conquered and controlled; and that nature could be divided into good and bad, useful and useless, flowers and weeds, game and varmints. The triumvirate of property, commodity, and market, along with a number of corollary attitudes, separated the settlers from the Native Americans, and though challenged by the post–World War II environmental movement, it has continued to play a role in shaping the environment of Indianapolis and Marion County.

The sons of Morris Morris were active in developing the city, including promotion of the railroad. Arrival of the railroad in 1847 initiated rapid transformation of Indianapolis. Railroads not only used coal, but they also transported it and made possible a far-reaching shift to fossil fuel. Fossil fuel in the form of coal, natural gas during the gas boom of the late 19th century, and petroleum in the 20th century provided exponentially increasing amounts of energy that powered the growth of the city in terms of size, commercial activity, and manufacturing. Population more than doubled between 1850 and 1860 and again between 1860 and 1870, climbing from 8,091 to 18,611 to 48,244.

The railroad and accompanying telegraph linked Indianapolis to an increasingly interdependent and interconnected nation and, of equal importance, bound the environmental histories of the city and the surrounding countryside into a common story. Aided by the interurban system that peaked in the 1910s and began to decline in the 1920s, the railroad expanded the markets served by wholesalers and retailers to include a multi-county region in central Indiana. In turn, commodities from the country streamed into the city to support a growing manufacturing base. Much of the industrial growth through the early 20th century depended on timber and on agricultural products such as wheat, corn, and hogs. Demand for coal, agricultural products, and lumber in the city (along with the rectangular survey) shaped the face of the land and the ecosystems of a large hinterland around Indianapolis. At the same time, products from the countryside literally became the city, in the form of raw materials for constructing buildings and infrastructure. They also contributed to its growing stream of wastes.

Rail transportation, a rising use of fossil fuel, expansion of manufacturing and commerce, and growth of the city's population produced a corresponding increase in air pollution, industrial effluents, sewage, and garbage. The capacity of air, land, and water to serve as sinks for wastes and still provide for competing needs such as fresh air and clean water was severely tested. In April, 1870, the *Indianapolis Journal* reported that a city councilman wanted a Mr. Schmidt enjoined "from continuing the nuisance occasioned by running the water from his brewery down the gutters of Wyoming street." In the last third of the 19th century the majority of the city's streets were unpaved, which produced dust when dry and mud when wet. Large numbers of horses and mules housed within the city added their wastes to the dust and mud of the streets. Flies not only found plenty to sustain them but also served as carriers of disease. White River, Fall Creek, the Central Canal, and Pogue's Run became repositories for garbage, effluents from manufacturers, and runoff from unpaved streets. In late May, 1870, the *Daily Sentinel* suggested that steps at once "be taken to clean out the bed of the canal, as the hot sun will soon cause a fearful stench." With the city's population growing exponentially between 1850 and 1870, a multiplying number of outhouses posed a range of problems, including likely contamination of groundwater.

During the mid–20th century, the Central Canal was a neglected site with low water levels and was frequently used for dumping trash. The downtown canal area has since been rejuvenated and is now a pedestrian park, making it a popular destination for downtown workers on their lunch breaks. [Indiana Historical Society, Bass Collection]

After 1870 Indianapolis installed an underground sewer system. In the long run, the unintended and unanticipated consequences of this attempted solution traded one set of problems for another. The system was not well constructed, it was not integrated, and like most other urban sanitary sewers of the time it dumped raw sewage into nearby waterways. A report of the Commercial Club in 1891 noted that the city needed a combined system that could handle street drainage and sewage; that the existing system leaked badly; and that the city's sewers conveyed street runoff and sewage to "the river, Pleasant run, Pogue's run, Fall creek and the canal." Pogue's Run was especially contaminated and in 1914 the city confirmed the stream's new status when it diverted the portion within the Mile Square into underground sewers. The *Indianapolis News* reported on May 23, 1925, that the city opened its first sewage treatment plant, which was the outcome of lawsuits filed by property owners on the White River below Indianapolis. The suits alleged that the river had become so foul that stock could not be watered from it and crops could not be grown along its banks. Water quality in the city's rivers and streams did not show significant improvement until the 1980s.

The white middle and upper classes who benefited disproportionately from economic growth in the city also possessed the means to relocate to more pleasant surroundings. One of

Morris Morris' sons, John, followed this trend and sold his property in the center of the city. He bought land in the College Corners subdivision; there, in 1864, he built a Second Empire–style home that still stands at 1204 Park Avenue. Both the land that he sold and the land he bought were divided into lots and blocks, which like the rectangular survey permitted efficient buying and selling of property. Undoubtedly John Morris and his family fled the smoke, dust, mud, smells, noise, and commotion of the city center in favor of the more pleasant surroundings and contact with nature offered by College Corners. With the advent of the mule-drawn streetcar after 1864, new homes like theirs in the suburbs offered the best of both worlds: a house near the country and ready access to the city. The Morrises' home remained fairly rural until the 1870s when new houses began to fill the subdivision. Unfortunately, in the aftermath of the Panic of 1873 John Morris was forced to declare bankruptcy and sell his family's home; Noble Butler purchased the house on Park Avenue in the early 1880s.

By the closing years of the 19th century the dust and dirt associated with the industrial growth of the city caught up with those who had fled to College Corners. A member of the Butler family remembered that "the town was full of coal dust," and "if you rocked on the back porch all morning and then went in for lunch, when you went out again after lunch you had to clean the chair thoroughly again." Ironically, as homes like the Butlers' joined apartments, businesses, factories, locomotives, and power plants in burning soft coal, thick, black clouds of smoke deposited soot and ash over the city, irritated and inconvenienced people, and endangered their health. Indianapolis passed anti-smoke ordinances in the late 1890s and again in 1904, thereby joining other industrial cities in attempting to abate smoke during the Progressive reform period. Stimulated by groups like the Indianapolis Smoke Abatement League, efforts at combating smoke continued through the 1930s; however, as use of coal increased, so too did the emission of smoke. By the 1940s, with petroleum replacing soft coal, the air over the city began to clear noticeably. But clearer air did not bring an end to pollution; in the future the problems would be far more intractable than elimination of smoke by substituting one fossil fuel for another.

When considering pollution caused by smoke from coal, it is worth noting that values have changed a great deal in the past few decades. Through the early 20th century many people saw smoke as a visible sign of progress. A "bird's-eye" map of Indianapolis from 1871 proudly depicts smoke pouring from the chimneys of factories, and shortly after the turn of the century the new Board of Trade Building (now demolished) displayed a mosaic titled "Industry" that illustrated the connection between smoke and progress. This was a point of view that was reinforced by the streetcar and the auto, which allowed the middle and upper classes to flee to more agreeable suburban environments.

If they let smoke pour into the air or effluents into waterways, manufacturers did not have to include the cost of cleanup in their prices. These costs were external to the price of the product; they were borne by the environment or by anyone who had to clean up the grime or who experienced inconvenience or annoyance or who suffered adverse health effects. In Indianapolis, as elsewhere, much of the history of regulating pollution has been one of persuading or forcing providers of goods and services (including government) to internalize costs and requiring consumers to accept the cost of cleanup in the prices of those goods and services.

Although descendants of Noble Butler lived on Park Avenue until the late 1950s, most of their middle class neighbors elected to move. As Indianapolis expanded those who could afford to do so moved ever farther from the city center, aided by the electric streetcar after 1891 and the auto after 1900. People were drawn to the suburbs by the lure of cheap land and country living and were pushed out of the city by environmental degradation and the changing composition of the population. The overwhelmingly white middle and upper classes who moved to the new developments helped transform farmland into suburbs. They left behind them industrial and wholesale districts, train yards, a central city that was devoted largely to business and commerce, and working class, immigrant, and minority groups who could not afford to move or who were not welcome in the suburbs. In common with most other American cities, the environmental experiences of residents of Indianapolis have been highly correlated with class and race. Not everyone has experienced the same environment, and that is a pattern that persists. And, so long as many women worked at home and most men traveled to work, there were differences in environmental experiences by gender as well.

By 1910 Indianapolis had become an industrial city with a population of 233,650. Urbanites who no longer had to wrest a living from the land began to mourn what they believed they had lost—opportunities for contact with an idealized version of nature, which had tested and tempered and shaped the character of pioneers like Morris Morris. This sense of loss contributed to a shift in attitudes toward nature, which nationally and locally revealed itself in nature appreciation, nature education, sport hunting and fishing, and conservation. These movements drew heavily on the kinds of people who were moving to the suburbs, the white middle and upper classes who believed they were protecting their natural heritage and their value system from the consequences of urban-industrial growth and an onslaught of immigrants. Inspired by the City Beautiful movement in the last decade of the 19th century and the first few decades of the 20th century, there were efforts to bring nature into the city in the form of parks and wide boulevards along Fall Creek, Pleasant Run, and White River. Aided by the streetcar and the auto, residents of Indianapolis also sought contact with nature outside of the city.

Jacob Piatt Dunn's history, *Greater Indianapolis* (1910), highlights both the evolution of the urban environment and a shift in attitudes between the first decades of settlement and the early 20th century. Dunn carefully chronicles the hunting and fishing paradise found in and around the city in the 1820s and 1830s. At the same time he also notes that "there was little need of skill or cunning in the early days," and "there was no 'letting a bass run.'" Living in a city and writing during the Progressive era and the first national conservation movement, Dunn observed that "the American people have shown a fearful lack of foresight in the exhaustion of natural resources." This perspective would have made little sense to pioneers like Morris Morris, who sought to settle and improve land they perceived to be a wilderness of almost unlimited abundance.

A great intellectual divide separated Dunn and his contemporaries from pioneers like Morris Morris. Despite the controversy that it created, Charles Darwin's *On the Origin of Species* (1859) had begun an intellectual revolution in the way people understood their relationship with nature. Evolution told us where we came from, demonstrated connections to other species, and challenged religion as the font of all knowledge. Nature appreciation, sport hunting and fishing, and conservation all drew on the post-Darwinian intellectual revolution. Despite exceptions like John Muir, who briefly lived in Indianapolis in 1867, the great shift in values during the late 19th and early 20th centuries was from a belief in unlimited natural abundance to conservation for use. Most people continued to place human beings above nature, to think of the natural world as a collection of useful and useless species, and to believe that nature needed to be conquered and controlled in the name of progress.

Dunn also documents the physical transformation of Indianapolis, as residents sought to adapt their surroundings to their needs. He describes a continuing process of filling low-lying and

Streetcars on West Michigan Street were stranded by floodwaters from the
great flood of March, 1913. [Indiana Historical Society, #C2589]

swampy areas, which he connects to a more irregular flow of the White River due to clearance of
land and other improvements that speeded runoff. As the city expanded in the 20th century,
drainage and filling of wetlands and channelization and relocation of streams contributed to the
ongoing modification of the physical environment. As Dunn observed, changes such as these
had an impact on the flow-rates of the White River and other streams in the city. Three years after
the publication of *Greater Indianapolis*, the city experienced its most devastating flood. The great
flood of March, 1913, was the result of unusually heavy precipitation and development on the
floodplain of White River, combined with drainage, filling, paving, and upstream agricultural
improvements that increased and accelerated runoff. Throughout the 20th century flooding in
the city remained as much a product of human attitudes and actions as a natural phenomenon.

In the 20th century electricity and the automobile contributed significantly to the creation
of the environment of Indianapolis and Marion County. Electrification of the city began in 1882
and before the 1930s was largely an urban development. Street lighting and indoor lighting progressively blurred the distinctions between day and night. Electricity permitted the city to reach
both up and out: Electric elevators allowed the construction of high-rise buildings on expensive
land downtown, and electric streetcars encouraged suburbs to expand over relatively cheap farmland on the periphery. Electric heating, refrigeration, and air conditioning helped to insulate people from the vicissitudes of nature and added to the impression that nature had been conquered
and controlled. At the same time, what began as a luxury became a necessity of life; its interruption can now have disastrous social and economic consequences. Rural electrification brought
power to the countryside beginning in the 1930s, and thereafter contributed to shifting land-use
patterns through accelerated suburbanization and dispersion of manufacturing.

More than any other technology the automobile has shaped the environment of city and
country alike. Although registration figures are not available, it is clear that residents of Indianap-

olis and Marion County embraced the automobile with the same passion as other Midwestern-ers. Ironically, at first the automobile appeared to offer a technical solution to the pollution generated by horses and mules. From the early 20th century through the construction of freeways in the 1960s and 1970s, Indianapolis has undergone major spatial reorganization and physical reconstruction to accommodate itself to the care and feeding of the automobile. Much of the Mile Square has been paved for streets, alleys, and parking lots, an action that lifted the city out of the mud but that also significantly affected drainage patterns and even local climatic conditions like temperature. Widespread paving now extends well beyond the Mile Square, symbolized by the huge parking lots of regional shopping malls that serve motorized consumers drawn from large markets inside and outside of the city. Along with the auto, the city has inherited a legacy of leak-ing underground storage tanks used for gasoline.

As the population of Indianapolis grew from 386,972 in 1940 to 744,624 in 1970 it spread out and occupied an environment that was shaped in form and function by the automobile. Along with the expansion of the automobile suburbs came a continuing process of channelizing and relocating streams and draining and filling wetlands, as was the case with Bacon's Swamp after World War II. The amount of farmland in Marion County offers a useful insight into the en-vironmental impact of the automobile. Farmland in the county peaked in 1900 when it reached about 240,000 acres. Thereafter the amount of farmland fell steadily, dropping below 180,000 acres by 1940; the decline then accelerated sharply until the late 1970s. By about 1975 the county had approximately 70,000 acres of farmland remaining, which was less than it possessed in 1850. While some of the decline in the early 20th century can be attributed to the street rail-way, these figures largely reflect the impact of a whole range of auto- and truck-related residential, commercial, and industrial developments, aided by the construction of freeways and the I-465 beltway. The net result has been suburban and exurban expansion into the county, with corre-sponding impacts on habitat, drainage, and air and water quality.

Thanks to the Interstate Highway Act of 1956, freeways and I-465 placed Indianapolis at the center of a nationwide system of superhighways, much as it had served as a hub for rail transpor-tation one hundred years earlier. Highways extended the city's commercial hinterland, and as trucks displaced the railroads in the 20th century they became the city's lifelines for food and for other necessities. Interstate roadways currently supply the city with fruits and vegetables, meat and dairy products. In so doing they bind Indianapolis to distant ecosystems upon which our dependence is disguised by the humanized environment that surrounds and insulates us.

In the 1960s popularization of ecology, a growing concern over environmental degradation, and an expanding interest in preserving and enhancing environmental quality stimulated the emergence of a broad-based environmental movement. The most important popularizer of ecol-ogy was Rachel Carson, in her seminal book *Silent Spring*, published in 1962. Carson built her arguments on things that people were already concerned about, like fallout from above-ground nuclear testing and widespread, indiscriminate use of nonselective pesticides like DDT. She en-couraged her readers to think of nature as an interconnected and interdependent web of life, to approach nature with humility rather than arrogance, and to coexist instead of conquer. *Silent Spring* was very controversial; it was also very popular. While Carson did not create the environ-mental movement, she did provide a focus, a vocabulary, and a scientific and philosophical under-pinning based on ecology. Environmentalists tended to talk in terms of protecting habitat or preserving ecosystems rather than conserving individual species or managing resources wisely and efficiently. Whether or not they called themselves environmentalists, people who understood the world around them in terms of ecology stood on the other side of an intellectual divide as great as the Darwinian revolution that separated Jacob Dunn and Noble Butler from Morris Morris.

The environmental movement of the 1960s and 1970s provided a largely middle class constituency for a host of new federal environmental statutes. As the *Indianapolis Star* observed in July, 1973, "few controversies have brought about more citizen involvement than has the recent 'ecology crisis.'" Backed by broad public support, between 1963 and 1980 Congress passed a series of environmental laws that had both anticipated and unanticipated consequences for cities like Indianapolis. Congress approved the Clean Air Act in 1963, the Water Quality and Solid Waste Disposal acts in 1965, and the National Environmental Policy Act (NEPA) in 1969. Among other things, NEPA created the Environmental Protection Agency (EPA) and the requirement for Environmental Impact Statements. Congress strengthened the Clean Air Act in 1970 and amended it again in 1977; it amended and toughened the federal Water Pollution Control Act in 1972, approved the Clean Water Act in 1977, and passed Superfund in 1980, which had a significant impact on real estate transfers in its effort to identify and clean up abandoned toxic waste sites. These federal statutes stimulated related regulatory activity at the state and city levels; they also sharpened and heightened differences among a range of groups, which placed conflicting and increasing demands on the same finite resources.

By the mid–1960s Indianapolis was taxing the ability of air, land, and water to absorb wastes produced by the growth of the city. In October, 1966, an article in the *Star* estimated that the water in White River was used six times over in the 80 miles between Anderson and Centerton. The waste-stream not only increased in volume but also consisted of new compounds such as synthetic, organic pesticides and herbicides; synthetic fibers; detergents; and aluminum and plastics. Many of these products represented the transfer of wartime technologies to the civilian economy. Much of the solid waste ended up in the Southside Landfill, which precipitated a waste-disposal crisis that was supposed to be addressed by the solid-waste-to-energy incinerator completed by Ogden Martin Systems, Inc., on the city's south side in the late 1980s. The controversy that surrounded this resource recovery facility before and after its completion reflected the importance and sensitivity of the solid waste issue in the city. The industrial, commercial, and domestic wastes delivered to the Southside Landfill have earned it designation by the EPA as a Superfund site.

By the early 1960s the deteriorating condition of White River made it clear that the city's aging sewage treatment facilities were inadequate. Not enough water existed in the river to dilute the effluent produced by the plant at Belmont Avenue. Even though the city added a second plant in 1966, five years later Indianapolis was failing to meet federal and state standards for the flow of sewage into the river. An increased population offset improvements in treatment facilities. By 1975 the *Star* was reporting that "the city has 'outgrown' White River," and the river "downstream from the city's Belmont Avenue treatment plant is almost 80 percent treated sewage." The addition of tertiary treatment at the city's sewage plants in the early 1980s began to yield improved water quality in the river, although the State Board of Health did not lift its ban on eating fish from the river due to contamination with PCBs and Chlordane until 1989.

Tertiary treatment did not completely solve the city's problems with sewage, and in 1986 the EPA was threatening to fine the city because its sludge-burning incinerators were in violation of the Clean Air Act. At that point, issues of air and water quality and solid waste intersected and demonstrated the complexity and difficulty of handling the wastes from a city the size of Indianapolis in a way that would satisfy competing interests and still protect and enhance environmental quality. Solid waste and air pollution intersected again as open-air burning of trash and yard waste became an issue by the late 1960s and remained so through the 1980s. In the humanized environment of the modern city, leaves and sticks and grass that once had been recyclable organic nutrients had become a solid waste problem of major proportions.

Federal laws dealing with clean air, clean water, solid waste, land use, and toxic contamination forced Indianapolis to confront the environmental consequences of its own growth. For a while in the 1970s it appeared as though the Clean Air Act would enforce *de facto* limits to growth on the city. From fall 1973 to spring 1974 the administration of Mayor Richard Lugar and a coalition of business, labor, and agricultural interests fought the EPA almost to a standstill over a plan to reduce air pollution by controlling transportation in the city. The bottom line for the Lugar administration and its allies was preserving the opportunity for continued economic growth. The issue of economic growth was sharpened by the oil embargo of 1973, which eliminated the cheap energy that had long fueled the growth of Indianapolis. As late as 1978 an official of the EPA's office in Chicago warned that "an unnecessary confrontation between clean air and growth" would occur if the city delayed in developing an adequate plan for cleaning up its air.

Growth had been an important theme in the environmental history of the city since the pioneer time of Morris Morris—growth in population, in size, in the use of energy and natural resources, in manufacturing and commerce, in markets, and in production of waste. The fact that growth became an issue at all demonstrated how much circumstances and values had shifted. In effect, the debate over growth was about confronting the consequences of the journey that created this place over time—a journey that began with the conversion of forests to farms, that continued with the expansion of streetcar and automobile suburbs over farmland, and that ultimately extended under I-465 and beyond, where industrial campuses and subdivisions sprout up amid cornfields and crumbling barns.

———

See also: AIR QUALITY; CLIMATE; FLOODING AND FLOOD CONTROL; FLORA AND FAUNA; GEOLOGY; GREEN-SPACE; LAND USE; PARKS; SOIL AND GROUNDWATER CONTAMINATION; WATERWAYS; and other individual topics.

VISUAL ARTS

Marion S. Garmel

Because it did not develop naturally but was carved from the center of the state to be its capital, Indianapolis evolved into a home for the visual arts differently than other midwestern art centers. Its growth did not result from a core of wealthy collectors who imported art and art appreciation, but from the efforts of the artists themselves, through public commissions, and from a handful of supporters who encouraged the study and appreciation of art. A strong tradition of self-help developed, with artists training one another and relying on local patrons for support. As a consequence, the Indianapolis art scene was more open—particularly to women—than in other cities. It was, simultaneously, more insular due to the isolation from outside influences.

The earliest artists were itinerant sign painters, mostly of German origin, who sought work in the new capital. The first was Samuel S. Rooker from Tennessee. He had some original notions about spelling and foreshortening: his first sign, for cabinetmaker Caleb Scudder, read "Kalop Skoddar, Kabbinet Maker." Commissioned to paint a sign for a tavern on the Michigan Road, he chose the figure of General Lafayette in full uniform. After finishing the head and the body, Rooker ran out of space for the legs; he solved the problem by attaching the feet to the knees.

Things changed in 1832 with the arrival of Jacob Cox and his brother Charles, both tinsmiths. Cox taught himself to paint and later shared a studio with John Gibson Dunn in Cincinnati, where he held a successful exhibit and sale of his paintings. Returning to Indianapolis, he announced in the *Indiana Journal* in 1844 that he had set up a studio on West Washington Street where "all are invited to call and examine his specimens of art."

Cox was the city's first art teacher and for a long time its only artist. Though his style was direct and lacked technical finesse, he managed to support a large family by painting and teaching until his death in 1892. Among his students were the young Lew Wallace, whose father was governor, and Henry W. Waugh, an actor and scene painter at Robinson's Athenaeum. A notable woman student was Lotta P. Guffin, who supported her family by painting portraits when her husband became ill.

Marion S. Garmel is former arts critic for the *Indianapolis News*.

In the 1840s, a number of artists arrived who had been portrait painters but transferred their allegiance to the new Daguerreotype. Thomas Worthington Whittredge was the first to arrive in 1843. He fell ill while living at Parker's Hotel and was taken in by clergyman Henry Ward Beecher, in whose house he recuperated for a year. In payment, he painted portraits of the entire Beecher family except for one son who was away.

In the 1850s, the great Panorama fever swept the United States, with artists exhibiting multi-panel narrative paintings for a fee in halls across the country. Indianapolis was considered "a great town for panoramas," both the making and the showing of them. In 1854, four local business-men paid Cox $1,500 to paint a temperance panorama, on which Waugh assisted. But the city's great panorama painter was J. H. Harris, who also painted the Indiana Banner for the Crystal Palace at the New York World's Fair of 1853.

The next important artist was Barton S. Hays, a self-taught artist who arrived in 1858 from Greenville, Ohio. He was notable not only for his portraits but for his work as a teacher. His students included William Merritt Chase, who became America's premiere Impressionist and the guiding light behind the Art Students' League in New York City, and John W. Love, cofounder of the first Indiana School of Art.

An epochal event occurred in 1869–1870, when Governor Conrad Baker persuaded the legislature to authorize him to secure "a true and life-like likeness of each of the Governors of the State and Territory, including the present incumbent." Thus was born the Governors' Portraits Collection, which brought enormous prestige to the visual arts in Indianapolis. Commissions went to artists such as Hays (William Henry Harrison), Cox (Boon, Ray, Noble, Wallace, Bigger, Wright, and Lane), and John B. Hill (Posey and Hammond). Subsequent governors selected their own portrait artists, with the result that many Indianapolis artists are represented in the collection.

The tradition of Indianapolis as a site for large art exhibitions began in 1852, when the State Fair mounted its first fine arts exhibition. In 1874, in conjunction with the fair, the first Indiana Exposition included 350 works by artists statewide, including Hays and Cox, and 17 portraits of Indiana governors.

Early artists exhibited mainly in downtown hotels or the state Senate chambers. Later artists congregated around two important art stores, Lieber's Art Emporium, established in 1854, and Lyman Brothers, established in 1900. For many years these were central points for supplying, ex-hibiting, and even supporting artists. Herman Lieber later financed T. C. Steele's stay in Munich; Lieber's son Carl became a major patron; and both Lieber's and Lyman's helped support the mental patient–artist John Zwara in the late 1930s.

The art scene took a more professional turn in 1877 when the first Indiana School of Art was opened by Love and James F. Gookins of Terre Haute. Both had trained abroad, Gookins at the Royal Academy in Munich, Love at the Beaux Arts in Paris. Both exhibited in the first Indianap-olis Home Exhibition the same year, causing Aloise E. Sinks, the city's acerbic first art critic, to note the superiority of the work of the foreign-trained artists.

The school lasted only two years, but it established a pattern of artists traveling to Europe or New York for advanced training. And from its students came a core of artists and patrons who would plant the seeds of art as an essential of life in the Hoosier capital. One outgrowth was the Bohe Club, founded by pupils who banded together to continue their studies. Members included F. A. Hetherington and T. E. Hibben, the first to produce etchings here, and William Forsyth, who became a major force for decades to come.

Richard B. Gruelle, American, 1851–1914. *The Canal, Morning Effect*, 1894.
[oil on canvas, 37 x 43 inches, John Herron Fund, from the exhibition: *Views of
Indianapolis: Artistic Perspectives*, collection of the Indianapolis Museum of Art.]

In 1880, five of the state's most prominent artists went to Munich to study at the Royal Academy: T. C. Steele, who studied with Gookins and Love; J. Ottis Adams of Muncie; Samuel Richards of Anderson and his wife, Carrie Wolff; and Augustus Metzner of Indianapolis. Forsyth joined them two years later. In addition to academic training, these artists spent their summers painting in the German countryside. They returned with a love of landscape and outdoor painting and the conviction that the Indiana landscape was as deserving of artistic attention as any other. A decade later Steele, Adams, and Forsyth, with the addition of Richard B. Gruelle, a self-taught artist, and Otto Stark, who studied in Paris, became known as the Hoosier Group from a successful 1894 exhibition of their paintings in Chicago.

These artists, with their early Impressionism, were the dominant force in the city at the turn of the century. Their works made Indianapolis an outpost of modernism in the heartland. They exhibited and won prizes at the World's Columbian Exposition in Chicago in 1893, the Louisiana Purchase Exposition in St. Louis in 1904 (for which Steele served as a juror), and the Panama Exposition at San Francisco in 1915. They were founding members of the Society of Western Artists (1895) and the Indiana Artists Club (1917). Moreover, the most avant-garde art journal in America, *Modern Art*, was published here by Joseph M. Bowles from 1893 to 1895, when it moved to Boston. Steele, Forsyth, Stark, and Susan M. Ketcham were among its first contributors. Their natural successors would flourish into the 1960s in the art colony that grew up in Brown County, where Steele moved in 1907.

While these artists were abroad, another important event took place. In 1883, May Wright Sewall, president of the Girls' Classical School, met with 17 women to sign the articles of incorporation of the Art Association of Indianapolis. The purpose of the organization was to arrange lectures and exhibits and establish a museum. In 1884, the association opened a school with Charles F. McDonald of Chicago and Susan M. Ketcham as instructors, but it lasted only two years.

For several years, the association's major activity was an annual show; the first consisted of paintings from the East, the second of Hoosier artists in Munich. For many years it hosted the annual exhibit of the Society of Western Artists, followed in 1908 by the annual Indiana Artists Exhibition. Its policy of purchasing the best pictures from these and other exhibits, including major international shows, resulted in some surprisingly contemporary pieces, including John Twachtman's *A Summer Day*, Dwight Tryon's *November Morning*, and Frank Duveneck's *Marine*.

When the Indiana colony in Munich returned—Steele after five years, the others soon thereafter—Steele established a studio and opened a school, later taken over by Forsyth. This grew into the second Indiana School of Art, which, reorganized by the art association, lasted six years (1891–1897).

At the same time, Indianapolis experienced a renaissance in the applied arts. Mainly to popularize the ideas of William Morris, leader of the British Arts and Crafts movement, the Portfolio Club was founded in 1895 and sponsored two major arts and crafts exhibits at Shortridge High School in 1898 and 1899. The movement was prominent into the 1920s, with Janet Payne Bowles becoming a nationally important metalsmith. Roda E. Selleck, first art teacher at Shortridge, was the outstanding ceramic artist. Brandt Steele was the most prominent designer. In photography, Mary Lyon Taylor gained a national reputation for her portraits.

Also in 1895, in an unexpected bequest, the art association fell heir to the fortune of John Herron, an Indianapolis real estate speculator who died in California. He left $250,000 with the provision that a school and museum be established in his name. With the prospect of money to build a school, the association did not reopen the Steele-Forsyth school and, for many years, the city's only art school was Forsyth's facility in the Union Trust Building.

In 1902, after years of wrangling over how to use its inheritance, the association purchased Steele's former home and studio, variously known as the Talbott, Talbot, or Tinker House, at 16th and Pennsylvania streets, and opened a school with Adams, Steele, Bessie Hendricks, and Brandt Steele among the teachers. In 1906 a museum building was added, and a year later a permanent school building was completed. After a few years, Adams retired and Forsyth took his place. Later instructors included Stark, Clifton A. Wheeler, a student of Forsyth's who also studied with Chase in New York and abroad, and children's instructor Tempe Tice.

Another important event in 1895 was the arrival of Wilhelmina Seegmiller, who altered the way art was taught in the public schools. Her idea was that the study of art should not be mere copying, but include all ways of expressing oneself with one's hands. She encouraged the schools to hire professional artists as instructors. Selleck at Shortridge, Stark at Manual, and later the illustrator Frederick W. Polley at Arsenal Technical High School would become mentors to generations of future artists and patrons. Seegmiller also persuaded the state legislature in 1909 to pass a law that allowed school boards in cities with art associations to split $1/2$ of one cent of each taxable $100 with the associations for art education. The money was used, among other things, for advanced training for promising public school art students.

All this was just part of a tremendous involvement of Indianapolis schools with Indianapolis artists. Parent-Teacher Associations commissioned artists to paint murals in the schools. Artists donated paintings, usually in honor of their graduating children. Parents and graduating classes presented paintings as gifts. There was a great spate of mural painting in the 1900s and 1910s, and again under the WPA projects of the 1930s and early 1940s. At Shortridge, students paid a fine arts fee for the purchase of paintings by Indiana artists, including Steele, Stark, and Wheeler. The collection was so prominent it now is on permanent loan to the Indiana State Museum.

Sculptors were less in evidence than painters in the early years. That would change in the 1880s, with the construction of the State House and the Soldiers and Sailors Monument on the Circle. Bruno Schmitz of Koblenz, Germany, who won the competition for architect of the monument, brought with him the Vienna-trained stone carver Rudolf Schwarz, who executed "The Return Home" and "The Dying Soldier" tableaus on either side of the monument and the sentry soldiers at its base. Schwarz settled here and maintained a bronze-casting foundry on East Raymond Street. Both he and his assistant, Walter Williams, taught at the Herron Art Institute.

Also important was the decoration of SS. Peter and Paul Cathedral in 1906 with a Byzantine-style mural by Edgar S. Cameron of Chicago (replaced by a glass mosaic in 1936) and statuary by the Italian sculptor Cesare Aureli. More than many cities, Indianapolis profited from the popularity of public sculpture in the late 19th and early 20th centuries. Statues popped up everywhere, prompting humorist George Ade to quip, in 1907, that "Indiana has more foundries than studios." The boom continued in the 1910s and 1920s with the statues and fountain in University Park. The construction of the World War Memorial in 1929 added to a downtown notable for its public statuary and green spaces.

All this provided inspiration for local artists, who painted many scenes of the city's monuments, buildings, and self-contained neighborhoods. A splendid example is Richard Gruelle's *The Canal—Morning Effect* (1894), with its shimmering view of the State House dome in the background.

Women artists, though never as numerous as men, have been part of the art scene from its beginning. Lotta Guffin exhibited at the first Home Exhibition, and women have been teachers and students at all the city's art schools. Prominent women included Ruth Pratt Bobbs and Lucy Taggart in portraiture, Dorothy Morlan, and Helene C. Hibben, the first major woman sculptor. These last worked on the mural project for the Burdsal Wing of City (now Wishard) Hospital.

This project, begun in 1914, was sponsored by St. Margaret's Guild of St. Paul Episcopal Church, which adopted the hospital's children's wards as its charity. To decorate the new wing, instead of buying paintings, Dr. T. Victor Keene, a member of the board of health, suggested the guild commission artists to paint murals. Wheeler and Carl Graf were commissioned, then Forsyth took over. Soon most of the city's artists and art students had commissions, including Steele, Stark, Wheeler, and portrait artists Wayman Adams and Simon Baus. Figure studies and landscapes predominated.

Another contributor was William Edouard Scott, the first black artist mentioned in city annals. He also painted murals in the schools. Like later African-American artists John W. Hardrick and Hale Woodruff, he settled elsewhere to make his fortune. In general, black artists remained invisible in the capital until the advent of Indiana Black Expo in 1971.

Indiana artists (left to right) Carl Graf, Clifton Wheeler, William Forsyth, and Otto Stark painted a large World War I era mural to help the War Chest Fund Drive. [Indiana State Library]

In the 1920s and 1930s, the most celebrated art schools in town were the life drawing school run by Elmer Taflinger, first in the Pierce Building downtown and then in the Propylaeum Carriage House, and the Circle Art Academy run by George Jo Mess and his wife, Evelynne, in their home in Broad Ripple. Taflinger's school was notorious for its night classes and nude models. Mess became one of the country's most prominent aquatint artists. His wife was a founding member of the Printmakers' Society of Indiana. Many graduates found work in local advertising.

In 1925, the Hoosier Salon was founded by expatriate Hoosiers in Chicago to spotlight the art of their native state. An annual juried exhibit was mounted in the Marshall Field Company picture galleries until 1941, when it moved to the William H. Block Company in downtown Indianapolis, where it became the art event of the season. Later it moved to L. S. Ayres and Company and then to the Indiana State Museum.

In the 1930s, most Indianapolis artists adopted the American Scene style of painting that was popular nationwide. Among these were Floyd Hopper, William Kaeser, and Cecil Head, who shared a studio on Market Street. Also, in the decade between 1928 and 1937, a colony known as the Irvington Society of Artists grew up in the prosperous suburb of Irvington, attracted by its wooded streets and streams. Forsyth was dean and members included most of the city's major artists. Another resident was Lucille Morehouse, second art critic of note, who wrote for the *Indianapolis Star* from 1913 until 1949.

In 1933, an upheaval at the Herron Art Institute turned the art scene upside down. Led by Caroline Marmon Fesler, an art association board member, an effort was made to acquire a faculty filled with winners of the prestigious Prix de Rome. Donald Mattison became head of the school. He dismissed such long-time instructors as Forsyth and Wheeler and recruited a faculty that would change Herron from a provincial institute for training art teachers to a school with a national reputation, turning out four Prix de Rome winners in approximately as many years.

Among Mattison's recruits were sculptor David Rubins and portrait artist Edmund Brucker. When Brucker arrived in 1938 he said he was surprised by the number of opportunities for artists here. Whereas Cleveland had one annual show, Indianapolis had the Hoosier Salon, the Indiana Artists Club Show, the Indiana Artists Exhibition, and the State Fair Fine Arts Exhibition.

Like artists elsewhere, Indianapolis' artists supported themselves during the Great Depression working for the federal government. Wilbur D. Peat, director of the Herron Museum, administered the post office mural project and sent the city's artists throughout the state. There were mural and painting commissions for schools and libraries. Another legacy was the Indianapolis Art League, which grew out of a WPA class taught by William Kaeser in 1934. Classes were modeled after those at New York's Art Students' League, with students pooling their money to pay the instructor. The league (recently renamed the Indianapolis Art Center) grew into the city's most important source of non-academic art instruction, with many of the city's best artists as instructors.

Following the upheavals of the 1930s, the postwar years were relatively quiet. Many artists, returning from the war, settled into domesticity and "normalcy." Prominent teachers at Herron were Harry A. Davis, who gained statewide fame for his paintings of historic buildings; Robert Weaver, who specialized in circus paintings; abstract expressionist Robert Berkshire; and sculptor Adolph Wolter.

More important nationally was Garo Antreasian, an Indianapolis native of Armenian descent, who set up one of the nation's first fine-art lithography presses at Herron. He also executed a number of murals, including a 750,000–piece mosaic mural in the lobby of the State Office Building. He later became director of the Tamarind Institute of Lithography in New Mexico.

The Herron Museum had several early directors, but none of note until Wilbur Peat accepted the job in 1929. Born in China, the son of missionary parents, he advised Eli Lilly, of the pharmaceutical family and firm, on the purchase of many Oriental art objects that became the core of a small but fine collection at the museum.

During the Peat years the museum hosted a number of important exhibits, including "Dutch Paintings of the 17th Century" in 1937 and "Turner in America" in 1955. These would not be matched until the 1980s, when senior curator Anthony Janson, whose father wrote the classic text *Janson's History of Art*, brought in such exhibits as "The Romantics to Rodin: French 19th Century Sculpture from North American Collections" and "Art of the Avant-Garde in Russia: Selections from the George Costakis Collection."

The late 1950s and 1960s saw the birth of a spate of galleries devoted to contemporary Indiana art. Spurred by the Association of Professional Artists, mainly Herron graduates and faculty, these included the 1444, Talbot, and Park galleries near Herron and the Whitehorse Gallery downtown. Artists included Rinaldo Paluzzi, Mary Beth Edelson, Amanda Block, and James Snodgrass. These galleries flourished for awhile, but died from lack of patronage or because their artists moved on. (Edelson became a prominent feminist artist on the East Coast.) The most popular artists were Joan T. (Joni) Johnson, who created wispy Victorian watercolors, and William

A. Eyden, Jr., retired from owning a gallery in New York City, who became the national authority on painting beech trees.

In 1961 the Alliance of the Herron Museum opened its Rental Gallery, which included works by local artists. In 1963, the museum's Contemporary Art Society began bringing in top art from New York galleries for its biennial "Painting and Sculpture Today" show, with tremendous impact on local artists and collectors. But, for the most part, artists had to move elsewhere to make their marks. The most famous expatriate was the pop artist Robert Indiana, who attended Tech High School. His original LOVE painting and sculpture are at the Indianapolis Museum of Art.

Outside the academy, the postwar years saw watercolor emerge as a favorite medium of city artists. Floyd Hopper was dean of the school, with Leah Traugott, Jean Vietor, and nature artist Paul Sweany prominent today. These also were years when art organizations proliferated. The nation's first mall art show was said to be the Eastgate Mile of Art established in 1958 by the Eastside Art Center. The great art fairs began in 1955 with the Talbot Street Art Fair, followed by the Broad Ripple Art Fair, and Penrod Day, founded by the Penrod Society, a latter-day Bohe Club.

By 1971, Indianapolis had three commercial galleries, mostly carrying original graphics by national or international artists. Local artists exhibited in the lobbies of cinemas, banks, and insurance companies. But in 1972, a trickle of galleries into Broad Ripple began with Joanne Chappell's Editions Ltd. and included the cooperative CCA Gallery, founded by artists who previously exhibited in mall or juried exhibitions.

In 1970, the Herron Museum and its school officially split. The school became part of Indiana University–Purdue University at Indianapolis. The Indianapolis Museum of Art was built on the former J. K. Lilly estate overlooking White River. The art association became the museum board. The Krannert Pavilion opened in 1970 and the Clowes Pavilion in 1971. The new building attracted a number of gifts to the museum, including the Clowes Fund Collection of Old Master Paintings and the Kurt Pantzer Collection of J. M. W. Turner Watercolors.

In the 1980s, there was renewed interest in Indiana art of the past. With the formation of the Hoosier Group, Inc., an effort was made to preserve the heritage of the Hoosier Group and Brown County artists. The Indianapolis Art League began recording oral histories of the art of the 1920s and 1930s. Interest in the Hoosier Group became so intense it led to a 1985 scandal involving bogus paintings attributed to Steele and Forsyth.

Also in the 1980s, with the revitalization of downtown, there was an influx of galleries in a transitional neighborhood on Massachusetts Avenue. Among the first in 1982 was Patrick King Contemporary Art, followed by the Ruschman and Engle galleries and the nonprofit 431 Gallery, a cooperative of Herron graduates that presents cutting-edge art. By 1991, nine galleries took part in the Fall Downtown Gallery Walk, and 11 in the Fall Gallery Tour in Broad Ripple. Artists also began renovating studio space in downtown warehouses, especially women in the Morris Building on South Meridian Street.

The 1970s and 1980s saw a proliferation of money coming into the arts from government and corporate sources. Most important was Lilly Endowment with its matching grants for civic and cultural programs. The Comprehensive Education and Training Act (CETA) funded the first director at the Herron Gallery, which became a center for contemporary art. The Metropolitan Arts Council sponsored two downtown murals as part of the national Urban Wall movement. In 1984, the Indiana Arts Commission began offering fellowships to visual artists.

Federal and state money also helped fund a Visiting Artists Series at Herron, which brought in such artists as Christo and the light sculptor James Turrell. The Indianapolis Museum of Art sponsored several important symposia. And the museum's affiliate groups—for contemporary, decorative, Oriental, and ethnographic art and prints and drawings—brought in exhibits and lecturers.

The publication of a statewide monthly arts magazine, now called *Arts Indiana*, also brought prestige to the visual arts. With Ann Stack as publisher, the magazine sponsored the annual Indiana Artists Postcard Series competition, which sent works by Indiana artists winging around the world on the fronts of postcards.

In 1987, when Indianapolis hosted the Pan American Games, the museum dropped its Indiana Artists Exhibition in order to organize a traveling exhibit of surrealist art from Latin America. In protest, the Coalition of Indianapolis Artists was formed and hosted its own show. Since then, corporations have taken up the slack, including American States Insurance with an annual juried exhibition of contemporary Indiana art.

The museum scene got a boost in the late 1980s when Harrison Eiteljorg, chairman of the board of trustees of the Indianapolis Museum of Art, donated his collection of western art to a museum to be built in the future White River State Park. The Eiteljorg Museum of American Indian and Western Art opened in June, 1989. Eiteljorg's African and Oceanic collections became the core of a 1991 expansion at the Indianapolis Museum of Art that doubled the museum's space and added the Hulman Pavilion. That same year the National Art Museum of Sport, now defunct, moved into the new Bank One Tower downtown.

The city has not been so lucky in its public sculpture. Mark DiSuvero's *Snowplow*, a gift from the Indianapolis Sesquicentennial Committee, ended up gracing the Department of Transportation garage when nobody else wanted it until the IMA purchased it in 1993. The few commissions that were made resulted in sculptures so minimal you could not find them or works that do not dominate their space.

Except for a brief period at the turn of the century, the Indianapolis art scene has been a mostly parochial environment from which artists had to travel for national attention. But since the late 1980s, with the revival of the Arts Council of Indianapolis, an effort has been made to recapture those earlier years. With two museums of national repute and a blossoming gallery scene, many artists have chosen to remain in, or return to, the city. As is true nationally, a variety of styles coexists, from the neo-Primitivism of recent Herron graduates to the surreal air brush paintings of James "Willie" Faust and the hard-edge space paintings of James Cunningham (killed in a helicopter crash in 1991), one of a handful of American artists selected by the National Air and Space Administration to document its space launches in art. In the 1990s, artists with developing national reputations included black photographer Carl Pope and Herron instructors Richard Nicholson and Gary Freeman. With its increasing activity and prominence, the visual arts in Indianapolis may yet experience its sought-after renaissance.

See also: ART DEALERS AND COMMERCIAL GALLERIES; ART EXHIBITIONS; PHILANTHROPY AND THE ARTS; SCULPTURE; and individual names, institutions, and organizations.

WOMEN

Nancy F. Gabin

The history of women in Indianapolis was ineluctably shaped by forces such as urbanization and industrialization, and by major events such as World Wars I and II. But that history was just as surely shaped by women themselves. The distinctive character of Indianapolis owes a great deal to the efforts of women regardless of class, race, and ethnicity to determine their own lives and to cross and blur the boundaries between the private and public spheres.

Women and men settled the frontier town of Indianapolis beginning in the 1820s. Like their counterparts elsewhere, women devoted themselves principally to sustaining their families. Yet even during the first two decades of settlement and certainly after Indianapolis became the state's commercial and industrial center in the 1850s, women did not pass their lives solely within the domestic sphere. They formed groups with a variety of purposes ranging from religious reform to cultural enrichment to social welfare. From its founding in 1835, the Indianapolis Benevolent Society, for example, distributed food and used clothing to the needy. As the city grew, the society created a central depository where goods for distribution were collected; members of the society canvassed the city for contributions of money and goods. The society also chartered and raised funds for the opening in 1855 of the Indianapolis Orphans' Home, among the first private orphanages in the state. Women's interest in the public sphere was further piqued in the antebellum era by the Women's Rights Association of Indiana, which sponsored a series of three lectures on women's rights by Lucy Stone and held conventions in Indianapolis in 1854 and 1855.

The activities of Indianapolis women in this early period also provide evidence of the city's social and economic diversity. A benefit performance of *Othello* in 1864 for the Sewing Women's Association of Indianapolis indicates not only that cultural entertainment was enjoyed by middle and upper class women but also that at least some women were economic providers for their families, working long hours for such little pay that their situation inspired charitable contributions. The establishment by women in 1867 of the German Protestant Orphans' Association reflects the city's ethnic diversity. The opening in 1871 of the Indianapolis Asylum for Friendless Colored Children and its operation by women of the Western Yearly Meeting of Friends similarly demon-

Nancy F. Gabin is Associate Professor of History at Purdue University, West Lafayette.

strate the presence of African-Americans in the city and their exclusion from white institutions as well as the important role played by these women in providing basic social services.

Between 1870 and 1920 the female experience in Indianapolis dramatically changed and diversified as the city expanded demographically, geographically, and economically. The changing urban environment invited greater collective action by Indianapolis women. Taken together, their diverse activities attest to the tremendous vitality of the era's "woman movement."

Much of the organizational activity was for self-improvement rather than social reform. Literary clubs, such as the charmingly named Over the Teacups, exemplified this approach. So, too, did the Indianapolis Woman's Club, founded in 1875 and the oldest of its type in Indiana, whose purpose was "to form an organized center for the mental and social culture of its members and for the improvement of domestic life." The clubs' expressed purpose challenged extant assumptions about the inferior intellect of women. The same was true for literary clubs of African-American women; these organizations, formed for self-improvement, also were responses to the denial of education to blacks of both sexes and expressed a more collective concern with racial survival and uplift.

Other women's groups combined self-improvement and sociability with benevolence, fulfilling a middle class commitment to social efficacy as well as acting on the prevalent notion of a special female nature and social purpose. Literary clubs often went beyond their stated purpose. Such groups engaged in a variety of private charitable activities, such as collecting and distributing food and clothing to the poor. The African-American women's Bethel Literary Society and the Allen Chapel Literary Society, for example, not only sponsored lectures and debates but also aided black migrants to the city from the South and provided other forms of community service. Other groups similarly operated under the aegis of churches and synagogues. To cite just one example, the Hebrew Ladies Benevolent Society, part of the Jewish Welfare Federation of Indianapolis that was established in 1905, provided social services to the poor in the Jewish immigrant community through financial support, employment opportunities, health care, and assistance in adjusting to American life. Secular women's organizations joined in taking on the task of providing social welfare and social services in a period when tax-supported poor relief was limited at best. The efforts of women in church groups, lodges, and clubs informed the Indianapolis community of the problems faced by urban residents and the need for their solution.

Some women regarded their collective group efforts with a heightened consciousness of their importance to the city, to women and children, and to themselves. Their efforts to expand and institutionalize private charity, raise public health and safety standards in the city, extend and improve the Indianapolis public school system, and increase urban residents' access to medical care created vital and durable institutions that transformed the quality of life for the city's citizens. At the same time, these efforts established a network of experienced women activists that improved the role and image of women in the city and enhanced their power and influence.

The prolonged financial panic that began in 1873 greatly expanded and institutionalized private charity in Indianapolis and began to professionalize the women who engaged in such efforts. So severe was the ensuing depression that even before the end of October in 1873 the Ladies Relief Society was making arrangements for a soup kitchen to feed the poor during the coming winter. The treasuries of the city's private charities proved inadequate to meet the need for assistance to the poor and unemployed. When the city council refused to coordinate charitable activities and appropriated only a small sum for poor relief, private charitable societies formed the Indianapolis Charity Organization (ICO) to serve as a clearinghouse for all charitable organizations and agencies. An office with a paid secretary and a staff of "visitors" opened; these visitors investigated the cases of all applicants for assistance and then referred "worthy" cases to appropriate organizations. Visitors were also to give advice and counsel to the poor and try to help them find employment. The ICO made the distribution of charity more efficient and helped professionalize women engaged in charitable activities.

A prominent example of women's political and social power in Indianapolis in this period was the Women's Improvement Club of Indianapolis (WIC). Organized as a literary circle in 1903, WIC became the group most responsible for attacking tuberculosis among the Indianapolis black population, which was excluded from the health care efforts and successes of white Indianapolis. Independent of any public funding or assistance, the WIC set up an outdoor tuberculosis camp, formed a nurses' training class for blacks (of particular value to the black community since young black women did not have access to the nursing schools at any of the city hospitals), and, lacking funding from major donors or the public coffers, raised money for supplies, groceries, and nursing care. When the WIC closed the camp in 1916 on account of lack of funds and a trend away from institutionalization toward home care for tuberculous patients, WIC members turned to home nursing, social work, and educational programs related to the tuberculosis problem. In the 1920s there were more preventive health services available to African-Americans in Indianapolis but still no place where black advanced tuberculous patients could go for extended care. The WIC thus began a successful campaign to secure such facilities. The WIC also expanded its social service activities, securing funds for undernourished black children to spend summers in the country and financially assisting poor blacks threatened with eviction.

In many other ways women demonstrated their importance in Indianapolis. The expansion of the public school system downward to the kindergarten level occurred in Indiana from 1880 to 1920 only after women working through their private charitable organizations introduced such programs in Indianapolis and other cities in the late 1870s and early 1880s. Prison reform also attracted the attention of Indianapolis women. In 1869 the state legislature voted to establish in Indianapolis the Indiana Reformatory Institution for Women and Girls as a combination prison for adults and reform school for girls. The first inmates were admitted in 1873; by 1875 there were 30 women in the penal department and 93 girls in the reformatory. The law creating the institution required that the officers be women. After 1877 all members of the governing board were women, too. Other urban institutions organized and operated by women included orphanages, homes for aged women, boardinghouses for single working women, and settlement houses such as Flanner Guild, the College Settlement (or Christamore House), and Foreign House/American Settlement.

By the 1890s the women's movement in Indianapolis was so well developed and institutionalized that it established its own building and organized a formal federation. The Indianapolis Woman's Club sponsored a project to erect a headquarters building owned and entirely operated by women—the Propylaeum, completed in 1891. Propylaeum stockholders also voted to form a council that would provide a forum for communication among the women's groups of the city. Begun in 1892 with 49 literary societies, charitable groups, and missionary and church associations, the Indianapolis Council of Women met monthly to address issues related to women and children such as women's suffrage and school matters. The group investigated conditions for women prisoners in jails and the presence of children in taverns, lobbied for municipal legislation regarding public health and housing, and campaigned for the appointment of women to local

Early telephone operators were primarily women, as this 1908 photograph
indicates. [Indiana Historical Society, Bass Collection, #14580]

commissions and government offices. The council, moreover, spawned other women's organizations such as the Indianapolis Consumers League in 1901.

Many of those involved in the Indianapolis women's movement were leisured, middle class women. But employment was another route for women out of the private and into the public sphere. In 1880 women composed 18 percent of the Indianapolis labor force. Two thirds of the 5,000 women employed in that year worked in the professional and personal services category, the vast majority as domestic servants. Another 29 percent worked in manufacturing where they constituted 14 percent of all workers in industry. These women worked in bookbinderies, clothing factories, laundries, pork packing houses, tobacco factories, chain and stamping works, and paper-box plants. Only 200 worked in trade and transportation in that year but the retail sector was still small-scale and clerk jobs had not yet been feminized. A study of working women in Indianapolis conducted by the U.S. Commissioner of Labor in 1880 described the wages of some women as "almost beggarly." Partly as a result of their low-waged status, nine tenths of the women working in the city (most of whom were native born) lived at home with their families rather than in rented rooms or boardinghouses.

The advance of commerce and manufacturing and the growth in population and urban development transformed and increased the number of jobs in the service sector between 1880 and 1920. The growth of office and retail clerk jobs contributed to the increased number of women in the city's labor force. Fully half of the 18,500 clerical workers in Indianapolis in 1920 were female. Women also comprised 16 percent of the 22,000 people employed in trade in that year. Most of these were retail salesclerks, a new occupation for women that reflected the emergence and expansion of department stores like L. S. Ayres and Company, which opened in 1872 and became one of the largest single employers of women in Indianapolis. Another new service occupation that was regarded as a female job was telephone operator: most of the 1,400 women employed in transportation in 1920 were phone operators.

The reorganization of the female labor market shifted the occupational distribution of women in Indianapolis. Most notably, the number of women employed in professional and personal service increased in absolute terms between 1880 and 1920, but their share of the female labor force dropped dramatically from 67 percent to 38 percent. The absolute increase, however, was significant in its own right. After 1880 middle class women gained access to new vocational space in the public sphere through the emergence of the so-called women's professions. The same groups that extended the public school system in the city also enlarged job opportunities for women. The Teachers College of Indianapolis, a private normal school founded in 1884 by Eliza Blaker under the auspices of the Free Kindergarten Society of Indianapolis, for example, trained kindergarten and primary grade teachers. The professionalization of nursing in Indianapolis similarly depended on women's social activism. Nurses' training programs were instituted in at least eight private hospitals before 1900. But the state's first school of nursing was organized in 1883 as part of the Indianapolis City Hospital under the auspices of the Indianapolis Flower Mission, a private charitable society started in 1876 to provide care for the sick and composed of women who visited the sick poor of the city. The Flower Mission further expanded and upgraded health services in 1890 when it set up a registry for private-duty nurses and became active in the movement to employ visiting nurses among the city's poor.

Another significant trend in the professional and personal service category is the occupational distribution of African-American women. In 1920, 83 percent of all employed black women worked in domestic and personal service; and black women comprised half of all women in this occupational category. After 1920 black women came to dominate these jobs as white women found employment in the expanding manufacturing and tertiary sectors. Yet a significant number of African-American women worked as professionals within the black community. Madam C. J. Walker is perhaps the most well-known but other black women worked as teachers, doctors, and small business operators. Beulah Wright Porter, a member of the WIC, in 1897 became the first black female physician to open practice in Indianapolis; by 1905 she was the principal of Public School 40 and represented black Hoosier schoolteachers at the Colored National Teachers Convention. A good number of WIC members were schoolteachers, many of them graduates of the Indianapolis Teachers College.

Working women were often the objects of middle class women's attention. But they also sought independently to ameliorate their working and living conditions. Working women certainly had grounds for complaint. In the late 1880s their average working hours were 9.4 per day and 56.3 per week and they earned an average weekly wage of $5.66. Saleswomen had to work for 13 hours or more on Saturdays, factory workers' hours were unregulated, and there were no laws regarding noise and dirt in workrooms, poor ventilation, or sanitary conditions. Evidence of working class women's collective action is scarcer than that for middle class women. But in the 1870s organizations of women workers formed to raise wages, insure members against sickness and death, provide legal assistance, and serve as employment bureaus. During the 1880s the Knights of Labor had six assemblies in four Indiana cities, including Indianapolis, made up en-

Women nurses marched in support of a World War I bond drive.
[Indiana Historical Society, Bretzman Collection, #C2274]

tirely of women. In Indianapolis, Assembly 4645 was composed of women workers in various trades and was organized in December, 1885; Assembly 6437, organized in April, 1886, was composed of sewing women and housekeepers. Women also formed an overall cooperative under the auspices of the Knights of Labor during the decade. Other women belonged to mixed assemblies of the Knights of Labor. The demise of the Knights of Labor and the rise of the skilled craft unions of the American Federation of Labor likely thwarted unionization by working women in Indianapolis. But even after the turn of the century, and despite a successful open-shop drive in Indianapolis which severely weakened unionism in the city, women formed unions. The bindery workers union, for example, provided a charter to an all-female local in 1903.

But working women as a group were vulnerable to exploitation, not nearly as well organized as men, politically weak, and unprotected by state or federal legislation regulating their employment. So they often welcomed middle class women's efforts to assist them. A singular example of the importance of middle class women's influence occurred before World War I when the WIC prevailed on the Van Camp Packing Company to alter its discriminatory hiring practices and staff an entire division of its plant with black female workers. A more typical form of assistance was the establishment of boardinghouses for single working women. As early as 1867 the Indianapolis Home for Friendless Women was incorporated to care for children and transient women. The Bertha Ballard Home was a nonsectarian boardinghouse for girls founded in 1890 by women of the Western Yearly Meeting of Friends. The Indianapolis YWCA, founded in 1894, helped young women living alone in the city; it sponsored educational, recreational, and religious activities, established a residence for single women, and organized a separate branch for black women, the Phyllis Wheatly Branch, which became a hub of cultural and educational activity in the black community.

Indianapolis resident May Wright Sewall served as president of the International
Council of Women between 1899 and 1904. Sewall, shown here in Berlin, is
seated at the middle of the table, with Susan B. Anthony on her right.
[Indiana Historical Society]

Also benefiting working women were the child care programs and employment services offered by some of the settlement houses and the YWCA, although these were not as well patronized because the element of social control was so apparent. The day nursery at Foreign House, for
example, took advantage of mothers' absence at work to Americanize the habits and ideals of immigrant children. Other settlements served as employment agencies. The best example of this
was the Flanner House Employment Department which by 1923 supplied work to 3,500 of the
4,000–5,000 black women estimated by the settlement as engaged in domestic work in Indianapolis. Flanner House did try to protect domestic workers from exploitation; the department
regulated hours and wages and had a graded pay scale based on experience. Yet like the child care
programs, the Flanner House employment agency extended help to working women that ironically tended to reinforce rather than undermine their dependence and vulnerability.

Capping a 70–year campaign, the enfranchisement of women in 1920 in many respects was
the inevitable consequence of the women's movement of the late 19th and early 20th centuries.
Even without the vote, women engaged in politics. As members of the Women's Christian Temperance Union, for example, women lobbied so vociferously in favor of prohibition during the
1874 Indianapolis city elections that the Democrats, having won control of the city council for
the first time in 14 years, attributed the Republicans' defeat to the "ill-conceived and misdirected
zeal of the so-called temperance people," especially women who were "conspicuous" at the polling places.

The women's suffrage movement for its part made little headway in Indiana until after the turn
of the century. But beginning in the 1870s Indianapolis was a center for suffrage agitation in the

state. Dormant in the Civil War era, the Woman's Rights Association of Indiana changed its name to the Indiana Woman's Suffrage Convention and affiliated with the American Woman Suffrage Association (AWSA) in 1869. In 1878 a group of Indianapolis residents, including Zerelda Wallace and May Wright Sewall, who felt that the Indiana Woman's Suffrage Convention was not pressing aggressively enough, formed the Equal Suffrage Society (ESS). The group lobbied with the AWSA for woman suffrage at the 1881 Indiana General Assembly and during the 1882 state elections.

The slow and uneven progress of the movement frustrated many, including Dr. Amelia R. Keller and Grace Julian Clarke of the ESS. In 1909 they organized a Woman's School League to seek election of a woman to the municipal school board in Indianapolis. When Mary E. Nicholson, principal of the Indianapolis Normal School from 1884 until 1909, indeed was elected to the Indianapolis Board of School Commissioners, the ESS extended its purpose to work for universal woman suffrage under the name of the Woman's Franchise League of Indiana. The organization became the leading feminist body in the state with 60 branches and 3,000 members by May, 1916. In 1917, to mobilize support for suffrage measures in the General Assembly, a Legislative Council of Women was formed under the presidency of Luella Frances Smith McWhirter of Indianapolis. The General Assembly deleted the word "male" from the state constitution's definition of voter qualifications and passed a partial suffrage bill for women that granted them the right to vote for presidential electors, municipal officials, and delegates to a proposed constitutional convention. And in 1920 the 19th Amendment was ratified.

Enfranchisement was not as effective in integrating women into party politics as some had hoped. The Woman's Franchise League dissolved and was replaced by the League of Women Voters (LWV) of Indianapolis in 1920. The new group was important in educating the electorate on political issues but its decision to remain nonpartisan like its predecessor prompted the organization in Indianapolis of the Women's Democratic Club and 7th District Women's Republican Club. These groups, however, did not serve very effectively in the short run as springboards for women seeking elective office. Of the total of 500 seats in the Indiana House from 1931 through 1939, for example, women held only five seats, although it is significant that three of these were by Indianapolis representatives Bess Robbins Kaufman and Roberta West Nicholson. Arcada Stark Balz parlayed a high profile role as president of the Indianapolis Federation of Women's Clubs into a successful campaign to become the first woman elected to the Indiana Senate in 1942 as a Republican representing parts of Marion and Johnson counties.

But Kaufman, Nicholson, and Balz were exceptions rather than role models. More women engaged in politics within the party organizations at the city and county levels, but here, too, there were obstacles and progress was slow. Until the 1960s, when different attitudes prevailed, women tended to participate in politics indirectly through organizations like the LWV. The investigative and lobbying efforts of such groups were important in ways not yet fully appreciated. They set agendas, drafted legislation, and mobilized support for political and institutional change. The LWV, for example, deserves a large share of the credit for the Unigov legislation of 1969 that consolidated city and county government and embodied many of the reforms the organization had sought since the 1920s. But because these groups had to work through male elected officials, their own significance as initiators and political activists often goes unnoticed.

Middle class women did not play as prominent a role in the delivery of social welfare and social services after 1920. With the professionalization and institutionalization of such work, middle class women's voluntary activities tended to emphasize fund raising and auxiliary support services. For example, one of the first projects of the Junior League of Indianapolis, a fund-raising and community service organization begun in 1921, was to organize, equip, finance, and initially maintain and staff the first occupational therapy clinic at Riley Hospital for Children. But there were some new concerns and opportunities for public activism, especially in light of the traditionally cooperative relationship between the private and public sectors in Indianapolis. The Central Indiana branch of Planned Parenthood, for example, was established in 1932 as the Indiana Birth Control League; it became the Maternal Health League of Indiana in 1934. The first clinic was established in 1933 in Indianapolis and served only married women with two or more children who were referred by a physician or social agency. By the mid–1950s the association expanded from traditional birth control services into the areas of premarital counseling, service to teens, and infertility services.

Although such activity was important not only for leisured, middle class women but also for the beneficiaries of their time and energy, one of the two most striking developments of the post–World War I era was the ever-increasing importance of employment for women. Particularly important was the tremendous expansion of the service sector after World War II that created demand for female labor at the same time that families, regardless of class, came increasingly to depend on more than one adult income. Women comprised a steadily increasing share of the Indianapolis labor force, from 29 percent in 1940 to 62 percent in 1990. They have gained greater access to male-defined occupations. In 1980, for example, there were 5,350 skilled tradeswomen and 337 female lawyers and judges in the city; these groups represented 8 percent and 11.7 percent, respectively, of people so employed. By the early 1990s one fifth of the membership of the Indianapolis Bar Association was female.

But their still small share of such jobs indicated that the ever-increasing number of women in the labor force have taken conventional "women's" jobs. In 1980 women comprised 40 percent of those in managerial and professional occupations; within this category there were 7,100 nurses and 12,800 elementary and secondary education teachers. The number of women exceeded the number of men employed in technical, sales, and administrative support occupations in 1980. Indeed, this category employed 48.7 percent of all working women in the city in that year. Still, the two most important jobs held by women in this category—and the two most important jobs for all 235,000 women employed in Indianapolis in 1980—were as salesclerks and secretaries.

Although the occupational distribution of women has not changed very much over the course of this century, their marital status has. In 1940, 39 percent of working women were married; in 1970, 59 percent of employed women were married. Increasing numbers of women with children worked. Half of all employed women in the city in 1970 had children under the age of 18. By 1990, 67 percent of all Indianapolis women with children under the age of six were in the labor force.

African-American women have experienced some improvement in their labor market status since 1920. Black women have gained access to clerical and manufacturing jobs; in 1980, 46 percent of all employed black women in the city held these jobs, which they had been almost completely denied in 1940. Also, about one quarter of all employed black women in 1980 worked as service and private household workers, compared to four fifths in 1940. Yet whereas just 15 percent of all white working women held service jobs in 1980, 27 percent of all black working women held such jobs in that year. Black women, moreover, made up a mere 7.6 percent of all saleswomen in the city in 1980, further demonstrating the persistence of racial and gender hierarchies in the labor market.

The importance of employment in women's lives was evident in the proliferation of professional women's organizations and in the increasing prominence of women in the labor movement in Indianapolis after 1920. Founded in 1912, the Indianapolis Business and Professional Women's Club represented white-collar women workers. The Indianapolis chapter of the American Society of Women Accountants (1938), the Indianapolis Association of Insurance Women (1942), the Indianapolis Credit Women's Breakfast Club (1954), and the Women's Construction League of Indianapolis (1955) reflect both women's increasing presence in male-dominated occupations and their marginal status within those occupations and the felt need to organize separate women's professional organizations in response to their exclusion from men's groups. The expansion of the industrial union movement from the 1930s through the 1950s brought more women into labor organizations as workers rather than into the auxiliaries as wives of male workers. Moreover, the unionization in the 1960s and 1970s of female-dominated occupations in the public sector—such as teachers, government employees, and health care workers—offered working women another arena for collective action and raised their public profile. Although serving different constituencies, professional women's organizations and labor unions have enabled working women to take care of themselves. The 19th-century tradition of middle class women's protection of working women has eroded in the face of greater employment and unionization.

The second most important theme in Indianapolis women's history after 1920 is the prominent role played by women in the civil rights and feminist movements. One of the most immediate challenges for the African-American community following World War I was the effort to segregate the city's high schools in the 1920s. Although Indianapolis elementary schools were generally segregated in 1920, largely due to residential patterns, the high schools were integrated. But in the 1920s, as the number of blacks in the city increased, whites demanded segregation. Under pressure from organizations including the white Federation of Women's Clubs, the Indianapolis Board of School Commissioners moved to divide the races in the city's schools. New boundaries for elementary schools further segregated white and black children. The school board also approved construction of a separate high school for blacks. Black opposition to segregation led to an unsuccessful suit against construction of the new high school. The one consolation was that the name of the new high school was changed from Jefferson to Crispus Attucks.

In the late 1940s, however, Indianapolis women spearheaded a successful and nationally important campaign for repeal of the state law permitting school segregation. The prominence of Indianapolis women in the civil rights movement has endured. The organization and influence of groups such as the Citizens Forum, founded by Mattie Coney in 1964 to secure an open housing ordinance in the city, and the Indianapolis chapter of the Coalition of 100 Black Women, a select group of African-American professional women, reflect the heightened consciousness of women's power within the black community and Indianapolis.

The feminist movement also has had an effective presence in Indianapolis. Two groups that formed in the 1960s—the Woman's Anti-Crime Crusade and the Mayor's Task Force on Women—signaled a changing political climate when they formed Women United Against Rape in 1973 and initiated 24–hour rape crisis centers at nine Indianapolis hospitals. Several older women's organizations as well as some newer ones similarly created the Greater Indianapolis Women's Political Caucus in 1972 to endorse and support female candidates and to lobby on issues of importance to women such as equal pay, child care, and equal access to credit. After participating in the campaign for state ratification of the Equal Rights Amendment (ERA), the Women's Political Caucus turned its attention to issues such as health care for women, domestic violence, rape, employment, and women in politics. The Indianapolis chapter of the National Organization for Women (NOW) also was established in 1971. From 1972 to 1975 it spearheaded an effort to expand employment opportunities for women and blacks in local radio and television stations. Then until 1982 the Indianapolis NOW chapter focused on winning state and national passage of the ERA. NOW also lobbied for passage of the state's rape shield law, funding for domestic violence shelters, and the spouse rape law and publicly opposed restrictions on women's access to abortion.

Not all women participated in the feminist movement or endorsed its strategies and goals. Many rejected feminism and gathered instead under the pro-family and other banners of the New Right beginning in the late 1970s. But one of the events that made Indianapolis notable if not notorious in the 1980s was the effort of antifeminists to take advantage of a 1984 feminist victory—the passage of a city law declaring pornography a form of violence against women and of sex discrimination. Spearheaded by Mayor William H. Hudnut III and city councilwoman Beulah Coughenour, the conservative effort seized on the law as a means of zoning against pornography. The city council further narrowed the intent and scope of the ordinance by limiting it to violent pornography (see *American Booksellers Association v. Hudnut*). Those who introduced and agitated for the original, broader, and more radical ordinance also were dismayed that not one local feminist group endorsed it at public hearings in 1984. The story of the ordinance—which was found to be unconstitutional by courts at all levels, including the U.S. Supreme Court in 1985—ironically bespoke women's collective strength and influence in the political arena even as it underscored the diversity of women's aims.

The history of women in Indianapolis demonstrates how blurry have become the boundaries between the domestic sphere of women and the public sphere of men. The well-established and permanent presence of women in the labor force regardless of age, marital status, class, or race, their increasingly important role in politics and government, and their greater social freedom and personal autonomy highlight the changes that have occurred in the last 200 years. Yet certain trends serve as reminders of the persistently unequal and vulnerable status of women. Indianapolis has witnessed an increase in the number of single-parent, female-headed households; 20 percent of all family households in the city in 1990 were headed by a woman with no husband present and 60 percent of these had children under the age of 18. Combined with occupational segregation by sex and women's low waged status as well as other factors, this has led to the feminization of poverty. In contrast to the past, the social safety net now frees poorer women from dependence on private charity administered for better or worse by middle and upper class women. Yet the characterization of these women as autonomous individuals with the freedom to make choices and be independent of men has cruel overtones and ignores the difficulty that all women regardless of class experience finding affordable child care and a secure, decent income. There are no easy solutions to these dilemmas. But the willingness of women to confront and address them is a legacy of the past and for the future.

See also: AFRICAN-AMERICAN WOMEN'S ORGANIZATIONS; EDUCATION, FEMALE; WOMEN IN POLITICS; WOMEN IN RELIGION; WOMEN IN THE PROFESSIONS AND BUSINESS; WOMEN'S CLUBS; WOMEN'S MOVEMENT (1960–PRESENT); WOMEN'S RIGHTS AND SUFFRAGE; WOMEN'S VOLUNTARY ORGANIZATIONS; and individual names, institutions, and organizations.

A. H. M. Graves. Real estate firm. Graves Realtors began in 1924 when A. H. Merriam Graves teamed with fraternity brother William L. Bridges to form the Bridges & Graves Company. The partnership lasted until 1948 when Graves organized A. H. M. Graves, Inc., serving as its president until his death in 1967. The company's current name, the A. H. M. Graves Company, Inc., dates to February, 1977, although as of the early 1990s the firm was still often called Graves Realtors.

Graves operates eight sales offices in the Indianapolis metropolitan area. Employing roughly 325 people, including some 280 real estate agents, Graves had a 1992 sales volume of $392 million, making it the second largest real estate firm in the Indianapolis area.

DEBORAH B. MARKISOHN

Acme-Evans Company (702 West Washington Street). Acme-Evans/ADM Milling Company evolved from two small mills of the antebellum era to the large milling company of today. Reputedly the oldest milling company in Indianapolis, it traces its heritage to Isaac Wilson, a Revolutionary War soldier who built his first mill along the WHITE RIVER in the 1820s, and to John Carlisle, who in 1840 constructed his first mill "only a short distance away," according to a company brochure. Carlisle's mill became the Acme Milling Company and Wilson's Mill became the Evans Milling Company. In 1909, the two firms merged to form Acme-Evans Milling Company. In 1946, the Early and Daniel Company acquired Acme-Evans. In May, 1988, Archer Daniels Midland Company (ADM) of Decatur, Illinois, took over Acme-Evans and changed the name to Acme-Evans/ADM Milling Company. Its product lines have included plain flour, self-rising flour, corn meal, cereal, and feed and grain mixtures for livestock. Its best-known product in Indiana is "E-Z Bake Flour."

The buildings at Acme-Evans illustrate the evolution of milling architecture since the 1880s. A two-story office building displaying Italianate architecture dates to the 1880s and was one of the primary buildings of the Acme Mill. After a fire in 1917, the Acme-Evans Company, as it was known

then, commissioned a modern mill to be built on its property along the river. NORDYKE AND MARMON, manufacturers of precision milling machinery in Indianapolis, constructed the nine-story mill building measuring 112 by 44 feet of reinforced concrete and steel in 1919. Built in Twentieth Century Functional style, the mill displayed many modern and innovative features, such as rounded corners to prevent the accumulation of flour dust and large sash windows to provide interior lighting for the "daylight" mill. As one of the first mills in the country to use reinforced concrete storage bins, Acme-Evans has modernized and expanded its system of bins and elevators several times since 1909. In July, 1994, demolition of the mill began after legal action failed to halt it. Because of urban space changes, especially the development of WHITE RIVER STATE PARK, Acme-Evans/ADM Milling Company relocated to the city's south side.

LINDA B. WEINTRAUT

Acme-Evans Company, *Acme-Evans, 1821–1919* (Indianapolis, 1919).

Acton. Southeastern Franklin Township community located near the intersection of Acton and McGregor roads. The town now known as Acton was platted in October, 1852, as a stop on the Indianapolis and Cincinnati Railroad. Originally called Farmersville, the village was later renamed, reportedly after General Acton, a resident. By the 1880s Acton boasted churches, stores, blacksmith shops, mills, and about 300 people.

Population swelled during the summer and fall months when thousands came to the Acton Camp Ground northwest of town. Purchased in 1859 and operated by the Southeast Indiana Conference of the Methodist Church, the campground featured daily prayer meetings, inspirational programs, and lectures, sometimes by noted politicians such as William Jennings Bryan. A 1,000–seat pavilion, the Acton Park Hotel, and guest cottages hosted campers who came by wagon or on one of the five trains that stopped daily at the gate. The camp buildings were rebuilt following several fires, but were abandoned after a disastrous 1905 blaze.

Acton grew slowly in the 20th century as an agricultural service center. By 1950 the town counted several small industries and about 900 residents. Acton was also touted as the hometown of Marjorie Main, a successful film actress.

Never incorporated, Acton became a part of Indianapolis under UNIGOV. In the 1990s it remains primarily rural, though future residential and commercial development is anticipated.

CATHLEEN F. DONNELLY

Indianapolis Star Magazine, Aug. 17, 1958, Nov. 30, 1980; Sylvia C. Henricks, "A Good and Profitable Occasion: The Story of Acton Camp Ground," *Indiana Magazine of History*, 66 (Dec., 1970), 299–317.

Adams, J. Ottis (July 8, 1851–Jan. 28, 1927). Hoosier Group artist. Adams was born in Amity, Johnson County, Indiana, the grandson of one of that county's pioneers. His visit to the 1869 INDIANA STATE FAIR in Indianapolis, which included the state's only regular display of art, inspired him to become an artist. He saw a memorable *Still Life with Watermelon* by young WILLIAM MERRITT CHASE, then of Indianapolis, that was so seductively painted that Adams returned to the family farm intent on doing his own versions. Three years later he sought formal training at London's South Kensington School of Art, returning in 1874 to set up his own portrait painting studio, first in Seymour and later (1876) in Muncie. In 1880 he joined T. C. STEELE, Carrie Wolff, and August Metzner of Indianapolis and Samuel Richards of Anderson for study at the Royal Academy of Painting in Munich. They were joined 18 months later by WILLIAM FORSYTH of Indianapolis.

The experiences and camaraderie shared for five years by Adams, Steele, and Forsyth in Germany continued when they returned to Indiana determined to paint its landscapes in preference to doing the portraiture for which they had been expertly trained. Soon termed the HOOSIER GROUP, they would lead Indiana painting for 40 years.

Adams returned to Muncie from Munich in 1887 where he and Forsyth opened the successful but short-lived Muncie Art School in 1889. After its close in 1891, Adams was at liberty for the first time to devote himself to independent landscape painting, which in subsequent summers he often did in the company of Steele. In 1898, Adams and Steele bought a historic house, soon dubbed the Hermitage, on the banks of the Whitewater in Brookville to serve as a seasonal studio, but which became Adams' permanent residence upon his marriage on October 1 to Winifred Brady, his former student.

Adams' finely wrought landscapes were well known in the capital city through exhibitions sponsored by the Art Association of Indianapolis; from the circuit exhibitions of the Society of Western Artists, an organization of midwestern painters of which Adams, Steele, and Forsyth had been the founding Indiana contingent in 1896; from the Home Artists exhibitions inaugurated in 1897; and from annual displays of his past season's work at the H. LIEBER COMPANY each December from 1900 to 1905.

Based on this reputation, the Art Association hired Adams in February, 1902, as its first instructor of painting and drawing at the newly established HERRON SCHOOL OF ART. Adams, responsible for the day, evening, and Saturday classes, bought a house nearby at 2022 North Pennsylvania. He died there on January 28, 1927, although he had rarely occupied it after his resignation from Herron in 1906 to return to paint full-time at the Hermitage.

MARTIN KRAUSE

Martin Krause, *The Passage: Return of Indiana Painters from Germany, 1880–1905* (Indianapolis: Indianapolis Museum of Art, 1990).

Adams, Wayman Eldridge (Sept. 23, 1883–Apr. 4, 1959). Portrait painter. Born in Delaware County, Indiana, young Adams was influenced as an artist by his father, Nelson Perry Adams, a stock breeder and self-taught painter of horses and other livestock. Adams came to Indianapolis in 1904 to study for four years with WILLIAM FORSYTH at the HERRON SCHOOL OF ART, where he supported himself by painting portraits. In 1910 he studied in Italy with WILLIAM MERRITT CHASE, returned to Indianapolis in 1911 to mount his first exhibition, and went to Spain in 1912 to study with Robert Henri. In 1918 he married Margaret Graham Boroughs, a native of Austin, Texas, whom he met in Italy while both studied with Chase.

Adams established himself as a portrait painter in Indianapolis in 1913, attracting many prominent citizens as sitters. In 1914 he was one of several local artists selected to execute paintings and murals for the children's ward of City Hospital (now WISHARD MEMORIAL HOSPITAL). Seeking a larger client base for his portraiture, Adams moved to New York City, teaching at the Grand Central School of Art. In 1933 he purchased a farm near Elizabethtown, New York, converting its old mill into his famous Old Mill Studio. Here he painted, taught students, and developed an interest in lithography. He returned to Indianapolis frequently, however, accepting many commissions in the Hoosier capital. After 1949 he moved to Austin, Texas.

Adams is best known as a portraitist, but he also created many small figure studies, porch scenes, and small landscapes, as well as occasional watercolors. He exhibited these works with success, receiving critical recognition such as the Dana Water Color Gold Medal. As a portrait painter many famous Americans sat for him; these included Indianapolis literary figures such as JAMES WHITCOMB RILEY and BOOTH TARKINGTON, as well as United States presidents Calvin Coolidge and Warren G. Harding. The Indiana Governors Portraits Collection, partially on display in STATE HOUSE offices, includes six canvases by Adams.

NED GRINER
Ball State University

Administration, Department of. Municipal government department. The Department of Administration is one of the six departments established under the original UNIGOV legislation in 1969. Its principal role is to perform administrative and miscellaneous functions of city and county government.

The department's director is appointed by, and serves at the pleasure of, the mayor. The director is advised by the City-County Administrative Board. Following reorganization in 1992–

1993 the department contains four divisions: the Director's Office, the Central Equipment Management Division, the Equal Opportunity Division, and the Human Resources Management Division.

The responsibilities of the Director's Office include providing staffing for the City-County Administrative Board, overseeing records management for city-county government, and providing an appeals process for denials of assistance by the township trustees.

The Central Equipment Management Division services and maintains the vehicles and equipment owned by the city. It purchases equipment, repair services, and fuel as needed.

The Equal Opportunity Division administers the city's nondiscrimination policies in conjunction with the Equal Opportunity Advisory Board. That board includes eight members appointed by the CITY-COUNTY COUNCIL and fourteen by the mayor. Division personnel respond to inquiries and receive and investigate discrimination complaints. Complaints are then referred to a panel composed of three members of the Equal Opportunity Advisory Board, who determine whether there is probable cause to investigate and pursue the allegations.

The Human Resources Management Division performs recruiting, interviewing and testing, and hiring and orientation of all city employees. It also administers and oversees wage and salary standards and classifications.

HEATHER ALYSE JAMES

Aesculapian Medical Society. African-American professional medical association. African-American physicians, dentists, and pharmacists originally banded together in Indianapolis around the turn of the 20th century when the Marion County Medical Society refused admission to blacks. This loosely organized group was more firmly established in 1929 when Dr. Edwin Moten took over leadership of the group, named after the ancient god of medicine and healing.

Like its white counterparts, the society transmitted professional information and established group cohesion and recognition. In addition, it was committed to self-protection against discriminatory practices within the local medical community. Members pushed for admittance of African-American doctors and patients into local hospitals, meeting success in 1953 when national forces converged with their efforts and city hospitals became integrated.

In the succeeding decades, the society supported the continued advances of African-American doctors into medical education and hospital administrative positions. The society has also pushed for better health care for African-Americans through such organizations as the Metropolitan Health Council, and since the 1960s it has contributed funds for medical school scholarships for African-American students. During the 1940s the society's dentists and pharmacists left to form their own organizations. As of 1993 there were approximately 60 members.

MICHELLE D. HALE

George Rawls, *History of the Black Physician in Indianapolis, 1870–1980* (Indianapolis, 1984).

Afflis, Richard, aka Dick the Bruiser

(June 27, 1929–Nov. 10, 1991). World champion professional wrestler. Born in Lafayette, Indiana, Afflis was raised in Delphi before moving with his family to Indianapolis. He attended SHORTRIDGE HIGH SCHOOL for two years before moving back to Lafayette, where he graduated from Lafayette Jefferson High School. He attended and played football at Purdue University for three years. After dropping out of Purdue, Afflis moved to Nevada and eventually enrolled at the University of Nevada–Las Vegas, where he continued to play football. He graduated in 1950 with a degree in engineering.

Afflis was drafted by the Green Bay Packers professional football team as an offensive lineman in 1951. While with the Packers he received his nickname, "Dick the Bruiser," for his physical style of play. Also during his playing days he was hit in his throat, giving him his distinctive raspy voice. After four seasons with the Packers he quit in 1955 and became a full-time professional wrestler, earning distinction as "The World's Most Dangerous Wrestler."

During his long wrestling career the Bruiser was five times world champion in the Worldwide Wrestling Association and the National Wrestling Alliance. He became well known throughout Indiana and the Midwest from his numerous appearances on Indianapolis-produced television programs like "Big Time Wrestling," "Championship Wrestling," and "All-Star Championship Wrestling." Bruiser, who lived most of his adult life in Indianapolis, was also known for his work on behalf of numerous charitable organizations, especially the Muscular Dystrophy Association.

RAY BOOMHOWER
Indiana Historical Society

Dick Wolfsie, "Requiem for a Heavyweight," *Indianapolis Monthly* (Jan., 1992).

African-American Businesses.

The African-American population of Indianapolis was quite small until the Civil War, numbering just under 500 residents in 1860. By 1870, however, the city's black population had increased dramatically to 2,931. Most of these people settled along the western edge of the MILE SQUARE. By 1900 the black population had increased to 15,931.

As part of this developing community, several African-Americans began businesses within the city; at least four of them were newspapers. The earliest on record was the INDIANAPOLIS LEADER, first published during the late 1870s by three educator brothers—James, Benjamin, and ROBERT BAGBY. The *Colored World* (Levi Christy and Alex-

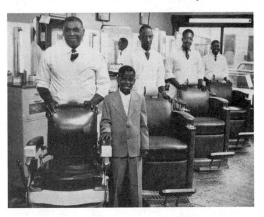

Small, locally owned businesses such as the Hayden barbershop, 912 W. Michigan Street, served a predominantly black clientele. [Indiana Historical Society, *Indianapolis Recorder* Collection, #C5312]

ander Manning, publishers); the *INDIANAPOLIS FREEMAN* (Louis Howland, Edward E. Cooper, and GEORGE KNOX, publishers); and the *INDIANAPOLIS RECORDER* (George P. Stewart and Will Porter, publishers) succeeded the *Leader*. Stewart represented the prototypical African-American businessman in Indianapolis during the late 1800s. He was politically and socially engaged in his community, and he used his activities to promote his newspaper and print shop. Several other newspapers started and folded during the first half of the 20th century, including the *Indiana Herald-Times* (Opal Tandy) in 1957 (changed to the *Indiana Herald* in 1960).

The late 19th century also gave rise to several individuals who built lucrative companies. Among the more successful were John Jones (cement and trucking), Henry L. Sanders (clothing, especially uniforms), Charles Webb (house moving), and Cassius M. C. Willis (funeral home director). By the beginning of the 20th century a substantial African-American business community existed as revealed in a list of business people complied and published by Stewart in the *Recorder* (December 21, 1901). Occupations included plumbers, dressmakers, shoemakers, contractors, junk dealers, grocers, barber and beauty shop owners, blacksmiths, carriage makers, morticians, paperhangers, physicians, attorneys, dentists, and musicians. Restaurants, newspapers, hotels, saloons, and other black-owned institutions were listed, as were less common occupations including a veterinary surgeon, a milliner, and a clairvoyant.

Traditionally, most African-American businesses were sole proprietorships. Service enterprises in particular enabled blacks to provide personal services and employment to other African-Americans, as well as create business opportunities for individuals. The first quarter of the 20th century witnessed the development of new businesses owned by blacks, as well as the continuation of earlier enterprises. In 1910 MADAM C. J. WALKER relocated her hair products and cosmetics company to Indianapolis where her lucrative business developed an international reputation. The company remained in the Walker family until it was sold in 1988. Another manufacturing company, Martin Brothers, incorporated in 1922. The company, owned by James, Samuel, and Jesse

Martin, manufactured and sold heavy cotton duck clothing, khaki and novelty uniforms, and other garments. Marion Stuart started his moving and storage business in 1936. The post–World War II period recorded the development of several groceries, service garages, cleaners, nightclubs, billiard halls, and restaurants owned by African-Americans. Winston Janitorial Service was founded in 1953; by 1992 it was Indianapolis' largest employer among minority-owned businesses.

According to the Bureau of the Census, African-American–owned businesses in Indianapolis exhibited several trends over the most recent 15–year period for which statistics are available. The number of firms showed a steady increase from 1,443 in 1972 to 2,686 in 1987. The selected services category—repair shops, recreation, barber and beauty shops, educational businesses, and legal and health professions, among others—rose from 522 in 1972 to 1,447 in 1987. These businesses accounted for 54 percent of all black-owned firms and 19 percent of gross receipts in 1987. Retail trade, the second largest area demonstrating growth in the economic censuses of 1972, 1977, and 1982, reflected a sharp downward turn in 1987.

Before the 1960s a highly segregated African-American community supported black-owned businesses, especially in service industries. Since the 1970s the decline of residential segregation and the increased integration of the black middle class have resulted in a dispersal of African-American purchasing power. Although it mirrors a national trend, Indianapolis blacks no longer exist in a tight knit business community that encourages economic strength. At times this change has led to racial conflict, such as in 1993 when the local Black Panther militia boycotted a Korean merchant's beauty supply store in a predominantly black neighborhood.

As is true elsewhere, an increasing number of blacks in Indianapolis own businesses, but these enterprises tend to be small. Larger, better capitalized businesses also exist and are financially healthy, but they remain relatively small. Among the 15 largest African-American employers in 1991 (ranked by number of employees), the largest, Winston Janitorial Service, employed 119 and counted assets of $1.5 million. Mays Chemical had assets of $5.8 million and employed 54. The 15th ranked company, a realtor, counted only 10 employees.

WILMA L. GIBBS
Indiana Historical Society

Wilma L. Gibbs, "African-American Businesses in Indianapolis, 1870–1950," *Black History News & Notes*, No. 51 (Feb., 1993), 4–7; Brian E. Frost, "Black Capitalism in Indianapolis," *Indiana Business Review* (Jan.–Feb., 1974); *Indianapolis Business Journal, 1993 Book of Business Lists* (Indianapolis, 1992), esp. p. 82.

African-American Churches. Churches have always occupied a central position within the Indianapolis African-American community. As the first institution that blacks controlled exclusively, African-American churches met religious needs, supplied community aid, fought for African-American rights, and allowed members to develop leadership skills and a sense of self-worth that often could be found nowhere else.

The founding and demographic trends of African-American churches in Indianapolis have reflected the growing diversity and dispersion of the local black population. African-American churchgoers attended white METHODIST and BAPTIST churches as early as the 1830s but were segregated from the rest of the congregation during services and were unable to participate in church governance or congregational life.

The first African-American churches in Indianapolis were Methodist and Baptist congregations founded by visiting black missionaries in what is now the Midtown area. The congregation that became BETHEL AFRICAN METHODIST EPISCOPAL (AME) CHURCH began in 1836 as part of a missionary tour of the West by Rev. Paul Quinn. SECOND BAPTIST CHURCH was organized in 1846 by Rev. Charles Sachel. Both Quinn and Sachel were Cincinnati-based missionaries.

After the Civil War, when southern African-Americans moved to Indianapolis in larger numbers, both the AME and Baptist denominations established new churches. AME congregations included Allen Chapel AME (1866) and Simpson Chapel (1875). Another branch of Methodism, the AME Zion church, appeared in Indianapolis after a group of black missionaries from New Albany, Indiana, organized Jones Tabernacle in 1872, followed by Lovely Lane Church (now St. Mark AME Zion) in 1886. Since many of the southern migrants were already Baptist, however, black Baptist churches soon claimed dominance in the number of churches and members, a lead which they have never relinquished. By 1900 the number of Baptist churches had grown to 18, including Olivet (1867), Mt. Zion (1872), New Bethel (1874), Corinthian (1881), and Barnes Chapel (1887).

The influx of southern blacks caused many white denominations to found mission churches for their "colored brethren." The first denomination to do so was DISCIPLES OF CHRIST, which in 1866 sponsored a mission and school led by white lay leaders. The congregation eventually became Second Christian (now known as LIGHT OF THE WORLD CHRISTIAN CHURCH) and soon attracted its own black minister. By the 1880s other white denominations had followed this lead. In 1881 local PRESBYTERIANS dissolved a white congregation, Ninth Presbyterian, and resurrected it as a black mission church. Two white Episcopal congregations established a mission for African-Americans in 1888, which later became St. Philip's. And CATHOLICS established a church school for African-American children in 1892 named St. Ann's.

The number of black Methodist and Baptist congregations continued to grow and diversify during the 20th century. By 1920 there were 10 AME and 7 AME Zion churches. Both denominations had some of the largest black congregations in the city, but had also reached their zenith in number of churches. The Colored Methodist Episcopal Church (CME), a southern brand of Methodism now known as the Christian Methodist Episcopal church, made its local appearance with the founding of Philip's Temple CME in 1907 and Trinity CME in 1924.

With over 30 churches by 1920, black Baptists began to experience divisions within their fellowship. A split nationally among African-American Baptists resulted locally in the establishment of two separate districts. In addition, three Freewill Baptist congregations were founded. Still, the number of Baptist congregations continued to rise, reaching over 60 churches by 1936 (the highest number of any one denomination in the city at the time). In 1943 the Central Baptist Theological Seminary was founded and located at South Calvary Baptist.

Indianapolis became the site of a new African-American Pentecostal denomination by the 1920s. Rev. GARFIELD T. HAYWOOD founded what became Christ Temple Apostolic Church, an integrated PENTECOSTAL congregation, in 1909. The church grew rapidly despite harassment by segregationist elements. When a national split among Pentecostals occurred in 1919, Haywood became presiding bishop of the predominately black Pentecostal Assemblies of the World denomination, which located its headquarters in the city.

White denominations continued to establish segregated mission churches well into the 20th century. United Presbyterians sponsored Witherspoon, an all-black congregation in 1907, and white Presbyterians renewed their mission efforts by establishing Senate Avenue Presbyterian (later Sutherland and now Immanuel) in 1908. The Roman Catholic church established St. Rita as a segregated black parish with a white priest in 1919. With sympathetic leadership during the 1930s, the church school grew past capacity and blacks began to be accepted at several other parishes. LUTHERANS sponsored a mission in 1938 which originally met at the PHYLLIS WHEATLEY YWCA. Both the First Colored Nazarene Church and First Free Christian (Disciples of Christ) were also organized during this time, but neither survived.

As the local African-American population grew beyond its traditional neighborhood boundaries after World War II, old congregations resettled farther north and new churches appeared. The more evangelical churches benefited the most from the population growth. While the AME and AME Zion denominations remained relatively stable in number, the number of CME congregations had grown to 13 as of the early 1990s. The number of black Baptist churches multiplied, and by 1960 there were 108 local congregations. As of the early 1990s, there were three separate associations of black Baptists in Indianapolis, representing over 180 churches, and an unknown number of independent storefront Baptist congregations.

The numbers of African-American Catholics have increased since World War II, especially since the 1970s. By the early 1990s there were three predominantly black congregations—St. Rita, St. Bridget, and Holy Angels—in addition to several other parishes with significant numbers of black congregants. Most of these parishes have African-American priests and nuns. Recently African-American Catholics have organized themselves and are seeking to be better represented in the church hierarchy and to express their culture within Catholic traditions.

To the dismay of many mainline denominational leaders, the modern era has witnessed a large increase in small independent and storefront churches within the African-American community. As the black population pushed north into neighborhoods abandoned by whites, some churches began to purchase the former buildings of white congregations or were able to build their own. However, under the pressure of needed services and low resources, many fledgling congregations resorted to using storefront properties. Already by 1959 there were almost as many storefront churches in Indianapolis as established denominational churches.

A new form of African-American worship, Islam, arrived in Indianapolis after World War II. African-American Muslim chapters were first organized in the 1940s, and by the late 1950s a significant group was allied with the Nation of Islam. Four mosques served the Indianapolis area in the early 1990s, and the ISLAMIC SOCIETY OF NORTH AMERICA was headquartered in nearby Plainfield.

As is true of mainstream white denominations and churches, African-American churches have always provided their congregants with spiritual sustenance and a world view. In a society where African-Americans have been enslaved or suffered discrimination, black ministers have preached eternal salvation—thus making the present life more bearable. Black churches and ministers have also consistently supported education, temperance, personal responsibility, and civil rights. Embracing all these ideas, local churches have traditionally sponsored an annual Emancipation Day celebration including a service and a parade. While this tradition lapsed during the early 20th century, it was revived in the 1940s and continues to be celebrated with a service and awards ceremony at a local black church.

Church buildings have provided space in which black community groups could meet and venues for social and cultural activities. Early African-American churches conducted revivals and quarterly Love Feasts and had sickness and burial provisions for their members. Many congregations sponsored benevolent societies, such as the Paul Quinn Missionary Society, as well as self-improvement, debating, and literary clubs, and temperance societies. Churchwomen's groups distributed food and clothing, organized and supported the ALPHA HOME for the aged, supervised young people's groups, raised money for church facilities and programming, hosted national speakers, and conducted vacation Bible schools. The local NAACP chapter and the Indiana State Federation of Colored Women's Clubs organized and met at Bethel AME. Other churches hosted community-wide social activities, speakers, and denominational conferences. Today local community groups hold meetings and sponsor Black History Month activities at many area black churches.

Education has always been a high priority of African-American churches. Since African-Americans were not allowed in local schools until the 1870s, churches offered classes to teach adults and children to read and write. In the 20th century, African-American churches have supported educational scholarships and started local colleges, including Central Baptist Theological Seminary (1943) and MARTIN UNIVERSITY (1969).

African-American churches often helped rural blacks assimilate to urban conditions through social welfare programs. Churches provided informal and later organized day care, employment services, housing assistance, food and clothing, as well as general health and welfare programs. During the 1950s and 1960s many local churches supported the efforts of the NAACP and the Urban League. Additionally, several ministers were heavily involved in organizing the local branches of Operation Breadbasket and the Southern Christian Leadership Conference.

While African-American churches have struggled with lack of financial and community resources and powerlessness outside the African-American community, they have provided sustenance and aid to their members and the community, as well as offered leadership in gaining civil rights and personal freedoms. Even today, when other institutions have taken over many church functions, a large number of the city's African-American residents still turn to black churches in times of crisis or need.

MICHELLE D. HALE

Ida Webb Bryant, *Glimpses of the Negro in Indianapolis, 1863–1963* (Indianapolis, 1963); C. Eric Lincoln, *The Black Church in the African-American Experience* (Durham, N.C., 1990); Emma Lou Thornbrough, *The Negro in Indiana: A Study of a Minority* (Indianapolis, 1957).

African-American Press. Newspapers have been part of the black community of Indianapolis since the 1870s. These publications offered black readers a distinctive perspective on local, national, and even international affairs and contributed heavily to the development of black communities in and outside of Indianapolis.

Indianapolis has been home to at least ten black newspapers, a fourth of the state's total. Two of them survive. The earliest was the *Leader*, established in mid–1879 by the Bagby brothers—Benjamin, James, and ROBERT BRUCE BAGBY—all of whom were educators. This strongly Republican weekly was published until 1890, although the Bagbys sold their interest in 1885. Other newspapers have been the *Argus* (published irregularly, ca. 1886–1887); the COLORED WORLD, renamed the *World* after the mid–1890s (a weekly that appeared from 1883 to 1932); the FREEMAN (a weekly published between 1888 and 1927); the *Courier* (put out irregularly between 1893 and the late 1890s); the *Ledger* (a weekly, 1913–ca. 1925); the *World Telegram* (printed irregularly, 1939–1940); and *Visions* (initially a weekly, later a monthly, 1985–1986). The *Indiana Herald*, currently published as a weekly, began in 1949 as the *Hoosier Herald*, which was possibly the successor of the *Mid-Western Post*. For a time in the late 1950s this newspaper was known as the *Indiana Herald-Times*. The INDIANAPOLIS RECORDER, a weekly established in 1897 by George P. Stewart, also survives, having the distinction as well of being published longer than any other African-American newspaper in Indiana and most others in the United States. Until 1988 its owners were members of the Stewart family.

In general, these newspapers—like their counterparts in the rest of the state—appeared irregularly and were short-lived. Some were weeklies, but none was a daily. Given the special economic and social circumstances facing black men and women who wished to publish a newspaper with a uniquely black perspective, the 40 years of the *Freeman* and near century of the *Recorder* represent remarkable achievements. Like other African-American newspapers in Indiana, Indianapolis' black press emerged as a tool of political parties—usually Republican, at least until the 1930s. Papers that lasted more than five years tended, like the *Recorder*, to shift to a self-defined independent status or, like the *Freeman* or the *World*, to strong support of the DEMOCRATIC PARTY. That black newspapers did not appear in Indianapolis until the late 1870s is attributable to such factors as the small size of the pre–Civil War black community, the modest number of African-Americans who were middle or upper class, and the limited amount of black political activity prior to the passage of the 15th Amendment. Financial support from white Republicans eager to capture the black vote undoubtedly aided these early newspapers.

Other characteristics of these early papers were repeated by later ones. The *World*, for instance, introduced a number of black writers to the public, maintained a print shop employing black printers, and complained of its support being taken for granted by its political sponsor. Most of these newspapers had local agents who sold the newspaper not only in the capital city but also in other cities and towns in Indiana. These individuals also wrote news columns for the Indianapolis black press. The *Freeman* was distinguished by having columns written by correspondents throughout the nation. Local agents were invariably leaders like Willis Rucker of Evansville, a barber, whose 1892 columns in the *Freeman* stressed the achievements of Evansville's black lodges and AME churches. These agents offered a wealth of news of local black society that emphasized self-help and economic

success. Agents also offered other kinds of news, including efforts of blacks to achieve racial justice.

The black newspapers' most striking feature was their special view of American society and politics. The *Freeman* of February 23, 1889, for example, included a lengthy article by Lucy Wilmot Smith on unique challenges to and contributions of black women who were journalists. An extensive piece on Isaac Myers, organizer of the first national black union and of numerous black cooperatives, appeared in the October 12, 1889, issue. For much of its history the *Freeman* annually provided a report on the number and location of lynchings across the nation. In a society in which news of blacks was limited to stories that reinforced images of blacks as either perpetual children or brutes, these papers offered ample evidence of black achievement. In addition to emphasizing racial progress through hard work and community self-reliance, the Indianapolis black press pointed with varying degrees of sharpness to the need for the ending of racial discrimination.

Through the 20th century, the Indianapolis African-American press continued to build on these patterns. Racial pride remains a focus, as news stories and editorials—especially in the *Recorder*—stress accomplishments of blacks in Indianapolis and elsewhere. In addition to developing and enhancing racial pride, black newspapers have provided leadership in the black community, especially in battles against segregation after World War II. These newspapers have been at once agents of change and mirrors of the many developments in race relations and community progress. Hence they became more aggressive in their exposure of discrimination and their demand for such reforms as the Voting Rights Act of 1965. They have also been a springboard for black writers. Opal Tandy, for instance, worked for the *Recorder* before launching the *Indiana Herald*, as did William Raspberry, currently a nationally syndicated columnist for the *Washington Post*. The *Recorder*'s 1992 circulation of almost 12,000 underscores the continuing vitality and relevance of the African-American press in Indianapolis. The ability of the black press to build a sales and news network outside as well as within the city has over time created a sense of racial solidarity and, as the success of the *Recorder* demonstrates, the financial base needed to survive and grow.

DARREL E. BIGHAM
University of Southern Indiana

John W. Miller, *Indiana Newspaper Bibliography* (Indianapolis, 1982); Emma Lou Thornbrough, *The Negro in Indiana* (Indianapolis, 1957); "Fit to Print," *Indianapolis Star*, Sept. 6, 1992, sec. F; *Black History News & Notes*, No. 18 (Aug., 1984), No. 42 (Nov., 1990).

African-American Women's Organizations.

Although African-American women have lived in Indianapolis since the 1820s, not until the 1870s do sources begin to reveal the organizations they formed. Six local African-American women in 1874 founded the Sisters of Charity, a relief and aid organization sustained by charitable donations. The Sisters helped pay for medical care, distributed clothing and food, and home-nursed the bedridden. Following a fund-raising campaign in 1912, they opened the 14-room Sisters of Charity State Hospital for blacks, operating it for nearly ten years before insolvency forced its closing.

On April 4, 1883, former slave Elizabeth Goff and several other women founded the Alpha Home Association. Goff's white employer, Pauline Merritt, donated a three-room house to the group, which opened the ALPHA HOME for impoverished former slave women on July 6, 1886. The Alpha Home picnic each July became a popular social event for black families in the city. First located on Oak Hill (now Hillside Avenue), the home began accepting male residents in the 1920s; after a series of moves Alpha Home opened a new 86-bed facility at 2640 Cold Spring Road in 1992.

Social and fraternal clubs helped to establish the African-American middle class in the city. Many of the women who joined these clubs were also active in other women's organizations. Huldah Bates Webb, of the Alpha Home Association, was simultaneously president of the Independent Daughters of Honor. Julia Johnson Reed led both the Alpha Home and the Court of Calanthe, a black lodge, for 25 years. Other African-American women's fraternal orders included the Magnolia Lodge, the Household of Ruth, and the American

Doves. The Young Ladies Excelsior Glee Club was a social organization. Members opened their 1879 season with a Thanksgiving "event" at the home of Mr. and Mrs. Andrew Herron. The following year the glee club became the Social Key Club and presented a "fine literary programme" at the home of Mrs. Jones Smith.

For women of all races, churches offered a venue for organizational activities. The Ladies Aid Society at SECOND BAPTIST CHURCH conducted festivals and suppers in the 1870s to raise money for the church. Corinthian Baptist's women's groups, such as the King's Daughters and the Sewing Circle, had combined memberships of nearly 600 women. In 1914 at Corinthian Baptist Julia Johnson Reed, Anna Walker, and others formed the Ladies Alliance, with Walker as president. Holding teas, recitals, lectures with nationally known black leaders, and baby contests, the alliance raised enough money by 1925 to pay for the congregation's new church.

In 1896 the women of Allen Chapel AME founded the Women's Mite Missionary Society; later the club became the Flora Grant Missionary Society. Its Mother's Department educated women about the social problems facing their homes and families. The society raised funds for the church, distributed fruit at the City Hospital—one of the few which accepted African-Americans—and visited residents at the Alpha Home. Members also joined the biracial Council of Church Women.

In 1903 LILLIAN THOMAS FOX, the first African-American reporter for the *INDIANAPOLIS NEWS*, was a member of the Bethel AME Church Literary Society and the principal mover behind the formation of the Women's Improvement Club (WIC). President Fox intended WIC to be for "higher class" women who represented the "Talented Tenth" of black society that African-American historian W. E. B. Du Bois believed should be its leaders. Most of WIC's members were Indianapolis school teachers, professionals, or homemakers, and eventually only relatives of the founding members were allowed to join.

Along with holding lectures and attending music recitals WIC members established an outdoor tuberculosis camp north of the city. Tuberculosis was a particular problem among the city's overcrowded African-American population, which also suffered from inadequate medical care. Fighting the disease served two purposes for WIC members: it aided the afflicted and it diminished rumors growing among the white population that blacks were responsible for the spread of the disease. Open until 1916, the camp was overseen by a matron and had a three-tent, six-patient capacity. In 1924 WIC opened a tuberculosis treatment cottage that functioned for many years before the City Hospital (now WISHARD MEMORIAL HOSPITAL) began accepting black tuberculosis patients. Later WIC employed a nurse to distribute clothing and food collected by the group.

The Thursday Afternoon Coterie, formed by Anna C. Moore in 1911, was originally a social club but soon found a mission in the community. Moore became a foster mother to a girl who was lured to Indiana on the pretense of gaining a domestic job with a white family, then forced into prostitution when the job did not materialize; her story mirrored the experience of other young black immigrants to the city. To help such girls, members of the Coterie volunteered as probation officers at the juvenile court. In 1919 member Lula Pate became the city's first salaried African-American woman probation officer.

Many organizations joined the Indiana State Federation of Colored Women's Clubs, a chapter of the National Association of Colored Women (NACW), after its formation in 1904. Fourteen women's organizations were represented at the first meeting, called by Lillian Thomas Fox. A venue for many club events, the federation's headquarters at 2034 North Capitol (since 1926) was placed on the National Register of Historic Places in 1987.

Before 1920 African-American women joined the Indianapolis suffrage movement in significant numbers. In 1917 the *Indianapolis News* reported that among black clubs discussing the "question of suffrage" were the 4th Ward League of North Indianapolis, the Women's Advance Franchise League, the Colored Women's Republican Club, and the Women's Suffrage League of the Second Baptist Church.

On January 19, 1923, a committee of 18 women held the charter meeting of the PHYLLIS WHEATLEY YWCA. May B. Belcher, a national organizer of Phyllis Wheatley Y's, was the local director for 21 years, and headed the 1937 citywide campaign to pay off the building's mortgage. The branch operated until 1959 when the YWCA ended its policy of segregated facilities.

In the 1940s and 1950s Indianapolis women played significant roles in organizing blacks to fight for desegregation. Roselyn Richardson, founder of the Browsers reading club, became a member of the national African-American sorority Alpha Kappa Alpha and energetically lobbied the state legislature during the 1940s for school desegregation. In 1949 her husband, HENRY RICHARDSON, wrote the desegregation bill that ended legal segregation in Indiana's public schools. In 1951 the founding principle of the Links, Inc., organized locally that year, was to "fight for social justice."

In the 1960s, although individual clubwomen were active participants in restaurant "sit-ins" and civil rights lobbying, women's organizations were primarily social in nature. The "socially prominent" Twelve-of-Us Club held dinners and travelogues. Another group, the Decor Club, involved women "whose emphasis is on 'gracious living.'"

Many women's organizations in the 1970s moved away from their tradition of philanthropic action toward monetary contributions to established African-American causes. Golden Circle members contributed to Alpha Home and underprivileged families, as did many of the 12 local clubs in the State Federation of Colored Women's Clubs in 1975.

By the 1980s and 1990s many African-American women's groups saw their role as one of mentoring the next generation. To that end the Indianapolis Section of the National Council of Negro Women published then–Purdue University professor Darlene Clark Hine's *When the Truth Is Told: A History of Black Women's Culture and Community in Indiana* (1981). In 1983 the recently formed Indianapolis Coalition of 100 BLACK WOMEN sponsored a role-modeling program between successful businesswomen and college students. Another group, Dialogue Today, was an alliance between African-American and Jewish women who met regularly, beginning in 1984, to discuss mutual concerns and fight negative stereotypes. By 1990 only five groups retained membership in the Indiana State Federation of Colored Women's Clubs. The National Council of Negro Women, founded nationally in 1936 and locally in 1947, held the largest membership among black women's groups in the city with 400 individual members and conducted educational programs in local schools addressing the concerns of all women.

Through the medium of women's organizations, African-American women forged a community. The organizations provided a means of addressing not only the needs of their gender, but also of their race. Members exemplified the growing black middle class, eased the burdens of racial prejudice by refuting negative stereotypes, and offered role models for future generations.

CONNIE J. ZEIGLER

Darlene Clark Hine, *When the Truth Is Told: A History of Black Women's Culture and Community in Indiana* (Indianapolis, 1981).

African-Americans in Politics. Although barred by Indiana's 1816 Constitution from voting and holding public office, African-Americans were nevertheless engaged in political activities to improve their status. As early as the 1840s African-American leaders in Indianapolis such as barber and Baptist layman John G. Britton made frequent appeals to white Hoosiers for the rights and privileges that their people were entitled to. During the 1840s and 1850s blacks from around the state occasionally met in Indianapolis prior to meetings of the Indiana General Assembly to petition for equal treatment under the laws. Since the state's new 1851 Constitution prohibited the future immigration of African-Americans into Indiana, however, these early political efforts failed to garner public sympathy and did little to improve their status.

In the years following the Civil War Indianapolis African-Americans pursued equal legal rights with whites. Black representatives from 30 Indiana counties met in Indianapolis in October, 1865, to seek the repeal of discriminatory laws. With the ratification of the 13th, 14th, and 15th amendments to the U.S. Constitution, local African-Americans felt that they finally had achieved the political rights for which they had struggled so long. They soon discovered that the right to vote and hold public office did not result in the immediate betterment of their condition. Painting Democrats as racists, Republican candidates regularly courted black voters, capturing them as a bloc until the 1920s. While the party routinely failed to support policies with special appeal to African-Americans, the Republicans did nominate four to the General Assembly between 1880 and 1896. In 1880 JAMES S. HINTON, an Indianapolis Republican, became the first African-American to be elected to Indiana's House of Representatives. Two years later, African-American physician SAMUEL A. ELBERT defeated Hinton in his bid for renomination, but Elbert and other Republican candidates were defeated in the general election. In 1896 Tennessee-born Gabriel L. Jones, an Indianapolis schoolteacher and advocate for equal educational opportunities for blacks, was elected to the House after serving as Marion County deputy recorder (1895–1897). Among the first African-Americans on the Indianapolis City Council were Henry Sweetland (1890–1892) and JOHN A. PURYEAR (1892–1897).

Traditionally, African-American ministers have played a conspicuous role in city politics. The Reverend MOSES BROYLES of the SECOND BAPTIST CHURCH was an ardent Republican supporter. Another Baptist minister, R. McCary, was one of two black delegates from Indiana to the Republican national convention of 1872. Other examples of local ministers involved in African-American politics over the years were J. P. Thompson, WILLIS REVELS, Benjamin F. Farrell, Henry L. Herod, Charles H. Johnson, Andrew J. Brown, and Landrum E. Shields.

In the late 19th century publishers and editors of local African-American newspapers, including the *INDIANAPOLIS LEADER*, *INDIANAPOLIS FREEMAN*, *Indianapolis World*, the *Recorder*, and the *Ledger*, also exhibited an interest in politics. Most of them, such as Levi E. Christy of the *World*, used their papers to shape the political attitudes of their readers. GEORGE L. KNOX, owner and publisher of the *Freeman*, never sought public office, but was the recognized leader of local African-American Republicans and an influential voice within the party during the 1890s. Some publishers used their newspapers as a springboard for public office. ROBERT B. BAGBY, founder of the *Leader*, became the first African-American elected to the Indianapolis City Council (1877–1879).

Despite a steady increase in the city's black population, between 1898 and 1932 no African-Americans from Indianapolis were elected to the state legislature. During the same period no legislation was sponsored at the municipal or state level by either party which might be regarded as having a special appeal for African-Americans. Instead, Indianapolis switched from a ward to an at-large system for the election of council members in 1909 in an apparent attempt to dilute the black vote. In spite of this maneuver, Dr. SUMNER FURNISS was elected to the City Council in 1918.

Dissatisfaction with the Republicans' deteriorating civil rights stance in the post–Civil War years did not produce an exodus of black voters from the party. However, an African-American Democratic club was active in the city from the late 1870s and particularly in the municipal elections of the late 1880s. Alexander E. Manning, lawyer and editor-publisher of the *World*, and JAMES T. V. HILL, Indianapolis' first African-American lawyer, were for many years the backbone of the African-American Democratic movement in the city and the state. Manning was the official courier for the Democratic national committee for 30 years, and served as president of the convention of the National League of Negro Democrats (1896). Although African-Americans resisted ongoing Democratic attempts to woo them nationally and statewide throughout the late 19th century, large numbers of Indianapolis blacks cast their votes for THOMAS TAGGART, a white Democrat, thereby helping him to win three successive terms as mayor.

The rise of the KU KLUX KLAN as a dominant force in Indiana politics in the 1920s temporarily aroused African-American voters in Indianapolis and weakened their long-time allegiance to the Republican party. In May, 1924, John Bankett of Indianapolis became the first black Democrat nominated for the Indiana General Assembly. George Knox and his previously pro-Republican *Freeman* newspaper encouraged local African-American voters to support the Democrats. But it was not until the mid–1930s, in response to Fran-

African-Americans Representing Indianapolis–Marion County in the Indiana General Assembly

James S. Hinton (R)	House, 1881
Gabriel L. Jones (R)	House, 1897
Henry J. Richardson, Jr. (D)	House, 1933–1935
Marshall A. Talley (D)	House, 1937
Theodore Cable (D)	House, 1939
Robert L. Brokenburr (R)	Senate, 1941–1947, 1953–1963
Wilbur H. Grant (R)	House, 1943–1947
Forrest W. Littlejohn (D)	House, 1949
William D. Mackey, Sr. (R)	House, 1951–1953
Patrick E. Chavis, Jr. (D)	Senate, 1965–1967
Daisy R. Lloyd (D)	House, 1965
Charles A. Walton (D)	House, 1965
Harriette V. Bailey Conn (R)	House, 1967–1969
Raymond P. Crowe (R)	House, 1967–1975
Choice Edwards (R)	House, 1969
William L. Alexander (D)	House, 1973–1974
Julia M. Porter Carson (D)	
	House, 1973–1976; Senate, 1977–1990
William A. Crawford (D)	House, 1973–
Joseph W. Summers (D)	House, 1977–1986
Glenn J. Howard (D)	Senate, 1993–
Billie J. Breaux (D)	Senate, 1990–
Vanessa Summers Barnes (D)	House, 1991–
Gregory W. Porter (D)	House, 1993–
Mae Dickinson (D)	House, 1993–

klin Roosevelt's New Deal, that African-Americans began defecting in large numbers to the Democratic party. During these years numerous black candidates from both major parties were elected to public office, thereby increasing the political power of the African-American population.

The Democrats' emphasis on CIVIL RIGHTS beginning in the late 1940s launched them as the principal party of African-American voters in the ensuing decades. While Republicans gained strength elsewhere, Indianapolis wards heavily populated by African-Americans continued to support Democratic candidates. Over the next decades, several African-Americans from Indianapolis were elected to the General Assembly, including Daisy R. Lloyd, the first African-American woman to serve (House, 1965, Democrat).

African-Americans made slow but gradual progress in winning election or appointment to local government positions. The position most commonly held by blacks over the years was that of Marion County deputy prosecutor, first held by Henry Brokenburr (1919–1931). MERCER M. MANCE served in that post (1939–1941) before becoming Indiana deputy attorney general (1941–1943) and judge of the Marion County Superior Court (1958–1978).

By 1968 City Hall seemed within reach of Indianapolis' African-Americans. But the redistricting which followed Unigov diluted blacks' voting power and reduced their proportional representation on the newly created City-County Council. Unigov dashed hopes for election of a black mayor in the foreseeable future, although African-Americans have been appointed deputy mayors in recent years; Joseph Slash, who served in the William H. Hudnut III administration, was the first. Many other local blacks held positions in Indianapolis–Marion County government, including Raymond P. Crowe (director, Indianapolis Department of Parks and Recreation, 1975–1979), Benjamin Osborne and Julia M. Porter Carson (Center Township trustee), and Joseph D. Kimbrew (first black fire chief, appointed 1987).

Today, African-American politics in Indianapolis remains as problematic as it was over a century ago. Since few blacks hold positions of responsibility or authority within either party, their movement into public offices has been somewhat slow. In 1992 James D. Toler became the first African-American appointed as chief of the Indianapolis Police Department. In 1993 African-Americans also held 7 of 29 City-County Council seats, 6 of 32 municipal judgeships, 4 of 7 seats on the Indianapolis Public Schools board, and 6 of 23 seats from Marion County in the Indiana General Assembly. At the same time voter apathy and indifference, coupled with an absence of grass roots political organizations and unity, have diminished African-American political power. The impact of this condition in Indianapolis in the 1990s remains uncertain.

MONROE H. LITTLE, JR.
Indiana University–Purdue University,
Indianapolis

Emma Lou Thornbrough, *The Negro in Indiana* (Indianapolis, 1957); Emma Lou Thornbrough, *Since Emancipation: A Short History of Indiana Negroes, 1863–1963* (Indianapolis, 1963); Alan F. January and Justin E. Walsh, *A Century of Achievement: Black Hoosiers in the Indiana General Assembly, 1881–1986* (Indianapolis, 1986).

Agricultural Fragments. In every corner of Indianapolis can be found fragments from the city's agricultural past. They remain in neighborhoods in the form of old farmhouses, occasional barns, and the remnants of orchards. With the adoption of UNIGOV in 1969, the boundaries of Indianapolis expanded to include all of Marion County. Residential and business areas do not fill the entire county, which has grown along north-south and east-west axes. Hence, much of the periphery of the city is characterized by active farms, often juxtaposed with the gradual outward movement of housing developments, industrial parks, recreational facilities, and shopping malls.

Fields of corn and soybeans are the most common agricultural fragments on the fringes of the city. Even in the densely populated areas near the city's northern boundary, corn and soybean fields are interspersed with stylish housing developments, condominiums, and strip malls. The southern boundary of Indianapolis is similar; SOUTHPORT and other small communities in Perry Township fan out toward GREENWOOD into land that was previously totally agricultural.

In Pike Township to the northwest, suburban residential areas are growing rapidly. In addition to fields, there are many large horse farms in the rolling hills, particularly near TRADERS POINT, the site of hunt activities. In the northeastern corner of Indianapolis, the development of GEIST RESERVOIR properties is causing existing farmland to disappear quickly.

The most rural segment of the city, southeastern Franklin Township, still has many active farms, some dominated by 19th-century farmhouses. Dairy farms, grazing cattle and horses, and large cornfields can be seen along Thompson and Southport roads. Westward toward Interstate 65 the atmosphere becomes less rural, with single rows of newer homes with fields behind them. Gradually neighborhoods with large homes carved out of recent cornfields appear. They overlook old farmhouses and land to the south that will soon be urbanized.

The southern and southwestern areas of Indianapolis are dotted with small truck farms and large greenhouses intermingled with corn and soybean fields. Many are still owned by families whose German forebears came to the city in the mid–1800s. The southwestern corner of the city is characterized by many farms and small, regularly spaced farming communities like Valley Mills, WEST NEWTON, Maple Ridge, and CAMBY.

Within more populated segments of the city, one can often find the original farmhouse surrounded by newer houses built when the farmer sold off his land. The Johnson house at 44th and Park is an excellent example. A farmhouse, barn, and outbuildings at 16th and Pershing represent an unusual agricultural fragment. Bounded by a stone fence and an acre or two of ground that originally stretched to the White River, the bungalow-style farmhouse looks out on busy 16th Street. An elegant horse barn and several outbuildings that belonged to the Lieber brewing family are located in Questover Circle at Lieber Road.

In another generation the outskirts will be swallowed by the city. But in the 1990s there is still considerable evidence of the importance of AGRICULTURE in the city's history.

JANE R. NOLAN

Agriculture and Agricultural Industries.

Agriculture was necessary for the survival of the city's first settlers. Early residents raised livestock, especially hogs; cultivated fruit trees such as apples, pears, and quince; and grew a variety of crops including corn, sweet potatoes, and Irish potatoes. By the mid–1820s residents harvested ginseng from the local woods and exported the dried roots.

During the 1830s several grist and flour mills were established in the city including the overly ambitious INDIANAPOLIS STEAM MILL COMPANY. Indianapolis' first brewery and the first tobacco factory opened in 1835, the same year that pork packing appeared in the city. However, meat processing was not very successful until the early 1840s when John H. Wright began a profitable pork-packing business. When the MADISON AND INDIANAPOLIS RAILROAD came to town in 1847, the city found increased markets for its agricultural surplus. During the ensuing decade, agriculture continued to flourish and agriculture-related industries became an important part of the local economy with pork packing, flour milling, and the manufacture of agricultural implements proving to be profitable ventures.

Dairies such as the Polk Sanitary Milk Company were an important part of the local economy, ca. 1911. [Indiana Historical Society, Bass Collection, #24464]

KINGAN AND COMPANY, one of the world's largest meat-packing houses in its day, opened in the city during the Civil War era. By the mid–1870s it employed hundreds of people. W. F. Piel & Co. began starch making operations in the 1860s; within a decade the firm employed 80 people who used 500 bushels of corn a day in its factory. During the 1870s Gilbert Van Camp and James Polk each pioneered the operation of small-scale canning in the Indianapolis area. The 1870 U.S. Census of Manufactures showed a highly diversified city economy with agricultural-related industries at the forefront. These included grist and flour mills, a woolen factory, soap factories, tanneries, breweries, tobacco manufacturers (including chewing, smoking, and plug tobacco as well as cigars), meat packers, a broom manufacturer, a plow factory, a starch factory, several bakeries, and fertilizer companies. The Union Stockyards did well in this environment when it opened in the late 1870s.

By 1880 Indianapolis was the third largest pork-packing city in the world, behind nearby Chicago and Cincinnati. During this decade cigar manufacturing became big business in the capital with 87 cigar makers in town by 1884. Nine flour mills operated, and important bakeries in town included Parrott & Nickum, Bryce's, and the Indianapolis Cracker Company. Also during this decade James T. Polk opened a dairy business, later incorporated as the Polk Sanitary Milk Company, and the Indianapolis Brewing Company was formed by the merger of three city breweries.

Indianapolis supplied 65 percent of the nation's starch market in 1890 through the National Starch Manufacturing Company (a merger of Piel's starch factory with several other firms). The Indianapolis STOCKYARDS were processing over a million cattle, pigs, and sheep each year by the early 1890s. Agriculture-related firms continued to be significant to the city's economy in 1900, with meat packing and flour milling recognized as leading industries. The state's largest bakery, the Taggart Bakery Co., was organized in Indianapolis in 1905.

During the next two decades meat packing continued to grow. By 1919 the value of products in this industry approached $105 million. Related products such as lard, glue, soap, tallow, fertilizers, and hides continued to be produced in the city. By 1920 the Indianapolis Stockyards received almost 600,000 cows, 3,000,000 pigs, and 136,000 sheep annually.

In the 1930s production of livestock, poultry, and dairy products remained an important part of the local economy. Marion County boasted 20 commercial dairies in addition to six commercial orchards. Principal agricultural crops of the decade included corn, wheat, hay, oats, Irish potatoes, peas, and tomatoes, with the latter two crops grown primarily for canning.

The 1939 U.S. Census of Agriculture reported that 169,045 acres of Marion County were farmland (66 percent). The 3,336 farms in the county averaged about 55 acres. Agriculture-related firms in Indianapolis during the decade included ACME-EVANS (flour), the COLUMBIA CONSERVE COMPANY (canned goods), National Starch (starch), Stokely Bros. (canned goods), several meat packers (including Armour, F. Hilgemeier Indiana Provision Co., Kingan, and Swift), two fertilizer manufacturers (E. Rauh & Sons Fertilizer Co. and Smith Agricultural Chemical Company), multiple breweries, a dozen bakeries, and over 15 dairy and ice cream companies.

Small family farms disappeared as the city expanded rapidly following World War II, resulting in a declining percentage of farmland in Marion County. The 1954 U.S. Census of Agriculture revealed that farmland accounted for just 52 percent of Marion County land use, although remaining farms were now larger in size, averaging 75 acres. By 1964 the census reported Marion County had 767 farms, averaging 120 acres. Farmland occupied 91,853 acres or 36 percent of the county's land. Just five years later, another 3 percent of the county's farmland was gone, along with 72 farms.

Following the 1970 consolidation of Indianapolis and Marion County through UNIGOV, the Department of Agriculture in 1974 declared Indianapolis to be the "biggest farm town in the United States" with a total of 602 farms occupying 29 percent of the county's acreage. Most of the city's farmland remained on the south side, producing crops such as corn and soybeans, and, to a much lesser extent, wheat, hay, and vegetables. Farmers continued raising cattle, but the number of pigs and chickens in the county had declined dramatically from previous levels. Small family farms were increasingly rare. Farms now averaged 123 acres and served as specialized farms, raising one or two crops or producing one variety of livestock.

During the 1980s farmland continued to disappear as new housing, shopping centers, and office parks sprang up around the outskirts of the city. Census figures recorded a declining number of farms in Marion County: 430 in 1978, 400 in 1982, and 361 in 1987. Average farm size grew during this time from 136 to 157 acres. With farmland accounting for 22 percent of the city's acreage in 1987, important crops included soybeans, corn, wheat, and oats.

A 1993 estimate of 45,000 acres of county farmland means that Indianapolis now has less than 18 percent of its land devoted to agriculture, with Franklin Township continuing to be the most rural area of the county. Corn and soybeans are principal crops with several nurseries and greenhouses adding to the city's agricultural production. Important agriculture-related industries in the city as of the early 1990s include Acme-Evans (flour), Continental Baking Co. (bread and cakes), Hebrew National Kosher Foods (meat processing), the Indiana Farm Bureau Co-op (feed and fertilizers), Maplehurst Farms (dairy products), and NATIONAL STARCH AND CHEMICAL CORPORATION (starch).

DEBORAH B. MARKISOHN

Jacob Piatt Dunn, *Greater Indianapolis* (Chicago, 1910); Berry R. Sulgrove, *History of Indianapolis and Marion County* (Philadelphia, 1884); U.S. Census; *Indianapolis Star*, Oct. 8, 1955, Aug. 21, 1977, June 4, 1978; *Indianapolis News*, Mar. 9, 1982.

Air Quality. There is little evidence that air pollution was ever considered a significant problem in Indianapolis from the late 1800s through World War II, although there were some organized efforts at smoke abatement. Indianapolis had a broad industrial base but never had the heavy industry found in other midwestern cities. A belching smokestack was a sign of prosperity and meant that people had jobs.

Coal was a major source of energy until the mid–20th century; it was burned to produce steam and also used for residential heating. During the winter months the smell of burning coal hung over most of the city. There was considerable fallout of soot and ash, yet most people did not view it as a health hazard. The soot that fell on laundry hung out to dry was undoubtedly viewed as more of a problem by many housewives.

After World War II air pollution became a major issue in many urban areas. This problem could not be approached state by state because air masses do not respect state boundaries. The federal Clean Air Act of 1970 (CAA), the first attempt to control air pollution nationally, set national standards for sulfur dioxide (SO_2), carbon monoxide (CO), ozone (O_3), total suspended particulate (TSP), and nitrogen oxides (NO_x). In addition an effort was to be made to control toxic air pollutants through the National Emission Standards of Hazardous Air Pollutants program. The implementation of the CCA was opposed by nearly all major Indiana industries, especially the steel and utility industries. Hoosiers also believed that cities should have control over their own affairs. Since the enabling legislation for the CCA permitted local air pollution agencies to have enforcement authority, the city established an Indianapolis Air

Pollution Control agency in 1967. Governed by the Indianapolis Air Pollution Control Board, it has authority to enact regulations and take enforcement actions.

Indianapolis has violated the SO_2, CO, lead (PB), and VOC (volatile organic compounds) standards at various times. The city has many sources of SO_2 since local utilities and large industries burn high sulfur coal. Indiana has an abundance of relatively cheap high sulfur coal that has been the fuel of choice for many years. Even so, there was only one violation of the SO_2 standard and that occurred in 1978.

Volatile organic compounds are a continual problem because of the wide variety of VOCs used by local industry. Automobiles, industrial operations that use organic solvents in cleaning operations, and chemical and pharmaceutical manufacturing are all sources of VOCs. VOC emissions are also related to the generation of ozone (O_3), which has been a continuing problem in the city. Marion County has been classified as an ozone nonattainment area since 1978. Since there have been no violations of the O_3 standards since 1988, application has been made to the EPA to have the county be declared in attainment of the O_3 standard. Marion County has never had to adopt highly unpopular mandatory automobile emissions testing.

Carbon monoxide (CO) has been a problem in a limited area of downtown. Automobiles are the major source of CO. Changes in downtown traffic patterns—for example, making Washington Street one way—causes traffic to move more rapidly through the area, thus reducing harmful emissions. Until the mid–1990s leaf burning also contributed to the problem and is believed to have resulted in violating the CO standard on at least one occasion.

One major industrial source of lead located on the west side of the city causes Indianapolis to be one of the few cities that remains in nonattainment status for lead. Odors are still a problem. However, there are no state or city regulations to control sources of odor even though many other states have adopted regulations to control odors from industrial and agricultural operations. Still, in recent years the air quality in Indianapolis has been relatively good and should continue to improve as the Clean Air Act of 1990 is implemented.

RICHARD M. VAN FRANK

———

Environmental Protection Agency, *National Air Quality and Emissions Trends Report 1989* (Washington, D.C.).

Aircraft Accidents. Indianapolis has witnessed over 100 air crashes since aviation came to the city in the early 20th century. The earliest known airplane accident occurred during the June, 1910, Indianapolis Aero Meet, the first licensed air meet in the United States. One of the "daring birdmen" crashed upon landing at the INDIANAPOLIS MOTOR SPEEDWAY field, and his plane burst into flames. A nearby group of pilots and "mechanicians" immediately pulled the uninjured pilot from the wreckage.

The city's first commercial aircraft accident was at STOUT FIELD on November 2, 1929. An Embry-Riddle mail plane, making a normal approach for landing, apparently suffered a control failure and suddenly nosed over and crashed. The pilot was killed and the plane burned beyond repair.

One passenger was killed when a Transcontinental Air Transport Ford trimotor hit a tree stump while landing at Stout Field in a blinding snowstorm on December 22, 1929. The plane, ironically christened *City of Indianapolis* by the airline, was repaired and continued in regular service. The snow-covered five-foot stump, one of several remaining from a recent tree clearing project, was later removed.

Several dramatic private plane crashes occurred through the years. Probably the most spectacular was the July 8, 1933, fiery entrapment by high-tension lines of a small craft approaching Hoosier Airport for landing. When the plane hit, gasoline spilled by the impact was ignited by the lines, resulting in the plane's catching fire and burning to its metal frame. Miraculously, the two women aboard the craft were not electrocuted, since the 33,000-volt line automatically cut off on impact. They were able to climb out and drop some 25 feet to the ground, surviving with burns and broken bones.

Just a week before, on July 1, a Bendix coast-to-coast air race pilot was killed on takeoff from Indianapolis Municipal. Losing control of the plane just after rising from the runway, he flipped inverted, then slid upside down along the runway for some 200 yards. He died two days later.

The Indianapolis metropolitan area experienced its worst air disaster on September 9, 1969, when an Allegheny Airlines DC–9 and a private plane collided in midair over Shelby County, just southeast of the city. Bodies and parts from the larger plane struck several mobile homes in a nearby court, but none of the residents or any of the students in two loaded school buses in the court were injured. The crash, apparently caused by pilot error, took the lives of 78 passengers and four crew in the airliner and the solo pilot of the private plane.

Another midair collision occurred September 11, 1992, just north of Greenwood Municipal Airport, when a business plane took off and collided with an inbound smaller plane. Apparently neither pilot saw the other plane, despite the clear weather. Four well-known community leaders— FRANK E. MCKINNEY, JR., MICHAEL A. CARROLL, JOHN WELIEVER, and ROBERT V. WELCH—were aboard the business plane; they and the pilots of both planes died, although two passengers in the small plane survived.

Military aircraft have been involved in numerous area crashes, the first at Schoen Field on October 3, 1926. An Indiana National Guard training plane spun in over the field, killing the pilot and seriously injuring a passenger. The most bizarre of all Indianapolis accidents was the November 14, 1948, ground collision of two Indiana Air National Guard planes at Stout. Two fighter aircraft in takeoff formation were still on the runway when the wingman's plane overran the leader's. The leader was killed, and his plane ran wild around the airport until it could be stopped by shooting out the tires.

A major tragedy occurred on October 20, 1987, when an Air Force jet fighter crashed into a Ramada Inn east of Indianapolis International. The plane's engine had flamed out some 15 miles southwest of the city, and several restart attempts failed. The pilot called Indianapolis air traffic controllers for his exact location (he was at 31,000 feet in the clouds), and was given a course to Indianapolis International. His options were to try for an Indianapolis landing or abandon the plane over open areas southwest of the city.

Electing Indianapolis, he broke out of the clouds just short of the field and tried to set up a landing pattern. When he saw that he could not make the runway he headed the plane away from buildings to the east. By this time the plane was sinking far too rapidly, so he pointed it toward an open area and ejected. However, the plane swung off his planned course and crashed into the front of the hotel, where it exploded and burned, killing nine hotel employees. Fortunately, the building was nearly empty, since most of the guests had checked out earlier that morning, thus preventing many more casualties.

JERRY MARLETTE

Airports. See Metropolitan Airports

Alice Adams (Garden City, N.Y., 1921). Novel by BOOTH TARKINGTON. *Alice Adams* is one of several Tarkington novels—among them *THE MAGNIFICENT AMBERSONS* (1918)—in which Tarkington offers a negative judgment of the rapid industrialization Indianapolis was undergoing at the time. In this book, which won the Pulitzer Prize in 1921, Tarkington depicted an Indianapolis polluted with smoke and social discrimination. Alice, a girl whose family circumstances offer little hope of her being a social success, invents what she considers a more desirable persona for herself and background for her family. As a result, she attracts a young man from the "proper" circle and is able to fascinate him for a time. Her fabrications break down in the end, however, leading her to a humiliating exposure and the loss of her suitor.

The most famous movie version of the book, made by RKO in 1935, starred Katharine Hepburn. The play adapted by Elizabeth Trotter from the novel was first performed at the CIVIC THEATRE in Indianapolis on March 7, 1946, about two months before the author's death in May of that year.

LEIGH DARBEE
Indiana Historical Society

Dorothy Ritter Russo and Thelma Lois Sullivan, *A Bibliography of Booth Tarkington, 1869–1946* (Indianapolis, 1949); James Woodress, *Booth Tarkington: Gentleman from Indiana* (Philadelphia, 1955).

Allison, James A. (Aug. 11, 1872–Aug. 4, 1928). Indianapolis industrialist; one of the founders of the Indianapolis Motor Speedway and Indianapolis 500–mile race. Allison also established a machine shop that became two divisions of General Motors Corporation, Allison Gas Turbine and Allison Transmission.

Allison was born in Niles, Michigan, the second of three sons of Noah and Myra Allison. His father, a native of Indiana, moved to Indianapolis in 1880 and was involved in various enterprises before establishing the Allison Coupon Company. James quit school at 12 to work in the family business. After his father's death in 1890 he and his two brothers took over the company.

In 1909 Allison formed a partnership with entrepreneur CARL G. FISHER and inventor Percy Avery to establish the Concentrated Acetylene Company, which compressed acetylene gas into canisters for use in automobile headlights. Subsequently, Fisher and Allison purchased Avery's shares and changed the company's name to PREST-O-LITE . Explosions at the plant prompted an ordinance prohibiting production of the volatile gas within the city limits. The operation thus moved, in 1912, to the vicinity of the newly established INDIANAPOLIS MOTOR SPEEDWAY. The track was another joint enterprise by Allison and Fisher in cooperation with FRANK H. WHEELER and ARTHUR C. NEWBY, and in 1911 it had been the site of the inaugural INDIANAPOLIS 500–MILE RACE.

The Allison Speedway Team Company, a machine shop located on the Prest-O-Lite grounds, was established by Allison in 1913, four years before Union Carbide and Carbon Corporation purchased Prest-O-Lite. Allison moved his remaining company to a new westside building in 1920 and it became the Allison Engineering Company. During World War I the company had provided the NORDYKE AND MARMON COMPANY with tools, jigs, fixtures, and gauges to be used in production of the Liberty aircraft engines. Subsequently, Allison received additional government contracts to build crawler-type tractors, whippet tanks, and tank tracks.

Although Allison established his Speedway Team Company primarily to work on race cars, he entered cars in the 500–mile race only once, in 1919, when Howard "Howdy" Wilcox drove one of Allison's two entries to victory. Allison later became sole owner of the track and in 1927 sold it to Eddie Rickenbacker.

After Allison's death in 1928, General Motors Corporation acquired the Allison Engineering Company. Under its guidance Allison's machine shop grew to become the second largest Indianapolis employer and a major supplier of aircraft engines and other aircraft hardware.

Allison was reputed to be a perfectionist. A hard-working businessman involved in many enterprises, he had vast real estate holdings in both Indianapolis and Florida. In the Indianapolis area he was largely responsible for the development of the town of Speedway; in Miami he built a hospital and an aquarium. He served on the board of directors in numerous industries and businesses, including banking. Though twice married, Allison had no children. His Indianapolis home on Cold Spring Road is now one of the MARIAN COLLEGE MANSIONS.

WANDA LOU WILLIS

Wanda Lou Willis, "James A. Allison: The Man and His Legacy," *Engineering Info* (June, 1990), 3–6; *Indianapolis Star*, Aug. 4, 1928; Indiana Biography Series, Indiana State Library.

Allison Divisions, General Motors Corporation. Major producer of aircraft engines and hardware and transmissions. JAMES A. ALLISON, a founding partner of the PREST-O-LITE Company and the INDIANAPOLIS MOTOR SPEEDWAY, established the Allison Speedway Team Company, a machine shop, in 1913. It was renamed the Allison Engineering Company in 1917. The firm began supplying tools, jigs, fixtures, and gauges initially to the NORDYKE AND MARMON COMPANY for use in the World War I Liberty engine. Allison received additional contracts for production models of superchargers, whippet tanks, and high-speed tractors.

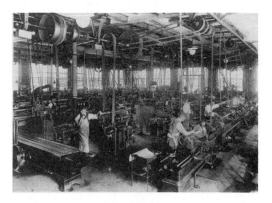

Interior of Allison's Plant 1 during the mid–1920s. [Indiana Historical Society, #C2550]

After the war the Army awarded Allison a contract to redesign and retool 3,000 surplus Liberty engines to improve their reliability and life. This resulted in the development of a steel-shell bearing with lead-bronze lining, a remarkable product that revolutionized the aircraft engine industry throughout the world and became the most profitable product of the company. By 1927 Allison's major products, in addition to its bearings, were airplane reduction gears and high speed superchargers.

After the death of James A. Allison, General Motors purchased the company (1929) for $592,000. During the early 1930s Allison began experimental development on a revolutionary idea, a 1,000–horsepower reciprocating, liquid-cooled aircraft engine, which would have a slimmer shape than an air-cooled engine, for use in military aircraft. On April 23, 1937, the engine, designated as the V–1710, passed all the tests required by the Army Air Corps to become the first aircraft engine in the United States qualifying at 1,000 horsepower.

Early in 1939 the War Department awarded Allison a $15 million contract for 524 V–1710 liquid-cooled reciprocating engines. This engine was so successful that the Allison Company received additional contracts from the United States as well as from Britain and France during World War II. Near the end of the war the company received a contract for the development and production of turbo-prop engines. Allison's total production for the war effort was 70,000 engines, both reciprocating and jet, and 10 million bearings. At its peak in 1943 the plant employed some 23,000 persons working three shifts seven days a week.

The physical size of the company also grew from one machine shop to three modern factory buildings, giving the company by 1943 total floor space of 3,843,690 square feet as well as 17 specially designed test cells for testing the new jet engines. An additional plant was built in 1951, at which time the Aeroproducts Propeller Company of Dayton, Ohio, became consolidated with Allison.

Allison entered the diesel industry in the late 1940s when it began providing bearings and gears for locomotives manufactured by General Motors' Electro Motive Engineering Corporation. Shortly thereafter General Motors moved its Transmission Engineering Section from Detroit to Indianapolis. As a result of this move, Allison Engineering was divided in 1946 into two General Motors operating units, Aircraft Operations and Transmission Operations.

In 1970 General Motors' Michigan-based Detroit Diesel Engine Division was consolidated with Allison Operations, which became Detroit Diesel-Allison and combined the production and development of diesel engines and transmissions with gas turbine engines. General Motors believed this merger would give Allison additional stability. General Motors' commitment to the increasingly strong diesel market, however, left Allison's position weak and insecure in the business world.

It was not until 1983 that the Detroit Diesel-Allison Operations and Transmission Operations were reorganized into two separate divisions, Detroit Diesel Allison Division (DDA), which included the transmission operations of Allison, and Allison Gas Turbine Division. The transmission portion of DDA was growing strong, though it was not being recognized by the diesel-dedicated corporation. Detroit Diesel began having problems and General Motors finally sold the diesel portion of the business to Roger Penske. GM retained the transmission portion, however, and in 1987 established it as the Allison Transmission Division.

By the early 1990s the machine shop that James A. Allison began had become two distinct General Motors divisions, Allison Gas Turbine Division and Allison Transmission Division. Both units faced an uncertain future as General Motors placed both divisions up for sale in 1991 in order to concentrate on the automotive business. In November, 1993, GM called off its sale of Allison Transmission to the German firm ZF Friedrichshafen AG following a suit by the U.S. Justice Department which claimed that it would dampen competition. On December 1, 1993, Allison Gas Turbine became Allison Engine Company following a reported $310 million sale to senior Gas Turbine managers. The company, with annual sales of about $700 million, employed approximately 4,700 at the time of the sale, down from 6,000 in the late 1980s.

WANDA LOU WILLIS

Phillip S. Dickey III, "The Liberty Engine, 1918–1942," *Smithsonian Annals of Flight*, Vol. 1, No. 3 (1968); Paul Sonnenburg and William A. Schoneberger, *Allison: Power of Excellence, 1915–1990: Allison Gas Turbine Division, General Motors Corporation* (Malibu, Calif., 1990) and *Allison: Power of Excellence, 1915–1990: Allison Transmission Division, General Motors Corporation* (Malibu, Calif., 1990).

Allisonville. Suburb centered near the intersection of 82nd Street and Allisonville Road, about ten miles northeast of downtown Indianapolis. John Allison brought his family from Kentucky to clear and farm the area in 1819. Fourteen years later he platted 40 town lots along the Winchester State Road, later renamed the Noblesville State Road and known today as Allisonville Road.

By the 1850s, Allisonville was a village of shopkeepers and craftsmen serving nearby farmers and travelers on the toll road. Dr. Ambrose Ruddell came in 1833 and practiced medicine in the village for 40 years. (In the 1970s, the Ruddell home was moved to CONNER PRAIRIE and interpreted as a 19th-century doctor's house.) The brick home (ca. 1830) of another early settler, John West, still stands at its original location along Allisonville Road, north of 75th Street.

The railroad bypassed Allisonville in the early 1850s and boosted CASTLETON, just three miles to the east. Although the village continued to serve travelers, it remained small. About 50 people lived there in the 1880s.

Post–World War II housing construction swallowed up Allisonville, then I–465 construction and the Castleton Shopping Mall brought traffic congestion and commercial development to the area. In the 1990s, there are few reminders of the little town of Allisonville.

JANE T. WALKER

Berry R. Sulgrove, *History of Indianapolis and Marion County* (Philadelphia, 1884), 641.

Alpha Home (1886–present). Elder care facility. Officially opened in 1886 and typical of black women's earliest organized reform efforts in the Progressive era, the Alpha Home still provides care for Indianapolis' elderly black citizens today. In 1879, former slave Elizabeth Goff first envisioned the Alpha Home for Aged Colored Women out of her deep concern for ex–slave women who found themselves plagued by old age, poverty, and ill health. By 1883, Goff founded the Alpha Home Association supported by several black clubwomen with whom she had previously worked in religious and social welfare projects. Goff's wealthy white employer, Pauline Merritt, donated the initial property for the venture in northeast Indianapolis, but for decades the Alpha Home's primary financial and administrative support came from the black community through the activities of its WOMEN'S CLUBS, fraternal and religious organizations, and businessmen and women.

Over the years the Alpha Home has embodied the concept of racial uplift and self-help in the African-American community. Its long tenure can be attributed to a continued need for the home's services, broadening its mission to include benefits to the whole community, and extending membership to individuals whose influence was beneficial to the home, regardless of gender or race. Having survived several fires, relocations, and financial crises, a much expanded version of the Alpha Home still provides care for Indianapolis' elderly citizens in its new facility at 2640 Cold Spring Road.

EARLINE RAE FERGUSON

Darlene Clark Hine, *When the Truth Is Told: A History of Black Women's Culture and Community in Indiana, 1875–1950* (Indianapolis, 1981).

Altenheim. Originally known as the German Home for the Aged of Indianapolis (Deutsches Altenheim von Indianapolis), the institution is still in existence today as the Altenheim Community. This home for the elderly traces its beginnings to the early 20th century; the present building, a spacious, modern, brick-and-glass structure on East Hanna Avenue, is in sharp contrast to the red brick Victorian mansion on Capitol Avenue that was the Altenheim prior to 1975.

The Altenheim was founded in 1909 by a group of prominent Indianapolis Germans affiliated with Zion Evangelical Church. They wanted to establish a home for aged persons, primarily childless widows and single women, not only for physical care but also for social benefits. The organizers then purchased the large William Elliott residence on Capitol Avenue at 20th Street and remodeled it for communal living. To manage the home, a board of directors was selected from the association, which in time came to number some 400 people.

Over the years, the old mansion was expanded with at least two additions. In 1918, only 15 persons were living in what was then known as the Old-Folks' Home, probably in deference to anti-German feeling at that time. Eventually, the home provided for 40 to 45 residents. Safety regulations and government health care mandates necessitated the move in 1975 to a more modern building. The Altenheim continues as a not-for-profit organization affiliated with the United Church of Christ.

HESTER ANNE HALE

Amateur Athletic Union (AAU). First national, amateur sports governing body to locate in Indianapolis. Established in 1888, the organization is the largest not-for-profit volunteer group for the promotion and development of amateur sports in the United States.

In 1969, desiring to be more centrally located in the United States, the AAU conducted a six-month study of possible relocation sites. Included in the cities studied by the group were: Indianapolis; Memphis, Tennessee; Salt Lake City, Utah; and Las Vegas, Nevada. Beurt SerVaas, publisher of the AAU magazine, *Amateur Athlete*, and FRANK

E. McKinney, Jr., a former Olympic swimmer, led the local campaign to promote Indianapolis. They organized the Sports Capitol Committee, and with promises of financing from local bankers, persuaded the AAU to choose Indianapolis as its new headquarters in May, 1970.

Since 1979 the annual James E. Sullivan award dinner has been held in Indianapolis, focusing national attention on the city. The award, given in the name of an AAU past president, recognizes outstanding amateur athletes based on character, sportsmanship, leadership, and ideals of amateurism. Former recipients include Olympic gold medalists Bruce Jenner, Tracy Caulkins, Carl Lewis, and Greg Louganis.

In 1990, the AAU had a membership of one million athletes, volunteers, coaches, and officials, and an annual budget of $3.5 million. Until the federal government passed the Amateur Sports Act of 1978, the AAU had been the governing body for 19 amateur sports. The Sports Act required that each Olympic and Pan-American sport create its own governing organization. Many of these governing bodies followed the example of their parent organization, the AAU, and also located in Indianapolis. (See Amateur Sports Governing Bodies.)

Connie J. Zeigler

Amateur Sports Governing Bodies.

The international and national governing bodies for eight Olympic sports are located in Indianapolis. The Amateur Sports Act of 1978 required each Olympic or Pan American Games sport to form its own governing body. Previously, the Amateur Athletic Union (AAU) held the United States international memberships for all of these sports. The legislation created eight governing bodies: the International Baseball Association (IBA), The Athletics Congress of the USA, since renamed USA Track and Field (USA/TAF), U.S. Canoe and Kayak Team (USCKT), U.S. Diving, U.S. Gymnastics Federation (USGF), U.S. Synchronized Swimming (USSS), U.S. Water Polo (USWP), and United States Rowing Association (USRowing). The founders of TAC/USA and U.S. Diving came to Indianapolis as part of the AAU in 1971 and chose to stay in the city when they

Amateur Sports Governing Bodies

Organization	Located or began operations in Indpls	Approximate number of members (1991)
U.S. Diving	1979	11,500 indiv.
USA/TAF	1981	2,500 clubs 50,000 indiv.
USGF	1983	160,000 indiv.
USSS	1983	5,000 indiv.
USRowing	1985	30,000 indiv.
IBA	1986	70 countries 200 indiv.
USCKT	1987	1,500 indiv.
USWP	1990	10,600 indiv.

formed separate organizations. In the 1980s, the Lilly Endowment funded the move to Indianapolis of five of the six remaining governing bodies. Finally in 1990, USWP moved its headquarters to Indianapolis with the help of a Lilly Endowment grant. The United States Olympic Committee (USOC), corporate sponsorships, and membership dues provide the operating funds for these eight governing bodies.

Connie J. Zeigler

Indianapolis Star, December 1, 1991, B–2.

American Association of University Women (AAUW).

Organization that promotes equity for women, education and self-development, and positive societal change. In 1921 the Association of Collegiate Alumnae (1889) joined with several other organizations to become part of the newly formed International Federation of University Women. AAUW accepts for membership any woman or (since 1987) man with a four-year degree from an accredited college or university. The Indianapolis branch promotes member education and self-development through programs and study groups. A national fellowships program encourages pursuit of graduate degrees and return to formal study by nontraditional students.

Study has led to service to Indianapolis through action projects, some of which have been continued by other groups. Noteworthy projects have included a book and toy exhibit at L. S. Ayres and Company (1925); a campaign to expand services of the public library to the entire county (1962), which state legislation made possible in 1963; an INTERNATIONAL FESTIVAL (1972), continued by the INTERNATIONAL CENTER; help with radio station WFBM's "Call for Action" (1972); development and distribution to libraries of a Child Care Directory (1979); and a conference for junior high school students, especially girls, on careers in the fields of math and science (1991).

JANET STEINHOFF
Indianapolis Branch, AAUW

The First Fifty Years of the American Association of University Women in Indianapolis, Indiana, 1889–1939 (Indianapolis: privately printed, [1940?]).

American Booksellers Association, et al. v. Hudnut. Action brought against the City of Indianapolis, challenging the constitutionality of a 1984 ordinance prohibiting "all discriminatory practices of sexual subordination or inequality through pornography." Based upon a similar ordinance passed in Minneapolis, Minnesota, but vetoed by that city's mayor, the ordinance was a widely publicized attempt to define pornography as the sexually explicit subordination of women and thus a discriminatory practice subject to regulation by the Indianapolis Human Relations Commission.

City-County councillor Beulah Coughenour sponsored the ordinance, which was supported by then Mayor William H. Hudnut III. It was also supported by several fundamentalist and evangelical Christian ministers who appeared at council hearings with dozens of members of their congregations to testify in favor of passage. A certain irony to that support was duly noted in news coverage of the proceedings: the alliance of so-called radical feminists with the religious right was considered a marriage of convenience, and it was widely assumed that the two groups were intent upon advancing quite different agendas. The INDIANAPOLIS URBAN LEAGUE and several other civil rights organizations opposed the ordinance on the grounds that it was a perversion of the mission of the city's Human Relations Commission as well as a threat to First Amendment freedoms.

The ordinance was signed into law on June 15, 1984, and suit was immediately filed on behalf of a large group of plaintiffs, including the American Booksellers Association, Inc., the Association for American Publishers, Inc., the Council for Periodical Distributors, Inc., and the Freedom to Read Foundation. The American Civil Liberties Union and its Indiana affiliate filed an *amicus* brief supporting the plaintiffs.

On November 19, 1984, Judge Sarah Evans Barker of the United States District Court for the Southern District of Indiana permanently enjoined enforcement of the ordinance and declared it unconstitutional. Judge Barker expressly rejected the contention by proponents of the ordinance that the production, dissemination, and use of sexually explicit works and pictures constituted subordination of women and thus should be considered conduct rather than speech. Instead, the Court agreed with plaintiffs that the First Amendment to the U.S. Constitution prohibited efforts to suppress speech even when the speech was alleged to cause a social evil. The Court also found the ordinance unconstitutionally vague.

The City of Indianapolis appealed the adverse judgment to the Seventh Circuit Court of Appeals, which affirmed the District Court's decision on August 27, 1985. The city persisted, appealing the Seventh Circuit decision to the U.S. Supreme Court. On February 24, 1986, the Supreme Court, without opinion, unanimously affirmed the lower courts, effectively concluding the debate with respect to the Indianapolis ordinance. The case has been widely cited, and copies of the opinions of the District Court and the Court of Appeals are found in numerous textbooks on constitutional law.

SHEILA SUESS KENNEDY
Indiana Civil Liberties Union

---

771 F.2d 323.

American Cabaret Theatre. Indianapolis-based professional, nonprofit theatre company. The American Cabaret Theatre (ACT) evolved from a summer theatre workshop at Sacred Heart University in Connecticut led by Yale Drama School graduate Claude McNeal in the early 1970s. By the end of the decade McNeal's theatre

group, based in Bridgeport, Connecticut, was known as the Downtown Cabaret. The group changed names again in 1980, becoming the American Cabaret Company and relocating to New York City. Three years later, now known as the American Cabaret Theatre, McNeal's group moved to Indiana where it played four successful seasons at the French Lick Sheraton Hotel. Coming to Indianapolis in 1987, the ACT performed at the Hilton Hotel on Monument Circle for two seasons before moving into the ATHENAEUM's renovated ballroom in 1990.

In 1993 over 20,000 patrons attended ACT's concept-centered original performances. A core group of four professionals appears in each show with additional talent provided by contract performers. The American Cabaret Theatre also sponsors Kabaret for Kidz in which ACT performers stage summer shows for children at the INDIANAPOLIS ZOO.

DEBORAH B. MARKISOHN

American Fletcher National Bank. See
Bank One, Indianapolis

American Legion. National veterans organization headquartered in Indianapolis. The idea for an American Legion began when Theodore Roosevelt, Jr., and a few officers met in Paris in February, 1919, to consider the postwar needs of American servicemen. By November the American Legion had emerged to lobby for rehabilitative services for veterans, patriotism, postwar national security, and legislation for protecting and caring for needy children.

The Legion chose railroad hub Indianapolis for its national headquarters site in 1919. Here volunteers gathered regularly in committees aided by a national staff to govern their organization. The Legion occupied a building built by the state for that purpose at the corner of Meridian and St. Clair streets (now the headquarters of the AMERICAN LEGION, DEPARTMENT OF INDIANA) before moving to the present structure at St. Clair and Pennsylvania streets.

An annual national convention governs the Legion, choosing new national officers and a new national commander. Between conventions a national executive committee representing the various "departments" meets to continue and complement the convention's directives. From its beginning the Legion has prided itself on being a cross section of America politically, religiously and, eventually, racially (though its constitution was non-exclusive).

The Legion has actively and successfully lobbied the federal government for veterans' medical and economic needs while practicing a wide variety of civic responsibilities. The GI Bill of Rights is a well-known result of its legislative agenda. The Legion's national legislative effort, along with its national security, defense, foreign relations, and economic functions, are housed at its office in Washington, D.C. All other program areas are administered at its national headquarters in Indianapolis. As mail hub, center of Legion travel activity periodically, site of news releases, the origin of a widely read national magazine, and with its archives-library-museum facility and its deposits in Indianapolis banks, the organization has an appreciable presence in the city.

THOMAS A. RUMER

Thomas A. Rumer, The American Legion: An Official History, 1919–1989 (New York, 1990).

American Legion, Department of Indiana. Statewide veterans organization affiliated with the American Legion and headquartered in Indianapolis. Indiana veterans of World War I joining the veterans movement popularized by Theodore Roosevelt, Jr., and others met in Indianapolis on April 24, 1919, before attending a national caucus at St. Louis. Another statewide gathering on June 6 voted to affiliate with the AMERICAN LEGION, which met in its first national convention in November in Minneapolis. The Indiana delegation convinced the convention to locate the Legion's headquarters in Indianapolis. This decision in turn prompted Indianapolis, Marion County, and the State of Indiana to construct the distinctive, five-block INDIANA WORLD WAR MEMORIAL PLAZA to include the Legion's headquarters at the corner of Meridian and St. Clair streets. The Department of Indiana initially

occupied an office in this building. In the early 1950s the national headquarters moved into a new building at the corner of St. Clair and Pennsylvania streets and the Department and the National Women's Auxiliary expanded throughout the original building.

The Department enrolled nearly 45,000 World War I veterans in 320 local posts its first year and implemented programs of service to hospitalized and disabled comrades and dependents of those who had died in war service. The posts provided honor guards for veterans' funerals, established women's auxiliaries, and adopted community projects and Boy Scout troops.

In the early 1950s the Department opposed the new INDIANA CIVIL LIBERTIES UNION using the state's World War Memorial auditorium. In 1973 the state Supreme Court ruled for the ICLU. More recently, the Department protested plans for the Cuban flag to be displayed on the American Legion Mall during the PAN AMERICAN GAMES in 1987. That ground had been dedicated, the Department stated, to American veterans, including the post commander in Havana executed in 1961 by a Cuban firing squad for alleged anti-Castro activities.

The Department offers Legion services to veterans, communities, and the nation, including aiding the Soldiers and Sailors Children's Home in Knightstown. Its ongoing child welfare activities include the state's Special Olympics, Hoosier Boys' State, American Legion baseball, and high school oratorical contests. Veteran-specific programming includes monitoring the POW-MIA and Agent Orange issues. The Department's lobbying efforts have produced many state laws providing benefits to veterans and their dependents and to children and the general populace. In the early 1990s the Department had approximately 140,000 members.

THOMAS A. RUMER

American Legion National Headquarters library and archives; Richard M. Clutter, "The Indiana American Legion, 1919–1960" (Ph.D. dissertation, Indiana University, 1974).

American Nonconformist (1879–1896). People's party (Populist) newspaper. Published in Winfield, Kansas, from 1879 until June, 1892, the *American Nonconformist* moved to Indianapolis under the ownership of the Vincent Brothers Publishing Company. The party arranged to move the paper after the Indiana branch of the People's party organized in July, 1891, and the party's executive committee met in Indianapolis that November. The paper had numerous owners but always retained its Populist stand. Leroy Templeton, People's party gubernatorial candidate in 1892 and part owner of the paper since 1893, became its sole owner in April, 1895, and continued publishing the *Nonconformist* until its demise.

The *Nonconformist* proclaimed itself to be "A Weekly Journal Devoted to the Interests of the Wealth Producing Classes" and followed the "principles advocated by the People's Party." The eight-page paper included national and state level news pertaining to the People's party and other related groups. It contained regular columns on farming and dairy production, women's interests, and featured excerpts from other Populist papers. In later years the *Nonconformist* included more state and local items as its readership became less regional. In 1893 and 1894 the paper sent a special correspondent to Washington, D.C., to cover congressional sessions.

As the Populist party lost supporters so did the *Nonconformist*. Although it previously had a circulation of 20,000, the paper in 1895 estimated its readership at approximately 5,000. Within a year the *Nonconformist* ceased publication.

JOAN CUNNINGHAM

John W. Miller, *Indiana Newspaper Bibliography* (Indianapolis, 1982).

American Red Ball Transit Company. Nation's first long distance moving firm. In 1914 Ward B. Hiner began selling automobile insurance in Indianapolis, soon adding insurance for motor transport shipments. Within a couple of years he organized his own group of livestock haulers under the "Red Ball Service" symbol. People frequently asked Red Ball drivers to move their household goods, and this apparent need for a household goods moving service prompted Hiner to found Red Ball Transit in 1919.

Although Red Ball initially served only Indianapolis and the immediate vicinity, the first branch office opened in Columbus, Ohio, in March, 1921. The next year the young company made a highly publicized move when ten vans traveled from Indianapolis to New York City, fighting poor road conditions to make the 700–mile trip in two weeks. Soon after, the company purchased a Frankfort, Indiana, plant to manufacture its specialized moving trucks. Red Ball had 20 branch offices in the East and Midwest by 1924. "American" was added to the company's name 15 years later.

Important industry firsts claimed by the company include insurance for household goods shippers and the drivers' percentage compensation system. American Red Ball continues to specialize in moving household goods, having moved a significant number of military and government personnel. By the early 1990s the privately held company operated in more than 167 countries and in addition to its Indianapolis offices had an international moving division based in Seattle, Washington. In 1992 American Red Ball made over 25,000 moves.

DEBORAH B. MARKISOHN

American Settlement. Social service agency. AMERICANIZATION, the instruction of foreign-born residents in English and United States history, government, and culture, was the primary purpose of American Settlement. The organization was created in 1923 as a charter member of the Community Chest by the consolidation of two older agencies: Foreign House (established by the IMMIGRANTS' AID ASSOCIATION) and Presbyterian (Cosmopolitan) Chapel, which had worked mainly with Bulgarians and ROMANIANS. MARY RIGG, a social worker whose thesis topic had been the immigrants in Indianapolis, became director in 1924 and stayed until 1961. In the 1920s, the settlement employed trained social workers and offered classes in citizenship and English, a supervised playground, and numerous clubs and activ-

Like other urban missions, the Presbyterian-affiliated Cosmopolitan Community Center, 511 W. Maryland, provided social services to area residents ca. 1920. [Indiana Historical Society, #C3163]

ities for children. Attendance in one week was said to be 5,785. A day nursery served working mothers, and a public health clinic offered health education and prevention of disease. Because Mary Rigg was sympathetic to immigrants and knowledgeable about foreign cultures, the settlement helped the immigrants preserve some aspects of their culture, and five nationality groups met there. However, its main thrust was Americanization. In 1939, because of declining numbers of immigrants, the settlement was relocated at 1905 West Morris Street after intensive study as to where need was greatest. It was now renamed the Southwest Social Center and worked mainly with native-born clients. In 1957, a donation of $12,000 from the Rotary Club provided the center with new buildings at 1917 West Morris Street. The agency, which continues to operate, was renamed the Mary Rigg Neighborhood Center after 1961.

RUTH HUTCHINSON CROCKER
Auburn University

American Settlement annual report (1928–1929); Mary Rigg, "My Own Record" (typescript at Mary Rigg Neighborhood Center).

American Trans Air (ATA). Charter airline company headquartered in Indianapolis. In August, 1973, several Indianapolis men founded Ambassadair, an air travel club providing reduced rates for air fares and tour packages. The Ambassadair group then incorporated American Trans Air to operate as its air carrier, furnishing aircraft and operational support. ATA began operations late in 1973 with a single four-engine Boeing 720 jet, serving limited destinations in the United States and overseas.

With airline deregulation in 1978, ATA was certified as a common carrier, which allowed it to fly public charter flights as well as club tours. To handle the growing demand, it acquired a second Boeing 720. In 1984, scheduled flights began from Indianapolis to four Florida cities. This service has since been greatly expanded, and other regular service added from Indianapolis to Las Vegas and from San Francisco to Hawaii.

By the end of 1991, American Trans Air club and charter flights had landed in some 490 cities in 100 countries. Contract charters had been operated for large tour operators, other major carriers, and, notably, for the federal government during Operation Desert Storm in 1991. ATA is now the nation's largest charter airline, flying more than 40 percent of all U.S. carrier revenue miles.

As a certified air carrier, the company has worldwide authority for domestic and international charter and scheduled passenger service. With a fleet of 25 Boeing 727s, 757s, and Lockheed 1011s, the airline in 1991 flew 2.6 million passengers a total of 5.4 billion miles.

JERRY MARLETTE

American United Life Insurance Company. Mutual life and health insurance company. American United Life, with $5 billion in assets at the end of 1992, is a diversified company with four major product lines. It has more than $3 billion of group annuity and pension assets under management and is one of the 50 largest providers of tax-deferred annuities and pension plans in the United States. It also offers a complete portfolio of individual and group life and health insurance products and is a leader in the specialized field of life and health reinsurance.

American United Life dates from 1877. In November of that year the Knights of Pythias lodge, which had its national headquarters in Indianapolis, created an insurance program called an endowment rank for its members as a way to attract new members to the lodge. In 1930, the lodge separated its insurance program from the fraternal order, creating United Mutual Life Insurance Company. In 1936, United Mutual merged with American Central Life Insurance Company, another Indianapolis insurer, which had been founded in 1899. The newly merged company took the name American United Life Insurance Company.

After the merger, American United Life, or AUL as it is frequently called, took over the old American Central offices at Fall Creek Parkway and Meridian Street. The building, a copy of the royal palace in Oslo, Norway, was built in 1930 and occupied by AUL until October, 1982, when it moved into its new home office, the AUL TOWER, in downtown Indianapolis. As of early 1993 the Indianapolis office was staffed by some 900 employees.

American Central entered the life reinsurance business in 1904, and the company has been in that business continuously since that time, making AUL today the oldest life reinsurer in the nation. The company is currently licensed to sell its other products in 45 states and the District of Columbia. It accepts life and health reinsurance from companies in all states.

JAMES R. HETHERINGTON
American United Life Insurance Company

From the Days of Knights: A History of American United Life Insurance Company, 1877–1977 (Indianapolis, 1977).

Americanization and Nativism. Although not recognized for its ethnic diversity, Indianapolis attracted periodic waves of immigrants. Local residents responded in contradictory fashion by promoting assimilation but also by expressing themselves at times in a protectionist, racist, and hateful manner.

Nativism, or an antipathy toward aliens, their institutions, and ideas, was clearly evident in Indianapolis during the 1850s. It appeared in the guise of the American party (also known as the Know-Nothings) that sought to protect the nation against an invasion of foreigners, paupers, and Catholics. Members were concerned that Irish and German immigrants (who were predominantly Catholic) were acquiring greater political power, especially within the Democratic party. Compared to cities like Cincinnati, however, Know-Nothingism in Indianapolis was fairly mild. Nativist sentiments were heightened briefly during the October, 1853, visit of exiled priest and Italian patriot FATHER ALESSANDRO GAVAZZI who warned Americans against the supposed Papist threat. Likewise, while naturalized Irish and German voters demonstrated against temperance legislation, Know-Nothing sympathizers called for electing only native-born Americans to political office and enacting more stringent naturalization and immigration restriction laws. In response the local Democratic party, which garnered political support from naturalized voters, condemned any organization "that would aim to disrobe any citizen, native or adopted, of his political, civil or religious liberty."

Although foreigners posed no threat to Indianapolis, nativism still permeated society. In 1856 the City Council adopted a resolution allowing German pupils in local schools to have instruction in their own language. School trustees opposed the policy and never implemented it. Consequently, Germans (primarily FREETHINKERS) organized the German-English Independent School in 1859 to educate their children in German and to preserve their native culture. Few Germans enrolled their children in the public schools—a decision that brought public criticism—but Germans defended their system of bilingual education as actually hastening the Americanization process. By 1869 the Indiana General Assembly recognized the value of German when it authorized German language instruction in public schools if parents petitioned for it.

The CIVIL WAR proved to be a unifying force in the city and allowed the GERMANS and IRISH to demonstrate their loyalty by raising companies of troops to serve in the Union army. During Recon-

struction, however, ethnic tensions resumed as the newly freed and enfranchised African-Americans (who supported the Republicans) confronted the predominantly Democratic Irish. The Democrats' anti-black sentiments were countered by anti-Irish attacks in the Republican-oriented *Indiana Journal*, which criticized the Democrats for importing "Irish tramps," "Hibernian heifers," and "Romanish herds" to vote in local elections.

The arrival of eastern European immigrants in the 1880s and 1890s intensified nativist sentiments in Indianapolis. Scattered incidents by the American Protective Association (APA), an Iowa-based organization devoted to excluding Catholics from public office, elicited responses from the secular press repudiating the use of religious intolerance in politics. Likewise, Rev. OSCAR C. McCULLOCH of Plymouth Church strongly condemned the prejudice against Catholics that many Protestants held.

By the early 20th century large numbers of southern and eastern Europeans had moved to Indianapolis to work in the city's industries, settling primarily in Ward 12, known as the "Foreign District." Local leaders, including JOHN H. HOLLIDAY and James A. Collins, founded the IMMIGRANTS AID SOCIETY (1909) and the Foreign House, a settlement house that served the needs of recent immigrants and assisted them in assimilating into American society. In his paper "The Life of Our Foreign Population," Holliday argued that immigrants should abandon their cultural separateness and assimilate quickly. Through the settlement house's Americanizing programs on domestic chores, personal hygiene, and cooking the immigrants could attain an "American" standard of living. The most successful program was the night school, which taught English, academic subjects, citizenship, and vocational education. While supporters of the settlement house clearly considered immigrant culture to be useless in American society, many immigrants resented the intrusion of the settlement into their family life and turned to their ethnic community to resist Americanization.

WORLD WAR I heightened nativist feelings that had lain dormant for some years. Many Indianapolis Germans chose to support their homeland in the conflict. Their decision fueled anti-

German rhetoric, symbolized by Lucius Swift's caustic anti-German paper read before the Indianapolis Literary Club in October, 1915. When the United States finally entered the war Americanization of the nation's foreign-born population became a top priority. The locus of that activity, however, shifted from the settlement house to the public school, thereby reflecting Americanization's change in emphasis from benevolence to patriotism. As schools fought to prevent disloyalty and sympathy for the German cause, citizens fiercely opposed the continued presence of German language courses in the schools. In January, 1918, the Board of School Commissioners passed a resolution declaring that "public schools . . . should not assist in perpetuating the language of an alien enemy in our homes and enemy viewpoints in the community." Shortly thereafter the Indiana General Assembly banned German from Indiana's schools.

Nativism intensified during the war and took its toll in the German community. The *Indianapolis Star* of December 7, 1917, filled two pages with the names of 800 unnaturalized German residents who resided near munitions production sites, thus suggesting their threat to national security. In June, 1918, the *Telegraph und Tribuene* (with roots back to 1865) suspended publication. Germans anglicized their names and those of their institutions (Das Deutsche Haus became the Athenaeum) to avoid the nativist-inspired vandalism of their property. To prove their loyalty and assuage their critics local Germans joined the U.S. military and actively participated in bond drives. Even after the war's end local opposition to German culture remained strong.

Among the largest public events held in Indianapolis during the war was the Americanization Day Parade of July 4, 1918. Organized by the Marion County Council of Defense, the parade was intended for "all loyal citizens, no matter of what extraction, to show their Americanism and patriotism." Thousands of people swelled Monument Circle where segments of the community, especially the foreign born, were symbolically placed within the parade to demonstrate their assimilation. Germans who had traditionally celebrated "German Day" in October marched with the American flag as the "Friends of German De-

mocracy." Slovenes attired in folk costume marched with the banner, "Slovenians: We Are For America First, Last, and All the Time." Romanians sponsored a float representing Uncle Sam's victory over autocracy.

The spirit of "100 Percent Americanism" permeated the city in the postwar years. Indianapolis became the home of the American Legion, a veterans organization founded in 1919 to foster patriotism. The Indiana State Board of Education declared October 24, 1919, to be "Americanization Day." With the 1920s "Red Scare" antiradical nativism evident in the war expanded to include anti-Semitism and increased the pressure for Americanization. Although the Federal Bureau of Naturalization called for communities to mount a "full, red-blooded American campaign" to convert adult foreigners to American citizens, the American Settlement (formerly the Foreign House) emphasized how immigrants already shared American values and had improved their lot in life. To show the success of Americanization, the local press reported in 1925 that "there is no unrest, no red [communist] problem at all among these people."

Thousands of Indianapolis residents joined the Ku Klux Klan in its "100 Percent Americanism" campaign, which appealed to patriotism, Protestantism, and racial purity. Although they opposed African-Americans, the Klan's principal targets were Catholics for their alleged immorality, antidemocratic tendencies, and allegiance to a foreign power, and Jews for their predominance in the economic sector. Upon gaining control of state and local governments in the mid–1920s, the Klan pursued a legislative agenda of Americanization and education, an effort that faded with the eventual demise of the Klan.

By the 1930s local leaders of Americanization no longer viewed immigrants, their cultures, and religions with grave suspicion. Given the marked changes in the foreign community, Americanization had apparently succeeded in instilling the proper values among the immigrant population and creating, as one newspaper reporter concluded, "a class of useful, loyal, and intelligent American citizens." This was most obvious during World War II as the number of antiforeign incidents were minimal compared to earlier decades.

Nativist sentiments have since continued to surface periodically, usually accompanying periods of national crisis—the KOREAN WAR, the Iranian hostage crisis, and the PERSIAN GULF WAR, for example. The marked absence of any organized Americanization campaign clearly points to the lack of a distinctive foreign element and the success of schools, businesses, and other institutions at incorporating all peoples into the American amalgam.

DAVID G. VANDERSTEL
Indiana University–Purdue University,
Indianapolis

John H. Holliday, "The Life of Our Foreign Population" (typescript, 1908?), copy in the Indiana State Library; Ruth Hutchinson Crocker, *Social Work and Social Order: The Settlement Movement in Two Industrial Cities, 1889–1930* (Urbana, Ill., 1992).

Ameritech. Telecommunications company, formerly known as Indiana Bell, serving Indianapolis and most of Indiana since 1920. Although Indiana Bell operated under that name after 1920, the telecommunications firm traces its origins to predecessors that began operating in the Hoosier capital in 1877, less than two years after Alexander Graham Bell invented the telephone in Boston in 1876.

Wales and Company, an Indianapolis coal supply firm, installed the first two telephones in the city in the fall of 1877 between its Pennsylvania Street office and its Market Street coalyard just west of West Street. A second coal dealer, Cobb and Branham, soon afterwards installed a telephone line from its office at Market and Delaware streets to its coalyard on South Delaware Street.

Indiana District Telephone Company, the state's first telephone firm, was organized in December, 1878, and established the state's first telephone exchange in March, 1879, in Room 66 of the Vance Block Building at the corner of Virginia Avenue and Washington Street. The company reorganized and changed its name to Telephone Exchange Company of Indianapolis in January, 1880.

Central Union Telephone Company, Indiana Bell's direct predecessor, was organized in 1883. By that time there were three telephone compa-

This 1930 reorientation of the eight-story, 11,000-ton Indiana Bell building was a remarkable engineering accomplishment. The building was shifted 52 feet south along Meridian Street and rotated 90 degrees to face New York Street. Using 100-ton lateral jacks, 18 workmen eased the building along a specially constructed concrete mat reinforced with heavy wooden timbers and steel rails. Every six strokes of the jack shifted the building three-eighths of an inch; in an hour it moved 15 inches. Gas, electric, steam heat, water, sewage, and elevator service were maintained through flexible hoses. The move began October 12 and lasted until November 14; throughout, the 600 workers inside sustained telephone service without disruption. (The building was demolished in 1963.) [Indiana Historical Society, #C2059]

nies serving Indianapolis and competition became increasingly fierce. In January, 1920, Central Union and four other Indiana telephone companies were consolidated into Indiana Bell Telephone Company. The new company was capitalized at $15 million, had 4,930 employees, operated 90 exchanges, and served approximately 170,000 telephones in the state.

Indiana Bell operated from headquarters in an eight-story red brick structure completed in 1907 at the corner of New York and Meridian streets. In 1930 the company's headquarters was set on rollers, moved 52 feet south, turned through a 90–degree arc, and moved 100 feet west. This internationally acclaimed engineering feat made room for construction of a seven-story limestone structure that was erected as the company headquarters in 1932. Five stories were added in 1948, and a 14–story annex addition was completed in 1961. The company built a 20–story annex and eight-story addition in 1967 and completed its building project with the construction of a 20–story office building just south of the site in 1975.

Indiana Bell converted all its exchanges to dial by the mid–1960s and completed installation of Direct Distance Dialing in 1973. In 1976 the company acquired 22 exchanges in Lake County in a property transfer with Illinois Bell. Two years later the company began offering Touch Tone service to its customers. In the 1980s the company changed virtually all of its exchanges to electronic digital switching and became a leader in the installation of fiber optics technology.

In January, 1984, Indiana Bell was divested as part of the judicially ordered AT&T breakup. The company became part of Ameritech, which is the Midwest holding company for the Bell operating companies in Illinois, Indiana, Michigan, Ohio, and Wisconsin. Ameritech announced a major reorganization in 1993 which largely eliminated use of the Indiana Bell name and divided the company into market segments for its business.

BILL BECK
Lakeside Writers' Group

Anacomp. Carmel-based micrographics firm. In 1968 Indianapolis native RONALD D. PALAMARA teamed with fellow Purdue professors Albert R. Sadaka and J. Melvin Ebbert to found the computer services firm Anacomp (*analyze* and *comp*ute). The firm grew rapidly through expansion and takeover of other companies, and by 1972 it specialized in micrographics (the conversion of computer data to microfilm or microfiche) and computer services for financial institutions and government agencies.

Under Palamara's leadership Anacomp grew from 1978 sales of $23.4 million to 1982 sales of $109.7 million. Reversals came in 1983 and 1984 with combined losses of $120 million before the company turned a small profit in 1985. With Palamara's death in January, 1985, Anacomp maintained its headquarters in Carmel but shifted its base of operations to Atlanta. The firm retained its profitable micrographics division but sold its unprofitable or unrelated subsidiaries including real estate, software development, and television station WXIN, Channel 59.

Two big 1987 acquisitions tripled Anacomp's size. However, the $372 million acquisition in 1988 of California-based Xidex Corp., manufacturer of microfilm and computer discs, resulted in a loss of $170 million in 1989 and nearly drove the company into bankruptcy before it rebounded to fend off a hostile takeover the next year. In 1991 a key Anacomp official paid a monetary penalty without admitting or denying allegations of insider trading concerning the 1988 Xidex acquisition.

Revenues for 1992 were $629 million, with international business accounting for almost a third. By 1993 Anacomp operated 50 COM (computer output to microfilm) centers nationwide and produced microfiche and microfilm readers. Anacomp employs some 4,500 people, with about 250 located in metropolitan Indianapolis.

DEBORAH B. MARKISOHN

Annexation. In Indianapolis annexation involved a struggle between those in city government who saw physical growth as progress and citizens who viewed absorption into the city as a loss of autonomy and an inevitable increase in taxes.

Although the city undertook a few annexations before the last decade of the 19th century, the city charter of 1891 opened the door for increased activity. Its controversial annexation provisions were the subject of protracted litigation until 1895 when the General Assembly passed an act validating them and effectively giving the City Council approval for expansion. During this decade the city annexed the towns of HAUGHVILLE, BRIGHTWOOD, WEST INDIANAPOLIS, NORTH INDIANAPOLIS, and Mount Jackson. Although residents of IRVINGTON and WOODRUFF PLACE prevented immediate annexations of their neighborhoods (both eventually succumbed, in 1902 and 1962, respectively), the other towns requested annexation as a means of either acquiring city services or having their debt absorbed by the larger urban entity. By 1900 the area of the city had grown from 12.4 to 27.21 square miles, the largest 10–year gain experienced before the adoption of UNIGOV.

In the 1920s to 1940s annexations continued, as did litigation to prevent them. While the citizens of BROAD RIPPLE welcomed their addition to the city in 1922, residents of nearby Primrose and Rosslyn avenues unsuccessfully sued to keep their neighborhoods from being taken into the city in 1942. In the 1950s, as a means of forcing neighborhoods to surrender to annexation, the city cut off garbage collection services to remonstrating areas. Portions of Emerson and Arlington avenues were annexed in 1952 over the protest of residents, and following litigation the Superior Court allowed the annexation of an area northeast of 38th Street. In 1952 the city grew by 180 acres due to ten successful annexations. In 1953, however, residents of LAWRENCE won a suit to deny Indianapolis the right to annex their town. Not long after this successful litigation, Lawrence itself began an annexation program hoping to envelop as much of the surrounding area as possible before Indianapolis could do so. As in the 1890s, in the 1950s there were areas of the county that requested annexation in order to acquire city services. In total, the first seven years of the decade saw six major annexations to the city adding 28,000 persons to Indianapolis' population. By 1959 Mayor CHARLES BOSWELL was urging annexation of the entire county. That year the city appointed its first annexation director, whose assignment was to create an "orderly annexation" plan and to "sell" annexation to citizens concerned about higher taxes and school redistricting.

In 1960 Indianapolis annexed 2,745 acres. The following year the state legislature settled long-time disputes between Indianapolis and Lawrence over which entity should be allowed to annex nearby lands by allowing Lawrence and other towns within four miles of Indianapolis to annex land if given permission by the Metropolitan Planning Commission. In April, 1962, the city annexed the last section of CENTER TOWNSHIP that lay outside municipal boundaries. That year the Indiana Supreme Court again upheld Indianapolis' right to annex outlying areas.

In 1966 the city appointed ALBERT H. LOSCHE, a former mayor, as annexation director, bidding him to conduct a "more vigorous" annexation program. School board president and annexation proponent Richard G. Lugar proposed a plan to separate the INDIANAPOLIS PUBLIC SCHOOLS system boundaries from those of the city. In order

to eliminate a major stumbling block in annexations, the school districts were frozen at their current boundaries. "Shoestring annexations," adding small strips of land at the owner's request, became the order of the day in the mid–1960s as a means of preventing remonstrances by unhappy citizens. This type of expansion allowed for land, usually owned by businesses, to be annexed even though it was not contiguous to the city. Although service provision for the "shoestrings" was difficult, the city utilized this method in order to avoid expensive lawsuits.

By the end of the 1960s Indianapolis covered 82 square miles, and it was clear to all parties that piecemeal annexations had reached the limits of their usefulness. When Mayor Richard G. Lugar took office in 1968 he aimed to eliminate the annexation question by merging the city and county. On January 1, 1970, UNIGOV became effective, and the remainder of Marion County was unified with the city. (Lawrence, SOUTHPORT, BEECH GROVE, and SPEEDWAY—the EXCLUDED CITIES—retained some separate governmental functions.) The bill prohibited annexations outside the county, thus closing the story of annexations in Indianapolis.

CONNIE J. ZEIGLER

Anniversary Celebrations. Periodically throughout the city's history Indianapolis residents commemorated significant events, including the founding of the Hoosier capital. Although they might have gathered occasionally to remember and honor the pioneers, there is no evidence of public observances of Indianapolis' founding prior to the centennial celebration in 1920. The city, however, did play a significant role in the commemoration of Indiana's centennial in 1916 (see HISTORICAL ORGANIZATIONS AND EVENTS), which may have been an inspiration in its own birthday observance four years later.

Influenced by the historical pageantry and centennial celebrations sweeping the nation during the early 20th century, Indianapolis marked its first 100 years with a six-day birthday party in June, 1920. The festivities began on Saturday, June 5 with a mass meeting at TOMLINSON HALL. Church services and an evening musical performance at the Indiana State Fairgrounds Coliseum featuring a 400–voice choir and the Cincinnati Symphony Orchestra comprised the next day's agenda. On the evening of Monday, June 7—the date when the state capital commissioners originally met at JOHN McCORMICK's cabin and voted to locate the new capital nearby—the city held a gigantic street parade which depicted events from the city's past and included 14 bands and 122 floats, many of them electrically lighted. The highlight of Tuesday's program was a pageant held at the Coliseum that told the story of Indianapolis. The day ended with an "elaborate ballet summarizing the progressive city of 1920." (The program was so successful that it was repeated on Thursday.) The grand finale took place on White River on Wednesday, June 9. Thousands of people lined the river banks between 16th and 30th streets to hear a band concert and to watch illuminated replicas of early riverboats journey upriver and to view a large display of fireworks.

To mark the sesquicentennial (150th year) of Indianapolis' founding the city embarked upon a year-long celebration in 1971. The Indianapolis Sesquicentennial Commission, chaired by George S. Diener, former state representative and senator from Marion County, coordinated the city's observances. The commission adopted a blue and orange logo of arrows pointing toward the center of a circle to symbolize the "Crossroads of America" slogan. Public celebrations began on January 6, commemorating the day when the General Assembly formally accepted the report of the capital commissioners in 1821, thereby creating Indiana's new capital city. Mayor Richard G. Lugar launched the festivities at an evening performance at the Murat Theater of the multimedia extravaganza, "We Celebrate Our City," based on Edward Leary's narrative history, *Indianapolis: The Story of a City* (1971).

During the ensuing months the city's museums sponsored several art exhibitions and special programs. The INDIANAPOLIS MUSEUM OF ART exhibited the works of state and local artists, while THE CHILDREN'S MUSEUM displayed CHRISTIAN SCHRADER's drawings of early Indianapolis. CONNER PRAIRIE hosted the pageant "Call This a Beginning," staged to commemorate the day in 1820 when Governor Jonathan Jennings and the ten

commissioners arrived at WILLIAM CONNER's trading post to begin their deliberations on a new capital site.

The summer months included numerous sesquicentennial events. A special commemorative float was entered in the 500 Festival Parade and the women's committee of the Sesquicentennial Commission issued a book of recipes, *Sesqui-Samplings*. In June nearly 2,000 Civil War reenactors encamped at FORT BENJAMIN HARRISON, and the Sesquicentennial Commission cosponsored the first INDIANA BLACK EXPO at the State Fairgrounds (June 18–20). On July 4 the commission sponsored the Sesquicentennial Free Street Fair and Fireworks Spectacular in downtown Indianapolis, attended by an estimated 100,000 people. The day also included the Central Indiana Council of Boy Scouts' recreation of the 1825 transfer of state government records from Corydon to Indianapolis by horse-drawn wagons. During August the CENTRAL CANAL was designated a National Waterways Landmark.

The fall brought assorted other festive programs. On September 26 the city's religious communities united in an interdenominational program, "Faith for a City." Designed as a reaffirmation of faith in God and mankind, the program was staged on the steps of the Indiana World War Memorial where 2,000 singers and 200 musicians under the baton of conductor Thomas Bricetti performed the world premiere of "A Song on Mankind." The INDIANAPOLIS MOTOR SPEEDWAY hosted an antique car and race program on October 10 to commemorate the influence of the automobile and the annual 500–mile race on the community. Finally, on November 7 the *INDIANAPOLIS STAR* issued a special 96–page sesquicentennial edition which included historical photographs, short business histories, biographical sketches, and stories about the city's past.

DAVID G. VANDERSTEL
Indiana University–Purdue University,
Indianapolis

Indianapolis Star, Nov. 7, 1971.

Anti-Picketing Ordinance of 1919. Labor ordinance passed by the Indianapolis City

Council September 19, 1919. This ordinance forbade all forms of picketing by striking workers in the city and imposed fines and prison terms on offenders. The ASSOCIATED EMPLOYERS OF INDIANAPOLIS, in its desire to make Indianapolis an "open shop" city, led the movement for the ordinance. In addition, both the INDIANAPOLIS NEWS and INDIANAPOLIS STAR supported the measure through their editorial policies. The INDIANAPOLIS TIMES, however, remained critical of the ordinance. All attempts by labor to repeal the ordinance failed. The Indiana Supreme Court upheld the constitutionality of the ordinance in 1924, and it remained in effect until rendered unenforceable by a pro-labor, anti-injunction law in 1933.

The ordinance should be considered in the context of national labor relations following World War I. In 1919, a national strike wave occurred as workers sought to maintain their wartime gains in wages and improved working conditions. Indianapolis business and political leaders, startled by violent strikes by telephone workers in Linton, Indiana, and Standard Steel Car Company workers in Hammond during 1919, and remembering the city's own STREET RAILWAY STRIKE OF 1913, believed that the ordinance would help combat the influence of unions in Indianapolis and keep similar strikes from occurring in the capital. The city ordinance, combined with the more general offensive by employers against labor unions, led to serious setbacks for the labor movement in Indianapolis during the 1920s.

SAMUEL WHITE

Antislavery Movement. Militant opposition to slavery was not widespread in Indianapolis because of the city's large southern population and general race prejudice. Antislavery sentiments were evident, however, among various groups and organizations, supported primarily by New Englanders, Quakers, and reform-minded individuals.

On November 4, 1829, the Indiana Colonization Society was established in Indianapolis. Its principal objective was to colonize free African-Americans in Liberia. Society officers were prominent civic leaders, including state Supreme Court judges JESSE L. HOLMAN, ISAAC BLACKFORD, and James Scott, attorney CALVIN FLETCHER, state treasurer SAMUEL MERRILL, and county clerk JAMES M. RAY. Although acknowledging that slavery was evil, the society believed that Indiana had to protect itself from a massive influx of indigent African-Americans. Colonization, it believed, was the best way to protect free blacks and to elevate their conditions. The society held regular meetings and often raised funds around July 4th to support colonization efforts. Few local African-Americans ever accepted the offer to relocate to Africa. In January, 1842, free blacks in Indianapolis held a meeting at the BETHEL AFRICAN METHODIST EPISCOPAL CHURCH to declare their opposition to colonization efforts.

The debate over slavery permeated the city's religious community. In 1840, the Presbytery of Indianapolis encouraged its clergy to deliver at least one antislavery sermon annually. The Reverend HENRY WARD BEECHER of Second Presbyterian Church was initially reluctant to preach against slavery among influential proslavery parishioners and residents. After learning about violence committed against African-Americans and abolition sympathizers in the capital city, however, Beecher declared in a May, 1843, sermon that slavery was a moral evil and that personal liberty should be extended to all people. Three years later several members left the congregation after Beecher delivered two antislavery sermons.

Other churches experienced disruptions and divisions as well. Among the Disciples of Christ, founder Alexander Campbell advised against Christians' involvement in the slavery debate. OVID BUTLER, a local Disciple, disagreed, claiming that slavery violated the universal brotherhood of man. At FIRST BAPTIST CHURCH, Reverend James Simmons preached emancipation in the late 1850s and later attributed the burning of his church on January 27, 1861, to his opponents.

In 1848, many local citizens, including the prominent Calvin Fletcher, supported the new Free Soil party that opposed the expansion of slavery into western territories previously held by Mexico. Indianapolis hosted a "Free Territory" state convention on July 26. Free Soilers also met August 30 to ratify the party's nominees and to establish the *Free Soil Banner*, a newspaper supported by Butler and edited by William Greer and LEW WALLACE in Indianapolis from 1848 to 1854. Other antislavery newspapers, namely the *Freeman*, *Western Presage*, and *Indiana American*, appeared in the city but were short-lived.

Reflecting the public's antipathy to African-Americans, the state constitutional convention, meeting in Indianapolis in October, 1850, drafted a proposal to prevent the migration of blacks and mulattoes into Indiana. Voters overwhelmingly approved it in a statewide referendum; Marion County voted 2,509 to 308 in favor of the proposal. The measure subsequently became Article 13 of the 1851 constitution.

Numerous antislavery groups met in Indianapolis during the 1850s and contributed to growing divisions among local citizens. Christian antislavery and political free soilers met May 28–29, 1851, to support repeal of the Fugitive Slave Law. In February, 1852, the Indiana Colonization Society encouraged increased state appropriations for its relocation program. Free soil advocates, led by Ovid Butler, founded the Free Democratic Association on January 12, 1853, and established the *Free Democrat* newspaper to promote their cause. Over 5,000 state delegates attended a RE- PUBLICAN PARTY convention at the State House in July, 1855, where they adopted resolutions opposing the extension of slavery and repudiating the DEMOCRATIC PARTY. Citizens also joined a local branch of the Kansas State Central Aid Committee to provide financial assistance to free-soil settlers in Kansas. In January, 1857, local groups sponsored a visit by international peace advocate Elihu Burritt, who presented his plans for freeing the slaves.

Local groups eventually acknowledged slavery as the principal cause of both the Civil War and political division within the state. Democrats, who considered Lincoln's preliminary Emancipation Proclamation (September, 1862) to be "unconstitutional and unwise," swept state offices in the fall 1862 elections. Pro-Union Republicans, however, retained Marion County offices and congressional seats. Local Republicans first considered emancipation to be "a measure of military necessity" to cripple the rebellion. By the end of 1863, however, many invoked moral and human-

itarian arguments favoring the slaves' freedom and a lasting peace in the nation.

On January 3, 1865, local African-Americans celebrated the anniversary of emancipation by parading with banners, flags, and a band through the streets of Indianapolis. Nearly 1,500 participated in a similar parade on January 1, 1866.

DAVID G. VANDERSTEL
Indiana University–Purdue University,
Indianapolis

Emma Lou Thornbrough, *The Negro in Indiana* (Indianapolis, 1957); Gwen Crenshaw, *"Bury Me in a Free Land": The Abolitionist Movement in Indiana, 1816–1865* (Indianapolis, 1986).

Arab-Americans. See Middle Easterners

Arsenal Technical High School. Tech High School, as it is now commonly known, officially became the third city high school in 1916. Its use as a school, however, began in 1904 when a group of citizens purchased the 75–acre state and federal arsenal grounds on Michigan Avenue for use as a technical training school. The founders dedicated the resulting Winona Agricultural and Technical Institute to education through the mechanical and manual arts, in perpetuity. When Winona became insolvent in 1909, the Indianapolis Board of School Commissioners sought to purchase the property. Litigation, complicated by multiple ownership and the educational restriction, dragged into 1916, when the state Supreme Court finally ruled in favor of the school board. That day, May 22, became known as "Supreme Day" in the subsequent history of Arsenal Technical High School.

While waiting for the legal resolution, school officials had opened the school in 1912 under the principalship of Milo Stuart, who was also principal of MANUAL HIGH SCHOOL. Stuart and one of the teachers canvassed local elementary schools and obtained promises of enrollment from 219 students. This initial enrollment mushroomed to over 7,000 by 1937, making Arsenal one of the largest high schools in the country. Subsequent students and faculty referred to the energy and dedication that carried the school through those interim years of 1912 to 1916 as the "Tech Spirit."

Opened as a manual and technical training school, Arsenal Tech's first classroom building, the Annex, was dedicated to general education rather than vocational subjects. Stuart, author of *The Organization of a Comprehensive High School* (1926), sought to create an exemplary modern high school that would be both academic and practical. Indeed, during its peak period from 1920 to 1940, Tech developed a reputation for academic excellence as well as vocational opportunity.

In its early years, Tech's freshman curriculum included English, algebra, ancient history, German, drawing, sewing, woodwork, shop science, Latin, music, and physical education. Throughout the 1920s, the curriculum expanded rapidly. By 1930 there were 242 teachers and 6,000 students in 12 buildings. The curriculum had expanded by 1948 to 413 different subjects, including many in "life adjustment," a national trend emphasizing general education and social skills. Tech was at the forefront of this innovation as it had been with vocational education.

Occupying its original site at 1500 East Michigan Street, Tech continues its role as a major city high school. Enrollment is considerably less than in the peak year of 1937, but a variety of academic and vocational courses are offered, including popular MAGNET SCHOOLS programs that draw students from around the city.

TED STAHLY
Indiana University, Bloomington

Fred N. Reeder et al., "Tech Through the Years: A History of the Arsenal Technical Schools from 1912–1948 (Indianapolis: typescript, 1948); Milo H. Stuart, *The Organization of a Comprehensive High School* (New York, 1926).

Art Association of Indianapolis (1883–1970).

Sponsor and founder of the John Herron Art Institute and the Indianapolis Museum of Art. Organized in March, 1883, through the efforts of MAY WRIGHT SEWALL and 17 other women, the Art Association of Indianapolis incorporated in October, 1883, with Albert E. Fletcher, son of CALVIN FLETCHER, serving as its first president. Its mission was to promote and study art in India-

napolis, a goal to be achieved through an annual exhibit, an art school, and a permanent museum.

The association's first exhibit in November, 1883, consisted of 435 paintings by 137 different artists and was held in the English Hotel. Its permanent collection began with the purchase of two paintings from that exhibit: *Running for an Anchorage* by Harry Chase, and *The Anxious Mother* by Percival DeLuce. From 1883 to 1896 exhibits were held in the Masonic Hall, the old Plymouth Church, and the H. Lieber Company Galleries. Then exhibits shifted to the PROPYLAEUM (1896–1902) and JOHN HERRON ART INSTITUTE (1906–1969). Among the more notable exhibits were an annual show by Indiana artists begun in 1908, a 1910 showing of works by sculptor Augustus Saint-Gaudens (attended by 56,000 people), and the first exhibit in the country of work solely by women artists (1912).

In January, 1884, the Art Association opened an art school in a parlor at the DENISON HOTEL with Charles P. McDonald of the Chicago Art League as head teacher, although financial difficulties forced its closure the next year. For much of the 1890s the Art Association managed the second Indiana School of Art founded by T. C. STEELE and WILLIAM FORSYTH in 1887. Then in 1895 the association received a bequest of $225,000 from the estate of John Herron to build an art museum and art school in his memory. In January, 1902, the Art Association purchased a house on the corner of 16th and Pennsylvania streets for $50,000 and opened the John Herron Art School. Increased enrollment prompted a temporary move to the Union Trust Building and construction of a larger facility. Designed by the Indianapolis firm of VONNEGUT AND BOHN, the John Herron Art Institute, housing both an art school and a museum, opened on November 20, 1906.

Initially housed in two rooms in the museum, the art school moved into its own building in 1907. The school was rebuilt in 1928 through a gift of $200,000 from Mrs. Caroline Marmon Fesler, daughter of the founder of the Marmon Motor Car Company and president of the Art Association from 1941 to 1947. Designed by architect Paul Phillipe Cret, the new building opened in 1929. Recognizing that the school's needs were expanding beyond its resources, the Art Association turned the school over to Indiana University in 1967.

In 1906 the association's art collection consisted of fewer than 100 paintings. Under the guidance of WILBUR D. PEAT, director of the museum from 1929 to 1965, the collection expanded by many thousands of items, necessitating extensive remodeling and reconstruction of the building in 1940–1941. In 1966 the Lilly family donated the 44–acre Oldfields estate, located at 1200 West 38th Street, to the Art Association. After turning over the John Herron Art Museum (now known as the Herron Gallery) to the Herron School of Art (a division of IUPUI), the Art Association of Indianapolis officially became the INDIANAPOLIS MUSEUM OF ART in 1970 with its relocation to the Krannert Pavilion.

JEFFERY A. DUVALL

"A Brief History of the IMA," *Indianapolis News*, Oct. 11, 1990; "The Way We Were," *Indianapolis Star Magazine*, Oct. 19, 1983; Clifton J. Phillips, *Indiana in Transition: The Emergence of an Industrial Commonwealth, 1880–1920* (Indianapolis, 1968).

Art Dealers and Commercial Galleries. The exhibition and sale of works of art has been a profession in Indianapolis for almost 150 years. One of Indianapolis' first professional art dealers was Herman Lieber, a printer by profession. His H. LIEBER CO., opened in 1854, also became a showcase for Indiana artists. Lieber's was the first Indiana venue to display T. C. STEELE paintings in 1885 and helped to promote the artist's popularity. H. Lieber Co. remained a prominent art gallery in Indianapolis until it closed in the 1950s.

Damien and Carl Lyman opened Lyman's Fireplace Gallery in 1933 with an exhibition by WILLIAM FORSYTH. The Fireplace Gallery was an offshoot from Lyman Brothers Art Store, which had been in existence since the turn of the century. The gallery and art store served the city for decades, closing in the early 1980s.

Beginning in the 1950s a contemporary gallery district began to form on Indianapolis' near north side. The 1444 Gallery opened in 1957, and by the mid–1960s five others had commenced business. Attendance at shows was high, but sales were low and most of the galleries on the near north side had closed by the end of the 1970s. However, the decline of this district did not signal the demise of galleries in the city.

In the 1970s the number of galleries increased and new gallery districts emerged. The Washington Gallery moved from Frankfort, Indiana, to the PYRAMIDS on the northwest side of Indianapolis in the 1970s, introducing the city to new forms of contemporary art work. In 1971 the BROAD RIPPLE gallery district began to grow when Editions Limited moved to a new location on Westfield Boulevard. Also that year, local artist Nancy Noel opened Gallery Noel in her Broad Ripple home. Numerous other galleries opened in the prospering Broad Ripple gallery district during the next 20 years. These included Byron & Sons, which offers works by HOOSIER GROUP, Brown County, Richmond School, and other Indiana artists, and the cooperative CCA Art Gallery.

In 1982, Patrick King Contemporary Art began operations at 427 Massachusetts Avenue, signaling the birth of a contemporary downtown gallery district. Within the decade several more innovative galleries opened in the area. In 1984, the 431 Gallery was the first in Indianapolis to bring an alternative to commercial galleries. Before closing in 1993, it offered a nonprofit setting for the display of budding Indiana artists following the example of similar not-for-profit galleries in Chicago. The downtown galleries operate independently but often coordinate showings, and together offer local, regional, national, and international art. In 1989 Patrick King Contemporary Art brought international acclaim to Indianapolis galleries when it was honored by the International Art Galleries Association for excellence in presentations.

New galleries and old-timers, such as the 28–year-old Winthrop Gallery, the oldest in the city, ensure the continuation of commercial exhibition and sale of art in Indianapolis.

SHARON L. CALHOON
CONNIE ZEIGLER

Art Exhibitions. The Art Association of Indianapolis had its first art exhibition in 1883.

Supervised by local painter and art instructor Sue Ketcham and held at the ENGLISH HOTEL on the Circle, this event brought fine American art to the attention of the average Indianapolis citizen.

In 1885, the emerging HOOSIER GROUP attracted local attention when the association showed works by WILLIAM FORSYTH and T. C. STEELE. "Ye Hoosiers Colony in Muenchen" was a turning point in the Indianapolis art world. Because attendance was high, the Art Association decided to hold annual exhibits thereafter. Also as a result of the exhibit, local art students filled the Hoosier Group's art classes.

In the early 20th century, the museum of the HERRON SCHOOL OF ART became an important venue for art exhibitions. Hoosiers experienced global art when they attended Herron exhibits showing everything from Japanese prints to paintings by Norwegian artists. However, the most popular exhibits in the Hoosier capital were those featuring American artists. Winslow Homer, John James Audubon, and Thomas Hart Benton exhibits drew large crowds. In 1938, Herron showcased another medium when it featured an Archipenko exhibit of contemporary sculpture, the first major showing of sculpture in the city. In addition to exhibits curated by its own staff, Herron also hosted traveling exhibitions which included works by Salvador Dali and Vincent Van Gogh.

In 1970, the INDIANAPOLIS MUSEUM OF ART (IMA), formerly the Herron Museum of Art, relocated to the former J. K. LILLY, JR. estate on West 38th Street. One of the first important exhibits at the new IMA was the 1973 showing of Max Beckman contemporary graphics. In 1987, almost 12,000 people attended the IMA's "Art of the Fantastic: Latin America 1920–1987," an exhibition in celebration of the Pan American Games.

The Herron Gallery opened at the former Herron Museum site in 1978. New and unusual programming at Herron Gallery included a film festival of contemporary, German-narrative films that later traveled throughout the state. A 1979 exhibit at Herron Gallery, "Fiberstructures and Fabric Surfaces," was a large traveling show that is still cited by art critics as an important exhibition of contemporary art.

Indianapolis' private galleries have also had important shows. The Washington Gallery exhibited avant-garde regional art, and in the 1970s was the first venue in Indianapolis to show installation and video art. In 1983, the Patrick King Contemporary Art Gallery presented "Modular Form," an exhibit of textile installation art. This was the first time a commercial gallery allowed an artist to rebuild the exhibition space to better suit their art. The success of the show influenced other commercial galleries in the city to allow similar major installations.

Other sites in Indianapolis have also housed significant exhibitions. The INDIANA STATE MUSEUM has showcased the work of Indiana artists. The 1990 exhibit "Robert Berkshire: A Retrospective" displayed the work of an Indiana University Herron School of Art professor to over 60,000 people. For many years L. S. AYRES, a downtown department store, hosted the annual HOOSIER SALON. This exhibit presented works of Indiana artists in an environment calculated to reach persons who might not visit an art gallery or museum.

Art exhibitions continue to play an important part in the cultural life of Indianapolis, and 1990 was a landmark year in the city's art world. To celebrate the opening of the Hulman Pavilion, over 26,000 people attended the IMA-curated "Seurat at Gravelines: The Last Landscapes." Two other exhibits in 1990 were "firsts" for the IMA. The Richard Pousette-Dart retrospective was the first exhibit at the museum to be reviewed by *Time* magazine. "The Passage: Return of Indiana Painters from Germany, 1880–1905" became the IMA's first international traveling show when it went to Indianapolis' sister city, Cologne, Germany. "The Passage" returned to the IMA in November, 1991, to an enthusiastic reception.

In addition to the IMA's successful shows in 1990, the Smithsonian Museum chose to display the largest traveling show ever curated by the Washington, D.C., institution at the EITELJORG MUSEUM OF AMERICAN INDIAN AND WESTERN ART. "Crossroads of Continents: Cultures of Siberia and Alaska," was viewed by 62,000 people in Indianapolis, the only midwestern city in its circuit, before traveling to other venues in Seattle, New York City, and Canada.

SHARON L. CALHOON

Art Fairs. Indianapolis has a long tradition of open air art exhibitions. These events, held in the city streets, allow the citizens of Indianapolis to view and purchase fine art in a venue very different from the art gallery. The Talbot Street Art Fair, the Penrod Society Arts Fair, and the Broad Ripple Art Fair are the city's three major art fairs.

Begun in the mid–1950s, the Talbot Street Art Fair is the oldest outdoor street fair in the Midwest and the only one of its size with free admission. Over 60,000 people attend annually. The fair held its first event in an alley between 14th and 16th streets. Currently, it occurs on the second weekend in June in an area of Talbot Street adjacent to HERRON SCHOOL OF ART. The fair is sponsored by Indiana Artists and Craftsmen, Inc., which selects the 240 exhibiting artists and craftspersons. Performing artists and a variety of food booths are part of the fair's attraction. Proceeds benefit the HERRON-MORTON PLACE Neighborhood Association and Indiana Artists and Craftsmen.

Dating to 1967, the PENROD SOCIETY Arts Fair is held on the grounds of the INDIANAPOLIS MUSEUM OF ART, traditionally at the beginning of September, with 250 artists and gallery booths. There are also performing artists and a variety of cultural groups represented. Proceeds from the juried exhibit benefit the Penrod Society. An estimated 20,000 people attend the paid-admission event annually.

The INDIANAPOLIS ART CENTER sponsors and benefits from the proceeds of the Broad Ripple Art Fair, which annually attracts an estimated 20,000 people. The paid-admission event, originally held in the streets of BROAD RIPPLE, is now located on the grounds adjacent to the Art Center offices at 67th and Ferguson streets. There are 200 artists and craftspersons selected to exhibit. The fair also has children's activities, live entertainment, and a variety of foods.

SHARON L. CALHOON

Artis, Lionel F. (Dec. 3, 1895–Sept. 1, 1971). African-American public housing manager and civic leader. Born in Paris, Illinois, Artis moved to Indianapolis as a youth. He attended BUTLER UNIVERSITY, and in 1933 earned a degree in social science at the University of Chicago. He went on to earn a master's degree at Indiana University in 1941.

Artis was the assistant executive secretary of the SENATE AVENUE YMCA from 1913 to 1937, leaving only to serve in the Army during World War I. During this time he also edited the journal of Kappa Alpha Psi, a Bloomington-based African-American fraternity. Between 1937 and 1969 he was the manager of LOCKEFIELD GARDENS, the first public housing facility in Indianapolis. He also served as manager of the War Housing Project during World War II.

Active as a volunteer, Artis sat on the boards of 23 civic and community organizations at his death. He was the first African-American appointed to a policy-making agency for Indianapolis, beginning service in 1944 as a member of the former Indianapolis Board of Health and Hospitals. He also held leadership positions with FLANNER HOUSE Homes, ALPHA HOME for the Aged, YMCA, Indianapolis Community Fund, URBAN LEAGUE, Council of Social Agencies, COMMUNITY SERVICE COUNCIL, and the Mayor's Race Relations Committee. In 1967, he was named "Man of the Year" by local service groups. The former Continental Hotel, now a low-income housing project serving elderly and handicapped persons, was named for him in 1974.

MICHELLE D. HALE

Indiana Biography Series, Indiana State Library; *Indianapolis Star*, Sept. 2, 1971.

Arts Council of Indianapolis. Nonprofit arts service organization, incorporated in 1987. Its mission is to champion creativity, innovation, artistic quality, and professional development; to strengthen the relationship of the arts to economic development and the business community; to broaden public and private support; and to introduce the arts to new audiences. The council has received financial support from the City of Indianapolis and the INDIANA ARTS COMMISSION, the National Endowment for the Arts, and local foundations and corporations.

In 1989, the Arts Council established a financial assistance program that provides annual organizational grants and artist fellowships for Indianapolis arts institutions, nonprofit service organizations and schools, and individual professional artists. Other programs and services consist of professional development workshops and seminars for arts administrators and artists; business and arts initiatives (annual "Start with Art" celebration); collaborative college and university arts promotions; and arts education projects ("Summer Arts for Youth").

The council's research reports and publications include *Climate for Creativity: A Vision and Strategy for Indianapolis Arts Tomorrow* (1987); *Profile of the Arts in Indianapolis, 1987* (1989); the annual *Indianapolis Arts Directory*; and *Arts Education Resource Guide, 1991–1992*, a listing of in-school and field trip opportunities for K–12 students. In 1992, the council facilitated and published *A Community Cultural Strategic Plan for the Arts in Indianapolis*, with the vision that "Indianapolis is recognized nationally and internationally as a cultural star of the Midwest." The plan outlines goals, objectives, and strategies for the development of the arts in Indianapolis through the year 2000.

NORMAN R. BRANDENSTEIN
Arts Council of Indianapolis

As Sounding Brass (1964). Novel by Indianapolis attorney Alan T. Nolan. The book, published by Houghton-Mifflin, focuses on the experiences of Adam Johnson, a probationary worker at the Faultless Pump Company, who is shot by police as a robbery suspect and becomes a paraplegic due to the bullet lodged in his spine. The author never reveals whether or not Johnson was guilty. Rather, the book is a chronicle of Johnson's trip through the criminal justice and social welfare systems of an "average" American city. Each group or organization Johnson encounters manages to pass his case on and rationalizes that nothing can be done for him. Adam Johnson's salvation is almost literally that, since the money to help him comes via Father Gleason, the "bingo priest."

Nolan based his book on a real case that had occurred in Indianapolis many years earlier. In in-terviews at the time of publication he emphasized that his intention was to tell a story that could have happened in any American city. Nevertheless, reviewers devoted much time and ink to matching up people and places in the book with Indianapolis equivalents.

LEIGH DARBEE
Indiana Historical Society

Associated Employers of Indianapolis. Organization of Indianapolis businessmen formed in opposition to labor unions. In 1904 local businessmen established the Employers Association of Indianapolis to combat labor strikes in the city. Membership grew steadily over the next decade. In 1914 the organization absorbed a similar antilabor group, the Commercial Vehicle Protective Association, formed in response to a 1913 teamsters' strike. Renamed the Associated Employers of Indianapolis, the group began publishing the *Associated Employers' Digest* in 1923 to review local and national business conditions relevant to its anti-union stance and to focus on wage trends and labor legislation. About 4,000 copies of the first issue announced goals of discouraging union practices, upholding open-shop principles, and encouraging law enforcement. In 1923 the Associated Employers claimed 500 anti-union employers as members, a significant number of the city's businessmen. They bragged that their organization had given Indianapolis an open-shop reputation that promoted business growth in the city.

The organization's minutes reflect an active group during the 1920s and early 1930s, with supporters including some of the city's best known firms: ELI LILLY AND COMPANY, INDIANA BELL, MERCHANTS NATIONAL BANK, KINGAN AND COMPANY, PREST-O-LITE, L. S. AYRES AND COMPANY. Based on the association's minutes, the organization had become less active by the mid–1930s. In 1939 the group appears to have changed its name to the Associated Employers of Indiana. Few public records from the organization exist for the 1950s and 1960s, although a 1961 pamphlet indicates the group had become a labor relations service specializing in personnel policies, arbitration, and cost of living figures. By 1974 the

Associated Employers of Indiana, Inc., no longer appeared in Indianapolis city directories.

DEBORAH B. MARKISOHN

Associated Employers of Indiana Collection, Indiana Historical Society; Clifton J. Phillips, *Indiana in Transition* (Indianapolis, 1968).

Athenaeum (401 East Michigan Street). German cultural and social center. The Athenaeum was constructed for the Socialer Turnverein Aktien Gesellschaft (Social Gymnastic Society Stock Association), founded in 1892 to raise money to build a home for the Socialer Turnverein and other liberal German societies of Indianapolis. Originally called Das Deutsche Haus (The German House), the building was constructed in two phases—the east wing in 1893–1894, the west wing in 1897–1898. The structure was renamed the Athenaeum in response to the anti-German sentiment prevalent during WORLD WAR I. The Turnverein later changed its name to the Athenaeum Turners.

The building is the design work of the prominent architectural firm of VONNEGUT AND BOHN. Both Bernard Vonnegut and Arthur Bohn were American-born of German immigrant parents and received architectural training in Germany. Vonnegut's father, Clemens, Sr., was one of the founders of the Turnverein in 1851 and Bernard's brother, Clemens, Jr., was an officer of the stock association. The building was equipped with a gymnasium, locker rooms, meeting rooms, restaurant, auditorium, bowling alleys, a concert hall–ballroom, and a wall-enclosed beer garden with concert pavilion.

An important cultural and social center of Indianapolis, the Athenaeum also became an important education center. In 1907 the building became the home of the oldest American institution (founded 1866) for training of physical education teachers when the NORMAL COLLEGE OF THE NORTH AMERICAN GYMNASTIC UNION moved from Milwaukee into the east wing of the Athenaeum, occupying the gymnasium and converting club rooms into classrooms. This change resulted in the alteration of other portions of the building as club and social functions were displaced from the

Designed by the architectural firm Vonnegut and Bohn, the Athenaeum was known originally as Das Deutsche Haus. [Indiana Historical Society, #KA2]

east wing. The Normal College attracted students from across the country and those graduates went on to be the pioneers of physical education departments in school systems throughout America. The Normal College merged with Indiana University in 1941, functioning as its school of physical education. The school vacated the Athenaeum in 1970, eventually settling in the Natatorium on the IUPUI campus. Thereafter much of the classroom space and the theater became the first home of the INDIANA REPERTORY THEATRE.

Architecturally the Athenaeum remains a significant example of the German Renaissance Revival style in America. It exhibits the hallmarks of the style with its decorated stepped gables, steeply pitched, massive roof, facade sculpture, limestone banding, and art-glass windows, some of which exhibit *Jugendstil* influence. The sculpted terra cotta and limestone is the work of local artist ALEXANDER SANGERNEBO. The building was listed on the National Register of Historic Places in 1973.

The Athenaeum, suffering from decades of neglect, has undergone repair and redevelopment since its ownership changed in 1991 to the Athenaeum Foundation, Inc. To date it houses the city's oldest restaurant (1894), gymnasium (1894), theater space (1898), and orchestra (1883).

WILLIAM L. SELM

David R. Hermansen, "National Register of Historic Places Inventory-Nomination Form" (copy available at the Division of Historic Preservation and Archaeology, Indiana Department of Natural Resources); Thomas M. Slade, ed., *Historic American Building Survey in Indiana* (Bloomington, Ind., 1983), 39–40.

Atkins, Henry Cornelius (Nov. 27, 1868–June 15, 1944). Industrialist and civic leader. Atkins was born at Atlanta, Idaho Territory, and moved to Indianapolis with his family at age two. He was one of the original pupils of the Indianapolis Classical School for Boys and graduated with honors. At 16, he entered Yale University and graduated in 1889 as one of the youngest in the class. He then became superintendent of E. C. Atkins and Company, a saw factory begun by his father in 1856. Upon his father's death in 1901 Atkins succeeded to the presidency of the company, which was reputed to be one of the nation's largest saw manufacturers.

A Republican, Atkins was involved in numerous business and charitable organizations in Indianapolis. He served on the board of directors of the YMCA for 36 years, and as president of the Indianapolis Community Fund. He was an early member of the Indianapolis BOARD OF TRADE, the Indiana Manufacturers' Association, the COMMERCIAL CLUB (later the CHAMBER OF COMMERCE), and the ASSOCIATED EMPLOYERS OF INDIANAPOLIS. Atkins also served as a director of the National Association of Manufacturers and the Fletcher Trust Company.

ELLEN TEVAULT

Indianapolis News, June 16, 1944; Jacob Piatt Dunn, *Greater Indianapolis* (Chicago, 1910), II, 1058.

Aufderheide, May Frances (May 21, 1888–Sept. 1, 1972). Ragtime composer. Daughter of John Henry and Lucy Deel Aufderheide of Indianapolis, May was raised in a middle class family. Her father owned the successful Commonwealth Loan Company and supported local arts organizations. As a youth May studied classical piano with her aunt, May Kolmer, a pianist with the Indianapolis Symphony. She later attended an eastern finishing school and traveled through Europe with her parents before returning to Indianapolis.

In March, 1908, May married architect Thomas Kaufman of Richmond, Indiana. Shortly thereafter she published her first composition, "Dusty Rag," issued by the Duane Crabb Publishing Company of Indianapolis. Sales of May's music encouraged her father to enter the music publishing business. Though criticized as a vanity press for his daughter's compositions, John H. Aufderheide and Company became an important publisher of Indiana composers between 1908 and 1913.

In her early 20s, May fit the youthful profile of RAGTIME composers. She published 19 pieces between 1908 and 1912, seven of which were financial successes. The New York–based *American Musician and Art Journal* reported in 1909 that the "talented Indianapolis girl is achieving [an] enviable reputation" for her classic rags. Her most popular tunes, composed during her residence in Richmond, were "Dusty Rag" (rag and song, 1908); "Thriller Rag," "The Richmond Rag," and "Buzzer Rag" (1909); "A Totally Different Song" (rag and song, 1910); "Blue Ribbon" (1910); and "Novelty Rag" (1911).

Around 1913 the Kaufmans left Richmond and returned to Indianapolis where Thomas gave up his architecture career and joined the Commonwealth Loan Company. For reasons unknown even to her family, May ended her music career at that time. The Kaufmans moved to Pasadena, California, in 1947, where May spent her last years confined to a wheelchair after suffering numerous strokes.

SHERYL D. VANDERSTEL

John E. Hasse and Frank J. Gillis, *Indiana Ragtime* (Indianapolis, 1981; booklet accompanying a record produced by the Indiana Historical Society); John E. Hasse, ed., *Ragtime: Its History, Composers, & Music* (New York, 1985).

Augusta. Town located just north of 71st Street on MICHIGAN ROAD, about 11 miles northwest of the Circle. Augusta was founded as a stopover for travelers on the Michigan Road. George Coble, Sr. and Jonathan Ingo first settled in the area in 1829, though the town was platted in 1832 by David G. Boardman. Augusta may have taken its name from the firm that built the road, the Augusta Gravel Road Company.

During the 19th century Augusta grew slowly. Most of its small businesses, such as grocers, blacksmiths, and dry goods purveyors, provided services for local farmers or travelers. Then, in 1852, the railroad bypassed the town. A depot was built a little over a mile away and NEW AUGUSTA sprang up around the railroad and eclipsed the older settlement.

In the 1950s, suburban sprawl reached PIKE TOWNSHIP. Shopping centers were built in 1957 and 1960 just south of Augusta at the intersection of 71st Street and Michigan Road. Entrepreneurs brought a few small factories to the area. Today, Augusta is a mix of residences, retail stores, and light industry; modernization has left only a few reminders of the 19th-century community.

CATHLEEN F. DONNELLY

Berry R. Sulgrove, *History of Indianapolis and Marion County* (Philadelphia, 1884), 605–606; *Indianapolis Star*, Sept. 16, 1956, Aug. 7, 1960.

AUL. See American United Life Insurance Company

AUL Tower. High-rise office building. At 38 stories, the American United Life Insurance Company Building (One American Square) surpassed the 1970 INB BANK TOWER and in 1982 became the tallest building in Indiana until BANK ONE TOWER superseded it in 1990. Designed by Skidmore, Owings & Merrill, architects of Chicago's ultra high-rise buildings, the Sears Tower and the John Hancock Center, the AUL Tower, with its facade of traditional Indiana limestone, faces toward MONUMENT CIRCLE. The main tower takes the plan of an elongated hexagon from which two wings of eight lower floors extend in a stair step, buttressing effect. Extending to the southeast corner, the main entry is located within a three-story, glass-covered atrium with a floor of Brazilian granite and walls of Italian marble. The ground floor was designed around an open interior courtyard landscaped like a garden. Public use of the adjacent cafeteria makes the courtyard more of a public space than the average interior court. The building is one of the most energy efficient high rises in the nation. Groundwater is used for a heat exchanger system to heat and cool the building, thereby reducing its energy costs by 60 percent. Encircling and enhancing the site are brick sidewalks and rows of linden trees. The building's location, on the square bounded by New York, Illinois, and Ohio streets and Capitol Avenue, has been criticized for closing off the first block of INDIANA AVENUE.

MARY ELLEN GADSKI

Automobile Culture. The automobile has changed every American city throughout the 20th century, those of middle size perhaps even more than the largest. Indianapolis felt the effects with full force, not only as its residents began to drive but as increasing numbers of them worked to build automobiles and auto parts. From 1911 onward the city's most popular public occasion was a spectacular 500–mile automobile race which attracted enormous crowds and was soon known nationwide as the "Indianapolis 500." Unlike Detroit, however, Indianapolis did not develop mass automobile production, requiring giant factories and a large force of semiskilled labor, and so it never attracted large numbers of European immigrants or developed strong industrial unions which would alter its traditional political structure.

The impact of the automobile was most clearly described by BOOTH TARKINGTON, the city's foremost novelist, who saw as early as 1918 that his beloved Indianapolis was changing almost beyond recognition. No American writer described so clearly or so early the overwhelming impact of the automobile on the nation's cities. In THE MAGNIFICENT AMBERSONS Tarkington created a family which prospered greatly from real estate investments during the 1870s and then lost everything during the 1910s as the automobile devastated established property values and shifted development to the suburbs. In a famous scene, the young and foolish George Amberson Minafer attacks Eugene Morgan, an automobile inventor who is courting his widowed mother. "Automobiles are a useless nuisance," says George. "They had no business to be invented." George's grandfather, the wealthy real estate investor, remarks that the growing number of automobiles would soon drive pedestrians and carriages from the streets. "We'll even things up by making the streets five or ten times as long as they are now," Eugene answers. "It isn't the distance from the centre of town that counts, it's the time it takes to get there. This town's already spreading; bicycles and trolleys have been doing their share, but the automobile is going to carry city streets clear out to the county line." In 1918 this seemed only a dream, but by the 1960s it was a reality on the north side of Indianapolis. As the old man feared, "real estate values in the old residence part of town are going to be stretched pretty thin."

Tarkington was no admirer of the automobile age, and he never mentioned the "500" in any of his many stories about Indianapolis. Nevertheless Tarkington gave to Eugene, the inventor and manufacturer, a wise and cautious answer for the brash young man who claimed that automobiles ought never to have been invented. "I'm not sure he's wrong about automobiles," Eugene replies. "With all their speed forward they may be a step backward in civilization. . . . But automobiles have come, and they bring a greater change in our life than most of us suspect. They are here, and almost all outward things are going to be different because of what they bring. . . . I think men's minds are going to be changed in subtle ways because of automobiles. . . . Perhaps, ten or twenty years from now, if we can see the inward change in men by that time, I shouldn't be able to defend the gasoline engine."

Tarkington received the Pulitzer Prize for *The Magnificent Ambersons*, but few readers took seriously his doubts about the automobile age. Indianapolis was booming with new automobile factories, bringing more jobs for its workers, more traffic on its streets, a building boom in its suburbs, and, as Tarkington feared, making it a place where "the streets were thunderous" and "a vast energy heaved under the universal coating of dinginess" in the "smoky bigness of the heavy city." For better or worse, Indianapolis was becoming an industrial center.

The CHAMBER OF COMMERCE boasted in 1921 that Indianapolis led the world in the manufacture of "better grade automobiles." Whether true or not this claim to leadership in an important part of the automobile industry shows clearly how the city's business leaders saw Indianapolis as the "Capital of the Land of Opportunity." Unlike the centers of low-priced automobile production in Michigan, Indianapolis took pride in its "almost

ideal" labor conditions and its high proportion of American-born residents. Immigrants and labor unions played no role in the business vision of Indianapolis.

The city's population more than doubled between 1900 and 1930, the years of the automobile boom in Indianapolis, but the number of wage earners in manufacturing increased by only 87 percent. Automobile workers outnumbered those in any other industry by 1919, but their share of the work force declined significantly during the 1920s, even before the Great Crash in 1929. Limited production luxury cars such as STUTZ, DUESENBERG, and MARMON drew attention wherever they appeared, but only a few thousand workers were employed to manufacture them. Indianapolis was famous for its fast and elegant cars, but they remained a rare sight even on their hometown streets.

Automobiles replaced horses with remarkable speed on city streets; the animals had almost disappeared by 1919. Automobile dealers created a prosperous new business district about ten blocks north of downtown on Capitol and Meridian streets. The annual auto show at the INDIANA STATE FAIRGROUNDS each winter attracted large crowds to see the new models, and service stations occupied a growing number of corner lots. By the early 1920s the automobile had become an inescapable part of city life in Indianapolis, even though most city residents did not yet possess cars of their own. Drivers seized control of the streets and pedestrians learned from childhood to "Look before crossing the street."

The automobile also brought noticeable changes to the city's network of streets. Although the fundamental Indianapolis street plan of a rectilinear gridiron with four diagonal avenues was fixed from the city's founding, GEORGE E. KESSLER developed a grand plan of improvements in 1908. Kessler, a landscape architect and city planner from St. Louis, worked as a consultant to the city park board for many years. He planned a comprehensive boulevard system along the city's waterways and directed much of its construction (see KESSLER'S BOULEVARD AND PARK SYSTEM). Kessler began with Fall Creek Parkway, and explicitly argued that it would improve traffic flow, although his reports never directly mentioned automobiles.

Within a few years Kessler reported significant residential construction along and near the new boulevards, although his long-range plan would require decades for completion. Both FALL CREEK and WHITE RIVER would have boulevards along both banks, as would Pleasant Run on the southeast side, with major improvements for Garfield and Riverside (later Tom Taggart) parks. On the northern edge of the city 38th Street would become a grand boulevard (alternatively called Maple Road and Parkway Boulevard), as would Capitol Avenue from downtown northward to Fall Creek. INTERURBANS and STREETCARS played no significant role in the development of these boulevards; they were designed to accommodate automobile traffic.

Kessler returned to Indianapolis in the early 1920s to plan an outer boulevard system for the spreading city. He began on the north side with a broad street extending from FORT BENJAMIN HARRISON westward to Big Eagle Creek and then southward, the route later known as Kessler Boulevard, but his ambitious plans were left unfinished after Kessler's death in 1923. Meridian Street north of 38th Street, which became the city's most elegant residential boulevard during the 1920s, was not part of Kessler's plan. Meridian Street was emphatically a creation of the automobile era and was never served by trolley cars.

Except for the incomplete boulevard system, which grew out of the pre-automobile City Beautiful movement, Indianapolis and Marion County lacked any sort of comprehensive street and traffic planning. By the early 1920s traffic congestion was a serious problem downtown, slowing trolley and interurban cars which shared the streets with growing numbers of automobiles. Traffic and parking problems were frequently discussed but never solved. Electric traffic lights replaced police officers to control traffic at busy intersections in 1925, and the city introduced comprehensive downtown parking restrictions in 1931, supplemented by hated parking meters in 1939 and one-way streets in the early 1950s.

As a national highway system developed Indianapolis became a vital crossroads. Local business leaders, particularly such auto men as CARL G. FISHER and JAMES A. ALLISON, played a leading role in the Good Roads Movement and were among the chief promoters of the Dixie Highway, extending from the Great Lakes to Florida. With the coming of the federal highway numbering system in 1925, Indianapolis was at the junction of two of the most heavily traveled cross-country routes—U.S. 40, which extended from the Atlantic to the Pacific, and U.S. 31, stretching from northern Michigan to the Gulf of Mexico—as well as three lesser federal routes.

Within Marion County, however, there was no planning and little improvement in the rural highway system as the growing population spread far beyond the slowly expanding city limits. A 1916 map showed only two road surfaces, "Gravel or improved roads" and "Ordinary or mud roads." By the early 1920s most of the traditional county section-line roads were paved with gravel, but no new roads were built. Not until 1942 was there an effort to expand the county road system with the construction of a belt-line box eventually known as State Road 100, extending north from U.S. 40 to CASTLETON on the east (Shadeland Avenue), and then westward to U.S. 52 along 82nd and 86th streets. The western and southern segments were never completed as suburban home builders worked more quickly than state and county highway officials.

Both city and county travel was revolutionized with the arrival of the interstate highway system in the late 1950s. More than ever before Indianapolis was the "Crossroads of America." Two of the most important interstate highways, I–65 and I–70, met two lesser routes at Indianapolis, I–74 and I–69, all feeding traffic into an unnamed circumferential highway known only as I–465. The two major interstates penetrated the city and formed an Inner Loop around the downtown area which required the demolition of hundreds of homes and businesses and disrupted the existing street system. Proposed north and northeast freeways were never funded, saving many of the city's better residential neighborhoods from further devastation, while the Madison Avenue Expressway (opened 1958) extending southward from downtown carried only limited traffic. Highway planners and downtown business interests of the 1960s imagined that the greatly improved highway system, not complete in Indianapolis until 1976, would make it easier for drivers to reach the traditional retail and office concentration downtown. By the mid–1970s, however, it was clear that people who lived in the suburbs and traveled only by automobile would reject downtown congestion for suburban shopping malls, which soon produced even greater congestion. By the 1980s suburban office complexes, many adjacent to I–465 interchanges north and northeast of the city, had largely replaced downtown office buildings. The nature of the city was changing beyond recognition as the automobile reigned supreme. Just as Tarkington had predicted a half century earlier, real estate values in older parts of town declined sharply. Rather than travel by trolley to the downtown stores, theaters, and restaurants, everyone who could afford an automobile drove to a suburban mall or shopping center, leaving downtown for daytime office workers, conventiongoers, sports fans, and the unfortunate poor who still rode the buses.

The most visible influence of the automobile in Indianapolis occurs each May with the 500–Mile Race, long considered the "greatest spectacle in racing." No American sporting event has enjoyed as many paying customers as the Indianapolis 500, which attracted crowds of 150,000 during the 1920s and triple that number in recent years. From 1919 this was the outstanding automobile race in the United States, and for many years it attracted European cars and drivers as well, just as its official name, the International Sweepstakes, suggested. For Indianapolis, the 500–Mile Race was the only sporting event of more than strictly local interest. The city was too small for major league baseball and its colleges were unknown among football fans. Daring race car drivers became heroic figures, and the danger of crippling injury or death on the track only added to their fame. The flamboyant Carl G. Fisher was the city's most famous businessman, presiding annually at the "500," the nation's longest automobile race and the only competition at the Speedway. Traditionally, only the great occasion on Memorial Day mattered, for parades and festival events outside the Speedway began only in 1956.

By 1970, when Unigov combined the governments of Indianapolis and Marion County for many purposes, the automobile dominated local transportation and an increasing share of public and private expenditure was devoted to roads, streets, and parking facilities. At last, however, all of Marion County had a single government department in charge of streets and roads, except for state-controlled highways. By then suburban expansion had extended beyond the county line and construction of new, wider roads meant enormous expense and determined opposition from affected property owners. Those who mattered socially and politically used their automobiles to travel everywhere they wished to go, and governments and businesses had little choice except to provide the facilities drivers demanded. Traffic congestion is the curse of the modern American city, and highway improvements only increase traffic even further. Indianapolis, like all American cities, is both dominated and devastated by the automobile. As Booth Tarkington warned in "The World Does Move," a short story of 1928 in which he reminisced about the early days of the automobile, "The quiet of the world is ending forever."

PATRICK J. FURLONG
Indiana University, South Bend

_____

Indianapolis Newspaper Index, Indiana State Library; Richard Hebert, *Highways to Nowhere: The Politics of City Transportation* (Indianapolis, 1972), esp. 65–96.

Automobile Industry. For a brief period early in the 20th century it seemed that perhaps Indianapolis would rival Detroit for leadership in the American automobile industry. About 1910 Indianapolis was considered the fourth most important city in automobile manufacturing, following Detroit, Toledo, and Cleveland. Unlike Michigan manufacturers, however, none of the Indianapolis firms ever achieved mass production. Three of America's most elegant automobiles of the 1920s were designed and manufactured in Indianapolis, but they were intended for the few and the rich, not the typical motorist. With very few exceptions the Indianapolis firms were seriously undercapitalized, for the automobile manufacturers of Indianapolis received little support from local bankers or men of wealth. Raising money was a constant worry, even for successful automakers.

Beginning with the pioneer efforts of CHARLES H. BLACK in the late 1890s, local inventors and promoters struggled to develop automobile manufacturing. For several decades they enjoyed considerable success. Waverly Electric was the first to produce more than a handful of vehicles, making battery-powered cars of limited range, suitable only for use in town, from 1898 to 1909. ARTHUR C. NEWBY and Charles E. Test, successful bicycle chain manufacturers, established National Auto and Electric Company in 1900 and three years later changed its name to National Motor Car Company. NATIONAL entered the business with an electric automobile in 1902, but suffered several financial reverses. Newby reluctantly introduced a gasoline-powered car in 1904, but continued to market electrics until 1911. National deliberately concentrated its efforts on high-quality, expensive cars and never attempted mass production. Despite its conservative design practices, National enjoyed great success on the race tracks between 1909 and 1912, but withdrew from competition after winning the second INDIANAPOLIS 500–MILE RACE.

Perhaps as many as 90 makes of automobile and five of motorcycles were manufactured in Indianapolis, most of them in small numbers for a brief span of years. The Atlas-Knight (1912–1913), Economycar (1914), Hoosier Scout (1914), and Pathfinder (1911–1918) were easily forgotten except by their owners, but Overland and Cole were important firms by any standard.

The Overland Auto Company began in Terre Haute and moved to Indianapolis in 1905 with the financial support of DAVID M. PARRY, a local buggy maker. Near bankruptcy during the financial panic of 1907, Overland was rescued by John North Willys, an ambitious automobile salesman from upstate New York who contracted for the firm's entire production. Willys became president, treasurer, general manager, and sales manager for Overland and launched an ambitious expansion program. Indianapolis financiers declined to support Willys, and in 1909 he purchased a vacant factory in Toledo and shifted Overland production to Ohio, renaming the car Willys-Overland. Willys hoped to challenge Ford's dominance of the low-priced field and produced 5,000 vehicles in 1909, the firm's last complete year in Indianap-

Automobile giant Henry Ford (far left) poses with Indianapolis Motor Speedway founders (left to right) Arthur Newby, Frank Wheeler, Carl Fisher, and James Allison on opening day at the racetrack in 1909. [Indianapolis Motor Speedway]

olis. Three years later Overland ranked second to Ford in production, but Willys' extravagant ambitions led eventually to financial disaster.

Although little noticed and never celebrated, the largest automobile producer in Indianapolis was ironically the most familiar name in the industry. Henry Ford developed an extensive network of branch assembly plants to "build" the Model T manufactured in his giant factories near Detroit. High railroad charges for finished vehicles encouraged the use of regional plants that could build cars for dealers within a few hundred miles. Twelve "semi-knocked-down" cars could fit in a standard boxcar, while special auto-carrying boxcars had space for only three or four fully-finished vehicles. Model T production in Indianapolis began in 1914, and during the early 1920s exceeded 25,000 vehicles a year. The plant shifted to Model A production in 1928, but branch manufacturing was no longer efficient in small plants so close to Detroit and the Indianapolis operation closed in 1933.

Joseph J. Cole was a successful carriage manufacturer who shifted into automobiles in 1908–1909. Harvey S. Firestone of the tire company provided much of the necessary capital for the COLE MOTOR CAR COMPANY, which pushed production to 2,000 vehicles a year by 1912. Cole promoted his cars in every way possible, from en-

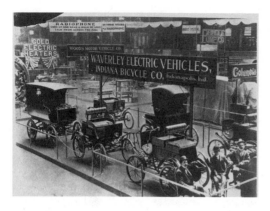

Waverly Electric Motor Vehicles were marketed by the Indiana Bicycle Company at the New York Electric Show, held in Madison Square Garden in May, 1899. [Indiana Historical Society, Bass Collection, #286322F]

tering road races to advertising on a giant balloon, and advertised them also as "The Man's Car That Any Woman Can Drive." Cole rejected offers from William Durant to become part of General Motors and competed directly with Cadillac in the luxury V–8 market, advertising the Cole as "The Pride of Indianapolis." In 1919 Cole began an expensive expansion program that drove the firm into serious financial troubles during the recession of 1920–1921. Sales dropped sharply and he closed the company rather than risk his fortune in a hopeless effort to compete with larger manufacturers. Production ceased in 1924 and the firm was successfully liquidated.

During the Roaring Twenties Indianapolis dominated the nation in the manufacture of luxury high-powered automobiles that often cost more than a new middle class house. Buyers of MARMON, STUTZ, and DUESENBERG models were people who regarded automobiles as they did their yachts, elegant playthings whose price did not matter. Depending upon the body design selected, a Duesenberg might cost nearly $20,000 in 1929.

HOWARD C. MARMON built his first automobile in 1902, using the facilities of NORDYKE AND MARMON, the nation's leading manufacturer of flour milling machinery. Commercial production began three years later. Marmons were always elegant and well-engineered machines, widely admired but never built in large numbers. Howard

Marmon was the chief designer and engineer while his elder brother Walter looked after finance and manufacturing. Marmons excelled in both road and closed-circuit racing between 1909 and 1911; in the latter year a Marmon Wasp won the first Indianapolis 500 at an average speed of 74.61 miles per hour.

Marmon advertised itself as "A Mechanical Masterpiece" and built virtually all of its own components, unlike most Indianapolis automobile manufacturers. The flour milling machinery business provided a solid financial and production base, and Marmon was successful as a car builder from its earliest years but not profitable. George M. Williams purchased a major interest in 1924 and two years later the flour milling machinery business was sold and the firm reorganized as the Marmon Motor Car Company. The smaller and cheaper Little Marmon lasted only one year, but the powerful and elegant 8–cylinder Marmon was a great success, with sales of 22,000 in 1929. The Great Depression hit Marmon very hard, and Howard Marmon's last design, a 16–cylinder model for 1931, was a magnificent machine that very few buyers could afford. Marmon closed in 1934.

Walter Marmon, meanwhile, joined with the inventor Arthur W. Herrington in 1931 to manufacture all-wheel-drive trucks under the MARMON-HERRINGTON name. Financial support came from New York, but many of the staff came from Marmon Motors. Marmon-Herrington specialized in heavy-duty trucks for special service, such as hauling oil field equipment. The firm flourished during World War II, manufacturing heavy trucks and light tanks. After the war it continued to produce heavy-duty trucks and from 1944 to 1956 was a major producer of trackless electric trolley buses. Marmon-Herrington purchased Ford's transit bus division and several school bus companies, but sank into financial troubles after Herrington's retirement. New corporate ownership diversified into other products and closed the Indianapolis factory in 1963, ending vehicle production in the city although automobile parts remain an important part of local industry.

Harry C. Stutz moved to Indianapolis from Ohio in 1903 and struggled in the auto parts business until 1911 when he hurriedly built a racing car to compete in the first 500–mile race. The Stutz finished only 11th, but it did finish and the new Ideal Motor Car Company advertised the achievement for years. The famed Stutz Bearcat appeared the following year, to immediate popularity. The Bearcat was fast, sporty, and uncomfortable, a "man's car" that could be raced competitively.

Known from 1913 as the Stutz Motor Car Company, Stutz expanded production to 2,200 cars by 1917 but suffered financial troubles and ownership changes which by the mid–1920s brought Charles M. Schwab to financial leadership and Frederick E. Moskovics to operating control. Moskovics improved both engines and body design and maintained Stutz's popularity among wealthy lovers of fast cars, even with a 1926 model known as the Safety Stutz. The Stutz Black Hawk of 1927 was America's fastest production car, but the Great Depression destroyed its market and sales dropped rapidly, falling to a mere six vehicles for 1934. Stutz suspended automobile production in January, 1934, and tried to keep in business with a delivery van called the Pak-Age-Car. The effort failed dismally and Stutz was liquidated following its 1937 bankruptcy.

Without question, the finest automobile ever built in Indianapolis was the Duesenberg Model J, usually ranked as the greatest of American automobiles. Brothers FRED AND AUGUST DUESENBERG advanced from making bicycles to building high-powered engines for boats and automobiles. During World War I they prospered building boat and airplane engines for military use, but with the return of peace they decided to enter automobile manufacturing and moved from New Jersey to Indianapolis in order to further their racing ambitions. Their Model A sedans were well-designed but unprofitable and the firm failed in 1924.

The Duesenberg brothers were more successful building race cars, winning the French Grand Prix in 1921 and the 500–mile race in 1924, 1925, and 1927. Fred Duesenberg became president of the reorganized Duesenberg Motors Company and solved his financial troubles by selling out to E. L. Cord's Auburn Automobile Company in 1926. Cord intended to challenge Stutz in the luxury high-performance field and Fred Duesenberg designed the elegant and carefully-engineered Model J, powered by a Lycoming

straight-eight engine that gave a top speed of 116 miles per hour (130 miles per hour for the supercharged Model SJ in 1932). Duesenberg built only the chassis of the Model J; buyers contracted the independent coach builders for the custom body they wished. Altogether only 481 of the legendary Model J Duesenbergs were built during five years of unprofitable effort (1929–1934) and the firm failed early in 1935.

The Great Crash of 1929 and the resulting depression destroyed the dream of automobile manufacturing in Indianapolis, but automotive parts and a single truck plant remained as important industries while the 500–mile Memorial Day race at the INDIANAPOLIS MOTOR SPEEDWAY flourished as the most popular one-day event in American sport. Collectors prize Marmon, Stutz, and especially Duesenberg automobiles, but Indianapolis lost its chance of leadership in the American automobile industry long before 1929. Detroit had no advantage in location, engineering talent, or skilled labor, but it did offer superior financial support and rapidly surpassed Indianapolis.

PATRICK J. FURLONG
Indiana University, South Bend

Automobile Quarterly, 8 (Spring, 1970) and 20 (Third Quarter, 1982), special issues about Stutz, and 30 (Summer, 1992), special issue about Duesenberg; George P. and Stacey P. Hanley, *The Marmon Heritage* (Rochester, Mich.: Doyle Hyk Publications, 1985, 1990); Beverly Rae Kimes and Henry Austin Clark, Jr., *Standard Catalog of American Cars, 1805–1942* (Iola, Wisc.: Krause Publications, 1985); John B. Rae, *American Manufacturers: The First Forty Years* (Philadelphia: Chilton Company, 1959).

Aviation. Indianapolis was introduced to the "air age" in the late 1800s with hot air balloon ascensions and parachute jumps. On July 15, 1889, five special trains carried hundreds of spectators from Indianapolis to BROAD RIPPLE to watch "this breath taking spectacle."

Aerostatic or balloon competition made its first appearance in 1909. On June 5 the first U.S. National Balloon Race launched from the as yet unfinished INDIANAPOLIS MOTOR SPEEDWAY. An estimated 75,000 persons watched six of the nine entries lift off, including the local favorite, the *Indiana*, piloted by CARL G. FISHER, one of the four

Speedway owners, and George Bumbaugh, Indianapolis balloonist. The *Indiana* was forced down near Ruskin, Tennessee, some 235 miles from Indianapolis. The race winner landed near Payne City, Alabama, 378 miles from the starting point. Another, much smaller balloon, the *Indianapolis*, piloted by GOETHE LINK, noted Indianapolis physician and scientist, and Russ Irvin, local aviator, won the handicap section of the event, landing at Westmoreland, Tennessee, about 40 miles northeast of Nashville. (Two more National Balloon Races started from the city on September 17, 1910, and July 4, 1923.)

The week of June 13–18, 1910, was "Aviation Week" in Indianapolis, the first licensed aviation meet in the United States. Attending were noted aviators from all over the country, including Wilbur (born near Millville, Indiana) and Orville Wright, who on December 17, 1903, had both flown the world's first successful airplane. Among the entries were three Indianapolis pilots: Russell Shaw and Melvin Marquette, who entered home-built planes, and Joseph Curzon, with a French-built craft. Included in the week's numerous events were demonstration flights of various models, speed record attempts, and several races of varying lengths. Notable among these was an event in which eight planes competed, at that time the largest number of planes ever in the air at the same time. Several records were set, including a new high for a plane carrying two persons when two men succeeded in remaining aloft for 12 minutes. The highlight of the meet, however, was the setting of a new world's altitude record. On June 13, the Wright brothers' demonstration pilot, Walter Brookins, reached a height of 4,384 1/2 feet above the ground, far exceeding the existing record.

Despite all the excitement of the balloons and the still relatively unproven airplanes, most Hoosiers were more interested in automobiles and auto racing. While the Aero Club of Indianapolis kept its clubhouse inside the Speedway track, and did a moderate amount of both airplane and balloon flying, no serious activity took place at the field until World War I. Early in 1918 the U.S. Army built a large aircraft and engine repair facility south of the track to repair all aircraft and engines east of the Mississippi and north of the Ohio

rivers. Two large shopbuildings, one for airplanes and one for engines, along with offices and barracks for military personnel, were set up on Main Street in Speedway City (now the town of SPEED-WAY) and new hangars were built on the flying field inside the track. Among the base's principal activities were the testing, repairing, and modifying of Liberty aircraft engines, many rebuilt by the Allison Engineering Company located across the street from the repair shops.

Probably the most exciting event in Indianapolis' early aviation history was the October 24, 1919, arrival at the Motor Speedway of the 18–passenger Lawson Airliner, at the time the world's largest passenger plane. On the return leg of a round trip from Milwaukee to New York and back, the plane carried nine passengers and a crew of two, including pilot Charles E. Cox (who would later become superintendent of the Indianapolis Municipal Airport). Large crowds of excited spectators braved ten days of continuing rain to inspect the giant plane, which, too large to be hangared, remained outside during the entire Indianapolis stay. The rain finally stopped, and on November 6 the plane and its weary passengers and crew finally made a slow and harrowing take-off from the water-soaked field.

The city's first public landing field was opened in July, 1920, by the Indianapolis Aerial Association. The company planned to offer flying instruction, passenger rides, and regular service to large cities within a 200–mile radius of Indianapolis. The venture, a few years ahead of its time, quickly faded into oblivion.

Crawford Field, an attempted revival of the Aerial Association, opened in 1922. The company had operated for almost a year when an unbelievable set of circumstances forced it out of business. Both of its planes were lost on the same day: one crashed near Bloomington and the second was lost when the company hangar burned down, the result of a hunter shooting at rabbits and igniting the grass around the hangar.

The first military field in Indianapolis was officially opened May 7, 1922. Located northeast of Lawrence at FORT BENJAMIN HARRISON, the field was named Schoen Field in memory of Army Lt. Carl J. Schoen, an Indianapolis pilot who was killed in action over France during World War I.

The facility served as an intermediate landing field and reserve airdome for years and also as a temporary home for the Indiana National Guard air unit in 1926–1927. It was closed by the army in 1945, but was reactivated by the Tenth Air Force in 1947. However, the short sod runways proved incapable of handling the large military craft using the field and it was permanently closed in 1950. The field later became the site of the U.S. ARMY FINANCE CENTER.

In 1922, the first air mail arrived in the city. On May 29, eight planes of the U.S. Air Mail Service flew in from Chicago to demonstrate the possibilities of direct air mail connections with other parts of the country. (At the time, the only government air route was New York–Chicago–San Francisco.) Their landing in a field just west of CUMBERLAND aroused considerable public interest, and numerous city and post office air service discussions ensued. However, another five and a half years would pass before Indianapolis would join the air mail system.

The first local scheduled air service began December 17, 1927, when the Embry-Riddle Company opened an air mail route between Cincinnati and Chicago via Indianapolis, operating from Cox Field. By the end of the year the company had carried 1,043 pounds of mail over the line; passenger service began early in 1928.

The second airline to serve the city was Capitol Airways, which on October 22, 1928, began an Indianapolis–Fort Wayne–Detroit passenger and express service from Capitol Airport. By February, 1929, the company added routes to Louisville via French Lick and to Chicago via South Bend. In the spring of 1929, however, all services were temporarily discontinued due to poor connections with other airlines at the three destinations, and permanently dropped in the fall for financial reasons.

The first major airline to serve the city was the highly promoted and long-awaited coast-to-coast Transcontinental Air Transport (TAT), which began scheduled service July 7, 1929. A novel operation, the new company sent its passengers overnight via the Pennsylvania Railroad from New York to Columbus, Ohio. (This rail segment bypassed the "killer stretch" over the Alleghenies, which had claimed the lives of many air mail pilots in the early twenties.) Early the next morning the passengers boarded the famous Ford trimotors for the air trip via Indianapolis and St. Louis to Waynoka, Oklahoma, where they transferred to the Santa Fe Railroad for the overnight trip to Clovis, New Mexico. Then, on the second morning, they boarded another Ford for the balance of the trip to Los Angeles.

The first westbound TAT trimotor landed at STOUT FIELD on the morning of July 8, and following an appropriate but short welcoming ceremony departed for St. Louis and the West Coast and its permanent niche in American airline history. Some three weeks earlier, on June 19, a TAT Ford on a route survey and pilot check flight stopped at Stout Field and was christened *City of Indianapolis* by the city's mayor, postmaster, and TAT officials. Ironically, the plane suffered a fatal crash on the same field while attempting a landing during a heavy snowstorm just six months later, on December 22, 1929.

To handle its Stout Field passenger and express operations (a mail contract was not obtained until September 30, 1930), TAT built a brick and concrete U-shaped terminal with two wings, one for offices and the other for a garage to store the "Aerocar" trailer used for local passenger transportation. A fireplace-equipped passenger lounge and ticket office occupied the central part of the building, and a metal canopied walkway extended from the lounge onto the concrete loading apron. Adjacent to the south was the large new hangar of the Curtiss Flying Service, where any required emergency maintenance could be performed. Both the former terminal and the hangar are still in use today by ground units of the Indiana Army NATIONAL GUARD.

In 1929, a new aeronautical mania, endurance flying, both solo and refueled, swept the country. Among the best known midwestern flights were those by two Indianapolis pilots, Lts. Walter Peck and Lawrence (Gene) Genaro, in the *Indianapolis Flamingo*, an all-metal plane similar to those used by the Embry-Riddle airline. Their two record attempts from Hoosier Airport came to naught when continuing fog and rain prevented refueling attempts. In the end, despite a perfectly functioning plane engine, the two pilots had to settle for a 149 hour and 36 minute mark, far short of the existing record.

New airlines began serving the city in the thirties. Embry-Riddle became part of American Airlines in November, 1930, and Eastern Air Lines began service in June, 1934. In 1939, the U.S. Civil Aeronautics Authority opened its Experimental Station at the Indianapolis Municipal Airport. The new technical center concentrated on development of improved aircraft radio equipment, radio ranges, instrument landing systems, and aircraft lighting.

During World War II, the Curtiss-Wright Corporation built one of the nation's largest propeller plants in the city, and the ALLISON DIVISION of General Motors added several new engine manufacturing plants. Allison also developed a flight test center at Weir Cook Airport for testing engines for numerous fighter and other aircraft.

Following the removal of World War II restrictions, local flying interest reached new highs. Attempting to fulfill the "plane in every garage" forecast, hundreds of former servicemen took flight instruction, private aircraft sales boomed, and several new commercial and private airfields were developed to handle the increased activity.

Commercial aviation grew apace as several new airlines began serving the city. These included a new type carrier, the air freight lines. Carrying cargo only, these companies hauled anything that would fit inside the planes, including flowers, heavy machinery, furniture, race horses, and perishable foods. In the eighties a new version of these lines developed—the small parcel carriers, offering overnight delivery services to points nationwide. Two of the country's largest, United Parcel Service and Federal Express, now serve the city.

Another new type of operation is the helicopter, which entered the local scene in the 1950s. Several law enforcement agencies and local companies have made extensive use of copters and the premier public heliport in the country now operates in downtown Indianapolis.

The Indianapolis Municipal Airport began operations in 1931. The field was renamed Weir Cook Memorial Airport in 1944 in honor of a World War I fighter ace. In 1976, with the opening of a new building to serve international flights,

the field was designated INDIANAPOLIS INTERNATIONAL AIRPORT. By the early 1990s the facility accommodated over 6 million passengers annually.

JERRY MARLETTE

Avondale Playhouse. Regarded as one of the Midwest's top professional summer stock theaters, the Avondale Playhouse (or "Avondale-in-the-Meadows") contracted nationally recognized stage and screen personalities to headline casts composed largely of local talent. A candy-striped tent erected at the Meadows Shopping Center on East 38th Street housed the 1,200–seat theater for most of its operating years, 1954–1966. Avondale regularly drew capacity audiences to popular light comedy productions in addition to award-winning modern classics. One of the nation's few theaters-in-the-round, the Avondale's stage afforded such stars as Myrna Loy, Cesar Romero, and Dorothy Lamour an unusual live performance experience, while its multiple viewing perspectives proved a challenge to directors and set designers.

Allen W. Clowes, who along with W. Taylor Wilson helped found Avondale, promoted the tent theater and its friendly rival, STARLIGHT MUSICALS, as the city's two best alternatives to summer boredom. In 1964, ticket prices ranged from $2.90 to $3.20. The Crown Room, located in the Meadows, advertised a dinner, cocktail, and Avondale show package for $6.95. Encouraged by the theater's success, Avondale's board of directors sought expansion to other midwestern locations, but the failure of a Louisville venture in 1965 forced the company to sell its assets. A proposed Avondale "Playhouse-on-the-Lake," scheduled to open June 20, 1967, at 116th and Keystone, never reached the construction stage.

CYNTHIA L. SNYDER
Princeton University

Ayres, Lyman S. (Sept. 4, 1824–May 7, 1896). Founder of L. S. Ayres and Company department store. Ayres was born and raised on a farm near Oswego, New York, and began his mercantile career at the age of 19 as a peddler of goods in Geauga County, Ohio. He owned and operated a general store for 15 years in Chardon, Ohio, and a dry goods store in Geneva, New York, for seven years. In 1872 Ayres accepted an offer to buy controlling interest of a leading dry goods store in partnership with N. R. Smith in Indiana's fast growing capital city.

The Trade Palace was a well-established dry goods retail store located in "Ray's Stone Front Building" at 26–28 West Washington Street. Ayres remained in New York as resident buyer for the Trade Palace for two years, then moved with his family to Indianapolis to assume management of the business. He changed the firm's name to L. S. AYRES AND COMPANY and within two years moved his store into a new and much larger three-story building at 33–37 West Washington Street.

Besides being a careful businessman Ayres was known for generosity and concern for his employees, personable customer service, and use of technological innovations. From 1874 to 1896 his staff grew from about 30 to 175 employees. He started new employees at a higher wage than did other retailers, was the first retailer in the city to have an annual employees' Fourth of July picnic, and closed on Saturday afternoons in the summer months so that his employees could take advantage of the city's new parks. Ayres greeted each em-

Lyman S. Ayres.
[Indiana State
Library]

ployee by name in the morning, as well as every customer at the door. His was the first store in the city to install electric lights and an elevator, and to use glass showcases to display merchandise.

Before Ayres' death in 1896 he had purchased Hubbard's Block at the southwest corner of Meridian and Washington streets. On this site in 1905 Frederic M. Ayres built the city's first modern department store and developed a successful retail business with his father's legacy.

ROBERT F. GILYEAT

L. S. Ayres and Company Collection, Indiana Historical Society.

B

Babe Denny Neighborhood. Near southside community bordered by South Street, Madison Avenue, and Morris and West streets. Settlement of the near south side began in the late 1830s and 1840s, when German and Irish immigrants arrived during a wave of railroad and canal construction. By the 1870s the BELT LINE RAILROAD at the northern edge of the neighborhood provided jobs for residents and spurred industrial and commercial growth. Mixed land use was an integral part of the neighborhood. Mills, warehouses, and meat packing firms were built alongside homes, shops, churches, and synagogues.

Irish, German, and Jewish immigrants predominated in the neighborhood during the late 19th and early 20th centuries. The JEWS, in particular, organized a self-sufficient community. Many of them were tradesmen who opened small businesses or grocery, meat, and poultry stores. Others worked at KAHN TAILORING COMPANY. They built five synagogues and established the Communal Building to provide English instruction for immigrants and to find housing for Jewish families. In 1946 the nonsectarian Concord Association formed to meet the changing needs of the neighborhood. The Communal Building became the Concord Center, which continues at a new location in the 1990s to offer recreational facilities, classes, and other services to area residents.

New groups migrated to the neighborhood after World War I as others moved out. Whites and African-Americans from the southern United States replaced prosperous ethnic families. Particularly after World War II, businesses expanded and demolished houses, while remaining homes fell into disrepair. Construction of Interstate 70 through the neighborhood accelerated the transition. In the 1980 census nearly 28 percent of the residents in some areas were below the poverty level, while up to one half of families in some tracts rented their homes.

Residents formed the Babe Denny Neighborhood Group in 1989, taking the name of a former Parks Department employee and longtime resident. Four years later the group successfully coordinated a partnership between Habitat for Humanity, local businesses, and the Concord Community Development Corporation to build two new homes in the neighborhood, the first in over 46 years. The association lobbies for changes in the zoning laws to limit commercial expansion and seeks to attract new residents and neighborhood services.

CATHLEEN F. DONNELLY

Maude Louvenbruck, *The Near Southside Community: As It Was and As It Is* (1974); Juanita Loundman Clay, "The Role of Concord Center, A Social Settlement, in Neighborhood Improvement" (M.A. thesis, Indiana University, 1959); *Indianapolis Star*, Nov. 11, 1979, July 10, 1993.

Bacon's Swamp. A large peat bog once extending several blocks west of today's Keystone Avenue between 54th Street and Kessler Boulevard. Named after its pioneer owner, Bacon's Swamp was possibly the only peat bog of its kind found this far south in the United States. It resulted from the retreat of the Wisconsin Glacier some 20,000 years ago. As the glacier receded it left in its wake a large crystal lake which slowly filled with organic growth that eventually evolved into peat.

The swamp's first notoriety came during the Civil War era when it served as a station on the Underground Railroad. "Stationmaster" Hiram Bacon hid fugitive slaves in a large grain bin in his barn on the east bank of the swamp. From there, under cover of darkness, they were moved to Westfield, the next stop on their way to Canada.

Through the years, particularly in the 1920s, 1930s, and 1940s, the bog became a living laboratory for college professors, amateur botanists, members of the Indiana Nature Study Club, bird watchers, and students. Taking daylong excursions to what were then the outskirts of the city, they studied the swamp's unusual flora and fauna and took soil borings and pollen samples from its depths to determine its natural history. Because the swamp abounded in wildlife, it also served as a hunter's delight.

Legend had it that the swamp was "bottomless" and never could be filled in. Two unsuccessful attempts to build a road across its ooze in 1914 and again in 1937 gave credence to the stories. Both roads sank as the waterlogged peat on which they were built became compressed under their weight.

Attempts to harvest and sell the peat were largely unsuccessful—not because of poor quality but because of the costly compressing procedures that were necessary to produce fuel peat. In later years a successful dredging industry did flourish, but this peat was sold to florists and nurseries to use as packing and mulch.

After World War II Bacon's Swamp was literally squeezed dry by encroaching housing developments and by "fill" dumped into it from nearby construction projects. Autumn brush fires and nearby drain installations had already lowered the water table considerably during the ten years preceding the war. The reptiles, amphibians, and aquatic mammals fled; and the marshy surroundings, where many wildflowers and other fauna not native to the area had flourished, disappeared.

The deaths of four children in two separate drowning incidents—one in 1947, another in 1956—caused nearby residents to mount a "fence and fill" campaign aimed at ridding the area of the "attractive nuisance." They also voiced constant complaints about the mosquito population.

At the same time, responding to pressures from nature lovers, various city, county, and even state agencies attacked the "problem" of Bacon's Swamp. Plans drawn up in the mid–1950s for a combined nature preserve and playground languished at the drawing board stage and eventually died—a scant ten or fifteen years before the ascendancy of the ecological movement. A retirement community, built in the 1980s, occupies the site and overlooks Bacon Lake, a small remnant of the original swamp.

ALICE ASHBY ROETTGER

Jacob Piatt Dunn, *Greater Indianapolis* (Chicago, 1910), I, 250; Stanley Cain, "Plant Succession and Ecological History of a Central Indiana Swamp," *Botanical Gazette*, 86 (Dec., 1928).

Bagby, Robert Bruce (1847–Jan. 24, 1903). African-American entrepreneur, politician, and teacher. Bagby's parents were born into slavery but purchased their freedom and eventually settled in Oxford, Ohio, a community known to be receptive to ex-slaves. Four of the Bagby children, including Robert, attended Oberlin College.

In the early 1870s, shortly after his arrival in Indianapolis, Robert Bagby became principal of Public School 17, one of the schools established for African-Americans. Brothers Benjamin D. and James D. followed his lead by also becoming principals of black schools in Indianapolis.

Though their primary occupations were in education, the Bagby brothers established the *INDIANAPOLIS LEADER*, a weekly newspaper that began publication in 1879. Because of its editorializing and Republican political connections, the *Leader* quickly gained a national reputation as one of the best African-American newspapers in the United States. As a result, the Bagby name become synonymous with success. Sale of the paper in 1886 allowed Robert Bagby to turn his talents to politics and law.

Bagby became the first African-American to serve on the City Council (1877–1879). He also conducted a successful law practice from his office in Indianapolis at 60 East Market Street.

STANLEY WARREN
DePauw University

Emma Lou Thornbrough, *The Negro in Indiana* (Indianapolis, 1957); *Indianapolis Freeman*, July 21, 1888, Jan. 11, 1890; *Indianapolis World*, June 4, 1892, Sept. 16, 30, 1893.

Bahr, Max A. (Mar. 21, 1872–Jan. 24, 1953). Physician and educator. An 1893 graduate of SHORTRIDGE HIGH SCHOOL, Bahr earned his medical degree from the city's Central College of Physicians and Surgeons in 1896. Following a residency, he became employed as the extern at CENTRAL STATE HOSPITAL in 1898. Realizing that American psychiatry was far behind that of the Germans, Bahr furthered his education and received a degree of Doctor of Psychological Medicine from the University of Berlin in 1908, subsequently returning to Central State Hospital as a clinical psychiatrist. Appointed superintendent of the institution in 1923, he served in that capacity until his retirement in 1952.

Bahr had a great interest in the relationship between crime and mental illness. He conducted the first clinical courses in America for lawyers in forensic psychiatry. With Bahr's encouragement, the hospital employed WALTER BRUETSCH, M.D., to head pathology and research for the hospital. In 1931, the hospital won international recognition for improvements in malarial therapy technique in syphilitic patients.

Bahr spent 54 years of his life demonstrating care, understanding, and kindness for the mentally ill. Even as superintendent, he routinely visited hospital wards to show his concern. Ten months following his retirement, Bahr died in January, 1953.

CHARLES O. HAZELRIGG, D.D.S.

Bailey, Robert L. (June 29, 1885–Mar. 4, 1940). African-American lawyer. Born in Florence, Alabama, Bailey attended public schools, graduated from Talladega College (Ala.) in 1906, and earned his LL.B. from Indiana Law School in 1912.

Bailey's first job was as a federal railway postal clerk. He helped found the National Alliance of Postal Employees in 1913 as Indiana's representative and subsequently served as the organization's general counsel. He then opened an Indianapolis law office in 1914 with ROBERT L. BROKENBURR, FREEMAN B. RANSOM, and later F. W. Littlejohn. He served as an assistant attorney general under state Attorney General James M. Ogden (1929–1933) and subsequently as judge pro tem of Marion County Circuit Court for Judge Harry O. Chamberlin.

Bailey was a member of both the Illinois and Indianapolis Bar Associations. He served on the Legal Aid Committee for the Indianapolis Bar and was its only African-American member in the late 1920s. Bailey was active with the Indianapolis branch of the NAACP, serving a term as president and acting as counsel. He was also chair of the Legal Redress Committee of the Indiana State NAACP.

MICHELLE D. HALE

Baltimore & Ohio Railroad. The large B&O Railroad system in 1927 acquired the 296-mile line from Hamilton, Ohio, to Springfield, Illinois, via Indianapolis, known as the Cincinnati,

Indianapolis & Western. Originally the CI&W consisted of two distinct railroads that were consolidated in 1888: the Cincinnati, Hamilton & Indianapolis (popularly referred to as the "Junction Railroad") and the Indiana, Bloomington & Springfield. The "Junction" or eastern segment of the line served as a comprehensive freight-passenger connection for the B&O between Indianapolis and more distant eastern points via Cincinnati. The western portion specialized in the hauling of agricultural commodities, and since the B&O used MONON RAILROAD tracks for carrying passengers between Indianapolis and Chicago, passenger traffic on this part of the total line was only nominal. Freight service in 1992 was still active between Indianapolis and the Cincinnati area; most of the line to Springfield between Indianapolis and Montezuma has been abandoned.

VICTOR M. BOGLE
Indiana University, Kokomo

John F. Stover, *History of the Baltimore and Ohio Railroad* (West Lafayette, Ind., 1987).

Balz, Arcada Campbell Stark (Dec. 31, 1879–Aug. 18, 1973). Politician and women's club leader. Born on a farm near Bloomington, Indiana, Arcada Stark's family moved to Colorado and Kansas before settling in Indianapolis. She attended MANUAL HIGH SCHOOL and Indianapolis Normal College, and later taught history, literature, and art in the Indianapolis junior high schools.

Balz served as president of the 7th district of the Federation of Women's Clubs, 1932–1935; president, 1935–1937, of the Indiana Federation of Women's Clubs; and director of the General Federation of Women's Clubs, 1937–1939. Club activities included purchasing radium for a free cancer clinic at Indianapolis City Hospital and developing orchestras in the city's schools.

Balz became politically active when she suggested the establishment of the New Harmony Memorial and served as president of the state commission, 1939–1947. As a Republican representing parts of Marion and Johnson counties, she became the first woman elected to the Indiana Senate in 1942 and was reelected in 1944. Her legislative interests included licensing nursing homes, developing school attendance requirements, improving the merit system for state employees, and regulating women's working hours and wages.

NORALEEN YOUNG

Bands, City/Municipal. Recognized as the first significant wind and percussion ensemble in the city's history, the Indianapolis Band (incorporated February 15, 1841) consisted of 27 charter members, including bass trombonist JAMES MCCREADY, the city's mayor from 1854 to 1856. A succession of short-lived bands followed the dissolution of this organization, among them the German Military Band, the Sax Horn Band, and the National Guard Band. The music of the Indianapolis City Band, an organization established in 1861, enlivened parades, balls, political rallies, and other events well into the 20th century. Other bands of this period included the Union Band, Beissenherz's Band, Bradshaw's Band, and the Indianapolis Ladies' Cornet Band.

JOHN T. BRUSH, the founder and owner of the When Clothing Store, formed the When Band in 1875. It quickly became one of the city's most popular ensembles. Comprised of musicians who held day jobs as When employees, the organization delighted audiences with its Saturday evening concerts. Its successor, the Indianapolis Military Band, enjoyed prominence for many years. Two of its members, cornetist Bohumir Kryl and euphonium virtuoso Noble Howard, later gained international fame. The *Indianapolis News* Newsboys Band (1900–1962) consisted of *News*

Musical groups such as the Frank Mayer Band were available for parties, parades, and funerals, although their services cost more on holidays. [Indiana Historical Society, #C5764]

carriers under the age of 18. Although it rehearsed three nights a week, the Newsboys Band attracted so many would-be members that a second band became necessary for the training of recruits. The Indianapolis Concert Band, under the direction of William Schumacher, also provided music for many local events.

Originally named "The Detroit Diesel Allison Concert Band" after the industrial plant that provided it with rehearsal space for over 30 years, the Indianapolis Municipal Band performs frequently at shopping centers, retirement homes, parks, and fairs. The Indianapolis Symphonic Band, brought to local attention in the 1960s by Robert Phillips, practices at Glendale Shopping Center where it presents several concerts a year.

SUZANNE G. SNYDER

Bank One, Indianapolis. The history of Bank One, Indianapolis, is long and complex, dating back to 1839. It includes the merger and acquisition of more than 30 independent banks.

STOUGHTON A. FLETCHER, SR., who arrived in Indianapolis from Vermont in 1831, opened a bank in a one-room office at 8 East Washington Street in 1839, with $3,000 of capital. The official name was S. A. Fletcher & Company, but the bank was known for years as Fletcher's Bank. A group of prominent Indianapolis businessmen founded the American National Bank in 1901. In 1910 this bank and the Fletcher National Bank, the successor to S. A. Fletcher & Company, merged to become Fletcher American National Bank with STOUGHTON A. FLETCHER II, grandson of the founder, as president. A series of business failures forced Fletcher to relinquish control of the bank and resign as president in 1923. The Fletcher American National Bank did not reopen after the federally imposed "bank holiday" in March, 1933. It was reorganized under federal trusteeship as the American National Bank.

Alexander Metzger, a German-born baker, went into banking in 1863 as Alexander Metzger & Sons. One of his sons, Albert E. Metzger, was instrumental in the merger of the Marion Trust Company and the German American Trust Company, the successor to the A. Metzger agency, into the Fletcher Savings & Trust Company in 1912.

The president of this new bank was Evans Wool-len, Sr. His son, Evans Woollen, Jr., was president of the Fletcher Trust Company (the name had been shortened in 1931) when it merged with the American National Bank on December 31, 1954. This new entity, the American Fletcher National Bank (AFNB), became the second largest bank in the state and Evans Woollen, Jr., was named its president.

On July 31, 1959, the Fidelity Bank & Trust Company merged with the American Fletcher National Bank. This created the largest bank in Indiana, which retained the name AFNB. Evans Woollen, Jr., died in February, 1959. FRANK E. MCKINNEY, SR., who acquired control of the Fidelity Bank in 1935 and built it into one of Marion County's leading banks at the time of the merger, was then named chairman of the AFNB board of directors.

The American Fletcher Corporation (AFC) was established in 1968. It was a one-bank holding company, one of the first of its kind in the country. The holding company would be the means to expand financial services opportunities into banking-related enterprises, and to do so in a wider geographical area. When Indiana bankers were allowed to expand beyond their own county borders, AFC was ready.

Under the leadership of FRANK E. MCKIN-NEY, JR., who was named president in 1972 and chairman of the board in 1973, AFC became the largest and most profitable bank holding company in the state. In addition to wanting to have the dominant banking institution in central Indiana, McKinney had two other goals: the construction of a new bank building and the reformation of Indiana's archaic banking laws. Both these goals were accomplished, but proved to be long and arduous in their attainment.

By May, 1986, AFC had acquired four banks in the state of Indiana, and had two other acquisitions in process. However, nine months before, in late summer of 1985, McKinney had begun to think about and analyze the question of interstate merger and acquisition. This led to a study of linkage partners within the Midwest. By the process of elimination, Banc One Corporation of Ohio seemed to be the organization that best suited AFC's requirements.

The merger of American Fletcher Corporation into Banc One Corporation was announced on May 11, 1986. McKinney became chairman and chief executive officer of Banc One, Indiana, with 12 affiliate banks throughout Indiana reporting to him. He remained chairman and CEO of American Fletcher National Bank, which was renamed Bank One, Indianapolis.

McKinney was responsible for creating this concept of a state holding company operating under the main holding company. All of the affiliate banks in Indiana would remain independent operating units, each with its own board of directors responsible to the board of directors of the state holding company, Banc One, Indiana Corporation. Banc One, Indiana Corporation in turn reported to the main holding company, Banc One Corporation. The affiliate banks in Ohio were then organized in like fashion. This model continues to serve well as Banc One Corporation expands throughout the country.

Bank One, Indianapolis, which employed approximately 2,500, was the largest bank in the city and state in 1992 with total assets exceeding $4.78 billion.

THOMAS L. PLIMPTON
Bank One, Indianapolis

Bank One Building (101 Monument Circle). First "curtainwall" building in Indianapolis, constructed by the George A. Fuller company of New York. The renowned Chicago architectural firm of Skidmore, Owings and Merrill designed this aluminum, concrete, and glass structure to house the main offices of the Fidelity Bank and Trust Company in the northeast quadrant of Monument Circle at Market Street. The building's developers razed the INDIANAPOLIS WATER COMPANY office, originally built in 1871 as a residence, and the 1875 Insurance Building to clear the site for construction. Fidelity was to occupy the first two floors; the remaining ten floors were to be leased for office space. By the time the building was completed in 1959, Fidelity had merged with AMERICAN FLETCHER BANK and Trust Company, forming the largest bank in Indiana. The new institution took the name American Fletcher (becoming BANK ONE after a merger in the 1980s) and kept the old Fletcher Bank building immediately east of the new one on the corner of Market and Illinois. A second-story bridge linking the two structures was built at the time of the merger.

The structure's main facade follows the curve of MONUMENT CIRCLE. The building's aluminum columns sweep upward in unbroken lines for 150 feet, expressing the verticality and lack of ornamentation typical of postwar commercial architecture. The non-load-bearing aluminum and glass exterior wall is not supported by the steel girders of the skeleton frame, hence the term "curtainwall."

GLORY-JUNE GREIFF

Bank One Tower. Tallest building in Indianapolis. FRANK E. MCKINNEY, JR., chairman of BANK ONE Indiana, began planning for the tower in 1969 when the financial institution was known as American Fletcher National Bank, but groundbreaking for the 701–foot high structure did not occur until June, 1987. It opened in 1990.

The tower occupies a full city block between Meridian and Pennsylvania streets, bounded on the north by Ohio Street. It has 51 stories, 48 of which are designated as office space. Massachusetts architect Hugh Stubbins of Stubbins Associates designed the building. The Indianapolis firm of Huber, Hunt and Nichols served as construction manager, and the Galbreath Company of Columbus, Ohio, was the original developer. Stubbins, who is most noted for his design of the Citicorp Building in Manhattan, expressed his desire for the Bank One Tower to serve as the terminus of the INDIANA WORLD WAR MEMORIAL PLAZA. The roof line of the tower reflects that of the World War Memorial. The exterior of the building is sheathed in granite quarried in Spain and Sweden and cut in Italy. The pyramidal roof is topped by twin antenna spires.

SUZANNE T. ROLLINS

Jeff Swiatek, "View from the Top," *Indianapolis Star*, Nov. 29, 1988; Kevin A. Drawbaugh, "Blueprints and Greenbacks" and "The Tower Trade," *Indianapolis News*, Sept. 19–20, 1990.

Banking Industry. In 1834 the General Assembly established the Second STATE BANK OF INDIANA with 10 (later 13) branches; the principal branch was the first bank to be located in Indianapolis. Two years later the Indianapolis Insurance Company organized with banking powers. It operated as a savings bank until it closed in 1840. In 1839 STOUGHTON A. FLETCHER, SR., opened an exchange banking office with $3,000 capital (eventually, after several mergers, it would become American Fletcher National Bank, the longest-lived bank in the city's history).

In 1851 the General Assembly created a new bank, the Bank of the State of Indiana, to replace the Second State Bank of Indiana, whose charter was to expire in 1857. In 1852 a "Free Banking Act," a general incorporation statute, permitted the establishment of other banking institutions that met the minimal requirements laid down by the General Assembly. Unfortunately many of the banks originating under the new law were unstable, resulting in frequent suspensions. Among the unsuccessful attempts was the newly reorganized Indianapolis Insurance Company, which opened in 1852 and remained in business for only six years before again suspending operations.

The Civil War put additional strains on already precarious banks. In 1863 Congress passed the National Banking Act, imposing a tax on state bank notes and effectively driving them out of circulation. This act, which also allowed for the chartering of national banks, regulated an obvi-

Interior of Indiana National Bank, 3 Virginia Avenue, in 1912. [Indiana Historical Society, #C5778]

ously distressed state banking system and provided the federal government with the capital needed to finance the war. National banks could issue notes backed by U.S. bonds and guaranteed by the federal government. Some of Indianapolis' banks (primarily those with over $75,000 capital) quickly secured charters as national banks.

The city's first nationally chartered bank was organized by WILLIAM H. ENGLISH and 10 associates as the First National Bank (FNB) of Indianapolis in May, 1863. FNB was the only national bank in the city for 18 months, followed by Citizens National and Indianapolis National in 1864, and Fourth National, Merchants National, and Indiana National (INB) in 1865. INB was, in effect, the successor institution to the former Indianapolis Branch of the State Bank of Indiana, gaining its president, George Towsey, and most of its business.

In 1869 a state law provided for the establishment of savings banks. Several of these new institutions soon sprang up in the city. In 1870 John Peter Frenzel, Merchants Bank's 16–year-old bookkeeper, and George A. Dickson started the Enterprise Building and Loan. The Western Savings and Loan, where members deposited $.50 to join and $.55 weekly, organized in 1884. The Dime Savings and Loan Association incorporated three years later. These businesses were popular because banking regulations allowed them to enter the mortgage loan field, an area prohibited to banks until after 1890.

The financial panics of 1893 and 1907 closed numerous savings and loans and national banks in Indianapolis as elsewhere. One survivor was Peoples Deposit Bank (later PEOPLES BANK). Chartered by Felix T. McWhirter in 1900, it was the first bank in the city with a woman on its board—LUELLA MCWHIRTER, the founder's wife. Another survivor was Indiana Trust Company. Organized in the 1890s by the Frenzels of Merchants National Bank, it had more total deposits in 1907—over $7.5 million—than all other trust companies in Indianapolis. In 1908 a group of southside businessmen organized the Fountain Square State Bank, the first neighborhood bank in the city.

By 1910 the banking industry had revived and 21 establishments were members of the Indianapolis Clearing House Association, a group of local bankers. That year American National Bank and Fletcher National Bank merged, becoming American Fletcher National Bank (AFNB). In 1912 Capital National Bank merged with INB, and Merchants National Bank constructed a new headquarters, the city's first skyscraper. Completed in 1913, it was the tallest building in Indianapolis for 50 years.

During World War I members of the Indianapolis Clearing House sold war bonds, earning $1 million in subscriptions at the end of their first drive. Merchants National Bank provided banking services to the U.S. Army at Fort Benjamin Harrison for the duration of the war.

By 1920 AFNB was the largest private banking establishment in Indiana. In 1921 local businessmen founded MORRIS PLAN as a lending establishment to serve working people. Another workingperson's organization, RAILROADMEN'S SAVINGS AND LOAN (established in 1888 by the Union Railway paymaster) was the largest building and loan association in the world in the 1920s.

The Great Depression proved fatal to many of Indianapolis' financial institutions. Between 1927 and 1933 ten local banks closed their doors—contributing to the national statistics of 10,000 failures. Still, the banks which entered the depression years with sizable assets remained healthy during the period, and sometimes profited from their competition's problems. In 1930 Merchants acquired the assets of the Continental National Bank and, the next year, reached nearly $14 million in deposits. Peoples Bank introduced the state's first auto drive-up window in 1931. In 1938 Peoples originated the state's first Federal Housing Administration (FHA) loan. Following a 1934 enabling law, Merchants opened its first branch on East 38th Street in 1939.

Locally and across the country banks shifted focus in the post–World War II years, offering a "department store" of financial services geared to the consumer. In the 1950s Merchants merged with Fountain Square State Bank, consolidated with the Indiana Trust Company, and acquired Co-op's State Bank in Beech Grove. Union Trust merged into INB in 1950. And in 1959 Union Federal merged with Colonel Savings and Loan. A

"Charge-It" system, first launched at a New York City bank in 1946, became a local phenomenon in 1953 when Morris Plan introduced its Free Charge Account. Eventually 23,000 customers subscribed, helping to make Morris Plan the nation's largest savings and loan without branches by 1958.

In 1961 Merchants constructed a $2 million ultra-modern banking office built around the tamper-proof vault that had been installed by the Indiana Trust Company in 1893. By 1965 the bank had 22 locations in the county and its services, like those of most local banks, included drive-up windows, storage vaults, safe deposit boxes, and community meeting rooms. By decade's end Indiana National Bank's assets had grown to $1 billion. The following year INB moved into its 37–story headquarters, then the state's tallest building.

During the 1970s local banks continued to expand services by adding branches and resources. Like banks nationwide Indianapolis banks also became much more aggressive in marketing, utilizing their banking symbols to advertise new products, services, and technology. Thus the Merchants green frog, the INB bison, and Railroadmen's locomotive, among others, came to represent Indianapolis banks to the city's residents.

The 1980s ushered in a period of high interest rates which adversely affected local savings and loans. Railroadmen's suffered a $6 million deficit, which it overcame with a stock issue. In 1984 Fort Wayne-based Waterfield Mortgage Company acquired Union Federal Savings and Loan for $6.1 million. At the time of acquisition Union Federal had a negative net worth of $20 million. Although in 1985 state banking laws finally reduced restrictions on cross-county acquisitions and mergers, the delay of this legislation for several years following similar laws in nearby states placed local banks at a disadvantage in acquiring the large asset bases of the Ohio and Michigan "super-regional" banks.

By the mid–1980s Merchants, AFNB, and INB were the "Big Three" of Indianapolis banking, but change was imminent. INB quickly jumped into out-of-county bank purchases, growing to $6 billion in assets. By May, 1986, American Fletcher

Corporation (AFC), a bank holding company formed by AFNB principals, had acquired four additional banks. A few days later AFC president FRANK MCKINNEY, JR., announced the bank's merger with Banc One Corp., a Columbus, Ohio, super-regional corporation. AFNB became BANK ONE, INDIANAPOLIS. At the end of the decade, of the larger banking institutions in the city, only Peoples retained its conservative attitude toward mergers, acquisitions, and loans. It was consistently listed among the nation's soundest banks.

By the 1990s commercial banks were active in insurance, investment and securities, mortgages, trade finance, venture capital, travel, and advisory work. As a further service, UNION FEDERAL SAVINGS BANK (formerly Union Federal Savings and Loan) and others opened branches at Indianapolis-area MARSH SUPERMARKETS. The merger trend of the 1980s climaxed in the 1990s, however, as out-of-state super-regional banks acquired one local bank after another. In May, 1992, Cleveland-based National City Corporation bought Merchants National Corporation in a $640 million transaction; Merchants became a NATIONAL CITY BANK. In September, 1992, shareholders of INB Financial Corporation sold the bank to NBD Bancorp of Detroit, making NBD BANK the largest bank in the state and the 16th largest in the nation. Society Bank Corporation, based in Cleveland, purchased Ameritrust Corporation, which had three branches in Marion County, and in November, 1993, shareholders of Railroadmen's voted to accept a merger with Huntington Bancshares, a Columbus, Ohio, firm in an $88 million deal. By 1993 seven midwestern banking powers were in business in Indianapolis. Together they controlled more than 80 percent of the $13 billion in deposits found in the city's financial institutions.

CONNIE J. ZEIGLER

James H. Madison, "Business and Politics in Indianapolis: The Branch Bank and the Junto, 1837–1846," *Indiana Magazine of History*, 71 (Mar., 1975), 1–20; *The City and the Bank, 1865–1965* [Merchants National Bank] (Indianapolis: privately printed, 1965); *Indianapolis Star*, Sept. 8, 1992, Feb. 28, Nov. 28, 1993.

Baptists. About 30 million Baptists reside in the United States, distributed among 28 national bodies or conventions and a host of nonaligned independent churches. Traditionally Baptists affirm the separation of church and state, the priesthood of all believers, local church autonomy, a high view of biblical authority, and believer's baptism by immersion.

The over 300 Baptist churches located in Greater Indianapolis belong to at least 13 groupings. Some are small: the Indiana Fellowship of Fundamental Baptists; North American Baptist General Conference, Chicago; the Primitive or Free Will Baptists; the Baptist Bible Fellowship; and the General Baptists. The General Association of Regular Baptist Churches has 16 affiliates in the Indianapolis area. Some churches are unaffiliated or only loosely organized. A prominent independent Baptist congregation in the city is the 6,000–member INDIANAPOLIS BAPTIST TEMPLE, founded in 1950. Under the longtime and present ministry of the Rev. Greg Dixon the traditional Baptist emphases of separation of church and state and freedom of speech have had their most vocal advocate. The Baptist Temple fellowships with the American Coalition of Unregistered Churches, an organization founded by Dixon, and it operates the Indianapolis Baptist Schools as part of its ministry.

The major limbs of the Baptist family tree, which together comprise around two-thirds of all Marion County Baptist churches, are the American Baptist Churches, USA, the Southern Baptist Convention, and the several black Baptist organizations.

American Baptist or ABC/USA churches in Marion County total 33 with close to 11,000 members. The FIRST BAPTIST CHURCH at 86th Street and College Avenue is the area's largest ABC church with nearly 700 members. It also holds the distinction of being the city's first Baptist church, founded September 21, 1822. Among its 17 charter members were Eliza and John McCormick and John's brother, Samuel, considered to be among Marion County's first white settlers. Benjamin Barnes, an itinerant minister, assumed the first pastoral charge. By 1841 the church had over 100 members. After a series of residences the church in 1864 erected a $35,000

meeting house at Pennsylvania and New York streets, its home for the next 40 years. After the Civil War the church's local mission efforts stepped up with the founding of the South Street Baptists, Garden Baptist Church, North Baptist, and River Avenue Baptist Church. Through its 170–year history First Baptist has fashioned or financially nurtured at least 16 congregations.

In 1904 the church burned. The 1,000 plus members in 1906 paid for a new $200,000, 1,200–seat, edifice, probably the state's largest, on the northeast corner of Vermont and Meridian streets. In this same year Frederick E. Taylor began his 26–year pastorate. Under his direction, and maintained by a well-to-do congregation, the church heavily supported missions, cared for the community's needy, and greatly expanded its Sunday school. By the late 1920s the church boasted a membership of 1,900. After World War II, as the city and its families pushed far outside the MILE SQUARE, the church, like other downtown churches, grappled with the focus of its mission. Diminishing parking space, and the state's persistent effort to purchase land around the Indiana World War Memorial, persuaded the church to sell its property to the state for over $725,000 and move to 86th Street and College Avenue in 1960 into a $1.25 million structure. The congregation eventually bought a surrounding 39–acre farm and orchard, on which today the church conducts a large athletic program.

First Baptist Church along with the other 32 ABC churches fellowship together in an association called the American Baptist Churches of Greater Indianapolis. Four of these ABC churches come from the ranks of the city's black congregations.

For much of the antebellum era Indianapolis blacks, usually Baptist or Methodist, worshipped in white churches, segregated in a balcony or rear pew, purposely denied active participation in the life of the congregation. In 1846 Rev. Charles Sachell, a former Cincinnati Baptist pastor turned missionary, assembled a group of like-believers in the house of John Brown at West and Ohio streets and launched the mother church of the city's black Baptists, known then and now as the SECOND BAPTIST CHURCH. A brick church went up in 1853 on Missouri Street between New York and

Ohio streets. In 1857 Second Baptist found an able preacher and pastor in MOSES BROYLES, an ex-slave who had been educated at Eleutherian College near Madison, Indiana. He came to a congregation of 30 and a four-year-old unplastered, pewless, and unpainted sanctuary. Broyles steadied the physical plant, increased its size, and as a result of his effort had to build a new church in 1867. The membership increased to 630 by 1875. Broyles also led in establishing a handful of other black churches in the area, including White Lick in Bridgeport in 1866, Lick Creek, now Olivet Baptist, in 1867, Mount Zion in 1869, Georgetown Baptist in 1872, New Bethel and Tabernacle in 1875. Broyles was instrumental in the formation in 1858 of an association of black churches, called the Indiana Baptist Association, which became by 1895 the Indiana Missionary Baptist State Convention. In 1880 Broyles witnessed the formation of the pioneering Foreign Mission Baptist Convention in Montgomery, Alabama, which evolved by 1895 into the National Baptist Convention. Broyles died in 1882 but his successors at Second Baptist soon built the church's membership to 1,900.

In the early years of the 20th century, Indianapolis' AFRICAN-AMERICAN CHURCHES grew rapidly as black migration to the northern cities increased. In 1908, 19 of 40 black congregations in Indianapolis were Baptist, including three Freewill, or "footwash," Baptists. In 1915 a schism in the National Baptist Convention split churches and created new ones throughout the country while in Indianapolis the upheaval resulted in the founding of two associations of churches. By 1923 there were 36 black Baptist churches in Indianapolis, a number that doubled by 1947. Meanwhile, Second Baptist, which built an edifice at Michigan and West streets between 1912 and 1920, continued to exert enormous influence in the black community until the post–World War II dispersion of population throughout the county substantially decreased the church's membership and, by the early 1990s, forced the congregation to relocate to 2300 West Washington Street.

The need for a school to train ministers led Rev. C. J. Dailey, pastor of St. Paul Baptist Church, to spearhead the establishment of the Central Baptist Theological Seminary in the fall of 1943.

Another formidable institution is the Edna Martin Christian Center, begun as the Eastside Christian Center in 1945.

Marion County contained 108 black Baptist churches by 1960, 15 of which belonged to a new national body, the Progressive National Baptist Convention, which Martin Luther King, Jr., assisted in establishing. The progressive churches blossomed for a few years in Indianapolis but few if any affiliates remain in the city.

Dr. James S. Wells, pastor of Zion Hope Baptist Church, founded the Baptist Bible College of Indianapolis in 1980 to provide a four-year program for minority, adult, and low-income students interested in full-time Christian vocations. The school, located at 2305 North Kitley Avenue, is the nation's only independent fundamentalist Baptist school offering a bona fide four-year Bible education to a primarily black student body.

In 1988, with the number of black Baptist churches nearing the 160 mark, not counting storefronts, a split in the National Baptist Convention of America created the National Missionary Baptist Convention, Inc. The Central District Association churches led by Dr. F. Benjamin Davis, pastor of New Bethel Church, joined the new convention almost en bloc. The Central Association changed its name to the Capitol City Fellowship Association. The old Central District is still intact but the number of churches staying with the association is unknown at this time. The old Union District Association remains together and is now the largest association of black Baptist churches in the city. The three associations annually meet together in a state convention.

The three city associations include the great majority of black Baptist churches but at least 40 black churches are singly or dually aligned with six other Baptist branches or are unassociated. Four of these churches are connected with the Southern Baptist Convention. In 1845 the southern Baptist churches broke from their northern brethren over the slavery issue and created the Southern Baptist Convention. In 1914 the Southern Baptists established their first church in Indiana in the Sullivan County town of Hymera. Some two dozen churches cropped up in the fertile Hoosier soil by 1953. In that year occurred the initial inroad of Southern Baptists into Indianapolis. Following the usual policy of determining receptivity in a new area, the Southern Baptists held a series of revivals in a tent at 3210 South Rural Street in July and August, 1953. Encouraged by the turnout, 24 charter members launched a mission Sunday school and services in a rented Youth for Christ building at 2011 North Meridian Street. In March, 1954, the church purchased nine lots in the 5500 block of East 38th Street. And in August the congregation broke ground for a new sanctuary. Even as the building underwent construction, the congregation began sponsoring the establishment of other area churches—five, in fact, between 1955 and 1958. In 1958 the church hosted representatives from throughout Indiana in the establishment of the Convention of Baptists in Indiana, the state organization of Southern Baptist churches.

By the end of its first decade in 1963 the First Southern Baptist church had a membership of 766. The founding of Northside Baptist Church in March, 1963, represented a milestone among Southern Baptists, as that Indianapolis church became the denomination's 1,500th church in the Great Lakes states. Working from a succession of judicious and well-directed plans in the next 25 years, the Southern Baptist churches in Indianapolis increased three-fold to number 30 with a total membership exceeding 6,500. In 1985 the mother church, First Southern Baptist, bought 75 acres in the 8900 block of Fall Creek Road and built a new church home. Northside Baptist's growth at 3021 East 71st Street spiraled until today with its nearly 1,600 members it is the largest Southern Baptist church in the city. Together the 26 churches and six missions of the Southern Baptists have around 7,500 members. These churches belong to the Metropolitan Baptist Association which, from Bloomington to Westfield, numbers almost 70 churches.

Except for some few instances of mutual help in years past, and the dual alignments of some of the churches, the Baptists in Indianapolis remain essentially separate denominations. No organization exists that brings all Baptist leaders together to address common concerns.

ROBERT M. TAYLOR, JR.
Indiana Historical Society

Harold Richard Hoffman, *A Light in the Forest: A History of the First Baptist Church of Indianapolis, Indiana, 1822–1966* (Indianapolis, 1966); E. Harmon Moore, *Hoosier Southern Baptists: Turning Points and Milestones, 1958–1983* (Indianapolis, 1983).

Bar Associations. The first bar association formed in Indianapolis in the early 1870s but was unsuccessful. Upon its organization in 1878, the Indianapolis Bar Association (IBA) assumed the library and treasury of the earlier group. The three objectives of the IBA have been to serve its members, maintain professional standards and practices within the legal profession, and provide law-related community service.

The 40 founding members grew to nearly 300 by the 1920s. Originally, the IBA gathered at the courthouse or a local club, even after it bought a clubhouse at Meridian and Ohio streets in 1933. It found a permanent location when it moved into the Loew's Theater building (33 North Pennsylvania) in 1955. The IBA remained at Loew's until 1970 when it moved into offices, which included a club dining facility, at the INB TOWER. Currently located at Market Tower (10 West Market Street), the IBA numbers over 3,000 members. The association admitted women members as early as the 1930s and its first African-American member in 1953, but neither group was present in significant numbers until after the 1970s.

Originally, the IBA's primary purpose was to serve its members by operating a law library and reading room housed in the courthouse. The association has always hosted annual social events and monthly meetings that include a dinner and presentation on a legal, historical, civic, or social topic. During World War I and World War II the IBA maintained the practices of members in the service. As IBA membership and the complexity of the practice of law increased, the organization expanded continuing education opportunities and organized sections specializing in various fields of law by the 1980s. Today, member services also include a lawyer referral service and informational publications.

The IBA has continually served the legal profession through committees that monitor the professional conduct of the bench and bar as well as investigate and recommend improvements in the system of justice in Marion County. The IBA constitution originally established five standing committees, which had grown to 29 committees by the early 1990s. Through committee intervention the IBA has worked to increase judges' salaries, recodify municipal law, recommend judicial appointments, monitor standards for legal education and acceptance to the bar, investigate racketeering, and improve various court systems and procedures.

Indianapolis has also benefited from IBA's volunteer legal services. The IBA early provided services to indigent clients on an informal case-by-case basis and in 1941 sponsored a Legal Aid Society. After the IBA hired an executive director in 1972, it chose to take on a more active educational and community role. In 1980 the IBA became the first bar association in the nation to provide extensive *pro bono* services using only volunteer resources. As of the 1990s community and *pro bono* programs include legal counseling, school programs, career talks, and a public grievance committee.

In 1924 a group of African-American lawyers founded the Marion County Lawyers Club, now known as the Marion County Bar Association, because they were excluded from the IBA. The group's original purpose was to act as an advocacy group for civil rights legal issues. In more recent years its focus shifted to providing professional services to members, supporting African-American attorneys and law students, and sponsoring legal programs for the African-American community.

As of the early 1990s the Marion County Bar Association supports nine standing committees that examine topics of special interest to minority lawyers. It has developed programs to encourage and support minority law students and to place minority attorneys in local law firms. The group is racially non-exclusive, although the majority of its less than 100 members has always been African-American.

The association also provides community-oriented services, such as a *pro bono* program and an annual awards program recognizing lawyers for their community service to the African-American legal or general community. It supports the CIRCLE CITY CLASSIC, and members give ca-

reer talks at local high schools. The association and its spousal auxiliary, active since the 1940s, hosted meetings of the National Bar Association held in Indianapolis in 1935 and 1991.

MICHELLE D. HALE

Indianapolis Newspaper Index, Indiana State Library; Indianapolis Bar Association Collection, Indiana Historical Society.

Barbasol. Shaving cream. In 1918 Frank Shields, an Indianapolis chemical engineer, began manufacturing a brushless shaving cream, naming it Barbasol after red-bearded medieval German emperor Frederick Barbarossa. Two years later Shields and partner L. R. Wasey incorporated the Barbasol company. Popularized through early radio broadcasts by "Singin Sam, the Barbasol Man" and his theme song "Barbasol, Barbasol, No Brush, No Lather, No Rub In," the product sold well. Despite the Great Depression, by 1936 Barbasol occupied four buildings at Senate Avenue and 9th Street and employed 400 people.

During World War II Barbasol was standard issue for combat troops. To keep up with increased demand the company employed 700 to 800 people on day and night shifts, with a special shift for housewives. In addition to shaving cream, Barbasol also manufactured razor blades, hair tonic, toothpaste, and cosmetics. In 1962 Wasey's heirs sold Barbasol to Charles Pfizer & Company, a drug manufacturer, which moved the business to New Jersey. Today Pfizer continues to manufacture Barbasol shaving cream in its familiar red, white, and blue barber-stripe packaging.

DEBORAH B. MARKISOHN

Barnhill, John F. (Jan. 2, 1865–Mar. 10, 1943). National pioneer in surgery of the head and neck; medical educator. A native of Flora, Indiana, Barnhill received his M.D. degree from the Central College of Physicians and Surgeons in 1888. He did postgraduate work at New York Eye and Ear Infirmary, the Central London Ear, Nose and Throat Hospital, the University of Vienna, and in Paris.

Barnhill was a member of the faculty of the Central College of Physicians and Surgeons and played an important role in the negotiations that led to the establishment of the INDIANA UNIVERSITY SCHOOL OF MEDICINE in 1908. He became Professor of Otolaryngology and served as first chairman of the department at Indiana University School of Medicine until his retirement. He created a course in anatomy of the head and neck that is still taught to physicians throughout the nation. Also, he was largely responsible for convincing Dr. Robert W. Long to provide funds for a teaching hospital for Indiana University. This was the first university-owned building and later the site of the INDIANA UNIVERSITY MEDICAL CENTER at IUPUI.

Barnhill was the author of numerous medical textbooks. He was an officer and a founder of several of the major national organizations in his field, serving as president of both the American Laryngological Association and the American Board of Otolaryngology.

GLENN W. IRWIN, JR., M.D.

Barton, John J., Administration of.

A native of Indianapolis (b. 1906) and a graduate of Cathedral High School, Barton earned an engineering degree from Purdue University in 1930. He served in the U.S. Navy during World War II and afterward joined the Indiana State Police. In 1961, after a three-year absence from the department spent working for a manufacturing company, he was appointed superintendent of the State Police by Governor Matthew Welsh.

Barton's reputation for honesty, earned during the years he worked with the State Police, helped him win the 1963 mayoral election. A political novice, he won the heated Democratic primary and defeated Republican Clarence Drayer and Independent candidate Samuel Unger in an election noted for its record voter participation. Barton campaigned on a platform that included promises to reform the troubled INDIANAPOLIS POLICE DEPARTMENT, involve the community in decision making, seek federal assistance for the city whenever possible, clear slums, and repair infrastructure. He served as mayor from 1964 through 1967.

Barton made the police department his first priority. The force had been racked the previous year by a series of bribery charges involving more than 27 officers. The mayor named Noel Jones, a tough disciplinarian, as chief of police. Jones reorganized the department, placing Vice Operations back under the uniformed division and cracking down on corruption. Barton cited the reorganization of the police department as one of his best achievements, but lamented that the General Assembly refused to authorize the stronger merit system he advocated.

In a break with his predecessors, Barton actively sought federal aid for municipal needs. He reactivated the INDIANAPOLIS HOUSING AUTHORITY and used federal funds to create low income housing for people displaced by the interstate highway system and slum clearance projects. By the end of Barton's term in office the city had completed a large portion of the planned 3,000 units. The mayor also led Indianapolis to participate in the HEAD START program, instituted a Community Action Against Poverty program (now COMMUNITY ACTION OF GREATER INDIANAPOLIS), and successfully lobbied the General Assembly to allow the city to receive federal matching funds for its urban renewal projects.

Barton also completed several projects that had languished under previous administrations. He pushed for the completion of EAGLE CREEK PARK, a downtown convention center, and a westside Indiana University campus. Both the INDIANA CONVENTION CENTER and what was to become IUPUI fit within his plans for urban renewal and his desire to attract businesses to Indianapolis. Eagle Creek Park and Reservoir were created to alleviate the flooding on the west side of the city and also to fill the need for more park and leisure space in Indianapolis. The Barton administration also changed the road system in the city to include more one-way streets and wider lanes. These improvements earned the city three national safety awards in 1966, including one naming it the "safest city in the United States."

The most lasting legacies of the Barton administration were the creation of the GREATER INDIANAPOLIS PROGRESS COMMITTEE (GIPC) in 1965 and the increased centralization of authority in Marion County. Barton advocated closer working relations and possible consolidation between city and county authorities that had overlapping jurisdictions. He hoped to give the mayor more control over municipal operations so that his as well as future administrations could actually make policy changes immediately. Most of the bills allowing for such control failed to pass in the General Assembly during his tenure, but passed in 1969 in the form of the legislation creating UNIGOV.

The major force behind the development of Indianapolis under Barton was the formation of a citizens advisory committee known as GIPC. During Barton's term the committee recommended a large park, development of expressways, better architecture, a downtown civic center, a capital improvement program, the fostering of racial integration, and intercity sports competition. Barton used GIPC recommendations and called the committee one of his greatest achievements, an assessment shared by his successors.

Despite all the accomplishments he could claim, Barton lost the 1967 mayoral election to Republican Richard Lugar in what many believed to be a protest vote against the national administration of President Lyndon Johnson. Governor Roger Branigin appointed Barton to the Indiana Parole Board in January, 1968, where he continued in public service until retiring in September, 1989.

BRADFORD W. SAMPLE

Barus, Carl (Oct. 12, 1823–June 7, 1908). Musician, conductor, and teacher. Born in Prussian Silesia, Barus studied organ and piano in Brieg and Breslau. In 1849 he immigrated to the United States because of political turmoil in Europe. Settling in Cincinnati after a brief attempt at farming in Saginaw, Michigan, Barus embarked upon a notable musical career, playing the organ at several prominent churches, conducting the Philharmonic Society and Carl Barus orchestras, and directing male choruses of several German singing societies. His prowess with the latter earned him an invitation to conduct the 1854 Saengerfest concerts of the North American Saengerbund (NASB), a federation of German

singing societies founded in Cincinnati in 1849. Gaining a national reputation at this event, Barus served as the musical director of four more NASB Saengerfests, including one held in Indianapolis in 1867. From 1858 to 1860, and again in 1868, Barus also conducted the Saengerfest concerts of the Indiana Saengerbund, a subfederation of the NASB.

In 1882 Barus came to Indianapolis at the invitation of the MAENNERCHOR. Under his direction the society enjoyed a period of great prosperity and musicality—staging operas and operettas, expanding its concert series, and operating a singing school for the children of its members. He exerted a positive influence on the musical culture of the community as well by conducting the festival chorus at the opening of TOMLINSON HALL in 1886 and instituting the Indianapolis May Music Festivals, events that for ten years brought many renowned artists to the city and attracted national attention. A great-grandson is novelist Kurt Vonnegut, Jr.

SUZANNE G. SNYDER

F. O. Jones, *A Handbook of American Music and Musicians* (New York, 1971; reprint of 1886 edition); Will Cumback and J. B. Maynard, eds., *Men of Progress. Indiana* (Indianapolis, 1899); Kurt Vonnegut, Jr., *Palm Sunday* (New York, 1984).

Base Hospital No. 32 (Lilly Base Hospital). Indianapolis-sponsored World War I evacuation hospital in France. It was founded in February, 1917, in expectation of U.S. involvement in the war. Following donations from JOSIAH K. LILLY, SR. and ELI LILLY AND COMPANY, Lilly Base Hospital was created by the Indianapolis chapter of the American Red Cross, which provided linen, bandages, and dressings to the hospital. It was named for Josiah's father, COL. ELI LILLY. The hospital was a volunteer unit, staffed by physicians including Indianapolis natives Drs. Edmund D. Clark, Orange G. Pfaff, and Carleton B. McCulloch, and was officially designated United States Army Base Hospital No. 32 when it was mustered into the U.S. Army service in September, 1917. After basic training at FORT BENJAMIN HARRISON, Indianapolis, in the fall, the unit embarked for Brest, France, in December, 1917.

Upon arriving the unit entrained for Contrexeville, a rail center east of Paris. The staff converted the hotels in town into the hospital. In 1918 Base Hospital No. 32 served as an evacuation unit, receiving patients from the field hospitals and preparing them for convalescent hospitals in the rear. It closed in January, 1919.

JAMES R. BISHOP

Benjamin Hitz, ed., *A History of Base Hospital 32* (Indianapolis, 1922); Alma S. Woolley, "A Hoosier Nurse in France," *Indiana Magazine of History*, 82 (Mar., 1986), 37–68.

Baseball. One of the nation's dozen largest cities without a major league baseball franchise, Indianapolis nonetheless points to a rich albeit somewhat hidden baseball tradition. No other city can brag of having at one time or another housed teams in all three among baseball's highest minor leagues (American Association, International League, Pacific Coast League), as well as in the early American and National leagues and the short-lived Federal League. The city boasts today one of the best preserved of the nation's old-style ballparks. Its long-standing American Association franchise, the INDIANAPOLIS INDIANS, has been the training ground for numerous big league stars and a surprising number of Cooperstown Hall-of-Famers. For three-plus decades one of the showcase teams of the barnstorming Negro League, the Clowns, called Indianapolis home, and the sport's greatest home run slugger, Henry Aaron, enjoyed his professional debut in the uniform of that famed Indianapolis team. And in recent seasons Indianapolis has become home to the thriving world of amateur baseball, hosting PAN AMERICAN GAMES tournament play in the summer of 1987 and housing the administrative offices of the International Baseball Association (the official governing body for world amateur play) since 1986.

Like the birth of the national pastime itself, the origins of baseball in the city of Indianapolis are now lost. The earliest printed record (found in the *Indianapolis Journal*) of a ballgame within the city limits dates from July 19, 1867. Two amateur clubs from Indianapolis reportedly shared a doubleheader on the Camp Burnside grounds with an outfit from Lafayette, as well as with the nation's most famous touring amateur ballclub of the time, the Washington Nationals. While America's first professional club would appear only two summers later with the birth of the famed Cincinnati Red Stockings, Indianapolis did not field its own pro team until the centennial summer of 1876. The Indianapolis Blues, as they were known, joined the organized International League the next season and are reported to have occasionally played and defeated teams from the more prestigious National League as well. Star pitcher for this first Indianapolis professional outfit was Edward "The Only" Nolan, who earned his nickname by hurling every contest. While the Blues soon disbanded, Indianapolis would field an entrant in the fledgling American Association by the 1884 season. The city's pro club was appropriately labeled the Hoosiers and played home games at the Seventh Street grounds, though also performing Sunday games outside the city limits at the Bruce Grounds to avoid the citywide ban on Sunday sporting events.

True major league status arrived when the Hoosier ballclub joined forces with the established National League for three seasons of big league play between 1887 and 1889. A light-hitting ballclub wracked by player dissension, the Hoosier ballclub finished last in its first campaign and only barely edged out Washington to remain free from the cellar the following two summers. The decade of the "Roaring Nineties" that followed witnessed seven improved seasons in the ambitious Western League, presided over by ex-sportswriter and creative baseball entrepreneur Ban Johnson, father of the American League. When Johnson's league expanded eastward in 1900 and renamed itself the American League, the Indianapolis entrant was still around long enough to enjoy one final season, runner-up behind a Chicago club managed by Charles Comiskey and a Milwaukee outfit piloted by a youthful Connie Mack.

Yet by 1902, as Ban Johnson's upstart "junior circuit" launched its modern century of major league play, Indianapolis was once more left behind, now a charter member of still another new minor league experiment, the American Association. This third marriage of an Indianapolis ballclub to a fledgling professional league would be a long and prosperous one, however. Indianapolis would remain a member of the circuit (which itself collapsed for a five-year span) down to the present.

Nine decades of American Association play have brought the city of Indianapolis numerous league titles (20 pennants in all), a host of famous managers and ballplayers, and one of the richest minor league traditions anywhere. Hall-of-Famers Napoleon Lajoie, Ray Schalk, and Luke Appling would all manage the club at one time or another, as would such future big-league skippers as Al Lopez, George "Birdie" Tebbetts, Les Moss, Vern Rapp, Roy Hartsfield, Buck Rodgers, and Don Zimmer. Future stars Herb Score, Luke Easter, Rocco Colavito (who slugged a still-standing club record 38 homers in 1954), Roger Maris, Wally Post, Mike Cuellar, Don Buford, Ken Berry, Tommy Agee, Dave Concepcion, and Hal McRae were among the numerous players who served their final minor league apprenticeships in Indianapolis during the 1950s and 1960s as farmhands of the Cleveland Indians, Chicago White Sox, and Cincinnati Reds. A short-lived financial collapse of the American Association during the nationwide decline of minor league baseball in the Vietnam era necessitated one International League season and five more Pacific Coast League campaigns for the Indians ballclubs of the 1960s, before a welcomed renewal of American Association play in 1969.

One of the most colorful figures in the history of Indianapolis baseball was the diminutive OWEN J. "DONIE" BUSH, manager in the heyday 1924–1926 seasons as well as in the war years of 1943–1944, long-time club owner in the decade of the 1940s, and franchise president in the mid–1950s as well. Bush's three American Association teams of the mid–1920s were league runners-up three straight summers before the ex-Detroit American League shortstop returned to the big leagues as manager at Pittsburgh the following summer. BUSH STADIUM, West 16th Street home of the Indianapolis minor league club since 1931 and formally rechristened on August 30, 1967, bears the name of the popular manager who was long known as "Mr. Baseball" to the citizens of Indianapolis.

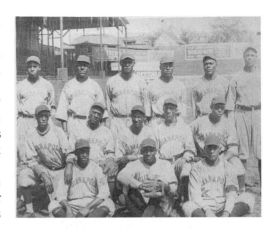

The Indianapolis ABCs, ca. 1922.
[Indiana State Museum]

Against the backdrop of nearly a century of minor league baseball in the Hoosier capital city, other professional baseball clubs would also call Indianapolis home from time to time. Nearly forgotten are two spectacular seasons enjoyed by baseball's only legitimate third major league of the 20th century—the ill-starred Federal League of 1913 (a minor league) and 1914 (a major league). Led by star pitcher Cy Falkenberg and batting hero Bennie Kauff (labeled "The Ty Cobb of the Federal League") Indianapolis provided a major chapter within the Federal League drama. For two straight mostly rocky seasons the Indianapolis ballclub (again called Hoosiers or even Hoosierfeds) waltzed away with the league crown. But the young circuit was already crumbling from within after only its second season and, despite two straight pennants, the Hoosier ballclub—forced to compete for fans with the equally attractive and more established American Association Indians—was barely solvent. A league realignment soon led to the transfer of the shaky Indianapolis franchise to Newark, New Jersey, for the league's abortive final campaign in 1915.

Another Indianapolis team to play in the shadows, though for a far longer span, was the Indianapolis Clowns of the Negro American League. The Clowns were the most famous black league team to play in Indianapolis, but not actually the first. The first formalized black league, the Negro National League, incorporated in 1920 with six midwestern cities, including Indianapolis. The Indiana team, known as the ABCs, was a holdover from the highly successful barnstorm club of the previous decade formed and managed by CHARLES I. TAYLOR, widely considered one of the most astute of early Negro baseball managers. The recast ABCs lasted only several seasons in the league, dropping out midway through the 1924 campaign. The ABCs posted a winning ledger in 1921–1923 and finished second place with a league high 46 wins in 1922 (all teams did not play an equal number of games, and standings were determined by winning percentage). The most illustrious player for the ABCs during both early independent barnstorming days and later Negro National League play was outfielder OSCAR CHARLESTON. An Indianapolis native known as "The Hoosier Comet," Charleston would enter the Cooperstown Hall of Fame posthumously in 1976.

In the heyday of Negro League play during the 1930s Indianapolis was again without representation, and the black leagues themselves remained across that era at best a loosely knit confederation of barnstorming teams. By the wartime 1940s black National and American Leagues had solidified, however, and Indianapolis joined with a league team in 1943. The colorful club, which would eventually call Indianapolis home during the zenith of Negro League play, began as a barnstorming outfit based in Miami and was first known nationwide as the Ethiopian Clowns. It was a team as devoted to showmanship and on-field clowning as to serious diamond play—a baseball equivalent of basketball's immensely popular Harlem Globetrotters. To bolster sagging gates some teams added novel attractions to their games, and the Indianapolis Clowns were the ultimate champions of such burlesque baseball, often wearing grass skirts, painting up their bodies to appear as African cannibals, and donning names such as "Selassie," "Mofike," "Wahoo," and even "Tarzan." Once admitted to Negro American League play the Indianapolis Clowns toned down these pranks and blatant showmanship, though they made the club one of the most popular in the circuit with fans, especially during barnstorming exhibition games in front of largely white crowds. Predictably, many Negro League players themselves deeply resented the comic image of the Indianapolis team.

Some remarkable players performed over the years for the Indianapolis Clowns, including future home run king Henry Aaron, who made his Negro League debut with Indianapolis as a teenage shortstop in 1951 and 1952. Aaron missed regular Negro American League play; his debut came the season after the league suspended action and resumed a nationwide schedule of barnstorming. By 1953, however, Aaron was a property of the Milwaukee Braves and was soon desegregating the South Atlantic League on his road to big league stardom. Meanwhile the Clowns were further spicing their roster with a female second basewoman named Toni Stone, a player talented enough to bat .243 while appearing in approximately 50 of the Clowns' 175 games that season. Throughout their earlier eight-season tenure in the organized Negro American League the Clowns had boasted some moderately successful teams as well—winning the Eastern Division title the final season of 1950 (when no championship playoff between Eastern and Western divisional winners was held), and finishing as league runner-up in both halves of a single-division split season during their second league campaign of 1944. The team actually divided time between Cincinnati and Indianapolis during the 1943–1945 seasons. Following the demise of the Negro League structure in 1950 the Indianapolis Clowns continued their barnstorming show across the nation for another two decades, only disbanding in the early 1970s.

While providing a site for exciting minor league play of both Triple-A and Negro League variety for three generations, Indianapolis and its environs has been home or nurturing grounds as well for a handful of the true immortals of professional baseball. Several living legends enshrined in Cooperstown once managed the Indianapolis minor league ballclub. The most noteworthy perhaps was one-time big-league .400 hitter Nap Lajoie, who was a playing manager in 1918 during the twilight of his incomparable career and steered the Hoosier club to a third-place league finish while himself batting a surprisingly low .282. Others were ex-catchers Ray Schalk, who directed the 1938–1939 teams, and Al Lopez, who skippered the 1949–1950 clubs, plus slugging shortstop Luke Appling, who piloted the

1962 team. Grover Cleveland Alexander (1910), Rube Marquard (1908), and Harmon Killebrew (1958) all served baseball apprenticeships on the minor league field in Indianapolis. A few were even native Hoosiers, the list including CHUCK KLEIN (Indianapolis), Amos Rusie (Mooresville), Edd Roush (Oakland City), Edgar "Sam" Rice (Morocco), Billy Herman (New Albany), Negro Leaguer Oscar Charleston (Indianapolis), Max Carey (Terre Haute), and Mordecai "Three Finger" Brown (Nyesville).

Amateur as well as professional baseball has been a popular spectator sport throughout the metropolitan Indianapolis area during recent decades. While the city actively promoted its reputation as the amateur sports capital of the nation, a premier showcase event became the 1987 Pan American Games baseball tournament. As expected, a powerhouse Cuban national team was the eventual gold medal winner, but not before a packed Bush Stadium witnessed a dramatic ninth-inning comeback 6–4 triumph by the USA team in a preliminary round game, which provided the Cubans with their first Pan Am Games defeat in 20 years. INDIANA HIGH SCHOOL ATHLETIC ASSOCIATION state tournaments in baseball have been a regular June feature in Bush Stadium in all but two years since 1967. And the administration of world amateur baseball is now centered in Indianapolis as well. With its founding in 1975, the International Baseball Association (IBA) provided an amalgamation of two world baseball organizations encompassing 39 baseball-playing nations and now stands officially as the governing body for all international amateur play. The IBA has maintained an Indianapolis home since 1986 and today coordinates and promotes such world-level events as the Senior World Championships, World Youth Championships, Intercontinental Cup Tournament, and IBA World All-Star Game. With the scheduling of the first official Olympic Baseball tournament in Barcelona in 1992, attention was further directed at IBA and its Indianapolis-based home as the central administrative arm of a growing international baseball movement.

PETER C. BJARKMAN
Society for American Baseball Research

Bill Heyward (with Dimitri V. Gat), *Some Are Called Clowns—A Season with the Last of the Great Barnstorming Baseball Teams* (New York, 1974); Marc Okkonen, *The Federal League of 1914–1915, Baseball's Third Major League* (Garrett Park, Md., 1989); David B. Reddick and Kim M. Rogers, *The Magic of Indians Baseball: 1887–1987* (Indianapolis, 1988).

Bash Seed Company. Popular seed business. In 1906 Daniel F. Bash started Bash Seed Store at 141 North Delaware Street as an extension of his father's Fort Wayne grain business, Bash and Eakin. Daniel owned and operated the store until 1932 when sons Jerome and Daniel K. Bash formed a partnership and bought the business. Following Daniel K.'s death in 1945, his brothers Jerome and Richard operated the store for a short time until Pauline, wife of eldest son S. Douglas Bash, purchased the business. She closed Quality Seed Company, which she began with her husband in the 1920s in Indianapolis, and in 1973 moved the store to its present location at 130 North Delaware Street, selling it in 1975. The small store, now something of an anachronism in its downtown location, caters mainly to suburban gardeners. Over 1,500 types of high quality seed are available, including heirloom and newer varieties.

JOAN CUNNINGHAM

Basketball. While particulars of the first basketball game played in Indianapolis have not been established, a game likely transpired at the Illinois Street YMCA in 1894. Reverend Nicholas McKay, an associate of Dr. James Naismith, basketball's inventor, reportedly introduced the game to the Crawfordsville YMCA in 1893, and the Indianapolis "Y" likely adopted the game soon thereafter. By the winter of 1897–1898 the local "Y" was hosting a four-team intramural league, and the Y All-Stars capped the season by defeating the University of Indianapolis (not the current University of Indianapolis).

The emergence of basketball as a major sport in Indianapolis occurred at TOMLINSON HALL on February 6, 1900. With over 1,000 fans present, Mayor THOMAS TAGGART tossed the first center jump as Yale University defeated the Indianapolis YMCA All-Stars 33–13. SHORT-RIDGE HIGH SCHOOL and MANUAL HIGH SCHOOL were to inaugurate their rivalry following the main event. Manual, however, showed up with two players who were not students at the school, so Shortridge was left to conquer the Yale reserves 6–4.

In the weeks following this historic event the Y All-Stars announced a six-game schedule that included bouts with BUTLER UNIVERSITY and Indiana Normal School, and with YMCAs in Cincinnati and Wisconsin. Prospects for the formation of a statewide college-YWCA basketball league were heartily advanced by local newspapers. Though a state league was still a few years removed, an Indianapolis city league began contesting games before average crowds of 500 in January, 1901. The Y All-Stars continued their customary dominance by going undefeated against Butler, Manual, and Shortridge in a six-game schedule. The league continued for many years.

Evidence of the passion generated by the new game is found in reports of a February, 1901, match. A member of the Butler squad took exception to being pelted with lemons hurled by Shortridge supporters. Entering the stands, he snatched a pennant from a Shortridge coed and made off with it. The ensuing riot reportedly resulted in considerable ill will.

In addition to YMCA and Butler games against regional foes, Shortridge held a home and home series versus Crawfordsville High School in 1901. Primarily on the basis of capturing both battles, Crawfordsville proclaimed itself the Indiana High School Basket Ball Champion. Crawfordsville followed the same course against Manual in 1905.

A virtual basketball explosion rocked Indianapolis during the first decade of the 20th century. Local sports pages featured ads placed by high schools, YMCA teams, the Turners Club, churches, neighborhood teams, and barnstorming semipro squads seeking games against "any fast basketball teams." A loosely organized Indiana College Athletic Association formed and by 1905 Butler was vying with Indiana University (IU), Indiana Normal, Wabash College, and Franklin College among others.

Indianapolis girls basketball experienced a more fitful genesis. Shortridge organized Indiana's first female intramural program in 1898. By 1901 the school was contesting Butler, Manual, the Girls Classical School, and the Indianapolis German House. Yet female basketball players of the era generated substantial controversy. Following a 1905 game between Shortridge and Butler, three high school boys were discovered hiding in the balcony. This violation of strict prohibitions against male attendance at female competitions resulted in threats to cancel all games featuring women athletes. Butler opened attendance to everyone the following season, and both schools continued to field popular girls basketball programs.

Interest in Indianapolis boys high school basketball grew unabated. By 1903 interscholastic athletic contests were so commonplace that a statewide governing body was needed. When the INDIANA HIGH SCHOOL ATHLETIC ASSOCIATION (IHSAA) was organized in 1904, Indianapolis Manual and Shortridge high schools were among the 15 charter members.

Despite this fact, neither school participated in the state's first official high school basketball tournament that was held in 1911. One team from each of the state's 13 congressional districts was invited to Bloomington by the IU Booster Club to compete for the championship. Since the IHSAA had not expressly sanctioned the tournament, and because board members believed that the games would distract from participants' studies, the Indianapolis School Board refused to allow local schools to compete.

Opposition to the tournament soon subsided and Indianapolis schools began vying for state honors. Manual advanced to the Final Four in 1915, Tech High School finished as state runner-up in 1929 and 1934, Shortridge reached the Final Four in 1933, and Broad Ripple High School followed suit in 1945. Tech's Emmett Lowery received the prestigious Gimbel Medal for mental attitude in 1929, while Shortridge's Jim Seward won the same honor in 1933. Broad Ripple's Max Allen earned the first Trester Award, which replaced the Gimbel Medal in 1945. Lowery and Tech's Leroy Edwards and Johnny Townsend won All-America honors at Purdue, Kentucky, and

Michigan respectively. Edwards and Townsend also pursued careers with the National Basketball League during the 1940s.

The local university mirrored the city's high school successes. Harlan "Pat" Page starred with powerhouse University of Chicago teams before becoming Butler's head basketball coach in 1920. During the next six seasons Page's Bulldogs compiled a 94–29 record, and his 1924–1925 team won the Amateur Athletic Union (AAU) National Collegiate Championship. In 1962 Page entered the Naismith Basketball Hall of Fame for his exploits as a collegiate player.

When Pat Page left Indianapolis to become head football coach at IU in 1926, his assistant, PAUL D. "TONY" HINKLE, succeeded him. Hinkle's tenure at Butler marked the most successful era in Indianapolis collegiate basketball to date. Led by future New York Yankee pitcher Oral Hildebrand, the 1929 Bulldogs compiled a 17–2 record and captured their second AAU National Collegiate Championship. All-Americans Frank Baird (1934), Jerry Steiner (1940), Bob Dietz (1941), Jimmy Doyle (1949), and Ralph "Buckshot" O'Brien (1949) produced expectations of success at the northside campus. All but Doyle pursued careers with pioneer professional basketball leagues of the period.

Butler's triumphs made attendance at the school's games a staple of the Indianapolis social scene. Interest became so intense the school constructed one of the nation's first great athletic fieldhouses. In an era of 5,000 seat gymnasiums, Butler Fieldhouse accommodated 15,000 fans at its March, 1928, inauguration. The fieldhouse was the site of the annual IHSAA Boys Basketball Tournament from 1928 to 1972, and hosted Indiana-Kentucky High School All-Star Games from 1940 to 1974. The first IHSAA Girls Basketball Finals were held at the arena in 1976. The fieldhouse hosted the first US-USSR basketball game, a U.S. Olympic Basketball Trial, an American Basketball Association All-Star Game, and was home to four professional basketball teams. Butler Fieldhouse was rechristened HINKLE FIELDHOUSE in 1966.

The foundation of professional basketball in Indianapolis is found in the Marion County Sunday School Basket Ball League and in Indiana's independent teams. Central Christian Church

The Em-Roes, originally known as the Detch Specials, posed for a 1916 team photograph. Al Feeney, second row, far right, later became mayor of Indianapolis. [Indiana State Museum]

dominated the Sunday School League, winning championships from 1914 to 1917. Likewise, the Detch Specials, sponsored by Indianapolis' Detch Wheel Company, reigned as Indiana Independent champions in 1913 and 1914. By 1916 several Central Christian teammates had joined a number of the Detch Specials to form a semipro barnstorming team. The squad added select high school and college players, gained the sponsorship of Indianapolis' Em-Roe Sporting Goods Company, and quickly became one of the dominant teams in Indiana sports history.

From 1912 to 1924 the Detch Specials or Em-Roes won over 90 percent of their 425 games against Indiana colleges, YMCA and high school teams, and the Original Celtics, Buffalo Germans, and other national barnstormers of the era. Future Indianapolis mayor AL FEENEY played for the team, as did Wingate High School legend Homer Stonebraker. Ward Lambert was with the Em-Roes prior to coaching Purdue to 11 Big Ten crowns.

World War I hampered the Em-Roes' ability to find players and competition, and the barnstormers' heyday ended during the 1920s. Professional teams began forming leagues with standard rules, rosters, and schedules. While Indianapolis' debut in such a league required the passing of a decade, the city's basketball reputation was established.

Grocer Frank Kautsky sponsored powerful AAU and semipro teams that played at the Dearborn gym in the 1930s. When a second incarnation of the National Basketball League (NBL) began in 1937, the Indianapolis Kautskys joined as a charter member. Teams from Akron, Buffalo, Cincinnati, Columbus (Ohio), Dayton, Kankakee, and Pittsburgh, as well as the Whiting Ciesar All-Americans and Fort Wayne Zollner Pistons were also original members. Chicago, Sheboygan, Detroit, Toledo, and the Anderson Duffy Packers soon came aboard.

With this amalgam of franchises in such disparate cities, the NBL had trouble establishing a major league identity. The NBL was nevertheless the genesis of the National Basketball Association (NBA), and Indiana teams formed the league bedrock throughout its 13–year existence. Fort Wayne won the NBL title from 1943 through 1945 and finished runner-up in 1947. Led by former Indianapolis Cathedral High School star Charley Shipp, Anderson reached the semifinals in 1948 and captured the last NBL crown in 1949.

While Indianapolis could not boast commensurate success, the franchise enjoyed its moments. IU All-America Ernie Andres signed in 1940 and became the Kautskys' star. Though military service and a season with baseball's Boston Red Sox interrupted his basketball career, Andres returned to coach the Kautskys to a 1947 NBL runner-up finish.

The end of World War II saw the return of a host of young athletes seeking employment and pro basketball men searching for larger markets. Ward Lambert left Purdue to become NBL commissioner in 1946. In one of his first moves he signed DePaul All-American George Mikan to a contract with the Minneapolis Lakers. Lambert disciple and future Indianapolis resident Doxie Moore succeeded his mentor as NBL commissioner in 1949 and immediately became immersed in one of America's great professional sports wars.

The Basketball Association of America (BAA), formed in 1948, was ready to challenge the NBL's Andersons and Oshkoshs with the likes of the Boston Celtics and New York Knickerbockers. The Kautskys, rechristened the Indianapolis Jets, abandoned the NBL for the BAA prior to the 1948–1949 season. The Jets floundered to a last-place 18–42 finish in their only BAA campaign. In the fall of 1949 NBL clubs from Anderson, Sheboygan, and elsewhere merged with the BAA to form the National Basketball Association. Doxie Moore was named the league's first supervisor of officials. Teams from Oshkosh, Dayton, and Hammond vanished and the Jets were replaced by yet another new franchise—the Indianapolis Olympians.

The Olympians are in many ways the most intriguing story in Indiana basketball history. The University of Kentucky claimed the 1948 and 1949 NCAA titles. As a reward, the core of UK's team represented the U.S. at the 1948 Olympics. Prior to the 1949–1950 NBA season the Indianapolis Jets fell into receivership. Kentucky stars Alex Groza, Ralph Beard, "Wah Wah" Jones, and Cliff Barker among others purchased the franchise and renamed it the Olympians in honor of their recent accomplishments. The Olympians packed Butler Fieldhouse. Groza trailed only George Mikan among league scorers, and the team won the NBA's first Western Division crown. Indianapolis' place in pro basketball appeared secure.

In January, 1950, a major point-shaving scandal rocked college basketball. Many players from collegiate powerhouses were implicated. Groza and Beard were banned from the NBA for life following the 1950–1951 season for shaving points while at Kentucky. A knee injury severely limited Jones' career. The heart went out of the team and the franchise collapsed following the 1953 season.

Just as Indianapolis' professional franchise disappeared, a local high school emerged to champion the city's basketball fortunes. Crispus Attucks High School, opened in 1927 to segregate Marion County's black students, was barred from playing in the IHSAA state tournament until

1943. The IHSAA also banned Indiana's parochial and institutional schools from state tournament play. Cathedral High School had assuaged the slight by capturing four Indiana Catholic championships and the 1933 National Catholic title. And the INDIANA SCHOOL FOR THE DEAF won seven Central States Deaf Schools championships and National Deaf Schools crowns in 1935, 1940, and 1987.

Attucks' vindication came soon after the school's admission to the IHSAA. Ray Crowe was named head coach in 1950 and he quickly established a high school dynasty. Crowe's teams compiled a 193–20 slate and won 1955 and 1956 State Championships. Bob Jewell earned the 1951 Trester Award, and several Tigers, led by Willie Gardner and Hallie Bryant, signed contracts with the Harlem Globetrotters.

Attucks' Bailey Robertson established numerous Indiana Central College (University of Indianapolis) scoring records during the 1950s. His brother, Oscar, was named Indiana's Mr. Basketball in 1956, was three-time College Player of the Year at the University of Cincinnati, became an eleven-time NBA All-Star, and with Kareem Abdul Jabbar led Milwaukee to the 1971 NBA crown. The "Big O" is ranked in the top ten in numerous NBA statistical categories and was inducted into the Naismith Basketball Hall of Fame in 1979.

When Ray Crowe became athletic director in 1958, Attucks continued to excel. Bill Garrett of Shelbyville, 1947 Mr. Basketball and All-American at IU in 1951, coached Attucks to the school's fifth Final Four and third State Championship of the decade in 1959. The Crispus Attucks example of discipline, organization, and success contributed significantly to the breakdown of racial barriers in Indiana athletics.

Attucks' legacy is an example of the city's high school basketball heritage. Joe Sexson became Indianapolis' first Mr. Basketball and third Trester Award winner when he led Tech High School to a 1952 state runner-up finish. Tech returned to the Final Four in 1966, falling in the title game. In 1961 Tom and Dick Van Arsdale took Manual to the championship game before succumbing in overtime. The twins were Indiana's first co–Mr. Basketballs and co–Trester Award winners. The

The Indianapolis Kautskys, named after their owner, Indianapolis grocer Frank Kautsky, played in the National Basketball League from 1937 to 1949. [Indiana State Museum]

Van Arsdales led IU to a 19–5 mark in 1965 and were named second team All-Americans. Both enjoyed lengthy NBA careers, with each being named to three All-Star Teams.

Shortridge made one last Final Four appearance, finishing runner-up in 1968, but it was Washington High School that ruled Indianapolis high school basketball in the 1960s. Bill Keller, Mr. Basketball, led Washington to the 1965 crown before teaming with Rick Mount on Purdue's 1969 NCAA runner-up squad. Keller excelled with the American Basketball Association's (ABA) Indiana Pacers during the 1970s.

George McGinnis soon surpassed Keller's achievements. With teammate Steve Downing, McGinnis led Washington to a 31–0 record and the 1969 state title. Named Mr. Basketball, McGinnis starred briefly at IU before embarking on an 11–year pro career. He won 1972 ABA Rookie of the Year honors, was voted to five ABA or NBA All-Star teams, and played for two ABA champions and a NBA runner-up.

Indianapolis' high school basketball legacy continues to grow. The IHSAA Tournament moved to MARKET SQUARE ARENA in 1975 and drew a then record 17,490 fans to the title game. Indianapolis Broad Ripple won the 1980 crown, Cathedral reached the Final Four in 1982, and Eric Montross led Lawrence North to the 1989 championship. In 1990, 41,096 fans crowded the HOOSIER DOME for the state finals, setting a national high school record. Southport reached the semifinals in 1990, while Brebeuf (1991) and Ben Davis (1993) have also made Final Four appearances in the Dome, both finishing as runners-up.

The story of Indianapolis girls high school basketball has become increasingly significant over the past two decades. For 76 years after the modest beginnings at Shortridge, progress in women's athletics was slow and sporadic. Manual fielded intramural teams in 1899 and an interscholastic squad in 1902. Tech and the Deaf School soon followed and by the 1920s Acton, Ben Davis, Broad Ripple, Castleton, Lawrence, New Augusta, Southport, and Valley Mills mounted spirited contests.

Games were contested according to "girls' rules," with guards remaining at the defensive end of the court, forwards at the offensive end, and the center covering the entire floor. Uniforms, often made by the players themselves, consisted of long bloomers, blouses, scarves, and over the knee stockings. Girls' games frequently served as curtain raisers to boys' contests.

Whether due to financial constraints brought on by the Great Depression or to the persistent notion that basketball was too strenuous and unladylike, girls' interscholastic basketball in Indiana disappeared during the 1930s. Scattered intramural squads persevered, and an occasional interscholastic game was contested, but a sanctioned IHSAA girls' tournament was not held until 1976.

Hinkle Fieldhouse hosted the 7,362 fans who witnessed Warsaw capture that historic championship. Indianapolis Tech advanced to the inaugural Final Four and North Central (1979), Brebeuf (1982), Howe (1983), Warren Central (1984), and Ben Davis (1992) reprised the feat. Southport won the 1980 State Championship behind Mental Attitude Award winner Amy Meth-

eny and Brebeuf followed *Parade* magazine All-America Vicky Hall to the title in 1988. Washington's Cheryl Cook was Miss Basketball in 1981, prior to winning All-America honors at the University of Southern California.

The IHSAA Girls' Basketball Tournament moved to Market Square Arena in 1980. By 1989, 16,662 spectators were on hand for the championship tilt. With recent commitments to gender equity in interscholastic sports, the future appears bright for the growth of Indianapolis girls high school basketball.

A codicil is necessary. Only two Indianapolis Public Schools (IPS) have ever made the girls' Final Four, and after sending 16 teams to the championship round during the tournament's first 58 years, only one IPS boys' team has reached the Final Four in the past 24 years. While competition from pro sports, videos, drugs, and other diversions has negatively impacted many Indiana schools, some IPS games are contested before but a smattering of fans. Whether due to declining budgets, decaying facilities, or social factors like urban violence, Indianapolis public school basketball has been overshadowed by suburban and private ventures.

Although interest in Marion County high school basketball has remained generally strong, the college game followed a more tortured path. Butler University was invited to the National Invitational Tournament (NIT) in 1958 and 1959, but the program fell into prolonged decline during the 1960s. As collegiate athletic budgets expanded exponentially, Butler attempted to maintain a major profile based on 1950s finances. By 1986, one season after a return to the NIT, a 9–19 Bulldog team drew only 2,406 fans per game to a dilapidated Hinkle Fieldhouse.

The university redressed the situation in 1989 with a $1.5-million renovation of the fieldhouse. Also, new head coach and former Butler captain, Barry Collier, received a 100 percent increase in the basketball budget. Recovery was rapid and dramatic. A 1978 charter member of the MIDWEST COLLEGIATE CONFERENCE (MCC), Butler went from league doormat to contender. A 1991 NIT appearance was followed by a 21–10 record and the school's first back-to-back, postseason invitations in 33 years.

The women's program at Butler was founded in 1975. An NCAA Division I charter member of the MCC, the women Bulldogs qualified for their first ever postseason appearance in 1992–1993, posting a 23 –8 record and finishing sixth in the women's NIT.

Butler's historic rival, the UNIVERSITY OF INDIANAPOLIS (Indiana Central College), fielded its first men's basketball team in 1913 and began an intercollegiate schedule in 1922. The NCAA Division II Greyhounds enjoyed their greatest success from 1947 to 1977 under Hall of Fame coach ANGUS NICOSON. In only its 15th year of existence, the U of I women's team hosted and qualified for the 1993 NCAA Division II National Tournament First Round. Both programs compete in the Great Lakes Valley Conference.

The men's and women's squads at IUPUI joined NCAA Division II in 1993. Both teams were founded on the new urban campus during the early 1970s and enjoyed some success as independent members of the National Association of Intercollegiate Athletics (NAIA). The men won the NAIA District 21 Championship in 1985 and advanced to the National Final 16 in 1990. The Women Metros won District 21 titles in 1987 and 1990 and reached the NAIA Final Four in 1991.

MARIAN COLLEGE began admitting men in 1954 and formed the school's first male basketball team the same year. The women's team, which had competed intercollegiately as the Maids since 1949, joined the men in becoming Knights. Marian is a member of the NAIA and competes in the Mid-Central Conference.

Professional basketball returned to Indianapolis in 1967 with the founding of the American Basketball Association (ABA). During the league's nine seasons, the INDIANA PACERS were a showcase franchise. The club won three league titles, produced three Most Valuable Players, hosted two All-Star Games, and annually led the league in attendance. When the chronically unstable ABA collapsed in 1976 the National Basketball Association (NBA) admitted the Pacers to membership. Concessions extracted by the established league and mismanagement, however, nearly destroyed the franchise. The club has habitually finished near the bottom of the league in wins and attendance. Locally owned since 1983, the club has

stabilized somewhat in recent years. The team has reached the NBA playoffs four successive seasons, and though still low by league standards, the Pacers drew a franchise record 12,949 fans per game in 1992–1993.

Indianapolis' place in basketball history is illustrated by recent example. In addition to setting the national high school attendance record, the 67,596 fans at the Hoosier Dome for the 1984 Olympic Team exhibition set the world record for the largest crowd to attend an indoor basketball game. An NBA single game record 43,146 witnessed the 35th All-Star game at the Dome in 1985, and in 1990 the three-session NCAA Division I men's basketball first and second rounds drew 117,199 fans.

R. DALE OGDEN
Indiana State Museum

Phillip M. Hoose, *Hoosiers: The Fabulous Basketball Life of Indiana* (New York, 1986); Stanley Warren, "The Other Side of Hoosier Hysteria: Segregation, Sports, and the IHSAA," *Black History News & Notes*, No. 54 (Nov., 1993).

Basketball, NCAA Finals. Indianapolis, the Midwestern Collegiate Conference, and Butler University hosted the 1980 and 1991 NCAA Men's Division I Final Four basketball tournament, and are scheduled to host the 1997 and 2000 championships. The city's ability to attract this prestigious tournament three times within a decade reflects the community's successful marketing of itself as a venue for amateur sports. It also demonstrates the suitability of the Indiana Convention Center and HOOSIER DOME complex for such events.

On March 24, 1980, Louisville defeated UCLA 59–54 before 16,637 spectators at Market Square Arena. UCLA fell for the first time in 11 Final Four appearances. (The Bruins later vacated their runner-up status due to the inadvertent use of an ineligible player.) The 1980 tournament featured the first 48- team field, and the lifting of the two team per conference limitation.

In its fifth Final Four appearance in six years, Duke beat Kansas 72–65 on April 1, 1991, with 47,185 fans in the Hoosier Dome. Duke was coached by Mike Krzyzewski, a former assistant coach under Bob Knight at Indiana University.

R. DALE OGDEN
Indiana State Museum

Basketball, Professional All-Star Games.
Indianapolis has hosted three professional basketball All-Star Games. The inaugural American Basketball Association (ABA) All-Star contest drew 10,872 fans to HINKLE FIELDHOUSE on January 9, 1968, to witness a 126–120 victory by the East team over the West. On January 24, 1970, the third ABA All-Star Game brought 11,932 spectators to the INDIANA STATE FAIRGROUNDS Coliseum. Resolution of a threatened player's strike over league recognition of the ABA Players Association allowed CBS-TV to broadcast the contest nationwide. The West squad won, 128–98. The 43,146 fans who packed the HOOSIER DOME for the National Basketball Association's (NBA) 35th All-Star Game on February 10, 1985, set professional basketball's one-game attendance record. The West won 140–129. Walt Bellamy, Roger Brown, Mel Daniels, Oscar Robertson, Tom and Dick VanArsdale, and George Yardley—all of whom had played basketball in Indiana at either the high school, college, or professional level—helped draw 16,665 to MARKET SQUARE ARENA for a "Legends of the Game" contest on All-Star eve.

R. DALE OGDEN
Indiana State Museum

Bass, Herbert L.
(Nov. 13, 1877–Apr. 8, 1926). Architect. A native and lifelong resident of Indianapolis, Bass designed numerous notable public residences, schools, commercial and industrial buildings, and post offices during his 23-year career. A graduate of MANUAL HIGH SCHOOL, he continued his training in several local architectural firms. At age 26 he began practicing architecture under the firm name of Herbert L. Bass & Company. In 1921 Lynn O. Knowlton, a consulting engineer, joined the firm, which was renamed Bass, Knowlton and Company. Bass designed the mansions of STOUGHTON A. FLETCHER II (now housing the HUDSON INSTITUTE), Charles B. Sommers, JAMES A. ALLISON, and James I. Holcomb (the latter three estates on Cold Spring Road). He was noted for several high schools across the state, including those at Lebanon (1908), Logansport (1912), and Greencastle (1914). Buildings of the COLE MOTOR CAR COMPANY plant on East Washington Street were among his industrial designs. One of his most architecturally significant buildings is the nine-story Test Building on Monument Circle, constructed in 1925. Within the design of a conventional urban building, it combined ground floor commercial spaces and offices with multilevel parking—an unusual example of mixed use for its time.

MARY ELLEN GADSKI

Paul D. Brown, ed., *Indianapolis Men of Affairs* (Indianapolis, 1923); Indiana Biography Series, Indiana State Library.

Bass Photo Collection.
Largest extant collection of photographs of 20th century Indianapolis. The W. H. Bass Photo Company, commonly known as Bass Photo, traces its beginnings to 1897 with the establishment of the James Bayne Company on South New Jersey Street, a satellite operation of its same-name parent in Grand Rapids, Michigan. The company advertised itself as commercial photographers, engravers, and printers of "fine catalogues," and sought to control the entire process of generating furniture trade catalogs from photography to printing. The enterprise failed, however, and in 1899 became Woodworth and Company after it was acquired by Walter T. Woodworth and William H. Bass. In 1912 Bass became the sole proprietor; his protege, Charles C. Branson, assumed ownership upon Bass's death in 1936. It remains a family business.

The firm's collection of historic photographs was acquired by the INDIANA HISTORICAL SOCIETY in 1987. Virtually all of the images, which were made between 1903 and 1971, are of Indianapolis and its environs. The collection, consisting of an estimated 40,000 prints and 180,000 negatives, is strong in architectural images (especially churches, hotels, residences, and schools), street scenes, aerial views, and transportation. Most of the architectural photographs have been indexed in a computer database. The vast majority of the images in the collection, however, exist only as negatives and are currently accessed through the company's numerical (essentially chronological) and client indexes.

STEPHEN J. FLETCHER
Indiana Historical Society

Indianapolis Star, Aug. 13, 1978.

Bates, Hervey (1795–July 6, 1876). Businessman and civic leader. Born at Fort Washington (now Cincinnati), Bates spent his formative years in Warren, Ohio. In 1816, Bates moved to Brookville, Indiana, and, following his marriage, to Connersville, Indiana.

In 1822, Bates moved to Indianapolis where he had been appointed the first sheriff of Marion County by Governor Jonathan Jennings. As sheriff he issued a proclamation calling for an election on April 1, 1822, the first election held in Marion County. Having served a single term as sheriff, Bates left politics in 1825 to become the first president of the Indianapolis branch of the State Bank, filling that office for ten years. As bank president, Bates was instrumental in forming both the first insurance company in Indianapolis and the Gas Light and Coke Company. He was also a shareholder in the first railroad to reach Indianapolis. In 1852, Bates began construction of the BATES HOUSE, long one of the city's finest hotels.

Known as a contributor to religious and philanthropic institutions, Bates worked tirelessly for the prosperity of the city, having played a role in nearly every local public enterprise.

MICHAEL C. ASHANIN

Jacob Piatt Dunn, *Indiana and Indianans* (Chicago, 1919); John H. B. Nowland, *Early Reminiscences of Indianapolis* (Indianapolis, 1870).

Bates House. 19th century hotel. HERVEY BATES, Indianapolis banker and businessman, built the Bates House in 1852–1853 on the northwest corner of Washington and Illinois streets. The four-story brick structure, completed at a cost of $75,000, was reputed to be the finest hotel in the Midwest. The lobby was spacious and luxurious, the rooms furnished in Victorian style. There was a separate entrance for ladies, a fashionable restaurant, and a large barber shop.

The hotel was a favorite of travelers and visiting celebrities, a community showplace, and a meeting place for Indiana politicians. Guests included presidents Abraham Lincoln, Andrew Johnson, and Ulysses S. Grant. Lincoln, traveling from Illinois to Washington, D.C., for his inauguration as president, delivered an address from the hotel's Washington Street balcony on February 11, 1861, making one of his earliest public statements on the preservation of the Union, only two months before the start of the Civil War.

After decades of success, the Bates House declined, hurt by competition from newer luxury hotels in the city. It was razed in 1901 to make way for the larger CLAYPOOL HOTEL that was built on the site.

RICHARD W. WORTH

Baus, Simon Paul (Sept. 4, 1882–Apr. 8, 1969). Landscape and portrait painter. Born in Indianapolis, Baus studied under OTTO STARK at MANUAL HIGH SCHOOL, and was a student of WILLIAM FORSYTH and J. OTTIS ADAMS at the HERRON SCHOOL OF ART.

In 1914, Baus joined a group of central Indiana artists to paint decorative murals for the children's ward of the Indianapolis City Hospital (now WISHARD MEMORIAL HOSPITAL). He is best known, however, for his portraiture, having painted the likenesses of such prominent Hoosiers as U.S. Senator James E. Watson, Governor Emmett Forrest Branch, newspaperman HILTON U. BROWN, and artists T. C. STEELE and WILLIAM KAESER. Thirty-minute portrait demonstrations by Baus were popular attractions at public art events.

Baus exhibited and won prizes for his paintings at the annual HOOSIER SALON, Art Association of Indianapolis, Indiana Artists Club, Art Association of Richmond, and INDIANA STATE FAIR juried competitions. His portraits are represented locally in the collections of the INDIANA STATE MUSEUM, the INDIANAPOLIS ART CENTER, the INDIANAPOLIS MUSEUM OF ART, and the INDIANAPOLIS SYMPHONY ORCHESTRA. Baus was a charter member of the Indiana Artists Club and held a membership in the Portfolio Club. A postal worker for 45 years, he retired in 1945.

FRANK N. OWINGS, JR.

Irvington Historical Society, *The Irvington Group* (Indianapolis, 1984); Flora Lauter, *Indiana Artists Active 1940* (Spencer, Ind., 1941).

Bayt, Philip Louis, Jr. (Sept. 29, 1910– May 10, 1989). Mayor of Indianapolis, Nov. 12, 1950–Nov. 24, 1951, Jan. 1, 1956–Jan. 1, 1959, Democrat. The second of 11 children born to Austrian parents, Philip Bayt, Jr. attended Holy Trinity grade school and Arsenal Technical and Washington high schools where he excelled in sports. After high school he worked for LINK-BELT COMPANY and then at KINGAN AND COMPANY in Indianapolis before enrolling in Lincoln Law School in 1933.

Bayt won the office of precinct committeeman in his westside neighborhood (HAUGHVILLE) in 1934 and held that position until 1942. In 1937 he became Marion County deputy sheriff and chief deputy in 1939. Shortly after this Bayt passed the bar examination.

Rejected for military service because of pulmonary tuberculosis scars from his childhood, Bayt became a U.S. Secret Service agent in 1943 and helped guard Franklin D. Roosevelt's train during the 1944 presidential campaign. That same year he returned to Haughville and worked as an inspector and then chief rent attorney for the Office of Price Administration (OPA). When OPA was abolished he became rent director for Marion and two other Indiana counties. On January 1, 1948, Bayt was appointed city controller when his best friend, ALBERT G. FEENEY, became mayor of Indianapolis. Bayt was often called the "Mayor of the Westside."

When Feeney died on November 12, 1950, Bayt, at age 40, became mayor. During his one-year term Bayt initiated or advanced the one-way streets program, a $1 million street repair plan, new playgrounds and parks, better city lighting, and an expansion of the city sewers. He also reorganized the police department under a merit system that provided salary increases without raises in taxes.

Bayt was the Democratic candidate for mayor in November, 1951, but lost to ALEX CLARK. He then resigned as mayor effective November 24, 1951, one month before the term ended, in order to accept appointment as judge of Municipal Court 3. The following year he became Democratic county and district chairman, positions he resigned in 1953, along with his judgeship, to accept a substantially higher paying position as manager of the Better Business Bureau of Indianapolis.

Bayt was elected mayor of Indianapolis in November, 1955. Accomplishments during his second stint in the position included continued expansion and improvement in the city's infrastructure, creation of several new city departments, and reduction of the workweek for police and firemen. Bayt also initiated a crackdown on gambling, narcotics, and vice, leading to national recognition of Indianapolis as a clean, safe city.

In November, 1958, while sitting as mayor, Bayt ran successfully for MARION COUNTY PROSECUTOR. He thus resigned as mayor on January 1, 1959, to accept the new position, serving as prosecutor through the end of 1962. From 1963 until 1968 Bayt was a member and chairman of the Indiana Public Service Commission. In 1968 he was a nominee for Congress from the Sixth Congressional District but did not win. In 1969 he opened a law office on the west side of Indianapolis and became a part-time judge for the Lawrence Magistrate Court, a post he held until he retired at age 65.

REBECCA M. MAIER
The Associated Group

Bean, Emmett James (July 28, 1897– Sept. 20, 1988). U.S. Army officer. A native of Erie, Pennsylvania, Bean entered the U.S. Military Academy as a member of the Class of 1919. His class graduated early to meet the needs of World War I, and Bean was commissioned on November 1, 1918, as a 2nd lieutenant of infantry. He was aboard a ship bound for Europe when the war ended. His class returned to West Point for further instruction, and Bean graduated a second time on

June 11, 1919. He served at various Army posts worldwide as an infantry officer until entering the U.S. Army Finance School in 1934 as a major. Promoted to colonel in 1942, he served as Commandant, Army Finance School, Fiscal Director of the Mediterranean Theatre, and as Assistant Chief of Finance.

In 1948 Bean was selected as the first commander of the Finance Center established in St. Louis. He coordinated the center's move to Indianapolis, which involved thousands of employees, rented office space, temporary housing, and construction of the second largest military office building in the United States (only the Pentagon is larger). Bean retired as a major general, commanding the Finance Center and FORT BENJAMIN HARRISON, in June, 1957. He then joined Merrill Lynch, Pierce, Fenner and Smith and remained active in local business and community affairs until his death. In the previous year, 1987, the Army renamed the Finance Center the Major General Emmett J. Bean Center, the first major U.S. military building ever named for a living soldier.

WILLIAM H. CARNES, JR.
Army Finance Corps Museum

Beard, Mary Ritter (Aug. 5, 1876–Aug. 14, 1958). Historian and suffragist. Mary Ritter was born into an affluent and education-minded Methodist family in Indianapolis. Her father, Eli Foster Ritter, was a lawyer with a strong temperance bent. Her mother, Narcissa Lockwood Ritter, had an academy education and taught school before their marriage. The Ritters provided their six children a comfortable and secure suburban home in the then exclusive residential area on Central Avenue near the family church, Central Avenue Methodist. The Ritters' involvement in church activities provided for Mary an atmosphere of social commitment and service that was reflected in her own later commitment to social activities and women's rights.

Mary left home in 1893 to attend DePauw University. There she met Charles A. Beard, also from Indiana. She graduated in 1897 and taught school in the state until her marriage to Charles in 1900. Both Beards became prominent historians and published many works separately and to-

gether. Mary's women's rights activities are reflected in many of her writings, including *Women's Work in Municipalities* (1915) and *Woman as Force in History* (1946). The best known of the books she cowrote with Charles are *The Rise of American Civilization* (1927) and *Basic History of the United States* (1944), both widely used as college texts.

LEIGH DARBEE
Indiana Historical Society

Ann J. Lane, ed., *Mary Ritter Beard: A Soucebook* (Boston, 1988).

Beebe Temperance Case. Famous case concerning prohibition in Indiana. Responding to pressure from local temperance advocates, the Indiana General Assembly passed a law in 1855 that banned the manufacture and sale of intoxicating liquors except for medicinal, chemical, or sacramental purposes. This effectively closed every tavern in the state. In Indianapolis the local German community was particularly hard hit, and many German-owned saloons and beer gardens remained open in defiance of the new law. As local authorities attempted to implement the law by closing saloons and arresting their owners, the city experienced a series of riots.

Organized legal resistance began on July 2, 1855, with the arrest of Indianapolis saloon keeper Roderick Beebe. Fined $50 in the mayor's court, Beebe refused to pay and was imprisoned. Following the arrest and imprisonment of a second Indianapolis saloon keeper, William Hermann, Beebe appealed to the state Supreme Court. Although arguments for the case were heard before the court adjourned for the summer, its final decision was postponed until the fall term. While the court was in recess, Hermann appealed to Supreme Court Justice Samuel E. Perkins to issue a writ of habeas corpus and release him from the county jail. In doing so, Perkins, a well-known opponent of prohibition, stated that the law was unconstitutional since the legislature could not completely prohibit the liquor business or the right of an individual to select what he or she chose to eat or drink.

During the November term, Perkins' decision in the Hermann case was confirmed when the state Supreme Court decided in Beebe's favor, holding that the law was unconstitutional on the grounds that it was destructive of property rights of manufacturers, sellers, and consumers. With the court's decision in the Beebe case, the law was overturned and prohibition in Indiana ended until the 18th Amendment to the United States Constitution was ratified in 1919.

MICHAEL ASHANIN

Jacob Piatt Dunn, *Greater Indianapolis* (Chicago, 1910); Emma Lou Thornbrough, *Indiana in the Civil War Era* (Indianapolis, 1965).

Beech Grove. Suburban town located about six miles southeast of downtown Indianapolis. Beech Grove was a quiet farming community in the 19th century. In 1837, Wesley Chapel was organized as the first church; the first school opened in 1868. F. M. Churchman, a banker who owned a large cattle farm in the area, convinced the railroad to build a shipping spur. The little station was named Beech Grove, reportedly after a nearby stand of old-growth trees.

Significant change came in 1906, when the NEW YORK CENTRAL RAILROAD purchased 640 acres to construct a $5 million locomotive shop and equipment plant. Cottages and businesses sprang up as workers arrived to build the shops. Beech Grove streets were laid out and named for cities served by the Big Four Railroad—Albany, Buffalo, Cleveland, and Detroit. Within two years, the railroad facility was touted as the "largest locomotive hospital in the world," with the capacity to service 48 engines at one time.

Beech Grove grew as the railroad shops expanded. The Main Street business district thrived and new companies were attracted to the area. ST. FRANCIS HOSPITAL was built in 1914 and later became one of Beech Grove's largest employers. By the 1950s, however, the steam locomotive shops cut the number of employees as new diesel engines were serviced elsewhere. In 1953, 2,000 workers were laid off, though 600 were later called back. Plans to convert the aging shops for diesel service were complicated when the owner, Penn Central, filed for bankruptcy. In the late 1970s Conrail and Amtrak took over the facility

and employed 700 workers. Although Conrail left in 1981, Amtrak continues to operate the shops today.

Despite these setbacks, the city of Beech Grove has stabilized by attracting new industry and diversifying its economy. Commercial development along I-465 and in a nearby industrial park brought new businesses into the area. In 1984, Main Street merchants took on an ambitious revitalization program funded by a grant from the state Department of Commerce. In an effort to attract shoppers, new sidewalks and streetlights were installed and exterior restoration work planned.

One of the EXCLUDED CITIES in the UNIGOV structure, Beech Grove remains one of the few self-governing cities in Marion County and has its own city council, mayor, police and fire departments, and school system. In the 1990 census, Beech Grove counted 13,400 residents.

CATHLEEN F. DONNELLY

Indianapolis Star, June 13, 1954; *Indianapolis News*, Sept. 21, 1906, Aug. 29, 1908, Jan. 13, 1977.

Beech Grove Railroad Shop. Once referred to as the "greatest locomotive hospital in the world," this installation in 1992 covered over 100 acres of former farmland in the community of BEECH GROVE in southeastern Marion County. It is the major repair facility of the National Railroad Passenger Corporation (Amtrak).

The Big Four Railroad, a major subsidiary of the former NEW YORK CENTRAL RAILROAD Company, constructed the multi-building complex (1906–1910) primarily for comprehensive repair work on its hundreds of steam locomotives. The locomotives were stripped down and overhauled along an extensive production line stretching throughout the commodious facility, with mules providing the temporary locomotion for the "ailing" machines over this internal rail network. Several large structures, some of them providing over 200,000 square feet of floor space, housed the several phases of the locomotive overhaul. Initial cost of this entire facility was $5 million. In 1910 there were 700 workers at the Beech Grove shop; during World War II the number reached 5,000.

Locomotive repair activity at Beech Grove during the postwar years paralleled the increase and later decrease in the nation's rail traffic.

Ownership of the Beech Grove facility went to the Penn Central Railroad Company in 1971 and four years later to Amtrak. A major reason Amtrak officials selected the Beech Grove site was its proximity to Chicago and the many rail lines converging there. This arrangement gave Amtrak's national "fleet" of locomotives and passenger cars optimum access to repair service. Having acquired a railroad repair complex with many positive features, Amtrak implemented changes at the Beech Grove shop in keeping with its requirements: overhauling diesel locomotives and passenger service rolling stock. However, much of the repair equipment designed and utilized by the Big Four Railroad continued to be used by Amtrak. Two dramatic changes have been the use of huge overhead cranes to lift locomotives and position them where crews can work on their underside and the replacement of mule power with tractor forklifts. A basic Amtrak policy at the Beech Grove shop is to renew rather than to discard its rolling stock. The cycle time required to overhaul equipment completely is 112 days for a diesel locomotive; for passenger, sleeping, and dining cars, 70 days. In 1992, the Beech Grove facility serviced 55 diesel locomotives and 185 passenger cars, employed 1,100 workers, and had an operating budget approaching $196 million. In early 1993, however, the facility faced layoffs and a reduction of services due to reduced federal funding for Amtrak.

VICTOR M. BOGLE
Indiana University, Kokomo

Ared M. Murphy, "The Big Four Railroad in Indiana," *Indiana Magazine of History*, 21 (June and Sept., 1925), 109–273; Robert M. Taylor, Jr., et al., *Indiana: A New Historical Guide* (Indianapolis, 1989).

Beecher, Henry Ward (June 24, 1813–Mar. 9, 1887). Presbyterian pastor. Beecher was born in Litchfield, Connecticut, son of the famous Presbyterian minister and revivalist Lyman Beecher (d. 1863). A graduate of Amherst College and Lane Theological Seminary, in 1837 Beecher

Henry Ward Beecher was the first pastor of Indianapolis' Second Presbyterian Church. [Indiana Historical Society, #C5893]

became pastor of the First Presbyterian Church in Lawrenceburg, Indiana.

In 1839 Beecher accepted a call from newly formed SECOND PRESBYTERIAN CHURCH of Indianapolis. He combined his father's pragmatic attitude toward theology and New School Presbyterian revival techniques with a more informal and personal style of preaching, which he believed was more suitable to western audiences. The combination was successful and helped make his church the largest Presbyterian congregation in the state. Highlights of Beecher's pastorate were the church's move to its first permanent facilities in 1840, his first ANTISLAVERY sermon on May 28, 1843, and his *Lectures to Young Men* during the winter of 1843–1844. Published in 1844, these lectures on morality first brought Beecher national recognition and reveal his distinctive blend of bold preaching about taboo subjects with a conservative concern for social order.

Beecher's activities were not narrowly confined to the ministries of Second Presbyterian. He was Stated Clerk of the Indianapolis Presbytery, served on the executive committee of the INDIANA HISTORICAL SOCIETY, was a member of the INDIANAPOLIS BENEVOLENT SOCIETY, and promoted the movements for temperance and common schools. On a statewide level he led revivals in several cities, served as a trustee of Wabash College, and was editor from 1845–1847 of the INDIANA FARMER AND GARDENER, renamed the *Western Farmer and Gardener* after a merger in 1846. On October 3, 1847, Beecher left Indianapolis to become pastor of Plymouth Congregational Church in Brooklyn, New York, where he would become one of the most famous orators and influential figures of 19th century America.

WILLIAM L. ISLEY, JR.

Jane Shaffer Elsmere, *Henry Ward Beecher: The Indiana Years, 1837–1847* (Indianapolis, 1973).

Beesley, Eugene Nevin (Jan. 29, 1909–Feb. 8, 1976). Former president and chairman of the board of Eli Lilly and Company and the Lilly Endowment. Born on a farm near Thorntown, Indiana, Beesley received his bachelor of arts degree from Wabash College (1929) before joining ELI LILLY AND COMPANY as a salesman. He began law studies at the University of Toledo but completed his degree at Indiana University School of Law (1943) after moving to Indianapolis. Beesley quickly ascended through the Lilly ranks, becoming associate director of sales (1949), vice-president for administration (1951), and executive vice-president (1952). In April, 1953, he became the fifth president of Lilly, the first from outside the Lilly family. Under his leadership Lilly expanded to more than 20,000 employees and constructed plants around the world to tap foreign markets. Beesley also served as director of Eli Lilly International Corporation and six Lilly foreign subsidiaries. As chair of the Pharmaceutical Manufacturers Association, Beesley was an important spokesman for the industry. Following the unsuccessful Bay of Pigs invasion of Cuba (1961), Beesley, at the request of U.S. Attorney General Robert F. Kennedy, coordinated the delivery of several million dollars' worth of drugs to ransom over 1,000 prisoners of war. In 1961 he also testified before the Subcommittee on Antitrust and Monopoly of the Senate Judiciary Committee, which resulted in the Drug Amendments of 1962 that increased FDA regulations over the industry. As a result, Lilly established a legislative liaison office in Washington, D.C.

Beesley sat on the LILLY ENDOWMENT board of directors from 1951 until his death, serving as vice-president (1960–1971) and president (1972–1976), again the first non–Lilly family member to hold that position. During his tenure as president Endowment grant payouts for education, religion, and community services/development increased from $10 million to more than $50 million.

Beesley was involved in many civic and business organizations, including the Associated Colleges of Indiana, SECOND PRESBYTERIAN CHURCH, the American and Indiana bar associations, and General Motors, where he served as a director.

SHELLY CHENOWETH

E. J. Kahn, Jr., *All in a Century: The First 100 Years of Eli Lilly and Company* (Indianapolis, 1976); Susan O. Conner, *Lilly Endowment Inc., '87* (Indianapolis, 1987); *Indianapolis Star*, Feb. 9, 1976.

Bell, Joseph E. (Nov. 28, 1865–Sept. 1, 1923). Mayor of Indianapolis, 1914–1918, Democrat. One of six children, Bell was reared on a farm in Union County, Indiana. His education included a term in high school, a year at a normal school in Lebanon, Ohio (followed by two years teaching in Union County), and graduation from the legal department of the University of Michigan in 1888.

Bell came to Indianapolis in August, 1888, to establish a law practice and a career in politics. He gave several speeches for the Democrats that fall, began an association with THOMAS TAGGART (then county chairman), and served as reading clerk of the House in the 1889 legislature. Appointed an assistant to the city attorney in 1893, he continued as deputy city attorney during Taggart's three mayoral administrations, 1895–1901. Bell methodically climbed the ladder of professional politics: precinct committeeman, ward and county chairman, and delegate to county, state, and national party conventions. His attention to politics enhanced his legal career; his law partners included former mayor THOMAS L. SULLIVAN, future U.S. senator JOHN W. KERN, and, after 1913, Walter D. Myers, a future Indiana House speaker and assistant U.S. postmaster general.

Bell won the mayor's office in an election unusual for attracting three major candidates and four minor ones. With 37 percent of the vote, Bell easily outdistanced his two major opponents, a Republican and a Progressive. Election irregularities led to the indictment of Bell, Taggart, and many others on charges of conspiracy to commit a felony, but the mayor was acquitted after a two-hour jury deliberation.

As mayor-elect, Bell promised to stamp out vice. While he did establish the first vice squad, his term was more notable for public improvements. POGUE'S RUN was transformed from an open sewer to an immense covered drain; a flood levee along the west bank of the WHITE RIVER was planned and constructed; RAILROAD TRACK ELEVATION permitting street crossings at grade, of great benefit to the south side, was begun; the boulevard system—Fall Creek, Maple Road (38th Street), Pleasant Run, Burdsal—was extended and developed; and the sunken gardens at GARFIELD PARK were constructed. In all, 281 miles of streets, sidewalks, and sewers were built. Bell also wanted to build a sewage treatment plant to relieve the White River of effluents, and blamed county Republicans in the legislature for the bill's failure.

Bell was a founder of the Indiana Democratic Club, a member of the Masons, Elks, Knights of Pythias, and many other organizations, and a deacon of Tabernacle Presbyterian Church. He died from an accidental, self-inflicted shotgun wound suffered at the Indianapolis Gun Club.

WILLIAM DOHERTY
Marian College

_____

Indianapolis Men of Affairs; *Indianapolis News*, Sept. 3, 1923.

Belt Line Railroad. Completed in 1878, this railroad over many decades has served as a supplemental track facility for other RAILROADS providing freight service to Indianapolis. Most of its 14–mile trackage resembles a large, partially closed letter "U" surrounding the inner city of Indianapolis on the northeast, the east, the south, and the west. UNION STATION is near the bottom of the "U." Since its construction the Belt Line has had multiple purposes. One was to prevent congestion on the city's downtown streets, which would likely result from many independent rail lines converging on Union Station. Another purpose, not fulfilled, was to avoid the piling up of freight at Union Station by establishing a series of freight depots on the "belt." Still another purpose was to provide convenient, inexpensive rail service that would promote industrial development in Indianapolis. The large stockyard and meat packing industries located for almost a century on the southwest side of the city are prime examples of how this purpose was carried out.

Whether the Belt Line in Indianapolis was actually the first such facility in the United States may be debatable, but certainly it was among the first built upon such a grand scale. Although the idea goes back at least to 1849 when OVID BUTLER broached it, serious planning did not begin until the economically troubled 1870s. The state of Indiana granted a charter to the Indianapolis Belt Railroad Company in 1873, but the financial panic later that year halted construction. Thomas D. Kingan, local meat packer, attempted construction a short time later but failed, as did another effort in 1876. A year later Indianapolis Mayor JOHN CAVEN guided still another effort which led to completion of the line. In promoting construction of the "belt line," Caven portrayed the facility as a large "navigable water" surrounding Indianapolis "into which poured eleven navigable rivers, navigable to every county in the state and to every state in the Union." A major portion of the original construction cost was defrayed by a $500,000 issue of Indianapolis city bonds, later repaid in full. As foreseen by Caven, the eleven rail lines (and others later) made extensive use of the "belt." By 1910 it was handling over a million freight cars a year; in 1920 it brought its company a net income of $250,000 and paid 11 percent dividends on its common stock.

Although the Belt Line has gone through title changes over the years (Union Railway Company; Union Railroad Transfer and Stock Yard Company; Belt Railroad and Stock Yards; Indianapolis Union Railway), until the late 1960s it retained two of its historic functions: providing shared track leading to Union Station; and the comprehensive stockyard–meat packing operations on the city's southwest side. With the departure of the latter, along with a general diminishing of rail freight business within the city, there has been a lessening of Belt Line activity. In the mid–1970s the Belt Line came under the control of the Consolidated Rail Corporation (Conrail), but other railroad companies have continued to use its tracks for entry into the Union Station complex and for switching purposes.

VICTOR M. BOGLE
Indiana University, Kokomo

Jacob Piatt Dunn, *Greater Indianapolis* (Chicago, 1910); Edward A. Leary, *Indianapolis* (Indianapolis, 1971).

Ben Davis. Westside community located about six miles west of the Circle near the intersection of High School Road and Minnesota Street. In the 1870s the community now known as Ben Davis was a small hamlet alongside the Vandalia Railroad. Local entrepreneurs petitioned the railroad superintendent, Benjamin Davis, for a station. In 1877, residents built a loading platform at Davis' suggestion and then named it for him. Two years later, John Pierson was authorized to build a regular railroad station.

The community suffered setbacks, including a tornado in October, 1911, that damaged many of the town's 100 homes and a December, 1968, fire that destroyed several businesses in the old section of Ben Davis. Despite a fire and location changes, the Mt. Olive Methodist Church, founded in 1870, retains its status as the oldest organization in the community. Ben Davis High School, known for its academic, technical, and extracurricular programs, is another area landmark, though the current school is located some $2^1/_2$ miles north of the community proper.

Ben Davis was never incorporated as a town; the only public buildings were WAYNE TOWNSHIP schools. When sewers were mandated in the 1950s the Indiana General Assembly permitted the formation of a special taxing unit, the Ben Davis Conservancy District. Under UNIGOV in 1970, the area became a part of the City of Indianapolis.

PAT WATSON

Indianapolis News, Jan. 11, 1979; *Indianapolis Star*, Feb. 11, 1979.

Benjamin Harrison Home (1230 North Delaware Street). Designed by architect Herman T. Brandt in the Italianate style popular in the late 19th century, the home of BENJAMIN HARRISON was built in 1874–1875. The 16–room, red brick house has a three-story bay window and the bracketed cornices typical of the style. A front porch was added by Harrison in 1895 (several years after his so-called "front porch campaign "). Inside are parquet floors, butternut woodwork, and a walnut staircase with oak trim. Harrison lived in the house before and after his term as president and died there in 1901. His move to the near north side set in motion a northward migration of the city's prominent families.

In 1939 the Arthur Jordan School of Music (now JORDAN COLLEGE OF FINE ARTS at BUTLER UNIVERSITY) purchased the house from Mary Lord Harrison, the president's second wife. The school turned the first floor into a museum, using the second and third floors as student housing. In 1966 the house became a National Historic Landmark, and in 1974 the Arthur Jordan Foundation renovated the building, turning it into a house museum. Now operated by the Benjamin Harrison Home Foundation, it contains many of the Harrisons' original furnishings and mementos and is visited by up to 35,000 people annually.

CONNIE J. ZEIGLER

Bethel African Methodist Episcopal (AME) Church. Oldest African-American church in Indianapolis. In 1836 a group of African-American Methodists organized and joined the AME Church. A circuit minister from Cincinnati first served the church, which remained the only AME congregation in Indianapolis for 30 years. By 1841 the members built a small frame building on Georgia Street between Senate Avenue and the CENTRAL CANAL.

During the 1850s Elisha Weaver became Bethel's first full-time minister, and its membership and influence within the African-American community grew. In 1857 it purchased the building that had housed the city's original Episcopal church and moved the structure to its Georgia Street location. By 1869 the church adopted the name Bethel AME Church, moved to its present site at 414 West Vermont Street, and built its current building.

Known as a stopover on the Underground Railroad, Bethel AME early became a center of social action for the African-American community. Both the State Federation of Colored Women's Clubs (1904) and the Indianapolis Chapter of the NAACP were founded there in the early 1900s. Throughout the first half of the 20th century the church sanctuary served as public meeting space and auditorium for the local African-American community.

Despite post–World War II highway construction and other development that erased many downtown neighborhoods and forced members to relocate, Bethel AME resolved to remain. Even as surrounding neighborhoods deteriorated, Bethel's congregation persisted. In 1974 members renovated the building and parsonage to provide more space and facilities for community outreach programming. Since then the church has continued to provide a variety of social services to the elderly, poor, and youth of the congregation and downtown community.

In 1991 the church building became the only African-American church in Indianapolis to be listed on the National Register of Historic Places. In the early 1990s Bethel's membership stood at roughly 1,200.

MICHELLE D. HALE

Beveridge, Albert Jeremiah (Oct. 6, 1862–Apr. 27, 1927). United States senator; author. Born in Highland County, Ohio, Beveridge moved with his family to Moultrie County, Illinois, in 1866. He attended the local common schools, graduated from high school in 1881, and matriculated that fall at Indiana Asbury (later DePauw) University in Greencastle, Indiana. Following his 1885 graduation from DePauw, where he had honed his considerable oratorical skills, he moved to Indianapolis, read law, and was admitted to the bar in 1887.

Beveridge had begun speaking on behalf of Republican candidates while still a college student, and he continued this partisan activity as he established his career. He also became increasingly prominent in the professional and social life

Albert J. Beveridge. [Indiana Historical Society, #C5894]

of his adopted city, with memberships in the Commercial Club, the YMCA, a Methodist church, the Art Association, and the Indianapolis Literary Club. Both his legal practice and his political ambitions grew during the 1890s, culminating with his election to the U.S. Senate by the Republican-controlled General Assembly in 1899. He was reelected in 1905.

In the words of his most noted biographer, Beveridge "came to the Senate a stalwart apologist for business America." But, gradually, he moved toward the progressive, Theodore Roosevelt wing of the Republican party, and away from the conservatism of the William Howard Taft majority. He supported, for example, such reforms as the direct primary and a national child labor law. Defeated for reelection in 1911 after the state legislature had gone Democratic, Beveridge cast his lot with the Roosevelt insurgents in 1912. When Taft won renomination at the Republican national convention, Beveridge joined Roosevelt's Progressive ("Bull Moose") party. He delivered the keynote address at the Progressive national convention, served as the convention's permanent chairman, and accepted nomination as the Progressive candidate for governor of Indiana.

The GOP-Progressive split in 1912 resulted in Democratic victories that fall; Beveridge, like Roosevelt, finished second in his contest. Twice more he sought a Senate seat—as a Progressive in 1914 and as a Republican in 1922—but he was unable to revive his political career.

Following his defeat for reelection in 1910 Beveridge returned to Indianapolis, though he subsequently spent much time on the Massachusetts North Shore. Increasingly, he devoted his energies to literary and historical pursuits, even becoming an active member of the American Historical Association. His four-volume *Life of John Marshall* (1916–1919) remains a standard biography of the chief justice; two volumes of a planned Lincoln biography were published posthumously as *Abraham Lincoln, 1809–1858* (1928). Beveridge died in the Hoosier capital and was buried in CROWN HILL CEMETERY.

ROBERT G. BARROWS
Indiana University–Purdue University,
Indianapolis

———————

John Braeman, *Albert J. Beveridge* (Chicago, 1971).

Bicycling. The earliest appearance of the bicycle in Indianapolis was a demonstration on the Circle of the high-wheeled "ordinary" in 1869. Within a few years hundreds of men were riding the contraptions around the city, but the invention of the safety bicycle with two equal-sized wheels in the 1880s, immediately followed by the adoption of pneumatic tires, initiated a national mania for the "wheel" embraced by men and women alike. A special dropped frame was soon designed that allowed modest ladies to ride in a skirt, but many women of the 1890s adopted shorter, divided skirts for cycling freedom.

In 1889 Harry T. Hearsey introduced the first safety bicycle to Indianapolis, which took to it immediately. Soon so many bicycles clogged the streets that in 1893 the City Council passed an ordinance requiring a $1 license fee. In the 1890s several popular bicycle models were manufactured locally, such as the Waverly and the Outing, and men who later became pioneers in the automobile field got a rolling start in bicycles, among them CARL G. FISHER, JAMES A. ALLISON, and ARTHUR NEWBY, all founders of the INDIANAPOLIS MOTOR SPEEDWAY but also all members of the Zig-Zag Cycle Club that began in Indianapolis in 1890. Both men's and women's clubs proliferated; their activities included "century rides" in which

cyclists would make a round trip of at least 100 miles a day. Bloomington was a popular destination for Indianapolis riders.

Bicycle racing was immensely popular in the 1890s, with most major events held at a track in BROAD RIPPLE until the construction of the Newby Oval near 30th and Central in 1898, which was large enough and sufficiently state-of-the-art to host national championship events sponsored by the League of American Wheelmen. Designed by Indianapolis architect HERBERT FOLTZ, the facility could and often did accommodate 20,000 fans. MAJOR TAYLOR, the city's renowned bicycle champion, raced there for an often unappreciative hometown crowd from the Oval's opening through 1900.

With the coming of the automobile (and with it, the motorcycle), the heyday of the bicycle was over. The depression of the 1930s saw a revival of popular interest with the staging of six-day bicycle races, often held in the Butler Fieldhouse. Because of gasoline and tire rationing, World War II stimulated a broad-based surge of bicycle commuters, who cried out for their own lanes and safety zones as they wove precariously through traffic on Indianapolis streets. To date, their cry remains largely ignored in the city, although recreational bicycle paths are set aside within several parks and parkways throughout Indianapolis.

GLORY-JUNE GREIFF

Big Brothers of Greater Indianapolis.
Social service agency. This voluntary, not-for-profit human service agency was organized in 1970 to foster the positive social development of boys, ages 7 to 18, through one-to-one friendships with men who volunteer to be Big Brothers. The professional social casework staff collaborates with other community services and schools to assess the needs of boys from single-parent homes, screens volunteers, and supervises the assigned relationships. Since 1987 the agency has doubled its service; in 1992 it served 767 pairs, putting it at the top of 500 federated agencies affiliated with Big Brothers–Big Sisters of America.

Big Brothers asks all members to be involved in fund raising and member recruitment. Typically boys wait six months to two years for assignment because they outnumber the men who volunteer. To increase the number of volunteers, the agency initiated a new membership campaign model that is now used nationally.

Because no fees are charged for program services, a 50–member volunteer board of directors organizes community appeals for financial resources. The 1993 budget was $698,000. Revenue comes from special events (50%), UNITED WAY (33%), foundations (16%), and endowment income (1%). A staff of 19 (an executive director, 14 program staff, 4 support staff) serves the eight-county metropolitan area.

CLAYTON I. BREWER
Big Brothers of Greater Indianapolis

Big Sisters of Central Indiana. Social service agency. Originally called Big Sisters of Greater Indianapolis, the organization grew out of a 1971 study by the Youth Service Bureau that indicated a need to provide at-risk girls with individual support and attention from caring adult volunteers. The agency was incorporated in 1974 with a staff of four. Initial funding came from a Law Enforcement Assistance Act grant and the JUNIOR LEAGUE. In 1975 it became a member of Big Sisters International, moved from its first location on 34th Street to the English Foundation building, and held its first major fund-raiser, an auction at Keystone at the Crossing. A merger at the national level in 1977 created Big Brothers–Big Sisters of America, but the local Big Sisters retained its discrete identity. The organization acquired its present name, Big Sisters of Central Indiana, in 1987.

Programs operated by Big Sisters serve 800 girls a year; the current staff of 19 is augmented by 550 volunteers, 400 of whom are involved in direct service to clients. Big Sisters' average annual income of $750,000 comes from UNITED WAY (25%), special events (50%), contributions (20%), and other sources (5%).

SALLY HERRHOLZ
Big Sisters of Central Indiana

Bindley Western Industries. Pharmaceutical wholesaler. Founded in Indianapolis in 1968 by Terre Haute native William E. Bindley, the company is the fifth largest supplier of pharmaceutical, health, and beauty products in the United States. Its nationwide distribution system serves two types of businesses: chain drug stores, such as HOOK'S DRUG STORES, and independent pharmacies, hospitals, and HMOs. In 1988, when one of its largest clients, Revco, filed for bankruptcy owing Bindley Western $16 million, the wholesaler began diversifying into the direct sales market. Following a 1985 federal investigation, four Bindley Western managers pleaded guilty to illegal purchasing practices and the company pleaded guilty to federal mail fraud charges. These problems prevented Bindley Western from acquiring much new business until the early 1990s. During the consolidation of drug companies in the 1990s Bindley Western purchased smaller wholesalers, won a contract to supply the Kroger Company, which included the Hook's and SupeRX drugstores, and began direct shipments to drugstores. In 1992 the company recorded sales of $2.91 billion and profits of $12.89 million, a 13.4 percent increase from the previous year. By 1993 Bindley Western operated 14 computerized distribution warehouses across the United States. The company, which employs 600, is traded on the New York Stock Exchange.

STACEY NICHOLAS

Bingham, Joseph Jenkins (Jan. 6, 1815–Jan. 12, 1897). Newspaper editor and alleged Copperhead. Born in New York City, Bingham migrated to the Midwest where he engaged in a wide variety of occupations. After serving as editor of the *Lafayette Journal* he moved to Indianapolis in 1856 and became editor-in-chief of the *INDIANA STATE SENTINEL*, purchasing an interest in the paper. He sold his interest in July, 1865, but returned as editor when in April, 1868, Richard J. Bright acquired ownership. Bingham retired from newspaper work in 1874. He later served as deputy auditor of Indiana for two years, compiled and published books on Indiana statutes and laws, and from 1871 to 1887 served on the Indianapolis Board of School Commissioners.

Bingham, who was chair of the Democratic State Central Committee during the CIVIL WAR, was critical of both President Lincoln's and Governor OLIVER P. MORTON's administrations. He briefly joined the Sons of Liberty, a group considered treasonous by the state. Bingham was arrested in the fall of 1864 along with several others allegedly involved in a plot against the state (see CIVIL WAR TREASON TRIALS). The charges against him were dropped prior to the trial, and he testified as a witness for the prosecution.

JOAN CUNNINGHAM

Jacob Piatt Dunn, *Greater Indianapolis* (Chicago, 1910); Emma Lou Thornbrough, *Indiana in the Civil War Era, 1850–1880* (Indianapolis, 1965).

Biskup, George Joseph (Aug. 23, 1911–Oct. 17, 1979). Third Catholic Archbishop of Indianapolis (1970–1979). Born in Cedar Rapids, Iowa, of Czech ancestry, Biskup was ordained in Rome on March 19, 1937. He was consecrated auxiliary bishop of Dubuque, Iowa, in 1957, was appointed bishop of Des Moines, Iowa, in 1965, and was named coadjutor archbishop of Indianapolis "with right of succession" on July 26, 1967. He served as pastor of Holy Cross parish, Indianapolis, until he automatically became archbishop on January 14, 1970.

During his short episcopate, Biskup began the reorganization of archdiocesan government and implemented changes authorized in the post–Vatican II era. In 1971 he authorized lay distribution of communion, established a personnel board to advise him on clerical appointments, initiated a program to place seminarians in parishes and agencies to experience clerical life, increased the number of Indianapolis deaneries from two to four, and established the Priests' Senate to advise him on archdiocesan policy. In 1972 he enlarged the personnel board by adding Senate nominees and reorganized the liturgical commission. He then established the ecumenical commission (1973) and Hispanic ministry (1974). He approved priests' retirement at age 70 and sponsored a $2 million archdiocesan drive to fund clerical pensions. He authorized communion in the hand (1977) and the renovation of SS. PETER AND PAUL CATHEDRAL.

Biskup was faced with a financial and enrollment crisis in Catholic education. During his time six high schools moved, closed, or merged, and Cathedral and Brebeuf high schools became coeducational. He also approved plans to close or consolidate some inner-city elementary schools.

In late 1975 the archbishop underwent surgery for malignant tumors. His health was never fully restored and he resigned effective March 26, 1979. He died in St. Vincent Hospital seven months later and was interred in the chapel of Calvary Cemetery mausoleum, construction of which he had authorized in 1972.

JAMES J. DIVITA
Marian College

Black, Charles H. (Oct. 5, 1852–Aug. 19, 1918). Carriage maker and automobile pioneer. Charles Black asserted that he built the first gasoline-powered automobile in the United States, but the evidence is frustratingly inconclusive. Born near Richmond, Indiana, Black became a blacksmith and carriage builder in Indianapolis. By the early 1890s the C. H. Black Manufacturing Company was the city's foremost carriage maker.

Automobile pioneer Charles Black.
[Indiana State Library]

A 1913 newspaper story credited Black with building America's earliest automobile and driving it on the city streets in the spring of 1891. His application to patent his "motor wagon" was rejected because another inventor filed two weeks before him. Black was offered patents on his designs for a differential and a floating axle, but angrily declined. The patent records have not survived, but this story ignores the notorious Selden patent, filed in 1879 and issued in 1895. Black said in 1913 that every part of his first car was built in his shop or to his special order, but apart from the wheels and body it bears a close resemblance to German-built Benz models of 1891 and 1893. The first contemporary report is a brief article in *The Horseless Age* for February, 1897, which announced his intention "to enter into the manufacture of motor vehicles propelled by a rotary gasolene [sic] motor."

Until his last years Black drove a one-cylinder vehicle of his own making, donated by his daughter to THE CHILDREN'S MUSEUM where it remains on display. He certainly attempted to manufacture automobiles in quantity and issued a catalog about 1897 which showed five distinct vehicles, but the illustrations appear to have been copied from Benz. Black was unsuccessful in raising money to open an automobile factory in Indianapolis and apparently made no effort to continue in the business after 1901.

PATRICK J. FURLONG
Indiana University, South Bend

Curatorial files of The Children's Museum and the private files of Jerry Jones and Brent Jones of Indianapolis, owners of the other known Black automobile; *Indianapolis News*, Dec. 27, 1913; Menno Duerksen, *Cars & Parts* (May, 1990); Murray Fahnestock, *The Horseless Carriage* Gazette (Jan.–Feb., 1965).

Black Hawk War (April to August, 1832). Black Hawk, chief of the Sac Indians, defied a treaty he had signed in 1830 by crossing the Mississippi River (June, 1831) to attack whites who had settled in Illinois. He was driven off but returned the following spring. MILITIA units throughout Illinois, Indiana, and surrounding territories mustered and prepared to defend their respective regions.

The 40th Regiment, Indiana State Militia, organized on June 14, 1826, was commanded by Alexander W. Russell at the time of Black Hawk's uprising. On June 3, 1832, McFarland was ordered to assemble an element of his regiment at the military grounds (MILITARY PARK) preparatory for a march into the northern part of the state. One hundred and fifty men assembled for the expedition, equipped with rifles, tomahawks, a pound of powder, and an ample supply of lead balls.

The entire campaign consisted of marching and maneuvering. During its time of service the force marched to the Lake Michigan area and back again. The only incident occurred when a cannon fired prematurely, causing a militiaman named William Warren to lose both of his arms. A few weeks after leaving the city, the volunteers returned and were disbanded.

WAYNE L. SANFORD

Blackburn, Cleo W. (Sept. 27, 1909–June 6, 1978). African-American minister and social work administrator. Born in Port Gibson, Mississippi, Blackburn came to Indianapolis in 1932 to attend BUTLER UNIVERSITY. After graduating from Butler's school of religion, he became an ordained minister in the CHRISTIAN CHURCH (DISCIPLES OF CHRIST). Blackburn then earned an M.A. in sociology at Fisk University and he worked as director of research and records at Tuskegee Institute.

Blackburn returned to Indianapolis in 1936 as executive director of FLANNER HOUSE, a social service center for the local black community. During his 40-year tenure, he worked to expand budgets, facilities, and programming to provide jobs, housing, and health services to the urban poor. He developed several unique self-help programs including Flanner House Homes, which became a national model for providing local and federal funding to help veterans build their own homes.

In 1948, Blackburn gathered a group of local community and business leaders and formed the

Board for Fundamental Education (BFE), for which they received a congressional charter in 1954. As executive director and later CEO of the BFE for 30 years, Blackburn used Flanner House and eventually 29 other test sites to develop programs to train and educate low-income workers.

While directing Flanner House, Blackburn was also president of Jarvis Christian College in Hawkins, Texas (1953–1964). He was a Rosenwald fellow at Indiana University in 1941 and received honorary doctorates from several universities. He also held leadership positions in numerous local organizations, including CHRISTIAN THEOLOGICAL SEMINARY and the URBAN LEAGUE.

MICHELLE D. HALE

Indianapolis News, June 7, 1978; Cleo Blackburn, *Board for Fundamental Education* (Indianapolis, 1959; copy in pamphlet collection, Indiana State Library); Michelle Hale, "Self-Help Moves from the Neighborhood to the Nation: Flanner House, 1936–1953," *Black History News & Notes*, No. 46 (Nov., 1991), 3–8.

Blackford, Isaac (Nov. 6, 1786–Dec. 31, 1859). Antebellum jurist. Born in Boundbrook, New Jersey, Blackford graduated from Princeton University. He read and practiced law in his home state until 1812 when he moved west, settling in Salem, Indiana. In Salem he was elected the first Washington County clerk and recorder in 1813. He won election for First Circuit Court judge in 1815, but resigned his term early to reenter private practice.

Governor Jonathan Jennings appointed Blackford to the Indiana Supreme Court in 1817 and he moved to Indianapolis soon after it became the capital. Only one session of the court had been held before he came to the bench and he remained a justice until 1852 when the position became an elected one. One of his most significant contributions as state Supreme Court justice was his *Blackford Reports*. Published between 1830 and 1850, the eight-volume *Reports*, shortened versions of most decisions made during his tenure, are the primary record for Supreme Court decisions of those years.

Blackford was a widower and considered a recluse. However, in addition to his duties on the court, he was an unsuccessful Whig candidate for the U.S. Senate in 1825 and served as president of the first state Common School Convention held in Indianapolis in 1847. He resumed his private practice in 1853. Two years later, President Franklin Pierce appointed him judge of the U.S. Court of Claims in Washington, D.C. Following his death, Blackford's body was returned to Indianapolis for burial. In 1868 his grave was moved to CROWN HILL CEMETERY.

CONNIE J. ZEIGLER

Blackwell, Francis "Scrapper" (Feb. 21, 1903–Oct. 7, 1962). African-American blues singer-guitarist-songwriter. Born in Syracuse, South Carolina, Blackwell arrived in Indianapolis at age three and was performing guitar professionally by his teens. In 1928 he began recording with pianist LEROY CARR on Vocalion Records. During the next seven years the duo's record sales totaled over a million copies, establishing them as pioneers in the newly emerging urban blues style. Blackwell also recorded with Bertha Hill, Georgia Tom Dorsey, Teddy Moss, Robinson's Knights of Rest, and other blues stars of the 1930s, his unique single-string accompaniment style influencing many guitarists including Robert Johnson, Muddy Waters, Johnny Shines, and T-Bone Walker. After Carr's death in 1935 Blackwell played infrequently around Indianapolis until the late 1950s when he was rediscovered by Indianapolis Jazz Club members and his old recordings were rereleased along with new albums on the 77 and Bluesville labels. In October, 1962, two weeks before a scheduled recording session, he was found in the alley behind a house at 527 West 17th Street suffering a gunshot wound; he died the following day.

LAWRENCE E. MCCULLOUGH
Indiana University–Purdue University,
Indianapolis

Sheldon Harris, *Blues Who's Who* (New Rochelle, N.Y., 1979).

Blackwood, Easley Rutland, Sr. (June 25, 1903–Mar. 27, 1992). Contract bridge expert and author. Born in Birmingham, Alabama, Blackwood spent most of his adult life in Indianapolis. After graduating from high school, Blackwood joined the Metropolitan Life Insurance Company and managed its offices in Decatur, Illinois, and Chicago before moving to Indianapolis in 1932. He continued in this capacity until retirement in 1964, when he opened the Blackwood Bridge Center, which he operated until 1976.

Having been taught to play at the age of 11, Blackwood became one of the nation's foremost authorities on the game of contract bridge. The author of a dozen books and numerous articles on the subject, Blackwood devised the bidding system that still carries his name, the Blackwood Convention. Originally intended as only a minor addition to a long-forgotten "perfect" bidding system, the Blackwood Convention remains a standard bidding technique for contract bridge players.

From 1948 to 1992 Blackwood wrote a syndicated daily column, "Blackwood on Bridge." After retirement he began a series of lectures aboard luxury cruises, which afforded him the opportunity to travel around the world eight times. He once estimated that he had taught over 10,000 students how to play contract bridge. Between 1968 and 1971 Blackwood served as executive secretary of the American Contract Bridge League. In 1984 he was named the "Bridge Personality of the Year" by the International Bridge Press Association.

JEFFREY A. DUVALL

Indianapolis Magazine, 16 (July, 1979), 18–21; *Indianapolis Monthly*, 10 (May, 1987), 54–57; *Indianapolis Star*, Mar. 28, 1992.

Blake, James (Mar. 3, 1791–Nov. 26, 1870). Early settler, businessman, civic leader. A native of York County, Pennsylvania, and veteran of the War of 1812, Blake was a wagon driver in his home state. Moving in July, 1821, to Indianapolis, where he resided until his death, Blake capitalized on the ginseng trade and established several drying houses (one in Indianapolis) to process the root for shipping.

From his arrival, Blake plunged into all aspects of life in the capital city. He established a successful wholesale dry goods store, founded the Indianapolis Rolling Mill, was a partner in the INDIANAPOLIS STEAM MILL COMPANY (1828), and president of the Indiana Mutual Fire Insurance Company (1837–1855). He was a member of the first board of directors of the MADISON AND INDIANAPOLIS RAILROAD and a director of the Lafayette and Indianapolis Railroad. Though never elected to public office, Blake served as a commissioner to accept plans for the first STATE HOUSE in Indianapolis. He also served as captain of the first militia company and the first fire company organized in town.

Devoted to numerous charitable endeavors, Blake was president of the INDIANAPOLIS BENEVOLENT SOCIETY for 35 years, helped organize the Indiana Colonization Society, established the first Sunday school in town and led its annual July 4th parade for 30 years, and promoted the cause of a state hospital for the insane. He also served as a trustee of Hanover College, Miami University (Ohio), and CROWN HILL CEMETERY, and at his death was the Indiana commissioner for the erection of a monument honoring Indiana's Civil War soldiers who fought at Gettysburg.

SHERYL D. VANDERSTEL

Indianapolis News, June 17, 1906, Nov. 7, 1968, Mar. 5, 1971; *Indianapolis Journal*, Nov. 28, 1870; Gayle Thornbrough, ed., *The Diary of Calvin Fletcher*, Vol. I (Indianapolis, 1972).

Blaker, Eliza Ann (Mar. 4, 1854–Dec. 4, 1926). Pioneer in child education. A native of Philadelphia, Blaker graduated from that city's Girls' Normal School and, in 1880, from the Centennial Kindergarten Training School, the first of its kind in the nation. Nineteenth-century kindergartens departed radically from conventional education. They were opposed to rote memorization, formality, and discipline, seeking instead to cultivate the preschool child's natural potential in a liberating atmosphere of play, aesthetics, and outdoor experiences.

With her husband, Louis Blaker (d. 1913), Eliza came to Indianapolis in 1882 to organize a kindergarten in connection with the Hadley Roberts Academy. Concurrently, a Free Kindergarten Society connected with the Indianapolis Free Kindergarten and Children's Aid Society persuaded Blaker to organize a free kindergarten to aid the community's charitable efforts toward its underprivileged children. She began to train teachers, and in 1883 established the Kindergarten Normal Training School, which in 1905 became the Teachers College of Indianapolis. All trustees, teachers, and students were women. The college affiliated with Butler College (now BUTLER UNIVERSITY) in 1926 and moved to the latter's campus in 1933.

Besides her work as college president, teacher, and lifetime superintendent of free kindergartens, Blaker instituted mothers' meetings in the schools and formed a Mothers' Council and a thrice-yearly Mothers' Mass Meeting. She led a victorious fight in 1901 for local tax support for kindergartens. She organized Saturday domestic training classes, the city's first, and was instrumental in founding and supervising Indianapolis' first directed playground, in MILITARY PARK. A member of numerous community organizations, Blaker helped establish the INDIANAPOLIS COUNCIL OF WOMEN. She lived to see her approach to kindergartens adopted throughout the nation. Hanover College awarded her an honorary doctorate in 1917 and an Eliza A. Blaker Club, formed in 1934, perpetuates the educator's philosophy. Indianapolis Public School 55 was renamed the Eliza A. Blaker School in 1958. Later, the Blaker Club established a memorial room at Butler in her honor.

ROBERT M. TAYLOR, JR.
Indiana Historical Society

Emma Lou Thornbrough, *Eliza A. Blaker: Her Life and Work* (Indianapolis, 1956).

Blankenbaker, Richard I. (1930–Nov. 18, 1988).

Indianapolis grocer, philanthropist, and public safety director. Born in New Albany, Indiana, Blankenbaker began his long career in the grocery business at age 12, working as a stockboy at a local store in order to help support his family. Moving to Indianapolis to take a job with Kroger, Blankenbaker later joined Stop & Shop supermarkets, managing one of the firm's stores. When Colonial Stores purchased Stop & Shop in 1955, Blankenbaker became district manager and eventually assistant to the president. In 1959 he married Virginia Murphy Blankenbaker, who worked as a public relations representative for Colonial and later became a state senator representing Marion County.

In 1961 Blankenbaker left Colonial to open his own grocery store at 52nd Street and Keystone Avenue. He eventually operated three Richard's Market Basket stores in Indianapolis. Blankenbaker was known for his charitable works, including an annual Thanksgiving turkey giveaway for needy families.

In December, 1980, Mayor William H. Hudnut III named his friend Blankenbaker as Director of Public Safety. During the years 1981–1983 Blankenbaker implemented an "austerity program" in the INDIANAPOLIS POLICE DEPARTMENT (IPD), which cut costs and personnel. By 1985 the program had produced a shortage of officers and secretaries and IPD was forced to increase its number of employees. Blankenbaker also implemented an in-service program on race relations and cultural understanding, as recommended by the mayor's Tanselle-Adams Commission. During his tenure Blankenbaker oversaw reorganizations of both IPD and the INDIANAPOLIS FIRE DEPARTMENT (IFD). Working with police chief Joseph G. McAtee, he introduced the "field command" approach which placed more supervisors and officers in the field and attempted to foster better police-community relations. In the area of fire protection services, Blankenbaker improved communications between IFD and township fire departments and implemented a joint training program for the county's firefighters.

The MICHAEL TAYLOR CASE, the 1987 shooting death of a 16–year-old black youth, caused trouble for Blankenbaker as both public safety director and businessman. Taylor, arrested on suspicion of car theft and with his hands cuffed behind his back, was found shot in the head in the back seat of a police car. Authorities said the youth shot himself with a gun he had hidden in his high-top tennis shoes. In November, 1987, a group called the Michael Taylor Justice Task Force, led by a group of black ministers, organized a boycott of Blankenbaker's grocery stores in an attempt to force him to release more information about the Taylor shooting. Following his death the next year, Blankenbaker's stores declared bankruptcy.

The police department memorialized Blankenbaker in 1989 by naming its north district headquarters at 42nd Street and College Avenue in his honor. He was also honored posthumously by the NAACP, INDIANAPOLIS URBAN LEAGUE, Indiana Christian Leadership Conference, and the MADAME WALKER URBAN LIFE CENTER in recognition of his food donations to the annual Rev. Mozel Sanders' Thanksgiving Dinner, his appointment of a black assistant public safety director, and other services to the African-American community.

RAY BOOMHOWER
Indiana Historical Society

The blizzard of January 25-27, 1978, dumped 15.5 inches of snow on the city, virtually eliminating city traffic for several days.
[Indianapolis Newspapers Inc.
Photo by Tim Halcomb]

Blizzard of 1978. The worst blizzard in Indianapolis history battered the city and most of Indiana on January 25–27. The "Great Blizzard of 1978" was part of a regional storm system that ravaged much of the Midwest and the eastern United States. Before it hit Indianapolis 5 inches of snow from an earlier storm remained on the ground. At 3:45 P.M., Wednesday, January 25, National Weather Service forecasters in Indianapolis issued a blizzard warning for the entire state—the only time such a warning was declared statewide. Snow began falling in the Indianapolis area about 5 P.M. When the storm abated 34 hours later, the city had received 15.5 inches of new snow, bringing the total snow depth to more than 20 inches. The total January snowfall of 30.6 inches set a monthly record for Indianapolis.

Strong, gusty winds that prevailed for nearly two days created snowdrifts as deep as 10 feet. At the blizzard's peak early Thursday, January 26, northwest winds reached 55 miles per hour, and the wind-chill temperature plummeted to −51°F. Although air temperatures near 0°F did not break any weather records, the combination of drifting snow, limited visibility, and bitter wind chills created severe conditions that eclipsed previous blizzards of January 29, 1977, and February 25, 1965.

The blizzard halted most forms of transportation. By early Thursday, travel on snow-clogged roadways was impossible. Airline, bus, and rail service ceased. Indianapolis International Airport was closed for a record three days from 11:45 P.M. Wednesday until 10 A.M. Saturday. Most businesses, industries, and nonessential services throughout the metropolitan area either closed or operated on a limited basis and with minimal staff.

The shutdown of land and air travel marooned thousands of people. Stranded travelers sought shelter at hotels, motels, Red Cross stations, National Guard armories, fire stations, public schools, hospitals, and homes of friends and relatives. Most state legislators, who had convened in Indianapolis for a session of the Indiana General Assembly, found lodging at downtown motels. Many of the city's service personnel and other snowbound employees remained at their workplace, some for as long as three days.

On Thursday Indianapolis Mayor William H. Hudnut III declared a snow emergency, mirroring the statewide emergency called by Governor Otis R. Bowen. The city's snow emergency remained in effect for three days, the longest such emergency ever issued for Indianapolis. Hudnut's declaration, coupled with his citywide curfew on Friday and Saturday nights, discouraged unnecessary travel, reduced the number of abandoned vehicles on roadways, and helped deter looting and vandalism.

Throughout the four-day ordeal, local officials, led by Mayor Hudnut, maintained essential services. Emergency personnel rescued stranded motorists and ferried the ill and injured to hospitals. Workers also delivered medical supplies to hospitals and homebound patients; provided food and fuel to the needy; and relayed information on the few local pharmacies and groceries that remained open. Because standard emergency vehicles could not negotiate the snow-clogged roadways, an array of trucks, snowplows, bulldozers, snowmobiles, and helicopters were called into service. On one segment of Interstate 465 a National Guard armored personnel carrier was required to break through massive snowdrifts. Civilian volunteers owning four-wheel-drive vehicles played a pivotal role in many emergency missions and service runs. Businesses, automobile dealerships, and hundreds of Indianapolis residents loaned four-wheel-drive vehicles to the city's emergency staff and helped transport workers to and from their posts. Snowmobile owners provided similar assistance, and networks of citizens band radio operators helped dispatch emergency personnel.

The state and city transportation departments faced a snow removal challenge of unprecedented scale. Although 60 snowplows and salt trucks were working on major thoroughfares in the metropolitan area, the city rented 29 heavy front- and end-loaders to break through snowdrifts and hired private contractors to supplement overwhelmed city crews. Although snow removal efforts were at first stymied by rapidly drifting snow, the city intensified its cleanup efforts early Saturday as high winds diminished. By Sunday, January 29, main roads in the metropolitan area were once again passable.

In the blizzard's aftermath Indianapolis experienced a surge in civic pride as residents reflected upon stories of personal sacrifice and acts of goodwill. Hudnut's hands-on approach and frequent media presence throughout the blizzard bolstered confidence in his leadership. He later characterized the blizzard as a defining moment in his administration. Tow truck drivers, heavy equipment operators, merchants of snow removal equipment, and four-wheel-drive dealerships enjoyed windfall profits.

After the blizzard Indianapolis reexamined its preparedness for future snowstorms. A boost in the transportation department's previously meager budget led to the purchase of heavier, more reliable equipment for snow removal. The city identified snow priority routes and eventually developed a comprehensive master plan for snow and ice removal. The police department improved its access to emergency vehicles, and the sheriff's department eventually purchased several four-wheel-drive vehicles to transport dispatchers and officers to their posts during heavy snows. Similarly, the city's major television stations began to purchase four-wheel-drive vehicles, which ten years later would become commonplace in the Indianapolis area.

CYNTHIA J. CLENDENON
Indiana Department of
Environmental Management

Indianapolis Star, Jan. 26–31, 1978; *Indianapolis News*, Jan. 26–28, 30–31, 1978; *Indianapolis Star*, Souvenir Edition, Feb. 5, 1978, section 5A–5B.

Block, William H. (ca. 1855–Dec. 11, 1928). Founder of the William H. Block Company department store. An immigrant from Trepezin, Hungary, Block came by steerage in 1874 to New York City. He worked for a brief period in New York before going to Cleveland, Ohio, to peddle goods in the mining districts. This venture was short-lived and he tried other jobs, such as telegraphy and farm work, only to return to peddling, with Cincinnati the center for his journeys through southwestern Ohio and eastern Indiana. Block and Abe Thalman, a Kokomo, Indiana, wholesaler, decided to pool their resources and in 1878 opened a store, Block & Thalman, in Kokomo. In 1894 Block withdrew from this partnership and two years later came to Indianapolis and opened a department store on Washington Street between Illinois and Meridian streets. The store prospered and in 1907 was incorporated as the WILLIAM H. BLOCK COMPANY. In 1911 the company moved to the completed eight-story modern department store at Illinois and Market streets.

Block, who established fixed prices with a small markup for his merchandise and encouraged quick turnover of goods, was seen by his peers as a progressive and visionary in the retail business. He was one of the founders of Merchant's Heat and Light Company. Also, he supported civic enterprises and was a generous contributor to the Community Chest, RILEY HOSPITAL FOR CHILDREN, and BUTLER UNIVERSITY.

CAROLYN S. BLACKWELL

Indianapolis News, Dec. 11, 1928.

Block Forum Lecture Series. A legacy from the estate of Edward A. Block, member of the INDIANAPOLIS HEBREW CONGREGATION, provided the endowment for this lecture series established in 1982 by the Indianapolis Hebrew Congregation Foundation. The traditionally sold-out series, held at the Hebrew Congregation, presents four nationally known speakers throughout the fall and spring. Over the past ten years the series has hosted such notables as Julian Bond, Ralph Nader, Alexander M. Haig, Jr., Abba Eban, Beverly Sills, Capt. Wally Schirra, Senator William Proxmire, and Dr. C. Everett Koop.

JOAN CUNNINGHAM

Blues. The African-American-originated folk music form known as "the blues" became popular in Indianapolis after World War I with the increased migration of southern blacks to the city. In the early 1920s popular local blues pianists included Jimmy Collins, Tom and Phil Harding, "Funky Five," Jesse Crump, and Arthur "Montana" Taylor. Crump (b. 1906, Dallas) arrived in Indianapolis in 1923 and performed at the Golden West Cafe on Indiana Avenue; he recorded as a soloist ("Mr. Crump's Rag," "Golden West Blues") and as an accompanist with vocalists Nina Reeves and Genevieve Stearns, later moving to Chicago to record and tour with singer Ida Cox. Taylor (b. 1903, Butte, Montana) played in Indianapolis at the Hole in the Wall, Goosie Lee's Rock House, and the Golden West Cafe. He recorded "Indiana Avenue Stomp" and several other sides for Vocalion in 1928 at an Indianapolis field recording session that was also the recording debut for pianist-singer LEROY CARR (1905–1935) and guitarist FRANCIS "SCRAPPER" BLACKWELL (1903–1962), the most successful and innovative blues duo of the period. Carr and Blackwell made over 100 records together and toured throughout the Midwest until Carr's sudden death from nephritis. Other local recording activity in the 1920s included Lulu Jackson singing and playing guitar for Vocalion in 1928 and pianist Herve Duerson performing several solo piano sides for Gennett in 1929 ("Naptown Special," "Avenue Strut").

Blues musicians residing in Indianapolis during the 1930s included pianist William "Champion Jack" Dupree, guitarist Amos Easton (aka Bumble Bee Slim), guitarist Bill Gaither (aka Leroy's Buddy), and pianist Pleasant Joseph (aka Cousin Joe). Dupree (b. 1910, New Orleans) began his five-decade recording career with several Okeh sides cut in 1940 while performing with singers Ophelia and Toots Hoy at the Cotton Club, Astoria, and Lincoln Theatre. Joseph (b. 1907, Wallace, Louisiana) entertained with Dupree and the Hoys in 1940 before moving to New York and recording for Savoy, Decca, and Bluebird. Easton (b. 1905, Brunswick, Georgia) performed in Indianapolis 1928–1930 before moving to Chicago to become one of the most popular blues singers of the 1930s. Louisville native Gaither was groomed by Decca Records as a successor to Carr and made 118 Decca and Okeh sides, often accompanied by Indianapolis pianist Honey Hill. Guitarist John Brim (b. 1922, Hopkinsville, Kentucky) spent 1941–1945 in Indianapolis before moving to Chicago and then to Gary, Indiana, where he recorded extensively for Chess and JOB. Guitarist Edward Lamonte "Pete" Franklin (1927–1975) was an Indianapolis native who traveled the United States in the 1940s and 1950s, recording for RCA Victor in 1947 and for Flyright and Blue Goose in the 1960s. Guitarist SHIRLEY GRIFFITH (1908–1974) moved to Indianapolis in 1928 from Mississippi and recorded albums for Bluesville, Blue Goose, and Flyright labels during the 1960s and 1970s. James "Yank" Rachell (b. 1910, Haywood County, Tennessee) is a mandolinist who recorded with several renowned country blues artists of the 1930s before arriving in Indianapolis in 1957. Other notable local blues figures included bassist Wilson Swain and harmonica player James Easley, guitarists William "Dollar Bill" Cox, John Tyler Adams, Raymond Holloway, Jessie Ellery, Harvey Cook, and William "Lefty" Bates.

After World War II, blues in Indianapolis was overshadowed by the city's burgeoning JAZZ scene and was less frequently heard in commercial venues until the 1970s when older blues performers such as Rachell, Griffith, and Bates began playing to younger audiences outside the traditional blues community, sparking an Indianapolis blues resurgence abetted by promotional groups like the Blues Society of Indiana, radio deejays, and a new crop of blues-oriented music bars throughout the city.

LAWRENCE E. McCULLOUGH
Indiana University–Purdue University,
Indianapolis

Sheldon Harris, *Blues Who's Who* (New Rochelle, N.Y., 1979); Duncan Schiedt, *The Jazz State of Indiana* (Pittsboro, Ind., 1977).

Board of Trade. Booster organization and grain exchange. In 1853, 36 of the city's leading businessmen formed the Indianapolis Board of Trade to promote the benefits of Indianapolis. The

The old Chamber of Commerce/Board of Trade building, ca. 1900.
[Indiana Historical Society, Bass Collection, #825].

next year the board published a circular detailing the city's many advantages for new businesses, primarily the extensive railroad network. It continued to publish similar promotional literature for the next several decades. By the 1870s the Board of Trade had its own building at the corner of Capitol and Maryland streets, renting out office space to grain dealers, freight line representatives, and others. The board also held a daily grain call at noon. When it incorporated in 1882, the Board of Trade consolidated all previously existing trade and commercial organizations in the city. In addition to promotional activities, it now sought to establish uniformity in commercial practices, promote business ethics, and arbitrate trade disputes. In 1907 the board moved to 143 North Meridian Street.

In June, 1946, the board reorganized again, becoming the Indianapolis Board of Trade, Inc., and eliminated the $1,000 mortuary benefit to encourage new younger members to join an organization whose average member was almost 60 years old. In September, 1977, the Board of Trade's shareholders voted to dissolve the organization, citing high operating costs, reluctance to raise rents in its building, and reduced downtown pedestrian traffic. Four years later the eight-story Board of Trade building was torn down to make way for the BANK ONE TOWER.

DEBORAH B. MARKISOHN

Indianapolis News, Apr. 28, 1923; *Indianapolis Star*, Sept. 25, 1977.

Bobbs, John Stough (Dec. 28, 1809–May 1, 1870). Pioneer surgeon and medical educator. Born in Greene Village, Franklin County, Pennsylvania, where he obtained his early education, Bobbs began the study of medicine in 1827 as an apprentice to Dr. Martin Luther in Harrisburg. His three-year stint included one complete course of formal lectures. After moving to Indianapolis in 1835, he returned to Pennsylvania later in the year to complete a second course of lectures at Jefferson Medical College (Philadelphia) and obtained his M.D. degree.

Bobbs served as one of the commissioners to establish the Indiana Hospital for the Insane. He was a founder and first secretary of the Indianapolis Medical Society (1848) and was instrumental in organizing the Indiana State Medical Society the following year. He was appointed professor of anatomy, and then professor of surgery and dean of Indiana Central Medical College (1848–1852). In 1856 he was elected a state senator from Marion County, and during the Civil War he served as a medical inspector and a commissioned surgeon.

Bobbs was concerned with maintaining an adequate supply of qualified physicians for the state. He founded the Indiana Medical College in 1869, oldest of the three proprietary schools that united in 1908 to form the INDIANA UNIVERSITY SCHOOL OF MEDICINE. The Bobbs' Free Dispensary, established as a result of his bequest, provided free medical care for thousands of patients and was a primary source of health care for the poor in Indianapolis during the late 19th and early 20th centuries.

CHARLES A. BONSETT, M.D.
Indiana University School of Medicine

Bobbs, Ruth Pratt (Sept. 3, 1884–Jan. 15, 1973). Portrait painter and Indianapolis socialite, born in the Hoosier capital. Bobbs' early art instruction was under Indiana artist and illustrator Mary Y. Robinson. She later attended the HERRON SCHOOL OF ART and studied at the Academie Julian in Paris and the School of Fine Arts (Boston), among other institutions. She was married to William C. Bobbs, president of the BOBBS-MERRILL PUBLISHING COMPANY, from 1912 until his death in 1926. Although she maintained a summer studio at Northport Point, Michigan, Bobbs lived most of the year in her Indianapolis studio-home at 11th and Delaware streets, and later at 14th and Delaware.

One of the leading women artists and portrait painters in Indianapolis from the 1930s through the 1950s, Bobbs was a frequent exhibitor at the HOOSIER SALON, the Indiana Artists Club, and the Art Association of Indianapolis annual shows. In 1933 she displayed her work in the state's exhibit at the Century of Progress Exhibition in Chicago. She was a member of the National Association of Women Artists, the Art Association of Indianapolis, the Hoosier Salon, and the Portfolio Club. Portraits by Bobbs include ROBERT H. TYNDALL, mayor of Indianapolis; Frank H. Sparks, president of Wabash College; THOMAS CARR HOWE, president of BUTLER UNIVERSITY; and writer Stephen Vincent Benet. Works by Bobbs can also be found in the permanent collection of the INDIANAPOLIS MUSEUM OF ART.

FRANK N. OWINGS, JR.

Mary Q. Burnet, *Art and Artists of Indiana* (New York, 1921); Peter Hastings Falk, ed., *Who Was Who in American Art* (Madison, Conn., 1985); Flora Lauter, *Indiana Artists Active 1940* (Spencer, Ind., 1941).

Bobbs-Merrill Company. Publishers. The firm's roots can be traced to a bookstore opened by SAMUEL MERRILL in 1850. (There has been some dispute over that date—JACOB PIATT DUNN's *Greater Indianapolis* gives two different years on the same page—but a preponderance of evidence favors the midcentury date.) Merrill's first publications were reprints of law reports in the early 1850s. He left the company to his son, Samuel Merrill, Jr., in 1855, and the younger Merrill, along with his brother-in-law Charles W. Moores, ran the business until the CIVIL WAR. In the absence of both men during the latter part of the war, Merrill's sisters, CATHARINE MERRILL and Julia Merrill Moores, wife of Charles, handled the firm's affairs. Catharine Merrill's *The Soldier of Indiana in the War for the Union*, published anonymously in 1866 and 1869, was apparently the first general title published by the firm.

The business suffered after the Civil War. Merrill's partners changed several times until

1885, when there was a major reorganization. The firm merged with competitor BOWEN, STEWART AND CO., forming the Bowen-Merrill Co. Thus revitalized, the company combined book publishing, a bookstore, and a wholesale business. By 1909 the company, which had become the Bobbs-Merrill Co. in 1903, was wholly a publisher of law and general books. The wholesale business had been sold in 1896, and in 1909 William K. Stewart purchased the bookstore.

Indiana authors, among them two of the state's great literary figures, MEREDITH NICHOLSON and George Ade, made Bobbs-Merrill a truly national publisher. However, it was JAMES WHITCOMB RILEY's first book of poems, *"The Old Swimmin'-Hole" and 'Leven More Poems*, reprinted by Merrill, Meigs and Co. in 1883, that provided the initial impetus for the firm's recognition on the national scene. Riley's exclusive domination of the firm's trade book sales ended with the publication of Shelbyville lawyer Charles Major's novel *When Knighthood Was in Flower* (1898), believed to be the first bestseller backed by a national advertising campaign. This success was followed in 1900 by *Alice of Old Vincennes*, by Maurice Thompson of Crawfordsville, and *The Redemption of David Corson* by another Hoosier, Charles Frederick Goss. These three books were among the nation's top ten sellers in 1900.

Meanwhile, in 1898, the firm acquired an extensive law list from Houghton Mifflin Co., and later added volumes from an Ohio publisher. Robert L. Moorhead, who was with the firm for 57 years, became manager of the law department in 1904. After a brief and unprofitable experience with magazine publishing from 1904 to 1908, the firm entered educational publishing. A series of readers called "Child Classics" was published in 1909, and in 1911 the education department was formally established.

By the turn of the century leadership of the firm had passed from the Merrills to William C. Bobbs. He served as president until 1926, with Hewitt H. Howland as trade editor and literary advisor. John Jay Curtis became eastern editorial representative in 1900 and opened a trade department office in New York. Moving to Hollywood in 1919, he opened a West Coast office for the firm, selling motion picture rights to moviemakers.

During the 1920s it is believed that Bobbs-Merrill sold more stories to the movies than all other publishers combined. Though Curtis continued to live on the West Coast, he became president of the firm in 1926.

DAVID LAURANCE CHAMBERS, a major stockholder and editor since 1925, gained full control of the company when he became president in 1935. The development of the "Childhood of Famous Americans" series, initiated in 1932, made CHILDREN'S LITERATURE a significant part of the trade department's lists. By the 1940s Bobbs-Merrill was recognized as the largest general publisher west of the Alleghenies. Chambers served as president until 1953, though he was active in the firm until it was sold to HOWARD W. SAMS of Indianapolis in 1958. By this time Bobbs-Merrill had published more than 100 Indiana authors.

Following the sale to Sams, Bobbs-Merrill ceased to be a closely held independent company. The educational publishing department grew with the acquisition of lists from other publishers, and the firm added a college textbook division in 1961. Publication continued under the Bobbs-Merrill imprint, even after International Telephone and Telegraph acquired Sams in 1966. The long history of the firm's imprint ended with the sales of the backlists to the Macmillan Company in 1985.

JOANNE LANDERS HENRY

Jack Wayne O'Bar, "A History of the Bobbs-Merrill Company, 1850–1940: With a Postlude Through the Early 1960's" (Ph.D. dissertation, Indiana University, 1975).

Boehringer Mannheim. Manufacturer of medical diagnostic devices. Boehringer Mannheim Corporation is part of an international group of privately held Boehringer Mannheim companies, the oldest and largest founded in Germany in 1859. Boehringer began U.S. operations in New York in 1964, selling biochemicals and reagent tests. In 1974 Boehringer acquired BioDynamics, moving its headquarters to Indianapolis the following year. With this acquisition Boehringer moved into the development of blood glucose monitoring devices for diabetics. These instruments still account for a large percentage of its diagnostics business.

Boehringer grew rapidly during the 1980s, constructing several new buildings on its 200–acre far northeastside campus. A 1988 estimate ranked Boehringer as the world's second largest medical diagnostic devices company. The firm's sales have increased rapidly during the last decade, from $285 million in 1985 to $500 million in 1988 to an estimated $2 billion in 1990. Employing about 2,000 people at its Indianapolis headquarters, Boehringer makes a variety of diagnostic products, tests for home and clinical use, and biochemicals.

DEBORAH B. MARKISOHN

Boetcher, Walter C. (Nov. 13, 1881–Oct. 5, 1951). Mayor of Indianapolis, 1937–1939, Democrat. A native of La Porte, Indiana, Boetcher spent most of his life in Indianapolis, moving to the capital as a child in 1888 and attending MANUAL HIGH SCHOOL and Wagner Business College. From 1911 to 1918 he held several governmental positions, including chief deputy in the Marion County treasurer's office. In 1919 he became the secretary-treasurer of the Meridian Service Company, a position he held for 14 years.

Boetcher served on the Marion County Council (1931–1933), as president of the city's Board of Works (1933–1934), and as city controller (1934). Following JOHN KERN's resignation as mayor in 1937, Boetcher became acting mayor of Indianapolis, serving from October, 1937, to early January, 1939. He was elected treasurer of Marion County in 1938 and again in 1940, and twice was chair of the Marion County Democratic Central Committee (1934–1936, 1946–1948).

JEFFREY A. DUVALL

Indiana Biography Series, Indiana State Library.

Bohlen, Diedrich August (Jan. 17, 1827–June 1, 1890). Architect. Born in Cadenberge in the kingdom of Hanover, Bohlen received his architectural training in Holzminden before immigrating to the United States in 1851 or 1852. After a year in Cincinnati, he arrived in

Architect Diedrich Bohlen designed many of the city's churches. [Indiana State Library]

Indianapolis and worked in the office of pioneer architect FRANCIS COSTIGAN. Bohlen established his own architectural practice in 1853. He designed such noted landmarks such as ST. JOHN CATHOLIC CHURCH (1871); ROBERTS PARK METHODIST CHURCH (1876); General German Protestant Orphans' Home (later called PLEASANT RUN CHILDREN'S HOME, 1872); Crown Hill Cemetery Chapel (1877); St. Paul's Lutheran Church (1883); Lockerbie Square United Methodist Church (1883); and the city's first theater, the Metropolitan (1858).

In 1884 Bohlen's son, Oscar D., became a partner in the firm, whose name changed to D. A. Bohlen and Son. This firm served the Midwest for four generations as Oscar's son, August C., joined the firm in 1910 and August's son, Robert L., joined in 1946. The firm's distinguished accomplishments include the design of all the structures on the St. Mary-of-the-Woods campus near Terre Haute, and the Franciscan convent and academy at Oldenburg. Its many Indianapolis projects included the CITY MARKET and TOMLINSON HALL (1886), MURAT TEMPLE (1910), the Big Four Building (1929), the MAJESTIC BUILDING (1896), and the facade of SS. PETER AND PAUL CATHEDRAL (1936). The firm specialized in churches and institutional buildings throughout the Midwest. D. A. Bohlen and Son merged with architect David V. Burns in 1961, becoming Bohlen and Burns until 1967 when the name changed to Bohlen, Burns and Associates despite the absence of any Bohlens in the firm.

D. A. Bohlen lived on Lockerbie Street and was active in the German-American community including the German-English Independent

School Association and the Gewerbeschulverein. He is buried in CROWN HILL CEMETERY.

WILLIAM SELM

Indiana Tribuene, June 2, 1890; Jacob Piatt Dunn, *Indiana and Indianans* (Chicago, 1919), Vol. 4.

Bohlen, Meyer, Gibson and Associates (BMG).

Architectural firm. Four generations of Bohlens practiced architecture in Indianapolis, and the firm, begun by the patriarch in the mid-19th century, is now one of the nation's oldest continuously operated architectural enterprises (some claim it is the oldest).

DIEDRICH AUGUST BOHLEN founded D. A. Bohlen, Architect on April 10, 1853. D. A. Bohlen designed the Charles Mayer Store facade (1853), the dome addition to the Odd Fellows Grand Lodge (1854), St. Mary-of-the-Woods Convent and Chapel (1858), the MORRIS-BUTLER HOUSE (1864), Crown Hill Cemetery Chapel (1877), the General German Protestant Orphans Home (1872), which still stands at 1404 South State Avenue, St. John's Catholic Church (1871), the Churchman House (1871), and the remodeled English Opera House and Hotel Auditorium (ca. 1897).

Diedrich's son, Oscar Diedrich Bohlen, joined his father in 1884 and the firm became D. A. Bohlen and Son. Together they designed the Indiana Dental College (1893), TOMLINSON HALL (1886), and the CITY MARKET (1886). On June 1, 1890, D. A. Bohlen died; he left a rich architectural legacy and was credited with introducing the German Neo-Gothic style to Indiana.

Oscar Bohlen became one of the first registered architects and registered engineers in Indiana. He designed the beautiful MAJESTIC BUILDING (1896), the first and tallest steel skeleton "skyscraper" west of the Alleghenies outside of Chicago, which still stands at the northeast corner of Pennsylvania and Maryland streets. He also designed the Indiana National Bank building (1895), the French Lick Springs Hotel (1898), Methodist Hospital (1901), St. Francis Hospital (1903), the former St. Vincent Hospital (located at Capitol Avenue and Fall Creek Parkway), and an addition to UNION STATION (1903).

Oscar's son, August Carl Bohlen, joined the firm in 1909. He was a coauthor of Indiana's original building codes. He designed the Stokely Brothers office building (1912) and the Indianapolis Star-News Building (1924).

Robert Lesh Bohlen, August's son, joined the firm in 1946. Together they worked on ongoing projects and he designed the Empire Life Building (now the LILLY ENDOWMENT headquarters) in 1950. Robert died suddenly in 1960, his father ten years later. In 1961 August incorporated the firm with a partner, David V. Burns, and the firm became Bohlen and Burns Architects. In 1967 it became Bohlen, Burns and Associates and in 1971 adopted its current name.

The National Register of Historic Places lists more than 20 Bohlen projects.

RICHARD W. SMITH
Smith-Brandt Associates

Bohlen, Meyer, Gibson Collection, Indiana Historical Society.

Bolton, Nathaniel

(July 25, 1803–Nov. 26, 1858). Coeditor of Indianapolis' first newspaper, the *Gazette*. Born in Chillicothe, Ohio, Bolton came to Indiana in 1820 when George Smith, his stepfather, established a print shop in Jeffersonville, Indiana. In 1821 Smith purchased land in Indianapolis and moved his family there. On January 28, 1822, Smith started the town's first newspaper, which was printed in the family's cabin located at Maryland and Missouri streets. Bolton, who had remained in Jeffersonville to finish some state printing work, came to Indianapolis shortly after the *Gazette's* inaugural issue and joined his stepfather on the paper.

Smith and Bolton published the paper together until 1823, when Smith left and Bolton ran it by himself until his stepfather rejoined the *Gazette* a year later. The duo continued their partnership until 1829, when George L. Kinnard became part owner and the newspaper's name was changed to the *Indiana State Gazette*. Bolton sold his interest in the paper to Alexander F. Morrison in March, 1830, and the paper's name was changed to the *INDIANA DEMOCRAT AND STATE GAZETTE*.

Bolton married Sarah T. Barrett in 1831 and the couple operated a tavern located on farmland once owned by Smith, who died in 1826. Bolton and his wife sold the property to the state in 1845 as the site for the Central Hospital for the Insane. In 1851 Bolton was elected as state librarian. He was appointed consul to Geneva, Switzerland, by President Franklin Pierce in 1855, remaining there until 1857, when ill health forced him to return to Indianapolis.

RAY BOOMHOWER
Indiana Historical Society

Bolton, Sarah T. (Dec. 18, 1814–Aug. 4, 1893). Pioneer poet and advocate of women's property rights. Born Sarah Tittle Barrett at Newport Barracks, Kentucky, she moved with her family to Indiana when she was three. When she was 13 years old, a Madison, Indiana, newspaper published one of her poems, and for the next four years her work appeared regularly in the papers of Madison and Cincinnati. In 1831 she married NATHANIEL BOLTON, publisher of the *INDIANAPOLIS GAZETTE*, a union that produced two children. The couple bought a farm, Mt. Jackson, on the National Road (West Washington Street), currently the location of CENTRAL STATE HOSPITAL. An advocate of property rights for women, she organized a women's group in 1850 that lobbied the Indiana Constitutional Convention concerning that issue. She also wrote a poem that year, "The Union," in which she predicted the Civil War.

The background of Sarah Bolton's most famous poem is briefly described by literary historian Arthur Shumaker: "While her husband served as state librarian and also the custodian of the statehouse, she sewed almost without help new carpets for the building . . . composing while she worked, her poem of courage despite odds, 'Paddle Your Own Canoe.'" Although written in the Victorian style of romantic images, the poem's message of hope, courage, and resolution was clear. It said, in part: "Nothing great is lightly won / Nothing won is lost / But if you succeed you must / Paddle your own canoe."

Nathaniel's appointment as consul at Geneva, Switzerland, in 1855, took the family to Europe for two years. Ill health led to his resignation, and he died in 1858. Sarah married Judge Addison Reese five years later, but the marriage did not succeed. Sarah purchased "Beech Bank" farm in 1871, located in what is now BEECH GROVE, and lived there until her death, by which time she had been considered Indiana's unofficial poet laureate for many years. She is buried with Nathaniel in CROWN HILL CEMETERY. Her achievements are commemorated by a bronze plaque in the rotunda of the STATE HOUSE.

NANCY GERARD

Arthur W. Shumaker, *A History of Indiana Literature* (Indianapolis, 1962); R. E. Banta, *Indiana Authors and Their Books, 1816–1916* (Crawfordsville, Ind., 1949).

Book, William Henry "Bill" (Nov. 22, 1891–Apr. 29, 1965). Civic leader. As executive vice-president of the Indianapolis CHAMBER OF COMMERCE from 1934 to 1963, Book was a significant force in the city's recovery from the GREAT DEPRESSION and its growth following World War II. His influence in the development of the city's government and as a key industrial center won him the nickname "Mr. Indianapolis."

After earning an A.B. degree at Franklin College in 1919, Book served on the staff of the *INDIANAPOLIS NEWS* as a reporter and assistant city editor until 1925, then joined the Chamber of Commerce as director of government research from 1926 to 1933. He served as director of unemployment relief for the State of Indiana from 1933 to 1934, when he returned to the chamber as its executive vice-president.

The period following the 1929 stock market crash was a grim time. Book got key business leaders put on the chamber board and then undertook the rebuilding of the city's economic base toward what became substantial industrial growth. Known as a conservative, he was both criticized and praised for his belief that, while federal funds might be used for interstate projects such as highways and airports, only private funds should underwrite housing and redevelopment. With a tight economy restraining the city at the end of World War II, however, he saw that his position was no longer practical, and he supported broader federal assistance.

Asked late in his career to list what he considered the chamber's primary achievements under his leadership, Book cited what he called "things that probably would not have happened otherwise." He listed a distinctive slum clearance program, a modern postwar sanitary system, adequate flood control legislation, countywide metropolitan planning, the new CITY-COUNTY BUILDING, a major fund drive for a modern hospital, a community attractive to business through fair taxation, and unparalleled business and industrial growth.

His many civic activities included service for 35 years as chairman of the Red Cross's Disaster Relief Committee. He was inducted posthumously into the Indiana Academy, an organization honoring the state's illustrious citizens.

JAMES E. FARMER

Hubert H. Hawkins and Robert R. McClaren, *Indiana Lives* (Indianapolis, 1967); George and Miriam Geib, *Indianapolis First* (Indianapolis, 1990); *Indianapolis Star*, Apr. 30, 1965 (obituary), May 1, 1965 (editorial).

Book Trade. Since the middle of the 19th century, Indianapolis has had important associations with the book world—for its publishers, book designers, and book collectors, as well as for its authors of popular literature.

Book Publishing. The book trade in Indianapolis began in earnest when the first bookstores appeared. W. E. Dunbar opened his shop in 1833, and SAMUEL MERRILL, founder of BOBBS-MERRILL, started the city's third bookstore in 1850. By 1873, when the Public Library first opened, Merrill's store was important enough to handle all of its initial orders.

Merrill was launched as a publisher ten years later through one of Indianapolis' most famous partnerships. Merrill's company decided to move away from its lawbook specialty by taking over JAMES WHITCOMB RILEY's *"The Old Swimmin' Hole" and 'Leven More Poems* for a second printing in 1883. The association of Merrill and Riley was an enormous success. The bookstore, now Bowen-Merrill, helped establish the market for Riley's books, and Riley's immense popularity turned the local bookseller into a major American publisher.

The company would sell half a million Riley titles in the next ten years, and more than three and a half million by 1949.

Bowen-Merrill did not find another bestselling author until 1898, when it brought out Charles Major's *When Knighthood Was in Flower*. The company had learned from its experience with Riley that publishers as well as authors make bestselling books, and it was John Jay Curtis, a company officer, who first suggested the title and then developed a sales plan to advertise the book in major newspapers throughout the country. The plan and the book were a great success, and *Knighthood* ended up as the second-best-selling American book of 1899.

Curtis was something of a genius as a publicist. He began the mass marketing of books to the general public by way of large newspaper advertisements. His dust jackets became the colorful sales-prompters of today. He was the first to commission likely authors—turning Maurice Thompson from a scholar into a bestselling fiction writer, for example. As a result, the firm had fiction bestsellers in all but two of the years between 1898 and 1914—sometimes two, three, even four on the list at once. Included among these bestsellers was the company's first children's book, *The Wonderful Wizard of Oz* by L. Frank Baum, published in 1900. Later triumphs included Maurice Thompson's *Alice of Old Vincennes* (1900), Emerson Hough's *The Mississippi Bubble* (1902), MEREDITH NICHOLSON's *The House of a Thousand Candles* (1905), Mary Roberts Rinehart's *The Man in Lower Ten* (1909), Vaughn Kester's *The Prodigal Judge* (1911), and Owen Johnson's *The Salamander* (1914). And of course new and regrouped Riley collections continued their phenomenal sales.

Though the company, renamed Bobbs-Merrill in 1903, would not monopolize the bestseller lists after 1914, it maintained its position as a major trade publisher. Such authors as Richard Halliburton (whose 1925 travel book *Royal Road to Romance* led to eight other books), Irving Bacheller, Earl Derr Biggers (author of the Charlie Chan stories), Talbot Mundy, and Julia Peterkin were all market successes. In 1926, the company again placed two outstanding titles on the year's bestseller list—John Erskine's novel, *The Private*

Life of Helen of Troy, and the first-place nonfiction book, Bruce Barton's *The Man Nobody Knows*.

During the 1930s Bobbs-Merrill's greatest commercial success was Irma Rombauer's *The Joy of Cooking*. First published in 1931, *Joy* sold some three million copies by 1958. The company also continued to publish lawbooks, the bestselling juvenile series "Childhood of Famous Americans," and a greatly expanded line of textbooks—especially the popular "Bobbs-Merrill Readers." By 1940, the School Book Department had sold millions of volumes.

During the next two decades, Bobbs-Merrill's trade press division would decline in importance, even though it published many notable titles. (Ayn Rand's *The Fountainhead* was one of these.) The company's fortunes had come to depend on its legal and educational publishing. It was the education division that was of primary interest when HOWARD W. SAMS bought Bobbs-Merrill in 1958. The purchase ended an era. As part of the Sams group, the firm would increasingly specialize in training materials and in school and college texts.

The Sams company is typical of another kind of book publisher that has come to occupy an important place in Indianapolis—the provider of training materials to business and industry. Howard Sams was an entrepreneur whose company had grown from 12 people in 1946 to over 500 when he acquired Bobbs-Merrill. It had begun by publishing radio and television technical service bulletins, but Sams saw education and technical training as the general purpose of all his enterprises. In this spirit, the Sams organization acquired Bobbs-Merrill, opened technical schools, and in later years became a substantial publisher of manuals for the microcomputer industry.

Sams did make an attempt to strengthen general-interest publishing at Bobbs-Merrill, hiring an experienced New York publishing executive as president, but those efforts were unsuccessful. The company finally passed out of local ownership in 1966 when Sams sold his companies to International Telephone and Telegraph (ITT). From that point, general book publishing was a relatively minor aspect of Bobbs-Merrill. ITT in turn sold the Sams companies to Macmillan in 1985, and Bobbs-Merrill was merged out of existence as a separate and distinct organization.

It is ironic but perhaps appropriate that Bobbs-Merrill, one of the country's oldest and most distinguished publishing houses, would cease as it was intermingled with the new wave of technological publishing that has become such a large part of the modern book industry. Indianapolis is still a publishing center, and the company that absorbed Bobbs-Merrill is still commissioning and selling millions of books; today, however, the books are for users of microcomputers rather than the general reader. A brief account of that "new" history illustrates the complexity, multinational character, and endless organizational changes that are now typical of the city's book trade.

Sams made a natural extension from electronics books to books for computer users in the late 1970s. In 1981, the Que Corporation in Carmel also started publishing computer books. A year after Macmillan acquired Sams (and Bobbs-Merrill) from ITT, it also purchased Que. Que went on to publish a national bestseller, though it never appeared on the *New York Times* bestsellers list—a software guide, *Using 1–2–3*, that sold a million copies by 1987.

Macmillan was itself acquired in 1988 by the London-based Maxwell Communications Corporation, and Sams and Que were merged. Shortly before Robert Maxwell drowned in a boating accident, with colossal consequences for his gigantic publishing empire, the Indianapolis entity was sold to Paramount Communications (owners of the movie studio). By then, Paramount also owned both the Simon and Schuster and the Prentice Hall publishing houses. The Indianapolis company then became Prentice Hall Computer Publishing, a part of Simon and Schuster, itself a subsidiary of Paramount. But at the end of it all, Indianapolis still had a major publisher, a descendant of Bobbs-Merrill, that sold more than seven million copies in 1991.

Book Retailing. The original Merrill bookstore would show the same continuity and staying power as the publisher. Known as Ober's for most of its history, it survived as Indianapolis' premier independent bookseller until 1983.

Ober's could trace its lineage continuously from 1833, when its first predecessor was opened. After a succession of owners, it became Bowen-Merrill in 1885, and then Bobbs-Merrill in 1903. It ceased to be part of the Bobbs-Merrill Company in 1909 when it was brought by William K. Stewart.

C. S. Ober acquired control of the bookstore in 1945, changed the name to Ober Bookstore, and moved it to its final location in the Ober Building. An Indianapolis cultural landmark until its closing, it found itself unable to compete with chain stores such as Waldenbooks and B. Dalton's, which offered many fewer titles but could provide shopping mall locations and discounted prices on trade books. It was believed at the time that independent bookstores were in permanent eclipse, but this proved overly pessimistic. A few years later there were several general-reader bookstores in Indianapolis, including Borders (opened 1987), a small chain that combined mall location and computerized operations with an immense inventory of more than a hundred thousand titles.

As for used and rare books, Indianapolis has improved since 1973, when a local magazine declared that "the last used bookstore has closed" after the Indiana Bookstore shut its doors. Aside from stores limited to paperbacks, there were in the early 1990s at least five dealers in used books with some antiquarian interests.

Book Design. Two of the most important names in book design and fine printing, BRUCE ROGERS and the Grabhorns, produced some of their early work in Indianapolis.

Bruce Rogers, claimed by some the best book designer of the early 20th century, was a native of Lafayette, Indiana, who studied art at Purdue University. In 1893, he worked for the Indiana Illustrating Company, where he designed a pamphlet, *Botany in Pharmacy*, for the Eli Lilly Company. This was the first published book designed entirely by him. His most substantial Indianapolis work was the catalogue of the Walters art collection done for R. B. Gruelle, produced in 1894, the first book with Rogers' name in the colophon. Rogers left the city for Boston in 1895, where he was to make his reputation.

Edwin and Robert Grabhorn, whose Grabhorn Press became one of the most honored private presses in the world, started as printers in Indianapolis. Edwin opened the Studio Press in Indianapolis in 1915 at the age of 25. His main business was advertising brochures, but he produced his first book the following year—*The Master of the Machine* by Temple Scott. Other booklets were to follow, and in 1918 his brother Robert joined him at the Studio. Together they produced in 1919 their first hardcover book, George C. Calvert's *A Defense of the Dilettante.* They were to produce only one more book in Indianapolis, a study of the typography in *A Midsummer Night's Dream* by Mark Liddell of the Purdue English Department. By the end of the year, the brothers decided to move to California, where their Grabhorn Press became world famous.

Book Collecting. Indianapolis' most famous book collector was JOSIAH K. LILLY, JR., who formed his collection over a 30–year period beginning in 1925. He started out with first editions of Indiana authors, but his first major acquisition was a rare copy of Edgar Allen Poe's *Tamerlane* (1827), which he bought in 1929 for $25,000. He went on to collect English and American literature generally, then Americana, and finally the history of science and medicine. In 1956, when he donated this collection to Indiana University, it contained over 20,000 volumes and was valued at $5 million.

Josiah seems to have inspired his father, J. K. LILLY, SR., to start collecting as well. Starting in 1930, J. K. assembled the most comprehensive collection of first and early editions of Stephen Foster, which he donated to the University of Pittsburgh in 1936.

Bibliographical Research. Indianapolis is also associated with important bibliographical research, most notably the work of CHARLES EVANS. Evans was the first librarian of the Indianapolis Public Library. After his retirement in 1892, he set out to record everything printed in the early years of the United States. In 1934, twelve volumes later, his *American Bibliography* had covered the years 1639 through 1799.

Dorothy and Anthony Russo were booksellers and bibliographers who began working with the INDIANA HISTORICAL SOCIETY in 1929. Over the next 30 years, Dorothy authored or co-authored four of the finest author bibliographies ever produced, all on Indiana authors—KIN HUB-

BARD, James Whitcomb Riley, George Ade, and BOOTH TARKINGTON.

The most important of Josiah Lilly's bibliographical projects was his support of the work of Jacob Blanck. Blanck was responsible for the comprehensive descriptive *Bibliography of American Literature* of the 19th century, which began appearing in 1955, as well as for assisting the Russos with their Riley bibliography.

DAVID VAPRIN
Indianapolis–Marion County Public Library

Connie Goddard, "Computer Books in Indianapolis," *Publishers' Weekly* (Oct. 4, 1991), 44–46; G. Thomas Tanselle, "The Hoosier House: Indianapolis in the World of Books," in *Indianapolis in the World of Books* (Indianapolis, 1974), 30–49; Theodore F. Vonnegut, *Indianapolis Booksellers and Their Literary Background, 1822–1860* (Greenfield, Ind., 1926).

Bookwalter, Charles Andrews (Dec. 7, 1860–Oct. 26, 1926). Mayor of Indianapolis, 1901–1903, 1906–1910, Republican. Bookwalter was born on a farm near Wabash, Indiana; his family moved to Fort Wayne when he was eight. A newsboy at ten, at thirteen a printer's devil at the *Fort Wayne Gazette*, he learned the newspaper trade over the next half-dozen years. After 18 months working and traveling through the West, Bookwalter, then 21, returned to Fort Wayne, worked two years as a locomotive fireman, rejoined the *Gazette*, and two years later became city editor. In 1886, endorsed by the KNIGHTS OF LABOR and the REPUBLICAN PARTY, he narrowly lost an election for state representative. The following year he was appointed clerk of the State Printing Bureau, 1887–1891, in Indianapolis.

By 1893 Bookwalter was secretary of the city's Republican committee and in 1899, with the support of the Marion Club, an organization of younger men, captured the mayoral nomination from party elders. Few thought he could contest popular Democrat THOMAS TAGGART's bid for a third term, yet Bookwalter, campaigning vigorously, lost by fewer than 350 votes, an inroad of 3,000 on Taggart's previous majorities. In all, Bookwalter ran for mayor five times, winning in 1901 and 1906. His losses came in 1903 and 1913. In 1917, he withdrew his candidacy after

the primary. His loss in 1903 was attributable to a party split, a drumbeat of hostile articles in the *Indianapolis News*, and the clergy's denunciations of his failure to close the city's wine rooms and gambling dens.

Highlights of Bookwalter's years as mayor include his battle against a smallpox epidemic in his first term; building a long-needed city hall; an extensive street paving program; and the appointment of Dr. Henry W. Jameson, "father of the Indianapolis park system," as president of the park board. During his administration the TRACTION TERMINAL was built, with Bookwalter drawing up the contracts for the INTERURBAN railways entering the city. A champion of vocational education, in 1902 the mayor appealed to residents for money to purchase the federal arsenal from the War Department; and when the technical institute established there fell into difficulty about 1909, Bookwalter was named receiver. His zealous leadership was a crucial factor in the founding of ARSENAL TECHNICAL HIGH SCHOOL in 1912.

His varied business interests ran to real estate, a building association, a large and successful garment manufacturing company, and a book printing firm. He was one of the founders of the Marion Motor Company, 1902, and business manager of Merchant's Heat and Light Company.

In 1922 Bookwalter managed the campaign of Henry S. New for United States senator. As an ardent supporter of the successful 1921 mayoral campaign of LEW SHANK, he was rewarded with appointment as president of the board of park commissioners, 1922–1926, years which saw the construction of Kessler Boulevard. A dedicated clubman—Masons, Elks, Knights of Pythias—Bookwalter was a fierce partisan and controversialist. Brilliant and bellicose, he was regarded as the best platform orator of his day.

WILLIAM DOHERTY
Marian College

Paul Donald Brown, ed., *Indianapolis Men of Affairs* (Indianapolis, 1923); *Indianapolis Star*, Apr. 30, 1905, Oct. 27, 1926.

Boone County. County adjacent to Marion County on the northwest and part of the Indianapolis Metropolitan Statistical Area. Boone County's proximity to the capital has been an important factor in the area's growth and development over the years. Transportation routes between Indianapolis and the northern part of the state spurred early settlement. In 1828 the state legislature authorized construction of the MICHI-GAN ROAD from Indianapolis to Lake Michigan. It passed through the eastern part of Boone County and became one of the most traveled highways in the state. White settlement began in the 1820s, though the area around Thorntown was the site of an Indian settlement and French trading post in the 18th and early 19th centuries. The Eel River tribe of the Miami Indians resided there before the federal government removed most of them in the 1830s. The county was organized in 1830 with 600 residents and named after Daniel Boone, the Kentucky pioneer. A site in the area's geographic center, Lebanon, became county seat in 1831.

Railroad development in the 1850s boosted Boone County towns. The first line, the Indianapolis, Cincinnati and Lafayette Railroad, was completed in 1852. ZIONSVILLE and Whitestown sprang up along its route, and Lebanon prospered. By 1875 Boone County listed 30,000 residents and 150 manufacturing establishments, in addition to a thriving agricultural economy.

In the early 1900s interurban tracks crisscrossed the county as part of the Indianapolis-Lafayette-Crawfordsville lines. Lebanon was the hub of a traction network, though the lines proved unprofitable by the late 1920s. About the same time, a Lebanon native, reportedly nostalgic for his hometown, decided to relocate his business to the area. Henry Ulen, who made his fortune in an east coast construction firm, brought

his company to Lebanon in 1929. North of the city he developed the model town of Ulen, featuring elegant homes, boulevard lighting, and a country club for Ulen executives.

Another transportation route, Interstate 65, has been a catalyst for development in the 1980s and 1990s. Service establishments, including hotels and restaurants, continue to open along the route, while commuters enjoy direct access to Indianapolis. Boone County development officials predict steady growth in the area, hoping for new high-tech manufacturing facilities and satellite industries from Lafayette's Subaru-Isuzu automotive plant. They also plan for additional residential development as Indianapolis commuters are lured by small-town ambience.

In 1990 about 38,000 people lived in Boone County, a 22 percent increase over the 1970 figures. The number of farms has declined slightly, yet the county ranked tenth in 1989 among all Indiana counties in market value of its crops. Although the area was a prime producer of dairy products for the Indianapolis market in the 19th and early 20th centuries, Boone County farmers today raise corn, soybeans, and hogs. Most Boone County residents now work in retail or service establishments and small manufacturing concerns. Of the working population, about 32 percent were employed outside the county in the late 1980s.

CATHLEEN F. DONNELLY

Indianapolis Star Magazine, July 26, 1959; *Indianapolis News*, Dec. 27, 1990.

Booth Tarkington Civic Theatre. See Civic Theatre

Bostwick, Mary Elizabeth (Feb. 11, 1886–July 29, 1959). Pioneer woman reporter. Bostwick was born in Denver, Colorado, and after dropping out of high school got her start in journalism in 1903 at the *Denver Post*, known for its lurid crime news and the stunts and crusades of its star women reporters. There she covered the police beat and wrote humorous features. Around 1912 the publishers of the *Post* sent her to bolster their struggling *Kansas City Post*.

Selected Statistics for Boone County, 1990

Population	38,147
Population per Square Mile	90
Percent African-American	0.2
Percent 0 to 17 Years	27.4
Percent 65 Years and Over	12.8
Percent 25 Years and Over with a High School Degree or Equivalency	82.5
Percent 25 Years and Over with a College Degree	22.2
Per Capita Income in 1989	$20,025
Unemployment Rate (%)	2.7
Married-Couple Families as a Percent of Total Households	68.6
Median Home Value	$71,100

Soon afterward she took a job at the *Indianapolis Evening Sun* and worked on one of the biggest news events of the decade, the 1913 flood. She also reported many sensational trials of the day with dramatic and emotional flair. In 1914, she went to work for the *INDIANAPOLIS STAR* where her byline was a staple until her retirement in 1958.

Bostwick was among the few women correspondents of WORLD WAR I. On leave of absence from the paper, she joined BASE HOSPITAL NO. 32 in Contrexeville, France, as a stenographer. A series of articles on her experiences ran on the front page of the *Star* in August, 1918. During the 1920s she became a stunt reporter. Disguised as a mechanic in a car driven by Howdy Wilcox, she was the first woman to ride in a race car during practice for the INDIANAPOLIS 500–MILE RACE. Her stories about flying, and sometimes crashing, in dirigibles, hot air balloons, gliders, and open-cockpit planes were avidly followed. In 1930s and 1940s she continued to cover most major trials and wrote a daily column called "Last Page Lyric" in which she composed a little rhyme about an event in the day's news.

JANET FRY SCHNEIDER
Indiana University, Bloomington

Indiana Biography Series, Indiana State Library; *Indianapolis Star*, Mar. 15, 1992.

Boswell, Charles H., Administration of. Democratic mayor of Indianapolis from 1959 to 1962, "Charlie" Boswell (b. Oct. 31, 1909, Henderson, Kentucky) had a hardscrabble youth in the city's HAUGHVILLE area. A graduate of Indiana University with degrees in sociology, he was, before taking political office, chief probation officer of the Marion County Juvenile Court. He served as city controller under Mayor PHILLIP L. BAYT, succeeding him when Bayt resigned on January 1, 1959, after being elected MARION COUNTY PROSECUTOR. Boswell won the mayor's office in his own right in a city election 11 months later.

The Boswell administration generated significant funds from the landmark action of depositing tax revenues in interest-bearing bank accounts, a practice later copied by county and state governments. Among other things, the financial windfall enabled the city to purchase land and begin an unprecedented growth in recreational facilities such as golf courses, swimming pools, and PLAYGROUNDS.

During the Bayt administration, a heavy flooding of EAGLE CREEK nearly devastated the town of SPEEDWAY. Boswell, as the city's financial officer, worked with Bayt in initiating a flood control project that was to become Eagle Creek Reservoir. The first phase of that improvement used bond financing through the city's Flood Control Board. Such a city tax base, Boswell noted later as mayor, was inadequate for recreational development at the site and for larger physical needs elsewhere. He went to local business leaders proposing the creation of countywide flood control, sanitation, parks, and airport authorities. He won their support, and laws creating the new governmental units were enacted by the Indiana General Assembly in 1961.

Federal aid for slum clearance and public housing was an issue during Boswell's term. Indianapolis newspapers and local business leaders adamantly opposed such aid. Boswell recalled years later that little federal money actually was available and that battles on the issue could have jeopardized other programs. Instead, Boswell worked with the CHAMBER OF COMMERCE and FLANNER HOUSE, a community self-help organization, in acquiring slum land and clearing it for new housing. The project attracted national attention because of its not-for-profit, go-it-alone concept, as well as the pride of home ownership created by construction labor that included people who were to live in the new dwellings.

Boswell continued sanitary and storm sewer construction and one-way street development started by Bayt. When he resigned as mayor on August 4, 1962, to become postmaster of Indianapolis, newspaper editorials commended him for a fiscally responsible administration without tax increases and for a drop in crime rates. After the reorganization that created the U.S. Postal Service, he became its district director for Indiana. He retired from that post in 1987.

JAMES E. FARMER

Bowen Site (ca. 1000 A.D.). Best documented of seven known Late Woodland village sites along White River in Hamilton and Marion counties that are included in the "Oliver Phase." The Oliver Phase was a cultural mixture between Late Woodland (Fort Ancient) and the Upper Mississippian influences between 800 and 1300 A.D. Pottery styles indicate a greater Fort Ancient (eastern) influence. The site was located on a glacial outwash terrace just north of WHITE RIVER and east of Keystone Avenue. Following a salvage excavation from 1959 to 1965 by Indiana University, the site area was mined for gravel.

The 0.78–acre excavation delineated a 200–foot diameter village and burial area with 120 features such as fire and refuse pits. No evidence of permanent habitation was found. Artifacts included pottery sherds, chipped stone, ground stone and bone, large amounts of unworked bone, and waste piles of mussel shells. Tools recovered on site included projectile points, hammers, axes, grinding stones, antlers, and other bones. The lack of permanent structures and the food-type distribution indicate that the Bowen Site was a transient, warmer weather habitation. The animal bone debris and the number of burials suggest a transient population of about 100 people over one generation. Thirty-nine of 42 burials were studied. The oldest burial was 70 years of age, the youngest 7 months. No male burials between ages 14 and 23 were found, while 5 female burials between ages 17 and 20 were found. This distribution of remains suggests young male death and burial away from the village, probably due to accidents and warfare, while young female deaths were likely due to first time childbirth trauma.

KEVIN STRUNK

John T. Dorwin, *The Bowen Site: An Archaeological Study of Culture Process in the Late Prehistory of Central Indiana*, Prehistory Research Series, Vol. 4, no. 4 (Indianapolis: Indiana Historical Society, 1971).

Bowers, Claude Gernade (Nov. 20, 1878–Jan. 21, 1958). Journalist, politician, orator, historian, and diplomat. Born and reared in rural communities in central Indiana, Bowers moved to Indianapolis at age 13 with his divorced mother. As a student at Indianapolis High School, he was a voracious reader and became a confirmed Democrat. In 1898 the youth graduated and also won the state oratorical contest, but lacked the money to attend college. Instead he worked for a publisher, the future BOBBS-MERRILL COMPANY. In 1900 he became the major editorial writer for the *INDIANA STATE SENTINEL*, Indianapolis' Democratic daily, and gave the first of hundreds of speeches for the Democracy. His rapid-fire delivery soon earned him the title "Gatling Gun Orator of the Wabash."

From 1903 until 1923 Bowers lived in Terre Haute, Washington, D.C., and Fort Wayne. He wrote editorials for the *Terre Haute Gazette* and *Star* advocating Progressive reforms and served on the Board of Public Works. Defeated for Congress in 1904 and 1906 by the Republican incumbent, Bowers went to Washington in 1911 as secretary to Senator JOHN W. KERN. During Woodrow Wilson's presidency Kern became the first party whip and shepherded New Freedom legislation through the Senate. Bowers handled many responsibilities for the overworked solon—important office duties, liaison work with constituents, and speeches in Indiana. Kern's defeat sent Bowers in 1917 to Fort Wayne where for six years he contributed editorials to the *Journal-Gazette*.

Bowers' national prominence followed his move to New York in 1923. He was an editorialist first for Pulitzer's *Evening World* and in 1931 for the *Evening Journal*, which distributed his signed columns in other Hearst newspapers coast to coast. He befriended and wrote speeches for Robert F. Wagner, Al Smith, and Franklin D. Roosevelt. At the 1928 Democratic convention Bowers delivered a memorable keynote address and in 1932 campaigned for FDR.

Bowers' historical works also brought him a national reputation. *The Irish Orators* (1916) was followed in 1918 and 1932 by laudatory biographies of Senator Kern and Hoosier Republican ALBERT J. BEVERIDGE; *The Party Battles of the Jackson Period* (1922), a vigorous defense of the seventh president; the charming *Spanish Adventures of Washington Irving* (1940); and *Pierre Vergniaud* (1950), praising this French revolutionary orator. Bowers' fame as a historian rests principally on two other works: *Jefferson and Hamilton* (1925) and *The Tragic Era* (1929). In the former the author applauded the Virginian for championing democracy while excoriating his opponent for defending aristocratic interests. In *The Tragic Era* the partisan historian blamed Radical Republicans for humiliating white southerners following the Civil War. *Jefferson in Power* (1936) and *The Young Jefferson* (1945) completed Bowers' trilogy on his democratic hero. Recent historians have taken issue with Bowers' interpretations of Jefferson and Reconstruction. Yet *Jefferson and Hamilton* has gone through 27 printings, and *The Tragic Era* probably has attracted a larger readership than any other study on Reconstruction.

In 1933 Bowers became important internationally. He was Roosevelt's ambassador to Spain, 1933–1939, and then served the New Deal and Truman as minister to Chile, 1939–1953. In Madrid Bowers sought to improve Spanish-American trade. During the Spanish Civil War, 1936–1939, he favored the Spanish Republic's unsuccessful fight to defeat General Franco's rebel forces, which were aided by Mussolini and Hitler. In Santiago the ambassador helped convince the reluctant Chilean government to break relations with the Axis in 1943. Bowers also worked to increase Chile's vital wartime exports of copper and promoted cultural exchanges and political cooperation during the Cold War.

Back in New York in 1953, the transplanted Hoosier continued his partisan Democratic activities, working with Eleanor Roosevelt and advising Adlai Stevenson. Bowers also wrote two volumes on his ambassadorships to Spain and Chile, and his almost completed autobiography was published posthumously.

PETER J. SEHLINGER
Indiana University–Purdue University,
Indianapolis

Claude G. Bowers, *My Life: The Memoirs of Claude Bowers* (New York, 1962); Holman Hamilton and Gayle Thornbrough, eds., *Indianapolis in the "Gay Nineties": The High School Diaries of Claude G. Bowers* (Indianapolis, 1964); Sabine Jessner and Peter J. Sehlinger, "Claude G. Bowers: A Partisan Hoosier," *Indiana Magazine of History*, 83 (Sept., 1987), 217–243.

Bowles, Janet Payne (June 29, 1872 or 1873–July 18, 1948). Metalsmith and jeweler. Born in Indianapolis, Bowles graduated from Indianapolis (later SHORTRIDGE) High School in 1890. After her marriage in 1895 to Joseph Moore Bowles, a graphic designer and printer, she moved to Boston, where she displayed her book illuminations at the second exhibition of the Society of Arts and Crafts (1899). During this time she began to study metalsmithing and established a metalworking studio in New York City.

J. Pierpont Morgan commissioned Bowles to make gold chalices, spoons, and plates. Another early order was from the painter and theatrical designer John Alexander, for the stage actress Maude Adams. Bowles reportedly made ecclesiastical metalwork for St. Patrick's Cathedral and the Cathedral of St. John the Divine in New York. Bowles exhibited in New York, Boston, London, and Paris, and regularly at the John Herron Art Institute (later the INDIANAPOLIS MUSEUM OF ART). In 1910 she displayed her metalwork at the fourth annual exhibition of the National Society of Craftsmen (New York). She won a bronze medal at the Panama-Pacific International Exposition in 1915 (San Francisco).

Bowles returned to Indianapolis in 1912, where she taught classes in jewelry, metalsmithing and, from about 1927, pottery at Shortridge High School for 28 years. In 1920 Bowles won the first prize offered by Bosselini, a Florentine art patron, for a gold chalice. Among artists who competed with Bowles for this prize was Rene Lalique, with whom she later studied. In 1924 Bowles exhibited her work at the Art Center in New York City where in 1929–1930 she had a solo exhibit. During this period Bowles created custom-made jewelry for Gorham's Fifth Avenue New York shop. In addition to her metalwork, Bowles was the author of *Gossamer to Steel* (1917) and *Complete Story of the Christmas Tree* (1918).

BARRY SHIFMAN
Indianapolis Museum of Art

Barry Shifman, with contributions by W. Scott Braznell and Sharon S. Darling, *The Arts & Crafts Metalwork of Janet Payne Bowles* (Indianapolis Museum of Art, 1993)

Bowling. Popular sport and recreational activity which evolved from European ninepins and skittles. Often associated with taverns and gambling during the early 19th century, bowling gradually became a respectable family pastime and debuted in Indianapolis in the 1880s with the opening of several establishments. Andrew Hermany installed two alleys in a shed behind his tavern at West and Washington streets, and the German Lyra bowling club opened a ninepin alley in Turner Hall, but later switched to the more popular tenpin version. Germans also built four alleys in Das Deutsche Haus (now the ATHENAEUM) in the 1890s. The sport quickly gained a local following, resulting in the American Bowling Congress's (ABC, organized 1895 as a sanctioning body) third ever tournament at TOMLINSON HALL in 1903. The competition attracted 78 five-man teams over seven days and offered a prize purse worth $4,137. Pins were set by hand on ten specially constructed alleys (known today as lanes) on the hall's second floor. Bowling's growing popularity led local aficionados to establish the Indianapolis Men's Bowling Association in 1906.

By the time the ABC tournament returned to Indianapolis in 1936, bowling had become so popular that a larger facility had to be secured. Tournament organizers installed 32 lanes in the Indiana State Fairgrounds Coliseum to accommodate 2,853 teams from across the nation that competed over 37 days for prizes totaling $108,928. There were two Indianapolis winners: Falls City Hi-Bru in the team event with a 3,089 three-game total, and John Murphy in all-events with a nine-game score of 2,006. Indianapolis hosted its third ABC tournament in 1974 at the Indiana Convention Center, where 40 lanes with fully automatic pinspotters were set up. The tournament ran 79 days; 6,138 teams vied for shares of a prize purse worth $793,055.

Following the creation of the Women's International Bowling Congress (WIBC) in 1916 as the official sanctioning body, local women formed their own governing body—the Indianapolis Women's Bowling Association (December, 1919)—which sponsored its first tournament that year. As women demonstrated growing support for bowling, the WIBC selected Indianapolis to host its tournaments three times. The ten-day 1924 competition saw 126 teams bowl at the 12-lane Central Lanes on West Ohio Street. Alice Feeney of Indianapolis won the singles title with a 593 score. The 1934 tournament, held at Pritchett's Recreation on East Maryland Street, drew 253 teams over 18 days to compete for $8,697 in prize money. Meadows Bowl hosted the 1975 tournament, which attracted 5,720 teams over 50 days to vie for $413,949 in prizes.

Over the years bowling establishments have come and gone. The heyday for bowling, according to the Greater Indianapolis Bowling Association, was the 1950s following the introduction of automatic pinspotters and the founding of the Indianapolis Junior Bowling Association (1958) to attract younger bowlers to the sport. Sport Bowl (opened 1941 and the oldest in the city) at 3900 South East Street became Indianapolis' first center to install the new pinsetting machinery. By 1955 there were 32 bowling establishments citywide with 412 total lanes; in 1964, there were 35 centers with 738 lanes; and in 1977, 29 with 916 lanes. As the population spread to the suburbs, bowling centers vanished from the downtown area; in 1993 there were 17 centers with 672 lanes scattered around the city. Indianapolis reportedly is the only city in the nation with three 80-lane bowling centers: Expo Bowl, 5261 Elmwood Drive; Western Bowl, 6441 West Washington Street; and Woodland Bowl, 3421 East 96th Street. The sport claims nearly 100,000 devotees locally.

Three Indianapolis bowlers have gained national prominence in the sport. Richard A. "Dick" Weber (b. 1929) learned to bowl at Sport Bowl and worked as a pinsetter at Carl Hindel's Indiana Alleys, 128 West Washington Street. Serving as Weber's mentor, Hindel advised him in 1955 to accept a job with the St. Louis–based Budweiser professional team. On March 12, 1958, Weber bowled 775 when his team set a world-record three game total score of 3,858, a record which still stands. That same year Weber became one of 33 charter members of the Professional Bowlers Association (PBA). During the 1965 Houston Open, Weber became the first pro to roll three perfect games in a tournament. He also was the first player to win PBA titles in five decades when he and Justin Hromek captured the PBA Touring

Pro-Senior Doubles title in 1992, Weber's 32nd title of his career (26 on the regular tour, 6 on the seniors circuit). Weber is a member of the ABC, PBA, Missouri, St. Louis, Indiana, and Indianapolis bowling halls of fame.

Pat Dryer (b. 1929) began her bowling career at age 12. She was the first Bowling Proprietors Association of America (BPAA) National Doubles champion with Marge Hitt in 1950 and had the highest average (200) in the nation for women that year. Dryer was a member of the Hickman Oldsmobile Whirlaway team that won a WIBC title in 1951. A member of the first women's professional tour, Dryer has been inducted into the WIBC, Indiana, and Indianapolis bowling halls of fame.

Mike Aulby (b. 1960) learned to bowl at Beech Grove Bowl and became a teenage phenomenon. At age 19 the lefthander joined the PBA Tour, and after winning his first title, the PBA National in June, 1979, was named PBA Rookie of the Year. In 1985 Aulby became the first PBA player to win more than $200,000 ($201,500) in one year and was named PBA Player of the Year. He also set a one-year earnings record of $298,237 in 1989 when he was named PBA Player of the Year and Bowler of the Year. With a victory at Green Bay, Wisconsin, in 1992, Aulby became only the seventh player to win 20 PBA titles.

Three Indianapolis bowlers have served as president of the American Bowling Congress: former mayor CHARLES A. BOOKWALTER, 1902–1903; former Indianapolis postmaster Robert H. Bryson, 1906–1907, 1909–1912; and Neil C. King, 1940–1941.

DICK DENNY
Indianapolis News

Boxing. Very little is known about boxing in early– and mid–19th century Indianapolis. Professional boxing was not yet organized. At that time there was a big difference between "professional prize fighting" and amateur "boxing." Prize fighting was a hooligans' sport promoted by gamblers and saloonkeepers. Boxing, or the "manly art of self-defense," was a gentlemanly form of exercise taught and practiced at YMCAs and private athletic clubs across the country.

Professional boxing's image changed in the early 1890s. James "Gentleman Jim" Corbett, a prominent San Francisco banker, gained national fame as a heavyweight contender and was the first professional fighter backed by a private athletic club. His knockout of hulking heavyweight champion John L. Sullivan in New Orleans in 1892 ushered in a new age of respectability for prize fighting. Big brawlers were out; lithe, crafty ring tacticians were all the rage. One boxer who took advantage of this new trend was Moscow, Indiana, native Norman Selby. Selby billed himself as Kid McCoy from Indianapolis and actually fought several bouts in the city in the early 1890s, but he never trained or lived in the capital. The popular expression "the real McCoy" is attributed to Selby's career.

Prize fights were illegal in most states until well into the 20th century. But by the early 1900s boxing was a popular sport nationwide and many tolerant cities permitted professional fights. In Indianapolis local promoters staged regular shows at the INDIANAPOLIS ATHLETIC CLUB. By 1912 fights between well-known contenders were being held at TOMLINSON HALL, the West Washington Street Ballpark, the Virginia Avenue Auditorium, and CADLE TABERNACLE. Several local fighters from this era became famous contenders and champions. Ray Bronson and Milburn Saylor fought championship bouts in several different weight classes and Jack Dillon, the "Hoosier Bearcat," became middleweight champion.

In the years preceding World War I, reformers pressured officials to enforce the state law against prize fighting. In 1913 Mayor JOSEPH E. BELL announced that he would permit only one boxing match in the city each year. Local promoters fought over the rights to the annual match, which was held on the eve of the INDIANAPOLIS 500–MILE RACE. Reports of bribery and political corruption were widespread and Governor Samuel Ralston stepped in to stop the match in 1916.

Concern about the evil effects of boxing diminished after the war, and by the 1920s Indianapolis had gained a national reputation as a good inland fight town. Louis Farb, who handled prominent fighters Jack Dillon and Kid Chissell, became one of the best known promoters in the Midwest. Farb was the first promoter to stage fights at Cadle Tabernacle and twice drew crowds of over 10,000 there.

Despite the legalization of boxing in 1931, local interest in professional matches waned in the 1930s and 1940s. In 1952 a group of businessmen formed the Hoosier Boxing Club (HBC) to promote professional boxing in Indianapolis and help develop young prospects. Within three months HBC President Robert Wormser arranged the city's first nationally televised fight. The 10–round exhibition match between lightweight champ Kid Gavilan and Fitzie Pruden took place at the INDIANA STATE FAIRGROUNDS Coliseum before 7,200 fans.

Local promoters continued to stage fights around Indianapolis, particularly at TYNDALL ARMORY, but local interest in professional boxing remained low. The early 1970s saw a new interest in the sport with the rise of local boxer Marvin Johnson. After winning several national amateur titles and a bronze medal at the 1972 Olympics, Johnson was considered one of the most promising young fighters in the nation. Two other local fighters, Norman Goins and Sammy Nesmith, achieved national fame as lightweight and middleweight contenders but neither made it to the top of the profession. Johnson was more fortunate, winning the light heavyweight crown with a knockout of Mate Parlov in Marsala, Italy, in 1978. In 1979 he defended his world title in a nationally televised bout against Matthew Franklin at MARKET SQUARE ARENA. Johnson lost the fight but went on to win the title two more times. His third championship victory, a TKO of champion Leslie Stewart at Market Square Arena in 1986, made him the only man to win the light heavyweight crown three times.

Widespread interest in amateur boxing began with the establishment of the Golden Gloves program in 1933. Local amateur boxers competed for championships in the annual state Golden Gloves tournament in Indianapolis. Held either at the armory or at the BUTLER UNIVERSITY fieldhouse, this tournament's final round regularly drew crowds of over 6,000. Today the state Golden Gloves tournament is held at the INDIANA CONVENTION CENTER.

During the early 1970s ring experts considered Indianapolis to have the nation's best amateur boxing. Two men responsible for the city's success were SARGE JOHNSON at Camp Atterbury and Colion "Champ" Chaney of the POLICE ATHLETIC LEAGUE clubs. Chaney began a long association with Marvin Johnson in 1969. U.S. National Boxing Coach Sarge Johnson became internationally famous for his work with the 1976 U.S. Olympic Boxing Team that won five gold medals at the Montreal games. He trained many local fighters, most notably Goins and Nesmith, before dying tragically in a 1980 plane crash that claimed the lives of the entire U.S. National Boxing Team.

WILLIAM D. DALTON

Boy Scouts of America, Crossroads of America Council.

The Boy Scout movement began in England in 1908 and was introduced in the United States in 1910. That same year, Indianapolis Troop One, Tuxedo Park Baptist Church, started with the Reverend U. S. Clutton as scoutmaster.

On November 17, 1914, the Indianapolis council was organized and chartered with a membership of 100 boys. The first scout executive of the council was F. O. Belzer, who served until 1940 and after whom Camp Belzer in northeastern Marion County is named. Homer T. Gratz succeeded Belzer but served for only six months before being drafted. Subsequent scout executives have been Delmer H. Wilson (1941–1950), Frank M. Chase (1950–1973), Robert L. Calvert (1973–1982), and A. John Bosio (1983–present).

The council has had a history of mergers, the most recent occurring in 1972 when councils headquartered in Indianapolis, Anderson, Muncie, and Richmond consolidated as the Crossroads of America Council, B.S.A., which includes 19 counties. Following a successful capital campaign and a generous gift from Edward J. F. and Fern Roesch of Indianapolis, the council opened its first owned headquarters in 1990 at 1900 North Meridian Street. Currently the council operates year-round camping and program centers at Indianapolis and near Anderson, Muncie, Connersville, Bloomington, and Martinsville. In 1991, its programs served 51,318 boys, young men, and young women and had 14,479 volunteers enrolled.

The scout mission, "to serve others by helping to instill values in young people and, in other ways, to prepare them to make ethical choices over their lifetime . . . ," is exemplified by programs like the "Good Turn" or service project, a long-standing scouting tradition. During WORLD WARS I and II, Scouts sold liberty bonds and war savings stamps, took a census of walnut trees to be used for gun stocks, and collected scrap metal, old tires, and newspapers. Later projects included collecting clothing for overseas relief in 1950, placing Liberty Bell doorknob hangers to get out the vote in 1952, planting trees in 1954, delivering handbooks prepared by the Office of CIVIL DEFENSE in 1958, distributing brochures on the need for donating human organs in 1986, and, annually since 1988, collecting food for pantries, kitchens, and food banks. The council's service orientation also is seen in its emphasis on serving special populations such as young people with disabilities, those in public housing and other low-income neighborhoods, and those in the Indiana Boys' School and the Juvenile Detention Center.

The council's annual budget of ca. $3 million comes from the UNITED WAY; Friends of Scouting; foundations, projects, grants; Bowl-A-Thon and popcorn sale; Scout Shop; and trust funds.

A. JOHN BOSIO
Crossroads of America Council
Boy Scouts of America

Boys and Girls Clubs of Indianapolis.

Social service organization focusing on youth. The organization was begun in 1893 as the Newsboys' Home by Thomas C. Day, CALEB S. DENNY (three-term mayor of Indianapolis), Mrs. Denny, and M. V. McGilliard, a local philanthropist. Influenced by the women of the Dashaway Club in Hartford, Connecticut, who in 1860 organized the first boys' club in the United States, the Indianapolis founders desired to get youth off the streets, provide them with a sense of belonging, and encourage values and skill development.

The Newsboys' Home became the Boys' Home and Employment Association after the first year, then the Boys' Club and Employment Asso-

ciation in 1895, and the Boys' Club Association in 1898. The local club was one of 53 charter clubs of Boys' Clubs of America, incorporated nationally in 1906.

Club members met in rented basement rooms until 1897 when heirs of John Maurice Butler donated the first clubhouse at Madison Avenue and South Meridian Street. Nearly 8,000 boys and girls are now served at six clubs and a camp near Noblesville. Membership is open to all youth regardless of race or religion, from kindergarten through high school.

The clubs currently are located in strategic areas of the city to serve at-risk youth. Programs of the national Boys and Girls Clubs of America and local programs offered by professional staff and volunteers include counseling and career development, cultural enrichment, social recreation, citizenship and leadership development, individual and team sports. The organization presents Youth of the Year awards and Horatio Alger and Outstanding Alumni awards.

The organization became the Boys and Girls Clubs of Indianapolis in 1991. Income support comes from endowments, the corporate community, service organizations, philanthropists, individual volunteers, and the UNITED WAY. In 1993, the 100th anniversary year, the organization completed a $4 million capital campaign, initiating major expansion at the six clubs and the Noblesville camp.

JAMES R. EAST
Indiana University–Purdue University,
Indianapolis

Bradford, James L. (1903–Apr. 26, 1960). Marion County Republican chairman, 1940–1944. Bradford graduated from ARSENAL TECHNICAL HIGH SCHOOL in Indianapolis in 1921 and in 1924 became a Republican volunteer by working at the polls. A year later he was elected a precinct committeeman. Bradford later served as secretary of the 7th district committee, head of the Republican registration committee, and ward chairman, prior to gaining control of the MARION COUNTY organization in 1940 by ousting Carl Vandivier as county chairman. When Bradford was reelected in 1942, he became the first county chairman in 40 years to receive that honor.

Following the defeat of his mayoral candidate, Henry E. Ostrom, in the 1942 primary, Bradford resisted pressure from hostile GOP officials to step aside; he agreed to do so only after his opponents accepted Ostrom as his successor as county chairman in 1944. In 1942, Bradford served as MARION COUNTY AUDITOR for six months, filling an unexpired term. From 1944 to 1946, he turned his interests to the state organization of the Republican party by serving as district chairman. He worked as a service area inspector of the Indiana Toll Road Commission from 1957 until his death. Bradford was a member of the Mystic Tie Masonic Lodge, SCOTTISH RITE, Murat Shrine, and the COLUMBIA CLUB.

GENE AUSTIN

Indiana Biography Series, Indiana State Library; *Indianapolis Star*, Apr. 27, 1960.

Brendonwood. Model residential subdivision situated between Fall Creek and East 56th Street at roughly the 5700–6300 blocks. Charles Lewis established Brendonwood Common, Inc., in 1917. It is a unique 350–acre self-regulated, nonprofit, country-styled residential park, eight miles northeast of downtown Indianapolis.

Formerly forest, brush, and farmland along FALL CREEK, Lewis acquired and developed the land into 110 single-family home plots plus common areas, all enhanced by their natural environment and plantings. Noted landscape architect and planner GEORGE E. KESSLER and civil engineer A. H. Moore helped design and oversee land clearance, grading, road construction, and utility installation. The curvilinear streets and scenic vistas of Kessler's plan reflect a suburban expression of the City Beautiful movement of the early 20th century. Initially, George U. Davis supervised field reforestation, special shrubbery plantings, plus seven rows of elm trees in the mall entrance (later damaged by disease), and installed a nursery for seedlings. The plantings, through time, have grown more beautiful. Lewis established protective guidelines concerning membership, a board of directors, assessments, and common and residential area maintenance while creating the park setting. For a time, an island in Fall Creek provided children with a private recreation area.

Residential plots and roads have names reflecting indigenous characteristics, like "Cloverhill." Architectural styles vary from Tudor to Ranch. No business can be established in the residential community. Roads, and recreational facilities such as the pool, tennis courts, and Common House, are owned by all residents for their private use. The nine-hole golf course became a victory garden during World War II.

JANE T. WALKER

Montgomery S. Lewis, *Brendonwood: A Dream— A Reality* (1943).

Bretzman, Charles (July 26, 1866–Jan. 19, 1934) **and C. Noble** (May 17, 1909–Nov. 24, 1986). Noted father and son photographers. Charles was born in Hanover, Germany, and came to America in 1885. He set up his photographic studio in Indianapolis in 1895, specializing in portraits. The studio's location on the top floor of the Fletcher Trust Building enabled Bretzman and his employees to use the roof for setting out printing frames to develop in the sun. Bretzman also served for a time as the first official photographer of the INDIANAPOLIS 500–MILE RACE. A member of several civic organizations, he cofounded the Indianapolis Photographers Association and was a member of the Daguerre Club of Indiana.

C. Noble Bretzman, born in Indianapolis, began his career sweeping the floors of his father's studio, though he soon became a journeyman retoucher and staff photographer. After graduation from SHORTRIDGE HIGH SCHOOL, he attended a school for professional photographers at Winona Lake, Indiana. He worked for a time in New York City, where he was Radio City Music Hall's first public relations photographer and took pictures of the Rockettes. Noble also set up his own studio specializing in illustrative photography. His business flourished as advertisers began to request photography instead of artwork to illustrate their products. He returned to Indianapolis in 1934 after the death of his father, took over the family business, and introduced his distinctive style to local advertisers.

Before signing an exclusive contract with L. S. AYRES, Noble took fashion photographs for a number of Indianapolis department stores. His photography was credited with inspiring the slogan, "The Ayres Look." He was also a noted portrait photographer.

In his later years, Noble became passionately interested in ballet. He was a cofounding board member of Indianapolis' first professional ballet company. He later served as vice-president and general manager for the INDIANAPOLIS BALLET THEATRE. Just before his death he founded Bravo Project, Inc., a not-for-profit corporation to interest school-age Marion County youngsters in the performing arts.

Noble Bretzman donated his negative files and his father's business records to the INDIANA HISTORICAL SOCIETY in 1980.

CATHLEEN F. DONNELLY

Indianapolis Star, Jan. 20, 1934, Nov. 26, 1986; *Indianapolis Star Magazine*, Dec. 14, 1980.

Brewing Industry. The brewing of beer in Indianapolis, as in the rest of the United States, was predominantly a German enterprise. William Wernweg, a contractor for the NATIONAL ROAD bridges, and John L. Young are credited with establishing the first brewery in Indianapolis in 1834. It lasted until about 1840, and Rene Faux then operated it for about two years. These and other early breweries produced what was called "strong beer"—neither ale nor lager.

The first successful brewery in the city was established in 1859 by Christian Frederick Schmidt and Charles Jaeger on Wyoming Street at High. In a few years Jaeger sold his interest to Schmidt, at which time the brewery had annual sales of about 1,500 barrels. Schmidt was the first to produce lager beer in any quantity. The marked superiority of this bottom-fermented beer, plus the concentration of troops in Indianapolis during the Civil War, were major factors in the success of the Schmidt Brewery. When C. F. Schmidt died in 1872 his widow, Caroline, operated the business with the help of her brother William Fieber until

Idealized view of the C. F. Schmidt Brewery's facilities. [Indiana Historical Society, #KC4]

his death in 1874, and then by herself until her death in 1877. Two sons, John W. Schmidt and Edward Schmidt, then operated the brewery, which by 1886 had agencies in Terre Haute, Crawfordsville, Columbus, Brazil, and Shelbyville, Indiana, and Danville, Illinois.

In 1863 Peter Lieber, in conjunction with his brother Herman and CHARLES MAYER, bought the Gagg & Company brewery that had been founded in 1859. In 1871 the Lieber Brewery was relocated to Madison Avenue, south of Morris Street. Lieber's beer was actually bottled by Jacob Metzger and Company, in a plant across the street from the brewery. (Prior to 1890 the Internal Revenue Department required that the bottling of beer had to be separated from the brewery proper by a street, and that the beer had to be barreled and a tax stamp applied before transporting it to the bottler.)

In October, 1889, the Schmidt and Lieber breweries combined with the Maus Brewery (established by Casper Maus in 1868) to form the Indianapolis Brewing Company, which was owned by an English syndicate. Initially, the three breweries all continued to operate, with the general office and bottling operations located at the Schmidt plant. In 1900 the Indianapolis Brewing Company's Dusseldorfer beer won a gold medal at the Paris Exposition. It also won the grand prize at the Louisiana Purchase Exposition at St. Louis in 1904 and the gold medal at Liege, Belgium, in 1906.

Other breweries emerged at the end of the 19th century, including the Home Brewing Company (1891) established by William P. Jungclaus,

August Hook, and others at Cruse and Daly streets, and the American Brewing Company founded in 1897 by Joseph C. Schaf at the corner of Ohio and Missouri streets.

All local breweries closed in 1918 with the adoption of national prohibition. Indianapolis Brewing reopened after prohibition ended in 1933, but closed for good when then-owner Lawrence P. Bardin went to prison for selling short-filled bottles during the 1940s. After a long drought, brewing in the Hoosier capital was revived in the early 1990s by a microbrewery (under 10,000 barrels) that adopted the proud name of one of its predecessors: Indianapolis Brewing Company. In addition, a brewpub (beer brewed and consumed on the same premises) called the Broad Ripple Brewpub began operations at 65th and Cornell.

JAMES C. TALLEY

Bridgeport. Westside community located eight miles from the Circle, along U.S. 40. In 1830, Samuel Barlow laid out the village at the site of a toll gate on the NATIONAL ROAD. Named for a bridge spanning White Lick Creek, Bridgeport was platted in May, 1831. Early businesses included a general store, wagon maker, shoemaker, and a public house, called the Wayside Inn, built about 1840. According to local lore, the inn hosted President Martin Van Buren when rain and mud halted his inspection of the National Road. The inn was razed in 1941 when the state widened U.S. 40.

Despite its location on a busy thoroughfare, Bridgeport grew slowly as a stopover for travelers and a local center for trade. In the 1920s about 250 people lived in the community, though as Indianapolis expanded westward that number increased to 2,000 by 1980. Never an incorporated town, Bridgeport became a part of Indianapolis under UNIGOV. On the outskirts of town, the Jameson Camp was founded in 1928 as a nutritional program to serve children at risk of contracting tuberculosis. In 1993, the camp continues to offer summer programs for children with minor health, emotional, or social problems. During the school year the camp's facilities are rented to community groups for special events and also house the Wayne Township Junior High School alternative programs.

PAT WATSON

Indianapolis News, Feb. 3, 1923, May 25, 1978; Berry R. Sulgrove, *History of Indianapolis and Marion County* (Philadelphia, 1884).

Bridges. Noted landscape architect George E. Kessler in 1922 proclaimed Indianapolis' greatest possessions to be its beautiful bridges. Many WATERWAYS, including WHITE RIVER, FALL CREEK, Eagle Creek, and Pleasant Run, pass through the county. Though unnavigable for commercial purposes, these streams interrupted overland travel and transport and required bridging. The resulting structures, first wood, then metal and, later, concrete, contributed to the growth, development, and attractiveness of Marion County.

White River presented the most formidable obstacle to early pioneers. The construction of the NATIONAL ROAD through Marion County in the early 1830s necessitated the construction of a wooden covered bridge over the river in 1834. Built by Lewis Wernweg and Walter Blake, the two-span structure served until 1872. Soon thereafter, a three-span structure built by the famed bridge-building Kennedy family of Rushville carried Southport Road over White River near West

The Capitol Avenue bridge over Fall Creek in 1916. The original St. Vincent Hospital building on Fall Creek Parkway is visible in the background. [Indiana Historical Society, Bass Collection, #49476F]

Newton. This bridge became one of the longest wooden bridges in the state.

Metal replaced wood as the preferred bridge material in the 1880s. Railroad companies constructed metal bridges over Marion County's waterways from the 1880s through the 1930s. The new material was both stronger and safer, since sparks from the increasingly massive railroad locomotives could set fire to wooden structures. Many metal bridges served Marion County's roads as well, often replacing older wooden bridges. The growth of the city stimulated the construction of many iron bridges including the Kentucky Avenue bridge (1894) over White River, which was important to the industrial growth of the southwestern part of the county.

In the early 1900s concrete bridges began to appear throughout Indianapolis. Following the disastrous flood of 1913, concrete spans replaced several bridges of both wood and metal that the raging waters had carried away. Some of the early concrete bridges were quite ornate; a good example is the Meridian Street bridge (1913) over Fall Creek. Probably the most imposing concrete span ever built in Marion County was the Emrichsville Bridge (1906) over White River south of present 16th Street. The bridge had a stone archway on one end, its corner tower giving the bridge a medieval appearance. The bridge was demolished following World War II because it delayed travelers to the INDIANAPOLIS 500–MILE RACE. In the 1930s the WPA provided employment and built several concrete bridges around Marion County, including the Shelby Street bridge (1938) over Pleasant Run and the New York Street bridge (1939) over White River. By this time bridges had become more functional in appearance.

After World War II new bridge construction altered the growth patterns for suburban Indianapolis. Most notable was the West 38th Street bridge (1962) over White River, which spurred development in the northwest sector of the city. The six-lane bridge linked that area of the county with new Interstate 465, and officials touted the bridge as the "gateway to the West."

Most of Marion County's early bridges are now gone. One covered bridge on private property in Pike Township, a few metal railroad trusses, and some early ornamental concrete spans are all that remain of the city's and the county's pre–World War I bridge-building legacy.

WILLIAM GULDE
North Central High School

James L. Cooper, *Iron Monuments to Distant Posterity* (n.p., 1987); Indiana Covered Bridge Society newsletters; "Bridges" clipping file, Indiana Division, Indiana State Library.

Bridges, Fall Creek. In 1899 a program of replacing Indianapolis' steel and iron BRIDGES with new "permanent" stone and concrete ones began. The first bridges to be replaced were on Fall Creek at Meridian and Illinois streets. The new bridges were designed by Henry W. Klaussman and constructed of stone-faced concrete with melan arches for support beneath the roadway. That same year the city added a third new bridge, built of stone, at Central Avenue. In 1905 the city erected the College Avenue bridge, a stacked stone construction that resembled a bridge in Scotland. It was considered an engineering marvel because its piers were set at an angle from the bridge, placing them in line with the flow of the creek rather than the roadway above. The 30th Street bridge spanned Fall Creek in 1906. According to legend, the two stone mermaids on its center buttresses were once young women trying to escape the smoke and noise of downtown Indianapolis by moving north. When they reached 30th Street they looked back at the city and were turned to stone. In 1911 a new bridge went up at Capitol Avenue and Fall Creek. It had massive supports and was decorated with concrete cascading flowers. Landscape architect George E. Kessler called these beautiful new bridges, also designed by Henry Klaussman, one of Indianapolis' greatest assets. Unfortunately, in 1913 both the Meridian Street and Illinois Street bridges were heavily damaged by the city's worst flood.

By 1917, however, the city had rebuilt the bridges in an even more ornate fashion. The new Meridian Street bridge was fashioned after the Victor Emmanuel span over the Tiber River in Rome. The concrete bridge featured decorative medallions, lamps on the balustrades, and flower boxes at each end. The new Illinois Street bridge was less ornate, but also of massive design. Today, only the Capitol Avenue and the rebuilt Meridian and Illinois streets bridges remain; the others have been replaced over the years because of structural damage or when increased traffic made it necessary to widen the crossings.

Although the Fall Creek bridges are architecturally important, they have an even deeper significance to the city of Indianapolis. Each new bridge, from Fall Creek Boulevard to 56th Street, heralded the city's progress northward. Development followed the construction of the new bridges. After 1917 Indianapolis' elite, and increasingly its middle class, moved out of the downtown area and migrated ever northward across the Fall Creek bridges.

CONNIE J. ZEIGLER

Brightwood. Located approximately 2.5 miles northeast of Monument Circle, this neighborhood is bounded by 30th Street, Sherman Drive, 21st Street and Massachusetts Avenue, and Keystone Avenue. The original 1872 plat for the area was signed by a group led by Clement A. Greenleaf, a manufacturer and the inventor of a turntable to rotate railroad cars and locomotives. After Greenleaf's business failed in the financial Panic of 1873, the remaining members of the group and several employees of the "Bee Line" Railroad submitted an amended plat in 1874 that outlined plans for a residential community surrounding planned industrial and commercial uses.

The community was incorporated as the town of Brightwood in 1876, perhaps in honor of local railroad figure John Bright. In 1877 the "Bee Line" opened a major yard and machine shop. In the 1880 census a majority of the adult men in the area identified themselves as skilled or unskilled workers; about 40 percent were either foreign-born or first-generation residents, predominantly of German, Irish, or British ancestry.

Brightwood was annexed into Indianapolis in 1897. Although it continued to serve into the mid–20th century as a residential area for the workers in nearby industries, its central role in railroad repair was supplanted in the years following the 1908 opening of the "Big Four" Yards in

BEECH GROVE. During the 1950s and 1960s Brightwood underwent transition as many working class white residents moved to newly built suburbs and the surplus housing they left behind became available to an in-migration of lower income black residents. By 1960 black residents accounted for almost half of the neighborhood's population of about 5,700. Recent figures indicate a black majority of over 90 percent of the current population of approximately 4,700.

In 1969 the Brightwood neighborhood was included as a major portion of the "Model Cities" area and a variety of federally funded efforts at urban renewal and rehabilitation were undertaken. Although some evidence of these efforts remains, such as the Martindale-Brightwood Neighborhood Association, and new efforts such as the adjacent Rural I–70 Industrial Park make progress, the Brightwood neighborhood continues to face the social and economic pressures common to many inner-city neighborhoods.

ROBERT CROSS

Timothy J. Sehr, "Three Gilded Age Suburbs of Indianapolis: Irvington, Brightwood, and Woodruff Place," *Indiana Magazine of History*, 77 (Dec., 1981).

Broad Ripple. Northeast neighborhood bounded by White River, Evanston Avenue, Kessler Boulevard, and Meridian Street. Broad Ripple began as two separate communities alongside the CENTRAL CANAL. In April, 1837, Jacob Coil platted Broad Ripple north of the canal. One month later, James and Adam Nelson established Wellington on the south bank. A few small businesses sprang up to serve the canal laborers and travelers coming by mule-powered boats from Indianapolis. In 1884 the two rival communities came together and incorporated as Broad Ripple with about 150 residents.

The canal, a commercial failure, passed into private ownership in 1851 and eventually became the property of the INDIANAPOLIS WATER COMPANY. Other transportation routes, such as Westfield Boulevard, were developed to link Broad Ripple with the capital. A rail line opened in 1883 and serviced a lumberyard and the KINGAN AND COMPANY ice storage facility. STREETCARS in the

1890s and INTERURBANS in the early 1900s brought city dwellers for riverside outings.

Broad Ripple became a summertime retreat for Indianapolis residents from 1890 to 1930. Steamers featuring onboard dining and dancing cruised the river. White City, now known as BROAD RIPPLE PARK, opened in 1906 and drew swarms of visitors with a variety of entertainment. The city of Indianapolis acquired the park in 1945, and today it is the site of a playground, swimming pool, and branch library.

Residential areas of Broad Ripple developed quickly as Indianapolis expanded northward. Many homes were built after 1900 in a variety of architectural styles, particularly bungalows. In the early 1990s about 5,000 people live in Broad Ripple.

A local landmark, Broad Ripple High School, was established in 1886. Though it was destroyed by fire ten years later, residents rebuilt and later enlarged the facilities. In 1993 it is part of INDIANAPOLIS PUBLIC SCHOOLS and has an enrollment of about 1,500 students.

Indianapolis annexed Broad Ripple in 1922, enabling residents to build higher levees along the river and modernize the fire department. The measures effectively eliminated fires from natural gas deposits and periodic flooding in the area. More recently, the Broad Ripple community has responded to new challenges. As shopping centers drew customers away from the business district along Broad Ripple Avenue in the 1950s and 1960s, specialty shops, nightclubs, and restaurants were opened. Additional parking was provided when a deck was constructed over part of the canal in 1961. A neighborhood group, the Broad Ripple Village Association, was formed in 1969 to revitalize commercial and residential areas.

Cooperative efforts by merchants and residents have made Broad Ripple in the 1990s a thriving, diverse community of homes, retail and service establishments, restaurants, and entertainment venues.

JANE T. WALKER

Berry R. Sulgrove, *History of Indianapolis and Marion County* (Philadelphia, 1884), 637–638; *Northside Topics*, Oct. 1, 1970; *Indianapolis Star*, June 27, 1987.

Broad Ripple Park (White City Amusement Park). Broad Ripple Park, located along the WHITE RIVER in Broad Ripple Village, served as a popular swimming and boating resort as early as 1890. Local businessmen W. H. Tabb and Dr. Robert C. Light, organizer of the Broad Ripple Transit Company, established the White City Corporation of Indianapolis to erect rides and amusements in the park. On May 26, 1906, White City Amusement Park, named after the monumental architecture of Chicago's 1893 World's Columbian Exposition, opened to the public.

Mechanical rides were White City's main attractions. A scenic railway roller coaster, the "Shoot the Chutes" waterslide, a reenactment of the eruption of Mount Vesuvius, a fire-disaster spectacle called "Fighting the Flames," and other midway rides were situated around a 500–foot center court. The park's most unusual attraction was a display of functioning baby incubators, copied from an exhibit at New York's Coney Island, that catered to the public's fascination with science and technology. White City also offered military band concerts, vaudeville shows, and boating. It proclaimed itself "the amusement park that satisfied."

At the beginning of its second season, the White City Corporation planned to improve the park's swimming facilities. It invested $40,000 to construct a pool, a concrete-lined "bathing beach," a broad promenade, and a two-story pavilion along White River. White City promoted

White City provided amusements at the Broad Ripple Park site from 1906 to 1908 when it was destroyed by fire. [Indiana Historical Society, #C5763]

this facility as "the largest affair of the kind in the country."

On June 26, 1908, a fire started in the "Mystic Cave" attraction and quickly spread throughout the park. Light estimated the park's loss at $160,000, none of which was covered by insurance. Only the pool, scheduled to open the next day, escaped the flames.

Three years later on March 6, 1911, Light and Tabb sold the property to the Union Traction Company, which restored and operated the park for 11 years. During that time, the company erected a new boathouse, dining hall, dance hall, and playground equipment. The 250 by 500–foot pool served as the park's principal attraction. The park hosted the National Swimming Event in 1922 and the Olympic tryouts in 1924, at which time Johnny Weissmuller, the soon-to-be Hollywood Tarzan, won the 100–meter freestyle qualification. The Olympic tryouts returned to Broad Ripple in 1952.

The new Broad Ripple Amusement Park Association, led by James H. Makin, later founder of the RIVIERA CLUB, purchased the park in May, 1922. The corporation planned major improvements including recreational facilities, athletic fields, and a large roller coaster. In 1927, Makin sold the park to Oscar Baur, a brewery executive from Terre Haute, who began an extensive modernization program. At its 1938 season opener, Broad Ripple Park boasted the "world's largest concrete pool," a variety of mechanized rides, a new ballroom, and "20 acres of free parking."

On May 18, 1945, the city's Board of Park Commissioners announced the purchase of the 60–acre Broad Ripple Park from Baur for $131,500. The rides were sold or demolished, and the park became a site for public recreation. (Only the Broad Ripple carousel survives, occupying a gallery at THE CHILDREN'S MUSEUM.) During the late 1980s Broad Ripple Park became the site of a new swimming pool and a new public library branch. A boat ramp provides access to White River.

DAVID G. VANDERSTEL
CONNIE ZEIGLER
Indiana University–Purdue University,
Indianapolis

Broadcasting, Educational and Public. Early in the development of radio, many groups and individuals realized the value of broadcasting for educational and non-commercial purposes. But commercial interests dominated radio and not until 1940 did the Federal Communications Commission (FCC) reserve FM frequencies for education. When television allocations were set in 1952, Indianapolis received two educational channels, 20 and 69.

However, radio and television in Indianapolis were used for education long before there were local stations established for this purpose. As early as 1938 Indiana University produced programs for AM station WIRE featuring various departments of the university, although the first program was a delayed broadcast of an IU basketball game. For more than ten years the university presented programs on state history as well as world issues. In the early 1940s, WIBC, WFBM, and WIRE, in cooperation with Indianapolis Public Schools, presented programs directly to elementary schools and later to high school students.

In the early days of television, WFBM–Channel 6 broadcast programs produced through Butler University, while WTTV–Channel 10 (later Channel 4) developed a relationship with Indiana University. Channel 6 also took part in a project with *Life* magazine, "*Life* Goes to School," a ten-part series that took a closer look inside some of the Indianapolis public schools.

Purdue University became involved with educational TV in Indianapolis in 1961 through the Midwest Program on Airborne Television Instruction. MPATI was based at Purdue and provided instructional programs to schools in six states by using transmitters on two DC–6 airplanes that circled over Montpelier, Indiana. The program, plagued by high costs, ended in 1968.

INDIANAPOLIS PUBLIC SCHOOLS (IPS) started its own radio station, WIAN (FM 90.1), in 1954. Originally housed at SHORTRIDGE HIGH SCHOOL, the station moved to the IPS Center for Instructional Radio and Television southeast of downtown in 1969. The station helped train students and also carried specialty programs, including classical music from the FINE ARTS SOCIETY OF INDIANAPOLIS. WIAN also became a National Public Radio affiliate in 1971. In 1985 IPS determined that WIAN was too expensive to operate and decided to sell the station. Although BUTLER UNIVERSITY offered $1 million for the facility, IPS transferred WIAN to public television station Channel 20, and the call letters were changed to WFYI-FM.

WFYI-TV, Channel 20, the city's first non-commercial TV station, overcame numerous obstacles to begin broadcasting in October, 1970. In the late 1960s Dr. Lynd Esch, president of Indiana Central College (now the UNIVERSITY OF INDIANAPOLIS) spearheaded efforts to put the station on the air. Attempts to tie Channel 20 to new transmitter locations for Channel 4, and then Channel 8, actually delayed the station because the FCC rejected both tower moves. After a group of women led by Ardath Burkhart raised almost $300,000 in the summer of 1970, WFYI-TV went on the air from a studio at the INDIANAPOLIS MUSEUM OF ART with the tower furnished by Channel 6.

The city's oldest university-owned radio station, WICR (FM 88.7), started in 1962. The University of Indianapolis station operates in conjunction with the school's communications department and has been home to the Fine Arts Society's classical programming since 1983.

The city's first educational station was also its first FM station. WAJC (FM 91.9, then 104.5), licensed to the Arthur Jordan Conservatory (which later became part of Butler University), began a limited schedule in September, 1949. WAJC provided training to students in the Department of Radio and Television, and added programming from National Public Radio in 1982. The station was also the local outlet for Metropolitan Opera broadcasts. After putting a television station on the air, Butler shifted the emphasis of its department and in 1993 sold WAJC to Susquehanna Broadcasting, owner of WFMS (FM 95.5).

Butler had been interested in television since the late 1950s, and considered applying for the Channel 20 license in 1961. However, the university waited until the 1980s to file for the city's second educational channel, 69. WTBU began operating in June, 1992.

In the 1960s and 1970s, four of the suburban school districts in Marion County started their own radio stations and added classes in broadcasting. The oldest of these is Ben Davis High School's WBDG (FM 90.9), which went on the air in 1965. Warren Central's WEDM (FM 91.1), operating from the Walker Career Center, followed five years later. In 1975 Washington Township's WJEL (FM 89.3) started from the J. Everett Light Career Center at North Central High School. The Warren and Washington township programs are vocational, while Ben Davis maintains an academic program. Students from the respective schools staff the stations, with juniors and seniors usually in charge. Faculty members oversee the operations. In addition to school news, all the stations broadcast their school's basketball and football games. Franklin Township's WRFT (FM 91.5) became the county's most recent high school station when it began in 1978. Carmel High School in Hamilton County has a broadcast department which oversees a 400 watt, 24 hour per day, student-run radio station (WHJE, FM 91.3, established August 16, 1963) and a television station airing local public information programs on the Carmel cable television system.

Although IPS no longer operates a radio station, it still offers vocational training in television. Some production is done at the Center for Instructional Television, while ARSENAL TECHNICAL HIGH SCHOOL opened its own facility in the fall of 1993. In addition, other instructional programs are offered through a closed circuit network linking all IPS schools. IPS also makes use of the cable educational access channel available on both the Comcast and American Cablevision systems. A federally funded program, "Homework Hotline," features teachers dealing with homework problems in all subjects.

MICHAEL SPILLMAN

Broadcasting Controversies. Radio and television broadcast licenses, issued by the Federal Communications Commission (FCC), are valuable business properties. Choosing the recipient for a new license or approving a license renewal or station sale, therefore, sometimes becomes a major legal issue. Though most radio and television stations in the city have had smooth relationships with the FCC, some of the most controversial cases before the commission have involved Indianapolis.

In 1948 a 14–year battle began to determine who would operate the city's last VHF television outlet, Channel 13. WIRE radio, owned at that time by *Indianapolis Star* publisher EUGENE C. PULLIAM, was the first applicant. When the FCC finally held hearings in 1954, other hopefuls included WIBC radio (operated by Richard Fairbanks, former owner of the *Indianapolis News*), Mid-West TV Corporation (headed by Union Federal president Charles Sadlier), and Crosley Broadcasting (owner of WLW radio and Channel 5 in Cincinnati). Pulliam and Fairbanks attacked each other's qualifications, and, in 1955, an FCC hearing examiner awarded the license to Mid-West. The losers appealed to the full commission, which voted in March, 1957, to give the license to Crosley. This ruling was controversial for a number of reasons. Not only did it give the last Indianapolis VHF station to a Cincinnati company, but the decision was leaked during a congressional hearing on a proposed bill to limit the authority of the FCC. In addition, the deciding vote was cast by a new commissioner who had not heard any arguments in the case. He also had worked for the engineering firm used by Pulliam.

WIBC took the FCC to court, but in the interim Crosley put Channel 13 on the air as WLW-I. In 1958 the District of Columbia Court of Appeals ruled the FCC decision was wrong and ordered the commission to reopen the case. Three years later the FCC gave the license to WIBC and ordered Crosley to shut down Channel 13. In the spring of 1962, though, Fairbanks and Crosley worked out their own settlement. Crosley agreed to sell Channel 11 in Atlanta to Fairbanks, and Fairbanks agreed to let Crosley keep Channel 13. The chief of the FCC's Broadcast Bureau balked at the agreement, as did some commissioners. Newton Minow, who as FCC chairman described television as a "vast wasteland," called this deal a "horse trade" that was an inappropriate way to choose a responsible licensee. However, the agreement was approved by the full commission. Fairbanks bought the Atlanta station for $2.2 million and sold it five years later for almost $13 million.

Another controversy occurred over the sale of WTTV. When Bloomington engineer SARKES TARZIAN put WTTV, Channel 10, on the air in 1949, Bloomington became the smallest city in the country with a television station. WTTV became Channel 4 a few years later, and was given a dual city of license, Bloomington and Indianapolis. Tarzian sold Channel 4 in 1977 for more than $26 million, at that time the highest price for a TV station not affiliated with a major network. The new owners, based in Detroit, decided to concentrate their efforts on Indianapolis. Concerned that Bloomington would be abandoned, Indiana University telecommunications professor Herbert Terry filed a petition with the FCC to stop the sale. The Detroit group backed down. They agreed to keep Channel 4's Bloomington studios and to originate some programs from there. Satisfied that Monroe County would keep its television service, Terry withdrew his petition and the FCC approved the sale.

WIFE's problems with the FCC started in 1964, just a few months after Don Burden's Star Stations, owners of stations in Omaha and Vancouver, purchased the former WISH AM-FM. The FCC charged WIFE with misusing ratings information to boost its sales, and gave the station a one-year renewal, rather than the usual three years. Over the next 11 years the FCC found evidence of false billings, fraudulent contests, and illegal political contributions, including giving free advertising time to Senator Vance Hartke. WIFE employees told the commission they had been ordered to destroy records, and the station's news director testified that he had been told by management to slant the station's news coverage to favor Hartke, who was seeking reelection in 1964. Still, the FCC continued to renew WIFE's license. However, in the early 1970s a local group filed a competing application for the WIFE-AM license. In 1973 an FCC law judge ruled in favor of that group, so Burden appealed to the full commission. The FCC stripped Burden of all his licenses in 1975, giving WIFE-FM to the local group, Indianapolis Broadcasting, and ordering WIFE-FM and all other Burden stations off the air. On September 2, 1976, WIFE-FM shut down, saluting Burden with the playing of Frank Sinatra's "My Way" before signing off. The FCC rejected requests to allow interim operators because Burden owned WIFE-FM's equipment. The station was off the air until 1984 when a new group, with its own studio and equipment, came on the air as WTPI.

The most recent broadcasting controversy concerned popular WFBQ's morning show hosts Bob Kevoian and Tom Griswold. The "Bob and Tom Show" featured adult humor that proved controversial. Decency in Broadcasting, a group organized by Carmel attorney John Price in 1986, charged the station with broadcasting vulgar and pornographic material. Following an unsuccessful appeal to the station's sponsors to withdraw their advertising, the group filed a complaint against WFBQ with the FCC. Although the FCC initially took no action, Decency in Broadcasting continued to monitor and document cases of alleged indecency on WFBQ. In 1990 the FCC levied a $10,000 fine against WFBQ (which the station chose not to contest) for broadcasting four questionable routines. Despite the penalty WFBQ continued to grow in popularity, becoming *Rolling Stone* magazine's "Station of the Year" in 1990.

MICHAEL SPILLMAN

Brokenburr, Robert Lee (Nov. 16, 1886–Mar. 24, 1974). African-American legislator, attorney, and civil rights leader. Born in Phoebus, Virginia, and encouraged by his parents to get an education, Brokenburr worked his way through Hampton Institute, graduating in 1906. He then attended Howard University, obtaining a degree in law in 1906. Brokenburr came to Indianapolis in the fall of 1909, having learned of opportunities available to men of ambition from publisher GEORGE L. KNOX. He gained admission to the bar in 1910.

As an attorney Brokenburr successfully pled landmark CIVIL RIGHTS cases challenging segregation in housing and theaters. He also served as counsel, general manager, and chairman of the board of the MADAM C. J. WALKER Manufacturing Company. From 1919 to 1931 Brokenburr held office as deputy prosecuting attorney, 19th Circuit of Indiana. He also served as judge pro tem in local courts and was a member of the Indiana Fair Employment Practices Advisory Board.

Brokenburr campaigned unsuccessfully for the Indiana House of Representatives in 1912,

1932, and 1934. In 1940 he ran as the Republican nominee for Indiana Senate and won the seat. His election made him the first African-American senator in the Indiana legislature. He was elected to four additional terms in 1944, 1952, 1956, and 1960, serving a total of 20 years before retiring from the General Assembly in 1964. During his tenure as state senator he authored bills that prohibited discrimination in employment, public accommodations, and education, as well as an act that established the Indiana Civil Rights Commission.

Brokenburr was an active participant in civic affairs, with affiliations that included the YMCA, the NAACP, and FLANNER HOUSE. He was a member of Jones Tabernacle AME Church. In 1955, President Dwight Eisenhower appointed him alternate delegate to the United Nations. Brokenburr Trails, a public housing community at 2300 Perkins Avenue, was named in his honor.

GEORGIA CRAVEY

Brough, John (Sept. 17, 1811–Aug. 29, 1865). Railroad pioneer. In addition to being a noted newspaperman, politician, and Civil War governor in his native Ohio, Brough was a conspicuous figure in the development of railroads in Indiana. Two of those roads, the Madison and Indianapolis and the Bellefontaine Line to Cleveland, terminated at Indianapolis. President of the former from 1849 to 1854 and of the latter from 1854 to 1863, Brough lived first in Madison and then in Indianapolis before returning to the Buckeye state. Along with CHAUNCEY ROSE of the Terre Haute and Richmond Railroad, he attempted, unsuccessfully, to establish a railroad linking Indianapolis and St. Louis. While president of the Madison and Indianapolis Brough joined Rose, OLIVER H. SMITH, Thomas Morris, and other early railroad executives in planning and constructing the city's original UNION STATION. He was a key figure in helping Indianapolis become known as "The Railroad City."

VICTOR M. BOGLE
Indiana University, Kokomo

Dictionary of American Biography; Osman Hooper, "John Brough," *Ohio Archaeological and Historical Publications*, 13 (1904), 40–70.

Brown, Demarchus Clariton (June 24, 1857–Aug. 22, 1926). College professor and state librarian. A lifelong resident of Indianapolis, Brown was the brother of HILTON U. BROWN, general manager of the *INDIANAPOLIS NEWS*. After graduating from BUTLER UNIVERSITY in 1879 he became tutor of Greek there and completed his master's degree at Butler in 1880. From 1882 to 1883 he studied at Tubingen University in Germany and then was professor of Greek at Butler until 1906. He taught at the American School of Classical Studies in Athens, Greece, from 1892 to 1893. In 1896, he published his translation of *Selections from Lucian*. He also compiled several editions of the *Indiana Legislative and State Manual*.

In 1906, Brown was appointed state librarian by Governor James Mount and the state board of education. He held this position until his death in 1926. In 1925, his title was changed by law to director of Indiana library work. As state librarian Brown was celebrated for his success in adding to the state's collection of original manuscripts, letters, state papers, and historical Indiana materials of all kinds.

From 1893 to 1921, Brown served as a member of the state board of charities and was president of the Indiana Conference of Charities in 1904. From 1910 to 1911, he was president of the National Association of State Librarians. He was also a member of numerous national, state, and local organizations, including the INDIANA HISTORICAL SOCIETY, ATHENAEUM, INDIANAPOLIS LITERARY CLUB, and CONTEMPORARY CLUB.

JEFFERY A. DUVALL

Brown, Genevieve (ca. 1885–Aug. 4, 1970). Court reporter and active Republican. A native of Winamac, Indiana, Brown graduated from Monticello High School and Indiana University, and subsequently attended Indiana University Law School. A member of the Indiana bar, Brown was elected reporter of the Supreme and Appellate courts and served from 1928 to 1932.

In 1936 Brown was sent on an extensive speaking trip to the Northwest by the Republican National Committee. Brown also served as a member of the Republican State Committee from 1924 to 1930. In 1945 Brown was appointed Indiana Supreme Court librarian by Chief Justice Mart J. O'Malley. She served in that position until 1951 at which time she was fired by the court in a political move that replaced her with a former secretary to U.S. Senator William Jenner. Active in many local groups, Brown's memberships included the Indiana Association of Women Lawyers, the State Assembly Women's Club, the Indiana University Women's Club, the BUSINESS AND PROFESSIONAL WOMEN'S CLUB, and the Indianapolis Women's Republican Club. Brown served as president of the latter two organizations.

KATHY INGELS HELMOND

Brown, George (June 19, 1835–June 29, 1913). United States Navy officer. Born in Rushville, Indiana, Brown moved to Indianapolis with his family at the age of one. He was appointed to the U.S. Naval Academy on February 2, 1849, beginning his service as a midshipman aboard the frigate USS *Cumberland*. After service in a variety of naval vessels, he rose to the rank of lieutenant prior to the outbreak of the Civil War.

Brown was promoted to the rank of lieutenant commander in July, 1862, and later commanded the ironclad USS *Indianola*, which was sunk by Confederate naval forces on February 24, 1863. He and his crew were captured but were later exchanged. Subsequently, Brown held various commands during the Battle of Mobile Bay and served in the Gulf of Mexico and Caribbean until the war's end.

Brown attained the rank of commander in 1866. In 1867, he delivered the Confederate ram *Stonewall Jackson* to Japan. The *Stonewall* was the first warship acquired by the Japanese, and Brown spent two years training them to operate it. The emergence of the Japanese navy dates from this visit.

Brown later held a variety of commands ashore and afloat, being promoted to the rank of captain (1878), commodore (1887), and rear admiral (1893), then the Navy's highest rank. Brown retired on June 19, 1897, and returned to Indianapolis, residing in IRVINGTON until his death.

THOMAS D. LUND

Indianapolis News, June 12, 1908, June 30, 1913; Indianapolis Star, July 1, 1913; Indianapolis Times, Feb. 21, 1938, July 23, 1945; Who Was Who in America (1942).

Brown, H. Dale (May 3, 1910–July 2, 1989). Chair of the Indiana and Marion County Republican party. A graduate of SHORTRIDGE HIGH SCHOOL, Brown attended Butler and Indiana universities, and the Benjamin Harrison Law School. From 1935 to 1940 he owned the H. D. Brown Casket Company.

Brown's political career began in 1932 when he was elected GOP precinct committeeman. From 1940 to 1948 he served as 7th Ward chairman. He was director of the state Bureau of Motor Vehicles from 1944 to 1948. In 1948, Brown ran unsuccessfully for state treasurer and from 1950 to 1958 he served as MARION COUNTY CLERK. In 1958, he ran unsuccessfully for COUNTY ASSESSOR. From 1954 to 1956 Brown was 11th District chairman and from 1956 to 1962 he served as chair of the Marion County REPUBLICAN PARTY. In November, 1962, Brown was elected state chairman of the Republican party but resigned in May, 1963, following months of conflict with conservative members of the state leadership. Having returned to his post of county chairman, Brown resigned in 1966, effectively ending his public career.

Brown's defining moment in politics came in the 1952 presidential election. He was the first public official in Indiana to support Dwight Eisenhower's nomination as the Republican candidate for president. This angered party insiders who had endorsed Robert Taft's nomination. Eisenhower's primary victory established Brown as a leader in state Republican politics, but it was also the first engagement in a sporadic feud between Brown and the conservative wing of the Republican party that continued to plague his public career.

MATTHEW BURRIDGE

Indianapolis Star, July 4, July 8, 1989.

Brown, Hilton Ultimus (Feb. 20, 1859–Sept. 20, 1958). Newspaper director and civic leader. Brown, an Indianapolis native, received a B.A. in 1880 and an M.A. in 1882 from BUTLER UNIVERSITY. In 1881, after one year as principal at Oaktown Academy, he began his 77–year tenure at the INDIANAPOLIS NEWS.

The acclaimed dean of Indiana journalism, Brown began his career as a reporter and subsequently worked as city editor, managing editor, secretary-treasurer, and served on the board of directors. He became vice-president of Indianapolis Newspapers, Inc., when it incorporated in 1948 and remained active in the position until his death. Brown also served on the board of directors of the American Newspaper Publishers Association from 1903 to 1935. He represented Indianapolis internationally as a correspondent at the Versailles peace conference and served as an escort for Queen Marie of Romania during her visit to the city in the late 1920s.

In 1885, at age 25, Brown became the youngest member ever elected to the Butler University board of trustees. He served on the board for 70 years, including 52 years as president. Upon his retirement in 1955 the board elected him president emeritus. Posthumously, in 1959, he received the Butler medal for distinguished service. The Hilton U. Brown Theater at Butler University and the IRVINGTON public library are named in his honor.

His motivation, leadership, copy desk rules, and knack for scooping the competition helped elevate the Indianapolis News into a major publica-

Hilton U. Brown in his 1880 photo as senior class president at Butler University. [Butler University Archives]

tion. He gained local, national, and international recognition at the annual Associated Press meetings. He is also noted for his series reflecting on Russia and industrial conditions in Europe after World War I. In 1939 he received the Indianapolis CHAMBER OF COMMERCE Staff of Honor for his contributions to the city through his journalism and service.

Brown resided in Irvington where he served as president of the town and school boards. A religious man, Brown also held positions as an elder of Downey Avenue Christian Church, president of the board of trustees of the Christian Foundation, and director of the Christian (Disciples of Christ) Board Publication. Brown's published works include *Fifty-four Forty or Fight* (1912), *Hilton U. Brown Jr., One of Three Brothers in Artillery* (1920), and his autobiography, *A Book About Memories* (1951). He is buried in CROWN HILL CEMETERY.

AMY GLOWACKI

Wayne Guthrie, "Hilton U. Brown Revered By News," *Indianapolis News*, Dec. 8, 1969; *Who Was Who in America* (Chicago, 1960).

Brown, Ignatius (Aug. 11, 1831–July 8, 1903). Historian. A native of Indianapolis, Brown received his early education at the Marion County Seminary. Upon graduating from the law department of Indiana University in 1852, he entered his father's law practice in Indianapolis. Following the latter's death in 1853, Brown continued with the general practice of law until 1868, thereafter specializing in real estate law.

In 1854, he served as a delegate to the first national convention of the Know-Nothing party. He later took part in organizing the REPUBLICAN PARTY in Marion County. From 1856 to 1857, Brown served as secretary to the state board of agriculture. In association with RICHARD J. GATLING, inventor of the GATLING GUN, Brown organized the city's first BOARD OF TRADE.

Brown's history of the city, which appeared in the 1857 city directory, was the first historical sketch of Indianapolis to be published. For the 1868 city directory he expanded this work into a 100–page essay covering the city's history from 1819 to 1867. In 1874, at the request of the City Council, he prepared a widely distributed pamphlet that set out the advantages of the town as both a commercial and a manufacturing center. In his later years, much of his leisure time was devoted to preparing a comprehensive abstract of the titles to all real estate in Marion County.

JEFFERY A. DUVALL

Indianapolis News, July 9, 1903; Donald E. Thompson, *Indiana Authors and Their Books, 1967–1980* (Crawfordsville, Ind., 1981).

Brown, Jessica Christian (Mrs. Demarchus) (Oct. 2, 1875–Jan. 10, 1941). Teacher, traveler, lecturer. A native of Madison, Indiana, Jessica moved to Indianapolis in 1890 with her parents. Following graduation from SHORTRIDGE HIGH SCHOOL, she attended BUTLER UNIVERSITY where she was a founder of a chapter of Pi Beta Phi. After graduation in 1897 she married DEMARCHUS C. BROWN, then professor of Greek at Butler and later state librarian for 20 years. She received her M.A. degree from Butler and taught French there from 1919 to 1923 and 1939 to 1941. In 1936 the university awarded her an honorary Doctor of Humanities degree.

Perhaps her greatest contributions to the city, however, resulted from her great love of travel. Brown made over 20 trips abroad, including journeys to Europe, Africa, Japan, India, Australia, and Jerusalem. These trips provided the material she used in lectures throughout Indiana and other states. She spoke on the Chautauqua circuit for several years and briefly had her own radio show, "Our Lovable Gadabout," on WIRE. Brown also offered a lecture series at Butler, sponsored by ELI LILLY, from 1936 to 1940, and held memberships in numerous women's organizations.

KATHY INGELS HELMOND

Indianapolis Star, Sept. 22, 1940, Jan. 12, 1941; *Indianapolis Times*, Oct. 1, 1938.

Browning Day Mullins Dierdorf (BDMD). Architecture and landscape architecture firm. Having won a silver medal at the World

Professional Figure Skating Championship in 1964, James Browning left athletics to begin a career in landscape architecture. He had a teaching position at Purdue University and a small practice of his own when he and his friend Alan Day cofounded a landscape architecture firm in Indianapolis in 1967.

Concentrating on ZONING and development issues in the early days, their work included areas of the city as diverse as Eagle Highlands and Castleton Square. By the late 1960s the practice grew to include four designers, and the firm found itself with early knowledge of many architectural projects. This led to the decision to expand into the practice of architecture. Richard J. Pollak AIA joined the firm as a principal in 1970, and the architecture practice commenced with the renovation of an AFNB Bank branch at 2829 North Meridian Street.

Since its start as a two-person firm, BDMD has experienced considerable growth, including the addition of an office in Louisville. In 1992, the INDIANAPOLIS BUSINESS JOURNAL listed it as the largest architecture firm in Indianapolis, as determined by 1990 fee billings. The firm's participation in design of the Indianapolis Sports Center, Indiana University Track and Field Stadium, and Natatorium led to a national practice in sports architecture. BDMD served as project architects on several downtown revitalization projects, including the HOOSIER DOME, PAN AMERICAN PLAZA, and Landmark Center. One of the firm's architects, Jonathan Hess, designed one of the city's most recognizable buildings, the southwestern style EITELJORG MUSEUM OF AMERICAN INDIAN AND WESTERN ART. The firm's design projects include the WTHR Channel 13 television studios, renovation of the UNION STATION and the ELI LILLY AND COMPANY corporate headquarters, and landscape architecture for MONUMENT CIRCLE, Obelisk Square, and part of the downtown CENTRAL CANAL renovation.

Having moved in 1974 to 116th Street and Meridian, and in 1979 to 124 South Meridian, in 1987 the firm renovated and moved into the Emelie Apartments building at 334 North Senate, a structure which is part of a thematic entry in the National Register of Historic Places. In 1991 the original partners began a transition of ownership to Craig Mullins, John Dierdorf, and Jonathan Hess, while remaining active participants in the work.

STEVEN W. ROBINSON AIA
Browning Day Mullins Dierdorf Inc.

Broyles, Moses (ca. 1826–Aug. 31, 1882). African-American Baptist minister. Broyles was born a slave near Centerville, Maryland, and sold to a master in Kentucky. In 1838 he became a Baptist preacher to local slaves. Soon after his emancipation in 1851, he came to Indiana to attend Eleutherian College in Jefferson County (later Craven Institute) from 1854 to 1857.

Broyles left college and moved to Indianapolis in 1857 to teach at one of the city's first schools for African-American children. The city provided a building in the 4th ward for the subscription school, funded by student tuition or subscriptions, in response to school superintendent ABRAM C. SHORTRIDGE's plea for education for African-Americans in the city. Broyles served as teacher and principal of the school for 12 years. In 1872 he was partly responsible for integrating the only high school in Indianapolis at the time.

Broyles joined the SECOND BAPTIST CHURCH of Indianapolis and became its ordained minister in 1857. During his ministry he rescued the church from debt and saw his African-American congregation multiply into the hundreds. Broyles ordained many local African-American ministers and helped to found several other Indianapolis congregations. Throughout his pastorate he was a vocal and active Republican, allowing many political meetings at the church. Broyles also encouraged the Indianapolis African-American community to be politically active through his preaching, such as his sermon responses to the Dred Scott decision of the U.S. Supreme Court (1857) and the ratification of the Fifteenth Amendment (1869). He helped organize the Indiana Association of Negro Baptist Churches (1858).

MICHELLE D. HALE

Moses Broyles, *The History of the Second Baptist Church of Indianapolis* (Indianapolis, 1876).

Bruetsch, Walter (Nov. 25, 1896–Jan. 31, 1977). Physician and neuropathologist. Born and educated in Heidelberg, Germany, Bruetsch became a scholar of Latin and Greek, but the outbreak of World War I interrupted his education. During the Battle of the Somme (1916), he suffered a paralyzing spinal wound and, after capture by the French, came under the care of the noted neurologist Babinski. He began premedical studies in Davos, Switzerland, after the war and received the M.D. degree at Freiburg, Germany, in 1922.

During the war researchers discovered that concurrent infection with malaria could cure syphilis of the brain, then the most common cause of insanity. Bruetsch, who immigrated to Indianapolis in 1924, inaugurated this method of treatment at CENTRAL STATE HOSPITAL the next year. His major contribution was demonstrating that malarial fever did not destroy the organism causing syphilis, as commonly believed, but rather that malaria triggered production of a type of white blood cell that then consumed both pathogens. During his some 30 years of service as a research pathologist at the hospital, he won international recognition for his studies of neurosyphilis and was appointed a consultant to the U.S. Public Health Service.

CHARLES A. BONSETT, M.D.
Indiana University School of Medicine

Brush, John Tomlinson (June 15, 1845–Nov. 26, 1912). Early major league baseball team owner. A native of Clintonville, New York, Brush came to Indianapolis in 1875 and founded the When Clothing Company. To help promote the firm, Brush became involved in ownership of a new Western League professional BASEBALL team in 1885, but the team folded after one season. Professional baseball didn't return to Indianapolis until 1887 when Brush was instrumental in moving a National League team from St. Louis. After that team lost its league membership in 1890, Brush became involved in baseball nationally, purchasing the Cincinnati Reds National League club in 1892 and in 1903 the National League New York Giants, which he owned and directed until his death.

Although Brush became prominent in the sport as owner of the Reds and Giants, he maintained his residence in Indianapolis and remained involved in local baseball. In 1894, Brush became majority owner of a new Western League team in Indianapolis and helped the team win the pennant in 1895 by supplying players from Cincinnati. His ownership of the team continued until fellow National League owners forced him to sell his interest in the minor league club in 1896.

THOMAS A. HARTON

Budget Process. The 1970 UNIGOV reorganization brought the budgets of several local governments in Marion County together, at least for review by the CITY-COUNTY COUNCIL. Combining the pre-Unigov budgetary review functions of the Indianapolis Common Council and the Marion County Council, the City-County Council reviews the budgets for all Indianapolis city departments and divisions, all Marion County government offices and agencies, and independent municipal corporations—the INDIANAPOLIS AIRPORT AUTHORITY, the CAPITAL IMPROVEMENT BOARD, the HEALTH AND HOSPITAL CORPORATION OF MARION COUNTY, and the Indianapolis–Marion County Library District.

The stages of the annual budget preparation and review process extend over the fiscal year, which matches the calendar year of January 1 through December 31. The first step is the development of budget requests from the Unigov departments, divisions, and districts, and the county offices and agencies. Preparation and revision of budget requests for the coming fiscal year begins as early as January of the preceding year, and lasts until July 1.

City government departments and divisions and the INDIANAPOLIS–MARION COUNTY BUILDING AUTHORITY submit their budget requests through the city controller's office. The controller, the MAYOR, and their staffs review, revise, and shape the request into a city budget ordinance during June and July. During the same period, the MARION COUNTY AUDITOR reviews the requests of county offices and agencies, and the other independent municipal corporations and compiles them into a budget ordinance.

The mayor introduces the city budget ordinance, and the Marion County auditor the county budget ordinance, at the first City-County Council meeting in August. During the remainder of August and most of September, the City-County Council's committees hold public hearings on the elements within the budget ordinances that fall within their jurisdictions. The city controller twice advertises budget ordinances in a local newspaper prior to the last City-County Council meeting in September, at which time the council finalizes and acts upon them. The ordinances passed by the City-County Council at its last September meeting may not exceed the levels advertised to the public. Then the council acts upon a combined city-county budget ordinance, along with separate budget ordinances for the independent municipal corporations.

Separate budget ordinances are also prepared for the Indianapolis Police and Fire SPECIAL SERVICE DISTRICTS and for the Solid Waste Collection and Solid Waste Disposal Special Service Districts. The respective Special Service District Councils, rather than the City-County Council, act upon these budgets.

The budget ordinances are presented to the mayor, who may approve or veto them in their entirety or may veto single expenditure items, except in the budgets for the Marion County courts, the constitutionally required county offices, and the independent municipal corporations. Vetoes by the mayor can be overridden by a two-thirds vote of the City-County Council members. The council and the mayor should have completed their actions on the budgets by October 1.

Budgets approved by the City-County Council and the mayor go to the Marion County Board of Tax Adjustment for review. This seven-member board consists of four persons appointed by the Marion County commissioners, one appointed by the mayor, one member of the City-County Council, and one member of the Indianapolis Board of School Commissioners. The Board of Tax Adjustment reviews the budgets at a public meeting. It can reduce budgets if the tax rates needed to fund those budgets will exceed limits imposed by state or local law, but it cannot increase budgets. The board is to complete its review by November 1. Budgets are then reviewed

by the Indiana Board of Tax Commissioners. The state board can reduce budgets or restore budgets and their accompanying tax rates on appeal from the decision of the county tax review board. The state board's decisions are final.

WILLIAM BLOMQUIST
Indiana University–Purdue University,
Indianapolis

Indianapolis League of Women Voters, *Unigov Handbook* (1985).

Burford, William B. (Nov. 18, 1846–Jan. 14, 1927). Businessman and state printer. A native of Independence, Missouri, Burford came to Indianapolis at age 15 to serve as a printer in the office of his brother-in-law, William Braden. In 1863 he returned to Missouri and joined the state militia, serving until the end of the Civil War. Following the war Burford entered a college in Missouri where he attended classes until 1867. He then returned to his job with Braden in Indianapolis.

In 1870 he became Braden's partner, forming the firm of Braden and Burford. Buying out Braden in 1875, Burford changed the name to WILLIAM B. BURFORD PRINTING COMPANY. Under his guidance the company, headquartered at 40 South Meridian Street, eventually grew to be the largest printing concern in the state. Serving for many years as the state printer, Burford also handled all printing incident to sessions of the state legislature for over 30 years.

An active member of the Indianapolis BOARD OF TRADE, the Commercial Club, the CHAMBER OF COMMERCE, the Masons, and the Meridian Street Methodist Episcopal Church, Burford continued working until his death.

JEFFERY A. DUVALL

Indianapolis Star, Jan. 15, 1927.

Burger Chef. Indianapolis-based fast food restaurant chain. In 1957 Frank P. Thomas opened a pilot restaurant at Little America Amusement Center to promote and sell the automated hamburger grill he had invented. Failing to sell the grill but successfully marketing his 15–cent hamburgers, Thomas instead opened the first Burger Chef at 1300 West 16th Street. By 1959 there were eight Burger Chefs in Indiana, Ohio, and Missouri. The national headquarters was located in Indianapolis adjacent to the West 16th Street restaurant.

In the early 1960s Thomas sold hundreds of Burger Chef franchises to owner-operators; the average return on an owner's $129,000 investment was 50 percent per year. The potential for profit and a training program for operators, developed by Indiana Central College (now UNIVERSITY OF INDIANAPOLIS), proved so popular that by 1966 there were 500 Burger Chefs in the Midwest. In 1968 Thomas sold his rights to the restaurant chain to General Foods Corporation for $16.5 million.

By the end of the 1970s, the Burger Chef system had 40 outlets in MARION COUNTY and over 650 nationwide. In 1978, the murder of four employees in a Speedway Burger Chef brought unwanted notoriety to the restaurant. Competition from other fast food chains, most notably McDonald's, caused a decline in Burger Chef profits. In 1981, General Foods sold Burger Chef to the Hardee's restaurant chain for $44 million. After the sale, the Burger Chefs were quickly converted into Hardee's restaurants, gaining business but losing their Burger Chef menu and distinctive building facades.

CONNIE J. ZEIGLER

Burger Chef Murders. Unsolved kidnapping and multiple murder. On November 18, 1978, an off-duty employee of the SPEEDWAY Burger Chef, 5725 Crawfordsville Road, discovered the back door of the restaurant open and the staff missing. Four youthful employees were evidently abducted from the restaurant and $500 stolen. The kidnapping had no eyewitnesses.

Over the next two days police and volunteers mounted an intensive search for the missing employees and their kidnappers. Police discovered one employee's car, which may have been used in the initial part of the abduction, near the Speedway Police Department. On Sunday, November 19, the bodies of the four employees were discovered in a rural wooded area in nearby Johnson County by a local property owner. Two victims had multiple gunshot wounds to the head, neck, and shoulders from .38–caliber slugs; a third had been stabbed to death with a hunting knife found in the body; the fourth died from severe head injuries.

The police organized a multiple-agency task force to investigate the murders. BURGER CHEF Systems, Inc., headquartered in Indianapolis, posted a $25,000 reward for information leading to the arrest and conviction of the murderers, and established a memorial fund for the families of the four victims. Despite thousands of hours devoted to the investigation, with leads pursued throughout the United States, the murderers remain unidentified. The Indiana State Police currently maintains the open case file.

VICKIE J. WEST

Indianapolis Star, Nov. 20–22, 1978.

Burkhart, Ardath Yates (Sept. 2, 1905–Dec. 8, 1983). Social and community leader. Born in Vincent, Indiana, Ardath Yates grew up in Oaktown. She graduated from DePauw University in 1927 with a B.S. in Music, and taught music and art in the public schools of Tipton, Indiana, and Indianapolis.

First active in GIRL SCOUTS as a leader, Burkhart served as a member of local, regional, and national Girl Scout committees and boards and as president of the Indianapolis council from 1951 to 1955. Elected to the Indianapolis School Board in 1962, she served until 1966. She was a DePauw University trustee from 1955 to 1978, when she became a life trustee. She served on the City Planning Commission, 1963–1965, and the GREATER INDIANAPOLIS PROGRESS COMMITTEE, 1971–1978. She also chaired the Indiana State Scholarship Commission, 1975–1977, and the City Charity Solicitors Commission from 1955 to 1965. She was named the first female member of the COLUMBIA CLUB in 1979.

Burkhart's philanthropic activities included the establishment of the United Fund League in 1957. She served on the UNITED WAY executive commission from 1958 until her death and was a trustee of the INDIANAPOLIS FOUNDATION from 1959 to 1969, during which time she was the only woman to serve on the board.

The arts and entertainment community was another focus of her skills as a community leader and fund raiser. "Ardath's Army" raised $300,000 to put WFYI, the city's first public television station, on the air in 1970. She also served on the boards of the INDIANAPOLIS OPERA COMPANY, the CIVIC THEATRE, and the HOOSIER SALON, of which she was president, 1978–1981.

NORALEEN YOUNG

Burns, Lee (Apr. 19, 1872–Jan. 8, 1957). Architect and author. Born in Bloomfield, Indiana, Burns graduated from Butler University and, as a young man, worked for the Bowen-Merrill Company. During the SPANISH-AMERICAN WAR he served in the 158th Indiana Infantry. Though not formally trained in architecture, in 1910 he founded Burns Realty Company specializing in the design and construction of fine country and town homes.

In 1926 Burns formed an architecture firm with Edward D. James. Utilizing traditional designs, Burns and James were responsible for many of Indianapolis' far northside homes, including several homes in the North Meridian Street Historic District. In 1929 the Indiana Society of Architects awarded the firm a gold medal for excellence in residential design. In 1949 the two men dissolved their partnership and Burns teamed with his son David V. Burns in a new architecture firm, Burns and Burns. The father-son partnership continued to design in traditional styles but shifted its emphasis to public structures. Among their Indianapolis works are several buildings at the INDIANA STATE FAIRGROUNDS and many Indianapolis Parks Department buildings.

Burns was active in Indianapolis civic affairs and wrote a number of books on Indiana history: *The National Road in Indiana* (1919), *Indianapolis—The Old Town and the New* (1923), *Life in Old Vincennes* (1929), and *Early Architects and Builders of Indiana* (1935). He also served for many years on the executive committee of the INDIANA HISTORICAL SOCIETY and was a member of the federal commission that built the George Rogers Clark

Memorial at Vincennes, Indiana. He was one of the founders of the Players Club and a director of the JOHN HERRON ART INSTITUTE.

CONNIE J. ZEIGLER

Indianapolis Star, Jan. 9, 1957.

Burns and James. Architects. In 1926 Lee Burns and Edward D. James formed a partnership. Both men were Butler University graduates, and although Burns had no formal training as an architect—he was a builder—James had graduated from Cornell University School of Architecture.

Burns and James' specialty was traditional residential design. In 1929 they won the Indiana Society of Architects' gold medal for best residential design for the William R. Teel home at 56th Street and Washington Boulevard. Other residences designed by them in the 1920s and 1930s include the Colonial Revival homes at 4919 and 5425 North Meridian Street and 3520 Washington Boulevard. In addition they were architects for the Georgian-style home at 4555 Broadway Street, the French Farmhouse–style home at 256 Buckingham Drive, and the Cape Cod–style residence at 4732 North Pennsylvania Street. Although the firm specialized in residential plans, in 1932 they designed a city fire station at 5555 North Illinois Street.

By 1949 James was working almost exclusively with Indiana University (IU) on buildings for its Bloomington campus, so the two principals dissolved Burns and James and formed two separate firms: Burns and Burns, with Lee and David V. Burns, his son, as principals; and Edward D. James Architect. Burns and Burns continued to employ traditional concepts: in the 1950s it designed the William E. English Foundation Building; the Broad Ripple branch of FLANNER AND BUCHANAN MORTUARIES; WIBC radio station; the conservatory at Garfield Park; and dormitories for IU. After his father's death in 1959, David Burns continued his architecture career, associating with August Bohlen in the firm Bohlen and Burns Architects in 1961. Shortly before Burns retired in 1967, the firm incorporated as Bohlen, Burns and Associates (today BOHLEN, MEYER, GIBSON AND ASSOCIATES).

During the 1950s the firm of Edward D. James Architect was very active. James took his IU commissions with him when he split with Burns, and the university was his primary client for many years. By 1956 he had gained other major clients; that year the firm designed the original terminal building at Weir Cook Airport (now INDIANAPOLIS INTERNATIONAL AIRPORT). The following year James offered associateships to three of the architects working for him and the firm became Edward D. James and Associates. The firm continued to design buildings for IU and added commissions in Indianapolis, such as Public School 2 and the Eastgate Christian Church. In the late 1950s the firm designed the Fall Creek branch of the YMCA and the Wabash Fire and Casualty Building on North Meridian Street.

The 1960s and 1970s were busy and profitable years for James and Associates and included designs for the Third Christian Church (1963) and PARK TUDOR SCHOOL (1964). Following James' death in 1969, James and Associates continued to thrive, with projects such as the U.S. Post Office at 125 West South Street.

One of the associates, H. Roll McLaughlin, became heavily involved in restoration projects in the 1970s and 1980s. Introduced to restoration by James, who had been a member of the American Institute of Architects' Committee for Preservation of Historic Buildings, McLaughlin gained skills in restoration and preservation at New Harmony and Madison, Indiana, in the 1950s and 1960s. Later he used these skills on several projects in the Indianapolis area, including the BENJAMIN HARRISON HOUSE, MORRIS-BUTLER HOUSE, CONNER PRAIRIE, and the JAMES WHITCOMB RILEY HOME.

In 1985 James Associates and Engineers, with 29 architects and 135 staff members, was the largest architectural firm in the city and had several other offices in the state. It counted the INDIANAPOLIS ZOO, renovations at the CITY MARKET, and additions at BUTLER UNIVERSITY among its most significant commissions. Annual billings reached $8.5 million. By the late 1980s, however, the principal partners had all retired from the firm and sold their interests to a group of younger architects who called themselves James Architects and Engineers. By 1990 the new group had gone

out of business and vacated the offices, leaving the retired partners to sell the firm's property and to bear the loss of the defunct buyout plan.

CONNIE J. ZEIGLER

Buses. Since 1975, most scheduled bus service between points in Marion County has been provided by the INDIANAPOLIS PUBLIC TRANSPORTATION CORPORATION—known as Metro—a municipal corporation with authority to tax real estate in the county outside Beech Grove, Lawrence, Southport, and Speedway, subject to approval by the CITY-COUNTY COUNCIL and the State Board of Tax Control. Earlier, three for-profit corporations had run buses on intensive schedules within the old city limits.

The Peoples Motor Coach Company operated scheduled, 24-seat buses between the Circle and Riverside Park beginning in December, 1923. Under the jitney ordinance, Peoples expanded steadily on routes not served by STREETCARS. The Indianapolis Street Railway Company also used buses beginning in 1925, extending its lines on Capitol and Central to points north of 54th Street. It added other routes and, in 1927, bought all of the shares in Peoples, creating an integrated system regulated by the Public Service Commission of Indiana. Buses went mostly to outlying areas, streetcars to densely populated areas.

The Railway Company operated in receivership from 1930 to 1932, when its system was bought by Indianapolis Railways, Inc. (renamed Indianapolis Transit System in 1953). This company began almost at once to replace the traditional streetcar—with its rails that were expensive to maintain and its lack of maneuverability in automobile traffic—substituting trackless trolleys on some lines, buses on others. The last streetcar lines were converted to bus lines in 1952 and 1953 so the streets involved could be made one-way. By then, trackless trolleys carried the most passengers.

But the bus—more maneuverable and lacking wires to build and maintain—was apparently the mode preferred by Frederick J. Johnson, leader of a group of non-local investors who bought control of the company in 1955. Buses entirely replaced trackless trolleys in 1957. Accused of weakening the company by such transactions as using surplus cash from the sale of the Traction Terminal to pay dividends, Johnson did manage to make a profit on operations every year from 1955 to 1969 and kept the system running until Metro could buy it (at a negotiated price) in 1975. The number of passenger rides had fallen from 118 million in 1946 to 12.4 million in 1974 as the company faced a cycle of losing passengers to the automobile, raising fares and cutting service to make ends meet, and losing more passengers as a result. The base fare was 12 cents in 1949, 50 cents in 1974.

Metro was launched with high hopes. The number of passenger rides rose from 12.8 million in 1975 to 15 million in 1980 because of public spirit and a gasoline shortage, but declined later. In 1990, there were 10.3 million passenger rides, which paid 30.5 percent of Metro's $23 million budget. The base fare in 1992 was 75 cents.

CHARLES JOHNSON TAGGART

James Farmer, "From Donkeys to Diesels," *Indianapolis Star Magazine*, Oct. 2, 1949; *Indianapolis News*, Nov. 26, 1952, Jan. 6, 1975.

Bush, Owen Joseph (Oct. 8, 1887–Mar. 28, 1972). Indianapolis Indians owner, manager, and player. A native of the east side of Indianapolis, Bush began his BASEBALL career playing for local amateur and semipro teams before beginning his professional career at Sault Ste. Marie, Michigan, in 1905. He was drafted by seven major league teams in 1907. The Detroit Tigers won his services and sent him to Indianapolis, where Bush helped the INDIANAPOLIS INDIANS win the American Association pennant in 1908. He then returned to Detroit and distinguished himself with his speed and fielding abilities as the team's primary shortstop for 14 seasons.

Bush became a baseball manager in 1923 and managed the Indians from 1924 to 1926. The following season, he managed the Pittsburgh Pirates to the National League pennant. He also managed the National League Cincinnati Reds and the American League Washington Senators and Chicago White Sox, making Bush at the time of his death the only man to have managed two teams in both major leagues.

Known as "Ownie" at home and "Donie" by baseball fans around the country, Bush returned to Indianapolis and, with local banker FRANK E. MCKINNEY, SR., bought the Indians in 1941. Although primary ownership of the club shifted to the Cleveland Indians in 1952 and to a broad-based group of community stockholders in 1956, Bush remained with the team as president or general manager until his retirement in 1969. The city-owned ballpark, Bush Stadium, was named in his honor in 1967.

THOMAS A. HARTON

Bush Stadium. Indianapolis Indians baseball park. After the 1930 season Norman Perry, INDIANAPOLIS INDIANS owner and president of INDIANAPOLIS POWER AND LIGHT COMPANY, announced plans to build a new baseball stadium on West 16th Street. The Indians played their first game in the 14,500 seat stadium before a disappointingly small crowd of 5,942 on September 5, 1931. Perry named the $350,000 park Perry Stadium in honor of his brother and previous team owner James Perry, who died in a plane crash in 1929.

After a string of unsuccessful seasons in the 1930s, Perry sold the Indians to FRANK E. MCKINNEY, SR., president of the Fidelity Trust Company, and OWEN J. BUSH, Indianapolis native and former major leaguer and Indians manager. The sale did not include Perry Stadium, which was to be leased to the new owners. McKinney and Bush promised a complete overhaul of baseball operations, and part of their plan was to rename Perry Stadium. One of Bush's first moves as club president was to conduct a vote among the fans to determine a new name, and in 1942 the Indians played their home opener at Victory Field.

On June 1, 1967, the city of Indianapolis bought Perry Stadium from the estate of Norman Perry. Victory Field was officially rechristened Owen J. Bush Stadium, in honor of the former Indians' star and long-time club president, during a pre-game ceremony on August 30, 1967.

Bush Stadium has hosted numerous minor league playoff and championship games during its years as the Indians' home. In 1987 it was the site of the PAN AMERICAN GAMES baseball tournament. In 1988, *Eight Men Out*, a movie about the infamous "Black Sox" scandal of 1920, was filmed at Bush Stadium.

In 1992 Major League Baseball inspected Bush Stadium and found that it did not meet the Minor League Baseball facility standards implemented in 1991. In July, 1993, the president of the National Association, Minor League Baseball's governing body, announced Major League Baseball's intention to move the Indians unless the city made a commitment to upgrade the facilities. Since necessary renovations were estimated at $12–14 million, the Indians in 1993 began negotiating with the CAPITAL IMPROVEMENT BOARD for the construction of a new stadium. These negotiations led to an announcement in late spring, 1994, of plans for a new downtown stadium to be built just west of the Hoosier Dome on land made available by White River State Park.

WILLIAM D. DALTON

David Reddick and Kim M. Rogers, *The Magic of Indians Baseball* (Indianapolis, 1988).

Business and Professional Women's Club.

The Business and Professional Women's Club was organized in 1926 as an offshoot of the WOMAN'S DEPARTMENT CLUB. It continued to meet at the department clubhouse until business club members bought a facility at 1101 North Delaware Street in 1936. One purpose of the club was to educate and support both young and mature women in their efforts to be active in the work force. To encourage careers for young women the club held an essay contest on "My Vocation" for high school girls and invited the winners to the clubhouse to read their essays. The club also formed a branch for young women called Contemporary Careers Club, which grew from 8 members to 50 within its first year. Its main purpose was to help young women with their concerns about the career world, especially after they were married. Annually BPW honored a top businesswoman, and in 1979 the club started an award to honor Indianapolis professional women.

ELLEN TEVAULT

Business Cycles.

In Indianapolis, as elsewhere, business cycles stem from shocks to the economy. In the 19th century, monetary panics begun by failures in the banking system gave rise to economic downturns. In the 20th century, oil price fluctuations have contributed to instability. An issue during both centuries has been the role of government as promoter of economic development through its regulatory powers and as an employer of last resort in the face of economic downturns. Indianapolis has been fortunate to have a diversified industrial base that has reduced the instability arising from national business cycles.

In the 19th century, insufficient financial capital for Indiana's growing economy led to state legislation in 1852 establishing the free banking system. The law made it easier to establish a bank through lower capitalization and reserve requirements. As a consequence, banks were rapidly established in Indianapolis and elsewhere and issued their own paper money. An oversupply of this paper currency soon depreciated the value of the money and caused runs on the banks which, in turn, reduced their ability to lend and thus contracted economic activity. The national Panic of 1857 further undermined the Indianapolis economy by eliminating even more free banks.

Following the Civil War, a boom in real estate encouraged a cycle of speculation and debt accumulation. Real estate values increased faster than the family incomes required to manage these debts. The result was a collapse of the speculative bubble in the nationwide Panic of 1873, the beginning of a six-year-long depression. In Indianapolis, some banks closed while others restricted withdrawals. Although a group of manufacturers urged firms to maintain payrolls and wage levels, individual firms ignored the plea and laid off workers. City and county government was called upon to become an employer of last resort, which it did by hiring men to work on the streets and roads. Controversy over the role of government in the economy was evidenced by a local newspaper that criticized a measure calling for direct relief as "wrong in principle and demoralizing in practice." The city council passed the measure despite the paper's opposition.

According to the National Bureau of Economic Research, the United States experienced 45 business cycles between 1790 and 1990. The bureau uses a variety of economic indicators, with inflation-adjusted Gross Domestic Product (GDP) being the most important. The standard U.S. Department of Commerce estimates of GDP were initiated in 1929. GDP has been estimated for the years before 1929 by using income payments and the value of finished commodities as they left the producer. For Indianapolis, estimates of income payments are available beginning in 1929.

During the GREAT DEPRESSION, personal income in the Great Lakes region declined more than in the nation as a whole. The declines focused on manufacturing and construction. During World War II, Great Lakes and Indianapolis manufacturing was stimulated by the conversion of automobile, machinery, and primary and fabricated metals industries to military durable goods production. Because there was no production of consumer durables such as appliances during the war, Great Lakes manufacturing benefited after the war from pent up demand.

The recessions of 1953–1954 and 1957–1958 slowed personal income growth, with weakness focused in manufacturing. During the 1950s earnings from Indianapolis manufacturing reached their largest share of total earnings. In the four national business cycles between 1948 and 1970, Indiana ranked second behind Michigan in having the greatest sensitivity to the national business cycle. The reason was the concentration in durable goods manufacturing, such as automobile parts, machinery, and steel, in both states.

Indianapolis has been well represented in durable goods manufacturing by companies such as Allison Gas Turbine, Allison Transmission, WESTERN ELECTRIC, FORD, General Motors, and CHRYSLER. A leading indicator of local economic activity has been the number of hours worked in durable goods manufacturing firms and the number of new unemployment insurance claims. If economic activity slows, the first place to indicate the slowdown has been these labor market measures.

In the back-to-back national recessions of 1980 and 1981–1982, Indianapolis' manufacturing firms, like their national counterparts, attempted to change their way of doing business and be more competitive in the emerging global economy primarily by cutting costs. Coming out of the 1980–1982 recession, Indianapolis did not regain its pre–1980 proportion of employment in manufacturing because of plant closures, reductions in size, and the substitution of electronically based machinery for employees. The occupations especially hard hit were machine operators, assemblers, and craftsworkers. These high wage jobs had provided the economic strength for many Indianapolis families. In the 1990–1991 recession, manufacturing did not contract as in prior recessions because of changes made earlier in production methods, better inventory control, and the growing importance of demand for exports produced by Indianapolis firms.

One consequence of the long-term employment shift out of agriculture and manufacturing and into services is that local recessions have become shorter and less frequent because the production of services is less volatile than the production of agricultural and manufactured goods. Services employment, however, is not immune to the business cycle. The two primary components of services are health and business services. As a primary health care center, Indianapolis employment in health care has increased and shown only slowed rates of increase during economic slowdowns. Business services consist of a range of activities, including temporary help agencies, computer programming, leasing, janitorial services, and management consulting. During recessions, firms tend to cut back on temporary help.

Another factor contributing to shorter and less frequent local recessions is the changing composition of personal income. Income support payments, such as unemployment insurance and welfare payments, and bank deposit insurance plans have been developed to support business and consumer confidence during recessions. In 1929, "transfer payments" like these represented 2.2 percent of Indianapolis' personal income. As Social Security benefits increased, transfer payments in 1982, a year of recession, had risen to 14.3 percent of personal income.

Indianapolis has developed a very diversified mix of industries. This characteristic moderates the influence of a national recession on the local economy as compared to the rest of Indiana. As a consequence of its diversification, and therefore its relative stability, the city of Indianapolis enjoyed a AAA bond rating for much of the 1980s.

As the capital city, Indianapolis has a concentration of government employment, a circumstance which, at times, shields the local economy from severe recessions. Some people argue that the business cycle is the result of the failure of the market to adjust, and they call upon the government to intervene in the market to reduce cyclical fluctuations. Others support a laissez-faire approach, believing that government should stay out of the market economy. During the recession of 1973–1975, government employment increased during the recession and, therefore, was countercyclical. During the 1980–1982 recession, however, government employment declined. Indiana state government, through the establishment of a "rainy day" fund, has assumed some responsibility for stabilizing Hoosier economics when the national economy contracts severely.

ROBERT J. KIRK
Indiana University–Purdue University,
Indianapolis

Butler, Noble Chase (Feb. 21, 1844–Oct. 7, 1933). Lawyer and civic leader. Born in Salem, Indiana, Butler attended Hanover College (1860–1863) before joining the 93rd Indiana Volunteer Infantry Regiment, serving in telegraphy and army intelligence. Following the Civil War he read law with his father, John H. Butler, and WALTER Q. GRESHAM, studied law at the University of Louisville (Kentucky), and joined his father's New Albany law practice. In 1867 U.S. Supreme Court Chief Justice Salmon P. Chase named him registrar in bankruptcy in New Albany. Butler moved to Indianapolis in July, 1879, to become clerk of the U.S. Circuit (until 1912) and District courts, a position he held until retiring in October, 1922.

A nationally recognized authority on bankruptcy law, Butler lectured on federal jurisprudence at the Indiana Law School (1902–1928) and the law school at Indiana University. Known as both orator and essayist, he contributed fre-

quently to the *American Law Review,* the *Atlantic Monthly,* and other literary reviews.

Butler was one of the incorporators of the National (American) Red Cross, the Indiana chapter of which was established in his home. He was a member of the INDIANAPOLIS LITERARY CLUB, COLUMBIA CLUB, and the American and Indiana bar associations. He died at his home at 1204 North Park Avenue, now the MORRIS-BUTLER HOUSE museum, and is interred in CROWN HILL CEMETERY.

SHERYL D. VANDERSTEL

Indianapolis Sentinel, May 30, 1904; *Indianapolis Star,* Oct. 26, 1922, Oct. 8, 1933.

Butler, Ovid (Feb. 7, 1801–July 12, 1881). Founder of North Western Christian (Butler) University and civic leader. Born in Augusta, New York, Butler moved to Jennings County, Indiana, in 1817. He taught school for a few years, read law, and settled in Shelbyville in 1825. He moved to Indianapolis in 1836, established a law practice, and quickly became partners with another well-known attorney, CALVIN FLETCHER.

In 1849 Butler retired from his law practice, but not from an active involvement with his adopted city. The following year he designed a university plan, drafted a charter, and sold 20 acres of his own property to be the site of a Disciples of Christ school, North Western Christian University (now BUTLER UNIVERSITY). The university was erected between 1854 and 1855 at the corner of current 13th Street and College Avenue. Butler also provided the school with a large en-

Ovid Butler served as president of North Western Christian (now Butler) University from 1851 until 1871. [Butler University Archives]

dowment. For 20 years, until 1871, he was president of the institution.

In addition to his work for the university, Butler was active in Indianapolis civic life. Politically, he was first a Democrat, then a Free Soiler, and finally a Republican. He was also an early residential developer. He platted the land around his home and the university (between current 11th and 16th streets) into residential additions, helping to create some of the more fashionable districts on the city's northside. He was a committee member and promoter of the Free School movement of the late 1840s and early 1850s. Part owner of the INDIANAPOLIS JOURNAL, he also was a financial backer of a local antislavery paper, the *Free Soil Banner*.

In 1877 North Western Christian honored its benefactor by adopting his name, becoming Butler College, and later, Butler University.

CONNIE J. ZEIGLER

Jacob Piatt Dunn, *Greater Indianapolis* (Chicago, 1910).

Butler Relays. National indoor track meet (1933–1942). Founded by BUTLER UNIVERSITY track coach Herman Phillips, the Butler Relays were a prestigious American track and field competition. Phillips had won three NCAA quartermile championships and was a member of the 1928 U.S. Olympic 1,600 meter gold medal relay team.

The event annually showcased 350–400 athletes representing 20–30 colleges and universities. From an attendance of 3,500, the games grew to attract over 10,000 spectators to Butler Fieldhouse each March. The college's fraternities and sororities vied in yearly ticket sales, parade float, house decoration, and Relay Queen competitions. The University Division "Governor's Cup" went to each year's victor, with Indiana University (IU) claiming the inaugural trophy and the University of Notre Dame taking the final prize. The University of Michigan captured the eight intervening awards. Butler claimed the College Division "Mayor's Trophy" between 1938 and 1941. In addition to the participation of legendary American Olympians Jesse Owens, Glenn Cunningham,

Indoor World Records Set at the Butler Relays

Athlete/School	Event	Year	Record
Ken Sandback/Purdue	60 yd high hurdles	1934	7.4 sec
Haye Lambertus/Nebraska	60 yd low hurdles	1934	6.7 sec
Milt Padaway/Wisconsin	pole vault	1939	14'
IU Relay Team	medley relay	1940	10:10.3
Bob Wright/Ohio State	60 yd high hurdles	1941	7.3 sec

Indoor World Records Tied at the Butler Relays

Athlete/School	Event	Year	Record
Jesse Owens/Ohio State	60 yd dash	1935	6.1 sec
Mel Walker/Ohio State	high jump	1937	6'9³/₄"
Harvey Woodstra/Mich. St.	60 yd high hurdles	1938	7.4 sec
Ed Smith/Wisconsin	60 yd high hurdles	1939	7.4 sec
Ed Smith/Wisconsin	60 yd high hurdles	1940	7.4 sec

Ralph Metcalfe, and IU's Don Lash, the Butler Relays saw ten world records set or tied during the meet's decade-long run.

When Phillips became head track and field coach at Purdue University in 1938, Lawrence Holmes directed the relays for one year. Butler alumnus and former world two mile record holder Ray Sears staged the games from 1939 until the fieldhouse was dedicated to military use in 1942. The Butler Relays were not reinstituted after World War II because of the expense and the basketball program's influence over fieldhouse scheduling.

R. DALE OGDEN
Indiana State Museum

"Butler Relays" Scrapbook, Division of Rare Books, Irwin Library, Butler University.

Butler Romantic Festival. A celebration of Romantic music at Butler University. An annual April or May event from 1968 to 1989, the Romantic Festival was founded by Frank Cooper, Butler music professor. Orchestral and vocal music, dance, lectures, and dining—all in a Romantic vein—were festival features.

Festival guests included Victor Borge, conducting the INDIANAPOLIS SYMPHONY ORCHESTRA (1969, 1977); violinist Isaac Stern (1986); and mezzo-soprano Marilyn Horne (1988). Funding sources varied over the years. Contributors included the National Endowment for the Arts, the INDIANA ARTS COMMISSION, and Indianapolis businesses, institutions, and citizens.

JOANNE KEATON

Butler-Tarkington. Northside neighborhood bounded by the Central Canal, Meridian Street (west side), 38th Street, and Michigan Road. Named for BUTLER UNIVERSITY and former resident BOOTH TARKINGTON, the area is a consolidation of numerous 19th-century farms, a few homes of which still stand.

Two key factors reflecting Indianapolis' urban growth in the early 20th century contributed to the development of the Butler-Tarkington neighborhood. The popularity of North Meridian Street as a prime residential address and Butler University's acquisition of and relocation to FAIRVIEW PARK in 1928 created a substantial area of desirable home sites located in between. The earliest homes constructed in the 20th century were typically middle class bungalows, located in the south central portion of the neighborhood, north of Maple Road (38th Street) and along Illinois Street, Capitol Avenue, and Boulevard Place. The development of the university and North Meridian Street, however, stimulated construction of homes reflecting the same diverse architectural styles as the Meridian Street mansions, though on a decidedly smaller scale. Although the neighborhood was essentially developed by 1940, scattered areas contain homes built after World War II.

Given the proximity of Butler University and CHRISTIAN THEOLOGICAL SEMINARY, education has traditionally played a central role in the neighborhood. In 1922 MARY STEWART CAREY established ORCHARD COUNTRY DAY SCHOOL, a progressive elementary school, in her home at 5050 North Meridian Street; it later moved to 610 West 42nd Street in 1927 where it remained until 1957. Two public schools also serve the neighborhood, as does St. Thomas Aquinas Catholic School. The Butler University campus is the neighborhood's cultural center.

Besides Booth Tarkington the neighborhood has been home to several influential individuals including LARUE D. CARTER, FRANK E. MCKINNEY, SR., Phillip R. Mallory, and DAVID LAURANCE CHAMBERS. Since 1975, when the State of Indiana acquired 4750 North Meridian Street for the official GOVERNOR'S RESIDENCE, the neighborhood has also been home to Indiana's governors. The Butler-Tarkington Neighborhood Association, established in 1956 to "conserve and improve" the neighborhood, serves the area. It is among the oldest continuously operating neighborhood associations in the nation.

SHERYL D. VANDERSTEL

David J. Bodenhamer et al., *The Main Stem* (Indianapolis, 1993); Butler-Tarkington Neighborhood Association files.

Butler University. Fully accredited, independent institution of higher education, chartered in 1850. Located in a residential area five miles north of the city's center, Butler occupies over 250 acres along the east bank of WHITE RIVER and the CENTRAL CANAL, combining the educational and cultural advantages of an urban area with the open vistas of its landscaped campus.

The university emphasizes the traditional liberal arts and sciences in innovative interdisciplinary approaches combined with diverse professional and preprofessional programs. Over 200 full-time faculty teach in five colleges: Liberal Arts and Sciences; Education, evolved from a merger in 1930 with Teachers College of Indianapolis, founded by ELIZA BLAKER; Business Administration, established in 1937; Pharmacy, from a merger that absorbed the old Indianapolis College of Pharmacy in 1945; and JORDAN COLLEGE OF FINE ARTS (formerly of Music), a merger with Arthur Jordan Conservatory of Music in 1951. A School of Religion, established in 1924, became independent CHRISTIAN THEOLOGICAL SEMINARY in 1958.

Enrollment from all parts of the country and abroad averages over 2,500 full-time students and 1,300 part-time. Three large residence halls and 14 national sororities and fraternities house residential students.

The university opened in 1855 as North Western Christian University, founded by members of the CHRISTIAN CHURCH (DISCIPLES OF CHRIST) though never controlled by the church, which had no central governing body. The charter written by OVID BUTLER, prominent city lawyer and leader of the founders, called for a nonsectarian institution free from the taint of slavery, offering instruction in every branch of liberal and professional education. Admitting women as well as men, North Western Christian was the first co-educational college in Indiana, and second or third in the nation. It made no restrictions on race or religious persuasion. Stockholders elected tri-ennially chose a board of directors who operated the university. In 1909 stock was called in and the board became self-perpetuating.

The university has occupied three campuses, the first of 25 acres at what is now 13th Street and College Avenue, land sold by Ovid Butler from his own estate. WILLIAM TINSLEY (later the architect of CHRIST CHURCH on the Circle) designed the build-ing in an innovative style that became known as Collegiate Gothic.

With Ovid Butler's endowment in 1869 of the Demia Butler Chair (the first endowed chair in the country specifically designated for a woman), the university established the first pro-fessorship in English literature and the first de-partment of English in the state. CATHARINE MERRILL, incumbent of the chair, became the sec-ond woman named to be a professor in an Amer-ican university.

After the Civil War, which had virtually emp-tied the college of male students, enrollments rose. A preparatory department (1853–1907), necessary for many colleges because of the lack of high schools, further crowded the old building. Expansion was necessary. Rising land values made campus acreage valuable. These factors, coupled with inducements of land and money from the village of IRVINGTON, offered an attractive enhancement of the meager endowment.

The university moved to Irvington, its sec-ond campus, in 1875. Here it became one of the state's respected small colleges, closely identified with literary figures, artists, and musicians who flourished in the suburban cultural enclave. In 1877 North Western Christian changed its name to Butler University to honor its long-time leader and major benefactor, Ovid Butler.

A short-lived and ineffective University of In-dianapolis, chartered in 1896, included Butler as its undergraduate college along with the city's for-merly independent colleges of medicine, den-tistry, and law, a combination that quietly expired by 1906. A more important alliance with the Uni-versity of Chicago, lasting from 1898 to 1908, fur-thered curricular development and offered special degree privileges to Butler students.

Butler University moved to its third and present campus, the extensive area of former FAIRVIEW PARK, in 1928. It had outgrown the re-stricted Irvington site. Moreover, it was respond-ing to a call from city leaders to develop the small college into a university that would serve the needs of a growing urban center.

This move was a turning point. Presidents Scot Butler (1891–1904, 1906–1907) and THO-MAS CARR HOWE (1908–1920) had effectively laid the groundwork for a greater Butler University. With the end of WORLD WAR II President Maurice O. Ross (1942 –1962) introduced an innovative University College, a two-year curriculum in gen-eral studies required of all students. His foresight and good management earned the confidence of the board, which had heretofore controlled all as-pects of the university. The directors henceforth entrusted administrative responsibilities to Ross and his successors.

Initial construction at the present campus in-cluded Arthur Jordan Hall and an impressive fieldhouse, earliest and largest of college field-houses in its time, now named HINKLE FIELD-HOUSE for Butler's legendary coach, PAUL D. "TONY" HINKLE. The fieldhouse became the site for the annual boys' basketball state tournament. In World War II it was temporarily converted into barracks and mess hall for Navy and Army Air Corps cadets. At Irwin Field in Irvington and later at Fairview teams coached by Orville "Pat" Page, George "Potsy" Clark, and Hinkle brought out crowds reflecting the rage for collegiate athletics that began in the 1920s.

Though slowed by the Great Depression and World War II, growth in the next half century added a score of buildings. Notable additions in-clude the strikingly modern Irwin Library and CLOWES HALL for the performing arts. Clowes Hall brought symphony, opera, ballet, noted speakers, and Broadway productions to the cam-pus and the public.

The school's graduates fill the ranks of the city's lawyers, teachers, businessmen, doctors, and dentists, as well as having achieved promi-nence in other endeavors at both state and na-tional levels. Butler students have become college presidents like Frank H. Sparks of Wabash; physicians and scientists like Harvey Wiley, father of the U.S. pure food and drug laws; government officials like Postmaster General Harry S. New; authors like James G. Randall, noted Civil War scholar; and newsmen like Edwin C. Hill, RALPH (LUKE) WALTON, Corbin Patrick, and HILTON U. BROWN. Other notable alumni include Todd Duncan, class of 1925, the original Porgy in Gershwin's *Porgy and Bess*, and bandsman NOBLE SISSLE.

An array of services now support new academic programs, the performing arts, and extracurricular organizations. Recommendations of a committee of 200 cultural, educational, and business leaders from around the country provide a guide for the university's future.

GEORGE M. WALLER
Butler University

———

Minutes, Board of Directors (after 1962, Trustees), 1852 to present; *Butler Alumnal Quarterly* (and successor alumni publications), 1912 to present; "A Source Manual Prepared for the Commission on the Future of Butler University," Butler University, 1985.

Butler University Architecture. The campus of Butler University occupies 290 acres on the city's north side, with its principal entrance on the east at 46th Street and Sunset Avenue. The present campus is the third location for the university. The first was on the city's near north side at the eastern edge of the present OLD NORTHSIDE Historic District, on land provided by lawyer and educator OVID BUTLER. Its buildings, none of which survive, had been designed by Irish-born architect WILLIAM TINSLEY, whose work also included Christ Church Cathedral.

In the mid–1870s the university, renamed for Ovid Butler, moved to the newly platted town of IRVINGTON, where it remained until 1928. The campus consisted of 25 acres and several buildings, including an observatory, most of which were demolished in 1939. The Bona Thompson Library (1902–1903) at the intersection of Downey and University avenues, designed by architects Dupont and Johnson, is the only extant university building in Irvington, although several dwellings that once housed faculty still remain, most notably the Benton House.

Increased enrollments following World War I prompted the administration to consider a new, larger campus location. The campus was ultimately laid out with assistance from noted landscape architect George Sheridan on the site of FAIRVIEW PARK, a former amusement park at a streetcar terminus on the city's northwest side.

At its present location Butler's first and for years its primary building was Arthur Jordan Memorial Hall, designed by ROBERT FROST DAGGETT and Thomas Hibben in 1927 and opened the following year. The structure's Collegiate Gothic style set the tone for subsequent buildings erected over the next three decades. Also in 1928 the Butler Fieldhouse (later renamed HINKLE FIELDHOUSE) by architect FERMOR SPENCER CANNON was completed. The building remained the largest indoor sports facility in the state until the mid–1960s.

The Williamsburg-inspired Religion Building and Sweeney Chapel (remodeled into Robertson Hall in 1966) designed by BURNS AND JAMES was completed in 1942. Other than that, there was little construction on the campus until after World War II, except for numerous fraternity houses, mostly along Hampton Drive. Postwar construction began with the Student Union Building (later, Atherton Center, remodeled and expanded in 1993) by MCGUIRE AND SHOOK, completed in 1950. In the mid–1950s the firm also designed the two large dormitories, Ross Hall, originally for men, and Schwitzer Hall for women, both on Hampton Drive. North of Jordan Hall the visually compatible Pharmacy Building, also designed by McGuire and Shook, was erected in 1954.

Along the Central Canal industrialist and philanthropist J. I. Holcomb in 1950 designed the gardens bearing his name, with assistance from Art Lindberg, Butler's superintendent of buildings and grounds. Safety concerns in recent decades have prompted the removal of several acres of woodland and the thinning of vegetation, diminishing somewhat the Romantic landscape envisioned by Holcomb. Lindberg, with help from Daggett, also designed the HOLCOMB OBSERVATORY, dedicated in 1955. Next to the fieldhouse the Hilton U. Brown Theatron, designed by Lennox and Matthews, was completed the same year, but without the roof that was added much later.

What had once been the Arthur Jordan Conservatory of Music moved onto the campus and into its new home, Lilly Hall, in 1962. The following year CLOWES MEMORIAL HALL, the cultural center of the campus and for years of the Indianapolis community as a whole, opened. It remains one of the finest works of architect Evans Woollen III, in association with John Johansen. The gleaming white Irwin Library, designed by Minoru Yamasaki, stirred even more comment when it opened in 1963.

For ten years there was no major construction on the Butler campus, until the science complex, consisting of the Holcomb Research Institute and Gallahue Hall, filled the gap between Jordan Hall and the Pharmacy Building to form a solid "U" at the terminus of 46th Street. Another decade passed before a new building to house the Special Instruction Division (formerly located on the Holcomb estate off Cold Spring Road) was constructed at the far northeast corner of the campus at 52nd Street and Boulevard Place. Recent years, however, have brought a major reconfiguration of the campus, with the conversion of the 4600 block of Clarendon Road into a grass-filled pedestrian mall and the construction at the corner of Sunset and Hampton of the innovative Residential College, designed by James and Associates, in 1990.

GLORY-JUNE GREIFF

Cable, Mary Ellen (ca. 1862–Sept. 18, 1944). African-American educator. Born and raised in Leavenworth, Kansas, Cable graduated from Leavenworth Teachers' Normal School in the 1890s and taught elementary school for a brief time in Topeka, Kansas, where she met her husband, teacher George Cable. The couple moved to Indianapolis ca. 1893, where George accepted a position at the post office and Mary began her 40 years of service with the Indianapolis Public Schools.

From 1903 to 1905 Cable successfully oversaw the African-American community's elementary school vegetable garden project, which ultimately caused residents in surrounding neighborhoods to plant gardens and improve property upkeep. In 1916–1917, with the support of several black women's clubs, Cable instituted the first "fresh air" classroom for tuberculous black children at Public School 4. During her tenure as director of practice teaching, the Indianapolis School Board certified 61 much needed African-American teachers. School 4, which was named in her honor, is now the Mary Cable Building on the IUPUI campus.

Cable was also an active member of various social and civic groups—among them BETHEL AFRICAN METHODIST EPISCOPAL CHURCH, Browning Literary Society, and SIGMA GAMMA RHO sorority. In 1912, as president of the Colored Women's Civic Club, a local philanthropic group, Cable provided the impetus for organizing the first Indiana chapter of the NATIONAL ASSOCIATION FOR THE ADVANCEMENT OF COLORED PEOPLE (NAACP), the organization's most western branch at that time. She served as Indiana's first NAACP president and for the first 13 months all other officers and members of the executive board were club women.

EARLINE RAE FERGUSON

Indianapolis News, Apr. 15, 1933, Sept. 19, 1944; *The Crisis*, July, Oct., 1912, Apr., 1915.

Cable Television. Cable television sends and receives television signals through coaxial cable instead of over the air. A master antenna or satellite dish receives a signal which is sent through wires to numerous receiving points. Boosters or amplifiers along the route maintain signal strength and quality. Cable originally was called CATV—community antenna television— and developed in the late 1940s in rural and mountainous areas of the country that suffered from poor reception of broadcast television. Urban systems emerged slowly over the next 30 years, and the industry's real growth came in the late 1970s and 1980s as cable programs became an alternative to broadcast television.

Two of the country's largest multiple system operators (MSO's) provide service to Indianapolis. American Cablevision, part of Time Warner Cable, is franchisee for the area within the pre-Unigov city limits, or the central city. It has subscribers in almost half the homes in its service area. Comcast Cable operates within the formerly unincorporated areas of Marion County, as well as Beech Grove, Speedway, Lawrence, and Southport. Its penetration level is near 60 percent.

While broadcast stations are regulated only by the Federal Communications Commission (FCC), cable systems are subject to regulation by both the FCC and local governments because cable operators must use local streets and utility poles to string their cable. Local governments issue franchises to serve particular communities. Cable operations in Indianapolis are governed by Chapter $8\frac{1}{2}$ of the Municipal Code. Originally enacted in 1979, this chapter calls for the development of cable television that is versatile and reliable, responsive to the needs of the community, and diverse in its information sources. Authority rests with a cable franchise board made up of five members, two of whom are appointed by the mayor, and three by the CITY-COUNTY COUNCIL. The board advises the council on cable policy and oversees franchising. A 1993 amendment created a cable communications agency to make sure cable companies operate within the law and according to their franchise agreements.

Chapter $8\frac{1}{2}$ also details all application renewal procedures for cable operators, as well as award and franchise fees. A new franchisee must pay an award fee of 20 cents for each home, apartment, motel, and hotel unit in its service area. The annual franchise fee is 3 percent of an operator's gross revenue, and is paid to the city each quarter. Franchise terms are 15 years.

Locally owned Metropolitan Cablevision was the original franchisee for Indianapolis, signing a 25–year agreement with the pre-Unigov Marion County commissioners in 1967. Wabash Cablevision and Metropolitan merged in 1978 to become Indianapolis Cablevision. The 1967 franchise was challenged by numerous parties in 1979, but was ruled valid; Indianapolis Cablevision's first customers received service later that year. In 1984 INDIANAPOLIS POWER AND LIGHT COMPANY purchased Indianapolis Cablevision, then sold it to Comcast, headquartered in Philadelphia, two years later.

Although the Metropolitan-Indianapolis-Comcast franchise was to expire in 1992, it was extended in 1984 to end the same year as American's agreement, 1996. American's 15–year franchise was awarded in 1981 after a political battle involving the City-County Council and the Board of Public Works.

As part of their service, both operators offer various cable networks, superstations, and premium services. American offered subscribers 42 channels in 1993, while Comcast had 37. Both companies also include three public access channels. Local government is featured on one channel and first offered live coverage of the City-County Council in 1984. A second channel is used for educational purposes, and the third is a public access channel where individuals or groups can produce and present their own programming.

Prior to 1993, cable systems were required to carry all local commercial broadcast stations. However, the federal Cable Act (1992) gave broadcasters the option of keeping their "must carry" status or negotiating payment from the cable systems for "retransmission consent." Locally, only Channel 23 chose "must carry." The other Indianapolis stations ran big advertising campaigns claiming they should be paid the same way as cable networks because local TV made cable more valuable. Cable companies countered with their own ads, charging that cable gave local TV more viewers, which allowed the stations to charge more for advertising. Some stations eventually reached agreements giving them access to another cable channel for other programming in lieu of payment. The other stations agreed to extend negotiations with cable operators into 1994.

MICHAEL SPILLMAN

Cadle Tabernacle. Revival and convention center. Constructed in 1921 on the northwest corner of Ohio and New Jersey streets at a cost of $305,000, the Cadle Tabernacle had a seating capacity of 10,000 with an additional 1,500 places in the choir loft. It was of Spanish design with a red-tiled roof and whitewashed exterior, the Ohio Street side being modeled after the Alamo. The tabernacle was purported to be the largest building in America devoted to religious services.

Two historical incidents were the occasion for the construction of the tabernacle. The first was the conversion of E. Howard Cadle (1884–1942), vividly recounted in his autobiographical *How I Came Back.* Cadle was born in the village of Fredericksburg, Indiana. After several years of a life of gambling and drunkenness, he was told by a doctor that he had Bright's disease and only six months to live. He returned to his family's home in Fredericksburg and there was converted to Christianity on March 14, 1914. He subsequently regained his health, and in a short time he made a fortune through his chain of shoe repair shops. The second incident was the highly successful 1921 evangelistic campaign in Indianapolis by the British evangelist Gypsy Smith. Cadle decided to build a tabernacle at his own expense in honor of his mother, to whose prayers he credited his salvation. Its purpose was to promote Christianity and to serve as a convention center for general cultural, civic, and educational events.

Due to internal disputes and financial difficulties, Cadle temporarily lost control of the tabernacle in the twenties. During that decade Klan rallies, dance marathons, and prize fights were held in the edifice. In 1931 Cadle, heading up the Peoples Church, Inc., regained control of the building and restored it to its original religious purpose. The permanent choir was said to be the largest of its kind in the world. In 1933 the organization's radio program, which had begun two years earlier, was picked up by WLW of Cincinnati and became the Nation's Family Prayer Pe-

Built in the early 1920s, Cadle Tabernacle, at the corner of New Jersey and Ohio streets, hosted religious services featuring such well-known evangelists as Billy Sunday, Aimee Semple McPherson, and Oral Roberts. [Indiana Historical Society, Bass Collection, #81061]

riod, the most popular religious program of its day. The tabernacle sponsored evangelistic campaigns throughout the nation and also distributed radios to pastorless churches in remote rural areas of southern states so that worship services could be conducted. Upon Cadle's death in 1942, his wife, Ola M. Cadle, became director and president of the board of trustees until her death in 1955. In 1952 a television program began. Later in 1963, a prayer chapel and office building were added.

Over the years famous evangelists such as Billy Sunday, Aimee Semple McPherson, Billy Graham, and Oral Roberts conducted campaigns at Cadle Tabernacle. Dignitaries such as Lloyd George and Marshal Foch were honored and musical concerts were conducted there. For many years the annual Indiana State Teachers Association convention and the graduation ceremonies of Shortridge High School took place in the tabernacle. In 1968 the property was purchased by INDIANA NATIONAL BANK and the tabernacle was razed to make space for a parking lot.

WILLIAM L. ISLEY, JR.

E. Howard Cadle, *How I Came Back* (Indianapolis, 1932).

Cadou, Eugene Jepson (Jep), Sr.

(Mar. 14, 1896–Dec. 2, 1968). Journalist. The dean of Indiana political reporters in the 1960s, the tall, courtly Cadou covered state government and politics for four decades. A 1917 Indiana University journalism graduate, he was one of the first college-trained journalists in the Hoosier press.

He first earned his credentials as a reporter for the *INDIANAPOLIS TIMES* covering the investigation and trial of D. C. STEPHENSON and the KU KLUX KLAN. In 1927 he joined the International News Service (INS) and in 1934, while continuing his reporting, became its Indiana manager. When INS was merged with the United Press, becoming United Press International (UPI), he went to UPI as a political reporter and worked there until his death.

Born in Philadelphia, Pennsylvania, Cadou lived at Vincennes and Washington, Indiana, during his early life. At Indiana University he was a classmate of songwriter Hoagy Carmichael and was editor-in-chief of the school's *Indiana Daily Student*. He served as a infantry lieutenant in France during World War I, and after the war attended the University of Lyons in France.

In 1968 Cadou was inducted into the Indiana Journalism Hall of Fame at DePauw University and also received Indiana University's Distinguished Alumni Award. He was a founding member of the INDIANAPOLIS PRESS CLUB and its president in 1944–1945. It gave him the Front Page Award as the outstanding newsman of the year in 1960.

JAMES E. FARMER

Indianapolis Star, Dec. 3, 1968.

Camby. Southwest Decatur Township community located near the intersection of Kentucky Avenue (S.R. 67) and Camby Road. In the 19th century the town now known as Camby was a farming area. In 1888 Don Carlos Morgan and his wife, Mary Alice, purchased land and settled there. Morgan could see potential in the site and donated property for a railroad depot. He also opened a grocery store and petitioned for a post office. When he was asked to name the town Morgan suggested the name Camby, reportedly after a Brazilian city. Morgan continued to serve the community in a variety of capacities, including postmaster, until his death in 1935.

Camby has remained small and rural, despite its location along the railroad and highway. In the 1990s residents anticipate development of the area, and have improved roads and installed sanitary sewers. Though it remains largely rural, Camby hopes to attract homes and businesses as Indianapolis expands southward.

CATHLEEN F. DONNELLY

Indianapolis News, Aug. 5, 1976, Aug. 10, 1988.

Camp Fire Inc. Youth organization. Founded in 1912 by Dr. and Mrs. Luther Halsey Gulick in New York, Camp Fire Girls first appeared in Indianapolis with the establishment in 1913 of the Chanktunoogi group at the Downey Avenue Christian Church in IRVINGTON. Eleanor Putnam served as the first guardian. The national organization granted Camp Fire Girls of Indianapolis (CFGI) its first charter on January 5, 1923. Putnam established Camp Delight, which first operated in HOLLIDAY PARK, later moved to Cicero Creek southwest of Noblesville, then to an area near Mooresville, and finally returned to southern Hamilton County (1935 to 1958). A second camp, Camp Wohelo, opened in 1944 near Versailles. A day camp program started in 1953. Camp Delight closed in 1958 and CFGI leased Camp Pioneer in Bradford Woods, located near Bloomington, Indiana, until Camp Towaki opened there in 1962. In response to changes in society, Camp Fire Girls became Camp Fire Inc. in 1971 and began accepting boys into the membership. Current programs include groups at day care centers and a group at a nursing home where residents and children can interact. Membership in the early 1990s stood at approximately 200.

NORALEEN YOUNG

Indianapolis Star, Sept. 27, 1953, Mar. 23, 1965.

Camp Morton. Civil War military training center and prisoner of war camp. Shortly after Fort Sumter fell in April, 1861, Governor OLIVER P. MORTON offered President Lincoln 10,000 Hoosier troops to fight for the Union. He then searched for a suitable place to house and train

Barracks at Camp Morton, located near today's 19th and Delaware streets, housed Confederate prisoners during the Civil War. [The George Wagner Collection, University of Georgia. From the Indiana Historical Society, #C1473]

these raw recruits on their arrival in Indianapolis. His selection was an auspicious one: the new IN-DIANA STATE FAIRGROUNDS, a 36–acre tract just north of the city (bounded today, approximately, by 19th and 22nd streets, Central Avenue, and Talbott Street). Formerly "Henderson's Grove," the estate of the city's first mayor, SAMUEL HENDERSON, this land would now become Camp Morton, appropriately named after the governor.

Turning the fairgrounds into a recruitment and training depot proved to be a colossal task, but within two days officials transformed horse and cattle stalls into barracks, erected scores of tents, and converted offices into guardhouses and the power hall into a hospital. When the first troops arrived on April 17, confusion reigned, as the camp overflowed with men who had to be clothed, fed, and adequately housed. Within weeks, however, the camp settled into a routine of drill and discipline, and Indianapolis residents found it a center of attraction.

Following the Union victory at Fort Donelson in February, 1862, Gen. Henry W. Halleck sought facilities to house captured Confederates. Governor Morton wired Halleck that the Indianapolis camp could take 3,000 prisoners; by February 22, some 3,700 Confederates arrived in the city. Having undergone the rigors of battle and capture, poorly clad and inadequately fed, and now exposed to the severity of a northern winter, many of the prisoners became ill, and, until summer, the death rate was high. Indianapolis folk responded to these conditions with considerable charity. They provided food, clothing, and volunteer nursing services, and the city converted several public buildings into temporary hospitals.

Equally fortunate was Governor Morton's appointment of Colonel RICHARD OWEN as the commanding officer of the prison. Upon taking command, Owen exhibited a combination of firm discipline and sympathetic rule. Among his benevolent innovations were a strict but humane code of rules, a bakehouse which provided prisoners with work and funds for some amenities, and the encouragement of music, ball games, and other recreational activities. Though occasionally criticized by local leaders, Owen's performance became a model for other camps, and his prisoners protested his reassignment to combat duty in May, 1862.

Later commandants did not share Owen's approach—or his good fortune. His immediate successor, Colonel David Garland Rose, imposed a more stringent set of regulations, thus departing from the virtual self-government the prisoners enjoyed under Owen. The result was a sharp increase in escape attempts in the summer of 1862. During the early months of 1863, the camp actually began to decline physically, with conditions growing steadily worse throughout the year. Indeed, a mid-summer inspection revealed serious overcrowding, verminous quarters, and an inefficient guard system. Under Commandant Ambrose A. Stevens, a camp reorganization ushered in some improved conditions, especially in the provision of food, blankets, and medical care. Idle prisoners, though, conjured up elaborate schemes for escape, including dozens of tunnels and several minor uprisings. In all, over 1,700 Confederates died at Camp Morton, a mortality figure appreciably lower than those of similar northern prisons.

LLOYD A. HUNTER
Franklin College of Indiana

W. H. H. Terrell, *Report of the Adjutant General of the State of Indiana*, Volume I (Indianapolis, 1869); Hattie L. Winslow and Joseph R. H. Moore, *Camp Morton, 1861–1865: Indianapolis Prison Camp* (1940).

Campaign for Healthy Babies. A public-private partnership formed in 1989 to reduce the high infant mortality rate in Indianapolis. In 1988, the City-County Council established the Marion County Task Force on Infant Mortality in response to statistics indicating that Indianapolis had led the nation in black infant mortality in 1984, 1986, and 1987.

In October, 1989, Mayor William H. Hudnut III and the CITY-COUNTY COUNCIL established the Indianapolis Campaign for Healthy Babies (ICHB) on a three-year basis to implement the recommendations of the task force. ICHB helped to develop an infrastructure for indigent, perinatal health care by working on: removing financial barriers to prenatal and pediatric care; increasing the availability of prenatal and pediatric care for low-income women; providing comprehensive, coordinated health care and social support to women and children; and expanding awareness of the importance of prenatal care, preventive health care, and healthy lifestyles. To coordinate patient care, ICHB initiated the installation of a computerized medical record system, which links all neighborhood health centers and hospitals, the Department of Families and Children, and the Marion County Health Department. To fund these initiatives, ICHB raised more than $6.5 million in public and private resources during its three-year existence.

By the end of 1992, most of the campaign's major initiatives had institutional homes and prospects for continued funding. The HEALTH AND HOSPITAL CORPORATION OF MARION COUNTY assumed leadership of "Healthy Babies" in January, 1993.

GARY R. MILLER

Campaigne, Jameson G. (Jan. 16, 1914–Jan. 23, 1985). Editor of the *INDIANAPOLIS STAR*, author, and columnist. A native of Brooklyn, New York, Campaigne received an A.B. degree from Williams College in 1936. He first came to the attention of EUGENE C. PULLIAM in 1945 after writing a provocative *SATURDAY EVENING POST* article, "What's the Matter with the USA?" Pulliam hired Campaigne in 1946, first as chief editorial writer, then editor of the editorial page, and eventually editor (1960–1969).

While at the *Star* Campaigne was known for forceful argument and keen insight. He warned about what he saw as excessive government growth, increasing taxation, overregulation, and rampant bureaucracy. Campaigne espoused a "new conservatism" promoting liberty, individualism, creativity, productivity, and limited government.

After he left the *Star* in 1969, Campaigne was an editorial writer for the *New York Daily News* and an editorial consultant. He was the author of two books, *American Might and Soviet Myth* (1960) and *Check-Off* (1961), and edited several others.

CATHLEEN F. DONNELLY

Eldon Campbell, ca. 1978. [Indiana State Museum]

Indianapolis Star, Jan. 25, 1985.

Campbell, Eldon (Jan. 8, 1916–Apr. 19, 1991). General manager of WFBM and WRTV–6. Born in Alert, Indiana, Campbell attended Hanover College before transferring to the University of Illinois to complete his bachelor's degree. He was program manager at WOWO radio station in Fort Wayne, Indiana, from 1938 to 1945. In 1945 he became sales and program manager at KEX radio in Portland, Oregon. From 1950 to 1956 he was an executive sales representative with Westinghouse Broadcasting Company in New York City. He joined Time-Life, Inc. in 1956, and the following year became vice-president and general manager of Time-Life-owned WFBM radio and television (now WRTV–6) stations in Indianapolis. The TV station garnered numerous local honors as well as a prestigious Peabody Award under Campbell's 15–year stewardship.

In 1962 Campbell was awarded a Doctor of Humane Letters from CHRISTIAN THEOLOGICAL SEMINARY in Indianapolis. For many years, while maintaining his position at WFBM, he also taught a radio and television management course at BUTLER UNIVERSITY. In 1965 he became a trustee of Hanover College. His retirement from radio and TV in 1973 signaled a new era in his life. In 1974 he became director of the Department of Commerce for the State of Indiana. During the next 13 years he was vice-president and advertising direc-

tor for HOOK'S DRUG STORES, then vice-president of community affairs and public relations for Indiana National Bank, and board chairman of Indianapolis Cablevision.

Campbell also had a significant impact on the city as a volunteer. He served on the Boy Scout Council, on the 500 FESTIVAL committee, was president of Crossroads of America and, as president of Junior Achievement, raised over $200,000 toward the purchase of the organization's building. In recognition of his contributions to the city the *Indianapolis Star* bestowed on Campbell the Jefferson Award for outstanding public service in 1987. Just before his death Campbell started Campbell Communications International, Ltd., a global business development company.

CONNIE J. ZEIGLER

Indianapolis Star, Dec. 27, 1987, Apr. 20, 1991; The Columbian [Columbia Club], 79 (Apr., 1987).

Canadians. From the mid to late 19th century many Canadians, reacting to economic change, stagnation, and depression in their homeland, migrated southward to the cities and frontier of the United States. The largest number of Indiana's Canadian-born inhabitants resided in counties bordering Michigan, although Marion County has experienced a steady increase since the 1870 census. At that time 346 individuals born in "British America" resided in the county (297 in Indianapolis). By 1900 there were 589 from Canada's English-speaking provinces. Although Canadians never comprised a large portion of Indianapolis' foreign-born population, their numbers grew steadily throughout the 20th century. There were 1,056 individuals of Canadian ancestry (825 foreign born) in 1910, 2,239 (735 foreign born) in 1930, and 3,038 (927 foreign born) in 1960. According to the 1990 census 2,474 residents of Indianapolis reported Canadian ancestry, 1,882 (76 percent) of whom claimed French Canadian ancestry. No distinct population clusters existed among the county's 2,706 residents of Canadian ancestry.

Canadians undoubtedly have been the most "invisible" of immigrants because of their language and North American background. Canadian immigrants have traditionally been white, middle class, and Protestant, while those from Quebec have mastered the English language and typically adhere to Catholicism. Canadians differ from other immigrants in one respect: many retain their Canadian citizenship. Some reside in Indianapolis for business purposes and intend to return to Canada upon reassignment or retirement. Others have chosen to leave the United States because of higher medical costs and fewer social services.

Canada is the largest trade partner of both Indiana and the United States. Through the North American Free Trade Agreement, Indianapolis and Marion County may experience an increase in Canadians' presence locally as well as in business and commercial transactions.

Unlike other ethnic groups in Indianapolis, social and cultural institutions are rare among the Canadian population; yet there is a Canadian presence. The Indiana Film Society has sponsored a Canadian Film Festival since 1988. The INDIANAPOLIS-SCARBOROUGH PEACE GAMES, an amateur sports event begun in 1973, promotes goodwill and cultural understanding between Hoosiers and Canadians. Franklin College, in adjoining Johnson County, maintains a Center for Canadian Studies, founded in 1984.

HELEN JEAN MCCLELLAND NUGENT
Franklin College of Indiana

Cannon, Fermor Spencer (Aug. 4, 1888–Dec. 11, 1973). Architect and businessman. A native of Indianapolis and graduate of SHORTRIDGE HIGH SCHOOL, Cannon studied architecture at the University of Illinois (B.S., 1911). Upon returning to Indianapolis, he worked two years for architect HERBERT L. BASS before establishing his own practice (1913–1929). As an architect, Cannon is noted for designing the FLANNER AND BUCHANAN MORTUARY on Fall Creek and Butler University's fieldhouse (HINKLE FIELDHOUSE). Cannon also assisted in designing the Interurban Freight Terminal, built in the early 1920s at 500 Kentucky Avenue by a partnership of four interurban lines. Reputed to be the largest in the country, the terminal consisted of two cement and brick fireproof buildings (one 928 feet long, the other 400 feet) surrounded by three miles of tracks and switches.

In the 1920s Cannon switched to a career in banking. He served as the president of RAILROADMEN'S FEDERAL SAVINGS AND LOAN ASSOCIATION of Indianapolis (1931–1954), a business founded by his father in 1887, and later became chairman of the board (1954–1958). A model train enthusiast, Cannon also served as president of the Indianapolis BOARD OF TRADE (1941).

STACEY NICHOLAS

John D. Barnhart and Donald F. Carmony, *Indiana* (New York, 1954), III, 268–269.

Capital Assets Management, Department of. See Transportation, Department of

Capital Improvement Board. One of six independent municipal corporations in Marion County, the Capital Improvement Board finances and operates public capital improvements within the county. Currently, the board operates the HOOSIER DOME and INDIANA CONVENTION CENTER, MARKET SQUARE ARENA, the City Center and PAN AMERICAN PLAZA, and Capital Commons.

The Capital Improvement Board was created by special state legislation in 1965 to oversee the construction of the Convention Center. Its organization and responsibilities were not affected by the UNIGOV reorganization in 1970. The board meets monthly and consists of seven non-salaried members appointed by the mayor (5) and by the Marion County commissioners (2).

In 1982 the board financed the construction of the Hoosier Dome through the sale of bonds backed by private grants and a 1 percent tax on food and beverage purchases in Marion County. This tax, along with a hotel tax, a portion of the cigarette tax, and facilities rentals, has since supported the acquisition and operation of the board's other public facilities. During 1991–1993, the board financed and supervised an extensive addition to the Convention Center.

LAURRY NEUFER

Carey, Mary Stewart (Mar. 5, 1859–June 14, 1938). Civic and social leader. Born in Greensburg, Indiana, Mary and her family moved to Indianapolis in 1862, where her father, Daniel Stewart, founded the Stewart Glass Company. Except for attending a private high school in the East, she lived in Indianapolis for the rest of her life. In 1879 she married John N. Carey, who then became president of STEWART-CAREY Glass Company. Mary traveled the world extensively, bringing ideas and artifacts back to Indianapolis. It is thought that John C. Olmsted, an associate in the famed Frederick Law Olmsted firm, designed her formal garden, and her home was an important gathering place for leading socialites during the first quarter of the 20th century.

Carey was responsible for the legislative approval of the state flag and helped to choose its design. She is best known as founder and benefactress of several local institutions. She let the privately run ORCHARD COUNTRY DAY SCHOOL use her orchard for their first home. After a visit to the Brooklyn Children's Museum in 1924, she spearheaded efforts to found THE CHILDREN'S MUSEUM of Indianapolis. She was elected chairperson of the original organizational committee, was its first board of trustees president, and remained a board member until her death. Her Meridian Street mansion housed the museum from 1927 to 1946.

Active in many civic and philanthropic organizations, Carey held leadership positions in the PROPYLAEUM, Women's Rotary Club, CHRISTAMORE HOUSE, DRAMATIC CLUB, Garden Club, INDIANAPOLIS CIVIC THEATRE, and both local and national branches of the Daughters of the American Revolution. She also collected art, especially Indiana artists, and donated 12 paintings to the John Herron Art Museum.

MICHELLE D. HALE

Nancy Kriplen, *Keep An Eye on That Mummy: A History of The Children's Museum of Indianapolis* (Indianapolis, 1982).

Carmel. Edge city located north of Indianapolis in southern Hamilton County, originally named Bethlehem and platted on April 13, 1837. The earliest settlers were primarily Quakers from North Carolina who arrived in the late 1820s. They began to have religious services under the supervision of a nearby meeting in 1830 and shortly thereafter established a school. In 1846 the town gained a post office that adopted the name Carmel because there was another Bethlehem in Indiana. Although accepted for the post office, Carmel did not become the official name until the town incorporated in 1874. A small farming community, Carmel boasted various businesses including a dentist, drugstores, blacksmiths, and a window sash maker.

By 1900 Carmel had a main street containing businesses and professional offices, a newspaper, three churches, and, within a year, its first bank. The town also got one of the first electric traffic signals in the nation when Carmel native Leslie Haines installed a stoplight at the main intersection in 1923.

At its centennial in 1937 Carmel reported a population of 682. By the late 1950s its population had doubled as it began to change from a small rural town to a suburban edge city. In the early 1960s most of Carmel's population could be found in its half dozen neighborhoods. By the end of the decade, however, following the northward extension of Keystone Avenue and construction of some luxury homes, the town had begun its rapid evolution into an affluent edge community. Carmel became a city in 1974 and elected its first mayor two years later. In 1970 its population was 6,568; by 1980 it had grown dramatically to

18,272. In 1993, partially as a result of annexation in surrounding Clay Township, the population exceeded 25,000, approximately half of whom were not born in Indiana. Contributing to this growth were Carmel's reputation as a prestigious place to live, highway construction and improvements in northern Marion and southern Hamilton counties, and the school desegregation controversy in Indianapolis from which Carmel was exempt. Ninety percent of the city's existing homes have been constructed since 1960; apartments account for a small but growing portion of the housing stock.

Carmel's population is homogeneous, with a minority population of less than 4 percent. Median family income in 1990 was $62,000, with 20 percent of the families having incomes over $100,000. The median house price was $142,500 compared to $61,100 for Indianapolis. Over 80 percent of the city's working population is employed in white-collar professions. Many of these professionals are corporate managers whose frequent transfers contribute to the community's high rate of transiency. The majority of workers commute to Indianapolis and over 90,000 cars pass daily through the U.S. 31 North (Meridian Street) and Interstate 465 intersection between Carmel and Indianapolis. Located along this corridor are several major employers including ANACOMP, CONSECO, Woods Wire Products, MAYFLOWER CORPORATION, and Delta Faucet Company.

JOAN CUNNINGHAM

Carr, Leroy (Mar. 27, 1905–Apr. 28, 1935). African-American blues singer-pianist-songwriter. The most popular male blues musician of his day, Carr was born in Nashville, Tennessee, and arrived in Indianapolis from Louisville in 1912. As a teenager he taught himself how to play piano after hearing Ollie Atkins, traveling Mississippi pianist. Following stints in the circus and the army, Carr returned to Indianapolis in the early 1920s and by 1927 had formed a duo with guitarist FRANCIS "SCRAPPER" BLACKWELL. In 1928 their first recording—"How Long, How Long Blues" on Vocalion—sold hundreds of thousands of copies, establishing the pair as innovators in the newly emerging urban blues style that blended contemporary pop and jazz elements with traditional country blues structures. Music historians have noted that Carr brought a new dimension to blues recording; he was far raunchier than the average vaudeville blues singer, and deeply influenced contemporary blues musicians. Carr and Blackwell recorded over 100 songs for Vocalion and toured throughout the Midwest until Carr's sudden death from nephritis. His music has been re-released on numerous blues anthology discs.

LAWRENCE E. McCULLOUGH
Indiana University–Purdue University,
Indianapolis

Sheldon Harris, *Blues Who's Who* (New Rochelle, N.Y., 1979).

Carroll, Michael A. (Feb. 9, 1941–Sept. 11, 1992). Indianapolis deputy mayor and Lilly Endowment official. An Indiana University graduate, Carroll received a master's degree in urban planning from the University of Illinois. In 1964 he joined Indianapolis' Metropolitan Planning Department, where he held posts as an assistant planner, deputy director, and director. He also served as the director of the Indianapolis Model Cities Program.

From 1970 to 1976 Carroll was a deputy mayor, playing a key role in securing public and private funds for the construction of MARKET SQUARE ARENA and MERCHANTS PLAZA and the renovation of CITY MARKET. Later he was on the staffs of Senators Richard Lugar and Dan Quayle. Although he had a long involvement with REPUBLICAN PARTY politics, Carroll ran for public office only once, losing to incumbent Democratic Congressman Andy Jacobs, Jr., in 1982.

After serving as vice-president for corporate development at James Associates, Architects and Engineers, in 1984 Carroll became vice-president for community development at LILLY ENDOWMENT. Carroll was active in civic affairs, serving on the board of directors for the GREATER INDIANAPOLIS PROGRESS COMMITTEE, the INDIANAPOLIS CONVENTION AND VISITORS ASSOCIATION, and the Catholic Youth Organization (CYO). He was board president of CYO, which honored him with its St. John Bosco Medal in 1984.

Carroll was one of four Indianapolis civic leaders who died on September 11, 1992, in an airplane crash in southern Marion County. The four men—FRANK E. MCKINNEY, JR., ROBERT V. WELCH, JOHN R. WELIEVER, and Carroll—were traveling to AmeriFlora '92 in Columbus, Ohio, to investigate ideas for the development of WHITE RIVER STATE PARK in Indianapolis.

RAY BOOMHOWER
Indiana Historical Society

Carter, Larue Depew (Mar. 17, 1880–Jan. 22, 1946). Neuropsychiatrist and neurology professor. Born in Westfield, Indiana, Carter graduated from the Medical College of Indianapolis in 1904. He interned at City Hospital (now WISHARD MEMORIAL HOSPITAL) and Philadelphia General Hospital and was a resident at Eastern Indiana Hospital for the Insane at Richmond. In 1914 Carter joined the faculty of the INDIANA UNIVERSITY SCHOOL OF MEDICINE as professor of neurology and served as chief of the neuropsychiatry staff at City Hospital. From 1916 to 1919 Carter served in the Medical Corps, first on the Mexican border with Pershing, then as division surgeon for the 39th Division and as commanding officer of Base Hospital 30 in France.

Carter returned to the School of Medicine faculty and served as a consultant at Methodist, St. Vincent, and Veterans hospitals, as well as the Norways Sanatorium. His medical contributions came principally through teaching and service to the state through participation on numerous committees, not through scientific discoveries. He was president of the Indianapolis (Marion County) Medical Association, Neuropsychiatric Association, Indiana Neurological Society, and Indiana Psychiatric Society, as well as a charter member of the Paul Coble Post of the AMERICAN LEGION.

In 1945 he served as chair of the Indiana Council for Mental Health and Governor Ralph F. Gates' committee for the construction of a new mental screening hospital at Indiana University, a facility that now bears his name, Larue D. Carter Memorial Hospital.

NANCY PIPPEN ECKERMAN
Indiana University School of Medicine

Castleton. Northeastside retail district located on East 82nd Street in Lawrence Township. The congested commercial district of Castleton today bears little resemblance to the village founded in 1852. In that year, Thomas Gentry sectioned off nine lots 12 miles northeast of the Circle; 23 years later, Dave Macy platted an additional 16 lots. The area these men pioneered became the town of Castleton.

The small town grew and prospered as a brick making and charcoal center, as well as a service center for farmers and travelers. Methodist residents built the first brick church in 1874. A gas well was first drilled in 1886 and the grain elevator and railroad depot did a brisk business. Castleton Grade School, built in 1910, became a landmark in northern Marion County. Just outside town, Alex Tuschinsky, a German immigrant, opened Hillsdale Nursery in 1917. The first recorded town board meeting occurred in 1906 and by 1950 Castleton claimed 268 residents. At the end of that decade, however, zoning for light industry brought the first hint of change to the town, although residents could not have anticipated the magnitude of those changes.

In 1965, the Indiana General Assembly passed a law creating a uniform zoning board for Marion County; Castleton was designated a commercial area. The construction of I–69 and I–465 at 82nd Street brought down the Methodist church, Masonic Temple, and Castleton Grade School. In 1970, Castleton became part of Greater Indianapolis when UNIGOV expanded the city's limits to include all of Marion County. Then, in 1972, the 104–acre Castleton Square Mall opened.

During the 1970s and 1980s Castleton rapidly developed into a commercial suburb. Indeed, by the early 1990s its 19 shopping centers within two square miles made it the most intensively developed retail district in the county. As commercial development moved in, townspeople moved out; by November, 1991, when the town council voted to dissolve, there were only 37 residents remaining. However, due to the construction of several large apartment complexes in the vicinity, the number of persons living in the Castleton area totaled over 10,000 in 1990.

LISA EHRET

Indianapolis Star, Nov. 2, 1941, Sept. 25, 1966; *Indianapolis Times*, Jan. 14, 1962; *Indianapolis News*, Sept. 12, 1972.

Cathedral Arts. Founded in 1969 Cathedral Arts presents a variety of arts-related activities in Indianapolis and throughout the state. Its mission is to promote the careers of young artists and, through the diversity of broadly popular and highly artistic events, to revitalize and enrich the culture of downtown Indianapolis.

From its beginnings as a small support organization for the CHRIST CHURCH CATHEDRAL CHOIR OF MEN AND BOYS, Cathedral Arts has grown to sponsor major events of local and international significance. Its quadrennial INTERNATIONAL VIOLIN COMPETITION of Indianapolis mobilizes nearly 1,000 volunteers and receives extensive media coverage locally and around the globe. In conjunction with the violin competition, Cathedral Arts coordinates the Juried Exhibition of Student Art involving 75,000 elementary through high school students statewide. The Midsummer Festival on MONUMENT CIRCLE is a popular festival of contemporary music that attracts 25,000 people annually. In 1991 Cathedral Arts launched a year-long celebration of the Cole Porter Centennial that included gala performances in New York City and London as well as Indianapolis. For several years Cathedral Arts has also presented the chamber music series of Suzuki and Friends; in 1982 it added a second chamber music series with the Ronen Chamber Ensemble.

Cathedral Arts is governed by a board of directors consisting of approximately 40 members of varying ages and areas of interest. Funding for the organization is provided by endowment income, personal gifts, and corporate contributions.

JOAN C. DALTON

Catholic Social Services. In 1919, Archbishop Joseph Chartrand founded the Catholic Community Center, a forerunner to Catholic Social Services (CSS), and appointed Father Maurice O'Connor as its first director. The services offered by the center included a day nursery, a cafeteria, and provision of food and clothing for the poor and destitute. The center was a charter member of the Indianapolis Community Chest, the predecessor of the local UNITED WAY.

During the 1920s, agency services grew to include a home for unmarried mothers; in the early 1930s, children's foster care was added, in response to a depression-induced increase in the number of broken homes, desertions, and delinquencies. These services continued to develop throughout the 1940s and 1950s.

Professional marriage counseling, psychological testing, school counseling, and family life education services were initiated in the 1960s. Additionally, CSS staff began to be involved in social action issues and to serve as advocates for persons in need. In the 1970s, agency staff helped to start what is now the HISPANIC CENTER and assisted in the formation of Indianapolis BIG BROTHERS.

CSS experienced major changes in 1983 when a reorganization resulted in the acquisition of six additional programs. These included congregate living for the elderly, a problem pregnancy hotline, refugee resettlement, sponsorship of the Retired Senior Volunteer and Senior Companion programs, and administration of the archdiocesan Campaign for Human Development. The preceding year CSS had assumed responsibility for an adult day care program. In 1985, CSS was first accredited by the Council on Accreditation of Services for Families and Children, Inc.

Today, Catholic Social Services operates twelve programs, serving 7,500 persons annually at four different sites. Income for its $2.8 million budget comes from the archdiocese, United Way, federal-state-local government, client fees, and fund-raising, primarily from individuals. While continuing to carry out its original mission to provide charity to the poor and destitute, its role has expanded to include advocacy and the provision of services designed to assist and to enable persons to help themselves.

THOMAS N. GAYBRICK
Catholic Social Services

Catholics. The largest Christian church in the Hoosier capital, comprising approximately 10 percent of Marion County's population and almost one quarter of the county's church membership. The city's first Catholics were IRISH canal workers and laborers and German artisans who arrived in the early 1830s. A priest periodically celebrated Mass in private homes or rented halls until 1840. Among these priests were Claude Francois, Logansport pastor; Michael Shawe, first priest ordained in Indiana; and French-born Vincent Bacquelin, pastor of St. Vincent's, Shelby County, who regularly visited Indianapolis beginning in late 1837.

The first parish in Indianapolis was Holy Cross, later renamed ST. JOHN THE EVANGELIST. Its church was located on the north side of Washington Street just west of West Street, on property near the present Eiteljorg Museum. Needing a larger worship space, the present St. John's site (Capitol Avenue and Georgia Street) was acquired in 1846.

A growing number of believers and ethnic divisions affected St. John's. Preferring the services of a priest who could preach in their own language, in 1858 GERMANS built their own church, St. Mary's, then located on East Maryland Street. Of the three new parishes organized as the city expanded south of Union Station and northeast along Massachusetts Avenue, St. Patrick (southeast, 1865) and St. Joseph (northeast, 1873) were English-speaking while Sacred Heart (south, 1875) was operated by German-speaking Franciscans. Irish and Germans were buried in separate sections when a cemetery opened along Pleasant Run at South Meridian Street in 1862.

Several religious communities were responsible for social services and education. In 1873 Good Shepherd Sisters organized an orphanage and Little Sisters of the Poor opened a home for the aged. Daughters of Charity started St. Vincent's Infirmary in 1881. Although Holy Cross Brothers (South Bend, Indiana) conducted a school for boys in 1847, Sisters of Providence (St. Mary-of-the-Woods, Indiana) opened the first permanent grade school (St. John's, 1859). Sisters of St. Francis (Oldenburg, Indiana) conducted a grade school and a girls' academy at St. Mary's parish after 1864, Brothers of the Sacred Heart (Mobile, Alabama) opened St. John's Boys School in 1867, and Sisters of St. Joseph (St. Louis, Missouri) taught at Sacred Heart after 1877.

An April, 1919, first communion class at St. Joseph's Church, one of the earliest Catholic parishes in the city. [Indiana Historical Society, #C4955]

The bishops charged with the spiritual development of Indianapolis resided in Vincennes after 1834. Because the Hoosier capital became a communications hub and the state's largest urban area, Bishop FRANCIS SILAS CHATARD took up residence in the city in 1878. The name, Diocese of Vincennes, was formally changed to Diocese of Indianapolis in March, 1898.

Chatard was preoccupied with the continuing process of forming parishes and finding priests to serve the burgeoning Catholic community. With the organization of St. Bridget's (northwest, 1880), he completed the circle of parishes around the original St. John's and St. Mary's. He then moved to develop a wider concentric circle of parishes: St. Francis de Sales (northeast in BRIGHTWOOD, 1881), St. Anthony (west in HAUGHVILLE, 1886), SS. PETER AND PAUL (the future cathedral, north, 1892), Assumption (southwest in WEST INDIANAPOLIS, 1894), and Holy Cross (east, 1895). By 1918, the year of Chatard's death, 31,000 Catholics were organized into 19 parishes in Marion County, 14 of which had been founded during his episcopate.

The Catholic share in the total population has varied in the 20th century. Catholics were 15.9 percent of Marion County's population in 1906, 10.5 percent in 1990. In 1906 they constituted 34.5 percent of the county's churchgoers. This figure is large when compared with the shares of the various Protestant denominations but small when compared to the over 60 percent share Catholics held in major immigrant centers like Chicago, Detroit, and Cincinnati. This percentage declined to 22.6 percent in 1936, increased to 27.2 percent in 1980, and stood at 23.3 percent of the county's church membership in the early 1990s.

The arrival of small contingents of southern and eastern European immigrants and southern African-Americans brought renewed ethnic consciousness, stronger lay leadership, fear of Protestant proselytization, and further organizational development. In 1892 St. Bridget's opened a second school, St. Ann's, for black children. Parishes were founded for SLOVENES (Holy Trinity, 1906), ITALIANS (Holy Rosary, 1909), and African-Americans (St. Rita, 1919). Mission churches existed in AUGUSTA, ACTON, and Valley Mills for several years. The ANCIENT ORDER OF HIBERNIANS appeared in 1870 and the first Knights of Columbus council organized in 1899. The German Roman Catholic *Central-Verein* (DRKCV) held national conventions here in 1878 and 1909. St. Elizabeth Maternity Hospital and Infant Home opened in 1915 and Catholic Charities was established in 1920 to serve the needy among the faithful.

Individual spiritual growth and greater educational opportunities concerned Catholics during the episcopacy of JOSEPH CHARTRAND (1918–1933). The bishop actively recruited young people for the clerical and religious life and encouraged the laity to receive the sacraments frequently. He welcomed the Carmelites, who established a cloister here in 1932. His founding of Cathedral High School (1918) increased both college attendance and Catholic participation in the city's professional community. A strong-willed individual, Chartrand set an example that encouraged pastors and lay people to emulate him. Consequently, they turned parishes into devotional, educational, and social centers, undoubtedly a response to the public intimidation and private prejudice against Catholics prevalent during the KU KLUX KLAN era of the 1920s.

The administration of JOSEPH ELMER RITTER (1934–1946) stabilized diocesan finances, which had been adversely affected by the Great Depression. Catholics became more outward looking: they formed lay organizations like National Coun-

cil of Catholic Women and Catholic Youth Organization and supported an outreach program to the black community. Catholic hospitals and schools began to admit black patients and students. The city's only Catholic institution of higher learning, MARIAN COLLEGE, opened as a college for women in 1937. Ritter became the first archbishop of Indianapolis in 1944 when Indiana was designated as an ecclesiastical province and the diocese was raised to an archdiocese.

Between 1940 and 1960 the number of Catholic residents more than doubled, from 44,000 to 92,000. Led by Archbishop PAUL C. SCHULTE (1946–1970), Catholics emphasized parish formation and educational expansion. The last concentric circle of parishes, now in suburban areas, was completed when St. Barnabas parish was established on the far south side in 1965. A $2 million school fund drive in the 1950s helped finance the building of four archdiocesan high schools: Scecina (east, 1953), Chatard (north, 1961), Ritter (west, 1964), and Roncalli (south, 1969). The Latin School opened to educate teenagers interested in the priesthood (1955); Benedictine Sisters conducted Our Lady of Grace Academy in Beech Grove (1956), and Jesuits opened Brebeuf on the far north side in 1962. Marian College admitted men after 1954. Marion County had 26 Catholic parishes at the end of World War II, 43 in 1970; six high schools at the end of the war, eleven in 1970. During these decades Indianapolis had three Catholic mayors— ALBERT G. FEENEY (1948–1950), PHILIP L. BAYT (1950–1951, 1956–1959), and JOHN J. BARTON (1964–1967).

The new emphases and reforms of the Second Vatican Council (1962–1965) affected the local church in the closing years of the Schulte era and during the episcopates of GEORGE J. BISKUP (1970–1979) and EDWARD T. O'MEARA (1980–1992). The number of priests and religious in parish life declined, Catholic education was reevaluated, and lay people found new avenues of service in the parish and in the classroom. Because of the emphasis on shared responsibility, parish councils were established to advise pastors on local needs, from the Sunday Mass schedule to financial policy. At the archdiocesan level clergy and religious formed their own groups (Indianapolis Priests Association, 1967, and Association of Religious in the Indianapolis Archdiocese, 1968) and new bodies advised the archbishop: Priests' Senate (1971, now Council of Priests), and Archdiocesan Pastoral Council (1990).

As the city's population growth resulted in the multiplication of parishes, the decline of the inner city affected existing parishes and institutions. Old St. Joseph's closed in 1949, St. Francis de Sales in 1983. St. Catherine and St. James consolidated as Good Shepherd parish (1993). Eight high schools closed, merged, or moved to a suburban location. Twelve elementary schools consolidated into three larger units: Holy Cross Central, All Saints, and Central Catholic.

In order to revitalize the Catholic presence and encourage interparochial cooperation in the inner city, the Urban Parish Cooperative was formed in 1984. Hispanic ministry was centered at St. Mary's. Situating the Catholic Center at 14th and Meridian streets (1982), renovating the Cathedral (1986), and establishing homes for senior citizens and abused women and a center for AIDS victims showed renewed commitment to the city.

Over the decades Catholics have encountered less hostility in the city than in other urban areas, despite the strong background of anti-Catholicism among Hoosiers. In the 1880s and 1890s there were scattered incidents by the American Protective Association (APA), an Iowa-based organization devoted to excluding Catholics from public office. While Protestant publications often denounced alleged Catholic political influence, the secular press repudiated the use of religious intolerance in politics. In an attempt to influence the election of city school commissioners in June, 1893, APA-backed candidates were soundly defeated. Rev. OSCAR C. MCCULLOCH of Plymouth Church also condemned the prejudiced opinions of Catholics which many Protestants held.

The greatest threat to Catholics, however, occurred during the 1920s when the Klan attacked them for their alleged immorality, antidemocratic tendencies, and allegiance to a foreign power. The INDIANA CATHOLIC AND RECORD, the Catholic Information Bureau (established 1924 in Indianapolis), and the American Unity League (headquartered in Chicago) refuted Klan propaganda through their own publications. For example, the Unity League's newspaper Tolerance published the names of over 12,000 alleged Klansmen who resided in Indianapolis. Catholic schools also faced exclusion, along with African-American schools, from the INDIANA HIGH SCHOOL ATHLETIC ASSOCIATION (IHSAA) until December, 1941.

In the early 1990s the 84,000 Catholics of Marion County were well integrated in the professional, business, and political worlds. Their spiritual leader is Indiana native Daniel Mark Buechlein, O.S.B., installed as fifth archbishop on September 9, 1992. They are organized into 41 parishes (of which 3 are predominantly African-American), a Byzantine congregation, and a Korean mission (founded 1991). They operate 29 elementary schools, 6 high schools, and Marian College, an undergraduate coeducational liberal arts institution. Two hospitals (ST. VINCENT and ST. FRANCIS) and two homes for the aged (St. Augustine and St. Paul Hermitage) serve the sick and elderly. Fatima Retreat House, Beech Grove Benedictine Center, and St. Maur Hospitality Center provide facilities for individual spiritual renewal. The weekly archdiocesan newspaper is the CRITERION, which succeeded the Indiana Catholic and Record (1910–1960) in 1960.

JAMES J. DIVITA
Marian College

Caven, John (Apr. 12, 1824–Mar. 9, 1905). Mayor of Indianapolis, 1863–1867, 1875–1881, Republican. Born near McKeesport, Pennsylvania, Caven attended a primitive log school. He worked as a laborer in his father's salt works, and in barging and coal mining, leaving home just before age 21. He reached Indianapolis in September, 1845, clerked in a shoe store for two years, then began the study of law in the office of Smith and Yandes. After a year in the coal business in Clay County, he returned to Indianapolis in 1851 or 1852 and opened a law practice with BERRY R. SULGROVE.

Elected to office a record five times, the first three unopposed, Caven served longer than any other mayor until William H. Hudnut III (1976–1991). Unlike his predecessors, Caven saw the mayor's role as leader and initiator. His first terms

John Caven.
[Indiana
Historical Society,
#C5902]

were marked by his drafting a street railway charter and inducing the parties to come and build it, by the printing of the council proceedings, and by the introduction and adoption in 1866 of an eight-hour ordinance for city workers. In his terms in the legislature (1869, 1871, 1887) Caven took a leading role in securing schools for black children, creating the city library, authoring the law establishing bipartisan election boards, and drafting a mechanics lien bill that was adopted after his service.

His last three terms as mayor coincided with the worst years of the depression of the 1870s and the dangerous social conflict it aroused. Caven exhibited genuine statesmanship: in May, 1876, his intervention ended an election day race riot; in June, 1877, he prevented a "blood or bread" uprising. Eliciting promises of no violence from a mass meeting of jobless workmen, Caven led a procession to the city's bakeries and distributed the bread at his own expense. He made good his promise that hundreds would find work next day on the construction of the BELT LINE RAILROAD and union STOCKYARDS. That project, whose bonds were guaranteed by the city, had been Caven's idea in 1876. When the great RAILROAD STRIKE OF 1877, reached Indianapolis, Caven's decision to enroll hundreds of striking railroadmen as special deputies prevented the widespread property destruction and loss of life experienced elsewhere.

Caven suffered financially after 1873, but recovered by the end of the decade. After his last stint as mayor, Caven became president and a director of the Indianapolis Brush Electric Light and Power Company, incorporated in 1881, which proposed to light the city with electricity. Had the

city council agreed to his plan, Indianapolis would have become one of the first cities in the world so lighted. In 1892 the Brush Company merged with others to form the INDIANAPOLIS POWER AND LIGHT COMPANY. Caven served as vice-president and a director until 1896 when he sold his interests. After his retirement, and before his health failed two years before his death, Caven often took long walks about the city. With a full beard and hair to his shoulders, completely white, his appearance was patriarchal. An assiduous Freemason and clubman, Caven never married.

WILLIAM DOHERTY
Marian College

William J. Doherty, "Indianapolis in the 1870s: Hard Times in the Gilded Age" (Ph.D diss., Indiana University, 1981); Men of Progress (Indianapolis, 1899).

Cemeteries. Prior to 1824 all cemeteries in Marion County were rural graveyards often adjacent to churches. Nearly 200 of these interment sites still dot the county; many line the streets of the city itself. Two examples are Pleasant Hill Cemetery in PIKE TOWNSHIP (south of 86th Street on Moore Road) and Round Hill Cemetery in PERRY TOWNSHIP (5300 South Meridian). Both are still used for burials.

Included in this grouping was a small burial grounds established in the summer of 1821, southwest of the city on an eminence overlooking White River. Here the community buried the first of its dead, residents who died from an outbreak of fever. On March 27, 1824, 71 citizens of Indianapolis signed a charter that established it as the city "bury grounds." This first city cemetery was located on the west side of Kentucky Avenue near White River about seven blocks southwest of the Circle. Among its administrators were Dr. ISAAC COE, NICHOLAS MCCARTY, JAMES M. RAY, DANIEL YANDES, and other local businessmen.

In February, 1834, Union Cemetery was laid out on the eastern boundary of the original burial grounds, increasing the overall size of the area to nine acres. Four years later a Philadelphia firm (Siter, Price and Co.) added another eight and one half acres to it, calling this addition Greenlawn Cemetery. Finally, in early 1852, seven and one half acres were given to the city by Edwin J. Peck, president of the Terre Haute and Indianapolis Railway Company, which expanded the City Cemetery complex to a total of 25 acres.

Although all of this region was commonly referred to as City Cemetery prior to and during the Civil War period, sometime thereafter citizens adopted the name of Greenlawn, so named from the third addition to it. Maps of the city published after the 1870s bear this change in identity. Prominent Indianapolis personages including CALVIN FLETCHER, SAMUEL MERRILL, Noah Noble, and James Whitcomb purchased lots at the old burial grounds. Other leading citizens, including Governors Noble and Whitcomb, were initially interred there but were removed to Crown Hill Cemetery during the 1890s.

During the CIVIL WAR, 1,281 Union soldiers and 1,616 Confederate prisoners of war (who died while confined at CAMP MORTON) were laid to rest within the boundaries of City Cemetery. Sadly, all documentation of the precise location of these burials, and of all lot owners and those burials within each family lot, was lost in a fire that occurred at the cemetery office sometime prior to 1866.

The city burial grounds began to lose its popularity soon after the dedication of CROWN HILL CEMETERY on June 1, 1864. According to Calvin Fletcher, the City Cemetery had become a public disgrace. Lack of care made it an embarrassment to the community; graves were sunken pits and many headstones lay on the ground. Families with loved ones buried in the old grounds purchased lots in Crown Hill, located 2.8 miles north of the city, and reinterred the remains in the rolling hills and valleys of the new rural facility. Additional interments continued to be made at City (or Greenlawn) Cemetery until 1890. That year marked the closing of the graveyard to any further burials. In 1920 E. H. K. McComb, principal of Manual High School, made an accurate listing of the gravestones and four years thereafter all remaining burials were removed to other cemeteries throughout the county—primarily Floral Park, Holy Cross, and Crown Hill. Today the region is an industrial area with DIAMOND CHAIN COMPANY as the largest of several firms at that location. Despite this, several graves are thought to still exist there.

One of the small country cemeteries incorporated into the city as it expanded eastward is Anderson Cemetery, located at 6500 East 10th Street. A check of burial records has established the first burial to have been in 1843, although earlier interments may have been made there. A large number of families from WARREN TOWNSHIP and several from IRVINGTON are buried there.

In 1856 the Jewish population of Indianapolis laid out the Hebrew Cemetery about two miles south of the city. This area is about a quarter mile north of Pleasant Run and is the burial place of several prominent Jewish families.

Catholics established a cemetery immediately south of the Hebrew grounds in 1860, which today bears the names of Holy Cross and St. Joseph cemeteries. Created first was Holy Cross, an interment area for Irish Catholic families on the west side of the complex. The latter, St. Joseph, was founded by the German community on the east side of Holy Cross. A third Catholic burial area was incorporated in 1945 as Calvary Cemeteries. Today the three operate as the Catholic Cemeteries Association.

The last of the 19th century cemeteries located in what is now the metropolitan area of Indianapolis is the Lutheran Cemetery, located about a mile south of the Holy Cross and St. Joseph area. It was created in 1879 when trustees of St. Paul Evangelical Lutheran Church purchased ten acres at this site. Known today as Concordia Cemetery, it has more than doubled in size.

Several, but by no means all, of the larger cemeteries which have come into existence during the 20th century are:

Floral Park Cemetery (1919), on Cossell Road; Floral Park West Cemetery (1919), at 9200 on West 21st Street; Forest Lawn Cemetery (1955), in Greenwood; Glenn Haven Cemetery (1927), north of what is now Kessler Boulevard, between Cooper Road and Michigan Road; Lincoln Memorial Gardens (1956), at Whitestown; Memorial Park Cemetery (1917), on the north side of East Washington Street, in the 9300 block; New Crown Cemetery (1900), at 2100 Churchman on the southeast side of the city; Oaklawn Memorial Gardens (1953), northwest of Castleton on Allisonville Road; Washington Park East (1927), at 10800 East Washington Stree; Washington Park North, originally Rest Haven Cemetery (1944), directly south of and attached to the Glenn Haven Cemetery.

WAYNE L. SANFORD

Center Township. Central Marion County township. When the county was organized into nine townships in 1822, Center Township was the site of a fledgling settlement and ALEXANDER RALSTON's plan for the new one-square-mile state capital.

Early growth was slow, despite the relocation of state government offices from Corydon in 1825 and the construction of the NATIONAL ROAD and the CENTRAL CANAL in the 1830s. Completion of rail lines to the city in the late 1840s and 1850s spurred intensive commercial and residential development. Packing houses, factories, and mills sprang up along the railroads, particularly to the south and west of the Circle. A thriving retail and commercial business district developed along Washington Street. The city continued to expand and grow through the Civil War and up to the early 1870s, when 48,000 residents were counted.

The Panic of 1873 put a temporary halt to development, but ten years later Indianapolis and Center Township were once again booming. The BELT LINE RAILROAD, constructed in the late 1870s, successfully channeled a number of rail lines south and west of the city to UNION STATION. The WHOLESALE DISTRICT on the city's south side expanded, while commercial and retail buildings were constructed north of the Washington Street corridor. Residential neighborhoods known today as the OLD NORTHSIDE, LOCKERBIE SQUARE,

CHATHAM ARCH, COTTAGE HOME, FLETCHER PLACE, and FOUNTAIN SQUARE grew and prospered as the demand for housing increased. Industrial neighborhoods such as STRINGTOWN, WEST INDIANAPOLIS, and BRIGHTWOOD housed employees of nearby railroads, packing plants, and foundries. The census counted nearly 81,000 township residents in 1880; by 1890, over 117,000.

In the early 20th century the city grew to the boundaries of Center Township and beyond. The development of streetcar lines and, later, a network of bridges and paved roads for automobiles, ensured residents access to developing suburbs. Between 1900 and 1950, township population increased from 168,000 to just over 337,000.

A congested Center Township began to lose residents in the post–World War II years as the demand for new housing created explosive growth in outlying townships. Between 1960 and 1970 population dropped from 333,000 to 274,000. Commercial, retail, and manufacturing firms also began to abandon the center city for the suburbs, lured by lower taxes, cheap land, and accessibility to interstate highways.

Efforts to reverse this trend began as early as the 1950s, then intensified in 1964 with the creation of the GREATER INDIANAPOLIS PROGRESS COMMITTEE (GIPC). Planners, policymakers, and city leaders began to focus their attention on downtown revitalization. In 1981 REGIONAL CENTER PLAN I was adopted, calling for joint public-private investment, growth in office space, a rejuvenated retail core, and a comprehensive transportation system.

Revitalization efforts coalesced in the 1980s, transforming the downtown. Six million square feet of new office space and $63.8 million in new amateur sports facilities were constructed between 1980 and 1988. New construction and rehabilitation of existing buildings added nearly 350,000 square feet of retail space and 1,400 new and rehabilitated housing units during the decade. Despite these gains, population dropped in the township; in 1990 just over 182,000 residents were counted. Planners predict high property tax rates in Center Township will encourage residents and businesses to relocate to the suburbs in coming years.

Selected Statistics for Center Township, 1990

Population	182,140
Population Per Square Mile	4,276
Percent African-American	40.9
Percent 0 to 17 Years	27.6
Percent 65 Years and Over	12.9
Percent 25 Years and Over with a High School Degree or Equivalency	57.3
Percent 25 Years and Over with a College Degree	8.0
Per Capita Income in 1989	$9,046
Unemployment Rate (%)	11.2
Married-Couple Families as a Percent of Total Households	35.3
Median Home Value	$33,400

In 1993 Center Township continues to be an employment center, with an estimated 100,000 people working in the downtown area. The largest employers include firms such as ELI LILLY AND COMPANY, AMERITECH, and the Associated Group, hospitals such as Methodist and Wishard, federal, state, and county governments, banks, and INDIANA UNIVERSITY–PURDUE UNIVERSITY AT INDIANAPOLIS. CIRCLE CENTRE MALL, scheduled for completion in 1995, will add hundreds of new jobs, as well as one million square feet of retail space.

Regional Center Plan II, adopted in 1990, carried planning initiatives forward to the year 2010. City leaders and planners call for continued growth in office space, completion of the Circle Centre Mall and WHITE RIVER STATE PARK, upgrading of residential areas, and an improved public school system.

CATHLEEN F. DONNELLY

Berry R. Sulgrove, *History of Indianapolis and Marion County* (Philadelphia, 1884); Department of Metropolitan Development, *Indianapolis Regional Center General Plan* (1981) and *Indianapolis Regional Center Plan 1990–2010* (1991); U.S. Census.

Central Canal. Pioneer waterway. The Central Canal, a fragment of which still runs from BROAD RIPPLE to downtown Indianapolis, once promised to place Indianapolis at the center of a statewide transportation network. In the early 1830s pioneer Hoosiers designed a comprehensive system of canals, ROADS, and RAILROADS to improve transportation and to orient the Indiana economy around its hub city, Indianapolis.

Natural WATERWAYS, especially the Wabash River and its short portage to Ohio's Maumee, marked important routes through early Indiana; however, the larger streams flowed away from the center of the state, drawing commerce into out-of-state markets. By connecting the upper reaches of the Wabash & Erie Canal with the southwestern river town of Evansville, a Whitewater Canal extension near Muncie, a "Cross-Cut" canal running east from Terre Haute to Worthington, a Madison railroad, and the MICHIGAN ROAD and NATIONAL ROAD in Indianapolis, the Central Canal was supposed to transform the disappointing WHITE RIVER waterway into the "main street" of Indiana commerce.

The Mammoth Internal Improvements Bill of 1836 authorized construction of the Central Canal as part of a $10 million program of internal improvements to be funded with state bonds. Preliminary engineering began at once under the supervision of Chief Engineer Jesse L. Williams, while state canal commissioners Jeremiah Sullivan, Samuel Hanna, and ISAAC COE peddled securities in New York. By year's end, the State Board of Internal Improvements reported final location of 24 miles of the Central Canal from Broad Ripple south to Port Royal Bluffs and the letting of construction contracts totaling $309,208.

Work progressed on the White River feeder dam, 11 locks, and 50 construction sections, guided by Resident Engineer Thomas A. Morris. On June 27, 1839, some nine miles of finished waterway opened for traffic, but by then fraud, ineptitude, and an international financial panic had undermined Indiana's mammoth loan. Cost overruns and revenue shortfalls forced the state to default on its interest payments and brought work to a halt on the Indianapolis Division (and most other projects as well). The finished fragment of canal provided some water power but it served no important transportation purposes.

In 1850 the state sold the Central Canal to private parties as part of a debt retirement program. After passing through several hands, the property in 1871 became the possession of the Water Works Company of Indianapolis, which hoped to employ it driving their pumps. The open ditch made a better sewer than a source of potable water, and faced with an 1873 suit for maintaining a public nuisance, the owners sold the lower portion for sewage removal. In 1881 the INDIANAPOLIS WATER COMPANY purchased the remaining canal. This firm developed FAIRVIEW PARK along the canal and doubled the waterway's usefulness by ferrying picnickers on the steam-powered *Cleopatra* from the Old Yellow Bridge at Indiana Avenue to CROWN HILL CEMETERY.

Off and on during the 20th century (once in 1938, again in 1966) the canal bed attracted the attention of developers seeking thoroughfares in a crowded city. Finally, in 1971, this surviving fragment of a once grand scheme of Hoosier public works received designation as an American Water Landmark. In 1976 the Indianapolis Water Company deeded the section south of 20th Street to the city, which in the 1980s redesigned the southernmost section into a downtown pedestrian park.

JOHN LAURITZ LARSON
Purdue University, West Lafayette

Paul Fatout, *Indiana Canals* (West Lafayette, Ind., 1972); Marjie Gates Griffin, *Water Runs Downhill: A History of the Indianapolis Water Company and Other Centenarians* (Indianapolis, 1981); Logan Esarey, *Internal Improvements in Early Indiana* (Indianapolis: Indiana Historical Society, 1912).

Central Indiana Area Library Services Authority (CIALSA).

The Indiana library community has established a statewide library information network to assist libraries in providing better service to the citizens of Indiana. The network provides regionally based support to local libraries for the purpose of sharing resources. CIALSA, established in 1974 as part of this network, provides supportive services to the libraries of central Indiana.

CIALSA member libraries are located in the eight central Indiana counties of Marion, Boone, Hamilton, Hancock, Shelby, Johnson, Morgan, and Hendricks and include approximately 140 member library corporations representing over 250 individual libraries. Public, school, academic, governmental, law and medical, and other special libraries comprise the membership. CIALSA is called a "multi-type" cooperative; both publicly and privately supported libraries are eligible for membership. Approximately 50 percent of the membership consists of the "special" libraries from business, industry, health, government, and law.

One of the most important services offered to member libraries for their patrons by CIALSA is interlibrary loan. Currently CIALSA subsidizes member library use of the interlibrary loan system through a contract with the INDIANAPOLIS–MARION COUNTY PUBLIC LIBRARY. CIALSA also negotiates discount purchasing agreements for its members and provides a consultation service, an extensive continuing education program of workshops and seminars, and book repair and bindery services.

JUDITH ELLYN

Central Indiana Council on Aging (CICOA).

In 1971 Mayor Richard G. Lugar and the GREATER INDIANAPOLIS PROGRESS COMMITTEE established the Mayor's Task Force on Aging to study the needs of older persons in the Indianapolis–Marion County area. In January, 1974, the Central Indiana Council on Aging (CICOA) was incorporated as the task force's successor to receive federal funds through the Indiana Commission on Aging. It continues to serve the elderly in Marion and surrounding counties. With government funds and private and client contributions, it provides services directly to the elderly and purchases services from community agencies. CICOA's annual budget in the early 1990s exceeded $11 million.

CICOA is governed by a voluntary board of directors, which sets policy for the agency, approves budgets, awards funds to community service providers, advocates for improved quality of life for the 190,000 persons 60 and older who reside in central Indiana, and is responsible for all the affairs of the corporation. It also has an advisory council, required by the Older Americans Act, from which it draws its designation as an area agency on aging. The council advises the board about the welfare of the area's elderly and about policy issues that affect the efficient management of the agency. Each of the eight counties has a county council on aging, staffed by CICOA, which provides information about and advocates for the needs of the county's elderly and advises CICOA on the quality of service delivered by providers.

In recent years CICOA's mission has expanded in response to administrative and funding decisions by the state of Indiana. CICOA processes screenings of nursing home applicants, regardless of age. It is the local administrative unit for Indiana's CHOICE (Community and Home Options to Institutionalized Care of the Elderly and Disabled) program in central Indiana, which serves all ages.

CICOA is preparing for the future by creating CICOA Foundation, Inc., which will enable it to diversify its funding base and be more responsive to the needs of the elderly without the restrictions that accompany government funds.

DUANE J. ETIENNE
Central Indiana Council on Aging, Inc.

Central Indiana Labor Council (originally the Indianapolis Central Labor Union). The industrialization of Indiana was accompanied by the emergence of an active and somewhat militant organized labor movement in which workers sought relief from economic distress through political activism. Meeting in 1873, state and local leaders of Indiana's craft unions began to organize city and state trade assemblies and to unify these unions into one brotherhood to protect workers' interests. The first citywide body of this kind in the state was the Indianapolis Trades Assembly, formed in July, 1880, by representatives of the printers, cigar makers, and iron molders. Under the presidency of Samuel L. Leffingwell of Typographical Union Local No. 1, the Indianapolis Trades Assembly became the focus for organized craft labor in the city. In 1883 the organization became known as the Indianapolis Central Labor Union (CLU). Within a decade it represented 83 local labor organizations and nearly 11,000 workers in Indianapolis. By 1894 it had affiliated with the American Federation of Labor.

Early in its existence, the Central Labor Union amended its constitution to prohibit endorsements of candidates or political parties and to exclude members who were candidates for or holders of elected or appointed public office. This provision sought to prevent office seekers from using the union to further their own political careers and platforms. The union generally refrained from political involvement unless it affected local craft unions.

Although serving to unify the city's diverse local unions, the Central Labor Union did not control individual locals. It did, however, recognize that the most powerful weapon at its command was the boycott. Merchants feared boycotts by organized labor since many firms had been closed and ruined by the use of such tactics. Given its importance in effecting changes in labor policies, no boycott was official without the endorsement of the Central Labor Union. With this proper sanctioning, the boycott became a very powerful tool of the local labor organizations.

The Indianapolis Central Labor Union became divided in 1923 when it departed from its stance of noninvolvement in political issues. Confronting the rising power and influence of the KU KLUX KLAN in the city and state, by a narrow margin the union approved a resolution which condemned the Klan as "un-American and unconstitutional." At least three local unions left the organization to protest labor's position on an issue which they considered not directly related to labor.

Now known as the Central Indiana Labor Council, the organization serves as one of 16 councils in Indiana organized under the Indiana State AFL-CIO whose purpose is to promote labor's agenda at the local level and to support its member unions. In 1993 the council represented nearly 100 unions and 28,000 members.

DONNA J. MUNDEN

Central State Hospital. Indiana's first state psychiatric institution, located on West Washington Street in Indianapolis. In 1844, the famous reformer Dorothea Dix inspected almshouses and jails near Indianapolis that housed mentally ill paupers. Her subsequent report helped persuade state legislators to approve funding for a "State Lunatic Asylum" to be located near Indianapolis so that legislators could oversee its operation. Even before its completion in 1848, the new institution's name was changed to the Indiana Hospital for the Insane. When the state legislature approved the establishment of three other regional psychiatric institutions in 1889, it became the Central Indiana Hospital; in 1929, its name was changed to Central State Hospital.

The 19th century was a turbulent period for the new institution. Like most such hospitals, Central State was chronically underfunded and poorly staffed. It admitted its first five patients on November 21, 1848, and expanded to 300 within ten years. When the legislature failed to allocate funds for the hospital in 1857, its superintendent,

James Athon, sent all of the patients back to their home counties. An appropriation was finally approved that autumn and the hospital reopened. Similar events recurred in 1863–1864 but this time monies for operating expenses were allocated from the general fund of the state and no inmates had to be discharged. Central State lacked a department for women until 1884; that year it also added its first female physician, Sarah Stockton, to the staff.

Nineteenth-century patients were offered a range of therapies. There was an initial commitment to the most popular antebellum treatment, moral therapy, but, as the hospital grew, its doctors increasingly relied on drugs to calm patients and substituted classification by ward for individualized treatment plans. Patient employment in farm and domestic work also was considered therapeutic. In 1885, a new superintendent, WILLIAM B. FLETCHER, burned the hospital's mechanical restraints in a public bonfire; he was subsequently fired and the hospital resumed its reliance on sedatives and restraints to control patients. Fletcher's dismissal suggests the extent to which, during the 1880s, Central State Hospital became a battleground for the partisan politics of the period. Its location in Indianapolis made the institution particularly vulnerable to political pressure. Increasingly, staff positions were awarded for political loyalty rather than professional competence. Superintendents changed with the governor. Eventually, in 1889, the legislature established a bipartisan Board of State Charities to oversee Indiana's benevolent institutions.

At the beginning of the 20th century, Indiana had four mental hospitals—Central (1848), Logansport (1888), Richmond (1890), and Evansville (1890)—scattered geographically so as to meet the needs of the various regions of the state. Central State, with an average population of 1,800, was by far the largest; the others held from 400 to 800 patients. Under the leadership of Superintendent GEORGE EDENHARTER, Central State had established a new pathology department in 1895 which, through its research and lectures, subsequently attracted international attention. But such innovations did not solve the perennial problems of patient abuse, overcrowding, and inadequate therapies. Throughout the 20th century,

periodic newspaper exposes shocked politicians and taxpayers but produced few substantive reforms. During the "deinstitutionalization" movement of the 1960s, Central State Hospital discharged many of its long-term patients and became involved in a broad range of mental health programs. During the early 1990s several patient deaths at the hospital once again brought Central State to public notice, and led to the Bayh administration's decision to close the hospital in 1994.

ELLEN DWYER
Indiana University, Bloomington

Indiana Medical History Quarterly, 9 (Mar., 1983; special issue on the history of mental health care in Indiana).

El Centro Hispano–The Hispanic Center. A nonprofit agency serving the Indianapolis Hispanic community. In 1968 HISPANICS primarily of Mexican, Cuban, and Puerto Rican descent organized in Indianapolis the Hispano-American Society in response to the needs of a growing and ethnically diverse Hispanic population in the city. Three years later, in 1971, the society, with support from the office of the mayor and several of the city's churches, founded the Hispano-American Center (now El Centro Hispano) at 617 East North Street in an abandoned parish hall donated by the Roman Catholic Archdiocese. Starting with a small paid staff, a board of directors, and contributions from many volunteers, the center quickly grew into the principal source of social services and a hub of cultural activities for the city's Hispanic community.

The COMMUNITY CENTERS OF INDIANAPOLIS (CCI) assumed control of the center in 1983. As the only member of CCI without a defined neighborhood, the center addresses the needs of all Hispanics in the greater metropolitan area by providing employment and immigration counseling, information and referral services, emergency assistance, and educational programs. The center continues its role as a facilitator of and focal point for cultural activities such as Fiesta Indianapolis, now an annual event in the life of the city.

HISPANIC INDIANAPOLIS ORAL HISTORY PROJECT
University of Indianapolis

Interviews conducted in the early 1990s and on deposit in the Indiana State Library.

Chamber Music. Immigrants from central and eastern Europe brought their love of music to Indianapolis in the 19th century, and no nationality was more passionate about chamber music than the Germans who had been raised on Bach, Beethoven, and Brahms. May festivals, sponsored by the German Club of Indianapolis, featured local chamber ensembles as well as recitalists and choral groups. During the 1890s the Schellschmidt family formed the Philharmonic String Quartet, one of the city's earliest professional chamber ensembles. The MAENNERCHOR of Indianapolis, a German choral group founded in 1853 and still in existence today, in its early years presented soloists and string quartets in addition to choral concerts. In the first half of the 20th century, under the auspices of the Maennerchor, violinists Joseph Szigeti and Georges Enesco, cellist Gregor Piatigorsky, as well as the Flonzaley and Budapest quartets, were frequent visitors to the city.

Other organizations presented artists of international stature in chamber music. The Ona B. Talbot Fine Arts Association, founded in 1899, arranged concerts at the Murat Theater. The Marten Concerts, first directed by NANCY MARTENS, presented some of the legendary names in music history, such as violinists Nathan Milstein, Fritz Kreisler, and Jascha Heifetz, in the 1930s and 1940s at the English Theatre on the Circle. The ENSEMBLE MUSIC SOCIETY, founded in 1944 by Leonard Strauss, is one of the longest continuously running chamber music societies in America. It presents the outstanding ensembles of the world, including the Juilliard, Cleveland, Tokyo, and Guarneri String Quartets. Filling yet another niche in the city's musical life, the FESTIVAL MUSIC SOCIETY was founded in 1967 to present music written before 1800, especially music of the Middle Ages and of the Renaissance, with period instruments.

With the permanent establishment of the INDIANAPOLIS SYMPHONY ORCHESTRA in 1930, professional resident musicians of the symphony often formed smaller groups to explore masterworks of the chamber repertory, thus broadening the community's musical fare. By the 1970s few resident ensembles were performing on a regular basis, but that tradition was revived in 1980 with the creation of "Suzuki and Friends" by ISO concertmaster Hidetaro Suzuki and his wife, pianist Zeyda Ruga Suzuki. Sponsored by CATHEDRAL ARTS, the success of this longest-running resident series in turn spawned a number of new groups such as the Ronen Chamber Ensemble, the Cameo Trio, the Indianapolis Brass Choir, the Faulkner Chamber Players, and the talented musicians of the Scott family whose performances echo those of the Schellschmidt family a century ago.

No fewer than 12 professional chamber groups were in existence in Indianapolis during the 1980s, featuring various string, wind, brass, and percussion combinations in the widest ranges of repertory. These groups often commission new works, thus enriching the repertory and making the city a vital center for chamber music in America.

THOMAS J. BECZKIEWICZ

Chamber of Commerce. Early organizations to promote economic growth in Indianapolis were a Board of Trade, founded in 1853 and reorganized in 1857 and 1870, and a short-lived Chamber of Commerce (1864–1870). In the late 1880s some members of the Board of Trade, led by COLONEL ELI LILLY, believed that a more active and forward-looking group was necessary to take on new initiatives. In 1890 they founded the Commercial Club of Indianapolis, with Lilly as its president and WILLIAM FORTUNE, his able young protege, as secretary.

One aim of the club was to operate as a regular men's club. To this end an eight-story building, housing club headquarters and renting office space, was built in 1893 at Meridian and Pearl streets. Another club function was to improve the city. A STREET PAVING EXPOSITION was held almost immediately and a report issued (1890). Studies were made, and reports printed, on sewerage (1901) and the need for a new federal building (1895). Successful efforts encouraged passage of laws providing for a new county jail, a new city charter, and a natural gas pipeline.

The Chamber of Commerce's current building at 320 North Meridian Street was dedicated in 1926. [Indiana Historical Society, Bass Collection, #204076F]

The club also worked to attract conventions and other visitors to the city. In 1893 the GRAND ARMY OF THE REPUBLIC had its national encampment in Indianapolis and hundreds of visitors stopped off on their way to the World's Columbian Exposition in Chicago. Other conventions followed. In 1894 the club established a commission to promote the elevation of railroad tracks in the city. Headed by Lilly and then by Fortune, the commission finally saw elevation completed in 1922.

In December, 1912, the Commercial Club joined several other commercial organizations in a new Indianapolis Chamber of Commerce, which continued many of the activities of the Commercial Club, such as persuading new industries to come to town and influencing national, state, and local legislation. It added new standing committees, such as a Good Roads Committee as automobiling developed, and a Clean-Up Paint-Up Committee.

In addition, the Chamber took steps to meet new situations. After a severe flood in 1913, a Flood Prevention Committee was instrumental in getting a state Flood Commission established. The Chamber spearheaded a War Chest drive in 1918. A Coliseum Committee worked for several years to answer the need for a city auditorium. The beginnings of the Great Depression called forth an Emergency Work Committee (1930–1933). A new 12–story CHAMBER OF COMMERCE BUILDING on North Meridian Street, designed by ROBERT FROST DAGGETT, was built in 1926. Women were admitted as members in the 1920s.

In more recent times, led by WILLIAM H. BOOK and Carl Dortch, the Chamber has worked for interstate highways, slum clearance and redevelopment, metropolitan planning, and UNIGOV. As the city has moved away from depending on a few heavy industries, the Chamber has followed the trend; 85 percent of its present membership is from small businesses (49 employees or fewer).

The Chamber continues to pursue its stated aim of giving direct service and directing the resources of its members toward maintaining a favorable business climate and creating economic growth.

CHARLES LATHAM, JR.
Indiana Historical Society

Commercial Club–Chamber of Commerce Collection, Indiana Historical Society; George H. Geib, *Indianapolis First* (Indianapolis, 1990).

Chamber of Commerce Building. Although it houses the CHAMBER OF COMMERCE offices and bears this name chiseled in ornate stone letters above the entrance, the building at 320 North Meridian Street has always been owned by others. The fondness of its first owner, Bowman Elder, for Gothic Revival architecture reputedly inspired its design. Indianapolis architect ROBERT FROST DAGGETT created a building featuring a massive base with the principal east facade relieved by five high arches that are repeated in the second-floor arched windows. From its base the structure rises in powerful vertical lines to a height of 11 stories. The building is of concrete and steel construction with a limestone exterior. Of special interest are the elaborate stone sculptures and detailing above the second floor. Included are representations of art, science, commerce, and industry, as well as brackets supported by gargoyles. The building's interior has changed little over the years. The long central hall at street level appears much as it did when the building was erected in 1926, with walnut beams, ornate wall sconces, and an assortment of shops and businesses.

RITA W. HARLAN

"The Chamber at 100," *Indianapolis News*, special section, Mar. 20, 1990.

Chambers, David Laurance (Jan. 12, 1879–Jan. 12, 1963). Publisher. Born in Washington, D.C., David Laurance Chambers graduated magna cum laude and Phi Beta Kappa from Princeton University in 1900 where he studied under Henry Van Dyke, Princeton's chief literary figure of the time. In 1901 he earned his M.A. from Princeton as a Charles Scribner Fellow in English and, after graduation, became secretary to Van Dyke and compiler with him of *Poems of Tennyson* (1903). He later wrote *Indiana: A Hoosier History, Based on the Mural Paintings of Thomas Hart Benton* (1933). Subsequent honorary degrees include the Litt.D. from Wabash College in 1937 and the LL.D. from Indiana University in 1948.

In 1903 Chambers went to work for the publishing firm of BOBBS-MERRILL in Indianapolis. Four years later he became a member of the firm, where for almost the next half century his guidance increasingly became a part of its daily operations. He was made vice-president in 1921, editor in 1925, and president in 1935. In 1953 he was elected chairman of the board, though as a major stockholder he remained active in the firm until its sale to HOWARD W. SAMS AND COMPANY of Indianapolis in 1958.

He knew many of the distinguished writers of his day, among them JAMES WHITCOMB RILEY and MEREDITH NICHOLSON, and published a number of them. On his lists were the popular novels of John Erskine, Earl Derr Biggers, Alice T. Hobart, Inglis Fletcher, Katharine M. Jones, and Ayn Rand. He also published Bruce Barton, Richard Halliburton, Elmer Davis, and Irma S. Rombauer's and Marion Rombauer Becker's *The Joy of Cooking*. His love for American history, especially Civil War history, was reflected in nonfiction books such as those by Henry Steele Commager, Bertita Harding, and Glenn Tucker. During his 28

years as editor, he produced not only ten best-sellers, but also eight books that won literary awards, among them three Pulitzer Prize winners. He was responsible for the development of the highly successful "Childhood of Famous Americans" series for children, after creating the position of children's book editor in 1946.

Chambers served as vice-president and director of the National Association of Book Publishers and was a member of the Council of the Princeton University Press. In 1910 he married Nora Taggart, daughter of THOMAS TAGGART, former mayor of Indianapolis and U.S. senator; they had three children. Eulogized as a relatively obscure great man, he left his personal imprint on almost every trade title Bobbs-Merrill published during the second quarter of the 20th century.

JOANNE LANDERS HENRY

Jack Wayne O'Bar, "A History of the Bobbs-Merrill Company, 1850–1940: With a Postlude Through the Early 1960's" (Ph.D. dissertation, Indiana University, 1975); Glenn Tucker, "Laurance Chambers: The Man Who Knew Books and Their Writers," *Indianapolis Sunday Star Magazine* (Apr. 20, 1975), 26–29.

Chapman, George Alexander (?-1850) and **Jacob Page** (ca. 1810–May 20, 1866). Newspaper publishers. Originally from Massachusetts, the brothers were publishing the *Wabash Enquirer* in Terre Haute by 1838. The newspaper folded following the statewide Democratic defeat of 1840 and in June, 1841, the Chapmans moved to Indianapolis where Jacob purchased the *Indiana Democrat*, renaming it the INDIANA STATE SENTINEL. The first issue, dated July 21, 1841, included a rooster atop the banner "Crow, Chapman, Crow!!!," which became a rallying cry for Democrats throughout Indiana and inaugurated the rooster as the state party's symbol.

The brothers divided duties, with Jacob assuming most of the editorial responsibilities. Known for its rabid political attacks, the *Sentinel* quickly became the state's leading paper and principal Democratic organ. It appeared each Wednesday, although the Chapmans published daily issues during the 1841–1842 legislative session, a practice they repeated for the next two General Assemblies. They moved their operations to new quarters on Illinois Street in 1844, and accepted John S. Spann as a partner in November, 1846.

George served on the city's board of trustees, 1848–1849, but died the following year. Jacob represented Marion County at the state Constitutional Convention in 1850 and later sold the *Sentinel* to Austin H. Brown. After retiring briefly, Jacob founded a new weekly, *The Chanticleer* (1853–1854), with son George H. and BERRY SULGROVE. That same year, Jacob was a candidate for president of the State Bank but lost to Ebenezer Dumont of Dearborn County. By 1855, Jacob's mental health deteriorated, and he was committed to an asylum.

SHERYL D. VANDERSTEL

Jacob Piatt Dunn, *Greater Indianapolis* (Chicago, 1910), I, 119, 389–391; *Indianapolis Star*, Sept. 8, 1940.

Charity Organization Society. Administrative, investigative, and referral service for affiliated charities. The establishment of the Charity Organization Society (COS) in March, 1880, marked a transition, in the words of the local *Year Book of Charities, 1889–1890*, "from the merely sentimental stage of alleviating want without question, into the scientific method of reformation and prevention." The "sentimental stage" was represented by the Indianapolis Benevolent Society (IBS), established in 1835 to provide relief for the needy. The Benevolent Society had administered aid by dividing the city into districts and assigning a man and a woman to each district to learn about residents' needs and to collect clothing, wood, and money for deposit in a central location, to be drawn on as needed. Among the prominent citizens who worked for the all-volunteer IBS were CALVIN FLETCHER, JAMES M. RAY, and JAMES BLAKE, IBS's president for its first 35 years.

By December, 1878, when the severe depression of the mid–1870s had put an estimated one fifth of the Indianapolis population on relief, the simple methods of the Benevolent Society were no longer adequate and it considered disbanding. However, members accepted a reorganization plan proposed by OSCAR C. MCCULLOCH, pastor

of Plymouth Congregational Church, and elected him president. McCulloch began the transition to a more "scientific method" of charity by hiring a full-time executive and instituting a confidential exchange of case information and centralized record keeping. At its annual meeting in November, 1879, following a speech about the charity organization society of Buffalo, New York, the Benevolent Society proposed an agency similar to Buffalo's; it would address problems of lack of coordination and "indiscriminate giving" by assuming administrative and investigative responsibilities for local charities.

A provisional council of the Indianapolis Charity Organization Society was formed in December, 1879; the first official meeting was held in March, 1880, with Mayor JOHN CAVEN as president. Oscar McCulloch, the primary force behind the establishment of COS, served as its third president from 1882 until his death in 1891. Income came primarily from "subscriptions" by local businesses. The Benevolent Society became solely a relief agency, funded by the Charity Organization Society and sharing an executive and board of directors with it.

The purposes of the COS were to provide relief to the deserving poor, reduce the causes of permanent dependency, and substitute work for relief. To fulfill its relief function, the society investigated requests for assistance, maintained a confidential exchange of information for cooperating agencies, requested aid from appropriate agencies, and kept case records. To eliminate dependency, it set up the Dime Savings and Loan Association to encourage regular saving, assigned "friendly visitors" to families to give advice about being thrifty and industrious, sponsored public lectures on the causes and cures of pauperism, and set up committees on the reduction of crime, municipal cooperation, penal and charitable institutions, and the cultivation of vacant lots. The Charity Organization Society's commitment to substituting work for relief led in 1880 to the Friendly Inn and Wood-Yard, operated by the Benevolent Society, to provide work as well as lodging for transients, and in 1907 to the Fairview Settlement project, which hired unemployed males to build cottages that were offered rent free to widows with children.

In November, 1922, the Charity Organization Society merged with the Benevolent Society, the Children's Aid Association, and the Mother's Aid Society to form the Family Welfare Society of Indianapolis (now the FAMILY SERVICE ASSOCIATION).

PATRICIA A. DEAN

Charity Organization Society, "The Organized Charities of Indianapolis" (copy in Indiana State Library); John T. Seeley et al., *Community Chest: A Case Study in Philanthropy* (Toronto, 1957); Thurman B. Rice, "The Beginnings of Organized Charity in Indianapolis," Indiana State Board of Health *Monthly Bulletin*, 55 (no. 9), 210–214.

Charles Mayer and Company. Gift store. In 1840 CHARLES MAYER settled in Indianapolis and opened a small store at 29 West Washington Street. A native of Germany, Mayer had learned retailing as an apprentice merchant. He left Germany at age 19 to start his own business, stopping in Baltimore and Cincinnati before coming to Indianapolis. In 1850 Mayer's began importing fancy items such as music boxes and doll buggies and soon was known as a gift store. In 1866 Mayer made his clerk of 11 years, William Haueisen, his partner, changing the business name to Charles Mayer and Company. About this time Mayer began a wholesale trade in addition to his retail business. The firm was well known outside of Indianapolis. In 1871 *Leslie's Weekly* called Mayer's one of the "curiosities of the West." Haueisen retired in 1888 and the founder's sons, Ferdinand L. Mayer and Charles Mayer II, became their father's partners.

In the early 1890s Mayer's employed 21 traveling wholesalers and a total of 80 employees. Founder Charles Mayer died in 1891. The wholesale business continued until 1902 when the company became strictly retail again. In 1925 Charles Mayer II was succeeded by his son, Charles Mayer III, as head of the firm. In January, 1955, the store closed, selling its inventory to L. S. AYRES AND COMPANY since there were no direct male Mayer heirs to take over the family business. In December, 1992, Charles Mayer and Company reopened in a new location in the BUTLER-TARKINGTON neighborhood. Several business partners, including the maternal great-great-grandson of the

Charles Mayer & Co.'s 1888 Christmas catalogue, distributed nationally, contained everything from dolls to xylophones. [Indiana Historical Society, #C5748]

founder, own the store, which offers home furnishings, accessories, and an art gallery.

DEBORAH B. MARKISOHN

Indianapolis Star, Nov. 18, 1940, Dec. 31, 1947; *Indianapolis Times*, Nov. 21, 1940.

Charleston, Oscar (Feb., 1896–Oct. 5, 1954). Professional baseball player. Born in Indianapolis, the seventh of eleven children, Charleston spent 33 seasons starring for or managing the Indianapolis ABCs, Chicago American Giants, Homestead Grays, and other Negro League teams. The legendary James "Cool Papa" Bell pronounced him the greatest BASEBALL player who ever lived.

In 1912, Charleston dominated opponents as a pitcher-outfielder for the U.S. 24th Infantry Division in Manila, the Philippines. Discharged in 1915, he signed with CHARLES I. TAYLOR's Indianapolis ABCs in the Negro Western League. Though reliable statistics from the era of the Negro Leagues are scarce, it is known that Charleston played in over 1,000 games with a batting average near .350. In 1921–1922, as a rookie in the Cuban winter leagues that featured numerous Major League ballplayers, the fleet centerfielder hit opposing pitchers at a .405 rate. A five-game exhibition series against the St. Louis Cardinals in 1922 produced five Oscar Charleston home runs. John McGraw, the New York Giants' Hall of Fame manager, was so impressed he attempted to sneak the Hoosier into the National League posing as a Cuban. The ruse failed.

Retired from the Negro Leagues in 1945, Charleston spent a number of years as a baggage handler for the Pennsylvania Railroad. He returned to baseball in 1954 as a manager of the famous Negro show team, the Indianapolis Clowns, but was felled by a fatal heart attack following the 1954 season. Charleston's contributions to the national pastime were recognized through his election to the Baseball Hall of Fame in 1976.

R. DALE OGDEN
Indiana State Musuem

John A. Mercurio, *Record Profiles of Baseball's Hall of Famers* (New York, 1990); Dale Ogden and Robert Collins, *Hoosier Sports Heroes* (Indianapolis, 1990); *Indianapolis Times* and *Indianapolis Recorder*, Oct. 9, 1954.

Charters, City. Between its founding in 1821 and its municipal incorporation in 1832, Indianapolis was governed by state laws which were enforced by county officers. From 1832 until 1970 Indianapolis functioned under five charters, each of which originated from particular municipal needs and which provided certain basic structures and guidelines for operating town and city governments.

Charter of 1832. The Indiana General Assembly adopted legislation on February 2, 1832, which changed the method of town incorporation. The new procedure required two thirds of eligible voters within the proposed town to sign a petition requesting county commissioners to approve incorporation and to call for public elec-

tions. Local citizens prepared a petition on September 3 and presented it the next day to the commissioners, who called for the first election of trustees on September 29, 1832. That day voters elected Obed Foote president and Josiah W. Davis clerk; they divided the town into five districts, each represented by one trustee. The newly elected town trustees drafted and adopted a general ordinance, known as the Charter of 1832, to govern Indianapolis. It defined the powers and responsibilities of the trustees and other town officials (including a clerk, assessor, treasurer, and marshal), prescribed taxes and special licenses, and listed local ordinances.

Charter of 1838. On February 5, 1836, the citizens of Indianapolis obtained a special charter from the state legislature. It allowed them to adopt any ordinances "necessary for the good government of the corporation." After two years residents sought a stronger charter, and on February 17, 1838, the legislature reincorporated Indianapolis. The new charter established a town council consisting of a popularly elected president and six trustees, one representing each of the six wards whose boundaries the charter established. The president possessed the powers of a justice of the peace, and the town marshal that of a constable. The council, whose members were elected annually, was authorized to appoint essential government officers and to tax property (one half of one percent of the valuation) for street and other improvements; taxation was limited to the MILE SQUARE even though the incorporation included the entire congressional land donation. The council also possessed powers to license and regulate markets and amusements, and to adopt any laws necessary to maintain the peace within the town's four square miles. The charter required adult males to work two days per year on street maintenance or pay a $1 tax. An 1840 legislative act increased council terms to two years and adopted alternate year elections for half of the councilmen.

Charter of 1847. Under a special act of the Indiana General Assembly on February 13, 1847, Indianapolis became an incorporated city, replacing its earlier status as a town. Local voters approved the charter 449–19 on March 27, and it became effective March 30. The council set citywide elections for April 24 to select a mayor (two-year term) and fill the seven-member Common Council (one-year term), elected from the newly redrawn wards. SAMUEL HENDERSON was elected mayor, an unsalaried position that carried the "jurisdiction of a justice of the peace," its attendant fees, and new veto powers. The charter established the corporate boundaries of the city and authorized the council to elect a secretary, treasurer, marshal, clerk, assessor, street commissioners, and other officers as needed. It imposed a local school tax, required adult males to work two days annually on streets and roads, and authorized taxation on all lands in the original donation at a rate not to exceed 15 cents per $100 valuation.

Charter of 1853. Following the adoption of a new state constitution in 1851, the Indiana General Assembly passed "an act for the incorporation of cities" (towns exceeding 3,000 in population) on June 18, 1852. The new charter, which the Indianapolis council adopted on March 7, 1853, established two councilmen per ward, designated the mayor president of the council, and limited all elected offices to one-year terms. The council was empowered to appoint city officers, pass ordinances for local governance, maintain and enforce sanitary regulations, annex property, and establish licensing procedures. The charter allowed the council to levy a property tax not to exceed 75 cents per $100 valuation, a poll tax of no more than 50 cents per adult male, and special taxes on carriages, hackneys, and dogs. By a legislative act of March 9, 1857, the Indiana General Assembly revised the incorporation laws, increasing the tax limit to $1 and the terms of the mayor and city judge to two years. An act of March 1, 1859, extended the two-year term to all city officers.

Charter of 1891. In March, 1890, the Indianapolis BOARD OF TRADE and the COMMERCIAL CLUB, both of which supported improvements on city streets, the creation of a Board of Public Works, and a more efficient and responsive government, met to discuss the revision of city government. Using the recently adopted charter of Brooklyn, New York (which utilized the federal plan of legislative, judicial, and executive divisions), and the Bullitt Law of Philadelphia (which allowed the mayor to appoint a Board of Public Works and other officers) as models, a committee met to draft a revised city charter. Key committee members included Augustus L. Mason, Samuel E. Morss, Mayor THOMAS L. SULLIVAN, George G. Tanner, and Granville S. Wright. Upon submitting the charter to the Indiana General Assembly both organizations lobbied the legislature, which approved the charter on March 3, 1891; the governor signed the legislation on March 6.

The new charter adopted a strong mayor-council form of municipal government. Authority was divided among the separate executive, legislative, and judicial branches with administrative responsibilities being concentrated in the office of the mayor. He was empowered to appoint a "cabinet" of six individuals to direct the departments of Finance (headed by a city comptroller), Law, Public Works, Public Safety, Assessment and Collection, and Public Health and Charities. The mayor, who received a salary of $4,000, could appoint other officers without approval of the common council. The council consisted of 21 members, one elected from each of the 15 wards and 6 at-large representatives. It possessed purely legislative functions to ensure public health and comfort, to maintain streets, to license and regulate occupations and businesses, to preserve the peace, to levy taxes (not to exceed 90 cents per $100 valuation), and to annex property, among other assorted responsibilities. The judicial branch consisted of a police court, headed by a police judge with the powers of a justice of the peace. He was assisted by a clerk and bailiff-constable. The charter specified that local elections would be held the second Tuesday of October of every alternate year.

Between each charter, state and local officials adopted revisions and amendments necessary to maintain the operation of municipal government: increasing tax rates; granting power to borrow; and redefining the powers of city offices. Over the years there were numerous amendments to the city charter. In 1895 the Indiana General Assembly created a board of park commissioners as part of the city's administrative structure; an amendment in 1909 increased the power of the board of park commissioners and appropriated tax revenues for park purposes. Other amendments addressed the annexation of property, assessment for public improvements, and salaries of city officers. A 1903 law established a juvenile court in Marion

County and modified the judicial division of city government. By the municipal corporations law of 1905, a system patterned after the Indianapolis model was adopted for Indiana's cities, which were divided into five classes according to size of population.

The Charter of 1891, as amended, remained the basis of municipal government in Indianapolis until implementation of the UNIGOV legislation in 1970.

GREGORY VOGEL
DAVID G. VANDERSTEL
Indiana University–Purdue University,
Indianapolis

_____

16th Session of the Indiana General Assembly (Indianapolis, 1832); An Ordinance for the Regulation and Government of the Town of Indianapolis (Indianapolis, 1848); An Act for the Incorporation of Cities (Indianapolis, 1853); Indianapolis City Charter (Indianapolis, 1891); Jacob Piatt Dunn, Greater Indianapolis (Chicago, 1910), esp. chapters 12, 16, and 27.

Chartrand, Joseph (May 11, 1870–Dec. 8, 1933). Second Catholic Bishop of Indianapolis (1918–1933). Born in St. Louis, Missouri, of French and Irish ancestry, Chartrand enrolled at St. Louis University, St. Francis Seminary in Milwaukee, and the University of Innsbruck. He completed his studies at St. Meinrad Seminary in southern Indiana (1891), and the next year Bishop FRANCIS SILAS CHATARD ordained him priest in the present Blessed Sacrament Chapel, SS. PETER AND PAUL CATHEDRAL. His entire clerical life was linked to the Cathedral. He resided there as secretary to the bishop and as rector supervised its construction (1905). Consecrated coadjutor to Chatard in 1910, he assumed administration of the diocese on behalf of the aged and ailing bishop. He founded Cathedral High School with a $50,000 purse presented him to mark his silver anniversary of ordination (1917) and succeeded Chatard as bishop on September 7, 1918.

Chartrand combined personal sanctity and interest in the welfare of parishioners with participation in ecclesiastical politics (four of his priests became bishops) and an unconcern for the financial condition of the diocese. He encouraged frequent reception of the Eucharist and devotion to the Virgin Mary, spent hours daily hearing confessions, attracted large crowds whenever he preached, and was generous to a fault. Convinced of the benefits of Catholic education, he required children to attend Catholic schools; in other matters, he willingly abrogated church laws for pastoral reasons. He personally distributed thousands of devotional books and increased the number of priests in the diocese from 246 to 345 during his episcopate. In 1925 Pope Pius XI appointed him Archbishop of Cincinnati, but he declined the appointment to remain in Indianapolis.

Suffering from diabetes and poor eyesight, Chartrand died of a heart attack at Cathedral rectory and was buried in the Cathedral crypt in the presence of 29 bishops. In 1976 he was reinterred in the mausoleum chapel of Calvary Cemetery.

JAMES J. DIVITA
Marian College

_____

James J. Divita, Under Mary's Guidance You Will Never Grow Weary—Remembering Bishop Joseph Chartrand of Indianapolis (Indianapolis: Marian College, 1983).

Chase, William Merritt (Nov. 1, 1849–Oct. 25, 1916). American Impressionist artist and art teacher. Born in Williamsburg (later renamed Nineveh), Indiana, William was the oldest of six children. He moved to Indianapolis in 1861 where his father opened a shoe store located near the studio of Indianapolis artist BARTON S. HAYS. Chase became a student of Hays and by the late 1860s was painting and selling portraits. Through Hays, Chase developed a friendship with JACOB COX, whom he called his "father in art." When Hays felt that Chase had learned all he could under his direction, he and Cox suggested to David Chase that he allow his son to study at the National Academy of New York. His father reluctantly agreed and Chase left for New York at the age of 21. The following summer he returned to Indianapolis and worked in Hays' studio on the Circle.

A business failure prompted the family's move to St. Louis, where in 1871 Chase won awards at the 11th St. Louis Fair. Recognizing the young artist's talent, a group of seven St. Louis businessmen sponsored his study at the Royal Academy in Munich in return for one painting each and help in acquiring European paintings.

From 1872 to 1878 Chase studied in Munich. He returned to New York to be an instructor at the Art Students League, a position he held for nearly four decades. In 1879, along with artists such as Thomas Moran, George Inness, and J. Alden Weir, Chase started the American Academy of Fine Arts and served as its president for nearly ten years. The group represented young artists rebelling against the National Academy's apparent lack of acceptance of their works. The academy was a leading force for other groups established for the advancement of American art.

Chase married in 1886 and a few years later acquired a summer home in Shinnecock, Long Island (near Southampton), where in 1891 he established the Shinnecock Hills Summer School of Art. In addition to teaching at the Art Students League and at Shinnecock, he accepted private students at his studio. From 1903 to 1913 he conducted classes in Europe. He also founded the Chase School of Art in 1896, which became the New York School of Art two years later. Many outstanding American artists studied under Chase, including George Bellows, Rockwell Kent, Edward Hopper, Joseph Stella, and Georgia O'Keeffe.

Chase joined the Ten American Painters group in 1905, and is recognized today as an outstanding American Impressionist. Although his time in the Midwest was limited to visits after 1878, his works are well known and represented in many Indiana collections.

RUTH B. MILLS-VARNELL

Art Association of Richmond, Indiana

Keith L. Bryant, Jr., *William Merritt Chase: A Genteel Bohemian* (Columbia, Mo., 1991); Mary Q. Burnet, *Art and Artists of Indiana* (New York, 1921).

Chatard, Francis Silas Marean (Dec. 12, 1834–Sept. 7, 1918). First bishop of the Roman Catholic Diocese of Indianapolis. The son of Ferdinand and Eliza Chatard was born and educated in Baltimore, Maryland. Following the path taken by his paternal grandfather and father, Chatard became a doctor. He served his residency at

Francis Silas Chatard directed the construction of SS. Peter and Paul Cathedral. [Catholic Communications Center, Archdiocese of Indianapolis]

the Baltimore Alms House. Feeling himself called to another vocation, however, in 1857 he entered the Urban College of Propaganda Fide in Rome, was ordained a priest in 1862, and stayed in Rome to work at the North American College.

On May 12, 1878, Pope Leo XIII appointed Chatard as bishop of the diocese of Vincennes, making him the first United States–born bishop in Indiana. He established his residence in Indianapolis in August of that year, although the see of the diocese was not officially transferred or the name changed to Diocese of Indianapolis until March, 1898. Chatard began an extensive reorganization of the diocese, and built SS. PETER AND PAUL CATHEDRAL. His efforts increased the number of parishes and missions and enlarged the ranks of the clergy and religious. He convened four synods. Demonstrating great concern for education, Chatard established a diocesan school board, mandated the building of a grade school in each parish, and made attendance at Catholic schools mandatory for all Catholic children. The bishop's stewardship of the new diocese increased the number of Catholics from about 80,000 to about 130,000 at the time of his death. Bishop Chatard suffered a stroke in January, 1899, from which he never fully recovered. Chatard High School, established in 1961, is named in his honor.

MARCUS EUGENE WOODS, II

R. Gorman, *The New Catholic Encyclopedia* (1967 ed.); Bernard Strange, "Francis Silas Chatard: First Bishop of Indianapolis, 1878–1918," *St. Meinrad Historical Essays*, 4 (Mar., 1934), 153–163; *Indiana Catholic and Record*, Aug. 30, 1935, pp. 56–57.

Chatham Arch. Near northside neighborhood bounded by I–65, College Avenue, East Street, and North Street. Platted between 1836 and 1871, the area now known as Chatham Arch was once a thriving working class community with Queen Anne, Gothic Revival, and Stick Style cottages. Along Broadway and East streets, the Italianate houses were grander, reflecting the prestige of the businessmen who owned them.

Chatham Arch was never exclusively residential. A five-acre railroad depot was in operation during the early years of development. Along Massachusetts Avenue, shops and light industry sprang up along the Citizens Avenue Railroad, while groceries and drug stores sprouted on busy corners. Several churches were built, including Allen Chapel, an African Methodist Episcopal church founded in 1867.

After 1900, apartments and commercial firms began to move in. The REAL SILK HOSIERY COMPANY opened the first of seven buildings between North Street and Massachusetts Avenue in 1922. Chatham Arch declined in the 1950s, when cottages were razed and larger homes subdivided into apartments. Construction of I–65 cut a swath through the neighborhood. Then in 1980 the area was placed on the National Register of Historic Places and designated Chatham Arch after a residential street and a commercial square. Many cottages have been restored and sites such as the Real Silk Company have been adapted to condominiums and offices. Art galleries and restaurants have revitalized Massachusetts Avenue. By 1993, Chatham Arch was one of the fastest growing historic neighborhoods in the city.

CATHLEEN F. DONNELLY

Chen, Ko Kuei (Feb. 26, 1898–Dec. 12, 1988). Pharmacologist with Eli Lilly and Company. A native of Shanghai, China, Chen came to the United States after graduating from Tsing Hua College in Peiping (now Beijing) in 1918. He received a B.S. in pharmacy (1920) and a Ph.D. in physiology and pharmacology (1923) from the University of Wisconsin, and the M.D. degree from Johns Hopkins University (1927). Chen remained at Johns Hopkins as an associate in pharmacology until 1929 when he joined the staff of ELI LILLY AND COMPANY. He directed Lilly's pharmacological division for 34 years. During that time he accumulated numerous awards for his research and became known for his discoveries of ephedrine and a cyanide poison antidote. Both the Philadelphia College of Pharmacy and Science and the University of Wisconsin awarded Chen honorary doctorates. Retiring from Lilly in 1963, Chen joined the INDIANA UNIVERSITY SCHOOL OF MEDICINE as a full-time professor and research scientist. In 1965 he was awarded the Remington medal by the American Pharmaceutical Association, presented annually to an individual who has given outstanding service to American pharmacy. Dr. Chen died in San Francisco at the age of 90.

KATHY INGELS HELMOND

Child Welfare. The historical development of child welfare programs and services in Indianapolis closely follows the pattern throughout the country; however, Indianapolis has lagged behind other cities in terms of trends, numbers, and severity of cases.

Public entities (county welfare departments, juvenile courts, and probation offices) have had legal responsibility for child welfare services, but private, not-for-profit, and church-sponsored agencies have played an important role in service delivery. In Indianapolis, such agencies include the CHILDREN'S BUREAU, LUTHERAN CHILD AND FAMILY SERVICES, PLEASANT RUN CHILDREN'S HOMES, FAMILY SERVICE ASSOCIATION, St. Elizabeth's Home, and many more.

Child welfare services in the early 19th century in Indianapolis were provided by township trustees, who by state statute were overseers of the poor. When trustees decided not to assist a needy child's family—often for arbitrary reasons—the child was either apprenticed, farmed out to the lowest bidder, or placed in the county poor asylum.

The first Indiana private institution for the care of destitute children, the Widows' and Orphans' Asylum of Indianapolis (now the Children's Bureau), opened in Indianapolis in 1851. The General Protestant Orphan Home (now Pleasant Run Children's Homes) was founded in 1867 to care for children whose fathers perished during the Civil War. Lutheran Child and Family Services began as an orphanage in 1883, was converted to a day care center during World War II, and evolved into a residential child care facility with the construction of Lutherwood in 1956.

During the 1800s, citizens of Indianapolis generally believed, as did the rest of the country, that childrearing decisions were the responsibility of parents. Parents' rights clearly took precedence over children's rights. Extreme cases of child abuse were handled by local courts on a case-by-case basis.

The first Indiana statute that mentioned cruelty to children was an 1889 law that authorized the appointment of a Board of Children's Guardians in Marion County. That board was charged with the responsibility of investigating cases of reported cruelty to children by their parents or custodians. The board was also authorized to take cases to the local judge when there was evidence to support the allegation of cruelty. Another 1889 state law made ill treatment of a child or cruelty to a child a misdemeanor.

In 1903 the state legislature provided for a separate system of JUVENILE JUSTICE in Marion County, including a juvenile court with paid probation officers. This court had responsibility for holding hearings on delinquency petitions and for making placements of delinquents. In 1907 the law was changed to include hearings and dispositions on dependent and neglected children.

Through the Welfare Act of 1936, the Marion County Department of Public Welfare was given the responsibility of providing direct care and services to dependent, neglected, and handicapped children and children in danger of becoming delinquent.

Throughout the years new theories, new knowledge, and changing value systems have led to the passage of a number of state and federal statutes pertaining to child welfare. A review of historical information on maltreatment in Marion County indicates a steady growth in the number of documented cases. As society has become more complex, so have the laws relating to child welfare, the problems presented by children coming into care, and the intervention strategies employed by service providers.

Increased numbers of seriously troubled teens and of very young children now are entering the system without corresponding increases in financial or professional resources to provide specialized help. Major new problems of the 1980s (dramatic increases in drug addiction, AIDS, teen pregnancy, and the like) have also placed new burdens on the child and family social services system, again without adding new resources.

In 1992 there were 5,100 reports of abuse and 3,700 reports of neglect in Marion County. In the same year there were 1,079 substantiated or indicated cases of physical abuse, 1,413 substantiated or indicated cases of sexual abuse, and 1,558 substantiated or indicated cases of child neglect. As of July 1, 1993, there were over 190 Indianapolis children placed in out-of-state institutions at an annual cost of over $12 million, due to lack of appropriate local treatment facilities.

Present Indianapolis child-serving agencies, in addition to the Marion County Division of Family and Children, include: Children's Bureau of Indianapolis, Lutheran Child and Family Services, Pleasant Run Children's Homes, The Villages, Family Service Association, St. Elizabeth's Family Works, and Visiting Nurse Service. Marion County public child welfare expenditures for 1993 are projected to be in excess of $45 million. Other sources of support include the UNITED WAY and contributions from foundations, religious groups, and businesses.

MARY KAPUR

Children's Bureau of Indianapolis.

Child welfare agency. Originally known as the Widows' and Orphans' Friends Society, this institution was founded in 1851 by 16 women who were members of the INDIANAPOLIS BENEVOLENT SOCIETY. Initially these volunteers solicited donations and provided rooms and jobs for indigent widows in the hopes of keeping families together and orphans out of the adult poorhouse.

In 1855 the society acquired its first residence, which housed and educated six orphans. There was such a need for services that by 1867 Marion County began regularly providing financial support to supplement private donations. The facilities were expanded in 1869 to house 70 widows and children.

By 1875 the society had limited its scope to orphans and changed its name to the Indianapolis Orphans' Asylum. The asylum rented the former North Western Christian University building in 1880 and purchased it in 1884. This building housed over 100 children and, with the help of ELI LILLY AND COMPANY, provided a daily clinic and immunization program staffed by a doctor and nurse. The institution relocated in 1905 to a site on East Washington Street where it maintained four buildings and a portable schoolhouse and served an average of 150 to 200 children. The young residents received highly regimented care, wore uniforms, kept their hair short, and attended classes in basic education, vocational training, and religion.

Changes in social work ideology soon shifted the asylum's focus from institutionalizing children to providing individualized care and/or placing children in foster or adoptive homes. The Child Welfare League of America, in conjunction with a grant from the INDIANAPOLIS FOUNDATION, provided a training program between 1928 and 1930 which resulted in the establishment of a professional social services staff that counseled families and placed children outside the institution. A women's auxiliary now known as the Children's Bureau Auxiliary formed in 1932 to provide additional fund-raising and volunteer support, as well as a yearly social work college scholarship.

The asylum became known as the Children's Bureau when it merged with the Children's Bureau of the FAMILY SERVICE ASSOCIATION in 1934 and hired its first professional director. The institution became a friendlier, less regimented place, and the boarding population dropped drastically throughout the 1930s as more children were placed in individual homes. The appearance of *The Reflector* in 1939, a newsletter for foster mothers, denotes this change. In 1941 the Children's Bureau turned over the orphanage to the General Protestant Orphan Home and focused its efforts on adoption placement and counseling for families, unwed mothers, and children. Meanwhile, the county's portion of financial support dropped and the local COMMUNITY CHEST began to fill the gap.

The need for foster care and adoption increased after World War II, but the staff also recognized a need for limited institutional care. During the 1960s the bureau pioneered the use of group homes, and by 1976 there were four residences that each housed a maximum of ten children and houseparents. In addition to an expansion of counseling programs, the 1980s witnessed the creation of several programs designed specifically for African-American children and for troubled teens.

Today the Children's Bureau provides adoption services, foster care, group home care, independent living programs, emergency and respite shelter, expectant parent services, counseling, and a child abuse hotline. The bureau's $5 million budget is supported mainly by government grants and contracts, the UNITED WAY of Central Indiana, private contributions, and the ongoing fundraising efforts of the Children's Bureau Auxiliary.

MICHELLE D. HALE

The Children's Bureau of Indianapolis Orphan Asylum History, 1851–1941 (Indianapolis, 1941).

The Children's Museum (TCM). Fourth oldest children's museum in the world and first general museum in Indianapolis. After a visit to the Brooklyn Children's Museum in 1925, MARY STEWART CAREY founded The Children's Museum of Indianapolis with the help of other like-minded civic leaders. With no collections or staff, the museum made its first home in the PROPYLAEUM's carriage house. Early collections were donations from school children and their families. Searching for a more permanent and spacious location, the museum moved to the Garfield Park community house in 1926, and the following year to the Carey mansion at 1150 North Meridian Street.

The museum hired its first curator-director, Arthur Carr, in 1926. During his tenure (1926–1942) the growing collections focused on natural history and social culture and eventually filled the entire Carey mansion. Permanent exhibits included the marine, pioneer, Japanese, archaeology, and natural history rooms, as well as a small nature study library. Programming through the 1930s included guided school tours, traveling classroom exhibits, after-school activities, and a few special events and programs such as summer Prairie Treks (1930–1947) to collect nature specimens.

Upon Carr's retirement, GRACE BLAISDELL GOLDEN assumed directorship of the museum from 1942 until 1964. She brought financial stability to the institution by cultivating the support of the LILLY ENDOWMENT, ELI LILLY, Ruth Lilly, and the INDIANAPOLIS FOUNDATION, as well as by implementing a corporate sponsorship program. The museum also purchased its first building in 1946, the Parry mansion located at 3010 North Meridian Street.

Golden steered the museum toward more active collection policies, no longer relying only on local donations. Solicited additions included a large collection of Indian and other local artifacts (1947), the mummy Wenuhotep, on permanent loan from the University of Chicago (1959), and a mid–19th century log cabin (1961). Golden also encouraged exhibits and school lending programs. Permanent exhibits in the new building focused on natural science, pioneer life, and ethnography. Subsequent building additions created the Prehistoric Gallery (1949), Transportation Gallery (1960), and Hall of Man (1962). A Junior Docent program, two weekly television shows, and interpretive activities added to the museum's repertoire.

MILDRED SARTOR COMPTON succeeded Golden as director in 1964, staying until 1982. Compton ran the museum more like a business, implementing long-range planning and cost-effective services. She prepared the museum for accreditation to the American Association of Museums by standardizing records, storage, and conservation procedures. She also waged a highly visible public relations campaign in 1965 to attract a wider audience and a larger financial base. Boosting museum attendance and exposure were the installation of a Physical Science Gallery (1967), the Reuben Wells steam engine (1968), a Model Train Gallery (1970), and more rotating special exhibits, as well as the Museum Guild's annual Haunted House.

A successful $8.78 million capital fund drive in 1973 permitted the razing of the Parry house facilities to make way for the core of the present

Skeleton of a giant ground sloth at The Children's Museum, ca. 1949. [Indianapolis Newspapers Inc.]

building. Completed in 1976, the new facility included modern collections, design, and conservation facilities and a separate schoolchildren's area. In addition to more than doubling the exhibit space, the new building also included classrooms, administration offices, and the 350–seat Ruth Allison Lilly Theater. Included in five floors of exhibits was a real mastodon skeleton, an operating carousel, and a simulated cave.

The 1980s witnessed continued growth, much of it under a new director, Peter Sterling (1982–). TCM added a restaurant and outdoor garden gallery (1983) and in 1984 received the 50,000 item Caplan folk art and toy collection, which almost doubled the size of the museum's holdings. A $14 million expansion project begun in 1987 resulted in a new atrium entrance and Welcome Center (1988); a 130–seat SpaceQuest Planetarium and additional classroom and temporary exhibit space (1989); and in 1990 the Eli Lilly Center for Exploration (CFX).

TCM also continued to add innovative exhibits and programming. Current galleries include computers, hands-on activities, and artifact-based exhibits focusing on physical and natural sciences, history, foreign cultures, and the arts. In 1982 TCM received Ritchey Woods, which now hosts seasonal nature education programs. The Youth Advisory Council, previously the Junior Board of Advisors, was revived in 1986 to allow child members to participate in museum programming. CFX, opened in 1990, sponsored the first news bureau in the Midwest staffed by teens, which writes the weekly "Children's Express" page in the *INDIANAPOLIS STAR*. A museum library opened in 1993.

As of 1992, TCM attracted approximately 835,000 visitors annually to its 4,000 programs and activities and maintains a collection of 140,000 artifacts. It operated in the early 1990s with a staff of roughly 165 full-time and 227 part-time employees, and over 850 volunteers. Admission fees (first charged in 1990), investments, corporate and individual donations, museum shop and restaurant revenues, and membership dues made up most of the annual operating budget ($12.4 million in 1992).

MICHELLE D. HALE

Chinese. Few Chinese settled in Indianapolis until the late 20th century. The first immigrants were recorded in the 1880 census: ten male sojourners, eight of whom were laundrymen. Because of national immigration restrictions and an inhospitable context for foreigners, the population grew slowly until after World War II. Throughout the first half of the 20th century, a defined Chinese community, though not a full-fledged Chinatown, existed in the vicinity of Fort Wayne and Massachusetts avenues; most businesses, located in family residences, were laundries and restaurants. Indianapolis city directories listed 36 Chinese laundries in 1930 and 25 in 1940, many of which were also located along IN-DIANA AVENUE and Washington and North Illinois streets. As late as the 1950s, directories still identified certain laundries as "Chinese." The community was predominantly male, and there was a scarcity of traditional Chinese families: the birth of the second Chinese girl in the city came only in the 1920s. The early years saw the community's informal selection of a "Chinese mayor" who represented the Chinese to the larger community. Early in the century there were reportedly some criminal tong (a secret Chinese fraternal society) activities, but these were linked to men who came to the city briefly from tongs in larger cities. In May, 1904, the visit of Chinese PRINCE PU LUN, rumored heir to the Manchu throne, excited the Chinese community whose elites participated in the ten-day city festivities.

By the mid–20th century there was no distinct locus for Chinese settlement; families lived on the north, west, and south sides of Indianapolis. Though many continued to establish laundries and restaurants, immigration from the 1960s to the 1980s, stimulated by turmoil in mainland China and liberalized U.S. immigration policies, brought highly educated and professional Chinese to the city. The Chinese population in Marion County rose from 98 in 1950 to 1,257 in 1990 (1,212 in Indianapolis). Men like K. K. CHEN, an outstanding pharmacologist with ELI LILLY AND COMPANY from 1929 until 1963, brought a different image to the community. Whereas early Chinese settlers had been sojourners, those who came in mid- and late-century became American citizens, desiring to contribute to their adopted community rather than to their Chinese homeland. Children of laundrymen and restaurateurs generally chose to leave their fathers' careers for higher education and entry into the professions.

In the 1980s and 1990s the two generational cultures tended to remain separate as the numbers of professional Chinese far surpassed those in the restaurant world. In 1984 an Indiana Chinese Professional Association was established. Two important cultural and social organizations were formed in the 1970s and 1980s. The Indianapolis Association of Chinese-Americans (IACA), with approximately 300 to 400 members in 1991, and the Taiwanese American Association (TAA), numbering 150 to 180, brought some cohesion to Chinese in the city while their names pointed to the importance of Americanization. Though both call themselves "non-political, non-religious, and non-partisan," the groups reflect differences based on political distinctions in China. IACA's elected leadership clearly comes from professionals, while TAA's comes from the general Taiwanese community; significantly, restaurateurs generally did not join these organizations.

One other important Chinese organization is the Chinese Community Church, established in 1974. The congregation met at the Meridian Street Methodist Church until 1982 when it purchased property at 56th and Broadway streets to expand its programs. Beginning in 1976, semi-monthly medical clinics operated at the church after services. The church also provides Saturday morning language and cultural programs for recent immigrants and Chinese-American children.

R. KEITH SCHOPPA
Valparaiso University

Indianapolis Star Magazine, Mar. 20, 1949; *Indianapolis Star*, Sept. 27, 1953, July 12, 1981.

Christ Church Cathedral. First Episcopalian church. In June, 1837, resident Episcopalians purchased a lot on the Governor's Circle (now MONUMENT CIRCLE) to build a church. Thirty individuals organized the Parish of Christ Church on July 13, with Rev. James B. Britton, recently of Louisville, as rector. By Christmas the congregation, which worshiped in a rented room on Washington Street, numbered 30 families and offered adult Bible and Sunday school classes.

Assisted by the fund-raising efforts of Episcopal Bishop DAVID JACKSON KEMPER, the sale of pews, and donations (including one from Christ Church Louisville), parishioners financed the construction of a small, frame, Gothic-style building, completed in November, 1838. The church's women subsequently held a fair in December, 1839, to raise money for a church bell.

Christ Church quickly assumed a leadership role in the community. It hosted the second annual convention of the Diocese of Indiana, May 31–June 3, 1839, and five others over the next 13 years. In November, 1839, Mrs. James (Susan B.) Britton announced the opening of a seminary for young ladies at Pennsylvania and Vermont streets; it was later succeeded by St. Mary's Seminary, chartered by the Indiana General Assembly on January 15, 1844. By 1850 Christ Church numbered 153 adult parishioners and 108 children, with a Sunday school of 80 scholars and ten teachers.

In March, 1856, the vestry appointed a committee to plan for a new church. They selected Irish-born architect WILLIAM TINSLEY, known for his work on North Western Christian University (now BUTLER UNIVERSITY) and Center Hall at Wabash College. Parishioners began a subscription drive to fund their building project, and sold their

Christ Church Cathedral, ca. 1895.
[Indiana Historical Society, Bass Collection, #42037]

old building in 1857 to BETHEL AME CHURCH, which relocated it to Georgia Street. After meeting in the STATE HOUSE during the construction period, on May 22, 1859, the Christ Church congregation held its first worship service in the new building, which cost $32,438—the same English Gothic structure seen on the Circle today.

Christ Church was not unaffected by the Civil War. In June, 1862, Rev. Horace Stringfellow, Jr., rector since 1860, resigned his post over unsubstantiated allegations regarding his southern sympathies. He returned to Indianapolis in 1866–1867 to lead the new St. Paul's Episcopal Church, which, composed primarily of Democrats, became known among opponents as "St. Butternut's, the Church of the Holy Copperheads" or "Holy Rebellion." In April, 1865, the Christ Church choir sang at memorial services for slain President Abraham Lincoln.

After adding a new spire in 1869–1870, the church endured the hard economic times of the 1870s and witnessed the migration of other congregations into northern sections of the city during the 1880s. By 1884 Christ Church was the last of five churches that had once occupied the Circle. Between 1888 and 1900 there were repeated efforts to remove the church from the Circle and join with either St. Paul's or Grace Episcopal churches, or move to a new northside location. A move appeared imminent in 1898 when the neighboring Columbia Club was given an option to buy the church for $66,900. Following a public outcry and a grant from the Diocese of Indianapolis, the vestry voted against any move and appropriated funds for needed renovations.

Located at the city's center, Christ Church became a focal point of wartime charity activities. During World War I women's auxiliaries met to sew garments for the Red Cross. Between 1942 and 1945, the church sponsored a servicemen's "Social Hour," later known as the Christ Church Canteen, which served thousands of servicemen and women who passed through wartime Indianapolis. With the outbreak of the Korean War the church reactivated the canteen and again assisted military personnel.

Since its founding Christ Church has conducted an active community ministry. It was the mother church for several missions and congregations, including St. Luke's (1863), Grace (1864–1865), St. Paul's (1866), St. George's (1872–1873), and St. Philip's (1888). Following a large-scale renovation in 1953, Christ Church was instituted as the pro-cathedral of the Diocese of Indianapolis on October 10, 1954. The church also received widespread recognition for its urban ministry programs established during the rectorship of Cathedral Dean Paul Moore, Jr., in the 1960s.

Since the mid–1800s, Christ Church has developed a reputation for its quality music program. In 1883 the parish established a boys' choir, the precursor of today's renowned Christ Church Cathedral Choir of Men and Boys. The church has consistently upgraded its organ and provides occasional noon organ concerts.

One of Christ Church's principal benefactors was ELI LILLY. He provided the diocese with $1 million in 1953 to support and maintain the church as the pro-cathedral and left an additional endowment at his death. He also wrote a history of the institution.

Christ Church Cathedral was entered on the National Register of Historic Places in 1973. Christ Church claimed over 750 members in 1993 and continued to serve as cathedral for the diocese, parish to members, and church to downtown Indianapolis.

WILLIAM D. DALTON

Eli Lilly, *History of the Little Church on the Circle* (Indianapolis, 1957).

Christ Church Cathedral Choir of Men and Boys. The Christ Church Cathedral Choir of Men and Boys, formed in 1883, has earned an international reputation for musical excellence. In addition to singing at church services, the choir presents an annual concert series at CHRIST CHURCH CATHEDRAL and makes regular appearances with the INDIANAPOLIS SYMPHONY ORCHESTRA. The choir has made several tours of Great Britain and Europe, appearing at St. Paul's Cathedral and Westminster Abbey in London, St. Mary's Cathedral in Edinburgh, the Cathedral of Notre Dame in Paris, St. Mark's Cathedral in Venice, and St. Peter's Basilica in Rome. It is the only fully professional church choir in Indianapolis and annually auditions boys from in and around the city, accepting between five and seven as probationers. Most of these boys become full choir members after three to six months of training and usually leave the choir when their voices change. Over the years the choir has produced several album, cassette, and compact disc recordings.

WILLIAM D. DALTON

Christamore House. Social service agency. In May, 1905, Butler College alumnae and urban missionaries Anna C. Stover (1870–1944) and Edith D. Surbey (ca. 1872–1972) began settlement work in a five-room house at 1718 Arsenal Avenue. Their long-term goal was to raise both the moral and material standards of the working class Atlas neighborhood. "Christamore: the College Settlement," as they called it, attracted teachers and nurses into a community of women reformers until by 1911 there were seven resident and six non-resident workers. Before the Indiana University School of Social Service was established, Christamore functioned as a "sociological laboratory" for BUTLER UNIVERSITY and Indiana University students and was briefly known as a "Training School for Social Workers." Its residents conducted surveys and compiled data on urban conditions, contributing to such Progressive era causes as housing reform, the Pure Milk campaign, and improved infant health. As demand for the settlement's services grew, it moved to 1908–10 Columbia Avenue in September, 1905, and then to a new 19–room building at 1806 East Columbia in 1909.

After Stover and Surbey resigned in 1911 the settlement altered direction: Olive Edwards (director, 1915–1947) and Martha Stewart Carey downplayed its religious programs, developing Christamore into a community center with a dozen resident workers and 75 part-time workers. Activities included a kindergarten, clubs for boys and girls, a pure milk station, and a baby clinic.

With the black migration of World War I, Christamore's board was forced to choose whether to integrate the settlement or close its doors. Olive Edwards advocated opening Christamore to blacks at certain times, but board members argued that Christamore should be moved to escape integration. In 1921, they sold Christamore's property on Columbia Avenue to the board of park commissioners (it eventually became the J. T. V. Hill Community Center), and in 1922 set about raising $100,000 for a new building. The building, at the corner of Tremont and West Michigan streets in HAUGHVILLE, was substantially complete by 1924 and a final wing was added in 1926. Renamed Christamore House in 1928, the settlement served mainly immigrants until the 1950s, when its clientele became predominantly AFRICAN-AMERICAN. Funding came mostly through the COMMUNITY CHEST. The Christamore Aid Association also raised funds and supplied volunteers. Under Pauline McCready (1950–55), Christamore was again used for training social workers and the Christamore Aid Society was revived. Under Ray Spencer (1955–1965), the practice of residence was abandoned. Christamore entered a social work federation, Indianapolis Settlements, Inc., in 1965.

RUTH HUTCHINSON CROCKER
Auburn University

James C. Clark, "The First Fifty Years at Christamore House, 1905–1955 (M.A. thesis, Division of Social Service, Indiana University, 1955); Ruth Hutchinson Crocker, "Christamore: An Indiana Settlement House from Private Dream to Public Agency," *Indiana Magazine of History*, 83 (June, 1987), 113–140.

Christian, Grant Wright (July 17, 1911–May 21, 1989). Commercial artist and fine arts painter. Born near Edinburgh, Indiana, Christian graduated from the HERRON SCHOOL OF ART in Indianapolis in 1933. His instructors included WILLIAM FORSYTH, CLIFTON A. WHEELER, DAVID RUBINS, and Frank Schoonover. In 1933 and 1934 he continued his art education at the Pennsylvania Academy of Fine Arts in Philadelphia.

In the 1930s Christian's art took on the Regionalist manner of painting, capturing the varied subjects of the "American scene" in his work. In the 1936 HOOSIER SALON exhibition his painting, *The Edge of Town*, won the Thomas Meek Butler Prize for Outstanding Landscape. Christian received federal commissions to paint the murals *Early and Present Day Indianapolis Life* and *Mail—Transportation and Delivery* for the old Indianapolis post office (now the FEDERAL BUILDING and Courthouse) in 1936, and the *Waiting of the Mail* mural in the Nappanee, Indiana, post office in 1938.

During World War II, Christian served in the U.S. Army with the Film Strip Preparation Unit. In 1944, he won the premium prize for his "Clock of Tomorrow" design in a national competition sponsored by the Seth Thomas Clock Company. Following the war, he held commercial art positions in several advertising firms, retiring from the advertising business in 1981.

Christian continued his design work and painting in retirement, winning first place for his design of the INDIANA STATE FAIR entrance in 1969 and receiving prizes and purchase awards in three consecutive Hoosier Salon exhibitions for his canvases *This Too Shall Pass* (1987), *Golden Glimpse* (1988), and *Blessed Sunset* (1989). Nationally, Christian's exhibition venues included the Corcoran Gallery, Washington, D.C., and the Grand Central Galleries and the Whitney Museum of American Art in New York City.

FRANK N. OWINGS, JR.

Indianapolis Art League, *The Edge of Town* (Indianapolis, 1989); Flora Lauter, *Indiana Artists Active 1940* (Spencer, Ind., 1941).

Christian Church (Disciples of Christ).

Mainline Protestant denomination with headquarters in Indianapolis. Along with Churches of Christ and "Independent" Christian Churches, the Disciples derive from the 19th-century Stone-Campbell movement. Early leaders called for preaching God's unconditional love for sinners made known in Jesus Christ unencumbered by extra-biblical doctrines such as Calvinist teachings of election and predestination. They taught that this message, received in faith (and not through mysterious actions of the Holy Spirit), breaks the sinner's rebellion against God. They called, too, for restoration of what they believed to be the apostolic (or ancient) order of the church, including congregational governance, the name Christian or Disciple, weekly observance of the Lord's Supper, and immersion as a divine promise of forgiveness. They asserted that acceptance of the "ancient gospel" and "ancient order" would result in the union of the church. This, in turn, would lead to conversion of unbelievers and usher in Christ's millennial reign of peace and justice.

The first Indianapolis congregation was organized June 12, 1833, as "the Church of Christ in Indianapolis" (now Central Christian). Early leaders included Butler K. Smith, a blacksmith, John H. Sanders, a physician, and ZERELDA WALLACE (wife of Governor David Wallace), a staunch advocate of temperance and women's suffrage. The organizing minister was John O'Kane, sent to Indianapolis by a missionary organization in Rush County. Other early ministers were Chauncey Butler and Love H. Jameson. In 1866 the congregation began a mission to African-Americans that became Second Christian Church (now LIGHT OF THE WORLD). Second Church conducted a school which became Public School 23. Rufus J. Conrad, the first pastor, was teacher of the school and a physician.

Along with others across the state, members in Indianapolis established North Western Christian University in 1855 (later named BUTLER UNIVERSITY in honor of Indianapolis attorney and Disciples leader OVID BUTLER). The location of the university's first campus at 13th Street and College Avenue led to the organization in 1868 of Third Christian Church. In like manner, Butler's move to IRVINGTON in 1875 sparked the development in that year of the First Church of Christ in Irvington (now Downey Avenue). Later, University Park and Northwood would benefit from the campus relocation in 1928 to former FAIRVIEW PARK.

By the mid–1870s there were six Indianapolis congregations. Meanwhile, conflict had begun that by the mid–1890s would result in the separation of a smaller group, the Churches of Christ, from the larger group, the Christian Church or the Disciples of Christ. The major issues were instrumental music in worship and the deployment of missionaries through missionary societies. Some opposed these practices as not authorized by the apostles; others promoted them as "expedients" for achieving ends that all agreed were apostolic. Members of the Churches of Christ refused Christian fellowship to supporters of the disputed measures. Members of the Christian Churches either advocated the disputed measures or refused to separate over these practices.

In 1878 Joshua Webb, a physician and former preacher, withdrew from Central over the use of an organ in worship. By 1885 a congregation (now Speedway Church of Christ) had been established in WEST INDIANAPOLIS that was opposed to all "innovations." In the 1890s a pro-instrument faction of newly formed North Church (now Emerson Avenue) took the non-instrumental faction to court over control of the property. The court decided for the non-instrumental faction. In 1892 the combined membership of West and North churches was only 135. By contrast the combined membership of the six churches that entered the Christian Church Union of Indianapolis and Marion County (a Disciples association) was 1,970. Notable numerical growth of Churches of Christ in Indianapolis began only after World War I.

Among the societies supported by Disciples was the Christian Woman's Board of Missions (CWBM), organized in 1874. Several early officers were Indianapolis women, including its first president, Mrs. P. H. (Maria) Jameson, and Indianapolis became headquarters of the organization. CWBM sponsored evangelistic and service ministries around the globe. From 1912 to 1923 it provided the primary support for FLANNER HOUSE, a social settlement. In the 1960s a successor organization provided support for similar ministries through the Broadway Mission.

During the late 19th and early 20th centuries, Indianapolis became the national headquarters for other Disciples activities. In 1895 the Board of Ministerial Relief (reorganized in 1928 as the Pension Fund) was established in Indianapolis. Howard Cale, a legal associate of Benjamin Harrison, was its first president.

In 1911 CWBM opened the College of Missions on the Butler campus in Irvington, but the college transferred operations to Hartford, Connecticut, in 1928. Simultaneously, the lease expired on the St. Louis offices of the United Christian Missionary Society (UCMS), an organization formed in 1919 by the union of the CWBM and other general organizations of the Disciples. Thus, in 1928, 222 Downey Avenue became headquarters of UCMS—the major Disciples denominational organization.

UCMS's move to Indianapolis coincided with the widening of a fissure in the Disciples which would result in the separation of the Independent Christian Churches and the Christian Church (Disciples of Christ). At issue was support of UCMS and the closely related International Convention of the Disciples of Christ. In 1927 opponents established the North American Christian Convention as an alternative to the International Convention and began a movement to support missions "independently" of UCMS.

Underlying this new split was a dispute over the communion's relation to the emerging ecumenical movement. Closely related was the stand of different leaders to the liberal theology and approach to the Bible also emerging among American Protestants. Theological liberals held that failure to recognize "the denominations" as churches was to promote denominationalism. Opponents of liberal theology argued that to recognize the denominations as churches was to condone denominationalism. They insisted that genuine Christian union could be achieved only by Christians rejecting their denominations for the apostolic (or New Testament) church as historically discerned by the Disciples.

The dispute focused on "open membership"—the policy of accepting into church membership Christians who had not received believer's immersion. "Independents" charged that UCMS missionaries practiced open membership and therefore they refused to support the organization. UCMS denied that missionaries practiced open membership, but acknowledged that some believed in it. Disciples (called "cooperatives") included advocates of open membership as well as opponents of that policy who were willing to cooperate in mission through UCMS.

Four decades later, in 1968, after a plan for restructuring denominational organizations supported by cooperatives was approved by the International Convention, more than a third of the congregations listed in denominational records formally withdrew from the Disciples. A widely propagated false assertion that unless congregations withdrew from the Disciples by a certain date they would lose control of their property impelled this action. The Independents asked to be listed as a separate body in the *Yearbook of American Churches* three years later.

Despite loss of the Churches of Christ, the Disciples grew in Marion County until the 1960s. In 1897 they reported 12 congregations with a total membership of 4,000. By 1919 there were 32 congregations with a total membership of 10,012. After 1919 much of the growth occurred in independent congregations, which grew at six times the rate of cooperative congregations. Following the formal separation, the Independents numbered 17,715 to the Disciples' 20,891. An early promoter of growth of the Independents was O. A. Trinkle, whose Englewood church increased to over 3,000 members and who supported the planting of Independent congregations.

Like "mainline" denominations nationally, the Disciples have declined numerically since the mid–1960s. In 1990 the Disciples in Marion County numbered 16,419, while the Churches of Christ and Christian Churches numbered 6,584 and 17,079 respectively.

Butler University remained a church related school through World War II. HILTON U. BROWN, president of the Butler board from 1903 to 1955, was an active Disciple. In 1925 Butler established a College of Religion (later named the School of Religion) to provide specialized education for ministry, with a new building (Robertson Hall) completed in 1942. After the war Butler increasingly gained support apart from the churches. In 1958 an amicable separation was negotiated between the School of Religion, which desired larger facilities and a definite relationship to the Disciples, and the university, which needed the school's building and surrounding property for other purposes. The former School of Religion incorporated as CHRISTIAN THEOLOGICAL SEMINARY and located on land adjoining the west end of the Butler campus. In the late 1970s Butler University officially severed its church relationship. The Seminary, which boasts an ecumenical character, has maintained close ties to the Christian Church (Disciples of Christ).

D. NEWELL WILLIAMS
Christian Theological Seminary

Christian Science. See Church of Christ, Scientist

Christian Theological Seminary. Graduate professional school for the preparation of persons for the ministries of the church; related to the CHRISTIAN CHURCH (DISCIPLES OF CHRIST). It was for many years the College of Religion (School of Religion) of BUTLER UNIVERSITY and in 1938 became a graduate school of the university. Twenty years later it separated from Butler and took the present name, Christian Theological Seminary. It soon built a campus near the university at 1000 West 42nd Street. A fully accredited member of the Association of Theological Schools and the North Central Association of Colleges and Secondary Schools, it enrolls graduates of colleges and universities from across the United States and every continent.

Orman L. Shelton presided over the development of the seminary. He had been dean of the School of Religion and first president of Christian Theological Seminary. The school's auditorium is named in his honor and is home to the EDYVEAN REPERTORY THEATRE.

The seminary speaks of itself as "an ecumenical seminary" and has deliberately widened its clientele beyond the Christian Church (Disciples of Christ). Its board of trustees, faculty appointments, and student body represent several Protestant denominations as well as the Catholic and Jewish traditions. The basic degree, Master of Divinity, is recognized among Protestant churches to meet the educational qualifications for ordination. Other master's degrees offer specialization in church music, religious education, pastoral counseling, and religious studies.

During the 1992–1993 academic year 344 students were enrolled—152 men and 192 women. They were graduates of 157 colleges and universities, came from 40 states and 5 foreign countries, and represented 40 religious denominations and faith traditions.

EDWIN L. BECKER
Christian Theological Seminary

Christmas. The popular celebration of Christmas in America developed slowly from a blending of diverse ethnic, folk, and religious traditions. Nineteenth-century authors like Washington Irving (*Knickerbocker History of New York*, 1809), Clement Moore (*A Visit from St. Nicholas*, 1823), and Charles Dickens (*A Christmas Carol*, 1842), and *Harper's Weekly* cartoonist Thomas Nast, creator of the rotund bearded Santa Claus in the 1860s and 1870s, provided the public with popular, sentimentalized images which became the basis for holiday observances. Although not regularly observed until the Civil War, Christmas gradually became a legal holiday. Alabama first recognized it in 1836; slowly other states joined the movement—Indiana in 1875—so that by 1890 all states had marked the day.

The diaries of Vermont native CALVIN FLETCHER provide the earliest evidence of Christmas observances in Indianapolis. Fletcher wrote that he gathered with his friends to drink hard cider, whiskey, and brandy (1821, 1823) and attended a party of 30 couples at Washington Hall tavern (1823). In 1829 he observed that there was "not the usual firing of guns and parade," referring to the Christmas celebration practices common in southern states, and that the state Senate "met as usual"; two years later, the General Assembly adjourned for Christmas for the first time.

Regular Fletcher family celebrations, which did not begin until the 1830s, became more elaborate by the 1840s. Fletcher's children attended their first Christmas Eve party in 1835 where they "spent the eve in singing & in plays." Governor Noah Noble hosted a party at his residence, but Fletcher noted that there was "very little parade about Christmas." By the 1840s Fletcher noted that the women joined in making cakes, and after the children retired to bed the adults filled the children's caps and stockings with cakes and gifts. On Christmas morning the family exchanged gifts, ate a turkey dinner, and celebrated by shooting off firecrackers and exploding water-filled hog bladders. Christmas 1846 marked the first account of a family Christmas tree upon which the Fletchers hung gifts. Subsequent Christmases included family dinners, exchanging gifts, attending church, and providing for the poor.

Christmas in Indianapolis became increasingly commercialized as its observance became more popular. Bookseller W. E. Dunbar advertised in the December, 1834, newspapers "a variety of beautiful Bibles, Testaments, and other books suitable for Christmas and New Year's presents." Newspapers of the late 1850s included advertisements for railroad watches and sapphire rings from Talbott's jewelry store, pianofortes from Williard & Stowell, and juvenile books and games from local bookstores. Stores during the 1900 holiday season promoted "all the popular new novels" including *Alice of Old Vincennes*, dolls, trains, wagons, and "all the things to make the visit of Santa Claus pleasant for the children." In 1905 CHARLES MAYER AND COMPANY printed a message from Santa Claus, postmarked in Nurnberg (Nuremberg), Germany, announcing a vast selection of toys and dolls "from this great Toy District." Marott Department Store on Massachusetts Avenue, touting itself as "the holiday store of Indianapolis" in 1910, enticed customers with refunds of rail fares and free trading stamps. By the early 20th century Indianapolis shoppers were truly caught up in the Christmas buying spirit.

Inspired by the elaborate Christmas window displays mounted by Macy's of New York in the 1870s and 1880s, Indianapolis retailers L. S. AYRES AND COMPANY, WILLIAM H. BLOCK COMPANY, and Charles Mayer and Company began in the 1920s to install special displays, which later included animated figures. H. P. WASSON AND

Union Station hosted this 50-foot, 4-ton Santa Claus display during the 1949 Christmas season. It took a crew 12 hours to assemble the 400 separate parts. It was wired for sound, and it played Christmas carols and chuckled. [Indiana Historical Society, Bass Collection, #C3128]

COMPANY unveiled its first window display in 1963. Although these popular displays ended with the closing of all downtown department stores by the early 1990s, the INDIANA STATE MUSEUM, which has many of the Ayres displays and the 1950s Santaland Express train in its collections, continues the tradition through special holiday exhibits.

Outdoor Christmas decorations grew in popularity after General Electric sold its first string of tree lights in the early 1900s and after New York City erected a giant lighted tree in 1912. The practice quickly spread to other cities with Indianapolis erecting its first municipal tree in UNIVERSITY PARK in 1913. Many towns and neighborhoods started residential decorating and lighting contests in the 1930s. By the 1940s Broad Ripple, Lawrence, and other communities began "Twelfth Night" ceremonies, an Epiphany-based observance involving the ceremonial burning of Christmas greenery, although Indianapolis ended this practice in the mid–1980s and encouraged mulching instead. One short-lived public display was a 50–foot, 4–ton Santa Claus which the Indianapolis Industrial Exposition erected in the main concourse of UNION STATION in 1949.

MONUMENT CIRCLE has been the focal point for parades and public celebrations since the early 20th century. In the late 1930s architect Edward D. Pierre proposed adding lights and decorations on the Circle to enhance the holiday spirit. Several organizations raised funds for the effort, and by the mid–1940s trees and other decorations adorned the Circle. The city's DEPARTMENT OF PARKS AND RECREATION also began scheduling choirs to provide evening concerts, a tradition that continues on the Circle to this day. While the Indianapolis Christmas Committee (now the Indianapolis Holidays Committee, Inc.) introduced new decorations over the years, its largest project was stringing lights on the SOLDIERS AND SAILORS MONUMENT to create the "World's Tallest (now Largest) Christmas Tree." This practice, first begun in 1962, has continued annually except during the late–1980s restoration of the Monument. "The Celebration of Lights," held after Thanksgiving, marks the lighting of the "tree," and attracts upwards of 75,000 people. For many years the Circle also provided public ice skating, which is now located at the PAN AMERICAN PLAZA building.

Santa Claus parades played major roles in the Christmas celebrations of New York, Detroit, and Philadelphia. For many years Indianapolis had its own parades. To begin the 1942 Christmas season, the William H. Block Company sponsored the mile-long "Parade of Giants," complete with 50 giant balloon figures. In 1954 Santa arrived by plane at Weir Cook Airport and led a parade along Washington Street to Block's store. Although the Downtown Merchants Association sponsored parades into the 1960s their popularity soon faded.

In the mid–1970s the JEWISH COMMUNITY RELATIONS COUNCIL and the INDIANA CIVIL LIBERTIES UNION filed a complaint with the city regarding the placement of a Nativity scene on public property, arguing that the city had violated the constitutional prohibition against mixing religious and governmental functions. Although the incident produced a public outcry, the parks department ended the Nativity scene in 1976.

Recently established holiday observances in Indianapolis include concerts offered by the INDIANAPOLIS SYMPHONY ORCHESTRA and TubaChristmas, featuring over 100 tuba players attired as Santa Claus. Several historic neighborhoods also sponsor candlelight home tours during December.

DAVID G. VANDERSTEL
Indiana University–Purdue University,
Indianapolis

<hr>

The Diary of Calvin Fletcher (Indianapolis, 1972–1983), passim; *Indianapolis News*, Dec. 20, 1913; *Indianapolis Star*, Dec. 16, 1976.

Chrysler. Major manufacturer of automobiles and trucks. Chrysler's most important enterprises in Marion County have been a factory at 2900 North Shadeland Avenue and a foundry at 1100 South Tibbs Avenue.

Construction of the Shadeland factory began in 1950 and, after changes of plans, production of automobile transmissions started in 1953. Distributors, starters, and other electrical parts for cars became the plant's focus after 1958. The main plant occupied about 80,000 square feet. A parts depot was built nearby. Employment reached 3,500 in the 1970s but had shrunk to 1,200 in 1987 when plans were announced to close the plant because of its obsolete tooling and dated and expensive product line. Most employees were transferred, but Chrysler, which had recently paid back a $32 million loan from the State of Indiana and had borrowed $3 billion on guarantees from the federal government, received much criticism.

Incorporated in 1946, the American Foundry Company succeeded an inactive corporation of the same name as owner of a foundry at 1535 Naomi Street and a scrapyard in the 500 block of South Warman Avenue. Wholly owned by Chrysler Corporation, it made nothing except engine blocks for Chrysler. It opened the plant on Tibbs Avenue in 1950, and formally merged with Chrysler on December 31, 1959. The Naomi Street plant closed later. The Tibbs plant remains open, quick to adopt new methods. The original American Foundry Company, incorporated in 1901, made engine blocks for many early automobiles on South Warman until a fire destroyed its plant in 1930. Later, it operated on Naomi Street until 1944.

CHARLES JOHNSON TAGGART

Church Federation of Greater Indianapolis.

White Protestant ministers, meeting monthly in their Indianapolis Ministerial Association at Roberts Park Methodist Episcopal Church, initiated an organizational meeting on June 7, 1912, for what became the Church Federation of Indianapolis. Representatives of 40 congregations were present. The organization was one of the first half-dozen church federations in the nation. For three decades its president was a layman from one of the member churches.

The agenda soon broadened to include programs on race relations, conducted through dialogue and exchange of pulpits and choirs. In 1926 an Interracial Committee was formed with ministers and lay leaders of African-American congregations participating and taking leadership in the federation. For over four decades the Interracial Committee addressed issues of discrimination in education, business, employment, housing, medical care, restaurants, and theaters.

A Social Service Department was established in 1922, first to work with youths assigned by the juvenile court judge and later to relate social agencies to the congregations. MARY RIGG, for whom a neighborhood center was named, was the first director from 1946 to 1954. Annual grants to the federation from the Community Chest–UNITED WAY were begun in 1920 and continue to the present day.

The federation has sponsored and coordinated cooperative programs in religious education and youth activities, in chaplaincies in hospitals and public institutions, and in planning for new congregations as the city grows. It has been called on to intervene when police-community relations have been tense. It has continued as a public witness and public service on behalf of mainline Protestant churches for over 80 years.

Since 1954 it has been known as the Church Federation of Greater Indianapolis and has its offices in the INDIANA INTERCHURCH CENTER at 100 West 42nd Street. Recent decades have seen a shift in the religious leadership of the city and a decline in the influence of white mainline Protestantism. The federation has reflected this change and is now governed by a board of 15 clergy and 21 laypersons including Catholics and African-American Protestants. In 1992 the organization operated with a staff of three and a budget of approximately $200,000, although declining donations during the early 1990s were a source of concern.

EDWIN L. BECKER
Christian Theological Seminary

Edwin L. Becker, *From Sovereign to Servant: The Church Federation of Greater Indianapolis, 1912–1987* (Indianapolis: Church Federation of Greater Indianapolis, 1987).

Church of Christ, Scientist (Christian Science).

Early Christianity first became known in many places through works of healing. In the 1880s the then new denomination Christian Science first became known to Indianapolis through its healing ministry. The denomination, begun in Boston in 1879, reflected this emphasis: to "reinstate primitive Christianity and its lost element of healing." Christian Scientists approach such healing not as a rare or inexplicable occurrence based on faith alone but as a normal part of Christian life that can be intelligently understood, studied, and practiced by all. Those who enter the public ministry of Christian Science healing—a ministry of individual prayer—are known as Christian Science practitioners.

In Indianapolis, a small group began studying and meeting for worship together after several residents turned to a visiting Christian Science practitioner, Dr. Silas Sawyer of Milwaukee, for help through prayer and were healed. Sawyer had studied with the denomination's founder, Mary Baker Eddy. Another Eddy student, John P. Filbert of Nebraska, taught three classes on Christian Science in Indianapolis in the same period, and one of his students, Frederick LaRue, became the first Christian Science practitioner in the city, while one of those healed under Sawyer's ministrations, Anna B. Dorland, later traveled to Boston herself to study with Eddy. Dorland returned to become the first authorized teacher of Christian Science in Indiana and in 1889 helped organize a group that became formally established as First Church of Christ, Scientist, Indianapolis, in 1897. For a time in the early 20th century the congregation met in the PROPYLAEUM.

As the church's membership in Indianapolis grew, a second congregation in the city was organized in August, 1903. In the early 1990s the Christian Science community in Indianapolis numbers six congregations, down from eight in the 1960s. Adherents come from all socioeconomic levels. Each branch church maintains a public Christian Science Reading Room, while the congregations jointly maintain a seventh reading room downtown. In addition to Sunday worship, each branch church holds Wednesday evening meetings that include a period for testimonies of healing from those in the congregation. Thirteen full-time Christian Science practitioners have offices in or near the city.

WADE HARDY, JR.
Christian Science Committee on
Publication for Indiana

Church of Jesus Christ of Latter-day Saints (Mormons).

In Indiana, as elsewhere in America in the 1830s, freedom of thought and an independent philosophy fostered by an absence of strict ecclesiastical control gave rise to many different religious ideas. Among these was the Church of Jesus Christ of Latter-day Saints (also called Mormons), founded in upstate New York in 1830 by Joseph Smith and a few followers. By 1831 the Mormons had begun to move away from New York toward the frontier.

Although early members did not choose to settle in large numbers in any part of Indiana in the decade of the 1830s, they crossed the state several times. Two church centers, one at Kirtland, Ohio, and another in Jackson County, Missouri, made it necessary for early leaders to travel in and out of Indiana preaching what they believed was the ancient gospel restored in modern times. Samuel Smith, Joseph Smith's brother, and Reynolds Cahoon were probably the first missionaries to preach in Indiana. These two and other early Mormon missionaries often attracted large numbers of curious frontierspeople who had heard of the Mormon belief in an indigenous American church and a new American scripture, *The Book of Mormon.*

Although there were several small branches of the church throughout the state in the 1830s, many converts were encouraged to "gather to Zion" in western Missouri to await the millennium. One of the earliest Indianapolis converts was Horace Eldredge who was comfortably settled on a farm near the city in 1836. Eldredge returned to Indianapolis several times before he left the state permanently in 1847 and traveled to Utah in the Mormon exodus.

The most dramatic crossing of Indiana came in 1834 when a group of Mormons known as Zion's Camp traveled from Ohio to Missouri to restore Mormon property that the Mormons believed had been confiscated illegally by the Missourians. Horses, supply wagons, provisions, and arms accompanied the group as it followed the old National Road across Indiana. As the party approached Indianapolis, local people spread rumors that the governor would stop it. But Joseph Smith directed the wagons to travel some distance apart and to scatter through different streets. In this way the group passed through Indianapolis without arousing extensive suspicion.

In the mid–1840s the Utah branch of the Mormon Church abandoned Indiana until 1882 when missionaries began to return to proselytize as a part of the Northern States Mission. By 1919 enough Mormons lived in the area for the church to reestablish an Indianapolis branch. In the 1940s many Indiana branches, including the Indianapolis branch, became wards (the equivalent of a parish).

In May, 1959, the first Indiana stake (the equivalent of a diocese) was organized with its headquarters in Indianapolis. Philip F. Low, a Purdue agronomy professor, was the first president of the Indianapolis Stake of Zion. On the day of its organization the stake population was 2,162; there were seven wards, two in Indianapolis.

In 1993 there were two Indianapolis stakes, the Indianapolis Stake which has 3 wards and the Indianapolis North Stake which has 7 wards.

MARTHA TAYSOM

Church Women United. Service organization. In 1898 a group of church women headed by Mrs. J. D. Forest and Mrs. W. H. H. Shank issued a call to other philanthropic church women's groups to form a Missionary Social Union similar to those in other cities. At a mass meeting held at the First Presbyterian Church, the group organized the Missionary Social Union of Indianapolis to serve as an umbrella organization for local evangelical women's societies. In 1908 over 1,500 women attended the tenth anniversary celebration in Indianapolis.

In 1929 the group helped sponsor the first Missionary Education Institute in the city. The Missionary Social Union became the Indianapolis Council of Federated Church Women in 1931 when it joined the state and national organizations of church women; in 1940 the word "Federated" was dropped from the local group's name. Open to all races, the Indianapolis Council of Church Women cancelled its plans for a 1947 national board meeting in the city when local hotels refused to provide accommodations to African-American members. Consequently, the INDIANAPOLIS RECORDER included the organization that year among its list of those that made outstanding contributions to racial understanding. In a 1966 national reorganization, the United Church Women separated from the Council of Churches and became Church Women United.

Longtime local projects of the organization have included support for FLANNER HOUSE, GOODWILL INDUSTRIES, WHEELER MISSION MINISTRIES, CENTRAL STATE HOSPITAL, and the Marion County Home. Annual celebrations include World Day of Prayer (first observed in 1922), World Community Day (first observed in 1944), May Fellowship Day (first observed in 1956) and the Spring and Fall Forums. Currently about 500 women from 300 churches of 15 denominations, primarily Protestant, are active members.

JOAN CUNNINGHAM

_____

Church Women United in Indianapolis Collection, Indiana Historical Society.

CIALSA. See Central Indiana Area Library Services Authority

Cinemas. According to some historians, the first movie theater in Indianapolis was the Bijou (ca. 1906) on East Washington Street. The Bijou showed Universal "short programs," half-hour films viewed during lunch hour.

One of Indianapolis' first theaters located outside the Mile Square was Northstar (ca. 1913), owned by Anzi Zaring who also owned Zaring Egyptian Theater (ca. 1925–1960s), reportedly one of the most beautiful theaters in the Midwest. Both theaters were located on Central Avenue. IRVINGTON was the last neighborhood to build a theater. Irving Theater (ca. 1915) initially showed little profit because adult residents wanted only educational films shown there. Refurbished in 1987, the theater currently runs contemporary independent art and foreign films.

The Alhambra (ca. 1913), 44 West Washington Street, was the first Indianapolis theater built specifically for "movies only." (Most theaters acted as multipurpose facilities, staging plays, vaudeville, and musical acts.) The Alhambra closed in 1922 to make room for the Apollo, which became the first local theater wired for sound. It closed in 1940.

The first sound film, "The Jazz Singer," played at the CIRCLE THEATRE (1916) in 1928. Placed on the National Register of Historic Places in 1980, it is now the home of the INDIANAPOLIS SYMPHONY ORCHESTRA.

The Murat Theatre (ca. 1910) showed the first real color film in 1911. In 1933 the Ohio Theater reportedly showed the first sound film containing a sex scene: "The Seventh Commandment." The INDIANA THEATRE and Indiana Roof Ballroom (ca. 1927) held a demonstration of television in 1936. That same year the Indiana Theatre showed its first 3–D cartoon, and in 1953 the first 3–D movie.

Movie houses thrived from 1930 to 1950. However, when television and drive-in movies became popular during the 1950s, only 12 out of 50 local movie theaters remained in full operation. For a time 3–D movies and wide screens helped attract audiences.

In 1965 seven new theaters or "hard-top drive-ins" ushered in a new era for movie business. Georgetown, Carlyle, and Regency cinemas, owned by Priority Theaters, featured adjustable, rocking seats, audience smoking areas, and lobbies with art gallery displays. General Cinemas (now Harcourt General, Inc.) opened theaters in Meadows Shopping Center and Glendale Mall. Glendale Cinemas I and II (ca. 1967) were the first local movie houses built adjacent to a shopping center. Vogue Theaters operated Nora Cinema (ca. 1973), as well as Vogue Cinema (ca. 1973) and Uptown (ca. 1926), which was once a major neighborhood theater. Prior to 1973 Vogue Cinema operated as Vogue Theater (ca. 1938). (Located in the BROAD RIPPLE entertainment district, the Vogue was transformed into a nightclub–concert venue by the early 1980s.)

As larger, corporate-owned theaters sprang up throughout Indianapolis, neighborhood and downtown theaters closed or changed. Emerson Theater (previously Eastland, ca. 1928) showed alternative films during the 1980s. Once considered a leading movie house in Indianapolis, the Ritz (ca. 1927) changed names and operated as a live burlesque, then rock hall before closing in 1972. The Rivoli showed films from 1927 to 1966. It later staged various acts and became a rock hall, then an X-rated theater in 1976.

Noted as the first local theater to play a stereophonic sound film, "Fantasia" in 1942, the Lyric closed in 1969. Loews Palace (originally Loews State in 1921) closed in 1970, one year before Loews Twin opened on North Keystone. Carmel Theatre (ca. 1949) struggled to remain in business after 1975, but closed in 1984. In 1985 the Eastwood Theater (38th Street and Pendleton Pike) operated as the only independent movie house in Indianapolis showing first run films. It also had the largest screen in the state.

As of 1993 there are a variety of movie houses operating in Indianapolis. The city's largest first run, multiscreen complexes are General Cinema's Clearwater Crossing 12, located at 82nd Street and Dean Road, and Regal Cinema's Village Park Plaza 12, located on U.S. 31 North in Westfield. Both opened in the summer of 1993 and each houses 12 screens. General Cinema, which has been in the area for 55 years, operates nine

other local theaters. (In 1982 there were more General Cinema theaters in Indiana than in any other state, with 30 screens in Indianapolis.) Village Park Plaza 12 marks Regal's first theater built in Indiana.

Loews operates five first run, multiscreen theaters in Indianapolis. Loews Norgate, at North Keystone and 73rd Street, shows foreign and alternative films as well as first run movies. Two other theaters, the Irving and General Cinema's Castleton Square, also show foreign and alternative films.

Cinemark Theatres operates Indianapolis' two largest second run, discount, multiscreen theaters. Two Movies 8 (eight screens each), located on East Washington Street and at U.S. 31 South and Stop 13 Road, opened in 1989 and 1990. CTS Theaters runs three smaller second run, discount, multiscreen theaters: Woodland, South Keystone, and Greenbriar. Two other discount theaters are General Cinema's Glendale Savings and Speedway Cinema.

The Hollywood Bar and Film Works, located at 245–247 South Meridian Street, is the only theater in the city where patrons may be served food and drinks while watching a movie. This theater, which opened in 1991, also operates as a discount theater.

LISA M. EHRET

Gene Gladson, *Indianapolis Theaters from A-Z* (1976); Edward Cotton, "Neighborhood Theaters . . . ," *Indianapolis Star*, Oct. 10, 1965.

Circle. See Monument Circle

Circle Centre Mall. Controversial downtown shopping mall development. On March 2, 1989, demolition of many historic buildings in downtown Indianapolis signaled the physical beginning of the Circle Centre Mall project that had been in the planning process for years. As the second part of a two-phase redevelopment of West Washington Street, Mayor William H. Hudnut's administration (1976–1992) and developer MELVIN SIMON AND ASSOCIATES saw the mall's proposed opening in December, 1993, as the completion of a project that had already seen the erection of the Claypool Courts and the Two West Washington Street building in phase one.

From its inception the mall was plagued with problems. Preservationists mourned the loss of many historic buildings and citizens decried the gaping holes created in the downtown landscape by the demolitions. Originally planned with Saks Fifth Avenue, L. S. AYRES, Nordstrom's, and The Limited as anchor stores, by September, 1990, the project had lost Saks. Two months later L. S. Ayres dropped its participation as a national recession caused the retail sales industry to "drown in a sea of financial troubles." When Simon and Associates experienced difficulty in funding the project, the city stepped in and financed $287 million with city bonds. Mayor Hudnut also convinced 14 Indianapolis-based companies, including Lilly Retirement Fund, Associated Group, MARSH SUPERMARKETS, and AMERICAN UNITED LIFE INSURANCE COMPANY, to enter as limited partners in the development for an additional $65 million. Finally, $72.5 million was borrowed from three European banks.

By 1993 delays had brought a redesign of the mall. New York architect Ehrenkrantz Eckstut's new plan included a "wintergarden" suspended over Washington Street; anchor stores for the 725,000–square-foot mall would be Parisian and Nordstrom. In August the mayoral ADMINISTRATION OF STEPHEN GOLDSMITH sought and received a reduction in the property "base" value of the project of over $33 million dollars. Although officials claimed this would provide more money to pay back the city bonds on the project, INDIANAPOLIS PUBLIC SCHOOLS officials worried that the lowered tax valuation would force the schools to seek a property tax increase. By the fall of 1993 the holes in the cityscape had become foundations covered by concrete and, in November, construction began on the skywalk across Washington Street intended to link the future shops. Encompassing an area south of the Circle almost to Union Station, primarily between Illinois and Meridian streets, Circle Centre Mall is now scheduled to open in August, 1995.

CONNIE J. ZEIGLER

Circle City Classic. Annual African-American college football festival. Patterned after the Bayou Classic held in New Orleans, the Circle City Classic is an annual autumn football match-up between two historically African-American colleges. With a $150,000 grant from LILLY ENDOWMENT as seed money, the INDIANA BLACK EXPO and other interested local African-American leaders organized the first Classic in 1984. Their goal was to provide a sports event in the Midwest for alumni of black colleges, as well as encourage black youths to attend college. The festivities originally included the game, held in the HOOSIER DOME, a parade, and several parties.

The Classic has grown in popularity each year, and since 1989 the game has had a sell-out crowd. Today, the Circle City Classic staff and advisory board organize the events in conjunction with Indiana Black Expo, the INDIANA SPORTS CORPORATION, and approximately 3,000 volunteers. While the game is still the focal point of the Classic, there are now over 25 official events in addition to numerous privately sponsored parties that occur over two weekends. Each year the Classic raises nearly $50,000 for scholarships at black colleges and attracts people from around the state and nation.

MICHELLE D. HALE

Circle Theatre (45 Monument Circle). Second oldest building on MONUMENT CIRCLE and currently home of the INDIANAPOLIS SYMPHONY ORCHESTRA. The Circle Theatre was the first building constructed in Indianapolis expressly for the presentation of feature-length motion pictures; indeed, it was one of the first such movie palaces in the Midwest. Until this time, movies were primarily shown in small storefronts of commercial buildings. Circle Theatre organizers, led by A. L. Block and Robert Lieber, invested over $500,000 in the project, which opened on August 30, 1916.

RUBUSH AND HUNTER, one of the most important architectural firms of Indianapolis during the early 20th century, took design inspiration from current trends in Neoclassical Revival architecture. What makes the Circle Theatre building unique is its expression of a style promulgated by late 18th century British architects Robert Adams and his brothers. Exterior elements, such as the classical Greek figures in the terra cotta facade's frieze and tympanum, and interior features, such as the richly detailed, bas-relief proscenium frieze and the plethora of intricate plaster moldings throughout the house, are characteristic of the style. Henry Behrens, the original interior designer, was also in charge of the 1930s renovation. The interior is of such significance that it is one of only two buildings in the city afforded design review under the aegis of the INDIANAPOLIS HISTORIC PRESERVATION COMMISSION.

Films were shown in the 3,100–seat Circle Theatre for 65 years, interspersed with stage shows, musical performances, and a variety of other forms of entertainment. Following the movie theatre's closure in 1981 and a brief period of vacancy, the building gained new life in 1984 as the concert hall of the Indianapolis Symphony Orchestra. The local architectural firm Archonics was in charge of its $6.9 million renovation.

MARY ELLEN GADSKI

The Shrine of the Silent Art (Indianapolis, 1917; copy in pamphlet collection, Indiana State Library); "Coming Full Circle," Indianapolis Star, Sept. 13, 1991.

Circle Tower (5 East Market Street). Premier Art Deco building in Indianapolis. Tower Realty Company's announcement in 1928 that it would construct a new modern office building in the southeast quadrant of the Circle at Market Street capped a construction boom of over a decade around the monument. RUBUSH AND HUNTER was the architectural firm responsible for most of the new buildings on the Circle in the 1920s, but this structure was to be a departure from their earlier styles.

In 1928–1929 the architects were in the midst of applying Egyptian-inspired motifs to their own Architects and Builders Building on North Pennsylvania; they developed the idea even further in the entrance details and lobby of the Circle Tower. The arched, two-story entrance on Market Street is an amalgamation of ornately carved granite and limestone, with bronze Egyp-

tian figures depicted in various work attitudes. Inside, the lobby walls are black travertine marble accented with typical Art Deco motifs in bronze: geometric flowers, stylized greyhounds, birds, zigzags, and concentric swirls. The doors of the three elevators are of solid bronze with medallions showing muscular figures of men as working parts of machines, a salute to the Machine Age that inspired many Art Deco architects. The floors in the lobby and in the corridors throughout the building are marble; the office floors are Italian terrazzo. Each office suite of two or three rooms originally contained a solid walnut booth containing a pedestal sink, but building managers have removed all these in recent decades.

On the second floor, the Circle Tower Barbershop remained virtually unchanged for 60 years. Its opulent black and silver decor featured motifs of stylized figures pursuing various sports as well as depictions of the shop's services accented with sunbursts and zigzags. In 1990 the shop was enlarged and altered somewhat to accommodate a modern hair salon, but most of the features remain intact.

Together with the former Coca-Cola Bottling Plant, the Circle Tower building on Monument Circle is the city's premier Art Deco building.
[Indiana Historical Society, #C5808]

The general contractor, WILLIAM P. JUNG-CLAUS COMPANY, erected the monumental building of Indiana limestone. Circle Tower's unusual shape is dictated in part by the odd trapezoidal lot on which it stands. It rises 14 stories with an additional two-story, stepped-back tower. Each floor above the tenth is set back from the one beneath, reflecting the influence of Mayan archaeological discoveries in the 1920s. All the parapets are accented at intervals with geometric floral motifs. Completed in 1930, Circle Tower was the first building in Indianapolis to feature setback construction, an idea that originated in the canyons of downtown Manhattan.

GLORY-JUNE GREIFF

Glory June, *Art Deco in Indianapolis* (Indianapolis, 1980).

Citizens Forum. Neighborhood improvement association. Begun as a citizens' group in July, 1964, the organizational meeting was coordinated by city councilmen Rufus Kuykendall, Rev. James L. Cummings, and school teacher Mattie Coney. Coney emerged as executive director and, joined by her husband Elmo, she officially guided the organization until 1981. Headquartered in the inner city of Indianapolis, the largely African-American organization sought to improve city neighborhoods through the formation of block clubs and community support. At its zenith during the late 1970s, Citizens Forum, touted for its philosophy of self-help and patriotism, claimed support from scores of neighborhood organizations.

Several programs were organized through the block clubs, as well as in cooperation with schools, businesses, and city and county agencies. Popular programs included the De-RAT-ication Campaign, Bloom-In, Dogwood Tree Caravan, Adopt-A-Park, and Rake-a-thons; the forum's most successful program, Helping Hands, encouraged adults to work with children to eliminate loitering, vandalism, and street crime and to provide children with "safe" houses during an emergency. The Citizens Forum model was expanded to several cities around the state and throughout the country, including Chicago; Co-lumbus, Ohio; Detroit; Milwaukee; New Orleans; New York; and Washington, D.C.

Through its Complaint Assistance–Referral Program, Citizens Forum aided block clubs in gaining improved services from governmental agencies by providing access for neighborhood health and safety concerns. The organization had a massive community education component that included open monthly meetings; speeches to block clubs, churches, schools, civic and labor groups, and other organizations; and the publication of a newsletter, *Citizens Forum Says*.

The Coneys, along with Citizens Forum, received many local, state, and national awards and commendations. Due to financial difficulties and the Coneys' retirement and failing health, the organization disbanded in 1984.

WILMA GIBBS
Indiana Historical Society

Citizens Forum Collection, Indiana Historical Society.

Citizens Gas and Coke Utility. Public utility serving manufacturing, commercial, residential, and transportation customers in Marion County. The municipally owned utility has more than 230,000 customers and assets of over $450 million. Its average daily sendout of gas is 129,224 dekatherms; peak day sendout is 434,127 dekatherms.

A strong interest in organizing a gas utility on the "trust" principle was evident as early as 1887 when the Consumers Gas Trust Company attempted to develop and market gas that had been discovered the previous year in east central Indiana. When those wells proved short-lived, the Citizens Gas Company was created in 1906 by the organizers of the original company. Both companies vested control in trustees to hold in perpetuity.

In 1935 an act of the Indiana General Assembly vested ownership of Citizens Gas and Coke Utility in the City of Indianapolis in the form of a public charitable trust. The beneficiaries of this unique trust are the consumers. There are no shares of stock; the utility raises capital through bonding authority. Tax money has never been used to purchase or fund the company. Control rests in a board of trustees (five members) who appoint a board of directors (seven members); the directors select and guide executive management. Members of the boards and the companies they represent are proscribed from benefiting from their association with the utility. The company pays payroll, property, gross receipt, and other miscellaneous taxes, but is not subject to federal income taxes.

As the name indicates, the utility's products include both gas and coke. The coke plant on Southeastern Avenue manufactures metallurgical coke by baking blends of coal at high temperatures. This product is marketed under the name Indianapolis Coke and is sold to foundries and blast furnaces nationwide. Net revenues from the operation of the coke plant are returned to gas customers unless required for capital and operating needs of the manufacturing division.

The coke plant originally provided all the gas (a by-product of the coking operation) for customers. After the arrival of natural gas in 1951, coke oven gas was combined with natural gas to produce a blend. In the early 1990s over 85 percent of sendout gas was natural.

An underground storage area in Greene County opened for operation in 1959 and the first gas stored there was returned to Indianapolis in 1961. The field stores natural gas in underground rock formations during times when contracted amounts of gas exceed sendout requirements. Natural gas received from the utility's two suppliers (Panhandle Eastern Pipeline Company and Texas Gas Transmission Corporation) is pumped underground, then retrieved and sent to customers when demand exceeds contracted supply. Two liquified natural gas plants using cryogenic techniques store gas in a liquified state for use when demand is high.

From time to time the need for municipal funds has encouraged various interests to attempt to sell the utility to private ownership. As of early 1994 those attempts had been unsuccessful.

H. RICHARD ROSENGARTEN

Thomas A. Rumer, *Citizens Gas and Coke Utility: A History, 1851–1980* (Indianapolis: privately published, 1983); Citizens Gas and Coke Utility annual reports, 1989–1991.

City Committee. Unofficial, self-selected group that worked behind the scenes to advance the city's revitalization initiatives. During the 1970s and 1980s a small clique of young Indianapolis business executives reportedly met privately to discuss ideas for the city's development. The group, whose existence was widely acknowledged but was never publicized, consisted of approximately 30 men. Membership was by invitation only. The City Committee had no women and State Representative William A. Crawford was the only minority member. The majority of the members were bankers, lawyers, businessmen, and civic leaders. Among them were former Lieutenant Governor John M. Mutz and former president of the Lilly Endowment James T. Morris.

The group disbanded sometime before the 1991 mayoral election and has since become associated with the WILLIAM H. HUDNUT III ADMINISTRATION. The City Committee has been credited with many of the revitalization schemes implemented in Indianapolis in the 1980s, including the HOOSIER DOME, WHITE RIVER STATE PARK, and the amateur sports strategy. Since 1991, however, the exclusivity of the group and its focus on development to the exclusion of the city's employment and educational problems have been criticized. One result of the criticism was greater emphasis by governmental officials and others on public participation in decision making.

WILLIAM D. DALTON

Indianapolis News, Nov. 14, 1989; *Indianapolis Star*, May 6, 1991.

City Controller. City financial officer. The controller directs the finance division of the city's DEPARTMENT OF ADMINISTRATION. That division also includes three deputy controllers and several assistant controllers.

The controller is responsible for management of the city's fiscal affairs. These responsibilities include preparing the city budget, managing accounting operations, overseeing payrolls, collecting revenue from traffic violations, tracking federal grant monies received by the city, and managing the city's debts. Many of these duties are performed by the controller in consultation and coordination with the MARION COUNTY AUDITOR. The controller also issues licenses on behalf of the city, and may make reasonable regulations concerning those licenses and investigate the qualifications of the applicants.

The city controller is appointed by the mayor and serves at the mayor's pleasure. The appointment is not subject to approval by the CITY-COUNTY COUNCIL.

HARRISON C. NEAL III

City-County Buildings. The first Marion County Courthouse, which was completed in 1825, also doubled as the State House until a separate capitol building opened a decade later. This first courthouse, constructed for $13,966, was a brick and frame building with a poplar-shingled roof.

The second Marion County Courthouse was designed by architect ISAAC M. HODGSON and dedicated on July 5, 1876. The building fronted on Washington Street and covered the block between Alabama and Delaware streets; it cost $1,422,000, almost twice the original estimate. It was an ornate Second Empire building with the mansard roof typical of the style, five three-story bays with a central clock tower, and red granite pillars on the second floor of the Indiana limestone facade. The style proved too elaborate for many Marion County citizens who especially decried the interior's "bewildering profusion of colors," frescoes, and intricate gingerbread trim. During the construction of the new State House in the 1880s, this building was the meeting place of the Indiana General Assembly.

The second courthouse remained in use for 85 years, but by the turn of the century city government needed a central location for its offices. When Mayor CHARLES BOOKWALTER took office in 1906 one of his priorities was to construct a real city hall. On September 30, 1908, the city opened a competition for the building's design and in November awarded the contract to the architectural firm RUBUSH AND HUNTER. The cornerstone, bearing the inscription "I am myself a citizen of no mean city," was laid on July 27, 1909. The building opened in December, 1910. By then its major

Completed in 1876, the elaborate Second Empire–style Marion County Courthouse was a city landmark until it was razed in the early 1960s.
[Indiana Historical Society]

proponent, Bookwalter, had left office and a new mayor, SAMUEL LEWIS (LEW) SHANK, presided at the opening ceremonies. Also present were Governor Thomas R. Marshall and six former mayors.

The new building, located at 202 North Alabama Street, was a fine example of the Neoclassical architecture that was a popular style for civic buildings of the period. The exterior of the four-story building was constructed of brick faced with large slabs of Indiana Bedford limestone atop a granite foundation. The first floor featured three double bronze doors with bronze torchieres on either side. A row of two-story Doric columns defined the seven central bays of the building's second and third stories. The interior was defined by a central rotunda which stretched 85 feet above the lobby and was capped by a 750–square-foot stained glass dome. The floors of all the lobbies and corridors were inlaid with colored marble. The Cincinnati art firm of William F. Behrens was commissioned to provide the murals that featured the symbols of the zodiac and wreaths of fruit, flowers, and ribbons. "Two high-speed electric passenger elevators," automated temperature controls, and "service connections" for telephones in every room were some of the "modern" features of the building. The Indianapolis City Hall (listed on the National Register of Historic Places in 1974) served as a source of civic pride as well as a central location for city offices until local government began to outgrow its capacity. Total cost of the construction was $699,239 plus $113,000 for the grounds.

In the 1950s, as an increasing number of city and county offices found it necessary to rent space outside the city hall and the courthouse, interest grew in consolidating the city and county offices in a single, new edifice. This consolidation occurred in 1962 with the dedication of the City-County Building at 200 East Washington Street. The new building, designed by the Indianapolis firm Wright, Porteous and Associates (see WRIGHT, PORTEOUS AND LOWE), was a 28-story rectangular, windowed box that one architectural critic called "almost a negative achievement." The former courthouse was demolished. In 1966 the old city hall building was occupied by the INDIANA STATE MUSEUM.

CONNIE J. ZEIGLER

Berry R. Sulgrove, *History of Indianapolis and Marion County* (Philadelphia, 1884); National Register of Historic Places nomination form for Indiana State Museum (old Indianapolis City Hall); *Indianapolis Architecture* (Indianapolis, 1975), 49.

City-County Council. Elected municipal and county government legislative body. When UNIGOV took effect in Marion County in 1970, the members of the former Indianapolis Common Council and the Marion County Council combined to form a new City-County Council. The first full 29–member City-County Council was elected in 1971.

The 29 councillors are elected in municipal election years and serve four-year, renewable terms. All councillors must be residents of Marion County, U.S. citizens, and at least 21 years old.

Twenty-five councillors are elected from districts within Marion County and must reside in the districts they represent. The boundaries of those districts are decided by the City-County Council after each decennial census, and the districts are required to be equal in population. The remaining four councillors are elected at large, or countywide.

The council is the legislative body for Marion County as well as for the city of Indianapolis. Its formal powers and responsibilities include: review and approval of ordinances or resolutions pertaining to the city of Indianapolis or Marion County; review and approval of the budgets of Indianapolis and Marion County government, as well as some of the independent municipal corporations within the county; review and approval of all appropriations ordinances for city and county government departments; appointment of the members of several local government boards and commissions; and, confirmation or rejection of the mayor's nominees to deputy mayor and department director positions.

The whole council meets on Monday evenings at least once and usually twice per month. Each year the council establishes a schedule of meetings for the coming year. Council meetings are open to the public and are televised.

To perform its tasks the City-County Council relies on officers, committees, and staff assistance. Four councillors are chosen each year to fill the offices of president, vice-president, majority leader, and minority leader. The president and vice-president are elected by a vote of all councillors. The president presides at council meetings and signs all ordinances and resolutions passed by the council. (As of December, 1993, Beurt SerVaas had served as the council's only president since the implementation of Unigov.) The vice-president performs these duties in the president's absence. The majority leader and minority leader are chosen by the members of their respective political parties on the council and preside over meetings of their party caucuses.

The City-County Council has three permanent committees and nine standing committees. The three permanent committees are: the Committee of the Whole, consisting of all councillors; the Committee on Committees, which assigns councillors to the other committees; and the Committee on Rules and Public Policy, which considers changes in council rules or operations.

The nine standing committees meet to consider proposed ordinances or resolutions concerning particular subjects. They are required to act on any proposal within 45 days of its referral. Each standing committee has at least three members, with one member designated as committee chair by the council president. Committee meetings are held at least once per month and are open to the public and to other councillors. Six standing committees correspond with the administrative departments in city-county government: Administration and Finance, Metropolitan Development, Parks and Recreation, Public Safety and Criminal Justice, Public Works, and Transportation. The other three committees are Community Affairs, Economic Development, and Municipal Corporations.

Some councillors also serve on Special Service District Councils that correspond with the Police and Fire Special Service Districts and the Solid Waste Collection and Disposal Special Service Districts. Councillors serve on these councils if the corresponding SPECIAL SERVICE DISTRICT contains a majority of the residents in their electoral districts.

The staff that assists the City-County Council includes, in addition to clerical support staff: the clerk of the City-County Council, who maintains the Council's records; a deputy clerk; the general counsel, who provides legal advice; the research director, who aids councillors in the preparation and review of ordinances; and the budget analyst, who provides fiscal advice.

WILLIAM BLOMQUIST
Indiana University–Purdue University,
Indianapolis

City Manager Proposal (1920s). Proposed change in city government structure. The Indiana General Assembly in 1921 authorized first-class cities such as Indianapolis to adopt a council-manager form of government following a special election that could be called after a petition bearing signatures equal to 20 percent of the voters taking part in the preceding municipal election had been filed with the city clerk's office. The law also stipulated that the city clerk would have five days to verify the petition's signatures.

Under this form of government the city would have seven elected commissioners who would appoint a city manager to serve an indefinite period at their pleasure. The city manager, rather than an elected mayor, would serve as the city's chief administrative officer. The manager would appoint department heads and direct them to appoint subordinates as needed. The manager

would also be responsible for preparing the city's annual budget and submitting it to the commissioners. City managers were to be appointed solely on the basis of their qualifications, and were not required to live in the city or state at the time of their appointment.

In April, 1925, a group known as the Citizens Committee of 1,000 gathered close to 32,000 signatures on a petition asking for a chance to vote on whether or not the city manager form of government should be introduced to Indianapolis. Before filing their petition, however, the Committee of 1,000 decided to postpone its campaign until it had time to better educate the public as to the merits of the council-manager form of government. In the spring of 1927, following a failed attempt by Mayor JOHN DUVALL and a majority of the city council to block the filing of another petition by refusing to allocate funds to the clerk's office to hire extra help to verify the petition's signatures, a second petition bearing over 33,000 signatures was successfully filed. On June 21, 1927, Indianapolis residents voted 53,912 to 9,954 in favor of adopting the council-manager form of government, set to go into effect on January 1, 1930.

Nevertheless, the council-manager form of government was never introduced to Indianapolis. In September, 1929, the Indiana Supreme Court ruled that the state law permitting this form of government was unconstitutional because it was a "physical and mental impossibility" for a city clerk to verify the signatures on a petition in a city the size of Indianapolis within five days. Having found this section (3) of the law to be an impossibility, the court deemed the law to be both "incomplete" and "impossible of performance" and thus unconstitutional.

HARRISON C. NEAL III
JEFFERY DUVALL

Laws of Indiana (1921), chapter 218; *Indianapolis Star*, Apr. 14, 1925, Sept. 25, 1929; *Indianapolis News*, Apr. 8, 14, June 22, 1927.

City Market (222 East Market Street). Erected in 1886, the building occupies the lot designated for the location of a market in the original 1821 plat of Indianapolis. The local architectural firm of D. A. BOHLEN AND SON designed the current market building, which replaced the original semi-enclosed wood and brick East Market House. The Bohlen firm also designed TOMLINSON HALL (1886), which stood immediately west of the market. The buildings were to work in tandem, with meat vendors in the market and produce vendors in the hall. The archway ruin on the West Plaza is all that remains above ground of Tomlinson Hall, demolished in 1958. The market was renovated from 1972 to 1977 as part of the city's downtown redevelopment program and was listed in the National Register of Historic Places in 1974. Today, the City Market houses more restaurant stands than meat and produce stalls, and it has experienced considerable vendor turnover and mixed financial success.

The market is constructed of brick with limestone details and a metal roof. Twin towers flanking the central entrance emphasize the front facade. A series of round arches pierce the walls, allowing very little solid wall space. These arches and the classical detailing harken to the *Rundbogenstil* (Round Arch style) popular in mid–19th century Germany for railway stations and other institutional buildings. The interior is significant for its large central hall and flanking side aisles. The cast-iron support system of trusses and columns is exposed. The clerestory windows flood the interior with natural light. The mezzanine around the periphery of the central hall allows for

Vendors line the street in front of the City Market ca. 1926. [Indiana Historical Society, Bass Collection, #97886]

additional stalls. The redevelopment project in the 1970s included the erection of twin wings in contemporary styling. The East and West Plazas flank the building and are popular lunchtime gathering places in fair weather.

WILLIAM L. SELM

Jacob Piatt Dunn, *Greater Indianapolis* (Chicago, 1910); Thomas M. Slade, ed., *Historic American Buildings Survey in Indiana* (Bloomington, Ind., 1983), 47, 133.

City Planning. The history of city planning in Indianapolis began with the founders' plat. As the plan for the capital city of Indiana, it was given impressive features not often seen in frontier towns. The original scheme still influences planning in the modern city.

Christopher Harrison, the commissioner charged with laying out the new capital, appointed ELIAS P. FORDHAM and ALEXANDER RALSTON as surveyors in April, 1821. Harrison and the surveyors immediately devised a plan for the city, and the surveyors had completed their work by October, 1821. The plat was roughly square, and each side of the square measured a mile, inspiring the enduring name MILE SQUARE for the city's central district. The plan was dominated by a central circular street and four diagonal avenues that radiated from near the center. The circle and the diagonal avenues, which local tradition attributes to Ralston, were imposed on a gridiron pattern of squares and streets. (For a reproduction of the 1821 plat, see the Mile Square entry.)

The planners of the capital anticipated the need for wide streets in the future. They bestowed a 120–foot width on Washington Street, the principal east-west street, and 90–foot widths on the diagonal avenues and other streets. In keeping with the infant community's purpose, the planners reserved whole or partial squares for government buildings and public institutions: State House Square, Governor's Circle, Court House Square, two half-squares for markets, and three squares set aside for "religious purposes."

Despite this auspicious beginning, no further governmental sponsorship of physical planning occurred in Indianapolis for the next 80 years, while the pioneer settlement grew from village to mid-sized city. Additions happened in a piecemeal fashion as individual real estate speculators purchased tracts of land and divided them into plats containing gridiron street patterns and rectangular lots.

Modern city planning, in which local governments took the initiative in making public improvements, began in the state capital during the 1890s. In that decade the city constructed a new sewerage system and established a park system. After 1900 Indianapolis became caught up in the "City Beautiful" planning movement in which municipalities across the United States undertook extensive improvements to beautify their appearances.

In 1908 the Board of Park Commissioners hired a noted midwestern landscape architect, GEORGE E. KESSLER, to design a system of boulevards to link the city's principal parks. In 1909 Kessler completed work on an ambitious boulevard plan that would create scenic drives along FALL CREEK on the north side of the city, Pleasant Run on the south side, Spades and Brookside parks on the east side, and WHITE RIVER on the west side. Over the following decade the park commissioners carried out much of Kessler's design for Fall Creek, Brookside, and Pleasant Run parkways.

The City Beautiful phase of city planning in Indianapolis reached its zenith during the 1920s with construction of the INDIANA WORLD WAR MEMORIAL PLAZA north of the central business district. Conceived by the AMERICAN LEGION as a memorial to World War I veterans, the plaza took shape over a five-block-long area between New York and St. Clair streets and between Meridian and Pennsylvania streets. The formal plan devised for the plaza by architects Walker and Weeks of Cleveland consisted of a monumental memorial hall, an Obelisk Square, and a two-block-long mall leading to a funerary cenotaph.

Also during the 1920s, Indianapolis joined a national movement to establish city planning as an official function of municipal government. The impetus to create an Indianapolis City Planning Commission in 1921 came from civic leaders concerned over the encroachment of industrial and commercial land uses into areas that had been exclusively residential. In 1922 Lawrence V. Sheridan, executive secretary of the new plan commission, and Robert H. Whitton, a planning expert from Cleveland, devised recommendations for a city ZONING ordinance.

The ordinance, which the city council adopted in November, 1922, provided for five categories of land use zones. The intention of Sheridan and Whitton was to fix current land use patterns and provide reassurance for residential property owners that undesirable land uses would not invade their neighborhoods and depreciate their property values. The city plan commission was to adjust the zoning district boundaries in response to changing trends in land use and act as a board of zoning appeals to which owners could petition for variances in the zoning uses designated for particular areas.

In 1935 the Indiana General Assembly passed a "master plan law." The legislation directed the Indianapolis City Plan Commission to prepare, at least every ten years, a long-term master plan for public improvements to the city. The 1935 law also authorized creation of a Marion County Plan Commission, which was to exercise the same powers as the city commission in areas of the county outside the city limits.

The approaching end of World War II in 1943 and 1944 stimulated interest in comprehensive city planning on the part of municipal and business leaders. In 1943 Mayor ROBERT H. TYNDALL appointed a COMMITTEE ON POST-WAR PLANNING to recommend physical improvements that would be needed in a peacetime community. The committee's report suggested a large-scale, $25 million physical improvement program, to take place over seven years. Despite endorsement of the report by community leaders, commitment to carrying out its recommendations faded in the economic boom that followed the end of the war.

During the late 1940s and early 1950s the effectiveness of zoning came into question as city and county boards of zoning appeals granted increasing numbers of variances in the land uses permitted by the zoning ordinances. The attention of public officials was also drawn to the inadequacy of the separate city and county planning and zoning systems in the face of mushrooming suburbs outside the city boundaries of Indianapolis. Master planning done by either the city or county plan commissions could not take into account developments outside their respective jurisdictions.

In 1955 the Indiana General Assembly created a Metropolitan Plan Commission, which combined the responsibilities of the former city and county plan commissions and conducted planning and zoning on a countywide basis. The merger was one of the first of its kind in the United States, and Calvin S. Hamilton, director of the new Metropolitan Planning Department, represented new thinking among the postwar generation of city planners.

Hamilton became particularly known for the visionary schemes that the planning department advocated for the downtown area of Indianapolis. A downtown master plan prepared by the department in 1958 recommended clearance of large sections of the central city that were declining in property value and their replacement with new public and private developments. Hamilton also called for the conversion of MONUMENT CIRCLE at the center of the Mile Square into a pedestrian mall and establishment of a "Lockerbie Fair" tourist development in the neighborhood where Hoosier poet JAMES WHITCOMB RILEY had lived. During the 1960s the Metropolitan Planning Department promoted two large-scale downtown urban renewal projects: a large new state university campus between West Street and White River (now INDIANA UNIVERSITY–PURDUE UNIVERSITY AT INDIANAPOLIS) and a projected apartment "city" north of North Street on Alabama Street (now known as Riley Center).

The expansion of the Indianapolis metropolitan area to the Marion County borders and beyond by the late 1960s helped precipitate completion of the consolidation of city and county governments that had begun with the creation of the Metropolitan Planning Department. In 1969 the Indiana General Assembly passed legislation that established UNIGOV in which most city and county agencies were merged. The Metropolitan Plan Commission became the METROPOLITAN DEVELOPMENT COMMISSION; the planning department became the Planning and Zoning Division of the new DEPARTMENT OF METROPOLITAN DEVELOPMENT (DMD).

In the years since consolidation DMD has turned much of its planning emphasis to preparing individual plans for neighborhoods and parks. Efforts begun in the 1940s to combat violations of the zoning ordinance have continued, along with struggles against excessive numbers of zoning variances. Large planned developments of the 1970s and 1980s have included construction of a pedestrian mall along Market Street and Monument Circle, construction of the HOOSIER DOME stadium, partial completion of WHITE RIVER STATE PARK at the west edge of the downtown, and the CIRCLE CENTRE MALL downtown.

What judgments can be made about the efforts of Indianapolis in city planning? The earliest instance of planning, the Mile Square plat of 1821, has not fared well. Since World War II developments sponsored by business and city leaders have truncated three of the four diagonal avenues, closed streets in the 1821 gridiron pattern, and narrowed Washington Street at the end of the Mile Square. The effect has often been to remove features that provided remarkable vistas or promoted smooth traffic circulation. With respect to the City Beautiful era of planning, the parts of KESSLER'S BOULEVARD AND PARK SYSTEM that were constructed have functioned effectively both as pleasant, aesthetic experiences for casual drivers and as efficient conveyors of traffic. The World War Memorial Plaza, although still a monumental presence in the downtown, has suffered since the 1960s from much deferred maintenance.

The experience of Indianapolis with respect to city planning commissions and zoning has been typical of many American cities. In general, planning has been supported by the public chiefly as a rationale for zoning, and zoning has functioned mainly to keep out undesirable land uses from particular residential neighborhoods and commercial areas. The master plans and downtown redevelopment plans prepared since World War II have also been similar to those pursued by other cities and, as in those other communities, frequently have not been carried out in many details.

Probably the most remarkable event in the history of city planning in Indianapolis was the consolidation of the city and county planning agencies in the 1950s. This occurrence helped lead to Unigov, an unusual development in its own right. Few other U.S. cities have achieved such a consolidation of planning efforts.

JAMES A. GLASS
Division of Historic Preservation
and Archaeology,
Indiana Department of Natural Resources

Jacob Piatt Dunn, *Greater Indianapolis*, Vol. 1 (Chicago, 1910); "Indianapolis—Planning" clipping files, Indiana Division, Indiana State Library; "Indianapolis—Planning" entries, Indianapolis Newspaper Index, Indiana Division, Indiana State Library.

City Securities Corporation. Indianapolis-based investment banking firm specializing in tax-free municipal bonds for public works projects. City Securities traces its origins to 1906 when municipal bonds salesman Dick Miller formed Miller & Company. Eleven years later Miller merged his business with the newly established City Trust Corporation, becoming the securities department of the bank. In 1924 this department incorporated as a separate entity, the City Securities Corporation. During the 1930s the firm kept busy reorganizing many bankrupt or near-bankrupt businesses. In 1953 City Securities managed negotiations for the $286 million bond issue for the Indiana Toll Road, one of the largest single bond issues in the state. Other public works the firm has helped finance include the old State Office Building and the CITY-COUNTY BUILDING. A change in ownership occurred in 1970 when minority stockholders bought out the majority stockholders. City Securities is the largest underwriter of municipal bonds in Indiana, employing about 110 people.

DEBORAH B. MARKISOHN

Civic Clubs. Civic clubs, such as Kiwanis, Rotary, Elks, Lions, and the Optimist Club, were originally a way to foster business and professional dealings, and their memberships were limited by occupation. As Indianapolis grew, placing more demands on government for social services, civic organizations proliferated and began to assist

in meeting social needs through voluntary activities and financial contributions.

In February, 1913, Rotarians traveled by train from Chicago, Louisville, Kansas City, Duluth, and Des Moines to attend the downtown Indianapolis club's first meeting. Attendees included Paul Harris, who had organized the first Rotary club in 1905. When the Indianapolis club was organized with 75 business and professional men as charter members, it became the 58th club in the United States. It met at the CLAYPOOL HOTEL for more than a half century. In later years, Rotary moved its meetings to the INDIANAPOLIS ATHLETIC CLUB and established administrative offices there. Membership doubled the first year; by its 25th year the club totaled 289 members, and on its Golden Anniversary the roster listed 500 Rotarians. By the 1990s, membership surpassed 600, making it the largest civic club in the city. Total membership for the metropolitan area is about 700 members.

Like other service clubs, Rotary has been committed to helping young people in Indianapolis. Rotary clubs throughout the state financed the Rotary Convalescent Hospital in the INDIANA UNIVERSITY MEDICAL CENTER, and contributed to funding for the adjoining RILEY HOSPITAL FOR CHILDREN. The local Rotary Foundation was incorporated in April, 1947; it had been launched the previous year with a $25,000 gift from Mrs. Isaac R. Holycross, the widow of a Rotarian. In 1954, the Indianapolis club purchased land and built facilities for the Southwest Social (Community) Center on West Morris Street. To commemorate its 50th anniversary, the club committed a gift of $25,000 to Junior Achievement of Indianapolis for a permanent headquarters. Other recipients of Rotary support have been the SALVATION ARMY, the INDIANAPOLIS CIVIC THEATRE, FLETCHER PLACE Community Center, and foreign exchange programs at Manual and the former Shortridge high schools. Average annual gifts to the community total $170,000.

When it was founded with 54 local business and community leaders on August 17, 1916, the Kiwanis Club of Indianapolis was the first Kiwanis club established in Indiana and the 18th in the nation. The club's charter was officially presented by International President George F. Hixson on

October 16, 1917. Membership quickly grew to 150 members, with club meetings held at the downtown Severin Hotel. In 1937, the club was the official host for the Kiwanis International Convention, an event which returned to the city in June, 1992. In the late 1940s, the club organized its first "Basketball Round-up" at the Hotel Antlers; other community programs became popular, including its annual football awards luncheon, a travelog program, the Abe Lincoln Awards, and the Indiana-Kentucky Academic Challenge. In 1974, club membership surpassed 400, making it the largest Kiwanis club in the world. Membership grew during the next few years to 500, a mark club members worked to stay above as a tribute to the INDIANAPOLIS 500– MILE RACE. Total metropolitan membership is over 1,000. KIWANIS INTERNATIONAL moved its headquarters to Indianapolis in 1982.

The club's foundation, incorporated in 1949, has participated with other local clubs in providing scholarships and programs for Indianapolis youth. The Kiwanis clubs of Downtown Indianapolis, Irvington, Riley-Lockerbie, East Central Indianapolis, Crossroads, and more than a dozen others form one of the largest metropolitan divisions of the organization; most of these clubs have raised funds for Riley Hospital for Children. Average annual gifts to the community come to over $140,000.

The Downtown Indianapolis Optimist Club was one of 11 original, independent clubs that formed Optimist International in 1919. Organized in May, 1916, and granted Charter No. 1, the Downtown club and later the Northside and Westside clubs focused their efforts on support of youth. In cooperation with the Indianapolis Baseball Club, Optimists hosted thousands of youths at INDIANAPOLIS INDIANS' home games. For many years the Optimists sponsored Port Optimist, the Explorer Scout base at 30th Street and White River Parkway, where thousands of spectators gathered each fall for the annual Boy Scout Regatta. The Optimists also organized the first Community Coordinating Council and supplied lockers for the Julia Jameson Nutrition Camp.

Lions clubs came to Indianapolis in 1921, soon after the founding of the international organization in Chicago. Melvin Jones of Chicago,

originator of Lions International, organized the first club in the city, and a second club soon followed in Irvington. Like the other service organizations, the Lions began organizing clubs in different geographic locations and by the 1990s had 21 chapters in the city, totaling almost 1,000 members.

Indianapolis clubs and clubs statewide established the Lions Cancer Control Fund of Indiana, Inc., which has purchased equipment for the radiation therapy building at the INDIANA UNIVERSITY MEDICAL CENTER. The Indiana Lions Eye Bank, also located in the hospital complex, makes the correction of eye problems possible, including cornea transplants. Local Lions also have donated used hearing aids to Riley Hospital for Children.

Another international organization, Sertoma, organized its first club in the city in 1938. Sertoma clubs were previously called Cooperative clubs until a national contest to change the name of the organization was conducted in the late 1940s. The winning entry was submitted by Indianapolis resident Noble Hiatt. Sertoma clubs have supported the Marion County Children's Guardian Home, Noble School, and the Campfire Girls' Activity Center. Other Sertoma projects included the purchase of equipment for the speech and hearing department of the Indiana University Medical Center and telecommunications devices for the deaf at GOODWILL INDUSTRIES.

As Indianapolis grew in size and diversity, smaller civic clubs were organized to supplement the work of larger clubs and organizations, while others were formed based on commonalities such as lifestyle, age, gender, or service in the military.

Founded at the Severin Hotel in 1922 to preserve the "barracks spirit" of World War I, the Service Club of Indianapolis was modeled after Rotary and Kiwanis. Club membership consisted of former servicemen who performed philanthropic work to supplement projects of the AMERICAN LEGION. Projects included providing funds for youth to attend Boys' and Girls' State and support for WHEELER MISSION MINISTRIES.

The focus of Jaycees, which organized in the city during the 1930s, was development of individual leadership skills through community involvement. The Jaycees, whose membership was limited to men ages 21 to 40, supported the Marion County Juvenile Center, the Marion County Children's Guardian Home, and the Marion County Retarded Children's Home. The nonprofit Indianapolis Jaycee Charities was incorporated in 1971 to increase the organization's fund-raising potential.

As the number of civic clubs grew, the need arose to improve communication and networking among the organizations. As early as 1909, a district federation of women's clubs was formed to promote understanding and cooperation among civic clubs. The Indianapolis Federation of Community Civic Clubs, a conglomerate of neighborhood civic clubs, was organized in 1922 and incorporated in 1933. By the mid–1950s, the Indianapolis Chamber of Commerce directory listed 49 major citywide organizations (38 for men and 11 for women), and there were scores of smaller groups supporting youth, the disadvantaged, and the needy.

Women in Indianapolis as elsewhere traditionally had either formed their own clubs to undertake philanthropic projects or joined auxiliaries of local men's organizations. That changed in 1984 when the U.S. Supreme Court ruled that Jaycees could no longer bar women from membership. The local Jaycees inducted eight women in the fall of 1984, and most of the city's other traditionally all-male service clubs, such as Kiwanis, Rotary, and Sertoma, changed their bylaws to admit women into membership. Women quickly moved into leadership positions in the organizations. In 1988, Downtown Sertoma Club elected, as its first female president, Sandra S. Wilt, vice-president of human resources for Goodwill Industries.

As in most metropolitan areas, Indianapolis service organizations established additional clubs to address the needs of outlying areas. Rotary chartered a Castleton club in 1984, followed by the Indianapolis-East club in 1989, and a club at the Indianapolis International Airport in 1990. Kiwanis organized an airport club two years later after its original club there failed. The Irvington Jaycees was reactivated in 1990, with club members organizing fund-raisers for the Marion County Children's Guardian Home. Civic clubs, with current membership in the thousands and financial contributions in the hundreds of thou-

sands, remain a strong philanthropic presence in Indianapolis.

MATTHEW C. MORRIS

Civic Theatre. In 1914, several community leaders formed the Little Theatre Society of Indiana, precursor to the Civic Theatre and the first volunteer-based theatre in the city. Artistic Director S. A. Elliot was hired away from the Chicago Little Theatre. No auditoriums were available, so a sculpture court at the HERRON ART INSTITUTE was pressed into service. Scenery had to be painted in a nearby barn and transported in hay wagons.

On October 30, 1915, the Little Theatre made its debut with an evening of four short plays. During its first two seasons the society presented a total of 43 shows. As years passed, however, the art school proved inappropriate for stage productions, so in 1925 the Little Theatre built a new, 340–seat playhouse at Alabama and 19th streets. The occasional participation of a famous Hoosier author resulted in a name change in 1929 to the Booth Tarkington Civic Theatre of Indianapolis, although "Indianapolis Civic Theatre" and then simply "Civic Theatre" became the common usage.

One of few arts organizations that survived the Great Depression and two world wars, Civic Theatre flourished for nearly 50 years. By the 1960s, however, attendance was down. The board of directors felt that the Civic's location had become undesirable, so a new, 700–seat theatre was built in 1973 on the grounds of the INDIANAPOLIS MUSEUM OF ART on West 38th Street.

The first season in the new complex was well received, but this renewed interest proved short-lived; attendance declined again. By 1978, a complete restructuring was necessary to ensure the theatre's survival. A board of directors was established to direct fiscal affairs; an executive director and an operations manager were hired to conduct day-to-day business; full-time positions were created for box office, publicity, marketing, and development; an artistic director and two backstage technicians were hired; designers, directors, musicians, and choreographers were contracted for each Mainstage show; and an education director was hired to stimulate youth programming. (Junior Civic now serves over 700 children each year.) In the late 1970s and early 1980s, Civic instituted two new programs: *Studio C*, a "showcase" where local artists can create experimental theatre; and *Kid Connection*, a group of adult actors who travel to Indiana schools presenting educational plays about social issues. This latter program annually reaches 110,000 schoolchildren.

Civic Theatre continues to present large-scale, mainstream entertainment on its *Mainstage*. Annual attendance has reached 50,000, and the annual student matinee series serves over 5,000 Indiana students. Musicals, rarely produced in Civic's early days, became the theatre's most popular ticket item in the 1980s. To enhance the musical product, a hydraulic orchestra pit was constructed in 1991 funded by a capital campaign. The 20–year-old sound, light, and fly equipment was also renovated, and the entire facility was redecorated.

MICHAEL KLASS

Civil Defense. Previously an uncoordinated citizens' movement, Civil Defense (CD) became part of the Department of Defense during WORLD WAR II. In the 1940s the CD organized fire fighters at the INDIANA STATE FAIRGROUNDS in Indianapolis, watched for sabotage, and participated in scrap metal and War Bond drives. A related organization allied with CD, the Passive Defense Force, organized Indianapolis industries to protect workers and ensure production.

During the 1950s hundreds of men attended fire fighting classes at neighborhood engine houses. The CD placed air raid sirens downtown and assigned wardens to the largest buildings. Indiana State Fairgrounds buildings housed radio equipment for emergency communications via several local radio stations.

In the early 1960s Indianapolis had one of the largest CD police training classes in the nation. Lessons ranged from combatting the supposed Communist menace to recognizing mentally disturbed persons. Directed from CD headquarters at 3951 North Illinois Street, 1,200 people in 1964 participated in Operation Alert, which simulated an enemy air attack. During the Cuban missile crisis (1962) CD encouraged the building of family fallout shelters in Indianapolis, but interest waned by the late 1970s when many private and public shelters were emptied of their stocks.

The ending of the Cold War required CD to shift emphases from military to non-military disaster readiness, a shift reflected in a 1991 name change to the Marion County Emergency Management Division. Today a full-time staff of four plans for all types of disasters. Warning sirens still sound for testing at 11 A.M. on Fridays and "bell and light" warning systems sound in many businesses and hospitals. Funding comes from state and federal governments.

MICHAEL WATSON

Clipping files, Indiana Division, Indiana State Library.

Civil Rights. The history of civil rights in Indianapolis is intertwined with that of the larger African-American struggle for equality in the United States. The points at which the two histories intersect can be found in the city's housing, schools, and public accommodations.

From 1816 until the Civil War African-Americans in Indiana, like those throughout the United States, were regarded as inferior. As such, the lives of African-American residents of Indianapolis were severely proscribed by prejudice, segregation, and other attributes of third class citizenship. They were denied the right to vote, excluded from the state militia, subjected to physical and verbal abuse, in peril of being kidnapped and sold into slavery, barred from public schools, excluded from trade union membership, and prevented from offering testimony in court.

Conditions such as these prompted the first efforts on behalf of civil rights in Indiana. The SOCIETY OF FRIENDS (or Quakers) frequently condemned racial discrimination in the city and state. In 1851 one of several African-American state conventions met in Indianapolis. Its president, John G. Britton, called upon whites to recognize African-Americans' entitlement to basic citizenship rights. Such efforts, however, had little effect.

The Civil War and emancipation changed this situation. Consequently, the years immediately following that conflict were marked by renewed action to secure rights heretofore denied African-Americans. In 1865 the first of two postwar African-American conventions met in Indianapolis to discuss ways of repealing "the unwholesome and tyrannical laws which have bereft us of the rights guaranteed other American citizens." The first fruits of their labors were the rights to present testimony in court and to serve on juries. This victory was followed in 1869 by the right to vote and hold public office. Legislation was also adopted which established public schools for African-American children. In Indianapolis African-Americans gained the right to equal treatment on city streetcars.

While the period 1865 to 1900 was marked by real progress in some areas, it was also clear that much remained to be done. In spite of constitutional guarantees and the adoption of a state civil rights law by the General Assembly in 1885, discrimination against African-Americans continued virtually unabated. Two cases involving prominent black residents JAMES T. V. HILL and Charles H. Stewart captured local attention. Hill, the first African-American attorney in the city, brought suit in 1890 when he was refused service in a "white" restaurant. Four years later, Stewart, an African-American newspaper publisher, sued an elevator operator in a local hotel for assault and battery while being forcibly removed from the elevator. Although both men won their cases, neither case resulted in a major test of the state's civil rights law.

Civil rights in Indianapolis worsened significantly in the 1920s with the rise of the KU KLUX KLAN. The Klan dominated city government, and the City Council, under pressure from white civic groups, adopted a zoning ordinance designed to prevent African-Americans from purchasing homes or living in white neighborhoods. Many public facilities were also segregated. Although the Indianapolis branch of the NAACP successfully challenged the constitutionality of the zoning ordinance, segregation in the city's housing, restaurants, parks, employment, theaters, hospitals, and public schools remained in force.

In the 1930s HENRY J. RICHARDSON, an African-American member of the state legislature from Indianapolis, initiated other challenges to

The local NAACP Youth Council staged sympathy strikes in 1960 at two Indianapolis Woolworth stores in support of southern blacks denied lunch counter service by the company. [Indiana Historical Society, *Indianapolis Recorder* Collection, #C5772]

segregation. At the 1933 session of the General Assembly Richardson proposed bills prohibiting discrimination in state public works projects and opening the state militia to blacks, both of which were passed; although voters approved the militia bill in 1936, obstacles remained to enrolling blacks in the National Guard until 1941. Richardson also cosponsored a bill with six other legislators in 1935 to prohibit racial discrimination. The attitudes and delaying tactics of white legislators defeated his bill, however.

By the 1940s Indianapolis had the reputation of being one of the worst offenders against equal rights among American cities. African-American workers encountered discrimination in job opportunities and union membership. During World War II black servicemen were barred from local USO facilities as well as from white restaurants and hotels. In one instance five African-American waitresses quit their jobs in an Indianapolis chili parlor when the manager refused service to black soldiers.

World War II also heightened black awareness of racial discrimination in employment and public accommodations. African-Americans demanded fulfillment of the freedoms for which they were fighting. Their improved overall economic situation at home and an expanded middle class also made African-Americans in the city and state more assertive of their rights. This more militant attitude paved the way for an all-out assault against racial discrimination in Indianapolis after the war.

The Indianapolis branch of the NAACP, under the leadership of Willard B. Ransom, played a particularly important role in the postwar fight for civil rights by virtue of its location in a city that was the state capital and had the largest African-American community in Indiana. Many members of the Indianapolis NAACP were also members of Starling W. James' FEDERATION OF ASSOCIATED CLUBS, a local organization with objectives similar to the NAACP.

In 1945 civil rights activists in Indianapolis scored their first postwar legislative success with the Indiana General Assembly's passage of the weak, noncompulsory, though much publicized Fair Employment Practices Act. This legislation authorized the State Labor Commission to work toward eliminating discrimination from the workplace, but did not specify penalties for noncompliance. Four years later, in 1949, activists scored their second major victory with a law abolishing segregation in public education.

Meanwhile African-Americans in the immediate postwar years undertook nonlegislative means of ending discrimination and winning access to places of public accommodation, spearheaded by the Indianapolis NAACP. It was joined by a loose coalition of NAACP branches in other Hoosier cities, the Federation of Associated Clubs, African-American social and fraternal organizations, labor unions associated with the Congress of Industrial Organization (CIO), the JEWISH COMMUNITY RELATIONS COUNCIL, and a variety of church-related groups. In the absence of strong government enforcement, these private groups began a largely indigenous, nonviolent campaign to secure compliance with the 1885 civil rights law. Meetings were held with managers of establishments that barred African-Americans to persuade them to observe the law. Unsuccessful negotiations were followed by nonviolent direct action, usually by racially mixed groups, to secure service in those establishments.

In 1946 the CIO mounted the first concerted attack on discrimination in local hotels and restaurants. The following year a local group, under NAACP leadership, began a more vigorous crusade against racial discrimination in the city's restaurants. There were also challenges to discrimination in places of recreation and amusement, such as RIVERSIDE AMUSEMENT PARK. The Federation of Associated Clubs opened many movie theaters to African-Americans through negotiations with the managers of these establishments.

The 1950s and 1960s witnessed increased local activity in the civil rights movement. Recognizing the need to address civil rights, the City Council in 1952–1953 created the INDIANAPOLIS HUMAN RIGHTS COMMISSION, an advisory group to the mayor on civil rights matters. Consisting of community leaders, the commission worked to promote "amicable relations" in the community, mediate disputes, and integrate local institutions. Others also joined in the push for civil rights. Local minister JAMES JONES, chair of the Human Rights Commission in 1961–1962, was a staunch advocate of integration. The Jewish Community Relations Council also participated actively in the civil rights movement. Likewise, the INDIANA CIVIL LIBERTIES UNION, dedicated to the protection of Bill of Rights guarantees, was founded in 1953 in response to the racial discrimination of the 1950s. Despite some success with challenging segregation, social activists recognized the need for a stronger civil rights law. Their efforts met with repeated frustration and failure until 1961, when the Indiana Conference on Civil Rights Legislation was formed in Indianapolis. By the mid–1960s intense lobbying by this group as well as public demonstrations in the city led to legislation creating the Indiana Civil Rights Commission, a stronger law banning discrimination in public accommodations, a fair housing law, and repeal of Indiana's prohibition against interracial marriage.

Despite the existence of a strengthened 1949 school desegregation law, patterns of racial segregation in the Indianapolis public schools persisted into the 1960s. The NAACP filed suit in 1968, and the resulting 1976 desegregation order by Federal Judge S. Hugh Dillin is still in effect today, although somewhat modified in 1993 by the school system's SELECT SCHOOLS program.

Although racism is not dead in the city and surrounding suburbs, its overt manifestations are not as visible and occur less frequently than in the past. That such is the case is due in large part to the Indianapolis civil rights movement.

MONROE H. LITTLE, JR.
Indiana University–Purdue University,
Indianapolis

Emma Lou Thornbrough, *The Negro in Indiana: A Study of a Minority* (Indianapolis, 1957); Emma Lou Thornbrough, *Since Emancipation: A Short History of Indiana Negroes, 1863–1963* (Indianapolis, 1963); Emma Lou Thornbrough, "Breaking Racial Barriers to Public Accommodations in Indiana, 1935 to 1963," *Indiana Magazine of History*, 83 (Dec., 1987), 301–343.

Civil War. News of the war reached Indianapolis in a telegraphed message from Charleston on April 12, 1861: "The ball has opened." Within two weeks Indiana's first 12,000 volunteer soldiers converged on Indianapolis. The city soon became the central recruiting station and the major military depot for Indiana during the American Civil War. In the next four years, 104 of 169 Indiana regiments were processed into military service at Indianapolis. The city itself sent an estimated 4,000 men. Eventually, there were 24 training camps in and around Indianapolis, a prison camp, a federal arsenal, an artillery practice field, a Soldiers' Home, a Ladies' Home, and three military hospitals.

But in April, 1861, there were no camps, no weapons, no supplies. Governor OLIVER P. MORTON summoned LEW WALLACE to Indianapolis and appointed him adjutant general, the top military office in the state. The INDIANA STATE FAIRGROUNDS was converted to an army training site and named CAMP MORTON. By the end of April, an arsenal was set up in a rented building on the STATE HOUSE grounds.

Six infantry regiments were organized at Indianapolis in compliance with President Lincoln's first call for volunteers. The six regimental commanders included one West Point graduate and five lawyers; one lawyer was an Indianapolis resident, EBENEZER DUMONT. There had been four MILITIA units headquartered in Indianapolis prior to the Civil War and all four were mustered into the 11th Volunteer Regiment. One of the militia lieutenants was FREDERICK KNEFLER, later the highest ranking Jewish officer in the Union army. Another militia officer, a lawyer and a West Pointer, was Francis A. Shoup, who went south and became a brigadier general in the Confederate army. Pvt. John C. Hollenbeck was the first Indianapolis resident killed in the Civil War, on June 27, 1861, near Romney, Virginia.

The seat of war preparation in Indiana was Camp Morton, an area roughly outlined today by 19th Street, Central Avenue, 22nd Street, and Talbott Street. Many of the first 6,000 trainees were crowded into the animal barns and stables for shelter. Bathing was performed in FALL CREEK, a half mile to the north. There was an abundance of army food, supplemented with overwhelming quantities of foodstuffs from home. The soldiers' families and friends clogged the Indianapolis streets, and it was reported that the visitors outnumbered the soldiers two to one.

More training camps became necessary as calls came for more men. The larger camps were Camp Carrington near 15th Street and Fall Creek, Camp McClellan at the site of today's Ellenberger Park, Camp Robinson on Cold Spring Road in (modern) Riverside Park, and Camp Sullivan at (modern) MILITARY PARK.

Camp Morton became the most historic military site in Indianapolis when it was converted to a Confederate prison in February, 1862. Governor Morton had indicated to the War Department on February 17 that Indiana could accommodate 3,000 prisoners of war. In a matter of days, the prisoners started to arrive and Camp Morton was encircled with a palisade wall, the reinforced gates, and sentry stations. By February 25, there were 4,800 prisoners in Indianapolis; another 1,000 arrived in early April. Many were sent on to Lafayette and Terre Haute.

Residents of Indianapolis responded immediately to the prisoners' needs. A hospital was improvised in the Athenaeum at Maryland and Meridian streets. The citizens donated food, blankets, and $5,400. Nevertheless, 144 prisoners died in March, 1862, the greatest number for any month in the prison's history. In August, 1862, all of the surviving prisoners were released (upon exchange for Union prisoners) and the prison was vacated.

In July, 1863, the prison reopened with an average population of 3,214 and a death rate of 50 per month over the next 24 months. The maximum population and death count for the same period was 4,999 and 133, respectively. The last prisoner was released on June 12, 1865. The total number of deaths at Camp Morton is debatable, although a monument was erected at Greenlawn Cemetery for "1616 Confederate Soldiers and Sailors Who Died Here While Prisoners of War." These bodies were later exhumed from Greenlawn, at West Street and Kentucky Avenue, and reinterred in a mass grave at CROWN HILL CEMETERY. The monument was moved to GARFIELD PARK (though there has been some discussion recently of relocating it to Crown Hill).

Despite the privations and sickness, the early Camp Morton survivors were appreciative of the care they had received. In an extraordinary salute, Southerners collected $3,000 to commission a bronze bust of former prison commandant RICHARD OWEN. The bust, dedicated on June 9, 1913, carried the engraved testimonial: "Tribute by Confederate prisoners of war and their friends for his courtesy and kindness."

For four years, soldiers thronged Indianapolis—sometimes as many as 12,000. They cluttered the Circle and slept at UNIVERSITY PARK. Massive military reviews were commonplace. On October 2, 1862, approximately 10,000 soldiers marched in a parade and staged a sham battle. Crime on the streets was a major problem, and it was necessary to ban liquor sales to soldiers. A visiting officer from Pennsylvania was found dead on the street, but the police were indifferent and never investigated the apparent murder. A list of dead and hospitalized soldiers was published almost daily, and military funerals were frequent. Corpses of deceased soldiers were laid out on the streets near UNION STATION, awaiting transfer to other cities by the express companies.

The West's first military execution for desertion occurred March 27, 1863, at the rear of Burn-

side Barracks just south of Camp Morton. Robert Gay, a 27–year-old former school teacher from Clay County, was shot by a 20–man firing squad. Three bounty jumpers were executed on the same parade ground in 1864.

A so-called Civil War battle occurred in Indianapolis on May 20, 1863, the "BATTLE OF POGUE'S RUN." During the Democratic state convention, a rumor circulated that the delegates were carrying firearms with the intent of an insurrection. Soldiers entered the hall and, in fact, did find concealed weapons. That night as the delegates departed Indianapolis, soldiers boarded two trains and confiscated more handguns. Some delegates chose to throw their side arms out the windows into a small creek, Pogue's Run.

Nothing during the war created more excitement in Indianapolis than the news of Confederate General JOHN HUNT MORGAN's crossing of the Ohio River into Indiana. On July 8, 1863, word spread that Morgan intended to capture Indianapolis and release all the prisoners. Bells rang, businesses came to a standstill, and saloons closed. Five regiments of trained soldiers defended the State House. Every able-bodied citizen was called to arms—and 65,000 showed up. The scare was temporary but during the excitement an ammunition caisson rushing down Indiana Avenue accidentally exploded and killed three soldiers, a boy, and two horses.

Indiana's only black Civil War regiment was enrolled at Camp Fremont, near Fountain Square. The 28th Colored Infantry was mustered for three years on March 31, 1864, and lost 212 men in their cause. A full company of 100 men had previously volunteered with the 54th Massachusetts Infantry, another all-black unit.

The favorite regiment of Indianapolis citizens was the 132nd Infantry, proudly referred to as "The City Regiment." Made up of young boys and old men, the 132nd was organized in May, 1864, to serve for 100 days as railroad guards in Tennessee and Alabama. The largest crowd ever assembled in Indianapolis to witness a regiment's departure escorted the 132nd to the depot. Twelve of the men died of disease before the regiment returned.

Indianapolis became recognized nationally for the care it provided servicemen and their families. The City Hospital was taken over by the federal administration and in a two-year period provided care for 6,114 government patients, 847 of whom were prisoners. A Soldiers' Home was built at West and Maryland streets to provide a place of relaxation for soldiers passing through Indianapolis. The home became the largest in the Midwest and accommodated 8,000 for meals and 1,800 for shelter. A Ladies' Home was built, convenient to Union Station, for needy wives and children of Civil War soldiers.

News of the Appomattox surrender reached Indianapolis at 11 P.M., April 9, 1865. The celebrations started immediately and the *Indianapolis Journal* reported the citizens became "demented" with excitement. Then came the black-bordered news accounts of Lincoln's assassination on April 15 and the city went into mourning. The former president's funeral train stopped in Indianapolis on April 30. More than 100,000 people filed by the bier in the State House in 18 hours.

Once again legions of Hoosier soldiers marched on the Indianapolis streets; this time they were going home. Formal receptions were conducted almost daily throughout June as Indianapolis welcomed the returning heroes. But not all the Indianapolis soldiers made it home. It is estimated, based on statewide data, that approximately 700 residents gave their lives in the Civil War. On July 25, 1865, the last military wagon train, 28 miles long, moved through the city. By fall, the soldiers and their camps were gone.

RICHARD S. SKIDMORE

John Hampden Holliday, *Indianapolis and the Civil War* (Indianapolis, 1909; reprint ed., 1972); Jacob Piatt Dunn, *Greater Indianapolis* (Chicago, 1910).

Civil War Camps and Installations. Indianapolis was well established as the commercial center of the state by 1860 and it was a major railroad hub from which troops and supplies could be quickly dispersed. Thus, the city was designated by the War Department as a place of rendezvous for troops. The first Civil War military installation in Marion County was *Camp Sullivan* (now MILITARY PARK), named for Col. Jerry Sullivan of the 13th Indiana Regiment. On May 24,

1861, Gen. George B. McClellan reviewed Indiana troops on its parade ground.

Next came *CAMP MORTON*. Named for Governor OLIVER P. MORTON, it was located on the site of the new fairgrounds (in the vicinity of today's 19th and Alabama) and was first used as a rendezvous point and training ground. After the fall of Fort Donelson in February, 1862, it became one of the Union's best known prison camps.

Located to the south of Camp Morton on Tinker Street (now 16th) was *Camp Burnside*, named for Union general Ambrose Burnside. It was home to the 71st Indiana (Col. Biddle) and later to the "Invalids" or "Veteran Reserve Corps." The first military execution in the West was carried out here on March 27, 1863, when one Robert Gay was shot as a spy and deserter.

Several other training camps were established around the city. *Camp Carrington*, located on the extreme northwestern corner of the city, became the largest in the state. An artillery camp, known as *Camp Noble*, was built by Col. W. W. Frybarger for the 3rd Battery. The 11th Regiment reorganized for three years service in a camp on the west bank of WHITE RIVER, near Cold Spring. Col. John A. Bridgeland's 2nd Cavalry was encamped near Fall Creek, four miles north of the city. An African-American regiment under Col. Charles Russell established *Camp Fremont* on wooded ground southeast of the city near Virginia Avenue. An artillery practice ground three miles south of the city, near the residence of a Mr. Paddock on Bluff Road, was a temporary camp for the 19th Regiment commanded by Lt. Col. King.

Both state and federal arsenals were located at Indianapolis. Frustrated by a shortage of ammunition, Governor Morton established the *Indiana State Arsenal* under Capt. Herman Sturm in rented quarters south of the STATE HOUSE. In the winter of 1861, the facility moved to the John Ott furniture factory and the next year to a site $1\frac{1}{2}$ miles east on Washington Street. In 1863, the federal government purchased a tract of land, now the site of ARSENAL TECHNICAL HIGH SCHOOL, and began construction of the *United States Arsenal*.

The *Indianapolis City Hospital*, established in 1856, became a military installation and remained so throughout the war. Closely allied to the hospital was the *Soldiers' Home*. Located on

West Street, south of Maryland, the home became a haven for traveling soldiers in need of rest, a hot meal, or medical treatment. The provost guard had its headquarters at the home and a permanent encampment of several hundred men lived on the grounds for many months.

Supplying the army was profitable and the city of Indianapolis thrived during the war years. Soldiers passing through the city brought home the reality of war in the stories they shared with their hosts. In turn, Indianapolis provided the soldiers with a variety of cultural attractions for their entertainment and enlightenment.

TONY L. TRIMBLE

John Hampden Holliday, *Indianapolis and the Civil War* (Indianapolis, 1909, reprint ed., 1972).

Civil War Round Table. Historical organization. On February 8, 1955, a small group of Civil War enthusiasts met to organize a Civil War study group. The objects of the resulting Indianapolis Civil War Round Table were identified as the study of the American Civil War, promotion and dissemination of knowledge concerning it, and preservation of Civil War battlefields, sites, memorabilia, and artifacts.

The organization meets the second Monday of each month, except July and August, currently in the auditorium of the INDIANA STATE LIBRARY AND HISTORICAL BUILDING. The meetings are open to the public and the membership includes both women and youth. Field trips to Civil War battlefields are organized each year, with bus transportation and tour guides provided. The group also has been active in providing financial and written support of preservation activities for sites related to the Civil War.

R. V. EARLE, JR.
Indianapolis Civil War Round Table

Civil War Treason Trials. Partisan politics in Indiana were unusually bitter during the Civil War. The state was overwhelmingly loyal to the Union, ranking high on the list of northern states in the percentage of its population that volunteered for federal military service. There was also a minority of dissenters, people who criticized the war, President Lincoln, and the policies of the Lincoln administration, including emancipation of the slaves. Governor OLIVER P. MORTON, a Republican, and his political allies indiscriminately attacked political dissenters as treasonable. Since the dissenters were often Democrats, the governor argued that all Democrats supported the Confederacy and were treasonous. Republican spokesmen contended that organizations known as the Sons of Liberty and the Order of American Knights had been established by the Democrats for purposes of forming a confederation of midwestern states that were to secede and become allies of the Confederacy. The membership of these organizations was highly exaggerated by the Republicans.

In the late summer and fall of 1864, as the state and national elections approached, the conflict between the Morton group and the Democratic critics of the war became unusually intense. With complicity of the national government and Governor Morton, the federal commander of the military district of Indiana carried out the military arrest of a number of prominent Indiana Democrats, including JOSEPH J. BINGHAM, the editor of the *Indianapolis Daily State Sentinel* who was also the party's state chairman, and Huntington lawyer Lambdin P. Milligan. They were charged with planning violent and treasonable activities in Indiana, Illinois, and Kentucky. Five of these men—William A. Bowles, HARRISON H. DODD, Stephen Horsey, Andrew Humphreys, and Milligan—were tried in Indianapolis before military commissions. There were improprieties in the conduct of the trials and the prosecution's effort to suggest that the Democratic party was treasonable. The trial was also surrounded by lurid publicity in the partisan press. Members of the commission made political speeches at Republican rallies while the trials were in progress.

In the course of the proceedings, Dodd fled and was convicted *in absentia*. Milligan and the others were found guilty on December 10, 1864. Dodd, Milligan, Horsey, and Bowles were sentenced to be hanged. Lawyers for Milligan, Bowles, and Horsey challenged the convictions in the federal courts in Indianapolis. Ultimately the case proceeded to the U.S. Supreme Court. On

April 3, 1866, Chief Justice Salmon P. Chase issued a writ of habeas corpus releasing the defendants. On December 17, 1866, the chief justice authored the majority opinion of the court that civilians residing in a state in which the civil courts were functioning could not be tried before a military commission. The government could not avoid the constitutional and legal protections available to defendants in the civil courts by creating a collateral jurisdiction, like a military commission, that did not observe those protections. Known as *Ex parte Milligan*, the decision of the Supreme Court is regarded as a landmark civil liberties decision.

Reaction in Indianapolis, insofar as it can be gleaned from the highly partisan press of the day, was predictably mixed. The pro-Republican *Indiana Journal* complained of the "reactionary dogmas" of the majority justices and argued that the decision was without moral force. The *Herald*, a Democratic organ, called it an "able opinion . . . probably the most important ever delivered by the Court" and recommended it to "the careful perusal of every citizen."

ALAN T. NOLAN

Alan T. Nolan, "Ex Parte Milligan: A Curb of Executive and Military Power," *We the People: Indiana and the United States Constitution* (Indianapolis, 1987), 27–53; Gilbert R. Tredway, *Democratic Opposition to the Lincoln Administration in Indiana* (Indianapolis, 1973); *Indianapolis Journal*, Jan. 2, 1867; *Indianapolis Herald*, Jan. 4, 1867.

Clark, Alex M. (Mar. 22, 1916–Feb. 14, 1991). Mayor of Indianapolis, 1952–1956, Republican. The son of Scottish immigrants and a lifelong resident of Indianapolis, Clark graduated from SHORTRIDGE HIGH SCHOOL in 1933. After attending DePauw University he received an LL.B. from Indiana University in 1939 and took a job as a Marion County deputy prosecutor. Following several years of military service in World War II, Clark returned to Indianapolis and was an unsuccessful candidate for the Republican nomination for prosecutor in the May, 1946, primary. In December, 1946, he became the youngest man in the county's history to be appointed a judge of the municipal court, a position he held until 1951.

Clark became one of the youngest mayors of Indianapolis when he assumed office on January 1, 1952. During his administration he continued many of the projects started by his predecessor, Democrat PHILIP L. BAYT, JR. Among his accomplishments were improvement of the city's infrastructure, approval for a new city-county building, restoration of Garfield Park, expansion of the sewer system, and construction of the Hilton U. Brown Theater to serve as the home for STARLIGHT MUSICALS. After leaving office at the end of 1956, Clark went into private practice with his brother, James C. Clark, and eventually formed the law firm of Clark, Quinn, Moses, and Clark. In 1967 he ran for mayor again, losing to Richard G. Lugar in the Republican primary.

Following the end of World War II Clark helped found the Marion County Republican Veterans of World War II, which became a powerful faction in the GOP. In 1949 he received the Outstanding Young Man of the Year Award from the Indianapolis Chamber of Commerce and in 1964 he was elected potentate of the Murat Shrine.

REBECCA M. MAIER
JEFFERY A. DUVALL

Who's Who in the Midwest (1955); *Indianapolis News*, Nov. 7, 1951, Jan. 1, 1952, Feb. 15, 1991.

Clarke, Grace Giddings Julian (Sept. 11, 1865–June 18, 1938). Clubwoman, author, editor, speaker, and woman suffragist. Grace Julian was born in Centerville, Indiana, the daughter of GEORGE W. JULIAN, abolitionist congressman from Indiana, and Laura Giddings Julian, daughter of Joshua Giddings, antislavery congressman from Ohio. Following Julian's retirement from Congress the family moved in 1873 to IRVINGTON, which had been platted three years before by Grace Julian's uncle, Jacob B. Julian, and Sylvester Johnson. Grace attended schools in Irvington and earned bachelor of philosophy and master of philosophy degrees from BUTLER UNIVERSITY in 1884 and 1885. In 1887 she married Charles B. Clarke, an Indianapolis attorney who had been U.S. deputy surveyor general under her father in New Mexico Territory.

Grace Julian
Clarke.
[Indiana State
Library]

Clarke was an active clubwoman in local, state, and national organizations. She founded the Irvington Woman's Club, and while president of that club helped to organize the 7th District Indiana Federation of Clubs. She was president of the Indiana Federation of Clubs from 1909 to 1911, and was a board member of the General Federation of Women's Clubs, which she served as national press chairman. She also served as president of the Local Council of Women.

Clarke's efforts as an author and editor were varied. For 18 years she wrote a weekly column for the INDIANAPOLIS STAR, and for a time also edited a woman's page for that newspaper. She wrote articles for various publications, including "Notes and Queries," a series of literary papers written for the Indianapolis Woman's Club. She wrote two books about her father—*George W. Julian, Some Impressions* (Indianapolis, n.d.) and *George W. Julian* (Indianapolis, 1923)—and edited his *Later Speeches on Political Questions, With Select Controversial Papers* (Indianapolis, 1889).

Well known as a speaker as well as a writer, Clarke often lectured on behalf of WOMEN'S RIGHTS AND SUFFRAGE. She supported that cause as an officer of the Woman's Franchise League and as the first president of the Legislative Council of Indiana Women, which lobbied the Indiana General Assembly in favor of suffrage legislation. She also traveled around the state giving "14–minute talks" for the Liberty Loan drives during WORLD WAR I.

Always loyal to the people and interests of Irvington, Clarke served her community and the city of Indianapolis in a number of ways. She was a member of the old Marion County Board of Charities and the City Plan Commission, she

headed the capital's first employment office under appointment by President Woodrow Wilson, and she was a member of the commission that chose the list of great authors whose names are carved on the outer frieze of the INDIANAPOLIS–MARION COUNTY PUBLIC LIBRARY.

Grace Julian Clarke died in the Julian home, which still stands at 115 South Audubon Road, and was buried in CROWN HILL CEMETERY.

MARTHA WRIGHT
Indiana State Library

R. E. Banta, *Indiana Authors and Their Books, 1816–1916* (Crawfordsville, Ind., 1949).

CLASS. See Community Leaders Allied for Superior Schools

Classical Music. The earliest cultivators of "classical" or "serious" music were vocal groups, specifically church choirs and amateur singing societies. One of the earliest choirs belonged to the FIRST BAPTIST CHURCH, which organized a chorus in 1822; another, the 50–voice SECOND PRESBYTERIAN CHURCH Choir, performed publicly with instrumental accompaniment during the 1839–1847 tenure of the church's famous pastor, HENRY WARD BEECHER. The Indianapolis Handelian Society, established in 1828, constituted the first of many secular amateur choral organizations formed in the city throughout the 19th century. Organized ca. 1851, the Handel and Haydn Society performed such masterpieces of the choral repertoire as Haydn's *The Creation* and *The Seasons*. The Indianapolis Choral Union introduced Handel's *Messiah* to Indianapolis audiences in 1874.

An influx of German immigrants stimulated the formation of over a thousand *Maennerchoere*, or male singing societies, across the nation, where they exerted a strong influence upon the musical culture of their communities. Founded in 1854, the Indianapolis MAENNERCHOR remains active to this day. Its 19th century musical offerings included choral and instrumental concerts; moreover, during the 1880s when CARL BARUS held the position of conductor, the society staged light opera and operetta productions. Financier John P.

Frenzel's support of the Maennerchor from 1906 to 1933 enabled the organization to import internationally known artists such as Artur Schnabel, the Flonzaley Quartet, Joseph Szigeti, Pablo Casals, and Efrem Zimbalist. In 1867 and again in 1908, the Maennerchor sponsored *Saengerfeste*, or singers' festivals, of the North American Saengerbund, a large Midwest-based federation of German male singing societies. The 1908 Saengerfest lasted several days and treated concertgoers to choral, symphonic, and operatic selections.

A series of music festivals took place during the last three decades of the 19th century. Patterned after the May Festivals of Cincinnati (themselves based on the German Saengerfest model), initiated by Theodore Thomas in 1873, these events typically lasted several days and featured a number of concerts at which patrons could hear symphonic, choral, and solo vocal works. The Choral Union and the Philharmonic Society sponsored the first May Festival (1874); the second (1875) was hosted by the Choral Union alone. Because the society performed essentially the same works as they had the previous year, few patrons attended, and plans for further festivals were discarded until the arrival of Carl Barus. In 1886 the GRAND ARMY OF THE REPUBLIC organized an "Indiana Music Festival" at TOMLINSON HALL to raise money for the construction of the SOLDIERS AND SAILORS MONUMENT. Barus directed soloist Lilli Lehmann, a festival chorus of 600 singers, and an orchestra of 60 pieces in a performance of Rossini's *Stabat Mater*. The event proved so successful that a May Music Festival Association was formed to organize future festivals. Between 1889 and 1898, ten festivals took place, a foundation of musical excellence having been laid in the early years by Barus, who conducted all the concerts in 1889 and 1890, assisted director Theodore Thomas in 1891, and led the festival chorus performances in 1892. Soloists participating in Indianapolis May Festival concerts in the 1890s included Victor Herbert, Nellie Melba, Madame Nordica, and Emma Eames; orchestras imported for the events included the Theodore Thomas Orchestra, the Walter Damrosch Orchestra, and the Cincinnati and Boston symphony orchestras. A deficit of $3,000 in 1898 convinced the city that the May Music Festivals had become too expensive to continue, and the Festival Association disbanded.

The city's earliest orchestras existed solely to provide singing societies with instrumental accompaniment at choral concerts. The first orchestra to break out of this mold was the Indianapolis Philharmonic Orchestra, created in 1871 for a benefit concert. Composed primarily of German-American musicians, the short-lived ensemble performed a series of Sunday concerts before its dispersal. Karl Schneider, a voice teacher, organized a 60–piece orchestra in 1896. The first Indianapolis orchestra to schedule a complete symphonic work for each of its concerts, the historically important Schneider ensemble stayed together for ten years. Several other orchestras were formed after the turn of the century; the Indianapolis Symphony Orchestra (a precursor of the present institution) proved to be the most enduring of these organizations. Financially solvent, the orchestra produced seven seasons of concerts between 1911 and 1917. It disbanded in November, 1917, when the anti-German sentiment spawned by WORLD WAR I threatened to endanger its members, many of whom were either German immigrants or could claim recent German ancestry.

The modern INDIANAPOLIS SYMPHONY ORCHESTRA (ISO) presented its first concert in 1930, under the direction of FERDINAND SCHAEFER, the orchestra's conductor until its eighth season (1937–1938) when FABIAN SEVITZKY took over directorship. Under Sevitzky the ISO earned a reputation for its performances of works by contemporary American composers, its recordings and radio broadcasts, and its neighborhood concert series. In 1956 IZLER SOLOMON replaced Sevitzky; during his 20–year tenure the orchestra reached new heights of international fame. John Nelson, Solomon's successor, took the orchestra on tour to Kennedy Center and Carnegie Hall where its concerts achieved critical acclaim. Following Nelson's retirement in 1987, the internationally renowned conductor-musicologist Raymond Leppard took over the baton, initiating the ISO's Promenade Concerts and Midwinter Festivals. In 1963 the ISO moved from the MURAT

THEATER, where it had presented concerts since its fourth season, to the newly built CLOWES MEMORIAL HALL on the BUTLER UNIVERSITY campus. The orchestra made the recently renovated CIRCLE THEATRE its home in 1984.

Other orchestras also call Indianapolis home. Founded by ISO percussionist Hermann H. Rinne, the PHILHARMONIC ORCHESTRA OF INDIANAPOLIS embarked upon its concert career in March, 1941. Rinne envisioned the community orchestra as a haven for players who wished to maintain a high level of proficiency on their instruments, yet did not have the time or the inclination to pursue a professional music career. The INDIANAPOLIS CHAMBER ORCHESTRA (ICO), a relatively recent addition to the Indianapolis classical music scene, performs symphonic works intended for smaller orchestras. Led by conductor Kirk Trevor, the ICO holds the position of orchestra-in-residence at Clowes Hall. The New World Chamber Orchestra provides aspiring instrumentalists with an orchestral learning environment. Besides performing several concerts a year, the youthful players attend weekend retreats where they work to enhance their musical skills. Additional professional instrumental groups include the Cameo Trio, piano-trio-in-residence at the Indianapolis Museum of Art since 1983, and the ENSEMBLE OUABACHE, which performs works from the 17th and 18th centuries on period instruments.

The INDIANAPOLIS SYMPHONIC CHOIR, a 160–member chorus established by Sevitzky in 1937, performs masterpieces of choral literature with the ISO each season. Comprised of young singers ages 8 to 14, the INDIANAPOLIS CHILDREN'S CHOIR is an audition-only group that presents several concerts of classical choral music throughout the year. CHRIST CHURCH CATHEDRAL's Choral Masterworks series consists of three annual concerts by the internationally recognized Cathedral Choir of Men and Boys, and the Cathedral Girls Choir. The series culminates with a festival devoted to the works of a single composer. CATHEDRAL ARTS, INC., a nonprofit cultural organization, sponsors the quadrennial INTERNATIONAL VIOLIN COMPETITION of Indianapolis, an event which since 1982 has attracted young violinists of remarkable talent and proficiency.

Although touring opera companies made frequent visits to the city, few operas gained local production until the late 20th century. The INDIANAPOLIS OPERA COMPANY, a professional organization founded in 1975, frequently draws sellout crowds to its performances. The Indiana Opera Theater, organized in 1983, stages new and less familiar works.

SUZANNE G. SNYDER

Martha F. Bellinger, "Music in Indianapolis, 1821–1900," *Indiana Magazine of History*, 41 (Dec., 1945), 345–362, and "Music in Indianapolis, 1900–1944," *Indiana Magazine of History*, 42 (Mar., 1946), 47–65.

Claypool Hotel. Downtown hotel at the corner of Illinois and Washington streets. Henry Lawrence built the Claypool Hotel in 1903 with the financial help of Connersville millionaire Edward Fay Claypool. Thomas Carter's tavern (1822) and the Bates House (1853) previously occupied the site.

Architect Frank Andrews designed a lobby that was reportedly the largest in the country. Meeting rooms were notable for their size and exotic motifs. The Claypool's proximity to the State House ensured its role as a headquarters for both political parties and the site for numerous political gatherings. Upstairs, the 450 guest rooms were elegantly furnished with mahogany dressers and brass beds. Lawrence insisted that each room

The Florentine Room on the second floor of the Claypool Hotel hosted elegant events.
[Indiana Historical Society, #C5777]

have a private bath, a new idea that was denounced by the National Hotelman's Association.

Two sensational murders took place at the Claypool. In 1943 Army nurse Naomi Riddings was found dead, a case that remains unsolved. In 1954 the body of 18–year-old Dorothy Poore was found stuffed in a dresser drawer; a suspect was arrested a week later, convicted, and sentenced to life in prison. Both crimes received national press coverage.

By the 1960s newer facilities had begun to attract much of the downtown hotel business. The Claypool closed following a fire in June, 1967, and the structure was demolished two years later. Claypool Court (an enclosed food court and retail mall) and an Embassy Suites Hotel opened on the site in the 1980s, continuing the tradition of a hotel operating at this location.

CATHLEEN DONNELLY

Indianapolis Star, Sept. 8, 1968, Dec. 4, 1977.

Clermont. Northwestside town located along Crawfordsville Road (U.S. Highway 136) at the Marion County line. In April, 1849, Percy Hosbrook laid out the town of Mechanicsburg alongside a proposed depot for the Indianapolis, Bloomington, and Western Railroad. The original name reflected its early settlement by craftsmen, though it became Clermont in 1853 to avoid confusion with another Mechanicsburg in the state. The little town grew slowly throughout the 19th century. The first church was organized in 1850; the first school in 1856. Fifty years later, Clermont counted only 205 inhabitants. Significant growth occurred in the post–World War II era, as Indianapolis expanded westward. In 1990, there were 1,678 residents.

Clermont was incorporated in 1903 and under UNIGOV has INCLUDED TOWN status. Residents elect a three-member town council and a clerk-treasurer.

In 1993, Clermont claimed a number of small retail shops, restaurants, and light industries. Miller Pipeline, which employs about 60 people locally and 600–650 statewide, moved its headquarters to Clermont in 1988. INDIANAPOLIS RACEWAY PARK, home of a number of drag racing

events and the U.S. Nationals, annually draws almost 500,000 visitors to Clermont.

PAT WATSON

Climate. Because of its continental mid-latitude location, Indianapolis has a temperate climate with very warm, humid summers and cool winters. Imposed on the daily and seasonal temperature fluctuations are changes occurring every few days as surges of cold continental polar air move southward, or warm tropical air moves northward. These changes are more frequent and pronounced in winter than summer. A winter may be unusually cold, or a summer cool, if the influence of polar air is persistent. Alternatively, a summer may be unusually warm, or a winter mild, if air of tropical origin predominates. The interaction between these two broad classes of air masses, with contrasting temperature, humidity, and density, results in the development of low pressure systems (cyclones) that generally move eastward over or close to the state, resulting in precipitation. These systems are least active in mid-summer, tending to move north of Indiana.

Climate data have been collected in Indianapolis since April 2, 1871. (Even prior to this, however, some excellent descriptive data are available, as in the antebellum diaries of CALVIN FLETCHER.) The first officially maintained climate instruments were installed at Blackford's Block, at the southeast corner of Washington and Meridian streets. Measurements were made of wind speed and direction; maximum and minimum temperatures; humidity, using a psychrometer; and precipitation, with both a tipping bucket and 8" rain gauge. Over the ensuing 70 years the instruments were moved four times within a three-block area. In terms of interpreting the climate record the most important move occurred on September 1, 1896, when the station was moved from its second site, Saks Building, at Washington and Pennsylvania streets, to the MAJESTIC BUILDING, at the northeast corner of Maryland and Pennsylvania. At this time the instruments were taken from street level and placed on top of the building's roof. On July 1, 1915, the station was moved again to the Consolidated Building, 115 North Pennsylvania Street, and back to street level.

Record Climatic Conditions

Temperature[1]		
Highest	July 25, 1934	107°F
Lowest	January 19, 1994	–27°F
	January 5, 1884	–25°F
Precipitation		
Maximum monthly	July 1875	13.12″
Minimum monthly	March 1910	0.07″
Precipitation intensity		
Maximum recorded 24-hour	September, 1895	6.80″
In last 40 years	July 1, 1987	5.32″
Snowfall		
Greatest winter season	1977–78	57.8″
Lowest winter season	1982–83	7.1″
Maximum monthly amount	January 1978	30.6″
Maximum daily amount	February 26, 1965	12.5″
Wind speed		
Greatest gust	June 1929 from northwest[2]	111 mph
	January 25th, 1950	90 mph
At the airport site April 6, 1988 from the northwest		74 mph

[1] Annual extremes recorded within the areas, not neccessarily at the airport site.

[2] During the early period of observations, wind speeds were measured using anemometers mounted on tall towers, well above the surface and thus higher wind speeds are to be expected. Wind speed is now measured much closer to the ground (20 ft.).

In June, 1954, the city office was closed and consolidated with measurements at Weir Cook Airport (now Indianapolis International Airport), approximately 7 miles to the southwest of downtown Indianapolis. The site at Weir Cook had opened at the Administration Building on April 1, 1931, and the instruments were moved to their current location at the southwest corner of the Administration Building on September 28, 1977. The specific site location is 3944N, 8616W; station elevation is 792 (WBAN number 93819). Currently measurements are made of maximum, minimum, and hourly air temperature, humidity, sunshine hours, and precipitation. The station is maintained as a National Weather Service Class 1 forecasting station. Climate records were switched from the city office to the airport in 1942.

When describing the climate of a location it is usual to discuss the "climatic normal," a 30–year average for the location of interest. In the United States this is computed and reported by the National Oceanic and Atmospheric Administration (NOAA). The climatic normal indicates the conditions to be expected at a given location and provides a reference against which to compare extremes. All of the average values presented here refer to the climatic normals calculated from the Indianapolis International Airport data for the period 1950–1980. The extreme values reported include data from other sites in the locality of Indianapolis. None of the data have been corrected for changes in the location of the climate station, or for changes in site conditions at any one of the locations through time. Based on the instrumental record, there appear to be no systematic changes in the climate of Indianapolis over the last century or so.

Average annual precipitation for Indianapolis is 39.12″. Precipitation is fairly evenly distributed throughout the year. Each month normally receives at least 3 inches, and the wettest months in spring–early summer only an inch or so more (May 3.66″; June 3.99″; and July 4.32″). Therefore, there is no pronounced wet or dry season. Nearly all rainfall is associated with cyclonic disturbances. The greatest number of days of precipitation occurs in February (15 days expected), followed closely by May, June, and December (14 days). April and November are the months with the fewest days of rain. As one would expect from this, cloudiness is greatest in February with only three perfectly clear days expected, and it is sunniest in July with an average of 11 clear days. Autumn is distinctly sunnier than spring. The maximum monthly precipitation on record was 13.12″ reported in July, 1875, and the minimum monthly precipitation was 0.07″ in March, 1910. In terms of rainfall intensity, an event of approximately 2.5″ in a 24–hour period can be expected about once a year. The maximum recorded 24–hour precipitation was 6.80″ in September, 1895, and in the last 40 years the maximum daily total was 5.32″ on July 1, 1987. Mild droughts may occur in the summer when evaporation is highest.

Indianapolis lies beyond the influence of the lake effect snows generated by Lake Michigan that affect the northern part of Indiana. For the city the average snowfall is approximately 20″; however, it is very variable because winter temperatures are commonly near the freezing point. Snowfalls of 3″ or more occur on average two to three times in a winter. The greatest snowfall on record occurred in the winter season 1977–78 with 57.8″; the lowest in the winter of 1982–83. The maximum monthly amount was 30.6″ in January, 1978, and the maximum daily snowfall was 12.5″ on February 26, 1965.

Average daily temperatures are 26.0°F in January, and 75.1°F in July. Average daily minimum temperatures are at their lowest in January (17.8°F), and highest in July (64.9°F). The average daily maximum is 34.2°F in January and 85.2°F in July. Annual extremes recorded within the area, not necessarily at the airport site, are: highest temperature 107°F on July 25, 1934; lowest temperature -27°F on January 19, 1994, superseding the earlier record low of -25°F on January 5, 1884. Residents of Indianapolis should expect to have 7 days in July and 4 in August with temperatures greater than 90°F; 21 days in December and 24 in January with minimum temperatures below freezing (32°F); and at least 2 days in December and 4 in January with minimum temperatures below 0°F. The average date of the first frost in autumn is October 20, and in the spring the average last occurrence April 22. Daytime relative humidity is highest on average in the winter (72% in December) because of the lower temperatures in this season, but high values in the summer (early afternoon average 56–61% May to August) exacerbate the high temperatures and result in high heat indexes.

Indianapolis is not a windy location. Surface winds are predominantly southwesterly in the summer, and on average less than 10 mph. Northwesterly winds are more frequent, although not predominant in winter. The windiest month is March with average speeds 11.7 mph; the least windy is August, with average speeds of 7.1 mph. Strong winds are uncommon and tend to be associated with thunderstorms and squalls. The greatest gust recorded in the Indianapolis area registered 111 mph from the northwest in June, 1929. However, it is important to note that during the early period of observations wind speeds were measured using anemometers mounted on tall towers, well above the surface, and thus higher wind speeds are to be expected. Wind speed is now measured much closer to the ground (20 ft.). A more recent record gust was 90 mph from the west, recorded on January 25, 1950, and at the airport site the maximum gust reached 74 mph on April 6, 1988.

Severe storms that damage property and cause loss of life are most frequent in the spring. Statewide, Indiana has an annual average of 11 days with tornadoes. In Indianapolis thunderstorm frequency is greatest from May to August, on average occurring on 6 or 7 days in each month, approximately 43 days in total per year.

There are no major topographic barriers or extensive water bodies within the city (other than small reservoirs, lakes, and rivers); therefore the major causes of microscale (neighborhood scale) variations in climate are due to the built environment of the city and the associated human activities.

CATHERINE SOUCH
Indiana University–Purdue University,
Indianapolis

———

Climates of the States: National Oceanic and Atmospheric Administration Narrative Summaries, Tables, and Maps for Each State, 2nd ed. (Detroit, 1980); *Local Climatological Data: Annual Summary with Comparative Data, Indianapolis, Indiana* (National Oceanic and Atmospheric Administration, 1990).

Clowes, Edith Whitehill Hinkel (Sept. 21, 1885–May 22, 1967). Patron of the arts. Born in Buffalo, New York, the daughter of Dr. and Mrs. Frank Whitehill Hinkel, Clowes attended Vassar College, married GEORGE HENRY ALEXANDER CLOWES in 1910, and moved to Indianapolis in 1918 when he took a position at ELI LILLY AND COMPANY. A well-known art collector, she served on the board of trustees of the ART ASSOCIATION OF INDIANAPOLIS. She helped found ORCHARD SCHOOL, the INDIANAPOLIS SYMPHONY ORCHESTRA, Indianapolis Officers Club, and served on various boards and committees including the Women's Committee of the State Symphony Association. Gardening was another interest, and her Indianapolis home, Westerley, featured an English country garden. In 1935, she initiated the Park School House and Garden Tour, an annual event that continues to benefit the school (now PARK TUDOR). In 1964, Clowes was named Woman of the Year by the *Indianapolis Times*.

She received an honorary Doctor of Humane Letters from BUTLER UNIVERSITY in 1962. CLOWES MEMORIAL HALL, a performing arts center on the Butler University campus, was named in honor of her husband, and she and her sons, Dr. George Henry Alexander Clowes, Jr. and Allen Whitehill

Clowes, provided generous support for the structure.

CYNTHIA FAUNCE

Clowes, George Henry Alexander

(Aug. 27, 1877–Aug. 25, 1958). Research director at Eli Lilly and Company. A native of Ipswich, England, Clowes attended the Royal College of Science, now London University. He earned his Ph.D. in chemistry at the University of Gottingen, Germany, then took six months of postgraduate studies at the Sorbonne, France. In 1901, he left England and came to the United States as co-director of what was then Gratwick Cancer Research Laboratories in Buffalo, New York. In 1919, he accepted a position as research associate at ELI LILLY AND COMPANY and two years later became research director. After the discovery of IN-SULIN in 1921, Clowes organized its mass production at the company. Before retiring in 1946 he directed research that developed protamine insulin, liver extract, hypnotic drugs, local anesthetics, antiseptics, and sulfonamides (organic sulfur compounds).

Clowes and his family established the CLOWES FUND, incorporated in 1952 for educational, religious, charitable, and scientific purposes. The fund underwrote the construction of CLOWES MEMORIAL HALL at BUTLER UNIVERSITY and the Clowes Pavilion at the INDIANAPOLIS MUSEUM OF ART. Clowes and his wife also contributed financially and artistically to Trinity Episcopal Church at Meridian and 32nd streets. An avid art collector, Clowes displayed masterpieces by El Greco, Goya, Holbein, Rubens, Titian, Clouet, and Rembrandt in his home. Mrs. Clowes left disposition of the collection to their sons, who donated it to the Indianapolis Museum of Art.

Clowes was a director of the JOHN HERRON ART INSTITUTE from 1933 to 1958, vice-president of the Art Association of Indianapolis, and president and a principal sponsor of the INDIANAPOLIS SYMPHONY ORCHESTRA. He was also a board member of ORCHARD COUNTRY DAY SCHOOL, a trustee of Park School (now PARK TUDOR), chairman of the Indianapolis Committee on Foreign Relations,

and a board member of the Indianapolis Council on World Affairs and the ENGLISH SPEAKING UNION.

PAT WATSON

Indiana Biography Series, Indiana State Library; A. Ian Fraser, *A Catalogue of the Clowes Collection* (Indianapolis Museum of Art).

The Clowes Fund.

A private foundation established in 1952 with gifts from EDITH WHITEHILL CLOWES and GEORGE H. A. CLOWES and their son, Allen Whitehill Clowes. Allen Clowes continues to oversee the fund as its president and treasurer, and several members of the Clowes family serve on the board of directors.

The Clowes Fund makes grants primarily in Indiana and Massachusetts in the fields of higher and secondary education, fine and performing arts, music, marine sciences, and social services. Grants are made for operating budgets, continuing support, building funds, endowment funds, scholarships, and research. The fund makes no grants to individuals or for publications or conferences.

Significant grants made in recent years include the Clowes Fund for Scholars in Medical Education (a graduate endowed scholarship fund at Harvard University), a research endowment for the American College of Surgeons, and major gifts to the University of Washington Medical School and New England Deaconess Hospital in Boston. The INDIANAPOLIS MUSEUM OF ART has been the recipient of several important grants from the Clowes Fund for the purchase of art as well as for operating expenses. BUTLER UNIVERSITY received major grants for the construction of a science building and for CLOWES MEMORIAL HALL, a performing arts center. The Boy Scout Council of Indianapolis also received major support from the fund for a construction project.

The Clowes Fund reported assets in 1991 (the most recent year available) of $43 million. Grants average between $5,000 and $50,000, although some have been for more than $1 million. No specific grant totals are made public.

NORA MCKINNEY HIATT

Clowes Memorial Hall (4600 Sunset Avenue). Performing arts hall. Built in the early 1960s at a cost of $3.5 million, its construction was made possible by major donations from members of the Clowes family in memory of GEORGE H. A. CLOWES and his devotion to the arts. When completed in 1963, this 2,200–seat hall ushered in a new era in the city's cultural history. Indeed, the headline of a contemporary feature article on Clowes Hall in the *New York Times Magazine* read: "'Culture' Comes to Indianapolis." Home of the INDIANAPOLIS SYMPHONY ORCHESTRA for 20 years until the symphony moved downtown to the CIRCLE THEATRE in 1984, Clowes has hosted the full spectrum of performing arts, from traveling Broadway shows and the ballet to chamber music concerts and grand-scale performances of the INDIANAPOLIS OPERA Company.

Sited at the principal entrance to BUTLER UNIVERSITY, the design of Clowes Hall relates to the 1920s Collegiate Gothic buildings on campus through its material and the massing of its towering forms. The reinforced concrete structure with steel truss roof is faced in Indiana limestone on the exterior; the interior finish is largely off-form poured concrete. Architects Evans Woollen of Indianapolis and John M. Johansen of Connecticut had three primary determinants of their design: the acoustical requirements for symphony—a shoe-box shaped hall with parallel sidewalls, high volume, and hard surfaces; the least possible distance for all seats for opera and drama (from stage to back row is only 113 feet); and Continental seating for more center seats, more leg room, and no interrupting aisles. Since the fire code for this seating demanded exits no more than 15 feet apart, the architects took this mandatory module and enclosed the sides with a series of staggered, boxlike wall elements, which are in turn expressed on the exterior. Safety requirements thus led to a design that unified interior and exterior in a novel way. The three balcony levels form a horseshoe around the main orchestra seating. Around the four-story main lobby, the layering of balconies enhances the act of theatergoing.

Called "formidable" on the exterior by some critics and "unfinished" on the interior by others, the design of Clowes Hall was praised and published in several European architectural journals

Clowes Memorial Hall accommodates almost 2,200 patrons with its Continental seating. [Butler University Archives]

and received considerable attention in the national press. The hall's acoustical design by Russell Johnson, with Bolt Baranek and Newman of Boston, has been widely acclaimed.

MARY ELLEN GADSKI

New York Times Magazine, Dec. 24, 1967; "Many-faceted Stage for the Performing Arts," *Architectural Forum*, 119 (Dec., 1963), 99–105.

Coats, Randolph LaSalle (Sept. 14, 1891–June 21, 1957). Fine arts painter and filmmaker. Coats was born in Richmond, Indiana, and studied art at the HERRON SCHOOL OF ART where he was a student of WILLIAM FORSYTH. He also enrolled at the Cincinnati Art Academy, where he remained to teach for four years. Returning to Indiana, he taught at the Art Association of Richmond from 1923 to 1928. Later, he traveled extensively throughout the United States and Europe, and kept a studio in Provincetown, Massachusetts, as well as in Indianapolis.

As a painter, Coats produced portraits of Indiana governors Ralph Gates and Henry Schricker, as well as assisting with a 1953 restoration of the Governors Portraits Collection. As a filmmaker, he produced the motion pictures *New England Art Colonies* and *One Hundred Years of Indiana Art and Artists*.

Coats exhibited and received various prizes at the HOOSIER SALON, INDIANA STATE FAIR, Art

Association of Richmond, and the Art Association of Indianapolis juried art shows. He was a charter member and president of the Indiana Artists Club and held memberships in the Chicago Art Galleries Association, the Cincinnati Art Club, and the Duveneck Society of Painters. Coats was elected to the Indiana Academy in 1976.

FRANK N. OWINGS, JR.

Art Association of Richmond, *Art in Richmond: 1898–1978* (Richmond, Ind., 1978); Mary Q. Burnet, *Art and Artists of Indiana* (New York, 1921); Flora Lauter, *Indiana Artists Active 1940* (Spencer, Ind., 1941).

Coburn, John (Oct. 27, 1825–Jan. 28, 1908). Lawyer, legislator, Civil War general, and U.S. congressman. Born in Indianapolis, Coburn received his education in the public schools and at the Marion County Seminary. He graduated with honors from Wabash College in 1846, studied law with his father, Henry Coburn, and was admitted to the bar in 1849. Elected in 1850 as a Whig to the Indiana House of Representatives from Marion County, he served one term in office.

In 1859 Coburn was elected judge of the Marion County Common Pleas Court. He resigned his judgeship with the outbreak of the Civil War, becoming a colonel with the 33rd Indiana Volunteer Infantry. Captured by Confederate forces during the war, Coburn was exchanged after a few months and later received the surrender of Atlanta from that city's mayor. Coburn was breveted a brigadier general at the conclusion of the war.

Coburn became Marion County Circuit Court judge in 1865 and, a year later, running as a Republican, was elected to the U.S. Congress. During his four terms Coburn served as chairman of the Committee on Public Expenditures and the Committee on Military Affairs. He was responsible for measures providing headstones for soldiers buried in Arlington National Cemetery and publishing Civil War records.

Coburn left Indianapolis briefly in 1884 when he was appointed as a Montana Territory supreme court justice. He returned to his India-napolis law practice in 1885 and remained in the city until his death. Coburn is buried in Crown Hill Cemetery.

RAY BOOMHOWER
Indiana Historical Society

Biographical Directory of the United States Congress; *Biographical Directory of the Indiana General Assembly*, Vol. 1 (Indianapolis, 1980); *Indianapolis Star*, Jan. 29, 1908.

Coca-Cola Bottling Plant (now IPS Service Center), 901 North Carrollton (800 block Massachusetts Avenue). Art Deco factory building. RUBUSH AND HUNTER, arguably the city's premier architectural firm of the interwar years, designed numerous bottling plants throughout the state for Coca-Cola in the 1920s and 1930s. For the capital city they created one like no other, a frothy white terra cotta–clad building lavishly ornamented with geometric fountains and flowers. The WILLIAM P. JUNGCLAUS COMPANY built the plant in 1931; after subsequent additions northeastward in the 1940s, it was said to be the largest Coca-Cola bottling plant in the world. The two-story trapezoidal building fronted on the 800 block of Massachusetts Avenue. The original main entrance (now closed, but intact) opens into a lavish two-story lobby featuring a circular stair, terrazzo floor, and brass-medallioned ceiling. The entrance on the southwest corner of the building at Massachusetts and Carrollton (formerly Ashland) leads into the former receiving room, which still boasts its long marble-topped counter and bright polychrome mosaics. Even the factory portion of the interior features Art Deco details on stair rails and doorknobs. Immediately southwest of the main building stands the one-story garage, also built in 1931 and only slightly less ornate than its companion. In 1969 Coca-Cola sold the building to the Indianapolis Public Schools, and since 1971 the building has housed the IPS Service Center.

GLORY-JUNE GREIFF

Glory June, *Art Deco in Indianapolis* (Indianapolis, 1980).

Cockrum, John Barrett (Sept. 12, 1857–Apr. 15, 1937). Attorney recognized as one of the city's leading corporate lawyers. Born in Oakland City, Indiana, Cockrum came to Indianapolis in 1889 after his appointment as assistant U.S. district attorney. Prior to this he was a partner in Handy, Armstrong, and Cockrum of Boonville, Indiana. He worked with the district attorney's office until 1893 when he became the assistant general attorney for the Lake Erie and Western Railway Company, headquartered in Indianapolis for many years. Two years later he was made general attorney and then general solicitor, a position he retained for 40 years.

During this time he also represented local firms, including an electric railroad company seeking to construct a route between Indianapolis and Anderson in 1899. That year he also served as receiver for the Indianapolis and Broad Ripple Rapid Transit Company. Upon his retirement he acted as advisory counsel to the Lake Erie and Western for a short time and in 1932 entered private practice. He retired from public life, due to illness, three years before his death. He was a delegate to the Republican national conventions of 1888 and 1908 and was a charter member of the COLUMBIA CLUB.

JOAN CUNNINGHAM

Jacob Piatt Dunn, *Greater Indianapolis* (Chicago, 1910), II, 658–660.

Coe, Isaac (July 25, 1782–July 30, 1855). Indianapolis' second physician and controversial commissioner for the state's canal building program. Born in Dover, New Jersey, Coe came to Indianapolis in May, 1821, becoming the second doctor to practice in the capital city. During a malaria epidemic that hit Indianapolis in the summer and fall of that year, he was one of the few physicians in the city able to minister to the sick.

Along with his work as a doctor, Coe was heavily involved in Indianapolis' early churches. In 1823 he helped found the Indianapolis Sabbath School Union, which offered religious instruction to the city's children, and was on the building committee for constructing the First Presbyterian Church. He served as church elder from 1823 to 1853.

From 1836 to 1839, Coe was on the board of fund commissioners for the massive Internal Improvements Act of 1836, which resulted in the state's financial collapse. An Indiana House committee investigating the situation recommended that the state sue Coe for alleged financial improprieties involving the Morris Canal and Banking Company. Although Coe was twice sued by the state for damages, both cases were ultimately dismissed.

RAY BOOMHOWER
Indiana Historical Society

Gayle Thornbrough et al., eds., *The Diary of Calvin Fletcher*, Vol. I (Indianapolis, 1972), 62n.

Coffin, George V. (May 18, 1875–Apr. 10, 1938). Political boss. A native of Jay County, Indiana, "Cap" Coffin settled in Indianapolis in 1901 after retiring from the U.S. Army. After working at CENTRAL STATE HOSPITAL, Coffin joined the INDIANAPOLIS POLICE DEPARTMENT as a patrolman in 1906. During the 1913 flood he was acclaimed for rescuing 500 people in HAUGHVILLE. Having risen to the rank of captain, Coffin was elected Marion County sheriff in 1914, a post he held until January 1, 1918, when he resigned in order to become chief of the Indianapolis Police Department. Following his resignation as chief of police in 1920, he went on to serve in a variety of roles within the local REPUBLICAN PARTY, including city chairman and district chairman. From 1924 to 1926, he was chairman of the Marion County Republican party.

Known among Republicans as "The Boss," Coffin's greatest community role was that of political kingpin. He avoided the limelight, preferring to maneuver behind the scenes, using patronage to benefit party loyalists and to build and maintain a strong constituency. His rapport with blacks delivered votes at a time when many Republicans were accused of being sympathetic to the KU KLUX KLAN. Conservative businessmen trusted him and contributed financially to his candidates. He was a strong family man, supported by local ministers for his stance against liquor traffic. Influential in virtually every area of Indianapolis politics, "Cap" Coffin was the quintessential power broker. He set a winning trend for his party's return to power following the Great Depression, laying important groundwork for a Republican organization that would remain viable for many years.

LINDA H. CROFTS

Jacob Piatt Dunn, *Indiana and Indianans* (Chicago, 1919), IV, 1876–77; Indiana Biography Series, Indiana State Library.

Cold Spring Murder Case. The bodies of Mr. and Mrs. Jacob Young were discovered along WHITE RIVER, near the intersection of today's Lafayette and Cold Spring roads, on September 13, 1868; the murder had actually occurred the previous day. Both victims had been shot in the head; Mrs. Young's body was also burned from the knees to the face, the shotgun blast having ignited her clothing. Even though the murder had occurred in a popular recreational area, apparently the shots were not heard or were not recognized for what they were.

William J. Abrams was the first person arrested in the case, on September 15, when it was discovered that he had purchased the murder weapon. This was followed by the arrests of Silas Hartman on September 21 and his sister Nancy Clem on October 7. The three were indicted for first-degree murder on October 23.

Clem had planned the murder. She had been involved in borrowing large amounts of money and paying it back at exorbitant interest rates by borrowing yet more money. She was deeply in debt to Jacob Young, and apparently the murders were to prevent Young from revealing the situation to Clem's husband, William F. Clem, a grocer "of good reputation" in the city. Mrs. Young had apparently unexpectedly accompanied her husband to Cold Spring, thereby making her murder necessary.

Clem was tried a total of five times. Between hung juries and appeals to the Indiana Supreme Court, she never served a sentence for the murders. She was in jail briefly for separate perjury and forgery charges, and during one of these periods her husband divorced her. Abrams was eventually pardoned, and Hartman committed suicide in jail after confessing to his part in the crime. Clem died in Indianapolis in 1897. She was selling patent medicines at the time of her death.

LEIGH DARBEE
Indiana Historical Society

The Cold Spring Tragedy (Indianapolis, 1869).

Cole Motor Car Company (1909–1925). Indianapolis automobile manufacturer. Joseph Jarrett Cole (1869–1925), a native of Connersville, Indiana, and a graduate of the Richmond Business College, first came to Indianapolis in 1888 as an employee of the Perry Manufacturing Company. From 1896 to 1904, Cole worked for the Moon Brothers Carriage Company of St. Louis. In 1904, he purchased the Gates-Osborne Buggy Company of Indianapolis and formed the Cole Carriage Company. The first Cole motor cars were built by the Cole Carriage Company in 1908. Realizing the great future of the "horseless carriage," Cole decided to concentrate his energies on auto production and formed the Cole Motor Car Company in 1909. The Cole was a luxury car in competition with GM's Cadillac. Unlike General Motors cars, which were manufactured solely with GM components, the Cole was assembled with parts from various manufacturers who upheld the highest standards in quality and craftsmanship. As a result, the Cole was coined "the standardized car."

To promote its product, Cole proved innovative in its advertising. Cole cars competed in various auto races including the 1911 INDIANAPOLIS 500–MILE RACE. In the fall of 1911, a Wright biplane equipped with a Cole engine participated in a coast-to-coast air race. In Indianapolis there was a Cole hot air balloon that hovered over area events; there also were Cole cigars, a Cole baseball team, and a Cole paced the field of the 1924 Indianapolis 500.

Despite such marketing efforts, both sales and auto production declined sharply during the post–World War I years to the point that Cole elected to liquidate while the company was still solvent. Cole closed in 1925. Throughout its 16 years of auto production, 40,717 Cole cars were assembled, most of them in the Indianapolis factory building at 730 East Washington Street, now listed on the National Register of Historic Places.

FRANK N. OWINGS, JR.

Howard R. Delancy, "The History of the Cole Motor Car Company" (D.B.A. dissertation, Indiana University, 1954).

Christopher Coleman. [Indiana Historical Society, Personal—C]

Coleman, Christopher Bush (Apr. 24, 1875–June 25, 1944). Historian, state government official. A native of Springfield, Illinois, where he was educated in the local schools, Coleman attended Laurenceville (N.J.) Academy, Yale University (B.A., 1896), and the University of Chicago (B.D., 1899). In 1900 he became professor of history at BUTLER UNIVERSITY and remained at this institution for the next 19 years as an instructor and an administrator, serving as vice-president of the university from 1912–1919. Interspersed with his work responsibilities were periods of study. In 1904–1905 he was in Europe studying at the University of Berlin and later he did graduate work at Columbia University where he was awarded his Ph.D. degree in 1914. In 1920 he moved to Meadville, Pennsylvania, to become chairman of the history and political science department at Allegheny College.

An invitation to become director of the Indiana Historical Commission (later INDIANA HISTORICAL BUREAU) brought Coleman back to Indianapolis in 1924, and shortly afterwards he also assumed the duties of secretary of the INDIANA HISTORICAL SOCIETY. He was to remain in both of these positions for the rest of this life. A strong proponent of popularizing history, he was tireless in his efforts to show the importance of history and historical figures to the public and the Indiana legislature. During his administration of the Historical Bureau he expanded the *Indiana History Bulletin* to include more news, articles, and information about upcoming historical events. In 1924 he was instrumental in having December 11 declared as "Indiana Day" by the General Assembly to commemorate the state's entry into the Union. Coleman was especially interested in seeing that recognition be given to George Rogers Clark for his victory over the British at Vincennes, and was one of the persons responsible for the establishment of a memorial commemorating this event. Other accomplishments credited to him were the establishment of the Indiana Junior Historical Society, the first state junior historical society in the nation, and the incorporation of a popular genealogy section within the Indiana Historical Society.

From 1936 to 1942 Coleman served as acting director of the INDIANA STATE LIBRARY in addition to his other responsibilities. While in this office he became a leading advocate for libraries at the state level as well as for the establishment of certification for librarians in the state. He also was active in a variety of professional, social, and civic organizations, including THE CHILDREN'S MUSEUM of Indianapolis and the Marion County Board of Charities.

Coleman contributed numerous articles to local, state, and national publications. He also authored several books including *Constantine the Great and Christianity* (1914); *The United States at War: Our Enemies and Our Associates* (1943); and a volume of essays, *The Undying Past and Other Addresses* (1946), which was published posthumously.

ROBERT L. LOGSDON
Indiana State Library

Lana Ruegamer, *A History of the Indiana Historical Society, 1830–1980* (Indianapolis, 1980); *Library Occurrent*, 14 (July–Sept., 1944), 285–286.

Coleman Adoption Services. Licensed adoption agency. The enterprise began in 1894 as a home for unwed mothers. Jointly sponsored by the Meridian Street chapter of the WOMEN'S CHRISTIAN TEMPERANCE UNION and local evangelist William C. Wheeler, its purpose was to provide "wayward girls" with seclusion, shelter, and medical assistance, as well as supervised moral reform. Originally part of Wheeler's Rescue Home and Mission (now WHEELER MISSION MINISTRIES), the girls shared space with the city's alcoholics and vagrants. That combination quickly proved untenable and Wheeler found a separate house for the Rescue Home. It incorporated as the Door of Hope in 1896 and the Indiana Door of Hope Rescue Home in 1906. In 1912 it affiliated with a national chain of similar institutions and took the name Florence Crittenden Home of Indianapolis. But in 1935, when the Crittenden chain insisted its affiliates stop offering mothers the choice of adoption, the local group separated and became the Suemma Coleman Home, named for a volunteer whose death prompted her parents to donate money for a new building.

Changes in medicine and social attitudes gradually refocused the institution's mission. Local hospitals eventually provided delivery services to the home's clients and unwed mothers no longer demanded seclusion. By 1975 the home gave up its residential facilities to specialize in counseling and adoptions, becoming the Suemma Coleman Agency. In 1985 the name again changed to Coleman Adoption Services. At one time a UNITED WAY agency, Coleman is now funded entirely by adoption fees.

KEVIN CORN
Indiana University–Purdue University,
Indianapolis

Floyd T. Romberger, M.D., "The Origin and Development of the Suemma Coleman Agency" (Indianapolis: Privately printed by Coleman Adoption Services, 1979 [updated 1987]).

Coliseum Explosion. One of the worst disasters in Indianapolis history, killing 74 people. On October 31, 1963, Shriners Night at the INDIANA STATE FAIRGROUNDS Coliseum, the Holiday on Ice performance ended abruptly when a propane tank in the concession area ignited and exploded. The concession area was located directly underneath the south side mezzanine seats. A faulty valve on an improperly stored LP gas tank allowed gas to leak near an electric popcorn warmer. The resulting explosion propelled the audience, seating, and slabs of concrete flooring from a 700–square-foot area around aisle 13 through the air and onto the ice. Victims landed up to 60 feet away. Chunks of concrete rained down upon crowded seating areas on all sides.

Some of the box seat spectators fell into the blast pit and were crushed when a damaged support wall collapsed and an additional 500 square feet of floor caved in. A few minutes later the remaining propane tanks created a secondary explosion. A fireball rose from the crater to the ceiling, burning those who had rushed to the area after the first explosion and incinerating those who had fallen into the blast pit.

The audience remained remarkably calm as it left the Coliseum. Some remained to assist the performers and staff in caring for the injured and to free trapped survivors. The police, fire department, Civil Defense, Red Cross, Salvation Army, and hundreds of volunteers used buses, ambulances, and private cars to transport the injured to area hospitals. Rescuers established a temporary hospital in the cattle barn, and the coroner's office set up a temporary morgue on the ice floor. After all other efforts failed, the fire department eventually brought a mobile crane into the Coliseum to lift the concrete slabs still covering victims.

Fifty-four people died outright from impact injuries, flying debris, and burns. The total number of deaths later reached 74. Approximately 400 others were injured, some permanently. The Marion County grand jury indicted the state fire marshal, the Indianapolis fire chief, the general manager and concessions manager of the Indianapolis Coliseum Corporation, and several officers of the LP gas supplier for charges ranging from dereliction of duty to involuntary manslaughter. However, the single conviction—the president of Discount Gas Corporation for assault and battery—was later reversed by the state Supreme Court, and charges against all other individuals were eventually dropped.

The Coliseum Disaster Relief Fund, sponsored by the *Indianapolis Star*, raised over $78,000 from public donations for victim assistance. Years of litigation followed. Over 413 lawsuits, for amounts totaling $70 million, were filed for damages against various insurance companies and the State of Indiana. The LP gas firm's insurance distributed $1.1 million among 379 victims and estates. An out-of-court settlement of $3.5 million resolved hundreds of other individual suits.

VICKIE J. WEST

Thomas E. Drabek, *Disaster in Aisle 13: A Case Study of the Coliseum Explosion* . . . (Columbus: College of Administrative Science, Ohio State University, 1968); *Indianapolis Star*, Nov. 1–7, 1963, Oct. 14, 1973.

Collins, Sid (July 17, 1922–May 2, 1977). Radio broadcaster and the original "Voice of the Indianapolis 500." Born Sidney Cahn in Indianapolis, Collins as a youth assisted his father in a family-owned store and attended Public School 66. His journalistic talents came to light as editor of the Shortridge High School *DAILY ECHO*. Intending to study medicine, he attended Indiana University and graduated with a bachelor of science degree. After serving in the U.S. Army during World War II, Collins began his broadcasting career at WKMO in Kokomo, Indiana.

In 1947 Collins joined the staff of WIBC, Indianapolis, to sell advertising, and soon became a radio announcer and host for "P.M. Party." He earned an assignment as a track announcer at the 1948 INDIANAPOLIS 500–MILE RACE and became the chief announcer in 1952 when WIBC went to lap-by-lap live coverage of the event. Tony Hulman, then owner of the INDIANAPOLIS MOTOR SPEEDWAY, called Collins the "Voice of the 500," a position he held for over 20 years. Collins, who achieved worldwide fame for his broadcasts, originated the phrase "the greatest spectacle in racing," which became synonymous with the race itself.

Besides serving as sports director at WIBC, Collins was a vibrant public speaker, master of ceremonies, and broadcasting personality. He received many honors, including Indiana Sportscaster of the Year, Sagamore of the Wabash, and

was the first broadcaster to receive the key to the City of Indianapolis.

Soon after being diagnosed with amyotrophic lateral sclerosis (Lou Gehrig's disease), Collins took his own life. He is buried at Indianapolis Hebrew Cemetery, South.

JACK D. MORROW
WIBC (retired)

Indianapolis News, Sept. 12, 1973, May 3, 1977.

Columbia Club. Prestigious downtown club. In 1888 a contingent of Indianapolis' most distinguished citizens united to help elect city resident BENJAMIN HARRISON as the nation's 23rd president. This group, the Harrison Marching Society, sporting decorative canes and attired in blue coats, gray vests, and silver derbies, welcomed dignitaries and delegations visiting Indianapolis during the campaign. Their grand processions to Harrison's home on North Delaware Street, where he addressed the crowds, soon became the talk of the town.

The enthusiastic members of the Marching Society decided to secure a clubhouse and increase their numbers from 150 to 400. At the suggestion of Harry S. New, one of the organization's original subscribers and a future U.S. senator and postmaster general, the club was renamed "Columbia" after the popular patriotic synonym for the United States. The Columbia Club was incorporated on February 13, 1889. One of the group's objects, according to an early constitution, was to advance "the science of political economy and of politico-legal historical criticism from the standpoint of the Republican party."

The club's third and present home, a ten-story architectural showpiece designed by RUBUSH AND HUNTER and located on MONUMENT CIRCLE, was dedicated in October, 1925. Listed on the National Register of Historic Places in 1983, the building boasts four floors of overnight guest rooms, banquet facilities for private meetings and parties, a library, billiards room, barbershop, fitness center, and two dining rooms. It has hosted scores of distinguished visitors, from political figures to celebrities, including every Republican president from Harrison through George Bush.

Although the Columbia Club has deep GOP roots, it has evolved over the years to become less exclusively white, male, and Republican. A resolution to end racial discrimination passed the club's board in the late 1960s, women were admitted to membership (and to the Harrison Dining Room, a male bastion) in the late 1970s, and a Democrat was elected president of the organization in 1979. Membership is currently limited to 3,500.

ROBERT L. GILDEA

Marjie Gates Giffin, *If Tables Could Talk* (Indianapolis: privately printed, 1988); Harry K. Stormont, comp. and ed., *A History of the Columbia Club of Indianapolis* (Indianapolis, 1925).

Columbia Conserve Company. Nationally known experiment in industrial democracy. The Columbia Conserve Company, located at 1735 Churchman Avenue (at the BELT LINE RAILROAD), canned a variety of soups and related items from 1903 until it was sold in 1953. Under the leadership of WILLIAM POWERS HAPGOOD, who served as Columbia's president throughout its history, the company in 1917 launched an experiment in workplace democracy that was to last a quarter of a century and achieved both national and international recognition.

Workplace democracy at Columbia was based on three innovations: (1) a workers' council; (2) a profit-sharing plan; and (3) a stock-purchase plan designed to bring about employee ownership and legal control of the company. The council made decisions on virtually all policy and operational matters, such as the selection of supervisory staff, the number of hours worked, salary scales, and physical plant. It alone had the authority to discipline or discharge an employee. Council participation was eventually opened to all workers and decisions were arrived at through discussion, debate, and majority vote at regular weekly meetings.

In 1925 a contract between stockholders and workers called for all profit after stockholders' dividends to be used to purchase common stock that would be held collectively by workers in a trust. As of 1930, 51 percent of common stock was owned collectively by workers who, accordingly, had legal control of the company. Workers owned 63 percent of common stock by 1937, making Columbia one of the earliest producer-cooperatives in the nation. In addition to a guaranteed annual salary, the list of workers' benefits at Columbia was impressive: free health care (including optometry and dentistry) for workers and dependents, a three-week paid vacation, an old age and disability pension, and educational benefits.

Although the Great Depression caused difficult times for Columbia in the 1930s, no employees were laid off; instead all workers accepted substantial pay cuts. By 1942, however, worker discontent resulted in a strike against the company. Late that same year workers sued for receivership against Columbia and its management staff, while trustees of the collectively held stock filed a countersuit to dissolve the trust. The Marion County Superior Court found in favor of the company in 1943 and ordered that the trust be dissolved and that stock be distributed to individual workers, thus ending Columbia's experiment in workplace democracy. In 1953 the company was sold to John Sexton and Company of Chicago.

KENNETH COLBURN, JR.
Butler University

Columbia Conserve Company Collection, Lilly Library, Indiana University, Bloomington; William P. Hapgood, *An Experiment in Industrial Democracy* (Indianapolis, [1933]); Kim McQuaid, "Industry and the Co-operative Commonwealth," *Labor History*, 17 (1976), 510–529.

Commerce and Industry, Architectural and Spatial Characteristics of. The architecture and location of commerce and industry in Indianapolis bear silent witness to the evolution of a small rustic town into a modern metropolis. In the early years, political activity lured visitors and residents to the capital city and sustained trade and manufacture. A landlocked city without a major waterway on which to transport its products to distant markets, Indianapolis awaited the development of mechanized land transportation to flourish commercially and industrially. Only after 1847, when the first rail line to Indianapolis was completed, did commercial and industrial expansion of the city begin in earnest. Numerous downtown buildings from the late 19th century and early 20th century reflect the eras of prosperity in the city's history and the architectural tastes of the times. Today, the commercial and industrial architecture of Indianapolis looks much like that of other cities of its size in the Midwest that have learned to cope with periods of decline, yet have emerged hopeful of the future.

The prominence of Washington Street as an avenue of trade was established early in the city's history. When ALEXANDER RALSTON platted the city, he clearly intended Washington Street to be a main east-west thoroughfare; Ralston drew Washington Street 120 feet wide. Lots on Washington Street—especially where it intersected with Meridian Street —commanded the highest prices at the land sales. The street became an avenue of hotels, dry goods stores, and taverns, especially after it became part of the National Road and later U.S. 40. The architecture of the street today does not suggest its early 19th century function—no buildings from that period remain—but this early route of trade set a pattern for the location of commercial buildings.

In the antebellum period, manufactures located their businesses along transportation routes and near a source of power. The WHITE RIVER, the major waterway flowing into the city, proved unnavigable most of the year, but it did provide power for industry. Early mills located along the falls of the White River where the drop in the river provided sufficient power to turn water wheels. In the 1830s, the CENTRAL CANAL began to furnish power for industry. Mills, tanneries, brickyards, and blacksmiths were counted among the earliest industrial endeavors. Many of these were either located in homes or in barn-like buildings of frame or brick.

While industry awaited a means of transporting its products to distant markets, the business of government stimulated trade. Governmental activity encouraged the establishment of taverns, boarding houses, and hotels to serve the needs of travelers and governmental workers. Barter as a means of trade diminished, the need for specie increased, and banking grew. It was during this period that the Second State Bank of Indiana was established in Indianapolis in 1834, and STOUGHTON FLETCHER began Fletcher Bank in 1839. In this period the association of Indianapolis and the insurance industry began; it was in 1836 that the Indianapolis Insurance Company was chartered with full banking powers. No wholesale district developed in the antebellum era and Indianapolis continued to function like a big small town. Construction materials evolved from crude logs to frame to brick, each change signifying more permanence and stability.

A turning point in the city's manufacturing history came in 1847 when the first railroad line reached Indianapolis from Madison, Indiana. With the construction of the MADISON AND INDIANAPOLIS RAILROAD, the capital for the first time gained easy access to shipping on the Ohio River. The presence of the Madison and Indianapolis depot on South Street dictated that industries relying on the rail transport to import raw materials or to export finished products be located on the south side of town. Along this and subsequent railroad lines many manufacturers built their factories. By the CIVIL WAR, ironworks, pork packers, lumber mills, cigar makers, and breweries were located along railroad lines to the east, west, and south of the commercial district.

As in much of the Midwest the period after the Civil War saw commerce and industry expand and small establishments consolidate into larger ones. A WHOLESALE DISTRICT developed south of Washington Street on Meridian, Pennsylvania, Delaware, Maryland, and Georgia streets, partly due to the location of train depots on the south side. Proof of the growth of the economy was the establishment of banks. Indiana National Bank (the successor of the Indianapolis Branch of the State Bank of Indiana) and Merchants National Bank were chartered during the 1860s. Retailers began to "modernize" their buildings, installing cast iron fronts painted to look like stone. New commercial buildings such as dry goods stores and hotels, with Italianate and Second Empire features, rose on Washington and intersecting street.

As adjuncts to downtown development, small service centers were built on major thoroughfares near residential areas. In an era of horse, foot, or bicycle travel, people lived close to their place of employment. Thus, residential areas developed around factories. These areas often began as separate towns until Indianapolis extended its city limits to include them. For example, the town of HAUGHVILLE, now part of Indianapolis, provided commercial services for working class immigrants who labored in foundries. In the area known as Haughville today, commercial buildings of Italianate and 20th century functional architecture—a small main street—suggest the life of the past.

Industrial buildings continued to locate along railroad lines, especially along the BELT LINE RAILROAD built in the 1870s. Companies such as NORDYKE AND MARMON and the Indianapolis Brewing Company built large factory complexes along the railroad lines. These multi-acre complexes of brick functional architecture frequently included office buildings and warehouses.

In decades that bracketed the year 1900, transportation and demographics continued to influence the location and kind of commercial buildings. The expansion of the street railway system provided Indianapolis residents more flexibility in terms of where they lived. Although some residential areas had been built along streetcar lines since the 1870s, more urban dwellers sought the atmosphere of the country in the suburbs. Invariably, entrepreneurs opened restaurants, groceries, and dry goods shops in one- and two-story brick buildings along the route of the street railway to serve commuters.

Proof of the growth of commerce and industry around 1900 was the construction of multi-storied commercial buildings downtown. Banks that had managed to survive the hard times of the 1890s constructed new facilities. In 1897, after a disastrous fire, Indiana National Bank built a new building on Virginia Avenue that recalled the classic lines of the Bank of England. The MERCHANTS NATIONAL BANK BUILDING at the corner of Washington and Meridian streets is another example of new multi-storied banks that were designed to evoke images of affluence and stability. Other large commercial buildings reflected the prosperity that was gripping the Midwest. Across the street from the Merchants Bank building arose the L. S. AYRES AND COMPANY department store. Ayres anchored the commercial block that included large stores such as L. STRAUSS AND COMPANY and Kresge's.

After 1900, commercial and industrial companies again began to consolidate or expand their operations. ELI LILLY AND COMPANY, a pharmaceutical firm begun in 1876, built a modern four-story building in 1905. Small mills began to merge with larger ones in order to manufacture flour or meal competitively with larger milling companies in neighboring states. In 1909, the Evans Milling Company and the Acme Milling Company, both along White River, merged to form the ACME-EVANS COMPANY and by 1919 had constructed a multi-story modern daylight mill. Commercial businesses, most notably grocery stores, began to form chain establishments that were experimenting with some uniformity of architecture as a means to building brand identification. In Indianapolis, grocers like Kroger, Piggly-Wiggly, Standard, and A & P built stores in neighborhood service centers. Although these buildings sometimes remain, they have often been remodeled and their original architecture disguised behind a false front.

Automobiles changed the face of the industry and commerce in Indianapolis. Several manufacturers of automobiles built large factories in the city after the turn of the century. The COLE factory in the 700 block of East Washington Street—beside the railroad tracks—and the STUTZ building in the 1200 block of North Capitol are two extant examples of automobile factories that utilize functional industrial architecture with stylized details. The consolidation of the automobile industry in the 1920s and the Great Depression of the 1930s dealt automobile manufacturers in Indianapolis a cruel blow; none survived the hard times, although automobile parts manufacturers continue to be a significant industry in the city. In addition to their industrial importance, the automobile manufacturers contributed to the commercial growth of the city. Entrepreneurs built automobile showrooms of art deco architecture on streets north of the Circle in the 1920s. Further, the proliferation of automobiles necessitated the construction of service stations to sell gasoline. Service stations located on street corners throughout the city to serve the commercial needs of an increasingly mobile population.

Increased mobility continued to characterize the post–World War II population, and entrepreneurs reacted to this change with modifications to the location and style of the commercial buildings. As new residential suburbs were constructed to accommodate returning servicemen and their families, strip SHOPPING MALLS and eventually enclosed malls simulated a small town shopping experience in a concrete and glass environment. In the 1950s, some 20 malls were constructed in suburban areas of Indianapolis with Glendale Mall (1958) the premier example of the new trend. Shopping centers generally prospered, while owners of downtown stores looked for customers and sought new ways to remain economically viable.

In the 1960s, commercial and industrial companies began to replace old downtown buildings with new ones along major highway routes, especially the I–465 beltway that encircles the city. Industrial parks such as Park Fletcher, built in the mid–1960s, signaled the pattern of the future. With the increase in truck transportation, factories, warehouses, and distribution centers located along highways. In addition, businesses such as life insurance companies built multi-storied office buildings along I–465. College Life (which constructed the PYRAMIDS) and Golden Rule are two examples of insurance companies along the beltway.

In the late 1960s, city planners began their attempts to halt the erosion of commerce and the service industry from the downtown area. In 1968, articles in the Indianapolis newspapers predicted a "changing skyline" and articulated the need for large skyscrapers as a statement that downtown was still a viable economic entity. Banks led the way with new monuments to their success. These modern buildings rejected the solid Romanesque and Classical architecture of the late 19th and early 20th centuries in favor of streamlined structures of glass and concrete. In 1967, the Indiana National Bank (now NBD Bank) built the first of these skyscrapers. American United Life Insurance Company joined this architectural revival of downtown Indianapolis in 1982. In the 1980s First Indiana Federal Savings Bank, Bank One, and Merchants Bank also constructed towers and in turn leased space to a variety of businesses.

In the 1990s Indianapolis is a mosaic of old and new. Next to a modern giant pharmaceutical company, Eli Lilly, at the corner of South and Delaware streets stands a small shop built in 1848 that once sold gingersnaps and beer to southside residents. Sandwiched in the midst of parking garages in the 400 block of North Illinois, there is a two-story building dating to the second half of the 19th century. At the corner of Washington and Meridian streets, the Merchants Bank building and the now abandoned L. S. Ayres building stand sentinel, silent reminders of the Indianapolis of the early 20th century when multi-storied commercial centers rose as testimony to the prosperity of the city and the times. A few blocks to the north, modern sleek towers rise vertically, hinting at the future of the city. From downtown the commercial and industrial buildings expand outward to the edges of the city and line modern highway routes. The architecture of 19th and 20th centuries co-mingle and co-exist, forging a story of resilience and hope.

LINDA B. WEINTRAUT

Commercial Club. See Chamber of Commerce

Commission for Downtown. See Indianapolis Downtown, Inc.

Committee of Public Safety. Organizing and oversight committee for a temporary local militia. In the summer of 1877 the nation experienced the most serious labor disruption in its history. On July 16 a spontaneous labor uprising against the BALTIMORE AND OHIO RAILROAD at Martinsburg, West Virginia, spread in a few days to paralyze nearly every railroad center from Baltimore to St. Louis. The strike was set off by a coordinated policy of wage cuts by railroad officials and other grievances, and in the beginning the public sided with the workers. When the strike reached Indianapolis on Monday, July 23, great destruction of property and loss of lives had already occurred.

Mayor JOHN CAVEN and the city's strike leader, Warren H. Sayre, secretary of the Brotherhood of Locomotive Engineers, shared a horror at the events that had taken place elsewhere. Sayre assured Caven that his men were law abiding and would not use force. In light of this promise, Caven met with railroad officials and swore in 200 railroad employees as special deputies to protect railroad property. At the Union Depot well-organized and disciplined strikers spoke to the crews of arriving trains, and passenger and freight cars, guarded by conductors and porters, piled up on the sidings. Caven, while noting the peaceableness of the strikers, convened a citizens meeting before the courthouse the evening of July 24, the strike's second day, to enroll a militia under a committee of public safety to act with the mayor and the sheriff. The results, however, were disappointing; only a hundred men enlisted the following day.

The strike brought the economy of the city to a near standstill: wholesale merchants did little business, the Board of Trade closed, KINGAN AND COMPANY and many other factories shut down. The community divided between sympathizers who hoped that local railroad officials would offer a compromise and strike opponents who believed that the strikers were a mob that threatened people's rights. WALTER Q. GRESHAM, federal judge for the District of Indiana, took the latter view. He placed the railroads in receivership, then under his jurisdiction, and authorized the U.S. marshal to arrest strikers interfering with the movement of the trains. He also called for the establishment of a militia, commanded by business and professional leaders, to break the strike and end the embargo at the depot.

On Thursday, July 26, with the support of BENJAMIN HARRISON, former governor Conrad Baker, former mayor DANIEL MACAULEY, and other notables, Gresham forced a merger with Caven's committee of public safety in which Gresham and four others held five of the seven leadership posts and Macauley was named brigadier general of the so-named Indiana Legion. Gresham's group held complete control of the city's military forces. The city council on Friday approved a Gresham resolution that empowered the committee to take any further steps it deemed essential. By week's end the city held 271 regular army troops, at least 750

more under Macauley, 72 Montgomery Guards under LEW WALLACE, and others—in all at least 1,100 men at arms and perhaps twice that number. Police, sheriff's deputies, and deputized strikers totaled another 400 to 600. In a city of 67,000, then, perhaps one of every four adult males was responsible for protecting the city and available to put down riots. Indianapolis had become an armed camp.

In fact, the strike had ended Friday evening. All but two companies of the Indiana Legion were mustered out Saturday and the mayor reiterated his statement of the previous day that no impediment existed in Indianapolis to the movement of trains.

Only employees of the Bee Line Railroad won rescission of the 20–percent pay cut and the promise of regular paydays. Other strikers lost their jobs or returned on their employers' terms. Judge Gresham outraged the mayor by bringing Sayre and 14 others to trial, with all but Sayre and one other striker convicted and sentenced to terms ranging from 30 days to 6 months. The Gresham committee of public safety wanted the voluntary legion to be made permanent, available to suppress mobs at their "first outbreak," but the circumstances hardly warranted it. At a time when 53 died at Pittsburgh, 18 at Chicago, and 11 at Baltimore, the only casualty in Indianapolis was a militiaman whose foot was stepped on by a horse. The city remained peaceful and orderly during the Great Railroad Strike because of the determination of the strikers to avoid bloodshed and the near unanimity of the city's elite which united itself against the strike however peacefully conducted.

WILLIAM DOHERTY
Marian College

William Doherty, "Indianapolis in the 1870s: Hard Times in the Gilded Age" (Ph.D. dissertation, Indiana University, 1981); Charles W. Calhoun, *Gilded Age Cato: The Life of Walter Q. Gresham* (Lexington, Ky., 1987); Jerry M. Cooper, *The Army and Civil Disorder* (Westport, Conn., 1980).

Committee on Post-War Planning. Citizen planning committee. Midway through WORLD WAR II civic leaders concluded that Indianapolis government had not kept pace with wartime industrial and population changes, resulting in a lack of badly needed public improvements and expanded services. In response, Mayor ROBERT H. TYNDALL in 1943 appointed a 150–member citizens' committee to recommend the city's postwar agenda. George Kuhn, former CHAMBER OF COMMERCE president, was appointed chairman of the committee.

Organized into subcommittees, the members spent a year studying individual problems. At a formal dinner hosted by department store owner William H. Block, the committee presented its plan calling for $25 million in expenditures over seven years to improve sewers, schools, recreation, government, and transportation systems. Also addressed were slum clearance and redevelopment, SMOKE ABATEMENT, railroad grade separations, property reassessment, and a new municipal building.

Having presented its plan the committee disbanded, leaving City Hall to work out the details. The following year a newly created Indianapolis Redevelopment Commission and the City Planning Commission were given the task of implementing the recommendations. Little of the plan was executed immediately. Five years later the city had just begun work on a $2 million sewer program, passed a new parking law, and bought 178 acres for slum clearance. Critics argued that the grandiose plan did not address immediate postwar needs and merely restated previous unfulfilled plans. The committee's recommendations did, however, guide local planning until a similar citizens committee, the GREATER INDIANAPOLIS PROGRESS COMMITTEE, was formed in the mid–1960s.

MICHELLE D. HALE

Indianapolis Newspaper Index, Indiana State Library; Indianapolis Chamber of Commerce, *The Post-War Plan for Indianapolis* (Indianapolis, 1944).

Common Council. Former legislative body of city government. From 1891 until 1970 the legislative branch of Indianapolis city government was the nine-member Common Council. This body had the power to approve city ordinances, the city government budget, and the issuance of city bonds. The council could override the mayor's veto of its actions by a two-thirds vote. The council also could fill a vacancy in the mayor's office with an acting mayor until the next election.

Members were elected to the Common Council by a system that combined district representation, party slating, and at-large voting. Each major political party presented voters with a slate of six council nominees—one from each of six districts in the city. Although nominated by district, councilmen were elected citywide. Each voter in the city could vote for up to nine of the candidates, and the nine with the highest vote totals became the Common Council. This six-nominee, nine-winner system usually meant a six-member council majority for the party that won the mayor's office, but the losing party was still guaranteed at least three councilmen.

When UNIGOV took effect in 1970 the Indianapolis Common Council was combined with the Marion County Council to form a CITY-COUNTY COUNCIL. The City-County Council has assumed the Common Council's former responsibilities.

WILLIAM BLOMQUIST

Community Action of Greater Indianapolis. Nonprofit program for low-income, disabled, and elderly persons. Community Action offers direct and referral services in the areas of education and development, energy assistance, housing rehabilitation, and nutrition and health. The organization focuses its efforts on the disabled and elderly low-income citizens of Boone, Hamilton, Hendricks, and Marion counties. It was established by Mayor John Barton and a group of concerned citizens called the Conference Group On Poverty as a result of the federal Economic Opportunity Act of 1964. Originally called Community Action Against Poverty, the organization served only Marion County until 1982. Some of its early programs were Operation Late Start, Legal Services Organization, GLEANERS FOOD BANK, Mapleton–Fall Creek Association, and the Near Eastside Multi-Services Center.

One of Community Action's most important services is HEAD START, a federally funded education program for low-income, preschool parents and children in Marion and Hamilton counties.

Other programs include the Community Action Youth Program for junior high and high school students; the Foster Grandparent program, which matches low-income, elderly adults with at-risk youth; and the TeenAge Parenting Program, which assists teenage parents through GED preparation, parenting training, money management, and other life skills. Community Action also provides food items to soup kitchens and food pantries. Other services include AIDS prevention programs, energy assistance, and housing services, including weatherization, housing rehabilitation, and Section 8 certification.

Community Action is governed by a board of directors representing the public (government) sector, the private sector, and the low-income population in the four-county area.

BRIDGET ROGERS
Community Action of Greater Indianapolis, Inc.

Community Centers. Centers providing a variety of social service programs to neighborhood residents. The history of Indianapolis community centers is rich and varied, some having their beginnings in local initiatives, others resulting from national trends.

Some of the earliest centers, such as FLANNER HOUSE (1898) and CHRISTAMORE HOUSE (1905), were founded as part of the settlement house movement. In the early days of settlements, well-to-do volunteers worked with low-income residents in the area. Emphasizing cultural and educational programming, settlements played an important role in integrating immigrants into the community. Other centers with roots in the settlement house movement are Concord Center (1875) and MARY RIGG Neighborhood Center (originally called the AMERICAN SETTLEMENT, 1911).

The neighborhood centers sponsored by religious groups have traditionally centered on recreational and educational programs for children, youth, and senior citizens. They also provide emergency assistance with food and clothing. The United Methodist church sponsors the FLETCHER PLACE Community Center and BRIGHTWOOD Community Center. Edna Martin Christian Center is connected with the American Baptist church. The Jewish Community Center was founded in 1924 to serve the growing Jewish population in Indianapolis. Originally in a downtown location, it moved to a large facility on the north side in the late 1950s. The SALVATION ARMY also has a long history of providing service in Indianapolis and currently operates facilities downtown, at FOUNTAIN SQUARE, and at 4400 North High School Road (Eagle Creek Center).

In the early 1970s, the City of Indianapolis used federal antipoverty funds to develop a number of multiservice centers, including Citizens, FOREST MANOR, Southeast, Southwest, Near Eastside, and the HISPANIC CENTER. Local neighborhood associations also played an important role in founding these centers. In the early years the program focus was on information and referral and on housing a variety of programs of other agencies in order to increase accessibility for local residents.

Several centers have been founded by the grassroots initiatives of neighborhood residents. Hawthorne Center was established in 1923 to provide service and recreational programs. Martin Luther King, Crooked Creek, and Greenleaf centers were founded in the 1970s by neighborhood residents who saw increasing needs in their communities.

The variety of centers operating under different auspices created challenges that led to the coordination of services among some centers. In the 1960s, Christamore, Concord, Mary Rigg, Hispanic Center, Hawthorne, and Butler-Tarkington (later renamed Martin Luther King Center) joined together to form Indianapolis Settlements, Inc. (ISI). In 1983, the major funders of human services in Indianapolis, in response to a study done by the COMMUNITY SERVICE COUNCIL, created Community Centers of Indianapolis, Inc. (CCI) as a federation of multiservice centers. The original members of CCI included all the ISI centers and centers established by the City of Indianapolis. They were later joined by FLANNER HOUSE, Greenleaf, and Crooked Creek.

The CCI annual budget of $8.5 million comes largely from five sources: UNITED WAY, city funds, state funds, CENTRAL INDIANA COUNCIL ON AGING, and Indianapolis Network for Employment and Training. It also receives foundation support for specific projects. Its programs serve 35,000 persons each year, primarily through the Access Program's counseling, referrals, and emergency assistance.

ROSEMARY DORSA
Community Centers of Indianapolis

Community Chest. See United Way of Central Indiana

Community Hospitals. City's largest health care network. With three hospitals, several MedCheck immediate medical care centers, and a variety of specialized services, Community serves thousands of area citizens every year.

After World War II, Indianapolis grew toward the suburbs. HOSPITALS were crowded, and most were far from the citizens of the city's eastside. To champion the cause of quality, accessible health care for the entire city, Edward Gallahue led a concerned civic group to form the Indianapolis Hospitals Development Association. Part of their challenge was to build a new eastside hospital on land donated by Gallahue for that purpose at 16th Street and Ritter Avenue.

Funding for the hospital came from business, industry, and private citizens. Volunteers conducted house-to-house campaigns. Employees in several companies donated funds through payroll deduction. The *East Side Herald* dubbed it "the swiftest, most effective fund raising campaign of our time." Vice-President Richard M. Nixon attended the groundbreaking for the newly named Community Hospital, which admitted its first patient on August 6, 1956.

Since then, the hospital has expanded seven times, has been renamed Community Hospital East, and has developed into part of a citywide health care network: Community Hospitals Indianapolis. In 1985, as the city's northeast side grew rapidly, the hospital built Community Hospital North, a full-service hospital at 82nd Street and Shadeland Avenue, to serve that area's expanding population. Also in the 1980s, Community opened five MedChecks, urgent care clinics for neighborhood residents' immediate medical needs.

In 1989 the city's south side had become another area of rapid growth and development, and Community again expanded into a growing population. On September 25, 1989, Community acquired University Heights Hospital, now Community Hospital South, with a commitment to expand services. This newest hospital sits at 1402 East County Line Road South, near Greenwood Park Mall. This hospital began a major expansion in 1992, adding maternity services, increased cardiology capabilities, and more.

Community Hospitals Indianapolis offers acute medical and surgical services at each hospital, as well as a variety of specialized health care programs. Services include the nationally recognized Regional Cancer Center; the Hook Rehabilitation Center; a full range of cardiovascular services; mental health services for all ages, both inpatient and outpatient; older adult services; Neurocare Services; and women's and children's services, including maternity care and pediatrics. Other services include outpatient surgery; Family Home Health Care; emergency services; laser surgery; and several other programs and services.

BETH A. DeHOFF
Community Hospitals Indianapolis

Community Leaders Allied for Superior Schools. A not-for-profit, business-education coalition dedicated to improving the education of Indianapolis youth. Dissatisfied with the quality of high school graduates entering their businesses, a cadre of Indianapolis business and civic leaders, headed by Andre B. Lacy and Thomas W. Binford, formed Community Leaders Allied for Superior Schools (CLASS) in 1989.

CLASS works for educational improvement in the city's public school system. Among its programs is the preparation of *Blueprint 2005—What Indianapolis Business Desires of Schools*, a document delineating 45 outcomes Indianapolis employers expect of high school graduates of 2005. The expected outcomes include being able to read at a 12th-grade level, knowing how to add, subtract, multiply, and divide, having a working knowledge of a foreign language, and understanding the basics of personal financial management. In addition, *Blueprint 2005* calls for high school graduates to exhibit life skills—knowledge of health and nutrition, cultural diversity, the fine arts, and literature.

Blueprint 2005 was formally adopted by the board of Indianapolis Public Schools (IPS) in July, 1992. Since then CLASS has disseminated the document to the public and is working with IPS and other Marion County school districts to implement it.

CLASS is funded by a 5–year, $5 million grant from the LILLY ENDOWMENT. Operating funds come from annual dues of the 46 Indianapolis executives who are members of CLASS.

PATRICIA L. BRENNAN
Community Leaders Allied for Superior Schools

Community Service Council of Central Indiana.

The Community Service Council (CSC), as well as the United Way of Central Indiana, evolved from the CHARITY ORGANIZATION SOCIETY (1880) and related efforts to coordinate charitable efforts to help the needy. The Indianapolis Council of Social Agencies, CSC's oldest direct antecedent, was established in 1923. According to the organization committee minutes, it was to be " . . . a means of advising together and planning the social work of the city so that the work of each organization will supplement the work of all other organizations."

The Council of Social Agencies was governed by delegates who represented social service agencies. As the organization became the Health and Welfare Council (1950) and, later, the Community Service Council (1961), governance fell to a citizen board of directors. The board over the years has included some of the city's most prominent civic and philanthropic leaders.

The Council, which originally operated under the aegis of the Community Fund, became an independent agency in the 1950s, and merged again with UNITED WAY in 1977. In the merger, a very unusual Council–United Way arrangement at the time, CSC retained its corporate identity and board of directors but became an operating division of United Way.

The Council historically has worked closely with funding and policymaking bodies, both as a resource and a grant recipient. Since 1978, CSC has provided staff support for the Coalition for Human Services Planning, an association of major public and private funders of human services.

The Community Service Council today conducts needs assessments, manages interagency coordination and planning initiatives, and promotes human service policy development, all very much in keeping with the purposes set forth for the Council of Social Agencies in 1923. Other functions historically associated with CSC have been spun off or abandoned over the years; among them: Information and Referral (now the Information and Referral Network); Volunteer Action Center, now a fellow division of United Way; and a library, abandoned in the 1970s with the emergence of the social work collection at the library of INDIANA UNIVERSITY–PURDUE UNIVERSITY, INDIANAPOLIS.

IRVIN S. KATZ
United Way of Central Indiana

John R. Seeley, et al., Community Surveys, Inc., *Community Chest: A Case Study in Philanthropy* (Toronto, 1957).

Composers.

Even though Indianapolis is not known as a music center, it has been home to a number of noteworthy 20th-century composers, especially in popular music, JAZZ, and BLUES. Perhaps the earliest of Indianapolis' well-known composers were brothers ALBERT AND HARRY VON TILZER. Harry, said to have written more than 3,000 songs, had his first success with "Only a Bird in a Gilded Cage." He also wrote "Nellie." Albert Von Tilzer is probably most famous for the music to "Take Me Out to the Ball Game" (1908). During this same period Indianapolis native Frederick "Fritz" Krull became well known for setting James Whitcomb Riley's poems to music, while Fred A. Jewell began to earn his sobriquet of "Indiana March King" by composing the earliest of what would grow to be nearly 200 marches.

A number of Indianapolis composers made significant contributions to ragtime music. MAY AUFDERHEIDE's popularity as a ragtime songwriter was at its height from 1909 to 1918. May's notable efforts included "Dusty Rag" (1908), "Buzzer Rag" (1909), and "Blue Ribbon Rag" (1910). She also collaborated with Indianapolis pianist Paul Pratt, whose rags "Vanity" and "Walhalla" were published in 1909 and 1910. Julia Neibergall published "Hoosier Rag" in 1907 and in 1911 "Horseshoe Rag." Glenn Leap, another Indianapolis rag writer, wrote "Stewed Chicken" (1912) and "That Demon Rag" (1911). One of his early successful vaudeville songs was "Everything He Does Just Pleases Me." Cecil Duane Crabb turned out several compositions after 1910 including "Klassicle Rag" and "Fluffy Ruffles" (1917). The most famous of the local ragtimers was J. RUSSELL ROBINSON, whose early hits included "Sapho Rag" (1909) and "Dynamite Rag" (1911). "Eccentric Rag" brought Robinson's ragtime career to its peak, and his hit song "Margie" followed in 1920.

One of the most famous Indiana composers of any era was Hoagland "Hoagy" Carmichael, who brought his orchestra to Indianapolis in the mid–1920s. One of his first successful numbers was "Washboard Blues"; Al Jolson made "Lazy Bones" popular, and "Stardust" achieved international renown. Hoagy's early influence was important for the introduction of "sock-time," a rhythmic innovation which was present in all the better hot jazz coming from campuses in the 1920s—the precursor of "swing."

In the fields of jazz and blues, Indianapolis produced composers such as LEROY CARR, whose works, including his song about Indianapolis, "Naptown Blues" (1929), were to have an impact upon both his contemporaries and future blues artists; FRANCIS HILLMAN "SCRAPPER" BLACKWELL; Frederick Dewayne "Freddie" Hubbard, whose 1972 album, "First Light," won a Grammy as best jazz performance of the year; Leroy Vinnegar, best known for his compositions "Hard to Find" and "For Carl," which was dedicated to the memory of fellow city native, pianist Carl Perkins; James Louis "J.J." Johnson, considered by most critics to be the "founder of the modern generation of jazz trombonists" and the composer of a number of extended pieces such as "El Camino Real, Sketch for Trombone and Orchestra"; Robert J. "Bobby" Sherwood, Edward Lamonte "Pete" Franklin and his mother, Flossie Woods Franklin, who wrote many songs for Leroy Carr and "Scrapper" Blackwell; and WES and MONK MONTGOMERY. Other notable blues and jazz composers with Indianapolis ties include William Thomas "Champion Jack" Dupree and James "Yank" Rachell.

In the area of pop-rock, Indianapolis' two best known composers are Henry Lee Summer and John Hiatt. Since the early 1980s Summer has released a series of albums including "Stay With Me" (1984), "Henry Lee Summer" (1988), and "Way Past Midnight" (1991). From the release of his first album, "Hanging Around the Observatory," in 1974, through 1993's "Perfectly Good Guitar," Hiatt has written over 600 songs which have been performed by well over 100 artists including Bob Dylan, Bonnie Raitt, the Neville Brothers, and Roseanne Cash.

In the 1970s Indianapolis-born composer Nancy Ford, along with her partner and fellow Hoosier, lyricist Gretchen Cryer, had the distinction of becoming the first women collaborators to have a show reach Broadway: *Shelter* (1973). Among their other works were the hit shows *The Last Sweet Days of Isaac* (1970) and *I'm Getting my Act Together and Taking it on the Road* (1978).

During the first half of the 20th century, the city's best known composers of orchestral and sacred music included Ellis Levey, ELMER ANDREW STEFFEN, Carl Hahn, Adolph Schellschmidt, Nicola A. Montani, and Charles F. Hanson. Contemporary composers include Indianapolis native Easley Blackwood, Jr., Butler University's Michael Schelle, and INDIANAPOLIS SYMPHONY ORCHESTRA Composer-in-Residence David Ott.

JEFFERY DUVALL
BETH HOLMES HAWKS

Compton, Mildred Sartor (July 18, 1917–Aug. 8, 1993). Former director of The Children's Museum (TCM). Born in Bicknell, Indiana, Compton earned undergraduate and graduate degrees in chemistry at the University of Michigan and Tulane University and from 1940 to 1946 was a research chemist for ELI LILLY AND COMPANY. In 1952 she joined TCM Guild, and by 1956 was elected Guild president. During her year as president she became very active in the museum's operation, and GRACE BLAISDELL GOLDEN hired her as executive secretary when Compton's husband died in 1961. Upon Golden's retirement in 1964, Compton became the third director of TCM.

Under Compton's leadership THE CHILDREN'S MUSEUM grew in size and recognition into a world-class museum. In 1971 she professionalized the institution's operations so that TCM became one of the first organizations accredited by the American Association of Museums (AAM). Compton orchestrated the $7 million capital fund campaign that resulted in building the core of the present facilities and broadening community support. Throughout her career Compton held many leadership positions within the museum community, including vice-president of AAM and president of the American Association of Youth Museums. Additionally, she helped found the Association of Indiana Museums and the Midwest Museums Conference. Compton also served on the boards of many local businesses and cultural institutions. She retired from TCM in 1982, and received AAM's Lifetime Achievement Award in 1988.

MICHELLE D. HALE

Nancy Kriplen, *Keep an Eye on That Mummy* (Indianapolis, 1982); *Indianapolis News*, Aug. 10, 11, 1993.

Congressional Medal of Honor Recipients. The nation's highest military award, first presented in 1863, is awarded "in the name of the Congress of the United States . . . for a deed of personal bravery or self-sacrifice above and beyond the call of duty. . . . " Twelve men born in Indianapolis, or who entered military service from the city, have been awarded the Medal of Honor:

Badders, William. Chief Machinist's Mate, U.S. Navy. Place and date: At sea, May 13, 1939. Awarded for attempting to save lives aboard a damaged submarine, the USS *Squalus*.

Brouse, Charles W. Capt., Co. "K," 100th Indiana Infantry. Place and date: Missionary Ridge, Tennessee, November 25, 1863, Civil War. Awarded for carrying ammunition under fire to his company.

Brown, Lorenzo D. Pvt., Co. "A," 7th U.S. Infantry. Place and date: Big Hole, Montana, August 9, 1877, Indian Campaigns. Awarded for continuing to "do duty in a most courageous manner" despite being severely wounded.

Davis, John. Pvt., Co. "F," 17th Indiana Mounted Infantry. Place and date: Culloden, Georgia, April, 1865, Civil War. Awarded for capturing the flag of a Confederate unit.

Davis, Sammy L. Sgt., Battery "C," 2nd Battalion, 4th Artillery, 9th Infantry Division. Place and date: West of Cai Lay, Republic of Vietnam, November 18, 1967, Vietnam War. Awarded for continuing to load and fire an artillery howitzer under near impossible conditions while protecting the lives of wounded comrades.

Fout, Fredrick W. 2nd Lt., 15th Battery, Indiana Light Artillery. Place and date: Near Harpers Ferry, West Virginia, September 15, 1862, Civil War. Awarded for returning to fire a gun that had been abandoned, doing so until the enemy surrendered.

Harris, David W. Pvt., Co. "A," 7th U.S. Cavalry. Place and date: Little Big Horn River, Montana, June 25, 1876, Indian Campaigns. Awarded for bringing water to the wounded at great danger to his life.

Holmes, William T. Pvt., Co. "A," 3rd Indiana Cavalry. Place and date: Sayler's Creek, Virginia, April 6, 1865, Civil War. Awarded for capturing an enemy regimental flag.

McGee, William D. Pvt., U.S. Army, Medical Detachment, 304th Infantry Regiment, 76th Infantry Division. Place and date: Near Mulheim, Germany, March 18, 1945, World War II. Awarded for continuing to demand that none of his comrades should enter a mine field to save his life after stepping on a land mine.

Scott, Norman. Rear Adm., U.S. Navy. Place and date: Savo Island (near Guadalcanal), October 11–12, 1942, World War II. Awarded for commanding a suicide attack of his naval group against a superior Japanese force, which resulted in the failure of the enemy to land reinforcements. Scott was killed.

Sterling, John T. Pvt., Co. "D," 11th Indiana Infantry. Place and date: Winchester, Virginia, September 19, 1864, Civil War. Awarded for passing artillery shells to his gun crew despite a serious wound.

Wigle, Thomas W. 2nd Lt., U.S. Army, Co. "K," 135th Infantry Regiment, 34th Infantry Division,

World War II. Place and date: Monte Frassino, Italy, September 14, 1944. Awarded for single-handedly clearing the enemy from a forward position. Mortally wounded.

WAYNE L. SANFORD

The Congressional Medal of Honor: The Names, The Deeds (Forest Ranch, Calif., 1984).

Conner, William (Dec. 10, 1777–Aug. 28, 1855). Early settler, fur trader, Indian interpreter, politician, and speculator. Born in the Moravian missionary village of Lichtenau in present-day Ohio, Conner and his family were removed by British troops to Detroit where they spent the latter years of the American Revolution. After the war, he and his brother John (1775–1826) entered the profitable fur trade in Michigan.

In October, 1800, the brothers moved to Indiana Territory and established a trading post among the Delaware tribes located along the west fork of WHITE RIVER south of present-day Noblesville. William married Mekinges, daughter of Chief William Anderson, in 1802, by whom he had six children. He soon began shipping furs to John's new trading post near Cedar Grove in the Whitewater River Valley of southeastern Indiana.

Territorial governor William Henry Harrison employed the Conner brothers as scouts and interpreters during the War of 1812. William accompanied Harrison at the Battle of the Thames (1813), where he allegedly identified the body of the great chief Tecumseh. He later served as a witness and/or interpreter at seven Indian treaty negotiations. Two years after the treaty conclave of St. Mary's, Ohio (October, 1818), which removed the Delaware and other tribes from central Indiana, including Mekinges and their six children, Conner married 18–year-old Elizabeth Chapman. They had ten children over the next 25 years.

Conner was a leading figure in pioneer central Indiana. The commissioners who selected Indianapolis for the state capital in 1820 convened first at his trading post. In 1823, Conner built a two-story Federal-style brick house overlooking his 1,000–acre farm along White River, which became the first seat of government and the first mail stop in newly established HAMILTON COUNTY.

Jacob Cox portrait of pioneer settler William Conner, ca. 1850. [Conner Prairie]

When Conner moved to Noblesville in 1837, he owned over 4,000 acres of land throughout the county.

Conner held several county offices and served three non-consecutive terms in the Indiana General Assembly (1829–1830, 1831–1832, 1836–1837), but devoted greater energies to his commercial ventures. He invested in general stores, mills, and artisans' shops in Indianapolis and other nearby towns and served as a subscription agent for the proposed Lawrenceburgh & Indianapolis Railroad in 1834. Conner speculated in land, including properties in Indianapolis, and platted the towns of Noblesville and Strawtown in Hamilton County, and Alexandria in Madison County.

After William's death in 1855, Elizabeth moved to Indianapolis in 1864 where she resided at 472 North East Street until her death in 1892.

DAVID G. VANDERSTEL
Indiana University–Purdue University,
Indianapolis

John Lauritz Larson and David G. Vanderstel, "Agent of Empire: William Conner on the Indiana Frontier, 1800–1855," *Indiana Magazine of History*, 80 (Dec., 1984), 301–328; Charles N. Thompson, *Sons of the Wilderness: John and William Conner* (Indianapolis, 1937, reprinted 1988).

Conner Prairie. Outdoor living history museum located in FISHERS, north of Indianapolis. Founded in 1964, its mission is to study and interpret the world of the early 19th-century settler in the Old Northwest by focusing on the Indiana experience. Through its research, collecting, and educational efforts, Conner Prairie attempts to preserve and present the material culture, lifeways, values, and history of these people and their times.

Conner Prairie is located on lands originally settled by WILLIAM CONNER, one of the first permanent white settlers in central Indiana. Born in Ohio in 1777 and raised in Michigan, William and his brother John migrated to central Indiana during the winter of 1800–1801. Establishing themselves among the Delaware Indians on the White River, both became licensed traders, married Delaware women, and led precariously balanced lives as traders, interpreters, and liaisons between two worlds.

William Conner remained in Indiana following removal of the Delaware in 1820. Marrying the daughter of an early white settler, Conner assumed a new role as a facilitator of settlement. His trading post became a stopping point for these migrating to the area. His brick home, built in 1823, quickly became a focal point of local activity.

Over the years Conner expanded his business interests, promoted settlement as a town founder, and entered the political arena when it suited his purposes. Conner moved from his home in 1837 to one of the towns he founded, Noblesville, where he died in 1855.

The Conner home and lands passed through many hands before being purchased by industrialist ELI LILLY in 1934. Following the lead of early preservation efforts like those at Colonial Williamsburg and Greenfield Village, Lilly oversaw an extensive restoration of the Conner house. The site also served as a model working farm. Lilly's keen sense of the property's historical significance impelled him to make other changes. A still house, loom house, and reconstructed trading post were added by 1940. He permitted the staging of historical pageants and visits by interested parties.

Lilly passed the stewardship of Conner Prairie to Earlham College in 1964, along with an endowment and continuing, generous financial support. One of his few provisos was that the site remain open to the public. In the early 1970s Earlham administrators decided to recreate a "typical" pioneer village. Period buildings from throughout Indiana were moved to Conner Prai-

rie and the village, Prairietown, featuring costumed interpreters, opened in 1974.

Conner Prairie is divided into three historic areas comprised of 39 buildings. The 1836 village is joined by the restored William Conner house and the Pioneer Adventure Area, where visitors may participate in activities such as weaving, woodworking, and candlemaking. A new museum center, opened in 1988, houses a collection of 15,000 artifacts, a 4,500–volume research library, and an exhibit gallery. It also contains administrative offices, classrooms, a theater, and a museum shop and restaurant. Other buildings on the 210–acre museum site include a historic craft and maintenance center and storage facilities. To ensure the William Conner house remained structurally sound and open to future generations, a multimillion-dollar "re-restoration" of the historic home occurred in 1992–1993.

Conner Prairie's historic areas and special programs educate and entertain nearly 300,000 visitors a year. Accredited by the American Association of Museums, the facility is administered by Earlham College and its board of trustees, an executive director, and is aided by a local advisory council. Its $3.7 million budget is derived from investments (45.8%), membership and admissions (16.1%), museum shop and restaurant receipts (15.1%), and contributions, grants, and sponsorships (10.5%).

TIMOTHY CRUMRIN
Conner Prairie

Conrad, Larry A. (Feb. 8, 1935–July 7, 1990). Indianapolis civic leader and former Indiana secretary of state. A native of Laconia, Indiana, Conrad graduated from Indiana University School of Law in 1961. Upon graduation he managed Birch Bayh's successful U.S. Senate campaign and then served on Bayh's Washington staff. In this capacity he became chief counsel for the Senate Judiciary Committee's Subcommittee on Constitutional Amendments and was an architect of the 25th and 26th amendments. Conrad managed Bayh's campaign in 1968 and then returned to Indiana to enter politics on his own.

After a failed bid for the Democratic nomination for governor, Conrad successfully ran for secretary of state and moved to Indianapolis in 1970. During his first term the media uncovered an alleged political manipulation "master plan" and office irregularities. He denied any involvement in a manipulation plan, but repaid the state over $7,700 for personal office expenses. Conrad was reelected secretary of state in 1974, but lost the gubernatorial election in 1976 to the incumbent, Otis R. Bowen.

After finishing his second term in 1978, Conrad ostensibly ended his political career and practiced law. In 1979 he joined MELVIN SIMON AND ASSOCIATES, a development firm, as vice-president of corporate affairs and chief spokesperson. Through this position he continued to influence state and local government by advising elected officials. More importantly for Indianapolis, Conrad became the leading advocate and catalyst for rebuilding the downtown area into a more livable and usable place as well as for developing the city as the nation's amateur sports capital. He cochaired the NATIONAL SPORTS FESTIVAL (1982) and the PAN AMERICAN GAMES (1987), both held in Indianapolis. Simultaneously, he became a vital member of many of the city's civic and charitable groups on whose boards he served. Some of these organizations included the INDIANAPOLIS URBAN LEAGUE, Committee for Downtown, INDIANAPOLIS PROJECT, INDIANAPOLIS CONVENTION AND VISITORS ASSOCIATION, and Indianapolis Growth Project.

In 1989, with three associates, Conrad left Simon and Associates to form a public affairs consulting and lobbying organization named The Conrad Group. The Conrad Group disbanded the following year upon his death. A memorial fund bearing his name supports an annual scholarship at ARSENAL TECHNICAL HIGH SCHOOL.

MICHELLE D. HALE

Indianapolis Newspaper Index, Indiana State Library.

Conseco. Carmel-based insurance holding company. In 1979 Stephen Hilbert and David Deeds started the Security National of Indiana Corporation. Four years later, after several acquisitions and mergers, the company changed its name to Conseco. Assets at that time were around $3 million. When cofounder Deeds left the firm in 1988 assets had grown to $3 billion.

During the 1980s and early 1990s, Conseco's explosive growth came through the aggressive acquisition of other insurance companies, often through highly leveraged transactions. By drastically cutting personnel and transferring home office operations to CARMEL, Conseco reduced operating expenses by avoiding duplication of services. As of the early 1990s Conseco operated eight major insurance subsidiaries in six states.

Critics charged that Conseco had too much debt, overstated profits through complex accounting practices, and had little tangible net worth. There were also concerns about extensive ownership of Conseco's stock by its subsidiaries. Conseco's records were investigated in 1991 by a congressional subcommittee looking into the financial reporting practices of the insurance industry. A private sector accounting standards firm, the Financial Accounting Standards Board, also reviewed Conseco's books and found nothing wrong. Despite these concerns Conseco's stock prices continued to climb. Conseco's earnings increased 16–fold from 1986 to 1992. The company's $15 billion in assets in 1992 made it the state's second largest insurance company and fourth largest corporation.

DEBORAH B. MARKISOHN

Construction Digest. Regional trade magazine serving the construction industry. Fred G. Johnston, Sr., a native of Bluffton, Indiana, and former Indianapolis bureau chief for United Press, launched Construction Digest in February, 1928. Genesis of the publication was the Indiana Clipping Service, a company Johnston started with EUGENE JEPSON CADOU, SR., the International News Service bureau chief, as a part-time partner, to publish business and building permits newsletters.

Johnston and his wife, Anna (Shea) Johnston, nurtured Construction Digest through the Great Depression and, with George C. and Argie N. Stewart as their first employees, the magazine's coverage was broadened to include Ohio and Illinois. Eastern Missouri and Kentucky were added later. When the Johnstons' two sons, Fred, Jr. and Jerry J., and son-in-law William Howard joined the business in the 1940s, the company launched two other regional magazines and, in subsequent years, acquired two other construction journals.

Construction Digest and its parent firm, Allied Publications, remained family-owned until 1987 when Fred Johnston, Jr., sold the business to Southam Communications, Ltd., Toronto, Canada. At the time, Allied also owned 11 truck and mining magazines, had more than 65 employees, and claimed gross annual revenues exceeding $10.5 million.

ARTHUR E. GRAHAM

Contemporary Club of Indianapolis.

Literary and social club. Organized at the home of Theodore and MAY WRIGHT SEWALL on June 27, 1890, the club's object was to cultivate sociability and intellectual activity among a membership open to men and women on equal terms. The club was to express no opinion on any subject, but all subjects were to be open for discussion.

The first meeting was held on September 25, 1890, with Prof. John M. Coulter, a renowned botanist then teaching at Wabash College, reading a paper on "The Physical Basis of Life." Early presidents included William Dudley Foulke, WILLIAM P. FISHBACK, DEMARCHUS C. BROWN, and CATHARINE MERRILL. Presidents in more recent years have had strong club roots, with several following a parent in that office.

The roster of speakers at the Contemporary Club over the years includes Woodrow Wilson, Booker T. Washington, and William Buckley. Cornelia Otis Skinner, Claude Rains, and Vincent Price came to entertain, and authors Edward Everett Hale, Henry James, and Gertrude Stein addressed the group. While the club is rooted firmly in tradition, that tradition includes concern with contemporary events and people.

MARY JANE MEEKER

Max R. Hyman, ed., *Hyman's Handbook of Indianapolis* (Indianapolis, 1897); clipping files, Indiana State Library.

Cook, Harvey Weir (June 30, 1892–Mar. 24, 1943). World War I ace and pioneer in commercial AVIATION. A native of Wilkinson, Indiana, Cook launched his celebrated career by joining Captain Edward Rickenbacker's famous "Hat in the Ring" squadron after taking flight training in France in 1917. As a member of this fighter squadron, Cook distinguished himself as an ace pilot, downing seven enemy aircraft. Promoted to flight commander of Rickenbacker's 94th Aero Squadron, he was one of eight aces in the unit. He received the Distinguished Service Cross with oak leaf cluster, for bravery under fire, in engagements near Bois-de-Dole, France, on August 1, 1918, and Crepion, France, on October 30, 1918.

In the years following the war, Cook continued his avid interest in aviation by becoming a pioneer of air mail delivery. He came to Indianapolis in the mid–1920s, serving for a time as an instructor with the 38th Division air corps. Although he resigned from the regular army in 1928, he retained his reserve commission and continued to advise the 38th Division and the Indiana Air Guard.

In the late 1920s Cook joined the managerial staff of Curtiss Flying Service, based in Indianapolis. He was primarily responsible for the selection of Indianapolis as a stop on the New York–St. Louis air mail route in 1934. He was actively involved in civic affairs, serving as a prominent member of the Indianapolis CHAMBER OF COMMERCE aviation committee. In this capacity he helped to select the site of the city's airport, which was christened "Weir Cook" in 1944 in his memory. Cook rejoined the army during World War II. He was promoted to colonel on June 22, 1942, and was killed the next year in a plane crash in New Caledonia.

JAMES R. BISHOP

Charles Funkhouser, "Weir Cook," *Indiana Freemason*, 40 (July, 1962), 10, 22; Harry A. Rider, *Indiana Book of Merit* (Indianapolis, 1932).

Coots, Charles E. (July 22, 1851–Apr. 24, 1930). Early 20th century fire chief. Coots was born at Hagerstown in Wayne County, Indiana, and grew up in Cambridge City. There he learned the iron molder's trade and came to Indianapolis to practice it in 1869. In 1878 he was hired as a substitute lineman with the INDIANAPOLIS FIRE DEPARTMENT at Engine House No. 6 and quickly worked his way up to station captain in the late 1880s and assistant fire chief in 1896. As a fireman, Coots battled many of the worst FIRES in the city's history including South Meridian Street (1888), Bowen-Merrill (1890), and Surgical Institute (1892).

Coots took over as Indianapolis fire chief in 1901 and distinguished himself as an excellent administrator and public official. During his 12–year tenure he expanded the city's force from less than 200 to 330 men and directed the transition from horse- to motor-powered fire engines. Coots' department was considered one of the best in the country, and he was admired for his excellent record of containing big fires. Indianapolis experienced only one major fire, the Meridian and Louisiana streets fire of 1905, during his career as chief.

WILLIAM D. DALTON

Indiana Biography Index, Indiana State Library.

Copperheads. Peace Democrats and political dissenters during the Civil War. Not all residents of Indianapolis were avid supporters of the Lincoln administration or of Governor OLIVER P. MORTON's rabid commitment to its war policies. Chief among the dissenters were the Peace Democrats. While essentially loyal to the Union, these conservatives feared that congressional Republicans were using the war to make revolutionary social and economic changes that would benefit northeastern industrialists at the expense of western farmers. As champions of constitutional liberties and states' rights, they also opposed the draft, the suspension of habeas corpus, and the denial of freedom of speech which characterized the Morton administration.

Because these Democrats sometimes openly displayed pro-southern sympathies, created secret societies that state officials viewed as disloyal, and occasionally wore pins that contained liberty heads cut from one-cent coins, Republicans scornfully labeled them "Copperheads" and painted them with the brush of treason. Governor Morton, supported by the INDIANA JOURNAL, publicly indicted all political opponents as traitors and attributed every sign of unrest to the action of Copperhead groups, thus heightening public distrust of any form of dissent. In the process, Copperhead, Democrat, traitor, and the INDIANA STATE SENTINEL (the Journal's chief competitor) became synonymous terms. Consequently, war hysteria reached such proportions in Indianapolis that many historians later concluded that the Copperhead threat was more a Republican-created myth than a genuine danger.

Nonetheless, a series of incidents during the war raised public apprehensions about allegedly treasonous Copperhead activities. On August 31, 1861, a band of Republicans and soldiers invaded a gathering of Marion County Democrats, verbally assaulting the speakers and threatening to pistol-whip anyone with disloyal views. Though violence was averted that night, subsequent evenings witnessed mobs of soldiers and citizens who dragged prominent Democrats from their homes and forced them to take a loyalty oath. The following summer, in the heat of state elections, a federal grand jury exposed a Copperhead organization, the Knights of the Golden Circle (KGC), as a hotbed of treason. These revelations, coupled with a Democratic victory at the polls, led to further Morton-inspired rumors and investigations—indeed, a veritable war on Copperheads.

A major crisis occurred in Indianapolis on May 20, 1863. As Democrats met in a statewide convention, Morton marshaled infantry, cavalry, and artillery throughout the city, and sent armed troops to the meeting hall. There, soldiers heckled speakers and even advanced on the podium with fixed bayonets; elsewhere fights broke out and many were arrested for uttering traitorous comments or carrying concealed weapons. That night, as conventioneers left the city, soldiers stormed their trains, boarded them, and began searching for weapons. In the so-called BATTLE OF POGUE'S RUN many passengers threw their weapons from train windows into the nearby stream.

The fallout from this event carried over into 1864, another election year. During that contest a Morton aide, General Henry B. Carrington, released a report which revealed a Copperhead plan to topple the government through subversive action. First hatched by the KGC, the plot was now being carried out, said Carrington, by the Sons of Liberty, a secret society recently launched in Indianapolis by printer HARRISON H. DODD, the order's local grand commander and the city's foremost Copperhead. The melodrama deepened when a state spy, Felix B. Stidger, claimed that Dodd and his cohorts had a scheme to free Confederate prisoners from CAMP MORTON, seize the arsenal, and stage an uprising in order to create a Northwest Confederacy. Though the plot was aborted by more sensible Democrats, Morton sought to link their party to Dodd's conspiracy. On August 20 the military raided Dodd's office, confiscating documents of the Sons of Liberty along with 400 revolvers and thousands of rounds of ammunition. Two weeks later soldiers arrested Dodd, but within a month he escaped and fled to Canada. Thus ended the Copperhead "threat" in Indianapolis, as much a creation of war hysteria and propaganda as of mystical conclaves of Peace Democrats.

LLOYD A. HUNTER
Franklin College of Indiana

Frank L. Klement, *The Copperheads in the Middle West* (Chicago, 1960); Gilbert Tredway, *Democratic Opposition to the Lincoln Administration in Indiana* (Indianapolis, 1973).

Corporate Community Council. Corporate council for support of community projects. In 1977 members of the GREATER INDIANAPOLIS PROGRESS COMMITTEE (GIPC), recognizing the need for future development in the city, formed a long-range planning committee. It was charged with the task of broadening the activities of GIPC to better serve community needs. From the work of the long-range planning committee came the idea to form an organization whose members would be chief executive officers of the city's leading business firms. The chair of LILLY ENDOWMENT, along with the chairs of three major banks, convened the first meeting. On September 14, 1977, those attending formed the founding group of the Council.

The purpose of the Council is to enhance the participation of corporate community leaders in identifying, understanding, and supporting significant needs and opportunities in the Indianapolis area, with special attention to cultural, economic, educational, and social concerns. All projects adopted for support are administered through existing community organizations such as GIPC, UNITED WAY, and the Indianapolis CHAMBER OF COMMERCE.

Staff support for the Council is provided by the Chamber of Commerce. The Council is governed by a 35–member board of directors including, as ex officio members, the governor of Indiana, the mayor of Indianapolis, the presidents of Indiana University and Purdue University, and the vice-president of INDIANA UNIVERSITY–PURDUE UNIVERSITY AT INDIANAPOLIS. The officers and chairs of standing committees (executive, finance, membership, program) are elected from the Council-at-large. All Council members are chief executive officers (some of whom are general managers—or the equivalent—of a branch of a national firm) and have committed their companies to financial support of and participation in the Council's projects.

The costs of Council projects and administration are provided by a combination of dues and a formula-based assessment, the latter determined by the Council's decision on projects for the ensuing year and their attendant costs. Each year, at the annual meeting in October, the financial assessment of the membership for the following year is determined by two-thirds majority vote of all Council members.

Among numerous projects the Council has supported, financially and through endorsements since its beginning in 1977, are: the 1982 NATIONAL SPORTS FESTIVAL, the 1987 PAN AMERICAN GAMES, relocation of the headquarters of KIWANIS INTERNATIONAL from Chicago to Indianapolis, and the community information campaign leading to construction of the HOOSIER DOME. The Council has also underwritten more than half of the operating expenses of the INDIANAPOLIS ECONOMIC DEVELOPMENT CORPORATION and the INDIANAPOLIS PROJECT.

MARJORIE C. TARPLEE
Central Newspapers Foundation

Costigan, Francis (Mar. 4, 1810–Apr. 18, 1865). Early Indianapolis architect. A native of Washington, D.C., Costigan studied to be a builder and an architect in Philadelphia and Baltimore. After moving to Madison, Indiana, he designed many homes in that city, including the Lanier Mansion (1844). When Madison entered a period of economic decline in the 1850s, Costigan moved to Indianapolis. He designed the former Odd Fellows Building on the northeast corner of Washington and Meridian streets, the Blind School, located on land now part of the INDIANA WORLD WAR MEMORIAL PLAZA, and the Oriental House Hotel at 121–125 South Illinois Street (later part of the Hotel Oxford). For a brief time he was proprietor of the Oriental House. He built, but did not design, the old Post Office on the corner of Pennsylvania and Market streets (1858).

Costigan employed a diversity of building styles, often using unusual and elaborate ornamentation. The Andrew Wallace Residence at 601 Fletcher Avenue, constructed in 1866 after his death, is the only building believed to have been designed by Costigan still standing in Indianapolis. Costigan died of consumption and was buried in Greenlawn Cemetery; his remains were later moved to CROWN HILL CEMETERY.

CONNIE J. ZEIGLER

Indiana Biography Series, Indiana State Library.

Cottage Home. Near eastside historic district bounded by 10th, Oriental, and Michigan streets and I–70. Cottage Home takes its name from the style of houses built in the neighborhood between 1870 and 1892. Residents built modest frame cottages in a variety of vernacular architectural styles, including gable front, L-plan, and cross gable. One brick Queen Anne style residence was the distinctive home of Frederick Ruskaup, the neighborhood's leading citizen. Ruskaup opened a prosperous grocery store, then built a Dorman Street commercial building, five duplexes, and his home, designed by the prestigious architectural firm VONNEGUT AND BOHN.

Like Ruskaup, many of the early residents of Cottage Home were German-Americans. The railroad nearby provided employment to some, while others worked as machinists, tradesmen, custodians, carpenters, and factory laborers. Irish and a small number of African-American families also lived in the area, which remained a working class community well into the 20th century.

Cottage Home was never exclusively residential, and land use is mixed even today. Few buildings have been demolished since the 1930s; many have retained their historic architectural integrity. In 1990, the area was placed on the National Register of Historic Places and named Cottage Home. This 150–home community experienced a restoration boom in the 1980s and early 1990s, spurred by rising property values and an active neighborhood organization.

CATHLEEN F. DONNELLY

Cottman, George S. (May 10, 1857–May 18, 1941). Historian, founder of *Indiana Magazine of History*. George Cottman was born in Indianapolis and spent his childhood on his parents' farm near Beech Grove where he attended the district school. In 1873, at the age of 16, he began a three-year tenure as an apprentice printer at the *Indianapolis Sentinel*, then moved back to the farm and began writing stories, plays, and nature pieces. Twelve years later he located in IRVINGTON and set up a printing office in his home. He published many of his own books and pamphlets.

After a few years in Irvington he turned from fiction to historical writing because he believed there was a market for it in the local newspapers. His research led him all over the state, and he became concerned with preserving Indiana's historical documents. He wrote articles for many local papers including the *News*, the *Star*, the *Sentinel*, and the *Indiana Farmer*. Cottman combined much of his historical work into scrapbooks that he later donated to the INDIANA STATE LIBRARY, where they are shelved under the title *Indiana Scrapbook Collection*. In 1905 he established the *Indiana Magazine of History* and served as its editor, publisher, printer, and author for two years. The INDIANA HISTORICAL SOCIETY took the publication over in 1907, with Cottman remaining as editor for several more years.

Cottman was a respected literary figure and counted JAMES WHITCOMB RILEY and T. C. STEELE among his close friends. He wrote two different pageants for the state centennial in 1916 and several books on Indiana history including *Indiana, Its History, Constitution, and Present Government* (1925), which was still used in public schools throughout the state at the time of his death.

WILLIAM D. DALTON

Indiana Biography Series, Indiana State Library; R. E. Banta, *Indiana Authors and Their Books, 1816–1916* (Crawfordsville, Ind., 1949).

Coulon, Charles G. (Feb. 16, 1825–Feb. 2, 1881). Mayor of Indianapolis, Nov. 8–22, 1856, Democrat. Coulon was born in Goettingen, Germany. He immigrated to the United States in 1847 to avoid military service, and moved from Boston to Indianapolis in 1852.

Once in Indianapolis, Coulon studied law with Robert L. Walpole and subsequently opened a real estate and law office. In 1856 he was elected to a four-year term as JUSTICE OF THE PEACE (JP). When Mayor HENRY F. WEST died in office, the COMMON COUNCIL unanimously elected him interim mayor until a special election could be held. Although elected as a Democrat, Coulon had refused to vote for that party after Democratic mayor JAMES MCCREADY found him guilty of playing pool on a Sunday in 1855.

After two weeks as mayor, Coulon resumed his term as JP. He subsequently returned to his law practice and remained active in Democratic politics. In 1858 he was secretary at a state meeting of Stephen Douglas Democrats. After an unsuccessful run for JP in 1860, he held public office again as school commissioner for the seventh ward (1863–1864) and as JP (1864–1868).

MICHELLE D. HALE

John H. B. Nowland, *Sketches of Prominent Citizens of 1876* (Indianapolis, 1877), 358–359; Jacob Piatt Dunn, *Greater Indianapolis* (Chicago, 1910), 162.

Country Clubs. By the late 1800s country clubs were popular social centers for the cultural elite in many American communities, including Indianapolis. The city's first country club, the Indianapolis Country Club, was incorporated June 4, 1891, and within a few decades was joined by a half dozen others.

The Indianapolis Country Club purchased land near the outskirts of the city, the current grounds of Woodstock Country Club, but soon found itself in search of a new location as Indianapolis grew. In 1912 the club purchased land on Crawfordsville Road for a golf course; golfing has been a popular activity at American country clubs since the 1890s. When its clubhouse burned in 1914, one group of members, who later organized the Country Club of Indianapolis, decided to concentrate on GOLF and move to the new land. Early members included BENJAMIN HARRISON, BOOTH TARKINGTON, JOSIAH K. LILLY, SR., and JAMES WHITCOMB RILEY. Another group decided to remain and rebuild, establishing Woodstock. Other early clubs included Highland Golf and Country Club (1908), Hillcrest Country Club (formerly Avalon Hills Country Club, 1926, reorganized 1933 as Hillcrest), Broadmoor Country Club (1921, begun as a Jewish club), and Meridian Hills Country Club (1923). Later clubs included Lake Shore Country Club (1935) and Westchester Country Club (1955, begun as a Jewish club).

Although now associated with private golf facilities, many clubs did not begin that way. Avalon Hills and Westchester initially were family swimming clubs, later adding golf courses. Woodland (1956), however, was originally established as a golf course and later incorporated as a private club. In the 1950s country clubs became connected with suburban real estate development and many, such as Hawthorne Hills (1959), included club membership with purchase of a lot. A related development was the family swimming and recreation club (no golf facilities); several were established in the mid–1950s, including Westwood Country Club (1954), Devon Country Club (1958), Dolphin Club (1959), and many others no longer in operation. Among the earliest of the family clubs was the RIVIERA CLUB (1933), well known for its swim teams. In 1967 the Sherwood Country Club was established for the teen crowd. Located on 34 acres, the club had 1,800 members by 1971 and sponsored dances and concerts at its clubhouse.

Established in 1969 and backed by African-American professional athletes and local businessmen, the Sportsman's Country Club was an unsuccessful attempt at an integrated club. Due to financial difficulties the club failed within a few years, reorganized as the Scenic View Country Club, and in 1973 sold its property to a church.

Local clubs have hosted many national and international tournaments including the Western Tennis Tourney and the Clay Court Championship at Woodstock, the U.S. Women's Open Golf Championship and the Mayflower Classic at Broadmoor, and the PGA and U.S. Women's Open golf championships held at Crooked Stick Golf Club.

Notable area clubs include Woodland Country Club (formerly Woodland Golf Club, 1956), Crooked Stick Golf Club (1964), Brookshire Golf Club (1979), and Twin Lakes Golf Club (1985) in Carmel, as well as Greenfield Country Club (1927), Ulen Country Club (1956) in Lebanon, Royal Oak Country Club (1962) in Greenwood, and Harbour Trees Golf Club (1972) in Noblesville. As of the early 1990s, the Country Club of Indianapolis and Meridian Hills Country Club had the highest initiation fees ($20,000), while the Riviera Club had the largest number of members (4,500).

JOAN CUNNINGHAM

Countrymark Cooperative (formerly Indiana Farm Bureau Cooperative Association). Major U.S. grain sales and agricultural supplies company, located at 950 North Meridian Street. In 1926 Indiana farmers founded the Indiana Farm Bureau Cooperative Association to improve their collective economic situation. I. Harvey Hull, a La Porte County farmer, was the first manager of the Indianapolis-based statewide co-op system that started with 27 local co-ops. The co-op was and continues to be owned and controlled by local member associations which, in turn, are owned and controlled by local farmer-members.

By the early 1950s, annual sales were $120 million; in 1970 they reached $250 million, making the co-op one of the largest businesses in the state. It was also one of the most diversified, marketing 80 million bushels of grain a year in addition to overseeing feed mills, lumber yards, fertilizer factories, refineries, and hatcheries. In the 1980s a shrinking base of farmers and low commodity prices forced the co-op to slash employment in half, discontinue several product lines, and suspend dividend payments. After three unprofitable years the co-op began an aggressive marketing strategy, showing a profit of $1.7 million in 1986 and $6.8 million the following year.

In 1991 Countrymark Co-op was formed, bringing together co-ops in Indiana, Ohio, and Michigan. Indiana Farm Bureau Co-op officials remained in charge of the new organization because of their successful turnaround in the mid–1980s. Countrymark is the sixth largest co-op in the country, with more than $2 billion in annual sales. Countrymark employs almost 2,000 people worldwide, with 500 working in Indianapolis at Countrymark's headquarters, grain terminals, feed mills, and soil testing facilities. In 1992 Countrymark was ranked as Indiana's largest privately held company.

DEBORAH B. MARKISOHN

Indianapolis Star, Sept. 8, 1991; *Indianapolis Business Journal*, May 25–31, 1992.

Cox, Jacob (Nov. 9, 1810–Jan. 2, 1892). Portrait, landscape, and still life painter. Cox was the major figure in the early development of visual arts in Indianapolis, maintaining a studio in the city from about 1840 until his death, a period of over 50 years.

Cox was born near Philadelphia and spent his youth in Washington, Pennsylvania, apprenticed to a tinsmith. In 1833 he and his brother Charles arrived in Indianapolis where they opened a stove, tinware, and coppersmith store. As business increased, Cox turned to painting until it became his only profession.

He gained recognition in 1840 for painting a large political banner carried by an Indianapolis delegation to the Tippecanoe battleground in support of William Henry Harrison. His first formal advertisement as a portrait painter appeared in the *Indiana State Sentinel* on December 30, 1841, and by 1843, a local editor asked, "Reader, have you visited Mr. Cox's painting gallery? If not, whether married or single, have your portrait painted." His

Jacob Cox, American, 1810-1892. *Landscape near Indianapolis,* 1860s. [oil on canvas, 33 1/2 x 43 inches, bequest of Mr. and Mrs. Hugo Fechtman, 63.204, from the exhibition: *Views of Indianapolis: Artistic Perspectives*, collection of the Indianapolis Museum of Art.]

portraits as well as landscapes and figure compositions soon found their way into numerous homes. Many of these pictures portrayed local scenes, for as Cox said, material at home was as good as could be found anywhere, nature was familiar, and the public more sympathetic.

He made two trips outside the city. In the winter of 1842, he opened a studio with John Gibson Dunn in Cincinnati, but returned home six months later. He traveled to New York in 1860 where he met eastern artists and took his first formal instruction at the National Academy of Design.

Cox had painted five Indiana governors prior to the formation of the Governors Portraits Collection in 1869. These were hanging in his studio as examples of his work. In 1869, Governor Conrad Baker commissioned him to paint Governor Henry Smith Lane, and this portrait and the other five are now part of the state collection.

Throughout his career, Cox generously took time to instruct aspiring artists. Students included Joseph O. Eaton, Lottie Guffin, Virginia Todd, Margaret Rudisill, India Kirkland, and Cox's daughter, Julia, who painted the full length portrait of Lovina Streight that hangs in the Indiana State House. WILLIAM MERRITT CHASE called him his "Father in Art" and T. C. STEELE said he was one of the most agreeable and lovable men he ever met. Cox was a trustee and town councilman and a vestryman at CHRIST CHURCH CATHEDRAL. His painting of a Madonna hangs in the library of the church.

Cox's portraits are direct, straightforward statements about the people who sat before his easel. His figure paintings, often inspired by other pictures, were usually referred to as "fancy pieces" since they were romantic and rather fanciful compositions of children and pretty girls.

Cox's paintings are included in collections at the INDIANAPOLIS MUSEUM OF ART, the INDIANA STATE MUSEUM, the Indiana STATE HOUSE, and the MORRIS-BUTLER HOUSE.

MARY JANE MEEKER

Wilbur D. Peat, *Pioneer Painters of Indiana* (Indianapolis, 1954).

Coy, Simeon (Oct. 13, 1851–Dec. 27, 1894). Controversial chairman of the Marion County Democratic party. A native of Greensburg, Indiana, Coy moved to Indianapolis in 1863. From 1866 to 1875 he worked as a painter at the Shaw Carriage Works; in 1875 he went into the saloon business. From 1878 to 1886 Coy served as a member of the City Council and in 1884 he became chairman of the Marion County DEMOCRATIC PARTY, a position to which he was reelected in 1886.

Known as a pleasant and affable man by many, behind the scenes Coy was tied to corruption during his years on the council. He made sure that saloons and gambling halls had the reassurance that they would remain open, regardless of their practices. Coy's corruption did not become widely known, however, until his tenure as chairman of the Marion County Democratic party. Following the election of 1886, Coy and 11 other party officials were accused of tampering with tally-sheets in order to secure the election of the Democratic candidate for judge of the criminal court. In February, 1888, Coy was convicted in the second of three trials that comprised the "TALLY-SHEET FORGERIES." Even though in prison, he remained a member of the council; upon his release he was reelected in October, 1889, for another term. That same year Coy published his account of the case, *The Great Conspiracy* (1889), in which he argued that the tally-sheet case had been manufactured by REPUBLICAN PARTY officials as a means of eliminating their more successful counterparts in the local Democratic party.

After leaving politics Coy went back into the saloon and gambling business, but laws that made gambling illegal left him virtually penniless. After his death the *Indianapolis News* called him "the most picturesque political character in the history of Indiana."

YANCY DEERING

R. E. Banta, *Indiana Authors and Their Books* (Crawfordsville, Ind., 1949); Jacob Piatt Dunn, *Greater Indianapolis* (Chicago, 1910).

Cram Company. See George F. Cram Company

Crawford, William (Bill) (June 26, 1917–Oct. 3, 1968). Early television weatherman. A native of Elkhart, Indiana, Crawford spent most of his youth in Wilmette, Illinois. A graduate of Beloit College in Wisconsin, he completed meteorological training at the University of Chicago prior to joining the U.S. Air Force in 1940. During World War II he served as a pilot and weather officer in the China-Burma-India theater. He remained in the military until 1949, resigning as a lieutenant colonel.

While attending Indiana University Dental School in the early 1950s, Crawford nervously

Bill Crawford was Indianapolis' first television weatherman. [Indiana State Museum]

auditioned for a weather announcer position on WFBM-TV (now WRTV). Soon he was providing evening weather reports. At one point his ratings were so impressive that the station had him doing weather at the start of a 30–minute newscast. His casual "Hi" to the television audience became a well-known trademark in Indianapolis.

Crawford started his dental practice in Indianapolis in 1953 but at the urging of the station he continued to provide both early and late evening weathercasts for another 11 years. In 1964 Crawford was stricken with cancer and forced to leave the air, but he wrote a weather column six days a week for the INDIANAPOLIS STAR until his death.

HOWARD CALDWELL
WRTV Channel 6

Crispus Attucks High School. African-American high school established in 1927. Created as a result of pressure to divide the races in city schools, Attucks consolidated the enrollment of black high school students at one location. The segregationist movement was so widespread that even black students entering their senior years at Manual, Arsenal Technical, and Shortridge high schools had to transfer to segregated Crispus Attucks High School when it opened. Attucks remained segregated into the 1970s, despite the passage of the 1949 Indiana school desegregation law and even after federal courts ordered the abandonment of segregated schools.

In the 1920s most of the city's elementary schools were already segregated but the lack of a separate secondary facility had forced the public school system to enroll blacks in existing high schools. Late in 1922 the school board recommended the construction of a separate high school for blacks, although it promised to encourage the "self-reliance, initiative, and good citizenship" of blacks with a "maximum educational opportunity." It also proposed to employ black teachers to make segregation seem less offensive.

The conservative social, economic, and political atmosphere which resulted in the city's segregated schools was exemplified by the 1924 election of KU KLUX KLAN members to state and local offices. In Indianapolis the Klan controlled the office of mayor and the city council, resulting in segregationist policies that alarmed the black community and set the stage for sharp racial divisions. Support for separate schools also came from the Federation of Community Civic Clubs, Chamber of Commerce, White Supremacy League, and the Mapleton Civic Association. In 1925 a "Klan-elected" school board appropriated funds for the construction of the new facility.

The NATIONAL ASSOCIATION FOR THE ADVANCEMENT OF COLORED PEOPLE (NAACP) filed a lawsuit in the name of Archie Greathouse, a black resident of the city, charging that students would not receive an equal education in a separate school. The NAACP lost the suit and an appeal, and construction proceeded. Although the school board had originally designated it the Thomas Jefferson High School, the black community successfully lobbied to name it after an African-American historical figure. The name Crispus Attucks honors a runaway slave who was one of the first martyrs of the American Revolution.

Matthias Nolcox, the first principal of Attucks, assembled a teaching staff of black professionals from around the country prior to the 1927 opening. Many of the faculty had advanced degrees in their subject areas and came from teaching positions at black colleges in the South. The rapid growth of the city's African-American population and a larger than expected number of pupils—1,350 rather then the anticipated 1,000—required an increase in the staff the next year.

At no time as a segregated high school did Crispus Attucks have the space and facilities to accommodate its student body and faculty. Additions to the structure occurred in 1938 and 1966, but rapid growth of the city's African-American population continued to place enormous pressure on the lone Indianapolis public high school for black students. At one point, when overcrowding became severe, the school board placed School 17, an elementary school adjacent to the high school, under the jurisdiction of Attucks' principal in the event there was a need for overflow space.

In 1930 Russell A. Lane moved from the English Department to the principalship. During his lengthy tenure (1930–1957) Crispus Attucks gained fame for both its athletic and academic programs. Although it could not participate in sporting events with other city schools, Attucks developed a vigorous athletic program. For many years the INDIANA HIGH SCHOOL ATHLETIC ASSOCIATION (IHSAA) banned membership of African-American schools, which it did not consider "public schools," and forbade competition between black and white teams. Attucks competed with other black-only schools, many from out of state, or with parochial schools. Finally, in December, 1941, the IHSAA accepted black schools as members. In 1955, under the leadership of coach Ray Crowe, Attucks captured both the all-city and the state basketball championships. Led by future NBA star Oscar Robertson the team won the state title against another black high school, Gary Roosevelt, in the first ever IHSAA-sponsored Indiana state championship between two African-American schools. Crowe's team repeated its victory in 1956, and coach Bill Garrett fielded another state championship team in 1959.

The Attucks curriculum was standard for IPS schools with one exception: Dr. Joseph C. Carroll introduced a course in black history. Other needs of the school were met in various ways. Spearheaded by FREEMAN B. RANSOM, a prominent black attorney, and a committee from the neighborhood's SENATE AVENUE YMCA, the school raised funds to purchase a pipe organ for its music and drama programs. Over the years the school's music program produced many well-known jazz musicians, including J. J. Johnson, Slide Hampton, JOHN LESLIE "WES" MONTGOMERY, Jimmy Coe, and Jimmy Spaulding.

As a result of an agreement between the U.S. Justice Department and IPS to integrate the school system, in 1969 several black teachers were reassigned from Crispus Attucks to other city high schools. Included in the 1969 plan was the gradual desegregation of elementary student populations. Also included in the preliminary plan was Attucks' relocation to a new site that favored school integration. That move, never favored by the black community, was later dropped.

During the mid–1970s the countywide busing program ordered by the U.S. district court increased the number of secondary schools in which black students were enrolled, including township schools in the suburbs. The result was a marked reduction in the number of black high school age students attending Indianapolis public schools. In addition the construction of the IUPUI campus and the I–65/I–70 inner loop eliminated much of the neighborhood that formerly housed Attucks students. In the late 1970s, after assigning city high schools to four attendance areas as part of the desegregation plan, Crispus Attucks became a magnet school specializing in the medical professions and health-related fields. In a final step, as the redirection of feeder schools to outlying areas reduced the enrollment of city high schools, Attucks became a junior high school in 1986, and in 1993 a middle school. By 1988 only 51 percent of the school's student body was African-American.

In 1992 the Crispus Attucks Museum and Center opened under the direction of the African-American History–Multicultural Education Office. The center and museum house memorabilia from the former Attucks High School and 14 black elementary schools. Crispus Attucks was included on the National Register of Historic places in 1989.

Stanley Warren

Stanley Warren, "The Evolution of Secondary Schooling for Blacks in Indianapolis: 1869–1930, Part II," *Black History News & Notes*, No. 30 (Nov., 1987); Phillip M. Hoose, *Hoosiers* (New York, 1986), ch. 4, "The Black and White of Hoosier Hysteria: Indianapolis Crispus Attucks High School."

Criterion. Religious newspaper. Father Raymond T. Bosler founded the *Criterion* in October, 1960, as the successor to the *Indiana Catholic and Record*. The paper focuses on the development and enhancement of Catholic living, with articles on events within the Indianapolis Catholic community, advice columns, and scriptural lessons. Circulation in 1993 totaled 53,600, of which 52,300 went to members of parishes within the Roman Catholic Archdiocese of Indianapolis. The tabloid-size *Criterion* is wholly self-supporting, receiving no funds from the Archdiocese. Its editorial pages generally articulate official Catholic positions and support measures allowing the parish members to participate actively in church business.

Stacey Nicholas

John W. Miller, *Indiana Newspaper Bibliography* (Indianapolis, 1982); *Criterion*, Oct. 7, 21, 1960, Apr. 23, 1965, Mar. 26, 1993.

Cropsey, Nebraska (1846–Mar. 8, 1916). Assistant superintendent of the Indianapolis schools for the primary grades, and one of the best known educators in the Midwest. A native of Pennsylvania, Cropsey came to Indianapolis with her parents while still a child. She became a teacher after Superintendent Abram C. Shortridge persuaded the school board to send her to Oswego (New York) Normal School for advanced instruction. Upon her return she served briefly as a critic in the training school for teachers and, in 1871 at age 25, became assistant principal of elementary education. She held this position, with a later title change to assistant superintendent, for 43 years.

During these years she supervised the primary schools of Indianapolis, fostered the cause of education, and worked for passage of the state's compulsory education law in 1897. She wrote several arithmetic textbooks—the first appearing in 1893—used in Indianapolis and other cities for a number of years.

Indiana University conferred an honorary degree on Nebraska Cropsey in 1913; she was the first woman and the fourth person so honored. Cropsey Auditorium in the Indianapolis–Marion County Public Library is named for her, as was Public School 22.

Laura Gaus

Crossroads Rehabilitation Center. Comprehensive outpatient rehabilitation facility. In 1936, Sarah F. (Mrs. William E.) Gavin learned that 12 disabled teenagers had formed a social club. She and Mildred C. (Mrs. P. R.) Mallory set out to aid the group by expanding its program to include profitable handicrafts.

In 1939 the group became formally organized under the leadership of the Indiana Society for Crippled Children. A year later it became an affiliate of what is now the National Easter Seal Society and leased a building at 30th and New Jersey streets. A curative workshop was established to prepare persons with disabilities for jobs in the community. In 1956 the organization moved to a new two-story structure at 3242 Sutherland Avenue and in 1958 it became a UNITED WAY affiliate. Expanded programs included physical, occupational, speech, and hearing therapy, developmental preschool, psychological and social services, and vocational evaluation, work adjustment, and training programs. In the late 1980s Lekotek, a toy lending library, extended the array of services for children, and a driver training program broadened opportunities for adults.

Today, Crossroads boasts one of the nation's most comprehensive rehabilitation programs and is headquartered in a five-story building (4740 Kingsway Drive) purchased and renovated in 1990. At another site, Crossroads operates a work center, which provides employment for adults with disabilities through subcontract jobs for industry. As part of its mission to assist individuals with disabilities to achieve maximum independence, it also offers supported employment programs to increase opportunities for mainstream community employment, and a consulting service to help employers comply with the Americans with Disabilities Act. Since the introduction of computer programmer training in 1979, Crossroads has become a recognized leader statewide in the use of technology to create opportunities for persons with disabilities.

Crossroads' annual budget of $7 million comes from fees for service (paid by third parties), federal and state agencies, and donations from United Way, Easter Seal, individuals, foundations, and corporations. By its 50th anniversary in 1986, it had served 50,000 clients; in 1991 it served over 1,700 clients.

JAMES J. VENTO
Crossroads Rehabilitation Center

Crown Hill Cemetery. Nation's third largest cemetery, located 2.8 miles northwest of Monument Circle. Crown Hill was incorporated as a nonprofit, nondenominational cemetery on September 25, 1863, at a time when Greenlawn Cemetery was the principal burial ground in the city. Concern over Greenlawn's limited acreage and lack of care spurred creation of a 30–member board of corporators that established Crown Hill. The land selected for the cemetery was considered some of the most beautiful in Marion County. From 750–foot Crown Hill, so named because it was the "crowning hill among all hills in Marion County," visitors encountered an extraordinary view of Indianapolis and the surrounding countryside.

The board contracted with Frederick W. Chislett, a landscape architect from Pittsburgh, to design the cemetery shortly after it purchased 274 acres of land for $51,000. The following spring Chislett supervised the development of seven burial sections. Lucy Ann Seaton became the first interment on June 2, 1864, one day following the cemetery's dedication.

Additional acreage was added to Crown Hill, the last being purchased in 1911. Today the cemetery includes 555 acres, with its southern boundary at 32nd Street and the northern limit at 42nd Street. The western border is Dr. Martin Luther King, Jr. Street and Northwestern Avenue (MICHIGAN ROAD), with both Clarendon Road and Boulevard Place on the east.

In 1866, 708 Union soldiers who died during the Civil War and were buried at Greenlawn were removed to Crown Hill and interred in a lot south of where the Gothic Chapel now stands. The United States government purchased this 1.37–acre lot to become the second of three national cemeteries in Indiana. Two years later the first Decoration Day service in Indianapolis was celebrated here, highlighted by a speech by Governor Conrad Baker. This traditional ceremony recurs each May on Memorial Day.

In 1875 an impressive limestone chapel, designed by DIEDRICH A. BOHLEN and built by German craftsmen, was erected in the very center of the cemetery. Originally a temporary storage vault for the dead, the Gothic Chapel is now used for funeral services, weddings, tours, and special events sponsored by the Historical Society of Crown Hill. The chapel was restored in 1971.

The principal entryway to Crown Hill, originally located on Michigan Road, was established in 1885 at what is now 34th Street and Boulevard Place. ADOLPH SCHERRER designed this elaborate limestone archway as a companion to a brick administration building (the "Waiting Station") that served as the cemetery office until 1969. A sentry house was constructed to the left of the entrance in 1904.

Two different homes once stood on the Crown Hill grounds, each constructed as a residence for the superintendent and his family. The first of these was erected in 1869 and stood until 1917; the second, built in 1914, was removed in 1950. Other dwellings, including employee quarters, barns, stables, and shops, were built throughout the cemetery grounds. Today only the service yard, constructed in the early 1920s, remains. Other major structures on the grounds include the Community Mausoleum (1949), the new Administration Building (1969), the Crown Hill Funeral Home (1993), 57 private mausoleums, and several garden crypt buildings (located on the north grounds). Art works include three statues (1875) that once stood atop the Marion County Courthouse in downtown Indianapolis, an Equitorial Sundial (1987) created by David L. Rodgers, and the Enkema Fountain (1989).

A brick and wrought iron fence, begun in 1914 and completed in the late 1930s, surrounds three sides of the south grounds as well as the southernmost end of the north grounds—both areas being separated by 38th Street. GEORGE E. KESSLER designed this fence, which underwent restoration from 1985 to 1992. In 1925 a bridge/subway was constructed beneath 38th Street (formerly Maple Road) so that cemetery visitors could access both sides of the cemetery without leaving the grounds.

More than 184,000 persons are buried and entombed at Crown Hill, including President BENJAMIN HARRISON and poet JAMES WHITCOMB RILEY, whose grave and monument stand atop the Crown Hill. The cemetery also contains the remains of three U.S. vice-presidents (THOMAS A. HENDRICKS, CHARLES W. FAIRBANKS, Thomas Riley Marshall), ten Indiana governors, fourteen mayors of the city, and over a dozen generals of the Civil War. Other notables include COL. ELI LILLY, movie actor James Baskett, and gangster JOHN DILLINGER. In 1933, 1,616 Confederate soldiers who died while prisoners of war at CAMP MORTON (1862–1865) in Indianapolis were reburied here from Greenlawn. Their graves are memorialized by one large granite monument and

Crown Hill Cemetery, East Entrance, ca. 1900. [Indiana Historical Society, #C5881]

ten smaller ones on which are mounted bronze plaques bearing the names and units of those interred at this location.

Crown Hill Cemetery was listed on the National Register of Historic Places in 1973. More than 25,000 people pass through the site annually, many on special occasions that include Memorial Day, Benjamin Harrison's birthday, Veterans Day, and a fall Victorian Day celebration.

Native to Crown Hill's rural setting are animals and birds including deer, squirrels, raccoons, foxes, and red-tailed hawks. Over 250 species of trees and shrubs adorn the grounds, 112 of which are identified on a tree map.

WAYNE L. SANFORD

Wayne L. Sanford, *The Crown Hill Cemetery: Past, Present and Future* (Indianapolis, 1988); Anna Nicholas, *The Crown Hill Story* (Indianapolis, 1928).

Crows Nest. Residential area located south of Kessler Boulevard, west of White River, and east of Lieber Road. The Hessongs, Lemings, and Krise families farmed the Crows Nest area (originally spelled "Crow's") in the first half of the 19th century. John Krise bought land about 1830 and built a mill just south of what would later be the intersection of Spring Mill Road and Kessler Boulevard. A one-acre cemetery off Sunset Lane contains the graves of more than two dozen 19th-century residents. Crows Nest was also a popular area for picnics, swimming, and fishing.

By the 1920s the area had become an enclave of private estates, ranging in size from 2 to 20 acres. In 1927, 37 of the residents petitioned for incorporation as the town of Crows Nest. Over the years some of the city's leading citizens, such as ELI LILLY, Nicholas Noyes, and the Ayres family, have owned homes in Crows Nest. At one time the area was dubbed "Pill Hill" because several executives of the Lilly pharmaceutical company lived there. An INCLUDED TOWN under the UNIGOV structure, it is governed by an elected council. In 1990 about 100 people lived in Crows Nest.

In 1934, six homeowners along WHITE RIVER, just north of Kessler and east of Spring Mill, incorporated as the town of North Crows Nest. About 60 people lived in the included town in 1990. Today, both communities retain their cachet as exclusive neighborhoods.

CATHLEEN F. DONNELLY

Indianapolis News, July 20, Oct. 14, 1959, Mar. 8, 1979.

CTS. See Christian Theological Seminary

Cumberland. Town located along U.S. 40 at the eastern edge of Marion County. On July 7, 1831, Henry Brady platted the town, naming it for Cumberland, Maryland. The village prospered as travelers passed through on the old NATIONAL ROAD. Little's Hotel and Tavern, constructed in the 1830s, served travelers into the 20th century, though it was demolished in 1968. Churches were organized in Cumberland at an early date. St. John's Evangelical and Reformed Church was established in 1855 by the area's German immigrants.

Local businesses have played an important role in the economic life of the community. Carl Sonnenschmidt and Herman Junge, German immigrants, founded Smith and Young Greenhouses in 1901. The firm was at one time the largest rose-growing nursery in Indiana before closing in 1972. Harlan, Sprague, Dawley, Inc. began in 1931 as a breeder of laboratory animals for scientific research. The firm has expanded its operations worldwide and in 1993 employed about 800 people, 120 of them in Cumberland.

As Indianapolis expands eastward, Cumberland continues to grow. In 1970, the town had a population of 1,500. By 1980 the number had more than doubled to 3,400, and there were some 4,500 residents counted in the 1990 census. Under UNIGOV, Cumberland has INCLUDED TOWN status and is governed by an elected council.

KRIS E. DAMAN

Rosalie Lewis, Cumberland Reflections, 1831–1988 (Nappanee, Ind., 1988).

Curtis Publishing Company. Publishing, licensing, and manufacturing firm. Cyrus Curtis founded Curtis Publishing in 1885 at Philadelphia. His first publication was Ladies' Home Journal. In 1897, he acquired the SATURDAY EVENING POST, begun by Benjamin Franklin in 1728 as the Pennsylvania Gazette.

In 1971, Indianapolis' Beurt SerVaas bought Curtis Publishing, eventually acquiring all its stock. His purchase included Country Gentleman, Jack & Jill, Holiday, and rights to the Post, which had ceased publication in 1969. SerVaas brought Curtis to his Review Publishing Company site on Waterway Boulevard, merging Review operations into Curtis. The Post resumed publication in 1971.

In 1982, SerVaas conveyed all the company's consumer magazines to the Benjamin Franklin Medical and Literary Society, a foundation formed in 1976 and headed by his wife, Indianapolis physician Cory SerVaas. The society has two divisions: the Saturday Evening Post Society publishes just the Post; the Children's Better Health Institute publishes a number of children's magazines, including Jack & Jill, Humpty Dumpty, Child Life, Children's Digest, and US Kids (The Weekly Reader). The foundation is not part of Curtis, but Curtis retains rights to pre–1982 magazine material.

Curtis Magazine Group publishes special-interest magazines such as Indiana Business Magazine and Trap & Field. Curtis also licenses art and editorial work, including its own and that of other publishing companies, and licenses names and likenesses of famous people, dead and alive. Some estates represented are those of Babe Ruth, Charlie Chaplin, and James Dean. Additionally, Curtis deals with engineering, pharmaceutical, and other technological licenses. The company operates factories in the United States, Canada, and Europe.

Curtis became a privately held company in 1991. It is under the umbrella of SerVaas, Inc., with independent companies in chemicals, pharmaceuticals, construction, and other fields. Curtis and Franklin Society employees total about 3,000, with 80 editorial people working at the *Post* and the children's and special-interest magazines.

JOANNE KEATON

A 1902 view of West Market Street shows the round Cyclorama building on the lower right.
[Indiana Historical Society, Bass Collection, #224832]

Curzon, Joseph (1813–July 7, 1896). Early architect. Born in Derbyshire, England, Curzon immigrated to Harrisburg, Pennsylvania, in the early 19th century. In 1851 he moved to Indianapolis and as one of six professional architects in the city in the 1850s quickly acquired a successful practice. He designed the UNION STATION in 1852, the first union station in America and predecessor to Indianapolis' current Union Station. Also in 1852 he designed additions to the State Hospital for the Insane. Curzon was the architect for the SECOND PRESBYTERIAN CHURCH at the corner of Pennsylvania and Vermont streets, where he was also a member of the congregation. Completed in 1870 at a cost of $105,000, the rubble limestone Gothic building was reputed to be one of the most attractive in the city. He also designed a number of local residences, among them the Vajen house (1864) and the Vinton Pierce Italianate mansion, which stood at 1415 North Meridian Street. Curzon is buried in CROWN HILL CEMETERY. None of the buildings known to have been designed by him in Indianapolis remains standing.

CONNIE J. ZEIGLER

Lee Burns, *Early Architects and Builders of Indiana* (Indianapolis, 1935).

Cyclorama. Turn-of-the-century exhibition structure. Located on the north side of Market Street just west of Illinois Street, the Cyclorama building exhibited life-size Civil War murals and served as a menagerie during its 15–year existence.

The dome-shaped structure was built in 1888 by a local cyclorama stock company to exhibit a massive mural portraying the Battle of Atlanta. The 50–foot high mural, painted in Milwaukee by German artists, stretched 400 feet in circumference around the inside of the building. Large crowds paid a modest fee to see the painting until the novelty wore off. Despite efforts to boost attendance, the cyclorama stock company folded and the painting was removed from the city in 1891; it is currently on display in Grant Park, Atlanta, Georgia. Because the depiction of Civil War battles was a popular artistic theme during this period, the Cyclorama was part of a national trend in the construction of such structures. Several other murals, including one of a religious nature entitled "Jerusalem," were featured in the Cyclorama building in the 1890s.

At the turn of the century, one of the nation's first horseless carriage exhibits was held in the structure. In the fall of 1900, the Cyclorama building was home to the Frank Bostock Zoo, a collection of wild animals resembling a circus. Lions, tigers, and bears were housed in cages, which were lined around the inner walls of the structure. Animal trainers entertained the large crowds that thronged to the zoo and an excursion to the facility became a prized outing until the zoo moved from town in 1901. The Cyclorama building was demolished in 1903 to make room for the new INDIANAPOLIS TRACTION TERMINAL.

JAMES R. BISHOP

D

Daggett, Robert Frost (Mar. 13, 1875–Sept. 6, 1955). Prominent Indianapolis architect. After graduating from Indianapolis High School (later SHORTRIDGE HIGH SCHOOL) in 1893, Daggett undertook the finest architectural education available in his day. He earned a degree in architecture at the University of Pennsylvania in 1896 and then studied at the Ecole des Beaux-Arts in Paris, receiving a diploma from the prestigious French school in 1901. On returning to Indianapolis he joined R. P. Daggett & Company, the architectural firm founded by his father, ROBERT PLATT DAGGETT. He assumed management of the firm around 1912 upon his father's retirement and continued the practice under his own name after his father's death in 1915.

An Army officer during World War I, Daggett was stationed in France for 16 months and was in charge of building military hospitals. Resuming private practice in 1919, he renewed his firm's association with ELI LILLY AND COMPANY, executing dozens of commissions for Lilly plants in Indianapolis and Greenfield, and with Purdue University, where he designed five buildings. He was architect also for Indiana, DePauw, and Butler universities. He designed several buildings for the INDIANA UNIVERSITY SCHOOL OF MEDICINE as well as Long, Riley, Coleman, Carter, and Community hospitals. He was supervising architect for Tabernacle Presbyterian Church (1921–1924) and was responsible for the INDIANAPOLIS ATHLETIC CLUB (1922), Consolidated Building, Chamber of Commerce Building (1926), Admiral Apartments (ca. 1930), and many Indianapolis public schools. Among his few residential works are the J. K. Lilly and Eli Lilly homes on Sunset Lane.

Daggett was active in numerous professional organizations, fraternal societies, and social clubs. The first president of the Indiana Construction League, he also was the first Indiana-born architect to be named a Fellow of the American Institute of Architects. The Indiana Society of Architects awarded him its Certificate of Merit in 1931 for his design of the Third Church of Christ, Scientist. Two of his buildings, Jordan Hall at BUTLER UNIVERSITY (with Thomas Hibben, 1928) and the Washington Hotel (1925), are listed in the National Register of Historic Places.

In 1948 Robert Frost ("Pete") Daggett, Jr. and F. Harold Naegele were named partners in the firm, which later became Daggett Naegele & Associates. The business was dissolved in 1977 upon the younger Daggett's retirement.

ANDREW R. SEAGER
Ball State University

Indianapolis Times, Sept. 6, 1955; Biography files, Drawings and Documents Archive, College of Architecture and Planning, Ball State University, Muncie, Indiana.

Daggett, Robert Platt (Jan. 13, 1837–Nov. 5, 1915). Founder of R. P. Daggett & Company, Architects. Daggett received his architectural training in New Haven, Connecticut, where he was born and raised. He moved to Indianapolis in 1868 and quickly established himself as one of the state's leading architects. He was in partnership with Matthew Roth for several years, ca. 1870–1874, and formed R. P. Daggett & Company with James B. Lizius in 1880.

A prolific and versatile architect, Daggett helped shape the appearance of late 19th century Indianapolis. He designed well over 100 residences, including the James Whitcomb Riley Home (528 Lockerbie Street, built for John R. Nickum, ca. 1872), and was responsible for several churches, public buildings, and schools. Among his school commissions were two high school buildings, the Girls' Classical School and Indianapolis Public School 3. A model of Public School 3 received first prize in Philadelphia at the Centennial Exhibition of 1876 for its "superiority of arrangement, ventilation and sanitary convenience."

Many of the city's leading businessmen sought Daggett's services. His firm produced several business blocks in the Indianapolis wholesale district, notably the McKee Building (200 South Meridian Street, 1889), and also Vajen's Block, the Lemcke Building, Sayles Building, Loraine Building, Marion Building, Wright's Market Street Block, the Indianapolis News Company, Lombard Building (22–24 East Washington Street, 1893, listed in the National Register of Historic Places), and H. Lieber Company Building (24 West Washington Street, ca. 1898). Major industrial commissions include the original Eli Lilly and Company laboratory, E. C. Atkins & Company saw works, Burford Printing Company, and Dean Brothers Steam Pump Works (323 West 10th Street, 1893).

Commissions undertaken by Daggett & Company outside Indianapolis include Stott Hall at Franklin College (ca. 1884) and many buildings on Purdue University's West Lafayette campus. Courthouses by Daggett in Shelby and Warren counties were destroyed by fire and have been replaced.

Daggett was named a Fellow of the American Institute of Architects in recognition of his distinguished career. He retired to California ca. 1912. The practice was continued under various names by his son ROBERT FROST DAGGETT and grandson Robert Frost Daggett, Jr. until the latter's retirement in 1977. At that time, it was the second oldest architectural firm in Indiana. Unfortunately, only a small fraction of the firm's early work survives.

ANDREW R. SEAGER
Ball State University

Indianapolis News, Nov. 6, 1915; Biography files, Drawings and Documents Archive, College of Architecture and Planning, Ball State University, Muncie, Indiana.

Daily Echo. Shortridge High School newspaper. The *Daily Echo* was the first and longest published high school daily newspaper in the nation. It was established at Indianapolis High School, which changed its name to SHORTRIDGE HIGH SCHOOL at the turn of the 20th century. Through the determination of a student, Fletcher Wagner, the newspaper survived two aborted attempts: a fortnightly paper, *Silent Spectator*, abandoned after seven issues, and *The Comet*, a weekly paper that lasted 21 issues. Wagner's perseverance resulted in the launching of the *Daily Echo* on September 27, 1898. It consisted of one page with advertisements on the back side. Wagner and two other students served as the paper's staff until their parents objected to their lengthy working hours. On November 3, 1898, production ceased. Fol-

lowing an all-school meeting held soon after the newspaper's demise a committee of faculty and students purchased and managed a printing press. On January 16, 1899, the *Daily Echo* reappeared as a four-page publication with an editorial staff for each day of the week. The *Echo* prospered as a daily for 72 years before the format changed during the 1970–1971 school year to an eight-page weekly. Publication ceased when Shortridge was converted to a junior high school in 1981. Former *Echo* staff members include authors Kurt Vonnegut and Dan Wakefield, and U.S. Senator Richard G. Lugar.

JUDY SCHWARTZ

Laura S. Gaus, *Shortridge High School* (Indianapolis, 1985).

Damien Center. AIDS support center. CHRIST CHURCH CATHEDRAL (Episcopal) and SS. PETER AND PAUL CATHEDRAL (Roman Catholic) founded the Damien Center in June, 1987, in response to the urging of Reverend Earl Conner. It was named for Father Damien, a Jesuit priest who ministered to a leper colony in Hawaii. The center's mission was to coordinate preexisting AIDS education and human service programs that had originated from efforts of public health officials, physicians, the gay community, and interested individuals.

Its current aims are to provide education, counseling, and psycho-social support for people affected with the HIV virus and their friends and families. Its services include case management, medical and dental referral, direct financial assistance, legal advocacy, client advocacy, transportation, the Buddy program, individual and group counseling, support groups, and interim housing.

The center is funded by state and federal grants, foundations, corporations, income from special events, and annual fund-raising.

LEE ANN VRIESMAN

Dance Bands. Professional bands of musicians hired to perform for public and private social dances began to flourish in Indianapolis during the 1880s when groups such as the MON-

TANI BROTHERS' Orchestra, Lyra Society Orchestra, First Turner Orchestra, and Catalano Family Orchestra played mixtures of European classical and American theatrical music to accompany waltzes, marches, polkas, and other popular period dance types. Instruments commonly used included brass and woodwind instruments, harp, violin, banjo, accordion, drums, and piano. Public venues included social clubs, hotels, theaters, saloons, and parks.

The 20th century saw the emergence of RAGTIME and JAZZ dance bands, which evolved into swing and big band ensembles through the 1930s, '40s, and '50s. Long-running venues for jazz-derived bands included Riverside Park, Broad Ripple Dance Pavilion, Casino Gardens, Jack-O-Lantern Gardens, Walnut Gardens, Southern Mansion, Indiana Roof Ballroom, Indianapolis Athletic Club, Columbia Club, Walker Ballroom, the Athenaeum, Tomlinson Hall, and all major hotels and movie theaters. Memorable bands included the Russell Smith Orchestra, Clay Military Band, Reginald Duvalle Orchestra, Hoosier Sextet, Wisdom Brothers, Patent Leather Kids, Brown Buddies, Varsity Red Hots, Columbia Club Orchestra (featuring Hoagy Carmichael), and orchestras headed by Laurence "Connie" Connaughton, Emil Seidel, Charlie Davis, Duke Hampton, Virgil Moore, Louis Lowe, Arnold Peek, Red Hufford, Danny Daniel, Charlie DeSautelle, and Amos Otstot.

Rock 'n' roll combos were popular ca. 1955–1970 at teen and young adult dances. Instrumentation included electric guitar, electric bass, trap drum set, electronic piano and organ, tenor or alto saxophone, and lead and background vocalists. Groups such as Johnny and the Pyramids, Downbeats, Crowns, Blue Angels, Danny Dollar, Five Stars, Gary Gillespi, Turbans, Rockin' Tones, Keetie and the Kats, Monograms, Swingin' Lads, Sir Winston and the Commons, Boys Next Door, Chosen Few, Dawn Five, and Sounds Unlimited performed at area nightclubs and for dances at Whiteland Barn, Westlake Beach Club, South Side Armory, and numerous drive-in theaters, restaurants, swimming pools, shopping centers, churches, and neighborhood community centers.

Youth-oriented local dance bands rapidly diminished in number during the 1970s and '80s as dance promoters increasingly used recorded music featuring national artists and teen popular music tastes fragmented into sub-genres of BLUES, soul, rock, punk, pop, thrash, and rap performed in venues where audience dancing was sporadic and secondary to the performance.

LAWRENCE E. MCCULLOUGH
Indiana University–Purdue University,
Indianapolis

Duncan Schiedt, *The Jazz State of Indiana* (Pittsboro, Ind., 1977); Larry G. Goshen, *Indy's Heart of Rock 'n' Roll* (Indianapolis, 1985).

Dance Kaleidoscope (DK). Professional contemporary dance company. YOUNG AUDIENCES of Indiana formed DK in 1972 to bring dance into the public schools. The company became a not-for-profit corporation in 1975 and Cherri Jaffee was hired as artistic director in 1977. In 1978, the group held its first concert; a board of directors was also created in 1978, and DK began its first official fund drive, with sponsorship from LILLY ENDOWMENT and the INDIANA ARTS COMMISSION. The company opened administrative offices and secured funds to pay salaries on a 43–week contractual basis. Corporate and individual fund drives were initiated in 1981.

A 1993 view of the dance company Dance Kaleidoscope taken on the grounds of the Indianapolis Museum of Art.
[Dance Kaleidoscope, David Hochoy, Artistic Director. Photo by Drew Endicott]

The company holds a three-concert subscription series at the INDIANA REPERTORY THEATRE. DK collaborates with the INDIANAPOLIS SYMPHONY ORCHESTRA in "Yuletide Celebration" each season, and performs for more than 25,000 children annually, presenting thematic concerts on the environment and anti-drug abuse. DK performed at the closing ceremonies of the Tenth PAN AMERICAN GAMES in 1987, at the Piccolo Spoleto Festival in South Carolina, and in New York City at the Riverside Dance Festival.

In 1990, the company established the Jaffee-Hall Emerging Indiana Artist Award, designed to give Indiana artists the opportunity to work with a professional company. In 1992, the company performed "Scheherezade," its first full evening work. The DK repertoire incorporates choreography from world-class artists, including Ohad Naharin, Fred Mathews, and Lambros Lanbrou.

BETH A. HAWKS
Dance Kaleidoscope, Inc.

Danes. The migration of Danes to America was sparse and slow, with the largest movement occurring late in the 19th century. Economic and political instability in Denmark and the lure of jobs and land in America were the principal reasons for emigrating. Most emigrants were rural peasants or members of the urban working class who quickly assimilated into American society because of their small, scattered numbers.

These patterns held true for the Indianapolis Danish community, which owed its existence to the city's well-established German community. In 1860 the German Lutheran congregation of St. Paul's contracted with a Cleveland, Ohio, firm to build a new church. Two recently emigrated Danes, Hans Peter Weis and Rasmus Svendsen, both from Fanefjord on the island of Moen, arrived in Cleveland in 1860 and joined the work crew sent to Indianapolis in the spring of 1861. Family members eventually joined the two men in the city. In 1865 Weis visited Denmark and returned with 40 young men and women from Moen and the neighboring island of Falster. By 1870 nearly 50 Danes lived in Wards 7 and 9 on the city's near southeast side. Most males were

employed in construction; others worked as tailors, shoemakers, and coopers.

In 1867 the Danish community, with the assistance of St. Paul's pastor, Carl Frinke, sought to establish a Danish Lutheran congregation. Since most Danes had joined Norwegian churches, they requested assistance from the Norwegian Lutheran Synod in locating a Danish pastor. Markus Weise, a student at St. Louis Concordia Seminary, arrived in 1868 and organized Trinity Lutheran Church, the first Danish congregation in the country. In 1872 parishioners purchased property at Noble and McCarty streets and erected a brick Gothic-style church that still stands today in the HOLY ROSARY–DANISH CHURCH Historic District. The congregation survives as First Trinity Lutheran Church, located on East 42nd Street.

In the late 19th century, doctrinal disputes within the Danish church divided the community, resulting in some Danes relocating to HAUGHVILLE and others to farms west of the city. By the early 20th century, Danes had moved farther south and northwest to the Riverside neighborhood.

Danish immigration to Indianapolis was always sparse. The 1880 census recorded 114 Danes in the city while the 1910 census showed a peak of 208 native-born Danes. Many worked in the building industry; others continued farming. The most successful of these was Carl Moller, owner of a dairy farm and milk delivery business located on present-day Moller Road.

The Danish church continued to be the religious and social center of most Indianapolis Danes. In the 20th century, however, the Swedish Lutheran Church and Grace Lutheran Church had small numbers of Danish members.

Fraternal organizations including the Danish Brotherhood (1905), the Danish Sisterhood (1911), and the Danish Sick Society (1910) offered both financial and cultural support to those Danes who settled in the city. Although other attempts were made to create Danish nationalist societies, none survived for any length of time, proof of the complete assimilation of the Danes into the Indianapolis population.

SHERYL D. VANDERSTEL

First Trinity Evangelical Lutheran Church (Indianapolis, 1943); *Indianapolis News*, July 18, 1931.

Day Nursery Association of Indianapolis. An advocator and provider of child care programs and services for children, parents, and the community. Begun in 1899 by the Kings Daughters Society, Day Nursery outfitted underprivileged children and provided food baskets for the needy. In 1901, it incorporated as an organization providing care for children of working mothers. By 1940, it had established modern child care standards in the nursery program. Stimulated by a need for quality child care, the program expanded; between 1977 and 1991, the average monthly enrollment rose from 335 to 628 children. The association's centers and programs now serve approximately 600 children at six centers and 882 children in sponsored licensed day care homes. Funding support comes from fees (50%), federal funds administered by state agencies (25%), UNITED WAY (6%), and other sources (19%).

The association's major focus is the development of the individual child, which is implemented in several ways. Day care centers provide preschool education supervised by professional, credentialed staff using curricular materials especially designed for young children in day care centers. Pediatric nurse practitioners provide health care, including immunizations, tuberculosis skin tests, physical examinations, vision screening, speech and hearing screening, dental screening, and sickle-cell anemia testing. Volunteers offer enrichment activities such as field trips, arts and crafts, languages, storytelling, and books on tape. A parent program fosters communication through parent-teacher conferences, newsletters, surveys, brochures, and curricular aids. It also offers financial aid to eligible parents. Training for day care providers and sponsoring of day care homes assures the availability of quality child care. Currently, Day Nursery sponsors 75 homes serving 959 children. A referral service helps parents to locate and evaluate child care; in 1991 it responded to 3,347 requests.

BARBARA BATCHELOR
Day Nursery Association

Dayspring Center. Homeless family shelter and food service for the hungry. Founded in 1989 by the Indianapolis Episcopal Metropolitan Council, whose member churches previously had each provided services, the Dayspring Center helps families with children and provides lunch for anyone in need of a meal. An average of 110,000 meals are served annually. The building, designed specifically as temporary housing for families in crisis, can accommodate 14 families. The average stay is about 24 days.

Assistance provided to families includes education and employment assessment and placement; individual and group counseling; medical, dental, and mental health care; substance abuse education; classes in parenting and nutrition; housing placement; and living skills counseling. Dayspring programs allow residents to identify—and to take responsibility for changing—the behaviors and conditions that contributed to their homelessness. Dayspring emphasizes community-based action as the most effective way to serve homeless families in crisis. It is the only shelter in the state to offer an on-site Head Start program.

Dayspring is Indianapolis' coordinating agency for handling inquiries and making referrals for homeless families seeking shelter. In 1993 it had a staff of 19 and over 250 volunteers. Its average annual budget of $480,000 comes, in roughly equal portions, from the federal government, grants, individual contributions, and churches.

SUSAN B. SKILLRUD
Dayspring Center

De La Matyr, Gilbert (July 8, 1825–May 17, 1892). Minister and congressman. Born in Philadelphia, New York, De La Matyr was licensed to preach by the Methodist church at age 20. He served as an army chaplain during the Civil War and preached in Brooklyn, Omaha, and Kansas City before coming to ROBERTS PARK METHODIST CHURCH in Indianapolis in 1874. Under De La Matyr's leadership the church constructed a new building at 401 North Delaware Street despite the economic depression of the mid–1870s.

De La Matyr became prominent in the city as an advocate of social justice, monetary reform, and lower interest rates. He was nominated in July, 1878 as the National (Greenback) party candidate from Indiana's 7th district to the U.S. House of Representatives, a nomination supported by the Democrats in August. After a lively campaign dominated by economic and fiscal issues, he defeated Republican incumbent John Hanna by a thousand votes. De La Matyr served one term in Congress, continuing to work for financial reform, including an unsuccessful bid for the issue of a billion dollars in greenbacks to be loaned by the government to private corporations in financial trouble. Returning to the ministry for a brief tenure in Denver, Colorado, he then joined the Northeast Ohio Methodist Conference in 1883, remaining there until his death in Akron in 1892.

ANNE HAUPT

Biographical Directory of the American Congress, 1774–1971 (Washington, D.C., 1971).

Decatur Township. Southwestern Marion County township. In 1819, three years before Decatur Township was organized and named for Stephen Decatur, a hero of the War of 1812, settlers had cleared dense hardwood forests and established farms along the White River or near the district's numerous springs. Many early residents were Quakers who moved to the area from the Carolinas. In 1827 they established the first Sanders Creek Meeting of Friends.

Small settlements sprang up along key roads or near rail lines. Northport was platted in 1839, though the name was changed to Fremont in 1856 and later to Valley Mills. The town prospered as a stop on the Indianapolis and Vincennes Railroad, constructed in 1867.

Farther south, Newton (later changed to WEST NEWTON) was laid out by Christopher Furnas in 1851. During the Civil War, the Mooresville Road was built through the community. Another settlement, Spring Valley, platted in 1848, survived only a brief time, though its rivals, West Newton and Valley Mills, boasted shops, schools, churches, and small businesses in the 1880s.

CAMBY was laid out and named by Don Carlos Morgan in 1890. Located along the railroad

Selected Statistics for Decatur Township, 1990

Population	21,092
Population per Square Mile	655
Percent African-American	1.1
Percent 0 to 17 Years	30.1
Percent 65 Years and Over	7.8
Percent 25 Years and Over with a High School Degree or Equivalency	74.4
Percent 25 Years and Over with a College Degree	8.3
Per Capita Income in 1989	$12,080
Unemployment Rate (%)	4.9
Married-Couple Families as a Percent of Total Households	65.2
Median Home Value	$61,300

and, later, a state highway, Camby served travelers and local farmers. INTERURBANS first came to Camby and other township communities in the early 1900s, though the lines were abandoned in the 1920s.

One impetus for growth was the opening of Indianapolis Municipal Airport (now INDIANAPOLIS INTERNATIONAL AIRPORT) in 1931 on the Decatur Township–Wayne Township line. Over the last 60 years the facilities have expanded and attracted satellite development, including warehouses, commercial firms, and Federal Express operations.

Improved motor routes also spurred township development. A state highway, S.R. 67 (Kentucky Avenue), constructed in the 1930s, was widened in the 1950s to accommodate increased traffic. In the 1960s and 1970s, I–465 and I–70 were built across the northern sector of the township.

Intensive residential development in some of the township's northern areas began after World War II when Indianapolis factories, such as Detroit Diesel Allison Division of General Motors, expanded the work force. Though a number of new subdivisions were built, the district did not experience the dramatic growth of other Marion County townships, in part because of a lack of key thoroughfares to Indianapolis and only limited access to the interstate system.

Throughout the 19th century, the township counted less than 1,600 residents. By 1940 that number had increased to nearly 4,000. From 1950 to 1980 population grew from about 6,000 to over 19,000. In the 1990 census, there were just over 21,000 residents, placing Decatur last among the nine Marion County townships in population.

In the early 1990s the largest employers in the township included Indianapolis Power and Light Company, Federal Express, and the Metropolitan School District of Decatur Township. District schools had a work force of 600 in the 1992–1993 school year, with 5,200 pupils enrolled in the four elementaries, one middle school, and one senior high school.

Decatur Township has retained its rural, residential character. Though much of the district is still farmland in the early 1990s, officials predict additional commercial and residential development as Indianapolis expands southward.

CATHLEEN F. DONNELLY

Berry R. Sulgrove, *History of Indianapolis and Marion County* (Philadelphia, 1884), 506–518; Department of Metropolitan Development, *Decatur Township Comprehensive Planning Study, Data Inventory* (1989); U.S. Census.

Deer Creek Music Center. Outdoor music-entertainment complex. Located southeast of Noblesville in Hamilton County, Deer Creek was completed in 1989 at a cost of $12 million and is owned and operated by SUNSHINE PROMOTIONS of Indianapolis. The 220–acre site features a main stage amphitheater with reserved seating for 6,200 patrons; another 14,000 patrons can be seated on the surrounding hillside. From May to September the center presents 50–60 concerts by national acts covering many contemporary musical styles. There is also a week-long country fair in June. The center was voted "Best New Concert Venue in North America" by *Pollstar* in 1989. Attendance at all events in 1992 totaled close to one half million.

LAWRENCE E. MCCULLOUGH
Indiana University–Purdue University,
Indianapolis

Mike Redmond, "Twenty Years of Sunshine," *Indianapolis News*, Sept. 18, 1991.

DeFrantz, Faburn E. (Feb. 9, 1885–Sept. 24, 1964). African-American YMCA director and civil rights activist. Born in Topeka, Kansas, DeFrantz continued his public school education by attending Washburn College and Kansas University. He also studied medicine for five years at Kansas Medical College but never practiced. Later, he studied at Indiana University School of Social Work and the YMCA College in Springfield, Massachusetts.

DeFrantz originally became interested in YMCA work during college when he worked as a physical director and janitor at the Topeka YMCA branch. He came to Indianapolis in 1913 to serve as physical director at the SENATE AVENUE YMCA and was promoted to executive secretary three years later. During his 35 years directing this YMCA, he was responsible for making it one of the most successful branches in the country. He instituted "Monster Meetings" for which he brought prominent African-American artists, writers, musicians, and educators to Indianapolis. He continually fought for an end to racism and was affectionately known as "The Chief" to all the local boys.

DeFrantz was a Madam Walker Company and FLANNER HOUSE board member, Howard University trustee, and member of Kappa Alpha Psi fraternity. He was active in the Committee of One Hundred, which raised college scholarship money for CRISPUS ATTUCKS HIGH SCHOOL graduates. He was also involved with the Academy of Political Science and State Social Workers Society.

MICHELLE D. HALE

Defrees, John D. (Nov. 8, 1810–Oct. 19, 1882). Printer and politician. Born in Sparta, Tennessee, Defrees was eight years old when his family moved to Ohio. At 13 he was apprenticed to a printer and later studied law in Lebanon, Ohio. Having passed the bar, Defrees moved to South Bend, Indiana, in 1831, where he became a newspaper publisher and represented St. Joseph County in the state legislature during the early 1840s. After selling his newspaper to Schuyler Colfax, his one-time apprentice, Defrees settled in Indianapolis in 1845 and purchased the *INDIANA JOURNAL*, later known as the *Indianapolis Journal*, a leading morning daily that he owned until 1854.

In 1859, he began publishing the *Atlas*, a daily which was absorbed by the *Journal* in 1861.

In 1852, Defrees served as chairman of the Whig state central committee and four years later he chaired the same committee for the REPUBLICAN PARTY. In 1855, he helped establish the Central Bank, serving as its president until it closed, and in 1858 he was defeated in the primary in a bid for election to Congress. Defrees left Indiana permanently in 1861 when President Abraham Lincoln named him government printer, a position he held until 1869 when he was ousted from office by Republican members of Congress. Reappointed by President Rutherford Hayes, Defrees served a third term as government printer from 1877 until his retirement in April, 1882.

Although he was a natural politician, ending arguments and uniting antagonisms through arbitration and humor, his first love was the press. As a publisher, he was the first Hoosier to use a caloric press engine, a metallic stretching machine for binding, the Bullock printing press, and the Edison light at a business place. He died in Berkley Springs, West Virginia, and was buried in CROWN HILL CEMETERY, Indianapolis.

JOE FROLLO, JR.

Indiana Biography Series, Indiana State Library; *Biographical Directory of the Indiana General Assembly*, Vol. 1 (Indianapolis, 1980).

Democratic Party. The oldest and only American political party in continuous existence in Indiana since it became a state in 1816. The Indiana and Marion County organizations are, in turn, parts of the national Democratic party that traces its origins to Thomas Jefferson. Jefferson and another Democratic president, Andrew Jackson, are recognized at local annual Jefferson-Jackson celebrations, especially dinners, that often serve as fund-raising events and highlight special guest speakers of national political prominence.

While the donkey is the symbol of the national Democratic party, the rooster is preferred by Marion County Democrats. It originated during the campaign of 1840 when Joseph Chapman, the Democratic candidate for state senator in neighboring Hancock County, was caricatured as a rooster in a local newspaper cartoon. Generally believed to be trailing his Whig opponent before the cartoon was published, Chapman went on to score an upset victory even though the national Whig ticket was led by the candidacy of adopted Hoosier William Henry Harrison for president. The rooster, variously known as Chapman or Chanticleer, survived as the local party symbol, although it never gained national recognition.

Party Structure. The Marion County Democratic party maintains a permanent organization known as the Marion County Democratic Central Committee. It is comprised of precinct committeemen elected by Democratic primary election voters and their appointed vice-committeemen in each of the county's 891 precincts (as of 1993). The typical precinct contains nearly 900 residents and more than 450 registered voters. From 12 to 15 precincts are grouped into wards or subwards. This contemporary organizational device has a long history. It derives from the 1838 reincorporation of Indianapolis by the Indiana General Assembly that divided the town into six wards, each of which was an election district for town trustee.

Marion County Democratic precinct committee members and vice-committee members meet every four years in convention to elect a chair, a vice-chair of the opposite sex, a secretary, and a treasurer. The chair and vice-chair maintain a party headquarters and are *ex officio* members of the congressional district Democratic central committee in each congressional district that is totally or partially within the county. The congressional district committee elects a chair and a vice-chair of the opposite sex who, along with their counterparts from other Indiana congressional districts, comprise the Indiana Democratic State Central Committee and elect the Indiana Democratic chair and vice-chair of the opposite sex.

The primary function of the Marion County Democratic Central Committee is electoral: the recruitment, nomination, election, and appointment of Democrats to public office. Party discipline, especially as regards political philosophy, is largely lacking because each level of party leadership elects the next higher level of leadership in the party's pyramidal structure. Real authority, then, is delegated from below rather than exercised from above, making a well-defined political philosophy enforced through party discipline virtually impossible.

Local Democratic Constituency. Location of the state capital made Indianapolis and Marion County an important political center only five years after Indiana achieved statehood. As the new state capital grew, the Marion County Democratic party benefited at various times from the electoral support of three primary ethnic or racial groups: African-Americans, Germans, and Irish.

Germans and Irish, both Catholic in religious preference, were major immigrant groups or nationalities in Marion County from the 1830s to the early 20th century. Both groups also voted Democratic. The construction of the canal system in the 1840s and the railroads in the following decades, both of which depended on an immigrant labor base, attracted numerous German and Irish immigrants to the Midwest generally and the growing Indiana capital at Indianapolis specifically. By the middle of the 20th century, more than three in ten Marion County residents claimed German heritage while nearly two in ten cited Irish ancestry.

Blacks have been another important constituency of the local Democratic party, especially since the 1930s. The African-American population increased greatly after the Civil War. It intensified after World War II as the Great Depression ended and urban industry became a magnet for black migration from the rural South. By 1990 the decennial census indicated that slightly more than 21 percent of the population in Marion County was black. The importance of blacks in the Democratic party increased after Unigov and the interdistrict busing that followed the end of *de jure* school segregation.

Of the remaining Democratic population, nearly all of it white Protestant, many derive from the post–Civil War South or from southern Indiana, a region that was particularly sympathetic with the aims of the Confederacy. Known as "copperheads," these southern sympathizers provided a social base for the KU KLUX KLAN and its Indiana leader, D. C. STEPHENSON, after World War I when more than 400,000 Hoosiers became affiliated with that organization. The Klan's anti-foreigner, anti-Semitic, anti-Catholic, and anti-Negro agenda briefly gave it the political balance of power in Indiana and Marion County during the early 1920s. It ended almost as quickly as it began when a Hamilton County jury convicted Stephenson of the 1925 murder of Madge Oberholtzer, a young State House worker who lived three blocks from Stephenson in the eastside Indianapolis neighborhood of Irvington.

Electoral History. Republicans have dominated party politics in Indianapolis and Marion County. Of the 20 Democratic governors in the state's history, only half carried a majority or plurality of the vote in Marion County. From the adoption of the city charter of 1847 through 1995, Democrats have controlled the office of Indianapolis mayor for only 48 years while Republicans have held sway for 94 years. The Whigs, forerunners of the Republicans, elected the first three Indianapolis mayors who served a total of seven years.

Democrats, then, have been a competitive minority political party that has enjoyed four periods of dominance in Marion County politics: immediately prior to the Civil War after the Whigs had virtually disintegrated and before the Republicans had supplanted them; between 1885 and the turn of the century when the Irish and the Germans buoyed the Democratic party; prior to World War I when the Republican party was split by Theodore Roosevelt's formation of the Bull Moose party; and during the four decades that began in the 1920s with the conviction of Klansman Stephenson and the onset of the Great Depression and ended with the consolidation of the Marion County and Indianapolis governments in 1969. By then the areas in Marion County outside the preconsolidation city of Indianapolis had gained enough population—most of it Republican—that county politics was dominated by the Republican party.

Henry Clay Whigs dominated Indianapolis and Marion County during the first half of the 19th century. The disappearance of the Whig party and the rise of the anti-foreigner American party (also known as the Know-Nothings) in its place around 1850–1854 pushed recently arrived German and Irish immigrants into the arms of the Democrats. The rise of the newly formed REPUBLICAN PARTY in the late 1850s, however, placed the

Democratic party in peril, and the antiwar sentiment attached to the Democratic party during the CIVIL WAR soon relegated it to its old minority status.

The end of the Civil War saw the beginning of substantial black migration to Indianapolis and Marion County, and black voters predictably formed an allegiance to the party of Lincoln. Not until the discrediting of the Ku Klux Klan in the middle 1920s and the economic collapse of 1929 would black voters shift from bloc-voting Republicans to bloc-voting Democrats.

During the Democratic resurgence in the 1880s, the first truly dominant Marion County Democratic politician emerged—THOMAS TAGGART. First elected county auditor for eight years (1887–1895), Taggart next served three two-year terms as mayor of Indianapolis beginning in 1895. Later elected chairman of the national Democratic party, Taggart was the first activist mayor of the capital city, spending the unprecedented sum of $4 million on public works, primarily for bridges over Fall Creek and land acquisitions for public parks. Born in northern Ireland, Taggart's base support came from recent German and Irish immigrants and their offspring whose lifestyles were threatened by the temperance movement and whose blue-collar livelihoods were threatened by the burgeoning black community. Taggart's public life was crowned by his appointment to a vacancy in the U.S. Senate where he served from March to November, 1916.

The Marion County Democratic party was competitive with the normally dominant Republicans until the end of World War I. The Democrats especially prospered after former Republican president Theodore Roosevelt formed the Bull Moose party and ran for president as its candidate in 1912. The passage of the Volstead Act at the war's end antagonized the German population, which interpreted prohibition as a Republican-inspired punishment for its ethnicity. The rise and fall of the Republican-oriented Ku Klux Klan and its agenda of hate threatened Jews, Catholics, foreigners, and blacks. The collapse of the economy in 1929—associated with President Herbert Hoover and the Republican party—confirmed the Marion County Democratic party as the dominant local political party for a period that lasted almost 40 years.

LOUIS LUDLOW, a congressman from Marion County, was the first local Democrat since Taggart to achieve almost mythical status. Elected to the United States House of Representatives in every even-numbered year from 1928 through 1942 as well as 1946, Ludlow set a record for longevity among Marion County politicians that was not broken until Andrew Jacobs, Jr., son of former congressman ANDREW JACOBS, SR., was elected in every general election from 1964 through 1970 and from 1974 through 1992. Another local Democrat who achieved his father's former office was REGINALD SULLIVAN, who served as mayor of Indianapolis from 1930 to 1935 and 1940 to 1943. First elected at the age of 53, Sullivan fused a coalition of Catholics and blacks to become the most popular Democratic mayor in the history of Indianapolis, winning his first term by 33,000 votes.

The Democratic coalition that provided the base for the careers of Ludlow and Sullivan—blacks, Catholics, and blue-collar workers —survived well into the 1960s. When Richard Lugar was elected mayor in 1967, he was only the third Republican to capture the Indianapolis City Hall in 40 years. By then, two of every five Marion County voters lived outside the Indianapolis city limits. The Republican opportunity for retaining control of Indianapolis city government required the enfranchisement of these suburban voters, most of whom were Republicans.

In early 1969 the state legislature, with an overwhelming Republican majority in each chamber, passed the consolidation statute that established UNIGOV. The legislative mandate to merge Indianapolis and Marion County governments bypassed the popular referendum that characterized all other city-county consolidations in the United States without exception during the 20th century. The Republican governor, whose nomination in the 1968 Republican state convention was dependent on the support of the Marion County Republican delegation, quickly added his signature. *The Wall Street Journal* later quoted Republican county chairman L. Keith Bulen as saying: "It's my greatest coup of all time, moving out there and taking in 85,000 Republican voters."

Indianapolis Democrats, for whom City Hall had provided sanctuary during the worst political times, now faced a franchise expanded to include the overwhelmingly Republican suburbs of Marion County. Broad, countywide, party victories by Democrats in Marion County were unusual; there have been only three such victories since 1950: the 1958 election that was in large part a reaction to the "Eisenhower recession" of that year; the 1964 election that was part of a national repudiation of the Republican candidate for president, Barry Goldwater; and the 1974 election that was a reaction to the Watergate scandal and the resignation of President Richard Nixon.

Lacking favorable demographics, Marion County Democrats have become more oriented to statewide and legislative elections. Statewide the Democratic party has a mixed record of success, winning five U.S. Senate contests and four races for governor since 1960. Marion County Democrats provided a majority for two of the five victorious Senate candidates and two of the four winning candidates for governor. In legislative politics, the 10th congressional district—comprising all of Marion County except the heaviest Republican suburbs—is safely Democratic as the record of 13 wins in the most recent 14 elections attests. The creation of single-member state legislative districts by the 1991 Indiana General Assembly guarantees some measure of Democratic success in Marion County since two of eight state Senate seats and six of fourteen state House districts possess very favorable demographic profiles for Democratic candidates. Finally, the existence of ten favorable single-member districts on the 29–member CITY-COUNTY COUNCIL offers political opportunity and visibility to a limited number of Democratic candidates who reside in the pre-consolidation portion of the city of Indianapolis.

WILLIAM M. SCHREIBER

John B. Stoll, *History of the Indiana Democracy, 1816–1916* (Indianapolis, 1917); Irving Leibowitz, *My Indiana* (Englewood Cliffs, N.J., 1964); *Indianapolis Star*, Nov. 5, 1971 (sesquicentennial edition).

Demographic Profile. In 1830 the population of Indianapolis was 1,900 and grew at a long-term rate equal to 5.8 percent per year to reach a population of 314,194 in 1920. During this period, most of Indianapolis' and Marion County's population was concentrated in CENTER TOWNSHIP. For example, in 1920 Center Township, with a population of 283,414, contained 90 percent of the Indianapolis population and 81 percent of the Marion County population of 348,061. Although measures of natural increase (the annual rate of population growth due to the excess of births over deaths) are not available until 1920, these figures suggest that natural increase did not contribute much to population growth between 1830 and 1920. In 1920 the crude birth rate in Marion County was approximately 18 births per 1,000 population, and the crude death rate was 14.7 deaths per 1,000 population, indicating a rate of natural increase of approximately 0.3 percent per year in 1920. Thus, most of the population growth between 1830 and 1920 was caused by high rates of in-migration. For example, in Marion County the number of in-migrants exceeded out-migrants by 57,583 between 1900 and 1910, and by 70,910 between 1910 and 1920.

Between 1920 and 1950 Marion County grew from a population of 348,061 to 551,777 (a rate of increase equal to 1.5 percent per year), Indianapolis increased from 314,194 to 427,173 (1.0 percent per year), and Center Township increased from 283,414 to 337,211 (0.6 percent per year). Suburbanization resulted in an increased proportion of the Marion County population residing outside of both Center Township and Indianapolis. In 1920, 81 percent of Marion County's population resided in Center Township and 90 percent in the city, but by 1950 only 61 percent of Marion County's population resided in Center Township and 77 percent in the city.

The population growth of Marion County and Indianapolis between 1920 and 1950 was fueled by high rates of in-migration, low rates of out-migration, declining death rates, and rising birth rates. In Marion County the number of in-migrants exceeded out-migrants by 51,200 between 1920 and 1930, by 24,500 between 1930 and 1940, and by 36,400 between 1940 and 1950. Furthermore, declining death rates and rising births rates in Marion County caused the rate of natural increase to rise from approximately 0.3

percent in 1920 to 1.5 percent in 1950. The crude death rate declined from 14.7 deaths per 1,000 population in 1920 to 10.6 deaths per 1,000 population in 1950. During these decades the crude birth rate increased from approximately 18 births per 1,000 population to 25.1 births per 1,000 population.

Between 1950 and 1990 the population of Marion County increased from 551,777 to 797,159 (a rate of increase equal to 0.9 percent per year), the population of Indianapolis increased from 476,258 to 741,952 (1.1 percent per year), and the population of Center Township declined from 333,351 to 182,140 (a rate of decline equal to 1.5 percent per year). Also during this period the Indianapolis metropolitan area expanded to include Boone, Hamilton, Hancock, Hendricks, Johnson, Madison, Marion, Morgan, and Shelby counties. This metropolitan area had a total population of 831,033 in 1950, with 66 percent of the population concentrated in Marion County. By 1990 the Indianapolis metropolitan area had a population of 1,380,491, with only 58 percent of this population residing in Marion County. Thus, between 1950 and 1990 the eight suburban counties had a rate of growth equal to 1.9 percent per year while the rate of growth of Marion County was equal to 0.9 percent per year.

Despite the slow rate of growth in Marion County between 1950 and 1990, the population of the Indianapolis METROPOLITAN STATISTICAL AREA continued to increase because of high rates of in-migration to the suburban counties and high, but declining, rates of natural increase. Leveling death rates and declining births rates in the metropolitan area caused the rate of natural increase to drop from 1.4 percent per year in 1950 to 0.8 percent per year in 1989. The crude death rate declined only slightly, from 10.6 deaths per 1,000 population to 8.5 deaths per 1,000 population, while the crude birth rate decreased dramatically, from 24.1 births per 1,000 population to 16.4 births per 1,000 population. Population figures reflect the rapid suburbanization of Marion County: In 1950, 61 percent of the Marion County population resided in Center Township, but by 1990 only 23 percent of the Marion County population resided there. The decline of Marion County population relative to the suburban counties resulted from a relatively higher rate of out-migration than in-migration in Marion County and a higher rate of in-migration than out-migration in the suburban counties. Between 1950 and 1960 in-migrants still exceeded out-migrants by 36,652 in Marion County, but out-migrants exceeded in-migrants by 2,009 between 1960 and 1970, by 89,535 between 1970 and 1980, and by 22,000 between 1980 and 1990. In contrast, among the suburban counties in-migrants exceeded out-migrants by 43,644 between 1950 and 1960, by 35,123 between 1960 and 1970, by 45,697 between 1970 and 1980, and by 9,900 between 1980 and 1990.

THOMAS J. COOKE
Indiana University–Purdue University,
Indianapolis

Denison Hotel. H. B. Sherman of Milwaukee built the prestigious hotel in 1880 at the corner of Ohio and Pennsylvania streets. The New-Denison, as it was originally known, was reportedly named for two of the investors, John C. New and a Cincinnati businessman named Denison. In the early 1890s, D. P. Erwin purchased the property and added more stories and a mansard roof. The six-story hotel boasted 250 rooms and a number of amenities, including a billiard room and bar. The dining rooms were popular with local residents, who could purchase Sunday dinners for 75 cents.

The hotel was well known for its political connections. Both the Republican and Democratic state organizations had headquarters there for a time. Before and during legislative sessions, the Denison was the site of party caucuses and closed-door negotiations. Political schemes were hatched in Parlor A on the second floor or in the "Amen Corner," a secluded nook in the lobby.

By 1920 the hotel had fallen on hard times and was closed shortly thereafter. The building was razed and later became the site of a parking garage.

CATHLEEN F. DONNELLY

Denny, Caleb Stone (May 13, 1850–Mar. 24, 1926). Mayor of Indianapolis, January 1,

Caleb S. Denny. [Indiana Historical Society, #C5892]

1886–January 1, 1890, October 12, 1893–October 10, 1895, Republican. Denny's father, born in Kentucky, was opposed to slavery, and so settled in Monroe County, Indiana, where Caleb, the youngest of 11 children, was born. The family moved to a farm near Boonville, Warrick County, in 1853, and then, upon his father's death in 1861, to town where Caleb was apprenticed to a tinsmith. He soon left his apprenticeship, attended graded schools in Boonville and Edwardsport, and entered Indiana Asbury (DePauw) University in 1866. Denny remained two years until, lacking funds, he turned to teaching in Warrick County and began to read law. Named assistant state librarian in 1870, he moved to Indianapolis. Continuing his studies with various lawyers, he was admitted to the local bar in 1872 and to state and federal courts in 1873. He was appointed assistant attorney general of Indiana, a new office (1873–1875), and then turned to the active practice of law. Elected city attorney in 1881 and reelected in 1884, Denny resigned in 1885 to wrest the Republican nomination for mayor from the party's incumbent and two other candidates.

Denny campaigned for a "strict enforcement of the laws" regarding Sunday closing, gambling, and prostitution. His 1885 victory was by a slim 60 votes from some 18,000 cast; his margin in 1887 was nearly 800. Denny did not run in 1889, but was persuaded to stand against a popular Democratic incumbent in 1892. He campaigned, as always, as the law and order candidate. His margin of victory, nearly 3,200 votes, the largest to that time, surprised the leaders of both parties.

Highlights of Denny's three terms as mayor include several court battles and city benchmarks.

In 1889 the Democratic General Assembly adopted two laws giving exclusive control of the public works of the city and the police and fire departments to boards appointed by the legislature. Mayor Denny fought this measure, and the Marion County Superior Court, and the state Supreme Court on appeal, agreed that the laws were unconstitutional. During the Pullman Railroad Strike of 1894, centered in Chicago, Denny took charge as mandated by the city charter of 1891, spending much of the crisis at the central police station. Only one train was delayed and no property damage occurred. True to his reformist impulses, the mayor in a lawsuit successfully defended the section of the 1891 charter requiring the testing of all job applicants. Members of his own party had urged him to disregard the civil service provisions. In the Denny years a test of asphalt street paving was made, horse and mule cars were abandoned for electric trolleys, and natural gas was introduced.

After 1895 Denny returned to his law practice but continued his public service: three terms as county attorney, 1905–1908; presidential elector for the 7th district, 1908; president of the trustees of the state normal school at Terre Haute after 1905; and secretary of the state pardon board, 1924 to his death. His son, GEORGE L. DENNY, city controller, became mayor for two years upon the death of the incumbent in 1947, making the Dennys one of three father and son mayors in Indianapolis history.

WILLIAM DOHERTY
Marian College

Charles W. Taylor, *Biographical Sketches and Review of the Bench and Bar of Indiana* (Indianapolis, 1895); Jacob Piatt Dunn, *Greater Indianapolis* (Chicago, 1910); *Indianapolis News*, Mar. 25, 1926.

Denny, George Littrell (July 7, 1878–Sept. 29, 1958). Mayor of Indianapolis, 1947–1948, Republican. A native of Indianapolis and the son of CALEB S. DENNY, former three-time mayor of the city, George Denny graduated from Princeton University in 1900 and Indiana University's School of Law in 1902. Denny specialized in corporation and tax cases and he represented ELI LILLY AND COMPANY for many years.

From 1910 to 1914, Denny served on the Indianapolis City Council. In 1934 he ran, unsuccessfully, as the Republican candidate for mayor, and he chaired the Republican state platform committee from 1938 to 1948. In 1939, he became the president of the Indianapolis BOARD OF TRADE. Appointed controller of the city of Indianapolis in April, 1947, Denny became the city's chief executive following Mayor ROBERT H. TYNDALL'S death in July of that year. Upon leaving office, Denny made an unsuccessful bid for Congress in 1948. In 1951, he became the inheritance tax administrator of the Indiana Department of Revenue.

In 1948, Denny was a delegate to the Republican national convention. He served as a director of the Indianapolis CHAMBER OF COMMERCE, a governor of the SOCIETY OF INDIANA PIONEERS, and as both trustee and president of the Boys Club of Indianapolis.

JEFFERY A. DUVALL

Indiana Biography Series, Indiana State Library; *Who's Who in the Midwest* (5th ed., Chicago, 1956).

Dentistry. Dental problems were a common affliction of early settlers of Indiana—casual references to dental ills abound in period newspapers and travel accounts—and facilities for obtaining dental treatment were indeed poor. Sufferers depended on home remedies or the visits of itinerant dentists. Traveling dentists usually had little formal training and only the crudest of techniques and instruments. Unless they caused pain, decayed teeth generally were not pulled or filled, though occasionally a tinfoil plug could be inserted in a troubled tooth. Few people replaced lost teeth with false ones.

One of the earliest appearances of a dentist in Indianapolis was by Dr. L. B. Bartle in December, 1825, who "pulled teeth without pain and made false teeth." In August, 1836, the *Indiana Democrat* advertised the services of George H. Parker, an itinerant dental surgeon from Philadelphia. Another early professional dentist in Indianapolis was Joshua Soule, who came to the town in 1833.

By the late 1840s the growing town began to attract permanent dentists. Dr. PHINIUS G. C.

HUNT, an Indianapolis native, learned dentistry through an apprenticeship, opening his own office in 1848. Two years later "Messrs. Jeffries and Allerdice, from Philadelphia" established an office for the manufacture of porcelain teeth and general dentistry, and in 1853 Dr. John F. Johnston began his practice after completing his training at the Ohio College of Dental Surgery.

In September, 1858, Johnston invited a small group of dentists to his office to form the Indiana State Dental Association, the first of its kind in the world. Later a committee of the association sponsored the Indiana Dental College (IDC; now the Indiana University School of Dentistry, or IUSD) and the Indiana Board of Dental Examiners, both formed in 1879. These two projects were very important in upgrading the status of dentistry in Indiana, and ultimately throughout the country. With the exception of the few years when a group of unhappy dental faculty members resigned from the IDC in 1897 to form the Central Dental College—which survived as a separate entity for five years before again merging with the IDC—Indiana's only dental school has been the IDC and its successor the IUSD.

Six students enrolled in the Indiana Dental College in 1879, its inaugural year. Enrollment gradually increased, as dentistry became more popular, and peaked in the mid–1920s. During the Great Depression and World War II class size dropped sharply. However, during the next three decades enrollments again increased, reaching a total of about 120 per class in the early 1970s, before leveling off at about 80 by the 1980s and 1990s. Three faculty members of the dental school have been presidents of the prestigious International Association for Dental Research: Maynard K. Hine, Ralph W. Phillips, and David Mitchell.

In addition to playing an important role in dental education, Indianapolis has been the site of important dental research, bringing changes in dentistry worldwide. In the 1940s Dr. Virgil D. Cheyne, an associate professor at the Indiana University Medical Center, experimented with a fluoride solution to prevent tooth decay. Another IUSD faculty member, Dr. Joseph Muhler, pioneered research on fluoride dentrifices that led to the development of Crest toothpaste.

In September, 1951, Indianapolis responded to these positive studies by fluoridating the city's water supply. The following year 12,000 Indianapolis school children were examined by 160 volunteers from the Indianapolis Dental Society. By the fifth year of these exams dentists found a 30 percent decrease in needed dental repair.

Over the years Indianapolis has attempted to make dental care available to all its citizens. As early as 1919 the Children's Aid Society operated the city's first free dental clinic staffed by volunteer dentists. In 1922 the clinic became a part of the Board of Health, but in the 1930s was kept open by the Jewish Federation when the city could no longer afford to fund it. Later clinics have been operated at the Fletcher Place Community Center and in Brightwood and Martindale, the last two financed by the Community Services Program of Indianapolis, a federally funded antipoverty program. In the 1980s and 1990s mobile dental units made oral health services available to patients in nursing homes and other institutions.

For decades dentistry remained a mostly male occupation in Indianapolis and across the nation. By 1967 Indianapolis had only six women dentists. For many years following the introduction of an IUSD training program for dental hygienists in 1952, women interested in the field of dentistry tended to enter the hygienists' program rather than dental school. In 1991, however, 30 of the 80 dentistry students enrolled at IUSD were women.

Although growth and development in dentistry in Indiana may have centered around the Indiana Dental College and its successor, the Indiana University School of Dentistry, the city's private-practice dentists, dental hygienists, and patients have also contributed to the legacy of Indianapolis dentistry.

MAYNARD K. HINE
CONNIE J. ZEIGLER

Jack D. Carr, "History of Dental Education in Indiana," *Indiana Medical History Quarterly*, 4 (Sept., 1978).

The Desperate Hours (1954). Popular novel, play, and movie set in Indianapolis. In Joseph Hayes' first novel, three men escape from federal prison in Terre Haute, flee to Indianapolis, and take a family hostage while they wait for a former girlfriend to bring money. Dan and Eleanor Hilliard, daughter Cindy, and son Ralphie, find their northside home and their lives at the command of the escapees. As days go by, and the money does not come, tempers grow short and the situation becomes tense as Dan tries to protect his family. The youngest fugitive flees and is killed in a highway accident. Dan succeeds in tipping off the police, Cindy's suspicious boyfriend becomes involved by sneaking into the residence, and even Ralphie tries to save his family by slipping a note to a teacher. As police piece clues together, a stake-out is set and the family is rescued. One of the remaining escapees is killed and the other is apprehended.

Made into a Broadway play starring Karl Malden as Dan Hilliard and Paul Newman as the escapees' leader, the production won a Tony award for Best Play in 1956. The novel has been made into a movie twice. The first, featuring Fredric March and Humphrey Bogart, had its midwestern premiere at the Circle Theatre in Indianapolis on October 26, 1955. (Hayes, a native of the city, explained to that audience that his story, while set in Indianapolis, was not based on any specific local incident.) The remake, set in Utah, was produced in 1990 starring Anthony Hopkins and Michael Rourke. The novel has been translated into many languages.

CYNTHIA FAUNCE

Diamond Chain Company. On Christmas Eve, 1890, ARTHUR C. NEWBY, Edward C. Fletcher, and Glenn Howe invested $5,000 to begin manufacturing bicycle chain in Indianapolis. They selected the diamond as their trademark because it symbolized perfection. Their firm, Indianapolis Chain & Stamping Company, started with four machines and four operators in rented rooms upstairs in a tinner's shop on South Street. Its only product was a chain to drive the power on a bicycle from the sprocket to the wheel. By 1895 the owners built a factory on the site of what is now the playing field of the Hoosier Dome. Wilbur and Orville Wright, owners of a bicycle shop in

Workers at the Diamond Chain Company in 1909. [Diamond Chain Company]

Dayton, Ohio, were agents for the company, and seven specially designed chains were used on their first successful flying machine at Kitty Hawk, North Carolina, in 1903.

In 1904 L. M. Wainwright of Noblesville, who had been plant manager since 1899, was able to arrange financing to buy the company, which he renamed Diamond Chain & Manufacturing Company. By 1917 he built a reinforced concrete factory building at Kentucky Avenue and West Street. This same building, with six major additions, continues to serve as the company's headquarters. In 1950 Diamond Chain became a part of AMSTED Industries of Chicago, Illinois.

Today Diamond Chain supplies roller chain to virtually every industry and has a worldwide reputation as the builder of high quality power transmission chain. In 1993 Diamond Chain had 600 employees in Indianapolis with an annual payroll and benefits of about $22 million. In September, 1993, the U.S. Department of Commerce honored the firm with the President's "E" award for excellence in exports.

EDWARD G. FLANINGHAM
Diamond Chain Company

Dick the Bruiser. See Richard Afflis

Diggs, Elder Watson (1883–Nov. 8, 1947). African-American educator. Born in Mad-

isonville, Kentucky, Diggs received a one-room school education in Louisville, where he helped to teach the younger children. He graduated from Indiana State Normal School in 1908, and later attended Howard University. He returned to Indiana in 1911 to earn a B.A. and later an M.A. in education at Indiana University. While at IU, he helped to found the Kappa Alpha Psi national fraternity.

Diggs began his career as a principal and teacher for "colored schools" in Bloomington and Vincennes in order to pay for college. He first came to Indianapolis in 1916 to fill a vacant principal's position at Public School 64 in Norwood, followed by a year at Public School 63 in HAUGHVILLE. After overseas service as an army officer in the 368th Infantry Regiment in World War I, Diggs returned to Indianapolis in 1919 to continue his career. He returned to the Haughville school as principal and was soon promoted to the larger Public School 42 in 1922. He saw this school grow from a four-room portable building and several outbuildings into a modern brick structure. After his death in 1947, School 42 was named in his honor.

MICHELLE D. HALE

Dillinger, John Herbert (June 23, 1903–July 22, 1934). Notorious bank robber. Born in Indianapolis to grocer John W. and Mollie Lancaster Dillinger, John grew up in the vicinity of 21st and Hillside streets. He attended public schools 38 and 55 but quit at age 16. He then worked briefly in a veneer mill, a westside machine shop, and as an errand boy for the Indianapolis BOARD OF TRADE. In March, 1920, Dillinger's family moved to Mooresville, hometown of his widowed father's new wife. Following his first crime (an auto theft) in July, 1923, Dillinger joined the Navy and was stationed at the Great Lakes Naval Training Facility. After being assigned as a fireman on the USS *Utah*, he deserted the Navy in December, returned home, and married.

Dillinger began his criminal career with an attempted holdup of a Mooresville grocer in September, 1924. Following his conviction he spent 1924–1933 in Indiana state prisons, during

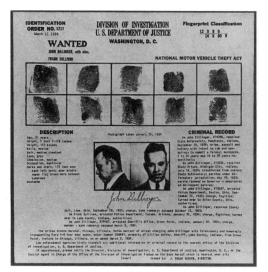

John Dillinger's "Wanted" poster, 1934.
[Indiana Historical Society, #C5823]

which time his wife divorced him (1929) and he strengthened his criminal connections. Paroled on May 22, 1933, within four months Dillinger successfully robbed numerous banks in Indiana, Ohio, and Michigan, including the Massachusetts Avenue State Bank in Indianapolis. On September 22 he was arrested and jailed in Ohio before escaping. Dillinger and his gang next robbed banks in Indiana and Wisconsin, and raided police stations for automatic weapons, bulletproof vests, and police identification before fleeing south where they were arrested in Tucson, Arizona. Extradited to Crown Point, Indiana, Dillinger achieved his most celebrated escape on March 3, 1934, when he allegedly used a fake pistol carved from wood to force his way past a dozen jail guards.

In the ensuing months, the Indiana AMERICAN LEGION offered to arm its 30,000 members to patrol Hoosier highways and the National Guard volunteered its aircraft for aerial patrols. Governor Paul McNutt agreed to increase expenditures for state police equipment while the *Indianapolis Times* informed the U.S. attorney general that the situation in Indiana was serious. In June, 1934, the federal government posted a $10,000 reward for Dillinger's capture.

After barely dodging the FBI in Minnesota and Wisconsin, Dillinger fell victim to a trap in-

volving Anna Sage, a friend and brothel madam who became known as the "Lady in Red." She drew him to the Biograph Theater in Chicago, and upon exiting he was shot to death. Dillinger was buried in CROWN HILL CEMETERY, despite protests from other plot owners.

AIMEE L. REX

Robert Cromie and Joseph Pinkston, *Dillinger: A Short and Violent Life* (Evanston, Ill., 1962, 1990).

Disciples of Christ. See Christian Church

Dispensaries. Precursors to hospital outpatient clinics and health clinics for the poor. During the Civil War civic leaders petitioned the Indianapolis City Council to establish a dispensary for those unable to pay for medical treatment and to provide a source of continuing education for medical students and practitioners. The first private dispensary was Bobbs' Free Dispensary, established around 1870 with a bequest from Dr. JOHN STOUGH BOBBS and associated with the Indiana Medical College. Soon thereafter WILLIAM B. FLETCHER, a prominent physician and son of CALVIN FLETCHER, established a city dispensary. Serving as its superintendent (1875–1879) Fletcher oversaw care for the poor and the city jail's prisoners, treated smallpox cases, and administered vaccinations. In 1875 alone dispensary physicians made 5,563 home visits, treated 4,210 patients at the dispensary, and filled 10,232 prescriptions.

The city dispensary's early years were filled with controversy (including a battle for control of the institution) and financial problems. Despite battles over whether the Indiana Medical College or private physicians would be more efficient in operating the dispensary, the city's Committee on Hospitals refused to cede control. Funds for the institution—half from city appropriations, half from private contributions—also proved inadequate and limited the purchase of medical supplies. In 1879 the City Council reorganized the dispensary as a government-funded agency with a full medical staff and imposed tighter controls to prevent abuse of medical services. The reform did not eliminate the dispensary's financial woes, win additional funds, or protect it from local politics. The council created another health board in 1891, placing the dispensary and City Hospital under its jurisdiction but with no increase in appropriations.

The need for the dispensary became most apparent during the 1893 depression. Cases treated rose from 7,313 in 1892 to 20,938 in 1893. After schools began requiring immunization of children, unemployed parents incapable of paying medical fees turned to the dispensary where one physician remarked that "the sidewalk . . . is crowded all the time with those who are waiting for the opportunity to be vaccinated free." When Superintendent Edward D. Moffett requested $30,000 for a new dispensary, he encountered a public that accused the city of being extravagant in its funding for the poor. Mayor CALEB S. DENNY recommended a $10,000 appropriation instead, noting that "We do not believe in making charities of any kind popular and thus destroying the sense of individual responsibility."

Over the next several years the dispensary continued to be a political battleground. Claiming no need for a new dispensary, Superintendent John F. Geis (May–August, 1894) criticized previous superintendents for prescribing expensive treatments for trivial ailments. Subsequent superintendents John Lambert (1894–1895) and Leonard Bell (1895–1897), however, described the facility as "unsafe, uncomfortable and unsightly" and a "counterpart of the poverty-stricken conditions of the patients." The Indianapolis Sanitary Association reported that "it is a disgrace to the city." While the dispensary received complaints about inadequate staffing and poor funding, conservative opponents claimed the majority of cases treated at the dispensary were those arising from "disgraceful causes, for which the public is not responsible and should not be called upon to treat."

In 1897 the city constructed a new dispensary on South Alabama Street, but it suffered the same problems of earlier years. While physicians were treating 20,000 patients annually by the early 1900s, some improvements were forthcoming. The City Hospital Training School for Nurses provided nurses for the dispensary's "house call"

program. The dispensary also established a tuberculosis clinic in 1908.

To give "proper attention to all cases of illness among the city's poor," the city dispensary merged with Bobbs' Free Dispensary (by now a part of the INDIANA UNIVERSITY SCHOOL OF MEDICINE) in 1909 and moved to new headquarters located at Senate and Market streets. Within a few years it had established clinics for tuberculosis patients, syphilitics, pediatrics, and obstetrics, among others. The dispensary was open 24 hours a day and provided ambulance service for the poor. Reaction to the reorganized dispensary was generally positive as the *Indianapolis Medical Journal* reported in 1911 that the dispensary "is now upon a higher plane than ever before." Critics, citing the December, 1910, death of an 8–year-old boy from improper medication prescribed by an intern, charged the dispensary with being in the hands of inexperienced medical students instead of experienced physicians.

Conflicts between the city and the university regarding the role of the dispensary continued. The medical school viewed the dispensary as a training facility for interns and a laboratory to gather statistics about social conditions and physical maladies. The city, however, considered the dispensary solely as a source of inexpensive health care for the poor. On October 31, 1915, the health board broke its contract with the university, assumed total control of the dispensary, and cancelled the school's privileges at City Hospital. Supporters of the medical school–operated dispensary argued that the university's association with local clinics had earned the school its "top five" status from the Carnegie Foundation in 1915. City and medical school officials eventually resolved their differences and resumed dual control of the facility. The dispensary remained a vital force in the care of Indianapolis' sick poor, providing smallpox vaccinations and public health nursing before being replaced by hospital outpatient clinics later in the 20th century.

KATHERINE MANDUSIC MCDONELL
DAVID G. VANDERSTEL

Dodd, Harrison H. (Feb. 29, 1824–June 2, 1906). Civil War–era conspirator. A native of

Brownville, New York, Dodd settled in Toledo, Ohio, where he ran unsuccessfully for mayor on the Know-Nothing ticket in 1855. Following relocation to Indianapolis in 1856 he became active in the DEMOCRATIC PARTY and established a printing business.

Dodd was openly critical of the Abraham Lincoln and OLIVER P. MORTON administrations and helped found the secret society known as the Sons of Liberty, assuming the title of grand commander in Indiana. During the summer of 1864 he engaged in a conspiracy with Confederate commissioners to release and arm rebel prisoners, capture arsenals, and separate the Northwest from the Union. Relying on information provided by the Morton administration, military authorities raided Dodd's offices on August 20, 1864, seizing several boxes of revolvers and ammunition marked "Sunday School books."

Dodd escaped confinement during his trial for conspiracy and fled to Canada. A military commission found him guilty in absentia, sentencing him to hang. Dodd's conviction is generally accepted to have been reversed by the U.S. Supreme Court decision in *Ex parte Milligan*, a related Sons of Liberty case in which convictions were overturned on jurisdictional grounds. Dodd returned to the United States following the Civil War and settled in Fond du Lac, Wisconsin, where he served several terms as Republican mayor.

DAVID A. LOCKE

Mayo Fesler, "Secret Political Societies in the North during the Civil War," *Indiana Magazine of History*, 14 (Sept., 1918), 183–286; G. R. Tredway, *Democratic Opposition to the Lincoln Administration in Indiana* (Indianapolis, 1973).

Donnan, Laura (1854–Aug. 21, 1930). A noted teacher and civic activist, Donnan was born in Indianapolis and lived her entire life in the house her father built at 232 North Capitol Avenue. She graduated from Indianapolis Normal School, taught grade school for a few years, and then went to the University of Michigan for A.B. and M.A. degrees. Returning to Indianapolis for a position at Indianapolis High School (later SHORTRIDGE HIGH SCHOOL), she taught history, civil

government, political economy, Latin, and geometry.

In 1887, Donnan founded the Indianapolis High School Senate, an institution which was to last nearly 100 years and be widely copied by schools around the country. Students took names of U.S. senators and debated the issues of the day, following the strict parliamentary procedure that Donnan insisted on. As "senators" graduated, their names became available to underclassmen who were eager to assume their roles. Membership was by permission of Donnan.

In 1899, Donnan became the first sponsor of the Shortridge *DAILY ECHO*, the nation's first daily high school paper. For three years she read proof every day, but after 1902 she shared that responsibility with other faculty members. During that same year, Donnan was instrumental in establishing the Shortridge Night School, which she served as principal. Its purpose was to make high school education available to working people who could not attend during the day. The first year 57 persons, black and white, ages 15–57, took advantage of the opportunity.

Donnan taught at Shortridge for 45 years. She was also active in civic affairs, a strong supporter of women's suffrage, and an advocate of civil rights. After retirement, she remained active until a few weeks before her death.

LAURA GAUS

Douglass, John (Nov. 12, 1787–Aug. 9, 1851). First state printer; newspaper editor. Douglass moved to Vevay, Indiana, from Philadelphia in 1820. He had learned the printing trade as an apprentice in Lancaster, Pennsylvania, in the early 1800s. After a year in Vevay, Douglass moved to Madison where he published a paper with William Carpenter. He soon left Madison for Corydon where he was elected state printer. In 1824 he and state treasurer SAMUEL MERRILL left Corydon for the new state offices in Indianapolis.

Upon his arrival in the capital Douglass became associated with DOUGLASS MAGUIRE and the *WESTERN CENSOR & EMIGRANTS GUIDE* through his purchase of a substantial interest in that weekly publication. The next year Douglass changed the newspaper's name to the *INDIANA JOURNAL*. He and

Maguire worked together at the *Journal* until Maguire sold his interest to Samuel V. B. Noel in 1835. During the 1830s the paper became increasingly pro-Whig and in 1840 Noel and Douglass published a Whig campaign paper called the *Spirit of '76*. Douglass sold his interest in the *Journal* to Noel in 1843 and lived in retirement until his death.

WILLIAM DALTON

John W. Miller, *Indiana Newspaper Bibliography* (Indianapolis, 1982); John H. B. Nowland, *Early Reminiscences of Indianapolis* (Indianapolis, 1870).

DowElanco. Major agricultural chemical firm. Formed in 1989 as a joint venture between the Dow Chemical Company and ELI LILLY AND COMPANY, DowElanco is the country's second largest agricultural chemical company and the world's sixth largest. Dow, which owns 60 percent, brings expertise in agricultural products to the partnership while Lilly, which controls 40 percent, has strength in the plant science business. Global sales in 1992 were approximately $1.6 billion. DowElanco would rank 250th on the Fortune 500 if it were listed. The company's product line includes pesticides, plant nutrition aids and growth regulators, fumigants, and seeds. Two of the firm's best-selling products are Lorsban, a corn and soybean insecticide, and Treflan, a soybean, corn, and cotton herbicide.

With an annual research budget of $160 million, DowElanco's research focuses on novel chemistries, biotechnology, and fermentation technology. A $100 million headquarters building occupies 325 acres on the far northwest side of Indianapolis and is home for about 1,000 of DowElanco's 2,900 employees worldwide. No manufacturing occurs in Indianapolis, which houses administration and research facilities. The headquarters also serves as operations base for DowElanco's North American market, comprising over half of its annual sales. Additional regional headquarters are located in Europe, Latin America, and the Pacific. DowElanco was lured to Indianapolis, in part, by the promise of property tax abatement and by road improvements made near the facility.

DEBORAH B. MARKISOHN

Downey, Nelle Bowman (July 12, 1876–Sept. 7, 1965). Civic and charity worker; state representative. A native of Knightstown, Indiana, Downey moved to Indianapolis as a child and attended SHORTRIDGE HIGH SCHOOL, Indianapolis Normal School, and Chicago University. She was an Indianapolis public school teacher (1897–1907), but quit teaching to marry Brandt C. Downey.

Downey was known especially for her successful fund-raising campaigns for the Indianapolis Community Fund. She also organized and headed its Women's and Junior Speakers Bureau. As a result of this work, she was appointed six times as state chairperson and Indiana representative for the National Women's Committee for the Mobilization of Human Needs (1929–1935), a national group charged with raising funds for local Community Fund organizations. During World War II Downey was chief of the block system of the Marion County Civilian Defense Council.

Downey represented Marion County in the General Assembly from 1941 to 1948 and again from 1951 to 1954. Her work in the legislature focused on public welfare and education. Among other accomplishments, she helped to modernize the state public school and child welfare laws. She was appointed the Indianapolis representative to the National Probation Association in 1947.

Among many other community organizations, Downey was long active in the YWCA, Home for the Aged, ALPHA HOME for Aged Colored Women, Parent-Teacher Associations, Women's Research Club, Daughters of the American Revolution, and Indianapolis Council of Affiliated Church Women.

MICHELLE D. HALE

Indiana Biography Index, Indiana State Library.

Downtown Development. Indianapolis has struggled with the issue of downtown development (or redevelopment) throughout much of the 20th century. The automobile's popularity in the 1920s and 1930s created a need for downtown parking, with older buildings knocked down for parking lots. By 1944, according to the Indianapolis Real Estate Board, the most significant problems included vacant tracts, high tax assessments, and low or nonexistent revenue among rental properties within the MILE SQUARE.

Indianapolis was not alone in the deterioration of its downtown area. But it was not until the 1970s that the city actively pursued downtown redevelopment in a budding revitalization movement. In 1972 the INDIANA CONVENTION CENTER opened its doors; two years later MARKET SQUARE ARENA, a major recreational and sports facility, opened downtown. Together these venues attracted concertgoers, exposition-attenders, and sports enthusiasts. In the 1970s business also made a new commitment to downtown when companies including Indiana National Bank (1970, now NBD Bank) and Indiana Bell (1975) constructed impressive new office complexes in the central business district. New hotels and commercial structures followed, among them MERCHANTS PLAZA with its Hyatt Regency Hotel (1976).

When William H. Hudnut III became mayor in 1976 the city entered a new phase of downtown redevelopment, focusing on a strategy which would establish a market niche for Indianapolis and further redevelop the downtown core as the cultural and economic center of the city and region.

An important element of the development plan involved marketing the city as a venue for sports events and as the headquarters for amateur sports organizations. This movement originated in 1970 when members of the Sports Capitol Committee persuaded the AMATEUR ATHLETIC UNION to locate in Indianapolis, but it was brought to completion during the Hudnut years. Equally important was creation of the INDIANAPOLIS PROJECT (IPI) in 1981. Jointly sponsored by the city, the CHAMBER OF COMMERCE, the INDIANAPOLIS CONVENTION AND VISITORS ASSOCIATION, and the Convention Center, IPI assisted and encouraged companies considering a move to or an expansion downtown. Within a few years IPI became an image-building organization with the goal of focusing positive local and national media attention on the city. The INDIANAPOLIS ECONOMIC DEVELOPMENT CORPORATION took over the development responsibilities of the IPI in 1983.

Indianapolis' plan fit important theories of development. There was a clear geographic focus: the downtown area. This emphasis capitalized on existing assets and several public investments, including a government center employing thousands of state and local government employees, a large private sector employer (ELI LILLY AND COMPANY), and a developing state university campus (INDIANA UNIVERSITY–PURDUE UNIVERSITY, INDIANAPOLIS, or IUPUI) with a hospital and health services center (INDIANA UNIVERSITY MEDICAL CENTER). During the Hudnut years public and private initiatives led to more than 30 major development projects for the downtown. Concurrently the investment in IUPUI totaled more than $231 million. In the late 1980s and early 1990s the State of Indiana provided additional stimulus by developing its new State Government Center at a cost of $264 million.

In addition, a specific industry—sports—created a market niche for Indianapolis, one with substantial symbolic value to society and the potential to attract future support. Five downtown projects were directly related to the sports identity Indianapolis had begun to establish with the construction of Market Square Arena. In 1984 the city opened the 61,000–seat HOOSIER DOME, which became the home of the INDIANAPOLIS COLTS and twice has served as a venue for the NCAA Men's Basketball Final Four. Other facilities included the Tennis Center, a stadium for the annual hardcourt championships; the Indiana University Natatorium; the Indiana University Track and Field Stadium; and the NATIONAL INSTITUTE FOR FITNESS AND SPORT. In addition the private and nonprofit sectors financially aided several amateur sports organizations to relocate in the city. By 1989 seven national and two international organizations had moved their governing offices to Indianapolis. While many located in the suburbs, their presence signaled local interest in the use of amateur sports as a means of attracting athletes and sports enthusiasts to downtown facilities.

The city also encouraged other development activity. The 1980s witnessed scores of downtown building projects. Among them were the first single-family residential structures constructed in the Mile Square in over 100 years; completion of several major buildings including Market Tower

(1988, 32 stories), AUL TOWER (1982, 38 stories), and BANK ONE TOWER (1990, 51 stories); rehabilitation of the CENTRAL CANAL adjacent to West Street (1991); and construction of the new INDIANAPOLIS ZOO (1985). Other projects were less successful, at least initially. The CIRCLE CENTRE MALL, for example, unveiled plans in 1982 but aside from site preparation no work began on the project until 1989.

Important lessons emerged from Indianapolis' downtown strategy of the 1970s and 1980s. There was a substantial commitment of funds targeted for a specific area and in support of a tightly focused policy. The decades saw $2.76 billion invested in downtown capital projects. There was extensive commitment of private funds to the strategy. Indeed, more than one half of the funds invested, 55.7 percent, came from the private sector. The nonprofit sector was also an active participant, responsible for almost one of every ten dollars invested, or 8.5 percent. Taken together, the private and nonprofit sectors were responsible for approximately two thirds of the investment in the amateur sports and downtown redevelopment strategies.

The City of Indianapolis' commitment amounted to less than one fifth of the total investment, 15.8 percent. The city successfully leveraged funds for economic development: a $2.76 billion investment for an economic development program required $436.1 million from the city. For every dollar it invested, the city was able to secure $5.33 from other sources. The State of Indiana and Indiana University actually invested more—$495 million—than did the city itself.

As a result of this successful strategy, downtown employment increased measurably between 1970 and 1980 and remained steady in the 1990s. The city also gained new and favorable exposure to national and international audiences. By the 1990s Indianapolis had redefined its skyline, gained a sports reputation, and polished its image as a commercial and business location. Secure in the success of earlier administrations' efforts, Mayor Stephen Goldsmith in 1992 began to shift the focus of development toward the neighborhoods while maintaining a healthy interest in completing long-planned downtown projects

such as the controversial Circle Centre Mall (scheduled to open in 1995).

MARK S. ROSENTRAUB
CONNIE J. ZEIGLER

Dramatic Club. Organization devoted to private theatrical performances. In 1889, 25 young women from the city's leading families formed an amateur theatrical group called the Matinee Club. The all-woman first performance was staged in a residential ballroom at 10th and Delaware streets. By the third play in 1890, men assisted in the production and joined the reorganized Dramatic Club. That year the club also adopted the policy of electing a male president and female vice-president. Membership included BOOTH TARKINGTON, who designed the group's logo.

The club held benefit performances for local charities beginning in 1890. Over the years the FLOWER MISSION, Orphans' Asylum, ART ASSOCIATION, and Red Cross received proceeds from Dramatic Club performances. The group's most ambitious charitable endeavor occurred immediately following WORLD WAR I when it "adopted" four French children and sent money abroad for their clothing, housing, and education.

In 1890 the club had 149 members, and grew to 400 by the early 20th century. Early plays were performed in private homes or at the PROPYLAEUM or ATHENAEUM. In the 1920s and 1930s, most were staged at the ENGLISH HOTEL AND OPERA HOUSE, the MURAT TEMPLE, and the Athenaeum, and by the 1950s at CIVIC THEATRE. Currently, spring and fall productions are performed at the Hedback Community Theatre and Civic Theatre. Plays are financed solely through club dues.

Social activities, including teas, dinners, and parties, have been a regular part of every play production. In 1950 the club's annual Christmas Cotillion became a debutante presentation, a tradition that continues today.

SHERYL D. VANDERSTEL

The Dramatic Club, 1889–1989 (Indianapolis, 1989); *The Dramatic Club: Fiftieth Year* (Indianapolis, 1940).

Drexel Gardens. Working class suburb. Located on Indianapolis' west side, Drexel Gardens is bounded by Minnesota Street on the north, Denison Avenue on the east, West Raymond Street on the south, and Lynhurst Drive on the west. In 1923 American Town Lot Company subdivided this area into 1,254 lots. The company's secretary-treasurer, Lafayette Perkins, promoted the subdivision as offering "two or three big beautiful lots for the price of one." Timed payments of $1 down and $1 a week for lots ranging from $149 to $300 made them affordable to the working class family. By September, 1923, the subdivision was almost sold out. With only 200 lots remaining, the real estate company offered free bus excursions to Drexel Gardens and a $25 coupon toward the purchase price of the remaining lots, which would be sold "to White People only." Attempting to appeal to workers in Indianapolis westside manufactories, the advertisement mentioned that Drexel Gardens was only six minutes from the Belmont Avenue area where Federal Foundry, LINK BELT COMPANY, and NORDYKE AND MARMON were located. Photographs showed that most of the homes already constructed in the subdivision were small craftsman bungalows.

Today, hemmed in by STOUT FIELD on the east and the INDIANAPOLIS INTERNATIONAL AIRPORT on the west, Drexel Gardens remains a predominately white, working class suburb. Many of the craftsman-style homes remain, although most have acquired aluminum siding or fake stone facades. Nearly all the large lots have been subdivided as in-fill homes were added in the 1940s, 1950s, and 1960s.

CONNIE J. ZEIGLER

Drive-In Restaurants. Henry Mewborn introduced the drive-in restaurant business to Indianapolis when he opened the Peacock in early 1930. Located at 38th Street and Massachusetts Avenue, it was the first restaurant in the city to serve patrons in their cars.

Indianapolis witnessed several successful drive-ins over the years. In 1932 A. R. McComb built the Wigwam, located next to the INDIANA STATE FAIRGROUNDS. Newly constructed in 1939

The Tee Pee restaurant, originally known as the Wigwam, stood by the Indiana State Fairgrounds until it was demolished in 1988. [Indianapolis Newspapers Inc.]

and renamed the Tee Pee, it became an Indiana landmark and stood until 1988.

Spencer's North Pole, built in 1937, changed its name and location in 1952 to the Pole at 16th Street and Lafayette Road. The Parkmoor, one of the largest drive-in restaurants of its kind, became Merrill's HiDecker in 1956. The Ron-D-Vu opened its doors to Butler University students in 1940. One of three Knobby's restaurants, built in 1955, still operates as a sit-down restaurant at 52nd Street and Keystone Avenue.

Al Green's drive-in opened on East Washington Street in 1947. In 1953 it became the nation's first drive-in to experiment with curb phone service. Although curb service and its outdoor movie screen have disappeared, Al Green's remains open in the early 1990s.

The popularity of drive-in restaurants reached its peak in the 1950s and continued through the 1960s when "cruising" was a common teen activity. Popular drive-ins included Hubbard's, the Blue Ribbon, Borky's, Northwood, Southwind, Southern Triangle, and the Steer-In. STEAK N SHAKE located its first drive-in at Lafayette and Tibbs roads in 1954.

Drive-in restaurant business began to decline in the 1970s as fast food business offering quick food at low cost began to rise, with drive-up windows a standard feature. However, drive-ins still have a following today. Restaurants such as Edward's and Mug 'n Bun have remained in operation since 1957 and 1960 respectively. Other drive-ins in the area include Buster's at South Holt

Road, B & K Root Beer at Mars Hill, and Bill's Fabulous 50s, which opened in 1983.

LISA EHRET

Duesenberg, Fred S. (Dec. 6, 1877–July 26, 1932) and **August S. "Augie"** (Dec. 11, 1879–Jan. 18, 1955). Automobile designers and engineers. Sons of Conrad and Kora Duesenberg of Lippe, Germany, the Duesenberg brothers immigrated with their family to the United States in 1885 and settled on an Iowa farm. In the late 1890s they opened a bicycle shop in Rockford, Iowa, where Fred became involved in bicycle racing and established several world records. After successfully building a racing motorcycle to pace his training, Fred joined the Mason motor and racing car company in Des Moines, Iowa, a venture in which Fred Maytag (of the Maytag Washer Company) and William Sears were involved. Duesenberg developed 12–cylinder motors for high speed motorboats, one of which was the first to break 60 mph (1914). The motors, produced at a plant in Elizabeth, New Jersey, gained notoriety during World War I, and were used in various water- and aircraft.

Eddie Rickenbacker drove the first Duesenberg automobile entered in the INDIANAPOLIS 500–MILE RACE in 1914. Shortly thereafter Fred began work on the straight-eight motor. Perfected in 1919, this engine became the basis for Duesenberg's domination of auto racing until his death. Duesenbergs won the race in 1924, 1925, and 1927, breaking the 100 mph mark in May, 1925, with a speed of 101.13 mph. A Duesenberg was the first American car to win the French Grand Prix (1921).

By 1920 Fred had opened a plant at Washington and Harding streets in Indianapolis to manufacture what became the world's most famous luxury cars. The Cord Corporation, producer of automobiles and aircraft, acquired the Duesenberg company around 1927, retaining Fred as a consulting engineer. He later became vice-president in charge of engineering. Suffering from injuries incurred in an auto accident, he died in Johnstown, Pennsylvania.

Augie, a resident of Indianapolis from 1921, assisted his brother in the production of their automobiles. In 1947 Augie proposed developing a new $25,000 model, but the venture never materialized and he remained in semiretirement at his Camby farm.

Both brothers are interred at CROWN HILL CEMETERY.

SHERYL D. VANDERSTEL

Indianapolis Star, July 27, 1932, Jan. 19, 1955; *Indianapolis Times*, Jan. 19, 1955.

Duesenberg. American automobile of the 1920s and 1930s, regarded as the most luxurious, best engineered motorcar of the classic era. Duesenberg Automobile and Motors Company, Inc., established in Indianapolis in 1920, built passenger cars at a factory on West Washington Street at Harding Street until 1937, when the company, by then a subsidiary of Cord Corporation, was sold and dissolved.

Both car and firm were named for FRED S. DUESENBERG (1877–1932) and AUGUST S. "AUGIE" DUESENBERG (1879–1955), brothers who emigrated from Lippe, Germany, to America as children. After establishing a bicycle shop in Iowa, the brothers built and raced bicycles, and later racing cars. WORLD WAR I brought production of aviation engines at Elizabeth, New Jersey. By 1920, the Duesenbergs relocated to Indianapolis and soon were manufacturing the Model A, a costly prestige car. Duesenberg pioneered the use of straight eight-cylinder engines and four-wheel hydraulic brakes. Model A production continued through 1926, when transportation industrialist Errett Lobban Cord purchased the company.

In 1928, Cord commissioned a massive, luxurious, high-powered automobile that would outclass all other American makes. The unsurpassed Model J, introduced in 1929, featured a Lycoming straight eight engine of 265 horsepower and attained speeds exceeding 115 miles per hour. Duesenberg manufactured the engine and chassis. Bodies were supplied by custom coachbuilders throughout the world, bringing the total price to $14,000–20,000.

Duesenbergs were favorites of movie stars, monarchs, and millionaires. Of the 480 made between 1929 and 1937, many survive today. They are prized by collectors and command prices exceeding $1 million.

GREGG BUTTERMORE
Auburn-Cord-Duesenberg Museum

Harold F. Blanchard, "265 Horse Power, 116 Miles Per Hour," *Motor*, 50 (Dec., 1928), 40–43+; Duesenberg, Inc., *The New Duesenberg 8* (Indianapolis, 1929), and *Duesenberg—The World's Finest Motor Car* (Indianapolis, 1929).

Duke, Phillip R. (May 24, 1935–July 22, 1986). Commercial real estate developer. A lifelong native of Indianapolis, Duke attended Public School 54 and ARSENAL TECHNICAL HIGH SCHOOL. He served in the Army and graduated from BUTLER UNIVERSITY with a bachelor's degree in accounting in 1959. In 1966 he worked as an accountant for the C. W. Jackson Construction Company, and eventually became a partner in the firm.

In 1972 Duke sold his share in C. W. Jackson and established a partnership with attorney John Wynne, creating P. R. Duke Construction and Duke Development companies. Their first project involved the development of Park 100, an industrial park on the northwest side of Indianapolis, co-developed with Waldemar Industries. In 1978 Duke formed the Keystone Crossing Development Company, purchased the foundering northside shopping center, and successfully rejuvenated it. Duke also developed One North Capitol in downtown Indianapolis. His interest in developing other industrial parks outside of Indianapolis resulted in projects in Cincinnati, Phoenix, and Decatur, Illinois.

Duke died of a heart attack while riding a bicycle near his condominium in Highland Beach, Florida. Earlier in the year he had sold his interests in his parent company, Phillip R. Duke and Associates, resulting in the creation of Duke Associates. Duke Associates includes the P. R. Duke Construction Company and P. R. Duke Realty.

Duke was a civic leader with many memberships in community organizations. At the time of his death he was chairman of the Indianapolis CHAMBER OF COMMERCE and vice-chairman of Butler University's board of trustees.

TIM MULHERIN

Indianapolis Star, July 23, 1986.

Duke Associates. Largest general commercial and industrial real estate developer in the city and state. Duke Associates was formed in 1972 by PHILLIP R. DUKE, John Rosebrough, and John Wynne. Shortly after its inception the firm developed its first major venture, the Park 100 industrial complex on the city's northwest side. Since that time, Park 100 has become one of the top ten business parks in the country with 1,630 acres of land and about 9.5 million square feet under roof. In 1976 Duke expanded into Cincinnati, Ohio, currently its other major market. Two years later, Duke began the northside development of Keystone at the Crossing, comprising high rise office buildings, restaurants, a hotel, and the Fashion Mall.

In the late 1970s and early 1980s Duke took on several new partners, expanding management to the current group of seven. Duke's management is unusual in the industry. Most property development firms are run by individuals rather than by a group of partners. Duke prospered in the 1980s, growing six-fold between 1982 and 1987. In 1985 Duke Realty Investments, a publicly owned real estate investment trust, was formed. In June, 1993, Duke announced that it would become a publicly traded company controlled by Duke Realty. The restructuring was believed to be an attempt to reduce debt.

As of the early 1990s Duke Associates controlled nearly 30 million square feet of property, with about 14 million square feet in Indianapolis. While many of Duke's properties are on the city's north side, the firm also has three downtown office buildings and a business park in Greenwood. With properties in several midwestern states, Duke's annual revenues are around $225 million.

DEBORAH B. MARKISOHN

Steve Kaelble, "The Dukes of Indiana," *Indiana Business Magazine* (June, 1992).

Dumont, Ebenezer (Nov. 23, 1814–Apr. 16, 1871). Born in Vevay, Indiana, Dumont graduated from Indiana University. He studied law and was admitted to the bar about 1835, after which he practiced in Dearborn County. He was elected to the Indiana legislature in 1838 and was also treasurer of Dearborn County (1839–45) and president of the State Bank (1852–59). During the Mexican War, he was elected captain and then lieutenant colonel of the 4th Indiana Regiment and distinguished himself at the battles of Huamantla and Puebla. In 1850 he was again elected to the Indiana House of Representatives (serving as speaker) and was chosen as a presidential elector for the DEMOCRATIC PARTY in 1852. He changed his residence to Indianapolis during that period.

In 1861 Dumont became a Republican, and in April he was appointed colonel of the 7th Indiana. Between July and September he participated in the western Virginia campaign, during which Dumont and his command fought well. Dumont was promoted to brigadier general in September. In January, 1862, he was given command of the 17th Brigade of the Army of the Ohio and in May defeated John Hunt Morgan at Lebanon, Kentucky. In October, he commanded the 12th Division of D. C. Buell's army during Braxton Bragg's invasion of Kentucky. In December, he was forced by ill health to return home and resigned his commission in February, 1863. Dumont was elected to Congress in 1863 and served until 1867, when he declined to run for a third term. In 1871, President Grant appointed him governor of Idaho, but he died before he could take the oath of office.

RAYMOND L. SHOEMAKER
Indiana Historical Society

William H. English Papers, Indiana Historical Society; Ezra J. Warner, *Generals in Blue: Lives of the Union Commanders* (Baton Rouge, La., 1964).

Dunlap, Livingston (1799–Sept. 10, 1862). Prominent physician who was the first major advocate of a city hospital. A native of New York, he came to Indianapolis in 1821 and established a practice with the city's first physician, SAMUEL G. MITCHELL. Dunlap was active in the community, serving as postmaster, adjutant general, physician of the Deaf and Dumb Institute, professor at the Central Medical College, and a member of the city council. Throughout his tenure on the council, he lobbied for the construction of a city hospital to care for the sick poor, as well as smallpox and cholera victims. Although the council approved the construction of such a facility, and a hospital was constructed during the 1850s, it remained vacant until the CIVIL WAR and was nicknamed "Dunlap's Folly."

KATHERINE MANDUSIC MCDONELL

Katherine Mandusic McDonell, "The Indianapolis City Hospital, 1833–1866," *Indiana Medical History Quarterly*, 9 (June, 1983), 3–13.

Dunn, Jacob Piatt, Jr. (Apr. 12, 1855– June 6, 1924). Historian, journalist, politician, and ethnologist. Born in Lawrenceburg, Indiana, Dunn came with his parents to Indianapolis in 1861 and attended the city's public schools. A precocious student, he graduated from Earlham College (B.S. 1874) at age 19 and from the University of Michigan (LL.B. 1876) at 21. After practicing law in Indianapolis for a few years, Dunn was sent by his father (along with two brothers) to Colorado in 1879 to look after investments in silver mines. He stayed for five years, prospecting for silver, researching Indian history, and working as a reporter for newspapers in the Denver and Leadville areas. Dunn returned to Indianapolis in 1884, where he made his permanent home.

Dunn first achieved public notice in 1886 with the publication of *Massacres of the Mountains: A History of the Indian Wars of the Far West, 1815– 1875*. The first scholarly treatment of the subject, based extensively on government documents, Dunn's book was quickly recognized as a minor

Jacob Piatt Dunn. [Indiana Historical Society, #C2261]

classic and is still respected by students of frontier history.

The reputation of *Massacres* prompted Houghton Mifflin to invite Dunn to write the Indiana volume for the *American Commonwealths* series. His *Indiana: A Redemption from Slavery* (1888; rev. ed., 1905), analyzing the history of the slavery issue in Indiana territorial politics, was well received. Meanwhile Dunn had joined with Indianapolis historians WILLIAM H. ENGLISH and Daniel Wait Howe to improve the dilapidated IN-DIANA STATE LIBRARY and to revive the comatose INDIANA HISTORICAL SOCIETY (IHS), organized in 1830. Dunn became recording secretary of IHS in 1886, leading to its revival and expansion. Elected state librarian by the state legislature for two terms, 1889–1890 and 1891–1892, Dunn was able to improve the library's condition notably. He also served on the Public Library Commission from its inception in 1899 until 1919 (president, 1899–1914).

Dunn, a Democrat, supported himself principally by his work as a journalist, writing political editorials for Indianapolis newspapers. His leadership of progressive reforms such as the Australian ballot (1889), the city charter, and the tax reform of 1891 had a significant impact on the city's politics. He also ran for Congress, unsuccessfully, in 1902, and he served two terms as city controller (1904–1906, 1914–1916).

Dunn produced a large number of historical works. He wrote five monographs for IHS and edited the first seven volumes of its *Publications*. He wrote for scholarly journals of history and political science and for biographical publications. His crowning achievement was *Greater Indianapolis* (1910), in two volumes (volume II is biographical). The first volume is among the finest of local histories, demonstrating an intimate knowledge of the city, a critical view of its development, and a lively appreciation for the personalities and events he describes. *Indiana and Indianans* (1919), in five volumes (three are biographical), also reflects Dunn's command of the sources and his evenhanded approach. Both works remain indispensable sources for Indiana history.

Dunn made contributions to Native American ethnology after 1905, when he began regular study of the Miami language with the aging Miami Indians Gabriel Godfroy of Peru and Kilsokwa, a granddaughter of Little Turtle. Supported in his studies by the U.S. Bureau of Ethnology (1908–1909, 1911–1913) Dunn created a dictionary that has helped to preserve the Miami language, though it died as a spoken language.

After a two-month trip to Haiti, prospecting for manganese in the winter of 1921–1922, Dunn joined the campaign staff of Samuel Ralston, who was elected to the Senate in 1922, and served as Ralston's chief aide in Washington until Dunn's death in 1924.

LANA RUEGAMER

Caroline Dunn, "Jacob Piatt Dunn: His Miami Language Studies," *Indiana Historical Society Prehistory Research Series*, I, No. 2 (Indianapolis, 1937); Lana Ruegamer, "History, Politics, and the Active Life: Jacob Piatt Dunn, Progressive Historian," *Indiana Magazine of History*, 81 (Sept., 1985), 265–283.

Dutch. The Dutch in Indianapolis, a mixed lot culturally and religiously, never totaled more than 500 persons. The first families arrived in the 1850s and 1860s, migrating directly from the Netherlands or residing first in New York, Pennsylvania, or Ohio. The 1850s contingent consisted of Reformed and Catholic craftsmen, especially carpenters and painters. In the 1860s itinerant Jewish merchants in clothing and cigarmaking settled in the city. Originally from the Jewish Quarter in Amsterdam, the largest Jewish center in Western Europe, they had previously done business in New York City, Philadelphia, and Detroit. A Roman Catholic, Herman Ryckhof, owned a liquor store and was the wealthiest Hollander in the city in 1870.

In the 1890s a second migration brought a group of Frisian dairy farmers to the city's outskirts. Among them was Cash (Kerst) Bottema, a milkhand who emigrated on a cattle boat in 1891 and who founded Bottema Farms, the Mutual Milk Dairy, and Brown Brothers Packing Company. He also served as president of the Holstein-Frisian Breeders Association of Indiana and was a founder of the Marion County Farm Bureau.

By 1910 Indianapolis counted nearly 300 persons of Dutch stock. The next year, 17 families organized the First Holland Reformed Church (now Christian Park Reformed Church) on the city's east side. Church elders reported in 1922 to the Chicago classis of the Reformed Church in America that some 200 Holland families in Indianapolis were "connected with no church at all, . . . who up to this time have been careless of religion and its demands." The classis provided an annual grant of $900 to the congregation to hire "a wideawake, energetic pastor" to "spend part of his time among them."

The evangelism strategy worked; the congregation outgrew its first two buildings and later erected a new facility on Wentworth Boulevard in 1948. A Dutch immigrant pastor, Reverend Herman Heeg, led the congregation from 1972 to 1989. Meanwhile, in 1961 a second Dutch congregation, the Indianapolis Christian Reformed Church, which currently has 125 members, was founded on the city's far northeast side.

A third immigrant wave arrived in the 1950s, including several dozen families expelled from the Netherlands East Indies (now Indonesia). By 1980, the number of Dutch-born in Marion County was the highest in 50 years, reaching 203.

The Dutch never maintained separate neighborhoods and assimilated rapidly. Practicing Catholics and JEWS worshiped in ethnically mixed congregations; only the Reformed maintained homogeneous churches for a generation or two. Apart from several first and second generation families in the Reformed churches, little remains of Dutch institutional life and culture.

ROBERT P. SWIERENGA
Kent State University

_____

Christian Park Reformed Church, *Dedication Services, September 11–12, 1949*; Kathleen Van Nuys, *Indy International* (Indianapolis, 1978), 9–11.

Duvall, John L. (Nov. 29, 1874–Feb. 25, 1962). Mayor of Indianapolis, 1926–1927, Republican. Born in Tazewell County, Illinois, Duvall entered Valparaiso University in 1886 and studied law. He later attended Chicago Law School, graduating in 1899. Admitted to the bar after moving to Arcadia, Indiana, he became a successful young attorney and served as the deputy HAMILTON COUNTY prosecutor. After moving

to Indianapolis in 1902, Duvall practiced law for seven years. In 1909 he organized the city's first suburban bank, the Haughville Bank, later called the Citizens State Bank. He went on to establish many other banks, most of which were later purchased by the AMERICAN FLETCHER NATIONAL BANK and Trust Company. He also organized and operated Leslie Duvall, Inc., a real estate firm.

Duvall served as Marion County treasurer in 1924–1925. The KU KLUX KLAN, then at the height of its political power in Indiana, supported Duvall in his mayoral campaign. This support guaranteed his nomination in May, 1925, and his election that November; he took office on January 4, 1926. Accused of having traded jobs for votes during the election campaign, Duvall was eventually convicted of violating the state corrupt practices act, sentenced to 30 days in jail, and fined $1,000. At the insistence of the city council, Duvall resigned on October 27, 1927. After two weeks of political upheaval, L. ERT SLACK was selected by the city council, on November 8, 1927, to fill out Duvall's remaining term in office. Following his political career, Duvall maintained an office in downtown Indianapolis and pursued work in real estate and investments.

KRIS E. DAMAN

_____

Indiana Biography Series, Indiana State Library; Duvall reminiscence, *Indianapolis Star*, Apr. 25, 1955.

Dye, Charity (1849–1921). High school teacher. A native of Kentucky, Dye studied at the Indianapolis Normal College in 1873 and received a bachelor of philosophy degree from the University of Chicago in 1900. She began teaching in 1874 at Public School 10, but soon transferred to Indianapolis High School (later renamed SHORTRIDGE HIGH SCHOOL). She gained a reputation as an excellent English teacher. An early success was the publication titled *Dawn*, a collection of the best work written by students under her direction. Both historian-diplomat CLAUDE BOWERS and industrialist ELI LILLY remembered Dye as a favorite teacher.

Following her attendance at a pageant in Oxford, England, in 1907, she began producing plays in observance of historical events. Her "Indi-

Charity Dye.
[Indiana State
Library]

ana Pageant," with a new segment produced each year, raised funds for high school projects. After preparing a successful pageant for the New Harmony centennial celebration in 1914, she was appointed to the Indiana Historical Commission the next year and helped plan the state's centennial celebration in 1916.

Active in civic affairs, Dye lectured on historical topics and organized the Browning Society of Indianapolis. She spoke in every county of the state in support of a memorial to pioneer women and was active in urging women's suffrage. When she retired in 1912, an issue of the Shortridge DAILY ECHO devoted tributes to her. Both Public School 27 and the library of the new Shortridge High School were named posthumously in her honor.

She was the author of *The Story Teller's Art* (1898) and *Some Torch Bearers in Indiana* (1917).

IRMA A. LINTON

Laura S. Gaus, *Shortridge High School* (Indianapolis, 1985); Frederick Gale, *A Biographical Study of Persons for Whom Indianapolis Schools are Named* (Indianapolis, 1965); R. E. Banta, *Indiana Authors and Their Books* (Crawfordsville, Ind., 1949).

Dyer, William A., Jr. (Oct. 23, 1902–Mar. 21, 1993). Newspaper executive. Born in Providence, Rhode Island, and educated at Brown University, Dyer worked as director of general advertising for the *Syracuse* (N.Y.) *Journal* before coming to Indianapolis in 1944 as vice-president and general manager of the INDIANAPOLIS STAR. In 1948 he became vice-president and general manager of EUGENE C. PULLIAM's recently formed Indianapolis Newspapers, Inc., and a member of the board of directors of Central Newspapers, Inc. He retained these positions until 1975 when he was promoted to president of both organizations as well as of Muncie Newspapers, Inc., positions which he held until his death.

Dyer served on the boards of the Bureau of Advertising, the Research Institute of the American Newspaper Publishers Association, and the Metropolitan Sunday Newspapers, Inc. A recipient of journalism awards and honorary degrees, Dyer was inducted into the Indiana Journalism Hall of Fame in 1982. The following year he was named a life member of the board of directors of the Community Health Services Foundation and received a distinguished service award from the Boys Clubs of Indianapolis.

Over the years Dyer was active in many local civic concerns, serving as director and former president of Goodwill Industries Foundation, vice-president of the COMMUNITY SERVICE COUNCIL of Indianapolis, president and board chairman of UNITED WAY of Greater Indianapolis, and a director of the Indiana Convention and Visitors Bureau. He also served on the boards of the INDIANAPOLIS MUSEUM OF ART and the Boys Clubs of Indianapolis. A trustee emeritus at Brown University, Dyer endowed the university with a $1 million academic chair.

JOAN CUNNINGHAM

Indianapolis Star, Mar. 23, 1993.

E

Eagle Creek Park. One of the largest municipal parks in the United States (and reputedly the largest non-landscaped urban park in the country situated entirely within the boundaries of its municipality). Though Indianapolis had a park in the 1930s and 1940s near Lynhurst Drive and Tenth Street called Eagle Creek, the park currently known by that name is bounded roughly by 79th Street, I–65, 56th Street, and the county line on the west. JOSIAH K. LILLY, JR. owned most of the property currently encompassed by the park. He maintained it as a private nature preserve and had a summer home there. In the mid–1950s Lilly offered the property as a gift to the city, but it was declined. He thereupon donated the property to Purdue University.

Serious flooding of Eagle Creek in 1957 prompted the city to purchase the land from Purdue for $1 in 1964 and to construct a reservoir for flood control. From the beginning plans also included constructing recreational facilities. Excavation for the reservoir began in 1964, and the water reached its present level in 1968. The dam was dedicated that year, with the park as a whole being dedicated on June 10, 1972. Throughout the 1980s more land was acquired; the current size is approximately 4,900 acres, 1,350 acres of which comprise the reservoir. Some land acquisition involved purchasing private property, some of which had been in the hands of the families involved for many years. This land acquisition has not always proceeded smoothly and without hard feelings.

The original development of the park cost approximately $22.5 million and involved a combination of federal and local funds. Facilities included picnic areas, shelters, playgrounds, hiking trails, and a gatehouse at the 56th Street entrance. Other plans from the late 1960s that were still not realized by the early 1990s included the construction of a lodge and restaurant.

Facilities added since the park opened include an 18–hole golf course, a beach, archery and pistol ranges, a marina, meeting facilities, a nature center, riding stables, an outdoor amphitheatre, and an arts center. A Water Sports Center, which includes training and competition facilities for rowing and sailing, was built for the NATIONAL SPORTS FESTIVAL in 1982 and renovated for the PAN AMERICAN GAMES in 1987.

Eagle Creek Park has dealt with many problems and continues to be concerned with some; these have included mining rights, timber harvesting, development adjacent to park boundaries, deer overpopulation, environmental stresses caused by a popular Christmas light show, and pollution of the reservoir from its feeder creeks.

In 1990 the DEPARTMENT OF PARKS AND RECREATION estimated that 10,000 people used the park on an average summer weekend, 90 percent of them being Marion County residents. Total park attendance for 1992 was approximately 300,000.

LEIGH DARBEE
Indiana Historical Society

Eagledale. Suburb centered near the intersection of 34th Street and Georgetown Road. In the 1950s a sudden demand for housing, particularly for working class families, led to the development of planned communities such as Eagledale. Lured by Veterans Administration loans, no down payment, and low-interest mortgages, westside workers eagerly bought prefabricated homes in the new suburb. Advertisements boasted the all-aluminum, maintenance-free exteriors of the houses, as well as the area's city services, sidewalks, and concrete streets. Buyers could choose among several model homes ranging in price from $10,000 to $15,000. Sales were brisk as soon as the development opened in 1955, and four years later an estimated 10,000 people lived in 3,400 homes. Additional homes continued to be built into the 1960s, and schools, churches, and the Eagledale Shopping Center were constructed to accommodate the influx of families.

The new development overshadowed the nearby village of Flackville, founded around 1900 at West 30th Street and Lafayette Road. Joseph Flack opened a grocery store near the Olive Branch Methodist Church and the post office, then later built a brickyard in the area. Flackville was a small community until the 1950s when suburbanization brought extensive commercial and residential development. It was annexed by Indianapolis in 1961.

In the 1990s little is left of the original Flackville, but Eagledale remains a stable, intact development. Though once almost exclusively white, Eagledale is now a racially integrated community for low to moderate-income families.

CATHLEEN F. DONNELLY

Indianapolis Times, Mar. 18, 1962 (*re* Flackville), Feb. 10, 1963 (*re* Eagledale); *Indianapolis Star*, Jan. 18, 1976.

Early, Maurice (June 14, 1890–Feb. 5, 1954). Journalist. A political writer for three decades, Early had more than an ordinary influence on the public scene because his column, "The Day in Indiana," appeared daily on page one of the INDIANAPOLIS STAR. He had a reputation as a fair and accurate reporter and in his writing looked beyond politics to a development's effect on government.

A native of Cleveland, Ohio, Early attended Wabash College and graduated in 1914 from Marquette University. He joined the *Star* as a reporter in 1916. After covering various governmental beats, he became the *Star's* first reporter assigned full time to politics. On his death, he had attended every Indiana and national Democratic and Republican convention since 1924.

His first-page column originated in January, 1939, when Early was covering a session of the General Assembly. It began as "The Day in the Legislature," and proved so popular that it continued as "The Day in Indiana" after the legislative session had ended. The column continued under the name until January 8, 1954.

The dean of Hoosier political reporters, Early was often called "Mr. Indiana" by fellow scribes because of his knowledge of Indiana government and politics. He wrote of the need for new state agencies and witnessed the creation of the state Tax Board, Public Service Commission, Highway Department, Conservation Department, and the Legislative Reference Bureau.

One of a small group of newspapermen who organized the INDIANAPOLIS PRESS CLUB in 1934, he was the club's first president. Both he and a younger brother, ROBERT P. EARLY, who was city editor and later managing editor of the *Star*, are members of the Indiana Journalism Hall of Fame.

JAMES E. FARMER

Indianapolis Star, Feb. 6, 1954.

Early, Robert P. (Oct. 3, 1905–Aug. 7, 1987). Journalist. Managing editor of the INDIANAPOLIS STAR from 1946 to 1979, Early was a crusading editor who directed investigations of government wrongdoing. The most notable of numerous awards won by the *Star* during his tenure was a 1974 PULITZER PRIZE for an expose of corruption in the INDIANAPOLIS POLICE DEPARTMENT. A story series in 1957 revealed a scandal in the State Highway Department which led to the conviction of ten persons. In 1969 he directed the newspaper's campaign that resulted in General Assembly action reforming the Marion County Municipal Court. Public service campaigns pushed by Early included an "every-yard-a-park" drive to beautify the city, a push for "running lights" on autos to improve highway safety, and the founding of the Crime Alert program in the police department.

Born in Indianapolis, Early was a 1923 graduate of Cathedral High School and entered journalism two years later with a job at United Press. He became a reporter on the *Star* in 1927, launching a 52–year career with Indiana's largest daily newspaper that included promotions to assistant city editor in 1940, city editor in 1944, and managing editor in 1946.

A charter member of the INDIANAPOLIS PRESS CLUB, he received its Indiana Newsman of the Year Award in 1969. He was a past president of the Indiana Associated Press Managing Editors Association. He was inducted into the Indiana Journalism Hall of Fame of the Society of Professional Journalists in 1979, receiving an honor also granted his brother, MAURICE EARLY, a political columnist for the *Star*.

JAMES E. FARMER

Indianapolis Star, Sept. 29, 1979, Aug. 8, 1987.

Eastern Orthodox Churches. After Roman emperor Constantine I legitimized Christianity in 313 controversies about religious doctrine and canonical law ultimately brought about a schism in 1054 that still divides the church into two separate denominations—the Eastern (Orthodox) and the Western (Roman Catholic). The organization of most Eastern Orthodox churches in the United States is based on nationalities. The history of many is complex and characterized by internal schisms, usually political in nature. Orthodox churches in Indianapolis have been and continue to be affected in varying degrees by world political events.

It is difficult to establish the number of Orthodox Christians in Indianapolis because church membership in the Orthodox parishes is counted not by individuals but by heads of households. In Indianapolis in 1993 there were six churches that professed Eastern Orthodoxy: SS. Constantine and Elena Romanian Orthodox Church (est. 1910); Holy Trinity Hellenic (Greek) Orthodox Church (est. 1910); St. Stephen Bulgarian Eastern Orthodox Church (est. 1907); St. George (Syrian) Orthodox Church (est. 1926); St. Nicholas Serbian Eastern Orthodox Church (est. 1950); and Joy of All Who Sorrow Eastern Orthodox Church (est. 1988). Holy Trinity was the largest Orthodox church in the early 1990s with about 1,000 families; St. George had moved most decisively toward pan-Orthodoxy.

Eastern Orthodox ROMANIANS, GREEKS, Bulgarians from Macedonia, and Serbians settled in

Indianapolis' largest Orthodox community, Holy Trinity, began as a small Greek parish at 27 South Meridian Street before moving to the north side in 1960. [Indiana Historical Society, #C1873]

Indianapolis as early as the first decade of the 20th century. They called their respective ethnic enclaves colonies and organized them into Orthodox parishes. The Indianapolis Orthodox churches had their origins in patriotic societies and clubs created to maintain each group's national and ethnic spirit and culture. Each group was interested in preserving its national cultural heritage and in worshiping in its own language. Because for centuries the Balkans had been dominated by the Ottoman Empire, for them nationality, ethnic culture, and church were inextricably bound. And since the Orthodox churches of each nation are autocephalous (self-governing) and a central Eastern Orthodox core such as the Vatican does not exist, each Eastern Orthodox church in Indianapolis had a closer affiliation with its national mother church and churches of the same nationality in other American cities than with the other Orthodox churches in Indianapolis. Their development is directly related to the development of their diocese in the United States rather than to the development of the other Orthodox churches in Indianapolis. Thus, the six Indianapolis Orthodox churches belong to six dioceses.

Since World War II the Indianapolis Orthodox Christians have held their ethnic conflicts in abeyance. Primarily they are interested in maintaining the Orthodox faith and only in purely cultural ethnic traditions. They prefer to live in cooperation with one another as Americans and to emphasize their religious, cultural, and ethnic similarities. Whereas prior to World War II intermarriage between members of these churches was discouraged, afterwards such unions became prevalent.

Developments in the Balkans in the late 1980s and 1990s have brought an influx of new immigrants and have set aflame old passions. In 1992 in an effort toward American pan-Orthodoxy and to highlight common ethnic characteristics instead of divisiveness, the Bulgarian, Romanian, and Serbian churches organized the first Balkan festival on the grounds of the Romanian church. The Greek church declined to participate, presumably because of Macedonia's delicate political situation and the fact that the majority of the Bulgarian church members are of Macedonian Bulgarian ancestry. The 1993 Balkan festival, again on the grounds of SS. Constantine and Elena Romanian Orthodox Church, received three bomb threats. On the day following the festival a number of Serbian and Macedono-Bulgarian graves in Floral Park Cemetery were vandalized.

OPHELIA GEORGIEV ROOP
Indiana University–Purdue University,
Indianapolis

Eastman, Joseph Rilus (Apr. 18, 1872–Nov. 29, 1942). Prominent Indianapolis physician and surgeon. Born in Brownsburg, Indiana, the son of Joseph Eastman, a prominent pioneer surgeon in Indiana, young Eastman attended Indianapolis public schools, Butler Preparatory School, and Wabash College. He graduated in 1894 from the Central College of Physicians and Surgeons, which his father had helped to establish. He also visited and studied surgery at many universities of the United States and Europe.

Eastman contributed numerous articles to U.S. and foreign medical journals. For many years, he was the director and owner of the Joseph Eastman Hospital in Indianapolis, a hospital established by his father in 1893. He was founder and governor of the American College of Surgeons, president of the Western Surgical Association, and president of the INDIANAPOLIS MEDICAL SOCIETY and the INDIANA STATE MEDICAL ASSOCIATION, among others. He was Professor of Surgery at the INDIANA UNIVERSITY SCHOOL OF MEDICINE and was active as a surgeon at the Indianapolis City Hospital beginning in 1900.

GLENN W. IRWIN, JR., M.D.

Echols, Roy C. (Apr. 22, 1903–Dec. 25, 1993). Business and civic leader. A native of Hubbard City, Texas, Echols began a 49–year career with the Bell system in 1919, working as a part-time clerk at Southwestern Bell Telephone Company in Dallas. After earning a degree at Southern Methodist University in 1925, Echols worked in Missouri, Arkansas, and Oklahoma before his 1954 appointment as vice-president and general manager of Indiana Bell. He served in this capacity for four years, then became vice-president of operations for American Telephone & Telegraph Company in New York for two years before returning to Indianapolis to serve as INDIANA BELL'S president from 1960 to 1968. He later was chairman of the INDIANAPOLIS WATER COMPANY and a business consultant. Upon his death a fellow businessman lauded him as "the soul of corporate responsibility and civic consciousness," citing his concern for corporate environmental accountability long before it became fashionable.

Echols was active in community affairs. He served as president of the Indianapolis CHAMBER OF COMMERCE, director of the INDIANAPOLIS ATHLETIC CLUB, and chairman of the UNITED WAY. Echols also held leadership positions with the Indianapolis Development Association, the GREATER INDIANAPOLIS PROGRESS COMMITTEE, the Indianapolis Center for Advanced Research, Clowes Memorial Hall, St. Vincent Hospital, 500 Festival Associates, and Starlight Musicals.

DEBORAH B. MARKISOHN

Indianapolis Star, Dec. 28 (obituary), 30 (editorial), 1993.

Economic Club of Indianapolis. Nonprofit public affairs club featuring nationally known speakers. Founded in 1974, the Economic Club of Indianapolis was begun by several PENROD SOCIETY members who patterned the organization after the Economic Club of Detroit. More than 50 top business and civic leaders formed the club's initial board of directors. Noontime addresses by prominent speakers are the organization's only formal functions. By the mid–1980s the club had brought more than 80 speakers to the city representing the fields of business, journalism, and government. Speakers have included syndicated columnist George Will, former United Nations Ambassador Jeane Kirkpatrick, and ex–British Prime Minister Edward Heath. The club sponsors five to ten luncheons each year; attendance averages about 1,000 people for each event.

DEBORAH B. MARKISOHN

Edenharter, George F. (June 13, 1857–Dec. 6, 1923). Physician. Born of German parents and educated in Ohio, Edenharter came to Indianapolis in 1878 and went to work in the John Rauch cigar factory. Leaving the cigar making trade in 1881, he graduated from the Physio-Medical College of Indianapolis in 1884 and received his M.D. in 1886 from the Medical College of Indiana. Following his graduation Edenharter served as chief of staff of the Marion County Infirmary, as a member of the medical staff of the city workhouse, and as superintendent of the City Hospital (1889–1893). In 1893 he was appointed superintendent of the Central Indiana Hospital for the Insane (CENTRAL STATE HOSPITAL), a position that he held until his death.

During his tenure at the Central State Hospital, Edenharter oversaw the establishment of one of the first pathology laboratories in the nation (1896). He was also responsible for an expansion of the hospital's teaching duties, culminating in a weekly lecture series on mental and nervous diseases and neuro-pathology offered to students of the Indiana Medical College. In 1905 the state legislature authorized the Southeastern Hospital for the Insane at Madison at his urging. Edenharter was also largely responsible for the establishment of the Indiana Village for Epileptics at New Castle and for the choice of Michigan City as the site for state's hospital for the criminal insane.

A lifelong Democrat, Edenharter served on the City Council (1883–1887) representing the eighth ward and in 1887 he was the Democratic nominee for mayor. He was a member of the American Medico-Psychological Association, the INDIANAPOLIS MEDICAL SOCIETY, the Marion County Medical Society, the INDIANA STATE MEDICAL ASSOCIATION, and the American Medical Association.

CHARLES O. HAZELRIGG, D.D.S.

Jacob Piatt Dunn, *Indiana and Indianans* (Chicago, 1919), V, 2051–2053; *Indiana Medical History Quarterly*, 7 (Sept., 1981), 10.

Edgewood. Perry Township suburb roughly bounded by Thompson Road, McFar-land Road, Edgewood Avenue, and U.S. 31. In August, 1907, Indianapolis realtor William Elder laid out the town of Edgewood, naming it for the nearby woods. It offered country living with an easy commute to Indianapolis via the interurban line that functioned through the early 1940s. Most homes, built for middle class families, were constructed in the 1920s and 1930s. One- and two-story bungalows were prevalent, as were a variety of vernacular styles. By the 1960s about 1,200 families lived in Edgewood. At the time it had attained a measure of local recognition as the home of the Kautsky Indians (a professional basketball team) and the Edgewood Wheelmen bicycle club. The town's business district on Madison Avenue boasted filling stations, eateries, retail and repair shops, and professional offices. Commuter traffic prompted county officials to spend $5 million in 1962 to improve a stretch of Madison Avenue through Edgewood.

Never incorporated, the community became a part of Indianapolis in 1970 under UNIGOV. Edgewood continues to be a stable, quiet suburb in the 1990s, though extensive commercial development elsewhere in the township has bypassed the business district.

CATHLEEN F. DONNELLY

Indianapolis Times, June 24, 1962.

Education, Early Childhood. Early childhood education programs provide children between ages two and six with planned experiences that encourage emotional, social, intellectual, and physical development. In Indianapolis, several types of programs are available for preschool aged children. Nursery schools generally accept three- and four-year-olds into half-day programs, which balance age-appropriate instructional activities with unstructured periods of play. Day care centers and day nurseries operate for the benefit of parents who need longer care for their children, while they work or attend school. Generally, day care services are offered 10 to 12 hours per day, 5 days a week, 12 months a year. HEAD START serves three-, four-, and five-year-old children of low-income families, providing educational experiences as well as health and social services. Kindergartens are usually attached to public schools, are instructionally oriented, and serve children five years old and older. Historically, kindergarten was the first form of early childhood education to arrive in Indianapolis.

Interest in the education of preschool-aged children was spread across Europe in the late 18th and early 19th centuries by individuals such as Robert Owen (a Scottish industrialist who eventually founded the first nursery school in the United States at New Harmony, Indiana, in 1826), Johann Pestalozzi, and Jean-Jacques Rousseau. These early efforts at preschool education were usually directed toward poor and working class children. But it was Friedrich Froebel who earned the epithet "Father of the Kindergarten" for the school he established in Blakenburgh, Germany, in 1837 for four- to six-year-old children of middle class parents. Froebel believed that, given a well-ordered environment, children should grow according to their own nature and potential, as do animals and plants—thus the metaphoric name, meaning "child's garden." Froebel's model was brought to the United States by German immigrants, who opened the first kindergarten in the United States in 1856.

As early as 1834, a teacher named Miss Sargent was operating a school for young children in the basement of the Governor's Mansion in Indianapolis. Both locally and nationally, interest in kindergarten increased because of the perceived neglect of preschool-aged poor and immigrant children. Churches and other charitable organizations viewed kindergartens as a way to provide much-needed educational and social services to these children. In 1881, OSCAR C. MCCULLOCH, pastor of the Plymouth Congregational Church, organized a free kindergarten, which was housed in the corridor of P.S. 12 during the summer and in the nearby mission church in fall and winter. Lois G. Hufford was the first teacher. The following year, McCulloch and others established the Indianapolis Free Kindergarten Society. Its first director was ELIZA BLAKER, who became Indianapolis' foremost crusader for early childhood education. Blaker also established the Indiana Kindergarten and Primary Normal Training School, which eventually became part of the teacher education program of BUTLER UNIVERSITY.

In March, 1889, the Indiana General Assembly approved an act for the establishment of kindergartens for all children aged four to six in the incorporated towns and cities of the state. By the next year, 17 kindergartens, funded and maintained by the Indianapolis Free Kindergarten Society, were operating in the city. Then, in 1901, the General Assembly passed an act that allowed part of the money for kindergartens to be raised through taxation, making Indiana one of the first states to appropriate public money for the maintenance of kindergartens. Over the next decade, the number of free kindergartens in Indianapolis grew, hitting a high of 60 in 1914. Up to this point, kindergartens had been enthusiastically endorsed by urban school leaders, but disaffection and decline soon began. Not only were kindergartens costly, but educators and kindergartners disagreed over whether kindergarten should be child-centered and developmental, as Froebel had envisioned it, or instructional and modificational, as such American educators as Dewey and Thorndike proposed. For Indianapolis, this debate effectively ended in 1949 when the Indianapolis Public Schools incorporated free kindergartens into the public school system, thereby determining that kindergartens would be instructional and modificational in approach.

Charitable organizations interested in the well-being of children helped bring other childhood education programs to the city. Established in 1901, the DAY NURSERY ASSOCIATION OF INDIANAPOLIS provided day care to indigent children. Settlement houses offered educational programs for preschool-aged children of immigrants, since early childhood education was viewed as an important part of the Americanization process. During the 1920s, for example, students from the local teachers college provided half-day programs in the Kingan Hill Settlement District. Children were instructed in saluting the flag, singing patriotic songs, and such "American" skills as bed making, table setting, and laundry sorting.

Federal involvement in early childhood education in Indiana dates to the mid–1930s, when the Works Projects Administration operated day nurseries for children ages two through six. With the expiration of the WPA legislation, the program was largely dismantled, but was resurrected in

1941 with the passage of the federal Lanham Act. Women entering the labor force needed care for their children, and in 1942 the Children's Division of the Indiana Department of Welfare published standards for day nurseries. These guidelines—some using the verb "must," but most using the verb "should"—mirrored an ongoing tension in federal involvement in early childhood programs, between quality, developmental child care and low-cost, welfare-based child care.

The end of World War II and the accompanying push for women to withdraw from the work force brought an end to federal funding for child care programs until the 1960s and the Johnson Administration's War on Poverty. The Head Start program for disadvantaged preschool children was authorized by the Economic Opportunity Act of 1964. Planners hoped that Head Start, in addition to providing early education for poor children, might stimulate community action by bringing parents together, help coordinate services to children and their families, better the life chances of disadvantaged youth, and even bring about school reform by encouraging schools to deal seriously with the needs of poor children. In Indianapolis, Head Start began as a summer program in 1965, and initially served over 1,000 five-and six-year-olds. It was extended to include three- and four-year-olds through the Indianapolis Pre-School Centers, which were also funded by the Office of Economic Opportunity.

Over the last several decades, early childhood education programs have expanded and multiplied in Indianapolis. Free, half-day kindergartens are available throughout the city, although free transportation is not provided. Programs are offered through both the public and private sectors and include nursery schools, cooperative nursery schools, day nurseries, Head Start, Montessori programs, and special programs that offer services to meet special needs, such as physical or mental handicaps and giftedness.

More recently, President George Bush's educational goals for the year 2000 again focused national attention on early childhood education. This is consistent with the historical pattern of federal interest in this issue in times of perceived national crisis. In order to "ensure that every child starts school ready to learn," Governor Evan Bayh proposed the Step Ahead plan, which he hoped to make available to all Indiana four-year-olds by 1995 to provide year-round, full-day instruction on a voluntary basis.

The Indiana Association for the Education of Young Children and the Day Nursery Association are two local organizations concerned with the quality of early childhood education programs. Both publish guidelines for parents seeking appropriate programs for their children. According to the Day Nursery Association, one pressing need in Indianapolis is care for working parents' children under the age of two. But perhaps even more pressing is the need for early childhood education programs to respond to national statistics which show that today one in five children is born into poverty, and which predict that in 1995 approximately one-third of all children in school will be children of color.

ELIZABETH SPALDING

Education, Female. Since the early 19th century, the methods and goals of female education in America have reflected dominant societal definitions of gender roles. As institutions and programs changed over time, one glimpses how gender itself is an historically constructed concept. The institutions established for educating women in Indianapolis over the years mirror these changes.

The Indianapolis Female School, founded in March, 1830, was the first school in the city exclusively for women. Its founder, a Mrs. Tichenor, offered a curriculum of spelling, reading, writing, English grammar, geography, astronomy, and needlework. Miss Hooker's Female School began four years later, adding history, natural philosophy, drawing, and painting to the curriculum developed in the Indianapolis Female School. Both institutions prided themselves on teaching women what were known as "accomplishments" rather than rigorous academic pursuits. Their goal was to give women the tools required to move in polite society and be a source of culture in the home. Society expected women to instill these finer values in their husbands and children.

Religious denominations were also instrumental in establishing female educational institutions in 19th-century Indianapolis. Like their secular counterparts, these schools sought to instill domestic and cultural values that would aid women in preserving domestic bliss. Added to this, of course, was religious education according to the beliefs of the sponsoring denomination. The Presbyterian church was the first religious group to establish a women's school in Indianapolis when it opened the Indianapolis Female Institute in 1837. After briefly occupying the second story of a building on Washington Street near Meridian, the institute moved to its own building on Pennsylvania Street but closed after 12 years because of the ill health of its director. The Presbyterian church continued its goals by founding the INDIANAPOLIS FEMALE SEMINARY in 1852, which it renamed McLean Seminary in 1860 and operated until 1865.

Other Indianapolis denominations founded female schools during this period. The Episcopalian church operated St. Mary's Seminary from 1844 to 1849; the Methodists opened the Indianapolis Female College in 1850; and the Baptist church maintained the Indianapolis Young Ladies Institute at the corner of Michigan and Pennsylvania streets from 1858 to 1872. By the late 1870s the Catholic church was also involved in female education through its three parochial schools for girls.

By the second half of the 19th century female education began taking on new meanings and precipitating unforeseen results. Ironically, it was the very segregation of women's schools and their emphasis on the supposed female ability to maintain moral standards that provided women with a means to break out of their constricted domestic sphere. Female schools provided the opportunity to hone skills such as public speaking, and to bolster self-esteem, while women used their reputed moral superiority to justify wider participation in public life. Beginning with the emancipation debate prior to and during the Civil War, and continuing into such issues as temperance, WOMEN'S RIGHTS AND SUFFRAGE, women's and children's labor regulations, and a wide variety of other morally charged causes, American women increasingly became more vocal in politics. For many, involvement in these public issues was a logical extension of their traditional role. Others

brushed gender boundaries aside by entering professions in which their unique attributes as women clearly meshed. Teaching, nursing, and social work were among the professions opened to Indianapolis women that combined traditional domestic values and broader social activism.

Exemplifying this shift in Indianapolis was a new school founded by MAY WRIGHT SEWALL in 1882. Sewall, a charter member of the Indianapolis Suffrage Society, had been active in Indianapolis community affairs for over 40 years. She opened the Classical School for Girls on the southeast corner of Pennsylvania and St. Joseph streets as a counterpart to the Classical School for Boys. Unlike earlier female schools, "accomplishments" gave way to serious academic study. The main goal of the Classical School for Girls until it closed in 1907 was to provide pupils with the background necessary to gain college admission.

Colleges and universities that admitted women were still very rare in the late 19th century. For the most part they were concentrated on the East Coast. Indianapolis, however, was home to North Western Christian University (later BUTLER UNIVERSITY), one of the first coeducational institutions of higher education in America, founded in 1855. Indianapolis women who were unable or unwilling to relocate to a distant college could earn a higher degree in their home city. Sixteen of the 66 students in 1856 were females, and 15 of the 51 college preparatory students were girls. Butler University further encouraged education for and by women when it instituted the Demia Butler Chair of English Literature in 1869. The endowment was the first academic chair in any U.S. university established specifically for a woman, and the first holder of the chair, CATHARINE MERRILL, became the second woman professor in the nation.

Teaching was the profession embraced by most women. Not only was it a socially acceptable job for women, teaching was economically unprofitable and, therefore, avoided by men. Ironically, the paltry salaries of teachers created openings into which women flooded. The Indianapolis public schools created a Normal School Department in March, 1867, to train students of the schools to become teachers in them. By 1884 over half of the Indianapolis public school teachers were graduates of the Normal School, and most of these graduates were women. Another opportunity for women's teacher education was initiated by ELIZA BLAKER, a pioneer in kindergarten education in Indianapolis. Blaker established the kindergarten Normal Training School in 1883, later renamed the Teachers College of Indianapolis, with an all-female staff and student body. The Teachers College affiliated with Butler University in 1926.

By the 20th century separate female educational institutions were no longer the norm in Indianapolis. Compulsory attendance laws and increasing acceptance of coeducational public schools and colleges diminished the role of gender-segregated schools at all educational levels. However, a handful of parochial and preparatory schools for young women continued to flourish in Indianapolis during the 20th century. Tudor Hall for Girls, founded in 1902, prospered until the 1960s when declining enrollments forced it to eliminate its lower grades and later merge with Park School for Boys in 1970 to become PARK TUDOR SCHOOL. There were also several Catholic girls schools in Indianapolis, including Ladywood, St. Agnes, St. Mary, St. John, and Our Lady of Grace. Declining enrollments in all of these schools also forced the Catholic Archdiocese to combine them in 1969, and in 1976 the Ladywood–St. Agnes campus became coeducational with the merger of Cathedral High School.

At the college level, while women increasingly enrolled in the local schools, traditional courses of study open to women, such as teaching, NURSING, home economics, and SOCIAL WORK, continued to appeal almost exclusively to women. As a result of the women's liberation movement in the 1970s, female students began making significant advances into fields of study not traditionally open to women, such as engineering and law. As of 1993 local colleges and universities reported slight female majorities in their overall enrollments and, with the help of outreach programs, still-growing numbers of women in traditionally male-dominated courses of study.

During the 1970s local colleges and universities also began to offer courses, academic programs, and even departments focusing exclusively on women's roles within society which had previously been ignored in most coeducational curriculums. A group of women educators at IUPUI organized the Continuing Education Center for Women in 1975, and merged its offerings with the Department of Women's Studies in the university's School of Liberal Arts in the late 1980s. In the early 1990s, Butler University began a Gender Studies program, signaling a new educational trend which emphasizes neither male nor female issues.

ALEXANDER URBIEL
Indiana University, Bloomington

Education, Special. Some Indianapolis children received special education services even before the city had a free, public school system. These services were made available by the Indiana state schools for deaf-mutes (est. 1843–1844), the blind (est. 1847), and the feebleminded (est. 1879). These services were inadequate, however, to meet the city's needs and by 1898 Indianapolis Public Schools (IPS) organized its first special education class, a separate (ungraded) class for grade-retarded pupils. This was followed in 1906 by the establishment of a "special school" (two classes) for truants and incorrigibles. The "school" label indicated that these classes were composed of students from the entire school system, but the clients were exclusively boys who typically were identified as hyperactive or as having behavioral problems. The curriculum emphasized practical subjects to encourage early employment.

There were two classes for grade-retarded students by 1908–1909, with Katrina Myers as head teacher. That same year, at least seven other teachers were assigned to various schools to provide individualized instruction to such students. By 1911 these teachers each saw 50–75 children per semester. That year also saw the opening of two "fresh air" classes, at least one of which was for tubercular students. The head teacher for the fresh air classes, Jeanette Williams, later administered much of the special education program for the entire school system.

By 1912, the special classes supervised and taught by Myers were referred to as classes for mentally defective children and the Simon-Binet intelligence tests were used to select the students.

Each class had a maximum of 16 students coming from throughout the school system. By 1913, the school for truants and incorrigibles had three teachers who together dealt with approximately 65 students at any one time and about 120 per year.

Programs for physically disabled students began to appear in the 1920s and 1930s. In 1925, for example, Superintendent E. U. Graff announced plans to construct a separate school for "crippled" children whose physical disabilities prevented them from attending regular classes. This school was to have two specially trained teachers and it was expected that 20–25 students would attend when it opened. By 1935, this school was replaced by the James E. Roberts School and had an enrollment of 200 students. A special class for the sight-impaired started in 1928 with a second class added in 1939. By 1952 there were five such classes. The first class for the hearing-impaired began in 1935. In each of these cases, the Indianapolis schools instituted these special programs for both the mentally and the physically disabled before the Indiana General Assembly formulated specific policy directives or made financial appropriations for such educational services.

During the 1920s, the Indianapolis school systems also appeared to be groping for terminology to describe these developing special educational services and for ways to administer them. The labels attached to both the classes and the students changed several times during this period. The classes for "truants and incorrigibles," for example, were folded into the classes for the "mentally defective" which, in turn, became classes for "atypical" students. Further, the "atypical" designation encompassed students with either physical or mental handicaps. By the early 1930s there were at least 17 classes for these "atypical" students as well as five fresh air classes, the several classes at the school for crippled children, and three other classes for various other "special" pupils.

Other than the designation of the head teacher of a group of special classes as "principal," the first general administrative appointment in special education was made in 1918 when Myers became the director of the "Department of Backward and Defective Children." This department was not mentioned again in the system's administrative directory for six years, but it reappeared in 1924. In 1926 Myers no longer appeared in the administrative directory and Williams was listed as the director of the "Department of Education of Exceptional Children." By 1929, Williams became the director of "Instruction of Exceptional Children." By 1934 the administration had settled on more current terminology and established an assistant superintendency for "Social Services and Special Education."

The next major expansion of special educational services took place in the 1950s and focused on both ends of the academic spectrum. After offering several experimental programs to certain elementary school pupils in 1951, the school system officially organized two classes for gifted students, one each in the fifth and sixth grades, for the 1952–1953 school year. Subsequently, students could continue in the gifted program through the eighth grade. Administered by the department of special education, this program enrolled 45 the first year. Within three years the Indianapolis schools offered eight classes for the gifted with a total enrollment of 205 students drawn from 60 schools. As with earlier special classes for students with mental and/or physical disabilities, the gifted classes were housed in designated schools to which students from other schools could be transported. The minimum entry requirement for the gifted classes was an IQ of 125.

In 1953, the administration announced plans to establish another separate school, this time for the very low IQ students with scores below 50, the minimum standard for public instruction. The curriculum in this school was to be largely vocational. Unlike the growth in services for the gifted students, however, by the end of the decade there was still only one class for these low IQ students.

Since the 1960s, the face of special education in Indianapolis as elsewhere has been shaped largely by the federal government. The present programmatic direction for the delivery of special educational services appears to be away from the separate facilities that characterized the system for over a century and toward mainstreaming all "special" children, whenever feasible, within the boundaries of the regular classroom. As of 1992, roughly 7,200 students in IPS (about 15 percent of the total) received special educational services. The vast majority of these students were categorized as "learning disabled." Some 500 staff, mainly teachers, were assigned to a program considered state of the art, thus continuing the city's tradition as a midwestern leader in the special education field.

JAMES L. FLANNERY
Indiana University, Bloomington

Ruth Knapp Heavenridge, "A History of Special Education for the Mentally Retarded in the Indianapolis Public Schools" (M.A. thesis, Indiana University, 1935); State of Indiana, Department of Public Instruction, *Twenty-Seventh Biennial Report of the State Superintendent of Public Instruction (1913–1914)* (Indianapolis, 1915).

Education, Vocational. Apprenticeship remained for hundreds of years the primary method of transmitting trade skills to new practitioners. It was not until the 19th century that vocational education as a component of schooling first attracted the attention of educators in the United States. Some vocational training was offered in juvenile asylums and orphanages as well as in private trade schools in the early 1800s. In the decades following the Civil War, however, vocational education began to assume a larger role in

Typing class at Manual High School in 1916.
[Indiana Historical Society, Bass Collection, #46343]

American education, especially in response to industrialization.

Vocational education in Indianapolis in general followed national patterns and trends. In 1888 the superintendent of the Indianapolis Public Schools recommended that manual training be included in the curriculum to provide practical and physical activities complementary to academic work. The school commissioners hired W. H. Bass to administer the program and made a $1,000 appropriation for books and equipment. Manual arts, in the form of woodworking and mechanical drawing, entered the curriculum as an elective for high school freshman the same year.

The growing interest in manual training led the commissioners in part to open the Indianapolis Industrial Training School (later MANUAL HIGH SCHOOL) in 1895. Under the principalship of CHARLES EMIL EMMERICH, the Industrial Training School, located at the corner of Madison Avenue and Meridian Street, was especially designed to integrate manual and industrial education into the Indianapolis public school curriculum.

Seventeen years after the opening of the Industrial Training School, the commissioners founded ARSENAL TECHNICAL HIGH SCHOOL on property acquired in 1904. The site's deed had specified that any educational institution established there should provide mechanical and manual training for both boys and girls. Classes offered over time at Tech (as it became known) were reflective of vocational education in general. Typical courses included graphic and commercial art, printing, and the building crafts. Classes in radio, automotive mechanics, and commerce later were added to the curricular offerings. Other public secondary vocational education was made available at Harry E. Wood High School, opened in the fall of 1953 with the specific purpose of providing vocational education at the secondary level. The school was closed in the spring of 1978.

Private and charitable vocational education also was found in Indianapolis during the late 19th and early 20th centuries. The Girls Industrial School of Indianapolis opened in 1890 with an enrollment of 20 children and by 1907 enrollment had climbed to 736. The school provided vocational training to girls from poor families between the ages of six and fifteen. The curriculum included stenography, sewing, typewriting, and home economics. The Winona Agricultural and Technical Institute was another early private trade school. Located on the arsenal property, which later became the site of Tech, the institute was founded in 1904 and offered several vocational classes. The school became insolvent in 1909.

Vocational schooling has continued to be an important part of Indianapolis education since the early part of the 20th century. Like other aspects of schooling, vocational education in the city has frequently been shaped by national developments. During World War II, for example, such war-related vocational offerings as aeronautics, map and military drawing, and code training made their way into the curriculum at Tech. Following the war another upsurge in vocational education occurred as large numbers of service personnel returned home. The Indianapolis Public Schools provided job training through the Educational Services For Veterans program to returning veterans who had not completed high school.

Vocational education today remains an integral part of the city's public school system. Vocational classes are found in each public secondary school's curriculum, but most secondary vocational training is conducted at the Indianapolis Career Education Center and the Health Professions Center at Arsenal Technical High School. Vocational subjects taught at these centers include electricity, carpentry, and house construction; cabinetmaking; architectural drafting; dry cleaning; alterations and tailoring; and painting and decorating. Those students who successfully meet course and program requirements receive a Vocational Certificate.

Post-secondary vocational education is available in programs offered by the INDIANA VOCATIONAL TECHNICAL COLLEGE. A number of private trade schools also offer vocational programs.

CHARLES TITUS
Eastern Illinois University

Lawrence A. Cremin, *The Transformation of the School* (New York, 1961); Marvin Layerson and W. Norton Grubb, eds., *American Education and Vocationalism: A Documentary History, 1870–1970* (New York, 1974).

Educational Radio and Television. See Broadcasting, Educational and Public

Educational Testing and Evaluation.
From the early 1850s, when the first free public school opened in Indianapolis, through the first decade of the 20th century, the responsibility for testing pupils was divided between the classroom teacher and the central school administration. One of the original duties of the school superintendent, for example, was the development and administration of promotional examinations in every grade.

As with other school systems around the country, these exams began as oral exercises but, as the numbers of students grew, printed questions were used and written responses required. The exams sought to be comprehensive, were pervasive in the system, and resulted in sifting of the student population. The January, 1885, list of printed high school examinations, for example, included at least 25 subject areas from arithmetic to Virgil. By 1876 the school system's "Manual of Instruction to Teachers" advised all teachers that they could expect up to four written exams a year, with questions developed by the Supervisors of Instruction. In 1879 J. B. Roberts, the high school principal, indicated that final course exams were the primary form of student evaluation and also the main reason for the high dropout rate among less well prepared ninth graders.

As with system-wide tests today, these early promotional examinations were used explicitly as evaluations of both the students and their schools and, implicitly, of the teachers. As a result, individual teachers not only taught the course content but also prepared students for promotional exams.

Because examinations were standard across the system, the curriculum taught by teachers needed to be uniform. From at least the 1870s, the central administration standardized curriculum by preparing lesson manuals and courses of study for virtually all subjects in virtually all grades. Many of these guides were very detailed and most were organized in the form of questions to be addressed by the teacher, questions that could form the basis of either lessons or tests. But the construction of such instructional tests was seen as the teacher's responsibility; they were generally not included in course manuals. The administration seemed to be aware that teachers might teach with an eye toward the promotional exams, and some of these manuals included explicit advice to the instructor that the best teaching gave the student love of reading and of books and did not rely on rote memorization. In the late 19th century, external observers commented that the methods of instruction in Indianapolis schools were characterized by humanistic and child-centered teaching and were not driven by the struggle for "results."

The 20th century brought both increased enrollment pressures on most school systems and the introduction of "scientific" methods of student evaluation. These methods included intelligence tests and a variety of standardized tests, which were soon incorporated into the examination system of the Indianapolis schools. By adopting these methods, the central administration relinquished some of its control over the development of tests for its pupils, and, to a lesser extent, over the content of the curriculum. The scientific tests, however, facilitated the classification of the ever-increasing numbers of students by academic abilities.

By 1913, the State Superintendent of Public Instruction commented that increased use of standardized tests in Indiana was in direct response to public demands for accountability in education. That same year, Indianapolis instituted its first class for mentally deficient students, relying, in part, on intelligence tests to select clients for this program. Intelligence and/or achievement tests were later used to determine, among other things, which children were mentally or emotionally unfit for schooling and therefore exempt from the compulsory education laws. By the 1930s, thousands of students in Indianapolis schools were being given a variety of standardized and intelligence tests on a regular basis. A full-time psychologist was hired in 1939 simply to deal with children whose academic difficulties had been identified by one or more of these tests.

Even within a regular class, the teacher could by the 1930s divide pupils into informal ability groups on the basis of "scientific" standardized test results. Course manuals, which the administration continued to develop, began to include specific enrichment and remedial activities for these various student groupings. The administration again cautioned teachers not to carry ability groupings too far and to be careful not to engage in instructional practices that might stamp any child with a mark of inferiority.

In 1953, however, Indianapolis began a more formal, systemic approach to ability grouping based principally on a pupil's scores on certain standardized tests. The Board of School Commissioners instituted a program for gifted students—one class in the fifth and sixth grades—with an IQ score of at least 125. That same year plans were announced for a separate public school for the students of very low academic abilities or an IQ score of 50 or lower. The reliance on standardized testing has continued to the present with the advent of the ISTEP examination program. As with the use of system-wide testing in the past, these tests are used not only to evaluate student performance but to evaluate their schools and, implicitly, teachers as well.

JAMES L. FLANNERY
Indiana University, Bloomington

Indianapolis Public Schools, *Indianapolis High School Examinations for Promotion* (Indianapolis, 1885); Indianapolis Public Schools, *Manual of Instruction to Teachers and the Graded Course Study of the Indianapolis Public Schools* (Indianapolis, 1876); J. M. Rice, "The Public Schools of St. Louis and Indianapolis," *Forum*, 14 (Dec., 1892), 429–444.

Edwards, Frank Allyn (Aug. 4, 1908–June 23, 1967). Radio and television newscaster, commentator, author. Edwards was born in Mattoon, Illinois, and grew up in Sullivan, Illinois, and New Albany, Indiana. His broadcasting career began in 1923 when he was hired as an unpaid announcer on KDKA, Pittsburgh. He also worked in radio in New Albany, Lexington, Kentucky, and Louisville. While in Louisville in 1943, Edwards began a weekly news and commentary program on the Mutual network. In 1944 he came to Indianapolis, working for WIBC radio, then moved to WISH in 1948. In 1949 he again took a job with Mutual, broadcasting first from Indianapolis, then

Washington, D.C.; he stayed with the network until 1954. Returning to Indianapolis, he was hired by WTTV Channel 4 to anchor its nightly newscast. He moved to WLW-I Channel 13 (now WTHR) in the early 1960s to host a late night talk show, and was working as a commentator for WXLW radio when he died.

While at Mutual in the early 1950s, Edwards attended a number of Air Force briefings on unidentified flying objects and became fascinated by the subject. He talked about UFOs on many of his programs, and also wrote six books on the subject. His most famous book, *Flying Saucers— Serious Business* (1966), was an international bestseller. Edwards wrote about his early radio career in his first book, *My First 10,000,000 Sponsors*, published in 1956. The title referred to membership of the American Federation of Labor, his sponsor on the Mutual broadcasts. Edwards was fired in 1954 by George Meany, leader of the AFL, in a dispute over censorship of Edwards' broadcasts.

Michael Spillman

Rory Stuart, ed., *The Strange World of Frank Edwards* (Secaucus, N.J., 1977).

Edyvean Repertory Theatre.

Incorporated November 9, 1971, as the Repertory Theatre at Christian Theological Seminary (CTS), the operation presented its first full season of dramas and musicals in 1968–1969. During celebration of its twentieth anniversary in 1991–1992 the theatre was renamed to honor its founder, Dr. Alfred R. Edyvean. It is the only community theatre in the United States with a full season sponsored by a theological seminary.

Its predecessor was Seminary Players of the School of Religion of Butler University. They performed short religious plays in Sweeney Chapel and in midwestern churches. Another forerunner was original television drama produced in cooperation with the Church Federation and local television stations, aided by a Lilly Endowment grant.

The theatre program moved to Shelton Auditorium on the new CTS campus in 1966 and received a $70,000 grant from Lilly Endowment to establish a repertory theatre for religious drama. The "theatre with a purpose" eventually developed a season of six full-length productions, with a concentration on "classics" by Shakespeare, Shaw, Ibsen, Chekhov, and others. While early participants were students and community volunteers, the group developed into a community theatre with a professional staff and is now a member of the League of Professionally Managed Theatres. Outreach efforts have included Jumping Mouse Players (for persons with disabilities), Matrix pre- and post-show discussions, and Epworth Forest Summer Theatre (for Methodist youth in northern Indiana).

Marian K. Towne
Indiana University–Purdue University, Indianapolis

Marian K. Towne, *Dreaming the Impossible Dream: The First Quarter Century of the Edyvean Repertory Theatre at Christian Theological Seminary* (1993).

Efroymson, Robert A.

(Sept. 27, 1905–Dec. 30, 1988). Businessman, philanthropist. A lifelong resident of Indianapolis and a graduate of Shortridge High School, Efroymson received a B.A. (1926) and LL.B. (1929) from Harvard University. He returned to Indianapolis, practiced law until 1942, served in World War II, and in 1945 accepted a vice-presidency with Real Silk Hosiery Mills. Succeeding his father as president of the company in 1946, Efroymson ended hosiery production by the mid–1950s and converted the business into an investment company, Real Silk Investments, Inc., which he operated until his death.

Named one of the 32 most influential people in the city in 1976 by the *Indianapolis Star*, Efroymson was noted for his involvement in numerous civic and philanthropic activities. From 1946 to 1988 he served as chairman of the board of the Indianapolis Foundation. As president of the Civic Progress Association during its first $3^{1}/_{2}$ years from 1955 to 1959, he was one of the first to envision the downtown redevelopment plan that became known as the Riley Center. As president of Community Hospital from 1952 to 1959, Efroymson oversaw a campaign that raised $15 million for local hospital construction, with $5.2 million earmarked for Community Hospital. In 1964 he helped found the GREATER INDIANAPOLIS PROGRESS COMMITTEE, and from 1964 to 1973 he chaired the INDIANAPOLIS HOUSING AUTHORITY; during his tenure most of the city's public housing projects were built.

Efroymson was a member of the board of directors of Indiana National Bank and Lincoln National Corporation. He served on the boards of the Marion County Child Guidance Clinic, the English Foundation, the JEWISH WELFARE FEDERATION, and PLANNED PARENTHOOD. He also served as president of the United Way of Indianapolis, and in 1986 he and his brother, Dr. Clarence W. Efroymson, established the MORIAH FUND, a private charitable foundation.

JEFFERY A. DUVALL

Indianapolis Star, Jan. 1, 1989; *Indianapolis News*, May 14, 1962.

Eiteljorg Museum of American Indian and Western Art.

Unique to the Midwest, the Eiteljorg is one of only two museums east of the Mississippi to combine collections of American western art and Native American objects. Opened in June, 1989, the museum sits just west of the city's downtown center at the main entrance to WHITE RIVER STATE PARK. Most of the museum's

Eiteljorg Museum of American Indian and Western Art. [Indianapolis Convention and Visitors Association]

collection was donated by Indianapolis businessman and philanthropist Harrison Eiteljorg, who went west after World War II in search of coal and fell in love with the people, the land, and the art. In addition, a large portion of the Native American objects were acquired as a result of a merger with the Museum of Indian Heritage, founded by Mr. and Mrs. James Lawton, which was previously located in Eagle Creek Park.

Three main galleries house the museum's permanent collections, which include approximately 400 paintings and bronzes and 2,000 artifacts. The Southwestern Gallery features paintings by members of the original Taos Society of Artists and includes works by Victor Higgins, E. Martin Hennings, and Ernest Blumenschein. The American Western Gallery exhibits nineteenth and twentieth century paintings and sculptures by such artists as Alfred Jacob Miller, Frederic Remington, and Charles Russell. The Native American Gallery houses the museum's permanent collection of Indian objects in the exhibition "Spirited Hands."

The Eiteljorg Museum is dedicated to preserving and interpreting the history of the American West through displays, exhibitions, and educational programs. Along with displaying and developing the permanent collection, the Eiteljorg brings to Indianapolis traveling exhibitions that explore particular historic or artistic themes, or display exceptional works of art. Tours, lectures, demonstrations, and classes are also held regularly. A not-for-profit organization, the museum relies on support from external grants, private donations, memberships, and revenue from admissions and the museum store. It attracted approximately 125,000 visitors per year in the early 1990s.

The museum building, an interpretation of southwestern culture, was born out of a collaboration between local architect Jonathan Hess and Harrison Eiteljorg. Designed to be an integral part of the museum experience, the building reflects the warm adobe pueblos so common in the southwestern region of the United States. Set in a circular base to represent a kiva (a sacred space used in Pueblo Indian communities), the museum blends ancient traditions with contemporary style. Construction costs were met through private grants and contributions, including major gifts from Eiteljorg himself and LILLY ENDOWMENT.

KAREN MCLEAN
Eiteljorg Museum of American Indian
and Western Art

Elbert, Samuel A. (Apr. 9, 1832–July 15, 1902). Prominent Indianapolis physician and the first African-American in Indiana to receive a medical degree. Born in Maryland of free parents, Elbert worked as a field hand and house servant in his youth and did not learn to read and write until his early twenties. During the Civil War he was a servant to a group of white Union officers. He subsequently attended Oberlin College in Ohio and moved to Indianapolis in 1866, teaching for a time in a private black school supported by Allen Chapel.

Elbert studied medicine privately with two white physicians, one of whom interceded to secure his admission to the newly opened Indiana Medical College in 1869. Although he paid tuition and completed the prescribed course of study, the college initially refused to grant him a degree. The faculty eventually reversed its position and Elbert received his M.D. in 1871. He was appointed to the Indianapolis Board of Health the following year and also developed a large private practice.

Prominent in the AME church, Elbert was also active in Republican politics. He was nominated for state representative in 1882 and, during the administration of William McKinley, was offered but declined a consular post in Brazil.

GLENN W. IRWIN, JR., M.D.

Emma Lou Thornbrough, *The Negro in Indiana* (Indianapolis, 1957); *Indiana Medical Journal*, 21 (Aug., 1902), 91.

Elder, John (Sept. 2, 1796–Nov. 3, 1857). Architect. Born in Harrisburg, Pennsylvania, Elder was one of the contractors for the Juanita division of the Pennsylvania canal. In 1831 he submitted drawings in the competition to design the Indiana STATE HOUSE. Although his design was not a winner, he came to Indianapolis in 1833 to take up permanent residence, becoming the first professional architect to make his home in the Hoosier capital. He designed HERVEY BATES' Washington Street retail buildings, CHARLES MAYER'S original store building, HENRY WARD BEECHER'S home, the Bank of Indiana Building (1840), the first Hospital for the Insane (later CENTRAL STATE HOSPITAL, 1848), and the Palmer House, one of Indianapolis' finest hotels. He drew the original plans of the Institute for the Blind (although FRANCIS COSTIGAN later embellished Elder's design) and was a contractor for the CENTRAL CANAL. In addition to his work in Indianapolis, Elder designed courthouses for Clinton, Bartholomew, and Rush counties in Indiana. Severely in debt, Elder left Indianapolis in 1850 before his last commission, the Blind Institute, was completed. He joined the Gold Rush to California and died seven years later in Sacramento. Elder's legacy to Indianapolis included his son, John R. Elder, publisher of the *INDIANA STATE SENTINEL*, and his grandson, William L. Elder, real estate developer.

CONNIE J. ZEIGLER

John Elder Papers, Indiana Historical Society; Kenneth Loucks, "John Elder: Pioneer Builder," *Indiana Magazine of History*, 26 (Mar., 1930), 25–33.

Election of 1860. As the state's largest city, Indianapolis was the site of unprecedented political activity during the presidential campaign of 1860. With the DEMOCRATIC PARTY in Indiana divided between supporters of Stephen Douglas and Hoosier Senator Jesse Bright, the six-year-old REPUBLICAN PARTY found itself better organized and at least as strong as its rival. Because of its population size, Indiana along with Illinois and Pennsylvania was considered a "must win" state by both parties, and carrying Indianapolis was viewed as a key to winning the state. The ensuing campaign was marked by innumerable torchlight parades, processions, speeches, and rallies in the capital city.

Following the defeat of his attempts to block Douglas' nomination at both the state and national Democratic conventions, Bright returned to Indianapolis in July and in partnership with Graham Fitch began publication of a triweekly paper,

The Old Line Guard, which quickly became known for being more anti-Douglas than anti-Lincoln. That same summer the Republican leadership engaged the services of Carl Schurz, for a fee paid by the Republican national committee, to stump the state's German voters in the belief that the outcome of the election might depend on Indiana's German population. As part of his tour of Indiana, Schurz gave a German language speech to a packed Metropolitan Hall in Indianapolis and enthusiastically endorsed Lincoln before being escorted to his train by a group of 200 uniformed campaign workers known as "Wide Awakes."

On August 29, the Republicans held a statewide rally in Indianapolis featuring a mammoth parade, an afternoon of political speeches, and an evening torchlight parade, drawing altogether an estimated 50,000 people, almost three times the city's population. A chief attraction in the parade was a large wagon filled with "pioneers" doing various tasks and drawn by 43 yoke of flag-decorated oxen, the whole outfit stretching more than 400 feet. The speeches in MILITARY PARK featured Republican notables from Indiana, Ohio, Missouri, Kentucky, and Virginia, speaking from four stands to large crowds. The torchlight parade of an estimated 5,000 torch bearers likewise drew enthusiastic throngs.

The Democrats held a comparable statewide rally on September 28. People jammed the sidewalks to watch the colorful parade of numerous floats, bands, and marching groups that escorted the featured speakers of the day, Stephen Douglas and his vice-presidential nominee, Herschel V. Johnson, to the Old Fair Grounds. There they spoke to an estimated 25,000 cheering Democrats. Downtown streets were lined that evening for the rally's climactic torchlight parade.

Following the Republican sweep of the state elections held in October, the outcome of the presidential election in November offered no surprises. Lincoln carried the state of Indiana with 139,033 votes to Douglas' 115,509, with an additional 12,294 votes going to Breckenridge and 5,306 to Bell. In Marion County, Lincoln won with 5,024 votes to Douglas' 3,252, while Breckenridge received 318 and Bell won only 161 votes.

NICHOLAS M. CRIPE
JEFFERY DUVALL

Emma Lou Thornbrough, *Indiana in the Civil War Era, 1850–1880* (Indianapolis, 1965); Reinhard H. Luthin, "Indiana and Lincoln's Rise to the Presidency," *Indiana Magazine of History*, 38 (Dec., 1942), 385–405; "Total Vote Marion County," *Indianapolis Journal*, Nov. 10, 1860; "Official Vote of Marion County," *Indianapolis Sentinel*, Nov. 9, 1860.

Election of 1896. Set against a backdrop of economic depression, the 1896 campaign focused on the resolution of a national debate concerning the metallic standard for U.S. currency. Republican presidential nominee William McKinley advocated preservation of the existing gold standard, while the Democratic platform demanded free and unlimited coinage of both silver and gold. Following the nomination of free silver candidate William Jennings Bryan, Democrats who favored maintenance of the gold standard bolted the party, forming the National Democratic party under the leadership of former Indianapolis Congressman William Dallas Bynum.

The free silver debate overshadowed all other issues on the Indianapolis political scene. Nearly 3,000 Democrats assembled at TOMLINSON HALL on July 18 to ratify Bryan's nomination. Ten days later the Indiana People's party (Populists) met in Indianapolis to endorse the national Populists' nomination of Bryan, initiating a troubled and incomplete alliance with the Democratic party. In September the NATIONAL DEMOCRATIC PARTY CONVENTION met in Indianapolis, nominating Senator John M. Palmer for president and former Confederate general Simon Bolivar Buckner for vice-president. While Republicans continued to concentrate on an anti-silver pamphlet campaign, Bryan engaged in a 600–stop speaking tour, crossing Indiana five times and making a speech in Indianapolis on October 6 reminiscent of his famous "Cross of Gold" address.

Interest in the free silver issue sparked a heavy turnout at the Marion County polls in November and McKinley carried Indianapolis by a margin of 22,405 votes to Bryan's 15,802. Having captured 12 of the 15 wards and four out of the nine townships, McKinley led a Republican sweep of both the city and the county. This marked the beginning of a decade-long period of

Republican hegemony in state politics and effectively ended Indiana's role as an evenly balanced and thus decisive state in presidential elections.

DAVID A. LOCKE

Edward A. Leary, *Indianapolis* (Indianapolis, 1971); Clifton J. Phillips, *Indiana in Transition: The Emergence of an Industrial Commonwealth, 1880–1920* (Indianapolis, 1968); *Indianapolis News*, Oct. 6, Nov. 4, 1896.

Election of 1925. Beginning with the May primary race for mayor in the Republican party, the city elections of 1925 were dominated by the presence of the KU KLUX KLAN. In May, 1925, JOHN L. DUVALL, former Marion County treasurer and Klan member, defeated anti-Klan candidate Ralph Lemcke for the Republican nomination for mayor of Indianapolis. Following his victory over A. G. Emhardt, former city attorney Walter Myers emerged as the Democratic nominee. Although the mayoral race that followed was labeled by political insiders as the most featureless in years, several important issues did emerge in the school board and city council races.

Operating under an at-large scheme for electing city councilmen, six pro-Klan Republican candidates were elected to the nine-member city council where their sympathy toward white neighborhood associations led to the passage of a residential segregation ordinance in 1926. Overturned by the courts before it could be put into effect, the ordinance gave whites the right to exclude black families from moving into their neighborhoods. The triumph of the Klan-supported United Protestant school board slate, however, seemed to be more a matter of widespread support for a proposed building and modernization program than sympathy for the Klan's racial agenda. In the mayoral race, Duvall ran on a combination of his record of efficiency as Marion County treasurer and allegations of Myers' involvement with the corrupt Bull Perrott Bush machine.

The resulting election in November was marked by low voter turnout, with only 95,872 out of the estimated 150,000 registered voters going to the polls. Capturing every ward except the 12th and 13th, Duvall won the mayor's race with about 52,000 votes to Myers' 43,000. More significantly, however, many Republicans on the ticket under Duvall surpassed his vote total in individual wards and his victory was due, at least in part, to his carrying the city's predominately black 5th and 6th wards.

MARK WYNN

Leonard J. Moore, *Citizen Klansmen: The Ku Klux Klan in Indiana, 1921–1928* (Chapel Hill, N.C., 1991), 144–150; *Indianapolis Star*, May 6, Nov. 4, 1925; *Indianapolis News*, Nov. 4, 1925.

Election of 1967. In the May mayoral Republican primary 35–year-old Richard G. Lugar, a former school board member, former vice-president of COMMUNITY ACTION AGAINST POVERTY (CAAP), and executive at Thomas I. Green & Co., defeated former mayor ALEX M. CLARK (1952–1956). Lugar's win over Clark was attributed primarily to support from the Republican Action Committee, a group of young Republican partisans who had organized following the party's defeat in the 1964 election in order to wrest control of the party from the regular Republican leadership. On the Democratic side, 61–year-old incumbent JOHN J. BARTON defeated county chairman James W. Beatty, whose challenge of an incumbent mayor was viewed by most as payback for Barton's attempt to unseat Beatty as county chairman in 1966.

The Lugar campaign, marked by the nearly 400 speeches that he made, was centered on a "series of local 'brushfire' problems rather than a concentrated attack [on] a single issue." Among the many problems addressed by Lugar were the open-dump burning of refuse, construction of the interstate highway inner loop, minority demands, and a lack of adequate recreation space. In his campaign Barton stressed his record on public housing and claimed that his administration had made the streets safer, improved the city's parks, and was responsible for the city's high rate of employment. As the campaign entered its final days, most long-time election observers predicted that Barton would be reelected in a close race.

In an upset, Lugar defeated Barton 72,278 votes to 63,284, and the Republicans gained control of the city council with a 6 to 3 majority. Lugar's surprise victory was attributed to a combination of low voter turnout among Democrats in Center Township and the strength of the Republican party's organization. In addition, Barton was hurt by Lugar's attacks on the issues of open-dump burning in several wards that Democratic candidates historically carried by large majorities, including wards 13, 14, 16, 17, 24, and 26. A final factor in Lugar's defeat of Barton was his strong showing in the African-American community, with a 10- to 15–percent increase in votes over the 1966 congressional elections. The 1967 election set the stage for the enactment of UNIGOV two years later and marked the beginning of a long period of Republican party domination in the city.

MATTHEW W. BURRIDGE

Indianapolis Star, Nov. 5, 10, 11, 1967; C. James Owen and York Willbern, *Governing Metropolitan Indianapolis* (Berkeley, Calif., 1985), 46–48.

Election of 1975. The 1975 mayoral election began with two contested primaries. Former congressman William H. Hudnut III easily won the Republican nomination over two other candidates. Businessman ROBERT V. WELCH won the Democratic nomination in a seven-man field, upsetting the favorite, Marion County chairman William Schreiber, with a strong grassroots campaign.

Hudnut and Welch battled for the mayor's office that fall along with three candidates from smaller parties. Jobs and crime control were the central issues of the campaign. Hudnut proposed improving the budget for convention and tourism promotion, fuller utilization of the Economic Development Commission, and the possibility of tax-free bonds, as means of enlarging the city's employment base. Having labeled crime the number one campaign issue, Hudnut called for strong leadership, better training for police, and more participation in crime fighting from residents of the city. Stressing the high rate of unemployment among those citizens between the ages of 18 and 30, Welch promised to call together all of the leaders of the community and to "put the full power of the mayor's office" behind their ef-

forts to improve the situation. Citing low morale as the major problem in the police department, Welch promised a new police chief if elected and called for more officers on the streets.

Hudnut won the mayoral race by a comfortable margin despite the lowest voter turnout in 13 years. Hudnut won the "new city" (the area added to Indianapolis by UNIGOV) 74,680 to 42,110. Welch won the "old city" 67,646 to 49,410. Hudnut's victory was attributed to a combination of the impact of Unigov (the expansion of the city to include the predominantly Republican suburban areas of the county) and the migration of people out of the Indianapolis area into the surrounding counties. The 1975 election marked the beginning of Hudnut's 16–year administration, the longest in the city's history.

AMY SMITH

Indianapolis News, Nov. 7, 1975.

Election of 1991. A decision in December, 1990, by Indianapolis Mayor William Hudnut III not to seek reelection following his unsuccessful run for secretary of state signaled the beginning of the 1991 mayoral campaign. In the May primaries Democrats chose Louis Mahern, a 15–year state senator, as their candidate. Republicans selected Stephen Goldsmith, a three-term Marion County prosecutor, over Virginia Blankenbaker, a state senator who had challenged Goldsmith's endorsement by the county Republican caucus and called for crossover votes from Democrats.

In a series of public forums, Mahern and Goldsmith debated a number of issues ranging from education and the CIRCLE CENTRE MALL to crime and the state of the city's infrastructure. On the subject of education, Goldsmith supported school choice, increased parental involvement, and stated that he would try to end court-ordered busing. Mahern advocated school choice and the need for the reestablishment of neighborhood schools. While both candidates supported the completion of the Circle Centre Mall, Goldsmith pledged not to spend any more public dollars on it. On the issue of crime, Mahern supported a waiting period for gun buyers, Goldsmith wanted to move some police administrators back to the streets, and both men supported the concept of community policing.

While agreeing that the city's infrastructure was in need of improvement, the candidates differed on both the costs and means of payment. Goldsmith argued that $100 million to $200 million could be cut from the $1.1 billion price tag outlined in an Indianapolis CHAMBER OF COMMERCE report on the subject. Mahern endorsed the report's findings. Both candidates opposed raising property taxes to pay the bill. Mahern, however, proposed a new storm water runoff tax, an increase in the city's sewer tax, and the creation of a tax on commuters who worked in Marion County but paid no local taxes. Goldsmith stated that he would endorse a debate on increased user fees to pay for the necessary repairs. Both candidates were in favor of selling certain city assets, such as INDIANAPOLIS INTERNATIONAL AIRPORT and golf courses, as another means of raising the necessary funds.

While engaged in one of the city's most negative mayoral campaigns, Goldsmith and Mahern together spent an unprecedented $2 million on TV, radio, and direct-mail advertising. By the fall of 1991, with polls indicating that Goldsmith had the lead over Mahern, the candidates turned increasingly to social issues to attract voters in the final weeks of the campaign. Mahern won support from the city's gay community and announced his support for the pro-choice side of the abortion issue, hoping to attract women voters. Goldsmith responded with ads promoting his views toward achieving equal employment opportunities and increased child support for women.

The final issue of the campaign surfaced after Goldsmith delayed announcing his support for an incentive package developed by Mayor Hudnut and Governor Evan Bayh to bring a UNITED AIRLINES MAINTENANCE FACILITY and 18,000 additional jobs to Indianapolis. Mahern immediately endorsed the plan and attacked Goldsmith's reluctant support. Goldsmith replied that he was protecting the taxpayers' interest against a possible future tax increase by exercising his patience.

Less than half of the 417,000 eligible voters turned out to vote on November 5. Goldsmith won with 110,545 votes to Mahern's 79,817. Ma-

hern lost much of the traditionally Democratic Catholic vote because of the abortion issue, yet he maintained the black community's vote. Goldsmith dominated the votes from the overwhelmingly white outlying precincts. Goldsmith's victory continued the Republican control of the city's government that had begun in 1968.

DAVID SABOL
JEFFERY DUVALL

"Steve & Louie: What's the Difference?" *NUVO*, Issue 34 (Oct. 30–Nov. 6, 1991); *Indianapolis Star*, Nov. 6, 1991.

Election Riot of 1876. In the early evening of May 3, 1876, the day of a special election for city councilmen, a disturbance broke out following a rumor that would-be African-American voters (overwhelmingly Republican) were being beaten and turned away from the polls in Ward 6 (a Democratic stronghold). As black residents of Ward 4 moved to investigate, they armed themselves with wooden spokes from the WOODBURN-SARVEN WHEEL COMPANY on South Illinois Street. The police tried to disarm them as they neared POGUE'S RUN and immediately a fight started between the African-Americans, the police, and Irish bystanders. Numerous blacks were injured, one of whom later died; no whites were reported seriously injured. Calm returned within an hour and the wounded were removed, but a large crowd remained in the area. Mayor JOHN CAVEN and others addressed the crowd from the balcony of the BATES HOUSE at the corner of Illinois and Washington streets. The mayor also spoke to fourth ward residents in their neighborhood and urged calm.

Press coverage of the incident reflected a divided community. The *Indianapolis News* blamed those who started the rumor for the rioting and criticized the police, but concluded that the African-Americans should not have gone to the sixth ward. The *Indianapolis Journal*, believing that the African-Americans had not sought a fight, criticized the police and reported that the Irish had taken an aggressive role in the incident. The *Sentinel* concluded that African-American voters had initiated the fighting and that they had been voting repeatedly for Republican candidates and inciting trouble in all the wards. In retrospect, the affair highlights, in its most extreme form, the agitation that sometimes resulted as the political process began to accommodate the participation of newly enfranchised African-American voters in the years following ratification of the 15th Amendment.

JOAN CUNNINGHAM

Jacob Piatt Dunn, *Greater Indianapolis* (Chicago, 1910), I, 252; *Indianapolis News*, *Indianapolis Journal*, and *Indianapolis Sentinel*, May 3–4, 1876.

Eli Lilly and Company. Eli Lilly and Company began in 1876 in a small two-story building on Pearl Street, just south of Washington Street. From the start it was a family business, with Civil War veteran COL. ELI LILLY at the head and JOSIAH K. LILLY, SR., his son, working alongside helping to make the syrups, elixirs, and pills. Although the business grew to employ about 100 workers by the late 1880s, when the firm relocated to larger facilities on McCarty Street, it was still one among hundreds of small pharmaceutical companies in America, most of which would not survive very far into the 20th century.

Lilly not only survived but prospered. It became one of the nation's leading pharmaceutical manufacturers by making fundamental transformations in production and in scientific research during the 1910s and 1920s. The company began

Eli Lilly and Company advertisement, ca. 1889.
[Eli Lilly and Company Archives]

an aggressive plant expansion in 1909 and, spurred by ELI LILLY and JOSIAH K. LILLY, JR., the two grandsons of the founder, also pioneered in introducing modern, systematic management methods that increased output and lowered unit costs.

Simply producing more and more of the same drugs would not have guaranteed survival or growth, however, for most of the pills and elixirs that came off the production lines were of little therapeutic benefit. The change, even revolution, that created the modern pharmaceutical company was the aggressive entry into scientific research and development. A major step came with the hiring in 1919 of GEORGE HENRY ALEXANDER CLOWES, whose biochemical expertise led him to cooperation with scientists at the University of Toronto to set up the world's first successful, large-scale production of INSULIN in 1923. Leadership in insulin production in the 1920s and long after brought huge profits. It brought also a large respect in the scientific community that enabled the company to attract other first-rate scientists.

Profits from insulin and other new products enabled the company to survive the Great Depression of the 1930s without laying off a single employee. It was during this decade also that Eli Lilly, who succeeded his father as president in 1932, instituted a variety of policies designed to increase the well-being of employees —policies that solidified "Lillys" reputation as one of the best places to work in central Indiana. World War II brought a return to full production in such products as blood plasma, Merthiolate, and, most important, penicillin, which contributed to major breakthroughs in antibiotics after 1945.

The growth of the 1940s brought large profits and the challenges of expansion, including the purchase in 1945 of a new plant on South Kentucky Avenue and growth in overseas markets. By 1948 sales exceeded $115 million and the company employed nearly 7,000 workers. There was another transition underway when the Lilly brothers shifted the presidency in 1953 to EUGENE N. BEESLEY, a long-time employee. The company was no longer a family-managed enterprise. The first public shares of stock were offered in 1952.

Beesley and his successors sought to maintain much of the spirit of the Lilly family even as the company continued to grow. Major plant expansion in Indiana came with the new Tippecanoe Laboratories, begun near Lafayette in 1950 to increase antibiotic production. A new plant opened in Clinton in 1969, and there were major expansions at the McCarty Street and Kentucky Avenue locations into the 1980s and 1990s. Increased attention to international sales and production led to Latin American, European, and Asian markets. A new division devoted to agricultural products, called Elanco, opened in 1954, with other diversification to follow, including, in the 1980s, medical instruments and diagnostic products. The company continued its interest in research by playing important roles in development of Salk polio vaccine, new antibiotics, and, in the 1980s, human insulin and the antidepressant Prozac.

The challenges of the pharmaceutical business increased substantially in the last decades of the 20th century. During the late 1950s and early 1960s public concern about the high costs of drugs led to new regulatory legislation, and by the early 1990s increased competition, the changing health care market, and proposed health care reform challenged the status quo of the industry and reduced its profitability. In 1993, under new leadership, Lilly streamlined its operations. The early retirement of 2,600 employees and other changes were aimed at maintaining the company's international position. Eli Lilly and Company was still a major force in the industry and in the city, but it was not as secure as it had long been.

JAMES H. MADISON
Indiana University, Bloomington

James H. Madison, *Eli Lilly: A Life, 1885–1977* (Indianapolis, 1989); E. J. Kahn, Jr., *All in a Century: The First 100 Years of Eli Lilly and Company* (Indianapolis, 1976).

Elliott, Byron K. (Sept. 4, 1835–Apr. 19, 1913). Lawyer, state supreme court justice, and law school founder. Born in Ohio, Elliott moved to Indianapolis with his father in 1850 and was elected city attorney in May, 1859. After serving as an adjutant general during the Civil War, he was again elected city attorney in 1865, 1867, and

1869, and judge of the Marion County Criminal Court in 1870. Two years later Elliott resigned to accept the new post of city solicitor. When that office was discontinued in 1873 he returned to the position of city attorney. Elliott was elected judge of the Marion County Superior Court in 1876 and judge of the Indiana Supreme Court, serving from 1881 to 1893. Although nominated in 1892, he was not reelected; he retired to private practice with his son, William F. Elliott, and coauthored several volumes on law.

A frequent contributor to law journals, Elliott served on the law faculty at North Western Christian University (later BUTLER UNIVERSITY) from 1871 to the mid–1870s. He helped establish the independent Central Indiana Law School in 1879, which closed shortly after his election to the Supreme Court. Following his retirement from the bench in 1893, Elliott, JOHN R. WILSON, Addison C. Harris, CHARLES W. FAIRBANKS, and WILLIAM P. FISHBACK opened the Indiana Law School on October 2, 1894. It merged in 1896 with the Medical College of Indiana, the Indiana Dental College, and Butler College to form the University of Indianapolis (which never fully developed). Elliott remained head of the school until 1899 and lecturer until 1903. Following a stroke he retired from public life.

JOAN CUNNINGHAM

Jacob Piatt Dunn, *Indiana and Indianans* (Chicago, 1919), IV, 1857; Donald E. Thompson, *Indiana Authors and Their Books, 1917–1966* (Crawfordsville, Ind., 1974).

Emerson, Charles Phillips (Sept. 4, 1872–Sept. 26, 1938). Physician, medical textbook author, and long-time dean of medicine at Indiana University. A native of Methuen, Massachusetts, Emerson received an A.B. degree from Amherst College in 1894 and an M.D. degree from Johns Hopkins University in 1899. He was an outstanding student and was an intern and faculty member under William Osler. He took extensive postgraduate work in Europe. At Hopkins he wrote two books, *Pneumothorax* and *Clinical Diagnosis*; the latter became the standard work in its field.

In 1911, Emerson was appointed dean of the INDIANA UNIVERSITY SCHOOL OF MEDICINE, a position he held until 1932. He was involved with the early development of the Medical Center, which included the Robert W. Long Hospital, the RILEY HOSPITAL FOR CHILDREN, the William H. Coleman Hospital, the Ball Residence of Nursing, and the Medical School building that now bears his name.

Emerson wrote several medical textbooks that were extensively used nationally. He was elected president of the Association of American Medical Colleges and served as president or officer of other national medical organizations.

GLENN W. IRWIN, JR., M.D.

Charles Emmerich was Manual High School's first principal. [Indiana Historical Society, #C5918]

Emhardt, Christian J. (Nov. 5, 1883–Sept. 4, 1971). Mayor of Indianapolis, 1951–1952, Democrat. Born in Pottsville, Pennsylvania, Emhardt and his family moved to Indianapolis when he was six months old. A MANUAL HIGH SCHOOL graduate, he received his law degree from the Indiana Law School and began an Indianapolis practice in 1906.

A longtime southside Democratic leader, Emhardt was Center Township justice of the peace from 1910 to 1914 and served on the Marion County Election Board. He served three terms on the City Council and, as president of that body, took over as interim mayor when Mayor PHILLIP L. BAYT resigned in 1951 to become a judge. Emhardt himself was elected a judge of the Marion Superior Court in 1959, serving a four-year term. He also was director of the Emhardt Memorial Hospital on the city's south side, which was founded by his brother, Dr. John Emhardt.

RAY BOOMHOWER
Indiana Historical Society

Edward A. Leary, *Indianapolis: The Story of a City* (Indianapolis, 1971).

Emmerich, Charles Emil (Aug. 25, 1845–June 6, 1911). Educator and school administrator. A native of Koblenz, Germany, Emmerich attended that city's public schools and then, at the urging of his Roman Catholic parents, studied briefly for the priesthood at a Jesuit seminary in

Fulda. Emmerich did not complete his course of religious studies with the Jesuits, however, instead leaving the seminary to join the Prussian army. He served in the artillery corps as a junior officer.

In 1865, at age 21, Emmerich immigrated to the United States. Joining the U.S. army, he was posted to assignments in Kansas and New Mexico. When his military service ended, he was offered a teaching position at a rural district school in Kansas.

Following a year of teaching in Kansas, he moved to the southeastern Indiana town of Madison. There he again taught in the district schools, and in 1871 joined the instructional staff at Madison High School. While serving as a faculty member in Madison, Emmerich authored an article concerning compulsory education, at the time a prominent issue in school reform. ABRAM C. SHORTRIDGE, superintendent of the Indianapolis Public Schools, read the article and invited Emmerich to join the faculty of Indianapolis High School (later SHORTRIDGE HIGH SCHOOL). Emmerich accepted Shortridge's offer in 1873 and remained at Indianapolis High School for the next 19 years.

In 1892 Emmerich became the first principal of Indianapolis High School Number 2 (later Calvin Fletcher High School). He remained there until early 1895 when he again became the first principal of another new educational facility, the Industrial Training School (later MANUAL HIGH SCHOOL). Emmerich remained as principal there for the following 15 years, until his retirement because of ill health in June, 1910. He died the following year in Indianapolis at his East Vermont Street home.

During his principalship, Emmerich organized a Visitor's Day, instituted a revised grading system through which pupils received grades at six-week intervals, and established academic requirements for participation in school athletic programs. A talented musician, he organized the school's first orchestra. The Manual Training High School was renamed Emmerich Manual Training High School (now Emmerich Manual High School) in his honor in 1916.

CHARLES TITUS
Eastern Illinois University

Frederic Gale, *A Biographical Study of Persons for Whom Indianapolis Schools Are Named* (Indianapolis: Indianapolis Public Schools, 1965); Carolyn Griffin, *A History of Emmerich Manual High School: 1895–1969* (n.p., n.d.; copy located in the Karl R. Kalp Teachers Library of the Education Service Center of the Indianapolis Public Schools).

Emmis Broadcasting Corporation.

Radio broadcasting and publishing company. Jeffrey H. Smulyan formed the company in 1979 with the expressed goal of acquiring underperforming radio properties in major media markets and turning them into more competitive and profitable operations.

Emmis Broadcasting Corporation (EBC) purchased its first station, WSVL-FM, Shelbyville, Indiana, in 1981. The station debuted in Indianapolis as WENS-FM on July 4, 1981. The city's only adult contemporary music format, it was an immediate success.

Over the course of the ensuing seven years EBC began acquiring other underperforming radio properties in markets significantly larger than Indianapolis. The first expansion purchase was in Minneapolis in 1982. By the summer of 1983, EBC embarked on an effort to buy stations in St. Louis and Los Angeles. This was the first of three multi-station purchases. The St. Louis station followed the rapid growth pattern of the original two stations. However, Los Angeles had only marginal growth. After extensive market research and a format change that targeted a young demographic audience in the Los Angeles market, the station

leaped from 26th position in the ratings to the number one station in the market. It has been at or near the top of the audience ratings ever since.

This series of successful turnarounds opened up new financial sources for EBC's expansion plans. By the close of 1988 it had additional operations in Washington, D.C., Boston, Chicago, San Francisco, Houston, and two stations in New York City. EBC also purchased INDIANAPOLIS MONTHLY magazine at this time. The total cost of the purchases over the seven years was $220 million. *American Radio* identified EBC as the most admired radio group in the industry in 1989.

In 1990, EBC began to sell properties that had matured in order to reduce debt and to prepare for the possibility that the Federal Communications Commission would allow multi-station ownership within a single market. By 1992, EBC had sold the stations in Houston, San Francisco, Minneapolis, Washington, D.C., and the AM operation in New York. The total revenue generated by the sales was $155 million. EBC planned to limit future radio expansion to the largest broadcast markets and other communications opportunities.

JAMES R. RIGGS

Engine No. 587.

Historic steam locomotive. In August, 1918, the Baldwin Locomotive Works completed the Lake Erie and Western engine No. 5541. When the Nickel Plate railroad obtained the engine in 1922, it was renumbered as the 587. Nickel Plate donated the engine to the city of Indianapolis in September, 1955, as a monument to the city's importance as a center for the railroad industry.

The 587 rested on permanent display near the entrance of BROAD RIPPLE PARK until October, 1983, when the INDIANA TRANSPORTATION MUSEUM moved it to BEECH GROVE for restoration. Refitting the engine required around a quarter of a million dollars in donated funds and materials. By July, 1988, the engine was fully operational, and it is now maintained as a part of the transportation museum's historic railroad collection in Noblesville.

The 587 was a product of the World War I federal control of the railroad industry. It is one of six extant examples of the United States Railroad Administration's light Mikado design, one of the period's most successful and influential designs. The 145–ton light Mikado has a 2–8–2 wheel arrangement and is a dual purpose engine that can haul either passengers or freight. The 587 was originally one of 625 such engines built, 15 of which were for the Lake Erie and Western railroad.

Today a volunteer staff operates the 587 during the summer months on public excursions in the Indianapolis area. The Nickel Plate 587 is on the National Register of Historic Places, and was the first locomotive to be so designated.

VICKIE J. WEST

Skip Sassmannhausen, "Nickel Plate Road 587," *Nickel Plate Road Magazine*, 17 (Fall, 1983), 4–7; Peter K. Shepherd "Unusually Sound, Reliable and Able," *ibid.*, 23 (Winter, 1989), 4–12.

English, William Eastin (Nov. 3, 1850– Apr. 29, 1926). Politician. The only son of WILLIAM HAYDEN ENGLISH, "Will" spent his early life in Lexington, Indiana, and moved to Indianapolis with his parents in 1865. An 1873 graduate of North Western Christian (BUTLER UNIVERSITY), English briefly practiced law before becoming involved in local Democratic politics. He represented Marion and Shelby counties in the Indiana House of Representatives, 1879–1880, and authored legislation limiting the indebtedness of Marion County.

Beginning in 1880, English managed English's Opera House (and later Hotel), which his father had built on the Circle. After serving in the U.S. House of Representatives, 1884–1885, he came home and reentered local Democratic politics. By 1892, English returned to national politics, serving as vice-president of the National Association of Democratic Clubs and as delegate to the Democratic national convention where he supported Grover Cleveland's renomination. He managed Indiana Governor Claude Matthews' bid for the Democratic presidential nomination in 1896. English later abandoned the party, supporting the Republicans and their position on protective tariffs.

After his father's death in 1896, English remodeled and expanded the English Theater, completed in 1897. When the Spanish-American War began in 1898, he declined a presidential appointment as an army paymaster and volunteered as an aide to Maj. Gen. Joseph Wheeler in Cuba. Crushed beneath his wounded horse, English survived and returned home, where he helped found the United Spanish War Veterans, serving as its first commander-in-chief, 1904–1905.

Upon returning to Indianapolis, English reentered politics, serving as president of the city's Board of Park Commissioners (1898–1900) and Safety (1904–1906). In 1904, he campaigned throughout Indiana for the Roosevelt-Fairbanks ticket. Later, he represented Hamilton, Hendricks, and Marion ccounties in the Indiana Senate, 1917–1923, and Johnson and Marion counties from 1923 until his death.

Active in numerous local organizations, English was a member of the Indiana Conservatory of the SCOTTISH RITE and author of *The History of Early Indianapolis Masonry and of Center Lodge* (1895) and *History of Masonry in Indianapolis* (1901). English also served as an officer of the Indianapolis COMMERCIAL CLUB, the INDIANAPOLIS BENEVOLENT SOCIETY, and the INDIANA HISTORICAL SOCIETY.

STACEY NICHOLAS

Biographical Directory of the Indiana General Assembly, Vols. 1 and 2 (Indianapolis, 1980, 1984); Indiana Biography Series, Indiana State Library.

English, William Hayden (Aug. 27, 1822–Feb. 7, 1896). Democratic politician and businessman. Born in Lexington, Indiana, English was the only son of Elisha G. and Mahala (Eastin) English. He completed three years at Hanover College before being admitted to the Indiana bar in 1840.

English practiced law only briefly before pursuing local political opportunities. He was postmaster at Lexington between 1842 and 1845, and served as principal clerk in the Indiana House of Representatives in 1843. From 1845 to 1849, he was a clerk in the U.S. Treasury Department.

English's political stature improved with his election as secretary of the state constitutional convention in 1850, a position requiring him to oversee publication of the convention's proceedings. He later won election to the Indiana House of Representatives from Scott County and served as speaker during the 1851–1852 session.

A Northern Democrat opposed to slavery, English was elected to the U.S. House of Representatives and served from 1853 to 1861. As a member of the House Committee on Territories, he worked on the Kansas-Nebraska Act (1854), which repealed the Missouri Compromise (1820) and allowed residents of western territories to decide on the slavery issue themselves. During the Civil War, English aided Governor OLIVER P. MORTON in disbanding the Knights of the Golden Circle, a secret society opposed to the policies of Morton and Lincoln.

On May 11, 1863, the First National Bank of Indianapolis, founded by English and other associates, opened its doors. As a result of this new enterprise, which he served as president until 1877, English moved his family to Indianapolis in 1865. During that same period, he secured a controlling interest in the Indianapolis Street Railway Company, which he retained until 1876. Upon resigning as bank president and selling his railway stock, English invested his money in real estate. This culminated in the construction of the ENGLISH HOTEL AND OPERA HOUSE, the city's finest; the Opera House opened first in September, 1880.

On Memorial Day, 1872, English suggested erecting a Civil War monument at CROWN HILL CEMETERY. Although his proposal failed to garner support, English eventually filled a vacancy on the Monument Commission in 1893 and helped to plan and finance the SOLDIERS AND SAILORS MONUMENT on the Circle.

In 1880, the Democratic party, holding its national convention in Cincinnati, nominated English for vice-president on a ticket headed by General Winfield Scott Hancock of Pennsylvania. After losing the election by less than 10,000 votes, English retired from politics.

In his later years English served as president of the INDIANA HISTORICAL SOCIETY (1886–1896), which holds a large collection of his papers. He also wrote *Conquest of the Country Northwest of the River Ohio, 1778–1783, and Life of General George Rogers Clark* (1896).

Upon English's death, Governor Claude Matthews decreed that his body lie in state in the Capitol, where over 15,000 citizens paid their respects. Known as one of the wealthiest men in Indiana, English is commemorated by English Avenue and the English Foundation Building in Indianapolis and the town of English in Crawford County.

STACEY NICHOLAS

Biographical Directory of the Indiana General Assembly, Vol. 1 (Indianapolis, 1980); Indiana Biography Series, Indiana State Library.

English. Though the English were among the earliest immigrants to arrive in Indianapolis, they never formed a very large proportion of the city's population. The census of 1850 enumerated only 59 English-born persons for Center Township, Marion County. This was only 4 percent of Indianapolis' foreign-born people and a mere 0.6 percent of the city's total population. At the same time the Germans in Indianapolis outnumbered the English by over 15 to 1; the Irish and Scots also outnumbered the English. By 1880 the numbers of English-born in Indianapolis approached 1,000 and then briefly exceeded that number in the early 20th century. At their peak number, the English accounted for roughly 7 percent of the city's foreign-born population. In more recent decades their numbers fell again, to only 70 by 1980. Available evidence suggests that during the period of highest English emigration, Yorkshire was the most common county of origin, followed by Lancashire and, in later years, the London area.

As limited as their numbers were, the English played a very significant role in the growth and development of Indianapolis. Throughout most of the 19th century Britain was the world's leading industrial nation, and hence the English brought with them certain skills and manufacturing techniques that served the city's economy well. The United States Encaustic Tile Works, for example, established in 1877 to make decorative floor tiles, was based very largely on the skills of English workers, and in the 1880s the firm's superintendent visited England and returned with more English workers who had the specialized skills that the factory needed. The English in Indianapolis also provided valuable skills and experience in engineering, machine-making, iron-making, and textiles, as well as many preindustrial craft occupations, particularly the building trades. Some became wealthy and highly prominent citizens, among them John Martin, a young skilled builder and slater who left Lancashire in 1848 and settled in Indianapolis in 1849. Martin was perhaps the city's most prominent builder ever, for among his buildings were the Grand Opera House, BUTLER UNIVERSITY, hospitals, libraries, and many of the largest mercantile establishments. He also was a generous philanthropist. Another English immigrant, George Marott, came to Indianapolis in 1875. Starting out in the shoe business, Marott eventually came to own many large businesses, including the Enterprize Hotel and the Marott Department Store Company, and by 1910 he was worth over $2 million. The English also entered the legal and other professions in disproportionately high numbers, and they were among the leading newspaper editors. James Swain, who came from Leicestershire to Indianapolis in the late 1830s, helped start the INDIANA STATE SENTINEL, and Elijah Halford, who left Nottingham and came to Indiana in 1861, later became the editor of the INDIANA JOURNAL.

What distinguished the English from other immigrant groups in Indianapolis was the fact that they shared the language and culture of the native-born people of the city. More than any other group, the English could "blend in" with the city's natives, and experience social integration and assimilation more quickly. The English did not form ethnic enclaves or neighborhoods as did non-English-speaking groups, and their rate of intermarriage with the native-born was noticeably higher. Generally, the English were seen as "cousins" rather than true foreigners.

After World War I, English immigration to Indianapolis waned as British emigrants turned their attention away from the United States as a destination and toward the Dominions. During the Great Depression probably more English people living in Indianapolis returned to England

than arrived, and thereafter English immigration remained very low. But those who did come to Indianapolis after World War II included higher proportions of skilled and professional people. They were part of the so-called "brain drain" from Britain to America. During the 1950s and 1960s, especially, English people with professional, technical, or managerial skills—mainly doctors, academics, nurses, engineers, and secretaries—found greener pastures in Indianapolis' expanding hospitals, universities, and corporations than they saw in England. Some left England because of the comparatively rigid hierarchical tradition in English society, while others were exasperated with the higher taxes under Britain's Labour governments and what they saw as progressive dependency in society. Today, organizations such as the ENGLISH-SPEAKING UNION of Indianapolis promote the "special" Anglo-American relationship by sponsoring exchange students between England and Indiana, and thereby contribute to the long tradition of interaction between the people of England and those of the city of Indianapolis.

WILLIAM E. VAN VUGT
Calvin College

English Hotel and Opera House. Fashionable hotel and theater. WILLIAM HAYDEN ENGLISH, Indianapolis businessman, congressman, and 1880 Democratic vice-presidential candidate, built his hotel and theater on the northwest quadrant of the Circle. He purchased and removed homes, commercial buildings, and a church to provide the site.

The theater, built first, was modeled after the New York Grand Opera House. It was four stories high, made of Bedford stone, with tall pillars, wide windows, and an exterior balcony where distinguished visitors to the city appeared before crowds on the street below.

The entrance corridor was 100 feet long, with frescoed walls and ceiling, marble pillars, mirrors, and a grand staircase. The auditorium contained 2,500 crimson plush and leather seats, carved woodwork, and ornate gas chandeliers. The stage was the largest in the city, permitting elaborate productions.

The English Opera House occupied the northwest quadrant of Monument Circle from 1880 until 1948. [Indiana Historical Society, Bass Collection]

The formal opening was held September 27, 1880, with famed actor Lawrence Barrett appearing in *Hamlet*. The opera house immediately became the city's leading theater and a favorite of Indianapolis society. It operated for 68 years, presenting drama, musical comedy, opera, ballet, concerts, minstrel shows, lectures, vaudeville, and films. The production of *Ben-Hur* played for ten weeks in 1902, thrilling audiences with eight horses running at full speed on a treadmill in the chariot race scene. Leading performers who appeared there included Sarah Bernhardt, the Barrymores, George M. Cohan, Helen Hayes, and Laurence Olivier. WILLIAM E. ENGLISH, son of the founder, was the theater's first manager. He later completed the construction of the English Hotel, begun by his father.

The hotel was built in two sections, encompassing the opera house. The first section, built in 1884, extended north to Meridian Street. The second section, extending south to Market Street, was completed in 1896, and required the removal of the English family mansion, which was on the property.

The hotel equaled the opera house in opulence. The front was curved to match the Circle, with towers and bas-relief sculptures depicting Indiana governors and members of the English family. The lobby had a sweeping marble staircase, large mirrors, marble pillars, potted plants, and a gilded iron elevator cage. The guest rooms were spacious and furnished in lavish Victorian style.

The English was the premier hotel in Indianapolis until age, deterioration, and changing style caused its decline. In 1948 both hotel and opera house were demolished to make way for a modern J. C. Penney building, which replaced them.

RICHARD W. WORTH

Ernestine Bradford Rose, *The Circle* (Indianapolis, 1957, rpt. 1971); Corbin Patrick, "A Theater to Remember," *Indianapolis Star Magazine*, Jan. 16, 1949.

English-Speaking Union. International cultural and educational membership organization. In 1918 British journalist Sir Evelyn Wrench founded the English-Speaking Union in London "to draw together in the bonds of comradeship the English-speaking peoples of the world." The English-Speaking Union of the United States was established in New York in 1920. Charles J. Lynn, the retired vice-president of ELI LILLY AND COMPANY, founded the Indianapolis Branch in 1949 and served as its first president until 1958. Later presidents included his wife, Dorothy B. Lynn, 1958–1973, and Robert S. Ashby, 1973–1989. The membership, drawn largely from central Indiana, numbered approximately 200 in the early 1990s.

The Indianapolis Branch has provided scholarships since 1951 for Commonwealth students to study at Indiana University in Bloomington and, since 1976, for teachers from Marion County schools to study at British universities. The branch regularly holds luncheon and dinner meetings with speakers such as Admiral Chester W. Nimitz (1950), British Ambassador Lord Harlech (1964), Margaret Thatcher (1969), General Maxwell D. Taylor (1973), and British Ambassador Sir Antony Acland (1990). Since 1988 the branch has sponsored an annual Shakespeare competition with contestants from Marion County high schools giving dramatic presentations. The winner each year has participated in the national competition in New York.

THOMAS A. MASON
Indiana Historical Society

Ensemble Music Society. Organized to encourage public presentation of CHAMBER MUSIC, the society was suggested during dinner conversation in December, 1943, by amateur violinist Leonard Strauss, who also had helped establish the INDIANAPOLIS SYMPHONY ORCHESTRA in 1929. Strauss and a core of local music enthusiasts presented the society's first concert on April 12, 1944, with the Musical Art Quartet, drawing close to 500 people to the Indiana World War Memorial auditorium. Strauss served as the society's first president. By the second season the society's subscription-only membership had a waiting list as it quickly gained a reputation for presenting the best in contemporary chamber music. Notable performers over the last half century have included the Budapest Quartet, Julliard String Quartet, Tokyo Quartet, Cleveland Quartet, Kronos Quartet, Amadeus Quartet, Beaux Arts Trio, New York String Sextet, and St. Paul Chamber Orchestra. No longer an exclusive members-only group, the society presents four concerts each season and sponsors several performances and master classes at area elementary and high schools.

LAWRENCE E. McCULLOUGH
Indiana University–Purdue University,
Indianapolis

_____

Indianapolis Star, Oct. 13, 1974; Ensemble Music Society, *25th Anniversary Program* (Indianapolis, 1969).

Ensemble Ouabache. Musical ensemble. Ensemble Ouabache is an Indianapolis-based chamber music ensemble that presents historically informed performances of baroque and classical music on period instruments. The word "ouabache" was the early French explorers' rendering of the name which the Native American people gave to the Wabash River. The group's Indianapolis debut occurred in 1987. The primary ensemble consists of four musicians playing baroque flute, baroque violin, viola da gamba, and harpsichord. Since joining the artist roster of Great Lakes Performing Artist Associates in 1991, the ensemble has given concerts in many midwestern cities. In addition to its commitment to the chamber music of 17th and 18th century

composers, Ensemble Ouabache has also performed newly commissioned compositions for historical instruments.

SUSAN J. ZURBUCHEN
Butler University

Environmental Records (Marion County).

TOPOLOGY

Size: 402 square miles, or about 257,681 acres

Developed acreage: 155,963 (1992)

Undeveloped acreage: 101,718 (1992)

Farm acreage: 48,000 (1991)

Number and acreage of wetlands: 1,447 totaling 8,435 acres (1990)

Wooded acreage: 13,000 acres (est.)

Largest contiguous wooded area: Fort Benjamin Harrison, 1,075 acres

Largest public land area: Eagle Creek Park, 4,574 acres

Largest body of water: Eagle Creek Reservoir, 1,383 acres

Highest elevation: 915+ feet above sea level, northwest corner of Pike Township (high point in Crown Hill Cemetery is 840 feet)

Lowest elevation: 635 feet above sea level, banks of White River at Johnson County line

Longest stream segment: White River, 31.3 miles

Shortest stream segment: Carmel Creek, 0.22 miles

Longest stream entirely within Marion County: Lick Creek, 15.64 miles

High flow, White River: estimated 70,000 cubic feet per second (CFS), March 26, 1913

Low flow, White River: 8 CFS, September 29, 1941

Average flow, White River: 1,398 CFS

Highest recorded flood stage, White River: 30.0 feet, March 26, 1913

CLIMATE

hottest day: 107°F, August 25, 1934

Coldest days: –27°F, January 19, 1994; –25°F, January 5, 1884

Mean temperature: 52.5°F (1962–1991)

Average annual number of days above 90°F: 18

Average annual number of days below 0°F: 8

Average annual number of cloudy days: 177

Average annual number of clear days: 89

Average annual number of precipitation days (0.01 inches): 125 (rain or snow)

Average number of days with at least 1 inch of snow: 8

Maximum 24–hour precipitation (rain): 5.32 inches, June 30–July 1, 1987

Maximum 24–hour precipitation (snow): 15.2 inches, January 25–26, 1978

Maximum snowfall in one month: 30.64 inches, January, 1978

Largest monthly cumulative rainfall: 12.69 inches, January, 1950

Smallest monthly cumulative rainfall: 0.21 inches, January, 1944

Average annual rainfall: 40.6 inches (1962–1991)

Lowest annual rainfall: 1988, 31.32 inches (1982–1991)

Maximum annual rainfall: 1989, 50.57 inches (1962–1991)

ENVIRONMENTAL INDEXES

Air quality, pollution standard index, days per category, 1991:

      Good (1–50): 225
      Moderate (51–100): 139
      Unhealthful (101–199): 1

Extremely hazardous substances (ehs) storage sites: 195 (1991)

Number of ehs chemicals reported: 4,030 (1991)

Superfund sites: Carter-Lee Lumber, Reilly Industries, Southside Landfill

Number of potential Superfund (CERCLIS) sites: 97 (December, 1991)

VEGETATION AND WILDLIFE

State Champion trees: Green Ash, 304 Buck Creek Blvd.: circumference, 194 inches; height, 85 feet; crown width, 32 feet. Downy Hawthorn, Indianapolis Museum of Art: circumference, 81 inches; height, 41 feet; crown width, 43 feet

Other big trees: "Kile" Bur Oak, Irvington; White Oak, 1500 E. Markwood; Chinquapin Oak, 2601 E. Brookside Pkwy., E. Dr.; Sycamore, 9300 Moore Road

State and federally listed endangered, threatened, and rare plants: Hardy Catalpa, Oblique Turtlehead, Tufted Hairgrass, Virginia Bunchflower, Purple-flowering Raspberry, Guyandotte Beauty, Speedwell, Wood's Sedge, Ginseng, Goldenseal, Wolf's Bluegrass

State and federally listed endangered, threatened, and rare animals: American Bittern, Least Bittern, Black-crowned Night-Heron, Cooper's Hawk, Red-shouldered Hawk, Broad-winged Hawk, Peregrine Falcon, King Rail, Loggerhead Shrike, Cerulean Warbler, Hooded Warbler, Eastern Sand Darter, Spotted Turtle, Kirtland's Watersnake, Badger, Indiana Bat

KEVIN STRUNK

Episcopalians. The principal characteristics which distinguish the Episcopal church from other denominations are: a hierarchical organization with bishops, priests, and deacons; membership in the worldwide Anglican communion; worship according to a liturgy contained in a common prayer book; and emphasis, particularly in recent years, on the sacrament of the Eucharist or Holy Communion.

The Episcopal Church has maintained a small but relatively important place in Indianapolis since the 1830s. Itinerant clergy occasionally appeared during the 1820s to perform baptisms and marriages, but not until 1835 did the national church declare the importance of missionary work and elect the Rev. DAVID JACKSON KEMPER bishop of Indiana and Missouri. Kemper was an indefatigable missionary, and Indiana remained for 15 years a part of his widespread diocese, which included most of the Midwest.

By the time Kemper made his second journey to Indiana in 1838, he found a fledgling congregation in Indianapolis, Christ Church (now CHRIST CHURCH CATHEDRAL). At first the church met in private homes, but in 1839 the congregation erected a simple wooden building on the Circle. The present stone Gothic church was built in 1859. For 30 years this was the only Episcopal church in Indianapolis, although in 1849 Indiana became a separate diocese.

Partisan feelings during the Civil War affected Christ Church, whose rector, the Rev. Horace Stringfellow, was forced to resign because of his sympathy for the plight of Confederate prisoners at Camp Morton. In 1866 a group of like-minded Episcopalians founded St. Paul's Church, erected a handsome building at New York and Illinois streets, and elected Stringfellow their rector. In the same year Grace Church was built at the corner of Pennsylvania and St. Joseph streets.

In 1865 Joseph Cruikshank Talbot, who had preceded Stringfellow at Christ Church and subsequently became missionary bishop of the Midwest, was elected bishop coadjutor. He succeeded George Upfold as Bishop of Indiana in 1872, and served until 1883. Under his leadership St. George's Church began (1873) as a mission of Christ Church at Morris and Church streets to serve the people on the south side. Finally organized as a church in 1880, it had a varied career as parish and mission until 1959. In 1875 the diocese adopted the cathedral system, and St. Paul's was made the pro-cathedral.

The next bishop, David Buel Knickerbacker (1883–1894), moved the denomination farther north. He relocated Grace Church, temporarily abandoned and rented out as a gymnasium, to the corner of 16th Street and Central Avenue, made it into a pro-cathedral, and developed a complex of buildings around it, used variously as a school (later Knickerbacker Hall), home for working girls, home for the aged, and bishop's residence. A new building on this site, All Saints Church (1911), remained the pro-cathedral until 1953.

In the late 1880s the denomination extended a mission to the African-American citizens of Indianapolis. Members of both Christ Church and St. Paul's helped establish St. Philip's on West Street in 1888, first as a mission (sometimes called St. Paul's Chapel), then in 1901 as an organized church.

White males led the Episcopal church in 19th-century Indianapolis. Women were welcome, within certain limits: to worship, to run the altar guild and the missionary society, and to do visiting and secretarial work. The election of Mrs. A. B. Mansur to the vestry of Christ Church in 1859 was a rare exception, one not to be repeated for many decades.

Apart from the continuing financial struggle to maintain buildings, pay the clergy, and run church schools, the principal issue for Episcopalians in this period was "churchmanship." The

Oxford Movement had rocked the Church of England with its efforts to rediscover the Catholic heritage and tradition of the Anglican church. Echoes of this occurred in the United States with efforts to bring Catholic ritual and practice—vestments, processions, genuflection, incense, signing the cross, frequent communion—into the heretofore largely Protestant American church. Bishops Kemper and Knickerbacker were both of this "high church" persuasion, and upon Kemper's death its adherents founded St. David's Church at 21st and Talbott streets. Led by the Rev. C. S. Sargent, this church lasted for over a decade, although without the approval of Bishop John Hazen White (1895–1899). White's term was so short because the diocese was soon split into a northern half, centering on Michigan City and headed by White, and a southern half which was henceforth called the diocese of Indianapolis.

The first bishop of Indianapolis, Joseph M. Francis (1899–1939), was essentially a "maintainer," though he served as a chaplain in World War I and spoke out for the League of Nations and against the Ku Klux Klan. In 1919 the Church of the Advent opened at 33rd and Meridian streets in a former Baptist building. Serving the growing community on the north side of the city, it prospered and 30 years later moved into a new building as Trinity Church. St. Matthew's opened in Irvington in 1924.

Richard A. Kirchhoffer (1939–1959) succeeded Bishop Francis. The church was heavily involved in many kinds of war work. After World War II came several important changes. In 1953 women were accepted for the first time as delegates to the diocesan convention. Christ Church became the pro-cathedral. The gift of $1 million in 1953 from ELI LILLY marked the beginning of a period of intense interest and influence on his part in church affairs. The diocese purchased Waycross as a conference center.

As the city grew, the Episcopal church made efforts to serve the expanding population. In 1949 St. Paul's moved from downtown to its present location at 61st and Meridian streets. In 1956 St. Alban's was founded in the northeast part of town, with help from Trinity Church, and the next year the Church of the Nativity began, with help from St. Paul's, on Lantern Road in the northeast corner of Marion County. St. Matthew's moved east from Irvington into Warren Township, and in 1959 St. Timothy's succeeded St. George's on the south side of the city.

John P. Craine (1959–1977) made perhaps more of an imprint on the local church than any of his predecessors as bishop. It was the era of agitation for civil rights and of civil disobedience, of Vietnam and community action. Craine, working with Archdeacon Frederic P. Williams and cathedral dean Paul Moore, and with the financial support of Eli Lilly, believed that the church should be in the forefront of action. During these years the Episcopal leadership was involved with the Southern Christian Leadership Conference and with the founding of a local chapter of the INDIANAPOLIS URBAN LEAGUE; Haiti was adopted as a companion diocese; a diocesan center was set up in connection with All Saints Church; and Episcopal Community Services was established, as well as the JULIAN CENTER for abused women.

Changes in the national church also affected Indianapolis Episcopalians. The first two regularly ordained female clergy in the nation were in Indianapolis, Jacqueline Means and Natalya Vonnegut. The local church backed experiments such as using theater as a form of worship and endorsed changes in the Prayer Book, providing alternative services, the passing of the peace, the use of laymen to pass the chalice, and a greater emphasis on the Eucharist. Canon Fred Williams was active on the commission which produced a new Hymnal in 1982. Not all these changes were universally popular, and many conservative members dropped away.

In 1960 Trinity Church founded ST. RICHARD'S SCHOOL, beginning with a kindergarten. The most successful of local efforts for a church school, St. Richard's by 1990 included eight grades, a new building, and 250 students.

Eli Lilly died in the same year as Bishop Craine and left generous bequests to Christ Church, Trinity, and St. Paul's, creating an endowment which challenged all three to make responsible use of their resources. Bishop Craine's successor was Edward W. Jones (1978–). During his tenure congregations became more accustomed to the new Prayer Book and Hymnal, and to the appearance of women as clergy, vestry

members, lectors, and chalice bearers. The church sought new areas for outreach: through John P. Craine House, an alternative to prison for women offenders; and to the elderly, the sick, and the homeless through the multidenominational Metro Council and through a new shelter for the homeless built in 1990 in connection with All Saints.

CHARLES LATHAM, JR.
Indiana Historical Society

Joyce Marks Booth, ed., *A History of the Episcopal Diocese of Indianapolis, 1838–1988* (Dallas, [1988]); Eli Lilly, *History of the Little Church on the Circle: Christ Church Parish Indianapolis, 1837–1955* (Indianapolis, 1957); James H. Madison, *Eli Lilly: A Life, 1885–1977* (Indianapolis, 1989), chapter 9.

Equal Rights Amendment. U.S. Senator Birch Bayh of Indiana in 1972 introduced the Equal Rights Amendment (ERA) in Congress. Both Indiana Democrats and Republicans endorsed the ERA in 1973 and Governor Otis Bowen (Republican) was elected on a platform that supported it. This apparent unity was short-lived, however, and in the next few years the Indiana Senate and House hearings on ratification of the amendment attracted overflow crowds of supporters and opponents in the INDIANA CONVENTION CENTER.

Early pro-ERA groups included the INDIANAPOLIS PRESS CLUB, the LEAGUE OF WOMEN VOTERS, Concerned Women Lawyers, and the Mayor's Task Force on Women. Opponents of the amendment's ratification included State Senator Joan Gubbins (R-Indianapolis), Stop ERA, Citizens to Oppose ERA, and Scratch Women's Lib.

On April 2, 1973, the Indiana House voted in favor of the amendment but the Senate voted against ratification. The measure was tabled until the 1975 session of the General Assembly. Again passing in the House, the ERA was killed when the Senate Governmental Affairs Committee voted not to report the bill out for passage. Senator Thomas J. Teague (D-Anderson) challenged the committee's action, claiming that a resolution proposing constitutional ratification was not legislation and therefore should not be subject to committee approval, but the decision stood.

In 1976 the Greater Indianapolis ERA Coalition, led by Cynthia Morse and Fran Moore, targeted ten state senators as "persuadable" and concentrated their efforts on lobbying them to vote for the amendment. Hoosiers for ERA, a statewide group, encouraged women to form local coalitions to work for ratification. The efforts of these groups were repaid on January 18, 1977, when Indiana became the 35th state to ratify the ERA under the titles of House Joint Resolution–1 and Senate Joint Resolution–1. A last-minute telephone call from President-elect Jimmy Carter persuaded State Senator Wayne Townsend (D-Hartford City) to vote against a procedural motion that would have killed the measure. Three Republicans joined 23 Democrats in ratifying the amendment in the Senate. In spite of Indiana's actions, when the time limit for national consideration of the ERA was reached in 1978 the amendment was still three states short of the number required for adoption.

FRANCES DODSON RHOME
Indiana University–Purdue University,
Indianapolis

Esch, I. Lynd (Nov. 17, 1905–Feb. 10, 1994). Minister and educator. Born in Flinton, Pennsylvania, Esch began working for B. F Goodrich Company at age 17, where he received an engineering education, advanced into the executive ranks, and became a professor at the Goodyear Industrial Institute. He left Goodyear in 1931 to enter the ministry and was ordained by the United Brethren Church in 1933. He subsequently received a bachelor's degree from Chapman College and a master of theology and doctor of philosophy at the University of Southern California. While in school he held pastorates in Oakland, San Diego, and Los Angeles, California.

Esch accepted the presidency of the UNIVERSITY OF INDIANAPOLIS, then known as Indiana Central College, in 1945 and served until 1970. During his presidency the college added evening and graduate divisions, constructed several academic buildings, and strengthened its academic reputation. Esch Hall is named after him, and each year the university awards the Esch Scholar-

ship to a senior student with outstanding character and scholastic achievements.

MICHELLE D. HALE

_____

Who's Who in the Midwest (1967); *Indianapolis Star*, Feb. 11, 1994.

Estonians. Before any Estonians arrived from their homeland by the Baltic Sea in northeastern Europe, an important part of their cultural heritage appeared in Indianapolis with the first log cabins, built in the early 19th century. This style of architecture spread throughout America from the colony of New Sweden. There the earliest documented cases of cabin construction involved Finnish builders, with ancestors from Estonia.

The first known Estonian immigrant in Indianapolis was the architectural sculptor ALEXANDER SANGERNEBO (1856–1930). Arriving in the early 1890s, he designed and produced adornments for many prominent buildings. These included the INDIANA THEATRE, MURAT TEMPLE, ATHENAEUM, COLUMBIA CLUB, National Guard Armory, and various churches, hotels, and high schools.

Most local Estonians came as political refugees following the Soviet invasion of their homeland in World War II. After spending years in displaced persons camps in West Germany, they gratefully accepted the opportunity to migrate to the United States. Between 1947 and 1959, at least 114 Estonian-born persons settled in Indianapolis. Two dozen more arrived in the next three decades, with First Lutheran Church as their main sponsor.

Though coming from a nation of farmers, these refugees were mostly well-educated townspeople. Yet difficulty with the English language forced many to take simple jobs as factory, slaughterhouse, dry-cleaning, or kitchen workers. Younger Estonians who studied in the United States and second-generation exiles born en route to or in the new land did well, however. Two-thirds finished college, and typically got high-status jobs as engineers, teachers, military officers, medical professionals, or laboratory technicians. Though the immigrants initially moved into low-rent apartments near downtown, they quickly saved enough to become homeowners and scattered into the suburbs. Thus no Estonian enclave developed.

Through their Estonian Society of Indianapolis (established 1952) and Congregation of (St.) Paul (founded 1964), local Estonians have organized a variety of ethnic activities. These include musical ensembles, folk dancing, a language school, support group for anti-Soviet dissidents, banquets celebrating the Estonian Declaration of Independence (February 24, 1918), Midsummer bonfires, INTERNATIONAL FESTIVAL displays, Estonian services at First Lutheran Church, and erection of a monument in CROWN HILL CEMETERY.

The group's small size meant extensive intermarriage and linguistic assimilation. Yet infusions of vitality have come from contact with Estonian scholars in Bloomington, participation in Estonian festivals elsewhere, and exchanges of visits with relatives in Estonia, which reasserted its independence on August 20, 1991.

AIN HAAS
Indiana University–Purdue University,
Indianapolis

Evans, Charles (Nov. 13, 1850–Feb. 8, 1935). Librarian and bibliographer. Born in Boston, Massachusetts, and educated in the public schools, Evans was assistant at the Boston Athenaeum Library from 1866 until his appointment in November, 1872, at the age of 22, as first librarian of the newly established Indianapolis Public Library. He was responsible for the early development of both the professional staff and the collection, and Indianapolis soon boasted one of the preeminent libraries in the country.

While most patrons found the collection and services satisfactory, and while Evans' work was consistently praised in the local press, influential members of the board of school commissioners—then the library's governing board—had personality conflicts with Evans. There was also some public dissatisfaction with his inflexible enforcement of the library's rules, and Evans was dismissed in August, 1878.

Several years passed, with an almost complete turnover in membership on the school board, and Evans was reappointed librarian in March, 1889. Much of Evans' work in the early years had not been continued by his successors, and development of the library collection had seriously lagged. Almost as soon as Evans had succeeded in revitalizing both the collection and the library's reputation, the school board divided over the proposed design for a new library building. That, along with recurring personality clashes with the politically minded board, led to Evans' second dismissal in 1892. Despite his Indianapolis experience, Evans had a distinguished career. He is primarily known as the compiler of the famous *American Bibliography*, a chronological listing of items printed in the United States from 1639 through 1799.

LEIGH DARBEE
Indiana Historical Society

Edward G. Holley, *Charles Evans: American Bibliographer* (Urbana, Ill., 1963).

Evans, John (Mar. 9, 1814–July 3, 1897). Physician and entrepreneur. Born in Warren County, Ohio, of Quaker parentage, Evans attended the Hicksite school in Richmond, Indiana, and received his M.D. degree from Cincinnati College in 1838. He married Hannah Canby, and the couple moved to Attica, Indiana, where Evans became concerned with the care and treatment of the mentally ill. During the early 1840s he urged the General Assembly to construct a hospital for the insane, a project that the legislature authorized during its 1845–1846 session. By visiting eastern mental hospitals at his own expense, Evans became knowledgeable about their special architectural requirements (massive firewalls, for example). In 1846, he and his family moved to Indianapolis, and for the next two years he supervised the construction of the Indiana Hospital for the Insane (later CENTRAL STATE HOSPITAL).

The Evans family moved to Chicago in 1848, where Evans became involved with building Chicago's first hospital and establishing the city's medical society, public school system, and parks. He was also actively involved in the founding of Northwestern University and the town of Evanston, Illinois, as well as with the promotion and construction of railroads.

In 1862, President Abraham Lincoln appointed Evans governor of Colorado Territory. Following the close of the CIVIL WAR, he once again began building railroads, this time to connect Denver to the transcontinental railroad via the Denver Pacific. Mount Evans, southwest of Denver, is named in his honor.

CHARLES A. BONSETT, M.D.
Indiana University School of Medicine

H. E. Kelsey, *Frontier Capitalist: The Life of John Evans* (Denver: State Historical Society of Colorado and Pruett Publishing Co., 1969).

Everett I. Brown Company. Indianapolis' largest architectural and engineering firm. Founded in 1914 in Bluffton, Indiana, by architect Everett I. Brown, the company moved to Indianapolis shortly thereafter. In the 1940s and 1950s the firm created the basic design for many of Indiana's National Guard armories. By 1960 E. I. Brown had designed over 200 schools throughout Indiana, and in Indianapolis was architect for North Central High School, the Marion County Juvenile Center, Warren Central High School, and 16 other school buildings.

In 1973 under the stewardship of Brown's sons, Eugene L. and Kenneth W. Brown, the firm designed the $11 million Braniff Place and Tucson Hotel in Tucson, Arizona, and planned the $25 million expansion at Weir Cook Airport (now INDIANAPOLIS INTERNATIONAL AIRPORT). By 1982 the company was the largest architectural and engineering firm in the city and 25th in billings nationally, with nine partners, five of whom were Browns. Pioneering in computer graphics, that year E. I. Brown contracted with the U.S. Army to provide computer-produced plans for standardized facilities at its bases.

In the late 1980s the firm moved to its current headquarters at 950 North Meridian Street. By 1993 E. I. Brown had $13.9 million in revenues, 156 employees, and, under the leadership of managing partner Joseph S. Brown, counted the USA Funds complex, CONSECO headquarters, and INDIANA VOCATIONAL TECHNICAL COLLEGE's new technology building among its most important projects.

CONNIE J. ZEIGLER

Excluded Cities. Municipalities left out of city-county consolidation. One of the compromises made to secure passage of the UNIGOV legislation was that all incorporated Marion County municipalities with populations of more than 5,000 would be excluded from the city-county consolidation. This exclusion reduced opposition to Unigov among the larger and more influential suburbs within the county. The municipalities originally excluded were the cities of BEECH GROVE and LAWRENCE and the town of SPEEDWAY. Just before Unigov took effect the city of SOUTHPORT annexed enough territory to meet the population requirement and attain exclusion.

These four municipalities remain part of Marion County but not of Indianapolis. They are essentially self-governing municipalities. Their residents are subject to all countywide ordinances, receive all countywide services, and pay all countywide taxes. They also vote in elections for the Unigov mayor and the CITY-COUNTY COUNCIL, in addition to their own municipal officials. Their municipal services are either self-provided or secured from Indianapolis or the township in which they are located.

HARRISON C. NEAL III

Executive and Legislative Department. Department of municipal government. The Executive and Legislative Department, created in 1993 as a spin-off from the Department of Administration, is the organizational umbrella for several administrative, intergovernmental, and oversight functions of city-county government. It consists of six major divisions or offices.

The OFFICE OF THE MAYOR—which includes the mayor, deputy mayors, and their staff assistants—is one component of the Executive and Legislative Department. The other components are the Office of the Controller, the Internal Audit Division, the Office of Corporation Counsel, the Office of Youth and Family Services, and the Office of Cable Communications.

The Office of the Controller contains the city controller and staff. This office is responsible for accounting, budgeting, purchasing, and revenue collection functions. It is also responsible for managing the city's debts, issuing licenses, and coordinating audits for federal programs. In discharging these responsibilities, the controller's office works also with the Marion County auditor.

The Internal Audit Division conducts audits of the administration of city and county services and programs and the expenditure of funds for those purposes. It is also responsible for auditing the expenditures of federal funds received by the city.

The Office of Corporation Counsel provides legal advice and assistance to the mayor, the CITY-COUNTY COUNCIL, county officials, and city and county departments and agencies. The division is administered by the corporation counsel, who is appointed by the mayor and serves at the mayor's pleasure. Attorneys in the office may represent the city or county in lawsuits. Office staff also analyze bills introduced in the Indiana General Assembly to determine their impact on city and county affairs. The office also includes the office of city prosecutor, who is responsible for prosecuting violations of municipal ordinances.

The Office of Youth and Family Services administers or oversees the administration of employment, training, and other human services programs supported with federal, state, and local funds. It receives and disburses federal funds under the Job Training Partnership Act (JTPA), administers funds for youth services programs, and oversees services provided at multiservice centers operated by Community Centers of Indianapolis, Inc.

The Office of Cable Communications administers the city-county government's own telecommunications operations, and oversees the city-county government's relations with companies providing CABLE TELEVISION service in Marion County. The office is advised by the five-member Cable Communications Advisory Board, with three members appointed by the City-County Council and two by the mayor. The office staff operate Government Cable Channel 16, which telecasts City-County Council meetings and other programming related to local government concerns. The office also reviews the compliance of cable television companies in Marion County with the terms of their franchise agreements.

WILLIAM BLOMQUIST
HEATHER ALYSE JAMES

Expositions. Large-scale public exhibitions. Various fairs and expositions were held in the northern states during and after the Civil War. Indianapolis held numerous expositions beginning in the 1870s. Before that decade, the primary venue for exhibitions had been the INDIANA STATE FAIR, which featured primarily small-scale shows.

The city's first Art Exposition opened on September 10, 1873. It highlighted the statuary of John Rogers, which first gained fame at the Sanitary Commission's Cosmopolitan Bazaar in Chicago during the Civil War. Before he displayed the statuary at the Philadelphia Centennial in 1876, Rogers sent it to the Indianapolis Art Exposition. Here it so inspired Indianapolis resident JOHN H. MAHONEY that he became a sculptor himself. Mahoney's bronzes of George Rogers Clark, William Henry Harrison, and James Whitcomb surround the SOLDIERS AND SAILORS MONUMENT on the Circle. The city hosted industrial expositions between 1890 and the 1920s. Among them were the STREET PAVING EXPOSITION, showcasing leading street paving firms and manufactures from around the nation (April, 1890); the Industrial Indianapolis Expo, featuring products made in Indianapolis (October, 1921); and the Broadcast Listeners' Radio Exposition, emphasizing the importance of radio (September, 1925). Of a nonindustrial nature, the INDIANAPOLIS HOME SHOW premiered at the fairgrounds in 1922, featuring items for the home as well as the home itself. The Home Show remains an annual event in the 1990s, over 70 years after its debut.

Although nearby Chicago hosted a number of significant expositions in the late 19th and early 20th centuries, including the World's Columbian Exposition in 1893, Indianapolis failed to attract national expositions, in part due to inadequate facilities. Indianapolis businessmen understood the need for increased space, but an exposition center proposed in 1922 was never built. It was not until 1939 that the construction of the new Coliseum at the INDIANA STATE FAIRGROUNDS on 38th Street offered increased exhibit space and allowed the promotion of additional expositions in the city.

In November, 1950, L. S. AYRES AND COMPANY was overwhelmed by the response to the National Rose Show that it hosted. In two days over 81,000 people viewed the world's largest display of roses on the sixth floor of the downtown department store, proving that flower exhibits could attract large crowds. Perhaps inspired by the success of the National Rose Show, another flower-themed exposition debuted in the city in March, 1959—the Flower and Patio Show. Held at the State Fairgrounds Exposition Hall, the show featured nine flower gardens and two "lavish patio settings" created by local landscape firms, and floral arrangements from foreign countries including England, France, Israel, and Japan. The fairgrounds also hosted the Indianapolis Boat, Sport, and Travel Show that opened in 1954. It is now Indiana's oldest sport show, offering hunting, camping, fishing, boating, and travel exhibits. The Capital City RV and Camper Show began in 1968. Recreational vehicles, campground and resort exhibits, and travel and tourism information remain among its popular features.

In 1971 INDIANA BLACK EXPO debuted. One of the nation's oldest and largest expositions dedicated to African-American life, it offers perspective on religion, politics, employment, health, education, and economic empowerment, and has sponsored popular sporting events, including the CIRCLE CITY CLASSIC. The exposition continues to be a well-attended event.

The construction of the INDIANA CONVENTION CENTER and MARKET SQUARE ARENA brought the Indianapolis exposition business increased space and new vitality in the 1970s. With these new facilities, later expanded with the addition of the HOOSIER DOME, it could be said that "Exposition Fever" struck again 100 years after it first appeared in Indianapolis. The number of new expositions has increased each year since the mid–1970s. In 1992 the Convention Center–Hoosier Dome alone hosted 46 shows, with attendance of over 213,000, and the city's other venues offered dozens of trade shows, exhibitions, and expositions ranging from the Entrepreneur Expo to the Hoosier Horse Fair.

CONNIE J. ZEIGLER

F. C. Tucker Company. Real estate company. Founded in 1923 by Illinois native and De-Pauw University graduate Fred C. Tucker, Sr., the firm is the largest real estate company in Indiana and (in the early 1990s) the 35th largest in the country.

Tucker, Sr., who moved to Indianapolis in 1918, worked in commercial and industrial real estate as a sole proprietorship, and in 1947 Fred C. "Bud" Tucker, Jr. joined the company. Tucker, Sr., died in 1958, and with three friends, John A. Wallace, Robert Houk, and Edward Joseph "Joe" Boleman, Tucker, Jr., led the company through dramatic growth. In 1986, F. C. Tucker III with two partners, H. James Litten and David W. Goodrich, bought the company from his father.

The Tucker company incorporated in 1972 and was involved in the development of downtown Indianapolis, including the Hilton at the Circle Hotel, which opened in 1970 as the first new hotel built in Indianapolis in 40 years. Other projects include what is now known as INB TOWER and the AUL TOWER.

The company, which now employs over 700, has eleven Indianapolis-area operations and eight franchises throughout the state. By 1991, the company reached $1 billion in gross sales and leasing volume, exceeding the company's previous records. In addition to real estate service, Tucker also operates a licensing program through the Tucker School of Real Estate, and other ancillary companies, including Service Mortgage Company, Tucker Referrals, and North Star Construction Company.

The company is also known for its "State of the Real Estate" presentation in January and extensive Indianapolis real estate market research. The familiar "Talk to Tucker" slogan has been used since the mid–1960s.

GRETA E. SHANKLE
Indianapolis Business Journal

"Tucker Reaches $1 Billion Milestone," *Indianapolis Business Journal*, Mar. 30–Apr. 5, 1992, 8B.

Fairbanks, Charles Warren (May 11, 1852–June 4, 1918). Attorney, state Republican leader, and vice-president of the United States,

1905–1909. Born in Unionville Center, Ohio, Fairbanks grew up in a strict Methodist farming family. After graduating from Ohio Wesleyan University in 1872, he worked as a reporter for the Western Associated Press before moving to Indianapolis in 1874 as an attorney for the Indianapolis, Bloomington, and Western Railroad. For the next 15 years Fairbanks amassed a personal fortune specializing in railroad bankruptcies.

Fairbanks began his political career in the late 1880s by supporting WALTER Q. GRESHAM over Senator BENJAMIN HARRISON for the 1888 Republican presidential nomination. Although a losing effort, it allowed Fairbanks to take a leadership role in the anti-Harrison faction of the party. Fairbanks built a grassroots political organization knowing that local politicians elected state legislators who (at that time) elected U.S. senators. Fairbanks became permanent chairman of the Indiana Republican Convention in 1892, presiding over election victories in 1894 and 1896. His position within state politics and his friendship with future president William McKinley helped him obtain a coveted Senate seat in 1897. With McKinley's death in 1901, Fairbanks lost his most powerful ally. Although he aspired to the presidency in 1904, his style of politics did not inspire national party leaders. He was viewed, however, as a good balance to Theodore Roosevelt and won a place on the ticket as vice-president.

Fairbanks subsequently failed to win renomination in 1908, due in part to an incident that occurred in 1906 at his Indianapolis mansion. Fairbanks hosted a lawn party for visiting President Roosevelt, unaware that alcoholic beverages had been served. A strict prohibitionist, Fairbanks was embarrassed by the subsequent newspaper references to "Cocktail Charlie." He made one last attempt at high office in 1916 as the vice-presidential running mate of Charles Evans Hughes but they lost the election to Woodrow Wilson and his Hoosier running mate, Thomas R. Marshall. Fairbanks retired in Indianapolis and died two years later.

JEFF TENUTH
Indiana State Museum

James H. Madison, "Charles Warren Fairbanks and Indiana Republicanism," in *Gentlemen from Indi-*

ana: National Party Candidates, 1836–1940, ed. Ralph D. Gray (Indianapolis, 1977).

Fairview Park. Amusement park. In August, 1889, the Citizens Street Railway Company purchased the 246-acre Adam Scott farm, located along the CENTRAL CANAL north of Indianapolis, to create a "suburban park." Company president John C. Shaffer wanted to provide a place for Indianapolis residents to picnic and play while also encouraging them to use the street railway. The first electric streetcar to Fairview premiered on June 18, 1890, carrying Cyrus H. McCormick and other Chicago capitalists. During its first decade, the park served as a popular rural retreat for bicyclists and streetcar riders.

Beginning in 1899, HUGH MCGOWAN, president of the newly consolidated Indianapolis Traction and Terminal Company, introduced amusements to Fairview to attract more visitors and increase streetcar ridership. "King and Queen, the diving horses," a pony track, canoeing, and a band shell were among the first attractions. The company later introduced a merry-go-round, electric fountains, moving pictures, and a miniature railway. One of the most popular attractions in the early 1910s was the annual visit of a group of Ojibwas who dramatized Longfellow's "Hiawatha" along the banks of the canal.

Fairview Park's principal attraction was its natural beauty. Trees, flowering shrubs, ponds, and freely roaming deer and peacocks provided a restful place for visitors. The park also hosted the

Butler University occupies the former Fairview Park grounds on the north side.
[Butler University Archives]

Fresh Air (or Summer) Mission, a philanthropic experiment providing rest and medical treatment for sick children and nursing mothers.

In November, 1922, BUTLER UNIVERSITY purchased the park from the Indianapolis Street Railway for $200,000 and relocated its campus there.

DAVID G. VANDERSTEL
CONNIE ZEIGLER
Indiana University–Purdue University,
Indianapolis

Fall Creek. Major tributary of White River within Marion County. The stream enters in the northeast corner of the county and flows southwest 19.66 miles to the WHITE RIVER, with an average discharge of 284 cubic feet per second (CFS). The original confluence was at Washington Street, but was moved to 10th Street following the 1913 flood (estimated discharge 22,000 CFS) to alleviate poor central city drainage. The confluence with the river was once a large wetland area.

The steep-walled Fall Creek valley was impounded in 1943 to form GEIST RESERVOIR, allowing up to 26.8 million gallons per day of drinking water to be withdrawn at the Keystone Avenue dam. Below Geist is a scenic valley extending into the urban area along which are many natural and recreation areas. These include FORT BENJAMIN HARRISON, Camp Belzer, Skiles Test and WOOLLEN'S GARDEN parks, and Fall Creek Parkway. Within the inner city, water quality deteriorates below the Keystone Dam, mostly due to urban stormwater and combined sewer overflows. The stream has been channelized downstream of Camp Belzer, with many meanders straightened. Downstream of the Keystone Dam the creek is contained within concrete walls and a levee system to its mouth.

Fall Creek was one of the earliest city "greenways" planned by GEORGE E. KESSLER in 1909. The city has systematically acquired land along the creek from its mouth to Woollen's Garden. The wetlands downstream of Geist dam are used as a wellhead protection area for drinking water wells.

KEVIN STRUNK

Fall Creek Massacre (1824).

Fall Creek Massacre (1824). Incident that established precedent for punishment in cases of white aggression toward Indians. On March 22, 1824, a band of nine Seneca and Miami Indians camped on FALL CREEK in nearby Madison County to hunt. Apparently not satisfied that the band's intentions were peaceful, and under the pretext of asking the Indians' help in locating lost livestock, a group of six white men slaughtered the males of the party and returned to their camp to kill the women and children.

Five of the six alleged murderers were captured within three days and held in Pendleton; the sixth escaped and was never apprehended. John Johnston, Indian agent for the region, with the backing of the War Department and the help of WILLIAM CONNER, maintained calm among Indians and whites alike. Johnston hoped for a conviction, in order to maintain the credibility of the United States government among the Indians.

An indictment for murder was brought against the five captured men on April 9, but, due to the illness of the presiding judge, the trials did not begin until the October court term. The proceedings attracted some of the leading attorneys in the central part of the state, including the young CALVIN FLETCHER from Indianapolis. Within three days, James Hudson was found guilty. Despite an appeal to the Indiana Supreme Court and an escape attempt by Hudson, he was hanged for his crime on January 12, 1825.

During the spring court term, three others, Stephen Sawyer and John Bridge, senior and junior, were tried and convicted. The two older men were hanged, but the younger Bridge was pardoned by Governor James Ray, who galloped up on horseback from the capital just as the sentence was about to be carried out.

These trials were a landmark in Indian-white relations in the United States. They likely represent the first significant acknowledgment of the civil rights of Native Americans. Two books were inspired by the case: *The Life and Confession of James Hudson*, published by Samuel Woodworth in Indianapolis in 1825, and Jessamyn West's 1975 fictional account, *The Massacre at Fall Creek*.

LEIGH DARBEE
Indiana Historical Society

George Chalou, "Massacre on Fall Creek," *Prologue*, 4 (Summer, 1972), 109–114; Oliver Hampton Smith, *Early Indiana Trials and Sketches* (Cincinnati, 1858), 51–57, 176–179.

Family Service Association of Central Indiana.

Family Service Association of Central Indiana. Social service agency focusing on families. The Family Welfare Society was formed in 1922 by a merger of the CHARITY ORGANIZATION SOCIETY, the Indianapolis Benevolent Society, the Mothers' Aid Society, and the Children's Aid Association. The Juvenile Protective Association and the SUMMER MISSION FOR SICK CHILDREN were included later. The Family Welfare Society functioned through two divisions: the Service and Relief Division, which had responsibility for family relief and rehabilitation, and the Children's Bureau, which cared for children outside their own homes. In 1934 the Children's Bureau was transferred to the Indianapolis Orphans Asylum, now known as the CHILDREN'S BUREAU OF INDIANAPOLIS.

Following the establishment of government relief programs during the Great Depression, the Family Welfare Society decreased its direct relief activities and focused on family casework. By 1939 it had established a homemaker service to keep families together when the mother was ill or incapacitated. That service operates today to prevent unnecessary removal of children from families and to prevent inappropriate institutionalization of elderly persons.

In 1945 the Family Welfare Society changed its name to Family Service Association and in 1947 began charging fees to those able to pay for counseling service. The association cautiously accepted government funding in the early 1970s, reaching a peak of 39 percent of its annual budget in 1984. The Program for Visually Impaired Elderly was acquired from the CHURCH FEDERATION OF GREATER INDIANAPOLIS in 1982 and a Friendly Guardianship Program was begun in 1991.

In January, 1993, the association reincorporated as the Family Service Association of Central Indiana. Its programs emphasize service for families with serious problems, such as domestic violence, alcohol abuse, child abuse and neglect, and inability to live in self-care arrangements without assistance. It now broadly defines family to include any couple or group forming bonds of kinship to fulfill the functions of the family. Paraprofessionals and volunteers supplement the work of professional counselors. Its budget of approximately $1.75 million is supported by UNITED WAY, the INDIANAPOLIS FOUNDATION, other foundations, government contracts, direct contributions, and employee assistance plans with business and industry.

JAMES N. MILLER
Family Service Association

Actress Frances Farmer hosted a popular TV show in Indianapolis in the 1960s.

Farm Bureau Insurance. Indianapolis-based insurance company. Farm Bureau Mutual Insurance Company of Indiana was chartered in 1934 by Hoosiers dissatisfied with insurance available through State Farm Mutual of Illinois. Automobile insurance for 3,341 cars and trucks was sold that first year to members of the Indiana Farm Bureau, Inc., a farm advocacy collective. The company added life insurance in 1937, and fire and tornado coverage became available in 1946. In the 1950s regional claims offices began to open to accommodate growing business. In 1954 Farm Bureau insurance was first offered to non-farm families; previously, it had been available only to voting members of the Indiana Farm Bureau.

By the early 1990s Farm Bureau had more than 700,000 active property and casualty policies and was the largest farm insurer in the state, as well as the second largest home and auto insurer. Farm Bureau Insurance is the collective name for several companies, including United Farm Bureau Mutual Insurance Co., United Farm Bureau Casualty Insurance Co., and United Farm Bureau Family Life Insurance Co. Statewide, Farm Bureau employs over 2,000 people, with more than 800 in its home office in Indianapolis. In 1992 the company relocated to a $40 million corporate headquarters that houses both Farm Bureau Insurance and the Indiana Farm Bureau in the renovated Indianapolis Rubber Company building on the southeast fringe of downtown.

DEBORAH B. MARKISOHN

George Geib, *Indianapolis: Hoosiers' Circle City* (Tulsa, Okla., 1981), 194.

Farmer, Frances (Sept. 9, 1914–Aug. 1, 1970). Movie actress and local television host. Born in Seattle, Washington, Frances Farmer graduated from the University of Washington and became a movie actress while still in her twenties. Although considered a major star in the 1930s and 1940s, she never enjoyed working in films. In 1942, Farmer quit acting and did not return to her craft for fourteen years. During this period she was institutionalized for eight years, diagnosed as schizophrenic.

In 1957 Farmer began touring in summer stock and played at the former AVONDALE PLAYHOUSE in Indianapolis. While in the city she accepted an offer from local television station WFBM to host its afternoon movie show. "Frances Farmer Presents" ran for seven tumultuous years; she was fired twice for erratic behavior and drunkenness. Although Farmer finally left the show in 1964, she remained in Indianapolis at her home on Park Avenue.

During the next five years Farmer acted in several productions of the Purdue University Drama Department, joined St. Joan of Arc Catholic Church, and opened a home decorating business with her friend Jean Ratcliffe. When Farmer's investment with Ratcliffe in a line of cosmetics soured, she lost all her money and her home. For the remainder of her life she rented a farmhouse at 6000 Moller Road.

Farmer's final years were spent writing her autobiography, *Will There Really Be a Morning?* (1972). The book chronicles her years in a state mental asylum as well as her life in Indianapolis. Before finishing her story Farmer died of cancer at the age of 57. The book's final chapter was written by Ratcliffe. In 1982, EMI Films released *Frances*, a movie account of Farmer's life starring Jessica Lange and Sam Shepard.

CONNIE J. ZEIGLER

Federal Buildings. There are two federal buildings in Indianapolis: the U.S. Court House and Post Office, located on Ohio Street between Meridian and Pennsylvania streets, and the Federal Office Building, 575 North Pennsylvania Street.

Indianapolis received its first clear expression of monumental Beaux-Arts classicism with the construction of the U.S. Court House and Post Office (1903–1905). Named for the Ecole des Beaux-Arts, an architectural training school in Paris, this style combined Roman, Greek, and Renaissance classicism into a bold and aggressive style. Hallmarks of this mode as represented by this building include symmetrical plans with projecting pavilions, large scale facades organized into expansive flat-roofed wings, heavy masonry construction, and richly detailed classical ornamentation. With its grand style, the massive Indiana limestone building set the trend for public architecture in Indianapolis for many years. Following suit were the Indianapolis City Hall (1910), INDIANAPOLIS–MARION COUNTY PUBLIC LIBRARY (1917), and, ultimately, the INDIANA WORLD WAR MEMORIAL PLAZA (1922–1950); all are variations on the style established by the U.S. Court House and Post Office. In a broad sense, this federal building is symbolic of America's emergence as a world power at the turn of the century. Federal architects and planners, inspired by the classical buildings displayed at the 1893 World's Columbian Exposition held in Chicago, adopted classicism as the official style of governmental buildings. Through imposing facilities like these, the government established what has been termed "the federal presence" across the country.

The U.S. Court House and Post Office has served as the headquarters of the federal government in Indianapolis since its completion. It houses several principal courtrooms and a variety of federal agencies. Prior to 1973 it was also the city's main post office, and from 1973 until 1991 a branch office was housed there.

Planning for the building began in 1900, when the federal government purchased the block for $626,000 and began to raze the commercial buildings that stood on the site. Between 1903 and 1905 $1,267,530 was spent on construction. Spanning a full city block, the building consists of four three-story wings arranged around a central light well. Projecting corner pavilions include pedimented entries. Engaged fluted Ionic columns articulate the principal facades. Flanking the main entries, the columns are free-standing but recessed. Bronze light standards, balustrades, and four allegorical figures sculpted by John Massey Rhinde (placed in 1908) decorate the grounds.

Originally, a one-story arcaded wing closed the north side of the building. This wing was razed in 1936, matching pavilions were added, and a new three-story section with Doric pilasters was erected. Of special interest on this 1936–1938 addition are the Art Deco bas-reliefs facing east and west over the round arched vehicle entries.

The interior of the U.S. Court House and Post Office retains many original elements. Corridors feature groin vaulting, marble wainscoting, and mosaics. Self-supporting spiral staircases of marble remain intact. Courtrooms have retained their ornate fittings, including large stained glass windows by Otto Heingke and murals by W. B. van Ingen.

Architects John Hall Rankin and Thomas Moore Kellogg of Philadelphia designed the building; the firm was known for its large governmental commissions, such as the Department of Agriculture buildings (1906) in Washington, D.C. The John Pierce Company of New York City was the contractor. Congress appropriated $1,300,000 for construction of the north wing in 1935. Indianapolis architect Wilbur Shook, of MCGUIRE AND SHOOK, designed the 1936–1938 addition to complement the old building and provide a suitably monumental facade to face the nearly completed World War Memorial Plaza. Great Lakes Construction Company of Chicago was the contractor.

The Federal Office Building, also known as the Minton-Capehart Building, is located a few blocks north of the Court House and Post Office.

Built to the designs of the Indianapolis firm of WOOLLEN AND ASSOCIATES in 1975, it is a frank expression of a recent phase of modern architecture known as "Brutalism." The cantilevered stories of this building (each being further out than the one below) are often noted. A similar project, the Boston City Hall (1962–1967) by the firm Kallmann, McKinnell and Knowles, may have inspired this design. Milton Glazer designed the colorful mural surrounding the lower level of the building.

PAUL C. DIEBOLD
Division of Historic Preservation and
Archaeology, Indiana Department of
Natural Resources

Bruce Goetzman, "United State Courthouse and Post Office," National Register of Historic Places nomination, Jan. 11, 1974; John Hall Rankin and Thomas Moore Kellogg, "U.S. Court House and Post Office," original working drawings, Indiana Historical Society.

Federal Theatre Project (FTP).

An agency of the Works Progress Administration from 1935 to 1939, under the supervision of Hallie Flanagan, that provided work for unemployed people in the theatrical profession. Lee Norvelle, chair of the Department of Speech and Theatre at Indiana University, directed the Indiana Project beginning in December, 1935.

Norvelle operated a company plus two vaudeville units in the B. F. Keith Vaudeville Theatre (built in 1875 as the Grand Opera House) at 117 North Pennsylvania Street, Indianapolis. He later helped organize a theatre for children in Gary. Norvelle ran the Indianapolis theatre as a stock company, changing productions every week or two. He avoided most controversial scripts and Living Newspaper Plays, innovations associated with the FTP. Most productions featured well-tested comedies, melodramas, or mysteries, frequently by Indiana writers such as BOOTH TARKINGTON. Norvelle also produced *It Can't Happen Here* by Sinclair Lewis. This play was simultaneously opened by 18 different Federal Theatre Projects on August 27, 1936. He also hosted the Black Harlem Company under the direction of Orson Welles in their touring production of the "voodoo" *Macbeth*, August 25–29, 1936.

Attendance was brisk in the beginning and local papers provided extensive coverage. Norvelle returned to his duties at Indiana University during the summer of 1936, although he continued to supervise the theatre. Audiences, however, began to dwindle and newspaper reviewers increasingly criticized play choices and the artistic quality of productions. Simultaneously Congress mandated cutbacks in all theatre projects. Faced with such adversity, Norvelle and Flanagan closed the operation in Indianapolis on July 15, 1937.

DOROTHY WEBB
Indiana University–Purdue University,
Indianapolis

Hallie Flanagan, *Arena* (New York, 1985); Library of Congress Federal Theatre Project Collection, George Mason University, Fairfax, Virginia; WPA Papers, Federal Theatre Project, Record Group 69, Box 59, National Archives, Washington, D.C.

Federation of Associated Clubs (FAC).

Black community organization. The Federation of Associated Clubs began on November 11, 1937. Initially, it consisted of nine local African-American social clubs. Within ten years its membership included representatives from 125 different black clubs in the Indianapolis area, enabling the organization to promote a wide range of activities in education, politics, civic projects, and employment for the black community.

FAC was founded by Starling W. James, who was its only president; the organization's philosophy always reflected his beliefs. Born in Pittsburg, Kansas, on October 10, 1893, James early demonstrated his ability as an organizer for the social betterment of black people. While in high school in Pittsburg he organized a group of young men into a civic organization called the Cosmopolitan Club. The club was the forerunner of the county branch of the NATIONAL ASSOCIATION FOR THE ADVANCEMENT OF COLORED PEOPLE (NAACP). Upon graduation from Lincoln University in Jefferson City, Missouri, James taught in several schools in Kansas, eventually becoming a principal in Kansas City, Kansas. While there he came under heavy criticism for his activities on behalf of civil rights for blacks and was forced to leave. He moved to Indianapolis in 1927 where his continuing organizational activities culminated with the founding of FAC.

The decade from 1939–1949 was the period of greatest activity for the federation. It provided scholarships to worthy graduates of CRISPUS ATTUCKS HIGH SCHOOL, promoted civic gatherings, circulated petitions, and met with policy-making bodies to advocate actions beneficial to the African-American community. FAC campaigned for black representation on the Indianapolis School Board, was successful in having downtown theaters desegregated, and worked to upgrade positions for blacks in Indiana Bell Telephone Company and other public utilities. Also, the club mounted voter registration campaigns, conducted public political forums, and sponsored appreciation banquets for friendly legislators.

The years 1950 to 1975 marked the accomplishment of objectives initiated during the earlier decade. These included the establishment of Negro History Week (which became African-American History Month), publication of a weekly column in the INDIANAPOLIS RECORDER, and active support of CIVIL RIGHTS legislation. There was much less activity in the years after 1975, and FAC ceased to exist with the death of Starling James on June 18, 1986.

DALLAS DANIELS, JR.

Feeney, Albert G. (Nov. 12, 1892–Nov. 12, 1950). Mayor of Indianapolis, Jan. 1, 1948–Nov. 12, 1950, Democrat. Feeney attended St. John's School and MANUAL HIGH SCHOOL in Indianapolis, then went to the University of Notre Dame where he played football (as a teammate of future coach Knute Rockne) and basketball. Following graduation in 1914 he played both sports professionally. Feeney retired from pro football in 1926 but continued coaching at Notre Dame, serving his former teammate as an advisory line coach until Rockne's death in 1931. He also directed Cathedral High School's football team in Indianapolis, where he lost only one game in three years.

In 1933 Feeney organized the State Board of Public Safety and became its first director. This appointment also made him superintendent of the Indiana State Police, director of the State Fire Marshal's Office, and in charge of the Department of Criminal Identification and Investigation. Although honored as Indiana's outstanding law enforcement officer, Governor Paul V. McNutt dismissed him in 1935 after a long battle between Feeney and the governor's patronage secretary, who used state policemen for political work despite Feeney's repeated prohibitions of such activity.

Feeney was elected sheriff of Marion County in 1938 and 1940. In this position he reduced juvenile delinquency, had all deputies study first aid, equipped department cars with two-way radios, improved conditions at the county jail, and required school bus inspections. Later in the 1940s he was the safety director for P. R. MALLORY AND COMPANY and a member of the Marion County Welfare Board.

Elected mayor of Indianapolis for the term beginning January 1, 1948, Feeney sought to improve the city's shaky financial situation. He directed that parking tickets and fines were to be paid rather than being "fixed" by friends. He also sold the mayor's car and fired his chauffeur to save money. He died unexpectedly before completing his term of office.

REBECCA M. MAIER

Notre Dame Alumnus, 25 (Dec., 1947), 15; Indianapolis Times, Nov. 13, 1950.

Fehrenbatch, John (1844–?). Labor leader. Born in Rochester, New York, Fehrenbatch went to work in a woolen factory in that city at age eight. In 1861 he moved to Indianapolis where he was elected president of the local Machinists' and Blacksmiths' Union No. 4. In 1865, following a WORKINGMEN'S PARTY convention in Indianapolis that he helped organize, Fehrenbatch was instrumental in forming Eight-Hour Leagues all over Indiana. In 1866 he became the leader of the Grand Eight-Hour League and was able to pressure both major parties to support the eight-hour workday in their 1866 campaign platforms. Having been elected president of the Machinists' and Blacksmiths' International Union in 1870, Fehrenbatch moved to Cleveland, Ohio, where he became the editor of the *Machinists' and Blacksmiths' Interna-*

tional Union Journal. In 1873 he served as the president of the Industrial Congress held in Cleveland, and in 1876 he was elected to a single term in the Ohio state legislature.

JEFFERY A. DUVALL

Emma Lou Thornbrough, *Indiana in the Civil War Era* (Indianapolis, 1965); David Montgomery, *Beyond Equality: Labor and the Radical Republicans, 1862–1872* (Urbana, Ill., 1981).

Fellowship of Christian Athletes. Parachurch organization. The Fellowship of Christian Athletes (FCA) is a not-for-profit, nondenominational, religious organization. Its goals are to instill in athletes and coaches a vital Christian commitment and to grow spiritually, mentally, emotionally, and socially. Conceived by Don McCleanen, the organization was formally established in 1954 in Norman, Oklahoma, and moved to Kansas City, Missouri, in 1956. FCA in Indiana is led by a state director and executive council of men and women from the business community. It is funded by contributions and depends on volunteers to organize and supervise events.

The core of the FCA is the "huddle," of which there are 95 in Indianapolis with a membership of 1,500. Huddle members are men and women athletes of junior high school, senior high school, and college age, as well as coaches. Huddles build friendships, feature group discussions, provide Bible study, furnish inspiring programs, and foster church and community involvement. FCA activities include camps, conferences, rallies, banquets, clinics, retreats, and tournaments. Huddle advisors are coaches, parents, and the clergy. Adult chapters consist of coaches, businessmen, clergy, parents, and teachers who encourage and support the huddles.

JUDY SCHWARTZ

Festival Music Society. Not-for-profit organization promoting early classical music for Indiana audiences. The society, established in 1966, presents concerts of music from the Medieval, Renaissance, Baroque, and Classic periods. The annual program, held in Indianapolis during the month of July, usually consists of seven concerts and three lectures. The society has sponsored over 200 programs, including performances of the Cologne Chamber Orchestra, harpsichordist Igor Kipnis, the Reger Trio, and the Paris Consort. Ensembles from Indiana University's Early Music Institute, the Smithsonian Institution, and Oberlin College have served as resident artists. In addition, the society has sponsored music competitions, educational training, and performance opportunities for young musicians.

The Festival Music Society is guided by a volunteer board of community leaders elected to three-year terms and by its music director, who proposes a theme and artists for each season. Frank Cooper, professor of music at the University of Miami, has served as the society's music director since 1973. The organization's annual budget is $65,000 and is supported by contributions and grants from businesses, individuals, and foundations. Formerly housed at the INDIANAPOLIS MUSEUM OF ART for 23 years, the society is now headquartered at St. Paul's Episcopal Church in Indianapolis.

DAVID VANDERSTEL
Indiana University–Purdue University,
Indianapolis

"Fit for a king: Festival Music Society tunes up with 'royal' patronage," *Indianapolis Star*, June 30, 1991.

Feuerlicht, Morris Marcus (Jan. 15, 1879–Nov. 30, 1959). Rabbi of Indianapolis Hebrew Congregation and leader in social and community services. Born in Tokay, Hungary, and raised in Chicago and Boston, Feuerlicht graduated from Hebrew Union College of Cincinnati (1897), the University of Cincinnati (1901), and pursued postgraduate studies at the University of Chicago. In the fall of 1904, Feuerlicht moved from a rabbinate at Lafayette, Indiana, to become the associate rabbi at the Indianapolis Hebrew Congregation. He later succeeded Rabbi Mayer Messing in November, 1907, and served the congregation until December, 1946.

Feuerlicht was very active in social and community services. He worked with Judge George

W. Stubbs of the Marion County Juvenile Court to promote the JUVENILE JUSTICE system throughout Indiana and served for 21 years as president of the Children's Aid Association (later the Indianapolis Family Service Society and then the Community Fund), an auxiliary of the juvenile court and voluntary agency for children's issues. He served on the County Board of Welfare, as president of the Indiana State Conference of Charities, and was the first Jew appointed to the State Board of Charities and Correction (1920–1931).

As a significant leader in the Indianapolis Jewish community, Feuerlicht drafted the constitution and bylaws of the newly established Jewish Federation of Indianapolis (1905) and served as the first editor-in-chief of the *Indiana Jewish Chronicle*, established in 1922. During the 1920s, Feuerlicht was the Jewish community's principal spokesman against the KU KLUX KLAN. In the 1930s, he condemned the Nazi government and appealed to the Indiana Pastors' Conference to combat Nazi propaganda. After World War II, Feuerlicht was a staunch critic of political Zionism.

Feuerlicht represented the Jewish community in numerous interfaith gatherings, debating attorney Clarence Darrow in 1928 and 1929 before large Indianapolis audiences. He also taught Semitics at BUTLER UNIVERSITY's School of Religion from 1926 to 1951.

A member of the Indiana Library and Historical Board (1942–1956), he served as its president from 1950 to 1956. He was a member of the INDIANAPOLIS LITERARY CLUB and author of *A Hoosier Rabbinate* (1974).

Feuerlicht is buried in the Indianapolis Hebrew Cemetery.

DAVID G. VANDERSTEL
Indiana University–Purdue University, Indianapolis

Morris Feuerlicht, *A Hoosier Rabbinate* (1974); *Indianapolis Times*, Dec. 4, 1946, Jan. 15, 1954.

The Fiery Cross. Weekly newspaper of the Ku Klux Klan. Originally appearing in Indianapolis in 1921 under the name *Fact!*, the paper was renamed in July, 1922 under the editorship of Ernest W. Reichard. Klan leader D. C. STEPHEN-

SON gained editorial control of *The Fiery Cross* in 1923.

At the beginning of Reichard's tenure, the KU KLUX KLAN claimed to have 5,000 members in Indianapolis. Initially, *The Fiery Cross* published relatively innocuous material—meetings, rallies, and other Klan activities—and the paper served as a medium for advertising. Merchants offered discounts to Klan members, and some advertisers put "TWK"—"Trade with the Klan"—signs in their shop windows.

Stephenson's takeover made the paper more ideological and political. Local Protestant ministers who supported the Klan had their sermons published. The paper reported negatively on Protestant clergy who refused to support the Klan. Names of prominent Catholic business figures were also published in *The Fiery Cross*, with a strong implication that Klansmen should boycott such firms.

After Stephenson took over circulation rose to some 50,000 copies, primarily in the Midwest. An annual subscription cost five dollars. By March, 1923, Stephenson claimed the paper's circulation numbered over 100,000 readers and in April *The Fiery Cross* expanded to a length of 12 pages. The paper had three editions, one each for Ohio, Illinois, and Indiana. Imperial Wizard Hiram Wesley Evans fought Stephenson for control of the paper. Although Stephenson was the victor, *The Fiery Cross* ceased publication in February, 1925, following his conviction for second-degree murder and the waning of Klan support in Indiana.

PATRICIA FOGLEMAN

M. William Lutholtz, *Grand Dragon: D. C. Stephenson and the Ku Klux Klan in Indiana* (West Lafayette, Ind., 1991); Richard K. Tucker, *The Dragon and the Cross* (Hamden, Conn., 1991).

Filipinos. Filipinos did not arrive in Indianapolis in significant numbers until the mid–1960s after U.S. immigration laws raised Asian quotas. The migration reached its peak between 1969 and 1974. As of the 1990 census there were 1,157 people living in Marion County who claimed Filipino ancestry.

Filipinos in Indianapolis tend to live among other Asian groups, with small clusters having formed near FORT BENJAMIN HARRISON and in the northwest corner of Indianapolis. Most Indianapolis Filipinos come from the northern Philippine islands. They tend to be college-educated, many having graduate training. A preponderance of Filipinos came to Indianapolis to train and/or work at the Indiana University medical facilities or ELI LILLY AND COMPANY. Roughly 70 percent of Indianapolis Filipinos work in health and medical fields, and an additional 20 percent represent other professions.

Filipinos throughout the United States do not create highly organized ethnic communities, and there is almost no institutionally distinct Filipino community in Indianapolis. Filipinos are very familial and express their native culture mainly within informal settings. Filipino holidays include Rizal Day, memorializing the Philippine revolution against Spain, and Santa Cruzan and Flores de Mayo, festivals celebrating harvest and Spring.

The leading Filipino institution in Indianapolis is the Barangay Club, founded in 1960, whose name means "mutual helpfulness." Activities of this club include a Christmas dance, Christmas caroling, a summer picnic coinciding with the Philippines Independence Day, and small social groups. The club also sponsors a Filipino contingent for the annual INTERNATIONAL FESTIVAL in Indianapolis, where club members dress in customary costume and perform traditional dances. The only other Filipino institution is the Indiana Philippines Medical Association, founded in 1977, which holds an annual dinner and dance.

Most Filipinos in Indianapolis are practicing CATHOLICS but they have not organized an ethnic church or congregation. For a short time in the late 1970s, however, there was a Filipino priest at St. Rita who performed traditional Filipino masses the nine days before Christmas. Black Rosary groups, organized through the Barangay Club, meet monthly in members' homes to pray and honor the Virgin Mary as well as to socialize.

MICHELLE D. HALE

Finance Center. See U.S. Army Finance Center

Fine Arts Society of Indianapolis. Public charitable trust established to promote the understanding and appreciation of the fine arts and performing arts. Financially supported by memberships and gifts, the society produces and broadcasts classical music on a privately owned, non-commercial radio station, currently WICR (88.7 FM) at the UNIVERSITY OF INDIANAPOLIS.

Founded in 1968, the society began broadcasting its "Second Program" on WIAN, then the radio station of the Indianapolis Public Schools, in November, 1969. Initially limited to 12 hours each weekend, the society expanded its broadcasts to six nights a week in November, 1970, and three years later introduced a morning edition of the "Second Program." In January, 1983, the society ended its 13-year association with WIAN and began broadcasting the "Second Program," as well as a new daily "First Program," from the University of Indianapolis. In 1986 the organization won a George Foster Peabody Award for excellence in broadcasting.

The society currently broadcasts classical music 104 hours weekly (with occasional modifications to accommodate University of Indianapolis broadcasts). It also sponsors fine arts and performing arts events, and awards educational and performing arts stipends. Commemorating the society's 20th anniversary in 1989, special "Diplomas of Honor" were inaugurated and are awarded annually to a civic leader for contributions to the cultural life of Indianapolis and central Indiana. In the early 1990s the society's membership was approximately 2,000.

NORBERT NEUSS

Fire Department. See Indianapolis Fire Department

Fires. The first fire in Indianapolis occurred on January 17, 1825, when Thomas Carter's tavern burned to the ground. There was no fire department at that time, but citizens rallied around the frame building opposite the courthouse on

Washington Street and managed to save most of the furniture and stock. The disaster persuaded the city to organize its first volunteer fire department in 1826. Since that time Indianapolis fire fighters have faced a number of major fires.

Kingan and Company, May 22, 1865. The fire, which completely destroyed the five-story pork packing plant, was the worst in the city's history to that time, causing over $200,000 in damages. The building was less than two years old and was equipped with the newest slaughtering and packing machinery. Thousands of pounds of pork and lard fed the flames, producing a heat so intense that firemen could hardly approach the building. They quickly abandoned the fire itself and concentrated their efforts on the surrounding buildings. Soaking these buildings prevented the fire from spreading; it finally died sometime after midnight. A subsequent investigation revealed that the building had been thoroughly cleaned of all shavings and flammable materials the day of the fire and, there having been no fire in the plant that day, the fire marshal concluded that it must have been an act of arson. However, Kingan's owners could name no suspects and the fire's origin remained a mystery.

The largest pork packing plant in the country, Kingan was one of the city's largest employers and several leading citizens had large quantities of pork and lard stored there. Initial reports indicated that the building, owned by a group of Irish-American businessmen, was not insured and there was concern as to whether or not the company would be able to rebuild. But two days after the fire Kingan's owners met in Indianapolis and announced that all but $20,000 of the damages were covered and that they intended to rebuild immediately.

Woodburn Sarven Wheel Company, March 11, 1873. Woodburn was a wooden wagon wheel factory located south of downtown at the corner of Illinois and Garden streets. The fire started in the machinery room, a large addition at the back of the building, when wood shavings scattered on the floor ignited. It spread quickly through the addition and a party of hose men led by fire chief DANIEL GLAZIER approached it from the second floor of the original building. While they were there, the fire wall of the addition fell onto the roof

of the original building, killing Glazier and injuring four of his men. By the time firemen brought it under control at 1:30 A.M., the fire had caused $75,000 of damage.

Chief Glazier's death was the INDIANAPOLIS FIRE DEPARTMENT's first fatality in the line of duty, and his funeral was one of the largest in the city to that time. Glazier, along with several of his brothers, had been a prominent member of the paid fire department since its founding in 1859. Among his survivors were several nephews and two sons who were also members of the department. One of the nephews, Ulysses Glazier, died while fighting the Bowen-Merrill fire in 1890.

South Meridian Street, January 13, 1888. This fire began at 11 P.M. in the four-story D. P. Erwin dry goods building on the east side of Meridian Street south of Georgia Street. The flames spread quickly and the fire department, hampered by freezing temperatures, was unable to contain them. The fire moved north to Stout's wholesale grocery house, then crossed the street and consumed Pearson & Wetzell's queensware house. By the time firemen brought the blaze under control at 3 A.M. it had destroyed six buildings on either side of Meridian in what was then the wholesale district. The loss of these buildings and damages to two others amounted to $1 million, making it the worst fire in the city to that date. Heat from the fire was so intense that much of the hose laid on Meridian Street was scorched and ruined. Unable to use ladders to reach the buildings' upper floors, firemen were forced to approach from the rear of the buildings. Much of their clothing was scorched, but no firemen were injured.

Bowen-Merrill, March 17, 1890. At 3 P.M. employees of the Bowen-Merrill Bookstore at 18 West Washington Street noticed smoke coming from the iron gratings in the sidewalk in front of the store and notified the fire department. Firemen arriving at the scene found nothing but a smoldering blaze confined to the basement, surveyed the building, and, thinking that things were under control, dispersed the crowd that had gathered out front. Owing to the flammable contents of the four-story building, firemen remained at the scene. At 5 P.M. they detected flames coming from the windows of the upper floors. They quickly doused them with a hose line and be-

Major Indianapolis Fires

FIRE	PROPERTY LOSS	FATALITIES
Kingan and Company May 22, 1865	$200,000	0
Morrison Opera House January 17, 1870	$200,000	0
Woodburn Sarven March 11, 1873	$75,000	1
Wright's Exchange Block March 22, 1874	$200,000	0
South Meridian Street January 13, 1888	$1,000,000	0
Bowen-Merrill March 17, 1890	$180,000	13
Surgical Institute January 21, 1892	$50,000	19
Meridian and Louisiana Streets February 19, 1905	$1,500,000	0
Coburn Warehouse January 28, 1908	$500,000	0
Romanian Rooming House July 3, 1915	$65,000	0
Livery Barn October 22, 1915	$8,000	53 Horses & Mules
Industrial Building January 13, 1918	$2,000,000	0
State Fair Stables February 19, 1922	$300,000	100 Horses
National Starch Products June 6, 1942	$200,000	0
Block's Department Store January 22, 1952	$1,000,000	0
TOMLINSON HALL January 30, 1958	$100,000	0
CLAYPOOL HOTEL June 23, 1967	$250,000	0
Hygrade Food Products July 17, 1967	$300,000	0
Midstate Chemical July 27, 1970	$150,000	0
Hilton Hotel January 7, 1972	$1,000,000	0
Grant Building November 5, 1973	$15,000,000	0
Indianapolis Athletic Club February 5, 1992	$250,000	3

lieved that they had brought the fire under control. But the building's cast iron facade had been hiding a growing fire from firemen stationed on the street and on the roofs of neighboring buildings. Without warning all four floors collapsed and over 20 firemen fell into the flames from their post on the roof of the adjacent Becker Building. Rescue and cleanup activities over the next 20 hours uncovered the bodies of 12 firemen. Over a dozen others were seriously hurt, and one died in the hospital from injuries received in the fall. The fire represents the highest death count in the fire

department's history and the fourth worst disaster in terms of loss of life in Indianapolis' history.

The city rallied to aid the injured firemen and the families of those who perished. On March 18 Mayor THOMAS L. SULLIVAN appointed a committee of seven, including COL. ELI LILLY and former Mayor CALEB S. DENNY, to receive funds and take charge of disbursements. As word of the tragedy spread, donations poured in from across the nation. By 1900 the fund had grown to $52,000. It purchased annuities for the nine widows and 22 orphans, bought homes for four of the widows, and paid all funeral and medical expenses. The tragedy spurred the state legislature to create the first statewide pension fund in 1891.

Surgical Institute, January 21, 1892. Shortly before midnight, a janitor at Dr. Allen's NATIONAL SURGICAL INSTITUTE noticed smoke coming from a secretary's office on the third floor. The institute building, located at the northeast corner of Illinois and Georgia streets, included the upper floors of several old buildings connected by narrow passageways. It was later discovered that the fire had started in an office on the ground floor and quickly spread to the upper floors. Over 300 people were in the building when the fire started, and by the time firemen arrived on the scene 194 patients were trapped on the top floor. With the help of firemen and volunteers, over 250 persons escaped the building unharmed. But many of the patients, mostly invalids and children, remained trapped on the top floor. Some died in desperate leaps from windows, while others died of smoke inhalation or were crushed when a section of the roof collapsed. In all, 19 patients were killed and 50 injured making the fire the city's third most fatal disaster.

The tragedy at the Surgical Institute did more to stir public interest in building safety than any other fire in the city's history. The building inspector had condemned the structure as a fire hazard in 1878, but few renovations had been made to meet the prescribed safety requirements. Indianapolis newspapers criticized the city government, the building inspector, and the fire department for allowing the institute to operate in violation of the safety codes. Public outcry spurred reform of the building code and the fire department.

Meridian and Louisiana Streets, February 19, 1905. Fire broke out just before 10 P.M. in Fahnley and McCrea's wholesale millinery house on South Meridian Street. Fueled by gas from several machines that the firm used to curl feathers, the fire quickly spread through the quarter square bounded by an alley and Meridian, Louisiana, and McCrea streets. Within 15 minutes the fire was so hot that firemen began dousing buildings across the street to prevent its spread. Despite these efforts, the fire moved north, abetted by the electrical wires that connected the buildings. Flames eventually reached the druggists' sundries and holiday goods house of the E. C. Dolmetsch Co., which had a large quantity of fireworks in stock. Their explosion, combined with explosive drugs from Keifer's drug store to the south, gave spectators the impression of battle artillery. The fire caused a then-record $1.2 million of damage, but there were no deaths or injuries. The newspapers praised the fire department's work in controlling the fire and attributed its spread and severity to the presence of gas and electrical wires rather than to the condition of the buildings.

Industrial Building, January 13, 1918. In 1918 the Industrial Building was a ten-year-old, five-story brick, stone, and cement structure containing over 400,000 square feet of floor space. It covered almost the entire block between 10th and 11th streets with Fayette Street to the west and the Indianapolis Water Company on the east. Twenty-three companies rented space in the building for storage or manufacturing. Many of these companies produced goods for the armed forces, then engaged in World War I.

As the nation was in the middle of a miners' strike, the owners, unable to obtain coal to heat the building, shut off the sprinkler system and drained the water from the pipes to prevent freezing. A night watchman discovered a fire on the evening of January 13 and, without the sprinklers to slow its progress, it quickly engulfed the building. The fire spread to the surrounding buildings, destroying a church, a saloon, and five homes and damaging a grocery store and 20 additional homes before firemen brought it under control. Total damage was estimated at $2 million.

Because many of the firms in the building were engaged in war production, rumors that the fire was set by German agents abounded. However, investigators were unable to find evidence to substantiate these claims.

Midstate Chemical, July 27, 1970. At 6:20 P.M. a two alarm blaze broke out in wooden shelving in the warehouse area near the office of the Midstate Chemical company at 2100 Greenbriar Lane on the city's northeast side. Two people were in the warehouse at the time, and fire department officials speculated that careless smoking could have been the cause of the fire. As the fire grew, it engulfed seventy 150–pound cylinders of liquid chlorine located in the warehouse. Investigators from Midstate, which sold liquid chlorine to the Indianapolis Department of Parks and Recreation for use in municipal pools, later concluded that only seven of the cylinders had actually leaked during the fire. The fire nevertheless emitted clouds of noxious, yellowish-green fumes that spread over an area from 25th Street to Roosevelt Avenue and from Keystone to Martindale avenues. The fire department ordered 1,200 people to evacuate homes in the affected area. Fire fighters brought the fire under control after five hours, but both the office building and the warehouse were destroyed at an estimated loss of $150,000.

Ten firemen, including Fire Chief David A. Russell, were hospitalized, and 50 others were treated at the scene for smoke inhalation. The Marion County disaster plan was ordered into effect, and ambulances, nurses, and Red Cross workers rushed to the scene and stood by to treat firemen and evacuees. Firefighters and toxicology experts from FORT BENJAMIN HARRISON declared the area safe sometime after midnight and evacuees returned to their homes.

Grant Building, November 5, 1973. Shortly before 1 P.M. several propane tanks exploded on the fourth floor of the Grant Building at 25 East Washington Street, triggering a general alarm fire that would prove to be the most costly in the city's history. No one was in the building as it had been vacant for some time and was being prepared for demolition. The structure collapsed after 15 minutes and the fire, aided by 20–mile-an-hour winds, spread to the 12–story Thomas Building at 15 East Washington, eventually destroying it as well. It also caused serious damage to the MER-

CHANTS NATIONAL BANK BUILDING, Kirk Furniture, Washington Tower Apartments, and Richmond Brothers before fire fighters brought it under control at around 3 P.M. In all, the fire caused over $15 million of damage.

One hundred and twenty fire fighters battled the blaze and the fire department ordered over 5,000 people evacuated from buildings in the downtown area. The city's disaster plan was ordered into effect, and 175 law enforcement officers were called in to handle crowd control and direct traffic around restricted areas. Six fire fighters suffered minor injuries during the fire.

Indianapolis Athletic Club, February 5, 1992. Sometime after midnight, employees called the fire department after detecting smoke coming from vents in the lobby of the Indianapolis Athletic Club building at 350 North Meridian Street. After checking the building, the manager began evacuating the 40 guests staying in the residential rooms on the sixth, seventh, and eighth floors. The situation seemed to be under control until an explosive flashover engulfed a third-floor lounge, killing two fire fighters and hospitalizing two others. A flashover—heat so intense (around 1,110 degrees Fahrenheit) that the entire surface area of a particular room catches fire at once—immediately consumed a lounge next to the third-floor dining room, overwhelming the two unsuspecting fire fighters. A third victim, a businessman from Illinois, was found dead in a stairwell between the fifth and sixth floors. All three fatalities were from smoke inhalation. The fire department sent 75 fire fighters and 16 vehicles to fight the fire, which caused $250,000 in damages to the nine-story building.

As a result of the three deaths, the city's public safety director organized an Indianapolis Fire Department panel to review equipment and procedures. The panel found that firemen acted properly. Both the IFD panel and investigators from the U.S. Bureau of Alcohol, Tobacco, and Firearms concluded that faulty wiring in a refrigerator in the lounge next to the third floor dining room caused the fire. The presence of the Mike Tyson trial jurors on the sixth floor led to speculation of arson and spurred Mayor Stephen Goldsmith's request for the ATF investigation. However, both investigations ruled out any possibility of arson.

WILLIAM DALTON

Jacob Piatt Dunn, *Greater Indianapolis* (Chicago, 1910), I, chapters 17, 25.

First Baptist Church. In August, 1822, 15 Indianapolis residents established a Baptist church at a schoolhouse, where they continued to meet once a month. In 1829 the congregation purchased a lot at the southwest corner of Meridian and Maryland streets and erected a one-story brick building that they eventually replaced with a two-story brick structure. This church burned in 1861 and the congregation, which had purchased land for a new edifice in 1858 at the corner of Pennsylvania and New York streets, dedicated a new building at this location in May, 1864. This building burned, was rebuilt, and was destroyed again by fire in 1904. The congregation purchased new land at Meridian and Vermont streets, where its large centrally located facility was the site for many public and church activities. The congregation vacated its sanctuary in March, 1960, to make way for the INDIANA WORLD WAR MEMORIAL PLAZA and relocated to their current complex at 8600 North College Avenue. Now encompassing 37 acres, the church includes a sanctuary seating over 600, 18 classrooms, a fellowship hall, gymnasium, baseball diamonds, a shelter house, and tennis courts. Canadian Prime Minister John Diefenbaker spoke at the dedication ceremony in June, 1960.

First Baptist's membership remained under 1,000 until shortly after 1900; then it began to grow, reaching a high of almost 2,000 in the early 1920s. The church experienced particular growth in membership under Rev. Frederick E. Taylor, pastor from September, 1906 until April, 1932. In 1923 he initiated the Winter Night College, a popular annual series of weekly lectures, which by 1960 had an enrollment of several hundred each year. Since the congregation's move to the suburbs membership has declined and in the early 1990s it stood at about 650.

Between 1869 and 1906 First Baptist supported eight missions that grew into full congregations, including South Street (1869), University Place (1889), and North Indianapolis (1906). First Baptist has also sponsored since 1968 a special mission to provide children with athletic opportunities within a Christian atmosphere. The program currently has nearly 2,000 participants.

JOAN CUNNINGHAM

Fishback, William Pinckney (Nov. 11, 1831–Jan. 15, 1901).

Attorney and businessman. A native of Batavia, Ohio, Fishback was educated at Miami University (Ohio) and Farmers College in Cincinnati. Graduating from the latter institution in 1852, Fishback studied law with his father and was admitted to the bar at 21. In 1857, he moved to Indianapolis and went into partnership with A. H. Conner. In 1858 and again in 1860 Fishback was elected prosecuting attorney of Marion County. In 1861, he was appointed agent for the United States in the payment of pensions, a post that he held for three years. In 1862, he went into practice with BENJAMIN HARRISON, forming the firm of Harrison and Fishback.

Leaving his practice in 1870, Fishback and his cousin, Lewis Hasselman, purchased a controlling interest in the INDIANA JOURNAL. From 1870 to 1872, Fishback served as the paper's editor. Selling their interest in the *Journal* in 1872, Fishback and Hasselman moved to St. Louis where they purchased the *St. Louis Democrat*. Following that paper's failure Fishback returned to Indianapolis and his law practice two years later. In 1877, he was appointed clerk and master of chancery of the United States courts for the district of Indiana. He held this position until his death.

From its founding in 1894 until his death, Fishback served as the first dean of the School of Law at the University of Indianapolis (a different institution than currently bears that name). He was also a member of the faculty. Fishback was author of several books including *A Plea for Honest Elections* (1886), urging an end to electoral corruption in the state; *The Lawyer in Literature* (1892); and *Recollections of Lord Coleridge* (1895). He was memorialized by JAMES WHITCOMB RILEY in his poem "William Pinckney Fishback."

TODD MCDORMAN

Jacob Piatt Dunn, *Memorial Record of Distinguished Men of Indianapolis and Indiana* (Chicago, 1912); R. E. Banta, *Indiana Authors and Their Books, 1816–1916* (Crawfordsville, Ind., 1949).

Fisher, Carl Graham (Jan. 12, 1874–July 5, 1939).

Early highway promoter and cofounder of the Indianapolis Motor Speedway. Born in Greensburg, Indiana, this flamboyant entrepreneur never let his poverty-stricken childhood nor his physical handicap (50 percent blindness) stand in his way. Although he quit school at 12 to help support his mother by selling candy on trains, Fisher's flair for promotion and his daredevil personality early brought him wealth and celebrity. At 17 he joined his brothers in a bicycle shop and became a champion bicycle racer and stuntman. Fisher quickly became interested in automobiles, and supposedly bought the first one in Indianapolis. He raced automobiles before and after the turn of the century, in 1904 setting a world's record of 2:02 for two miles on a dirt track. An enthusiastic promoter of the new invention, Fisher opened an automobile showroom at 330 North Illinois Street, a three-story structure built to his specifications about 1902. There he sold and serviced Premiers, which were manufactured in Indianapolis, and Wintons. A few years later Fisher moved his operations to 400 North Capitol Avenue, a building that still stands.

In 1904, along with engine manufacturer JAMES A. ALLISON and inventor P. C. (Fred) Avery, Fisher established the PREST-O-LITE Storage Battery Company, which soon made him a fortune. Using compressed acetylene, the system provided a means to light automobile headlamps. Since the manufacturing facilities were prone to explosions, Prest-O-Lite moved to farmland south of the Crawfordsville Road. The plant was located across from the new motor speedway that Fisher, Allison, and partners ARTHUR NEWBY and FRANK WHEELER built in 1909 for testing automobiles. A balloon race, in which Fisher participated (but did not win), was the first event held at the track. The town of SPEEDWAY, which the partners platted in 1912, grew rapidly on the remaining acreage west of the track and the Prest-O-Lite plant.

Fisher helped to found the HOOSIER MOTOR CLUB in 1902, a group which, among other things, sent out automobiles to scout miles of roads in search of the best routes, with sign erection crews close behind. In the early 1910s the organization joined with Fisher in helping to form the Lincoln Highway Association, which platted and marked the first improved transcontinental road suitable for automobiles. The highway crossed Indiana about 130 miles north of Indianapolis.

In 1909 Fisher married 15–year-old Jane Watt and established her as hostess of Blossom Heath, the estate he created on Cold Spring Road. (It survives in much-altered form today as part of MARIAN COLLEGE.) But at the same time he was trumpeting the Lincoln Highway, the restless Fisher found new challenges in a Florida mangrove swamp out of which he began to carve the resort of Miami Beach. He promoted and developed the Dixie Highway north to south, terminating in Miami Beach where he and Jane built a new mansion. The Fishers kept Blossom Heath for a time, finally selling in 1922.

In 1926 a hurricane destroyed Fisher's Florida development, which had been his security for financing a new summer resort on Long Island, New York. Fisher and Jane divorced; a year later he remarried. His fortune dissipated, Fisher died of a gastric hemorrhage in Miami Beach at age 65.

GLORY-JUNE GREIFF

Fishers. Initially a settlement near an Indian post, in the early 1990s the Hamilton County town of Fishers, which is centered between I–69/S.R. 37 and Allisonville Road northeast of Indianapolis, was the fastest growing area in the metropolitan region. The settlement was named after Salathiel Fisher, an influential resident, in 1872, the same year the Peru and Chicago Railroad located a stop at Fishers Station (or Landing).

In 1893 when the town's population was 250, its homes were clustered around the intersection of Lantern Road and 116th Street. The first substantial housing development occurred in the mid–1950s when several modest ranch-style homes, a few storefront businesses, and a school

were constructed. Still, by 1960 the population was only 344 and the town offered neither sewers nor fire and police protection.

The construction of I–69 brought a building boom to Fishers in the 1970s. In 1972 the three-person town board government annexed 1,400 acres of surrounding land. Housing developments and schools grew up concurrently. The number of residents in 1980 reached 2,000. In the mid–1980s the 3,000–home Sunblest Farms development brought an instant surge in population. The number of local businesses grew from 30 in 1980 to over 250 by 1991, including the 1,300–employee USA GROUP complex located along I–69. Traffic congestion and concerns over future development increased.

In the early 1990s the town board added two additional members and appointed a steering committee to define town needs, problems, and future expansion. They hired a national consulting firm to create a plan to retain Fishers' small-town atmosphere, while encouraging controlled growth.

In 1993 the town continues to grow through annexation and development. Residents' median income is $52,100, and typical home prices range from $90,000 to $250,000. Increasing by 50 percent since the 1990 census, Fishers' predominately white population stands at nearly 13,000 in 1993.

CONNIE J. ZEIGLER

Fitton and George. Architects. In 1917 architect and "real estate packager" Lawrence George formed a partnership with architect-contractor Harry R. Fitton. By this time George had already designed several northside homes, and Fitton's Builder's Realty firm had constructed a number of residences on North Delaware Street.

The firm Fitton and George was responsible for two of the city's finest early 20th century apartment buildings. In 1917 the team designed, constructed, and temporarily managed the Delaware Court apartments at 1000–1015 North Delaware Street (National Register of Historic Places, 1983). Their short partnership also produced The Balmoral Court at 3055 North Meridian Street (ca. 1920). With keystone-topped windows, dormers, and entrances facing a center courtyard, The Balmoral was the first Georgian Revival–style apartment complex in the city.

In 1921 Fitton and George dissolved their firm. Forming new partnerships, the two men continued to design and construct Indianapolis buildings. The new firm Mothershead and Fitton specialized in industrial buildings. George and MacLucas's work included the Seville apartments (National Register of Historic Places, 1987) and the northside homes of Sol Meyer and two other officers of the Meyer-Kiser bank, which had been the primary financial backer of The Balmoral Court.

CONNIE J. ZEIGLER

Indianapolis Historic Preservation Commission file "George MacLucas and Fitton."

500 Festival. Newspaper editorials and civic leaders began advocating a festival to celebrate the INDIANAPOLIS 500–MILE RACE soon after its inaugural running in 1911, but the first 500 Festival did not occur until 1957. In February of that year a group of civic leaders led by Howard S. Wilcox and backed by the mayor, the CHAMBER OF COMMERCE, and the Merchants Association formed 500 Festival Associates, Inc. to promote downtown Indianapolis and provide entertainment for visiting race fans. The organization has planned and financed the festival for the past 36 years.

Festivities surrounding the Indianapolis 500-Mile Race include a large downtown parade, seen here in 1992. [Indianapolis Motor Speedway. Photo by Mike Young]

The first festival, planned in just 60 days, included a parade, a square dance on MONUMENT CIRCLE, an invitational ball, and a Memorial Day service. Two hundred volunteers helped organize the events. The festival added a Mayor's Breakfast and Governor's Reception for visiting dignitaries in 1958 and began selecting a 500 Festival Queen in 1959. In 1960 the Professional Golfers Association sponsored the first 500 Festival Open. The $50,000 purse, the third largest of any tournament at the time, brought the world's best professional and amateur golfers to SPEEDWAY. Despite the presence of famous names like Arnold Palmer and Gary Player, the tournament lost money every year and was discontinued after 1968. Other events that were formerly part of the festival included a gin rummy tournament, a baton twirling contest, UNITED STATES AUTO CLUB sprint and midget car races, American Motorcycle Association championship motorcycle races, and a hot air balloon race.

The parade has always been the highlight of the month-long festival. Planned by the Indianapolis Chamber of Commerce, the Downtown Merchants Association, Convention and Visitors Association, Murat Temple of the Mystic Shrine, and the 33–member board of 500 Festival Associates, the first parade had more than 2,000 participants, was more than two miles long, and was seen by more than 200,000 spectators. It is now the second largest parade in the country, and planning for the next year's events begins as soon as the prior year is complete. The parade has been nationally televised since 1967, and in 1992 the Festival Parade was seen by 30 million viewers in the United States, Canada, and South America.

Josephine Hauck was executive director of 500 Festival Associates from 1962 through 1992. Under her direction the festival grew into a month-long celebration including nine separate events. Two thousand corporations sponsor the festival and 1,600 people have individual memberships in 500 Festival Associates. Over 5,000 volunteers help organize and run events. The 500 Festival Associates' board of directors elects a new president each year, and he or she determines a theme that will inspire and unite the various events. For the past ten years the annual theme has inspired and united the Festival Queen's Coronation Dinner, the Mayor's Breakfast, the Festival of the Arts Exhibition, Kid's Day, the Mechanics Banquet, the Indy Mini-Marathon, Memorial Services, the 500 Festival Parade, and the Victory Dinner. An estimated 260,000 attend 500 Festival events each May. The festival generates over $1 million in revenues annually which 500 Festival Associates, a nonprofit organization, uses to finance the next year's activities. The organization will also plan an annual 400 Festival to celebrate the Brickyard 400 NASCAR race beginning in August, 1994.

GRETA SHANKLE
WILLIAM DALTON

Five Points. An early settlement in Franklin Township, so called for its location at the intersection of Southeastern Avenue (formerly Michigan Road, S.R. 29, and U.S. 421), Troy Avenue, and Five Points Road.

In the 1820s and 1830s Belles' Tavern was located just east of the intersection. With the building of the MICHIGAN ROAD, Major John Belles' log house, eight miles southeast of Indianapolis, became a station for changing horses. A few years later Belles built a large log house with guest quarters.

In 1881 the H. A. Waterman Company, one of Marion County's oldest businesses, was established. Henry A. Waterman was an apprentice blacksmith in New Palestine before he opened his own shop. In 1914 he enlarged his original 20 by 50 foot building to include a garage, and added a hardware department and a truck and machinery repair building. The business, later run by his four sons and daughter, added farm tractors and machinery and lawn and garden equipment.

The Marion County Fairgrounds is north of Five Points. Nearby are Nativity Catholic Church and St. John Lutheran Church.

SYLVIA C. HENRICKS
Franklin Township Historical Society

Berry R. Sulgrove, *History of Indianapolis and Marion County* (Philadelphia, 1884); *History of New Bethel/Wanamaker* ([Indianapolis]: Franklin Township Historical Society, 1984).

Flanner, Francis William (Frank) (Dec. 5, 1854–Feb. 17, 1912). Indianapolis mortician. Flanner was born in the Quaker village of Mount Pleasant, Jefferson County, Ohio. At the age of nine he moved with his family to Indianapolis, where he attended the public elementary schools and SHORTRIDGE HIGH SCHOOL. In 1881 Flanner engaged in the undertaking business. In 1886–1887 he and Charles J. Buchanan established the firm of FLANNER AND BUCHANAN funeral directors. The original headquarters of the crematory and the business were located at 172 North Illinois, later moving to the 300 block of that street. When Flanner engaged in the funeral business in 1881 his firm had the only crematory in the state.

Aside from his funeral business, Flanner was involved with many community organizations. He was especially interested in the development of the public park system of Indianapolis, and was actively identified with the Civic League, the Indianapolis Art School, the Taxpayers' League, the May Music Festival Association, and the COMMERCIAL CLUB. Flanner was also active in several charitable enterprises. He assisted, for example, in securing the enactment of the original law permitting the establishment of boards of guardians for the various benevolent, charitable, and penal institutions of the state. He also supported the CHARITY ORGANIZATION SOCIETY.

The year 1903 brought the incorporation of Flanner Guild, an organization that worked for the settlement and education among the African-American population of the city. In 1912 it was renamed FLANNER HOUSE. This service center expressly for blacks began with Flanner's gift of a small property on Rhode Island (later Colton) Street. At his death by suicide in 1912, the trustees of Flanner House were fortunate to gain the support of the Christian Women's Board of Missions. That group in 1918 bought four buildings at West and St. Clair streets and remodeled and equipped them for the use of the institution. Flanner is buried in CROWN HILL CEMETERY.

AIMEE L. REX

Jacob Piatt Dunn, *Greater Indianapolis* (Chicago, 1910); Hester Anne Hale, *Indianapolis: The First Century* (Indianapolis, 1987).

Flanner, Janet Tyler "Genet" (Mar. 13, 1892–Nov. 7, 1978). Foreign correspondent and essayist. Janet Flanner was the second child of Mary Hockett Flanner and FRANCIS (FRANK) FLANNER. The parents were active in the business, civic, and cultural life of Indianapolis: Mary as a poet, playwright, actress, and platform reader, Frank as a founder and partner of FLANNER AND BUCHANAN MORTUARIES and a benefactor of the settlement house that bears his name.

Flanner's education started in the public schools, but at age 11 she transferred to Tudor Hall where she was undistinguished academically but a popular member of the class of 1909. After high school, Flanner joined her family in a year-long visit to Germany. Soon after the family returned to Indianapolis, Frank Flanner committed suicide.

After less than two years at the University of Chicago and a brief stint in Philadelphia working at a girls' reformatory, Flanner returned to Indianapolis and was hired by Frank Tarkington Baker, the drama editor of the INDIANAPOLIS STAR, to review vaudeville and burlesque shows. That job soon led to a promotion to assistant drama editor and a column, "Impressions in the Field of Art." (During some of this period Flanner used the name "Jeannette.")

In April, 1918, Flanner married and immediately left for New York, but she was back in Indianapolis a month later writing "Comments on the Screen" for the *Star*. Within months Flanner was back in New York and never returned to Indianapolis except for brief visits.

In New York Flanner was on the edges of artistic and literary groups and earned some distinction as a wit; however, it was not until she moved to Paris (1922) and accepted an assignment for *The New Yorker* (1925) that she began to find her niche in American literature. Her marriage ended during this period.

Harold Ross, editor of *The New Yorker*, asked Flanner to write a semimonthly "Letter from Paris" in which Flanner would describe what the French thought was happening. Since Flanner was part of the "Lost Generation" group of authors who gathered in Paris' Left Bank literary colony and the Parisian artistic scene, she was a natural for this assignment. For the next 50 years, often

using the pseudonym "Genet," Flanner wrote "Letters," "Profiles," and "Reporter at Large" pieces for *The New Yorker*. Her writing style was lean but descriptive, and personal comments were omitted. During World War II Flanner spent some time in New York, but she returned to Europe with the U.S. Army in 1944. She remained in Paris until her retirement in 1975, when she moved to New York.

Flanner wrote one novel, *The Cubical City*, published in 1926. Other books by Flanner were *An American in Paris* (1940); *Petain: the Old Man of France* (1944); *Men and Monuments* (1957); *Paris Journals, 1944–1965* (1965; winner of the National Book Award for Arts and Letters in 1966); *Paris Journals, 1965–1971* (1971); *Paris Was Yesterday, 1925–1939* (1972); *London Was Yesterday, 1934–1939* (1975); and *Janet Flanner's World: Uncollected Writings 1932–1975*.

Flanner was honored by the Indiana Arts Commission in 1975. She received an honorary Doctor of Literature degree from Smith College and was awarded the French Legion of Honor.

CATHERINE GIBSON
Indianapolis–Marion County Public Library

Brenda Wineapple, *Genet: A Biography of Janet Flanner* (New York, 1989).

Flanner and Buchanan Mortuary. Indianapolis-based mortuary and crematorium. Early in 1881, using $500 borrowed from his mother, FRANCIS W. (FRANK) FLANNER opened a funeral parlor at 172 North Illinois Street in partnership with city hack driver John Hommown. Flanner, who had trained with local undertaker David Kregelo, probably offered the first embalming services in Indianapolis. In 1884, the partners sold one-third interest in the business to Peter Wright, who resold his interest to Flanner. Charles J. Buchanan, Flanner's brother-in-law, purchased the Hommown interest in 1887 and the firm became Flanner and Buchanan.

By 1893, the business acquired the Kingan residence at 320 North Illinois and remodeled it as a mortuary. In 1909, Flanner and Buchanan purchased the first motorized ambulance in the city. Upon incorporating in 1911, the firm razed its old mortuary and constructed a new building containing the city's first crematorium and columbarium (vaults for urns). When Flanner died in 1912, Buchanan became president of the organization. The Buchanan family continues to own and operate the business.

Flanner and Buchanan moved to 25 West Fall Creek Parkway in February, 1927, where its business offices are still located. The structure, designed by FERMOR S. CANNON, included a study for clergy, crematory, crypts, chapels, and pipe organ. Over the last 40 years Flanner and Buchanan has expanded its operation throughout suburban Indianapolis, opening its first branch in Broad Ripple (1953) and adding others in Lawrence (1973), Carmel (1983), and far east Indianapolis (1990). Flanner and Buchanan also has acquired existing mortuaries, including Zionsville's Phillippi Mortuary (1955) and Farley Funeral Homes (1967).

SHERYL D. VANDERSTEL

History of Flanner and Buchanan (Indianapolis: Flanner and Buchanan, n.d.); *Indianapolis Star*, Dec. 31, 1947; *Indianapolis News*, Mar. 15, 1961.

Flanner House. African-American social service agency. Flanner House, originally a black branch of a white settlement house organized by the CHARITY ORGANIZATION SOCIETY of Indianapolis, began in a cottage that FRANK FLANNER donated for the use of black children in 1898. Meager funding limited most early programs to self-help efforts featuring lectures and classes by local volunteers. Successful activities included an employment agency that placed female domestics and a day nursery.

In 1911 the Christian Women's Board of Missions took over the funding and administration of Flanner House. They kept the name and moved the institution to 802–814 North West Street in 1918. Under Charles O. Lee's active direction, the new settlement facilities soon housed a branch tuberculosis clinic and other health programs. A larger budget, increasingly from the Indianapolis Community Chest, allowed Flanner House to increase its efforts to train and employ domestics and provide other self-help classes.

In 1936 Flanner House hired CLEO BLACKBURN as director. By 1944 he had built a new headquarters at 333 West 16th Street to house a cannery, workshop, and health center, reorganized the staff into five divisions, and greatly increased the budget. Flanner House continued to hold a variety of social service classes, group meetings, employment services, vocational training, health services, and a day nursery. New self-help activities included cannery use, family gardening, cooperative ventures, work camps, and a furniture and home-building program.

The success of the cooperatively built Flanner House homes in the 1950s and 1960s gave the settlement national recognition. As a result, Blackburn organized the Board for Fundamental Education as a social service think-tank to devise similar programs that could be tested at Flanner House and implemented nationally. Congress chartered this group in 1954, and it subsequently implemented many job training and educational programs.

In 1967 Flanner House moved to 2110 North Illinois, leaving behind the health center and the canning facilities. After Blackburn's 1975 resignation, the institution moved to its present location at 2424 Dr. Martin Luther King, Jr. Street in 1979, scaled programming back down to the community level, and joined with the consolidated Community Centers of Indianapolis (CCI) in 1987. Today, Flanner House is a multiservice center that administers federal and state welfare programs, houses a branch library, and conducts its own senior citizen, youth, and daycare programs.

MICHELLE D. HALE

Ruth Hutchinson Crocker, *Social Work and Social Order* (Urbana and Chicago, 1992), ch. 3; Michelle Hale, "Self-Help Moves from the Neighborhood to the Nation: Flanner House, 1936–1953," *Black History News & Notes*, No. 46 (Nov., 1991).

Fletcher, Calvin (Feb. 4, 1798–May 26, 1866). Early settler, lawyer, banker, civic leader, and diarist. Born in Ludlow, Vermont, the 11th of 15 children, Fletcher attended local academies before moving to Urbana, Ohio, where he taught school to support his study of law. After residing

Calvin Fletcher, with his wife, Sarah.
[Indiana Historical Society, #C5891,
Courtesy Bradford F. Hodges]

briefly in Lynchburg, Virginia (1820), he returned to Urbana where he was licensed to practice law in January, 1821. Seeing few opportunities locally, he married and in October, 1821, moved to Indianapolis.

Fletcher's law career spanned only two decades. He defended those accused in the FALL CREEK MASSACRE (1824–1825) and represented an African-American woman who sued for her freedom (1829). Joined by OVID BUTLER in 1835 and Simon Yandes in 1839 Fletcher handled civil and criminal cases, although the collection business proved especially profitable. Fletcher dissolved the partnership in March, 1843, telling his partners that he wished to "finish my days as a husbandman [like] my father."

Local politics also occupied Fletcher's attention. At the formation of county government in April, 1822, he was appointed township overseer of the poor and county prosecuting attorney. He also served as attorney for the fifth judicial circuit (1825–1826). Fletcher's only elected office was that of state senator representing Boone, Hamilton, Hancock, Hendricks, Madison, and Marion counties (1826–1833). An opponent of Jacksonian Democrats, and later a Whig, Fletcher declined an 1836 invitation to run for the U.S. Congress. By the late 1840s he was ardently antislavery and chaired the state's Free Soil committee (1848). By 1855 he was an active Republican.

Fletcher supported economic development in Indianapolis and Indiana. In 1834 the General Assembly elected him as one of the founding directors of the STATE BANK OF INDIANA. His association included serving as sinking fund commissioner (1834–1841), director of the Indianapolis branch of the State Bank (1841–1844), and branch president (1843–1858). In 1857 Fletcher founded the Indianapolis Branch Banking Company with Thomas Sharpe and acquired banking interests in Madison, Indiana. He also promoted canal and railroad construction and in 1855 was appointed director and president of the Indianapolis and Bellefontaine Railroad.

Numerous benevolent, reform, and cultural organizations benefited from Fletcher's involvement. He was a founder of both the Indiana Colonization Society (1829) and the INDIANA HISTORICAL SOCIETY (1830), and was active in the Indiana Temperance Society, INDIANAPOLIS BENEVOLENT SOCIETY, and Irish relief effort of the 1840s. A friend of Sabbath schools, Fletcher was for 10 years school superintendent for Roberts Chapel. Denominationalism proved no concern for him as he contributed to numerous church treasuries and building funds. Regretting his limited schooling, Fletcher was also an active supporter of free education. He served on the board of superintendents for Indianapolis schools and as a school trustee (1851–1858), and as trustee of the Marion County Seminary and the Indiana Female College (1850).

Arriving in Indianapolis almost penniless, Fletcher soon began investing in land. Between 1826 and 1830 he acquired 450 acres northeast of town, which became one of many farms that he owned in Marion County. As his holdings grew so did his interest in farming. He was elected the first treasurer of the Marion County Agricultural Society (1835) and helped form the Indiana State Horticultural Society (1840). In his later years Fletcher wrote extensively about agriculture, breeding, and raising livestock. By the 1860s he was among the largest landowners in Marion County, with property in 1861–1862 assessed at $137,155.

Apart from his role in early Indianapolis Fletcher is best known for his diary, which he started before leaving Vermont and which extends to May 13, 1866, only days before his death. His wife Sarah also kept a journal, although her life as mother of 11 prevented her from the extensive writings of her spouse. Fletcher left all of his and

Sarah's diaries and personal papers to their family, stipulating that they be given to the Indiana Historical Society. Fletcher is buried at CROWN HILL CEMETERY.

SHERYL D. VANDERSTEL

Indianapolis Journal, May 28, 1866; *Diary of Calvin Fletcher*, 9 vols. (Indianapolis, 1972–1983).

Fletcher, Stoughton A., II (Nov. 24, 1879–Oct. 8, 1957). Banker, businessman. Grandson of bank founder STOUGHTON A. FLETCHER, SR., and a native of Indianapolis, Fletcher attended local public schools and graduated from Princeton University. He became assistant cashier (1898) in the Fletcher National Bank, directed by his father Stoughton J., before becoming vice-president and later succeeding his father as president in 1907. On September 3, 1910, the bank merged with American National Bank, and Fletcher became president of the new Fletcher American National Bank. On May 19, 1923, however, he resigned "to discharge [his] liability to personal creditors."

Over the years Fletcher was involved in numerous business transactions, including one which resulted in the loss of his personal fortune. In 1912 he was instrumental in merging the Marion Trust Company (1895) and the German American Trust Company (1906) into the Fletcher Savings and Trust Company. He attempted unsuccessfully to corner the sugar market during World War I. Fletcher also invested in Remy Electric Company and the American Creosoting Company, which he later relinquished, and pledged his personal resources to organize the Midwest Engine Company (a merger of the Hill Pump Company of Anderson and Lyons-Atlas Engine Company of Indianapolis) in 1918. The armistice, however, resulted in the cancellation of government contracts to manufacture turbine engines, leading to the company's demise and the forced sale of its assets in July, 1922. Two years later Fletcher filed for bankruptcy. He subsequently lost his 40,000-square-foot, 32-bedroom mansion, Laurel Hall (built ca. 1911–1912), having pledged it to finance his industrial operations.

(Since 1986 the former Fletcher mansion has served as the home of the HUDSON INSTITUTE.)

Following his 1923 resignation Fletcher served as a financial consultant but led a life of relative obscurity, spending the last four years of his life in Saranac Lake, New York. Fletcher is buried in CROWN HILL CEMETERY.

SHERYL D. VANDERSTEL

Paul D. Brown, ed., *Indianapolis Men of Affairs* (Indianapolis, 1923); *Indianapolis News*, May 19, 1923; *Indianapolis Star*, Oct. 10, 1957.

Fletcher, Stoughton A., Sr. (Aug. 22, 1808–Mar. 17, 1882). Banker. The youngest of 15 children, Fletcher remained on the family farm in Ludlow, Vermont, until his father's death in February, 1831, and later joined his brother Calvin who had moved to Indianapolis ten years earlier. By February, 1833, Fletcher operated a general store with Henry Bradley on Washington Street east of Meridian Street. Purchasing Bradley's portion in 1837, Fletcher resumed business with cousin Timothy Richardson Fletcher, son of Michael Fletcher, another of Calvin's brothers who moved to Indianapolis.

Possessing an interest in banking, Fletcher became a director of the Indianapolis branch of the STATE BANK OF INDIANA in 1839. With cousin Timothy he opened a broker's office and private bank at 8 East Washington Street in 1840, later known as S. A. Fletcher & Co. The bank flourished and remained Fletcher's principal occupation until his death. A private bank until 1898, it then became Fletcher National Bank. In October, 1864, Fletcher convinced brother Calvin and Thomas H. Sharpe of the Indianapolis Branch Banking Company (founded 1857) to join in organizing the Indianapolis National Bank, located at Washington and Pennsylvania streets, with Stoughton and Calvin among the directors, and Calvin's son Stoughton A. as president. The bank was capitalized at $1 million.

Known to have amassed large fortunes and estates in Marion County, Fletcher was considered among the wealthiest individuals in Indianapolis as well as Indiana. In 1853 he acquired substantial stock in the Indianapolis Gas Light and Coke

Company (predecessor to Citizens Gas), and also in the Indianapolis and Bellefontaine Railroad, for which he was elected a director in 1855. Fletcher's Center Township property was assessed in November, 1862, at $107,244—fourth highest in the township; properties in other townships were valued at $25,580.

Despite his vast wealth and influence Fletcher never held public office and his benevolence was questionable. He did, however, advance $51,500 in 1863 to acquire Martin Williams' farm for the creation of CROWN HILL CEMETERY. That same year, responding to Mayor JOHN CAVEN's call for a house of refuge for prostitutes who were flocking into the city during the Civil War, Fletcher provided seven acres of land south of Indianapolis on which to build a women's reformatory. The war halted construction in 1864 and the city proposed donating the land to the Catholic church for a women's refuge, which elicited harsh anti-Catholic protests. The city eventually gave the land in 1873 to a Catholic sisterhood, which established the House of the Good Shepherd female reformatory.

Fletcher was a member of SECOND PRESBYTERIAN CHURCH and is buried in Crown Hill Cemetery.

SHERYL D. VANDERSTEL

Diary of Calvin Fletcher (9 vols., Indianapolis, 1972–1983); Indianapolis Journal, Mar. 18, 1882; Berry R. Sulgrove, History of Indianapolis and Marion County, Indiana (Philadelphia, 1884).

Fletcher, William Baldwin (Aug. 18, 1837–Apr. 25, 1907). Physician, educator, and state senator. Fletcher, the son of pioneer Indianapolis lawyer CALVIN FLETCHER, was born in the capital city. In 1859, he graduated from the College of Physicians and Surgeons in New York City and two years later, after returning to Indianapolis, he enlisted in the Union army. During his first year of service he was captured, placed in solitary confinement, wounded during the second of two escape attempts, and ordered to be executed. General Robert E. Lee granted Fletcher a reprieve pending further investigation, but before the investigation could take place, the Confederates lost

his paperwork. No longer aware that he was considered a special prisoner, they paroled him. In 1862, he returned to Indianapolis and married.

In 1866–1867, Fletcher studied at many of the famous hospitals in Europe. Upon his return to Indianapolis, he became a professor at the Indiana Medical College and the Central College of Physicians and Surgeons. He established the Indianapolis City Dispensary in 1870.

In 1882, the citizens of Marion County elected Fletcher as their state senator. The following year he became superintendent of the Indiana Hospital for the Insane. In addition to hiring the hospital's first female physician, Fletcher abolished the use of mechanical restraints for patients, abandoned secret burials, and instituted dental care for patients. He lost his position in 1887 after calling attention to political abuses in the state hospital system.

In 1888, Fletcher opened a private sanatorium, Neuronhurst, for the treatment of mentally ill women. He immediately employed MARY A. SPINK, M.D., who later became superintendent of the institution. Neuronhurst, also called Fletcher Sanatorium, offered patients exercise, daily therapeutic baths, and individual care.

CHARLES O. HAZELRIGG, D.D.S.

Indiana Medical History Quarterly, 7 (Sept., 1981).

Fletcher Place. Southeastside historic district bounded by East Street, I–65/70, the Conrail tracks, and Virginia Avenue. Fletcher Place took its name from one of its first residents, CALVIN FLETCHER, SR. In 1839, he and his family moved to Wood Lawn, a farm at the edge of the city. In 1853–1854 he sold half of the farm to a group of Ohio businessmen, with his son STOUGHTON A. FLETCHER, SR. serving as the sale agent. The remainder of the farm was sold and platted shortly after Calvin moved in 1855. By 1872 the subdivision was known as Fletcher Place.

Many of the first residents were Irish and German immigrants who built worker cottages along the north-south streets. By the 1860s, businessmen were constructing large, comfortable homes on the east-west street, Fletcher Avenue. Andrew Wallace, a successful wholesale grocer, hired noted architect FRANCIS COSTIGAN to design his home at 601 Fletcher Avenue. Later in the 19th century, immigrants arrived from Central Europe and Italy. They purchased existing homes and built additional cottages. Architectural styles in the neighborhood range from Italianate, Federal, and Gothic Revival to Queen Anne and Eastlake–Stick Style.

Fletcher Place was not exclusively residential. A commercial district developed along Virginia Avenue linking Fletcher Place with the MILE SQUARE to the north and FOUNTAIN SQUARE to the south. Retail and commercial establishments and apartments were built on the avenue, which got an added boost when the Virginia Avenue Viaduct was completed in 1888.

Fletcher Avenue Methodist Episcopal Church, an area landmark, was erected 1872–1880 on the site of the old Fletcher home. SECOND BAPTIST CHURCH and Sixth Christian Church were located nearby, as was Calvin Fletcher School 8, built in 1857. Once one of the preeminent southside churches, the Methodist church still stands, now serving as the Fletcher Place Community Center. As an integral part of the neighborhood, the center has offered educational programs and community services for a number of years. GOODWILL INDUSTRIES of Indianapolis was an outgrowth of these programs during the Great Depression.

Like nearby areas, Fletcher Place declined when residents moved to new suburbs. Then industrial encroachment and construction of Interstates 65 and 70 took land and houses in the area. The founding of a neighborhood organization in 1977 marked the revival of Fletcher Place. Community leaders worked to encourage preservation and protect the integrity of the neighborhood. In 1982, Fletcher Place was listed on the National Register of Historic Places and continues to undergo restoration by residents.

CATHLEEN F. DONNELLY

Flooding and Flood Control. Because flood-producing precipitation is highly variable, floods may occur on a section of a single stream, or on many streams over a large geographic area. Although flooding can occur at any time, major floods on the WHITE RIVER primarily occur in winter and early spring as the result of heavy rains and/or snowmelt over large areas. Flood conditions along the White River in Indianapolis may continue for several days. Floods on other streams and drainageways typically result from localized thunderstorms during the summer and fall. These "flash floods" rise and subside quickly, sometimes within a few hours.

Flooding in Indianapolis has been aggravated by activities associated with urbanization. The presence of buildings, roadways, and other relatively impervious surfaces decreases the holding capacity of underlying soil and increases storm runoff. Drainage of upland areas also increases runoff, which is rapidly delivered to drainageways through networks of ditches, culverts, drains, and other artificial channels. The dredging, clearing, widening, and straightening of natural waterways and the construction of levees and floodwalls further increase drainage efficiency, but may intensify flooding in downtown areas.

The development of floodplains also increases potential flood hazards. Riverfront areas that once were sparsely populated or used only as summer resorts now are fully developed for year-round residences and businesses. Any construction, filling, or dumping within the floodplain that reduces its cross-sectional area can obstruct flood flow, especially where high embankments impede overbank flows and where bridge openings are much smaller than the normal channel area.

In early Indianapolis floods were of little concern because there was virtually no riverfront development. But as floodplains were converted to agricultural, commercial, industrial, and residential uses, the economic and social losses from floods increased. The adverse impacts of floods include property damage, erosion and deposition of sediments, sewer and drainage backwaters, crop losses, and occasionally the loss of human lives. Indirect damage includes the interruption of business, transportation, and commerce, and the associated loss of receipts and wages.

The most disastrous flood in Indiana history swept the state in March, 1913. It was part of a regional flood disaster that devastated much of the Midwest and Ohio River valley, particularly Ohio and the central two thirds of Indiana. Six

A West Indianapolis streetcar stranded during the March, 1913, flood.
[Indiana Historical Society, #C3275]

inches of rainfall drenched Indianapolis over a five-day period that began Easter Sunday, March 23, 1913. Five-day rainfall amounts north of Indianapolis totaled up to 12 inches. Because the ground was already saturated from previous rains, the excess water quickly made its way to creeks and rivers.

The flood's crest on White River near downtown Indianapolis was estimated at 31.5 feet, or 19.5 feet above flood stage; its exact height is unknown because the gauge washed away when the river reached 29.5 feet. The estimated peak discharge was 70,000 cubic feet per second (cfs), or 50 times greater than the average discharge of 1,398 cfs. (The second highest discharge of record on the White River at Morris Street was 37,200 cfs, which occurred during the May, 1943, flood.) At the height of the 1913 flood, earthen levees along White River, FALL CREEK, Eagle Creek, and Little Eagle Creek failed, sending torrents of water rushing through the city, especially the area formerly known as WEST INDIANAPOLIS (roughly bounded by West Washington Street, White River Parkway, Raymond Street, and Belmont Avenue). Nearly all bridges, including the West Washington Street bridge, were washed away or irreparably damaged. The city's public water supply was shut down for nearly four days, and normal transportation ceased in the flooded areas. Some areas in West Indianapolis were under 30 feet of water, and only the roofs of two-story houses were visible above the floodwaters.

In Indianapolis about 7,000 families lost their homes, and as many as 25 deaths were reported but unconfirmed. Statewide the flood claimed 200 lives and left 200,000 homeless. A massive relief effort organized at both the local and state levels continued throughout the year as cities and residents rebuilt. In the capital a General Relief Committee for Flood Sufferers operated for several months to assist those left in need with food, fuel, clothing, and temporary housing.

After the 1913 flood, the City of Indianapolis and later the federal Works Progress Administration began implementing a comprehensive flood protection plan. The long-range plan included the construction of earth levees, concrete floodwalls, and associated facilities such as pumping stations and detention basins. The plan also included channel work such as dredging and straightening, bridge reconstruction, channel relocation, and utility alterations.

From the 1920s through the 1960s extensive flood protection projects and associated structures were completed along segments of the White River, Fall Creek, and Eagle Creek. Additional projects were conducted along Little Eagle Creek, POGUE'S RUN, Pleasant Run, and other tributaries. Most large-scale projects were coordinated by the Indianapolis Flood Control District, a predecessor of the present-day DEPARTMENT OF PUBLIC WORKS. The Works Progress Administration and the U.S. Army Corps of Engineers participated in several major projects, and the Indiana Flood Control and Water Resources Commission provided regulatory oversight and some financial assistance.

The construction of Eagle Creek Reservoir greatly reduced flooding on lower Eagle Creek by storing incoming floodwaters and slowly releasing excess flows. GEIST RESERVOIR in northeastern Indianapolis and Morse Reservoir in Hamilton County were designed primarily for water supply purposes, but can have some flood control benefits.

Channel modifications are notable along several streams. The major portion of flood flows from Dry Run on the city's west side are diverted to Little Eagle Creek through Dry Run Diversion Ditch, which helps relieve flooding near the INDIANAPOLIS MOTOR SPEEDWAY. On the north side of

Indianapolis about 35 percent of the flood flows on White River near Williams Creek are diverted through the Williams Creek Cutoff. In the downtown area the lower 2.2 miles of Pogue's Run are enclosed in an underground box culvert that carries runoff from low-intensity storms to its outlet at the White River near Kentucky Avenue. However, the culvert cannot carry peak flows from high-intensity storms, and floodwaters overflow at the culvert entrance.

In recent decades many channel improvements, realignments, and bridge modifications have been completed as part of highway and interstate construction programs, although these projects generally affect only short segments of the city's watercourses. Since the 1960s most flood protection projects have focused on correcting drainage and flooding problems along selected reaches of tributary creeks.

In addition to structural measures, city and state agencies also use nonstructural means to alleviate flooding. The Indianapolis Flood Control District's countywide zoning ordinance gives the Department of Public Works the authority to regulate any development within the identified floodplains of Indianapolis. Because the city participates in the National Flood Insurance Program (NFIP), this ordinance contains not only local building requirements but also all state and federal requirements. Through NFIP, residents of Indianapolis are eligible to purchase federal flood insurance.

CYNTHIA J. CLENDENON
Indiana Department of
Environmental Management

Federal Emergency Management Agency, *Flood insurance study, City of Indianapolis, Marion County*, 2 vols. (rev. ed. 1988); Thomas H. Russell, *Swept by Mighty Waters—The Great Tornado, Flood and Fire* (Chicago, 1913); Snell Environmental Group, *Marion County flood control works study*, 2 vols. (1990, prepared for Indianapolis Department of Public Works); *The Indianapolis Flood, March 25, 1913: The Report of the Indianapolis General Relief Committee for Flood Sufferers* (Indianapolis, 1913).

Flora and Fauna. The biological landscape of Indianapolis is a product of both postglacial climatic change and human activity, set in the varied terrain left by the last ice sheet. Although plant and animal patterns may seem static at human time scales, they have been and still are changing in response to changes in natural and human environment.

The history of the present landscape began less than 20,000 years ago, with retreat of the Wisconsin ice sheet from its terminus just south of present-day Indianapolis. Fossil pollen from midwestern lakes and bogs suggests that tundra, spruce woodland, and spruce forest invaded rapidly in the glacier's wake. These plant communities apparently supported diverse assemblages of large mammals, including northern species such as white-tailed deer; and species now extinct, such as mastodon and giant beaver.

By 10,000 years ago conifers were being replaced by many of the broadleaved trees of the present deciduous forest, including oaks, hickories, elms, ashes, and maples. The deciduous forest did not arrive as a unit, as once thought, but species by species from various directions. For example, the sugar maple may have reached central Indiana from the south by about 10,000 years ago, but beech arrived from the east some 4,000 years later. Thus, the beech-maple forests of central Indiana are not more than a few thousand years old, and some scientists have argued that they are still changing in response to postglacial climate change. The accompanying animal migrations are less well documented, but most evidence suggests that mammal communities have become less diverse since early postglacial time. This decline was due partly to emigration of species still extant elsewhere, such as the caribou, but many large mammals (including the mastodon and giant beaver) became entirely extinct around 10,000 years ago. Central Indiana animal communities are thus also recent assemblages.

People arrived early in this story, but little is known about their effects on biological patterns in prehistory. Some paleontologists believe that early hunters caused the large mammal extinctions just mentioned, though others attribute their demise to natural climate change. NATIVE AMERICANS are known to have set fires in some midwestern forests, but there is little record of human-set fire in central Indiana, perhaps because many forests stayed too wet to burn. It is known that Amerindian agricultural groups introduced crops (maize, beans, squash, Indian tobacco) and weeds (annual sunflower) from tropical America and western North America, and that they cleared patches of bottomland forest around villages for cropland. When the first whites arrived, one Delaware town at the southern edge of Marion County reportedly was cultivating fields on the WHITE RIVER floodplain. Such clearings, however, were a minor part of the total landscape, and the introduced crops and weeds may have remained closely confined to village sites.

White settlers thus entered a landscape that, while not pristine, was still almost entirely forested. The 1819 General Land Office survey, which provides a systematic sample of Marion County vegetation just before settlement, shows forest broken only by scattered brushy openings, streams, and swamps. There were apparently no prairies, though open wetlands such as BACON'S SWAMP contained some wet-prairie plants.

Upland forests were predominantly beech-maple communities: more than half of all trees in the 1819 survey were American beech or sugar maple. Many other species were present, including white and green ashes, Ohio buckeye, black walnut, American and slippery elms, shagbark and bitternut hickories, and several oaks. Black cherry, sassafras, and other fast-growing trees of forest openings were uncommon, judging from their rarity in the survey.

Forest composition varied with local topography. The 1819 witness-tree patterns and remaining forest stands in and around Marion County suggest that swamp white oak, bur oak, hackberry, and other wet-site trees were important around seasonally flooded upland depressions. White oak, chinquapin oak, and the hickories were prominent on dry hills and ridges, such as those west of EAGLE CREEK. The floodplain forests of White River and other large streams comprised a distinctive suite of fast-growing, disturbance-tolerant trees: eastern cottonwood, silver maple, black willow, sycamore, and box elder.

The General Land Office survey did not describe animal patterns, but we can infer that the terrestrial animals were mostly forest species. Many of these would have been characteristic of closed forest, including bobcat, timber wolf, black bear, turkey, ruffed grouse, and passenger pigeon. In *A Home in the Woods*, Indianapolis pioneer Oliver Johnson recalls shooting wild turkeys at the edge of the family cornfield and helping tree a bear near the present state fairgrounds. There would also have been species characteristic of forest edges and openings, such as opossum, fox squirrel, rabbit, and goldfinch. Rivers and other wetlands provided habitat for waterfowl, turtles, muskrat, beaver, and other wetland species.

Biological patterns may not have been in equilibrium when whites arrived, but white settlement dramatically increased the pace and scope of biological change. The most drastic change was forest clearing. Historical surveys indicate that forest cover was reduced to about 40 percent of Marion County by 1876, 10 percent by 1952, and perhaps 1 percent by 1986. These surveys underestimate the extent of tree cover (for example, they ignore urban trees), but they confirm the near-complete elimination of the original forest. What remain are mostly scattered farm woodlots around the edge of the county and narrow streamside corridors on land too steep or wet to farm. None of these stands has escaped alteration by logging, grazing, Dutch elm disease (introduced from Europe in the 1930s), or other human influences. Most woodlots are dense young secondary forest with at most only scattered old trees, and their composition has changed with cutting of oak and black walnut and increases in "weed" trees such as hawthorn, black locust, and redbud. The best remaining examples of what presettlement forests might have looked like are found in small stands at FORT BENJAMIN HARRISON and in four small nature preserves: Eagle's Crest, Spring Pond, Marott Park, and WOOLLEN'S GARDEN.

Settlers soon eliminated most of the large mammals native to Marion County, including the timber wolf, black bear, bison, bobcat, white-tailed deer, and beaver. Many of these animals were hunted even before settlement and disappeared before 1850. Deer and beaver have been successfully reintroduced, but the large predators have not. Several prominent birds were also eliminated fairly early: the ruffed grouse, turkey, Carolina parakeet, and passenger pigeon. Although hunting is now restricted, some small animals may still be disappearing because of habitat loss.

For example, the continued decline of small migratory songbirds in the Midwest has been linked to fragmentation of the forest into small, isolated islands with little or no deep-forest breeding habitat.

Loss of forests and of wetlands such as Bacon's Swamp has greatly reduced the abundance of many plant species, though few are known to have been entirely eliminated. The most conspicuous local plant extinction is an inconspicuous trailing herb named running buffalo clover, a plant apparently closely associated with bison trails and formerly known from Marion County, but now rare, like the bison, and federally protected.

The presettlement forests have been replaced by fields, pastures, parks, vacant lots, lawns, and gardens. These herbaceous communities are human created and human maintained, prevented from returning to forest by continual expenditure of human energy. They are also ecologically open communities, with dry, sunny microclimates and biological interactions continually disrupted by human disturbance. By all of these measures they are less stable than the forests they replaced.

Alien plants and animals commonly dominate these new communities. Most of our important crop plants and livestock animals, most lawn and forage plants, and probably most ornamentals and weeds are Old World species introduced, intentionally or accidentally, since settlement. Although some remain under human control, many have become naturalized and are now easily mistaken for natives. The starling, house sparrow, honeybee, Queen Anne's lace, and Kentucky bluegrass (native to Europe, not Kentucky) are conspicuous examples from a long list. As botanist Edgar Anderson put it, we are surrounded by "transported landscapes."

Native plants and animals have also moved into all of these communities, but they are mostly species of open, disturbed habitats, not closed forest. Some (chipmunk, opossum, giant ragweed) were probably present in naturally open sites when white settlers arrived; others have invaded since settlement, often from the prairie region to the west (coyote, brown-headed cowbird, windmill grass).

It is not clear how historical invasion and extinction have affected overall biological diversity; plant diversity has likely increased, whereas mammal and bird diversity may have declined. Regardless, this biological turnover has created a more generic biological landscape of widespread weedy species. Homogenization will probably continue as urbanization encroaches on the remaining woodlots and wetlands and agriculture becomes ever more narrowly focused on uniform crops and clean fields. Above all, the biological landscape will continue to change, if not always in directions foreseen.

TIMOTHY S. BROTHERS
Indiana University–Purdue University,
Indianapolis

Marilyn B. Blewett and John E. Potzger, "The Forest Primeval of Marion and Johnson Counties, Indiana, in 1918," *Butler University Botanical Studies*, 10 (1951), 40–52; Indiana Department of Natural Resources, *Directory of Indiana's Dedicated Nature Preserves* (Indianapolis, 1988); Alton A. Lindsey, ed., *Natural Features of Indiana* (Indianapolis: Indiana Academy of Science, 1966); Donald R. Whitehead, "In the Glacier's Wake: Patterns of Forest Development Following Glaciation," in a book edited by Marion Jackson, forthcoming from Indiana University Press.

Flower Mission. Private organization devoted to providing health care and social welfare services to the city's indigent. The idea for this nonprofit organization dates to 1876 when a group of young women took flowers to City Hospital (now WISHARD MEMORIAL HOSPITAL) patients. Founded by Alice Wright and officially incorporated in 1892, the Flower Mission's major activity was visiting the sick poor in their homes and providing necessary assistance to them. During its history the organization undertook a number of projects and raised money for these projects through lawn fetes, fairs, parades, doll fairs, and balls.

In the course of their work, Flower Mission members saw individuals who needed nursing and medical care. In 1883 they convinced City Hospital to establish a training school for nurses. Two years later, the Flower Mission hired a district nurse to provide medical care for the sick poor.

In their work, Flower Mission members became distressed at the lack of proper care for sick children. With a major donation from COLONEL

ELI LILLY, the Flower Mission opened Eleanor Hospital in 1895 to care for poor children under age 15. The hospital was named in memory of Lilly's daughter, Eleanor. Operating the hospital, however, was expensive and in 1909, upon the recommendation of a medical advisory board, Eleanor Hospital closed its doors.

Beginning in 1901, the Flower Mission focused on providing care for the terminally ill (usually cancer or tuberculosis patients) and in 1903 built a hospital to accommodate them. The hospital was torn down in 1923 to make room for a new wing for City Hospital, and the Flower Mission temporarily used a nearby building for these purposes. When the fire marshal condemned the structure in 1930, the Flower Mission raised money for a new facility. The 100–bed Flower Mission Memorial Hospital was dedicated in 1937 to treat tuberculosis patients and continued to operate into the early 1960s. (The building now houses the Bell Flower Clinic.)

After the construction of this hospital, the Flower Mission became less active. It continues to support new health care concepts by donating funds to various projects at Wishard Memorial Hospital. Today, the organization is primarily an advisory group to the HEALTH AND HOSPITAL CORPORATION OF MARION COUNTY and provides items that are outside the Wishard budget to patients and staff.

KATHERINE MANDUSIC MCDONELL

Indianapolis Flower Mission Collection, Indiana Historical Society; Health and Hospital Corporation of Marion County, 1976 annual report.

Folklore. Folklore manifests itself in various genres or categories; for example, folktales, legends, proverbs, riddles, folksongs, regional speech, beliefs, customs, festivals, folk architecture, and folk crafts. Legends are among the most fascinating genres of folklore and are readily collectible in urban settings. The legend is a secular belief tale; an apparently factual account, believed to be true, of an unusual or extraordinary event in the lives of otherwise ordinary people.

Urban belief legends have the remarkable ability to migrate from one location to another, attaching themselves to local places and people. Few legends or folk tales are unique to Indianapolis. For example, the Indianapolis couple who "adopts" a puppy while in Florida discovers, after the violent death of their cat, that their new pet is an Australian swamp rat; it is now housed in the Indianapolis Zoo. The same legend is found in Chicago, except the animal is in the Brookfield Zoo.

CROWN HILL CEMETERY is the location of several legends of local interest, although these stories too have counterparts in other American cities. One narrative describes a young woman with a baby in her arms who was unable to find her way out of the cemetery at closing time. She finally wandered to the fence on 38th Street, but no passersby came to the aid of the wailing woman within the cemetery. Another early 20th century legend describes the cemetery night watchman making his rounds one dark night with his collie, Shep. When the dog stepped off the path as if allowing someone to pass, the watchman felt a warm breeze as the unseen "visitor" went by. The dog returned to the path, and the watchman completed his route, knowing they probably were not alone.

A third Crown Hill Cemetery legend concerns the Caleb B. Smith sandstone mausoleum, erected in Egyptian architectural style. It is believed by some that its "fire-blackened" appearance was caused by members of the black community at the turn of the century, when they gathered at the gravesite and lit fires believing that this would keep the spirit of a conspirator in the Lincoln assassination from coming out and haunting the city. Interestingly, no Hoosier is known to have been involved in the Lincoln assassination. Instead history records that Caleb Smith was Indiana's first presidential cabinet member—Abraham Lincoln's Secretary of the Interior and his friend. Although the mausoleum bears his name, Smith's remains were never placed there. Adding further mystery to the mausoleum's history and legend, his exact place of burial is unknown.

Another Crown Hill ghost story, also noted in other cemeteries, is "The Legend of the Gypsy King." According to the legend, the Gypsy King instructed his relatives to leave a bottle of wine on his grave every night after he died, which they did. And every night the bottle of wine disappeared.

"The Ghost of Crown Hill Cemetery," "The Woman in White," or "The Ghostly Hitchhiker" are other local variants of widespread folk ghost stories. In nearly all of the versions, a teenage girl dressed for the prom is standing near the corner of 38th Street and Northwestern Avenue soaking wet from the falling rain, when a young man offers her a ride home. She accepts and gets into the back seat of the car. The girl gives the boy an address, and upon arrival the boy turns around and the girl has disappeared, but the back seat is still wet. The driver goes to the door and explains the situation to the woman of the house, who becomes disturbed when the boy points to a photograph of the girl. The woman says that was her daughter and she died the night of the prom six years ago.

Legends of haunted houses in Indianapolis are recounted regularly. Many of the narratives about these structures consist of unexplained phenomena: footsteps, moans and groans, strange odors, or corners that defy heat. Occasionally reports suggest that a poltergeist haunts the structure, peppering the exterior of the house with rocks or tossing about the interior contents of the house.

Hannah House on the south side of the city is said to have been used as a station on the Underground Railroad for smuggling slaves out of the South to Canada prior to the Civil War. One account claims that a fire spread through the basement when a lantern was overturned, killing many of the slaves before they could escape. Another version has the slaves dying in the basement without any mention of the fire. In both versions, the slaves were buried in the basement or on some of the original acreage. Legend has it that these souls still roam the house and grounds, restless and frustrated that they were never able to attain their goal of freedom.

Perhaps the most famous haunted house in Indianapolis is "THE HOUSE OF BLUE LIGHTS," where millionaire Skiles E. Test lived. Rumors and legends about the house began in the 1930s and include narratives about an old man who preserved his first wife in a glass coffin surrounded by blue lights. Another version has Mr. Test's wife on a sarcophagus in an airtight room. Despite all efforts to play down the validity of the legends, the narratives continue to be recounted, even after the house was demolished in 1978.

The INDIANAPOLIS 500–MILE RACE, with its festival-like atmosphere, produces colorful legends and anecdotes. There is, for example, "The Mobbed Motorist," who while passing through town is unexpectedly caught in race day traffic and pulled by the stream of cars into the infield. Or the "500 Festival Princess," who poses nude for a magazine photographer in a Gasoline Alley garage. Another anecdote describes "The Good Luck Rabbit" that regularly appears on the track at starting time.

Scholars characterize Hoosier folklore as "a part of the main," a regional variant of American folklore. Likewise, legends and stories of Indianapolis reflect its state and midwestern roots and especially its similarities with the folk culture of the region's cities.

SUSANNE S. RIDLEN
Indiana University, Kokomo

Ronald L. Baker, *Hoosier Folk Legends* (Bloomington, Ind., 1982); Linda Degh, ed., *Indiana Folklore: A Reader* (Bloomington, Ind., 1980); Steve Bell, "Ghost Stories: A Ghoulish Gallery of Indianapolis Haunts," *Indianapolis Monthly* (Oct., 1983), 46–53.

Foltz, Herbert Willard (Feb. 23, 1867–July 6, 1946). Architect. A native of Indianapolis, Foltz graduated from SHORTRIDGE HIGH SCHOOL before attending Rose Polytechnic Institute (now Rose-Hulman Institute of Technology), from which he graduated in 1886. After a stint at the Chicago Art Institute and an apprenticeship in structural engineering with the Illinois Steel Company, he returned to Indianapolis in 1891 and began an architectural career.

Foltz designed many structures around the city, including the BOBBS-MERRILL building, the 1928 Shortridge High School (Neoclassical style; now Shortridge Junior High School), Tudor Hall School for Girls, and the Indiana Reformatory in Pendleton. Foltz also designed the Broadway Methodist Church, the Irvington United Methodist Church (1926, English Gothic style), and the

Meridian Heights Presbyterian Church. Foltz served on the Indianapolis Public Schools' board of commissioners from 1917 to 1920 and was the organization's president in 1918–1919. A member of the First Presbyterian Church, Foltz's interest in amateur dramatics led him to found the Little Theater Society of Indianapolis.

STACEY NICHOLAS

Jacob Piatt Dunn, *Indiana and Indianans* (Chicago, 1919), Vol.4; *Indianapolis News*, July 6, 1946.

Football. Butler and DePauw played the state's first intercollegiate game at the old 7th Street Baseball Grounds in Indianapolis in the spring of 1884. Butler senior John F. Stone compiled the rules for the game. He combined association (soccer) rules with eastern intercollegiate rules to form the western intercollegiate rules, which were published by Charles Mayer of Indianapolis. Butler won the game by a score of four goals to one.

Association rules dominated the intercollegiate games held in Indianapolis until 1886. In that year four Ivy League graduates—Merrill Moores, Clinton Hare, Pirtle Harrod, and William Bradshaw—formed the Indianapolis Athletic Association (IAA) for the purpose of introducing rugby football in Indiana. The IAA sponsored all intercollegiate games, supplying players with train tickets for the games in Indianapolis. Butler, Hanover, Wabash, and Franklin colleges competed for the state championship with Wabash coming out on top. The IAA also sponsored games in 1887, but in 1888 the presidential campaign of native

A 1923 football game at Irwin Field between Butler University and Wabash College resulted in a 9-7 win for the host Bulldogs. [Butler University Archives]

son BENJAMIN HARRISON absorbed everyone's interest and no football games were played.

Games resumed in 1889 under the auspices of the newly formed Indianapolis Intercollegiate Athletic Association (IIAA). This group, composed of each institution's president, guided college football through the 1890s. During that decade numerous independent athletic club football teams developed throughout the state (two of Indianapolis' more famous clubs were the Light Artillery Eleven and the Zig-Zag Club). Many top college teams dropped IIAA opponents to schedule games with these athletic clubs. This problem came to a head in 1894 when Butler scheduled a Thanksgiving Day game against the Indianapolis Light Artillery Eleven at the old Ohio Street ground that clashed with the traditional Thanksgiving Day game between Purdue and DePauw at the State Fairgrounds. Bitter feelings over lost gate receipts nearly resulted in Butler's expulsion from the IIAA.

The IIAA held an emergency meeting in Indianapolis in December, 1894. The athletic club controversy, as well as a general outcry against the roughness of the game, led them to drop football until the rules were reformed. In 1895 the IIAA adopted new rules banning rough play and games against non-collegiate teams. It also called for officials with more stamina and authority to enforce these regulations.

Most Indiana colleges built their own football fields during the 1890s and, during the first quarter of the 20th century, Butler was the only college team playing in the city. Indiana Central College began playing football at its southeastside campus in 1924. Its program struggled for seven years before disbanding in 1932.

On October 13, 1928, Butler College played Franklin College in the first game at Butler Bowl. Originally planned as a 75,000–seat stadium, the Bowl as finished held only half that number. It lost another 16,000 seats to STARLIGHT MUSICALS' Hilton U. Brown Theater in 1955. Today the stadium seats 18,000.

In 1971 Indianapolis became the site of the annual Top Dog game played on the last day of the season between the Butler University Bulldogs and the UNIVERSITY OF INDIANAPOLIS Greyhounds (formerly Indiana Central College, which reinstated football in 1945). The two schools' alumni associations developed the trophy to focus attention on the intracity rivalry. For most of the Top Dog game's history the schools have played in the same conference. However, in 1992 Butler joined another conference, marking the probable end of the series after the 1993 game.

The first high school football games in Indianapolis were played between Indianapolis High School and Indianapolis Training High School, later known as Shortridge and Manual, in the late 1890s. However, neither school played a formal annual schedule until after the founding of the INDIANA HIGH SCHOOL ATHLETIC ASSOCIATION (IHSAA) in 1903.

In 1920 the newspapers began naming an unofficial city football champion based on won-loss record. Also in that year Shortridge, Manual, and Tech began vying for the School Board Trophy. The award was to go to the first five-time undisputed city champion. By the time SHORTRIDGE HIGH SCHOOL claimed it in 1935, Broad Ripple, Washington, and Cathedral had joined the citywide competition. By 1955 eight public schools and four parochial schools competed for the city championship. At this time there were plans to establish a formal city football league and abolish the traditional method of naming an unofficial champion, but scheduling conflicts prevented the plans from materializing.

Today the city's seven public and five parochial high schools vie for the city championship that is voted on by the 12 head coaches at the end of the regular season. Since the establishment of the state high school football tournament in 1973, all Indianapolis high schools have gone on to compete for the state football championship in their respective classes under the auspices of the IHSAA.

Indianapolis has a long history of minor league professional football. The city's first professional team was the J. J. Cuming All-Stars, who played in a statewide league in the 1920s. In 1961 the Indianapolis Warriors played a ten-game schedule in the newly formed United Football League. They played their home games at Victory Field, now Bush Stadium, and hosted the UFL championship game in 1964. A year later, having lost money every year, the franchise moved to Fort

State Football Champions from Marion County

Year	School
1966[1]	Indianapolis Washington
1969[1]	Indianapolis Washington
1974	3A–Indianapolis Washington
1977	1A–Ritter
1980	2A–Franklin Central
1981	2A–Franklin Central
1982	2A–Franklin Central
1983	2A–Chatard
1984	4A–Warren Central
	2A–Chatard
1985	4A–Warren Central
	3A–Roncalli
1986	3A–Cathedral
1987	5A–Ben Davis
1988	5A–Ben Davis
	3A–Roncalli
1990	5A–Ben Davis
	4A–Franklin Central
	2A–Secina
1991	5A–Ben Davis
	2A–Secina
1992	3A–Cathedral
1993	3A–Roncalli

[1] The IHSAA instituted the classification system and the state football tournament in 1973. Previously, AP and UPI rating systems determined the state football champion.

Wayne. From 1968 to 1980, Indianapolis was home to a professional football team called the Capitals. The Capitals played in several different leagues and moved their home venue from BUSH STADIUM to Indiana Central University's Key Stadium during their 13 year history.

The city's first venture into the National Football League came in 1933. In September of that year the Indianapolis Football Indians played only three games, all lopsided losses, before management disbanded the team. In 1984 the Baltimore Colts became the INDIANAPOLIS COLTS, playing in the newly built HOOSIER DOME, and Indianapolis has been an NFL city ever since.

WILLIAM DALTON

Footlite Musicals. Community theater. Footlite Musicals is a nonprofit organization founded in 1956 to bring the finest in musical theater to the Indianapolis area. Starting with two productions a year, Footlite's season now includes four shows plus a summer teenage show. Footlite also sponsors a children's workshop, the Hiliters song-and-dance group, and a dance company. By 1992 the company had performed 128 productions of 87 different musicals. Footlite used rented facilities until 1974 when it found a permanent home at the renovated Hedback Theatre.

Footlite Musicals is an all-volunteer organization administered by a board of directors chosen from the membership. The organization's activities are financed principally through ticket sales. In July, 1991, Footlite Musicals became America's "Number One Community Theatre" by winning the national competition of the American Community Theatre Association for *Into the Woods* by Stephen Sondheim; this production then competed in international competition in Toyama, Japan, in August, 1992, where it won several awards.

JEAN CONES
Footlite Musicals

Forbes, Gilbert (May 20, 1904–Sept. 18, 1961). Radio and television newscaster. Blessed with a resonant voice, Forbes was the original news anchor on the city's first television station, WFBM-TV (now WRTV), beginning in May, 1949. He provided local news on TV and for years continued his daily noon, early evening, and late evening newscasts on radio. He also was the creator and quiz master of "Test the Press," one of the city's top local TV attractions from 1949 to 1955.

Prior to joining the radio station in 1937, Forbes had been a newspaper reporter in Chicago during the 1920s. He switched to broadcast news at WIL in St. Louis and was news editor at WKBB in Dubuque, Iowa, three years before joining WFBM. A native of St. Louis and a graduate of the University of Dubuque, he also was an organist graduate of Chicago's American Conservatory.

In 1944 Forbes became a war correspondent for his station, landing at Omaha Beach shortly after D-Day. He reported combat experiences of Hoosier servicemen with the 82nd Airborne Division and the 4th Bomber Group of the 8th Air Force, in addition to those of the 735th Tank Battalion during the battle for Metz, France.

In 1957 Forbes turned primarily to radio after eight years of serving both radio and television. At the time of his death he was the radio station's news editor, chief anchor, and analyst.

HOWARD CALDWELL
WRTV Channel 6

Ford Motor Company. Automobile and truck manufacturer with Indianapolis factories at 1315–1325 East Washington Street and 6900 English Avenue. In 1903, when Ford began taking orders for its legendary Model-T, the Indiana Auto Company at 34–36 Monument Place in Indianapolis processed one of the earliest orders. In 1914, as part of a plan to decentralize operations and save shipping costs, Ford erected the buildings on Washington Street as a regional center where cars would be assembled, sold, and repaired. Retail sales ended in 1916, but cars were assembled on the site until 1932 and Ford used the buildings for administrative purposes until 1942. Subsequent occupants have been the P. R. MALLORY COMPANY and INDIANA VOCATIONAL TECHNICAL COLLEGE.

In 1956–1957 Ford made plans to resume assembly operations in Indianapolis and constructed the factory on English Avenue to make steering gear assemblies for all its North American cars. The main building occupied 1,645,000 square feet of ground and later was expanded to 1,900,000 square feet. The plant also made bolts and steering gears for trucks.

In 1992 Ford upgraded part of the plant so that it could supply power steering units for cars made in Europe. Ford spent $150 million on the improvement and received a $40,000 state grant for job training and $20 million in tax abatements over a five-year period. Ford employed over 3,000 hourly and salaried personnel in mid–1993.

CHARLES JOHNSON TAGGART

Indianapolis News, Sept. 7, 1957, Sept. 12, 1972, Sept. 28, 1992.

Fordham, Elias Pym (1787–unknown). Surveyor of Indianapolis. Born on his family's ancestral estate in eastern England, Fordham was one of two sons and seven children of Elias and Mary Clapton Fordham. He trained as a civil engineer under George Stephenson, British inventor of the steam locomotive.

In 1816, Fordham considered migrating to America. Morris Birkbeck, an English Quaker, planned to establish an English colony in the Illinois Territory, and Fordham's uncle by marriage,

George Flower, was involved in the venture. In 1817, Fordham and his sister Maria joined Birkbeck and his family on the trip to America and across the country to southern Illinois. He immediately acquired a plot of land in what became known as "the English Prairie," surveyed the surrounding lands, and assisted Birkbeck in constructing buildings and mills for the settlers.

Between July, 1817, and fall, 1818, Fordham traveled through southern Indiana on business for Birkbeck. He passed through Salem, possibly meeting ALEXANDER RALSTON who resided there, and on one occasion stayed with Judge Christopher Harrison, later appointed a commissioner for the survey of the new state capital. In April, 1821, Fordham and Ralston received joint appointments as surveyors of the capital city. After completing the survey in the fall of 1821, Fordham left Indianapolis, probably returning to his home in Illinois.

Little else is known about Fordham. His writing, evidenced by his *Personal Narrative of Travels . . . 1817–1818* (1906), reflects a man of superior education and keen intellect. Family members reported that Fordham eventually returned to England where he pursued a career in civil engineering and worked for Stephenson on assorted projects.

SHERYL D. VANDERSTEL

Jacob Piatt Dunn, *Greater Indianapolis* (Chicago, 1910), I, 28; *Hyman's Handbook of Indianapolis* (1909).

Forest Hills. Northside residential area bounded by Kessler Boulevard, the Monon railway corridor, Northview Avenue, and College Avenue. A curvilinear street pattern, hilly terrain, and a cohesive architectural style make the Forest Hills neighborhood unique to the city. Known originally as "Stevenson's Woods," the land was developed by Benjamin Stevenson, who built a home there in 1911 as a gift for his wife. The majority of the 237 homes were built from 1924 to 1935, with a few constructed as late as 1945. Most of the homes are in the English Tudor Cottage style. Leaded windows, arched doorways, brick construction, and high pitched slate roofs are typical features. Other styles prevalent in the

area include American and Dutch Colonial and Cape Cod. There are similar houses nearby, yet Forest Hills is set apart by its distinctive winding streets, older-style streetlights, and brick columns flanking the entrances.

Over the years, bank presidents, professionals, and business executives have lived in the area. The Forest Hills Neighborhood Association, incorporated in 1922, is one of the oldest such associations in the city. Residents have successfully defended the neighborhood against intrusive construction and commercial expansion. In June, 1983, Forest Hills was placed on the National Register of Historic Places.

CATHLEEN F. DONNELLY

Forest Manor. Northeastside neighborhood bounded by 38th Street, Hawthorne Lane, 30th Street, and Parker Avenue. The popularity of the automobile in the 1920s promoted the development of suburbs such as Forest Manor. In 1921 the Security Trust Company opened the area to middle class commuters eager to build homes. Bungalows and cottages were constructed on the wooded lots and in two later additions. By 1953 Forest Manor was home to 15,000 people.

Black families purchased homes in Forest Manor in the 1960s. Over the next few years many white residents sold their homes and left. To ease tensions, Forest Manor United Methodist Church founded the Forest Manor Neighborhood Association in 1967. The group became an effective voice during the transition and later took on challenges such as an urban homesteading program and street resurfacing in cooperation with the city.

Despite early successes, Forest Manor faced problems common to many urban neighborhoods in the 1990s. Hawthorne Place, a public housing project opened in 1968 that provides housing for 330 residents, needed extensive renovations. Homeowners were concerned about the area's crime rate and vacant buildings. They listed youth recreational programs and services for the elderly as priorities and looked to city government to help resolve complex issues facing Forest Manor.

CATHLEEN F. DONNELLY

Forsyth, Constance E. "Connie" (Aug. 18, 1903–Jan. 22, 1987). Artist and teacher. Forsyth was the oldest of three daughters of William and Alice (Atkinson) Forsyth of IRVINGTON. Her father was recognized as one of the foremost Hoosier artists and art teachers; she inherited and learned from his talents. Forsyth graduated from SHORTRIDGE HIGH SCHOOL. She received an A.B. degree in chemistry from BUTLER UNIVERSITY and studied art at JOHN HERRON ART INSTITUTE, the Pennsylvania Academy of Fine Arts in Philadelphia, and Broadmoor Art Academy in Colorado Springs.

Forsyth's art won numerous Indiana State Fair ribbons for watercolor landscapes and composites, and her watercolors have been exhibited in England, Scotland, France, and India. Besides watercolors she did oil painting, lithography, and etchings. Some of her etchings—especially *Dunes Beach*, *Delaware Bridge*, and *Canal Bridge*—were inspired by the Indiana area. She was also active in the Society of Print Makers and a member of the HOOSIER SALON.

Forsyth left the Indianapolis area in 1940 to accept a teaching position at the University of Texas at Austin. She retired from that institution as Professor Emeritus of Art in 1973.

REBECCA M. MAIER

Indianapolis News, Feb., 22, 1978, Jan. 24, 1987; Indianapolis Star, Nov. 8, 1931, Sept. 7, 1940.

Forsyth, William (Oct. 15, 1854–Mar. 29, 1935). Hoosier Group artist. Born in California, Ohio, Forsyth moved to Indianapolis as a young man. He enrolled in the first class of the Indiana School of Art (1877), organized by John Love and James Gookins in the Fletcher-Sharpe Block at the southwest corner of Washington and Pennsylvania streets. The school failed in 1879 for lack of pubic support, but its students, including Forsyth, Thomas E. Hibben, and Fred Hetherington, occupied the school's rooms and pursued sketching and etching on their own under the name of the Bohe Club, abbreviated from Bohemian. In December, 1881, with underwriting from Hibben, Forsyth joined a contingent of Indiana artists—T. C. STEELE, J. OTTIS ADAMS, and Samuel Richards—already at the Royal Academy of Painting in Munich.

Of the group, Forsyth was the last to return, coming home in the fall of 1888. By the next spring, faced with tight finances, he joined Adams in Muncie to teach and organize the Muncie Art School. From that time until his death, teaching was his profession. The summer months, often spent in southernmost Indiana, were reserved for his own painting. Forsyth won a bronze medal for his oil painting and a silver for his watercolor at the St. Louis World's Fair in 1904, another medal at the 1910 International Fine Arts Exposition in Buenos Aires, and two more at the Panama-Pacific International Exposition in San Francisco in 1915.

When the Muncie Art School folded in the spring of 1891, Forsyth joined Steele for the fall term of the second Indiana School of Art, which occupied the former SECOND PRESBYTERIAN CHURCH on the northwest corner of Market Street and the Circle in Indianapolis. Among his students was Alice Atkinson, whom he married October 14, 1897. That same year the school closed because of the expansion of the ENGLISH HOTEL AND OPERA HOUSE; Forsyth then took private students until October, 1906, when he replaced Adams as principal instructor of painting and drawing at the HERRON SCHOOL OF ART.

Though combative in temperament and severe as a teacher, Forsyth was highly regarded by his students. When in May, 1933, the new dean of the art school, DONALD M. MATTISON, forcibly retired the 78–year-old Forsyth, an event still vividly and hotly remembered, the students hung Mattison in effigy. The last surviving member of the HOOSIER GROUP, Forsyth died two years later in the rambling house at 15 South Emerson in IRVINGTON that had been his home and where he had raised his family since 1906.

MARTIN KRAUSE

Martin Krause, *The Passage: Return of Indiana Painters from Germany, 1880–1905* (Indianapolis: Indianapolis Museum of Art, 1990).

Fort Benjamin Harrison. U.S. Army installation established June 28, 1904, in LAWRENCE

TOWNSHIP, MARION COUNTY. Shortly after the conclusion of the SPANISH-AMERICAN WAR of 1898, Secretary of War Elihu Root included Fort Harrison among those new military installations responsible for maintaining an expanded national army of nearly 100,000. The federal government purchased the original site consisting of 1,994 acres for $279,238.01. At the request of President Theodore Roosevelt, Root named the post after Benjamin Harrison, resident of Indianapolis and 23rd president of the United States.

The U.S. Army constructed Fort Harrison to garrison one regiment of infantry, but during World Wars I and II the post became one of the nation's largest training and mobilization sites. Its convenient location on some of the nation's major highways and railroads made the Indiana post easily accessible for troop units and individuals called to duty from the Midwest. During World War I, the post hosted three large officer training camps, and became the training ground for hundreds of medical and engineering specialists.

During World War II, Fort Harrison proved adaptable to a variety of missions essential to a wartime army. Used largely for the purpose of inducting thousands of young Americans into the Army during the war, the post also became a training ground for Army cooks and bakers, chaplains, finance specialists, and medical technicians. In addition, Fort Harrison became the site of one of the Army's largest general hospitals, used to treat thousands of wounded American servicemen. In the latter stages of the conflict, the induction center was converted into a branch disciplinary barracks of the main facility at Fort Leavenworth, Kansas. With the knowledge that Fort Harrison was too small to resume its prewar infantry training mission, the War Department decided in July, 1947, to close the post. Secretary of War Kenneth C. Royall rescinded that decision and turned the Army post over to the Air Force. The 10th Air Force briefly occupied the installation before returning it to the Army in January, 1950.

In March, 1951, two Army branch service schools, the Adjutant General's School and the Finance School, moved to the post to make Fort Harrison the training base for Army personnel and finance specialists. A third school, the De-

World War I troops trained at Fort Benjamin Harrison in 1917. Indiana Historical Society, Bass Collection, #61285F]

fense Information School, moved to Fort Harrison in January, 1966, to train public affairs specialists for all the nation's military services. One part of a major Army reorganization in 1973, which centered around the training mission of the three schools at Fort Harrison, established a coordinating and planning agency for wartime personnel, finance, religious, legal, medical, and public affairs support activities. Initially, the new command was named the U.S. Army Administration Center. On July 1, 1980, officials redesignated it the U.S. Army Soldier Support Center to more accurately reflect a mission that had grown beyond the limited features of Army administration.

For residents of Indianapolis and Marion County, the U.S. ARMY FINANCE CENTER became the most recognizable landmark at Fort Benjamin Harrison. Completed in October, 1953, the huge complex centralized all of the Army's related pay and disbursing activities that had been scattered across the country since the end of World War II. The completed structure covered more than 14 acres, measured 996 feet long and 612 feet wide, and stood second only to the Pentagon as the largest building owned by the defense establishment. On March 1, 1958, the new building also became the home of the U.S. Army Enlisted Records and Evaluation Center, an agency responsible for recording and evaluating the performance of the Army's enlisted soldiers for purposes of pay and promotion. In the hope of increased efficiency, the

Department of Defense, in November, 1990, consolidated all military finance and accounting agencies into one organization called the Defense Finance and Accounting Service (DFAS). Accordingly, the Army's Finance and Accounting Center at Fort Harrison became a Department of Defense activity under the new DFAS organization.

On October 12, 1973, officials dedicated the William D. McGee U.S. Army Reserve Center, a $1.5 million complex located on the eastern edge of the post. Architects designed the center to house the Headquarters, 123rd U.S. Army Reserve Command (ARCOM) and to accommodate the training requirements of the six local Reserve units under its authority. Following the dedication of the Reserve Center, the Fort Harrison mission centered around the activities of the Soldier Support Center, the Defense Information School, the Defense Finance and Accounting Service, the Enlisted Records and Evaluation Center, and the 123rd Army Reserve Command.

With the end of the Cold War and the dismantling of the Soviet Union in the late 1980s and early 1990s, congressional pressure to decrease the size of the military led to a series of Defense Department initiatives to streamline some military organizations and eliminate others. One side of the military "drawdown" caused the elimination of a number of active military units and installations around the world. In April, 1991, the Department of the Army listed Fort Benjamin Harrison as one of several Army installations slated for closure during the 1990s. The closure plan called for most of the major activities at the post to move to other locations. The 123rd ARCOM was left in place, because of its importance to the Army Reserve program in central Indiana. State and local politicians, certain of the closing's potentially damaging impact on the Marion County economy, immediately began lobbying to keep the Defense Finance and Accounting Service and its 2,500 civilian jobs in the Indianapolis area. Whatever the outcome of that effort, the Department of the Army planned to phase out the Fort Harrison operation over a period of six years with officials closing the post for good in October, 1997.

STEPHEN E. BOWER
U.S. Army Soldier Support Center

Stephen E. Bower, *The History of Fort Benjamin Harrison, 1903–1982* (Fort Benjamin Harrison, Indiana, 1984); Dorothy Riker, *The Indiana Training Ground* (Bloomington, Ind., 1952).

Fortune, William (May 27, 1863–Jan. 28, 1942). Newspaperman, executive, and civic leader. Born in Boonville, Indiana, Fortune was largely self-educated through intense reading and through boyhood work as a printer's helper and reporter on the *Boonville Standard*. At 17 he wrote a history of Warrick County. In 1881 he began a lifelong interest by interviewing several people in nearby Spencer County who had known Abraham Lincoln during his Indiana years (1816–1830).

Moving to Indianapolis in 1882, Fortune worked for the *Indianapolis Journal* as a reporter, then as city editor. Through his work he became a friend of several Hoosier writers, notably JAMES WHITCOMB RILEY and MEREDITH NICHOLSON. He also developed a close relationship with COL. ELI LILLY. Briefly in 1888 Fortune edited the weekly *Sunday Press*; he then joined the INDIANAPOLIS NEWS as a reporter and editorial writer.

Fortune worked with Colonel Lilly in 1890 to launch the COMMERCIAL CLUB, which envisioned a broader program than the existing BOARD OF TRADE. He became the salaried secretary of the club (until 1894), while Lilly was president. One major club objective was to get the city's streets paved with something other than cobblestones and gravel; a STREET PAVING EXPOSITION in 1890 brought in exhibitors of new methods and mate-

William Fortune. [Indianapolis Chamber of Commerce]

rials. For 20 years (1890–1910) Fortune published a paving trade magazine called *Municipal Engineering*; he also wrote an authoritative article on paving in *Century Magazine* (October, 1892). Another successful Commercial Club effort gave the city a new charter (1891) providing expanded powers for the City Council. The club began a 30–year campaign, led by Fortune after 1898, to elevate the city's railroad tracks. In 1893 the club opened an eight-story office building, the city's first "skyscraper," and led in bringing over 100,000 veterans to a GRAND ARMY OF THE REPUBLIC encampment, Indianapolis' first large convention. Fortune did much of the detail work for all these enterprises.

An automobile enthusiast, Fortune founded the local auto club and was active in the Indiana Good Roads Movement. He served as host for Chinese PRINCE PU LUN on his visit to Indianapolis in 1904 and maintained contacts in China thereafter. From 1910 to 1924 Fortune was president of several independent telephone companies; his company installed automatic dialing several years before the Bell system. On the board of ELI LILLY AND COMPANY (1913–1927), he chaired the board's finance committee (1916–1921).

In his later years Fortune became an expert organizer and fund-raiser for civic causes, including the local chapter of the Red Cross (founder; president 1916–1942) and the War Chest ($3 million in a week in 1918).

CHARLES LATHAM, JR.

Who Was Who in America (Chicago, 1943).

Foster, Robert Sanford (Jan. 27, 1834–Mar. 4, 1903). Civil War general. Born in Vernon, Indiana, Foster came to Indianapolis at age 16, learning the tinner's trade and later working in his uncle's store. In 1861 he joined the Indianapolis Greys militia company and subsequently raised and became captain, then lieutenant colonel, of a company which joined Colonel LEW WALLACE'S 13th Indiana Regiment.

Foster became a brigadier general in June, 1863, and thereafter commanded almost continually at the division level. His engagements and outstanding services all occurred in the eastern theater in the sieges of Richmond and Petersburg, Virginia, and later in the Appomattox campaign under General John Gibbon. He became brevet major general in March, 1865.

After the Confederate surrender Foster declined a regular army appointment, choosing instead to return to Indianapolis where he entered the brokerage business, maintaining offices in the Board of Trade Building. He served as city treasurer (1867-1872) and as U.S. marshal for the district of Indiana (1881–1885). In 1876 he served as president of the Indianapolis BOARD OF TRADE and at the time of his death was the quartermaster general of the INDIANA NATIONAL GUARD. In addition to serving as Indiana's first GRAND ARMY OF THE REPUBLIC department commander, Foster was a member of the COLUMBIA CLUB, the Scottish Rite Masons, and the Odd Fellows.

JAMES A. TRULOCK

Charles W. Smith, "Life and Military Services of Brevet-Major General Robert S. Foster" (Indianapolis: Indiana Historical Society *Publications*, Vol. 5, No. 6, 1915); *Indianapolis Sentinel*, Mar. 4, 1903.

Foundations and Trusts. Nongovernmental, nonprofit charitable funding entities. Indianapolis has enjoyed a lengthy and impressive tradition of philanthropy, beginning with the INDIANAPOLIS BENEVOLENT SOCIETY in 1835. It continued with creation of the nation's second community foundation—the INDIANAPOLIS FOUNDATION—in 1916 and the establishment of LILLY ENDOWMENT, now the nation's fourth largest foundation, in 1937. Major foundations emerging later in the 20th century included the CLOWES FUND (1952), the KRANNERT CHARITABLE TRUST (1960; now dissolved), and the MORIAH FUND (1985). Indianapolis also boasts a sizable number of smaller foundations established by community-minded individuals or families, including the W. C. Griffith Foundation (1959), the Arthur Jordan Foundation (1928), and the NICHOLAS H. NOYES, JR. MEMORIAL FOUNDATION (1951).

Early giving in Indianapolis emulated national trends by grappling with social problems of the times. The Indianapolis Foundation's first action, for example, was to underwrite the salary of a nurse for crippled children. An examination of the Foundation's archives reveals that its direction and management have been remarkably consistent over the years. In its emphasis upon innovative projects and capital expenditures contributing to the health and well-being of Marion County residents, the Indianapolis Foundation has been a pacesetter in local philanthropy.

After founding ELI LILLY AND COMPANY in 1876, COL. ELI LILLY set an example as a thoughtful philanthropist by helping to organize the CHARITY ORGANIZATION SOCIETY, forerunner of the UNITED WAY, and by providing relief and employment during economic downturns in the late 1800s. His grandson, ELI LILLY, conceived the idea of a Lilly Endowment "to continue the family tradition of being generous in public affairs." This led to gifts of Lilly stock by young Eli, his father, J. K. LILLY, SR., and his brother, J. K. LILLY, JR., in 1937. In its first 50 years, the Endowment disbursed approximately 10,000 grants, valued at just under $700 million, to about 5,800 charitable organizations. In the mid–1970s, acknowledging the deterioration of Indianapolis, the Endowment became partners with organizations from the public, private, academic, and nonprofit sectors, including the GREATER INDIANAPOLIS PROGRESS COMMITTEE, the Commission for Downtown, and the CORPORATE COMMUNITY COUNCIL. In its largest capital project, the Endowment gave $25 million for an enlargement of the INDIANA CONVENTION CENTER that included construction of the HOOSIER DOME. The facility impelled redevelopment of the city's decaying warehouse district and attracted hundreds of thousands of people to the downtown area each year. By the end of the 1980s a striking change in Indianapolis' appearance and vitality was readily apparent, and the city was garnering international attention for its dramatic turnaround and commitment to amateur sports and community development.

While Indianapolis has only one Fortune 500 corporation, it has been blessed with significant charitable organizations. Of approximately 24,000 active grantmaking foundations in the United States, fewer than 200 have assets of $50 million or more. Four of those 200 have an Indianapolis connection (the Lilly Endowment, Mo-

riah Fund, LIBERTY FUND, and the Indianapolis Foundation).

A variety of types of foundations are represented in Indianapolis. Independent foundations (e.g., the Clowes Fund, the W. C. Griffith Foundation, etc.) receive funds from a single source, usually an individual, family, or group of individuals; community foundations (e.g., the Indianapolis Foundation) receive funds from many contributors and distribute funds to benefit a specific community; company-sponsored foundations (e.g., Eli Lilly and Company Foundation) receive funds from the profits of the corporation but usually function independently of the corporation; organizational foundations (e.g., the James Whitcomb Riley Children's Hospital Foundation) receive funds from a variety of sources, sometimes including income-producing activities, and serve a single institution; and operating foundations (e.g., Walther Cancer Institute Foundation) usually receive funds from a sole funder and serve a single purpose, often through internally managed programs.

LINDA BRIMMER

Fountain Square. Near southside historic commercial district. Located at and near the intersection of three busy thoroughfares—Virginia Avenue and Prospect and Shelby streets —Fountain Square has been a commercial center for over 100 years. The Citizens Street Railway Company laid tracks down Virginia Avenue and located a turnaround at the intersection in 1864. Settlement, sparse at first, increased significantly in the 1870s as German families built homes in nearby FLETCHER PLACE. Additional traffic from the Virginia Avenue viaduct gave the area a second boost after 1892.

German entrepreneurs were the first to arrive, opening groceries, bakeries, jewelry stores, and saloons in the square. Irish, Italian, and Danish immigrants followed, but Fountain Square retained a distinctive German character well into the 20th century.

The original fountain in the square was erected in 1889 by area merchants. According to lore, the fountain toppled some 30 years later when an advertising banner was anchored to it. The second fountain was constructed as a memorial to Ralph Hill, an Indiana congressman. Local artist MYRA REYNOLDS RICHARDS sculpted the fountain piece, *The Pioneer Family*. Dedicated in 1924, the fountain was removed in 1954 as part of a plan to alleviate traffic congestion in the square. A community organization petitioned for the fountain's return from GARFIELD PARK, and it was restored in 1979.

Fountain Square prospered into the 1920s, especially when it became the city's first cinema theater district. As many as seven theaters operated at one time, including the Sanders (Apex) Theater (1914–1952) and the Fountain Square Theatre (1928–1960).

Fountain Square fell on hard times after World War II when newer shopping centers emerged and suburbs drew away residents. Interstate 65/70 construction razed many homes in the 1960s, but when the district was listed on the National Register of Historic Places in 1983, corporate support, city grants, and private donations initiated a revitalization program that continues today.

CATHLEEN F. DONNELLY

Indianapolis Historic Preservation Commission, "Fountain Square Historic Area Preservation Plan," January, 1984.

Fox, Lillian Thomas (1866–1917). African-American journalist, club woman, and civic leader. Lillian Thomas was born in Chicago to the Reverend Byrd Parker, pastor of Quinn African Methodist Episcopal Church, and Jane Janette Thomas, a schoolteacher. She was raised in Oshkosh, Wisconsin, moving to Indianapolis in the early 1880s. She began writing at an early age and by the late 1880s achieved recognition for her work as reporter and correspondence editor for the *INDIANAPOLIS FREEMAN*, a nationally prominent black newspaper. She also made several speaking tours in the Midwest and South for various political and religious organizations.

In 1893 Thomas retired from the *Freeman* after her marriage to James E. Fox, a Jamaican merchant tailor from Pensacola, Florida, who relocated his business to Indianapolis. Although she curtailed her career, Fox continued her work

Lillian Thomas Fox was the first African-American reporter for the *Indianapolis News*. [Indiana Historical Society, #C3441]

with community and national civic organizations such as the Afro-American Council, the Atlanta Congress of Colored Women at the 1895 National Exposition, and the National Association of Colored Women's Clubs.

After separation from her husband in the late 1890s, Fox returned to journalism. In 1900 the *INDIANAPOLIS NEWS* hired her as the first African-American to write a regular news column in any white Indiana newspaper. For the following 14 years Fox used her contacts with the white community and her position at the *News* to further the social and political agendas of many black community organizations, among them the Woman's Improvement Club, founded by Fox in 1903. That club not only provided its members with an opportunity for self-expression and growth, but between 1905 and 1935 provided health care to black tuberculosis patients and scholarships and assistance to indigent black citizens. A superb organizer, Fox also founded the Indiana State Federation of Colored Women's Clubs and had memberships in other community organizations, including BETHEL AFRICAN METHODIST EPISCOPAL Literary Society and the ALPHA HOME Association.

EARLINE RAE FERGUSON

Earline Rae Ferguson, "Lillian Thomas Fox: Indianapolis Journalist and Community Leader," *Black History News & Notes*, No. 28 (May, 1987), 4–8.

Franklin Township. Southeastern Marion County township. Laid out by the county commissioner in 1822, Franklin Township became a separate political unit with its division from PERRY

Selected Statistics for Franklin Township, 1990

Population	21,458
Population per Square Mile	511
Percent African-American	0.5
Percent 0 to 17 Years	30.8
Percent 65 Years and Over	7.2
Percent 25 Years and Over with a High School Degree or Equivalency	85.3
Percent 25 Years and Over with a College Degree	16.9
Per Capita Income in 1989	$16,111
Unemployment Rate (%)	2.9
Married-Couple Families as a Percent of Total Households	72.0
Median Home Value	$75,600

TOWNSHIP on May 12, 1824. Approximately 42 square miles in area, with a 1990 population of 21,458, it is rapidly changing from farmland to home sites, with some commercial development.

The earliest settler is believed to have been William Rector, whose land lay along Buck Creek where Michigan Road (later S.R. 29, U.S. 421, and now I–74 and Southeastern Avenue) enters the township. The first election was held at his cabin where he was chosen justice of the peace on June 19, 1824.

The first settlement was New Bethel, platted along the MICHIGAN ROAD in 1834. There was a store, a pottery, a blacksmith, and wagon maker. Smither Tavern, just west of the village, was an early stage stop, about 12 miles from Indianapolis. In 1889, needing a name for the newly established post office (there was already a Bethel, Indiana), the town chose WANAMAKER, honoring Philadelphia merchant John Wanamaker, then U.S. postmaster general.

ACTON was platted in 1852 along the nearly completed Cincinnati and Indianapolis Railroad. Originally called Farmersville, the town was renamed when the post office was opened in 1854. (The origin of the name is unknown). Acton developed as a busy trading center with general stores, blacksmith shops, a lumber yard, feed mill, canning factory, a bank, three lodge halls, churches, and homes.

The Acton Camp Ground, a 40–acre tract at the corner of Southport and Acton roads, was established as a Methodist campground in 1859. Visitors came from a wide area for the late summer programs, and many well-known clergymen, educators, and politicians spoke there. Families rented or owned cottages on the grounds,

some staying all summer. The grounds burned in 1905, destroying the large pavilion and 115 cottages.

In 1902 the Indianapolis and Cincinnati Traction Company began service through the township, along Michigan Road through Wanamaker, then following the train tracks through Acton. The interurban line, which extended to Greensburg, was discontinued in the mid–1930s.

Wanamaker is now the business center of the township. There is commercial growth along the township's western edge. Beech Grove annexed some land that was originally Franklin Township, including the Beech Grove Shops (Amtrak) and commercial property along Emerson Avenue. In the 1990s development centered on Emerson Avenue at Southport Road and Stop 11 Road.

The FIVE POINTS area includes the H. A. Waterman Company, a century-old business, a few stores, and the nearby Marion County Fairgrounds.

The Franklin Township Community School Corporation operates five elementary schools, one middle school, and Franklin Central High School. Lutheran High School is located on Arlington Avenue. The Franklin Township Civic League oversees community development and supports a weekly newspaper, the *Franklin Township Informer*. Other community organizations include the Franklin Township Chamber of Commerce, Acton Community Council, Franklin Township Historical Society, and the Buck Creek Players.

SYLVIA C. HENRICKS
Franklin Township Historical Society

Berry R. Sulgrove, *History of Indianapolis and Marion County* (Philadelphia, 1884), 519–534; *The Trail of a Century, Being a History of the New Bethel Baptist Church and Community from 1827–1927* (Wanamaker, Ind., 1927); Sylvia C. Henricks, "A Good and Profitable Occasion: The Story of Acton Camp Ground," *Indiana Magazine of History*, 66 (Dec., 1970), 299–317; U.S. Census.

Fraternal Organizations. From the earliest days of the city fraternal organizations have been an important part of community life, providing members with opportunities to socialize and serving as important sources of mutual aid. They have also been active in philanthropic work for the benefit of the whole community. While most began as men's organizations, the term *fraternal* also applies to some women's groups, both those auxiliary to men's organizations and those that are independent. Some fraternals have given support and structure to particular racial, religious, and ethnic communities, and others have worked with the Anglo-Protestant mainstream, giving members a sense of participation in national and international organizations, as well as opportunities to acquire local status and recognition.

The Free and Accepted Order of Masons was the first of the city's fraternal organizations, coming in 1824. Affiliated with them are the Scottish and York Rites, as well as two girls' organizations—Job's Daughters and Rainbow Girls—and a boys' group, De Molay. The Order of the Eastern Star is a Masonic women's organization that functions independently of the men's lodges. The Murat Temple of the Ancient Order of Nobles of the Mystic Shrine (organized in Indianapolis in 1884), and the Sahara Grotto draw their members entirely from Freemasons but maintain independent organizations. By 1994 the city had over 13,000 Freemasons in 23 separate lodges. The Independent Order of Odd Fellows, which came to Indianapolis in 1844, retains four lodges in the city, but its membership has declined since the 1960s. The Benevolent and Protective Order of Elks, which came to town in 1881, and the Loyal Order of the Moose, which arrived in 1907, both maintain a ritual tradition but have adopted a less formal style. Local Elks in 1993 numbered about 300, while the Moose have over 5,000 men and about 4,000 women enrolled in the area. All the groups own or lease space for a variety of social activities. Some maintain bar and restaurant facilities for their members. Most sponsor regular social gatherings that promote long-standing social relationships between members.

Besides social and ritual activity, most Indianapolis fraternal groups have provided some type of material benefits to their members. Much of the early popularity of beneficial fraternal orders came from the death benefits they provided to widows and orphans of deceased members. For some groups this evolved into a full range of insurance services, and many mutual insurance companies have their roots in these groups. This was especially important for groups that catered to immigrant populations in the years surrounding the turn of the century, but even the mainstream Freemasons provide for a Masonic funeral service for members. Some local Odd Fellows lodges continue to provide death benefits, but many have had to curtail such activities as their finances declined. The Elks made care of widows and orphans of members one of their central concerns in their early years, but have since given it up as insurance has become nearly universal among their members. Health care is still a major concern of the Moose. Its Indianapolis lodges have frequently used Mooseheart, a facility for the care of widows and orphans in Aurora, Illinois. Local Moose members have also made use of their retirement home, Moosehaven, located near Jacksonville, Florida. One organization that has made material benefits central to its mission is the Independent Order of Foresters, which set up its first lodge in the city in 1889. While it once had social and ritual facilities like most Indianapolis fraternals, this group has abandoned most of that and rents space for its monthly social gatherings. Its main focus is to provide an extensive network of financial services including full-range insurance, mutual funds, and various investment opportunities. It also maintains a local credit union and a scholarship fund for its members, which include men, women, and children. Its local membership stood at about 5,000 in 1993.

Philanthropy and charitable activity have gained an increasing role in the work of many Indianapolis fraternal organizations. As the character of modern society has made social and ritual activities less attractive, and many of the mutual aid benefits less necessary, giving something to the community has become an important part of the purpose of most fraternals. Both nationally and locally, nearly every group has adopted at least one cause or organization to support. The Murat Shrine supports a pediatric hospital and burn unit. Local Elks have given several million dollars for cancer research at IUPUI. The Odd Fellows support research into diseases of the eye. Most Indianapolis fraternals sponsor youth athletic programs, and many support efforts to discourage drug use among young people. Volunteer service also has become a major part of the program for many fraternal organizations.

Indianapolis once had many fraternal societies oriented to the needs of particular ethnic and religious groups. The city's once large German-speaking population boasted several such organizations. The German Order of Harugari came in 1875 and was followed by the Sons of Herman in 1896. Both groups were founded to protect German-Americans and their culture from the depredations of the American nativists. GERMANS also formed separate lodges within mainstream fraternal groups such as the Ancient Order of Druids, a society that originated in England but had an entirely German-speaking membership when it came to town in 1854. When the Knights of Pythias demanded its rituals be conducted exclusively in English, seven local lodges with 13,000 German-speaking members seceded and helped found the Improved Order of the Knights of Pythias in 1893. Church bans and ingrained religious tensions forced Roman Catholics to form their own fraternal organizations. The Knights of Columbus came to town in 1899 and promoted adult education and provided insurance to its members. It currently maintains an insurance office in the city and six chapters in the Indianapolis area. Irish Catholics brought the ANCIENT ORDER OF HIBERNIANS to Indianapolis in 1867. It provided its members with mutual aid and social opportunities, and it promoted the ideal of a Catholic Ireland among its members. A number of Jewish fraternal organizations once flourished in the city during the late 19th and early 20th centuries, including the Order of B'rith Abraham, the Independent Order of the Sons of Benjamin, and the Knights of Joseph. B'nai B'rith came to town in 1867 and continues to have a presence in the city.

Of all the barriers between residents of Indianapolis, race has been the most enduring. In recent years most of the large mainstream fraternal organizations have admitted African-Americans, but over the years the black community has produced its own fraternal groups. These organizations have always been an important social outlet, a forum for the development of leadership skills, and a mechanism of self-help and mutual aid by providing insurance benefits and charity

to group members and the city's larger African-American community. Prince Hall Free-masonry—a black version of Masonry—came to the city in 1847, and by the turn of the century there were 14 such lodges in Indianapolis and two black Order of the Eastern Star chapters for women. African-American versions of the Odd Fellows, the Elks, and the Knights of Pythias also assumed a prominent place in the city's black community. As with all fraternal groups, many of those oriented to the black community began to decline in the 1960s. Several Prince Hall Masonic groups remain active, as well as the Knights and Ladies of St. Peter Claver, a black Catholic order. The Masonic groups sponsor two annual parades and Emancipation Day activities. Most of the lodges make contributions to local black churches and run programs to help the needy. They also engage in philanthropy of special interest to African-Americans, sponsoring scholarships and youth programs and donating to the NAACP, the United Negro College Fund, and sickle cell anemia research.

Fraternalism in Indianapolis peaked in the years around the turn of the century and went through another resurgence in the 1920s. During that time even the politically oriented KU KLUX KLAN attempted to present itself as a fraternal organization and gained a huge local membership. But political involvement has never been a popular feature of local fraternals. Several local fraternal organizations dedicated themselves to the cause of temperance, but these too disappeared rather quickly. In keeping with the national trend, Indianapolis' fraternalism has declined since the 1960s, but several groups continue to grow by adapting to the needs of contemporary society. Over the years these groups have provided the community with a wide range of services and have been important vehicles for the spread of mainstream social values. Even fraternal groups that catered to the needs of particular racial, religious, and ethnic groups have fostered mainstream social values and helped move their membership into the city's middle class.

KEVIN CORN

Jacob Piatt Dunn, *Greater Indianapolis* (Chicago, 1910).

Free University. Established in Indianapolis in 1964, the Free University provided a variety of courses on different topics to as many people as possible at limited or no cost. Free universities were a very popular idea in the 1960s. Many were associated with "counterculture" movements that sought to provide alternative learning experiences outside of formal education settings such as public schools or colleges.

From 1964 to 1969, Free University was a loosely structured set of classes overseen by the nonprofit Experimental Education Foundation of Indianapolis, Inc. to "provide complementary and continuing education" to the Indianapolis area. The Indianapolis Free University was a leader in the free university movement in both course offerings and enrollment. The university catalog published in 1977 offered courses from hypnosis to candlemaking to astrology to metaphysics. In 1978, the Indianapolis Free University was the fourth largest free university in the United States, enrolling 15,000 people in noncredit courses administered by a staff of 14. Free University catalogs distributed in 1982 listed over 100 different courses.

Control of the Free University transferred from the Hoosier Educational Resource Exchange to the Athenaeum Turners group in the mid–1980s. The name changed to Turners Free University and the headquarters moved to the Athenaeum Turners building in downtown Indianapolis. Free University continues to offer a wide variety of courses and programs.

ROBERT SCHWARTZ

———

Free University catalogs; *Indianapolis Star Magazine* (Feb. 7, 1982).

Freeman, John, Fugitive Slave Case of (1853). The Fugitive Slave Law of 1850, part of the Compromise of 1850, amended the 1793 Fugitive Slave Law by giving the federal government sole jurisdiction over fugitive slave cases. Following a summary hearing, special commissioners could issue warrants for the arrest of fugitive slaves and certify their return to their masters. An affidavit by the claimant was accepted as sufficient proof of ownership. To entice commission-

ers to return suspected slaves, commissioners received $10 for each return certificate and half as much if return was denied. Fugitives claiming to be free men were not entitled to a jury trial and could not testify on their own behalf. Likewise, those who interfered with the law were penalized. Marshals refusing to execute warrants were fined $1,000 and citizens interfering with the arrest of a suspect were fined $1,000, with a possible six-month jail term.

A native of Georgia, John Freeman came to Indianapolis about 1844, where he was a painter and owned a restaurant. On June 20, 1853, United States marshals arrested him on an affidavit sworn by Reverend Pleasant Ellington, a Methodist minister from St. Louis, Missouri. Ellington claimed that 17 years earlier, while a resident of Kentucky, his slave Sam ran away and that Freeman was the escaped slave. Hearing of Freeman's predicament, Indianapolis attorneys John L. Ketcham, Lucian Barbour, and JOHN COBURN came to his aid. The attorneys successfully petitioned the U.S. commissioner for additional time to prepare their case but lost their request that Freeman be released on bond during that time.

Freeman's lawyers found witnesses in Georgia who were prepared to testify that Freeman had lived in Georgia as a free man from 1831 to 1844. The lawyers also located the real Sam residing in Canada under the alias of William McConnell, but understandably he refused to return to Indianapolis for the trial. Witnesses who met Sam testified that his physical characteristics did not resemble Freeman's. For his part, Ellington produced three witnesses who, after stripping Freeman to examine his body, claimed he was Sam. The case was dismissed when Ellington's son could not identify Freeman as the former slave.

Released from jail after nine weeks, Freeman retained his freedom but lost his savings in the process. He brought a civil suit against both Ellington and the arresting federal marshal, John L. Robinson. Freeman sued Ellington for $10,000; the court ruled in Freeman's favor, but reduced the award to $2,000. Ellington, however, had fled Indianapolis, leaving no means to collect the settlement. Freeman also brought suit in the Marion County Circuit Court against Robinson for $3,000, charging him with assault, forcing the prisoner to strip, and extorting $3 per day for protection while imprisoned. The Indiana Supreme Court agreed in December, 1855, that Robinson had acted improperly, but dismissed the case because it had been filed in Marion County instead of Rush County where Robinson resided.

Freeman sold much of his property to pay his debts and when the Civil War erupted, he moved his family to Canada.

STACEY NICHOLAS

Charles H. Money, "The Fugitive Slave Law of 1850 in Indiana," *Indiana Magazine of History*, 17 (June, 1921), 180–198; Emma Lou Thornbrough, *The Negro in Indiana* (Indianapolis, 1957), 115–117.

Freemasonry. Oldest fraternal order in Indianapolis. The Freemason's Grand Lodge of Indiana, with its doctrine of self-knowledge and service, was chartered in 1823 and met in various cities before finding a home in Indianapolis that same year. Shortly thereafter, HARVEY GREGG, SAMUEL HENDERSON, and others founded Center Lodge, which first met in the Washington Hall tavern on October 7, 1823. Many prominent Indianapolis citizens became Masons. Governor James Whitcomb was a Royal Arch Mason. Indianapolis businessman Alexander Franco was reputedly the first known Jewish Mason.

Interest and membership waned during a strong anti-Masonic movement between 1826 and 1840. A supposed "expose" of Freemasonry led to public opposition; Indianapolis membership fell from 654 to 513. Remaining Indianapolis members held their ground until persecution died out in the early 1840s. From that point growth of Masonry followed the growth of Indianapolis, with nine lodges chartered between 1848 and 1877. Membership doubled between 1857 and 1865 but fell again after the Panic of 1873. By 1901 Indianapolis claimed 2,042 members. Citizens gathered to watch Masonic parades and funeral processions. New Masonic temples were built of stone as examples of the trade of masonry. The first Masonic Hall in Indianapolis (constructed 1848–1850) was for many years the city's principal venue for public lectures and concerts; it also hosted the state's second Constitutional Convention in 1850–1851. The SCOTTISH RITE CATHEDRAL is currently the city's premier Masonic building.

Locally, Masonry is practiced by a variety of groups which, though united by a desire for self-improvement and service, practice different rites. The most prominent groups are the Ancient Accepted Scottish Rite, Order of the Eastern Star, Sahara Grotto, and the Ancient Order of Nobles of the Mystic Shrine. Most African-American members are aligned with Prince Hall Masonry.

In 1993, when Indiana Freemasons celebrated the 175th anniversary of Freemasonry in the state, Indianapolis had 13,229 Masons in 23 lodges.

MICHAEL WATSON

Jacob Piatt Dunn, *Greater Indianapolis* (Chicago, 1910), I, 371–377; Will E. English, *A History of Early Indianapolis Masonry and Center Lodge* (Indianapolis, 1895); Dwight L. Smith, *Goodly Heritage: One Hundred Fifty Years of Craft Freemasonry in Indiana* ([Franklin, Ind.], 1968).

Freethought. Freethought aims to approach all matters objectively and rationally, although this definition oversimplifies. Principally antireligious, thus its atheistic and humanistic cast, the movement encompasses a wide range of thinkers and doers: social activists, radicals, iconoclasts, liberal religionists, and ideologues. Their ideas and activities often have, in time, become public policy. Freethought came to the United

the Athenaeum in 1905. [IUPUI Archives]

States through English Deism and German Rationalism, the latter being particularly relevant in Indianapolis. The large German component in Indianapolis in the mid- to late–19th century practically guaranteed the presence of freethought.

Although some freethought stirrings occurred before 1870 (the *Freie Presse von Indiana*, Indianapolis, 1853–1866, is considered a freethought newspaper), the organization in that year of the Indianapolis Freidenker-Verein or Freethinkers' Society is generally recognized as the origin of Indianapolis freethought. This group, led by such urban professionals as CLEMENS VONNEGUT, Herman Lieber, and PHILIP RAPPAPORT, sought to instill progressive and modern ideas in their children and their community. They instituted lectures, a "Sunday School," and social programs, and they challenged conventional wisdom through their advocacy of women's rights, health insurance, and vocational education. Clemens Vonnegut's *A Proposed Guide for Instruction in Morals: From the Standpoint of a Freethinker: For Adult Persons / Offered by a Dilettante* (Indianapolis, 1889) is one known freethought tract from this era. Through its 20–year existence, membership in the Freidenker-Verein never exceeded 80. The group faded in the 1880s from lack of volunteer effort and funding, and it disbanded in 1890.

Organized freethought in Indianapolis stalled after the collapse of the German society. Dr. Jasper Roland Monroe's Indianapolis weekly, *Ironclad Age*, advocated freethought issues in the 1890s, but most freethinkers wanting an organizational structure had to go out of state. In 1909, however, Indianapolis hosted the first convention of the newly formed Indiana Rationalist Association. This group established its headquarters in Indianapolis and many of its officers and members came from the capital city. In 1911 it published an important compilation of its activity entitled *The Light of Reason*. Its purpose was almost exclusively antireligious: it sought to expose the fallacy of revealed religion, oppose the union of church and state, and disprove the existence of the supernatural. A leading spokesperson was Dr. James A. Houser, an Indianapolis physician, who lectured widely and disseminated his orthodoxy, called the New Science of Life. A lack of dues-paying members spelled the end in 1913 for the Indiana Rationalist Association, which then evolved into a national body, though not headquartered in Indianapolis. A few short-lived groups, the Truth Seekers, the Scientific Educational Society, and others, attempted to carry on the work, but organized freethought in Indianapolis for all practical purposes ceased by the mid–1920s. Individuals, afterwards, practiced freethinking with memberships in national or regional humanistic and atheistic bodies.

ROBERT M. TAYLOR, JR.
Indiana Historical Society

Marshall G. Brown and Gordon Stein, *Freethought in the United States: A Descriptive Bibliography* (Westport, Conn., 1978); Robert M. Taylor, Jr., "The Light of Reason: Hoosier Freethought and the Indiana Rationalist Association, 1909–1913," *Indiana Magazine of History*, 79 (June, 1983), 109–132.

Freetown Village. Living history museum that symbolically represents predominantly black settlements located throughout Indiana after the Civil War. "Residents" are composite characters based upon the approximately 3,000 African-American men, women, and children living in Indianapolis around 1870. Issues of education, family life, religion, politics, economics, and society are addressed through interactive educational programs, including first-person interpretive programs, touring history plays, craft and heritage workshops, and special events.

Founded in 1982 to teach black history to wider audiences, Freetown Village received a planning grant from the Indiana Humanities Council to implement a pilot project at the INDIANA STATE MUSEUM. Subsequent funding has come from memberships, gifts, and foundation and corporate grants. Approximately 400,000 individuals participate annually in Freetown Village programs offered at schools, state parks, museums, and other locations. Freetown Village is governed by a board of directors and administered by an executive director. Long range plans call for development of a permanent museum and village site in the downtown area.

OPHELIA UMAR WELLINGTON
Freetown Village

Frenzel, John P., II (Dec. 21, 1853–May 29, 1933) and **Otto N., I** (Sept. 8, 1856–June 23, 1925). Indianapolis bankers and businessmen. Sons of the engineer responsible for driving the first locomotive from Madison to Indianapolis, John P. Frenzel II was born in Madison, Indiana, while Otto N. Frenzel I was born in Indianapolis in the family home on South Street.

Having studied at the German-English Independent School, John enrolled in North Western Christian University (later BUTLER UNIVERSITY) at age 11. In January, 1867, he became the first Frenzel to work at MERCHANTS NATIONAL BANK when he became the bank's messenger at age 13. In 1870 John and George A. Dickson formed Enterprise Building & Loan, the city's first building and loan association. When John was promoted by management to bookkeeper and teller in 1871 the bank took his recommendation and hired his younger brother, Otto N., to take over his former job as messenger. In 1872 Otto and John founded a steamship booking agency, called Frenzel Brothers, which operated out of the bank building. Three years later, when John became cashier, Otto took over as bookkeeper and teller and a third Frenzel brother, Oscar F., joined the bank as messenger.

When Volney T. Malott retired as president of Merchants National Bank in 1882, John and Otto Frenzel purchased his stock holdings. John took over as president and Otto became bank cashier. The two brothers were also involved in other financial institutions, forming such firms as the Western Savings & Loan Association of Indianapolis, the National Trust and Safe Deposit Company, the South Eastern Savings & Loan Association, and the Indiana Trust Company.

In 1883 John was elected to the city's Board of School Commissioners, serving as a member and president for 14 years. It was his recommendation that led to the construction of MANUAL HIGH SCHOOL. In 1887 John joined with other local businessmen to found the Consumers Gas Trust Company, the predecessor to the CITIZENS GAS Company. In 1892 he was elected treasurer of Marion County and served as a delegate to the Democratic national convention in Chicago in 1896.

Following John's resignation in 1902 to devote more time to the Indiana Trust Company, Otto became president of Merchants National Bank. As president, he oversaw the firm's move into the city's first skyscraper, the MERCHANTS NATIONAL BANK BUILDING, a 17–story structure. He was an active member of the Indianapolis BOARD OF TRADE and served for many years as president of the Indianapolis Clearing House Association. In addition to his position with Merchants, Otto also served as a vice-president and member of the board of directors of the Indiana Trust Company and as a member of the board of directors of the Indiana Hotel Company, which owned the CLAYPOOL HOTEL. The brothers were long-time supporters of the Indianapolis MAENNERCHOR, a German-American male chorus; during WORLD WAR I both John and Otto served on the general committee for Liberty Bond drives.

After Otto's death, John served as president of Merchants National Bank (1925–1928) and as chairman of the board of directors until his own death in 1933. An active member of the Democratic party, he served many years as treasurer of the county organization. He was a member of the first Board of Metropolitan Police Commissioners of Indianapolis and both president and chairman of the board of the Indianapolis Street Railway Company.

RAY BOOMHOWER
Indiana Historical Society

The City and the Bank, 1865–1965 (Indianapolis: privately printed, 1965); *Indianapolis Star*, June 24, 1925.

Frenzel, Otto Nicholas, II (May 6, 1899–May 28, 1989). Banker. The son of Otto N. Frenzel I, the nephew of John P. Frenzel II, and a native of Indianapolis, Frenzel attended Cornell University after graduating from SHORTRIDGE HIGH SCHOOL. While a student at Cornell he enlisted in the Naval Reserve and served in the United States Navy during World War I. Returning to Indianapolis, Frenzel began his career in banking as a messenger boy in his father's MERCHANTS NATIONAL BANK in 1919. Progressing through all offices, he served as the bank's president from 1945 to 1966, chairman of the board from 1966 to 1969, and retired as chairman of the executive committee of Merchants National Bank and Trust Company two weeks before his death. He also served as president of the Indiana Bankers Association and as a member of the executive committee of the American Bankers Association.

Throughout his banking career Frenzel was a director of many Indianapolis companies including INDIANAPOLIS POWER AND LIGHT, STOKELY–VAN CAMP, AMERICAN UNITED LIFE INSURANCE, and American States Insurance. He also served as a director of the PENNSYLVANIA RAILROAD and Youngstown Sheet and Tube. From 1936 to 1945 Frenzel served as president of the Indiana Trust Company.

In civic service, Frenzel served as a director for a number of groups: the Indiana State Chamber of Commerce, Indianapolis Hospital Development Association, United Fund of Greater Indianapolis (now UNITED WAY), Indianapolis Civic Progress Association, and the Indianapolis CHAMBER OF COMMERCE. He was also a trustee of both Park School (now PARK TUDOR) and BUTLER UNIVERSITY. A member of the Traders Point Hunt Club, Frenzel served as its president from 1936 to 1938. During World War II he served on the War Finance Committee and in 1954 he was appointed to a four-year term as chairman of the Indiana Toll Bridge Commission.

In recognition of his many civic contributions, Frenzel was awarded an honorary Doctor of Laws degree from Indiana Central College (now UNIVERSITY OF INDIANAPOLIS) in 1965.

PAT WATSON

Indiana Biography Series, Indiana State Library.

From Dawn to Daylight (1859). A controversial autobiographical novel, set principally in Indianapolis, by Eunice White Bullard Beecher. Born on August 20, 1812, in Massachusetts, Eunice Bullard was a schoolteacher who married HENRY WARD BEECHER in 1837 and moved with him to Indiana. Beecher, who became one of the most influential clergymen of his time, served two Presbyterian churches in Indiana between the years 1837 and 1847, First Presbyterian in Lawrenceburg and SECOND PRESBYTERIAN in Indianapolis.

Twelve years after leaving Indiana, Eunice Beecher, under the pseudonym "A Minister's Wife," published *From Dawn to Daylight*, a thinly veiled autobiographical novel about her years in Indiana. (The volume was subtitled *The Simple Story of a Western Home*.) Second Presbyterian Church in the state capital was the major subject of the book. Using the fictional names of Glenville and Norton for Lawrenceburg and Indianapolis respectively, Mrs. Beecher's portrayal of the cities and congregations outraged Indianapolis residents, particularly members of Second Presbyterian. Especially troublesome were allegations that both congregations, and notably Second Presbyterian, had been remiss in paying Mr. Beecher's salary. Also offensive were depictions of Indianapolis as a primitive, disease-infested backwater, devoid of culture or modern sensibilities.

In the novel, the character of Mary Leighton stands for Mrs. Beecher and her husband is represented by George Herbert. Mary, a vital, educated woman, follows her young clergyman husband to the frontier. There she endures profound loneliness and isolation, chronic illness, and the deaths of several children. In addition, she suffers the daily indignities peculiar to a minister's wife. She is little more than a domestic servant, at the constant disposal of judgmental parishioners.

Such unflattering depictions caused the novel to be banned by public sentiment in Indianapolis for decades after its publication. In 1872 copies disappeared from the shelves of the newly established city library and the school board passed a resolution officially withdrawing it. Twelve years later, when a new librarian put it back in circulation, the novel again disappeared.

Scholars have corroborated the events described in the novel and consider the characters and chronology to be an accurate representation of the Beechers' years in Indiana. Whatever its literary merits, *From Dawn to Daylight* has value for its portrayal of events and personalities from Indianapolis in the 1830s and 1840s.

JEANETTE VANAUSDALL

Jane Shaffer Elsmere, *Henry Ward Beecher: The Indiana Years, 1837–1847* (Indianapolis, 1973); Arthur

W. Shumaker, *A History of Indiana Literature* (Indianapolis, 1962).

Furniss, Sumner A. (Jan. 30, 1874 –Jan. 18, 1953). African-American physician. Born in Jackson, Mississippi, Furniss moved to Indianapolis with his family as a small child. He attended public schools and the University of Missouri. Before graduating he returned to Indianapolis and began studying medicine in 1891 under Dr. E. S. Elder, a white physician. Concurrently, he attended the Medical College of Indiana, graduating second in his class in 1894. That same year he successfully competed for a City Hospital internship, becoming the first African-American professional to serve at the hospital. He started his own practice the following year, eventually moving his office to 401 INDIANA AVENUE. "Doc" Furniss continued his general practice for over 50 years.

Furniss held memberships in the Marion County and Indiana medical societies and the American Medical Association. He was a lifetime member of the FLANNER HOUSE board and was a charter member and first president of the SENATE AVENUE YMCA. Also active in politics in the early 1900s, Furniss served as the second African-American on the City Council and as a member of the Marion County Republican executive committee. His brother Dr. Henry Furniss, who was briefly associated in practice with him in Indianapolis, served as consul to Bahia during the McKinley administration and in 1906 was appointed as minister to Haiti.

MICHELLE D. HALE

Indiana Biography Series, Indiana State Library; *Commemorative Biographical Record of Prominent and Representative Men of Indianapolis and Vicinity* (Chicago, 1908).

Fusion Movement (1854–1856). Political coalition that evolved into the Indiana REPUBLICAN PARTY. The Kansas-Nebraska dispute of 1854 triggered an effort in Indiana to bring together such diverse groups as Old Whigs, antislavery Free Soil men, anti-Nebraska Democrats, Know-Nothings, and supporters of temperance legislation. These groups successfully coalesced, temporarily, in the so-called Fusionist movement.

The state Fusion convention, which met in Indianapolis in July, 1854, called for restoration of the Missouri Compromise and repeal of the Kansas-Nebraska Act and opposed the extension of slavery into the territories. The delegates to the convention nominated an entire slate of candidates for state offices and announced support for candidates in all of Indiana's 11 congressional districts. The Fusion ticket, running under the banner of the People's party, captured state offices by margins of about 13,000 votes and won 9 of the 11 congressional seats. Fusionists won overwhelmingly in the northern two-thirds of the state.

In 1856, an effort was made to hold together the coalition that had won so decisively two years before. The People's party continued to oppose the Kansas-Nebraska Act and sent delegates to the first Republican national convention in Philadelphia. At the state convention the Fusionists selected OLIVER P. MORTON (a Democrat until 1854) as their nominee for governor. In spite of Morton's intense and able campaign, Democrat Ashbel Willard defeated him by nearly 6,000 votes. The Democrats won back four and retained two congressional seats, while People's party candidates were successful in five districts. But the emerging German vote, especially in Marion County, moved toward the People's party in 1856, and became a critical factor in Republican victories in the future. Fusion was thus a transitional stage that provided a vehicle for many politically disaffected individuals in the mid–1850s to find their way into the emerging Republican party.

ALLEN SHARP

Emma Lou Thornbrough, *Indiana in the Civil War Era* (Indianapolis, 1965), 61–76; Justin Walsh, *The Centennial History of the Indiana General Assembly* (Indianapolis, 1987), 184–186 (see esp. note 38).

G

Gallahue Plan. Strategy for recruitment of nurses. In an attempt to help alleviate the shortage of nurses following WORLD WAR II, Edward F. Gallahue, president of American States Insurance Company and a Methodist layman, decided to recruit nurses for METHODIST HOSPITAL "like we sell insurance." He enlisted the cooperation of the church hierarchy and visited Methodist summer youth camps. After a film and a short talk on nursing as a career, he distributed cards and asked the girls to indicate interest. Using the cards as a prospect file, ministers paid calls and follow-up mailings went out regularly. In 1949 Gallahue's efforts resulted in the largest graduating nursing class in the history of the hospital. The recruitment program, called the Gallahue Plan, was so successful that it became the subject of national attention and an article in *Reader's Digest*.

MARY BETH MOSTER
Methodist Hospital

GAR. See Grand Army of the Republic

Garfield Park and Conservatory. Oldest public park in the Indianapolis park system. Located 2.7 miles southeast of MONUMENT CIRCLE, its main entrance is at 2450 Shelby Street. In 1874 the Jeffersonville Railroad sold a 98–acre tract along its right of way to a group of entrepreneurs who built Southern Riding Park, a harness racing track. The venture was short-lived and the park was sold to Sheriff N. R. Rucker, who resold it to the City of Indianapolis for $109,500. The

The sunken gardens at Garfield Park, formerly the Southern Driving Park, on the south side were a popular attraction during the early 1900s.
[Indiana Historical Society, Bass Collection, #51093]

city renamed it Southern Park until President James A. Garfield was assassinated in 1881 when it was renamed in his honor. Two additional land purchases were made in the early 1900s, bringing the total area of Garfield Park to 128 acres.

Garfield provides generously equipped playground and picnic areas as well as extensive athletic facilities, a large outdoor pool, and a community center. Unique features include a large greenhouse and conservatory. The 10,000 square foot conservatory boasts the country's first welded aluminum, glass roof structure. The temperature controlled building includes a 15–foot granite waterfall set against a background of orchids and other tropical plants. A rain forest and desert area provide a varied educational opportunity for visitors. The conservatory faces another unusual park feature, the Sunken Garden, a large landscaped formal garden. Both the conservatory and garden are popular wedding sites.

The park's Pagoda is an imposing oriental-style concrete, rock, and wrought iron open structure with a curved copper roof. Built in 1903 at the height of opera popularity, it has been used for musical performances throughout the years. An open air theater provides staging for various theatrical events, including the annual Shakespeare Festival plays (threatened with closure after 1993 due to decreasing attendance).

Three separate war memorials are in Garfield Park: a large bronze statue of Major General Henry W. Lawton, a Fort Wayne native and Civil War veteran who later was credited with the capture of the Apache chief Geronimo; a granite shaft inscribed with the names of 1,616 Confederate soldiers who died while imprisoned at CAMP MORTON; and the Grove of Remembrance, with a tree planted for each of the 387 Marion County men and women who lost their lives in World War I.

A drive through the park and over the limestone bridges which span the flowing streams of Pleasant Run and Bean Creek and over "Tickle Belly Hill" reveals a beautiful rolling landscape. Although a 1992 tornado destroyed 20 percent of the park's trees, many stately oaks and sycamores are included in the still beautiful stand of trees.

VI WALTON

Garfield Park Neighborhood. District bounded by Raymond Street and Pleasant Run Creek, I–65, Troy Avenue, and Madison Avenue. Proximity to the city's first major park encouraged little growth in the vicinity of Southern Driving Park (renamed Garfield Park in 1881) before the first streetcar reached the leisure spot in 1895. Residential development remained slow into the 20th century, primarily because of the difficulty of negotiating railroad crossings on Indianapolis' south side. Between 1915 and 1918 the city annexed much of the former Yoke farmstead around the park. Elevating railroad crossings allowed easier access to the area, and by 1916 a neighborhood had sprung up east of the spot. Although much of the nearby land remained as small truck farms until the 1950s, by 1960 the area had become a mixed residential, commercial, and industrial district. In 1962, when there were 13,000 residents in the neighborhood surrounding the park, the district had reached its population apex. Construction of the Madison Avenue Expressway and I–65 in the late 1960s increased traffic through the area and also resulted in the demolition of a number of residences east of the park.

In the early 1990s the neighborhood is a predominately white, middle class district with a relatively stable population. Housing ranges from the 1842 Yoke farmhouse to 20th-century bungalows and duplexes, and the continuing presence of storefront businesses lends a small-town atmosphere to the neighborhood.

CONNIE J. ZEIGLER

Garrigue, Jean (Dec. 8, 1914–Dec. 27, 1972). Award-winning poet. Born in Evansville, Indiana, to Allan Colfax and Gertrude (Heath) Garrigus, Jean later changed her surname to the original French spelling of Garrigue. Her father was a U.S. postal inspector in Indianapolis for many years, and she graduated from SHORTRIDGE HIGH SCHOOL in 1931. She attended BUTLER UNIVERSITY, graduated from the University of Chicago in 1937, and received a master's degree from the University of Iowa in 1943. Apart from brief teaching engagements, travel, and visits to artists' colonies, she lived the remainder of her life in New York City.

Although she wrote short stories and published a study of the poet Marianne Moore, Garrigue was best known for her own poetry. Her numerous awards included a Rockefeller grant in creative writing (1954), a *Hudson Review* poetry fellowship (1957), and a Guggenheim fellowship (1960–1961). Her *Country Without Maps* (1964) was nominated for a National Book Award. Other publications included *The Monument Rose* (1953) and *New and Selected Poems* (1967).

CATHERINE SWANSON

Donald E. Thompson, comp., *Indiana Authors and Their Books* (Crawfordsville, Ind., 1974); *Indianapolis Star*, Jan. 22, 1973.

Gatch, Willis Dew (Oct. 27, 1877–Jan. 24, 1962). Surgeon and medical educator; inventor of the Gatch hospital bed. A native of Aurora, Indiana, Gatch received an A.B. degree from Indiana University in 1901. He graduated from Johns Hopkins Medical School in 1907, remaining there until 1909 as an intern and resident. While at Hopkins he devised the first hand-cranked "hospital bed" or Gatch bed. This bed was divided into sections for the independent elevation of a patient's head and knees.

Following a residency at Washington University in St. Louis, in 1912 Gatch became associate professor of surgery at INDIANA UNIVERSITY SCHOOL OF MEDICINE. He also maintained a large private practice in Indianapolis. In 1928, as head of the surgery department, he established the first residency programs recognized by the Board of Surgery in Indiana.

Dean of the School of Medicine from 1931 to 1946, Gatch established the school's clinical laboratories and medical illustration department. He presided over a critical period for the school, attempting to conform to national standards in medical education at a time of scanty Depression-era budgets. During World War II, facing a depletion of the staff at the same time the number of students was growing, he arranged deferments for School of Medicine faculty in order to help meet the medical needs of the armed forces. Following the war he continued his studies on surgical shock.

NANCY PIPPEN ECKERMAN
Indiana University School of Medicine

J. Stanley Battersby, *Dr. Gatch As I Knew Him* (Indianapolis, 1989).

Gatling, Richard J. (Sept. 12, 1818–Feb. 26, 1903). Inventor of the Gatling Gun. Born in North Carolina, Gatling became an inventor as a teen. His first important device was a wheat drill invented in 1843. It drilled wheat seeds into the earth, revolutionizing agricultural methods that had previously relied on inefficient broadcast sowing. In 1848 Gatling traded territoral sales rights for his drill to Mayor SAMUEL HENDERSON in exchange for Indianapolis real estate.

Gatling completed a medical degree from Cincinnati College before moving to Indianapolis in 1854, but he never practiced medicine. He dabbled in real estate and was unsuccessful in railroad speculation; he also continued to experiment with inventions. In 1862 he completed and patented his first GATLING GUN. Firing 250 (later up to 1,000) shots per minute the gun was a formidable weapon. Because it fired as many rounds as 100 men, Gatling believed it would reduce the number of soldiers needed to fight the Civil War and thereby lessen the number of Union casualties. He also said that his gun would serve as a deterrent by making war more "terrible." Governor OLIVER P. MORTON persuaded the federal government to purchase the gun for Union troops. Unfortunately for Gatling, his first factory located in Cincinnati, Ohio, burned down before completing the order. Although he rebuilt in Hartford, Connecticut, only two guns were completed and used by U.S. troops before the end of the war. Gatling also took his gun to the Paris Exposition in 1863, meeting and selling his invention to many of the crowned heads of Europe. Consequently the Gatling Gun was used in nearly every major armed conflict over the next 50 years.

In the mid–1860s Gatling moved from Indianapolis to Hartford, Connecticut. For many years he was president of the American Association of Inventors. His last invention was a motor-

ized plow, patented when he was 82. Gatling died in New York City but was buried with his wife in Crown Hill Cemetery.

CONNIE J. ZEIGLER

Indiana Biography Series, Indiana State Library.

Gatling Gun. Early rapid-firing weapon, or machine gun, invented by Dr. RICHARD J. GATLING. Gatling was a physician and real estate broker who settled in Indianapolis in 1854. His early inventions included a rice sowing machine, a wheat drill, and a steam plow, the latter developed in 1857.

In November, 1861, Gatling attended an Indianapolis exhibition at which a Mr. Hatch of Ohio demonstrated a breech loading cannon. It was made like a revolver and fired 25 shots per minute. In a few weeks Gatling developed a hand-cranked, rapid-fire weapon with ten rotating barrels capable of firing over 250 shots per minute. (Eventually, the standard firing rate of the Gatling gun was improved to about 1,000 rounds per minute.) In November, 1862, Gatling received U.S. Patent No. 36,836 for his weapon. Two sites later claimed to be the location where the first Gatling gun was manufactured: Gatling's Indianapolis factory and a metalsmith shop in Freeport, Shelby County.

The U.S. Navy adopted the gun in 1862, placing it aboard several federal gunboats on the Ohio and Mississippi rivers. The U.S. Army, however, experienced mechanical problems with its models and did not adopt the weapon until 1866. The Gatling gun was the military's principal rapid-firing weapon for more than 40 years, although the patent was sold to the Colt Company of Hartford, Connecticut, in the mid–1870s. The gun gave one of its greatest performances on July 1, 1898, when it provided support for the infantry charge up San Juan Hill in Cuba.

Manufacturers modified and greatly improved Gatling's original rapid-firing technique, but the principle never changed. During the Vietnam War the U.S. Army used a cannon (in 20mm and 30mm calibers) called the "Vulcan Automatic Gun." It utilized six rotating barrels and operated on the order of the original gun. The Air Force incorporated a similar design in one of its fighter aircraft used during the Persian Gulf War.

WAYNE L. SANFORD

Arville L. Funk, *Hoosiers in the Civil War* (Chicago, 1967); John Quick, *Dictionary of Weapons & Military Terms* (New York, 1973).

Gavazzi, Father Alessandro. After the fall of Rome to French troops in 1849, Catholic priest and Italian patriot Gavazzi escaped to England where he began a vigorous campaign against the Catholic Church and the Jesuit order. He later toured Quebec, where his criticisms of papal abuses and injustice provoked riots among the heavily Catholic population. Aided by anti-Catholic and Know Nothing groups, Gavazzi traveled through the United States warning audiences against Catholicism. Following an engagement in Cincinnati, he visited Indianapolis and spoke at the Masonic Hall on October 29–30, 1853.

In his lectures Father Gavazzi, who was introduced by Reverend Love H. Jameson of Central Christian Church, described the Church of Rome as a system of "hideous deformity and unmitigated evil," which neglected social problems and deprived people of their liberties. He criticized American women for wearing crosses as fashion ornamentation, urging them instead to "take the American Eagle." An avid nationalist, Gavazzi chastised Americans for patronizing Catholic schools and urged them to support the schools where "the mothers of Washington, Jefferson, Franklin, Webster and Clay [received] their education."

The *Indianapolis Journal* reported that Gavazzi's "patriotic outbursts were eloquent in the highest degree, and [he] elicited enthusiastic cheers from his auditors." Following his well-received appearance, Gavazzi continued his speaking tour and later returned to Italy where he continued to fight for Italian independence and religious liberalism.

DAVID G. VANDERSTEL
Indiana University–Purdue University,
Indianapolis

Indianapolis Journal, Oct. 26, Nov. 1, 1853; *Cambridge Biographical Dictionary* (Cambridge, Eng., 1990), 571.

Geisendorff Mill. 19th century woolen manufacturers. In 1847 Maryland-born brothers Christian E. and George W. Geisendorff opened a woolen mill in the abandoned INDIANAPOLIS STEAM MILL COMPANY building. Five years later they left the site and built the Hoosier Woolen Factory on West Washington Street near the WHITE RIVER bridge. The mill produced flannel, cassimeres, satinetts, blankets, pants, and stocking yarns. In 1861 they opened a salesroom and dry goods store at 63 West Washington Street. After the Civil War the Geisendorffs enlarged the mill, adding the Hoosier State Flouring Mills to the family business by 1867. In 1870 the company incorporated, listing Jacob C. Geisendorff, Christian E. Geisendorff, Isaac Thalman, and William W. H. MacCurdy as directors and shareholders. By 1880 the Geisendorff Mill was no longer producing flour, concentrating instead on woolen goods. During the early 1890s it employed more than 50 workers, produced an average of 8,000 yards of fabric each week, and opened branch mills in New York, Chicago, and St. Louis. In 1897 bankers S. A. Fletcher and Co. bought the company. The business apparently closed or changed its name soon after, since it does not appear in city directories after 1898.

DEBORAH B. MARKISOHN

Jacob Piatt Dunn, *Greater Indianapolis* (Chicago, 1910); *Hyman's Handbook of Indianapolis* (1897).

Geisse, John F. (1921–Feb. 22, 1992) Discount retailer. A native of Madison, Wisconsin, Geisse was a leader in the emerging high volume discount store industry and cofounder of several discount chains. In 1962 Geisse joined with Douglas Dayton of the Dayton Hudson Corporation, headquartered in Minneapolis, to found Target stores, which has become the third largest discount chain in the nation. In 1968 Geisse cofounded Venture Stores, a discount chain for the May Department Stores located in St. Louis.

After retiring from May Company to establish his own consulting business, Geisse invested in Ayr-Way Stores, the discount arm of L. S. AYRES AND COMPANY. He moved to Indianapolis in 1976 and served as chief executive officer of Ayr-Way from 1976 to 1978.

In 1982, following another brief retirement, Geisse founded the Indianapolis-based Wholesale Club, a no-frills, members-only discount store. By 1990 it had grown to 27 stores in six states. The next year, the Wholesale Club, valued at over $160 million, merged with Wal-Mart stores and reopened as Sam's Clubs. Geisse was inducted into the Discount Hall of Fame in 1984.

STACEY NICHOLAS

Indianapolis Star, Feb. 23, 1992.

Geist Reservoir. In 1941 the INDIANAPOLIS WATER COMPANY built a dam across FALL CREEK and flooded 1,900 of its 5,727 acres of land in northern Marion, southeastern Hamilton, and northwestern Hancock counties. The dam backed up water for 7.5 miles and covered 535 acres of woodland and 45 homesteads including the small village of Germantown. The water company, realizing that the WHITE RIVER could not continue to meet the growing city's water demands, had purchased the land in the 1920s. Geist Reservoir, named after Clarence H. Geist (president of the Indianapolis Water Company, 1913–1938), began supplying Indianapolis with water in 1943.

The reservoir was a popular fishing and recreation spot during the 1940s and 1950s. Motor boats and swimming were prohibited, but the Indianapolis Sailing Club had its headquarters at Geist and held races there. Bank fishing yielded thousands of local fishermen some of the largest crappies and catfish in the state.

In 1961 the Indianapolis Water Company announced its intention to convert the property around Geist into an exclusive subdivision. The company transferred 2,782 acres of land to its newly created subsidiary corporation, Shorewood, which proposed to close all of the land around the lake to bank fishing and picnicking and sell it as private lots.

The Marion County Council, led by president and frequent Geist fisherman John Kitley, opposed the water company's plan. In May, 1961, the County Board of Commissioners adopted a resolution to condemn the land around Geist for a public park. But when surveyors estimated the value of the land at $3.9 million the commissioners voted to rescind their resolution. This vote marked the end of official opposition to the water company's plan. Despite these events, little changed at Geist during the 1960s. The land remained undeveloped. Bank fishing was prohibited after 1961, but a public dock accommodated fishers. No boats with motors larger than 5 horsepower were permitted.

In 1970 the Indiana Public Service Commission ordered the water company to dispose of its excess reservoir land. Shorewood was made an independent, private corporation and given the land around Geist in exchange for 1,069,000 shares of its stock. Later that year the water company bought the rights to control boating and fishing on Geist from the County Line Dock Corporation. It renovated the docking facilities and in 1971 opened Geist to water skiing and speedboats with unlimited horsepower.

In September of that year Governor Edgar Whitcomb announced the state's plan to participate in the Army Corps of Engineers' $52 million project to expand Geist. The plans included two new dams that would double the reservoir's size. The proposed project delayed development for almost a decade, but was eventually scrapped in 1978 when U.S. Senator Birch Bayh refused to support it.

Shorewood finally began construction of its first two housing developments, Beamreach and Masthead, in 1980. Now under the ownership of the Meritor Financial Group of Philadelphia, Shorewood continues to sell lots around Geist in the early 1990s. Development has expanded farther from the shore as 500 homes now line the reservoir's banks. The reservoir itself is controlled by the state's Department of Natural Resources.

WILLIAM D. DALTON

Geology. The general geology of Marion County, gently dipping sedimentary rocks overlain by glacial deposits (see Figure 1), is quite similar to that in many other parts of the Midwest. The details of the local geology, however, are more specific to Marion County. The surface of the county is part of the physiographic province called the Tipton Till Plain. This is a flat to gently rolling land surface that is named after Tipton County (two counties north of Marion County) and is underlain by glacial deposits, the most common type being "till." In Marion County, the rolling surface is at elevations between about 650 and 900 ft. (about 200 and 275 m) above sea level.

The West Fork of WHITE RIVER and its tributaries drain most of Marion County; Buck Creek drains a narrow part of the southeastern margin of the county. White River enters the county at the north-central county line and flows south-south-westward as it passes near downtown Indianapolis to exit the county at the southwest-central county line. FALL CREEK, the largest tributary on the east side, enters the county in the northeast corner and flows southwestward until it joins White River at 10th Street near downtown Indianapolis. In fact, the original site selected for the new city in 1820 was located on the east bank of the White River at its junction with Fall Creek. (At that time Fall Creek joined White River farther south, near Washington Street.) The largest tributary on the west side is Eagle Creek, which enters the county in the northwest corner and flows southeastward until it joins White River in the southwestern part of the city.

Surficial Geology. About 2 million years ago an Ice Age began that resulted in several continental glaciers spread over Canada and the United States north of approximately the Ohio and Missouri rivers. In central Indiana this glaciation eventually extended to the Martinsville area about 35 miles (60 km) south of Marion County, with other lobes of the glacier extending much farther south in the southeastern and southwestern parts of Indiana. About 22,000 years ago the glacier retreated northward, leaving the county about 18,000 years ago. The evidence that the glacier once covered Marion County are the various deposits of materials that had been carried by the glacier as it advanced over the area but were left behind when the glacier melted away.

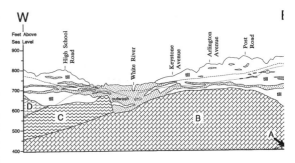

Fig. 1. Geologic cross section of Marion County.

These surficial materials are of utmost importance because they are the basic materials on which other factors act or depend. Thus, the soils that have supported agriculture from the beginning of settlement are developed from the weathering of the parent surficial materials. The surficial materials, especially those composed of sand and gravel, are a primary repository of underground well water, as well as being a prime source of sand and gravel for the construction industry throughout Marion County.

Most of the surficial materials in Marion County consist of glacial deposits that range in thickness from 16 to 350 ft. (5 to 107 m). Regionally, these deposits are related to Pleistocene (2 million years to 10,000 years ago) glaciation, although only Wisconsinan deposits (about 75,000 to 18,000 years ago) are exposed in the county. The main glacial deposit is a widespread *till* (material ranging in size from clay to boulders that had been carried by the glacier, but that was laid down under the glacier when it melted away or that flowed out from the margins of the glacier). This till blankets the upland surfaces in the county between major streams. The second most widespread glacial deposit is *outwash* (material that is washed out from the margins of the glacier by meltwater as the glacier is melting). The outwash consists of sand and sandy gravel, which typically occurs along the major streams as terraces. The original site of Indianapolis was on such a terrace as is much of the downtown area of the modern city. Other small and isolated deposits of sand and gravel called *kames*, that were entrapped in pockets along the ice margin or in crevasses on the glacier, occur mostly in the southern part of the county. Relatively minor amounts of sand, silt, and clay occur along the major stream valleys, deposited there over the centuries by the running water.

Soils. The soils in Marion County are developed mostly from glacial deposits, and to a lesser extent from the alluvial strips along the major valley bottoms. The most widespread soils in the county are the Brookston silty clay loam and the Miami and Crosby silt loams, which develop from glacial till on the upland gentle slopes. Other soils include Fox and Ockley silt loam, which form on outwash terraces along the White River valley and parts of the Eagle Creek valley, and Genessee silt loam which forms on the alluvial bottomlands of these valleys. The Brookston and Crosby soils are poorly drained, whereas the other soils are well drained.

Bedrock Geology. The bedrock structure of Indiana is geologically simple: from an axis trending from the southeastern to the northeastern corners of the state, the rock formations dip gently southwestward into the Illinois Basin or northward into the Michigan Basin. Marion County lies on the southwestward-dipping area, but, because of the glacial cover, bedrock is not exposed anywhere in the county (see Figure 1) except where quarrying and underground mining activities have removed the covering material.

The youngest bedrock unit in Marion County (D in Figure 1) is the Borden Group of sandstone and shale of Early Mississippian age (about 350 million years ago). The next older unit (C in Figure 1) is the New Albany Shale of Late Devonian to Early Mississippian age (about 370–350 million years ago); this formation is a potential source for petroleum products in the future. The next older bedrock unit (B in Figure 1) consists of several limestone and dolomite formations of Middle Devonian age (380 million years ago) and Silurian age (420 million years ago); the limestone is quarried or mined at several places in Marion County for use as crushed-stone or aggregate in the construction industry, and at deeper levels is a major bedrock aquifer for well water. The next older bedrock unit (A in Figure 1) is shale of Late Ordovician age (about 440 million years ago), which is underlain by about 4,000 ft. (about 1,220 m) of limestone, dolomite, shale, and sandstone extending back to the Late Cambrian age (about 525 million years ago). All of these sedimentary rocks rest on a basement complex of granitic rocks.

Geologic History. Beginning about 525 million years ago a shallow sea moved across Marion County, which had been undergoing erosion of a basement complex. During the interval until about 350 million years ago, the sea fluctuated over Indiana with Marion County being the site for the deposition of various types of sediments depending on the relative position of the shoreline. The evidence for what happened next is missing. The tilting of the bedrock formations occurred sometime after 350 million years ago, probably during the earth movements associated with the development of the Appalachian Mountains, ending about 250 million years ago. There may well have been more sediments deposited, but erosion stripped away any such deposits sometime before the onset of glaciation. About 2 million years ago an ice age began with glaciation gradually expanding until about one third of North America, eventually including Indiana and Marion County, was covered by an ice sheet. Marion County was quite hilly, with relief up to 425 ft. (about 130 m), but as the glaciers moved back and forth across the area they gradually filled in the valleys with glacial deposits and covered the hills. The glaciers left the county about 18,000 years ago, leaving the landscape pretty much what we see today, taking into consideration the modifying effects of climatic changes and weathering that follow a shift from a polar to a temperate climate.

ARTHUR MIRSKY
Indiana University–Purdue University,
Indianapolis

Edwin J. Hartke et al., "Geology for Environmental Planning in Marion County, Indiana," *Indiana Geological Survey*, Special Report 19 (1980); Arthur Mirsky, "The Geology of Water: The Limiting Factor in Urban Development," *Proceedings of the Indiana Academy of Science for 1972*, 82 (1973), 310–317.

George F. Cram Company. Indianapolis-based globe and map manufacturer. In 1862 George F. Cram enlisted in the Union Army, where he probably worked as a topographer. After the war he returned to Chicago and in 1867 joined his uncle's map business, eventually branching out on his own. In the 1920s Indianapolis-based National Map Company acquired Cram and moved it to the city, keeping the name because it was well known. Cram began making globes in the early 1930s.

The company continued to expand for the next several decades, moving to increasingly larger quarters and hiring more employees. Cram changed hands again in the 1960s. During the mid to late 1980s, business tripled as retail sales began to catch up with school sales. Previously, about 80 percent of the firm's products were for classroom use.

As of the early 1990s, Cram employed about 70 workers. All calculations and drawings for its maps are done by hand, with scale being determined by the size of the paper on which it is printed. Cram sells large wall maps for classroom use primarily in the United States and Canada; its globes, both machine made and handmade, are sold worldwide. Cram is the second largest producer of globes in the world.

DEBORAH B. MARKISOHN

German-English School Society.
After several attempts to establish schools for German-American children, a group of prominent, non-sectarian, liberal German-Americans in Indianapolis founded the German-English School Society (Deutsch-Englischer Schulverein) in 1859. The main reasons for the founding of the society were the deplorable conditions of the public schools of the time, the perceived undesirable stress on religion in public and parochial schools, and the desire to provide instruction in German language and culture as well as in English. The first meetings were held in February of that year. The German-English Independent School began operation toward the end of 1859 with Theodore Hielscher and Julius Schumm as teachers. Hielscher was also editor of the liberal German language newspaper *Die Freie Presse*. Both he and Schumm had previously conducted private schools of their own. In May, 1860, the school had 110 pupils. A three-story building on Maryland Street between Alabama and Delaware was designed by renowned architect DIEDRICH A. BOHLEN, who also served as one of the school's trustees.

The school enjoyed wide support from the German community, and in 1871 there were 252 children attending. By 1882, however, most German-Americans apparently believed that because the public schools had improved sufficiently and because German was now included in the curriculum it was no longer necessary to pay tuition for a separate school. Thus the bilingual school, which had educated well over a thousand children, ceased operations.

GILES R. HOYT
Indiana University–Purdue University, Indianapolis

George T. Probst, *The Germans in Indianapolis, 1850–1914*, rev. ed. by Eberhard Reichmann (Indianapolis, 1989); Theodore Stein, *Historical Sketch of the German-English Independent School of Indianapolis* (Indianapolis, 1913).

German-Language Press.
For thousands of German immigrants moving to the city in the mid–19th century, the press became part of a support structure that included churches, schools, *Vereins* (clubs, societies), and, in part, ethnic neighborhoods. This combination provided a comforting cultural continuity and kept the German language alive. Between September, 1848, when Julius Boetticher founded the weekly *Indiana Volksblatt* (Indiana People's Paper), and 1918, when the daily *Telegraph und Tribuene* closed due to wartime anti-German sentiments, German-language publications, which catered to the political and social diversity of the German-Americans, were the only foreign language press in the city.

The German-language newspapers were highly political in their focus. The conservative, Democratic-oriented *Volksblatt* (1848–1875) opposed the liberal 1848 revolution in the German states and criticized many recently emigrated leaders who sought to represent the local German community. The *Freie Presse* (Free Press, 1853–1866), founded by Theodore Hielscher, a supporter of the German revolution, was an uncompromising human rights voice embracing free soil, abolition, and the new Republican party. With key figures from the German-American community as editors (Karl Beyschlag, Valentine Butsch, Konradin Homburg, Herman Lieber, and E. J. Metzger), it fought against the largely anti-German nativist and prohibitionist factions and for personal freedom.

Eventually the original papers were absorbed by successors. The Democratic *Taeglicher Telegraph* (Daily Telegraph, 1865–1907) acquired the *Volksblatt* in 1875, and later merged with the *Indiana Tribuene* (1877–1907) to form the independent daily *Telegraph und Tribuene* (1907–June 1, 1918). The Gutenberg Company, which had published both the *Telegraph* and the *Tribuene* separately since 1903, reported that this last Indianapolis German daily had a circulation of 11,000 by 1915; its Sunday edition, the *Spottvogel* (Mockingbird), begun in 1865–1866, reached 11,979. News coverage ranged from local to international. The lighter side, with anecdotes, jokes, and installment novels, nurtured the cultural tradition. Advertising in both languages played its role, too.

The German community supported a variety of other publications. The religious press included the monthlies *Bote* (Messenger) and *Huelfe* (Help), and *Die Glocke* (The Bell, 1882–1905), "the Catholic weekly for truth and justice" with a circulation of 3,600. FREETHINKERS enjoyed the radical treatises of German revolutionary Karl Heinzen, published by the Society for the Dissemination of Radical Principles and distributed locally by its president Herman Lieber. *Gesundheits-Bote* (Health Messenger) was a practical health journal (1886–1899?). "Education! Progress! Freedom!" was the motto of the *Die Zukunft* (The Future), published by the Gutenberg Company for the North American Turners (1867–1882). Organizational and professional journals moved with their headquarters from city to city, including the German-American Typographical Union's semimonthly *Buchdruckerzeitung* (Printers Newspaper, 1873–1926) and the monthly *Carpenter* (1904?-1917) with its German section. Around 1900 anniversary observations of the Soziale Turnverein and the MAENNERCHOR resulted in beautiful

Festschrifts (festival publications) now available in translation.

EBERHARD REICHMANN
German-American Center, Indianapolis

George T. Probst, *The Germans in Indianapolis, 1840–1918*, rev. ed. by Eberhard Reichmann (Indianapolis, 1989); Jacob Piatt Dunn, *Greater Indianapolis* (Chicago, 1910), I, 395–396.

German Mutual Aid Societies. In post–1850 cities, *Unterstuetzungs-Vereins* (UVs) or mutual aid societies played a central support role for immigrants and their descendants by recreating elements of the supportive functions of the Old World village community. These societies, which often took the form of fraternal orders, promoted sociability among kindred groups and preservation of German language and culture, offered financial assistance in sickness and death, and helped ease the problems of adjusting to American life.

In 1916 the Indiana State Federation of German Vereins listed 56 affiliated *Vereins* for Indianapolis alone; church-based *Vereins*, largely unaffiliated with the state federation, provided additional groups for the Germans' associational life. These societies mirrored the diversity of the city's German-speaking population. Many were organized on the basis of the German state or province from which its members emigrated, such as the *Verein Bavaria*, *Badischer UV* (Baden), *Pfaelzer UV* (Palatinate), *Preussen* (Prussians), and *Plattdeutsche* (Low Germans). Supraregional societies included *Allemania Kranken-UV*, *Deutscher UV*, and *Germania UV*. Others were chapters of national UVs.

Typically, the societies were male organizations with women's auxiliaries, or *Damenverein*. Through dues and contributions they provided social and cultural services for specific sectors of the German population. Of greatest importance were health benefits (approximately $5 per week for 13 weeks) and death benefits ($100 for members, $50 for spouse). Indianapolis brewers, bakers, and butchers had their *Bierbrauer UV*, *Brauer Internationale Arbeiter-Union*, *Baecker UV*, and *Metzger Verein*. Workers could join the *Arbeiter Kranken UV* or the *Hermann Arbeiter Kranken UV*.

Old soldiers had the German-American Veterans of the Civil War and the *Deutsche-Militaer Verein*. Large church-related UVs included *St. Bonifacius, St. Franziskus, St. Joseph, Deutscher Roemisch-Katholische Central Verein*, and the German General Protestant Orphanage Association, which claimed nearly 700 members. Fraternal lodges like *Pythiasritter* (Knights of Pythias), *Germania* (Odd Fellows), *Cherusker, Schiller*, and *Koerner* constituted another large segment. Organizations like the *Heimath UV, Preussen UV*, and *Gaertner UV* continue the practice of providing health and death benefits for members. Through annual fund-raising *Fests*, and in earlier days masked balls, the UVs, especially the music and sports *Vereins*, brought and still bring entertainment to the city at their Summer and October Fests.

In 1932 twenty *Vereins* founded the Federation of German Societies, headquartered at GERMAN PARK (1934) on South Meridian Street. The organization's membership reflected how the German population had suffered a dramatic reduction in its once diverse and flourishing associational life. In one case, however, a society recorded its *Protokoll* (minutes) in German until 1975. The federation reported 13 *Vereins* as members in 1992.

EBERHARD REICHMANN
German-American Center, Indianapolis

George T. Probst, *The Germans in Indianapolis, 1840–1918*, rev. ed. by Eberhard Reichmann (Indianapolis, 1989); Johann Glaesser, *Deutsch-Amerikanisches Vereins-Adressbuch f.d. Jahr 1916–1917* (Milwaukee, 1917).

German Park. Privately owned park located at 8600 South Meridian Street. In 1881 the Indianapolis German Park Association purchased the 30–acre Old Germania Park, which included a clubhouse, dance pavilions, bowling alleys, tennis courts, and baseball diamonds. With the advent of World War I the group changed the name to Columbia Park. In 1934, 22 German-American societies under the recently formed FEDERATION OF GERMAN SOCIETIES purchased the park and renamed it German Park. Federation members worked on weekends and donated materials to improve the site. The Indianapolis Street Railway Company donated an old streetcar to serve as the park's first kitchen. Successful German Day celebrations, held in 1936 and 1937, raised funds for ongoing improvements and mortgage payments. Festivals were cancelled during World War II and many societies ceased their activities at the park until the formation of "Edelweiss," a youth group, which reintroduced park activities. Groups raised money through dances and parties and made the last loan payment in 1945. Improvements to the park over the next few decades included a bridge over Buffalo Creek, a shelter, and sports fields. In the early 1970s the federation began to plan construction of a cultural center, which opened a decade later. The park has been the site for many annual events including a July 4th picnic, begun in the early 1930s, the Oktoberfest held since the mid–1970s, and the annual picnics of federation societies.

JOAN CUNNINGHAM

German Societies, Federation of (Verband deutscher Vereine von Indianapolis). A Federation of German Societies existed in the Hoosier capital during the late 1800s through the end of World War I. In 1910 it consisted of 56 German-American societies. Its board of directors at that time included, among others, prominent German-American businessman Joseph Keller, architect Armin Bohn, and attorney PHILIP RAPPAPORT. Member societies ranged from educational to veterans organizations and included Turners, GERMAN-ENGLISH SCHOOL SOCIETY, MAENNERCHOR, Musikverein, SAENGERCHOR, Prussian Benefit Society, Germania Lodge–Order of the Sons of Hermann, German-American Veterans Society, German Gardeners Society, and German General Orphans Society, among others.

The federation ceased to function during the anti-German hysteria of WORLD WAR I. Well after the war, in 1932, the 22 societies that then formed the federation purchased land for GERMAN PARK and maintained it through the Great Depression and World War II. There was sufficient interest in the German heritage in the period after World War II that new societies were formed—for example, the German-American Klub and the Indianapolis Soccer Club (1954), a successor to the

Deutscher Fussball Club. The renewed interest in ethnic heritage gave impetus to the societies' growth, as did the German women who married men from Indianapolis while the latter were stationed in Germany.

The federation's 12 current member societies are: German-American Klub, German-American Klub Auxiliary, Greenhouse Growers Association, Heimaths-Preussen-Unterstutzungsverein, Indianapolis Gardeners Benefit Society, Indianapolis Liederkranz, Indianapolis Liederkranz Ladies Society, Indianapolis Maennerchor, Indianapolis Saengerchor, Indianapolis Soccer Club, Indianapolis Vegetable Growers Association, and South Side Turners.

GILES R. HOYT
Indiana University–Purdue University,
Indianapolis

George T. Probst, *The Germans in Indianapolis, 1850–1914*, rev. ed. by Eberhard Reichmann (Indianapolis, 1989).

Germans. People with ancestral ties to Germany, Austria, Switzerland, Liechtenstein, Luxembourg, and other German-speaking provinces of central and eastern Europe constitute the largest ethnic group in Indianapolis and have since the city's formative years. There were 1,045 persons of German ancestry (802 German-born, 243 of German parentage) in Indianapolis in 1850, or 12.9 percent of the total population. The area bounded by New York, Noble (now College), Market, and East streets was known as "Germantown" because of the concentration of Germans living there. Over the decades the German-born population declined while the ancestral population grew steadily. The 1870 census listed 6,536 German-born in Marion County compared to 1,940 in Indianapolis in 1980. The 1890 enumeration counted 19,154 residents of German ancestry (18 percent of population), and the 1990 census reported 175,101 individuals of German ancestry (23.6 percent of total population), the largest proportion for any ethnic group.

German-Americans hardly comprised a monolithic group and were more diverse than, for example, the IRISH. Consequently, they never functioned as a cohesive political or social unit. Originating in provinces that had very diverse cultures, Germans retained their regional loyalties even after German unification in 1871. There were also religious differences: Protestants of various persuasions from the North, Catholics from the Rhineland and Bavaria, Anabaptists from southwest Germany and Switzerland, and Jews from urban areas. Even after settling in America, ethnic and cultural homogeneity was not a given, especially in urban areas. Although Germans organized *Vereine* (societies) and churches to maintain their ethnic identity and provide for the mutual assistance of fellow countrymen, they tended to be identified either with the church (*kirchendeutsch*, or church German) or with the more secular lodges (*vereinsdeutsch*, or club German), which contributed to the diversity and fragmentation of the community.

Events in Europe always influenced German immigration. Except for the Harmonist settlement (1814–1824) in southwestern Indiana, early immigration to Indiana occurred during the post-Napoleonic period (1815–1848). The peace following Napoleon's defeat did not bring prosperous times. Economic hardship, loss of liberty under an authoritarian government, and the forced merger of Lutherans with the Reformed churches in Prussia all served as an impetus for hard-working, religious, and rather conservative German families to immigrate to America.

Arrivals in Indianapolis after the abortive democratic revolutions of 1848 were generally well educated, liberal, anti-clerical, and dedicated to applying their ideals of freedom and progress through education to their adoptive country. They believed that American democracy reflected their own ideals of individual freedom combined with social responsibility. Many were dedicated to the teachings of Friedrich Jahn (1778–1852), a political liberal and "father" of the Turner movement that espoused the classical ideal of *mens sana in corpore sano* (a healthy mind in a healthy body), a motto engraved on the INDEPENDENT TURNVEREIN building on North Meridian Street. Several young progressive followers of Jahn—August Hofmeister, CLEMENS VONNEGUT, and John Ott, all future prominent and prosperous civic leaders—established the Indianapolis Turngemeinde (later Socialer Turnverein, now Athenaeum Turners) in 1851.

Another indicator of a vibrant culture was the German press, established as a means of communication and cultural preservation for the growing population. The first journal was the conservative *Das Volksblatt*, founded in 1848 by Julius Boetticher. Its progressive counterpart was *Die Freie Presse*, edited and published by Theodore Hielscher beginning in 1854. Over time Indianapolis had 26 German-language periodicals, some of which reported remarkable circulations (nearly 11,000 for the *Telegraph-Tribuene* in 1910).

By the 1860s German immigrants and their offspring had become an integral part of the Indianapolis business community. Clemens Vonnegut established a hardware business, Henry and August Schnull a wholesale grocery, John Ott a furniture business, Peter Lieber a brewery, Hermann Lieber an art supplies and frames store. George Meyer dealt in wholesale tobacco products, Wilhelm Langsenkamp established a train repair business, and Albrecht Kipp dealt in wholesale products. By 1875 there were 91 German-American businesses in the three blocks on Washington Street between Illinois and Delaware. German-Americans were also involved in banking and capital ventures, such as the Frenzel family and MERCHANTS NATIONAL BANK (1865). One of the state's largest insurance firms was the German Mutual Insurance Company (1854). On a smaller scale, mutual aid societies (*Unterstuetzungsvereine*) helped small businesses and families in need. Although now less important for their financial activities, four German-American mutual aid societies remain in Indianapolis.

During the Civil War the Indianapolis German community actively opposed slavery, favored the Union, and volunteered in large numbers to fight for the new fatherland. The Freimaenner Verein (Freemen's Society) agitated against slavery in the early 1850s, while the liberal, activist Turners advocated the necessity of opposing the Confederacy. Prominent Germans received permission from Governor Oliver P. Morton in 1861 to establish the 32nd (First German) Regiment, commanded by General August Willich, which served with distinction at Shiloh and Missionary

The Turners believed gymnastics were an excellent form of exercise. Here, students from the Normal College do gymnastics in the courtyard behind the Athenaeum. [IUPUI Archives]

Ridge. The Germans' role in the Civil War was indicative of their relationship to their new country. German intellectuals, if not the greater majority, believed that since the United States was still in its formative stage, they had a particular role in infusing the best of their own cultural and intellectual traditions into the American mainstream.

German-Americans played a strong part in the development of the arts in Indianapolis. The oldest continuously existing men's choir in the United States is the Indianapolis MAENNERCHOR, founded in 1854; under directors Eduard Longerich, CARL BARUS, and Alexander Ernestinoff the chorus received wide acclaim. Karl Schneider founded a local symphony orchestra in 1895. Hermann Lieber, a great patron of the arts, made it possible for artists of the "Hoosier Group," including T. C. STEELE and OTTO STARK, to study in Munich and get their start back home. Wilhelm J. Reiss, who arrived in Indianapolis from Berlin in 1884, painted scenes of the West and Indian life.

German-American architects designed many of the city's churches and public buildings. ANTON SCHERRER, of Swiss-German origin, completed the design of the present Indiana STATE HOUSE. George Schreiber designed the SCOTTISH RITE CATHEDRAL. The architectural firm of VONNEGUT AND BOHN was responsible for the ATHENAEUM and the HERRON SCHOOL OF ART, among others. DIEDRICH A. BOHLEN (later D. A. Bohlen & Son) designed many public buildings, including CITY MARKET, TOMLINSON HALL, the MURAT TEMPLE, ROBERTS PARK METHODIST CHURCH, and the MAJESTIC

BUILDING. Bruno Schmitz of Berlin designed the SOLDIERS AND SAILORS MONUMENT, the tallest such monument in the United States at its completion in 1902; RUDOLF SCHWARZ created the accompanying sculptures depicting Civil War scenes.

The Germans' emphasis on preserving their intellectual and cultural traditions affected the development of education in Indianapolis. Liberal-minded German-Americans, including Valentine Butsch and Adolph Seidensticker, who sought an alternative to inadequate public schools and German Lutheran and Catholic parochial schools, established the German-English Independent School in 1859. It survived until 1882 when parents considered public schools sufficiently improved and German instruction was made available. By 1900 Indianapolis was a center for German language pedagogy, and the major second language was German. Dr. Robert Nix, author of numerous textbooks, served as director of German language instruction for the city schools (1894–1910). New industrial training schools, based upon the German *Gewerbeschule*, originated through active lobbying by the German community. CHARLES E. EMMERICH, an active FREETHINKER, was the first principal of MANUAL HIGH SCHOOL, which was later renamed for him. Prominent *"vereinsdeutsch"* freethinker and philosopher CLEMENS VONNEGUT served as head of the Indianapolis School Board for many years. In 1907 the NORMAL COLLEGE OF THE AMERICAN GYMNASTIC UNION, which promoted physical education in school curricula nationwide, moved from Milwaukee to Indianapolis. The college became a part of Indiana University in 1941, making the School of Physical Education of INDIANA UNIVERSITY–PURDUE UNIVERSITY AT INDIANAPOLIS the oldest in the United States.

Around 1910 there were 56 German societies in Indianapolis providing social, cultural, and educational opportunities. Only 16 societies, or 17 including the FEDERATION OF GERMAN SOCIETIES, an umbrella organization to which 13 societies belong, existed in 1993. The Federation and the German-American Klub have maintained headquarters in GERMAN PARK on South Meridian Street since the 1930s. The Indiana German Heritage Society, a statewide organization located in Indianapolis, was formed in 1985 and supports research on German-Americans.

The social service infrastructure of Indianapolis also felt the impact of the German presence. Concern for Civil War orphans resulted in the founding of the German General Protestant Orphans' Home (1867). German-Americans also helped establish City Hospital and the DEPARTMENT OF PUBLIC WORKS. Reverend Christopher Peters of Zion Evangelical Reformed Church (now Zion Evangelical United Church of Christ) organized the Protestant Deaconess Society in January, 1895, which later established Deaconess Hospital with its nurses' education program and the ALTENHEIM (now Altenheim Retirement Community).

Reflecting the desire for religious self-determination, inspired in part by the religious persecutions in Prussia, Germans contributed to the diversity of religious life in Indianapolis. Many churches claim a German-American heritage, including First Lutheran, Zion Evangelical U.C.C. (which still holds services in German), Friedens U.C.C., St. John's Lutheran, St. Peter's Lutheran, Emmaus Lutheran, St. Paul's Lutheran, St. Mary's Catholic, Sacred Heart Catholic, and First German Evangelical Church (now Lockerbie Square United Methodist). Congregations like Ebenezer Lutheran (1836–1970s) and Mt. Pisgah (1837, later First) Lutheran date from Indianapolis' earliest German settlement. Relative latecomers are the Mennonites (1951) and the Wisconsin Evangelical Lutheran Synod (Divine Savior Lutheran Church, 1971).

In the early 1900s German-Americans suffered three distinct blows to their way of life: WORLD WAR I, Prohibition, and the Great Depression. The war brought German-Americans into direct conflict with the Anglo-American majority who used the occasion to seek a leveling of overt German cultural influence. Such chauvinism was reminiscent of nativistic outbreaks witnessed as early as the 1840s. To maintain the economic and other gains they had made, and since they had become a part of "mainstream" society, many German-Americans abruptly stopped using the German language. The war had a highly disruptive effect on social activities and in some instances on family life. Prohibition had a further deleterious effect by removing a staple from their social and economic lives. Economically, like all Americans, local German-Americans suffered from the effects of the Depression.

Immigration from Hitler's Germany during the 1930s and the subsequent postwar period added to the city's German population. By 1990 nearly one quarter of Indianapolis' population claimed German ancestry. Unlike in Cincinnati, there has not been a distinctly German section of the city since the earliest immigration. Yet German business interests, such as BOEHRINGER MANNHEIM, have added a new dimension to Indianapolis' relationship to Germany.

The 150–year presence of Germans in Indianapolis continues to be evident through their numerous festivals and celebrations. Oktoberfest in German Park, the Athenaeum Turners' St. Benno Fest, the concerts, dances, and dinners sponsored by the LIEDERKRANZ, Maennerchor, and SAENGERCHOR, and the observance of German-American Day on October 6th all reflect the strong German heritage of the urban population. Indianapolis and Cologne have established a sister city relationship that provides an official link to a major German city. German continues to be taught in almost all of the township schools, in some of the Indianapolis Public Schools, and all of the city's major colleges and universities, testifying to the continued impact of German immigrants since the 1840s.

GILES R. HOYT
Indiana University–Purdue University,
Indianapolis

George T. Probst, *The Germans in Indianapolis, 1840–1918*, rev. ed. by Eberhard Reichmann (Indianapolis, 1989); Theodore Stempfel, *Fifty Years of Unrelenting German Aspirations in Indianapolis, 1848–1898*, ed. and trans. by Giles Hoyt et al. (Indianapolis: German American Center & Indiana German Heritage Society, 1991).

Germans in Politics. Although Germans had been in Indianapolis since at least the 1840s, their political influence did not become significant until the mid–1850s. Many of the early immigrants were liberals who left their homeland after the failed democratic revolutions of 1848 and found the ideals of Jacksonian Democracy much to their liking. This group also included a number of liberal FREETHINKERS who did not believe in organized Christian religions and relied instead on scientific explanation. The German community of Indianapolis supported the DEMOCRATIC PARTY in the 1854 election, primarily for its opposition to prohibition. The simultaneous rise of the American party (also known as the Know Nothings), which publicly opposed Germans, provided another reason for Germans to unite in order to preserve their political freedom. Combating nativist sentiments, Germans joined with the Democrats and became active office seekers. The 1856 Indianapolis city election saw Germans Frederick Stein, John B. Stumph, and CHARLES G. COULON winning the offices of clerk, assessor, and justice of the peace, respectively. When Mayor HENRY WEST died in office, the Common Council elected Coulon interim mayor, a position he held for two weeks in November, 1856.

The Democratic party's stance on slavery created divisions with the local German community and forced many to disassociate themselves from the party. The *Freie Presse* (established 1853) expressed the views of many liberal Germans when it advocated the total abolition of slavery rather than simply opposing its expansion into the territories. While the Germans continued to support Democratic opposition to the prohibition of alcohol, they could not continue to vote for a party that did not value the freedom of all people. The presidential election of 1856, however, revealed the extent of divisions among the Germans. Some of the more established members continued their support of the party; the Turngemeinde favored the Free Soil party; and the *Freie Presse* chose to endorse John C. Fremont and the newly created REPUBLICAN PARTY. In response, *Freie Presse* editor Theodore Hielscher formed the German Republican Society in 1856, and by 1860 the Indianapolis German community strongly supported Abraham Lincoln's candidacy for president. Germans were not merely Republican supporters, they sided with the most liberal factions of the party. In 1860 Hielscher played a significant role in defeating the presidential candidacy of the more conservative Republican judge Edward Bates. Coming from an autocratic and oppressive system of government in their homeland, local Germans played an active role in recognizing the rights of all people.

Germans remained united in their support of the Republicans throughout the 1860s and early 1870s. In an 1868 Turnerbund convention in Boston, however, 17 delegates from the Indianapolis Turnverein were thrown out for their objections to the organization's support of enfranchisement for African-Americans. New divisions within the local German political community began to appear with the 1876 election. The *Zukunft*, a previously pro-Republican, Turner-supported newspaper, endorsed the Democratic ticket of Samuel Tilden and THOMAS A. HENDRICKS. In 1878 a new German Republican paper, the *Indiana Tribune*, made its first appearance, while the *Telegraph* (founded 1865) presented the views of the independent Democratic party within the German community.

The 1882 election saw prohibition reemerge as an issue, and Germans worked actively against its introduction. Not only did Germans like their beer and maintain that within limits there was nothing wrong with its consumption, they also argued that prohibition was an infringement upon the rights of all citizens. Germans supported the Democrats in this election and were instrumental in the defeat of prohibitionist legislation.

Nationally, Germans were often politically linked by religion, with Catholics favoring the Democrats and Protestants favoring the Republicans. German immigrants in Indianapolis, originating primarily from the northern regions, were mainly Protestant in their religious beliefs and tended to support the Republicans. The liberal German community was very supportive of the labor movement as it related to political issues.

Germans continued to be politically active as a group until the United States' entrance into WORLD WAR I. While Germans nationwide were generally sympathetic toward Spain during the Spanish-American War, local Germans supported President William McKinley's policies. As a result, the *Indianapolis News* reported, "No truer Americans walk the soil or breathe the air than the Germans that have made this land their home." Many joined the local German-American Alliance to promote German culture and better education, and to lobby against laws restricting personal freedoms. Local German merchant Joseph H. Keller

served as president of the Indiana German-American Alliance and vice-president of the national Alliance and used his position to attack prohibitionist efforts. With the war in Europe, however, Indianapolis Germans demonstrated both through their press and political organizations their loyalty to the homeland and dissatisfaction with the United States' neutrality and its initial threat to sever diplomatic relations with Germany. No evidence exists to determine if local Germans were involved in the national German-American Alliance movement that worked for the defeat of President Woodrow Wilson in 1916 because of his alleged bias toward Britain, although they did abandon the Democratic party. Following the declaration of war, most Germans affirmed their loyalty to America by participating in local bond drives and working in war relief efforts, but continued to face social persecution for their German sympathies. Indiana Governor James P. Goodrich acknowledged their support by appointing as his military secretary German-born RICHARD LIEBER, who helped rally German-American opinion to the American cause. The war, however, hastened assimilation of the German population and effectively eliminated them as a unified political voice in the ensuing decades.

PAUL BROCKMAN
Indiana Historical Society

George T. Probst, *The Germans in Indianapolis, 1840–1918*, rev. ed. by Eberhard Reichmann (Indianapolis, 1989).

Gholson, Robert Lee, Jr. (Jan. 23, 1931– Dec. 7, 1993). African-American jazz pianist, singer, and piano technician. A native of Aberdeen, Mississippi, Gholson moved with his family to Gary, Indiana, in 1938. At age nine he was permanently blinded in an accident and enrolled in the INDIANA SCHOOL FOR THE BLIND where he learned to play trumpet, drums, organ, and piano and mastered piano tuning and repair. A 1957 School of Education graduate of Indiana University and member of the campus NAACP, Gholson performed in Bloomington during the mid–1950s as the leader of The Blue Notes, working with several future JAZZ stars including David Baker, Eddie Harris, Freddie Hubbard, and Larry Ridley.

From 1957 to 1984 he taught industrial arts and piano tuning at the Indiana School for the Blind and for much of that time also served as a piano tuner–technician with the Riddick, Wilking, and Wurlitzer companies, maintaining pianos at Indianapolis' major performance venues including STARLIGHT MUSICALS, Indiana Roof, MARKET SQUARE ARENA, and MURAT TEMPLE. Influenced stylistically by Indianapolis pianists ERROLL GRANDY and Earl Van Riper, Gholson performed in Indianapolis nightclubs for 35 years as a soloist and jazz combo leader, displaying a remarkable technical facility and vast repertoire spanning gospel, rhythm-and-blues, soul, swing, bebop, contemporary jazz, popular standards, boogie-woogie, and RAGTIME.

LAWRENCE E. MCCULLOUGH
Indiana University–Purdue University,
Indianapolis

Indianapolis Recorder, Dec. 1, 1990; *Nuvo*, Apr. 29, 1992; *Indianapolis News*, July 2, 1993.

Gibson, Louis Henry (Mar. 17, 1855–Nov. 1, 1907). Indianapolis architect, author, and art critic. Born in Aurora (Dearborn County), Indiana, Louis moved to Indianapolis in 1862 when his father, David Gibson, acquired what is known today as the ACME-EVANS flour mill on West Washington Street. He attended Indianapolis public schools, graduated from North Western Christian University (later BUTLER UNIVERSITY), and apprenticed with Edwin Peckham, a local architect, for several years before graduating from Massachusetts Institute of Technology in 1874 with a degree in architecture. While at MIT, Gibson probably met the famous Chicago architect Louis Sullivan; Gibson's brother described the two as "intimate friends."

After traveling in Europe for 15 months, Gibson found employment in Boston before returning to Indianapolis in about 1878 and becoming a draftsman in the office of Edwin May. From 1880 to 1883 he briefly managed the Gibson Flour Mills on West Washington Street. Upon his father's death, Gibson returned to architectural practice in partnership with Edwin Ketchum. By the late 1880s, he had established his own practice.

Gibson designed a number of important buildings in Indianapolis, including the original portion of Public School 38 (2050 N. Winter Street) and the Law Building (now PEOPLE'S BANK AND TRUST COMPANY on E. Market Street). However his most significant legacy is as an author and domestic architect. Gibson's *Convenient Houses* (1889) and *Beautiful Houses* (1895) are the only known nationally published building pattern books written by a Hoosier architect. In these two books he advocated practical houses suited for middle class families. Having been trained and educated on the East Coast during the formative years of the so-called Shingle Style, Gibson was influenced by the relative simplicity of this style, as reflected in both books. His friendship with Louis Sullivan also influenced the florid style of surface ornament in his designs. Gibson introduced central Indiana to these new architectural trends. Unfortunately, his domestic work is poorly documented. His own house at 1636–40 N. Pennsylvania Street illustrates a typical design from *Convenient Houses*.

PAUL C. DIEBOLD
Division of Historic Preservation
and Archaeology, Indiana Department
of Natural Resources

Indiana Biography Series, Indiana State Library; *Indianapolis News*, Nov. 2, 1907; *Indianapolis Times*, Nov. 19, 1937.

GIPC. See Greater Indianapolis Progress Committee

Girl Scouts. Anna Marie Ridge established the first local troop on July 27, 1917, in IRVINGTON after corresponding with Juliette Low, national founder of Girl Scouts. With nine troops in Indianapolis by 1919, the Indianapolis Leaders Association was established to offer support and training for adults.

The formal organization of a council, Girl Scouts, Inc., came in 1921. In the same year Selma Harry organized the first African-American troop with 20 girls from School 17. In 1922, girls could go camping at Camp Ada-Boy-Holliday along Williams Creek at College Avenue and 75th Street. The scouts soon outgrew this site and Dorothy Dell Moffet donated land on the west side of Indianapolis along EAGLE CREEK. Camp Dellwood opened in the summer of 1926. That year also marked the formation of troops at the Indiana School for the Blind. Cookies were sold for the first time in 1926, and the council realized a profit of almost $700. The council hosted the National Girl Scout Conference in 1930. Scouts received title to what became known as the "Little House" on April 15, 1935, after meeting the challenge of getting 75,000 people to visit the structure (a home remodeled by the Construction League in conjunction with the Better Housing Program) in less than four months. During World War II, Girl Scouts baked cookies for the Serviceman's Center, participated in war bond drives, and demonstrated cooking meatless meals on the Circle. By 1952, there were 8,000 scouts in Marion County.

March 5, 1958, marked the formation of the Hoosier Capital Girl Scout Council (HCGSC). With 950 troops and 14,385 members, the new council included scouts in Boone, Hamilton, Hancock, Hendricks, and Marion counties. In 1960, Girl Scouts United States of America, Inc. added Johnson, Shelby, and the northern half of Morgan County to HCGSC. Dudley R. Gallahue donated 400 acres in Brown County to establish Camp Gallahue, which opened in the summer of 1961.

Beginning in 1965 the Special Area Services project, funded by grants from the LILLY ENDOWMENT, the INDIANAPOLIS FOUNDATION, and INDIANA BELL, brought scouting to areas not traditionally served by regular troops. In 1967 the council sponsored a Senior Scout national conference on the inner city and the future of youth. The World of the Arts was an international event offered by the council in 1970. The acquisition of Hawthorne Trails in Boone County (1962) and Camp Ada (1971) provided additional camping sites for the growing council.

During the 1980s the council stressed career exploration and community service to the membership. In 1983 HCGSC sponsored an international workshop, called Arts in Action, which explored career opportunities in the arts. Cookie sales topped one million boxes in 1986, with the profits going into camping and assistance programs. In 1990, the Girls at Risk program targeted girls who had been brought into the juvenile court system and placed them in special troops to provide positive peer support. On the eve of the 75th anniversary of Girl Scouting in Indianapolis, the HCGSC had over 18,000 members.

NORALEEN YOUNG

Noraleen Young, "On My Honor, I Will Try: A History of Hoosier Capital Girl Scout Council" (M.A. thesis, Indiana University–Purdue University, Indianapolis, 1992).

Girls Incorporated. Youth organization. In 1969 five mothers banded together to provide alternative after-school activities for girls, converting an empty school in the FOUNTAIN SQUARE neighborhood into a clubhouse. In 1970 Girls Clubs of America granted national affiliation to the club and two matching grants from the LILLY ENDOWMENT and the INDIANAPOLIS FOUNDATION helped to meet expenses. The Model Cities Girls Club opened in the MAPLETON–FALL CREEK area in 1971. The two clubs merged to become the Girls Clubs of Marion County in 1975 and established the Fountain Square and Mapleton–Fall Creek clubs as branches. The name changed in 1978 to Girls Clubs of Greater Indianapolis (GCGI), and the organization received a grant from the Lilly Endowment to conduct a long-range study in 1980. In 1982–1983 the GCGI raised $1.2 million dollars to build a new facility for the Fountain Square area and remodel the Mid-North branch (formerly Mapleton–Fall Creek).

Beyond providing supervised recreational activities in the neighborhood facilities, members have also participated in programs to expand career opportunities and create self-esteem. In 1987 GCGI initiated the Campus Cruisers program to encourage 5th- and 6th-grade girls to stay in school and plan for college. In 1988 this program received one of eight Outstanding Program Awards from the Girls Clubs of America. Other programs included the "Kid Ability!" program (1989) aimed at preventing child abuse and "Operation SMART" (1989) to foster interest in science among girls.

In June, 1981, the Girls Clubs of America National Resource Center opened along the Central Canal near downtown Indianapolis. The Resource Center, initially funded by a grant from the Lilly Endowment, studies the problems of young women in today's society and provides a coordinated effort to develop programs based on the needs of girls. The organization's name was changed to Girls Incorporated in 1990.

NORALEEN YOUNG

Glazier, Daniel (July 1, 1835–Mar. 11, 1873). Fire chief and the first Indianapolis fireman to die in the line of duty. Born in Uniontown, Maryland, Glazier moved to Marion County with his parents in 1838. In 1850 he became a resident of the city and five years later joined the volunteer fire company named The Unions. The volunteer companies disbanded in favor of a municipal fire department in 1859, and in 1860 Glazier became engineer of the INDIANAPOLIS FIRE DEPARTMENT'S (IFD) Fire Engine No. 3, located at the former Unions' firehouse. In 1870 Glazier was elected Chief Fire Engineer in consideration of his "fearlessness of danger, efficiency, and generous conduct."

On March 11, 1873, Glazier led his men into a fire at the WOODBURN SARVEN WHEEL COMPANY building. Glazier was killed and several firemen were injured when one of the building's walls collapsed on top of them. The funeral, held at Glazier's home at 185 South New Jersey Street, was one of the largest in the city to that time. Glazier's legacy included two sons who became firemen.

CONNIE J. ZEIGLER

Gleaners' Food Bank of Indiana. A food bank incorporated on April 14, 1980, to solicit, collect, and redistribute donated food to IRS-designated 501(c)(3) charities. Initial funding came from the Office of Economic Opportunity through Community Action Against Poverty, and Gleaners hired its first full-time staff person in February, 1981. Grants from LILLY ENDOWMENT and Christ Church Cathedral's Lilly Memorial Trust in 1981 and 1982 allowed Gleaners to expand food banking statewide, helped create the nation's first affiliate food bank network, and funded the development of an equitable allocation system based upon poverty population percentages. The affiliate and allocation concepts spread across the country through Second Harvest, the National Food Bank Network.

In 1980, 83,021 pounds of food were distributed to 35 agencies; in 1992, 6.5 million pounds were distributed to over 250 soup kitchens, pantries, shelters, and other people-feeding charities. The Indiana Food Bank Network created by Gleaners has ten banks serving over 1,500 Indiana charities.

Gleaners' 1992 income of $1 million came from gifts, grants, and direct mail solicitation. It has received support from the CHURCH FEDERATION OF GREATER INDIANAPOLIS, its first fiscal agent, and from the INDIANAPOLIS FOUNDATION, which renovated Gleaners' first building and holds joint ownership in its present building. Gleaners had 26 employees in 1992, and volunteers contributed an additional 28,843 hours of service.

PAMELA ALTMEYER
Gleaners' Food Bank of Indiana

Going All the Way. Publication of *Going All the Way* (New York: Delacorte Press, 1970) was of particular significance to Indianapolis. The novel's author, Dan Wakefield, was born in the city in 1932 and grew up at 6131 Winthrop Avenue. He was a frequent user of the Broad Ripple Library, attended Public School 80 next door to the library, and graduated from SHORTRIDGE HIGH SCHOOL. *Going All the Way*, Wakefield's first novel, came out of his Indianapolis experience and created something of a frisson in the city.

The novel explores the narrow-minded and confining attitudes in the Indianapolis of 1954 through the lives of two friends, Sonny Burns and Tom "Gunner" Casselman. Sonny is introverted and awkward and Gunner is the popular athlete, one of Shortridge's (Shortley High in the book) "Big Rods." Out of college and back from serving in the armed forces, they spend a summer in Indianapolis searching for more in life than just drinking and cruising for girls.

Life in Indianapolis is vacuous, marked by the self-contentment of a society convinced of its moral superiority. McCarthyism, Moral Rearmament, racism, and bigotry surround the two protagonists. In a memorable scene, a bearded Gunner is not allowed to swim in a country club swimming pool because he will "contaminate" it and "get the water dirty." A number of Indianapolis landmarks, such as Shortridge High School, the HERRON SCHOOL OF ART, the RED KEY TAVERN, and the RIVIERA and Meridian Hills clubs, are immortalized in the book.

In Indianapolis rumors persisted that the book satirized the author's classmates and acquaintances. Wakefield denied this, but the subsequent ire and hostility toward him in the city kept the author away from Indianapolis in self-exile for 15 years. Wakefield wrote about this reaction to Going All the Way in a subsequent memoir, Returning: A Spiritual Journey (1988), a work that marked the author's reconciliation with the city. In spite of the hometown reception, the novel quickly climbed the best-seller list and Kurt Vonnegut proclaimed it the "midwestern Catcher in the Rye."

OPHELIA GEORGIEV ROOP
Indiana University–Purdue University,
Indianapolis

Golden, Grace Blaisdell (June, 1899–Jan. 11, 1966). Director of The Children's Museum. Born in Indianapolis, Golden gained experience in writing, fund raising, public relations, and education through nonprofit and freelance work locally. In 1928 THE CHILDREN'S MUSEUM (TCM) hired her as executive secretary in charge of fund raising and public relations. She also developed new exhibit techniques for children and started a museum lending program with local schools. She supervised WPA workers assigned to TCM, and in 1938 was appointed field supervisor of the WPA Statewide Museum Program.

Once at TCM, Golden developed an expertise in folklore and antiques. She wrote articles for national magazines and published a children's book, Pueblo People (1935). In the late 1930s she began writing "Know Your Heirlooms," an Indianapolis Star column, and taught courses on antiques at BUTLER UNIVERSITY. Golden also received a Carnegie Institute grant to travel to Eastern Europe to study costumes, folklore, and customs.

In 1942 Golden became the second director of TCM. She believed that collections, instead of being hidden away, should be used for museum education and promotion. An energetic and dynamic leader, she increased TCM's collections, attendance, facilities, and financial stability during her 22 years as director. She gave the museum national and international exposure through her leadership positions in the Midwest Museums Conference, American Association of Museums, and International Council of Museums. In 1947 she was one of six Americans chosen to work with UNESCO on museum problems. She also published two more children's books, Made in Iceland (1958) and Seven Dancing Dolls (1961). Golden retired as director of TCM in 1964. Upon her death TCM created the Grace Golden Memorial Scholarship which, until the early 1980s, provided grants to students interested in the museum field.

MICHELLE D. HALE

Nancy Kriplen, Keep an Eye on That Mummy: A History of The Children's Museum of Indianapolis (Indianapolis, 1982); Indianapolis Star, Jan. 12, 1966.

Golden Age of Indiana Literature. A period extending roughly from 1880 to 1920 in which Hoosier authors, including several from Indianapolis, achieved national prominence and a wide audience in the field of popular literature.

At the end of the 19th century, the Midwest was in ascendance as a literary region. Indiana, and especially Indianapolis, became a publishing and literary center by catering to readers who preferred writing that idealized traditional values or offered escape from contemporary social problems. This writing took a variety of forms, including the local color poetry of JAMES WHITCOMB

RILEY; the historical romances of LEW WALLACE, Maurice Thompson, and Charles Major; the humor of George Ade and KIN HUBBARD; the fantasy of George Barr McCutcheon; the nature writing of Gene Stratton-Porter; and the mild realism of BOOTH TARKINGTON and MEREDITH NICHOLSON.

Indianapolis resident Riley was the most popular poet in America in the 1890s. Later, another Indianapolis writer, Tarkington, would become equally well known with the publication of *The Gentleman from Indiana* (1899) and his Pulitzer Prize winning novels, *THE MAGNIFICENT AMBERSONS* (1918) and *ALICE ADAMS* (1921). While Riley's homespun dialect rhymes revolved around such sentimental and nostalgic themes as the wonders of childhood, the love of parents, and the yearnings of youth, Tarkington deftly captured in realistic detail the changes wrought on midwestern manners and morals by urban industrial growth. Nicholson was another Indianapolis-based writer who made a national reputation with essays and novels that explored Indiana themes.

Midwestern writing and publishing rose to such national prominence in part because of a broad desire for reunification after the Civil War and in part because of the sheer geographical vastness of the country. Unlike their New England predecessors of the 1850s whose regional concerns could also be interpreted broadly as American concerns, the postwar writers of the 1880s and 1890s could not attain such a national tone. America was simply too big and too diverse. In this period New England and New York were but regions and were best treated in literature in the same way as Richard Malcolm Johnston's Georgia, Bret Harte's California, and Riley's Indiana.

Indiana literature in particular eclipsed the popularity of that from other states during this period. One often-cited 1947 study determined that Indiana authors ranked second in the number of bestsellers produced in the previous 40 years only to their counterparts from New York, and the difference between the two was small. Reasons for the success of Hoosier authors abound. Indiana had a strong tradition of oratory, writing, and publishing that preceded the Golden Age period and helped to foster the development of those with literary inclinations. Also by the last decade of the 19th century, a general belief existed on the part of

Authors (standing, left to right) James Whitcomb Riley, Meredith Nicholson, (seated, left to right) George Ade, and Booth Tarkington helped establish the capital's literary reputation. [Indiana Historical Society, #C108]

Hoosiers and non-Hoosiers alike that people from Indiana were more typically American than people in other parts of the country and that writing by the state's authors was more truly American literature. An expanding number of middle class readers in rapidly changing urban environments relished the nostalgic and sentimental writings of Riley and Stratton-Porter, which evoked traditional values and portrayed images of rustic simplicity and wholesomeness. They identified as well with the precarious condition of Tarkington's protagonists, whose established ways of life were threatened by industrialization and urban growth. Moreover, they escaped from the social ills of the Gilded Age through the romances, fantasies, and thrillers of Hoosier authors such as Wallace, Thompson, Major, McCutcheon, and Nicholson.

Aside from Riley, Nicholson, and Tarkington, Indianapolis' most important contribution to Indiana's literary Golden Age was through its publishing firm, which under the successive names of Merrill, Meigs and Company, Bowen-Merrill Company, and BOBBS-MERRILL COMPANY produced more bestselling titles during this period than any other publisher in the country. Beginning with the publication of Riley's "*The Old Swimmin'-Hole*" *and 'Leven More Poems* in 1883 the reputations of Riley and his Indianapolis publisher were inseparably linked. By the centennial of the poet's birth in 1949, the firm had published more than 90 different Riley titles and sold around 3.5 million copies of his books.

In the years following its initial association with Riley, the publisher mastered the techniques of marketing sentimental literature. Capitalizing on a trend established by the immense success of Anthony Hope's *The Prisoner of Zenda* (1894), Bowen-Merrill produced a string of bestseller adventure romances, many of them by Indiana authors. When William Dean Howells visited Indianapolis on a lecture tour in 1899, he found it a stronghold of what he called "neoromantic best-sellerdom." Lew Wallace's *Ben-Hur* (1880) sold 1.2 million copies by 1900, and Charles Major's *When Knighthood Was in Flower* (1898), the first big hit of the Bowen-Merrill Company outside of Riley, was the second best-selling book of 1899. Major's book too sold over a million copies, a fact that influenced Maurice Thompson in Crawfordsville to write *Alice of Old Vincennes*, published by Bowen-Merrill in 1900. By 1915 the firm, which became Bobbs-Merrill in 1903, had produced a total of 26 titles that made the annual lists of top ten bestsellers, a record surpassing that of any other publisher in the country during this period. These titles included, among many others, Nicholson's *The House of a Thousand Candles* (1905), L. Frank Baum's *The Wonderful Wizard of Oz* (1900), and numerous collections of Riley's poetry.

The luster of Indiana's literary Golden Age began to diminish as changes in the economic and social order accelerated after World War I. Traditional values, simple pleasures, nostalgia, and romance were less important to a postwar society preoccupied with business prosperity and technological advancement. Automobiles, radios, household appliances, and prepared foods placed the ideal of an American "good" life in the future rather than in the past. Easy credit and installment-plan purchasing rendered obsolete such time-honored virtues as hard work and self-denial. Popular literature competed for increasing leisure time with movies, sports, and jazz. Rural and small-town Americans, including many Hoosiers, resented the secularism and materialism of the age and became increasingly less tolerant. The KU KLUX KLAN, the Red Scare, immigration restriction, fundamentalism, and Prohibition re-

flected their discontent. The pride that Hoosiers had taken in being typical Americans before the war manifested itself afterward as nativism. Literature became the province of Lost Generation writers who could identify with neither the materialism nor the intolerance of the modern age. Though Tarkington and Nicholson continued to write and publish in the 1920s and though many talented Hoosier writers established themselves in later years, the Golden Age of Indiana literature had passed.

J. KENT CALDER
Indiana Historical Society

Arthur W. Shumaker, *A History of Indiana Literature* (Indianapolis, 1962); G. Thomas Tanselle, "Indianapolis in the World of Books," in *Indianapolis in the World of Books* (Indianapolis, 1974).

Golden Hill. Exclusive northwestside neighborhood bounded by Woodstock Country Club, Clifton Street, 36th Street, and White River. Originally platted as early as 1872, the area was not developed until Indianapolis industrialist DAVID PARRY acquired the properties between 1900 and 1907 to develop his personal estate. He hired Scotch-born landscape architect George MacDougall to design the grounds; MacDougall also designed Indianapolis properties for ELI LILLY, Walter Marmon, and Nicholas Noyes. At Parry's death in 1915 his family subdivided the estate and hired MacDougall to plan the neighborhood. Today, Golden Hill remains much as originally designed with curving streets, circles, and greenspaces providing a parklike setting for elegant homes. The area is characterized by architectural diversity; period revival styles predominate, reflecting the affluence of the original owners. Parry's home and gatehouse serve as reminders of the area's original developer. The district was added to the National Register of Historic Places in 1991.

Golden Hill has been home to many of the city's wealthy and influential families, among them the Parrys, Dr. and Mrs. GEORGE H. A. CLOWES, WILLIAM B.. STOKELY, and William A. Atkins, heir to E. C. Atkins and Company. Until recently homes were not placed on the open market but passed along to family members or sold to friends. As of 1983, 72 percent of the area's homes had been acquired in this manner.

The neighborhood is also known for a now-vanished curiosity. Following the 1904 St. Louis World's Fair, Parry received a gift of an Alaskan totem pole displayed at the exhibition. He raised the pole on his estate where it remained until a storm toppled it in 1948. The pole, which has since vanished, is memorialized by the naming of Totem Lane.

SHERYL D. VANDERSTEL

"National Register Nomination, Golden Hill Historic District," 1990; Historic Landmarks Foundation of Indiana, *Center Township, Marion County, Interim Report, Indiana Historic Sites and Structures Inventory* (Indianapolis, 1991).

Goldsmith, Stephen, Administration of.

Stephen Goldsmith, a Republican and formerly prosecuting attorney of Marion County, entered the office of mayor of Indianapolis in January, 1992. His campaign had focused on three main themes: redirecting attention from downtown redevelopment to the city's neighborhoods; reorganizing the delivery of government services; and resisting local tax increases. Changes early in his administration attracted national attention and stirred controversy within the city.

The Goldsmith administration began as national interest in "reinventing government," especially privatizing its services, was rising rapidly. Scrutiny of city-county government began almost immediately. Within months private firms had contracts for some administrative functions, such as large-quantity printing and the microfilming of government documents and records. Vacant lots owned by local government were sold or converted to more productive uses. Departments and divisions developed cost estimates of each activity or service as a first step to opening government services to potential competition. Also in 1992 the mayor appointed a nine-member Service Efficiency and Lower Taxes for Indianapolis Commission (SELTIC), charged with bringing a business perspective to governmental operations. By the end of its first year SELTIC claimed $5 mil-

lion in savings through changes in service delivery and asset management practices. By mid–1993 over 40 governmental services were open to competition, including street repair, management of municipal golf courses, and animal control operation.

Reorganizations and privatization initiatives resulted in more than 160 employees being laid off, with hundreds more positions eliminated through attrition. By 1993 the mayor admitted that inadequate attention had been given to communicating with city-county workers, and he distributed a videotaped message to allay fears and encourage employees to work with him. The city's new two-year collective bargaining agreement with city-county workers in 1993 contained assurances that employees could compete in any future bidding of city-county government services and offered them training on contracting and bid preparation. But early in 1994 the Goldsmith administration essentially privatized wastewater treatment without going through a bidding process.

Early in his administration Goldsmith targeted the DEPARTMENT OF METROPOLITAN DEVELOPMENT for extensive reorganization and many layoffs. It was the only city-county department for which he chose not to appoint a full-time director. The changes and layoffs confused some neighborhood association leaders, worried others, and infuriated a few. As they perceived it, the mayor had visited maximum disruption upon the very department with which many neighborhoods had their greatest contacts.

At the same time, the administration pushed aggressively to acquire property for private redevelopment along the upper portion of the downtown CENTRAL CANAL. The canal issue quickly became a focus for neighborhood leaders' unhappiness with the administration. Although the upper canal area contained relatively few residents, many of them were elderly or the working poor who became known as "the canal people" the city was trying to push out of their homes.

For the remainder of its first year and well into its second, the Goldsmith administration found many of its suggestions for neighborhood improvements received coldly by neighborhood leaders. During 1993 the administration was able to communicate its initiatives more successfully. The improved atmosphere between the administration and the neighborhoods was silently underscored when the METROPOLITAN DEVELOPMENT COMMISSION met in June 1993 to approve the acquisition of 11 more properties in the upper canal area; no individual or organization attended to speak against the move.

The administration had mixed success in its efforts to remedy problems with the city's public housing projects. In April, local news reports revealed that the city's public housing division had left millions of dollars of federal funds for maintenance of the projects unclaimed or unspent. Administration suggestions that the operation of the projects be transferred to private firms encountered quick criticism, although SELTIC approved transfers for 2 of the city's 11 projects. Early anticipation that Indianapolis could be released from the U.S. Department of Housing and Urban Development's (HUD) "troubled housing" list for the first time in ten years—a change that would ease federal oversight and speed the delivery of federal funds—led to disappointment in May, 1993, when the revised HUD list still included the city. The city's public housing administrator resigned under pressure, and a new public housing administrator was appointed, with a commitment to get the city off the HUD troubled list within a year.

The concern with the city's public housing projects and the administration's focus on redevelopment in Center Township reflected an effort to shift Indianapolis economic development policy from large-scale projects and downtown redevelopment to improving the quality of life at the neighborhood level through smaller-scale changes. The new approach to economic development featured four identifiable components: avoidance of further increases in property tax rates, especially in the pre-Unigov portion of Indianapolis; regulatory reform; infrastructure improvements; and modification of tax abatement polices.

Infrastructure improvement was an especially complex and costly component of this economic development policy. In 1991 the Indianapolis CHAMBER OF COMMERCE issued a report of its two-year study of the status of public infrastructure in Marion County and its recommendations for improvements, which included projects estimated to cost up to $1.1 billion if undertaken by the year 2000. The chamber strongly linked the status of the city's transportation, water and sewer, and solid waste disposal facilities to the city's ability to attract and accommodate future economic development. In 1992 Goldsmith announced a three-year, $500 million program of improvements and repairs targeted primarily at the city's roads, bridges, sewers, and stormwater drainage. The program was funded from savings generated by reorganization initiatives, refinancing the city's outstanding debt obligations, and sale of approximately $150 million in new bonds. Refinancing took advantage of lower interest rates available in 1992–1993 and allowed the city nearly to double its outstanding debt without increasing the annual debt repayment obligations of property taxpayers or jeopardizing the city's AAA bond rating.

The Goldsmith administration also modified the city's property tax abatement policies. These abatements had been used often in Indianapolis to attract large-scale development projects, in many cases with little regard to where the projects were located or their impact on the city's low income or hard core unemployed residents. The new policy targeted future property tax abatements toward development or expansion projects within Center Township that would increase high wage employment opportunities for inner-city residents.

Goldsmith made no secret of his reservations about some of the city's previous large economic development projects, such as the downtown CIRCLE CENTRE MALL and the financial arrangements supporting the UNITED AIR LINES INDIANAPOLIS MAINTENANCE CENTER. He announced, for example, that the city would refuse to pay for the construction or the maintenance of the redesigned "Wintergarden" entrance to the Circle Centre Mall. But some of the changes in economic development policy were also products of necessity. Large-scale projects involving public-private partnerships, similar to the ones that sustained downtown redevelopment during the 1970s and 1980s, were harder to finance and implement in the 1990s since the city had lost several corporate headquarters and local ownership of its largest banks. Several earlier projects had received large commitments from local public resources, which limited the city's ability to undertake additional ones. For instance, Marion County taxpayers by 1993 were supporting about 60 percent, or $187 million, of the anticipated $300 million cost of the Circle Centre Mall project. Over $111 million in bonds were sold to support the city and county's share of the United Air Lines base, to be repaid from increased property tax revenues in a tax-increment financing district on the westside. Meanwhile, several completed downtown redevelopment projects from the 1970s and 1980s, such as UNION STATION, the CITY MARKET, and MERCHANTS PLAZA, continued to lose money in the 1990s.

Despite these outstanding obligations, the disappointing performance of past projects, and the mayor's distaste for the "big deal" approach to economic development, another large economic incentive package had to be assembled in the winter of 1992–1993 to respond to the possible loss of the U.S. Department of Defense finance center at FORT BENJAMIN HARRISON. And in the summer of 1993 the city received an ultimatum from professional baseball to either build a new ballpark to replace Bush Stadium or face the loss of the INDIANAPOLIS INDIANS baseball franchise.

The economic development experiences of the Goldsmith administration highlight a fundamental observation concerning its first two years. Changes in government operations and policies may be pursued vigorously, and even with vision, but they will always be received and implemented within the legacy of the past.

WILLIAM BLOMQUIST
Indiana University–Purdue University,
Indianapolis

Golf. In 1896 Philip Watson, J. A. Barnard, Robert Martindale, and Alvin S. Lockard laid out a two-hole golf course on land northwest of the city known as Martindale's addition. Lockard, who had witnessed the game on a trip to India, purchased a set of clubs, a box of practice balls, and a guide book in England on his way home. In the spring of 1897 the four men built a nine-hole, 2,400 –yard course in a field adjoining the India-

napolis Country Club at 38th Street and Northwestern Avenue. The course was accessible by horse and buggy, and only country club members were permitted to play.

As interest in the game grew, more private golf and country clubs began building courses. Highland Golf and Country Club opened links on West 30th Street (now Coffin municipal golf course) to members in 1908 and moved to its present location on West 52nd Street in the mid–1920s. In 1914 the original Indianapolis Country Club split into two clubs, Woodstock (located at the original site) and the Country Club of Indianapolis on Crawfordsville Road, both of which had golf courses. Other early private golf clubs were Broadmoor (1921), Meridian Hills (1923), and Avalon (now Hillcrest, 1926).

In 1900 Mayor THOMAS TAGGART and the Board of Park Commissioners established Riverside, the city's first municipal golf course and the fourth in the nation, in Riverside Park. In 1901 the board opened a second nine-hole course called South Grove in Riverside Park. Over the next three decades the city built four more courses: Coffin (1904), Pleasant Run (1921), Sarah Shank (1925), and Douglass (1928). By the mid–1950s all of the municipal courses except Douglass had been expanded to 18 holes.

On September 11, 1900, Francis Herd, president of the Country Club of Indianapolis, held a meeting of golf devotees from private clubs in seven cities around the state at the DENISON HOTEL in Indianapolis. The group, which included former President BENJAMIN HARRISON and humorist George Ade, established the Indiana Golf Association (IGA) and scheduled its first state tournament for October 11–13 at the Country Club of Indianapolis. Twenty-five players participated in the tournament, which the IGA has sponsored every year since with the exception of 1918. Originally a private organization, the IGA, in partnership with the Professional Golfers' Association (PGA), is now open to both private and public courses throughout the state. Of Indianapolis' 12 municipal courses, only Thatcher is not an IGA-PGA member. Eleven of the city's twelve private courses are also members.

In 1914 a group of local golfers founded the Indianapolis District Golf Association (IDGA) to

**National PGA, LPGA, and USGA Tournaments
Held in Indianapolis**

Year	Event	Site
1935	Indianapolis Open	Highland
1935	National Public Links	Coffin
1955	National Public Links	Coffin
1960–1968	500 Festival Open	Speedway
1972	National Public Links	Coffin
1977–1980	LPGA Mayflower Classic	Harbour Trees
1981–1988	LPGA Mayflower Classic	Country Club of Indianapolis
1982	National Public Links	Eagle Creek
1982	USGA Junior Amateur	Crooked Stick
1983	USGA Senior Amateur	Crooked Stick
1989-	GTE North Senior Open	Broadmoor
1991	PGA Championship	Crooked Stick
1993	U.S. Women's Open	Crooked Stick

From 1960 through 1968 the Speedway Golf Club hosted the 500 Festival Open, a PGA tournament that initially attracted many of the world's best golfers. But the tournament, once the world's third largest with a $50,000 purse, suffered financially throughout its nine year history and disbanded after 1968.

In 1991 the PGA Championship was played at Crooked Stick in Carmel. The tournament received great attention locally and nationally as unknown John Daly claimed the first title of his career. Crooked Stick also hosted the U.S. Women's Open in 1993.

WILLIAM DALTON

promote the sport in the city and surrounding area. Any golf club within 60 miles of Indianapolis was eligible to join the association, which sponsored an annual tournament open only to residents of the Indianapolis district. The tournament, held from 1914 through 1988, was a multisite event played at different Indianapolis district clubs from year to year. The IDGA disbanded in the 1980s and its tournament, taken over by the IGA-PGA, became the IGA Match Play Tournament in 1989.

In 1964 the IGA-PGA established the Indiana Golf Hall of Fame and Broadmoor Country Club hosted the first annual Hall of Fame tournament and induction dinner. Since then, several Indianapolis clubs have hosted the annual ceremony, which travels to the home cities of each year's inductees. The IGA-PGA is currently working on plans to establish a permanent home for the Hall of Fame at its headquarters near Franklin.

In October, 1935, Highland hosted the Veterans of Foreign Wars Indianapolis Open, the city's first national tournament. Many of the nation's top professional golfers, plus several members of the British Ryder Cup team, competed for $5,000 in prize money. Later that year the United States Golf Association chose Coffin as the site of its annual National Public Links amateur championships, a tournament for amateur golfers who do not hold a membership in a private club. Coffin hosted the tournament again in 1955 and 1972. In 1982 the tournament was held at Eagle Creek, making Indianapolis the only city to host four National Public Links championships.

Goodman, Sarah Wolf (Mar. 25, 1886– Nov. 4, 1975). Civic leader and humanist, born in Vienna, Austria. Goodman's family moved to the United States and settled in Ashland, Kentucky, while she was still an infant. After graduating from the St. Louis (Mo.) Teachers College she divided her time between teaching kindergarten and doing volunteer work. She was instrumental in organizing 13 community centers in the public schools and also helped organize the St. Louis Municipal Outdoor Theater.

In 1924, she married Jack Goodman and moved to Indianapolis. She became active in the MATINEE MUSICALE and the Little Theater, which became known as the Booth Tarkington CIVIC THEATER. In 1926, she was named vice-president in charge of arts for the Kirshbaum Community Center, which later became the Jewish Community Center. The origin of the INDIANAPOLIS SYMPHONY ORCHESTRA can be traced to a small orchestra hired by this group for one of its art programs. She was the third president (1946–1949) of the Woman's Committee of the Indiana State Symphony Society and also served on the Symphony Society Board. She later cofounded the ENSEMBLE MUSIC SOCIETY and the Aspen Scholarship Association.

As a member of the National Committee on Youth of the United Jewish Appeal, she traveled to gain support for children and immigrants in Israel after World War II. In 1956, the Indianapolis COMMUNITY CHEST and B'nai B'rith named her Woman of the Year. She served as the national chair of the Woman's Division of the United Jewish Appeal (1957–1961) and later served on the group's national cabinet. In 1966, the Jewish Welfare Federation campaign was dedicated to her as a tribute for her work to help in Israel after the war. During her lifetime, she was the only woman to be president of the JEWISH FEDERATION OF GREATER INDIANAPOLIS and the first woman to hold such a position in the United States. She also served as the national vice-president of Hadassah and remained on its national board for 18 years. At the time of her death, Goodman was a member of the National Council of Jewish Women as well as a member and trustee of the Indianapolis Hebrew Congregation.

ELLEN TEVAULT

Indianapolis Star Magazine, Mar. 31, 1963, Jan. 2, 1966; *Indianapolis Star*, Nov. 5, 1975.

Goodwill Industries of Central Indiana. Social service agency. Founded nationally by the Rev. Edgar J. Helms in 1902 in Boston, Goodwill Industries came to Indianapolis under the auspices of the Methodist church. In 1930 a fledgling Goodwill program was begun at the Fletcher Place Methodist Church and the community center that served the neighborhood. Like the Boston model, the local agency accepted donations of used clothing, shoes, toys, and household items that were repaired and sold by Goodwill employees. Sales income paid wages and provided jobs for Fletcher Place residents.

In 1934 Rev. HOWARD LYTLE became executive secretary, a post he held until 1969. Under his leadership the Goodwill program expanded to serve the larger Indianapolis community. The agency incorporated in 1937 and relocated from Fletcher Place to new headquarters at 220 South Senate Avenue in 1943. Goodwill moved to its current location on Michigan Street west of White River in 1960.

Since 1945 the agency has won recognition for innovative programs that teach independent living skills and provide vocational testing, rehabilitation, and job placement. Clients have included people with physical and developmental disabilities and those with social or emotional barriers to employment.

In 1974 the organization reincorporated as Goodwill Industries of Central Indiana, Inc., to reflect the regional nature of the agency's operation. A branch facility opened in Muncie in 1978, followed by donation centers and/or stores in 30 counties in central Indiana.

The agency is supported by earned income from a variety of entrepreneurial operations, as well as by contributions, including those from the United Way and the Goodwill Service Guild. In 1990 Goodwill served nearly 1,800 people by providing vocational assessment, training, and employment opportunities.

CATHLEEN F. DONNELLY

Governor's Residence. There have been five official residences for Indiana's chief executives since Indianapolis became the state capital in 1825. At times, notably between 1865 and 1919, governors owned or rented private quarters. The five official residences have been:

Governor's Circle (1827–1839). In 1827 the General Assembly appropriated funds for a governor's residence on the Circle. Contractors built a large two-story yellow brick building with low hipped roof and a square platform on top. In fact, the mansion never housed a first family; Esther Ray, wife of then-Governor James Brown Ray, refused to live in it. At different times the state bank, state auditor, state library, state engineer, Supreme Court judges, Supreme Court clerk, debating societies, and several private individuals occupied the rooms. By 1857 the building had fallen into decay; the city council sold the structure and the new owner razed it for building materials.

This home, at Illinois and Market streets, served as the second official Governor's Residence in the city. [Indiana State Museum]

Northwest corner of Illinois and Market streets (1839–1864). In 1839, the legislature purchased Dr. John Sanders' home for the governor's mansion. Eight governors occupied the two-story brick house that had been built in 1836. CHRISTIAN SCHRADER's drawing from memory depicted a five-ranked Colonial style house. The state sold the home in 1865 after Governor Oliver P. Morton refused to live in it, declaring that it was damp and poorly heated.

101 East 27th Street (1919–1945). The Indianapolis Park Board purchased the Henry Kahn home in 1917 and leased it to the state for a governor's residence. HERBERT FOLTZ had designed the English Tudor country home in 1908. The mansion had multiple front gables and a steeply pitched roof. A parapeted central brick gable and a half-timbered gable with stucco infilling comprised the north facade. The property once extended to FALL CREEK, but became an island surrounded by traffic as Fall Creek Parkway developed. Dust from the street and the lack of privacy caused state officials to move the governor's residence to a new site in 1945. The home was demolished in 1962.

4343 North Meridian Street (1945–1973). In 1945 the state bought the home from the Trimble family. FRANK B. HUNTER designed the Colonial revival home in 1920 for William N. Thompson, president of the STUTZ Motor Car Company. The two-and-one-half-story buff-colored brick home had a variegated slate hipped roof. Four bays with paired French doors flanked the entrance to the north and south. The Adam style entry porch had a semi-circular wrought iron roof railing above it; similar railings surrounded balconies on the second story. Eventually the mansion proved inadequate for family living and official entertaining. It was sold at public auction in 1973.

4750 North Meridian (1975–present). In 1974 the state bought this 1928 Tudor revival home for the governor's residence. Designed by RUBUSH AND HUNTER for Scott Wadley, the two-and-one-half-story red brick house clad with a Flemish rowlock bond has a steeply pitched roof covered with variegated slate. A two-story bay with a flat, castellated parapet and a main gable with a high pitched roof and grouped tall, narrow windows dominate the east facade. The original main door

opening had renaissance details with tabs of cut stone that projected into the brickwork. Recent alterations north of the doorway transformed a porte-cochere into a compatible, formal entrance.

JANE R. NOLAN

Virginia and Lee McAlester, *A Field Guide to American Houses* (New York, 1986); Ignatius Brown, *History of Indianapolis* (Indianapolis, 1868); *Indianapolis Star*, Aug. 19, 1909, May 26, 1916, Feb. 14, 1943, Mar. 15, 1964, Dec. 28, 1974.

Grabill, Harvey A.

Grabill, Harvey A. (Jan. 8, 1890–Sept. 25, 1977). Attorney. Born in Ohio, Grabill moved to Indianapolis and attended the Benjamin Harrison Law School (later absorbed into Indiana University Law School). He was admitted to the Indiana bar in 1918 and joined the firm of Denny and Miller. He served as the county attorney for Marion County in 1931 and in 1937 established the law firm of Grabill and Baker. Governor Henry Schricker appointed him in 1949 to serve as chair of the Indiana Probate Code Study Commission created by the Indiana General Assembly to recodify the probate laws of the state. His efforts resulted in the first major changes in the Indiana Probate Court in over a century when a new Indiana Probate Code was passed by the General Assembly in the early 1950s. Grabill served as the president of the Indianapolis Bar Association in 1943, a member of the board of directors of the SALVATION ARMY, and a lecturer at Indiana University Law School.

JOAN CUNNINGHAM

Indiana Biography Series, Indiana State Library; *Who's Who in the Central States* (1947).

Grand Army of the Republic (GAR).

Grand Army of the Republic (GAR). Organization of Union veterans of the Civil War. The GAR was founded on April 6, 1866, mainly through the efforts of Dr. Benjamin Franklin Stephenson, former major and surgeon in the 14th Illinois Infantry. Membership was open to honorably discharged veterans who had served in the Union forces sometime between April 12, 1861, and April 9, 1865. "Fraternity, Charity, Loyalty," the slogan of the GAR, expressed the organi-

The 1893 GAR Encampment featured a replica of a Union gunboat, the *Kearsarge*, displayed on the Indiana State House lawn.
[Indiana Historical Society, Bass Collection, #17805]

stamp to observe the occasion. The last GAR member died seven years later.

DAN M. MITCHELL

Robert B. Beath, *History of the Grand Army of the Republic* (New York, 1888); Oliver M. Wilson, *The Grand Army of the Republic Under Its First Constitution and Ritual* (Kansas City, 1905).

zation's purpose. It sought to win such benefits as pensions (for widows and orphans, as well as veterans themselves), job preferments, and medical attention, and to secure recognition of the contributions of Union soldiers.

Indiana played a key role in the early history of the GAR. Governor OLIVER P. MORTON recognized the political opportunities of such an organization and sent representatives to visit Stephenson. With Morton's encouragement Indiana served as unofficial national headquarters for several months. Indiana posts took a lead in organizing the order by printing the charters, rituals, and constitutions to be distributed to prospective members, and Indiana (especially Indianapolis) veterans enlisted new recruits at the Pittsburgh Convention of Soldiers and Sailors held in September 1866.

The first national encampment of the GAR was held in Indianapolis on November 20 and 21, 1866. The Hoosier capital would host the national encampment seven more times (1881, 1893, 1920, 1921, 1942, 1946, 1949), more than any other city in the nation. The 1893 encampment, marked by the construction of a replica of the Union gunboat *Kearsarge* on the State House lawn, was the largest held in Indianapolis. The most memorable encampment, however, may have been the one in 1949—attended by only six members. It was the organization's final meeting, and the U.S. Post Office issued a commemorative

Grand Army of the Republic Encampments.

Civil War reunion and veterans' groups often chose Indianapolis for meetings after reunion groups became popular in the late 1870s. Indiana "reunion regiments" met individually in small and medium-sized towns in Indiana, but when they met at the brigade level, or desired a larger reunion, they gathered in the state capital, posing in front of some imposing building like the State House. Several regiments, for example, came to dedicate the SOLDIERS AND SAILORS MONUMENT in 1902 and held individual reunions in its basement and nearby hotels.

Indianapolis, proud of its contribution to military and political successes in the Civil War, called itself the "home of patriotism" in the years following the conflict. The Grand Army of the Republic (GAR) had been founded in Decatur, Illinois, in 1866, with Indiana men taking a leading role, and its first national meeting was held in Indianapolis later that year. Squabbles about leadership and factional fighting almost marred the meeting, but the GAR continued to grow and prosper in Indiana as well as in the nation.

The GAR's Fifteenth National Encampment was held again in Indianapolis, June 15–16, 1881, and another large "campfire" occurred in the Hoosier capital in 1893. Collateral groups such as the Army War Nurses and Mississippi Marine Brigade would convene at these national encampments, as well as individual brigades, and the 1893 meeting brought an estimated 75,000 visitors to the city. Many of them no doubt took an opportunity to review a replica of the Union ship *Kearsarge* constructed on the lawn of the State House.

A national encampment held in Indianapolis in 1920 was such a success that the GAR decided to return in 1921. The gray-haired veterans, some of whom had served in the Union Army at CAMP MORTON and the Confederate prison camp in the vicinity of 19th and Alabama streets, toured the site of the camp and prison, the Confederate burial ground, and the Soldiers and Sailors Monument on the Circle. Adjunct women's organizations, the Woman's Relief Corps and the Ladies of the GAR, met at the same time. When they were not in meetings the veterans visited the statue of Governor OLIVER P. MORTON, a Republican who had given President Lincoln unyielding political support in the North's darkest days, and trekked to the old Confederate burial site and monument, by 1920 blackened by industrial smoke. They were driven to the location of Camp Robertson in RIVERSIDE PARK, where LEW WALLACE and his Zouaves had carved their initials in a beech tree before departing for the front.

After other meetings in the Hoosier capital in 1942 and 1946, the final encampment of the GAR returned to Indianapolis in 1949. Six veterans, all over 100 years old and including the sole surviving black veteran, Joseph Clovese (105), were all that remained of the great army that had at the end of the war totaled some 200,000 soldiers. Nine other federal soldiers were too infirm to attend. On August 31, 1949, these last members of the Union Army, with the U.S. Marine Band stepping out before them, were taken in open cars on a final parade through the downtown and around MONUMENT CIRCLE. Then, at the Indiana Roof Ballroom, they held their last business meeting, sang "Tenting Tonight on the Old Camp Ground" one last time, and moved for adjournment.

NANCY NIBLACK BAXTER
Guild Press of Indiana

Grandy, Erroll (Jan. 1, 1918–June 12, 1991). Jazz pianist affectionately nicknamed the "godfather of Indianapolis jazz" in deference to his influence on the city's jazz scene from the 1940s to the 1960s. Born Lucas Erroll Grandy near Norfolk, Virginia, he began playing hymns on the piano at age three and later starred in his own local radio show. He moved to Indianapolis in 1936 when his father, Thomas Leroy Grandy, became pastor at Witherspoon Presbyterian Church. He

graduated from CRISPUS ATTUCKS HIGH SCHOOL in 1940.

Though afflicted by chronic eye disease, Grandy earned a B.A. in music from Jordan Conservatory (now JORDAN COLLEGE OF FINE ARTS) in 1944, working his way through college by playing for $15 a night at the Boulevard Kitchen at 21st Street and Boulevard Place. After a brief tour with the Jim Coe Band, he settled into the Indianapolis club circuit backing visiting musicians such as Dinah Washington, Billie Holiday, Lionel Hampton, and Count Basie, and serving as a mentor to aspiring local players WES MONTGOMERY, Pookie Johnson, Flo Garvin, Leroy Vinegar, J. J. Johnson, and Freddie Hubbard. Grandy's musical contributions were recognized by a mayoral proclamation of Erroll Grandy Day on May 6, 1984, highlighted by a marathon benefit concert featuring 14 leading Indianapolis jazz groups. He continued to perform regularly until moving to the ALPHA HOME in 1986, where he died five years later.

LAWRENCE E. MCCULLOUGH
Indiana University–Purdue University,
Indianapolis

Phil Oldham, "Erroll Grandy Benefit: A Great Community Effort," *Jazz Notes* (June, 1984); Eunice McLayea-Trotter, "Indianapolis Jazz 'Godfather' to Get Appreciation-day Jam," *Indianapolis Star*, Apr. 29, 1984.

Great Depression. During the ten months preceding the stock market crash in October, 1929, the *Indiana Business Review* concluded that there was a high level of industrial activity in Indianapolis and that most lines of business had improved over the previous year, except for the building trades. By early 1930 the situation had changed dramatically. The U.S. Bureau of the Census reported that almost 17,000 of Marion County's work force of 182,000 (9.3 percent) were looking for work. By September, employment in the city was 17 percent under the 1929 level, compared to a statewide drop of 15 percent. "Help Wanted" advertisements for December in the capital's three newspapers decreased 23 percent from pre-Depression levels. By May, 1931, most factory employees were working on a part-time basis. Without unemployment benefits or other features of the modern welfare system, the unemployed faced serious financial problems. Finding a job was particularly difficult for middle-aged men, since men over 45 were considered past their prime.

In February, 1930, local business leaders formed a commission "to study and act for the stabilization of employment in Indianapolis." For the remainder of the winter the commission worked to persuade employers to reduce layoffs and to increase their support of relief efforts. That summer the group planned for the winter of 1930–1931 by organizing a relief program which would require relief recipients to work for their benefits. Winters were especially bad times because seasonal unemployment peaked then.

The nonprofit Emergency Work Committee operated the make-work program, beginning its efforts in early fall 1930 and incorporating in December. A benefit football game between Shortridge and Cathedral high schools provided the initial $10,500 the committee used to pay wages to unemployed people recommended by the Family Welfare Society, the Catholic Community Center, the Jewish Welfare Federation, and the public schools' social service department. Workers received 30 cents an hour for three eight-hour days of work.

When funds ran out in early January, 1931, the Indianapolis Community Fund gave $42,500 for relief. The Indianapolis chapter of the American Red Cross provided funds earmarked for World War I veterans and many Marion County employees donated 1 percent of their salaries to the committee. The program was expanded so that those receiving relief from township trustees could participate. The committee decreased its level of relief support during the summer months, citing reduced need as the reason. By August, 1931, relief recipients were almost evenly divided between African-Americans and whites.

The Emergency Work Committee held various fund-raising activities such as firewood sales, baseball games, and vaudeville performances to continue funding relief efforts. As economic conditions worsened, the committee was able to provide less relief, decreasing from three days' work for cash to three days' work for cash and food to two days' work for food. During the final phase, the committee gave relief recipients a card with their work assignment, usually in a city government department. In exchange for 16 hours of work, workers' cards were approved and returned to the township trustee where they could be redeemed for a basket of groceries valued between $2.00 and $5.00 depending on family size.

After its first year of operation the Emergency Work Committee drew up guidelines to determine who should receive aid and in what order. Relief cases were graded good, fair, or poor on the basis of the applicant's need, physical condition, moral character, and ability to be self-supporting if given a small wage. Those graded as good in all categories received assistance first, whereas previously recipients had been selected randomly. Based on committee minutes from January, 1932, most aid recipients resided in Center Township, particularly downtown and on the near west side between the Central Canal and White River. They painted and cleaned, repaired streets and sidewalks, removed trash, mowed grass, and performed clerical work. By March, 1932, the Emergency Work Committee had provided relief compensation for almost 2.3 million hours of work.

Beginning in July, 1931, the *Indiana Business Review* reported new record lows in Indianapolis employment and business activity for 22 straight months. In November, 1931, employment in the city was more than 25 percent under 1929 levels. By April, 1932, it had dropped off 30 percent. The manufacturing work force was hit especially hard, declining by half (59,000 to 30,000) from 1930 to 1933. Other midwestern cities had even higher total unemployment rates, with 50 percent out of work in Cleveland and 90 percent without jobs in Gary. Indianapolis avoided such extremes because of its diversified economic base; however, its unemployment rate continued to climb until April, 1933, when it reached 37 percent.

For Indianapolis, the years 1932 and 1933 were the most severe. The construction industry was down dramatically with the building index in May, 1933, almost 90 percent under pre-Depression norms. The number of Indianapolis building permits issued in the period from 1931 to 1934 was one quarter the number issued from 1927 to

1930; only 27 homes were built in the city in 1933. The real estate business also suffered, with the number of deeds and mortgages recorded bottoming out in 1932 and 1933. The city's cost of living index reflected the hard times, declining almost 9 percent in 1932 alone. In the first six months of 1933, the index dropped another 2.7 percent to a level 25 percent lower than the pre-Depression years.

Both private and public sectors of the economy suffered during the early to mid–1930s. The STUTZ Motor Car Company closed in 1934 and the COLUMBIA CONSERVE COMPANY forced employees to take substantial pay cuts, but ELI LILLY AND COMPANY and MERCHANTS NATIONAL BANK managed to retain all their employees during the hard times. The Marion County sheriff was forced to cut 17 deputies from his staff in January, 1932. During early 1932 charities such as the Sunshine Mission, 744 Virginia Avenue, fed 300 people each day and distributed 6,000 garments, yet still failed to meet demand. In 1933 Second Presbyterian Church's Mayer Chapel on the south side provided food, clothing, and coal to over 200 church families.

In early 1933 the Indiana General Assembly created the Governor's Commission on Unemployment Relief (GCUR). In November of that year the Women's Work Division of the GCUR was organized under the federal Civil Works Administration. This division recognized that "in many family groups the potential wage earner was a woman . . . [and] large numbers of unattached women were in need." In Marion County women engaged in clerical work, cataloged and indexed books in libraries, cleaned public buildings, participated in large sewing projects, and served as public health nurses. Previously women had been certified for work relief only if there were no employable men in their families. Women who found private employment during the Depression often were forced into accepting similar lower-paying, pink-collar jobs. Black women had even fewer opportunities; many who received relief jobs worked as domestic or personal servants.

By fall, 1933, New Deal programs were having an impact on the Indianapolis economy. Employment picked up, in part because of regulations by the National Recovery Administra-

tion. In November, a decline in private employment was more than offset by employment on Civil Works Administration projects. The Women's Prison, Naval Armory, Fall Creek Parkway, Howe High School, and LOCKEFIELD GARDENS were local examples of public works projects.

Indiana's 28 Civilian Conservation Corps camps were coordinated from FORT BENJAMIN HARRISON. Fort Harrison also hosted the Citizens' Military Training Camp during the 1930s to train young men for the Officers' Reserve Corps. These camps were very popular, no doubt in part because the month-long training session included free food, clothing, laundry, and transportation for participants. Enrollment for the 1933 camp was filled in a day.

In May, 1934, the GCUR conducted a survey of relief recipients. Men comprised nearly 77 percent of recipients and women about 23 percent. Most recipients were white (65 percent); blacks accounted for almost 34 percent of those receiving aid. Aid recipients were most common in the 51+ age bracket (34 percent), as opposed to those in the 41–50 (23 percent), 31–40 (24 percent), or 21–30 (15 percent) age categories. Sixty-four percent were married. Over half of public assistance recipients had no better than an eighth grade education. Households receiving the most public assistance were those consisting of 2 people (24 percent) and those with 6 or more individuals (20 percent). The average worker on relief labored 22 hours a week for 30.8 cents an hour for a total of $6.78 per week.

The Indianapolis economy showed marked improvement by July, 1934, even though total industrial employment was 20 percent under the 1929 peak. In March, 1935, new car sales picked up considerably as dealers sold more vehicles than at any time since August, 1929. In the spring of 1935 the *Indiana Business Review* began publishing statistics on public relief by county. Although figures did not include those who never applied, transients, or persons receiving help under programs such as college student aid, emergency education, or rural rehabilitation, the reports are useful in approximating the extent of public relief in Indianapolis. In March, 1935, almost 19 percent of Marion County's residents received public relief. This number declined steadily over the next year to 6 percent reported in March, 1936.

February, 1936, marked the first time the city's general business cycle showed above-normal activity since mid–1930. In 1937 INTERNATIONAL HARVESTER built a huge truck engine facility and H. P. WASSON AND COMPANY opened a new downtown department store on the corner of Meridian and Washington streets. Newspaper advertising also surpassed pre-Depression levels. By August, 1938, business payrolls increased, reflecting more full-time work than previously available.

An analysis of manufacturing trends in Indianapolis shows that the city did not recover as quickly as the country did on the whole. Nationally, the average number of wage earners and wages paid in 1937 were both 87 percent of the 1929 level. In Indianapolis, the number of wage earners in the city was only 77 percent of the 1929 level and wages were just 58 percent of what they had been in 1929. The country's 1937 value of manufactured products was 81 percent of the 1929 figure while in Indianapolis the value was 68 percent of what it had been in 1929.

DEBORAH B. MARKISOHN

Greater Indianapolis Helicopter.

Pioneering effort to implement aerial ambulance service. In 1968 Indianapolis and Marion County officials launched the Greater Indianapolis Helicopter program. Spearheaded by County Council president Beurt SerVaas and Sheriff Lee Eads, the service was designed to provide helicopter evacuation of accident victims from areas remote from local hospitals. Six metropolitan government agencies—Marion County Sheriff, Health and Hospital Corporation (General Hospital), Indianapolis Police and Fire departments, Mass Transportation Authority, and Indianapolis Airport Authority—operated the service with costs shared equally among them.

In August the program purchased a five-passenger, litter-equipped Bell Helicopter Jet-Ranger, "N 3399. " Indianapolis-based Allison Division of General Motors donated the turbine engine for the craft to reduce the initial outlay, and Indiana Helicopter Corporation was contracted to handle all operation and maintenance. Entering service on December 6, 1968, the copter was assigned to regular morning and evening rush hour traffic patrols, offering what was considered the first scheduled aerial ambulance service in the United States. It also remained on call 24 hours a day, 365 days a year.

By 1979 commercial helicopter operators were developing aerial ambulance programs for area hospitals, and 3399 was retired from its regular ambulance runs. During its ten and a half years of rescue operations, the craft flew over 300 accident victims to area hospitals. Federal Department of Transportation standards credited the copter with definitely saving some 90 lives and probably saving another 140; more conservative figures from local doctors reported 40 saves and 70 probables. The Indianapolis service was recognized as a national leader in air ambulance work, gaining considerable experience in both medical and flight operations.

JERRY MARLETTE

Greater Indianapolis Progress Committee (GIPC).

A private, not-for-profit, nonpartisan civic improvement organization funded by foundation grants and private contributions. GIPC (pronounced "gypsy") functions as an advisory arm to the mayor's office. Unlike the earlier Indianapolis Civic Progress Association, which it supplanted, the Greater Indianapolis Progress Committee has had from its beginning a loosely defined relationship with the city's executive branch. The small professional staff is located in the CITY-COUNTY BUILDING.

GIPC had its origins in the fall of 1964 when Democratic Mayor JOHN J. BARTON appointed an advisory committee of business and civic leaders to "formulate a program of progress that makes use of the city's full potential." The committee's name was adopted by the end of the year and the first executive director, John W. Walls, assumed his position in March, 1965. FRANK E. MCKINNEY, SR. served as the first president, and his address to the membership in June of that year, outlining the organization's goals, is often cited as the committee's true beginning. In this prescient talk, McKinney outlined many of the projects that were to be undertaken by the city during the next two decades.

Republican mayors Richard G. Lugar, William H. Hudnut III, and Stephen Goldsmith not only left GIPC in place but expanded its scope and membership. In its early years the organization initiated the development of Eagle Creek Park and Reservoir and led the drive for a downtown convention center. The committee also provided leadership in planning the government reorganization that became known as UNIGOV. In the 1980s GIPC was involved in various downtown revitalization projects (INDIANA THEATRE, WHITE RIVER STATE PARK, etc.), as well as in establishing the ARTS COUNCIL OF INDIANAPOLIS and the CENTRAL INDIANA COUNCIL ON AGING. In the words of a former committee chair: "GIPC's approach to problem solving . . . is to form a task force, gather facts and opinions, recommend a course of action, and see to it that the right organization is either created or delegated to carry out the recommended action."

GIPC's strength has been its ability to marshal the talents of private sector leaders and volunteers in support of public endeavors. A broad-based organization—in 1992 there were roughly 90 persons on the board of directors—it includes representatives of business, education, labor, government, religious bodies, social service organizations, and neighborhood groups. (Under the recently amended article of incorporation, the mayor nominates individuals to serve on the board of directors; the board itself then elects new members from those nominees.) In spite of its diverse membership, GIPC has occasionally been subject to criticism that it is controlled by a business elite. The organization has also been faulted for being an unelected "shadow government"—an institution with tremendous influence on the city's agenda but accountable to neither the electorate nor their representatives on the City-County Council. GIPC officials maintain, however, that in practice the committee is reactive rather than proactive, with its initiatives originating either in the mayor's office or the broader community.

ROBERT G. BARROWS
Indiana University–Purdue University,
Indianapolis

Greater Indianapolis Women's Political Caucus. In February, 1972, 17 women active in civic affairs met to organize an Indianapolis chapter that would discuss political issues important to women and encourage their involvement in politics. Soon 80 bipartisan members had collected statistics on the number of women holding political office, organized instructional programs to train women in politics, and identified women to assist in political campaigns and run for public office. Platform issues included the problem of displaced homemakers, equal pay, child care support, inheritance tax laws, and discrimination in access to credit.

From this core chapter, a state conference gathered in late 1972 for the purpose of organizing other chapters. Some 800 women attended and later formed chapters in Anderson, South Bend, Bloomington, Columbus, Lafayette, and Muncie. The Indianapolis chapter became heavily engaged for four years in pressing for state passage of the Equal Rights Amendment, accomplished in 1977. Additional issues of importance to the Indianapolis chapter were health care for women, wife and child abuse, rape, and employment opportunities. The organization spurred many women of both major parties to become more active in politics, attend political conventions, and learn more about lobbying and the legislative process.

In 1980 the organization ceased to exist as a separate entity and joined the Gender Fairness Coalition, a network of local women's organizations that continues to hold annual legislative awareness seminars, meetings with local government officials, and instructional sessions on issues pertinent to women.

FRANCES DODSON RHOME
Indiana University–Purdue University,
Indianapolis

Greeks. The Greek community of Indianapolis was established in the 1890s and early 20th century. The initial immigrants, from the Peloponnesus region, migrated to the city in search of economic advancement. The typical Greek immigrant to Indianapolis in the early years was an adolescent male of peasant stock with little formal education. However, ambition and persistence more than compensated for an apparent lack of skills.

Many Europeans viewed the United States as a land of opportunity where the streets were "paved with gold." Letters home from earlier immigrants and advertisements by ship lines helped maintain that perception and the continuous flow of immigrants. Most Greeks who emigrated intended to return home after making their fortunes here. However, as they established families, opened successful businesses, and witnessed the disruption in Europe following World War I, many decided to remain. The Greek community of Indianapolis developed in this manner.

According to the 1900 census, 82 Greeks resided in Indiana; 29 lived in Indianapolis. Despite the small size of the community, the Greeks formed a council to establish an Orthodox church. In 1905 the parish reestablished, and in 1910 it incorporated under state law, adopting the name of Holy Trinity. By 1914 the church, previously located at 27 South Meridian Street, relocated to the 200 block of North West Street where it remained until 1960. The church is now located at 4011 North Pennsylvania Street. In the United States, Greek Orthodoxy and Hellenism, a devotion to Greek culture and nationalism, became synonymous. The establishment of a church and community provided the immigrants with a source of religious and cultural continuity and comradeship in their new environment.

Initially, Greek immigrants earned their livelihoods as common laborers or peddlers. By 1906 Greeks in Indianapolis had established numerous businesses since entrepreneurship was viewed as the quickest route to financial success. Most of the Greek-owned enterprises, usually sole proprietorships or partnerships, were located along the major streets of downtown Indianapolis. Greeks operated service-oriented businesses such as shoe shine stands, confectioneries, restaurants, florists, bakeries, groceries, theaters, billiard parlors, tailoring shops, dry cleaning shops, hardware stores, an employment agency, and taverns. One educated immigrant became a lawyer.

The pioneer Greeks usually lived communally near their places of employment. As they established families, they settled next to other Greeks in the city. By the 1920s, they inhabited

Owner Pantelis Cafouros (far left) and staff in front of the oddly named Paradise and Devil's Cafe, 108 W. Maryland Street, ca. 1910. Originally, it was called Devil's Cafe. Cafouros' wife (seated, third from left), who did not speak English, believed "Devil" corresponded to the French "de ville," *of the city*. When she found out what the word meant, she objected. Cafouros then remodeled the business into two cafes, one called the Paradise, where Mrs. Cafouros worked, and the other retaining the original name.
[Indiana Historical Society, #C88]

three areas of the city: the Balkan neighborhood around MILITARY PARK, the near east side, and the emerging northside neighborhoods. One wealthy Greek restaurateur and businessman, John G. Zazas, built a mansion at 4356 North Meridian Street. The old neighborhoods began to disintegrate, however, after World War II.

The social and cultural life of Indianapolis Greeks centered on the home and church. Their main affairs were church picnics and celebrations that brought the growing community together. Over time, they established various Greek social clubs to supplement the community's social calendar with dances and plays. Greek parents who wanted to preserve their language and culture provided afternoon Greek schools in the church to instruct their children in Greek history, culture, and language. The parish continues such instruction today for the next generation.

Greek immigrants were patriotic to both Greece and the United States. Greeks from Indianapolis returned to fight for their homeland in the Balkan Wars (1912–1913). During both World Wars local Greeks served in the United States armed forces and joined in assorted war fund drives.

Indianapolis Greeks remain involved with Greek domestic politics. Civil strife in Greece resulted in a bitter schism in Holy Trinity parish from 1923–1940. The schism pitted Royalists against Venizelists in numerous legal battles for control of Holy Trinity. The schism in Indianapolis ended during World War II when local Greeks united to aid Greece in its battles with the Axis Powers.

Hellenism is alive in Indianapolis. The 1990 census reported 1,465 individuals of Greek ancestry in Marion County. The Greek community constructed a new church in 1960 and a cultural center in 1981. The parish conducts educational, philanthropic, and ecumenical programs and has sponsored since 1974 the annual Greek Food Festival, an event that allows everyone who attends to enjoy the Greek zest for living.

CARL C. CAFOUROS

Carl C. Cafouros, *Seeds of Faith* (Indianapolis, 1980); Carl C. Cafouros, "The Community of Indianapolis: A Microcosm of the Greek Immigrant Experience" (M.A. thesis, University of Illinois, 1981).

Greenough, Katharine Croan (1889–Dec. 12, 1977). Women's rights and good government advocate. A native of Iowa, Greenough grew up in Anderson, Indiana, and graduated Phi Beta Kappa from Indiana University in 1911. In 1912, she married Walter S. Greenough, a 1910 Indiana University graduate, and moved to Indianapolis. Her involvement in the women's suffrage movement began in 1916, and her interest in women's causes became a lifelong commitment—part of an overall commitment to civic welfare.

In 1919, Greenough served as state organization chair of the Woman's Franchise League of Indiana, which organized support for women's suffrage throughout the more than 1,000 Indiana townships. After the committee's whirlwind campaign, the Indiana General Assembly ratified the 19th Amendment in 1920. Greenough then headed the first Citizenship School in Indiana, a school designed to instruct women in the proper use of their newly acquired voting privilege. From then on, she was a tireless worker for the intelligent use of the vote by both men and women.

Active in the foundation of the national LEAGUE OF WOMEN VOTERS (established 1921), she became the second president of the Indiana league in 1922. She also served twice as president of the Indianapolis league and was on the state board of directors continuously until 1955.

From 1932 to 1939, Greenough was a board member of the national league, first as secretary, and later as chair of the national Department of Government and Its Operation. During the 1930s, she edited the league's national publication, *The Woman Voter,* and wrote numerous league pamphlets and study kits for national distribution. Particularly popular were two informal studies of local governments, "Know Your County" and "Know Your Town."

In addition, Greenough served on the executive council of the National Civil Service League and on the board of the National Municipal League. She also organized the Indiana Merit System Association, which sponsored legislation to improve the quality of personnel in Indiana state government, serving as its vice-president from 1940 to 1955.

Greenough's interests were not limited to governmental issues. From 1945 to 1950, she served as an executive board member of the Health and Welfare Council of Indianapolis, and in 1948–1949 chaired the Family and Child Welfare Division of the Indianapolis Council for Social Agencies (forerunner of the COMMUNITY SERVICE COUNCIL).

A strong advocate of education, Greenough maintained a lifelong devotion to her alma mater. In 1938, she was named to the Indiana University Alumni Council, a position she held for many years. At the time of her death in 1977, memorial contributions were requested for the Katharine Croan Greenough Award Fund in Government, a scholarship fund administered by the Indiana University Foundation.

LAURA GAUS

Greenspace. Planning of greenspace areas within Marion County has been part of every land development plan since ALEXANDER RALSTON laid out the MILE SQUARE in 1821. Traditionally, the acquisition and maintenance of publicly owned

Greenspace has been the primary responsibility of the DEPARTMENT OF PARKS AND RECREATION (DPR), with the DEPARTMENT OF METROPOLITAN DEVELOPMENT (DMD) sharing planning duties. Today, many constituencies work on greenspace goals. These groups include neighborhood and environmental groups such as the Nora-Northside Community Council and the Audubon Society working together as GAUGE (Groups Advocating Urban Greenspace Environments), the city-sponsored White River Greenway Development Board, and state and federal agencies.

A "greenspace" can be defined as any partially or wholly undeveloped tract of land that is available for uses other than construction of manmade structures (although some greenspaces have park-style buildings and recreation facilities). Greenspaces can be any size and shape and have any combination of vegetation, water, topography, and uses. Examples of greenspaces within Marion County include EAGLE CREEK PARK, Fall Creek Parkway, White River Greenway, the proposed Monon Trail, commercial golf courses, corn fields, small woodlots preserved within a subdivision, and wooded vacant lots in the inner city. Greenspaces can be privately and publicly owned. Their continued existence may be tenuous due to development pressures, or perpetual if preserved by intent (master planning, zoning, public ownership, and/or deed restriction). Developed areas can also be returned to greenspace use.

The original 1821 Mile Square city plan by Alexander Ralston incorporated planned open areas such as MONUMENT CIRCLE and what is today the INDIANA WORLD WAR MEMORIAL PLAZA. The design intentionally included streets radiating diagonally out from the Circle to provide some relief from the monotony of a flat grid of streets. The diagonal streets now continue to the edges of the county and beyond, hooking up with state roads. The Ralston plan was updated and expanded in 1870 to include much of the area toward the White River.

In 1885 the first City Board of Park Commissioners was formed and prominent landscape architect John C. Olmsted was hired to survey the city's park needs. Olmsted's plans called for a central city area for public buildings, a series of small public parks, a series of large local parks, one or more large rural parks on the outskirts of the city, one or two great public reservations, and parkways connecting two or more of the parks. His plan led to the purchase of Brookside and Riverside parks, Morris and Indianola squares, and McCarty Place.

In 1905 city planner and landscape architect GEORGE A. KESSLER was hired to update and further implement Olmsted's plan. Kessler's 1909 plans consisted of lining the city's streams with boulevards which would link major parks. This resulted in White River, Fall Creek, and Pleasant Run parkways. Kessler also laid out the scenic, wide, tree-lined boulevard which meanders through Washington and Wayne townships and now bears his name. In 1929 the Council of Social Agencies and the INDIANAPOLIS FOUNDATION conducted a study resulting in a 571–page document, "The Leisure of a People," which called for more park expansion, the involvement of many civic, church, and business groups, and the setting aside of open areas by land developers and realtors. Numerous city park and open space plans have been developed by the city planners since 1929, the most recent being issued in 1991.

Greenspace and park acreage acquisition within Marion County has declined markedly since World War II. Prior to the war the city actively solicited and coerced land developers to set aside portions of new subdivisions, resulting in many small neighborhood parks (called "tot lots") used primarily by neighborhood residents. Much land was given to the city by families of early residents; an example is WOOLLEN'S GARDENS. During the post-World War II building boom, the political climate favored land developers, and the city's need to keep up with infrastructure demands of the new suburbs resulted in no funding for major park acquisition. At the same time many of the best natural areas, such as BACON'S SWAMP, and logical park locations were being developed. The city received some new parkland—Marott and Eagle Creek—as gifts, but it did not purchase land as aggressively as it had in the past. This decision resulted in the old city having the most park land (exclusive of Eagle Creek Park), while newer areas are relatively park poor. The county as a whole had 9,657 acres of park in 1991, with a ratio of 12.0 acres:1,000 population. This figure compares unfavorably to Columbus, Ohio, 21.2; Cincinnati, 12.6; St. Louis, 26.6; Kansas City, 17.2; and Minneapolis, 17.2. The county is also far behind National Park Service standards. However, Eagle Creek (4,574 acres) is one of the largest municipally owned parks in the nation, containing nearly half of the total county park acreage.

The future of greenspace in Indianapolis appeared brighter in the early 1990s than at any time in decades. New initiatives under consideration included the White River Greenway as a major hike, bike, and canoe system, a National Park Service recreational corridor study of all streams and abandoned railroads, development of the now city-owned Monon rail corridor as a bike and hike trail, transfer of undeveloped city-owned properties from other departments to the DPR, and a major fund-raising campaign through the new Indianapolis Parks Foundation (1991). A major opportunity for a greenspace expansion opened with the U.S. Army's decision to close the 2,500–acre FORT BENJAMIN HARRISON in 1995. "Fort Ben" contains the largest contiguous wooded tract in central Indiana (1,075 acres), along with many untilled fields, lakes, ponds and Fall Creek, and a large golf course.

KEVIN STRUNK
Wabash Resources and Consulting

Greenwood. Northernmost city in Johnson County, located just south of the Marion County line. The community is bounded by I–65 on the east and S.R. 135 on the west. The area was first settled by Anglo-Americans around 1824 when Jacob Smock and the Brewer family took up residence. Initially called Smockton, the settlers later designated their town Greenfield. In 1832 they changed its name to Greenwood to eliminate confusion with the Greenfield in nearby Hancock County.

Greenwood, with a population of 300, incorporated under a town board in 1864. By that time it had become an important shipping point on the MADISON AND INDIANAPOLIS RAILROAD. In 1872 J. T. Polk opened a canning factory which became the largest cannery west of Baltimore and the town's biggest employer, bringing in workers who became residents. In 1930 the Stokely Company (later STOKELY–VAN CAMP) purchased the former Polk canning factory and operated it until 1959 when it moved to Indianapolis.

On January 1, 1900, the Indianapolis, Greenwood, and Franklin Railroad sent its first interurban into Indianapolis from its Greenwood shops. The interurban further facilitated settlement in Greenwood, allowing easy and inexpensive access to Indianapolis jobs for people who chose to live in the smaller town.

For many years Greenwood remained a small town. In 1960, when it became a 5th class city, its population was only 7,200. However, following the creation of UNIGOV in 1970, the 1973 court-ordered desegregation of Indianapolis schools through busing, and the related flight out of Marion County, Greenwood's population increased rapidly. Builders throughout the 1970s averaged 400 new home starts per year. Although that growth slowed somewhat in the following decades, by 1990 the city encompassed approximately 10 square miles and had a predominately white population of 26,265, with a median age of 32.6 years.

In 1993 Greenwood's housing stock varies from Victorian homes in "Old Towne" to half-million-dollar, custom-built homes in new subdivisions; the median home price in 1990 was $74,400. The city, with three major hospitals, three school districts, and shopping areas ranging from downtown specialty shops, to strip malls, to hundreds of shops at Greenwood Park Mall, considers itself more than a bedroom community for Indianapolis. Its primary employers are Noblett-Sparks, Arvin North American Automotive, Endress + Hauser, NACHI Technology, and Alpine Electronics; residents' median income in 1990 was $39,639.

CONNIE J. ZEIGLER

Indianapolis Monthly (July, 1993).

Gregg, Harvey (Mar. 5, 1792–Apr. 3, 1833). Early settler, lawyer, and newspaperman. Arriving in Indianapolis in December, 1821, from Henry County, Kentucky, Gregg was admitted to practice law at the initial meeting of the First Circuit Court in Marion County in September,

1822. The next year he formed a law partnership with fellow Kentuckian Gabriel J. Johnston.

On March 7, 1823, Gregg and DOUGLASS MAGUIRE, also from Kentucky, began publication of the WESTERN CENSOR & EMIGRANTS GUIDE, the second newspaper established in Indianapolis. Gregg sold his interest in the paper in late 1824 to JOHN DOUGLASS and turned to his law practice. During the mid–1820s and again in the early 1830s he served as the prosecuting attorney for the judicial circuit that included Marion County. He lost a bid for state auditor in 1828.

JOAN CUNNINGHAM

Gayle Thornbrough, ed., *The Diary of Calvin Fletcher*, Vol. I (Indianapolis, 1972); Leander J. Monks, *Courts and Lawyers of Indiana* (Indianapolis, 1916).

Gregory and Appel. Long-standing family-owned insurance agency. Fred A. Gregory and John J. Appel formed an insurance and real estate business in 1884, sharing a desk in an office at the corner of Market and Pennsylvania streets. In July, 1909, the two men and their sons, Fred Appel and Frank Gregory, formed Gregory and Appel Incorporated. In addition to selling real estate and insurance the men were also rental and loan agents. One of their early insurance clients was L. S. AYRES AND COMPANY department store in downtown Indianapolis.

John and Fred Appel purchased the interest of Fred Gregory in 1916, making the company a single-family business. In 1928 Fred Appel became president of the company when John Appel died. Gregory and Appel entered real estate development, constructing and selling six houses on North New Jersey Street in 1936. By World War II the company had built over 250 homes in Indianapolis. After the war, in 1947, Fred Appel passed the company presidency along to his son John C. Appel. Two years later the company moved to its own office building at 120 East Vermont Street, adding extra office space in 1973 as the number of employees grew. Additional growth brought another move in 1987; the current 50–person staff is located at 333 North Penn-

sylvania Street where the company now specializes exclusively in insurance.

CONNIE J. ZEIGLER

Gresham, Walter Quintin (Mar. 17, 1832–May 28, 1895). Soldier, judge, and cabinet officer. A native of Harrison County, Indiana, Gresham attended Indiana University one year before reading law. Admitted to the bar in 1854, he practiced at Corydon and took a leading part in the local REPUBLICAN PARTY.

Gresham served in the state House of Representatives at the tumultuous session of 1861, during which he clashed with Governor OLIVER P. MORTON over the state's response to the pending sectional crisis. In the Union army Gresham was colonel of the 53rd Indiana Infantry and won promotion to brigadier general before a severe leg wound ended his service in 1864. Taking up residence at New Albany, he ran unsuccessfully for Congress in 1866 and 1868.

In 1869 President Ulysses Grant appointed Gresham federal district judge for Indiana. Court duties frequently took him to Indianapolis, and he moved to the city in 1875. Among his notable actions on the bench was his injunction against strikers at Indianapolis during the great RAILROAD STRIKE OF 1877. He urged President Rutherford Hayes to send troops to the city and headed a company of citizens militia designed to overawe the strikers.

Politically, Gresham remained at odds with Morton and with Morton's successor as state Republican leader, BENJAMIN HARRISON, who easily outdistanced Gresham's bid for the U.S. Senate in 1880. In 1883–1884 Gresham served in the cabinet of President Chester Arthur as postmaster general and briefly as secretary of the treasury. In 1884 he returned to the bench as circuit judge for Illinois, Indiana, and Wisconsin, with his headquarters and residence at Chicago. Gresham was a dark-horse presidential possibility in 1884. Four years later he mounted a serious campaign only to lose the Republican nomination to Hoosier rival Harrison.

Gresham's labor views mellowed, and, disenchanted with the Republicans' high tariff policy, he won considerable favor for the Populist presidential nomination in 1892. He declined, however, and backed Democrat Grover Cleveland against Harrison. In March, 1893, President Cleveland appointed him secretary of state, a post he held until his death. As secretary he opposed territorial expansion, gave little support to economic imperialism, and spearheaded the administration's rejection of the annexation of Hawaii.

CHARLES W. CALHOUN
East Carolina University

Charles W. Calhoun, *Gilded Age Cato: The Life of Walter Q. Gresham* (Lexington, Ky., 1988); Matilda Gresham, *Life of Walter Quintin Gresham, 1832–1895* (2 vols., Chicago, 1919).

Griffith, Shirley (Apr. 26, 1908 –June 18, 1974). Blues singer-guitarist-songwriter. A native of Brandon, Mississippi, Griffith learned the guitar at age ten. He moved to Indianapolis in 1928 bearing the stylistic influence of popular Mississippi bluesmen Tommy Johnson and Ishmon Bracey. In Indianapolis he played locally with guitarists FRANCIS "SCRAPPER" BLACKWELL, John Tyler Adams, Edward Lamonte "Pete" Franklin, and mandolinist Yank Rachell, while maintaining steady employment as an automotive plant worker. During the 1960s and 1970s Griffith toured the blues festival circuit and recorded albums for Bluesville, Blue Goose, and Flyright labels. His best known compositions include "King of Spades," "Shaggy Hound Blues," and, with Adams, "Bright Street Jump" and "Indiana Avenue Blues."

LAWRENCE E. MCCULLOUGH
Indiana University–Purdue University, Indianapolis

Sheldon Harris, *Blues Who's Who* (New Rochelle, N.Y., 1979).

Grubbs, Daniel Webster (May 19, 1835–Feb. 5, 1917). Mayor of Indianapolis, May 12, 1881–January 1, 1884, Republican. Born in Henry County, Indiana, Grubbs learned the printing business at the *New Castle Courier*. He came to Indianapolis in 1857, studied law, and was admitted to the bar. Briefly a private in the Civil War, he

later helped organize and served as secretary of two insurance companies in the city. Elected alderman in 1878, he resigned that position in the spring of 1881 during his campaign for mayor. Regarding the condition of the CITY MARKET as discreditable to the city, in a November, 1881, message to the Common Council Grubbs proposed to use a bequest by Stephen D. Tomlinson to build a new market that became known as TOMLINSON HALL. In his role as police court judge, Grubbs supported enforcement of the Sunday closing law, but criticized police raids of houses of ill-fame; such raids, he argued, simply displaced prostitution from the better-run houses to rooms throughout the city and increased the evil. Grubbs preferred that the police go after those landlords, many reputed to be "upstanding citizens," who profited from the high rents paid by such houses.

Rather than stand for reelection, Grubbs moved to Parral, Mexico, immediately following his term to manage the mining and banking interests of his wife's family, retiring from active business in 1903. He died at Harrodsburg, Kentucky, his residence for a number of years.

WILLIAM DOHERTY
Marian College

Indianapolis News, Feb. 5, 1917; Daniel W. Grubbs, "Scrapbook," Indiana Division, Indiana State Library.

Gruelle, John Barton "Johnny" (Dec. 24, 1880–Jan. 9, 1938). Illustrator and author; creator of Raggedy Ann and Andy dolls and stories. Born in Arcola, Illinois, the son of Alice and RICHARD GRUELLE, Johnny moved to Indianapolis in 1882, where the family resided first in the Lockerbie Street area and later settled on the city's east side. Johnny grew up surrounded by music, literature, and the arts. His artist father eventually became known as a member of the HOOSIER GROUP of Impressionists, and writers such as JAMES WHITCOMB RILEY were regular visitors to the Gruelle home.

Rather than follow his father's fine-art career, Johnny Gruelle honed his skills as a cartoonist. Around 1900, he took his first regular newspaper job with the *Indianapolis People*. In 1903, Gruelle joined the staff of the newly founded INDIANAPOLIS STAR, where he provided scores of political, sports, stock-market, and headline cartoons. During those years Gruelle also worked briefly for the IN-DIANAPOLIS SENTINEL and INDIANAPOLIS SUN.

Johnny Gruelle already was an established newspaper cartoonist when he and his young family finally left the Hoosier capital in 1907 to move east—first to Cleveland, Ohio; several years later to Norwalk, Connecticut. It was in the East that Johnny became well known for his "Mr. Twee Deedle" comic in the *New York Herald*. He also illustrated children's stories that appeared in women's magazines, and his satirical "bird's-eye-view" cartoons ran regularly in national humor magazines such as *Judge*. In 1915, Johnny Gruelle created and patented his Raggedy Ann doll. In 1918, he published *Raggedy Ann Stories*, followed two years later by a Raggedy Andy volume. Until his death in 1938, Johnny Gruelle wrote and illustrated, on average, one Raggedy Ann and Andy book per year.

Although Gruelle's creation of his famous rag dolls occurred nearly a decade after he had left Indiana, legend has it that it was his mother's Indianapolis attic that yielded the family-made rag doll that later served as the inspiration for Raggedy Ann. Throughout his life, Gruelle continued to think of himself as a native Hoosier, incorporating into his many books, magazine illustrations, and cartoons the friendly characters, idyllic scenery, and down-to-earth values and humor he so associated with growing up in Indiana.

PATRICIA HALL
Nashville, Tennessee

———

Martin Williams, "Some Remarks About Raggedy Ann and Johnny Gruelle" (transcript of talk presented at the University of Connecticut, Oct. 25, 1973), in *Children's Literature: Vol. 3* (Philadelphia: Temple University Press); Jack Zipes, "Johnny Gruelle," in *American Writers for Children, 1900–1960*, ed. John Cech, Vol. 22 of *Dictionary of Literary Biography* (Detroit, Mich.: Gale Research Co., 1983); R. E. Banta, *Indiana Authors and Their Books, 1816–1916* (Crawfordsville, Ind., 1949).

Gruelle, Richard Buckner (Feb. 22, 1851–Nov. 8, 1914). Artist and author; one of the HOOSIER GROUP of Indiana painters. Born in Cynthiana, Kentucky, Gruelle spent his boyhood years in Arcola, Illinois, where an apprenticeship with the village painter took the place of formal art training. He lived in Illinois, Ohio, and Florida before settling in Indianapolis in 1882. The largely self-taught painter supported his family with the sale of landscape paintings and commission work, most notably illustrations for "When The Frost Is On The Punkin" and "The Old Swimmin'-Hole" by Hoosier poet JAMES WHITCOMB RILEY. In 1892, Gruelle undertook the writing of a book based on the nationally recognized art collection of Baltimore industrialist William T. Walters. The resulting 217–page *Notes: Critical & Biographical* was published in 1895.

In Gruelle's later years, his artistic life was split between family in Indianapolis and annual painting trips to the East Coast shoreline. There he would fill sketchbooks and canvases with marine landscapes that would share the spotlight with scenes from around the Hoosier capital in his annual winter shows. In 1910, Gruelle moved to Connecticut, setting up a family home with his children and their spouses near the historic town of New Canaan. His eldest son, illustrator JOHNNY GRUELLE, subsequently became the creator of Raggedy Ann. Even though he had located on the East Coast, Gruelle still maintained ties with Indianapolis. He continued to write occasional articles about art for the INDIANAPOLIS NEWS as well as holding yearly exhibits of his New England work, usually in the galleries of H. LIEBER COMPANY.

A member of the Society of Western Artists, the Art Association of Indianapolis, and the New Canaan Society of Artists, Gruelle was known primarily for his pastoral landscapes. With the exception of the 1894 Hoosier Group show in Chicago, the 1904 Louisiana Purchase Exposition at St. Louis, and Society of Western Artists annuals, he rarely displayed his work in national shows. Instead, he focused on one-man exhibitions in Indianapolis and New Canaan. Gruelle died in Indianapolis while visiting his wife's family.

JUDITH VALE NEWTON

———

Judith Vale Newton, *The Hoosier Group: Five American Painters* (Indianapolis, 1985).

Guaranty Building (20 North Meridian Street). The local architectural firm of RUBUSH AND HUNTER designed the Guaranty Building in 1922, with construction completed in 1923. The building's design was born out of the height restriction controversy of 1921–1922. The 1920s was a decade of new commercial construction that transformed the downtown, particularly MONUMENT CIRCLE. A local ordinance of 1905 limited the height of buildings fronting the Circle to 86 feet or approximately seven stories in an attempt to protect the prominence of the SOLDIERS AND SAILORS MONUMENT. After much debate, an ordinance passed in 1922 permitting Circle-fronting buildings to rise to 108 feet and allowing for an additional 42 feet through a series of facade setbacks. Rubush and Hunter's final design conforms to the 1922 ordinance; however, two earlier design proposals for the Guaranty in 1921 called for building twelve-story and seven-story heights. The Guaranty set the standards that decade for other near-identical Circle buildings constructed with Renaissance Revival styling, limestone facades, and nine-story height.

The Guaranty Building was built by WILLIAM P. JUNGCLAUS COMPANY as an office building with retail use on the first two floors. Early tenants included Western Union Telegraph Company, numerous law offices, and insurance companies. Over the years the Guaranty has retained most of its original design and fabric. The sculpted bas-reliefs on the facade are the work of local Estonian-born sculptor ALEXANDER SANGERNEBO. The curved limestone facade continues to underscore the importance of its location on Monument Circle.

WILLIAM L. SELM

Mary Ellen Gadski, James A. Glass, and William L. Selm, "Guaranty Building, Indianapolis–Marion County Register of Historic Properties Nomination Form," July, 1983, copy in the files of the Indianapolis Historic Preservation Commission.

Gustafson, Nellie Margaret Gilroy (Jan. 1, 1916–Nov. 6, 1987). Social worker. As a college student Nellie M. Gilroy aimed toward a career in social service. The Atlanta, Georgia, native graduated cum laude from Agnes Scott College, Decatur, Georgia, and earned her master's degree in social work from Western Reserve University, Cleveland, Ohio. She pursued her career in Cleveland, Chicago, Houston, and the Virgin Islands before coming to Indianapolis in 1952 with her husband, Howard F. Gustafson, who served as executive director of the COMMUNITY SERVICE COUNCIL of Metropolitan Indianapolis, and their three children.

Gustafson served as associate director of the INDIANAPOLIS URBAN LEAGUE from 1966 to 1975 when she became executive director of the YOUNG WOMEN'S CHRISTIAN ASSOCIATION OF INDIANAPOLIS (YWCA). She came at a time of change; the organization was in temporary quarters on Fort Wayne Avenue, having closed the deteriorating headquarters at 329 Pennsylvania Street that it had occupied since 1909. Gustafson oversaw the move to the former Dolphin Club at 4460 Guion Road and the modification of the facilities there for the YWCA's use. She initiated many other changes, adding new programs and spurring successful drives for increased membership and activities. She retired for health reasons in 1982.

Gustafson was active in many other civic endeavors, receiving a number of honors for her work. She was named Woman of the Year by B'nai B'rith in 1969 and by the YWCA in 1975. The CHRISTIAN THEOLOGICAL SEMINARY honored her with its Outstanding Civic Achievement Award in 1975. She was a recipient of the Indiana Jefferson Award in 1977 and was named Indiana Social Worker of the Year in 1981.

MARTHA WRIGHT
Indiana State Library

Guthrie, Richard Wayne (Mar. 19, 1926–Apr. 14, 1993). Attorney, speaker of the Indiana House of Representatives, and Indianapolis Public Schools board member. Born in Indianapolis, Guthrie graduated from Thomas Carr Howe High School. He received a bachelor of science degree from the Indiana University School of Business in 1949 and graduated from the IU School of Law four years later. He served in the U.S. Army Air Corps during World War II.

Long active in Republican party politics, Guthrie was a precinct committeeman, ward chairman, and a delegate to the GOP state convention in 1950 and 1952. He served as Marion County Probate Court clerk from 1950 to 1952, becoming assistant commissioner in 1953.

Elected to the Indiana House of Representatives in 1955 and 1957, Guthrie lost his seat in the 1958 election. He won his seat back in 1960 and, with the Republicans controlling the chamber, announced his candidacy for the speaker's post. Guthrie ran against James D. Allen, a former House speaker, and Ralph W. Waltz. With Allen dropping from the race after the fourth ballot, Guthrie defeated Waltz by a 33 to 29 count on the subsequent ballot. With his election, the 35–year-old Guthrie became the second youngest person to hold the speaker's post in Indiana General Assembly history. He ran unopposed for the same position in 1963, his last term in the legislature.

Following his legislative career, Guthrie became a partner in the Indianapolis law firm of Stewart, Irwin, Gilliom, Fuller & Meyer. He also lobbied the General Assembly on behalf of the Indiana Association of Certified Public Accountants, the American Mutual Insurance Alliance, and the Indiana State Medical Association.

Elected to the INDIANAPOLIS PUBLIC SCHOOLS Board of Commissioners in 1980, Guthrie served as its president, 1982–1983, 1992–February, 1993, and presided over the debates about the SELECT SCHOOLS initiative.

RAY BOOMHOWER
Indiana Historical Society

Indianapolis Star, Apr. 15, 1993; *Biographical Directory of the Indiana General Assembly*, Vol. 2 (Indianapolis, 1984).

H. Lieber Company (1854–1979). Retailer of art works and art and photo supplies. Herman Lieber immigrated to Cincinnati, Ohio, from Dusseldorf, Germany, in 1853. He moved to Indianapolis in 1854 and opened a stationery and bookbinding establishment. As his business increased Lieber expanded with a stock of pictures. Eventually, in addition to selling paintings, he established a factory that manufactured picture frames and decorative moldings. In 1900 Lieber became one of the first local exhibitors of the paintings by the Indiana artists known as the HOOSIER GROUP. By this time the bookbinding portion of the business no longer existed. In 1902 the enterprise incorporated under the name H. Lieber Company as a wholesaler in frames and retailer in paintings. After Herman Lieber's death in 1908 his sons retained control of the company, located downtown on East Washington Street. In the ensuing years H. Lieber Company gained a national and international reputation for its moldings and frames, while maintaining the art gallery.

As photography gained popularity in the early 20th century the Liebers moved away from manufacturing frames to sales of photographic equipment and supplies and photofinishing. By 1954, in addition to the art gallery, the firm had four retail stores in Indianapolis that sold camera and artists' equipment. Within the decade the company officers closed the art gallery and focused on their professional photo supply and photofinishing departments, adding a fifth location for these services. In 1979 HOOK'S DRUG STORES bought the assets of the 125–year-old company. Only the 440 North Capitol location remained a Lieber store. In 1984 Hook's sold the photographic supply division of H. Lieber Company to Hoosier Photo Supplies, Inc., for an undisclosed price, retaining the photofinishing division.

CONNIE J. ZEIGLER

H. P. Wasson and Company. Department store. In 1870 the Bee Hive Dry Goods Company opened at 2 West Washington Street. The store underwent several changes in ownership before Hiram P. Wasson bought into the business in 1874. Nine years later Wasson be-

came sole owner, moved the store to 12–14 West Washington Street, and changed the name to H. P. Wasson and Company

With the death of the founder in 1910 and his son, H. Kennard Wasson, two years later, the family sold the company to G. A. Efroymson and Louis Wolf in 1912. Wasson's opened a new downtown store at the corner of Washington and Meridian streets in 1937 and suburban stores in the Eastgate (1957) and Eagledale (1961) shopping centers before changing hands again in 1967. In December, 1979, Goldblatt Brothers, Inc., closed the downtown Wasson's store. Four months later Wasson's suburban stores closed, citing annual losses of $400,000.

DEBORAH B. MARKISOHN

Haag Drug Company. Retail drugstore chain. In 1876 German-born brothers Louis and Julius Haag opened a moderately successful drugstore at 802 Massachusetts Avenue. To increase sales they turned to high volume business, cutting prices on popular items by 10 to 20 percent. The formula worked and their strategy of "cut-price drugs" was soon copied nationwide. By the early 1900s the firm had four stores in the downtown area, open from 7 A.M. to 11 P.M. seven days a week. After the founders died, nephew Herbert Haag took over the business before selling it in 1929. During the next two decades additional stores opened in the city, particularly in residential neighborhoods.

Haag drugstores, this one at the corner of Alabama Street and Massachusetts Avenue, originated the phrase "cut-price drugs." [Indiana Historical Society, Bass Collection, #93956]

In 1950 Sam B. Moxley purchased the chain and began a policy of modernization and expansion that resulted in the closing and sale of many older stores. Haag opened new larger suburban stores with increased variety of merchandise and ample off-street parking, a move fueled by high downtown rents and consumer demands for more product diversity. By 1959 Moxley's program of modernization had resulted in a 250–percent increase in business. Haag changed hands again in 1970 and the new owners doubled the chain's size from 40 to 80 stores by purchasing additional drug store chains. Since 1980 Haag's Indianapolis-area drugstores have changed ownership three times, becoming Peoples (1980), Reliable (1989), and most recently, Osco (1993).

DEBORAH B. MARKISOHN

Haas, Thomas (Dec. 7, 1937–Feb. 21, 1991).

Artistic director of the INDIANA REPERTORY THEATRE (IRT). Haas graduated from Montclair State College and subsequently received a master's degree from Cornell University and a doctorate from the University of Wisconsin. He taught drama at Emerson College in Boston and headed the drama and acting programs at Yale School of Drama, where his students included Meryl Streep, Sigourney Weaver, and Michael Gross. He was also associate director of Yale Repertory Theatre.

Haas joined IRT in 1980, succeeding Ed Stern. He came to Indianapolis from PlayMakers Repertory Theatre in Chapel Hill, North Carolina, which he founded. He also was a cofounder of the Weathervane Theatre in Whitfield, New Hampshire, and served as its artistic director for more than 25 years.

During his tenure at IRT, Haas created the Upperstage for experimental works and the Cabaret Stage for musical revues. He directed numerous productions on the Mainstage, including the self-written *Operetta, My Dear Watson,* a musical thriller in which Sherlock Holmes meets characters out of Gilbert and Sullivan operettas.

Haas died following a jogging accident near his home.

SUSAN GUYETT

Indianapolis Star, Feb. 23, 1991; *Indianapolis Star Magazine,* Feb. 28, 1982.

Hadassah.

Women's Zionist organization of America. The largest women's voluntary organization in the world, Hadassah has 385,000 members. Founded in 1912 by Henrietta Szold, the Jewish organization established and operates two nonsectarian hospitals of healing, research, and teaching in Israel. Other projects include Hadassah-Israel Education Services, Youth Aliyah, Jewish National Fund, and Hadassah's Zionist Youth Movement, Young Judaea.

The Indianapolis chapter, organized in the early 1920s, now has over 1,200 members. As it grew, its composition changed and in 1992 consisted of three groups, each with its own board of directors and coordinated by the chapter board: Henrietta Szold Group, the oldest and largest; Ha'Ima (the Mother), established in 1957; and P'Ninat (the Pearls), originated in 1985. In 1991 the 40–year-old Business and Professional Group was absorbed by the other groups.

Education of members and the community, voluntarism, and fund raising for its national projects are the focus of the chapter's activities. A chapter donor event culminates the annual fundraising campaign. In 1991 the Indianapolis chapter received the 370th "Point of Light" distinction from President George Bush for its ongoing volunteer staffing of the Infant Developmental Play Program at RILEY HOSPITAL FOR CHILDREN. Membership is open; dues are $25 per year or $250 for life membership.

JUDY SCHWARTZ

Hadley, Paul (Aug. 5, 1880–Jan. 31, 1971).

Art designer and watercolorist. Born in Indianapolis, Hadley attended MANUAL HIGH SCHOOL, studying art under OTTO STARK. Upon graduation, he attended the Pennsylvania Museum and School of Industrial Art in Philadelphia.

Hadley designed stained glass windows for churches and did interior decorating before joining the faculty of the HERRON SCHOOL OF ART in 1922. At Herron, he taught classes in watercolor and interior design for ten years and later served as Assistant Curator to the John Herron Art Museum.

Hadley is best known for his creation of Indiana's state flag in 1916. In celebration of the state's centennial, the Indiana Daughters of the American Revolution sponsored a juried flag competition. Hadley's flag won the top prize and was officially accepted by the Indiana General Assembly in 1917.

Hadley's watercolors brought him many awards in the annual HOOSIER SALON, Indiana Artists Club, and INDIANA STATE FAIR art exhibitions. His work is located in the collections of SHORTRIDGE HIGH SCHOOL (now housed at the INDIANA STATE MUSEUM), Manual High School, and the INDIANAPOLIS MUSEUM OF ART. Mooresville, Indiana, named its junior high school after the celebrated artist, who was a long-time resident of the community.

FRANK N. OWINGS, JR.

Flora Lauter, *Indiana Artists Active 1940* (Spencer, Ind., 1941); Henry Wood, "Hoosier Artist—Modest in Success," *Indianapolis Star*, Apr. 29, 1951.

Hahn, E. Vernon (Oct. 23, 1891–Oct. 16, 1959). Neurosurgeon, psychiatrist, and educator. Born in Indianapolis, Hahn attended Public School 32 and SHORTRIDGE HIGH SCHOOL before graduating from Wabash College in 1913. After teaching chemistry at Shortridge High School (1914–1915), Columbia University (1915–1916), and Indiana University (1916–1917), he was awarded the Ravdin medal for scholarship and graduated cum laude from Indiana University Medical School in 1920. Upon graduation Hahn entered private practice in Indianapolis.

From 1920 to 1922 he continued his training at Robert Long Hospital and from 1922 to 1927 he was an instructor in surgery at his alma mater. In 1925 Hahn became professor of surgery at the Indiana University School of Dentistry and following World War II he became clinical professor of psychiatry at the Indiana University Medical School. During his career Hahn also served as neurosurgeon to the Indianapolis City Hospital, consulting surgeon to the Sunnyside Sanatorium, staff member at ST. VINCENT HOSPITAL, and president of the medical staff of METHODIST HOSPITAL.

He was on the boards of examiners of the American Psychiatric Association and American College of Surgeons and served as an officer of the Central Neuropsychiatric Association. From 1953 to 1955 Hahn served on the governor's medical advisory board and took an active role in the administration's program to improve the state's mental hospitals. He was a member and former president (1946–1947) of the INDIANAPOLIS MEDICAL SOCIETY, a fellow of the American Medical Association, a member of both the INDIANA STATE MEDICAL ASSOCIATION and the Indianapolis Medical Association, and a member of the Indianapolis Society of Neurology and Psychiatry. Hahn was awarded the honorary degree of Doctor of Science by Wabash College in 1937.

CHARLES O. HAZELRIGG, D.D.S.

Indiana Biography Series, Indiana State Library; *Indianapolis News*, Oct. 16, 1959.

Hamilton, Francis F. (Feb. 21, 1891–Sept. 3, 1960). Radio pioneer. Hamilton is credited with getting the first Indianapolis radio station on the air on election night in November, 1920. The station signed on as 9ZJ (WLK) from Hamilton's garage at 2011 North Alabama Street. On New Year's eve of 1921 Hamilton invited a few friends, including Mayor LEW SHANK, to join him in greeting the new year with a wireless salute. That same night also produced what was probably the city's first remote broadcast. Hamilton installed an ordinary telephone receiver on the stage of B. F. Keith's theater in downtown Indianapolis. It provided listeners with the sound of vaudeville acts appearing there at the time.

Hamilton was the son of Lucius Hamilton, a founder of the Hamilton-Harris Company of Indianapolis. He learned about radio while earning an electrical engineering degree at Purdue University. Purdue had become a partner with the U.S. Army Signal Corps in the instruction of radio operators during World War I. Hamilton became part of the program and in the process completed what was considered to be an advanced and efficient long range receiver.

In 1922 the INDIANAPOLIS NEWS joined forces with Hamilton in his new broadcast venture, with the latest equipment installed on the tenth floor of the newspaper's office building on West Washington Street. Programming included concerts by the

News' Glee Club and the Newsboys' Band and readings by *News* feature writer William Herschell. A few weeks later, at the insistence of the U.S. Department of Commerce, the station became WLK.

Hamilton expanded his operation when L. S. AYRES AND COMPANY joined him in April, 1922. WLK became the *News*-Ayres-Hamilton station. Ayres opened a radio room that offered the latest radio sets and spare parts and provided records that could be played and promoted.

By 1923 the enthusiasm waned. Expenses exceeded income, which apparently went primarily to Ayres; surprisingly, Hamilton was not charging for air time. In an effort to raise money, he tried to interest 5,000 Hoosiers in subscribing to a proposed magazine for $3 a year but didn't get enough response and WLK folded. The city's first fling with broadcasting was over, as was Hamilton's involvement as a broadcast entrepreneur.

HOWARD CALDWELL
WRTV Channel 6

Hamilton County. County adjacent to Indianapolis–Marion County on the north and part of the Indianapolis Metropolitan Statistical Area. WILLIAM CONNER was one of the first white settlers to arrive in the area now known as Hamilton County. Conner opened a trading post with the Delaware Indians about 1801 near White River, four miles south of present-day Noblesville. More settlers began arriving after the Indians were removed in 1818. Five years later the county was organized and named after the early American statesman Alexander Hamilton.

Transportation routes determined the location of the first settlements. Strawtown, on White River, was once an Indian village, but was laid out by white settlers in 1819 to serve travelers. Westfield was platted by Quakers in 1834 at the intersection of two roads. Farther north the town of Cicero, founded in 1835, developed as a service center for local farmers.

When railroads were constructed in the early 1850s Hamilton County towns prospered. Noblesville was chosen as the county seat in 1823, but it was not until the Peru and Indianapolis

Selected Statistics for Hamilton County, 1990

Population	108,936
Population per Square Mile	274
Percent African-American	0.6
Percent 0 to 17 Years	29.0
Percent 65 Years and Over	8.3
Percent 25 Years and Over with a High School Degree or Equivalency	88.7
Percent 25 Years and Over with a College Degree	36.2
Per Capita Income in 1989	$23,928
Unemployment Rate (%)	2.7
Married-Couple Families as a Percent of Total Households	70.6
Median Home Value	$106,500

Railroad was completed in 1851 that the town attracted a number of warehouses and tradesmen. Arcadia (established 1849) was also on the Peru and Indianapolis line, while Atlanta (founded 1850s) was laid out alongside the Lake Erie and Western Railroad. The Chicago and Indianapolis Airline (Monon), completed in 1882, attracted mills and factories to Sheridan (platted 1860). The interurban arrived just after 1900, when the Union Traction Company constructed a line through Carmel, Noblesville, Cicero, Arcadia, and Atlanta. Also on the line was a new community, HOME PLACE, platted in 1914 near College Avenue and 106th Street.

When natural gas was discovered in the eastern part of the county in the 1880s, industries moved to areas such as Noblesville to take advantage of the cheap fuel. The gas wells gave out after 1900, though some of the industries remained.

Despite moderate growth, Hamilton County was primarily rural until after World War II. In 1950 there were 28,500 residents. Ten years later the population had increased by 41 percent, followed by a 35–percent jump between 1960 and 1970. From 1970 to 1990 the number of residents doubled from 54,000 to nearly 109,000. Officials project 134,000 residents by 2000.

Southern Hamilton County, adjacent to Indianapolis, has experienced the greatest amount of commercial and residential development. As Indianapolis expanded, suburban sprawl spilled over the county line. The improvement and extension of major thoroughfares, such as Meridian Street and Keystone Avenue, and the construction of I–465 in the late 1960s and early 1970s made Hamilton County accessible. More recently, I–69 has spurred extensive commercial growth for

FISHERS, while CARMEL has benefited from intensive development along U.S. 31. Northwest of Noblesville, Morse Reservoir, constructed 1953–1956, attracted its first residential subdivisions in 1971.

Change has come suddenly and dramatically for once tranquil communities such as Carmel (established 1837) and Fishers (platted 1872). In 1960 Carmel counted about 1,400 residents; by 1990 its population was 25,000. Fishers posted a population of about 600 in 1970, 2,000 in 1980, and over 7,500 in 1990. Within the next decade an additional 10,000 new residents are expected to settle in Hamilton Proper, a development on the east side of Fishers. As available land continues to be converted to homes and offices, Noblesville and Westfield are predicted to be the next boom towns, along with areas near the MICHIGAN ROAD (U.S. 421) in the county's southwestern section.

Not only is Hamilton County the fastest growing county in the state, in 1989 it also ranked first in median family income ($51,000) and median price of homes ($106,000). Most residents are employed in service industries, followed by the retail trade, and finance, insurance, and real estate. Over 53 percent commute to jobs outside the county, particularly to Marion County.

In the 1990s explosive development has created problems such as an overloaded infrastructure and crowded schools, yet Hamilton County residents hope future growth can be controlled and managed.

CATHLEEN F. DONNELLY

Historic Landmarks Foundation of Indiana et al., *Indiana Historic Sites & Structures Inventory, Interim Report, Hamilton County* (1978); U.S. Census.

Hampton Family. African-American family of jazz musicians whose individual members and various ensemble configurations have contributed greatly to Indianapolis musical life since the 1930s. Clarke F. "Deacon" Hampton (1877–1951) was born in Batavia, Ohio, and attended a military school in nearby Xenia, where he learned to play the bugle. In 1908 he married Laura Bur-

The Duke Hampton Band appeared in Indianapolis during the 1940s. [Indiana Historical Society, Duncan Schiedt Collection, #C5913]

ford (1891–1967) and by World War I had organized their children into Deacon Hampton's Family Band, a Middletown, Ohio–based ensemble that toured the rural Midwest performing at fairs, tent shows, parties, and clubs with a varied repertoire of square dance tunes, polkas, blues, jazz, minstrel numbers, and pop ballads.

After a successful engagement at Indianapolis' Sunset Ballroom in 1938, the Hamptons settled in Indianapolis, where Marcus, Russell, Maceo, and Slide attended the McArthur School of Music, and changed the Family Band into a swing-style ensemble, the Duke Hampton Band. Members in the mid–1940s included Virtue (double bass), Aletra (harp, piano), Marcus (trumpet), Dawn (alto sax), Russell "Lucky" (baritone-tenor-alto saxes), Carmalita (banjo, guitar, tenor-baritone saxes), Locksley "Slide" (trombone, flugelhorn), Clarke, Jr. "Duke" (saxophones, drums, timpani, vibraharp), and Maceo (trumpet). The group recorded on the King and Aladdin labels, but disbanded after having appeared at Carnegie Hall, the Apollo Theatre, and the Savoy Ballroom in New York City.

In the 1950s Virtue, Aletra, and Carmalita formed the Hampton Sisters Trio after Dawn went to New York and became an established cabaret singer and songwriter. Slide Hampton moved to New York in the mid–1950s and to Europe in the 1960s, where he became a prolific composer, arranger, and performer, appearing with jazz vibraharpist Lionel Hampton (a distant cousin),

Maynard Ferguson, Freddie Hubbard, Lloyd Price, Woody Herman, Ron Carter, Art Blakey, and others. Third-generation Hampton family performers include several of Virtue Whitted's children (Tamar, vocals; Pharez, trumpet, flugelhorn; Thomas, trombone; Henry, saxophone; L'Overture, trumpet) and Aletra's daughter Paula Hampton, a drummer.

LAWRENCE E. MCCULLOUGH
Indiana University–Purdue University,
Indianapolis

Duncan Schiedt, *The Jazz State of Indiana* (Pittsboro, Ind., 1977); *Indianapolis Star*, Feb. 29, 1988.

Hancock County. County adjacent to Indianapolis–Marion County on the east and part of the Indianapolis Metropolitan Statistical Area. The families of Andrew Evans, John Montgomery, and Montgomery Call settled along Blue River in what is now Hancock County around 1818. They had established farmsteads by the time the U.S. government surveyed the area in 1819. However, the county itself was not created until 1828 when it was set off from Madison County and named after John Hancock. There were about 400 people living on scattered farmsteads throughout the county at that time. Most were Methodists, with settlers organizing a class meeting in the area by 1820. Greenfield became the county seat in 1828, and has always been the largest town in Hancock County. The other early towns in the county were Fortville and New Palestine.

Much of the land in the new county was low and swampy. Farmsteads were scattered on the few hills and knolls above Blue River and Sugar Creek. Gradually the county was drained through the use of tiled ditches and made into rich farmland. Residents exported large quantities of wheat, corn, oats, hogs, cattle, and sheep, and many county residents earned extra income by feeding or boarding travelers along the NATIONAL ROAD. Greenfield especially benefited from the Dayton coach, a passenger coach that made weekly trips between Indianapolis and Dayton, Ohio. The construction of railroads through Hancock County in the 1850s and 1860s spurred agricultural production and strengthened the connection between Greenfield and Indianapolis. The Indiana Central Railroad, completed in 1851, provided regular passenger service from Greenfield to the capital. Shortly after its completion Greenfield was incorporated as a town, and, in 1876, it became a city with 2,023 residents. Access to Indianapolis and its stores and markets improved in 1900 with the completion of the interurban line to Greenfield. An interurban line that ran from Indianapolis to Anderson through Fortville was completed in 1901.

The demise of the railroad and interurbans in the first quarter of the 20th century halted the rapid late 19th century growth of Greenfield and Hancock County. The county has remained predominately rural and agricultural. The growth of Indianapolis during and after World War II, however, spurred suburban development in the western part of the county, and its total population nearly tripled between 1940 and 1980. This rate slowed considerably after 1980, and the 1990 figure of 45,527 was an increase of less than 2,000 from ten years earlier. Agriculture is still the county's main economic interest, but farmland has been converted to residential subdivisions in some areas.

The 1990 population of Greenfield was 11,657. The city has maintained a population of around 10,000 for the past 20 years. Both Greenfield and Hancock County are perhaps best known as the birthplace of Indiana poet JAMES WHITCOMB RILEY.

WILLIAM D. DALTON

J. H. Binford, *History of Hancock County, Indiana* (Greenfield, Ind., 1882); U.S. Census.

Selected Statistics for Hancock County, 1990

Population	45,527
Population per Square Mile	149
Percent African-American	0.1
Percent 0 to 17 Years	27.6
Percent 65 Years and Over	10.4
Percent 25 Years and Over with a High School Degree or Equivalency	80.1
Percent 25 Years and Over with a College Degree	14.9
Per Capita Income in 1989	$17,328
Unemployment Rate (%)	3.7
Married-Couple Families as a Percent of Total Households	71.4
Median Home Value	$72,000

Hanly, J. Frank (James Franklin) (Apr. 4, 1863–Aug. 1, 1920). Republican politician, governor (1905–1909), and reformer. Born near St. Joseph, Illinois, Hanly moved to Warren County, Indiana, in 1879. Admitted to the Indiana bar in 1889, he won election the next year to complete the term of George W. Cronk in the Indiana Senate, where he gained a reputation as a vigorous orator and debater.

From 1895 to 1897, Hanly served in the U.S. House of Representatives. Gerrymandered out of his district, he returned to Lafayette, Indiana, to practice law. He was one of five Republican candidates in 1899 for the U.S. Senate, but lost to eventual winner ALBERT J. BEVERIDGE.

Hanly reentered state politics in 1904 by defeating Democrat JOHN W. KERN in the gubernatorial race. A political maverick who often acted independently of his party, Hanly embarked upon a major reform of state government. He secured legislation that halted gambling at State Fair horse races, urged creation of the Indiana Railroad Commission (1905), and reorganized charitable and correctional institutions along nonpartisan lines (1907).

Despite his support for a broad progressive program, Hanly was most concerned with TEMPERANCE. In 1908, he convened a special session of the General Assembly to enact a "county option law," enabling residents to decide through popular referendum whether to permit the sale and distribution of alcoholic beverages.

Hanly remained active in the prohibitionist cause until his death. He founded and edited in Indianapolis the prohibition-oriented NATIONAL ENQUIRER (1915–1920), a weekly organ of the prohibition crusade. Recognizing the fragmentation of the movement, Hanly formed the Flying Squadron of America to promote prohibition nationwide. In 1916, he declined the Progressive party's nomination for governor to accept the National Prohibition party's presidential nomination. After losing the election, Hanly continued to speak on behalf of prohibition. He died in an auto-train accident while on a speaking tour in Ohio.

STACEY NICHOLAS

Jan Shipps, "J. Frank Hanly: Enigmatic Reformer," in *Gentlemen from Indiana: National Party Candidates, 1836–1940*, ed. Ralph Gray (Indianapolis, 1977), 237–268.

Hapgood, Mary Donovan (1886–June 24, 1973). Political activist and labor organizer. Mary Donovan Hapgood was born in North Brookfield, Massachusetts. She graduated from the University of Michigan in 1912, returned to Brookfield where she taught school until 1914, and then became a factory inspector for the Massachusetts Department of Labor.

Hapgood became well known in the 1920s for her involvement in the defense of Sacco and Vanzetti and the unsuccessful campaign for their release. She became their corresponding secretary in 1924, and after their execution in 1927 she delivered their eulogy. In his book, *Boston*, Upton Sinclair referred to her as the "Joan of Arc" of the defense. During her involvement in the case she met her future husband, POWERS HAPGOOD, who had also gone to Boston to campaign for release of the condemned men.

Mary Hapgood became active in the Socialist party and in 1928 she was nominated as its candidate for governor of Massachusetts. In 1940, after settling in Indiana with her husband Powers, she was the party's candidate for governor of Indiana, making her the first woman to be nominated for the Hoosier state's highest office. In 1932 she was proposed for, but did not accept, the party's nomination as its candidate for vice-president of the United States. Instead she campaigned in 1932 for Powers, who ran as the party's candidate for governor of Indiana.

Along with her husband, Mary Hapgood was involved in the founding in 1936 of the Committee of Industrial Organizations, later the Congress of Industrial Organizations (CIO). She was also involved in the American Civil Liberties Union and the labor movement, and helped to found the INDIANA CIVIL LIBERTIES UNION after her husband's death in 1949. She remained politically active, working in the 1960s peace movement, helping to form the Women's International League for Peace and Freedom, and being involved in the presidential campaigns of Eugene McCarthy in 1968 and George McGovern in 1972.

KENNETH COLBURN, JR.
Butler University

Hapgood, Norman (Mar. 28, 1868–Apr. 29, 1937). Writer and editor. Born in Chicago, Norman Hapgood graduated from Harvard College in 1890, where he also received his master's and law degrees in 1893. After a brief stint at a law firm in Chicago, Hapgood worked for the *Chicago Evening Post* in 1894 and, later, the *Milwaukee Sentinel* and the *New York Evening Post*. He became editor of *Collier's National Weekly* magazine in 1903; under his direction until 1912, it assumed a leading role in several reform movements of the time. He edited *Harper's Weekly* magazine from 1913 to 1916. An ardent supporter of Woodrow Wilson's presidency, he served as ambassador to Denmark for one year in 1919. From 1923 to 1925 he was editor of *Hearst's International Magazine*; in 1936 he became editor of the *Christian Register*, a post he held until his death.

Hapgood was the largest outside stockholder in the Indianapolis-based COLUMBIA CONSERVE COMPANY, managed by his brother, WILLIAM POWERS HAPGOOD. He went to work at the concern in 1932 for a year to help in advertising and publicity, and he also served periodically in an advisory capacity. Columbia was widely known and regarded as a leading example of workplace democracy during the 1920s and 1930s. Norman Hapgood discussed the company and its ideals in his autobiography *The Changing Years* (1930). He died in New York.

KENNETH COLBURN, JR.
Butler University

Michael D. Marcaccio, *The Hapgoods: Three Earnest Brothers* (Charlottesville, Va., 1977).

Hapgood, Powers (Dec. 28, 1899–Feb. 4, 1949). Union organizer. Powers Hapgood, son of WILLIAM POWERS HAPGOOD, was born in Chicago and raised in Indianapolis where he attended Shortridge High School. He graduated from Harvard University in 1921 and then lived and worked as a coal miner, first in the United States and thereafter for two years in England, France, Germany, and Siberia.

Hapgood was active as a union organizer and administrator, beginning in the 1920s as a member of the United Mine Workers, and he was often arrested and jailed for his participation in labor strikes and demonstrations. He unsuccessfully opposed John L. Lewis for leadership of the UNITED MINE WORKERS OF AMERICA, and was one of the three founders of the Committee of Industrial Organizations (later the Congress of Industrial Organizations or CIO) in 1935. In 1937 he organized the New England branch of the CIO and was regional director in Indiana from 1941 through 1948, when he became assistant to the national director of the CIO. In between his service for the CIO in New England and Indiana, Hapgood served as president of the United Shoe Workers of America where he helped to organize southern sharecroppers.

Hapgood went to Boston in 1927 to assist in the unsuccessful campaign to save the anarchists Sacco and Vanzetti from prison and execution. He made several speeches on their behalf, for which he was arrested. In Boston he met his future wife, MARY DONOVAN HAPGOOD, who was also working in the defense of Sacco and Vanzetti. Hapgood was the Socialist party's candidate for governor of Indiana in 1932, as was his wife in 1940.

KENNETH COLBURN, JR.
Butler University

Hapgood, William Powers (Feb. 26, 1872–July 30, 1960). Pioneer in workplace democracy. Born in Chicago, Hapgood graduated from Harvard University in 1894 and worked for several years in Chicago with a wholesale grocer. He moved to Indianapolis in 1903 to manage his father's newly acquired COLUMBIA CONSERVE COMPANY, which he served as president from 1903 to 1953.

The first dozen or so years at Columbia were difficult ones, and William's father died in 1916 without ever having seen his canning company make a profit. The year 1917 was a prosperous one for the company, however, and at that time

William, along with his mother and brothers, Hutchins and NORMAN HAPGOOD, initiated an innovative and progressive plan of workplace democracy. It began with two important features: a workers' council and a profit-sharing plan. The council eventually included all workers and made decisions on virtually all operations and policy for the company.

A contract between the Hapgoods and workers in 1925 established a plan whereby most of the company's profit would be used for the purchase of common stock by workers. Workers reached this goal in 1930 when they acquired control of 51 percent of Columbia stock (increased to 63 percent by 1937), making it one of the first producer-cooperatives in the nation. Columbia's workers also enjoyed benefits such as guaranteed employment throughout the year, several weeks of paid vacation, free health care for themselves and their dependents, and pensions.

Workplace democracy at Columbia came to an end in 1943 as a result of an employee suit against the company and a countersuit by the trustees of the workers' commonly held stock. Hapgood continued as president until 1953, when the company was sold to John Sexton and Company of Chicago.

KENNETH COLBURN, JR.
Butler University

Columbia Conserve Company Collection, Lilly Library, Indiana University, Bloomington; Michael D. Marcaccio, *The Hapgoods: Three Earnest Brothers* (Charlottesville, Va., 1977).

Hardrick, John Wesley (1891–Oct. 18, 1968). African-American visual artist. Born in Indianapolis, Hardrick attended Harriet Beecher Stowe Public School 5, MANUAL HIGH SCHOOL, and HERRON SCHOOL OF ART. His artistic ability became evident in elementary school and was developed under the tutelage of OTTO STARK at Manual. Through encouragement from Herman Lieber, owner of H. LIEBER COMPANY art supply store, Hardrick enrolled in the Herron children's classes while in elementary school. The public became aware of his talent early as 1904 when he won awards for his works exhibited at the INDI-

ANA STATE FAIR. He entered Herron Institute in 1910, taking day drawing and painting classes, and in September entered 53 works at the Indiana State Fair and won eight awards. While he received a scholarship for one term at Herron, he worked at a foundry to earn additional money for his schooling. He graduated from Herron in 1918.

Hardrick's first major exhibit was in January, 1914, at Allen Chapel, A.M.E. Church, consisting of 56 paintings and drawings. After establishing himself in the community as a capable artist, he did not paint for two years but worked as a laborer to support his family. In 1927 he shared a studio at 541 INDIANA AVENUE with fellow Herron alumnus HALE WOODRUFF. In 1927 his painting *The Little Brown Girl* was one of five paintings that won second place in the Harmon Foundation awards for black artists. The same painting was purchased by a group of black citizens in 1929 and donated to the John Herron Art Institute; after a decades-long disappearance, the painting was rediscovered and returned to the Indianapolis Museum of Art in 1994. Hardrick's work is represented by landscape paintings in the collections of both the INDIANA STATE MUSEUM and the INDIANAPOLIS MUSEUM OF ART.

WILLIAM E. TAYLOR
Indiana University–Purdue University,
Indianapolis

Charles J. Ferruzza, "Two Indiana Black Artists Remembered," *Arts Insight* (Dec., 1980); taped interview with Rowena Tucker (Hardrick's daughter), Aug., 1988, in author's possession.

Harrison, Benjamin (Aug. 20, 1833–Mar. 13, 1901). United States senator and president. Born at North Bend, Ohio, Harrison was the grandson of President William Henry Harrison. He attended Farmers' College in Cincinnati and graduated from Miami University (Ohio). After reading law Harrison was admitted to the bar in 1854 and moved to Indianapolis where he steadily advanced in the legal profession. A committed Christian, he became an elder in the First Presbyterian Church at age 28.

With the Whig party's demise, Harrison took an active part in Indiana Republican politics. He served as city attorney in 1857 and three years later was elected reporter of the state Supreme Court. He lost the post when he left to fight in the Civil War as colonel of the 70th Indiana Infantry. Serving in the Army of the Cumberland, Harrison emerged with the rank of brevet brigadier general.

In 1865 Harrison returned to Indianapolis and the job of Supreme Court reporter, which he had regained in the previous year's election. Upon completing his term, he turned to full-time private practice. By 1875 his great success allowed him to build a large new residence on North Delaware Street. Courtroom triumphs, addresses before veterans' groups, and effective stump-speaking brought him increased political prominence, and he moved steadily up through the ranks in the Republican party. In 1876, when the party's gubernatorial nominee retired from the race amid allegations of financial misdealings, Harrison stepped into the breach and waged a gallant, though losing, campaign.

When the great RAILROAD STRIKE OF 1877 reached Indianapolis in late July, Harrison took command of a citizens militia company to maintain order, but he also argued that the workers had legitimate grievances that ought to be addressed once they returned to work. The incident underscored his reputation as a defender of law and order, but many labor organizations subsequently saw him as an enemy. Even so, his political career flourished. When OLIVER P. MORTON died in late 1877, Harrison succeeded him as leader of the state's Republicans. In 1881 he easily won election to the U.S. Senate.

Harrison's single term in the Senate enhanced his national prominence. In 1888 the Republican party nominated him for president, and Indianapolis became the focus of the campaign. First at his Delaware Street house and later at UNIVERSITY PARK, Harrison daily addressed visiting delegations. Reporters recorded his remarks, which appeared in newspapers across the country. Harrison defeated Grover Cleveland and served as president from 1889 to 1893. Working with a Republican Congress his first two years, he presided over one of the 19th century's most activist administrations. Its accomplishments included the

Former President Benjamin Harrison posing after a duck hunting trip in the early 1890s.
[Benjamin Harrison Home]

McKinley Tariff Act, the Sherman Anti-Trust Act, the Meat Inspection Act, federal aid to veterans, and increased naval expenditures.

Harrison lost an electoral rematch with Cleveland in 1892 and lived his last years in Indianapolis, working at the law, engaging in church work, and making occasional political speeches. At the end of the century he spoke out against American overseas expansionism. Harrison is buried in CROWN HILL CEMETERY.

CHARLES W. CALHOUN
East Carolina University

Charles W. Calhoun, "Benjamin Harrison, Centennial President: A Review Essay," *Indiana Magazine of History*, 84 (June, 1988), 135-160; Harry J. Sievers, *Benjamin Harrison* (3 vols., New York and Indianapolis, 1952–1968); Homer E. Socolofsky and Allan B. Spetter, *The Presidency of Benjamin Harrison* (Lawrence, Kan., 1987).'

Harrison, Caroline Lavinia Scott (Oct. 1, 1832–Oct. 25, 1892). Wife of President Ben-

Caroline Scott Harrison in an 1889 photograph by a Washington, D.C. photographer.
[Benjamin Harrison Home]

jamin Harrison (1889–1893), and first president-general of the National Society of the Daughters of the American Revolution. Caroline Scott was born in Oxford, Ohio, and educated at Oxford Female Institute. In 1853 she married BENJAMIN HARRISON and the next year moved with him to Indianapolis, where he established a law practice and later entered politics. Mrs. Harrison busied herself as a homemaker and mother to the couple's two children. She was an active member of the First Presbyterian Church, teaching the infant class, playing the organ, and teaching the children to sing. For many years she was a member of the board of managers of the Indianapolis Orphans' Asylum. While her husband served in the Civil War, Mrs. Harrison was a leader in the Ladies' Patriotic Association, the Ladies' Sanitary Committee, and other local groups concerned with the welfare of wounded soldiers.

During her residence in Washington, D.C., as wife of the nation's 23rd president, Mrs. Harrison was chosen the first president-general of the Daughters of the American Revolution. She and President Harrison brought prestige to the organization in its early years, at a time when many hereditary patriotic societies were being founded. When the DAR's first Indiana chapter formed in Indianapolis in 1894, it was named in her honor.

Mrs. Harrison died in the White House during her husband's administration, the second First Lady to do so (Mrs. John Tyler was the first). She was buried in CROWN HILL CEMETERY following a funeral procession during which thousands of Indianapolis residents lined the streets to pay their respects.

MARTHA WRIGHT
Indiana State Library

Harriet McIntire Foster, *Mrs. Benjamin Harrison* (n.p., 1908); *Notable American Women, 1607–1950* (Cambridge, Mass., 1971), II, 145.

Harrison and Turnock (Russ and Harrison). Architects. Merritt Harrison, a graduate of Indianapolis Manual High School (1906) and Cornell University School of Architecture (1911), worked for architect HERBERT L. BASS before opening his own office in the Board of Trade Building in 1916. Within a few years he was designing residences on the city's north side. Between 1919 and early 1923 his designs included the homes at 4611, 4605, and 4025 North Meridian Street.

By 1923 Harrison had formed Harrison and Turnock, a brief but important partnership, with Llewellyn Turnock. During their association they were architects, as a team or separately, for the Tudor Revival home at 4041 North Meridian Street (1924–1925), the Colonial Revival Brookside Park Community Building (1927), CRISPUS ATTUCKS HIGH SCHOOL (1927), the Gothic Revival Irvington Presbyterian Church (1929), and the INDIANA SCHOOL FOR THE BLIND (1930).

In 1934 Harrison, who had dissolved his partnership with Turnock, formed a new architecture firm with William Earl Russ, a graduate of Columbia University. Russ had been a partner in an Ohio architecture firm before moving to Indianapolis in 1913. Some of his early work included schools and industrial buildings in Ohio and Indiana and the Sunnyside Tuberculosis Sanitarium in eastern Marion County (1917). In 1923 Russ won 3rd prize ($10,000) in the international competition to design the World War Memorial in Indianapolis. In 1926 he was architect for the Piccadilly Apartments at 28 East 16th Street.

Russ and Harrison designed many important buildings in Indianapolis and elsewhere in the state. In the 1930s their work encompassed both private and public buildings including clubhouses for Hillcrest and Broadmoor country clubs, LOCKEFIELD GARDENS housing complex, and the $1 million State Fair Coliseum (1939), voted the most "outstanding recent building in Indianapolis" in a 1940 survey conducted by the *Architectural Record*. During the 1940s the firm designed many industrial buildings in the city and elsewhere, and in 1950 it designed the Meridian Street Methodist Church, a Colonial Revival structure.

By 1959 other Indiana architects had dubbed Harrison the "Dean of Indiana Architects" in recognition of his contributions to their field. Although less active in his later years, Harrison maintained an office in the Architects and Builders Building in downtown Indianapolis until he retired in 1971.

CONNIE J. ZEIGLER

Indiana Biography Series, Indiana State Library; *Indianapolis Star Magazine*, June 28, 1959.

Hartman, Grover L. (Aug. 3, 1914–Nov. 13, 1988). State and national ecumenical leader. Hartman was born on a farm near Brookston, Indiana, and reared in a United Brethren family. He graduated from DePauw University with honors in history, earned the Ph.D. from American University, and spent his career working in ecumenical church bodies. He was director of the Wartime Services Committee of the Washington, D.C., Council of Churches and from 1944 to 1946 was assistant to the secretary of the Department of International Justice and Goodwill of the Federal Council of Churches.

Hartman returned to Indiana in 1946 to head the Social Service Department of the Indianapolis CHURCH FEDERATION. He developed a network among social service agencies and per-

sonnel and organized a Fellowship of Church Social Workers. He later was elected president of the National Conference of Church Social Workers and participated in the Mid-Century White House Conference on Children and Youth. While with the federation he completed a master's degree in social work.

In 1954 Hartman became executive secretary of the St. Joseph County Council of Churches in South Bend. Six years later, he headed the Indiana Council of Churches. For 20 years he represented the Protestant community throughout the state, was active in legislative affairs, and developed relations with Catholics, members of EASTERN ORTHODOX CHURCHES, and JEWS. For 22 years he was a member of the governing board of the National Council of Churches. Following retirement in 1979, he was made director of the Ecumenical Institute at CHRISTIAN THEOLOGICAL SEMINARY and consultant to the National Council of Churches Commission on Regional and Local Ecumenism. He planned and led ecumenical leadership seminars at the seminary and at other centers in the nation. He was active in this work at the time of his death.

EDWIN L. BECKER
Christian Theological Seminary

Haughville. Westside neighborhood roughly bounded by 10th Street, Belmont Avenue, Michigan and Vermont streets, and Tibbs Avenue. In 1880 Benjamin Haugh moved his iron foundry from downtown Indianapolis to farmland west of White River. A village grew up around the foundry and was incorporated in 1883 as Haughville. By 1890 Haughville was home to 2,100 residents, and Indianapolis annexed the growing community in 1897.

Many Haughville residents were European immigrants. The IRISH settled in the southern part of the area and worked at KINGAN AND COMPANY or the local railyards. Eastern European immigrants, particularly SLOVENES, began to arrive in the 1890s, recruited by George Lambert, a Slovenian-born agent for National Malleable Castings Company. The Malleable foundry paid the immigrants' passage in return for a set period of employment. A third foundry, which in 1906 be-

A double funeral at Haughville's Holy Trinity church during the Spanish flu epidemic that claimed almost 1,000 lives in the city. The funeral was well attended by Slovenian members of St. Joseph Lodge No. 45; absentees would have been fined.
[Indiana Historical Society, #C2204]

came known as the LINK BELT COMPANY, also employed local workers.

Slovene religious and social organizations became an integral part of the Haughville community. Holy Trinity Roman Catholic Church, built in 1906–1907 at the corner of Holmes and St. Clair streets, served the spiritual needs of residents. The SLOVENIAN NATIONAL HOME on West 10th Street was organized in 1918 as a social club and offered choir concerts, plays, and recreational sports. Three Slovenian societies, St. Aloysius, St. Joseph, and Preseren lodges, provided insurance coverage and social and athletic activities for members.

Although Slovenes were the most numerous of the eastern European immigrants, Haughville residents also came from Poland, Romania, Macedonia, and Hungary, among other countries. They built small, usually $1\frac{1}{2}$-story frame cottages on narrow lots. Single men often boarded with relatives or found cramped accommodations in Haughville apartments. Iron workers put in long hours at the foundries under harsh conditions, but enjoyed time off drinking beer at the neighborhood's numerous saloons. They also took part in athletic contests and impromptu accordion concerts.

Following World War II the close-knit Haughville community began to change. Chil-

dren of immigrants were moving out for better-paying jobs and larger homes, industries such as Malleable closed down, and new residents, including whites from Appalachia and blacks, moved in. By 1992 an estimated 60 percent of the residents were African-Americans.

The City of Indianapolis, social service agencies, and Neighbors for Historic Haughville worked together to solve community problems in the 1990s. Government programs combat drugs and crime, recruit and train new community leaders, and stimulate economic revitalization. The city also planned to rehabilitate Concord Place, a housing project built in Haughville in 1967. CHRISTAMORE HOUSE, relocated to Haughville in 1925, continues to offer a wide range of programs for residents, while Holy Trinity provides day care for neighborhood children and the elderly. A section of Haughville was designated a historic district and placed on the National Register of Historic Places in 1992.

CATHLEEN F. DONNELLY

James J. Divita, *Slaves to No One* (Indianapolis, 1981); *Indianapolis Star*, July 16, 1992; National Register of Historic Places nomination form (copy on file at Division of Historic Preservation and Archaeology, Indiana Department of Natural Resources).

Hays, Barton Stone (Apr. 5, 1826–Mar. 14, 1914). Portrait, landscape, and still-life artist. Hays was born in Greenville, Ohio, but settled in Montgomery County, Indiana. He traveled in the vicinity of Wingate, Covington, and Attica, making likenesses of relatives and friends. He arrived in Indianapolis in 1858 and with William Runnion established the firm Hays & Runnion, soon the principal daguerreotype establishment of the city. During his years in Indianapolis he would leave the city for months at a time, returning with landscapes and other pieces. These he would exhibit for a while, and afterwards sell at auction. He worked in Cincinnati from 1871 to 1873, returned to Indianapolis until 1883, then moved to Minneapolis, where he lived until his death.

Hays was especially kind to young artists and taught groups of aspiring students, including WILLIAM MERRITT CHASE, who became nationally known, and John Love, who played an important part in starting the first art school in Indianapolis.

As one of the leading painters in Indianapolis in 1869, Hays received a commission to paint the portrait of William Henry Harrison for the newly begun Governors Portraits Collection. He apparently copied a portrait by an unknown artist that is now in the collection of the Bowdoin College Museum of Art. In addition to his portrait of Harrison, which can be seen in the Indiana State House, the INDIANAPOLIS MUSEUM OF ART owns two portraits and a still life by him.

MARY JANE MEEKER

Haywood, Garfield Thomas (July 15, 1880–Apr. 12, 1931). African-American minister and major leader in the Pentecostal Assemblies of the World. Born in Greencastle, Indiana, Haywood moved with his family to Indianapolis as a child, locating in the HAUGHVILLE neighborhood. He was educated at School 52, attended SHORTRIDGE HIGH SCHOOL, and worked as a cartoonist for both the INDIANAPOLIS FREEMAN and INDIANAPOLIS RECORDER.

As a young man Haywood was very active in religion, serving as Sunday school superintendent for the Methodist and Baptist churches. In 1907, Haywood attended a gathering of PENTECOSTALS in Indianapolis and became part of that movement. Two years later, he founded the Christ Temple Apostolic Faith Assembly. Haywood, who published numerous articles and tracts on behalf of his faith, rose to become Presiding Bishop of the Pentecostal Assemblies of the World. On July 22, 1980, the City of Indianapolis named a stretch of Fall Creek Parkway, from Riverside Drive to Keystone Avenue, Bishop Garfield Haywood Memorial Way.

RAY BOOMHOWER
Indiana Historical Society

Bishop Morris E. Golder, *The Life and Works of Bishop Garfield Thomas Haywood* (Indianapolis, 1977).

Head Start. Early childhood education program. The Head Start project was created by the federal Economic Opportunity Act of 1964 to provide early childhood education and other services to children of low-income families, including children with special needs or handicapping conditions. In Indianapolis, Head Start officially began in 1965 as a summer program staffed mainly by volunteers. Soon after, the Indianapolis Pre-School Center, already operating under the aegis of Community Action Against Poverty of Greater Indianapolis, complied with federal guidelines and became a Head Start program. It enrolled 1,350 children at 23 centers throughout the city.

Head Start of Indianapolis was developed to meet specific needs within the community. Accordingly, the local program provides free of charge: a daily, half-day education program for three-, four-, and five-year-olds; health services, including speech, hearing and vision screenings, dental exams, and immunizations; services to children with handicapping conditions; opportunity for parent involvement at all levels; social services to Head Start families; bus transportation to and from assigned classrooms; and daily hot lunch and snack.

The Head Start educational program focuses on developing motor, cognitive, language, and social/emotional skills. The curriculum includes health, safety, and nutrition education. Language development is evaluated twice yearly and parents receive progress reports at mid-year and at the end of the term, which runs from September to June. Each class is conducted by a teacher, a teaching assistant, and a classroom aide. Parents and community volunteers also serve in the classroom. After children have completed a one- or two-year program, Head Start personnel assist families who wish to enroll their children in kindergarten.

In the early 1990s Head Start served approximately 1,500 children and employed a staff of 190. Headquartered in School 36 at 2801 Capitol Avenue, the program operated at five locations on a $3.8 million budget (1991) granted to COMMUNITY ACTION OF GREATER INDIANAPOLIS by the U.S. Department of Health and Human Services. All centers are licensed by the State of Indiana and all teachers must possess a Child Development Associate credential.

ELIZABETH SPALDING

Community Action Against Poverty of Greater Indianapolis, *Head Start Parent Handbook* (Indianapolis, 1990); Leland D. Melvin, "A Study of Head Start Programs in Indiana" (Ed.D. dissertation, Indiana University, 1966).

Health and Hospital Corporation of Marion County (HHC).

Independent municipal corporation. The growth and diffusion of population in Marion County after World War II created demands that went unmet by existing public health bodies. In 1948 the Health and Welfare Council, a consortium of public and private health agencies, began to investigate Marion County's health needs. Its recommendations resulted in the creation of the HHC by the Indiana General Assembly in 1951, a consolidation of the Indianapolis Health and Hospital Board, the Marion County Health Board, and the board of managers of Sunnyside, the county poorhouse. The HHC was given jurisdiction to provide public health protection and services throughout Marion County as well as the power to raise bonds and levy property taxes.

Due to a suit challenging the HHC's constitutionality, it did not exist legally until 1954. At that time, the Indiana Supreme Court declared HHC a constitutional body by removing Sunnyside from its control. The status of the corporation was again threatened with the implementation of UNIGOV in the early 1970s, but a powerful political bloc successfully fought to retain the corporation's independent status.

The Health and Hospital Corporation was originally governed by a board of five members who served four-year terms. As of the early 1990s the board consists of seven members, three being appointed by the mayor, two by the county commissioners, and two by the City-County Council. Municipal bonds pay for capital improvements, while property taxes provide funds to pay for indigent patients who do not qualify for financial assistance from other governmental agencies. Other sources of income include patient revenues, Division of Public Health licenses, and federal grants.

The corporation has two independent divisions that work cooperatively. The Division of Public Health, also known as the Marion County Health Department, offers preventive health services through neighborhood clinics, provides health education programs, monitors environmental factors, maintains health-related statistics, and issues birth and death certificates. Currently, four bureaus provide these services.

The Division of Public Hospitals provides curative services mainly through WISHARD MEMORIAL HOSPITAL (formerly Marion County General), which is staffed by the INDIANA UNIVERSITY SCHOOL OF MEDICINE. Also housed at Wishard is the Midtown Community Mental Health Center, a statewide service, and the Regenstrief Health Center, which provides outpatient care. As of 1990, Wishard assumed operation of five community health centers previously administered by the county health department.

MICHELLE D. HALE

Indianapolis League of Women Voters, *Unigov Handbook* (1985); Indianapolis Newspaper Index, Indiana State Library.

Henderson, Samuel (ca. 1800–1883).

First mayor of Indianapolis, 1847–1849, Whig. A native of Kentucky, Henderson was among the first settlers in the new capital and immediately became a leading citizen. Appointed by the Monroe administration as the first postmaster of Indianapolis in 1821, he held that post until removed by the Jackson administration in 1829—and then served again in 1844–1845. He was a founding officer in 1823 of Center Lodge, Masonic Order, and a Whig presidential elector in 1832. In September, 1832, a citizens' meeting incorporated Indianapolis and elected Henderson one of five town trustees. Chosen president of the board by his peers, he served from October, 1832, to September, 1833.

Henderson earned a living from real estate and innkeeping. In addition to a 160–acre farm, he owned land in the MILE SQUARE, many odd lots, and property around the state. By 1835 he was one of the town's wealthiest citizens. The first bank in Indianapolis, a branch of the State Bank, opened in 1834 with Henderson one of eight directors. The directors advanced large loans to themselves, leaving Henderson, the bank's third largest debtor, in straitened circumstances during the economic depression of the late 1830s and early 1840s.

With the railroad from Madison nearing completion in 1847, civic leaders determined to install a more vigorous government and sought a city charter from the legislature. The resulting Charter of 1847 provided for election of a mayor. Henderson defeated two other candidates for the post in April, 1847, winning 249 of 500 ballots cast. The office carried the responsibilities, powers, and fees of a justice of the peace.

Ironically, by the end of his term in 1849 the first mayor of Indianapolis had lost confidence in the city's future. Henderson believed that the growth of RAILROADS would relegate Indianapolis to a "way station," a place where passengers would not stop long enough for "a drink of water." Selling off his holdings at reduced prices, he joined the California gold rush; he died in that state in 1883.

WILLIAM DOHERTY
Marian College

John H. B. Nowland, *Early Reminiscences of Indianapolis* (Indianapolis, 1870); Jacob Piatt Dunn, *Greater Indianapolis* (Chicago, 1910).

Hendricks, Thomas Andrews (Sept. 7, 1819–Nov. 25, 1885). Governor of Indiana, U.S. senator, and vice-president of the United States. Hendricks was born in Muskingum County, Ohio, and moved with his family to Indiana in 1820. After schooling in Shelby County and graduation from Hanover College, Hendricks read law and opened a legal practice in Shelbyville. In 1860 he moved his family to Indianapolis, where he formed a legal firm with Oscar Hord, and later with other well-known Hoosiers. For 25 years Hendricks was one of the city's leading attorneys. A prominent statesman and accomplished orator, he was called upon often in his later years to make addresses on commemorative occasions, such as the laying of the cornerstone for the STATE HOUSE.

Hendricks launched his political career in 1848 by winning election to the Indiana General Assembly. Although he declined to stand for reelection, he served in the state constitutional convention of 1850–1851, the U.S. House of Representatives (1851–1855), and as commissioner of the General Land Office under presidents Pierce and Buchanan. The state legislature elected him in 1863 to the U.S. Senate, where he anchored a small band of Democrats who opposed the Radical Republicans. Nominated three times as the Democratic candidate for governor, Hendricks won in 1872 and presided as the state's chief executive for four years marked by economic depression, labor turmoil, and anti-liquor agitation. Hendricks' status among Democrats spread beyond Indiana, a prominence manifested in efforts on three occasions to nominate him as the party's presidential candidate. His standing among Democrats, coupled with Indiana's strategic position in the nation's closely balanced electoral system, gained him the second spot on the Democratic national ticket behind Samuel Tilden, who lost the disputed election in 1876, and with Grover Cleveland in the election of 1884. Nine months into his term as vice-president, Hendricks died at his home in Indianapolis.

BALLARD C. CAMPBELL
Northeastern University

John W. Holcombe and Hubert M. Skinner, *Life and Public Services of Thomas A. Hendricks* (Indianapolis, 1886); Ralph D. Gray, ed., *Gentlemen from Indiana: National Party Candidates, 1836–1940* (Indianapolis, 1977), 119–139.

Hendricks County. County adjacent to Indianapolis–Marion County on the west and part of the Indianapolis Metropolitan Statistical Area. In 1820 the families of Bartholomew Ramsey, Harris Bray, John W. Bryant, James Dunn, and Ezekiel Moore settled along the White Lick River in what is now Hendricks County. They came to the area by the Terre Haute Trail, a path that led to settlements along the Wabash River. Soon Hendricks County had a population of over 1,000. The county, organized in 1824, chose Danville, near its geographic center, as the county seat, opening a courthouse there in 1826. The land in northeastern Hendricks County was swampy and uninhabitable, but the rest of the county had been settled by 1840.

Selected Statistics for Hendricks County, 1990

Population	75,717
Population per Square Mile	185
Percent African-American	0.9
Percent 0 to 17 Years	27.9
Percent 65 Years and Over	9.7
Percent 25 Years and Over with a High School Degree or Equivalency	84.1
Percent 25 Years and Over with a College Degree	18.2
Per Capita Income in 1989	$17,361
Unemployment Rate (%)	2.7
Married-Couple Families as a Percent of Total Households	71.9
Median Home Value	$75,700

The Cumberland Road, later called the NA-
TIONAL ROAD, came through the southern part of
the county in 1830 and contributed to the rapid
settlement and development of that area. Businesses established along the National Road served
the constant stream of travelers and hog drovers.
By the late 1830s, 150,000 hogs passed through
Hendricks County annually. Residents profited
from these drives by operating stock stands and
renting rooms to travelers. In 1839 the Quakers
who originally settled the area platted the town of
PLAINFIELD on the National Road in the southeastern part of the county. The small town quickly became an important Quaker center, and the
Western Yearly Meeting of Friends was established there in 1858 to serve Quakers in northwestern Indiana and Illinois. In the 1840s
Hendricks County citizens hired a group of Irish
immigrants to drain the swampy land in the
northeastern townships. The workers constructed wood-lined ditches employed in their
native land to channel water off the land. The area
was quickly transformed into excellent farmland
and soon was traversed by railroads and interurbans. The Indianapolis and Terre Haute Railroad, also called the Vandalia Line, connected
Plainfield to Indianapolis in the 1880s and provided Guilford Township farmers with easy access
to Indianapolis STOCKYARDS. Four interurban lines
provided Hendricks County residents easy access
to Indianapolis in the early 1900s, and area farmers used the interurbans to ship livestock and produce to markets all over the Midwest.

The completion of the Indianapolis and St.
Louis Railroad through Danville in 1880 spurred
economic growth in the county seat. In 1878 ambitious Danville citizens lured Central Normal
College from its home in Montgomery County.
The school grew steadily in Danville, peaking at
1,500 students in the late 1890s. Central Normal
College continued with enrollments over 1,000
through the first quarter of this century, but its fortunes declined shortly before World War II. The
school went bankrupt and closed its doors in
1951.

In the early 1990s Hendricks County (population 75,717) is changing from a rural-agricul-
tural to a suburban area. As Indianapolis
expanded after World War II, suburban tracts developed throughout the eastern half of the county.
Danville, once the largest town in the county, has
not grown as quickly as its neighbors to the east.
It had 4,345 residents in 1990 compared to 7,628
in Brownsburg, historically a smaller and less important community. In 1990 Plainfield was the
largest town in Hendricks County with a population of 10,433.

WILLIAM D. DALTON

History of Hendricks County, Indiana (Chicago,
1885); John R. McDowell, ed., The History of Hendricks
County, 1914–1976 (Danville, Ind., 1976); U.S. Census.

Herff Jones. Manufacturer of scholastic,
recognition, and motivational products for the
scholastic and commercial markets. Incorporated
in 1920 by Indianapolis residents Harry J. Herff
and Randall H. Jones, Herff Jones has been in continuous operation for almost 75 years. Initially
manufacturing insignia jewelry, Herff Jones products have expanded to include class rings, medals,
pins, awards, diplomas, graduation announcements and accessory items, yearbooks, caps and
gowns, senior portraits, underclass school pictures, photography finishing for the professional
photographer, classroom instructional materials
including maps, globes, anatomical models, and
multimedia teaching programs, and jewelry and
award items for the commercial market.

There are approximately 3,000 employees
and 700 sales representatives serving the needs of
education and business at all levels throughout
the United States, its territories, Puerto Rico, and

Canada. The company has 20 manufacturing and distribution centers in 13 states and Canada.

Herff Jones provides support for many well established educational, youth, health, ethnic, and general civic programs. The company is the founding sponsor of the Principal's Leadership Award, a national scholarship award program for deserving student leaders, and has consistently provided support programs to meet ongoing motivational needs of schools throughout the nation.

MICHAEL S. WILLIAMS
Herff Jones, Inc.

Herron-Morton Place. Residential area bounded by 22nd Street on the north, Central Avenue on the east, 16th Street on the south, and Pennsylvania Street on the west. Herron-Morton Place was an undeveloped wooded area when a part of it was purchased in 1859 by the Indiana State Board of Agriculture as a home for the INDIANA STATE FAIR. During the Civil War, Governor OLIVER P. MORTON requisitioned the area to induct and train soldiers. Later, CAMP MORTON housed captured Confederate troops.

Some parts of Herron-Morton Place were developed as residential lots as early as 1870. However, the state fairgrounds took up much of the area until a new site was selected on Maple Road (38th Street) in 1890. Willard W. Hubbard, Edward F. Claypool, and Elijah B. Martindale bought the old fairgrounds, renamed it Morton Place, and sold upscale residential lots.

Between 1900 and 1930, Herron-Morton Place was home to some of the city's leading citizens in politics, business, and the arts. Senators ALBERT J. BEVERIDGE and JOHN W. KERN lived there, as did Governor Samuel Ralston, retailers Frederic Ayres and WILLIAM H. BLOCK, and Dr. WILLIAM N. WISHARD. The HERRON SCHOOL OF ART, established in the area in 1907, and the Booth Tarkington CIVIC THEATRE were important cultural resources for the neighborhood.

Affluent families built imposing homes in the Queen Anne style, although there are also a few examples of Italianate, Tudor Revival, and American Four Square styles. Many of the homes displayed extensive detailing and fine craftsmanship.

A number of apartment buildings were also built in the area as early as 1907.

From 1930 to 1970, the area deteriorated as new suburbs to the north drew residents and original owners died. Many of the homes were subdivided into apartments. Decay, neglect, and demolition claimed a considerable number of homes.

In the 1970s, new residents began to purchase and restore remaining structures, and Herron-Morton Place was listed on the National Register of Historic Places in 1983. The Herron-Morton Place Association continues to revitalize the area and provide support for restoration efforts.

CATHLEEN F. DONNELLY

"Historic Area Conservation Plan, Herron-Morton Place" (Indianapolis Historic Preservation Commission, 1986).

Herron School of Art. Indiana's oldest and largest art school. Through its faculty, students and alumni, facilities, and programs, Herron School of Art has defined and shaped the visual arts culture of Indianapolis for a century. The John Herron School of Art, now Herron School of Art of Indiana University, operates a campus at 16th and Pennsylvania streets and provides an intensive program training individuals for careers in fine art, commercial art, and teaching. Herron's 2,000 alumni are active in Indianapolis, around the United States, and abroad. The school is accredited by the National Association of Schools of Art and Design.

A bequest in 1895 by Indianapolis businessman John Herron gave the fledgling Art Association of Indianapolis funds to establish an art museum and art school. Instruction at Herron School of Art, also referred to as the John Herron Art Institute, began at the Tinker House (or Talbot Place) in January, 1902. In 1907 the school occupied its own building, a modest frame structure designed by the architectural firm VONNEGUT AND BOHN. HOOSIER GROUP artists J. OTTIS ADAMS, WILLIAM FORSYTH, and OTTO STARK were principal instructors, conducting classes in painting, drawing, composition, and design. RUDOLF

Herron School of Art students in a life drawing class, ca. 1925. Well-known artist William Forsyth (second from left) was the instructor. [IUPUI Archives]

SCHWARZ taught sculpture. By 1913 fine art, commercial art, and teacher training were the three departments of instruction. Herron offered classes for Indianapolis school children and their teachers. Study of the collections in the neighboring John Herron Art Museum reinforced studio training.

In the 1920s several endowments, most notably the Mary Milliken Fund, provided scholarships, and in 1928 degrees were first conferred. A gift underwrote construction of a permanent art school building. This important two-story brick structure, designed in the Beaux Arts style by Paul Philippe Cret, opened in 1929. The building provided increased space for studio work, lectures, and art exhibitions. Relations with Butler and Indiana universities helped train art teachers, an important school mission. PAUL HADLEY taught commercial art; WAYMAN ADAMS, fine art; and Herron alumni CLIFTON WHEELER and Oakley Ritchie, fine art and scenic design.

The appointment of DONALD M. MATTISON as director in 1933 gave new impetus to the school's fine arts program. Dismissing the old faculty, including William Forsyth, Mattison appointed young, award-winning artists such as DAVID RUBINS to teach a curriculum structured to produce completely trained artists. A five-year program led to a Bachelor of Fine Arts degree. From 1937 to 1940 Herron graduates won important competitions, garnering the Prix de Rome in four successive years. Students and faculty entered local and national art exhibitions and secured government art commissions, particularly for post office murals. During World War II many Herron men and women served in the armed forces, some as illustrators and combat artists.

Enrollment burgeoned in the postwar years, leading to increases in faculty and growth of programs, particularly printmaking. Herron graduates won prestigious awards such as Guggenheim, Fulbright, and Whitney fellowships. Students and faculty showed work nationally, presentations by guest artists reinforced the curriculum, and an alumni association conducted programs benefiting instruction. In 1958 a major bequest established the Wolcott scholarships, awarded to seniors for postgraduate study. A legacy from Caroline Fesler funded construction of another building, Fesler Hall, designed by Evans Woollen and opened in 1962.

In 1966 the Art Association board of directors decided to separate the art school from the art museum. Negotiations led to Herron's acquisition by Indiana University in 1967, with Mattison serving as the school's first academic dean. Joining Indiana University increased Herron's faculty, academic, and support resources. Student enrollment rose and new faculty members developed programs in art history, ceramics, photography, and woodworking design. An enlarged sculpture foundry was equipped with new metal working machinery. The commercial art program obtained typographic equipment and in the 1980s installed a large computer graphics laboratory.

With the art museum's departure from the Herron campus in 1970, the school acquired the museum building and converted it to classrooms, studios, the Herron Library, and the Herron Gallery. The library houses an important collection of art reference material. Herron Gallery, Indianapolis Center for Contemporary Art, opened in 1971. During the 1980s its annual program of contemporary art exhibitions brought to Indianapolis important new work not otherwise seen in Indiana. The gallery commissioned, and in 1989 premiered, *Dromos Indiana*, a work of video art examining the INDIANAPOLIS 500–MILE RACE.

Through its visiting artist lecture series, Saturday school for children, and summer art workshops Herron extends the reach of its programs to the Indianapolis community. In 1990 Herron received its largest legacy gift, a $200,000 scholarship bequest from Marilyn Redinger Van Sickle honoring the parents of her husband Joseph, a Herron alumnus. Plans were being made in the early 1990s for the relocation of Herron School of Art to a major new facility on the IUPUI campus.

JOHN J. COONEY

M. Dolorita Carper, "A History of the John Herron Art Institute" (M.A. thesis, Butler University, 1947); *A History of the Art School, 1891–1972* (Indianapolis, 1972; copy in Herron Collection, IUPUI Archives).

Herschell, William Miller (Nov. 17, 1873–Dec. 2, 1939). Journalist and poet. A native Hoosier, Herschell for 37 years was a reporter for the *INDIANAPOLIS NEWS*. His poems and verses, which appeared in the paper each Saturday, were reminiscent of the work of his friend JAMES WHITCOMB RILEY. Literary historian Arthur W. Shumaker noted that Herschell "received the mantle of Hoosier folksy poetry from Riley; yet the mantle fitted awkwardly." Herschell's best-known work is the poem "Ain't God Good to Indiana?," inscribed on a bronze plaque in the rotunda of the STATE HOUSE.

Born in Spencer, Herschell was the son of Scottish immigrants John and Martha Herschell. His father was a railroad mechanic and machinist and the family lived in several Indiana towns. Herschell attended school in Huntingburg, but left in the seventh grade to work in a machine shop. He began his journalism career with the *Huntingburg Independent*, moving to the *Princeton News* after meeting the paper's editor, James McCormick, during a visit home. In 1902 he joined the *Indianapolis News* staff as a feature writer. He married Josephine Pugh, who also worked at the *News*, in 1908.

While at the Indianapolis newspaper, Herschell—along with humorist KIN HUBBARD, creator of cartoon philosopher Abe Martin, and cartoonist Gaar Williams—was a member of what was known as the "idle ward." After finishing their morning work for the afternoon paper, the men would congregate in the *News* building to talk and fill the wall with their drawings and verse.

Along with his poems, during WORLD WAR I Herschell wrote a number of war songs. His pop-

ular song "Long Boy" contributed the doughboy refrain, "Goodbye Ma! Goodbye Pa! Goodbye mule with your old heehaw!," to the nation's vocabulary. In 1917 Wabash College awarded him an honorary master of arts degree for his war verses.

Herschell's poetry from his *News* days is collected in several books published between 1915 and 1928. A posthumous collection by his widow, *Song of the Morning and Other Poems*, appeared in 1940.

RAY BOOMHOWER
Indiana Historical Society

Arthur W. Shumaker, *A History of Indiana Literature* (Indianapolis, 1962); Ray Banta, *Indiana Laughmakers* (Indianapolis, 1990).

Hervey, James Walter (Apr. 5, 1819 or 1820–Jan. 5, 1905). Prominent Indianapolis physician considered the father of the State Board of Health. Born near Brookville, Indiana, Hervey received his primary education in Ohio. He was an early student in the medical department of Indiana Asbury College (now DePauw University) and served as a surgeon for the 50th Indiana Regiment during the Civil War. Hervey wrote extensively on medical hygiene, sanitation, temperance, and the need to create a State Board of Health, which was accomplished in 1881. He was a Republican representative from Marion County in the state House of Representatives in 1855. He is also considered the first Indiana writer to attempt "horror stories," publishing *The Scroll and Locket; or the Maniac of the Mound* in 1858.

GLENN W. IRWIN, JR., M.D.

Biographical Directory of the Indiana General Assembly, Vol. 1 (Indianapolis, 1980).

Heslar Naval Armory. Home of the Indiana Naval Reserve at Indianapolis, located on the east bank of WHITE RIVER at the 30th Street bridge. Work began on the $550,000 project in February, 1936, and the building was dedicated October 29, 1938.

The four-story structure was built of reinforced architectural concrete with steel roof trusses. It housed a navigation bridge, signal hoist, magazine, battle telephones, boiler room, radio communication, watertight bulkheads, ship's ladder, and gallery. It also included a 50–foot swimming pool, gymnasium, rifle range, classrooms, and mess and quarters for officers and staff. The outer halls were decorated with oil murals 12 by 15 feet, each depicting historic naval events and famous words of naval heroes.

On November 20, 1939, Capt. O. F. Heslar (1891–1970) took command of the armory and the USS *Sacramento*, the gunboat aboard which the naval reserve force trained on Lake Michigan each summer. Captain Heslar remained in this capacity through November, 1940, when he was ordered to take his ship and its Indianapolis crew to Boston, Massachusetts. Here the vessel was transferred to the U.S. Navy and was docked at Pearl Harbor when that base was attacked by Japanese forces on December 7, 1941.

Throughout World War II, the Naval Reserve Armory remained a vital facility where radio and yeoman recruits trained for sea duty. Following that conflict it returned to a peacetime reserve function. In 1946, the U.S. Marine Corps reactivated a battalion and assigned it to the armory for training. This unit was called for Korean duty in July, 1950.

The center was renamed the Heslar Naval Armory in 1965 to honor its first commanding officer. It has undergone considerable interior change and today continues to be an excellent facility for the training of Naval and Marine reservists. The Heslar Naval Armory celebrated its 50th anniversary in October, 1988.

WAYNE L. SANFORD

Hibernians, Ancient Order of. National Irish Catholic organization founded in New York (1836), with the first Indianapolis division (chapter) formed, according to tradition, on St. Patrick's Day, March 17, 1870. Its purpose was to provide "mutual support in sickness and distress" and to advance the principles of Irish nationality. To be eligible to join a male had to be of IRISH background and a practicing Catholic. Bishop FRANCIS SILAS CHATARD, however, banned the wearing of the order's regalia in church (1882) because the Hibernians sponsored fund-raising dances. He lifted the ban during the Hibernians' national convention in Indianapolis in 1908.

Despite the existence of several other local Irish societies, the Hibernians experienced impressive growth. Two divisions were organized by 1874, four by 1877. In the early 1920s, county headquarters in Morrison Hall coordinated five divisions of men and ten auxiliary divisions of women. Probably the most important annual parade and program marked St. Patrick's Day, 1923, at which Hibernians publicly protested the religious intolerance fostered by the KU KLUX KLAN.

The order dwindled to two active men's divisions and a women's auxiliary during the Great Depression (1932) and no longer sponsored a parade. Then on October 28, 1958, Irish-born James J. Heneghan organized the Kevin Barry Division #3. Named for an Irish martyr, the division grants scholarships to deserving young people and recognizes local Irish American leaders. It helped reintroduce the annual St. Patrick's Day parade and program (1980). In conjunction with the Irish American Heritage Society, it erected an ornate limestone Celtic cross at St. John's Catholic Church in 1990 in memory of Indiana's Irish immigrants.

JAMES J. DIVITA
Marian College

Hickam, John Bamber (Aug. 10, 1914–Feb. 9, 1970). Distinguished physician, medical investigator, teacher, and administrator. His father was Colonel Horace M. Hickam, for whom Hickam Air Force Base, Hawaii, was named. Born in Manila in the Philippine Islands, Hickam graduated summa cum laude from Harvard University in 1936 and received his M.D. degree cum laude from Harvard in 1940. He had an internship and medical residency at the Peter Bent Brigham Hospital in Boston and additional residency at Emory University. He joined the medical faculty of Duke University in 1947 where he remained until he was appointed professor and chairman of the Department of Medicine at INDIANA UNIVERSITY SCHOOL OF MEDICINE in 1958.

Hickam was widely known for his original research on pulmonary function in heart and lung disease. He published extensively, wrote several chapters in the leading *Cecil-Loeb Textbook of Medicine*, and was one of the authors of the 1964 Surgeon General's "Report on Smoking and Health." He was president of the Central Society for Clinical Research, president of the Association of Professors of Medicine, trustee of the Thomas A. Edison Foundation, and a member and officer of many other national organizations. As chairman of the Department of Medicine, he greatly expanded the faculty, research, and teaching of medical students and resident physicians. An outstanding administrator with a probing intellect, he helped the department achieve top rank among the nation's medical schools.

GLENN W. IRWIN, JR., M.D.

A Shortridge High School lunchroom menu from 1907. [Indiana Historical Society, #C5758]

High Schools. Early in its history Indianapolis was dubbed the "railroad city," in reference to its location at the intersection of several important rail lines. The appellation suggests a broader metaphor—Indianapolis as a crossroads and representation of American culture. This metaphor is particularly apt when applied to the development of the American high school. From the inception of Indianapolis High School in 1853 to recent debates over the SELECT SCHOOLS plan, the development and practice of secondary education in Indianapolis have mirrored and sometimes anticipated trends that spread across America.

The rapid rise of the urban high school during the mid–19th century as a showplace of urban pride and civic-mindedness; the resulting intracity battles over the establishment and placement of subsequent high schools and the burgeoning rivalry between these high schools; the battle over the curriculum and the new "needs" of students and society at the turn of the century; the rapid expansion of the high school population, curriculum, and facilities in the first two decades of the 20th century; the first wave of suburbanization as major cities rapidly expanded, requiring still more high schools; the renewed efforts to "modernize" the curriculum in the forties; the backlash against these developments in the fifties; the second wave of suburbanization in the fifties and sixties, often

taking the form of "white flight," and the use of busing to overcome the historical effects of both legal and *de facto* segregation; the steady decline of urban high schools in the late 20th century as they were caught in the seemingly intractable problems endemic to urban centers—these developments are all well represented in the historical development of high schools in Indianapolis. Events in Indianapolis during each of these episodes echo themes both from other American localities and from other historical periods. Stripped of their immediate context, contemporary arguments over the purpose and practice of secondary education, while sometimes original in detail, often are strikingly similar to debates of the past.

In the 1990s INDIANAPOLIS PUBLIC SCHOOLS operated seven high schools—Arsenal Technical, Manual, Broad Ripple, Arlington, Northwest, Howe, and Washington—with a total secondary enrollment of approximately 10,000. This number has shrunk steadily for over two decades because of demographic changes, including a declining fertility rate (one-half that of the 1950s) and rapid suburbanization. With flight to the suburbs has come a shrinking tax base, inadequate to compensate for educational problems connected to contemporary urban culture. These concerns range from the purely educational to life-threatening violence. Between these extremes lie a panoply of woes, including declining SAT scores, at-risk students, lack of career opportunities, lack of parental and community involvement, disruptions in the classroom, low attendance rates, aging school plants, and inadequate finances.

Some problems, such as declining SAT scores, weapons in the schools, and lack of community involvement, represent historically new conditions. A 1993 meeting of the GREATER INDIANAPOLIS PROGRESS COMMITTEE on a variety of governmental issues drew no attendance for a session on education. This lack of interest stands in stark contrast to the community involvement of earlier decades, such as during Education Week, 1936, when over 10,000 patrons visited ARSENAL TECHNICAL HIGH SCHOOL alone. Numerous recent efforts to revive community involvement are more representative of the depth of the problem than the achievement of a solution. Other contemporary issues—financial pressures, dropouts, and concern for career preparation—reflect long-standing concerns. Citizens' groups such as the Committee for Efficient and Effective Schools, a 1990s team of business people that aided the central administration in its attempt to operate more economically, have their parallels in former eras, specifically during the battle over school funds in the 1890s and again during the Great Depression.

The citizens who founded Indianapolis High School in 1853 would have been bewildered by the notion that it could ever be viewed as anything but the "crowning glory" of a newly founded common school system. The high school was begun as a result of legislation that allowed incorporated towns and cities to levy taxes for the support of public education. A state Supreme Court decision in 1858, however, made such taxation illegal, and only with the appointment of ABRAM C. SHORTRIDGE as superintendent of schools in 1863 did Indianapolis High School open its doors again. Not until an 1867 reenactment of the earlier law was declared constitutional in *Robinson v. Schenk* (1885) was the legality of urban school funding assured.

While many concurred with the original negative Supreme Court decision, including William Larrabee, state Superintendent of Public Instruction in 1858, who claimed that the original legislation gave undue educational advantage to wealthier urban dwellers, most Indianapolis residents took pride in their newly formed high school. W. A. Bell, president of the school board in 1879, boasted that even the humblest citizen could get an education that would allow him "to compete even-handed in the battle of life with the child of a millionaire." While there was some truth in this statement in terms of the quality of education available by then, few residents were able to take advantage of even a free high school education at the time. There were only 11 teachers in the high school, with an average class size of 38. Each successive year the entering class lost one quarter or more of its enrollment as many students, especially males, entered the labor force. School officials made a special effort to find part-time work for children of the poor so that they would not have to terminate their education. This combination of part-time work with high school attendance was common through World War II.

By the late 19th century, the teaching staff of Indianapolis High School had developed a reputation for dedication and excellence. This reputation would grow as LAURA DONNAN, RODA E. SELLECK, CHARITY DYE, and many others became well-known figures in the community. Chemistry teacher George Benton spent his summer vacations visiting other high schools around the country in order to investigate their programs and innovations. Many extracurricular activities were begun at this time, including student government, the nation's first daily student newspaper, the *DAILY ECHO*, athletics, and unofficial social "clubs." These extracurricular activities and organizations combined to create a high school culture that would remain remarkably consistent well into the 20th century.

By the 1890s two connected developments altered secondary education in Indianapolis and elsewhere—the rapidly expanding high school population and the introduction of new curricular offerings spurred by a widespread interest in manual training. Superintendent L. H. Jones in his 1888 report embraced this latter trend with caution, pointing out with remarkable foresight that many of the claims for this new curriculum were overblown or specious. He then listed benefits that he thought applicable to Indianapolis, among them that manual training would develop the muscles of the arms and chest "much needed in city life," and that it would reawaken and strengthen the virtues of self-reliance and inventiveness endangered by modern, industrial society. In Indianapolis the German community was instrumental in promoting this new curricular direction, which they introduced in their own *Gewerbeschule* in the form of drawing and drafting. At first they succeeded only in persuading the school board to provide them with a manual training teacher, William H. Bass. By 1888, however, Indianapolis High School had a manual training department. In 1891 special legislation authorized a special tax dedicated to the establishment of a manual training high school. This school, the Industrial Training School, was built in 1895 but soon renamed Manual Training High School because of its less negative connotations. Indianapolis High School was renamed Shortridge.

Although the establishment of the second school was justified on the basis that it met the needs of a different and increasingly diverse population, southside residents looked upon Manual as their high school rather than as a different kind of education. Manual training courses were offered, but three fourths of the curriculum remained academic. While the new curriculum attracted students who otherwise would not have attended high school, broad social and economic trends, especially decreasing employment opportunities for youth and urbanization, combined to create a larger potential population for the high school regardless of its curricular offerings. Certainly the residents of the south side would have vigorously protested the philosophy of H. S. Tarbell, whose superintendent's report of 1879 called for a more practical education for the "lower classes" because "if a boy is going to make a bad man, the less we do for him intellectually, the better."

Rivalry between the two high schools began almost immediately. Shortridge students wasted no time in exploiting the ideology that was responsible for the creation of their rival; one couplet referring to Manual's colors went like this: "White and red, white and red. They're the gals who bake the bread." The superintendent's report a decade later went to some length to illustrate the democratic character of the high schools by listing the number of parents in each school representing various occupations. Among bankers and brokers, 20 were parents at Shortridge and 6 at Manual. Among lawyers, 45 were parents at Shortridge and 12 at Manual. There were 35 physicians who were parents at Shortridge, 16 at Manual. Ironically, this listing of occupations illustrated the potential for breaking down social barriers within schools, but it also revealed the social and economic distance between the two schools.

The differing emphases between Shortridge and Manual emerge in the respective principals' reports for 1909. George Benton's report for Shortridge pointedly referred to more academically rigorous course offerings aimed at preparing students for college. Manual training still offered at Shortridge had become a craft and drawing activity rather than a technical-industrial preparation. Benton also emphasized the renewed interest in Latin and claimed that physics was the proper bridge between academic and "real" life—clearly making a comparison with Manual, where shop classes fulfilled this function. For his report, Manual principal CHARLES E. EMMERICH emphasized that high school should be only incidentally preparatory for college. Yet his larger educational goals were the same as those claimed for Shortridge: to get students to think clearly and reason logically. He also made a point of the need for English classes to develop clear, unadorned expression rather than "special graces of literary skill." Despite the similar concerns, the two schools represented different and at times antagonistic cultures, as witnessed in the heated football rivalry between them, a rivalry so intense that it was abandoned after a 1907 match between them resulted in a riot.

Over capacity from its opening, Manual, as well as Shortridge, continued to expand. The period around 1900 was one of great activism among Indianapolis schoolmen, many of whom were also members of the COMMERCIAL CLUB. While the population of the city grew by 19 percent, school expenditures increased 66 percent.

When the former United States Arsenal property became available in 1909, the school board eagerly sought it for a third city high school. Begun provisionally in 1912 and officially in 1916, Arsenal Technical High School soon eclipsed both Shortridge and Manual in terms of growth. By 1910 the original manual training concept had evolved into a more explicitly vocational approach to education. "Tech" took full advantage of this new concept, expressed nationally in the Seven Cardinal Principles of Secondary Education report issued by the National Education Association in 1918. High schools were now to promote social efficiency. They were to assess the strengths, weaknesses, and needs of their students scientifically and structure the curriculum accordingly. What they found was that there were thousands of potential students who "needed" sheet metal and barbering courses rather than Virgil. Tech flourished on this discovery. By 1926 there were over 5,000 students; by 1940, 7,539. In 1912 there were 16 courses; by 1948 there were 413. Milo Stuart, Tech's first principal, helped to create one of the nation's premier "comprehensive" high schools, a concept he outlined in a book and which persists as the model for high schools today—although no longer on such a grand scale. While Tech based its growth on the wide variety of vocational courses, it also offered, just as Manual had previously, an academic program comparable to that of crosstown rival Shortridge. Tech has graduated many who have distinguished themselves in nontechnical careers. Its rivalry with Shortridge is immortalized in Indianapolis native Dan Wakefield's novel, GOING ALL THE WAY.

The 1920s and 1930s marked the zenith of high school expansion, with the annexation of Broad Ripple (1923), the addition of George Washington High School (1927), and the construction of Crispus Attucks (1927) and Thomas Carr Howe (1938). In 1920 only about one third of all 14- to 17–year-olds were in high school. By 1930 this group increased to one half and by 1940 to three fourths. As Indianapolis expanded, the west, north, and east sides demanded separate high schools just as the south side had done earlier. The need was obvious: when Washington was built, 670 westside students were commuting to one of the three existing high schools.

During the years of the GREAT DEPRESSION all of the city's high schools were severely overcrowded as students unable to find employment continued their schooling. Shortridge and Tech even had postgraduate students. Despite the overcrowding, the desire to expand educational opportunities remained strong. In 1933 a school survey completed under the supervision of Tech principal Milo Stuart recommended the further expansion of the curriculum to meet the needs of the expanded school population, a reversal (and result) of the previous policy of expanding the curriculum in order to attract a larger population.

Life adjustment education found its way into Indianapolis high schools in the 1940s as it did across the nation. This was the apotheosis of the curricular expansion begun earlier in the century. Where academic preparation had made way for vocational training, now VOCATIONAL EDUCATION was no longer considered appropriate for everyone. Nonacademic students were offered "general" courses that would prepare them for life. The 1950s saw a continuation of this policy in the form of the "Four Diploma Plan." Initiated in 1958, this plan created separate high school programs, with academic, fine and practical arts, vocational, and general orientations. A major emphasis was to limit the number of electives that could be taken, especially for the academic diploma. Anyone who could not maintain a C– average or take a sufficient number of traditional core courses would receive a diploma stamped "general" so that employers could readily see what level of training the student had received.

Vocationalism also peaked during the fifties with the conversion of the former Manual building into the Harry E. Wood High School. Its first principal, Dick Emery, known to students as "Big Daddy," maintained that a society that carefully sorted and graded everything from olives to cars should also be doing this with high school graduates. Students who could not get a traditional diploma were given certificates of vocational competence in areas such as cleaning and pressing, cosmetology, fountaineering, shoe rebuilding, and greenhouse production. He assembled a teaching staff who he said were willing to "love the unlovely."

It was also during the fifties that first steps were taken toward desegregating the nation's schools, beginning with the 1954 U.S. Supreme Court case *Brown v. Board of Education of Topeka, Kansas.* Indianapolis had a checkered past in terms of school segregation. While an 1869 state law provided for separate schools for blacks, Superintendent Shortridge in 1871 personally escorted an African-American student, Mary Ann Rann, to Indianapolis High School in defiance of existing law. H. S. Tarbell in his superintendent's report of 1879 spoke highly of the "colored population's" eagerness to learn in night schools—a desire he did not see in many of the white youths who attended.

Even though the idea of a separate black high school was raised at a school board meeting in 1908, blacks continued to attend city high schools, representing as much as 15 percent of the student population at Shortridge, until the school board created a separate black high school in 1927. CRISPUS ATTUCKS HIGH SCHOOL opened with 1,350 students and a distinguished faculty, some of whom had Ph.Ds. There was considerable pride in the black community for Attucks during these early years in spite of the fact that it had been initially forced upon them. From 1927 until 1949, when the state legislature prohibited legal segregation, blacks in Indianapolis were required to attend Attucks regardless of how far away they lived or of their need for a special program available at another high school.

Although legal segregation was eliminated with the 1949 law, *de facto* segregation continued as whites fled to the suburbs, first to the newly constructed Arlington, Northwest, and Marshall high schools, and then to outlying township schools as court-ordered busing and demographic shifts altered the racial balance at Indianapolis schools in the 1970s. Data sheets prepared for each high school and neighborhood by the High School Facilities Task Force illustrate the failure of the Indianapolis desegregation plan. Arlington in 1971 was 32 percent black, with a total population of 3,287 and attendance rate of 92 percent. By 1980 these figures had changed to 71 percent, 2,022, and 80 percent, respectively. To a greater or lesser degree, all schools showed this surge in black school population, reduction in white (total) population, and decline in attendance rate. The schools increasingly became troubled by violence and apathy.

Subsequent attempts to improve the city high schools failed to reverse the racial imbalance. The decline of Shortridge in the 1960s prompted the "Shortridge Plan," which designated the high school as academic. This plan improved the racial balance somewhat, but at the expense of other city high schools. It resulted more in denying access of neighborhood blacks to the school than it caused whites to reenter from outlying areas. Similarly, magnet programs tended to concentrate whites in several schools, doing little to alleviate overall racial imbalance. Nor did busing help, since it transported students only one way—blacks to outlying districts.

The latest scheme to combat the many problems of urban high schools, the Select Schools plan launched in 1992, seems to ignore the issue of *de facto* segregation. The goals of this choice plan are laudable—parental involvement, student commitment, and educational excellence—but it is uncertain whether parental choice of the school their child will attend will significantly alleviate the problems that led to this massive restructuring effort. While it will allow for a reconnection of neighborhood and school, it continues to offer magnets and school specialties such as the "Mind-Body Program" at Washington and the "Agricultural Science Program" at Manual. Such an approach suggests that "community" can be rebuilt on the fragile and tenuous framework of school curriculum.

Whatever the fate of Select Schools, it follows in the footsteps of many other reform efforts in the history of Indianapolis high schools. All have claimed to meet the needs of students while at the same time better serving the interests of the community. Since the latter part of the last century, all have spoken the language of business efficiency and the need to train an increasingly specialized work force. Finally, all have dutifully responded to the suggestion that the problems of society follow from deficiencies in the schools.

TED STAHLY
Indiana University, Bloomington

A. C. Shortridge, "The Schools of Indianapolis," *Indiana Magazine of History*, 8 (Jan., 1912); Alfred P. Smith, "Industrial Education in Indianapolis High Schools," *Industrial Arts and Vocational Education*, 43 (Mar., 1954); William Henry Wenning, *Brief Sketch of the Indianapolis Public School System* (n.p., 1936).

Higher Education. Indianapolis boasts a large array of post-secondary institutions, extending from traditional four-year colleges to a major urban university to populist academies. In the early 1990s over 60,000 students were enrolled annually in area colleges and universities.

By the mid–1800s Indianapolis was developing into a major metropolitan area. Businessmen, lawyers, physicians, other professionals, even the occasional entrepreneur hoped Indianapolis would achieve the status of a significant midwestern hub comparable to Cleveland, Detroit, or Pittsburgh. Higher education, however, did not seem to be a part of the plan. Ovid Butler's development of North Western Christian University (later renamed BUTLER UNIVERSITY) in 1855 marked the only successful establishment of a major college or university in the city in the 19th century. The reasons for this lack of development are interesting to consider, especially given the common practice of college "boosterism," using the promise of a college or university to promote a town or city to outside investors.

Indiana retained a very rural flavor well into the 20th century. Most of its citizens lived outside of any city of significant size. In contrast to the westward migration common to most midwestern states, large sections of Indiana were settled from the South, not the East. These southern-born Hoosier settlers brought with them an agrarian orientation toward family, land, and virtue coupled with a strong rural distrust of cities. A city, they believed, was inappropriate as a center for learning and serious study. The tradition of locating institutions of higher education in rural areas had started with Oxford and Cambridge in England, and most colonial colleges followed the example. It was no accident that the first state institution, Indiana University, was established as Indiana Seminary in 1820 in the isolated town of Bloomington. Even

Butler, originally sited on the fringe of the MILE SQUARE, was relocated to the quiet suburb of IRVINGTON, far removed from the center of urban distraction.

Although an attempt was made to move Indiana University from Bloomington to Indianapolis in 1840, strong arguments were raised in opposition. For one, the cost of living in the city was much greater. Board alone was estimated to be at least 50 percent higher. A second argument was straightforward—a relocation would cost at least $20,000, a very large amount of money at that time. Third, young men living in the city would have more "inclination to extravagance." The fourth and concluding argument was simply that Bloomington was a "healthy" location while Indianapolis was "wicked." Three more efforts to relocate Indiana University were made during the 19th century but none was successful.

When the idea of a land-grant agricultural college was first proposed in 1863, Indianapolis seemed a probable location, especially as the old STATE HOUSE was vacant and appeared to offer a suitable building. But heavy lobbying by Tippecanoe County legislators, the existence of several available buildings there, and the donation of $100,000 by John Purdue for the college persuaded the legislature to locate the institution in present-day West Lafayette. The preference for rural isolation continued. In 1870 Terre Haute was chosen as the site for the first major teacher training institution in the state, the Indiana State Normal School. Even 50 years later, when a branch site for teacher education was proposed in 1918, it was located in Muncie, 60 miles northeast of the capital city.

Boosters mounted a brief effort in 1896 to create a University of Indianapolis as a merger of Butler, the Medical College of Indiana (1878), the Indiana Law School (1893), and the Indiana Dental College (1894). The experiment actually began in 1902, foundered, and eventually failed in 1906. Two other local colleges did emerge in the early 20th century, however: the UNIVERSITY OF INDIANAPOLIS—known as Indiana Central College for much of its history—was founded by the Church of the United Brethren in 1902 (its present affiliation is with the United Methodist Church); and in 1937 MARIAN COLLEGE, a Roman

Catholic institution, moved to Indianapolis from its original home in southeastern Indiana.

Professional schools were more attractive to 19th-century Indianapolis leaders. These schools have reflected a long-standing interest of Indianapolis citizens in creating a city which would be a center for the development of business and commerce. Schools were established for the training of lawyers, businessmen, physicians, dentists, musicians, kindergarten teachers, veterinarians, and even telegraph key operators. As a railroad hub and the state capital, Indianapolis was a natural location for business-related activity in the state. The numerous schools dedicated to the professions mirrored the ambitious goals of the city at large.

By 1922 Indiana University and Purdue University accounted for 35 percent of the total college enrollment in the state, a figure that rose to 39 percent by 1939, just prior to World War II. Private institutions around the state, both in number and diversity, accounted for a sizable proportion of the remaining college students. Even so, some 26 percent of Hoosier college students attended schools in other states. Indiana did not place great emphasis on the development of education during much of the 19th century and well into the 20th. By the late 1800s Indiana ranked sixth out of ten midwestern states in length of school term and ninth of ten in the literacy of its population. It is not surprising, then, that the city experienced no stronger effort to pursue a major college or university; higher education in the state was not overly important through the mid–1900s.

The "G.I. Bill," which emerged from World War II as one of the most significant entitlement programs in the history of American education, changed the nature of higher education in Indiana and Indianapolis. Not only were veterans given unprecedented opportunity to gain a higher education, but their offspring, the much-studied "baby boomers," grew up with the expectation of attending college. As a result, the demand for higher education increased exponentially throughout the state during the 1950s and 1960s. But nowhere would the increase grow faster and be felt more strongly than in Indianapolis.

The presidents of the two largest state universities, Herman B Wells at Indiana and Frederick L. Hovde at Purdue, used the demand for higher education as an entrepreneurial opportunity to expand their respective institutions while also expanding the scope of state commitment and investment in the "Big Two." Although extension courses had been offered by both Indiana and Purdue universities in Indianapolis since 1891, the new demand was unprecedented. Enrollments and campus size had increased so much by 1968 that Elvis Stahr, Wells' successor at Indiana, recommended a separate chancellor to oversee the newly created INDIANA UNIVERSITY–PURDUE UNIVERSITY AT INDIANAPOLIS (IUPUI).

Owing to the ready student population in the metro area and the vast opportunities for degrees, the IUPUI campus became the third largest in the state in a matter of a few years. The Indianapolis campus absorbed several of the professional schools in the Indianapolis area, notably the HERRON SCHOOL OF ART, the NORMAL COLLEGE OF THE AMERICAN GYMNASTIC CENTER and the Benjamin Harrison School of Law, to name several examples. The medical complex of six hospitals and training centers connected with the IUPUI Medical Center boasts one of the largest medical training programs in the United States.

INDIANA VOCATIONAL TECHNICAL COLLEGE (Ivy Tech) is mandated to provide "occupational training of a practical, technical and semi technical nature." The school began regular operation in Indianapolis in 1966 and has offered programs in the capital continuously since that time. Ivy Tech's Region VIII, which includes Indianapolis, enrolled almost 6,100 students in the fall semester of 1992. Several of the college's programs of study are available at the region's campus complex on North Meridian Street at Fall Creek Parkway, where the institution moved in 1983.

In the 1970s and 1980s increasing numbers of older, nontraditional students and women students further ensured the sustained growth of higher education in Indianapolis. Enrollments spurred the growth of traditional schools such as Butler and Marian as well as the nontraditional MARTIN UNIVERSITY and the "LEARN AND SHOP" and "Weekend College" programs offered by IUPUI. As higher education became an opportunity for lifelong learning, the expansion of post-secondary education throughout the city at both state-supported and private institutions became less an afterthought and more a necessity. Despite a slow start, higher education in Indianapolis, in the latter years of the 20th century, has expanded rapidly. Indianapolis residents today can find classes, courses, and colleges to meet a wide range of educational needs.

ROBERT SCHWARTZ

Highland-Brookside. Eastside neighborhood bounded by I–70, Sherman Drive, the east-west railroad tracks just south of Washington Street, and the east leg of the I–65/I–70 inner beltway. In 1819–1820 GEORGE POGUE moved his family from Connersville to a log cabin located above the stream later known as POGUE'S RUN in what is now the Highland-Brookside neighborhood. For the next 40 years farmsteads were the only form of residential development in the area. The Civil War brought an economic boom and a demand for housing to Indianapolis, and a portion of the southwest corner of the area was platted for residential development in 1863. Nine years later INDIANAPOLIS WATER COMPANY director James O. Woodruff purchased and platted a 77–acre tract of land northeast of the first platted area. Subsequently known as WOODRUFF PLACE, this subdivision became the area's most prestigious address during the early 1900s.

The completion of the BELT LINE RAILROAD in 1877 spurred Indianapolis' eastward expansion, and the period between 1870 and 1900 saw much residential and industrial development in Highland-Brookside. The development of the street railway system in the late 19th century shaped residential and commercial development throughout the area. Developers platted subdivisions near the trolley lines, and these subdivisions spurred commercial development. East Washington Street housed businesses of all types along its Highland-Brookside extension. The trolley lines brought the neighborhood a prosperity that lasted up to the Great Depression of the 1930s.

Prior to 1880 Highland-Brookside supported a large German population, as evidenced by the use of the German language in the area's public schools. The growth of the construction and transportation industries in the 1880s and 1890s brought an influx of IRISH immigrants to the area. In 1886, 300 of these newcomers founded Holy Cross Roman Catholic Church. By the end of its first year the congregation had grown to over 900 members.

Highland-Brookside reached a population zenith in 1940 with 41,856 residents. The population has decreased in each subsequent decade, stabilizing at approximately 27,000 in the mid–1980s. During this 40–year period the opening of Indianapolis' outskirts for suburban development crippled Highland-Brookside. Businesses followed wealthier residents out, draining the neighborhood of much of its economic base by the mid–1960s. The construction of I–70 East and the I–65/I–70 inner beltway, a decrease in birth rates, and the desegregation of the public schools have all contributed to the area's deterioration since that time.

By the early 1990s rental housing units were predominate in Highland-Brookside and the neighborhood supported a disproportionately high number of economically disadvantaged groups. Neighborhood organizations have upgraded the area's housing stock, however, and the development of the I–70/Rural Industrial Park has increased its economic base. These developments, along with the efforts of organizations such as Eastside Community Investors and the Near East Side Community Organization, offer Highland-Brookside the promise of future revitalization.

WILLIAM D. DALTON

Hill, James T. V. (Oct. 27, 1854–Feb. 20, 1928). Attorney. Born at Chillicothe, Ohio, where he attended local schools, Hill arrived in Indianapolis in 1874, finding employment as a barber and later as a railway postal clerk. Hill attended Central Law School, the first African-American to enroll, and graduated in 1882. He promptly opened a legal practice, establishing himself as the first African-American attorney in Marion County. In 1890 he was the first African-American to serve on a grand jury in the state. He served as deputy prosecutor for four years, 1911–1915, and also acted as special judge in local courts. An active Democrat and civic leader, he practiced law until his death. He was one of the first directors of the board of the SENATE AVENUE YMCA and a charter member and trustee of Simpson M.E. Church. The J. T. V. Hill Recreation Center at 1806 North Columbia Avenue is named in his honor.

GEORGIA CRAVEY

Hines, Felrath (Nov. 5, 1913–Oct. 3, 1993). African-American artist and conservator. Born in Indianapolis, Hines attended Saturday classes at the JOHN HERRON ART INSTITUTE while attending P.S. 42 and graduated in January, 1931, from CRISPUS ATTUCKS HIGH SCHOOL. In 1945 he enrolled at the Art Institute of Chicago, then he went to New York in 1948 where he worked as a fabric designer and attended night design class at Pratt Institute. His next job was in a frame shop where he stayed for ten years and worked for little pay to learn how to conserve art.

Hines continued to paint and in 1957 exhibited in the 50th anniversary show at the John Herron Art Institute. He was part of three New York exhibits in the 1960s and early 1970s including "Afro-American Artists New York and Boston" (1970). A *New York Times* critic wrote that Hines was one of the four best mainstream artists in the exhibit. He participated in the first major African-American Los Angeles exhibition, "Two Centuries of Black American Art." His abstract paintings, which he called "Geo-Cubist" in style, can be found in gallery, private, and corporate collections.

In 1964 Hines began work as an art conservator at the Museum of Modern Art in New York City. In 1972 he became chief conservator of the National Portrait Gallery, and then worked at the Hirshhorn Museum in Washington, D.C., until his retirement in 1984.

WILLIAM E. TAYLOR
Indiana University–Purdue University,
Indianapolis

William E. Taylor, "The Abstract Art of Felrath Hines," *International Review of African American Art*, 10 (No. 3, 1993), 12–19.

Hinkle, Paul Daniel "Tony" (1898–Sept. 22, 1992). Coach and athletic director. Born in Logansport, Indiana, Tony Hinkle attended the University of Chicago where he was named to the All-Western Conference (Big 10) basketball team in 1919 and 1920 and won All-America honors in the latter season. An end on the Maroon football team, he earned three letters playing for the legendary Amos Alonzo Stagg. While pitching in Chicago's semi-pro leagues, he won a tryout offer from the New York Giants.

Hinkle joined the BUTLER UNIVERSITY coaching staff in 1921 as an assistant to Stagg disciple Harlan Page. When Page took over the Indiana University football program in 1926, Hinkle succeeded his mentor as head coach of Butler's athletic teams. Except for a 1942–1944 stint as coach of the powerhouse Great Lakes Naval Training Station squads, Hinkle remained at Butler until his retirement in 1970. His Bulldog football teams claimed a 171–100–12 mark and nine Indiana Collegiate Conference titles. His baseball teams finished 325–305–4 and Hinkle's basketball charges achieved a 572–403 slate. A 1929 national college championship, National Invitational Tournament appearances in 1958 and 1959, and a 1962 NCAA berth highlighted his tenure as basketball coach.

On March 7, 1928, Hinkle and his team dedicated their new basketball arena with a 21–13 victory over Notre Dame. Butler Fieldhouse remained America's largest gymnasium until after World War II, and Hinkle was still head basketball coach when the hall was christened Hinkle Fieldhouse in 1965. Named Butler's athletic director in

Butler University's Tony Hinkle during the late 1920s. [Butler University Archives]

1932, Hinkle also ran fieldhouse concessions for a brief period. He was known to do groundskeeping on the football field and to polish the basketball floor himself.

Hinkle's greatest impact on national athletics may have been his invention of the "Hinkle System." A basketball strategy based on motion, passing, picks, and screens, the system was a precursor of offenses later perfected by Indiana University coach Bob Knight and others. Hinkle's success at teaching athletics led over 200 of his lettermen to pursue coaching careers at the secondary school or collegiate levels.

Tony Hinkle served on the NCAA Basketball Rules Committee (1937–1938, 1942–1950), including a term as chairman (1948–1950), and during 1954–1955 was president of the National Association of Basketball Coaches (NABC). He received the 1962 National Collegiate Basketball Coaches Association Award and the 1986 NABC Golden Anniversary Award. Hinkle was a member of the Indiana and Helms Foundation football and basketball halls of fame and was inducted into the James Naismith Basketball Hall of Fame in 1965.

R. DALE OGDEN
Indiana State Museum

Howard Caldwell, *Tony Hinkle: Coach for All Seasons* (Bloomington and Indianapolis, 1991).

Hinkle Fieldhouse. Nation's oldest college basketball arena. The construction of Butler (later Hinkle) Fieldhouse in 1928 thrust BUTLER UNIVERSITY'S basketball team and its coach PAUL D. "TONY" HINKLE, into the national spotlight. Along with Madison Square Garden, the 15,000–seat fieldhouse was considered the nation's premier basketball venue. The mystique of the large structure attracted defending national champion Notre Dame to play Butler, with the Bulldogs' subsequent victory in the building's inaugural game propelling them to the 1928 national championship.

The fieldhouse, designed by Indianapolis architect FERMOR SPENCER CANNON, served as a prototype for other large indoor athletic complexes. The brick structure is six stories high and covers over three acres. Its innovative construction techniques, such as an arched steel truss system that supports the roof, allows spectators to view events unobstructed by posts or pillars. Butler Fieldhouse was also the first arena to employ a ramp system to get people to upper level seating. The original basketball court ran east and west. This design was changed in 1933 to provide more seating and because athletes complained about facing the late afternoon sun when attacking the western basket.

The building quickly became the focal point for high school basketball in Indiana. The INDIANA HIGH SCHOOL ATHLETIC ASSOCIATION held its annual basketball championships there beginning in 1928, and Butler Fieldhouse became a coveted destination as "Hoosier Hysteria" swept through small towns throughout the state every March. The destination remained the same, but after 1965 the arena was called Hinkle Fieldhouse in honor of the legendary Butler coach. The IHSAA moved its basketball tournament finals from Hinkle to Indiana University's Assembly Hall in 1972 (and later to other sites), but the fieldhouse continued to host sectional play through 1993. The IHSAA's decision to move the sectional to Lawrence North High School in 1994 ended Hinkle Fieldhouse's long association with IHSAA basketball.

Aside from basketball, the fieldhouse has hosted numerous important athletic, religious, political, and entertainment events, including the BUTLER RELAYS of the 1930s and 1940s, professional tennis tours, and circuses. It also served as a convention center, hosting such prominent figures as Wendell Willkie, Herbert Hoover, Dwight D. Eisenhower, Gerald Ford, and Billy Graham. The final scene of the 1986 movie *Hoosiers*, the fictional story based on the 1954 IHSAA champion Milan High School basketball team, was filmed at Hinkle Fieldhouse. The structure was listed on the National Register of Historic Places in 1983; as of 1993 it was one of only 21 National Historic Landmarks in Indiana.

WILLIAM D. DALTON

Howard Caldwell, *Tony Hinkle: Coach for All Seasons* (Bloomington, Ind., 1991); National Register of Historic Places nomination form.

Hinton, James Sidney (Dec. 25, 1834–Nov. 6, 1892). African-American politician and legislator. James Hinton was born in Raleigh, North Carolina, to free parents. By 1848 the Hinton family moved to Terre Haute, Indiana, where James attended a subscription school and worked part-time as a barber. At age 16 he furthered his education at a Quaker school in Hartford (Vigo County), Indiana. Upon graduation he enrolled in a course of collegiate training at the Greenville Institute in Greenville, Ohio.

During the Civil War, Hinton went to Massachusetts to recruit for the 54th and 55th United States Colored Troops. When he returned to Indiana in 1863 he was commissioned to the rank of second lieutenant to recruit for the 28th Indiana Colored Volunteer Infantry at Camp Fremont in Indianapolis.

His political career got underway in the postwar period. Extensive involvement with the Masonic lodge and the African Methodist Episcopal Church, before and after the war, gained him notoriety, and caused him to be a much sought after public speaker. The REPUBLICAN PARTY, anxious for black votes, enlisted him to speak at campaign rallies. He was elected as a delegate-at-large to the 1872 Republican national convention. His appointment as trustee of Indiana's Wabash and Erie Canal Fund from 1873 to 1877 made him the first African-American to hold an Indiana state office. In 1880 he reached the height of his political career, being elected for one term to the Indiana House of Representatives. He was Indiana's first African-American legislator.

Remaining a faithful and staunch GOP supporter, James Hinton collapsed and died mo-

James S. Hinton, the first African-American elected to the Indiana General Assembly, served in the House of Representatives in 1881.
[Indiana State Library]

ments after delivering a speech in Brazil, Indiana, during the 1892 Republican campaign.

ETTA RUSSELL

Alan F. January and Justin E. Walsh, *A Century of Achievement: Black Hoosiers in the Indiana General Assembly, 1881–1986* (Indianapolis, 1986); Ronald D. Snell, "Black Spokesman or Republican Pawn," *Negro History Bulletin*, 32(7): 6–10.

Hispanic Center. See El Centro Hispano

Hispanics. Hispanic presence in Indianapolis is recorded as far back as 1870 in the city's federal census. Hispanic immigration to Indianapolis remained very limited before World War I, and the small increase in numbers during the interwar years was overshadowed by the thousands of Hispanics who settled farther north in Lake County to work in the steel and railroad industries. By the 1930s, however, the Hispanic presence in Indianapolis was more evident. Many of these individuals were educated professionals or semi-professionals from various Latin American countries who worked for ELI LILLY AND COMPANY at a time when its operations had begun to expand into Latin America.

Since World War II, Indianapolis has experienced sharp increases in Hispanic immigration. According to the 1990 census, Marion County's 8,450 Hispanic residents constitute the state's second largest concentration of Hispanics among Indiana's counties, an increase of 24 percent over the 1980 count. Only two Lake County cities (East Chicago and Hammond) surpass Indianapolis in the number of Hispanic residents. Mexican-Americans account for the majority, followed by Puerto Ricans and Cuban-Americans.

Hispanics in Indianapolis have origins almost as diverse as their reasons for coming. Mexicans and Mexican-Americans were attracted in the late 1940s and early 1950s by work on the railroads and by a variety of opportunities in the city's expanding economy. At first limited in number, many of these workers settled as renters on the near eastside, close enough that they could visit, socialize, and support one another as they confronted the challenges of succeeding in a new environment. About the same time, the city's Puerto Rican population was expanding. The status of Puerto Ricans as U.S. citizens had enabled them to move freely from their island nation to the mainland in response to the abundant postwar economic opportunities. In addition, some were U.S. Army personnel drawn to this city by their work at FORT BENJAMIN HARRISON. Cuban immigration to Indianapolis, steady but limited for several decades, intensified in the late 1950s as the Batista government gradually succumbed to revolutionary forces.

Indianapolis' Hispanic population is spread throughout the city. Its small numbers, diverse origins, and range of social and economic levels discouraged concentration in one geographical area and at the same time encouraged assimilation. Even though in later years population clusters did appear in the city, an identifiable ethnic neighborhood characteristic of the city's early German and Italian settlement never developed. This dispersed pattern of residence has affected the character of Indianapolis' Hispanic community. Even as recently as the 1950s Hispanics knew little about themselves. Rarely did the press or media announce their presence to the community. There was no common work experience such as that provided by the steel mills in Lake County, and no Catholic services in Spanish to unite them through religious experience. Limited but vital informal networks had served the basic needs of employment, adaptation, and cultural maintenance. As their numbers grew, however, they gradually began to meet in the public arena—in the workplace, at worship, at occasional parties and dances. The formation of the Mexican Social Club in 1958, the first formal Hispanic organization in the city, reflected this increasing activity among a small population of Mexican descent concentrated on the near eastside. This, too, went largely unnoticed by other Hispanics in the city.

The dramatic arrival in Indianapolis in the early 1960s of approximately 200 Cuban refugees fleeing Fidel Castro's revolution had a transforming effect upon the Hispanic community as well as the city of Indianapolis. In a sense, this event marks the beginning of the Indianapolis Hispanic community's public chronology. As the city's churches, businesses, community groups, and in-

dividuals reached out to help settle these new arrivals, a flood of press and television coverage contributed to a growing public awareness of the larger Hispanic community. The Cuban Association, established in the early 1960s, helped ease the transition of these new arrivals and maintained their national identity as the Mexican association had done some years before. In 1965 the naming of a Hispanic to serve as detective in the Indianapolis Police Department became an occasion of some symbolic significance as the first to occupy a position in the public sector.

In 1967 St. Mary's Church in Center Township began offering Sunday Mass in Spanish, evidence of a growing Spanish-speaking community. A year later the Hispano-American Society was formed to deal with special interests common to the Hispanic community. Members of this society, with support from city leaders, founded the Hispano-American Center (now EL CENTRO HISPANO) in 1971 to provide Hispanics with social services and cultural experiences. As its responsibilities grew, the center, located in the city's downtown, became the most permanent and visible symbol of the Hispanic community in Indianapolis.

The 1970s and 1980s were decades of accelerated growth for the Hispanic community, both in terms of population and of institutional growth. The city's increased media coverage of the Hispanic community reflected that growth. Several Protestant denominations organized Spanish-speaking congregations. The Greater Indianapolis Hispanic Chamber of Commerce was formed in 1984 to assist Hispanic-owned businesses. Several new activities and organizations appeared on the Indianapolis cultural scene. Fiesta Indianapolis, an annual community-wide event organized in 1981 by the Hispano-American Center featuring Hispanic food, music, dancing, singing, and other cultural activities, offered one of the few opportunities for this ethnically diverse and geographically dispersed community to interact. At about the same time, the formation of several new Hispanic national associations contributed to a growing awareness among Hispanics of their numbers and diverse national origins. A need for communication within this emerging community was reflected in the development of radio and television programs aimed principally at a Hispanic audience, and in efforts in 1985 to establish a monthly newspaper, *Estrella Hispana*. Indianapolis' hosting of the PAN AMERICAN GAMES in 1987 highlighted the presence of the local Hispanic community and drew upon its resources.

Today peoples of Hispanic origin, while limited in number and dispersed throughout the greater Indianapolis area, are nonetheless represented in all facets of the city's life and constitute an important addition to the city's rich ethnic composition.

HISPANIC INDIANAPOLIS ORAL HISTORY PROJECT
University of Indianapolis
DAN BRIERE
CHARLES GUTHRIE
MARY MOORE

Historic Landmarks Foundation of Indiana.
Private historic preservation organization. Founded in 1960, Historic Landmarks Foundation of Indiana has grown from an all-volunteer group to become the largest nonprofit, statewide preservation organization in the United States.

From its state headquarters in Indianapolis, the award-winning Heritage Preservation Center, Historic Landmarks Foundation stimulates efforts at the grassroots level to save historic buildings in neighborhoods, cities, and towns across Indiana. Regional offices in Cambridge City, Jeffersonville, South Bend, and Terre Haute bring the foundation's programs and services closer to the people who need them. The foundation also operates a separate regional office in Indianapolis.

Each year Historic Landmarks' staff assists individuals and groups in nearly 150 communities to save Indiana's architectural heritage. The organization's diverse programming aims to save endangered historic buildings, preserve and restore significant structures and neighborhoods, and educate the public about the benefits of preserving older sites and structures. Among Historic Landmarks' statewide programs are revolving loan and grant funds; Landmark Tours, a guided tour service; county-by-county architectural surveys of historic sites and structures; informational and educational workshops; and a variety of publica-

tions including a magazine, the *Indiana Preservationist*.

In Indianapolis and throughout the state, Historic Landmarks Foundation's philosophy of preservation centers on the importance of local interest and initiative. Historic Landmarks, therefore, has supported the creation and nurtured the growth of more than 200 local groups, commissions, and historic neighborhood associations in Indiana.

Historic Landmarks owns restored historic properties throughout the state. Its Indianapolis properties include the Morris-Butler House Museum, the Kemper House, Michigan Road Toll House, and the Heritage Preservation Center (Charles Kuhn House). The MORRIS-BUTLER HOUSE, a museum of Victorian decorative arts, was Historic Landmarks' first restoration project in the mid–1960s. The KEMPER HOUSE serves as the foundation's Indianapolis regional office.

In Indianapolis, Historic Landmarks Foundation rescues vacant buildings and lots in historic areas through its Fund for Landmark Indianapolis Properties (FLIP). FLIP buys and resells endangered historic properties with protective covenants that ensure appropriate restoration. The fund grew out of an earlier program developed by Historic Landmarks to restore the Lockerbie Square Historic District. In the 1970s and 1980s Historic Landmarks purchased approximately one third of Lockerbie's houses and a majority of its vacant lots using this revolving fund technique.

Through its Indianapolis regional office, Historic Landmarks Foundation nominated most of the city's historic districts to the National Register of Historic Places. In 1990 Historic Landmarks also completed an architectural survey of Marion County. Both the National Register listings and the published survey bring attention and investment to historic properties.

SUZANNE ROLLINS
Historic Landmarks Foundation of Indiana

Historic Preservation.
The goal of historic preservation is to preserve and maintain significant structures or groupings of structures for present and future use. It goes beyond efforts to memorialize historical events or sites and at-

tempts to assure a degree of cultural continuity between past and present in the built environment.

Although there are earlier examples of efforts to preserve buildings associated with significant historical figures, historic preservation in Indianapolis in its present, more programmatic form dates from the late 1950s. In 1958 Marion County's DEPARTMENT OF METROPOLITAN PLANNING proposed the creation of "Lockerbie Fair," a tourist magnet which was to include a complete restoration of Lockerbie Street near the former home of JAMES WHITCOMB RILEY and a recreation of a late 19th century streetscape on the adjacent blocks of New York Street. While never adopted, the plan reflected a growing awareness that increased development activity threatened to remove all vestiges of the city's past.

The historic preservation movement in Indianapolis received impetus in early 1960 when a small but influential group of Indianapolis residents and local planning officials, with substantial financial support from ELI LILLY, organized the HISTORIC LANDMARKS FOUNDATION OF INDIANA (HLFI). This statewide organization combines direct involvement in the preservation process with educational and consulting activities. At the local level it has encouraged the formation of such groups as the umbrella advocacy group Historic Urban Neighborhoods of Indianapolis.

Although HLFI had significant resources, as a private organization its efforts to affect the fate of a historic structure were limited to persuasion or situations where it was able to become the owner. In order to fill this gap, in 1967 many advocates who formed and continued to direct HLFI supported the passage of legislation to create an INDIANAPOLIS HISTORIC PRESERVATION COMMISSION (IHPC). The resulting seven-member commission (since increased to nine) was given the power to prepare plans of historically significant districts for zoning adoption by the Planning Commission and County Council. It was also given the power to acquire and dispose of property; to exercise the right of eminent domain; and to control the construction, rehabilitation, and demolition of property within a designated district through the issuance of "certificates of appropriateness." While the commission did not receive financial or

staff support from local government until 1975, it prepared a preliminary LOCKERBIE SQUARE plan which was adopted in 1968 by the Metropolitan Planning Commission (the pre-Unigov predecessor to the METROPOLITAN DEVELOPMENT COMMISSION). The first certificate of appropriateness, authorizing owners to proceed with work on a property in Lockerbie Square, was issued in 1972.

After the commission obtained staff and financial support from local government, work began on a countywide survey of historic structures, undertaken to fulfill a condition for the city's receipt of federal Housing and Community Development funds. Building on the results of the survey and further research, and in response to requests from neighborhood residents, eight residential districts, one commercial district, and several individual structures have subsequently come under the review authority of the IHPC. Proposed construction and rehabilitation in these districts result in over 300 certificates of appropriateness annually.

At least some of the impetus for increased local preservation activity can be traced to the passage of federal legislation, including the Historic Preservation Act of 1966, the Tax Reform Act of 1976, and the Revenue Act of 1978. A key element of the 1966 law was the inclusion in most federal aid programs of a formal review process, similar to that required to assess environmental impact. This review is conducted prior to expenditure of funds to determine the effect of a proposed action on a site or building "that is included in or eligible for inclusion in the National Register of Historic Places." It is this requirement which led to a local historic survey in 1975 and increased local governmental involvement in historic preservation. The act also created an Advisory Council on Historic Preservation that must be given the opportunity to comment on any federally funded activity that might affect a site listed, or eligible to be listed, in the National Register. In the late 1970s, State Historic Preservation Officers were given formal responsibility for making the initial determination of National Register status. In Indianapolis, agreements have made this a cooperative process with the IHPC.

The Tax Reform Act of 1976 reduced some of the tax advantages associated with development projects if they involved demolishing historic buildings, while the Revenue Act of 1978 added tax credits (since substantially reduced) to encourage the rehabilitation of historically significant commercial structures. Since other factors such as increasing costs of new construction and changing architectural tastes also contributed to increased rehabilitation activity, it is difficult to determine precisely the economic impact of these initiatives. However, several million dollars of rehabilitation activity in Indianapolis since the mid–1970s has been performed under historic preservation guidelines in order to qualify for the favorable tax treatment.

In some instances, local historic preservation efforts have generated controversy. Philosophical objections to government intrusion and fears of financial hardship have sometimes been aroused by the belief, substantially unfounded, that designation as an historic district would lead to mandated property improvements. Perhaps more noteworthy were the debates in the mid–1970s to the early 1980s over whether historic preservation displaced lower income, largely minority residents in favor of middle class, usually white "gentrifiers." No one disputed that many of the neighborhoods undergoing revitalization had experienced significant declines in the numbers of low-income residents. What was at issue was whether the decline was the result of the disinvestment, housing abandonment, and demolition typical throughout the central city, or if it was caused by the preservationists' intervention. Although there is some anecdotal evidence that the reconversion of structures from low-income apartments back to single-family houses did occur, no systematic study has yet provided a definitive answer to the underlying causal question.

Historic Districts of Marion County Listed in the National Register of Historic Places (1993): CHATHAM-ARCH; COTTAGE HOME; FLETCHER PLACE; FOREST HILLS; FOUNTAIN SQUARE Commercial Areas (Laurel and Prospect District, State and Prospect District, Virginia Avenue District); GOLDEN HILL; HAUGHVILLE; HERRON-MORTON PLACE; HOLY ROSARY–DANISH CHURCH; INDIANA AVENUE; Indianapolis Union Station–Wholesale District; IRVINGTON; LOCKERBIE SQUARE; Massachusetts Avenue Commercial District; Meridian Park; NEW AUGUSTA; NORTH MERIDIAN STREET; OLD NORTHSIDE; RANSOM PLACE; ST. JOSEPH; WOODRUFF PLACE.

ROBERT CROSS

Historical Organizations and Events.

The earliest organized effort to preserve local history appears to have been the founding of the INDIANA HISTORICAL SOCIETY (IHS) on December 11, 1830. Prominent state figures including John Hay Farnham (principal founder) and JESSE L. HOLMAN, as well as Indianapolis residents ISAAC BLACKFORD, JAMES BLAKE, BETHUEL F. MORRIS, SAMUEL MERRILL, CALVIN FLETCHER, and WILLIAM CONNER, were among the society's first leaders. A rather inactive organization during its formative years, the IHS collected historical records, developed a library collection, and sponsored publications on local history. John B. Dillon, the Virginia-born editor of the *Logansport Canal-Telegraph* (1834–1842) and author of the first history of Indiana (1843), served as state librarian (1845–1851), thereby developing the principal repository of the state's historical materials in Indianapolis. In an 1853 program for the historical society new state librarian NATHANIEL BOLTON delivered what may have been the first lecture on Indianapolis' early history; the IHS subsequently published the lecture in 1897.

Reflecting the growing historical awareness of the period (as well as a desire to preserve their place in the annals of local history), several of Indianapolis' founding families formed the Marion County Old Settlers Association, which met for the first time on June 6, 1854, at the home of MORRIS MORRIS. Established "to perpetuate the names of the first settlers of Marion County, to embody the history of the early times, and transmit the same to future times," the group, which elected Calvin Fletcher president, claimed 55 members who had settled in Indianapolis between 1820 and 1825. By 1856, when James Blake hosted the annual meeting, nearly 600 people attended. In 1857 the association met at the INDIANA STATE FAIRGROUNDS where several hundred attendees heard memorial addresses, viewed exhibits of artifacts and daguerreotypes of the early settlers, and ate dinner. As local attention turned to the Civil War, the regular commemoration of the pioneer years faded until being resurrected by the SOCIETY OF INDIANA PIONEERS during the state's centennial (1916).

Two key events at midcentury proved to be significant for local history in the capital city. In 1857 Indianapolis-born lawyer IGNATIUS BROWN wrote the first comprehensive history of the city, which he later expanded for *Logan's Indianapolis Directory, 1868–1869*. This document provided Indianapolis with a detailed timeline of its past. The other significant event was the death in 1866 of Calvin Fletcher, who had kept a diary since his arrival in Indianapolis in 1821 and also had saved and bound a series of local newspapers. By bequeathing these items to the Indiana Historical Society Fletcher left a valuable historical record, one which provided a detailed view of daily life in early Indianapolis.

Although July 4th observances had been a continuous part of Indianapolis' public celebrations since the 1820s, the nation's centennial (1876) inspired local citizens to mark the occasion in a magnificent manner. Organizers mounted a large parade with marching bands and elaborate floats representing "The Discovery of America," "The Landing of the Pilgrims," and "Emancipation," most of which were sponsored by local German organizations. Young women staged tableaux representing the 13 colonies and the Goddess of Liberty, while men from German and French fraternal societies portrayed George Washington and other Revolutionary War generals. The day concluded with commemorative speeches and balloon ascensions.

The nation's centennial coupled with the emergence of the historical profession renewed interest in the study of local history. In 1884 BERRY R. SULGROVE, editor of the *Indianapolis Journal*, published *History of Indianapolis and Marion County, Indiana*, a comprehensive political and biographical narrative. Two years later JACOB PIATT DUNN, JR., WILLIAM HAYDEN ENGLISH, Daniel W. Howe, and others helped to reorganize the Indiana Historical Society; with a restricted membership, however, the focus of the IHS was elitist and filiopietistic and emphasized the state's "great white men" and their families. Another major accomplishment was the publication of Dunn's

monumental two-volume history, *Greater Indianapolis* (1910), which has served as the definitive resource on early Indianapolis history.

During the following decade Indianapolis participated in two major celebrations. Indiana observed its centennial in 1916 with statewide celebrations coordinated by the Indiana Historical Commission. There were scattered observances (pageants, historical markers, lectures, pioneer exhibits) throughout Marion County, including an elaborate pageant prepared by historian GEORGE S. COTTMAN for the town of IRVINGTON. The principal state observance, however, was the Centennial Jubilee, held October 2–15, 1916, in Indianapolis. For two weeks sites around the city hosted expositions, parades, athletic contests, concerts, drama and dance programs, and commemorative addresses by politicians including former President William Howard Taft and President Woodrow Wilson. The most ambitious commemorative program was the "Pageant of Indiana." Written and directed by New York pageant expert William Chauncy Langdon and staged at Riverside Park, the pageant used 3,000 performers to trace Indiana's history beginning with French explorer La Salle's visit in 1679. As with all of the centennial celebrations this presentation emphasized progress from pioneer to industrial society and instilled a sense of confidence about the future.

Four years later Indianapolis marked its own centennial with a week-long schedule of parades, pageants, music concerts, and special events. Resembling the elaborate festivities of the state centennial, Indianapolis' program was highlighted by concerts at the State Fairgrounds, parades, fireworks, and a historical pageant.

Designating and marking historic sites has been another method of remembering the past. In February, 1917, the Indianapolis Park Board considered a proposal to mark the spot of JOHN MC-CORMICK's cabin on White River, to which the *Indianapolis Star* responded, "Other cities take great pride in preserving places of historical importance. Why not Indianapolis?" Historical marker programs administered by the INDIANA HISTORICAL BUREAU and the MARION COUNTY–INDIANAPOLIS HISTORICAL SOCIETY continue to designate historically significant locations. In the early 1990s there were other efforts to document and mark sites of architectural, religious, and ethnic significance.

The emergence of historic preservation and the creation of museums have also served to increase public awareness of and appreciation for the city's history. In 1934 ELI LILLY, inspired by John D. Rockefeller's restoration of Colonial Williamsburg, purchased the William Conner house in Hamilton County to preserve the site where state capital commissioners first met in 1820 and to recreate pioneer Indiana for the visiting public. Lilly also helped found HISTORIC LANDMARKS FOUNDATION OF INDIANA (1960), which acquired the MORRIS-BUTLER HOUSE in 1962 and later opened it to interpret mid to late 19th century decorative arts and life in Indianapolis. Similarly, the creation of historic house museums like the BENJAMIN HARRISON HOUSE and the JAMES WHITCOMB RILEY HOME demonstrate a desire to document and preserve the history of Indianapolis' important and influential citizens. At the same time, ironically, urban renewal and redevelopment led to the demolition of many significant historic structures in the downtown and surrounding neighborhood areas, thereby severing the present's tie with the past.

During the 1960s and 1970s three key events—the demolition of downtown's historic buildings, the city's sesquicentennial in 1971, and the nation's bicentennial in 1976—contributed to increased public interest in local history and resulted in the formation of several local historical societies. The Marion County–Indianapolis Historical Society (1961) organized to preserve local history materials and to oppose the proposed demolition of the old county courthouse. The Irvington Historical Society (1964), which occupies the restored Ohmer-Benton House, started as an effort to preserve that neighborhood's vibrant history. The Franklin Township Historical Society (1975) occupies the former Big Run Primitive Baptist Church (1871). The Beech Grove Historical Society (1978) began as a result of a local school project to prepare a history for Beech Grove's diamond jubilee. Decatur, Pike, and Wayne townships also maintain historical societies.

Despite the presence of numerous historical organizations Indianapolis' collective sense of its historical past has waned over the decades. Public commemorations and celebrations, like those surrounding Memorial Day and July 4th, once possessed a strong historical focus and invited people to consider their place in time. Even the city's largest commemorative event—the dedication of the SOLDIERS AND SAILORS MONUMENT in May, 1902—proved to be a joint memorial service–history lesson. Few public observances today, although patriotic in tone, actually evoke a sense of the historical past. This condition may reflect the dominance of a culture of entertainment and leisure and the absence of a public historical identity. Consequently, local historical organizations have attempted to preserve the city's history and to improve civic historical awareness which, unlike many other American cities, seems to be sorely lacking in modern Indianapolis.

DAVID G. VANDERSTEL
Indiana University–Purdue University,
Indianapolis

Harlow Lindley, ed., *The Indiana Centennial 1916: A Record of the Celebration of the One Hundredth Anniversary of Indiana's Admission to Statehood* (Indianapolis, 1919); John Bodnar, "Commemorative Activity in Twentieth-Century Indianapolis: The Invention of Civic Traditions," *Indiana Magazine of History*, 87 (Mar., 1991), 1–23.

Histories of Indianapolis. The historiography of the Hoosier capital begins with a "Historical Sketch of Indianapolis" prepared by IGNATIUS BROWN for *A. C. Howard's Directory, for the City of Indianapolis* (1857). In his preface Howard called Brown's effort "the only history written of Indianapolis since its settlement" in the early 1820s. While cautioning that "want of space and want of time prevented full examination, and cut off opportunities for information," Brown defended his work as "the most complete and accurate sketch of the history of the city yet published." His focus was on the capital's first 20 years and his narrative is replete with the community's "firsts"—first marriage, first post office, first physician, and so on.

Brown expanded his manuscript a decade later and a 100–page "History of Indianapolis from 1818" appeared in *Logan's Indianapolis Directory* (1868). This version, twice the length of its predecessor, carried the story into the post–Civil War years and added several tables that had not been included in the first edition (e.g., "Town Corporation Officers from 1832 to 1847"). Brown was the first historian of Indianapolis, but by no means the last, to acknowledge "the use of the files of papers collected and left by [CALVIN FLETCHER], from which, far more than from any other source, the facts were secured on which this article is founded."

Brown's work, too, became a foundation upon which others built. WILLIAM R. HOLLOWAY admitted that he had made "free use" of Brown's "excellent history" in his own *Indianapolis: A Historical and Statistical Sketch of the Railroad City* (Indianapolis, 1870). But this work, appearing at the end of the frenetic Civil War decade, was a major advance in writing about the city's history. Whereas Brown had produced what amounted to extended essays, Holloway had published a bona fide book. Almost 400 pages long, it contained both chronological and topical chapters, illustrations, statistical tables, and a rudimentary index. Like much 19th-century historical writing, there was often a boosterish quality to Holloway's work—as when he referred in his preface to the progress of Indianapolis from "a village full of trees to a city full of the bustle of business." And it is difficult to defend his description of Indianapolis, even in 1870, as *the* Railroad City. Still, if used with awareness of its occasional hyperbole, Holloway's *Indianapolis* remains a very valuable source for the city's first 50 years.

The nation's centennial celebration in 1876 unleashed a flood of historical writing that crested in the 1880s. In Indiana dozens of county histories were published during that decade. So, too, was one of the most well known histories of the state's capital, BERRY R. SULGROVE's *History of Indianapolis and Marion County, Indiana* (Philadelphia, 1884). It is clear from his prefatory remarks that Sulgrove struggled to decide how best to organize the mass of material he wished to present; readers have struggled with his solution ever since. The volume begins by presenting, as the author put it, "a general history of the city and the county up to the outbreak of the civil war, throwing together in it all incidents which have a natural association with each other or with some

central incident or locality, so as to make a complete affair of that class of incidents." But for the city's post–Civil War history he thought it best to abandon "the form of a continuous narrative . . . and divide it into departments." The awkwardness of this scheme, compounded by the lack of an index, makes the volume difficult to use. (A 1974 reprint edition with a name index, as well as an index to several Marion County histories prepared by the Works Progress Administration, mitigated the problem somewhat.) Sulgrove did break new ground by compiling a complete list of city and county officeholders (everyone from mayor to city janitor), as well as providing separate histories of all nine Marion County townships. His work remains indispensable to the serious student of Indianapolis' 19th-century history.

Perhaps daunted by Sulgrove's 666–page tome, no one attempted a full-scale history of the city for the next quarter century. Then JACOB PIATT DUNN, JR., issued a two-volume set that remains the most frequently cited general history: *Greater Indianapolis: The History, the Industries, the Institutions, and the People of a City of Homes* (Chicago, 1910). Dunn—newspaperman, author, and secretary of the INDIANA HISTORICAL SOCIETY—explained the timing of his publication by noting that since the mid–1880s Indianapolis had "developed from an overgrown town to one of the leading cities of the country." In addition, earlier histories had relied on Ignatius Brown, "errors and all"; Dunn claimed to have gone over "the entire ground . . . from the beginning, with consultation of original authorities, a number of which were not in reach of previous writers." Finally, contrasting his work with Sulgrove's, Dunn observed that he had placed the biographical entries in his second volume and that the organization of volume 1 was "strictly topical, the chapters being arranged as nearly in chronological order as practicable."

Dunn consciously sought to give "especially full treatment" to "disputed questions." He thus devoted an entire chapter to reviewing the evidence concerning the area's first settlers. And he dealt with topics little examined by earlier chroniclers of the city's past, such as ethnicity ("The Germans in Indianapolis") and the development of the greater metropolitan area ("The Suburban Towns"). The language in his discussion of the city's African-American community may seem anachronistic or even offensive to modern readers—the chapter is titled "The Colored Brother"—but Dunn deserves credit for being the first historian to acknowledge that the city had an African-American community. And while the biographical sketches appearing in volume 2 would hardly be judged "critical" treatments of their subjects by today's standards, Dunn did compile a huge amount of material in a compact and usable format. In spite of its interpretive inadequacies, *Greater Indianapolis* remains a significant achievement and a useful source for students of the city's past.

Less useful overall than Dunn's volumes, but valuable for some topics, is KATE MILNER RABB and WILLIAM HERSCHELL, *An Account of Indianapolis and Marion County* (published as a companion volume to Logan Esarey, *History of Indiana from Its Exploration to 1922* [Dayton, Ohio, 1924]). Written in a breezy style that reflects their experience as journalists, the authors' treatment of the city's history is notable for its lack of balance. For example, separate chapters on "The John Herron Art Institute" (a single institution) and "Schools and Teachers of Indianapolis" (a large and complex subject) are both the same length. On the positive side, Rabb and Herschell did address some subjects that had been little noted by their predecessors; Indianapolis artists and social service organizations, among other topics, first received extended treatment in their pages.

The account by Rabb and Herschell appeared just a few years after the capital's centennial. The next one-volume narrative history of the city was not issued until 1971 when local publisher BOBBS-MERRILL brought out Edward A. Leary's *Indianapolis: The Story of a City* for the community's sesquicentennial. This relatively short and highly readable volume carried the story up to the implementation of Unigov. Its strength was its accessibility to the general reader; its weakness was the cursory treatment given to the years after 1930. (Of the 232 pages of text, only 25 pages concern themselves with the period following the onset of the Great Depression.) Leary's second book dealing with the city, *Indianapolis: A Pictorial History* (Virginia Beach, Va., 1980), also devoted relatively little text to the more recent decades. This latter volume is, however, one of the best collections of historical visual material concerning the city ever collected between two covers.

Another well-illustrated volume, one that combines both historical and contemporary photographs with a brief but thoughtful text, is George Geib's *Indianapolis: Hoosiers' Circle City* (Tulsa, Okla., 1981). Part of a formulaic series of community histories published by Continental Heritage Press, the book concludes with a series of one-page corporate "biographies" of those institutions that supported the publication.

The story of the city's first 100 years is the focus of Hester Anne Hale's *Indianapolis: The First Century*, published in 1987 by the MARION COUNTY–INDIANAPOLIS HISTORICAL SOCIETY. Although the volume was organized primarily as a chronological narrative, Hale included several topical chapters that allowed her to explore some subjects in greater depth. "The Story of One Man," for example, details the Indianapolis career of James Woodruff and his creation of WOODRUFF PLACE. Likewise "An Architectural Record" provides a discussion of the 19th-century city's built environment.

Although the books of both Leary and Geib include brief discussions of the modern city, the history of post–World War II Indianapolis remains largely unwritten. An attempt to begin addressing that gap in the historical literature is an essay by Robert G. Barrows, "Indianapolis: Silver Buckle on the Rust Belt," which appeared as chapter 7 in *Snowbelt Cities: Metropolitan Politics in the Northeast and Midwest since World War II*, ed. Richard M. Bernard (Bloomington, Ind., 1990).

Several diaries and reminiscences stand out as being particularly important for students of Indianapolis history. Among the former is the unparalleled *Diary of Calvin Fletcher*, 9 vols. (Indianapolis: Indiana Historical Society, 1972–1983), an essential source for the antebellum city. Fletcher's entries, which cover the years 1817 to 1866, describe both the significant and the commonplace. The editors' superb job of annotation greatly enhances the published diary's value. Other volumes in this genre include Howard Johnson, *A Home in the Woods: Oliver Johnson's Reminiscences of Early Marion County* (Indianapolis, 1951; rep. Bloomington, 1978), in which grandson Howard tells his grandfather's stories of pioneer life on the outskirts of the Hoosier capital (see JOHNSON WOODS); and Eli Lilly, ed., *Schliemann in Indianapolis* (Indianapolis, 1961), a view of the city in the late 1860s by the man who later discovered ancient Troy. The Indianapolis of the late 19th and early 20th centuries comes alive in *Indianapolis in the "Gay Nineties": High School Diaries of Claude G. Bowers*, ed. Holman Hamilton and Gayle Thornbrough (Indianapolis, 1964); Charlotte Cathcart, *Indianapolis from Our Old Corner* (Indianapolis, 1965); and Walter B. Hendrickson, *The Indiana Years, 1903–1941* (Indianapolis, 1983). Neither diary nor reminiscence, but also useful for the turn of the century, is *Hyman's Handbook of Indianapolis*, a historical, industrial, and commercial review of the city edited and published by MAX R. HYMAN that went through four editions between 1897 and 1909.

The ethnic communities of Indianapolis, although relatively small, have been the subject of considerable attention. The place to start is with James J. Divita's *Ethnic Settlement Patterns in Indianapolis*, prepared in 1988 for the Indiana Division of Historic Preservation and Archaeology. Copies of this spiral-bound typescript are on deposit in the principal Indianapolis libraries. The city's largest ethnic group is the subject of George Theodore Probst, *The Germans in Indianapolis, 1840–1918*, rev. ed. by Eberhard Reichmann (Indianapolis, 1989), while Judith Endelman has told the story of *The Jewish Community of Indianapolis: 1849 to the Present* (Bloomington, 1984). The settlement houses that served some of the city's immigrants are discussed in detail in Part I of Ruth Hutchinson Crocker's *Social Work and Social Order: The Settlement Movement in Two Industrial Cities, 1889–1930* (Urbana, Ill., 1991). Finally, three M.A. theses completed at Indiana University, although now out of date, can provide a starting point for additional research: Myra Auerbach, "The Jewish Settlement in Indianapolis" (1933); Charles R. Parks and Elavina S. Stammel, "The Slavic Peoples in Indianapolis" (1930); and Mary Rigg, "A Survey of the Foreigners in the American Settlement District of Indianapolis" (1925).

There is as yet no book-length study of the African-American community in Indianapolis. Several articles that treat aspects of blacks' experience in the capital city will be found, however, in Wilma L. Gibbs, ed., *Indiana's African-American Heritage* (Indianapolis, 1993), as well as in many of the back issues of the Indiana Historical Society's *Black History News & Notes*. See, too, the relevant material in Darlene Clark Hine, *When the Truth Is Told: A History of Black Women's Culture and Community in Indiana, 1875–1950* (Indianapolis [?], 1981), as well as the material pertaining to Indianapolis in Emma Lou Thornbrough's *The Negro in Indiana: A Study of a Minority* (Indianapolis, 1957; rep., Bloomington, 1993).

There is currently no general survey of the Indiana capital's religious history, but there are many fine studies of individual congregations. Among the best are Eli Lilly, *History of the Little Church on the Circle: Christ Church Parish Indianapolis, 1837–1955* (Indianapolis, 1955) and George Geib, *Lives Touched by Faith: Second Presbyterian Church, 150 Years* (Indianapolis, 1988). James J. Divita, the preeminent scholar of the city's Catholic community, has authored the following four parish histories (all published in Indianapolis): *A History of Assumption Parish . . . 1894–1969* (1969); *Slaves to No One: A History of the Holy Trinity Catholic Community in Indianapolis . . .* (1981); *The Italians of Indianapolis: The Story of Holy Rosary Catholic Parish, 1909–1984* (1984); and *Rejoice and Remember: A Centennial History of the Catholic Community of St. Anthony of Padua* (1992).

Three specialized but frequently cited studies are JOHN HAMPDEN HOLLIDAY, *Indianapolis and the Civil War* (Indianapolis, 1911; rep. 1972), which needs to be updated and supplemented but remains the best brief discussion of a time in the city's history when, as the author put it, "change was over all"; Ernestine Bradford Rose, *The Circle: "The Center of Our Universe"* (Indianapolis, 1957), which traces the evolution of Monument Circle; and David J. Bodenhamer, Lamont Hulse, and Elizabeth Monroe, *The Main Stem: The History and Architecture of North Meridian Street* (Indianapolis, 1992), which traces the development of the residential corridor that has been designated the North Meridian Street Historic District.

Much useful research and writing about the Hoosier capital exists in the form of theses and dissertations. Among the best are Frederick Doyle Kershner, Jr., "A Social and Cultural History of Indianapolis, 1860–1914" (Ph.D. diss., Univ. of Wisconsin, 1950) and Eva Draegert, "Indianapolis: The Culture of an Inland City" (Ph.D. diss., Indiana Univ., 1952). Somewhat more narrowly focused either chronologically or topically, but nonetheless useful, are the following dissertations all completed at Indiana University: James H. Madison, "Businessmen and the Business Community in Indianapolis, 1820–1860" (1972); David J. Bodenhamer, "Crime and Criminal Justice in Antebellum Indiana: Marion County as a Case Study" (1977); William J. Doherty, "Indianapolis in the 1870s: Hard Times in the Gilded Age" (1981); Robert G. Barrows, "A Demographic Analysis of Indianapolis, 1870–1920" (1977); and Richard M. Ugland, "The Adolescent Experience during World War II: Indianapolis as a Case Study" (1977).

Finally, aspects of the capital city's history are treated in scores of journal articles, a literature too extensive to be reviewed here. The single richest source of such articles is the *Indiana Magazine of History*; the three published indexes that cover the first 75 volumes contain many Indianapolis entries.

ROBERT G. BARROWS
Indiana University–Purdue University,
Indianapolis

Merica Evans Hoagland. [Indiana Historical Society, Subject Collection Hi-Hy]

Hoagland, Merica Evans (1858–Aug. 16, 1933). Founder of Indiana's first year-long library school. Hoagland, a native of Fort Wayne and a prominent club woman, viewed the library as an agent for social change. After attending a summer course at Melvil Dewey's New York State Library School in 1898, she worked as an itinerant library organizer and in 1901 became state organizer of libraries for the recently established Public Library Commission of Indiana. Hoagland's agenda was very similar to that of her counterparts in other states: to circulate traveling libraries, organize public libraries, and instruct librarians. Field visits convinced her of the need for the systematic training of Indiana librarians.

In 1905 Hoagland opened a library school in Indianapolis at the Winona Technical Institute, a privately funded manual training school sponsored by the Presbyterian-based Winona Assembly and Summer Schools. As her involvement with the library school deepened, she severed her connections with the Public Library Commission. When the institute experienced financial difficulties in 1908, Hoagland moved the library school to the Indianapolis PROPYLAEUM and incorporated it as a private venture. Hoagland appealed to club women, influential friends, and Andrew Carnegie for contributions to maintain the Indiana Library School until state support could be secured. She also appointed an executive board consisting of such prominent Hoosiers as author MEREDITH NICHOLSON, historian JACOB PIATT DUNN, and Butler College president THOMAS CARR HOWE.

Although Hoagland persuaded friends in the legislature to introduce a number of bills on behalf of the school, the state's librarians did not support her efforts. Her advocacy of social reform and the aggressive tactics she employed to promote the passage of library school legislation alienated many Hoosier librarians and made her school an irritant. Opponents cited the small number of library positions available each year, low salaries, and the presence of recognized library schools in neighboring states as reasons why such a school was unnecessary. The school closed in 1912 when Hoagland finally withdrew her energy, time, and financial backing. Of the 11 library schools in existence at this time, hers was the only one to fail.

Hoagland died in 1933 after spending the last years of her life engaged in personnel work at the DIAMOND CHAIN COMPANY. Although she fully expected her school to reopen, the state was without a year-long library school until 1938 when one began at Indiana University.

JOANNE E. PASSETT
Indiana University, Bloomington

Joanne E. Passet, " 'The Open Door of Opportunity': The Indiana Library School and Its Students, 1905–1912," *Libraries & Culture*, 23 (Fall, 1988), 474–492.

Hockey. Indianapolis' first professional hockey team, the Capitols, made its debut in October, 1939, as a member of the International American Hockey League. The team was affiliated with the Detroit Red Wings of the National Hockey League (NHL) and played in the newly constructed Indiana State Fair Coliseum. Arthur W. Wirtz, an executive in the Red Wings organization and president of the Coliseum Corporation, was largely responsible for introducing professional hockey in Indianapolis. The Caps won three divisional titles (1940, 1942, 1946)

INDIANAPOLIS CAPS — 1949-1950

The Indianapolis Capitols were league Calder Cup champions of the American Hockey League in 1950. Goalie Terry Sawchuck (#1) became an NHL Hall-of-Famer with the Detroit Red Wings and the Toronto Maple Leafs. [Indiana Historical Society, #C5759]

and were the league's Calder Cup champions in 1942 and 1950. Future NHL stars who played for the Caps included goalie Terry Sawchuck (20 seasons, Detroit Red Wings and Toronto Maple Leafs) and Hall-of-Famer Alex Delvelecchio (24 years, Detroit). The team ceased operations in October, 1952, after the Red Wings and the State Fair Board were unable to reach a long-term lease agreement for the Coliseum.

The Indianapolis Chiefs of the newly formed, semiprofessional International Hockey League (IHL) debuted in October, 1955. This locally owned team also played at the Coliseum but had no NHL affiliation. Although the team never won a divisional title, it was the league's Turner Cup champions in 1958. The team lost money in all seven of its seasons in Indianapolis and ceased operations in 1962. A second team called the Indianapolis Capitols began play in October, 1963. A member of the newly formed Central Hockey League (CHL), the Capitols were again the minor league affiliate of the Detroit Red Wings and also played in the Coliseum. The team had played only eight games in Indianapolis before the October 31 COLISEUM EXPLOSION resulted in a mutually agreed upon termination of the lease and the team moved to Cincinnati.

In 1974 Indianapolis was awarded a franchise in the newly formed, major league World Hockey Association (WHA). The team, which was named the Racers, began play in the newly built MARKET SQUARE ARENA (MSA) and was owned by Indiana Pro-Sports, Inc. In 1976 the Racers won the league's eastern division under coach Jacques Demers, and the following year reached the championship round of the postseason playoffs. The Racers led the WHA in attendance in the 1976–1977, averaging over 9,000 fans. After several changes in ownership, financial losses, and the departure of Demers, the team came under the control of Canadian businessman Nelson Skalbania in October, 1977. In May, 1978, Skalbania signed 16–year-old Wayne Gretzky to a Racer contract. Gretzky played his first eight games in Indianapolis, scoring three goals and three assists. Financial problems continued to plague the Racers, and in a desperate move to keep the team in operation Skalbania sold Gretzky and two other top-flight players to the

Edmonton Oilers for $850,000. This measure also failed and the team ceased operations in December, 1978.

The following year the New York Islanders of the NHL moved their top affiliate in the Central Hockey League from Fort Worth to Indianapolis. The team was named the Checkers and began play at MSA in October, 1979. Financial disagreements between the team and MSA management resulted in the return of professional hockey to the Coliseum for the 1981–1982 season. The Checkers won the Adams Cup in 1982 and 1983. In 1984 the CHL folded, but the team was able to join the International Hockey League, with players coming from the Islanders, Minnesota North Stars, and New Jersey Devils. In 1985 the Checkers moved back to MSA and were primarily a North Stars affiliate. The Checkers suspended operations after the 1986–1987 season when the North Stars changed their affiliation to Kalamazoo.

The Indianapolis Ice, also of the Central Hockey League, began play in 1988 at the Coliseum under the ownership of two Chicago businessmen. The team, without an NHL affiliate for its first season, compiled a 26–54–2 record. The following season they reached a five-year agreement with the Chicago Black Hawks to move their top minor league affiliate from Saginaw to Indianapolis. In 1989–1990 the Ice set an Indianapolis hockey franchise record with 53 victories in addition to winning the Turner Cup. The Ice will continue to serve as the Black Hawks top affiliate at least through the mid–1990s, having signed a three-year extension of its agreement with the parent club in 1993.

Amateur hockey has been active in Indianapolis since 1958 when a program was initiated at the Coliseum for youths ages 8 –18. Participatory interest in the sport continued to grow in the city with an additional and larger league emerging at the Carmel Ice Skadium in the 1970s. Leagues also were formed in Perry Township and at Ellenberger Park and PAN AMERICAN PLAZA. Boys and girls ages 4–18 continue to participate in these programs. Hockey has been played at the high school level since 1975 with several Indianapolis area schools combining talent to form one team. The city also supports a junior hockey league

team, the Indianapolis Junior Ice, for amateur players ages 18 –20. A member of the North American Junior League since 1989, the Junior Ice play their home games at the Pan Am Plaza rink. There are also senior leagues in Indianapolis for men aged 18 to late 50s. Two women's hockey teams have played in Indianapolis; both Ms. Skates and the Race-Hers participated in national women's leagues in the 1970s.

PAUL BROCKMAN
Indiana Historical Society

Hodgson, Isaac (Dec. 16, 1826–May 17, 1909). Architect. Born in Belfast, Ireland, Hodgson attended the Royal Academy. At age 16 he entered the office of Sir Charles Lanyon, architect of the Palm House at the Belfast Botanical Gardens and of Killyleagh Castle. Hodgson immigrated to New York in 1848. One year later he moved west to Louisville, Kentucky, where he was assistant architect for several state government buildings. Hodgson relocated to Indianapolis in the 1850s, becoming one of six professional architects working in the city at that time. He designed the stone and brick buildings for the United States Arsenal in 1863 (now ARSENAL TECHNICAL HIGH SCHOOL), as well as the original structures for the Indiana Female Reformatory (1870) and several residences. His greatest Indianapolis accomplishment was the Marion County Courthouse. The most elaborate courthouse in the state, the Second Empire –style building cost $1.5 million to erect in 1876, and stood for 90 years. He was also the architect for the Rose Polytechnic Institute (now Rose-Hulman) in Terre Haute, Indiana, and for several courthouses and prisons throughout the Midwest. In May, 1884, he and eight others chartered the Indiana Chapter of the American Institute of Architects.

CONNIE J. ZEIGLER

Holcomb Observatory and Planetarium. Largest telescope in Indiana. Millionaire James Irving Holcomb funded the building of BUTLER UNIVERSITY'S $500,000 observatory and planetarium, named in his honor and opened in 1954. The observatory's 38–inch Cassegrainian telescope, constructed by the J. W. Fecker Co. of Pittsburgh, Pennsylvania, was then the ninth largest in the United States and remains the largest in Indiana.

Architect ROBERT FROST DAGGETT planned the observatory with the assistance of Butler's superintendent of buildings and grounds. Built of Indiana limestone, the observatory features a lobby, lecture room, and clock room, with 13 clocks displaying half of the world's 24 standard time zones and Indianapolis time. The lobby floor, designed by Garo Z. Antreasian, a former Indiana University HERRON SCHOOL OF ART instructor, is made of colored terrazzo.

Armand N. Spitz, a leading designer and manufacturer of planetariums, designed the Holcomb Observatory's planetarium. Renovations of the facility throughout the years have included replacing the planetarium's wooden dome with aluminum, installing a new projector, and resilvering the telescope's 600–pound main mirror. The telescope is supported by a 21–ton concrete pad resting on four steel columns, preventing it from swaying.

Holcomb Observatory is central to Butler's astronomy program, with students operating the facility. Public tours are still conducted, as are planetarium shows.

TIM MULHERIN

Susan McMullin, "Butler's Own Star Search," *Butler University Alumni Quarterly* (Winter, 1991), 11.

Holiness Churches. Historically and theologically most Holiness churches trace their roots to the Methodist tradition; that is, they attempt to maintain the combination of radical social witness and theological commitment to developmental spirituality which traces its formulation to the teachings of John Wesley, founder of Methodism.

Holiness denominations include: Christian and Missionary Alliance, Church of God (Anderson), Church of the Nazarene, Free Methodist Church, Holiness Christian Church, Pilgrim Holiness Church, Salvation Army, Volunteers of America, Wesleyan Church, Central Yearly Meeting of Friends, and numerous independent Holiness congregations. Several of the Holiness denominations are the result of mergers of smaller groups. Two of these denominations have their international headquarters in Indianapolis (Free Methodists and Wesleyans), while that of the Church of God (Anderson) is within the Indianapolis metropolitan area in nearby Anderson. The interdenominational Holiness mission organizations and OMS International both have international headquarters in the Indianapolis suburb of Greenwood. The Holiness churches in Indianapolis served about 25,550 constituents in the early 1990s.

Churches which are Holiness but with Pentecostal doctrinal structures, including the Church of God (Cleveland, Tennessee), Church of God in Christ, and Holiness-Pentecostal Church, are discussed in the article entitled PENTECOSTAL CHURCHES. Other Holiness persons maintain memberships within the United Methodist Church, AME, AME Zion, and the Christian Methodist Episcopal Church.

Holiness churches did not arrive in Indianapolis until the first decade of the 20th century, a date quite later than in northern and southern Indiana. The Wesleyan Methodists Connection of America (precursors to today's Wesleyan Church) organized nationally in 1844 as a protest against the Methodist Episcopal churches' refusal to condemn slavery or recognize women's rights. Efforts to organize a Wesleyan Methodist presence in Indianapolis (1853–1857) failed and the church was not established here until 1918. The Free Methodists (founded 1860) did not organize churches in Indianapolis until 1906. The arrival of these churches in central Indiana was slow because: (1) the Methodist Protestant Church (from the South) with its strong Holiness commitment had several flourishing congregations; (2) the Evangelical United Brethren (which merged with the Methodist Episcopal Church in 1965) had a large Holiness constituency; and (3) the Methodist Episcopal Church in Indiana, and especially Indianapolis, had retained a strong Holiness emphasis up to the 1890s. National Holiness leaders, including Bishop Matthew Simpson and Samuel Brengle, had strong connections to Indiana. Roberts Park and Meridian Street Methodist Episcopal churches were nationally recognized as centers of Holiness activism. Holiness believers perceived no need for separate organizations.

The Methodist Episcopal Church in Indianapolis, as elsewhere, began to force Holiness clergy from the church by the late 1890s. Perhaps the most celebrated case was that of G. D. Watson, an evangelist who had been pastor at Meridian Street Methodist Episcopal Church and who became president of the National Holiness Association, a loose organization of Holiness activists and denominations today known as the Christian Holiness Association. Watson was forced to resign from the Methodist Episcopal Church in 1896.

The Indianapolis Presbyterian churches also had significant Holiness connections but by the late 1890s Presbyterian Holiness believers were being forced outside to form Christian and Missionary alliance groups under the leadership of A. B. Simpson, who visited Indianapolis frequently during this transition period. The (Christ) Cumberland Presbyterian Church is the Indianapolis representative of that Holiness denomination. Among the Quakers, the Holiness influences led to the founding (1912) of the Central Yearly Meeting of Friends with headquarters in nearby Westfield, Indiana, where a school, campground, and college (Union Bible College and Seminary) are maintained. Holiness evangelists also had determinative influences on the ecclesiology, ministerial structures, and theology of both the Indiana Yearly Meeting (Richmond) and Western Yearly Meeting of Friends with headquarters and archives at nearby Plainfield.

The first Holiness organizations in Indianapolis were para-church developments or independent congregations such as the Original Methodist Church (1890). These included the International Holiness Union and Prayer League (1897), founded by M. W. Knapp and C. W. Ruth, and the Pentecost Bands (1898), established by Vivian Dake. The Young Men's Holiness League, with headquarters at the corner of New York and Alabama streets, was also active during the decade and counted more than 3,000 men converted to the Holiness tradition during the decade 1897–1907. Cadle Tabernacle had a strong Holiness constituency, with Pilgrim Holiness ministers (James DeWeerd, for example) serving occasion-ally as pastors and radio preachers for that downtown center.

Independent Holiness Missions, Chapels, and Congregations have been a rapidly changing feature of the city's landscape. Some, such as Holiness Tabernacle, founded ca. 1950 by Mary Johnson and husband on Beauty Avenue, were the target of takeovers by roving evangelists who had little respect for established leadership. Many independent Holiness churches, such as the Holiness League of Roy and George Golay (Washington and West streets), were displaced by the urban renewal of downtown and the IUPUI campus area. There were over 20 independent churches in Indianapolis in 1993, with average Sunday attendance of around 4,800 and a constituency of perhaps 6,500. Some of these are part of the International Holiness Convention, a loose association of independent Holiness churches.

The *Wesleyan Church* is a result of the merging of the Wesleyan Methodist Church with the Pilgrim Holiness Church, which was in turn the result of a merger in Indiana of the Holiness Christian Church, Apostolic Holiness Union of Indiana, the International Holiness Union and Prayer League, the Trinity Tabernacle Association, and the Missionary Bands of the World (Pentecost Bands). The Wesleyan Methodist Church began (1844) as a protest against the refusal of the Methodist Episcopal Church to oppose slavery. The other groups were formed as the Methodist Episcopal Church and Quakers (in Indiana) took stands against the Wesleyan doctrines of sanctification and ceased to take reformist social positions. The denomination has about 200,000 members worldwide. In Indianapolis there were 13 congregations in 1992 counting 900 members with a constituency of approximately 1,500. Juridically, the churches are part of the Indiana Central District of the Wesleyan Church. The international headquarters (with library and archives) moved from Marion, Indiana, to Indianapolis (6060 Castleway Drive West) in 1986.

The Pentecost Bands and the Pilgrim Holiness Church were the major merging elements that formed the Wesleyan Church. The Pentecost Bands, groups of youth devoted to short-term evangelistic and missionary endeavors, were founded (1882) by the Free Methodist Vivian

**Holiness Churches in Indianapolis:
Statistical Summary of Constituencies (1993)[1]**

Free Methodist Church	1,800
Christian and Missionary Alliance	500
Church of God (Anderson)	6,200
Church of the Nazarene	7,000
Independent Holiness Churches	6,500
Pilgrim Holiness Church	300
Salvation Army	1,500
Volunteers of America	250
Wesleyan Church	<u>1,500</u>
	25,550

[1] These numbers reflect the churches' constituencies, which include members (all limit membership to adults) and children of members.

Dake. They arrived in Indianapolis (1887) and established a center at 3400 West Washington Street. In 1898 these incorporated independently of the Free Methodist Church as Pentecost Bands of the World. The international headquarters of the organization was in Indianapolis at the Salem Park Campgrounds. When the group merged with the Wesleyan Church (1958), the constituency had declined to about 200 in two churches in Indianapolis: Salem Park (3400 West Washington Street) and St. Clair (719 East St. Clair). The Salem Park Church later withdrew (1966) from the Wesleyan Church and is independent with a membership of about 150 with a school (K–12). The group was very active in providing medical and social services to indigents and in evangelistic and missionary work around the world.

The eventual First Pilgrim Holiness Church in Indianapolis was founded in 1890 as the (independent) Original Methodist Church. It then joined (1902) the Christian Holiness Church which merged in 1919 (82 Indianapolis members) with the International Apostolic Holiness Church. This church evolved through other mergers into the Pilgrim Holiness Church (1922), with offices scattered around the nation. These offices were consolidated with the establishment of the denominational headquarters and publishing company (1930) at 839 North Capitol Avenue, Indianapolis, then moved to 1609 North Delaware Street and later (1945) to 226–230 East Ohio Street. In 1930 there were four churches with an average attendance of 237. When the denomination merged with the Wesleyan Methodists (1968), there were 12 churches with an average

attendance of around 900. Two Indianapolis congregations did not merge.

The *Free Methodist Church* began (1860) as a protest against the secularization of the Methodist Episcopal Church, the issues being freedom from slavery, sin (positively stated in Wesleyan terms of sanctification), the influence of secret societies, pew rents, and freedom for women to preach. The Pentecost Bands, then part of the Free Methodist Church, arrived in Indianapolis in 1887, but withdrew to form a separate denomination in 1898. The next official Free Methodist presence was not established until 1906, and then the development was slow until around 1910 when a congregation was established. The international headquarters and archives moved from Marion, Indiana, to Indianapolis (770 North High School Road) in 1990. There are now six congregations in Indianapolis with a combined membership of about 1,385 and a constituency of about 1,800.

The *Church of the Nazarene* in Indianapolis has 21 congregations with a membership of about 3,800 and a constituency around 7,000. Juridically these congregations are part of the Indianapolis District of the Church of the Nazarene. The district office is at the Nazarene Campground in nearby CAMBY. An annual "Assembly Journal" reports statistics, clergy assignments, and minutes of judicatory meetings.

The first congregation of the then Pentecostal Church of the Nazarene was organized (1907) with 60 charter members in the Young Men's Holiness League building at New York and Alabama streets. The league, despite having a "membership" large enough to attract numerous nationally prominent Holiness personalities as speakers, had not been structured as a church and had few churches to which it could refer its numerous converts. C. W. Ruth, peripatetic Indianapolis-based evangelist and organizer on a national level for the Church of the Nazarene, served briefly as pastor (1908). The church was initially part of the Chicago Central District of the new denomination.

The first appointed pastor was C. A. Imhoff, who moved the congregation to its own quarters at 16th and Delaware streets. First Church of the Nazarene grew slowly and moved frequently before it obtained a building at 1621 West Washington Street ca. 1914 where it remained until it moved to its present site at 601 North Shortridge Road. The building on West Washington Street houses an innovative Nazarene Church, Shepherd Community (1961), that does significant ministry to the poor and homeless of the city. The most prominent pastor at First Nazarene was probably Haldor Lillenas, author of more than 4,000 songs and hymns, who during his tenure (1923–1926) founded a music publishing company, Lillenas Publishing Company, at the corner of East Washington Street and Arlington Avenue. Before the company was sold (1930) to the Nazarene Publishing House, Kansas City, Missouri, more than 700,000 hymnals and songbooks were published and sold. The church has published its own periodicals including *The Nazarene Informer*. Throughout its history the Church of the Nazarene has provided services to the poor of the city. Among its programs were an extensive system of vegetable gardens provided to the inner city poor on land owned or leased by the churches. This continued through the 1950s when the price of renting land became prohibitive.

The other large Nazarene church is Westside Church of the Nazarene. Its origins are to be traced to a revival meeting held at the corner of West 10th Street and North Holmes Avenue in 1915. The church was finally organized on July 17, 1916, with 82 charter members. In 1919 a church building was constructed at the intersection of 11th and King streets. The building was expanded on that site until the congregation moved (1981) to its present location at 8610 West 10th Street. The church has a retirement village as well as a school (K–12) and an extensive day care program.

These, as well as the other 19 congregations founded between 1907 and 1992, give significant funds to the missions budget and universities of the denomination, maintain a number of social ministries within Indianapolis, and provide a flow of clergy and leaders to the national church.

The *Church of God (Anderson)* uses the geographical denominator to distinguish it from the Pentecostal "Church of God, Cleveland, Tennessee." In 1993 the Church of God (Anderson) had 11 congregations with a membership of 2,314 in Indianapolis and a constituency around 6,200, a large number of whom are associated with Church at the Crossing. The state offices of the Church of God are in Carmel. The national offices, publishing house, archives, national campground (held annually), and largest university are in the Indianapolis metropolitan area in nearby Anderson.

Technically, the Church of God (Anderson) considers itself a "restoration [of New Testament Christianity] movement" rather than a denomination, but it has all the structures of a denomination. The movement was founded by Hoosier evangelist Daniel Warner, a former member of the (Winebrenner) Church of God and former vice-president of the Indiana State Holiness Association. He used the periodical *The Gospel Trumpet*, now *Vital Christianity*, as a forum to define the tradition and as a communication device to connect the local groups of adherents into a national body. Warner left the North Indiana Eldership of the (Winebrennerian) Church of God in 1881 but it is unclear when the first congregation of the new group was formed in Indianapolis since records were not kept and the anticlerical nature of the "reformation movement" avoided early institutionalization. However, already from September, 1881, through September, 1882, Warner and J. C. Fisher published *The Gospel Trumpet* in Indianapolis, first at 70 North Illinois Street then at 625 West Vermont Street. But local resources were not sufficient to maintain the leadership; the paper and headquarters, after several moves, were transferred to Anderson.

The *Pilgrim Holiness Church* is a remnant of the 1968 merger of the Wesleyan Methodist and Pilgrim Holiness churches. There are two congregations in Indianapolis—Pilgrim Chapel and Fountain Square Pilgrim Holiness—with a combined constituency of about 300.

The SALVATION ARMY is best known as a social service agency, but it is also a Holiness church with four congregations (Corps) in Indianapolis. The membership of about 300 persons (full adult members committed to the ministry of the Salvation Army) is augmented with a much larger constituency, perhaps as many as 1,500. From the city-state headquarters at 1919 East 52nd Street it administers numerous thrift stores, a rehabilitation center, a Family Service Center, and other ministries. The Salvation Army arrived in Indianapolis in 1889. It has had headquarters and ministry sites at a number of Indianapolis locations.

The *Volunteers of America* split off from the Salvation Army in 1896. The discipline and methods of the Salvation Army were maintained until 1984 when a corporate structure, complete with a CEO, was adopted. However, they still view themselves as a church but with a radical social as well as a religious mission. The Volunteers began work in Indianapolis at least as early as 1902 with "90 sustaining members," but the Indianapolis "post" was not officially founded until 1922. There is one "post" in Indianapolis with about 60 members and a constituency of perhaps 250.

The *Christian and Missionary Alliance* in Indianapolis had its origin in the ministry of George N. Eldridge, an Anderson Methodist Episcopal minister who was expelled from the North Indiana Conference for teaching the Wesleyan-Holiness doctrines of healing and sanctification. The "Gospel Tabernacle" was opened in 1883 on East Street north of its intersection with Massachusetts Avenue. In 1907 many members of the congregation became Pentecostal, despite the efforts of Eldridge, who also eventually became Pentecostal, and several visits by A. B. Simpson, founder of the Alliance. There were three congregations in Indianapolis in 1993 with a membership of around 300 and a constituency of about 500. The national denominational headquarters and archives are in Colorado Springs, Colorado.

DAVID BUNDY
Christian Theological Seminary

Hollenbeck Press. One of the earliest printers in Indianapolis. Symbolized by a griffin, Hollenbeck Press was founded in 1864 as Carlon and Hollenbeck and located at the southeast corner of Meridian Street and the Circle. New York native Charles E. Hollenbeck bought controlling interest in the company in 1898, changing its name to Hollenbeck Press. The company was the first printer in Indianapolis to do fine art and artistic printing. When Hollenbeck died in December, 1901, the company reorganized with William C. Bobbs, Charles W. Merrill, and Merrill B. Barkley as directors and controlling stock owners. In 1904 they erected a new plant at the northwest

corner of Market and New Jersey streets and installed the latest printing and binding machinery.

Hollenbeck Press produced many of the city's historical pieces, city directories, and local newspapers, such as the INDIANAPOLIS NEWS and the INDIANAPOLIS JOURNAL. It also printed corporate promotional materials for ELI LILLY AND COMPANY, Marmon Motor Car Company, and Fletcher Savings and Trust Company. By 1941 the company had relocated to 126 North Noble Street (later College Avenue) where it existed until ca. 1981.

STACEY NICHOLAS

Holliday, John Hampden (May 31, 1846–Oct. 20, 1921). Founder of the *Indianapolis News* and the Union Trust Company; civic leader and philanthropist. The grandson of Samuel Holliday, an Indiana Territory pioneer, he was born in Indianapolis to the Rev. William A. and Lucia Shaw Holliday. He began his education in the local public schools, continued at North Western Christian University (now BUTLER UNIVERSITY), and earned an A.B. degree from Hanover College in 1864. He served in the 100–day 137th Regiment, Indiana Volunteer Infantry, and then returned to Hanover where he was awarded an A.M. degree in 1867.

After graduation Holliday studied law briefly, but abandoned it to take up journalism. He served on the staffs of the Indianapolis *Sentinel*, *Herald*, and *Gazette* and was correspondent for several Cincinnati, Chicago, and New York newspapers. In 1869, at age 23, he founded the INDIANAPOLIS NEWS, which maintained a small size through condensation of news and sold in the beginning for two cents. Holliday reasoned that a paper with a low price would enjoy a large circulation, which would in turn produce the large advertising revenues on which success depended.

The first issue of the *News* was scheduled for December 7, 1869. However, Holliday determined to "scoop" the competing papers with an extra edition on the 6th reporting President Grant's first message to Congress. Difficulty with the telegraph service delayed release of the extra until 6:30 P.M. The weather was bitterly cold, the streets were nearly deserted, and no more than 50 copies were sold. From this inauspicious beginning the *News* grew to a circulation of more than 25,000 in the 23 years of Holliday's ownership and control. At age 46, because of concern over his deteriorating health, he resolved to sell his interest in the *News* and to retire. He announced his retirement on May 12, 1892, in the 6,981st issue of the paper.

Within a few months of his retirement, Holliday recovered his health. In May, 1893, he organized the UNION TRUST COMPANY and became its first president. In 1899 he set this position aside to found the *Indianapolis Press*, in competition with the *News*. Early in 1901 he concluded that the *Press* would not thrive and it was consolidated with the *News*. Shortly thereafter he resumed his position as president of the Union Trust Company and retained it until 1916, when he became chairman of the board of directors. The Union Trust Company was later merged with the INDIANA NATIONAL BANK.

Holliday served as director of numerous financial and industrial corporations and on the boards of several educational and benevolent institutions including the local CHARITY ORGANIZATION SOCIETY. His memberships ranged from the GRAND ARMY OF THE REPUBLIC to Phi Beta Kappa, and he was a 33rd-degree Scottish Rite Mason. He was the first president of the SOCIETY OF INDIANA PIONEERS and was active in the INDIANA HISTORICAL SOCIETY, which published his *Indianapolis and the Civil War* (1911). In 1916 Wabash College conferred upon him an honorary LL.D. degree.

In 1892 Holliday and his wife Evaline acquired an 80–acre country estate on the west bank of WHITE RIVER near CROWS NEST. In 1916 they donated it to the City of Indianapolis for use as a park, subject to their life estate. After Evaline died in 1929 it became HOLLIDAY PARK.

RICHARD G. GROOME

Indianapolis News, Oct. 21, 1921, Jan. 7, 1929; *Indianapolis and the Civil War* (n.p.: Society of Indiana Pioneers, 1972 reprint ed.), v-vi.

Holliday Park. City park located at 6349 Spring Mill Road. JOHN H. HOLLIDAY, founder of

the *Indianapolis News*, and his wife Evaline, both active in philanthropic activities, deeded their 80–acre estate to the city in 1916 for use as a public park. The land became part of the city park system in early March, 1932, although it was never formally opened and financial difficulties delayed early plans for the park. An arboretum and botanical garden opened in early 1940 after four years of work by BUTLER UNIVERSITY professor and botanist William Clute. The Holliday House served as a botanical museum and library until 1955 when it burned.

In 1958 Holliday Park became home to the three *Races of Mankind*, sculpted by Karl T. Bitter. An Indianapolis native, Bitter designed the five-foot-tall statues of three kneeling men to adorn New York City's St. Paul Building, erected in 1898–1899. When Western Electric Company decided to raze the building in 1958 to make way for their new headquarters, they arranged with the former Committee to Preserve American Art to donate the sculptures. A national committee selected Indianapolis over bids by the United Nations, several universities, and the New York airport. The city commissioned local artist ELMER E. TAFLINGER to design a grotto for the statues; the grouping later became known as "The Ruins." Changing city and park administrations delayed development of Taflinger's plans until the 1970s. When dedicated in 1977, "Constitution Mall," as Taflinger called his design, included three limestone tablets representing the three races of mankind and the three branches of government, a reflecting pool with fountains, 25 Grecian columns from the former Sisters of the Good Shepherd Convent, and four allegorical female statues from the old Marion County Courthouse, all situated amidst a tree-filled landscape.

Beginning in the 1970s, problems with vandalism, drug dealing, public indecency, and lack of maintenance contributed to the decreasing use of the park by neighborhood families. Established in 1990, The Friends of Holliday Park, a nonprofit foundation, began to raise money for a family recreation area and to renovate the park's trails, gardens, and structures. In 1992 the group opened a playground and picnic area on the south edge of the park.

JOAN CUNNINGHAM

Holloway, William Robeson (Dec. 6, 1836–Dec. 10, 1911). Journalist-politician. Born in Richmond, Indiana, Holloway was the son of David P. Holloway, editor of the *Richmond Palladium* and commissioner of patents during the Lincoln administration. Educated in the Richmond public schools, Holloway learned the printing business in his father's office and worked as a compositor for the *Cincinnati Times* from 1852 to 1857. Returning to Richmond in 1858, Holloway married future governor OLIVER P. MORTON's sister-in-law. Admitted to the bar in 1860, Holloway served as Governor Morton's private secretary from 1861 to 1863.

Having spent a year on business in New York City, Holloway returned to Indianapolis in 1864 and purchased an interest in the INDIANA JOURNAL. Holloway retained both an editorial and a financial interest in the paper until 1872. In 1875, he repurchased his interest in the *Journal* but sold it within a few months. In 1880, Holloway established the INDIANAPOLIS TIMES. This venture, however, turned out to be a failure and the *Times* was merged with the *Journal* in 1886.

In 1869, Holloway was appointed postmaster of Indianapolis, serving until 1881. Later he was United States consul general at St. Petersburg, Russia (1897–1904) and Halifax, Nova Scotia (1904–1907). Holloway authored *History of Richmond and Wayne County* (1858) and *Indianapolis: A Historical and Statistical Sketch of the Railroad City* (1870).

JEFFERY A. DUVALL

Indiana Biography Series, Indiana State Library; R. E. Banta, *Indiana Authors and Their Books, 1816–1916* (Crawfordsville, Ind., 1949).

Holman, Jesse Lynch (Oct. 24, 1784–Mar. 28, 1842). Author, lawyer, clergyman, Indiana legislator, and judge. Born near Danville, Kentucky, Holman was one of 14 children; his father died in 1789 while attempting to rescue his wife and children during an attack by Indians. After teaching school for a time, tradition has it that Holman read law in Henry Clay's office. Admitted to the Kentucky bar in 1805, he practiced the lawyer's trade in New Castle, Port William, and Frankfort, Kentucky.

Holman married in 1810 and that same year published a novel, *The Prisoners of Niagara, or Errors of Education*, which he later tried to find and destroy as he was convinced that the work was bad for young people's morals. A year after his book's publication, he and his wife moved to the Indiana Territory, settling near what is now Aurora. Holman built a house, which he named Veraestau, on a bluff overlooking the Ohio River. This handsome structure is listed in the National Register of Historic Places.

In 1816, after earlier service in the territorial legislature and judiciary, Holman became one of the first three Supreme Court justices for the new state of Indiana. He was reappointed in 1823, and two years later the court moved from Corydon to the new state capital. With Governor James Brown Ray's refusal to reappoint him to the court in 1830, Holman turned to other activities. He served on a committee selected to write the INDIANA HISTORICAL SOCIETY's constitution, was ordained a Baptist minister, and helped found Franklin College and Indiana College (now Indiana University). In 1835 President Andrew Jackson appointed Holman as judge of the United States district court for Indiana, which was located in Indianapolis. He held this post until his death.

RAY BOOMHOWER
Indiana Historical Society

I. George Blake, *The Holmans of Veraestau* (Oxford, Ohio, 1943).

Holtzman, John W. (Apr. 23, 1858–Mar. 6, 1942). Mayor of Indianapolis, 1903–1906, Democrat. Born in Berks County, Pennsylvania, Holtzman moved with his family to White County, Indiana, ca. 1864. In May, 1883, he came to Indianapolis, read law, and was admitted to the bar in 1885, his profession for the rest of his life. After an unsuccessful bid for city council, Holtzman was named county attorney for the poor in January, 1886, but resigned in November to accept appointment as assistant county prosecutor, 1886–1890. He was elected and reelected prosecutor in 1890 and 1892, leading the ticket both times. He became Democratic county chairman in 1894.

The mayoral elections of 1903 and 1905 between Holtzman and CHARLES A. BOOKWALTER were notable for their bitterness. During his term Holtzman began a systematic RAILROAD TRACK ELEVATION program (delays and deaths were the bane of the city from the many downtown trains operating at street level); established the first filter beds of the water company, thus ensuring purer drinking water; and fought successfully to create the city-owned gas company. Additionally, his police chief experimented with the "Paris system" of controlling vice by registering prostitutes and adopting a policy of non-interference with orderly houses. Doubtless Holtzman is the only Indianapolis mayor to be decorated by the Emperor of China, in 1904 when PRINCE PU LUN visited the city. Holtzman also served on the state conservation commission, 1917–1924, and as city corporation counsel, 1928.

WILLIAM DOHERTY
Marian College

Pictorial and Biographical Memoirs of Indianapolis (Chicago, 1893); *Indianapolis News*, Mar. 6, 1942.

Holy Cross–Westminster. Near eastside neighborhood bounded by Michigan Street, Hamilton Avenue, Washington Street, and I–65/I–70. The area now called Holy Cross –Westminster was purchased in the 1830s by Governor Noah Noble (1831–1837). His son-in-law constructed one of its first homes atop the knoll now called Highland Park. In 1873 the INDIANA WOMEN'S PRISON located on the neighborhood's eastern border. By the 1880s many of the city's IRISH immigrants had settled along the area's western edges near IRISH HILL. To meet the needs of these Irish Catholics, in 1886 Holy Cross Roman Catholic Church (125 North Oriental Avenue) opened its doors. The initial congregation of 300 increased to 900 before the church's first anniversary. (Westminster United Presbyterian Church at 445 North State Avenue also lends its name to the neighborhood.) The surrounding community saw continuous growth in both residential and business development.

After 1940 residents, then businesses, began to move out of the neighborhood to the suburbs, leaving behind empty, decaying structures. Further population decline followed the demolition of homes for the construction of the I–65/I–70 loop in the early 1970s. By 1988 nearly one half of the 929 homes in the Holy Cross–Westminster neighborhood were rentals. In the 1990s many of the two-story, early 20th-century frame structures, some deteriorating from lack of maintenance, remain rental units. Others are being revitalized by optimistic owners who are tapping the resources of an umbrella organization, the Highland-Brookside Neighborhood Association, in an attempt to arrest their neighborhood's decline.

CONNIE J. ZEIGLER

Holy Rosary–Danish Church. Historic district bounded by Virginia Avenue and Wright, Buchanan, and East streets. The neighborhood is located approximately one-half mile southeast of MONUMENT CIRCLE. Originally platted in 1854, the area contained rental cottages constructed and inhabited originally by skilled German, Irish, Scots, and Welsh laborers. Subsequent tenants included DANES who arrived after 1867 and then ITALIANS in the early 1900s.

The Danish influence was most apparent between 1870 and 1890: 63 Danes resided there at the 1880 census, most of them skilled laborers in the building industry. In 1872 Danish Lutherans erected a simple Gothic Revival brick church and parsonage on McCarty Street, which housed their societies and cultural events even after parishioners had departed the neighborhood. They sold the church, parish hall, and parsonage in 1956.

Italian immigrants, mostly of Sicilian origin, replaced the Danes and comprised nearly 90 percent of the neighborhood by 1910. They first attended St. Mary's Catholic Church on Maryland Street, but when Methodists established an Italian mission in the neighborhood the Catholic archdiocese authorized the creation of an Italian national parish. Located at Stevens and East streets, Holy Rosary Church, an Italian Renaissance structure (begun 1911, completed 1925), was the first of three Italian national parishes in Indiana. A school, established adjacent to the church in 1924, educated parish children until its closing in

1957. The Latin School, founded in 1955 to prepare boys for the priesthood, occupied the building from 1957 to 1977.

The neighborhood, located close to the city's rail lines, markets, and warehouses, provided an ideal residence for the Italians who were employed almost exclusively in produce businesses. Although the area possesses few Italian residents today, it remains the Italian center of the city. The Italian Festival, held at Holy Rosary each June since 1984, raises money for ongoing building maintenance. When the archdiocese proposed closing the church in 1991–1992, parishioners successfully rallied to prevent its discontinuation.

Neighborhood houses, which date primarily from the late 19th century, are small working class cottages: the earliest house dates from 1857, the most recent from the 1940s. Commercial corridors along Virginia Avenue and East Street retain scattered historic commercial structures, while the ELI LILLY AND COMPANY complex looms along the western edge. The district was listed on the National Register of Historic Places in 1986.

SHERYL D. VANDERSTEL

"Holy Rosary–Danish Church National Register Nomination" (Indianapolis, 198?); James J. Divita, *The Italians of Indianapolis: The Story of Holy Rosary Catholic Parish, 1909–1984* (Indianapolis, 1984); Historic Landmarks Foundation of Indiana, *Center Township, Marion County, Interim Report, Indiana Historic Sites and Structures Inventory* (Indianapolis, 1991).

Home-News (1922–early 1930s).

Weekly neighborhood newspapers. In November, 1922, Reverend Clay Trusty incorporated the *East Side News* (1918), the *Christian Visitor* (1914), and *South Side News* (1919) into a chain of neighborhood papers produced by the Home-News Publishing Company.

The *Christian Visitor*, begun by Trusty and Cecil Stalnacker for Seventh Christian Church which Trusty pastored, focused on NORTH INDIANAPOLIS. After its incorporation into the Home-News chain, the *Visitor* continued to print mainly religious news. The *East Side News* became the *Home-News, East Side*, covering an area including IRVINGTON and WOODRUFF PLACE. The *South Side News* was renamed *Home-News, South Side* and included the Shortridge and FOUNTAIN SQUARE areas. The *Home-News, North Side* edition covered the area north of 38th Street, including BROAD RIPPLE east of Washington Boulevard.

Home-News printed news regarding "local civic affairs, society news, church news, personal items, club and business news and anything of interest to local people." The contents of each edition varied slightly; there were many columns such as "A Page Devoted to Indianapolis Theaters Owned, Operated and Managed by Indianapolis Men," as well as serialized fiction. The eight-page paper was heavily laced with advertisements, particularly after changing its policy to one of free distribution in 1924. It had a circulation over 40,000 by 1925.

JOAN CUNNINGHAM

John W. Miller, *Indiana Newspaper Bibliography* (Indianapolis, 1982).

Home Place. Hamilton County suburban area, centered at the intersection of 106th Street and College Avenue. Before 1914 the area now known as Home Place was called Pleasant Grove, a small farming community of a few homes, a school, two sawmills, and the Pleasant Grove Methodist Episcopal Church. In 1914 the Orin Jessup Land Company purchased farmland in the area and platted Home Place along the Kokomo interurban line. The company hoped College Avenue would be developed as U.S. 31, but Meridian Street became the federal highway and development moved west of the town. Lot sales slowed and the area never incorporated, although two later additions were platted.

Primarily residential, Home Place counted only about 200 residents in the 1940s when a few small businesses, a general store, and a filling station made up the business district. In the 1970s and '80s, as CARMEL and Indianapolis expanded, a number of subdivisions were built near Home Place. According to estimates, about 5,000 residents lived in the area in 1989.

New commercial and residential developments continue to encroach on Home Place in 1993. A few shops and businesses remain in operation at the intersection of College Avenue and

106th Street, though little is left of the old community.

CATHLEEN F. DONNELLY

Jack L. Edwards, *A View of Home Place, Indiana* (Noblesville, Ind., 1992).

Home Rule. The concept of "home rule" permits local communities within a state to provide for their own governments and to exercise all powers not prohibited by state law or by the state or U.S. constitutions. Historically, the home rule authority of local governments in Indiana has been limited. State officials specify the government structure and many of the powers of Indiana cities and towns. One of the principal arguments made in favor of the 1851 Indiana Constitution was that the original 1816 Constitution had involved the state government too much in the affairs of local communities.

Even under the 1851 Constitution the Indiana General Assembly has exercised considerable control over cities and towns, defining their powers and establishing their governmental structures under a classification system that categorized municipalities as towns or as first-, second-, or third-class cities. Cities such as Indianapolis could not substantially alter any aspect of their governmental organization or finances without state legislative approval.

The number of state laws regulating local governments accumulated for more than a century until the General Assembly created a Local Government Study Commission in the 1970s. The commission's recommendations led to the rewriting and recodification in 1980 and 1981 of many state laws concerning local governments. The new laws, gathered under Title 36 of the Indiana Code, included a home rule statement of the relationship between state power and local government autonomy. The state legislature declared that local units of government could exercise any powers not specifically denied to them.

In spite of the home rule declaration, the state still specifies municipal government structure in Indiana. The state divides municipalities into towns and three classes of cities, based on their populations. State laws prescribe the size, powers, and length of terms of the city council or town board and the mayor for each class of municipalities.

In a first-class city (Indianapolis is currently the only first-class city in the state), state law sets the size of the city council at 29 members and specifies that 25 will be elected from districts and four at-large. State law further provides that both the council members and the mayor serve renewable four-year terms.

The list of powers that the state specifically denies to municipalities is substantial. The Indiana Constitution restricts the borrowing authority of municipalities. State law regulates the incorporation and annexation actions of municipal governments, and in Title 36 cities and towns are denied the power to: impose any tax except as expressly granted by statute; impose a license or other fee greater than that reasonably related to the administrative cost of exercising a regulatory power; impose a service charge greater than that reasonably related to the cost of the service provided; invest money except as expressly authorized by statute; prescribe a penalty of imprisonment for violation of a municipal ordinance; prescribe a fine of more than $2,500 for violation of an ordinance; regulate conduct that is regulated by a state agency, except as expressly granted by statute; impose duties on another local jurisdiction, unless expressly granted by statute; condition or limit their civil liability, except as expressly granted by statute; regulate or restrict rents; or prescribe the laws governing civil actions between private persons.

GREGORY M. VOGEL

Homecroft. Perry Township community roughly bounded by Banta Road, the Conrail tracks, Tulip Drive, and Shelby Street. In 1923 Indianapolis realtor Frank Gates and his son Oliver bought 150 acres in the area now known as Homecroft. A decade later they worked with the federal Works Progress Administration to drain the swampy area and install a storm sewer. The new development was dubbed Homecroft, reportedly because the name implied a desire to own a home. Sales of lots in the first 80 acres were brisk, as the area proved to be a popular commuter suburb. In the 1930s and early 1940s quick interurban service made a trip to the city inexpensive; in the 1950s and 1960s Madison Avenue offered a convenient motor route. A second addition of 40 acres and a final addition of 30 acres were also developed by the early 1950s. Designed to be exclusively residential, Homecroft featured homes in a variety of vernacular styles, including ranches and bungalows. Portions of the neighborhood, identified in a 1991 historic properties survey, are being considered for nomination to the National Register of Historic Places.

Incorporated in 1949, Homecroft counted over 800 residents in the 1950s. Since that time only a few additional homes have been built and the population has hovered around 800. The community assumed the status of an INCLUDED TOWN under UNIGOV and continues to be self-governed by an elected four-member town council and clerk-treasurer. The community employs its own police force with a town marshal and eight part-time reservists. Local concerns in the 1990s have included street maintenance and zoning issues, particularly commercial encroachment along Madison Avenue.

CATHLEEN F. DONNELLY

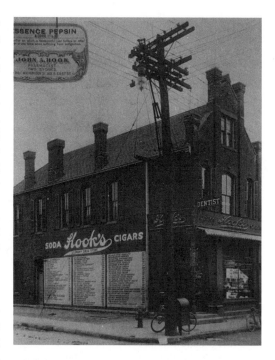

The first Hook's Drug Store stood at the corner of South East and Prospect streets until it was demolished in 1941.
[Indianapolis Newspapers Inc.]

Hook's Drug Stores. In October, 1900, John A. Hook opened the first Hook's Drug Store at the corner of South East and Prospect streets in Indianapolis' German community. Hook, a recent graduate of the Cincinnati College of Pharmacy, hired Edward F. Roesch in 1905 to run a second store at New Jersey and Washington streets. Together with Roesch, Hook expanded the chain to 12 stores by 1912.

Hook died in 1943 and Roesch then ran the company. But when Roesch was killed in an automobile accident, Hook's son, August F. "Bud" Hook, became president. Hook recognized the need for change in locations and service, and he hired Norman Reeves to head store operations for 56 locations. Reeves eventually became chairman; Roesch's sons, Edward and John, joined the company in later years.

Between 1946 and 1972 all but two of the old stores had been closed and replaced by 150 new ones, with room for parking and a new self-serve design. In 1963, Hook's constructed a 152,966–square-foot headquarters and service center at 2800 Enterprise Street on the city's east side. (Such heavy rain and hail occurred at the groundbreaking that bulldozers had to construct a road of crushed stone before the 1,000 guests could leave.) Three additions and the acquisition of two adjacent buildings expanded the complex to its present 596,470 square feet covering 33 acres.

The Kroger Company acquired Hook's in 1985 but divested the firm a year later. Then Hook's became a division of the privately held Hook-SupeRx, Inc. In 1988, the company added the Brooks Drug chain.

The company is one of the oldest drugstore chains in the country and operates over 400 stores in Indiana and the contiguous states. The chain also includes 30 Convalescent Aids Centers, which were established in 1977. Most stores are managed by registered pharmacists and the chain has over 5,000 employees.

In 1994 Revco D.S. Inc. signed a definitive merger agreement to acquire Hook-SupeRx, a move that would create the nation's second largest drugstore chain.

GRETA E. SHANKLE
Indianapolis Business Journal

Hook's Historical Drug Store (1202 East 38th Street). Located in the INDIANA STATE FAIRGROUNDS, the Hook's museum was opened in August, 1966, as part of HOOK'S DRUG STORES' effort to commemorate the 150th anniversary of Indiana's admission to the Union as the 19th state.

The turn-of-the-century drugstore, which is housed in the former Indiana State Board of Health Building at the State Fairgrounds, features furnishings and other paraphernalia originally purchased from a Cambridge City, Indiana, drugstore. Other pharmaceutical items were obtained from collectors and drugstores. The restored building's two rooms display drugs, patent medicines, advertisements, apothecary bottles, mortars and pestles, cameras, pens, and other items usually sold in a turn-of-the-century drugstore. Museum visitors can also purchase candies, sundries, or ice cream treats from an old-fashioned soda fountain. Admission is free.

RAY BOOMHOWER
Indiana Historical Society

Robert M. Taylor, Jr., ed., *Indiana: A New Historical Guide* (Indianapolis, 1989), 420.

A Hoosier Chronicle (1912). Novel by MEREDITH NICHOLSON. This is a powerful novel of politics and society set in central Indiana, particularly Indianapolis, in the early 20th century. Published during the height of Nicholson's reputation, it marked his most ambitious effort at a serious, factually based analysis of politics, the role of legislative bosses, and the efficacy of progressive reforms then being promoted within the Hoosier state. Nicholson drew some of the characters from life, particularly the feisty older woman, Aunt Sally Owens, and outdoorsman-minister John Ware, and the dramatic selection of a senator to fill a vacancy was based upon events during Governor Thomas Marshall's administration. Nicholson always considered this novel, his ninth, as his best.

The story chronicles the life of a young woman from Madison (Wabash) College and her mysterious background and relations with the two most powerful political figures in the state following her arrival in the state capital. Brimming with insights regarding Indiana's political and cultural history, and mentions of a few of its actual people, it reveals not only a great deal of Nicholson's own political philosophy and his support of women's rights, but also much about life in the capital city at the dawn of the automobile age. Nicholson described the physical layout of the city at the end of the 19th century, its major thoroughfares and fine homes, the pleasures and pastimes of the people, and various historical curiosities. Quite consciously accepting a responsibility to posterity to record things about the city accurately in his more serious literary works, he noted, for example, that cattle were still being driven "through" Washington Street en route to the railroad yards until 1888, when "the cobbles yielded to asphalt." And he recorded that, "what later historians may be interested to learn from these pages," the station wagon, drawn by a single horse, was for years "the commonest vehicle" of Indianapolis, a byproduct of the financial panics of 1873, 1884, and 1893. The city's resultant label as a "one-horse town" persisted into the 20th century.

RALPH D. GRAY
Indiana University–Purdue University,
Indianapolis

Dorothy Ritter Russo and Thelma Lois Sullivan, *Bibliographical Studies of Seven Authors of Crawfordsville, Indiana* (Indianapolis, 1952); *Indianapolis Star*, Mar. 8, 1912.

Hoosier Dome. Located in the southwest corner of the MILE SQUARE, the Hoosier Dome was completed in May, 1984, as a part of the Indiana Convention Center. Built at a cost of $82 million, the structure was partially financed by major grants from the LILLY ENDOWMENT and the KRANNERT CHARITABLE TRUST. A municipal bond issue,

Hoosier Dome, ca. 1991.
[Indianapolis Project. Photo by Rob Banayote.]

funded by a controversial 1-percent food and beverage tax levied only in Marion County restaurants, also financed the project. A joint venture of the architectural firms BROWNING, DAY, POLLAK, MULLINS, DIERDORF, INC. and Howard, Needles, Tammen, and Bergendoff, it has a massive eight-acre roof consisting of two layers of fabric supported by 100 horsepower fans that create an inside pressure 5 to 15 pounds per square foot greater than the outside air. One unique feature of the dome is its sprinkler system consisting of a grid of 26 laser beams and photo-electric rays designed to activate four water cannons located around the dome's perimeter. When activated by fire or smoke the system will drench the stadium floor in minutes without injuring the spectators. Dome facilities include 99 private luxury suites, a 95,000 square-foot stadium floor, 60,500 permanent seats, and state-of-the-art communications facilities. The dome, one of only a handful of such structures, is home to the National Football League's INDIANAPOLIS COLTS and has hosted numerous events including local commencement exercises, national religious conventions, the Tenth PAN AMERICAN GAMES, the NCAA men's basketball and indoor track and field finals, the INDIANA HIGH SCHOOL ATHLETIC ASSOCIATION'S boys basketball finals, and the World Gymnastics Championships.

RITA W. HARLAN

Hoosier Group. Informal association of Indiana painters. Artists J. OTTIS ADAMS, WILLIAM

FORSYTH, RICHARD B. GRUELLE, OTTO STARK, and T. C. STEELE became known as members of the Hoosier Group after participating in a holiday art exhibition, "Five Hoosier Painters," sponsored by the Central Art Association in Chicago during December, 1894. Chicago writers applauded the vitality and freshness of approach shown by this group of Indiana artists, heralding their work as a distinctly American vision from the country's heartland. Despite such collective praise, the five men never formally associated as a group. Although their paths often crossed, each artist maintained his individual painting style.

The Hoosier Group held a common interest in interpreting the Indiana landscape. Images of the Brown County hills spilled from Steele's canvases, as did his earlier scenes of turn-of-the-century Indianapolis. Adams was intrigued by the sparkling waters of the Whitewater River near Brookville, and Forsyth explored the scenery around Pleasant Run Creek near his home in IRVINGTON. Stark delighted in using the neighborhood children as models for his out-of-doors work in SOUTHPORT, and Gruelle gravitated toward water in his compositions, finding inspiration in the Indianapolis canal for his pastoral landscapes. Even though the five never exhibited together again as a group, the Hoosier Group artists have become synonymous with early twentieth century Indiana landscape painting. Today they are seen as having developed their own variant of Impressionism during that period.

JUDITH VALE NEWTON

Judith Vale Newton, *The Hoosier Group: Five American Painters* (Indianapolis, 1985); Martin Krause, *The Passage: Return of Indiana Painters from Germany, 1880–1905* (Indianapolis, 1990).

Hoosier Motor Club. In 1902 CARL G. FISHER and a circle of local automobile enthusiasts organized a driving club called the Flat Tire Group. Recognizing that motorists needed political representation in order to promote a system of paved roads, the Flat Tire Group reorganized in 1911, changing its name to the Hoosier Motor Club. In 1917, with nearly 500 members, the club affiliated with the American Automobile Association (AAA). This affiliation allowed the local organization to expand its services greatly. With home offices located in Indianapolis, during the following years the organization became the largest automobile club in Indiana.

By the 1960s AAA Hoosier Motor Club served 50 of the state's 92 counties and was one of 3 AAA affiliates in Indiana. By 1973 the club had over 140,000 members, and services included specialized Triptik maps, emergency road service, foreign and domestic travel arrangements, bail bonds, and safety education. In 1980 the Hoosier Motor Club became one of the first AAA affiliates to offer the AAA credit card, and in 1982 it became an official distributor of state license plates under contract to the Bureau of Motor Vehicles—although in 1990 the BMV canceled this contract.

In 1993 AAA Hoosier Motor Club has 21 branch offices, 8 in Marion County, and 275,000 members.

CONNIE J. ZEIGLER

Hoosier Salon. Annual art exhibition. The first Hoosier Salon was held in the galleries of Chicago's Marshall Field & Co. on March 9–19, 1925. Organized by the Daughters of Indiana, a group of women living in Chicago, the juried exhibition was designed to foster interest in the artists of Indiana. Encouraged by their success, the women organized the Hoosier Salon Patrons Association in 1926, and made plans to continue the show on an annual basis. The association established its headquarters and a gallery featuring the work of Indiana artists in downtown Chicago in 1928.

After the 1941 show, the association relocated its operations to Indianapolis. From 1942 to 1977, the Hoosier Salon was held at the WILLIAM H. BLOCK CO.; from 1978 to 1989, at L. S. AYRES AND CO.; and most recently, at the INDIANA STATE MUSEUM. In celebration of its 25th anniversary, the 1949 Hoosier Salon was mounted in the Freer Gallery of Art of the Smithsonian Institution in Washington, D.C., as well as in Indianapolis.

Individual patrons and a variety of organizations have supported the Hoosier Salon by providing cash awards and purchase prizes. The WOMAN'S DEPARTMENT CLUB of Indianapolis, the Indiana Federation of Clubs, Kappa Kappa Kappa

sorority, and Psi Iota Xi sorority were among the first groups to furnish the association with both leadership and funding. The generous awards make the show one of the richest in the country.

Characterized as an exhibition favoring traditional entries—that is, those treated in a representational fashion—the Hoosier Salon has offered a forum for some 2,500 Indiana artists. Notable artists to exhibit at the Salon include JACOB COX and Daniel Garber, four of the HOOSIER GROUP painters (J. OTTIS ADAMS, WILLIAM FORSYTH, OTTO STARK, T. C. STEELE), and many painters of Brown County landscapes. Prominent contemporary artists whose works have graced the Salon include Rosemary Browne Beck, Harry Davis, FLOYD D. HOPPER, Wilbur Meese, Nancy Noel, K. P. Singh, and ELMER TAFLINGER.

JUDITH VALE NEWTON

Judith Vale Newton and Carol Weiss, *A Grand Tradition: The Art and Artists of the Hoosier Salon, 1925–1990* (Indianapolis, 1993).

Hoover, Robert L. (Jan. 6, 1898–Dec. 30, 1981). Journalist. A newspaper reporter who covered the JOHN DILLINGER era of bank robberies in the 1930s, Hoover was still chasing down police stories in the 1970s as a radio newsman. The septuagenarian broadcaster delighted radio listeners through reports laced with crime cliches from earlier eras.

The colorful Hoover, a graduate of MANUAL HIGH SCHOOL, started his journalistic career in 1919 with the INDIANAPOLIS NEWS, where he worked for more than 30 years as both reporter and photographer. On leaving the *News* in 1949, he became publicity director for the State Department of Conservation and editor of its magazine, *Outdoor Indiana*. In 1953 he joined the Indiana Motor Truck Association as publicity director. He became a broadcaster in 1957 when radio station WIBC employed him to cover police news; although his reports finally were infrequent, he was still a WIBC employee when he died 24 years later.

A free-lancer for several newsreel services, Hoover was the first to capture a confession on motion picture film while covering the 1954 "dresser drawer" murder case. A founding member of the INDIANAPOLIS PRESS CLUB and its president from 1934 to 1939, Hoover is in both the Indiana Journalism Hall of Fame and the Indiana Broadcasters Hall of Fame.

JAMES E. FARMER

Indianapolis News, Dec. 31, 1981; *Indianapolis Star*, June 7, 1970, Dec. 31, 1981.

Hopper, Floyd D. (Nov. 1, 1909–July 2, 1984). Artist regarded as the dean of Indiana watercolorists. Born in Martin County, Hopper attended the HERRON SCHOOL OF ART in Indianapolis from 1929 to 1933, studying under WILLIAM FORSYTH, CLIFTON WHEELER, PAUL HADLEY, and DONALD MATTISON. Hopper's art of the 1930s and early 1940s strongly resembles the American Scene style of painting practiced by midwestern Regionalists Thomas Hart Benton (Missouri), John Steuart Curry (Kansas), and Grant Wood (Iowa). Through such works as *Thirteenth and Roosevelt* (1935), *A Summer Rain* (1936), *Red Farm* (1937), *Our Alley* (1939), *Railroad Yard* (1939), and *Wash Day* (1940), Hopper depicted Indiana during the latter years of the Great Depression in his oils, watercolors, and lithographs.

When the United States became involved in World War II, Hopper exchanged his paint brushes for industrial tooling that would aid the war effort. In 1941, he joined the Indianapolis steel fabricator Hetherington and Berner and later helped found the Noblesville Casting Company. In 1958, he returned full-time to the easel to paint, teach, and exhibit.

During this second artistic phase, Hopper specialized in the medium of watercolor—both painting and teaching. For over 20 years, he taught watercolor classes at the INDIANAPOLIS ART LEAGUE and at his Cherry Hill Studio in Noblesville. His watercolor paintings were annual prize winners at the HOOSIER SALON, Indiana Artists Club, and INDIANA STATE FAIR art shows. Through his teaching and painting, Hopper influenced two decades of Indiana watercolorists. He was elected to membership in the Indiana Academy in 1979 and in 1987 was posthumously recognized as a major Indiana artist by a concurrent resolution of the Indiana General Assembly.

Hopper's work can be found in many private collections and in such public institutions as the INDIANAPOLIS MUSEUM OF ART, the Fort Wayne Museum of Art, Indiana University, Franklin College, DePauw University, Ball State University, and the Brown County Art Guild.

FRANK N. OWINGS, JR.

Indianapolis Art League, *The Edge of Town* (Indianapolis, 1989); Indianapolis Art League, *Floyd D. Hopper Retrospective Exhibition 1935–1969* (Indianapolis, 1986); Flora Lauter, *Indiana Artists Active 1940* (Spencer, Ind., 1941).

Hornbrook, Henry Hallam (Feb. 15, 1870–Sept. 20, 1935). Attorney and civic leader. Born in Evansville, Indiana, Hornbrook graduated from DePauw University in 1892 and studied at Harvard Law School the following year. He practiced law in Evansville for a year before moving to Indianapolis and joining the firm of Duncan and Smith. He remained with the firm until his death, at which time it was known as Smith, Remster, Hornbrook and Smith. An authority on the organization of gas companies, Hornbrook had been on the board of directors of CITIZENS GAS AND COKE UTILITY since 1918 and for the last 12 years was a member of its executive committee. He was recognized throughout the United States as an authority on constitutional law, particularly the constitutionality of bond issues for governmental units.

Hornbrook was a director at Indiana National Bank, treasurer of Meridian Street M.E. Church, board member for Union Trust Company, and a trustee for CROWN HILL CEMETERY and Tudor Hall School. He served as DePauw University board secretary from 1908 until his death, and during this time he secured the gift that made the construction of Asbury Hall possible. He had been a member of the YMCA board of directors since 1918 and board vice-president for 6 years. From 1926 until his death, Hornbrook was president of the INDIANAPOLIS FOUNDATION.

JOAN CUNNINGHAM

Who Was Who in America; *Indianapolis Star*, Sept. 21, 24, 1935.

Hospital Guilds. Volunteer organizations supporting hospitals with fund-raising and patient services. In the late 1800s, religious and other volunteer organizations in America led the way in addressing educational, human service, and health needs. One such group, the Needlework Guild of Philadelphia, was organized in 1885 to contribute clothes to the needy. This provided a model for the hospital guild, or auxiliary, movement in Indianapolis in the early 1900s.

Through fund-raising activities such as operating gift shops, conducting bazaars, and holding charity balls, Indianapolis guilds have raised millions of dollars over the years for new equipment and programs. For example, the annual Decorators' Show House, sponsored by St. Margaret's Hospital Guild, raised more than $3 million over a 30–year period for WISHARD MEMORIAL HOSPITAL. Guild members have also contributed thousands of volunteer hours in services such as writing letters for patients and staffing book carts and reception areas.

St. Margaret's Hospital Guild was founded in 1907 by the Reverend Doctor Lewis Brown to serve City Hospital (now Wishard). Sunnyside Guild, originally founded to support the Sunnyside Sanitarium, is now also based at Wishard. In 1924, the forerunner of the Cheer Guild of Indiana University Hospitals was founded by a charter group of 30 women to serve the new RILEY HOSPITAL FOR CHILDREN. Affiliated chapters were formed around the state to support fund-raising efforts. ST. FRANCIS HOSPITAL Center Auxiliary (originally Hospital Guild) was organized in 1929. White Cross Guild, founded by Mrs. Edgar Blake in 1932 with 80 charter members, grew out of the original METHODIST HOSPITAL Guild. ST. VINCENT HOSPITAL Guild was founded in 1933 with 22 charter members. The Women's Auxiliary of COMMUNITY HOSPITAL was organized with 80 charter members by Mrs. Louis Bruck in 1956, the same year the new hospital opened. The Memorial Hospital Auxiliary was organized in 1961 by 55 charter members, directed by Mrs. John Coleman, to serve Memorial Clinic (later WINONA MEMORIAL HOSPITAL).

STEPHEN E. KIRCHHOFF

Susan J. Ellis and Katherine H. Noyes, *By the People: A History of Americans as Volunteers* (San Francisco, 1990).

Hospitals. During much of the 19th century hospitals offered few advantages to the sick and suffering. Doctors treated most patients in their own homes. Early hospitals had evolved from almshouses and were little more than welfare institutions. The medical care at these institutions was minimal, and the death rate from infection was high (approximately 10 percent). Patients in these early hospitals were poor and had been abandoned by family and friends.

By the mid–19th century most municipal hospitals abandoned their welfare functions and began operating as true hospitals, offering primarily medical care to the poor. A number of private, or voluntary, hospitals also provided care to the poor. Not until the late 19th and early 20th centuries did the middle class use hospital facilities.

Indianapolis opened its first hospital during the CIVIL WAR. The Indianapolis City Hospital (now WISHARD MEMORIAL HOSPITAL) was used by the federal government to care for sick and wounded soldiers. After the war, the city assumed control of the facility and operated it as a charity hospital that provided care for the indigent. Like city hospitals elsewhere, the institution was constantly overcrowded and chronically underfunded.

The late 19th and early 20th centuries witnessed the expansion of City Hospital and the opening of a number of other hospitals to provide better care for those considered the worthy poor, as well as for paying patients. The Daughters of Charity of the St. Vincent de Paul Society established the St. Vincent Infirmary (later ST. VINCENT HOSPITAL) in 1881. In 1899 Protestant Deaconess Hospital and Home for the Aged (later known as the Indiana Christian Hospital and Clinic) opened. The Epworth League dedicated its 65–bed Methodist Episcopal Hospital (now METHODIST HOSPITAL) in 1908. Although all these institutions initially accepted charity cases, the majority of the patients paid for care and consequently the care at these institutions was superior to City Hospital. These new hospitals and hospital addi-

An early City Hospital (now Wishard Memorial Hospital) ambulance.[Indiana Historical Society, #C4148]

tions employed the latest techniques in hospital architecture. Most were laid out in a pavilion style, which maximized ventilation, minimized the crowding of wards, and reduced the risk of infection. Pavilion hospitals usually were sprawling structures, one or two stories in height.

By the early 20th century much of the stigma attached to hospitals had subsided. Hospitals began offering specialty services such as care for contagious patients, obstetrics-gynecology, ophthalmology, gastroenterology, neurology, and urology. Hospitals were also influenced by the tremendous growth of medical science (especially the development of the germ theory and bacteriology) and medical technology, improvements in medical education, and the professionalization of nursing. For the first time, hospitals had the potential for providing better care than could be received at home. They also became an integral part of the medical education system and important facilities for training medical students and nurses, as well as major research centers.

As the demand for hospital services rapidly increased, Indianapolis hospitals could not keep pace with the need for bed space. In 1914 the Poor Sisters of St. Francis Seraph of Perpetual Adoration founded ST. FRANCIS HOSPITAL. This 75–bed charity hospital served the city's rapidly expanding south side and eventually accepted mostly paying patients.

The 1910s and 1920s also witnessed the growth of a number of specialty hospitals funded through private philanthropy. The Robert Long Hospital opened in 1914 as a 138–bed hospital for the care of the rural poor. Although Long donated the original gift for the hospital, the institution relied on the state for operating support. Because of a generous gift from William H. Coleman and his wife, the William H. Coleman Hospital for Women opened in 1927 to provide obstetrical and gynecological services. Through contributions collected by the Riley Memorial Association, the James Whitcomb Riley Hospital for Children opened in 1924. Long, Riley, and Coleman were all used as teaching hospitals for the INDIANA UNIVERSITY SCHOOL OF MEDICINE.

During this time two hospitals served the needs of the mentally ill. The Indiana Hospital for the Insane (later CENTRAL STATE HOSPITAL) opened in 1848 as a state-funded hospital. This hospital remained open continuously to the early 1990s. In 1992, after several scandals and patient deaths at the institution, the governor ordered the facility to close. In 1899 the city opened the Marion County Insane Asylum (known as Julietta) and operated it until 1938. Norways Sanatorium, founded by Albert Sterne, operated in the city's near east side from 1898 to 1957 as a private facility to care for nervous and mental disorders. The latter was the first institution in the state to employ insulin, metrazol, and electric-shock therapy.

Despite all the hospitals in the city, the black population failed to receive proper health care, since Indianapolis City Hospital was the only institution until the 1940s which admitted them. Unable to gain admission to existing hospitals, African-Americans established their own hospitals, including Lincoln Hospital (1909), Charity Hospital (1911), Dr. Ward's Sanatorium (late 1910s; later Dr. Batties' Sanitorium), and Provident Hospital (1921). All these institutions were short-lived since they lacked money and proper facilities to practice modern medicine. In 1927 the black physicians of Indianapolis approached the INDIANAPOLIS FOUNDATION to study the state of black health care in the city. The foundation's report in 1930 concluded that Indianapolis City Hospital's facilities were woefully inadequate to care for blacks, and it urged that City Hospital construct a separate hospital for them.

The Great Depression had an adverse effect on the city's hospitals, with resources strained to the limit as charity care increased dramatically. Some hospitals were unable to withstand economic hardships. In 1935, after a number of reorganizations, Protestant Deaconess closed its doors. Other hospitals began considering accepting hospitalization insurance, although the state and local medical associations initially opposed it. In 1944 Methodist Hospital became the first Indianapolis hospital to sign an agreement with the Blue Cross Hospital Service.

The world wars also had an effect on local hospitals, especially with staff shortages. After World War I, many individuals became aware of the need for a hospital to care for the veterans. WILLIAM FORTUNE donated land on the near northwest side of the city (on Cold Spring Road) for such a facility. Originally called the General Medical and Surgical Hospital, it opened in 1932 as a model veterans hospital. In 1952 a new veterans facility opened near the medical school complex. The Cold Spring facility was used briefly for the care of tuberculosis patients. Both facilities currently are used for veterans and, although federally funded, both are an integral part of the Indiana University Medical School complex.

The end of World War II marked the beginning of the baby boom, which resulted in a need for more bed space. Demand for hospital bed space also occurred because of the growth of hospital insurance and the advances made in surgery.

Concerned about the lack of hospital bed space, the INDIANAPOLIS MEDICAL SOCIETY urged the community to take action. In 1951 a group of local businessmen formed the Indianapolis Hospital Development Association and named Edward Gallahue as its president. This represented the first attempt to systematize hospital development within Indianapolis. After assessing the city's hospital needs, the association undertook a $12 million campaign to add 825 hospital beds by 1975. To participate in the campaign, however, hospitals could not discriminate by race. Hospitals which had previously not admitted blacks (e.g., Methodist, St. Francis, Norways) began admitting them. The 1963 explosion at the Coliseum also pointed to the need for additional hospital bed space within the city.

Out of this campaign, many local hospitals added bed space. Also, COMMUNITY HOSPITAL

Hospitals, 1992	Year Founded	Number of Licensed Beds
Methodist Hospital of Indiana Inc.	1908	1,120
St. Vincent Hosp./ Health Care Center[1]	1881	892
Community Hospital East	1956	804
Indiana University Medical Center	1914	692[2]
William N. Wishard Memorial Hospital	1859	618
Richard L. Roudebush V.A. Medical	1932	553
St. Francis Hospital Center	1914	540
Winona Memorial Hospital	1965	405
Community Hospital North	1985	225
Humana Women's Hospital– Indpls.	1983	182
Community Hospital South	1963	150
Westview Hospital	1961	120
Lifelines of Indianapolis	1987	59

[1] Includes Indianapolis, Carmel, and Stress Center hospitals; statistics are for fiscal year 7/1–6/30.

[2] Excludes newborn treatment. Sources: Individual hospitals and the Indiana State Department of Health

opened in 1956 as a 300–bed facility. The money for that hospital was raised exclusively through private donations from eastside residents. In 1952 the state opened the first psychopathic hospital, LaRue Carter, and opened a new facility on the medical school campus in 1971. Also in 1956 Dr. Joseph E. Walther founded Winona Memorial Clinic (now WINONA MEMORIAL HOSPITAL), a voluntary hospital funded totally through private donations. Winona specialized in medical and surgical cases. In 1964 construction was begun on a much larger facility (280 beds) just north of the clinic. Although the construction of Winona Hospital increased the bed space in Indianapolis, it was not part of the citywide fund-raising campaign for hospitals.

In the 1960s, with the enactment of Medicare (1965), the health care industry witnessed dramatic growth. The government paid for the medical care of the elderly, and physicians set fees arbitrarily. The result was increased hospital admissions, new clinics, and skyrocketing medical costs. Health insurance premiums rose dramatically.

To control costs the federal government in 1983 set prices in advance based on the expense of medical procedures. To implement this they established diagnosis related groups (DRGs). DRGs created problems for the hospital and for the physician. If a person took a longer period of time to recover from an illness, the hospital paid the difference. As a result, hospital admissions declined and the city was left with excess bed space.

Thus, 1983 and 1984 were very lean years for local hospitals; many cut staff or downsized their operations. Other hospitals sought new markets, offering specialized medical care and wellness programs. Methodist, the largest hospital in Indiana, became known for its treatment of heart disease, cancer, and diabetes, its emergency medicine and trauma center, the Midwest Eye Institute, and organ transplantation. Indiana University Hospital and Medical Center specialized in cancer, cardiac, and neonatal care, treatment for hypertension, neurosurgery, and rheumatology. St. Vincent Hospital became recognized for its heart institute, family life center, vascular center, and the specialties of sports medicine, oncology-biotherapy, geriatrics, and occupational health. Community Hospital's specialties include neurology, cardiovascular programs, and oncology. Wishard Hospital's burn and trauma units are among the best in the nation. The Winona Memorial Hospital has the Walther Cancer Institute, adult, child, and adolescent psychiatric services, and a diabetic unit.

The 1970s and 1980s also saw the development of a number of specialty hospitals including Westview (opened in 1975) for osteopathic medicine, New Hope of Indiana (a treatment facility for mentally and physically handicapped children that opened in 1978), Humana Women's Hospital (the first for-profit hospital, which opened in 1983, now the Women's Hospital–Indianapolis), Lifelines Hospital (opened in 1987 as a pediatric rehabilitation hospital), Fairbanks Hospital (which opened in 1982 to replace the Cornelia Cole Fairbanks Home) for the treatment of alcoholism, and Charter Hospital (a private hospital specializing in mental health and substance abuse treatment). The major hospitals like St. Vincent and Community opened "branch" hospitals in high-growth areas of the city and surrounding counties. They also opened community health centers and began utilizing outpatient departments to make their health care services more accessible.

KATHERINE MANDUSIC McDONELL

House of Blue Lights. Folk legend. Millionaire Skiles Edward Test (1889–1964) was president of Indianapolis Motor Inns, part-owner of the Test Building on MONUMENT CIRCLE, and heir to the DIAMOND CHAIN COMPANY fortune. In 1913 Test bought the farmhouse at 6700 Fall Creek Road as a home for himself and his first wife. (Test eventually owned hundreds of acres on the northeast side of Indianapolis and donated the land for the Skiles E. Test Elementary School.) An amateur inventor and architect, Test sided the farmhouse in white opaque tile, added glass brick additions, and decorated the interior with glass as well. The trees around the house he strung with blue lights. He also added a three-story bathhouse, with basement, sun deck, and elevator, and a 40–by–80–foot swimming pool, with solar heating system, three-story diving complex, and motorized surf board. Extremely fond of animals, Test created separate dog and cat parks for his hundreds of pets and also maintained a private pet cemetery.

Test was already known for his lavish parties when, in the early 1940s, the "House of Blue Lights" legend began to circulate. In the most common variant, Test was a recluse who kept the body of his wife in a glass coffin surrounded by blue lights and guarded by vicious dogs. Adolescents invaded the property at night to investigate the story in what became a local initiation ritual. Test tolerated the trespassing until the 1950s when the vandalism forced him to erect a fence around the property. As the House of Blue Lights legend spread, vandalism increased. Trespassers set fire to the outbuildings, broke into the house, injured the animals, and on several occasions exploded dynamite on the property.

Following Test's death, a three-day public estate auction in May, 1964, drew over 50,000 souvenir seekers who vied for such items as hundreds of pet caskets, cases of canned food, pairs of shoes, record albums, and nail kegs. The Test estate bequeathed the property, including the house and 86 heavily wooded acres, to the Department of Parks and Recreation. Despite widespread public protest and interest in the structure by the Historic Landmarks Foundation of Indiana, the Board of Parks and Recreation razed the house and all outbuildings on the property in 1978. The site is now being developed as Skiles Test Park.

VICKIE J. WEST

Linda Degh, "The House of Blue Lights in Indianapolis," in *Indiana Folklore: A Reader*, ed. Linda Degh (Bloomington, Ind., 1980), 179–195; Lisa Levin, "The Estate to Top All Estates," *Indianapolis Magazine*, 18 (Feb., 1981), 113–117.

Howard, Roy Wilson (Jan. 1, 1883–Nov. 20, 1964). Internationally known newspaperman. A native of Gano, Ohio, he was the son of a railroad trainman. The family moved to Indianapolis when Howard was 7; at 13, he carried the morning and afternoon newspapers to supplement the family income. During his final two years at MANUAL HIGH SCHOOL, Howard covered scholastic and sports events for the *INDIANAPOLIS NEWS*.

After graduation in 1902 he became sports editor of the *INDIANAPOLIS STAR*. Then, in rapid succession, he became assistant telegraph editor for the *St. Louis Post-Dispatch* (1905), assistant managing editor of the *Cincinnati Post* (1905), and the New York correspondent for Scripps McRae's Ohio newspapers (1906). Several months later Howard was named New York manager of Publishers Press, a struggling wire service purchased by Scripps to compete with the Associated Press. In 1907 he became general news manager of the United Press, a wire service formed that year by consolidating three Scripps news-gathering services.

By 1912 Howard was president of United Press, a position he held until 1920 when he became chairman of the board and business director of the Scripps newspapers. On November 2, 1922, E. W. Scripps, the controlling stockholder of all the properties, changed the concern's name to Scripps Howard. Until his retirement in 1952, Howard worked to expand the newspaper group coast to coast and to strengthen the wire service, which became known as United Press International.

Though he gained respect for his business acumen, he remained a newspaperman. His byline frequently appeared above interviews with the world's foremost leaders. His legend is memorialized today at the Roy W. Howard Archive at Indiana University and perpetuated by Scripps Howard through the annual presentation of the Roy W. Howard Awards for Public Service.

SUSAN J. PORTER
Scripps Howard

Scripps Howard Handbook (1948, 1967, 1981); *Scripps Howard News* (1964); *Current Biography: 1940*.

Howard W. Sams and Company. Technical publications firm. Howard W. Sams started his Indianapolis-based publishing company in 1946 when he was unable to convince his employer, the P. R. MALLORY COMPANY, that technical documentation would be a lucrative field. The firm grew with the rise of electronic and computer technology. Its first success was the electronic parts catalog *Photofact*. Used by repair technicians and hobbyists, *Photofact* provided standardized information through detailed photographs and schematic diagrams that took apart and analyzed new technologies. Within four years the company had annual sales of $1 million.

In 1953 Sams began producing books on electronics and by the early 1960s was publishing computer books. During this time Sams also was growing by acquisition, purchasing the Indianapolis-based BOBBS-MERRILL COMPANY in 1958. In 1966 Howard Sams sold his company to New York-based International Telephone and Telegraph. Macmillan purchased Sams from ITT in 1985. Three years later Macmillan became part of British publishing magnate Robert Maxwell's empire. During the late 1980s annual sales were more than $30 million. In February, 1990, Sams was taken private in a leveraged buyout by two top Sams executives, Richard Hauser and Damon Davis. Located on the city's west side, the firm employed some 160 persons in the early 1990s.

DEBORAH B. MARKISOHN

Howe, Thomas Carr (Aug. 5, 1867–May 4, 1934). College president. A native of Clark County, Indiana, Howe moved to Indianapolis in 1889. He received a bachelor's degree from Butler College (now BUTLER UNIVERSITY) in 1889 and an

A.M. degree in 1893. From 1890 to 1892 he attended the University of Berlin and earned a Ph.D. from Harvard University in 1899. From 1890 to 1910 Howe was Armstrong Professor of Germanic Languages at Butler and was dean of the college from 1907 to 1908. In 1908 he became the college's president, serving in this position until 1920. After his retirement, he became president of the Armstrong-Landon Hardware Company of Kokomo.

Throughout his career Howe was active in local Republican politics. In 1905 he represented MARION COUNTY in the Indiana General Assembly. In 1921 he was an unsuccessful mayoral candidate and from 1921 to 1925 was vice-president of the Indianapolis City Planning Commission and Board of Zoning Appeals. He served as president of the state Teachers Retirement Fund Board from 1921 to 1933. Howe was also director of the INDIANAPOLIS WATER COMPANY, member of the Board of Public Health, president of the Disciples of Christ Pension Fund (1932–1934), and president of the CHURCH FEDERATION OF GREATER INDIANAPOLIS (1933). In 1914 he helped sponsor the organization of the local BOY SCOUTS council and served as its first president until 1921. In 1937 Thomas Carr Howe High School was named in his honor.

JEFFERY A. DUVALL

Jacob Piatt Dunn, *Greater Indianapolis* (Chicago, 1910); Indiana Biography Series, Indiana State Library.

Howland, Louis (June 13, 1857–March 26, 1934). Journalist, author, and longtime *Indianapolis News* editor. Born in Indianapolis, Howland was the son of John D. and Desdemona (Harrison) Howland, who had moved to the city from Brookville. An 1879 graduate of Yale University, Howland returned to Indianapolis to study law under John T. Dye. In 1888 Howland moved to New York, where he worked for the Reform Club and later joined the staff of *Forum* magazine.

Howland returned to Indianapolis in 1892 and became an editorial writer for the INDIANAPOLIS NEWS. He was named *News* editor in 1911 and remained in the job until 1934, when he became the newspaper's editor emeritus. Along with his duties as editor, Howland wrote the column "Case and Comment" that appeared each Saturday on the *News'* editorial page. One column, involving the Panama Canal's construction, caused President Theodore Roosevelt to sue the newspaper for libel. A federal court dismissed the charge. Howland is also credited with being the first to suggest Woodrow Wilson as a possible presidential candidate in a 1902 letter to the *News* that was signed "Old-Fashioned Democrat."

Howland, who never married, helped found the INDIANAPOLIS LITERARY CLUB and served as the organization's treasurer from 1883 to 1887, as its secretary from 1895 to 1898, and as its president from 1898 to 1899. He wrote such books as *Day Unto Day* (1911), *Stephen A. Douglas* (1920), *The Mind of Jesus* (1926), *Case and Comment: Meditations of a Layman on the Christian Year* (1927), and *Autobiography of a Cathedral* (1927). He died in Indianapolis.

RAY BOOMHOWER
Indiana Historical Society

Arthur W. Shumaker, *A History of Indiana Literature* (Indianapolis, 1962).

Hubbard, Frank McKinney (Kin) (Sept. 1, 1868–Dec. 26, 1930). Newspaper artist and creator of Abe Martin, the fictional cracker-barrel philosopher whose folksy sayings graced the back page of the *INDIANAPOLIS NEWS* for 26 years. Hubbard's creation was syndicated nationally, appearing in approximately 300 newspapers.

Born in Bellefontaine, Ohio, Hubbard was the youngest of six children born to Thomas and Sarah Jane (Miller) Hubbard. Hubbard's father was editor and publisher of the *Bellefontaine Examiner*, while his mother's father, Capt. John B. Miller, managed a theatrical group. Both men had a strong influence on Hubbard's career.

Hubbard quit school before finishing the seventh grade, going to work in a paint shop. With the election of Grover Cleveland in 1884, Hubbard's father—a staunch Democratic supporter—became Bellefontaine's postmaster. The young Hubbard worked on and off for five years as a clerk in the post office, but also found time to tour the South as a silhouette artist. Encouraged by his mother, Hubbard entered the Jefferson School of Art in Detroit, but dropped out after only a short time.

In 1891, he sent an Indianapolis friend some thumbnail sketches of a minstrel show he had organized in Bellefontaine; the sketches caught the eye of JOHN H. HOLLIDAY, founder of the *Indianapolis News*, who hired Hubbard as an artist for his newspaper at $12 per week. Fired by a new managing editor after three years at the *News*, Hubbard had stints as an artist for the *Cincinnati Tribune*, *Mansfield (Ohio) News*, and INDIANAPOLIS SUN. Rehired by the *Indianapolis News* in 1901, he returned to Indianapolis and four years later married Josephine Jackson.

In his early days on the *News*, Hubbard was chiefly a political caricaturist, furnishing the newspaper with drawings of Indiana legislators, lobbyists, and staff members. While covering the 1904 presidential election, Hubbard began to draw the country character that he would make famous. "Abe Martin"—a smiling fellow with whiskers, big shoes, a black coat, and a hat—first appeared in the newspaper on December 17, 1904. By February, 1905, Hubbard had moved Abe Martin to the fictitious town of Bloom Center in the rugged hill country of Brown County.

Abe Martin was soon delighting the public with such sage wisdom as "It's no disgrace t' be poor, but it might as well be" and "When a fellow says it hain't the money but the principle o' the thing, it's th' money." Through the years, Hubbard populated Bloom Center with other country characters, including spinster Miss Fawn Lippincut; senior citizen Uncle Niles Turner; teacher Professor Alexander Tansey; and editor and publisher of the *Bloom Center Weekly Sliphorn*, Hon. Ex-Editor Cale Fluhart.

In 1910, following an *American Magazine* article by Hoosier humorist George Ade praising the Abe Martin feature, Hubbard received numerous offers to syndicate his character. He eventually signed with the George Matthews Adams Syndicate. A year later, Hubbard began a regular Saturday column in the *News* called "Short Furrows." The feature, which was also syndicated nationally, featured comical stories from Abe Martin and other Bloom Center townspeople.

Kin Hubbard's character Abe Martin first appeared in the *Indianapolis News* on December 17, 1904. [Indiana Historical Society, #5579]

Abe Martin's sayings were first put in book form in 1906, when Hubbard started a yearly tradition by issuing a collection culled from the *News* in time for the Christmas season. Hubbard's creations live today in Brown County State Park, where the park's lodge is named for Abe Martin and each guest cabin features the name of a character from Bloom Center.

RAY BOOMHOWER
Indiana Historical Society

Fred C. Kelly, *The Life and Times of Kin Hubbard* (New York, 1952); David S. Hawes, ed., *The Best of Kin Hubbard* (Bloomington, Ind., 1984).

Hudnut, William H., III, Administration of (1976–1992). William H. Hudnut III, former Second Presbyterian Church minister and 11th

District congressman, became mayor of Indianapolis after a closely contested campaign against Democrat ROBERT V. WELCH. Hudnut succeeded Republican Richard G. Lugar, and became chief executive of a city with a newly merged Indianapolis–Marion County government (UNIGOV), the beginnings of downtown redevelopment, a corrupt police department, and a lackluster image. The city, as Hudnut often repeated, had been "India-NO-place," and he was determined to turn it into "India-SHOW-place."

During the 16 years that Hudnut served as mayor, his personality set the tone for his policy. He was not only a flamboyant showman and promoter, but also a skilled deal maker and conciliator. As mayor, he was equally comfortable playing with children in a city sprinkler as he was performing other duties. However, he was uncomfortable with discord and worked diligently to avoid or diffuse it.

Hudnut's philosophies on municipal administration tested and largely defined Indianapolis governance under Unigov. Above all, he believed that the mayor should formulate policy and delegate its implementation to others. In his annual State of the City address, given to the Chamber of Commerce and Rotary Club, he set broad goals and then monitored how his department directors reached them. With those not directly under his authority, Hudnut acted as a willing bargaining partner in order to achieve his vision of the city.

Corresponding to the most up-to-date municipal governance theories, Hudnut's policies often took on a consciously "entrepreneurial spirit," adopting some of the aggressive tactics of private business. By carefully analyzing the city's assets, his administration sought to create a "market niche" for Indianapolis in attracting economic development. He also encouraged taking calculated risks and was not afraid of raising taxes and issuing municipal bonds to pay for worthwhile capital improvement projects. Yet he maintained a watchful eye on the city's AAA bond rating and did not believe in running the city government on a deficit budget. He also instituted better management, public employee training, and fiscal review policies for all city departments.

Hudnut played advocate for the city's needs and conducted extensive public relations campaigns among state and federal government officials as well as private business and social leaders. Rising to the presidency of the National Association of Cities and Towns, Hudnut was not only successful in forming extensive contacts for the city, but he also won national media attention for Indianapolis. The INDIANAPOLIS ECONOMIC DEVELOPMENT CORPORATION and the INDIANAPOLIS PROJECT, which he organized soon after taking office, were also very successful in building national recognition and partnerships.

Another characteristic of the Hudnut administration was a penchant for coalition building. Often labeled "public-private partnerships," these coalitions provided funding and expertise for city development projects, programs, and services during an era of declining federal grants and subsidies. One of the most influential of these coalition groups was the CORPORATE COMMUNITY COUNCIL, a group of business leaders who also served as financial advisors.

Hudnut also expanded the use of the GREATER INDIANAPOLIS PROGRESS COMMITTEE (GIPC) as a consultative body. GIPC, originally organized by Mayor John J. Barton in the 1960s, consisted of a select group of Indianapolis business and civic leaders whose committees and related taskforces conducted studies and made recommendations to Hudnut on all the major issues during his tenure as mayor. Hudnut was often criticized for this closed-door process of decision making, even after he attempted to make it more inclusionary toward the end of his tenure.

As mayor Hudnut focused much of his effort on projects that provided visible gains in jobs, broadened the tax base, and maintained law and order. In this way, economic development became the first and primary goal of his administration. He paid special attention to the downtown area, to keep the city, he said, from becoming a doughnut with development only in the suburban ring and with an empty hole in the middle. To retain downtown businesses and attract new ones the city devised competitive benefit packages, including tax incentives, job training programs, and infrastructure improvements, and aggressively sought development projects. This focus on downtown development drew many critics, however, who argued that other geographic areas were ignored and that the amount spent on these projects did not produce a good return on the city's investment.

During Hudnut's four terms as mayor, there were over 30 large downtown building and beautification projects, including the renovation of MONUMENT CIRCLE and UNION STATION, the expansion of IUPUI and the IU Medical Center, additions to the INDIANA CONVENTION CENTER, and the construction of several office buildings, all of which transformed the downtown skyline. Additionally, several large businesses, including Eli Lilly and Company and American United Life, committed to building and staying in Indianapolis, while the Hudnut administration attracted a U.S. Postal Service mail sorting hub and a United Airlines maintenance center to the city. Possibly reaching development saturation by the early 1990s, the much-touted CIRCLE CENTRE MALL project was stalled in the funding stage when Hudnut left office in 1991.

Tied to downtown development, a second economic development tool was the marketing of Indianapolis as a "sports capital." After forming the INDIANA SPORTS CORPORATION to direct and implement the sports strategy, Indianapolis succeeded in building several sports-related structures, such as the HOOSIER DOME, Indianapolis Sports Center (now the Indianapolis Tennis Center), IUPUI Natatorium, and the Major Taylor Velodrome, all of which hosted annual national events and allowed the city to attract huge amateur sporting events, including the NATIONAL SPORTS FESTIVAL (1982) and the PAN AMERICAN GAMES (1987). Hudnut also lured the NFL Baltimore Colts as well as many national sports headquarters, such as the U.S. Gymnastics Association and U.S. Rowing. While these sports projects brought exposure to Indianapolis, Hudnut's critics argued that, for all the cost to city taxpayers, the revenue produced by the projects reflected a small portion of the city's total economy and attracted only low-paying service jobs.

In order to ensure the image of a "city that works," public safety was a constant concern of the Hudnut administration. Hudnut quickly reorganized the police department upon becoming mayor, focusing on professionalizing the department by removing waste and politics from its operation. New programs, such as Crime Watch and the Citizens Taskforce on Crime, began to show a commitment to decentralized policing. While he implemented an affirmative action policy citywide, Hudnut set specific goals for the police and fire departments, targets which brought a substantial number of minority and women officers to both forces by the end of his fourth term. Despite all the changes he brought, Hudnut and the department faced several charges of police brutality as evidenced by the MICHAEL TAYLOR CASE (1987).

The Hudnut administration put a high priority on environmental issues. Early on, it created a Clean City Committee and implemented a city beautification program. It was the first in the nation to institute a full-time environmental court in 1978, and that same year the wastewater treatment plant was updated. After community dissatisfaction with a proposed new garbage dump in 1984, the administration sponsored the construction of the state-of-the-art waste-to-energy incinerator, completed in 1988. The city also built a sludge handling facility and implemented a sewer maintenance program. By the end of his administration, Indianapolis had greatly lowered air and water pollution levels and in some areas bettered federal compliance rates.

Other city responsibilities—health and human services, neighborhoods, public transportation, housing, parks, and education—fell lower in the Hudnut administration's priorities. These issues were addressed most often when problems could no longer be ignored or when necessary to attract economic development. Infant mortality did not become a priority until Indianapolis was cited as having the highest rate in the nation, but then the city coordinated an effective CAMPAIGN FOR HEALTHY BABIES. Hudnut allocated very few resources to joint projects with the independent board of school commissioners and became directly involved only when disputes arose, such as with the desegregation busing plan, or when the future reputation of INDIANAPOLIS PUBLIC SCHOOLS threatened economic development. Similarly, the Hudnut administration placed less emphasis on neighborhood issues such as in community services, neighborhood infrastructure, and low-to-moderate income housing.

The 16–year Hudnut administration adopted priorities that favored downtown economic development, big business, bricks-and-mortar projects, sports, and public relations, sometimes at the expense of human services. While his efforts brought mixed results, Indianapolis during the Hudnut administration earned the reputation of a well-run, progressive, and livable city. Hudnut, who served longer in the office than any other Indianapolis mayor, chose not to run for a fifth term after losing to Joseph H. Hogsett in the race for Indiana secretary of state in 1990.

MICHELLE D. HALE

William H. Hudnut III and Theresa Kenworthy-Bennett, eds., *The Hudnut Years in Indianapolis* (Bloomington, Ind., 1995).

Hudson Institute. Center for public policy research and analysis. The institute has no partisan political positions; its main tenets are skepticism about conventional wisdom, belief in free markets and free institutions, and optimism about mankind's ability to solve its problems.

The Hudson Institute moved to Indianapolis in 1984 from Croton-on-Hudson, in New York, where it had been located since its founding in 1961 by the late Herman Kahn. After Kahn's death in 1983, Hudson's trustees felt that the institute's future depended on its relocation to "a community more supportive of the organization and its mission." So when Indianapolis leaders in the business and political sectors, backed by strong support from Indiana and Purdue universities and LILLY ENDOWMENT, made an appealing offer to Hudson's trustees, they accepted.

Hudson operated out of offices on the INDIANA UNIVERSITY–PURDUE UNIVERSITY AT INDIANAPOLIS campus until permanent headquarters were found in 1986 in the historic STOUGHTON FLETCHER II mansion in the Windridge area on the city's northeast side. Originally called Laurel Hall when it was built for $2 million in 1916 by the scion of the Indianapolis banking family, the mansion served as home for Ladywood School and R. V. Welch's Manor House before welcoming 50+ staffers and researchers into its spacious quarters and being rechristened "The Herman Kahn Center of the Hudson Institute."

The institute's work originally centered upon predicting future trends and building a strong national defense capable of effective nuclear deterrence. It now has expertise in subjects ranging from economic development and health care to global food policy and urban affairs. In the 1990s Hudson has lent technical assistance to former Soviet bloc European countries. Hudson scholars regularly publish briefings, reports, articles, and books. One of the institute's major projects for the 1990s is "The Modern Red Schoolhouse," an effort to revitalize American education by building innovative schools in several school districts in Indiana, Arizona, New York, and North Carolina.

The Hudson Institute's funding comes primarily from government contracts and private sector grants from corporations, foundations, and individuals. The organization also has offices in Washington, D.C., and Montreal, Canada.

WILLIAM H. HUDNUT III
The Hudson Institute

Hugh J. Baker and Company. Fabricator of structural and reinforcing steel and reinforced concrete. In 1910 Hugh Baker, an Ohio native, established a consulting engineer's office in Indianapolis. The following year he formed the Fireproofing Company, a structural steel firm, with his brother-in-law, J. Ralph Fenstermaker. In 1918 the two businesses consolidated as Hugh J. Baker and Company. The firm furnished steel building products for many Indianapolis buildings; among them were the Hume-Mansur Building and the CIRCLE THEATRE. In 1921 the company began Baker Forms, which constructed wood forms for concrete joists for such buildings as L. S. AYRES AND COMPANY, the Test Building, and the CIRCLE TOWER. When Baker died in 1938 Fenstermaker continued the business, which grew into a multimillion-dollar company based at 602 West McCarty Street. During World War II Baker and Company devoted 95 percent of its production to war-related products, supplying the army with treadways for infantry support bridges.

By 1980 the company was one of the largest independent fabricators of structural and reinforcing steel in the country. Its structural steel supports many of Indianapolis' most prominent buildings, among which are the Indiana University Natatorium and the INDIANAPOLIS MOTOR SPEEDWAY.

In 1986 the company sold Baker Forms to a Cincinnati, Ohio, firm and the following year it sold a second division to a New Jersey corporation. Baker and Company executives purchased the remaining assets in 1987 and formed Farnsworth Steel. The new firm retained many of the former employees, as well as Baker's Farnsworth Avenue plant. In 1993 Farnsworth Steel remains a successful steel fabrication firm with annual sales of $10 to $11 million.

CONNIE J. ZEIGLER

Humane Society of Indianapolis. Animal shelter. In 1905, a group of concerned citizens founded the Indianapolis Humane Society to prevent cruelty to children, animals, and other sentient beings. The society functioned for many years with limited funds and low visibility. A bequest from the estate of Mary Powell Crume provided the means to purchase the grounds of the Indiana Society for the Prevention of Cruelty to Animals on North Michigan Road and in 1967 the Humane Society had its first shelter facility. Focusing only on animals, the society began kennel operations, adoption and education programs, and rescue and investigation services. In 1990, a new facility was built and a new mission adopted that called for providing shelter to lost and homeless animals, educating the community about the humane care and treatment of all animals, and advocating animal welfare.

An average of 13,000 animals are brought to the society annually, with 30 percent finding new homes. Expanded services include 24–hour rescue, dog obedience classes, animal behavior seminars, resources for all animal-related problems, and cooperative programs with veterinarians to provide health care and reduce the overpopulation of domestic animals. Income for an annual budget of $920,000 comes from donations, fees for service, trusts, and an endowment.

MARSHA SPRING
Humane Society of Indianapolis

The Hungarian Club held its 1926 Grape Harvest Dance in Gasnik Hall in the Haughville neighborhood.
[Indiana Historical Society, #C5803]

Hungarians. Before World War I over 1,000 Hungarians and their children lived in Indianapolis. Like other eastern European immigrants they found work at KINGAN AND COMPANY meatpackers or in the foundries of HAUGHVILLE. About one half of them lived around Kingan's where a Protestant chapel stood nearby on Geisendorff Street; about one quarter of the Hungarians resided in Haughville. In 1904 Hungarian Catholics donated the St. Elizabeth of Hungary stained-glass window, which bears the city's only public inscription in the Hungarian language, to St. Anthony's Catholic Church. The Hungarian Reformed community also donated a baptismal font to the church.

In 1920 over 3 percent of the state's Hungarian-born lived in Indianapolis. Thereafter the Hungarian community moved out of the pocket near Kingan's and from the MILITARY PARK area to Haughville. By 1940 community life centered on Hungarian Hall at 1019 Sharon Avenue, home of the Arpad Society. Enlarged after refugees from the 1956 revolution arrived here, the society welcomed Ferenc Nagy, Hungary's last non-Communist premier, when he addressed a Marian College convocation in 1967. In 1990 approximately 3,000 Marion County residents are Hungarian immigrants or their descendants.

JAMES J. DIVITA
Marian College

Hunt, George Edwin (Apr. 29, 1864–July 11, 1914). Dentist and second dean of the Indiana Dental College. Born and educated in Indianapolis, Hunt completed a two-year course in civil engineering at Indiana Asbury (now DePauw) University. After attending the University of Michigan and working with railroad construction in Florida for four years, he returned to study at the Indiana Dental College, graduating in 1890. He also obtained his degree in medicine from Indiana Medical College in 1892. Hunt established a dental practice in the city and joined the board of the Indiana Dental College, which was begun and directed by his father, PHINIUS G. C. HUNT. In 1895 he assisted his father in acquiring the college's stock, and became secretary of the school as well as professor of dental pathology and therapeutics.

Following his father's death Hunt became dean of the college, which became part of the newly established University of Indianapolis (a short-lived confederation of Butler College, the Medical College of Indiana, and the Indiana Law School). In 1898 he founded the *Indiana Dental Journal*, a monthly publication which he edited until December, 1900; he later edited the *Journal of Oral Hygiene*. In 1904–1905 colleague and college co-owner Dr. Harry Hicks sued Hunt, charging him with fraudulent issuance of stock. Resulting from an out-of-court settlement, Hunt acquired the school's stock and its equipment, while Hicks obtained the title to the school building. Hunt continued as dean of the college until his death; his widow retained ownership of the school.

Besides his involvement in professional organizations, Hunt was active in numerous civic and fraternal groups. He was secretary of the Commercial Club (July, 1901–February, 1903) during which time he assisted in securing the establishment of FORT BENJAMIN HARRISON. Between 1902 and 1906 he helped found and direct the Citizen's League, which promoted the election of honest and responsible public officials.

MAYNARD K. HINE
Indiana University–Purdue University,
Indianapolis

Jack D. Carr, "History of Dental Education in Indiana," *Indiana Medical History Quarterly* (Sept., 1978); Jacob Piatt Dunn, *Greater Indianapolis* (Chicago, 1910).

Hunt, Lester M. (Nov. 21, 1894–June 14, 1962). Former political editor and writer for the *Indianapolis Star*. Born in Minneapolis and educated in New York City, Hunt had a colorful career spanning 48 years on newspapers in several states. Among fellow journalists, he was known as a "newspaperman's newspaperman," someone who could cover any kind of story with skill and thoroughness.

Hunt began his career with the *Daily Chautauquan* in New York, then worked for papers on the east and west coasts. He spent 20 years in the state of Washington covering top stories and writing exposes on local crime and corruption.

In 1941 he moved to Indianapolis and became editor of the Teamsters' magazine. EUGENE C. PULLIAM hired him in 1948 at the *INDIANAPOLIS STAR*, where he worked as chief political writer until his death. Hunt attracted national attention in the early 1950s in a series of articles campaigning against the secrecy of welfare records. This series (the accuracy of which was challenged) prompted passage of the Hughes Anti-Secrecy Act, which opened state and local documents to the public. He also wrote about highway scandals in the administration of Governor George Craig and election frauds in Lake County.

CATHLEEN F. DONNELLY

Indianapolis Star, June 15, 1962; *Indianapolis Times*, Feb. 8, 9, 19, 1951.

Hunt, Phinius George Canning (June 16, 1827–Apr. 24, 1896). Dentist; founder of the Indiana Dental College and professional dental associations. A native of Champaign County, Ohio, Hunt moved with his family to Wayne County, Indiana, in 1830. At age 19 he apprenticed under his brother David, a dentist in Indianapolis. After David's death in 1848, Phinius continued the practice located on the Circle. Interested in elevating the state's dental standards, Hunt was a founder of the Indiana State Dental Association in 1858 and served as its president (1861–1864, 1871). In 1879 he helped to establish the Indiana Dental College, located at 147 East Market Street, and became its first dean. In 1895 Hunt joined with his son, Dr. GEORGE EDWIN HUNT, and Dr.

Harry Hicks and his sister, Mary, to acquire the college through a stock purchase. Elected as president of the board, Hunt oversaw the implementation of a progressive dental curriculum, which included studies in porcelain work, prosthetic techniques, and bacteriology. He was instrumental in organizing the State Board of Dental Examiners to monitor dental practice statewide and served as its first president (1879–1895). He also was president of the American Dental Association (1872–1873).

MAYNARD K. HINE
Indiana University–Purdue University,
Indianapolis

Jack D. Carr, "History of Dental Education in Indiana," *Indiana Medical History Quarterly* (Sept., 1978); *Indianapolis News*, Apr. 24, 1896.

Hunter, Frank Baldwin (June 17, 1883–Jan. 5, 1958). Indianapolis architect and swimming pool designer. Born in Covington, Kentucky, Hunter moved to Indianapolis in 1889 with his parents. His father, George F. Hunter, was a sales representative for a commercial printer in Cincinnati and had found employment with the BURFORD PRINTING COMPANY in Indianapolis.

Frank Hunter attended public high schools, the Classical Art School, and MANUAL HIGH SCHOOL specializing in art. After a brief employment with Preston C. Rubush (who with Frank's brother, Edgar O. Hunter, soon formed the architectural firm RUBUSH AND HUNTER), he became a draftsman in the office of J. W. Gaddis, Vincennes, Indiana, and assisted Gaddis in designing the current Huntington County and Putnam County courthouses.

Frank returned to Indianapolis and established his own practice in 1907. Although never achieving the reputation of his brother's firm, he did make several important contributions to the built environment of Indianapolis. Some of his larger commissions include the FOUNTAIN SQUARE Theatre, the Ambassador Apartments, and the St. James Courts Apartments. In 1922 he was appointed "official architect" of the City of Indianapolis, although the significance of this title is unknown.

Frank Hunter is best remembered as a residential architect. He designed over 600 such buildings and specialized in stucco construction and the use of insulation. Interior features such as patented wallboard and modern kitchens (including electric refrigerators) were advanced for the period. Most of his residences are located in the MERIDIAN-KESSLER and BUTLER-TARKINGTON neighborhoods. Hunter's work cannot be classified as any particular style; instead, he was equally talented at all the architectural styles of the early 1900s. Hunter even custom-designed an imitation of a Frank Lloyd Wright house for one client (the Shea-Markun House, 4366 N. Meridian Street) while providing Tudor Revival designs for others.

Frank Hunter is also remembered as the inventor of the Hunter Seashore Pool, a saucer-shaped pool with sand beach. Along with his brother Edgar, he built a number of public pools to this design in Indiana as well as neighboring states.

Frank Baldwin Hunter retired from architectural practice in 1942; in 1948 he moved to Nashville, Indiana, becoming an amateur artist. Although retired, he designed several buildings in the Nashville area before his death.

PAUL C. DIEBOLD
Division of Historic Preservation
and Archaeology,
Indiana Department of Natural Resources

Paul Donald Brown, *Indianapolis Men of Affairs* (Indianapolis, 1923).

Hurty, John Newell (Feb. 21, 1852–Mar. 27, 1925). Pharmacist, medical educator, public health advocate, state legislator. Born in Lebanon, Ohio, Hurty attended both the Philadelphia College of Pharmacy (1871–1872) and the Franklin Institute (1871–1873) before graduating from the Medical College of Indiana (1891). Settling in Indianapolis in 1873, he served as chief chemist and drug foreman at Johnston & Lilly until 1879. In 1879 Hurty opened a drugstore (Hurty's Drugstore) at the corner of Ohio and Pennsylvania streets. In the basement below and later in an extra room to the north, he set up a chemistry laboratory, the first of its kind in Indiana.

Following his appointment as secretary of the State Board of Health and as state health commissioner in 1896, Hurty wrote the first comprehensive pure food and drug law passed by any organized government. Covering all medicines, antiseptics, disinfectants, and cosmetics, as well as confectionery, condiments, and all "articles used for food or drink by man," the law provided for a multitude of practices or offenses through which a food or drug might be deemed "adulterated." It was passed by the Indiana legislature in 1899 and preceded federal food and drug legislation by seven years. His efforts led to many other advances, including: methods for recording vital statistics adopted as a model by the Department of Health in Washington; the passage of more than 20 public health laws by the Indiana General Assembly; a silver medal for excellence in health programs awarded to the Indiana State Board of Health at the Paris International Exposition in 1900, a bronze medal at the St. Louis Exposition in 1904, and the gold medal in 1907 at the Jamestown Exposition.

Having served 26 years as both secretary of the State Board of Health and as state health commissioner, Hurty retired in 1922 in order to run for the Indiana House of Representatives, where he served one term. In 1911 he served as vice-president of the American Medical Association and in 1912 he became the president of the American Public Health Association. He was the author of *Life with Health* (1902).

LUCRETIA ANN SAUNDERS
Indiana State Board of Health (retired)

Thurman B. Rice, *The Hoosier Health Officer: A Biography of Dr. John N. Hurty* (Indianapolis, 1946).

Hyman, Max Robinson (Mar. 16, 1859– Apr. 28, 1927). Journalist and publisher. Born in Edinburgh, Indiana, the son of Robert and Helena Hyman, he moved to Indianapolis with his family in 1862. Hyman began his journalism career as a reporter for the *Indianapolis Herald*, which he later operated with his brother Ben from 1887 to 1889. Before that acquisition, the Hyman brothers published *The Scissors* (1883–1884), a local weekly humorous digest that printed early works of the WESTERN ASSOCIATION OF WRITERS, including those of JAMES WHITCOMB RILEY and Edward Eggleston. He later worked for the *INDIANA STATE SENTINEL* and *INDIANA JOURNAL* in editorial and advertising positions. Before his death, he served as editor of the homebuilders' section of the *INDIANAPOLIS STAR*.

Hyman was active in publishing local histories. Between 1897 and 1909, he edited and published four editions of *Hyman's Handbook of Indianapolis*, a historical, industrial, and commercial review of the city. His publishing business, M. R. Hyman Co., also printed *Indianapolis; an Outline History and Description of the Hoosier Capital* for the state's centennial in 1916.

Hyman was keenly interested in civic improvements for Indianapolis. He was an early advocate for a downtown municipal "coliseum" and one of the founders of the Indianapolis Military Band. Hyman was a charter member of the Monument Masonic Lodge and a member of the Indianapolis Hebrew Congregation.

SHERYL D. VANDERSTEL

R. E. Banta, *Indiana Authors and Their Books* (Crawfordsville, Ind., 1949); *Indianapolis Star*, Apr. 29, 1927.

Ice, Harry T. (Oct. 17, 1904–Sept. 8, 1982). Born in Paulding, Ohio, Ice moved to Indianapolis in 1918, graduated from BUTLER UNIVERSITY in 1926, and earned his law degree at Harvard University and passed the Indiana bar in 1929. He joined the firm that became Ice Miller Donadio & Ryan in 1929 and became a partner in 1934, a position he retained until 1982. Ice Miller Donadio & Ryan is recognized in major financial markets as a leading bond counselor and its activities have affected the city and the state. In 1972, Ice served as special counsel to the Indiana attorney general in successful defense of the state financing plan for public schools against a lawsuit challenging its constitutionality. He served on the boards of many local, state, and national businesses, organizations, and philanthropic concerns. He was vice-president of the United States Chamber of Commerce (1937–1938), trustee of the Indiana State Reformatory at Pendleton (1939–1942), trustee of the Boys School at Plainfield (1945–1949), and president of FLANNER HOUSE (1950–1952). Directorships included the Associated Colleges in Indiana, UNITED WAY of Greater Indianapolis, GREATER INDIANAPOLIS PROGRESS COMMITTEE, Crossroads of America Council of Boy Scouts of America, YWCA, Indiana Chamber of Commerce, and Indianapolis CHAMBER OF COMMERCE. He was a member of the Constitutional Revision Commission, Indiana Commission on Higher Education, Commission on State Taxation and Financing Policy, and chairman of the Indiana Ethics and Conflicts of Interests Commission.

JOAN CUNNINGHAM

Indianapolis Star, Sept. 9, 1982; *Who Was Who in America.*

ICLU. See Indiana Civil Liberties Union

IFD. See Indianapolis Fire Department

IHSAA. See Indiana High School Athletic Association

Illinois Central Gulf Railroad. The section of this large railroad system serving Indianapolis is a composite of several short coal roads extending from southeastern Illinois through southwestern Indiana to Indianapolis. Completed to Indianapolis in 1907, the line enters the city from the southwest, follows the east side of White River, and continues almost due north along the bed of POGUE'S RUN to its Wisconsin Street yards. Although during the early years trains on this line hauled passengers and many other commodities besides coal, it was and is today essentially a coal road. An early Indianapolis city ordinance stipulated that the predecessor of this line was obliged to deliver Indiana-mined coal to Indianapolis at a rate not to exceed one-half cent per ton-mile. Along with coal, grain is a principal commodity hauled into Indianapolis over this line.

VICTOR M. BOGLE
Indiana University, Kokomo

J. David Baker, *The Postal History of Indiana* (Louisville, Ky., n.d.).

IMAGIS. The Indianapolis Mapping and Geographic Infrastructure System (IMAGIS) was established in 1987 as a consortium of public and private agencies to create a shared computerized map of Indianapolis. The map consolidates above- and below-ground information on the 492 square miles of Marion County and parts of surrounding counties. The area is mapped with an accuracy of a two-foot contour interval that includes 310,000 parcels of land and approximately 3,900 miles of roadway. The satellite-referenced map contains many layers, each of which includes a relational data base with the land fabric of political boundaries, streets, property lines, and physical features. Some of the other layers are dedicated to soils, census data, and zoning. IMAGIS maintains its staff offices and data at INDIANA UNIVERSITY–PURDUE UNIVERSITY, INDIANAPOLIS. The consortium in 1993 had 13 voting member agencies, primarily Unigov departments, county offices, and public utilities.

The geographic data base is one of the largest of its kind in North America.

FREDERICK L. BEIN
Indiana University–Purdue University,
Indianapolis

IMCPL. See Indianapolis-Marion County Public Library

Immigrants' Aid Association. Social service agency. Civic leaders meeting at the Indianapolis COMMERCIAL CLUB in January, 1911, established the Immigrants' Aid Association in response to the needs of the city's growing foreign-born population. Organizers included JOHN H. HOLLIDAY, Judge James A. Collins, and Dr. C. S. Woods, and represented reform movements including housing, public health, juvenile court, and the CHARITY ORGANIZATION SOCIETY. Although foreigners comprised only 8 percent of the Indianapolis population at the time, in the 13th ward they made up one-third, and civic leaders associated this unassimilated alien community with crowding, crime, and disease. The association's efforts for the foreign-born combined protection and coercion: it worked to counteract the influence of the saloon and to eradicate fraudulent savings banks and straw bondsmen who exploited the aliens. It also sought to counteract socialist influences and to integrate the aliens into American life.

In October, 1911, the association opened a settlement, Foreign House, at 617 West Pearl Street. About 60 men a night attended the Foreign House night school, which was staffed by students from the Disciples of Christ Missionary College. In 1913, the association hired social worker Ellen P. Hanes to work with immigrant families, and started a kindergarten and classes in English and domestic science.

The settlement functioned simultaneously as a social service agency and an agency of AMERICANIZATION and Protestant evangelism. However, cultural events and ethnic festivals drew large crowds so that the settlement also helped to keep immigrant culture and customs alive. With the outbreak of the Balkan Wars (1912–1913), the Foreign House went into decline as many foreigners returned to their homelands. Its Americanization and other programs would be taken up vigorously again after 1923, when it was renamed AMERICAN SETTLEMENT and later the MARY RIGG Neighborhood Center.

RUTH HUTCHINSON CROCKER
Auburn University

———

Immigrants' Aid Association annual reports (1911–1912, 1912–1913); John H. Holliday, "The Life of Our Foreign Population" (typescript in Indiana State Library).

INB. See NBD Bank

INB Tower. The INB Tower opened in 1970 on the site of the KNIGHTS OF PYTHIAS BUILDING (demolished, 1967). Designed by Thomas E. Stanley, the structure sits on the south half of the block bounded by Pennsylvania, Ohio, Delaware, and New York streets. The INB Tower was sold to JMB Realty Company of Chicago in 1983. The 33–story aluminum, glass, and marble tower rises from the northeast section of its 4–story colonnaded base to a height 1,221 feet above sea level. Until completion of the AUL TOWER in 1982, it was the state's tallest building. Besides the Indiana National Bank offices, the structure housed a heliport, an observation tower, an auditorium, office space, an 8–level parking garage, several shops, and restaurants. Its walls were a gallery of American artists born after 1834 (the bank's founding date).

Over the years numerous changes have altered the tower. At one time Robert Indiana's LOVE sculpture, a statute of Mercury and two goddesses from atop the bank's old building at 3 Virginia Avenue, and a fountain graced the north plaza. Later a wire-sculpture bison, the bank's logo, sat there. The Picasso tapestry "Volutes" was removed during the marble lobby's 1982 remodeling.

By 1974 several thousand slabs of exterior Italian marble had to be reattached. Then in 1982 Vermont marble, better suited to Indiana's temperatures, was installed. In 1992, following INB's acquisition by NBD BANK, a year-long renovation began and metal panels replaced the marble between the 5th and 36th floors. Atop the tower a band of blue light under an extended cornice highlighted on the east and west facades by a band of white light replaced the Indiana National Bank name. Seven vertical strips of white light extend between the cornice and lighted medallions on the 34th floor.

RITA W. HARLAN

Clipping file "Indiana Banks," Indiana State Library.

Included Towns. Municipalities included in city-county consolidation. The special status of "included towns" was extended to 16 municipalities in the UNIGOV legislation that consolidated the city of Indianapolis and Marion County. Those towns were: Castleton, Clermont, Crows Nest, Cumberland, High Woods, Homecroft, Lynhurst, Meridian Hills, North Crows Nest, Ravenswood, Rocky Ripple, Shore Acres, Spring Hill, Warren Park, Williams Creek, and Wynnedale. Most of these communities originally opposed being included in Unigov.

The included towns are permitted to maintain local governments, adopt and enforce local ordinances, provide local services, and impose local property taxes. The local ordinances of included towns must be consistent with ordinances of the city of Indianapolis and Marion County. In addition, the CITY-COUNTY COUNCIL must approve the issuance of any general obligation bonds by the included towns.

Many of the included towns have chosen not to maintain active governments. Some, such as Castleton, have dissolved. The others generally have town boards that meet informally and infrequently. Most local services are provided by contracting with a private company, a township, the city of Indianapolis, or Marion County. Few of the towns still impose a separate property tax. The included towns receive revenues from distributions of state funds and from the city-county government. Where an active town government is not maintained, a clerk-treasurer usually serves to receive and put to use revenues received by the

town; otherwise, those funds revert to the city-county government.

HARRISON C. NEAL III

Independent Colleges of Indiana Foundation (formerly Associated Colleges of Indiana). Pioneering concept in collective fund raising for independent colleges and universities when founded in 1948 by Frank Sparks, president of Wabash College, Tom Jones, president of Earlham College, and local attorney KURT PANTZER. Sparks, an industrialist from Columbus, Indiana, and one of the founders of Noblitt and Sparks, sold his interest in that firm in early 1930 and came to Indianapolis to study at BUTLER UNIVERSITY. After earning his Ph.D. in economics from the University of Southern California in 1941, he returned to Indiana, at the urging of a group of Indianapolis businessmen, to be president of Wabash College in Crawfordsville. As he stumped the state looking for money for Wabash's all-male student body of 500, he found that he didn't have a broad appeal to businesses.

Sparks' vision of a consortium of private colleges and universities telling their story in the aggregate was realized in the Independent Colleges of Indiana Foundation, a model which has been replicated in many similar associations across the United States. Located in Indianapolis, the organization, formed with 12 charter members, had 29 members in July, 1992, and had raised over $78 million beneficially for independent higher education in the state of Indiana.

The purpose of the foundation is to raise unrestricted operating funds from corporate and foundation entities to keep the dual systems of public and private higher education strong and viable in the Hoosier state. The foundation also administers a continuing education program for independent college development staff, and owns and operates the Indiana Academy, which promotes charitable, scientific, literary, and educational purposes.

HUGH J. BAKER III
Independent Colleges of Indiana Foundation

Independent Turnverein Building (902 North Meridian Street). Architectural landmark. The Independent Turnverein building was constructed in 1914 by architect ADOLPH SCHERRER. Exhibiting both Renaissance and Prairie Style elements, the building is red brick with elaborately carved, arched limestone entrances. Its features include a red tile roof, recessed windows, and an extended eave. The building was originally the headquarters of the Independent Turnverein, a German athletic and social club begun in 1879. In 1921 the Independent Turnverein changed its name to the Independent Athletic Club; later it became the Hoosier Athletic Club. The club experienced serious financial problems in the 1940s, and in 1943 the building was sold at a sheriff's auction for $77,000. Its new owner, George J. Marott, gave the Turnverein to Purdue University two years later. For many years, it housed administrative offices and classrooms for INDIANA UNIVERSITY–PURDUE UNIVERSITY, INDIANAPOLIS.

In the 1980s Stenz Construction Corporation purchased the building and invested over $3 million in its renovation, adding a center atrium. Stenz turned the original ballroom, natatorium, and gymnasium into a full-size penthouse and 52 apartments; many retain the original stained glass windows and walnut woodwork. In 1991 Van Rooy Property purchased the Turnverein Apartments. Home to many professionals who work in or near the MILE SQUARE, the Independent Turnverein building was added to the National Register of Historic Places in 1983.

CONNIE J. ZEIGLER

Indiana Arts Commission. State funding agency for the arts. The Indiana Arts Commission (IAC), headquartered in Indianapolis, was created in July, 1969, to encourage and stimulate the cultural arts in Indiana. Its existence is an outgrowth of the mid–1960s establishment of the National Endowment for the Arts (NEA), which guaranteed state agencies a block grant for operational expenses or program revenues. The IAC is composed of 15 commissioners appointed by the governor to serve without pay for four-year terms. The commissioners are selected to provide representation from various areas of the state and vari-

ous fields of the performing, literary, and visual arts. The IAC establishes the agency's policies and goals, makes final decisions on grant awards and programs, and sells the state legislature on the need for financial support of the arts before each budget session. It elects one of its members yearly to serve as chairman and chief executive officer and is empowered to select an executive director to administer the agency and hire staff as needed. With the monies from the Indiana General Assembly and the NEA, the IAC provides grants and programs of assistance to community arts councils, community groups, cultural organizations, and individual artists.

The IAC has a significant impact on the arts community of Greater Indianapolis. For fiscal year 1993 the commission awarded almost 40 percent of its $2.6 million in grants to organizations in Marion County. Recipients in 1992 included some of the city's largest and most prestigious cultural institutions (INDIANAPOLIS MUSEUM OF ART, INDIANAPOLIS SYMPHONY ORCHESTRA), but also many smaller, less well known arts organization for which IAC support is particularly welcome.

CAROL WEISS

Carol Weiss, "The Indiana Arts Commission," *Arts Indiana*, 11 (Feb., 1989); *1991–92 Annual Report of the Indiana Arts Commission.*

Indiana Avenue. As it evolved, Indiana Avenue became the focal point of the local African-American community's needs, identity, and changing relationship with the rest of the city. Initially called Indiana Street, Indiana Avenue appears on ALEXANDER RALSTON's original plat of the city (1821) as one of four diagonal thoroughfares. It extended northwest from the intersection of Illinois and Ohio streets to end at the corner of the MILE SQUARE. By the early 20th century it extended as far north as 16th Street; its present terminus at 10th Street resulted when the section north of Fall Creek was renamed Stadium Drive.

Early settlers avoided the area because of its proximity to the White River; they considered it a breeding ground for disease-carrying insects. By the mid–1830s the Avenue's residents, mostly

Opened in 1927, the Walker Building on Indiana Avenue, now called the Madame Walker Urban Life Center, Inc., housed several retail shops, restaurants, a theater, and professional offices. [Indiana Historical Society, Bass Collection, #209274F]

German or Irish immigrants plus a few African-Americans, were from poor laboring families who could afford to live nowhere else. For the next several decades most of the businesses along the Avenue were operated by and for the dominant German and Irish majority.

By 1870, however, with 974 African-American residents, one third of the city's total black population, the Avenue was on its way to becoming the premier site for black entrepreneurship and cultural development. The first businesses owned by African-Americans appeared on the 500 block in 1865: Samuel G. Smothers' grocery and William Franklin's peddler shop. Starting in the 1870s the INDIANAPOLIS LEADER, the city's first successful black-owned newspaper, carried ads for a wide variety of Indiana Avenue businesses.

During the early 1900s waves of southern migrants moved into the area and whites increasingly moved out. Most Indiana Avenue residents were employed as domestics or as unskilled laborers in local foundries, factories, or processing plants. A smaller number were middle class housewives, teachers, white collar workers, and professionals. Regardless of class, black residents took a growing pride in "their" Avenue, which was fast becoming a world unto itself in an increasingly segregated Indianapolis.

Correspondingly, African-American owned businesses continued to fill in the blocks nearer to downtown, and newer buildings were constructed heading northward through the 1920s. The 500 block of the Avenue, however, had become the shopping and social center for African-Americans citywide. The more upscale of these businesses served a white clientele too.

The businesses along the Avenue provided all the goods and services available downtown, and some served as residences. By 1916 there were 142 residential units, 33 restaurants, 33 saloons, 26 grocery stores, 17 barber shops and hair stylists, 16 tailors and clothing stores, 14 shoemakers, 13 dry goods stores, several undertakers, a bicycle repair shop, Ward's Sanitorium (a medical facility), and the Plaza Hotel. Some businesses, such as the Martin Brothers' National Jacket Company, Henry L. Sanders' Clothing Manufacturers, and MADAM C. J. WALKER's beauty products company, also employed area residents. There were a few entertainment establishments, including the Two John's Theatre, and professional offices of doctors, lawyers, and a photographer. The INDIANAPOLIS RECORDER relocated its offices to the Avenue in 1920.

Saloons disappeared with the coming of prohibition in 1919, but the Avenue did not become "dry." Soft drink establishments, restaurants, pool halls, smoke shops, and even barber shops served as well-known fronts for gambling and selling bootlegged liquor, patronized by whites and blacks citywide. There were few raids; officials turned a blind eye to illegal activities in return for votes in the next election. Thus, the Avenue developed its own government and home rule with the help of the African-American staffed fire station and police station.

The Walker Building, erected in 1927 on Indiana Avenue at the intersection of West and North streets, crowned the area's development. Named for the millionairess who started the Indianapolis-based hair care company, it housed the Casino and Theatre, professional offices, a beauty college, a drugstore, and the Walker Coffee Pot, a popular restaurant. The building proved to be the centerpiece of the neighborhood; it not only provided a magnificent venue for entertainment but also embodied the residents' ethnic pride and sense of accomplishment.

The Great Depression hastened the turn to entertainment when the economic downturn forced many businesses to close, and residents along the Avenue began to vacate their homes. By the mid–1930s and into the 1940s the Avenue came to be known as "Funky Broadway," "The Yellow Brick Road," and "The Grand Ol' Street," reflecting a new focus on food and entertainment.

Avenue businesses of the time included Joyner's Chili Parlor; the Marble Palace, a hair salon that shared its building with the Masonic temple; Palmer Richardson's P&P Club, featuring miniature golf; Ma Smothers Eatery, serving everything from chitterlings to pumpkin pie; and Henry Flemming's Smoke House, a tobacco shop. There was also Kid Edwards' Record Shop, Floyd Stone's Jumbo Donut Shoppe, Brown's Beanery, and Porter Jones' barbecue stand. In 1938 LOCK-EFIELD GARDENS, a low-income public housing complex, opened, along with a grocer, barber, cleaners, and playground.

At the same time the number of lounges and clubs multiplied, with over 25 clubs on the Avenue by 1940. Indiana Avenue became a stop on the national African-American entertainment circuit thanks in large part to Denver and Sea Ferguson, proprietors of F. Brothers Booking Agency and owners of the Sunset Terrace, the Cotton Club, and Trianon Ballroom. Internationally recognized musicians soon began appearing regularly on the Avenue. These musicians developed the exciting "Indy Sound"— JAZZ that demanded an eclectic ear and informed audiences who knew when to fall silent.

The entertainment establishments centered on the 400 and 500 blocks of Indiana Avenue, many attracting integrated audiences. The Lido, Columbia, Washington, and Hills Indiana theaters all offered live shows, as well as movies, many with African-American casts. At the Cotton Club, Trianon Ballroom, Sunset Terrace, "Dee" Paradise, the Rainbow Palm Gardens, the Mitchellyn, Danny's Dreamland, and others one could hear Count Basie, Jimmie Lunceford, Billy Eckstein, Sarah Vaughn, Cab Calloway, Josephine Baker, Lucky Millinder, Erskine Hawkins, Lionel Hampton, Pooky Johnson, Slide Hampton, David Baker, Freddie Hubbard, and scores of others. Among the hometown legends there was NOBLE SISSLE, ERROLL "Groundhog" GRANDY, WES MONTGOMERY, J. J. Johnson, Leroy Vinnegar, Jimmy Anderson, Earl Walker, and the Inkspots.

By 1950 the Avenue's pace had slowed considerably, and even the legendary Sunset was in financial trouble. In addition to disruptions from World War II, local segregation was lessening and African-Americans were already moving into new neighborhoods farther north, shopping at malls and stores nearer their homes and being entertained elsewhere. Once the lounges and clubs disappeared all that was left on the Avenue was vice, gambling, a few one-night stands by local musicians, and mostly poor residents living in increasingly dilapidated housing.

Starting in the 1950s the city had begun to buy property to the east of the Avenue, eventually clearing it to make way for redevelopment. Meanwhile, the newly formed IUPUI campus was buying residential property to the west of the Avenue, which the city eventually condemned. Despite reassurances to residents and business owners that revitalization would take place, the city rezoned the area for commercial uses and proceeded to build university buildings, parking lots, and interstates.

By 1970 the housing stock had been reduced by half. With the sharp reduction in the number of neighborhood residents, merchants and professionals also moved out. The once-thriving nine-block Avenue was soon reduced to several clusters of structures on the 400 and 500 blocks. In 1968 local businessmen, headed by Willard B. Ransom, established the Indiana Avenue Association. A local community leader, John Ivy Lands, also tried to organize local residents to salvage the neighborhood. Both efforts ultimately failed.

Segments of the African-American community rallied, however, at the threatened closing of Lockefield Gardens in 1973. Local residents formed the Midtown Economic Development and Industrial Corporation (MEDIC) and the MA-DAME WALKER URBAN LIFE CENTER, Inc., and bargained with the city. In 1980 only part of Lockefield Gardens was demolished, with the land being sold to IUPUI, but the money from the land purchase going toward renovating the Walker Building.

Since 1980 MEDIC, the Urban Life Center, and others have become involved in several projects to revitalize Indiana Avenue. In 1987 a local historic preservation group successfully nominated the 500 block to the National Register of Historic Places. The register nomination did not prevent further demolition—the Sunset Cafe was "accidentally" demolished later that year—but it did signal the beginning of serious efforts to preserve and rebuild parts of the Avenue.

Other projects along the Avenue during the 1980s and early 1990s included a housing complex for the elderly, a new headquarters building for SIGMA THETA TAU nursing sorority, restoration of the Ferger Building, rehabilitation of area homes, and several business and residential projects along the CENTRAL CANAL. The Walker Plaza, a three-story office building, was completed in 1987 and was soon fully rented. "500 Place," a retail-office building, and Stewart Center, named to commemorate George Stewart, founder and publisher of the *Indianapolis Recorder*, were both completed in the early 1990s. In all of these projects, black-owned businesses such as Business Opportunities Systems, Inc. (BOS), Oscar Robertson Construction, and architect Walter Blackburn have been partners with outside investors and the neighborhood not-for-profit organizations in planning, construction, and ownership.

MICHELLE D. HALE

Clyde Nickerson Bolden, "Indiana Avenue: Black Entertainment Boulevard" (M.A. thesis, University of Cincinnati, 1981); clipping files, Historic Landmarks Foundation of Indiana state headquarters; Michael Regenold, "An Analysis of the Displacement of the Midtown Community by an Urban Campus" (SC 1881) and Marlene Potter, "Should Indiana Avenue Be Preserved as an Historic Landmark for the Black Community?" (SC 1877), Indiana Historical Society; Duncan Schiedt, *The Jazz State of Indiana* (Pittsboro, Ind., 1977).

Indiana Bell. See Ameritech

Indiana Black Expo (IBE). Nonprofit organization that celebrates African-American history and achievement. Local civic leaders Rev. Andrew J. Brown, Jr., Willard B. Ransom, Jr., and James C. Cummings founded Indiana Black Expo in 1971, modeling it after a similar event initiated by Operation Push in Chicago. It soon grew to surpass the Chicago Expo in size and scope. Headquartered in Indianapolis, the organization has a staff of 18 and is governed by a 35-member board. Expo also relies on hundreds of volunteers, especially during its summer celebration. There are 13 Expo chapters around the state. In 1993 the organization purchased a headquarters building in the 3100 block of North Meridian Street.

The focal point of Indiana Black Expo is the summer celebration held every year in the middle of July. Its various events attract a total attendance of approximately 500,000; it is billed as the largest black event of its kind in the United States. The week-long celebration at the Indiana Convention Center, which concludes IBE, attracts 65,000 people from across the nation. It features symposia, seminars, corporate and organizational booths, educational, economic, religious, and youth forums, a corporate luncheon, employment opportunity fair, talent show, boxing tournament, and a wide variety of entertainment.

Other IBE programs include the Indiana Black Expo Scholarship Fund, established in 1984 to recognize and assist deserving minority students who are pursuing higher education, and the Youth and Telecommunications Workshop, a nine-month communications program developed in 1983 to train youths between the ages of 13–19 in the rudiments of television and cable production. In association with Indiana Sports Corporation, IBE also sponsors the CIRCLE CITY CLASSIC, one of the best attended black collegiate football games in the nation, and cosponsors the "We Can Feed the Hungry" program during the Christmas season.

AUDREY S. GADZEKPO

Indiana Catholic and Record. Religious newspaper. The first *Indiana Catholic* was issued by Joseph P. O'Mahony for the Indiana Catholic Printing and Publishing Company on February 4, 1910. This weekly paper published news for the dioceses of Indianapolis and Fort Wayne. When the company absorbed the *Catholic Columbian-Record* of Columbus, Ohio, in March, 1915, the paper became the *Indiana Catholic and Record*. The journal survived under a series of editors until September, 1960, when it was succeeded by the *Criterion*. Circulation at the time it ceased publication was approximately 42,000.

The *Indiana Catholic and Record*, although privately published, was dedicated to keeping the Catholic family abreast of the principal events, movements, and activities of the church both locally and abroad. Beyond diocesan concerns, the journal sought to incorporate news from outside the church that might affect Catholic life and thought. It was the opinion of O'Mahony and his successors that the lives of many Catholic faithful were being influenced too greatly by the papers that were read and discussed regularly among religious families. It was the job of the diocesan newspapers to introduce subtle religious influence into the home and thus preserve Catholic values.

WILLIAM D. DALTON

Indiana Central University. See University of Indianapolis

Indiana Civil Liberties Union. Private, nonprofit organization concerned with issues related to the Bill of Rights. The Indiana Civil Liberties Union (ICLU), an affiliate of the American Civil Liberties Union (ACLU), was founded in Indianapolis in 1953 and has always maintained its headquarters in the city. Although the group boasts local chapters and members in many areas of the state, Indianapolis has served as the source of many of its leaders, a frequent site for its major meetings, and a generator of a variety of issues on which its efforts have focused.

One of ICLU's most celebrated cases resulted from its efforts to hold its organizational meeting at the Indiana World War Memorial in downtown Indianapolis in November, 1953. The group was banned from the facility as a result of protests by the AMERICAN LEGION and other patriotic groups that alleged ACLU disloyalty and links to communism. Showcased on Edward R. Murrow's CBS television program "See It Now" in 1953, the conflict continued for 20 years until the Indiana Supreme Court ordered the facility opened to the group in October, 1973.

ICLU efforts to publicize and protect Bill of Rights guarantees during the past 40 years have made it both controversial and respected. Its efforts to protect rights of the accused have included instructing local police forces in Indianapolis and negotiating for the establishment of Citizens Review Boards of Police Actions. Many cases undertaken by the ICLU have focused on the rights of individuals, ranging from battles against racial discrimination in the 1950s (which prompted the formation of a local Indianapolis chapter of the ICLU) to suits in behalf of rights of public school students and other juveniles in the 1960s and 1970s. Volunteer attorneys acting for the ICLU have defended rights of conscientious objectors, victims of sexual harassment, and prisoners in local, state, and federal institutions. In the 1980s the group became the first ACLU affiliate in the country to have a task force on the rights of gays and lesbians.

Through the years the ICLU has also undertaken major lawsuits alleging violation of constitutional protections by various governing bodies in the state. A reapportionment case begun in 1959 led to a plan for more equitable distribution of legislative districts. In 1983 the ICLU filed a class action suit which brought to an end the links between political patronage and the state license branch system. One of the group's best known efforts pitted it against the City of Indianapolis in *AMERICAN BOOKSELLERS ASSOCIATION V. HUDNUT* (1984). Arguing for First Amendment guarantees of freedom of the press, the group persuaded Federal District Judge Sarah Evans Barker to overturn a city ordinance banning pornographic materials as violating the civil rights of women. The group's position ultimately prevailed through an appeal to the U.S. Supreme Court.

As the ICLU became more activist in the 1980s, Executive Director Michael L. Gradison and attorney Richard Waples, hired as the group's first full-time legal director in 1986, spearheaded efforts dealing with issues such as the rights of AIDS patients (most notably Indiana native RYAN WHITE), opposition to capital punishment, restricting police use of deadly force, and limiting religious displays on public property. The naming of Gradison's successor, Sheila Suess Kennedy, in 1992 resulted from the group's desire to expand its organizational and financial bases.

REBECCA S. SHOEMAKER
Indiana State University

ICLU newsletter, 1954–present, published under several titles; most complete collection located in Indiana Division, Indiana State Library.

Indiana Convention Center (100 South

Capitol Avenue). The Indiana Convention Center (ICC) opened in 1972 at a cost of $26.1 million in an effort to increase the city's capacity to host large meetings and events. The next year, 19 conventions were held at the ICC. The facility continued to attract an increasing number of events during the next decade until expansion became necessary 12 years after its opening.

The 1984 expansion added the 60,500–seat HOOSIER DOME to the complex, making the Indiana Convention Center & Hoosier Dome (ICCHD) one of two convention centers in the nation that is directly connected to a domed stadium. Two exhibit halls were also added, bringing the total cost to $94.7 million.

By the early 1990s the ICCHD had reached a practical maximum occupancy and again needed to expand its facilities. The $43 million, two-story expansion, begun in January, 1992, and completed in September, 1993, significantly enlarged facilities and upgraded the ICCHD exterior. Meeting space was increased to 127,595 square feet (in 52 meeting rooms), a new lobby and registration area were added, and exhibit space was expanded

The Indiana Convention Center and Hoosier Dome, ca. 1993. [Indianapolis Convention and Visitors Association. Photo by Rob Banayote.]

to 301,500 square feet (including five exhibit halls). The ICCHD now houses the state's largest ballroom, the 36,000–square-foot Sagamore Ballroom, along with two smaller ballrooms.

The 1993 expansion also added skywalks to the Indianapolis Westin and Hyatt Regency hotels, providing conventiongoers with direct access to over 1,000 hotel rooms and 2,700 parking spaces. The expansion and renovation provided the ICCHD with greater flexibility to host multiple large-scale events simultaneously.

In 1992 over 1.7 million people attended events at the ICCHD, including 113 conventions and trade shows. Important events held at the ICCHD include the CIRCLE CITY CLASSIC, INDIANA BLACK EXPO, and the NCAA Final Four. The ICCHD is managed by the CAPITAL IMPROVEMENT BOARD, a public agency.

DEBORAH B. MARKISOHN

Indiana Democrat and State Gazette

(1830–1841). Democratic newspaper. Alexander Morrison, who came to Indianapolis as a state representative from Clark County where he also published the *Republican Statesman*, began publication of the *Indiana Democrat* in April, 1830, in support of President Andrew Jackson. Shortly thereafter he purchased a share of the *Indiana State Gazette*, a pro-Democratic paper, and merged the two under the name *Indiana Democrat and State Gazette*. He later dropped "State Gazette" from the title.

As editor, Morrison was known for a sarcastic style that made opponents wary of challenging him. A four-page weekly, the *Democrat* printed political and foreign news under his direction and occasionally included local items, fiction, and poetry. Morrison sold and repurchased his share in the paper a few times before retiring in May, 1836.

The paper had several owners before NATHANIEL BOLTON, a previous owner, and George Pattison purchased it in May, 1840, and merged it with their *Constitution* in August, 1840. They sold the paper, then named the *Indiana Democrat and the Spirit of the Constitution*, to GEORGE A. AND JACOB P. CHAPMAN in June, 1841, who renamed it the *INDIANA STATE SENTINEL*.

JOAN CUNNINGHAM

Berry R. Sulgrove, *History of Indianapolis and Marion County* (Philadelphia, 1884); John W. Miller, *Indiana Newspaper Bibliography* (Indianapolis, 1982).

Indiana Donors Alliance. A statewide association of grantmakers. The Indiana Donors Alliance (IDA), which is headquartered in Indianapolis, was organized after a 1983 meeting at which representatives of foundations and other grantmaking organizations met to discuss the condition and potential of the state's philanthropic community. Initially guided by a volunteer steering committee composed of executives from Indiana's largest and most active philanthropic organizations, IDA hired its first staff member in 1989, instituted a board of directors in 1990, and acquired 501(c)(3) status under federal tax laws in 1992. IDA's goals are to foster interaction among members of the community of donors, to enhance the quality and quantity of grantmaking, to stimulate development of new foundations and corporate giving programs, to inform and educate grantseekers, and to raise public awareness.

IDA has sponsored statewide conferences and focused workshops; funded a survey of giving and volunteering in Indiana; coordinated the state Give Five program; and launched a pilot program to build community foundations. It publishes the *Directory of Indiana Donors* and a newsletter as well as other informational publications, maintains a resource library, and provides technical assistance. Under the auspices of the Council on Foundations, IDA works with the other regional grantmaking associations in the United States to improve grants management and programs.

In 1993 IDA had a staff of six and an annual budget of $150,000, with approximately 50 percent coming from members' dues, 30 to 40 percent from grants, and the remainder from income-producing activities.

CAROL S. WARNER
Indiana Donors Alliance

Indiana Farmer and **Indiana Farmer and Gardener.** Agricultural journals. Under the sponsorship of the State Board of Agriculture,

the *Indiana Farmer* began in Indianapolis in March, 1836, promoting improved agricultural methods among Hoosier farmers. Moses M. Henkle, formerly publisher of the *Indiana Aurora*, a weekly agricultural journal, served as editor; he was later succeeded by John W. Osborn and Jacob S. Willets. The paper became the *Indiana Farmer and Stock Register* in 1837 and ceased publication in 1841. The *Indiana Farmer and Gardener* began February 1, 1845, as a semimonthly agricultural and horticultural journal and a subsidiary of the INDIANA JOURNAL, published by Samuel Vance B. Noel. HENRY WARD BEECHER, pastor of Second Presbyterian Church, was its first editor. Issued in a 16–page octavo form, the paper kept subscribers apprised of agricultural developments, breeds of animals, improved implements and machines, and horticulture. It also served as the medium through which Beecher criticized Hoosiers for maintaining slovenly habits and for failing to adopt modern methods and implements that would improve the productivity of their farms. Beecher's growing fame added to the popularity of the paper and helped it gain a national reputation. Indianapolis benefited indirectly from Beecher's editorship since he received samples of non-native seeds and nursery stock which he planted in his orchards and flower beds. On January 1, 1846, the *Indiana Farmer and Gardener* merged with the Cincinnati-based *Western Farmer and Gardener*, which allowed Beecher to issue papers under the same name in both cities. The Indianapolis paper garnered over 1,200 subscribers by year's end, but ceased publishing in 1847 when Beecher departed Indianapolis for New York.

A second *Indiana Farmer*, published by J. G. Kingsbury and Company of Indianapolis, ran weekly from April, 1871, to 1916.

SHELLY CHENOWETH

Jane Shaffer Elsmere, *Henry Ward Beecher: The Indiana Years, 1837–1847* (Indianapolis, 1973); *Indiana Farmer and Gardener*, Feb., 1845.

Indiana Federation of Trade and Labor Unions (IFTLU). Statewide federation of labor unions. Originating with members of the INTERNATIONAL TYPOGRAPHICAL UNION No. 1, of

Indianapolis, the IFTLU was organized in the Hoosier capital on September 9, 1885. Only representatives from Indianapolis locals of the KNIGHTS OF LABOR, Moulders, Cigar Makers, and Typographical unions attended this organizational meeting designed to promote cooperation among all Indiana unions. Under the initial leadership of Samuel L. Leffingwell of Indianapolis, the IFTLU sought to improve relations among the state's labor unions, form new locals, lobby for improved factory and labor legislation, and obtain better wages. The second session of the federation met in Indianapolis in June, 1886, following Chicago's Haymarket riot, and attracted 33 delegates from 24 unions who heard Leffingwell criticize labor's indulgence in lawlessness and violence. Up to 1891 the federation held all conventions at Indianapolis; thereafter, annual conventions met in different cities. In 1900 the IFTLU represented over 80 unions, up from 6 in 1885, and had organized more than 60 new locals in Indiana.

Following the creation of the American Federation of Labor (AFL) in 1886, Indiana labor leaders made repeated efforts to affiliate with the new organization, though many members feared the loss of local autonomy. When the IFTLU became the Indiana Federation of Labor (IFL) and joined the AFL on October 8, 1903, membership changed from unrestricted union participation to those affiliated solely with the AFL. Over the ensuing years the IFL became increasingly active in social legislation and political education and action. The IFL was most vocal in 1935 when it accused Indiana Governor Paul McNutt of strikebreaking and establishing a "Fascist-Military-Dictatorship in our state."

When the AFL and the Congress of Industrial Organizations (CIO) merged in 1958, the Hoosier federation became one of the constituent parts of the Indiana State AFL-CIO on May 24 of that year. Currently located in Indianapolis at 1403 West 18th Street, the state organization continues to represent over 180,000 members of 57 international unions.

LARRY HENNINGER

Ralph Walden Van Valer, "The Indiana State Federation of Labor," *Indiana Magazine of History*, 11 (Mar., 1915), 40–58; Dallas Sells, "Organized Labor," in Donald F. Carmony, ed., *Indiana: A Self-Appraisal* (Bloomington, Ind., 1966).

Indiana Gas Company. Indianapolis-based distributor of natural gas. Indiana Gas Company, 1630 North Meridian Street, was organized in September, 1945, by its parent company, PUBLIC SERVICE INDIANA (PSI). The parent company was forced to divest itself of its gas subsidiary to comply with the Public Utilities Holding Company Act (PUHCA) of 1935.

Indiana Gas Company traces its origins to the coal gas era in Indiana. Early predecessors provided manufactured gas to Lafayette (1852) and Terre Haute (1856). Most Indiana cities in the latter half of the 19th century had manufactured gas (also called town gas) plants, and the predecessors of Indiana Gas provided service to communities in the central and southern parts of the state. The discovery of natural gas in the area northeast of Indianapolis during the 1880s created a natural gas distribution industry in the state 30 years prior to the development of the industry elsewhere in the country. The shallow Indiana wells, however, went dry shortly after the turn of the century, and the industry in Indiana returned to a mixture of natural gas from Appalachia and manufactured gas.

By 1912 the predecessors of Indiana Gas had been organized into the gas division of the Interstate Public Service Company. Interstate operated the interurban electric railway between Indianapolis and Louisville and was a part of the Chicago-based utility empire of Samuel Insull. Insull bought up small-town electric and gas utilities across the Midwest. Interstate Public Service was headquartered in the Traction Terminal Building at Market and Illinois streets, and when the first natural gas pipeline from the Kansas and Texas Panhandle gas fields entered Indiana in 1931 the holding company began converting many of its towns to natural gas. The Insull empire, however, was one of the major casualties of the Great Depression, entering bankruptcy in 1932.

The receivership and subsequent passage of the PUHCA dictated that the gas properties would be divested from the electric properties. That occurred in September, 1948, and three years later, the company—then known as Indiana Gas & Water Company—moved to its present offices. Indiana Gas sold its water properties during the early 1960s. The company expanded its service territory dramatically during the 1960s and 1970s, meeting additional gas demand by building underground gas storage fields around the state. In 1973 it purchased the Central Indiana Gas Company from American Natural Resources in Detroit and expanded the company's service territory into east central Indiana.

Like all gas utilities in the United States, the company struggled with late–1970s gas shortages and the resulting run-up in price. Indiana Gas reorganized itself in 1990, partly in response to federal deregulation of the natural gas industry. Indiana Energy, Inc., the new holding company, continued to grow as the decade began by acquiring natural gas companies in Richmond and Terre Haute, expanding its territory to cover 48 counties throughout the lower two thirds of the state. Serving some 357,000 residential, commercial, and business customers, the company employs 1,200 workers in both its Indianapolis and regional offices throughout Indiana.

BILL BECK
Lakeside Writers' Group

John Heiney, *The Story of Indiana Gas Company* (Indianapolis, 1970).

Indiana Gear Works. Manufacturer of precision gears, mainly for helicopters. The company began in 1933 as a partnership of Louis C. Buehler, formerly of the Indianapolis Tool and Manufacturing Company, and his son John L. Buehler, newly graduated from Purdue University. The small firm, located at 1458 East 19th Street, received contracts for airplane gears and in the 1940s became a pioneer maker of gears for helicopters built by Sikorsky Aircraft. From then on a majority of its gross income came from Sikorsky, despite efforts to diversify. Incorporated in 1949, the firm was renamed Buehler Corporation in 1960, shortly before moving most of its operations to a large factory at 3051 North Post Road. The name change reflected a move into turbo-powered boats and racks for storing nu-

clear waste. By 1966 the firm employed 1,500 persons.

After John Buehler retired in 1971 delays in production became a problem, and Sikorsky, while changing product lines, reduced orders. In 1977 the company merged with Maul Technology, Inc., a New Jersey manufacturer of machines for bottle factories. Reorganization specialists made Indiana Gear Works, Inc., later IGW Systems, a subsidiary of Maul in 1980 and sold it to a Chicago-based holding company. The gear works prospered early in the decade, then faltered. Purchased by a Cleveland-based turnaround firm in 1986, IGW Systems went bankrupt in 1988.

CHARLES JOHNSON TAGGART

Indiana Government Center. State office complex including State Office Building North, State Office Building South, Indiana State Library and Historical Building, State House, and parking garages. Completed in 1888, the State House initially accommodated the two legislative chambers, courtrooms, the State Library, and offices for the governor, members of the Supreme Court, legislators, and other state officials. In 1934 the library moved from the STATE HOUSE and, along with the INDIANA HISTORICAL BUREAU and the INDIANA HISTORICAL SOCIETY, relocated to the newly completed INDIANA STATE LIBRARY AND HISTORICAL BUILDING at 140 North Senate Avenue.

In 1953 the Indiana General Assembly passed an enabling act for the construction of a state office building. The new structure, dedicated on December 20, 1960, was the largest state office building in the nation, and it brought to a central location agencies that had formerly been at 22 different sites. Designed by the Chicago architectural firm Graham, Anderson, Probst & White, and Raymond Kastendieck of Gary, Indiana, the $30 million structure at 100 North Senate featured 2,000 windows, a 900–seat cafeteria, and a large plaza. It was connected by tunnels to the State House, the State Library, and nearby parking facilities.

By 1975 state bureaucracy had outgrown this building, and the structure was deteriorating; legislators allotted $1.5 million that year for emergency renovation work. Ten years later, projecting substantial savings in office space rental fees over a 25–year period, the General Assembly approved the $103 million funding for construction of a new office structure and renovation of the existing building and grounds in order to create a complex of state buildings.

In 1988 the Washington Street parking facility became the first completed building in the new complex. With a ground floor of Indiana limestone and a tower at the northeast corner, the garage foreshadowed the architectural themes of the new office center.

Beginning in 1988 CSO Architects and Cole Associates, two Indianapolis firms, reconfigured the 1960 structure, completely refacing its exterior, reorienting its entrance to Government Place (facing the south building), and renovating its interior. Concurrently, HNTB architects and Walter Blackburn of Indianapolis, and Edmund L. Hafer of Evansville, designed and began construction on the south building.

The E-shaped south building's spine faces Washington Street. It is a four-story, limestone structure with five-story, copper-roofed towers at each corner. The building's over 1 million square feet of space includes a cafeteria, central atrium, training center, conference area, and office space. The facade also encompasses the former Employment Security Building, which was completely renovated. A loggia facing Washington Street runs the full length of the south building. In 1991 completion of the Senate Avenue parking garage completed the new construction. The garage echoes the structural components of the south office building. Completed in 1991, the overall appearance of the compound is one of unity in which the new construction complements and repeats features of the State Library and the State House.

The design of the Indiana Government Center accommodates the people who work and carry on business there. Three courtyards around the south building provide outdoor vistas to employees and visitors. The north building cafeteria opens onto the renovated CENTRAL CANAL, presenting workers a picturesque dining spot and providing joggers and walkers along the canal a lunch site. In 1993 plans are proceeding to create a day care center for children of state employees within the building, which now provides nearly 70 percent of the state's office space.

CONNIE J. ZEIGLER

"State Offices" and "State Office Building" clipping files, Indiana State Library and Indianapolis-Marion County Public Library.

Indiana High School Athletic Association (IHSAA). Regulatory association for junior high and high school athletics. In 1899 a meeting in Indianapolis of high school principals from eight Indiana cities resulted in the formation of the Indiana Interscholastic Athletic Association, whose purpose was to regulate state high school athletics. In addition to promoting uniform standards in athletics, this organization was also intended to prevent abuses such as enrolling college and professional players on high school teams. By 1904 five similar organizations had formed elsewhere in the state.

Recognizing the need for a statewide central organization, school principals gathered in Anderson, Indiana, on December 29, 1903, and adopted a constitution and Board of Control to administer the affairs of the newly formed IHSAA. Fifteen high schools joined the organization. The first commissioner was Arthur L. Trester, who retained the position until his death in 1944. Since that time five other men have held the office. In 1976 the IHSAA incorporated with the stated primary purpose of managing and fostering high school athletics "on a high plane."

At first the association concerned itself primarily with track and FOOTBALL. By 1975, however, the role of the IHSAA had expanded to encompass the regulation of nine boys' sports and nine girls' sports. The need for additional space prompted the organization's move from its headquarters in the CIRCLE TOWER BUILDING to new offices at 91st and Meridian streets in 1977. In 1992, IHSAA's membership stood at 389 high schools and 21 junior high schools. State championships for all boys' sports and eight girls' sports are held annually in the capital city at locations including the HOOSIER DOME, MARKET SQUARE ARENA, BUSH STADIUM, and the Natatorium and

Track and Field Stadium at INDIANA UNIVERSITY–
PURDUE UNIVERSITY, INDIANAPOLIS.

CONNIE J. ZEIGLER

Ward Brown, *IHSAA Membership History* (Indianapolis, 1984).

Indiana Historical Bureau. State agency
that promotes the study of Indiana history. In
1915 the General Assembly created the Indiana
Historical Commission to celebrate the centennial
of statehood. The commission continued its work
with a major project to collect records from World
War I, and by 1921 it was considered a permanent agency of state government. In 1925 the legislature established the Indiana Historical Bureau
in its present configuration as a part of the Indiana
Library and Historical Department. The agency
has always had an educational focus, with books
and other publications, historical markers, archaeological surveys, public programs, and
school-oriented initiatives.

According to the present mission statement,
"The Indiana Historical Bureau provides programs and opportunities for Indiana's citizens of
all ages to learn and teach about the history of
their state and its place in the broader communities of the nation and the world." Current major
programming includes two monograph series (*Indiana Historical Collections* and *Indiana History Resource Series*), the *Indiana History Bulletin* (a
newsletter), *The Indiana Historian: Exploring Indiana History* (a magazine on local history topics
and research for use in schools and other venues),
classroom publications and materials, administration of the state historical marker program, care of
the Indiana Governors' Portraits Collection, administration of two educational programs (Indiana Close Up and Indiana History Day), and co-
sponsorship of the Indiana Junior Historical Society and the REACH Program.

PAMELA J. BENNETT
Indiana Historical Bureau

Indiana Historical Society. On December 11, 1830, civic leaders met in Indianapolis to
form the Indiana Historical Society (IHS). They
established as "objects" the "collection of all materials calculated to shed light on the natural, civil
and political history of Indiana, the promotion of
useful knowledge and the friendly and profitable
intercourse of such citizens of the state as are disposed to promote the aforesaid objects." The following year the General Assembly granted the
basic charter under which the IHS still operates.
The institution barely survived its infancy. Two of
the organizers died within the next few years, and
Hoosiers kept alive the idea of a statewide historical society with sputters of enthusiasm at meetings of the membership held in only 12 years
between 1830 and 1886.

In 1886 JACOB PIATT DUNN and some close
associates reorganized the IHS. Since then the
members have met annually and publications
have appeared with increasing regularity. Lawyers, writers, professional historians, editors, librarians, and Hoosiers from many walks of life
gradually transformed a state-chartered corporation that received a few small appropriations from
the General Assembly into a multifaceted, privately financed 20th-century institution. Democ-
ratization came slowly. For example, Dunn's
motion at the 1888 annual meeting to admit
women into membership failed. The first female
to be elected a member very likely was Eliza
Browning, an editor, in 1906.

Through the years the IHS has adjusted its
mission to the changing fortunes of Indiana's State
Library, State Museum, and Historical Commission (later Bureau). From 1924 to 1976 the executive secretaries of the IHS also served as directors
of the Bureau. That organization's *Indiana History
Bulletin* went out to IHS members, as did (and still
does) the *Indiana Magazine of History*, published at
Indiana University.

When DELAVAN SMITH in 1922 willed a collection of books and a sum of money to honor his
father, the opportunity came for the IHS to establish a library. Under terms of an arrangement with
the state, the William Henry Smith Memorial Library opened its doors within the new INDIANA
STATE LIBRARY AND HISTORICAL BUILDING in 1934.
In 1993 the library held more than 60,000 books

and pamphlets, 3,500 manuscripts collections, 1,500,000 visual images, 1,000 maps, as well as ancillary material relating to Indiana and the Old Northwest.

The IHS also began publishing solid, readable books—studies of Native Americans, monographs, and regional documentary material. R. Carlyle Buley's *The Old Northwest* (1950) set high standards when it won a Pulitzer Prize. In observance of the 1966 sesquicentennial of Indiana's statehood and in cooperation with the Bureau, the IHS engaged scholars to prepare a multivolume history of Indiana. In addition to books, the IHS publishes *Traces of Indiana and Midwestern History*, *IHS News*, *The Hoosier Genealogist*, *Black History News & Notes*, *Prehistory Research Series*, and occasional record albums.

During the 1960s members came to annual meetings and to genealogy and other special interest programs in increasing numbers. By 1975 the IHS had strong library and publications programs, a staff of a dozen, and a membership of 5,000. ELI LILLY (1885–1977), a longtime trustee with avid interests in Indiana archaeology and history, provided capital funds to enable the IHS to move into a 1976 addition to the State Library building (315 West Ohio Street). He also willed a portion of his estate to the IHS, an endowment that has made possible unprecedented growth.

A board of 18 trustees establishes policies for the central administration, four divisions, a staff of 50, and an active membership of 10,000 (1993). The IHS reaches out to its own members and to the general public through a variety of conference and workshop opportunities. It administers and provides leadership for the Indiana Junior Historical Society, exhibitions, a program to record material for the blind, grants programs to support research in Indiana history, and efforts to assist Indiana's county and local historical organizations. Finally, the IHS supports a program to microfilm newspapers and other historical sources.

Though the IHS is an institution with a statewide focus, its influence on and relationship with Indianapolis is significant. A law approved by the General Assembly in 1992 enables the State of Indiana to provide a building site for the IHS in Marion County. The society has always been headquartered in the capital, its annual meeting

and some other programs are held there, and roughly 40 percent of IHS members live in the Greater Indianapolis area.

PETER T. HARSTAD
Indiana Historical Society

Lana Ruegamer, *A History of the Indiana Historical Society 1830–1980* (Indianapolis, 1980); James A. Woodburn, "The Indiana Historical Society: A Hundred Years," in *Indiana Historical Society Publications* (Indianapolis, 1930), Vol. 10, No. 1, pp. 5–79.

Indiana Interchurch Center. In the 1950s Protestant church leaders and two ecumenical agencies, the CHURCH FEDERATION OF INDIANAPOLIS and the Indiana Council of Churches, explored building a center to house their offices. Their aims were "to witness to the unity which God has given the churches in Indiana" and to "nurture the spirit and practice of cooperation" among the churches.

Plans were realized when the building was opened July 5, 1967, at the corner of Michigan Road and 42nd Street. The ground was part of the campus of CHRISTIAN THEOLOGICAL SEMINARY and donated to the Indiana Interchurch Center Corporation. Its owners and chief tenants are the Church Federation of Greater Indianapolis; the Indiana Council of Churches; the Christian Church (Disciples of Christ) of Indiana; the Episcopal Church, Diocese of Indianapolis; the United Church of Christ, Indiana Conference; the United Methodist Church, Indiana Area; and the United Presbyterian Church, Synod of Lincoln Trails. It also houses offices of other religious and community-serving organizations, including the JEWISH COMMUNITY RELATIONS COUNCIL and the INDIANA INTERRELIGIOUS COMMISSION ON HUMAN EQUALITY. Facilities at the center include a printing office and dining and conference rooms.

EDWIN L. BECKER
Christian Theological Seminary

Edwin L. Becker, "The Story of the Indiana Interchurch Center, Twenty-Fifth Anniversary" (1991), copy of typescript available at the Indiana Historical Society Library.

Indiana Interreligious Commission on Human Equality (IICHE). Interfaith organization to promote civil rights and social justice. In 1968 the national Presidential Advisory Commission on Civil Disorder (the "Kerner Commission") concluded that the United States comprised two separate and unequal societies, one black, the other white. In response to that report the Jewish, Catholic, and Protestant faiths in Indianapolis founded IICHE to design and implement programs to promote social and racial justice and interreligious dialogue.

The commission is comprised of 21 institutional members ("judicatories") that include church conferences, dioceses, synods, and organizations. These members, plus ten at-large representatives with strong roots in the Indiana faith community, form the board of directors. Each judicatory contributes an annual gift toward the commission's operating expenses.

In September, 1968, the commission addressed employment discrimination against blacks through Project Equality. The organization's first statewide program, Project Commitment, led to a series of interracial discussion groups. Other programs included Interreligious Consultations (1973–1975) and Education: The Unfinished Revolution (1976–1977), both focusing on school desegregation. The commission sponsors the Dr. Martin Luther King, Jr. Essay Contest for Indiana schoolchildren, and conducts numerous public forums on issues ranging from human rights violations in Central and South America and apartheid in South Africa to Jewish-Christian dialogues and discrimination in social services.

STACEY NICHOLAS

Indiana Journal (1825–1904). Indianapolis newspaper. First published January 11, 1825, by JOHN DOUGLASS and DOUGLASS MAGUIRE after they purchased, enlarged, and changed the name of the WESTERN CENSOR & EMIGRANTS GUIDE (1823). The paper was anti-Jacksonian, then pro-Whig, and later a voice for the REPUBLICAN PARTY.

The Journal alternated between tri-weekly, twice-weekly, and daily issues during the early 1840s and produced dailies during legislative sessions after 1842. On April 21, 1851, it became the first paper in Indianapolis to publish a permanent daily issue. Until the late 1850s it consisted mainly of political news but then regularly began to include local items.

On November 8, 1864, the paper, then the *Indianapolis Daily Journal*, under editor WILLIAM R. HOLLOWAY was the first to carry the news of Sherman's burning of Atlanta. Other newspapers reprinted the story but mainly discounted it because Indianapolis was not a center for war news. Holloway received a visit from a member of General Grant's staff wanting to know the source of his information. Holloway refused to name the officers who had given him the information and claimed that the War Department also had plans for a similar investigation which outranked Grant's probe. The matter was dropped shortly thereafter.

The *Journal* purchased many of the early papers in the city including the *Atlas* in 1861, the *Evening Gazette* in 1867, the *Evening Commercial* in 1871, the *Daily Times* in 1879, and the *Indianapolis Times* in 1886. The *Evening Commercial* became a short-lived evening edition after its purchase.

The paper changed owners, editors, and names frequently until June, 1904, when Charles S. Henry, owner of the paper for less than two years, sold it to the Indianapolis Star Company. Although published briefly under the name *Star and Journal*, by October *Journal* had been dropped from the title.

JOAN CUNNINGHAM

Jacob Piatt Dunn, *Greater Indianapolis* (Chicago, 1910); John W. Miller, *Indiana Newspaper Bibliography* (Indianapolis, 1982).

Indiana Medical History Museum. Organization dedicated to preserving the historic Old Pathology Building at CENTRAL STATE HOSPITAL, as well as the history of medicine. The museum offers tours, maintains a collection of over 15,000 artifacts, and displays interpretive exhibits in a changing exhibit gallery.

Constructed in 1895 and opened the following year, the 19–room Old Pathology Building

The old Pathology Department at Central State Hospital now houses the Indiana Medical History Museum. [Indiana Medical History Museum]

(originally known as the Pathological Department of Central State Hospital) was a state-of-the-art psychiatric teaching and research facility. Conceived by hospital superintendent George F. Edenharter, M.D., and designed by architect ADOLPH SCHERRER, this two-story brick structure contained a lecture hall (or amphitheater), autopsy room, library, photography room, anatomical museum, and modern research laboratories for the scientific study of mental illness.

In 1900, the Medical College of Indiana and the Central College of Physicians and Surgeons held classes in neurology and psychiatry in the building's amphitheater. This tradition continued after these two schools merged in 1908 with INDIANA UNIVERSITY SCHOOL OF MEDICINE. Indiana University held classes there until 1956.

The most significant research at the facility occurred in the 1920s and 1930s under the direction of WALTER BRUETSCH. Bruetsch was primarily interested in central nervous system syphilis, one of the leading causes of mental illness. By the 1930s, however, scientific psychiatry was in decline; most psychiatric research facilities closed their doors in the 1940s. Central State Hospital did not close its pathology department; the facility continued in use until the 1960s.

Remarkably, the interior of the Old Pathology Building remained virtually unaltered, and all the research records remained intact. In 1969, the Indiana Medical History Museum was incorporated as a private, not-for-profit organization to preserve this building, with the structure placed on the National Register of Historic Places in 1972. The organization also collects artifacts pertaining

to all aspects of the history of health care. In 1990 the museum opened a changing exhibits gallery in the Old Pathology Building.

KATHERINE MANDUSIC MCDONELL

Katherine Mandusic McDonell, "The Old Pathology Building: The Indiana Medical History Museum's Most Priceless Artifact," *Indiana Medicine*, 80 (Dec., 1987), 1190–1194.

Indiana National Bank. See NBD Bank

Indiana National Guard. The state MILITIA, also known since the 1860s as the Indiana Legion, was renamed the National Guard by an 1895 state law. It was not until the early 20th century, however, with passage of the National Defense Act of 1916, that the Indiana National Guard was more formally integrated into the federal defense establishment. In that year Governor Samuel M. Ralston was commander-in-chief of the Guard, while day-to-day control was exercised by Adjutant General Franklin L. Bridges.

Preparations for the December, 1916, celebration of Indiana's centennial as a state were suddenly interrupted in June when President Woodrow Wilson issued a call to mobilize the National Guard for active federal service on the Mexican border in response to an anticipated invasion of Texas by the Mexican army. At Bridges' direction Guardsmen from throughout the state were mustered in at FORT BENJAMIN HARRISON near Indianapolis. They were mustered, moved, and were in an Indiana encampment at Llano Grade, Texas, by early July. A war with Mexico never materialized, and by late 1916 troops began to return to Indiana and other home states.

The following year the Guard faced another mobilization. War Department instructions were issued in May, 1917, even while some Indiana troops were still returning from Texas, and effective the following August 5 the entire National Guard was "drafted" into federal service for World War I. One regiment was ordered to Fort Benjamin Harrison and became part of the new 42nd (Rainbow) Division. The remainder of the Indiana Guard went to Camp Shelby, Mississippi, and became part of the new 38th (Cyclone) Division. While the Indiana National Guard was in federal service, a brigade of State Militia was organized with headquarters in Indianapolis.

Following the war, Headquarters 38th Division was organized in 1923 at Indianapolis with Maj. Gen. ROBERT H. TYNDALL in command. A new permanent military armory was needed for a headquarters of this size, and as a result the Indianapolis Armory (later TYNDALL ARMORY) at 711 North Pennsylvania Street was constructed and was occupied in late 1926. Prior to that the division headquarters had occupied rental space in the Chalfant Building on the northwest corner of Michigan and Pennsylvania streets. In 1926 the Guard also installed STOUT FIELD as its air facility.

In 1933 the state purchased the Capitol Warehouse at 2000 South Madison Avenue and reconfigured it as the Indianapolis Motor Armory. The field artillery of the Indiana National Guard was horse-drawn at the time, and many of its horses were kept at the Indiana State Fairgrounds on East 38th Street. But in 1935 the Guard began conversion from horse-drawn to truck-drawn artillery, and other facilities were needed. A new Indianapolis Artillery Armory was built at 2015 South Pennsylvania Street immediately west of the motor armory and was occupied in early 1940. An adjunct to the Indiana National Guard that also operated under the governor and the adjutant general was the Indiana Naval Forces. In late 1937 they relocated from rental facilities in the Cole Motor Car building at 730 West Washington Street into the new HESLAR NAVAL ARMORY on the east bank of White River at the 30th Street bridge.

On January 17, 1941, the Indiana National Guard was called into federal service again for subsequent combat duty during World War II in the Southwest Pacific Theater. The adjutant general's office remained and was headquarters for the Indiana State Guard during the war. Starting in Indianapolis in 1946, following the war, the National Guard began a three-year period of organization again, this time with an Army National Guard and a new Air National Guard.

Indianapolis served as the central coordinating headquarters location for subsequent mobilizations for active federal service in 1951 for units of the Army and Air Guard during the Korean War, in 1961 for the Air Guard during the Berlin Crisis, and in 1968 for an Army Guard ranger unit during the Vietnam War.

December, 1960, saw the office of the adjutant general relocated from the State House to the new State Office Building immediately west across Senate Avenue. Four years later to the month the office relocated again, this time to its current permanent headquarters at Stout Field. In December, 1977, the largest armory constructed in the nation to that date since World War II was opened at 3912 West Minnesota Street just north across the street from the original Stout Field proper. The following year both the motor armory and the artillery armory on the city's south side were sold.

Throughout the years, during peacetime and wartime alike, senior National Guard headquarters in Indianapolis have acted as command and control centers for statewide emergency assistance operations as a result of severe flooding, devastating tornados, winter blizzard conditions, and countless other instances of rescue efforts and community assistance programs for Indiana citizens.

ROBERT T. FISCHER COLONEL, AUS (RET)

Reference Files, Military History Section, Military Department of Indiana, Stout Field, Indianapolis; William J. Watt and James R. H. Spears, eds., *Indiana's Citizen Soldiers* (Indianapolis: Indiana State Armory Board, 1980).

Indiana Opera Theatre (MacAllister Awards and Festival Opera Theatre). Formed in 1981 by a group of opera enthusiasts, the Indiana Opera Theatre quickly gained a reputation for its creative staging of rarely heard works. A district courtroom in the City-County Building served as the site of a 1984 production of Gilbert and Sullivan's popular operetta *Trial by Jury*. A winter performance of Stanley Silverman's *Hotel for Criminals* took place in a truck barn at MacAllister Machinery Company. Past productions have included a variety of offerings.

In 1992 Indiana Opera Theatre directors renamed the organization the MacAllister Awards and Festival Opera Theatre. Intended to eliminate possible confusion between the Opera Theatre and the similarly titled INDIANAPOLIS OPERA COMPANY, the name change also emphasized the Opera Theatre board's connection with the nationally recognized MACALLISTER AWARDS competition for aspiring opera singers.

SUZANNE G. SNYDER

Indiana Pacers. Professional basketball team. In February, 1967, six Indiana businessmen, including sports agent Chuck Barnes and *Indianapolis Star* sports editor Bob Collins, met at the Lafayette Country Club and agreed to pool $6,000 to purchase a franchise in the proposed American Basketball Association (ABA). With George Mikan as commissioner the ABA embarked on its inaugural season with National Basketball Association (NBA) castoffs, players banned from the NBA, and unknown youngsters looking for a break. League gyms were cramped and occasionally leaked. While the ABA did employ a number of future NBA luminaries, the association struggled financially and organizationally. A distinctive red, white, and blue basketball and a radical innovation—the three-point shot—were two of very few league constants. So was the dominance of Indianapolis' entry in the league, the Pacers.

Rejected by established Hoosier stars like Oscar Robertson and the Van Arsdale twins, the Pacers signed Roger Brown as their first player. Brown was peripherally linked to a college point-shaving scandal in 1961 and banned from the NBA. Freddie Lewis and Bob Netolicky were obtained in early drafts and 1967 ABA Rookie of the Year Mel Daniels was received in a trade with the floundering Minnesota Muskies. During the first several seasons the team also signed an assortment of Hoosier basketball players, including Jimmy Rayl, Ron Bonham, Rick Mount, Bill Keller, and 1969 Indiana high school Mr. Basketball George McGinnis, who joined the Pacers after his sophomore season at Indiana University.

Over the course of the league's nine tumultuous seasons the Indiana Pacers became the ABA's showcase franchise. Under the stewardship of coach Bobby "Slick" Leonard, the club won three league titles (1970, 1972, and 1973), produced three MVPs (Mel Daniels, 1969 and 1971, and

George McGinnis, 1975), hosted the first and third ABA All-Star Games, and habitually led the league in attendance. While most ABA teams attracted fewer than 5,000 fans per game, the Pacers averaged over 8,000 at the Indiana State Fairgrounds Coliseum.

When the administration of Mayor Richard Lugar constructed a 17,000–seat downtown arena as a centerpiece of urban renewal, the foundation for true major league basketball was laid. The Pacers moved to MARKET SQUARE ARENA in 1974 and drew an ABA record 8,604 spectators per game.

The chronic instability of the ABA led to the league's demise following the 1975–1976 season. Indiana, Denver, San Antonio, and the New York Nets were admitted to the NBA for a fee of $3.2 million per franchise. The ABA expatriates were also required to pool $3 million to pay off investors in other ABA franchises, were denied television money in 1976–1977, and agreed to forego first round draft choices in the 1977 college draft.

The resultant financial difficulties nearly destroyed the Pacers. Unable to meet increasing salary demands, the team lost several top players, including McGinnis, to free agency. A telethon in 1977 helped to keep the club afloat and, after a series of ownership changes, the franchise was sold to California businessman Sam Nassi in 1979.

A legacy of injuries, poor drafts, bad trades, and constant threats to move the franchise followed. In 1982–1983 a 20–62 team attracted 4,814 fans per game, last in the NBA and lowest in franchise ABA-NBA history. The Pacers' long-term prospects appeared to improve in 1983 when Indianapolis shopping mall magnates Melvin and Herbert Simon purchased the club. While the team has employed several head coaches in the past decade (including 1981 NBA Coach of the Year Jack McKinney and Hall of Famer Jack Ramsey), the consistent support of local ownership has lent a semblance of stability to the organization.

The team won its first NBA playoff game in 1987 and by 1993 the club had reached the league playoffs in four consecutive seasons. In 1994, under new coach Larry Brown, the Pacers reached the division finals. This was the first time the team had moved beyond the initial round of the playoffs, an achievement that heightened the enthusiasm of area residents.

The 1990s brought dramatic changes to pro basketball, including an explosion in players' salaries, and the future of the franchise remains in question. Indianapolis represents one of the NBA's smallest television markets. Although a 1992 city study placed the franchise's financial impact on Marion County at $36 million a year, the club lost $4 million that year on revenues of $25 million. Gate, radio-TV, souvenir, and arena advertising receipts all ranked well below the NBA average. So did attendance, although the club did draw a franchise record 12,949 fans per game in 1992–1993. While *Financial World* magazine recently placed the Pacers' market value at $43 million (last in the NBA), Toronto investors reportedly offered the Simons $100 million for the franchise—a relative bargain considering the $125 million Toronto eventually paid in 1993 for the NBA's latest expansion opportunity.

R. DALE OGDEN
Indiana State Museum

Indiana Repertory Theatre (IRT).

Professional Equity theatre. The Indiana Repertory Theatre (IRT) is a not-for-profit professional theatre, the only Indiana resident theatre that produces a full season of plays using full-time professionals. IRT, which employs both a resident repertory company and guest artists, offers a varied repertoire of classics, enduring popular favorites, and recent plays by American and British authors. IRT often presents Indiana, American, and world premieres.

IRT was founded in 1972 by Benjamin Mordecai, Edward Stern, and Gregory Poggi, who developed plans for a new theatre while doctoral students at Indiana University–Bloomington. To choose a site for their theater, they wrote to the mayors of 99 American cities. Of the cities responding, Indianapolis was chosen because of the enthusiasm and interest expressed. Mordecai and Stern served together as IRT's first artistic directors, with Stern eventually filling the role alone. The premier production opened during October, 1972, at the ATHENAEUM on East Michigan Street. IRT held its productions in the facil-

ity's 396–seat auditorium, a converted ballroom, for eight seasons.

In 1979, playing to near-capacity crowds at the Athenaeum, IRT began the search for a larger performing space that would allow for future growth. In 1980, IRT moved to its present location, the INDIANA THEATRE on West Washington Street near the State House. The new, larger facilities also gave the theatre the capacity to produce plays using more than one set. That year, IRT appointed TOM HAAS as artistic director, a position he held until his death in 1991; he was succeeded by Libby Appel.

Before being taken over by IRT, the Indiana Theatre had been scheduled for demolition. A Spanish Baroque movie palace that also has Indian, Spanish, and Egyptian motifs, the building was constructed in 1927 and is listed on the National Register of Historic Places. With over $5 million in funding from private as well as federal and local government sources, IRT renovated the theatre, restoring the lobby to its original condition, dividing the theatre into three performing areas, and creating rehearsal rooms.

IRT's regular season performances are held in the 600–seat Mainstage theatre, which features a variable-thrust proscenium stage. The 250–seat Upperstage, above the Mainstage, is used for some performances by DANCE KALEIDOSCOPE, seminars, and IRT Junior Works productions. The building also houses a 150–seat Cabaret Club, and IRT's production facilities and administrative offices.

In 1991, IRT inaugurated the Education Outreach Program. The program includes Classic Theatre for Youth, which makes a Mainstage production of a classic available each year to high school students from around the state; Junior Works, annually offering three productions geared to young audiences; and student matinees of Mainstage plays for junior high and high school students. IRT also has technical and administrative internship programs.

In addition to ticket sales, IRT productions are supported by funding from arts organizations, corporations and foundations, and a large base of individual donors.

JOYCE K. JENSEN

Indiana School for the Blind. In 1845 the Indiana General Assembly appropriated $5,000 to purchase land to build a school for the blind. A three-member committee selected an eight-acre site on North Street between Meridian and Pennsylvania streets in 1848; that same year the legislature appropriated another $5,000 for construction. While the school temporarily operated from rented quarters, construction on a three-story brick building began. This first building, intended for temporary use, was completed in 1850 and construction began on what would be the permanent building at the site.

William H. Churchman, a blind man who was the school's first superintendent, provided trustees with ideas for the building based on his study of buildings in use by the blind. Local architect JOHN ELDER made the early drafts under Churchman's direction. FRANCIS COSTIGAN made several exterior ornamental changes to the plans, raising the main entrance to the second floor, adding three Corinthian cupolas, removing the third and fourth floor porches, and setting the building farther back from the street. Surrounded by an iron fence, the main building was five stories, with two four-story wings. Of the original three cupolas, only the one on the main building remained by 1930. The main building was built primarily of brick faced with sandstone; the Ionic portico and the verandas were of sandstone. Four large stone scrolls bordered the broad staircases of the main

entrance. Occupied in 1853, the total cost of the buildings and grounds was $110,000. The original three-story brick building on the site remained in use as a workshop. Additions to the property over the years included a barn, laundry, bakeshop, greenhouse, and dormitories.

In 1920 the state legislature authorized the INDIANA WORLD WAR MEMORIAL PLAZA and in 1923 approved a plan for a new blind school. A commission selected a 60–acre site at 75th Street and North College Avenue and construction began on its facilities under the direction of Harrison and Turnock, a local firm. The state legislature appropriated $400,000 in 1927 to continue construction on the boys' dormitory, the industrial building, and music hall. Another appropriation in 1929 enabled completion of the property. All the buildings were two stories, connected by tunnels. The school opened in September, 1930. The stone scrolls, columns from the cupola, and iron fence from the old building were incorporated into the new property. Later additions to the current property include the superintendent's residence, garden and arboretum, Lambert Hall, greenhouse, the track and field facility, and the natatorium.

JOAN CUNNINGHAM

Indianapolis Star, May 22, 1927, Mar. 3, 1929, Nov. 9, 1990.

The Indiana School for the Blind occupied this downtown building on North Street from 1853 until 1930 when plans for the Indiana World War Memorial Plaza forced it to relocate to the city's north side.[Indiana State Library]

Indiana School for the Deaf (1843 to present). In 1843 the Indiana General Assembly enacted a property tax to finance the education and housing of the state's deaf population. The Indiana State Asylum for the Deaf and Dumb opened that year in rented quarters. In 1849, the state hired architect Joseph Willis to design and build the first permanent residence of the asylum. Opened in 1850, the construction was completed the following year by Colonel Andrew Brouse. The finished asylum, located east of the MILE SQUARE in the vicinity of today's Willard Park (Washington Street and State Avenue), consisted of two stucco buildings constructed in the popular Greek Revival style. The buildings were classic examples of public buildings of their period. The main building was 265 feet long with a five-story center section and two recessed, three-story wings ending with projecting four-story wings. It had a slate roof, Doric columns, and a copper-roofed portico. An octagonal cupola, also roofed in copper, sat atop the building. Behind this main edifice was the two-story Greek Revival building that housed the schoolrooms and chapel.

In 1905 plans were drawn up for a new school to be located at 1200 East 42nd Street, its present location. The Indianapolis architectural firm of RUBUSH AND HUNTER designed this campus, which opened in 1911. Seven buildings of one or two stories were constructed in an Americanized French design of red brick laid in red mortar. Each had stone trim and a red tile roof. In 1907, the legislature renamed the asylum the Indiana State School for the Deaf. A final name change took place in 1961 when the institution became the Indiana School for the Deaf. The campus now consists of over 21 buildings, and the staff of 346 serves approximately 300 students yearly.

CONNIE J. ZEIGLER

Indiana Sports Corporation (ISC).

Sports marketing agency. Incorporated in December, 1979, this private, not-for-profit entity was initiated by a coalition of government and business leaders in order to implement the city's objective of becoming a national sports capital. The ISC's governing board consists of approximately 75 people, some of whom represent a broad spectrum of community organizations and others who serve as members-at-large. The LILLY ENDOWMENT provided initial support; current funding is primarily through memberships (both corporate and individual), events, and contributions.

Under the direction of Sandy Knapp, president from 1980 to 1991, the ISC worked to bring major sporting events to Indianapolis and to encourage sports organizations to locate in the city. The agency's goals include stimulating the Indianapolis economy; improving the city's image, both nationally and internationally; enhancing the city's quality of life; and providing opportunities for youth.

Within the first ten years of its existence, the ISC was a key factor in what proved to be a successful marketing strategy for the city. During that time, $165 million in sports facilities were constructed and 230 major amateur sporting events were staged in Indianapolis. Estimates of economic impact of this sports strategy ranged upward to $400 million.

The first major event the ISC landed was the 1982 NATIONAL SPORTS FESTIVAL, now known as the U.S. Olympic Sports Festival. Other events followed, including many national and world championships in various sports and the 1987 PAN AMERICAN GAMES. The ISC also attracted many sports organizations to locate in Indianapolis, including seven national governing bodies and one international federation (see AMATEUR SPORTS GOVERNING BODIES). The volume of sports activity generated a great deal of attention nationally, prompting *TV Guide* to write, "Indianapolis never met a sport it didn't like."

In 1988, the Indiana Sports Corporation created a for-profit subsidiary, Sports Marketing of Indiana. This organization assists professional sporting events in much the same way the ISC assists amateur events on behalf of the community. The subsidiary's first clients included the GTE Tennis Championships, INDIANAPOLIS COLTS, and 1991 PGA Championship.

JUDY KEENE

Sandy Knapp, "Indianapolis: A City with a Sporting Spirit," *Olympian* (Nov., 1990), 62; Indiana Sports Corporation annual report (1989).

Indiana State Archives. Repository for

the official records of the State of Indiana. The origins of the State Archives are somewhat tangled, snared in a web of bureaucracies formed and reformed, but its history can be simply characterized: for the most part, the rest of state government has shown a notable disinterest in its mission.

During the 19th century, each office of the state cared, or did not care, for its own records. The INDIANA STATE LIBRARY took the initiative in 1906, forming a department called the Indiana Archives. A variety of reorganizations followed, culminating in 1979, when the Archives split from the Library and became a division of the newly created Commission on Public Records.

Until that point, no standard policy governed the preservation of historical records; a statute passed in 1937 allowed every official "at his discretion" to turn over materials not in use. After 1979, though, the Commission on Public Records created schedules regulating the retention of government records and the State Archives became the single repository of all materials of historical and legal significance.

Despite its heritage of neglect, the State Archives, located in the State Library building adjacent to the State House, constitutes an invaluable resource for the history of Indiana and its capital. Not only does it house the official records of the state government and state agencies, but it has acquired large quantities of federal records, including military, census, and land office materials, as well as most of the 19th century records of Marion County government. No other institution can provide a comparable range of governmental records for research on social, political, or economic questions regarding the city and state.

ROBERT HORTON
Indiana State Archives

Indiana State Fair. Annual agricultural exposition. Concerned about the state of agriculture in Indiana, the General Assembly created the State Board of Agriculture in February, 1851. The board first met on May 27, 1851, with Governor Joseph Wright as president, and appointed a com-

These sculptures from the 1949 Indiana State Fair were made of solid lard, promoting the shortening as "digestible, flavorful, and nutritious."
[Indiana Historical Society,
Larry Foster Collection, #16763]

mittee to consider holding a state agricultural fair in the fall; they later recommended waiting until fall, 1852.

Conceived as a venue for the exchange of ideas and to stimulate improved agricultural productivity, the first Indiana State Fair ran October 20–22, 1852, at present-day MILITARY PARK in Indianapolis. An estimated 30,000 people paid 20 cents each to see 1,365 exhibit entries featuring an array of agricultural products and machinery. From the beginning the fair focused on improved agriculture and stock production, highlighted the mechanical arts and farm technology, and offered plowing contests, horse pulls, and harness racing. A Women's Department sponsored exhibitions and competitions in sewing, needlework, cooking and baking, and other domestic arts.

During its early years the fair was held in different communities—Lafayette (1853), Madison (1854), Indianapolis (1855–1858), and New Albany (1859). In 1860 the State Board of Agriculture, with the financial assistance of Indianapolis-area railroads, bought 30 acres called Otis Grove (bounded by today's 19th, Talbott, and 22nd streets and Central Avenue) as a suitable permanent location for the fair. A year after opening the new site, the board sought other space to accommodate the fair as the outbreak of the Civil War rendered the grounds more valuable for other purposes. The fairgrounds, renamed CAMP MORTON, was used by Indiana troops, housed Confederate prisoners of war, and served as the site for a Union hospital.

The State Fair returned to Military Park for the years 1862–1864; Fort Wayne and Terre Haute hosted the exhibition in 1865 and 1867, respectively. In 1868 the State Fair returned to its rebuilt Indianapolis location which, by 1872, included a two-story brick Exposition Building for the 30–day fair and exposition. During these years, however, the state board expressed increasing concern over the quality and reputability of side shows, vendors, and auctioneer stands, which resulted in the licensing of exhibitors. In 1870 the board barred "all side shows, auction stands, fat women, white negroes, snake shows, and all classes of similar exhibitions."

With Indianapolis' continued northward growth the Board of Agriculture found it needed more space for the annual fair. In November, 1891, the board sold its former Camp Morton grounds for $275,100 to three Indianapolis businessmen, and purchased the Jay G. Voss farm, located two miles northeast of the old fairgrounds (at present-day East 38th Street and Fall Creek Parkway). In February, 1892, the board hired the J. F. Alexander and Son architectural firm to supervise construction of the fair's facilities. The new fairgrounds, containing 72 buildings, a 6,000–seat grandstand, and a mile race track, officially opened on September 19, 1892.

Over the decades the State Fair captured and showcased the latest in science and technology for fairgoers. Developments in aviation led to appearances of a dirigible (1906), monoplane demonstrations (1914), and hot-air balloons. The first annual balloon race was launched in 1975. Growing public fascination with the automobile brought auto exhibits, auto polo (1918), and in the 1930s auto daredevil thrill shows and midget auto races. The Hoosier Hundred, a 100–mile dirt track race, premiered in 1953. Another feature was the Better Babies Contest, begun in 1920 to encourage improved hygiene and education for young children; by the early 1930s this had evolved into a regular health exhibit. In 1983 the INDIANA TRANSPORTATION MUSEUM introduced the FairTrain, which carried fairgoers on restored railroad cars to the fairgrounds.

Musical entertainment has always been a significant part of the annual fair. During the late 19th and early 20th centuries military bands, including John Philip Sousa's, made numerous appearances. In recent decades the fair hosted popular entertainers and musicians of the day, including the Beatles (September 3, 1964). It continues to offer a full schedule of popular and country-western performers.

The agriculture board guided fair operations until 1925 when the Indiana General Assembly created the Indiana State Fair Board. A new fair board, established in 1947, included representatives elected from 11 agricultural districts and 5 members appointed by the governor. To address the financial problems and deteriorating facilities at the fairgrounds in the 1980s, the legislature acted on a December, 1989, recommendation from the Indiana State Fair Advisory Commis-

sion. It abolished the old fair board (1990) and created the Indiana State Fair Commission to operate the fairgrounds and an Indiana State Fair Committee (later renamed the Indiana State Fair Board) to run the annual State Fair.

The sixth oldest state fair in the nation and winner of the 1952 "Finest Agricultural Fair in the Nation" trophy, the Indiana State Fair has been an important asset to the state and the community. The 1992 fair attracted 722,218 people, the highest attendance on record; the 1993 fair drew 689,924. A 1990–1991 economic impact study of the fairgrounds' contribution to Indianapolis showed over $609 million in total direct and indirect sales and a total fairgrounds visitation in excess of 5 million.

RAY BOOMHOWER
Indiana Historical Society

Paul Miner, *Indiana's Best: An Illustrated Celebration of the Indiana State Fairgrounds, 1852–1992* (Indianapolis, 1992).

Indiana State Fairgrounds. Since 1852, the INDIANA STATE FAIR has served as an annual showcase for agricultural productivity and innovation. During the rest of the year, the fairgrounds provide a location for educational, sporting, and entertainment events. The fairgrounds are currently located on the northeast side of Indianapolis, bounded by 38th Street, Fall Creek Parkway, 42nd Street, and Winthrop Avenue.

The present location is the third permanent site for the fairgrounds in Indianapolis. In 1852, the State Board of Agriculture hosted the first fair at MILITARY PARK along West Street. For the next eight years the fair traveled to other cities throughout the state, but gate receipts seemed to be highest when Indianapolis hosted the event. In 1860, the Board of Agriculture decided to locate the fair on 36 acres north of the city in "Otis Grove," the area bounded by 19th and 22nd streets between Delaware and New Jersey streets. The CIVIL WAR halted further development and it was not until 1872 that construction actually began. Twenty years later, the Board of Agriculture decided to relocate the fair at a larger site, which it acquired in 1891.

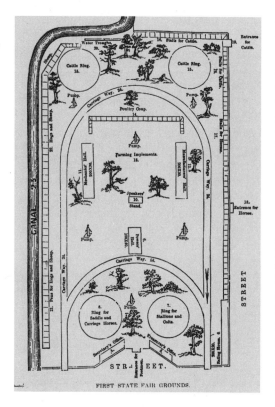

FIRST STATE FAIR GROUNDS.

Military Park was the site of the first Indiana State Fair in October, 1852. [Indiana Historical Society, Bass Collection, #91510]

The new grounds on the northeast side of the city had 214 acres for permanent buildings. Animal barns of vernacular architecture with monitors (raised center sections of the gable roof) were quickly erected to provide shelter for mules, horses, swine, and cows. By 1908, exhibition buildings, a race track, and a coliseum with 12,000 seats had been built at the new location.

The fairgrounds have hosted a variety of attractions over the years. One of the prime locations for these events has been the coliseum. In 1939 the federal Public Works Administration constructed a second coliseum using both federal and local bond money. During the past 50 years, this Art Deco building has held events ranging from public ice skating to professional ice hockey, from rock concerts and basketball games to political conventions. In addition, the Fair Board leases its facilities at the fairgrounds for educational and recreational exhibits, such as automobile, flower and patio, and boat shows. Further, drivers com-

pete in car races, such as the Hoosier Hundred, at the race track.

Today, the Indiana State Fairgrounds is a large complex of buildings that hosts events throughout the year. Fifty-two permanent buildings, plus race tracks, parking lots, and fields for the yearly midway, occupy 238 acres of land. Although people use the fairgrounds year round, its central function remains the Indiana State Fair, an annual celebration of the state's agricultural prowess.

LINDA B. WEINTRAUT

Indiana State Library. One of the oldest libraries in the state, this institution was established in 1825 to provide library service to the legislature, state government officials and their staffs, and other governmental personnel. At the time of its establishment the secretary of state served as the state librarian and, along with the state auditor, treasurer, and the governor, made up the Board of Library Commissioners. In 1841 the library was designated as a separate agency and an office of librarian established. This position was a political one and selection was made by the General Assembly for a three-year term. Candidates for this office were normally members of the majority party in the legislature; the position was viewed as a reward for party loyalty and/or service. Because of high turnover in the office (21 librarians between 1841 and 1897) and lack of consistency and direction, the library achieved only minimal success in its intended purpose. Another change occurred in 1895 when the library was placed under the auspices of the State Board of Education, which, in 1897, assumed responsibility for selecting the state librarian. In that year the first non-political librarian, William E. Henry, was appointed and the institution began to establish itself as a unique and important library.

In 1925 the governance of the State Library was again changed when the library and the Public Library Commission were merged and placed under the direction of the newly created Library and Historical Board. This body continues to oversee the agency and is composed of five members who are appointed by the governor.

Throughout most of its early history the library was housed in the State House but in 1934 it moved, along with the INDIANA HISTORICAL BUREAU and the INDIANA HISTORICAL SOCIETY, to a new facility located on the corner of Ohio Street and Senate Avenue. It remains at this site, with an addition to the building completed in 1976.

Over the years the services of the library have expanded beyond its original responsibility to state government. Beginning in the early part of this century it circulated reading material to the blind and continues to do so. The Division of Indiana History and Archives, created in 1913, has acquired an outstanding collection of manuscripts, pamphlets, maps, books, and magazines pertaining to the state. The library also has an extensive Indiana newspaper collection. A genealogy section was established in 1934 and remains one of the most popular areas in the agency. The library serves as a regional depository for U.S. government documents and has a large Indiana state documents collection as well. Since its merger with the Public Library Commission the library has worked closely with the state's public libraries and has been instrumental in the development of a strong library network in Indiana.

ROBERT L. LOGSDON
Indiana State Library

Larry Joe Brown, "The Indiana State Library, 1825–1925" (Ph.D. dissertation, Indiana University, 1976); Esther U. McNitt, "Short History of the Indiana State Library," *Library Occurrent*, 10 (Jan.-Mar., 1931), 21–30.

Indiana State Library and Historical Building

(140 North Senate Avenue). PIERRE & WRIGHT, Architects, designed the original (east) wing, the first permanent home of the INDIANA STATE LIBRARY, the INDIANA HISTORICAL BUREAU, and the INDIANA HISTORICAL SOCIETY. The commission was awarded by a competition jury including eminent New York architect Raymond Hood. Construction began in 1932; the dedication was held December 7, 1934. The building was conceived as the first of a series of state buildings extending from the State House toward WHITE RIVER—a planning concept that only recently was realized.

The east wing is formal and dignified: a square block, four stories high. Major reading rooms are on the second floor, flanking a stately vaulted foyer and exhibition hall. The exterior is classical, restrained, Greek in detail. The interior is Moderne in spirit but with details drawn from a variety of period and contemporary sources. Stained glass windows and mural paintings by J. Scott Williams and relief sculptures by Leon Hermant represent the advance of civilization, the history of Indiana, the attributes of knowledge, and the means by which knowledge is transmitted.

Materials native to Indiana predominate. The exterior is of Bedford limestone. Interior walls are faced with Monte Cassina sandstone from St. Meinrad, paneling of Indiana walnut, or Indiana-made glazed tiles.

An addition to the west, shared with the Indiana Historical Society (which moved its operation to this new wing), was designed by Burkart, Shropshire, Boots, Reid & Associates and dedicated in 1976.

ANDREW R. SEAGER
Ball State University

Pierre & Wright, Architects, "Indiana State Library & Historical Building," architectural drawings, 1932, Drawing Archives, College of Architecture and Planning, Ball State University, Muncie, Indiana; "State Library," clipping files, Indiana Division, Indiana State Library, Indianapolis.

Indiana State Medical Association.

Formed as the Indiana State Medical Society (ISMS) in 1849, the organization's purpose was, and remains, to educate physicians about scientific and clinical developments in medicine. Among the founding members was Indianapolis physician John H. Sanders.

Since its inception the association has held annual meetings at which physicians have presented papers about health and medical issues. During the Civil War topics included camp diarrhea and military surgery. By 1868 the organization had designated all county medical societies as auxiliaries.

In 1903 the ISMS changed its name to the Indiana State Medical Association (ISMA) in conformance with the guidelines of the American Medical Association. In 1924 the ISMA secured its first full-time executive secretary, and in 1927 wives of association members formed the Women's Auxiliary. By 1946 the association's annual three-day convention attracted 2,000 attendees. In 1950 it formed committees to hear grievances against its members, and to study poliomyelitis.

Headquartered in Indianapolis since 1924, today the ISMA remains a federation of county and district medical societies. In 1993 it boasted 7,000 members. In addition to its traditional services to members, the ISMA lobbies for public health initiatives and serves as a patient advocate by distributing brochures promoting better health and health care. It also funds a scholarship program for medical students and accredits medical education institutions and programs in the state.

CONNIE J. ZEIGLER

Charles N. Combs, "History of the Indiana State Medical Association," in Dorothy Ritter Russo, ed., *One Hundred Years of Indiana Medicine, 1849–1949* (n.p., 1949).

Indiana State Museum. A museum of Indiana's cultural and natural history. The State Museum existed for years more in name than in reality. After its relocation to the former Indianapolis City Hall, the museum developed into an institution worthy of the challenge to preserve the state's cultural and natural history.

The museum began as a cabinet of minerals and curiosities that State Librarian R. Deloss Brown set up in 1862. The General Assembly recognized the collection in 1869 with a law directing the state geologist to collect and preserve examples of Indiana's geology and animal and plant life.

State Geologist James Maurice Thompson moved the collection in 1888 from the library to a spacious room on the third floor of the new STATE HOUSE. He improved the exhibits by labeling and arranging the objects in scientific order. Most were natural history specimens, with native American artifacts, war trophies, and oddities from Indiana and foreign countries accounting for the remainder of the collection.

The institution did not fulfill its early promise. Governmental reorganization in 1919 moved the museum to the State House basement where it languished for over 45 years. Displays were arranged in no conceivable order with few labels. The most notable item was the carcass of Hoosier Jumbo, "the largest hog in the world." For several years in the 1920s, the state closed the museum to make room for the needs of the growing automobile license department.

Deplorable conditions led to calls for better quarters. The dirty, cramped space prompted many to seek a separate building that would allow for development of a modern institution. The administration of Governor M. Clifford Townsend (1937–1941) initiated talk of a new facility, but there were no serious moves until after World War II.

For almost 20 years, officials periodically debated the future of the State Museum. Most agreed that they should do something; but indecision and lack of funds stalled action. Shifting the museum from Geology to State Parks in 1945 brought little progress, despite an attempt to add professional staff. Although a study in 1948 recommended construction of a structure north of the Indiana State Library, the legislature refused to appropriate the necessary funds. A decade later a new commission concluded that Indiana had the poorest state museum in the nation and that the only hope would be to move it into a separate building. The sole result of the study was relocation of the collection to a slightly larger basement room.

Interest in the state's sesquicentennial and encouragement from Governor Matthew E. Welsh (1961–1965) laid the basis for a modern, professional institution. The desire for an acceptable home for the museum as a lasting legacy of the sesquicentennial coincided with attempts by the City of Indianapolis to find a use for the recently vacated City Hall.

Constructed in 1909, the former City Hall is a limestone structure designed in the Neoclassical style by the architectural firm of RUBUSH AND HUNTER. A stained glass canopy rises above a four-story rotunda with inlaid marble floors. The state leased the property in 1963 and after renovating it, officials dedicated the new museum in January,

1967. Six years later state ownership of the building became permanent.

The new facility encouraged professional development. The museum became a separate division in the Department of Natural Resources in 1970. Additional staff brought the institution up to contemporary museum standards and secured accreditation by the American Association of Museums. The collection consists of artifacts related to the state's cultural and natural history with concentration in fossils, furniture, household items, political and sports memorabilia, costumes, quilts and coverlets, and Indiana art. Permanent exhibits along with temporary and traveling shows fulfill a mission to collect, preserve, and interpret Indiana's history.

RICHARD A. GANTZ
Indiana State Museum

Donald F. Carmony, "The New Indiana State Museum," *Indiana Magazine of History*, 64 (Sept., 1968), 191–208.

Indiana State Museum, Fine Arts Department. A collection of regional American art, comprised of over 2,000 paintings, works of art on paper, and sculpture by Indiana artists. The mandate of the INDIANA STATE MUSEUM (ISM) is to collect, preserve, and interpret the natural and cultural history of the state. By focusing on art created by Indiana artists or relating to Indiana, the museum has amassed a significant collection of American regional art dating from the early 18th century to the present. The collection centers on the turn-of-the-century flowering of regional American Impressionism known as the HOOSIER GROUP.

The Selma N. Steele Collection is the most important and comprehensive component within the department. Upon her death in 1945, Mrs. Steele donated to the state over 300 paintings and drawings by her late husband, T. C. STEELE, dean of the Hoosier Group. Also included in the donation are the Steele Archives, a comprehensive collection of paisley shawls, and decorative arts. The Steeles' Brown County home, known as the House of the Singing Winds, and its 211 acres of adjacent property

were included in her bequest. ISM maintains the home, large studio, and outbuildings as the T. C. Steele State Historic Site and the property as the T. C. Steele Nature Preserve.

With the museum's 1967 move from the STATE HOUSE to the former City Hall on Alabama Street, a concerted effort was made to acquire a fine arts collection. Governor Roger Branigin designated funds to acquire works of art from the family estates of Hoosier Group artists J. OTTIS ADAMS and WILLIAM FORSYTH. Twenty-four paintings by Adolph Shulz, founding member of the early 20th century Brown County art colony, were donated by his second wife Alberta.

The most innovative means of ISM acquisition involved the works of Frank V. Dudley, the "Painter of the Indiana Dunes." Dudley found the changing seasons and shifting sands of the Indiana dunes to be an endless source of inspiration. In 1923, a coalition of conservation groups successfully preserved over 2,000 acres of Indiana dunesland as a state park. In the transition Dudley was forced to give up his studio-home to the new state park. In lieu of monetary payment, the artist rented his former cabin from the state for one large oil painting a year. This unique arrangement lasted for 19 years.

As a regional center for contemporary and historical art, ISM has made a commitment to recognizing, collecting, and exhibiting the works of Indiana artists. Art exhibitions have become a vital part of the museum's programs. The landmark 1985 exhibition "The Best Years" contributed to the renewed interest in the Hoosier Group artists. Other significant exhibitions recently organized by the museum include "Photographs: Carl Robert Pope Jr. and Dorinth Doherty," "Robert Berkshire: A Retrospective," "Cibachromes by Linda Adle Goodine," "Francesc Torres' Dromos Indiana," and "Cottage 108 Revisited: The Painting and Drawings of Frank V. Dudley."

CLAUDIA KHEEL

Indiana State Sentinel (July, 1841–February, 1906). Indianapolis newspaper. First published by brothers GEORGE A. AND JACOB P. CHAPMAN after they purchased the INDIANA DEMOCRAT (1830) and renamed it the INDIANA STATE

SENTINEL. The paper remained a supporter of the DEMOCRATIC PARTY throughout most of its history despite its many ownership and name changes.

Published as a bi-weekly by 1844, the morning paper became a daily in 1851. The *Sentinel* published daily during the legislative sessions from 1841 to 1844 and thereafter tri-weekly during the sessions. Originally the paper printed political news almost exclusively and only occasionally local news, but beginning in the late 1850s it included local items on a regular basis. It had numerous owners until 1861 when purchased by John R. Elder and John Harkness of the *Indiana State Guard*, who merged the two papers under the *Sentinel*'s name. The paper changed hands frequently from 1865 to 1888 but achieved financial stability under the strong editorial direction of Samuel E. Morss, the owner from 1888 to 1903. While Morss served as United States consul general to Paris from 1893 to 1897, historian JACOB PIATT DUNN directed the editorial section of the paper. After it failed to take a stand on the 1896 "Free Silver" issue, the *Sentinel* lost advertisers and subscribers. Continued party division over the issue and a prolonged advertising boycott resulted in irreversible financial problems for the paper.

In 1903 Morss was forced to produce the *Sentinel* as a one-cent evening edition. The Associated Press franchise was sold a few days later to the founders of the *INDIANAPOLIS STAR*. After Morss' death in 1903 the paper declined and in 1906 was sold, with the *Star* purchasing the Sunday *Sentinel* and the *INDIANAPOLIS NEWS* acquiring the daily edition and the printing plant.

JOAN CUNNINGHAM

Jacob Piatt Dunn, *Greater Indianapolis* (Chicago, 1910); John W. Miller, *Indiana Newspaper Bibliography* (Indianapolis, 1982).

Indiana Theatre (140 West Washington Street). In 1927 the Circle Theatre Company, which owned the Circle Theatre on MONUMENT CIRCLE, built the Indiana Theatre on West Washington Street as a movie palace. The Spanish baroque theatre was designed by the Indianapolis architectural firm of RUBUSH AND HUNTER. The F.

E. Gates Marble and Tile Company supplied travertine marble and terra cotta and utilized sculptor ALEXANDER SANGERNEBO's design for facade ornament. The firm of William Herman & Sons prepared all the plaster work, including friezes, figures, and ceiling panels, as well as custom woodwork and furniture. Joseph Wollenberg designed the interior decoration.

The six-story concrete frame structure has side and back walls of red brick and a south facade of glazed white terra cotta tile divided into three bays. The marquee, at mezzanine level, extends the entire width of the facade. Above the marquee, simple side bays flank a central bay decorated with high relief churrigueresque ornament. The entrance lobby features travertine marble walls and floors and an elaborate plaster ceiling. Beyond the entrance lobby the two and one half story main lobby, with vaulted ceiling and mezzanine promenade, extends the full width of the building. The west end of the lobby contains a multitiered fountain of green Rookwood tile, set in a mirrored niche framed by a Moorish arch. The freestanding grand stairway at the east end of the lobby rises to the mezzanine.

Originally the Indiana Theatre contained a luncheonette, soda fountain, bowling alleys, billiard rooms, candy-, tobacco-, and barber shops, and a 3,200–seat auditorium, the largest cinema ever built in Indianapolis. The top floor of the building houses the Indiana Roof Ballroom. The ballroom resembles a Spanish town square, with a promenade arcade one step above the dance floor. A balcony with a simple iron railing surrounds this composition. The deep blue elliptical domed ceiling is studded with small electric "stars." Four projectors created "clouds" which moved across the ceiling, adding to the effect of a night sky.

In 1927 the Indiana Theatre represented the height of technology. The building's unique "weather system" made it one of the first structures in Indianapolis to feature air conditioning. In the ballroom a "sea breeze" was provided for dancers by passing outside air over iced salt water in the summer and warmed salt water in the winter. The resilient dance floor used a suspension system. Later, the Indiana Theatre was the first theatre in the state to adopt stereophonic sound,

Panavision, 3–D projection, closed-circuit television, and Cinerama facilities.

The theatre ceased operation as a cinema in 1975 but was acquired by the INDIANA REPERTORY THEATRE and remodeled in 1979–1980. The Indiana Theatre is listed on the National Register of Historic Places (1979) and the Historic American Buildings Survey.

AMY H. WILSON

Thomas M. Slade, ed., *Historic American Buildings Survey in Indiana* (Indianapolis and Bloomington, 1983).

Indiana Transportation Museum. Institution dedicated to Indiana's transportation heritage, with a focus on railroads. The not-for-profit museum, located northeast of Indianapolis in Noblesville's Forest Park, preserves, restores, operates, and interprets historic transportation equipment, including many examples of railroad rolling stock and several locomotives. Three transportation enthusiasts founded the museum in 1960 with a small inventory that now exceeds 100 pieces. A small professional staff and numerous volunteers manage and operate the predominately outdoor facility, which also houses a gift shop and administrative offices in an old depot.

Visitors can view dozens of examples of railroad equipment, some dating to the late 19th century and restored according to federal regulations. A trolley ride is another popular feature, as are excursions such as the Fair Train to the INDIANA STATE FAIR. Acquisitions come from liquidation of corporate assets and auctions, as well as donations from RAILROADS and private investors. The museum's most ambitious project has been the five-year $250,000 restoration in the late 1980s of three urban cars for the National Park Service. In an attempt to acquire its own track museum officials secured an option to purchase from Norfolk Southern Corporation the last north-south rail line into the center of Indianapolis, which runs south from Tipton and passes adjacent to the museum. Negotiations were continuing as of early 1994.

JUDY SCHWARTZ

Indiana University Center on Philanthropy. Supports education, research, and public service in philanthropy. A university-wide policy committee governs the center; a national board of visitors, representing government, business, and the nonprofit sector, serves as an external advisory body.

The Center on Philanthropy was established at INDIANA UNIVERSITY–PURDUE UNIVERSITY AT INDIANAPOLIS in November, 1987. The next year, Robert L. Payton, former president of the Exxon Education Foundation, became the Center's first director. Initial support for the center came from a core grant of $4.1 million from LILLY ENDOWMENT; in 1990 the Endowment gave an additional $11.4 million and anonymous donors $3.7 million to support center programs.

A leader in developing the new field of philanthropic studies, the center works to integrate philanthropic studies into the liberal arts curriculum and professional programs at undergraduate and graduate levels. To support the development of philanthropic studies, the center (1) offers curriculum development grants to Indiana University faculty and research grants to scholars in the United States and abroad, (2) sponsors a doctoral fellows program, (3) operates a series of ongoing seminars for faculty members, nonprofit executives, and community leaders, (4) publishes two reference tools, *Research in Progress* and *Philanthropic Studies Index*, (5) funds library acquisitions and archive development, and (6) explores ways of cooperating with existing and developing degree programs in related fields throughout the university.

The center's primary public service activity is The Fund Raising School, the only university-based, national program in fund-raising education. The school offers general and tailored workshops internationally, which combine philanthropic theory and ethics with practical techniques of the profession, furthering the center's aim of improving the practice of philanthropy while connecting practice with theory. Other public service activities are center-sponsored lectures, workshops, symposia, and conferences; the publication of books, monographs, topical bibliographies, and a periodical (*Philanthropy Matters*); the Jane Addams Fellows Program, which introduces recent college graduates to voluntary sector issues and activities; and facilitation of programs that support student voluntary service at the eight Indiana University campuses, Butler University, DePauw University, Earlham College, the University of Notre Dame, and Valparaiso University.

PATRICIA A. DEAN

Indiana University Medical Center (IUMC).

Internationally known medical training and treatment facilities located on 85 acres of what is now the INDIANA UNIVERSITY–PURDUE UNIVERSITY AT INDIANAPOLIS campus. The IUMC is home to the facilities of the Indiana University Schools of Medicine (IUSM), Nursing, Dentistry, and Allied Health, and six hospitals with over 2,100 beds. Three of the hospitals—Riley, University, and Long—are owned by Indiana University. Other hospitals associated with IUMC include WISHARD MEMORIAL HOSPITAL, formerly Marion County General, managed by IUSM since 1975; Larue D. Carter Memorial, a state mental health facility; and the Richard L. Roudebush Veterans Administration Medical Center. The Indiana State Board of Health Building is also located within the IUMC boundaries. IUMC is the center for the Indiana Statewide Medical Education system with programs in several Indiana communities.

Established by the Indiana General Assembly in 1909, the IUMC united three proprietary medical schools—Indiana Medical College, Fort Wayne College of Medicine, and Central College of Physicians and Surgeons. This allowed Indiana University to create a first-class, four-year school of medicine—the first year offered at Bloomington, the remaining three years in Indianapolis. The IUSM, originally located downtown at the corner of Senate Avenue and Market Street, moved to the Medical School Building (now Emerson Hall) on the IUMC grounds in 1919. Now students may complete their four-year degree at IUMC, or take up to two years toward their degree at Indiana University-Bloomington or any one of the university's regional campuses. The final two years of the degree must be taken on the Indianapolis campus. By 1990 two-thirds of the physicians in Indiana had received their diplomas from IUSM.

Upon its dedication in 1924, the JAMES WHITCOMB RILEY HOSPITAL FOR CHILDREN joined the IUMC campus as Indiana's only children's hospital. A pioneer in research on childhood diseases, Riley serves 83,000 patients annually and has an international reputation for its burn and bone marrow transplant units. Some families of patients being treated at Riley are provided with temporary housing at the Ronald McDonald House, which is supported by donations from private sources including local McDonald's restaurant owners. The other two Indiana University hospitals, Long and University, serve 20,000 inpatients annually and operate solely with service fees and contributions; they receive no state funds. The Coleman Center for Women—formerly located at Coleman Hospital, a center for obstetric-gynecologic research and care—now operates within University Hospital. Ten percent of Indiana University hospitals' patients now come from outside the state of Indiana, some from outside the country.

IUMC has gained an international reputation for its medical training and research in advanced techniques. Pioneering work in prostate gland surgery and the treatment of thyroid disease and testicular cancer have added to the center's prestige. In 1963 a team of IUMC physicians developed the echocardiograph (EKG). An advanced bone marrow transplant program, in-vitro fertilization, the nation's only noncommercial DNA bank, heart and kidney transplants, and the largest pediatric cardiology program in the United States keep IUMC a leader in medical research and training.

NANCY L. ECKERMAN
Indiana University School of Medicine

Indiana University–Purdue University at Indianapolis (IUPUI).

The third largest institution of higher education in Indiana with nearly 28,000 students, IUPUI employs over 1,400 full-time faculty and nearly 7,000 full-time staff and an additional 3,450 part-time faculty and staff. Located on 289 acres on the west side of downtown Indianapolis, the university offers over 170 degree programs through an array of academic schools that include Liberal Arts, Science, Allied

Health, Engineering and Technology, Medicine, Dentistry, Nursing, Law, Education, Public and Environmental Affairs, Business, Social Work, Physical Education, and the Herron School of Art. IUPUI was the fourth largest employer in Indianapolis in 1993.

As an institution, the university can trace its roots to 1891 when a young economics professor, Jeremiah Jenks, traveled the 50 muddy miles to Indianapolis from Indiana University (IU) in Bloomington to deliver a series of lectures. Sponsored by the Indianapolis chapter of the Association of Collegiate Alumnae, the series spanned 12 weeks. Students who completed all of the prescribed readings, met with Jenks for weekly recitations, and passed the written examinations were granted two university credits. The concept proved to be extremely popular with Indianapolis residents and other courses soon followed.

By 1916 the growing number of courses offered in Indianapolis spurred IU to establish an Extension Teaching Center in the city. Originally located on the 10th floor of the MERCHANTS NATIONAL BANK BUILDING, the center moved in 1920 to a new location on North Senate Avenue and later to North Pennsylvania Street. In 1928 the center relocated in the former Bobbs-Merrill Building on East Michigan Street until after World War II.

The number of students enrolled in these extension courses rose rapidly, climbing from just over 1,000 in 1920 to 3,500 by the mid–1930s. Enrollment continued to mount in the postwar years of the 1940s, expanding even faster after passage of the Servicemen's Readjustment Act, the "GI Bill," which gave returning World War II veterans unprecedented opportunities for a college degree.

Purdue University had established a strong presence in the area as well, and returning veterans found the lure of engineering and the sciences quite attractive. As the demand for higher education continued into the 1960s, course offerings and academic programs at the Indianapolis extensions of both Indiana and Purdue expanded rapidly. Although competition was keen between the two universities, they managed to operate under terms Chancellor Herman B Wells of IU referred to as a "host-guest" relationship. If either university already had established a substantial program of courses and services, it served as "host" to the other university and provided the administrative and other necessary services for both. This arrangement was the case in Indianapolis until the late 1960s.

The demand for courses in the capital city was incessant. Growth was so impressive that in 1968 Wells' successor, Elvis Stahr, recommended that a separate chancellor be appointed for the Indianapolis campus. In 1969 the boards of Indiana and Purdue officially merged the operations of their respective Indianapolis extensions to create Indiana University–Purdue University at Indianapolis, reflecting the vested interests of both institutions.

Local politicians and partisans within the Indianapolis metropolitan area have often argued that a separate, state-funded institution should have been created independent of the established universities. At least four efforts had been mounted in the 19th century to relocate Indiana University from Bloomington to Indianapolis. Similarly, a legislative bill proposed the old State House in Indianapolis as a site for an agricultural college in 1857. The bill failed when John Purdue's offer of land and money tipped the scales in favor of Tippecanoe County. The argument for a separate state institution in Indianapolis persists, even though it has weakened in recent years.

IUPUI actually represents, within its institutional framework, the amalgamation of several other schools. For example, the School of Physical Education embraces the former NORMAL COLLEGE OF THE AMERICAN GYMNASTIC UNION. The HERRON SCHOOL OF ART, begun in 1877 as an independent institution, merged with the Indiana University system in 1967. The Benjamin Harrison Law School had operated on its own until its merger within the IU system in 1944; it became an independent college within the university in 1968. The INDIANA UNIVERSITY MEDICAL CENTER was first organized as a medical center in 1909; it now consists of 6 buildings and 90 clinics on the IUPUI campus. The medical center is the second largest in the United States in terms of enrollment and campus size. Some of it now sits on land near the White River which was notorious for mosquitoes and malaria epidemics in the late 1800s and early 1900s.

The physical expansion of IUPUI, especially the move to its current location, an area near the historic center of the city's African-American population, has not been without controversy. Especially troublesome to neighborhood advocates was the 1983 decision to expand the campus into an area known as LOCKEFIELD GARDENS, which housed one of the first federal public housing projects in the 1930s. Although it contained substandard housing, some African-Americans protested the decision to construct campus facilities in this historically significant neighborhood. Rehabilitation and renovation by local developers preserved only 200 of the original residential units in the area, most of them as part of the refurbished Lockefield Gardens Apartments.

As an institution, IUPUI is still governed cooperatively by both Purdue and Indiana universities. The various schools and faculties are aligned according to their respective institutional systems, e.g., the faculty within the School of Engineering and Technology is associated with Purdue. Other programs, departments, and academic schools are governed only by the Indianapolis campus. As such, IUPUI is able to draw upon the strengths of both major university systems while maintaining a unique institutional mission and purpose of its own.

Because of its urban setting and easy access for thousands of Indiana citizens, Indiana University–Purdue University at Indianapolis has a long history of reaching out to the community in terms of course offerings and unique programs. LEARN AND SHOP, a program which offers college courses in area shopping malls, and Weekend College are two examples of the IUPUI tradition of creating opportunities for the nontraditional students who comprised 25 percent of the university's total enrollment. By the 1990s almost half of IUPUI's student population was over 25 years of age.

The rapid expansion of the Indianapolis area as a national center for amateur athletics has also enabled the university to expand athletic facilities, such as the nationally recognized natatorium, the track and field facilities, and other sports and recreation areas. Many of these facilities were built for the 1987 PAN AMERICAN GAMES and are often open to the public as well as to students, staff, and faculty. By working cooperatively with the city, state, and federal governments, private developers, and local philanthropies such as the LILLY ENDOWMENT, IUPUI also has been able to continue its expansion of academic buildings. New science and technology buildings in the late 1980s and early 1990s housed most of the campus offerings at the downtown campus—many of the Purdue programs had been located in the Krannert Building on 38th Street—with only a planned move by the Herron School of Art needed to complete consolidation of the university's physical plant.

In both 1992 and 1993 IUPUI attracted more grant and contract income than either IU or Purdue. Although state appropriations have decreased from 23 percent to 18 percent of the school's annual budget in the last four years, the budget has increased by an annual average of over $95 million. Thus external revenue sources including student tuition and fees, contracts, and grants play an increasingly important part in the school's funding. IUPUI's grant and contract income rose from $58.2 million in 1988 to $89.4 million in 1993.

With an annual budget of over $852 million, IUPUI's economic impact significantly contributes to the stability of central Indiana's economy. The educational impact has been even more important, with nearly 12 percent of metropolitan-area residents between 18 and 54 taking at least one course at the university between 1988 and 1993. IUPUI's contribution to Indianapolis has been and continues to be profound both educationally and economically.

ROBERT SCHWARTZ

Indiana University School of Medicine.

Until the 1890s most medical education was based at proprietary schools. At that time basic science courses were added to the curriculum, requiring expensive equipment and full-time instructors that strained the finances of the proprietary schools. University-based schools with access to state funding and endowments became the model for medical education, with Johns Hopkins University leading the way in 1893. Indiana University joined the movement in 1903 by establishing the School of Medicine (IUSM) in Indianapolis. University president William Lowe Bryan recruited outstanding faculty for the new school, which at the time was one of only four schools in the country to require at least two years of college for admission.

Students were admitted immediately and, in 1905, friends of the university purchased and remodeled the former Central College of Physicians and Surgeons building for the clinical years of study. In 1908 the Indiana Medical College, a consolidation of three proprietary schools that had affiliated with Purdue University in 1905, merged with IUSM, which then moved to the old Medical College of Indiana building.

Dr. Allison Maxwell became the first dean of the medical school in Indianapolis in 1908. He was succeeded by Dr. CHARLES P. EMERSON (1911–1932). During Emerson's tenure the medical social service program began (a forerunner of what eventually became the School of Social Work). In 1911 the General Assembly accepted Dr. Robert Long's offer to provide funding for a new hospital, and a site near the City Hospital was selected. Ironically, this location was originally swampland and considered the most unhealthy part of the city. The new Long Hospital opened in 1914, and in 1919 the first medical education building, later to become Emerson Hall, was completed nearby.

By 1920 the freshman class reached 100 students, one of the largest classes in the country. In 1924 the JAMES WHITCOMB RILEY HOSPITAL FOR CHILDREN opened as the state's only children's hospital. The Coleman Hospital for Women opened in 1927, the first hospital in Indiana built exclusively for obstetrics and gynecology.

Dr. WILLIS GATCH served as dean from 1932 to 1946, introducing a laboratory for experimental surgery during his term, but not until the appointment of Dr. JOHN VAN NUYS (1947–1964) did IUSM have its first full-time dean. During this period there was a major increase in outside grants for research and buildings, allowing the development of a true medical center. New facilities completed at Riley Hospital in the 1950s became the focus for major research on children's diseases and disabilities, including innovative health care

delivery methods. The Medical Science Building opened in 1958, providing space for laboratories and research facilities and allowing all four years of study to be completed in Indianapolis for the first time.

Many specialized research centers have been developed since the 1960s, including those for cancer, arthritis, diabetes, psychiatry, hypertension, medical genetics, alcoholism, Alzheimer's disease, general clinical research, and sexually transmitted diseases. The Krannert Institute of Cardiology, created in 1963, has an international reputation for its cardiovascular research. Research is conducted in most of the basic science and clinical departments as well as in the specialized centers. The Division of Allied Health Sciences, which provides instruction in health care occupations such as physical therapy and radiography, was established within the IUSM in 1959.

Under Dr. Glenn Irwin's leadership (1965–1974) the first phase of the new University Hospital opened (1970) and IUSM initiated an extensive curriculum revision, the "Indiana Plan," which established new residency programs in leading hospitals throughout the state and became a national model. Dr. Steven Beering became the sixth dean of the IUSM in 1974. During his term the second phase of University Hospital was completed (the Regenstrief Health Center, which consolidated medical center outpatient clinics). Also opened was the world's largest Ronald McDonald House, a home-away-from-home for families of children being treated at Riley and other area hospitals.

Dr. Walter Daly became dean in 1983. A major new addition to Riley Hospital was completed in 1986, the new Medical Research and Library Building opened in 1989, and in 1992 a major new wing was opened in University Hospital, consolidating campus-wide ambulatory health services. During this period IUSM developed a model contract for managing the professional responsibilities of WISHARD MEMORIAL HOSPITAL, the city-owned hospital. By the late 1980s the entering class size had reached 300 students. The medical center campus currently includes six hospitals and 25 buildings on a 90–acre campus, including state, federal, and city-county facilities, all managed under the medical direction of the School of Medicine.

The IUSM can claim a number of "firsts" in Indiana medical history. These include the state's first kidney transplant (1964), first adult (1980) and pediatric (1983) cochlear implants, first liver transplant (1988), and first pancreas transplant (1990). The school is also recognized for its pathbreaking research on testicular cancer and for work on voice restoration in cancer patients.

STEPHEN KIRCHHOFF

Charles A. Bonsett, M.D., ed., *The I.U. Physician* (Indianapolis, 1978); Dorothy Ritter Russo, ed., *One Hundred Years of Indiana Medicine, 1849–1949* (Indianapolis, 1949).

Indiana Vocational Technical College (Ivy Tech).
Post-secondary technical institution. Indiana Vocational Technical College is a public institution that offers a wide range of technical, semi-technical, and vocational programs in 13 regions throughout Indiana. The school, popularly known as Ivy Tech, awards Associate in Science and Associate in Applied Science degrees, and technical certificates. It is accredited by the North Central Association of Colleges and Schools, the Indiana Commission on Vocational Technical Education, and other appropriate agencies for specific programs. Statewide enrollment for the fall semester, 1992, was approximately 33,000.

The Indiana General Assembly founded Indiana Vocational and Technical College in 1963 with a two-year $50,000 appropriation for planning and development. Legislation establishing the college specified that a seven-person board of trustees (later 13) govern the school. The initial board, appointed by Governor Matthew Welsh, included representatives of specific constituencies as well as the general public, and the state superintendent of public instruction as an ex officio member.

From 1963 to 1965, Dr. J. M. Ryder, the director of Purdue University's Indianapolis regional campus, acted as the school's part-time interim administrator. In 1965 the institution's board of trustees appointed Frederic M. Hadley, a former executive at Eli Lilly and Company and a vice-president with Wabash College in Crawfordsville, as the school's first president. The school began classes the same year. The state legislature also provided a $2.8 million budget and authorized the creation of 13 districts, each with its own board of trustees, in order for the college to offer vocational training statewide.

Though Indiana Vocational Technical College was created by the Indiana General Assembly to provide "occupational training of a practical, technical and semi-technical nature for the citizens of Indiana," there was strong initial resistance to the college within the state educational bureaucracy. Between 1966 and early 1969 opponents vigorously protested that public vocational and technical education should be controlled by the state's department of public instruction rather than by a separate board of trustees. Despite this bureaucratic conflict, the school continued to grow. Twelve of the college's 13 regions had been issued charters by 1969 and enrollment continued to increase.

The Central Indiana region, Region VIII, in which Indianapolis is located, was formally chartered in June, 1969. But Ivy Tech first offered classes in the city in 1965, when the school assumed operation of the Mallory Technical Institute under a contract with the Indianapolis Board of School Commissioners. The P. R. MALLORY COMPANY had given the building housing the institute, located at 1315 East Washington Street, to the Indianapolis Public Schools. So until Region VIII was chartered, the administrative and instructional staff at the institute were technically employees of the public school system. Mallory Technical Institute officially became a part of Indiana Vocational Technical College in 1969. The college had also signed a contract in 1965 with the state Vocational and Technical Education Board to assume responsibility for the Manpower Training Program at the city's major air terminal, Weir Cook (now INDIANAPOLIS INTERNATIONAL AIRPORT). The college's regular operation in Indianapolis began in September, 1966, with ten full-time and 357 part-time students. Warren F. Haase served as the first director of Ivy Tech programs in Region VIII. He later became Region VIII's vice-president-dean. Ivy Tech has offered programs in Indianapolis continuously since that time, and Region VIII's fall enrollment in 1992 approached 6,100 students. Several of the college's programs of study are available at the region's campus complex on North Meridian Street at Fall Creek Parkway, where the institution moved in 1983. A new Technologies Building opened at this site in 1990.

CHARLES TITUS
Eastern Illinois University

Laura A. Gaus, *Ivy Tech: The First Twenty-Five Years* (Indianapolis, 1990).

Indiana Women's Prison. The Indiana Reformatory Institution for Women and Girls opened in Indianapolis on October 8, 1873, when 17 prisoners transferred from the State Prison South at Jeffersonville. A female three-member board oversaw the first prison built in the United States to house female criminals. Divided into two sections, adult criminals went to the prison and those younger than 15 to reformatory school. When the Girls School opened near CLERMONT in 1907 the name became the Indiana Woman's (and later Women's) Prison. Situated on 15 acres at 401 North Randolph Street, it remained in one building until the late 1930s when an administration building, residential cottages, hospital, and chapel were added. In 1975 the prison board was disbanded and control assigned to the Indiana Parole Board, which developed a master plan and renovated several buildings. In

A 1916 view of the poultry yard at the Indiana Women's Prison on the city's near east side. [Indiana Historical Society, Bass Collection, #46278-F]

the early 1990s the prison houses some 350 inmates and it has a staff of approximately 240 full-time employees.

Emphasis has always been placed on rehabilitation and education. In early days, sewing, laundry, and knitting occupied time and provided skills which could be used as a means of support upon release. Later an accredited high school education program with diplomas issued by ARSENAL TECHNICAL HIGH SCHOOL was available. A nurses aid program, business classes, beauty school, and the GED program also exist at the prison, and more recently MARTIN UNIVERSITY has been making collegiate instruction available to the women incarcerated there.

CYNTHIA FAUNCE

Indiana/World Skating Academy and Research Center. Ice sports facility. The Indiana/World Skating Academy and Research Center (I/WSA) is a not-for-profit foundation founded in Indianapolis in 1987 and governed by a board of directors chosen by several civic organizations and local universities. I/WSA offers extensive competitive training in figure skating, HOCKEY, and speed skating. Daily patch and freestyle sessions and Olympic training camps are conducted for figure skaters. Hockey competition is offered through the Indiana Select Youth Hockey Association, known as "Team Indiana." Also, the Indianapolis Junior Ice play an elite level of Junior "A" Hockey in the North American Junior Hockey League. The Indy Speed Skating Club hosts meets. A "Learn-to-Skate" program guides students of all ages in basic skating skills through advanced moves in figures, freestyle, ice dance, power skating, and precision skating.

The I/WSA facility, located at Pan American Plaza, houses two rinks that have been used by skaters from all over the world. The Olympic Rink is one of the few 100 by 200′ international-sized ice surfaces in the United States. The American Rink is an 85 by 200′ National Hockey League–sized surface bordered by seating for 1,000 spectators. The facility is also available for recreational skating.

The Human Performance Laboratory in the research center is the site of the sports medicine and science programs. The latest techniques in biochemics, fitness and conditioning, nutrition, and sports psychology help the skaters achieve their potential.

JUDY SCHWARTZ

Indiana World War Memorial Plaza.

Plaza and monument originally dedicated to the veterans of World War I, and now honoring Indiana veterans who have served in any conflict since then.

In 1919 Indiana waged a campaign to bring the national headquarters of the AMERICAN LEGION to Indianapolis. Founded in 1919 at the close of World War I, the American Legion temporarily located in New York City. Later that year, following successful lobbying and campaigning, the American Legion selected Indianapolis to be the site of its national headquarters.

To make good on their promise to construct a memorial to the veterans, in January, 1920, a Citizens Planning Committee set aside two city blocks (Vermont to North streets between Meridian and Pennsylvania). Within these blocks were SECOND PRESBYTERIAN CHURCH, FIRST BAPTIST CHURCH, the Indianapolis Elks Lodge, and office buildings. The two designated blocks, along with St. Clair Park and the public library to the north and UNIVERSITY PARK to the south, would form a five block civic plaza that would incorporate the memorial, the American Legion headquarters, and public buildings along Meridian and Pennsylvania streets. The plan thus called for the removal of several buildings in the southern block of the plaza, as well as the INDIANA SCHOOL FOR THE BLIND south of the library. The formal setting, civic center concept, and Neoclassical design clearly reflect the tenets of the City Beautiful Movement. This movement had rooted itself in American culture in the late 1880s when planners and architects began to think of beautifying cities along classic lines. The 1893 World's Columbian Exposition, held in Chicago, focused attention on this principle.

Preliminary work began on the plaza in early 1921. Announcing a nationwide competition for an architect, the War Memorial Board requested a design to commemorate valor and the sacrifices of soldiers, sailors, and marines while also providing meeting, office, and archival space. Funding for the site purchase and continued maintenance was to be provided by city funds, with the state paying for the memorial construction. In 1923 the War Memorial Board selected Frank B. Walker and Harry E. Weeks of Cleveland, Ohio, to serve as architects of the plaza. Walker & Weeks' original plans included the main memorial, two auxiliary buildings, the cenotaph, mall, and obelisk.

Advertisement for bids for the western Legion building—the first of two auxiliary buildings in the Walker & Weeks plan—began in 1924. The Craig-Curtiss Company of Cleveland, selected as contractor, began construction on the two-story limestone building in 1925. The building displays typical Neoclassical elements such as pilasters and a monitor roof. Its style clearly echoes that of the INDIANAPOLIS–MARION COUNTY PUBLIC LIBRARY immediately to the north. The eastern auxiliary building reflects a similar Neoclassical design. Although it was part of the plan by Walker & Weeks, this building was not constructed until 1950.

Located in the sunken garden between the two Legion buildings is Cenotaph Square, a memorial to the war dead. Constructed of black granite, the cenotaph rests on a base of red and dark green granite. Completing the square are four black granite shafts surmounted by eagles.

In early 1926 work began on the World War Memorial. The buildings on the site, including the Elks Club, Haugh Hotel, Cambridge Apartment Building, and Bobbs-Merrill Building, were demolished or moved. This left only the two churches, which remained on each side of the memorial until demolished in 1960.

The actual superstructure construction for the memorial began in early 1927, and on July 4 General John J. Pershing laid the cornerstone "consecrating the edifice as a patriotic shrine." Work continued steadily on the memorial until 1928 when a delay in the appropriation of state funds slowed the completion of the interior. In September, 1931, the Thomas A. Moynahan Company of Indianapolis received the contract to complete the interior of the memorial. In 1936 the federal Public Works Administration completed $195,000 worth of additional work, but there was much left to do including the removal of the churches, landscaping, and construction of the east and west steps on the memorial.

In April, 1949, the first newspaper accounts of the memorial's deterioration appeared. Leaks, cracked plaster, peeling paint, and eroding limestone led people to believe the memorial would deteriorate before its completion. Accounts of deterioration continued into the 1960s. Finally, in 1965, work was finished on the structure. The complete memorial is a high-style example of Neoclassical architecture. As a reflection of the significance of ancient classical forms, the memorial resembles the tomb of the Turkish king Mausolus at Halicarnassus. This great marble tomb, one of the seven wonders of the ancient world, consisted of a rectangular base upon which sat a colonnade similar to that of the World War Memorial. Because of its size and scale, the memorial is the most imposing Neoclassical structure in the city and is the focal point of the World War Memorial Plaza.

On the southern steps of the memorial is *Pro Patria*, a sculpture by New York artist Henry Herring. At the time of installation in 1929, the 25–foot-tall, seven-ton statue was described as the largest sculptured bronze casting ever made in America. In addition to *Pro Patria*, Herring also sculpted the stone figures on the memorial and the panels on the obelisk.

The obelisk and fountain in the center of the plaza were completed in 1930 as part of Walker & Weeks' original design. The obelisk is a 100–foot-tall shaft faced in Berwick granite with four bronze bas-relief panels at the base sculpted to represent law, science, religion, and education. The fountain consists of two basins with spray rings and multi-colored lights. The square was originally paved, as called for in the plans, but some citizens felt it would be more attractive if it were landscaped, and a beautification campaign was mounted in 1973. In 1975 the firm of Browning, Day and Pollack was awarded a contract to replace the paving with lawn, trees, and brick walkways. One area has been set aside for the flying of state flags.

As one of the most prominent buildings in downtown Indianapolis and an important design and planning element of the MILE SQUARE, the World War Memorial and surrounding plaza play host to numerous civic and military activities throughout the year. Included among the celebrations and memorials are a Fourth of July festival, Veterans Day and Memorial Day services, and use of the meeting rooms and auditorium by civic organizations as well as state and federal agencies. The plaza, which was added to the National Register of Historic Places in 1989, is also frequently used for athletic and recreational events.

The War Memorials Commission, which maintains the plaza grounds and memorial, plans to construct a memorial on the plaza to honor Korean and Vietnam veterans. The memorial currently houses exhibits relating to the Korean and Vietnam wars with plans to include the Persian Gulf War in the future.

SUZANNE T. ROLLINS

American Legion Weekly, 6 (Aug. 29, 1924), 4+; National Register of Historic Places nomination form (copy in the files of Historic Landmarks Foundation of Indiana).

Indianapolis, Music about. Cities and towns have always been a favorite topic of songwriters and composers, and Indianapolis is no exception. This music tends to be formulaic: song texts differ little except for the name of the locale and a few salient details, and most are sentimental and patriotic. Boosterism is a common theme, and tunes are of a musical style popular in the period they were written. Even though these topical pieces offer little that is unique, they do encapsulate contemporary feelings about a city, as shown by the following representative pieces about Indianapolis.

An early piece of music about the city is entitled "The Indianapolis Waltz." Written by S. Ehrlich and dedicated to Alfred Moses, it is very much a piece of its time. Published in Philadelphia, it is undated, but the highly ornamented engraving style was common in music published between 1850 and 1875. Ehrlich and Moses do not appear in Marion County histories, so it is difficult to link this parlor piano piece to the city by anything other than its name.

Written in 1916 in honor of the state's centennial, Stella Hall Millikan's "Indianapolis" is a booster song, promoting the positive attributes of the city. [Indiana Historical Society, #C5836]

Isaac Doles (ca. 1853–1927), a well-known Indianapolis composer and performer on organ and piano, wrote "Back to Dear Old Indianapolis" in 1905. The highly sentimental song, subtitled a "patriotic waltz song and chorus," could have been written about any city whose young men went off to war leaving hometown and sweethearts behind, only to die "on some distant island." The piece, presumably about service in the Philippines or Cuba, was republished again in 1918 because it described World War I equally well.

State and city anniversaries are common themes for songs and music, as illustrated by Stella Hall Millikan's "Indianapolis." Written in 1916 to honor the centennial of Indiana's statehood, the song is dedicated to "Indianapolis, No Mean City." The cover artwork shows an outline of the state overlaid with U.S. flags and governors' portraits from 1816 and 1916. The subtitle, "a booster song for the capital of Indiana," accurately describes the contents of the text. In nine verses, Millikan mentions the Soldiers and Sailors Monu-

ment, celebrated authors, educational, cultural, and entertainment venues, business institutions, and the *News*, *Times*, and *Star* newspapers. Unsurprisingly, two verses are devoted to the INDIANAPOLIS MOTOR SPEEDWAY and the INDIANAPOLIS 500–MILE RACE.

"Indianapolis, My Home Town," a similar booster piece, was written by local organist and composer Charles F. Roberts (ca. 1878–1936) and playwright Henry K. Burton (1884–1947). Published in 1921, it was the official song of the Indianapolis Industrial Exposition. Dedicated to the Indianapolis Chamber of Commerce, the cover art depicts the Soldiers and Sailors Monument. Beyond this image, the song could be about any city celebrating its civic pride, growth, and modernity; the text mentions nothing specific to the city. Even so, the song became extremely popular, and over 30,000 copies were sold in Indianapolis.

In 1920 Isaac Doles composed and published the "Indianapolis Centennial March," dedicated to "Dear Old Indianapolis, Largest and Most Beautiful City in the World." Doles, a master of hyperbole, was also skilled at getting multiple publications from one piece of music, a common practice of the time. It was first written in 1883 as the "St. George Commandery March" for the Knights of St. John in Chicago, appeared again dedicated to Commandery 31, Greensburg, Indiana (Dole's home lodge), and again as a supplement to the *Indianapolis Sentinel* Sunday edition, June 29, 1902.

Doles republished the piece in 1920 to take advantage of the centennial sales market and seems to have poked fun at it simultaneously. The cover art includes similar pictures of Doles, supposedly in 1820 and 1920, and the publication information states that it was "copyright 1820, by Isaac Doles," and "copyrite [sic] 1920, by Isaac Doles." The cover notes that the march was written originally in 1820 as the "St. George Commandery March," the "best march published since the Flood," and the satire is continued by the statement that the author is "124 years old and never told a lie *yet*, Not Yet??" Each edition of the tune was printed from original plates with different title engravings.

The most recent booster song for Indianapolis differs little from Millikan's tune. "Indianapolis, Indeed," written in 1988 with words by Gloria Gaither (and sung at the State Fair and other events by popular country singer Sandi Patti), paints a sentimental and romantic but contemporary vision of the city that includes St. John's Catholic Church, Starlight Musicals, Union Station, the Circle, City Market, the Indianapolis Symphony Orchestra, and the 500. The tune is similar in emotional content to Millikan's picture of a growing, modern, culturally aware city.

The city also has been treated musically by other than popular writers. The most recent and unique piece of music written about the city is a symphonic work commissioned by the Indianapolis Symphony Orchestra, written by David Ott, composer-in-residence for the ISO and a faculty member at DePauw University. Premiered by the orchestra in September, 1993, the *Indianapolis Concerto* uses aural images instead of words to evoke the sights and rites of the city. The six movements depict the composer's drive into the city through the factory areas toward the growing skyline; the beauty of a sunrise reflected off a glass skyscraper; the fast pace and excitement of the Speedway; the solemnity of the Soldiers and Sailors Monument; the peaceful beauty of Holcomb Gardens at Butler University; and the city's May festivities.

Even though the pieces examined are separated by over 125 years of time, represent many different musical styles, and range from the mundane to the outstanding, all evoke the fondness residents have for the city.

SALLY CARR CHILDS-HELTON
Indiana Historical Society

Indianapolis Airport Authority (IAA).

Independent municipal corporation. As air traffic increased after World War II, additional airports were needed to divert small aircraft from Weir Cook Airport (now INDIANAPOLIS INTERNATIONAL AIRPORT), and such sites could not be found within the city limits. Therefore, the Indiana General Assembly created the IAA in 1961 to administer an air transportation system with jurisdiction over Marion County and the seven surrounding counties. Despite initial problems in establishing

the satellite airports, by the early 1990s the IAA owned and managed the Indianapolis International Airport, Eagle Creek Airpark, the downtown Heliport, and the Metropolitan, Mount Comfort, and Speedway airports.

IAA, which replaced the Board of Aviation Commissioners, is a five-member board, four of whom are appointed by the mayor and one by the county commissioners. The volunteer board meets bi-monthly and serves four-year terms. In addition to its policy and management functions the IAA sets its own budget, which is reviewed annually by the City-County Council. The IAA has taxing authority but has issued bonds only for large capital improvements. Revenue for operating expenses comes from federal airport funds, user fees, and service contracts.

MICHELLE D. HALE

League of Women Voters, *Unigov Handbook: A Citizen's Guide to Local Government* (Indianapolis, 1985); Marion County Metropolitan Planning Committee, *Metropolitan Airport System Plan, Summary Report* (Indianapolis, 1975).

Indianapolis Art Center (formerly Indianapolis Art League). Nonprofit visual arts organization focusing on teaching and exhibitions. The institution began in 1934 as a Works Progress Administration (WPA) project. An adult education art study group with ten founding women members met with artist-instructor William Kaeser, a native Austrian and HERRON SCHOOL OF ART graduate, at Public School 72. The group formally organized in 1938 as the Indianapolis Art Students' League, patterned after the New York Art Students' League. Classes were at first dispersed widely throughout the city due to gasoline rationing and later consolidated at Public School 66. By the 1950s space was at a premium, with classes held in various locations including the Rauh Memorial Library and the Governor's Residence, until the Holliday House at HOLLIDAY PARK was offered for use. It served as the first real home for the Indianapolis Art League (as it was now named) until it burned in 1958.

The fire spurred the efforts to raise funds for the Art League's own facility, and in 1960 the organization incorporated as the Indianapolis Art

League Foundation. With a gift of land at 3103 North Pennsylvania Street from John and Marguerite Fehsenfeld, and significant funds from the INDIANAPOLIS FOUNDATION and the Elsie Sweeney Foundation along with gifts from members, corporations, and the community, the league built its first new facility with two studio classrooms and a lobby. In 12 years it was again out of space. In 1976 the league raised $300,000 from members, foundations (especially the Indianapolis Foundation and LILLY ENDOWMENT), and corporations to build a facility with five studios, a gallery, offices, and a library along the White River at Broad Ripple. In the new location classes doubled during the first year to 40 a week; by 1993 the league offered 100 classes a week with 55 part-time artist-faculty. With burgeoning enrollment, the organization hired its first executive director in 1976 and began to build a professional staff.

In 1994, after a successful fund-raising campaign ($7.6 million), the league changed its name to the Indianapolis Art Center to coincide with expansion into a new facility designed by Michael Graves, a leading national architect and a native of Broad Ripple. This new building tripled the space and programs, with 13 studios, three galleries, a sales gallery, three courtyards, and offices. The Riverfront Performance Terrace, which in 1989 was Phase I of the expansion, allowed the league to introduce performance arts—music, dance, storytelling, film—as an enhancement to its previous visual arts mission.

The league's exhibitions program, begun in 1937, features the work of Indiana and regional producing artists. The first annual competition was held at Lyman Brothers and continued under various titles and at various locations: "The Indianapolis Art Students' League Annual Exhibition" (WILLIAM H. BLOCK COMPANY auditorium for 15 years), "500 Festival of Arts" (downtown storefronts until 1973), "Art 500" (Convention Center), and the biannual "Indiana Directions and Regional" (since 1976 at its own galleries).

The traditional Eurocentric approach to teaching art in the league's early days has been continually broadened to include more accessible media such as woodworking, glass, plastics, steel fabrication, and computer art, in addition to classes in ceramics, metalsmithing, textiles, and

photography. Also, in response to a growing awareness and celebration of diverse local and global communities, the league has expanded its audience, culminating in 1989 with ArtReach, a program for youth at risk. Begun in public housing communities, it currently serves 300 youth and extends into public parks, schools, and mental health community centers through innovative private-public partnerships that have become national models.

JOYCE A. SOMMERS
JOHN DAVID HOOVER
Indianapolis Art Center

Indianapolis Art League. See Indianapolis Art Center

Indianapolis Asylum for Friendless Colored Children. Orphanage for black children. Begun in 1870, it was then the sole orphanage in the state to care for African-American children, and one of a handful in the country. Orthodox Friends (or Quakers) established the home in a simple brick house located at 317 West 21st Street. Numerous additions to the home attempted to meet changing needs, and the asylum housed children at the same location throughout its existence.

The SOCIETY OF FRIENDS maintained the orphanage until 1922 when it was turned over to the Marion County Board of Commissioners. The home received funds from both private donations and county governments, particularly Marion County. The Quakers ran the orphanage through a Board of Women Managers who directed the daily activities of the asylum and a male Board of Directors who managed the home's finances. The orphanage accepted dependents from infancy to 14 years of age. At the end of the home's first year it had housed 18 children; by 1922 it had sheltered more than 3,000. Although most of the children came from the Indianapolis area, the home accepted orphans from all over Indiana.

In 1922, after management of the orphanage changed hands, the asylum's closing balance of $4,304.22 became the basis of a Friends Educational Fund for Negroes, a scholarship fund for black students that is administered by the First Friends Meeting of Indianapolis. The county commissioners operated the home until 1939, when the county welfare department took it over and cleared the home of children within a year. It closed a few years later.

THOMAS W. COWGER
Purdue University, West Lafayette

Indianapolis Asylum for Friendless Colored Children Manuscript Collection, Indiana Historical Society Library; Thomas W. Cowger, "Custodians of Social Justice: The Indianapolis Asylum for Friendless Colored Children, 1870–1922," *Indiana Magazine of History*, 88 (June, 1992), 93–110.

Indianapolis Athletic Club.
Sport and social club. The Indianapolis Athletic Club (IAC) was incorporated in 1920 by a group of Indianapolis businessmen to "promote clean sports, amusement, and sociability" among members. The clubhouse, a nine-story structure at Meridian and Vermont streets, was completed in January, 1924.

Although established as an athletic and social club, the IAC also became known for its professional and political (especially Democratic) connections. Members have included businessman ELI LILLY, *Indianapolis Star* and *News* publisher EUGENE C. PULLIAM, Democratic national committeeman FRANK MCHALE, and Governor Paul McNutt. The club has included several U.S. presidents among its guests. The institution has remained faithful to its athletic origins, however, winning several AMATEUR ATHLETIC UNION swimming championships during the 1950s and sending four swimmers to the 1960 Olympics—including FRANK E. MCKINNEY, JR., son of the chairman of the Democratic national committee and an IAC member.

During the 1970s and 1980s the IAC made a number of changes. In addition to extensive renovations, the club admitted its first African-American members in 1972 and gave the first voting membership to a woman in 1980. More recently, the club made national headlines in February, 1992, when a faulty refrigerator caused a fatal fire while jury members for the rape trial of world heavyweight boxing champion Mike Tyson were sequestered in the guest facilities.

ANNE HAUPT

Indianapolis Bail Bond Project.
Bail screening and pretrial services. Judge William T. Sharp, presiding judge of the Marion County Municipal Court, and representatives from the legal community organized the project on a trial basis in 1970 in response to bail bond abuses during the 1960s. The program paralleled others in operation elsewhere in the United States. Organizers sought to lessen the need for bail bondsmen as well as render judges' bail recommendations both reasonable and equitable.

The Indiana University Law School in Indianapolis provided staff and administrative facilities for the project, while the Indiana Criminal Justice Planning Agency provided most of the funding through a federal grant. Senior law school students acted as bail commissioners, interviewing misdemeanor defendants upon their arrest. Based on verifiable information from jail interviews, commissioners made bail recommendations to the court. A majority of defendants were then released on their own recognizance, saving time and money for defendants and reducing the jail population. Project staff also monitored defendants who were released with restrictions, investigated those who missed court dates, and diverted some defendants to non-jail rehabilitation programs.

In 1976 the various municipal courts adopted a 10 percent cash bond system to allow the program to become self-sustaining. The new bond system allowed certain civil and criminal defendants to deposit 10 percent of the bail amount with the court instead of paying the high fees of private bondsmen. Upon appearing for trial, most of the bond deposit was returned to the defendant, and the remainder was used to fund the bail bond project. While project staff consistently reported a 97–percent court appearance rate, by the mid–1980s rising costs and a rearrest controversy fueled investigations and the project's reorganization.

The CITY-COUNTY COUNCIL transferred the bail bond program's operation to the Marion County Justice Agency in 1988. Expanded but nearly identical services are now carried out by a professionally staffed 24–hour Pre-Trial Service Division that has four subdivisions: lock-up services, diversion program, fail-to-appear office, and office of the jail ombudsman. These services are funded by the City-County Council and the County Corrections Fund. An electronic monitoring system for restricted defendants is operated by a separate agency and is funded by defendant fees.

MICHELLE D. HALE

Indianapolis Ballet Theatre (IBT).

Indiana's only professional touring ballet company. Formed in 1973 as an outgrowth of the Civic Ballet Society of Indianapolis (which had been founded in 1959), IBT initially performed only to Indianapolis Public Schools' audiences. The programs for school children were so successful that they were expanded and eventually received funding from the American Heritage Program, LILLY ENDOWMENT, and state and local agencies. The troupe's current budget is funded by individual donations and income from touring.

In 1978 George Verdak, a former member of the Ballet Russe de Monte Carlo, was hired as full-time artistic director. In 1983 Aleksandr "Sasha" Agadzhanov, a 1969 graduate of the Kiev State Academy, who performed with the Moscow Ballet Company and the New York Dance Theatre, was appointed ballet master. He stayed with the company less than a year and was replaced in July, 1986, by world-renowned dance instructor George Montague.

In 1976 the IBT opened its season at the IN-DIANAPOLIS MUSEUM OF ART, moving to CLOWES HALL in 1984. A fire destroyed most of the troupe's costumes and scenery in 1980. By 1986 the IBT was composed of 20 professional dancers from across the United States as well as Canada, Japan, and China, who performed in front of 65,000 in over 50 cities across North America. From 1985 to 1990, attendance increased from 4,000 to 14,000. After being headquartered in the ATHENAEUM for 11 years, the IBT moved to a converted office building at 502B North Capitol Avenue in fall, 1992.

BILL ELLIOTT

Susan Lennis, "IBT: Coming on Strong," *Indianapolis Star Magazine*, Jan. 4, 1976; *Indianapolis Business Journal*, Sept. 22, 1986; *Indianapolis Star*, Apr. 14, Dec. 18, 1991.

Indianapolis Baptist Temple Church.

Founded in 1950, Indianapolis Baptist Temple had humble beginnings on the south side of the city. The congregation remained relatively small until 1955 when the Rev. Greg Dixon became the pastor. From 1955 until about 1976 Baptist Temple grew by a reported 300 members per year. After 1976 membership stabilized until the late 1980s when it began a slight decline. At its largest size in the 1970s Indianapolis Baptist Temple claimed more than 8,000 members.

Baptist Temple has been an active congregation with a wide variety of ministries, including a school for kindergarten through grade 12 founded in 1971, day care for preschoolers, a college founded in 1979, and a wide-ranging bus ministry. At one time the church owned a nursing home, but it was forced to declare bankruptcy.

Under the ministry of the Rev. Dixon Baptist Temple has emphasized traditional Baptist tenets of separation of church and state and freedom of conscience. Dixon was at one time the national secretary and Indiana chairman of the Moral Majority, a fundamentalist, evangelical religious and political organization under the leadership of the Rev. Jerry Falwell of Virginia. Dixon left that group in 1983 to found and head a new organization called the American Coalition of Unregistered Churches. The organization opposes any sort of government regulation and interference in church concerns. In keeping with this stance the congregation dissolved the incorporated Indianapolis Baptist Temple on January 1, 1984. The church was reorganized and renamed the Indianapolis Baptist Temple Church, an unincorporated church. Dixon has spearheaded the fight against licensing for schools and daycare centers operated by churches throughout the country.

Baptist Temple worship services have been televised in all 50 states. The church also sponsors a radio program in the Indianapolis area.

TOMMY L. FARIS

Indianapolis Magazine (Dec., 1986); *Indianapolis Monthly* (Feb., 1987); *Indianapolis News*, Sept. 17, 1983, June 23, 1990.

Indianapolis Benevolent Society. See Charity Organization Society

Indianapolis Business Journal. Weekly business newspaper. Believing that local businesses and businesspeople demanded more thorough coverage of business news than daily newspapers provided, John Burkhart, founder of the College Life Insurance Company in Indianapolis, and Mark Vittert, a St. Louis businessman, began the *Indianapolis Business Journal* (*IBJ*) in May, 1980. As *IBJ*'s circulation rose, it became the prototype for other business weeklies that Burkhart and Vittert started in St. Louis, Philadelphia, Pittsburgh, Cincinnati, and Baltimore.

During the *IBJ*'s first decade, circulation grew steadily to approximately 15,000. In 1986, however, Burkhart and Vittert sold the paper and its sister publications to American City Business Journals, Inc., a Kansas City, Missouri, company. Because of financial difficulties associated with the stock market crash in October, 1987, ACBJ sold the *Indianapolis Business Journal* and six other publications to Minneapolis-based publisher MCP, Inc., in 1988. Two years later MCP accepted Indianapolis attorney and businessman Michael Maurer's offer to purchase the paper. By 1993 *IBJ* reported a circulation of 16,744.

THOMAS A. HARTON

Indianapolis Business Journal, May 10–14, 1990 (10th anniversary issue).

Indianapolis Chamber Orchestra (ICO). The Indianapolis Chamber Orchestra was formed in April, 1984, initially taking the name "Musicians of the Cloister" after the medieval cloister garden of Trinity Episcopal Church, where it played its first concerts. It incorporated in March, 1985, and changed to its current name in March, 1987.

ICO's founder, David Urness, modeled the orchestra on the Academy of St. Martin-in-the-Fields of London, one of the most highly regarded chamber orchestras in the world. ICO's original members were recruited mainly from local freelance musicians who were not employed by the INDIANAPOLIS SYMPHONY ORCHESTRA; many of these musicians were trained at Indiana University. The ICO is a not-for-profit corporation supporting itself through performances and donations from individuals, corporations, and foundations.

ICO's first subscription series took place in the fall of 1985 at the Indiana Repertory Theatre's Mainstage. Its inaugural concert featured world-renowned pianist Menahem Pressler as soloist. The orchestra moved to the INDIANAPOLIS MUSEUM OF ART for the beginning of the 1986–1987 season. Urness conducted the orchestra for its first two seasons, being replaced by British-born conductor Kirk Trevor in the spring of 1988.

For the 1988–1989 season, the 32–piece orchestra moved to CLOWES HALL where it currently stages an annual six-concert subscription series.

BILL ELLIOTT

Tom Aldridge, "Carving a Niche," *Arts Indiana* (Mar., 1990).

Indianapolis Children's Choir. Music performance and education program. Founded in 1986 by Henry H. Leck, the Indianapolis Children's Choir (ICC) is known for its performances at civic and cultural events in the city in addition to its own concert series. The choir also has performed concert tours in Wales, England, France, Austria, and Germany in 1989; Canada and the Northeastern United States in 1991; and Australia and New Zealand in 1992.

Over 650 children participate in the program in seven choirs. Singers range in age from 9 to 14 and are admitted to the choir by audition. While classical music literature forms the foundation for instruction, the choir's repertoire includes folk, ethnic, sacred, and secular music.

In 1990 the Indianapolis Children's Choir made its debut at Carnegie Hall in New York City. The choir regularly performs with area symphonies such as the INDIANAPOLIS SYMPHONY ORCHES-

TRA and the INDIANAPOLIS CHAMBER ORCHESTRA. Local civic performances have included the opening and closing ceremonies of the PAN AMERICAN GAMES, the International Indoor Track and Field Competition, and the opening and closing ceremonies of the 1992 World Gymnastics Competition. ICC has also performed for the Music Educators National Conference, American Choral Directors Association, and several other music organizations.

JULIE PRATT MCQUISTON
Indianapolis Children's Choir

Indianapolis Colored World. African-American newspaper. Begun in 1883 by Edward E. Cooper and Edwin F. Horn, this newspaper, initially Republican, soon became one of the outstanding publications of its kind. Under Levi E. Christy, a teacher who published it from 1888 to 1896, it introduced many new black writers to the reading public and maintained its own print shop, thus employing and training black printers. More independent than most of the AFRICAN-AMERICAN PRESS, it provided national as well as local news and reports on the conditions of blacks nationwide. After its rival, the INDIANAPOLIS FREEMAN, became unabashedly Republican, it openly supported Democratic candidates. When Christy left journalism for the ministry, ownership passed to Alexander E. Manning, a Virginia-born (1860) businessman who had arrived in Indianapolis in 1883 and shortly thereafter became a Democratic loyalist. The weekly, renamed the *Indianapolis World*, initially supported William Jennings Bryan and took a more militant stand on race matters. For 30 years, until his death in January, 1925, Manning was "Official Courier" of the Democratic National Committee. White Democrats subsidized his paper, which became increasingly conservative in politics and ambiguous on race issues. Manning's widow, Melvina, was publisher and editor until the Depression ended the paper's life on March 25, 1932.

DARREL E. BIGHAM
University of Southern Indiana

Indianapolis Colts. Professional football team. The Indianapolis Colts National Football League (NFL) franchise traces its lineage to December, 1946, when the Miami Seahawks of the All-American Football Conference (AAFC) moved to Baltimore, Maryland. The rechristened "Colts" completed three seasons in the AAFC before the league merged with the NFL in 1950. The franchise succumbed to bankruptcy in January, 1951.

In 1953 a partnership headed by Carroll Rosenbloom purchased the Dallas Texans, transferred the team to Baltimore, and renamed it the Colts. The team soon became one of the NFL's premier franchises. Led by coaches Weeb Ewbank and Don Schula and featuring eight Hall of Fame players, the Colts won 1958 and 1959 NFL championships and the 1971 Super Bowl. The team finished as league runners-up in 1965, 1972, and 1975–1977. A 23–17 overtime victory against the New York Giants in the 1958 NFL title game is considered by many to be the greatest pro football game ever played, and the 1969 Super Bowl loss to the New York Jets was a pivotal game in NFL history.

In 1972 Chicago businessman Robert Irsay exchanged his ownership of the Los Angeles Rams for Rosenbloom's interest in the Colts. Irsay's relationship with Baltimore was less than amicable. Colts fans and the Baltimore media saw the new owner as an irascible meddler who was responsible for the team's declining fortunes. Irsay grew increasingly hostile toward what he viewed as unwarranted criticism.

Indianapolis, meanwhile, had launched an aggressive urban renewal effort featuring sports as a primary vehicle for the city's redevelopment. The administration of Mayor William H. Hudnut III successfully endorsed a $94.7 million expan-

Indianapolis Colts Won-Lost Record, 1984–1993

Year	Won-Lost Record	Coach
1984	4–12	Frank Kush, Hal Hunter
1985	5–11	Rod Dowhower
1986	3–13	Rod Dowhower, Ron Meyer
1987	9–6	Ron Meyer
1988	9–7	Ron Meyer
1989	8–8	Ron Meyer
1990	7–9	Ron Meyer
1991	1–15	Ron Meyer, Rick Venturi
1992	9–7	Ted Marchibroda
1993	4–12	Ted Marchibroda

sion of the INDIANA CONVENTION CENTER that included construction of a domed stadium. In March, 1984, citing decaying facilities and decreasing attendance in Baltimore, and lured by generous financial incentives (including a guarantee by the CAPITAL IMPROVEMENT BOARD of $7 million a year in ticket sales for the first seven years), Irsay removed his team to Indianapolis. The move, which occurred in the middle of the night of March 28, 1984, became known in sports circles as the midnight ride of the Colts.

The Indianapolis Colts have a checkered history since moving to the Hoosier capital. In 1984 over 143,000 fans applied for season tickets. In 1989 a mediocre team drew nearly 60,000 spectators per game to the Hoosier Dome. A legacy of poor drafts, questionable trades, and injuries eventually resulted in noncompetitive teams and an ensuing drop in attendance. In 1992 Ted Marchibroda returned to coach the Colts, 11 seasons after his first tour as the head coach of the franchise had ended. The team's 9–7 record in 1992, following a 1–15 debacle the previous year, tied the NFL record for the greatest turnaround in one season.

R. DALE OGDEN
Indiana State Museum

Beau Rissenburgh, *The Official NFL Encyclopedia* (New York, 1985); Dale Ogden and Robert Collins, *Hoosier Sports Heroes* (Indianapolis, 1990); *Indianapolis Star*, Mar. 30, 1984; Bob Collins, "Instant Replay," *Indianapolis Monthly*, 17 (Nov., 1993), 92–98.

Indianapolis Commercial. Local business newspaper. Citing the absence of adequate commercial reporting in local papers and the need to promote the interests of the Indiana Banking Association, Arthur F. Hall and stocks and bonds salesman Joseph T. Elliott, Jr., started the *Daily Reporter* in September, 1895. Although its title was changed to the *Commercial Reporter* in May, 1903, the paper continued its focus on markets, legal proceedings, and other business issues.

In April, 1908, Fred L. Purdy, formerly of the *INDIANAPOLIS SUN*, acquired the *Commercial Reporter*, enlarged its coverage, and dropped *Reporter* from the title. Over the ensuing decades the paper passed through numerous owners including

the Enquirer Printing and Publishing Company of which former governor J. FRANK HANLY was president and editor (1919–1920), and ROBERT V. WELCH (1972–1979). The Indianapolis Daily Legal, Inc., acquired the paper in 1985 and continues publishing it as a daily. A standard size paper, the *Commercial* devotes sections to recent law suits filed in the county, mortgages, building permits, sheriff sales, bankruptcies, and general articles on topics of commercial interest.

PAUL BROCKMAN
Indiana Historical Society

John W. Miller, *Indiana Newspaper Bibliography* (Indianapolis, 1982).

Indianapolis Convention and Visitors Association. Not-for-profit organization that markets Indianapolis as a convention and tourism destination. The Indianapolis Convention and Visitors Association (ICVA) traces its origins to 1923 when local businessmen founded the Indianapolis Convention and Publicity Bureau (ICPB) in an effort to attract business from the fledgling convention industry to the city. Within its first nine months of operation, the ICPB hosted 69 conventions with 36,125 delegates. By 1932 conventions generated over $5 million for the city's economy.

During World War II, the convention business dropped off dramatically as the government discouraged all nonessential meetings. When tourism increased after the war the ICPB created a tourism department, adding group sightseeing tours to its services. By 1947 the ICPB had changed its name to the Indianapolis Convention and Visitors Bureau (ICVB).

The convention industry continued to pump millions of dollars into the local economy during the 1950s and 1960s. Tourism generated $7 million in 1950, $16 million by 1958, $20 million by 1961, and $36 million by 1968.

In 1977 the ICVB was reorganized. During the next four years the bureau's budget increased five-fold as it implemented a major marketing campaign. Revenues from conventions and tourism jumped dramatically from $50 million in 1978 to $192 million just two years later. In 1983 the ICVB changed its name to its current designation as the ICVA. By 1985 ICVA-related business had a $358.3 million impact on the local economy. During this decade Indianapolis was becoming an increasingly popular destination for both religious and minority-related conventions.

In 1989 ICVA officials filed a lawsuit against Indianapolis Newspapers, Inc., after a reporter requested access to the ICVA's financial records. Eventually, the Indiana Supreme Court ruled that the ICVA's records were subject to the state's public records law since over half of the association's funding came from tax money provided by the CAPITAL IMPROVEMENT BOARD. ICVA records revealed that the association had spent several thousand dollars entertaining clients in pursuit of convention business for the city, a practice the organization defended as necessary to attract convention business. Later, both the State Board of Accounts and an independent auditor found ICVA accounts in order.

As of the early 1990s, ICVA-related conventions and tourism claimed to generate over $1.2 billion for Indianapolis' economy and provide more than 37,000 full-time jobs. The ICVA employs 36 people who market Indianapolis, schedule events for the INDIANA CONVENTION CENTER, and publish *This Is Indianapolis*, an award-winning visitors guide to the city. Over 600 local businesses and organizations are ICVA members, providing partial financial support for ICVA activities.

DEBORAH B. MARKISOHN

Indianapolis Newspaper Index, Indiana State Library.

Indianapolis Council of Women. Federation of women's groups. In 1891 PROPYLAEUM stockholders, led by MAY WRIGHT SEWALL, voted to form a council to accomplish at the local level what the National Council of Women was trying to do for the country. Begun in 1892 with 49 Indianapolis literary clubs, charitable institutions, missionary and church societies, and other associations, the group was originally known as the Local Council of Women.

Sewall had been instrumental in the founding of the national and international organizations in 1888. Local councils, like the Indianapolis group, provided a forum for communication among the various women's groups so that they could learn from and provide assistance to each other for civic betterment. Organizations belonging to a local council were to be equally represented and maintain their autonomy.

The Indianapolis Council of Women incorporated in 1902 and later survived its founder's death in 1920. Until 1923 the council met monthly in the Propylaeum. The council took most interest in those moral and civic issues that related to women and children, such as women's suffrage and improved conditions in the schools. These women made their influence felt by conducting investigations, making resolutions, and pressuring authorities in local government and private organizations. During its early years, it studied jail conditions for women prisoners, investigated the presence of children in "wine rooms," pushed for women on local governmental boards and commissions, and became active for municipal legislation regarding public health and improved housing. It also donated time and money to causes such as setting up free milk stations and paying for police matrons and juvenile probation officers.

Several groups were founded through this local council, including the Indianapolis Consumers League (1901) and the Indiana Council of Women (1921). Social programs were also a part of the council's activities. Besides a Founder's Day luncheon the women regularly had lunches and dinners featuring music programs, literary readings, or local speakers.

The council celebrated its centennial in 1992 by hosting several historical programs. It currently has 135 participating groups, representing roughly 45,000 people. They now meet for seven lunches a year to host speakers on topics of community interest. These women continue to make an impact on the community, most recently by providing assistance to the city's homeless and abused people.

ANN MAUGER COLBERT
Indiana University–Purdue University,
Fort Wayne

Indianapolis Downtown, Inc. A nonprofit, nonpartisan downtown management corporation. Begun in 1977 as the Commission for Downtown, Inc. (CFD), the group focused on facilitating growth in Indianapolis and beautifying the downtown area, especially MONUMENT CIRCLE, Market Street, and Meridian Street. Initially the CFD's major project was to complete the bricking of Monument Circle, which was accomplished in the late 1970s. Its mission statement from the 1992–1994 strategic plan emphasized that the strengths of downtown Indianapolis would be promoted on a variety of fronts, including social, cultural, commercial, and residential. To accomplish this the CFD entered into partnerships with the public and private sectors, raising funds from memberships, grants, and various activities. At the end of 1992 the CFD's budget was around $465,000, with almost half of that amount coming from city funds and the remainder from business memberships.

In January, 1993, the name changed to Indianapolis Downtown, Inc. (IDI) after Mayor Stephen Goldsmith and the GREATER INDIANAPOLIS PROGRESS COMMITTEE decided that a downtown management association was needed. IDI retained the public-private component but expanded its focus to include downtown management, planning, and safety as well as retail and business retention and recruitment. Its starting budget was an estimated $890,000, of which $300,000 was a contribution from the CORPORATE COMMUNITY COUNCIL. Mayor Goldsmith's goal was for IDI to earn more income and eventually become self-supporting from services provided to downtown, particularly in the areas of public safety, transportation, and parking.

IDI's policy-making arm is a board of directors that meets monthly and is comprised of representatives of local government as well as business and civic organizations. In addition, an advisory group meets at least twice a year to give input to the board. IDI's marketing component, Indianapolis Downtown Marketing, Inc., is a separate subsidiary whose board of directors meets bimonthly.

SHELAINE MARIE NEELY
BARBARA L. WALDSMITH

Indianapolis Economic Development Corporation. Established in 1983, the Indianapolis Economic Development Corporation (IEDC), a nonprofit organization responsible for business development in Indianapolis, stemmed from a GREATER INDIANAPOLIS PROGRESS COMMITTEE suggestion that a nonprofit agency coordinate business development.

IEDC has a 30–member board of directors. Eighteen are appointed by public and private funding sources, including the CORPORATE COMMUNITY COUNCIL, City of Indianapolis, Indiana Department of Commerce, and Indianapolis CHAMBER OF COMMERCE. Twelve other members from related business areas in Indianapolis are appointed by the board. The term is for three years, and one third of the members are up for election each year. In addition, there is a president, vice-president of development services, and a vice-president–assistant treasurer and controller. The IEDC has a contract with the city to provide services for and to promote Indianapolis.

IEDC is concerned with business development. One priority is dealing with companies located in Indianapolis that have expansion capabilities. IEDC also assists companies looking to locate in Indianapolis and helps to retain existing business. The IEDC also manages the Mid City Pioneer Corporation, a fixed asset financing program for small and medium-sized business.

SHELAINE MARIE NEELY

_____

Indianapolis Economic Development Corporation, *1990 Annual Report.*

Indianapolis Female Institute/Seminary. Nineteenth-century Presbyterian women's school. In the early decades of the 19th century, American society placed increasing importance on the home and, concurrently, on the paramount role of women in preserving and passing on moral and cultural values. As the national economy shifted from agricultural to industrial, bringing about changes in the workplace and community life, the home became an idealized place in which escape could be found from the increasingly complex world. Educators and churchmen recognized this shift and in these years established many secular and religious educational institutions specifically to train women for their newfound role. The Indianapolis Female Institute was typical of many of the gender-based educational institutions of the time.

The institute opened its doors in June, 1837, under sponsorship of the Presbyterian church in Indianapolis. After briefly occupying the second story of a building on Washington Street near Meridian, the institute was housed in its own building on Pennsylvania Street. To run the new school the board of directors hired two sisters, Mary J. and Harriet Axtell, who were previously teachers at a female academy in Courtlandville, New York. The students, who boarded with families in Indianapolis, were taught a variety of subjects including math, science, and history. A large part of the curriculum, however, concentrated on "cultural" subjects such as music, drawing, and languages. The institute closed its doors in 1849 because of the ill health of Mary Axtell.

In 1852, the PRESBYTERIANS founded the Indianapolis Female Seminary as a continuation of the institute's goals of educating women. In addition to the curriculum established by the institute, an increased emphasis was placed on charity and community service. The new three-story brick school at the southwest corner of Meridian and New York streets was under the direction of Dr. C. G. McLean, a Presbyterian clergyman from Pennsylvania and an Irish immigrant. McLean, his wife, and his two daughters comprised the original staff of the seminary, which had an initial enrollment of 150 young women from Indianapolis and the surrounding area. As enrollment grew, McLean hired a number of teachers trained in East Coast colleges to bolster his small staff. Unlike the earlier institute, many of the students boarded at the seminary although enrollment was also open to women living with their own families in Indianapolis.

After McLean's death in 1860, the church renamed the institution McLean Seminary and appointed as director Professor C. N. Todd, McLean's son-in-law. The seminary operated under its new name for five more years. In 1865 the Presbyterian church closed the institution and sold the building to the Methodist-operated Indiana Female College, which continued at the site until 1868.

The Indianapolis Female Institute and Seminary exemplified some of the main characteristics of educational institutions for women in 19th-century America. An unforseen result of schools that trained women for their domestic role was that they also exposed them to broader social roles and responsibilities including church and community service. Despite the primary emphasis on domesticity in these gender-segregated schools, women who attended them were provided with some means to break out of their isolated domestic world.

ALEXANDER URBIEL
Indiana University, Bloomington

Indianapolis Fire Department (IFD).

The first recorded fire in Indianapolis (a newly built wooden tavern opposite the courthouse on Washington Street, January 17, 1825) found the city without a firefighting force. Not until June 20, 1826, almost a year and a half later—under a state law of 1821 which permitted 40 or more citizens to organize a company, make rules and regulations, and collect fines for violations—was a volunteer fire company established. Its equipment was limited to leather buckets and ladders, its alarm the church bell. To protect the new State House, an 1835 law obligated the state to purchase fire buckets and ladders and erect an engine house, an offer conditional on city residents paying half the cost of a "first-rate fire engine" and the necessary hose. A second-hand engine purchased for $1,800, named the "Marion," arrived in September, 1835. Five public wells were dug and the bucket company merged into the new organization, the Marion Fire, Hose, and Protection Company. A second volunteer company was organized in 1841, and six more by 1859. Nearly 600 men were listed on the rolls, and members were exempt from militia and jury duty, poll and road taxes.

The undue, and fractious, political influence of the volunteer companies through their Fire Association prompted the shift to paid firemen, as did the anticipated purchase of a newly invented and expensive steam fire engine. An additional factor was the habit of the volunteer companies, acting as moral guardians of the community, to burst into houses of prostitution, hosing down the occupants and ruining the interiors. Unable to control the volunteer companies, city councilmen passed an ordinance to establish the paid force on November 14, 1859. Unlike most cities, the change in Indianapolis was remarkably free of rancor.

The Indianapolis Fire Department (IFD) began existence with two hand engines and a hook and ladder company. The first steam engine arrived in March, 1860, and two more before the end of the year. Two members of each engine company remained at the station at all times and received $300 a year; the others, who served only at fires, were paid $25. A watch tower was erected atop one of the taller buildings and a man with a field glass was stationed there to spot fires and give the alarm. In 1870 at a cost of $350,000, fifteen miles of pipes and water mains were laid in the MILE SQUARE. The Holly System, designed to do away with reservoirs, used immense pumps. Thus the future of fire fighting eventually lay with hose companies, not steam engines, although that future still lay some decades ahead.

The annual report to the council for the year ending May 15, 1864, listed three steam engines, one hook and ladder company, and 15 horses. The total cost to the city was just under $16,500. The 28 men (including the fire chief) who made up the force counted three engineers, seven drivers, two tower watchmen (in 1882 watchmen moved to a tower atop the courthouse), and 12 hosemen. Forty-five cisterns dotted the city, though some of the newer neighborhoods lacked them. The department was called out 54 times to 47 fires, and there were seven false alarms. All firemen lived at the firehouses. Given no days off, they could not leave their posts except for one meal, sickness in the family, or on department business—and then for no longer than strictly necessary. Under the 1859 ordinance the chief fire engineer and his two assistants could arrest persons supplying firemen with liquor, and no card or dice games were permitted in the stations at any time. Badges had served to distinguish firemen from civilians after 1843, and later leather hats were worn both for

Members of Fire Station #1, located at 443 Indiana Avenue, in 1926. [Indiana State Library]

protection and identification. Indianapolis firemen were uniformed in 1874, but not until 1928 was a regulation uniform adopted, with service stripes and summer caps the following year. Until 1943, when the first clothing allowance was paid ($60), firemen bore the cost of their clothes and equipment.

The growth of the department in the years after the Civil War was rapid and substantial. In 1877, 79 men operated 7 steamers, 11 hose reels, and 2 hook and ladder companies, drawn by 34 horses. The cost of the IFD had risen to over $96,000, nearly a sixfold increase in 14 years. The number of alarms, 189, was three times the 1864–1865 total. Water lines—50 miles by 1880 (599 hydrants)—were supplemented by 144 cisterns. An electric alarm system was installed in 1868, and the engine, reel houses, and the fire chief's home were connected by telephone in 1880. The fireman's week remained 7 days, 24 hours a day, but from the late 1870s he could sleep one night at home. By 1894 firemen received a week's vacation with pay, and by 1912 one day a week off. A two-platoon system (one of 10 hours, the other 14) was inaugurated in 1921, with the men rotating shifts every two weeks. A year later this confusing arrangement was dropped for one of 24 hours on and 24 off, a workweek of 84 hours. In 1948 firemen got an extra day off every seventh working day and a 72 hour week. With the adoption of the three-platoon system in 1966 (24 hours on, 48 off), 56 hours has remained the weekly stint.

Further improvements and expansion took place under the Charter of 1891. In 1893 the water company supplied 107 miles of mains and 931 public hydrants over the 21 square mile area, including WEST INDIANAPOLIS, that comprised the IFD district. By 1909 the department consisted of 264 men (with a payroll of $227,000), 12 engines, 27 hose reel wagons, 4 chemical engines, 10 hook and ladder companies, and 121 horses. Fire hydrants numbered 2,371 and were supplemented by 177 cisterns. (Cisterns were not abandoned until 1932.) A Gamewell system of 280 pull boxes replaced the older electric alarms after 1901 and remained in use until 1955.

The threat of higher rates by fire insurance companies also spurred improvements. After 1894 the Fire Inspection Bureau, maintained by the insurance companies, inspected buildings and premises and used higher rates to gain compliance from property owners. After 1904 no new frame buildings were to be built in the Mile Square, crowning efforts dating from May, 1859, to mandate brick construction in the city's center. In 1919 an ordinance created a division of fire prevention with a director and four firemen. A training class held by the fire chief instructed each member of the force in inspections and abatement orders.

Political influence and public employment went hand in hand in the 19th century and later. While the annual report of 1876–1877 stated that firemen were to take no active role in politics, the office of fire chief was always political, a circumstance recognized in the Charter of 1891 which stipulated that the department (and the police) be divided equally between Republicans and Democrats. From time to time fire chiefs asserted that politics would play no part in the department, but family influence was usually crucial in gaining appointment and promotion invariably depended on political affiliation. In 1943 a captain, retiring after 44 years, said that he would not make the same career decision: "Too much confinement and too much politics in our business." In 1973 the fire chief, citing political interference, quit after only six months in office.

Until 1929 the department offered no significant training to its firemen. Appointed by a ward chairman and assigned to a station, new firemen learned on the job. Applicants attended drill school at their own expense with no guarantee of employment. Standards were minimal: 21 to 30 years old, average weight, a character check in the neighborhood, clean record with the police. Standards improved after World War II: in 1948 the 62 men who vied for 15 vacancies received 80 hours of instruction. The recruit class of July, 1969 was the first to be appointed to the department and paid while attending six weeks of class. By 1989 training extended to 17 weeks and included instruction in hazardous materials, firefighting, and emergency medical service.

The department's shift from horses to motor vehicles began in 1908 with the purchase of a Marion roadster for the chief. But not until 1921 was IFD fully motorized; by 1928 the last horses had been auctioned. ("Spot," the last of the firehouse dogs, was killed in 1967.) HARRY E. VOSHELL, fire chief from 1928 to 1935, installed the first radio receivers in the chief's car and in the fire stations in 1932. (Two-way radios on fire equipment appeared only in 1947.) Voshell, who retired from the department in 1940 at age 70, served one of the longest stints as chief and was perhaps the most notable of the 30 men who have headed IFD. He established the policy of building, rather than buying, the department's fire engines; improved the living quarters for firemen (every engine house was remodeled); and won a reputation for IFD as the department that "fights fires from the inside."

Until March, 1968 when the first arson squad was established, suspicious fires were handled by the Fire Prevention Bureau with a police officer assigned to "arson detail." In 1970 the arson squad was separated from the bureau and a joint investigative team created with the INDIANAPOLIS POLICE DEPARTMENT. Despite an estimated one arson fire a day, prosecutions fell and in 1984 the system was reorganized with fire investigations combined into one agency. Command of the team rotates between police and firefighters and all members receive extensive training in the other specialty. Arson is easy to detect, but the arsonist is the most difficult criminal to identify. In July, 1993, IFD acquired its first arson-sniffing dog, a method found useful in other departments.

In the last 25 years the work of IFD has undergone a revolution as provision of emergency medical aid made extraordinary inroads on traditional firefighting. Through 1969 the great majority of the city's rescue runs were handled by the police department. After 1970 IFD was given primary responsibility for delivering first aid. This shift grew out of a 1966 federal highway act that charged the U.S. Department of Transportation with developing standards of emergency medical care in prehospital settings. A curriculum soon emerged for certifying emergency medical technicians (EMTs). Rescue runs soon dwarfed fire and other emergency responses of IFD. The six EMT-trained firefighters of 1976 grew to 320 in 1985 when training was required of all recruits. Emergency medical service runs grew from 6,468 in 1980 (fire emergencies, 5,904) to 41,331 in 1989, while fire runs less than doubled. Forty-six percent of all IFD responses in 1979, EMT runs constituted 80 percent of incidents in 1989. IFD further upgraded its emergency medical capabilities to provide life support care, graduating its first class of paramedics in March, 1992.

Proposals to unify the fire departments in the county have been rumored for over 50 years. In 1941, for example, the Board of Public Safety discussed a plan to have IFD provide fire service countywide, augmented by the township volunteer companies. Given the number of entities involved—twelve (versus only two for a police-sheriff merger)—and the Unigov requirement of a petition of a majority of property owners or the owners of three quarters of the assessed property affected, such a merger of departments is difficult. A State Senate bill in 1982 to give the CITY-COUNTY COUNCIL greater authority to consolidate IFD and the 11 township fire departments died in committee. While similar mergers have proved cost effective in Los Angeles, and in Jacksonville and Orlando, Florida, its adoption in Indianapolis appears unlikely in the near future. In the absence of merger, the Indianapolis Fire Department has a mutual aid agreement with surrounding townships, and since 1991 "dual response" pacts with Perry, Washington, and Warren townships (the closest apparatus responds regardless of boundary lines).

With the smallest taxing district in the city (93 square miles), inexorably rising costs and a declining tax base (its budget grew from $29.7 million in 1988 to $40.2 million in 1994, while property tax revenues in the service district rose only $1.9 million), and an electorate adverse to tax increases, IFD has searched for ways to cut costs. For years the department has consolidated administrative posts and deferred maintenance of station houses and equipment. The number of firefighters fell from 869 in 1977 to 719 in November, 1993. Nevertheless, the department exceeded its budget by $1.1 million in 1993 (mostly overtime costs attributable to shortages in personnel). In 1993 it began a pilot program to co-staff ambulances (housed at selected fire stations) with WISHARD MEMORIAL HOSPITAL to free 21 firefighters for other emergencies. It has shuffled equipment and personnel (its first recruit class since 1989 is scheduled for 1994), and contemplated new service fees for hydrants, special events, and inspections.

WILLIAM DOHERTY
Marian College

Indianapolis 500-Mile Race. The best known motor race in the world was first held on May 30, 1911, during the INDIANAPOLIS MOTOR SPEEDWAY'S third year of operation. Long known simply as the "500," it has been conducted continuously since its inception except for 1917–1918 and 1942–1945, when the United States was at war. Its 75th running occurred in 1991.

After nine days of racing in 1910, each packed with dozens of events and spread over the holiday weekends of Memorial Day, Fourth of July, and Labor Day (some of which were poorly attended), track founders CARL G. FISHER, JAMES A. ALLISON, ARTHUR NEWBY, and FRANK WHEELER decided in 1911 to experiment with a single event of marathon proportions, offering a huge purse. After briefly weighing the merits of a 24–hour event, they reasoned that something lasting around seven hours would be far more acceptable to spectators. They agreed upon a 500–mile race with a purse of $25,000 for the first 12 finishers.

The track was available for practice for the entire month of May, 1911, although many con-

Start of the 1993 Indianapolis 500.
[Indianapolis Motor Speedway.
Photo by Ron McQueeney]

testants did not arrive until the third and fourth week. Time trials were conducted on May 27 and 28 in order to sort out the slower cars. An average speed of 75 miles per hour (from a flying start) for a quarter of a mile down the main straightaway was required in order to earn a starting position.

Forty cars met the requirements, lining up for the race in rows of five (rather than the later three) and in the order in which each had been entered. The first row actually contained only four starters, with Carl Fisher occupying what would become known as the "pole" position (inside, front row) with a Stoddard-Dayton passenger car. Fisher felt that 40 cars were too many for the customary standing start, so his plan was to lead the field around on a single unscored lap at about 40 mph to begin the race. This is believed to have been the first mass rolling start for an automobile race anywhere in the world and quite possibly the first use of a pace car at a major event.

The 1911 race was won in just over six hours and 42 minutes by Ray Harroun (with about an hour of midpoint relief driving by Cyrus Patschke) in a locally built MARMON. But already Fisher's original concept for the track's competitions was being circumvented. Although the second-placed Lozier was a standard production car, modified only slightly for the race, Harroun's winner was largely a "one-off" or specially created racing car, built in one corner of the Marmon passenger car factory. Because no rule required a riding mechanic (which everyone used routinely),

Harroun designed a streamlined, single-seat body, and on four rods above the cowling he installed what may well have been the first rearview mirror ever used on an automobile. As far as the public was concerned, however, the car was a standard Marmon, and passenger car sales picked up so appreciably that the firm decided to end its racing program with this notable victory.

For 1912 prize money doubled to $50,000, with the winner guaranteed $20,000. In fact, several accessory companies were already posting additional amounts, contingent upon use of their products; Harroun actually earned $4,250 above the Speedway's prize in 1911. Although only 24 cars started in 1912, a new formula limited the size of the field. Based on a standard of one car for every 400 feet of race track, no more than 33 were now permitted to start, a limit lifted for only five subsequent 500s. Joe Dawson's winning NATIONAL was much closer to its street version than had been Harroun's Marmon and, for the second year in a row, a local manufacturer had triumphed. National also withdrew from racing following the resulting boost in sales.

While foreign cars and drivers had participated in the first two 500s, the cars had been American-owned and the drivers all immigrants. In 1913, however, several foreign teams made the transatlantic trip specifically to compete in the race, and Jules Goux in a French Peugeot was triumphant. The following year continental drivers piloted French cars to the first four places, while overseas cars and drivers also won in 1915 and 1916. Howard "Howdy" Wilcox of Indianapolis won in 1919, but his car was foreign, although locally owned. It was a Peugeot entered by the Indianapolis Speedway Team Company (actually, Fisher and Allison) and prepared during the spring on Main Street in Speedway in what is now known as Allison's Plant One. American cars began winning again in 1920, but racing had become very specialized and even firms like DUESENBERG (which had relocated from Elizabeth, New Jersey, to Indianapolis in 1921) were now building 100–percent racing cars for competition. The most successful and prolific builder of both cars and engines was Harry Miller of Los Angeles, a racing specialist who did not offer a passenger car in any form at all.

Engine sizes were reduced several times in an attempt to curb speeds, but seemingly at a slower rate than the progression of technology. Cubic inch displacement (cid) was cut from a maximum allowable 600 cid in 1911 and 1912 down to 450 for 1913 and 1914; then to 300 for 1915–1919, 183 for 1920–1922, and 122 for 1923–1925. Seven drivers turned single-lap qualifying runs in excess of 100 mph in 1919, and after the introduction of four-lap qualifications in 1920, a single lap at almost 115 mph was attained in 1925. Riding mechanics were eliminated in 1923, which coincided with the initial appearance of superchargers, a method of achieving additional power used by brothers FRED AND AUGUST DUESENBERG on their winning cars in 1924 and 1925. In terms of speed, the first three finishers in 1925 each completed the 500 miles in under five hours, thus averaging better than 100 mph for the entire distance.

Practically every car was supercharged by 1926 as engine size was reduced still further to only $91^1/_2$ cubic inches. Frank Lockhart responded by lapping at 120 mph in 1927 and in 1928 Leon Duray (real name: George Stewart) managed a qualifying lap at over 124 mph. A 60 cid formula was discussed for 1930, but drastic changes took place instead. In an attempt to lure back the automobile companies (now mostly located in Detroit), supercharging was eliminated (except for two-cycle engines) and the cubic inch displacement was increased to 366 so as to encompass most passenger car engines of the day. Riding mechanics were reintroduced and the starting field increased to 40.

Of the 38 cars that started in 1930, however, not one was factory-backed. The field consisted of detuned racing cars of the previous years (modified to carry a mechanic), and a few inexpensive, privately entered production efforts. Studebaker (of South Bend, Indiana) fielded a five-car team in 1932 and 1933, while Ford ambitiously teamed up with Harry Miller to build ten cars for 1935; but it was the older Millers that kept winning during the Great Depression years. Studebaker did place a few cars within the first ten, topped by a third in 1932, but Ford managed to qualify only four of its cars in 1935 and none of them finished. The factories were out of it for the time being by

1937, and supercharging was permitted once again. Jimmy Snyder turned a qualifying lap at over 130 mph. A year later the riding mechanics were gone for good.

Among drivers, Tommy Milton became the first two-time victor by winning in 1921 and 1923. Louis Meyer, the 1928 champion, won his second 500 in 1933, then became a *three*-time winner in 1936. WILBUR SHAW quickly duplicated Meyer's feat and, with triumphs in 1937, 1939, and 1940, was the first to score in consecutive years.

Following a number of victories by cars utilizing front wheel drive, including the 500s of 1947–1949, lightweight rear-drive cars began to succeed, ushering in a trend of low-slung creations with engines offset to the left and driver cockpits offset to the right. Because their front portions in particular strongly resembled road-going sports cars, these cars were nicknamed "roadsters," something they most certainly were not. Beginning with 1957 came several successful experiments at tilting the perennially victorious four-cylinder Offenhauser engine (derived from the Miller) on its side for a lower center of gravity.

While a smattering of rear-engined cars appeared between 1937 and 1951, only a few qualified and none ever finished. Then, in 1961, Australian Jack Brabham (defending two-time World Champion at the time) placed ninth, driving a British Grand Prix–based Cooper powered by a Coventry-climax engine mounted behind the driver. Two years after that, Scotsman Jim Clark placed second with an American Ford-powered, British rear-engined Lotus, and in 1965 Clark won. By 1966 all but one of the starting cars were rear-engined.

A variety of factors, including turbocharged engines, considerably wider tires, computer designed aerodynamic bodies, and front- and rear-mounted stabilizer wings, caused speeds to soar after the mid–1960s. From a lap of 150 mph by Parnelli Jones in a front-engined car in 1962, Tom Sneva was able to record 200 mph in 1977. By 1990 Rick Mears had officially exceeded 225 mph. The race record itself, down to two hours, 41 minutes by Arie Luyendyk in 1990, represented an average speed of 185.981 mph for 500 miles.

Notable advancements were made for the safety of drivers, once a widely publicized negative of the 500. During the race itself, 13 drivers lost their lives through 1964, but only one race day–related driver fatality has occurred since then and none at all since 1973.

Prize money also made extraordinary leaps in the 1980s. The total purse in 1970 exceeded $1 million for the first time. It then topped $2 million in 1982, $3 million in 1985, $4 million in 1986, $5 million in 1988, and $6 million in 1989, at which time Brazilian winner Emerson Fittipaldi's first-place prize alone exceeded $1 million. Even 33rd (last) place was worth over $100,000. Attendance figures, although unofficial (the Motor Speedway does not release this information), are similarly impressive; the race is reputed to be the largest single-day sporting event in the world, with estimates of the crowd size ranging as high as 500,000.

As worldwide exposure of the 500 increased, hand in hand with technological advances, rising speeds, and increased involvement in recent years by both automotive and non-automotive international corporations, a variety of socially intriguing "firsts" have taken place. In 1977, the year in which A. J. Foyt became the first *four*-time winner, the field included its first female driver, Janet Guthrie. (A second woman, Lyn St. James, qualified in 1992.) When Al Unser (later to join Foyt as a four-time winner) lined up against Al Unser, Jr., in the 1983 race, it marked the first instance of a driver appearing in a 500 with his son. Back in 1937 Billy Devore had been the first second-generation driver to compete in a 500; in 1988 Billy Vukovich III followed in the footsteps of his father and grandfather to become a *third*-generation 500 driver. And for the 75th running in 1991, the field expanded its horizons still further by containing its first African-American driver, Willy T. Ribbs, as well as its first from Asia, Hiro Matsushita from Japan.

DONALD DAVIDSON
Statistician and Historian
United States Auto Club

Indianapolis Foundation. A publicly supported philanthropic institution whose purpose is to promote the welfare of residents of Indianapolis. It was created January 5, 1916, by a joint resolution of trust adopted by the Fletcher Savings and Trust Company, the Indiana Trust Company, and the UNION TRUST COMPANY. The Indianapolis Foundation was among the earliest community foundations in the country and was the first to utilize the multiple trusteeship concept whereby several banks and trust companies adopt the same resolution of trust and receive and administer gifts and bequests to generate investment income. The trustee banks then make the investment income available for charitable distribution in the form of grants. The Indianapolis Foundation's assets are made up of combined gifts and bequests from hundreds of donors. The foundation now has seven trustee banks, including successors of the original three. On December 31, 1991, its assets totaled $89,171,884.

Judge Frederick H. Goff established the first community foundation in Cleveland in 1914 as a mechanism to free philanthropic interests from the "dead hand" that governed outmoded or overly restricted private trust funds. Evans Woollen, Sr., president of the Fletcher Savings and Trust Company and a friend of Goff, brought the idea to Indianapolis. He and attorney Henry Hornbrook were primarily responsible for the Indianapolis Foundation's inception.

While the trustee banks administer funds to generate income, a six-member board of trustees determines how this income is to be expended. These private citizens are chosen for their knowledge about the community and their ability to represent the public interest. They serve six-year terms without compensation, and they may be reappointed. Two appointments each are made by the mayor of Indianapolis, the judge of the Marion Circuit Court, and the federal court judges exercising jurisdiction over the Southern District of Indiana. The board of trustees meets five or six times a year to consider grant requests and to determine Foundation policies.

Other than the geographic limitation that confines grants to those that benefit the residents of Indianapolis (Marion County), there are few restrictions governing the expenditure of income. The foundation makes grants only to not-for-profit organizations, not to individuals, or for sec-

**The Indianapolis Foundation
Grants Distribution by Purpose**

	1991		1924–1991	
Youth	$418,807	13%	$7,716,674	19%
Family and Community Services	1,543,488	46%	14,922,340	36%
Education	699,929	21%	4,764,228	11%
Civic and Cultural Activities	351,929	10%	5,658,029	14%
Health, Handicapped, and Rehabilitation	318,887	10%	8,405,441	20%
Total	$3,333,040	100%	$41,466,712	100%

tarian or religious purposes. Because the foundation has a higher percentage of unrestricted funds than any other community foundation, its board of trustees has the flexibility to direct the foundation's resources to the most urgent community needs. In 1987 the foundation adopted a mission statement that committed it to providing donors a way to help "where the needs are greatest, and the benefits . . . most substantial," as changing conditions dictate.

The foundation issued its first grant in 1924 to the Public Health Nursing Association for a nurse for crippled children. Among organizations that have received major grants are: GLEANERS FOOD BANK, GOODWILL INDUSTRIES, INDIANA REPERTORY THEATRE, INDIANAPOLIS ART LEAGUE, INDIANAPOLIS PUBLIC SCHOOLS (the scholarship fund), Indianapolis Senior Citizens Center, INDIANAPOLIS SYMPHONY ORCHESTRA, Marion County library services, and UNITED WAY. By the end of 1991 the Foundation had expended $41,466,712.

The WILLIAM E. ENGLISH Foundation is a support organization to the Indianapolis Foundation. It was organized in 1932 to carry out provisions in English's will for a facility to house community service agencies. In 1953 it opened the English Foundation Building at 615 North Alabama Street, which houses tenant agencies on a shared maintenance cost basis that results in substantial savings over commercial office space rates. At the time of its construction, the building was the largest structure anywhere specifically designed to house community service agencies. The English Foundation's sole purpose is the ownership and operation of the building. It does not make financial grants.

The English Foundation is governed by a nine-member board of directors, six of whom serve concurrently as trustees of Indianapolis Foundation. The English Foundation also shares offices and staff with Indianapolis Foundation, enabling each foundation to operate at lower costs than would otherwise be possible.

GREGORY E. LYNN
Indianapolis Foundation

Indianapolis Freeman. Black newspaper. Edward E. Cooper, formerly with the *Indianapolis World*, launched the *Freeman* in 1888. He claimed it to be the only illustrated African-American journal and poured large sums into making the *Freeman*, with its Democratic party proclivities, the "Harper's Weekly of the Colored Race." Financially strapped, he sold the paper in 1892 to GEORGE L. KNOX. Under Knox, the paper supported the Republican party, gave full play to Booker T. Washington's Tuskegee philosophy of accommodation, became known for its theater coverage, and professed to having the largest circulation of any black paper in the United States. After World War I, inflation, competition from the more locally attuned INDIANAPOLIS RECORDER, and increased price doomed the *Freeman*; it ceased publication in 1926.

ROBERT M. TAYLOR, JR.
Indiana Historical Society

Willard B. Gatewood, Jr., ed., *Slave and Freeman: The Autobiography of George L. Knox* (Lexington, Ky., 1979).

Indianapolis Gazette. Indianapolis newspaper. The original *Gazette* was Indianapolis' first newspaper, appearing on January 28, 1822, with NATHANIEL BOLTON as editor and publisher. Initially the *Gazette* was issued at irregular intervals due to poor lines of communication between Indianapolis and its neighboring cities. During these early years the paper was politically neutral. On October 22, 1829, George L. Kinnard became editor and the name was changed to the *Indiana State Gazette*. Soon the paper took a pro-Democratic political stance by supporting the beliefs of Andrew Jackson. In March, 1830, Alexander F. Morrison acquired Bolton's interest and the paper became known as the *INDIANA DEMOCRAT AND*

STATE GAZETTE. In the early 1840s it was renamed the *INDIANA STATE SENTINEL*.

The second *Gazette* appeared in 1862 and was issued by Johnson H. Jordan, J. C. Burnett, and Company. This publication had formerly been the *Indiana American* and supported the Republican party. In 1866, Jordan sold the paper to the Gazette Company, owned by Abraham Smith, J. H. Tilford, and E. W. Halford. The paper changed hands several times before Charles P. Wilder acquired it in 1867. The journal halted publication later that year. The third *Gazette* was also a pro-Republican paper, founded in 1862 by Joseph A. Dynes and Company. The paper was terminated in the early 20th century after changing owners several times. A fourth *Gazette*, inaugurated by Elmer S. Lenz in 1966, survived for only two months.

WILLIAM D. DALTON

Indianapolis Hebrew Congregation.

First Jewish congregation in Indianapolis. Soon after the first Jewish settlers arrived, 14 men organized the Indianapolis Hebrew Congregation (IHC) on November 2, 1856. IHC early adhered to Reform Judaism, the most liberal of American Jewish religious movements. Throughout its existence IHC has been a source of civic and charitable leadership and a strong promoter of interreligious understanding.

The founders immediately purchased land for a Jewish burial ground that they established on the city's south side. During IHC's early years the tiny congregation worshiped in rented rooms with a series of short-term rabbis. In 1865 the congregation purchased a permanent home on Market Street near East Street and soon attracted a long-term rabbi.

During Rabbi Mayer Messing's 40 years at IHC (1867–1907), the growing congregation became financially and numerically stable. IHC members laid the foundations for a variety of Jewish social and welfare groups, and Messing helped to found the Indianapolis Red Cross chapter and the Humane Society. In 1899 IHC built a new temple at 10th and Delaware streets. Subsequently, the Hebrew Ladies Benevolent Society founded the Jewish Shelter House, the Nathan

Morris Settlement House, and a foster home. The Jewish Federation, founded by IHC members in 1905 (becoming the JEWISH WELFARE FEDERATION in 1948), later took over management of these organizations.

IHC hired its first associate rabbi in 1904, and Rabbi MORRIS FEUERLICHT became senior rabbi in 1907. Feuerlicht's 40–year rabbinate (1904–1946) was marked by the observance of few traditional customs, but an emphasis on education and welfare work. Members organized the Temple Brotherhood and Sisterhood during World War I. Both organizations early provided aid to Jewish war victims and afterward served as the major IHC sponsors of temple and community service projects and fund raisers. During the 1920s Feuerlicht led the IHC in active protest against the KU KLUX KLAN.

Rabbi Maurice Goldblatt first came to IHC in 1938 and succeeded Feuerlicht as senior rabbi in 1946. Goldblatt re-introduced many traditional observances into IHC services, but his rabbinate was continually involved in conflict over his conservative interpretation of Reform Judaism as well as the Zionist issue. Still, the congregation doubled in size during the 1950s. While Goldblatt successfully elicited more lay involvement he was unable to reconcile everyone to changes in the religious school curriculum, and a group of dissidents left IHC in 1953.

Rabbi Maurice Davis (1956–1967) reunited the congregation by focusing energies on a building fund drive. In 1958 IHC moved to its present modern facilities at 65th and Meridian streets. The congregation became more active in youth, elderly, and civil rights issues in the Jewish and non-Jewish communities. During the 1960s, in addition to expanded IHC youth programs, IHC spearheaded the creation of a Jewish youth camp and nonprofit elderly housing.

Under Rabbi Murray Saltzman's leadership (1967–1977), IHC instituted a variety of family programs and members continued to sustain social action and community programs such as interfaith forums and the Concord Center, an inner-city social welfare center. Rabbi Jonathan Stein became senior rabbi of IHC in 1977, introducing more traditional rituals into congregational life, expanding IHC programming, encouraging more women and lay participation, and increasing community social welfare and inter-faith activities. In recent years IHC has founded an ecumenical organization called Inter-faith Alliance and an annual community lecture series.

MICHELLE D. HALE

Ethel and David Rosenberg, *To 120 Years!: A Social History of the Indianapolis Hebrew Congregation (1856–1976)* (Indianapolis, 1978).

Indianapolis Historic Preservation Commission.
Government commission that functions in cooperation with the City of Indianapolis to preserve both the character and fabric of historically significant areas and structures in Marion County. The commission identifies and protects historic properties through the creation of historic area preservation plans and issues certificates of appropriateness for land use changes, building alterations, new construction, and demolition of buildings in those areas.

The commission was formed in 1967 by state legislation, with its seven commissioners appointed by the mayor. It gained its first task of architectural review in 1968 when an historic district zoning ordinance was adopted for LOCKERBIE SQUARE. New legislation in 1975 strengthened the legal and financial base of the commission. Funding from the city's 1975 Community Development Block Grant and from the Comprehensive Employment Training Act provided for the hiring of staff and the establishment of an office in the City-County Building.

Since 1975, the commission has adopted historic area preservation plans for additional properties and districts: Lockerbie Square (revised 1976, 1987); eight individual buildings including UNION STATION and CIRCLE THEATRE, 1979–1981; OLD NORTHSIDE, 1980; FLETCHER PLACE, 1981; CHATHAM-ARCH, 1982; FOUNTAIN SQUARE, 1984; LOCKEFIELD GARDENS, 1985; HERRON-MORTON PLACE, 1986; WHOLESALE DISTRICT, 1990; ST. JOSEPH, 1991.

In 1982 the commission's state legislation was again amended. The number of commissioners was increased from seven to nine and one commissioner was required to be a resident of an historic district. The commission has since developed policies and procedures to ensure timely and fair review. Published guidelines in adopted preservation plans encourage compliance with nationally and locally accepted standards. The commission and its staff, now part of the DEPARTMENT OF METROPOLITAN DEVELOPMENT, work in cooperation with neighborhood associations, preservation groups, and the general public in pursuing the community's preservation goals.

DAVID L. BAKER
Indianapolis Historic Preservation Commission

Indianapolis Home Show.
Largest home show in the nation. In April, 1922, more than 67,000 people attended the first Indianapolis Home Complete Exposition sponsored by the local real estate board at the INDIANA STATE FAIRGROUNDS to promote home ownership. The show's centerpiece home, a five-room bungalow, was awarded to the winner of an essay contest on "Why One Should Own His Home in Indianapolis." At the show's conclusion, the house was moved to 13th Street and Emerson Avenue where it still stands. Within a few years the show boasted nearly 150 exhibitors.

During the height of the Great Depression financial considerations forced the show to forgo its trademark centerpiece home display, and it mounted a garden display instead. The next year the Indianapolis Real Estate Board dropped its

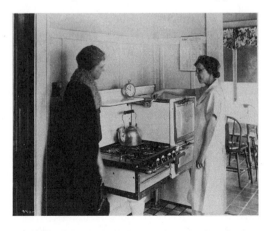

The 1924 Indianapolis Home Show introduced city housewives to gas range cooking.
[Indiana Historical Society, Bass Collection, #87317F]

sponsorship of the show. Since that time the Indianapolis Home Show, Inc., has run the annual event.

The show's founder, Indianapolis resident J. Frank Cantwell, developed the home show concept in the United States, using it to introduce variety and innovation into American home building. Cantwell directed the exposition for almost four decades. During this time the show held design competitions for its centerpiece homes, which were often luxurious.

From 1942 to 1945 the Home Show was temporarily suspended due to shortages of building materials, manpower, and available space since the fairgrounds were used by the army during the war. By the mid–1940s the show's name was changed to the Indianapolis Home Show. It received national exposure in 1947 when *Better Homes & Gardens* magazine carried a nine-page spread on that year's centerpiece home.

The Home Show has been used to introduce new products such as electric refrigerators, dishwashers, garbage disposals, and central air conditioning to Indianapolis residents. It also helped popularize the ranch style home in the city during the 1950s. By the early 1960s annual attendance at the show had increased to 100,000 people. The show continued to grow during the next several decades. In 1993 more than 150,000 people viewed the 700 Home Show exhibits, located in three buildings at the fairgrounds.

DEBORAH B. MARKISOHN

Indianapolis Star, Nov. 16, 1959; "Heading for Home," *Indianapolis Monthly* (Jan., 1992).

Indianapolis Housing Authority (IHA).

Federally sponsored municipal agency. Organized during the GREAT DEPRESSION, the original IHA operated low-income and temporary postwar housing projects. It disbanded in 1958, having incurred large debts. Mayor CHARLES BOSWELL revived the IHA by city ordinance in 1964 to provide low-cost rental housing when highway construction displaced poor residents. Critics from the real estate, development, and building professions and the CHAMBER OF COMMERCE argued that the IHA was socialistic and not needed

in Indianapolis. Claiming that it was improper to take federal money, they believed that private builders could satisfy existing housing needs.

The IHA has the power to design, construct, maintain, and manage public housing for low-income, elderly, and handicapped residents. The mayor appoints, and can remove, the five housing commissioners, who serve four-year terms, set policy, and appoint the IHA director. The commissioners are not subject to review by the City-County Council. Most of the IHA budget comes from grants and subsidies from the U.S. Department of Housing and Urban Development (HUD) and tenant rents. Tenant rents are based on family size and income. The IHA's jurisdiction extends five miles beyond the old (pre-Unigov) city limits, but public housing has never been constructed outside of the old city boundaries.

During the 1960s, IHA managed LOCKEFIELD GARDENS and constructed six low-income housing projects. The IHA also provided single-family homes, scattered throughout the city, for lease with the option to purchase. Under Mayor Richard G. Lugar, the IHA became one of ten authorities selected as part of President Nixon's experimental federal housing program, "Operation Breakthrough." Sixty-five percent of the units created by Operation Breakthrough were eventually sold, however, to Adult Student Housing, Inc., to pay for a $5 million deficit.

Due to huge deficits, mismanagement, and low occupancy rates by the late 1970s, the IHA became one of HUD's "troubled authorities." A late 1970s court ruling by federal judge S. Hugh Dillin prohibits the IHA from encouraging segregation by building facilities within the Indianapolis Public Schools district. In 1980 Mayor William H. Hudnut III ordered the GREATER INDIANAPOLIS PROGRESS COMMITTEE (GIPC) to study public housing conditions. As a result of GIPC's findings, the IHA made management changes and was temporarily taken off the troubled authorities list in 1983, only to be re-listed as a troubled authority later that year. The City-County Council transferred IHA management to the DEPARTMENT OF METROPOLITAN DEVELOPMENT (DMD) in 1985.

As of the early 1990s, the IHA retains limited independence within the DMD as the Division of Housing. There have been recurring administrative problems and disagreements over privatization of property management and maintenance as well as resident homeownership and empowerment policies. As of 1993, the IHA manages five high-rise facilities for senior and handicapped citizens and ten family community projects with units ranging from efficiencies to five-bedroom apartments. IHA facilities also house day care centers and health care clinics.

MICHELLE D. HALE

Indianapolis Newspaper Index, Indiana State Library.

Indianapolis Human Rights Commission (1952–1982). Municipal civil rights body. Organized in 1952 as an advisory group to Mayor ALEX M. CLARK on CIVIL RIGHTS matters, the City Council passed an ordinance the following year that made the advisory board an official commission within city government. The original commission consisted of volunteer business, labor, religious, and civic leaders appointed by the mayor and City Council. The commission, which had no legal authority, was empowered to mediate and educate citizens in "conditions which strain relations." While often inactive during the 1950s, it has been credited with helping to integrate local hospitals, neighborhoods, parks, and businesses, as well as the city's fire, police, and sanitation departments.

In 1958, the City Council approved a director and secretary to administer the commission. For the next two years Alex Kertis, also the city's personnel director, worked as a part-time executive secretary. He was followed by Rev. JAMES JONES (who years after leaving Indianapolis led the members of his Peoples Temple to mass suicide in Guyana). A full-time professional director, J. Griffin Crump, was not hired until 1963 as a result of increased state and national civil rights legislation, as well as local agitation under the leadership of commission co-chair HENRY J. RICHARDSON.

As the commission became more of an investigatory body its caseload multiplied, especially in regard to employment and housing discrimination. During the 1970s when the commission's jurisdiction expanded to include all of Marion County in the areas of schooling, housing, employment, education, public facilities, and gender discrimination. The CITY-COUNTY COUNCIL also granted it the power to initiate investigations and complaints, as well as obtain temporary injunctions, subpoenas, and court decrees to aid its investigations and enforce decisions.

In 1982, Mayor William H. Hudnut III fired executive director Charles Guynn and reorganized the office after an investigation revealed internal conflicts, unqualified staff, and office supplies being used for personal work. By the end of the year the commission was disbanded and its work became the responsibility of the Office for Equal Opportunity within the city's Legal Division. The new administrator also served as the city's affirmative action officer and was advised by a newly created Equal Opportunity Board. The division was arranged into four committees: internal employment practices, contract compliance, handicapped accessibility, and complaint adjudication. Today, that office has become a separate division in city government.

MICHELLE D. HALE

Indianapolis Newspaper Index, Indiana State Library.

Indianapolis Indians. Professional baseball team. A charter member of the American Association (baseball's most prestigious minor league) since its inaugural season of 1902, the Indianapolis Indians BASEBALL club has provided nearly a full century of exciting professional minor league play for baseball fans throughout central Indiana. Known as the Indians throughout its history and playing in a variety of leagues in addition to the venerable American Association, the Indianapolis club has enjoyed 20 league or divisional titles and provided training grounds for several future major league stars (Roger Maris, Herb Score, Rocco Colavito, Eric Davis) and a handful of future Hall-of-Famers (Grover Cleveland Alexander, Al Lopez, Harmon Killebrew, Rube Marquard). The working agreement between the Indians and the National League Montreal franchise resulted in four consecutive

American Association playoff championships (1986–1989) and two victories in the Triple-A Alliance World Series contested between American Association and International League champions. Other franchise highlights include a 1917 first Junior World Series sweep over the reigning International League champion Toronto Maple Leafs, a second Junior World Series triumph against the International League Rochester Red Wings in 1956, the 1963 International League pennant season (during the club's only campaign in that circuit), and a 1948 American Association ballclub that topped 100 victories for the only time in franchise history.

Indianapolis Indians major league affiliations were formally launched during the 1939–1941 seasons with a working agreement between Indianapolis and the National League Cincinnati Reds. Indianapolis also served as a farm team for the National League Boston Braves (1946–1947) and Pittsburgh Pirates (1948–1951) before joining forces with the Cleveland Indians between 1952 and 1956. It was the latter Cleveland affiliation which lent the team its first cluster of future big-league stars, as Cleveland pitching prospect Herb Score won 22 games while Rocco Colavito cracked a club record with 38 homers in 1954. The 1952–1956 campaigns brought two American Association titles to Indianapolis, as did the power-packed 1954 ballclub under manager Kerby Farrell, considered by many baseball historians the finest minor league outfit in the nation during that decade. Additional major league working agreements included the American League Chicago White Sox (1957–1959, 1962–1967) and National League Philadelphia Phillies (1960), as well as once again with the Cincinnati Reds (1961, 1968–1983). A 16–year Cincinnati affiliation was acrimoniously broken after the 1983 season, however, when the Indians front office under long-time general manager Max Schumacher lost patience with the parent club's steadfast policy banning use of the designated hitter at the minor league level. Following a decade-long association with Montreal, the Cincinnati affiliation was reestablished in 1993.

The largely successful saga of hometown Indians baseball has not been without its low points, and none was more critical than the financial woes that almost sunk the ballclub at the conclusion of the 1956 season. A baseball-loving community saved the franchise when 6,672 community shareholders contributed $205,000 in desperately needed operating capital. A second crisis arose when the proud but cash-short American Association temporarily folded after the 1962 season. The Indianapolis franchise, which had captured a first AA title flag in 1902 and a last league pennant in 1962, was suddenly forced to join forces with the International League for a single season, and then with the geographically distant Pacific Coast League for five additional summers (1964–1968). Reformation of the American Association in 1969 quickly brought a happy renewal of Indianapolis membership in America's second oldest minor league circuit.

Owen J. BUSH STADIUM is the most recent name for the near downtown ballpark on West 16th Street that has served the club continuously since 1931, first under the name of Perry Stadium (honoring James Perry, brother of owner Norman Perry) and later as Victory Field (1941–1967). This quaint stadium, now sporting the name of one-time popular manager and long-time club owner "Donie" Bush, is one of America's last remaining minor league architectural treasures from an earlier age of intimate steel-and-concrete urban ballyards. The park itself gained considerable national attention in 1987 when selected as the setting for filming the popular movie *Eight Men Out*, based on the 1919 Black Sox World Series scandal. It also drew wide international notice that same season as host site for the PAN AMERICAN GAMES baseball tournament, as well as a national audience a season later as the setting for an inaugural two games of the first-ever Triple-A Alliance championship series between the International League Rochester Red Wings and host American Association Indians. In 1993, however, Major League baseball advised Indians' management that the aging facility must be either thoroughly refurbished or replaced in order to meet present day standards. In spring, 1994, the city's CAPITAL IMPROVEMENT BOARD approved financing for the Indians' plan to build a downtown stadium just west of the Hoosier Dome.

PETER C. BJARKMAN
Society for American Baseball Research

Mike Blake, *The Minor Leagues: A Celebration of the Little Show* (New York, 1991); Robert Obojski, *Bush League: A History of Minor League Baseball* (New York, 1975); David B. Reddick and Kim M. Rogers, *The Magic of Indians Baseball: 1887–1987* (Indianapolis, 1988).

Indianapolis International Airport.

During the summer of 1928 the Indianapolis CHAMBER OF COMMERCE and the Indianapolis City Council held several discussions about developing a municipal airport. State-owned Cox Field (later STOUT FIELD) was satisfactory at the time, but the group believed that the city should own its airport ground.

In August, a committee of Indianapolis businessmen, formed to recommend a site for the proposed airport, established general site requirements and published a questionnaire in local newspapers. Considering the opinions of civil and military pilots, existing airport operators, real estate appraisers, and others, the committee eventually whittled the 43 proposed sites down to two. Most proposals favored a site west of High School Road and north of West Washington Street, even though this location was close to the Ben Davis schools on the east and was bounded by a high railroad embankment on the west.

After much discussion the committee settled on the present site, and in 1929 the city brought 320 acres on South High School Road for a landing area plus another 627 acres for future expansion. Here, in an area unhampered for decades to come by any industrial or residential obstructions, the city built the new Indianapolis Municipal Airport, the first in the area with concrete runways. The field was renamed Weir Cook Municipal Airport on March 28, 1944, in honor of H. WEIR COOK, a Hoosier fighter ace during World War II. (Cook died in a plane crash in New Caledonia on March 24, 1943.) In 1976, coincident with the opening of a new building to serve international arrivals and departures, including full customs services, the field was renamed Indianapolis International Airport. Operations at the facility are supervised by the INDIANAPOLIS AIRPORT AUTHORITY.

Airline traffic first operated from the field on February 16, 1931, when Transcontinental Air Transport moved from Stout Field. American Airways followed on April 1, and the field was officially dedicated on September 25, 1931. Indianapolis jet operations began April 30, 1961, when Trans World Airlines inaugurated non-stop service to New York City. Since 1931 some 68 different scheduled airlines have operated from the field, in addition to numerous nonscheduled passenger, cargo, and military operators. Passenger traffic has increased apace. In 1981 the field served just over 2 million passengers; in 1992 that figure stood at 6.3 million, an 11.5 percent increase over the previous year.

The field's original 2,000–foot runways have been expanded to over 10,000 feet, capable of handling any aircraft now flying or planned in the foreseeable future. The field's size has also been increased to over 6,000 acres, with plans for further additions. In early 1994 work was progressing on two major airport projects: a multi-state sorting hub for U.S. Postal Service airmail handling and a $1 billion aircraft maintenance facility for United Airlines.

JERRY MARLETTE

Indianapolis Leader.

African-American newspaper. Benjamin D. Bagby and Company began publishing what is purported to be the first black Indianapolis newspaper in August, 1879. The four-page weekly was distributed on Saturdays and cost five cents per issue or two dollars per year. The *Leader's* motto was "An Equal Chance and Fair Play." The weekly supported the Republican party and the Frederick Douglass philosophy of the self-made man. The paper was active in the politics of the day, reported on events at the 1880 Republican convention, and presented petitions to the governor of Indiana. The journal also carried national and local news of the previous week, church information, society news, meeting dates of various clubs, and announcements about special events.

The *Leader* gave its readers biographical sketches of famous Americans, articles and stories about African-American success in America, philosophical anecdotes, and Sunday school lessons. The "Leader Thinks" column commented on current political and social happenings. The paper dedicated a special column to activities in the Cincinnati area. In 1882 the paper published a debate between Frederick Douglass and a Dr. Blyden on whether Africa or America would be the best place for the advancement of the Negro race. Benjamin Bagby sold the newspaper to A. J. and L. H. Johnson in 1886, who in turn sold the paper to John Medert in 1889. Medert hired T. J. Sharp to serve as editor until the *Leader* ceased publication around 1890.

BRADFORD W. SAMPLE

John W. Miller, *Indiana Newspaper Bibliography* (Indianapolis, 1982).

Indianapolis Life Insurance Company.

Indianapolis Life was organized on July 4, 1905, by brothers Charles, Edward, George, and Joseph Raub, Frank Manly, and Albert Goslee. Six days later it incorporated as a mutual life insurance company, meaning that policyholders, not stockholders, owned the company. This was unusual since most insurance companies are founded as stock companies, evolving into mutual companies when the stock is retired. By November, 1905, the company had sold the 250 life insurance policies required to engage officially in business. Indianapolis Life's first office was located in the INDIANAPOLIS TRACTION TERMINAL building with a clerical staff of one. In 1907 the company moved to larger quarters in the newly constructed BOARD OF TRADE building and purchased the mansion of former Vice-President CHARLES WARREN FAIRBANKS at 30th and Meridian streets for its home office in 1923, to which additions were made in 1951, 1966, 1980, and 1985. The company purchased the adjoining Levey mansion in 1978.

Indianapolis Life specializes in individual life, annuity, and disability income insurance, selling policies in 44 states and the District of Columbia through more than 500 sales agents. About 40 percent of the company's business is in Indiana and four surrounding states. Indianapolis Life reported assets in excess of $1 billion for 1993 with more than $11 billion in life insurance policies, ranking it among the country's 45 largest mutual life insurance companies based upon admitted assets and total life insurance in force. In the early

1990s it was the state's third largest insurance company.

DEBORAH B. MARKISOHN

"A 'Plain Vanilla' Company," *Indianapolis Business Journal*, Apr. 2–8, 1990; George Geib, *Indianapolis: Hoosiers' Circle City* (Tulsa, Okla., 1981), 201.

Indianapolis Literary Club.

Men's club founded January 10, 1877, by John D. Howland, clerk of the federal courts; Charles Evans, city librarian; William A. Bartlett, pastor of Second Presbyterian Church; and attorneys George H. Chapman, William P. Fishback, and Jordan W. Gordon. Modeled after the Chicago and Cincinnati men's literary clubs and the Indianapolis Woman's Club (established 1875), the club's stated purpose is "social, literary and aesthetic culture." Its only requirements for membership (which is limited to 150) are intellectual curiosity and a willingness to serve periodically as the "essayist of the evening." Special programs during the year include two "ladies' nights" and the annual dinner.

Over the years the club has met in various locations. Beginning initially in the homes of its members, the club later convened at the Denison Hotel, Plymouth Church, the Propylaeum, a chapter house of the Daughters of the American Revolution, and, most recently, Robertson Hall at Butler University.

Many prominent men representing various professions have been members of the Literary Club, including educators William Lowe Bryan and David Starr Jordan, authors LEW WALLACE, BOOTH TARKINGTON, JAMES WHITCOMB RILEY, and JACOB PIATT DUNN, JR., journalists MEREDITH NICHOLSON and HILTON U. BROWN, and attorneys BENJAMIN HARRISON, Alvin P. Hovey, and NOBLE C. BUTLER. Artist members included T. C. STEELE, WILLIAM FORSYTH, and CLIFTON WHEELER; the club owns a number of their paintings, which are on loan to the INDIANAPOLIS MUSEUM OF ART. The club's historical records, including copies of essays delivered by members, are located in the Indiana Historical Society Library.

CHARLES E. MEYER
Indianapolis Literary Club

Francis H. Insley, comp., *Indianapolis Literary Club* (Indianapolis, 1977).

Indianapolis–Marion County Building Authority.

Independent municipal corporation that owns, finances, and operates land and buildings for the use of city and county government operations. It was organized under special state legislation in 1953 to oversee the construction and financing of the CITY-COUNTY BUILDING.

The authority has no separate taxing power, so it repays its bonds and pays its operating expenses through rents collected under long-term leases with the city of Indianapolis and Marion County. In addition to the City-County Building, the authority owns and operates the Marion County Jail addition, the Juvenile Detention Center, the sheriff's roll-call site, the City Maintenance Garage, and the Environmental Services Building. All projects financed by the authority are subject to the approval of the City-County Council.

The building authority is governed by a five-member board of directors. Two members are appointed by the mayor of Indianapolis, two by the City-County Council, and one by the Marion County commissioners. The members serve four-year terms without salary and may be reappointed.

LAURRY NEUFER

Indianapolis–Marion County Public Library.

The best known early efforts to foster reading and libraries in Indianapolis were the Union Sabbath School founded in 1823; the Marion County Library, a subscription library established in 1844 under the provisions of the 1816 Indiana constitution and housed in the county courthouse; and township libraries set up through a school law passed by the Indiana legislature in 1852. None of these early libraries achieved much success since they were poorly housed, frequently had no one responsible for their care, and no money was provided for their maintenance and expansion. The real impetus came on Thanksgiving Day, 1868, when the Reverend Hanford A. Edson, pastor of the SECOND PRESBYTERIAN CHURCH, delivered a sermon in

School children using the Haughville branch library, ca. 1920. [Indiana Historical Society, Bass Collection, #69043]

which he issued a plea for a free public library in Indianapolis. As a result, 113 citizens formed the Indianapolis Library Association on March 18, 1869, with subscribers paying $150 each in annual installments of $25 for stock shares in the association.

The next year, under the leadership of ABRAM C. SHORTRIDGE, the superintendent of public schools, eight public-spirited citizens drafted a revision of the existing Indiana school law to provide for the maintenance of free public libraries controlled by a board of school commissioners. Their effort met with success when the Indiana General Assembly passed the School Law of 1871 empowering school boards to levy an additional tax for the purpose of establishing and maintaining public libraries.

In July, 1872, the public library committee of the school board hired Cincinnati librarian William F. Poole to compile a list of 8,000 titles as a nucleus collection for the new Indianapolis library. The committee also selected CHARLES EVANS of the Boston Athenaeum as the first librarian.

The library, located in one room of the high school building at the northeast corner of Pennsylvania and Michigan streets, opened on April 9, 1873. It had 12,790 volumes ready for 500 registered borrowers, including the collection of 3,649 volumes given by the Indianapolis Library Association. Later locations of the library were the Sentinel Building on the Circle (1876–1880) and the

Alvord House at Pennsylvania and Ohio streets (1880–1893).

Evans served as librarian until 1878, and again from 1889 to 1892. His outstanding contribution to scholarship was his *American Bibliography*, a chronological guide to all publications printed in the United States from 1639 to 1820. Evans' successors were Albert B. Yohn (1878–1879), Arthur W. Tyler (1879–1883), and William deM. Hooper (1883–1889). Eliza G. Browning, a member of the library staff since 1880, succeeded Evans in his second tenure, holding the position of librarian from 1892 to 1917. In 1893 the library moved to the first building constructed primarily for its use, located on the southwest corner of Ohio and Meridian streets.

In December, 1896, the first branch library opened. Between 1910 and 1914 five branch libraries were built with a grant of $100,000 received from Andrew Carnegie. Two of these libraries—Spades Park and East Washington branches —are still in use. Prior to her resignation Browning completed work on a new Central Library located on land donated by James Whitcomb Riley at St. Clair between Pennsylvania and Meridian streets. Designed by Philadelphia architect Paul Cret this impressive Greek Doric style structure, built of Indiana limestone on a Vermont marble base, opened October 8, 1917, and remains in use today. The main reading room (100 feet by 45 feet) just inside the main entrance is noteworthy for its two flights of Maryland marble stairs, two 30–foot diameter bronze light fixtures, and the ornamental ceiling, designed by C. C. Zantzinger, which includes oil-on-canvas medallions and printers ' colophons accompanied by a series of bas-relief plaster plaques portraying the early history of Indiana. Reading rooms at the top of each staircase have wood paneling above oak bookcases, and large leaded glass windows.

Charles E. Rush succeeded Browning, serving as librarian from 1917 until 1927. His successors were Luther L. Dickerson (1927–1944) and Marian McFadden (1944–1955). During this 38–year period, eight new branch libraries were opened, films (1944) and phonorecords (1948) were added to the library's borrowing collection, bookmobile service began (1952), and newspapers on microfilm became available for public use (1940s). Harold J. Sander, who served as the director from 1956 to 1971, undertook a reorganization of the Central Library in 1960 that departmentalized all adult materials and services. He also presided over the opening of ten new branch libraries.

Prior to 1966 the library served only the School City of Indianapolis (that is, the area served by INDIANAPOLIS PUBLIC SCHOOLS). Over 200,000 Marion County residents outside of the city limits had no access to free public library services. From 1966 to 1968 a newly formed Marion County Public Library Board contracted with the Indianapolis Public Library for service to county residents. In June, 1968, the Indianapolis Board of School Commissioners divested itself of the responsibility for library service that it had held since 1873. The city library then merged with the county library, establishing the new Indianapolis-Marion County Public Library as a separate municipal corporation serving all of Marion County except Beech Grove and Speedway.

Raymond E. Gnat succeeded Sander as library director in 1972. A 40,000 square foot Central Library Annex was completed in 1975, a major branch library building program began in 1982 and continued through that decade, a Central Library restoration fund drive was launched in 1984 with restoration work (which included cleaning and repainting the main room ceiling) completed in 1988, and computerization of major library functions was completed between 1982 and 1991.

In the early 1990s the Indianapolis-Marion County Public Library is comprised of a Central Library, 21 branch libraries, and three bookmobiles. In 1991 some 7,038,000 items were loaned to 470,000 registered borrowers, and 3,402,000 inquiries were answered. Also in 1991 there were 1,691,000 books and other library materials in the collection, and a full-time equivalent staff of 410. A seven-member board governs the library: two members are appointed by the City-County Council, two by the Indianapolis Board of School Commissioners, and three by the county assessor, auditor, and treasurer acting jointly as an appointing authority under UNIGOV provisions. Funding for library services is derived from property tax, financial institution tax, vehicle excise tax, fines and fees, and other miscellaneous income.

LAWRENCE J. DOWNEY

Lawrence J. Downey, *A Live Thing in the Whole Town: The History of the Indianapolis-Marion County Public Library, 1873–1990* (Indianapolis, 1991).

Indianapolis Matinee Musicale. One of the oldest music organizations in the United States. The group gives November 20, 1877, as its founding date, when nine young women gathered informally to spend a musical afternoon together. Two years later, with 20 members, the group had outgrown its "parlor club" origins, drawn up a constitution, and adopted the name Ladies Matinee Musicale. In addition to performing for one another, they studied composers and different styles of composition. In 1883 they established active and associate (non-performing) memberships and began meeting in a club room at the DENISON HOTEL.

The organization presented its first artist concert in 1885 and six years later inaugurated an artist concert series. In 1895 the group added a new student section, admitted men as associate members, and began holding auditions for active membership by secret ballot. It became affiliated with the National Federation of Music Clubs in 1910 and a decade later helped to establish the Indiana Federation of Music Clubs, both groups being dedicated to fostering American music and American composers. The professional associate section was added in 1922, a choral section in 1929, and an alumnae section now accommodates retired members. A scholarship fund for students was established in 1958 and an active program for granting scholarships has since been implemented.

JEROME DONAHUE

"Indianapolis Matinee Musicale: A Brief History" (pamphlet available from the organization).

Indianapolis Medical Society. Nonprofit professional medical association, also known at times as the Marion County Medical So-
ciety. The Indianapolis Medical Society (IMS) was founded in 1848 as the city's first local medical organization. With an initial membership of 20 physicians, Dr. John Sanders served as the first president. The organization experienced several divisions and reorganizations during the 1850s, 1860s, and 1870s, until it was restructured as the Marion County Medical Society in 1875 when several competing groups merged.

By 1902 the group's name was changed to Indianapolis Medical Society: The Medical Society of Marion County. In 1924 the 400–member organization was legally incorporated as the Marion County Medical Society. Membership doubled during the next 25 years, increasing to 860 physicians by 1949. By 1974 the group had almost 1,100 members and a full-time staff of four workers.

In 1990 the society purchased a building at 631 East New York Street for its headquarters and again changed its name, returning to the original Indianapolis Medical Society. As of 1994 a staff of eight people serves the approximately 2,000 physicians who hold membership in the IMS. Membership in the local society serves as a steppingstone to membership in the INDIANA STATE MEDICAL ASSOCIATION and the American Medical Association. The IMS also operates a public referral service which provides the names of area physicians who are currently accepting new patients.

DEBORAH B. MARKISOHN

Indianapolis Monthly. Magazine focusing on the Indianapolis metropolitan area. Founded in 1977 by John and Sally Mayhill and Jim and Nancy Cottrell, the magazine's original name was *Indianapolis Home & Garden*. It underwent changes in 1980 and was renamed *Indianapolis at Home*. A third name change to *Indianapolis Monthly* occurred in 1981 after Tom Mayhill (John's father) of Mayhill Publishing took ownership. At that time, Deborah Paul became editor-in-chief–copublisher and Jack Marsella became advertising director–copublisher. Jeff Smulyan, chairman and principal owner of Emmis Publishing, became the third owner in 1988.

Indianapolis Monthly celebrated its fifteenth year in September, 1992, boasting a circulation over 45,000 in central Indiana. Articles contained within 160 pages per copy include everything from issues to fashion, personalities to politics and business. The magazine has become known for its annual "Best and Worst of Indianapolis" awards (started in 1983), as well as its Dining Awards and People's Choice Awards.

CHRISTY M. MCKAY

Nancy Comiskey, "Evolution of a City Magazine," *Indianapolis Magazine* (Sept., 1987); *Gale Directory of Publications and Broadcast Media*, Vol. 1 (1992); interview with Deborah Paul, May 27, 1992.

Indianapolis Motor Speedway. Site of the Indianapolis 500 and the Brickyard 400 automobile races. The track was the concept of flamboyant entrepreneur CARL GRAHAM FISHER, born in Greensburg, Indiana, who in 1902 established himself in Indianapolis as a pioneer in the business of selling automobiles. By 1905 the many local automobile manufacturers were finding the rutty, virtually undeveloped public roads no longer adequate for testing an automobile's performance, and even the brand-new, one-mile oval dirt track at the INDIANA STATE FAIRGROUNDS was becoming outmoded for speed runs. Fisher proposed a much larger, sprawling track for both private testing and occasionally races in which manufacturers would compete against each other. He believed that success on the track would translate into showroom sales.

Three years after the failure of his ambitious plan to build a five-mile track at French Lick, Indiana, in 1906, Fisher formed the Indianapolis Motor Speedway Company (later Corporation) and in 1909 opened a $2^{1}/_{2}$-mile, rectangular track laid out on farmland about five miles northwest of Indianapolis. His three partners were ARTHUR NEWBY (of the prominent National Motor Vehicle Company on East 22nd Street), FRANK WHEELER (of Wheeler-Schebler Carburetor Company), and JAMES A. ALLISON, Fisher's partner in the successful PREST-O-LITE Company.

The track's inaugural motorcycle and automobile races in August, 1909, were consistently hampered by accidents caused by the original surface of crushed rock and tar. In September the company resurfaced the entire speedway in an amazing 63 days with 3,200,000 ten-pound paving bricks, mostly Culver Blocks, imported from several locations near the Illinois border. Changes also occurred in the track's racing program. Poor attendance at a trio of three-day meets in 1910 (with as many as 42 races in three days) led management to present a one-day "extravaganza" for 1911, paying a huge purse. Thus, the INDIANAPOLIS 500–MILE RACE was born.

In 1927 Fisher and Allison sold the track to a Michigan group headed up by World War I flying ace Eddie Rickenbacker, formerly a racing driver who had competed in most of the pre–World War I 500s. Although Rickenbacker carried out many notable renovations and improvements during his tenure, the track deteriorated dreadfully during four years of total inactivity during World War II. Three-time race winner WILBUR SHAW rescued the track by arranging for Terre Haute businessman Anton "Tony" Hulman to purchase it from Rickenbacker's group in November, 1945.

Hulman and his colleagues immediately embarked upon an ambitious six-month renovation program in order to get the facility ready for a 1946 race. Patches of asphalt had begun to be applied to the turns in the spring of 1936, and by the time the track was closed for World War II all but the greater portion of the main straight was of Kentucky rock asphalt. The remaining bricks were retained as long as feasible for reasons of nostalgia but finally were covered over—except for three feet at the start/finish line—following the 1961 race. The old wooden grandstands began to be replaced when a huge double-deck stand of steel was erected outside of turn one in 1949, soon to be followed by several more, similar in appearance, to its north. VIP suites were built as an experiment on the outside of turn two in 1973 and were so well received by corporations that many more were added later on either side of the main straight at the north end. The garage area ("Gasoline Alley"), which has taken several different forms on the current location since 1915, was completely torn down and rebuilt as a modern complex in time for the 1986 race.

Until 1956 all year-round Speedway business had been conducted in offices on North Capitol

Avenue near downtown Indianapolis rather than at the track itself. That spring, however, a combination office building and museum opened on the track grounds at the corner of West 16th Street and Georgetown Road. This structure eventually was superseded by a much larger building and museum on the inside of the track between turns one and two. Upon completion of this new facility in April, 1976, the main entrance—at the southwest corner of the property since 1909—was moved to its current location on West 16th Street. The 1956 building, used for years as a security headquarters and more recently as a credentials office, was razed in July, 1993, to make way for a new three-story office. The INDIANAPOLIS MOTOR SPEEDWAY HALL OF FAME MUSEUM, displaying nearly 100 vehicles, was not affected by this move and remains on the inside of the track.

An 18–hole golf course, originally installed in 1929 with nine holes on the infield and nine outside of the backstretch, was expanded to 27 holes in 1965 during the period when the track was hosting the PGA-sanctioned 500 Open. Internationally renowned designer Pete Dye, an Indianapolis native, completely revamped the course between 1991 and 1993. Now designated Brickyard Crossing, the new 18–hole course more than accommodates current PGA tour standards.

After years of speculation and anticipation, track management announced in the spring of 1993 that a NASCAR stock car race, the Brickyard 400, would be held on August 6, 1994, finally ending the one-race-per-year policy that had been in effect since the Harvest Day Classic drew a disappointing crowd in September, 1916.

Attention generated by the Indianapolis Motor Speedway seems to grow continuously, and it is generally accepted that its economic impact on central Indiana now exceeds hundreds of millions of dollars annually.

DONALD DAVIDSON
Statistician and Historian
United States Auto Club

Indianapolis Motor Speedway Hall of Fame Museum. The museum was established in 1956 by the late Tony Hulman, then track owner, and Karl Kizer, first museum director, to house the Hall of Fame, created in 1952 to honor outstanding personalities in racing and the auto industry. The museum was located outside Gate 1 and displayed a few vintage racing cars.

A larger museum was built within the Speedway oval in 1975. This 96,000–square-foot building houses the museum, administrative offices, Speedway ticket office, and Speedway gift shop. The Louis Chevrolet Memorial, located adjacent to the museum, exhibits a bronze bust of Chevrolet and highlights his automotive accomplishments.

The displays are regularly rotated in the museum, exhibiting approximately 70 of the cars included in the collection of more than 200 vehicles. In addition to winning cars from the INDIANAPOLIS 500–MILE RACE, the museum displays vintage passenger cars. Inductee medals and portraits are displayed in the museum, which is also assembling tapes and films to be used for researching cars and drivers' careers.

One of the most noted exhibits is the car that won the 1911 race, a MARMON Wasp driven by Ray Harroun. Another popular exhibit features the four cars driven by A. J. Foyt the four times he won the race.

The museum includes a collection of trophies, uniforms, goggles, and other race-related items, documenting the changing styles and safety standards throughout the years since the race's beginning. One of the most notable trophies is the Wheeler-Schebler trophy created by Tiffany. An exhibit of the timing and scoring methods is a recent addition to the museum. The Tony Hulman Theatre provides visitors with a look at historic footage from the first race in 1911, private footage of the track in 1945 when it was purchased by Hulman, and highlights from many races. The museum is open every day except Christmas.

SHELLY CHENOWETH

Indianapolis Motor Speedway Hall of Fame Museum press kit (1992); "Museum shows Hulman will 'Never Give Up,'" *Indianapolis Star*, Oct. 20, 1975; Welton W. Harris II, "Racing history documented via old films," *Indianapolis News*, May 24, 1990; Donald Davidson, "Pole Position," *Auto Week* (Mar. 9, 1992), 21–23.

Indianapolis Motor Speedway Radio
Network. World's largest radio network. The Indianapolis Motor Speedway (IMS) Radio Network was established in 1952 with WIBC and 26 stations broadcasting the INDIANAPOLIS 500–MILE RACE live. The network has grown to over 600 stations in the United States and Canada, and Armed Forces Radio beams the broadcasts to several hundred more stations worldwide.

From 1946 through 1950 a Mutual Broadcasting System (MBS) staff of five covered the Indianapolis 500 with brief reports every hour of the race. In 1951 WIBC broadcast the event live, with MBS picking up the final 30 minutes. In 1955 SID COLLINS, who had first participated in the broadcast in 1948, became known as the "Voice of the 500." He was synonymous with the IMS Radio Network until his death in 1977 and coined the famous description of the Indianapolis 500: the "Greatest Spectacle in Racing."

Paul Page followed his mentor in 1977 as the "Voice of the 500; Bob Jenkins became the chief announcer in 1989. Other members of the current IMS Radio Network staff include Donald Davidson, historian, and Howdy Bell, statistician. Nine additional professional announcers provide coverage from around the track as well as from the pits and garage area.

JUDY SCHWARTZ

Indianapolis Museum of Art (IMA).
One of the oldest art museums in the United States, established in 1883. The IMA functions both as an art museum and a 152–acre botanical garden. It contains five pavilions, a lecture hall, theatre, concert terrace, restaurant, shops, and greenhouse.

In 1883, MAY WRIGHT SEWALL held a meeting in her home to discuss the organization of a society for the study and promotion of art. On October 11, 1883, as a result of this and subsequent meetings, the ART ASSOCIATION OF INDIANAPOLIS was incorporated; its goal was to establish a permanent art museum and art school in Indianapolis. The first step in reaching this goal took place in 1895 when John Herron bequeathed almost $250,000 to the association. Herron stipulated that the money be used to build a museum and art school bearing his name.

The Indianapolis Museum of Art, ca. 1991. [Indianapolis Museum of Art. Photo by Wilbur Montgomery W M Photographic Services]

The John Herron Art Institute opened in 1902 in the Tinker House (or Talbot Place), once the studio of T. C. STEELE, at 16th and Pennsylvania streets. In 1905–1906 the institute constructed a new building on the site. The museum and art school continued to expand and the institute erected a second building in 1929 to house the HERRON SCHOOL OF ART. This enabled the museum, now sole occupant of the original building, to augment its collection and professionalize its staff.

The first professional director of the John Herron Art Museum was WILBUR D. PEAT, who began his 36 years with the museum in 1929. During his tenure the institution increased its holdings through purchases, gifts, bequests, and permanent loans. By 1942, the museum had acquired 350 paintings by 260 artists.

In 1965, Peat retired and Carl J. Weinhardt, Jr., became the new director of the museum. The following year, the children of Mr. and Mrs. JOSIAH K. LILLY, JR. donated their parents' estate, Oldfields, to the Art Association. For the next three years, the Art Association worked to convert the estate into a new home for the art museum. The Lilly mansion became Lilly Pavilion of Decorative Arts, and the construction of new exhibition buildings on the Oldfields estate began.

The John Herron Art Museum took a new name when it moved into these new quarters at

1200 West 38th Street in 1969: Indianapolis Museum of Art. This change signified the divergence of the Herron School of Art, which affiliated with INDIANA UNIVERSITY–PURDUE UNIVERSITY AT INDIANAPOLIS, and the new museum of art.

In the years following the move the IMA continued to expand. It opened the Krannert Pavilion in 1970, the Clowes Pavilion in 1971, and the Showalter Pavilion in 1973. When Weinhardt resigned as director of the IMA in 1974, he left a flourishing museum to his successor, Robert A. Yassin.

Yassin enlarged the IMA's curatorial department to keep pace with the expanding facility. In 1985, plans for yet another expansion were announced. The Mary Fendrich Hulman Charitable Trust made a gift of $3.5 million to the IMA for a new four-story Hulman Pavilion. When this pavilion opened on October 14, 1990, it increased the museum's exhibition space by about 75 percent.

Bret Waller became director in 1990. He currently oversees the museum's substantial collection of American, Asian, African, and pre-Columbian art, including Old Master, Classical, and Renaissance paintings, American and European furniture, silver, textiles, and special exhibitions. Some of the IMA's finest permanent collections include the J. M. W. Turner Collection of watercolors and drawings, the Holliday Collection of Neo-Impressionist Art, the Clowes Fund Collection of Old Master paintings, the Eli Lilly Collection of Chinese Art, and the Eiteljorg Collection of African Art.

In addition to exhibition space, the IMA also houses the Alliance Museum Shop, the Alliance Rental and Sales Gallery, and the Indianapolis Civic Theatre. The outdoor Concert Terrace is the site of summer concerts, films, and special programs. The IMA greenhouse cultivates and sells flowers, herbs, and plants. The Lillys' recreation house has become the Garden on the Green Restaurant, and Newfields, a second Lilly residence on the estate, is now the location of the IMA Alliance's Better-Than-New Shop. Expanding the range of the facilities in Indianapolis, the IMA opened the Indianapolis Museum of Art–Columbus at the Visitors' Center in Columbus, Indiana, in 1974.

In the mid–1990s, the IMA had a yearly budget of around $8 million and over 11,000 members. There are some 200,000 annual visitors to the museum and grounds.

HARRIET G. WARKEL
Indianapolis Museum of Art

Indianapolis Music Promoters. The Indianapolis Music Promoters Club was founded in 1919 as a branch of the National Association of Negro Musicians. Adelaide Thornton Riley and Ellen Thomas Merriweather, who served as first president, established the branch after attending an organizational meeting of the national association in Washington, D.C. The purpose of the club was to pursue musical study and foster youthful talents. Many of the club members directed musical groups at local churches, schools, and businesses. Programs were performed regularly at Caleb Mills Hall, Phyllis Wheatley YWCA, the Indiana World War Memorial, Clowes Memorial Hall, and Christian Theological Seminary.

Since 1979 the Indianapolis Music Promoters, in conjunction with THE CHILDREN'S MUSEUM, has sponsored the annual Music Stars of Tomorrow program. Open to advanced junior and senior high school music students, the program hails individual accomplishments and exposes participants to various cultures. Other activities of the organization include conducting workshops and clinics and the identification and development of musical talent.

WILMA GIBBS
Indiana Historical Society

Indianapolis Neighborhood Housing Partnership (INHP). Nonprofit agency focusing on the city's housing needs. In 1987 Mayor William Hudnut appointed a Housing Strategy Task Force to study the city's growing housing problems. The task force found that approximately 30,000 substandard housing units existed within Marion County and recommended that every Indianapolis resident have access to safe and decent housing by the year 2000. It also recommended the creation, in 1988, of the Indianapolis Neighborhood Housing Partnership.

The INHP, a nonprofit agency headed by a board of directors, develops and coordinates comprehensive housing and neighborhood renewal strategies. It targets inner-city neighborhoods, primarily in Center Township, and its objective is to bring together efforts of the city, public agencies, financial institutions, businesses, developers, and foundations to meet the need for affordable, decent housing by those city residents with low and moderate incomes.

Part of the INHP's focus includes working toward the development of affordable homeownership and home rehabilitation financing through a cooperative loan pool and other funding such as grants. In 1990 the partnership acquired enough money from the city and local lending institutions ($1.25 million) to begin a loan assistance program with three different types of loans at varied interest rates. In 1993 the housing partnership, with substantial support from the major local banks, put together an $8 million pool for the development of apartments for low-income families.

The INHP is involved with other areas of the housing effort as well. Focal points include long-term planning and program development in all phases of the community housing system; assisting with rehabilitation and development of rental properties and housing units; providing housing counseling for needy families (in 1993 the agency was counseling some 1,400 people regarding their housing needs); and working with human service agencies to ensure their support.

LISA EHRET

Indianapolis News, Feb. 20, 1993; Indianapolis Star, July 23, 1993.

Indianapolis News. Daily newspaper. The city's oldest newspaper, the Indianapolis News was established December 7, 1869, by 23–year-old reporter JOHN HAMPDEN HOLLIDAY. At two cents, the News was a penny cheaper than its competition. Its price, plus clean makeup and condensed form, made it popular. Three months after its founding, the News had a circulation of 2,500 and had absorbed the weekly Mirror. Holliday stuck to his commitment to publish a politically independent newspaper, although the paper traditionally has been considered conservative in its editorial position.

The News' circulation had grown to 25,000 when the ailing Holliday sold it in May, 1892, to William H. Smith, his son DELAVAN SMITH, and his son-in-law Charles N. Williams. In 1909 the News' editors were indicted on criminal libel charges, later dismissed, for reprinting an article critical of the Theodore Roosevelt administration's actions that resulted in the United States taking possession of the Panama Canal. CHARLES W. FAIRBANKS, United States vice-president under Roosevelt and former U.S. senator from Indiana, had owned part of the News since 1892, although it was never revealed until his death in 1918. When Delavan Smith died in 1922, the Fairbanks children bought complete ownership of the News, with sons Warren, Frederick, and Richard serving terms as publisher through 1944.

Known as the "Great Hoosier Daily," the News enjoyed its heyday during the first half of the 20th century and was the state's most widely read paper. In May, 1932, the News was awarded a PULITZER PRIZE for a series of stories and editorials on wasteful spending by city and state government.

The News continued to dominate its closest competitor, the morning INDIANAPOLIS STAR, into the 1940s. But in 1944 EUGENE C. PULLIAM bought the Star and started intense competition, calling off an unwritten truce that the Star would not challenge the News' circulation if the News would not start a Sunday paper. The News edged the Star in circulation in 1945, 151,640 to 133,600. But by the end of World War II, squabbling among the Fairbanks heirs was hurting the News, and by 1947 the Star had overtaken the News in circulation. In August, 1948, Pulliam bought the paper for $4 million and formed Indianapolis Newspapers, Inc. (INI).

When the city's other afternoon paper, the INDIANAPOLIS TIMES, folded in 1965, the News picked up some of its following. By 1970 the News' circulation had rebounded to 183,026, and the paper employed 103 reporters and editors. However, the News could not escape the trend of declining afternoon circulation and lost 40,000 subscribers between 1970 and the 1980s, when circulation hit 143,141. As newspapers moved into the technological age, INI and the *News* converted to word processors, offset printing, and an electronic library later than most big-city newspapers, waiting for the technology to prove itself.

In 1950 the *News* began one of the early newspaper consumer columns, Herman Hoglebogle, which continues today. Another continuing tradition is the Blue Streak, the latest daily edition, sold only as single copies. It debuted in 1956 with a jagged blue line running down the edge.

Among the paper's most famous employees were FRANK MCKINNEY "KIN" HUBBARD, creator of the "Abe Martin" character that ran in 300 newspapers, and HILTON U. BROWN, who worked there for 77 years. The *News* marks its December anniversary yearly with "The News Proposes," which outlines long-range goals the paper and community can work toward together. Some realized goals were a domed stadium and restoration of UNION STATION.

During the 1980s the *News* initiated successful investigations of state government, including two that led to the resignation of the heads of the Department of Education and the Department of Correction. In 1988 the *News* broke the story of how U.S. vice-presidential nominee Dan Quayle avoided military service in the Vietnam War, despite the fact that Quayle is the nephew of current *News* publisher Eugene S. Pulliam and has stock holdings in the paper's parent company.

The *News* shares advertising, production, and an expanded building at the corner of New York and Pennsylvania streets with the *Star*, but editorial and reporting staffs are separate. The *News* continues to publish daily except Sundays, with circulation at 102,000 in 1990.

BETH MURPHY

Russell Pulliam, *Publisher Gene Pulliam: Last of the Newspaper Titans* (Ottawa, Ill., 1984); John W. Miller, *Indiana Newspaper Bibliography* (Indianapolis, 1982).

Indianapolis Opera (Indianapolis Opera Company). Formed September 29, 1975, through the efforts of Miriam Ramaker of Indiana Central University and other opera enthusiasts, the Indianapolis Opera Company (IOC) began modestly as a not-for-profit corporation with an initial budget of less than $8,000 and a season limited to a one-night performance of two short works: Douglas Moore's *The Devil and Daniel Webster* and Gian Carlo Menotti's *The Telephone*. Over the next five years the fledgling organization experienced steady growth, staging numerous opera favorites. IOC's success came to an abrupt halt in March of 1981, however, when the organization suffered financial collapse amidst allegations of misappropriation of federal funds.

Convinced that a market for opera existed in Indianapolis, a new board of directors appointed James Caraher musical director and Robert Driver artistic director. Driver, who continued to hold the same position with the Syracuse (N.Y.) Opera, ushered in a new period of cooperative production ventures for the two companies. The Indianapolis Opera, as it now called itself, shared rental scenery sets, singers' fees, costumes, and other production costs with the Syracuse organization. A third opera company, Opera Memphis of Memphis, Tennessee, joined the partnership in 1984. For the next three years the Indianapolis Opera, as part of this triumvirate, staged three operas a season. In 1987 the Syracuse Opera dropped out of the cooperative alliance. The following year the two remaining companies initiated a highly successful four-production season format which the Indianapolis Opera continues to the present. Between 1988 and 1992 (after which time Opera Memphis left the partnership), the Indianapolis Opera staged highly praised, creative presentations of *The Magic Flute*, *Don Giovanni*, *Cosi fan tutte*, *Lucia di Lammermoor*, and *Porgy and Bess*, starring such internationally recognized singers as Nova Thomas, Robert Orth, Arthur Woodley, Stella Zambalis, and Kenneth Cox. In 1992 Nando Schellen, a native of Holland and former managing director of the Netherlands Opera, succeeded Robert Driver, who had accepted the artistic directorship of the Opera Company of Philadelphia.

Formed in 1989 as part of the Indianapolis Opera's educational and touring outreach program, the Indianapolis Opera Ensemble presents short programs for school children. This resident company also provides opportunities for young opera singers to gain professional experience. Lectures, Discovery Guides, and full-script libretti with translations present background information on each opera. English translations projected above the stage also facilitate operagoers' understanding of foreign-language performances.

The Indianapolis Opera maintains a collaborative relationship with the INDIANAPOLIS SYMPHONY ORCHESTRA, which has provided instrumental accompaniment for more than ten years. One opera each season is also accompanied by the INDIANAPOLIS CHAMBER ORCHESTRA. Talented local singers comprise the Indianapolis Opera Chorus and fill supporting roles.

SUZANNE G. SNYDER

Indianapolis Police Department (IPD).

Residents of early Indianapolis prided themselves on the orderliness of the community. The peace was kept with a town marshal, the sheriff and a few deputies, a volunteer night watch, and a handful of constables and justices of the peace. But with the growth of population and the rise of nativist fears at the influx of Irish and German immigrants, the coming of the railroad, and the deep split over the liquor question, the 1840s and 1850s produced a perception that Indianapolis was in the grip of a crime wave.

Attempts in 1854 and 1856 to establish a paid city police force under a state law of 1852 proved temporary and the department was twice disbanded. In May, 1857, the city council finally succeeded in creating a permanent Indianapolis Police Department (IPD). Paid $1.50 a day, a worker's wage, a man patrolled each of the seven wards from evening to early morning, his only badge of office a silver star. A "watch captain" ("chief of police" in 1861) mustered the force daily and reported the number of arrests to the council. In July, 1862, the police received uniforms—dark blue coat, light blue trousers with a cord along the seam, and a blue cap. The force, which doubled to 14 in 1861, the first year of the Civil War, grew to 47 by the war's end, with a chief, two lieutenants, a detective branch, and patrolmen divided into day and night shifts in the nine wards.

City politicians early used the police department as a source of patronage and to control law enforcement policies, especially on election day. After February, 1866, a three-member board elected by and from the council had complete discretion in appointments and removals. Denied any influence over the department for all but two of 20 years, in 1883 a Democratic majority in the state legislature enacted a metropolitan police bill. Applicable only to Indianapolis, the law approved the appointment of police at a ratio of one officer per thousand citizens, with the proviso that the force include an equal number of Democrats and Republicans. The City Charter of 1891 preserved this practice of dividing the spoils. It established a Department of Public Safety with three commissioners appointed by the mayor, only two of whom could be of the same party, and specified that the men of the police and fire departments be appointed on a bipartisan basis, a principle retained in the Cities and Towns Act of 1905. With the parties guaranteed representation on the police department thereafter, and despite the Indiana Merit Law of 1935, the dominant party influenced appointments, controlled promotions, and named the chief and high ranking officers. A citizens' report in 1917 recognized one consequence of this overtly political system of appointments: the failure to discipline officers who failed to follow departmental policy.

In 1900 the city's population reached almost 170,000, nine times what it had been at IPD's founding. The size of the force kept pace, growing to 166, approximately one sworn officer per thousand residents. Paid $2.25 a day and required to purchase their own uniform and equipment, patrolmen worked 12 hours a day, seven days a week, with seven days vacation after two years on the force.

In the late 1800s, IPD, like its counterparts elsewhere, sought measures, equipment, and new technologies to increase its ability to combat crime. In 1883 the department procured two horse-drawn carts as an alternative to commandeering private wagons or conveying drunks to the station in a wheelbarrow. Mounted horse patrols and bicycle squads were employed before 1900 (and again in 1983 and 1990, respectively) and motorcycle police from 1909. In 1904 the department was a pioneer in the use of motor vehicles and in 1906 trucks supplanted horse-drawn paddy wagons. To replace telephone booths first used in the late 1870s to keep street officers in touch with headquarters, the city in 1897 spent $60,000 on a Gamewell call box system, installed throughout the city. Beat policemen for the next half-century reported hourly and could summon help from headquarters. Although obsolete by the 1930s, the system was not abandoned until 1955. The city trailed only Detroit and Cleveland in installing radio receivers in patrol cars (WMDZ began broadcasting Christmas Day, 1929). Two-way car radios appeared in 1939.

The department was equally quick to adopt the latest methods of criminal identification. In the 1890s and for many years thereafter IPD used the Bertillon system—a file collection of body measurements, photographs, and fingerprints—to identify criminals. London's Scotland Yard in 1901 was the first to rely on fingerprints, but Indianapolis in 1908 organized a Criminal Identification Bureau using fingerprints as the main tool after Albert G. Perrott (IPD, 1903–1949) witnessed a demonstration by Scotland Yard at the 1904 St. Louis Exposition. Innovations continued in the 1930s under reforming Chief MICHAEL F. MORRISSEY: IPD's first crime laboratory (1932), "drunk-o-meter" or breathalyzer (1937), polygraph machine (1938), and the department's first formal training school for recruits.

In the 1950s IPD began to substitute lower paid civilians for sworn personnel in clerical and administrative posts, a process pursued every decade since. From 1970 to 1991 total strength increased modestly from 1,211 to 1,362, but fundamental shifts took place in departmental structure: sworn officers, comprising 89.8 percent of IPD in 1970, declined to 71.7 percent in 1991. The department more than compensated for this decline by shifting sworn officers from administration to "outside law enforcement" and filling more positions with civilians. Thus the 702 patrol officers in 1977 rose to 760 in 1991. Civilian employees, 10.2 percent of IPD in 1970, grew to 28.3 percent in 1991. With the decrease of population in the service district, the estimated ratio of sworn officers to residents actually rose—1 to 449 (1970), 1 to 404 (1980), and 1 to 364 (1990)—despite the decline of sworn officers from a high of 1,067 in 1978 to 979 in 1992.

Police officers from Station No. 1 on E. 17th Street patrolled the streets via bicycle ca. 1910.
[Indiana Historical Society, Bass Collection, #27565]

Among the innovations introduced after 1945 were walkie-talkies and the establishment of a juvenile division (1948); radar (1951); one-officer patrol cars with three-way radios permitting communication with other cars as well as headquarters (1957); canine unit (1960); helicopters (1968); a Special Weapons Action Team (SWAT, 1975); computer-aided dispatch (1978); automated fingerprint identification (1989); 911 emergency communications system (1967), enhanced 911 (1990); and a countywide radio system linking all emergency agencies (Metropolitan Emergency Communications Agency, 1992). Despite such technologies or perhaps because of them, the reported violent crime rate increased from 7.3 to 18.1 per 1,000 residents from 1970 to 1991, giving rise to the belief that radio patrol cars and overcentralization of IPD had isolated police from citizens.

To enlist residents in the struggle against crime and to establish closer ties between the department and the community, IPD in 1976 initiated a neighborhood crime watch program and "community-based team policing" in 1977. Continuing efforts to decentralize service, in the late 1980s quadrant headquarters were moved out of the City-County Building, and in January, 1992, the new mayor, Stephen Goldsmith, heralded a program to reorient IPD to "community policing," which assigns more officers to neighborhood beats. Expected to develop expert knowledge and greater rapport with an area's law-abiding citizens, beat patrol officers have greater discretion to solve problems. Detectives, no longer seen as specialists in certain crimes, have been relocated to the districts, and mini-stations have been established in problem housing complexes and shopping malls.

Intended to be in place in 1993, the shift of IPD to community policing was marked by delays and criticism, especially by police rank and file. Community policing is personnel-intensive and in 1993 IPD found its human resources stretched to the limit. To find the needed personnel the department continued its decades-long practice of moving sworn officers out of headquarters and substituting civilians. A new Public Safety Corps, cadets 18 to 21 and 21 years of age and over (the latter will be armed), is being developed for 1994. After six weeks of training an initial group of 30 cadets will work as evidence technicians, park security officers, and accident investigators, as well as transporting prisoners, further relieving sworn officers for neighborhood beats.

Given the nature of police work, corrupt practice by some officers is endemic and, as in other big cities, charges of systemic corruption in IPD have been leveled from time to time. In 1915 three officers and the chief were found guilty of election fraud; in the 1920s Prohibition proved a baleful influence and it was routine for gamblers and after-hours houses to pay protection in every decade through the 1960s; in 1956 a traffic-fixing scandal hit the department; and in 1964, 22 police were indicted for being on the pad of the kingpin of the city's numbers racket. In 1974 three *Indianapolis Star* reporters won a PULITZER PRIZE for a myriad of articles alleging police brutality, pervasive political influence in appointments and promotions, shakedowns, defalcation of funds, ghost employment, and unsavory connections with brothels, known burglars, and fences. What was unusual about the 1974 expose was that over 50 officers violated the "code of silence" and supplied information to the reporters. The results of such allegations of malfeasance in the department historically are that few or none are convicted, some retire or resign, and some are demoted or reassigned in a departmental shakeup. At the end of his term in 1975 Mayor Richard G. Lugar confessed that reform of IPD had eluded his best efforts. If mayors and the ju-

dicial system have had little effect, discipline within IPD, as in other paramilitary organizations, is stringent. From 1982 through 1991 a disciplinary board of captains found guilty over 98 percent of the 1,453 officers brought up on departmental charges ranging from tardiness to crimes.

Since the 1970s IPD's most serious problem has not been scandal but police-community relations. Critics have focused on controversial police shooting fatalities, harassment and excessive force, the citizen complaint process, and the absence of credible civilian review. Mirroring national trends, Indianapolis police action shootings and shooting fatalities reached their height in 1974–1976 (averaging 25 shootings and 8.3 deaths in those years), and then declined. Over the period 1970–1991, IPD averaged 10.4 shootings and 2.8 fatalities per year. Despite the downward trend and the absence of any pattern of white officer–black suspect fatal shootings, controversial deaths of black suspects outraged the local African-American community. In November, 1980, police fire killed a 15–year-old running from an officer; in September, 1987, a 16–year-old suspected of auto theft, although handcuffed and in a police car, shot himself, an apparent suicide; in July, 1990, a young man of 25 was killed after a robbery and high-speed chase; and in June, 1991, a suspected shoplifter, age 27, was fatally wounded. Except for the suicide, all victims were unarmed and were shot by white male officers. Furthermore, many citizens did not accept the suicide verdict despite the unanimous finding of a half-dozen agencies, including the investigation by a retired African-American IPD deputy chief. Black ministers and officeholders organized demonstrations around IPD headquarters, carried out economic boycotts, and called for the resignation of the mayor, the police chief, and other city officials.

For their part, police officers were embittered by the shooting death of an officer in August, 1988. What began as a complaint about a dog escalated when police forcibly entered the house of Fred Sanders, a white school teacher. In the ensuing melee the teacher fired a shotgun at the officers, striking one who died ten days later. Police retaliated by beating Sanders at the scene. The teacher pled guilty to involuntary manslaughter;

one officer pled guilty to excessive force and resigned from the department; another was acquitted of the same charges by a jury. Many citizens supported the teacher in the affair and a jury found for him in a suit against the city, circumstances that the police found especially galling.

When controversies arose regarding police, city administrations have turned to blue ribbon committees to suggest reforms. Rising criticism of the use of deadly force and complaints of brutality led a human relations task force in October, 1989, to recommend, and the city to adopt, a nine-member (six civilians, three IPD) Citizens Police Complaint Review Board. The board, lacking a budget, staff, and legal counsel, never operated effectively. When the City-County Council in December, 1990, explicitly removed its power to review police shootings, a mandate the board and the public assumed it had, it became moribund. By March, 1992, there were four vacancies and it sometimes lacked a quorum. Some observers, many sympathetic to police, believe civilian review to be in IPD's interest. The Goldsmith administration, in an attempt to improve trust between citizens and police, convened a 22–member task force on "police performance assessment" in August, 1992. In its report a year later it recommended establishing a Police Professional Standards Board composed of four citizens elected by residents in each of the four police districts, and four police officers, with a non-voting chairperson selected by the director of public safety. It would hear police misconduct cases—including police-action shootings—and while evidentiary hearings and some records would be closed, its deliberations and votes would be public. Its recommendations would go to the police chief. The citizens' police complaint review board, firearms review board, and board of captains would be eliminated. The eight police officers on the task force, reluctant to have civilians review deadly force and opposed to open hearings, submitted a minority report. The issue remained unresolved in early 1994.

Recent studies of hazardous occupations rank police work among the ten most dangerous. Since 1883, when the first IPD policeman was killed, to December, 1993, 50 officers have died in the line of duty (34 by gunshot, 16 in acci-

dents), an average of one every two years. The 1910s, 1920s, and 1970s were the most dangerous decades, with five, seven, and five policemen murdered respectively. In 1993 the first policewoman was killed in the line of duty, the result of a vehicle accident.

The blatant political interference so characteristic in IPD as recently as the 1970s is much reduced, as are the scandals and the common perception of endemic, if often minor, corruption. High salaries (base salary for a third-year officer in 1994 is over $34,000), good benefits, and an excellent pension attract a far larger pool of better-educated applicants than ever before. For example, the 24 members of the recruit class of October, 1993, came from more than 3,200 applicants. More sophisticated and more extensive training has been developed: IPD trainees in 1993 spent 19 weeks (over 750 hours) in class gaining instruction in firearms, managing a crime scene, rescue and water safety, radio, interrogation and interview techniques, making an arrest, conducting a search, transporting prisoners, peace keeping, cultural diversity, written communications, preparing for court, driving, and equipment maintenance. Since 1980 completion of the course is followed by 15 weeks of field training working with experienced officers on the street.

IPD in 1994 bears little resemblance to the department of 40 years ago. As a typical police department of the 1950s it was marked by nepotism, low pay, and little prestige. Today it is much more professional. Ironically, as IPD has improved, public scrutiny and expected standards of performance have risen commensurately.

WILLIAM DOHERTY
Marian College

Clipping files, Indiana Division, Indiana State Library; IPD Staffing Statistics (1970–1991); IPD Annual Reports (1990, 1991).

Indianapolis Power and Light Company. Local public utility. The first company to introduce electric service to the city was the Indianapolis Brush Electric Light and Power Company, a predecessor to Indianapolis Power and Light, incorporated on June 17, 1881, with ex-mayor JOHN CAVEN, George W. Stokely, and Horace P. Clough as directors. A subsidiary of the Brush Company of Cleveland, Ohio, the Brush Electric Company proposed erecting electric arc lamps on high towers to light city streets, but lost the contract to the gas company. After establishing the first generating station at 224 South Pennsylvania Street, the company used the old UNION STATION for the first display of arc lighting on January 11, 1882, and later provided service to the new State House.

While Brush Electric developed the downtown market, Jenney Electric Company, affiliated with NORDYKE AND MARMON, Inc., erected light towers in WEST INDIANAPOLIS. Later known as the Marmon-Perry Light Company, directed by Daniel W. Marmon and CHARLES C. PERRY, it was the first utility to bring Thomas Edison's incandescent lighting to Indianapolis. Thanksgiving Day, 1888, saw the lighting of the Park Theatre with 741 16-candlepower lights. Marmon-Perry also provided the first incandescent lighting of a private residence in 1889.

The Indianapolis Light and Power Company, organized May 20, 1892, acquired control of Brush Electric Company, consolidated with the Marmon-Perry Company, and constructed a 1,120 kilowatt capacity generating plant at Kentucky Avenue and West Street in 1892–1893, a plant later used by Indianapolis Power and Light. Over the next several years other electric utility companies entered the field: Merchants Heat and Light Company, founded by William C. Bobbs, Hiram P. Wasson, FERDINAND S. MAYER, Frederic M. Ayres, and Henry Kahn in 1902; and Home Heating and Lighting Company in 1902, reorganized as People's Light and Heat Company in 1905. Fierce competition among the utilities produced wildly fluctuating rates and extensive advertising campaigns. In 1912 Merchants and People's merged, retaining the Merchants Heat and Light name until 1926.

Indianapolis Power and Light Company (IPL) was incorporated on October 27, 1926, by Utilities Power and Light Corporation, an out-of-state holding company which owned utilities in 410 cities and towns in 12 states. Under the leadership of chairman Walter C. Marmon and president Norman A. Perry, the company acquired Indianapolis Light and Heat Company (a consolidation of Indianapolis Light and Power Company and the Marion County Hot Water Heating Company) and Merchants Heat and Light. The merger, which raised concern among citizens about non-local ownership, streamlined operations into one efficient and cost effective electric delivery service. In 1927 the company eliminated 125 miles of duplicate lines and revamped the meter system.

During the 1930s the federal government dissolved interstate utilities to decrease costs to consumers and increase efficiency. Utilities Power and Light Corporation formed a separate organization in 1939 to acquire IPL common stock and transfer ownership to the public. On April 3, 1940, over 8,000 new shareholders made Indianapolis Power and Light Company one of the nation's first large electric utilities to have its ownership transferred from a holding company to individual investors. The new regulated, investor-held public utility was limited to providing service to the Indianapolis-Marion County area.

On August 30, 1983, the utility formed IPALCO Enterprises, Inc., with Indianapolis Power and Light Company as its principal subsidiary, to provide diversified revenues. Mid-America Capital Resources, Inc., was formed July 31, 1984, as a subsidiary of IPALCO Enterprises to create a holding company for all non-utility subsidiaries.

Electricity production has increased tremendously over the past decades. Beginning in the 1890s with a capacity of 1,120 kilowatts, the company had a daily generating capacity of 160,000 kilowatts by 1940, 2.5 million kilowatts by 1977, and 2,900 megawatts in 1992. IPL served 400,000 customers and reported $633.2 million in operating revenue for 1992.

On March 15, 1993, IPALCO made an unsolicited offer to purchase PSI Resources, Inc., of Plainfield, Indiana, for $1.52 billion. Seeking to prevent the planned merger of PSI, which serves 69 counties in central and southern Indiana, with Cincinnati Gas & Electric Company of Ohio, IPALCO argued that the merger would save customers $1.6 billion over 10 years and maintain Hoosier ownership of the utility. IPALCO's hostile takeover of PSI was not successful.

MARCUS EUGENE WOODS II

Zane G. Todd, *Electrifying Indianapolis: A History of Indianapolis Power and Light Company* (New York: Newcomen Society in North America [Newcomen Publication No. 1077], 1977).

Indianapolis Press Club. A social and professional club for working journalists and allied crafts. Its attractive quarters are across from the STATE HOUSE in the lower level of 150 West Market Street. Featuring the Ernie Pyle Dining Room and a room equipped for news conferences, the facility's walls display historic newspaper headlines and other mementoes that constitute a "living museum of journalism."

The organization was founded on April 10, 1934, in the pre-radio and television days when the word "press " referred only to the newspaper profession and to men and not women. Over the years since, it has not only embraced both broadcasters and women journalists but elected them to leadership positions. Its 1992 membership of nearly 800 persons included a variety of practitioners in the communications arts, public officials, and other individuals deemed "assets" to the club.

On its 1934 incorporation, the club's objectives were stated as: "To promote the social enjoyment and fellowship among its members, and to encourage and foster the ethical standards of the newspaper profession." Its first president was MAURICE EARLY, then a political reporter for the *INDIANAPOLIS STAR*. It was 1967 when its first broadcaster president was named, James R. Hetherington of WFBM-TV. The first woman president was HORTENSE P. MYERS of United Press International, who served in 1976.

Over the years the club has been a meeting place for both the newsmaker and the news reporter. Governors, mayors, legislators, political party chairmen—all appear at the club. Especially during the January-to-April months when the General Assembly is in session, the club is alive with activity. Its main social event is the Gridiron Dinner at which public officials are roasted. Activities also include the annual 500 –Mile Race "Last-Row Party," numerous other parties, and monthly speeches by public figures.

The club's educational services include scholarship grants to college journalism students and awards to promising writers who are chosen in the annual THOMAS R. KEATING feature writing competition. Its affairs are overseen by a 16–member Board of Governors and administered by a full-time executive director.

JAMES E. FARMER

Indianapolis Project. The Indianapolis Project began in 1981 as a three-year, $4 million public relations campaign sponsored by the city of Indianapolis, the CHAMBER OF COMMERCE, the INDIANA CONVENTION CENTER, and the INDIANAPOLIS CONVENTION AND VISITORS ASSOCIATION to enhance the city's reputation and attract new businesses. The Chamber of Commerce supplied the project's staff and paid its bills for 18 months, but in July, 1983, the project was incorporated as two separate but affiliated not-for-profit organizations—the Indianapolis Project, Inc. (IPI) and the Indianapolis Growth Project, Inc. (IGP). Less than a year later a review panel found that IPI's and IGP's development functions overlapped those of several other organizations and their focuses were tightened. The IGP became the INDIANAPOLIS ECONOMIC DEVELOPMENT CORPORATION and the IPI forfeited its development functions to concentrate solely on public relations and image-building through its two remaining branches, the Indianapolis City Center and the IPI media relations division.

The Indianapolis City Center on MONUMENT CIRCLE became a department of the Indianapolis Project in 1982. The project initially used it to provide visitors to the city with information during the NATIONAL SPORTS FESTIVAL. The center, which moved into the PAN AMERICAN PLAZA in 1987, has developed into an important promotional tool, providing current information for visitors and residents alike. It offers many services including over 300 free brochures, a multimedia presentation promoting Indianapolis, an interactive model of the downtown area, and various city tours. In the first six months of 1993 the City Center's small full-time staff and over 200 volunteers served 47,000 visitors and answered 25,700 phone and mail requests for information about Indianapolis.

The media relations division operates out of the IPI's offices in the HOOSIER DOME. Its main function is creating and updating files on all aspects of the city and providing members of the national and local media with current information. From 1981 to 1993 the media relations division placed, or provided information for, over 1,600 local, national, and international articles about Indianapolis. It also assisted with news features on the "Today" show, "Good Morning America," ESPN, and CNN.

WILLIAM D. DALTON

Indianapolis Public Library. See Indianapolis-Marion County Public Library

Indianapolis Public Schools (IPS). Largest school system in the state. The Indianapolis Public Schools system traces its origin to the city's first free public school in 1853. Today, the school system serves students who live within the old city boundaries as they existed prior to the 1970 city-county consolidation known as Unigov. IPS is one of eleven public school districts within Marion County.

Between 1980 and 1990, IPS enrollment dropped from more than 66,000 students to approximately 48,000 students. In 1993 IPS served approximately 47,000 students plus an additional 5,700 students who are required by a court order to be bused to township schools. Approximately 53 percent of the current IPS student population is African-American. The school system had a 1993 graduation rate of 66.79 percent of its senior class, with six of every ten graduates going on to attend college or vocational school.

During the mid- to late 1980s, instructional costs per student rose from about $2,800 to $3,700. As of 1993 IPS spent $4,993 per pupil. During the 1980s the teacher to student ratio improved from 1 teacher for every 18 students to 1 teacher for every 15 students. By 1990, 79 percent of IPS teachers were female and 28 percent of teachers were African-American.

IPS employs a total staff of approximately 6,300 persons, including almost 3,000 teachers, to operate 62 elementary schools, 17 middle schools, 7 high schools, and 3 alternative schools. IPS also provides instructional programs at Methodist Hospital, Riley Hospital for Children, and the Juvenile Detention Center. Additionally, IPS offers vocational education, special education, adult education, classes in English as a second language, a GED program, and a variety of magnet programs which offer an educational emphasis. Food service is provided at all schools and students pay yearly book rental fees.

Administratively, IPS is governed by a seven-member board of school commissioners which appoints a superintendent, determines the annual budget, and sets school policies and procedures. Voters elect five district commissioners and two at-large commissioners who comprise the board. IPS is not part of the consolidated city-county government.

IPS had a 1993 budget of $352,132,757. Funding for this budget came from the following sources: local sources, especially property taxes (42.76 percent), state sources (47.31 percent), and federal sources (9.93 percent). As IPS approached the mid–1990s, the school district faced an estimated $12 to $15 million deficit and likely budget cuts.

Under Superintendent Shirl E. Gilbert II, IPS initiated random metal detector scans in 1991 to deter students from bringing guns and other weapons onto school property. Gilbert also introduced grade-level curricular standards for the system. IPS' most notable recent change was the 1992 implementation of the SELECT SCHOOLS plan in an effort to promote parental involvement in school choice. Each school within the system offers a focused program, with the plan's overall aim to improve the quality of education and to further the racial desegregation of IPS schools.

DEBORAH B. MARKISOHN

Indianapolis Public Transportation Corporation (Metro). Municipal bus system. The Indianapolis Public Transportation Corporation owns and operates the Metro bus system to provide public transportation for Marion County. It was created by ordinance of the City-County Council in 1973, and began service in 1975 after assuming the assets of Indianapolis Transit System, Inc., a private corporation.

The Indianapolis Public Transportation Corporation is an independent municipal corporation governed by a five-member, unpaid, bipartisan board of directors. Three members are appointed by the City-County Council, and two by the mayor. The members serve renewable four-year terms. At its regular public meetings, the board receives information from the Metro management and sets policy for the corporation concerning the structure, operation, and financing of the bus system. The board approves the corporation's budget, which is subject to direct review by the Marion County Board of Tax Adjustment and does not have to be approved first by the City-County Council and the mayor.

Bus fares account for about 35 percent of the corporation's revenues. It also receives federal, state, and city transportation funds. As an independent municipal corporation, it can levy its own property tax and issue bonds. Like many large city public transit systems, Metro has had recurring financial problems, and its management and operations have been subject to substantial review during the early 1990s in an effort to balance ridership, revenues, and expenses.

In 1990, nearly 7 million miles were driven on Metro's 50 routes. Total ridership was 10,298,111, or about 14 rides for each person in Marion County. These rides were provided by Metro's fleet of 245 diesel coaches, seven of which have wheelchair lifts. Metro employs about 500 people, including 300 drivers.

CHARLES AUDRITSH

Indianapolis Raceway Park. Motorsports complex. The 300–acre Indianapolis Raceway Park (IRP) is located on U.S. 136 west of CLERMONT. A joint venture by local businessmen, IRP was conceived in 1959 as a recreational complex focused on automobile racing. The owners built two tracks in 1960: a 15–turn, 2.5–mile road course and a 4,400–foot drag strip incorporated into the main straightaway of the road course. A .686–mile paved oval was completed in 1961 and renovated in 1988 to yield greater speed for the cars. The oval has seen the most use

by midget, sprint, and stock cars, the road course by sports cars, go-carts, and motorcycles, and the drag strip by cars and motorcycles in amateur and professional competition.

The first IRP road race was held in 1961, and the early 1960s saw both IndyCar and USAC stock car races on the road course. The 2.5–mile course accommodates many sports car road races by the Sports Car Club of America (SCCA). The season's highlight is the Indy Grand Prix, drawing club racers from distant parts of the United States to compete on a fast and favored track. Two annual motorcycle road races are sanctioned by Western Eastern Racing Association (WERA), go-carts compete in an "enduro" event, and International Motor Sports Association (IMSA) hosts the 3–hour Firestone Firehawk Endurance race. The Skip Barber Racing School holds numerous classes that use the road course.

The drag strip was begun to buffer IRP finances whenever the other tracks did not make a profit. Since its inaugural race in the fall of 1960, the track has generated interest and income beyond initial expectations. The quarter-mile drag strip has hosted the National Hot Rod Association (NHRA) U.S. Nationals drag race since 1961. The largest professional drag racing event in the world, the "National Drags" draws over 150,000 spectators and 1,000 racing teams sharing a $1.5 million purse. A yearly schedule of sportsman and amateur racing culminates in the world's largest amateur drag racing event, the NHRA Firestone-TNN E.T. Racing Tournament.

The NHRA purchased Indianapolis Raceway Park in 1979 and invested heavily in renovations to improve track surfaces and spectator convenience. Events are produced by a full-time staff supported by 300 part-time employees. Currently, IRP annually schedules additional races, shows, and swap meets catering to specific groups. These annual events include the Super Chevy Show, Indy Hot Rod Happening, Mopar Nationals, and Corvette Nationals.

MICHAEL WATSON

Indianapolis Recorder. African-American newspaper cofounded by George Pheldon Stewart and Will Porter in 1895. The longest con-

The Stewart family, including founder George P.
Stewart (second from right) and his son Marcus
Stewart (child), controlled the *Indianapolis Recorder,*
Indiana's oldest African-American newspaper, from its
beginning until the late 1980s.
[Indiana Historical Society, #C5317]

tinuously operated African-American newspaper
in Indiana, the *Recorder*, like most of its predecessors,
promoted racial pride through stories about
the achievements and accomplishments of blacks.
Unlike its early competitors, the *Freeman* and the
Colored World, however, the *Recorder* regularly
provided a forum for local news that appealed to
both an Indianapolis and a statewide black community
during a period of racial uplift. In 1899
Porter sold his share of the newspaper to Stewart.
Eunice M. Trotter's purchase of the newspaper in
1988 marked the first time in the paper's history
that the George P. Stewart family did not own the
controlling interest. William G. Mays bought the
Recorder in 1990.

The *Recorder* first located its office at 122
West New York Street. In 1900 it moved to 414
Indiana Avenue, then relocated to the KNIGHTS OF
PYTHIAS BUILDING at 236–240 West Walnut Street.
By the summer of 1918 the newspaper had
moved to 518–520 Indiana Avenue; there it
would remain for over half a century until relocating
to its current home at 2901 North Tacoma Avenue
in 1975.

With a weekly circulation of approximately
15,000 in the early 1990s, the newspaper continues
to focus on local news stories with a bent
toward analysis of issues affecting the African-American
community. As part of a long tradition
it reports church announcements and religious
news stories, and contains a religion column and
a local church directory. In addition to religion
and local news stories, the paper features arts and
entertainment, sports, business, and syndicated
columnists. The *Recorder* claims nationally
known journalist William Raspberry among its
former employees. It has been honored with the
Human Rights Award of the Indiana Education
Association and a 1992 CASPER award for general
reporting.

WILMA GIBBS
Indiana Historical Society

Indianapolis Retirement Home. A
modern retirement community that traces its history
to the Indianapolis Home for Friendless
Women. The original institution was established
in 1867 as a temporary shelter for soldiers' widows
and orphans, left homeless by the Civil War.

CATHARINE MERRILL and Jane Chambers
McKinney Graydon founded the Indianapolis
Home for Friendless Women with the assistance
of banker STOUGHTON A. FLETCHER, SR. and other
civic-minded Indianapolis residents. The city's
most prominent families were represented on the
all-male board of trustees and the all-female board
of managers. The association's constitution stated
that "the object of this society shall be, to protect
unprotected women, house the homeless, save the
erring and help the tempted."

The original facility was a three-story structure
at the corner of what was then Ninth and
Tennessee streets (later renamed 18th and Capitol).
In its early years the home relied upon annual
appropriations from both the city council and
county commissioners, in addition to private donations.
Funding for the home was always tenuous.
Members of the board of managers were
assigned districts to canvass for donations of food,
fuel, clothing, and money. All work necessary to
the home itself was performed by the residents.
During the late 1800s the home routinely cared
for 400–500 persons in an average year.

After the turn of the century, other charitable
institutions began to assume more responsibility
for young women with children and in 1913 the
home became the Indianapolis Home for Aged
Women. In 1936 its name was changed to the In-

dianapolis Home for the Aged to permit male residents, and in 1976 it became the Indianapolis Retirement Home. It now offers independent retirement living and some assisted living to 55 residents on a monthly rental basis and operates in part from an endowment fund, contributions, and bequests.

JEANETTE VANAUSDALL

Jeanette Vanausdall, "'A Worthy History': The Indianapolis Retirement Home, 1867–1992," *Traces of Indiana and Midwestern History*, 4 (Fall, 1992), 34–43.

Indianapolis/Scarborough Peace Games.

Annual international amateur sporting event. On January 27, 1973, Indianapolis and Scarborough, Ontario, Canada, officially agreed to conduct an annual multi-sport, international athletic competition. The event was named the Indianapolis/Scarborough Peace Games in honor of the Vietnam Peace Treaty which was signed that same day. The purpose of the games, held annually during the second week of August, is to promote friendship and cultural understanding between the residents of the two cities.

Beginning with the first Peace Games in 1973, the event has been held every other year in Indianapolis, with Scarborough hosting in alternate years. During the competition, visiting athletes stay in the homes of the host city's participants. Approximately 800 athletes from each city compete in 15 sports: athletics (cross country and track), badminton, baseball, basketball, bowling, chess, bicycling, horseshoes, soccer, softball, swimming, table tennis, tennis, volleyball, and wrestling.

Each year, approximately 5,000 Indianapolis-area residents of all skill levels, from former college athletes to beginners, compete in the local preliminaries. Anyone may compete, but only Marion County residents can qualify for the international competition with Scarborough. Local competition begins in April and continues for approximately four months until the top teams and top three finalists in each sport and age group emerge.

The Indianapolis DEPARTMENT OF PARKS AND RECREATION organizes and conducts the Peace Games, with the event funded by the parks department, corporate sponsorships, and athletes' entry fees.

DELORES J. WRIGHT

Indianapolis Star. Daily newspaper. The *Indianapolis Star* debuted June 6, 1903, as a seven-days-a-week newspaper, the brainchild of Muncie industrialist George McCulloch. The first two days of the *Star's* existence McCulloch distributed 50,000 free copies of the one-cent newspaper; six months later paid circulation was 70,000.

The *Star* challenged the two older morning papers, the INDIANA JOURNAL and the INDIANA STATE SENTINEL, and a year after the *Star's* debut it had absorbed the *Journal*. In 1907 the *Star* bought the Sunday *Sentinel* and the daily *Sentinel* stopped publishing, leaving the *Star* the city's lone morning paper. The paper moved twice in its first year, then in 1907 to its current site, a new building at the corner of New York and Pennsylvania streets.

McCulloch's one-cent price drained his finances, and he sold the paper in 1904 to tin-plate millionaire Daniel G. Reid of Richmond, who hired *Chicago Post* publisher John Shaffer to the same position at the *Star*. Shaffer emerged as the major stockholder during a 1908 court battle and served as editor and publisher from 1911 until his death in 1943. During his tenure the paper became known as "the businessman's paper" and also led campaigns for social and economic reforms. Among the earlier colorful *Star* employees were MARY E. BOSTWICK, a woman journalist of the Nellie Bly tradition, and MAURICE EARLY, a political columnist who wrote "The Day in Indiana," a page one column, until his death in 1954. Hoosier author BOOTH TARKINGTON was a frequent contributor to the Sunday *Star*.

EUGENE C. PULLIAM, newspaper and radio station owner, fought off competitors to buy the *Star* and the *Muncie Star* for $2.35 million in 1944. The publisher spiritedly took on the *Star's* larger afternoon rivals, the *Indianapolis News* and the INDIANAPOLIS TIMES. He began a women's section, built up the sports page, and started a Sunday magazine. He also hired the *Times'* popular columnist, LOWELL NUSSBAUM. Pulliam never shied from controversy, writing impassioned front-page editorials that made his paper popular with readers and an exciting place to work. By 1947 the *Star* was dominating the city's other newspapers, leading the *News* by a margin of 177,390 to 171,000. The paper has been the city's and state's largest circulation newspaper since.

By then the *News*, owned by the Fairbanks family, was for sale. In another battle, Pulliam dueled with *Times* publisher ROY W. HOWARD for the rights to own it. He won for $4 million, merged the *Star* and the *News*, and formed Indianapolis Newspapers, Inc. (INI). The *Star's* circulation continued to grow with the city, and with readers' penchant for a morning newspaper, to 228,565 daily and 411,377 Sundays in 1990. It is among the nation's top 50 newspapers in circulation. Pulliam died in 1975 and his son, Eugene S., became publisher.

Throughout the years, *Star* features have come and gone. The *Star's* Sunday magazine, which Pulliam started in 1947, aimed at covering Indiana on a more featured basis than the daily paper. It ceased publishing in 1985; though popular with readers, it failed to attract advertising. Joe Crow, a daily front-page feature that had provided weather and humorous looks at the issues since the early 1900s, was retired in 1985 when the newspaper was redesigned. For 14 years, writer TOM KEATING won a loyal following with his daily columns about the city's people before he left the *Star* in 1985, shortly before his death. In 1972 Keating had started an annual poll of readers to name the *Indianapolis Star's* Man and Woman of the Year, a practice that continues.

As investigative journalism became the rage in the 1970s, the *Star* won its first PULITZER PRIZE in 1975 for a series that began in February, 1974, on Indianapolis police corruption. The newspaper's second Pulitzer Prize came in 1991 for a June, 1990, series on Indiana doctors who continued to practice despite losing multiple malpractice lawsuits and receiving no punishment. Although INI and the *Star* generally moved slowly toward new newspaper technology, the malpractice series was completed using the most modern form of investigative reporting—computer-assisted journalism.

The *Star* and the *News* share advertising, production, and the building at 307 North Pennsylvania Street, but the editorial and reporting departments remain separate and competitive. In 1990 the *News'* managing editor Frank Caperton took over the same position at the *Star*, the first time a top editor has moved from one paper to the other during the Pulliam era.

BETH MURPHY

Russell Pulliam, *Publisher Gene Pulliam: Last of the Newspaper Titans* (Ottawa, Ill., 1984); John W. Miller, *Indiana Newspaper Bibliography* (Indianapolis, 1982).

Indianapolis Steam Mill Company.

Saw, grist, and carding mills. In 1828 several leading citizens of early Indianapolis, including JAMES BLAKE, NICHOLAS MCCARTY, Noah Noble, JAMES M. RAY, William Sanders, and DANIEL YANDES incorporated the Indianapolis Steam Mill Company. The state legislature provided the business with additional assistance by selling it a choice seven-acre site on the WHITE RIVER just above the National Road bridge (built in the early 1830s) and by granting the company permission to cut timber on state-owned land.

Construction of the three-story mill was completed in September, 1831, with the saw and flour mills soon in operation. The following spring the mill began processing wool and opened a dry goods store to sell its products. The mercantile business closed in 1833 and the mill was abandoned two years later. Since the facility produced more than three times the local demand for flour and since inadequate transportation facilities prevented operators from shipping surplus elsewhere, the mill often operated at less than full capacity. Too large for the early Indianapolis market, the mill proved to be one of the biggest business failures in the city's history. The building remained vacant until sold in 1847 to the Geisendorffs, who refitted it as a woolen mill and used it until 1852. The vacated mill burned down the next year.

DEBORAH B. MARKISOHN

Jacob Piatt Dunn, *Greater Indianapolis* (Chicago, 1910); Berry R. Sulgrove, *History of Indianapolis and Marion County* (Philadelphia, 1884).

Indianapolis Sun. Indianapolis newspaper. The first *Sun*, begun by Joseph A. Dynes and a Mr. Seifert, was an independent advertising sheet that lasted less than one year. On September 6, 1873, a second *Sun*, known also as the *Daily Sun*, was started by John O. Hardesty, who served as editor. The publication was sold to the Indianapolis Sun Company in 1874 and became a National (Greenback) party journal under the direction of proprietor Edward S. Pope and editor T. R. Buchanan. In 1879, Pope became the sole owner and J. K. Speer took over the editorial department. The paper remained a National party publication in 1882 when it was acquired by H. W. Burtch, but was discontinued in 1884. A third *Sun* appeared in 1888, and was run by the Sun Company, whose principal owners included Fred L. Purdy, the paper's editor. This *Sun* was an independent daily publication.

Both the ownership and editorial duties changed hands several times between 1888 and 1912, with Purdy serving as editor on three separate occasions. In 1913 the paper was sold to G. H. Larke and W. D. Boyce. Under their ownership the paper's title was changed to the *Evening Sun*. In 1914 Larke sold his interest to Boyce and J. W. Banbury, but not before a legal battle and much ill feeling had ensued. On July 20, 1914, the new owners changed the title yet again and the paper became the *Indiana Daily Times* (later the *INDIANAPOLIS TIMES*). A fourth and short-lived *Sun* was issued in 1936 with A. G. Buchanan as editor.

WILLIAM DALTON

Indianapolis Symphonic Choir. Founded by Indianapolis Symphony Orchestra (ISO) conductor FABIEN SEVITZKY, who required a trained chorus for the finale of Beethoven's Ninth Symphony to close the symphony's 1937–1938 season, the Indianapolis Symphonic Choir (ISC) possesses a long history of critically acclaimed choral performances in conjunction with the ISO and other orchestras. ELMER ANDREW STEFFEN, director of music for the Catholic diocese of Indianapolis and a papal knight of the Order of St. Gregory, served as the ISC's first director. Subsequent directors have included Donald Neuen, Charles H. Webb, John W. Williams, and Robert Porco.

Despite its long association with the INDIANAPOLIS SYMPHONY ORCHESTRA, the ISC functions as an independent organization with its own board of directors. Debt free since its inception, the choir meets its annual budget through the efforts of members and the services of a part-time development director. Its approximately 120 experienced singers are selected through yearly auditions.

Besides annual performances of choral masterworks with the ISO, the ISC presents an annual Festival of Carols during the Christmas season. The choir has performed at Carnegie Hall, Kennedy Center, and the Cincinnati May Festival, as well as many locations and events in Indiana and surrounding states. As a contribution to the community the ISC produces "Symphonic Choir Presents," a weekly radio program broadcast Sundays at 5:30 P.M. over station WICR 88.7 FM. The program features choral music by the ISC and other world-renowned choral organizations.

SUZANNE G. SNYDER

Indianapolis Symphony Orchestra (ISO). One of the few orchestras in the nation with a 52–week schedule, the 88–member Indianapolis Symphony Orchestra (ISO) performs nearly 200 concerts for more than 300,000 listeners a year. Its first concert took place November 2, 1930, in Shortridge High School's Caleb Mills Hall under the baton of FERDINAND SCHAEFER, the orchestra's conductor until the 1937–1938 season when FABIEN SEVITZKY assumed directorship. Under Sevitzky the ISO earned praise for its performances of American works and its recordings and radio broadcasts. In 1956 IZLER SOLOMON replaced Sevitzky; during Solomon's 19–year tenure the orchestra gained heightened international fame. Under John Nelson, who succeeded Solomon in 1976, the ISO's Kennedy Center and Carnegie Hall concerts achieved critical acclaim. Internationally renowned conductor, musicologist, and composer Raymond Leppard took up the baton in 1987, successfully combining musicality, scholarship, and creative marketing strategies to advance the ISO's proud heritage.

The Indianapolis Symphony Orchestra's broadcasting history extends from the mid–1930s when Admiral Richard Byrd's Antarctic expedition team received a special broadcast directed by Ferdinand Schaefer. It was not until 1937 under Fabian Sevitzky, however, that the ISO initiated a series of regularly scheduled national broadcasts over the Mutual Broadcasting System. By 1940 the orchestra had concluded over 80 broadcasts.

The following year marked the Indianapolis Symphony Orchestra's debut in the recording industry. Between 1941 and 1953 the ISO could be heard on 20 different 78 rpm vinyl discs bearing the RCA Victor and Capitol labels. Many of these recordings, which featured rarely heard Russian compositions as well as standard orchestral works, were later rereleased in 33 rpm format. Under Izler Solomon the ISO courted the broadcasting medium, exchanging taped concerts with other cultural centers worldwide as a "goodwill ambassador" for the U.S. Information Agency's "Voice of America" program (1957–1965). The sole recording venture of Solomon's directorship was a live performance in Carnegie Hall under the Project Skylark label.

Contracts with public radio and public television in the 1980s enhanced the ISO's reputation. So did two 1985 New World albums, one of which received the distinguished Arturo Toscanini Music Critics Award for the recorded performance of Ellen Taaffe Zwilich's Pulitzer Prize–winning Symphony No. 1. Compact discs of Schubert and Elgar works, under the Koss Classics label, have garnered high praise from music critics. Recent ISO releases include Vaughan Williams' *Sinfonia antartica* and Schumann's Symphony No. 1 in B-flat major.

The Indianapolis Symphony Orchestra provides an extensive selection of musical programs throughout the year. Its acclaimed 18–week Classical Series, geared toward the performance of works representing the classical elements of proportion, balance, and accuracy, showcases the talents and musicality of the ISO's 88 members. Seasonal offerings include "A Yuletide Celebration," the lavish New Year's Eve Viennese Gala, and the thematically based Mid–Winter Festival. Summer fare consists of the Symphony Promenades in June, the six-week "Symphony on the Prairie" outdoor series at CONNER PRAIRIE, free public concerts in parks and community centers as part of the

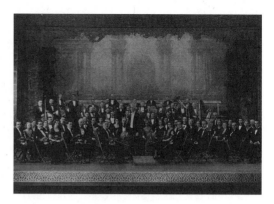

The 1930 Indianapolis Symphony Orchestra. [Indianapolis Symphony Orchestra]

ISO's Sound of the City and Indiana series, and a Pops Series directed by world-renowned pops conductor Erich Kunzel. The ISO utilizes a number of educational formats. Its innovative Studio Series combines analysis by Raymond Leppard with full performances of masterpieces. The Words on Music pre-concert discussions feature interviews with guest artists and presentations by musical authorities. Lollipop, Discovery, and High School concerts introduce preschool through high school age students to orchestral music and instruments. The Partners and Side by Side programs allow Indianapolis-area music students to gain onstage rehearsal experience with ISO mentors.

One of only two American orchestras currently operating without debt, the ISO possesses a strong endowment fund of over $50 million managed by the Indianapolis Symphony Orchestra Foundation. In 1992 ticket sales to 15,000 subscribers accounted for 67 percent of the ISO's income. More than 2,000 volunteers also work on its behalf, including members of the largest symphony women's organization in the United States.

In 1963 the ISO moved from the MURAT THEATRE, where it had presented concerts since its fourth season, to CLOWES MEMORIAL HALL on the Butler University campus. The orchestra made the recently renovated CIRCLE THEATRE its home in 1984.

SUZANNE G. SNYDER

Samuel Wasson Siurua, "History of the Indianapolis Symphony Orchestra" (D.M.E. dissertation, Indiana University, 1961).

Indianapolis Times. Daily newspaper published from 1888 to 1965. The *Times* received a Pulitzer Prize in 1928 for "exposing political corruption in Indiana, prosecuting the guilty and bringing about a more wholesome state of affairs in civil government." The award winning series appeared in 1927 and exposed KU KLUX KLAN activities in Indiana, helping to break the strength of that organization in the state.

The newspaper was founded as the INDIANAPOLIS SUN on March 12, 1888, by five newspapermen who had worked together in Cleveland, Ohio. They were led by Fred L. Purdy, city editor of the *Cleveland Press* and founding editor of the *Sun*. J. S. Sweeny was the paper's principal stockholder and chief financial backer. The *Sun* maintained ties with the Cleveland newspaper and with the Scripps-McRae (later Scripps-Howard) telegraph service.

The *Sun* was sold to Rudolph Leeds of Richmond, Indiana, in 1910. Three years later W. D. Boyce bought the paper and changed its name to the *Evening Sun*. In 1914 Boyce and his partner, J. W. Banbury, changed the paper's name to the *Indiana Daily Times*. Scripps-Howard bought the paper in 1922 and changed its name to the *Indianapolis Times* in 1923.

The *Sun* was first located at a plant on the south side of Ohio Street, between Pennsylvania and Delaware streets; its second location was on Georgia Street, between Meridian and Pennsylvania streets. The third and last location was at 214 West Maryland Street (where a plaque now marks the spot). The *Times* building on West Maryland was erected in 1924 and expanded in 1950, increasing the floor space from 28,000 to 52,000 square feet at a cost in excess of $1,150,000.

Indianapolis native ROY W. HOWARD served as president of the *Times* from 1922 to 1964 and built the United Press International into a worldwide news service. His son Jack, who served as president of Scripps-Howard, began his career on the *Times*. Other names associated with the paper include Lee Hills, later executive editor of the *Detroit Free Press* and the *Miami Herald*; author and diplomat JOHN BARTLOW MARTIN; and Norman Isaacs, later executive editor of the *Louisville Courier-Journal* and the *Louisville Times*.

Known for "lively and sometimes courageous journalism," the *Times* was frequently engaged in crusades against injustice and corruption on both a city and a state level. In addition to its coverage of Klan activity in the 1920s, the *Times* also played a key roll in exposing the state highway scandals of 1957–1958, voter fraud in the 5th district during the election of 1960, and a scandal involving mechanics' liens in 1961–1962. In 1961 the *Times* found local jobs for nearly 4,000 unemployed Hoosiers by running help wanted ads for free, and in 1962 the paper's exposure of errors in the reporting of crime statistics in Indianapolis, a practice that disguised the city's growing crime rate, led to enlarged street patrols by police. From 1960 to 1964 the *Times* waged a successful campaign to persuade the Indianapolis Public Schools to provide better school lunches through use of the federal surplus food program. The paper also took pride in its long-term coverage of such issues as humane treatment of the mentally ill, urban renewal, and hospital development.

Although increased circulation led to the introduction of a Sunday edition in 1948 and building expansion in 1950, by the 1960s the *Times* proved unable to compete with its two rivals, the INDIANAPOLIS STAR and the INDIANAPOLIS NEWS. When the paper ceased publication on October 11, 1965, the *Times* ranked third in its local market with a daily circulation of only 89,374 and a Sunday circulation of 101,000.

JOHN SHERMAN

John W. Miller, *Indiana Newspaper Bibliography* (Indianapolis, 1982); *Indianapolis Times*, Oct. 11, 1965; *Indianapolis Star*, Oct. 12, 1965, Oct. 6, 1990.

Indianapolis Traction Terminal. Hub of the statewide interurban (electric railway) system, and reputed to be the largest traction terminal in the world. The introduction of INTERURBANS in the Hoosier capital at the beginning of the 20th century created serious traffic congestion due to loading and unloading in the city streets. Since each line had its own station, traffic delays occurred in three different blocks by 1901. With six additional lines under construction, corrective action was necessary. Thus, seven interurban companies signed an agreement by early 1902 for use of the city street railway tracks and construction of a joint interurban terminal.

On August 4, 1902, the Indianapolis Traction and Terminal Company incorporated to operate the city railway and to build and operate the new terminal. In December the new company bought half of a block just east of the State House (the 100 block of West Market Street). The existing buildings, including the famous CYCLORAMA, which had housed the giant mural "The Battle of Atlanta," were razed, and terminal construction began in July, 1903. The station was completed in September, 1904.

The terminal complex contained an office building and a train shed. The nine-story building had 250 offices (most of the traction companies located there), nine storerooms on the first floor, and a ticket office and waiting room. West of the building was the giant, nine-track train shed. The interurban cars entered and left the shed via access tracks from Ohio and Market streets. City STREETCARS entered the shed only on rare special occasions.

On July 1, 1905, the Indianapolis Joint Ticket Agency, the first of its kind in the country, opened in the terminal. An immediate success, the agency offered tickets to all points on interurban lines in Indiana, Ohio, Kentucky, and Michigan that could be reached from Indianapolis.

The freight terminal, located in the northwest quarter of the block, included three large brick sheds served by nine tracks and four loading areas. Freight traffic saw a spectacular increase, from a dozen cars per day in 1905 to an average 71 per day in 1916. The small and crowded freight area at the terminal could not properly handle this traffic, and in 1918 the Terre Haute, Indianapolis and Eastern line moved to a new, much larger terminal of its own on Kentucky Avenue. This new freight terminal relieved the original station's problems to some extent, and in 1924 the remaining lines also moved to new facilities adjoining those of the THI&E. The old buildings became an express terminal, and later a coach storage yard.

In the late 1930s, as interurbans began to be abandoned, several of the station's tracks were paved over for bus service. Early in 1941, the entire shed floor was paved for exclusive bus op-

The Traction Terminal, which stood on Market Street between the Indiana State House and Monument Circle, had nine tracks to handle interurban traffic. [Indiana Historical Society, Bass Collection, #315278]

eration, and the sole remaining electric line, Interstate's run from Indianapolis to Seymour, turned on a wye north of the shed.

In October, 1968, following construction of a new bus station nearby, the giant shed was torn down. The terminal building itself was razed in April, 1972. The sole surviving mementos of the former terminal are the two large stone eagles from the south side of the old shed, now located in front of the INDIANA STATE MUSEUM.

JERRY MARLETTE

Jerry Marlette, *Electric Railroads of Indiana*, 2nd ed. (Indianapolis, 1980).

Indianapolis Urban League. Nonprofit organization concerned with eliminating discrimination, especially racial. Incorporated in December, 1965, the Indianapolis Urban League (IUL) succeeded the Association for Merit Employment, a local organization founded by the American Friends Service Committee in 1952 as a part of the Job Opportunity Program. IUL is an interracial, interfaith, nonpartisan organization affiliated with the National Urban League. Sam H. Jones has been the president of the Indianapolis chapter since its establishment.

IUL has worked since its beginning to ease racial tensions and promote further understanding between blacks and whites. It provides services in the areas of health, welfare, economic development, housing, advocacy, and criminal justice; encourages minority businesses and nonpartisan participation in the political process; disseminates information about public policy issues; and provides services ranging from help with school problems to job counseling.

The Indianapolis Urban League's programs have changed over the years in response to community needs. Early special programs continued from the predecessor Association for Merit Employment included Project Thrive (1961–1980), which addressed child abuse and neglect. The Human Relations Consortium (1964–1979) dealt with school desegregation and busing issues. The Clearstream Garden Multi-Service and Youth Project (1964–1982) took social services to the residents of a public housing project and aided youths in finding summer employment.

In the 1990s, the Indianapolis Urban League has specific goals to help the black community economically and socially. Project NEAT is designed to heighten citizens' awareness of drug problems. Concerned Males of Indianapolis provides mentors and role models for black males. The IUL has made a concerted effort to get black parents involved in education; it sponsors five scholarship programs in conjunction with various organizations for youths. The IUL has taken a stand against police brutality against all citizens, especially blacks. Close ties with the corporate community have made the IUL a force in improving job opportunities for blacks and other minorities.

The Urban League is a United Way agency. Its broad mission allows it to receive funding from both private and public sectors.

JANE NOLAN AND LINDA WEINTRAUT

Paul Brockman, "Indianapolis Urban League," *Black History News & Notes*, No. 44 (May, 1991), 1, 3; *Indianapolis Star*, Aug. 13, 1985, June 14, 1990; *Indianapolis Recorder*, June 15, 1991.

Indianapolis Water Company. Water utility serving Indiana's capital city since 1871. The Indianapolis Water Company (an investor-

owned subsidiary of IWC Resources Corporation) traces its roots to the formation of the Water Works Company of Indianapolis. Chartered by the City Council in 1869 to use the Indianapolis Division of the CENTRAL CANAL, not as the source of potable water for city residents but as a power source to drive the pumps of its Washington Street station, the Water Works Company began operations on June 1, 1871. Incorporated by James O. Woodruff of Rochester, New York, also the founder of WOODRUFF PLACE, the company soon ran out of capital and was succeeded by the Indianapolis Water Company, formed by a group of local businessmen in April, 1881. As the company began to identify and use additional water sources other than its wells near Washington Street, in 1904 the company placed its White River Station Treatment Plant into operation. That facility, located east of FALL CREEK near 16th Street, obtains its water supply from the river at BROAD RIPPLE via the old Central Canal, and still serves as the foundation of the IWC system.

The water company's first president was Thomas Armstrong Morris, a civil engineer who settled in Indianapolis in 1821 with his father, MORRIS MORRIS. He spearheaded the construction of the Riverside pumping station north of Fall Creek in the 1890s and the sand filtration beds at the White River Station near the canal aqueduct, which made Indianapolis one of the first large cities to treat its water.

The company remained in local hands until 1912 when it was purchased by Clarence H. Geist, a Philadelphia-based utility investor who controlled electric, gas, and water utilities across the nation in the 1920s. During his 26–year ownership, the water company erected Fall Creek Station in 1915; located northeast of downtown on Fall Creek near the Keystone Avenue bridge, the station obtains its water supply from the creek. As early as the 1920s the company developed plans for a reservoir upstream from the treatment plant to ensure a dependable supply of water even in drought years.

Howard S. ("Scotty") Morse's tenure as general manager and chairman (1925–1949, 1953–1961) produced great gains for the company, including the construction of GEIST RESERVOIR. Completed and filled in 1943, it together with

Fall Creek is capable of providing an average of 26.8 million gallons a day (MGD). In the 1950s the White River Station Treatment Plant was greatly enlarged, more than doubling its capacity. Additionally, Morse Reservoir, located near Noblesville in HAMILTON COUNTY, was completed in 1956, becoming an integral part of the metropolitan area's water supply. Combined with natural flows in White River, Morse Reservoir provides 87.6 MGD of dependable yield to the IWC system. Following the flooding of 1958, the City of Indianapolis constructed a flood-control and water-supply reservoir on Eagle Creek in northwestern Marion County, completed in 1968. Through its Eagle Creek Station, now known as the Thomas W. Moses Station, completed in 1976, the IWC supplies customers in the northwestern part of its system.

Attorney THOMAS W. MOSES came to Indianapolis in 1956 to manage IWC for the Dallas-based Murchison family, which had recently purchased control of the utility. Following transfers by the Murchisons to Philadelphia in 1959 and later Minneapolis, Moses returned to Indianapolis as chairman and president of the Indianapolis Water Company in 1970. Shortly afterward plans for the city and IWC to build a reservoir in northeast Marion County were shelved in favor of a proposed joint U.S. Corps of Engineers–State of Indiana project known as Highland Reservoir. The Indiana General Assembly authorized this project, but the U.S. Congress did not. The demise of the Highland project made it evident that maximum use of existing sources along with the development of groundwater supplies were needed to ensure adequate supplies in the future.

New high-capacity wells in both the Fall Creek Valley and the southern part of the county added to the supplies available in 1989, and in 1991 the new White River North Station came on line to serve northern Marion and southern Hamilton counties. However, in June, 1992, a severe wind- and rainstorm caused a breach in the water company's canal wall near the Michigan Road bridge, cutting off water to a large portion of the city's population and indicating how dependent the city is on the White River, via the canal, for its water supply.

The company maintains eight booster pumping stations to distribute water to city residents through more than 2,500 miles of water mains. Water use averages approximately 120 MGD (or 43 billion gallons annually); the utility is capable of providing an average of 139.8 MGD with its current facilities. As the overall use of water continues to grow, IWC is already planning to meet its water supply requirements through the year 2050.

In December, 1976, the company deeded the canal south of 20th Street and the Washington Street Station to the city. This corridor, the southern portion of which has been redeveloped, has been the focal point for residential and commercial development as well as for the WHITE RIVER STATE PARK.

THOMAS M. BRUNS
Indianapolis Water Company

BILL BECK
Lakeside Writers' Group

Marjie Gates Giffin, *Water Runs Downhill: A History of the Indianapolis Water Company and Other Centenarians* (Indianapolis, 1981); J. Darrell Bakken, "Evolution of a Regional System," *Journal of the American Water Works Association*, 73 (May, 1981), 238–242.

Indianapolis Woman. Women's magazine launched by C. E. Publishing in September, 1984. Connie Rosenthal and Linda Eder published *Indianapolis Woman* for women with a wide variety of interests. The magazine profiled an Indianapolis woman each month and ran regular articles on shopping, working, cooking, and decorating. The magazine also carried articles on craft making and raising children, and reviewed books, movies, and restaurants.

Late in 1988, C. E. Publishing made an agreement with Media Management Group, owner of *City* magazine, to provide advertising and circulation services for *Indianapolis Woman*, also know as *IW*, and the associate publisher of *City* became publisher of *IW*. Since *Indianapolis Woman* was aimed at such a large population group, the publishing companies hoped the agreement would expand the 20,000 circulation by offering both magazines to advertisers.

Publication halted, however, with the August, 1989, issue. The contract with Media Management was canceled when EMMIS BROAD-CASTING bought *City* and folded it into its own publication, *Indianapolis Monthly.* The sale agreement between Emmis Broadcasting and Media Management canceled the advertising and distribution contract, and *IW* ceased publication.

ELLEN R. TEVAULT

Indianapolis Woman's Club. Founded February 18, 1875, the purpose of the organization is "to form an organized center for the mental and social culture of its members, and for the improvements of domestic life." The club encourages a liberal interchange of thought by means of papers and discussions. Early programs of the club centered on women and domestic concerns, but the programs evolved eclectically, members having the option to choose any topic for the mandatory papers they prepare and read.

Although the club is socially traditional, its members were innovators and have included throughout the years many women prominent in civic affairs. Among the founders, for example, were reformer MAY WRIGHT SEWALL and Laura Giddings Julian, wife of abolitionist GEORGE WASHINGTON JULIAN. Club committees helped to form the General Federation of Clubs and the PROPYLAEUM, the latter to assure a regular meeting place that they still use. Members have included teachers, journalists, and writers, the majority being housewives with access to libraries. Some authors expanded club papers into books, notably Laura Fletcher Hodges (*Early Indianapolis,* 1918), Ernestine Bradford Rose (*The Circle: The Center of Our Universe,* 1955), Blanche Stillson, artist and museum curator (*Wings,* 1954), and Alice Usher (*The Sunny Hours,* 1983). Current published members include Laura Gaus, Vesle Fenstermaker, Martha Berman, Nancy Kriplen, and Martha Waller. Club membership has remained stable for over a century at the constitutional maximum of 100 active members set by the founders.

BARBARA E. ZIMMER

Indianapolis Zoo. LOWELL NUSSBAUM, newspaper columnist for the *INDIANAPOLIS TIMES* and later the *INDIANAPOLIS STAR,* first proposed a zoo for Indianapolis in the early 1940s. Nussbaum obtained community support, and the Indianapolis Zoological Society, Inc., was incorporated in 1944. Progress on the project was slow. In 1955, with the assistance of the Indianapolis Jaycees, a site was selected, and in 1960 a lease was signed with the city to build a zoo in Washington Park on the northeast side. On April 18, 1964, the original Indianapolis Zoo opened to the public, culminating 20 years of preparation. The original zoo operated on 24 acres with 500 animals in its collection and was host to over 6.5 million visitors in 23 years.

In 1979, the society commissioned a study to determine the possibility of moving the zoo to a more accessible, larger site. During this same period the Indiana legislature proposed the development of a state park just west of the downtown business district. On June 21, 1982, the Zoo Society signed a letter of intent to relocate the Indianapolis Zoo to the WHITE RIVER STATE PARK. This was the first entirely new zoo built in the United States in many years, and the decision to choose an urban site as opposed to a suburban or rural setting was unusual.

To help prepare for this undertaking, the Indianapolis Zoo hosted an international symposium on the "Future of Zoos" in December, 1982. International authorities on zoos, aquariums, and wildlife gathered for two days to help set the goals for this new modern zoo. Based on the results of this symposium, the zoo trustees, staff, architects, construction managers, and consultants formed a design team to create the master plan for the zoo.

In July, 1983, host Marlin Perkins of the popular "Wild Kingdom" television show kicked off the capital campaign drive on MONUMENT CIRCLE with several thousand persons in attendance. With major support from the LILLY ENDOWMENT and the KRANNERT CHARITABLE TRUST, as well as thousands of donations from area corporations and individuals, the Zoo Society raised over $63 million by December, 1987. On September 8, 1985, in a ceremony attended by more than 5,000 supporters, the official groundbreaking ceremony took place. In April, 1986, construction began and by December, 1987, there were 57 exhibit buildings, holding areas, and support buildings on the new site.

During 1987 the zoo management staff had the unique challenge of operating and closing down the original zoo while overseeing the preparation of the new facility. The Washington Park Zoo closed on November 1, 1987, as a part of the transfer to the new Indianapolis Zoo in White River State Park. In late November and early December, 1987, the actual move of the zoo's 500 animals took place. The community again affirmed its support when charter memberships were offered in the spring of 1988. Membership at the original zoo had risen to 11,000 by 1987, and the society expected that membership would increase to 20,000. Instead, over 74,000 enrolled, giving the new zoo the second largest membership in the nation at the time of its opening. The zoo officially opened on June 11, 1988.

By 1991, the Indianapolis Zoo had evolved from a mid-sized zoo in a city park to a major metropolitan zoo with "state of the art" facilities. Its design was based on the bioclimatic concept— grouping animals found in particular environments ("biomes") such as deserts, plains, forests, and waters. The Marine Mammals Pavilion featuring whales and dolphins was the largest totally enclosed, environmentally controlled structure of its kind in the nation when it opened in February, 1989. July, 1990, marked the opening of the "Deserts of the World" exhibit, and other new exhibit areas are planned on a periodic basis.

In 1991, the Indianapolis Zoo had over 2,500 animals on 64 acres and employed over 300 people during the height of the season. It hosts nearly 900,000 visitors annually and is one of a few major zoos in the United States that receive no direct tax support, deriving its income from attendance, membership, foundation, corporate, and community support. A planning effort by the board of trustees culminated in 1993 with a reorganization of the society. The plan also addressed the challenges of funding a major zoological park, renewed the institution's commitment to science education, and suggested the future construction of additional exhibit areas.

RICHARD M. HURST
Indianapolis Zoo

Indians, American. See Native Americans

Indians, Asian (aka Asian Indians, East Asians, Indo-Americans, Indian-Americans). The 1990 census recorded 1,538 Asian Indians in Greater Indianapolis, or 22 percent of the state total. Most Asian Indian immigration to Indianapolis occurred after the passage of the 1965 immigration law that eliminated national quotas. The driving force behind this immigration was economic. The Asian Indians constituted a special group of immigrants who spoke English, were highly educated, and looked for jobs in universities, research centers, hospitals, and manufacturing plants. In Indianapolis as elsewhere, they came to be a "reference community" rather than an ethnic group living in a single neighborhood.

Members of the Indianapolis Asian Indian community follow different religions, for example, Hinduism, Jainism, Buddhism, Sikhism, Islam, Christianity, Judaism, Zoroastrianism, and Bahaism. They also speak many languages, among them Assamese, Bengali, Gujarati, Hindi, Kannada, Kashmiri, Malayalam, Marathi, Oriya, Punjabi, Sindhi, Tamil, Telugu, and Urdu.

Home-keeping and family-oriented, Asian Indians are socially conservative, academically motivated, and generally politically inactive. (Local artist Kanwal Prakash [K. P.] Singh, however, has both documented the city's rich architectural heritage and worked actively to preserve it.) The India Community Center, Indian restaurants, and Indian dance and musical programs in Indianapolis are evidence of the cultural contributions of Asian Indians to the city.

H. S. BHOLA
Indiana University, Bloomington

Arthur W. and Usha M. Helweg, *The Immigrant Success Story: East Indians in America* (Philadelphia, 1990); Joan M. Jensen, *Passage from India: Asian Indian Immigrants in North America* (New Haven, Conn., 1988).

Industrial Expositions. Held in conjunction with a national convention of purchasing agents, the Indianapolis Industrial Exposition opened on October 10, 1921, in the Manufacturer's Building at the INDIANA STATE FAIR-GROUNDS. It promoted Indianapolis as a desirable and stable hub of industry because "there is less wobble at the hub." This phrase became the industrial slogan of Indianapolis. During "a week of exploiting the industrial bigness of Indianapolis," 400 displays showed 780 articles manufactured for domestic and foreign trade. Samples were given away, and many articles were made on-site. Also displayed were a gold plated miniature printing press and the DUESENBERG in which Tommy Milton had traveled "the fastest mile ever" by a human being—135 mph on a Florida beach.

After a change in name, the Indianapolis Exposition moved to UNION STATION in November 7, 1946, with a ceremony attended by Governor Ralph F. Gates and Mayor ROBERT H. TYNDALL. Built at a cost $100,000, it was the country's only exposition housed in a railroad station and was open 24 hours a day, 7 days a week. The products of 74 manufacturing firms were displayed in aluminum and glass cases intended to simulate the observation cars of streamliner trains. A radio drama, "Indianapolis Industry in Review," carried by all Indianapolis radio stations, accompanied the exposition opening.

Sponsored by the Indianapolis CHAMBER OF COMMERCE, this permanent exhibit had up to 90 displays. It offered guided tours and was viewed daily by thousands of people waiting for trains. Exhibits included aircraft and truck engines, candy, construction machinery, electronic devices, and jewelry. The exposition was eventually removed as railroad passenger traffic declined.

The primary objective of the Indianapolis Industrial Exposition was to inform the public of the benefits of industrial progress. During the 1960s the objective changed and expositions served to match the industrial buyer with suppliers of products and services. Today, Indianapolis hosts a number of industrial exhibitions, held in venues such as the INDIANA CONVENTION CENTER and the Indiana State Fairgrounds. These separate annual events fulfill the needs of different groups; some exhibitions feature a variety of industrial products and services, while others focus on machine tools and machining services.

MICHAEL WATSON

Indianapolis Star, Oct. 10, 1921, Mar. 13, 1955; clipping files, Indiana State Library.

Indy's Child. Parenting magazine. *Indy's Child* was started in 1984 "to make parenting easier in Indianapolis." The magazine, owned by publisher Barbara S. Wynne, is issued monthly. It is distributed free of charge at retail stores, libraries, doctors' and dentists' offices, day care centers, preschools, schools, and at local grocery stores. Some subscriptions are also sold. Circulation in January, 1994, was 70,000. Articles focus on education, recreation, health, and family issues. *Indy's Child* has won three national awards when judged against 58 other parenting publications in the United States, including best feature article, best cover, and best reporting.

SHELLY CHENOWETH

Infrastructure (Public Utilities). The term infrastructure is typically used to describe the technological systems that support urban life, including transportation and communication systems and public utilities. Commonplace today, these services are of fairly recent origin, gradually evolving into their current form over the last century or so. Indianapolis developed its infrastructure when its population grew large enough to need these services. Gas lighting came first, in 1851. A rudimentary sewer system was built and a water company formed 20 years later. The telephone appeared very soon after its invention in 1875, and incandescent electric lighting followed in 1888.

Gas. Indianapolis was a rapidly growing railroad hub in 1851 when gas lighting made its first appearance in the city. Two years later the city contracted with the newly organized Indianapolis Gas Light & Coke Company (IGL&C) to light several blocks of Washington Street. The coal gas lights worked well, and by the end of the decade most downtown streets were illuminated by gas. Gas was in demand for domestic and commercial use, too; unlike wood, coal, or whale oil, its burning produced neither ashes, smoke, nor soot. IGL&C was the city's only gas producer until 1876 when Citizens Gas Light & Coke Company began operation. The new company met a sudden end, however, when its gas works exploded in 1877.

Discovery of an enormous natural gas field near Muncie in 1886 shifted Indiana gas companies' focus from manufacture to distribution. IGL&C promptly organized the Indianapolis Natural Gas Company and began laying pipelines to the city. In early 1887 public dissatisfaction with IGL&C's past service gave rise to the idea of a consumer-oriented gas company organized as a public trust. Many in the community rallied to the new utility, purchasing enough stock from its promoters to enable Consumers Gas Trust Company to begin operation in 1888.

In 1890 IGL&C and Indianapolis Natural Gas Company merged to form the Indianapolis Gas Company (IGC), which, in competition with Consumers, served the city for over a decade. By 1902 the gas field was nearly dry, prematurely depleted by widespread waste, and customer rolls shrank drastically as the public resumed burning wood and coal. Its product gone, Consumers Trust fought a lengthy court battle for the right to reorganize as an artificial gas producer. The trust won its case in 1906 and was incorporated as Citizens Gas Company (not be confused with the ill-fated Citizens Gas Light & Coke Company). By 1909 its new, state-of-the-art Prospect Street plant was operational and the company began to prosper, becoming strong enough to weather the changes wrought by creation of the state's Public Service Commission in 1913. IGC, less lucky, ended its independent existence that year and merged with Citizens Gas.

Over the years the strategy of Citizens Gas has been to pay for gas production by selling coke and other by-products, but market fluctuations have frequently caused operating losses—a situation partly remedied by aggressive promotion of gas appliances. Unstable profits, combined with rising natural gas prices, consumer resistance to rate increases, and demands for expanded service have made the utility's existence a strenuous one. Renamed CITIZENS GAS & COKE UTILITY after coming under municipal trusteeship in 1935, the company moved its offices to its present location at 2020 North Meridian Street in 1956.

Electricity. Electricity first came to Indianapolis in 1882 when the Indianapolis Brush Electric Light and Power Company demonstrated this lighting innovation at the railroad depot on South Illinois Street. By contrast with oil and gas lamps, the newly developed carbon arc lighting used electric current to produce a safe, clean light of unprecedented brilliance. Public ardor for electricity was undampened by the failure of arc street lighting, and by 1892 the streets of Indianapolis and West Indianapolis were artificially brightened by the Brush Electric and Jenney Electric companies. Indoor lighting, however, continued to be provided by gas and coal oil lamps.

Thomas Edison's demonstration of incandescent lighting in 1882 manifested its superiority over petroleum-based competitors. First used in Indianapolis on Thanksgiving Day, 1888, "Edison service" quickly proved an effective source of illumination for both interior and exterior spaces. It could also be used for heating, as could the steam its plant boilers produced.

Electricity generated a great deal of entrepreneurial activity; between 1892 and 1912 ten electric utilities were organized in Indianapolis. By 1927 only two survived, each serving roughly half the area of the city; their consolidation that year by a large out-of-state holding company created the INDIANAPOLIS POWER AND LIGHT COMPANY (IPALCO or IPL).

The new company merged its predecessors' electric and heating systems, established a new operating center near Morris Street and Kentucky Avenue, and opened administrative headquarters at 48 Monument Circle. IPL soon pioneered the combination of electric service and high pressure steam for industrial power, leading to steam sales second only to New York City's.

At the time of the merger, IPL's existing power plants were well able to serve its customers, but as their numbers continued to grow rapidly the need for greater generating capacity became apparent. The Harding Street plant, begun in 1929, was a "super-power" plant whose high capacity and efficiency enabled local industries to set military production records during World War II and to meet the demand for electricity of a population swollen by an influx of war workers.

After the war the demand for electricity soared due to population growth, suburbanization, and the increasing use of electric appliances, furnaces, and air conditioning. IPL responded with new power plants and equipment. At the end of 1991 the company was serving nearly 390,000 customers in Marion County and had a system generating capability of 2,829 megawatts.

Telephony. The telephone made its debut in Indianapolis in 1877, two years after its invention, when the city council allowed a local coal dealer to run a telephone wire between the company office and its coal yard. In 1878 the usefulness of the still rudimentary new invention increased dramatically when the first workable exchange was developed. This made possible switched calls among any number of subscribers rather than direct connections between only two or three parties. Entrepreneurs promptly established an exchange in Indianapolis, but it failed to attract enough customers to survive. The following year Ezra Gilliland, one of these entrepreneurs who also owned a small electric shop, became one of a number of licensed manufacturers of Bell Telephone Company equipment in the United States.

By 1883, however, Indianapolis had enough telephone users to justify publication of its first directory, and like many other cities was served simultaneously by multiple telephone companies. The intense competition kept rates low, but was otherwise inconvenient because the systems were not interconnected. By 1906 only two telephone companies remained: an American Bell licensee, Central Union Telephone Company, and an independent, New Telephone Company. Each had about 10,000 customers, with several thousand duplications. Central was later dissolved after a reorganization in American Telephone and Telegraph, of which it had become a subsidiary. In 1916 New Telephone and the expansion companies to which it had given rise were merged to create the Indianapolis Telephone Company.

During World War I the federal government took control of telephone and telegraph communications under the postmaster general, who ordered consolidation of local companies nationwide. As a result, Indianapolis Telephone Company was purchased by the Bell System in 1918. Indiana Bell was organized in 1920, and by the end of the year was operating 65,000 telephones in the city.

The number of telephone subscriptions has steadily increased since that time, accompanied by improvements in equipment and service. In 1949 Indianapolis, recently converted to an all-dial city, saw the installation of its 200,000th telephone. Three years later Indiana Bell adopted a two-letter, five-digit telephone numbering system to accommodate its expanding customer base. During the next decade touch-tone telephones and all-digit telephone numbers were introduced, and direct dialing replaced operator-assisted long distance calls. The city's local calling area, expanded by 1962 to cover many communities in the surrounding counties, as of March, 1993, had 691,976 lines.

Water Supply. Well water was safe for the tiny population of early Indianapolis, but had become dangerously contaminated by the 18,000 people living there in 1860. The city had no water system until 1871 when James Woodruff's Water Works Company (WWC) dug wells, built the city's first pumping station nearby (the present headquarters of the White River State Park Commission), and began laying mains. WWC soon found, however, that few people were willing or, after the Panic of 1873, able to pay for piped water.

In spite of poor water quality, low water pressure that hampered fire fighting, and a small customer base, WWC managed to stay in business until 1881 when its assets were purchased by the newly organized INDIANAPOLIS WATER COMPANY (IWC).

IWC gradually began to improve service. In 1889 it built a second pumping station (Riverside) to raise pressure, and dug deep wells to improve water quality, but there was simply not enough water underground to supply the city. In 1904 newly constructed slow sand filtration beds began purifying water from WHITE RIVER, making Indianapolis one of the first large American cities to treat its water supply.

During the next three decades IWC expanded the water system by building the Fall Creek pumping station, converting to a metered system, adopting improved purification techniques, and constructing raised water tanks to maintain pressure at higher elevations where the city's new suburbs were being developed.

Growth continued during World War II as IWC added a filter plant to Fall Creek Station, and in 1943 completed GEIST RESERVOIR—a seven billion gallon impounding reservoir. In 1948 IWC construction doubled the capacity of the Fall Creek filtration plant, which purified FALL CREEK water for the city's northeast side. (All other parts of Indianapolis drank purified White River water that had come from the CENTRAL CANAL or from pumps near the river.) In 1955 the company built Morse Reservoir—named for Howard Morse, the IWC president who had planned it—on Cicero Creek. The Eagle Creek water filter and pumping station was added in 1973 to serve northwest Marion County.

IWC currently serves over 200,000 households, businesses, and industrial customers in Marion and parts of Boone and Hamilton counties.

Sewer System. Early Indianapolis was drained by culverts and assorted above-ground wooden gutters that haphazardly carried wastewater and sewage to the White River. The city sorely needed an underground sewer system, but the city council shrank from so costly an undertaking until the late 1860s when the growing city's inhabitants began to demand clean streets and elimination of the dreadful odors that marred Indianapolis' burgeoning prosperity.

In 1870 the city did construct a sewer system, but it was built piecemeal and never completed. Some 20 years later, when the COMMERCIAL CLUB made a thorough study of the city's sewerage, it found the old system in a state of collapse, dumping sewage into all watercourses within the city limits and frequently causing many streets to be flooded with sewage and wastewater. The club's thoughtful recommendations for a new, adequate sewer system were, unfortunately, ignored by elected officials who feared raising taxes high enough to pay for one.

By 1909 the unabated pollution of White River caused communities along its banks to seek court injunctions against upstream towns for dumping raw sewage into its waters. Indianapolis needed a sewage treatment plant, but prior to 1915 municipalities could not legally incur the level of indebtedness required for so expensive an operation. That year a bill was enacted by the state legislature enabling cities to establish sanitary districts separate from the municipal corporations with the authority to issue bonds to finance infrastructure development.

By 1925 the Belmont sewage disposal plant began operation on the city's southwest side. It was the first large activated sludge plant in the United States. In 1966 the city added a second facility, the Southport Treatment Plant, to accommodate further growth. By 1981 the southside plants were updated and expanded to meet both continued urban growth and state and national mandates to further improve White River's water quality. Sewerage meanwhile has not fared as well as water treatment. An extensive investment will be needed in the 1990s and beyond to replace the combined storm and sanitary sewers whose overflow during heavy rainfall frequently pollutes White River with raw sewage.

CELESTE JAFFE

Thomas A. Rumer, *Citizens Gas & Coke Utility: A History, 1851–1980* (Indianapolis, 1983); John Longsdorf, *Electrifying Indianapolis* (Indianapolis, 1960); Marjie Gates Giffin, *Water Runs Downhill: A History of the Indianapolis Water Company* . . . (Indianapolis, 1981); Commercial Club, *Sewerage of Indianapolis* (Indianapolis, 1891); *Wastewater Treatment for Indianapolis, Indiana: A Short History* (Indianapolis: Department of Public Works, n.d.).

Inland Container Corporation. Manufacturer of corrugated boxes. In March, 1925, HERMAN KRANNERT founded the Inland Box Corporation in Indianapolis, operating out of the old NORDYKE AND MARMON factory until the company's new plant and offices at 700 West Morris Street were ready the next year. Within two years business had more than doubled and the plant employed 600 people working both day and night shifts.

Inland purchased the Gardner Harvey Container Company of Middletown, Ohio, in 1930 and changed its name to Inland Container Corporation, a company that became the country's third largest corrugated box manufacturer by 1952. In 1960 Inland went public. When Krannert stepped down in 1970 annual sales were $197 million and the company operated 27 plants. By

1978, when publishing giant Time Inc., purchased Inland and made it a wholly owned subsidiary, annual sales had grown to $397 million. In 1981 Inland closed its original West Morris Street plant due to increasing costs of operating the outdated facility. Two years later Inland became a subsidiary of Temple-Inland, a Texas-based holding company, although Inland's corporate headquarters remained in Indianapolis.

Inland prospered during the 1980s, with annual sales reaching $1.1 billion by 1989. That year Inland moved to new corporate headquarters on the city's far northwestside, a site close to other Inland facilities, including the company's new $17 million graphics facility on the city's far westside. As of 1992 Inland operated seven paper mills which produced 2.3 million tons of containerboard and 39 corrugated box manufacturing plants. Ranked as one of the country's top four corrugated box manufacturers, Inland posted annual sales of $1.25 billion, providing about half of the revenues for parent company Temple-Inland.

DEBORAH B. MARKISOHN

Insulin. Indianapolis became a leading center for insulin manufacture in 1922, immediately after the hormone's discovery at the University of Toronto (Canada). Insulin is secreted in the pancreas and essential to the metabolism of carbohydrates and fats; insulin deficiency leads to the development of diabetes. Many diabetics require regular injections of insulin to maintain life and health. When the Canadians had difficulty making more than small laboratory batches of the hormone, they accepted an offer of collaboration from GEORGE H. A. CLOWES, the research director of ELI LILLY AND COMPANY. Under a formal agreement signed in May, 1922, Lilly and the University of Toronto fully shared their knowledge of insulin, with the company being given a one-year exclusive license for the U.S. market.

The focus of insulin production immediately shifted to Indianapolis. The Lilly product, Iletin, initially prepared from beef or hog pancreas, was exported to Canada and used in clinical trials that signaled a milestone in treatment for millions of diabetics. Eli Lilly and Company subsequently made important advances in insulin isolation and

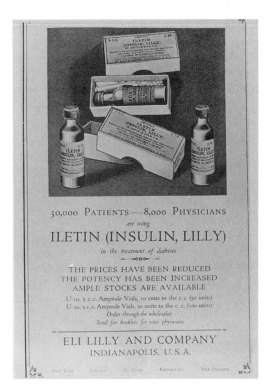

Advertisement for Iletin, manufactured by Eli Lilly and Company, ca. 1923. [Eli Lilly and Company Archives]

purification, and used its head start to dominate the U.S. market for insulin, a position it has never relinquished. Insulin has been the most important product in the company's history, and Lilly has continued to be a world leader in insulin research. Lilly's introduction in the early 1980s of synthetic human insulin (Humulin), made by techniques of genetic engineering, was another milestone in the history of science and therapeutics, and guaranteed that the central role of Indianapolis in the insulin story would continue into the 21st century.

MICHAEL BLISS
University of Toronto

Michael Bliss, *The Discovery of Insulin* (Chicago, 1983).

Insurance Industry. With its central location and favorable legal climate, Indiana has long been headquarters for a number of life and property/casualty insurance companies in disproportion to its population. For example, the 54 life insurance companies in the state are only two less than the 56 companies headquartered in California. Indianapolis in particular has a lengthy history as an insurance capital, rivaling better known centers such as Hartford, Connecticut, during much of the 20th century. In 1992, 94 of Indiana's 186 life, health, and property/casualty insurance companies were headquartered in Indianapolis.

Life insurance in the United States began in the East in the 1840s and 1850s and soon appeared in the Midwest. One of the first insurance companies to locate in Indianapolis was the German Mutual Insurance Company founded in 1854. Many more insurance companies began to organize in the 1870s and later. Most of these enterprises were mutual companies, with the assets owned by policyholders instead of shareholders. The word mutual usually appeared in the company name, as typified by the United Mutual Life Insurance Company founded in Indianapolis in 1877. (United Mutual Life merged with American Central Life Insurance Company in 1936 to form AMERICAN UNITED LIFE INSURANCE COMPANY.) These companies originally served limited interests, often growing out of an association formed for broader purposes. For instance, the Grange, a late 19th century farmers' organization, established Indiana Farmers Mutual (1877) to provide insurance for farm properties. The Indiana State Fire Insurance Company (1907) began as a mutual company to protect manufacturers in Indiana. Insurance brokers also began to appear in late 19th century Indianapolis, as witnessed by the 1884 establishment of GREGORY AND APPEL, a firm still doing business over a century later.

Prior to 1899 the legality of legal reserve insurance companies was in some dispute in Indiana. The Indiana Compulsory Reserve Deposit Bill of 1899, drafted by Wilbur Wynn, corporate secretary of State Life Insurance Company of Indianapolis (established in 1894) and a former clerk of the Indiana Supreme Court, cleared up ambiguities and allowed for the expansion of these companies in Indiana. Among the companies which located in Indianapolis following the bill's passage were American Central Life Insurance Company (1899), INDIANAPOLIS LIFE INSURANCE COMPANY (1905), and Standard Life Insurance Company of Indiana (1934).

Early insurance companies in Indianapolis often invested premium money in real estate, making mortgages on property in the years before that practice became widespread in the savings and loan and banking industries. State Life Insurance Company, for example, reported real estate assets of $2.5 million in 1905; many of those properties were located in metropolitan Indianapolis.

One of the reasons that Indiana has been such a popular state for locating insurance company headquarters is that the state government worked closely with its insurance companies during the Great Depression of the 1930s. While neighboring states like Michigan forced many companies into insolvency, the State of Indiana attempted to establish rules and regulations that allowed the industry time to work through its financial difficulties. The completely rewritten Indiana Insurance Code of 1935 was a major contributor to the health of the industry in later years.

In the 1980s the downtown construction of the 38–story AUL TOWER, headquarters of American United Life, signaled the importance of the industry to the city. By the mid–1990s the insurance industry in the Indianapolis area employed thousands and counted assets in billions of dollars. Its continuing growth was epitomized by Carmel-based CONSECO, an insurance holding company that in 1993 was the state's fourth largest corporation with assets of $15 billion.

BILL BECK
Lakeside Writers' Group

International Center of Indianapolis.

Established in 1972, the International Center of Indianapolis (ICI) provides services to local ethnic groups and acts as a resource center for international information. ICI was the first group responsible for promoting various ethnic organizations in central Indiana and creating higher visibility for international groups in the community. Originally located on the campus of Christian Theological Seminary, the organization began sponsoring in 1974 the event that evolved two years later into the INTERNATIONAL FESTIVAL. ICI now maintains offices in One American Square; the NATIONALITIES COUNCIL has assumed responsibility for the festival.

ICI is actively involved with many multicultural services and programs. The most widely used service, the International Hotline, provides extensive information on practically every international topic, from foreign embassies to local translators and interpreters. From the Hotline came several other services: the International CORPs, a group of linguistic and cultural specialists; a flag-loaning service; and country-specific information packets. In addition, ICI offers a variety of cross- cultural programs. ICI assists Indianapolis-based companies through cross-cultural business seminars for local professionals and cultural orientation and English-as-a-Second Language classes for visiting businesspeople and their families. ICI also conducts citizenship preparation classes for future Americans and presents a youth education outreach program to central Indiana middle school students.

BARBARA P. GRAHAM
KRISTIN E. SVYANTEK
International Center of Indianapolis

International Festival. Annual event celebrating ethnic heritage. Established in 1976 as part of the nation's Bicentennial celebration, the International Festival was under the management of the INTERNATIONAL CENTER OF INDIANAPOLIS for its first 12 years, the last 9 years in partnership with the Promotion Company. In 1988 management shifted to the NATIONALITIES COUNCIL. The International Festival was modeled after similar events held in Cincinnati and Milwaukee. The INDIANA STATE FAIRGROUNDS was the site of the festival from 1976 through 1978, and in 1992; from 1979 to 1991 the event was held in the INDIANA CONVENTION CENTER.

Management principles have remained the same throughout the life of the festival. The cultural focus of the event is provided by the ethnic member groups of the Nationalities Council. The members participate by establishing a cultural booth for the cost of a performance bond; the groups then are eligible to buy booth space to sell ethnic food or merchandise. Remaining booth space is made available to not-for-profit organizations or commercial groups. National and local ethnic groups provide entertainment. The three-day event traditionally takes place in late October. During the early 1990s the festival attracted approximately 22,000 visitors annually.

NIKKI MARTIN
Nationalities Council of Indiana

International Harvester. See Navistar

International Typographical Union (ITU). Workers in the printing trade were among the first in the nation to organize trade unions. After several attempts to create a national body, representatives of local journeyman printers unions from 14 cities (including Indianapolis) met in Cincinnati on May 3, 1852, and organized the National Typographical Union. Through a random drawing, the Indianapolis local became Typographical Union No. 1, which still exists. Following the admittance of Canadian locals in 1869–1870, the union became the International Typographical Union.

Although struggling through its formative years, Typographical Union No. 1 gradually built strength. It struck the *Indianapolis Sentinel* for a wage increase in 1863, but lost when the paper replaced union employees with nonunion workers. Samuel L. Leffingwell, head of the local around 1880 and member of the KNIGHTS OF LABOR, led the union as a sponsoring member of the Indianapolis Trades Assembly (1880; after 1883, the Indianapolis Central Labor Union) and the Indiana Federation of Trade and Labor Unions (1885). Leffingwell also represented the ITU at a conference in Pittsburgh in November, 1881, which established the Federation of Organized Trades and Labor Unions of the United States and Canada, predecessor of the American Federation of Labor (1886).

The ITU originally represented many areas of the printing trade. Increased craft consciousness and resentment against a group of compositors who dominated the ITU produced a splintering of the membership in the early 1900s. By 1910 the ITU was primarily a craft union of typesetters.

In 1888 the ITU, seeking a more central location, moved its national headquarters from New York City to Indianapolis where it published its national organ, the *Typographical Journal*, and the local's paper, *The Appeal*. The union moved its offices to the former Van Camp mansion at 2820 North Meridian Street in 1925, where it remained until relocating to Colorado Springs, Colorado, in 1961–1962. The ITU held its 72nd national convention in Indianapolis (August 8–13, 1927), marking the 75th year of the union's existence.

JOAN CUNNINGHAM

Diamond Jubilee of the International Typographical Union, 1852–1927 (Indianapolis, 1927); International Typographical Union of North America, *A Study of the History of the International Typographical Union, 1852–1966*, 2 vols. (Colorado Springs, Colo., 1964–1967).

International Violin Competition.

Among the most prestigious violin competitions in the world, the event began in 1980 when CATHEDRAL ARTS, the competition's sponsor, asked noted Indiana University violinist and teacher Josef Gingold to be the founding jury president of a quadrennial violin competition based in Indianapolis. Gingold accepted the position and in 1982 Indianapolis debuted the first two-week-long competition. In 1985, through the generosity of the KRANNERT CHARITABLE TRUST, the Josef Gingold Fund was established to ensure the future of the event.

There are six place laureates awarded in the competition (totaling more than $200,000 in cash prizes and engagements), and 18K gold medals go to the top three contestants. Monetary awards range from $20,000 for first laureate to $500 each to the ten semifinalists who are not named laureates. (Approximately 45 contestants begin the competition.) There are also cash awards for best performance of the following: an original work commissioned for the competition, a Bach partita, the Paganini Capriccio, an Ysaye sonata, a Mozart concerto, and a Beethoven sonata. In addition there is a Carnegie Hall recital for the gold medalist and more than 50 other engagements in recitals and with other major orchestras in North America and Europe.

The 1982 winner was Mihaela Martin from Bucharest, Romania; in 1986 it was Kyoko Takezawa of Japan; and in 1990 Russian Pavel Berman won the competition.

JOAN C. DALTON

Interurbans. Intercity electric railways. Interurbans developed in the late 19th century as a result of technological breakthroughs in small electric motors and long-distance electrical transmission systems. Frank J. Sprague, a naval engineer from the East, played a major role in developing, first, the new technology for streetcar systems within cities (Richmond, Va., and Chicago had early electric streetcars), and then for intercity systems. Given the pent-up demand for cheap, efficient intercity travel, a demand partially met by the bicycle in the 1890s and later by the automobile in the early 20th century, interurban systems spread rapidly throughout the nation. Indiana had one of the earliest and most extensive systems in the country, by which the capital city was connected with every other part of the state (except for Evansville in the southwestern "pocket") long before World War I.

Indianapolis' first interurban was the Indianapolis, Greenwood and Franklin Railroad. This line's inaugural trip from Greenwood arrived in downtown Indianapolis at 11:30 A.M. on January 1, 1900. The first trip was a trial run; more line work was needed in Indianapolis before regular service could begin. Regular service to Greenwood began January 16 on an hourly schedule. The line was a success, carrying 330,000 passengers during its first year of operation. The one-way fare was 20 cents; round trips cost 30 cents.

A second line also entered the city in 1900; the Indianapolis and Greenfield Rapid Transit Company began service from Greenfield on June 19. By 1910, when the last interurban line was completed into the city, 12 separate companies operated direct routes to all major cities within 120 miles of Indianapolis, and, by connection, to all others within 200 miles.

With the local interurban operations constantly increasing during the early 1900s, Indianapolis street traffic faced major congestion. To combat this problem, the companies entering the city began planning a terminal station for off-street passenger handling. The new complex was completed in 1904 and opened on September 12, the first day of State Fair week. During its first week the INDIANAPOLIS TRACTION TERMINAL handled an average of 10,000 passengers a day, with a maximum of 25,000. In 1906, the first year for which complete figures are available, the terminal handled 4,469,982 passengers on 87,730 round trips.

During the next ten years traffic in the terminal, the world's largest interurban station, grew steadily, with a reported 7,208,747 passengers in 1916, carried on 694 cars in 462 trains per day. As the passenger traffic increased so did the number and length of the various intercity runs. By 1910 long-distance runs included Indianapolis to Fort Wayne via Muncie, 123 miles, or via Peru, 136 miles; Indianapolis to Louisville, 117 miles; and Indianapolis to South Bend via Peru, 170 miles. An even longer run, covering the 248 miles from Indianapolis to Zanesville, Ohio, began in 1916. This tiring nine-hour trip, however, could not compete with the faster steam railroad service between the two cities, and the run was soon dropped.

During their heyday interurban lines greatly affected Indiana travel habits in general and the habits of Indianapolis residents in particular. Before electric lines, steam RAILROADS offered intercity transportation of people and goods throughout the state. This service, however, often operated only two or three times a day, usually to major cities and then not always at convenient hours. The interurbans, on the other hand, ran frequent service—10 to 12 trains per day between the major cities—and at hours desired by the traveling public, usually between 6 A.M. and 11 P.M. or midnight. Except for the limiteds, interurbans made all stops en route, including the country road crossings, and from the late 1920s most trains made all stops. Road names such as Stop 10 and Stop 11 in southern Marion County are present-day reminders of this bygone form of transportation.

The traveling public liked the comfortable, quiet, and clean ride and the cheaper fares. With lower ticket prices the Indianapolis-Franklin line by 1902 had captured 98 percent of the local traffic from the Pennsylvania Railroad. The steam railroads retaliated with excursion bargains to points as far away as Niagara Falls; ironically, many excursions were joint fares with competing interurbans.

Originally, Indianapolis merchants objected to the "noisy, dirty freight cars" on the city streets. But objections ceased with the beginnings of small package dispatch freight, an interurban service that allowed businessmen to ship orders quickly and economically to customers along the various lines. This service often allowed one-day order and delivery, an obvious selling point. Although this hurt smaller town merchants initially, soon they began using same-day delivery to compete with big city stores.

Larger orders required cars devoted exclusively to package freight, and these cars soon were hauled in scheduled freight trains. Other industries followed the trend, and carload shipments of logs, syrup, paper goods, auto parts, and livestock became common on most roads. Interchange of freight cars with steam railroads, however, was the exception rather than the norm because of differences in car equipment and objections from steam railroads.

As Indiana's largest city, Indianapolis quickly became the center of this frenzied activity, and the large passenger and freight terminals were built to accommodate ever increasing traffic demands. Indiana companies also were among the industry's innovative leaders, offering pioneer train order dispatching, varied passenger equipment including parlor-diners and sleepers (one of only three sleeper operations in the country), special cars (express, railway post office), and the world's largest traction terminal station in Indianapolis.

The 1920s started promisingly for the Indiana interurbans. The companies provided the traveling public more comfortable and safer equipment, including all-steel limited cars, parlor-diners, and sleepers. Roadbeds were improved for faster and smoother riding, and freight services were expanded with the addition of heavy locomotives, fast express service, and specialized freight cars. But other factors worked against the continued success of interurbans. The private automobile and the paved highway system caused a decline in interurban passenger traffic: almost 40 percent by the end of the 1920s. Several smaller lines either went out of business or merged into larger and stronger companies.

All the companies serving Indianapolis, however, survived the decade in fairly strong financial positions until the stock market crash of 1929. The resulting widespread financial failures severely affected the interurbans and their parent, the electric power industry. Many companies abandoned operations, although some managed to keep operating for a few more years, hoping vainly for a revival that never occurred.

Early in 1930 two large companies serving Indianapolis, Union Traction and Interstate Public Service (successor to the original Indianapolis, Greenwood and Franklin), combined forces to combat their developing financial problems. On August 1, 1930, the new company, Indiana Railroad (IR), began operation of all the properties. It quickly disposed of over a hundred miles of unprofitable line (none serving Indianapolis) and dropped the parlor-dining service between Indianapolis and Louisville.

The other two companies serving the city, Terre Haute, Indianapolis and Eastern Traction Company (which had merged several of the smaller companies in west central Indiana) and Indianapolis and Southeastern Railroad, successor to Indianapolis and Cincinnati Traction, continued to operate independently. But Terre Haute, Indianapolis and Eastern abandoned most of its Indianapolis service on October 31, 1930, dropping routes to Martinsville, Danville, Crawfordsville, and Lafayette.

Eight months later Indiana Railroad took over the THI&E line from Indianapolis to Terre Haute, plus other tracks in the Terre Haute area. These acquisitions gave IR a total interurban trackage of 850 miles, by far the largest of any company in the entire United States. The company also operated another 100 miles of city lines. Still, the losses continued. 1932 brought abandonment of the IR's Indianapolis-Dunreith line (forcing rerouting of the Indianapolis-Dayton service via New Castle and Dunreith), the Indianapolis and Southeastern lines from Indianapolis to Greensburg and Connersville, and the cessation of sleeper service between Indianapolis and Louisville.

Interior of an interurban car, ca. 1920.
[Indiana Historical Society, #C2351]

The final blow to the interurbans was the passage in 1935 of the Public Utility Holding Act, which required holding companies to restrict their operations to a single integrated system and to "reasonably incidental or economically necessary activities." This provision required the separation of power and railway operations, effectively leaving the railways without access to utilities' resources. Although delayed in court for several years, the act was eventually upheld by the U.S. Supreme Court and the utilities began cutting back their railway operations.

In 1937 the suburban Beech Grove line failed, after many years of struggling with declining revenues and harassment by creditors. The INDIANAPOLIS POWER AND LIGHT COMPANY, frustrated by continuing nonpayment of its bills, simply cut the power one morning and the line was no more.

The January, 1937, floods on the Ohio River and its many tributaries caused several breaks in service on the Indianapolis-Louisville line. In May, IR abandoned its Indianapolis-Dayton service. Ironically, just as the company was beginning to show a profit it suffered a long and difficult strike. By the time the strike was resolved the company had lost all it had gained over its short but active life.

Other abandonments continued the downward trend: 1938, Indianapolis–Fort Wayne via Peru; 1939, Seymour to Louisville (leaving only the short Indianapolis-Seymour stub of the once prosperous Indianapolis-Louisville route); 1940,

Indianapolis–Terre Haute; and 1941, Indianapolis–Fort Wayne via Muncie, and the final segment, Indianapolis-Seymour (following a fatal accident that wrecked two of the last four cars still in service).

Thus went the interurban in Indiana. From its tiny beginnings the industry had grown to an extensive system connecting most of the major cities and villages in the state. Through the years, 111 different interurban companies operated more than 3,000 cars over the state's 2,100 miles of line (a mileage figure second only to that of Ohio, a much more populous state).

JERRY MARLETTE

Jerry Marlette, *Electric Railroads of Indiana* (2nd ed., Indianapolis, 1980); Glen A. Blackburn, "Interurban Railroads of Indiana," *Indiana Magazine of History*, 20 (Sept., Dec., 1924); Jerry Marlette, *Interstate—A History of Interstate Public Service Rail Operations* (Polo, Ill.: Transportation Trails, 1991).

IPD. See Indianapolis Police Department

IPL. See Indianapolis Power and Light Company

IPS. See Indianapolis Public Schools

Irish. Second largest ethnic group in Indianapolis. Individuals of Irish ancestry were among the earliest settlers in Indiana's capital. Over the ensuing decades, however, emigrants from Ireland came via eastern cities to central Indiana in response to increased employment opportunities. As early as 1832 the *Indiana Journal* advertised the need for "canal hands" to work on the Wabash and Erie Canal near Fort Wayne. Canal company agents in the East specifically recruited Irish immigrants with inducements of "$10 per month for sober and industrious men" and Indiana land at favorable rates. Following the General Assembly's passage of the overly ambitious Mammoth Internal Improvements Bill (1836), contractors hired Irish workers for massive road and canal construction projects. While many Irishmen set-

tled near their work in small towns like Peru and Logansport, where they quickly developed a reputation for hard drinking and brawling, others moved to Indianapolis to dig the CENTRAL CANAL and build the NATIONAL ROAD. With the Panic of 1837 and the subsequent end to the public works projects, Irish workers found themselves unemployed within a community unable to absorb them financially.

As their numbers in Indianapolis increased, the Irish began to establish a distinct community. Irish Catholics first assembled for Mass in a West Washington Street tavern around 1837 and later helped found Holy Cross Catholic Church in 1840 (known as ST. JOHN CATHOLIC CHURCH after 1850). By the early 1840s Irish clustered in the same poor area of Indianapolis as African-Americans—an area straddling Washington Street and bounded by the Central Canal and White River—which indicated the groups' similar low status.

Facing a growing Irish presence, Indianapolis residents became more aware of events in Ireland, particularly the great potato famine of the late 1840s. In February, 1847, some 30 residents met to begin a relief effort for those affected by the blight that was sweeping Europe. Attorney CALVIN FLETCHER, elected treasurer of the group, noted that there was "n[o]t as much interest as the starving condition of the country requires." By April he reported greater success in raising monies and relief supplies, including socks and corn.

In the years preceding the Civil War the Irish, who comprised the second largest immigrant group in Indiana, became a more visible and vocal part of Indianapolis. Irish contractors filled the town streets in May, 1845, when jobs were let for work on the Indianapolis to Edinburgh railroad. Street skirmishes between the Irish and other groups also became more prevalent. In April, 1852, newly naturalized Irishmen and GERMANS rallied at the county courthouse to oppose temperance legislation. Their increased visibility led to the emergence of "Know-Nothings," a nativistic organization suspicious of political activities by foreigners.

By the early 1860s the Irish primarily resided in two sections of town. A nine-block area known as IRISH HILL, bounded north and south by railroad tracks and by Dillon (Shelby) and Noble (College) streets on the east and west, attracted numerous Irish working class families and saloons, which earned it a reputation as being the tough part of town. The FOUNTAIN SQUARE neighborhood, located at the end of the Virginia Avenue streetcar line, also attracted the Irish where they established St. Patrick's Catholic Church in 1865. Residents of these neighborhoods found work in the railroad yards, on construction jobs, or at KINGAN AND COMPANY, an Ireland-based pork packing company, which opened a facility on Maryland Street near White River in 1863 and employed local and imported Irishmen. Women needing employment found work in factories like NATIONAL STARCH or Clune Mattress or as domestics in private homes.

With the coming of the CIVIL WAR the Irish quickly responded to the call for volunteers. They raised an Irish regiment (the 35th), commanded by Colonel John Walker of La Porte, and used St. John's parish school as a recruiting station; the regiment was later consolidated with the 61st or Second Irish Regiment. Members of the Irish Republican (or Fenian) Brotherhood, a national organization founded in 1857 and dedicated to a free Ireland, saw the war as an opportunity for Irishmen to gain military experience for their forthcoming confrontation with Great Britain.

Immediately following the war local Irishmen joined in the Fenians' efforts to seize Canada from Britain and win freedom for Ireland. One of two rival Fenian lodges in the city subscribed money to the abortive effort and equipped 150 men under the command of Captain James Haggerty. Marching in May, 1866, the unit joined with other groups to invade Canada from Buffalo, New York. On June 6, President Andrew Johnson ordered an end to the "unlawful proceedings" and the arrest of all offenders.

During the 1860s the Irish became more active in local politics. Primarily Democratic in their political orientation, the Irish generally opposed the Republican party for its temperance and pro-business and anti-labor stances. Two of the first Irish-American political leaders in Indianapolis, however, were Republicans—JOHN CAVEN and DANIEL MACAULEY. Both elected as mayor, Caven served 1863–1867 and 1875–1881, while

Macauley served 1867–1873. Their elections showed the emerging political influence of the Irish. Over 3,300 foreign-born Irish resided in Indianapolis (3,760 in Marion County) in 1870, comprising 31 percent of the city's foreign-born population.

Following ratification of the 15th Amendment, which guaranteed African-Americans the right to vote, Indianapolis residents encountered mounting ethnic conflict at the local level. During the 1875 city election, the Democrats' anti-black sentiments were countered with vicious anti-Irish attacks in the Republican-oriented *Indiana Journal*. On election eve, the *Journal* accused the Democrats of importing Irishmen to vote for the party, and lashed out against the "Irish tramps," "Hibernian heifers," and "Romanish herds." Quickly, African-Americans and the Irish became political rivals. The next year, on May 3, 1876, a special election for city councilmen, clouded by Republican accusations of Democratic gerrymandering, revealed the underlying political and ethnic tensions in Indianapolis. After hearing reports of Democrats intimidating would-be African-American voters in heavily Irish Democratic Ward 6, nearly 100 African-American residents of Ward 4 marched south into the Irish stronghold. Upon reaching the WOODBURN SARVEN WHEEL COMPANY near Pogue's Run and South Illinois Street, the marchers seized hickory sticks from the factory yard and confronted the Irish Democrats. Following an exchange of gunfire and the intervention by police and Mayor Caven, the crowds were dispersed, leaving several African-Americans injured, one of whom later died. Despite the labor unrest of the period, this election incident stood out as the city's worst riot.

The Irish, who were predominantly Catholic, made the church with its parish societies, special events, and religious celebrations the center of their social life. Several parishes opened over the years to serve the increasing numbers of Irish families—St. Peter's (1864–1865, renamed St. Patrick's, 1870); St. Joseph's (1873); St. Bridget's (1880); St. Francis de Sales (1881); and St. Anthony (1891). Likewise an Irish Catholic school located on Tennessee between Maryland and Georgia streets served the local children. In 1879 an Irish Delegate Assembly held in Indianapolis attracted representatives from Irish societies and churches statewide. Following a St. Patrick's Day parade, they heard Bishop FRANCIS SILAS CHATARD speak on "The Social Mission of the Irish Race."

Irish associational life was centered in the sixth ward, clustering in the vicinity of St. John's church. The ANCIENT ORDER OF HIBERNIANS, a local chapter of the secret society devoted to mutual assistance and Irish independence, formed in 1870 and flourished locally despite opposition from Bishop Chatard. By 1910 it maintained eight divisions with 1,000 male members and nine female auxiliaries with 1,100 members. In subsequent years the Hibernians protested the intolerance of the KU KLUX KLAN in the 1920s and sponsored an annual St. Patrick's Day parade (cancelled during the Great Depression but revived in 1980). Other organizations included the Emerald Beneficial Association, the Knights of Father Matthew, St. Augustine Ladies' Total Abstinence Society, and the United Irish Society. The first local council of the Knights of Columbus was established in June, 1899.

One of the most influential Irishmen in Indianapolis was Democratic politician THOMAS A. TAGGART. Born in County Monaghan, Ireland, Taggart worked his way up through the political ranks to head the local and state Democratic party. He was elected mayor in 1895, 1897, and 1899, became chairman of the Democratic National Committee in 1904, and was appointed to fill a vacancy in the U.S. Senate in 1916.

By 1910 the Irish were the second largest ethnic group in the city, numbering approximately 12,225 (3,255 foreign-born, 8,970 native-born of foreign parents), and comprising 5 percent of the total population and 15 percent of the foreign population. This group, while affirming its loyalty to the United States during WORLD WAR I, generally supported the local German population and the German cause out of antagonism toward Britain. One of the most pro-German journals in the state was Joseph Patrick O'Mahony's *Indiana Catholic* (*INDIANA CATHOLIC & RECORD* by 1916) which carried anti-British editorials. In 1915 the Irish rallied with Germans in several Hoosier cities to protest America's partiality toward the Allies.

While the Irish had resided primarily on the near east, south, and west sides of the city, by 1920 there was considerable movement out of the downtown neighborhoods of St. John's and St. Bridget's. Irish-born residents, who numbered 2,414 or 33 percent of the state's Irish-born population, established new enclaves on the east side around Holy Cross Parish (Oriental and Ohio streets, 1895), St. Philip Neri Church (North Rural Street, 1909), and St. Therese (Little Flower) Parish (established 1926).

The ensuing decades witnessed a declining immigration of Irish to Indianapolis, although individuals of Irish ancestry still comprised the second largest ethnic group in the city. Catholic parishes continued to attract the Irish to the surrounding neighborhoods, but increased evidence of Irish assimilation reduced their distinctive presence of earlier years. In 1970 there were 2,752 persons of Irish stock (427 Irish-born, 2,325 native-born of foreign parents) in the city, placing the Irish fourth behind Germans, ENGLISH, and CANADIANS. Among Marion County's residents in 1980 over 18 percent (138,407 individuals) reported an Irish ancestry; by 1990, 64,771 Indianapolis residents (8.7 percent) reported Irish ancestry, placing them second behind the Germans and just ahead of the English.

Since the founding of Indianapolis numerous individuals of Irish ancestry have played leading roles on the local scene, including pioneer WILLIAM CONNER; mayors John Caven, Daniel Macauley, REGINALD H. and THOMAS L. SULLIVAN, JAMES L. MITCHELL, ALBERT G. FEENEY, and JOHN J. BARTON; police chief MICHAEL MORRISEY; and bankers and politicians FRANK E. MCKINNEY, SR. and FRANK E. MCKINNEY, JR.

To commemorate the contributions of the Irish to Indiana and Indianapolis, the Irish American Heritage Society and the Ancient Order of Hibernians on March 17, 1990, dedicated a Celtic limestone cross in the churchyard of St. John Catholic Church. The inscription reads: "In memory of the faith and determination of the Irish people who settled in Indiana, we dedicate this Celtic Cross to challenge Irish Americans to keep that faith and determination and to build a better tomorrow."

DAVID G. VANDERSTEL
Indiana University–Purdue University,
Indianapolis

James J. Divita, *Ethnic Settlement Patterns in Indianapolis* (Indianapolis, 1988); Emma Lou Thornbrough, *Indiana in the Civil War Era, 1850–1880* (Indianapolis, 1965); Jacob Piatt Dunn, *Greater Indianapolis* (Chicago, 1910).

ture of ethnic groups, including newcomers from the Appalachian South.

CATHLEEN F. DONNELLY

Indianapolis Star, Feb. 23, 1930, Mar. 17, 1988; *Indianapolis Times*, Aug. 14, 1947, Jan. 14, 1962.

Irish Hill. Near southside residential area once the center of Irish-American life in the 19th and early 20th centuries. There is little agreement on the boundaries of Irish Hill: some say Shelby Street on the east, College Avenue on the west, and the railroad tracks on the north and south, while others extend the east-west boundaries to State and Delaware streets. Most agree the neighborhood's name came from Irish who escaped the potato famine of the 1840s and labored to build RAILROADS, canals, and roads in the Indianapolis area. Later male immigrants found maintenance work in the railyards or meat-packing jobs at KINGAN AND COMPANY adjacent to "The Hill." The choices were fewer for neighborhood women. They worked at Kingan, found jobs as domestics in wealthy homes, or wrapped chocolates at Hershey Candy Company.

A closely knit community, Irish Hill took care of its own. Neighbors welcomed new immigrants arriving from Ireland and helped them find jobs and homes. Baptisms, weddings, and St. Patrick's Day festivities were occasions for the community to celebrate. Family life centered on the church, where residents attended Mass, went to school, and took part in parish programs. Three churches served the large Catholic population of Irish Hill—St. Patrick's, St. John's, and Holy Cross. Residents enjoyed sporting events, card parties, ice skating on POGUE'S RUN, and Thursday evening "breakdowns," where revelers played and danced traditional jigs. Neighborhood saloons offered spirited political discussion and a place to drink and eat.

Just as the railroads helped to create Irish Hill, they also contributed to its demise. In 1918, the PENNSYLVANIA RAILROAD razed a number of homes to build elevated tracks through the neighborhood. Later, as the railroads declined, employment opportunities became scarce and families moved away. Today, Irish Hill residents are a mix-

Irish in Politics. Politics enabled the Irish and their descendants to rise to positions of prominence in Indianapolis as mayors, police chiefs, judges, city councilmen, and party officials. Denied political freedom in their homeland, Irish immigrants took a keen interest in politics when they arrived in America. Political power brought patronage to Irish communities—party positions, city government jobs, and police and fire department appointments. Politics afforded the Irish a certain legitimacy in Indianapolis, since most lacked the capital, education, or skills that would have allowed them to advance immediately in business or the professions. Moreover, political power assured Irish saloon keepers of their livelihood, even as temperance forces sought to close them.

The prolabor, antitemperance stance of the Democratic party attracted most Irishmen in the late 19th and early 20th centuries. They began as precinct workers and ward bosses in IRISH HILL, a near southside community, and in the near westside neighborhoods served by St. Bridget's and St. John's parishes.

The first Indianapolis mayors of Irish descent were popular Republicans—JOHN CAVEN (1863–1867, 1875–1881) and DANIEL MACAULEY (1867–1873), but the election in 1873 of Democrat JAMES L. MITCHELL marked the crossover of Irish support to the Democratic party. By 1890, when THOMAS L. SULLIVAN became mayor, the Irish played a significant role in city politics.

Perhaps the best-known Irish politician was THOMAS A. TAGGART, who came to Indianapolis in 1877 and enjoyed great success at the local, state, and national levels. A gifted political organizer, Taggart became local chairman of the Democratic party in 1888, state chairman in 1892, and served as mayor from 1895 to 1901. Taggart was a member of the Democratic national committee in 1900 and became chairman in 1904. He built a formidable party machine, dubbed the "Tammany of the Middle West," and brokered political deals until the 1920s.

Irish organizations provided Democratic politicians such as Taggart with financial support and votes. A local chapter of the ANCIENT ORDER OF HIBERNIANS, formed in 1870, sponsored the city's annual St. Patrick's Day parade and by 1910 boasted a membership of 1,000 Irishmen. A colorful incident in 1903 underscored the political and financial clout of the local group. An escaped Irish convict, James Lynchehaun, was arrested in Indianapolis and faced extradition to Great Britain. Prominent Hibernians called mass meetings at TOMLINSON HALL, solicited the state's two senators and Mayor CHARLES BOOKWALTER to speak, and hired one of the city's top lawyers for Lynchehaun's defense. In an Indianapolis courtroom packed with Irish supporters, a U.S. commissioner denied extradition on the grounds that Lynchehaun originally had been convicted of a political crime.

Irish immigration slowed in the 20th century and the percentage of foreign-born residents in Indianapolis declined from 9.5 percent of the total population in 1900 to 2.7 percent in 1940. Second-generation Irish began moving out of Irish Hill to establish new communities, particularly on the city's east side. Gone were the popular saloons such as Kelly's on East Maryland Street, where "you could poll the whole precinct without leaving the place," or Jim Reilly's at Georgia and Pine streets, a spot to dispense both liquor and patronage.

Irish politicians, however, continued to enjoy success at the polls, partly because of a new alliance between African-American and Irish voters in the Democratic party. In 1930 REGINALD H. SULLIVAN, son of former mayor Thomas Sullivan, took office as mayor after serving as county and state Democratic chairman. Also in the 1930s, FRANK E. MCKINNEY, SR., was elected treasurer of Marion County. McKinney went on to become a national force in the Democratic party, serving as party chairman in 1951–1952 at the request of President Harry S Truman. Democrats ALBERT G. FEENEY (1948–1950) and JOHN J. BARTON (1964–1967) served as mayor when the city faced new challenges as neighborhoods changed and sec-

ond- and third-generation Irish moved to the suburbs. In 1970 Unigov brought predominantly Republican suburban wards into the city election process and further diluted the political clout of traditional Irish and Democratic neighborhoods.

Politicians of Irish descent continue to play an active role in local Democratic politics. In 1991 Democratic state senator Louis B. Mahern ran unsuccessfully for mayor of Indianapolis. In 1994 Thomas P. O'Brien and Cathline Mullin serve as chair and vice-chair of the Marion County Democratic party.

CATHLEEN F. DONNELLY

Indianapolis News, Aug. 28, 1903; *Indianapolis Times*, Mar. 16, 1940; *Indianapolis Star Magazine*, Feb. 18, 1973.

Irvington. Eastside neighborhood bounded roughly by 10th Street, Arlington Avenue, Brookville Road, and Emerson Avenue. In November, 1870, Jacob B. Julian, president of the First National Bank of Centerville and a former state legislator, and Wayne County auditor Sylvester Johnson purchased 300 acres of farmland along the National Road four miles east of the Circle. The men, joined by Dr. Levi Ritter, owner of 80 acres west of Ritter Avenue, planned to develop a community of "refinement and culture" near Indianapolis. They platted the town of Irvington, named in honor of 19th-century author Washington Irving, with 109 randomly sized lots situated along meandering curved streets. Incorporated in March, 1873, and annexed by Indianapolis on February 17, 1902, Irvington was a community of substantial homes and thriving culture from its beginning.

A 25-acre donation of land and a $150,000 grant from the town of Irvington inspired North Western Christian University (now BUTLER UNIVERSITY) to relocate there in 1873. Faculty members purchased and built homes throughout the town and the college became the focal point of Irvington life before it moved in 1928.

A commercial center emerged in the late 19th century around the Penn Central Railroad depot on South Audubon Road. By 1900 businesses began moving to Washington Street near Emerson

Avenue, as well as a public library, theater, Masonic lodge, and fire station. Several original buildings still exist.

Children attended Mrs. Paul Hopkins' private school until a public school opened on Irving Circle in 1874; it moved to the corner of Ritter and Washington by 1904. Our Lady of Lourdes Catholic Church began a grade school in 1909. Irvington High School opened briefly in the late 1800s; by 1900 students attended Shortridge or Manual high schools or Butler's prep school (closed 1905). Thomas Carr Howe High School opened at 4900 Julian Avenue in 1938.

The neighborhood initially possessed a professional, middle class character. According to the 1880 census over 50 percent of resident males were professionals, highly skilled laborers, or students. Following Butler College's removal the neighborhood lost its professional distinctiveness and now a more diverse population resides there.

Irvington has been home to many prestigious and renowned individuals: Allen R. Benton, DEMARCHUS BROWN, HILTON U. BROWN, GRACE JULIAN CLARKE, GEORGE S. COTTMAN, WILLIAM FORSYTH, Helene Hibben, THOMAS CARR HOWE, FRANK MCKINNEY "KIN" HUBBARD, David Starr Jordan, GEORGE W. JULIAN, Dr. Robert Long, FREDERICK POLLEY, and CLIFTON A. WHEELER. Ku Klux Klan leader DAVID CURTIS (D. C.) STEPHENSON also made his home in Irvington at 5432 East University Avenue in the mid–1920s.

Irvington Historic District was placed on the National Register of Historic Places in 1987.

SHERYL D. VANDERSTEL

Timothy J. Sehr, "Three Gilded Age Suburbs of Indianapolis: Irvington, Brightwood, Woodruff Place," *Indiana Magazine of History*, 77 (Dec., 1981), 305–332; Gertrude Winders, *A Glimpse of Irvington Then and Now, 1870–1970* (Indianapolis, 1970); *Indianapolis Architecture* (Indianapolis, 1975).

Irvington Group. Colony of artists residing in IRVINGTON during the 1920s and 1930s. From 1928 to 1937 the Irvington Union of Clubs sponsored ten exhibitions of Irvington artists. Seventeen professional artists displayed their works during these annual shows. The Irvington Group exhibits were not juried art competitions but group shows exhibiting the varied mediums of the artists who lived in the community. The exhibits, usually held in December, were popular and profitable. Even in the midst of the Great Depression, 24 of 90 paintings were sold.

Lectures, gallery talks, and art demonstrations further enhanced the exhibits from year to year. WILBUR D. PEAT, director of the John Herron Art Museum, was a contributing speaker, as were artists WILLIAM FORSYTH, DOROTHY MORLAN, and FREDERICK POLLEY. The 30–minute portrait demonstrations of SIMON BAUS were especially popular attractions during the shows of the 1930s.

As individuals, the artists of the Irvington Group found varying degrees of success. Most notable were the careers of William Forsyth, dean of the Irvington Group, renowned instructor at the John Herron Art Institute, and a member of the HOOSIER GROUP; CLIFTON A. WHEELER, art teacher at Herron and SHORTRIDGE HIGH SCHOOL, and painter of the mural above the marquee of the CIRCLE THEATRE in Indianapolis; and WILLIAM KAESER, celebrated Regionalist artist and painter of the Pendleton, Indiana, post office mural.

FRANK N. OWINGS, JR.

Irvington Historical Society, *The Irvington Group* (Indianapolis, 1984); Flora Lauter, *Indiana Artists Active 1940* (Spencer, Ind., 1941); Lucille Morehouse, "Supper Party Winds Up Sixth Annual Exhibition of Irvington Artists' Work," *Indianapolis Star* (Nov. 27, 1933).

Irvington War. School board dispute. In 1877 a dispute arose over the qualifications of the newly elected members of the Irvington school board. Old board members GEORGE W. JULIAN and J. O. Hopkins refused to relinquish their positions and new members Sylvester Johnson and Dr. James A. Krumrine formed a rival board.

When the old board reemployed the previous year's school teacher, Lydia Putnam, for the 1877 term, the new board disputed the appointment. In the meantime, Hopkins resigned from the old board and was replaced by William H. H. Shank, who aligned with the new board members. Now in the majority, the new board changed the locks on the school to deny access to Putnam.

School was scheduled to begin September 3, 1877. When Putnam arrived the new school board dismissed her, but she refused to leave. The frustrated board members forcibly removed her from the school; Johnson and Krumrine held her by the arms while Shank "brought up the rear 'boosting with his knee.'" Putnam reentered the building through the back door and hung onto a staple on the wall until the men could pry her loose and force her from the building. Putnam filed assault and battery charges against the men and sued them for damages, winning an $800 award. The board members appealed the case to the Indiana Supreme Court, but the justices upheld the lower court's decision. In its coverage of the events the *INDIANAPOLIS NEWS* gave the episode its popular name—the Irvington "war."

CONNIE J. ZEIGLER

Jacob Piatt Dunn, *Greater Indianapolis* (Chicago, 1910), I, 435–436.

Islam. Among the 30,000 estimated Muslims in Indiana, approximately 4,000 live in Indianapolis. By region of origin these Muslims are 55 percent African-American, 27 percent Middle Eastern/North African, 8 percent Eastern European, 5 percent Asian, and 5 percent Subsaharan. Islam has six obligatory beliefs and five obligatory actions. The Muslim must believe in (1) Allah, (2) angels, (3) the prophets (from Adam to Muhammad), (4) revealed scriptures (Torah, Psalms, Gospels, and Qur'an), (5) the hereafter (heaven, hell, and judgment day), and (6) predestination. Muslims should practice the five pillars of faith: (1) profess faith in Allah and Muhammad's prophethood (shahada), (2) pray five times daily (salat), (3) fast during Ramadan (sawm), (4) pay a $2\frac{1}{2}$ percent tithe (zakat), and (5) make the pilgrimage (hajj).

Organizationally, Indianapolis African-American Muslims form three groups: those linked to Louis Farrakhan, those linked to Warith (Wallace) Muhammad, and the al-Fajr mosque. All three groups were antedated in Indianapolis by the proto-Islamic Moorish American Science Temple Movement. Immigrant Muslims generally associate with the ISLAMIC SOCIETY OF NORTH AMERICA (ISNA) located in Plainfield, Indiana. The immigrant Muslims were preceded by the heterodox Ahmadiyya of Qadianis originating in India.

The African-American Muslims originated in the Moorish American Science Temple movement, Indiana chapters of which appeared in the 1940s in Indianapolis and Indiana Harbor. A temple led by Grand Governor J. Blakely-Bey was at INDIANA AVENUE in Indianapolis until the 1960s. By the late 1950s the principal indigenous Muslim group was the Nation of Islam, led nationally by Elijah Muhammad. The Indianapolis leader was Daniel Green (Brother Minister X), who was murdered in 1971 after a rift among members. With Elijah's death in 1975, his son W. D. Muhammad moved the group toward orthodoxy. In March, 1981, W. D. Muhammad brought Muhammad Siddiq to Indianapolis to lead the city's Muslims. Louis Farrakhan, unhappy with the new orthodoxy, broke from the movement in 1978. In the early 1990s a group of Farrakhan sympathizers was led by James 2X. Another independent African-American Muslim group was established at Sherman Avenue in 1973. In 1986 it moved to Leon Street and in 1992 built a mosque on Cold Spring Road. A small African-American Muslim group, the Bilalian Student Alliance, was formed at INDIANA UNIVERSITY–PURDUE UNIVERSITY, INDIANAPOLIS (IUPUI) in the early 1990s.

Orthodox immigrant Muslims were preceded by the heterodox Ahmadiyya. The small Pakistani Ahmadiyya group formed at Yandes Street by 1960 and was led by Aminullah Khan. In 1975 the Muslim Students Association (MSA), founded in Peoria, Illinois, by Sunni foreign students in 1963, moved its national headquarters from Gary to Indianapolis. A small MSA chapter was formed in the early 1960s at IUPUI by Arab and Pakistani Muslims. MSA became the major national conservative Islamic organization and by 1982 became ISNA. Allegedly led by Muslims in the Muslim Brotherhood and Jammat Islami, ISNA is an umbrella organization incorporating a proselytizing wing, three professional organizations, a youth movement (MYNA), and Malaysian and Arab student groups (MISG and MAYA). Its financial wing, the North American Islamic Trust, encompasses book publishing and distributing, audiovisual facilities, and a mutual fund.

STEVE A. JOHNSON
Indiana University–Purdue University,
Indianapolis

Islamic Society of North America. Orthodox Muslim organization. In 1976 the Islamic Society of North America (ISNA), a conservative Islamic organization, bought 123 acres of land between I–70 and old State Road 267 near Plainfield and moved its offices into existing buildings. In January, 1978, the organization announced plans to build a mosque and other facilities to house the North American Islamic Trust, which deals with the organization's finances and mailorder book sales, and the Muslim Students Association of the United States and Canada. The 42–acre compound was to include a mosque, classrooms, cafeteria, library, residences, gymnasium, and a recreational area open to the public.

Many local residents, believing the plans violated a residential zoning ordinance, contested the society's plans; 960 people signed a petition against the proposed center and took their case to the circuit court of appeals. The protest also had racial overtones. While the appeal was pending, a sign at the entrance to the property was knocked down and painted over with the letters "KKK."

The appeal eventually was denied and construction began in 1980. Completed in January, 1983, the center serves as the Islamic Society of North America's headquarters and houses the five department offices of the General Secretariat and several specialized organizations including the Muslim Students Association. ISNA, led by the Muslim Brotherhood, serves Orthodox immigrant Muslims in the United States and Canada. It describes itself as a grassroots organization focusing on developing Muslim identity and supporting Muslim communities in North America.

WILLIAM D. DALTON

Italians. The largest demographic element of southern and eastern European heritage in Marion County. The 1990 federal census estimated that 2.3 percent of the county's residents

(18,589) have an Italian ancestor, a statistic which ranks Marion County second only to Lake County among Indiana counties.

By 1860, 19 Italian-born persons resided in Indianapolis. One family of seven operated a grocery; three others worked as "plaster of paris image makers." As the Italian population grew to 1,137 by 1910 (of which Sicilians comprised the largest single contingent), the food industry and the arts dominated the employment of immigrants. Italian fruit peddlers in the late 19th and early 20th centuries operated stands at busy intersections like Illinois and Washington streets, and several natives of Genoa ran a confectionery nearby. Frank Mascari from Termini Imerese opened a fruit store on Virginia Avenue near Washington Street in 1882 and was soon joined by several members of his family. By 1910, 33 of the city's 54 fruit and vegetable dealers were Italian. They reputedly introduced the banana to the city, which earned several dealers the nickname "the banana kings." Their descendants still dominate the city's produce industry.

Italians were also prominent in the arts in 19th century Indianapolis. The MONTANI BROTHERS orchestra played for special events and at local parks in the early 1900s. Fresco painter Giovanni Gioscio, from Calvello in Basilicata, decorated local churches, notably old St. Joseph's Catholic Church at College Avenue and North Street, and prominent citizens' homes.

Numbering over 2,000 by 1930, Italian immigrants and their children settled in the city by region of origin and employment. Sicilians in the produce business resided around the intersection of Virginia Avenue and South and East streets. Calabrians who worked for the gas or rubber companies lived along South College Avenue while those working for KAHN TAILORING lived on the near northside. Neapolitan barbers and Calabrian shoemakers dispersed around the city. Friulan installers of terrazzo floors and marble artwork lived on the northeast side. Successful merchants and professionals in medicine and law resided on the fashionable northside.

Despite these differences, the Italian community attempted to enhance its solidarity by organizing associations and clubs. The early ones were social outlets and provided insurance: Umberto

An Italian family's stand in the City Market, ca. 1920. [Indiana Historical Society, #M377]

Primo (1891), Regina Margherita for women (1908), and Francesco Crispi for men (1918). Later organizations, like the Italian-American Society (1960s) and Sons of Italy (1974), were primarily social.

Religion was a key component of community life. Nominally Catholic, Italians attended German and Irish parishes until Methodists opened an Italian mission (1908–1920) around the Virginia Avenue–East Street triangle. In response, BISHOP FRANCIS SILAS CHATARD authorized Father MARINO PRIORI to organize an Italian national parish called Holy Rosary (1909) in the Sicilian district on the southeast side. The parish school operated from 1911 to 1957. A brick and stone church, designed by Kopf and Wooling with bell towers modeled after Rome's San Giorgio in Velabro, was constructed 1923–1925. A focus of the community's social life, Holy Rosary Church attests to its faith and self-pride.

Economic advancement through self-employment was always an immigrant goal. Many Italians established produce firms and in 1954 organized the Indianapolis Produce Terminal. Calabrian native Fred Iozzo opened Garden of Italy, the first important downtown Italian restaurant, in the 1930s. Hardworking, ambitious, competitive, and tightfisted immigrants bought their own homes, and several amassed fortunes by investing in the deflated real estate market of the Great Depression. Their ordinary lifestyle was unostentatious; only at weddings and funerals was family

wealth truly evident. Politically, many Italians were Republican until the 1920s when KU KLUX KLAN support of Republican candidates led Italians to vote Democratic.

Local Italians strongly supported American efforts in both world wars. In 1917–1918 they registered for military service, established a relief association to aid war victims, and participated in patriotic rallies. During the interwar period, many Italians supported Mussolini. They accepted his government's gift of textbooks for local Italian language instruction (1932) and cheered his Ethiopian victory (1936). When Mussolini allied with Hitler, Indianapolis Italians proclaimed their support for the Allies as over 100 Holy Rosary men and women served in the U.S. armed forces.

After 1945, the death of immigrant parents, economic improvement, and veterans establishing their own families elsewhere affected the cohesiveness of the Italian community. Many moved to southern Marion County or to the far northeast side. Holy Rosary Parish, with 1,011 members in 1950, reached its nadir with 160 members in 1977.

New arrivals appeared alongside the old traditional families. One group was professional/managerial, transferred by their companies to Indianapolis, or doctors, lawyers, and teachers who found employment here. Usually from large urban centers, they settled at the city's northern outskirts and looked to the city for leisure and cultural pursuits. Recent immigrants who came as war brides or to pursue professional and middle class occupations were a third element. They particularly treasured old world traditions and language.

These new elements brought a revived ethnic consciousness that coalesced around Holy Rosary Church and in the Columbus '92 Commission. This sense of identity coincided with the 1978 closing of the Latin School (established 1955) adjoining Holy Rosary Church, an event that resulted in the revival of parish life and a more than doubling of membership. Parishioners, relatives, and friends now join to feed and entertain thousands of visitors at a two-day summer festival. In 1986 the listing of the HOLY ROSARY–DANISH CHURCH HISTORIC DISTRICT on the National Register of Historic Places recognized the role of Italians and other immigrants in Indianapolis history. The commission, founded in 1989, planned appropriate observances of the quincentenary of the discovery of America including a gala dinner dance, Mass, and rededication of the Columbus bust on the State House grounds in October, 1992. The commission subsequently reorganized as the Italian Heritage Society of Indiana.

JAMES J. DIVITA
Marian College

James J. Divita, *The Italians of Indianapolis: The Story of Holy Rosary Catholic Parish, 1909–1984* (Indianapolis, 1984).

Ittenbach, Gerhard (Mar. 20, 1828–Jan. 16, 1899). Stonecutter, builder, and stone contractor, responsible for the stonework of many local 19th century landmarks. Born in Koenigswinter, Germany, Ittenbach learned his trade in nearby Cologne, at the great cathedral then nearing completion.

Ittenbach emigrated in the revolutionary year 1848, arriving in New York City, then working in Philadelphia, Wheeling, Cincinnati, and Madison, Indiana. He arrived in Indianapolis in 1851 and worked on the Deaf and Dumb Asylum as an employee of James Muerson. He bought out Muerson in 1860 and formed a partnership with J. C. Schmid. After Schmid's retirement in 1869, the firm was named G. Ittenbach & Company and became one of Indiana's largest and most active stoneyards. Ittenbach retired in 1892; his sons, Frank, John, and Gerhard, continued the business. The stoneyard, on the city's southside, continued as a family business until its demise in the mid–1950s.

Ittenbach and his firm were responsible for the stonework of numerous landmarks including the BATES HOUSE Hotel, the Blind Asylum, and Indiana National Bank (all demolished), the John W Schmidt house (the PROPYLAEUM), the ATHENAEUM, ROBERTS PARK METHODIST CHURCH, St. Mary Catholic Church (both the original and the present), and St. Mary-of-the-Woods Convent and College near Terre Haute.

WILLIAM L. SELM

Pictorial and Biographical Memoirs of Indianapolis and Marion County (Chicago, 1893); *Indianapolis Journal* and *Indianapolis News*, Jan. 17, 1899.

IUPUI. See Indiana University–Purdue University at Indianapolis

Ivy Tech. See Indiana Vocational Technical College

Marjorie Jackson Murder Case. The widow of former Standard Grocery Company president Chester H. Jackson was found murdered in her residence at 6490 Spring Mill Road on May 7, 1977. She had been killed with a .22 caliber rifle during a burglary of her residence. A recluse since her husband's death in 1970, Jackson had withdrawn her entire fortune, totaling $9 million, from Indiana National Bank by May of 1976 and kept the cash scattered throughout her home.

Jackson had been robbed of $800,000 in cash and jewelry on May 16, 1976, but refused to press charges when the suspects were arrested. Three men were later prosecuted in connection with this robbery. On May 2, 1977, Howard Willard and Manuel Lee Robinson robbed Jackson of approximately $160,000. They returned two days later, apparently surprising and then killing her. The two men started a fire, which evidently smoldered for some time, in an unsuccessful attempt to conceal their crime; Jackson's body was eventually discovered when firemen were summoned. Police found $5 million in cash in the home and eventually recovered several million dollars after the robbery.

Within a month authorities arrested Willard and Marjorie Pollitt, his former wife, in Tempe, Arizona, attempting to buy a motor home with money from the robbery. Willard was subsequently convicted of Jackson's murder and sentenced to life in prison. Arrested while purchasing a new car with robbery money, Robinson was found not guilty of murder and armed robbery but convicted of six counts in connection with the crime. Pollitt was convicted of conspiracy to transport stolen money interstate and sentenced to five years.

The Jackson home remained vacant and neglected for many years, a continual reminder of the tragic death of the eccentric woman who lived there with a fortune in cash.

JOAN CUNNINGHAM

Jackson, William N. (June 6, 1809–Dec. 9, 1900). Union Station executive. As a youth Jackson worked in his family's small foundry at Elk Forge, Maryland, and later as a skilled iron worker he moved to Cincinnati to pursue this occupation. Shortly thereafter, ca. 1834, he came to Indianapolis to start his own iron works. Not successful in this venture, he obtained a job in the Terre Haute office of the NATIONAL ROAD. He left this position in 1840 to become assistant to the U.S. postmaster in Indianapolis, and 11 years later moved to Madison to become secretary of the MADISON AND INDIANAPOLIS RAILROAD during the presidency of JOHN BROUGH. With the building of UNION STATION in Indianapolis (1853) he once again took up residence in the capital and assumed the role of secretary-treasurer of the Union Station Company.

Jackson had strong managerial skills, fiscal knowledge, and sensitivity to the needs of the traveling public. He eased the inconveniences of rail travel by expediting ticket purchases and arranging passenger transfers to other rail lines. Over a period of almost 50 years "Uncle Billy" Jackson transformed both the initial and the second (1888) Indianapolis Union Station into relatively hospitable places. Although not a wealthy man he contributed extensively to local charities, particularly institutions designed to aid little children.

VICTOR M. BOGLE
Indiana University, Kokomo

Indiana Biography Series, Indiana State Library.

Jacobs, James Andrew, Sr. (Feb. 22, 1906–Dec. 17, 1992). Attorney, judge, and congressman. Born in Perry County, Indiana, Jacobs attended Benjamin Harrison Law School (later incorporated into the Indiana University School of Law) in Indianapolis. He was admitted to the bar in 1927 and started practicing with a local firm prior to graduating at the top of his class in 1928. Jacobs served as public defender in Marion County Felony Court from 1930 to 1933. During the 1937 automobile industry unrest in Anderson he defended workers who were arrested for their attempts to organize unions, thus earning a reputation as a labor lawyer.

Jacobs represented Indiana's 11th Congressional District from 1949 to 1951 and served as a

Congressman
Andrew Jacobs, Sr.
[Andrew Jacobs, Jr.]

member of the House Committee on Education and Labor and chair of the subcommittee on Democracy in Unions. In 1950 he made an unsuccessful bid for the Democratic Senate nomination and that fall failed to win reelection to the House. After an unsuccessful attempt to win the Democratic nomination for mayor in 1952, he returned to private practice.

Jacobs was elected to the Marion County Superior Court in 1974 and assigned to the criminal division. He quickly earned a reputation as a tough judge, causing many defendants to seek reassignment from his courtroom. During 1975 he tried 127 jury trials in 131 days. He resigned in protest when ordered by the Indiana Supreme Court to grant a change of judge to three defendants, but Governor Otis Bowen persuaded him to reconsider. Jacobs presided over 157 jury trials in 159 days during 1976 and in April of 1977 again resigned in protest after the Supreme Court once more refused to modify the change of judge rule. The following year Jacobs lost as the Democratic candidate for Marion County prosecutor to Stephen Goldsmith, later mayor of Indianapolis. As a longtime civil rights advocate, he served on the Indiana Bar Association Committee on the Bill of Rights and Labor Law. Jacobs was the father of Andy Jacobs, Jr., a U.S. congressman who represented portions of Indianapolis–Marion County 1965–1973 and 1975–present.

JOAN CUNNINGHAM

Biographical Directory of the American Congress (1981); Indianapolis Star and Indianapolis News, Dec. 18, 1992.

James Whitcomb Riley Home (528 Lockerbie Street). JAMES WHITCOMB RILEY, the "Hoosier Poet," was born in 1849 in Greenfield, Indiana. He moved to Lockerbie Street in 1893 and lived there as a paying guest of friends, the Charles L. Holsteins, until he died in 1916.

In 1872 John R. Nickum, Mrs. Holstein's father, built the two-story red brick home for the family. It is an excellent example of the high-style Italianate architecture popular in the neighborhood in the 1860s and 1870s. The low-pitched hipped roof with wide overhanging eaves and decorated brackets beneath is covered with slate shingles. The three-ranked south facade has a central tower that contains paired doors with oval glazing. Tall narrow windows with segmental arches and hooded masonry crowns flank the doorway to the east and west. To the west is a porch with wooden archways and carved balustrades. Inverted U-shaped upper story windows have hooded masonry crowns.

WILLIAM FORTUNE bought the property from the Holstein estate in 1916. Five years later he transferred it to the newly formed James Whitcomb Riley Memorial Association, which has continued to oversee the site. Designated a National Historic Landmark in 1963, the home since the 1970s has served as an anchor for the LOCKERBIE SQUARE Historic District, the first designated historic district in Indianapolis.

JANE R. NOLAN

Japanese. Censuses from 1880 to the present have identified Indianapolis as one of the urban centers of the small Japanese presence in the state. With only 14 residents in Marion County by 1910, the Japanese population of Indianapolis did not grow until the post–World War II years when a number of Japanese (primarily Nisei, the American-born children of Japanese immigrants) came to Indiana from detention camps in the West. Many of these Nisei were college students whose only escape from the camps was to attend schools like Earlham College in Richmond. By 1950, 46 Japanese lived in Marion County, 37 in Indianapolis. Over the next decades the city's Japanese population (foreign born and native born of foreign parents) increased from

263 in 1960 to 753 (824 in Marion County) in 1990.

In 1905 and 1906 the *Indianapolis Sentinel* and the *Indianapolis Star* investigated several "representative" Japanese-Americans who had settled in the city. The papers questioned why they came here and whether they intended to remain as permanent residents. While the press was not entirely negative, it questioned whether the Japanese were here simply to learn American industrial methods for the purpose of transporting these new technologies back to Japan.

With the advent of restrictive immigration laws beginning in the 1920s, the Indianapolis-based AMERICAN LEGION was one of several national groups that lobbied successfully to bar Japanese-Americans (including those born in the United States) from rights of citizenship. The Japanese attack on Pearl Harbor on December 7, 1941, only seemed to vindicate the Legion's stance.

During World War II, however, not all Hoosiers supported anti-Asian sentiments. In 1944 the *Indianapolis News* commended a Legion post in New York for admitting several Japanese-American soldiers (calling them "patriots") who had been rejected by a post in Oregon. The year before another *News* article had discussed the availability of Japanese from relocation camps who could be recruited to fill a number of jobs, provided that the community was willing to accept them.

In many ways the Japanese experienced less discrimination in the Midwest than they did along the Pacific Coast. Through the years in Indianapolis societies such as the Japanese-American Citizens League (1970s), Japan-America Society of Indiana (1988), and the Minyo Dancers have worked to combat racial discrimination and to provide programs of intercultural awareness.

JUSTIN LIBBY
Indiana University–Purdue University,
Indianapolis

Jazz. Music created primarily by African-Americans in the early 20th century reflecting an amalgamation of African and European-American music and improvisation. Although not a principal originator of jazz music like New Orleans, New York, and Chicago, Indianapolis possesses a rich jazz heritage, centered especially in the city's African-American community. At the turn of the 20th century the capital city was a favorite place for touring musical shows of all kinds, and there was much work for local musicians. The city also was a major ragtime center and was home to such important composers and performers as MAY AUFDERHEIDE, Will B. Morrison, Abe Olman, Paul Pratt, J. RUSSEL ROBINSON, and the young black composer Russell Smith.

In the 1910s and 1920s the African-American community had its share of gifted brass bands, itinerant pianists, singers, and instrumentalists. Indianapolis venues such as the Washington Theatre attracted a steady stream of top black performers who played the circuit. Among them were The Pickaninny Band (comprised of youths), Frank Clay's Military Band, and The Kioda Barber Band. Local bands included the Reginald DuValle Orchestra, the Russell Smith Orchestra, and the Harry Farley Orchestra which included a young NOBLE SISSLE.

During the late 1920s and the 1930s, Indianapolis musical venues continued to host performers such as cornetist Frank Clay at the Washington Theatre; Nina Reeves and pianist Jesse Crump at the Golden West; blues specialists FRANCIS "SCRAPPER" BLACKWELL and LEROY CARR at the Paradise; and Zack Whyte's Chocolate Beau Brummels, Louis Armstrong, Fats Waller, Alphonse Trent, Bennie Moten, and Andy Kirk at Denver and Sea Ferguson's Cotton Club on Indiana Avenue.

Several important local bands came to prominence in the 1930s. They were The Brown Buddies, originating at CRISPUS ATTUCKS HIGH SCHOOL and including Beryl Steiner, Roger Jones, Renuald Jones, and James "Step" Wharton; Fred Wisdom's Merrymakers; The Patent Leather Kids, featuring trumpeter Raymond "Syd" Valentine, and saxophonists Buddy Bryant and Cleve Bottoms; and the HAMPTON FAMILY, comprised of talented musicians from one of Indianapolis' most important musical families. Led by Clark Hampton, Sr., the band included sons Clark, Jr. (Duke), Marcus (Buge), Maceo, Russell (Lucky), and Locksley (Slide) and daughters Aletra, Virtue, Carmalita, and Dawn.

Those early years were exciting, fruitful, and undeniably important years for jazz in Indianapolis. However, even though Indianapolis musicians were active on both the local and national levels, by and large they did not have the impact that those from the 1940s, 1950s, and early 1960s did. These decades constituted a golden age for jazz in the city, producing jazz artists who achieved national and international recognition and created an unprecedented stream of great and near great innovative, high level, exciting jazz.

The venues for jazz during this period were many and varied widely in the audiences they attracted. Jazz groups appeared in clubs that served blacks primarily, clubs that served whites, black and tan clubs, theaters, lounges, art galleries, dance halls, and after hours clubs. A major center of jazz activity was INDIANA AVENUE, sometimes referred to simply as "The Avenue." It stretched blocks from LOCKEFIELD GARDENS, a New Deal housing project, to Ohio Street, the beginning of Indianapolis' downtown area, and boasted many jazz venues including the Cotton Club, the Sunset Terrace, George's Bar, Henri's, the Red Keg, the Red Rooster, the Ritz Lounge, the Sky Club (after hours), the Trianon Ballroom, and the Walker Casino. Off Indiana Avenue on West Street (now Dr. Martin Luther King, Jr. Drive) could be found the Missile Room (after hours) and on Capitol Avenue the Pink Poodle. Downtown were the Circle and Indiana theatres, both of which featured jazz bands on a semiregular basis; the 500 Bar; the Beachcomber; the 1444 Art Gallery; and TOMLINSON HALL. Sixteenth Street, a main cross street, boasted the 16th Street Gallery, the 16th Street Tavern, and the Turf Bar. Located at 11th Street and Capitol Avenue was the Ferguson Hotel, owned by entrepreneurs Denver and Sea Ferguson who also owned the Cotton Club and the Sunset Terrace. On the near northside were such clubs as the Cactus Club, Mr. B's, the Hub-Bub, the 19th Hole on 30th Street, the Topper on 34th Street, Stein's on North Meridian, and the Tropic Club on East 10th Street. In these clubs, theaters, and bars, and at countless private jam sessions, Indianapolis' jazz musicians, some destined for worldwide fame and others who would remain

Jazz clubs were popular along Indiana Avenue. [Indiana Historical Society, Duncan Schiedt Collection, #C5919]

unknown outside of local circles, practiced and sharpened their often considerable skills.

The years between 1945 and 1965 represent the period during which the impact of jazz musicians from Indianapolis was the most obvious and quantifiable. The following categories include some of the Indianapolis musicians who achieved national or international recognition as attested to by their peers, critics, historians, and other major chroniclers of jazz, as well as other noteworthy musicians who played regularly in Indianapolis. Numerous other figures of comparable skill, imagination, and abilities chose to remain and perform in Indianapolis and developed a local following.

Guitarists. JOHN LESLIE (WES) MONTGOMERY is usually considered the most influential jazz guitarist, after Charlie Christian. Floyd Smith (1917–1982), who was born in St. Louis but spent much of his creative life in Indianapolis, played the first electric guitar solo on record, "Floyd's Guitar Blues," with Andy Kirk in 1939. Other notable guitarists include Paul Weeden and Ted Dunbar, originally from Port Arthur, Texas, who was a creative force in Indianapolis for many years and remains a leading jazz educator.

Bass Players. WILLIAM (MONK) MONTGOMERY, brother of Wes, pioneered the electric (Fender) bass ca. 1951–1953 while in the Lionel Hampton band and was the first to specialize and record on it (1953). Indianapolis-born Leroy Vinnegar, a specialist in "walking" bass, was one of the major voices in jazz on the West Coast and is among the most recorded of jazz bassists, along with such artists as Andre Previn, Shorty Rogers, and Harold Land. Laurence "Larry" Ridley, another Indianapolis native, worked with Thelonious Monk, Horace Silver, Art Blakey, Sonny Rollins, and others, and became an important figure in jazz education at major universities.

Pianists. Charles (Buddy) Montgomery, younger brother of Wes and Monk, was the vibist with The Mastersounds and pianist with Miles Davis and Kenny Burrell; he remains a recording artist of great stature in his own right. Indianapolis-born Carl Perkins (1928–1958) performed or recorded with Jay McNeely, Miles Davis, Illinois Jacquet, Chet Baker, Clifford Brown, and Max Roach. ERROLL GRANDY, a native of Virginia and long-time resident of Indianapolis, was the legendary "godfather" of jazz players of the 1940s, 1950s, and 1960s. Lanny Hartley played and recorded with The Fifth Dimension; Melvin Rhyne was pianist and organist with the Wes Montgomery Trio, Slide Hampton, and others; Tipton native John Bunch played piano with Tony Bennett, Benny Goodman, Woody Herman, Buddy Rich, Gene Krupa, and Maynard Ferguson.

Drummers. Earl "Fox" Walker was the mainstay of one of Lionel Hampton's most famous bands (with Charles Mingus). Sonny Johnson was a member of the Montgomery-Johnson Quintet and in Lionel Hampton's band with Clifford Brown, Quincy Jones, Art Farmer, Jimmy Cleveland, and others; "Killer Ray" Appleton worked and recorded with Freddie Hubbard, Slide Hampton, Jimmy Spaulding, and others; and Paul Parker played with Wes Montgomery and David Young, among others.

Trombonists. J. J. Johnson, the single most important trombonist in contemporary music, jazz or otherwise, revolutionized the approach to the instrument. Locksley "Slide" Hampton played with Lionel Hampton, Maynard Ferguson, Dizzy Gillespie, Art Blakey, Lloyd Price, and many others, and currently leads Slide Hampton & The Jazz Masters; he is also a major jazz composer and arranger. David Baker played with Lionel Hampton, Quincy Jones, Stan Kenton, and George Rus-

sell, and became Distinguished Professor of Music and chair of the Jazz Department at Indiana University. Phil Ranelin worked with Freddie Hubbard and others.

Trumpeters. Roger Jones played with Count Basie, Duke Ellington, Tiny Bradshaw, Earl Bostic, Don Redman, and Cab Calloway. Freddie Hubbard was a contemporary giant of the trumpet. Virgil Jones played with Lionel Hampton, Billy Taylor, and others; he appears on countless small group recordings. Alan Kiger recorded with George Russell and John Lewis; Lee Katzman recorded with Stan Kenton and also The Baja Marimba Band; and Joe Mitchell played with Earl Bostic when John Coltrane was in the group.

Saxophonists. Indianapolis native Jimmy Spaulding performed and recorded with Freddie Hubbard, Sun Ra, Duke Ellington, Max Roach, Art Blakey, Horace Silver, and others. Jimmy Coe worked with Jay McShann, Buddy Bryant, and Tiny Bradshaw; he is also a jazz educator. Charles Tyler, a major figure in the jazz avant garde, performed and recorded with Albert Ayler, Dewey Redman, David Murray, Cecil Taylor, and Billy Bang. David Young performed and recorded with Lionel Hampton, Mercer Ellington, George Russell, and others. Les "Bear" Taylor, who worked with Slide Hampton and Bill Doggett, also was a jazz educator.

Groups. Several musical groups having roots in Indianapolis included The Ink Spots (1930s–1940s); The Mastersounds (1957–1960) with Richard Crabtree, piano, and Benjamin Barth, drums; The Wes Montgomery Trio; The J. J. Johnson Quintet; The Four Freshmen (a quartet from Columbus, Indiana, and Butler University, 1940s–1950s); and The David Baker Quintet (which became The George Russell Sextet).

The mid–1960s and early 1970s saw the beginning of a decline of jazz as a force in the musical life of Indianapolis. A number of factors contributed to this phenomenon; among the more important were the dispersal of the black population, the death of the jam session as a learning place and proving ground, the loss through attrition of many of the mentors and master players, and the demise of Indiana Avenue as a focal point of jazz and black culture, including the closing of most of the traditional jazz venues.

Although the high visibility and continuing impact of Indianapolis jazz and jazz musicians has lessened considerably since the mid–1960s, as of 1993 a few downtown clubs and others in suburbia and local neighborhoods still feature jazz. It is also noteworthy that there are a number of promising youngsters making their presence felt on the local scene, many of whom, whether by accident, choice, or design, have not chosen to try to make their mark outside of Indianapolis.

DAVID N. BAKER
Indiana University, Bloomington

Duncan Schiedt, *The Jazz State of Indiana* (Pittsboro, Ind., 1977).

Jeffries, Allen, Sr. (1910–Dec. 5, 1980). Broadcast newsman and commentator. A native of Roachdale, Indiana, Jeffries graduated from DePauw University in 1930 and was a broadcast journalist for radio stations in Fort Wayne, Kokomo, and Marion before coming to Indianapolis in 1947 as commentator for WIRE radio. The station was owned by Indianapolis Newspapers, Inc., and Jeffries' newscasts originated for awhile from the city room of the *Indianapolis Star.* Later he moved to the WISH radio news operation and by 1961 had become a part of the WFBM (now WRTV) news staff where he was assignment editor and newscaster.

During the 1950s Jeffries was honored by both the Indianapolis CHAMBER OF COMMERCE and the Indianapolis Safety Council for his contributions to traffic safety. While at Channel 6 he won separate news writing awards from both the NBC and CBS networks for documentaries he researched and prepared. He also became a member of the Indiana Journalism Hall of Fame. Jeffries died in Atlanta, Georgia, where he resided following his retirement in 1975.

HOWARD CALDWELL
WRTV Channel 6

Indianapolis News, Dec. 6, 1980.

Jehovah's Witnesses. In the early 1870s founder Charles Taze Russell organized the International Bible Student's Association (IBSA), an offshoot of the 19th-century Adventist movement. The group adopted its current name in 1931. The Witnesses hold many distinctive beliefs including the rejection of the Trinity, refusal to salute the American flag or participate in the armed services, lack of celebration of Christmas, and refusal to receive blood transfusions. Witnesses attend weekly meetings in Kingdom Halls, which are similar to churches, and canvass new members through house-to-house visitation and distribution of their literature. The Jehovah's Witnesses are organized under the Watchtower Bible and Tract Society, a publishing house headquartered in Brooklyn, New York.

Early Russellites were known by various names including the Millennial Dawn Church, which appeared in the Indianapolis city directory as early as 1905. By April, 1918, the Associated Bible Students sponsored free lectures entitled "The World Has Ended—Millions Now Living May Never Die." That same month, 20 members of the local IBSA were arrested for distributing the "Kingdom News" bulletin protesting the suppression of another IBSA publication, "The Finished Mystery," which the federal government had banned as a violation of the espionage law.

The movement continued to grow during the next two decades and by 1938 the city directory listed the first Indianapolis Jehovah's Witnesses congregation at 725 East 27th Street. Two years later a local Witness was arrested for refusing to salute the American flag. He was charged with desecrating the flag and released on $100 bond.

In August, 1950, local Witnesses again were arrested, this time for holding religious meetings in Brookside Park. They were jailed for violating a city ordinance which prohibited meetings on park property without consent of the park board. The next month a judge ruled that the constitutional rights of free speech and assembly superseded local ordinances and the Witnesses could continue to meet. By 1956 ten congregations of Jehovah's Witnesses were meeting in the city and local Witnesses were hosting district convention meetings. City residents continued to be wary of the Witnesses, with several zoning requests for construction of new Kingdom Halls denied in the late 1950s.

During the 1960s and 1970s the Witnesses expanded their presence in Indianapolis, adding new congregations and hosting district conventions. In 1978 the Witnesses purchased the former Church of Christ Scientist structure at 1201 North Delaware to provide a permanent meeting place for central Indiana Witnesses.

By the 1980s Jehovah's Witnesses in Indianapolis were estimated to number between 4,000 to 5,000 members. A 1988 newspaper article counted 27 city congregations. As of 1993 the Indianapolis Yellow Pages listed 14 Indianapolis Jehovah's Witnesses congregations in addition to the Indianapolis Assembly Hall of Jehovah's Witnesses at 1201 North Delaware.

DEBORAH B. MARKISOHN

Indianapolis Newspaper Index, Indiana State Library.

Jenn-Air Corporation. Manufacturer of ventilation equipment and kitchen ranges. Founded by Ohio native Louis J. Jenn in 1947, following his move to Indianapolis, Jenn Industries produced self-ventilating, overhead exhaust fans for factories. After experiencing great success with the product, Jenn diversified and created the Jenn-Air Corporation in 1961. This division, located on North Shadeland Avenue in Indianapolis, incorporated the advanced ventilation technology into the first self-ventilating kitchen range/oven with smokeless grill.

During the late 1970s, Jenn sold both divisions to Carrier Corporation for $88 million. Five years later Carrier divested itself of the Jenn divisions, which the Maytag Company purchased for $50.8 million. Maytag introduced refrigerators, dishwashers, and freezers to the Jenn-Air line of products. In 1989 Maytag retained the Jenn appliance division and sold the industrial ventilation division to Dallas-based Snyder-General Corporation, a national manufacturer of air quality control products.

Jenn later turned his attention to the restaurant business and to the development of "quadraminiums," a quadrangle of condominiums with an enclosed atrium. Chairman of the Jenn Foundation, a private charity, he was an active community leader. He died March 18, 1993.

STACEY NICHOLAS

Indianapolis Business Journal, July 12–18, 1982; *Indianapolis Star*, Apr. 12, 1985, June 28, 1987, Mar. 20, 1993.

Jewett, Charles W. (Jan. 7, 1884–Apr. 28, 1961). Mayor of Indianapolis, January 7, 1918–January 4, 1922, Republican. As the son of a Methodist minister, much of Charles Jewett's youth was spent in frequent moves throughout rural southern Indiana until the family settled in Indianapolis in 1902. Jewett's education included attendance at various public schools, Franklin College, DePauw University (A.B., 1907), and Harvard Law School (LL.B., 1910).

In 1910 he returned to Indianapolis, opened a law practice with a boyhood friend, and failed to win his party's nomination for the state legislature. In 1913 he was one of the founders of the Republican Union in Marion County, its purpose being to heal the breach between the party's conservative and progressive wings. He was elected county chairman in 1914 and 1916. The electoral success of local Republicans in those years won Jewett the party nomination for mayor in 1917 over former mayor SAMUEL (LEW) SHANK. In the election the maverick Shank, running on a "Home Rule" ticket, drew votes from the Democratic candidate, while Jewett campaigned vigorously against the "Shank Menace" and won with 42 percent of the vote.

Jewett's accomplishments were substantial, given the city's financial problems, which included lost liquor license revenues from the onset of Prohibition. In finance, comprehensive budgets were carefully drawn and matched to appropriations and city purchasing was centralized; in public safety, the platoon system for police and firemen was instituted, the fire department completely motorized, wages increased, and a women's branch in the police department created; in city services, a systematic plan for the collection and disposal of garbage and refuse was begun as was the construction of the first sanitary and garbage disposal plants. Jewett, tireless in giving speeches to put Indianapolis "over the top" in war bond drives, helped persuade the AMERICAN LEGION to establish its national headquarters in the city and was instrumental in getting the INDIANA WORLD WAR MEMORIAL PLAZA project underway.

After his term as mayor Jewett returned to the law. He had been a delegate to the Republican national convention in 1920 and continued his interest in politics after 1922. He failed to win the nomination for governor in a crowded field of ten in 1928, ran unsuccessfully for Congress in 1938, and was active in support of Robert Tyndall's campaign for mayor in 1942. He made his living from the law, as vice-president of Jewett and Company, a bond house, owned a cattle farm, and was a director of the Fletcher bank. A 32nd degree Mason, Jewett belonged to the leading fraternal, business, social, and literary clubs in the city.

WILLIAM DOHERTY
Marian College

Paul D. Brown, ed., *Indianapolis Men of Affairs* (Indianapolis, 1923); *Indianapolis News*, Apr. 29, 1961.

Jewish Community Relations Council.

In 1939 the Indianapolis Jewish Federation organized a public relations committee in an effort to inform the non-Jewish community about Judaism and the Jewish situation in Nazi Germany. In 1947 this committee became the Jewish Community Relations Council (JCRC). Its goals were to promote interfaith activities, maintain good relations between Jews and non-Jews, promote high ethical standards among Jews, protect Jewish rights, support civic and community welfare programs, and publicize Jewish contributions to American life. Since its inception, the goals have been expanded to include defense and support of Israel, support for Soviet Jewry, and educational programs on the Holocaust. The JCRC also cooperates with other community groups on domestic issues that appear to undermine civil liberties and social and economic justice. The council works to develop and maintain interreligious coalition ties on various community projects. In recent years the JCRC has worked closely with many general community leaders and groups (for example, the

NAACP and the INDIANA CIVIL LIBERTIES UNION) to respond not only to the needs and problems of the Jewish community, but the community at large.

The JCRC is headed by an executive director and governed by an elected delegate board that represents all parts of the community—synagogues, women's groups, men's groups, and Jewish Federation agencies. Though the group is diverse and expressive of differing views, it is united in preserving Jewish identity and resisting anti-Semitism.

CAROLYN S. BLACKWELL

Judith E. Endelman, *The Jewish Community of Indianapolis* (Bloomington, Ind., 1984).

Jewish Federation of Greater Indianapolis.

Established in 1905 as the Jewish Federation of Indianapolis. The Federation movement started in Boston in 1895 as an organization of Jewish charities. In Indianapolis, as in other cities, JEWS of German heritage controlled the Federation, although Eastern European immigrants were the main recipients of services. The goals of the Federation were to centralize fund-raising, support local and national Jewish organizations, and provide educational opportunities. During the early years, the Federation's efforts were directed primarily toward financial assistance, employment, health care, and legal aid for new immigrants. As immigration decreased, it turned to community projects, including a Jewish community center (October, 1913), adult education classes, and social gatherings.

The Jewish Welfare Fund was established in 1927 as an autonomous agency of the Federation. Its purpose was to support projects not supported by local and national organizations. By intent, the Welfare Fund's board was more representative than the Federation's board and included members from Zionist, Sephardic, and Orthodox communities. In 1948 the Jewish Federation and the Jewish Welfare Fund merged to form the Jewish Welfare Federation. The organization continues fund-raising activities for national and local projects, such as the Bureau of Jewish Education, Jewish Community Center, Jewish Family and

Child Services, Jewish Social Services, Park Regency (retirement housing), and Hooverwood (home for the elderly). The Federation has addressed contemporary issues by establishing, for example, the New Americans Committee to assist Russian resettlement.

CAROLYN S. BLACKWELL

Jewish Post and Opinion. Weekly newspaper. The Spokesman Company, founded by Gabriel Cohen in 1932, currently publishes three newspapers, all edited and composed in Indianapolis, that report on local, national, and international Jewish-related events and issues. The *Indiana Jewish Post and Opinion*, with a circulation in the early 1990s of roughly 5,000, covers organizations, institutions, and life cycle events of local Jewish residents as well as highlighting other Jewish communities in the state. Several special issues are published each year on the occasion of Jewish holidays and Brotherhood Week. The *National Jewish Post and Opinion*, another of the Spokesman Company's papers, is included in toto in the Indiana paper and publishes columns by national writers on such topics as genealogy, women's issues, sports, and religion.

JUDY SCHWARTZ

Jews. Throughout its history, the Jewish community of Indianapolis has comprised approximately 1 percent of the city's total population. Jewish immigration to the city, however, occurred in distinct waves over time, each representing people of different national origins who possessed different cultural and religious practices. The first Jewish residents in the capital city appear to have been Polish-born merchant Alexander Franco and English-born clerk Moses Woolf, who arrived in 1849. Other Jews of predominantly German origin took advantage of the city's first railroad, which linked Madison with Indianapolis in 1847, and moved here in the 1850s. Many were peddlers turned small merchants or residents of small Indiana towns who shared a pride in German culture and achievements through their support of local German associations. Jewish merchants soon dominated the

city's clothing business, operating 10 of 18 clothing stores in 1860. By the 1880s one half of the German Jews were shopkeepers, retailers, and wholesalers; others were involved in peddling, tailoring, and assorted professions.

The Jewish population, which grew from 180 in 1860 to more than 500 by the 1870s, was quick to establish ethnic enclaves on the near south and east sides of Indianapolis. Fourteen male Jews from Knightstown, Kokomo, and Indianapolis (most of whom resided in the area bounded by Washington, Alabama, New York, and East streets) organized INDIANAPOLIS HEBREW CONGREGATION, the city's first synagogue, in 1856. The founders erected their first temple in 1865 on East Market Street between New Jersey and East streets, and it quickly became the focal point of a close-knit community. They started clubs, benevolent associations, a cemetery at South Meridian and Kelly streets, and a school. With an established community Jews began to take an active part in local politics; Leon Kahn was the first Jew elected to the Indianapolis Common Council, serving eight years between 1869 and 1884. Civic and business leaders also emerged from this group, including WILLIAM H. BLOCK, Gustave A. Efroymson, and Henry Kahn; the *Indianapolis News* of December 6, 1894, counted Jewish merchants Herman Bamberger and Leopold Strauss among the city's leaders. With increased affluence and assimilation, however, German Jews moved from the south side to the emerging residential areas along North Meridian Street south of Fall Creek.

During the late 1880s central and east European (particularly Hungarian, Polish, and Russian) Jews, known as Ashkenazim, began to arrive. Speaking different Yiddish dialects though possessing similar cultural and religious practices, these Jews were divided according to national or regional origins. The Ashkenazim settled on the south side in an area bounded by Morris Street, Capitol Avenue, Union Street, and Washington Street. They became a visible minority, characterized by cultural practices, Orthodoxy, language, and separate institutions. These east European Jews were commonly employed as artisans, garment workers, carpenters and cabinetmakers working for automobile and furniture manufacturers, or hucksters and pushcart vendors.

In 1906 a small wave of Sephardic Jews from the Ottoman Empire (Salonika and Monastir, now Bitola, in Macedonia) came to Indianapolis. Their principal language, Ladino, made communication with the eastern Ashkenazim impossible except by using English. Labeled derogatorily as "Turks" and considered "not really Jewish," the Sephardim lived among the east European Jews along South Illinois and South Meridian streets, but maintained their own unique institutions. Until after World War II, intermarriage between Ashkenazim and Sephardim took place rarely if at all.

Northside Jewry and southside Jewry differed in many ways. The predominantly German Jewish north side practiced Reform Judaism and attended the Indianapolis Hebrew Congregation; the east European Jews on the south side practiced Orthodoxy, a more strict observance of Jewish law and customs, and maintained several ethnic congregations (Shara Tefila, Polish, 1882; Ohev Zedeck, Hungarian, 1884; and Knesses Israel, Russian, 1889). Reform Jews tended to oppose political Zionism, arguing that JUDAISM was a religion and that Americans of the Jewish faith should pay allegiance to the United States. Most Orthodox Jews, while not agreeing with all aspects of political Zionism, supported the concept of an eventual return to Zion and the possibility of creating a Jewish state.

Both nationally and locally based Jewish organizations helped the eastern Ashkenazim and Sephardim adapt to American life. In 1901 the national B'nai B'rith established the Industrial Removal Office to disperse Jewish immigrants throughout the United States. This resulted in the formation of the local Jewish Welfare Federation (1905, now JEWISH FEDERATION OF GREATER INDIANAPOLIS), designed to consolidate fund-raising efforts and to dispense relief to the poor. Indianapolis Jewish leaders like rabbis MORRIS FEUERLICHT and Mayer Messing, industrialist Samuel Rauh, and merchant Gustave A. Efroymson were among the many prominent Jews who were devoted to local civic life as well as to assisting recent immigrants to assimilate into American society. Other groups like the NATIONAL COUNCIL OF JEWISH WOMEN and the Nathan Morris House provided educational and social service programs for recent arrivals.

Sarah Harris and Joseph Solomon (seated, on wife's right) were married in the city's first public Jewish ceremony in 1860.
[Indiana Historical Society, #C1857]

Although strong nativist sentiments and restrictive immigration laws deterred Jewish immigrants in the post–World War I years, Indianapolis recorded 42 percent of the state's Jewish population in the 1920s. With the rise of Nazism and Hitler's persecution of the Jews, however, central European (German and Austrian) Jewish refugees began arriving in Indianapolis in 1938; by 1941 there were about 250 in the city. Unlike their skilled and unskilled predecessors, these refugees were primarily professionals or businessmen. Local Jews put aside their own cultural differences to assist these refugees in adapting to American life. By this time only the Sephardim lived exclusively on the south side; the majority of the Jewish population lived in the rapidly growing north side above 38th Street. By 1948 over 11 percent of employed Jews were professionals; 19 percent in sales; 43 percent proprietors; and 27 percent manufacturers and other workers.

Following World War II the Indianapolis Jewish community joined the nationwide United

Jewish Appeal to raise funds for the surviving European Jews. Local contributions rose from $196,000 (1945) to $625,000 (1946) and $1,004,600 (1948). After the creation of the state of Israel in 1948, larger portions of local funds went to support local synagogues, homes for the elderly, hospitals, and Jewish community centers.

In the 1970s Soviet Jews comprised the fifth wave of Jewish immigration to the city. They were, for the most part, non-practicing Jews who considered themselves Jews by reason of birth. Many of the synagogues and community organizations, including the Jewish Community Center (established 1926), assisted the Soviet emigres by providing language education, housing, and employment assistance. Since the breakup of the Soviet Union in 1991, several hundred Jews who emigrated from the former Soviet republics to escape increased anti-Semitism have settled in Greater Indianapolis.

Throughout the city's history the Jewish population faced minimal discrimination, due in part to their small numbers and early involvement in Indianapolis' civic, economic, and cultural life. By the 1920s, a period of rampant xenophobia and nativism, Jews were being excluded from private clubs, certain neighborhoods, and jobs. The KU KLUX KLAN directed its campaign of hate against Catholics, African-Americans, and Jews, and targeted Jewish-owned businesses as a threat to American society. The Jewish community adopted various methods to combat Klan propaganda. The editor of the *Indiana Jewish Chronicle* (established 1921, Indianapolis) advocated "silent contempt"; a B'nai B'rith lodge favored exposing Klan businessmen and voting against Klan candidates; the Jewish Federation promoted Americanization programs; and Rabbi Morris Feuerlicht became the community's principal and most vocal anti-Klan spokesman. By the 1940s any existing anti-Semitism was rather discreet, although some Jewish leaders attributed anti-Semitism to Jewish economic mobility and affiliations with socialist or liberal organizations. During the 1950s Jews established ties with local organizations to promote civil liberties and interfaith cooperation. Incidents of anti-Semitism, sparked by the JEWISH COMMUNITY RELATIONS COUNCIL'S (JCRC) challenge of religious practices in city schools and CHRISTMAS displays

on public property, continued in the 1960s and 1970s. In recent years JCRC and the Indiana Anti-Defamation League have combated anti-Semitism through public education programs.

Within the contemporary Indianapolis Jewish community the diverse groups are held together by common aspects of Jewish American life. There has been a drastic decline in the use of Yiddish and Ladino and a high rate of intermarriage with non-Jews. These factors have helped to diminish cultural boundaries within the Jewish community and to stimulate the replacement of social institutions unique to each group in favor of organizations which serve the total Jewish community.

CAROLYN S. BLACKWELL

Judith E. Endelman, *The Jewish Community of Indianapolis, 1849 to the Present* (Bloomington, Ind., 1984); Ethel and David Rosenberg, *To 120 Years! A Social History of the Indianapolis Hebrew Congregation* (Indianapolis, 1979); Indianapolis Hebrew Congregation Archives.

John Birch Society. Anticommunist organization. The John Birch Society is a nationwide organization dedicated to freeing the United States from the threat of a communist takeover. Robert H. W. Welch, Jr., founded the society in Indianapolis in 1958, meeting with 11 other men from various states at a northside home on December 8 and 9. The exact size of the organization has never been known due to its policy of semisecrecy.

During the early 1960s the society was the object of much controversy, its activities even being viewed with concern by the U.S. Justice Department. Although Indianapolis was not the center of those activities, local conservative leaders frequently expressed doubts about the society's tactics to the local newspapers. Over the protests of the INDIANAPOLIS HUMAN RIGHTS COMMISSION, the John Birch Society was one of several groups included in a lecture series offered to Indianapolis police trainees from 1966 to 1969. In 1965 union officials in Indianapolis claimed that the John Birch Society was attempting to infiltrate local affiliates of the AFL-CIO. By the end of the decade, however, the society was no longer considered to be a serious factor in Indiana politics.

In 1993 the John Birch Society still maintained a telephone number with an address in a downtown Indianapolis office building.

AMY SMITH

Indianapolis Times, Mar. 30, 1961, Oct. 21, 1962, June 30, 1965; *Indianapolis Star*, May 20, 1966, Dec. 6, 1968; *Indianapolis News*, Aug. 26, 1969.

John Herron Art Institute. See Herron School of Art

Johnson, Thomas L. "Sarge" (Mar., 1922–Mar. 14, 1980). Amateur boxing coach. Born in Millikin, Louisiana, Johnson was undefeated in 30 amateur fights as a lightweight with the United States Army prior to World War II. In the 1970s, he became one of the most influential amateur sports coaches in America.

Master Sergeant Thomas Johnson had called Indianapolis home for 25 years when he retired from the Army in 1965. Following his separation from the military, Sarge Johnson served as BOXING coach for the Camp Atterbury Job Corps Center at Edinburgh, Indiana. He also worked with the ROTC program at CRISPUS ATTUCKS HIGH SCHOOL and with the Indianapolis POLICE ATHLETIC LEAGUE. Coaching Indiana's Amateur Athletic Union boxing team, Johnson tutored 1970s national Golden Gloves champion Marvin Johnson. An assistant with the 1976 U.S. Olympic Boxing Team, Sarge counted Ray Leonard, Leon and Michael Spinks, and Howard Davis among his pupils. Representing the U.S. State Department, Johnson organized Indonesia's national boxing team, and in 1978 conducted a 17–day boxing clinic in Kenya. His American teams competed in over 40 countries during the 1970s.

On March 14, 1980, Sarge Johnson and all 21 U.S. National Boxing team members were killed in an airplane crash near Warsaw, Poland. Johnson was eulogized as an American goodwill ambassador and as a minister, taskmaster, psychologist, and shining example to America's youth. The Indianapolis Parks Department boxing club at Riverside Park was rechristened the Sarge Johnson Boxing Club in 1981.

R. DALE OGDEN
Indiana State Museum

Indiana Biography Series, Indiana State Library.

Johnson County. County adjacent to Indianapolis–Marion County on the south and part of the Indianapolis Metropolitan Statistical Area. In 1818 Jacob Whetzel determined to blaze a trail from Franklin County to Greene County, but settled instead on the bluffs of White River in what is now Johnson County. This trail, known as Whetzel's Trace, was used by many early settlers of Marion, Johnson, Morgan, and Shelby counties.

Johnson County was organized in 1822. Whetzel's Trace, the Ancient River Trail, and the Madison and Indianapolis State Road all facilitated settlement of the county, which was traversed by the White and Blue rivers and Sugar Creek. A site for the county seat was chosen near the geographic center of the county, with the town of Franklin platted there in 1823. It grew rapidly and was incorporated as a city with over 2,000 residents by the time of the Civil War.

The second important town in early Johnson County was Edinburgh. Platted in southern Johnson County in 1825, Edinburgh grew slowly until the MADISON AND INDIANAPOLIS RAILROAD was completed there in 1845. The population quickly doubled and Edinburgh became the leading grain and pork market in central Indiana, with merchants coming from as far away as Danville, Spencer, and Bloomington. Edinburgh's growth slowed with the completion of the Madison and Indianapolis Railroad to Indianapolis in 1847, but it continued to be the manufacturing center of the county throughout the 19th century.

Before the railroad arrived, Johnson County was served by a stagecoach line that ran from the capital to Madison along the Madison and Indianapolis State Road. Taverns were constructed in the county at five-mile intervals along the route to serve travelers and provide fresh horses. The coach was abandoned in the late 1840s.

Selected Statistics for Johnson County, 1990

Population	88,109
Population per Square Mile	275
Percent African-American	1.0
Percent 0 to 17 Years	27.0
Percent 65 Years and Over	10.6
Percent 25 Years and Over with a	
High School Degree or Equivalency	80.4
Percent 25 Years and Over with a College Degree	16.7
Per Capita Income in 1989	$17,562
Unemployment Rate (%)	3.6
Married-Couple Families as a	
Percent of Total Households	66.0
Median Home Value	$72,200

In 1835 the Indiana Baptist Education Society founded the Indiana Baptist Manual Labor Institute at Franklin. The IBES operated the institution until May, 1872, when it declared bankruptcy. During the summer of that year the Franklin College Association, a group of local residents who wanted to save the school, assumed the institute's debts and managed to reopen it in September. The name was officially changed to Franklin College, and the Franklin College Association operated it successfully until 1907 when it was incorporated as Franklin College of Indiana. As of 1993 Franklin College is recognized throughout the state and the Midwest as an excellent small liberal arts college.

The town of GREENWOOD was established in northern Johnson County in 1864. It had a population of around 350 for many years, but grew rapidly with the completion of the electric railway from Indianapolis in 1900. By 1902 Greenwood, Franklin, and Edinburgh were all connected to Indianapolis by INTERURBANS, and all were prosperous towns.

The demise of the RAILROADS and interurbans crippled Edinburgh. Already replaced as a market, the town lost its industry as well. Its population has declined since 1970 even though the population of Johnson County increased by over 25,000 during the same period. Franklin, with a 1990 population of 12,907, has remained a successful small college city.

Greenwood, a city of 11,869 in 1970, has far outstripped its former rivals in recent years. The growth of Indianapolis has led to much suburban residential and commercial development along U.S. 31 in Greenwood, including Greenwood Park Mall, the largest shopping center in the Indianapolis area. In 1990 Greenwood had a population of 26,265.

WILLIAM D. DALTON

Elba L. Branigin, *History of Johnson County, Indiana* (Indianapolis, 1913); U.S. Census.

Johnson Woods. Small northside neighborhood bounded by 44th and 46th streets, College and Central avenues. Oliver Johnson, a prosperous farmer, lived his entire life in the area. Born on his father's farm, now the site of the INDIANA STATE FAIRGROUNDS, he later built an impressive farmhouse (ca. 1862, 4456 North Park Avenue), which remains a testament to the family's early influence in southern WASHINGTON TOWNSHIP. As Indianapolis expanded northward at the turn of the century, the aging Johnson and his sons saw the advantage of subdividing the family property. In 1905 they filed an intention to convert a quarter section of land into town lots. The new suburb of "Oliver Johnson Woods" consisted of large properties lining four wide, boulevard-like streets. Indianapolis annexed the area in 1912, and by World War II the wooded lots were filled with architecturally diverse and impressive middle class homes.

During its early decades Johnson Woods was home to numerous executives and business leaders. Surrounded by the much larger MERIDIAN-KESSLER neighborhood, Johnson Woods has attracted the professional–white-collar middle class and remains the quiet, wooded, residential retreat Oliver Johnson intended.

SHERYL D. VANDERSTEL

Paul Diebold, "History of the Architecture of the Meridian-Kessler Neighborhood" (M.S. thesis, Ball State University, 1988); Howard Johnson, comp., *A Home in the Woods: Oliver Johnson's Reminiscences of Early Marion County* (Indianapolis, 1951).

Jones, James Warren "Jim" (May 13, 1931–Nov. 18, 1978). Founder of Peoples Temple Full Gospel Church and a colony at Jonestown, Guyana, where over 900 participated in mass murder-suicide. Born in Lynn, Indiana, Jones graduated from Richmond High School, worked at Reid Memorial Hospital, and later married. After attending Indiana University, Bloomington (1949–1951), he moved to Indianapolis where he intended to continue his studies and enter law school.

In June, 1952, Jones became student pastor at the southside Somerset Methodist Church where he began healing services and a campaign for racial integration. Around 1954 he established "Community Unity," an integrated congregation at Hoyt and Randolph streets, and preached occasionally at Laurel Street Tabernacle (Assembly of God), drawing large crowds. By 1956 he moved his church, renamed "Wings of Deliverance" and later "Peoples Temple," to 15th and North New Jersey streets, attracting defectors from his previous congregations. That June, Jones organized a massive religious convention at CADLE TABERNACLE, which drew a racially mixed audience exceeding 11,000 people. He later moved his church to the former Hebrew synagogue at 10th and Delaware streets and invited Archie Ijames, an African-American, to serve as associate pastor in his effort to integrate the church fully. Jones quickly attracted followers through psychic discernment, prophecy, speaking in tongues, and healing. He also began a social ministry, opening a soup kitchen that served nearly 3,000 meals a month, providing nursing care for the elderly, and unsuccessfully promoting a Cuban refugee relocation program for Indianapolis. In 1960 the Temple became affiliated with the Indianapolis-based CHRISTIAN CHURCH (DISCIPLES OF CHRIST), which applauded Jones for his ministry among the poor. Mayor CHARLES BOSWELL named Jones to chair the INDIANAPOLIS HUMAN RIGHTS COMMISSION (1961–1962) where he garnered great publicity for his promotion of neighborhood and public facility integration. During this time, Jones took classes at Butler University, from which he later received an education degree.

In 1962, following a rash of racist attacks on his home at 2327 Broadway and an alleged vision of nuclear destruction, Jones began a search for a new site for Peoples Temple. He took his multiracial "rainbow family" to Brazil, South America, but returned home to his foundering church in December, 1963, and was later ordained by the Disciples of Christ (1964).

Racial integration was an important, if unusual, element of Jim Jones' Peoples Temple Sunday School, 1502 N. New Jersey, in 1956. [Indiana Historical Society, Indianapolis Recorded, #C5766]

The next year, casting himself as a prophet who envisioned impending nuclear war, Jones led over 140 church members from Indianapolis to settle and establish their church in Redwood Valley, California. By 1972 Jones had established congregations in San Francisco (where he served on the city's housing authority) and Los Angeles, as well as followings in a dozen smaller cities. Jones also established Jonestown, a commune outpost in Guyana where most Temple members fled in 1977 following adverse newspaper coverage and government probes. During a congressional investigation of the Temple, U.S. Representative Leo J. Ryan of California and several reporters were murdered in Guyana as defectors attempted to leave the commune on November 18, 1978. Later that day Jones led his followers to mass suicide by drinking cyanide-laced fruit drink in a previously rehearsed ritual.

In the aftermath, Jones received mixed reviews from the Indianapolis public and press. Many praised his work among the city's poor and homeless and his crusades against racism and discrimination. Others portrayed him as an unbalanced, power-hungry fanatic who believed himself to be God. Following his October, 1971, return to Indianapolis to conduct a healing crusade, the INDIANAPOLIS STAR launched an investigation of Jones' ministry, focusing on alleged abuses, fake healings, and mass hypnosis. In early 1972, *Star* reporter Carolyn Pickering contacted the *San Francisco Examiner* for information about Jones' transplanted church, which led to a long-term *Examiner* investigation of Peoples Temple. Analyses in the Indianapolis press compared Jones with other notorious Hoosiers—mass murderer Charles Manson and Symbionese Liberation Army terrorist William Harris.

MARIAN K. TOWNE
Indiana University–Purdue University,
Indianapolis

Tim Reiterman with John Jacobs, *Raven: The Untold Story of the Rev. Jim Jones and His People* (New York, 1982); Sara Buchwald and Marian K. Towne, *The Onliest One Alive* (videotape available from the Church Federation of Greater Indianapolis and the Indiana Humanities Council); *Indianapolis Star*, Oct. 14, 1971, Nov. 19–26, 1978.

Jordan, Arthur (Sept. 1, 1855–Sept. 3, 1934). Businessman and philanthropist. Born in Madison, Indiana, in 1855, Jordan came to Indianapolis in his teens. In 1876 he purchased a small wholesale company dealing in eggs and butter and soon added a full range of poultry products. He expanded his market by packing perishable products in ice, later pioneering the use of refrigerated railroad cars to open the eastern market to midwestern poultry producers. By 1894 the Arthur Jordan Company had over 50 packing and cold storage plants in Indiana and Illinois; from that base, Jordan started other businesses. Locally, these included the Keyless Lock Company, the City Ice and Coal Company, and the Meridian Life Insurance Company.

Jordan believed strongly that wealth brought with it community responsibilities. In 1926 he gave BUTLER UNIVERSITY $1 million to build Jordan Hall on its new northside campus. He also arranged for the consolidation of the city's four music conservatories in the Arthur Jordan Conservatory of Music, forerunner to the present JORDAN COLLEGE OF FINE ARTS at Butler University. Jordan contributed land for buildings to the local YMCA and YWCA; a prominent Indianapolis YMCA bears his name.

In 1928 he established the Arthur Jordan Foundation with an endowment of $2 million, which has since grown to $11 million. The foundation supports projects in Marion County that carry on Jordan's interests in music and the YMCA, and it operates the BENJAMIN HARRISON HOME, which once served as the conservatory's dormitory. Jordan died in New York City.

KEVIN CORN
Indiana University–Purdue University,
Indianapolis

Jacob Piatt Dunn, *Indiana and Indianans* (Chicago, 1919), III, 1489–1491; *Who Was Who in America*.

Jordan College of Fine Arts, Butler University. On April 13, 1895, the Metropolitan School of Music (MSM) was founded by four private music teachers and opened for the summer at 134 North Illinois Street. By 1907 the success of the school required the construction of its own building at the intersection of Fort Wayne and North streets. That same year Oliver Willard Pierce, one of the original founders of the school, left MSM and established the College of Musical Art (CMA). CMA began in a building at 824 North Pennsylvania Street, adjacent to the then new city library on St. Clair Street. For several years there was keen competition between the two schools.

With the retirement of Pierce in 1918, CMA and its building were sold and the name of the school changed to the Indiana College of Music and Fine Arts (ICM&FA). MSM affiliated with BUTLER UNIVERSITY in 1924, followed by ICM&FA's Butler affiliation in 1927.

In June, 1928, ARTHUR JORDAN purchased the two schools and consolidated them into the Arthur Jordan Conservatory of Music. The following November, Jordan, a successful businessman and philanthropist, purchased two large homes and properties at 1116 and 1204 North Delaware Street as the site for the construction of a costly conservatory of music building. (The two homes had previously been owned by founders of two Indianapolis department stores, H. P. WASSON AND COMPANY and L. S. AYRES AND COMPANY.) In December, 1928, Jordan established the Arthur

Jordan Foundation, with assets of over $2 million. The foundation served as the board of trustees for the conservatory.

Radio studios and a certificate program were established in 1939, which led to the initial broadcast by WAJC-FM as the university radio station in 1950. The year before, 1949, the conservatory's name was changed to Jordan College of Music (JCM). This was followed by the merger of JCM with Butler University in 1951 to become a college within the university. The college's departments were dance, music, radio and television, and theater. Major construction occurred on the Butler campus in the early 1960s, including a small broadcasting and transmitter building, a 400–foot tower for WAJC-FM, Lilly Hall as the home of the four academic departments, and CLOWES MEMORIAL HALL, then home of the INDIANAPOLIS SYMPHONY ORCHESTRA and site of the major performances by the college. The availability of Clowes Hall during the next 30 years made possible numerous performances of instrumental and vocal ensembles and regular full evenings of ballet, including annual performances of *The Nutcracker*. In addition there were 22 consecutive Romantic Festivals, performances of Leonard Bernstein's *Mass* and Shakespeare's *A Midsummer-Night's Dream*, and most recently a Soviet Arts Week.

The name of the college changed again in 1978 to the Jordan College of Fine Arts to reflect its wider scope plus the addition of art history offerings. In 1992 the radio and television department's opportunities were greatly enhanced by the establishment of WTBU-Channel 69, Butler's new television station. In 1993 the radio station was sold to promote better fund-raising for more popular television offerings.

Over the past 98 years Jordan College and its predecessors have graduated over 3,500 undergraduate majors and nearly 900 graduate students in the fields of dance, music, radio–television, and theater.

JACK L. EATON
Butler University

Judaism. The term Judaism refers to the religion, philosophy, and way of life of the Jews. Judaism has developed and adapted to changing circumstances over its long history. Although Judaism cannot be thought of as monolithic, it can be considered to be based on three concepts—belief in God, God's revelation of the Torah to Israel, and Israel as the people who live by the Torah in obedience to God. Jews have interpreted adherence to these beliefs in many ways.

Judaism requires a community and communal organizations. Wherever Jews settled in the United States in sufficient numbers they formed Jewish organizations, usually beginning with a burial society, a synagogue, then benevolent and charitable associations, Hebrew schools, and so forth. While many Jews would consider the synagogue to be the focus of their Judaism, others might view their activity in Jewish charitable or educational organizations as their expression of Judaism.

Jews first settled in Indianapolis in 1849. Attracted to the growing commercial expansion of the city, which followed the completion of the first rail line to Indianapolis in 1847, these Jews were part of a movement of German Jewish immigrants who spread out across the country in the mid–19th century. Often beginning as peddlers, these migrants eventually settled down to life as storekeepers in dozens of midwestern, western, and southern communities. Many Jewish communities trace their origins to these mid–19th century merchants.

Seven years after the arrival of the first three Jewish residents—Alexander and Sarah Franco and Moses Woolf—a group of 14 men founded the city's first synagogue, the INDIANAPOLIS HEBREW CONGREGATION, on November 2, 1856. Within two years the congregation had purchased land for a cemetery, rented rooms, hired S. Berman to act as cantor, sexton, and ritual slaughterer (to provide kosher meat), and ordered prayer books, a Torah scroll, and other religious artifacts. The congregation modified Orthodox Jewish practices fairly quickly and was an early adherent of Reform Judaism.

As the Jewish community in Indianapolis grew and prospered, so did its synagogue. Most of the city's Jews were in the clothing trade—about 70 percent of the clothing businesses in Indianapolis were Jewish-owned—and the Civil War brought increased orders for uniforms. The congregation dedicated its first building, located on East Market Street, in 1868. The congregation's rabbi, Mayer Messing (1845–1930), remained with the synagogue for 40 years and was active in the city's charitable and civic life, as was his assistant and then successor, MORRIS M. FEUERLICHT (1879–1959). Other Jewish organizations established during the 1860s and early 1870s included charitable organizations such as the Hebrew Ladies Benevolent Society (1859), men's social clubs, of which only B'nai B'rith Abraham Lodge No. 58 (founded 1864) survives, and mutual benefit societies such as the Tree of Life Mutual Benefit Association (founded 1870).

Eastern European immigration substantially increased the size of the Indianapolis Jewish community. In 1870 around 500 Jews lived in the city. In 1894 the *Indianapolis News* estimated that there were 2,125 synagogue members in the capital. The local Industrial Removal Office estimated the number at between 6,000 and 7,000 in 1910. The Jewish population has generally remained at 1 percent of the city's population, except for the period immediately following World War I, when it rose to 2.5 percent. In the early 1990s the Jewish Federation of Greater Indianapolis estimated the population at 11,000.

Impoverished Jewish immigrants from eastern Europe brought diversity and change to an increasingly middle class and Americanized community. These newcomers settled on the south side where they created a series of synagogues, each founded by Jews from a particular part of Europe. Sharah Tefilla, originally known as Chevro Bene Jacob, came first, founded by Polish Jews about 1870. The Hungarian Hebrew Ohev Zedeck Congregation followed in 1884. In 1899 Ohev Zedeck purchased the vacated building of the Indianapolis Hebrew Congregation on East Market Street. (The congregation, following its members, had moved north to 10th and Delaware streets; it moved farther north in 1958.)

Immigrants from Russia established the third Orthodox immigrant synagogue, Knesses Israel, in 1889. Although the founders of the United Hebrew Congregation (1903) were all Galician immigrants, they wanted to overcome the divisiveness of "old country" attachments and establish a "modern" Orthodox synagogue. Ezras Achim, founded in 1910 and known as the peddlers' synagogue, was the last of the eastern European immigrant synagogues.

Jews from Monastir, then a part of Turkish Macedonia, began settling in Indianapolis in 1906. Sephardic Jews, primarily from Turkey, Greece, and Syria, formed a small proportion of the Jewish immigration to America. Like all Jews, their language and customs had been influenced by the cultures in which they had lived and thus the eastern European majority perceived them as "different." Indianapolis was one of a handful of American cities with a Sephardic Jewish community. The original group from Monastir attracted more newcomers and in 1913 they founded Congregation Sepharad of Monastir. The name was changed to Etz Chaim Congregation in 1919.

A Jewish community requires more than synagogues to sustain it. In the late 19th and 20th centuries Indianapolis Jews established a wide range of organizations, including benevolent societies, charities, and Zionist organizations. United Hebrew Schools, a community-supported afternoon Hebrew school, began in 1911. It became the Jewish Educational Association and an affiliate of the Jewish Federation in 1924 (since 1980, the Bureau of Jewish Education). The Jewish Federation, founded in 1905, established a unified method of fund-raising and distribution of funds to support local and national Jewish organizations. The federation provided direct relief to poor Jews, established relief giving agencies such as the Communal Building, a southside settlement house previously known as the Nathan Morris House, and made allocations to both national organizations and local groups. It became the Jewish Welfare Federation in 1948 and, more recently, the JEWISH FEDERATION OF GREATER INDIANAPOLIS.

After 1924 and the imposition of strict national immigration quotas, the growth of the Indianapolis Jewish community slowed considerably. The existing community prospered, however, and Jews began moving out of the south side. Some of these former southsiders founded Central Hebrew Congregation in 1923. Other than that, synagogue development from the 1920s on involved relocations and mergers rather than new congregations. As the community became increasingly native-born, the importance of national origins and allegiances declined.

As early as 1915 a group of former southsiders and leaders of Sharah Tefilla had established a synagogue, Congregation Beth El, on the north side. Beth El merged with the Hungarian Congregation Ohev Zedeck in March, 1927, and became Congregation Beth-El Zedeck. Under the guidance of an early rabbi, Milton Steinberg, it became a liberally oriented Conservative congregation. Today it is affiliated with both the Conservative and Reconstructionist movements. Beth-El Zedeck moved to new facilities on the far north side in 1958.

Central Hebrew Congregation and United Hebrew Congregation, still located on the south side, merged in 1957 to become the largest Orthodox Jewish congregation in Indiana. A year later, the congregation, renamed Congregation B'nai Torah, moved to its present location on the city's far north side.

Sharah Tefilla, Knesses Israel, and Ezras Achim merged to become United Orthodox Hebrew Congregation and left the south side in 1966. Membership in United Orthodox Hebrew Congregation preserves a link to the past and the old southside community. Many of the members also belong to one of the three major synagogues: Indianapolis Hebrew Congregation (Reform), Beth-El Zedeck (Conservative-Reconstructionist), or B'nai Torah (Orthodox). Etz Chaim Congregation, the synagogue of the Sephardic Jews, moved to the far north side in 1963. Membership in Etz Chaim is seen as a way for the members to preserve their Sephardic heritage and identity, although many also belong to one of the major synagogues.

Indianapolis Judaism reflects the contradictory trends of American Jewry as a whole. The Hebrew Academy of Indianapolis, a Jewish day school that opened in 1971, spoke to the desire of many Jews to strengthen Jewish identity and Jewish education through private education. Conversely, the number of Jews who marry non-Jews has increased from 10 percent in the 1960s to nearly one third today. Outreach, a support group for religiously blended couples, meets at the Indianapolis Hebrew Congregation and attempts to help intermarried couples identify with Judaism. Jewish activities in Indianapolis also center on support for Israel and, in recent years, resettlement of Soviet Jews. Between 1989 and 1991 over 200 Soviet Jews settled in Indianapolis.

JUDITH E. ENDELMAN
Henry Ford Museum & Greenfield Village

Judith E. Endelman, *The Jewish Community of Indianapolis, 1849 to the Present* (Bloomington, Ind., 1984).

Steven T. Judy Case. Sensational murder trial that resulted in the reimposition of capital punishment in Indiana. Judy (1956-March 9, 1981) was tried and convicted by a Morgan County jury for the 1979 rape and murder of Terry Lee Chasteen and the drowning of her three small children. An Indianapolis native, Judy's childhood was characterized by parental drunkenness, abuse, and neglect. His first documented sex crime occurred when he was thirteen and during the next eight years he committed at least three other savagely violent sexual offenses. At the time of the Chasteen murders he was free on a $75,000 bond for a 1977 supermarket robbery.

Judy, whom a psychiatrist labeled a "dangerous sadist" and a "sociopath," confessed to the Chasteen killings but pleaded not guilty by reason of insanity. When convicted, he asked the judge to impose the death penalty, apparently because he believed in reincarnation. The case attracted an enormous amount of attention in the state in general, and the Indianapolis metropolitan area in particular, because it resulted in the first execution in Indiana in 20 years. Indeed, from 1972 to 1977 the state had had no death penalty at all following a U.S. Supreme Court ruling that struck down many states' capital punishment laws. Judy died in the electric chair at the Indiana State Prison while the INDIANA CIVIL LIBERTIES UNION and others opposed to capital punishment held a candlelight vigil outside the site of the execution.

PATRICIA FOGLEMAN

Julian, George Washington (May 5, 1817–July 7, 1899). Politician. Born in Wayne

County, Indiana, and educated in the common schools, Julian entered the teaching profession at age 18. Admitted to the bar in 1840, he practiced successively in New Castle, Greenfield, and Centerville. In 1845, he was elected to the Indiana House of Representatives as a Whig; two years later he was defeated in his attempt to receive the Whig nomination for state senator. Opposed to repudiation of the state debt and a staunch abolitionist, he joined the Free Soil party in 1848 and was elected to Congress. Defeated in his bid for reelection in 1850, Julian became the Free Soil vice-presidential running mate for John P. Hale in 1852.

Having attended the Pittsburgh convention that organized the Republican party in 1856, Julian was elected to Congress on its ticket in 1860. From 1861 to 1871 he served in Congress, where he became known as an advocate of abolition, civil rights, and WOMEN'S RIGHTS AND SUFFRAGE. As chairman of the committee on public lands, Julian played a significant role in the passage of the Homestead Act. He was also a member of the committee on the conduct of the war. In 1867, Julian was one of the committee of seven appointed by the House to prepare articles of impeachment against President Andrew Johnson. In 1868, he proposed an amendment to the Constitution in support of women's suffrage. Defeated in the 1870 election, Julian joined the Liberal Republicans in 1872.

Leaving politics in 1873, he moved to the new Indianapolis suburb of IRVINGTON where he practiced law. Having joined the Democratic party, Julian was appointed surveyor general of New Mexico by President Grover Cleveland in 1885. He served in this capacity until 1889. Julian published several notable works concerning the politics of the era, including *Political Recollections* (1884) and his father-in-law's biography, *Life of Joshua R. Giddings* (1892).

MOLLY HIPSKIND

Patrick W. Riddleberger, *George Washington Julian: Radical Republican* (Indianapolis, 1966).

The Julian Center. Human services agency for women, established in 1975 by the Episcopal Diocese of Indianapolis. It became an affiliate of UNITED WAY in 1981, after the staff of the counseling center, the agency's first division, documented the need for expanded services, particularly for adult female victims of sexual abuse in childhood, rape, and domestic violence. In 1982, in response to a COMMUNITY SERVICE COUNCIL study that established the need for a local battered woman's shelter, The Julian Center opened Sojourner. The center moved twice between 1984 and 1989 to meet a continually growing demand for services.

Since 1990 the agency has increased its emphasis on the prevention of violence against women by developing educational programs and materials that can be used with a variety of populations. By 1992, Sojourner, the shelter for battered women, was providing safe shelter, counseling, and educational services to over 700 women and children annually; the counseling center was providing group and individual counseling services to over 400 women.

NAOMI TROPP
The Julian Center

Junior League of Indianapolis. Community-oriented volunteer organization of women. The Junior League of Indianapolis (JLI) began in 1921 as part of the Association of Junior Leagues International, an organization which now includes 274 leagues with 180,000 women throughout North America and Great Britain.

Women between the ages of 21 and 37, regardless of race, religion, or ethnic origin, may join as provisional members. After completing one year of training women become active members until age 45 when they must become sustaining members. JLI membership, as of June, 1993, included 105 provisional, 459 active, and 804 sustaining members; of the active and provisional members 83 percent were married, 64 percent were parents, 94 percent held a college degree or higher, and 65 percent were employed outside the home.

The mission of JLI is to train volunteers as community leaders to improve local social, economic, educational, and civic conditions. Headquartered in the historic Schnull-Rauch House at

3050 North Meridian Street, JLI acts as a local advocacy group on issues relating to voluntarism, children, aging, domestic violence, and women. In responding to community needs, JLI identifies and brings together other local agencies to implement the necessary programs. Trained JLI volunteers initiate, develop, and fund the projects temporarily, with the goal of recruiting and training volunteers within the community to staff and maintain the programs. JLI volunteers and funds are phased out when the community develops the means to perpetuate the projects.

The first of the major service projects undertaken by JLI involved the creation of the initial occupational therapy clinic at RILEY HOSPITAL FOR CHILDREN in 1924. The women organized, staffed, equipped, financed, and maintained the department. The success of the program led to the development of two more clinics at the Robert W. Long Hospital. JLI also helped establish the James Whitcomb Riley Child Guidance Clinic in cooperation with INDIANA UNIVERSITY MEDICAL CENTER in 1949 to provide treatment for emotionally disturbed children and training for child psychologists. JLI established a trust fund in 1924 to aid handicapped children. It also initiated an endowment fund in 1988 to provide long-term funding for the organization.

In 1976 and 1977, collaborating with the HISTORIC LANDMARKS FOUNDATION OF INDIANA and the INDIANAPOLIS HISTORIC PRESERVATION COMMISSION, JLI helped produce pamphlets and walking tours of historic homes in the OLD NORTHSIDE and LOCKERBIE SQUARE neighborhoods. Other community projects have included the INDIANAPOLIS SYMPHONY ORCHESTRA, Children's Theatre, Indianapolis Children's Zoo, Ronald McDonald House, Heritage Place, and the Greater Indianapolis Literacy League. More recently the group has provided assistance for the Ryan White Foundation and the Indiana chapter of the Nature Conservancy.

AMY GLOWACKI

Indianapolis Junior League, *400 Women We'd Like You to Know* (Indianapolis, 1952); Junior League of Indianapolis, *Junior League of Indianapolis* (Indianapolis, 1990); Indianapolis Junior League, *Volunteer Service Headlines Our Story* (Indianapolis, 1954).

Justices of the Peace. From the earliest settlement of the state, justices of the peace (JPs) were constitutional officers who served five-year terms as part-time magistrates. Each township in Indiana elected a JP, who did not have to be a lawyer. JP courts were designed to be easily accessible to every citizen, who could bring a claim without an attorney. JPs had countywide jurisdiction over marriages, petty crimes, civil cases involving real and personal property of small value, and, later, traffic violations. A JP could also issue "peace bonds," similar to a temporary restraining order. Township constables worked in tandem with JPs to serve summonses and enforce court orders.

By 1939 the Marion County JP courts were so heavily used that two countywide common pleas courts were added to handle traffic and misdemeanor cases. In the 1950s, however, there were several attempts to reform or abolish the JP courts due to money scandals and the outdated nature of the system. The General Assembly enacted legislation calling for statewide changes in the JP system in 1957 and 1959, but both laws were found unconstitutional. In Marion County, common pleas, municipal, and criminal courts effected their own reforms by simply assuming more and more JP responsibilities, leaving the JPs primarily responsible only for marriages by the 1960s.

A 1970 statewide referendum removed JPs as constitutional officials and led to a 1975 state law that abolished all JP courts. Only in Marion County were the JP courts replaced with eight township small claims courts (Franklin Township voted against the idea) supervised by the Marion County Circuit Court judge. These courts, commonly referred to as "people's courts," function much like the earlier JP courts and deal mainly with landlord-tenant disputes, unpaid bills, and property damage amounting to less than $1,500.

MICHELLE D. HALE

Juvenile Justice. Prior to the 20th century Indianapolis juvenile delinquents were treated the same as adult criminals. By the 1890s local "progressive" thinkers began to object to handling children, who they thought were products of bad environments, in the same manner as adults. They argued that the state had a special responsibility to save wayward children.

Judge George W. Stubbs, judge of the city police court, spearheaded the creation of the juvenile justice system in Indianapolis. He began holding separate sessions for child offenders in 1901, eventually acquiring secluded offices in the basement of the courthouse. By taking children out of police court he hoped to protect them from further negative influences and to prevent the stigma of being branded a criminal, as well as to provide each child with proper guidance and supervision.

After visiting the Chicago juvenile court, Stubbs and local reformers drafted a juvenile court law and successfully steered it through the state legislature in 1903. This state law, which affected only Indianapolis at the time, became the nation's second juvenile court law. The Indianapolis court was organized separately with a full-time judge, two paid probation officers, and a system of volunteer probation officers. The judge had the authority to hold informal investigations and hearings and to determine punishment on a case-by-case basis, unlike adult criminal proceedings. The law further prohibited the incarceration of juvenile delinquents with adults. Subsequent legislation in 1905 and 1907 extended the court's jurisdiction to include cases involving contributory delinquency and neglected and dependent children.

Since the original intent of the juvenile court law was to reform rather than punish child offenders, early judges usually scolded the child and either dropped the charges or sentenced particularly troubled youth to supervised probation. Probation officers were middle class men and women recruited by the Children's Aid Association to supervise a single child weekly. The majority of early delinquency cases involved boys who committed petty larceny or status crimes (truancy or incorrigibility, for example), and the court reported few repeat offenders. More serious offenders were sentenced to a state or private reform school, such as the Indiana Boys' School, where they stayed until they were considered rehabilitated. Dependent and neglected children became wards of the court and were placed in state institutions or private homes.

During its first two decades the Indianapolis court was emulated nationally, and locally the court received many resources and much community support. By 1910 the court leased a detention home at 28 West North Street for temporary care of children whose cases could not be immediately processed. A Citizens Juvenile Court Bi-Partisan Committee, the first of several such organizations, began in 1918 to help oversee the court's growing operation. In the early 1920s legislation provided for more professional probation staff, one of whom had to be an African-American.

By the 1930s individualized informal attention began to give way to impersonal processing of cases. A 1937 CHARITY ORGANIZATION SOCIETY study of Indianapolis juvenile delinquency cited major problems with the court: meager investigations; referees hearing cases without the judge; perfunctory probationary supervision; insufficient coordination with social welfare agencies; and inadequate facilities. Despite a growing number of programs for juvenile delinquents conducted by the Marion County Welfare Department, Indianapolis Police Department, Indianapolis Public Schools, and a number of private social welfare organizations, rates of repeat offenders continued to rise.

The social disruption and growth in urban population that occurred during and after World War II brought increased incidence of violent juvenile crimes, which by the 1950s were making the headlines of local newspapers. Citizens began demanding retribution rather than reform of juvenile delinquents. One result was the creation of the Youth Advisory Council of Marion County and the Citizens Committee on Juvenile Delinquents in the 1940s and 1950s. These groups studied the juvenile justice system and made recommendations for improvement. Responding to these suggestions, a new juvenile court law, enacted in 1941 and reenacted in 1945, made the court tougher on juvenile crime. The law lowered the age at which juveniles could be transferred to adult criminal courts and introduced more formal court procedures, but did not significantly alter the court's social welfare mentality. With the move to the site of the present juvenile justice center (located at 25th Street and Keystone Avenue) in 1958, court officials promised increased effectiveness in the combined detention home and juvenile court facilities.

During the 1960s public dissatisfaction continued to mount over what some believed were the Indianapolis court's too lenient policies. Reinforcing this call for strictness in handling juvenile offenders were several decisions by the U.S. Supreme Court in the 1960s that required juvenile courts to ensure due process, but also forced the local court to adopt more of the procedures of adult criminal courts. A juvenile caseload that topped 10,000 cases annually tended to nullify these conservative reform attempts, since police, social workers, and court officials struggled simply to process cases rather than mete out tougher sentences. Police officers abandoned counseling programs and increased arrest efforts, a circumstance that forced the court increasingly to invoke automatic probation with little or no supervision and counseling. Commitments to reform school also rose but became progressively short and ineffectual. Juvenile delinquency rates in Indianapolis continued to rise, and bewildered citizens blamed families, schools, churches and "the community."

When Indianapolis became a Model Cities site in the 1970s, the juvenile court began to sponsor federally funded youth work training, education, counseling, and family programs. But these programs often focused on serious repeat offenders and involved institutionalization rather than prevention as the way to satisfy the community's need for security. A new juvenile code in 1978, while it upheld the ideal of the court as child protector and reformer, acknowledged that there was a class of unredeemable delinquents who should be treated as adult criminals. Major changes in the law included forcing parents to participate in rehabilitation programs, regular delinquent evaluation, lowered age limits for youth waivers to adult criminal court, more standardized court procedures, and limited public access to juvenile records.

The number of annual juvenile delinquency cases continued to climb throughout the 1980s, stressing the juvenile justice system's limited resources and blocking officials' ability to deal with cases effectively. As of the early 1990s most youth offenders receive little personal rehabilitation or counseling unless they are serious repeat offenders. Rates of repeat offenders have reached 70 percent, with the incidence of violent crime committed by younger and female delinquents rising. Additionally, the worst areas of delinquency in Indianapolis have remained essentially the same central-city neighborhoods as those of the 1930s. Problems within the system today are compounded by larger social trends relating to poverty, drug usage, gangs, and changing family lifestyles.

MICHELLE D. HALE

Indianapolis Newspaper Index ("Juvenile Court"), Indiana State Library; James A. Collins, "The Juvenile Court Movement in Indiana," *Indiana Magazine of History*, 28 (Mar., 1932), 1–8; National Youth Administration of Indiana et al., *Juvenile Delinquency in Marion County, 1924–1934* (1936); William A. Kerr, "Foreword: Indiana's New Juvenile Code," *Indiana Law Review*, 12 (No. 1, 1979), 1–30.

Kaeser, William F. (Oct. 31, 1908–July 17, 1987). Commercial artist and fine arts painter. Born in Durlach, Germany, Kaeser came to the United States in 1923. He attended the Leonardo da Vinci Art School in New York City and was a graduate of the HERRON SCHOOL OF ART and Indiana University. Among his art instructors were WILLIAM FORSYTH, CLIFTON WHEELER, PAUL HADLEY, and Frank Schoonover.

Kaeser was a founder and the first teacher of the INDIANAPOLIS ART LEAGUE in 1934 and president of the Indiana Artists Club from 1936 to 1938. In 1939 he painted the mural *Loggers Clearing the Land* for the Pendleton, Indiana, post office; and his award-winning still life, *Rubber Plant*, was one of four works from Indiana in the American Art Exhibition at the New York World's Fair in 1939.

Kaeser was instrumental in the founding and promotion of The Twenty and The Hoosier Five—two groups of Indiana artists who exhibited their work in various locations throughout the state in the 1950s, 1960s, and 1970s. He had an extensive exhibition record with over 30 HOOSIER SALON art exhibitions; and his paintings appeared in numerous juried competitions, including those at the Carnegie Institute (Pittsburgh), the Midwest Arts Exhibition (Kansas City), the Pennsylvania Academy of Fine Arts (Philadelphia), the Cincinnati Art Museum, and the Corcoran Gallery (Washington, D.C.). In Indianapolis his works are in the permanent art collections of Indiana University–Purdue University at Indianapolis, the Indianapolis Public Schools, the Jefferson National Life Insurance Company, the Second Presbyterian Church, the Indianapolis Art League, the Irvington Historical Society, the Indiana Employment Security Division, and Ameritech.

FRANK N. OWINGS, JR.

Indianapolis Art League, *The Edge of Town* (Indianapolis, 1989); Irvington Historical Society, *The Irvington Group* (Indianapolis, 1984); Flora Lauter, *Indiana Artists Active 1940* (Spencer, Ind., 1941).

Kahn Tailoring Company. Tailoring and retail clothing business. The son of Alsatian Jewish immigrants, Henry Kahn (1860–1934) attended BUTLER UNIVERSITY and trained as a tailor with his father. In 1886 he opened a small tailor shop at 14 East Washington Street. The business soon thrived and by 1898 filled a four-story building at the northwest corner of Meridian and Washington streets. By the early 1910s Kahn Tailoring maintained offices and production rooms at 800 North Capitol and a retail store at 2 West Washington Street, which later moved across Meridian Street to the Kahn Building.

Kahn employed newly arrived European Jewish immigrants and operated a social welfare office, which provided a physician, health care, and night school for them. The company also maintained a social center that sponsored evening and weekend activities for employees and an orchestra that played during lunch.

The tailoring firm was a principal manufacturer of uniforms for the United States military during World War I and remained a major supplier through World War II. Following Kahn's death in 1934, son-in-law Mortimer C. Furscott succeeded as company president and directed a steady expansion. By 1948 the business encompassed its Indianapolis factory and 12 retail stores nationwide, including a Washington, D.C., store near the White House that outfitted Mrs. Harry Truman and daughter Margaret in 1947. Over 2,000 dealers reportedly carried Kahn's clothing by the late 1940s.

In November, 1954, Kahn merged with Globe Tailoring of Cincinnati, which became the

Kahn Tailoring Company, at the northwest corner of Washington and Meridian streets, in 1906.
[Indiana Historical Society, Bass Collection, #6546]

new base of production. Kahn maintained a retail tailor shop at 7 North Meridian Street, and became Hilton-Kahn Tailors on East Market Street in the late 1960s. By 1970 the Kahn name had vanished from the local tailoring trade.

SHERYL D. VANDERSTEL

Indianapolis Star, Aug. 15, 1934, Nov. 2, 1954; Indianapolis Times, Jan. 1, 1948.

Kaufman, Bess Robbins (Jan. 9, 1905– May 3, 1961). Legislator and attorney. A native of Anderson, Indiana, Bess Robbins came to Indianapolis as a young girl. She attended the Indianapolis public schools, graduated from MANUAL HIGH SCHOOL, attended the Indiana Law School, Indianapolis, and received a bachelor of laws degree from Indiana University. Following admission to the bar in 1925, she opened a law office in Indianapolis. She continued to practice under her maiden name after her marriage in 1936.

Kaufman became interested in politics at an early age, serving as a delegate to the Democratic state convention and belonging to the Marion County Democratic Women's Club prior to her election to the Indiana General Assembly. Her campaign for a seat in the Indiana House of Representatives in 1928 was unsuccessful, but in 1932 she became one of the first Democratic women to be elected to the Indiana House. She served in the sessions of 1933, 1937, and 1939.

Kaufman was an active legislator, particularly in the 1937 session when she served as chair of the Committee on Public Morals, ranking member of one of the judiciary committees, and introduced or cosponsored 30 bills, 10 of which became law. Though somewhat less active in the other sessions, she supported bills that concerned women's rights, humanitarian affairs, and matters relating to courts and the law, among other subjects.

Defeated in her bid for reelection in 1940, Kaufman continued her law practice until her death.

MARTHA WRIGHT
Indiana State Library

Keating, Thomas R. (Oct. 11, 1939–Aug. 23, 1985). Newspaper columnist. An Indianapolis native, Keating graduated from Cathedral Grade School and High School on the city's near north side and attended Ball State and Indiana universities. He was a real estate salesman before joining the INDIANAPOLIS STAR in 1966 as a police reporter. By virtue of his flair for the human interest story, he was awarded a regular column in 1971 and became an institution through his daily chronicles of the city's ordinary lives.

Over the following 14 years and approximately 3,500 columns, Keating conveyed anecdotes and character sketches drawn from throughout the world and all levels of society; his specialty, however, was the local common man and woman. He won numerous journalistic and civic awards and published a book of selected columns, Indiana Faces and Other Places, in 1982.

Keating left the Star in January, 1985, to become director of communications for LILLY ENDOWMENT. He died suddenly eight months later. The Thomas R. Keating Memorial Scholarship Fund, endowed in 1986 with corporate and private contributions and grants from the Lilly Endowment and the INDIANAPOLIS FOUNDATION, assists college students interested in feature writing.

DAN CARPENTER

Thomas R. Keating, Indiana Faces and Other Places (Indianapolis, 1982); Barbara Hager, "In Focus: Thomas R. Keating," The Indiana Publisher, 37 (Dec., 1972), 10; Indianapolis Star, Jan. 11, 1985, Aug. 24, 1985, Aug. 22, 1986, Dec. 9, 1986.

Keller, Amelia R. (Jan. 12, 1871–Jan. 28, 1943). Physician and suffragist. One of the first women physicians to practice in Indianapolis, Keller was born in Cleveland, Ohio, but came to Indianapolis while a young girl, where she lived for the rest of her life. She graduated from Indianapolis High School (later SHORTRIDGE HIGH SCHOOL), attended the Woman's Medical College of Chicago, and earned her medical degree from the Central College of Physicians and Surgeons in Indianapolis in 1893. In addition to a busy general practice, she served as associate professor of diseases of children at the INDIANA UNIVERSITY

SCHOOL OF MEDICINE and lectured on eugenics and public health.

Keller was best known for her leadership in the movement for WOMEN'S RIGHTS AND SUFFRAGE. As the first president of the Woman's Franchise League of Indiana, serving from 1911 to 1917, she broadened the league's work to cover the entire state of Indiana, with thousands of members and an efficient statewide organization. (The league played a significant role in the General Assembly's ratification of the 19th Amendment in 1920.) Keller also served as editor of the suffrage department of the Citizens League of Indiana's monthly magazine, *The Citizen*.

After the suffrage battle was won Keller became active in the REPUBLICAN PARTY, working with many women's organizations within the party and making speeches for party candidates. She also continued her club work, serving as first vice-president of the Indiana Federation of Clubs and president of the Indianapolis Local Council of Women.

MARTHA WRIGHT
Indiana State Library

Kemper, David Jackson (Dec. 24, 1789–May 24, 1870).

Episcopal priest and missionary bishop of Indiana and Missouri. A native of Pleasant Valley, New York, and graduate of Columbia College (1809), Kemper was ordained as deacon (1811) and priest (January 23, 1814) and spent 20 years as assistant to William White, bishop of Philadelphia and presiding bishop of the Episcopal Church in America. From 1831 to 1835 Kemper served as pastor of St. Paul's Episcopal Church in Norwalk, Connecticut. In September, 1835, the General Convention of the Episcopal Church, meeting in Philadelphia, appointed Kemper its first missionary bishop, assigning him to the diocese of Indiana and Missouri (which was later expanded to include Kansas and the Upper Midwest). During his 14 years as acting bishop of the Diocese of Indiana, Kemper oversaw the creation of 23 parishes throughout the state and advocated the election of a full-time bishop, which occurred with the appointment of the Reverend George Upfold of Pittsburgh in 1849. Kemper continued to serve as bishop of the Northwest and later as bishop of Wisconsin (1860–1870).

Concerned with the shortage of Episcopal churches in the West, Kemper toured the diocese and raised funds for new congregations. He visited Indianapolis in January and February, 1837, and spoke at the Methodist and Presbyterian churches to raise money for CHRIST CHURCH, organized in 1838 as the first Episcopal church in the city. Throughout 1841–1842 he substituted at the parish while the congregation searched for a pastor. Moved by the dearth of clergymen willing to serve in the West, Kemper later founded the Nashota Mission, west of Milwaukee, Wisconsin, in 1840 to train young men for the ministry. He is memorialized with a statue and the east window of the north transept of Christ Church.

DAVID G. VANDERSTEL
Indiana University–Purdue University,
Indianapolis

Eli Lilly, *History of the Little Church on the Circle: Christ Church Parish, Indianapolis, 1837–1955* (Indianapolis, 1957); *History of the Episcopal Diocese of Indianapolis, 1838–1988* (Dallas, Texas, 1988).

Kemper House (Pierson-Griffiths House).

Historic house located at 1028 North Delaware Street; Indianapolis office of Historic Landmarks Foundation of Indiana. It is often referred to as "the wedding cake house." Businessman Charles Pierson constructed the house in 1873 for his new bride, Mary Alice Scofield. An undocumented architect designed the house, incorporating elements of the Greek Revival and Italianate styles. The Piersons occupied the house nine months before selling it. Subsequent owners of note, Mr. and Mrs. John Lewis Griffiths, owned the house from 1897 to 1914. Mr. Griffiths served in the Indiana House of Representatives and as consul general in Liverpool and London.

Following a series of owners and a variety of uses, the house was saved from demolition when philanthropist and industrialist ELI LILLY purchased it in 1962. After renovation of the house Lilly donated it to the Episcopal Diocese of Indianapolis for use as a curate's residence and meeting space. It was dedicated as the Kemper House, in honor of Reverend DAVID JACKSON KEMPER, Indiana's first Episcopal bishop (1835–1849). In 1977 the Episcopal diocese gave the Kemper House to HISTORIC LANDMARKS FOUNDATION OF INDIANA, a nonprofit historic preservation organization founded by Lilly in 1960. Today it serves as the Indianapolis Regional Office of Historic Landmarks Foundation.

SUZANNE T. ROLLINS

Robert F. Kennedy Speech (April 4, 1968).

On the evening of April 4, 1968, as more than a hundred cities erupted in violence following the murder of Martin Luther King, Jr., Senator Robert F. Kennedy (D-N.Y.) stood before a mostly African-American audience in Indianapolis and made a moving personal appeal for calm. Kennedy had come seeking votes in Indiana's May presidential primary. Since state Democratic leaders opposed his candidacy, Kennedy's staff

Robert F. Kennedy announced the murder of Martin Luther King, Jr. to a stunned Indianapolis crowd on April 4, 1968. Kennedy's plea for a peaceful response to the tragedy is credited with helping keep the city calm in the days that followed.
[Indiana Historical Society, *Indianapolis Recorder* Collection, #C3254]

had arranged a campaign appearance in the heart of an Indianapolis African-American neighborhood to cement backing from black voters who valued the senator's support for minorities and the disadvantaged. Fearing violence, city officials unsuccessfully urged Kennedy to cancel his speech. When he arrived at 17th Street and Broadway, the festive crowd of about 2,500 had not heard of King's death. Speaking extemporaneously from the back of a truck, Kennedy began with the shocking announcement. He recalled that he had a member of his family killed by a white man and asked the crowd to join him in prayer for the nation and in the determination to replace savageness with gentleness in the world. It was a defining moment for both Kennedy and the city. Kennedy won the Indiana primary but fell victim himself to an assassin in California on June 6. His remarks of April 4 became an epitaph proclaiming his vision for America: a portion of the speech is inscribed on a memorial wall adjoining his gravesite at Arlington National Cemetery. For Indianapolis, the speech helped preserve the city as an island of restraint in the turbulent aftermath of the King assassination.

DAVID L. ANDERSON
University of Indianapolis

Arthur M. Schlesinger, Jr., *Robert Kennedy and His Times* (Boston, 1978).

Kentucky and Whitewater Factions.

Early political coalitions. The development of strong, organized political parties in Indianapolis occurred during the 1830s. Until then, voters aligned themselves with loosely structured factions forged either around individual politicians or geographical regions. The two Indianapolis factions in the 1820s, dubbed the Whitewater faction and the Kentucky faction, reflected the geographical origins of the candidates and their supporters. The Whitewater faction, originally based in southeastern Indiana, was the most resilient, perhaps because its leaders, including the astute Jonathan Jennings, had gained experience battling William Henry Harrison and a proslavery faction located in the lower Wabash valley region centered in Vincennes, the territorial capital. As Indiana's population grew, and when the state constitution prohibited slavery, the Wabash valley faction declined as a major political force. However, the Whitewater faction remained active and, in the early 1820s, a number of settlers with links to the faction moved to Indianapolis. At the same time settlers from Kentucky also moved to Indianapolis, and almost immediately the two groups fielded candidates for a variety of local offices. In one of the more hotly contested elections, the 1822 county clerk's race, MORRIS MORRIS of the Kentucky faction opposed JAMES M. RAY, the Whitewater candidate. Ray won the election, and the Whitewater faction, supported by early Indianapolis luminaries such as CALVIN FLETCHER, continued to occupy a preeminent position throughout the 1820s. Eventually, both factions were rendered meaningless when durable, well-managed political parties took root in Indianapolis during the 1830s.

STEPHEN L. COX
Conner Prairie

Kern, John Worth, Jr. (July 7, 1900–Jan. 29, 1971). Mayor of Indianapolis, 1935–1937, Democrat; United States Tax Court judge. Born in Indianapolis, Kern was the son of JOHN WORTH KERN, SR., who was vice-presidential candidate with William Jennings Bryan in the 1908 presidential election, twice Indiana gubernatorial candidate, and former U.S. Senate majority leader. When he was eight years old, the junior Kern was stricken with polio, leaving both of his legs paralyzed for life. In 1920, after only three years there, he graduated from Washington and Lee University in Virginia. Kern received his law degree from Harvard University in 1923.

Returning to Indianapolis, Kern started a private practice and also was named as a U.S. commissioner, a post he held until 1931. He taught law at the Indianapolis branch of the Indiana University School of Law and served as Indianapolis Bar Association secretary from 1924 to 1930.

In 1924, Kern was the Democratic nominee for Indiana supreme and appellate courts reporter. Although unsuccessful in his first try for public office, Kern had better luck six years later when he was elected Marion County Superior

Court judge. His electoral success continued 10 years later when the then 34–year-old Kern was the Democratic nominee for Indianapolis mayor. In the election, he defeated Republican opponent Walter Pritchard by approximately 14,000 votes.

Reelected as the city's chief executive in 1936, Kern did not serve his entire second term. Instead, he resigned from office on September 2, 1937, when he was named to the 16–member U.S. Board of Tax Appeals by President Franklin D. Roosevelt. (Roosevelt, who had also been a victim of polio earlier in his life, appeared in Indianapolis on Kern's behalf during the 1936 mayoral campaign.) City Controller WALTER C. BOETCHER filled out the rest of Kern's term, which ended in 1939.

During his years in Washington, D.C., with the federal tax court, Kern was named Harvard Law School Alumni Association president and was a member of the University of Virginia's law faculty. Kern retired from the bench in 1961, having served three successive terms as the tax court's chief judge. However, he was subsequently recalled to his post and continued to serve on the court until his death.

RAY BOOMHOWER
Indiana Historical Society

Kern, John Worth, Sr. (Dec. 20, 1849–Aug. 17, 1917). Democratic politician, vice-presidential nominee, U.S. senator, and Senate majority leader. A native of Howard County, Indiana, Kern was reared in Indiana and Iowa. An avid Democrat, he was a schoolmaster in Indiana and a law student at the University of Michigan before opening his attorney's office in Kokomo.

Throughout his adult life he sought elective office as a Democrat in a strongly Republican state, winning the voters' support only twice in nine contests. After failing to win a seat in the state legislature in 1870, Kern was elected reporter of the Indiana Supreme Court on the victorious state ticket in 1884. He moved to Indianapolis as the court reporter and also practiced law. Defeated for reelection in 1888, he was sent to the state Senate in 1892. There he defended labor unions and supported the passage of child labor legislation. THOMAS TAGGART, Indianapolis'

Democratic mayor, made Kern city attorney, and in 1900 and 1904 he was his party's unsuccessful candidate for governor.

In 1908 Kern first gained national prominence. Although a "gold" Democrat, the Hoosier actively supported William Jennings Bryan in the 1896 presidential campaign, gaining the lasting friendship of the Nebraskan. When Bryan ran for the White House for a third time in 1908, Republican William Howard Taft's victory appeared all but certain, so few Democrats were eager to join Bryan on his ticket. With Taggart's backing and Bryan's approval, Kern was chosen vice-presidential nominee by acclamation. His pro-labor record and his progressive views in favor of civil service reform, a graduated income tax, and a lower tariff made him an attractive running mate. Despite a very active Democratic campaign, Taft won an overwhelming victory.

Kern's major contribution to American political life came in the U.S. Senate. The Republican split between Taft and Roosevelt in 1908 gave Hoosier Democrats control of the State House, and in 1911 the legislature elected Kern to the Senate. In Washington he quickly gained a national reputation as a progressive. Following Woodrow Wilson's election in 1912, Kern's Democratic colleagues made him majority leader. From 1913 to 1917 Kern developed this position into an efficient instrument for translating administrative policies and party goals into legislation. By appealing to party loyalty, employing the president's influence, and convincing his colleagues to respect decisions reached at Democratic caucuses as binding, the Hoosier solon helped to win Senate approval for Wilson's New Freedom program.

Following the enactment of the 17th Amendment, Kern faced the general electorate in his 1916 campaign and met defeat. He died from tuberculosis the following summer.

PETER J. SEHLINGER
Indiana University–Purdue University,
Indianapolis

Claude G. Bowers, *The Life of John Worth Kern* (Indianapolis, 1918); Virginia F. Haughton, "John Worth Kern and Wilson's New Freedom: A Study of a Senate Majority Leader" (Ph.D. dissertation, University of Kentucky, 1973); Peter J. Sehlinger, "John W. Kern: A Hoosier Progressive," in *Gentlemen from Indiana: National Party Candidates, 1836–1940*, ed. Ralph D. Gray (Indianapolis, 1977), 189–217.

Kessler, George Edward (July 16, 1862–Mar. 19, 1923). Architect of the city's system of parks and boulevards. Born in Frankenhausen, Germany, Kessler moved to the United States with his parents when he was three years old. He attended schools in New York and Dallas until 1878 when he returned to Europe to train at the Grand Ducal Gardens in Weimar. He then entered the Charlottenburg Polytechnicum and received special instruction in civil engineering at the University of Jena.

Kessler began his professional career in the U.S. in 1882 working on a pleasure resort near Kansas City, Missouri. In 1892 he designed Kansas City's park and boulevard system and became the secretary and landscape architect of the city's newly created park board. He retained his position as landscape architect until his death. In 1902 Kessler laid out the grounds for the Louisiana Purchase Exposition in St. Louis (1904). At that time he established offices in St. Louis, and moved to that city in 1910.

In 1908 the Indianapolis Board of Park Commissioners hired Kessler as landscape architect, a position he held until 1915. Kessler's parks and boulevards design for Indianapolis, presented in 1909, featured a "chain of parks brought to the doors of all sections of the community" linked by wide, sweeping boulevards. While under contract to the city Kessler also redesigned the GARFIELD PARK plan, adding the sunken gardens and new bridges, and designed scenic bridges at Brookside Park. In 1917 he planned the suburban enclave of BRENDONWOOD, with its curvilinear streets, homes sited on wooded hills, and golf links.

Internationally known, Kessler also designed park systems, boulevards, and other improvements for cities such as Memphis, Cincinnati, Dallas, Houston, Salt Lake City, Denver, and Mexico City, Mexico. Just before his death he completed plans for the park and boulevard system in Terre Haute, Indiana, and an addition to the boulevard system in Indianapolis, which when completed in 1929 was named Kessler Boulevard. Although never a resident of Indianapolis, Kessler died in the city following surgery for kidney disease.

CONNIE J. ZEIGLER

National Cyclopedia of Biography, Vol. 20; Michael Maloney and Kenneth J. Remenschneider, *Indianapolis Landscape Architecture* (Washington, D.C., 1983); *Indianapolis News*, Mar. 20, 1923.

Kessler's Boulevard and Park System. The first comprehensive plan for parks and boulevards in Indianapolis. Landscape architect and urban planner GEORGE EDWARD KESSLER (1862–1923) of St. Louis, Missouri, created the plan in 1909 and assisted in its implementation. It provided a sound framework for the expansion of the city well into the 20th century and remains a vital part of the city's infrastructure.

Although Kessler should be given credit for the design and success of the plan, the park movement in Indianapolis predates his plan by several decades. In 1894, the Commercial Club (forerunner of the CHAMBER OF COMMERCE) hired landscape architect Joseph Earnshaw of Cincinnati, Ohio, to prepare a park plan for the city. Earnshaw recommended that a new boulevard, lined with parks, parallel WHITE RIVER and FALL CREEK from Washington Street to the current site of the INDIANA STATE FAIRGROUNDS. Although his plan was rejected as too extravagant, the Park Board in

Construction of Kessler Boulevard, completed in 1929, was still in the early stages in this 1924 view. [Indiana Historical Society, #A67]

1895 endorsed a similar plan initiated by the firm of Olmsted, Olmsted, and Eliot from Brookline, Massachusetts. A new state law in that year enabled cities of 100,000 or more to create park agencies.

The Park Board and the Olmsted plan came under attack almost immediately. The issue of cost was the subject of much debate, and residents of the east and south sides argued that while the entire city would be assessed for the improvements, the plan would benefit only the north side. Then, in 1897, the state enabling law was declared unconstitutional. Passage of a new state law in 1899 did not resolve the local controversy, and the progress of the parks and boulevard system was sporadic until 1907. The most important events were the acquisition of Riverside Park (not recommended in the plan) and the replacement of several old iron BRIDGES with stone-clad arched spans. J. Clyde Power, city engineer, designed these handsome bridges which cross White River and Fall Creek. Several still stand today; and, in 1912, Kessler would design a similar bridge to carry Capitol Avenue across Fall Creek.

By 1907, the city clearly needed a single guiding vision for its boulevard and park system. From 1908 until 1915 the Parks Department retained Kessler, a well-recognized planner, as landscape architect. He was born in Frankenhausen, Germany, raised in Dallas, Texas, and formally trained at the Grand Ducal Gardens in Weimar and the University of Jena. He had designed park and boulevard plans for Kansas City, Missouri (1892), and Cincinnati (1907), as well as planning the Louisiana Purchase Exposition grounds in St. Louis (1904).

Kessler retained aspects of both the Earnshaw and Olmsted plans, including the concept of a linear park lined by boulevards along White River and Fall Creek. The Kessler plan, however, was far more comprehensive in scope than its predecessors. It linked all the public open spaces in the city with a system of broad parkways to follow the four major waterways in Marion County: White River, Fall Creek, Pleasant Run, and POGUE'S RUN. The plan took advantage of those features that the city offered: picturesque, meandering streams, broad vistas, and fine stands of timber. Kessler's plan was also practical, since it protected waterways from pollution and acted as a flood control device. In addition, it tied existing thoroughfares, such as Meridian Street, Washington Boulevard, and 38th Street (Maple Road), to the boulevard system and called for their beautification. Kessler quelled the opposition shown to previous plans by dividing the city into separate taxing districts, a strategy also incorporated into a new state park law (1909).

Over the next several years, Kessler's firm produced designs for new and existing city parks, including UNIVERSITY PARK (1914), GARFIELD PARK (1915), and RIVERSIDE PARK (1916). In October, 1922, the Board of Park Commissioners once again hired Kessler to plan extensions to the boulevard system on the north side. He recommended that FORT BENJAMIN HARRISON be connected to the northwest side of town by a leisurely route. Following parts of existing Cooper Road, 59th, and 56th streets, the thoroughfare was to include a 100–foot roadbed and bridle paths. Work had just begun on the boulevard when Kessler died in March, 1923, in Indianapolis. The parkway, named Kessler Boulevard in his honor, was completed by 1929.

By placing parks and boulevards in strategic locations, Kessler's plan fostered residential growth in sparsely populated areas and reinforced the tendency of citizens to regard the north and east sides of the city as desirable neighborhoods. Ideas first presented in the Kessler plan still influence planning in Indianapolis today. It was Kessler who recommended that a public court of government buildings and park land extend west of the STATE HOUSE in 1909; this idea has recently been followed in spirit with the completion of the INDIANA GOVERNMENT CENTER South building and planning for WHITE RIVER STATE PARK.

PAUL C. DIEBOLD
Division of Historic Preservation
and Archaeology,
Indiana Department of Natural Resources

James R. O'Day, "George Edward Kessler and the Indianapolis Park System: A Study of its Historical Development during the City Beautiful Era, 1895–1915" (M.S. thesis, Historic Preservation, Ball State University, October, 1988); Michael Maloney and Kenneth Remenschneider, *Indianapolis Landscape Architecture* (Washington, D.C., 1983).

Ketcham, Susan Merrill (June, 1841–Feb. 2, 1930). Professional artist. The granddaughter of SAMUEL MERRILL, Indiana's first state treasurer, Susan Ketcham was born in Indianapolis and received her early art education at the Indiana School of Art under John Washington Love and James F. Gookins. As a founding member and director of the ART ASSOCIATION OF INDIANAPOLIS in 1883, she was responsible for selecting superior paintings for a major art loan exhibition, a role that required travel to Chicago and New York. When the Art Association's school was established, she not only selected the painters for the faculty, but also taught at the school until it closed in 1886.

Ketcham studied music and art in Italy and Switzerland for over two years. Afterward she moved to New York and continued her education at the Art Students' League, of which she was a member and later served as vice-president. She established and maintained a studio at Carnegie Hall for 29 years and also studied with WILLIAM MERRITT CHASE at the Shinnecock Hills Art School on Long Island. Her interest in interpreting and painting the sea led to the establishment of her own summer studio in Ogunquit, Maine, where she was a pupil of Charles Woodbury, the noted marine painter.

For over three decades Susan Ketcham made her home in the East, and her paintings were shown in many New York exhibitions. She became well known internationally as a marine and portrait painter. The JOHN HERRON ART INSTITUTE sponsored a memorial exhibition in 1930 and her work is represented in many private and public collections, including the INDIANAPOLIS MUSEUM OF ART and Indiana University.

SHARON A. SMITH-THEOBALD
Greater Lafayette Museum of Art

Mary Q. Burnet, *Art and Artists of Indiana* (New York, 1921); Wilbur D. Peat, *Pioneer Painters of Indiana* (Indianapolis, 1954).

Key School. Magnet option program in INDIANAPOLIS PUBLIC SCHOOLS. The first school in the country based upon psychologist Howard Gardner's theory of multiple intelligences, Key School provides equal attention in its curriculum to Gardner's seven avenues of intelligence: linguistic, logical-mathematical, musical, spatial, bodily-kinesthetic, intrapersonal, and interpersonal. Eight IPS teachers founded this nationally acclaimed school in 1987 after three years of research, a planning grant from the LILLY ENDOWMENT, and support from IPS Superintendent James A. Adams.

In addition to learning state-mandated subjects, students at Key School take Spanish, music, computers, art, and gym. They also participate in unorthodox activities such as "pods" and the "Flow Center." Children join a multi-age interest group or pod, and complete projects throughout the year based upon school-wide interdisciplinary themes that change every nine weeks. Projects are videotaped, and the tapes are used to assess each child's development. In the semi-structured Flow Center students choose their own activities, such as puzzles and games.

A staff of 15 serves 160 students from preschool through fifth grade. Applicants are admitted by lottery without qualifications, limited only by federally mandated desegregation guidelines. The school uses age groupings combined into primary or intermediate levels and qualitative assessment instead of traditional class structure and grading systems. All but a small minority of students have performed well in standardized achievement tests. In 1993 IPS extended the program, opening the Key Renaissance School for grades six to eight.

MICHELLE D. HALE

Lynn Olson, "Children 'Flourish' Here," *Education Week* (Jan. 27, 1988), 1.

Kinder, Trustin B. (July 27, 1822–Feb. 23, 1847). First war hero from Indianapolis. Kinder was born on the family's farm near the small village of Indianapolis. He was educated locally, read law, and was admitted to the bar in 1845. Kinder practiced his trade in Paoli, Indiana, prior to volunteering for military duty during the MEXICAN WAR. Commissioned a captain of Company B, 2nd Indiana Volunteer Infantry, Kinder died in action at the Battle of Buena Vista. Upon learning of his son's death, the captain's father, despite his advanced years, made a hazardous journey to Mexico to bring his son's remains back to Indianapolis for burial. Kinder's body lay in state in the Capitol rotunda, and on July 12, 1847, was the object of what observers reported was the largest funeral in the city to that time and for years afterwards. After an initial burial in City Cemetery, where members of his company laid him to rest with full military honors, Kinder's mother reinterred his body at CROWN HILL CEMETERY in October, 1864.

WAYNE L. SANFORD

Kingan and Company. Meat-packing company in operation 1862–1966 at Maryland and Blackford streets along White River. In 1845 Samuel Kingan opened a meat-packing plant in northern Ireland and began a lucrative trade supplying salt pork to British ships. After plants in Brooklyn and Cincinnati burned, he opened an Indianapolis facility in 1862. Thomas Kingan, Samuel's brother, was the first manager of the Indianapolis plant. In 1875 Kingan merged with another Belfast, Ireland, firm, J & T Sinclair. Family member W. R. Sinclair came to Indianapolis in 1906 and later directed the American operation for 16 years.

Many of Kingan's original workers were Irish; some were recruited by the company in Ireland. Housing was scarce in the growing Irish community around the plant, so Kingan built an apart-

An 1893 advertisement for Kingan and Company. [Indiana Historical Society, #C5897]

ment house for workers in 1872 and helped to establish a Presbyterian church. Employment at Kingan became a tradition among the city's Irish-American and Eastern European immigrants, with jobs passed from generation to generation.

Since much of the plant's output was shipped overseas, Kingan adopted a nautical trademark in 1877. It pictured a yellow-slickered pilot at the wheel of an ocean-going clipper ship. For more than 70 years it served as a symbol of the Kingan "Reliable" brand. By the 1920s, however, most of the firm's products went to American consumers, so the company incorporated as a United States concern. Kingan diversified its products and offered a variety of fresh, preserved, and processed meats. Presliced bacon was a new product developed for the American market.

Innovations in meat processing allowed the Indianapolis facility to remain competitive for over a century. The company's pioneering use of ice to preserve meat allowed year-round operation. Initially the ice was cut from the WHITE RIVER, but later Kingan manufactured artificial ice. The plant also made use of refrigerated railroad cars to ship fresh products across the country. Chain conveyors, moving tables, and on-the-line meat-cutting were new processing techniques developed by employees at the plant.

By the time of Kingan's 100th anniversary in 1945, the Indianapolis facility covered 27 acres and employed 3,000 people. It had grown from a small meat-packing plant to one of the ten largest in the country. Additional plants were operated in several states, including Virginia, South Carolina, Iowa, Nebraska, and Florida.

In 1952 the Hygrade Corporation of Detroit, Michigan, purchased Kingan. Citing increasing costs and low profits, Hygrade closed the plant in August, 1966. A fire destroyed the vacant plant in 1969.

CATHLEEN F. DONNELLY

Indianapolis Times, Aug. 13–15, 1947; *Indianapolis Star Magazine*, Apr. 3, 1960; *Indianapolis News*, May 23, 1966.

Tony Kiritsis Case. Kidnapping and hostage incident. The morning of February 8, 1977,

Anthony G. "Tony" Kiritsis, 44, entered the office of Richard O. Hall, an executive of the Meridian Mortgage Company, and took him hostage with a sawed-off 12–gauge shotgun. Kiritsis wired the shotgun to Hall's neck, with a "deadman's switch" from the trigger to his own neck. Kiritsis forced Hall out of the building and through downtown streets in near-zero weather, the entire walk surrounded by police and journalists. Kiritsis then commandeered a police car and forced Hall to drive to Kiritsis' Crestwood Village apartment. He told police the apartment was rigged with explosives, chained Hall in the bathroom, and held him captive for nearly 63 hours.

Kiritsis had purchased a 17–acre westside property in hopes of developing a shopping center. His $130,000 mortgage with Meridian Mortgage was due on March 1, 1977, and he accused the company of having deliberately sabotaged his project. For Hall's release Kiritsis demanded an apology and $5 million compensation from Meridian Mortgage, as well as a promise of no state, federal, or civil prosecution.

On February 10, when assured his demands had been met, Kiritsis led Hall at gunpoint to the building's lobby where he delivered an obscenity-filled, 23–minute monologue carried live during prime time by all Indianapolis television stations. Afterwards he released Hall and was immediately taken into police custody.

Eight months later Kiritsis was tried on charges of kidnapping, armed robbery, and armed extortion. On October 21, 1977, he was found not guilty by reason of insanity and two weeks later was declared incompetent and turned over to the State Department of Mental Health for commitment to an institution. In December Kiritsis was found in contempt of court for refusing to submit to a psychiatric examination.

From November, 1977, to June, 1981, Kiritsis was held in various state hospitals. He was then sent to the infirmary of the Indiana State Reformatory on another contempt citation for refusing to be examined; January 1, 1985, was the deadline set for compliance with the court order. Following a new court order that he submit to medical examination with or without his consent, the Indiana Supreme Court ruled in January, 1985, that Kiritsis could not be forced to undergo such examinations against his will. Following two more years of detention in state hospitals, in 1987 he agreed to see a psychiatrist outside the state system.

Released in December, 1987, after spending 11 years in state custody, Kiritsis continued to live in Indianapolis in the early 1990s. He returned briefly to the public eye in 1990 when he filed 101 lawsuits in Marion County Superior Court against virtually everyone who had been involved in his case since 1977.

VICKIE J. WEST

Newsweek, Feb. 22, 1977; Indianapolis Star, Feb. 9–11, Oct. 22, 1977, Apr. 14, 1985, Dec. 4, 1987; articles by Walter B. Jaehnig, F. Thomas Schornhorst, and Herbert A. Terry in Indiana Law Journal, 53 (Summer, 1978).

Kiwanis International. Worldwide service organization. Founded in 1915, Kiwanis International had grown to more than 300,000 members, with youth programs serving 100,000 college and high school students, when its board started deliberating about a move in 1977. In January, 1981, the board of trustees of Kiwanis International voted to move its national headquarters from its cramped quarters in downtown Chicago to a building to be constructed in Indianapolis.

In spring, 1981, trustees exercised an option on 6.84 acres of land owned by Indiana Lumbermen's Mutual Insurance Company in the College Park subdivision. An Indianapolis firm, BOHLEN, MEYER, GIBSON AND ASSOCIATES, was selected to draw plans for the building. Financing for the facility and moving costs were underwritten in part by the city of Indianapolis, LILLY ENDOWMENT, and the Kiwanis Club of Indianapolis Foundation. The three-story, 60,000–square-foot building, constructed by Indianapolis-based contractor Jungclaus-Campbell, was completed in the fall of 1982.

In June, 1992, Indianapolis hosted the Kiwanis International convention, which was attended by nearly 14,000 members and their families. It was the second time the city had hosted the organization's convention, the first being in 1937, when 4,009 official delegates attended.

There were 145 full- and part-time staff at the international office as of August, 1992.

MATTHEW C. MORRIS

Klein, Charles Herbert "Chuck" (Oct. 7, 1904–Mar. 28, 1958). Professional baseball player. Indianapolis-born Chuck Klein spent 17 seasons in the major leagues. Career statistics that include 2,076 hits, 1,201 RBIs, 300 home runs, and a .320 batting average won the "Hoosier Hammerer" election to the Baseball Hall of Fame in 1980.

Following his 1922 graduation from SOUTH-PORT High School, Klein played for several local amateur and semipro squads, including Indianapolis Power and Light. Failed tryouts with minor league teams in Indianapolis and Evansville led to a job as a steel catcher in an Indianapolis mill. Laid off in 1927, Klein attempted a second, and this time successful, tryout with Evansville's Three-I League entry. In 1928, Evansville sold him to Fort Wayne's Central League franchise for $200. A mid-season tryout with the Philadelphia Phillies resulted in the beginning of a long tenure with the National League's Phillies, Pittsburgh Pirates, and Chicago Cubs.

In 1929, the right fielder set a National League record with 43 home runs in a single season. Klein led the league in fielding average six times, was league MVP in 1931 and 1932, played in Major League Baseball's first two All-Star Games (1933 and 1934), and starred for the Cubs' 1935 World Series team.

Following his retirement in 1944, Klein went into the tavern business in Philadelphia. Alcoholism and chronic malnutrition led to a failed marriage, severe heart disease, and a return to Indianapolis in 1947. The Southport Little League complex is named in his honor.

R. DALE OGDEN
Indiana State Museum

John A. Mercurio, Record Profiles of Baseball's Hall of Famers (New York, 1990); Indianapolis Times, Apr. 14–16, 1957 (three-part series).

Knabe, Helene (Dec. 22, 1875–Oct. 24, 1911). Physician and medical illustrator. Born in Germany, Knabe emigrated to Indianapolis in 1896. She attended BUTLER UNIVERSITY and obtained her M.D. degree from the Medical College of Indiana in 1904. The next year she was appointed assistant pathologist at the State Laboratory of Hygiene, where her work in the microscopical recognition of rabies attracted considerable attention. She also was noted for her drawing skills and illustrated a number of medical textbooks. She resigned from the state laboratory in 1908 to enter private practice, and was subsequently elected to the faculty of the Indiana Veterinary College. Knabe was found murdered in her combination office-apartment on October 24, 1911, a crime that remains unsolved.

CHARLES A. BONSETT, M.D.
Indiana University School of Medicine

Journal of the Indiana State Medical Association (Nov. 15, 1911), 495; *Indianapolis News*, Oct. 24, 1911.

Knefler, Frederick (Oct., 1833–June 14, 1901). Soldier and attorney. Born in Arad, Hungary, Knefler took part in the great Magyar uprising at the age of fifteen. With his physician father he came to America in 1849. They settled briefly in New York, where Frederick learned the carpentry trade, before migrating west to Indianapolis.

In Indianapolis, Knefler secured a position in the office of the court clerk and read law. When the CIVIL WAR began, he joined the 11th Indiana Regiment as a lieutenant. Knefler became captain of Company H when the regiment enlisted for three years service. Appointed colonel of the 79th Indiana in August, 1862, Knefler led his regiment in battle at Perryville, Stones River, Chickamauga, Missionary Ridge, Atlanta, and Nashville. He mustered out with his men on June 7, 1865. Retiring with the brevet rank of brigadier general, he was among the highest ranking officers to come from Indianapolis.

Following the war, Knefler entered the practice of law as the partner of John Hanna, former U.S. District Attorney. President Rutherford B. Hayes appointed him pension agent for the district to succeed W. H. H. TERRELL. After eight years in this position, Knefler became president of the board of regents of the SOLDIERS AND SAILORS MONUMENT.

TONY L. TRIMBLE

Berry R. Sulgrove, *History of Indianapolis and Marion County* (Philadelphia, 1884).

Knight, Etheridge (Apr. 19, 1931–Mar. 10, 1991). Poet. A native of Corinth, Mississippi, Knight was an off-and-on resident of Indianapolis from the 1950s until his death. He began writing while incarcerated in the Indiana State Prison, observing: "I died in Korea from a shrapnel wound and narcotics resurrected me. I died in 1960 from a prison sentence and poetry brought me back to life."

Knight's early work was encouraged by poets Gwendolyn Brooks and Dudley Randall. His 30–page chapbook, *Poems from Prison*, was published by Randall's Broadside Press in 1968. He edited the work of other prisoners in *Black Voices from Prison* (New York: Pathfinder Press, 1970). This editing activity was the first in Knight's career-long concern with the poetry of prisoners (in 1990 he served as a visiting writer in the Indiana Women's Prison), and with the idea of poets forming a community. He conducted three different Free People's Poetry Workshops in Indianapolis (the first in the early 1970s, the last from 1989 until his death), and began other Free People's Workshops in Boston, Memphis, Philadelphia, and elsewhere.

Formally, Knight served as poet-in-residence at the University of Pittsburgh, Lincoln University, and the University of Hartford and worked with the BUTLER UNIVERSITY Writer's Studio in 1990. He was named the poet laureate of Indianapolis' MARTIN UNIVERSITY and in 1990 was awarded a B.A. degree from that institution. Knight won fellowships from the National Endowment for the Arts and the Guggenheim Foundation and received the Shelley Memorial Award from the Poetry Society of America in 1985. *The Essential Etheridge Knight* (Pitt Poetry Series, University of Pittsburgh Press, 1986) earned him the Before Columbus American Book Award in 1986. Knight's other books of poems are: *Belly Song and Other Poems* (Broadside Press, 1973) and *Born of a Woman* (Houghton Mifflin, 1980).

Knight's poems have often been anthologized, notably "Hard Rock Returns to Prison from the Hospital for the Criminally Insane," "The Idea of Ancestry," and "For Black Poets Who Think of Suicide." Knight was acknowledged for his performance of poetry and his belief that poetry was essentially an oral art. As Brooks wrote in her preface to *Poems from Prison*: "Since Etheridge Knight is not your stifled *artiste*, there is air in these poems. And there is blackness, inclusive, possessed and given; freed and terrible and beautiful."

The Etheridge Knight Festival of the Arts was staged in Indianapolis in 1992 and 1993. Knight was posthumously awarded a Governor's Arts Award by the INDIANA ARTS COMMISSION in 1993.

JIM POWELL
Writers' Center of Indianapolis

———

Susan Neville, "Free Singers Be," *Arts Indiana*, 13 (Apr., 1991), 22–27; Lamont B. Steptoe, "A Deity of the Spoken Word," *Painted Word* (Winter, 1992).

Knights of Labor. Labor organization active in Indianapolis in the 1880s. Founded as a secret organization of Philadelphia garment cutters in 1869, the Knights of Labor had formed more than 15,000 local assemblies by 1889, and had a peak membership of more than 7,000,000 in 1886. Between 1875 and 1890 the Knights organized more than 330 local assemblies in 170 communities in Indiana, including 36 in Indianapolis. The first Indianapolis assembly, No. 141, was led by Calvin Light, a printer and the editor of the *Workingman's Map*. Light and Lycurgus P. McCormack, who became Master Workman of L.A. 141 in 1880, were active in the Workingmen's party and leaders of protests by the unemployed in Indianapolis in 1876 and 1877.

During the early 1880s the Indianapolis Knights expanded to 18 local assemblies under the leadership of Samuel H. Leffingwell, also a printer and editor of the labor paper *Our Organette*. The local Knights were active supporters of a national strike of telegraphers in 1883–1884, and joined International Typographical Union Local No. 1 in strikes against the *Indianapolis Journal* in 1884 and the *Journal* and the *Sentinel* in 1887. The following trades organized local assemblies in

Indianapolis during this period: coopers, printers, telegraph operators, barbers, varnishers, plumbers, iron workers, stonecutters, horseshoers and blacksmiths, bakers, machinery molders, hod carriers, machinists, furniture workers, salesmen and clerks, saw makers, wheelmakers, and bookbinders. In 1886 they helped organize the first LABOR DAY CELEBRATION and parade in Indianapolis.

As the Knights grew in strength they became increasingly involved in politics. Under the leadership of Thomas Gruelle, editor of the *Labor Signal*, they campaigned vigorously against Republican BENJAMIN HARRISON in the 1888 presidential campaign, and helped persuade the majority of voters in his home county, Marion County, to vote Democratic. The Knights also elected 14 members to the state legislature in 1888, and were largely responsible for a substantial amount of reform legislation, including enactment of an eight-hour day in 1889.

The Knights exhibited considerable strength in Indianapolis from 1886 to 1889, and cooperated with the local trade unions belonging to the newly formed American Federation of Labor. However, Indianapolis members also became disenchanted with the national leadership of the Knights, partly because the national leaders had supported Harrison in 1888, but even more because of their reinstatement of J. P. Kelleher, a retail merchant who had been expelled for breaking an early closing agreement with the assembly to which his employees belonged. By 1890 all but six local assemblies had turned in their charters, and most of them became Federal Labor Unions or local unions of affiliates of the American Federation of Labor.

JOHN W. BENNETT
Empire State College

———

Jonathon Garlock, comp., *Guide to the Local Assemblies of the Knights of Labor* (Westport, Conn., 1982); Minute Books of International Typographical Union Local No. 1 (Indiana State Library); *Labor Signal* (Indianapolis, 1888–1889).

Knights of Pythias (Stokely–Van Camp) Building. White ceramic building at 941 North Meridian Street. The architectural firm McGUIRE AND SHOOK designed this Gothic Revival building in 1925 to house the insurance department of the Supreme Lodge of the Knights of Pythias. The steel-skeleton, three-story structure features elaborate ornamentation with glazed crosses along its roof perimeter and a different horizontal design along the base of each story. The entrance is flanked by large brass lanterns.

At the time of its construction the building's interior was opulently appointed. The lobby and vestibule walls were yellow Verona marble with alpine green marble bases. The lobby ceiling was intricately detailed, gold-painted plaster. The second and third floors walls were wainscoted with white Alabama marble.

In 1946 STOKELY–VAN CAMP purchased the building to use for offices. During remodeling the company removed the marble paneling and wainscoting and installed a dropped, acoustic tile ceiling throughout. In 1958 the company added a plain limestone extension at the rear of the original building. A major renovation occurred in 1987 after Stokely sold the building in 1985 to Everett I. Brown/Mid States Engineering. A new lobby was added and the original lobby was divided into a vestibule and conference room. Where marble once covered the walls, now wallpaper and oak accent the first and second floors, mahogany the third.

CONNIE J. ZEIGLER

Knox, George L. (Sept. 16, 1841–Aug. 24, 1927). African-American publisher and businessman. Knox embodied Booker T. Washington's values of economic uplift and self-reliance. Born a slave in Tennessee, he came to Indiana in 1864 when a Hoosier officer in whose regiment Knox served, as a runaway, was furloughed. Learning the barber's trade, he opened a shop in Greenfield in 1865—the same year he married. Highly successful, he became a prominent Hancock County Republican and an organizer of the town's first black Methodist congregation, public school, and Sunday school. He also gained the friendship of JAMES WHITCOMB RILEY.

By the time Knox moved to Indianapolis in 1884 he had established patterns of business and civic values that characterized the remainder of his life. By the mid–1890s he owned a number of barber shops and had 50 employees. Knox gained substantial income and secured the friendship of prominent whites—chiefly BENJAMIN HARRISON. Holder of the INDIANAPOLIS FREEMAN's mortgages, he purchased the paper in 1892 and made it a mouthpiece for Harrison. He was a delegate to Republican conventions in 1892 and 1896. Beginning in December, 1894, his paper published a series that became his remarkable autobiography, *Slave and Freeman* (1895), the appearance of which supported the message that Booker T. Washington gave at the Atlanta Exposition.

With the Republican abandonment of blacks, however, Knox retreated from political activism. At first he supported national Republicans and independents at the state and local levels, but eventually he endorsed the national Democratic ticket. He espoused Booker T. Washington's economic message of self-help, although in later years he also supported the NAACP. Most consistent was his devotion to Methodist church programs.

After his first wife's death in 1910, Knox remarried and his only surviving child, Elwood, took over managing the *Freeman*. The paper fell on hard times, however, and filed for bankruptcy in 1926. George Knox was promoting black newspapers in Richmond, Virginia, when he suffered a stroke. He never abandoned his hopes for the advancement of African-Americans. He was buried in CROWN HILL CEMETERY.

DARREL E. BIGHAM
University of Southern Indiana

Willard B. Gatewood, Jr., ed., *Slave and Freeman: The Autobiography of George L. Knox* (Lexington, Ky., 1979).

Korean War (June, 1950–July, 1953). When North Korea invaded South Korea in June, 1950, and President Harry S. Truman committed United States armed forces under the authority of the United Nations, Indianapolis eagerly joined the war effort. As many interpreted the invasion, including the *Indianapolis News*, the lessons of recent history justified the call to arms. But support for the war quickly took on partisan tones. At the Republican state convention in Indianapolis, U.S. Senator William E. Jenner urged Indianans not to shrink from their patriotic duty. Nevertheless, sounding themes that would intensify later in the war, the senator insisted upon the resignations of Truman and Secretary of State Dean Acheson because both men had forced the crisis. Local Democrats, however, praised Truman. Despite partisan differences the U.N. force generally enjoyed support in the capital city.

The call-up of national guardsmen and reserves followed. The Indiana Air Guard mobilized and trained at Stout and Baer fields, but never deployed. Mobilized and deployed but hardly trained, the 16th Marine Reserve Infantry Battalion suddenly, and disastrously, found itself under attack when the Chinese army entered the war in November, 1950. Some of the battalion had not fired weapons in recent training. Captain Robert M. Moore, Jr., became the first of 171 casualties from Marion County. Posthumously awarded the Purple Heart, Moore was buried in Crown Hill Cemetery.

Editorials in the *News* and *Indianapolis Star* reflected the city's support for the U.N. during the early stages of the war. Many residents wrote letters praising Truman and calling for firm statesmanship rather than negotiation. The public believed that the situation in Korea paralleled pre–World War II Europe and was adamant that the forces of democracy deal with aggression properly this time. As the city prepared for war the papers ran editorials calling for patriotism over politics and denouncing greedy consumers who were buying and hoarding rubber products, canned goods, sugar, and other items that had been rationed during World War II. The city began a "Clothes for Korea" drive in 1951. Several local churches, most notably Brookside Evangelical United Brethren, contributed greatly and sponsored relief drives of their own. In June, 1953, Governor George Craig formed a statewide committee to aid suffering Koreans in compliance with a request from the American-Korean Foundation. The committee met at the COLUMBIA CLUB and proclaimed an "Aid to Korea" week throughout the state to help raise funds.

China's invasion and the U.N. forces' retreat to the 38th parallel frustrated Indianapolis residents and diminished the patriotic optimism of June, 1950. Truman's "limited war," based on his belief that Russia's power in Europe posed a greater menace than China's in Asia, found wide disfavor because it did not permit assaults on China proper, including the use of the atomic bomb. The *News* believed that U.N. Commander General Douglas MacArthur, not Truman, should decide whether or not to use the bomb. A local minister identified Moscow as the source of America's agony and recommended bombing it. Occasional letters advocating peaceful negotiations with the Communists appeared in local papers, but most of the city believed that Truman and the U.N. should let MacArthur take the offensive and force communism out of Korea entirely.

The city's feelings about the war changed after Truman removed MacArthur from command. On April 11, 1951, the *News* conducted an unscientific random survey of public opinion about the president's decision. Its interviews did not produce a single vote of sympathy for the president. Local residents viewed MacArthur as the only man who was willing to achieve victory in Korea. With his dismissal the city became disillusioned with, and eventually disinterested in, the war effort. Convinced that the U.N. and our allies would never let us win the war, the *Star* began calling for withdrawal from Korea. Editorials and letters demanded that American troops be sent home and that the U.N. enforce its policies without aid from the U.S. military. By 1952 editorials and letters concerning Korea had virtually disappeared from local newspapers.

The war's end in July, 1953, brought mixed reactions in Indianapolis. There were no celebrations, and an *Indianapolis Times* survey showed that most people were glad that the fighting was over but felt that the truce would be only temporary. Young men of draft age were particularly happy, some stating that they had been concerned about being drafted to serve a senseless cause. An editorial in the *Star* blasted the truce as a negotiated defeat and asserted that our government should boycott the U.N. as long as it recognized Red China as a member. The perceived failure of democratic forces in Korea left Indianapolis fearful of both the external and the internal threat of communism.

THOMAS KEISER
WILLIAM D. DALTON

Indianapolis Newspaper Index, Indiana State Library.

Koreans. Although first immigrating to the United States in the 1890s, by 1960 there were only 16 Koreans in Indianapolis. The population grew slowly and steadily following the 1965 immigration act, which abolished quotas based on national origin. By 1990 there were 1,144 immigrants and people of Korean ancestry in Marion County, 927 in Indianapolis.

Koreans came to Indianapolis for many reasons, among them for educational and economic opportunities, as wives of American servicemen, and as orphaned children adopted by American families. Doctors, scientists, engineers, entrepreneurs, and assembly-line workers are some of the most common professions of Koreans in Indianapolis. The small community, centered principally in the vicinity of FORT BENJAMIN HARRISON, also supports a variety of groceries and restaurants.

The Korean community is relatively cohesive, promotes a strict work ethic, and emphasizes a strong family structure. A number of Korean organizations exist, the most important of which are churches. Around 1971 Koreans founded a non-denominational church on the city's east side, which spawned separate Baptist, Catholic, Methodist, and Presbyterian congregations during the 1980s. The Korean Society, founded in 1971 primarily as a social organization, provides services for newly arrived immigrants. A Korean language school, also established in 1971, teaches Korean-American children the language and culture of their ancestral homeland.

In May, 1993, the local Black Panther Militia launched a boycott of a Korean-American beauty supply business on the city's eastside, arguing that the store channeled money away from the black community. The Korean Association of Indiana, in turn, worked with community and business leaders to end the boycott, which the City-County Council and the mayor condemned, and to reduce the tensions between the two minority communities.

ELISABETH E. ORR
Indiana University, Bloomington

Kossuth, Louis, Visit of (1852). During the United States tour of Louis Kossuth, exiled leader of Hungary's failed attempt to escape the Austro-Hungarian Alliance, Indiana's Governor Joseph Wright issued the first invitation to visit a western state. Kossuth, in America to raise funds to renew his country's effort to be free of its alliance with Austria, accepted the invitation, and a delegation of state legislators and their families journeyed to Cincinnati to welcome him. Local merchants began promoting Kossuth items, the most popular being the Kossuth hat, described as round with a low crown resembling a loaf of bread.

Kossuth arrived in Indianapolis Friday, February 27, to cheering throngs and streets filled with American and Hungarian flags. There were numerous speeches, a levee on Friday night, presentation to the legislature and groups who donated to the freedom fund, and visits to churches and Sunday schools. Monday evening, Kossuth addressed the State Association of Friends of Hungary and accepted a donation from SARAH BOLTON on behalf of the city's women. However, not everyone was pleased by the visit. The February 27 *Indianapolis Journal* carried only a small item in its "Local Matters" column stating that if Kossuth wanted to be interviewed he could visit the office since the reporter wasn't interested in pushing his way through the crowd just to see him. Theresa Pulsky, a member of Kossuth's party, described the hotel and its service as poor and the city as small, without means to drain or pave its streets. When discussing the governor's reception she called the house uncomfortable and decried the diversity of the guests and their attire. Nevertheless, when Kossuth left Indianapolis the fund for Hungarian freedom was $800 richer.

RITA W. HARLAN

Indianapolis Journal, Feb. 27, 1852; *Indianapolis Locomotive*, Mar. 6, 1852; Francis and Theresa Pulsky, *White, Red, Black* (New York, 1853).

Krannert, Herman Charles (Nov. 5, 1887–Feb. 24, 1972). Founder of Inland Container Corporation. A native of Chicago, Krannert graduated from the University of Illinois in 1912 with a B.S. in mechanical engineering. He began his career in the paperboard and container industry in 1914 with Sefton Manufacturing Company of Chicago. In 1917 he became manager of its plant in Anderson, Indiana, where he married the former Ellnora Decker in 1919. In 1925, Krannert moved to Indianapolis and founded the INLAND CONTAINER CORPORATION, serving as president, treasurer, and director of the company from its founding until 1952 when he became chairman of both the board and the executive committee. Krannert was also a director of the INDIANA NATIONAL BANK as well as several companies outside of Indianapolis. He also served as president of the board of trustees of the INDIANAPOLIS–MARION COUNTY BUILDING AUTHORITY, trustee of BUTLER UNIVERSITY and Indiana Central College (now UNIVERSITY OF INDIANAPOLIS), and as a director of the Indianapolis Civic Progress Association.

In 1952 the Krannerts established the Robert M. Moore Heart Clinic at Indianapolis City Hospital (now WISHARD MEMORIAL HOSPITAL). This became the Krannert Institute of Cardiology, part of the HEALTH AND HOSPITAL CORPORATION, Wishard Hospital, and INDIANA UNIVERSITY SCHOOL OF MEDICINE. He endowed Krannert Tower at METHODIST HOSPITAL and the Krannert Pavilion at INDIANA UNIVERSITY MEDICAL CENTER. *Krannert on Management*, a collection of his lectures at the Krannert Graduate School of Industrial Administration, Purdue University, was published in 1966; a second edition, including additional lectures, was published in 1974. Krannert established a course in legal techniques at Indiana University School of Law, Bloomington.

The Krannerts established the Krannert Foundation and the KRANNERT CHARITABLE TRUST. Among their joint major gifts were grants for the Krannert Center for the Performing Arts and the Krannert Art Museum, both at the University of Illinois; the Krannert School of Management and Graduate School of Management at Purdue University; and the Krannert Building at IUPUI on East 38th Street, Indianapolis. They also donated the Krannert Room at CLOWES MEMORIAL HALL; Krannert Hall, a women's dormitory at the University of Indianapolis; the Krannert Memorial YMCA; and a Memorial Parlor at Meridian Street Methodist Church.

The Krannert Pavilion at the INDIANAPOLIS MUSEUM OF ART (IMA) was named in their honor. A supporter of the Art Association of Indianapolis, Krannert was chairman of the board of trustees of the IMA during the development and building of the new museum. He set up an endowment and challenge grant program which raised construction funds. The Herman C. Krannert Memorial Fund was used to purchase decorative arts for the IMA.

In recognition of his many business and civic contributions, Krannert was awarded numerous honorary degrees including a Doctor of Humane Letters from Butler University in 1960, a Doctor of Industrial Administration from Purdue University in 1962, and a Doctor of Laws from Indiana University in 1957.

PAT WATSON

Krannert Charitable Trust. The Krannert Charitable Trust was established in 1960 by a million-dollar gift from Indianapolis philanthropists Ellnora and HERMAN KRANNERT. The Krannerts' aim was to fund major projects, creating "Centers of Excellence" in the fields of education, medicine, youth services, and the performing arts. Unlike most philanthropic foundations, however, the Krannert Charitable Trust was designed to dissolve within 15 years after the deaths of Mr. and Mrs. Krannert. He died in 1972; she died two years later. The trust gave its last grant and was legally dissolved in 1987. During its 27–year existence, it received $62 million from the Krannerts and paid out $200 million in grants.

Herman Krannert (1887–1972) was born in Chicago and moved to Indiana in 1917, where he managed a paperboard facility in Anderson. In 1925, Krannert and his wife, Ellnora, moved to Indianapolis to found Inland Container Corporation, a manufacturer of corrugated packaging. During the four decades of his leadership the firm grew to a worldwide operation encompassing 25 factories.

The Krannert Charitable Trust supported numerous institutions of higher education, most of them in the Midwest. Recipients include Indiana University, Purdue University, University of Illinois, University of Evansville, INDIANA UNIVERSITY–PURDUE UNIVERSITY AT INDIANAPOLIS, Anderson College (now University), Indiana Central College (now UNIVERSITY OF INDIANAPOLIS), and Harvard Business School.

Medicine was another important focus of the Krannert Trust. Gifts funded buildings at METHODIST HOSPITAL and at the INDIANA UNIVERSITY MEDICAL CENTER. The trust also established the Krannert Institute of Cardiology at WISHARD MEMORIAL HOSPITAL, one of the nation's top cardiac research and teaching facilities.

In the area of community and youth development, the trust made generous gifts to Junior Achievement, the Krannert YMCA, and THE CHILDREN'S MUSEUM, as well as to the HOOSIER DOME, PAN AMERICAN PLAZA, and the University Place Conference Center. In the arts, the trust contributed substantially to the INDIANAPOLIS SYMPHONY ORCHESTRA and to the renovation of the INDIANA THEATRE and the CIRCLE THEATRE. Its contributions to the INDIANAPOLIS MUSEUM OF ART, where Mr. Krannert served as chairman of the board of trustees, included the major gift for the Krannert Pavilion.

NORA MCKINNEY HIATT

Ku Klux Klan. Populist, white Protestant social and political movement of the 1920s. Based on white supremacist, anti-Catholic, and anti-Semitic beliefs, support for prohibition enforcement, and a wide range of traditional social, religious, and family values, the Klan became the largest social organization in Indianapolis and the dominant force in city politics between 1921 and 1928. At least 27 percent and perhaps as many as 40 percent of all native-born white men in the city paid ten dollars to become official members of the Klan during this era. A separate women's organization (Women of the Ku Klux Klan) also existed, and may have been quite large, although the actual extent of its popularity is not known. Political candidates openly supported by the Klan captured Marion County's congressional seat in 1924,

and the mayor's office, the city council, and the board of school commissioners, among other offices, in 1925. Throughout the state one quarter to one third of all native-born white men became members and Klan politicians gained control of the state Republican party, many of the major local party organizations (both Democrat and Republican), the state legislature, and virtually all of the state's major elected offices, including that of governor.

The Klan movement of the 1920s, distinct from the southern terrorist Klans of the Reconstruction era (1865–1877) and the civil rights era (1954–1968), had its beginnings in Atlanta, Georgia, in 1915. For a number of years it barely survived as a regional fraternal organization prone to vigilante violence and devoted to the idea that sinister forces—primarily Catholics, Jews, and blacks—threatened American institutions. In 1920, however, after the onset of national prohibition, Klan leaders began a national marketing campaign that turned the organization in a new, more successful direction. While retaining its bigoted ideological orientation, the Klan now promoted itself as an organization of patriotic citizens determined to use politics and other law-abiding means to support prohibition enforcement, traditional moral and family values, patriotism, public education, civic responsibility, and various other concerns.

Millions of Americans rushed to join the Klan or support it with their votes between 1920 and 1925. At least three million and perhaps as many as six million men and women joined from every region of the nation, with the most success coming in areas that were most homogeneously white and tied culturally to a strong evangelical Protestant tradition. The most popular state organizations were in the Midwest. By all accounts Indiana's Klan was the largest and most politically powerful in the nation and its original Grand Dragon (state leader), DAVID CURTIS (D. C.) STEPHENSON, was one of the most well-known Klansmen of the era.

The Klan established its first Indiana chapter in Evansville in late 1920 and quickly organized chapters in every Indiana county. In March, 1921, the Klan opened an office in Indianapolis and began soliciting members locally. By summer, 1922, the Klan, claiming some 5,000 members, had begun publishing THE FIERY CROSS, a weekly newspaper headquartered in the Century Building and supported by local business advertising. Within a year the paper reported a circulation of 125,000 throughout the Midwest.

The Indianapolis men who joined the Klan came in large numbers from every area of the city and represented a wide cross-section of the city's white Protestant society. This was also true throughout the state and in other areas around the nation where the Klan flourished. Klan members were highly representative of Indianapolis' occupational spectrum. Men at the upper end of the spectrum—successful businessmen, shop owners, and professionals—could be found just as frequently in the Klan as they could among the population at large. Less affluent white collar workers and skilled blue collar workers joined the Klan at a slightly higher rate than other occupational groups. Semiskilled and unskilled workers were somewhat less likely to join the Klan, but even they were well represented. Only the very rich and the very poor failed to belong in significant numbers. For many individuals the ten dollar initiation fee (easily a quarter of a week's pay for well-paid workers) represented an important barrier to Klan membership. Klansmen also came in representative numbers from virtually all of the city's major Protestant churches as well as from that segment of society that did not attend any church. Many of the city's Protestant ministers were openly sympathetic to the Klan and became active organizers and leaders in the movement.

At the same time many Indianapolis citizens—including many white Protestants—reacted with anger and alarm to the Klan's great popularity. Naturally, those sentiments ran strongest in the city's Catholic, black, and Jewish communities. The INDIANA CATHOLIC AND RECORD, the INDIANAPOLIS FREEMAN, and the Indiana Jewish Chronicle, all published in Indianapolis, relentlessly attacked the Klan's bigotry, expressed outrage at its political influence, and encouraged their readers to do everything in their power to stop the Klan. The city's leading anti-Klan newspaper, the INDIANAPOLIS TIMES, battled the Klan throughout the 1920s and received a Pulitzer Prize in 1928 for its detailed reports on the Klan's

involvement in bribery and corruption in city, county, and state politics.

One of the bolder anti-Klan actions of the era occurred in April, 1923, when Klan opponents— thought to be led by Catholic members of the Indianapolis police force—broke into the city's Klan headquarters in Buschmann Hall (located at 11th Street and College Avenue), stole a membership list, and later published it in the Chicago-based anti-Klan newspaper, Tolerance. Publication of the list came as something of an embarrassment to a number of prominent individuals such as Indiana Secretary of State Edward Jackson, who would be elected governor a little more than a year later. But the list's publication, like other anti-Klan activities, did virtually nothing to slow the Klan's rapidly increasing popularity. Membership almost certainly tripled in Indianapolis within a year and a half after its appearance.

Another opponent of the Klan, the city's Republican mayor, SAMUEL LEWIS SHANK, also tried to stem the organization's power, although he, too, failed. Shank prohibited masked parades, refused the use of TOMLINSON HALL for a Women of the Ku Klux Klan rally, and enforced the Board of Public Safety's ban on cross burnings. In July, 1923, a cross burning in West Indianapolis attracted several thousand people and produced a rock-throwing incident when city firemen attempted to extinguish the fire. The Klan threatened to impeach Shank, accusing him of aiding bootleggers and criminals.

In an effort to break the Klan statewide, Shank entered the Republican gubernatorial primary against the Klan's candidate, Ed Jackson. In the May 6 primary election, Jackson easily gained the nomination over Shank and other anti-Klan Republicans, defeating the Indianapolis mayor in Marion County by a total of 38,668 to 20,306 votes. Following his defeat, Shank reluctantly capitulated to the Klan's political power. He allowed the Klan to hold a massive victory parade which saw more than 7,000 triumphant Klansmen and Klanswomen march from the INDIANA STATE FAIRGROUNDS on the north side of Indianapolis, through the black neighborhoods along Indiana Avenue, into the center of the city.

In November, 1924, the Klan reached the zenith of its political power in Indiana. Klansman

Ed Jackson was elected governor along with a full Klan-endorsed slate of state officials, a Klan-backed majority in the state legislature (including State Senator William T. Quillen of Indianapolis), and all but a handful of the state's 13 congressional representatives (including Congressman Ralph E. Updike of Indianapolis). In Marion County, Jackson defeated his anti-Klan Democratic opponent, Carleton B. McCulloch, by a total of 85,740 to 71,876 votes. In the following year the Klan assumed control of Indianapolis city government. The discredited Shank was replaced by Klansman JOHN L. DUVALL, who defeated Democrat Walter Myers in the November, 1925, municipal election. A significant number of traditionally Republican voters abandoned the party as the Klan gained control. The largest bloc of disaffected Republicans came from the city's black community. Black voters turned overwhelmingly to the Democratic party during the Klan elections of 1924 and 1925; few would ever return to the Republican ranks.

Local opposition stemmed primarily from the Klan's reputation as an organization that fomented danger, division, and violence. Klan demonstrations, rallies, and parades—usually culminating in ceremonial cross burnings—certainly underscored this concern. So too did the frequently tumultuous pro- and anti-Klan political demonstrations that accompanied elections. In reality, however, the Klan was a mainstream movement oriented toward politics, not an organization of vigilantes operating on the fringes of society. Perhaps even more significant, its ideology was far from aberrant in Indianapolis or the rest of American society in the 1920s. Indeed, the widely held view that white Protestant cultural values should be dominant in society, and that white Protestants could be legitimately viewed as America's chosen people, lay at the heart of the Klan's popularity. This mainstream, "populist" message explained the Klan's successful political insurgency.

In Indianapolis, as throughout the state, the issue of prohibition enforcement was the primary catalyst for white Protestant concerns. While liquor had been outlawed by federal and state law, a vast underground market flourished in Indianapolis just as it did elsewhere. Not only was pro-

At the height of its power, Indianapolis' Ku Klux Klan rallied at the fairgrounds in June, 1924. As many as 40 percent of the city's native-born white men joined the organization. Women and children also participated in Klan activities as members of auxiliary organizations. A local fireworks company commissioned the photograph, presumably for advertising purposes. [Indiana Historical Society, Bass Collection, #86797]

hibition enforcement an abysmal failure, but law enforcement officials themselves were corrupt. When the Klan-backed city council and Mayor Duvall were elected in 1925, "law enforcement" was their central message. But the city's Klan politicians proved just as ineffective as their predecessors at enforcing the liquor laws—and just as corrupt in other areas. A series of scandals forced Duvall and the entire Klan city council out of office before the completion of their terms.

The Klan's populist politics spilled over into other areas as well. The Indianapolis Klan became deeply involved in a complex and controversial battle over the expansion of the city's public school system during the 1920s. In the early part of the decade, the school system was the target of public criticism for its poorly maintained, overcrowded facilities. In 1921 and 1923, Indianapolis voters passed bond issues to support the construction of new elementary and high schools. Throughout these years, however, city business leaders who controlled the Indianapolis Board of School Commissioners through an organization known as the Citizen's School Committee blocked these construction projects. Combining its support for the building program with anti-Catholic rhetoric directed at board president Charles W. Barry, the Klan slated five candidates (known as the Protestant School Ticket) in the 1925 election and swept the Citizen's Committee off the school board. Over the next four years the school board carried out the building program that the previous board considered "extravagant." One of the schools built during this era was the racially segregated CRISPUS ATTUCKS HIGH SCHOOL. The Klan-dominated school board naturally favored this development. But so too did its opponent, the Citizen's Committee, which originally devised the segregation plan and maintained it while controlling the school board from the late 1920s into the 1950s. Higher school taxes were controversial in Indianapolis during the 1920s; segregation was not. The Klan-dominated city council subsequently passed a law to segregate the city's residential neighborhoods, but federal courts threw out the law before it ever went into effect.

After 1925 the Klan declined abruptly in Indianapolis and throughout the nation. The conviction and subsequent imprisonment of former Indiana Grand Dragon D. C. Stephenson on the charge of second-degree murder in 1925 played an important part in discrediting the organization. So too did other criminal charges against Klan leaders and politicians in Indianapolis and elsewhere. Growing public disillusionment with prohibition by the mid–1920s also contributed significantly to the Klan's decline. Once Klan politicians demonstrated that they were just as unable as other government officials to stop the flow of illegal liquor, many supporters simply gave up on the idea that the prohibition laws were enforceable. Remnants of the 1920s Klan movement would linger into the 1930s, and small, sometimes violent hate groups bearing the Klan's name continue to exist. None of these groups, however, would match the massive, mainstream popularity of the Indianapolis Klan of the early 1920s.

LEONARD J. MOORE
McGill University

Kenneth T. Jackson, *The Ku Klux Klan in the City, 1915–1930* (New York, 1967); Leonard J. Moore, *Citizen Klansmen: The Ku Klux Klan in Indiana, 1921–1928* (Chapel Hill, N.C., 1991); Emma Lou Thornbrough, "Segregation in Indiana during the Klan Era of the 1920s," *Mississippi Valley Historical Review*, 47 (1961), 594–618.

L. S. Ayres and Company. First modern department store in Indianapolis and long one of the city's major retailers. In 1872 LYMAN S. AYRES bought controlling interest in the Trade Palace, a well-established dry and fancy goods store at 26–28 West Washington Street. He stayed in New York as a resident buyer until 1874 when he moved his family to Indianapolis to assume management. In 1875 he relocated his store across the street to 33–37 West Washington Street in a new three-story building. His progressive concern for the welfare of his employees and personable customer service was coupled with his early use of gas and incandescent lighting, telephones, and the first elevator to be used by a retailer in the city, as well as the state's first glass merchandise showcases.

Frederic M. Ayres, Lyman's son, assumed control upon his father's death in 1896, incorporated the store as L. S. Ayres and Company with himself as president, and began a period of internal expansion. He built a new eight-story store at 1–15 West Washington Street on land purchased by his father in the heart of the shopping district. Opened on October 2, 1905, Ayres was the first retailer in Indianapolis to use the modern concept of a department store.

The original arrangement of the store began with six departments of less expensive dry goods in the economy basement, which included a soda fountain with 125 varieties of sodas. The main floor sold dry goods such as cravats, collars, and combs, underwear, laces, and nightshirts, perfume, jewelry, and walking sticks. On the second floor were goods by-the-yard and millinery; on the third floor, ready-made garments for men, women, and children; and interior decorations on the fourth floor. The fifth floor's elegant Tea Room, with its monogrammed china and seating for 300, soon became a popular meeting place. On the sixth floor up to 180 dressmakers made ready-to-wear clothing and special orders, while seventh-floor carpenters manufactured picture frames and cabinets, as well as did upholstering. The eighth floor was the receiving and marking room.

The store arrangement and size grew and changed over the years. This was due in part to Ayres' ability to attract, hold, and develop talented employees. A store newsletter, originally called *El-Es-A-Log*, appeared in 1914, and an in-store training program began in the early 1920s. The store provided employee benefits such as vacations, insurance, and Christmas bonuses and continued them even during the Great Depression.

L. S. Ayres and Company early became an innovative retailer. Frederic Ayres and nine other leading national department store retailers founded the Retail Research Association to exchange ideas and information. This organization evolved into the Associated Merchandising Corporation, which bought goods cooperatively and opened several buying offices in Europe and one in Asia. Beginning with its golden anniversary in 1922 the company held annual special events and sales, often emphasizing its connection with the city. In 1936 "That Ayres Look" was first used as an advertising slogan to define Ayres' philosophy of fashion leadership. That same year the company installed the five-ton electric clock, designed by Arthur Bohn, on the store's corner at Washington and Meridian streets; the clock, which could be read at 500 feet, soon became a familiar city landmark. In 1937 Ayres distributed "Charga-Plates" to its charge customers, and in 1939 it provided the city's first "Audichron Service" to give time-of-day by telephone to customers.

Christmas was a special time at Ayres. In 1922 the Ayres Christmas Carollers first sang from the balcony overlooking the main floor during the week of Christmas, and in 1926 its traditional five-story Christmas Candle was placed on the North Building fronting Washington Street. On Thanksgiving Eve, 1947, a 1,200–pound bronze cherub sculpted by DAVID K. RUBINS was first placed atop the Ayres' clock, to be removed every year at midnight on Christmas Eve. Below the clock the corner show window displayed the L. S. Ayres store in the 1930s with moving mechanical figures clothed in period costumes. Inside the store's eighth-floor auditorium a Santa Claus Express train carried thousands of children annually through a mountain tunnel and around an ice-covered pond scene to deliver them to Santa Claus.

After World War II Ayres expanded beyond Indianapolis by building and buying stores throughout Indiana, Kentucky, Ohio, and Illinois.

Ayres also developed a number of specialty stores. The acquisition of the local CHARLES MAYER AND COMPANY store in 1954 introduced fine china, silver, and jewelry to Ayres' shoppers. Lyman S. Ayres II became president of the company in 1954 and opened Ayres' first suburban store in the new Glendale Mall in 1958. Eventually ten more branches were opened in Indiana and in the Indianapolis metropolitan area. In 1961 Ayres began Ayr-Way, a discount store chain.

In 1972 Associated Dry Goods acquired L. S. Ayres and Company, made Ayres and Ayr-Way separate subsidiaries, and dissolved the Indianapolis company. Target bought Ayr-Way in the early 1980s and the May Company acquired Ayres in 1986. The downtown store reported a loss of $2.2 million in 1988. A dispute with the city over the proposed CIRCLE CENTRE MALL resulted in the flagship store finally being closed in January, 1992, ending 120 years of business in downtown Indianapolis. Ayres stores, however, continue to operate in metropolitan area malls. The city of Indianapolis bought the downtown Ayres buildings with its clock and holiday cherub to become a cornerstone of Circle Centre Mall.

ROBERT F. GILYEAT
MARCUS EUGENE WOODS, II

———
L. S. Ayres and Company Records, Indiana Historical Society.

L. Strauss and Company. Clothing retailer. In 1853 Jewish tailor Max Dernham and German clothier John Gramling purchased the stock of G. Simon & Co. (founded 1853) and opened the Eagle Clothing Company on Washington Street, promoting themselves as "manufacturers and dealers of ready-made clothing and gent's furnishing goods." After two German Jewish brothers, Louis and Morris Greisheimer, purchased the store in 1865–1866, Leopold Strauss, a young tailor from Chronberg, Germany, joined the company as a clerk. Within five years Strauss had become a partner, and by 1879 he had acquired the Greisheimers' interests. Eagle Clothing became one of the city's leading retailers and reputedly pioneered the concept of fixed prices for customers. In 1899 Strauss formed a partnership with friend and New York merchandiser Abram

L. Strauss's 33 W. Washington Street store operated from 1905 until 1946. [Indiana Historical Society, Bass Collection, #35384]

L. Block and later changed the firm's name to L. Strauss and Company. As Strauss' health failed, Block assumed control and directed the company after Strauss' death (March 11, 1914) until 1935.

In April, 1946, the company relocated from 33 West Washington Street, its home for 41 years, to the Occidental Building at the corner of Illinois and Washington streets. A $750,000 remodeling of the building, including air conditioning and escalators, made Strauss one of the largest retail clothing stores for men and boys in the state. During the 1950s Strauss opened branch stores in Broad Ripple (1956) and Glendale Center (1958).

In February, 1969, Genesco Corporation, a conglomerate based in Nashville, Tennessee, and owner of such upscale stores as Bonwit Teller, acquired L. Strauss and hired Minnesota native and clothing retailer Thad Larson as president. Seeking to return the store to local ownership, Larson purchased Strauss from Genesco in August, 1979, and opened stores in Fort Wayne (1984) and Cincinnati (1987). After moving Strauss' downtown store to Claypool Court in 1985, Larson relocated Strauss to MONUMENT CIRCLE in October, 1991, citing delays in the CIRCLE CENTRE MALL project. The company declared bankruptcy for purposes of reorganization in March, 1993.

SHERYL D. VANDERSTEL

Indianapolis Star, Mar. 18, 1928, Mar. 14, 1946; *Indianapolis News*, Aug. 1, 1979, Apr. 14, 1987.

Labor Day Celebrations. Indianapolis first observed Labor Day on Sunday, September 19, 1886. Originally scheduled for Monday, September 6, organizers accommodated their guest speakers by changing the festivities to Sunday, despite objections from local ministers. Labor supporters hoped to make the occasion a statewide celebration; however, the refusal of railroads to reduce rates for traveling laborers limited participation to local workers. The dominance of the KNIGHTS OF LABOR and the Typographical Union among Indianapolis workers was most evident in the day's parade. The 45–minute parade concluded with a large picnic at the Exposition Grounds (later the old INDIANA STATE FAIRGROUNDS) with nearly 6,000 attending the afternoon festivities.

Indianapolis Mayor CALEB S. DENNY issued the first Labor Day proclamation in Indiana in 1887, designating Monday, September 5, as a day to commemorate the contributions of the city's laborers. Following New York's lead, Indiana sanctioned the observance of Labor Day in 1891. In response to a nationwide movement President Grover Cleveland signed legislation in June, 1894, making Labor Day an official national holiday.

Between 1894 and 1922 annual Labor Day celebrations varied in scope. There were parades, races, picnics, speakers (including ALBERT J. BEVERIDGE and LEW WALLACE), theatrical productions, and a "spectacular" called "The Last Days of Pompeii." The 1921 festivity attracted thousands of workers representing 95 local unions who paraded through the streets to TOMLINSON HALL where they heard speeches and concluded with an evening ball.

From 1923 to 1936 there were no official observances of Labor Day, due in part to local antilabor sentiment and the Great Depression. The traditional Labor Day parade returned in 1937 but was marked by antagonisms between the AFL and CIO. The CIO refused to participate in the parade, which was sponsored by the Indianapolis Central Labor Union comprised of some 23,000 members of 135 AFL locals. During World War II official observances of Labor Day were cancelled to keep the factories open. For the next several decades there were no official Labor Day observances. The Central Indiana Labor Council, the United Auto Workers, and the Teamsters jointly sponsored parades during the 1980s. In 1992 over 5,000 people attended local Labor Day festivities.

MICHAEL E. WISKER

Labor Militancy. In one of the earliest documented labor struggles in Indianapolis, members of the typographical union went on strike in 1863 after failing to secure a 20–percent wage increase from the publishers of the *Indianapolis Sentinel*. The paper dismissed union workers and promptly advertised for new employees, announcing, "no member of a typographical union need apply." The next year, the Blacksmiths and Machinists Union went on strike over wage issues.

Indianapolis experienced the first tremors of national labor disputes in the late 1860s. Local foundries shut down in 1866 during a nationwide dispute between the Iron Molders Union and foundry owners. Union members accused owners of locking out workers in an effort to destroy the union, while owners insisted that the union was on strike over wage issues.

During the 1870s Indiana and Indianapolis faced the most serious threats to labor peace and stability when workers shut down railroad lines. In the midst of the Panic of 1873 the PENNSYLVANIA RAILROAD cut wages by 10 percent, precipitating a general strike that became the largest strike in the nation to that date. Beginning in the East and making its way west to Indiana, the strike affected most of the rail lines passing through Indianapolis. While there were many strikers and sympathizers in the capital city, there was surprisingly little violence. The relative calm of Indianapolis allowed Governor THOMAS A. HENDRICKS to use the city as a staging area from which he dispatched the militia to trouble spots. On December 27, 1873, Hendricks ordered 66 militiamen under the command of General Daniel Macauley to depart from the Massachusetts Avenue train station for Logansport to deal with striking rail workers. The *Indianapolis Journal* criticized the governor for not taking more drastic action, especially in Indianapolis where transportation was seriously impeded.

The national railroad strike in the summer of 1877 was larger and more serious. Despite the absence of significant disorders, rail owners convinced Judge WALTER Q. GRESHAM of the Seventh District Court to ask President Rutherford B. Hayes to dispatch 200 U.S. Army regulars to Indianapolis to control striking rail workers. Rail workers ended their strikes by early August and returned to work without a wage increase, all before the arrival of the federal troops. This marked the first strike in Indiana in which regular army troops were authorized for use against citizens in a labor dispute.

The early 20th century witnessed an increase in labor violence. Indianapolis' first strike-related bombings occurred during a construction workers' strike in September, 1909, when job sites in the city were dynamited. In April, 1911, John J. McNamara, secretary-treasurer of the Bridge and Structural Iron Workers Union, was arrested at the union's international headquarters on MONUMENT CIRCLE and extradited to California to stand trial with his brother for dynamiting the *Los Angeles Times* building in Los Angeles. His extradition brought protests from the Indianapolis Central Labor Union and Indiana Federation of Labor. The subsequent indictment of 51 others, mostly members of the Iron Workers Union, on charges of transporting dynamite resulted in a lengthy trial in federal circuit court in Indianapolis (Oct.-Dec., 1912). Despite efforts by prolabor senator JOHN W. KERN, SR., who served as defense attorney, the jury found 38 of 40 brought to trial guilty, including union president Frank M. Ryan. The U.S. Supreme Court upheld the convictions, which was a blow to organized labor and gave a boost to local antilabor campaigns by manufacturers.

Between October 31 and November 7, 1913, 800 Indianapolis streetcar operators stopped work to obtain union recognition, higher wages, and better working conditions. Mob activity resulted in three deaths and destruction of rail company property, which the Central Labor Union condemned. Governor Samuel Ralston mobilized the National Guard to reestablish order. This strike, followed in late November by a violent Teamsters' walkout, served to weaken labor's support in Indianapolis.

In light of the 1913 strikes, the 1919 national steel strike, and the antilabor campaign led by ASSOCIATED EMPLOYERS OF INDIANAPOLIS, the City Council enacted an antipicketing ordinance on September 19, 1919. This measure, which remained in effect until the mid–1930s, prohibited all picketing by striking workers, marking yet another setback for the local labor movement.

During the REAL SILK HOSIERY MILLS STRIKE of April–May, 1934, dynamite again made the headlines of Indianapolis newspapers as bombings were attempted at the homes of strikers and strike-breakers. There were numerous reports of violent encounters between strikers and scabs and between strikers and the private security police hired by the company.

In 1976 officials of LINK-BELT COMPANY accused members of the United Steel Workers of America Local 1150 of planting dynamite at a power substation and propane tanks at the Rockville Road plant and at loading docks of trucking firms that had refused to honor the union's picket lines. Since none of the dynamite was exploded (no blasting caps or fusing were found), no charges were filed. Union members insisted that management had planted the explosives in an effort to discredit the union.

Labor-related violence in Indianapolis has waned in recent decades. A declining number of organized workers and fewer organizational drives in the city have diminished labor's strength. Violent action, once considered a viable though risky and questionable tactic, has been replaced by more sophisticated methods of arbitration and negotiation.

MARK J. KEEFE

Frederick Doyle Kershner, Jr., "A Social and Cultural History of Indianapolis, 1860–1914" (Ph.D. dissertation, University of Wisconsin, 1950); Emma Lou Thornbrough, *Indiana in the Civil War Era, 1850–1880*

(Indianapolis, 1965); Clifton J. Phillips, *Indiana in Transition: The Emergence of an Industrial Commonwealth, 1880–1920* (Indianapolis, 1968).

Labor Newspapers.

Newspapers representing the interests and concerns of working men and women have been published in Indianapolis since the 1870s. Although some papers appealed to the general laboring community, most were sponsored by specific unions and reported news and labor activities locally and nationwide.

The first labor paper in Indianapolis was *The Union*, started in late 1873–early 1874 by the INTERNATIONAL TYPOGRAPHICAL UNION, No. 1, Indianapolis. Begun as a daily by the Union Publishing Company, it became a weekly by July and ceased publishing later that year. *The Workingmen's Map*, published by labor radical Calvin A. Light, George S. Bonnel, and Joseph G. Charlton, was a general labor paper that lasted from March, 1876, until May, 1877. *The Labor Signal* (later *The Signal*), published 1881–1896 and edited for several years by Thomas M. Gruelle, was the official organ of the Central Trades and Labor Union, Indianapolis' federation of local unions.

Several other labor papers appeared in the city for short periods of time and addressed the particular needs of blue collar workers. *The Appeal* and *The Union Standard* were published briefly in 1887 and 1896, respectively. The *Indiana Labor Bulletin* (1908–1926), which became the *Union Labor Bulletin* in 1916, changed from weekly to twice-monthly publication and addressed labor issues facing unions throughout the state.

Since Indianapolis was home to numerous national and international unions, many union publications originated in the Hoosier capital. The UNITED MINE WORKERS OF AMERICA, headquartered here from 1898 to 1934, published Italian, Slovak, and English editions of the weekly *United Mine Workers Journal* until the 1910s. The *Buchdrucker-Zeitung*, published for German members of the Typographical Union, was the only other Indianapolis paper providing labor news in the workers' native language. Other union papers included the *Locomotive Fireman and Engineman's Magazine* (ca. 1885), the *Typographical Journal* (ca.

1893), *Bricklayer and Mason* (ca. 1898), *Teamster* (ca. 1903), the *Carpenter* (ca. 1905), and *Journeyman Barber* (ca. 1905). Another paper for the general working community was the *Indiana Labor Tribune* (1955–1974), launched by Maury E. Rubin and later edited by Harry Berns.

Serving as the voice of the Indiana Federation of Labor and the CENTRAL LABOR UNION of Indianapolis, *The Union*, founded by Edwin F. Gould in 1888, probably had the greatest impact in the city. Initially opposed to the candidacy of Benjamin Harrison, *The Union* endured several controversies during its 80–year run. In the 1890s the International Typographical Union No. 1 placed the paper on its "do not patronize" list for failing to use union printers. During a subsequent competition among local labor papers, *The Signal* accused *Union* publisher Harry W. Bassett of being Mayor Joseph E. Bell's personal secretary and an opponent of union projects. This allegation appeared in a three-inch block of every *Signal* edition between March 16 and August 25, 1916. Bassett responded with a notice on page one of his paper, showcasing a statement of support and endorsement from the Indiana Federation of Labor. *The Union* ultimately survived the tumult of union politics and became the official voice of the Indiana State AFL before ceasing publication in 1968.

In 1974 *Labor News* became the official voice of the local labor community. Sponsored by the Indiana State AFL-CIO and published by Marty and Fred Levin, the 20–plus page paper utilized a paper-within-a-paper format to highlight local unions and their activities. Amid differences over content and advertising procurement practices, the state AFL-CIO terminated *Labor News* as its official publication in 1992.

LARRY HENNINGER

_____

Jacob Piatt Dunn, *Greater Indianapolis* (Chicago, 1910); Clifton J. Phillips, *Indiana in Transition: The Emergence of an Industrial Commonwealth, 1880–1920* (Indianapolis, 1968); John W. Miller, *Indiana Newspaper Bibliography* (Indianapolis, 1982).

Labor Unions (National Headquarters).

Beginning in the mid–1800s, Indianapolis served as a locus of the state's growing labor activity. By the early 20th century the city had become headquarters for several national and international unions and the center of operations for such legendary labor leaders as Samuel Gompers, John L. Lewis, William L. "Big Bill" Hutcheson, William Green, and Daniel J. Tobin. Indianapolis' central location and its elaborate rail system made the city more accessible to the rest of the country than most cities. At least 12 major unions selected Indianapolis for their headquarters, thus establishing the city as the "labor capital of America" by the early 1900s.

The roots of organized labor activity in the city can be found as early as June, 1850, when Indiana artisans founded the Mechanics Mutual Protections. The group sought increased wages, better educational opportunities, and security for families of members unable to work because of illness. In November, 1865, advocates for an eight-hour workday met in Indianapolis to launch a statewide movement. JOHN FEHRENBATCH, president of the local Machinists' and Blacksmiths' Union and future president of the international union (1870), led the effort. Delegates representing various Indiana unions convened in Indianapolis in April, 1873, and founded a trades assembly to promote the interests of laborers statewide. Another meeting on September 8, 1885, resulted in the organization of the Indiana Federation of Labor, led by Samuel L. Leffingwell; in 1903 it affiliated with the American Federation of Labor.

By the 1880s Indianapolis reportedly was one of the largest union cities in the nation with nearly 10,000 union members. The 1880 census listed 77 labor unions in the state, most represented in Indianapolis, with the KNIGHTS OF LABOR constituting the largest group. In July, 1880, local unions formed the Indianapolis Trades Assembly (known as the Indianapolis Central Labor Union after 1883), which comprised 83 locals and 11,000 members by 1892. This high degree of labor activity attracted many national and international unions to Indiana's capital city.

One of the earliest national unions to locate in Indianapolis was the Journeymen Stonecutters' Association of North America. Around 1875 the union established its headquarters at 8 East Market Street and remained until ca. 1968 when it merged with the Laborers' International Union of North America, headquartered in Washington, D.C. The Brotherhood of Locomotive Firemen (organized 1873) maintained headquarters in Indianapolis from 1876 until 1880 when it relocated to Terre Haute.

Typographical Union No. 1, organized in 1852 as part of the National Typographical Union to represent pressmen, typesetters, and others in the printing trades, remains as one of the oldest unions in the city. The national union, which became the INTERNATIONAL TYPOGRAPHICAL UNION in 1869, moved its headquarters from New York City to Indianapolis in 1888. It acquired the Van Camp mansion at 2820 North Meridian Street in 1925 for its new offices, staying there until 1961–1962 when it moved to Colorado Springs, Colorado.

The American Federation of Labor, founded in Columbus, Ohio, in 1886, moved its headquarters from New York City to Indianapolis around 1894, apparently in retaliation against eastern leadership. AFL president Samuel Gompers kept offices with the International Typographical Union in the old DeSoto Block on East Market Street. He later relocated the federation's headquarters to Washington, D.C.

Mine workers comprised one of the largest organized labor bodies in the United States in the early 1900s. On September 8, 1885, union representatives met in Indianapolis and founded the National Federation of Miners and Mine Laborers. After reorganizing as the UNITED MINE WORKERS OF AMERICA in 1890, the union selected Indianapolis for its headquarters in 1898, citing the city's geographical location near the center of the coal-mining region. Under the leadership of John L. Lewis, the UMWA maintained offices on the 11th floor of the MERCHANTS NATIONAL BANK BUILDING in the 1920s. At a January, 1934, meeting in TOMLINSON HALL, 1,800 UMWA delegates voted to relocate union headquarters to Washington, D.C.

The United Brotherhood of Carpenters and Joiners, organized in Chicago in 1881, designated Indianapolis as its headquarters around 1901. A new building constructed at 222 East Michigan Street in 1909 housed the union's administrative offices as well as those of the Barbers, Teamsters, and other unions.

The Journeymen Barbers, Hairdressers, and Cosmetologists International Union of America, founded in Buffalo, New York, in 1887, moved from Cleveland to Indianapolis where it remained from 1902 until the late 1970s. Union leaders helped to establish state licensing standards for new barbers and to regulate barber and beauty schools. In 1933 the JBHCIU opened and operated a nonprofit barbers' and beauticians' school in Indianapolis.

Several other unions maintained headquarters in Indianapolis at one time. Among them were the International Brotherhood of Teamsters, known as the TEAMSTERS UNION (1903–1953); the Laundry Workers International Union (?-1930s); International Brotherhood of Bookbinders (ca. 1915); the Bricklayers, Masons, and Plasterers International Union of America (ca. 1905); and the Bridge and Structural Iron Workers Union (ca. 1910).

While unions were principally concerned with building membership in their early years, they gradually became more active in lobbying for national labor legislation. During the 1930s several of the national and international unions left Indianapolis for Washington, D.C., to be closer to the nation's political activities. Mergers between unions, such as the Journeymen Barbers International Union (the last international union in the city) and the United Food and Commercial Workers, also led to the removal of union headquarters from Indianapolis. Likewise, the long history of antilabor sentiment exhibited by the city's business leaders may have affected unions' decisions to leave the city. Indianapolis continued as headquarters for the newly formed Indiana State AFL-CIO following the national merger of the American Federation of Labor and the Congress of Industrial Organizations in 1955, but by the mid–1950s the city had lost its place as the nation's labor capital to Washington, D.C.

MICHAEL E. WISKER

Emma Lou Thornbrough, *Indiana in the Civil War Era, 1850–1880* (Indianapolis, 1965); Clifton J. Phillips, *Indiana in Transition: The Emergence of an Industrial Commonwealth, 1880–1920* (Indianapolis, 1968); *Indianapolis Star*, Sept. 27, 1953; *Indianapolis Times*, July 30, 1961; Gary M. Fink, ed., *Labor Unions* (Westport, Conn., 1977).

Lacy, Edna Balz (Sept. 21, 1906–Dec. 30, 1991). Manufacturing executive and civic leader. A native of Indianapolis, Lacy graduated from SHORTRIDGE HIGH SCHOOL and later earned a B.A. in education from the University of Michigan (1928). She returned to Indianapolis and taught introductory language courses and science in the Indianapolis Public Schools for five years before marrying Indianapolis industrialist Howard John Lacy II in 1934 and beginning a family.

After the unexpected death of her husband in 1959, Lacy became president and chairman of the board of U.S. Corrugated-Fibre Box Company, a firm that her father-in-law founded in 1912.

Under her direction the company became a national leader in corrugated box production and expanded into several other industries, becoming Lacy Diversified Industries in 1972.

Lacy was active on the boards of numerous Indianapolis business, civic, and charitable organizations, including THE CHILDREN'S MUSEUM and STARLIGHT MUSICALS. She was elected in 1973 as the first woman board member of the Indianapolis CHAMBER OF COMMERCE. One of her most significant contributions to the city was the creation in 1976 of the STANLEY K. LACY EXECUTIVE LEADERSHIP SERIES, memorializing a son killed in an automobile accident. The annual program provides training for young executives in community leadership skills.

Lacy's leadership in the city brought numerous awards and recognition. Three governors named her a Sagamore of the Wabash. The Indiana Republican Mayors' Association and Women in Communications selected her in 1976 as

Businesswoman Edna Balz Lacy. [Lacy Diversified Industries]

Woman of the Year. In 1993 she was named post-humously to the Indiana Business Hall of Fame. Lacy also received the Madam C. J. Walker Award for leadership in creating minority-owned enterprises and for promoting minority participation in the Lacy Leadership Program.

STACEY NICHOLAS

George and Miriam Geib, *Indianapolis First* (Indianapolis, 1990); *Who's Who in the Midwest* (1963–1964, 1990–1991); *Indianapolis Star*, Dec. 31, 1991.

Lake Central Airlines. Indianapolis-based local service airline. Lake Central Airlines was established in May, 1949, as Turner Airlines to provide short-haul service from its base at Weir Cook Airport. The flamboyant Roscoe Turner had a vision of air service for smaller communities, but he could not overcome the financial difficulties. By December, 1950, Turner sold his controlling interest in the fledgling airline and it changed its name to Lake Central Airlines. The new corporation was organized under Delaware law, but its offices and chief maintenance base were always located in Indianapolis and it was generally identified as a "Hoosier airline," at least within Indiana.

Service began on November 12, 1949, on a route from Indianapolis to Grand Rapids, Michigan. Within two years Lake Central operated regular service over a region extending from Louisville and Cincinnati on the south to Chicago and Grand Rapids on the north. Ownership and management were unstable for several years. Turner sold control to the Weesner family from Nebraska, which had conflicts with the Civil Aeronautics Board (CAB) over other airline operations. Control passed temporarily to an Indianapolis insurance executive, Harry V. Wade, under a voting trust arrangement. Both Wisconsin Central and Ozark airlines attempted to take over Lake Central when a CAB examiner found the current management unfit to continue operations. Not until September, 1954, were all of the disputes resolved through the purchase of 97 percent of the voting stock by a majority of the airline's employees, who used payroll deductions to pay $81,000 for their shares.

Lake Central operated successfully under the regime of detailed federal regulations, winning permission to expand service to a total of 50 cities. It flew as far west as Chicago and St. Louis, and as far east as Buffalo and Baltimore, but concentrated its service in Indiana and Ohio. Passenger and freight traffic increased rapidly through the 1950s and early 1960s, but Lake Central remained dependent upon its federal subsidy. In 1960 Lake Central began flying 52–passenger Convair aircraft no longer needed by larger airlines but replaced their conventional piston engines with faster and more efficient turboprop engines manufactured in Indianapolis by the ALLISON DIVISION of General Motors.

Lloyd Hartman became president in 1962 and energetically expanded Lake Central's routes and improved its service. Meanwhile the CAB began to implement a policy of reducing subsidy requirements by assigning busier and presumably more profitable routes to the smaller airlines. Hartman agreed completely with the policy, but soon faced a very difficult financial problem because the additional and often competitive routes required larger, faster, and more expensive aircraft. The entire local service industry had for years sought a replacement for its aging DC–3s, and Hartman bound Lake Central's future to the Nord–262, a newly designed turboprop aircraft imported from France. Not only would Lake Central be the first North American airline to fly the Nord, it also secured exclusive sales rights for most of North and South America. The 27–passenger Nords cost $550,000 each and Lake Central went deeply into debt to finance the purchase of 12 of the aircraft to serve its lightly traveled routes. For its busiest routes Hartman announced plans to acquire 111–passenger Boeing 737 twin-jet aircraft by 1968, at a cost of $3,000,000 each. Indianapolis banks declined to finance the new aircraft purchases, so Lake Central turned to out-of-town banks.

Unfortunately, the untried Nord–262s soon developed serious troubles with in-flight engine failures that injured several passengers. All 12 planes were withdrawn from service in August, 1967, for major overhaul. This well-publicized operating problem, combined with continuing financial difficulties beyond the resources of the employee ownership program, revived rumors of a merger to save the airline. In April, 1967, Hartman was suddenly removed as president by the Bass family of Dallas, which had quietly acquired ownership of the common stock from the employee group. The newly installed president, L. Thomas Ferguson, soon announced ambitious plans for continued expansion financed by additional bank loans and began an extensive advertising program to restore Lake Central's tarnished reputation. Within six months, however, the new owners announced a merger with Allegheny Airlines (now USAir), the largest of the nation's nine local service carriers. Ferguson returned to his old position as a vice-president at Allegheny when the merger became effective on July 1, 1968. Lake Central, often called "Late Central" by disappointed passengers, quickly faded from memory when Allegheny closed its Indianapolis base and sold its ill-fated Nord–262s.

PATRICK J. FURLONG
Indiana University, South Bend

Indianapolis Newspaper Index, Indiana State Library; *Aviation Week*, passim; *CAB Reports*, particularly the *Great Lakes Local-Service Investigation* (31 CAB 442 [1960]) and the *Allegheny-Lake Central Merger Case* (48 CAB 664 [1968]).

Land Use. Marion County contains nearly every conceivable land use within a mixed urban-suburban-rural environment that has no unique geography. The county contains 402 square miles, or about 257,681 acres. As of 1992 about 60 percent of this land was developed in some manner (155,963 acres). The remaining 40 percent (101,718 acres) consisted of about 48,000 tilled acres, (18.6 percent), 1,447 wetlands totaling 8,435 acres (3.3 percent), about 13,000 wooded acres (5 percent), with the remaining 32,000 acres (12.5 percent) a mixture of bodies of water, non-tilled agricultural lands, odd parcels, and other land uses. Most of the undeveloped land in the early 1990s was within the corner townships of Lawrence, Franklin, Decatur, and Pike, with large undeveloped areas within Warren, Wayne, and Perry townships. There are 9,657.2 acres of park land.

The original 1821 city plan by ALEXANDER RALSTON and the WHITE RIVER valley have been the two most important overall controls on land use within the county. Since the area had few topographic features, the Ralston design intentionally included streets radiating diagonally out from the CIRCLE to provide relief from the monotony of a square grid of streets. The diagonal streets, as well as major gridded streets, now continue to the edges of the county and beyond, hooking up with state roads. With few geographical barriers to confine the direction of development, state roads acted as conduits of commerce along which commercial and residential development occurred, extending the city away from the MILE SQUARE into the outlying townships.

The mistaken perception that White River was truly navigable downstream to the Wabash River led both to the city being platted initially, and later to the development of extensive highway, rail, and air service to accommodate the growth of commerce. The river was of no commercial use, and it became an open sewer within the inner city. Because the river valley was wide, swampy, prone to flooding, and thus difficult to cross with bridges, the city developed along the eastern highlands of the river, slowly extending northward along the high ground, with only the original city and the older towns such as BROAD RIPPLE and HAUGHVILLE exposed to flooding. Areas west of the river were largely cut off from the growing city, while the scenic valley, especially within Washington Township, became the location of many finer homes. Extensive sand and gravel mining has occurred along White River and FALL CREEK, resulting in the creation of many lakes which have become popular sites for residential and recreational development.

The adoption of UNIGOV in 1970 led to distinct delineation of land use within the city by formalizing boundaries of the old city with the county. Unigov allowed the four smaller towns of Lawrence, Beech Grove, Southport, and Speedway to maintain local control over land use. Many small villages also have some local jurisdiction. Various infrastructure, social, and political policies, including school busing, the extension of municipal services outside of the old city, and the construction of four interstate highways, have led to a mixture of increased residential and commercial building in the outlying townships, but for many different reasons.

Center Township is the original Indianapolis. As the core of the city its central business district, the Regional Center, contains commercial, institutional, and governmental buildings. The Mile Square had declined greatly in appearance and vitality by 1972 when then Mayor Richard G. Lugar initiated downtown rebuilding projects involving substantial public and private investment. These efforts continued under the Hudnut and Goldsmith administrations, resulting in the building of MARKET SQUARE ARENA, the new CITY MARKET complex, the HOOSIER DOME and Convention Center complex, numerous large office buildings, and the CIRCLE CENTRE MALL. The largely new INDIANA UNIVERSITY–PURDUE UNIVERSITY AT INDIANAPOLIS complex lies to the west adjacent to WHITE RIVER STATE PARK. To the south and southwest, extending into Wayne Township, is a major industrial complex along and west of the river. Several landfills and the city waste disposal incinerator are also located here. Center Township also has a large residential population broken into three groups: downtown highrise apartments, older and poorer inner-city, and renovated historic districts. Interstate highways 65 and 70 intersect near the center of the township. CROWN HILL CEMETERY and many of the older and larger parks are within Center Township.

The old city of Indianapolis extends in all directions into the outlying townships, but the city grew chiefly along the major north-south and east-west roads, and also within the most scenic areas. These two factors have led to the development of major residential and commercial areas in Washington, Lawrence, Wayne, and eastern Perry, southern Pike, and western Warren townships. Northern Pike, eastern Warren, western Perry, and all of Franklin and Decatur townships have remained largely rural in nature, with mostly scattered housing and limited commercial development. A distinct population concentration in the far north and south exists in the well-developed adjacent out-of-county towns of Carmel (Hamilton) and Greenwood (Johnson). The smaller out-of-county towns of Brownsburg (Hendricks) and Zionsville (Boone) are becoming increasingly attractive for development.

Four large land uses are found in outlying portions of the county: the INDIANAPOLIS INTERNATIONAL AIRPORT, Eagle Creek Reservoir and Park, FORT BENJAMIN HARRISON, and GEIST RESERVOIR. The airport, located in western Wayne and northern Decatur townships, dominates the land use patterns in that portion of the county by discouraging residential uses, while concentrating commercial and industrial land uses that rely upon convenient access to air traffic. These uses will continue to expand. Eagle Creek Reservoir and EAGLE CREEK PARK dominate western Pike Township. The scenic Eagle Creek area has attracted upscale housing, and the densely wooded, popular park has made Pike Township a fast-growing area that has retained much of its rural quality. The reservoir is used for flood control, water supply, and recreation. Fort Benjamin Harrison is located along scenic Fall Creek downstream of Geist Reservoir. The 2,500–acre Army property has been an important economic and social influence on all of Marion County. It has especially influenced use within Lawrence Township by preserving a uniquely large tract of public land with a substantial forest, while allowing for the growth of the city of Lawrence. Fort Harrison is slated to be closed in 1995, and the longterm potential for new land uses of the property are unknown. Geist Reservoir, partially within extreme northeastern Lawrence Township, was long a scenic wooded rural water supply source until the early 1980s when much of the land adjacent to the reservoir was developed for residential purposes.

Perhaps the greatest modern impact on Marion County land use patterns has been the creation of several centralized shopping mall-commercial office-residential complexes built at major road intersections or interstate exits. The Castleton Square Mall vicinity in northeastern Marion County is a prime example of this type of development. Following the building of the Allisonville Road and 82nd Street exits on I–465 and I–69, real estate speculators purchased large blocks of rural land in the vicinity of the small farm town of Castleton. The main mall complex was built first in the early 1970s, followed by the first commercial structures in the mid–1970s, with substantial and continuing residential development beginning in the late 1970s. Fill-in commercial and light industrial development also exists. The village of CASTLETON, once a true community with a high school, has completely disappeared and was dissolved in 1992.

KEVIN STRUNK
Wabash Resources and Consulting

Landers, Julia E. (June 19, 1874–Apr. 12, 1953). Suffragist and active Democrat. A native of Indianapolis, Landers was born in her family home at 802 North Pennsylvania, later the site of Central Library. After attending MAY WRIGHT SEWALL's Girls Classical School, Landers graduated from Bryn Mawr College in Philadelphia. Returning to Indianapolis, she served as assistant to Sewall until the school's closing in 1907. At that time, Landers established a girls school known as Knickerbacker Hall, at 15th Street and Central Avenue, which she operated until World War I. Appointed acting chair of the woman's committee of the Indiana State Council of Defense in 1917, Landers mobilized more than 5,000 Indiana women in the production of shirts and bedding for soldiers. She achieved many firsts for the women of Indiana: first woman appointed district chairman of the Democratic party; first woman to serve on an election board; and first woman from Indiana elected Democratic national committeewoman. An ardent suffragist, Landers worked for passage of the 19th Amendment and was an organizer of the LEAGUE OF WOMEN VOTERS. Other memberships included the Woman's Franchise League, the WOMAN'S DEPARTMENT CLUB, and the Indiana Women's Democratic Club.

KATHY INGELS HELMOND

Landscape Design. Upon her arrival in Indianapolis in 1837, minister Henry Ward Beecher's wife, Eunice Bullard Beecher, noted that the town's homes were not close together (by New England standards) but rather separated by wide backyards, with front lawns facing tree-lined streets. Although the availability of land made these spacious lawns possible, it was their aesthetic appeal which impressed Mrs. Beecher. Signifi-

cantly, her descriptions suggest that Indianapolis fit the ideals of the national "village improvement movement" of the 1850s, which sought to beautify towns with parks, parkways, and tree-lined drives. In turn, the movement probably motivated Indianapolis' first "pleasure garden," which John Hodgkins developed around 1850 at the corner of Tennessee and Georgia streets. Hodgkins planted the grounds with fruit trees and flower beds, built bowers for flowering vines, and placed seats in advantageous spots.

In 1864 Indianapolis made a noteworthy advance in beautifying the city when it purchased the land which became CROWN HILL CEMETERY. Frederick Chislett designed the area's original layout of winding carriage paths; as one of only a few public green spaces, the cemetery quickly became the city's most popular spot for picnicking.

The 1870s were a landmark decade for landscape architecture (then a newly coined term) in Indianapolis. In August, 1872, Horace W. S. Cleveland, a landscape architect from Massachusetts, designed the eastside subdivision of Oakhill as a wealthy residential neighborhood with expansive lots and parks. But the Panic of 1873 prevented the sale of the large lots, which were subsequently subdivided into smaller, cheaper sites. In 1872–1873 James Woodruff platted WOODRUFF PLACE. Woodruff's 77–acre residential park featured three drives centered with grassy esplanades and elaborate fountains and statuary. It was designed as a suburban haven for Indianapolis' wealthy families, but nonresidents were also allowed Sunday excursions in the town. In 1873 Jacob Julian and Sylvester Johnson platted the town of IRVINGTON. This middle class community introduced Indianapolis to the curvilinear streets and natural plantings that renowned landscape architects Frederick Law Olmsted and Calvert Vaux employed in 1869 in their planned community of Riverside, Illinois.

The 1870s also saw a brief focus on the purchase and improvement of public park lands. In 1873 Indianapolis purchased Southern Park (now Garfield Park), and the following year annexed the land in the neighborhood surrounding it. Also in the 1870s, John S. Spann led a movement which beautified UNIVERSITY PARK with walkways and a fountain surrounded by benches, and George Merritt donated time and money toward major improvements at MILITARY PARK, including trees and shrubs, walkways, and a central limestone fountain.

Toward the end of the 19th century, inspired by the 1893 World's Columbian Exposition in Chicago, Indianapolis and cities throughout the United States joined in the "City Beautiful" movement, which promoted municipal improvements, well-tended flower gardens, and landscaped parks as solutions to urban problems. Although city government did not immediately act on the perceived need for green spaces, private groups did so. Four years after the Columbian Exposition opened, William Tron introduced Fairbank Park, located on Illinois Street along FALL CREEK (later the site of ST. VINCENT HOSPITAL). Fairbank's many colorful flower beds were planned by a Mr. Thorpe, designer of the plantings at the Chicago Exposition. The park featured rustic benches and overflowing planters, large trees, exotic plants, bicycle paths, and fountains. Its cafe was the city's first "drive-in" where park visitors could stop for refreshments, including alcoholic beverages, ordered from and delivered to their carriages.

In 1892 the Commercial Club (later the CHAMBER OF COMMERCE) pressed for a City Beautiful–type plan which would promote "sidewalks smooth and even" in a city where "beautiful parks are everywhere." Four years later the newly appointed Board of Park Commissioners hired John C. Olmsted (stepson of Frederick Law Olmsted) to report on the city's park and parkway needs. Inspired by Olmsted's report, Mayor THOMAS TAGGART purchased hundreds of acres of park land, including the land for Riverside Park.

By the beginning of the 20th century cities across America were constructing parks and boulevard systems. By 1903 Seattle, Minneapolis, Baltimore, Detroit, Milwaukee, and Chicago all had their own systems in place. After designing the Kansas City plan, landscape architect GEORGE E. KESSLER came to Indianapolis in 1905 to design a parks and boulevard system. Calling for small and large parks connected by boulevards, the plan—true to City Beautiful ideals for solving urban problems—would also serve as a flood control system. Along Fall Creek, Kessler designed attractive bridges, wide streets, and walkways border-

Early landscape design: One of Woodruff Place's three scenic, tree-lined boulevards, ca. 1900. [Indiana Historical Society, #C5804]

ing the water. Kessler and Riverside boulevards were planned as broad, winding drives highlighting the natural beauty surrounding the city. These boulevards and parkways offered attractive clean-air retreats from the smoke-filled downtown, enhanced the value of adjoining property, and swelled tax revenues. They also were a source of pride to citizens when Indianapolis' system became a model for other cities.

Kessler came to epitomize landscape architecture in Indianapolis. Hired by the park board in 1908, he designed the sunken gardens at GARFIELD PARK AND CONSERVATORY in 1915, as well as bridges for both Garfield and Brookside parks, and in 1917 he planned the BRENDONWOOD subdivision's spacious lots and winding drives. One of his plans which never saw fruition was a proposed public plaza along the WHITE RIVER. In the 1980s the city set aside this area for the WHITE RIVER STATE PARK.

By 1910 city planners were shifting from a City Beautiful ideal to the "City Practical," aiming more specifically at remedying urban congestion and planning for the benefit of large populations. In Indianapolis this movement was supported by the Commercial Club, in conjunction with the city government, in its 1914 "vacant lot cultivation" plans and its 1916 "clean-up, paint-up" campaign. Both aimed at creating a more livable city for everyone rather than beautifying specific areas used by only a few.

Beautification of public spaces also became a strong component of Indianapolis landscape design in this period. In 1919 University Square received a facelift when J. Sterling Calder's Depew Fountain was placed at its center and sculptures of Schuyler Colfax, Benjamin Harrison, and Abraham Lincoln graced the outer perimeter. In the 1920s the INDIANA WORLD WAR MEMORIAL PLAZA was begun with its border of limestone buildings and Obelisk Square embellishing the memorial.

In the 1920s landscape design became an important component of private home planning. As the city's wealthy entered the "country place era," they hired famous landscape architects to prepare their estate grounds. The Hugh McK. Landons employed the Olmsted Brothers firm in 1920 to develop the grounds at their Oldfields estate (now part of the INDIANAPOLIS MUSEUM OF ART). The firm created greenswards, fountains, and intimate areas utilizing massed plantings and statuary; much of their plan is still apparent today. In 1922 Jens Jensen landscaped the F. D. Stalnaker estate near BUTLER UNIVERSITY with a cascading waterfall, reflecting pool, and a council ring for campfires (later this became his trademark). Frederic M. Ayres hired LAWRENCE SHERIDAN to design his estate, Walden, in a manner which retained its natural character with formal gardens extending into woods, a rock-rimmed pool, and a stone terrace.

The Great Depression ended the era of estate designing in Indianapolis. During the 1930s and 1940s landscape design shifted to playgrounds, "make-work" programs, and public buildings. Landscape design included projects such as the construction of new channels for Pleasant Run Creek and rock gardens for the slopes of Riverside Park, both funded by the Works Progress Administration, and the Public Works Administration's LOCKEFIELD GARDENS.

In the 1950s and 1960s landscape architects were again active in city planning. Lawrence Sheridan was a member of the City Plan Commission, and in 1968 landscape architect Calvin S. Hamilton directed the DEPARTMENT OF METROPOLITAN DEVELOPMENT planning agency which purchased EAGLE CREEK PARK.

By the 1970s residential landscape design in Indianapolis was used most often on the grounds of apartment and condominium complexes. In public spaces, office parks became a popular arena for design. In 1971 the American States Insurance Company created Indianapolis' first office minipark on property next to its new seven-story office at Meridian and North streets. This park, with its small pool, water jets, and trees and benches, inspired other businesses to similar enhancements of work environments. In 1972 Browning Day Pollak and Mullins, Inc. designed the Lilly Industrial Center's sweeping green spaces, winding drives, and plantings of canopy trees. In 1983 American United Life's new headquarters featured an atrium with small fountains, a bridged pool of water, and plantings.

Indianapolis landscape design in the 1990s mirrors the national green movement. The work of local landscaping companies such as Engledow, Inc., is visible on every downtown street, with beds of bright annuals contributing variety to the scene. Urban green spaces like the Westin Plaza offer city workers and tourists cool fountains amidst perennial plantings and bowers of climbing roses. Even highway interchanges have been touched by the increasing interest in conservation and landscape design. In 1993 public-private cooperation created prairies at I–465 and North Meridian Street and a series of plantings and brick pavings at 21st Street and I–65. In 1994 plans were underway to complete Kessler's original plans and to extend the park and boulevard system to all parts of the county. Upon completion, the Indianapolis Greenways Project will create a network of nature and fitness trails linking over 100 destinations along 14 rivers, streams, and abandoned railroad corridors.

CONNIE J. ZEIGLER

Michael Maloney and Kenneth J. Remenschneider, *Indianapolis Landscape Architecture* (Washington, D.C., 1983).

Lapenta, Vincent A. (July 4, 1883–Apr. 20, 1946). Surgeon, scientist, and Royal Italian consular agent for Indiana before World War II. Born on the island of Ischia in the Bay of Naples, the son of an army officer, Lapenta lived in Naples' English colony. After receiving his medical degree from the University of Naples in 1906, he emigrated to the United States to continue medical studies at Harvard and in Chicago.

Recruited by local Italians to serve their community, Lapenta moved to Indianapolis ca. 1911 and for the next 30 years served its medical needs. Although a recognized specialist in abdominal surgery, who became senior surgeon at St. Francis Hospital, he was best known for his discovery of a serum to control hemorrhage. Marketed commercially, it had great practical value during World War I and for controlling hemophilia.

Recipient of various honors, Lapenta was the most distinguished member of the local Italian community. He became a fellow in the Royal British Society of Arts and Sciences (1922) and was appointed a knight (1923) and knight officer (1930) of the Royal Crown of Italy. He was also chairman of the board of trustees and on the council of examiners for the United States chapter of the International College of Surgeons. Locally, he was a benefactor of Cathedral High School.

Lapenta was appointed Italian consular agent for the state in 1921. He encouraged the formation of Italian societies and lectured on Italian foreign and domestic policy. In June, 1941, he was ordered deported and, when Italy declared war six months later, he was interned as an enemy alien at FORT BENJAMIN HARRISON. He remained there for 16 months, devoting time to experiments on artificial blood plasma. A war casualty without going to battle, Lapenta died in BEECH GROVE and was buried in St. Joseph Cemetery, Indianapolis.

JAMES J. DIVITA
Marian College

James J. Divita, *The Italians of Indianapolis* (Indianapolis, 1984); *Journal of the International College of Surgeons* (Sept.–Oct., 1946), 609–610.

LaSalle Street Murders. Unsolved triple homicide. On December 1, 1971, three men were murdered in a house at 1318 North LaSalle Street. Robert A. Gierse, 35, Robert W. Hinson, Jr., 27, and James Barker, 26, had been bound and their throats were slashed. There were no signs of a struggle and no weapon was found.

Evidence at the scene and interviews during months of intense investigation in 1971 and 1972 provided police with a sketch of the events of that night. Three men seen drinking beer in a cream-colored car across the street from the house on the night of the murders are believed to have committed the crime. These alleged perpetrators are believed to have ambushed the three victims as each entered the house.

A number of motives have been suggested over the years. Some of these speculated a mafia hit or revenge for murders with which one of the victims may have been involved. The most likely motive for the killings is that one of the victims was involved with the ex-wife of a jealous man. Too many motives and too few clues prevented police from finding a solution.

When a freelance journalist obtained the identity of the supposed killer from a man she had interviewed in the fall of 1992, a solution to the crime appeared imminent. As of mid–1993, however, the Marion County prosecutor claimed that insufficient evidence existed for an arrest and that the case remained open.

MARCUS EUGENE WOODS, II

Indianapolis Star, Dec. 2, 3, 1971; *Indianapolis News*, Nov. 29, 1991, Apr. 3, 1993; Carol Schultz, "Out in the Cold," *Nuvo*, Apr. 7, 1993.

Latvians. Earliest records indicate the presence of Latvians in North America around 1680. The greatest migration of Latvians to the United States, however, came following World War II pursuant to provisions of the Displaced Persons Act of 1948. Organizations such as Church World Services, the Indiana Economic Council, and Catholic and Lutheran churches sponsored the resettlement of Latvian immigrants to Indiana. The decision to settle in Indianapolis was determined by proximity to family members, job opportunities, and other considerations. The U.S. Census showed 1,526 persons of Latvian heritage in Indiana in 1960 and 1,587 in 1980. The Latvian-born population of Indianapolis has been quite small, numbering 779 in 1960 and 577 in 1970. They have not maintained distinct neighborhoods but reside throughout the urban area.

Despite its small numbers, the Latvian community flourishes with a variety of supporting cultural organizations: Latviesu Biedriba and Daugavas Vanagi (Latvian welfare associations); ILJOP (Latvian Youth Organization Board); a choir, a folk dance group, and a language school. The Latvian Evangelical Lutheran Church, organized in April, 1957, still offers Latvian-language services. The Latvian Community Center, founded in 1962, houses various activities of local Latvian residents. A regional Latvian Song Festival was held in the city in 1960, as was the eighth national Latvian Song Festival in 1988.

Latvia declared its independence from the Soviet Union on August 21, 1991. Members of the local Latvian community have responded by providing technical, medical, and financial aid through their welfare associations for the rebuilding of their ancient homeland.

LIGITA KRUMKALNS
University of Indianapolis

Laughner's Cafeterias. Indianapolis-based restaurant chain. In 1888 Jonathon Wesley Laughner opened a candy store, the Boston Confectionery, at 4 Indiana Avenue. About 1900 the confectionery was remodeled and renamed Laughner's Dairy Lunch. The restaurant was unusual because of its new cafeteria-style service, one of the first in the Midwest. Customers selected meals from a glass cabinet where the food was displayed. Novelty, convenience, and increased public concern about cleanliness combined to make this new style of service a success.

Jonathon's son and daughter-in-law, Claude and Flora Laughner, expanded the family business in the 1920s, opening the Central Cafeteria. During the 1930s the Laughners had cafeterias, usually two or three at a time, in a variety of Indianapolis locations. They also operated concession stands at the State Fair, the INDIANAPOLIS MOTOR SPEEDWAY, and RIVERSIDE AMUSEMENT PARK. There were a half-dozen stands at Riverside, each with a different menu featuring such treats as homemade root beer, caramel corn, and chocolate-dipped "polar clubs" or scoops of ice cream on a stick. The family also sold candy door-to-door.

In 1957 the Laughner Brothers Corporation was formed. The company introduced free-standing suburban cafeteria buildings with ample parking in response to decreased downtown dinner traffic. In the late 1950s the Laughners experimented unsuccessfully with drive-in restaurants before concentrating on suburban cafeterias in the 1960s and 1970s. By the 1990s Laughners operated ten Indianapolis-area restaurants, with additional cafeterias in Kokomo and Terre Haute.

DEBORAH B. MARKISOHN

Jane and Michael Stern, "A Reporter at Large: Cafeteria," *The New Yorker* (Aug. 1, 1988), 37–54.

Law Schools. Legal education in the early 19th century consisted of studying as an apprentice under a practicing lawyer. One of the earliest opportunities for formal course work in law in Indianapolis was at North Western Christian University (now BUTLER UNIVERSITY). When the university opened in 1855 it offered law as an optional subject outside the regular curriculum, a practice that continued until the mid–1870s. Early proprietary law schools in the city emphasized the close proximity of the city, county, state, and federal courts as well as student access to the state law library, the Indianapolis Bar Association library, and the general city library. These schools generally occupied one floor, containing classrooms and moot courtrooms, in an office building. Some, such as the Lincoln College of Law (1934–1941), remained open only a few years.

Judge BYRON K. ELLIOT and Charles P. Jacobs, both of whom previously taught law through North Western Christian University, and others organized the Central Law School of Indiana, which incorporated in 1879 with former governor Conrad Baker as president of the board of directors. Although successful for a time, offering a postgraduate course as well as a two-year course and featuring a well-stocked law library, the school lost ground following Elliot's departure in 1881 and it closed a few years later.

In 1894 Elliot and four others, including CHARLES W. FAIRBANKS, organized the Indiana Law School. The school opened in October with a class of advanced students from local offices. It offered a two-year course of study using regular and special lecturers until 1899 when it changed to the textbook and case method. In 1896 Indiana Law, along with the Indiana Dental College, the Medical College of Indiana, and Butler College, formed the short-lived University of Indianapolis, but each retained separate administration of its own school. In 1916 the law school offered a three-year curriculum and raised the requirements for admission. James A. Rohback, who joined the Indiana Law School in 1899 as a professor of law and the school's secretary, became dean in 1901. He retained this position until his death in 1930.

The Benjamin Harrison Law School was formed in 1914 when the American Central Law School of Indianapolis (ca. 1900) and Indianapolis College of Law (1898) merged. It offered a two-year course of study, three years after 1931, which included lectures, the case method, and textbook instruction. Students submitted a thesis for graduation. The Harrison school offered only evening classes in both part-time and full-time programs and in 1935, after a steady growth in enrollment, began offering a postgraduate course.

In 1936 the Benjamin Harrison Law School merged with the Indiana Law School in order to obtain approval from the American Bar Association (ABA). By the end of the year the new school, under the name Indiana Law School, had 300 students and ABA approval. It offered both day and night classes with three full-time and several part-time instructors. In 1940 Indiana Law School became affiliated with Butler University but remained separate and in 1944 merged into the Indiana University School of Law to become the Indianapolis Division of the Indiana University School of Law. It operated as a part-time division of the Bloomington law school, offering courses in 16 subjects. In January, 1968, the school became autonomous under the name Indiana University–Indianapolis Law School, with plans for full-time day courses. Later that year it broke ground for its new building located on the IUPUI campus. Currently, the Law School has both part-time and full-time divisions for its student body of approximately 760 students. Included among its over 5,000 alumni are state and federal judges and state and federal legislators.

JOAN CUNNINGHAM

Lawrence. Marion County city located about ten miles northeast of the Circle. Lawrence was originally platted in 1849 as the town of Lanesville. Named for a prominent resident, Lanesville was sited near the Bee Line Railroad and Pendleton Pike. In 1866 county commissioners changed the name to Lawrence, after the township post office south of the town. About 20 years later Lawrence, with a population of nearly 150, prospered as a trading center for farmers and merchants supplied by the highway and the railroad.

In 1903 the federal government purchased 2,000 acres north of the town to establish FORT BENJAMIN HARRISON. The fort played a vital role in the economic life of Lawrence, particularly after 1953 when the U.S. ARMY FINANCE CENTER opened on the base. In the early 1990s the fort was the largest employer in Lawrence with nearly 10,000 civilian and military employees. Although the Defense Department announced in 1991 it would close the base, the city submitted a bid to retain the Finance Center and in 1994 received word from the federal government that the center would remain open.

Lawrence experienced tremendous growth from 1950 to 1980. As WESTERN ELECTRIC, FORD, and CHRYSLER plants opened on nearby Shadeland Avenue in Indianapolis, subdivisions sprouted in Lawrence. In 1950 the town counted about 2,000 residents; in 1960, 10,000; in 1970, over 16,000; and by 1980, more than 25,000. The 1990 census counted 27,000 residents of Lawrence. Some of the growth resulted from annexation. The decision by Lawrence officials to annex Indian Lake and OAKLANDON was initially controversial, though it was later upheld in court. Fort Benjamin Harrison was annexed in 1970, despite objections from the U.S. Army. The GEIST RESERVOIR area was not annexed, yet extensive residential and commercial development there and in nearby CASTLETON also contributed to growth on the north side of Lawrence.

Incorporated in 1929, Lawrence has the status of an excluded city under UNIGOV. A mayor and a city council oversee police and fire departments, a municipal water company, and a parks department. Despite the loss of manufacturing jobs on Shadeland Avenue and the impending closure of Fort Harrison, Lawrence continues to grow, primarily as a middle class residential suburb.

CATHLEEN F. DONNELLY

Lawrence Township. Northeastern Marion County township, roughly bordered by 96th Street, County Line Road, 38th Street, and Emerson and Graham avenues. Settlers moved into the area now known as Lawrence Township just after it was organized in 1822. The first community, Germantown, was laid out in 1834 along the Marion County–Hamilton County line. Two small hamlets, Lanesville (later LAWRENCE) and OAKLANDON, were platted in 1849 along Pendleton Pike, a well-traveled highway cut through the township in 1825–1826.

RAILROADS provided the strongest impetus to growth in early Lawrence Township. The "Bee Line" Railroad was built during the winter of 1850 and served Oaklandon and Lawrence. To the northwest, Vertland was laid out in 1851 around a switching facility for another rail line. When the town foundered the facilities were moved a short distance south to CASTLETON, platted in 1852. Lawrence Township grew slowly and by 1900 counted 3,200 residents.

In 1903 the federal government purchased land for FORT BENJAMIN HARRISON, a sprawling facility that would later become the township's largest employer. Shortly thereafter the increasing popularity of the automobile stimulated the development of affluent suburbs such as BRENDONWOOD (1917) along FALL CREEK. By the 1950s

---

Selected Statistics for Lawrence Township, 1990

Population	94,548
Population per Square Mile	1,954
Percent African-American	24.1
Percent 0 to 17 Years	27.5
Percent 65 Years and Over	7.3
Percent 25 Years and Over with a High School Degree or Equivalency	86.1
Percent 25 Years and Over with a College Degree	30.3
Per Capita Income in 1989	$17,420
Unemployment Rate (%)	4.5
Married-Couple Families as a Percent of Total Households	53.4
Median Home Value	$83,700

---

middle class and working class residents commuted by car from homes in new developments, such as Devington, to work in the industrial plants along Shadeland Avenue or at the U.S. ARMY FINANCE CENTER.

Ten years later construction of I–465 stimulated additional development, particularly in Lawrence and Castleton. Apartment complexes were built near the east 56th Street interchange in the 1970s and 1980s. Castleton Square Shopping Mall, opened in 1972 just off the interstate, brought explosive growth to the east 82nd Street corridor. Later, construction of I–69 spurred development north to the county line. By 1990 Castleton had become the most intensively developed retail district in Marion County.

In the northeastern section of the township at GEIST RESERVOIR, residential construction began in 1978. Delayed by years of political squabbles, initial development was begun by a subsidiary of the INDIANAPOLIS WATER COMPANY, which had dammed Fall Creek in 1941 to create the reservoir. Though Germantown was flooded, the rising waters of the reservoir created valuable waterfront property. Today the area has been developed primarily and extensively with homes and condominiums for affluent families.

With development came a significant population increase. Between 1960 and 1986 Lawrence Township's population grew from 34,400 to 83,000, or 141 percent. In the 1990 census there were just over 94,500 residents.

As the school-age population increased, the Metropolitan School District of Lawrence Township expanded to nine elementaries, three middle schools, and two high schools. In the 1992–1993 school year about 12,000 students were enrolled in the district, which also boasts a progressive centralized kindergarten.

Despite 40 years of dramatic growth, Lawrence Township faced challenges in the early 1990s, particularly the closure of Fort Harrison and the threatened loss of the Finance Center. In 1994 the Department of Defense chose to keep the Finance Center open. Local officials are studying ways to use the fort's facilities while attracting new employers to the township.

CATHLEEN F. DONNELLY

Berry R. Sulgrove, *History of Indianapolis and Marion County* (Philadelphia, 1884), 534–575; Department of Metropolitan Development, *Lawrence Township Comprehensive Planning Study* (1988); U.S. Census.

Leadership Training Programs (United Way).

United Way of Central Indiana is an organization that is volunteer-driven and volunteer-dependent. To enhance volunteers' ability to serve the community, UNITED WAY created three leadership training programs.

The Ardath Burkhart Series, begun in 1986, provides education and experience in nonprofit board leadership. Named in memory of the late ARDATH Y. BURKHART, an Indianapolis community volunteer and philanthropist, the series prepares emerging community leaders for nonprofit board membership. It graduates 20 persons a year.

Leadership Training Development, begun in 1989, trains minorities with the potential to assume leadership roles in their work, organizations, and communities. It graduated about 40 persons a year until 1993 when it reduced that number to 25. Its funding came initially from the Kellogg Foundation; since 1991–1992 it has been supported by small matching grants from United Way and the INDIANAPOLIS FOUNDATION, with staff and other in-kind support from United Way.

Executive Women's Leadership Program, begun in 1990, trains women to be leaders in philanthropy, in United Way, within their businesses, and in other community organizations. It serves 25 persons a year.

Each program's curriculum includes experiential education as well as workshops. Upon graduation, all program alumni are expected and encouraged to continue to serve United Way of Central Indiana and the community through volunteer and philanthropic activity.

ANN T. DALY
United Way of Central Indiana

League of Women Voters of Indianapolis.

Nonpartisan organization devoted to promoting informed and active citizen participation in government. On April 16, 1920, the Woman's Franchise League of Indiana, Indianapolis Branch, voted to disband and to establish a League of Women Voters in its place, carrying the members of the Franchise League on its roster for six months. These actions followed similar ones by the National American Woman's Suffrage Association and the state Woman's Franchise League since the primary purpose of those organizations, securing the vote for women, was certain of accomplishment. The new organization had as its purposes "fostering education in citizenship and supporting needed legislation."

In the early 1920s, under the leadership of KATHARINE C. GREENOUGH, the League conducted classes on citizenship, later establishing citizenship courses at BUTLER UNIVERSITY in 1926 and 1927. The League ran intensive "Get-Out-the-Vote" campaigns and biennial voter registration drives and in 1926 began its candidate forums, which continue to be a feature of League activity. Also, candidate questionnaires were reprinted in the newspapers in advance of each election. The League held voting machine demonstrations downtown in 1941 and continued this activity at various locations for three decades, except for a brief period in 1942 when the county commissioners would not allow them the use of a machine. In 1946 the first monthly radio show hosted by League members aired on WISH; in 1952, under the leadership of Elaine Thomas, the League began to use television, first for voting machine demonstrations and eventually for candidate forums. The League continually sought ways to reach out to all citizens, conducting massive registration drives and educating citizens about local government in advance of local elections in 1963 and again in 1967, and sponsoring an inner-city registration drive in 1964, all under the leadership of Jean Tyler. Registration drives and candidate forum sponsorship continue to the present day.

As to "needed legislation," typically the League identified a governmental problem, studied the problem and possible solutions, discussed the issues and reached consensus on a plan of action, and then worked to educate the citizenry so that reforms could be enacted. As soon as Indianapolis League women became aware of inequity in the election and registration laws or inefficiency in local government, they began working for change. The League supported the "50–50 law," designed to give men and women equal representation in the political parties, which passed in 1925, and a permanent registration law that passed in 1933.

During the Great Depression years of the 1930s the League worked to educate its members and the public about the cost of government and began a 20–year campaign to support the merit system and eliminate patronage. In the 1940s, League members surveyed city government and attached themselves individually to each of the 15 departments, often being appointed to specific advisory committees. Working throughout the 1950s toward consolidation of city and county services, in 1959 the League began publication of *Who's In Charge Here?*, a booklet designed to help citizens understand their local government so they could work to change it. Finally, in 1969, the General Assembly passed the UNIGOV legislation consolidating city and county government and embodying many of the reforms the League had long sought.

Success came more swiftly when reforms concentrated on issues traditionally associated with women—for example, strengthening the juvenile court in the 1930s and school board nominating procedures in the late 1950s—and when the League gained cooperation from other community organizations. The study of the juvenile court, begun in 1931, led to successful efforts in the 1935 General Assembly to strengthen the Probation Department and clarify the law establishing the Juvenile Court of Marion County. Finding that the administration of the court was inadequate, the League helped to form the Marion County Bi-Partisan Juvenile Court Committee in 1938 to arouse citizen interest in attracting able candidates. Recent decades have seen the League continue its interest in JUVENILE JUSTICE and local government, with some emphasis also on broader national issues such as international affairs, equality of opportunity, and the environment. Until the 1980s League members were predominantly college-educated wives of business and professional men, but the leadership has sought to recruit women (and, since 1974, men) from all walks of life.

Supporting positions of the national League, especially in the area of international relations, sometimes was difficult in the conservative Indianapolis of the 1950s. Controversy resulted from the League's national position on the Bricker Amendment and efforts to have flags of the United Nations displayed in the AMERICAN LEGION plaza. Generally, however, the League's work has been supported by community leaders, and League members have consistently been appointed to boards and commissions that deal with traditional League concerns.

BARBARA E. ZIMMER

Barbara E. Zimmer, "A History of the League of Women Voters of Indianapolis, 1920–1970" (M.A. thesis, Butler University, 1970).

Learn and Shop. Program offering higher education classes at shopping centers. The idea of offering college credit courses and degree programs at retail malls originated at INDIANA UNIVERSITY–PURDUE UNIVERSITY AT INDIANAPOLIS (IUPUI) in the spring of 1979 as the Learn and Shop College Credit Program. Since then, the idea has been adapted by colleges and universities in 25 American states and Canada. There have been more than 40,000 IUPUI student enrollments in Learn and Shop classes, which are offered in training rooms provided by major retailers in five suburban shopping malls in the Indianapolis area. Enrollments typically exceed 2,000 each semester. In this program, a person can go to a nearby shopping center on personal business and while there take college credit courses that fulfill the requirements for three Indiana University degrees: Bachelor of General Studies, Associate of General Studies, and Associate of Arts. As of fall, 1993, some 223 different courses had been offered in 40 academic areas.

ROBERT SCHWARTZ

James R. East, *Teaching on Weekends and in Shopping Centers*, 2nd ed. (Indianapolis, 1991).

Leedy Manufacturing Company. Manufacturer of drum and percussion instruments and equipment. Ulysses G. Leedy (1867–1931), the trap drummer for English's Opera House, established a shop in the Cyclorama Building in 1895 with Sam Cooley to manufacture drums, stands, and sound effects. In 1903 Leedy built a new factory at the corner of Barth Avenue and Palmer Street; additions in 1910 and 1920 resulted in 78,450 square feet of floor space. The firm considered itself the world's largest manufacturer of percussion instruments, with over 900 items in its catalog, including drums, tympani, marimbas, and chimes.

Products were made on site from raw materials; departments included a tannery and drum head plant, lumberyard, chrome plating works, and shops for making cases and custom tools. The company was responsible for numerous innovations and improvements, including the first vibraphone, but is best remembered by Hoosiers for making Purdue University's first giant bass drum in 1921.

C. G. Conn, Ltd., bought the company in 1929 and sold it to the Slingerland Drum Company in 1955, keeping the Leedy name alive until 1958. In Indianapolis, Leedy and Cecil H. Strupe formed the General Manufacturing Company in 1930 to manufacture Leedy and Strupe (L&S) drums, and Leedy's family ran the business until 1940 when it was sold to the Indiana Drum Company.

SALLY CARR CHILDS-HELTON
Indiana Historical Society

_____

Indiana Biography Index, Indiana State Library; *Indianapolis Star*, May 19, 1929.

Leibowitz, Irving (Aug. 5, 1922–Apr. 28, 1979). Columnist and managing editor of the INDIANAPOLIS TIMES. During his 17–year career with the *Times*, Leibowitz enlivened its pages as a writer of a daily column focusing heavily on Indiana politics. He also had the concurrent duty of directing the paper's news coverage, first as city editor and later as managing editor.

A native of New York City and son of Rumanian immigrants, Leibowitz attended public schools and Bordentown Military Institute before enrolling in New York University. During World War II, he was an Army combat correspondent and photographer in North Africa, Italy, and France, for which he received the Bronze Star.

Following a brief stint at small newspapers in Virginia and Ohio, "Leibo," as he became known in the profession, joined the *Times* in 1948 as a reporter and introduced his column "Hoosier Headlines" in 1951. He served as columnist (1951–1961), assistant managing editor (1954–1960), and managing editor (1960–1965) until the *Times* ceased publication. Leibowitz became the editor of the *Lorain (Ohio) Journal* in 1966 and turned that paper into one of Ohio's most aggressive newspapers.

Leibowitz is known for his book *My Indiana* (1964), a tribute to his adopted state consisting of a collection of stories and essays about Indiana history, personalities, and culture. Leibowitz served as president of the INDIANAPOLIS PRESS CLUB and the Indiana Chapter of the Society of Professional Journalists. He also was a member of the board of directors of the 500 FESTIVAL and founder of the Indiana Press Institute at Indiana University.

JUDY SCHWARTZ

_____

Irving Leibowitz, *My Indiana* (Englewood Cliffs, N.J., 1964); *Indianapolis Star*, Apr. 30, 1979.

Liberty Fund. Educational foundation. Begun in 1960 "to encourage the study of the ideal of a society of free and responsible individuals," Liberty Fund is one of the nation's largest private operating foundations. Program activities emphasize liberal education in the "Great Books" tradition and open discussion of enduring intellectual issues as the best ways to sustain liberty. The organization does not engage in political action or public policy research.

Liberty Fund was founded by Pierre Frist Goodrich (Sept. 10, 1894–Oct. 25, 1973), son of Indiana Governor (1917–1921) James Putnam Goodrich. Born in Winchester and educated at Wabash College and Harvard Law School, Goodrich moved his law practice to Indianapolis in 1923. His extensive business and ownership interests included Ayrshire Collieries, Indiana Telephone, Peoples Loan and Trust, and City Securities. Goodrich was an active director or trustee in various civic and educational organizations locally and nationally, including the Indiana State Symphony Society, Wabash College, the Great Books Foundation, and the Foundation for Economic Education.

Goodrich left most of his considerable estate to Liberty Fund. Shortly after 1973 Liberty Fund expanded its efforts to reach scholars and professionals. Each year Liberty Fund conducts some 90 small, private, discussion-style conferences throughout the United States, Canada, Latin America, and Europe. These conferences focus primarily on history, philosophy, law, literature, political thought, and economics. Liberty Fund annually publishes four to six books. They are new scholarly and accessible editions of classic works, including the writings of Adam Smith, Lord Acton, George Washington, and F. A. Hayek.

All of these programs focus on the place liberty has had in human affairs, from Classical and Judeo-Christian thought through such rich intellectual periods as the Scottish Enlightenment and the American Founding era. In this way, Liberty Fund endeavors to make a "hopeful contribution" to a better understanding of the complex nature of a free society and its preservation.

CHARLES H. HAMILTON
Indiana University–Purdue University,
Indianapolis

Libraries and Archives. The first efforts to establish libraries in Indianapolis were made shortly after the founding of the city, although it was not until after the Civil War that libraries began to flourish. The idea of public libraries was not new in the 1820s. Community libraries supported by a combination of tax dollars and private subscriptions had become common in New England at the end of the 18th century, and served as an inspiration for the provision in the 1816 Indiana Constitution allowing for county libraries financed by the sale of town lots.

In spite of the provision for public funding, the first attempts to make books available to the public were private subscription libraries, beginning with the Indianapolis Library in 1828. This library, like the other subscription libraries, lasted only a few years before waning interest and lack of funds forced it to close. Two more successful efforts to start libraries used public funds. Indianapolis attorney Henry P. Coburn started the Marion County Library in 1841, using a small amount of money that had been set aside from the sale of town lots as provided for in the 1816 Constitution. The money was not as much as it might have been, since the state legislature had diverted the Marion County monies to other purposes, but it was enough to purchase books and begin operations. After some initial interest, use of the library declined because it charged a subscription fee and was open only for a few hours on Saturdays. In 1868 the library reported fewer than 100 subscribers, and while it continued to function into the 1910s, usage remained low.

In the early 1850s the state legislature approved funding for a system of township libraries as part of a new system of township schools. Through this program, supported by Indiana educational reformers Caleb Mills and Robert Dale Owen, the state government purchased and distributed collections of about 500 books for each township. The collections were used heavily in Indianapolis, as well as throughout the rest of the state, but as there was neither continued funding nor a local institution to maintain the program, the township libraries eventually closed.

The city's principal library before the Civil War was the INDIANA STATE LIBRARY. The library was created to support the work of the legislature and state government officials, but it played an important role in the intellectual life of the town. Its collections of historical, geographical, and literary works were widely read; novelist LEW WALLACE remembered reading James Fenimore Cooper and Washington Irving in the State Library's reading room, while HENRY WARD BEECHER used its collections heavily when he was editor of the INDIANA FARMER AND GARDENER. In spite of its importance to the young city, the State Library was inadequate to serve as a city library. Its books did not circulate to the general public, and despite Wallace's experience it contained very few popular works.

The absence of an adequate library was remarked upon by a number of writers. Libraries were seen as an essential continuation of the public school system, for without a library adults were limited in how they could improve their reading and broaden their understanding of the world. Moreover, a strong public library was considered to be a mark of a city's cultural interests and hence a sign that the city had arrived. During the pre–Civil War period, though, the city had neither the size nor the prosperity to support a successful library.

Following the Civil War there was renewed interest in establishing a public library, resulting in the creation of the Indianapolis Public Library in 1873. It came into existence as part of school reform legislation prepared by Indianapolis School Superintendent ABRAM C. SHORTRIDGE. The legislation allowed the state's largest cities to use property taxes in support of a public library placed under the control of the school board. Public funding made the library a significant cultural force in the community from its beginning. At the time the library opened it had more than 12,000 books, the city's largest collection; it had a professionally trained librarian from the East, CHARLES EVANS; and it was open from 9 A.M. to 9 P.M. every day, including Sunday. People in Indianapolis were clearly ready for a library. They borrowed more than 100,000 books in 1874, the library's first year of operation, and more than 300,000 ten years later, making it one of the most heavily used libraries in the country. Moreover, the library played an active cultural role in the city, as numerous literary societies formed around the institution, including the still-active Indianapolis Literary Club.

In spite of being under the jurisdiction of the Board of School Commissioners, the Public Library did not offer any special programs for children until the early 1880s when it printed its first juvenile books catalog and set up reference libraries in many of the schools. Under the administration of Eliza Browning (1892–1917), the children's programs began to play an increasingly large role. A separate children's book section was established in the late 1890s, and shortly thereafter the library began holding after-school story hours. By 1917 the library circulated nearly as many children's books as adult books.

Browning also inaugurated the extension of library services into the city's neighborhoods. The first four branch libraries opened in 1896, and by the end of her administration there were 12 branches, including five funded by gifts from Andrew Carnegie. The branches played an important role in providing reading material to the city; more than 60 percent of the library's book circulation was through the branch libraries by 1920. The library saw the branches as neighborhood educational and social centers as much as book distribution points. This educational role was especially important in immigrant neighborhoods, where the libraries ran language and culture classes and provided reading materials in people's native languages. The HAUGHVILLE branch library, one of the city's busiest in the 1920s, provided books and newspapers in 14 languages, and the librarian made house visits throughout the neighborhood to encourage immigrants to come to the library.

Although the Indianapolis Public Library was the dominant library in the city in the late 19th and early 20th centuries, there were numerous other libraries. The two largest of these, the State Library and the Supreme Court Library, were run by the state government, and their primary users were state officials, court officials, and local lawyers. The state government also supported small libraries at a number of public institutions, including the Women's Prison, the Central Indiana Hospital for the Insane, and the INDIANA SCHOOL FOR THE BLIND. By the turn of the century there were also small but growing libraries at the increasing number of colleges and private professional schools. These had only small collections, though, ranging from a few hundred volumes at the HERRON SCHOOL OF ART to about 15,000 at BUTLER UNIVERSITY in 1910. Because of their own limited book collections, these institutions expected their students to make use of the much more extensive collections of the Public Library.

The growth of the libraries in the city was slowed by the Great Depression and World War II, but the demand for books continued to be high. Throughout the 1940s and 1950s the Indianapolis Public Library consistently ranked among the top five city libraries nationally both in number of borrowers and number of books circulated per capita.

Since the mid–1950s libraries in Indianapolis have experienced remarkable growth and change. The Public Library expanded in the mid–1960s by extending its services into the rapidly growing Marion County suburbs. As a result of the creation of a new INDIANAPOLIS–MARION COUNTY PUBLIC LIBRARY, the institution added seven branches in the county between 1967 and 1971 and saw its budget for book buying more than double. In the process of expanding to the suburbs, the library separated from the Indianapolis Public Schools. The library had operated a School Services Division since 1917 to coordinate the provision of books for the city's schools. The division closed in 1968, and since that time the schools have been responsible for their own libraries.

The academic libraries in the city have also grown dramatically since the 1950s. In part this is the result of the growth of the schools themselves, particularly the Indiana University and Purdue University schools. More important was the changing nature of academic work, requiring faculty and students to have greater access to recent research, particularly in the scientific, technical, and professional fields. To house these growing collections, substantial new library buildings have been constructed on nearly every campus in the city since the early 1960s.

The increasing public need for specialized information resources has led the libraries in the city to devote increasing attention to sharing resources. In 1974 a group of 44 libraries in Indianapolis and the surrounding counties formed the CENTRAL INDIANA AREA LIBRARY SERVICES AUTHORITY (CIALSA) to improve services by sharing collections, expertise, and continuing education for staff. By the early 1990s there were nearly 150 participating academic, public, school, and business libraries, and they were providing more than 1,000 books per month to patrons of the other member libraries.

The coming of automation in the 1970s led to substantial changes in the services libraries offer and in the way the libraries operate, making them increasingly connected to national and international information resources. By the late 1970s most of the city's major libraries were connected to OCLC (Online Computer Library Center), a national database of cataloging records that allowed them both to increase their cataloging efficiency and to have access to information about library holdings throughout the country. In 1983 the Public Library was the first in the city to replace its card catalog with an on-line catalog, and the State Library and the Indiana University libraries followed a few years later. By the early 1990s the trend of library automation was to make information about library resources, and ultimately the resources themselves, available to the public without going to the library.

The history of archives and historical collections in Indianapolis is primarily the story of two institutions, the Indiana State Library and the private INDIANA HISTORICAL SOCIETY. As with libraries, several efforts were made before the Civil War to establish a collection of printed and manuscript materials on the history of the city and state, principally through the Indiana Historical Society. Lack of consistent funding and interest doomed these efforts, and most of the materials collected by the society before the Civil War were lost by the 1870s. The State Library began to collect state historical records only in the late 1890s, coinciding with both the removal of the library from the direct control of the legislature and the growing national movement to preserve state historical records. By the time the State Library formally established its Division of Archives and History in 1906 it had already become the principal repository in the state for historical manuscripts and printed materials on Indiana history.

In the 1920s the Indiana Historical Society reentered the field of historical collections as the result of a bequest of money and a historical library from newspaper publisher DELAVAN SMITH. The Historical Society's search for a location for its new library coincided with the State Library's campaign for a separate library building for its collections, and when the new INDIANA STATE LIBRARY AND HISTORICAL BUILDING opened in 1934 it included an area for the Historical Society's library. Although efforts were made before 1934 to unite the two libraries administratively, they remained separate. The opening of the new State Library building was also the occasion for splitting the Division of Archives and History into three new divisions: the INDIANA STATE ARCHIVES, responsible for the records of state and local government; the Indiana Division, responsible for printed materials and manuscripts on state history; and the Genealogy Division.

Over the following 30 years the collections of both institutions grew slowly, as inadequate funding made it impossible for either of them to mount aggressive collecting programs. In the mid–1960s the State Library was able to hire a field agent and began actively collecting the papers of modern Indiana politicians and contemporary organizations. Since the late 1970s, though, the State Library has played a smaller role in preserving archival records on state history. In 1979 the Archives Division was separated from the State Library and merged into the new Indiana Commission on Public Records, and the gradual reduction of funding for the library during the 1980s caused the Indiana Division to curtail most of its active collecting of archival materials. During these same years, however, the Indiana Historical Society significantly expanded its collecting of 20th-century historical records following ELI LILLY's bequest to the organization that allowed for the substantial expansion of the society's staff and programs.

ERIC L. PUMROY
Indiana University–Purdue University,
Indianapolis

Lawrence J. Downey, *A Live Thing in the Whole Town: The History of the Indianapolis–Marion County Public Library, 1873–1990* (Indianapolis, 1991); Lana Ruegamer, *A History of the Indiana Historical Society, 1830–1980* (Indianapolis, 1981).

Lieber, Richard (Sept. 5, 1869–Apr. 15, 1944). Businessman and naturalist. Born into a well-to-do family in St. Johann, the Saarland, Germany, Lieber attended the Royal Lyceum in Duesseldorf. Because of illness, however, he received much of his education from private tutors. After studying the mercantile trade in England in 1890, he visited his uncles Herman and Peter Lieber, who had immigrated to Indianapolis after the 1848 political uprisings in Germany and become successful businessmen. Richard worked as a salesman and accounts collector at Franke and Schindler's hardware store, became a partner in

Richard Lieber is best known for his role in creating Indiana's state park system. [Indiana State Library]

the Western Chemical Company (1892), and served as an art critic for the *Indianapolis Journal* (1890s). In August, 1893, he married Emma Rappaport, daughter of well-known German-American lawyer and newspaper editor PHILLIP RAPPAPORT.

Lieber became involved in the business and civic communities of Indianapolis. Bankrolled by cousin Albert Lieber, he began a soft drink and charged water business (the Richard Lieber Company). Mayor LEW SHANK appointed him chairman of the city's public utilities in the 1910s. Lieber founded the Merchants and Manufacturers Insurance Bureau of Indianapolis, serving as its president (1912–1939) while working to improve the city's fire insurance and protection. He also was vice-chair of a local relief committee following the flood of 1913.

An avid conservationist, Lieber was a delegate to a White House conference (1908) to discuss the nation's natural resources and attended the Fourth National Conference on Conservation held in Indianapolis (1912). He advocated the creation of state parks, and in March, 1916, became chairman of the State Parks Committee, established as part of the Indiana Historical Commission's state centennial celebration. Lieber's lengthy report outlined plans for acquiring and preserving land throughout Indiana and became the basis for the Department of Conservation (now Department of Natural Resources) and the state park system. McCormick's Creek and Turkey Run were the first state parks created during the centennial year. In March, 1917, Governor James Goodrich appointed Lieber secretary of the state's forestry board.

Following the United States' entrance into WORLD WAR I, Goodrich named Lieber his military secretary at the rank of colonel to serve as a liaison between the State of Indiana and the U.S. War Department. The appointment was remarkable considering Lieber's prominent role in the German-American community and the rampant anti-German hysteria that gripped the nation, including Indiana.

After the Indiana General Assembly passed a conservation bill in 1919, Lieber became the first director of the Department of Conservation, a position he held until resigning in 1933. During his tenure the department created other parks and took responsibility for several state memorials and historic sites. Lieber also served as chairman of the Board of the National Conference on State Parks (1939–1944) and as an advisor for the National Park Service for many years. His ashes are buried at Turkey Run State Park, and the Richard Lieber State Recreation Area near Cloverdale is named in his honor.

GILES HOYT
Indiana University–Purdue University,
Indianapolis

Emma Lieber, *Richard Lieber* (n.p., 1947); Richard Lieber, *America's Natural Wealth: A Story of the Use and Abuse of Our Resources* (New York, 1942).

Liederkranz. German-American male singing society. On July 4, 1872, the male singing sections of two German secret fraternal organizations, the Druiden Lodge and the Rothmaenner ("Red Men"), merged to form the Indianapolis Liederkranz, which means "wreath of songs." The initial group consisted of 45 "active" or "singing" members under the direction of August Mueller. By 1908 the Liederkranz possessed 60 active members and 250 "passive" or "non-singing" members who joined in the social events of the society, and, with their families, constituted the bulk of the audience at Liederkranz concerts. The society participated in the choral festivals or "Saengerfeste" of the North American Saengerbund (NASB), a federation of German-American singing societies, and assisted the MAENNERCHOR in hosting the NASB's 1908 Saengerfest in Indianapolis.

Involved in many community celebrations as well, the Liederkranz took part in the dedication ceremonies of the SOLDIERS AND SAILORS MONUMENT in 1902, and the city's 1916 commemoration of the centennial of Indiana statehood. In the 1930s the formation of a theatrical group, headed by Wilhelm Pitschler, supplemented the society's musical activities. The Liederkranz presents two annual concerts, in addition to dances, holiday celebrations, and a summer picnic at GERMAN PARK. It continues to participate in Saengerfeste of the NASB.

SUZANNE G. SNYDER

George Theodore Probst, *The Germans in Indianapolis: 1840–1918*, rev. ed. by Eberhard Reichmann (Indianapolis, 1989).

Light of the World Christian Church.

First African-American CHRISTIAN CHURCH (DISCIPLES OF CHRIST) in Indianapolis. Central Christian congregation, a predominately white fellowship, sponsored a missionary church and school for their "African brethren" in 1866. This school and congregation originally met in a building at what was then Second Street and soon became known as Second Christian Church. In 1867 the church received its first full-time minister. During the remainder of the 19th century, however, the nascent congregation was often without a pastor, the tiny membership fluctuated greatly, and the church moved several times.

Second Christian experienced a rebirth when Rev. H. L. Herod became pastor in 1898. During his 37–year pastorate, Herod encouraged members to value education and take active leadership roles in the African-American community. He organized the National Christian Missionary Convention to teach African-Americans how to be leaders. During this time, the 375–member congregation became known as the elite church of the African-American community in Indianapolis.

Rev. R. H. Peoples became pastor of Second Christian in 1943 and ushered in an era of social ministry. The church moved to a former white Christian church at 29th Street and Kenwood Avenue in 1948, enlarged its staff, and expanded its philanthropic and community outreach programs. It remained predominantly nonwhite, drawing its 800 African-American members from throughout the Indianapolis area.

Dr. T. Garrott Benjamin succeeded Peoples in the pastorate in 1969 and remains pastor as of the early 1990s. A dynamic evangelist, he spurred phenomenal growth and national interest. Throughout the 1970s the congregation was recognized as one of the largest and fastest growing Disciples of Christ churches. It purchased its current facilities at 5640 East 38th Street in 1982 and changed its name to Light of the World Christian Church in 1984 to accommodate its 3,000–member, evangelistic congregation. The church began a local cable television ministry in 1986 named "Heaven on Earth Ministries." By 1988 this ministry was broadcast nationally and reached over 35 million viewers. The church also provides many community and youth programs.

MICHELLE D. HALE

History of Second Christian Church, 1866–1966 (Indianapolis, 1966).

Lighthouse Ministries. Homeless shelter. The Reverend Charles Oldham founded Lighthouse Mission in 1952, and the small gospel mission began operations in the 500 block of East Washington Street. It was incorporated in Indiana on June 16, 1955, as a nonprofit, Christian, nondenominational rescue mission caring for indigent men of the inner city. In the 1950s, the mission moved to 126 South Delaware Street, in 1963 to 343 Market Street, and in 1969 to its present location at 520 East Market Street. In January, 1989, the old building was demolished to make way for the present facility. In 1991, the name was changed to Lighthouse Ministries to better reflect its expanded mission.

Lighthouse annually serves 85,000 meals, provides 25,000 nights lodging, and gives over 23,000 clothing items. During the holidays hundreds of food baskets are distributed to the needy. As a leading service provider to the homeless and poor of Indianapolis, Lighthouse constantly assesses the needs of the homeless and provides emergency and long-term programs offering transient care and residential training, with case man-

agement, which enables clients to reenter the mainstream of society.

Affiliated with the International Union of Gospel Missions and the Evangelical Council of Financial Accountability, Lighthouse acquires funds for its over $1 million budget solely from private contributions.

REVEREND JERRY D. JONES
Lighthouse Ministries, Inc.

Sylvia Likens Murder Case. Indianapolis torture-murder. In July, 1965, Lester and Betty Likens, traveling fair concessionaires, left two of their children, Sylvia Marie, 16, and Jenny Fay, 15, as boarders in the home of Gertrude Baniszewski (alias Gertrude Wright), 37, divorced mother of seven. On October 26, 1965, police called to the East New York Street house discovered Sylvia Likens' body lying on a soiled mattress on the floor of an empty upstairs bedroom. Her body was covered with cuts, severe bruises, and a variety of open sores—some from over 100 cigarette burns, peeling scald marks, and missing skin. She had two black eyes, shredded lips, and fingernails broken backward. Further, Likens' body showed evidence of malnutrition. A "3" was branded on her chest, and the words "I am a prostitute and proud of it" were etched into her stomach. The official cause of death was a subdural hematoma from a blow to the temple, but shock and extensive injuries contributed to her death.

Jenny Likens approached the investigating officers and offered to make a statement, provided she was immediately removed from the home. Over the next several days, police took the entire Baniszewski family and eight neighborhood children into custody. Anna Cisco, 13, Michael Monroe, 11, Randy Lepper, 11, and Judy Duke, 12, were charged with injury to person; all would later be released under subpoena as state witnesses. Baniszewski's youngest children Marie, 11, Shirley, 10, James, 8, and Dennis Wright, Jr., 1, were placed in separate foster homes.

In December, 1965, a grand jury indicted Gertrude Baniszewski, her daughters Paula, 17, and Stephanie, 15, and her son John, Jr., 12, and two neighbors, Coy Hubbard and Richard Hobbs, both 15, on charges of first-degree murder. The highly publicized April, 1966, murder trial drew national attention. The testimony revealed that Gertrude Baniszewski had supervised and assisted her own and other neighborhood children in the daily torture of Likens. Sylvia Likens spent the last weeks of her life shut in the basement of the house without access to food or water. Neighbors who were aware of Likens' condition in the Baniszewski household had not interfered.

Gertrude Baniszewski pleaded not guilty by reason of insanity. She was found guilty of first-degree murder and sentenced to life imprisonment. The judgment was reversed on appeal in 1970, and a new trial ordered with a change of venue. The 1971 retrial again found her guilty of first-degree murder. In 1985 she was granted parole, despite a public petition protest that raised over 40,000 signatures.

Paula Baniszewski was found guilty of second-degree murder, and was sentenced to life imprisonment. Also granted a new trial on appeal in 1970, she pleaded guilty to involuntary manslaughter in the 1971 retrial, and was sentenced to 2 to 21 years. She twice escaped from prison, and was granted parole two years later. Stephanie Baniszewski, who voluntarily testified for the state, was granted a separate trial, found not guilty, and released. Coy Hubbard, Richard Hobbs, and John Baniszewski, Jr., were all convicted of manslaughter and sentenced to 2 to 21 years. They served 18 months and were released on parole in 1967.

VICKIE J. WEST

Kate Millett, *The Basement* (New York, 1991 [1979]); Linda G. Caleca, "House of Torture," *Indianapolis Star*, Sept. 15, 1985.

Lilly, Eli (Apr. 1, 1885–Jan. 24, 1977). Pharmaceutical entrepreneur, civic leader, and philanthropist. Eli Lilly was the son of JOSIAH K. LILLY, SR., and Lilly Ridgely Lilly; the grandson of COLONEL ELI LILLY; and the brother of JOSIAH K. LILLY, JR. His marriage in 1907 to Evelyn Fortune produced two sons who died in infancy and a daughter who died in 1970. This first marriage ended in divorce in 1926. His marriage in 1927 to Ruth Allison Lilly lasted happily until her death in 1973.

Eli Lilly.
[Eli Lilly and Company Archives]

Lilly was educated in the Indianapolis public schools and graduated from the Philadelphia College of Pharmacy in 1907. He immediately joined the pharmaceutical company founded by his grandfather and remained associated with the business until his death, serving as president from 1932 to 1948 and then as chairman of the board. Lilly played a dominant role in the growth and maturation of the company. He successfully applied the techniques of mass production to drug manufacturing, setting up in the 1920s a straight-line production system far more complex than Henry Ford's auto assembly line. He led the company into sophisticated research in its own laboratories and into close cooperation with university scientists, beginning with insulin in the 1920s and extending to penicillin and a range of antibiotics. In the 1930s and 1940s, he also devoted great attention to employee morale and welfare, making "Lillys" one of the most attractive places to work in the city. The American Pharmaceutical Association awarded him the Remington Honor Medal in 1957 for distinguished service to pharmacy.

Among Lilly's many interests outside the business were the history and archaeology of Indiana. He was president of the INDIANA HISTORICAL SOCIETY from 1933 to 1947 and was thereafter a member of its Executive Committee and Board of Trustees. His book *Prehistoric Antiquities of Indiana*, published in 1937, was a major contribution to the field, as was the report on the Walam Olum, published in 1954. His direction and financial support preserved the prehistoric Angel Site in southern Indiana and led to the construction of the Glenn A. Black Laboratory of Archaeology at

Indiana University, Bloomington. His *History of the Little Church on the Circle: Christ Church Parish Indianapolis, 1837–1955*, published in 1957, is a model church history. Lilly's attraction to the past led also to his strong support for historic preservation, evident in the development of CONNER PRAIRIE, support for the restoration of several houses in Indianapolis, and the founding of the HISTORIC LANDMARKS FOUNDATION OF INDIANA.

Lilly's wealth and humanity led him to become a major philanthropic benefactor. He and his family established the LILLY ENDOWMENT in 1937. He played an active role in focusing the endowment's support in the areas closest to his own concerns—religion, education, and community development, with special attention to Indianapolis and Indiana. Lilly also made large personal contributions to many projects and organizations, usually with the insistence that they be anonymous. Among the Indianapolis institutions that were major beneficiaries of his estate were the Indiana Historical Society, the Historic Landmarks Foundation of Indiana, THE CHILDREN'S MUSEUM of Indianapolis, CHRIST CHURCH CATHEDRAL, St. Paul's and Trinity Episcopal churches, Conner Prairie, the INDIANAPOLIS MUSEUM OF ART, BUTLER UNIVERSITY, and the foundations of ORCHARD COUNTRY DAY SCHOOL and PARK TUDOR SCHOOL.

Lilly enjoyed sailing at Lake Wawasee, woodworking, and visiting with a small circle of close friends, particularly friends from Indianapolis and those who shared his historical interests. He was modest and unassuming, though he set high standards for himself. He was never actively involved in politics, but he became generally recognized as one of the most powerful men in the city, the consequence not simply of his wealth but also of his intense concern and affection for the place of his birth.

JAMES H. MADISON
Indiana University, Bloomington

James H. Madison, *Eli Lilly: A Life, 1885–1977* (Indianapolis, 1989); E. J. Kahn, Jr., *All in a Century: The First 100 Years of Eli Lilly and Company* (Indianapolis, 1976).

Lilly, Eli, Col. (July 8, 1838–June 6, 1898). Founder of Eli Lilly and Company pharmaceutical firm. Eli Lilly was born in Maryland but soon thereafter moved with his family to Kentucky and then, in 1852, to Greencastle, Indiana. In 1854 he began working at the Good Samaritan Drug Store in Lafayette, learning the business as an apprentice. He returned to Greencastle to open his own drugstore in early 1861. At the same time he married the daughter of one of the town's merchants. Their son, JOSIAH K. LILLY, SR., was born November 18, 1861, when Eli was away at war.

Lilly enlisted immediately with the outbreak of the Civil War in 1861. He soon organized the 18th Indiana Light Artillery Battery. Composed of Hoosier farm boys, clerks, and college students, the battery members elected Lilly as their captain. As part of John T. Wilder's Lightning Brigade, they saw action at Hoover's Gap and Chickamauga. Lilly later joined the 9th Indiana Cavalry as a major. Captured by Confederates, he was mustered out at the end of the war as a colonel. Like many others of his generation, his Civil War title stayed with him, used even after his death to distinguish him from his grandson of the same name. In 1893 he served as chairman of the GRAND ARMY OF THE REPUBLIC's annual encampment, which brought thousands of Union veterans and their families to Indianapolis.

With peace Lilly tried business in several places, including operating a cotton plantation in Mississippi. It was during this unsuccessful business venture that his wife died (August 20, 1866), contributing to his return to Indiana where in 1868 he filed for bankruptcy. A year later he remarried and moved to Paris, Illinois, and a new and more successful drugstore business.

Seeking larger opportunity, Lilly returned to Indianapolis and on May 10, 1876, opened a pharmaceutical laboratory on Pearl Street, just off Washington Street. Above the door of the small two-story building he hung the sign "Eli Lilly, Chemist." His pills, elixirs, and syrups soon sold well in the city and surrounding towns, and by the late 1880s the company had become one of the prominent businesses in Indianapolis, with sales exceeding $200,000 and a work force of 100. Growth brought a move to McCarty Street on the growing industrial south side.

By 1890 Col. Lilly was a wealthy man. Less interested in the pharmaceutical business than civic affairs, he turned over much of the running of the company to his son, Josiah. His civic interests had been apparent as early as late 1870s when he served as a sponsor for Oscar McCulloch's CHARITY ORGANIZATION SOCIETY. His primary interest was in promoting the economic and general development of the city through commercial organizations. Most notable was the COMMERCIAL CLUB of Indianapolis, of which he was the major founder in 1890 and served as president from 1890 to 1895. One of the Commercial Club's first projects was promotion of a STREET PAVING EXPOSITION. The organization played a major role in encouraging other civic improvements, particularly sewers and elevated railroad crossings, and generally promoted the economic advantages of the city to outside investors. Lilly's interest in civic affairs also led to leadership in providing relief for unemployed workers during the harsh depression of 1893.

Lilly became an enthusiastic fisherman and sailor, particularly after he built a family cottage on Lake Wawasee in northern Indiana in 1887. He died of cancer at age 60, one of the most well-known men in the city. His son and two grandsons (ELI LILLY and JOSIAH K. LILLY, JR.) would often refer to the Colonel's business and civic example as models in their lives.

JAMES H. MADISON
Indiana University, Bloomington

Roscoe Collins Clark, *Threescore Years and Ten: A Narrative of the First Seventy Years of Eli Lilly and Company, 1876–1946* (Indianapolis, 1946); John W. Rowell, *Yankee Artillerymen: Through the Civil War with Eli Lilly's Indiana Battery* (Knoxville, Tenn., 1975).

Lilly, Josiah Kirby, Jr. (Sept. 25, 1893–May 5, 1966). Businessman, philanthropist, collector. Born in Indianapolis, the younger son of JOSIAH K. LILLY, SR., "Joe" earned a pharmacy degree from the University of Michigan. He entered the family business, ELI LILLY AND COMPANY, in 1914, and focused on the fields of personnel and marketing.

During his more than 50 years with the company, Joe Lilly did much to reorganize the firm internally, with increased efficiency and improved business procedures as tangible results. Shortly after joining the company he wrote a lengthy report on the subject of employment practices, which established the groundwork for the company's personnel philosophies and practices: fair wages, reasonable hours, favorable working conditions, and good benefits. He stressed the importance of the human side of business. He also formed a sales research department, and inaugurated sales training courses at regular intervals. After serving as vice-president in the marketing area and then vice-president of the company, in 1944 he was named president of the newly formed Eli Lilly International Corporation, a position he held until becoming president of Eli Lilly and Company in 1948.

At the same time he was attaining business success, Joe Lilly found time to devote to many personal interests. From his childhood love of books Lilly developed an interest in collecting first editions and manuscripts. Eventually he amassed a superb collection of rare books, which he later donated to Indiana University. (This collection formed the core of the Lilly Library of rare books and manuscripts on the Bloomington campus.) Another interest was the formation of a set of miniature soldiers representing every regiment that ever served in the United States armies up to 1900, with accurate uniforms, flags, insignia, and arms.

Other hobbies included collecting gold coins, stamps, firearms, and 18th-century paintings. After his retirement in 1953, his hobbies occupied most of his time, and he built a special house where he could retreat and spend his days with all the treasures he loved.

In 1934, Joe Lilly began acquisition of land northwest of Indianapolis that eventually totaled 3,469 acres and included a private residential retreat, a 1,000–acre forest in which he planted thousands of trees over a 20–year period, and a 1,000–acre farm. He donated the estate to Purdue University in the mid–1950s. A decade later the city of Indianapolis purchased the property to develop what is now EAGLE CREEK Park.

ANITA MARTIN
Eli Lilly and Company Archives

David A. Randall, *J. K. Lilly—America's Quiet Collector* (Bloomington, Ind., 1966); Eli Lilly and Company, *The Lilly Review* (June, 1949).

Lilly, Josiah Kirby, Sr.

Lilly, Josiah Kirby, Sr. (Nov. 18, 1861–Feb. 8, 1948). Businessman, philanthropist, humanist. Born in Greencastle, Indiana, the only child of COL. ELI LILLY and Emily Lemon Lilly, "J. K." was 14 years old when his father founded ELI LILLY AND COMPANY in Indianapolis in 1876. The young man joined his father to learn the pharmacy trade through apprenticeship. After resolving to make pharmaceutical manufacturing his lifework, J. K. entered the Philadelphia College of Pharmacy, graduating in 1882 *cum laude*. Following his return to the company, he became superintendent and proceeded to make changes which would have a positive effect on the firm.

Upon the death of his father Lilly became president of the company in 1898 and, with a far-sighted vision of the possibilities of the business, began instituting changes in research and marketing methods. Under his direction the sales force soon covered the entire United States and later much of the world. Around 1918 he led discussions among the management of the company, including his two sons, on the importance of expanding the research effort. A few years later, when INSULIN was discovered at the University of Toronto, Lilly signed a contract with the university to make insulin commercially available to the world.

J. K. Lilly's way of business and his way of life reflected a creed of civic involvement and charity. "Every man should, in addition to his endeavors for personal and family gain and comfort, unselfishly perform some duties as a citizen for the community in which he and others live, move and have their beings," he once wrote. He was active in the Indianapolis COMMERCIAL CLUB, the YMCA, Red Cross, the INDIANAPOLIS FOUNDATION, CROWN HILL CEMETERY, James Whitcomb Riley Memorial Association, and CHRIST CHURCH CATHEDRAL. He also served as a trustee for Purdue University and the Philadelphia College of Pharmacy.

As he grew older, fondness for the melodies of Stephen Collins Foster stirred in him an interest to collect memorabilia on the composer. According to Lilly, "What started as a diversion soon became a passion and now is an obsession." The collection, containing more than 10,000 items and said to be one of the finest examples in existence of collections pertaining to one author or composer, was presented to the University of Pittsburgh.

ANITA MARTIN
Eli Lilly and Company Archives

Eli Lilly and Company, *The Lilly Review* (Feb., 1948); E. J. Kahn, Jr., *All in a Century* (Indianapolis, 1976).

Lilly Center Museum and Archives.

Lilly Center Museum and Archives. Repository for historical records of ELI LILLY AND COMPANY and the Lilly family. The museum includes a replica of the original laboratory, built in 1934 to honor the company's founder, COL. ELI LILLY. There are also three museum rooms featuring displays of memorabilia from the three generations of Lillys who led the company through the first 100 years, as well as artifacts from the early years of research, manufacturing, and marketing. The archives of Eli Lilly and Company contains records of the company's history dating back to the founding on May 10, 1876; and the archival collection includes family papers from the 1800s, as well as genealogical data to 1291.

Eli Lilly and Company was first opened on Pearl Street in downtown Indianapolis. In 1934, a photograph of the original building was enlarged to determine the size of the building so a replica could be constructed. The two-story building measures 20 by 40 feet and has much of the original equipment, representing the pharmaceutical business of more than a century ago—percolators, drug mills, evaporating pans, and a still. There is Col. Eli Lilly's own invention, a device for gelatin-coating pills. In the beginning, working hours were ten hours per day, six days a week. Telephones and typewriters were not available. Letters were copied soon after writing by placing them between tissue paper and waterproof cardboards, and inserting in a letter press for a half hour. The letter press is on display beside Col. Lilly's original desk and chair. The same stuffed blackbird that was discovered mounted on the wall in the original structure watches over all visitors to the little replica building.

The seeds of the Lilly Archives go back before the founding of the company. The Lillys were a history-minded family, and heirlooms, portraits, and memorabilia were saved that date to the early 19th century. Generations of Lillys continued to be conscious of the value of saving records representative of the growth of the company, as well as items pertinent to the life surrounding the business.

In 1949 JOSIAH K. LILLY, JR., requested the librarian to proceed with cataloging the historical material. Archives became an official department of the company in 1956. Records representing more than a century of operation include journals and ledgers, manuals and handbooks, significant files and reports, advertising materials, corporate publications, speeches, employee records, and photographs. The purpose of the archives is to preserve the corporate memory and to supply authentic documentation of company activities.

With the exception of the laboratory replica, the museum rooms and archives are located in Lilly Center, opened in 1969 as a visitors' center. The building also includes an exhibit hall that conveys the research and discovery story of modern medicine and health-care products. A theater using 21 projectors and 1,200 visual images tells of Eli Lilly and Company's commitment as a research-based organization to help improve the quality of life throughout the world.

ANITA N. MARTIN
Eli Lilly and Company Archives

Lilly Endowment. Founded in 1937, Lilly Endowment grew to become one of the nation's major philanthropic institutions. Although its gifts have reached across the nation and around the world, the Endowment's primary giving has focused since its founding on Indianapolis and Indiana.

The Lilly family had long made major contributions to the well-being of their city and state. In the late 19th century COL. ELI LILLY supported the CHARITY ORGANIZATION SOCIETY and led in organizing civic improvements through the Indianapolis COMMERCIAL CLUB. His son and grandsons actively carried on this tradition through private giving in these and other areas. As the pharmaceutical company profits grew and as the external environment changed, however, the family decided a more formal manner of philanthropy was necessary.

The primary mover in creating the Endowment was ELI LILLY, then president of ELI LILLY AND COMPANY. He told his father, JOSIAH K. LILLY, SR., and his brother, JOSIAH K. LILLY, JR., that a formal philanthropic institution was essential if they wished to continue their large charitable gifts and if they wished to retain family control of the pharmaceutical company. A primary impetus in Eli Lilly's thinking and the thinking behind the origins of many other new foundations in the 1930s and 1940s was the changing federal tax law that accompanied Franklin D. Roosevelt's New Deal. Eli Lilly was especially fearful that he and his brother would need to pay large inheritance taxes on their father's company stock at his death and that these taxes might require selling some of the family's shares and thereby risk losing control of the business. The Lilly Endowment formed, then, in an effort to continue and expand the family's philanthropy, to lessen income and inheritance taxes, and to maintain control of the family pharmaceutical business.

In the early years Eli Lilly ran the Endowment from one of his office desk drawers. He received and studied requests for contributions and made recommendations to the board, which consisted of his father, brother, and wife, Ruth Allison Lilly, plus Nicholas Noyes, treasurer of the company. The board approved the first grants in December, 1937, the largest of which was $10,500 to the Indianapolis Community Chest, forerunner of UNITED WAY, thereby setting an enduring pattern of giving concentrated on the city.

The Endowment experienced its first significant change following J. K. Lilly, Sr.'s death in 1948 and his bequest of company stock, which increased assets from $9 million in 1947 to $39 million in 1948. Grants in the years 1948–1957 expanded to an annual average of $2 million, compared to $200,000 in the previous ten years. Eli Lilly soon concluded that this increased size required more attentive management by a full-time staff. J. K. Lilly III and G. Harold Duling became the first staff. The two men began in 1951 to publish an annual report and attempted to specify more formal policies and procedures, including requiring written grant requests rather than the informal oral requests that had often been received earlier. Family members, particularly Eli Lilly, continued nonetheless to operate on an informal basis that thwarted some of these efforts toward more professional procedures, so much so that J. K. Lilly III resigned in 1954. The tension between family influence and staff professionalism would continue into the 1970s.

During the 1950s the Endowment formalized its areas of concentration to focus on education, religion, and community service. Indianapolis charities, such as the United Way, formed with Endowment encouragement in 1957, and local institutions, such as THE CHILDREN'S MUSEUM and the Boys' Club, received significant contributions. Support was substantial also for the family's CHRIST CHURCH and other Episcopal causes, but included many other Protestant institutions as well. Indeed, the Endowment's special identity among foundations by the 1950s was its unusually large support for religion. The Endowment also made major contributions to higher education, particularly to church-related, liberal arts colleges in Indiana, with special family affection for Wabash and Earlham colleges. Support for other projects followed personal interests of the two Lilly brothers. J. K. Lilly, Jr.'s fondness for American literature and rare books led to special grants in these areas. Eli Lilly's much wider interests stimulated support for a long list of causes and endeavors, ranging from the United Negro College Fund, to research in prehistoric archaeology, to Indiana history projects.

While the Endowment maintained its central focus on education, religion, and community service, some notable changes occurred during the turbulent 1960s. At the urging of John S. Lynn, who became general manager in 1961, and who was actively backed by J. K. Lilly, Jr., the Endowment began to make grants to very conservative political and religious causes. Annual reports preached the wisdom of free markets, anticommunism, and evangelical Christianity. There was also concern about the upheaval on college campuses in the 1960s, resulting in a shift of grants away from higher education. This shift to the right caused concern among foundation watchers and led to some criticism of the Endowment, most notably in Waldemar A. Nielsen's *The Big Foundations* (1972).

In the early 1970s, however, the Endowment purposefully moved away from the aggressive conservatism of the 1960s. At the instigation of Eli Lilly, Landrum Bolling replaced Lynn as executive vice-president and began to respond to Lilly's urging that the Endowment needed to find broader and more important projects. Lilly also hired Bolling, then president of Earlham College, because he knew that the criticism of foundations generally and the Tax Reform Act of 1969 particularly had created challenges requiring the large talents and vision of a leader of Bolling's stature. The 1969 legislation forced the Endowment to diversify some of its stock holdings and to increase significantly its grant payouts. As a consequence of this legislation and also because of an increase in assets from a family trust, annual grants rose from about $9 million in the late 1960s to over $50 million by the mid–1970s. The staff increased from 6 to 75 and moved to large quarters on North Meridian Street. The board now included members not part of the Lilly family, though all were friends of Eli Lilly, including Indiana University's former president, Herman B Wells, former Indiana governor Roger D. Branigin, and Wabash College president Byron K. Trippet. The Endowment restated its commitment to the trinity of religion, education, and community service in the early 1970s, but also began to make more grants outside Indiana and even outside the United States, partly in response to Bolling's own international interests.

The interest in Indianapolis intensified too, however, particularly after Eli Lilly met with Mayor Richard Lugar in 1972 to discuss their concerns about the deterioration of the downtown. Three days later Lilly told Lugar that the Endowment would renovate the CITY MARKET to save it from the wrecker's ball. A few months later Lugar's aide, James T. Morris, moved from city hall to the Endowment to administer Indianapolis projects. At an Endowment retreat in 1976, a year before his death, Lilly urged his colleagues to intensify their commitment to the city.

The late 1970s and early 1980s witnessed a substantial increase in the Endowment's investment in the city, with contributions totaling about $300 million between 1975 and 1987, as the institution became a major partner in public and private ventures to rebuild and revitalize downtown. This new Indianapolis initiative meant that the Endowment moved away from its reluctance both to support capital projects and to become closely involved with public, tax-supported development. Thus the Endowment contributed $25 million to the expansion of the INDIANA CONVENTION CENTER and construction of the HOOSIER DOME. It supported other major downtown construction projects, including the CENTRAL CANAL, Market Street repaving, and the beautification of the American Legion Mall. The Endowment contributed to restoring the INDIANA THEATRE and CIRCLE THEATRE, and made substantial grants to build the new INDIANAPOLIS ZOO, the EITELJORG MUSEUM OF AMERICAN INDIAN AND WESTERN ART, the sports complex on the INDIANA UNIVERSITY–PURDUE UNIVERSITY AT INDIANAPOLIS campus, the velodrome at Sullivan Park, and other sports facilities that attracted the PAN AMERICAN GAMES in 1987. Endowment support also helped revitalization of the areas around the Walker Building, FOUNTAIN SQUARE–FLETCHER PLACE, and other near-downtown neighborhoods.

The Endowment continued its nationwide programs in religion during the 1980s and 1990s, expanding to include Catholic as well as Protestant concerns and supporting major attention to African-American churches. Support for higher education also continued, with special emphasis on Indiana's colleges and universities. The Endowment's largest grant (a seven-year, $50 million allocation fund) was made in 1987 to assist more students to gain a college education. And the Endowment began in the mid–1980s for the first time to offer major assistance to public schools. Other new initiatives focused on helping nonprofit organizations function more effectively, including the establishment of the INDIANA UNIVERSITY CENTER ON PHILANTHROPY.

At the end of its first half century, 1937–1987, the Endowment accounts showed assets of $2 billion, ranking it fifth largest among American foundations. In those first 50 years the philanthropy had paid out $698 million in grants, most to Indianapolis and Indiana recipients, a total that exceeded $1 billion by 1991.

In the late 1980s and early 1990s, recognizing that the physical revitalization of Indianapolis was on a course of its own, the Endowment refocused its attention on human needs and its statewide initiatives. These included the unique $60.1 million GIFT (Giving Indiana Funds for Tomorrow) program that helped establish some 30 community foundations and strengthened existing community foundations in Indiana, the $10 million Giant Step initiative to bolster the network of United Ways around the state, more than $25 million to address the issue of housing in Indianapolis and at the national level, and an additional $12 million in allocations for the state scholarship program.

JAMES H. MADISON
Indiana University, Bloomington

Lilly Endowment Inc. 1987: A Family Legacy for 50 Years (Indianapolis, 1987); James H. Madison, *Eli Lilly: A Life, 1885–1977* (Indianapolis, 1989).

Lilly Endowment Building (2801 North Meridian Street). Construction began on this late Art Deco building in the fall of 1949, with the cornerstone laid in 1950. It was originally the home office of one of Indiana's oldest insurance companies, the Empire Life and Accident Insurance Company. Initially planned as four stories (only two of which were built), the structure underwent considerable design changes from the original sketches by the architectural firm of D. A. BOHLEN AND SON. This firm designed numerous other postwar Art Deco buildings in Indianapolis, such as branch offices of (then) Indiana National Bank, the CROWN HILL CEMETERY mausoleum, and several buildings at MARIAN COLLEGE. The general contractor, Carl M. Geupel Construction Company, completed the structure in January, 1952, at a cost of $450,000. In the fall of 1972, subsequent to its major program expansion, LILLY ENDOWMENT moved into the building, which the foundation now owns.

The building is an excellent example of the Art Deco concern with contrast of materials, texture, and linear emphasis. Features of the Bohlen design include the use of black Vermont granite for the giant central first story entrance and third story clock tower, contrasting with the Indiana limestone of the main block. The design also incorporates application of vertical window fins on the first story facade and second story central pavilion alternating with horizontal banding in the second story parapet.

GLORY-JUNE GREIFF

Lilly Industries. Manufacturers of paints, varnishes, lacquers, and other specialty surface coatings. Lilly Industries is the outgrowth of a varnish company started in 1865 by Henry B. Mears. Two years later J. O. D. Lilly (no relation to the pharmaceutical family) joined the firm and the name was changed to Mears, Lilly & Company. In the 1870s Mears sold his interest to Lilly and his two sons, Charles and John, and the firm was renamed J. O. D. Lilly & Sons. In 1888 the business incorporated as the Lilly Varnish Company.

In 1921 the Lilly family sold the business to a group of men with an industrial coatings background. Under the new owners Lilly's 20 employees specialized in the formulation, manufacture, and sale of industrial finishes. Beginning in 1935 Lilly opened its first out-of-state manufacturing facility, building a factory in High Point, North Carolina, to serve the area's furniture manufacturers. One of Lilly's many innovations was the enamel finish used to coat home appliances, replacing the older porcelain finishes.

The firm changed its name again in 1965 to Lilly Industrial Coatings, and in 1984 moved its headquarters near those of Eli Lilly and Company headquarters. The two firms are not related. Lilly moved into retail paint sales with the 1988 acquisition of Perfection Paints' four area retail stores and a plant at Maryland Street and College Avenue. Previously, its coatings were sold exclusively to manufacturers. In 1991 the firm shortened its name to Lilly Industries. By 1993 the company employed over 1,200 people—300 in Indianapolis—in 18 plants in the United States, Canada, Taiwan, Germany, and Malaysia.

DEBORAH B. MARKISOHN

Indiana Business & Industry (Jan., 1966); *Indiana Business Journal*, Apr. 26–May 2, 1982; George Geib, *Indianapolis: Hoosiers' Circle City* (Tulsa, Okla., 1981), 204.

Abraham Lincoln's Funeral Cortege.

The Lincoln funeral train arrived in a rainy Indianapolis at 7 A.M. on Sunday, April 30, 1865. The coffin was transferred to a hearse drawn by four white horses, and a procession led by Governor OLIVER P. MORTON and Maj. Gen. Joseph Hooker formed to accompany the remains to the State House. A long procession through the city was canceled due to the weather.

Soldiers from Indianapolis camps lined both sides of the procession's route. Upon arrival at the Capitol, the coffin was placed on an elaborate dais in the rotunda and the upper third of the lid was opened so that mourners might see the face of the president. The public viewing began at 8 A.M. and continued until 10 that night. There is no accurate figure for the number of people paying their respects in the rotunda, but both the *Indianapolis Sentinel* and *Indianapolis Journal* estimated the crowd at "not less than 50,000"—slightly more than the entire city population five years later.

Torrential rains prevented photographers from recording Abraham Lincoln's cortege as his body lay in state on April 30, 1865. This image was staged the following day.
[Indiana Historical Society, Bass Collection, #31199]

Between 10 and 11 P.M. the guard of honor returned the coffin to the hearse, and a procession accompanied the coffin to the waiting train. The *Sentinel* reported: "This was the most solemn and imposing of all the pageantry that has attended the remains in this city. The wailing sadness of the music, the fitful glare of the lamps, the deep silence unbroken except by the heavy tramp of the soldiers and muffled rumbling of carriage wheels, made it the most impressive scene of all, in the mournful occasion."

LEIGH DARBEE
Indiana Historical Society

_____

George S. Cottman, "Lincoln in Indianapolis," *Indiana Magazine of History*, 24 (Mar., 1928), 1–14; *Indianapolis Sentinel* and *Indianapolis Journal*, Apr. 30, May 1, 1865.

Abraham Lincoln's Visits to Indianapolis.

President-elect Lincoln's trip to Washington, D.C., in February, 1861, for his inauguration as chief executive was a "progress" rather than a quiet journey. The railroads that controlled the Springfield, Illinois, to Washington route had offered Lincoln a special train that would travel on any schedule he chose. Lincoln made stops of varying length along the way, one of them in Indianapolis.

Though he was the first president-elect to visit the city, it was not Lincoln's first visit to Indianapolis. That had occurred on September 19, 1859, when Lincoln delivered a campaign speech to a full house at the Masonic Hall.

Lincoln's more well-known visit began with his arrival at about 5 P.M. on Monday, February 11, 1861, when he was welcomed by Governor Oliver P. Morton at the Lafayette and Indianapolis Railroad's crossing at Missouri and Washington streets. After Lincoln responded briefly, the party moved on to the BATES HOUSE. That evening, Lincoln made a speech from the hotel balcony to a crowd that local newspapers estimated at anywhere from 10,000 to 45,000 people.

The speech at Indianapolis was Lincoln's first major policy statement as president-elect, and it was quoted and analyzed in newspapers around the country. In it, he made clear that he considered

preservation of the Union his primary duty. One passage, as quoted in the *Indianapolis Sentinel*, summed up his message: ". . . where is the mysterious, original right, from principle, for a certain district of country with inhabitants, by merely being called a State, to play tyrant over all its own citizens, and deny the authority of everything greater than itself?"

LEIGH DARBEE
Indiana Historical Society

_____

George S. Cottman, "Lincoln in Indianapolis," *Indiana Magazine of History*, 24 (Mar., 1928), 1–14; Paul Fatout, "Mr. Lincoln Goes to Washington," *Indiana Magazine of History*, 47 (Dec., 1951), 321–332; *Indianapolis Journal* and *Indianapolis Sentinel*, Feb. 12, 1861.

Lindner's Dairy.

David and Hannah Lindner operated a dairy in Dayton, Ohio, for 9 years before moving to Indianapolis in 1929, where David and brother Carl opened an ice cream business, originally Lindner's Brothers, in May of that year. The store could not support both families and Carl withdrew after a short time. The family kept the business following David's death in 1940, and in 1949 Lindner's opened its first successful branch. By 1968 it had 27 locations. During the year the store produced nearly 100 flavors of ice cream, with 25 always available. Memorable flavors included "006 7/8," "purple fink," and "Batman."

In 1982 there were 36 Lindner's stores in Marion County and the surrounding area when son David Lindner, who owned the business, sold it to Roberts Dairy as a subsidiary. Roberts filed for bankruptcy reorganization in May, 1987, and while Lindner's was not included in the bankruptcy, the debt incurred by acquiring Lindner's was among Roberts' liabilities. Lindner's filed for Chapter 11 reorganization in October, 1989, and Friendly Foods, also a subsidiary of Roberts, began operating the 15 remaining stores in December. Friendly Foods terminated the agreement less than a month later and seized the properties in late January, 1990, as payment for its secured debt. The last seven Lindner's stores closed in January, 1992.

JOAN CUNNINGHAM

Link, Goethe (May 20, 1879–Dec. 31, 1980). Surgeon. Link was born in Selvin, Warrick County, Indiana; his father, a teacher turned physician, influenced his choice of profession. By the time Link entered medical school, he had earned a bachelor's degree (Indiana University, 1898), and also had become a registered pharmacist. He received his M.D. degree from the Central College of Physicians and Surgeons (Indianapolis) in 1902.

Following an internship at City Hospital (now WISHARD MEMORIAL HOSPITAL), Link entered the private practice of medicine with his father in a downtown office on Virginia Avenue. He also had been appointed to his medical alma mater's teaching faculty, in the department of anatomy. This opportunity enabled him to master the vascular intricacy of the thyroid gland, basic knowledge that enabled him to perfect surgical procedures for correction of certain thyroid disorders. He performed over 22,000 such surgeries.

Dr. Link also achieved recognition as an aeronaut (winner of the 1909 National Balloon Race), herpetologist, ornithologist, and amateur astronomer. He presented his Link Observatory, located south of Mooresville, to Indiana University in 1948. An asteroid was named in his honor in 1968.

CHARLES A. BONSETT, M.D.
Indiana University School of Medicine

Link-Belt Company. In 1874 William Dana Ewart, an Iowa agricultural tool dealer, patented his idea of a detachable square link chain for harvest equipment that could be easily repaired by farmers in the field. The next year he organized the Ewart Manufacturing Company in Chicago and moved the business to Indianapolis in 1885. Three years later he formed the Link-Belt Engineering Company to produce chain elevating and conveying machinery and in 1890 created the Link-Belt Machinery Company to build accessory parts. Business and sales manager Edward A. Turner coined the term "Link-Belt" for advertising purposes. Ewart consolidated the three companies in 1906 as the Link-Belt Company.

Link-Belt built several plants in Indianapolis: the Dodge plant, 519 North Holmes Street (1901),

the Ewart plant, 220 South Belmont Avenue (1913), and a facility at 7601 Rockville Road (1959). Employment at Link-Belt increased steadily from 100 persons in 1888 to 2,500 persons in 1929 to 3,400 workers by the mid–1950s. In June, 1967, the company merged with Chicago-based FMC Corporation, a machinery and chemical manufacturer. At the time of the merger Link-Belt operated 22 plants worldwide in addition to its Indianapolis facilities. In 1969 Link-Belt was the fifth largest employer in Indianapolis with more than 4,000 employees.

In 1981 Indianapolis-based PT Components was formed in a leveraged buyout of FMC's Power Transmission Group, obtaining the former Link-Belt Bearing Division and the Link-Belt Chain Division. Manufacturing power transmission equipment, PT Components employed 1,000 people in Indianapolis with annual sales around $200 million. In 1988 the firm merged with the mechanical power division of Rexnord Corporation, a Wisconsin-based industrial equipment manufacturer. Rexnord's division in Indianapolis retains the Link-Belt name.

DEBORAH B. MARKISOHN

Literacy. Census data show a continuous decline in the percentage of Indianapolis residents reported as illiterate or presumed to be functionally illiterate due to inadequate educational attainment. Literacy crises or campaigns, then, do not reflect a demonstrable rise in illiteracy, but rather a perception that illiteracy has increased or a conviction that the number of illiterate or poorly educated adults is unacceptably high, given school attendance rates and higher occupational and social requirements for literacy abilities.

Unfortunately, the federal census has used different measures for literacy in different years, so reliable comparisons are hard to make. The illiteracy data for Indianapolis from 1840 to 1880 are especially sketchy. In 1850, 965 (4 percent) Marion County adults over 20 were reported as illiterate (unable to read and write); in 1870, 2,426 (probably around 10 percent) Indianapolis residents over 20 were counted as unable to write. The increase has been attributed primarily to improved reporting methods.

Beginning in 1890 all those reported as "unable to write" were counted as illiterate, since data had shown that almost all those able to write were also able to read. (However, about 20 percent of those counted as illiterate in Indianapolis that year could read but could not write.) Based on those ages 10 and over unable to write, then, Indianapolis (6.1 percent) and Indiana (6.3 percent) scored below the national percentage of 13.3 percent. Indianapolis' illiteracy percentage was comparable to that in other midwestern cities.

Illiteracy continued to decline in Indianapolis and the state during the last four census years in which the literacy question was asked (1900–1930). By 1930 only 1.2 percent of Indianapolis residents 10 and over were reported as illiterate, compared to 1.7 percent for Indiana and 4.3 percent for the United States. Despite those decreases national and state commissions on illiteracy were appointed in 1930. The *Indianapolis Star* expressed alarm that year over the high number of native white illiterates in the state, concluding that "the larger centers of population apparently have failed to utilize their supposedly superior school systems." But a 1932 article reported that Indianapolis had one of the lowest illiteracy rates among 93 large cities in the United States.

Beginning in 1940 the census started asking about educational attainment rather than literacy per se. The correlation is not exact, but the shift from rudimentary literacy to a more functional definition probably has helped promote a sense of concern about illiteracy. Still, the percentage of adults with less than a ninth grade education provides only a rough gauge of functional literacy. In 1940, 51 percent of Marion County residents 25 and over had completed less than nine years of school; by 1950, that figure had dropped dramatically to 38 percent. The next ten years saw a smaller decline, to 33 percent in 1960.

Early in 1962 President John F. Kennedy requested $50 million for a "massive attack" on adult illiteracy; in Indianapolis literacy institutes sponsored by Laubach Literacy Action (a training program for volunteer literacy instructors) led to the formation of the Central Indiana Literacy Council. After a few years the council seems to have faded away, but another Indianapolis literacy group was formed sometime in the early 1970s,

working through CHURCH WOMEN UNITED. This group was the first incarnation of the Greater Indianapolis Literacy League (GILL). Meanwhile, the percentage of Marion County adults with less than nine years schooling dropped to 23 percent in 1970 and 15 percent in 1980, compared to 17 percent in the United States.

By the early 1980s GILL had become inactive. Recognizing the need for a revived organization to coordinate literacy efforts for adults at the lowest reading levels, a group of concerned citizens reorganized GILL in 1984 and established a coalition with the INDIANAPOLIS–MARION COUNTY PUBLIC LIBRARY. The library provides support services, including a full-time Manager of Literacy Services who serves as executive director of GILL. Serving primarily those with less than a fourth grade reading level, GILL has worked with 1,958 students since 1984. In 1985 the Marion County (now Indianapolis) Adult Literacy Coalition was established to coordinate literacy efforts in the city and secure funding for literacy projects. IALC was instrumental in setting up an Adult Education Referral Network.

Of course, the oldest continuous providers of literacy services in the area are the adult education programs of the various school districts. In 1967 INDIANAPOLIS PUBLIC SCHOOLS opened the Day Adult School, one of the first in the country. Today, IPS offers adult literacy training at over 50 sites including schools, social agencies, jails, halfway houses, and mental hospitals. About 80 percent of adult eduction funds go to classes for adults with less than a sixth grade education. Enrollment in adult literacy classes has increased from 4,020 in 1985–1986 to over 7,000 in 1992–1993.

In the early 1990s over 118,000 adults (23 percent of adults 25 years and over) in Marion County had no high school diploma (in the United States it is 25 percent); over 35,000 (7 percent) had less than a ninth grade education (U.S., 11 percent). Thirty adult literacy programs in Indianapolis tried to meet the diverse needs of this heterogeneous group—or rather, of the uncountable subgroup whose lack of literacy skills interfere with workplace and personal functioning. A profile of GILL students, for example, revealed a median age of 41; 76 percent had no high school diploma, most had fewer than 9 years of schooling, and their average reading level upon entry to the program was 1.8 (less than second grade). Only 50 percent were employed full time, most of those in low-skilled jobs. GILL students were predominantly male (62 percent) and half are African-American. Illiteracy in Indianapolis is interwoven with poverty, discrimination, inadequate schooling, learning disabilities, and family problems; literacy programs and campaigns, however effective, will never of themselves solve the persistent problem of illiteracy.

STEPHEN FOX
Indiana University–Purdue University,
Indianapolis

Literary Organizations and Events.
Literary clubs have had great popularity in Indianapolis. Particularly in the last decades of the 19th century, paralleling to some extent the GOLDEN AGE OF INDIANA LITERATURE, both men and women founded societies to study and discuss literary works. As in other parts of the nation at that time, learning and culture were in much demand. Books and magazines were increasingly popular. Public lectures or lyceums were well attended. Women wanting to broaden their minds as well as their daily lives organized literary clubs. Men, many of them in the professions, also formed clubs in order to pursue their literary interests, at least within their own social circle. Several of the organizations begun during that era have continued to the present day.

Although their period of greatest growth was the 1880s and 1890s, literary clubs had for many years been important to the city's cultural life. The Young Men's Literary Society was begun in 1835, intended for composition, debate, and the general improvement of its members. Incorporated in 1847 as the Union Literary Society, it donated its library of several hundred books to the YOUNG MEN'S CHRISTIAN ASSOCIATION at the time it was established in 1854. The YMCA maintained the library and continued the literary society's program of public lectures. A later organization, the Hesperian Club for women, included among its members CATHARINE MERRILL and MAY WRIGHT SEWALL, two of the city's most admired teachers.

In 1872, the residents of the old Butler College neighborhood north of the MILE SQUARE organized the College Corner Club. When the college in 1874–1875 moved to IRVINGTON, newspapers of the period named it the "classic suburb" because of its academic atmosphere. A. R. Benton, president of the college, served also as president of the Irvington Literary Society, whose members came from the town as well as the college. Meetings were held on moonlit nights so that members would have no difficulty in finding their way home. In 1900, a later president, Scott Butler, founded the Irvington Atheneum, with members from Indianapolis as well as Irvington. The club brought such eminent speakers as Charles Eliot and Henry James to the Butler College Chapel.

Literary clubs were formed in other neighborhoods as well, such as the Paragon Literary Society for young people in the southwest part of the city. Churches and schools also sponsored literary organizations. The Aristotelian Club met at Plymouth Church, while the Agiliar Literary Society was a Jewish organization. In the black community, the Garnett Literary Society, open to both men and women, was founded in 1883 and, in the same decade, the Parlor Reading Club and the Douglass Literary Society.

The most prestigious of the city's 19th-century literary societies was the INDIANAPOLIS LITERARY CLUB (1877), which counted among its members some of the city's most prominent men. Sometimes called the Gentlemen's Literary Club, its stated objective was to advance "social, literary, and aesthetic culture." The Century Club was another highly regarded men's literary organization, whose membership at the time of its founding was younger than that of the Indianapolis Literary Club. Among its charter members were such Indianapolis notables as HILTON U. BROWN, WILLIAM FORTUNE, and Evans Woollen.

The INDIANAPOLIS WOMAN'S CLUB, organized in 1875, while not specifically designated a literary club, required for its programs papers written and presented by its members. Many of the papers dealt with literary topics. Several Woman's Club members were published writers, among them Anna Nicholas, Laura Fletcher Hodges, and Ernestine Rose. The Catharine Merrill Club (1885) began as an association of the Butler teacher's students who wanted to continue their study of literature with her. Founded in the same year, the Fortnightly Literary Club had as its goal "literary culture, the search of knowledge to be unlimited, the field universal." These women's clubs are still active today, in many cases with second and third generation members. The Indianapolis German Literary Club (1889–1917), like the Catharine Merrill Club, began with a group of students and expanded to include others interested in German literature. It was mandatory that all papers and discussions be presented in the German language. In 1890, four Indianapolis clubs joined the Indiana Union of Literary Clubs, and two Indianapolis women were among its early presidents.

Literary organizations continued to be popular as the old century closed and the next began. Many new literary clubs appeared, but not all survived. The names chosen for the clubs were interesting. Some simply stated their purpose, such as the Culture Club and the Late Book Club. Other names made connections: the Busy Bees became the Minerva Club, named for New Harmony's Minerva Society; the Ladies' Literary Union became the New Century Club. Still others sought originality. Organized in 1905 and still active today, the Zatathea Club chose for its name a Greek word meaning "seekers of knowledge."

LUELLA (MRS. FELIX) MCWHIRTER is credited with beginning the WOMAN'S DEPARTMENT CLUB in 1912. Organized with a broader base than many of the literary clubs, this organization was composed of several departments, or areas of study, one of which was literature and drama. In addition to instruction of its own members, this department invited well-known writers to speak. The Woman's Department Club was one of the few organizations to have its own clubhouse until the building, at 1702 North Meridian Street, was sold in 1960.

The focus of many of the literary clubs gradually broadened to include other topics of cultural interest, not only literature and other fine arts, but history, philosophy, and social issues. While the usual practice was for members to present original papers, a number of organizations began to bring in guest speakers, many of whom were nationally known. The CONTEMPORARY CLUB (1890) had as its goal to consider and discuss many top-

ics, literature being but one. Primarily an organization of artists, the Portfolio Club, formed the same year, also included in its membership persons interested in literature and music. These clubs continue today.

Libraries, public lectures, and other forms of activity also fostered an appreciation of literature in Indianapolis. A Presbyterian minister's sermon in 1868 led to the establishment of a public library for the city, and in 1872 CHARLES EVANS was appointed its first librarian. At that time, there were many bookstores in Indianapolis and a number of excellent private libraries. Two of the more prominent of these booksellers later, through several mergers, became the book publishing firm of Bowen-Merrill (later BOBBS-MERRILL).

Lecture series were sponsored as early as 1831 by the Indianapolis Lyceum or Atheneum and, later, by the Young Men's Literary Society and the YMCA. In the 1860s Ralph Waldo Emerson came to speak in Indianapolis on two occasions. Local organizations, such as the Chautauqua Literary and Scientific Circle, sponsored the lecture courses of the 1880s. The Irvington Woman's Club (1892) maintained a public reading room in 1894 and, two years later, invited the newly organized Irvington Tuesday Club and Irvington Fortnightly Club to join in sponsoring a series of public lectures. William Dean Howells, editor of the *Atlantic Monthly* magazine, was impressed by his Indianapolis audience when he came here as a lecturer in 1899, particularly after being entertained at a dinner in his honor by Haute Tarkington Jameson, sister of the young novelist Booth Tarkington.

Indianapolis also had literary journals, although most were of short duration. The earliest were the *THE LOCOMOTIVE,* a weekly newspaper in the 1840s, and *The Saturday Evening Mirror,* begun in 1867. Directed chiefly to a feminine audience, *The Telephone*, later renamed *Midland Monthly,* appeared in 1882–1883. *Hoosier* (1889–1891) was a weekly with comic illustrations; another illustrated journal was *The Pen* (1895). Hewitt H. Howland, later connected with the Bobbs-Merrill firm, edited *The Ishmaelite* from 1896–1899. His brother Louis and MEREDITH NICHOLSON, both then writers for the *Indianapolis News,* were among the magazine's contributors. *The Reader,* begun in 1902, became the property of Bobbs-Merrill in

1904 and was edited by Howland. Four years later, the magazine merged with *Putnam's Weekly* in New York.

In an early effort by authors to help and encourage each other, the WESTERN ASSOCIATION OF WRITERS was founded in Indianapolis in 1886. Begun as the American Writers' Association, it proved to have more appeal in the Midwest than in the East. Years later, during the Depression era, a similar idea of shared support and encouragement for local writers resulted in the Story-a-Month Club, an outgrowth of Works Progress Administration writing classes and possibly the Federal Writers Project (1935). For several years, the Indianapolis Writers Club (1946) was active. Today, the Writers' Center, through its meetings and publications, gives local authors a means of contact with others interested in writing. Currently the city's only non-college-affiliated organization for writers, the Center developed from a creative writing workshop at the FREE UNIVERSITY in 1978. In addition to its regular meetings where writers read their stories and poems, the Writers' Center sponsors festivals and workshops on writers and writing.

The lecture series of earlier years also have modern-day counterparts. The Indiana Center for the Book, affiliated with the Library of Congress, was established at the Indiana State Library in 1987 to stimulate interest in all aspects of books and reading. In the same year, the INDIANAPOLIS–MARION COUNTY PUBLIC LIBRARY began its annual MARIAN McFADDEN LECTURE. Named in honor of a former librarian, this lecture series invites to the city an outstanding author, alternating each year a writer of adult literature and a writer for children. Indiana authors gain recognition from the Friends of Indiana Literature (1980) at a summer festival which, depending on the author chosen, may include films or drama in addition to lectures. Its purpose is to remind Indiana residents of the state's important literary past. Every year since 1988, the Visiting Writers Series of BUTLER UNIVERSITY has brought several poets and writers of fiction to the school each semester. These readings, held on the campus, are open to the public. The Christamore Aid Society's annual Books and Authors Luncheon is another highly regarded literary event held each April. Four writers of cur-

rently published books are invited to Indianapolis to discuss not only the topics on which they write but the craft of writing as well.

Today, both readers and writers are provided a variety of literary events. While the impact of these on the community is less dynamic than were the lectures and club programs of a century ago, the quality is high. In earlier years, the smaller city, its limited society, and the strong influence of its leading citizens were important factors. The mid–19th-century common school issue was a likely stimulant in the development of private library associations, lyceums, and literary clubs in Indianapolis and elsewhere in Indiana. Later, here and in other parts of the Midwest, when cities and towns were expanding, clubs and public lectures helped shape the community's cultural growth. In a time when a significant part of the population belonged to literary clubs, the city benefited directly. There were perhaps as many as 50 of these clubs by the end of the 1870s, and their popularity continued for some time. In the late 20th century, however, when literary clubs are fewer in number and smaller in membership, their direct effect on the community is limited, and it is the members who are enriched through their programs on literature.

HESTER ANNE HALE

Eva Draegert, "Cultural History of Indianapolis: Literature, 1875–1890," *Indiana Magazine of History*, 52 (Sept., 1956), 221–246, (Dec., 1956), 343–367; J. C. Croly, *The History of the Woman's Club Movement in America* (New York, 1898); Jacob P. Dunn, *Greater Indianapolis* (Chicago, 1910).

Literature, Children's. Indianapolis has long been a center for children's literature, primarily because of the activities and influence of the BOBBS-MERRILL COMPANY. The firm became nationally known through its publication of the works of JAMES WHITCOMB RILEY, Maurice Thompson, and other children's writers who flourished from 1871 to 1921, a period often referred to as the GOLDEN AGE OF INDIANA LITERATURE.

To the audience that still reads and enjoys his verse, James Whitcomb Riley (1849–1916) epitomizes Indianapolis' contribution to children's literature during the "Golden Age" years. He was idolized by children, and his Lockerbie Street home, in Indianapolis, was visited annually by schoolchildren on the occasion of the poet's birthday. His first book of collected poems, *"The Old Swimmin'-Hole," and 'Leven More Poems*, was printed in 1883. Much of his work, including *The Raggedy Man* (1907) and *The Orphant Annie Book* (1908), was published by Bobbs. Many years after the poet's death, *The Gobble-uns 'll Git You Ef You Don't Watch Out!* appeared (Lippincott, 1975). It is one of the few Riley poems set in a colorful picture-book edition. JOHN BARTON GRUELLE (1880–1938), a cartoonist with the *Indianapolis Star*, also gained popularity with themes reminiscent of Riley's work. In 1918, after leaving the city, he published his first *Raggedy Ann* book, which by the time of his death had sold three million copies. His work remains popular: the *Orphant Annie Story Book* (1921) recently appeared in a facsimile edition.

Themes of adventure, nature, and mystery became of increasing interest during this period. Maurice Thompson (1844–1901) of Crawfordsville was one of the first to highlight nature studies and outdoor life in his essays. He worked in other genres as well. His *Alice of Old Vincennes* (1900), a historical romance in which a brave young woman defends the flag at Fort Sackville, was the first Indiana novel published by Bobbs to stand at the top of the nation's reading list. Indianapolis-born Charles Major (1856–1913) tells the tale of a boy and his brother who meet up with a notorious one-eared bear in *The Bears of Blue River* (New York, 1901). Another author of stories from nature was Gene Stratton-Porter (1863–1924). Although she spent most of her life in northern Indiana, and many of her books were placed with a New York publisher, her earliest works—*Song of the Cardinal* (1903) and *What I Have Done with Birds* (1907)—appeared under the Bobbs imprint.

Two famous Indianapolis authors, MEREDITH NICHOLSON (1866–1947) and BOOTH TARKINGTON (1869–1946), wrote several novels that appealed to children and adolescents. Nicholson's *House of a Thousand Candles*, a mystery story still appreciated by present-day youth, was a bestseller for Bobbs in 1905. One of the most distinguished and popular Indiana authors, Booth Tarkington

stands at the close of this early period. His works, concentrating on the Midwest and the mores of the time, have held the interest of young and old for many years: *PENROD* (1914) and *Penrod and Sam* (1916) are humorous; *Seventeen* (1916) is a wry look at adolescence.

During the 1930s the Bobbs-Merrill Company initiated a new program in which a group of related publications appeared as part of its Childhood of Famous Americans (COFA) series. Each volume had the same number of pages, a simple vocabulary, and an attractive typeface, with primary emphasis on well-known Americans whose lives would be of interest to children. Often the little books presented the only information of this kind available to eight- and nine-year-olds and served as a bridge to the more difficult biographical works on presidents, scientists, and other leading historical figures.

The first author to publish in this series was Augusta Stevenson (ca. 1869–1976), a schoolteacher who had lived in Indianapolis since she was a small child. Her *Abe Lincoln: Frontier Boy* (1932) was followed by many titles, ranging from George Washington Carver to Paul Revere. Stevenson's 23rd book in the series was *Israel Putnam: Fearless Boy* (1959), which deals with the courage displayed by a young man and how it prepared him for adult life. She observed in a Bobbs-Merrill questionnaire that her purpose in writing the volumes was "to develop in young children a feeling of patriotism or love of country, through childhood stories of great American patriots."

Miriam E. Mason (1900–1973), who lived briefly in Indianapolis during the early 1920s, contributed to the series from 1931 to 1968; she wrote on Mark Twain, John James Audubon, Dan Beard, *Frances Willard: Girl Crusader* (1961), and other historical figures. Julia Ward Howe and Jessie Fremont became known to many young readers through the work of Jean Brown Wagoner (b. 1896), a lifelong Indianapolis resident who concentrated on books about women.

Helen Boyd Higgins (1892–1971), who was born in Columbus, Indiana, but spent most of her life in the capital city offered her first story to the COFA series in 1942: *Alec Hamilton: The Little Lion*, which was followed by *Noah Webster: Boy of Words* (1961). An Indianapolis native, Gertrude

Hecker Winders (b. 1897), added seven titles during the almost 20 years she was part of the series. Two of her well-known publications were *James Fenimore Cooper: Leatherstocking Tales* (1951) and, her last effort, *Harriet Tubman: Freedom Girl* (1969). One of the few male writers in the series, Guernsey Van Riper (b. 1909) was book editor at Bobbs from 1940 to 1950. He contributed stories about sports figures and his *Knute Rockne: Young Athlete* (1952) is still enjoyed by many readers, as are his books concurrently published for Garrard. An interesting pairing of topics came from Ann Weil (1908–1969): *Franklin Roosevelt: Boy of the Four Freedoms* (1947) and *Eleanor Roosevelt: Courageous Girl* (1965). In all, she contributed five titles to Bobbs, and others to New York publishers.

From Bloomington, Ellen Wilson (1902–1976) added to the COFA series with her story of a famous Hoosier—*Ernie Pyle: Boy from Back Home* (1956). Wilson also published sketches of Annie Oakley and Robert Frost. Howard H. Peckham (1910-), a former executive secretary of the Indianapolis-based INDIANA HISTORICAL SOCIETY, presented a story of the ninth president of the United States—*William Henry Harrison: Young Tippecanoe* (1951). Other titles of his in the series are life histories of the Ottawa Indian chief Pontiac and the Revolutionary War General Nathanael Greene. In the 1960s two capital city residents came forth with one book each: Martha E. Schaaf (b. 1911), a cataloger in the Wallace Collection of the Indiana Historical Society, published *Lew Wallace: Boy Writer* (1961); Helen R. Speicher (b. 1915) coauthored *Allan Pinkerton: Young Detective* (1962). Elisabeth P. Myers (b. 1918), a Bloomington, Indiana, resident who was associated with the series from 1961 to 1974, contributed eight titles, several on the theme of business and financial leaders such as *F. W. Woolworth: Five and Ten Boy* (1962).

The Childhood of Famous Americans series published approximately 100 titles by some 50 authors from 1932 to 1985 when Macmillan assumed ownership of the Bobbs catalog. The authors in the COFA series were well educated, and many of them earned their livelihood in various professional fields. Often almost by accident they found themselves filling a niche in the publishing world.

The work of four prolific authors stands as a link between the early and more recent periods in Indianapolis literature. Clara Ingram Judson (1879–1960) moved with her family to the capital city when she was six, graduating from the Girls' Classical School in 1898. Judson never published with an Indiana publisher; most of her 79 volumes of juvenile fiction were placed with Rand McNally. In 1944 she published *They Came from Scotland*, her only work set in Indianapolis. Two of her biographies won Newbery Honor Book awards and, in 1960, she received the Laura Ingalls Wilder Award for her lasting contribution to children's literature.

Well known in Indianapolis, JEANNETTE COVERT NOLAN (1896–1974) placed her *Hoosier City: The Story of Indianapolis* (1943) and *James Whitcomb Riley, Hoosier Poet* (1941) with Julian Messner, which published most of her 48 titles. Mabel Leigh Hunt (1892–1971), a librarian with the Indianapolis Public Library for 12 years, wrote 30 books between 1934 and 1963, some of which are about Quakers. Two of her titles are: *Lucinda: A Little Girl of 1860* (1934), which tells the reader of Lucinda's visit to Indianapolis to meet the publisher SAMUEL MERRILL, and *Better Known as Johnny Appleseed* (1950), a documentary of John Chapman's life.

The long writing career of Eth Clifford (Ethel Clifford Rosenberg, b. 1915), known for both fiction and nonfiction, began in 1959 when she edited and wrote for the David-Stewart Company of Indianapolis. Her book *Help! I'm a Prisoner in the Library!* (1979) won the Young Hoosier Book Award, and *Rocking Chair Rebellion* (1983) was adapted for an "After-School Special" by NBC television. Her earlier historical fiction, *The Year of the Three-Legged Deer* (1972), was based on the FALL CREEK MASSACRE, the first known conviction and hanging of a white man for murdering Indians. The book received a Friends of American Writers Award in 1973. Another children's author who focused on local history was Ann Mallett (b. 1906), who brought the capital city's past to a youthful audience with *Indianapolis, Now & Long Ago* (1953) and *A Child's History of Indianapolis* (1966).

Literary works appearing in the 1980s and 1990s represent a new generation of Indiana authors writing for children and young adults.

Themes are wider in scope and greater in depth, appealing to a more sophisticated readership. A new publisher based in Indianapolis, the Guild Press of Indiana, added a fresh element to the changing milieu.

Joanne Landers Henry (1927–), who worked as an editorial assistant at Bobbs in the 1950s, wrote two books about early Indianapolis, set near where she grew up on the north side: *Log Cabin in the Woods* (1988) and its sequel, *Clearing in the Forest* (1992). Bobbs-Merrill had earlier published her *Bernard Baruch, Boy from South Carolina* (1971), *Andrew Carnegie, Young Steelmaker* (1966), and other titles in its Childhood series.

Nancy Niblack Baxter (1934–), a native of Indianapolis and former English teacher at Cathedral High School, wrote on Native Americans, *The Miamis* (1987), and compiled and edited a collection of letters under the title of *Hoosier Farmboy in Lincoln's Army* (1992), both published by Guild. Another offering from Guild, copublished with the Conner Prairie Press, is *The Conners of Conner Prairie* (1989), a colorful history of two brothers and their involvements with American Indians, the fur trade, and Indiana statehood. It was written by Janet Hale, who was born and raised in Indianapolis.

An established writer of more than 17 books, Kathryn Lasky (1944–) produced one book with an Indianapolis setting: *Pageant* (Four Winds, 1986). It is an account of a young Jewish girl at a private school. Details of trips made to Ayres and Blocks department stores and Clowes Hall place the action in the Hoosier capital.

Phyllis Reynolds Naylor (1933–), who grew up in Indianapolis, published a trilogy on witchcraft—*Witch's Sister* (1975), *Witch Water* (1977), and *The Witch Herself* (1978)—and two mysteries, which are light and appealing to young readers. She has the honor of being the only Hoosier author to win the prestigious Newbery Medal, which she received for *Shiloh* (1992), a novel about a boy trying to protect his dog. Literary critics have described the book as having all the elements of distinguished fiction.

RUTH JEANNETTE GILLIS

R. E. Banta, *Indiana Authors and Their Books, 1816–1916* (Crawfordsville, Ind., 1949); Donald E. Thomp-

son, *Indiana Authors and Their Books, 1917–1966* (Crawfordsville, Ind., 1974); Donald E. Thompson, *Indiana Authors and Their Books, 1967–1980* (Crawfordsville, Ind., 1981); Arthur W. Shumaker, *A History of Indiana Literature* (Indianapolis, 1962); Marie T. Wright, "Augusta Stevenson and the Bobbs-Merrill Childhood of Famous Americans Biographies," *Indiana Libraries*, 12 (No. 1, 1993), 11 –21; D. Laurance Chambers, "The Genesis and Continuing Success of a Well-Known Juvenile Series," *Publishers Weekly* (Oct. 29, 1949).

The Little Red Door. Provides services to cancer patients and their families. The agency began operation in 1945 in a World War II barracks with a red front door. Because cancer carried a social stigma, those needing assistance were referred to "the little red door."

Initially, the agency provided information on cancer symptoms. Later developments in public education and medical technology have challenged the agency to improve and enhance its programs and services; however, its central belief in the importance of providing direct services to cancer patients and their families has remained constant.

Agency programs serve 5,000 persons annually. Present services include transportation to treatments, equipment and supplies for recuperation, financial assistance for medications, and a summer camp for young patients. The agency also focuses on prevention by providing educational materials, cancer screenings, and an informational program targeting the African-American community, which is especially at risk.

Funds for its annual budget come from UNITED WAY, investments, and individual contributions in various forms.

TERI LEMPKE
The Little Red Door
Cancer Agency

Lockefield Gardens. The first major public housing project in Indianapolis. In the mid–1930s New Deal era, the federal Public Works Administration (PWA) made funds available for projects in about 20 states to clear slums and develop low-rent housing. The goals of the national program were to provide jobs in the hard-hit construction industry and improve the housing available to low-income citizens.

Under the program in Indianapolis, the firm of Russ and Harrison designed a development of 748 units on 22 acres bounded by INDIANA AVENUE and Blake, North, and Locke streets. It was considered one of the finest developments of its kind in the country. The land on which the complex was built was originally occupied by 363 residential structures. A contemporary report indicated that only one of the existing houses was habitable.

Based on the PWA Housing Division's "strip," "corner," and "tee" models for public housing units, the development was marked by low-density apartment groups, high-quality construction, and plentiful natural light and ventilation. There were 24 buildings, two to four stories tall. The overall plan incorporated such amenities as spacious rooms, pleasant views, a central mall, a small shopping arcade within the complex, playgrounds, and an existing public school incorporated into the plan. The total cost of the project was approximately $3 million.

Opened in February, 1938, Lockefield Garden Apartments offered comfortable apartments at a reasonable price. Monthly rents ranged from $20.80 for a three-room apartment to $30.10 for a four-room group house. Initially Lockefield was racially segregated, but it offered black residents a community-oriented place to live. The apartment complex formed the heart of the African-American community just northwest of the MILE SQUARE.

Lockefield maintained this central role until the 1950s, when there was national pressure to make housing available to blacks in what had traditionally been white residential areas. With new housing options open to more affluent members of the African-American community, and with many residents being excluded from Lockefield by new income restrictions, the development gradually lost residents, units became vacant, and the development fell into general disrepair. In the 1970s the city attempted to devise a redevelopment program for the complex, but federal judge S. Hugh Dillin interpreted the plan as a means of perpetuating residential—and thus educational—segregation.

The spacious, open areas of Lockefield Gardens were not typical of public housing projects elsewhere. [Indiana Historical Society, Bass Collection, #333354]

In 1980, as part of a general proposal billed as a revitalization of Indiana Avenue, the neighborhood-based Midtown Economic Development Industrial Corporation (MEDIC), IUPUI, and WISHARD MEMORIAL HOSPITAL agreed to a plan to vacate some of the land the development occupied, primarily for the expansion of the university. Under this plan, all but seven of the original buildings would be demolished, replaced with new construction, and the remaining original buildings renovated. Despite determined opposition from local preservationists and interested citizens, the planned demolition occurred in 1983. The seven remaining original buildings were rehabilitated and 11 new buildings were constructed with 493 total units, 199 of which are in the historic structures.

LEIGH DARBEE
Indiana Historical Society

Indianapolis Historic Preservation Commission, *Historic Area Preservation Plan: Lockefield Gardens* (Indianapolis, 1985).

Lockerbie Square. Historic district bounded (since 1987) by Michigan, Davidson, New York, and New Jersey streets. In 1830 Janet and Thomas McQuat settled approximately five eighths of a mile east of the CIRCLE on property known today as the western portion of Lockerbie Square. Janet named Lockerbie Street in honor of her father, George Murray Lockerbie, a Scottish immigrant and well-known citizen of Indianapolis who moved to the area in 1831.

People began moving to Lockerbie Square during the Civil War. Expansion of the German neighborhood south of Lockerbie created the building of 45 new homes on property subdivided by Timothy R. Fletcher and Janet McQuat during the 1860s.

By 1900 Lockerbie Square contained larger residential homes and smaller cottages mixed with buildings for commerce and light industry. During this time Indiana poet JAMES WHITCOMB RILEY lived at 528 Lockerbie Street. From 1893 until his death in 1916 Riley boarded in the home of Major and Mrs. Charles Holstein.

After World War I increased industry downtown caused many middle class residents to move to the suburbs. Rooming houses and absentee landlords increased in the 1930s. By 1950 many homes in the neighborhood required attention and repair.

In 1958 the Metropolitan Planning Department proposed a revitalization for the 500 block of Lockerbie Street to be called Lockerbie Fair. The department proposed a memorial to James Whitcomb Riley through restoration of the area's appearance as it looked in Riley's lifetime. The plan included an 1890s Midwestern Main Street complete with horsedrawn carriages and specialty shops, as well as a children's park.

Revitalization of the neighborhood under the Lockerbie Fair plan never materialized. However, ELI LILLY and architects Edward D. Pierre and Edward D. James participated in the restoration effort, which resulted in the founding (1960) of HISTORIC LANDMARKS FOUNDATION OF INDIANA. The foundation worked to have the Indiana General Assembly adopt legislation that set up the INDIANAPOLIS HISTORIC PRESERVATION COMMISSION (1967). One of the first tasks of the preservation commission involved working with Historic Landmarks Foundation to establish Lockerbie Square as a historic district. The area was added to the National Register of Historic Places in 1973.

Lockerbie Square Historic District grew into a successful revitalized neighborhood. The restoration of private homes began in the 1960s. Young professionals and their families moved into the neighborhood in the 1970s. In the 1980s the former Indianapolis Glove Company on Park Avenue was converted into condominiums. In 1990 Lockerbie Square had a population of over 1,200.

LISA EHRET

The Locomotive (1845–1860). Antebellum weekly newspaper. On August 16, 1845, Daniel B. Culley, John H. Ohr, and David R. Elder printed the first copy of *The Locomotive*. Financial problems plagued the paper and forced the owners to suspend publication after a few issues. Publication resumed for three months beginning with the April 3, 1847, issue and again for a 13–year run beginning January, 1848. John Harkness and John R. Elder became proprietors in March, 1850. They enlarged the paper from its original 7 x 10 dimensions to typical newsprint size. *The Locomotive* was a nonpolitical newspaper focusing on gossip, original stories, and poems. Especially popular were the poetic tributes to local girls sent in by Indianapolis authors. It had the largest circulation in the county and printed the coveted "letter list," which gave the names of citizens who had letters waiting at the post office. *The Locomotive* was the first local newspaper to carry society reporting.

On July 17, 1860, Elder and Harkness began *The Old Line Guard*, a political newspaper that supported John Breckinridge in his bid for the presidency. On November 10, 1860, in its final issue, *The Locomotive* announced its merger with *The Old Line Guard*, which was then renamed the *Indiana State Guard*. The following year, Harkness and Elder discontinued publication of the *Indiana State Guard* when they purchased the INDIANA STATE SENTINEL.

CONNIE J. ZEIGLER

John W. Miller, *Indiana Newspaper Bibliography* (Indianapolis, 1982). An index of *The Locomotive* is located in the Newspaper Section, Indiana Division, Indiana State Library.

Loonsten, Frits (Feb. 24, 1909–July 26, 1989). Landscape architect. Born in the Netherlands, Loonsten studied at the Royal School of Horticulture and Landscape Architecture in Boskoop, Holland. He came to the United States in 1928 to visit his brother in Chicago where he then took up residence for many years. He soon met and became partners with Erick Bushholtz, a prominent landscape architect. Together they designed landscapes for many Wisconsin estates. When Bushholtz retired, Loonsten gained control of the firm.

In the 1930s Loonsten came to Indianapolis, having heard that the city needed landscape architects and was less hard hit by the Great Depression than many other urban areas. His first work in the city was the design of the Flowering Walk at Westerley, the Allen W. Clowes estate on Spring Hollow Road. In 1938 he designed a village street to complement a Colonial Williamsburg–style home at the INDIANAPOLIS HOME SHOW. Loonsten's Home Show work so impressed Indiana University president Herman B Wells that he recruited Loonsten as the landscape architect for IU.

After moving to Indianapolis, Loonsten worked in both commercial and estate design. His local work included the plaza outside the original IUPUI library, MARIAN COLLEGE's Japanese Tea Garden, the ELI LILLY estate, the period plantings at the BENJAMIN HARRISON HOUSE, and a traditional knot garden at Trinity Episcopal Church. For 31 years, beginning with the first show, he displayed a garden at the Flower and Patio Show. Loonsten also worked in tandem with other landscape architects on the design for the grounds of the Harrison Eiteljorg estate and ST. VINCENT HOSPITAL's landscaping. When possible, Loonsten worked with architects on building placement and attempted to retain the area's natural trees. He said that "a good landscape architect must be first a good gardener."

In addition to his work in the city, his company, Frits Loonsten, Inc., was responsible for all the land planning throughout the IU system, including designing the grounds for Indiana University–Purdue University, Fort Wayne. In the early 1970s, he received a national award at the White House for his work on a West Lafayette, Indiana, estate. Loonsten was active in many civic organizations in Indianapolis and served for 30 years on the Indiana University Planning Board.

CONNIE ZEIGLER

Michael Maloney and Kenneth J. Remenschneider, *Indianapolis Landscape Architecture* (Washington, D.C., 1983).

Losche, Albert H. (Jan. 6, 1891–Nov. 22, 1966). Mayor of Indianapolis, 1962–1963, Democrat. The grandson of German immigrants, Losche was a lifelong resident of Indianapolis. Upon graduating from MANUAL HIGH SCHOOL he worked his way through college, first attending BUTLER UNIVERSITY and then graduating from Hanover College. He later attended Indiana University Law School, receiving an LL.B. in 1944. Losche was the founder of the Albert H. Losche Insurance Agency and president of the Grower's Automobile Insurance Company. He also served as the secretary-treasurer of the Losche Securities Company.

Losche entered politics in 1922, winning election as county clerk. He later lost his bid for reelection. In 1930, he joined city government as the city purchasing agent. He held this position for a total of 21 years, serving under every Democratic mayor from 1930 to 1958. After unsuccessful races for county clerk (1950) and Marion County Council (1954), he was appointed city controller in 1959. Following the resignation of Mayor CHARLES BOSWELL, Losche was appointed mayor of Indianapolis on August 7, 1962. After announcing plans to run for nomination as mayor in the Democratic primary, Losche withdrew in February, 1963, following defeat at a meeting of the Marion County Democratic party and allegations (which he denied) of KU KLUX KLAN membership in the 1920s. Under his successor, JOHN J. BARTON, Losche served as annexation director until his retirement in October, 1966.

Losche was on the board of directors of the General Protestant Orphans Home, JOHN HERRON

ART INSTITUTE, and INDIANAPOLIS SYMPHONY OR-
CHESTRA.

JEFFERY A. DUVALL

Indiana Biography Series, Indiana State Library;
Indianapolis Times, Feb. 20, 1963; *Indianapolis Star*,
Feb. 27, 1963.

Lost Indianapolis. The idea of a Lost Indianapolis embraces a recognition of and a yearning
for past values of beauty, substance, and craftsmanship. Often viewed narrowly in terms of a list
of notable historic buildings that have been demolished, a broader vision is one of change over
time in land use and values. Individual structures
and whole streetscapes that no longer exist offer a
study in disappearing neighborhoods, obsolete
commercial enterprises, dated amusements, and
antiquated institutions as well as outmoded building styles.

The individual buildings that most people
mourn were high style and highly visible. They
disappeared because their architectural styles fell
out of favor, their original functions were no
longer needed, and adaptive reuse was either impractical or not considered. Although some modern developers see adaptive reuse as a viable
alternative to new construction, with or without
tax credits, it remains the road less traveled to urban revitalization, especially downtown, where in
the past decade numerous historic commercial
buildings have fallen to make way for the speculative Circle Centre mall. Among the most notable
losses, both at Illinois and Washington streets,
were the Roosevelt Building by Vonnegut, Bohn,
and Mueller and the terra cotta–clad Occidental
Building, the work of RUBUSH AND HUNTER. Aside
from the INDIANA THEATRE and the CIRCLE THE-
ATRE, no movie palaces downtown survive.

What is now lost encompasses large areas as
well as single lots or buildings. These areas represent changes in the use of space in response to the
growth of the city. What was once residential may
now be commercial or industrial owing to expanding needs—or the perception thereof. Recalling past structures is a means of calling
attention to the transition over time of entire
neighborhoods. Once substantial houses existed

along lower Meridian Street north of the Circle
(and Illinois and Capitol), a fact that reminds us of
how small the city once was. Those houses (which
included BOOTH TARKINGTON's family home at
272 North Meridian) were rapidly replaced after
the turn of the 20th century by what became
known as Automobile Row, blocks of three- and
four-story dealers' showrooms, on both Capitol
and Meridian. In turn, the showroom buildings
on Meridian have largely disappeared over the
years because of interstate highway construction
in the 1970s and new office building construction
in the 1980s. After World War II, accelerated suburbanization led dealerships to locate in sprawling one-story showrooms surrounded by huge
lots near or beyond the city limits. Downtown
space was too cramped and too expensive in comparison. Some vestiges of the Row on Capitol
Avenue remain—for example, a former Ford
dealership in the 600 block—but the buildings'
original functions are largely forgotten and they
now serve primarily as warehouses.

Similarly, remembering a school like Oscar
McCulloch School 5 on West Washington Street
that until its demolition in 1985 was located on
what had become the industrial west side recalls
the fact that here once was a thriving neighborhood of families with children. Now the industries are themselves disappearing as WHITE RIVER
STATE PARK develops.

A neighborhood in this "City of Homes," as
Hoosier author MEREDITH NICHOLSON called Indianapolis, was often most identified by and with
its public school, and a few of these buildings
survive in isolation but with a new purpose, such
as old School 7 (renovated into office space) in
the former IRISH HILL and School 12 (now Lilly
Industries, Inc.) on South West Street in what
had been a neighborhood of workers' cottages
around the now demolished KINGAN AND COM-
PANY meat packing plant. Scarcely a house is to be
seen in either area; the industries that fed the occupants declined, but the majority of the dwellings disappeared with the construction of I–70
and I–65.

The loss of several large factories and heavy
industries, including railroad shops and stockyards, on the traditionally blue collar south and
west sides of Indianapolis left huge gaps where

their facilities once stood, as well as in their accompanying neighborhoods. Not even the school buildings remain in what was once the heart of HAUGHVILLE, a town in its own right for over 20 years in the late 19th century. Long after the ironworks of the brothers Haugh disappeared, the identity of this neighborhood lingers around its churches, particularly Holy Trinity.

In still another example of change in use over time, the American Legion Mall–INDIANA WORLD WAR MEMORIAL PLAZA replaced residences and institutional buildings alike in a burst of City Beautiful enthusiasm later blended with the patriotic fervor of the post–World War I years. Among the losses: the original PROPYLAEUM on North Street, the Institute for the Blind between Meridian and Pennsylvania south of St. Clair, and the second SECOND PRESBYTERIAN CHURCH. (The congregation's first building, on the northwest quadrant of the Circle, was displaced by the ENGLISH HOTEL.)

Few may mourn the old fairgrounds around 19th and Alabama streets that was long ago replaced by residential development in the late 19th century, but that neighborhood itself became endangered in the post–World War II flight to the suburbs. HERRON-MORTON PLACE is today a historic district, but not without several substantial gaps in the streetscape.

Whole towns have been "lost" as Indianapolis stretched and grew over the years. Indianola has disappeared even in the discussions of historians; it was real enough, having been founded in 1853 across the river from the still young state capital. Indianapolis annexed it in 1873, but its memory lived on in the popular name of its neighborhood school as the westside industries sprawled beyond and to the south of it. Most of the remaining fragments of the village were demolished for the present INDIANAPOLIS ZOO.

In more recent decades the city's suburbs have gobbled whole farming communities, swallowing agricultural land and the sprinkling of hamlets that remained in Marion County. CASTLETON today defines a congested sprawl of shopping malls and office parks, not the original town that has faded into oblivion with only scattered scraps of visible evidence to suggest there ever was such a place. Also in Lawrence Township, OAKLANDON underwent tremendous transformation in the

1980s owing to the boom in development around GEIST RESERVOIR. Today it is scarcely recognizable as the agrarian village it had been for over 130 years.

We are perhaps more conscious today of the loss of rural spaces in and around Marion County, with new office complexes, commercial centers, and upscale housing projects sprouting from land that only a year or two before had grown corn. For many decades the city's outward expansion had conquered formerly agricultural land; now we no longer see such land as a commodity of virtually infinite supply.

Improvement and change in modes of transportation are among the strongest agents of transformation of the land and the streetscape. In the latter 19th century RAILROADS cut through and defined industrial areas and stimulated a wealth of buildings and structures related directly and indirectly to their tracks. Today much has disappeared along with the rails themselves. Most outlying depots are long gone, such as the ones that served Oaklandon and IRVINGTON, but survivors include those in NEW AUGUSTA and BROAD RIPPLE (adapted for other uses) as well as downtown's UNION STATION, itself a replacement for the first Union Station built in the 1850s. The loss of railroad tracks has caused such seemingly mundane alterations to the cityscape as the removal of several cramped underpasses that were the bane of motorists for many years.

The rise of the INTERURBANS in the 1890s hastened suburban development around Indianapolis. They too spurred the construction of numerous depots and other related structures, most now gone. No less important an architect than Daniel Burnham designed the INDIANAPOLIS TRACTION TERMINAL that formerly stood at Illinois and Market streets. Built in 1904, it was the first and the largest in the country, graced with two limestone eagles crafted by architectural sculptor ALEXANDER SANGERNEBO. The building survived for a few more decades after the heyday of the interurbans, functioning as a bus terminal, but the shed came down in 1968, with the building demolished in 1972 to create the present minipark on the site. The eagles now guard the entrance to the former City Hall, currently the INDIANA STATE MUSEUM. The ubiquitous trolley tracks largely disappeared during the Great Depression and most of the remainder went for scrap metal during World War II. Occasionally a chuckhole reveals a gleam of surviving rail, along with a layer of the brick paving blocks (or even earlier ones of treated wood) that once topped the city's streets.

Along with the trolleys Indianapolis no longer has "streetcar stops" and the commercial blocks that developed around them by the 1920s. Although many of these are still visible along former major lines such as College Avenue, their original purpose is now served by outlying malls, and the surviving blocks contain alternative businesses such as antiques shops and restaurants. Numerous fine buildings of this type have not endured, however, such as the Maco Block at 38th and College, an Art Deco gem designed by PIERRE AND WRIGHT.

The automobile, itself an agent of change, is fast losing the visible remnants of its own history. The massive Emrichsville Bridge, built in 1906 across WHITE RIVER near 16th Street, by 1948 could no longer serve increasing demands of traffic. Wooden covered bridges long ago became outmoded in Marion County; today we have lost nearly all of the metal truss bridges that replaced them. Encroaching development threatens the last remnant of rural highway in the county, Bluff Road, formerly S.R. 37. The roadside architecture is disappearing as well; gone are many of the familiar DRIVE-IN RESTAURANTS of the 1950s, such as the Pole on 16th Street, the southside TeePee on Madison Avenue, and the one at the State Fairgrounds off Fall Creek Parkway, which had been listed on the National Register of Historic Places. Missing, too, or greatly altered, are most of the outdoor theaters so popular in the first decades after World War II. Also gone are most of the independent motels with their fanciful signage that once flourished along the highways on the city's outskirts.

Changes in travel habits led to the decline, especially after World War II, in the need for downtown hotels, which originally catered primarily to railroad travelers. Ironically the city has seen a renaissance in recent years of downtown hotels geared toward the convention trade, and some of the few surviving older buildings have been renovated, such as the Canterbury and the Omni Severin. But this development was too late for the Lincoln Hotel, a flatiron building that stood at the site of the present Hyatt Regency, formerly Washington and Kentucky. (Several blocks of that latter avenue have been lost as well.) Across the street once stood the CLAYPOOL HOTEL, built on the site of the earlier BATES HOUSE where Abraham Lincoln had spent the night. Most missed, perhaps, is the ENGLISH HOTEL and its adjacent English Theater on the Circle, demolished in 1949 to make way for retail space. The new structure, which had housed J. C. Penney's, twice has been so greatly remodeled as to be a completely different building today, combining office with retail.

The commercial face of Indianapolis as seen in its buildings has undergone perhaps the greatest change. Few tenants appear to be interested in "Class B" (that is, older) office space downtown. The few remaining older commercial structures survive precariously. Gone are the Hume-Mansur by Rubush and Hunter and the BOARD OF TRADE, a fine example of the Chicago School of architecture, both demolished to make way for the BANK ONE TOWER. Long demolished is the neoclassical Indiana National Bank building on Virginia Avenue at Pennsylvania; near this site once stood the Pembroke Arcade with facades on both Virginia and Washington.

The preservation movement came far too late to save many of the fine houses of the early movers and shakers of Indianapolis that were close to the growing downtown, let alone the more modest neighborhoods that succumbed both to industrial expansion and decline. Despite greater appreciation for their design and craftsmanship, early apartment buildings still are regularly demolished, such as the terra cotta–bedecked Richelieu at 16th and Illinois. Preservationists and community members fought to save LOCKEFIELD GARDENS, a model public housing project that was the nation's best-preserved example of such New Deal efforts. Only about a third of the complex was spared, with a loss of all the townhouses and the imaginative siting of the buildings.

The expanding needs of government have demanded ever more spacious facilities. The magnificent Marion County Courthouse built in 1876 gave way in 1962 to the present CITY-COUNTY

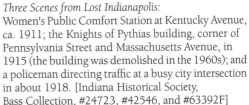

Three Scenes from Lost Indianapolis:
Women's Public Comfort Station at Kentucky Avenue,
ca. 1911; the Knights of Pythias building, corner of
Pennsylvania Street and Massachusetts Avenue, in
1915 (the building was demolished in the 1960s); and
a policeman directing traffic at a busy city intersection
in about 1918. [Indiana Historical Society,
Bass Collection, #24723, #42546, and #63392F]

BUILDING. As has been the case with a number of demolished structures, the courthouse's heroically proportioned sculpted ladies survive at various sites around town. While the spatial shortcomings of the present STATE HOUSE, completed in 1888, were met with additional buildings rather than replacement, still it is the second such structure to occupy that site. Not a few citizens of the 1880s indicated a preference for the earlier building. Today changes in government policy threaten FORT BENJAMIN HARRISON with its many historic buildings as well as its expanses of woods and fields.

New educational practices have spurred the elimination of most remaining 19th century school buildings and a large share of those constructed between 1900 and 1930. Besides School 5, among the most notable were the Theodore Potter Fresh Air School 74 on 10th Street and the Thomas R. Gregg School 15 on East Michigan. Gone, too, is the city's first high school, the original Shortridge on Pennsylvania Street. When the public library and school administrations were one, they occupied an office building at the southwest corner of Meridian and Ohio. Only its allegorical sculpture group survives, standing northwest of the current Central Library. Parochial schools have suffered even more, victims of declining enrollment and neighborhood changes. Once, nearly every parish had its own elementary school; over the years the majority have closed and most have been demolished, most recently the former Sacred Heart School on South Union in 1993.

Expansions and moves of some of Marion County's institutions of higher learning have created tremendous changes in some neighborhoods. The siting of INDIANA UNIVERSITY–PURDUE UNIVERSITY AT INDIANAPOLIS caused mass demolition of an entire neighborhood south and west of Lockefield Gardens and, indirectly, the loss of one of the city's finest examples of German architecture, the MAENNERCHOR, which had housed the School of Law. Conversely, the original campus of what became BUTLER UNIVERSITY is now an old residential area that had itself been in decline for many years. Today it is the College Corners area of the OLD NORTHSIDE. Butler's second campus in Irvington is today a neighborhood of relatively modest homes that offers virtually no trace of its former life save for the Bona Thompson library building on University Avenue. Butler's present campus was once a sizable park that had been developed by the streetcar company.

Religious structures tend to be more stable than most, but Indianapolis has lost many through the years, reflecting changing neighborhoods and disappearing congregations. Long ago the Circle boasted four churches; now only CHRIST CHURCH CATHEDRAL remains, a charming anomaly amidst its towering neighbors. Gone is the once-famous CADLE TABERNACLE, a huge auditorium that stood at Ohio and New Jersey.

Religious or not, the great halls of yesteryear were overshadowed by today's gigantic arenas; the INDIANA CONVENTION CENTER eventually took over the functions of TOMLINSON HALL, which burned in the 1950s. Buildings housing fraternal organizations, often resembling churches themselves, have disappeared, especially in the downtown area. Probably the most notable was the KNIGHTS OF PYTHIAS BUILDING, an ornate flatiron structure on Massachusetts Avenue at Pennsylvania. Even the intersection no longer exists.

The disappearance of certain places of entertainment may have something to do with the transient nature of social amusements. The short-lived fad for bicycle racing stimulated both the construction of the Newby Oval at Central and

30th in 1898 and its subsequent demolition before World War I. FAIRVIEW PARK was well past its prime when Butler University moved there in the mid–1920s. Economic woes and fires beset WONDERLAND on East Washington and White City in Broad Ripple. RIVERSIDE AMUSEMENT PARK hung on until 1970, but real or imagined health threats finally demanded its demolition some ten years later. The Traction Terminal, itself mourned, replaced the CYCLORAMA, its heyday over with the advent of moving pictures. The death knell for the English Theater and others had begun ringing by then. But the movie houses that replaced them, like the Apollo Theater, the Lyric, Loew's, and numerous others are gone now, too. So are nearly all the neighborhood theaters, from the Old Trail Theater on West Washington near Morris to the Uptown on North College. The restaurants of old—and their buildings—have disappeared, from the highly affordable little brick White Castles and streamlined Downey Dunker Donuts that peppered the 1930s city to basic cafes like Troy's at Pennsylvania and Market to the more elegant Ayres Tea Room.

Indianapolis has changed—and it is reflected in our losses—from a walking city to one of streetcar suburbs to an urban sprawl accessible primarily by automobile. Its struggling downtown, largely held together by its government functions, is ringed on the edges of the county with shopping malls, commercial and industrial "parks," and apartment complexes and subdivisions. The concept of Lost Indianapolis is hardly a stable one; today's city will be lost to tomorrow's citizens as perceptions of what is valuable change in response to new modes of commerce, transportation, housing, education, and government.

GLORY-JUNE GREIFF

Ludlow, Louis Leon (June 24, 1873–Nov. 28, 1950). Journalist and U.S. congressman. Born in a log cabin in Fayette County, Ludlow graduated from high school in Connersville, Indiana, in 1892, and moved to Indianapolis where he became a newspaper reporter for the INDIANAPOLIS SUN. After a brief stint in New York, Ludlow returned to Indianapolis and wrote for the INDIANAPOLIS SENTINEL and the INDIANAPOLIS JOURNAL.

In the fall of 1899 Ludlow became head of the political department for the *Indianapolis Press*. When that newspaper ceased publication in 1901, he returned to the *Sentinel* and became its correspondent in the nation's capital. Over the next 28 years he served as the Washington correspondent for a number of newspapers in Indiana and Ohio. He also authored such books as the autobiographical *From Cornfield to Press Gallery* (1924), the historical *In the Heart of Hoosierland* (1925), and the satirical *Senator Solomon Spiffledink* (1927).

In 1928 Ludlow became the first correspondent to journey from the press gallery to a seat in Congress when he defeated Republican incumbent Ralph E. Updike by approximately 6,000 votes in the race to represent Indiana's 7th District (which included Marion County). Ludlow, who continued to serve in the House of Representatives until 1948, was best known for championing an equal rights amendment for women and his unsuccessful campaign to pass a constitutional amendment requiring a national referendum to declare war, except in case of an attack.

RAY BOOMHOWER
Indiana Historical Society

Louis Ludlow, *From Cornfield to Press Gallery* (Washington, D.C., 1924); Walter R. Griffin, "Louis Ludlow and the War Referendum Crusade, 1935–1941," *Indiana Magazine of History*, 64 (Dec., 1968), 267–288.

Lugar, Richard G., Administration of

(1968–1976). The 1960s were years of large-scale urban programs, with youthful activist mayors pursuing abundant federal grants for planning and infrastructure needs. Indianapolis was not among the cities seeking such funding, at least not to any large extent, until the mayoral administration of Richard G. Lugar reversed the city's antipathy to federal grants. Pursuing an agenda to redevelop the city, Lugar's administration marked the emergence of a modern mayoralty for Indianapolis. Also under Lugar the most notable event in the governmental history of the city and county occurred with the adoption of Unigov.

In the early 1960s Richard G. Lugar—Eagle Scout, Rhodes Scholar, Navy veteran, and local businessman—gained civic prominence following his election to the Indianapolis school board. In 1967 he decided to run for mayor, supported by L. Keith Bulen, new chairman of the Marion County Republican party and a leading force in the drive to consolidate city and county governments. Lugar's campaign, based on objections to politics as usual, emphasized urban redevelopment and the need for some city-county consolidation while assuring neighborhoods that their concerns would not be neglected. Disarray in the Democratic party between its younger and older members cleared the way for Lugar's defeat of incumbent mayor John J. Barton (see BARTON, JOHN J., ADMINISTRATION OF).

After World War II Indianapolis mayors had focused on reversing the suburbanization that diminished the city's tax base, but they insisted on accomplishing this without federal assistance. Instead they relied on the private sector to provide employment and assigned beautification, redevelopment, and building tasks to various citizen committees. The mayor, limited to one term until the early 1960s, had no control over certain boards and commissions, and the Chamber of Commerce served as the real center of power in the city. WILLIAM H. BOOK, executive president of the Chamber of Commerce from 1934 to 1964, effectively blocked attempts to secure federal aid for planning and development projects. His death in the mid–1960s opened the way for Barton, who founded the GREATER INDIANAPOLIS PROGRESS COMMITTEE (GIPC) to seek federal funds for development.

Lugar continued Barton's initiatives and launched new ones. In the process he confirmed a more active role for the mayor and began a new era of confidence in and authority for the office. The new mayor quickly established a nonpartisan approach to the office by appointing John W. Walls, executive of the Greater Indianapolis Progress Committee and an advisor to Barton, as his chief administrative assistant (later deputy mayor). Another early Lugar appointee was James T. Morris, a campaign assistant. Morris was responsible for follow-up on the scores of campaign promises made by candidate Lugar to neighborhood groups. The first key department appointment by the new mayor was also nontraditional.

Lugar opened applications for police chief to all officers and selected Winston Churchill as the new chief, bypassing older, higher ranking personnel.

Lugar's election coincided with the success of a wider campaign to consolidate city-county government. Known as UNIGOV, the merger dramatically expanded the city's population, greatly enlarged its revenues, and enhanced its stature as a major American city. Unigov gave the mayor control over the six administrative departments it created, thrusting the mayor into the role of full-time administrator and marking the emergence of the modern mayoralty in Indianapolis. (As late as the mid–1960s the tradition of a "part-time" mayor was strong in the city; John J. Barton, for example, was paid $12,000 to manage a government serving over 500,000 people.)

The federal award of a "Model Cities" grant in 1968 to aid neighborhood planning and renewal signaled the Lugar administration's decision to pursue federal urban renewal funds. This strategy, begun tentatively in the Barton administration, represented a clear break with the practice of previous Republican administrations. The "Model Cities" program focused on creating local planning committees rather than on building and developing. Money from the grant helped Community Action Against Poverty fund new programs such as Head Start, created the Brightwood-Martindale Neighborhood Association, and funded several studies of the urban area. The city also received federal funding for a program called "Operation Breakthrough," which resulted in new housing units built with innovative construction techniques east of the Indianapolis Motor Speedway. Soon Indianapolis was in the top rank of all U.S. cities in numerous federal grant programs.

Many city construction initiatives during Lugar's first term involved improvements in roads, streets, and sewers, but there were also numerous private developments such as the downtown Hilton Hotel, suburban motor inns, and new commercial and office buildings. Using a combination of public and private funds, Lugar initiated a major downtown project involving renovation of the CITY MARKET (1972–1977) and development of MARKET SQUARE ARENA (1974). (One key factor in this successful initiative was the interest of ELI LILLY in making a gift to the city to help preserve the City Market.) Lugar administration support for the development of MERCHANTS PLAZA (1974–1977) also succeeded in creating another hotel and office building near the new INDIANA CONVENTION CENTER.

Although the Unigov consolidation of some city and county functions and the success in attracting federal funds were the premier achievements of Lugar's first term, he also accomplished another important objective—gaining recognition for the city. Richard Nixon's presidential victory in 1968 brought Republicans to the White House and increased the visibility of the few Republican mayors of large cities. Emphasizing the political importance of Lugar—whom Nixon called his favorite mayor—and Indianapolis, the president scheduled a 1969 cabinet meeting in the mayor's office. Key federal leaders involved with urban problems attended. The resulting publicity benefited the city and its young chief executive. Symbolic of this new visibility was Lugar's election in 1970 as president of the National League of Cities. Also significant in promoting a new image for the city was a 1971 conference on cities sponsored by the North Atlantic Treaty Organization (NATO) and held in Indianapolis. Several hundred municipal officials from western Europe joined their counterparts in the United States to discuss urban problems. The National Municipal League and *Look* magazine gave their imprimatur to the city for its successes by designating it an "All American City" in 1971.

One reason for the city's attractive image was the absence of major civil disturbances that plagued other American cities during the late 1960s and early 1970s. Although Indianapolis experienced racial tension and antiwar protests, there were few confrontations and no serious riots. Lugar's personal involvement with African-American community leaders effectively calmed volatile situations. Help from business and program gifts from the LILLY ENDOWMENT assisted the mayor in these efforts. Lugar's commitment to children and young people created recreation, entertainment, and jobs programs, and also fostered positive community attitudes. Many of these activities were a part of the mayor's "Upswing" initiative, which sponsored cultural and leisure opportunities for all citizens.

In 1971 Lugar became the first mayor of Indianapolis in the 20th century to successfully seek reelection. (Until the early 1960s state law prohibited the city's mayors from serving consecutive terms.) He campaigned on a platform calling for support of Unigov and for continuation of his redevelopment efforts. Voters gave him an overwhelming victory.

Lugar's second term witnessed increased activity in support of urban redevelopment. New key staff members, including deputy mayors Michael DeFabis, Thomas Hasbrook, and MICHAEL A. CARROLL, replaced those who left for other career options. This new cast helped Lugar push for a major university in Indianapolis, a role assumed by newly created INDIANA UNIVERSITY–PURDUE UNIVERSITY AT INDIANAPOLIS (IUPUI). Completion of Market Square Arena achieved Lugar's goal of helping the INDIANA PACERS professional basketball franchise. The mayor's desire to preserve public transportation for Indianapolis resulted in the city's decision to replace the defunct bus company with METRO. He created a Task Force on Women that in 1973 released a report on the status of women and girls in Marion County showing lingering discrepancies in job availability and pay levels. During his second term Lugar continued to emphasize detailed performance and worked long hours in his efforts to improve the city. His ability to articulate his ideas and positions added to his stature in Indiana and nationally.

Not everything was positive during the second term, however. The *Indianapolis Star* in 1974 ran a lengthy series detailing alleged police corruption. Although no police officers were convicted, Lugar took the unprecedented step of naming an outsider to head the department. The scandal damaged Lugar's reputation and doubtless weakened his bid that same year to unseat Birch Bayh as U.S. senator. Following his second term as mayor in 1976, Lugar succeeded in his second statewide race by defeating incumbent U.S. Senator Vance Hartke.

By the end of Lugar's term in office Indianapolis had been named the "City with the Healthiest Economy in the Nation" (1974) by the National Council on Municipal Performance. In addition, the city's bond rating had risen to the highest possible mark ("Triple-A"), an achievement matched by only six other major American cities. During his two terms the local economy gained 57,000 jobs, property values in Marion County surpassed $2 billion, the city ranked sixth in the nation in the total value of new building permits issued (1974), an average of 112 miles of city streets and roads had been resurfaced each year, and Indianapolis received an unprecedented amount of federal funding compared to previous decades.

With the exception of Unigov, the Lugar administration's most long-lasting impact came from the city's aggressive pursuit of and participation in various federal public housing and urban renewal projects. By breaking with the traditional pattern of avoiding federal funding and by using fully the new executive powers of his office under Unigov, Lugar succeeded in redefining the office of mayor and elevating Indianapolis once again to the status of a major American city.

JOHN W. WALLS

Clipping files, Indiana State Library; C. James Owen and York Willbern, *Governing Metropolitan Indianapolis: The Politics of Unigov* (Berkeley, Calif., 1985).

Prince Pu Lun, Visit of. In May, 1904, Prince Pu Lun, twice rumored to be heir to the Manchu throne, visited Indianapolis for ten days on his trip to the Louisiana Purchase Exposition in St. Louis. He was invited to the city by Wong Kai Kah, Chinese government commissioner to the exposition, who made Indianapolis his United States base at the behest of his friend WILLIAM FORTUNE, newspaperman and civic leader. Indianapolis social and political elites feted the prince daily, worrying over what he was fed and noting his personal habits; he appeared before women's groups and participated in a German House male "smoker." The city's small Chinese community participated at several social events. The prince's stay included visits to schools, industries, and public institutions (prisons, institutes for the blind and deaf, and an asylum). Speeches at public gatherings touted what China could learn from Indiana and, most importantly, how trade could be expanded. Perhaps the high point of the visit was an automobile caravan from the capital to West Lafayette. There were two low points. Some local Christian ministers, upset that the prince's schedule did not include a worship service, protested. And Miss Wong Ah Mae, who had planned to arrive from Toronto to be with the prince's Chinese host, was initially turned back when she tried to enter the country, even though her papers were in order. She was eventually allowed to enter, but the episode underscored anti-Chinese sentiment.

R. KEITH SCHOPPA
Valparaiso University

Indianapolis News, May 18–27, 1904; _Indianapolis Star Magazine_, Nov. 25, 1979.

Lutheran Child and Family Services.

Founded in 1883 by a Bible society of St. Paul and Trinity Lutheran churches, Lutheran Child and Family Services, Inc. (LCFS) was originally "an asylum for orphans and aged people." The first orphanage, incorporated under the name of Evangelische Lutherische Waisenhaus Gesellschaft, was a nine-room residence on East Washington Street, housing three orphan children, foster parents, and staff. In June, 1893, the board of directors dedicated a new building that would be its care center for the next 63 years. After WORLD WAR I the agency became the Evangelical Lutheran Orphans' Home Association of Indianapolis, Indiana and in July, 1945, the Lutheran Child Welfare Association of Indiana.

Lutherwood, a multi-building complex and 16–acre site at East 16th Street and Ritter Avenue, was dedicated on May 20, 1956. In January, 1981, the official name became Lutheran Child and Family Services of Indiana and Kentucky. LCFS operates offices in Louisville, Kentucky, and in Carmel, Evansville, Kokomo, Noblesville, Richmond, Seymour, and Zionsville, Indiana. Financial support for its annual budget of ca. $1.75 million comes primarily from Lutheran congregations, organizations, and individuals, and from government, UNITED WAY, and private foundations.

LCFS programs include residential care and treatment for emotionally disturbed children, individual and family counseling, adoption and foster care services, parenting education, and elder care. In addition, its "Sharing Places" provide food and clothing (free or discounted) to disadvantaged persons. Annually, LCFS assists approximately 12,000 persons.

RUDOLPH F. REHMER

Lutherans.

Although Lutherans from Maryland settled in Marion County around 1830, the first Lutheran churches did not appear until 1836 when Pastor ABRAHAM RECK arrived in the vicinity and organized Ebenezer Lutheran Church on the Millersville Road and Hopeful Evangelical Lutheran Church (now Salem Lutheran) at NEW AUGUSTA. A year later the earliest Lutheran church organized in the city itself was constituted when the heads of 20 Lutheran families residing in Indianapolis became charter members of Mt. Pisgah (now First Lutheran). Thus this venerable form of Christianity that initiated the Protestant Reformation first appeared in central Indiana.

The Lutheranism over which Pastor Reck presided was not that of the state churches of northern Europe, however, for Reck had come to terms with denominationalism. He advocated the "new measures" being employed by Baptist, Methodist, and Presbyterian revivalists to attract church members, and he functioned as a sort of religious entrepreneur, organizing and serving as many as six congregations simultaneously. Liberal in doctrine and liturgical practices, Reck's Indianapolis area congregations initially affiliated with the Synod of the West. This supervisory judicatory was connected, in turn, to the General Synod, a body that, in its acceptance of other forms of Protestantism, was more comparable to other denominational structures in the new nation than other more conservative Lutheran synods.

In 1844 an English congregation made up of pioneers from Maryland and Pennsylvania established Pleasant View under the guidance of Jacob Scherer, who also pastored the Mt. Pisgah and Ebenezer churches after Abraham Reck left the Indianapolis area. These three churches were among those represented two years later in a meeting at First Lutheran that formed an Indiana judicatory, the Olive Branch Synod, in Indianapolis.

In Europe Lutheranism existed as part of an establishment that integrated church and state. Not surprisingly, therefore, the Lutheranism that appealed to recently arrived immigrants reflected the European pattern of an official church rather than simply one of several denominations. But the European pattern was by no means uncomplicated. In some states Lutheran and Reformed churches were brought together in the same establishment while in others confessional Lutheranism held fast to the historic Lutheran doctrines—the "real presence," for example —and such traditional practices as catechizing Lutheran children.

The sequence of church formation in the decades following the organization of the initial Lutheran congregations in the area reveals that the larger trends in Lutheranism in America were played out in the Indianapolis area. The diversity within American Lutheranism created complications for local churches. Early in the 1840s a second Lutheran pastor, Theodore J. G. Kunz, came to Indianapolis and attempted to organize a single parish composed of adherents of both the German State Church (which brought Lutheran and Reformed congregations together in a single body) and Confessional Lutherans. Although his effort at amalgamation was unsuccessful, the church Pastor Kunz organized in 1841 gave rise to two important Indianapolis churches, Evangelical German Zion's Church, which eventually became Zion Evangelical, and St. Paul German Evangelical Lutheran Church, which at one time was the largest Lutheran congregation in the city. Each of these congregations affiliated with a different synod: in 1862 Zion's Church joined the Western Synod, which included Reformed as well as Lutheran churches in the Midwest, while in 1847 St. Paul's affiliated with the Missouri Synod, which held to a strict Lutheran confessionalism.

The arrival in the city of increasing numbers of immigrants from Germany and other parts of northern Europe complicated the relationship of local Lutheran bodies to the various synods and to each other. While certain congregations such as St. John's developed independently, others were assisted by existing congregations. Indeed, if German Lutheran churches were not as comfortable with denominational status as other Protestant churches in the area, especially as far as the use of

revivalistic techniques for building church membership was concerned, their history shows that the practice of church planting functioned as an alternative procedure for spreading the Christian gospel. St. Paul's, for instance, grew so rapidly that it became the mother church to Trinity Lutheran in 1872 and Trinity, in turn, directly contributed to the founding of St. Peter Lutheran in 1896. Emmaus Lutheran organized in 1904 was also a daughter church to St. Paul's. The city's Danish immigrants initially worshipped at St. Paul's. In 1869, however, they organized their own congregation, First Trinity Danish Lutheran Church.

Outside the German community, congregations were often organized at the behest of one of the various Lutheran synods. A notable effort of the Olive Branch Synod was founding Saint Mark Lutheran in 1891. At the turn of the century the city had no Lutheran church representing the Evangelical Lutheran Joint Synod of Ohio; in 1908 the Western district of the Synod worked for the founding of St. Matthew Lutheran Church. Nearly a half century later, this congregation sponsored both Faith Lutheran Church and Hope Lutheran Church. Bethany Lutheran resulted from a canvass made by a group of men from St. Mark's; Bethlehem, first named Reformation Lutheran Church, came into being following a canvass by the men of First Lutheran Church. One hundred and twenty laymen of the Federation of the Missouri Synod Lutheran Churches made house calls in several areas of the south side of Indianapolis. Calvary Lutheran Church was founded in November of 1929 as a result of such efforts. What is clear here is the existence of what might be called a mission pattern. While the Great Depression hindered the construction of churches, it did not entirely impede the mission impulse: In 1938 the PHYLLIS WHEATLEY YWCA was pressed into service for the establishment of a "Negro Mission," providing the genesis of a bond that would grow between Caucasian Lutherans and African-Americans.

Seeking to start new congregations was but one example of the service mission of Indianapolis Lutherans. The LUTHERAN CHILD AND FAMILY SERVICES was founded in 1883 by members of the Bible Society from St. Paul's and Trinity Lutheran. Dedicated as "an asylum for orphans and aged people," the first orphanage housed three orphan children, foster parents, and support staff. During their first decade both St. Paul's and Zion's churches established parochial schools which served their immigrant members well as they settled into the Indianapolis scene. Attention to education and social service continued throughout the 19th century and remains critically important to Indianapolis Lutheran churches. In 1922 the Lutheran churches affiliated with the Missouri Synod organized as a federation to encourage support of the Haughville Mission (which became Grace Lutheran) and cooperation in educational and social services. The Federation of Lutheran Churches of Greater Indianapolis gave rise to an association for parochial education at the secondary level and this association began operating the Lutheran High School of Indianapolis in 1976.

During the 1970s and 1980s merger talks between the Lutheran Church of America (LCA), the American Lutheran Church (ALC), and the Lutheran Church–Missouri Synod took place. When the latter opted out of the discussion, more than 100 former Missouri Synod churches organized the American Evangelical Lutheran Church (AELC). The AELC provided support for two Indianapolis Lutheran congregations, Our Redeemer and Pilgrim Lutheran, thereby continuing the mission emphasis of Indianapolis Lutheranism.

Carrying on in the ecumenical spirit of the Lutheran church, the AELC joined in a dialogue between the LCA and the ALC which resulted in the formation of the Evangelical Lutheran Church in America (ELCA) in 1988. The Indiana-Kentucky former Synod of the Lutheran Church in America became the Indiana-Kentucky Synod of the ELCA, whose offices are in Indianapolis. Although more liberal than the Wisconsin and Missouri synods, the ELCA is attractive for those who want to maintain a tie with historic Lutheranism.

A record of a European church that became an American denomination without losing its character as the religion of a particular people, the history of Lutheranism in Indianapolis provides a picture of a very different form of American Protestantism.

RUDOLPH F. REHMER
ROBERT WAUZZINSKI

George Theodore Probst, *The Germans in Indianapolis, 1840–1918,* rev. ed. by Eberhard Reichmann (Indianapolis, 1989); Henry G. Waltmann, ed., *History of the Indiana-Kentucky Synod of the Lutheran Church in America* (Indianapolis, 1971); R. F. Rehmer, *Lutherans in Pioneer Indiana* (Lafayette, Ind., 1972) (reprint of an article published in the *Concordia Historical Institute Quarterly,* 40 [Apr., 1967], 13–29).

Lynn, Charles J. (Jan. 17, 1874-Sept. 22, 1958) and **Dorothy B.** (July 14, 1902–July 19, 1989). Pharmaceutical company executive; philanthropists. In a career of nearly 50 years with ELI LILLY AND COMPANY, Charles J. Lynn helped turn the firm into a worldwide pharmaceutical empire. Lynn began as a salesman for Lilly in 1895 and later became the company's vice-president and a member of its board of directors. The company stock he acquired became the basis of a fortune that he dedicated to numerous philanthropies. Among Lynn's many beneficiaries were METHODIST HOSPITAL, the YOUNG MEN'S CHRISTIAN ASSOCIATION, the Public Health Nurses Association, and SECOND PRESBYTERIAN CHURCH. Having established Lynnwood Farms just north of Indianapolis to pursue an interest in animal breeding, Lynn deeded the property to Purdue University as an experimental station in 1942. He later established the Lynn Fund in the Purdue Research Foundation. For his work with the ENGLISH SPEAKING UNION, Queen Elizabeth II awarded Lynn the Honorary Order of the British Empire in 1956. He bequeathed half his multimillion-dollar estate to various philanthropic institutions. The balance went to his wife Dorothy, who continued many of his civic and charitable activities.

Dorothy Black Lynn was born in Indianapolis and graduated from BUTLER UNIVERSITY in 1923. She served as secretary to Charles and married him after the death of his first wife, Celestia, in 1942. Active in the support of Butler University, the Visiting Nurses Association, HISTORIC LANDMARKS FOUNDATION OF INDIANA, and many other local institutions, Dorothy Lynn was an important Indianapolis philanthropist who avoided publicity. When she died auditors valued the Lynn estate at $150 million. It was the second largest fortune ever to pass through Marion County's probate courts, surpassed only by that of ELI LILLY.

KEVIN CORN
Indiana University–Purdue University,
Indianapolis

Indiana Biography Index, Indiana State Library; *Indianapolis News*, Sept. 23, 1958, July 24, 1990.

Lytle, Howard G. (Oct. 4, 1903–Oct. 31, 1993). Community service leader and Goodwill Industries executive. Lytle was born in Pennsylvania but moved to Evansville, Indiana, in 1918. He graduated from the University of Evansville in 1923 and from Boston University School of Theology in 1926. He began his career as a minister in Massachusetts, later moved to Ohio, and then to Indianapolis in 1934 to take a position as pastor at Fletcher Place Methodist Church. While at FLETCHER PLACE he worked with the city's four-year-old Goodwill program. Enlisting the aid of other community leaders as a board of directors, Lytle became Goodwill's chief executive in 1934 and began changing the program from merely offering relief to training the disabled.

After retiring in 1969 from his position with GOODWILL INDUSTRIES OF CENTRAL INDIANA, Lytle served on the national boards of both the National Association of Sheltered Workshops and Goodwill Industries of America. In 1981 he was recognized by the Indiana Academy for his contributions to the cultural, educational, civic, and social life of the state. Lytle was inducted into the national Goodwill Hall of Fame in 1991.

CONNIE J. ZEIGLER

Indianapolis Star, Nov. 2, 1993.

MacAllister Awards. Vocal competition. Named for P. E. MacAllister, Indianapolis businessman and philanthropist, the first competition was held in 1979 and is now an annual event. Through a series of nationwide auditions, finalists are chosen to compete in Indianapolis for the largest nonrestricted monetary awards in North America for young opera singers, age 36 and under. Judges are usually managers or artistic directors of nationally recognized opera companies or singers with international careers. Applicants in the professional division must have performed a staged role and be citizens of the United States. The top 20 finalists receive awards; first prize is $10,000.

A youth division, ages 13 to 18, began in 1987; a college division, 25 years of age and younger and enrolled in college, followed in 1988. The youth division is open to Indiana residents only. The event is sponsored by Indiana Opera Theatre and cosponsored by a broad base of community support from individuals and corporations.

JEROME DONAHUE

McCarthy's List. Novel by Indianapolis native Mary Mackey. *McCarthy's List* (1979) tells the story of Rinda Sue McCarthy, born in Indianapolis at the precise moment of the atomic bombing of Hiroshima and now imprisoned in Mexico for a murder she did not commit. Rinda Sue has, however, murdered five men and one woman, most of "Them" from Indianapolis and all members of an insidious organization she is not at liberty to name but who abused her and her sensibilities in her youth.

In the course of Rinda Sue's recounting of the stories of her relationships, the reader is treated to a feminist and surrealistic rendering of a young woman's coming of age. The notion of "Them" and the ensuing list for McCarthy's revenge has been given to Rinda Sue in a vision by her dead grandmother, a former Joe McCarthyite, and the dark parable that ensues offers a slapstick social commentary on the nature of male-dominated Indianapolis (and American) culture in the 1950s, '60s, and '70s.

JIM POWELL
Writers' Center of Indianapolis

McCarty, Nicholas, Sr. (Sept. 26, 1795–May 17, 1854). Pioneering Indianapolis merchant. Born in Moorefield, Hardy County, Virginia (now West Virginia), McCarty grew up in Pittsburgh, Pennsylvania, where his family moved after the death of his father. As a young man he moved to Newark, Ohio, where he worked in a store for one of the state's leading merchants. With savings from this job, the 28–year-old McCarty moved to Indianapolis in the fall of 1823 to establish one of the city's first and most successful general stores.

McCarty located his business on the southwest corner of Washington and Pennsylvania streets, an area that became known over the years as "McCarty's Corner." A success in Indianapolis, McCarty also opened branch stores in Covington, Cumberland, Greenfield, La Porte, and Waverly. Along with his stores, McCarty was involved with numerous real estate transactions; produced and distributed ginseng, hemp, and silk; built the city's first steam flour mill in partnership with JAMES M. RAY and JAMES BLAKE; and was one of the founders of the Indianapolis Orphans Home.

From 1832 to 1836, McCarty served as Canal Fund commissioner for the state. He resigned from the post following the 1836 passage of Indiana's Mammoth Internal Improvements Act—legislation he predicted would hurt the state financially. In 1847 McCarty, who supported the Whig party for most of his life, was nominated by that party to run for Congress. Although unsuccessful in his first try for public office, he managed to win election to the Indiana Senate in 1849. He also served as Indianapolis city councilman from 1853 to 1854.

McCarty resigned from his Senate seat in 1852 after being nominated at the Whig party's state convention to run as its gubernatorial candidate. In the general election, McCarty was defeated by incumbent Democratic Governor Joseph A. Wright by approximately 10,000 votes. McCarty is buried in CROWN HILL CEMETERY.

RAY BOOMHOWER
Indiana Historical Society

William Wesley Woollen, *Biographical and Historical Sketches of Early Indiana* (Indianapolis, 1883).

McCauley (Macauley), Daniel (Sept. 8, 1839–Apr., 1894). Mayor of Indianapolis, 1867–1873, Republican. A native of New York, McCauley was orphaned at age ten. He came to Indianapolis in 1861 and was a bookbinder at Bingham & Doughty. During the Civil War he joined the 11th Indiana Regiment under the command of LEW WALLACE and ultimately attained the rank of brigadier general. In 1867, at the age of 28, he became mayor of Indianapolis. He served three terms.

In other ventures, McCauley was a stockholder in WOODRUFF PLACE and during his term as mayor Woodruff Place, IRVINGTON, and BRIGHTWOOD were platted. After leaving office McCauley was superintendent of the water company, and later manager of the Academy of Music in Indianapolis. In 1877 he commanded federal troops in Indianapolis during the RAILROAD STRIKE. He left the city in 1880 to pursue other business ventures, including a mine operation in Mexico and hotels in New York City and Columbus, Ohio. He also served in the Treasury Department under President BENJAMIN HARRISON. His final venture was with the Maritime Canal Company in Nicaragua, where he died. He is buried in Arlington National Cemetery.

WILLIAM F. GULDE

John H. B. Nowland, *Sketches of Prominent Citizens of 1876* (Indianapolis, 1877); Jacob Piatt Dunn, *Greater Indianapolis* (Chicago, 1910).

McConnell, Charles Bruce (Sept. 26, 1902–Jan. 31, 1976). Founder of WISH AM-FM and WISH-TV. Born in Scipio, Jennings County, Indiana, McConnell lived in Indianapolis for more than 50 years. In the 1920s he worked as a route salesman for Hamilton-Harris and Company, a tobacco and candy wholesaler in the city, and became sales manager of the company in 1931.

Pleased with the response to radio advertising of his company's products, McConnell decided to build his own radio station in Indianapolis. He formed Capitol Broadcasting in 1940, and WISH (1310 AM), the city's fourth station, went on the air in August, 1941. In the next six years McConnell's group started a station in South Bend, and also bought stations in Anderson and Fort Wayne.

In 1947 Universal Broadcasting, headed by FRANK E. MCKINNEY, SR., bought WISH. McConnell continued with Hamilton-Harris, becoming president of that company. However, he again became involved with WISH after a number of stock sales made him the majority stockholder of Universal.

McConnell founded WISH-TV, Channel 8, in July, 1954, and in June, 1956, bought Channel 15 in Fort Wayne. Later that year he sold WISH-AM-TV and the two Fort Wayne stations to financier J. H. "Jock" Whitney for $10 million, but remained majority stockholder of the new company.

McConnell helped found the Indiana Broadcasters Association in 1948, and served as its first president. He also was chairman of the Indiana State Library and Historical Building Expansion Committee ca. 1973–1976, as well as a trustee of both Wabash and Marian colleges.

MICHAEL SPILLMAN

McCormick, John (Sept. 25, 1791–Sept., 1825). One of the two pioneers credited with being the first settler in Indianapolis. A resident of Connersville, Indiana, around 1813, McCormick left in February, 1820, and led his family, two brothers, and nine employees along the Whetzel Trace to Rushville and then into the newly opened lands of central Indiana, arriving at the confluence of Fall Creek and White River on February 26.

An idealized depiction of Indianapolis showing early settlers at the time John McCormick was there. [Indiana Historical Society, #C5746]

Family tradition holds that 12 men in the party raised a cabin that first day and greeted the GEORGE POGUE family which arrived days later. McCormick, who kept a tavern there until his death, hosted the state commissioners who met in June, 1820, and selected the site for the new state capital. McCormick was elected a Marion County commissioner in the first county elections of April, 1822. Later that September he was indicted, found guilty, and fined one cent for obstructing the White River with a mill feeder dam. Public sentiment so strongly favored McCormick and the other indicted millers that the court suspended its sentence on the grounds that the millers had dammed only a small portion of the river.

In his *Greater Indianapolis* (1910), JACOB PIATT DUNN examined the dispute regarding who was the first settler in Indianapolis, McCormick or George Pogue. After sorting through each family's oral histories, Dunn concluded that McCormick was most likely the first permanent settler in the White River–Fall Creek area (February, 1820), whereas Pogue was probably the first to settle permanently within the boundaries of the °congressional donation lands (March, 1820).

SHERYL D. VANDERSTEL

Jacob Piatt Dunn, *Greater Indianapolis* (Chicago, 1910); John H. B. Nowland, *Early Reminiscences of Indianapolis* (Indianapolis, 1870).

McCoy, William D. (Nov. 14, 1853–May 16, 1893). African-American educator and diplomat. Born in Cambridge City, Indiana, but educated in the Boston, Massachusetts, public schools, McCoy served as county superintendent of schools in Helena, Arkansas, and later moved to Indianapolis where he served as principal of Public Schools 23 and 24 from 1879 to 1890.

An aspiring politician, McCoy was one of five Republican candidates for the Indiana House of Representatives in 1890, all of whom were defeated by their Democratic opponents. In 1892, President BENJAMIN HARRISON appointed McCoy as minister and consul-general at Monrovia, Liberia, over three other well-known black Indianapolis professionals: SAMUEL ELBERT, physician; Levi Christy, school principal; and JAMES S. HIN-

TON, politician and former state legislator. Only four months after his appointment, McCoy became gravely ill. The rigors of Liberia and the combination of poor health and the extreme climate caused his death. His widow, Celeste McCoy, dedicated $1,500 from his estate to establish The McCoy Fund for black pupils in Indianapolis, still administered by the Indianapolis Public Schools. The school board also named School 24, McCoy's first principalship formerly located at 908 West North Street, in his memory.

STANLEY WARREN
DePauw University

Emma Lou Thornbrough, *The Negro in Indiana* (Indianapolis, 1957); *Indianapolis Freeman*, Oct. 23, 1890, Jan. 9, 1892, July 1, 1893.

McCready, James (Feb. 22, 1816–Oct. 9, 1909). The fourth mayor of Indianapolis (1854–1856), and the first Democrat. McCready came to Indianapolis in 1836 from New York City. A tailor by trade, he worked in Indianapolis as a cloth cutter and in time opened his own store. Gregarious and popular, McCready threw himself into the social life of the town: he joined the "Independent Reliefs," one of the half dozen fire companies; was a charter member of the Indianapolis Band; and was a leading member of the Indianapolis Thespian Corps, the first amateur theatrical group in the city. In his forties McCready's resemblance to pictures of Napoleon Bonaparte was frequently noted, and he enjoyed striking suitably Napoleonic poses.

A justice of the peace from 1850 to 1854, McCready handily defeated the incumbent mayor, CALEB SCUDDER, in May, 1854, and won reelection in 1855 over a Know-Nothing candidate in a close election. He ran again in 1859 but lost. In 1861 McCready became the bookkeeper for the Indiana National Bank, a job he held for more than 30 years until he retired in his mid–70s. In 1893 he moved to Los Angeles, returning to Indianapolis in 1908 to live with his only son. When he died the following year at age 93 all the city offices closed in his memory during the funeral.

WILLIAM DOHERTY
Marian College

Jacob Piatt Dunn, *Greater Indianapolis* (Chicago, 1910); Indiana Biography Series, Indiana State Library.

McCulloch, Oscar Carleton (July 2, 1843–Dec. 10, 1891).

Social gospel minister and advocate of organized charity. Born in Fremont, Ohio, the eldest of five children, McCulloch received his education in Portage, Wisconsin, and at Eastman Business College in Poughkeepsie, New York. He worked as a government clerk in Springfield, Illinois, and as a salesman for a wholesale drug firm in Chicago before entering Chicago Theological Seminary in 1867. In 1870 McCulloch became minister of the First Congregational Church in Sheboygan, Wisconsin.

In 1877 McCulloch arrived in Indianapolis to assume the pastorate of PLYMOUTH (CONGREGATIONAL) CHURCH and immediately began leading the congregation toward a social gospel mission. Among the programs he organized was the Plymouth Institute; created in 1884, the institute offered classes to expand the educational and cultural opportunities for young people in Indianapolis. Indiana University would later provide these courses as part of its extension program.

McCulloch's understanding of the poor came, in part, from visits to the homes and institutions in which they resided. As a result of these visits he undertook a ten-year study of the environmental and genetic factors affecting poverty. His examination of the so-called TRIBE OF ISHMAEL, published in 1888, reflected the Social Darwinism popular in McCulloch's time and argued that ill-informed public relief and private benevolence fostered pauperism.

McCulloch played a critical role in the evolution of charity in Indianapolis, moving it from informal, private charity toward organized philanthropy based on scientific principles. When members of the Indianapolis Benevolent Society (IBS) talked of disbanding, McCulloch persuaded them to reorganize to be more effective. He drafted the reorganization plan that IBS adopted in 1879 and was elected to its presidency, a post he held until his death in 1891. Under McCulloch's leadership the Benevolent Society developed a system of "friendly visiting" to the homes of the poor, oper-

ated an inn for transients, and ran an employment bureau. His efforts to coordinate the relief activities of IBS and other Indianapolis charitable organizations led, in 1880, to the creation of the Indianapolis CHARITY ORGANIZATION SOCIETY (COS), based on the principles of "scientific" philanthropy.

McCulloch was president of COS from 1882 until his death. In his position as a leader of both the Indianapolis Benevolent Society and the Charity Organization Society, McCulloch contributed to the development of other philanthropic enterprises, among them the FLOWER MISSION Society's training school for nurses (1883), the Dime Savings and Loan Association (1887), and the Board of State Charities. His social welfare work brought him national recognition, culminating in his presidency of the National Council of Charities and Correction in 1891. In that position he advocated a national registration of needy persons and the implementation of scientific methods of investigation to understand better the plight of the poor.

J THOMAS FORBES

Genevieve C. Weeks, *Oscar Carleton McCulloch, 1843–1891: Preacher and Practitioner of Applied Christianity* (Indianapolis, 1976); Oscar C. McCulloch, *The Tribe of Ishmael: A Study in Social Degradation* (Indianapolis, 1888).

McDonald, David (May 4, 1803–Aug. 25, 1869).

Attorney, judge, and legal educator. Born in Kentucky, McDonald moved with his family to Daviess County, Indiana, in 1817. Despite receiving only a grammar school education, he was admitted to the Indiana bar in 1830 after reading law for two years. McDonald represented Daviess County in the Indiana General Assembly in 1833, and then served as prosecuting attorney for the 7th judicial district (1834–1837). Two years later he became circuit judge for the 19th judicial court, a position he held for two terms. In 1842, while residing at Bloomington, McDonald was appointed professor of law at the founding of the Indiana University Law School and served as the school's only faculty member until 1847. In 1852 he ran on the Whig party ticket as a candidate for the state Supreme Court. He lost the election but received 5,000 more votes than any other Whig candidate.

In 1854 McDonald moved to Indianapolis to practice in the federal courts. Shortly after his arrival he joined old friend Albert G. Porter and announced the firm McDonald and Porter. In 1856 he published what became known as *McDonald's Treatise*, a large volume designed to provide constables, justices of the peace, and other inferior officers with a guide to the performance of their duties. The *Treatise* proved valuable to lawyers as well and ran through many editions under different editors. In 1864 President Abraham Lincoln appointed McDonald as judge of the federal district court, a position he held at the time of his death.

JOAN CUNNINGHAM

Donald E. Thompson, *Indiana Authors and Their Books, 1967–1980* (Crawfordsville, Ind., 1981); Burton Dorr Myers, *Trustees and Officers of Indiana University, 1820 to 1950* (Bloomington, Ind., 1951).

Macedonians. Immigrants from the border region of northern Greece, southern Serbia, and Bulgaria. Wars, political oppression, and economic instability caused Macedonians of eastern Europe to immigrate to the United States after 1900. By 1915 there were approximately 1,000 in Indianapolis where they worked at KINGAN AND COMPANY meat packers, in the railroad yards, and at National Malleable Castings in HAUGHVILLE. Predominately men who planned to earn money and return home, they established small businesses such as restaurants, bakeries, and markets along the 400–600 blocks of West Washington Street. Some took English classes at the AMERICAN SETTLEMENT on Pearl Street and studied to obtain U.S. citizenship. Subsequently, families were sent for or marriages arranged.

In 1915 St. Stephen Bulgarian (Eastern) Orthodox Church began serving their religious needs in a remodeled house at 226 North Blackford Street. During the 1940s the Macedonians began moving out of the MILITARY PARK and Haughville areas to West 16th Street and Kessler Boulevard. A new church edifice was built at 1435 North Medford Street in 1955 and consecrated in 1962. A center of religious, cultural, and social life, the church sponsors folk dances, picnics, fund-raisers, and charitable projects, hosts diocesan conventions, and cosponsors an annual Balkan Festival with the SERBS and ROMANIANS in the city. There were approximately 450 Macedonians in the city in 1993.

LUBA KAZACOFF

McGinnis, George (Mar. 19, 1826–May 29, 1910). Union army general. McGinnis' mother died shortly after he was born in Boston, and he was sent to live with an aunt in Maine. At age 12 he went to live with his father in Chillicothe, Ohio. His father was a hatmaker, and George went to school and worked as his apprentice. He enlisted in Company A, Second Ohio Volunteers at the outset of the Mexican War and was promoted to captain in 1847 at the age of 21.

In 1850 McGinnis moved to Indianapolis and opened a hat shop on East Washington Street. When the Civil War began he enlisted as a private in Company K, Eleventh Indiana Regiment, and quickly won promotions to colonel (1861) and brigadier general (1863). He participated in the battles of Fort Henry and Fort Donelson and the siege of Corinth. During the Vicksburg campaign he commanded troops in the battles of Port Hudson and Champion's Hill.

McGinnis returned to his hat shop in Indianapolis after the war and became an active Republican, serving a term as county auditor and two terms as county commissioner in the late 1860s and early 1870s. He was city postmaster from 1900 to 1905, and lived in retirement in Indianapolis from 1905 until his death.

WILLIAM D. DALTON

McGowan, Hugh J. (Jan. 25, 1857–Dec. 19, 1911). Electric railway entrepreneur. Born of Irish immigrant parents on a farm near Liberty, Clay County, Missouri, McGowan became a mule tender for the street railway company in Kansas City in 1876 before returning home because of illness. About 1880, he joined the Kansas City police force, eventually serving as acting captain before becoming marshal of Jackson County. In 1890, he became an agent for the Barber Asphalt Company in Kansas City. Philadelphia financiers

Randall Morgan and George Widener and their associates noted McGowan's work, and, at their request, he reorganized and consolidated the gas utilities in Kansas City, saving their investments.

Acquaintances of Morgan and Widener, bondholders of Indianapolis' troubled Citizens Street Railroad Company, brought McGowan to Indianapolis to save their own investments. He organized the Indianapolis Street Railway Company, which bought Citizens, and was credited with major improvements in service. Hoping to build a strong, efficient system of electric railways, McGowan established the Indianapolis Traction and Terminal Company in 1902, which leased the assets of the Indianapolis Street Railway Company and built the INDIANAPOLIS TRACTION TERMINAL (1904) as a convenient interchange for INTERURBAN railways. Aided by W. Kelsey Schoepf of Cincinnati, he worked to consolidate small interurban companies into a larger system, founding the Union Traction Company of Indiana (1902), the Fort Wayne and Wabash Valley Traction Company (1904), the Terre Haute, Indianapolis & Eastern Traction Company (1907), and several interurbans in Ohio.

The interurbans were never as profitable as he had hoped, but because of diversified holdings, largely in utilities, he left a large fortune to his wife, Kate F. McGowan. During his life, McGowan contributed to the YMCA, the SENATE AVENUE YMCA, and the YWCA, and provided charitable contributions to numerous local families. He is buried in Holy Cross Cemetery.

CHARLES JOHNSON TAGGART

_____

Indianapolis News, Dec. 20, 1911; *Indianapolis Star*, Dec. 20, 1911.

McGuire and Shook. Architectural firm. In 1916 Rushville native William C. McGuire, born in 1888, and Wilbur Briant Shook, born in Versailles in 1889, formed their lifelong partnership as Indianapolis architects. McGuire was a graduate of Purdue University while Shook received his degree from the then–Rose Polytechnic Institute. Probably the most lasting legacies of the firm's first 25 years in Indianapolis are the numerous schools they designed. Starting in 1924 with

the Calvin N. Kendall School 62 on West 10th Street, these include a new structure for Clemens Vonnegut School 9 (1926) near present LOCKERBIE SQUARE, Frances E. Willard School 80 (1929) in BROAD RIPPLE, the Georgian Revival Christian Park School 82 (1931) southwest of IRVINGTON on English Avenue, and the James E. Roberts School (originally School for Crippled Children, 1936), an Art Deco structure on West 10th. The schools exhibit a wide variety of styles, culminating, perhaps, with Thomas Carr Howe High School, constructed in three phases from 1938 to 1954 in the Collegiate Gothic mode. McGuire and Shook also designed the Southport, Pike Township, and Wayne Township high schools during the Great Depression, as well as over a score of others around the state within the partnership's first quarter century of existence.

Among McGuire and Shook's early projects related to health care was the Masonic Home in Franklin, with which they have continued to be associated in expansion and renovation projects over the years. In the 1930s the firm was especially noteworthy for the number of institutional buildings that it designed around the state, many of which were Public Works Administration (PWA) projects. Besides a residence building at CENTRAL STATE HOSPITAL, McGuire and Shook were the architects for buildings at the Indiana State Sanitarium at Rockville and a group of 18 structures at what was then known as the Muscatatuck Colony for the Feeble-Minded near Butlerville. In Indianapolis the architects took on the task of creating a compatible addition of 78,000 square feet on the north side of the U.S. Court House and Post Office building in 1938.

The years after World War II saw the firm heavily involved in church design in Indianapolis, including Trinity Episcopal on North Meridian Street, patterned after a 12th century English church, the huge SECOND PRESBYTERIAN CHURCH, also on North Meridian, and the Beth-El Zedeck Temple. McGuire and Shook did not forsake educational facilities, however; the Alpha Chi Omega house at BUTLER UNIVERSITY is another of their school-related structures. They also designed the Marion County Jail. In 1958 the firm became McGuire and Shook, Compton, Richey and Associates, adding as partners two longtime employees, Donald E. Compton and Gilbert T. Richey. The newly christened company moved immediately into offices in the new Indiana State Teachers Association Building, which it had designed. The two original partners died not long after, McGuire in January, 1960, Shook almost a year to the day later.

The firm continued true to its tradition of designing institutional buildings, such as a major addition to George Washington High School and the St. Vincent Wellness Center in Carmel (and later, St. Vincent's Carmel Hospital). In 1975 the company incorporated as the McGuire and Shook Corporation, winning an American Institute of Architects Design Award in 1981 for its innovative Avon Middle School. In 1986 the firm completed the huge maximum security addition to the Marion County Jail. Some of the firm's projects for private enterprises have included the Blue Cross-Blue Shield Building on the Circle (now the Associated Group), the Allison Pointe Office Park, and the Wavetek offices and factory. The firm name changed once again in 1989 when the corporation merged with The Odle Group out of Bloomington to become the Odle McGuire and Shook Corporation. It continues its main focus on designing buildings to house educational and health care facilities.

GLORY-JUNE GREIFF

McHale, Frank Martin (Mar. 4, 1891–Jan. 26, 1975). Attorney, businessman, state and national Democratic leader. The child of Irish immigrants and a native of Logansport, McHale earned a law degree from the University of Michigan where he also played football. A veteran of World War I, McHale maintained his legal residence in Logansport but spent much time in Indianapolis.

Although he held no popularly elected office, McHale was a powerful figure in state and national politics for decades. From 1937–1952 he served as Democratic National Committee chairman. He organized the gubernatorial campaigns of Paul V. McNutt (early 1930s) and Roger D. Branigin (mid–1960s). During legislative sessions, McHale and McNutt's advisors held evening meetings at the INDIANAPOLIS ATHLETIC CLUB to draft legislation. McHale wrote the state's Public Service Commis-

sion Act (1933) and the Gross Income Tax and Utility Tax acts (both 1949).

Besides being senior partner at the Indianapolis law firm McHale, Cook and Welch, McHale was active in banking and transportation. He founded and chaired the National Bank of Logansport, directed the Norfolk and Western Railroad Company, and co-owned and served as chairman of the board of the Southern Indiana Railway. He was also director and executive committee member of the American Fletcher Corporation.

A member of SS. PETER AND PAUL CATHEDRAL of Indianapolis, McHale ardently opposed the KU KLUX KLAN. When the Klan planned a march in Logansport, McHale stood in the street with a baseball bat, forcing them to parade around him. Citing his exemplary Catholic behavior and generosity, Pope John XXIII initiated McHale as a knight in the Order of St. Gregory in 1961.

McHale served on many civic boards, including the INDIANAPOLIS FOUNDATION. He was inducted into the Indiana Football Hall of Fame in 1974.

STACEY NICHOLAS

Indiana Biography Series and clipping file, Indiana State Library; *Who's Who and What's What in Indiana Politics* (Indianapolis, 1944).

McIntyre, Jim (ca. 1925–Sept. 6, 1983). Sportscaster. Born in Ohio County, Kentucky, McIntyre launched his broadcast career in 1945 at WAVE in Louisville where he was baseball announcer for the Louisville Colonels, a member of the American Association. He came to Indianapolis in 1956 when he joined WISH radio and television as a sports show host and play-by-play radio announcer for the INDIANAPOLIS INDIANS baseball and BUTLER UNIVERSITY basketball teams. He joined WFBM radio and television in 1960 and during the next five years anchored sports shows and did play-by-play radio for Purdue University football. He also covered the INDIANAPOLIS 500–MILE RACE, and he was a frequent contributor to CBS and ABC network sports shows.

McIntyre's goal was to become a major league baseball play-by-play man on radio, which he achieved in 1966 when hired by the Cincinnati

Reds. He broadcast for the Reds for five seasons including the 1970 championship season.

When McIntyre left the Reds in 1970, weary of all the travel, he returned to Indianapolis and for awhile joined WNDE, the former WFBM radio station. He also did Indianapolis Indians baseball in 1971 before leaving broadcasting in the early 1970s for a business career.

HOWARD CALDWELL
WRTV Channel 6

_____

Indianapolis News, Sept. 7, 1983.

McKinney, Frank Edward, Jr. (Nov. 3, 1938–Sept. 11, 1992). Banking executive, community leader, athlete. Born in Indianapolis, Frank McKinney, Jr., grew up close to success. His father, FRANK E. MCKINNEY, SR., was chairman of AMERICAN FLETCHER NATIONAL BANK (AFNB). As the junior McKinney moved into adulthood, competitive swimming provided the first forum for successes of his own. While a junior at Cathedral High School he won the bronze medal in the 100 meter backstroke at the 1956 Olympic Games in Melbourne. As a freshman at Indiana University he won the first of nine Big Ten Conference swimming titles. McKinney's early athletic career culminated with a silver medal in the 100–meter backstroke, and a gold medal as part of the 400–meter medley relay team at the 1960 Olympics in Rome.

After receiving his B.S. from Indiana University in 1961, and his M.B.A., also from IU, the following year, McKinney served in U.S. Army Intelligence (1962–1964) before beginning a banking career as an assistant cashier for the First National Bank of Chicago. In 1967 he left Chicago for a position with AFNB. In 1972 he was named president of AFNB, and then chairman of the board in 1973. He became president of the American Fletcher Corporation in 1983, and the corporation came fully under his leadership in 1984 when he was named chairman and CEO. In 1987 the American Fletcher Corporation merged with Banc One of Columbus, Ohio, and became Banc One Indiana Corporation. McKinney was named chairman of the board, a position he held until his death.

Outside the area of banking, McKinney's accomplishments were numerous and diverse. He was responsible for bringing the AMATEUR ATHLETIC UNION's headquarters to Indianapolis, and he headed the effort to create the Indianapolis Sports Center. He served as a senior advisor in the Export Promotion Program, and as co-chair of the Indiana Democratic Business Council. He also served on the board of governors for the United Way of Central Indiana.

McKinney died in 1992 in a midair collision that also killed community leaders ROBERT V. WELCH, JOHN R. WELIEVER, and MICHAEL A. CARROLL.

GREG PERRY

_____

Indianapolis Star, Sept. 12–15, 1992.

McKinney, Frank Edward, Sr. (June 16, 1904–Jan. 9, 1974). Banker and Democratic politician. The son of an Indianapolis fireman, McKinney quit Sacred Heart High School at 14 to become a messenger for the Meyer Kiser Bank in Indianapolis. He took home study courses from the Indiana University Extension and the LaSalle Institute of Accounting. From 1922 to 1935 he was auditor and cashier for Peoples State Bank and in 1934 was elected MARION COUNTY TREASURER.

In December, 1934, McKinney borrowed $100,000 to buy a large block of Fidelty Trust Company stock and became president of Indianapolis' smallest bank in January, 1935, at age 30. After acquiring six small banks, Fidelty merged with the much larger American Fletcher National Bank (now BANK ONE) in 1959, and McKinney became chairman of the state's largest bank.

McKinney co-owned the Louisville Colonels (1938–1940), bought the INDIANAPOLIS INDIANS (1941), and co-owned the Pittsburgh Pirates (1946–1950). He also was a director of the Indianapolis Warriors professional football team.

McKinney served (without pay) as Democratic national chairman in 1951–1952. President Harry Truman later called him the best national chairman the Democratic party ever had. In 1940 McKinney had been vice-chairman of the Democratic National Finance Committee. In 1962 he was chairman of President John Kennedy's committee to rewrite the nation's banking laws, and in 1968 President Lyndon Johnson appointed McKinney U.S. ambassador to Spain. He was confirmed by the Senate but resigned before taking the post due to ill health.

DAVID MANNWEILER
Indianapolis News

Irving Leibowitz, *My Indiana* (Englewood Cliffs, N.J., 1964); *Indianapolis News*, Jan. 9, 1974.

McMaster, John Lennox (Feb. 9, 1843–May 29, 1914). Mayor of Indianapolis, January 1, 1884–January 1, 1886, Republican. Born at Rutland, Ohio, McMaster worked at his father's mill and was educated at the village school. He joined the Union army in 1861, serving more than three years. After his military service he attended Ohio University at Athens, graduating in 1869. He completed work at the Cincinnati Law School the next year and opened a law office in Indianapolis, McMaster and Boice. His first attempt at elective office—superior court judge—failed, but the following year he was elected mayor. He lost his party's nomination in 1885 to CALEB S. DENNY, the incumbent city attorney, and also lost for Marion County state senator in 1890.

Elected to the superior court bench in 1894, McMaster was reelected three times, serving 16 years in all, until defeated in 1910. He was a leading member of a citizens' group instrumental in securing the compulsory education law of 1897, and was an active member of the GRAND ARMY OF THE REPUBLIC in the effort to build the SOLDIERS AND SAILORS MONUMENT. McMaster was a devoted Mason, and a member of the COLUMBIA CLUB and the Marion Club. He was regarded as an able lawyer, a profession he pursued to the end of his life.

WILLIAM DOHERTY
Marian College

Indianapolis News, May 30, 1914; *Eighteenth Annual Report of the Indiana Bar Association* (1914).

McWhirter, Luella Frances Smith (Oct. 1, 1859–Dec. 10, 1952). Clubwoman, leader in

women's suffrage and temperance movements, and bank director. Luella Smith was a member of a pioneer Indianapolis area family; her father, Rev. Hezekiah Smith, Jr., came with his parents to Marion County in 1820. Educated at East Tennessee Wesleyan University (Athens) and DePauw University, she married Felix T. McWhirter in 1878 and moved with him to Indianapolis, where he founded the predecessor of PEOPLES BANK AND TRUST COMPANY. Luella was one of the institution's directors.

McWhirter soon became involved in the TEMPERANCE and WOMEN'S SUFFRAGE movements, serving as president of the Indiana WOMEN'S CHRISTIAN TEMPERANCE UNION (1896–1900) and editing its monthly magazine *The Message* into the 1940s. She was vice-president of the Indiana Dry Federation (1917), and co-organizer and vice-president of the Woman's Franchise League of Indiana (1911–1916). In addition, she was an organizer and president of the Legislative Council of Indiana Women, a group of eight women's organizations that lobbied for the passage of legislation of interest to women and children.

Active as a clubwoman, McWhirter served as president of the Indiana Federation of Clubs (1911–1913) and founded and was president (1922–1926) of the WOMAN'S DEPARTMENT CLUB of Indianapolis. She was appointed by Governor J. FRANK HANLY in 1908 to represent Indiana at the National Congress of Mothers (a group of women working for child welfare), and was elected a national director from Indiana. In addition to these numerous service and civic commitments, she reared four children.

MARTHA WRIGHT
Indiana State Library

Luella Frances Smith McWhirter. [Peoples Bank & Trust Company]

Madame Walker Urban Life Center.
The Walker Building was erected in 1927, eight years after the death of MADAM C. J. WALKER. The four-story, 48,000–square foot flatiron building was the world headquarters of a cosmetics manufacturing company founded by Walker. The steel and reinforced concrete building was constructed with hydraulic pressed brick and polychrome terra cotta trim. Originally designed by the architectural firm of RUBUSH AND HUNTER, the building is located at 617 Indiana Avenue, at the northwest corner of the MILE SQUARE. For several decades, it operated as the nerve center of INDIANA AVENUE, a busy corridor of homes, businesses, churches, and community organizations. Its mix of businesses included theaters, restaurants, a community newspaper, billiard halls, taverns, and furnished rooms. There was a myriad of barber and beauty, shoe repair, cigar, and jewelry shops. The building served as a social, cultural, educational, and business center for a segment of the city's black community. It contained the Walker Manufacturing Company, professional offices, a beauty school, a barber and beauty shop, a pharmacy, a restaurant, meeting rooms, a ballroom, and the Walker Theatre.

In 1979, the Madame Walker Urban Life Center, Inc., was created as a not-for-profit organization to save the historic Walker Building from deterioration and demolition. The directors commissioned Robert LaRue, an architect with WRIGHT, PORTEOUS, AND LOWE, to update the building. The first executive director of the center began work in 1981.

The triangle-shaped building is listed in both the national and state registers of historic places. The Madame Walker Urban Life Center, Inc., funded by grants, public-private partnerships, and community support, owns and manages the building. There are several service-oriented businesses and community organizations located on the first three floors of the building, which reopened in 1984 with offices, commercial space, and the Casino Ballroom. The center celebrated the renovation and the opening of a 950–seat capacity theatre in 1988. Later the theatre billed itself as Indianapolis's only downtown theatre. The Walker Center offices are located on the top floor of the building, along with the Casino Ballroom and Lounge, and the Madam C. J. Walker Memorial Room.

In keeping with its mission of cultural, economic, and educational development of the community, the center offers several programs and engages in cooperative business ventures. It sponsors Jazz on the Avenue, a children's arts program, and an annual writers' symposium and film festival. Youth in Arts is designed as an outreach program to expose young people to drama, dance, creative writing, music, and the visual arts. The writers' symposium and film festival are held yearly to bring together professionals, educators, students, and those interested in learning about various techniques of writing and filmmaking.

Two major business ventures include the development of Walker Plaza in 1989 and 500 Place in 1992. The former, a three-story office complex, was a joint commercial venture between the Walker Center and Browning Investments, Inc.; Business Opportunities Systems, Inc. (BOS), a community development corporation founded by the Center; Midtown Economic Development and Industrial Corporation (MEDIC); and FLANNER HOUSE. The latter, also an office complex, was a joint venture between the Walker Center, BOS, and MEDIC.

WILMA GIBBS
Indiana Historical Society

Madison and Indianapolis Railroad.
The first operable steam railroad completed in Indiana (October, 1847), and one of the first west of the Allegheny Mountains. Construction began under auspices of the state as part of the comprehensive Internal Improvements Act of 1836. The project encountered serious financial problems, particularly in constructing the line over the ridges rising above Madison. In 1842 the state turned the M&I Railroad project over to a private company, the terms of the agreement later becoming controversial. Under the presidencies of Nathan Palmer (1842–1844) and SAMUEL MERRILL (1844–1848) work on the 86.5–mile line continued, and the first through train arrived at Indianapolis on October 1, 1847. By hauling surplus farm commodities southeastward to Madison and "merchandise" in the direction of

Indianapolis, the M&I Railroad was remarkably successful for about six years. This initial success encouraged the speedy construction of other "pioneer" RAILROADS in the state, and the completion of some of these, particularly the Jeffersonville and the Indianapolis & Cincinnati, brought crippling competition to the M&I. Under the presidency of JOHN BROUGH (1848–1854) the M&I Railroad reached its peak as a freight carrier. The competition from other lines, financial overextension, and continuing problems on the "Madison Hill" paved the way for its takeover by the rival Jeffersonville Railroad (1866) and its later merger into the PENNSYLVANIA RAILROAD system (1872). Only the segment of the original M&I from North Vernon to Columbus has been totally abandoned. Conrail uses the Indianapolis-Columbus portion, and the City of Madison Port Authority has access to the 25.8 miles of track from Madison to North Vernon.

VICTOR M. BOGLE
Indiana University, Kokomo

George H. Burgess and Miles C. Kennedy, *Centennial History of the Pennsylvania Railroad* (Philadelphia, 1949); Wylie J. Daniels, *The Village at the End of the Road* (Indianapolis, 1938).

Madison County. County northeast of Marion County and part of the Indianapolis Metropolitan Statistical Area. The first white settler in the area that is now Madison County was Irishman John Rogers, who settled with his family one and a half miles east of present-day Pendleton in December, 1818. Two years later, eight families left their homes in Clark County, Ohio, and settled in the area around the Rogers' homestead. More families from the Clark County area arrived in the early 1820s. The county was organized in 1823, and after four years of negotiations Andersontown was made the county seat. During the county's first four years justice was administered at Pendleton, but it was never officially the county seat.

Andersontown was located on the site of Delaware chief Anderson's village along the White River. John Berry laid out the first plat of Andersontown in 1823 and in 1827 donated 32 acres of

Selected Statistics for Madison County, 1990

Population	130,669
Population per Square Mile	289
Percent African-American	7.6
Percent 0 to 17 Years	24.8
Percent 65 Years and Over	14.0
Percent 25 Years and Over with a High School Degree or Equivalency	73.5
Percent 25 Years and Over with a College Degree	11.7
Per Capita Income in 1989	$15,558
Unemployment Rate %()	6.4
Married-Couple Families as a Percent of Total Households	57.5
Median Home Value	$43,700

land in Andersontown to Madison County on the condition that it become the county seat. At the time it was a village of around 200 people. In 1837 the decision to build a canal through Madison County connecting the Wabash and Erie Canal to Indianapolis spurred growth in Andersontown and throughout the county. The Central Canal that was to go through Andersontown was never completed and the town reverted to a small village. In the 1840s the name was officially changed to Anderson, and it remained a small village until the arrival of a railroad in 1852. The completion of the Indianapolis and Bellefontaine Railroad in that year connected Anderson to the state capital for the first time. The railroad brought new life to Anderson, and in 1865 it was incorporated as a city with 1,300 residents.

Anderson, Alexandria, and Elwood all benefited greatly from the discovery of natural gas in Madison County in the 1870s and 1880s. Large factories flocked from eastern cities to take advantage of the cheap and abundant energy source. Anderson grew rapidly after the discovery of gas there in 1887, and became home to many glass and rubber producing factories. The gas boom was followed by the birth of the interurban railroad in Anderson in 1897. Within two years all of the county's towns and cities were connected by INTERURBAN lines, and in 1901 the first interurban car ran between Anderson and Indianapolis.

The year 1912 brought disaster to Madison County. The large gas well in Anderson ran out, as did many of the wells throughout the county. Factories moved out and the county population dropped. Since that time the county, and particularly Anderson, has experienced many ups and downs. The county seat managed to keep some of its major employers and attracted many automobile plants. However, the crisis in the American automobile industry in the late 1970s left Anderson with the nation's highest unemployment rate, almost 20 percent, by 1980.

Today Madison is the second largest of the METROPOLITAN STATISTICAL AREA'S nine counties, with a population of over 130,000. Much of the county is still farmland, but large industries are its main employer. Most of these are located in Anderson, which in 1990 had a population of 59,459.

WILLIAM D. DALTON

Maennerchor. German-American male singing society. Seven young GERMANS who liked to gather by candlelight to sing popular male choruses of their fatherland organized the Maennerchor in 1854. The group rapidly developed into

During the late 19th century, the Maennerchor held masked balls just prior to the beginning of the Lenten season. Invitations to these lavish events were highly prized. [IUPUI Archives]

an amateur music society of distinction that influenced the musical culture of Indianapolis for over a century. The Maennerchor belonged to the North American Saengerbund (NASB), a federation of German singing societies that held choral festivals throughout the Midwest. In 1867 the Maennerchor hosted the NASB's Fifteenth National Saengerfest, a four-day event that consisted of three concerts, a parade, a Grand Ball, and a picnic. In June of 1908, with the assistance of other Indianapolis German-American organizations, it again hosted a NASB Saengerfest. Walter Damrosch conducted the festival's five concerts, which featured four eminent soloists: Marie Rappold, Ernestine Schumann-Heink, Adolf Muehlmann, and David Bispham.

In the late 1800s the Maennerchor's concerts, masked balls, and operetta productions earned the society high praise from the community. The patronage of John P. Frenzel, president from 1906 to 1933, enabled the Maennerchor to present over 200 guest artists in its concert series. The Maennerchor continues to delight audiences with its performances, including its notable Triad Concerts with the Knights of Columbus Columbians and the MURAT TEMPLE Chanters.

SUZANNE G. SNYDER

George Theodore Probst, *The Germans in Indianapolis: 1840–1918*, rev. ed. by Eberhard Reichmann (Indianapolis, 1989).

Magnet Schools. The "Magnet" and "Option" programs of the Indianapolis Public Schools (IPS) allow students to pursue a variety of individual learning needs. The original nine programs, begun in 1971 and heavily funded by the federal government, had grown to 22 in 1993.

Admission to Magnets, for middle school and high school students, and to Options, for elementary school students, is by application. Academic performance, artistic portfolios, and auditions are the principal criteria for admission. During most of their existence, however, an excess of qualified applicants over openings has necessitated a lottery system for magnet admissions.

Elementary options programs include Cold Spring Academy, Back to Basics (2), Montessori

(3), Continuous Progress, Open Concept, and KEY SCHOOL. These programs use a variety of innovative instructional methods that cultivate students' different learning styles.

Middle school magnet programs include the Center for Foreign Language and Global Studies, the Center for Math, Science, and Technology, Crispus Attucks Academic Academy, Pre-International Baccalaureate, and Key Renaissance. High school magnets are the Health Professions Center, Applied Academics for Technology, and the centers for Humanities, Performing Arts, Math-Science, Foreign Language, and Business-Finance. The Arlington College Preparatory Academy and the Science and Technology of Agriculture and Its Resources (STAR) Academy will open in 1994. These programs allow students to develop their own skills and interests.

Since their inception Magnet and Option programs overall have been successful in improving racial integration and academic achievement in IPS. Instead of using magnet schools as a tool to continue segregation, as in other cities, IPS magnet enrollments have met federal desegregation guidelines for the past 15 years. According to standardized test scores, IPS magnet students overall have performed on a par with the best public and private schools in the Marion County area. Additionally, attendance rates and parental involvement are higher than in the standard schools, while dropout and expulsion rates are almost nonexistent. The middle school and high school programs also encourage community involvement through advisory committees and contributions.

As of 1993 there were approximately 6,000 students enrolled in Magnet and Options programs, accounting for 13 percent of total IPS enrollments. With the introduction of the IPS SELECT SCHOOLS program, calling for all schools to adopt a focus area or teaching style, Magnet and Option programs may become indistinguishable from the typical IPS educational experience.

TED STAHLY
Indiana University, Bloomington

The Magnificent Ambersons (Garden City, N.Y., 1918). BOOTH TARKINGTON's novel set in turn-of-the-century Indianapolis. *The Magnificent Ambersons* was the second work in Tarkington's *Growth*, a trilogy of novels that included *The Turmoil* (1914) and *The Midlander* (1924). The three novels address the dark side of economic growth—the dangers of unchecked industrialism and the blind pursuit of progress. In *The Magnificent Ambersons*, Tarkington faithfully records the decline of an old, aristocratic family as industrialization changes the social and economic character of a small midwestern town.

Old Major Amberson makes a fortune in land speculation after the Civil War and settles back to enjoy his position as the arbiter of style and the chief wielder of political power in his small community. Of his three children, only his daughter, Isabel, produces an heir, George. The young man is arrogant and overbearing, a product of his mother's overindulgence and his family's social prominence. George's one redeeming quality is his love for Lucy Morgan, but his contempt for Lucy's widowed father, Eugene, an increasingly successful automobile manufacturer, complicates their attraction. A self-made man, Eugene represents changes in the social order that George cannot accept. After his father's death, his mother's interest in Eugene so compromises George's sense of position and privilege that he deliberately destroys their relationship and, in the process, his own with Lucy.

George and a grief-stricken Isabel take an extended trip abroad, returning only when she is seriously ill, whereupon they discover their beloved community to be irreparably changed. The quiet town is now a sooty, sprawling city whose industrial section has encroached upon the once-exclusive neighborhoods. The Amberson fortune has evaporated, while Eugene Morgan has risen to a position of wealth and prominence. After Isabel's death, George is bereft of both money and position, the old Major's legacy having been eroded by the idle disregard of two generations and the emergence of a new work ethic. The Ambersons' "magnificence" has become obsolete. At the end of the novel George is redeemed only by the necessity of taking up "honest work," by which means he is reconciled with Lucy and her father. In this way the marriage of the old and new social orders is finally achieved.

Like his central character, Tarkington had returned from a lengthy sojourn in Europe to find his hometown ravaged by the effects of industrialization. While the community depicted in *The Magnificent Ambersons* could pass for any sizable midwestern town of the period, the author patterned it after his own beloved Indianapolis. When first published, residents enjoyed matching the book's fictional settings with actual city landmarks. Amberson Addition, for example, the Ambersons' gracious and exclusive neighborhood, was generally regarded as a thinly disguised WOODRUFF PLACE. The mansion itself was reputed to be modeled after a house that still stands as the Knights of Columbus headquarters at 13th and Delaware streets. The novel is rich in historical detail, a vivid record of midwestern landscape and architecture, styles of dress and home decor, mores and manners.

Published in 1918, *The Magnificent Ambersons* was an immediate popular and critical success. It won the Pulitzer Prize for Literature, the first of two for its author. A popular film version, produced and directed by Orson Welles, earned several Academy Award nominations in 1942, including that for best picture. Though the *Growth* novels represent a shift for Tarkington from romance to a measure of realism and social commentary, *The Magnificent Ambersons* is most significant as a portrait of a community in transition, recorded with the honesty, optimism, and gentle humor typical of Tarkington.

JEANETTE VANAUSDALL

Keith J. Fennimore, *Booth Tarkington* (New York, 1974); Robert Cortes Holliday, *Booth Tarkington* (New York, 1918); James Woodress, *Booth Tarkington: Gentleman from Indiana* (New York, 1955).

Maguire, Douglass (Apr. 29, 1799–Oct. 13, 1857). Journalist and politician. Born in Fayette County, Kentucky, Maguire came to Indianapolis in 1823. On March 7, 1823, Maguire and fellow Kentucky lawyer HARVEY GREGG established the city's second newspaper, the WESTERN CENSOR & EMIGRANTS' GUIDE. A supporter and friend of politician Henry Clay, Maguire and his newspaper strongly opposed Democratic candidate Andrew Jackson's campaign for the White House in 1824, and continued its opposition to Jackson and his followers after the election.

Gregg sold his interest in the newspaper to JOHN DOUGLASS on October 29, 1824. Douglass and Maguire operated the *Western Censor & Emigrants' Guide* together until January 11, 1825, when its name was changed to the INDIANA JOURNAL. Maguire left the newspaper in January, 1826, only to return as editor three years later. He continued in that post until 1829. A year later he married Rebecca Porter of Bainbridge, Ohio.

Along with his newspaper career, Maguire was active in business and politics. He served as president of the first insurance company in Indianapolis, which was organized on March 16, 1836, and was selected by the Indiana legislature to be state auditor for the years 1847 to 1850. Maguire also was a Marion County delegate to the 1850 Indiana constitutional convention and was on the Indianapolis COMMON COUNCIL from 1853 to 1856.

RAY BOOMHOWER
Indiana Historical Society

John H. B. Nowland, *Early Reminiscences of Indianapolis* (Indianapolis, 1870).

Mahoney, John H. (June 24, 1855–Sept. 13, 1919). Sculptor. Born in Usk, Wales, Mahoney came to Indianapolis with his parents in 1868. His earliest work was a marble statue of Benjamin Franklin done in 1874 for the Franklin Building at the southeast corner of Market Street and the Circle. He studied at the English Academy in Rome under Randolph Rogers from 1878 to 1880, then worked for several years on the East Coast. By 1889 he had returned to Indianapolis, where his best known works are the bronze statues of Governor James Whitcomb (1893), General William Henry Harrison (1895), and General George Rogers Clark (1898) on the SOLDIERS AND SAILORS MONUMENT. He also modeled the tablet of COLONEL ELI LILLY that is displayed in the CHAMBER OF COMMERCE BUILDING. Additional sculptures include WILLIAM E. ENGLISH (1891), with castings for the cities of English and Scottsburg, Indiana; two statues representing "freedom" and "law" for the Pilgrims Monument in Plymouth, Massachusetts; and numerous other works.

MARY JANE MEEKER

Jacob Piatt Dunn, *Greater Indianapolis* (Chicago, 1910); Mary Q. Burnet, *Art and Artists of Indiana* (New York, 1921).

Majestic Building (47 South Pennsylvania Street). City's first skyscraper. Immediately after a fire destroyed the Indianapolis Gas Company's building in November, 1894, architect Oscar D. Bohlen of the local firm D. A. BOHLEN & SON prepared plans for a new office building at the northeast corner of South Pennsylvania and East Maryland streets. He employed a type of structural steel "skeletal frame," pioneered a decade before in Chicago, that allowed the building to reach 10 stories, making it the first tall building in Indianapolis. (Not until 1912 was its height exceeded by the MERCHANTS NATIONAL BANK BUILDING.) The richly carved facades of Bedford oolitic limestone—exhibiting Roman arches, engaged columns, deeply recessed window openings, swagged spandrels, and a garlanded attic frieze—substantiated the choice of the name "Majestic." General contractor WILLIAM P. JUNGCLAUS completed the Majestic Building in August, 1896, at a cost of $350,000. The Indianapolis Gas Company and its successor firm, the CITIZENS GAS Company, were headquartered on the lower floors of the building until 1958, when the Indiana Farm Bureau Co-op, which had purchased the structure (ca. 1940) for use of its upper floors, occupied the entire building. Today the Majestic is known as the home of numerous arts organizations. The Majestic Oyster Bar and the Architectural Center occupy the ground floor.

MARY ELLEN GADSKI

Majors, William (1930–Aug. 30, 1982). African-American painter and graphic artist. Majors was a dropout from CRISPUS ATTUCKS HIGH SCHOOL. His schooling was completed and his artistic ability developed under teacher Helen Mowray while he was being treated for tuberculosis at Sunnyside Sanitorium. In 1952, Majors enrolled

in the HERRON SCHOOL OF ART and then the Cleveland School of Art. A 1960 Whitney Foundation fellowship enabled him to study in Florence, Italy. Majors returned to the United States in 1963 and settled in New York City with jobs as a guard at the Museum of Modern Art and as an evening art instructor.

While his early paintings were in the vein of abstract expressionism, after returning from Italy Majors went from painter to graphic artist. This led him to his most ambitious undertaking, the 18–print portfolio *Etchings from Ecclesiastes*. This 1966 work earned the grand prize at the First World Festival of Negro Arts, held in Dakar, Senegal, and was purchased for the Herron Art Institute. He received an award for his work shown in the United States pavilion at the 35th Venice Biennale in 1970. In 1974 he received a Guggenheim Award.

Majors' final years were divided between creating art from a studio in Portsmouth, New Hampshire, and teaching at northeastern universities and art schools.

WILLIAM E. TAYLOR
Indiana University–Purdue University, Indianapolis

Christine Temin, "Majors' Posthumous Show Is An Affirmation of Life," *Boston Globe*, Jan. 22, 1987; Susan Stedman Majors, taped interview with author, Aug., 1990, New York City.

Mallory and Company. See P. R. Mallory and Company

Mance, Mercer M. (Dec. 23, 1910–Oct. 17, 1990). Indianapolis attorney and the first African-American elected as a judge in Indiana. Born in Beaufort, South Carolina, Mance was educated in the schools there and received a B.A. degree in 1931 from Howard University in Washington, D.C. He graduated from Harvard University Law School in 1934, and moved to Indianapolis shortly afterward to set up a law practice.

A Democrat, Mance served as state supervisor for the federal government's National Youth Administration from 1936 to 1938, Marion County pauper attorney from 1938 to 1939, Marion County deputy prosecuting attorney from 1939 to 1941, and Indiana deputy attorney general from 1941 to 1943. Also during his career he was city attorney, an Indianapolis Board of Public Safety member, an Indiana Public Service Commission hearing examiner, and served on the Mayor's Commission on Human Rights and the Marion County Social Health Council's board of directors.

In 1958, Mance was elected as Marion County Superior Court judge, becoming the first African-American to be elected to such a post in the state. After serving three more terms as judge, he returned to his private law practice in 1978 and retired in 1989.

During World War II, Mance served in the Army Signal Corps. He was on the BETHEL AME CHURCH's board of trustees, an Alpha Phi Alpha Fraternity member, a Fall Creek YMCA board of management member, an Elk, and a 33rd degree Mason. He was honored as Alpha Phi Alpha's Man of the Year in 1958, was on the *Indianapolis Recorder*'s Race Relations Honor Roll in 1959, received Howard University's alumni recognition award in 1984, the National Association for the Advancement of Colored People's appreciation award in 1984, and the Rufus C. Kuykendall Freedom, Justice, and Equality award in 1985 and 1988.

RAY BOOMHOWER
Indiana Historical Society

Manual High School. Although the Emmerich Manual Training High School benefited from the wave of enthusiasm for manual training in education in the latter part of the 19th century, its early supporters were equally motivated by a desire to have a neighborhood high school that was on the city's south side. When the old Baptist Female Seminary building, which housed Indianapolis High School, was declared unsafe, a new building was erected in 1884. This created resentment among southside residents, who felt it was unnecessarily distant from them. As a result of their protests, a second, temporary high school was created in the old Calvin Fletcher Primary School at 520 Virginia Avenue. Students could

Boys learning automotive repair at Manual High School in 1916.
[Indiana Historical Society, Bass Collection, #46204]

complete two or three years at that location, finishing at Indianapolis High.

Influenced by the widespread manual training movement of the 1880s, Indianapolis High School offered mechanical drawing and woodworking classes in 1888. These were very popular and, together with southside pressure, brought about the passage of state legislation in 1891 authorizing a tax levy for the construction of a second high school. Although the levy did not cover expenses, and despite objections from some southsiders that their high school was to be "manual" rather than academic, school board member John Frenzel pushed for construction that was completed in 1895.

Among the first high schools in the United States inspired by the manual training ideal, "Manual" was meant to be exemplary. The building's design resulted from a national competition won by an architectural firm in Philadelphia. Located on a triangle of land at Meridian and Merrill streets, and crowned by twin bell towers representing the academic and vocational wings, Manual exceeded the expectations of its early enthusiasts. It was designed to accommodate 500 students, and 278 boys and 248 girls showed up on opening day. This was the first time in decades that boys outnumbered girls in a high school population, a demographic shift that would not occur again until the 1930s.

"Big Chief" CHARLES EMMERICH, the first principal, soon quelled the fears of southsiders that their high school would be strictly vocational. Three-fourths of the required curriculum was traditionally academic, with Emmerich himself teaching two courses on Virgil. Uneasiness over the vocational question created pressure to change the school's name from the Industrial Training School to Manual Training School several years after its opening. In 1910, upon Emmerich's retirement, the name was changed again to Emmerich Manual Training High School. The word "Training" was eventually dropped and today the facility is generally referred to simply as Manual High School.

Mind and Hand, the first student periodical, echoed Emmerich's emphasis on both academic and practical education. Significantly, this publication was dedicated to the *belles lettres*. Manual's popularity in the early part of the 20th century, along with a generally increasing demand for high school education, contributed to the establishment of ARSENAL TECHNICAL HIGH SCHOOL in 1916.

Manual High School relocated to 2405 Madison Avenue in 1953. The newly formed Harry E. Wood Vocational Training School utilized its former buildings and carried on the vocational curriculum as Manual moved into the mainstream of urban, comprehensive high schools.

TED STAHLY
Indiana University, Bloomington

Carolyn Griffin, "Emmerich Manual High School, 1895–1969" (IPS, typescript, 1969); Harry E. Wood, "History of Art, Practical Arts and Vocational Education in the Indianapolis Public Schools" (IPS, typescript, 1950).

Mapleton–Fall Creek. Northside neighborhood bounded by 38th Street, Fall Creek Parkway, and Meridian Street. The area now encompassed by the Mapleton–Fall Creek neighborhood was once two separate developments, the village of Mapleton on West 38th Street and residential subdivisions between Fall Creek Parkway and Meridian Street.

In the 1870s, Mapleton was a streetcar stop along West Maple Road (now 38th Street). Ten years later about 300 residents lived in the area, which included a church, post office, school, general store, and blacksmith shop. Annexed by Indianapolis in 1902, Mapleton grew quickly as a residential suburb.

To the southeast, GEORGE E. KESSLER designed Fall Creek Parkway as a scenic boulevard in the early 1900s. Affluent residents built homes near the parkway and motored to the city, easily accessible by a series of BRIDGES spanning Fall Creek. Most homes were built between 1900 and 1930 and featured such architectural styles as Tudor Revival, Colonial Revival, and Arts and Crafts. In addition to single-family homes, duplexes and apartment buildings were constructed in the neighborhood.

Meridian Park, a sub-area bounded by 34th Street, Washington Boulevard, 30th Street, and Pennsylvania Street, boasted residences designed by prominent local architects and built by affluent families between 1892 and 1930. The district was listed on the National Register of Historic Places in 1990.

Commercial nodes developed along the main thoroughfares, such as 38th Street, where restaurants and retail shops were constructed. Churches, including Trinity Episcopal, Tabernacle Presbyterian, Broadway Methodist, and Our Redeemer Lutheran also were built in the peak years of development and continue to play prominent roles in the community. North United Methodist Church, located at 38th and Meridian streets, was founded in 1855 as Sugar Grove Methodist Episcopal Church.

In the 1960s the Mapleton–Fall Creek area began to change as newer suburbs attracted residents and businesses. The racial makeup of the area changed as well. Two percent of the residents were black in 1960; by 1983, 87 percent of the approximately 12,000 residents were black.

Mapleton–Fall Creek Neighborhood Association, formed in 1962, brought the two neighborhoods together by providing social services and a forum for residents to discuss problems. The group also cofounded the Mapleton–Fall Creek Housing Corporation with five area churches in 1988. The corporation sponsors home improvement programs, including handyman training for residents and rehabilitation assistance. Five mini-neighborhoods have been adopted by a partnership of churches and neighborhood groups in the corporation's Adopt-A-Block Program. Funds pay for low-interest loans to homeowners, neighborhood clean-up campaigns, and crime-watch programs.

CATHLEEN F. DONNELLY

Neighborhood files, Social Sciences Reference Division, Indianapolis–Marion County Public Library.

Marian College. Independent, coeducational, comprehensive liberal arts college. Affiliated with the Roman Catholic church, the college is located on a 114–acre campus on Cold Spring Road, a 10–minute drive from downtown Indianapolis. Its property comprises the former estates of three of the four founders of the Indianapolis Motor Speedway: JAMES A. ALLISON, FRANK WHEELER, and CARL G. FISHER.

Marian's emergence as a liberal arts college parallels similar developments in other Catholic women's colleges. In January, 1851, Father Francis Joseph Rudolph brought Sister Theresa Hackelmeier from her Franciscan convent in Vienna to found the Congregation of the Sisters of Saint Francis in Oldenburg, Indiana. The sisters provided Germans of Oldenburg and the vicinity with properly trained teachers, versed in Catholic pedagogy, to teach the growing number of children in that area.

In 1910, the Indiana Department of Education approved the St. Francis Normal School as an institution qualified to prepare the sisters to teach in both parochial and public elementary schools. The congregation then established Immaculate Conception Junior College at Oldenburg, a two-year junior college with a normal school department, which the state approved in 1924. In 1936, the two schools merged under the name of Marian College, dedicated to the Virgin Mary.

Under the direction of Mother M. Clarissa Dillhoff, the college relocated to the Allison estate on the west side of Indianapolis and was chartered by the state in 1937 as a four-year institution. The entire faculty and student body, 16 sisters and 24 women students, relocated into the two main buildings on the former estate. Archbishop JOSEPH E. RITTER named Father John J. Doyle to serve as college chaplain and full-time professor.

The college significantly expanded its acreage in 1963 with purchase of the Wheeler estate (then owned by the Stokely family). Two years later the board of trustees physically united the school by purchasing the Fisher property (then the Park School for Boys), which had divided the Allison and Wheeler estates.

In 1954, Marian College initiated a series of "firsts." The administration, auditorium, and science building were used for the first time, the new chapel was completed, and Father Francis J. Reine became the first priest-president of the college. Perhaps the most noticeable change was in the student body which, for the first time, included male students. Marian became the first coeducational Catholic college in the state and one of only five in the nation.

In 1968, the board of trustees appointed the first lay president, Dr. Dominic Guzzetta. Within a matter of months, the board itself was reorganized. Although still chaired by the congregational minister of the Sisters of Saint Francis following the reorganization, the board consisted of a preponderance of lay persons rather than sister members. In 1987, the board elected the first lay chairperson.

In 1993, Marian's 1,233 students had available 54 programs of study and degrees in 26 subject areas. A substantial majority of the students are female, many attracted to well-established programs in nursing and teacher education. Only 44 percent of the students are Catholic. The college maintains a student to faculty ratio of 14 to 1, a strong selling point for prospective students, many of whom are the first generation in their family to attend college. The institution is an active member of the National Association of Intercollegiate Athletics.

The school's 29 buildings include a library, three residence halls, a student center, and the Allison and Stokely mansions, which are used as conference centers. In response to the consistently increasing enrollment, in 1989 the 28 sisters who lived in St. Francis Hall exchanged their quarters for two new apartment buildings.

Despite its small size Marian is surprisingly cosmopolitan, in part because of the English Language School (ELS) that is housed in part of the former Fisher estate. A component of the campus since 1960, ELS teaches an average of 50 to 60 foreign students from countries such as China, Indonesia, South Korea, Vietnam, Taiwan, Mexico, France, and Central and South America, who come to the school to learn English.

Marian strives to be recognized as the "College that Mentors." In 1990, the college, with financial support from the LILLY ENDOWMENT, established a "Mentor-Leader Certificate." Students, through a close relationship with the faculty, are instructed how to motivate, coach, instill confidence, and serve as advocates for fellow students.

ROBERT A. SCHWARTZ

Indianapolis News, May 10, 1989; Marian College catalogs.

Marian College Mansions.

JAMES A. ALLISON, CARL G. FISHER, and FRANK WHEELER, partners in the creation of the INDIANAPOLIS MOTOR SPEEDWAY, each built or remodeled homes in the 3200 block of Cold Spring Road. All are currently owned by MARIAN COLLEGE.

Wheeler made his fortune in the automotive industry as owner of the Wheeler-Schebler Carburetor Company and the Langsenkamp-Wheeler Brass Works. His home, Hawkeye, was designed by William Price of the Philadelphia architectural firm of Price and McLanahan and built during 1912–1913. The Wheeler estate included a 320–foot covered walkway, 7–car garage, Japanese teahouse, and two houses for gardeners and servants. The exterior of the house reflects the architectural influences of the Mediterranean Revival and Craftsman styles. Both the interior and exterior are ornamented with decorative Arts and Crafts style Moravian tiles from the Mercer Tile Works in Pennsylvania. A later owner, G. Monty Williams, filled the lake and added a swimming pool. In 1937 William B. Stokely, Jr., of the STOKELY-VANCAMP COMPANY, purchased the house. The Stokelys sold the property to Marian College in 1963, and the house, now referred to as the Stokely Mansion, is used as a conference and events center.

Allison was also a pioneer in the automotive industry, having cofounded the PREST-O-LITE COMPANY to manufacture headlights. In 1910 he hired HERBERT L. BASS to design an estate he called Riverdale. Bass planned a complex that included a powerhouse, garage, servants' quarters, greenhouses, and a gardener's cottage. In midstream, however, Allison dismissed him and hired William Price, who had worked on the nearby Wheeler mansion. In order to facilitate construction of the steel and concrete structure during the winter, workers erected a barn around the building.

Riverdale was completed in 1914; its architecture reflects the eclecticism typical of the early 20th century. The exterior contains elements of Italian Renaissance Revival combined with the horizontality of the Prairie style. Interior features include an aviary on the first floor and an indoor swimming pool in the basement. The Sisters of St. Francis purchased the house in 1936, originally using it for classrooms and dormitory space. Today it serves the college as a conference and events center. Usually referred to simply as the Allison Mansion, the structure was listed on the National Register of Historic Places in 1970.

Little is left of Blossom Heath, the estate of Carl Fisher. He purchased the house in 1909 and adapted it to meet his penchant for sports. The estate featured a gymnasium, indoor tennis court and swimming pool, clay and grass tennis courts, stables, and polo grounds. In 1921 the Fishers moved to Florida and the house became part of Park School for boys in 1928. Marian College purchased the house in 1965 and used it for classroom space.

SUZANNE ROLLINS

Marian College, "The Mansions of Marian" (undated pamphlet); Jane C. Sprague, "Allison Mansion National Register of Historic Places Inventory-Nomination Form," June 25, 1970 (copy available in the files of the Division of Historic Preservation and Archaeology, Indiana Department of Natural Resources).

Marian McFadden Lecture Series.

Upon her death in 1975, Marian McFadden, director of the INDIANAPOLIS–MARION COUNTY PUBLIC LIBRARY from 1944 to 1955, left over $150,000 to the library's foundation. Desiring to recognize her contribution to the city, foundation officials established in her name an annual memorial lecture series, which features an outstanding author of either adult or children's literature. Saul Bellow gave the first lecture in 1978. The program committee has since adopted an alternating schedule with authors of adult literature featured in even years and children's authors featured in odd years. The lectures, free and open to the public, are held at the North Central High School auditorium. Other authors who have made presentations include Norman Mailer, James Baldwin, Kurt Vonnegut, John Updike, Maurice Sendak, and Chris Van Allsburg.

JOAN CUNNINGHAM

Marion County. Indianapolis' home county. Named in honor of Revolutionary War General Francis Marion, the county was organized in 1821. The first white families had come to the area only two years earlier, but the decision to move the state capital to the vicinity of WHITE RIVER in central Marion County attracted optimistic settlers to this swampy wilderness.

The earliest residents of Marion County spent much of their time hunting deer and bear, which were plentiful throughout the area. Hides and pelts were tanned and sold or traded, first at Indian posts and later at Indianapolis, and hundreds of pounds of meat were smoked and cured for winter. As more settlers came to the area, some residents began making bricks and selling them to prospective builders in Indianapolis. Since the land was heavily forested and swampy in many areas, agriculture was slow to develop in the county. Ginseng grew abundantly, however, and although not valued in the United States the Chinese used it for medicinal purposes. In the late 1820s JAMES BLAKE opened a shop on Delaware Street near POGUE'S RUN where he dried and prepared ginseng roots. Blake sent his product overland to Philadelphia, from which it was shipped to China. His business prospered for several years, and his shop provided an important market for many Marion County residents.

Transportation has been a central theme in the county's history. Indianapolis' early hopes of becoming a large inland market center were dashed when the White River proved unnavigable and work on the CENTRAL CANAL halted after the state's program of internal improvements went bankrupt in the late 1830s. Marion County residents relied on the NATIONAL ROAD and the MICHIGAN ROAD for shipping, and many made a living serving travelers as hotel and tavern keepers. However, the price of shipping goods overland was prohibitive (it cost more to ship freight from Madison, Indiana, to Indianapolis than it did from Boston to Madison), and early attempts at manufacturing in Marion County failed.

The advent of the railroad in Indiana was a turning point in the history of Indianapolis and Marion County. The completion of the MADISON AND INDIANAPOLIS RAILROAD to the state capital in 1847 made large scale manufacturing economically viable. By 1852 Indianapolis had six different railroad lines connecting it to all of the large midwestern markets. Easier and cheaper access to more cities made Indianapolis a more attractive market than Madison, and in the 1850s population growth in the capital city outpaced that in the Ohio River cities for the first time. By the end of the decade Indianapolis had replaced Madison as the state's most populous city.

Outside of Indianapolis the railroads spurred agricultural development in what would become the most fertile and productive county in the state. Farmers were paying less to ship their crops and livestock and investing their profits in improving more farmland and developing more advanced methods of farming. Indianapolis' many pork packing plants catered to the county's hog breeders, and made hog raising one of the most profitable occupations in central Indiana. The construction of the BELT LINE RAILROAD in the 1870s routed 13 different rail lines around the perimeter of the city and opened space downtown for the development of the famous Indianapolis STOCKYARDS, which provided yet another convenience for Marion County farmers.

The development of the interurban railway system in the early 20th century had a dramatic impact on Marion County as well. It offered all county residents easy access to Indianapolis and other cities in central Indiana. The introduction of freight service on the INTERURBANS changed the nature of farming in those areas of Marion County

Selected Statistics for Marion County, 1990

Population	797,159
Population per Square Mile	2,011
Percent African-American	21.3
Percent 0 to 17 Years	25.5
Percent 65 Years and Over	11.6
Percent 25 Years and Over with a	
High School Degree or Equivalency	76.8
Percent 25 Years and Over with a College Degree	21.4
Per Capita Income in 1989	$17,730
Unemployment Rate (%)	4.5
Married-Couple Families as a	
Percent of Total Households	47.3
Median Home Value	$61,400

nearest Indianapolis. Express delivery into the city meant that large quantities of fresh dairy products could be shipped daily. Poultry farming increased to keep up with the demand for eggs, and dairy farms cropped up all around the periphery of the city.

The mode of transportation that has had the most impact on Marion County is the automobile. Throughout its history the county had been predominantly rural and agricultural with an urban area at its center. Villages and suburbs developed around train stations and along interurban lines, but the overwhelming majority of acreage in the county was in farmland. In 1922 more than 80 percent of the over 260,000 acres of land in Marion County was farmland; as late as 1953 this figure was still over 72 percent. Marion County was the richest agricultural county in the state and had the largest 4–H program of any county in the nation.

Rapid suburbanization of the county in the 1960s and 1970s changed the landscape dramatically. Housing subdivisions, strip malls, and shopping centers sprang up throughout the county on what was once productive soil. But the interstate highway system has been the key factor in the transformation of Marion County. By 1968 only 106,000 acres of land in the county were classified as agricultural. During the 1970s and 1980s development along I–65 in Pike Township claimed much of the farmland that remained in northwestern Marion County. Development in the CASTLETON area had likewise covered most of the productive soil in the northeastern portion of the county. In the early 1990s fewer than 48,000 acres of farmland remained, almost all of it in

Franklin Township in the southeastern corner. Urban planners and agricultural experts predict that there will be no farmland remaining in the county by the year 2050.

Politically, Indianapolis has been the focal point of Marion County since the first elections in 1822. In 1970 UNIGOV merged city and county government by bringing all unincorporated areas under the jurisdiction of the mayor of Indianapolis and the 29–member City-County Council. All county residents are eligible to vote for the mayor and council. The county is divided into nine TOWNSHIPS and has four incorporated cities, 11 public school districts, and several incorporated towns. The total population in 1990 was 797,159.

WILLIAM D. DALTON

Berry R. Sulgrove, *History of Indianapolis and Marion County* (Philadelphia, 1884); Howard Johnson, *A Home in the Woods: Oliver Johnson's Reminiscences of Early Marion County* (Indianapolis, 1951; rep. Bloomington, Ind., 1978).

Marion County Assessor. The assessor is responsible for the general assessment of real property subject to taxation throughout the county, which occurs periodically as mandated by the Indiana General Assembly. The assessor's office also determines the value of taxable personal property, and appraises inherited property—such as the amounts in bank accounts and the items in safe deposit boxes—to determine the proper amount of estate taxes.

The assessor's office processes petitions for real estate tax exemptions and approves all mortgage exemptions on taxable real estate in the county. The assessor is responsible for implementing directives of the Indiana Board of Tax Commissioners and serves as president of the Marion County Board of Tax Review. The Board of Tax Review oversees the procedures for assessment of taxable real property in the county. The Marion County assessor meets annually with the nine elected township assessors to assure countywide uniformity and equity in property assessments.

The assessor is elected to a four-year term by all voters in the county and may be reelected to any number of terms. The Marion County assessor serves ex officio as one of the three Marion County commissioners, and as president of the commissioners on alternate years with the MARION COUNTY TREASURER.

LAURRY NEUFER

Marion County Auditor.

The office of county auditor is required by the Indiana Constitution. The Marion County auditor is elected to a four-year term by all voters in the county and may serve no more than two terms within 12 years.

The Marion County auditor serves formally as the manager of the county's financial affairs. The auditor prepares the annual city-county government budget for action by the CITY-COUNTY COUNCIL and monitors the fiscal performance of city and county agencies. The auditor's office maintains all financial ledgers and accounts involving county revenues and expenditures and is responsible for making sure that all payments made by the county or its agencies conform to applicable laws, regulations, and generally accepted accounting practices.

The auditor identifies delinquencies in the payment of taxes owed to the county, and may direct the MARION COUNTY SHERIFF to seize property on which taxes are owed. Each year the auditor conducts a sale of such property.

The Marion County auditor serves ex officio as a member and the secretary of the Marion County commissioners. The auditor also serves on the Marion County Board of Tax Adjustment and the Marion County Board of Tax Review.

LAURRY NEUFER

Marion County Board of Voter Registration.

Implements and administers voting rules established under state and local law. The board and its staff also register voters, coordinate registration activities with civic and political organizations such as the county political parties and the League of Women Voters, and maintain voter registration records.

The Board of Voter Registration consists of one Republican and one Democrat, appointed for two-year terms by their respective county chairs.

The board maintains an office in the City-County Building where its duties are executed by a staff of 22 workers split evenly between the two major parties. Funding for the board's operations comes from the Marion County general fund and is approved by the same budget process used for most other county agencies.

GREGORY M. VOGEL

Marion County Clerk.

The office of Marion County Clerk, officially titled the Clerk of the Marion County Circuit Court, is required by the Indiana Constitution. It was one of the original offices elected by Marion County voters in 1822. The clerk is elected to a four-year term by all voters in the county in even-numbered, non–presidential election years. The clerk may be re-elected, but no person may serve in the position for more than eight years in a twelve-year period.

The clerk's office supports the operations of the Marion County courts by maintaining records, collecting fees and fines, and collecting and disbursing child support payments. The clerk also serves as the clerk to the MARION COUNTY COMMISSIONERS and maintains the commissioners' public records, supervises the administration of elections in the county, and serves as the secretary to the MARION COUNTY ELECTION BOARD. Certified election returns and related records are maintained in the clerk's office.

Several public records of Marion County governmental activities, as well as statistical information on the county and its residents, are maintained by the clerk's office, which meets citizens' requests for information and documents. The many duties of the office make it necessary for the person serving as clerk to appoint others to act on his or her behalf, which is permitted under state law.

THOMAS C. KENNEDY

Marion County Commissioners.

County government executive committee. Under Indiana's system of local government most counties do not have an individual county executive officer but a group of elected county commissioners who serve as a collective executive body.

MARION COUNTY voters elected their first three Marion County Commissioners in 1822, and the commissioners met for the first time on April 15 of that year. Each commissioner's seat was filled by the voters until 1970 when the UNIGOV reorganization of local government in Marion County ended the practice of separately electing the Marion County Commissioners. Since then the elected MARION COUNTY ASSESSOR, MARION COUNTY AUDITOR, and MARION COUNTY TREASURER have also served as the three county commissioners, and many of their previous functions as the county's chief executive body have been assumed by the Unigov MAYOR.

Most functions retained by the commissioners concern county government finances. In addition to their responsibilities as county assessor, auditor, and treasurer, the commissioners must approve and sign any county-backed bonds. The commissioners also appoint individuals to 11 county government boards, including the CAPITAL IMPROVEMENT BOARD, the HEALTH AND HOSPITAL CORPORATION Board, and the METROPOLITAN DEVELOPMENT COMMISSION. The commissioners are formally responsible for the administration of the Marion County Home for the Aged and Indigent.

THOMAS C. KENNEDY

Marion County Coroner. An elective office provided for by the state constitution. Each county has a coroner who serves part-time for a four-year term, not to exceed two consecutive terms. The coroner's office conducts inquiries into the cause and manner of death in cases of violent or questionable death or where there is no personal physician to sign the death certificate. Such cases include accidental death, suicides, homicides, and infant deaths. The coroner's office has the power to issue subpoenas and conduct cases within its jurisdiction as part of a federal investigation. The chief coroner, the only official who can arrest or replace the sheriff, is not required to have any medical qualifications.

Originally, the coroner's offices were housed in the City-County Building, while autopsies and lab work were done at WISHARD MEMORIAL HOSPITAL. In 1986 the entire coroner staff moved to the basement of the county jail where they now have both offices and a pathology lab. Cases are referred to the coroner's office by health officials, physicians, and police agencies. Upon referral, deputy coroners conduct investigations in cooperation with the police, and bodies are subsequently sent to the morgue for further examination and, if necessary, an autopsy. The chief coroner makes the final death determination based upon all the evidence gathered and is responsible for signing the death certificate.

MICHELLE D. HALE

Marion County Courts. Indianapolis is a center of justice as the site of federal, state, and county courts. During Marion County's founding decade all three judicial branches—the U.S. District Court, the Indiana Supreme Court, and the local trial court—shared the county's first courthouse. The city's only public building from 1825 to 1835, it also was the meeting place for the Indiana General Assembly. Indianapolis in 1994 was the site for the deliberations of five federal district judges, 21 state appellate-level judges, and 32 trial court judges. The complexities of modern society are reflected in matters of life, liberty, money, and property which they decide. Over 4,400 local attorneys practiced in the courts of Marion County in 1992 compared to the five lawyers who resided in the county when its Circuit Court held its first session on September 26, 1822 in a double log cabin home.

As the state capital, Indianapolis has figured in a distinctive way in the evolution of law. Since the General Assembly meets here, tests of its enactments, such as the sales tax of 1961, have originated in the local Circuit Court and been resolved on appeal by the state Supreme Court. When federal issues have been involved, such as with reapportionment of the General Assembly, they have been decided by the local U.S. District Court.

Also, as the state's most populous county, Marion County has been in the vanguard of change at the trial court level. The legislature gave the county the state's first Criminal Court in 1865; its first Superior Court in 1871; the first Juvenile Court in 1903; and the first Municipal Court with appointed judges in 1925. In addition, Marion

County has been an incubator of innovation with such agencies as the Domestic Relations Counseling Bureau and special mental health and environmental divisions of its Municipal Court.

The first judge to preside over the Circuit Court in Marion County was William W. Wick, and the horseback-riding jurist had 10 counties besides Marion in his jurisdiction. It was not until the state capital was formally moved from Corydon to Indianapolis in 1825 that judges of the two other levels of frontier justice arrived on the scene. The first federal judge was Benjamin Parke, an appointee of President Thomas Jefferson. The first judges of the Indiana Supreme Court doing business in Indianapolis were ISAAC BLACKFORD, James Scott, and JESSE L. HOLMAN.

The roots of the judicial systems are in the United States and Indiana constitutions, which set out the basic jurisdictions of their respective courts. While the state Constitution established the Indiana Supreme Court and the local Circuit Court as constitutional entities, the local Superior Court and Municipal Court were created by acts of the General Assembly.

United States Judiciary. The U.S. District Court moved to Indianapolis in January, 1825. It still was under its first judge, Benjamin Parke of Vincennes, who had been named originally in 1808 when Indiana was a territory and who was to serve 27 years. Senior Judge William E. Steckler in 1992 had served a record 42 years on that bench. When appointed in 1950 he was the sole judge for the district which covers 60 central and southern Indiana counties. In 1992 there were five full-time judges with four of them, as well as Senior Judge Steckler, sitting at Indianapolis.

The court has original jurisdiction in all civil actions arising under the U.S. Constitution and laws of the United States. It hears alleged violations of federal criminal laws and civil actions that include matters in controversy exceeding $50,000 and are between citizens of different states. Three federal bankruptcy judges and three federal magistrates also sit at Indianapolis.

State Appellate Judiciary. The docket of the Indiana Supreme Court for its first year at Indianapolis in 1825 showed its three judges decided 44 cases, all but two of them civil. That compares with 1,015 cases, more than half of them crimi-

Interior view of Marion County Superior Court, Room 3, June, 1917. At far left is Will Remy, the Marion County prosecutor who put Ku Klux Klan leader D. C. Stephenson behind bars in 1925. Due to his youthful appearance, Remy was nicknamed the "boy prosecutor."
[Indiana Historical Society,
Louise Carpenter Stanfield Collection, #C5798]

nal, considered by the current court's five justices in 1991.

Under the 1816 Constitution, the earliest judges were appointed by the governor. The 1851 Constitution directed that they be elected for six-year terms by popular vote. In 1970 a constitutional amendment removed them from political election, made them appointive by the governor for 10–year terms, and had them stand unopposed on general election "yes or no" retention ballots. Besides being a court of last resort for appeals on constitutional issues, in death penalty and long imprisonment cases, and in civil disputes, the Supreme Court oversees admission to the practice of law and the disciplining of lawyers and judges.

Two other appellate tribunals that sit at Indianapolis are the Court of Appeals and Indiana Tax Court. The former court dates from 1891 when such a panel was created to help with an overflow of cases in the Supreme Court. Its 15 judges sit in three-judge panels and handle all civil appeals and appeals of criminal sentences of 50 years or less. The Tax Court came into being in 1986 and its single judge takes appeals of administrative rulings involving sales, income, and property taxes.

Trial Courts. The first circuit judge to sit in Marion County, William W. Wick, was called "president judge" and served with two associate judges. Their Fifth Circuit included 10 counties besides Marion in 1821, and was not to become a one-county circuit until 1889. While Judge Wick heard a full range of civil and criminal cases, the docket of Marion County's 1992 circuit judge is almost totally civil. Besides a one-judge Circuit Court, the county now has a 15–judge Superior Court and a 16–judge Municipal Court. Serious criminal felony cases are heard by six of the Superior Court judges, and Class D felonies, misdemeanors, and infractions by nine of the Municipal Court judges.

The three courts disposed of 165,123 cases in 1991. This figure included 78,376 traffic cases, or infractions, decided in Municipal Court. The latter court also handles mental health cases, with a specially assigned judge hearing them at Wishard Memorial Hospital.

Marion County formerly had separate Criminal, Superior, Juvenile, and Probate courts, but a 1975 statute joined them under one Superior Court. The reorganization provided for a presiding judge, elected by the other judges, who was responsible for the operation and conduct of the court under rules adopted by the court. There are civil, criminal, probate, and juvenile divisions, although judges are elected without any specific division being named on the ballot.

Previously the judges were elected on partisan ballots but, after complaints that irrelevant national issues, such as Watergate and the Vietnam War, could sweep an entire sitting bench out of office, a 1975 law adopted a bipartisan plan for the election of the Superior Court's then 13 members. The plan called for the Republican and Democratic parties each to nominate seven candidates to be voted on in the general election. The 13 receiving the highest number of votes were declared elected, meaning seven of the majority party and six of the minority party. The Circuit Court, as a constitutional court, was outside of the reorganization and its judge continued to be elected by party ballot.

The Municipal Court originated in 1925 as a bipartisan court, with persons of both political parties appointed by the governor. The judges operated independently of each other until a 1969 act placed a presiding judge over the 10 trial judges to seek the "speedy, economical and uniform disposition of cases."

That reorganization was followed in 1971 by a law creating a Judicial Nominating Commission for the Municipal Court. Established in response to charges that some judges should be removed because of cronyism with lawyers, the panel saw that they were not reappointed through its function of screening candidates and nominating the "most highly qualified" for appointment by the governor. In 1992 Paul H. Buchanan, Jr., who was judge of the Court of Appeals, ended 21 years as the first and only chairman of the commission.

The Circuit and Superior courts have general, concurrent jurisdictions. While also a court of record, the Municipal Court has a limited jurisdiction. Besides Class D felonies, misdemeanors, infractions, and ordinance violations, it hears civil cases involving claims not exceeding $25,000.

Small Claims Court. Since pioneer times JUSTICES OF THE PEACE held court to handle small claims and minor offenses. The JPs often were persons untrained in the law, and their compensation was dependent on fees and fines they might assess. Those courts were abolished in 1975 and a Small Claims Court for Marion County was created effective January 1, 1976. Divisions of the court sit in each of the county's townships and hold informal hearings on claims that do not exceed $6,000. The court decided 67,278 small claims in 1991.

JAMES E. FARMER

Leander J. Monks, *Courts and Lawyers of Indiana* (Indianapolis, 1916); Supreme Court of Indiana, *1991 Indiana Judicial Report* (Indianapolis, 1991).

Marion County Department of Public Welfare. County human services department. The Marion County Department of Public Welfare was established by the state's Welfare Act of 1936. It is organized and administered under the authority of the Indiana Department of Public Welfare and was not affected by the implementation of UNIGOV.

The department distributes federal, state, and local public assistance throughout the county. It is divided into three divisions: family services, child welfare services, and food stamps. The family services programs include Aid to Families with Dependent Children (AFDC) and special assistance for the elderly, blind, and disabled. The child welfare services include foster homes, adoption programs, and the guardian home, as well as assistance for children of abusive parents, and assistance in obtaining medical care for disabled children of poor families. The food stamps division distributes food stamps to qualifying applicants (over 25,000 households in July, 1991).

The department is governed by a five-member Board of Public Welfare appointed by the judge of the Marion County circuit court. Members serve four-year terms. No more than three members may be of the same political party, and all members must have been residents of the county for at least two years prior to selection. The board meets monthly to determine policies and approve transactions of the department.

HARRISON C. NEAL III

Marion County Election Board.

Responsible for selecting voting places and overseeing the administration of elections in Marion County. Its responsibilities also include ensuring that each voting place has proper materials and correctly labeled and properly functioning voting machines; distributing and overseeing the distribution of absentee ballots; and assisting agencies and individuals who distribute ballots to hospitalized and institutionalized voters.

The election board consist of three members: the MARION COUNTY CLERK and one representative each from the county Republican and Democratic parties, who serve at the pleasure of their respective county chairs. The election board maintains office space in the City-County Building and has a staff of four full-time and several part-time employees. During election periods the board adds other temporary workers. The board's operations are financed from the Marion County general fund through the ordinary budget process.

GREGORY M. VOGEL

Marion County Fair.

The first Marion County Fair was held in 1835 under the auspices of the Marion County Agricultural Society. Early fairs were held on the county courthouse grounds and offered prizes in animal, home manufacture, and agriculture categories. Economic hard times forced the fair to disband by 1837. Another short-lived attempt to hold a county fair came in 1873 when the Marion County Agricultural and Horticultural Association held its first annual fair southwest of Indianapolis at Valley Mills. Prizes were awarded in livestock, grain and vegetables, horticulture, poultry, home manufactures, flowers, and stock animal categories.

The present Marion County Fair began as a fund-raiser for the New Bethel Baptist Church in 1931. This street fair was so successful that within two years the festival moved to the Franklin Township High School grounds. By 1937 it had moved to a 16–acre site near WANAMAKER. At this time the Marion County extension agent and 4–H clubs became involved in the fair, and it grew to be a countywide attraction. The main events promoted 4–H and agriculture and included animal, produce, and handicrafts contests, as well as farm equipment exhibits and carnival entertainment.

The fair moved to its present site in 1953 when the nonprofit volunteer organization purchased 80 acres southeast of the city on Troy Avenue at Five Points. By the early 1990s the fair commission had expanded the grounds to include 143 acres and built 16 permanent structures. Admission was free during the 32–year presidency of Marion County building commissioner Ray Fisher, and fees remained nominal until the 1980s.

Starting in the 1950s the fair commission added attractions to draw an urban as well as rural audience, including music concerts, midway rides, and special shows. In the early 1990s the fair was a 10–day operation offering daily entertainment to complement educational exhibits and the traditional livestock, crop, and craft competitions. In attendance second only to the State Fair in Indiana, the 1992 Marion County Fair drew an estimated 165,000 visitors and operated with a budget of approximately $130,000.

MICHELLE D. HALE

Marion County Healthcare Center.
Founded in 1832 as the Marion County Farm, the
county's poorhouse, this institution now functions as an extended care facility for the poor and
elderly. During much of the 19th century, the
Marion County Farm housed not only the poor
but also the mentally ill, the elderly, and the
chronically ill cases refused by City Hospital and
the City Dispensary.

In 1869 the county constructed a new poorhouse and renamed it the Marion County Infirmary. The infirmary continued to care for the
mentally ill until the county-run Asylum for the
Incurably Insane was opened in 1899 at Julietta
(on Brookville Road at the eastern edge of the
county). By the early 20th century the infirmary
cared primarily for the elderly.

In 1924 a new building was constructed on
Tibbs Avenue, and in 1938 the infirmary moved
to the Julietta facility and became the Marion
County Home for the Aged. The state took over
the Tibbs Avenue facility and assumed responsibility for the care of the mentally ill, who were
moved to Tibbs Avenue from Julietta.

The infirmary suffered from constant overcrowding. Although the county completed a new
$500,000, three-story wing to the infirmary in
1944, it was not occupied until 1946 following an
Indianapolis Times investigation and charges of
mismanagement. Grand jury investigations in
1948 and 1950 into charges of graft and corruption preceded the passage in 1951 of the "Julietta
bill," which replaced supervision by the county
commissioners with a nonpartisan, independent
board of managers and made the superintendent's
job competitive instead of a political appointment.

A 1964 renovation project included a new
employees' building, a new wing, and remodeling
of the wing completed in 1944. The infirmary's
name was then changed to the Marion County
Home and Julietta Convalescent Center. In 1982
the center opened one of the first Alzheimer's
units in the state; the following year it changed its
name to the Marion County Healthcare Center.

The average occupancy rate in the 1990s has
been 270 persons. More than three-fourths of its
residents are elderly Medicare or Medicaid patients. The internal medicine group of INDIANA
UNIVERSITY MEDICAL CENTER provides the medical
staff for the facility. Following a two-year study of
how to cut financial losses due to inadequate
Medicaid reimbursements, a plan was approved
in 1992 for Marion County HEALTH AND HOSPITAL
CORPORATION to assume ownership and to relocate the care center in a new 240–bed facility to be
built near WISHARD HOSPITAL.

KATHERINE MANDUSIC MCDONELL

**Marion County–Indianapolis Histori-
cal Society.** Local historical organization. The
society fosters public awareness of Marion
County and Indianapolis history through publications, programs, and an annual conference.

Community leaders and local historians
founded the society on December 3, 1961, to collect and preserve local history materials, mark historic sites, and promote the preservation of
historic structures in Indianapolis. Faced with the
demolition of the old Marion County Courthouse
in 1962, the society was one of the first local organizations to oppose destruction of the city's historic structures. Its largest public program, held in
August, 1965, at the Van Camp Mansion on
North Meridian Street, attracted over 30,000 people who visited the house before its demolition.
The society has helped to save public sculptures
and assisted in restoring the WOODRUFF PLACE
Town Hall, in which the society maintained its
headquarters for seven years.

The society, now a non-collecting historical
organization, provides occasional public programs and tours of historic sites. It is a volunteer-
operated, not-for-profit organization led by
elected officers and a board of directors. Total
membership in 1993 was approximately 200.

DAVID G. VANDERSTEL
Indianapolis University–Purdue University,
Indianapolis

Marion County-Indianapolis Historical Society
Archives; "County Historical Society Formed At Meet-
ing In State Library," *Indianapolis Star*, Dec. 4, 1961;
"Doomed Van Camp Mansion Has Its Largest Party,"
Indianapolis Times, Aug. 22, 1965.

Marion County Prosecutor. Elected county government office. Provided for by the state constitution, the prosecutor's office represents the State of Indiana for the 19th judicial circuit in offenses against state laws occurring in Marion County. The prosecutor is elected by the voters of Marion County to a four-year term and has few checks on his/her power other than impeachment or being voted out of office. The CITY-COUNTY COUNCIL must approve the prosecutor's budget annually.

The prosecutor's office consists of five major departments: felony, municipal, and juvenile court divisions, the family advocacy center, and the grand jury. Once law enforcement officials make an arrest or a citizen files a charge the case is referred to the appropriate division of the prosecutor's office so that a formal charge can be made. Most cases are then filed with the court and assigned to a judge and deputy prosecutor, while the remaining cases are sent for further investigation to the grand jury. During the trial and sentencing process deputy prosecutors present the state's case based upon facts from police investigations.

In addition to prosecuting cases, the prosecutor's office provides community services. The Family Advocacy Center can file charges on behalf of clients and acts as a clearinghouse for family social services. The Juvenile Court Division enforces court orders for child support. The office also assists victims and handles citizens' complaints. In the early 1990s the prosecutor created an environmental crime section.

The grand jury consists of six summoned citizens who serve for three months at a time. The grand jury was originally created to conduct investigations into all murder and treason cases and any other cases referred to it by the prosecutor to determine if there were enough evidence for indictment. The grand jury also has the power to investigate misconduct concerning public facilities and officials. The jurors are dependent upon the prosecutor's staff for their job training, legal advice, and witness testimony, and they have no budget or authority to conduct their own investigations. Since 1973 use of the grand jury is totally at the discretion of the prosecutor's office. Despite much criticism, the grand jury remains intact in Marion County but it now reviews very few cases.

MICHELLE D. HALE

Marion County Recorder. The office of county recorder is required by the Indiana constitution. The recorder is elected by all voters in the county in even-numbered, non–presidential election years. The recorder serves a four-year term and may be reelected, but no person may serve in the position more than eight years in a twelve-year period.

The primary responsibility of the recorder's office is preserving public documents. The office maintains records of property boundaries and property ownership, including deeds and liens. The office also maintains articles of incorporation, bankruptcy notices, records of discharges from the armed forces, and other records as needed or as specified by law. The recorder collects fees from individuals filing such documents and transmits those fees to the county treasurer.

THOMAS C. KENNEDY

Marion County Sheriff. County law enforcement office. The office of county sheriff is established by the Indiana Constitution. The first sheriff of Marion County, HERVEY BATES, was appointed by the state legislature when the county was established in 1821. The Marion County Sheriff is an elected official responsible for law enforcement throughout the county. The sheriff is elected to four-year terms by the voters of the entire county, and cannot serve more than eight years in a twelve-year period.

The duties of the sheriff are: to keep the peace; apprehend, arrest, and confine lawbreakers; maintain order in the courts; enforce county election laws; and supervise the county jail facilities and prisoners. The sheriff or a designated deputy must attend all meetings of the CITY-COUNTY COUNCIL and the Marion County Commissioners. The sheriff's authority to enforce laws and apprehend persons extends everywhere in the county except to FORT BENJAMIN HARRISON, which is a federal reservation. However, the Marion County Sheriff ordinarily does not provide law enforce-

The Marion County Jail stood on the northwest corner of Alabama and Maryland streets ca. 1905. [Indiana Historical Society, Bass Collection, #820]

ment services within the jurisdictions of the INDI-ANAPOLIS POLICE DEPARTMENT, the cities of BEECH GROVE, LAWRENCE, and SOUTHPORT, and the town of SPEEDWAY.

The sheriff may employ deputies and other staff to assist in fulfilling the several responsibilities of the office. The Marion County Commissioners determine the number of deputies and other staff available to the sheriff. Sheriff's deputies are appointed by the sheriff, with the approval of the sheriff's merit board. In addition to receiving a salary, the sheriff is authorized to keep a percentage of overdue state taxes collected. (The maximum amount of such fees that the sheriff is permitted to keep is limited in the state's most populous counties, including Marion.)

The Marion County Sheriff's Department is organized into divisions. The Civil Division collects delinquent taxes, serves legal process papers as directed by the county courts, and serves legal process papers on behalf of the county election board and the county board of tax review. The Corrections Division administers the Marion County jail. The Personnel Division includes the merit board, which consists of four members appointed by the sheriff. The merit board sets personnel standards and handles employment-related complaints.

HARRISON C. NEAL III

Marion County Surveyor.

A constitutional official elected by all voters in the county in presidential election years. The surveyor serves a four-year term and may be reelected to any number of terms.

The surveyor is responsible for surveying and keeping detailed records of all section corners in the county. The surveyor's office maintains record books containing detailed depictions of all grants, tracts, and subdivisions within the county. In addition, the surveyor serves as the county's supervising engineer, overseeing the construction and maintenance of roadways, bridges, and storm-water ditches and drains. The surveyor may appoint assistants to aid in the performance of the duties of the office.

THOMAS C. KENNEDY

Marion County Treasurer.

The office of county treasurer is required by the Indiana constitution. The Marion County Treasurer is elected to a four-year term by all voters in the county and may serve no more than two consecutive terms.

The treasurer collects and accounts for all county monies. County taxpayers are billed by, and make payments to, the treasurer's office for real and personal property TAXES, inheritance taxes, and county excise, license, and wheel taxes. The treasurer is responsible for investing surplus revenues until they are needed, and for issuing payments to individuals with approved claims to county funds. In addition, the treasurer responds to requests from citizens for tax clearance searches and for title and lien information on properties and businesses in the county.

The Marion County Treasurer serves ex officio as treasurer of the city of Indianapolis, treasurer of the Indianapolis Board of School Commissioners, member of the MARION COUNTY COMMISSIONERS, and president of the county commissioners in alternate years with the MARION COUNTY ASSESSOR. The treasurer also serves on the Marion County Board of Tax Review.

LAURRY NEUFER

Market Square Arena.

Market Square Arena (MSA) opened on September 15, 1974, as the fifth largest sports arena in the United States. The structure's completion concluded efforts, spurred in part by the INDIANA PACERS' search for a new home, by civic leaders and city officials to revitalize the downtown area with a sports facility. The arena eventually became part of the Market Square Complex, centered around the CITY MARKET. Financed by a combination of public and private funds, construction began in the fall of 1971 and cost $23.5 million. Huber, Hunt, & Nichols managed the construction of the building designed by Architects 4, a group of four firms.

The building is 150 feet from arena floor to ceiling and has a clear span diameter of 364 feet with what was in the early 1970s the largest Swedler dome ever constructed. The once rare convex roof was constructed by the American Bridge Division of the United States Steel Corporation. Support of the dome was designed to provide an unobstructed view from all seats. Festival seating is no longer allowed and maximum capacity is now 18,178. A restaurant, Market Square Gardens, originally planned as a private club, sits atop the seven-story structure. Over the years MSA has been the site for concerts, circuses, midget auto races, and evangelists, as well as Indiana Pacers basketball and Indianapolis Racers hockey games. In 1986 the CAPITAL IMPROVEMENT BOARD, a municipal corporation that owns the arena, leased the facility and property for 40 years to Melvin and Herbert Simon, owners of the Indiana Pacers.

JOAN CUNNINGHAM

Marmon, Howard C. (May 24, 1876–Apr. 4, 1943). Pioneer automotive engineer and designer. Marmon designed the Wasp, which won the first 500–mile race at the INDIANAPOLIS MOTOR SPEEDWAY. He also designed the Marmon 16, which earned him a medal from the American Society of Automotive Engineers.

The Marmon family moved to Indianapolis when Howard was two years old. After graduating from SHORTRIDGE HIGH SCHOOL in 1891, he attended Earlham College (1892–1894) and graduated from the University of California in 1898 with a mechanical engineering degree.

After returning to Indianapolis he became associated with his father, Daniel W. Marmon, in NORDYKE AND MARMON, Inc. When the company was absorbed by the automotive industry,

Howard managed the designing and mechanical department. In 1913 and 1914 he served as president of the American Society of Automotive Engineers. His automotive reputation led to his assignment to head the airplane engine experimental station at McCook Field in Dayton, Ohio, during World War I as a captain in the Army Air Corps. He participated with other engineers in the designing of the Liberty aircraft engine. After the war he moved to North Carolina to pursue other industrial activities.

ELLEN TEVAULT

Indiana Biography Series, Indiana State Library; *Indianapolis Star*, Apr. 5, 6, 1943.

Marmon (1902–1933). A superbly engineered automobile produced in Indianapolis, often called "the nearest American approximation to the Rolls-Royce." The Marmon was produced by Marmon Motor Car Company, a division of NOR-

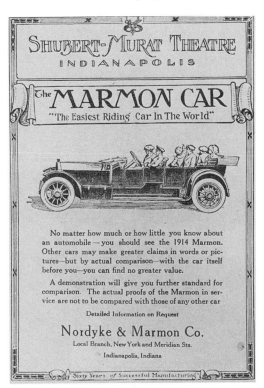

Advertisement for 1914 Marmon luxury automobile. [Indiana Historical Society, Bass Collection, #286716-3]

DYKE AND MARMON COMPANY on West Morris Street. It was part of an elite group of cars that did not start from a horse-drawn carriage plant but rather from established machinery builders. Marmon engineers pioneered modern pressure lubrication, designed air-cooled V–4 engines, and built "systems engineered" cars that incorporated driver, car, road, and tire interface in the design. Other firsts for the company were side entrances, all-aluminum cars, and factory-installed radios.

Marmon gained national prominence when its entry became the first winner of the INDIANAPOLIS 500–MILE RACE in 1911. By scoring highly or winning various other early road races, the Marmon earned a reputation for reliability and comfort. In 1916, the French government purchased a fleet of Marmons for its political and army officials, the French automobile industry having been disrupted by World War I. Marmon, which as early as 1920 employed 5,000 people, produced innovative and stylish autos throughout the 1920s. In the late 1920s, Marmon introduced two unique autos, the Little Marmon (1927), a compact; and the Roosevelt (1929), the first eight-cylinder car in the world to sell for under $1,000.

Despite its reputation and the introduction of more reasonably priced cars, Marmon was unable to weather the stock market failure of 1929 and the ensuing economic depression. Decreased sales forced the company to close its automotive activities. The Marmon name lives on, however, through the distinctive and well-engineered line of Marmon-Herrington trucks produced initially in Indianapolis but more recently in Knoxville, Tennessee.

WILLIAM GULDE
North Central High School

———

George and Stacey Hanley, *The Marmon Heritage* (Rochester, Mich.: Doyle Hyk Publishing Company, 1985).

Marmon-Herrington. Truck manufacturer. Formed on March 13, 1931, the Marmon-Herrington Company, Inc., was the continuation of the truck division of the Marmon Motor Car Company. Production took place in a separate part of the plant at York Street and Kentucky Avenue. Partners in the company were Walter Marmon, Colonel Arthur W. Herrington, and F. E. Moskovics. After some patent and financial controversy, Moskovics released his interest and the company reorganized in December, 1931. The company specialized in the manufacture, assembly, and sale of heavy-duty, all-wheel-drive trucks. Because of their off-road capabilities, the trucks were of particular use in the construction of Middle East oil pipelines. In 1935 Marmon-Herrington began converting Ford 1.5 ton, V–8 trucks to all-wheel drive. In 1937 the company purchased and moved into the former Duesenberg Company plant on West Washington and Harding streets. During World War II the company produced trucks and armored vehicles such as half-tracks and light tanks for the United States and its allies. These vehicles were especially effective in desert warfare. At its peak during World War II, the company employed 1,500 workers.

After the war, the company added a line of on-road vehicles that included a Delivr-All, designed for house-to-house delivery, trolley buses, and transit buses. In 1960 an HDT (highway tractor) was added to the line. A. H. Roop acquired the company in July, 1963, and moved the operation to Denton, Texas.

PAUL BROCKMAN
Indiana Historical Society

———

George and Stacey Hanley, *The Marmon Heritage* (Rochester, Mich.: Doyle Hyk Publishing Co., 1985).

Marott Hotel. The Marott Hotel first opened November 25, 1926, under its original owner, George J. Marott. The rooms in the two 10–story towers were as elegant as those in hotels found in much larger cities at that time. The one-floor lobby featured an open-air Spanish garden, dining and ball rooms with marble pillars, and crystal chandeliers. The hotel, located at 2625 North Meridian Street, was a community in itself, with a pharmacy, delicatessen, beauty shop, and the city's first studio devoted to the game of auction bridge.

Located next to what then was the GOVERNOR'S MANSION, the Marott hosted many political functions and social events. Winston Churchill, Herbert Hoover, Clark Gable, and Marilyn Monroe are among the prominent people who once stayed at the hotel.

After George Marott died in February, 1946, the Marott began to decline from its original grandeur. Various owners renovated the building, added two new dining rooms and a pool, turned lawns into parking lots, changed the Spanish garden into a covered patio, and replaced the marble columns with steel girders. By 1978 fewer than 12 permanent residents lived in the hotel's 78 apartments. In April, 1981, the power was disconnected from the decaying building and the windows were boarded.

Almost two years later, a group of local businessmen invested $16 million to renovate the building, which reopened in 1983 as an apartment building. It currently has 240 units.

GRETA E. SHANKLE
Indianapolis Business Journal

Nancy L. Comiskey, "Check-out Time at the Marott Hotel," *Indianapolis Monthly* (Feb., 1983), 24–25, 91; Sheri Massa, "Marott: Grand Dame of North Meridian Corridor on the Way to Vitality," *Indianapolis Business Journal*, June 30–July 6, 1986, 10A–11A.

Mars Hill. Southwestside suburb in the vicinity of the Holt Road and Kentucky Avenue intersection. Mars Hill was founded in 1911 with high hopes and an ambitious scheme. A group of Indianapolis businessmen planned to make the picturesque farming community a new industrial suburb with factories and 50,000 residents. They formed the Greater Indianapolis Industrial Association and purchased several farms, including a large horse farm owned by Sterling Holt. Reportedly the new town took its name from a hill dubbed "Marr's" for a 19th-century settler.

To finance construction of the new city, the group proposed to sell 8,000 lots to the public. Proceeds were to be used to move out-of-state factories to the new site and pay for city services. At a mass meeting in February, 1911, civic-minded citizens were urged to invest in the future and buy lots for $400 each. Within a few months, however, the association had not sold the required number of lots and the scheme failed. The group

reorganized as a stockholding company in 1912 and met with some success, though not enough to implement original plans.

In the years that followed, some small factories moved to Mars Hill, but the promised city did not develop. The area was never incorporated and roads were not paved, nor were sewers or water provided. Since there were no building codes, residents built whatever they could afford, including tar-paper shacks and half-houses (basement dwellings). Mars Hill enjoyed a small building boom during World War II, when many found work at the nearby Allison plant. Problems continued to plague the area in the 1950s and 1960s. With the area's inclusion into the city under UNIGOV, Indianapolis officials were forced to deal with Mars Hill's sewage, trash, abandoned buildings, and unpaved roads. Despite efforts to solve these problems, Mars Hill remains a community in need of improved infrastructure and services.

CATHLEEN DONNELLY

Indianapolis Star, Feb. 19, 1911, May 2, 1912; *Indianapolis Times*, Feb. 25, 1962.

Marsh Supermarkets. Indiana supermarket chain. Wilber Marsh opened the first Marsh grocery store in 1922 in North Salem, Indiana. By the 1930s the family-owned business had opened a chain of stores throughout Indiana and later Ohio, with the first true supermarket appearing in 1947. Marsh stores incorporated as Marsh Foodliners in 1952, later known as Marsh Supermarkets.

The first Marsh supermarket in Indianapolis, located at 53rd Street and Keystone Avenue, opened in 1957. Since then Marsh has increased its presence in Indianapolis to include 33 supermarkets and 66 Village Pantry convenience stores. Battling fierce competition from Kroger and Cub Foods, Marsh has developed large one-stop-shopping stores which include specialty foods and services and as of 1993 claimed 30 percent of the Indianapolis market.

In 1991, with roughly 40 percent of its stores in the Indianapolis area, Marsh moved its headquarters to nearby FISHERS. Currently the nation's 38th largest food retailer, Marsh Supermarkets does about $1.3 billion in annual sales. In 1993 Marsh employed over 4,000 people from the Indianapolis area in its Marion County warehouse, stores, and corporate offices.

Throughout its history in Indianapolis, Marsh has been very active in local philanthropic and civic affairs. Marsh has contributed to the arts and amateur sports, as well as Indianapolis schools, churches, and museums, by sponsoring such programs and events as Symphony on the Prairie, WHITE RIVER PARK STATE GAMES, and Computers for Education. Marsh has also aided local charities in fund-raising and food donation programs and has developed progressive environmental recycling and human services policies.

AIMEE L. REX
MICHELLE D. HALE

Marshal Foch Day. Visit to Indianapolis by Ferdinand Foch, Marshal of France, November 4, 1921. Marshal Foch, commander in chief on the western front during World War I, toured the United States in 1921 as a guest of the AMERICAN LEGION. The city, county, and state jointly planned for the visit, in cooperation with the American Legion. Legion and National Guard units statewide participated, and Governor Warren McCray invited dignitaries from across the nation.

Governor Warren T. McCray (left) and American Legion National Commander Hanford MacNider (right) joined Marshal Foch (center) in reviewing the Marshal Foch Day festivities on November 4, 1921. [Indiana Historical Society, Bretzman Collection, #C5767]

Foch's special train arrived at Union Station at 9 A.M. The official reception committee and 200 citizens greeted him while thousands waited outside. The day's events began with a reception at the CLAYPOOL HOTEL and included a 25–mile race at the Speedway, the governor's luncheon at the Indianapolis Country Club, a mammoth parade, dedication of the cornerstone of the planned INDIANA WORLD WAR MEMORIAL, a brief visit to the American Legion National Headquarters, and a banquet at the Claypool. A mass meeting at CADLE TABERNACLE climaxed the day's events, with 12,000 seated and 2,000 standing. The marshal's party arrived at 9 P.M. to a wild demonstration. Governor McCray and Mayor CHARLES W. JEWETT spoke, and the marshal responded through an interpreter. Foch then returned to UNION STATION and departed the city.

Surviving mementos of Marshal Foch Day include a stone salvaged from a destroyed bridge over the Marne, dedicated on that day as the cornerstone of the future War Memorial, and a 16th-century pillar from the Belleau Cathedral that was used as an altar during the cornerstone dedication. Both may be seen at the American Legion Museum. The actual cornerstone of the Indiana War Memorial was laid by General John J. Pershing in 1927.

RICHARD G. GROOME

Indiana Historical Commission, *Marshal Foch Day, November 4, 1921* (Indianapolis, 1922).

Martens, Nancy McCann (May 27, 1881–Sept. 11, 1940). Impresario who brought classical music and dance to Indianapolis during the 1930s as president of Martens Concerts, Inc. Orphaned early in life, Martens was reared in a convent school in Ohio and attended the Cincinnati Conservatory of Music before coming to Indianapolis to join the staff of the College of Music, later known as the Arthur Jordan Conservatory of Music (now JORDAN COLLEGE OF FINE ARTS). She married fellow teacher Christian Frederick Martens in 1906.

Following her husband's death in 1918, Martens worked for 12 years for the ONA B. TALBOT Fine Arts Enterprises. She organized her own company in 1930 after Talbot left the city and brought a steady stream of classical music and dance artists to Indianapolis during the Depression decade. Martens paid famed pianist Paderewski in cash during the bank holiday in March, 1933, saving the artist's cashless American tour.

Martens took care of aspiring local musical artists by giving them ushering jobs and discounted tickets. A theatrical publication in 1935 called her a top-notch "Lady Barnum." She died following a long illness, several months after the January, 1940, appearance of famed contralto Marian Anderson.

SUSAN GUYETT

Indianapolis Times, Nov. 15, 1935, Sept. 12, 1940; *Indianapolis News*, Sept. 11, 1940.

Martin, John Bartlow (Aug. 4, 1915–Jan. 3, 1987). Journalist, author, and U.S. ambassador to the Dominican Republic. Born in Hamilton, Ohio, Martin and his family came to Indianapolis when he was three years old. The eldest and only survivor of three brothers, Martin lived with his family in a house on Brookside Avenue. Although his family life was troubled (his parents would eventually divorce), Martin found comfort in books and decided at an early age he wanted to be a writer, despite his contractor father's disapproval.

Expelled from DePauw University near the end of his first year for drinking, Martin worked as a night copyboy for the Indianapolis bureau of the Associated Press. He returned to DePauw in 1937, edited the school's newspaper, and was a stringer for the INDIANAPOLIS TIMES. He accepted a full-time reporter's position with the *Times* before graduating from DePauw, and completed his courses in absentia. Starting on the police beat, Martin moved up to covering city hall for the newspaper. He eventually moved to Chicago and worked as a free-lance writer producing articles for a number of true-crime magazines.

Over the years, Martin advanced to writing for such prestigious publications as *Harper's*, SATURDAY EVENING POST, *Esquire*, *Life*, and *Look*. Earning distinction as one of America's best reporters,

Martin returned to Indiana in 1946 to research a book on the state. Published in 1947, *Indiana: An Interpretation*, although not bitter in tone, painted a less than flattering portrait of the state.

A lifelong liberal Democrat, Martin worked as a speech writer for Adlai Stevenson's losing presidential campaigns in 1952 and 1956. He had better luck in 1960, when he worked for John Kennedy's successful run for the White House. Kennedy would later appoint Martin as ambassador to the Dominican Republic, a post he held until February 15, 1964.

Martin returned once again to Indiana in 1968 as an advisor to Robert Kennedy's successful campaign in the state's Democratic presidential primary. In 1969 he began teaching journalism at Northwestern University's Medill School of Journalism, a post he held for ten years.

RAY BOOMHOWER
Indiana Historical Society

John Bartlow Martin, *It Seems Like Only Yesterday: Memoirs of Writing, Presidential Politics, and the Diplomatic Life* (New York, 1986).

Martin University (Martin Center College). A unique institution within the Indianapolis area, Martin Center officially began in 1977. Its founder, Benedictine priest Boniface Hardin, named the school in honor of two Martins, Martin Luther King, Jr. and St. Martin DePorres. (The latter, the first mulatto Catholic saint, worked with the poor in Peru in the 16th and 17th centuries.) The college became a university in 1990, the name change a reflection of increased enrollment and an expanding number of degree programs.

The origins of Martin University can be traced to 1969, when Father Hardin and Sister Jane Schilling opened a center on North College Avenue to address significant community issues, especially racial concerns and the inherited disease sickle cell anemia. Five years later, in 1974, the center conducted a study in cooperation with the Union of Experimenting Colleges and INDIANA UNIVERSITY–PURDUE UNIVERSITY, INDIANAPOLIS, on the difficulties experienced by low-income adults and minority students who wished to attend traditional colleges or universities. To provide an alternative for these target populations, the state of Indiana allowed Hardin to begin a college in 1977. Seven students attended Martin Center in its first year. The experiment was successful and by 1990 enrollment stood at 1,100 students on three campuses. The average age of a Martin University student is 40, and a large number of the students are minorities, a reflection of Hardin and Schilling's original target populations for the institution.

Although the original site on College Avenue remains, a branch campus at 2171 Avondale Place, first opened in 1987, has become the main campus. A third location, the Lady Elizabeth campus, is actually an education building located inside the Indiana WOMEN'S PRISON.

From its beginnings in 1969 to its college status in 1977 and ultimately its university designation in 1990, Martin has expanded dramatically. By 1990, the faculty had increased to 72 members, 45 percent of whom had doctorates. Course offerings include bachelor's degrees in African-American studies, accounting, addictions, biology, business administration, chemistry, child development, communication, computer technology, counseling, criminal justice, English, gerontology, history, humanities, management, marketing, mathematics, music, political science, physics, psychology, social services administration, religious studies, and sociology.

In 1992, Martin University was authorized by the North Central Association of Colleges and Schools, an accrediting body for the region, to grant master's degrees. Martin offers graduate programs in community psychology and urban ministries. The psychology program emphasizes substance abuse, addiction, AIDS, and stress in the urban setting. The M.A. degree in urban ministries is unique in the state and is targeted to the special needs of work within the community.

ROBERT A. SCHWARTZ

Indianapolis News, Apr. 19, Nov. 23, Dec. 5, 1990.

Martindale. Eastside neighborhood bounded by 30th Street, Keystone and Massachusetts avenues, and the NORFOLK SOUTHERN RAILROAD (Monon) tracks. The Martindale area was settled by Frederick Ruschaupt and Gustave Zschech in 1873, the same year that developers platted Brightwood along the district's eastern border. Never an incorporated town, the area now known as Martindale grew up around Ruschaupt and Zschech's Indianapolis Car Works railroad machinery factory, located north of present-day 19th Street. Within a few years Car Works went out of business and for many years Atlas Machine Works, manufacturer of the Corliss Steam Engine, occupied the failed company's buildings. While the nearby MONON RAILROAD aided the area's industrial growth it hindered high-grade residential development and the district quickly became a working class suburb.

By 1878 African-Americans were making their homes and building churches in the area around Beeler Street. In 1895 Beeler Street became Martindale Avenue (since 1987 Dr. Andrew J. Brown Avenue) and lent its name to the surrounding neighborhood. By the 1920s most of Martindale was developed as a residential-industrial area.

In the 1960s, suffering from lower-than-average incomes and increasing crime, citizens formed the Martindale-Brightwood neighborhood association and, in 1969, received Model Neighborhood designation as a "most in need" district in a federal rehabilitation program.

In the 1990s Martindale remains an area of small African-American owned, working class homes intermixed with industry. Ertel Manufacturing now occupies the former Atlas Machine Works grounds and is the area's largest employer with 350 workers.

CONNIE J. ZEIGLER

"Martindale-Brightwood Neighborhood Plan" (Indianapolis Department of Metropolitan Development, 1985).

Mattison, Donald M. (Apr. 24, 1905–July 28, 1975). Artist and art educator. Born in Rockford, Illinois, where his father invented machine tools and his mother taught school, Donald Mattison grew up in North Carolina. He showed an early interest in art and enrolled in the school of fine arts at Yale University, excelling as a draftsman and painter. After completing bachelor and master of fine art degrees, Mattison moved to Chicago in 1927 where he worked as an assistant to the muralist Eugene Savage and married. In 1928 he won the Prix de Rome and held a three-year fellowship in painting at the American Academy in Rome. Returning to New York City in 1931 with his wife and daughter, he taught and accepted commissions until he became director of HERRON SCHOOL OF ART in May, 1933.

Charged with developing a distinguished fine arts program, Mattison swiftly replaced the school's faculty and dealt tactfully with protesting students who hung and burned his effigy. Curriculum changes he inaugurated aimed to produce completely trained and experienced artists. Mattison hired DAVID RUBINS to build a sculpture program and invited guest artists to teach special media such as lithography. With his encouragement Herron students entered and won the Prix de Rome competition in four successive years from 1937 to 1940.

Enrollment burgeoned following WORLD WAR II and despite limited resources Mattison continued to develop Herron's programs, particularly printmaking. His profile appeared in a national art magazine and in 1958 the Herron Art Museum mounted a 25–year retrospective honoring his achievement.

Mattison's success as an administrator matched the demand for his artwork. Focusing on portraits and paintings of the American scene, an art movement chronicling everyday life in America, Mattison exhibited locally and nationally, won prizes, and accepted commissions. He completed post office murals in Tipton and Union City, Indiana.

The 1960s opened with Herron receiving a major scholarship bequest and the gift of a new school building. The sudden death of his wife in 1961 and debates within the Art Association about the future of the Herron Museum and School made the decade a difficult one for Mattison. Despite his eloquent pleas for a continuance of the partnership, the Art Association's board of directors severed the school and museum. In 1967 Herron School of Art joined Indiana University. Mattison's skill in negotiating this transfer preserved the school's heritage. He became its first

dean, serving until retirement in 1970. Afflicted with poor health, he remained active as a painter until he succumbed after a long illness.

Mattison mentored the professional development of two generations of artists and he created an important body of artwork. His portrait commissions included U.S. Supreme Court justices Thurgood Marshall and Sherman Minton, Indiana governors Paul McNutt and Harold Handley, author BOOTH TARKINGTON, and many social, business, and community leaders. His work is in the collections of the Smithsonian Institution, the INDIANAPOLIS MUSEUM OF ART, Yale, Princeton, and Indiana universities, and many private collections.

JOHN J. COONEY

M. Dolorita Carper, "A History of the John Herron Art Institute" (M.A. thesis, Butler University, 1947); Indiana Artist Files, Indianapolis Museum of Art Library.

Maxwell, Samuel D. (Feb. 19, 1803–July 3, 1873). Mayor of Indianapolis, 1858–1863, Republican. Born in Garrard County, Kentucky, of Scots ancestry, in 1820 he moved with his family from Hanover, Indiana, to Marion County, locating close to FALL CREEK near present-day INDIANA AVENUE. Only GEORGE POGUE and the JOHN MC-CORMICK family were then resident in or near what would become Indianapolis.

In 1822 Maxwell moved to Montgomery County (not yet organized), married that December (the first marriage license issued in Marion County), and was appointed sheriff of Montgomery County in April, 1823. He moved to Clinton County where he was the first county clerk, 1830. Returning to Indianapolis in 1854 or 1855, Maxwell practiced law and owned ice houses on the canal above 16th Street. In January, 1857, he chaired the Marion County Republican convention. A lifelong Presbyterian, he was active in the work of the Indianapolis Benevolent Society and the ward schools.

Maxwell won three mayoral elections: 1858, 1859 (from 1853 to 1858 elections were annual), and 1861. During the Civil War he presided over a city swollen with Union recruits and was a member of the United States Sanitary Commission. By 1863 his health had failed and while certain of a fourth nomination for mayor Maxwell gave up public life. After the war he moved to Grand Gulf, Mississippi, returning to Indianapolis in his last illness about February, 1873. This last of the "first settlers" had spent only a dozen of his 70 years in the city.

WILLIAM DOHERTY
Marian College

Indianapolis News, July 5, 1873; Jacob Piatt Dunn, _Greater Indianapolis_ (Chicago, 1910).

May, Edwin (July 23, 1823–Feb. 27, 1880). Architect of the current Indiana State House and numerous county courthouses. May was prominent among the first generation of architects working in Indiana. Born in Boston in 1823, he moved with his carpenter father first to Madison, Indiana, and then to Indianapolis in 1842 at the age of 18. After working as a carpenter for eight years, he studied architecture informally. May served as contractor of the former Johnson County Courthouse in Franklin, designed by JOHN ELDER in 1849, but his career as an architect is believed to have begun with the Franklin County Courthouse in Brookville in 1852. That same year he designed the former Sullivan County Courthouse in Sullivan and Shelby County Courthouse in Shelbyville. Three other courthouses to his credit are the Decatur County Courthouse in Greensburg (1854); the Allen County Courthouse in Fort Wayne (1860); and the Knox County Courthouse in Vincennes (1872).

May designed a variety of other public buildings throughout the state, including the Horace Mann School in Indianapolis (1873) and several buildings in the 1870s at the Central Hospital for the Insane in Indianapolis, most prominent among them the Women's Building costing over $700,000. May also had considerable experience in designing fireproof buildings, for which he held three patents granted by the U.S. Patent Office in 1869.

By the late 1870s Edwin May was well known as a designer of courthouses in Indiana. In 1877 he was the architect of the Hamilton County

Courthouse in Noblesville, his last project of this kind. This building, which has been called "one of the most lucid expressions of the classical French Renaissance mode to have been constructed in the Midwest," played an important role in his development of the design of the STATE HOUSE. The county commissioners summarily fired May as architect in January, 1878, in a dispute instigated by the building's contractor. The courthouse was completed in July, 1879.

From a field of 27 entrants in an intense competition, May's design for the new Indiana State House was chosen in early 1878. When construction on this project began in August of that year, May was paralyzed and later traveled to Jacksonville, Florida, to recuperate. He died there in February, 1880, leaving the immense project in the hands of ADOLPH SCHERRER, a Swiss architect in his office. Because the Capitol was not completed until 1888, it is uncertain how the building would have differed if May had remained to supervise its construction and make revisions to his original plans.

MARY ELLEN GADSKI

Lee Burns, _Early Architects and Builders of Indiana_ (Indianapolis, 1935); _Who Was Who in America_.

Mayer, Charles (June 6, 1862-Nov. 30, 1925) and **Ferdinand L.** (Dec. 9, 1860–Mar. 13, 1915). Merchants of fine china, silverware, jewelry, imported artware. The Mayers were an old Indianapolis family. In 1840, Charles Mayer, a German immigrant, opened a store on the Washington Street site where CHARLES MAYER & COMPANY was later located. In their home at North and Illinois streets, where the Masonic Temple is today, the Mayers had the city's first private floral conservatory.

Ferdinand and Charles Mayer were educated in a Moravian academy at Prangins, Switzerland, and at Greylock Institute, South Williamstown, Massachusetts. They joined the family business in 1879; nine years later the older son became a partner. On the father's death in 1891, the sons assumed full management. Both were active in business, civic, and social organizations. Ferdinand was appointed by Mayor CHARLES A. BOOK-

WALTER to the city park board and was a "corporator" of CROWN HILL CEMETERY from 1897 to 1915.

Mayer Chapel was begun in 1894 as a mission of SECOND PRESBYTERIAN CHURCH to young people in the area of the stockyards and the BELT LINE RAILROAD. Ferdinand Mayer's generous financial support paid a large portion of the construction costs. The chapel honored his father, a longtime member of Second Presbyterian Church and a Sunday school teacher, trustee, and elder.

HESTER ANNE HALE

Mayer and Company. See Charles Mayer and Company

Mayflower Transit Company. Carmel-based moving company. In 1927 trucker Conrad M. Gentry, formerly of Red Ball Transit Company, and International Harvester truck salesman Don F. Kenworthy started the Mayflower Transit Company in Indianapolis with two trucks. Within a year the company desperately needed capital, and investors Burnside Smith and Parke Cooling helped reorganize the company as the Aero Mayflower Transit Company. By 1932, despite the Great Depression, Mayflower's business topped $500,000.

In 1940 Mayflower became the first trucking company in the industry to receive operating rights in all states. The company's revenues reached $10 million by 1947 and $45 million by 1958. Mayflower went public in 1976 and three years later the company began moving electronic, computer, and trade show exhibits.

Seeking to stabilize the cyclical profits of the moving business, which peaks during the summer months, Mayflower began operating buses for schools, companies, and transit authorities in September, 1984. Two years later, after fending off a hostile takeover bid by Laidlaw Transportation of Canada, Mayflower management took the company private in a debt-laden leveraged buyout. In 1990 Mayflower Transit formed a joint venture with Sovtransavto, the largest trucking company in Russia, to become the first moving company in the former Soviet Union. Mayflower

filed for bankruptcy in December, 1991, emerging from bankruptcy reorganization in early 1992.

As of the early 1990s, Mayflower Transit, Inc. is a wholly owned subsidiary of Mayflower Group, based in Shawnee Mission, Kansas. Mayflower Transit handles approximately 150,000 shipments each year, having made over two million moves to date. It employs 800 workers at its Carmel headquarters.

DEBORAH B. MARKISOHN

Mayor, Office of. The mayor of Indianapolis is the head of the executive branch of city and county government and is elected by all voters in the county to a renewable four-year term. The mayor's salary is fixed by the CITY-COUNTY COUNCIL, and vacancies in the office are filled by temporary appointment approved by the council. The responsibilities of the office include: enforcing city ordinances and state laws; appointing, supervising, and removing heads and employees of city government departments, agencies, and divisions; appointing, supervising, and removing deputy mayors, with appointments subject to City-County Council approval; reviewing and either approving or disapproving, in writing and within 10 days, ordinances or appropriations passed by the City-County Council, with the mayor's vetoes subject to being overridden by a two thirds vote of the councillors; communicating and coordinating with the City-County Council and the Marion County Commissioners concerning the financial condition and budget of the city and county; and setting the salaries of city officers and employees, subject to City-County Council approval for salaries of police and fire employees. The mayor can veto individual items in budgetary appropriations passed by the City-County Council, but this veto power does not extend to the funds for the constitutionally required county offices of auditor, coroner, prosecutor, recorder, sheriff, surveyor, and treasurer, or to the Marion County courts, or to the independent municipal corporations: the INDIANAPOLIS AIRPORT AUTHORITY, the Indianapolis–Marion County Library District, and the HEALTH AND HOSPITAL CORPORATION of Marion County.

Mayors of Indianapolis

Samuel Henderson (Whig)	1847–1849
Horatio C. Newcomb (Whig)	1849–1851
Caleb Scudder (Whig)	1851–1854
James McCready (Democrat)	1854–1856
Henry F. West (Democrat)	1856
Charles G. Coulon (Democrat)	Nov. 8–22, 1856
William J. Wallace (Republican)	1856–1858
Samuel D. Maxwell (Republican)	1858–1863
John Caven (Republican)	1863–1867
Daniel McCauley (Macauley) (Republican)	1867–1873
James L. Mitchell (Democrat)	1873–1875
John Caven (Republican)	1875–1881
Daniel W. Grubbs (Republican)	1881–1884
John L. McMaster (Republican)	1884–1886
Caleb S. Denny (Republican)	1886–1890
Thomas Sullivan (Democrat)	1890–1893
Caleb S. Denny (Republican)	1893–1895
Thomas Taggart (Democrat)	1895–1901
Charles A. Bookwalter (Republican)	1901–1903
John W. Holtzman (Democrat)	1903–1906
Charles A. Bookwalter (Republican)	1906–1910
Samuel Lewis (Lew) Shank (Republican)	1910–1913
Harry R. Wallace (Republican)	1913–1914
Joseph E. Bell (Democrat)	1914–1918
Charles W. Jewett (Republican)	1918–1922
Samuel Lewis (Lew) Shank (Republican)	1922–1926
John L. Duvall (Republican)	1926–1927
Claude E. Negley (Republican)	Oct. 27–Nov. 9, 1927
L. Ert Slack (Democrat)	1927–1930
Reginald H. Sullivan (Democrat)	1930–1935
John W. Kern, Jr. (Democrat)	1935–1937
Walter C. Boetcher (Democrat)	1937–1939
Reginald H. Sullivan (Democrat)	1939–1943
Robert Tyndall (Republican)	1943–1947
George L. Denny (Republican)	1947–1948
Albert G. Feeney (Democrat)	1948–1950
Philip L. Bayt, Jr. (Democrat)	1950–1951
Christian J. Emhardt (Democrat)	1951–1952
Alex M. Clark (Republican)	1952–1956
Philip L. Bayt, Jr. (Democrat)	1956–1959
Charles H. Boswell (Democrat)	1959–1962
Albert H. Losche (Democrat)	1962–1964
John J. Barton (Democrat)	1964–1968
Richard G. Lugar (Republican)	1968–1976
William H. Hudnut III (Republican)	1976–1992
Stephen Goldsmith (Republican)	1992-

The office of mayor of Indianapolis experienced several changes from the mid–1960s through the mid–1980s, especially because of the 1969–1970 UNIGOV reorganization of local government in Marion County. During the 1800s Indianapolis mayors served two-year terms but could be reelected. At the turn of the century the mayor's term was extended to four years, but the mayor was barred from seeking reelection to another term. The restriction against serving consecutive terms weakened the office politically. The expansion in the number of appointed boards

and commissions responsible for local public services also weakened the mayor's office. By the early 1960s the Indianapolis mayor could appoint only a fraction of the board members responsible for such key public services as parks, thoroughfares, libraries, public health, and major public works such as the airport and the CITY-COUNTY BUILDING.

In 1964 the Indiana General Assembly modified the laws governing first-class cities such as Indianapolis and permitted the mayor to serve two consecutive terms. In a 1983 act known popularly as the "Hudnut forever" bill, this restriction on the number of consecutive terms was lifted, and Indianapolis mayors currently may serve an unlimited number of terms. The mayor's ability to seek reelection adds to the political power of the office, since a mayor's days in office are no longer numbered from the moment he or she takes the oath.

Unigov added considerably to the powers of the mayor's office. The mayor is the chief executive of Marion County government as well as Indianapolis city government. This dual role accounts for the fact that the Indianapolis mayor is chosen by all voters in Marion County, even from the "excluded cities" that separately elect mayors of their own. Unigov also brought some local agencies that had been separate municipal corporations within a "cabinet" of departments under the mayor's control and extended the mayor's authority over county and city financial affairs.

The Unigov law also provided for the mayor to appoint one or more deputy mayors, subject to City-County Council approval, and to define their duties. The three mayors who have served since 1970 have assigned the responsibilities of deputy mayors in slightly different ways, but there has usually been one deputy mayor whose primary responsibility is handling the city and county's relations with the federal, state, and other local governments, and another deputy mayor whose primary responsibility is for some aspect of city and county policies or services. There were three deputy mayors during the last term of Mayor William H. Hudnut III, and two during the first years of Stephen Goldsmith's administration.

With these changes the mayor's office has emerged as a crucial, central position of leadership in local politics and local government in Indianapolis and Marion County.

JOHN C. WHITHAM

Maywood. Wayne Township neighborhood centered near the intersection of Kentucky and Tibbs avenues, about three miles southwest of downtown Indianapolis. Maywood began as a steam grist- and sawmill operation owned by Fielding Beeler and CALVIN FLETCHER. In 1854 the two men purchased machinery from a Decatur Township mill and moved it to the Wayne Township site. They built nine homes for their workers, and soon a cooper and blacksmith set up shops. When the Indianapolis and Vincennes Railroad was completed in 1869 the depot was named Beeler's Station. The mill, however, proved unprofitable, so Beeler sold the enterprise in 1873. Later, the machinery was removed and the building dismantled. Platted as Maywood in 1873, the village by the 1880s counted about 100 residents, 20 homes, a post office, shops, a school, and a Methodist church.

In the 20th century several large Indianapolis firms established plants near Maywood, though only REILLY TAR AND CHEMICAL and Detroit Diesel Allison remain open in the 1990s. Numbering around 300 residents, many of them from Maywood Manor, a nearby subdivision, Maywood was never incorporated and became a part of Indianapolis in 1970 under UNIGOV.

CATHLEEN F. DONNELLY

Berry R. Sulgrove, *History of Indianapolis and Marion County* (Philadelphia, 1884); "A Post Office Grows Up," *Indianapolis Star Magazine*, Jan. 20, 1957.

Mazzini, Louis Yolando (June 3, 1894–June 23, 1973). Serologist. A native of Lima, Peru, Mazzini attended the University of Wisconsin, BUTLER UNIVERSITY, and Indiana University. Because of political unrest in Peru, he moved to the United States permanently in 1916.

Mazzini's association with the INDIANA UNIVERSITY SCHOOL OF MEDICINE (IUSM), as professor of serology and pathology, began in 1924. From 1933 to 1947 he served the Indiana State Board of Health as a laboratory scientist and serologist. He began his own laboratory in 1947, although he continued to lecture on serological methods at IUSM.

In 1939, he developed the Mazzini test for syphilis (lipoidal flocculation test), which was faster, cheaper, and more sensitive to all stages of syphilis than the commonly used Wassermann Test. Mazzini donated the patent rights for his test, which was employed by the Armed Forces during World War II, to the Indiana University Foundation. In 1950 he developed a more accurate syphilis test, the Mazzini cardiolipin test, which was adopted by the United States Public Health Service.

Mazzini also owned the College Inn on Michigan Street, across from Long Hospital. The inn was a popular gathering place for medical and dental students; today a plaque honoring Mazzini occupies a spot at its former location.

NANCY PIPPEN ECKERMAN
Indiana University School of Medicine

MCL Cafeterias. Largest privately held cafeteria chain in the country. MCL was founded in 1950 by Indianapolis cousins Charles McGaughey and George Laughner. A third partner, Charles Chandler, later joined the cofounders. MCL opened its first restaurant, which no longer exists, in 1950 at 38th Street and Sherman Drive, then on the city's northside. Two years later a second cafeteria was opened on the eastside. During the 1960s MCL continued to expand, opening out-of-town and out-of-state cafeterias. In 1973 Laughner retired from the business, and the next year McGaughey bought out Laughner's share of the enterprise. Chandler sold his interest in the company in 1984, at which point MCL became wholly owned by the McGaughey family. In 1987 Craig McGaughey, son of the cofounder, purchased all outstanding shares of the company from relatives to became MCL's sole owner. In 1993 MCL had 28 cafeterias in four midwestern states—Indiana, Ohio, Illinois, and Michigan.

DEBORAH B. MARKISOHN

Meadows. Eastside neighborhood bounded by Fall Creek, Sherman Drive, and 38th and 46th streets. FALL CREEK and the railroad originally hindered commercial and residential development in the area now known as Meadows. A sudden demand for housing after 1945, however, brought significant development as single-family homes and multi-family apartment complexes were built for middle and upper class residents. The largest of the apartment complexes was Meadowbrook (1953), a 40–acre development with 56 buildings. Shops and offices were also constructed, such as the Meadows Shopping Center (1956–1957) on 38th Street. It was the first of its kind in Indianapolis, offering branches of downtown department stores, a supermarket, retail shops, and parking spaces for 2,000 cars.

By the 1980s the Meadows neighborhood was in decline as newer suburbs and SHOPPING MALLS drew residents. A neighborhood organization, the Meadows–Fall Creek Civic League, pressed city officials and business leaders to infuse new life into the community. In 1989–1990, the HEALTH AND HOSPITAL CORPORATION purchased a vacant building for offices and clinics and the area was designated as an urban enterprise zone. Pentecostal Assemblies of the World Church, a property owner, announced plans to build a new shopping complex with a Cub Foods anchor store, and in the early 1990s governmental leaders continued to seek ways to revitalize the area.

CATHLEEN F. DONNELLY

Medical Research. In the late 1800s, Louis Pasteur and Robert Koch led successful efforts by European scientists to identify specific disease organisms, which laid the basis for further research in preventing and curing these diseases. In America, pharmacology was developing as experiments were conducted to determine the effects of specific drugs on cells. In Indianapolis, ELI LILLY AND COMPANY (Lilly), founded in 1876, joined these research efforts in 1886 with the hiring of the company's first full-time chemist. Lilly introduced a new drug for treating venereal disease and invited hospitals to provide information on the drug's effectiveness, marking initial efforts in clinical research.

INDIANA UNIVERSITY SCHOOL OF MEDICINE (established in 1903) also conducted research early in its history, including studies by Dr. George Bond on electroencephalography and by Dr. WALTER BRUETSCH on malaria treatment for syphilis. LOUIS MAZZINI developed a test for syphilis. A laboratory for experimental surgery was established by Dr. WILLIS D. GATCH.

In 1922, Lilly and University of Toronto scientists worked collaboratively to develop INSULIN, which was soon in worldwide use for the treatment of diabetes. In 1926 the Lilly Laboratory for Clinical Research (now based at WISHARD MEMORIAL HOSPITAL) opened as a site for clinical testing of new drugs on patients in collaboration with major medical research institutions around the world. Lilly played a major role in the development and production of the first penicillin in the early 1940s and the Salk vaccine for polio in the mid–1950s.

After 1950, medical research in Indianapolis expanded to include a broad range of basic, clinical, and applied studies conducted in university, independent nonprofit, and corporate settings. External research funding at the INDIANA UNIVERSITY MEDICAL CENTER grew rapidly; in FY 1992 over $63 million in external funding, including grants and contracts, was awarded to the School of Medicine alone. New facilities completed at RILEY HOSPITAL FOR CHILDREN in the 1950s became the focus for major research on children's diseases and disabilities, including innovative health care delivery methods. Specialized research centers were developed for cancer, arthritis, diabetes, psychiatry, hypertension, medical genetics, alcoholism, Alzheimer's disease, general clinical research, and sexually transmitted diseases. The Krannert Institute of Cardiology, created in 1963, developed an international reputation for its cardiovascular research. The Regenstrief Institute, founded in 1969, conducts research in improved treatment programs using industrial engineering and computer techniques. The Oral Health Research Institute was founded in 1971 at the School of Dentistry to conduct preventive research. In the 1970s, testicular cancer research at the IUMC resulted in increasing the cure rate to more than 90 percent for the once-deadly disease, while research on voice restoration in cancer patients led to the development of an internationally recognized voice prosthesis.

METHODIST HOSPITAL'S Department of Medical Research, founded in 1956, conducted studies leading to the development of an artificial kidney in 1966, one of the first of its kind in the country. Other research led to the first kidney transplant in Indiana in 1972, the first heart transplant in the country by a non-university hospital in 1982, the first clinical research on the lithotripter (kidney stone crusher) by an American hospital in 1984, and Indiana's first artificial heart transplant in 1987.

Lilly developed the world's first cephalosporin antibiotic in 1964, introducing a whole new class of drugs, and the world's first pharmaceutical product based on recombinant DNA technology in 1982, its human insulin product. In recent years research at Lilly has focused on treatments for cancer, cardiovascular disease, central nervous system disorders, diabetes, pulmonary conditions, skeletal diseases, and infections. Lilly has also diversified its research efforts since the late 1970s to include the development of medical instruments and diagnostic products.

Medical research centers in Indianapolis developed rapidly in the 1970s and 1980s. The Indianapolis Center for Advanced Research, founded in 1972 as an independent nonprofit research center, conducts medical instrumentation research and is a national leader in ultrasonic research. The WALTHER CANCER INSTITUTE, founded in 1985, conducts basic, clinical, and patient care research in cancer through affiliations such as the Walther Oncology Center at the IUMC. The Biomechanics and Biomaterials Research Center, a recent collaborative effort by the schools of Medicine, Dentistry, and Science at IU and the Purdue School of Engineering and Technology, conducts bone and biomaterials research, including experiments on a recent space shuttle flight. The BOEHRINGER MANNHEIM CORPORATION began Indianapolis operations in 1974 and conducts research on enzyme technology, proteins, and genetic engineering related to its production of chemical reagents and biochemicals for research use by universities and bioengineering firms. CardioVascular Laser Systems, a subsidiary of Biomet, USA, which specializes in the research

and development of medical lasers, and Marion Merrell Dow, which conducts pharmaceutical research, recently entered the Indianapolis market.

The work being done in the various settings combines to make Indianapolis a nationally important center for medical research. It also makes a very substantial contribution to the economy of central Indiana.

STEPHEN E. KIRCHHOFF

Charles A. Bonsett, M.D., ed., *The I.U. Physician* (Indianapolis, 1978); E. J. Kahn, Jr., *All in a Century* (Indianapolis, 1976); Kenneth E. Reed and Edward A. Leary, *A Mission of Compassionate Health Care* (Indianapolis, 1984).

Medical Schools. Medicine was taught by the preceptor (apprenticeship) system in Indiana throughout most of the 19th century. The state's first successful medical school commenced in 1841 at La Porte, and existed until 1856. Its graduates included William Henry Wishard, father of WILLIAM NILES WISHARD, SR., for whom WISHARD MEMORIAL HOSPITAL is named; William Mayo, who would later found the Mayo Clinic in Minnesota; and William Lomax, whose bequest would provide for construction in 1895 of a modern medical school building. The Lomax Building, located on Senate Avenue at the northwest corner of Market Street, was variously the home of Indiana University School of Medicine (1908–1918), the State Board of Health, and the State Highway Commission. It was razed in 1961.

The first proprietary school in Indianapolis was Indiana Central Medical College (1849–1852), associated with Asbury College (now DePauw University) and located in a brick structure on East Washington Street. JOHN S. BOBBS, a pioneer city physician, served as dean, and an 1851 graduate was Joshua T. Belles, maternal grandfather of Britain's prime minister from 1956 to 1963, Harold Macmillan.

There were no medical schools in Indiana between 1852 and 1869. Bobbs and others launched a more successful school in 1869, the Indiana Medical College. Its initial session was held in the old STATE HOUSE, and following sessions were held in a building that existed until 1969 at the northwest corner of Delaware and

The Medical College of Indiana was an early proprietary school in the city.
[Indiana Historical Society, #C5747]

Court streets. An early graduate of this Delaware Street school (1871) was Harvey W. Wiley, author of the U.S. Pure Food and Drug Act.

In 1874 dissident faculty members from Indiana Medical College established the College of Physicians and Surgeons. The two schools reunited in 1878 under the name Medical College of Indiana. Its location, until the construction of the Lomax Building, was the northeast corner of Pennsylvania and Maryland streets.

In 1879 another dissident group formed the Central College of Physicians and Surgeons (1879–1905). In 1905 this group reunited with the Medical College of Indiana, and joined with the Fort Wayne College of Medicine (1879–1905), the name of the united schools being the Indiana Medical College. The purpose of the union was to create a state-supported medical school, which was initiated with Purdue University (1905–1907).

Indiana University began developing a medical school in 1903, achieving an excellent program for the first two years—the basic science years. By incorporating the teaching staff of the In-

diana Medical College into their program, Indiana University created an excellent four-year program, one of the few in the nation to receive praise in the 1910 Flexner report on medical education. (See INDIANA UNIVERSITY SCHOOL OF MEDICINE.)

Other medical schools in Indianapolis included the Physiomedical College (1873–1909), the Indiana College of Medicine and Midwifery (1877–1888), Indiana Eclectic Medical College (1880–1890), Beach Medical College (1883–1886), Eclectic College of Physicians and Surgeons (1890–1894), American Medical College (1894–1897), the University of Medicine (1897–1898), the Eclectic Medical College of Indiana (1900–1908), and the State College of Physicians and Surgeons (1906–1908), the latter being identified with Indiana University. Other Indiana medical schools were located in New Albany, Vincennes, Evansville, Marion, and Valparaiso. This plethora of schools was typical for the age. They varied from very good to very bad. The New Albany school, for example, was a fraudulent diploma mill. At the other extreme was the Physiomedical College, which was held in high esteem.

CHARLES A. BONSETT, M.D.
Indiana University School of Medicine

Medicine, Alternative. Because of the harsh remedies of bloodletting and purging employed during the early 19th century, many Indianapolis residents avoided physicians altogether. Home remedies passed down through the generations provided treatment for these people and also for those who could not afford medical fees or lived too far from a physician. Roots, herbs, and materials from surrounding forests and kitchen gardens were used to heal the sick or injured. Some settlers also employed Native American medical therapies.

Self-treatment was popular during the Jacksonian era. Indianapolis residents may have used home remedy books like Dr. C. Vanhook's *The Sick Man's Companion* (1832) published in Vincennes, Indiana. Samuel Thomson's (1767–1843) *New Guide to Health* also offered self-help to an estimated one of every six Americans in the

1830s. Thomson's botanical system of medical treatment featured use of steam baths and herbal medicines to restore the patient's loss of body heat, which he thought to be the cause of disease. Dr. Abner Pope, who came to Indianapolis in 1836, sold Thomsonian products like *Lobelia inflata*, cayenne pepper, prickly ash, and other botanicals at Pope's Drug Store. He prescribed steam baths and encouraged the formation of Thomsonian "Friendly Botanic Societies" to promote Thomson's course of treatments.

By adopting some of the practices of traditional medicine that were successful in treating disease, the Thomsonians spawned two sects that gained adherents in Indianapolis and elsewhere. The Eclectics used methods of medical treatment from any source if it was effective and the Physio-Medicals used highly concentrated doses of botanic medicine in treating illness. Both shunned mineral-based medicines, use of toxic materials, and bloodletting. However, they agreed that formal medical education was desirable. Both groups published medical journals and formed medical societies in Indiana and had practitioners in Indianapolis. The Eclectic Medical Association was organized in Indianapolis in 1857. In 1878 it began the *Indiana Medical Eclectic Quarterly* and three years later established a medical college at Indiana Avenue and California Street. The Physio-Medicals convened in 1874 and decided to publish the *Physio-Medical Journal*. The editor, Dr. George Hasty, was the founder of the Physio-Medical College in Indianapolis.

One of the first physicians to practice medicine in pioneer Indianapolis was Dr. ISAAC COE. He was a traditional practitioner who converted to the practice of homeopathy later in his career. Homeopathy promoted exceedingly small doses of medicine prescribed on the "like cures like" principle. Medicines consisted of botanical substances instead of minerals, narcotics, or alcohol. Coe introduced Indianapolis to cinchona bark, the source of quinine, for treatment of the malarial fevers rampant in the community. Since epidemics were frequent and fevers always a menace, homeopathy offered a safer way to treat contagious illnesses than the allopathic methods of harsh chemicals and bloodletting. In an attempt to stop homeopaths from legally practicing medicine,

regular physicians refused homeopaths hospital privileges. Not until the 20th century did local Indianapolis homeopathic physicians gain hospital privileges and then these privileges were only available at ST. VINCENT HOSPITAL.

Despite regular medicine's attempt to limit homeopathy, it remained the second most popular form of medical care into the 20th century with its own medical schools and medical societies. The Indiana Institute of Homeopathy was formed in 1867 while the Marion County Homeopathic Society was organized in 1871. Both were located in Indianapolis.

The prevalence of endemic and contagious diseases in the Indianapolis area provided a climate for the sale of over-the-counter patent medicines advertised as cure-alls. These products were available and popular in the city from its earliest days until the advent of the Pure Food and Drug Act of 1906 and the Food, Drug and Cosmetic Act of 1938.

Promoting the control of patent medicines proved easier than control of osteopathy and chiropractic medical treatments, practices opposed by regular physicians and the American Medical Association. Chiropractic and osteopathic medical treatments depend upon manual manipulation of the muscles, tissue, and bones of patients by their practitioners. Osteopathists, who counted African-Americans and women in their ranks, first appeared in the Indianapolis city directory in 1904, with eight listings including the Spaunhurst Institute of Osteopathy in the State Life Building. Although the American Medical Association fought hard to eliminate the legal practice of osteopathy from its inception, the practitioners eventually accepted the system of regular medicine and added it to their educational requirements. Today osteopathists prescribe medications and perform surgery, unlike chiropractics. WESTVIEW HOSPITAL, the first osteopathic hospital in Indianapolis, opened in 1975.

Chiropractic treatment was based on the theory that the misalignment of the nervous system caused disease. Realignment by chiropractic manipulation of the vertebrae was the prescribed cure. By 1906 a school had been established in Davenport, Iowa, for chiropractic training. Chiropractors first appeared in Indianapolis soon afterward and by the mid–20th century chiropractic treatment was widely available to local residents. Although orthodox medicine also branded it a quack cure, chiropractic medicine today is well established.

Other nontraditional health care systems that claimed to cure disease also made their appearances in Indianapolis. Mesmerism was based on the notion that disease stemmed from an imbalance of an invisible electrical magnetic fluid in the patients' bodies. Mesmerists gained considerable popularity in the 19th century and expanded their following in the 20th century when various electrical devices like the Radioclast and the Master Violet Ray Kit were used to treat patients. These devices eventually became illegal when their effectiveness and safety could not be demonstrated to the scientific community. The followers of Mesmer in Indianapolis in the 1840s gave lectures and demonstrations of cures for illnesses by the use of magnetized rods. The subjects responded to the ritualistic method of mesmerism by becoming hypnotized. Elaborate claims of cures for disease were attributed to this hypnotherapy along with other cures which seemed to hold promise.

By the late 19th century hydropathy, or water-cure therapy, increased in use as an alternative to the bloodletting of the conventional physicians in Europe and the United States. Water cures originally consisted of wrapping patients in wet sheets. Practitioners also promoted treatment such as imbibing pure water as well as mineral water and applying water externally through ice pack treatment, wet pack treatment, steam bath treatment, and sitz baths. Late in the century Indianapolis residents could take the waters at Mudlavia in Warren County, French Lick, West Baden, or Trinity Springs in Martin County, and numerous other spas throughout the state. Adherents drank both pure and mineral bottled water. Bottled water offered a safer source of drinking water than the public water supply until the Indianapolis Water Company succeeded in offering safer drinking water around the turn of the century. In 1899 the Mount Jackson Sanitarium opened in Indianapolis on West Washington Street. The owners claimed that the mineral well located there could cure rheumatism, dyspepsia, and nervous prostration, as well as liver, blood, skin, and stomach troubles.

Phrenology was another alternative medical practice available in 19th century Indianapolis. This movement postulated that a direct relationship existed between personality and the shape and size of the brain. CALVIN FLETCHER, the prominent Indianapolis pioneer and attorney, was familiar with the ideas of phrenology. He and his family and friends attended numerous lectures by phrenologists who traveled to Indianapolis to analyze the heads of local citizens. HENRY WARD BEECHER, minister at Second Presbyterian Church, was an early convert to phrenology through Orson and Lorenzo Fowler, founders of the movement. (Orson Fowler was Beecher's classmate at Amherst College.)

Two significant religious movements claimed to be able to cure disease if members followed their belief systems. By the 1880s Mary Baker Eddy formalized as Christian Science her metaphysical healing by the "Divine Mind" cure for disease. The first listing for Christian Science practitioners in Indianapolis city directories appeared in 1911. Women were trained as practitioners and many women's names appear in Polk's directory through subsequent editions. Another religious healing movement that attracted adherents in Indianapolis was Seventh-Day Adventism, which established a church in 1863. Founder Ellen G. White's program of healing required Adventists to abstain from meat, tobacco, alcohol, and drugs, and from all but minimal sexual activity. White wrote books about her religious health reform principles, lectured on the American temperance circuit, and established health retreats and hospitals in the United States and beyond.

Mutual skepticism has characterized the relationship between conventional medicine and alternative health care theories from the early days of settlement in Indianapolis to the present. In spite of the vast improvement of conventional medicine, alternative health care treatment is still extremely popular. Major Indianapolis bookstores now have special sections to sell alternative health care information alongside information on traditional health care, and city directories list a wide range of alternative health care providers.

ANN BLUNK

Katherine Mandusic McDonell, *Medicine in Antebellum Indiana: Conflict, Conservatism and Change* (Indianapolis, 1982); Paul Starr, *The Social Transformation of American Medicine* (New York, 1982).

Melvin Simon and Associates. Real estate development and management corporation. By the early 1990s the Simon company was one of the largest and most successful developers of SHOPPING CENTERS in the country, owning and managing more than 147 centers in 30 states from its Indianapolis headquarters.

Melvin and Herbert Simon were born in Brooklyn and grew up in the Bronx, where their father was a tailor. Melvin, stationed with the army at FORT BENJAMIN HARRISON, remained in Indianapolis after service and accepted a $100 per week job leasing store space for the Eastgate Shopping Center, a mall which he would purchase in later years. In 1960, with his brother, he founded Melvin Simon and Associates.

The new company developed shopping plazas, and within five years was developing enclosed malls in communities throughout the country. Through the early 1980s the company focused on shopping center construction, then diversified into mixed-use projects, which are various combinations of retail stores, offices, hotels, restaurants, and entertainment components in a single complex. The Simons' first mixed-use project was the Two West Washington center in downtown Indianapolis, completed in 1983. Other notable examples include: A & S Plaza, a reconstruction of the former Gimbel's department store in Manhattan; Newport Centre, a $2 billion residential, office, and shopping community in New Jersey, across the Hudson River from New York City; Hollywood Promenade, which erected a hotel, stores, and museums on Hollywood Boulevard; and The Fashion Centre at Pentagon City, in suburban Washington, D.C.

The company is the managing partner in the Mall of America, which opened in 1992 in Bloomington, Minnesota, as the largest retail, hotel, and entertainment complex in the United States. It includes eight department stores, over 400 smaller shops, a seven-acre indoor amusement park, and a 1.2 million-gallon walk-through aquarium among its attractions.

Melvin Simon and Associates has shopping centers in more than a dozen Indiana cities. It owns or has an interest in numerous Indianapolis centers, including public-private partnership with the city in the development of the downtown CIRCLE CENTRE MALL.

RICHARD W. WORTH

Merchants National Bank. See National City Bank

Merchants National Bank Building. From its completion in 1913 until 1962 the Merchants National Bank was the tallest building in Indianapolis. Situated on the southeast corner of Meridian and Washington streets, the 17-story Chicago School building was designed by Daniel H. Burnham. Built of Kittaning brick, Indiana limestone, and architectural terra cotta over a steel skeleton, it was constructed in two phases beginning in 1904. The original four-story structure forms the banking hall and first three floors of the building, with the principal facade facing west on Meridian Street. The north (Washington Street) facade incorporated the Merchants National Bank Annex built in 1938 by F. W. Woolworth from two earlier buildings. At that time an Art Moderne limestone facade was added; it was altered in 1969 by the Kirk Furniture Company. The structures are connected to the original building on the upper floors. By the early 1990s the facade was in a state of deterioration. The roof was once used by city firemen to check the area for fires and is the site of the tower used to transmit the first television broadcast in Indiana in 1949.

Of particular interest is the extensive use of green Georgia marble and ornamental bronze in the banking hall. The bank counters are formed of marble, as are eight Doric columns supporting the coffered ceiling and second story balcony. Ornamental bronze is found in six globe ceiling lights, teller cages, and counter screens of statuary bronze decorated with shields and rosettes. The U-shaped structure also contains a 16-story open well, an ornamental iron and marble stairway with the original marble wainscoting, as well as many other original interior details designed by Burnham. The Merchants National Bank Building was listed on the National Register of Historic Places in 1982.

RITA W. HARLAN

The City and the Bank, 1865–1965 (Indianapolis: privately printed, 1965).

Merchants Plaza (115 West Washington Street). High-rise office building with hotel, restaurants, and shops. Located on the site of the Lincoln Hotel, demolished in 1973, the Merchants Plaza complex, designed by J V III of Houston, was built over the vacated right-of-way of Kentucky Avenue at Washington Street. At the time the largest single privately developed project in the state's history, the square-block complex consists of twin 15–story office towers, trapezoidal in plan, offices of NATIONAL CITY BANK (formerly Merchants National Bank, hence the name of the complex), the 535–room Hyatt Regency Hotel, underground parking, and restaurants and shops on the first three levels. Groundbreaking occurred in November, 1974, with construction completed in early 1977.

At the time it was built, the atrium—the 19–story-tall inner lobby which is a Hyatt trademark—was one of the largest enclosed spaces in the country. Through the use of angular exterior walls and entrances positioned on the diagonal, the project reflects the flow of traffic that once traveled over this block. A triangular landscaped plaza sits at the mid-block Washington Street entrance. The 20th floor's revolving circular restaurant affords one of the few public places to enjoy a panoramic view of the city's downtown.

MARY ELLEN GADSKI

Meridian Hills. Northside town bounded by Williams Creek, College Avenue, 71st/64th streets, and Spring Mill Road. Residential development in Meridian Hills began as early as the 1920s and 1930s, when affluent families built homes in the countryside to escape Indianapolis taxes and traffic. Residents voted for incorpora-

tion in 1937, seeking stricter ZONING laws to keep out nonresidential development. Since then the town has been governed by a three-member council consisting of a president and two members elected to serve four-year terms. Meridian Hills maintains its special status as an INCLUDED TOWN under UNIGOV.

In the 1950s and early 1960s, several religious organizations battled opposition from the zoning board to build in Meridian Hills. Two cases eventually went to the Indiana Supreme Court, which permitted construction. Today, the Indianapolis Hebrew Congregation, SECOND PRESBYTERIAN CHURCH, First Congregational Church, and St. Luke's Catholic Church are integral parts of the community.

Most of the land has been developed exclusively for residences, though the town also boasts the campus of PARK TUDOR SCHOOL and Meridian Hills Country Club. Built in 1924–1925, the club serves as an unofficial town hall and a meeting place for the council. Today, Meridian Hills counts 1,800 residents. The town continues to retain its status as a quiet enclave of upper middle class homes.

CATHLEEN F. DONNELLY

Meridian-Kessler. Northside neighborhood bounded by Kessler Boulevard, the former Monon Railroad corridor, 38th Street, and the east side of Meridian Street. The neighborhood's name, derived from its western and northern boundaries, originated in 1965 when residents established the Meridian-Kessler Neighborhood Association (MKNA) to halt "white flight" caused by African-American families moving into the all-white area.

As Indianapolis was being platted in 1821 farmers established farms and orchards in this region north of the nascent city. The area flourished throughout the 19th century. Although the rural population remained small, direct roads—Sugar Flat Road (Central Avenue), the Indianapolis Road (Meridian Street), and Westfield Road (Westfield Boulevard)—connected the area to the capital city. Two homes remain from those earliest years—the Hardin House, ca. 1832 (4644 North Central Avenue), and the Oliver Johnson House, ca. 1862

(4456 North Park Avenue). Twenty-seven homes constructed prior to 1900 still exist in the neighborhood.

Indianapolis residents moved steadily northward after 1900. By the 1920s the area was subdivided although not completely built. By this time, however, the emerging neighborhood had become a prestigious address for community and business leaders as well as for those aspiring to influence. The neighborhood's western edge boasted large homes, many of near mansion proportions, on sizable wooded lots. Homes become more modestly middle class toward the eastern edge where bungalows are predominant. Meridian-Kessler also has a number of small apartment buildings located primarily along the major thoroughfares of 38th Street and College Avenue but also scattered along Washington Boulevard, Central Avenue, and Pennsylvania Street.

Commercial centers developed at 49th and Pennsylvania streets and along College Avenue at each major intersection to Kessler Boulevard, providing local residents with groceries, shops, and service stations. Neighborhood businesses continue to occupy many of the original structures.

Education has been a part of the neighborhood from the 1820s when a Mr. Hawkins held classes in his log cabin at 46th Street and Central Avenue. Since 1854 a public school has been located at that site, including the present Mary Nicholson School No. 70. Henry Coburn School No. 66, built at 38th Street and Broadway Street in 1914, served the area until 1979 and was converted to senior citizens housing (1991). Joseph J. Bingham School No. 84, located at 57th Street and Central Avenue, opened in 1928. Two parochial schools serve the neighborhood—St. Joan of Arc (1921) and Immaculate Heart of Mary (1948).

Influential members of Indianapolis' professional and business communities have resided in Meridian-Kessler, including HERBERT L. BASS, ALBERT J. BEVERIDGE, LEE BURNS, E. Howard Cadle, FRANCES FARMER, FRANK MCKINNEY "KIN" HUBBARD, JOSIAH K. LILLY, JR., and MEREDITH NICHOLSON. Meridian Street between 40th Street and Kessler Boulevard, which bisects the Meridian-Kessler and BUTLER-TARKINGTON neighborhoods, was placed on the National Register of Historic Places in 1986.

In recent years Meridian-Kessler has embarked upon extensive redevelopment activities in its southeastern quadrant. MKNA secured a police precinct station and fire station at 42nd Street and College Avenue, and has sponsored numerous neighborhood stabilization programs.

SHERYL D. VANDERSTEL

Paul C. Diebold, "History of the Architecture of the Meridian-Kessler Neighborhood " (M.S. thesis, Ball State University, 1988); David J. Bodenhamer et al., *The Main Stem* (Indianapolis, 1993); *Indianapolis Architecture* (Indianapolis, 1975).

Merrill, Catharine (Jan. 24, 1824–May 30, 1900). Teacher and author. Born at Corydon, Indiana, the old state capital, Catharine Merrill was the daughter of SAMUEL MERRILL who, as state treasurer, helped move the state offices to the wilderness capital of Indianapolis. Primarily noted as a teacher, and revered by three generations of Indianapolis students, Merrill first operated a private school from the family home. She followed in the footsteps of her father, who—in addition to his civic duties—volunteered as a pioneer schoolmaster at the first Indianapolis Merrill home near the site of the Grand Hotel. The family later moved to an 80–acre farm that extended from 10th Street to North Indianapolis, along the MICHIGAN ROAD. The Catharine Merrill School was built on the site of the family home. She is also credited with arousing interest in the housing of women prisoners, and her efforts led to the Home for Friendless Women.

After teaching for a time at Cleveland, Ohio—where a number of her Indianapolis pu-

Catharine Merrill at age 27. [Indiana Historical Society, #C170]

pils followed her—Merrill spent two years of study in Europe. Many of her letters from this period were saved by the Catharine Merrill Club and later published in a volume arranged by Katharine Merrill Graydon in 1934.

During the CIVIL WAR she was actively involved in war work, including service as a nurse in the field. After the war Governor OLIVER P. MORTON personally recruited her to write a history of Indiana's soldiers in the conflict. *The Soldier of Indiana in the War for the Union* (2 vols., 1866, 1869) contains biographical material not available elsewhere and has been ranked as the most comprehensive history of the state's part in the Civil War.

In 1869, OVID BUTLER endowed the Demia Butler chair of English literature at North Western Christian University (now BUTLER UNIVERSITY). The endowment was to provide funds for a woman teacher and was named in honor of his daughter, the first female graduate. Butler invited Merrill to accept the position; she did so and taught at the college until 1885. At that time, she resumed teaching the private classes so in demand by old and new students, continuing to do so until April, 1890.

MEREDITH NICHOLSON described Merrill as a "Bringer of the Light" in *The Hoosiers* (1915); David Starr Jordan, who taught at Butler College in 1879, wrote that Merrill's "uplifting influence" lived beyond her generation; and JOHN MUIR, who called Merrill's gifts "rare," credited her with being a "builder of character" and observed that to know her "was a liberal education." Muir's comments and some short literary studies appear in the posthumously published *The Man Shakespeare and Other Essays by Catharine Merrill* (1902).

ANN COLBERT
Indiana University–Purdue University,
Fort Wayne

———

Charity Dye, *Some Torch Bearers in Indiana* (Indianapolis, 1917); Katharine Merrill Graydon, *Catharine Merrill: Life and Letters* (Greenfield, Ind., 1934).

Merrill, Samuel (Oct. 29, 1792–Aug. 24, 1855). Politician and businessman. Born in Peacham, Vermont, Merrill attended Dartmouth College from 1812 to 1813, then left to teach school and study law at York, Pennsylvania. In 1816, he moved to Vevay, Indiana, where he was admitted to the bar in 1817.

Merrill represented Switzerland County in the Indiana General Assembly from 1819 to 1822. In 1822, he was elected state treasurer and moved to Corydon, the temporary state capital. He held this position until 1834. After the legislature chose a permanent capital site, Merrill suggested the name "Indianapolis," although the name is formally attributed to Jeremiah Sullivan. In October, 1824, Merrill took 11 days to move state documents, silver from the state treasury, and a printing press from Corydon to Indianapolis. From 1834 to 1843 he served as president of the State Bank. Merrill was president of the MADISON AND INDIANAPOLIS RAILROAD from 1844 to 1848, one of whose trains was the first to enter Indianapolis.

In his leisure time, Merrill compiled the third edition of the *Indiana Gazetteer* (1850). He purchased Hood and Noble's Bookstore in 1850 and began the Merrill Publishing Company, which evolved into the BOBBS-MERRILL COMPANY. Merrill was the founder of both the Young Men's Literary Society and of the city's first Athenaeum. He was a cofounder of SECOND PRESBYTERIAN CHURCH and served as president of the INDIANA HISTORICAL SOCIETY, the Indiana Colonization Society, and the Indianapolis Temperance Society. Merrill was also a trustee of Wabash College.

DAVID SABOL

———

Biographical Directory of the Indiana General Assembly, Vol. 1 (Indianapolis, 1980).

Mess, George Jo (June 30, 1898–June 24, 1962). Artist and teacher. Mess was born in Cincinnati but grew up in Indianapolis, where his family settled in 1899. He attended ARSENAL TECHNICAL HIGH SCHOOL, graduating in 1916. While still in high school he became a scholarship student at the HERRON SCHOOL OF ART, where he came under the influence of the respected teacher MARIE C. TODD and Indiana artists OTTO STARK and WILLIAM FORSYTH. Following high school, he continued to paint in Forsyth's night classes at Herron.

Further training eventually included the study of design under Arthur W. Dow at Columbia University's Teachers College. In the summer of 1929 Mess studied fresco, landscape, and figure painting in France. Back in the United States he won a Louis C. Tiffany Fellowship for a summer of painting at the Tiffany estate in 1931, and subsequently studied at the School of Design in Chicago.

Possibly Mess's most practical instruction in art came from Evelynne Bernloehr (b. 1903), whom he married in 1925. Self-taught in printmaking until she studied etching at Fontainebleau with the French master engraver-printer Achile Ouvre, she was well qualified to pass on her knowledge of the craft. Indeed, the two were partners in art for the rest of their years together, with Evelynne often providing technical assistance during George's printmaking. Between 1935 and his death in 1962, he created 164 aquatints, one etching, one mezzotint, and three block prints.

Mess also taught drawing and oil and watercolor painting privately and at the Circle Art Academy in Indianapolis (with emphasis on commercial art), as well as at the couple's Ox Bow Acres Art Studio in Brown County, Indiana. In addition, he taught at the Wayman Adams summer school in the Adirondacks, INDIANAPOLIS ART LEAGUE, John Herron Art Institute, and the Indianapolis campus of Indiana University.

For the most part Mess portrayed familiar, everyday scenes, persons, and places. His style found favor both within the region and elsewhere, and he received numerous awards over a 25-year period. His works may be found among the collections of many institutions, including: Philadelphia Museum of Art, Library of Congress, Cleveland Museum of Art, Metropolitan Museum of Art (New York), INDIANAPOLIS MUSEUM OF ART, INDIANA STATE MUSEUM, INDIANA UNIVERSITY MEDICAL CENTER, and Broad Ripple High School, Indianapolis.

JUNE DuBOIS

June DuBois, *Indiana Artists George Jo and Evelynne Bernloehr Mess* (Indianapolis: Indiana Historical Society, 1985).

Metal Processing and Fabrication.
Blacksmiths and toolmakers were some of the earliest metal workers in Indianapolis. They shod horses, manufactured agricultural implements, and forged iron tools for the agrarian economy. By 1835 Robert Underhill established a successful iron foundry at Pennsylvania and Vermont streets which produced plows, andirons, and skillets, and later cast iron products, steam engines, and parts for railroad cars. With the arrival of the MADISON AND INDIANAPOLIS RAILROAD in 1847 the city's previously limited markets became much more accessible. Metal-related enterprises, in turn, increased dramatically as Indianapolis responded to the railroad industry's need for iron products and repair facilities.

Attorney CALVIN FLETCHER noted in October, 1852, that "some 5 or 6 machine shops and foundries" were in the city. The *Indianapolis Locomotive* in November, 1852, reported that these new establishments, "which employed some two hundred men," had increased Indianapolis' population and its contribution to the industry. Among the principal manufacturers of the period were the Eagle Machine Works (threshing equipment and agricultural implements), the Washington Foundry (steam engines and threshing machines), along with other machine works, boilermakers, and stove manufacturers. Although it initially floundered, the Indianapolis Rolling Mill, which began shaping iron railroad rails in 1857, became an important industry within a decade.

By the 1860s iron manufacturers constituted the largest of all Indianapolis industries in capital invested, number of workers, value of product, and value added. The local economy supported blacksmiths, wagon makers, machine shops, a stove manufacturer, and toolmakers. In response to the CIVIL WAR, a cartridge production facility was set up on the State House grounds. Work began in April, 1861, to supply Hoosier troops, as well as those from other states, with ammunition. The next year the arsenal moved to East Washington Street. The 1870s showed continued diversification of the city's iron industries, with several new ventures—a pump manufacturer, brass works, tinware shops, plow makers, lightning rod manufacturers, railroad car production, hardware manufacturers, and a lamp maker.

During the ensuing decade industrialization increased rapidly. The 1880 manufacturing census recorded that the city's iron and steel–related industries produced over $3.8 million worth of products and employed over 2,200 people. By 1884 Indianapolis boasted 48 blacksmiths, 14 tinware manufacturers, 4 ornamental iron works, several copperware makers, and a cutlery specialist. Numerous metal-related businesses began or expanded operations during this decade, including E. C. Atkins and Company saw works, Parry Manufacturing, Indianapolis Frog and Switch Company, National Malleable & Steel Castings Company, Pioneer Brass Works, Atlas Engine Works, William Langsenkamp's copper business, and C. & G. Potts & Company, an iron and steel foundry. NORDYKE AND MARMON, which specialized in gristmill machinery, employed 300 people and reported annual production worth over $600,000. By this time many of the companies recruited and employed immigrants to work in the factories, thereby contributing to the rapidly growing economy as well as to the emerging ethnic enclaves surrounding the places of employment.

Indianapolis again proved important in the transportation industry in the 1890s, producing both bicycles and bicycle parts at nine local shops. By the early 1900s the city's automobile manufacturers such as Cole, MARMON, and DUESENBERG had become principal consumers of metal and metal products. The industry generated a vast complementary industry of automotive parts manufacturing which continued to be a significant part of the city's economy for many years despite the loss of automobile manufacturers and the emergence of Detroit as the nation's automobile capital.

Metal industries had clearly become more diversified by the 1930s. Principal manufacturers included the Akron Surgical House (surgical instruments), the Baur Tack Company (tacks and staples), Central States Bridge and Structural Company (structural steel), DIAMOND CHAIN COMPANY (chains and sprockets), Indiana Canning Machine Company (canning equipment), Isley Manufacturing Company (concrete machinery), and Universal Gear Corporation (transmissions, clutches, and machine parts). In the early 1940s the city geared up to meet wartime demands. The Bridge-port Brass facility opened on the city's west side, producing ammunition for the U.S. Army. STEWART-WARNER's Indianapolis plant manufactured field stoves, aircraft heaters, and bomb detonating mechanisms for the military.

By the 1950s machinery manufacturing and the automotive parts and accessories business were Indianapolis' leading industries. Important metal-related industries included the Indianapolis Drop Forging Company (tanks and specialty metal products), Sonith Industries (specialty iron castings), heating equipment manufacturers Hall-Neal Furnace Company and the Peerless Furnace and Foundry, the INDIANA GEAR WORKS (transmissions and other aircraft equipment), the Merz Engineering Company (jet aircraft), and Hetherington & Benner (boilers, fabricated structural steel, and road construction equipment such as asphalt mixing machines). City foundries produced steel, iron, copper, brass, magnesium, and aluminum during the decade and more than 160 machine shops were in operation.

By the 1960s national economic trends strongly affected Indianapolis. National Malleable and Steel Castings closed and hundreds of city residents were out of work. CHRYSLER and WESTERN ELECTRIC soon followed. By the early 1980s other large manufacturing facilities in the city had closed, and jobs were lost in the automotive and machine tool industries although both businesses continued to employ many Indianapolis workers.

As of the early 1990s important Indianapolis firms involved in metal processing and fabrication included Allison Gas Turbine Operations (gas turbine engines), Allison Transmissions (heavy duty transmissions), GM Truck and Bus Operations (body stamping for trucks), FORD MOTOR COMPANY (automotive components), NAVISTAR INTERNATIONAL (diesel engines), Carrier Corporation (heating and cooling equipment), Amtrak (rail car maintenance and refurbishing), Chrysler Corporation Foundry (engine blocks), Jenn-Air (ventilating equipment, ovens, ranges), OLIN BRASS (brass and copper products), Rexnord (chains and bearings), Best Lock (locks), and Diamond Chain Company (roller chains).

DEBORAH B. MARKISOHN

Methodist Hospital of Indiana. Largest hospital in Indiana. Methodist began as, and remains, a ministry of the Methodist church. In July, 1899, Indianapolis hosted the Fourth Annual International Convention of the Epworth League of the Methodist Episcopal Church, which brought more than 10,000 delegates to the city. The convention was such a success that after all the bills were paid, $4,750 (a substantial sum in those days) remained in the convention fund. The convention committee donated the money to a building fund for the construction of a new hospital for the city of Indianapolis, an action approved by the Indiana Conference. Rev. Leslie J. Naftzger was elected the first president of the board of trustees.

The cornerstone for the first building was laid on October 25, 1905, at the building site at Capitol Avenue and 16th Street (then Tinker Street), earlier a baseball park for the Indianapolis Indians. Completed in April, 1908, at a cost of $225,000, the new hospital had 65 beds, 37 private rooms, four large wards, and three small wards. The three-story fireproof structure boasted modern surgical rooms with floors and walls of white glass. The hospital had portable bathtubs, plumbing equipped with pedal action, dumbwaiters operated by pushbuttons, and a call system of signal lights that "eliminated the continuous noise of clanging bells." Singled out for special praise, the new "plunger type" hospital elevator worked by means of water pressure and was large enough to hold a patient litter. A handwritten report in 1909 declared that 880 patients were cared for at Methodist in its first full year of operation. The hospital's emphasis on training also began early, with two interns and a group of nurses in training the first year.

The hospital opened its first X-ray department in 1909. Dr. Albert M. Cole installed one of the earliest X-ray machines in a tiny, unused hospital room. The device used a Crookes gas tube and heavy glass plates. Because the hospital had no facilities for developing the plates, they had to be taken downtown, usually by a messenger on the electric streetcar, to Dr. Cole's office for processing. Methodist Hospital's long and continuing relationship with the INDIANAPOLIS MOTOR SPEEDWAY was also established early when doctors and

Completed in 1908, this brand new Methodist Hospital building (since demolished) had 65 beds. [Indiana Historical Society, Bass Collection, #C884]

nurses from Methodist were stationed at the track in case of emergencies.

Almost before the first building was completed Methodist Hospital needed to expand its facilities. In 1910 the board of trustees voted to add two pavilions at a cost of $250,000. By 1916 both of the pavilions were in operation and the number of beds had increased to 250, making the hospital the largest in the state, a ranking it retained in the early 1990s with over 1,100 beds. In 1933 Mary Hanson Carey donated the hospital's most famous landmark, the Lighthouse of Health Beacon which sits atop one of the older buildings.

In concert with ELI LILLY AND COMPANY, Methodist Hospital was one of the primary centers for clinical research in the use of INSULIN to treat diabetes mellitus, beginning in August, 1922, when the first units of insulin were given to its patients. Clinical research in diabetes was only the beginning of many areas of research achievement for the institution. On October 30, 1982, the hospital recorded its first heart transplant (the first in a private hospital anywhere in the world). On February 23, 1984, the hospital was site of the nation's first use of an extracorporeal shock wave lithotripter, a device that pulverizes kidney stones using shock waves. Methodist remains a world leader in lithotripsy and other innovative treatments for kidney stones. In the early 1990s the institution began to decentralize some of its services by locating several outpatient centers near the I-465 beltway. Through the years such innovative programs have given Methodist a leading role in health care in the community, the state, and the region.

MARY BETH MOSTER

Kenneth E. Reed and Edward A. Leary, *A Mission of Compassionate Health Care: The History of Methodist Hospital of Indiana, Inc.* (Indianapolis, [1984]).

Methodists. This Protestant movement had an early and formative influence on Indianapolis. In several forms local Methodists helped create community life for the city's white middle class, its German-speaking minority, and its African-American population. As they established extensive networks of churches and missions, organized Methodists also founded many major Indianapolis institutions, including METHODIST HOSPITAL and the UNIVERSITY OF INDIANAPOLIS. Today, local Methodist churches and agencies provide city residents with a wealth of social services in addition to ministering to their spiritual needs. While in recent years the local membership has declined along with that of most mainline churches, when taken together the various Methodist congregations constitute the city's largest single Protestant grouping.

Four different Methodist denominations have churches in Indianapolis: the African Methodist Episcopal Church, the African Methodist Episcopal Zion Church, the Christian Methodist Episcopal Church, and the United Methodist Church. Together they have 84 churches and missions in Marion County and approximately 37,500 members. In addition, several Indianapolis churches are affiliated with Holiness denominations, which share a Methodist heritage.

All Methodist denominations have roots in the work of John Wesley, an 18th-century Anglican reformer. Wesley directed his emotional evangelism primarily at the poor, emphasizing religious experience and moral conduct over doctrinal sophistication and ritual. He preached free will and the obligation to strive for holiness and Christian perfection. The lay organization Wesley set up in England spread to America in the 1760s and became the Methodist Episcopal Church in 1784, after the Revolution made continued connection with the Church of England impossible. The core of this new church was a tightly knit group of itinerant preachers who maintained an expanding network of preaching circuits projecting far into the frontier.

The Methodist Episcopal Church (M.E.) is the direct forerunner of the present United Methodist Church (U.M.) and was the first Methodist group in Indianapolis. M.E. itinerant preacher William Cravens reached Indianapolis in 1821 and organized a local society or class meeting as part of a central Indiana circuit. Beginning with only seven members, it was the town's first religious congregation of any kind and provided early residents with a base of social and religious life.

An emphasis on evangelism characterized local Methodism in the early 19th century. Local M.E. clergymen such as John Strange, Alan Wiley, and James Havens won fame as powerful evangelists at frequent camp meetings and other extended revivals that swelled church membership. In 1828 the Indianapolis congregation was taken off the circuit and given its own minister. The next year it built Wesley Chapel on the corner of the Circle and Meridian Street. In 1842, when local membership topped 600, Indianapolis got its second Methodist Episcopal congregation, which erected Roberts Chapel in 1846 at Pennsylvania and Market streets. More churches and missions quickly followed.

As the Methodist Episcopal Church grew and prospered with Indianapolis, it gradually came to represent the values of the upwardly mobile middle class. Churches acquired choirs, organs, and stained glass windows. Congregations began to demand an educated clergy. By the end of the Civil War the rough evangelism of frontier Methodism was giving way to a quieter, more formal religiosity. Many members dissented and tried to preserve the older traditions, dividing some local congregations between rich and poor, but the more affluent and modernist elements prevailed. From the 1860s local Methodist growth was offset slightly by defections to other denominations, especially HOLINESS CHURCHES, that attempted to maintain the style of old-fashioned Methodism.

From the 1880s through the 1920s the M.E. Church devoted much of its energy to reforming society. Indianapolis Methodists espoused causes from public education to Sabbatarianism. Above all, they battled against the use of alcoholic beverages and became deeply entwined in the TEMPERANCE AND PROHIBITION movements. Local

Methodist leaders played major roles in most of the large prohibitionist organizations, including the WOMEN'S CHRISTIAN TEMPERANCE UNION, the Anti-Saloon League, and the Prohibition party.

The M.E. Church and its successors have also tried to improve city life by providing services to the larger community. In 1908 Methodist Hospital, now the largest health care facility in the state, opened with 65 beds. Local Methodists brought GOODWILL INDUSTRIES to Indianapolis in 1928, and in 1937 established Fletcher Place Community Center on the city's southside. More recently, United Methodists established another community center in the BRIGHTWOOD area. In 1970 they opened the Lucille Raines Residence for Women, which houses a variety of women with special needs in a downtown apartment building.

To accommodate people outside its mainstream, the M.E. Church created ethnically distinct congregations. In the late 19th century it segregated Indianapolis African-Americans into several all-black congregations responsible to their own conference organization. This arrangement persisted until 1968 when the black churches joined the South Indiana Conference, along with the rest of the city's U.M. churches. While only three city congregations are significantly integrated, six predominantly black U.M. congregations remain active. They maintain a distinct identity, and relate their activities to the needs and culture of the city's African-American community. The Methodist Episcopal Church also had two German-speaking congregations in Indianapolis, attached to a German conference organization, but by 1940 these were integrated into the mainstream. Today, in addition to the black organizations, the United Methodist Church has one local Korean church.

Over the years a number of schisms rent the M.E. Church. Some persist in the form of competing Methodist denominations. Others mended in two major mergers that transformed the Methodist Episcopal Church into the United Methodist Church, Indianapolis' largest Protestant denomination. In 1830 the Methodist Protestant Church split away to set up a more democratic form of church government. In 1939, with these issues resolved, they reunited with their parent body along with the Methodist Episcopal Church, South, which had formed in 1844 when the issue of slavery divided the church. While Indianapolis had no Southern Methodist congregations, the Methodist Protestants brought two local churches into the newly formed Methodist Church.

In 1968 the United Methodist Church was created by the merger of the Methodist Church with the Evangelical United Brethren. The E.U.B. Church was itself the result of a merger of the Evangelical Church (formerly the Evangelical Association) with the Church of the United Brethren in Christ. Both these groups were formed early in the 19th century by German-speaking Americans who shared a similar style, theology, and organization with English-speaking Methodists. The first United Brethren congregation formed in 1850 and built its first church the following year at Ohio and New Jersey streets. In 1905 they established Indiana Central College—now the University of Indianapolis—just south of the city. The Evangelical Association's first local congregation came together in 1853 and erected a church on Ohio Street near its intersection with New Jersey in 1855. The two German denominations combined in 1946 to form the E.U.B. Church and later brought four Indianapolis congregations into the United Methodist fold.

As noted, the United Methodist Church remains the largest Protestant denomination in Indianapolis. In 1992 it included 62 churches in Marion County with approximately 29,000 members. Each local church sends its clergy and an equal number of lay delegates to the South Indiana Conference, which formally holds title to the local church property. The Indiana Area Bishop also has offices in the city, from which he presides over both the South and North Indiana Conferences. These bodies both send delegates to the quadrennial General Conference to make policy for the denomination. The U.M. Church is an important member of the CHURCH FEDERATION OF GREATER INDIANAPOLIS, through which it shares projects with many other Indianapolis Protestant groups. Indianapolis Methodists' active role in the National Council of Churches of Christ brought criticism by local fundamentalists unhappy with the NCCC's liberal policies. Like other mainline denominations, the United Methodist Church's local and national membership has declined since the late 1960s. Suburbanization has forced many church closures, moves, and consolidations. Nevertheless, new churches continue to flourish in outlying areas, and the bulk of Indianapolis United Methodists are in these white, suburban congregations.

Despite the M.E. Church's creation of all-black congregations, most of the city's African-American Methodists belong to predominately black denominations. Created in the 19th century in response to racism by white Methodists were the African Methodist Episcopal Church in 1816; the African Methodist Episcopal Zion Church in 1821; and the Colored Methodist Episcopal Church in 1870.

The first black church in Indianapolis was BETHEL AFRICAN METHODIST EPISCOPAL CHURCH, founded in 1836 as a station on the AME Church's Western Circuit. Bethel quickly became a major focus of community life for Indianapolis blacks. Prior to the Civil War the church reputedly served as a station on the Underground Railroad. The building burned in the early 1860s, was rebuilt at its current location at Vermont and Toledo streets, and in 1867 a school was started for local blacks. Bethel remains a large and active congregation. The African Methodist Episcopal church currently has seven local congregations with about 4,000 members. The African Methodist Episcopal Zion Church set up Jones Tabernacle, its first Indianapolis congregation, in 1872. Today there are five Indianapolis AMEZ congregations with about 1,500 members. The Colored Methodist Episcopal Church, now known as the Christian Methodist Episcopal Church, erected Phillips Temple on the near west side in 1906. Now at 34th and Washington Boulevard, it remains the largest of the ten local CME churches, which altogether have about 3,000 local members.

Significantly, while the local membership of the United Methodist Church continues to erode, all three African-American denominations have shown recent growth. All the black Methodist churches share a common liturgical tradition that maintains many of the older usages of 19th century Methodism. They have also maintained emphasis on evangelism as well as a strong commitment to improving the Indianapolis African-American community. Many local black Methodist churches provide day care centers, youth recreation and mentoring programs, adult literacy training, and senior citizen services. Following cuts in government programs in the 1980s, black Methodists have increasingly tried to provide relief programs such as clothing banks and food pantries. Black Methodist clergy of all four denominations united in 1990 in the Black Methodist Ministerial Forum to address the concerns of the city's black residents on such issues as police shootings and racism.

Despite denominational divisions, all Indianapolis Methodists share a common history of deep community involvement and religious commitment. They helped lay the foundations of Indianapolis community life and have helped guide its development. Religiously and socially, Methodism continues to play a major role in Indianapolis.

KEVIN J. CORN
Indiana University–Purdue University,
Indianapolis

Ferdinand Holliday, *Indiana Methodism* (Cincinnati, 1873); Frederick Doyle Kershner, Jr., "A Social and Cultural History of Indianapolis, 1860-1914" (Ph.D. dissertation, University of Wisconsin, 1950).

Metro. See Indianapolis Public Transportation Corporation

Metropolitan Airports. Beginning in the late 1920s Indianapolis became home to a number of small airports, in addition to its major municipal airport, known as INDIANAPOLIS INTERNATIONAL AIRPORT since 1976. The city's first airport, established in 1927, was Cox Field, named in honor of a local World War I pilot; in 1929 the name was changed to STOUT FIELD in memory of Lt. R. H. Stout of the Indiana National Guard, who died in a plane crash in 1926.

In the mid–1920s a group of prominent Indianapolis businessmen led by J. A. Goodman formed the Indianapolis Airport Corporation, an organization committed to bringing an airport to the city. The IAC leased the 254 acres of farmland southwest of the city that became Stout Field to the Indiana State Armory Board in October, 1926. The site was operated by the Indiana National Guard as a joint commercial-military field.

Embry-Riddle was the first airline to operate from the field, opening a Cincinnati-Indianapolis-Chicago airmail route on December 17, 1927. In July, 1929, Transcontinental Air Transport began using Stout as a stop on its coast to coast air-rail passenger service. The two airline operations moved to the new municipal airport in 1931, and Stout reverted to a military field, although limited commercial and state government operations continued for several years.

The most successful private landing field from the 1920s to the 1940s was Hoosier Airport, owned by Bob Shank, one of the U.S. Post Office's four original airmail pilots. Offering complete fuel and maintenance service, flight instruction, and aircraft sales, the field was also a popular destination for transient pilots. Other local fields were Sky Harbor and Capitol, the latter being one of the few active fields in the country to be owned by a pilots' association instead of a commercial operator.

Following World War II, urban expansion closed many private airports. Hoosier moved to a new site on West 38th Street (Bob Shank Airport), which was planned as an aviation community with homes and private hangars adjoining the field. The old Hoosier Airport became a large housing development in what is now the EAGLEDALE neighborhood on West 30th Street. Capitol also became a victim of low-cost housing, and Sky Harbor eventually moved its operation to the new Eagle Creek site.

A number of small private fields were constructed during the postwar years. These fields served individuals or small groups of owners for pleasure and limited business use. During the late 1960s and early 1970s the INDIANAPOLIS AIRPORT AUTHORITY bought or built several smaller fields, thereby drawing considerable light traffic away from the busy airline airport. In 1993 the eight-county metropolitan area has 16 airports and air fields, with one more under construction in Hendricks County.

In the early 1980s the FAA selected Indianapolis as one of four sites for a new type of urban heliport designed to facilitate urban helicopter travel and landing. The first one completed was the Indianapolis Downtown Heliport, which opened on May 9, 1985. It has been highly successful and has served as the model for similar active and proposed ports across the nation.

JERRY MARLETTE
WILLIAM D. DALTON

Metropolitan Development, Department of. Municipal government department. The primary objective of the Department of Metropolitan Development (DMD) is to improve the quality of life of Marion County residents by encouraging and regulating orderly growth and development within the county. It performs several functions that relate to the built environment and neighborhood life.

The organization and operation of the Department of Metropolitan Development have undergone many changes since its creation, some of them initiated by changes in the federal programs administered locally by the department, others motivated by efforts to improve services or reduce operating costs. It experienced the most extensive organizational changes of any UNIGOV department during the ADMINISTRATION OF MAYOR STEPHEN GOLDSMITH. Although appointed by and serving at the pleasure of the MAYOR, DMD's director has usually operated separately from the mayor's office. During the first two years of the Goldsmith administration, however, the Deputy Mayor for Neighborhoods also served as the director of the Department of Metropolitan Development.

The director's office oversees four divisions: Financial Services, Neighborhood and Development Services, Planning, and Public Housing. Among these divisions, the Neighborhood and Development Services Division is the most visible. Its Administration Section, also known as "the Core," executes the licensing and permitting functions for construction, demolition, and rehabilitation in the county. Other sections promote the development and rehabilitation of low-income housing and other development and redevelopment projects throughout the county, monitor zoning and building codes, and perform liaison between the city administration and neighborhood organizations throughout the county. This division also administers federal funds received by the city from the U.S. Department of Housing and

Urban Development's Community Development Block Grant (CDBG) and housing programs.

The INDIANAPOLIS HISTORIC PRESERVATION COMMISSION is located within Neighborhood and Development Services. It is a semiautonomous agency of city-county government, with responsibility for designating and overseeing local historic areas, offering technical assistance on historic preservation to property owners and residents, and promoting the preservation and restoration of historic properties.

Other divisions of DMD support the development and updating of the Marion County Comprehensive Plan, engage in long-range forecasting of population, housing, and land use in Marion County, and administer the city's public housing properties.

WILLIAM BLOMQUIST
Indiana University–Purdue University,
Indianapolis

Metropolitan Development Commission.

Municipal government board. The Metropolitan Development Commission is the policy-making body for the DEPARTMENT OF METROPOLITAN DEVELOPMENT. It has nine appointed members—four by the mayor, three by the CITY-COUNTY COUNCIL , and two by the Marion County Commissioners—who serve renewable one-year terms. Although the commission's current name and structure date from the 1970 UNIGOV reorganization, it is the successor of the Metropolitan Plan Commission which was created in 1955. That commission combined the planning and zoning decision making for the city and county.

The Metropolitan Development Commission has more extensive policy-making authority than do the boards associated with other Unigov departments. In addition to reviewing departmental policies and budget requests, the Metropolitan Development Commission adopts the Marion County Comprehensive Plan, which is prepared by department staff in consultation with residents. The plan is the basis for local governments' development strategies and land use regulations. The commission has the power to designate boards that hear and decide requests for variances or rezoning of parcels of land, and to review those de-

cisions on appeal. The commission also is authorized to declare portions of Marion County as redevelopment areas, to approve redevelopment plans for those areas, and to acquire and sell property within those areas as part of the implementation of the redevelopment plans.

WILLIAM BLOMQUIST
Indiana University–Purdue University,
Indianapolis

Metropolitan Indianapolis Board of Realtors.

Voluntary trade association for Indianapolis area real estate professionals. In January, 1912, 43 real estate brokers organized as the Indiana Real Estate Board to pool resources and provide guidelines for local realtors. In 1914 the board introduced the city's first multiple listing service, which revolutionized the local market with a centralized listing of properties for sale. It also organized and sponsored the first INDIANAPOLIS HOME SHOW in 1922 and continued sponsorship until 1933. The board incorporated in 1924; and in the late 1920s, by which time it had been renamed the Indianapolis Real Estate Board, served approximately 400 active members. During the next several decades membership grew steadily, with women being admitted in 1947; in 1962 there were over 800 members.

In 1972 the board changed its name to the Indianapolis Board of Realtors. Five years later, it expanded into Hamilton County and changed its name to the Metropolitan Indianapolis Board of Realtors (MIBOR). The organization subsequently added Johnson County (1983), Morgan County (1989), Hancock County (1992), and Boone County (1992). As of the late 1980s the 4,000 MIBOR members handled about 80 percent of the sales of existing homes within their areas of jurisdiction.

DEBORAH B. MARKISOHN

Metropolitan Statistical Area (MSA).

Historically the boundaries of an urban area coincided with the political boundaries of one city. The rapid suburbanization of population and economic activity during the 20th century meant that previously separated cities became socially and economically connected to large central cities.

Selected Statistics for the Indianapolis MSA, 1990[1]

Population (000s)	1,249
Population Per Square Mile	407
Percent African-American	13.8
Percent 0 to 17 Years	26.3
Percent 65 Years and Over	11.1
Percent 25 Years and Over with a High School Degree or Equivalency	78.6
Percent 25 Years and Over with a College Degree	21.1
Per Capita Income in 1989	$15,159
Unemployment Rate (%)	4.7
Married-Couple Families as a Percent of Total Households	54.6
Median Home Value	$66,900

[1] The Indianapolis MSA included Boone, Hamilton, Hancock, Hendricks, Johnson, Marion, Morgan, and Shelby counties.

Termed a metropolis, this late 20th century form of urbanization consists of areas of intense social and economic interdependence which encompass the boundaries of one large city (the "central city") and a number of smaller cities (the "suburbs").

In 1950 the U.S. Office of Management and Budget, in cooperation with other federal agencies, devised standard criteria for metropolitan areas. The criteria for identifying the boundaries of an MSA have changed only slightly since then. Currently, an MSA consists of at least one county, within which there is a city of at least 50,000 residents, and any contiguous counties that are urban in character and have a significant degree of economic interaction with the central county. Each MSA is identified by the name of its central city and state. While the MSA definitions are intended only for statistical purposes, a number of federal programs specifically target metropolitan areas.

The metropolitan status of the Indianapolis MSA was first designated in 1950 and consisted only of Marion County. In 1966 the Indianapolis MSA was expanded to include Marion, Hamilton, Hendricks, Hancock, Shelby, and Johnson counties. Boone County was added to the MSA in 1971, and Madison County in 1991. In December, 1990, Indianapolis was the 31st most populous MSA in the United States with 1,250,000 residents. In January, 1993, following the addition of Madison County to the MSA in 1991, Indianapolis was the 28th most populous MSA, with 1,405,000 residents.

THOMAS J. COOKE
Indiana University–Purdue University, Indianapolis

Mexican War (May 13, 1846–Mar. 10, 1848). On May 16, 1846, Gov. James Whitcomb was given a federal quota to supply three regiments of infantry or riflemen for service in the opening phase of the war with Mexico. During the conflict Indiana provided five infantry regiments, including three companies from the Indianapolis area.

The first unit from Marion County was Company H, 1st Indiana Volunteer Infantry, organized June 4, 1846. This element was stationed near the mouth of the Rio Grande River for the entire war. Although it saw no combat it suffered greatly from disease. The company was commanded by Capt. James P. Drake who was elevated to regimental commander when the unit arrived at New Albany, Indiana. Lt. LEW WALLACE was an officer in this company.

The second and third Indianapolis companies were mustered in the following year. Company D, 4th Indiana Volunteer Infantry, organized April 24, 1847, was commanded by Capt. Edward Lander. Company F, 5th Indiana Volunteer Infantry, mustered into federal service on August 31, 1847, had John McDougall as its captain. The Fourth joined Gen. Winfield Scott's army near Vera Cruz and participated in the final operations of the 1847 campaign. The Fifth moved down the Gulf and went into garrison duty where they endured the routine of camp life, interrupted occasionally by skirmishes and menacing guerrillas.

The city's first war hero was a casualty of the Mexican War. Capt. TRUSTIN B. KINDER, a native of Indianapolis, commanded Company B, 2nd Indiana Volunteer Infantry. His unit originated at Paoli, in the southern part of the state, where Kinder had established a law practice prior to hostilities. Kinder was killed during the Battle of Buena Vista, February 23, 1847, and on hearing the news, his father, Isaac, traveled from the city to Mexico and returned his son's body to Indianapolis for a well-attended public burial in City Cemetery. Kinder's body was removed to CROWN HILL CEMETERY in October, 1864.

Another Indianapolis citizen, Joseph Stretcher, thought to be the first established undertaker in the city, was called upon to return the remains of Gen. Tilghman A. Howard, from Texas to his home in Rockville, Indiana. With the exception of Gen. Howard, Capt. Kinder, and other officers, most of the war dead remained in Mexico and were eventually buried in a national cemetery at Mexico City.

Two individuals who would one day have ties to Indianapolis—Lew Wallace and EBENEZER DUMONT—established themselves as efficient officers during their Mexican War service. Both became generals during the CIVIL WAR.

WAYNE L. SANFORD

William J. Watt and James R. H. Spears, *Indiana's Citizen Soldiers: The Militia and National Guard in Indiana History* (Indianapolis, 1980); William R. Holloway, *Indianapolis: A Historical and Statistical Sketch of the Railroad City* (Indianapolis, 1870).

Michigan Road.

Early state road linking the Ohio River to Lake Michigan. Using federal funds earmarked for transportation improvements, Indiana in the 1820s embarked on a program of state road construction to link the principal towns and settlements to one another and to the new state capital at Indianapolis. By far the most ambitious project was the Michigan Road. Running the length of the state from Madison to Michigan City (which was platted as the road's northern terminus in 1832), it traversed southeastern Indiana via Versailles, Greensburg, and Shelbyville to Indianapolis. The northern leg skirted the worst of northwestern Indiana's marshlands by way of Logansport and South Bend. Scarcely more than a muddy lane by today's standards, the Michigan Road was essentially completed by the late 1830s. In 1837, because of the state's inability to appropriate funds for further maintenance, the legislature shifted responsibility for upkeep to the counties through which the road passed.

A few roadside dwellings from the Michigan Road's heyday still stand in Marion County, especially in Washington and Franklin townships. A former tollhouse of the Augusta Gravel Road Company, just north of WHITE RIVER, marks the years after the Civil War when private companies undertook to improve the road surface and recoup their investment through user fees. With the popularization of the automobile, the road (called Southeastern Avenue south of Washington Street)

took on new life in the 1920s as State Road 29, later U.S. Highway 421, which lasted until the federal highway was routed onto the completed I-465 in the 1970s.

GLORY-JUNE GREIFF

General Prather, "The Construction of the Michigan Road, 1830–1840," *Indiana Magazine of History*, 40 (Sept., 1944), 243–279; Geneal Prather, "The Struggle for the Michigan Road," *Indiana Magazine of History*, 39 (Mar., 1943), 1–25.

Middle Easterners.

Immigrants from the Arabic-speaking regions of the Middle East, ranging from western Asia through northern Africa (i.e., Iraq through Egypt to Morocco), began arriving in the United States and Indiana during the late 19th century. In 1890 there were only 216 individuals of Middle Eastern ancestry among Indiana's 2.2 million inhabitants. However, given the irregular categorization of ethnic groups in subsequent censuses because of changing national or political boundaries and religious differences, it is difficult to trace those of Arab ancestry with any consistency over the years.

Indianapolis did not attract Middle Eastern immigrants initially. Urban areas such as Chicago, Cleveland, Detroit, and the Indiana cities of Fort Wayne and Terre Haute reported some of the earliest communities. Syrian Christians, originating primarily from the Mount Lebanon area (the Mediterranean coastal area between Beirut and Tripoli), appeared to be the first arrivals in Indiana during the late 19th century. Primarily peddlers, small business owners, and factory and farm workers, they eventually moved to Indianapolis to capitalize on opportunities offered at the state's industrial and railroad center. Francis Riszk, a peddler, resided on Broadway Street; David and Saada Kafoure opened a dry goods business on Willard Street in 1892; Nick Shaheen owned a rug store on the Circle; and a Jewish Syrian operated Dayan's Linen Store. Others maintained warehouses and provided assorted services, such as Dr. Waheeb Zarick who established a general practice in 1920. There were other Middle Easterners who came to Indianapolis during the early 20th century but, excluding Syrians, they numbered less than ten.

By the 1920s Syrians inhabited the city's east and southeast sides and the area surrounding KINGAN AND COMPANY. Many had organized the Syrian-American Social Club (1919) on North Davidson Street and the Knights of St. George (1925), a men's religious society from which St. George Syrian Orthodox Church was founded in January, 1926. (The congregation later moved from its original location at 2700 North Sherman Drive to a new building at 4020 North Sherman Drive in 1961.) By 1930 there were 443 Syrians (178 foreign born) in the city. Approximately 76 individuals of Turkish ancestry resided in an area encompassed by INDIANA AVENUE, West, and West Washington streets.

The World War II years and subsequent decades witnessed a steady growth in the "other than Syrian Christian" population. Indianapolis' institutions of higher education, the development of its medical centers and research facilities, the substantial growth of international business activity, and the industrial operations of corporations requiring engineering and management skills attracted Egyptians, Turks, Armenians, and others with marketable skills and professions. Students and scholars from nations such as Kuwait, Saudi Arabia, Iraq, and Yemen continue to come to work, study, and live in Indianapolis, though many return to their homelands upon completion of their education or research.

By 1960 the Middle Eastern population of Indianapolis had become somewhat more diverse. There were 174 Turks (77 foreign born), 170 Lebanese (79 foreign born), 288 Egyptians (85 foreign born), and 273 Syrians (74 foreign-born) in the city. In 1970 those from "West Asia," including Turkey, numbered 463 (327 foreign born). In the early 1990s there were a modest number of Indianapolis residents with ethnic ties to Middle East regions; the 1990 census noted 1,541 individuals in Marion County and 1,450 in Indianapolis who reported Arab ancestry.

Those who emigrated from or who have forebears who emigrated from Afghanistan, Iran, Palestine, Israel, Kuwait, Saudi Arabia, Egypt, Syria, Lebanon, Turkey, Assyria, and Armenia, while not comprising a large group, have contributed to many segments of the Indianapolis community. Despite the presence of an Orthodox church, Islamic mosque, and assorted ethnic observances and holidays, it appears that Middle Easterners have assimilated into the Indianapolis mainstream. There are no apparent Arab enclaves and few ethnic clubs or institutions to maintain their cultural identity within the urban setting. Ethnic identity may well be fragmented, reflecting the geographic and sectarian divisions within the larger Arab world.

FRANK W. BLANNING

Middleton, Harvey Nathaniel (Feb. 15, 1895–Mar. 18, 1978). African-American physician. Born in Denmark, South Carolina, Middleton graduated from Benedict College in 1919. After brief service in the Army during World War I (1918–1919), he attended the School of Medicine at Boston University (1920–1922) and graduated from Meharry Medical College with an M.D. (1926). A cardiologist, Middleton completed postgraduate work in the diagnosis and treatment of heart disease at Harvard Medical School, Michael Reese Hospital in Chicago, University of Michigan, University of London, and the Indiana University Medical School.

In 1928, after a brief practice in Springfield, Tennessee, Middleton joined the staff of St. Joseph Hospital in Anderson, Indiana. He moved to Indianapolis in 1935, where he unsuccessfully applied to become the only black doctor on the staff of City Hospital (now WISHARD MEMORIAL HOSPITAL). He was allowed to volunteer in the outpatient clinic at the facility. He purchased a portable cardiette machine and went into private practice making electrocardiograms. He subsequently received a staff appointment at City Hospital in 1942 and later served on the staffs of St. Vincent, Methodist, Community, and Winona Memorial hospitals.

The author of several scientific papers and journal articles, Middleton was affiliated with numerous professional medical organizations. As a civic leader in Indianapolis, Middleton was active with the YOUNG MEN'S CHRISTIAN ASSOCIATION (YMCA), serving on the metropolitan board for three years, chairing several committees of the SENATE AVENUE YMCA, and working as a delegate at the International YMCA conference in Paris in 1955.

WILMA GIBBS
Indiana Historical Society

Harvey Middleton Collection, Indiana Historical Society.

Midtown (Indiana Avenue Area).

Historically African-American neighborhood bounded by 16th Street, Dr. Martin Luther King, Jr. Drive, Ohio Street, and University Boulevard. Blacks began to settle in this area, originally known as "Bucktown," prior to the Civil War. By 1870 the residents had erected two churches in the district, and INDIANA AVENUE, which bisected the area, had become the core of the African-American community. The area experienced its greatest period of population growth between 1875 and 1890. Residents bordered the streets with one- and two-story frame homes in styles ranging from shotgun to foursquare.

By the 1920s Indiana Avenue was an eight-block business district serving the African-American clientele of the area. In 1927 the Madam C. J. Walker Building opened at the corner of Indiana Avenue and West Street. The edifice housed professional offices, a drug store, beauty shop and beauty college, the Walker Casino and Theatre, and a restaurant, and offered employment and services for Midtown residents.

Between 1935 and 1938 the Public Works Administration and the Advisory Committee on Housing of Indianapolis began a "slum clearance" project in a financially depressed part of the district. The 24–building LOCKEFIELD GARDENS project replaced 363 residences with low-income housing, playgrounds, and courtyards. Opening in February, 1938, the 748 units in Lockefield were filled by September of that year. Public School No. 24, the only original building left standing after the demolition, continued to serve the area as a neighborhood school.

Between 1930 and 1950 Indiana Avenue began to lose its business district as it became an entertainment area where well-known JAZZ musicians such as WES MONTGOMERY and NOBLE SISSLE played at neighborhood clubs. In the 1950s

and 1960s, following a series of court decisions prohibiting discrimination in housing and the deterioration of Lockefield Gardens, many residents moved out of the housing project and the surrounding area and away from the city center. In the 1970s expansion of INDIANA UNIVERSITY–PURDUE UNIVERSITY AT INDIANAPOLIS and the continuing deterioration of Lockefield resulted in further population decreases in the area.

In 1980 the city of Indianapolis, Indiana University, the Health and Hospital Corporation, and the Midtown Economic Development Industrial Corporation (MEDIC) united in an effort to revitalize what had become known as the Midtown area. The group supervised the demolition of 18 Lockefield Gardens buildings and restoration of the 6 remaining; in 1983 these were placed on the National Register of Historic Places. Also placed on the register were the Walker Building (1980) and the 500 block of Indiana Avenue (1987). Construction of new apartments on former Lockefield land and the renovation of the nearby CENTRAL CANAL signaled renewed growth and interest in the Midtown area in the 1990s.

CONNIE J. ZEIGLER

Midwestern Collegiate Conference.

Collegiate sports league. Representatives of BUTLER UNIVERSITY, the University of Evansville, Loyola University of Chicago, Xavier University, Oklahoma City University, and Oral Roberts University formed the Midwestern Collegiate Conference, then known as the Midwestern Cities Conference, in 1979 to enhance the athletic reputations of the schools. The conference opened a part-time headquarters office in Champaign, Illinois, in 1980, and in 1984 relocated to Indianapolis and hired its first full-time commissioner.

From its inception, the conference pursued national recognition through its flagship sport, men's basketball. The MCC champion was guaranteed participation in the prestigious NCAA men's basketball tournament beginning in 1983, and the conference and its Indianapolis member, Butler, also hosted the tournament finals in 1980 and 1991. Conference realignments across the nation affected the MCC in 1991 and 1993 as various schools departed for other conference affiliations. As of June, 1994, member schools include

Butler, Xavier, Detroit Mercy, Loyola of Chicago, LaSalle, Wright State, Cleveland State, Northern Illinois, Wisconsin–Green Bay, Wisconsin–Milwaukee, Illinois–Chicago, and Notre Dame (which remains independent in football and men's basketball).

THOMAS A. HARTON

Migration Patterns. Immigrants, defined for the purpose of this essay as those not native to Indiana, always have contributed to the growth of Indianapolis' population. Although they constituted the vast majority of the city's earliest population, immigrants became an ever declining source of population growth over subsequent decades. Recent expansion of the metropolitan region, however, has been fueled by arrivals from outside the city and state.

Indianapolis is, in some ways, a microcosm of Indiana. Both city and state possess a fairly limited diversity of immigrants, especially those of foreign birth, which gives each a reputation of being rather homogeneous. The immigration history of Indianapolis, however, differs from that of Indiana because in-migrants generally, and specifically those from foreign countries, comprised a greater proportion of the city's population than the state's. Indeed, Indianapolis throughout its history has been more ethnically diverse, particularly with respect to foreign-born settlers, and more racially diverse, than has Indiana. But the sources and proportions of the city's immigrants have not differed dramatically from the state's.

In 1850, the first year in which the federal census recorded state or country of birth, Indianapolis already contained proportionally more foreign-born immigrants and African-Americans than resided in the rest of Indiana. Slightly over 65 percent of the immigrants were U.S.-born natives; 17.1 percent originated in the east south central region (Kentucky, Tennessee, Alabama, Mississippi) with Kentucky supplying 15.4 percent. The states of Ohio, Illinois, Michigan, and Wisconsin—the east north central region—supplied the next largest group (16.1 percent) with 15.2 percent born in Ohio. South Atlantic states followed at 15.6 percent (North Carolina, 6 percent; Virginia, 5.6 percent); Middle Atlantic states (Penn-sylvania, New Jersey, New York) provided 13.6 percent; and New England, 2.1 percent. Those of foreign birth accounted for 35 percent of the immigrants (more than twice the statewide average), with Germans constituting 20 percent and the Irish 12 percent; those of Scotch and English birth accounted for approximately 1 percent each. African-Americans, who comprised 6.5 percent of the city's population, immigrated from beyond Indiana, primarily from North Carolina (38.5 percent), Kentucky (22.3 percent), Virginia (13.2 percent), Tennessee (7.2 percent), and Ohio (4.9 percent).

The U.S.-born and foreign-born proportions of Indianapolis' 1880 population were similar to 1850, with few changes occurring in the sources of migrants. The greatest differences were an increase in immigrants from the east north central region (from 16.1 percent in 1850 to 24.1 percent in 1880, with Ohio accounting for 19.7 percent) and a decrease in Middle Atlantic natives to 7.1 percent. Minor changes occurred among the foreign-born immigrants, with a slight decrease in German natives and a comparable increase in English natives. African-Americans comprised 8.7 percent of the population.

During the early decades of the 20th century Indianapolis witnessed significant changes in the sources of its immigrants, influenced primarily by changes occurring at the national level. The United States experienced its greatest numerical influx of foreign immigrants between 1900 and 1910. By the early 1920s the federal government had enacted a series of increasingly restrictive immigration policies. The character of the city's population reflected both factors.

In 1910, 36.1 percent of Indianapolis' population had been born beyond Indiana; 20 years later that percentage had declined to 30.1 percent. More significantly, the foreign-born portion of the immigrant population was cut nearly in half—23.5 percent in 1910 to 12.7 percent in 1930—reflecting the overall decrease in immigration and the impact of immigration restriction. Germans continued to comprise the largest group of foreign born, although their actual numbers decreased noticeably and their proportion of immigrants fell from 8.9 percent in 1910 to 3.6 percent in 1930. The Irish also experienced a decline—3.9 percent in 1910 to 1.6 percent in 1930. Natives of England and Canada also decreased but not as dramatically, while those born in Scotland and Italy held steady in percentage and numbers.

Among immigrants born in the United States, natives of the east south central region increased in number and percentage during the period—from 25.8 percent of the in-migrants in 1910 to 43.7 percent in 1930; natives of Kentucky dominated but Tennessee's portion expanded as well. The portion of the population from other U.S. regions or states varied over the years: natives of South Atlantic states increased from 5.2 percent to 6.8 percent; those from the east north central region remained about the same, 29.5 percent in 1910 and 30.7 percent in 1930; the Middle Atlantic states contributed 7.4 percent in 1910 and 5.8 percent in 1930. Natives of Ohio, the largest source after Kentucky, accounted for 18.1 percent of the immigrants in 1910 but 13.7 percent in 1930. African-Americans comprised 12.1 percent of the city's 1930 population. Over two thirds of the blacks were native to states other than Indiana; Kentucky accounted for 43.4 percent, Tennessee, 24.4 percent, and Georgia, 7 percent.

The 1940 census gathered different population origin information. For those born outside the U.S., country of birth continued to be listed. For natives of the U.S., instead of identifying state of birth, individuals were asked to identify the state in which they resided five years previously, thus complicating any comparison with earlier birthplace data. Censuses after 1970 include some combination of broad geographical groupings of birthplaces (regions in the U.S. or a general "Foreign" category) and identify the population by "race."

Immigrants from other parts of the U.S. and abroad comprised 26.4 percent of Indianapolis' population in 1940, slightly below the 30.1 percent of 1930. Foreign-born residents comprised 10.3 percent of the immigrants (compared to 12.7 percent in 1930), with Germany (2.5 percent), Ireland (1.6 percent), and Russia (0.8 percent) supplying the largest segments. Natives of the U.S., based on residence five years previously, continued to come from the same general areas: the east north central region (43.6 percent) with Ohio

supplying 14.4 percent; the east south central region (24.3 percent) with 16.8 percent from Kentucky; and the Middle Atlantic (7.9 percent) and South Atlantic (6.1 percent) regions.

Sources of U.S. immigrants to Indianapolis between 1955 and 1960 shifted, in some cases dramatically but in others only slightly, from the 1935–1940 sources. Natives from the east north central region declined from 43.6 percent to 34.4 percent, with Ohioans comprising 11.5 percent; those from the east south central region rose from 24.4 percent to 28.6 percent, due in part to an increase in natives from Tennessee (4.9 percent to 8.1 percent); immigrants from the South Atlantic region increased from 6.1 percent in 1935–1940 to 13.5 percent in 1955–1960. By 1970 the foreign-born portion of Indianapolis' immigrant population had fallen below 5 percent, while most immigrants from within the U.S. were native to the east south central (38.8 percent) or the east north central (23.8 percent) regions. African-Americans comprised 18 percent of the population, most of whom were Indiana born, in contrast to the pre–World War II years. However, blacks who immigrated from beyond Indiana continued to originate in the same regions as previously—the east south central (68.7 percent) and the South Atlantic (11.4 percent).

Not only did the percentage of foreign-born immigrants to Indianapolis decline after 1940, the sources of those people shifted. Countries such as Germany, Ireland, and England, which traditionally accounted for most of the foreign born, sent proportionally fewer to the city while members of ethnic groups who before rarely settled in Indianapolis arrived in increasing numbers. In 1990 there were 7,681 Hispanics (1.1 percent of the population), whereas in 1910 there were only 33 in the city and as recently as 1970 they comprised only 0.1 percent of the total population. Their leading countries of origin in 1980 (in descending order) were Mexico, Cuba, Colombia, and Argentina. Persons of Asian origin had settled in Indianapolis since the late 19th century, but always in small numbers. The 1910 census reported 54 Asians in the city (0.02 percent); by 1990 natives of Asia comprised 0.9 percent of the population, an increase from 0.5 percent in 1980. Leading countries of origin (in descending order) were India, China, the Philippines, Korea, Japan, Vietnam, and Cambodia. American Indians were 0.2 percent of the 1990 population and African-Americans 22.6 percent, the largest number and percentage for both groups recorded in any census to date.

While immigrants constitute proportionally less of Indianapolis' population today than in the past, the city's ethnic and racial diversity is increasing. African-Americans and American Indians are a larger part of the city. Reflecting general trends in immigration to the U.S., greater numbers of Asians and Hispanics are evident today. In addition, U.S.-born immigrants also help diversify the city. Although the proportional impact of immigrants and their cultural diversity have not been as great in Indianapolis as in larger, more industrialized cities of the Midwest and beyond, both U.S.- and foreign-born immigrants have provided and will continue to provide the city with a rich economic and cultural heritage.

GREGORY S. ROSE
The Ohio State University, Marion

Gregory S. Rose, "Hoosier Origins: The Nativity of Indiana's United States-Born Population in 1850," *Indiana Magazine of History*, 81 (Sept., 1985), 201–232; Gregory S. Rose, "Upland Southerners: The County Origins of Southern Migrants to Indiana by 1850," *Indiana Magazine of History*, 82 (Sept., 1986), 242–263; Gregory S. Rose, "The Distribution of Indiana's Ethnic and Racial Minorities in 1850," *Indiana Magazine of History*, 87 (Sept., 1991), 224–260.

Mile Square. The area comprising Indianapolis' original plat created in 1821 by surveyor ALEXANDER RALSTON, who worked under Pierre L'Enfant in the planning of Washington City (now D.C.). Ralston was chosen by a commission to devise a layout for a capital city for the young state of Indiana in a four square mile area of dense forest provided by the federal government. Doubting that the city would ever encompass four square miles, Ralston planned one square mile bounded today by North, South, East, and West streets in Indianapolis' central business district. The Ralston plan is distinguished by diagonal arteries—Massachusetts, Virginia, Kentucky, and Indiana streets (now avenues)—connecting the corners of a mile square gridiron with four centrally located blocks.

The original plat of the town of Indianapolis (1821). [Indiana State Library]

Unusual in American city planning, diagonal streets derive from Renaissance "ideal cities" that reflected thinking on universal order, and from the baroque period's use of diagonals to emphasize prominent buildings, monuments, and squares important to a ruling nobility. The most notable applications of diagonals predating the Mile Square are Versailles, St. Petersburg, and Washington, D.C. Versailles used diagonals laid out by garden designer Le Notre in the baroque grand fashion highlighting the royal palace and for visibility of hunting parties at points of diagonals' convergence. St. Petersburg —influenced by Peter the Great's desire for a "window on Europe," and planned by Le Notre pupil Le Blonde—intentionally mimics Versailles. Appropriately, in this case, diagonals converge on the Admiralty. The plan for Washington by L'Enfant, who was the son of a painter to the royal court at Versailles, uses diagonal boulevards to emphasize points of convergence in the baroque tradition, namely at the Capitol, the White House, and numerous monuments.

Clearly extending the lineage of Versailles, St. Petersburg, and Washington, but of much more modest proportions, the Mile Square departs from typical Renaissance and baroque use of diagonals. The Mile Square's diagonals originally terminated at blocks bounded by Washington, Illinois, Ohio, and Pennsylvania streets, rather than at key buildings, monuments, or squares. This condition was offset, however, with the addition of the Soldiers and Sailors Monument in 1901.

Other key features of the original plat include a central circle intended for the governor's house which subsequently became the location of the monument. Ralston also designated two blocks on Washington Street for the State House and county courthouse. In outer portions of Massachusetts, Kentucky, and Indiana streets three additional squares were located for religious purposes. Halves of two blocks on Market Street were reserved for market places. Typical of the era, streets were broad, with Washington Street the widest at 120 feet.

The POGUE'S RUN area in the southeast corner of the Mile Square deviates from the symmetrical gridiron plan. The origin of its irregular layout is unclear but Ralston may have intended it for uses requiring water (such as mills) or for park land.

The plan's impact on Indianapolis' development was initially sporadic. Early 19th century development was concentrated on Washington Street between Illinois and Delaware streets. Introduction of the railroad and location of UNION STATION south of Washington Street in the pre–Civil War era resulted in considerable development. These additions offset east-west oriented growth on Washington Street, which had become part of the National Road, and spurred industrial development to the south, residential to the north, and commercial activities around Union Station. The pattern and location of these land uses is virtually intact today, with the Mile Square currently comprising the heart of Indianapolis' downtown. The principal alteration of the original plan has been the truncation of three of the four diagonals (Indiana, Massachusetts, and Kentucky avenues) so that they no longer terminate at the block surrounding the Circle.

THOMAS W. SCHURCH
Ball State University, Muncie

Wolfgang Braunfels, *Urban Design in Western Europe* (Chicago, 1988); Albert E. Dickens, "The Growth and Structure of Real Property Uses in Indianapolis" (M.A. thesis, Indiana University, 1939); Jacob Piatt Dunn, *Greater Indianapolis* (Chicago, 1910); John W. Reps, *The Making of Urban America* (Princeton, 1965).

Military Park. Bounded by West, New York, and Blackford streets and the CENTRAL CANAL, the 14–acre park is the oldest in the city. Originally referred to as the Military Ground, then Military Park, it was renamed Camp Sullivan by Governor OLIVER P. MORTON after Col. J. C. Sullivan of the 13th Indiana Regiment, during the Civil War. The name was changed to Camp Sullivan Park in 1916. It is now once again known as Military Park. The ground on which it is situated was donated to the State of Indiana by Congress in 1827 for militia training purposes and is referred to in the 1851 Indiana Constitution (Art. 15, sec. 9).

From the very early days of Indianapolis this park has had a varied use. The city's first recorded July 4th celebration was held there in 1822. In 1836 militia gathered there to prepare for the BLACK HAWK WAR. Organized into three companies, they marched to Chicago and then turned around and came back. For this less than glorious achievement, they became derisively known as the "Bloody Three Hundred."

In October, 1852, the first INDIANA STATE FAIR was held at this location and, except for years when the fair traveled, it was held in the park until 1860. A large board fence surrounded the site and exhibition buildings and stalls were present. In 1863 the fair was held for the last time in Military Park.

At the outbreak of the Civil War the park quickly became a military camp used for the recruitment and training of troops. The Indianapolis Greys, the Guards, the Zouave Guards, and others encamped there. They were the first of thousands of men who formed regiments in the park, by now called Camp Sullivan. Senator Stephen A. Douglas of Illinois visited the camp, and the future commander of the Army of the Potomac, General George B. McClellan, reviewed troops there.

Visitors to Military Park around 1900 could view Civil War relics as well as a reflecting pool and fountain. [Indiana Historical Society, #C5916]

The park suffered much physical damage during the war years and was, in general, "a deplorable tract of land." A civic-minded nearby resident, George Merritt, guided its restoration. A pool with a large rock formation and fountain were added, as well as playground equipment and Civil War relics. A pavilion (which still stands) was built and a circular drive constructed. The park in the late 19th and early 20th centuries received heavier use than at present.

Between the world wars and through the ensuing decades the park slowly deteriorated, its beauty and historical importance largely forgotten. In 1980 it was given a facelift with funds granted by the LILLY ENDOWMENT and the KRANNERT CHARITABLE TRUST. In recent years Military Park has been used for gatherings of social and political groups such as labor union rallies and Earth Day celebrations. Now a part of WHITE RIVER STATE PARK, its expansive greenspace and mature trees constitute a visual reminder of the rich heritage of the city.

JAMES A. TRULOCK

Militia. Organized initially to protect expanding settlements in the Northwest Territory, the militia played a significant role in the development of Indiana and its communities. The state's first constitution (1816) declared all white males ages 18 to 45 members of the militia. With the removal of Native Americans across the Mississippi River by the 1830s, the threat to local settlements passed, and interest in the militia disappeared.

From the 1830s to 1860, Indiana, like many states, maintained a dual militia system. Adult males were obligated to serve in an organized district militia. Following 1842, however, state law permitted males to volunteer in "independent companies." Although some men still met for organized musters in Indianapolis into the 1840s, only the independent companies remained viable. They were usually small infantry units, 20 to 40 members, and always uniformed, which the organized militia was not. Stylish uniforms, regular meetings, and occasional commissions from the governor ensured the continuation of these companies. Two such groups, the Marion Guards (1837) and the Marion Riflemen (1842), lasted longer than most independents, surviving until 1845 and serving as a core for future military recruitment.

Following the MEXICAN WAR (1846–1848) interest in military affairs faded briefly. No militia existed in Indianapolis until the City Guards (1852) and Mechanic Rifles (1853) were established. The late 1850s witnessed a renewed interest in the militia with the formation of the National Guards (1856), the City Greys and the City Greys Auxiliary Company (1857), and the Marion Light Dragoons (1858), the only cavalry unit in Indianapolis. With the organization of the Independent Zouaves and the Zouave Guards by 1860, there were over 300 active militiamen in Indianapolis. Each unit was independent of state control and possessed its own drill hall and handsome uniforms.

At the beginning of the CIVIL WAR in April, 1861, local units (except for the City Greys, which consisted of men beyond military age) became part of General LEW WALLACE's elite Indiana Zouaves, the 11th Indiana Volunteer Infantry. In May, 1861, the General Assembly created additional regiments for state service and passed the Militia Act, which divided the militia into the active and sedentary militia, or those males subject to serve. The active militia, which included volunteers in recognized companies, became the Indiana Legion, a name that was retained until 1895 when it became the INDIANA NATIONAL GUARD. During the summer of 1861, enthusiasm in Indianapolis ran high, and large numbers enrolled in the Legion. Lacking sufficient arms and equipment, many units disbanded with some individuals entering federal service.

The Legion languished until July, 1863, when Confederate cavalry leader General John Hunt Morgan crossed the Ohio River and began his famous Indiana raid. Governor OLIVER P. MORTON mobilized the Legion, with Indianapolis furnishing 20 companies. Only three companies left Indianapolis for the field, skirmishing with the enemy and advancing as far as Batavia, Ohio, before returning home to be mustered out after several exciting days. MORGAN'S RAID proved to be a great stimulus to recruiting. After July, 1863, the Legion was large enough that Marion County was divided into an Indianapolis regiment and a county regiment. The Indianapolis regiment contained 24 companies and provided most of the men for the 132nd Indiana Volunteer Infantry in May, 1864.

Although the Civil War was followed by declining interest in militia activities, the adjutant general reported in 1870 the formation of the independent Emmett Guards and Company A, Indianapolis National Guards, both of which joined the Indiana Legion in the 1880s. These small militia units, however, proved valuable during the labor unrest of the 1870s. During the RAILROAD STRIKE OF 1877, nine companies of volunteer militia were mustered and served for five weeks, helping to keep the peace throughout the state. Five companies were commanded by former Civil War officers, including former general and future president BENJAMIN HARRISON.

In the ensuing years, the Legion grew slowly in Indianapolis. In 1882 the state was divided into regiments, and Indianapolis became the headquarters for the second regiment and four infantry companies. Following the organization of the second regiment, all companies bore letter designations instead of names; Indianapolis companies were labeled A, D, E, and M.

Seeking to modernize the militia in 1895, the General Assembly approved the reorganization of the Indiana Legion as the Indiana National Guard, which retained the original dual militia system. As tensions mounted with Spain over its oppression of Cuba, local interest in the new National Guard peaked. After the United States declared war on Spain in April, 1898, the second

regiment became the 158th Volunteer Infantry Regiment; Indianapolis furnished three companies of infantry and one battery of field artillery. The local infantry companies never left the country, however; the old Curtis Artillery battery, which went to Puerto Rico, was the only Indiana National Guard unit to serve on foreign soil. Despite a constitutional ban on blacks in the militia, Indianapolis had two independent African-American companies in existence from the mid–1880s which sought inclusion in the SPANISH-AMERICAN WAR and became the nucleus for two separate companies of the Guard.

The National Guard revitalized quickly after the war. Following a devastating storm and accompanying floods in March, 1913, four Guard companies aided flood victims and operated a field hospital in Indianapolis. In November, they mobilized in response to the Indianapolis traction workers strike. The Guard's greatest test came in June, 1916, when President Woodrow Wilson federalized the Indiana National Guard and ordered it to the Texas-Mexican border to protect the United States against raids by Mexican revolutionaries. (The National Defense Act of 1916 had more formally integrated state guards into the federal defense establishment.) Although they saw no action, three infantry companies, one artillery battery, and one signal company from Indianapolis spent the winter in Texas before returning home in April, 1917. Within the month, the United States entered World War I, whereupon the Guard was federalized again.

With the professionalization of U.S. armed forces and reorganization of the National Guard, the importance of the "citizen soldier" was somewhat diminished. As provided by Article 12 of Indiana's 1851 constitution, however, the non-enrolled, able-bodied manpower of the state remains as a potential source of local defense and disaster relief.

JAMES R. H. SPEARS

William J. Watt and James R. H. Spears, eds., *Indiana's Citizen Soldiers: The Militia and National Guard in Indiana History* (Indianapolis, 1980); *A History of the National Guard in Indiana* (Indianapolis, 1901).

Millersville. Northeastside neighborhood centered near the intersection of Millersvile Road and East 56th Street. Millersville grew up along Fall Creek at the site of grist mills. Peter Negley and Seth Bacon built one of the first mills in 1826. William Winpenny's mill served in 1852 as the first meeting place of the local Masons. The group later built two temples, the second of which still stands, that served the community in a variety of capacities. At its busiest in the mid–1800s, Millersville boasted a general store, blacksmith shops, and a few businesses. About 90 people lived in the area by the 1880s.

Millersville was known to city dwellers as a popular destination for hiking and picnicking in the early 1900s. It was also the site of dairy farms that supplied the Indianapolis market, including the Hornaday Milk Company and the nearby Roberts Dairy. Across the creek from Millersville, STOUGHTON FLETCHER II's 19th-century mansion, Laurel Hall, became a Catholic girls' school, Ladywood, in the 1920s. The Windridge development purchased the house to use as an entertainment center in the 1970s, but later sold it to the current occupant, the HUDSON INSTITUTE. Cathedral High School has operated in some of the former Ladywood facilities since 1976.

In the 1950s and '60s subdivisions and shopping centers surrounded Millersville, which had never incorporated. By 1990 only a few homes and an old store served as reminders of the village.

CATHLEEN F. DONNELLY

Berry R. Sulgrove, *History of Indianapolis and Marion County* (Philadelphia, 1884); *Indianapolis Times*, Apr. 8, 1962.

Minigov. Neighborhood government plan. When UNIGOV was considered during the 1969 session of the Indiana General Assembly, State Representative E. Henry Lamkin, Jr. (R-Indpls.) introduced a companion bill to allow for smaller scale community governments within the new Consolidated City. This so-called Minigov bill proposed the creation of organized communities within Indianapolis, with community councils elected to decide certain neighborhood affairs. Its sponsor and supporters promoted Minigov as en-

hancing representation and preserving neighborhood identification, while Unigov extended the scale of the city of Indianapolis and its governmental structure.

Under the original Minigov bill community councils would have had the same general powers as town boards of trustees, except for those powers that were specifically denied to them by either the Unigov law or actions of the CITY-COUNTY COUNCIL. Among other things, community councils would be authorized to: adopt traffic flow and parking regulations for residential side streets; spend funds appropriated to them by the City-County Council or raised from other sources; contract with city-county government or with private organizations for neighborhood services such as supplemental police and fire protection, community improvements, and park and recreation facilities; and propose changes to the county's Comprehensive Land Use Plan and hear and decide upon requests for zoning variances.

The Minigov bill passed the House but did not come up for a final vote in the Senate during the 1969 session. It was reintroduced in 1971, but its passage was neither pursued nor opposed vigorously, largely because the attention of local officials and political groups in Marion County was focused on the initial implementation of Unigov.

During the 1972 legislative session, a modified version of the Minigov bill passed both chambers and became law. The modifications stripped the councils of their authority to decide zoning and traffic issues, leaving them only the right to be advised of and comment on proposed traffic or zoning changes in their neighborhoods. The 1972 law kept the community councils' powers to receive and spend funds and contract for supplemental services. The law contained an expiration date of April 1, 1979, after which Minigov would remain in effect only if reauthorized by the state legislature.

The Minigov law directed the METROPOLITAN DEVELOPMENT COMMISSION to prepare and submit to the City-County Council a community plan, dividing the entire area of the Consolidated City into communities. Each community was to contain at least 5,000 persons and at least two precincts, and was to conform as nearly as possible to existing natural and political boundaries. At the primary elections in May, 1974, voters in each community would indicate in a referendum whether they wanted to elect a community council and exercise the powers of a Minigov community. If a majority in the primary voted in favor, the first community council elections would be held in November.

More substantial and organized opposition to Minigov mobilized during the remainder of 1972. Some existing neighborhood organizations and political party officials feared that their influence in city-county government would be diminished by the elected community councils. Several members of the City-County Council perceived themselves to be the proper representatives of residents' interests and concerns and thus opposed Minigov.

During the 1973 legislative session, State Representative Doris Dorbecker (R-Indpls.) introduced a bill to repeal Minigov. The bill's original sponsor, Rep. Lamkin, avoided the repeal by introducing and obtaining passage of additional amendments to the Minigov law. Township advisory boards were inserted into the process of developing the community boundaries, community boundary lines were required to conform to precinct boundary lines, and the minimum size for a community was increased to three precincts. Community councils were redefined as advisory to the township advisory boards, and any contracts for services proposed by a community council had to be approved by its corresponding township advisory board. Funding allocations could come only from the City-County Council, and expenditures would have to be administered through the city's Purchasing Department.

Despite these changes, Minigov was not implemented. The City-County Council refused to approve any submitted community plans or to recognize and appropriate funds to any community council. The provisions of the Minigov law expired in 1979. The Unigov law still authorizes the City-County Council to designate community councils within the Consolidated City and to define their powers, but there has been no widespread attempt to revive Minigov.

WILLIAM BLOMQUIST
Indiana University–Purdue University,
Indianapolis

Mitchell, James L. (Sept. 29, 1834–Feb. 22, 1894). Mayor of Indianapolis, 1873–1875, Democrat. Mitchell was born in Shelby County, Kentucky, and lived in Monroe County, Indiana, before moving to Indianapolis in 1859. There he read law and was married in 1864 to Clara E. Carter. During the Civil War he served as an officer in the 70th Regiment of the Indiana Volunteer Infantry, attaining the rank of major. In 1873 he became the first Democratic mayor of the city since the mid–1850s. Mitchell served only a single two-year term and then resumed his law practice. In 1886 and 1888 he was elected prosecuting attorney for Marion and Hendricks counties. He also served as an Indiana University trustee in the 1880s.

WILLIAM F. GULDE

Mitchell, Samuel Grant (1783–1837). First physician to locate in Indianapolis (April, 1821). Mitchell had practiced medicine in Kentucky for 15 years but had never attended a course of medical lectures. His brother-in-law, SAMUEL HENDERSON, the city's first postmaster and eventually its first mayor, persuaded him to move to Indianapolis, at the time only a village in the forest. Mitchell's office and home were situated on the northwest corner of Washington and Meridian streets. Dr. LIVINGSTON DUNLAP (father of Indianapolis City Hospital), who came to the city during the summer of 1821, became his partner. Mitchell published an interesting account of the epidemic of fever that affected virtually the entire population of the town during 1821–1822. He was active in local and state medical societies and was an early president of both.

GLENN W. IRWIN, JR., M.D.

Monasteries and Retreat Houses. A monastery is home to a group of religious believers who reside in seclusion to pursue a life of contemplation. The monastic life is characterized by asceticism and self-denial. The general physical property of a monastery includes the church, cloister, work area, and individual cells—usually forming a quadrangle. An Indianapolis example of this lifestyle and architecture is the Carmelite

Monastery on Cold Spring Road. Five sisters from Iowa founded their Indiana mission in New Albany, Indiana, in 1922. Ten years later, the sisters relocated to a newly constructed monastery on Indianapolis' near west side. J. D. Kopf designed the medieval, castle-like building. The Carmelite Sisters are a cloistered order, meaning they seldom leave the confines of their monastery. Sixteen sisters resided in the monastery in 1993, leading a contemplative life of prayer.

A retreat house provides opportunities for the faithful to pursue personal prayer, meditation, devotions, and spiritual exercises. Increasingly popular following changes suggested by the Second Vatican Council in 1965, Indianapolis has numerous retreat houses. The program at Alverna Retreat House, established in 1948 by Franciscan brothers from St. Louis, traditionally stressed one's relationship with God through a special emphasis on prayer, meditation, and silence. In 1991, the brothers were forced to close the 40–acre facility because of high maintenance costs. (RESORT CONDOMINIUMS INTERNATIONAL, a time-sharing brokerage, purchased the property and restored the mansion.) The Benedictine Sisters of Our Lady of Grace in Beech Grove own and operate a similar retreat house. Since 1981 the programs sponsored by the sisters have focused on the monastic practices of prayer, work, community formation, and hospitality. Fr. James Moriarty founded the Fatima Retreat House in 1950. Originally the retreat house served the spiritual needs of women, but expanded its mission in 1963 to include men. Its programs are directed toward reflection and spiritual enrichment. Franciscan brother Justin Belitz founded the Hermitage in 1984 on East 46th Street. The retreat house and educational center emphasizes personal development as a lifelong process.

STACEY NICHOLAS

Monetary Conventions. Series of meetings supporting the gold standard and opposing the "free silver" movement, 1896–1898. During the latter decades of the 19th century, monetary policy—especially the continued maintenance of a "gold standard"—was a hotly debated issue. John P. Frenzel and John R. Wilson, both of Indi-

anapolis, were prominent among organizers of "Gold Democrats" into the National Democratic party, which held its convention in TOMLINSON HALL, September 2–3, 1896. Their involvement spurred a local manufacturer, Hugh H. Hanna, to persuade the Indianapolis BOARD OF TRADE to invite other midwestern commercial organizations to send delegates to a conference which met December 1, 1896. Commercial groups in 26 states and the District of Columbia responded to the conference's call for delegates to a convention—commonly called the Indianapolis Monetary Convention—that met in Tomlinson Hall, January 12–13, 1897, and authorized its executive committee to create a Monetary Commission of experts if Congress failed to do so. The executive committee, of which Hanna was chairman, appointed a commission which proposed a law affirming the gold standard. But the commission also sought to create a more flexible currency by allowing federally chartered banks to issue notes against their own assets and to insure these notes by gold coins the banks would have to deposit in the U.S. Treasury.

The executive committee called a second convention, representing mostly the same organizations as its predecessor, which met in the Opera House in Indianapolis on January 24–25, 1898. This convention approved the Monetary Commission's proposals and authorized the executive committee to call future conventions. But the second Indianapolis Monetary Convention would be the last. Congress disregarded the commission's proposal, and new discoveries of gold ended the crisis that had made currency such an emotional issue.

CHARLES JOHNSON TAGGART

Clifton J. Phillips, *Indiana in Transition* (Indianapolis, 1968), 54–56; *Report of the Monetary Commission of the Indianapolis Convention . . .* (1898).

Monon Railroad. The Monon Railroad's Indianapolis branch dates to 1865 when the Indianapolis, Delphi, and Chicago Railway, later the Indianapolis and Chicago Air Line, was incorporated. Operation began in 1878 as a narrow gauge line between Rensselaer and Monticello. Following conversion to standard gauge, the Louisville, New Albany, and Chicago Railway acquired it in 1881.

The line reached Indianapolis in 1882, the year after it had arrived in Chicago, but until 1888 it used the Lake Erie and Western tracks (later the Nickel Plate and Norfolk and Western) south of Howland's Junction, near 34th Street and Fall Creek Parkway. Passenger service began in 1883 and by 1889 had been expanded to four round trips daily, including an overnight train carrying sleeping cars. Trains carried through cars that continued to Cincinnati over what is now CSX.

The railroad reorganized as the Chicago, Indianapolis and Louisville Railway in 1897 and in 1956 formally adopted its long-time nickname, Monon, for the White County junction of its two main lines. Lacking a strong freight base in Indianapolis, the Monon emphasized passenger service and in 1922 built Boulevard Station on East 38th Street to serve the city's north side.

In 1947, the railroad, which was the shortest line to Chicago, re-equipped all trains with rebuilt army hospital cars, but as travelers turned to other modes of travel it eliminated all service on April 10, 1959. The Louisville and Nashville Railroad acquired the Monon in 1971 and in 1985 its successor, Seaboard System, abandoned the Indianapolis-Frankfort segment and removed the rails. The track bed through northern Marion County has been proposed for several uses, including light rail transportation and a linear "greenway" park.

RICHARD S. SIMONS
National Railway Historical Society

George W. Hilton, *Monon Route* (Berkeley, Calif., n.d.); Gary and Stephen Dalzell, *Monon: The Hoosier Line* (Glendale, Calif., 1987).

Montani Brothers. Popular musical group. Originally from Italy, the family immigrated to Utica, New York, in 1878 and moved to Indianapolis in 1881. The five sons of local businessman Ferdinand Montani, owner of fruit and confectionery stands throughout the city, formed an orchestra in 1890 and played throughout the Midwest until the 1920s. With Guy (1865–1907)

The Montani Brothers Orchestra played at city social gatherings from the 1890s until the 1920s. [Indiana Historical Society, #C1084]

as leader and violinist, Domenico (1867–1957), harpist, Pasquale (1874–1955), flutist, Antonio (1875–1948), violinist, and Nicola (1880–1948), cornetist, the group specialized in performing at weddings, receptions, banquets, recitals, and commencements. Locally they played the ENGLISH HOTEL, Germania Hall, the MAENNERCHOR, the COMMERCIAL CLUB, the COLUMBIA CLUB, masonic lodges, parks, and private homes. The Montanis appeared at the opening of the CLAYPOOL HOTEL in 1903 and at the 29th National Gymnastic Festival of the North American Gymnastics Union in 1905. The group frequently hired other area musicians and routinely traveled to Greencastle, Bloomington, Rushville, and Muncie. While waiting for trains at UNION STATION they would play impromptu concerts to supplement their income. Both Guy and Domenico helped organize the first musicians' union in the city, the Indianapolis Protective Musicians' Union, in 1890, the third such union in the country. The brothers continued their musical careers as teachers and musicians after they ceased playing together. The most notable, Nicola, became a well-known composer of Catholic liturgical music and was knighted in 1926 by Pope Pius XI.

JOAN CUNNINGHAM

Montani Family Collection, Indiana Historical Society; *Indianapolis Star Magazine*, Nov. 25, 1956.

Montgomery, John Leslie (Wes) (Mar. 6, 1923–June 15, 1968). Jazz guitarist. Born John Leslie Montgomery in Indianapolis, Montgomery took up the guitar in 1943, joining the Lionel Hampton Big Band in 1948 for a two-year stint of touring and recording. Returning to Indianapolis, he played the local club circuit with his brothers Monk and Buddy, making his first recording, *The Wes Montgomery Trio*, for Riverside in 1959. Four more Riverside albums and a brief sojourn in San Francisco established his primacy among jazz aficionados; his 1965 Verve album, *Goin' Out of My Head*, won a Grammy Award, and his next album, *A Day in the Life* (A&M Records), was the best-selling jazz LP of 1967. Considered by critics as the most influential jazz guitarist since jazz guitar pioneer Charlie Christian, Montgomery developed a unique right-hand "thumbing" style that allowed him to use his fingers for a seemingly infinite variety of melodic, rhythmic, harmonic, and timbrel embellishments. Montgomery died in his home of a heart attack just before he was to depart on a tour of Japan. Over 2,000 persons attended his funeral, and a new park at 34th Street and Hawthorne Lane was named after him in 1972. Each summer Jazzline, Inc., presents the Wes Montgomery Jazz Festival, featuring local jazz performers, at Washington Park.

LAWRENCE E. McCULLOUGH
Indiana University–Purdue University,
Indianapolis

Barry Kernfeld, ed., *The New Grove Dictionary of Jazz* (New York, 1988); *Indianapolis Star*, June 19, 1968.

Montgomery, William Howard (Monk) (Oct. 10, 1921–May 20, 1982). Jazz musician. Born William Howard Montgomery in Indianapolis, Monk toured with Lionel Hampton in the early 1950s and in 1953 became the first jazz musician to record on the electric bass. He returned to Indianapolis and played with his brothers, WES and Buddy, before moving to Seattle, San Francisco, and Las Vegas, where he died in 1982. Monk was known for playing with Cal Tjader, Red Norvo, and other jazz notables.

Another Montgomery brother, Buddy, a pianist and vibraharpist, was born Charles F. Montgomery (Jan. 30, 1930–) in Indianapolis and first played professionally with Indianapolis groups led by Slide Hampton and Roy Johnson in the early 1950s. He performed in various bands with his brothers into the early 1960s, settling in Milwaukee in 1969 and moving to Oakland in the early 1980s.

LAWRENCE E. McCULLOUGH
Indiana University–Purdue University,
Indianapolis

Barry Kernfeld, ed., *The New Grove Dictionary of Jazz* (New York, 1988).

The Wes Montgomery Trio, featuring the jazz legend on the guitar. [Indianapolis Newspapers Inc.]

Monument Circle. The circular street in the very center of the Mile Square is one of the city's shortest yet most famous thoroughfares. Planned as the focal point of the original city plan, the circular street stands in sharp contrast to the standard grid of other streets and is further emphasized by the four radiating angular streets leading to but not meeting the Circle.

The 1821 Plat of the Town of Indianapolis identifies the circular street as Circle Street; it surrounded the intended site of the Governor's House. The four blocks framing the Circle were called the Governor's Square. A temporary market building was soon constructed in the center of the Circle facing south amid the many trees. The governor's residence, depicted in the sketches of local artist CHRISTIAN SCHRADER, was added in 1827, although no governor ever resided there. Instead the brick house served a variety of uses—including state library, state bank, and ballroom—before its demolition in 1857. By this time the character of the Circle was residential, with houses interspersed among four churches constructed between 1829 and 1843: in chronological order, Wesley Chapel (Methodist), Second Presbyterian Church, First Presbyterian Church, and Christ Episcopal Church. A fifth church, Plymouth Congregational, did not face the Circle but was immediately north, opposite Christ Church, which is the only surviving church on the Circle.

The English Hotel and Opera House dominated Monument Circle in this 1930s photograph. [Indiana Historical Society, Bass Collection]

After the demolition of the Governor's House the Circle deteriorated into a livestock grazing area and rubbish dump. Following the Civil War the site was improved and renamed Circle Park. In this period the character of the Circle began to change from religious and residential to commercial. Hotels, office buildings, and stores began to front the right-of-way of Circle Park with arched facades, in sharp contrast to the front lawns of the buildings belonging to the previous period.

The erection of the SOLDIERS AND SAILORS MONUMENT between 1888 and 1901 changed the Circle from an open, forested park to a setting for an elaborate obelisk ornamented with fountains and statuary. The monument's design carried the motto, "The symbol of Indianapolis," and the structure became just that. The monument, physically defined by the Circle, in turn shaped the development of the Circle. After its construction the street name was changed from Circle Street to Monument Place and later to the current Monument Circle, a merger of the two previous names.

In 1905 the City Council enacted a pioneering urban design ordinance to preserve the skyline of the Circle. The ordinance limited the height of all buildings fronting the Circle to 86 feet, the height of the existing COLUMBIA CLUB Building. After World War I commercial interests pushed for the allowance of greater building heights. A 1922 ordinance capped the height at 108 feet with an extra 42 feet permitted by using a setback from the facade line. The uniqueness of the Circle inspired local architect William Earl Russ in 1921 to advocate not only the height restrictions, but also uniform height, style, and materials for buildings to be constructed facing the Circle. Russ' ideas apparently helped to shape the appearance of both the Guaranty and Test buildings and two others since demolished.

The 1920s saw Monument Circle reshaped as larger office buildings and the present Columbia Club replaced the smaller 19th-century structures. In that decade four major office buildings were constructed, ending with the completion of the Art Deco CIRCLE TOWER. No new additions were made for the next two decades because of the Great Depression and World War II. Two major buildings, the J. C. Penney and Fidelity Trust buildings, appeared in the 1950s. The 1970s brought the bricking of the Circle pavement as a symbol of urban revitalization. In the 1980s the CIRCLE THEATRE was renovated, as was the Penney's building (now Associated Group headquarters) in the 1990s. Also in the 1990s construction began on the CIRCLE CENTRE MALL, with one of its entrances opening onto the Circle.

The Circle has been the scene of numerous public celebrations, parades, rallies, and ceremonies. Independence Day celebrations were staged here in the 19th century. The Circle and Washington Street comprised a common parade route earlier in this century, while today Monument Circle has been incorporated into the route of the annual 500 Festival Parade.

WILLIAM L. SELM

Ernestine Bradford Rose, *The Circle: The Center of Indianapolis* (Indianapolis, 1971); Mary Ellen Gadski, James A. Glass, and William L. Selm, "Indiana State Soldiers' and Sailors' Monument, Indianapolis–Marion County Register of Historic Properties Nomination Form," June 27, 1983, copy in the files of the Indianapolis Historic Preservation Commission.

Moores, Merrill (Apr. 21, 1856–Oct. 21, 1929). Attorney and politician. A native of Indianapolis, Moores was the grandson of SAMUEL MERRILL, state treasurer and founder of BOBBS-MERRILL COMPANY. As a child he was educated by his aunt, CATHARINE MERRILL, at her private school. After attending both Butler and Willamette universities, Moores graduated from Yale University in 1878. In 1880 he graduated from the Central Law School of Indiana, was admitted to the bar, and commenced practice in Indianapolis.

From 1899 to 1906, Moores served as secretary of the Indiana State Bar Association; in 1907 and 1908 he served as its president. In 1908, Moores was also president of the Marion County Bar Association. From 1909 to 1921, he acted as Indiana commissioner for the National Conference on Uniform State Laws. Although Moores was associated with the law firm of Pickens, Moores, Davidson and Pickens prior to entering Congress, he practiced alone after his retirement from politics in 1925. At the time of his death, Moores was also serving as vice-president of the American Systems and Audit Company.

From 1890 to 1894, Moores served as chairman of the Marion County Republican Committee and from 1894 to 1903 he was the assistant attorney general of Indiana. In 1914, Moores was elected to the U.S. House of Representatives from Indiana's 7th District, the first of five successive terms. In 1924 and again in 1926 he was defeated in his bid for renomination. While in Congress, Moores was a member of the House committee on foreign affairs, and in 1919 he served as a member of the executive council of Interparliamentary Union.

JEFFERY A. DUVALL

Biographical Directory of the American Congress, 1774–1971 (Washington, 1971); Indiana Biography Series, Indiana State Library.

Moorhead, Robert Lowry (Sept. 15, 1875–Mar. 15, 1968). Spanish-American and World War I officer, state legislator, and veterans' affairs advocate. A lifelong resident of Indianapolis, Colonel Moorhead was extensively involved in military matters throughout his life. During the Spanish-American War, he served as a sergeant major of the Indiana Volunteer Infantry. With the outbreak of World War I, he received a promotion to lieutenant colonel and then colonel of the 139th Field Artillery, American Expeditionary Force. After the war, Moorhead remained in the NATIONAL GUARD, serving a total of 46 years in both branches. His association with publisher BOBBS-MERRILL was also lengthy; he joined the firm as a clerk in 1893 and left as a director in 1958.

Moorhead's interest in military affairs carried over into his service as a state legislator from 1921 to 1932. He served on the Indiana Senate's Military Affairs Committee, was on the State Armory Board, and was a key figure in the founding of the state's armory system. He also was actively involved in numerous civic functions and charitable organizations in Indianapolis, serving on the Warren Township advisory board and as a director of the Salvation Army. Perhaps his greatest contribution, however, was helping to bring the AMERICAN LEGION National Headquarters to Indianapolis in 1919.

JAMES R. BISHOP

Biographical Directory of the Indiana General Assembly, vol. 2 (Indianapolis, 1984).

Morgan County. County adjacent to Indianapolis–Marion County on the southwest and part of the Indianapolis Metropolitan Statistical Area. Settlers began entering land in the area that is now Morgan County in 1820. The county was organized in 1821, with Martinsville platted as the county seat in March, 1822. The northern part of the county, including the town of Mooresville (platted in 1824), was settled by Quakers. The county's first white settler, Asa Bales, a North Carolina Quaker, later founded the town of Westfield in Hamilton County (1834). Samuel Moore built an excellent grist mill on White Lick Creek near Mooresville that contributed greatly to the town's development during the 1830s.

Through the 1830s Martinsville relied on the whiskey trade for much of its modest wealth and growth. By the mid–1830s there were eight distilleries producing corn and rye whiskey and apple and peach brandy and dozens of taverns in and around Martinsville. After 1835, however, the economic focus switched to the pork trade. Hogs were driven from all over central Indiana to slaughterhouses at Martinsville. The carcasses were packed during the winter and floated on flatboats down the West Fork of White River to the Ohio River, arriving in New Orleans by the spring. This trade system flourished until the development of railroads in Indiana after 1850.

In 1853 the Martinsville and Franklin Flatbar Railroad was completed to Martinsville, but operated for less than five years. The completion of the Indianapolis and Vincennes Railroad in the late 1850s spurred growth in the county seat. The pork packing and shipping business continued to flourish, and the town added a large woolen factory. The completion of the Indianapolis and Vincennes Railroad to Mooresville in 1867 spurred the pork shipping industry as farmers took advantage of the large stock pens just south of town while waiting for trains. An INTERURBAN line constructed to Mooresville in 1901 and hourly trains into Indianapolis gave residents easy access to the capital city's shops and department stores. By 1903 the interurban line extended to Martinsville. Speed and convenience made the interurban the top choice for both freight and passenger service, and the Indianapolis and Vincennes Railroad was all but abandoned by 1920.

By the 1930s Morgan County farmers were using trucks to haul their produce to market and cars for personal travel. With the railroad used sparingly and the interurban abandoned, business slowed in the county's two largest towns. Today Morgan County is a predominately rural area with a population of almost 56,000 (1990). Agriculture is an important economic factor in the county, but more residents in and around Martinsville and Mooresville work in factories and offices than farm. Martinsville, the county's only city, had a population of 11,677 in 1990, while Mooresville had 5,541 residents.

WILLIAM D. DALTON

Charles Blanchard, ed., *Counties of Morgan, Monroe, and Brown, Indiana* (Chicago, 1884); Clara S. Richardson, *A Brief History of Mooresville* (Mooresville, Ind., 1974); U.S. Census.

Selected Statistics for Morgan County, 1990

Population	55,920
Population per Square Mile	138
Percent African-American	0.0
Percent 0 to 17 Years	27.8
Percent 65 Years and Over	10.3
Percent 25 Years and Over with a High School Degree or Equivalency	73.6
Percent 25 Years and Over with a College Degree	10.0
Per Capita Income in 1989	$14,822
Unemployment Rate (%)	5.3
Married-Couple Families as a Percent of Total Households	62.0
Median Home Value	$59,700

Morgan's Raid. On July 8, 1863, Gen. John Hunt Morgan and about 2,500 Confederate cavalrymen crossed the Ohio River south of Corydon. The next day they moved north, stealing horses, looting the communities of Corydon and Salem, and sending shock waves throughout southern Indiana.

On July 10 Governor OLIVER P. MORTON called out the Indiana Legion and asked loyal citizens to enroll in their counties as minutemen to resist the invaders. He appointed Gen. LEW WALLACE to command the resistance against Morgan.

The *Indianapolis Daily Evening Gazette* of July 13 reported that the State House yard was thronged with companies reporting from different parts of the state, as were the Governor's Circle and the Soldiers' Home. The sound of fifes and drums was incessant as troops marched and drilled in the streets. On Saturday, the Soldiers' Home fed 12,000 to 15,000 men. It was rumored that local banks were transferring their money to Chicago.

Was Indianapolis Morgan's objective? Certainly the 5,000 Confederate prisoners at CAMP MORTON and the vast quantities of war material in the city were inviting. Unconfirmed telegraphic reports filtering into the capital placed his strength at 5,000 to 10,000, stated that Camp Morton was his objective, and claimed that Nathan Bedford Forrest had followed Morgan across the Ohio with another Confederate division.

Morgan turned east at Salem, probably because of his desire to stay near the Ohio River. He left the state at Harrison on July 13 and Indianapolis breathed a sigh of relief.

HARRY M. SMITH

Indianapolis Daily Evening Gazette, July 12, 13, 1863; Kenneth M. Stampp, *Indiana Politics During the Civil War* (Indianapolis, 1949), 205–209.

Moriah Fund. The Moriah Fund was established in 1985 by Robert and Clarence Efroymson to carry on the philanthropic commitment of their father, Gustave, owner of H. P. WASSON AND COMPANY department store and REAL SILK HOSIERY MILLS.

Robert, a graduate of Harvard University and Harvard Law School, joined Real Silk in 1945. His older brother, Clarence, a graduate of Harvard and the University of Vienna, was part owner in the mill and taught economics at BUTLER UNIVERSITY for 35 years. The Moriah Fund was created from earnings of an investment trading firm (now Real Silk Investments, Inc.) to which the mill transferred its assets after suspending operations in 1956.

Valued at $165 million at the end of fiscal 1991, the fund makes grants in five areas: promoting the well-being of the Jewish people; improving the quality of life in Indiana; stabilizing population growth and promoting reproductive health; conserving natural resources; and fighting the causes and effects of poverty.

The fund allocated the largest portion of its 1991 grants ($2.4 million) to programs in Israel, including $1.9 million to the New Israel Fund. Emphasis in this area was placed on the development of Israeli organizations that promote pluralism, democracy, and educational and economic opportunities; concern for the environment; and improved relations among Israel's diverse communities. Also funded were efforts to aid in the resettlement of Russian and Ethiopian refugees.

Grants of $1.3 million were made in 1991 to Indiana-based programs that supported housing, community development, the environment, family planning, and economic and educational opportunities for less advantaged citizens.

Another component of the Moriah Fund supports national and international programs that promote reproductive health and abortion rights and that improve health care for women, adolescents, and other under-served populations. The environmental program area targets the sustainable management of natural resources and promotes energy conservation, alternative fuels, and research into natural resources economics and policies. The newest area of interest, accounting for $310,000 in grants in 1991, focuses on poverty and housing.

NORA McKINNEY HIATT

Morlan, Dorothy (May 25, 1882–Oct. 25, 1967). Landscape painter. Born in Salem, Ohio, Morlan lived most of her adult life in the eastside suburb of IRVINGTON. She was one of relatively few recognized women painters in Indianapolis.

Her art education included instruction under J. OTTIS ADAMS and WILLIAM FORSYTH in the Brookville, Indiana, area; formal art classes at the HERRON SCHOOL OF ART in Indianapolis; a course of study at the Pennsylvania Academy of Fine Arts, Philadelphia; and painting under the guidance of Robert Henri in New York.

Morlan was elected to the Society of Western Artists in 1908; and in 1914, she was one of the artists selected to paint murals for the Indianapolis

City Hospital (now WISHARD MEMORIAL HOSPITAL). In 1925, at the first HOOSIER SALON exhibition in Chicago, she received the Mrs. Preston M. Nolan Prize for Landscape Painting for *Frosty Morning*. A modernist in painting style, Morlan often gave her large canvases of the 1930s and 1940s titles that reflected their unorthodox themes: *Harmony in Gray, The Marching Tree, The Hounds of Heaven*, and *The Burning Bush*.

The last collected exhibition of Morlan's work was at the Herron Art Institute in 1946. Today, her paintings can be found in private and public collections alike. Some of the Indianapolis institutions housing her art are the INDIANA STATE MUSEUM, the INDIANAPOLIS MUSEUM OF ART, and the Irvington Historical Society.

FRANK N. OWINGS, JR.

Mary Q. Burnet, *Art and Artists of Indiana* (New York, 1921); Virginia Lucas Finney, "Dorothy Morlan: Dreamer of Landscapes" (unpublished manuscript dated Apr., 1976, in Indianapolis Museum of Art library); Irvington Historical Society, *The Irvington Group* (Indianapolis, 1984).

Mormons. See Church of Jesus Christ of Latter-day Saints

Morris, Bethuel F. (Sept. 6, 1792–Feb. 1, 1864). Early settler and circuit court judge. Morris was born in Washington County, Pennsylvania, and moved to Ohio at age 18. He attained the rank of orderly sergeant in the Ohio Company during the War of 1812 before moving to Brookville, Indiana, in 1816, where he became county recorder.

In 1822, the Indiana General Assembly elected Morris state agent to survey, map, and oversee the sale of the remaining lots in the capital donation lands. Morris moved his family to Indianapolis in 1823 and established a law practice, including a brief partnership with CALVIN FLETCHER. He also became one of the first teachers of the interdenominational Indianapolis Sabbath School Union, established in 1823.

In January, 1825, Morris became president judge of Indiana's Fifth Circuit Court. In a controversial decision (1829), he handed down one of the nation's first rulings against a slaveholder's right to transport slaves through a free state, finding that a slave woman and three children passing through Indiana with their owner were free. Morris served on the executive committee of the Temperance Society of Marion County (1830), as an Indiana University trustee (1828–1836), and as a founding member of SECOND PRESBYTERIAN CHURCH (1838). He retired from the circuit court to become the first cashier of the Indianapolis branch of the State Bank of Indiana (1834–1845). When failing eyesight forced his retirement from the bank, Morris withdrew from public life and spent his remaining years on his 40–acre farm on the east side of Madison Avenue. Present-day Morris Street marks the northern boundary of what once was his property.

CONNIE J. ZEIGLER

Jacob Piatt Dunn, *Greater Indianapolis* (Chicago, 1910); Gayle Thornbrough, ed., *The Diary of Calvin Fletcher*, Vol. I (Indianapolis, 1972).

Morris, Morris (Dec. 18, 1780–Aug. 16, 1864). Indianapolis pioneer. Born in Monogalia County, Virginia (now West Virginia), Morris moved to Kentucky as a child and later practiced law there. When he became a Christian, Morris gave up his law practice, believing it was no longer a suitable career. In 1821, desiring to live in a state without slavery, he moved his family to Indiana. They arrived in Indianapolis not long after it was platted, and Morris began acquiring large landholdings in and near the town. He ran unsuccessfully for county clerk in 1822 and for sheriff in 1824. Two years later, he was elected to the Indiana General Assembly's House of Representatives, serving for one year (1826–1827). In 1828 Morris began a 16–year career as elected state auditor (1828–1844). During this period he also served as one of three commissioners who supervised the construction of the first STATE HOUSE in 1832. After leaving the auditor's position, he was an Indianapolis city councilman (1847–1848). In 1848 he and his sons constructed a steam mill on South Meridian Street near the site of the future UNION STATION. When his term on the City Council expired, Morris retired at age 68. In 1854 he hosted the first Old Settlers' Meeting of Indianapolis pioneers, which became an annual event thereafter.

CONNIE J. ZEIGLER

Berry R. Sulgrove, *History of Indianapolis and Marion County* (Philadelphia, 1884); *Biographical Directory of the Indiana General Assembly*, Vol. 1 (Indianapolis, 1980).

Morris-Butler House. House museum. Named for its original residents, the Morris-Butler House, located at 1204 North Park Avenue, is operated by HISTORIC LANDMARKS FOUNDATION OF INDIANA.

John D. Morris (1815–1895) moved to Indianapolis from Kentucky in 1821. In 1864 he purchased Lot 112 in Ovid Butler's subdivision and erected an upper middle class home of molded brick, designed by DIEDRICH A. BOHLEN and built by John Clements. Morris' family lived in the 16–room home until 1878 when an economic depression contributed to Morris' default on a loan that ended in bankruptcy. NOBLE CHASE BUTLER (1844–1933) purchased the house in October, 1881, living there with his family until 1933. A daughter, Florence, continued to live in the house until her death in 1958.

Park Avenue (art) Gallery operated in the home until owners sold the property to Historic Landmarks Foundation in 1962. The foundation's goal was to restore an example of fine Victorian architecture remaining in Indianapolis. The museum opened in 1969 and foundation offices in the house relocated as the collection grew. The entire building now serves as a nationally recognized museum of Victorian decorative arts and preservation education.

TIFFANY C. H. SALLEE
Morris-Butler House
Historic Landmarks Foundation of Indiana

Morris Plan. Savings and loan institution. Arthur J. Morris originated the Morris Plan in Virginia in 1910 to lend money to working people at reasonable rates. This idea proved so popular that Morris Plans grew up in cities across the nation. In 1921 a group of Indianapolis community leaders, including Charles F. Coffin, president of State Life Insurance Company, and L. M. Wainwright, president of Diamond Chain and Manufacturing, organized the Indianapolis Morris Plan. For several years Coffin and Wainwright served as officers of the locally owned institution, located throughout most of its history at 110 East Washington Street.

In 1936 Morris Plan merged with Schloss Brothers Savings and Loan, with William L. Schloss as president. By the end of 1946 the institution's assets totaled $2.5 million. In 1953 Schloss introduced the Morris Plan Free Charge Account and, by the following year, counted 23,000 individuals as holders of the charge plates, which were accepted at over 400 local and outlying stores. By 1958, with assets now over $36 million, Indianapolis Morris Plan was the largest savings and loan institution, without branches, in the nation. One third of Marion County families were members.

In 1967 the state legislature allowed Morris Plan to organize branch offices for the first time. Within two years the institution opened four branches in the city. By 1973 it had over 125,000 customers and 500 employees.

In the mid–1970s Firstmark Corporation purchased Morris Plan, but by 1987 Firstmark was experiencing serious financial problems and attempted to curb its losses by selling the parent company's subordinated debentures, which were really unsecured loans, to Morris Plan depositors. When Firstmark filed Chapter 11 bankruptcy on August 26, 1987, Morris Plan customers lost their funds in these uninsured investments and some filed civil suits against the parent company. On December 7, Summcorp, parent company of Summit Bank, purchased most of Morris Plan's assets and changed the institution's name to Transition Bank Asset Corporation.

CONNIE J. ZEIGLER

Morrissey, Michael F. (July 21, 1898–Mar. 25, 1985). Police chief, June 16, 1931–January 1, 1943. A son of Irish immigrants from Limerick and Kerry, and at 32 the youngest police chief in the city's history, Morrissey also held the position longer than anyone, a record made possible by an unbroken line of Democratic mayors from the late 1920s to 1943.

His tenure was marked by devotion to efficiency, the latest methods, recruitment of better educated officers, and improvements in training (he established a 14–week police school). When a survey of police departments elsewhere convinced him of the need for a crime laboratory, Morrissey secured private support for a skilled technician until the city council appropriated the funds. By 1940 a fully equipped lab was directed by a trained scientist with the rank of criminologist. Among Morrissey's innovations were painting the patrol cars with stripes to increase visibility, and substituting a "rubber slapper," his own invention, for the flexible, weighted leather clubs then in use. But Morrissey also wiretapped prison cells, created a Red Squad to develop a list of names and addresses of suspicious persons, and boasted of his "Indianapolis system" in which "known criminals" were arrested, released, and rearrested until they left the city.

More positively, Morrissey raised standards for recruitment and seems to have supported the goals of the Merit Law of 1935. He wanted intelligent and quiet-spoken police, and by 1938 he could report that most new officers were high school graduates with a sprinkling of college men. Applicants had to pass background checks and physical and psychological exams. Morrissey required officers to account for every minute of their day and kept statistics to identify high crime areas and thus deploy the department's resources more effectively. A president and vice-president of the International Association of Police Chiefs, Morrissey sent officers for training to the FBI and other police departments, and used Indiana University to improve recruitment and promotion tests.

In 1945 Morrissey married, left Indianapolis to head the private police of the Pullman Company in Chicago, and later was chief of security for a General Electric plant. He returned to the city after retirement in 1964.

WILLIAM DOHERTY
Marian College

Indiana Biography Series, Indiana State Library.

Mortality and Morbidity. The Indianapolis Board of Health began publishing annual health statistics, including statistics on death and disease, in the 1890s. Such statistics were not regularly collected before then, but frequent epidemics of malaria, cholera, and typhoid fever were described in public accounts, sometimes inconsistently. For example, an epidemic (possibly malaria) in the summer of 1821 was reported by Dr. SAMUEL G. MITCHELL, the city's first physician, as claiming 72 lives in one account, but only 25 lives in his second account.

Official health statistics for the past century reflect the progress made in achieving PUBLIC HEALTH standards as well as advances in medicine. Successful efforts to provide a clean water supply, promote the use of vaccinations, and develop new medications correlate with a gradual decrease in the incidence of many contagious diseases such as tuberculosis. Corresponding with this decrease in deaths from contagious diseases and a gradual aging of the population, chronic illnesses such as heart disease and cancer have become the leading causes of death.

In 1891, the three leading causes of death in Indianapolis were tuberculosis, diseases of the circulatory system, and stomach and intestinal diseases, together accounting for 596, or 28 percent, of the 2,128 deaths. Diphtheria and typhoid fever, two common contagious diseases related to poor sanitation, caused 183 deaths, or nearly 9 percent of the total. There were 1,180 cases of measles recorded in 1891, resulting in 9 deaths.

In 1939, approximately 50 years later, the top three causes of death had become heart disease, stroke, and cancer, accounting for 2,372 or almost 44 percent of the 5,418 deaths. By comparison, diphtheria and typhoid fever together accounted for only 14 deaths and measles for only one death in 1939. Tuberculosis still accounted for 215, or 4 percent, of all deaths in 1939. By the 1950s, tuberculosis was no longer a leading cause of death, although 239 cases were recorded in 1953.

In 1990, the three leading causes of death in Marion County remained heart disease, cancer, and stroke, accounting for 4,518, or 62 percent, of the 6,656 deaths. By contrast with 1891, only one case of measles and 70 cases of tuberculosis were recorded in 1989.

STEPHEN E. KIRCHHOFF

Ruby M. Grosdidier and Maria Rosado, eds., *Marion County Health Department, Indianapolis, Indiana (1820–1983)* (Indianapolis, 1984); Thurman B. Rice, M.D., *One Hundred Years of Medicine: Indianapolis, 1820–1920* (Indianapolis, 1949).

Morton, Oliver P. (Aug. 4, 1823–Nov. 1, 1877). Civil War governor and United States senator. A Wayne County, Indiana, native, Morton spent two years at Miami University (Ohio) and one term at Cincinnati College Law School. He read law and established his practice at Centerville.

Morton was originally a Democrat but abandoned that party in 1854 over the Kansas-Nebraska issue. He helped launch the state RE-PUBLICAN PARTY and was its first nominee for governor in 1856. Four years later he won election as lieutenant governor. When Governor Henry Lane resigned to enter the U.S. Senate in early 1861, Morton became governor.

In the secession crisis Morton opposed any compromise with the rebellious southern states. At the fall of Fort Sumter he offered 10,000 troops to the federal government. Thereafter he worked tirelessly to fill Indiana's quotas. The rendezvous point at Indianapolis for soldiers headed for federal service was CAMP MORTON.

Earning the sobriquet "the soldiers' friend," Morton took deep interest in the welfare of Hoosier troops and devised ingenious ways of supplying their needs when regular channels failed. To keep them in ammunition, the governor, on his own authority, established an arsenal at Indianapolis that not only supplied Indiana soldiers but also sold ammunition to the federal government.

After the Democrats won the 1862 legislative elections, the General Assembly sought to transfer the governor's military powers to other, Democratic, state officials, but at Morton's urging a sufficient number of Republican legislators abandoned Indianapolis for Madison, thus preventing a quorum and frustrating passage of the obnoxious proposal. When the legislature adjourned without making appropriations, Morton operated the state on his own with funds generated by the state arse-

Oliver P. Morton served as Indiana's governor during the Civil War. [Indiana Historical Society]

nal, appropriated by county governments, and borrowed from a variety of sources, including the federal government. Never one to miss a political opportunity, Morton tended to magnify the threat from allegedly treasonous secret societies, especially during election years, and countenanced the suppression of opposition newspapers and the arrest and trial of individuals critical of his and Lincoln's administrations.

In 1864 Morton won a second term as governor, and three years later he was elected U.S. senator. In the Senate he supported Radical Reconstruction and championed the rights of blacks in the South long after other Republicans cooled on the idea. Originally a hard-money man, he advocated inflation in the wake of the Panic of 1873. With strong support from southern Republicans, Morton sought the 1876 presidential nomination but lost to Rutherford B. Hayes in the convention.

CHARLES W. CALHOUN
East Carolina University

William Dudley Foulke, *Life of Oliver P. Morton Including His Important Speeches* (2 vols., Indianapolis, 1899); Kenneth M. Stampp, *Indiana Politics During the Civil War* (Indianapolis, 1949); Emma Lou Thornbrough, *Indiana in the Civil War Era, 1850–1880* (Indianapolis, 1965).

Moses, Thomas William (June 30, 1919–Mar. 21, 1986). Water utility executive and civic leader. Moses was born in Benton, Illinois, graduated from high school in Gary, West Virginia, received an undergraduate degree from Washington and Lee University (1939), and a law degree from Yale Law School (1942). After service in the U.S. Navy (1942–1945), he practiced law in Charleston, West Virginia, and Pittsburgh, Pennsylvania. The wealthy Murchison family of Dallas noticed him when he litigated a lawsuit against them, and in 1955 they made him executive assistant of their Investment Management Corporation in Dallas. The Murchisons—majority holders of the INDIANAPOLIS WATER COMPANY, 1953–1956, minority holders, 1956–1965—sent Moses to Indianapolis as assistant to the company's president in 1956. Moses became president later that year. In 1962, he moved to Minneapolis as president of the Michigan-owned Investors Diversified Services. From 1964 to 1969, he was president of the First Interoceanic Corporation in Minneapolis. Named chairman of the board of CURTIS PUBLISHING in Philadelphia in 1969, Moses arranged for its conversion into a nonprofit society in Indianapolis. In 1970, Moses became chairman of the board of the Indianapolis Water Company. He promoted its non-utility subsidiaries, notably the Shorewood Corporation, which developed land near the company's reservoirs. He also gained a reputation for civic activities, including a term as chairman of the local UNITED WAY, and he was widely regarded as the most important influence in bringing the HUDSON INSTITUTE and the INDIANAPOLIS COLTS to the Hoosier capital.

CHARLES JOHNSON TAGGART

Muir, John (Apr. 21, 1838–Dec. 24, 1914). Conservationist. Born in Dunbar, Scotland, Muir immigrated with his family to the United States in 1849, settling on a farm near Portage, Wisconsin. In the fall of 1860 Muir exhibited several mechanical inventions at the Wisconsin State Fair. Although his formal education ended at age 11, he was able to gain admission to the University of Wisconsin in 1861 on the strength of his designs. In 1863 Muir left the university without a degree and began the first of what would be a series of foot tours of the United States dedicated to the study of nature. In March, 1864, Muir went to Canada in order to avoid the draft.

At age 28, Muir returned to the United States and settled in Indianapolis. He chose the capital because of its industrial potential and the fact that it was surrounded by forests of deciduous hard-woods. From April, 1866, to March, 1867, he worked for Osgood and Smith, manufacturers of the Sarven carriage wheel. Initially hired as a sawyer, Muir was soon promoted to foreman and made several mechanical innovations in addition to doing a time-and-motion study to determine how productivity might be increased. After making his report in December of 1866, Muir began implementing many of his timesaving suggestions throughout the factory. But after one of his eyes was injured in an industrial accident, Muir decided that he would not devote his life to mechanical inventions but rather that he would pursue the study of nature. In April, 1867, he resigned his job and in June returned to Wisconsin. In August he began his epic thousand-mile walk to the Gulf of Mexico, then settled in California the next year.

The remainder of Muir's life was devoted to the study of nature and the preservation of natural resources. In 1890 he was instrumental in getting the Yosemite National Park bill passed by Congress. In 1892 he founded the Sierra Club and in 1908 Muir Woods National Monument north of San Francisco was created in his honor.

JEFFERY A. DUVALL

———

Frederick Turner, *Rediscovering America: John Muir in His Time and Ours* (San Francisco, 1985); Catherine E Forrest Weber, "'A Genius in the Best Sense': John Muir, Earth, and Indianapolis," *Traces of Indiana and Midwestern History,* 5 (Winter, 1993), 36–47.

Multi-family Residential Architecture. Multi-family dwellings have been erected since early in the city's history, despite the capital's deserved reputation as a community of single-family homes. The double appears to have been the earliest type of multi-family dwelling, dating from about 1840. By 1850, the city had a number of small doubles. The earliest double residences still existing in the city date from the 1860s. The William Keely Double (ca. 1867) at 335–337 North East Street is similar to earlier doubles, suggesting that this two-story, four-bay type may have been duplicated for several years. Another early double type is represented by the Greenwalt Double (ca. 1864) at 322–324 North College Avenue.

During the 1880s and 1890s, coinciding with the city's dramatic population increase, the double residence became more common. Doubles were built close to job sources. Indicative of this trend are the Ruskaup Doubles (ca. 1890), 702–720 Dorman Street (VONNEGUT AND BOHN, architects), built for grocer Frederick Ruskaup as an investment. The basic plan is similar to the Keely Double, but the architects applied fashionable Late Victorian detailing.

With the rapid development of Indianapolis during the early 1900s, the double became a popular investment property. Many older houses were converted to doubles or multi-units during the early 1900s. Principal streets and nearby side streets on nearly every side of town were considered good sites for doubles. The double began to shed its working-class image and became oriented to the middle class. The F. M. Bartholomew House at 4044–4046 North Central Avenue (1925) is a typical double of the era both in its design and location. Bartholomew, a contractor, built the house for his family and as an investment. Fewer doubles were built during the GREAT DEPRESSION, but by that time apartments were becoming more popular.

The rowhouse was another early type of multi-family housing in Indianapolis. Rowhouses were probably first built during the 1850s and 1860s. Very few exist today. Unlike eastern rowhouses, most in Indianapolis were erected as a single large development rather than individual units. The ST. JOSEPH neighborhood has the largest collection of rows in the city, including the large Apollo-Aurora rows at 1101–1103 North Alabama Street (1904).

Rowhouses were less common during the 1920s and virtually ceased to be built after 1940. Condominium development in Indianapolis, though legally distinct from rows, revived the rowhouse building concept. Lake Forest Condominiums, College Park Estates (1972), is an early instance of this modern development trend.

The apartment became the most popular form of multi-family housing after 1900. Several trends affected the development of apartments in Indianapolis. Throughout the 1800s, the average Indianapolis family had decreased in size. Young men and women left the shelter of their parents'

homestead and sought opportunities in Indianapolis. Both young childless and elderly couples needed an alternative to the large old family home. Apartments satisfied this demand for a new housing type. Shopkeepers had probably rented out vacant rooms for many years prior, but the Delaware (1885, demolished) is often cited as the first true apartment block. These early apartments combined commercial use on the first floor with flats on the upper levels. Flats had all the luxuries of a house, but apartments might have only several rooms without kitchen and dining rooms. By about 1920 the distinction was not so apparent, and the term flat was seldom used.

The Blacherne, 402 North Meridian Street, made apartment living acceptable and even fashionable. Hoosier author LEW WALLACE had the building erected in 1895 using royalties from his popular novels. The seven-story, red brick, Romanesque Revival style building created a sensation; apartment blocks of this size were previously unknown here.

By 1910, the near north side became "the flat district." Within easy reach of trolley lines to downtown jobs, this area was also desirable for its prestigious northside location. Increasing land values led developers to erect multi-story apartment buildings. A most common form of apartment was the eastern flat, consisting of a two- or three-story building with two large units per floor. The Sylvania, 801 North Pennsylvania Street (1906), is a typical example.

During the early 1900s, a new apartment type was created by eastern developers. Known as the "garden apartment," it was a two- or three-story, H- or U-plan building placed in a suburban context. Many examples still exist on North Meridian and Pennsylvania streets. The Buckingham, 3101–3119 North Meridian Street (1910, RUBUSH AND HUNTER, architects), and Oxford Gables, 320 East 38th Street (1927, PIERRE & WRIGHT, architects), are fine representatives.

Government involvement in apartment construction in Indianapolis began with the erection of LOCKEFIELD GARDEN Apartments at 900 INDIANA AVENUE (1937, Russ and Harrison, architects). The project was intended to mitigate poor housing conditions for one of the city's black neighborhoods, and its innovative design received much national attention. A subsidized housing project on this scale was not attempted locally again until 1968, when the JOHN J. BARTON Apartments, 555 Massachusetts Avenue (WOOLLEN ASSOCIATES, architects), were completed.

Private apartment construction of the scale seen during the 1920s was not surpassed until the 1970s and 1980s. Taking advantage of access to I–465, developers erected apartments, many on the same plan, on the outskirts of the city. Both local and national developers rehabilitated many historic downtown apartment blocks, returning them to use as rentals for young professionals and couples. Often, former residents were displaced, and the precise effect of this on the city has not been calculated. Another significant downtown event during the 1980s was redevelopment of portions of the CENTRAL CANAL and construction of several large apartment complexes adjacent to this waterway.

With ample building sites, Indianapolis never had need of the modern high-rise apartments of larger cities. Instead, apartment complexes are more popular with builders and occupants. Apartments were once an anomaly in Indianapolis, but today they provide housing for a large portion of its population. (See also SINGLE-FAMILY RESIDENTAL ARCHITECTURE.)

PAUL C. DIEBOLD
Division of Historic Preservation
and Archaeology,
Indiana Department of Natural Resources

Karen S. Niggle, Samuel Roberson, and Sheryl Roberson, "Apartments and Flats of Downtown Indianapolis," National Register of Historic Places nomination, Sept. 15, 1983.

Municipal Gardens. City park located at 1831 Lafayette Road. Established ca. 1920 as Casino Gardens, a private canoe and yacht club, and later a popular dance hall, the four-acre property and clubhouse were acquired by the city of Indianapolis during the summer of 1927 and renamed Municipal Gardens. Initial plans called for tennis, horseshoe and croquet courts, a playground, and a picnic area. By the mid–1960s the park included a community building, softball diamond, volleyball court, and playground. Since the 1970s

it has served as headquarters for the mayor's garden program, which leases small garden plots at other locations to citizens.

Under grants from the Urban Park and Recreation Recovery Act of 1978 and the U.S. Department of Housing and Urban Development Act of 1974, Municipal Gardens underwent an extensive $500,000 renovation beginning in 1979. The park includes fishing facilities, a hiking trail and bike path, a renovated community center, and rebuilt boat docks to serve the span of White River between 16th and 30th streets known as "Lake Indy." It also sponsors numerous activities, including Special Olympics programs, for the disabled.

Municipal Gardens is best known for its youth basketball program, begun in 1958, which allows over 300 inner-city and suburban youths to play in regularly scheduled league games. It entered teams in the summer AMATEUR ATHLETIC UNION (AAU)–USA Junior Olympics basketball competition beginning in 1973. Since that time Municipal Gardens' teams have won nine national championships (1979, 1983, 1985–1988, 1990–1991) and have been national champion runner-up six times (1975, 1980, 1982, 1985, 1988–1989) in different age categories. Many former Gardens players have played for the Indiana High School All-Star teams and major universities. Within amateur sports circles Municipal Gardens has earned a reputation as one of the top junior basketball programs in the nation.

JOAN CUNNINGHAM

Murat Temple (510 North New Jersey Street). Local headquarters for the Ancient Arabic Order, Nobles of the Mystic Shrine, more popularly known as the "Shriners." Designed by Oscar D. Bohlen (son of DIEDRICH A. BOHLEN and himself a Murat Shriner) and built by WILLIAM P. JUNGCLAUS COMPANY in 1909, the building draws on Middle Eastern and Egyptian designs. The four-story structure is distinguished by its yellow and brown brick banding, terra cotta trim, minarets, and stained-glass windows. The tower at the southeast corner is 208 feet high. The firm of RUBUSH AND HUNTER designed the 1922 addition to the building to blend with the original structure. It features a minaret intended to balance the tower on the original structure, as well as the Egyptian Room, an auditorium with motifs taken from tombs in Upper Egypt. (Though the theme of the room coincided with the discovery of the tomb of Tutankhamen by Howard Carter and Lord Carnarvon in 1922, it had been designed earlier.) An attempt was made to integrate an architecturally unsympathetic 1968 clubhouse addition by decorating it with a mosaic of Arabs crossing a desert.

The Murat is the only Shrine temple to bear a French name. It was named for "Bir Murat," an oasis in the Nubian desert, which was in turn named for Joachim Murat, a general in Napoleon's Egyptian campaign. The Indianapolis Temple was chartered on June 4, 1884; its first Ceremonial Class (1885) included LEW WALLACE and THOMAS TAGGART. By the time of its centenary in 1984, Murat was the second largest Shrine temple in the world in membership.

Many Indianapolitans know the Murat best for its theater (1910), the oldest surviving downtown stage house. The Shuberts leased the theater from 1910 to 1930 and brought in a variety of events and shows, ranging from a 1932 speech by Winston Churchill to Broadway musicals. After the English Theatre closed in 1948 and until

Opened in 1910, the Murat Temple at the corner of North and New Jersey streets was modeled after an Islamic mosque. [Indiana Historical Society, Bass Collection, #82280]

CLOWES MEMORIAL HALL opened in 1963, the Murat Theater was the only venue available for road shows. The theater has also served as a home for the Indianapolis Symphony Orchestra (pre-Clowes) and, briefly in the 1980s, the Indianapolis Opera Company.

The Temple has been active in Indianapolis in other ways: It is responsible for establishing the 500 Festival Parade; it gave the first animal—appropriately, a camel—to the Indianapolis Zoo; and it allowed the Indianapolis Symphony Orchestra to use the theater for a nominal charge during the Great Depression, a gesture that helped ISO survive.

The building was threatened by a 1988 fire in the 1968 addition. Though damage to the building was comparatively slight, 15 firefighters were injured when part of the building collapsed.

LEIGH DARBEE
Indiana Historical Society

Murat: One Hundred Years, 1884–1984 (Indianapolis, 1984).

Museums. The Indianapolis area boasts a variety of museums, many of them nationally acclaimed. A few of these originated in the 19th century, but most developed and flourished during the 20th century. Their development paralleled that of museums nationwide, with public-spirited community leaders, museum pioneers, and major benefactors working together to create outstanding institutions.

Establishing museums and other cultural institutions was obviously not a priority for early Indianapolis settlers. By the time Indianapolis museums emerged, strategies for museum management, funding, and education had matured. In fact, most historians believe that museums took their modern form during the watershed decades of the 1870s and 1880s, the very years that witnessed the early development of Indianapolis museums. By that time museums had generally become more professional and educational, and had abandoned excessive forms of entertainment. They had abandoned their total dependence on a paying public as well. Instead, they were formed by public-spirited citizens (a growing number of them women) who were intent on educating the community and who understood that major collections could be financed in part by the growing fortunes of industrialists and wealthy community members.

Like other larger industrializing cities, Indianapolis was developing a class of business and community leaders whose newly acquired wealth would soon serve as the foundation for museum collections, buildings, and publications. One of its most prominent institutions, the INDIANAPOLIS MUSEUM OF ART (IMA), originated as the ART ASSOCIATION OF INDIANAPOLIS, founded by MAY WRIGHT SEWALL in 1883. Thanks to the active promotion of art by Sewall and others, John Herron, an English immigrant who had settled in Indianapolis, bequeathed the Art Association close to a quarter of a million dollars to build an art school and museum in his name.

One of the oldest Indianapolis institutions found new direction and stability during the important decade of the 1880s. The INDIANA HISTORICAL SOCIETY (IHS), established in 1830, had faltered for over 50 years, lacking both an active leadership and interested membership. But in 1886, shortly after the founding of the Art Association, JACOB PIATT DUNN, JR., and others revamped the IHS.

The IHS and the IMA stand alone as successful cultural institutions in the 19th century. Although the INDIANA STATE MUSEUM was established as early as 1862, the absence of a permanent location doomed it to secondary status for almost a hundred years. But during the first half of the 20th century a number of newly created Indianapolis museums joined the IHS and the IMA as cultural and educational landmarks. All relied on visionary founders, generous benefactors, and highly motivated, public-spirited citizens. For instance, THE CHILDREN'S MUSEUM (1926) was pioneered, like the Art Association, by a resourceful woman determined to launch an institution that would serve the people of Indianapolis. MARY STEWART CAREY not only proposed the idea of a children's museum but garnered support among benefactors and fellow advocates who helped fund it. Similarly, a score of writers and admirers of JAMES WHITCOMB RILEY, including George Ade and BOOTH TARKINGTON, purchased the house in

which the Hoosier poet last resided and preserved it as a memorial (1921) for the general public.

Although public-spirited individuals and generous benefactors were central to most museum ventures in Indianapolis, one family—and in particular, one man—looms large as a major force in vision and funding for many cultural institutions. ELI LILLY, businessman and philanthropist, contributed countless resources to a number of museums in the greater Indianapolis area, as did his wife, Ruth. The Lillys' involvement in the city's museum community was so extensive that few institutions were untouched by the family's generosity.

Lilly's range was remarkable. A long-time advocate of Indiana's history, he served on the Indiana Historical Society's board of trustees and bequeathed a portion of his estate to the organization. This gift allowed the IHS to develop into one of the preeminent state historical societies in the country, with a significant library and a sophisticated publications program. Lilly's interests also encompassed historic preservation. In 1934 he purchased the deteriorating WILLIAM CONNER house, on the site where state commissioners had met to determine the location for the new capital. Influenced by Williamsburg, Lilly hoped to recapture some of Indiana's pioneer heritage by restoring the Conner House and occasionally opening the grounds to the public. Eventually he presented the house and property to Earlham College, which incorporated them into CONNER PRAIRIE, the area's first living history museum. Lilly also purchased the KEMPER HOUSE, a property he had long admired, restoring and furnishing it in 1962. He helped endow HISTORIC LANDMARKS FOUNDATION OF INDIANA (1960) and provided additional money for the organization to purchase the MORRIS-BUTLER HOUSE. Then he and Ruth helped to furnish the 1864 structure as a house museum.

Other Lilly family members also contributed to the financial health of Indianapolis-area museums. The descendants of JOSIAH K. LILLY, JR., donated Oldfields, the family estate, to the IMA. On several occasions Ruth and Eli each donated funds to the IMA, and Ruth Lilly actively supported The Children's Museum. The Lillys' influence was so great that the NATIONAL ART MUSEUM

OF SPORT, founded in 1959 at New Haven, Connecticut, relocated to Indianapolis 30 years later in large part due to the proximity of the LILLY ENDOWMENT, the private foundation funded by the family in 1937.

Even when other benefactors provided the catalyst for new museum creations, the Lillys or the Lilly Endowment usually became involved. For instance, Indianapolis businessman Harrison Eiteljorg donated his important collection of western art to what would become the EITELJORG MUSEUM OF AMERICAN INDIAN AND WESTERN ART (1989). At the same time, he contributed funds designated for construction of the museum building. But to complete the construction of the architecturally significant building, the museum relied heavily on resources from the Lilly Endowment.

The Lilly family and the Lilly Endowment have not been the only forces responsible for the development and transformation of Indianapolis museums. Major changes in historical thinking also have inspired and refocused the interpretive framework for many museums since the 1970s. The burgeoning field of social history profoundly influenced several museum presentations. Important insights by social historians have served as the bases for interpretive efforts at Conner Prairie and FREETOWN VILLAGE, an organization of African-American interpreters who portray the black experience in 1870s Indianapolis. The INDIANA MEDICAL HISTORY MUSEUM began concentrating not only on important physicians and medical institutions but also on the social impact of disease, medical education, and medical ethics on the larger community. Historically, house museums have often been utilized as stages for narrowly highlighting the one important man, woman, or family who lived in the structure. But their interpretive focus within the last 20 years has been directed toward larger issues. The Morris-Butler House has not focused exclusively on the families that lived there, but on the larger 19th-century society of which they were a part. Likewise, the BENJAMIN HARRISON HOUSE, while delving into the life of the Hoosier president, began interpreting broader issues within the political culture of the 19th century.

Like the city itself, many museums launched building campaigns in the 1980s and 1990s. A variety of institutions including the INDIANAPOLIS ZOO, Conner Prairie, the INDIANAPOLIS MOTOR SPEEDWAY HALL OF FAME MUSEUM, and the Eiteljorg Museum of American Indian and Western Art—to name only a few—built new structures and, since 1990, others made plans to move into the White River State Park area or began to develop plans for larger facilities elsewhere.

Most not-for-profit museums in Indianapolis have been accredited by the American Association of Museums, and most have professional staffs. As these staffs assume more educational responsibilities, and as the educational missions of museums become even more pronounced, Indianapolis museums will continue to play a role in the cultural life of the city.

STEPHEN L. COX
Conner Prairie

Music, Nineteenth-Century. Indianapolis residents in the 19th century enjoyed an active and participatory musical life. Music was more than entertainment: it was a shared activity that helped to build community and foster civic pride. Voluntary music associations flourished, as did the serious study of music by ordinary citizens. During the second half of the century performances took place in more than two dozen concert halls and typically involved both amateur and professional musicians. Programs were usually made up of many short works or excerpts, and included classics of the Western European repertory intermingled with American patriotic music, folk songs, and hymns.

The earliest musical activity in the city was the informal singing of hymns and folk songs. The first music organizations were church choirs, including those of the First Baptist Church from 1822, and the highly regarded choir of the Second Presbyterian Church during the pastorate of HENRY WARD BEECHER. The Society for the Cultivation of Church Music was in existence by 1824.

The first secular music organization was the Indianapolis Handelian Society, which performed on July 4, 1828, and included both voices and instruments. The Indianapolis Band was organized in 1840 and is reported to have included many of the city's leading citizens. Over the next half century more than 50 choirs, orchestras, bands, and other ensembles were formed. Some of these grew out of particular ethnic groups, such as the ensembles established by the city's German-Americans and, to a lesser extent, by members of the African-American community. These were important vehicles for preserving ethnic heritage; at the same time the combining of ensembles for festivals and holiday celebrations united the city's disparate ethnic populations.

The city's most long-lived music organization is the MAENNERCHOR, which has existed since 1854. Also established in the early 1850s was the Handel and Haydn Society, which flourished for two decades or more and which rehearsed Haydn's oratorio *The Creation* in 1851 with a large chorus and an assortment of available instruments.

In the 1860s concerts were offered by numerous ensembles, most prominently the Mendelssohn Society, the Philharmonic Society, and the Philharmonic Orchestra. The Mendelssohn Society was established as a chorus in 1867; an orchestra was added later. The society and its director organized performances for the benefit of the YMCA building fund in 1886, including concerts featuring a chorus of 600 girls.

The Philharmonic Society offered weekly concerts. In 1870 the Philharmonic Orchestra consisted of three violins, one double bass, one flute, one clarinet, one horn, and one trombone. The orchestra's small size did not prevent it from performing works by Beethoven and Wagner. Also active around this time was the Concordia, a short-lived vocal ensemble not to be confused with a drama society of the same name. Other ensembles included the Druid Maennerchor, Frohsinn, Beethoven Society, and Musicale. The Musicale, unlike the others, reportedly gave private parlor concerts in preference to public performances.

Musical life reached its peak during the 1870s and 1880s when an increasing number of music societies engaged ordinary citizens in semiweekly rehearsals and regular concerts. The Choral Union was the leading ensemble of the Anglo-American segment of the community. It presented many oratorios, including the city's first performance of Handel's *Messiah* in 1874. By 1877 it had over 100 members, including an orchestra.

The LIEDERKRANZ was the second leading German-American ensemble, after the Maennerchor. The INDIANAPOLIS MATINEE MUSICALE, believed to be the second oldest surviving women's music club in the United States, was established in 1877 to encourage music education and appreciation, performance, and friendship.

In the early 1870s a small group of German-Americans established the Lyra Society for the purposes of study and performance. The group developed into a mixed choir with an orchestra that was generally regarded as the best in the city; it offered frequent performances of Gilbert and Sullivan operettas.

Another orchestra was the Academy of Music orchestra, a professional ensemble that was criticized for playing too much music from the standard repertory and too few folk tunes. The Indianapolis Orchestra, a community group, gave its first performance in 1876 together with the Indianapolis Glee Club.

The Indianapolis Opera presented a full schedule of operettas in the 1880s, in addition to the premiere of the opera *Magnanon* by local composer Barclay Walker. It also offered an ambitious production of J. S. Dalrymple's *Naiad Queen*, with costly scenery and machinery that enabled hundreds of children cast as fairies to fly above the stage.

Other community ensembles that flourished during these two decades were the A. B. Clifford String Band, reported to have included two violins, double bass, flute, and cornet; the Cecilian Glee Club, a small but active singing society; the Harmonic Society, a breakaway group from the Choral Union; the Harmonie Society, a German-American men's chorus; the Euterpean Society, named after Euterpe, the Greek Muse of music, in which Mayor Daniel McCauley played the flute; the Harugi Maennerchor; the Indianapolis Chorus; the When Band, an ensemble sponsored by the WHEN STORE; the Socialist-Labor Saengerbund, and other choirs, orchestras, and bands. "Literary concerts" were popular among the city's African-American residents. These featured both solo and ensemble singing and dramatic recitations, often on biblical subjects.

In 1895 the German-born teacher and conductor Karl Schneider organized the Indianapolis

Symphony Orchestra, an ensemble unrelated to the orchestra founded in 1930. Two years later the Musikverein was formed as part of the German House; it included a men's choir, mixed choir, and 60–piece orchestra.

Music festivals were an important part of the city's civic life. A large number of music teachers' conventions, festivals of the German singing societies, African-American music festivals, and spring festivals featuring huge choruses brought together musicians and families from many different church and community ensembles.

Although music-making was to a large extent an activity of amateurs, as many as 131 professional musicians and music teachers may have been working in the city by 1880. Prominent among them were CARL BARUS; James S. Black, who conducted the Choral Union; Thomas N. Caulfield, who conducted the Mendelssohn Society; William Horatio Clarke, an organ builder who directed the Harmonic Society; Alexander Ernestinoff, who conducted the Maennerchor, Liederkranz, and Lyra; Max Leckner, a pianist who also directed the Maennerchor, Philharmonic Society, and Cecilian Glee Club; organist Peter Robuck Pearsall; tenor Ora Pearson, who organized the Indianapolis Orchestra and Indianapolis Opera; Hubert J. Schonacker, a pianist, organist, and composer; and Emil Wulschner, conductor of the Lyra and Choral Union orchestras and owner of the state's largest music store.

Guest artists frequently traveled to Indianapolis and surrounding towns. Violinist Ole Bull gave a recital in Indianapolis in 1853 together with pianist Maurice Strakosch and 10–year-old Adelina Patti. In 1859 Cooper's English Opera Troupe staged the city's first full opera production. Before 1867 pianist Sigismond Thalberg, violinist Henri Vieuxtemps, and American pianist Louis Moreau Gottschalk had all performed in Indianapolis. Anton Rubinstein and Henryk Wieniawski presented a recital in Indianapolis in 1872, and Hans von Buelow gave piano recitals in 1876. Soprano Lilli Lehmann was the soloist with a festival chorus in 1886. The Theodore Thomas Orchestra was a frequent visitor, and many traveling opera troupes introduced Indianapolis audiences to favorites from the German, Italian, and French repertories. Soloists with May festivals in the

1890s included Nellie Melba, Eugene Ysaye, and Edward MacDowell.

Local, national, and international music activity was followed in a number of local publications, including *Benham's Musical Review*, which was connected with Benham's music store and appeared originally as the *Western Musical Review* in 1866. Music lovers could also read about musical developments in *Willard's Musical Visitor*, established in 1870, and in reviews and essays by BERRY R. SULGROVE and others.

ANITA HEPPNER PLOTINSKY

Martha F. Bellinger, "Music in Indianapolis," *Indiana Magazine of History*, 41 (1945), 345–362; *Benham's Musical Review* (aka *Western Musical Review*), 1866–1879; Eva Draegert, "Cultural History of Indianapolis: Music, 1875–1890," *Indiana Magazine of History*, 53 (1957), 265–304; Ona B. Talbot, "A Sketch of Musical Life in Our City, Past and Present," in the program of the 32nd National Saengerfest N.A.S.B. (1908), 54–60.

Myers, Charles Wesley (Dec. 16, 1890–May 13, 1985). Physician and hospital administrator. Born in Marysville, Pennsylvania, and a graduate of the University of Maryland School of Medicine in 1915, Myers served in the Army Medical Corps during World War I and received the Distinguished Service Cross and the Croix de Guerre (twice) from France. Following the war he became a surgeon for the U.S. Veterans Bureau in Indianapolis before moving to City Hospital (later Marion County General Hospital, predecessor to WISHARD MEMORIAL HOSPITAL). During his tenure as superintendent and medical director (1931–1952), Myers opened new wards for African-American patients, appointed blacks to the hospital staff, and oversaw the construction of improved special care facilities. He was instrumental in creating the HEALTH AND HOSPITAL CORPORATION of Marion County, serving as a trustee from 1952 to 1968. In September, 1968, General Hospital dedicated a $12–million, seven-story addition designated as the Dr. Charles W. Myers Building.

Myers was a fellow of the American College of Surgeons and a former president of the Indiana Hospital Association and the Indianapolis Board of Health. He also served as a professor of gynecology in the INDIANA UNIVERSITY SCHOOL OF MEDICINE.

DAVID G. VANDERSTEL
Indiana University–Purdue University,
Indianapolis

Myers, (Mary) Hortense Powner (July 15, 1913–June 25, 1987). Journalist. An Indianapolis native, Hortense Myers graduated from Ben Davis High School in 1932. Her first newspaper position, with the *Old Trail News*, began in 1934. In 1942, she became the first woman to join the International News Service, which later merged with United Press to form United Press International. She completed a journalism degree at BUTLER UNIVERSITY in 1953. A well-respected political reporter, her three regularly published columns were "Statehouse Views," "Hoosier Politics," and "Feminine Horizon."

The numerous awards she collected during her career include the Frances Wright Award for outstanding contribution to Indiana journalism (1960); Woman of the Year, National Federation of Press Women (1966); and Indiana Newsman of the Year (1972). In 1975 she was named to the Indiana Journalism Hall of Fame. She was president of the Indiana chapter of Sigma Delta Chi and in 1976 became the first woman president of the INDIANAPOLIS PRESS CLUB. She retired in 1981 after 39 years with UPI. In 1982, Ball State University created the Hortense Myers Award in journalism in her honor.

Myers served on several governor's committees and coauthored seven books, including *Robert F. Kennedy: The Brother Within* (1962).

CYNTHIA FAUNCE

Indianapolis Star Magazine, Nov. 26, 1972; *Indianapolis News*, June 26, 1987.

NAACP. See National Association for the Advancement of Colored People

National. Indianapolis-produced automobile. The National Automobile and Electric Company was founded in Indianapolis (1900) by L. S. Dow and Philip Goetz. Until 1902 the company produced electric vehicles as well as horse-drawn carriages. The company reorganized as the National Vehicle Company after sale of the carriage manufacturing operation to the Gates-Osborne Carriage Company of Indianapolis. In 1904 the company, renamed the National Motor Vehicle Company, introduced a gasoline-powered vehicle. By then, except for a commercial model, production had ceased on electric passenger vehicles.

ARTHUR C. NEWBY, a promoter of six-day bicycle races in Indianapolis, joined the firm as a director and eventually became president of the factory located at 1105 East 22nd Street, along the Belt Line Railroad. In 1906 National introduced one of the nation's first 6–cylinder automobiles. Later, upon completion of the INDIANAPOLIS MOTOR SPEEDWAY in 1909 (Newby was a founding partner), the National did quite well, winning the second INDIANAPOLIS 500–MILE RACE in 1912. Illness forced Newby to relinquish control of the company to G. M. Dickinson in 1916.

After 1912 the company produced 4– and 6– cylinder cars, with a 12–cylinder model added in 1915. In the early 1920s the firm produced 6–cylinder cars only. A merger with Jackson, Michigan, and Louisville, Kentucky, firms ca. 1922–1923 resulted in the Associated Motor Industries, with Clarence A. Earl in charge. Automobiles continued to be produced under the National name only, but the company failed in 1924.

ALAN CONANT

Beverly Rae Kimes and Henry Austin Clark, Jr., *Standard Catalog of American Cars, 1805–1942* (Iola, Wisc., 1985).

National Art Museum of Sport. America's largest and most diversified collection of sporting art. Artist and former national squash champion Germain G. Glidden founded the museum in 1959, and it subsequently held its first exhibition in 1961 in the IBM Gallery of Science and Art in New York City. Not until 1968 did the museum find a permanent home at Madison Square Garden. Ten years later the museum moved to the campus of the University of New Haven in West Haven, Connecticut.

In September, 1988, the museum announced plans to move to Indianapolis due to the city's growing reputation as a sports center. Several local civic leaders, including James Morris, FRANK McKINNEY, JR., J. Joseph Hale, David Shane, and representatives of the LILLY ENDOWMENT helped precipitate the move. The Endowment assisted relocation with a $625,000 grant, and the museum opened in January, 1991, on the mezzanine level of Bank One Tower. Its initial exhibition, "Sport in Art from American Museums," displayed 68 artworks from 50 of the nation's most prestigious art museums and marked the museum's 75th exhibition mounted since its founding.

In September, 1993, the museum closed at the Bank One Tower location. Reasons cited included a poor location, an absence of marketing, and the failure to raise sufficient operating funds. The status of the collection, which includes over 250 paintings, drawings, and sculptures, plus 1,400 photographs, and ranges from a fifth-century-B.C. Greek sculpture to contemporary works, remained in doubt for several months. Then in July, 1994, it was announced that the museum would be relocated to the University Place Conference Center and Hotel on the IUPUI campus.

HEIDI K. MARTIN

Indianapolis Star, Jan. 30, 1994; *Indianapolis Business Journal*, July 11–17, 1994.

National Association for the Advancement of Colored People (NAACP). Civil rights organization. The Indianapolis chapter of the NAACP began in 1909, one year after the inception of the national organization. Its early meetings were informal and held wherever space was available. Formerly located on INDIANA AVENUE, offices of the local NAACP moved to 111 East 34th Street before relocating at its current address at 4155 Boulevard Place. Governed by a 24–member board and operated by volunteer staff who take and investigate complaints, the organization meets the first Thursday of every month.

Like the national organization, the local NAACP is committed to obtaining equal rights for African-Americans. The Indianapolis chapter unsuccessfully sued in the early 1920s to prevent the creation of the all-black CRISPUS ATTUCKS HIGH SCHOOL. Later in the decade the NAACP fought a successful legal battle to overturn an ordinance enforcing residential segregation. In the 1930s interest in the chapter declined, but revived in the 1940s. In the late 1960s and early 1970s the chapter fought to end segregation in Indianapolis' public schools. While they advocated two-way busing, NAACP members considered it a victory when in 1981 Judge S. Hugh Dillin ordered the one-way busing of 6,000 inner-city students to six township schools in Marion County. Afraid that the desegregation order was in danger of being circumvented, in 1993 the chapter threatened a lawsuit against Indianapolis Public Schools to prevent it from implementing a "SELECT SCHOOLS" plan. The plan, later accepted by Judge Dillin, allows IPS parents to choose from a group of schools which school their children would attend.

Today, the chapter continues to fight for civil rights, particularly in the areas of job and housing discrimination, and against bigotry. The NAACP office receives numerous complaints each week from members as well as non-members of the organization. The local chapter also seeks to empower blacks through the ballot box and is responsible for registering many black voters in the city. In the early 1990s the chapter came under criticism for being inactive and in need of new leadership. While recognized as a watchdog of the African-American community, the chapter has had difficulty attracting young members. Still, the city hosted the NAACP national convention in July, 1993.

Like other chapters across the country, the Indianapolis chapter is governed by a constitution issued by the national NAACP office in Baltimore. All major decisions must be cleared through the national office and there can be no action—boycotts, strikes, lawsuits—without the approval of

headquarters. The local chapter is comprised of several committees such as the youth committee, the voter registration committee, and the life membership committee. A new administration is elected every two years and any member in good standing is eligible to serve on the board.

AUDREY GADZEKPO

National City Bank (formerly Merchants National Bank). Fourth national bank in Indianapolis. Businessmen David Macy, Volney T. Malott, Alexander Metzger, and brothers Henry and Augustus Schnull founded Merchants National Bank on January 17, 1865, with Henry Schnull as president of Merchants' first office at 23 North Meridian Street. In 1867 the bank hired a thirteen-year-old messenger, John Peter Frenzel, the first of several generations of Frenzels to figure prominently with Merchants. Frenzel served in various capacities before being elected president in 1882 at age 28, then the nation's youngest national bank president. Merchants' offices changed locations several times until 1884 when it moved to the southwest corner of Washington and Meridian streets, later the site of the L. S. AYRES AND COMPANY building, where the bank installed the city's first safety deposit vault.

In the early 1890s Frenzel successfully lobbied the Indiana General Assembly to charter trust companies in Indiana. (Trust companies were for individuals, whereas banks primarily served businessmen.) He organized the Indiana Trust Company in April, 1893, and actively sought minority business by featuring a women's department, providing savings passbooks printed in German, and employing foreign language speaking lobby guards during busy Saturday banking hours.

Merchants built Indianapolis' first downtown skyscraper in 1913. The 17–story MERCHANTS NATIONAL BANK BUILDING at the southeast corner of Washington and Meridian streets remained the city's tallest structure for 50 years until surpassed by the CITY-COUNTY BUILDING in the 1960s. In 1918 the Frenzels and associates organized three neighborhood banks, forerunners of the institution's later branch banking system, including the State Bank of Massachusetts Avenue, site of a robbery by JOHN DILLINGER in the 1930s. In 1934 Merchants opened its first branch bank in the old Mustard Pot restaurant on East 38th Street. The firm then acquired former neighborhood banks and quickly converted them to branch offices.

In 1953 Merchants National Bank and the Indiana Trust Company consolidated as the Merchants National Bank and Trust Company of Indianapolis. The institutions previously had been closely allied through management and stock control. During the 1960s Merchants doubled its assets from $232 million to more than $500 million, and by 1965 had 22 banking offices in the Indianapolis area. In 1971 the Merchants National Corporation, a bank holding company, became the bank's parent organization. Six years later the $50 million MERCHANTS PLAZA complex opened at Washington Street and Capitol Avenue, housing Merchants' headquarters and the Hyatt Regency Hotel. The bank put together a $12.5 million loan package to lure the Colts professional football team to Indianapolis in 1984.

Aided by a new state banking law that allowed statewide and limited interstate banking, Merchants launched an aggressive acquisition campaign in 1985. Targeting banks that were first or second in market share, Merchants purchased 20 banks in four years and doubled its assets from $2.6 billion to $5.5 billion. In 1987 Merchants won a lucrative contract from the U.S. Defense Department to provide banking services to military personnel abroad.

In May, 1992, the Cleveland-based holding company National City Corporation acquired Merchants National Corporation in a transaction valued at $640 million. Merchants became National City Bank, Indiana the following October. The merger gave National City, with $30 billion in assets, the largest share of the combined banking markets of Indiana, Ohio, and Kentucky and ranked National City among the top 25 U.S. bank holding companies. Prior to the acquisition, Merchants employed 3,500 statewide. By 1993 National City Bank, Indiana employed approximately 2,000 people statewide, of which 1,500 worked in Indianapolis.

DEBORAH B. MARKISOHN

The City and the Bank, 1865–1965 (Indianapolis: privately printed, 1965).

National Council of Jewish Women (NCJW).

The oldest volunteer Jewish women's organization in the United States (established 1893). The goals of the NCJW embody Jewish values and democratic principles by advocating human welfare through volunteerism and participation in education, service, and advocacy programs. Special focus is placed on family issues involving women and children.

Women from the Indianapolis Hebrew Congregation formed the Indianapolis council of the NCJW in 1903. It began as a religious study group and attempted some social service projects. In its first year the members organized an industrial school that trained young women in darning, patching, and sewing. In December, 1904, under the supervision of Rabbi MORRIS FEUERLICHT, the council reorganized, placing more emphasis on social service work.

Both before and after World War II, the Indianapolis members assisted federal immigration authorities in resettling Eastern European immigrants and in providing guidance regarding American life and culture. During the 1930s, the women provided lunch money for refugee children and paid night school tuition for adults. In 1939, the Indianapolis council assisted in opening and managing a Refugees' Handicraft Exchange where refugees could sell the products of their trade. Indianapolis members also organized the Home Institute to instruct married refugee women in child care, budgeting, cooking, and homemaking. In the 1980s, with the increasing number of Jewish immigrants from the Soviet Union, the Indianapolis council reorganized its immigration efforts to help alleviate problems faced by the Soviet Jews.

The national organization established its social services utilizing scientific principles of social welfare. At the turn of the century, the Indianapolis council furnished a cottage in the Tuberculosis Colony of City Hospital (now WISHARD MEMORIAL HOSPITAL). Forty years later, the Polio Committee helped administer polio immunizations in public schools. Other volunteers assisted patients at Larue Carter Hospital, a mental health facility, with gardening projects and provided the hospital with a bus for patient outings.

Initiated in the 1980s, the "Sundries for Sojourner" program provides personal items for the families of battered women and it renovated the interior of a women's shelter. The Indianapolis council also founded "Rape and Its Aftermath," an educational program concerning rape.

The NCJW strives to serve youth by providing both assistance and protection. In 1906, in conjunction with the Jewish Federation, Indianapolis members agreed to act as juvenile court probation officers, overseeing all Jewish and some non-Jewish cases. During the first year NCJW handled 14 cases; only six involved Jewish children. Nearly 80 years later, this program developed into the Guardian *ad litem* Project, a UNITED WAY agency providing and training volunteers to represent the best interests of children in the court system.

One of the council's early preventive works was developing playgrounds to provide children an alternative to playing in the streets. The first playground was built at School 6 and monitored by NCJW volunteers. These volunteers estimated that over 150 children used the playground weekly. In response to the GREAT DEPRESSION, the Indianapolis council initiated milk lunch programs for undernourished school children. Coinciding with the lunches, the Personal Services Committee provided medical attention and clothing for the children.

To furnish religious instruction to Jewish children who attended public schools, NCJW opened the "School in Jewish History" in 1908 at the Nathan Morris House. Still in operation, it is now called the Council Religious School. Volunteers teach classes in Judaism and Jewish history to approximately 200 children.

The council works toward improving the life of the elderly, too. During the 1960s, Indianapolis members founded the "Hoosier Helper" volunteer program. This senior citizens program was the precursor to the Volunteer Bureau of Indianapolis. The women also manage the Golden Age Program that includes social services and two hot meals per week. Other programs organized senior

citizens to visit patients in the CENTRAL STATE HOSPITAL, a mental health facility.

STACEY NICHOLAS

Judith E. Endelman, *The Jewish Community of Indianapolis: 1849 to the Present* (Bloomington, Ind., 1984).

National Democratic Party Convention (1896). Convinced that the demonetization of silver was the primary cause of the nation's economic difficulties, advocates of the unrestricted coinage of silver succeeded in having their leader, William Jennings Bryan of Nebraska, nominated for president at the 1896 Democratic convention. Following Bryan's nomination, however, Democrats who favored maintaining the gold standard chose to form their own party. Led by former Indiana congressman William Dallas Bynum, the National Democratic party met in convention on September 2–3 in Indianapolis.

Held in TOMLINSON HALL, the convention was attended by 824 delegates from 41 states and was marked by great enthusiasm and little dissension. The delegates centered the party's platform around their opposition to silver coinage and support for a gold standard. Senator John M. Palmer of Illinois, a former Union general, became the party's presidential candidate; a former Confederate general, Simon Bolivar Buckner of Kentucky, was his running mate. Bynum and fellow Hoosier John A. Wilson were both on the new party's executive committee.

Despite the success of the National Democratic party's convention, the Gold Democrats, as they soon became known, failed to attract much support and in November, 1896, the Republicans carried both Indiana and the nation in the general election.

TODD McDORMAN

Clifton J. Phillips, *Indiana in Transition* (Indianapolis, 1968), 38–49; John B. Stoll, *History of the Indiana Democracy* (Indianapolis, 1917).

National Enquirer (1915–1933?). Prohibition newspaper. J. FRANK HANLY, former Indiana governor and strong prohibition supporter, organized and published the *Enquirer*. The weekly publication, using the motto "Truth without Fear," focused primarily on prohibition but also included articles relating to women's suffrage and family and religious news. By 1916 the paper claimed at least one subscriber in every state as well as the territory of Alaska and over the years maintained a limited national circulation. Oliver W. Stewart, associate editor, became editor in 1920 after Hanly's death. That year the format changed from 8 to 16 pages and by the mid–1920s reported a circulation of 4,000. Both Stewart, a former member of the Illinois House of Representatives, and Hanly were officers in the Flying Squadron Foundation, an organization devoted to the promotion of prohibition, and later editions of the paper were published by the foundation. By 1927 the paper had experienced financial difficulties and editions shrank to four pages. Around 1928 the paper became a monthly and later publication lapsed. Stewart renewed publication from June, 1932, to 1933 to support efforts of a national campaign organizing local prohibition societies.

JOAN CUNNINGHAM

John W. Miller, *Indiana Newspaper Bibliography* (Indianapolis, 1982).

National Institute for Fitness and Sport (NIFS).

National research/education center for fitness and sport. In June, 1983, the President's Council on Physical Fitness and Sport announced that Indianapolis was one of the cities being considered as the site for a United States fitness academy. In 1984, the academy staff decided to pursue development in California. Indianapolis business and community leaders, however, made a commitment to go forward with plans for a major center for health and physical fitness research and education.

The establishment of the National Institute for Fitness and Sport was part of the city's strategy to position Indianapolis as a national and international leader in amateur sports and physical fitness. The institute was a public/private project funded by LILLY ENDOWMENT ($6 million), the State of Indiana ($3 million), and the City of Indi-

anapolis ($3 million). The $10.5 million center opened on November 1, 1988. The 117,000–square-foot facility is located near the Indiana University Natatorium on land owned by Indiana University and leased to NIFS. A not-for-profit organization, NIFS continues to be funded by corporate, agency, and individual contributions.

The mission of the institute is to be a national center for research, education, and service, through which the latest information on human health, physical fitness, and athletic performance can evolve and benefit both aspiring and elite athletes. The institute is a comprehensive resource for fitness and sport development and human performance research. It offers a professional staff and extensive health and fitness programs for people of all ages and abilities.

DELORES WRIGHT

Indianapolis Star, Jan. 16, 1994.

National League of American Pen Women (NLAPW), Indianapolis Branch.

Founded by Grace Porterfield Polk in 1923 as the Indiana Branch of NLAPW, its name changed to the Indianapolis Branch in 1944 when a second group organized in Muncie. The national Pen Women's group began in 1897 in Washington, D.C., when women were excluded from the all-male Washington Press Club. Thereafter the national and local groups, like the Indianapolis Branch, have brought together professional women artists, journalists, and musicians to provide contacts, information, and mutual support.

Pen Women contribute to the cultural life of Indianapolis by providing regular programs and workshops for members and guests in the areas of art, letters, and music. The group also sponsors state and local art and writing competitions. The most numerous and active of the members within the local branch are the journalists, followed by artists. Throughout its existence, this professional association has benefited and promoted the careers of many local women journalists and artists. Several Indianapolis members have been highly active in the national organization.

SHIRLEY VOGLER MEISTER
Indianapolis Branch, NLAPW

Indianapolis Branch of National League of American Pen Women yearbooks and newsletters, Indiana State Library; Shirley Vogler Meister, "Pen Women: Creative in art, letters, and music," *Village Sampler* (Broad Ripple), May, 1992.

National Organization for Women.

Law student Norma Bradway Card convened the Indianapolis chapter of the National Organization for Women (NOW) in March, 1972. It was the second chapter in Indiana, Muncie-Delaware County NOW being the first. A civil rights advocacy organization for women, it seeks "to bring women into full participation" in American society.

In 1972–1975 NOW examined local radio and television station Federal Communications Commission license applications for sex and race discrimination patterns. NOW then met with station managers and successfully urged them to expand employment opportunities for women and minorities. In 1973–1975 the chapter dealt with gay and lesbian rights, child support, education, and employment issues. However, the proposed federal EQUAL RIGHTS AMENDMENT (ERA) was NOW's primary focus until 1982. President Marion Wagner led Indianapolis NOW in organizing to elect pro-ERA legislators in 1975–1976. The success of this strategy resulted in Indiana's ratification of ERA on January 18, 1977. Chapter members worked for an extension of the ratification period and went as ERA missionaries to unratified states until the extended deadline ended without full ratification on June 30, 1982.

Through the years Indianapolis NOW also worked successfully for passage of the state's rape shield law, domestic violence shelter funding, the spouse rape law, and the Indiana Sexual Harassment Task Force. It also opposed restrictions on abortion rights and helped establish the annual conferences on Women and the Legislative Process. In the early 1990s the Indianapolis chapter continues to monitor issues dealing with women's rights, especially during sessions of the General Assembly.

JILL LOUGH CHAMBERS

National Road.

First federal road through Indianapolis. Initially constructed 1811–1818 from Cumberland, Maryland, to Wheeling, (West) Virginia, the National Road was the first federally funded road planned across the United States. By connecting the Potomac River to the Ohio River, the road linked Washington, D.C., to the nation's interior. Further extension to St. Louis proceeded much more slowly as the political climate changed, but by 1827 surveys platting the road across Indiana were essentially completed. The road was entirely open across the state by the end of the 1830s. Covered bridges spanned major rivers along the road, including the White River in Indianapolis, where the route followed Washington Street through the heart of town. In 1848 Congress turned the National Road over to the states to maintain. During the 1830s and 1840s the National Road through Indianapolis carried a constant stream of stagecoaches, freight wagons, animals being driven to market, and westward-bound Conestogas, but its importance outside the city dwindled after railroad construction in the 1850s duplicated the route.

The road, known as the National Old Trails Road, experienced a renaissance as an automobile route in the 1910s, and the new State Highway Commission designated it a "main market road" in 1919. In 1927 it became U.S. 40, one of the first federal highways. The completion of I–70 in the 1970s again reduced the importance of the former National Road. Lengthy stretches of strip development in Marion County have obliterated

The National Road passed over White River through this covered bridge on Washington Street. The bridge was torn down in 1902. [Indiana Historical Society, Bass Collection, #223747]

virtually all vestiges of the National Road's mid–19th century past, but roadside diners and motels from its early years as an automobile highway survive in scattered remnants.

GLORY-JUNE GREIFF

Philip D. Jordan, *The National Road* (Indianapolis, 1948); Thomas J. Schlereth, *U.S. 40: A Roadscape of the American Experience* (Indianapolis, 1985).

National Sports Festival IV (July 23–31, 1982). Largest Olympic-style multisport event in the United States (renamed United States Olympic Sports Festival in 1986). In 1978 the United States Olympic Committee (USOC) announced its decision to implement a new national multisport event that would help develop and prepare the athletes who would eventually represent the United States in the Olympic Games. Held in non-Olympic years, the festival would also be a showcase for the country's finest amateur athletes. At that time, Indianapolis was in the early stages of its campaign to use amateur sports as a way to enhance the city's image and boost its flagging economy. Success in hosting an event of the magnitude of the National Sports Festival would generate positive national publicity and help establish Indianapolis as a major international amateur sports capital.

In 1980, Sandy Knapp, executive director of the INDIANA SPORTS CORPORATION (ISC), a not-for-profit organization charged with attracting national and international sports events to the city, went before officials of the USOC on behalf of Indianapolis in a bid for the 1982 National Sports Festival. In February, 1981, the USOC notified Indianapolis that the city had been selected to host the event. Factors influencing the decision included the support shown by the ISC and city leadership, existing sports facilities along with the commitment to build new ones, proven organizational abilities, long-standing volunteer spirit, and a reputation for Hoosier hospitality.

The $2 million event was financed through ticket sales totaling $1 million, six corporate underwriters, and 250 companies that made charitable contributions. In addition, with substantial financial assistance from the LILLY ENDOWMENT,

several new venues were built for the event, including the Indiana University Natatorium ($21.5 million), the Indiana University Track and Field Stadium ($5.9 million), and the Major Taylor Velodrome ($2.5 million).

During the eight days of competition, an unprecedented crowd of 250,000 spectators saw more than 2,600 U.S. athletes compete in 33 sports, breaking 58 National Sports Festival records in track and field, swimming, and archery.

Indianapolis was the first host city in the festival's history to present the USOC with a profit. Net proceeds were $132,000, with 50 percent going to the USOC.

DELORES J. WRIGHT

National Sports Festival-Indianapolis (Indianapolis, 1982).

National Starch and Chemical Company. The first starch plant in Indianapolis was begun as Union Starch Company in the near downtown area by William F. Piel, Sr., in 1867. This small facility had a grind capacity of 3,000 bushels of corn per day, but production halted on October 8, 1868, when it was destroyed in a fire. Piel rebuilt the plant at the same location, but an expansion in the customer base caused its relocation in 1872 to a site on the east bank of White River south of Morris Street.

Piel dissolved the Union Starch Company the next year, in 1873, and reorganized it as the William F. Piel Company, with a grind capacity of 5,000 bushels a day. For the next quarter century the company provided customers in Indianapolis and central Indiana with starch products. In 1899 it merged with a number of other small midwestern starch manufacturers to form the National Starch Manufacturing Company. The next year National Starch Manufacturing merged with Union Starch to form National Starch Company.

Piel's three sons soon after withdrew from the company and built a new plant on the west bank of the White River. Piel Brothers Starch Company operated from 1900 to 1939 and had a grind capacity of approximately 7,800 bushels a day. In 1902 National Starch acquired several other small plants and changed its name to the Corn Products Company. The name was later changed to the Corn Products Refining Company, and in 1939 a subsidiary, the National Adhesives Corporation, bought Piel Brothers for $225,000 and began producing starch under the name National Starch Products, Inc. An explosion and fire leveled the central manufacturing portion of the plant in May, 1942, but the company rebuilt the damaged facility.

The company changed its name to National Starch and Chemical Corporation in 1959 to reflect the widening scope of its manufacturing efforts, and in 1965 its Indianapolis plant underwent a major expansion, with a 30–percent increase in plant capacity. National Starch built its Raymond Street plant in another major expansion in 1978, and the company again changed its name to National Starch and Chemical Company. In 1993 the company, with headquarters in Bridgewater, New Jersey, had approximately 600 Indianapolis employees.

BILL BECK
Lakeside Writers' Group

The National Surgical Institute promised to treat a wide variety of diseases, as this 1889 advertisement suggests. [Indiana Historical Society, #C5751]

National Surgical Institute. Dr. H. R. Allen established the National Surgical Institute at Indianapolis in 1858. The institute, committed to the treatment of all surgeries and chronic diseases, was the first of its kind in the United States. It specialized in deformities of all sorts (particularly club feet, harelips, and hip and spinal deformities) and the manufacture of surgical and mechanical appliances for the treatment of these cases. Patients were housed at the institute's two four-story buildings on the northeast corner of Illinois and Georgia streets.

By the 1870s the National Surgical Institute had expanded to include four regional divisions located in Indianapolis, Philadelphia, Atlanta, and San Francisco. The national headquarters remained at Indianapolis, and the original institute was the nation's largest and most respected. In 1876 the Indianapolis division displayed samples of Dr. Allen's many patented surgical and mechanical appliances in a 36–foot, $1,200 glass case at the Philadelphia Centennial Exhibition. The display was the largest of its type and took highest premium at the exhibition.

On January 21, 1892, a fire in the facility killed 19 patients, wounded 30 others, and caused over $30,000 damage to the two buildings. At the time of the fire, the institute housed 316 patients. Since the buildings had been declared fire hazards more than ten years earlier, the tragedy created a public outcry and spurred building code and safety reform in the city.

Allen decided to construct a new building across the street from the State House. Building costs forced him to raise fees dramatically, and the institute lost patients and ran into financial trouble. It went into the hands of a receiver in November, 1898, and the Medical College of Indiana moved into the new building the next month. Allen continued to live and work in Indianapolis, while most of his staff moved on to St. Louis and founded the McLain Sanitarium in 1899.

WILLIAM D. DALTON

Indianapolis Star Magazine, July 31, 1966; *Indianapolis News*, Jan. 22, 1892.

Nationalities Council of Indiana. Not-for-profit organization devoted to educating the public about international cultures. Growing from the informal meetings of people from various ethnic backgrounds, the Nationalities Council became a standing committee of the INTERNATIONAL CENTER OF INDIANAPOLIS (ICI), established 1972. The council's major function was to provide authentic ethnic representation at events sponsored or supported by the ICI, primarily the INTERNATIONAL FESTIVAL, first held in 1974. It also provides a structure for organizing and promoting nonpolitical and nonreligious cultural and ethnic activities; promotes and increases communication and cultural exchange among ethnic groups in Indianapolis; and supports cultural and ethnic activities of member groups and other cultural and international organizations. The principal fundraising activity of the council is the annual International Festival, which attracted over 25,000 to the Indiana State Fairgrounds in 1992. The council also publishes the *Ethnic Hoosier* newsletter and provides educational materials on international affairs and cultures to schools.

Most ethnic groups participating in the council are stable organizations functioning under their own leadership, with an additional number of small transient groups. A growing desire for self-governance among council delegates led to a separation from ICI, with incorporation as the Nationalities Council of Indiana, Inc., in January, 1988. The council is governed by 15 directors, with 12 elected from council membership and 3 from the community. As of 1993 the council listed over 50 active organizations.

NAOMI MARTIN

Native Americans. Original inhabitants in the vicinity of Indianapolis. Disruptions and movements of Native American peoples during the proto-historic period of the 1600s makes it difficult to ascribe settlement in Marion County to a specific historic tribe. As the area of present-day central Indiana became better known to Europeans in the 1700s, speakers of Central Algonquian languages were reported as inhabitants of the Wabash/Maumee region. In all probability, they also utilized the WHITE RIVER drainage lands. The Miami, Wea, and Piankashaw, speakers of dialects of a single Central Algonquian language, were in the general region throughout the 1700s. Kickapoo, Mascouten, Shawnee, and Potawatomi were also reported in central Indiana periodically during that century. At the Treaty of Greenville in 1795, Little Turtle, the Miami war chief, claimed a broad area that included the future site of Indianapolis. The Miami continued to assert the primacy of their claim to the region throughout the treaty period of the early 1800s.

The first solid records of occupancy along the West Fork of the White River date to the early 1800s. Between ca. 1795 and 1821 a number of Delaware villages and one Nanticoke village existed along the White River from its forks to east of present Muncie, Indiana. Both the Delaware and Nanticoke spoke Coastal Algonquian languages and, having lost their original lands along the Atlantic seaboard, moved into the region at the invitation of the Miami. Most of the Delaware villages along the White River were upriver from present-day Indianapolis. At least one of these villages was in northern Marion County near the Hamilton County line.

In 1818, in separate treaties negotiated at St. Mary's, Ohio (the New Purchase treaties), both the Delaware and Miami alienated their claims to the greater part of central Indiana south of the Wabash River, including the area that would become Marion County. In their treaty, the Delaware agreed to move to an area west of the Mississippi and most of the Delaware who had not already departed were removed in 1821.

During the 1820s, as the Indianapolis vicinity was in transition from Native American to Anglo-American occupancy, a declining American Indian presence was still recorded. The existence of WILLIAM CONNER's trading post in present-day Hamilton County ensured some continuation of nearby Indian trade. Village and camp sites were noted during surveys of the county confirming both present and past occupancy and use by Native Americans. At least one early Indianapolis resident, CALVIN FLETCHER, reported that he was supplied with game in the city by a group of Wyandot in 1823. However, by the end of the 1820s, the Native American presence in the immediate area of Indianapolis was negligible.

In recent times there has been a different trend in the relationship between American Indians and Indianapolis. As an urban center, Indianapolis has attracted Native Americans from many tribes and regions. In the 1980 census, the diverse Native American population of Marion County numbered 1,437. This count includes 105 Miami, the first documented American Indian claimants of the area.

ELIZABETH J. GLENN
Ball State University

William C. Sturtevant (General Editor), *Handbook of North American Indians*, Vol. XV, *The Northeast*, ed. Bruce G. Trigger (Washington, D.C.: Smithsonian Institution, 1978).

Naval Air Warfare Center (formerly Naval Avionics). Avionics research and development facility for all U.S. armed forces. Commissioned in 1942 and operated under sole contract by the Lukas-Harold Corporation, the Naval Ordnance Plant (NOP), as it was then called, manufactured the famous World War II Norden Bombsight. This bombsight, invented by Carl L. Norden and Theodore H. Barth and fitted on all Army Air Corps and Navy bombers engaged against Axis targets, allowed American bombers to strike targets from high altitudes. The aircraft that dropped atomic bombs on Hiroshima and Nagasaki had Norden bombsights. The mechanical workings of the bombsight were kept "Top Secret" for 15 years; most Indianapolis residents were unaware of the plant's mission until well after war's end. NOP also repaired and shipped into combat many varieties of fire control instruments, flight instruments, and gunsights. For its wartime record of service NOP received the Navy "E" flag for excellence in 1943, 1944, and 1945.

The plant reverted to full Navy control in September, 1945, was designated the Naval Ordnance Plant, Indianapolis (NOP,I), and continued its manufacturing and repair roles throughout the KOREAN WAR. Rechristened the Naval Avionics Facility, Indianapolis (NAF,I) in 1956, its major mission changed primarily to avionics research and development for all military services.

In 1977, in recognition of the facility's service, NAF,I received an upgrade to full Naval Avionics

Center and the commensurate responsibility for research and development for all U.S. armed forces. While focusing on research and development, the facility still designed and built many prototype avionics and electronic countermeasure devices—"black boxes"—for mass production contractors. These included guidance packages for Polaris missiles as well as "smart bombs" like the Walleye, a camera-guided missile. The 1980s found NAC's avionics mission expanded to include anti-submarine warfare, weapons, and platforms (aircraft) research and development for the F–14 and the F/A 18. One of NAC's most recent efforts has been on the complex guidance system for the Tomahawk Cruise Missile, used with great success in the Persian Gulf War.

The plant's 3,000 employees have put weather and ship positioning satellites into orbit; fielded a space-based radio global positioning system; and worked on the Carrier Aircraft Inertial Navigation System for navigation, weapons delivery, and guidance. The facility was renamed the Naval Air Warfare Center Aircraft Division Indianapolis in 1992.

JOHN WARNER

NAFI (Indianapolis: Naval Avionics Facility, 1957); *Annual Report FY 1990* (Indianapolis: Naval Avionics Center, 1990).

Naval Armory. See Heslar Naval Armory

Navistar International Transportation Corporation (formerly International Harvester). Diesel engine plant. Chicago-based International Harvester grew out of Cyrus Hall McCormick's 1831 invention of the mechanical reaper. In 1904 the farm machinery business began manufacturing trucks, and in 1937 Harvester consolidated motor production by building a foundry and an engine plant on a 75–acre site on the southeast side of Indianapolis. Employing 1,100 people, the plant produced its first engine in 1938. During World War II the plant operated around the clock, manufacturing engines for military vehicles, mounts for Navy antiaircraft guns, and track shoes for Army personnel carriers. By 1946 plant employment had increased to 4,450 people.

The Indianapolis plant continued manufacturing engines during the 1950s and 1960s, but by the late 1970s Harvester began losing its competitive edge. Financial troubles forced it to stop production of vehicles using engines made at the Indianapolis plant. In 1981 engine production in Indianapolis dropped to 28,000 as compared to over 200,000 annually in the early 1970s. Employment also dropped, from over 3,400 to less than 1,000. A 172–day strike in late 1979 and early 1980 caused company officials to consider abandoning the plant and moving production to Mexico in favor of lower labor costs. To save the plant, the city and state chipped in $2.1 million in loans and job training and the union agreed to wage and benefit concessions. Rejuvenated, the plant began production of a new engine, used by the FORD MOTOR COMPANY in vans and pickup trucks, and became a money-maker for Harvester. In 1986 International Harvester changed its name to Navistar International, reflecting the sale of its farm equipment business. In 1991 the plant's foundry, now known as the Indianapolis Castings Corporation, became a wholly owned subsidiary of Navistar. As of the early 1990s, Navistar's Indianapolis engine plant employed over 1,900 people (700 at Indianapolis Castings) and had annual sales of more than $350 million.

DEBORAH B. MARKISOHN

"International Harvester . . . ," *Indiana Business and Industry* (Oct., 1963); *Indianapolis Star*, Jan. 8, 1986.

NBD Bank (formerly Indiana National Bank). Major Indianapolis bank that traces its roots to the antebellum era. In 1834 the Indiana General Assembly granted a 25–year charter for the Second State Bank of Indiana. Branches were located around the state, including Indianapolis, to provide currency and short-term commercial and agricultural loans. The charter for the Second State Bank expired in 1857 and many of the same investors sought a charter for the third state bank, the Bank of the State of Indiana. In 1865, after investors of the Indianapolis branch secured a national charter under the National Banking Act of

Indiana National Bank, corner of Virginia Avenue and Pennsylvania Street. [Indiana Historical Society, Bretzman Collection]

1863, the charter of the third state bank was allowed to expire. The new bank was called the Indiana National Bank of Indianapolis.

Indiana National, located at Washington and Meridian streets, enjoyed quiet growth during the rest of the 19th century. In 1882 Volney T. Malott purchased the bank, moved it to 11 East Washington Street, and expanded its customer base. In 1895 a massive fire destroyed the building, and two years later Indiana National opened the doors to its Neoclassical building at 3 Virginia Avenue. Indiana National acquired Capital National Bank in 1912. The bank continued its conservative management during the Great Depression and not only survived but grew during this period, acquiring the assets of Continental National Bank in 1933.

Indiana National took advantage of the economic vitality that occurred during World War II and the postwar period. Indianapolis experienced rapid growth, and Indiana National reached out to potential customers by establishing branches, the first on Maple Road (38th Street) in 1947. Indiana National also augmented its financial and customer base through acquisition of other banks in the community, including Madison Avenue State Bank in 1948, Union Trust in 1950, and New Augusta State Bank in 1958. By 1968 INB had identified itself as the "Billion Dollar Bank."

In 1969 Indiana National Bank came under the umbrella of Indiana National Corporation, which allowed the bank to engage in a wider range of activity. Aware of its stature as the largest bank in Indianapolis, Indiana National moved into the 37–story INB TOWER at One Indiana Square in 1970. The new tower symbolized the development of a corporate identity—a one-bank holding company—and Indiana National's investment in the community. During the mid–1970s the bank also became involved in urban development, forming a bank community development corporation.

The economic conditions of the 1980s contributed to restructuring of banking institutions nationally. In 1986 INB began an aggressive program of acquisitions throughout the state as a result of the legislative changes at the state level that allowed banking across county lines. Indiana National Corporation became INB Financial Corporation in 1989. In 1992 NBD Bancorp, Inc., of Detroit, a regional bank holding company, purchased INB; it changed the name to NBD Indiana, Inc., in October, 1993.

NORALEEN A. YOUNG

Negley, Claude E. Mayor of Indianapolis, October 27–November 9, 1927, Republican. Born in northern Marion County, Negley was in the real estate business when he won a seat on the Indianapolis Common Council in 1925 in an election that saw Republicans sweep city offices, with JOHN L. DUVALL elected as mayor. In 1927 a Marion County court convicted Duvall for violating the Corrupt Practices Act by taking bribes from KU KLUX KLAN leader DAVID CURTIS (D. C.) STEPHENSON in exchange for allowing the Klan to pick members of various city boards. Barred from holding office, Duvall resigned on October 27, 1927, a few days after appointing his wife city controller. With Duvall's resignation, his wife became mayor for 15 minutes. During her short tenure, she named Ira Holmes as city controller and then resigned; Holmes took over as mayor. The Common Council, however, selected Negley, its president, as acting mayor.

On November 8, 1927, the council met and, on the 33rd ballot, elected Democrat L. ERT SLACK as mayor. Later that month, a Marion County grand jury returned indictments against Negley

and three other council members for soliciting bribes from Duvall in exchange for their votes in impeachment proceedings against the mayor in August, 1927. Negley and other council members pleaded guilty, were fined, and resigned from the council.

RAY BOOMHOWER
Indiana Historical Society

"City Had Four 'Mayors' at One Time, Back in '27," *Indianapolis Times*, Oct. 18, 1959.

Nehrling, Wally A. (1910–May 26, 1980). Radio personality. Known as "Uncle Wally" to thousands of central Indiana radio listeners for four decades, Nehrling, a native of Normal, Illinois, began his career as a would-be radio singer in South Bend while attending the University of Notre Dame. Radio singing jobs were scarce, however, so he turned to announcing. Nehrling later worked at radio stations in Fort Wayne and Gary before joining WIRE in Indianapolis in 1938 as its morning announcer. He remained in that position for almost 30 years, retiring from the air in 1967. Nehrling was a broadcasting original, a man whose warm, folksy style and sometimes corny jokes coaxed two generations of listeners out of bed, even though he confessed that he kept two alarm clocks at his own bedside to get him up at 4 A.M.

In addition to his "Wake Up With Wally" morning show, Nehrling gained fame as the host of the "Funny Paper Party" each Sunday morning. The program first was broadcast from the WIRE studios, but Wally soon took it "on the road," reading the Sunday morning comics from homes

Wally A. Nehrling, known to Indianapolis children as "Uncle Wally," read the Sunday comics over the radio for his "Funny Paper Party" show. [Indiana Historical Society, Bretzman Collection, #C5806]

all across the listening area. As a father of four, he found it easy to relate to the youngsters who gathered around him as he read the adventures of the Lone Ranger and other cartoon heroes from the pages of the Sunday *Indianapolis Star.*

Following his retirement from active broadcasting in 1967, Nehrling served as WIRE's public service director until 1974.

MIKE AHERN
WISH-TV

___

Indianapolis News, Sept. 29, 1967, May 27, 1980.

New Augusta. Town located in northwest Marion County, just northeast of Georgetown Road and 71st Street. The Indianapolis & Lafayette Railroad built Augusta Station in 1852 as a link to the village of AUGUSTA, a short distance to the east. In the next few years, a town grew up around the depot. It was named Hosbrook for one of the commissioners who platted the town. Some referred to the town as Augusta Station, while others called it Hosbrook. The U.S. Post Office settled the question in 1878, dubbing the area New Augusta.

The town has grown slowly over the years, numbering at its peak 200–300 residents. New Augusta celebrated its centennial in 1955 and counted three grocery stores, a feed and grain store, a small manufacturing plant, and a number of specialty shops. The New Augusta State Bank was a fixture in the town until it was purchased by Indiana National Bank (now NBD BANK) in 1958.

Under UNIGOV, New Augusta became a part of Indianapolis. Today, housing developments and shopping centers have almost enveloped the town, yet the community retains a number of original structures. The Salem Lutheran Church, founded in 1836, is one of the oldest buildings (1880) in New Augusta. The railroad depot, though closed, also still stands, as do many old homes. In July, 1989, New Augusta was listed on the National Register of Historic Places.

CATHLEEN F. DONNELLY

___

Berry R. Sulgrove, *History of Indianapolis and Marion County* (Philadelphia, 1884); *New Augusta*

Community Centennial, 1855–1955 (pamphlet; copy in Indiana State Library).

New York Central Railroad. Beginning in 1850, RAILROADS that later comprised parts of the New York Central (NYC) began operating to St. Louis and Cleveland; Chicago and Cincinnati; and Peoria, Illinois, and Springfield, Ohio.

The forerunner of this system was the Indianapolis and Bellefontaine, chartered in 1848, which, in December, 1850, began service to Pendleton, 28 miles northeast of the capital. In January, 1853, tracks reached Union City, an important junction. After mergers in the 1860s, it was extended to Galion, Ohio, on a route to Cleveland and became known as the Bee Line. After an 1889 merger, it became the Cleveland, Cincinnati, Chicago, and St. Louis (Big Four).

Meanwhile, roads reached Cincinnati and Chicago. In late 1852 service began over the Lafayette and Indianapolis Railroad (L&I), and in November, 1853, the first train, which utilized a short Ohio River boat connection, ran the length of the Indianapolis and Cincinnati Railroad. After its president, Henry C. Lord, failed to gain control of the L&I, he began to construct a competing line via Crawfordsville. By 1867, his threat had forced the L&I to sell and he abandoned the incomplete Crawfordsville line. (Other companies extended it to Peoria, Illinois, in 1869 as the Indianapolis, Bloomington, and Western.) The new road became the Indianapolis, Cincinnati, and Lafayette and in 1873 it was extended to Chicago via trackage rights over the Illinois Central beyond Kankakee, Illinois. Among four roads connecting Indianapolis and Chicago, it dominated the post–World War II passenger business with six daily round trips. Nevertheless the line was abandoned beginning in 1976.

In 1867, the Indianapolis and St. Louis Railroad was incorporated to parallel what became the PENNSYLVANIA RAILROAD. It was opened in 1870 to Terre Haute and by lease extended to St. Louis. It also became part of the 1889 Big Four merger, and with the one-time Bee Line now forms Conrail's busy St. Louis–East Coast freight route. To serve it, NYC built the $3^3/_4$-mile-long Big Four Yard near Avon in the late 1950s. It moved

49 trains daily (as of 1989) through its 55 classification tracks.

In 1880, the Indianapolis and Ohio State Line Railroad was projected to Columbus, Ohio. Following a merger, it reached Springfield, Ohio, in 1882 and leased an extension to Columbus. Following two reorganizations, the combined Peoria-Springfield routes emerged as Peoria and Eastern Railroad (P&E) in 1890. The Big Four then acquired the Springfield line and leased the Peoria road. The NYC absorbed the Big Four system after leasing it in 1930.

Penn Central interests, successors to NYC, abandoned virtually the entire Springfield line in Indiana in 1976–1977. Conrail, Penn Central's successor, abandoned the P&E from Crawfordsville west to Olin (near Covington) in 1982. Amtrak, however, operates its daily Chicago round trip and its thrice-weekly New York-Washington-Cincinnati-Chicago service over the Crawfordsville line and CSX freight trains also have trackage rights.

RICHARD S. SIMONS
National Railway Historical Society

Alvin F. Harlow, *The Road of the Century* (New York, 1947); A. Maurice Murphy, "The Big Four Railroad in Indiana," *Indiana Magazine of History*, 21 (June, Sept., 1925), 109+.

Newby, Arthur C. (Dec. 29, 1865–Sept. 11, 1933). Early bicycle and automobile manufacturer and cofounder of the Indianapolis Motor Speedway. Born on a farm near Monrovia, Indiana, Newby came to Indianapolis seeking employment about 1881 and eventually settled in at NORDYKE AND MARMON, where he worked his way from office boy to middle management. Succumbing to the bicycle craze that swept the country in the late 19th century, Newby helped found the Zig-Zag Cycling Club in the 1890s. That same decade, Newby, along with Charles E. Test and Edward Fletcher, formed the Indianapolis Chain and Stamping Company, precursor to the DIAMOND CHAIN COMPANY. By the end of the 1890s the company was supplying about 60 percent of American-made bicycle chains. Newby was also associated with the Hay and Willits Manufacturing Company, makers of Outing bicycles, from 1894 to 1899.

Newby became heavily involved in the promotion of bicycle racing with the construction in 1898 of the Newby Oval, a quarter-mile wooden track set on 15 acres near Central Avenue and 30th Street. Among his partners in this venture were JAMES A. ALLISON and CARL G. FISHER, both of whom he later joined in founding the INDIANAPOLIS MOTOR SPEEDWAY in 1909. By the turn of the century Newby had redirected his attention to automobiles, founding, with others, the NATIONAL Motor Vehicle Company, which built first electric, then gasoline-driven cars. In later years Newby, who never married, became known as the "quiet philanthropist," giving several hundred thousand dollars without fanfare, primarily for hospitals and higher education.

GLORY-JUNE GREIFF

Newcomb, Horatio Cooley (Dec. 20, 1821–May 23, 1882). Second mayor of Indianapolis, 1849–1851, Whig. Born in Wellsboro, Pennsylvania, Newcomb in 1833 moved with his widowed mother from Cortland, New York, to Vernon, Indiana, where her brother, William Avery Bullock, had opened the first law office in Jennings County. Young Newcomb studied law under his uncle's direction, passing the bar in December, 1844. He married Eliza Pabody in 1845 (they had seven children) and moved to Indianapolis in December, 1846, to form a partnership with OVID BUTLER, Eliza's uncle and a prominent lawyer. Newcomb rapidly became a leader of the local bar. He won election as mayor in April, 1849, at age 27 (he remains the youngest mayor in the city's history). Reelected in April, 1851, he resigned six months later to devote more time to his law practice.

For a man "never known to seek office" (the accepted pretense of the day), Newcomb's subsequent career was filled with elective and appointive offices and other responsible posts: Indiana House of Representatives (1855, 1865, 1867) and Senate (1861); city councilman (1853, 1854) and president, Indianapolis board of aldermen (1877, 1878); president, state sinking fund (1861–1863); director, City Hospital (1870, 1871); Marion County Superior Court judge (1871–1876); and state Supreme Court commissioner (1881, 1882). He also served as political editor of the IN-DIANA STATE JOURNAL from 1864 to 1868. New-comb declined appointment as assistant secretary of the U.S. Department of the Interior in 1874 and failed at election to the state Supreme Court two years later.

WILLIAM DOHERTY
Marian College

———————

John H. B. Nowland, *Sketches of Prominent Citizens of 1876* (Indianapolis, 1877); *A Biographical History of Eminent and Self-Made Men of the State of Indiana* (Cincinnati, 1880).

News Broadcasting. In November, 1924, the city's first permanent radio station, WFBM, devoted its introductory night of operation to election returns. Actual newscasts were not common during the early days of radio, however; most stations left news reporting to the daily papers. By the early 1930s broadcasting's immediacy and competition for advertising began to challenge the print media. Newspapers subsequently pressured the major wire services—Associated Press (AP), United Press (UP), and International News Service (INS)—not to provide radio with news reports. By 1936, however, UP had established a special radio wire service, and AP began one five years later.

WFBM's Ken Ellington became the city's first regular newscaster in 1933–1934. He was a popular reporter and became known for leading his station's five day, 24 hours a day coverage of the Ohio River flood in January, 1937. Following Ellington's departure for WBBM in Chicago the next month, WFBM hired GILBERT FORBES who became one of Indiana's most famous newscasters during his 24–year tenure. The local voice of World War II news, Forbes served as a war correspondent in France after D-Day, reporting on Indiana troops involved in the fighting. It was during the war and postwar years that modern news broadcasting was born.

During the 1950s all five Indianapolis radio stations had organized news staffs. Reporting on a newsmaker or an event became easier as recording technology improved, though it still proved to be difficult because the equipment remained rather bulky and cumbersome. By the end of the decade some stations had acquired the capability to report live from the site of a news story. WXLW's Bill Anderson and Bob Rutherford often broke into regular programming with reports from their "newsmobiles." Both WFBM and WIBC had mobile news units; WIBC's was manned by former newspaper reporter ROBERT (BOB) HOOVER, who became legendary for his field reports.

While broadcast news had been the exclusive domain of radio, television entered the local picture by the 1950s. The earliest television news programs were essentially radio scripts read on camera, and most ran no longer than 15 minutes. Forbes anchored newscasts on WFBM-TV (later WRTV) Channel 6, while WISH-TV Channel 8's first newscasters were John Fraim and then Vince Leonard. When WLW-I (later WTHR) Channel 13 first aired in 1957 former WIBC news reporter Gordon Graham handled the anchor duties. WTTV Channel 4 also aired news with former WIBC and WISH newscaster Frank Edwards, who had returned to Indianapolis in 1955 following a stint with Mutual Radio in Washington.

With the arrival of the 1960s radio newsgathering demonstrated a growing dependence on new technologies. Recorders were smaller, and live radio transmissions improved in quality. Remote radio broadcasts were routine by October, 1963, when Bob Hoover drove the WIBC mobile unit onto the bloodstained ice of the State Fairgrounds Coliseum following the tragic explosion that killed 74 and wounded hundreds. Television remained hampered by existing technology. News stories were shot on film, which required lengthy processing and editing. During the decade, however, local television news, like the networks, came of age and gained sophistication. To cover the news of the day the major networks expanded their news programming; local stations quickly followed. WFBM's "early report" with Ken Beckley and Howard Caldwell expanded to one hour in 1966. WISH-TV Channel 8 began its own one-hour news program in 1968 anchored by former WIRE radio news reporter Mike Ahern.

A larger public appetite for news and a greater maturity in the industry followed in the 1970s.

Live reports and expanded news staffs drove the increasingly competitive Indianapolis market. The personality of broadcasters, and attention to the cosmetics of sets, graphics, and lighting, also became important for the success of news programming. In 1975 competition for viewers became stiffer when the new owners and management of WTHR Channel 13 selected Paul Udell to anchor their news program.

The 1970s saw legitimate news departments disappear from all but a few radio stations. WIBC, led by news director Fred Heckman and a full complement of reporters, built its reputation on local news and information. WIRE and WTLC also maintained full news staffs, while WNTS operated a news-talk format on its daytime-only programming. One of the city's major news events, the 1977 abduction of Richard Hall by Tony Kiritsis, directly involved Heckman with whom Kiritsis kept in contact. The Kiritsis story also showed how television technology had changed; electronic news gathering (ENG), satellite technology, and the advent of the videotape camera all gave television the power of immediacy.

During the 1980s the business of news broadcasting began to drive decision making at the stations. News promotion became part of the tactics of the operation, as did the use of consultants, research teams, talent development coaches, and graphic design specialists. Once again newscasts, responding to public desires for more news and information, expanded in length, with WRTV and WISH-TV adopting 90-minute early evening programs in 1987 and 1989, respectively. Male-female anchor teams also became the norm at all three network affiliates, as did sending local personnel to cover national stories. In 1989, for example, WTHR used its satellite truck to broadcast live each night from Washington, D.C., during the celebrations surrounding Dan Quayle's inauguration as vice-president. The changing economics of radio, however, resulted in further thinning of staffs. WIFE adopted an all-news format in 1981, but abandoned it two years later. At the end of the decade only WIBC and WTLC had viable news operations.

By the early 1990s most Americans were getting their news from television, and local stations responded with more changes. Besides the regular midday news program, the stations produced morning news shows to precede the networks' morning programming. WRTV began producing a nightly half-hour newscast at 10 P.M. on WTTV after that station dropped its news department. WISH-TV started a 24-hour headline service and expanded its full-time news staff to 55 (up from 8 in 1963). WTHR adopted a news and public affairs format on its low-power facility, Channel 27, in January, 1994. WXIN Channel 59, which produced a short-lived newscast in 1984, reestablished a news department in 1991 and offered a nightly newscast at 10 P.M. Demonstrating the importance of news programming to the stations' success, in the early 1990s the three main stations derived an estimated 33 to 38 percent of their profits from local newscasts.

Anchor teams for the stations in the early 1990s included Clyde Lee and Diane Willis on WRTV Channel 6, Mike Ahern and Debby Knox on WISH-TV Channel 8, Tom Cochrun and Anne Ryder on WTHR Channel 13, and Bob Donaldson and Caroline Thau on WXIN Channel 59. WRTV's longtime anchor Howard Caldwell retired in 1994 after 35 years with the station. In radio, WTLC cited money as the reason for scrapping its news department, while Fred Heckman resigned from WIBC in 1993 after disputes with new management over changes in the news department. By 1994 only WIBC and WFMS presented any locally originated news on radio.

As of the early 1990s Indianapolis television stations boasted great stability in their news anchor positions. Compared to the industry's average of five years, many local anchors had held their positions much longer, which lent credibility to their reporting of local news. At the same time, however, communication critics have claimed that local stations lack the aggressive journalism and "hard news" capabilities of earlier years. Nevertheless, local broadcast news provides an important service to the community, offering quick coverage of breaking news and valuable information to the city's residents.

THOMAS DECKER COCHRUN
WTHR News Channel 13

MICHAEL SPILLMAN

Burk Friedersdorf, *From Crystal to Color: WFBM* (Indianapolis, 1964); *Indianapolis Star*, August 12, 1990.

Newspapers, Alternative. In the 1960s discontented writers around the country, and around Indianapolis, went into the publishing business. They started so-called underground newspapers, which often more closely resembled pamphlets, frequently to protest the VIETNAM WAR and the actions of the Nixon administration. These papers were scantily financed projects, sometimes operating out of the publisher's kitchen. The writers had day jobs, and in many cases they wrote for free. Most such papers published weekly, though some came out monthly and others were issued irregularly. The underground papers fed off the antiwar movement; Indianapolis, where the antiwar movement was smaller than in some parts of the country, thus had a comparatively small underground press.

When the war ended, the undergrounds survived as "alternative" newspapers. Publishers of alternatives still give their papers away, but today they aggressively pursue advertising dollars. They have become viable businesses, replete with a corps of advertising sales representatives and bookkeepers. Still, alternative journalism is more free-flowing, more subjective, than the mainstream newspapers. Although devoting considerable attention to entertainment-related stories, alternatives continue to practice highly interpretive journalism and to promote controversial social causes.

There are no official records of the comings and goings of Indianapolis' roughly 20 alternatives. The first paper seems to have been *An Indiana Liberal*, which came and went in 1966. It was the first of many alternatives to be published by Ron Haldeman. The following year Haldeman was at the helm of *The Participant*, which billed itself as "an Indiana Subterranean Journal of Change." The largest of the city's underground papers of the 1960s was the *Indianapolis Free Press* (1966–1970). Its circulation reached 75,000. Once, the *Free Press* drew the ire of some Indianapolis residents by publishing a cartoon that depicted President and Mrs. Nixon naked. Police tried to halt distribution, but the INDIANA CIVIL LIBERTIES UNION interceded and the paper went out. Later, Haldeman merged his *Participant* with the *Free Press*, and the papers died together. Soon Haldeman was back, this time with *Expecting Rain* (from a Bob Dylan lyric). Among the more noteworthy things *ER* did was to publish poems by local poet Jared Carter, who later won the prestigious Walt Whitman Award.

The trend toward entertainment news can be traced to the launch of *Second City*, in 1974. The work of Kim Huegel and Tom Harper, *SC* soon became political, sending a reporter to Wounded Knee, South Dakota, to do a story on the aftermath of the Indian uprising. The paper folded within months. The next year M. William Lutholtz's *City Lights* started, determined to restrict itself to entertainment. David Letterman, then a recent Ball State graduate, was a contributor. The paper lasted for 17 issues. There was a pause in the action until monthly *Radio Free Rock* came along, in the late 1970s. It was exclusively entertainment-oriented, noteworthy for its introduction of the column "Kiwi Tracks." Written by Allen Deck, "Tracks" was a long, yet entertaining gossip column that concentrated on the local entertainment scene. After *RFR* folded, Deck took "Tracks" to Terry Lowe's *Hot Potato*, a new monthly entertainment paper. In 1983, under the leadership of Mike Jacque Griffin, *HP* merged with *Express* to form *The Alternative*, which lasted until June, 1984.

Indianapolis' longest running alternative is *The New Times*, published by Stephen Sylvester. It started as *Steppin' Out*, in May, 1984, and was heavy on entertainment. In 1987 it began to emphasize news. *TNT* gained national acclaim in 1988 when it published vice-presidential candidate Dan Quayle's law school grades. The grades had been a closely guarded secret until *TNT* tapped into Indiana University's computer and obtained the information. *NUVO*, the latest entry into Indianapolis' alternative newspaper scene, was launched in March, 1990. Today it is the city's largest such paper and is known for its investigative reporting on such topics as police brutality.

WILL HIGGINS

Niblack, John Lewis (Aug. 14, 1897–June 16, 1986). Judge of Marion County Municipal, Superior, and Circuit courts (1941–1974). Born and reared in the small farm town of Wheatland, Knox County, Niblack graduated from Indiana University in 1922 (Phi Beta Kappa) and Benjamin Harrison Law School, Indianapolis, in 1925. He was successively a school teacher, newspaper reporter, lawyer, deputy prosecutor, state senator, judge, and author. His autobiography, *The Life and Times of a Hoosier Judge* (1973), affords a window on Indianapolis life and politics throughout much of the 20th century.

As a newspaper reporter for the INDIANAPOLIS TIMES (1922–1925) Niblack reported daily on the criminal trials and political activities at the Marion County Courthouse. He also exposed many activities of the powerful KU KLUX KLAN, which had endorsed and supported many local political figures, mostly Republicans. As deputy prosecutor Niblack assisted in all the grand jury investigations and sensational trials brought from 1926 through 1928 against a number of Klan officeholders for bribery, corrupt practices, and malfeasance of office. Often at odds with the county Republican organization because of his anti-Klan activities, he won the offices of state senator (1929), superior court (1946), and circuit court (1956) without its official support. Additionally, in 1929 Niblack spearheaded a newly formed Citizens School Committee to elect a nonpartisan slate of candidates to the Indianapolis School Board and until 1964 supported its efforts to improve the quality of education in the city.

In 1966, Niblack, with the help of prominent Republican finance people and incumbent officeholders, organized the Republican Action Committee (RAC), which endorsed a complete slate of candidates for county and township offices against the regular Republican county organization. The RAC candidates won overwhelmingly, and as a result the county Republican chairman, H. Dale Brown, relinquished control of party. The RAC loyalists took over undisputed control of the party for a great many years thereafter. Niblack remained a key advisor and mentor to the new Republican leadership until 1974, the year he lost his first election, when all county Republican officeholders were defeated. Niblack moved to Washington, Indiana, in 1975, where he engaged in the part-time practice of law until his death.

WILLIAM MERCURI

George P. Rice, Jr., "Introduction" to John L. Niblack, *The Life and Times of a Hoosier Judge* (n.p., 1973).

Nicholas H. Noyes, Jr. Memorial Foundation. Foundation established in 1951 by Nicholas H. Noyes, Sr. and Marguerite Lilly Noyes as a memorial to their son, who died at age 27. The purpose of the foundation is to assist organizations, predominantly in Indiana, that are involved with education, performing arts, museums, health, social services, and youth.

Nicholas Noyes, Sr. was a member of the board of directors of ELI LILLY AND COMPANY from 1913 to 1976, campaign chairman of the Indianapolis Community Fund, and vice-chairman of the board of governors of the INDIANAPOLIS MUSEUM OF ART. His contributions to health and education include grants to METHODIST HOSPITAL for the Children's Pavilion and to Earlham College for the science complex. Noyes deeded his estate on Sunset Lane to BUTLER UNIVERSITY in 1956.

Marguerite Lilly Noyes, also a noted philanthropist, was one of two daughters of Evan Frost Lilly, a cousin of COLONEL ELI LILLY. Her contributions emphasized service to children. She took special interest in THE CHILDREN'S MUSEUM and international organizations such as CARE and HOPE. She also contributed to the INDIANAPOLIS SYMPHONY ORCHESTRA and the INDIANAPOLIS MUSEUM OF ART.

ANNE M. MAJEWSKI
Indiana University–Purdue University, Indianapolis

Nicholson, Mary E. (Mar. 27 or 29, 1839–Sept. 20, 1928). Prominent Indianapolis educator. Born in Greene County, Ohio, Nicholson attended Antioch College and College Hill Seminary for Young Ladies before moving to Indianapolis in 1867. She began her teaching career at the First Ward School, at Vermont and New Jersey streets. The following year, 1868, Nicholson began teaching at the new high school at Market Street and the Circle. In 1884 she became principal of the Indianapolis Normal School and held that position until 1909, when she resigned. In 1910, she became the first woman elected to the Indianapolis Board of School Commissioners, serving until 1914. Active in the National Education Association, Nicholson served as that group's vice-president in 1890 and 1891. She was a frequent contributor to the publication of the National Education Association, earning renown as a writer and lecturer. In honor of her more than 40 years of service with the Indianapolis public schools, the school board named School 70 at Central Avenue and 46th Street the Mary E. Nicholson School. Her home at 1233 Park Avenue often served as a gathering place for school leaders to engage in philosophical discussions. After retiring, Nicholson served on the board of directors of the JOHN HERRON ART INSTITUTE.

KATHY INGELS HELMOND

Nicholson, Meredith (Dec. 9, 1866–Dec. 22, 1947). Indiana essayist and novelist. The author of 29 books plus countless shorter works, this prolific Indianapolis-based writer is best known for his popular light romances. His most valuable writings, however, are his historical essays and his analyses of current events published in newspapers and magazines. Nicholson was a dauntless booster of his home state and an ardent Democrat politically, although he never sought elective office. In his later years, he accepted appointment from President Franklin Roosevelt to be the American minister in Paraguay (1933–1934), Venezuela (1935–1938), and Nicaragua (1938–1941).

Born in Crawfordsville, Indiana, the son of a prosperous farmer, Nicholson moved to Indianapolis in 1872, where he discovered that schools "didn't fit" him, and his formal education ended at an early age. His subsequent attempts to enter college failed because he could not meet the "mathematical requirements." Consequently, he entered upon his life's work "without benefit of college," the title of one of his better essays, but his personal study habits served him well. He worked as an office boy in a print shop, clerked in a drug store,

studied shorthand and became a court reporter, and then became an apprentice in a law office. His talents were literary and journalistic rather than legal, and from 1885 until 1897, he held various editorial positions on the INDIANAPOLIS NEWS.

He began to contribute verses to the local press, and in 1891 a book of his poetry, *Short Flights*, appeared. His talents clearly lay elsewhere, and in 1897, after his marriage to Eugenie Kountze, the daughter of a wealthy Omaha, Nebraska, banker, Nicholson tried a career in business. This occasioned a move to Denver, where he found success but not happiness. His first narrative book, *The Hoosiers* (1900), a history of the state with emphasis upon its literary culture, appeared during his Colorado years and was also the catalyst which brought him back to Indianapolis and a career as a full-time writer. Between 1903 and 1925 he published an average of one book a year, most of them novels, but there were also three collections of essays, a second book of poetry, and even a co-authored play. Several of these volumes achieved bestseller status. His most famous novel was *The House of a Thousand Candles* (1905), a thrilling but scarcely believable mystery-romance set in northern Indiana. A more powerful novel, *A HOOSIER CHRONICLE* (1912), explored changes in midwestern society at the turn of the century. His last book, the author's personal favorite, was a collection of biographical sketches titled *Old Familiar Faces* (1929).

For reasons associated with both the onset of the Depression in 1929 and the death of his wife in 1931, Nicholson was unable to complete any more books. His work as a diplomat was more demanding than expected, but he proved effective as a representative of the United States and its governmental system in which he believed so firmly. Recurring health problems prompted Nicholson's retirement from the foreign service in 1941, but he continued to write for the local newspapers and to support the Allied effort during World War II.

A warm, gregarious, fun-loving man, Nicholson contributed both to the political and literary culture of his time. A member of Indiana's "Big Four" men of letters (with Riley, Ade, and Tarkington) during the early part of the 20th century, Nicholson was considered the dean of Indiana writers at the time of his death in 1947. Although his romantic novels have not aged well and Nicholson is but slightly read and studied now, his essays of political and social commentary and his richly textured biographical sketches remain a valuable resource for the study of midwestern culture at the turn of the century.

RALPH D. GRAY
Indiana University–Purdue University,
Indianapolis

Dorothy Ritter Russo and Thelma Lois Sullivan, *Bibliographical Studies of Seven Authors of Crawfordsville, Indiana* (Indianapolis, 1952); R. E. Banta, *Indiana Authors and Their Books, 1816–1916* (Crawfordsville, Ind., 1949); Jean Butler Sanders, "Meredith Nicholson: Hoosier Cavalier" (M.A. thesis, DePauw University, 1952).

Nicholson, Roberta West (Jan. 17, 1903–Nov. 6, 1987). Legislator; advocate of social justice for women and children. A native of Cincinnati, Ohio, Roberta West graduated from the University of Cincinnati in 1924 with majors in both history and French. She came to Indianapolis in 1926 following her marriage to Meredith Nicholson, Jr., the previous year.

Roberta Nicholson had been brought up in a Republican family, but she found Indiana Republicans of the 1920s heavily influenced by the KU KLUX KLAN. Her husband came from a staunch Democratic background and she became an active Democrat. Appointed to the Liquor Control Advisory Board in 1933 by Governor Paul V. McNutt, she was elected secretary to the Indiana convention that ratified the 21st Amendment, which repealed prohibition.

In 1934, Nicholson was elected to the Indiana General Assembly and served in the 1935 session and the special session of 1936. She made worldwide headlines for her "anti-heart balm" bill, which made it illegal for Indiana women to sue men for breach of promise. The bill passed and was promptly copied by eleven other states.

In the 1930s Nicholson was active in numerous civic organizations and events, serving as a member of the LEAGUE OF WOMEN VOTERS, Council of Social Agencies, board of managers of the Indianapolis Orphans' Home, JUNIOR LEAGUE, Parent-Teacher Association, Mayor's Advisory

Committee on Recreation, and state advisory committee on child welfare. She also served as state chairwoman for the New York World's Fair, the President's Birthday Ball, and a committee for aid to Chinese orphans.

During World War II, Nicholson established recreational facilities for servicemen stationed at Camp Atterbury. She found businesses magnanimous in donating goods and services for white soldiers, but mostly unwilling to do the same for blacks. Outraged and determined, she finally located a facility for black soldiers, paid for by private funds. She then prodded and shamed businesses into providing support.

In 1943, she became the first director of the Indianapolis Social Hygiene Association, later the SOCIAL HEALTH ASSOCIATION OF CENTRAL INDIANA, a position she held until her retirement in 1960.

One of Nicholson's principal causes was the improvement of the system of JUVENILE JUSTICE. She was a founder and long-time member of the Juvenile Court Bi-Partisan Committee, an organization that worked within both political parties for the nomination of qualified candidates, and of the Juvenile Court Advisory Committee, child welfare activists who met monthly with Juvenile Court judges to provide advice and support. Another cause was the CHILDREN'S BUREAU OF INDIANAPOLIS. She served on its board from 1935 until her death in 1987—the last 20 years as an honorary member.

In 1957, Nicholson received the Distinguished Public Service Award of the Indiana Public Health Association for outstanding achievement in the field of PUBLIC HEALTH. She was elected to the Indiana Academy in 1973.

LAURA S. GAUS

Nicoson, Angus J. (Sept. 30, 1919–May 23, 1982). Basketball coach and sports administrator. Born in Clay County, Indiana, Nicoson coached Indiana Central College (now the UNIVERSITY OF INDIANAPOLIS) to 483 basketball victories. He retired in 1977 as the seventh most winning college coach in history to that time.

After graduating from Ashboro High School in 1938, Nicoson captained Indiana Central to 16 consecutive wins and a ninth-place national ranking in 1942. He coached basketball and taught physical education at Franklin Township High School (now Franklin Central) from 1942 to 1947. Named head basketball coach at Indiana Central in 1947, "Nick" also coached football, baseball, track, cross country, and tennis squads. He became the school's athletic director in 1949.

After earning his Master's degree from Indiana University in 1952, Nicoson served on U.S. Olympic, PAN AMERICAN GAMES, International Federation, and AMATEUR ATHLETIC UNION basketball committees. A seven-time Hoosier College Conference and three-time National Association of Intercollegiate Athletics (NAIA) District 21 Coach of the Year, he was NAIA president in 1966–1967. Nicoson toured Europe and the Soviet Union as an assistant coach with the 1969 U.S. National Basketball Team, and he received the 1977 National Association of Basketball Coaches Honor Award.

From 1952 to 1965, and from 1969 to 1971, Nicoson coached the Indiana High School Boys' Basketball All-Stars to a 19–12 record against their rivals from Kentucky. In 1977, he was inducted into both the Helms Foundation and Indiana Basketball Hall of Fame. The University of Indianapolis renamed its physical education/basketball facility Nicoson Hall that same year.

R. DALE OGDEN
Indiana State Museum

Nizamoff, Christo N. (Sept. 2, 1903–May 25, 1989). Editor of the *Macedonian Tribune* and advocate for an independent and democratic Macedonia. Born in Yankovetz near Resen, Macedonia, and educated in Sofia, Bulgaria, Nizamoff escaped Serbian oppression by immigrating to the United States in 1921. After working in a Connecticut cotton mill he moved to New York City in 1922 where he directed the Macedonian Press Bureau during the formative years of the Macedonian Patriotic Organization (MPO), founded in Fort Wayne and headquartered in Indianapolis. At the request of MPO leadership Nizamoff moved to Indianapolis in 1930 on a temporary assignment for the Bulgarian-language weekly *Makedonska tribuna/Macedonian Tribune* (founded

February 10, 1927). He remained with the paper for 41 years, serving as its editor-in-chief from April, 1966 to March, 1971.

Nizamoff wrote articles and editorials regularly for the *Tribune* for which he received two Freedom Foundation awards (1968, 1970). He was a founding member of the INDIANAPOLIS PRESS CLUB in 1934 and was named its Man of the Year in 1966. Nizamoff was inducted into the Indiana Journalism Hall of Fame in 1974. Considered an expert on Balkan affairs, Nizamoff recounted his life in the pursuit of Macedonian independence in his autobiography, *A Struggle for Freedom*.

VIRGINIA NIZAMOFF SURSO

Christo N. Nizamoff, *A Struggle for Freedom: Reflections and Reminiscences* (Indianapolis, 1985).

Noble Centers. Organization providing educational and vocational programs for children and adults with developmental disabilities. In 1953, more than 100 parents of children with developmental disabilities met at the World War Memorial, where they created Parents and Friends of Retarded Children, Inc. to provide formal education for their children. The first "Noble School" opened in September of that year; by 1960, it was providing job opportunities to persons with disabilities through sheltered workshops. In 1965, the group reorganized as the Marion County Association for Retarded Children, Inc. (MCARC). At that time, the agency operated the Noble Sheltered Workshop for Retarded Adults at 752 East Market Street.

The 1970s was a period of astounding growth for MCARC, including the construction of a facility at 2400 North Tibbs Avenue to serve preschool and primary aged children. By 1973, however, state mandates required children ages 6–18 to receive formal education through the public schools. In response, MCARC expanded services to preschool children and adults.

In 1974, Noble Industries relocated to its present Tibbs Avenue site, offering persons with developmental disabilities job opportunities that include packaging, sealing, and light assembly work. With funding assistance from the Department of Vocational Rehabilitation, MCARC opened the Noble Greenhouse in 1980, providing additional employment opportunities.

Founded in the mid–1980s, Noble's Supported Employment program works with the Indianapolis business community to assist persons with developmental disabilities to secure jobs in a variety of occupations. In 1992, when the state mandated public schools to serve children three through five years old, Noble focused on meeting the needs of children from birth through age three and continued its commitment to adult services.

Initial financial support came from individual gifts, tuition, and fund-raising events. Of its current budget of $10.5 million, approximately 75 percent comes from federal, state, and local government, with the remainder from the UNITED WAY, businesses, foundations, and individuals. Today, Noble has a staff of 240 and programs throughout Marion County, annually helping about 1,000 persons with developmental disabilities.

ERVIN PICHA
Noble Centers

Nolan, Jeannette Covert (Mar. 31, 1896–Oct. 12, 1974). Indianapolis author of 50 books, including adult fiction, detective stories, and 31 histories and biographies for children. Born in Evansville, Indiana, Jeannette Covert came from a long line of journalists. Her grandfather owned a newspaper in Washington, Indiana, before the Civil War, and later in Evansville. At the age of 17 she went to work for the *Evansville Courier* as a reporter and feature writer. In 1917, she married and devoted herself to domestic duties and the rearing of three children. Writing down the stories she told the children and selling them to magazines occupied her for many years. The family moved to Indianapolis in 1933.

Her first book, *Barry Barton's Mystery*, was published in 1932. *The Young Douglas* (1934), her third book, was the first of three Junior Literary Guild selections. The other two were *Hobnailed Boots* (1939) and *The Story of Clara Barton and the Red Cross* (1941). *New Days, New Ways*, an adult novel, was published in 1936, in England as well as the United States.

The death of her husband in 1940 made writing a necessity for Jeannette Nolan. In 1941 she published three books including *James Whitcomb Riley, Hoosier Poet*, which was introduced at a party for the poet's birthday on Lockerbie Street. *Hoosier City: The Story of Indianapolis* was published in 1943. *Gather Ye Rosebuds*, published in 1946, was made into a motion picture musical called *Isn't It Romantic?*. From 1946 to 1973, she published 30 books, including biographies of Florence Nightingale, Daniel Boone, Abraham Lincoln, and Benedict Arnold.

Jeannette Nolan directed Indiana University's summer workshop on writing for children for five years. In 1954 she received the Indiana University Writers Conference award for *George Rogers Clark: Soldier and Hero*, chosen as the best children's book by an Indiana author. In 1961 she won the award again for *Spy for the Confederacy: Rose O'Neal Greenhow*.

Indiana University awarded her the Doctor of Humane Letters in 1967, and in 1968 Jeannette Covert Nolan was elected to the university's Writers Conference Hall of Fame.

NANCY GERARD

Nora. Northside suburb originally centered in the vicinity of Westfield Boulevard and 86th Street. The Nora Community Council, the area's prominent neighborhood association, defines its current boundaries as 96th Street, White River, Williams Creek, and Township Line Road. Peter Lawson, a Swedish immigrant, founded the town in 1871. His general store and post office stood near the rail station, sawmill, blacksmith shop, and grocery, all now demolished. The origin of the name "Nora" is uncertain, although most versions report that Lawson named it after his hometown in Sweden.

Though Nora had rail and INTERURBAN service for a time and was later near the intersection of busy motor routes—S.R. 431, U.S. 31, and S.R. 100 (86th Street)—it remained small and quiet until the 1950s. Then it seemed that Nora would be overwhelmed by the sudden influx of new businesses and homes as Indianapolis expanded northward. A large shopping mall, Nora Plaza, opened in 1959 and additional commercial developments were planned. Roads and sewers were inadequate to handle the new growth.

In response to the problems, residents organized in 1967 as the Nora Community Council, an umbrella organization for a number of small neighborhood groups. Since its founding, this effective and powerful organization has fought to control development patterns and to enhance residential neighborhoods. The council's efforts have contained commercial development within designated nodes, such as Keystone at the Crossing and 86th and Westfield Boulevard. The group has also worked with the Department of Transportation on engineering designs for area roadways. Due to this cooperative planning, original designs for widening 86th Street were altered significantly to retain residential corridors.

CATHLEEN F. DONNELLY

Nordyke and Marmon. Mill equipment and automobile manufacturer. In 1851 Ohio-born Ellis Nordyke started a flour mill equipment factory in Richmond, Indiana. His son Addison H. joined the firm in 1858. Daniel W. Marmon purchased an interest in 1866, and the business became Nordyke and Marmon. Upon Ellis Nordyke's death in 1871, Addison assumed his father's interest and led the company until 1902. The need for more production space and better transportation outlets resulted in a relocation from Richmond in 1876 to the former Quaker City Works factory, located in an area bounded by

Nordyke & Marmon's 1891 advertisement displayed several of the company's extensive line of mills. [Indiana Historical Society, #C5745]

Kentucky Avenue, Morris Street, and the BELT LINE RAILROAD in WEST INDIANAPOLIS. The company produced a wide variety of machinery for corn, rice, flour, and other cereal mills worldwide.

Marmon's sons, Walter and Howard, joined the company in 1897 and 1899 respectively. Both graduates of engineering schools and keenly interested in the automobile, they helped establish a subsidiary of Nordyke and Marmon which in 1901–1902 produced a motor car featuring an improved lubricated crankshaft and rod bearings. In 1911 the Marmon Wasp became the first winner of the INDIANAPOLIS 500–MILE RACE. During the late 1910s the Marmon Model 34 gained recognition for its use of aluminum, making it much lighter than its competitors. In 1926 Nordyke and Marmon dropped its production of milling equipment and became known as the Marmon Motor Car Company. The Nordyke name and the milling equipment were sold to Allis-Chalmers, which gradually phased out the name yet continued to take orders for Nordyke parts.

The original (pre–1915) Nordyke and Marmon factory has been replaced by the ELI LILLY AND COMPANY complex. Portions of the 1919 plant additions have been incorporated into the Lilly facility.

PAUL BROCKMAN
Indiana Historical Society

George P. and Stacey Pankiw Hanley, *The Marmon Heritage* (Rochester, Mich., 1985); Jacob Piatt Dunn, *Greater Indianapolis* (Chicago, 1910).

Norfolk Southern Railroad. The one line of this railroad system that has direct connection with Indianapolis was originally (1849) known as the Peru & Indianapolis. The line entered Indianapolis from the northeast via the tiny village of CASTLETON and then followed a south-southwesterly direction to UNION STATION. Once it extended to Michigan City this line became an important link between Indianapolis and Chicago (1873). In the course of its long history it has been identified with several major rail systems, including the Lake Erie & Western, the "Nickel Plate," the Wabash, St. Louis & Pacific, the Norfolk & Western, and ultimately the Norfolk Southern. For many years prior to 1909 the PENNSYLVANIA RAILROAD leased the Indianapolis-Kokomo segment as part of its mainline to Chicago. It was abandoned as a through line after World War II. Today some trackage from Indianapolis to Argus continues to provide limited rail service, mainly the hauling of grain.

VICTOR M. BOGLE
Indiana University, Kokomo

William R. Holloway, *Indianapolis: A Historical and Statistical Sketch of the Railroad City* (Indianapolis, 1870); J. David Baker, *The Postal History of Indiana* (Louisville, Ky., n.d.).

Normal College of the American Gymnastic Union.

Oldest college of physical education in the United States. Physical education professional training did not begin in America until the North American Turnerbund, the national governing body of gymnastics societies created by German gymnastics enthusiasts, established the Normal College of the American Gymnastic Union (NCAGU) in 1866. Its purpose was to train qualified gymnastics instructors, first for the country's turnvereins and later for public school programs. New York City became the site of the first NCAGU because that city had a Turner hall large enough for the school and because there were plentiful job placement opportunities for students. Chicago (1871), New York (1871–1875), and Indianapolis (1889–1891) were early locations of the Normal College. It achieved a relatively permanent home when it moved to Milwaukee and stayed for 16 years (1891–1907). In 1880 the national convention of the North American Turnerbund launched a campaign for compulsory gymnastics in the public schools. By 1898 several major American cities, including Indianapolis, had adopted school physical education programs, a result that the U.S. Commissioner of Education attributed to the Turners' efforts.

In 1907 the American Turners moved the Normal College back to Indianapolis where the city's German community received it enthusiastically. It became part of the Indiana University extension in 1941, although it remained in the east wing of the Athenaeum Turners building on Michigan Street until 1971. It is now part of the School of Health, Physical Education, and Recreation at IUPUI.

ALIDA J. MOONEN

NCAGU Collection, University Archives, IUPUI; Emil Rinsch, *The History of the Normal College of the American Gymnastic Union of Indiana University, 1866–1966* (Bloomington, Ind., 1966).

North Indianapolis.

Industrial suburb. The boundaries of North Indianapolis, which was platted in 1873, were Congress Street, Michigan Road, 21st Street, and Harding Street. Although never incorporated, the suburb developed around the Udell Ladder Works, the North Indianapolis Wagon Works, and the Henry Ocow Manufacturing Company. When the BELT LINE RAILROAD was constructed in the 1870s, North Indianapolis became its western terminus. By 1890 North Indianapolis' population was 1,479. An electric streetcar line to the area in the early 1890s increased its popularity as a residential location for middle-income, working class families. In 1895 residents of North Indianapolis requested annexation to Indianapolis in order to receive its lower natural gas rates, becoming one of six communities annexed to the city during the decade 1890 to 1900.

Today the official designation of North Indianapolis no longer exists, but the neighborhood remains a residential and small business area contained within the United Northwest Area, Inc., an association of neighborhood organizations. Most homes are two-story frame buildings, dating primarily from the late 19th and early 20th centuries. Once a middle-income, white community, it became a predominately African-American neighborhood as whites moved to the suburbs.

CONNIE J. ZEIGLER

Jacob Piatt Dunn, *Greater Indianapolis* (Chicago, 1910).

North Meridian Street Corridor.

Historic residential district located between 40th Street and Westfield Boulevard. Once an area of orchards and dairy farms, Meridian Street north of 38th Street was platted as early as the 1890s, yet intensive development did not begin until the 1920s. Over half of the district's 173 homes were built in the period 1910–1930. Though the Great Depression and World War II slowed construction, additional residences were built between 1945 and 1966 on remaining lots. Most homes were individually designed and built by speculators familiar with buyers' tastes and requirements. Despite a variety of architectural styles, the street has a generally cohesive appearance thanks to deep setbacks, large lots, and carefully designed landscaping.

Meridian Street south of 16th Street had been the address of choice for Indianapolis' socially prominent families in the 1880s and 1890s, and the cachet extended north as the new area was developed. Many leading citizens lived on North Meridian Street, including professionals, bankers, and corporate executives, but the district's best known resident was author Booth Tarkington, who lived at 4270 from 1923 to 1947. Two different North Meridian homes—4343 (1947–1971) and 4750 (1975–present)—have served as the Indiana Governor's Residence.

When commercialization threatened 40th Street homes in the 1960s, residents established the Meridian Street Foundation to preserve the neighborhood. Protection was assured with formation of the Meridian Street Preservation Commission in 1971 and the district's 1986 inclusion on the National Register of Historic Places.

CATHLEEN F. DONNELLY

View of North Meridian Street taken from the Monument Circle area, looking north, ca. 1900. [Indiana Historical Society, Bass Collection, #941]

David J. Bodenhamer, Lamont Hulse, and Elizabeth Monroe, *The Main Stem: The History and Architecture of North Meridian Street* (Indianapolis: Historic Landmarks Foundation of Indiana, 1992).

North Western Christian University.
See Butler University

Nursing. Professional nursing in the United States dates to the last quarter of the 19th century. Prior to that time religious orders provided nursing care in Catholic and Protestant hospitals. Untrained, and often unscrupulous, former patients functioned as nurses in most municipal hospitals. American women became aware of the atrocious conditions in city hospitals and the need for trained nurses through the work of Englishwoman Florence Nightingale. During the Civil War women demonstrated their ability to nurse the sick and the wounded. The movement to create professional nurse training schools, however, lost momentum until after the Civil War. The first nurse training school in the United States did not open until 1873.

Indianapolis played a leading role in the development of professional nursing within the state. In 1883 the first nurse training program opened in the city. The Flower Mission Training School for Nurses (later the WISHARD MEMORIAL HOSPITAL School of Nursing), which was opened by the FLOWER MISSION, supplied nursing care for the Indianapolis City Hospital (now Wishard) and provided nursing care for the community through its system of district nursing. Nursing students from the hospital also worked in private duty practice, providing nursing care for patients in their homes. During this period nursing required long hours and offered little pay.

As hospitals grew and developed in Indianapolis, so did the number of nurse training schools. ST. VINCENT HOSPITAL opened its program in 1896; Protestant Deaconess in 1899; Methodist in 1908; and the Indiana University Training School for Nurses in Indianapolis (now Indiana University School of Nursing) in 1914. As was common in other parts of the United States, black women were denied admission to the nurse training schools well into the 20th century. In the 1910s black women trained at Indianapolis' two black hospitals, the Lincoln Hospital and Sisters of Charity State Hospital. These hospitals closed in the 1920s, however, and Wishard Hospital's School of Nursing began to accept black women into its program. Not until 1953 did the first black woman graduate from Indiana University School of Nursing.

The formation of professional nursing associations and nurse registries (organizations providing the names of nurses for employment) closely followed the establishment of nurse training schools. In 1885 local nurses formed the "Nightingales of Indianapolis," which functioned as a nurse registry. The Marion County Nurses Association formed in the early 20th century. In 1904 the Indiana State Nurses Association was officially incorporated with headquarters in Indianapolis. That group played a leading role in formulating standards for the profession, establishing a registry for nurses and developing a standard nursing school curriculum. By 1913 a bill passed the Indiana state legislature requiring a minimum of three years training for nurses.

Leaders in nursing education stressed the benefit of baccalaureate degree nursing programs over diploma programs. The 1923 Winslow-Goldmark report, supported by the Rockefeller Foundation, substantiated this view. The report's authors urged that nursing schools affiliate with institutions of higher learning and that universities improve postgraduate education for nurses. The Indiana University School of Nursing already was affiliated with a university. In the 1930s Wishard Hospital's program and METHODIST HOSPITAL'S program respectively affiliated with BUTLER UNIVERSITY and DePauw University. The need for qualified nursing instructors led Indiana University in 1932 to offer nursing education courses. A doctorate in nursing at Indiana University, however, was not available until 1978.

In 1922, six student nurses at Indiana University School of Nursing in Indianapolis founded SIGMA THETA TAU, the first national nursing honor society. The organization's national headquarters opened in Indianapolis in 1974. Today, that association is an international society which

Public health nursing, focusing on tuberculosis, maternal, and child health, became increasingly important in the early 20th century.
[Indiana Historical Society, #4151]

actively supports nursing research and grants nursing scholarships.

Originally the focus was on hospital and private duty nursing. By the late 19th and early 20th centuries, public health nursing became increasingly important. In 1890 Indianapolis employed a public health nurse to care for the poor of the city. Yet, these nurses had no specialized training. In 1912 local nurses formed the Indianapolis Visiting Nurse Association (renamed the Visiting Nurse Association of Indianapolis in 1947) to address the special needs of these nurses. Finally, in 1917, under the leadership of Abbie Hunt Bryce (who had served as the first superintendent of nurses at City Hospital and was instrumental in forming an Indianapolis Visiting Nurse Section), the Indiana State Nurses Association formed a public health nursing section.

The official recognition of public health nursing as a separate nursing specialty led private duty nurses to lobby for similar recognition. Frances M. Ott, a graduate of Wishard School of Nursing, was one of the leading advocates for the establishment of a private duty section of the state association. In 1920 the state association formed a private duty section and fought for the establishment of a 12–hour work day (rather than a 20–hour one) for nurses.

In 1939 the Indiana State Nurses Association established an industrial section. The development of this specialty coincided with the growth of industrial jobs and interest in occupational and industrial diseases in the 1930s.

The world wars gave impetus to the profession, although the Great Depression hurt nursing. World War I brought a decline in the number of nursing students, and many Indianapolis nurses were recruited through the Red Cross. A number of Indianapolis nurses served at BASE HOSPITAL NO. 32. In 1921 the state association undertook a nurse recruitment campaign to meet the demand for nurses which resulted from increasing numbers of hospital patients.

The Great Depression, however, hit the nursing profession hard. Earlier campaigns had increased the number of nurses, but the number of jobs declined during the 1930s. Although some nurse training schools throughout the state closed, the Indianapolis nurse training schools remained open.

The outbreak of World War II brought an increased need for nurses. In July, 1942, the U.S. Congress passed the Bolton Act to prepare nurses in large numbers for the armed services. Indiana University also began an accelerated nurse training program to allay the shortage. Although these efforts helped increase the number of nurses, Indianapolis suffered from a severe nursing shortage after the war. Edward F. Gallahue, the president of the American States Insurance Company, provided a solution to the nurse shortage by aggressively recruiting young people—particularly Methodist youth—through a year-round recruitment campaign, which became known as the Indiana Plan (or GALLAHUE PLAN). This effort was aided by the Indianapolis CHAMBER OF COMMERCE, which established a nurse enrollment week, and the local newspapers, which sponsored a public awareness campaign.

During the 1940s the Indiana State Nurses Association realized the need for auxiliary personnel to assist nurses: by 1947 it published regulations for trained attendants and formed a practical nurses association in 1949. In 1950 a school, operated under the public school system, opened in Indianapolis to train practical nurses.

In the 1940s and 1950s nurses became increasingly specialized—surgery, pediatrics, and psychiatry all had specially trained nurses. Whereas nurses once performed more menial tasks, today they have assumed greatly increased responsibilities, some of which traditionally belonged to physicians. Also, nursing was dominated by women in the 1940s; only 2.3 percent of nurses were male. Today, an increasing number of nurses are male (approximately 5 percent), but the profession remains predominantly a female one.

In the 1960s the nursing shortage continued, despite federal subsidies to nurse education. In the mid–1960s a survey of nursing resources in the Indianapolis metropolitan area was conducted by the consulting firm of Booz, Allen and Hamilton at the request of the Indianapolis Hospital Development Association. This report revealed that the demand for nurses would soon exceed the supply if existing nursing programs were not expanded and others were not created. It also urged that existing programs be improved and suggested that nursing schools affiliate with universities. The decision of Methodist Hospital in 1966 to close its diploma nursing program and of St. Vincent Hospital to phase out its diploma program magnified the potential nursing shortage. As a result of the report, MARIAN COLLEGE (which had been affiliated with St. Vincent) began a baccalaureate degree program in nursing using St. Vincent's clinical resources. To increase the supply of nurses, Indiana University established an associate degree in 1965.

In 1980 Wishard Memorial Hospital closed its nursing program. With DePauw University's decision to close its nursing program in 1993, Indianapolis has only two baccalaureate degree nursing programs in the city—Indiana University School of Nursing and Marian College School of Nursing. The demand for nurses within Indianapolis remained high in the early 1990s.

KATHERINE MANDUSIC MCDONELL

Indiana State Nurses Association Collection (1930–1979) and Marion County General Hospital Collection, Indiana Historical Society; Marie D'Andrea Loftus, *A History of St. Vincent's Hospital School of Nursing* (Indianapolis, 1972); Dotaline Allen, "History of Nursing in Indiana," *One Hundred Years of Indiana Medicine*, ed. Dorothy Ritter Russo (Indianapolis, 1949), 124–137; Dorcas Irene Rock, *A History of the Indiana University Training School for Nurses, 1914–1946* (Indiana University, 1946); Ann Marriner-Tomey, *Nursing at Indiana University: 75 Years at the Heart of Health Care* (Indiana University School of Nursing, 1989).

Nussbaum, Lowell (Nov. 6, 1901–Nov. 19, 1987). Journalist. Born in Marion, Indiana, Nussbaum began his journalistic career while still in high school, working as a part-time reporter for both town papers as well as the *Chicago Journal*. Later he became city editor of the *Marion Chronicle* and in 1927 left for a job as reporter at the INDIANAPOLIS TIMES. Nussbaum later became city editor at the *Times*, and then author of a column entitled "Inside Indianapolis." In August, 1945, he moved to the INDIANAPOLIS STAR and began writing "The Things I Hear," a daily human interest column. He retired in October, 1971, but continued the column as a Sunday feature until November 26, 1976.

His column was widely read and he used it to promote his favorite causes, especially the city's need for a zoo. He made mocking references to a "mythical" Indianapolis Zoological Society, helped in such a society's creation, and then started a fund drive that resulted in the city's first zoo in 1964. The zoo has officially recognized Nussbaum as the "guiding force and visionary" for its establishment.

He was a long-time member of the board of directors of the Zoological Society and served as its president. He was also a founding member of the INDIANAPOLIS PRESS CLUB and its president in 1941–1942. Nussbaum was inducted into the Indiana Journalism Hall of Fame in 1975.

JAMES E. FARMER

Indianapolis Star, Nov. 21, 1987; *Indianapolis Star Magazine*, Nov. 14, 1982.

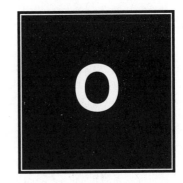

Oaklandon. Suburb located approximately 15 miles northeast of downtown Indianapolis along Pendleton Pike (S.R. 67) and the Conrail tracks. In 1849, John Emery platted Oakland alongside the approaching railroad tracks and named it for the surrounding oak forest. The post office changed the name to Oaklandon when it was established there in 1870. By then the town's bustling railroad depot served local farmers as a shipping point for livestock and grain. The village's first homes were built along what became the New York Central Railroad tracks.

Churches played an important role in the community. The Universalist Church, built in 1850 in Oakland, was among the first congregations in Lawrence Township. It survives in 1993 as the Unitarian-Universalist Church of Oaklandon.

Oaklandon developed slowly in the late 19th and early 20th centuries. Never incorporated, the village had no local government or police department. A civic group addressed community needs, such as raising funds to purchase street lights. In 1979, Lawrence annexed Oaklandon. By the mid–1980s suburban sprawl from GEIST RESERVOIR development had reached the town. The population of the area, which had been only about 500 in 1960, grew to roughly 2,600 by the beginning of the 1990s.

KRIS E. DAMAN

Berry R. Sulgrove, *History of Indianapolis and Marion County* (Philadelphia, 1884); *Indianapolis News*, Jan. 12, 1963, Aug. 22, 1988, June 11, 1990.

Old Northside. Near northside neighborhood bounded by 16th Street, Bellefontaine Street, I–65, and Pennsylvania Street. The area now known as the Old Northside began as two communities that grew into one neighborhood. In the 1850s OVID BUTLER provided a campus for North Western Christian University (later BUTLER UNIVERSITY) on farmland near 13th Street and College Avenue. A small town known as College Corner grew up around the school building, and served the university from 1855 to 1875. The second neighborhood was an outgrowth of the affluent residential development north of the city's MILE SQUARE, primarily along Meridian Street.

Imposing homes in the Gothic Revival, Italianate, Second Empire, Queen Anne, Eastlake, and Stick styles were built between 1870 and 1914 on the northside. Politicians such as BENJAMIN HARRISON and THOMAS TAGGART were northside residents, as were businessmen LYMAN S. AYRES, Hiram P. Wasson, and Herman Lieber. Authors BOOTH TARKINGTON and MEREDITH NICHOLSON also lived in the neighborhood.

After World War I the near northside began to decline as the commercial district expanded northward and residents built new, more fashionable homes north of 38th Street. This trend accelerated during World War II, when housing pressures prompted the subdivision of large homes into apartments and rooming houses. By the 1960s and '70s, the neighborhood suffered from poverty, neglect, and commercial intrusion. A small group of homeowners seeking to reverse the trend, began to restore residences in the early 1970s. They founded Old Northside, Inc., in 1975 and sponsored home tours to raise funds and focus attention on the area's architectural significance. In 1978 the district was listed on the National Register of Historic Places. Old Northside, Inc., and its policies were controversial, however, with lower-income residents, who were represented by the Citizens Neighborhood Coalition. They felt excluded from the neighborhood organization and feared displacement by new property owners. In 1979 an IUPUI study concluded that minimal displacement had taken place through historic preservation, though renters could be forced to leave if apartments were converted into condominiums. The issue was defused as rental units remained available.

By 1993 approximately 80 percent of the housing stock had been renovated in the 36–square-block area. The Old Northside, Inc., and its nonprofit foundation raise funds for new trees, streetlamps, and neighborhood parks. What was once a neighborhood in decline has again become a fashionable address.

CATHLEEN F. DONNELLY

Indianapolis Star, Dec. 8, 1979.

Olin Brass (formerly Bridgeport Brass). Bridgeport Brass was founded in 1865 in Bridgeport, Connecticut, and remained in that state until the early 1940s when it designed and built the Indianapolis westside plant. Bridgeport operated the facility for the U.S. Army, employing 2,500 people around the clock during WORLD WAR II to produce ammunition. After the war Bridgeport purchased the plant from the government and converted it from defense to commercial manufacturing, although it continued to produce shell cases in the 1950s and 1960s for the Korean and Vietnam wars.

In 1980 the Bridgeport, Connecticut, facility was shut down and all brass was manufactured in Indianapolis. The company's fortunes declined in the 1980s. Sales fell from $400 million in 1981 to a loss of $6 million in 1986. Employment also dropped during this time from 1,200 people in 1982 to fewer than 750 in 1987. After several changes in ownership, Indianapolis entrepreneur Beurt SerVaas bought the plant in 1986. Workers approved wage and benefit concessions in order to keep the plant running. Current owner Olin Corporation purchased the operation in 1988, renaming it Olin Brass. As of 1990 metals produced by Olin Brass comprised about 20 percent of the parent company's sales. The 1.3 million square foot facility at 1800 South Holt Road produces brass, copper, and other metals for use in the automotive, electronics, and communications industries as well as for use by the U.S. Mint and the U.S. Department of Defense. In 1993 it employed approximately 1,000 workers.

DEBORAH B. MARKISOHN

Oliver, John H. (Apr. 16, 1859–Oct. 16, 1927). Prominent Indianapolis surgeon and medical educator. Oliver was born in Clermont, Indiana, attended Butler and Wabash colleges, and received an M.D. degree from the Medical College of Indiana in 1881. He also studied in London, Berlin, Paris, and Vienna. Appointed professor of anatomy at the Indiana Dental College in 1881 and professor of surgery at the Medical College of Indiana in 1899, he became professor of surgery at the INDIANA UNIVERSITY SCHOOL OF MEDICINE in 1908 and later first chair of the Department of Sur-

gery. He was also a visiting surgeon at ST. VINCENT HOSPITAL, where he served as chief of staff in the 1920s.

Oliver was prominent throughout the country for his work in industrial surgery and orthopaedics. In 1902 he operated on President Theodore Roosevelt, who was passing through Indianapolis on a western trip, when the president suffered complications from an old leg injury. Oliver was also very active in medical organizations, serving as president of the INDIANAPOLIS MEDICAL SOCIETY in 1906 and of the INDIANA STATE MEDICAL ASSOCIATION in 1917.

GLENN W. IRWIN, JR., M.D.

Indianapolis News, Sept. 24, 1902.

Olympic Exhibitions. Since 1924 Indianapolis has hosted 18 Olympic exhibition events in ten different sports. The 1980s saw an increase in these events with the city's push to become recognized as the amateur sports capital of the world. In 1984 alone Indianapolis hosted five different Olympic team trials, more than any other city in the United States.

Records Set in Indianapolis Olympic Trials

Date	Event	Venue
June 5–7, 1924	Swimming & Diving	Broad Ripple Pool
Dec. 21–22, 1951	Ice Skating	Fairgrounds Coliseum
July 4–6, 1952	Swimming & Diving	Broad Ripple Pool
April 24–27, 1984	Synchronized Swimming	Natatorium
June 24–27, 1984	Swimming	Natatorium
July 4–8, 1984	Diving	Natatorium
July 9, 1984	Women's Basketball	Hoosier Dome
July 9, 1984	Men's Basketball	Hoosier Dome
April 18–23, 1988	Synchronized Swimming	Natatorium
May 25, 1988	Men's Soccer	Kuntz Stadium
June 9–12, 1988	Canoe/Kayak	Eagle Creek Park
June 22–26, 1988	Rowing	Eagle Creek Park
July 15–23, 1988	Track & Field	IU Track Stadium, IUPUI
August 10, 1988	Baseball	Bush Stadium
August 17–21, 1988	Diving	Natatorium
March 1–6, 1992	Swimming	Natatorium
June 17–21, 1992	Diving	Natatorium
June 26–28, 1992	Rowing	Eagle Creek Park

Records
1924: Johnny Weismuller, Olympic, 100–yd. freestyle (59.4 sec.); World, 50–yd. freestyle (25.2 sec.).
1952: Gail Peters, American, 200–yd. breaststroke (3:02.6 min.); Evelyn Kawamoto, American, 400–yd. freestyle (5:17.4 min.).
1988: Jackie Joyner-Kersee, World, Heptathlon, 7,215 pts.; Florence Griffith-Joyner, World, 100 meters (10:49 sec.).

DOUGLAS T. WILSON
WILLIAM D. DALTON

O'Malia Food Markets. Grocery store chain. Founder George J. "Joe" O'Malia had worked in the retail grocery business since 1938 before opening his own chain of grocery stores in and around Indianapolis. He started with Kroger as a stock boy and worked his way up to store manager before moving on to the locally owned Stop and Shop stores. After the Stop and Shop stores were sold, O'Malia co-owned Roth's Food Market and then Preston's Market.

At the age of 46, O'Malia opened his own store in March, 1966, at 104th Street and College Avenue. In 1986, O'Malia opened the only full-service grocery store in the downtown area, housed in the former Sears Roebuck building on North Alabama Street. By 1993 the chain had grown to eight stores and one bakery, located primarily on the north side of Indianapolis. Corporate headquarters are in Noblesville.

MARCUS EUGENE WOODS, II

Indianapolis Star, Apr. 13, 1988; Terri McMahon Stiegman, "Expect the Best: 25 Years of Excellence, 1966–1991" (O'Malia's Food Market, 1991).

O'Meara, Edward T. (Aug. 3, 1921–Jan. 10, 1992). Fourth Archbishop of Indianapolis. A native of St. Louis, O'Meara was ordained there in 1946 by Archbishop (later Cardinal) JOSEPH RITTER, who had served earlier as the first Archbishop of Indianapolis. After graduate study in Rome and a variety of pastoral and administrative assignments in St. Louis, in 1956 O'Meara was named national assistant director for the Society for the

Edward T. O'Meara. [Catholic Communication Center, Archdiocese of Indianapolis]

Propagation of the Faith, then headed by Archbishop Fulton J. Sheen. Thus began a highly visible national and global career, ultimately taking him to 70 countries. In 1967 he became national director of SPF, which is in charge of missions throughout the world. In 1987 O'Meara became chairman of Catholic Relief Services, the largest private voluntary relief agency in the world. Thereafter, he used much of his vacation time traveling to Third World countries to see first hand how CRS carries out its mission to help people in the Third World help themselves.

Shortly after consecration as Archbishop of Indianapolis in 1980, O'Meara launched a sweeping reorganization of archdiocesan administration. Ultimately, 22 scattered agencies and offices were consolidated under seven secretariats. These were relocated to the Catholic Center, across from SS. PETER AND PAUL CATHEDRAL. An innovative administrator, he provided a support system for religious personnel, streamlined fiscal procedures, and broke with tradition by naming women to key posts.

Gregarious and community-minded, Archbishop O'Meara was a familiar presence at civic events. He especially relished delivering the blessing of the INDIANAPOLIS 500–MILE RACE.

ANN WAGNER ELY

Criterion, Jan. 17, 1992.

100 Black Men. Civic organization serving the African-American community. Established in 1984, the Indianapolis chapter of 100 Black Men promotes the advancement of the black community in Indianapolis through charitable programs, with a special focus on youth.

The organization sponsors four programs for students of Indianapolis Public Schools 14, 27, and 45: the Summer Academy, offering mathematics, reading, computer training, and physical education from June through August; a nationally recognized mentoring program which enlists black male mentors; a Saturday recreation and basketball program that recognizes good behavior, attendance, and scholastic achievement, as well as athletic performance; and a motivational program.

Other programs sponsored by 100 Black Men are: the Beautillion Militaire, a military ceremony for black males in their junior or senior years of high school; the Jerry Harkness Award (named for a member of 100 Black Men who was captain of the 1963 Loyola University NCAA championship basketball team and an Indiana Pacer), which honors a high school basketball player for academic standing, athletic ability, and community service; and health programs, which include free health services, workshops to explore solutions to health problems, and forums on health-related topics. With the exception of a paid executive director, the work of the organization is carried on by volunteers.

MOSES GRAY
100 Black Men of Indianapolis

100 Black Women. Founded in October, 1982, the Indianapolis chapter of this national coalition works in political, economic, and cultural arenas to promote the well-being of its members and of the African-American community, with a special focus on women's issues.

100 Black Women sponsors programs in education, economic development, political action, arts and culture, and personal and professional development. These have included seminars on financial planning, work, and family issues; women and minority vendor fairs; women's forums with nationally recognized African-American speakers; career days; and legislative forums with the Indiana Black Caucus.

Funds raised from its projects are used to support coalition and non-coalition projects consistent with its mission, such as a black infant mortality project in conjunction with Homes for Black Children and the CHILDREN'S BUREAU OF INDIANAPOLIS, and a teen pregnancy and parenting project in conjunction with the Marion County Prosecutor's Office. Organizations to which it has contributed are: United Negro College Fund, Martin Luther King Multi-Service Center, Christamore House Achievement Program, Ruth Lilly Center for Health Education Headstart Program, Sojourner Women's Shelter, Arlington High School Teen Pregnancy Program, and the Center

for Leadership Development in Indianapolis. The organization cosponsors a minority intern program with UNITED WAY of Central Indiana and has participated in a mentoring program with Spelman College students. Volunteers carry out the work of the organization.

JAN CLARK

Orchard Country Day School. Private day school. In 1922 nine local women, including Evelyn Fortune Lilly, EDITH WHITEHILL CLOWES, Martha Carey, and Mary Carey Appel, established an experimental first grade based on Marietta Johnson's "Organic School Model." MARY STEWART CAREY, mother of two of the school's founders and later founder of THE CHILDREN'S MUSEUM, donated her home and apple orchard at 5050 North Meridian Street for the school, which opened October 2, 1922, with 20 students. The founders initially arranged for the Indianapolis Public Schools to operate the parent-funded school under its auspices. When the school board mandated that only neighborhood children could attend the school, thereby excluding founders' children, Orchard's executive committee severed its ties with the Indianapolis school system.

Orchard Country Day School moved to a larger building at the corner of West 42nd Street and Byram Avenue in 1927. It remained at that location until 1957 when it relocated to a 50–acre site at 615 West 63rd Street. A building program in 1976 doubled the size of the school.

From its inception Orchard School has offered a progressive curriculum in its lower school (through grade four) and upper school (grades five through eight). It provides classes for children as young as $2^1/_2$ years old and transitional pro-

Students at the Orchard Country Day School, 5050 North Meridian Street, ca. 1925.
[Orchard Country Day School]

grams for kindergarten and first grade. Orchard emphasizes individual educational goals for each student and uses standardized testing to help determine such goals. Periodic performance reports rather than letter grades are used for children through grade six; students in the upper grades receive quarterly letter grades.

Orchard School is operated by The Orchard School Foundation, established in 1950 and directed by a board of governors. One of its principal benefactors was ELI LILLY, who gave the foundation 20,000 shares of Lilly stock in 1950 and 123,961 shares at his death in 1977. The school, unclassified by the Indiana Department of Education, is a member of the Independent School Association of Central States, National Association of Independent Schools, and the Indiana Association of Independent Schools. Enrollment for the 1993–1994 school year was 590; tuition was $5,800.

HELEN JEAN MCCLELLAND NUGENT
Franklin College of Indiana
DAVID G. VANDERSTEL
Indiana University–Purdue University,
Indianapolis

Caterina Cregor, *The Path Well Chosen: History of the Orchard School, 1922–1984* (Indianapolis, 1984).

Osborne, Benjamin A. "Doc" (Nov. 15, 1898–Aug. 30, 1986). Center Township trustee. Born in Guyana, South America, Osborne came to the United States in 1922. He became a chiropractor, graduating from the United States College of Chiropractic in 1926. He came to Indianapolis in 1932 and set up a practice.

Osborne was the Center Township trustee in Marion County from 1965 until 1986. A Democrat, he served five consecutive terms of four years each. A bid for an unprecedented sixth term ended when he died before the election. At the time of his death, Osborne held the longest service record of any black official in Indiana and was the oldest active trustee in the state.

During his tenure as trustee, Osborne led constant campaigns to raise local spending and improve services for the poor. He expanded the trustee's staff and budget and purchased the former Mayflower building to provide educa-

tional services. Other local officials and clients continually accused Osborne's administration of poor management and inefficiency. Due to his overspending in 1969, the federal government cut off poor relief funds to 26 Indiana counties, and the CITY-COUNTY COUNCIL had to replenish his budget several times.

REBECCA M. MAIER

Indiana Herald, Sept. 6–10, 1986; *Indianapolis News*, Aug. 30, 1986; *Indianapolis Star*, Mar. 25, 1979.

Owen, Richard (Jan. 6, 1810–Mar. 24, 1890). Commanding officer of CAMP MORTON, leading scientist, and educator. Born in New Lanark, Scotland, Owen was the youngest child of utopian theorist Robert Owen. In 1828, he came to the socialist community recently launched by his father at New Harmony, Indiana. There he taught school and engaged in scientific farming.

Drawn to the military life, Owen left New Harmony in April, 1847, to fight in the Mexican War, after which he became a professor of natural science at the Western Military Institute in Nashville, Tennessee. As the sectional crises of the late 1850s intensified, however, Owen found himself increasingly uncomfortable in his southern surroundings and returned to Indiana to assist his brother, David Dale Owen, in his work as state geologist.

When war erupted in 1861, Owen received a commission as colonel of the 60th Indiana Volunteers. In February, 1862, Governor OLIVER P. MORTON selected him to be commandant of Camp Morton in Indianapolis, one of the North's major prisoner of war installations. Owen's service elicited praise from both federal officials and his Confederate prisoners. He established disciplinary measures that were firm yet humane, and which allowed for virtual self-government among the 3,700 prisoners. His benevolence led to several reforms, including building a camp bakery to give prisoners work and to generate funds for their care. Reassigned in May, 1862, Owen later fought in the Vicksburg campaign.

In 1864 Owen relinquished his commission and joined the science faculty at Indiana University, where he would teach and write for the next

15 years. He served briefly as the first president of Purdue University in 1873. Twenty years after Owen's death, former prisoners of Camp Morton erected a bronze bust of the colonel in the Indiana State House in appreciation for his courtesies as their commandant.

LLOYD A. HUNTER
Franklin College of Indiana

Victor Lincoln Albjerg, *Richard Owen: Scotland 1810–Indiana 1890* (West Lafayette, Ind., 1946); *Indianapolis News*, Mar. 25, 1890.

P. R. Mallory and Company. Producer of timer switches; electrical, electronic, and metallurgical components and parts; and dry battery systems and semiconductors. A native of Brooklyn, New York, Philip Rogers Mallory (1885–1975) resigned as general manager of the Commercial Research Company, a manufacturer of incandescent lamps, and founded his own company in Port Chester, New York, in 1916. Starting with nine employees, Mallory's first produced a tungsten filament wire used in light bulbs. Following a successful 1924 patent infringement suit by General Electric, Mallory diversified its product line to remain solvent. The company acquired the Elkon Works, an alloy manufacturer, and contracted with Samuel Ruben to develop a dry electrolytic condenser, which reduced the size of capacitors and lowered overall manufacturing costs. In 1928 Mallory joined with General Electric to create Carboloy Company, a producer of a tungsten carbide cutting tool. Seeking larger manufacturing space, in 1929 Mallory opened a new production facility at 3029 East Washington Street in Indianapolis, which became the firm's new headquarters.

P. R. Mallory and Company suffered heavy losses during the Great Depression and sold its Carboloy division, although it retained its Indianapolis facility. In subsequent years the company developed the Mallory Vibrator and purchased Yaxley Manufacturing, a leading manufacturer of radio parts and switches. During the 1940s Mallory produced assorted articles for the war effort, including condensers, noise filters, electrical contacts, ceramic capacitors, and the mercuric oxide battery. Mallory-developed timing devices were later used in space satellites and air-to-surface missiles.

Boasting a growing list of products, in 1959 Mallory established P. R. Mallory International, a subsidiary that owned and operated production facilities in ten states, England, and Japan. By 1966 Mallory reported more than 8,000 employees, 1,500 in Indianapolis alone, and by 1975 ranked 507th among U.S. companies with sales of $322.8 million. In 1978 Dart Industries of Los Angeles acquired Mallory and later sold it to Black & Decker, which broke up the Mallory divisions in the late 1980s. Mallory Controls, a manufacturer of timers

owned by Emerson Electric, and North American Capacitor Company are the only Indianapolis-based remnants of the original company.

Conscious of the importance of vocational education, Mallory presented a four-story industrial building at 1315 East Washington Street to the Indianapolis Public Schools in December, 1964, for use as an occupational and practical arts education center. IPS later leased the property to INDIANA VOCATIONAL TECHNICAL COLLEGE.

BETH HOLMES HAWKS
STACEY NICHOLAS

Indianapolis Star, Nov. 17, 1975.

Page, Ruth (Mar. 22, 1899–Apr. 4, 1991). Choreographer and dancer. The daughter of an Indianapolis brain surgeon and a pianist, Page studied dance at an early age. In 1914 the Russian ballerina Anna Pavlova invited Page on a tour of South America and she accepted, becoming the first American woman to dance with Pavlova's company. She finished her scholastic studies in New York. After performing a lead role in Carpenter's *The Birthday of the Infanta* in Chicago and New York, she toured internationally with Adolph Bolm's Ballet Intime, then scored another success in Irving Berlin's *Music Box Revue*. She made her Metropolitan Opera debut in 1927 in Smetana's *The Bartered Bride* and danced for several seasons with that ballet ensemble. In 1928 she toured Japan and was guest artist in the enthronement ceremonies for Emperor Hirohito. At various times she was principal dancer for opera companies in Buenos Aires and Ravinia (suburban Chicago) and maintained an international career.

Page began choreographing in the late 1920s and was a pioneer in using American themes in a Russian-dominated field. Her collaboration with Bentley Stone in 1945 led to the birth of the Page-Stone Ballet Company, which toured the United States for nearly a decade. In 1975 she founded the Ruth Page School of Dance in Chicago. Her awards include membership in the Indiana Academy (1975), Dance Magazine Award (1980), the Illinois Gubernatorial Award (1985), and honorary degrees from Indiana University, De Paul University, and Columbia College of Chicago. She was the author of *Page by Page* and *Class*.

JEROME DONAHUE

Indiana Biography Index, Indiana State Library; *Indianapolis News*, Apr. 9, 1991.

Palamara, Ronald D. (Jan. 13, 1939–Jan. 23, 1985). Entrepreneur and founder of Anacomp. An Indianapolis native, Palamara graduated from Cathedral High School before earning his bachelor's degree in mechanical engineering at General Motors Institute in Flint, Michigan, in 1960. Following two years at General Motors, where he worked on the Apollo space program, Palamara completed a master's and doctorate in engineering mechanics at Wayne State University in Detroit.

In 1964 Palamara returned to Indianapolis, working as an engineer at GM's ALLISON DIVISION until the following year when he became associate professor and coordinator of graduate programs at Purdue University's Indianapolis campus (later INDIANA UNIVERSITY-PURDUE UNIVERSITY AT INDIANAPOLIS). In 1968 he teamed with fellow Purdue professors Albert R. Sadaka and J. Melvin Ebbert to found ANACOMP, a computer services firm. Two years later Palamara became president and chairman of the company. Anacomp proved highly successful, reaching annual sales of $172 million in 1983 before encountering financial difficulties. His personal net worth estimated at $10 million, Palamara spent the next two years working to restore financial stability to his company.

Active in numerous community organizations, Palamara was a director of the Indianapolis CHAMBER OF COMMERCE and a director-at-large of the INDIANAPOLIS MUSEUM OF ART. In the early 1980s he attempted to bring a USFL professional football franchise to Indianapolis before withdrawing his backing due to lack of support.

DEBORAH B. MARKISOHN

Indianapolis Magazine (Nov., 1983); *Indianapolis News* and *Indianapolis Star*, Jan. 24, 1985.

Palm Sunday (1981). An autobiographical collection of nonfiction and fiction by Indianapolis native Kurt Vonnegut, Jr. *Palm Sunday*, subtitled *An Autobiographical Collage*, is a collection of essays, letters, speeches, reviews, and fiction. Throughout the book, especially in the chapter titled "Roots," Vonnegut—perhaps the best known Indianapolis author of the mid/late 20th century—explores his family's history in Indianapolis. The "Roots" chapter features excerpts from attorney John Rauch's manuscript, "An Account of the Ancestry of Kurt Vonnegut, Jr., by an Ancient Friend of His Family," which examines the lives of such Vonnegut ancestors as great-grandfather CLEMENS VONNEGUT, Sr., who established the VONNEGUT HARDWARE COMPANY, and grandfather BERNARD VONNEGUT of the architectural firm VONNEGUT & BOHN, which designed such Indianapolis landmarks as the John Herron Art Museum, the ATHENAEUM, and the L. S. Ayres and the Fletcher Trust buildings.

Along with the Vonnegut family genealogy, the book includes a letter from Vonnegut to a school committee in North Dakota where his books were burned; a chapter titled "Embarrassment" detailing his Indianapolis relatives' lack of enthusiasm for his fiction; and a musical comedy version of the Dr. Jekyll and Mr. Hyde story.

Born on November 11, 1922, Vonnegut is the second son of Kurt and Edith (Lieber) Vonnegut. He attended Indianapolis' Public School No. 43 and SHORTRIDGE HIGH SCHOOL, graduating in 1940. While at Shortridge, Vonnegut was an editor for the school's newspaper, the *DAILY ECHO*. He attended Cornell University before enlisting in the Army. Vonnegut served with the 106th Infantry Division and was captured by the Germans during the Battle of the Bulge. As a prisoner of war, Vonnegut witnessed the Allied firebombing of Dresden, an experience recreated in his bestselling book, *Slaughterhouse-Five* (1969).

After the war, Vonnegut worked in the public relations department of General Electric in Schenectady, New York. He left that job in 1950 to write full time and has authored *Player Piano* (1952), *The Sirens of Titan* (1959), *Cat's Cradle* (1961), *Breakfast of Champions* (1973), *Slapstick* (1976), and many others.

RAY BOOMHOWER
Indiana Historical Society

Donald E. Thompson, *Indiana Authors and Their Books, 1917–1966* (Crawfordsville, Ind., 1974).

Pan American Games (August 7–23, 1987). Second-largest multisport event in the world (the Olympics is largest). Since 1951 the Pan American Games have been held every four years in the summer preceding the Olympics. The games are staged by the Pan American Sports Organization (PASO), which was formed in 1950 by the National Olympic Committees in the Western Hemisphere. Their mission is to pave the way for cultural exchange, mutual understanding, and the strengthening of Olympic ideals throughout the Americas.

By 1984 Indianapolis was well into its campaign to become an international sports capital. Since the 1987 Pan American Games had already been awarded to Chile, Indianapolis set its sights on hosting the 1991 competition. However, when Chile, and then Ecuador, backed out of hosting

Opening ceremonies of the Pan American Games were held at the Indianapolis Motor Speedway. [Indianapolis Newspapers Inc.]

the 1987 games because of economic considerations, Indianapolis seized the opportunity. In November, 1984, at the request of the United States Olympic Committee, Mayor William H. Hudnut III, led a delegation of city leaders to Mexico City to meet with PASO president Mario Vazquez Rana to present a bid.

Several factors weighed heavily in favor of Indianapolis. The city had already demonstrated success in hosting national and international sports events; more than $136 million worth of first-class sports facilities were already in place, so little construction would be needed to prepare; and Indianapolis was headquarters for the AMATEUR ATHLETIC UNION and for several national AMATEUR SPORTS GOVERNING BODIES.

On December 18, 1984, PASO announced that Indianapolis had been selected as host. Normally, the event is awarded five to six years in advance, but because of the circumstances, Indianapolis had only two and a half years to prepare. A local organizing committee, Pan American Ten/Indianapolis (PAX/I), was formed to carry out the planning and staging of the games. Eighteen operational divisions, involving a paid staff of 300 and 37,000 volunteers, assumed responsibility for every aspect of the games, from arranging housing, transportation, and security to ticket marketing, sponsor sales, public relations, and parking.

The U.S. Department of Defense agreed to allow PAX/I to use a section of FORT BENJAMIN HARRISON as an Athletes Village. The village provided visiting athletes with lodging, a practice track, a nightclub, and dining facilities staffed with volunteers who served more than 300,000 meals during the week. A new shooting range was built, and several sports facilities, including the William Kuntz Soccer Center and the Eagle Creek Park regatta course and archery range, were refurbished for the games.

The games cost approximately $30 million. The revenue came from several sources, including 22 corporate sponsors who contributed a minimum of $500,000 each; 83 corporate suppliers, whose support varied from several thousand dollars to more than $2 million; companies who were licensed to market products bearing the protected marks of the games; individual and corporate charitable contributions; and the sale of broadcast rights. About $7 million was received in dedicated grants, federal government support, and Athletes Village per diem. In addition, spectators bought 905,813 tickets worth $9,007,587.

Approximately 62 arts and community organizations spent about $4 million to produce the Pan American Arts Festival. The festival consisted of 1,104 separate events and activities designed to help residents of Indiana and visitors to the games learn about and experience the artistic heritage of the participating countries. Activities covered a wide range—from music to literature, from theater to design arts, from dance to the visual arts. The INDIANAPOLIS MUSEUM OF ART conducted classes in Latin American culture and presented a special exhibit. Hundreds of Indianapolis residents studied Spanish in anticipation of the arrival of thousands of Spanish-speaking guests.

On August 8, approximately 80,000 spectators converged at the INDIANAPOLIS MOTOR SPEEDWAY to see the opening ceremonies, which proved to be the largest outdoor live entertainment show ever staged in the United States. Produced and staged by Walt Disney World Productions, the event involved more than 6,500 volunteer performers with an additional 23,000 volunteers in the card section.

During the next three weeks, 4,453 athletes from 38 PASO nations competed in 30 sports ranging from archery to yacht racing. CBS televised 26 hours of the event on three successive weekends, and 2,100 journalists representing 628 news organizations from 36 nations covered the action.

According to a study by Indiana University, the event added about $175 million to the city's economy. In addition, Indianapolis earned the distinction of being the first Pan American Games host city to break even financially.

DELORES J. WRIGHT

Pan American Plaza. Block bounded by UNION STATION, the Hoosier Dome, Georgia Street, and Illinois Street. The Pan American Plaza, designed by BROWNING DAY MULLINS DIERDORF, opened in 1987 and served as the media center for the 10th Quadrennial PAN AMERICAN

GAMES. The INDIANA SPORTS CORPORATION, owner of the plaza, promoted it as a permanent tribute to the Pan American Games and a symbol of Indianapolis' claim to be the amateur sports capital of the world. Contributions from the local business community and the city itself made the multimillion dollar project possible.

The cornerstone of the Pan Am Plaza (as it is commonly known) is the 12–story office tower on the northwest corner which houses the Indiana Sports Corporation, the headquarters of five separate Olympic sports governing associations, and several commercial establishments. Walkways connect the tower and an underground parking garage to two indoor skating rinks. These facilities—The Indiana/World Skating Academy—have attracted some of the nation's finest ice skaters, and Indianapolis has become a major training site for youth figure skating and hockey.

Aside from these buildings, the plaza provides over two acres of public space. This open area is covered with brick pathways and benches. During the summer the plaza's outdoor stage is used for public performances, festivals, and street fairs, and an outdoor skating rink is set up during the winter. The plaza flies the flags of every Pan American nation as a tribute to the peaceful competition that brought them together in Indianapolis.

WILLIAM D. DALTON

Pantzer, Kurt F. (Aug. 21, 1892–July 8, 1979). Attorney. Born in Indianapolis, Pantzer attended Wabash College and received both his A.B. and his law degree from Harvard. He practiced for two years in New York City and, after returning to Indiana in 1922, associated with two Indianapolis law firms before becoming a partner in 1940 at Barnes, Hickman, Pantzer, and Boyd, where he remained until his death. Nationally known for his legal expertise, Pantzer served on the National Conference of Commissioners on Uniform State Laws, was chair of the Indiana Commission on a Uniform Commercial Code and the Indiana Commission on Uniform State Laws (including a special committee of the latter on Uniform Acts to Prevent Organized Crime), and co-chair of the Joint Committee of the American Bar Association. He also chaired the Committee of Twenty-One, which introduced and lobbied the Indiana General Assembly in 1949 to adopt the Uniform Partnership Act, Uniform Limited Partnership Act, Uniform Divorce Act, and amendments to the Business Corporation Act. He served on the boards of many corporations, and educational, civic, and cultural institutions.

Pantzer owned the world's largest collection of J. M. W. Turner watercolors in private hands, a collection now on display at the INDIANAPOLIS MUSEUM OF ART. He was active in the formation of the Meridian Street Preservation Commission to preserve the character of the corridor between 40th Street and Westfield Boulevard. That commission successfully opposed the proposed widening of Meridian Street in the early 1970s.

JOAN CUNNINGHAM

Who Was Who in America, Vol. 7; Indianapolis Star and Indianapolis News, July 9, 1979.

Park Tudor School. This private school, located at 7200 North College Avenue, took its present name and form in 1970 as the result of a merger between Tudor Hall School for Girls (est. 1902) and Park School for Boys (est. 1914).

Fredonia Allen established Tudor Hall in 1902 to satisfy the need for a college preparatory school for girls in Indianapolis. With the Reverend James C. Smith, a Presbyterian clergyman, she founded the school and named it for her mother, Ann Tudor Allen. Previously on the teaching staff of the Classical School for Girls, Allen remained as principal and proprietor of Tudor Hall until her death in 1927. Whenever possible she hired graduates of eastern women's colleges as instructors in order to introduce the "culture" of the East Coast to the Midwest. Tudor Hall, which followed the lead of the eastern schools in establishing residence quarters for boarding students, attracted students from the Midwest, the eastern states, and foreign nations.

Following Allen's death the school suffered financial difficulties and, in 1936, incorporated as a nonprofit institution. After World War II enrollment outgrew its facilities at 3171 North Meridian Street and in 1959 the day school and boarding facilities moved to 3650 Cold Spring Road.

Brooks School for Boys began in 1914 at 1535 Central Avenue to meet the college preparatory needs of young men. Financial problems threatened in 1920, and a group of local businessmen purchased the assets and changed the name to Boys Preparatory School. Graduates of eastern colleges filled most faculty positions, and the school admitted both day and boarding students. In 1929 the institution moved to facilities at 3050 Cold Spring Road near Thomas Taggart Park and changed its name to Park School. When Tudor Hall eliminated lower grades in 1964, Park School responded by admitting girls through grade six. In 1966 the school relocated to the College Avenue site.

Upon the merger of the two schools in 1970, Park School's northside facilities served the consolidated institution. Boarding was discontinued due to declining interest. The present institution is operated by Park Tudor Foundation through an elected board of directors. The pre-kindergarten through grade twelve curriculum falls into lower, middle, and upper school components, each administered by a director under the overall administration of the headmaster. Enrollment in 1993–1994 was nearly 800 students, and tuition ranged from $6,000 to $7,630.

Park Tudor holds membership in the Independent Schools Association of the Central States and the National Association of Independent Schools, and certification by the Indiana Department of Education. Park Tudor has been a full member of the INDIANA HIGH SCHOOL ATHLETIC ASSOCIATION since 1979.

HELEN JEAN MCCLELLAND NUGENT
Franklin College of Indiana

Parks. During the early planning and development of the city there seemed no need for planned public parks. ALEXANDER RALSTON'S original plan of the MILE SQUARE did not include any designated public spaces. Early residents used pastures, cemeteries, and all the undeveloped land about them as recreational areas. As the Civil War approached and the city experienced congestion for the first time, however, citizen action in favor of public parks began slowly to build. In 1859 Timothy Fletcher donated a plot of land to the city with the provision that it be improved and used as a public park. The City Council, believing Fletcher's gesture was a ruse to elevate the value of his adjacent land, refused his offer. Other private donations also were viewed with suspicion, and the council chose not to act upon them.

Using a different tactic, George Merritt was responsible for the first public park in Indianapolis. He repeatedly petitioned state and local authorities for donation of state land for use as a public park. Governor OLIVER P. MORTON offered the land now known as MILITARY PARK for use as a recreation area, and in 1864 the City Council took over protective control of Military Park as well as University Square and the Governor's Circle.

By the 1870s citizens became more vocal in their desire for public parks, and the City Council launched a tentative program of park purchases. In 1870 the city purchased Brookside Park from the heirs of CALVIN FLETCHER. Three years later a group of northside residents petitioned the council for a park along FALL CREEK, with seven citizens donating 91.5 acres. The northside project failed to gain council support, but similar efforts by a group of southside residents ultimately led to the purchase of Southern Park, later renamed GARFIELD PARK. Again the council did not develop this property, and the city leased it to the Indiana Trotting Association between 1877 and 1880.

By the 1880s residents privately and in combination with the city improved all these park lands. Merritt funded Military Park's original improvements and subsequently installed a playground. Neighbors of the University Square property voluntarily landscaped the park, and the Odd Fellows of Indiana erected a statue of Vice-President Schuyler Colfax there. Citizens planted trees in Garfield Park and carried out other improvements funded by the council. Additionally, residents in the area of St. Clair Square created their own park, collecting subscriptions, laying walks, and planting trees.

These 19th-century public parks were intended for use as passive recreation areas where middle class and wealthy citizens could relax and enjoy nature. It was not until 1895 that the City Council, under a new CITY CHARTER (1891), created a public park commission which subsequently developed a system of public parks in Indianapolis. The Commercial Club, forerunner of the CHAMBER OF COMMERCE, drafted the legislation creating a five-member Board of Park Commissioners to administer the six previously established parks.

City officials immediately consulted with nationally prominent park landscape designers to guide park development. The Commercial Club had hired parks consultant Joseph Earnshaw in 1894, who recommended that sites be purchased and developed along White River and Fall Creek, connected by a chain of small parks and interconnecting parkways. Once established, the park board conducted a survey of possible park sites and commissioned John C. Olmsted, stepson of famed landscape designer Frederick Law Olmsted, Sr., to develop a plan for future parks. The Olmsted plan, like the Earnshaw plan, recommended that local waterways be the focus of a system which would include small parks, boulevards, several larger local parks, and a large public reservation.

Mayor THOMAS TAGGERT, who assumed office in 1895, was a strong supporter of parks and was instrumental in laying the foundations of the park system. At his behest the council approved a limited version of the Olmsted plan and authorized the purchase of over 1,100 acres of land, including much of what is now Riverside Park, during the early 1900s. Much of the land bought at this time had previously been used as unauthorized dumping grounds. The park department saw its job as ridding the city of unclean and unhealthy areas as well as providing beautiful recreation spaces. Park improvements included landscaping, building water features, and adding walking paths and benches, with the bulk of the work focusing on Riverside and Garfield parks. Parks also began to provide entertainment such as the 18–hole golf course, zoo, and steamboat cruises on White River at Riverside Park.

In 1908 the park board hired nationally known park planner GEORGE E. KESSLER as a consulting landscape architect, ushering in an era of greater park presence throughout the city. Kessler, already at work on planning the city's boulevard system, helped pass a new park law in 1909 which allowed the department to levy taxes for park purchases and improvements. Much public debate surrounded the law since not all citizens agreed that public parks should be a municipal responsibility. Successive park laws in 1913 and 1919, however, further increased the department's autonomy and taxing power. The new legislation made possible department expansion, purchase of new properties, and the beginnings of boulevard construction. Despite the city's official sponsorship, citizens continued to actively support park development during the early 1900s by donating property or funding park improvements. The bequests of Alfred Burdsal and George Rhodius in 1911 funded the purchase and development of Willard Park, Burdsal Parkway, and Rhodius Park. Other citizens financed memorials placed on park property, such as the Depew Memorial Fountain and the Benjamin Harrison and Lew Wallace statues.

During World War I the city suspended most park activities and funding. As a result, almost all park contracts and improvements were discontinued except for those completed by a specially formed Park Construction Force. Simultaneously, the department supported the war effort by opening park property for use as vegetable gardens to help alleviate general food shortages.

In the 1920s the department resumed park purchases and expansion. The park system grew to include 24 parks and parkways, with land totaling approximately 1,900 acres. This acreage included three large parks outside the downtown area: Riverside to the northwest, Garfield to the south, and Brookside to the northeast. The parks also continued to be a venue for memorials, and after World War I several structures and gardens were donated and dedicated to Marion County soldiers and veterans.

The idea that public parks should provide active as well as passive recreation originally surfaced before the war, but recreational programming did not become a high priority until later. As early as 1910 the park board joined with public school and library officials to provide recreational programs, gradually accepting more of this responsibility. In 1919 a new park law transferred the recreation division from the city's public health department to the public parks department, which began constructing a system of playgrounds, pools, and community recreational cen-

ters in the parks. Parks soon provided a variety of year-round athletic programming, classes, clubs, and special events. The centers also provided bathing facilities, day nurseries, dental clinics, and served as a neighborhood headquarters for welfare agencies.

Although some residents opposed the expanded definition of public parks, these new activities were a large success, greatly multiplying park attendance. This programming also expanded the department's presence within the city, establishing close links with other community groups such as the school board, Southside Turners, settlement houses, YMCA, and the Girl Scouts.

During the 1930s the system of neighborhood parks, playgrounds, boulevards, and recreation areas in Indianapolis grew despite the Great Depression. The department, however, began to charge fees for some of its operations, such as the golf courses, swimming pools, and community houses, to make them self-sustaining. At the same time volunteers from women's groups, civic organizations, and WPA and CWA workers augmented the parks' work force. Park activities focused on city beautification projects and year-round recreational activities: completing Lake Sullivan, constructing wading pools, staffing summer playgrounds, landscaping the boulevards and public properties, and sponsoring dances. Park community houses became popular, low-cost centers of activity during the 1930s, housing many clubs and classes as well as providing space for other groups.

Despite the expansion of park facilities and programs, a CHARITY ORGANIZATION SOCIETY study in 1937 found that only 20 percent of public park acreage was within a two-mile radius of half of the residential population. The park department's major strategies for land acquisition had been to receive donations or purchase cheap land on the outskirts of town; the intended policy of buying small parcels of land within walking distance of all residents throughout the city remained largely unimplemented by the 1940s. Additionally, the African-American population felt particularly ignored because of the department's segregation policies.

The World War II years added temporary new responsibilities for the public parks—running canteens and clubs for servicemen and providing land for postwar veteran and emergency housing. After the war and into the 1950s, however, the park department again turned its attention to recreation and city beautification. The playground system expanded, and parks continued to sponsor a growing number of clubs, classes, and "teen canteens." Although the parks had long hosted festivals, the 1950s saw the increase of music festivals, carnivals, and dances, many of which were revenue producing projects.

By the late 1940s the city renewed its efforts to beautify and restore its 52 parks. Much of the park property and existing facilities had not had significant improvements made to them in at least 20 years, and large bond issues in the early 1950s helped pay for much of the renovation.

Athletics became increasingly important after the 1940s and the parks provided the sites for many boxing, basketball, and baseball leagues and tournaments, including some of national significance. For example, the purchase of BROAD RIPPLE PARK in 1946 with its Olympic-size pool led to the AAU national championship swimming meet in 1958. Golfing also became a high priority during these years, with the parks department even hiring golf pros to assist patrons and oversee the courses.

Rising rates of suburbanization and competition with private sources of recreation during the 1960s forced park officials to change the focus of public parks. Downtown properties increasingly received less attention as the park department devoted resources to parks nearer the suburbs and purchased park land in suburban townships. Financed by Indianapolis and Marion County taxes, the park department purchased Northwestway, Northeastway (now Sahm Park), Southeastway, and EAGLE CREEK PARK. Not all downtown efforts were forsaken, however, as the department began what would become a perennial effort at park promotion by encouraging neighborhoods, clubs, and civic groups to "adopt" and help maintain a park. Also, in 1964 Washington Park became the site of a new city zoo.

Changes continued during the 1970s. Unigov expanded the Indianapolis service boundaries to include all of Marion County and created a reorganized DEPARTMENT OF PARKS AND RECREATION.

Citizen interest in parks fell as suburbanization and park vandalism increased. Public parks also competed for space and resources with urban expansion and renewal efforts. The parks department responded by experimenting with new programs and projects. Using millions of dollars from federal grants and local bond issues, it constructed a system of small, special use parks known as "tot lot" and "vest pocket" parks along highways, refurbished deteriorating facilities, built new facilities, expanded recreational programs, and made extensive improvements to Eagle Creek Park, which opened in 1974. The parks department also renamed many central city parks after notable local and national African-Americans, reflecting the changing nature of park visitors.

While these efforts resulted in notable successes, such as the institution of the INDIANAPOLIS/ SCARBOROUGH PEACE GAMES, a general lack of park usage, inadequate maintenance, and vandalism became serious problems, especially for central city parks. Several park officials were prosecuted for mismanagement and fraud, further lowering the public's confidence. Parks on the outer edges of the city, especially Eagle Creek Park, and the golf courses, however, offered first-rate facilities and programs.

A new parks administration began a greater focus on amateur sports during the 1980s, which inspired a resurgence in park usage and image. The department, in an effort to supply a unique recreational need in the community, began to phase out smaller central city parks in favor of large natural-setting parks and linear parks equipped with fitness and bike paths. Eagle Creek became the showcase of the park system during the 1980s, offering a lake, nature trails, and many recreation facilities. Large bond issues funded amateur sports facilities, such as the Lake Sullivan Sports Complex and the Major Taylor Velodrome, which along with the 11 golf courses became venues for special events as well as local and national competitions. The INDIANAPOLIS ZOO also relocated from Washington Park in 1986 to the new WHITE RIVER STATE PARK.

As of the early 1990s the Indianapolis Department of Parks and Recreation continues to fight vandalism and public apathy. While the department offers a wide variety of traditional recreational and nature programs, many are underused due to competition from private and commercial providers of recreational activities. Popular new park programs are those tied to the city's environmental efforts, including "Tox-Away Day," recycling centers, and urban forestry programs. An important focus for the parks department in the future will be the development of the "Indianapolis Greenways Project." In an undertaking built upon Kessler's acquisition of waterway corridors, department officials and city planners hope to develop approximately 150 miles of recreation and fitness trails along local waterways and abandoned railroad rights-of-way. These trails would connect recreational and cultural sites throughout the city.

The park system of the early 1990s claimed 73 properties, 16 community recreation centers, 13 pools, and 12 golf courses. Most of these properties were located in Center Township but continue to compete for space with other governmental agencies. Segments of the community continue to be committed to public parks, however, as is evidenced by the 1991 organization of the Indianapolis Parks Foundation, a private citizen funding group, and the use of neighborhood advisory councils in park planning.

MICHELLE D. HALE

Parks and Recreation, Department of.

This department of municipal government oversees recreational facilities and provides leisure time activities throughout Marion County. The department also enforces all city ordinances and state laws pertaining to parks and recreational facilities.

A five-member board, administered by a director, oversees department policies, reviews its annual budget, and approves all contracts. Two members are appointed by the CITY-COUNTY COUNCIL and two by the MAYOR. These four members serve renewable one-year terms. The director, who is appointed by the mayor and serves at the mayor's pleasure, is the fifth member and the chair of the Board of Parks and Recreation.

The department is organized into five divisions. The Division of Administration includes sections for data processing, planning and design,

property and construction management, and marketing.

The Eagle Creek Division operates Eagle Creek Park and Nature Preserve. One of the largest municipal parks in the United States, it covers 4,500 acres and draws nearly 300,000 visitors each year. The park and preserve surround Eagle Creek Reservoir, so this division also provides some water recreation activities.

The Golf Division has managed and operated the city's extensive system of municipal public golf courses. The division conducts public tournaments and golf education programs, including classes for children. In 1992 the Golf Division entered into contracts for the private management and maintenance of the city's golf courses, but it still oversees golf operations.

The Parks Management Division operates and maintains over 130 parks and the facilities within them (excluding Eagle Creek Park). Division personnel also operate or oversee support operations at the city's parks, such as concessions, aquatics, and amateur athletics. This division maintains all trees along the streets of Marion County.

The Recreation Division contains three sections. Its Arts Services Section provides art and cultural programs and activities, which served over 240,000 people in 1990. Its Special Populations Section focuses on recreational activities for the elderly and disabled residents of Marion County. Its Regional Districts Section includes north, east, west, and south offices that plan and conduct special recreational events and ongoing classes in their portions of the county.

LAURRY NEUFER

Parkways and Boulevards.

In part a response to the "City Beautiful" ideal popularized by the 1893 World's Columbian Exposition in Chicago, Indianapolis initiated a number of expansions and improvements in its city parks around the turn of the 20th century. With the idea of reserved GREENSPACE came the notion of attractive thoroughfares, usually winding alongside streams, connecting various points within the town. The thoroughfares were intended to be largely recreational, providing pleasant drives around the city with occasional benches and suitable picnic spots provided.

The prospect of a boulevard following FALL CREEK from Capitol Avenue to the then-new INDIANA STATE FAIRGROUNDS on Maple Road (38th Street) arose as early as 1901 in discussions of the Indianapolis Board of Park Commissioners, itself only in its seventh year. By 1906 Fall Creek Boulevard was completed between Capitol and Central Avenue, as was most of a section of Pleasant Run Boulevard (later Parkway) between Raymond and Beecher streets. Other boulevards in progress were along the levee on the east bank of WHITE RIVER north of Michigan Street, and another northward through Riverside Park from the stone dam (still extant), near where the Emrichsville Bridge had recently been built, to 30th Street. From the beginning Indianapolis planned parks for its boulevards. City engineers did not lose sight of this link in succeeding decades, thereby seeking and ultimately achieving, to a degree, a true system of wide parkways with broader intermittent expanses of parks like green beads on a cord.

The original park-boulevard plan was the work of George Kessler, a landscape architect hired by the park board. Among the plan's most enthusiastic proponents was Dr. Henry Jameson, who became chairman of the park board in 1908. Among other things he successfully urged that the location of the new ST. VINCENT HOSPITAL be moved back several hundred yards from its originally planned spot on the bank of Fall Creek, thus allowing space for the boulevard and streamside improvements.

The construction of FORT BENJAMIN HARRISON in 1906 brought a proposal from the federal government to build a boulevard connecting the army post with the city. The park board suggested it could easily be an extension of Fall Creek Boulevard. Ultimately, the plan came to fruition in the 1930s, when workers of the Federal Emergency Relief Administration and Works Progress Administration fulfilled the dreams of the early park planner and completed lengthy stretches of Fall Creek Parkway, Pleasant Run Parkway, Riverside Drive, and KESSLER BOULEVARD.

As the city rapidly expanded after World War II, some advocates, such as Mayor PHILIP BAYT in the late 1950s, urged the creation of a parkway along lower EAGLE CREEK on the west side of the city. At the same time, many of the neighborhoods along Fall Creek were beginning to change and the parkway, with its picnic shelters and benches placed all along the creek, began to deteriorate. In the 1980s the city undertook a massive Fall Creek restoration program, the most noticeable result of which has been the beautification of the parkway upstream from State Road 37 along the stream's north bank.

GLORY-JUNE GREIFF

Parry, David M. (Mar. 26, 1852–May 12, 1915). Indianapolis businessman and foe of organized labor. Elected president of the National Association of Manufacturers in 1902, Parry led the businessmen's fight against unions during the Progressive era. Despite never holding elective office, Parry, a lifelong Republican, was an influential figure in the careers of such Indiana politicians as ALBERT J. BEVERIDGE, CHARLES W. FAIRBANKS, and BENJAMIN HARRISON.

Parry was born in Allegheny County, Pennsylvania, near Pittsburgh. In 1853 Parry's father moved his family to a farm near Laurel, Indiana. At the age of 16 Parry took his first job as a clerk in a Laurel store. In 1872 he moved to Columbus City, Iowa, where he worked in a store owned by his brother Edward. Parry later was a bookkeeper for the New York Enamel Paint Company in New

One of the Parry Manufacturing Company's many buggy styles depicted in an 1891 advertisement. [Indiana Historical Society, #C5756]

York City before returning to Indiana in 1873 to open a hardware store in Connersville.

Forced to sell the store in order to help his financially troubled father, Parry became a traveling salesman based in Cincinnati. With money saved from that job he bought a Rushville hardware store, selling it in 1882. Although he had planned to travel to South America to sell farm implements, the death of his wife caused Parry to cancel those plans. Instead, he purchased a Rushville carriage firm.

In 1886 Parry moved his business to Indianapolis where he and his brother Thomas created the Parry Manufacturing Company, which built a variety of carriages. With the coming of the automobile, Parry turned from building carriages to manufacturing cars. He established the Parry Auto Company in 1909 and also founded the Overland Automobile Company, which was later sold to John Willys who moved the firm to Toledo, Ohio.

Parry, who had served as president and director of the Indianapolis BOARD OF TRADE and the COMMERCIAL CLUB, led the fight against unions and for the open shop at the beginning of the century from his post as head of the National Association of Manufacturers. Parry's antilabor writings and speeches drew the ire of such labor leaders as Samuel Gompers.

Upon his return from a trip to study economic conditions in such countries as New Zealand, Australia, China, and Japan, Parry became ill. He died at his estate, GOLDEN HILL, located northwest of the city, and is buried in CROWN HILL CEMETERY.

RAY BOOMHOWER
Indiana Historical Society

___

Milton Rubincam, "David M. Parry," *Indiana Magazine of History*, 34 (June, 1938), 165–174; John Bartlow Martin, *Indiana: An Interpretation* (New York, 1947).

Parvin, Theophilus (Jan. 9, 1829–Jan. 29, 1898). Obstetrician-gynecologist and medical writer. A native of Buenos Aires, Argentina, with degrees from Indiana University (B.A.) and the University of Pennsylvania (M.D., 1852), Parvin

practiced medicine in Indianapolis from 1853 to 1883.

Parvin edited the *Cincinnati Journal of Medicine*, 1866–1867, the *Western Journal of Medicine*, 1868, and the *American Practitioner*, 1869–1883. He became the first Indiana physician to enter medical journalism when he began publication of the *Indiana Journal of Medicine* in 1870. He held the presidencies of the Indiana (1862) and American Medical Associations (1879), and served on the faculties of the Medical College of Ohio, 1864–1869, the University of Louisville, 1869–1876, the College of Physicians and Surgeons (Indianapolis), 1878–1883, and Jefferson Medical College (Philadelphia), 1883–1898.

Parvin's major work, *Science and Art of Obstetrics* (1886), although published after he left the state, is often cited as the first medical textbook written by an Indiana physician.

NANCY PIPPEN ECKERMAN
Indiana University School of Medicine

___

Morris Fishbein, *A History of the American Medical Association, 1847 to 1947* (Philadelphia, 1947).

Paxton, James (July 1, 1792–Apr. 5, 1829). Early settler, militia leader, and state representative. A native of Virginia and veteran of the War of 1812, Paxton came to Indianapolis in October, 1821, and constructed several early buildings in the new village. He was a contractor on the first Marion County Courthouse, completed in the fall of 1824. This structure also served as the state capitol for several years.

Paxton was elected colonel of MILITIA when MARION COUNTY officers balloted for leadership on September 7, 1822. He assumed command of ten infantry companies and one company each of artillery, rifles, and cavalry (the 40th Regiment, Indiana State Militia). His citizen soldiers trained in what is now known as MILITARY PARK, land he was instrumental in obtaining from the federal government. The companies drilled and paraded there, generally for little more than the amusement of citizens. He held this post until 1826 when he was succeeded by ALEXANDER W. RUSSELL.

Paxton was also active in politics and business. He was a representative from Marion and other nearby counties to the 1823–1824 and 1825 –1826 sessions, and he sponsored legislation that facilitated removal of the capital from Corydon to Indianapolis. The following year he became president of a local Clay for President club. He invested in some of the city's early business ventures and counted among his closest friends two other pioneer citizens of Indianapolis, CALVIN FLETCHER and DANIEL YANDES. Paxton is buried at CROWN HILL CEMETERY.

WAYNE L. SANFORD

John H. B. Nowland, *Early Reminiscences of Indianapolis* (Indianapolis, 1870); *Biographical Directory of the Indiana General Assembly*, Vol. 1 (Indianapolis, 1980); Gayle Thornbrough, ed., *The Diary of Calvin Fletcher*, Vol. I (Indianapolis, 1972).

Peanut Butter Press. Monthly children's newspaper. The *Peanut Butter Press* (*PBP*) is a newspaper written by children in grades five and six for children ages 7 through 13. It is published as a 12–page tabloid insert in the *INDIANAPOLIS NEWS* on the second Tuesday of every month during the school year. Barbara Poore, acting as editor, founded *PBP* in 1980 as a product of the Children's Educational Foundation, Inc., a not-for-profit organization she also served as president. When the newspaper became part of the *News* in 1986 a new editor was appointed, but the original format was retained.

Student reporters from area schools are selected each month by their school administrators to cover topics on local businesses and events and to interview celebrities and community leaders. The newspaper also contains student-written book reviews, puzzles, and creative writing, as well as comics, crafts, and recipes that are created by adults.

PBP has received a 1984 Casper Award for outstanding community service, national awards for excellence in educational journalism, and national television coverage. Because *PBP* is a part of the *News*, it enjoys the same circulation as the daily newspaper, in addition to its school subscriptions, which totaled 75,000 during 1990–1991.

JUDY SCHWARTZ

Peat, Wilbur David (Nov. 8, 1898–Dec. 14, 1966). Art museum director, artist, and art instructor and historian. Peat was born in Chengtu, Szechuan, China, to parents of English descent. He was a student at Ohio Wesleyan University and graduated in 1923 from the Cleveland School of Art where he received the Agnes Gund portrait scholarship for study abroad. He further studied at the National Academy of Design and the Art Students League in New York City, and traveled to Paris for instruction at the Colarossi Academy in 1924. Later, Peat received a master of arts degree from the University of Chicago and honorary doctorate degrees from Hanover College in 1944 and Indiana Central College (now UNIVERSITY OF INDIANAPOLIS) in 1956.

From 1924 to 1929 Peat served as director of the Akron Art Institute, Akron, Ohio, and was art instructor at the University of Akron and the Western Reserve Academy during 1926 and 1927. In 1929 Peat became director of the John Herron Art Museum in Indianapolis; he remained in that capacity until 1965 and as a consultant until his death. While at Herron, Peat brought national recognition to the museum through the major art exhibitions that he assembled. The museum's permanent collection was rounded out under Peat's supervision, acquiring examples of most of the European schools as well as promoting the contemporary American artist. To judge the annual Indiana Artists exhibitions that were held at Herron, Peat was instrumental in bringing to Indianapolis such well-known American artists as Thomas Hart Benton.

Peat was a member of the American Association of Museums, the Midwest Museum Conference, and the Indiana Artists Club. His publications include *Portraits and Painters of the Governors of Indiana, 1800–1943* (1944), *Pioneer Painters of Indiana* (1954), *Indiana Houses of the Nineteenth Century* (1962), and, as coauthor, *The House of the Singing Winds: The Life and Work of T. C. Steele* (1966).

FRANK N. OWINGS, JR.

Indiana Biography Series, Indiana State Library; *Who Was Who in America.*

Pennsylvania Railroad. One of the four major northeastern rail systems that served Indianapolis. The oldest predecessor line, the MADISON AND INDIANAPOLIS (M&I), was completed to Indianapolis in 1847. Following a brief period of prosperity, the M&I was absorbed by its rival, the Jeffersonville Railroad. The Jeffersonville was chartered in 1832 as the Ohio & Indianapolis. Completion to Columbus in 1852 was followed by bitter confrontation with the M&I, culminating in an agreement giving the Jeffersonville access to Indianapolis over the Madison road's line. The Jeffersonville merged the reorganized Madison and Indianapolis in 1866 to form the Jeffersonville, Madison & Indianapolis (JM&I), which was leased by the Pennsylvania interests in 1871.

Chartered in 1847 to bisect the state from east to west, the Terre Haute & Richmond (TH&R) built east from the Wabash River. When support for the line east of Indianapolis languished, the Richmond-Indianapolis portion was separately rechartered as the Indiana Central in 1851. The TH&R (renamed the Terre Haute & Indianapolis in 1865) was finally completed to Indianapolis in 1852.

The Indiana Central line was completed to Richmond in 1854 as a link to Cincinnati, Dayton, and Columbus. The company formed an alliance with the Columbus & Indianapolis Railroad in 1863 which blossomed one year later into a merger creating the Columbus & Indianapolis Central. After further consolidations the company emerged in 1868 as the Columbus, Chicago, & Indiana Central (CC&IC), and was leased in 1869 to the Pennsylvania-owned Pittsburg [sic], Cincinnati & St. Louis ("The Panhandle").

The Indianapolis & Vincennes Railroad (I&V) was chartered in 1865 and attracted the sponsorship of former Union general, Rhode Island politician, and railroad promoter Ambrose E. Burnside, who quickly enlisted the support of the Indianapolis, Cincinnati & Lafayette and the Pennsylvania interests. The Pennsylvania soon assumed complete financial responsibility, and with an eye to also acquiring a Burnside-promoted extension from Vincennes to Cairo, Illinois, opened the line to Vincennes in 1869. The Cairo line was never acquired, leaving the I&V a perennial loser

until coal mining developed on-line in Greene County in 1884.

By 1871, the Pennsylvania System had nearly assumed its ultimate dimensions. The Terre Haute & Indianapolis, strengthened by heavy traffic in Brazil-area coal and dominated by its Terre Haute owners, eluded direct control until 1893. The Pennsylvania consolidated the CC&IC and JM&I with the Panhandle in 1890, and the TH&I, I&V, and other lines were merged to form the Vandalia Railroad in 1905. The Vandalia disappeared into the Panhandle in 1916, and the Panhandle itself ceased independent operations with a lease to the Pennsylvania in 1921. In 1918, the Pennsylvania opened the Indianapolis & Frankfort (I&F), replacing running rights acquired in 1882 between Indianapolis and Kokomo over the line of the former Indianapolis, Peru & Chicago.

The Pennsylvania's Indianapolis-area lines operated intact until its unsuccessful 1968 merger with the NEW YORK CENTRAL. Collapse of the new Penn Central in 1970, and the rocky start-up of successor Conrail, culminated in the abandonment of former Pennsylvania lines east to Richmond and west of Terre Haute, leaving at present the I&V to Sandborn, JM&I to Louisville, and the I&F to Frankfort and Logansport as survivors.

RICHARD T. WALLIS

S. H. Church, comp., *Corporate History of the Pennsylvania Lines West of Pittsburgh* (Baltimore, 1899–1927), vols. 3–5, 7, 13, 15.

Penrod (Garden City, N.Y., 1914). Popular juvenile fiction by BOOTH TARKINGTON based, in part, upon the author's own experiences growing up in Indianapolis. First serialized in magazines in 1913, the Penrod stories were collected and published in book form in 1914. *Penrod* was followed by two other collections, *Penrod and Sam* (1916) and *Penrod Jashber* (1929). The Penrod stories made Tarkington a major figure in juvenile literature. Though they did not impress the critics, the stories were enormously popular with the average reader who felt them to be honest and endearing. The stories enjoyed a double audience, captivating both young readers and adults. Twelve-year-old Penrod Schofield and his bemused dog,

Duke, make high adventure of everyday occurrences—dance class, school pageants, girls' birthday parties. Though Penrod and his companions are never exactly bad, their energy, inventiveness, and lack of foresight cause every episode to end in disaster. Because Tarkington's boyhood in the Hoosier capital had been a happy one, the Penrod stories are charmingly nostalgic. In them Tarkington admonishes his readers to remember what it was like to be a middle class, midwestern boy "in the days when the stable was empty but not yet rebuilt into a garage."

JEANETTE VANAUSDALL

Keith J. Fennimore, *Booth Tarkington* (New York, 1974); Robert Cortes Holliday, *Booth Tarkington* (New York, 1918); James Woodress, *Booth Tarkington: Gentleman from Indiana* (New York, 1955).

Penrod Society. Philanthropic organization for the promotion of arts in Indianapolis. The Penrod Society holds its annual Penrod Arts Fair the Saturday after Labor Day on the grounds of the INDIANAPOLIS MUSEUM OF ART (IMA). Conceived in 1966 by William J. Mead and John A. Roberts, along with Carl Weinhardt, late director of the IMA, the group derives its name and merry style from Penrod Schofield, boy hero of BOOTH TARKINGTON'S *Penrod* stories. Proceeds from the first fair, "An Afternoon at Oldfields," helped construct the new art museum shortly after the ART ASSOCIATION had acquired the Oldfields mansion and 154–acre grounds. Subsequent Penrod fairs have featured over 200 booths selling local arts, crafts, and foods, and various performance stages showcasing jazz, classical, bluegrass, rock, and ethnic music. In 1986, the fair's 20th anniversary, the society launched the Pan-American Arts Festival for which sculptor Michael Helbing created a "crawl-through" version of the Pan-Am logo, and acclaimed vocalist Pia Zadora performed with the INDIANAPOLIS SYMPHONY ORCHESTRA (ISO). By 1991 the society had raised in excess of $1,000,000 in continuing support to the IMA, the ISO, and the INDIANA REPERTORY THEATRE, in addition to over 35 grants each year to such beneficiaries as the FESTIVAL MUSIC SOCIETY, the INTERNATIONAL VIOLIN COM-

PETITION, DANCE KALEIDOSCOPE, INDIANAPOLIS BALLET THEATRE, and Drums of Africa. In 1992 the group refocused priorities to increase support to fledgling art ventures. The all-male society holds two legal meetings and four planning sessions annually; each year the society invites between three and twelve carefully selected new members.

CYNTHIA L. SNYDER
Princeton University

Pentecostal Churches. Pentecostal denominations include: Assemblies of God, Church of God (Cleveland, Tennessee), Church of God of Prophecy, Church of God in Christ, Church of the Living God, Foursquare Gospel Church, Pentecostal Assemblies of the World, and the United Pentecostal Church. In addition there were at least 127 independent congregations with no formal denominational identification in 1993. All of the denominations, except for the Assemblies of God and Charismatics, can also be identified as Holiness denominations, identifying as they do with the 19th-century revivals and/or Wesleyan theology.

Pentecostalism, today the second largest branch of world Christianity, had its beginnings in a Los Angeles revival in early 1906 that began at the Azusa Street Mission. One of the persons involved early on in the Los Angeles revival was Glenn A. Cook, described by the *Indianapolis Star* as having been "at one time a barber in Indianapolis." He returned to Indianapolis in January, 1907, where he began to develop a group tagged by derisive reporters as "gliddy-gluks" and then by the shorter "gluks," or later, "bluks." The initial converts were members of Methodist and Church of God (Anderson) congregations as well as the Christian and Missionary Alliance and the local chapter of John Alexander Dowie's Christian Catholic Church located in Fountain Square.

From that beginning, Pentecostalism in Indianapolis developed national and international influence. A few items will illustrate that point: (1) the periodical which evolved into the *Pentecostal Evangel*, the periodical of the Assemblies of God, U.S.A., was founded in Indianapolis; (2) the earliest successful American effort to develop denominational structures for the fledgling Pentecostal churches happened in nearby Plainfield, primarily through the efforts of individuals from Indianapolis; (3) early missionaries from Indianapolis Pentecostal churches had significant roles in the development of Pentecostalism and related phenomena in India, China, Iceland, South Africa, Zaire, Mexico, and Egypt; (4) the "oneness" (nontrinitarian) Pentecostal movements drew their early leadership from Indianapolis; (5) the international headquarters of an African-American denomination, Pentecostal Assemblies of the World, is in Indianapolis; and, (6) the two leaders who dominated the first eight decades of the history of the Assemblies of God, U.S.A., J. Roswell Flower and Thomas F. Zimmerman, were both from Indianapolis. Finally, the first American author of a Pentecostal Sunday school curriculum, Alice Reynolds Flower, was a graduate of Shortridge High School and attended Butler University.

The early numbers of adherents in Indianapolis are difficult to ascertain. Attendance at meetings fluctuated wildly and there were no membership rolls. Sites of the meetings changed frequently. Newspaper accounts of 1907 suggest that crowds of 300 were not unusual. The congregations during the first decade were small, with the exception of the church of GARFIELD T. HAYWOOD (see below). By its second decade pentecostalism was beginning to split into various factions, each with its own history in the city.

The "Oneness" Pentecostal Churches. In 1913 the liturgical observation that Acts 2:38 called for "baptism in the name of Jesus" rather than in the later trinitarian formula split the Pentecostal movement into what are traditionally, albeit inaccurately, described as "trinitarian" and "oneness" Pentecostalism. Indianapolis quickly became the major international center for the "oneness" persuasion. Again it was Glenn A. Cook who brought the concept from California to Indianapolis where two prominent pastors, L. V. Roberts and Garfield T. Haywood, accepted the idea. Haywood rebaptized 465 members of his congregation in 1915 according to the new formula. The leading opponent of "oneness" was Indianapolis native J. Roswell Flower, who more than any other was responsible for the retention of a traditional trinitarian theology within the Assemblies of God.

With "oneness" Pentecostals excluded both from the Assemblies of God and the Church of God in Christ, in 1918 they joined the Pentecostal Assemblies of the World, a California-based church, and moved the international headquarters to Indianapolis where Haywood became the presiding bishop (1925–1931). The annual conferences of the denomination were normally held at Indianapolis under the leadership of Haywood.

Haywood, who attended Shortridge High School for two years and worked part time as a cartoonist for the *Indianapolis Freeman* and the *Indianapolis Recorder*, began his career as pastor in 1909 with 13 persons in a storefront church. His successful ministry led in 1924 to the erection of a large building, Christ Temple Apostolic, on Fall Creek Parkway. Through the 1970s it was the only genuinely interracial church in the city. The congregation now has a constituency of about 3,000 persons. In 1993 there were 18 congregations, the largest of which were Christ Temple Apostolic, Grace Apostolic Church, and Christ Church Apostolic, with about 12,500 constituents. The international headquarters of this 500,000–member, predominantly African-American denomination are at 3939 Meadows Drive. The primary educational institution of the denomination, Aenon Bible College, is also at 3939 Meadows Drive. The college maintains a number of branch campuses across the nation, and attracts students from around the world.

United Pentecostal Church. The Pentecostal Assemblies of the World was biracial after the union of the West Coast and Midwest congregations. However, racial tensions in the larger society made it difficult to maintain this structure. In 1924 the Pentecostal Ministerial Alliance, Emmanuel's Church of Jesus Christ, and Apostolic Church in Jesus' Name split off as primarily white denominations which merged by 1945 to form the United Pentecostal Church.

The largest United Pentecostal church in Indianapolis is Calvary Tabernacle. This congregation was founded in the early 1930s as Pleasant Street Assembly under the leadership of Oscar Hughes. The congregation moved to its current address on Fletcher Avenue in 1934. Among the internationally renowned pastors were Raymond G. Hoekstra, Nathaniel A. Urshan, James Larson, and Paul D. Mooney. The congregation also supports Indiana Bible College, since 1988 at 3350 Carson Avenue. About 250 students from across the nation attend this program, which primarily trains individuals for ministry in the United Pentecostal Church. In 1993 there were eight United Pentecostal churches in Indianapolis with a constituency of about 4,000, the vast majority being related to Calvary Tabernacle.

Church of God in Christ. The largest North American Pentecostal church and fastest growing church nationally (1992), this African-American denomination became the nation's first Pentecostal denomination after its leader, Charles H. Mason, leader of the Holiness denomination, accepted the Pentecostal version of Christianity in 1906 at Los Angeles. He returned to Memphis to discover that Glenn A. Cook, on his way to Indianapolis, had already converted his (Mason's) congregation to that perspective. At first most white Pentecostal ministers also joined that denomination. The earliest records of the annual conferences include participants from Indianapolis. However, after the movement split racially, and the Assemblies of God was formed, and after the "oneness" split, there were few Church of God in Christ persons left in Indianapolis. In 1993 there were 19 congregations in the city with a constituency of approximately 9,700.

Church of God (Cleveland, Tennessee). Founded in the South under the leadership of A. J. Tomlinson, a native of Westfield, Indiana, who was heavily influenced by the Holiness Quakers of the Central Yearly Meeting, this interracial Wesleyan Holiness Pentecostal church had five congregations in Indianapolis in 1993 with a constituency of about 900 persons.

Among the earliest persons with a local connection to join the church was Lucy Leatherman, who left Indianapolis in 1907 as a faith missionary to Egypt and Palestine. She joined the Church of God in 1916. Tomlinson made various evangelistic tours to Indiana, but it is uncertain whether any converts were organized into congregations in Indianapolis. Certainly the local constituency was strong enough to host the 1952 General Assembly of the Church of God (Cleveland), one of the few meetings of that body to be held outside the South.

Church of God of Prophecy. This denomination was founded by A. J. Tomlinson after his removal from the leadership of the Church of God (Cleveland). It is also Wesleyan, Holiness, and Pentecostal. There were two congregations in Indianapolis with a constituency of approximately 250 persons in 1993.

International Church of the Foursquare Gospel. Founded by Aimee Semple McPherson in Los Angeles, this Wesleyan, Holiness, Fundamentalist, and Pentecostal denomination has a worldwide membership of more than 1.2 million. Women continue in prominent roles and more than 40 percent of the clergy are women. There has been a "Foursquare" presence in Indianapolis since the early 1940s. In 1993 there were three congregations with a constituency of about 460.

Church of the Living God, Christian Workers for Fellowship. Founded as a Holiness church in Wrightsville, Arkansas, in 1889, this African-American denomination converted to Pentecostalism. The church shares features of theology and liturgy with the Church of God (Cleveland) and Church of God in Christ. With international headquarters in Cincinnati, the worldwide membership is about 55,000. In Indianapolis in 1993 there were five congregations with a constituency of approximately 1,800 persons. In addition there was the Church of the Living God, Pentecostal Gospel of Truth, an offsplit of the above, with three congregations in Indianapolis, having a constituency of around 470 persons.

Assemblies of God. Several prominent leaders of the national Assemblies of God came from Indianapolis, including J. Roswell Flower, Alice Reynolds Flower, and Thomas F. Zimmerman. Also missionaries such as Zelda Flower Mussen went to China under Assemblies of God aegis. However, after the restructuring which followed the racial and theological schisms among the early Pentecostals in Indianapolis, the Assemblies of God might have faded from the city except for the efforts of Maria Beulah Woodworth-Etter.

Woodworth-Etter had been part of the Winebrennerian Church of God, General Conference, until she was forced out because of her holiness and healing tent campaigns. She became a Pentecostal and, although she never joined the Assemblies of God, she was instrumental in spreading

Pentecostal revival across the nation before she "retired" to Indianapolis in 1912. In 1918 she built the 500–seat Woodworth-Etter Tabernacle at the corner of Miller Street and Belmont Avenue and pastored there until her death in 1924.

Woodworth-Etter was succeeded by a former assistant, Thomas Peino, Sr., who moved the church to its present site renamed as Lakeview Christian Center. This church, with a constituency of about 3,500 persons in 1993, became the parent church for numerous Indianapolis congregations. There are now 19 congregations in the Assemblies of God, serving a constituency of approximately 5,900.

Independent Pentecostal Churches. A street by street survey conducted between 1991 and 1993 identified 127 independent Pentecostal groups and ministries in Indianapolis. This number is doubtless inaccurate because it was impossible to keep up with the changing meeting places, leaders, and constituents. Reexamination of particular areas suggested a 29–percent change during the survey period. The groups visited varied from 8 to 550 in attendance. The majority of visible attendees are adults, since children are frequently, but not always, kept in separate quarters for Sunday school instruction. About 60 percent of the congregations are African-American, another 30 percent are European-American, and the rest are Korean, Hispanic, Chinese, Russian, and other ethnic groups. It is estimated that there are at least 8,450 persons who regularly attend these churches and ministries, with a constituency of perhaps 12,000.

Charismatic Groups in Other Denominations. Few mainline denominations have not experienced significant influence from the Pentecostal churches in the form of the Charismatic renewal. In Indianapolis the groups most influenced include Catholic parishes, St. John's Episcopal Church in Speedway as well as other Episcopal parishes, LIGHT OF THE WORLD CHRISTIAN CHURCH (Disciples of Christ), which disdains the labels of Pentecostal or Charismatic but which teaches Pentecostal doctrines and engages in a Pentecostal worship style, as well as Methodist, Presbyterian, and Lutheran congregations.

Pentecostals in Indianapolis: Statistical Summary. Most Pentecostal churches have no formal

Pentecostal Churches in Indianapolis: Statistical Summary, 1993	
Pentecostal Assemblies of the World	12,500
United Pentecostal Church	4,000
Church of God in Christ	9,700
Church of God (Cleveland, Tennessee)	900
Church of God of Prophecy	350
International Church of the Foursquare Gospel	460
Church of the Living God, Christian Workers for Fellowship	1,800
Church of the Living God, Pentecostal Gospel of Truth	470
Assemblies of God	5,900
Independent Pentecostal and Charismatic Groups and Ministries	12,000
Total:	48,080

reporting system for either attendance or constituency. All membership is limited to full adults or teenagers. Therefore, an effort was made to define the "constituency" of each congregation, including members, regular attendees who are not members, and children, with estimates compiled through site visits and/or conversations with either pastors or laity of the individual congregations and verified, where possible, through judicatories. Preliminary research suggests that there may be an additional 9,000 Charismatics in non-Pentecostal congregations in Indianapolis.

DAVID BUNDY
Christian Theological Seminary

People. Weekly newspaper. Enos B. Read started *People* in 1870 as a Sunday weekly dedicated to politics, literature, society, and news. He also used the paper to publish his own literary pieces and poems. It was the first Indianapolis newspaper to use illustrations, in the form of woodcuts created with a butcher knife by artist Fred Hetherington. But *People* became known mainly for its own form of yellow journalism, stories of sensationalized crimes and scandals. The front-page articles often featured bizarre court cases. Newsboys hawked the paper by yelling out about the murders it covered. The paper also carried gossipy columns, such as the one on the Indiana General Assembly called "Legislative Small Talk."

After Read's death, James B. Wilson became publisher of *People* in the 1890s. Wilson also edited a liquor newspaper called *Freedom and Right.* Wilson and *People* appeared to be doing a good business when the U.S. government objected to some of his other publications. In December, 1895, he was sent to a federal penitentiary for two years following his conviction for sending obscene matter through the mail. Wilson revived the paper after his release but *People* ceased publication in the early 1900s.

BETH MURPHY

John W. Miller, *Indiana Newspaper Bibliography* (Indianapolis, 1982); *Indianapolis Times*, May 6, 1938.

Peoples Bank and Trust Company.
Oldest state bank in Indianapolis and as of 1993 the city's only locally based commercial bank. In 1891 Tennessee native Felix Tony McWhirter opened an office at 122 East Market Street, providing banking operations for clients awaiting real estate transactions. McWhirter soon focused exclusively on banking, receiving a state charter in 1900 to conduct business as the Peoples Deposit Bank. That same year Peoples became the first Indiana bank to appoint a woman, LUELLA FRANCES SMITH MCWHIRTER, to its board of directors. In 1905 the bank moved to larger offices next door at 130 East Market Street, purchasing the building 15 years later.

After the founder's death in 1915, son Felix Marcus McWhirter took over the bank and added a trust department to the institution's services. Peoples introduced the state's first auto drive-up window in 1931 and originated Indiana's first Federal Housing Administration loan seven years later. The bank opened its first branch in Lawrence in December, 1951.

When new state banking laws reduced restrictions on acquisitions and mergers in 1985, Peoples was one of the few banks in Indiana to resist such activity. Peoples instead increased its customer base by marketing services to small and medium-sized businesses, professionals, and people concerned about spending money with local companies. The bank's small size, conservative management, and focus on Marion County have given it financial stability: Peoples consistently has

Original office of Peoples Bank, ca. 1900.
[Indiana Historical Society, #C4938]

been listed among the nation's soundest banks by various rating services.

As of the early 1990s, Peoples had total assets exceeding $350 million, posting record earnings of $3.47 million in 1992. The McWhirter family controls over half of the company's voting stock and the founder's great grandson serves as bank president. With 13 Indianapolis locations, Peoples has about 250 employees and accounts for about 4 percent of the city's banking market.

DEBORAH B. MARKISOHN

Peoples Bank and Trust Company annual reports, 1990, 1992; *Indianapolis News*, Apr. 24, 1990, Apr. 17, 1992.

Perry, Charles Coffin (Dec. 15, 1857–
Sept. 23, 1924). Businessman. A native of Richmond, Indiana, Perry attended Earlham College. After working first as a messenger boy and then as a telegrapher for the Pittsburgh, Cincinnati, Chicago, and St. Louis Railway, he became the manager (1880–1884) of the Central Union Telephone Company's Richmond exchange and then district

superintendent of the Northern Indiana & Ohio Telephone Company in Fort Wayne, Indiana (1884–1886).

In 1886 Perry became the Indianapolis representative of the Jenney Electric Company and oversaw the electric street lighting of the city's west side. In 1888 Perry and Daniel W. Marmon formed the Marmon-Perry Light Company. Among other accomplishments the Marmon-Perry Light Company was responsible for the electrification of the Park Theater (1888), the installation of the first watt-hour meter in the city, the first incandescent lighting of a private residence (1889), and the construction of the first incandescent lighting–central steam heating plant in Indianapolis (1889).

After forming the Indianapolis Light & Power Company in May, 1892, Perry and Marmon acquired control of the Brush Electric Company and merged both it and the Marmon-Perry Light Company with the Indianapolis Light & Power Company. In 1902 the partners formed the Marion County Hot Water Heating Company, which was later merged with the Indianapolis Light & Power Company to form the Indianapolis Light & Heat Company (1904). Following Marmon's death (1909) Perry became president of the company, a position that he held until his retirement. In 1910 Perry made an unsuccessful attempt to consolidate all of the city's light and heat companies, something that did not occur until the formation of the INDIANAPOLIS POWER AND LIGHT COMPANY (IPALCO) in 1926.

IPALCO's plants on Kentucky Avenue and West Washington Street were renamed the C. C. Perry Plant in his honor in 1937.

JEFFERY A. DUVALL

Perry Township. Southern Marion County township. In 1822 county commissioners defined boundaries for the township they named after naval hero Commodore Oliver Hazard Perry. Among the first to settle was Jacob Smock, who farmed the area now known as SOUTHPORT in 1822. Southport was platted in 1849 and incorporated in 1853 as the township's first community; it was served by the MADISON AND INDIANAPOLIS RAILROAD.

Selected Statistics for Perry Township, 1990	
Population	85,060
Population per Square Mile	1,853
Percent African-American	1.0
Percent 0 to 17 Years	24.4
Percent 65 Years and Over	12.8
Percent 25 Years and Over with a High School Degree or Equivalency	79.5
Percent 25 Years and Over with a College Degree	16.9
Per Capita Income in 1989	$14,969
Unemployment Rate (%)	3.4
Married-Couple Families as a Percent of Total Households	56.1
Median Home Value	$69,700

At the toll gate where Bluff and Morgantown roads met, Archibald Glenn founded the settlement of Glenns Valley in the 1820s. The community counted about 80 residents and a few businesses by 1923.

In 1905 track elevation was mandated on the south side of Indianapolis, relieving congestion and opening up Perry Township to intensive development. Realtor William Elder planned two residential neighborhoods in the district. In 1902 he donated land and a campus building for a church-affiliated college (now known as the UNIVERSITY OF INDIANAPOLIS). In exchange, members of the Church of the United Brethren in Christ sold lots in Elder's nearby subdivision, incorporated in 1907 as UNIVERSITY HEIGHTS. At the same time Elder platted the town of EDGEWOOD, originally Stop 7 on the interurban line, and promoted it as a quiet residential community with a small business district along Madison Avenue, the township's main north-south thoroughfare.

German-Americans built greenhouses, nurseries, and truck farms along Bluff Road and South Meridian Street in the early 20th century. Refrigerated railroad cars transporting southern produce later led to the decline of the local farms, yet some still operate in the 1990s.

A mammoth Big Four locomotive shop was opened in 1907 in Franklin Township, while the adjacent town of BEECH GROVE was platted across the boundary line in Perry. Beech Grove grew as the railroad shops expanded and prided itself as an independent community, a role it retained in the 1990s as one of the EXCLUDED CITIES under UNIGOV.

Developer Frank Gates laid out the town of Homecroft in 1923. Most of the bungalow-style homes were constructed between 1930 and 1950. Incorporated in 1949, HOMECROFT has the status of an INCLUDED TOWN under Unigov.

The increasing popularity of the automobile in the 1950s and 1960s led to improvements in existing roads and the construction of new highways, with Madison Avenue widened and the northern segment transformed into an expressway in the 1950s. South Meridian (S.R. 135), S.R. 37, and U.S. 31 accommodated increased commuter traffic, while I–465 and I–65, constructed in the 1960s and 1970s, offered easy access to Indianapolis.

The township's peak period of growth coincided with the emergence of GREENWOOD in adjacent JOHNSON COUNTY as a population center. From 1950 to 1970 Perry Township's population nearly tripled, from 25,000 to 74,000. In 1990 there were just over 85,000 residents. While many residents commute, others are employed in local commercial establishments. The district's largest employer is the Metropolitan School District of Perry Township, which employed about 1,600 people in the 1992–1993 school year. About 11,500 students were enrolled in the district's nine elementaries, three middle schools, and two high schools in 1992–1993. Perry Township has retained its residential character and in the early 1990s prided itself as a community of small, quiet neighborhoods.

CATHLEEN DONNELLY

Berry R. Sulgrove, *History of Indianapolis and Marion County* (Philadelphia, 1884), 575–596; Department of Metropolitan Development, *Perry Township Comprehensive Planning Study, Data Inventory* (1988); U.S. Census.

Perry Township Weekly. Community newspaper. Originally established ca. 1945 as a four-sheet, letterhead-size tabloid by the daughter of Mrs. Allen Goddard of BEECH GROVE, it began as a high school paper for Beech Grove High School. It was not until 1953, when it was purchased by Beech Grove businessman Louis A. Lukenbill and his wife, Clara, that it became a full-scale community newspaper.

The Lukenbills operated from a small back room behind a gas station at Fifth and Main streets. They later moved to larger quarters behind the Driskolis Restaurant, also on Main Street. In 1963, they built the present building at Third and Main streets, making it one of the first structures in the Midwest to be built exclusively for a community newspaper. Circulation reached over 40,000 each Thursday. Coverage extended to ACTON on the east side, South Meridian Street on the west, GREENWOOD on the south, and Raymond Street on the north. It was the largest free circulation newspaper in Indiana.

The Lukenbills sold the paper to Jerry Sargent, Joe Cline, and Ernie Lester in April, 1968. It changed hands again in April, 1982, when it was purchased from Jerry and Frances Sargent by the Reporter-Times, Inc., publisher of several MORGAN COUNTY papers. After several years in the early 1980s as *The Perry Weekly*, the newspaper returned to the name *The Perry Township Weekly* in January, 1987.

JERRY L. SARGENT

Persian Gulf War (Operation Desert Shield–Desert Storm), August, 1990, to February, 1991. In September, 1990, the first mobilized U.S. Army Reserve unit arrived at FORT BENJAMIN HARRISON from Ohio for service in the war. The local affiliates of the three major television networks, CNN, radio stations, the *Indianapolis Star* and *Indianapolis News*, and weekly papers filmed or reported the arrival, an early indication of Marion County's popular support of the conflict. Ultimately, the fort processed 2,725 Reserve or National Guard soldiers in 25 units, mostly from the Midwest, 2,384 of whom deployed to Saudi Arabia.

Two Reserve units from Indianapolis mobilized at Fort Harrison: the 425th Adjutant General Company and the 21st Theater Army Area Company, each headquartered at the Robert M. Moore Reserve Center on Kessler Boulevard. Both deployed to Saudi Arabia. Five other city Reserve units mobilized either at Fort Harrison or in other states but never deployed to the Saudi Arabian desert.

The community soon involved itself in the mobilization. Military units brought their transportation with them—tractor trailers, pickups, cranes, petroleum tankers, and bulldozers, all appropriately painted green for a European or jungle war but not for a war in the sand. Thus the federal government purchased 2,000 gallons of desert tan paint for $50,000 and hired nine body shops for $300,000 to spray 1,000 vehicles.

Rail lines also became involved. Army truck drivers drove the vehicles (tanks, 5–ton pickup trucks, tank retrievers) to Conrail's Hawthorne Yards on South Emerson Avenue for transport to the East Coast for shipment to the desert. CSX Transportation Company also moved heavy vehicles by rail from the Belmont Yard on North Belmont Avenue. Too heavy even for the rails and denied passage by Ohio officials through that state, one 54–ton tank retriever was driven from Camp Atterbury through the city around I–465 and to Grissom Air Force Base for shipment overseas. It may have been the oddest vehicle ever seen on I–465.

Although the city's residents did not support the war unanimously, enthusiasm soared before and after deployment to the desert. Civilian volunteers painted the homes of departed soldiers. Family-support groups offered moral support to spouses left behind, and the wives of the Indiana Pacers professional basketball team catered to the support groups. The Pacers and other professional teams, the Ice and Indians, as well as the sponsors of an all-star professional basketball game, the zoo, and the symphony gave away $114,506 worth of tickets. After the announcement of the accelerated departure of one unit, Taco Bell served 600 tacos to soldiers in the 3rd Battalion in their very act of leaving the fort on buses. Upon the return of one unit, Monarch Brewery gave away 100 cases of beer. Ultimately, city businesses offered $138,006 in products, services, and cash donations to the Directorate of Personnel and Community Activities at Fort Harrison for soldiers and their families.

The city's patriotism knew no bounds. At I–465 and Washington Street on the eastside, WIBC Radio erected the "World's Largest Greeting Card," an 8–by–14–foot billboard inscribed "A Show of Hands in Support of Our Troops" and "signed" with at least 5,000 handprints, including that of Governor Evan Bayh. AT&T provided military families with "Desert FAX." Students called Fort Harrison to obtain soldiers' names, "adopted" the soldiers, and wrote thousands of letters addressed to "Any Soldier." ("Any Soldier" temporarily broke down the military postal service in Saudi Arabia.) Community groups mailed soldiers canned meat, cookies, cakes, flyswatters, and bug spray. Representatives from Pepsi-Cola and the Salvation Army met at Fort Harrison every unit arriving home from the desert, except the first two.

Largess from outside the city also flowed into Indianapolis. In nearby Carmel, the American Legion invited 5,000 soldiers and family members to a gigantic pig roast prior to deployment. The Mars Candy Bar Company of Ohio sent 20,000 pieces of candy to Fort Harrison. Charles O. Finley, a former owner of a professional baseball team, personally delivered 120 footballs, with yellow markings to glow at night, to the 1015th Postal Company.

In 1991 sponsors of the Indianapolis 500–Mile Race invited Gen. H. Norman Schwarzkopf, commander-in-chief of the U.S. and allied forces during the war, to participate in the pre-race ceremonies. Ending the celebration on July 4, Indianapolis and Lawrence hosted a "Hoosier Hero Homecoming" parade.

Only one resident of Indianapolis died as a result of the mobilization: Otha B. Squires, a 23–year-old National Guardsman, expired of cardiac arrest in Dhahran, Saudi Arabia, three months after the conflict ended. His body was returned and buried in the city.

THOMAS KEISER
Historian
Fort Benjamin Harrison

Pharmacy. The first pharmacy practitioner in the territory that became Indianapolis was probably an Indian medicine man who compounded medications from known indigenous flora. The pioneer settlers of the 1820s relied upon patent medicines and home remedies as there were so few physicians. In the mid–19th century the only prerequisite to opening an apothecary was sufficient business capital; some practitioners trained by apprenticeship, but formal professional education was unavailable. Apothecaries, which also stocked paint, glass, lumber, dyes, and tobacco to supplement meager prescription compounding incomes, became known as drugstores. By 1840 Indianapolis had a drugstore on almost every corner. Noteworthy pharmacy practitioners of the 19th century were COL. ELI LILLY and JOHN N. HURTY. Louis and Julius Haag founded HAAG DRUG COMPANY in 1876, and John A. Hook founded the Indianapolis retail pharmacy chain of HOOK'S DRUG STORES in 1900.

In the 1870s surrounding states adopted pharmacy practice acts to restrict sales of patent medicines and protect the public from untrained pharmacy practitioners. Indiana had no such law; patent medicine hawkers moved here in droves. Thus, on May 9, 1882, 200 pharmacists met in Indianapolis as the Indiana Pharmacists Association (IPA) to provide a professional forum and promote a pharmacy licensure. Four years later, in 1886, Hurty, Lilly, Joseph Perry, and Arthur Timberlake organized the Indianapolis Association of Retail Druggists for a similar purpose. Finally, in 1899 the legislature established a Board of Pharmacy and required one year of apprenticeship for licensure.

The average turn-of-the-century pharmacy stocked 350 to 400 tinctures, syrups, elixirs, fluid extracts, emulsions, powders, solutions, narcotics, chemicals, and herbs. The pharmacist served as the neighborhood chemist who could compound elegant prescriptions, soft drinks, perfumes, shoe polish, furniture waxes, inks, and cosmetics. Unfortunately, many foodstuffs and drug products of the day contained contaminants and dangerous ingredients. Inaccurate labeling and exaggerated claims of superior healing powers characterized patent medicines. Thus, in 1906 Congress passed the Food and Drug Act to protect the public from misbranded and adulterated products. In 1907 the Indiana Board of Pharmacy regulations required that an applicant for licensure pass a written examination.

Local pharmacy education began in April, 1904, when John Gertler organized the pharmacy department of Winona Technical Institute at the site of the former United States Arsenal and the current ARSENAL TECHNICAL HIGH SCHOOL. The program consisted of two sessions of 26 weeks each leading to the Ph.G. degree (Pharmacy Graduate). In 1911 regulations lengthened the pharmacy program to two sessions of 36 weeks each. Economic hardship resulted in dissolution of the Winona Institute and the Indianapolis Public Schools incorporated the pharmacy department for a time. In December, 1914, a board of prominent citizens chartered the Indianapolis College of Pharmacy (ICP). The program included two sessions of 32 weeks each.

In 1924 the ICP bought the Indiana Veterinary College grounds on East Market Street, where it remained for 25 years. The program changed to a three-year course in 1925, and if a student wished to attend an extra ten weeks of classes, he would receive a Ph.C. degree (Pharmaceutical Chemist). The college's curriculum changed again in 1930 when Indiana law required a four-year course of training. The addition of liberal arts classes to the professional curriculum upgraded the program, and graduates received the Bachelor of Science degree. Pharmacy regulations changed in 1932, adding one year of internship to the didactic education. The onset of World War II placed additional demands on the profession as the Pharmacy Corps drafted pharmacists. The ICP adapted to create accelerated programs that condensed a four-year curriculum into three years. In the late 1930s independent colleges of pharmacy sought merger with larger institutions due to liberal arts course requirements. On October 13, 1945, the ICP merged with BUTLER UNIVERSITY to become the Butler University College of Pharmacy (BUCOP).

Medical advancements of the late 1930s produced more potent but dangerous medications. Amendments to the federal Food and Drug Law in 1941 required a physician's prescription for the sale of dangerous and addictive drugs, a practice that established pharmacist control and distribution of restricted classes of drugs. Large pharmaceutical firms produced more drug products in the late 1940s and 1950s, so the emphasis of community pharmacy practice shifted from compounding drug dosages to the accurate and safe dispensing of manufactured products. In 1952 amendments to the federal Food, Drug, and Cosmetic Act required physician authorization of prescription refills, restricted dangerous drugs to prescription status only, and created an over-the-counter class of drugs.

The importance of merchandising increased as community pharmacy evolved into a retail business. In 1953, 425 independently owned pharmacies served the city, but competition from supermarkets and the chain pharmacies of Haag Drugs and Hook's Drugs began to deplete their numbers. Pharmacy chains purchased many independent operations, with the previous owners electing to continue their practice as employees of the chain. In 1950, 90 percent of pharmacists were independent store owners. Forty years later most practitioners were employee pharmacists. Of the licensed pharmacies in Marion County in 1993 over 208 were chain or corporately owned pharmacy operations.

Since its inception hospital pharmacy had received little regulatory attention. A hospitalized patient in the early 20th century received drugs from a "drug room" commonly staffed by a nurse. Local hospitals, however, report the presence of pharmacy services as early as 1915 to 1920. Hospital practice was similar to community practice in that compounding of prescriptions then commanded much of the pharmacist's attention and effort. In 1946 Indiana passed the Hospital Pharmacy Licensing Act to provide standards for facilities, drug storage and preparation, and uniform labeling of drugs in hospitals. Pharmaceutical science developed injectable medications and perfected intravenous fluid therapies, and hospital practice included the control and preparation of these therapies. Hospital practitioners needed a forum to address their unique practice and chartered the Indiana Society of Hospital Pharmacists in 1952.

In 1960 the Butler University College of Pharmacy instituted a mandatory five-year program in response to increasing practice demands and accreditation requirements. Local pharmacists initiated drug abuse education and poison prevention programs in the 1960s. They also developed patient medication recording systems to prevent allergic reactions and to avoid interactions between drugs. In the late 1960s hospital pharmacists introduced the practice of clinical pharmacy, wherein the pharmacist functions as a therapeutic advisor. Hospital-based drug information services and drug dosing services focused on individualizing drug therapy for specific patients. In community pharmacy many practitioners exercised this therapeutic advisory capacity by providing patient education with each prescription. Butler's program incorporated patient education courses into the curriculum. The profession experienced a gender shift during this era. In March of 1969, 29.5 percent of the Butler pharmacy class was female. By 1978, 58 percent of the freshman pharmacy class was female, and the figure rose to 70 percent in 1992.

In the 1970s and 1980s technological advances produced drugs that exhibited greater disease specificity and generated a variety of drug administration devices that permit home delivery of intensive therapies such as intravenous nutrition, cancer chemotherapy, and pain management. Computers provided rapid access to drug information and alerted the pharmacist to potential drug therapy problems. In the 1990s increasing societal demands require highly trained pharmacists who are patient oriented and responsible for the outcomes of drug therapy. Thus, in 1990 the Butler program initiated an optional six-year Doctor of Pharmacy program. It is anticipated that by the year 2000 the Doctor of Pharmacy degree will be the entry-level professional degree.

KENNETH E. ROBERTSON, PHARM.D.
Butler University College of Pharmacy

K. L. Kaufman, "A Brief History of the Pharmacy College of Butler University," *Proceedings of the Indiana Academy of Science*, 75 (1965), 216–219; E. H. Kraus, "The Development of Pharmaceutical Education," *Indiana Pharmacist*, 12 (July, 1930), 12–15; special issue of *Indiana Pharmacist*, 21 (Mar., 1939), 71–104, for the Indianapolis Association of Retail Druggists.

Philanthropy and Business. Throughout the formative years of Indiana's capital city, representatives of Indianapolis' business community were actively involved in all aspects of charitable and philanthropic endeavors. Many of its early leaders, like JAMES BLAKE, CALVIN FLETCHER, and JAMES M. RAY, came from New England or the eastern United States, bringing with them concepts of social responsibility and community stewardship. They considered themselves to possess special responsibilities because of their stations in life and acquired major roles in politics, benevolent societies, religious institutions, and economic and community development. From the 1840s Irish famine relief efforts to support for the Union during the Civil War, and from the efforts to establish the INDIANAPOLIS STEAM MILL COMPANY in the 1820s to involvement in the city's school system and the founding of schools for the blind and deaf, these individuals demonstrated their commitment to the community and its citizens and established a precedent for philanthropic pursuits by future generations of business leaders.

The Panic of 1873 and the succeeding years proved to be a watershed in the development of Indianapolis. It ended the exuberant speculation of earlier years and caused the loss of many personal fortunes. The magnitude of economic losses in the 1870s, however, nurtured a lasting conservative attitude that valued self-reliance and independence. The panic also stimulated greater social awareness, organized charitable endeavors, and encouraged involvement in various agencies, directing the attention of many to the larger needs of the community.

During the 1890s COL. ELI LILLY emerged as an enduring influence in the city's development. He possessed strong convictions about the obligation of businessmen to be responsible to and for the community where they resided. Lilly endorsed and practiced a "stewardship of wealth," which held that it was appropriate and wise to use a portion of personal (and business) income for community improvement. Indianapolis continues to benefit from institutions created by the benevolence of the Lilly family and pharmaceutical company, such as the Eli Lilly and Company Foundation, CATHEDRAL ARTS, the Christ Church Cathedral Fund and, most notably, the LILLY ENDOWMENT.

Numerous voluntary associations originated during the 1890s, which allowed the business community to define by example what it meant to be a "good" business and a responsible citizen in Indianapolis. Among them was the COMMERCIAL CLUB, founded in 1890 by 27 prominent businessmen. With Col. Lilly as president and WILL-IAM FORTUNE, a writer for the *Indianapolis News*, as secretary, the organization literally paved the way for progress and made civic beautification a high priority. The club sponsored a STREET PAVING EXPOSITION in spring, 1890, to arouse local interest in the latest techniques of paving. It also promoted the cleanup of the downtown area, endorsed a revision of the city charter, and pushed for the creation of a city park system.

Under Lilly's leadership in 1893 the Commercial Club and Indianapolis hosted the 27th National Encampment of the GRAND ARMY OF THE REPUBLIC (veterans of the Union Army of the Civil War). Over 250,000 attended, making it the largest event of its kind in the city's history and one of only a few national encampments to finish "in the black." Thirty committees consisting of 3,000 local volunteers planned and coordinated the activities, and in the process successfully publicized the city.

Through the encampment and other events the business community formulated unwritten, but understood, criteria for future philanthropic contributions. First, there must be an emphasis on good financial planning with a sound monetary base. Second, the project should include economic advancement and a well-conceived promotion of the city. Third, effective management and leadership should be identified and charged to get results and not seek personal credit for accomplishments. Such factors remain primary considerations for business participation even today. Even so, Indianapolis is distinguishable from cities of similar or greater size by the relative absence of facilities, structures, and institutions bearing the names of individual benefactors.

Philanthropy and business became stronger partners during the golden age of the 1920s, a period of civic growth and improvement. It was, however, the personal and voluntary spirit, not monetary affluence, that enhanced the quality of life locally. Author and editor MEREDITH NICHOLSON captured that sense in 1920 when he wrote, "The continuing charm of Indianapolis lies in the sturdy Americanism and broad democracy of its founders. A certain folksiness and neighborliness of pioneer life retained is the secret of the real Indianapolis atmosphere." Likewise, in a 1926 advertisement an anonymous businessman called for business and citizens to "work together—for Indianapolis first, last, and always." One of the early cooperative efforts to promote the city and the use of the automobile was the Citizens' Speedway Committee, established by the CHAMBER OF COMMERCE in 1920 to raise funds to pay lap prize money for the INDIANAPOLIS 500–MILE RACE. Still active in 1993, the committee is one of numerous 500 FESTIVAL organizations, most of which are led by business volunteers.

Despite the seriousness of the stock market crash and the ensuing Great Depression many local business leaders sustained their philanthropic contributions over the years. Work relief committees focused on a system of public works. BUTLER UNIVERSITY lent 70 acres of land to promote efficient home food production. Chamber of Commerce leaders looked to solve the problems of adequate housing for workers and the homeless. In 1934 they also organized a successful campaign, led by corporate executives and supported by corporate donations, to save the INDIANAPOLIS SYMPHONY ORCHESTRA from collapse. It was also during this period that perhaps the most significant philanthropic action occurred: the Lilly Endowment was founded in 1937, not with money but with shares of stock in the pharmaceutical company.

The years following World War II may have been the time when Indianapolis' public and private sectors experienced the least interaction. Business leaders seemed more focused on preserving American free enterprise against attacks by ideological opponents and those who had suffered from the depression. Nevertheless, voluntary action by business for charitable and community causes continued. The Chamber of Commerce initiated several programs to improve local education and launched programs of inner-city renovation. It also worked to promote amateur and professional athletics and continued its support of local cultural institutions. In the early 1950s local business leaders, confronting the critical need for hospital beds and services, contributed substantially to a $12 million hospital development campaign and raised an additional $13 million just ten years later.

The years 1965 to 1990 brought significant changes for Indianapolis, many of which resulted from the commitment of human and financial resources from business. Under mayors John J. Barton, Richard G. Lugar, and William H. Hudnut III, both government and business leaders adopted a strategic plan that required cooperation and collaboration at new levels. The phrase "public-private partnership" became the community's buzzword and elevated the nation's awareness of Indianapolis. Chief executives became the major fund raisers, cheerleaders, and volunteers in local efforts. Most importantly, they also worked to encourage the Lilly Endowment to redirect its focus toward local needs and development projects.

For Indianapolis to become recognized as the "amateur sports capital of the world" required construction of "world class" facilities and sponsorship of sporting events. It also necessitated enhancement and expansion of existing facilities, institutions, and recreational opportunities. The Lilly Endowment, several corporations, and the INDIANAPOLIS FOUNDATION (one of the nation's largest community foundations) championed these projects and carried the vision to reality. The city soon became known as a "can do" community, which motivated business to raise the seed money to assure the construction of MARKET SQUARE ARENA, the HOOSIER DOME, the INDIANA CONVENTION CENTER, and sports venues to accommodate the Tenth PAN AMERICAN GAMES in August, 1987. During the games nearly 40,000 volunteers contributed ten times that many hours. Employees used vacation time to volunteer, and business leaders served at the forefront of many activities, raising more money than ever before.

During the 1965–1990 period business and philanthropy developed different mechanisms for working more closely. They created several 501(c)(3) community-based nonprofit organizations to serve and promote the community's development. These include, but are not limited to, the GREATER INDIANAPOLIS PROGRESS COMMITTEE (GIPC), the INDIANAPOLIS ECONOMIC DEVELOPMENT CORPORATION (IEDC), INDIANAPOLIS DOWNTOWN, INC. (IDI), the INDIANAPOLIS CONVENTION AND VISITORS ASSOCIATION (ICVA), the INDIANAPOLIS PROJECT (IP), the ARTS COUNCIL OF INDIANAPOLIS, COMMUNITY LEADERS ALLIED FOR SUPERIOR SCHOOLS (CLASS), and the CORPORATE

COMMUNITY COUNCIL (CCC). The majority of the board members and operating funds for all of them come from the corporate and business community. In 1985 the Chamber of Commerce established the 2%-5% Club to recognize businesses that donated at least 2 percent of pretax profits to community organizations, philanthropic projects, or other civic causes. Unlike similar clubs in other cities the local club continues to grow although members receive no public recognition. The Chamber also established the Society of Retired Executives (SRE), which now has a wide variety of programs that provide skilled professional volunteers to serve the needs of nonprofits, small and minority businesses, and youth and educational groups.

Businesses provide extensive leadership for the UNITED WAY of Central Indiana, the COMMUNITY SERVICE COUNCIL, COMMUNITY CENTERS of Indianapolis, the INDIANAPOLIS URBAN LEAGUE, and the network of human service providers. In 1992, when other United Way chapters suffered due to troubles in the national organization, the Indianapolis chapter was one of only a few to meet its fund-raising goals. Not only do business leaders serve on United Way boards and committees and head the campaigns, they provide loaned executives to United Way and its agencies, and many give employees time off with pay to volunteer, especially for "The Day of Caring."

Indianapolis businesses and labor organizations also have contributed generously with in-kind donations. Construction costs for the Pan American Plaza Building and the first newly built Ronald McDonald House were greatly reduced through such gifts. Volunteer labor is also responsible for the annual transformation of the SOLDIERS AND SAILORS MONUMENT into the "World's Largest Christmas Tree." Small businesses actively participate by giving time and career guidance through educational programs like Partners in Education, Junior Achievement, and the Center for Leadership Development.

Indianapolis may face its greatest challenges as it approaches the 21st century. Loss of corporate headquarters, manufacturing, and substantial Lilly Endowment funds have diminished the city's financial resources. Most large businesses are "downsizing" and many are no longer locally or state owned, including the major banks. The arrival and/or emergence of new business leaders, however, like the Associated Group, United Airlines, DOWELANCO, THOMSON CONSUMER ELECTRONICS, as well as Indianapolis' legacy of self-reliance and commitment to the good of the community, provide opportunities for a continued and beneficial partnership. In addition, more than 50 foundations exist in the city, with most of their assets directed toward grants that benefit central Indiana. Provisions have been made for the training and development of future business and philanthropy partnerships through community leadership programs such as the STANLEY K. LACY EXECUTIVE LEADERSHIP SERIES, the Ardath Burkhart Series, and the Leadership Training and Development Program. All of these, and many others, focus on keeping business and professional people actively involved in activities for the common good.

ANDREA L. MARSHALL

Philanthropy and Community Development. Community development can be viewed as a form of philanthropy that strives to improve the quality of life within the local public domain. Views differ as to what constitutes improvement in the quality of life: some people emphasize human services and development; others, the physical and economic environment. Where the emphasis has been placed in Indianapolis has varied over time. In the 1980s public attention was focused on physical and economic development, but in the early 1990s human development needs such as unemployment, homelessness, single-parent households, and children in poverty commanded public attention. Whether for economic development or human development, community development efforts in Indianapolis have been enhanced by three factors: partnership across sectors, the city's manageable size, and strong volunteer spirit.

The intersector partnership among nonprofits, corporations, and government agencies is commonly cited as the key to community development in Indianapolis. That partnership evolved because each sector wanted a role in shaping the city's future, but no single sector had adequate resources to meet the community's needs. The partnership has become formalized through the creation of facilitating organizations such as the GREATER INDIANAPOLIS PROGRESS COMMITTEE, the CORPORATE COMMUNITY COUNCIL, the INDIANAPOLIS ECONOMIC DEVELOPMENT CORPORATION, the INDIANA SPORTS CORPORATION, the INDIANAPOLIS PROJECT, and the INDIANAPOLIS NEIGHBORHOOD HOUSING PARTNERSHIP.

The achievements of the intersector partnership include the downtown tennis complex, built with $4 million of public money, $1.5 million from the LILLY ENDOWMENT, $1.5 million from business, and a lease of campus land from INDIANA UNIVERSITY–PURDUE UNIVERSITY AT INDIANAPOLIS (1979); the Indianapolis Neighborhood Housing Partnership, established in 1988 by for-profit lending institutions, nonprofit funders, human service providers, and community development corporations to increase available housing for low and moderate income families; and the "Dream Wall" project at 40th and Boulevard Place, which, with assistance from the Arts Council, foundations, businesses, and neighborhood children, transformed a graffiti-covered wall into a community landmark (1993).

A second factor in Indianapolis' development, its medium size, makes contributions to community development more visible and thus more rewarding than in a larger city. The city's size also facilitates cooperation, as when local radio and television stations cooperated in 1992 to simulcast primetime coverage of the United Way campaign.

A third factor contributing to community development, volunteer spirit, is evident in the hours of voluntary time given to nonprofit organizations like the Greater Indianapolis Progress Committee, INDIANAPOLIS DOWNTOWN, INC. (formerly the Commission for Downtown), the Coalition for Human Service Planning, and the neighborhood associations. Events such as the NATIONAL SPORTS FESTIVAL and the Tenth PAN AMERICAN GAMES were made possible because thousands of volunteers provided crucial services. The practice of volunteering is given an impetus by Indianapolis churches, which encourage voluntarism by church members and offer space to voluntary groups, and by corporations that give employees time off for voluntary activities and expect their upper-level managers to donate time to community affairs.

The beginning of community development in Indianapolis, in its modern, planned, comprehensive form, is commonly associated with the establishment of the Greater Indianapolis Progress Committee (GIPC) in 1965 during the administration of Mayor JOHN J. BARTON. GIPC has served as sounding board, advisory council, and primary mover of major projects (e.g., Eagle Creek Park, Unigov, the Convention Center). Its task forces have studied and reported on salient public issues (e.g., highway construction, jail overcrowding, the Regional Center plans, and government reorganization); its studies have stimulated the establishment of organizations to respond to community needs (e.g., the Economic Development Corporation). Although a prominent example of intersector cooperation, GIPC has been criticized as not sufficiently representative of the general population because it is a privately funded, nonelective body, initially appointed and now nominated by the mayor. In recent years, however, it has expanded its membership, board, and executive committee to provide more diversity and more turnover.

The creation of UNIGOV (1970) and increased interaction among government, business, and nonprofits during the mayoral administration of Richard G. Lugar in the late 1960s and early 1970s put in place formal and informal mechanisms essential to community development. Confidence in the city's prospects—another important ingredient in community development—grew as Indianapolis received national attention through its involvement in the Model Cities Program and Lugar's heading the National League of Cities. During this period community development included buildings (MARKET SQUARE ARENA, CITY MARKET) and legislation supporting the expansion and merger of the Indiana University and Purdue University regional campuses in Indianapolis into a full-scale university (IUPUI). Proponents of IUPUI believed that a large public university, complementing established professional schools such as medicine and law, was an essential resource for community development.

During the administration of Mayor William H. Hudnut III the pace of community development increased. Hudnut's ability to build coalitions and to engender enthusiasm for his image of the new Indianapolis mobilized support for an array of bricks-and-mortar projects, which included the HOOSIER DOME, the INDIANAPOLIS ZOO, the natatorium, Capitol Commons, PAN AMERICAN PLAZA, the EITELJORG MUSEUM, and renovation of UNION STATION and the Indiana and Circle theatres. Although the development of the urban center received the lion's share of public attention, the Hudnut administration also supported community development corporations, worked for legislation that would permit more aggressive action in blighted neighborhoods, and established the Indianapolis Neighborhood Housing Partnership. By the late 1980s neighborhoods were receiving virtually all of the community development block grant money, with the production of new and renovated housing almost tripling since the beginning of the decade.

In spite of hefty expenditures of money and time on neighborhoods, some neighborhood and minority groups questioned the decision makers' commitment to social welfare, noting that social service and neighborhood development programs were relying heavily on federal funds for support. In response, proponents of downtown development emphasized the need for a prosperous downtown private sector to attract new business and investment, to provide new jobs for inner city employees, and to balance the large percentage of downtown occupants that paid no tax. They also argued that it was important for Indianapolis residents to be proud of their community, especially the downtown space which all shared.

Specific objections were raised to projects such as the Hoosier Dome and the tennis complex, which were designed to promote Indianapolis as the amateur sports capital of the nation. Critics doubted the projects' value to the community as a whole. While admitting that economic benefits, in the form of income and opportunities for building corporate relationships, were a primary objective, defenders of the sports emphasis argued that nationally recognized sports events also foster the civic pride and cohesion that undergird all forms of community development. Subsequent evidence reveals that economic benefits have in fact been widespread; a 1992 evalua-

tion ("Beyond the Games") indicates that sports promotion accounted for a total impact of $1.89 billion on the Indianapolis economy between 1977 and 1991.

Human service projects received steady support during the 1980s from some funding agencies, notably the INDIANAPOLIS FOUNDATION and UNITED WAY, as well as from the city. During the latter half of the 1980s the city initiated its CAMPAIGN FOR HEALTHY BABIES, and allocated annually a half million dollars to multiservice centers and human service programs, an amount left intact when other items were slashed during the recession. Lilly Endowment also supported social welfare during the 1980s through grants to United Way, by underwriting the Local Initiatives Support Corporation (LISC) grants in Indianapolis, and by providing seed funding to Community Centers, Inc., and the Family Support Center.

Between 1977 and 1988 Lilly Endowment devoted approximately $160 million of its community development grants to Indianapolis building projects and about $8.7 million to neighborhood improvements. Although an economic boom allowed a freer use of public monies and more generosity on the part of the corporate community, undeniably the endowment could make or break community development projects. In some instances, such as WHITE RIVER STATE PARK, public funds appeared to be committed to projects only because Lilly proffered matching funds.

It should be noted that Lilly Endowment support for community development has been evident in other than monetary ways. Its commitment to Indianapolis—even expanding its professional staff to better support its community development activities—has set a standard for community involvement by others. The endowment has also moved projects forward by serving as neutral territory for antagonistic factions to meet to resolve their disagreements.

Because of the extraordinary size of its endowment and its willingness to support community development, Lilly Endowment has overshadowed other important contributors. The Indianapolis Foundation, for instance, has carried out its role in community projects and has been a mainstay of cultural organizations and human service programs by supporting areas of need not covered by Lilly. The United Way continued to expand its combined campaign and, since absorbing the COMMUNITY SERVICE COUNCIL in 1978, has provided crucial planning and research services to identify and respond to community needs. The Corporate Community Council has underwritten projects and organizations with wide community impact: the Tenth Pan American Games, the Indianapolis Project, the Indianapolis Economic Development Corporation, and Vision Indianapolis Tomorrow. And the broader corporate community was responsible for a substantial portion of the $6.5 million raised for the Campaign for Healthy Babies and for most of the $2.5 million secured from private funds prior to the issuing of bonds for the Convention Center.

Near the end of the Hudnut administration, as the glamorous projects of the 1980s were completed, the economy took a downturn; social problems such as poverty and unemployment appeared intractable, and enthusiasm for community development waned.

Soon after Mayor Stephen Goldsmith took office in 1992 he appointed a deputy mayor for neighborhood services, convened a Neighborhood Roundtable to discuss neighborhood needs, and targeted funds for rehabilitating homes, strengthening the physical infrastructure, and improving human services. Also contributing to heightened attention to neighborhoods has been the Lilly Endowment's decision to increase its support for housing, community development corporations, and education. To support an expanded base of responsibility for community development, the United Way's Community Service Council and the city of Indianapolis worked together to open a Neighborhood Resource Center in late 1993, with the backing of a coalition of community leaders and agencies. The center's objective is to assist neighborhood organizations bring about positive change in their neighborhoods by helping them to acquire the resources needed to respond to residents' needs.

An emphasis on neighborhoods and human development may alter the way philanthropic individuals and organizations answer the central question of community development: What constitutes an improvement in the overall quality of life? An answer that focuses on human development will consider the means as well as the ends, and means involve methods of decisionmaking. A series of articles in the *Indianapolis News* in November, 1989, criticized the decisionmaking process of the 1980s as highly centralized, involving a small coalition of government, business, and nonprofit leaders. Cited as an example of a closed circle of influence was the so-called CITY COMMITTEE, a self-appointed group of men who successfully promoted a number of community development projects in the 1970s and 1980s. Although interested in communal as well as personal benefits, committee members chose to apply their influence at key points, bypassing a public airing of issues.

More inclusive methods of community development, however, typically require more time and more complicated strategies for gathering different points of view, as demonstrated by the 1992–1993 Indianapolis project "Vision Tomorrow." Moreover, the neighborhood focus is confronting differences among neighborhoods, e.g., the inner city's concern with small business development and home rehabilitation and the suburbs' concern with land use planning.

The approach of the Goldsmith administration supports some decentralization, as in its implementation strategy for home rehabilitation, which offers neighborhoods more control over the assistance they receive. In 1992–1993 three federal programs—HOPE 3, Community Development Block Grants, and HOME—provided funds for rehabilitation and construction of affordable housing, primarily in seven targeted neighborhoods. All three programs were monitored by the Department of Housing and Urban Development and implemented by the local Department of Metropolitan Development, working with the Indianapolis Neighborhood Housing Partnership and a coalition of community development corporations. Under the HOPE 3 grant community development corporations in the targeted neighborhoods were responsible for identifying, acquiring, and rehabilitating properties for homeownership. Total expenditures for all three programs—an anticipated $12 million—will support renovation or construction of an estimated 1,290 housing units. In addition, a $530 million outlay planned for physical improvements throughout the city from 1993 through 1995, will benefit the business community as well as the local neighborhoods.

The city continues to work with a variety of partners—the Indianapolis Economic Development Corporation, local utilities, the INDIANAPOLIS AIRPORT AUTHORITY, Indianapolis Downtown, Inc., and others—to promote existing industry initiatives, international ties, and natural business strengths in areas like motorsports. For the Goldsmith administration, as for the Hudnut and Lugar administrations, community development requires a dual focus on economic development and neighborhood revitalization.

PATRICIA A. DEAN

Philanthropy and Education. Indianapolis has approximately 50 foundations, representing a variety of types and sizes, which sponsor programs for schools. FOUNDATIONS that award educational grants in Indianapolis fall into five categories: family, corporate, community, advocacy, and religious.

Indianapolis family foundations include, among others: the CLOWES FUND (1952), LILLY ENDOWMENT (1937), and the Moore Foundation (1960). In 1991, Lilly Endowment awarded $47 million (36 percent of its total grants) to education. A significant portion of those grants were awarded to Indiana's educational institutions, including pre-collegiate and collegiate institutions located in Indianapolis. Program emphases included community guidance programs, special programs for the INDIANAPOLIS PUBLIC SCHOOLS, and school reform at the elementary-secondary school level. In HIGHER EDUCATION, the emphases included grants for curriculum, faculty, and institutional development. BUTLER UNIVERSITY, INDIANA UNIVERSITY–PURDUE UNIVERSITY AT INDIANAPOLIS, MARIAN COLLEGE, and MARTIN UNIVERSITY all received grants. The Moore Foundation, with assets of $7 million, awards approximately 19 percent of its annual grants for educational purposes, and they are concentrated in Indianapolis and central Indiana. The Clowes Fund allocates approximately 30 percent of its grants to education; however, only a small percentage of these awards goes to institutions located in Indianapolis.

Two examples of corporate foundations are Inland Container Corporation Foundation and ELI LILLY AND COMPANY Foundation. Inland Container Corporation Foundation's annual awards budget has been about $1.35 million; approximately 30 percent of this amount is dedicated specifically to education, but only a portion of that amount funds programs in Indianapolis. The foundation's awards include scholarships to children of employees, programs for at-risk inner city youth in Indianapolis, and grants to elementary and secondary schools and private colleges. It does not award education grants to individuals. In 1991, Eli Lilly and Company Foundation's grants for educational purposes totaled $4 million and were given to organizations in Indianapolis and across the country. Examples of its local grants include funds for science equipment at Martin University, matching gifts to pre-collegiate and collegiate institutions based upon contributions made by their employees and retirees, and a grant for the Fund for Hoosier Excellence. Other local programs assisted by the Lilly Company Foundation include COMMUNITY LEADERS ALLIED FOR SUPERIOR SCHOOLS (CLASS), the Central Indiana Honors Academy at PARK TUDOR SCHOOL, the RUTH LILLY HEALTH EDUCATION CENTER, and the Science Education Foundation of Indiana.

The INDIANAPOLIS FOUNDATION, a community foundation established in 1916 by a group of local business persons, exists to promote the welfare of individuals residing in Indianapolis. In 1991, of the $3.3 million it awarded in grants, $100,000 went to education. Recipients included 29 high school libraries and the Indianapolis Public Schools Scholarship Program. Historically, approximately 10 percent of its annual grants have been for educational purposes, usually focused at the elementary-secondary level, although grants have been awarded to Indiana University–Purdue University at Indianapolis and Martin University, among other higher education institutions. The foundation's educational funding objectives are flexible in order to meet demonstrated and emerging needs in public education.

Advocacy foundations and organizations are formed to promote a particular cause, organization, or constituency group. In Indianapolis they include several organizations that promote education. The Indianapolis Public Schools Foundation, founded in 1985, has a 22–member board. Characteristic of relatively new advocacy foundations, this one is in the process of raising money to build its endowment, while concurrently awarding a few grants. All of its grants are for projects associated with the Indianapolis Public Schools. The Indianapolis–Marion County Public Library Foundation, founded in 1969, had assets of about $1.2 million as of December 31, 1991. The foundation funds programs of $1,000 to $30,000 that are supportive of the library's programs, including volunteer recognition, trustee and employee education, and professional development. Free public education programs include lectures, concerts, and book-related discussion groups.

Community Leaders Allied for Superior Schools (CLASS) is an example of an independent community organization that represents a joint venture between the business community and a private foundation (the Lilly Endowment) to provide direct and in-kind services to schools. CLASS works with its primary constituency, the Indianapolis Public Schools, in a collaborative relationship to help the system develop the leadership and management skills of teachers and administrators, using the services of local business leaders and experts. It does not award grants unless they are directly related to its programs. The Rotary Foundation of Indianapolis has awarded grants in the $1,000 to $14,000 range to organizations that support education, such as the Indiana Council for Economic Education. Junior Achievement of Central Indiana provides program support to Indianapolis elementary and secondary schools through materials and volunteers from the business sector. Junior Achievement's primary objective is to provide young people with practical economic education programs and experience in the competitive private enterprise system through a partnership between the business and educational communities. Indianapolis CHAMBER OF COMMERCE sponsors the Partners in Education program whereby businesses volunteer to pair off with an Indianapolis public school. Employees of the firms volunteer their time for a variety of tasks, such as reading and tutoring.

The Catholic Community Foundation, representing the fifth type of foundation, is focused on a particular set of religious institutions and organizations, but it also serves the entire community through social service programs supported by endowment funds within the foundation. Created in 1987 and governed by a 25–member board appointed by the Archbishop of Indianapolis, the foundation's grants are designed to strengthen and support Catholic religious education in and through its elementary and secondary schools.

Grant program emphases change periodically within all foundations because of the changing needs in the area they serve. However, some foundation programs can and do remain constant for many years. In the aggregate, the presence of a wide range of foundations in the city serves to enrich the quality of life and education of Indianapolis citizens.

RALPH E. LUNDGREN

Philanthropy and Government. Since its earliest years Indianapolis has provided social services through a combination of government and nonprofit agencies. In 1835 the Indianapolis Benevolent Society (IBS) was formed to supplement the assistance provided by the township trustees. Through the CHARITY ORGANIZATION SOCIETY (COS), which was initiated in 1879, the township trustees cooperated with private charitable agencies to share information about persons in need of assistance and to assign cases to the appropriate agency. Government and nonprofit agencies cooperated also in financing charitable institutions such as the Home for Friendless Women, which built a new structure in 1870 with combined funding from city, county, and private sources.

When the Family Welfare Society was organized in 1922, from a merger of IBS, COS, Children's Aid Association, and Mother's Aid Society, some services that had been provided by private agencies were transferred to public agencies. The Catholic Charities Bureau announced in its 1939 annual report the need to coordinate its caseworkers with public and private agencies supporting families receiving Aid to Dependent Children. By

1950 the Department of Welfare's Children's Division had adopted interagency agreements with many institutions, including the FAMILY SERVICE ASSOCIATION and the CHILDREN'S BUREAU OF INDIANAPOLIS. The COMMUNITY CENTERS of Indianapolis was created collaboratively in 1983 to be the consolidated solicitor for government dollars for 14 community centers providing direct assistance, referrals, and case management for needy individuals.

Currently, in Indianapolis as elsewhere in the nation, philanthropy and government are related both by law and practical necessity. Government determines which organizations are charitable entities and thus tax-exempt and able to receive tax-exempt gifts. At the practical level, government agencies and philanthropic organizations cooperate in the provision of social services. The Step Ahead process, initiated in 1991, seeks to provide comprehensive, seamless service delivery to children from birth to age 13, through ensuring coordination of services among government agencies and nonprofits, which mutually sign funding contracts.

As providers of social service programs, both sectors share an interest in finding the most effective and responsible ways to offer those services. In Indianapolis this issue goes back at least to the mid–19th century, when the IBS cautioned against careless almsgiving that encouraged "pauperism." When the COS was formed in 1879, its explicit intention was "to distinguish between poverty and pauperism, to relieve the one and to refuse the other; . . . and to do what it could to substitute work for alms." Transients who stayed at the Friendly Inn operated by IBS were offered the chance to earn their meals and lodging by cutting wood in the inn's woodyard.

In the 1990s government and nonprofit organizations continue to face the issue of how to help individuals become self-sustaining. The Indianapolis Network of Employment and Training (INET), the INDIANAPOLIS NEIGHBORHOOD HOUSING PARTNERSHIP, and the Marion County Council on Youth work to create capable and responsible citizens.

Social services provided by nonprofits may supplement, complement, or substitute for governmental services. Supplemental assistance is provided by nonprofits like Meals on Wheels, the SALVATION ARMY, and the DAY NURSERY ASSOCIATION. When organizations like GIRLS, INC., and BOYS AND GIRLS CLUBS work to instill attitudes and skills that students are not acquiring in the public schools, their efforts may be seen as an implicit or, in some cases explicit, judgment of government's educational programs. Nonprofits may also complement government by serving as advocates for groups whose voices need to be heard by policymakers.

Other nongovernmental providers are under contract with the government to provide services on behalf of the government. Providers in this category serve as proxies, or substitutes, for government, offering services that government has chosen not to offer. Of almost $300 million of government funding spent in Marion County for human services, about two thirds is contracted with nonprofit agencies. Agencies with government contracts include Community Centers of Indianapolis, NOBLE CENTERS, INET, and others.

MARK BUCHERL

Philanthropy and Health Care. Voluntary giving of time and money in the health-related, nonprofit sector. In the early 1800s, interest in health issues was sporadic, peaking during epidemics. In 1847 an early Indianapolis board of health raised $1,000 to construct a hospital for smallpox victims, but interest passed when the epidemic subsided. It was not until 1859 that the first city hospital was finally constructed.

In the late 1800s, religious and other volunteer organizations in Indianapolis led the way in addressing health needs, with hospitals becoming a major focus for philanthropy. The women of the Indianapolis FLOWER MISSION Society, formed in 1876, delivered flowers and provided volunteer nursing services to the patients in City Hospital. In 1883 the Flower Mission raised funds through fairs, bazaars, and elegant balls for a training school for nurses, the first of its kind in Indianapolis. The Eleanor Home, a hospital for children made possible by contributions from Mr. and Mrs. ELI LILLY, and also supported financially by the society, opened in 1895, operating for several years on the current site of METHODIST HOSPITAL.

Early clinics often gave health care assistance to city residents
[Indiana Historical Society, #C2221]

In 1881 four sisters from the Daughters of Charity of St. Vincent de Paul came to Indianapolis to operate St. Vincent Infirmary, the forerunner of ST. VINCENT HOSPITAL, supported with $50 donated by the local bishop, SILAS CHATARD. Through the efforts of OSCAR MCCULLOCH and JOHN HOLLIDAY, the Summer Mission for Sick Children opened near the current site of BUTLER UNIVERSITY in 1890. Free medical care for mothers and their children was provided by volunteer physicians. In 1901 Methodist church members began four years of fund-raising efforts, collecting $200,000 for the new Methodist Hospital, which opened in 1908. ST. FRANCIS HOSPITAL was founded in 1913 by Father Killian of the Holy Name Catholic Church, supported by the order of the Poor Sisters of St. Francis Seraph of the Perpetual Adoration. Long Hospital was completed in 1914 on the INDIANA UNIVERSITY SCHOOL OF MEDICINE campus, made possible by $240,000 donated by Dr. and Mrs. Robert Long. Following the death of Hoosier poet James Whitcomb Riley in 1916, his close friends decided to commemorate his life by building a pediatric hospital for all Indiana children. The James Whitcomb Riley Memorial Association was formed and conducted a statewide campaign, raising $1.2 million for the new RILEY HOSPITAL FOR CHILDREN, that opened in 1924.

The hospital guild movement began in Indianapolis in the early 1900s, with members supporting hospitals through fund-raising and volunteer service. In 1907 the St. Margaret's Hospital Guild was founded to serve the City Hospital. Guilds were formed at Riley, St. Francis, St. Vincent, and Methodist hospitals in the 1920s and 1930s.

By the early 1900s, philanthropy was becoming more scientific and foundations were developing. The INDIANAPOLIS FOUNDATION was begun in 1916 and in its early years provided funds to support visiting nurse services and a study on the continued hospital bed shortage. In 1937 the Flower Mission Society contributed its own endowment fund and campaigned to build the Flower Mission Hospital for tuberculosis patients.

After World War II there was renewed philanthropic interest in health and hospital campaigns. Complementing the federal aid programs were substantial corporate and private gifts. In addition, major medical discoveries during the war led to a renewed interest in medical research and to an expanded development of voluntary health organizations. Many voluntary health agencies were formed in Indianapolis, involving volunteers in service, education, and fund-raising activities. Local chapters included the National Foundation for Infantile Paralysis in 1938, the American Cancer Society in 1945, the LITTLE RED DOOR in 1945, the American Heart Association in 1948, the Marion County Mental Health Association in 1949, the Muscular Dystrophy Association in 1952, United Cerebral Palsy in 1953, and the Multiple Sclerosis Society in 1954.

Hospitals in the city especially benefited from charitable contributions. The Indianapolis Hospital Development Association (IHDA) was formed in 1950 by a group of civic, medical, business, and industrial leaders to raise funds both to build new hospitals and provide for the expansion of existing hospitals. In 1953 the IHDA launched a citywide campaign to raise $12 million in contributions. Financing was provided for Methodist Hospital, St. Francis Hospital, and the new COMMUNITY HOSPITAL, which opened in 1956. In the mid–1960s, a second campaign was conducted, raising $15.5 million. The Winona Memorial Foundation of Indianapolis, formed in 1956, completed the new Winona Memorial Hospital in 1966 on North Meridian Street. The internationally known Krannert Institute of Cardiology was founded in 1963 through the financial support of Mr. and Mrs. HERMAN C. KRANNERT.

Before World War II, philanthropy and public subsidy accounted for more than half of hospital revenues in the United States, but by the 1970s only 9 percent of hospital construction funds came from philanthropy. Despite this trend, ongoing development activities continued to be an important part of hospital fund-raising in Indianapolis during the 1970s and 1980s. Foundations have also continued to play an important part in supporting health care. In 1990 the Indianapolis Foundation distributed approximately 29 percent of its more than $3 million in grants to health, handicapped, and rehabilitation organizations. The Eli Lilly and Company Foundation has provided support for health and welfare grants, including $300,000 for the community health centers in 1989. Although the LILLY ENDOWMENT does not generally support health care projects, the foundation provided $1.2 million for the city's CAMPAIGN FOR HEALTHY BABIES in 1989. The Health Foundation of Greater Indianapolis has supported projects in adolescent health, geriatrics, health education, and mental health. Life/Leadership Development, founded through the cooperative efforts of six Indianapolis service clubs, provided financial support for the RUTH LILLY CENTER FOR HEALTH EDUCATION, which opened in 1989.

A study conducted in 1991 by the CENTER ON PHILANTHROPY at Indiana University showed that 27.5 percent of the people in Indiana reported volunteer activity in the health sector, and almost half had made monetary contributions. In 1991 in Indianapolis, nearly 25,000 volunteers served the seven largest health-related agencies of UNITED WAY.

STEPHEN E. KIRCHHOFF

Indiana Gives, Volunteering and Giving in Indiana: 1991 (Indianapolis, 1992); John R. Seeley et al., *Community Chest: A Case Study in Philanthropy* (rep., New Brunswick, N.J., 1989); Nathan Weber, ed., *Giving USA—1991* (New York, 1991).

Philanthropy and Recreation. Parks and recreation are key components of the human service system and therefore have been, and continue to be, the recipients of philanthropy in Indianapolis. Public parks and open spaces counterbalance the effects of an industrial society, preserve natural beauty, and contribute to the quality of life.

During Indianapolis' earliest decades, citizens had few places for public recreation and leisure except for the WHITE RIVER and the surrounding countryside. Private interests and enlightened individuals, however, were the earliest catalysts for the development of recreational spaces within the growing city. Abel C. Pepper, a former Indian agent and director of the State Bank of Indiana from Lawrenceburg, sponsored a resolution at the state's 1850–1851 constitutional convention to designate unsold lands in the capital as "public grounds," although local officials failed to express interest in his proposal. In 1859 Timothy Richardson Fletcher, local businessman and nephew of CALVIN FLETCHER, donated a lot to the city for a park, but it remained untouched until 1884–1885 when, following Fletcher's petition for its return, the city sold the property. The heirs to Calvin Fletcher's estate also offered 30 acres for use as a public park, an offer that the City Council rejected. Unsuccessful in their dealings with the city, residents in other sections of Indianapolis gathered contributions, planted trees, and developed several neighborhood parks on their own.

Despite the popularity and success of New York's Central Park (ca. 1860) Indianapolis did not formulate and adopt a comprehensive park system until the mid–1890s. Influenced by the emerging City Beautiful movement and public calls for recreational space, the COMMERCIAL CLUB and Mayor THOMAS TAGGART eventually supported the creation of a city parks department to develop "greenspaces" for residents. Only after individuals like BOOTH TARKINGTON (who donated land for Tarkington Park in the 1890s) and groups like the Commercial Club took the lead in promoting public recreational space did the city follow. Over the years individuals continued to provide park lands for public recreation. These benefactors included newspaper publisher JOHN H. HOLLIDAY, who donated his 80–acre estate on Spring Mill Road (1916); heirs of former postmaster Henry W. Bennett, who deeded land in 1937 for Brookside Park; and businessman George J.

Marrott, who gave a 46–acre tract on North College Avenue to the city in 1945.

During the early 20th century local businesses and organizations provided leadership in hosting national hot air balloon races and the first clay court TENNIS competition and in staging the INDIANAPOLIS 500–MILE RACE. The ensuing years, however, were filled with problems caused by war, depression, and urbanization which preoccupied government and business leaders. Recreation, therefore, became an important outlet for the urban population. Beginning in 1919, R. Walter Jarvis, recreation supervisor for the park system, urged local youth organizations and their supporters to coordinate community recreational and athletic programs through his office. By the early 1920s many parks had become social service centers, providing day nurseries, clinics, and athletic programs in newly constructed community centers. During the 1930s a Civil Works Administration project operating through the parks department recruited recreation workers and volunteers to organize and supervise recreational activities at the community houses.

From the late 1940s through the 1960s there were numerous efforts to improve public parks, recreational facilities, and programs citywide. This led the *Indianapolis Star* of May 10, 1955, to comment that "An expanding city can hardly have too many parks, too many facilities for the recreation of its people, both young and old." The 1970s and 1980s, however, brought a shift in commitment by Indianapolis' community leaders to amateur sports as part of a larger economic development strategy. During this period philanthropy played a significant role in the development of new athletic facilities such as the Major Taylor Velodrome, the Natatorium and Track and Field Stadium at IUPUI, and the Bill Kuntz Soccer Stadium. These facilities represented important community assets, not only for amateur and professional athletes but for recreational purposes as well.

Since recreational opportunities are considered to be a critical component of the focus on neighborhoods, families, and children, the 1990s will likely be characterized by a major shift in philanthropic efforts from facilities to programs. For example, the INDIANA SPORTS CORPORATION'S

ten-year strategic plan adopted in 1992 is largely directed toward youth. The Sports Corporation provides Champs grants to sports organizations that serve youth and to its own Youth Sports Development Program, itself a recipient of support from the LILLY ENDOWMENT. Likewise, the 1992–1993 study *Beyond the Games: The Indianapolis Amateur Sports Strategy*, commissioned by the Indianapolis CHAMBER OF COMMERCE, also emphasized increased recreational and sports programs and greater utilization of the city's parks and recreational facilities.

Philanthropic support for youth programs is not a new concept. Nonprofit organizations such as the BOYS AND GIRLS CLUBS, the YMCA, and the YWCA have long depended on the community's generosity. The modern challenges of juvenile delinquency, teen pregnancy, drug abuse, and poor academic performance make such support important. The Sports Corporation's Champs grants have emphasized partnerships between youth groups (like the POLICE ATHLETIC LEAGUE clubs) and other organizations (like USA Track and Field) to create opportunities for at-risk youth. Long-standing philanthropic entities such as the Indianapolis Foundation are directing important support to programs emphasizing recreational opportunities for inner-city and disadvantaged youth. The goal of these new partnerships and directions is prevention through intervention.

The private sector plays an increasingly important role in the stimulation of sports and recreation opportunities. Corporations consider these programs not only as a constructive means of giving something back to their communities, but also as a way to gain recognition for the services and products they provide. Examples of this new corporate giving strategy are common in Indianapolis. Corporate sponsors of the INDIANAPOLIS/SCARBOROUGH PEACE GAMES, the annual Youth Links golf tournament, and the Mazda Indy Games (track and field) exemplify the marriage between commercial identification and community service for corporate sponsors.

The creation of the National Junior Tennis League (1968; Indianapolis branch, March, 1976) and the Indiana Amateur Baseball Association heralded another trend, the development of a nonprofit sector dedicated to sports and recreation.

Organizations such as these and the Indiana Sports Corporation solicit and dispense funds to support a variety of programs serving a broad spectrum of society. The Indianapolis Parks Foundation, established in 1991, seeks philanthropic and corporate support for the maintenance of park property and facilities, the continuation of ongoing programs, and the development of new services.

Support also comes from the local sports community. Opportunities for children to interact with professionals from the INDIANAPOLIS INDIANS, the INDIANA PACERS, the INDIANAPOLIS COLTS, and the Indianapolis Ice are a regular part of the franchises' community activities, each of which lends time, facilities, and money to support community sports and recreation. National AMATEUR SPORTS GOVERNING BODIES headquartered in Indianapolis, such as the United States Gymnastics Federation, USA Track and Field, the United States Rowing Association, United States Synchronized Swimming, the United States Diving Association, and the U.S. Canoe and Kayak Team, put into practice their commitment to youth development by donating time and expertise to the community.

DEBORAH SMITH
Indiana University, Bloomington
MILTON O. THOMPSON

Indianapolis Chamber of Commerce, *Beyond the Games: The Indianapolis Amateur Sports Strategy* (Indianapolis, 1992–1993); Indianapolis Department of Parks and Recreation, "A Look Back: A Historical Review of the Department of Parks and Recreation of the City of Indianapolis" (unpublished manuscript, n.d.).

Philanthropy and Religion. From the city's founding, religious bodies have been active in various levels of philanthropy. Congregations raised money for the local poor while church women sewed and knitted clothing for the needy. During the late 1840s Indianapolis residents gathered relief supplies and funds for victims of the Irish potato famine. Many congregations sponsored mission churches for the poor, African-Americans, and immigrants who settled in the rapidly growing city. Churches played an important role during periods of war by providing assistance to local families of servicemen and offering

food and recreational opportunities—such as Christ Church's Servicemen's Canteen in World Wars I and II—to those individuals in uniform.

Indianapolis has been home to a variety of explicitly religious philanthropies. The SALVATION ARMY is one example of a group whose character as both an evangelical movement and an organized charity remains as obvious today as when it began operations in Indianapolis in 1889. LUTHERAN CHILD AND FAMILY SERVICES, founded in 1883 as "an asylum for orphans and aged people," and the JULIAN CENTER, established in 1975 by the Episcopal Diocese of Indianapolis as a human services agency for women, are other examples. Religiously based philanthropies in the city range from comprehensive agencies like the (Protestant) Church Federation, Catholic Social Services, and the Jewish Welfare Federation, to more focused operations such as the Damien Center, a ministry to victims of AIDS.

Religion was also important in the creation of what are now considered secular philanthropies. The PLEASANT RUN CHILDREN'S HOME began its life as the General German Protestant Orphan Home in 1867, founded in part by the German Zion Evangelical Church (later Zion United Church of Christ). The FLOWER MISSION, a Christian women's group, started in 1876 with the purpose of bringing flowers to those in the hospital and eventually evolved into the sponsor of a tuberculosis sanitarium, a children's hospital, and the state's first school of nursing. GLEANERS FOOD BANK, incorporated in 1980 by religiously motivated leaders, provided an organized means for getting food to charities that feed the hungry.

Another way religion fosters philanthropy in Indianapolis occurs within the lives of individuals. It is impossible to calculate accurately how much giving and volunteering is motivated by the religious convictions people hold. But in the case of the most prominent philanthropic organization in Indianapolis, the impact of personal religious conviction is well documented.

Pharmaceutical executive and philanthropist ELI LILLY guided the development of the foundation that bears his family name. From its founding in 1937, the LILLY ENDOWMENT has pursued grantmaking in the areas of community, education, and perhaps most significantly, religion. Although direct grants to religious organizations and for religious research have rarely exceeded 25 percent of any year's grants, Lilly's own philanthropic interests, which drove the Endowment's policies, were fundamentally religious in orientation. Lilly himself made many substantial gifts of money to programs and causes of the Episcopal church. From 1927 onward, he served as a vestryman at Christ Church Cathedral, a role in which he took his duties seriously, to the point of personally cleaning out the church's furnace room during his term in the 1950s as the junior warden in charge of church property. Materialism, in Lilly's view, needed to be opposed by religion and education so that people might be taught "that it is not what we have but what we are that is of real importance." For the rest of his life he shaped the programs of the Endowment to find and support "character education." Thus, many grants made by the Endowment to this day are premised on a belief that better communities are made by enhancing individual character through educational settings suffused with religious and spiritual values.

Indianapolis has been the site of periodic debates over how to organize community benevolence. Religious persons and ideals have figured prominently in those debates. One of the key episodes in the development of Indianapolis' philanthropic sector occurred in the late 1870s. After several years of economic depression, the Indianapolis Benevolent Society's (IBS) approach to relief for the needy was falling apart under the strain of the area's poverty and the limitations of an all-volunteer relief system. The Reverend OSCAR C. MCCULLOCH, pastor of Plymouth (Congregational) Church, convinced the IBS leadership that it was time to reorganize charity relief using a "scientific method" whereby professionals would be employed to investigate cases and coordinate the assistance individuals might receive from any local agency. The Indianapolis CHARITY ORGANIZATION SOCIETY (1879) was the result of the reorganization.

Religious reasons supported both the old and the new patterns of philanthropy. The IBS had been controlled since its founding in 1835 by prominent Protestant elders and deacons and had dispensed assistance on the principle of material

want. McCulloch, on the other hand, was deeply influenced by the Social Gospel movement and its assertion that it was more Christian to be concerned with issues of prevention and education and to help persons break their patterns of dependence and avoid future misery. The Charity Organization Society eventually evolved into the present-day COMMUNITY SERVICE COUNCIL and the UNITED WAY OF CENTRAL INDIANA. But the debate over the best way to meet human needs and to work for the common good of the community continues to this day, and religious convictions and precepts lie behind many of the positions concerned persons take in that debate.

Religion is also the recipient of much local philanthropy. National surveys of individuals repeatedly show that approximately two thirds of every charitable dollar given by individuals goes to a church or other religious institution. Likewise, churches and synagogues are the principal recipients of volunteer activity. The collateral societal benefits of religious activity can be seen throughout Indianapolis. Second Presbyterian and Westminster Presbyterian churches have cooperated in a ministry of service—across lines of class, neighborhood, and race—to the residents of the near eastside neighborhood in which Westminster is located. Through this partnership, persons unable to afford counsel may receive free legal advice, an elementary school student has a place to go after school, and persons learning to read are tutored. In another program, a group of African-American congregations, with the encouragement of the CHURCH FEDERATION OF GREATER INDIANAPOLIS, has taken on the ministry of relating to individuals confined in Indiana Women's Prison and to ex-offenders in transition to life after prison. On the city's north side, the Indianapolis Hebrew Congregation sponsors a public lecture series that brings major thinkers, authors, and performing artists to Indianapolis.

Even the buildings of religious congregations serve philanthropic ends as when Alcoholics Anonymous and ALANON chapters and other support groups meet there. After-school programs, aging adults day care programs, and feeding programs for hungry and poor persons are increasingly prevalent in Indianapolis congregations. Countless Head Start, preschool, and mother's morning-out programs meet in churches, as do Boy Scout and Girl Scout troops. Bethlehem Lutheran Church houses the Meridian-Kessler Neighborhood Association and works with local groups to assist in neighborhood redevelopment. Tabernacle Presbyterian and First Baptist churches offer extensive athletic and recreational programs for city and neighborhood youths, as do other congregations.

The relationship of philanthropy and religion is a mutually supportive and interdependent one. As the source of philanthropic ideals and behaviors, religion plays an important role in the community life of Indianapolis. As the recipient of voluntary effort and financial support, religion benefits from the philanthropy of Indianapolis residents. As community institutions, religious congregations also provide a context for the expression of philanthropic activity.

JAMES HUDNUT-BEUMLER
Columbia Theological Seminary

Jacob Piatt Dunn, *Greater Indianapolis* (Chicago, 1910); John R. Seeley, ed., *Community Chest: A Case Study in Philanthropy* (Toronto, 1957).

Philanthropy and Social Services.

"Relief" for the poor was among the earliest forms of organized philanthropy in Indianapolis. Among the more prominent of such efforts was the INDIANAPOLIS BENEVOLENT SOCIETY (IBS), which was organized in 1835, predating the better-known New York Association for Improving the Conditions of the Poor (1843) by eight years. At the time, public assistance was available in Indiana through government-sponsored poor farms and township trustees. However, the IBS, recognizing that public assistance was insufficient, offered supplemental aid. It provided wood, clothing, and grocery store vouchers of $1.50 per family per week. JAMES BLAKE led the society for its first 35 years. Among other notable leaders were the Reverends John L. Richmond and James W. McKennan, JAMES M. RAY, Albert G. Willard, Alfred Harrison, SARAH T. BOLTON, SAMUEL MERRILL, and CALVIN FLETCHER.

Several institutions were established to assist widows and orphans, who were often the focus of

The Flanner House home-building program received national attention in the 1950s and 1960s. [Indiana Historical Society, #C5272]

mid–19th century relief efforts. Those institutions included the Widows' and Orphans' Asylum of Indianapolis and St. Vincent's School, an orphanage, both of which were established in 1851, and the Home for Friendless Women, founded in 1867. During the same period, Indianapolis philanthropy moved into other arenas with the founding of the YMCA in 1854, the Young Men's Library Association in 1863, and the Indianapolis Chapter of the American Red Cross in 1864.

In Indianapolis as elsewhere, the depression of the 1870s dramatically increased the need for social services. In 1870, some 300 families in the city received township trustee assistance; by 1873, the number had doubled; and by 1879, it had increased tenfold. This was an era in which there was growing demand for government involvement in meeting the needs of the population. Ironically, it was also a time of concern in Indianapolis that relief efforts might be too generous, covering "tramps" and other undeserving individuals. In 1873, the *Indianapolis Daily Journal* and the city council opposed public funding for a soup kitchen and a commissioner of charity, proposals for dealing with the growing number of needy persons and charitable organizations. Instead, the council invested in public works projects to increase employment. It allocated only a small sum to poor relief ($2,000), leaving the care of the needy primarily to the township trustees and private charities.

Reverend OSCAR C. MCCULLOCH, pastor of PLYMOUTH (CONGREGATIONAL) CHURCH, assumed the leadership of IBS in 1879 when the organization lacked a sense of direction. Under McCulloch's leadership, IBS instituted an employment bureau and a lodging house with a woodyard (for transients to earn their keep), a system of "friendly visits" to the homes of the poor (to identify the "deserving" and the "undeserving" poor), and a Confidential Exchange—later the Social Service Exchange—to share information about clients with other relief agencies (to verify need and prevent duplication of effort).

McCulloch was attracted to the concept of organized charity—also known as scientific charity—which originated with the London Charity Organization Society. Organized charity emphasized the investigation of cases to validate the need, a centralized exchange of case information to avoid duplication, the referral of cases to the appropriate agency, regular visitation to encourage changes in lifestyle, and the study of the causes of pauperism. The first organization built on this model in the United States was established in 1877 in Buffalo by an Episcopal rector, S. H. Gurteen. At McCulloch's urging, the Benevolent Society brought Gurteen to Indianapolis in November, 1879, to meet with local leaders. Plans for the Indianapolis CHARITY ORGANIZATION SOCIETY (COS) were initiated in December, 1879, and Mayor JOHN CAVEN was elected its first president in February, 1880. McCulloch later became president of COS, serving from 1882 to 1891.

COS was not without opposition in the community, including that of William Bartlett, minister of SECOND PRESBYTERIAN CHURCH, who objected to organizing existing charities under one umbrella. Others regarded the investigation of clients' needs as a form of espionage. Still, the prevailing sentiment supported the society's formation.

During this early period, social service needs were addressed in two ways: direct relief programs and the development of an infrastructure to manage relief programs. The former included the direct relief agencies cited earlier, as well as: FLOWER MISSION SOCIETY (1876); Newsboys' Lodging House (1879); Free Kindergarten Society (1881); ALPHA HOME, one of the first local agencies for African-Americans (1883); Evangelical

Lutheran Orphans Home (1883); SALVATION ARMY (1889); Boys' Club Association (1892); WHEELER MISSION (1893); YWCA (1895); Flanner Guild and FLANNER HOUSE (1898); Indianapolis DAY NURSERY (1901); Shelter House, for Jewish relief (1902); CHRISTAMORE HOUSE (1905); and numerous others. Some agencies founded during the late 19th and early 20th centuries formed the foundations of agencies that continue to operate today, among them the CHILDREN'S BUREAU OF INDIANAPOLIS, the FAMILY SERVICE ASSOCIATION, Indianapolis Day Nursery, and LUTHERAN CHILD AND FAMILY SERVICES. The INDIANAPOLIS FOUNDATION was also founded during this period, in 1916. Its aim was "the relief of the needy poor and the improvement of living conditions . . . the care of the sick or aged . . . educational and philanthropic research in Indianapolis."

During WORLD WAR I, the Indianapolis Chapter of the Red Cross, under the leadership of WILLIAM FORTUNE and Frank D. Stalnaker, surpassed its local quota of $300,000, raising almost $600,000 for war-related relief efforts. The success of the Indianapolis campaign attracted national attention; it also attracted the attention of JOSIAH K. LILLY, SR., chairman of the Chamber of Commerce committee on charities, who noted that the cost of fund-raising for the Red Cross campaign was much lower than the cost of fund-raising for 60 local charities individually. Lilly and other community leaders formed the War Chest in April, 1918; by May, 1918, the Chest had raised $2,793,070 from 100,000 subscribers.

The success of the War Chest firmly established the case for federated fund-raising in Indianapolis. In 1922, the War Chest dissolved and transferred all of its assets to the Community Chest, which had been organized in 1920. In 1923, the Community Chest was reconstituted as the Community Fund, formalizing its guidelines for federated fund-raising and establishing a plan for a Council of Social Agencies to promote cooperation among local agencies. During World War II, Eli Lilly brought the United War Fund and the Community Fund into a single unified campaign. The Community Fund was reorganized as the Indianapolis Community Chest in 1950, and the Council of Social Agencies, which had been a part of the fund organization, became the independent Health and Welfare Council. In succeeding years, the Chest would become the United Fund and then the UNITED WAY. The Health and Welfare Council became the COMMUNITY SERVICE COUNCIL in the 1960s, re-merging with United Way in 1977 to become a division of the larger organization.

Other federated fund-raising entities developed to serve the needs of specific religious and ethnic groups, the JEWISH FEDERATION OF GREATER INDIANAPOLIS and Catholic Charities among them. Though not federations per se, organizations sponsoring major activities and raising funds on behalf of the African-American community emerged in the 1970s; among them were Youth Links, which raises funds from corporations for programs benefiting African-American youth, and INDIANA BLACK EXPO, which hosts a large annual African-American exposition. The latter underwrites social services and scholarships with proceeds from the exposition and other events.

Some organizations not associated with a federated fund-raising program have conducted their own annual campaigns; these have included the American Heart Association, the Red Cross, the Tuberculosis Association, and the March of Dimes. The number of such organizations has grown over the years, although a few, such as the Red Cross and the American Heart Association, now participate in the United Way campaign. Historically there have also been, and continue to be, drives for specific causes like the flood relief drives of 1913 and 1937.

One cannot adequately cover the subject of philanthropy's contribution to social services in Indianapolis without discussing the contributions of certain individuals and families as well as of foundations, guilds, and voluntary service organizations. While all of them cannot be cited here, a few examples will suggest the extent of their contributions.

With respect to individuals and families, the Lilly name is one that appears from the late 19th century, with the construction of Eleanor Home, a hospital for children funded by Mr. and Mrs. Eli Lilly, to the present, with the ongoing contributions of Ruth Allison Lilly. Gustave Efroymson and his descendants have played important roles in the work of the Indianapolis Foundation and other philanthropic efforts, including the establishment of the MORIAH FUND.

Relief and social welfare programs were among the first to benefit from local foundations, and foundations continue to be important in the development of new programs, capital projects, and other efforts. The most prominent foundations have been the LILLY ENDOWMENT and the Indianapolis Foundation. Other foundations, most of them family or corporate (e.g., Griffith, Glick, Baxter, Jordan, Eli Lilly and Company), provide large and small sums to an array of local social service programs. One of the newer foundations, the Health Foundation, was created from the proceeds of the sale of a health maintenance organization and supports only health-related programs. Although it is a private foundation, it is similar to a community foundation in that it is not affiliated with a family or company and is governed by a community board.

Clubs and voluntary organizations, from the Knights of Columbus to Rotary, have been instrumental in marshaling dollars and volunteers for human services. A notable example of the power of these groups was the creation in the 1980s of what eventually became the RUTH LILLY CENTER FOR HEALTH EDUCATION. The concept of a sophisticated, interactive health education center for use by the local school systems was jointly and successfully championed by six service clubs.

Women's service organizations, including the Christamore Aid Society, the JUNIOR LEAGUE, the NATIONAL COUNCIL OF JEWISH WOMEN (NCJW), and the Coalition of 100 BLACK WOMEN, have been instrumental not only in generating funds but also in initiating social welfare programs. For example, NCJW developed preschools for poor children, leading to the Indianapolis HEAD START program; the Junior League was responsible for the creation of the Volunteer Bureau (now the Volunteer Action Center) and the Family Support Center for abused and neglected children; and the Coalition of 100 Black Women established a mentoring program for pregnant and parenting teenagers.

As social work in Indianapolis became more professionalized, as evidenced by the establishment in 1923 of the Council of Social Agencies and the Indianapolis Chapter of the American Association of Social Workers, functions once performed by volunteers were increasingly the province of paid staff. Yet volunteers continue to undergird the operations of Indianapolis' non-profit social service organizations. In individual service agencies and in intermediary organizations, such as United Way and Catholic Charities, volunteers have responsibilities for governance and development, engaging in prioritizing needs, allocating resources, ensuring accountability, and other functions. Leadership training and development, especially in philanthropy and social services, are the focus of special programs, such as the TRUSTEE RENEWAL PROJECT, established by the Lilly Endowment, and the Ardath Burkhart Series, the Executive Women's Leadership Program, and Leadership Training and Development for members of minority communities, sponsored by United Way.

The philanthropic support of social services in Indianapolis has been generous, but it has been tempered by Hoosier skepticism about the worthiness of the causes and the recipients. This skepticism may explain why Indianapolis was among the earlier communities to adopt the investigative and coordinating mechanisms of the Social Service Exchange, the Charity Organization Society, and the Community Chest. That coordination has continued to evolve, even though social services are fragmented in Indianapolis, as in other communities, by the multiplicity of government programs and independent agencies. Indianapolis business and civic leaders historically have placed a high value on working cooperatively, through the Community Service Council and in other ways, to develop solutions to problems through the combined efforts of public and private social services.

IRVIN S. KATZ
United Way of Central Indiana

Philanthropy and the Arts. Philanthropy in its various forms has played a major role in shaping the arts and cultural life in Indianapolis. Having one of the country's largest foundations, the LILLY ENDOWMENT, in Indianapolis has been a major force in cultural growth, and individuals, corporations, volunteer groups, and grassroots endeavors also have contributed significantly to progress in the arts.

The Lilly Endowment, with its primary focus on its hometown, has touched almost every arts endeavor since its founding in 1937, giving an estimated $169 million to 23 arts, culture, and preservation organization in Indianapolis. Of the total, $136.1 million has funded 191 grants to six major Marion County institutions: THE CHILDREN'S MUSEUM, EITELJORG MUSEUM OF AMERICAN INDIAN AND WESTERN ART, INDIANAPOLIS MUSEUM OF ART (IMA), INDIANAPOLIS ZOO, INDIANA REPERTORY THEATRE (IRT), and INDIANAPOLIS SYMPHONY ORCHESTRA (ISO).

KRANNERT CHARITABLE TRUST has also made substantial contributions to the arts in several fields, including the performing arts. From its inception in 1960 until its dissolution in 1987, the Trust advocated developing "Centers of Excellence." It participated in renovations of the INDIANA THEATRE (1980) for the IRT and the CIRCLE THEATRE (1982) for the ISO.

Another of the city's major arts foundations is the CLOWES FUND, established in 1956 by Dr. GEORGE HENRY ALEXANDER CLOWES. The CLOWES FUND financed the Clowes Pavilion at the IMA to house the Clowes art collection. The fund, as well as the Clowes family, has given generously to The Children's Museum, CONNER PRAIRIE, the INDIANAPOLIS BALLET, the INDIANAPOLIS OPERA, the Indianapolis Zoo, and other organizations.

EDITH WHITEHILL CLOWES, with her sons Allen Whitehill Clowes and the late Dr. George H. A. Clowes, Jr., was a major donor to the building of CLOWES MEMORIAL HALL, the center for performing arts at BUTLER UNIVERSITY, which opened October 18, 1963. Other arts facilities carrying the Clowes name include the Clowes Garden Gallery at The Children's Museum, the Clowes Pavilion at the IMA, and the Clowes Common at Conner Prairie. Allen Whitehill Clowes continues to contribute personally to the same arts institutions which captured his family's interest and support.

Some individuals have enhanced the arts through the contribution of their collections. Harrison Eiteljorg contributed his extensive collection to found the Eiteljorg Museum of American Indian and Western Art, which opened in 1989. His gift to the museum that bears his name was appraised at $20 million and was supplemented by a building fund gift of $1.5 million. Eiteljorg also contributed his collection of African art to the IMA. Other important art collections contributed to the IMA carry donor names of Fesler, Pantzer, Holliday, Lilly, and Herzman.

Some philanthropists have channeled their support into facilities for the arts. Those gifts include, in addition to Clowes Hall, the Circle Theatre, and the Indiana Theatre: Oldfields, given by Josiah K. Lilly III and his sister Ruth Lilly to the IMA (1967) to be used as a center for decorative arts; the WILLIAM CONNER home, given by ELI LILLY to Earlham College (1964) to be operated as a living history museum; the MORRIS-BUTLER HOME (1969) and the KEMPER HOUSE (1977) given by Eli Lilly to HISTORIC LANDMARKS FOUNDATION OF INDIANA; and a church, given by J. Scott Keller (1988) as a home for the PHOENIX THEATRE.

Others have contributed through their leadership and vision to the cultural life of Indianapolis. MARY STEWART CAREY envisioned a children's museum in Indianapolis (1925); John Herron left a bequest to build an art gallery and art school (1895); and LOWELL NUSSBAUM proposed a zoo (1946).

In recent years corporate sponsorships of arts events and activities have added greatly to the viability of the arts in the city. The steady support of Symphony on the Prairie by MARSH SUPERMARKETS, since the concerts began in 1982, is an example of corporate stewardship. Encouraging individual contributions through corporate matching gifts is exemplified by ELI LILLY AND COMPANY. The firm matches $2 for $1 the contributions of Lilly employees to the arts through its Patrons program, established in 1989 "to express [the company's] belief in the significance of the arts and culture to the enrichment of life in our communities."

CATHEDRAL ARTS was begun in 1968 by a volunteer group which, with a series of fund-raisers, aspired to "further the careers of young artists and the economic development of Indianapolis through arts programming." Indianapolis also has a number of women's volunteer groups, which have raised a considerable amount of money for the arts. Among those are the Children's Museum

Clowes Memorial Hall opened in 1963 at a cost of $3.5 million. [Butler University Archives]

Guild (1933), the Symphony Women's Committee (1937), the Alliance of the IMA (1958), Clowes Hall Women's Committee (1963), Indianapolis Zoological Guild (1964), and many others. The Children's Museum Guild, for example, has contributed over $2 million to the museum since its inception.

The PENROD SOCIETY, founded in 1966, supports the arts through an annual fair, currently raising about $80,000 each year. All proceeds of the event are granted to Indianapolis arts institutions. By 1991 the total accumulated grants surpassed $1 million.

Grassroots support, too, has been strong in Indianapolis. The children of the community gave their collections of treasured objects to help establish The Children's Museum, as well as their pennies for membership. Children's monetary contributions also were important in the establishment of the Indianapolis Zoo. One of the best examples of adult grassroots support, known as "Ardath's Army," was a group of 7,000 volunteers who rallied to the call of ARDATH Y. BURKHART to generate $275,000 to put WFYI, Indianapolis' public television station, on the air.

POLLY JONTZ
Conner Prairie

Philharmonic Orchestra of Indianapolis.

Conceived by Herman H. Rinne, local businessman and former INDIANAPOLIS SYMPHONY

ORCHESTRA member, the Philharmonic Orchestra began with three members in October, 1940. Open to all who played an instrument, the organization grew until it claimed 31 musicians by April, 1941. It established itself as one of the few symphonies that limits board membership to orchestra members. That same month the orchestra held its first concert at MANUAL HIGH SCHOOL. During World War II the Philharmonic performed only one or two concerts annually and donated proceeds to organizations such as the Navy Relief. In 1946 the group began performances outside Indianapolis, traveling to Danville and Anderson. The next year it incorporated under its present name. A decade later, LaVerne E. Newsome, first violin, became the first African-American member. The orchestra has provided scholarships and financially assisted its young players, and continues to donate monies above operating expenses to civic causes.

After the death of Rinne in 1949, the orchestra hired its first professional leader, Ernst Hoffman, music director of the Indiana University opera and philharmonic, although guest conductors occasionally have led the ensemble. The Philharmonic has made its home in Shortridge Junior High School, Marian College, and Arsenal Technical High School. The orchestra plays a mixture of subscription and free concerts during the year, including performances at Glendale Shopping Center each June.

JOAN CUNNINGHAM

Phoenix Theatre. Professional Equity theatre. The not-for-profit Phoenix Theatre opened in the fall of 1983 under the leadership of founding artistic director Bryan Fonseca. Actors and crew generally are local residents and include both vocational and avocational artists.

The Phoenix's first five seasons were performed in a converted 93–seat theatre in the Ambassador building in downtown Indianapolis. In 1988, Indianapolis developer J. Scott Keller donated a historic church to the theatre, and Phoenix productions have been staged there since October of that year. Built in 1907, the former church is located in the CHATHAM ARCH neighborhood northeast of downtown Indianapolis. Resto-

ration and renovation of the building were completed in August, 1992. A main stage, seating 150, was constructed in the gabled nave; the smaller Underground theatre downstairs seats 75. Both stages are used for Phoenix productions.

The Phoenix presents issue-oriented, contemporary American drama, usually in local, regional, or national premieres. In 1984 the Phoenix sponsored the Indiana New Plays Festival for Indiana playwrights. The following year the contest became national in scope and was renamed the Festival of Emerging Theatre, now an annual event. Winning plays are chosen from submissions of original, unproduced manuscripts, and receive full productions at the Phoenix during July and August. The Phoenix also offers beginning and advanced playwriting classes, as well as a regular schedule of acting and improvisation classes for adults and children.

Phoenix productions are supported by individual donors as well as corporations, foundations, and arts organizations.

JOYCE K. JENSEN

Phyllis Wheatley YWCA. The central YMCA of Indianapolis began in 1895, but a separate YWCA for African-Americans was not established until the 1920s. The idea for a black YWCA in Indianapolis was born from a desire of African-American Christian women to make a contribution to society. Their goal was finally realized when the Phyllis Wheatley Branch for Negro Women and Girls (named for a colonial era black woman poet) held its charter meeting on January 28, 1923. May B. Belcher, nationally known in YWCA circles for organizing a number of Phyllis Wheatley branches throughout the country, was the first executive director of the Indianapolis branch, serving from 1923 to 1944.

Following a vigorous two year fund-raising campaign, a new building, located at 653 North West Street, was dedicated in 1929. In keeping with goals and objectives expressed in the bylaws and constitution of the YWCA, the Phyllis Wheatley Branch sought to demonstrate its Christian purpose and ideals by its outreach to industrial, business, professional, and home women, as well as teenagers. This outreach consistently resulted in the use of its building for a variety of social and cultural activities sponsored by the YWCA and other civic, religious, and fraternal groups.

A decision by the board of directors of the Indianapolis YWCA to integrate the organization brought about the termination of the Phyllis Wheatley Branch in 1959. The building was sold to Prince Hall Masonic Temple in 1960 and was demolished in 1983 for the widening of West Street (later renamed Dr. Martin Luther King, Jr. Street).

ETTA RUSSEL

Pierre and Wright. Indianapolis architectural firm from 1925 to 1944. The partnership of Edward Dienhart Pierre (May 22, 1890–Mar. 27, 1971) and George Caleb Wright (Apr. 25, 1889 – Feb. 27, 1973) was one of the most important in Indianapolis during the first half of the 20th century.

Both men were young professionals when they relocated to Indianapolis and each had a significant impact on the growth and development of the capital during the next five decades. Pierre, a native of Fort Wayne, Indiana, moved to Indianapolis in 1919 and soon opened an architecture office. Wright, born in Libertyville, Illinois, worked for a Chicago architectural firm before settling in Indianapolis in 1923. The merging of their talents and energies in 1925 resulted in a series of substantial commissions during the late 1920s that allowed them to take leadership roles in the Indianapolis construction community.

The design contributions of Pierre and Wright to Indiana, particularly to Indianapolis, are important because of the wide variety of architectural styles in which they worked, such as Tudor and French Eclectic revival-styles and Art Deco; the high quality of construction; enduring buildings such as the INDIANA STATE LIBRARY AND HISTORICAL BUILDING and Williams Creek Estates; and the number of structures which remain, including Milo Stuart Hall, Oxford Gables, and Perry Baseball Stadium (now BUSH STADIUM).

Pierre handled the clients and the design process while Wright oversaw business operations and dealt with engineering matters. The commis-

sion which made their reputation was the 1925 *Indianapolis News* Ideal House Project at Williams Creek Estates, which featured five large houses designed in distinct revival-styles. This project exposed the firm to the clientele who would use their services for the coming two decades.

Pierre and Wright designed numerous commercial structures, including a suburban style grocery store at 46th and College Avenue (1931–1932). Surrounded by parking, it is thought to be the first "drive-in" store in Indiana. The largest commercial structure designed by the firm is the Old Trails Insurance Building (1928), which is located across the street from the Indiana State House and displays exceptional terra cotta with an American Indian design motif.

To promote the firm, Pierre and Wright entered various design competitions, including those for the George Rogers Clark Memorial (1930), ARSENAL TECHNICAL HIGH SCHOOL's Milo Stuart Memorial Building (1938), and the Indiana State Library and Historical Building (1932). The latter was the most substantial commission Pierre and Wright won and supposedly this was the first time an Indiana architect had won a national competition. The State Library was a model of modern library design and technology and was constructed using mainly Hoosier materials.

In 1937 Wright was appointed by President Franklin Roosevelt as the chief architect of the Federal Housing Administration in Indiana. He served in this position until 1940. Both partners had a longstanding interest in low-cost housing and were involved in many efforts to rid cities of slums. The firm was involved with the Purdue Housing Research Foundation and through the INDIANAPOLIS HOME SHOW and the Indianapolis Construction League developed numerous examples of quality, affordable housing. During World War II, Pierre and Wright helped organize Indiana's architects to work for the war effort. At this time the firm worked as Allied Architects and Engineers and obtained commissions for several military air fields and ammunition depots, as well as several public or low-cost housing projects in Indiana cities.

The partnership ended in 1944, but both men continued their careers as architects in Indianapolis. Pierre and Wright worked throughout their careers to enhance their profession and their community. They believed it was their professional and moral responsibility to be involved with the serious construction and design issues facing a changing city. Their most obvious contribution in Indianapolis is the many buildings that they designed, but more important is the impact they had on the design and construction professions in Indiana. Examples of their lasting influence include their work with government agencies to develop slum clearance laws and standardized building codes; developing lines of communication among individuals in the construction industry by organizing activities such as the Indianapolis Construction League and the Indianapolis Home Show; and advocating issues of urban planning, with Pierre creating a 1953 master plan for downtown development ("The Crossroads of America Plan") and a comprehensive parking study in the late 1940s, while in the 1960s Wright served as chairman of the first Metropolitan Indianapolis Planning Commission.

JEFFREY L. HUNTINGTON

Edward Pierre Collection, Indiana Division, Indiana State Library; Pierre and Wright Collection, Drawings and Documents Archives, College of Architecture and Planning, Ball State University, Muncie, Ind.

Pike Township. Northwestern Marion County township. Named for General Zebulon Pike, a hero of the War of 1812, Pike Township was organized in 1822. The first settlers chose sites on Eagle Creek or near the Michigan and Lafayette roads that were cut through the district in 1828 and 1829. George Coble, Sr., and

Jonathan Ingo founded AUGUSTA in 1829 on the MICHIGAN ROAD. Farther west along the Lafayette Road and Big Eagle Creek, TRADERS POINT was organized in 1834. These settlements were eclipsed by another community, NEW AUGUSTA, platted in 1855 as a stop on the Indianapolis and Lafayette Railroad. Known as both Hosbrook and Augusta Station until 1887 when the post office dubbed it New Augusta, the town prospered as a shipping point for agricultural products.

Throughout the 19th and early 20th centuries, Pike Township was largely undeveloped. The 1900 census counted 2,000 residents; in 1950 there were 3,400. In the 1960s, however, several improvements opened the township to intensive development. A bridge spanning White River at 38th Street was completed in 1962, and within a few years construction of I–465 and I–65 provided access to all parts of the city. A sewer construction project in 1969 and the completion of Eagle Creek Reservoir also spurred commercial and residential development.

Between 1960 and 1970 population increased 125 percent to 15,000 residents. By 1990 hundreds of new homes and 46 apartment complexes boosted the number to about 45,000. As the fastest-growing township in the county, Pike grew in the 1980s at a rate of 7 to 8 percent per year, roughly twice the county's average.

With the influx of families, the Metropolitan School District of Pike Township continued to expand. In the 1992–1993 school year the district served nearly 6,000 students in six elementaries, two middle schools, and one high school. Two new schools are under construction for completion in 1994.

In addition to residential development, sprawling commercial complexes emerged along West 86th Street and Zionsville Road. The Park 100 commercial and industrial park, begun in 1974, expanded to cover 1,800 acres by 1990. In the same area, two additional office parks were under construction in the early 1990s. The Dow Venture Center is the site of DOWELANCO, Marion Merrell Dow, and DowBrands, while the Northwest Business Center continues to develop a 72–acre complex of warehouse, retail, and commercial space. College Park features the PYRAMIDS, three office buildings that have become a focal point of

Selected Statistics for Pike Township, 1990	
Population	45,204
Population per Square Mile	1,030
Percent African-American	19.7
Percent 0 to 17 Years	23.0
Percent 65 Years and Over	7.9
Percent 25 Years and Over with a	
High School Degree or Equivalency	91.2
Percent 25 Years and Over with a College Degree	38.9
Per Capita Income in 1989	$20,420
Unemployment Rate (%)	3.4
Married-Couple Families as a	
Percent of Total Households	44.6
Median Home Value	$85,300

the area near Michigan Road and 86th Street. Extensive development along Guion Road includes warehouse and light industrial facilities, as well as the new Nabisco Foods Group complex.

In 1993 the township's largest employers included DowElanco, DowBrands, Golden Rule Insurance, Epson America, and Rock Island Refinery. Lafayette Square Shopping Center and nearby retail shops and restaurants employ additional residents.

Pike Township faces new challenges in the 1990s. Rapid growth has strained the township's fire protection, roads, and sewers, and in late 1993 Marathon Oil Company shut down Rock Island Refinery with its 255 jobs and lucrative tax base. City officials and residents believe controlled growth and improvements to the infrastructure are the key to future township development.

CATHLEEN F. DONNELLY

Berry R. Sulgrove, *History of Indianapolis and Marion County* (Philadelphia, 1884), 596–612; Department of Metropolitan Development, *Pike Township Comprehensive Planning Study Data Book* (1987); U.S. Census.

Plainfield. Hendricks County town, located west of Indianapolis along U.S. 40. Quakers from the Carolinas were the first to settle in the Plainfield area in 1823. A post office opened in 1835, and four years later Levi Jessup and Elias Hadley platted Plainfield alongside the NATIONAL ROAD, which opened in 1830. Within a short time businesses were serving travelers, though the road was often nearly impassable with mud. In 1842 a stagecoach carrying former president Martin Van Buren reportedly was tipped over in the mud east of Plainfield by a local driver to protest Van Buren's veto of a federal road improvements bill.

In 1850–1851 the Vandalia Railroad was constructed just north of the town. The depot served for many years as a shipping point for local agricultural products. The Terre Haute Interurban Line arrived in 1907 to transport passengers to and from Indianapolis and points west.

Correctional, medical, and educational institutions opened in Plainfield at an early date. The House of Refuge for Delinquent Boys (now known as the Indiana Boys School) was built in 1867.

From 1891 to 1918 the Plainfield Keeley Institute treated nearly 4,000 patients addicted to alcohol and nicotine. More recently the Indiana Youth Center, a minimum security facility for first-time offenders, opened in 1971. The first public school was organized in 1878, while Quakers set up a secondary school, Central Academy, in 1881. Today nearly 3,500 pupils are enrolled in Plainfield public schools, including three elementaries, a middle school, and one high school.

There was little industry in Plainfield until after World War II when PUBLIC SERVICE INDIANA built its headquarters in the town. New factories on the west side of Indianapolis also employed Plainfield workers. In 1960 the town counted nearly 5,500 residents; by 1970 the number had reached 8,000. Growth slowed slightly from 1980 to 1990, when the population increased from 9,000 to 10,400.

Public Service Indiana (now known as PSI Energy) brought hundreds of workers to the community in 1951. Forty years later the utility employs about 1,000 people in Plainfield. Other local employers include Oak Rite Manufacturing, Foto Lab, Jeco Plastics, and Rhoades Beverage Company, as well as the numerous restaurants and motels that line U.S. 40.

Within a few years employees transferred to the new United Airlines facility at Indianapolis International Airport are expected to settle in the Plainfield area. Additional commercial and residential growth, including a proposed theme park in southern HENDRICKS COUNTY, is predicted as Indianapolis expands westward in the 1990s.

CATHLEEN DONNELLY

Margaret Moore Post and Joe Lease, *Plainfield, Indiana: A Pictorial History* (privately published, 1986).

Planned Parenthood. A family-planning organization. The organization now known as Planned Parenthood of Central Indiana, Inc., was founded as the Indiana Birth Control League on February 4, 1932, headed by Anna Ray Burns. The League was established to serve only married women with two or more children, who had to be referred by a physician or a social service agency. No one able to pay for a physician was allowed access to the League. Publicity was studiously avoided. The first clinic opened in 1934 with daily operating costs between $18 and $19 a day.

In the 1940s, the League abolished its strict requirements for patients, undertook an aggressive publicity campaign and, in the 1950s, changed its name to Planned Parenthood. The organization, with new offices in the English Foundation building, provided extended hours to accommodate working women and added marriage counseling to its services. The U.S. Food and Drug Administration's approval of the birth control pill in 1960 and a changing social climate made it necessary for Planned Parenthood to open new clinics to accommodate an increasing number of clients. New challenges and controversy arose in the 1970s with the growing polarization of the "pro-choice" and "right-to-life" movements, fueled by the U.S. Supreme Court's guarantee in 1973 of the right to an abortion.

Services offered by Planned Parenthood grew to include birth control and pregnancy testing; health screening, including screening for sexually transmitted diseases; patient education; education and training programs for youth and adults in the community; counseling; and a resource center.

Planned Parenthood serves 33,000 clients annually. Its $4 million budget comes from patients' fees, federal and state funds, and private contributions. Its headquarters, known as the Education, Counseling and Resource Center, are at 3219 North Meridian Street.

JOHN SHERMAN

Playground and Pool Movement. The push for public playgrounds and swimming facilities in Indianapolis was part of the national progressive movement to save urban children. As early as the 1880s national and local reformers believed that supervised play and recreation helped build character and citizenship in children and protected them from playing in the dangerous and immoral environment of city streets.

In Indianapolis the development of pools and playgrounds was originally a private effort. In 1905 the Children's Aid Society started the first supervised bathing program at the Taylor Bath-

One of the earliest pools in the city was located at Washington and Delaware streets.
[Indiana Historical Society, Bass Collection, #29676]

house at Fall Creek and Senate Avenue and opened the Schissel Bathhouse at West Street and Central Canal near MILITARY PARK in 1907. The support and interest of the Indiana Federation of Women's Clubs helped to garner special appropriations from the city so that five additional free bathhouses opened along Fall Creek and White River in 1911.

These groups pushed for the passage of the original state playground law in 1913, which allowed local municipalities to set up playgrounds. Indianapolis had already committed police to patrol non-swimming areas and was operating six bathing places and nine playgrounds. The following year, 1914, the CHAMBER OF COMMERCE sponsored a study of recreational conditions and needs, hiring an agent of the National Playground Association of America (NPAA) to conduct the study. As a result of recommendations to expand facilities and supervised programming, the following year there were 7 bathing beaches, 3 swimming pools, 10 school grounds maintained by the city, 12 swimming holes and bathhouses, and 28 playgrounds in operation. Critics argued that such expenditure on public recreation was wasteful.

Momentum for playgrounds continued, however, so that in 1916 the Indiana University Extension Division, along with the NPAA, sponsored a statewide recreation conference in Indianapolis. The extension division then established a training program for playground leaders administered by Dr. Henry Curtis, who had experience in establishing playgrounds in other cities.

By 1920 the recreation division of the Indianapolis Park Board had assumed much of the responsibility for pools and playgrounds. Under R. Walter Jarvis the park board operated 40 playgrounds, arranged according to a survey of the population to serve children within a half-mile radius of their homes. The park board also took over the training of playground leaders and lifeguards. The playground law in 1925 legalized this arrangement; two years later another state law allowed cities to collect taxes for local recreation.

By 1930 many people believed that there was no more room for additional playgrounds in Indianapolis, yet a 1929 recreational survey, sponsored by the Indianapolis Council of Social Agencies and conducted by the NPAA, called for more and better playgrounds and further cooperation with schools. The council study was virtually the last act of the "playground movement" in Indianapolis, with the municipal Park Board assuming total control thereafter. As of 1993 there are 56 playgrounds and 16 pools in operation in Indianapolis.

Throughout these formative years pools and playgrounds were open and supervised six days a week, eight hours a day. There were segregated playgrounds for African-American children that, along with facilities in the poorer districts, were not usually well equipped or supervised. The standard playground equipment included swings, slides, sandboxes, maypoles, seesaws, and athletic fields. Play leaders organized sports, such as baseball leagues for both boys and girls, and conducted structured activities including weekly storytelling, sand pile contests, sewing for girls, crafts, swim lessons, and pageants.

MICHELLE D. HALE

Chamber of Commerce, *Indianapolis Recreation Survey* (Indianapolis, 1914); Children's Aid Association, *Report of the Public Recreation Committee of the Children's Aid Ass'n of Indianapolis* (Indianapolis, 1908); Council of Social Agencies, *The Leisure of a People: Report of a Recreation Survey of Indianapolis* (Indianapolis, 1929).

Pleasant Run Children's Homes. Residential treatment facility for children and young adults. Pleasant Run Children's Homes (PRCH), one of the oldest children's homes in the nation, was founded in 1867 as the (German) General Protestant Orphan Home. Children orphaned by the Civil War were housed in a building at 1404 South State Avenue, which remained the PRCH residence until 1981.

The home's first constitution stated that "the orphanage is to receive all poor children of Marion County, Indiana, who are without parents, for education without compensation." Between 1867 and 1941, over 2,000 children received care. On November 1, 1941, the Indianapolis Orphans' Home and the Evangelical Lutheran Orphans' Home merged with the General Protestant Orphan Home. All the orphans lived in the South State Avenue residence. Support came from the Indianapolis Community Fund.

In 1971 the General Protestant Orphan Home became Pleasant Run Children's Home, so named because Pleasant Run Parkway borders the property. The name change reflected the transition from serving a declining orphan population to serving a growing population of abused, abandoned, and neglected children. All residents were now wards of the court.

In response to the treatment needs of the children of the 1980s, the transition from a single residence to several group homes began in 1981. Five group homes, with a total capacity of 48, serve children ages 6–18. Treatment programs range from foster care and home-based services to family reunification and long-term care. In addition, 18- to 21–year-olds participate in an Emancipation Apartment Project, which teaches independent living skills.

PRCH is state licensed, nonprofit, and nonsectarian. Its annual budget of ca. $3 million comes from state and federal funds, UNITED WAY, local fund-raising, and grants from charitable organizations.

RICHARD W. SMITH
Smith-Brandt Associates

Ray C. Enmeier, *Pleasant Run Children's Home* (Indianapolis, 1980).

Plymouth Church. Organized in 1857 as the first Congregational church in Indianapolis, Plymouth's 31 original members met in a private home and the Senate chamber of the State House until their first church building on the northwest corner of Monument Circle was finished in 1859. Rev. Nathaniel Alden Hyde served as the first full-time pastor. In 1867 a 500–seat auditorium was added to the church.

Plymouth underwent a transformation in 1877 when Rev. OSCAR C. MCCULLOCH assumed leadership of the church. McCulloch was a proponent of the Social Gospel, a liberal theology that emphasized social action. Plymouth's small, heavily indebted membership was initially indifferent to his views, but soon supported a plan to transform Plymouth Church into an "institutional" church which offered a variety of social services. Early programs included the Plymouth Christian Union for "general charitable and relief purposes" and the Plymouth Friendly Society, a woman's relief organization.

Plymouth sold its first church building on the Circle to William H. English around 1880 but continued to lease it until January, 1883. The church was later torn down and replaced by the ENGLISH HOTEL AND OPERA HOUSE, although a small chapel with stained glass windows was kept intact. The congregation then rented space in the Grand Opera House at Pennsylvania and Ohio streets until its new church building on the southeast corner of New York and Meridian streets was completed in January, 1884.

Membership grew at the new location, with attendance at the morning service averaging 500 people. Sunday evening services were quite popular, attracting as many as 1,000 people each week. Aimed at the laboring class, McCulloch enlivened his evening sermons with Stereoptican slides of well-known religious paintings. Plymouth's new building included upgraded facilities such as a 1,200–seat auditorium, classrooms, a gymnasium, a library, and office space which was leased to charitable organizations.

In 1884 the congregation adopted a policy of not requiring belief in a particular creed as a prerequisite to joining the church, a policy which markedly increased church membership. That same year Plymouth instituted one of its most successful social programs, the Plymouth Institute, which provided educational and cultural opportunities to the city's young adults. Early classes covered literature, bookkeeping, French, and drawing. Another popular social program was the Plymouth Savings and Loan Association, formed in 1885 to provide investment opportunities and loans for mortgages. It was so successful that a second savings and loan was added a year and a half later.

When McCulloch died in 1891, Plymouth Church lacked the forceful leadership to continue many of his social programs. In 1903 its property was purchased by the government for construction of a FEDERAL BUILDING on the site. Five years later Plymouth merged with Mayflower Church to form First Congregational Church, which met at 16th and Delaware streets. In 1957 First Congregational Church left the downtown area, relocating to 7171 North Pennsylvania Street.

DEBORAH B. MARKISOHN

Genevieve C. Weeks, *Oscar Carleton McCulloch* (Indianapolis, 1976); *Indianapolis Star*, Dec. 22, 1907, Nov. 14, 1942; *Indianapolis Star Magazine*, Jan. 19, 1958.

Pogue, George (ca. 1765–1821). One of the two pioneers credited with being the first settler in Indianapolis. When state commissioners convened at JOHN MCCORMICK's cabin in June, 1820, to select a new state capital, about 15 families resided in the area. Among them McCormick and George Pogue are considered to be the area's first permanent white settlers. Family histories claimed that Pogue, a blacksmith, and his family of seven left Connersville, Indiana, in February, 1819. They cut a trail in line with present-day Brookville Road, arrived at the future site of Indianapolis on March 2, and settled approximately where POGUE'S RUN crossed today's Michigan Street.

Pogue's place in the local lore of Indiana's state capital was enhanced by his mysterious disappearance. In April, 1821, Pogue ventured into the woods near the settlement searching for lost horses he believed to have been stolen and never returned.

Historian JACOB PIATT DUNN argued in his *Greater Indianapolis* (1910) that Pogue actually arrived March 2, 1820, one year later than family recollections indicated, noting that Pogue's widow registered at an 1854 old settlers meeting as having arrived in 1820, not 1819. Dunn claimed that in early 1819 Ute Perkins arrived in the area and built a cabin along a creek, known briefly thereafter as Perkins Creek. Depressed by the isolated life, Perkins returned to Rush County, and the Pogues, who arrived the following year, occupied Perkins' vacant cabin. After Pogue's disappearance settlers renamed the creek Pogue's Run, memorializing him as the first permanent settler within the congressional donation lands.

SHERYL D. VANDERSTEL

John H. B. Nowland, *Early Reminiscences of Indianapolis* (Indianapolis, 1870); Jacob Piatt Dunn, *Greater Indianapolis* (Chicago, 1910).

Pogue's Run. Small stream which broke the Mile Square's grid pattern. GEORGE POGUE and his family were among the first permanent settlers in the Indianapolis area. In the spring of 1821 some of Pogue's horses disappeared. When he failed to return from his search for them, his neighbors began calling the stream beside his family's cabin Pogue's Run.

In 1821, when ALEXANDER RALSTON platted Indianapolis, he had to modify the overall grid pattern on the southeastern corner of the town where Pogue's Run flowed. The land around the stream was swampy and the stream itself was mosquito infested in the warm months. Before the state legislators moved to the city in 1825, they appropriated $50 to clean out Pogue's Run, "a source of pestilence."

In 1863, soldiers stopped a train carrying men who had protested against the Lincoln government at a Democratic convention. As they searched the passengers in one train car those in a second car discarded their guns and knives into the waters of Pogue's Run, which ran alongside the track. This event, which dramatized Indiana's Civil War tensions, became known as the BATTLE OF POGUE'S RUN.

In 1914, the city ran the portion of the stream inside the MILE SQUARE into the storm sewers, finally making it possible for continuous platting of the area. Outside of the Mile Square, city planner GEORGE E. KESSLER turned the land beside the creek into one of the city's parkways. Pogue's Run still flows along Brookside Parkway, northeast of downtown, in part dictating Brookside Park's linear layout.

CONNIE J. ZEIGLER

Pogue's Run, Battle of (May 20, 1863). Derisive name given by the REPUBLICAN PARTY to events surrounding a stormy session of the state Democratic convention in Indianapolis in May, 1863. The meeting occurred shortly after President Abraham Lincoln had issued the Emancipation Proclamation and during difficult times militarily. Nevertheless, some 10,000 Democrats assembled near the STATE HOUSE on May 20, literally under the guns of a large military force commanded by Col. JOHN COBURN. The tensions of the period and unruly men on both sides, including soldiers home on furlough, led to repeated disturbances that threatened to develop into open rioting, something that finally happened about 4 P.M., shortly after Senator THOMAS A. HENDRICKS had begun to speak to the convention. That evening, as many of the delegates were leaving the city by railroad, an incident occurred that gave a name to the entire day's proceedings. Armed soldiers and others stopped the trains in order to search the passengers for weapons, which prompted many Democrats to toss knives, pistols, and rifles out the car windows, some of which landed in the small creek, POGUE'S RUN, that flows through the southeastern MILE SQUARE. Estimates of the number of arms collected following the "Battle of Pogue's Run" varied from 500 to 2,000. According to Republican accounts of the episode, the soldiers had halted a meeting of traitors to the Union cause; the Democratic version described the day's events as still more assaults upon constitutional rights by the supporters of President Lincoln and Governor OLIVER P. MORTON.

RALPH D. GRAY
Indiana University–Purdue University,
Indianapolis

Poles. In 1875 Polish immigrants, probably Kashubes from the Pomerania–Baltic coast region of Germany, were involved in organizing Sacred Heart Catholic Church on Indianapolis' south side. By 1900 Catholics and Jews born in Poland constituted the seventh largest foreign-born group in the city. Some lived on Eddy Street south of Union Station and others near KINGAN AND COMPANY meatpackers. Poles from Galicia in Austria resided on the west side, worked in area foundries, and attended Holy Trinity Catholic Church in HAUGHVILLE with the Slovenes. Although the Polish-born generally settled in St. Joseph, La Porte, and Allen counties, by the end of World War I almost 400 resided in Indianapolis. Among them was Alex Tuschinski, a young immigrant who in 1917 founded Hillsdale Nursery on 80 acres south of Castleton.

The 1930 census indicated that 1,195 inhabitants of the capital were of Polish background. Some belonged to a lodge which sponsored social activities and offered insurance coverage (the Polish National Alliance of Chicago). After World War II displaced persons and migrants from northern Indiana enlarged the local Polish contingent to almost 1,500 by 1970. Over 5 percent of the state's Polish-born lived in Indianapolis in 1980. According to the 1990 census approximately 1 percent of Marion County's population had a Polish ancestor.

The Polish Cultural Society of Indiana was founded in 1976 as an outgrowth of Polish ethnic participation in the nation's bicentennial observance. It also sponsored a statewide relief campaign for Poland during the early 1980s. The Polish Century Club organized later. Local Polish groups observe "Koleda" (Epiphany), Dyngus Day (Easter Monday), and "Dozynki" (harvest festival), and represent Polish culture and serve traditional foods at the annual INTERNATIONAL FESTIVAL.

JAMES J. DIVITA
Marian College

Police Athletic League. Police-sponsored youth organization. Officer Forrest Higgs organized the first PAL club at Rhodius Park (southwestern Indianapolis) in 1941 as part of a new crime prevention program. The Kiwanis Club underwrote the project during its first year, but in 1942 it was taken over by the INDIANAPOLIS POLICE DEPARTMENT's Juvenile Aid Division. PAL clubs sponsored athletic leagues for boys ages six to 18. By 1947 Indianapolis had nine PAL clubs with a full-time police officer assigned to supervise them and an annual participation of nearly 5,000 boys.

The PAL clubs split with the Juvenile Aid unit in 1952. As a result, the Indianapolis Police Department created a PAL board of directors and assigned an officer to each of the nine PAL clubs. The organization grew rapidly over the next decade. By 1963 there were 13 PAL centers serving 10,000 regular members. Monthly attendance at each center exceeded 30,000.

In 1972 differences between PAL and the DEPARTMENT OF PARKS AND RECREATION led to the removal of the 11 PAL centers from city parks to five public housing projects. PAL continued to operate centers in the city's public housing projects throughout the 1970s.

Today PAL operates seven centers located in city schools, public housing projects, and community centers. These centers provide organized sports and other activities for over 2,000 underprivileged children each year. The Indianapolis Police Department employs the league's ten staff members; the PAL board of directors, an entirely civilian group since the late 1980s, provides an executive director.

WILLIAM D. DALTON

Police Department. See Indianapolis Police Department

Police Mutiny (November, 1913). Occasioned by a streetcar strike, the mutiny was the most serious breach of police discipline and the greatest breakdown in public order ever seen in Indianapolis. The Amalgamated Association of Street and Electric Railway Employees, attempting to organize the 900 workers of the Indianapolis Traction and Terminal Company, called for a strike of motormen and conductors on October 31, 1913. Determined to continue operations, the company dismissed union men and summoned 300 professional strikebreakers ("sluggers" and Pinkertons) from Chicago.

Saturday morning service was near normal, but throughout the day more crews joined the strike or fled their posts. Unruly crowds stoned and wrecked six trolley cars, cut overhead trolley wires, and frightened passengers away. A police squad protecting repair crews met a hail of brickbats and stones, forcing its retreat. The strike disrupted the interurban system that connected Indianapolis with many communities in the state. When the afternoon train carrying the strikebreakers arrived at UNION STATION, police cleared a passage through a large, hostile crowd to strikebreakers' headquarters in the Louisiana Street car barns, but for the most part the police refused to interfere.

On Saturday afternoon Mayor SAMUEL (LEW) SHANK told Governor Samuel M. Ralston that order could not be restored without the state's intervention. He also asked the Marion County sheriff to deputize 200 men to aid police, but the sheriff refused, claiming he lacked authority.

The issue that led to the mutiny of 33 policemen was the traction company's demand that police ride the cars to protect the strikebreakers. Among the 200 patrolmen were many former craftsmen and workingmen. Only 20 arrests were made the first day, and there were reports of police standing by while crews were intimidated and cars vandalized. On Sunday a patrolman resigned rather than ride the cars as ordered. Shank, who witnessed the scene, supported the officer's action and pledged to defend him in any future hearing, a statement that was widely reported. On Tuesday Chief Martin Hyland again ordered police to ride the cars, but 29 turned in their badges rather than do so. Short of men and fearing the complete disintegration of the force, Hyland did not accept their resignations; he placed them in other duties, promising to charge them with insubordination later.

The worst affray took place Wednesday when rioters in a crowd of 8,000 wrecked a car on Illinois Street. Thirty were injured, seven strikebreakers and two policemen seriously. The next day Governor Ralston quietly assembled 2,000 guardsmen at armories and in the basement of the State House. On Friday the traction company bowed to public opinion and pressure from Ralston and accepted arbitration by the Public Service Commission. Within three hours the strikebreakers were on a train to Chicago. The next day trolley service resumed.

On November 12 Hyland charged 33 officers with insubordination. When the public safety board next day suspended the accused there was talk among police of a general walkout. At the trial—the board acted as a court—Mayor Shank supported the men: to ride the cars would have dangerously worsened matters. All but one of the men claimed they had been asked to volunteer or they argued the mayor's policy superseded the chief's orders. All acknowledged a refusal to ride with strikebreakers. Petitions condemning the officers came from business organizations; petitions in support, one with 4,000 signatures, from labor. The board voted 2 to 1 for acquittal; Hyland, a 29–year veteran, then resigned, as did the minority board member. With labor troubles impending among the teamsters of the city, angry businessmen called on Shank to resign or face impeachment. To head off the latter, the mayor promised to resign if the teamsters struck. When his mediation efforts failed to prevent a strike, Shank resigned on November 28, barely a month before the end of his term.

WILLIAM DOHERTY
Marian College

Indianapolis Star and *Indianapolis News*, Nov., 1913.

Political Journalism. Politics has often been called Indiana's second favorite indoor sport after basketball. So it was a natural evolution that political journalism in Indiana and its capital city would become a spirited, partisan endeavor. Since 1804, when Elihu Stout's (Vincennes) *Indiana Gazette*, Indiana Territory's first paper, announced a popular referendum for representative territorial government, Hoosiers have practiced intensely competitive politics, and newspaper coverage has followed.

In January, 1822, George Smith and NATHANIEL BOLTON began the *INDIANAPOLIS GA-*

ZETTE, the newly designated capital's first paper. It covered the Indiana General Assembly meeting in Corydon and printed laws adopted by that body. Although the *Gazette* initially took a nonpartisan stance, it later put legislators on notice that the press would be watching their activities. Beginning with the General Assembly's first session in Indianapolis in 1825, Indianapolis newspapers possessed a particular responsibility to cover legislative activities for the state. Likewise, the legislature, acknowledging the importance of the press to the public and to its own political well-being, began providing accommodations for journalists representing state and local newspapers.

As political factionalism increased newspapers joined the fray by attacking opposing party leaders and editorializing when necessary, thus giving each paper a distinct political overtone and readership. The *Indianapolis State Sentinel* (formerly *Gazette*) became the leading Democratic organ under the editorship of GEORGE AND JACOB CHAPMAN. Subsequent publisher Austin H. Brown used the paper to attack and expose the secrecy of the Know-Nothings. The *INDIANA JOURNAL*, originally a Whig paper, joined the Republican ranks in 1856 and retained that affiliation until the 20th century. *The Family Visitor* promoted the temperance cause for two years, and the *INDIANAPOLIS FREEMAN* and the *Free Soil Banner* both battled the slavery issue. During campaigns candidates relied heavily on the newspapers as vehicles of party propaganda and as a means of disseminating their messages to the voters.

The printing of the state's official documents also took on a political flavor locally. In 1825 JOHN DOUGLASS, publisher of the *Indiana Journal*, was named state printer. Beginning in 1851, however, the contract became a lucrative prize every session, alternating between the *Indianapolis State Sentinel* (Democrat) and the *Indianapolis Journal* (Whig/Republican) depending upon which party held the legislative majority. Facing a divided legislature in 1883, the state awarded the contract to the nonpartisan WILLIAM B. BURFORD PRINTING COMPANY.

Journalists played significant roles in monitoring politicians and espousing party positions in their writings. LEW WALLACE, the Brookville native and later author of *Ben-Hur*, covered the legislature for the *Indianapolis Journal* at age 18 and co-edited the *Free Soil Banner* (c. 1848). Schuyler Colfax, later vice-president under Ulysses S. Grant, worked as a legislative reporter for the *Indiana Journal* (1842–1843, 1847). Neither Wallace nor Colfax was unusual for his time since partisanship of the press was the norm well into the 20th century.

Three newspapers clearly represented the political spectrum of the late 19th and early 20th centuries. The *INDIANAPOLIS NEWS* began as an independent newspaper in December, 1869, and became a Republican organ when William Henry Smith and CHARLES W. FAIRBANKS acquired it in the 1890s. By the 1920s the *News* was among the state's most influential papers. The *INDIANAPOLIS STAR*, begun in June, 1903, as a Republican daily, later absorbed the *Journal* (1904) and the *Sentinel* (1906). The *INDIANAPOLIS SUN* began as a Populist newspaper in 1888, but in 1914 became the *INDIANAPOLIS TIMES*, supporting the Democrats who controlled the State House and the White House. When the Scripps-Howard newspaper chain acquired the paper in 1923 it espoused Republican sentiments on national issues, voiced a Democratic perspective on state and local issues, and was, in subsequent years, the closest thing in the capital to a liberal newspaper. Journalist LOUIS LUDLOW characterized the press during this period, however, as a classic example of "partisan journalism of the slapstick variety."

Political journalism heated up in Indianapolis when EUGENE C. PULLIAM bought the *Star* (1944) and later the *News* (1946). Pulliam unabashedly used both papers, clearly perceived as Republican mouthpieces, to promote his strident conservatism. For managing editor of the *News* Pulliam retained C. Walter McCarty (1944–1965), who was less Republican and conservative than the state GOP and who advocated objective coverage of politics. Beginning in 1948, however, Pulliam assigned LESTER M. HUNT, described by *Times* political reporter Charles M. Maddox as "a hatchet man," to cover the State House and to do his political bidding. Responding to Pulliam's desire to expose county welfare fraud and secrecy, Hunt prepared a story with false charges and highly slanted reporting, which were refuted and condemned by the journalistic community.

Several journalists played key roles in covering the local political scene. Hunt's primary nemesis was IRVING LEIBOWITZ, a New Yorker whom the *Times* hired in the late 1940s and who launched a journalistic war on Pulliam and the *Star.* While Leibowitz had his share of enemies, he generally was respected for his political coverage. His departure for Ohio following the *Times'* demise in 1965 was mourned by many, especially Democrats who lost an important sympathetic voice. MAURICE EARLY joined the *Star* in 1916 and covered the police beat and City Hall before moving to cover the General Assembly in 1921 (which he did until 1953). Known for his column "The Day in the Legislature" (called "The Day in Indiana" following the legislature's recess) which ran 1939–1954, Early developed a reputation for his fairness and for writing with more authority than his colleague Hunt.

In the late 1920s former *Times* reporter EUGENE JEPSON "JEP" CADOU, SR., who had covered the DAVID (D. C.) STEPHENSON trial, joined the Indianapolis bureau of International News Service, which later merged with United Press to form UPI. Cadou, who covered every biennial legislative session from 1925 to 1967, began a tradition of addressing the General Assembly at the end of each session; he was named an honorary member of the State Senate in 1963.

EDWARD ZIEGNER, hired by the *News* as State House reporter in 1946, became director of the paper's legislative bureau in 1953 and its political editor in the 1960s. Taking the legislative beat when Cadou died in 1968, Ziegner continued until retiring in 1985. Dubbed the "dean of the State House press corps," he held court in his news shack with lawmakers and other state officials who sought his counsel. Although respected by both parties, Ziegner represented the end of the line for such advocacy journalism. His peers, notably Gordon Englehart of the *Louisville Courier-Journal*, Patrick J. Traub of the *Star*, Jack Colwell of the *South Bend Tribune*, and Bob Ashley of the *Gary Post-Tribune*, clearly rejected reporting that was not an arm's length away from the decision makers. After Pulliam's son Eugene S. became publisher of the *News* and the *Star* in 1975, both papers dropped partisan biases from their news pages. Partisan editorial associations, while still functioning in the 1990s, wield considerably less clout than they once did, particularly among newspapers that regularly cover the State House.

The press corps of the 1990s is more diverse than ever. Many women and members of racial minorities are full-time reporters. But perhaps because they enjoy less influence and are more removed from the political process, modern reporters come and go from the State House beat, sometimes with dizzying speed. Some may argue that that means political journalism's heyday has passed; others, however, would argue that objectivity is more desirable, more ethical, and certainly more appropriate.

MARY E. DIETER
Louisville Courier-Journal

Political Power. Power is the ability to get things done that would not otherwise happen. Since about 1960 in Indianapolis persons in both the public and private sectors have shared power in differing degrees at different times. A generation ago a small elite ran Indianapolis. Most important decisions were either made or approved by EUGENE C. PULLIAM, publisher of the INDIANAPOLIS STAR and INDIANAPOLIS NEWS, WILLIAM BOOK, president of the CHAMBER OF COMMERCE, FRANK MCKINNEY, SR., chairman of the old American Fletcher National Bank, or FRANK MCHALE, a prominent Democratic attorney.

After the 1960s this circle widened tremendously, to the city's benefit. UNIGOV merged the suburbs (predominantly white and Republican) into the old city (predominantly black and Democratic). Criticized as a Republican power grab and as an effort to restrict African-American participation in the city's governance, it brought a younger leadership into the life of the city and enabled those who lived in the suburbs to identify with what was going on downtown. Also, under the leadership of EUGENE N. BEESLEY, the LILLY ENDOWMENT turned its attention to helping the city develop a vision of its future. The endowment made significant grants for that purpose, supporting many projects that promoted neighborhood and downtown revitalization. Public/private partnerships in the 1970s and 1980s, such as the CORPORATE COMMUNITY COUNCIL, the Mayor's La-

The Claypool Hotel hosted the Democratic
State Convention in June, 1940.
[Indiana Historical Society,
Larry Foster Collection, #763]

bor Advisory Council, the COMMISSION FOR
DOWNTOWN, the INDIANAPOLIS PROJECT, and the
Indianapolis ECONOMIC DEVELOPMENT COMMIS-
SION, expanded the decision-making process.
Neighborhood and community-based organizations became more vocal and effective participants: through such groups as the GREATER
INDIANAPOLIS PROGRESS COMMITTEE, task forces,
and Unigov with its numerous appointed boards
and large legislative body, a consensus-building
process emerged that broadened citizen participation in the city's affairs.

The public and private sectors have joined
forces on most important decisions in Indianapolis
since the 1960s, as witnessed by the formation of
Unigov and large economic development projects.
The decision to build the HOOSIER DOME offers an
example of this public-private partnership. The
mayor asked the Indianapolis Chamber of Commerce to undertake a study of its feasibility and de-
sirability; the implementation of the idea involved
ever widening circles of political and business
leadership, including public hearings at the city
and state levels. The same process occurred with
the CIRCLE CENTRE MALL and UNITED AIRLINES IN-
DIANAPOLIS MAINTENANCE CENTER projects in the
1980s and the infrastructure projects and community-based policing in the 1990s. Less often, public input is sought initially and not simply in
response to a leader's ideas. The decision by the

governor and mayor in the late 1970s not to
extend I–69 downtown to the inner loop was
made after public hearings were held and citizens
had the opportunity to express their concerns
about the cost of the project and displacement of
residents.

Full-time political officeholders possess more
power than the average citizen, but it is counter-
balanced by economic power, which has always
been an important source of influence in Indianapolis. This condition may change in the 1990s
since buyouts and mergers have reshaped the Indianapolis economy. Twenty-eight major local corporations either disappeared or were purchased
by out-of-state interests from 1990 to 1993—and
with turnover occurring more frequently in the
city's corporate leadership, the mayor's office has
gained more power. Also, the suburbanization
and professionalization of the city have so dif-
fused people's energies and allegiances that real
power-sharing in the modern city is extraordinar-
ily difficult to achieve. Nonetheless, the heads of
the large corporations, particularly ELI LILLY AND
COMPANY, the banks, utilities, and newspapers,
plus the local philanthropies, most notably Lilly
Endowment, the INDIANAPOLIS FOUNDATION, and
the former KRANNERT CHARITABLE TRUST, still possess enormous capacity to make projects go or to
stop them. Without the support of Eli Lilly and
Company chairman Richard Wood, the Circle
Centre Mall project would have foundered. Nor
would the Hoosier Dome have been built without
support of the city's newspapers.

At best, Indianapolis has benefited from a
partnership between those with economic and
those with political power, although criticism has
sometimes been leveled that it was not sufficiently
inclusive or open. The so-called CITY COMMITTEE
was an informal group of bright, young, second-
tier leaders in Indianapolis during the 1980s who
supported and promoted the idea of using sports
to leverage economic development opportunity;
after its existence became public knowledge, however, its members were criticized for being too se-
cretive and exclusive. Such criticism has never
been leveled at the Corporate Community Council, a similar organization of top business leaders,
with the mayor, governor, and university presidents as ex officio members.

Throughout these decades of change the city's leadership remained overwhelmingly white and male. Women and minorities have made advances since 1960; the percentage of African-Americans and women in the city's police and fire departments, for example, increased markedly in the officer ranks, and blacks and women gained a larger percentage of seats on mayorally appointed boards and agencies. The city had its first black fire and police chiefs and deputy mayors during these years. Yet in a 1993 survey of the 20 top power brokers in town, only two were black and none was a woman.

Empowerment of others has become an important part of the city's governance. Community-based organizations, neighborhood associations, minorities, and advocacy groups have assumed an increasingly greater role in recent years. In the late 1980s neighborhood forums were held in each township to receive citizen input about needed services; in the 1990s scores of citizens were involved in a visioning process to capture a picture of where Indianapolis needed to be improving as the century comes to a close. The vitality of such constituencies will constitute an important check on the tendency of political and economic leaders to aggregate too much power or to decide public matters in secret.

WILLIAM H. HUDNUT III

Politics, Antebellum. Politics in Indianapolis in the decades before the Civil War reflected the stresses of a growing city against a background of national issues and changing political parties. Disintegration of the Whig party about 1854 created opportunities for minority factions before the Republicans emerged to become, along with the older DEMOCRATIC PARTY, one of the two major parties in the state.

After Indianapolis secured its city charter in 1847, local political battles revolved around electing officials and providing adequate governmental services. The first charter provided for a mayor to serve a two-year term and a city council of seven members to serve one-year terms. Revisions to the charter in 1853, 1857, and 1859 doubled the councilmen from each ward, changed the terms

of all officials first to two and ultimately to four years, and increased the taxing limit.

The Whigs successfully secured the charter and elected the first mayors. The demise of the Whigs in the mid–1850s allowed Democrats to carry most of the elections until 1858 when the Republicans elected their first mayor and a majority of the city council.

By 1850 Indianapolis was the state's largest community; ten years later its population had more than doubled. The growth placed a great burden on basic services which the young community could ill afford. Although the first city election approved a tax for a free school system, subsequent levies for street improvements, gas lights on the streets, a hospital, and full-time police and firemen were not always successful.

At times reform issues such as TEMPERANCE touched Indianapolis. Local temperance advocates achieved a temporary victory in 1853 when the legislature gave each township the option to prohibit alcohol sales. After the Indiana Supreme Court declared this law unconstitutional, temperance supporters made it a political issue. Former Whigs and members of the American or Know-Nothing party campaigned as the People's party in 1854 on a prohibition plank, while Democrats, including many GERMANS, condemned the "intemperate" position of their opponents. The victory of the People's party brought a new law that prohibited the manufacture and distribution of alcohol except for medical purposes. German saloon keepers in Indianapolis opposed the law, and the newly created police force had to quell a series of beer riots in 1855. In the BEEBE TEMPERANCE CASE (1855) the state Supreme Court struck down the law and the city disbanded its police force.

Less popular was the women's rights movement. The state constitutional convention in 1850–1851 defeated Robert Dale Owen's proposals to improve the legal standing of women. Although a women's rights convention met in Indianapolis in October, 1855, and in 1859 Dr. Mary F. Thomas presented a women's rights petition to the legislature, the major parties continued to ignore the issue.

The antislavery movement attracted the greatest interest. Indianapolis became increasingly caught up in the slavery question, especially as it related to the territories. While a number of Quakers and settlers from New England opposed slavery, many Hoosiers from the South did not object to it and racism remained strong in Indiana. The Fugitive Slave Law of 1850 brought new concerns. While Hoosiers disliked its provisions, leading politicians supported it and the Compromise of 1850 as the best way to preserve the Union.

A notorious case in Indianapolis emphasized the dangers of the Fugitive Slave Law. A bogus claim from a Missourian led officials in 1853 to arrest John Freeman of Indianapolis as a fugitive slave. Freeman was a free black who had come north in 1844 from Georgia and through hard work had become a businessman. His arrest aroused many citizens. A lawyer proved that the charges were groundless, but Freeman had to sell much of his property to pay legal fees (see FREEMAN FUGITIVE SLAVE CASE). The incident led many to view slavery in a new, alarming light. Other national crises over slavery in the territories continued to agitate politics in Indianapolis throughout the 1850s.

Indiana was a key state in the ELECTION OF 1860, and Indianapolis witnessed a number of political rallies. Republicans sent German immigrant Carl Schurz to woo Indiana's large German vote. Democratic candidate Stephen Douglas appeared at the state fairgrounds. Democrats appealed to racism while Republicans downplayed their radical image by emphasizing their economic program and willingness to accept slavery where it already existed. Conservative Know-Nothings and Whigs supported the Constitutional Union party as the only way to preserve the Union. The result was a victory both statewide and local for Abraham Lincoln and the Republican state ticket. Lincoln carried Marion County with 5,024 votes to 3,252 for Douglas.

Although Hoosiers had doubted that the southern states would secede if Lincoln were elected, they were uncertain about the future. At an Indianapolis rally in late November, Governor-elect Henry S. Lane and others called for calm; however, incoming Lieutenant Governor OLIVER P. MORTON declared that the choice was between disunion and war and he favored war. Debate

continued until the firing on Fort Sumter released a wave of unionism that temporarily obliterated political divisions in the city and the state.

RICHARD A. GANTZ
Indiana State Museum

Polley, Frederick (Aug. 15, 1875–Sept. 9, 1957). Painter, etcher, printmaker, writer, and teacher. Polley was born in Union City, Indiana. His art instruction included study at the Corcoran Art School, Washington, D.C., and the HERRON SCHOOL OF ART, under WILLIAM FORSYTH. He was also a student of James Hopkins in Provincetown, Massachusetts.

As an art teacher, Polley began his career at the Herron School of Art. Later, for over 20 years, Polley taught art at ARSENAL TECHNICAL HIGH SCHOOL in Indianapolis, becoming head of the Graphic Arts Department. Perhaps Polley is best known for the weekly art editorial features that he contributed to the INDIANAPOLIS STAR. Through illustration and text, Polley highlighted hundreds of state landmarks from 1924 to 1947.

Polley's paintings and lithographs were exhibited at the annual art shows of the HOOSIER SALON, the IRVINGTON GROUP, and the Indiana Artists Club, from which he received the First Selection Purchase Prize in 1939. His work is located in such permanent collections as the INDIANAPOLIS MUSEUM OF ART; the National Museum, Washington, D.C.; the Irvington Historical Society, Indianapolis; and the Indianapolis Public Schools.

FRANK N. OWINGS, JR.

Peter Hastings Falk, ed., *Who Was Who in American Art* (Madison, Conn., 1985); Irvington Historical Society, *The Irvington Group* (Indianapolis, 1984); Flora Lauter, *Indiana Artists Active 1940* (Spencer, Ind., 1941).

Polly of Pogue's Run (1917). A one-act play by William Oscar Bates, set in the office of Governor OLIVER P. MORTON. First performed in 1917 by the Little Theatre Society of Indianapolis, the play is described by one literary historian as "a slender one-act patriotic composition." The plot draws on the turmoil in Indiana during the CIVIL

WAR. Republican Governor Morton is pitted against the Knights of the Golden Circle, a secret society of "Peace Democrats" and southern sympathizers, as he seeks financing to send Indiana soldiers to war. The Knights deputize young Polly Trowbridge from the governor's home county of Wayne to assassinate him. She and her aunt are arrested in the company of several like-minded young rebels on a train near POGUE'S RUN. Undaunted, she faces the governor with gun poised to fire, but relents when confronted with the force of his arguments against slavery. Her capitulation is so wholehearted that she hands him a list of potential assassins and begs him to let her stay on in his service.

The author, a graduate of North Western Christian University (now BUTLER UNIVERSITY) and Cornell University, wrote for a number of newspapers, not only in Indianapolis, but in New York, Ohio, and Minnesota. He also wrote dialogue for *The Indianapolis Centennial Pageant* (1920), as well as other plays.

SARAH JANE BATT
Indianapolis–Marion County Public Library

Arthur W. Shumaker, *A History of Indiana Literature* (Indianapolis, 1962).

Post, Margaret Moore (Aug. 16, 1909–Oct. 31, 1987). Journalist, civic activist, educator. Born Margaret Stephenson in Plainfield, Indiana, she earned her first byline on the Plainfield High School newspaper. While studying journalism at Louisiana State University she interviewed Governor Huey Long; her coverage of his 1929 impeachment trial a short time later received national attention. Following graduation Post returned to Indiana as a reporter for the *Logansport Press*. Within a short time she was city editor. Later, as editor of the *Mooresville Times*, she again garnered national attention reporting the exploits of notorious Indiana criminal JOHN DILLINGER. In 1932 Post married and began her long career with Indianapolis Newspapers, Inc. She continued an association with either the INDIANAPOLIS STAR or the INDIANAPOLIS NEWS in various capacities until her 1983 retirement.

Margaret Moore Post.
[Indianapolis Star/News Library]

While working in the *Star/News* public relations department in 1959, Post first served on the U.S. Chamber of Commerce Crime Control Panel. Subsequently she was associated with a variety of crime control efforts, including Indiana's first Child Abuse Conference, the Indianapolis Anti-Crime Crusade, Women Against Rape, and the Presidential Crime Prevention Commission. The mother of two daughters, Post was also concerned with social reform and education. She was a member of the United Cerebral Palsy board of directors, and a founding member of Big Sisters and the Indiana Association for the Prevention of Blindness. As an educator Post headed the journalism department of Franklin College, taught journalism at IUPUI and FORT BENJAMIN HARRISON Defense Information Center, and was a faculty member of the University of Louisville School of Police Administration.

She received numerous awards, including 50 first place awards from the Women's Press Club of Indianapolis, seven community service CASPERs, the Sagamore of the Wabash twice, and Indiana Mother of the Year. Post also received the Freedom Foundation award, the General Federation of Women's Clubs first place award, plus two Clarions and a Headliner award from Women in Communication. She authored four books, among them *The Lawbreakers: America's Number One Domestic Problem* (with M. Stanton Evans; 1968) and *First Ladies of Indiana and The Governors* (1984).

RITA W. HARLAN

Indiana Lives 1967; *Who's Who in the Midwest, 1986–1987*.

Potter, Theodore (Nov. 29, 1861–Feb. 8, 1915). Physician and medical educator. Potter was an early exponent of the germ theory of disease, a pioneer in the cause and treatment of tuberculosis, and author of *Essays on Bacteriology and Its Relation to the Progress of Medicine* (1898), as well as many articles on the subject. A native of Hamilton County, Ohio, Potter graduated with honors from Princeton University (1882) and Ohio Medical College (1887), and spent a year studying in Germany.

Potter came to Indianapolis in 1889 as demonstrator of microscopy and bacteriology in the Medical College of Indiana. In 1891 he was named professor of bacteriology; and he retained his professorship when the Indiana Medical College merged with the INDIANA UNIVERSITY SCHOOL OF MEDICINE.

An active member of the local, state, and national medical societies, Potter served as editor of the *Indiana Medical Journal*. He was a consulting pathologist to the Indianapolis City Hospital (now WISHARD MEMORIAL HOSPITAL) and an attending physician for chest diseases, especially at the City Dispensary. He was largely responsible for a fresh air school being established in 1914 on the grounds of ARSENAL TECHNICAL HIGH SCHOOL. The school was expanded and named for Potter 20 years later.

LUCRETIA ANN SAUNDERS
Indiana State Board of Health (Retired)

Indianapolis News, Feb. 8, 1915; Donald E. Thompson, *Indiana Authors and Their Books, 1967–1980* (Crawfordsville, Ind., 1981).

Prehistory—Archaeological Evidence. Over 600 archaeological sites are recorded in Indianapolis and Marion County. The majority of these sites are prehistoric, dating from 10,000 B.C. to the 17th century A.D. Despite the number of recorded sites, there is no satisfactory description of the details and cultural chronologies of the prehistoric cultures in the area. Until recently most archaeological investigations occurred along the West Fork of WHITE RIVER and major creeks and runs in Marion County. Urban expansion has destroyed many of the large sites.

Although a few descriptions of sites in the county were prepared in the late 19th century, archaeological investigations of any extent began only in the 20th century. ELI LILLY, archaeologist Glenn A. Black, and in particular John C. Householder—archaeologist with the INDIANA HISTORICAL SOCIETY—recorded and described a number of prehistoric sites. Black, Householder, Paul Weer, Vernon Helmen, and John Dorwin excavated sites in the county. Recent fieldwork includes work by avocational archaeologists, university researchers, and private archaeological contractors. Large field surveys have also taken place on FORT BENJAMIN HARRISON property.

The earliest occupations in the county are Paleoindian (10,000–8000 B.C.). Paleoindians were small, nomadic bands who hunted and gathered wild foods after the last major glacial retreat in Indiana. Paleoindian sites are scarce; they are characterized by surface scatters of chipped stone and well-made lanceolate stone projectile points.

After 6000 B.C. the climate warmed, and deciduous forests replaced boreal and pine forests. Early Archaic (8000–6000 B.C.) occupations followed, marked by an increase in the number and dispersal of sites and a variety of new stone projectile point types, often beveled along the sides by resharpening, and with new hafting techniques. Middle Archaic (6000–3000 B.C.) occupations are associated with higher temperatures and less moist conditions. Sites are characterized by projectile points with side notches. Also appearing are stemmed and notched points which continue into the Late Archaic. Few of these sites are recorded in Marion County.

Late Archaic (ca. 3000–1000 B.C.) sites are the most frequently recorded occupations in central Indiana, partly due to research interests. Late Archaic people—still hunting and gathering for a living—exploited such natural resources as deer, nuts, and mussels on a seasonal basis. Terminal Archaic and Late Archaic–Early Woodland transitional sites (ca. 1500–700 B.C.) are recorded in the county, although in low frequencies. The latter are characterized by distinctive Turkey-tail projectile points.

Woodland sites are distinguished by the presence of pottery, evidence of ceremonialism, and increasing use of cultivated plant foods. Earthen mounds are often characteristic of this tradition, but few mounds are reported in Marion County. Early Woodland (700–200 B.C.) groups still relied upon the harvesting of wild foods. The few Early Woodland sites recorded in the county are usually marked by Adena projectile points. Middle Woodland (200 B.C.-600 A.D.) occupations in Indiana show evidence of localized groups participating in extra-regional Hopewell trade of exotic goods and ideas, along with complex social behavior and increasing horticulture. The present-day Indianapolis area is between the Scioto and Havana Hopewell cultural areas, to the east and west respectively. In general, Middle Woodland sites along the West Fork of the White River often show influences from Havana Hopewell. Few definite Middle Woodland sites have been recorded in the county, although documented ones are identified by distinctive, broad-bladed Snyders projectile points.

Triangular arrow points are indicative of Late Woodland culture (ca. 700–1700 A.D.). During Late Woodland, use of the bow and arrow occurred, and maize agriculture became common. In central Indiana, sites with triangular projectile points occur frequently. Grit-tempered and cord-impressed ceramics sometimes occur on these sites.

A unique cultural manifestation found in Marion and Hamilton counties and along the forks of White River in central Indiana is the Oliver Phase. These sites contain local Late Woodland ceramics which include Early Mississippian Fort Ancient vessel motifs—such as broad incised lines and curvilinear designs—from distinctive cultures to the east and southeast. Dates for these sites range from approximately 950 to 1300 A.D. Well-known Oliver Phase sites in Marion County include Oliver, BOWEN, Jose, Bosson, and Haueissen.

The Mississippian prehistoric tradition (1000–1700 A.D.), characterized by shell-tempered pottery, large-scale maize agriculture, and planned towns and villages, is unknown in Marion County. However, there is a suggestion that

Huber Phase shell-tempered ceramics are present in central Indiana, such as at the Strawtown site in Hamilton County.

RICK JONES

Prelude Awards. Annual awards made to Marion County high school students in visual, performing, and fine arts. Begun in 1985, the Prelude Awards are sponsored by the PENROD SOCIETY, THE CHILDREN'S MUSEUM, and The Children's Museum Guild. The program identifies, encourages, and rewards students who show great potential in dance, instrumental music, literature, theater, visual arts, and vocal music.

Marion County high schools nominate students in each of the six disciplines. After preliminary judging at the JORDAN COLLEGE OF FINE ARTS at Butler University, finalists perform at a public competition at The Children's Museum. Judges include both local and nationally known artists. Six students—one from each arts discipline—receive $2,000 scholarships sponsored by local corporations and private donors.

In June of each year The Children's Museum sponsors the Prelude Academy. The top 16 students in each of the six arts areas from the preliminary round are invited to attend a one-week, non-competitive arts experience. Students take part in workshops and discussions with practicing artists, attend cultural events, and meet with local artists in their work environments.

CATHLEEN F. DONNELLY

Presbyterians. This Protestant denomination was already well recognized in the state when surveyors platted Indianapolis, and the first church building erected in the new city was Presbyterian. Although they usually numbered less than 3 percent of the city's population, Presbyterians have shared substantially in religious and community leadership.

Presbyterian members profess their faith in the lordship of Jesus Christ and their decision to be his followers. Presbyterian government is by elders elected by the members. Ministers are selected through calling and training for a variety of special services. Elected elders meeting with the

Henry Ward Beecher preached at Second Presbyterian Church on the northwest corner of Market Street and Monument Circle. [Indiana Historical Society, Bass Collection, #95670F]

minister as a "session" direct the local congregation. The ministers and elders elected from each of the churches in a designated area constitute a "presbytery." Each presbytery ordains and installs ministers and provides oversight of its congregations. Elders and ministers elected from the presbyteries constitute the regional "synod" and the national "general assembly."

Physician ISAAC COE convened one of the first Presbyterian groups in Indianapolis, a Bible class at the home of a Methodist citizen, in February of 1822. From this group grew a union Sunday school the following April which gathered scholars and teachers across denominational lines and taught many village children to read. The Sunday school met in Caleb Scudder's carpenter shop on State House square. On Saturday, July 5, 1823, First Presbyterian Church was organized there, and Scudder and Coe were elected elders. On the following Sunday the congregation celebrated communion in their partially completed building.

The union Sunday school was the only one in town for five years. When the Methodists and other denominations formed schools beginning in 1828, the original school dropped the name "union" and became Presbyterian. JAMES M. RAY, first Marion County clerk, was Sunday school superintendent for 25 years, and pioneer merchant

JAMES BLAKE was associated with the institution for three decades. Presbyterians also provided weekday schools for pioneer Indianapolis. The libraries of the church and the union Sunday school were probably the earliest in the city for public use.

America's Presbyterians split in 1837. Old School Presbyterians were more conservative; New School Presbyterians more experimental. Fifteen Indianapolis Presbyterians took action to become New School in November, 1838, electing DANIEL YANDES and BETHUEL F. MORRIS as elders. By the end of 1840, when Indianapolis reported 2,662 citizens, the Presbyterians had two churches with two impressive young pastors. Phineas D. Gurley, at First Church (Old School) 1840–1849, would eventually become a prominent Washington pastor, chaplain of the U.S. Senate, and minister to Abraham Lincoln. HENRY WARD BEECHER, at SECOND PRESBYTERIAN CHURCH (New School) 1839–1847, would move to New York and national prominence as a pulpiteer.

Both churches steadily expanded. Parishioners would open a new Sunday school, and if it prospered they would build a chapel. Eventually some members of the mother church would transfer to become the nucleus for a new church. On that pattern First Presbyterian formed Third Presbyterian (later Tabernacle) in September of 1851. Second Presbyterian formed Fourth Presbyterian only a few weeks later. Officers of Third Presbyterian helped a mission Sunday school in an ammunition warehouse become Fifth Presbyterian in 1867. Pastor Hanford Edson of Second Church led his mission workers to form Olivet Church (later Sixth Presbyterian) also in 1867. And First Presbyterian moved its mission, begun in Peter Routier's carpenter shop, into its own building as Seventh Presbyterian the same year. Eighth Presbyterian (later West Washington Street) was at Indianola west of town. BENJAMIN HARRISON was among First Church elders who made the "Saw Mill Mission" into Ninth Presbyterian in 1872. Old School and New School Presbyterians reunited in 1869; the mission formed by Second Presbyterian as part of the reunion celebration became Memorial Church in 1873. Seventh Church members were the nucleus for the new Eleventh Church in 1887; its later names were Olive Street and Troub Memorial. The "West End Mission" Sunday school became Twelfth Church in 1876. In 1888 some 87 persons transformed a mission of Tabernacle into East Washington Street Presbyterian.

This informal growth pattern gradually gave way to church development planned by the denomination's national mission agencies. Expansion continued with Home (1897), Grace (1897), Irvington (1906), Immanuel (formerly Sutherland, 1908), Meridian Heights (1909), Fairview (1924), Wallace Street (1925), and Christ (formerly Prentice, 1929). Following World War II churches paid off indebtedness and expanded facilities. New congregations in that vital period were Northminster (1945), Covenant (1949), St. Andrew (1955), Orchard Park (1956), and Faith (1960, from historic New Providence–Southport, 1833). The Korean Church was organized in 1981.

Indianapolis had Presbyterians in Scottish psalmsinging tradition, Covenanters and Seceders who united to form the United Presbyterian Church of North America (UPCNA) in 1858. There were 988 UPCNA members in four congregations in 1958: First (1849), Eastminster (formerly Woodruff Avenue, 1892), Witherspoon (1907), and Trinity (1955). That year the UPCNA merged with the larger Presbyterian body. Indianapolis listed only one Cumberland Presbyterian (CPC) congregation with 34 members for 1906, the year in which most of the CPC merged with the larger Presbyterian body. Cumberlands gathered a new Indianapolis congregation named Christ Church in 1942. A new conservative body, formed in 1973 as the Presbyterian Church in America (PCA), enlisted existing Indianapolis congregations which became Grace Church and Rawles Avenue Church of the PCA.

Presbyterian women of Indianapolis conducted much of the church's enterprise in their home congregations and served in nearly every public charity in the city. They also sent missionaries to Iran, Africa, Japan, Korea, and India through their Woman's Foreign Missionary Society after 1870. Through the Woman's Board of Home Missions, formed in 1879, they offered assistance to African-Americans, Hispanics, Native Americans, and mountain poor. Presbyterian

women became eligible for ordination as elders in 1930 and as ministers in 1956. There were 168 women and 241 men serving as elders on the sessions of Indianapolis churches in 1990. Contributions from 14,306 Presbyterians in 23 congregations for missions beyond local church expense amounted to $2,087,932 that year. Presbyterian women added another $47,262 for mission projects of their own.

Presbyterians made modest progress among African-Americans in Indianapolis. Ninth Presbyterian changed location to become a black church but did not survive. Witherspoon and Immanuel churches became the widely recognized predominantly black congregations. Presbyterians of Indianapolis intended that all their churches become racially integrated, an ideal only partially achieved.

Indianapolis became a natural center for Presbyterian administration. There was an Indianapolis Presbytery from 1830 to 1972 when the name became Whitewater Valley Presbytery with its office continuing in the capital city. Indiana Synod made Indianapolis an administrative center beginning in 1924. When Indiana and Illinois synods united in 1973 to become the Synod of Lincoln Trails, the offices of that new synod located in the Indiana Interchurch Center at Indianapolis.

General assemblies of the national church met at Indianapolis in 1859 (Old School) and in 1923. Two Indianapolis pastors were moderators of a national general assembly. They were J. P. Cowan of Woodruff Avenue Church in 1903 and Roy Ewing Vale of Tabernacle in 1944. Clinton Marsh of Witherspoon and Herbert Valentine of Troub Memorial won election as general assembly moderators in 1973 and 1991 respectively, having earlier been Indianapolis pastors. Mayor William H. Hudnut III, former pastor of Second Presbyterian (1963–1972), welcomed the Presbyterian general assembly to Indianapolis for its meeting in June, 1985.

L. C. RUDOLPH
Indiana University, Bloomington

Centennial Memorial. First Presbyterian Church, Indianapolis, Ind. (Greenfield, 1925); George W. Geib, *Lives Touched by Faith: Second Presbyterian Church 150 Years* (Indianapolis, 1988); *Historical Sketches of Eighty-*

eight Churches (compiled by the History Committee of Whitewater Valley Presbytery; Indianapolis, 1976).

Prest-O-Lite. Automobile headlight and battery manufacturer. In 1904, partners CARL G. FISHER, JAMES A. ALLISON, and P. C. Avery formed the Concentrated Acetylene Company to assemble and fill acetylene cylinders then used to power automobile headlights. When Avery, the inventor of the system, withdrew from the company in 1906, Fisher and Allison changed the name to Prest-O-Lite Company.

Compressing the acetylene in the tanks often caused explosions in the two early factories at 28th and Pennsylvania streets and 229 E. South Street. After a major explosion at the South Street factory in 1908 and subsequent passage of an ordinance prohibiting the manufacture of explosives within city limits, a new factory was built near 16th Street in SPEEDWAY in 1912. Prest-O-Lite entered the storage battery field in 1914 with the purchase of the Pumpelly Battery Company. It also became a recognized leader in the acetylene field with a nationwide system of charging plants and international distribution.

In 1917, Fisher and Allison sold the company to Union Carbide and Carbon Corporation. The Prest-O-Lite unit continued distributing automotive batteries from the Speedway plant until 1927 when the battery interest of Union Carbide and the name Prest-O-Lite were sold to a subsidiary of Electric Auto-Lite Company of Toledo. Electric Auto-Lite continued making batteries in part of the Speedway factory until 1947, when the Indianapolis plant closed.

JOAN HOSTETLER

"Prest-O-Lite Battery to Close Plant Here," *Indianapolis News*, May 12, 1948; Jane Fisher, *Fabulous Hoosier* (New York, 1947); Speedway Civic Committee, *The Story of Speedway* (1976).

Printing and Publishing Industries. In the early 19th century, the demand for printed information in new Indiana settlements often led to the establishment of printing offices; Indianapolis was no exception. Besides job work (billheads, broadsides, cards, posters, and the like), which was the fledgling companies' "bread-and-butter," newspapers represented the most significant printing and publishing activity.

The first newspaper in Indianapolis was the INDIANAPOLIS GAZETTE, appearing on January 28, 1822, and published by George Smith and NATHANIEL BOLTON. This and subsequent early newspapers were typically four pages with three or four columns to the page. They were printed on handpresses using paper imported from eastern suppliers. Few newspapers before 1860 had more than 1,000 subscribers, and most had half that number or fewer. Bolton later recalled that he applied ink to the locked forms of composed type using ink balls made of dressed deerskin stuffed with wool. He kept them soft with raccoon oil when not in use.

Subsequent names of the *Gazette*, which often also signaled a change in ownership, were the *Indiana State Gazette* (October 22, 1829), the INDIANA DEMOCRAT AND STATE GAZETTE (April 14, 1830), the *Indiana Democrat* (August 14, 1830), the *Indiana Democrat and Spirit of the Constitution* (August 21, 1840), and the INDIANA STATE SENTINEL (July 21, 1841), which finally expired on February 26, 1906. For other long-lived Indianapolis newspapers, similar changes in ownership, periodicity, and name were the rule, not the exception.

Other important Indianapolis newspapers included the WESTERN CENSOR & EMIGRANTS' GUIDE (March 7, 1823), later the INDIANA JOURNAL (January 11, 1825), and the *Indiana State Journal* (about 1844), which merged with the INDIANAPOLIS STAR on June 8, 1904; the INDIANAPOLIS NEWS (December 7, 1869), which is one of the two newspapers in 1994 being published as part of Indianapolis Newspapers, Inc.; the *Daily Reporter* (September 3, 1895), which became the *Commercial-Reporter* on May 20, 1903, and later the INDIANAPOLIS COMMERCIAL (April 14, 1913); and the *Indianapolis Star* (June 6, 1903), which was sold to EUGENE C. PULLIAM in April, 1944, and in 1994 is the second newspaper published by Indianapolis Newspapers, Inc.

Indianapolis had witnessed the publication of at least 185 different newspapers through 1980, many for only an issue or two. Some of longer duration include school newspapers (the *Butler Col-*

legian [ca. 1885] and the *DAILY ECHO* [1898] from Shortridge High School); German-language newspapers (*Indiana Volksblatt* [September, 1848], which later became the *Indiana Volksblatt und Telegraph* [April, 1875], the *Telegraph und Tribuene* [March, 1907], which ceased publication in early June 1918, and the *Freie Presse von Indiana* [September, 1853–1866]); and African-American newspapers (*Hoosier Herald* [1949–1957], which became the *Indiana Herald-Times*, and the *INDIANAPOLIS RECORDER* [1896]).

Early book publishing in Indianapolis took place in newspaper offices. The first book was probably *The Indiana Justice, and Farmer's Scrivener*, written anonymously by CALVIN FLETCHER and the clerk of the Marion County Circuit Court and published by Smith and Bolton in 1822. Since literature was more easily imported from eastern publishers via Cincinnati dealers, the subsequent subject matter of local productions was usually official. Minutes and proceedings of meetings, speeches, reports, sermons, college catalogs, and city directories were the most common imprints. More substantial histories, music, maps, and textbooks, however, began to appear by midcentury.

After the Civil War, an increase in the number of settled communities in Indiana without bookstores prompted a significant rise in subscription book publishing in Indianapolis. Firms such as Fred L. Horton & Company on East Market Street, and Beckworth & Waite, 42 Vance Block, acted as surrogates for outstate publishers such as Henry Howe of Cincinnati, and the American Publishing Company of Hartford, Connecticut, and they might best be described as book distributors.

At midcentury, many Indianapolis newspaper printers published the occasional book. Relying on paper and type supplied from outside Indiana, including the Franklin Type and Stereotype Foundry in Cincinnati, these firms included Cameron & McNeely, whose Capitol Steam Printing Office also published the *Daily Citizen*; the Indiana State Journal Steam Printing Establishment; and the Indiana State Sentinel Steam Printing House. City directories were the stock in trade for Henry N. McEvoy (whose city directories were printed at the Sentinel office), A. C. Howard, and others,

whose efforts were largely replaced in 1878 by R. L. Polk & Company.

Indianapolis has had its share of non-newspaper printers and/or publishers since the mid–19th century; three firms, however, stand out. The WILLIAM B. BURFORD PRINTING COMPANY evolved out of a partnership between Miles Burford and William Braden in the 1860s. Miles' son, William, took over the business in 1875 and built it into one of the largest and most successful printing concerns in Indiana. Burford served as the state printer for many years, and for three decades in the late 19th and early 20th centuries handled all printing incident to sessions of the General Assembly.

John Carlon and C. E. Hollenbeck founded the printing firm of Carlon & Hollenbeck, later THE HOLLENBECK PRESS, in 1867. Located on the southeast corner of the Circle at Meridian Street, Hollenbeck came as close to fitting the definition of a "fine printer" as any operating in Indianapolis in the late 19th century. The firm's advertising proclaimed its interest in the "unseen specification," which "stood for the *addition* of higher characteristics to printed things," where ink, paper, and metal were not the end products but merely "the instruments through which our real product is expressed."

Begun in 1838 as Merrill & Company, a book and stationery store owned by E. H. Hood and SAMUEL MERRILL, the publishing firm of BOBBS-MERRILL COMPANY was a happy exception to a 19th-century publishing rule—a successful, long-lived trade publisher located outside the eastern publishing centers of New York, Boston, and Philadelphia. The firm changed its name several times: Merrill, Meigs & Company after the Civil War; the Bowen-Merrill Company in 1884, when it merged with Bowen, Stewart & Company; and finally the Bobbs-Merrill Company in 1903. Volume 5 of the *Indiana Reports* (state Supreme Court decisions) was the firm's first publication. In 1899 it amplified its interest in legal publishing by purchasing the law book list of Houghton Mifflin, and 13 years later it purchased from the American Publishers Company of Norwalk, Ohio, the right to publish 125 titles in law.

The firm published many Indiana authors. JAMES WHITCOMB RILEY's first collection of poetry, *"The Old Swimmin' Hole" and 'Leven More Poems*

(1883) and MEREDITH NICHOLSON's *Short Flights* (1891) found notable success through their association with Bobbs-Merrill. The firm's greatest success began in the early 20th century when it issued books of national interest such as *When Knighthood Was in Flower* (1898) by Charles Major; L. Frank Baum's *The Wonderful Wizard of Oz* (1900); and Mary Roberts Rinehart's *The Circular Staircase* (1908). Bobbs-Merrill also supported psychology and other emerging social sciences with multivolume series such as The Childhood and Youth Series.

Bobbs-Merrill remained a major publishing firm until its demise, and its list included the phenomenal bestseller, *The Joy of Cooking* (1931, and subsequent editions). In its later years the firm discontinued its wholesale paper and retail bookselling departments and focused on the publication of trade, law, and schoolbooks.

After about 1970 numerous offset lithographic printers (the so-called "quick" or "instant" printers) appeared, and Indianapolis today has no shortage of such firms. Several, however, offer many additional services, such as design and color printing. Among these are Shepard Poorman Communications Corporation, noted also for its full-color calendars; Alexander's Standard Printing; Design Printing Company; and White Arts.

In 1994 Indianapolis has regional offices and distribution centers for several national publishers headquartered elsewhere in the country. Indianapolis publishing itself has taken on a regional or specialist aura. Hackett Publishing Company, founded in 1972, specializes in college textbooks and scholarly books. Que Corporation, a division of Macmillan Computer Publishing, is riding the wave associated today with the rise of the personal computer and the consequent demand for books to explain software documentation. And the Guild Press of Indiana, founded in 1987, specializes in books about Indiana and the Midwest.

BRUCE L. JOHNSON
Indiana Historical Society

John W. Miller, *Indiana Newspaper Bibliography* (Indianapolis, 1982); Donald F. Carmony, "The Pioneer Press in Indiana," *Indiana History Bulletin*, 31 (Oct., 1954); Mary Alden Walker, *The Beginnings of Printing in the State of Indiana* (Crawfordsville, Ind., 1934); *The Unseen Specification* (Indianapolis: Hollenbeck Press, n.d.).

Priori, Marino (Mar. 24, 1878–June 11, 1946). Founding pastor of Holy Rosary Catholic Parish, organized in 1909 for Italian immigrants. Born at Montefalcone Appennino in the Marches, at age 17 Priori became a Franciscan and was ordained in 1901. In 1908 he emigrated to the United States and served Italian quarry workers in Bedford, Indiana. Shortly afterward, Protestant proselytization among Indianapolis Italians resulted in his transfer to the Hoosier capital.

For a quarter century Priori served at Holy Rosary. He registered parishioners for the draft and helped organize relief efforts for Italian war victims during World War I. He became an American citizen (1922) and was incardinated into the Indianapolis Diocese (1931). Under Bishop Joseph Chartrand's patronage, he constructed the present church, adjoining convent, and grade school in 1923–1925. Priori also published *Eternal Light*, a local religious magazine, and amassed a small collection of religious art.

Priori's parishioners did not respond well to his financial appeals, for traditionally the state or wealthy landlords supported the Church in Italy. When the Great Depression further reduced parish income despite his best efforts, Chartrand's successor, Bishop JOSEPH E. RITTER, transferred Priori to Troy, Indiana, in 1934.

Priori received several honors for his activities among Indianapolis Italians. Pope Pius XI created him a monsignor (1933) and awarded him *Pro Ecclesia et Pontifice* (1924) and *Benemerenti* (1938). King Victor Emmanuel III made him a knight of the Royal Crown of Italy (1932). Retiring in 1941, Priori helped bolster Indianapolis Italians' loyalty to the United States during World War II. He died in Louisville, Kentucky, and was buried in St. Joseph Cemetery, Indianapolis.

JAMES J. DIVITA
Marian College

Eternal Light (July, 1932), 84–87; James J. Divita, *The Italians of Indianapolis: The Story of Holy Rosary Catholic Parish, 1909–1984* (Indianapolis, 1984).

Propylaeum. Literary and cultural club for women. The Propylaeum, meaning "gateway to higher culture," was built through a stock company (1888) composed of Indianapolis women interested in a place for club meetings. The original structure on North Street was razed in 1923 for the INDIANA WORLD WAR MEMORIAL PLAZA. That same year, members purchased the Schmidt-Schaf home at 1410 North Delaware Street, which continues to serve as the organization's headquarters.

A committee of seven women met April 30, 1888, to find a suitable home for the INDIANAPOLIS WOMAN'S CLUB, established in 1875. They were surprised at a proposition from their chairperson MAY WRIGHT SEWALL: "that they should at once reorganize themselves into a voluntary committee to consider the feasibility of forming, among the women of Indianapolis, a stock company for the purpose of erecting and owning a building which should be specially adapted for the use of various clubs." Originally from Wisconsin, Sewall based her idea on a successful model facility in Milwaukee.

Two months and ten meetings later, the scheme secured the necessary support; and the Indianapolis Propylaeum incorporated June 6, 1888, with a capital stock of $15,000. The Articles of Association provided that stock might be acquired, purchased, and held only by women. They also specified that the building would be used for "literary, artistic, scientific, industrial, musical, mechanical and education purposes" for the public, but particularly for the women of Indianapolis. Among the incorporators were Sewall, Mary N. Walcott, Harriet McIntire Foster, and Carrie F. Milligan.

From its beginning, the Propylaeum has been home to many Indianapolis clubs, including the Indianapolis Woman's Club, the Fortnightly Literary Club, the INDIANAPOLIS LITERARY CLUB, the ENGLISH SPEAKING UNION, the Daughters of the American Revolution, and the Portfolio Club, a cultural group for writers and artists. During World War I, the original building housed numerous relief and recreation programs for soldiers and their families. The Propylaeum became the key cultural meeting center for Indianapolis women where they could focus their cultural and literary activities and foster civic responsibility.

The Victorian elegance of the Propylaeum is carefully maintained. Built in 1890, the brick home has been offered as part of the OLD NORTH-SIDE Victorian Home Tour. It has a combination of Romanesque Revival, Neo-Jacobean, and Queen Anne styles of architecture. Notable are the elegant windows and leaded-glass doors, Rookwood fireplace tiles, intricate Italian carvings, and grand staircase. The Propylaeum is listed on the National Register of Historic Places (1973).

ANN MAUGER COLBERT
Indiana University–Purdue University,
Fort Wayne

Caroline Dunn, *Indianapolis Propylaeum, 1888–1938* (Indianapolis, 1938); *Indianapolis Woman's Club, 1875–1975* (Indianapolis, 1975).

Public Defender System. Traditionally, courts in Marion County provided attorneys to "paupers" on an informal, case-by-case basis at the discretion of each judge. But by 1968 a series of U.S. Supreme Court decisions guaranteed indigents' right to a defense in all felony cases and, as of 1972, all misdemeanor cases involving the possibility of incarceration. These developments led to separate public defender (PD) staffs in the several levels of Marion County's multi-layered court system, including the Municipal Courts, the Superior Courts, and the Appellate Courts. Additionally, PDs have provided services in special areas like environmental court, protective order court, probation violations, drug court, and mental health commitment reviews.

In Marion County each PD staff was organized and administered differently. The presiding judge of the Municipal Court created a PD office administered by a chief PD and financed by the Municipal Court budget. The presiding judge appointed a chief PD, and together they hired the PDs. Since the late–1980s the majority of Municipal Court PDs have worked full time. Judges determined defendants' indigency based upon an informal set of guidelines, passed the case on to the chief PD, who in turn assigned it a staff PD. Support staff, including an investigator, secretaries, paralegals, and interviewers, aided the PDs.

Superior Court judges funded and appointed their own staff of PDs. The Criminal Court judges continued to hire PDs as part-time independent contractors. Judges determined defendants' indigency based on subjective criteria and then appointed a PD based on a rotation formula. These judges provided little or no office and staff support, so PDs had to petition the court for resources in mounting their defense. The Juvenile Court presiding judge, however, created a staffed PD office similar to the Municipal Court PD office.

A separate staff of PDs handled the municipal and superior court appeals. The lower court judges appointed and financed these PDs in addition to their regular PD staff. One PD was appointed supervisor, and appellate PDs were assigned cases by the judge for whom they worked.

Since the early 1970s critics have found many flaws with the PD system in Marion County. Practical problems have included inadequate salaries, support services, investigatory resources, indigency screening, defender supervision, as well as excessive caseloads and delayed appointments of counsel. The overriding problem, however, was the lack of independence from the judges before whom the defenders served.

Several investigations of the public defender system have attempted to address these criticisms. An Indianapolis Bar Association (IBA) investigation of the PD system (1976) and an IBA Public Defender Committee study (1979) both recommended major overhauls. Another IBA committee (1985) proposed the creation of a nonprofit corporation which would contract defender services out to the courts. Little court or legislative reform followed, and Marion County's system became known as one of the worst in the country.

Attempting to find governmental solutions, a fourth IBA study began in 1990, and soon after the City-County Council selected an IBA committee member to devise the council's own reform plan. In the absence of legislative reform, the Indiana Civil Liberties Union filed a lawsuit with the Indiana Supreme Court in 1992 asking for judicial reform using court-issued rules. In 1993, however, the City-County Council adopted an ordinance creating the Marion County Public Defender Agency, a version of the nonprofit organization that the IBA had supported.

After much political controversy, the nonpartisan, independent agency was implemented in mid–1993, encompassing all former PD staffs. The agency is governed by a nine-member board appointed by the City-County Council (4), the presiding Municipal Court judge (2), the Superior Court (2), and the mayor (1). The board sets the budget, approves policy, and nominates the chief public defender of Marion County, subject to City-County Council approval. The chief PD has direct responsibility over agency administration, personnel, and policy. While the agency renders PDs independent from the courts and centralizes PD administration, it has yet to provide lasting solutions to issues like defender caseload limits, determination of defendant indigency, and adequate PD salary and support.

Michelle D. Hale

Public Health. Early Indianapolis residents lived under conditions which led to frequent bouts with malaria, typhoid fever, and cholera. Families were often large and lived in crowded cabins, with no windowpanes or screens to keep out insects. Streams were often polluted, and there were no sewage or trash collection systems. Nearby swampland was a breeding ground for disease-carrying mosquitoes.

Epidemics were common. According to one report a malaria epidemic in the summer of 1821 claimed 72, or one of eight, residents. In 1832 a cholera epidemic killed 62 people in one month. In these early years half the children under 14 lost at least one parent to disease. Since germ theory was unknown, diseases were believed to be God's punishment or the result of "miasmas," invisible substances thought to rise from damp soil and night air. Draining the swamps to reduce these miasmas did reduce the number of mosquitoes, the unsuspected carriers of malaria.

Antebellum interest in public health was very sporadic, peaking only when an epidemic struck. For example, in 1833 Dr. Livingston Dunlap first proposed a hospital for victims of cholera and smallpox. In 1847 an early board of health raised $1,000 to construct such a hospital, but interest again waned with the demise of the smallpox epidemic. Dunlap persisted in his efforts until the first city hospital was finally constructed in 1859.

The Shattuck Report (1850), a survey of sanitary conditions in Massachusetts, became a blueprint for public health efforts for decades to come.

Its more than 50 recommendations on issues such as water and air pollution, control of communicable diseases, and housing construction were gradually implemented over the next century. Possibly influenced by this report, the Common Council created the first official and permanent board of health for Indianapolis in 1859. In 1863 the board adopted food inspection standards and rules for keeping and disposing of animals, and in 1871 required sewer hook-ups for hotels, restaurants, hospitals, saloons, and boardinghouses. However, in the 1880s sanitary conditions remained extremely poor. Drinking water samples were very bad, hogs and cattle were allowed to wander the city streets (until banned by city ordinance in the late 1880s), and household wastes and garbage were often thrown directly into the streets. To deal with such conditions the city adopted standards for well and water inspection in 1893 and for plumbing and garbage in 1904 and 1906.

The late 19th and early 20th century also witnessed the creation of public health agencies and associations. In 1879 the FLOWER MISSION, an organization of women who served the poor and sick, offered the first nursing services in the city. The Public Health Nursing Association was formed in 1912 as a voluntary agency, with initial efforts focused on maternal and child health, tuberculosis, and school health issues. Early efforts in maternal and child health focused on improving milk quality. The Indianapolis Pure Milk Association members maintained the first well-baby clinics during the summers; a successor organization, the Children's Aid Association, expanded to year-round well-baby clinics and added children's dental clinics. The city began a school health program in 1906, added vision and hearing screening in 1911, and employed the first school nurse in 1914.

In 1896 the WHITE RIVER was seriously polluted, resulting in a typhoid epidemic. Having a clean surface water supply was critical since wells alone could not supply a city the size of Indianapolis. For this reason the INDIANAPOLIS WATER COMPANY began constructing a modern filtration system in 1904 and settling basins in 1908, and first used liquid chlorine in 1916. The typhoid rate remained high for years, however, because a

Children suffering from tuberculosis often attended "fresh air schools" where the constant circulation of fresh air was believed to restore health. [Indiana State Library]

majority of the families in Indianapolis continued to use wells and privies. Eventually the general improvement of sanitary standards effectively eliminated diseases such as cholera and typhoid fever.

In the early 1900s certain contagious diseases such as tuberculosis remained widespread. Controlling tuberculosis by quarantining its victims in a "pest house" was replaced by treatment in sanitariums. In 1945 streptomycin was first used for the successful treatment of tuberculosis and by the 1950s the incidence of this disease was greatly reduced.

The Board of Health and Charities, formed in 1905, hired the city's first full-time health officer, Dr. Elijah Elder (later secretary of the State Board of Health). Dr. Herman Morgan served in this role from 1912 until 1946 and played a major role in changing public attitudes toward public health; he helped to establish pure food regulations and supported the construction of a city sewage disposal plant. During his term much progress was made in controlling venereal disease and in reducing the pneumonia and infant death rates. From 1941 to 1946 the infant mortality rate declined from 125 to 46 per 100,000 population.

In 1948 the Health and Welfare Council, a group of 115 agencies, recommended the merger of the public health and hospital services of the city and Marion County. Three years later the General Assembly created the HEALTH AND HOS-

PITAL CORPORATION OF MARION COUNTY. Before this occurred, the 110,000 county residents outside the city limits had received very few public health services.

Modern efforts in public health have focused on infants and children. In 1954 the Division of Public Health began a polio vaccination program among school children, effectively eliminating this disease. The division began decentralizing public health services to neighborhood centers in 1960, and in 1969 implemented the nation's first successful rubella vaccination program. In 1987 the National Children's Defense Fund issued a report on infant mortality that cited Indianapolis as the city with the highest black infant mortality rate in the country. The Marion County Task Force on Infant Mortality formed by the City-County Council in 1988 to study this issue led to the CAMPAIGN FOR HEALTHY BABIES in 1990, which focused on comprehensive prenatal care, financial accessibility, good transportation, care coordination, and education and outreach. By the early 1990s black infant mortality had not declined significantly, but the groundwork had been laid to remove barriers to prenatal care.

Acquired Immune Deficiency Syndrome (AIDS) became a very critical public health issue in the 1980s. In Marion County the first case was reported in 1982, with 737 cases reported through 1992. Major environmental health issues in the 1980s were the control of hazardous materials and ground water quality.

STEPHEN E. KIRCHHOFF

Ruby M. Grosdidier and Maria Rosado, eds., *Marion County Health Department, Indianapolis, Indiana (1820–1983)* (Indianapolis, 1984); Thurman B. Rice, *The Hoosier Health Officer* (Indianapolis, 1946).

Public Housing. Although the federal public housing program has roots in Indianapolis, the city's support for and level of involvement in federally supported housing for low-income individuals and families has a remarkably inconsistent and politically charged history. The LOCKEFIELD GARDENS project, begun in 1934 and completed in 1937, was a joint project of the Housing Division of the Federal Emergency Administration of Public Works and the Advisory Committee on Housing of Indianapolis. One of over 50 Public Works Administration projects for low-cost housing and the eighth to be completed, Lockefield Gardens served as a model for federal housing assistance under the federal Housing Act of 1937. It was billed as a slum clearance project and cost over $3 million to construct. Described in its initial promotional brochure as "a modern low rent housing project developed in a residential area occupied by negro families," Lockefield consisted of 24 buildings providing 748 three- and four-room units with hot and cold running water, steam heating, and electric lighting and appliances. The complex also included club rooms, laundries, and storage areas. Rents were not to exceed one-fifth of a family's monthly income and averaged about $20.00 per month.

Another example of public-supported housing in Indianapolis was Tyndall Towne, built in 1946 under the mayoral leadership of ROBERT TYNDALL. It consisted of 738 apartments at four sites around the city. Constructed as temporary housing for returning veterans, it was completely demolished by 1955. Because housing and neighborhoods were strictly segregated during this time, Lockefield Gardens was for African-American families and Tyndall Towne for white families.

Although states had been encouraged to pass legislation enabling localities to create local housing authorities to develop, own, and manage apartment projects for low-income families under the federal Housing Act of 1937, Lockefield Gardens and Tyndall Towne remained the only public-supported housing projects in Indianapolis for the next 25 years. In 1949 the INDIANAPOLIS HOUSING AUTHORITY (IHA) was established under Mayor ALBERT G. FEENEY; he appointed a board of commissioners, but little was accomplished. In 1952 Mayor ALEX M. CLARK worked to reenergize the housing authority, which purchased property to proceed with additional public housing in Indianapolis. Carl Beck, who had been the manager of Tyndall Towne since 1948, was appointed director in 1953. That same year, however, the newly elected City Council passed Ordinance 13 prohibiting the housing authority to function. Subsequent mayors and city councils were opposed to the principle of public housing and supported the ban. In 1957 the Federal Housing Authority, which had managed Lockefield Gardens since its inception, pressed the city of Indianapolis to take responsibility for the complex. Mayor PHILIP L. BAYT, JR., refused and the Indianapolis Housing Authority was disbanded in 1958.

In 1964 Mayor JOHN J. BARTON was elected on a platform of using federal aid "when needed." He worked with the City Council to reestablish the Indianapolis Housing Authority in March of 1964. With urban renewal and the construction of the interstate highway system around and through Indianapolis forcing the relocation of many families, Indianapolis finally found the impetus to participate in earnest with the federal public housing program. The IHA assumed management of Lockefield Gardens on December 31, 1964. Between 1964 and 1974, 14 of the 15 current public housing communities were constructed, with 2,622 apartment units developed for low-income families and the elderly and/or handicapped. Private developers built or refurbished the communities and rapidly turned the keys over to the IHA, thus coining the phrase "turn-key" housing.

Beginning in the 1970s IHA experienced the same social and financial problems as did many urban housing authorities. Costs for maintenance and management increased while changes in rent calculations mandated by the federal Department of Housing and Urban Development (HUD) caused income to fall. By 1972 IHA was in debt and apartments were not being properly maintained. The situation at Lockefield Gardens was especially severe and residents were relocated to other public housing sites in 1974. The vacant apartments deteriorated rapidly and were health hazards as well as a roadblock to the rapidly expanding INDIANA UNIVERSITY–PURDUE UNIVERSITY AT INDIANAPOLIS (IUPUI). Various plans were presented to renovate the apartments, which had been listed in the National Register of Historic Places in 1976. In partnership with the city of Indianapolis, private development, IUPUI, and IHA eventually agreed upon a plan that combined the demolition of several of the original Lockefield apartments, the private development of new apartments with the renovation of the remaining original units to be included under private man-

agement, and construction of new public housing units for the elderly/handicapped to the north of the Lockefield site. The most recent public housing community, located on Indiana Avenue adjacent to the Lockefield Gardens site, was completed in 1987 and currently provides 107 units of low-income housing to elderly/handicapped residents. This plan provided inhabitable buildings and economic development for the neighborhood, but it also removed public housing from the culturally significant Lockefield site with a net loss of public housing units for Indianapolis.

Public housing, nationally as well as locally, has been inhabited mostly by African-American families. Despite some attempts here to integrate the communities, public housing remained segregated and became known as "housing of last resort." The number of white applicants declined sharply in the late 1960s as racial tensions increased around the city. In response to this increased segregation in Indianapolis public housing, Judge S. Hugh Dillin included a ban on developing family public housing units in the Indianapolis Public Schools district as a part of his desegregation order of 1973. That ban remained in effect in the early 1990s.

High rates of vacancy and overwhelming social problems continued to plague the Indianapolis public housing communities into the 1980s and were repeatedly cited by HUD management reports. Indianapolis appeared on HUD's "Troubled Housing" list in 1981. A series of directors attempted to rectify the problems and improve the deteriorating condition of the units and the financial stability of the agency. In 1984, under threat of withdrawal of fiscal support from HUD, the CITY-COUNTY COUNCIL and Mayor William H. Hudnut III developed a plan to accept administrative responsibility for public housing in Indianapolis. On January 1, 1986, public housing became a division of the city's DEPARTMENT OF METROPOLITAN DEVELOPMENT.

Today the Division of Housing operates 2,729 units of public housing in ten family and five elderly/handicapped communities. One of a very few housing authorities under a city's direct jurisdiction, the Division of Housing has made slow but continuous progress in repairing and modernizing units, implementing an inventory system for materials, and maintaining reasonable levels of occupancy. The Division of Housing continues to be a political issue, making headlines and headaches for the mayoral administrations of Hudnut and his successor, Stephen Goldsmith. The four administrators since 1984 have met with varying success in addressing the problems of public housing in Indianapolis. Despite the changes in administration there has been a notable emphasis on the quality of life of residents, with the reactivation of a Resident Services Department to assist residents in attaining economic self-sufficiency through HUD-funded initiatives to develop resident management and resident-owned businesses. Although in 1993 the Division of Housing remained on the "Troubled Housing" list, its removal appeared imminent.

LISA E. MCGUIRE
Indiana University–Purdue University,
Indianapolis

Public Radio. See Broadcasting, Educational and Public

Public Safety, Department of. Part of the executive branch of Indianapolis-Marion County government, the Department of Public Safety (DPS) is one of six departments created under UNIGOV. It is charged with keeping order and protecting citizens and their property. Before Unigov, similar functions were the responsibility of the Board of Public Safety. In addition to a director and three advisory boards, the department has five divisions: Police, Fire, Emergency Management Planning, Animal Control, and Weights and Measures.

The director, appointed by the MAYOR and approved by the CITY-COUNTY COUNCIL, appoints the police and fire chiefs and is responsible for major policy decisions, budgeting, planning, and coordination of the departmental divisions. The director supervises hiring, promotion, affirmative action, and discipline within the department. The Police Merit Board and the Fire Merit Board, each with six members appointed by the director, help implement the merit system for their respective departments. The director also

manages the Marion County Justice Agency, previously the DPS Marion County Criminal Justice Coordinating Council, which maintains the criminal and civil court computer system and provides pretrial services.

The Board of Public Safety advises the director and is responsible for reviewing departmental contracts, approving the budget, and studying relevant issues. It consists of four members serving one-year terms, two of whom are appointed by the mayor and two by the City-County Council. The Public Safety Committee of the City-County Council also advises the director and approves the budget.

The INDIANAPOLIS POLICE DEPARTMENT (IPD) has jurisdiction within the old Indianapolis city limits. Through several restructurings IPD has evolved into a department consisting of the Office of the Chief and six other divisions, each headed by its own deputy chief, including Administration, Investigative Management Division, and four neighborhood service districts. It operated a police radio station until 1992, when the Metropolitan Emergency Communication Agency (MECA) began operating a radio channel that serves all local emergency and law enforcement agencies.

The IPD Operations Division, formerly organized on a citywide basis, was decentralized in 1993 in an effort to provide community-oriented services. The city is currently divided into four geographic service districts: North, South, East, and West. Each district has its own main office and provides police services to the public, including uniformed patrol officers, special investigators, traffic control, and community relations programs like Neighborhood Crime Watch (formerly its own division within the DPS until 1992). Some functions remain centralized: traffic control, tactical air patrol, mounted police, S.W.A.T., scuba diving, bomb squad, and hostage negotiation.

The IPD Investigative Management Division, formerly the Criminal Investigations Division, currently has five main branches in addition to a crime laboratory. These divisions handle all reports of criminal activities and most investigations, including narcotics and vice, homicide and robbery, sex offenses and family violence, and juvenile crime among others. It also traces missing children and manages the Metropolitan Gang Taskforce.

The INDIANAPOLIS FIRE DEPARTMENT'S (IFD) mission is to provide fire, medical, and other emergency services, as well as public prevention and education programs. The IFD's jurisdiction encompasses the old city limits, but it coordinates services with the Marion County township and volunteer fire departments through MECA. It also provides services to contracted commercial and industrial sites outside its jurisdiction. The IFD has five divisions, each administered by a deputy chief: Administration, Education, Suppression Operations, Technical Services, and Communications.

The fire chief is responsible for management, policy, and budget decisions for the entire department, and provides public information and neighborhood liaison services. Reporting directly to the chief is the Fire Investigations Unit, which is responsible for investigating cases of suspected arson. The IFD Suppression Operations Division, also known as Field Operations, oversees the management and operation of all fire houses and their staffs, as well as Emergency Medical Service (EMS), Rescue, and Hazardous Materials (HAZMAT) Units. Operations is divided into four districts or battalions, each supervised by an assistant fire marshal. EMS operates an ambulance service affiliated with Wishard Hospital and provides its services at special events. The Fire Department also trains personnel, operates the Fire Dispatch Center which works in tandem with MECA, promotes fire safety education programs, and enforces municipal fire codes through annual building inspections.

The Department of Public Safety is also responsible for emergency management planning, formerly known as civil defense, that prepares and implements comprehensive disaster plans for the metropolitan area and coordinates local resources for emergency relief services. Animal control is another function of the department. It assumed these responsibilities from private agencies in the mid–1970s, but as of 1994 was negotiating with the Indianapolis Humane Society to take over both kennel and enforcement services. Finally, DPS serves a consumer protection function by checking all weighing and measuring devices for accuracy. Inspectors routinely check measuring devices and measured commodities such as gas pumps, produce scales, and pre-weighed turkeys.

MICHELLE D. HALE

Public Safety, Women and African-Americans in. African-American males appeared on the rolls of the INDIANAPOLIS POLICE DEPARTMENT (IPD) and INDIANAPOLIS FIRE DEPARTMENT (IFD) in 1876, yet until well after World War II their numbers were few: 5 of 71 policemen in 1890; 16 of more than 400 in 1934. Also, blacks invariably served in lower ranks. Not until 1973, for example, did an African-American hold a top administrative position in IPD.

Both IPD and IFD were also segregated. Until the 1960s African-American policemen worked in what were then the two predominately black areas of the city and black firemen were restricted to all-black Fire Station No. 1 at 1445 West Michigan Street. Integration of the fire stations began January 1, 1960, when four black firemen transferred to two other stations. Two years later six whites (including a captain and a lieutenant) moved to Station No. 1. By 1974, 18 of the then 33 fire stations were integrated.

The impetus for employing women in police work dates to 1845 with the successful agitation of the American Female Reform Society to place matrons in New York City jails. After the 1880s the Women's Christian Temperance Union (WCTU) led the campaign and by 1900 most major cities employed jail matrons. The duties of such "policewomen" were limited strictly to juveniles and women, a clientele universally held to be suited to their "maternal instincts." The matrons—policemen's widows or, more commonly, trained social workers—were often paid wholly or in part by private groups.

In Indianapolis the office of police matron was established as part of the police force by the board of public safety in April, 1891. The first matron, Annie Buchanan, operated from a room furnished by the local WCTU on the second floor of the station house. Buchanan counseled boys under 15, girls, and women, and decided whether to send them to institutions such as reform school, the Home for Friendless Women, or Children's

Guardian, or whether to hold them for trial. Buchanan's success led to an 1895 state law mandating matrons in every city and a similar law in 1901 for county jails. By 1914 Indianapolis employed three matrons and a female probation officer.

In 1917 a report by the New York Bureau of Municipal Research advocated the appointment of Indianapolis policewomen to operate outside the station house. The following year Clara Burnside, an experienced social worker and for 12 years a juvenile court probation officer, was given the rank of sergeant and appointed supervisor of 13 women police (two blacks). In mufti and unarmed, their beats were the dance halls, movie houses, parks, restaurants—places where children and women might come into contact with vice. By 1920, 16 women under Lieutenant Burnside (captain in 1921) dealt with shoplifters, runaways, and young girls on the streets. Counseling continued to be emphasized with arrest the last resort. By 1939, however, the 23 policewomen of 1921 had declined to 14 who performed only as matrons, clerks, or telephone operators.

The shortage of manpower during World War II brought a breakthrough for women in IPD, as was true for women's employment generally. In November, 1943, two armed, uniformed policewomen were assigned to traffic posts on MONU-MENT CIRCLE. The gains did not last: although about 30 women were hired during the war, in 1947 the number on the force fell to 26, of which six worked "on the street" and were armed. Even these officers were usually not in uniform.

Policemen's hostility to policewomen and notions that women could not handle real police work—as late as 1968 typing was a requirement for female officers—continued unabated through the 1970s. Starting pay was equal, but policewomen, believing it a useless exercise, did not sit for promotion exams. When IPD became the first department in the nation to assign women to patrol cars (the announced purpose was to free men for crime fighting), officers Betty Blankenship and Elizabeth Robinson were given one day's notice, no training, and limited to service runs. A 1972 Police Foundation study of policewomen in seven cities found Indianapolis represented both the best and the worst: IPD led in assigning women to patrol cars (eight by 1972), but 60 of 74 had office jobs, with more than half working as secretaries. Moreover, disdain for women within IPD was marked.

The real revolution for minorities in public safety in Indianapolis began with the 1975 lawsuit alleging discrimination filed by seven black policemen. In January, 1976, the new ADMINISTRATION OF WILLIAM H. HUDNUT III voluntarily inaugurated an affirmative action program for all city departments, and in 1978 and 1979 it signed consent decrees on race and sex with the U.S. Department of Justice which made hiring goals for minorities in public safety legally binding on the city.

One of the effects of the consent decrees was to bring women into the fire department. Women having a permanent presence in IFD dates to 1980 with the appointments of Valarie High and Nancy Sweeney. Still in 1992, while 145 women constituted 14.7 percent of IPD, they were only 2.8 percent (21) of the city's firefighters, a circumstance attributable to the even greater competition for selection to IFD, greater physical demands, and a longer "male only" tradition (the first woman, a civilian clerk, was hired in 1950, 60 years after the first jail matron).

Affirmative action in hiring and promoting minorities has been accompanied by charges of favoritism from white males, countercharges by blacks and women of persistent discrimination, and lawsuits. Yet the changes in race and gender in public safety institutions remain remarkable: From 1978 to 1992 minorities in IPD rose from 18 to 29.3 percent; in IFD from 9.3 to 21.8 percent. In 1990 Indianapolis ranked fifth among 18 big cities in the proportion of black police officers compared to the size of the African-American population.

WILLIAM DOHERTY
Marian College

Public Schools, Religion in. In the middle decades of the 19th century reformers urged the building of common schools across America as part of an effort to promote shared values and offset sectarian divisions. Overwhelmingly Protestant, these reformers advocated Bible reading in the schools, but without any commentary that might favor the views of particular denominations. The rhetoric of the common school crusade outlasted the movement's initial drive and shaped the language of educators for decades following the Civil War.

Rebuilding and expanding during and after the Civil War, the Indianapolis public schools reflected the concern for a generalized moral and religious education that had been a founding principle of the common school movement. The Indianapolis public school manuals of the 1880s spoke to this concern by calling for morning exercises that included reading or reciting Bible verses or "other appropriate matter," possibly followed by the Lord's Prayer and "appropriate singing." Further echoing the earlier common school reformers, the manuals instructed teachers to guard against introducing sectarian or partisan issues into the classroom.

The language of the Indianapolis school manuals matched the opinion of many educators across the United States in the post –Civil War decades. Both the National Education Association and its forerunner, the National Teachers' Association, strongly advocated nonsectarian religion in the public schools. Nevertheless, this position was coming under increasing attack in the late 19th and early 20th centuries. Leading the opposition were the growing numbers of Catholic and Jewish immigrants to the United States, whose version of the Bible differed from that of Protestants. In Indianapolis between 1913 and 1915 controversy over a proposed course to teach the Bible as history and literature showed the weakening of consensus over the role of religion in public education. Here, as elsewhere, increasing cultural diversity was a factor in the dispute.

In 1913 the Indiana State Board of Education devised a syllabus for high school students based on a North Dakota course that used the Bible for historical and literary, not theological, study. Perhaps reflecting growing demands for separation of church and state, the Bible program was not to take place in school buildings, and public school teachers were not to be the principal instructors. School authorities, however, would examine the pupils and award credit. After the state superintendent of schools discovered that the state board did not have the authority to initiate or order courses of study, a committee of representatives from state educational associations devised an outline for the course, which the state board approved.

By the fall of 1915 nearly 20 towns in Indiana had adopted the course for their schools. Indianapolis, however, was not among these, despite requests from Protestant church representatives that the city do so. The debate before the Indianapolis board of school commissioners revealed growing discontent with Protestant-defined Bible education. Although the commissioners themselves generally favored the course, they feared encouraging religious strife among Protestants, Catholics, and Jews by implementing the program. Furthermore, the involvement of school representatives in examining, though not directly teaching, pupils elicited declarations that the course violated the principle of church-state separation.

Despite increasing recognition of the principle of the separation of church and state, devotional Bible reading continued in many classrooms across the country. In fact, 11 states and the District of Columbia enacted legislation after 1913 requiring daily Bible reading in the public schools. Although Indiana was not among these states, a group supporting "AMERICANIZATION and education" in the Indiana House of Representatives attempted in 1925 to make Bible reading compulsory in the state's school system.

During these same decades another means for introducing religion into the daily life of public school students appeared. In 1914 Superintendent William Wirt of Gary, Indiana, began a program of "released time" providing weekday religious education within the public schools. Other communities adopted similar programs in the 1920s and 1930s, sometimes offering separate classes for Catholics, Jews, and Protestants. To many, released time seemed to be a way of offering religious instruction without offending minority religious groups.

The number of released time programs expanded rapidly in the 1940s. In 1941 the Indiana education department laid plans to encourage released-time programs throughout the state. Within a few years weekday religious education developed in the Indianapolis schools. Although in the *McCollum* case (1948) the U.S. Supreme Court ruled against the use of school property for released-time classes, in the *Zorach* case (1952) the high court allowed such programs to continue off school grounds. An organization called Weekday Religious Education of Indianapolis and Marion County used mobile chapels to offer religious training to fourth and fifth graders. Interdenominational Protestantism shaped the program throughout Marion County, where in 1962–1963 about 21,000 children enrolled in the course; in 1973 the number was close to 18,000.

A more short-lived Indianapolis project to provide religious education, but within classrooms, also appeared in the postwar period. In the 1950s there was increasing concern to offer moral and religious education in order to counteract a perceived growth of secularization and juvenile delinquency in society. A group of Indianapolis citizens, with contributions from Catholics, Protestants, Jews, and Christian Scientists, devised a plan aimed at teaching fundamental religious values while eschewing indoctrination. In the fall of 1954 courses were introduced for seventh and eighth graders in 11 of the city's schools. According to their syllabi, the classes were to examine the religious influences on the founding and development of the United States. Although the program was to have been expanded to other grades, it quickly came under fire. In early 1955 the school board voted to discontinue the classes the following September, proposing however to incorporate certain elements of the courses into the social studies curriculum. The board claimed fear of lawsuits, though some suggested at the time that personal conflicts with Superintendent Herman L. Shibler, a proponent of the plan, also played a role in the board's decision.

In the 1960s the Indianapolis schools were forced to respond to major rulings of the U.S. Supreme Court. As a result, morning devotions using the Bible and prayer lost official sanction in the city in 1963. In November of that year the Indianapolis board of school commissioners replaced its rule that morning exercises in the public schools might include Scriptures and the Lord's Prayer with a rule that permitted patriotic songs, the Pledge of Allegiance, and poetry or prose promoting cultural appreciation or ethical character.

The decision was in response to the U.S. Supreme Court decisions in *Engel v. Vitale* (1962) and *Schempp v. Board of Abington Township* (1963), the former striking at prayer in the public schools and the latter at Bible reading.

The Supreme Court decisions were ignored, or at least not fully complied with, in many parts of the country. Out of about 227 school corporations in Indiana surveyed in 1964, about one-third continued to permit devotional Bible reading and nearly half continued to use the Lord's Prayer. In recent years the INDIANAPOLIS PUBLIC SCHOOLS have generally complied with the major Supreme Court decisions; however, from time to time citizens have raised concerns about such issues as Christmastime activities and pressure on students to participate in before- or after-school religious clubs. Although released time programs continue in some rural districts of the state, they are no longer in operation in the Indianapolis Public Schools.

AMY C. SCHUTT
Indiana University, Bloomington,
and *History of Education Quarterly*

Public Service Indiana. Indianapolis-based electric utility. Public Service Indiana, one of the state's largest electric utilities, was headquartered at the Traction Terminal Building in Indianapolis for four decades after 1912. In 1951 the company began to move to new headquarters in nearby Plainfield.

The predecessors of Public Service Indiana were the small, central light plants and electric street railways that sprouted up around Indiana between 1880 and 1900. By 1913 there were 210 central electric stations operating in Indiana. In 1912 Samuel Insull (d. 1938) of Chicago organized the Interstate Public Service Company in Indianapolis. Insull, a British native and early employee of Thomas A. Edison, was a proponent of centralized control of electric and gas utilities. He established Interstate to operate the Indianapolis, Columbus and Southern Traction Company, which provided interurban electric railway service between the Hoosier capital and Louisville. He also consolidated numerous electric and gas utilities from New Albany to Lafayette into Interstate, and as the 1920s advanced the electric and gas utilities increased in size while the interurban railway waned. Insull's empire across the U.S. was overextended, and in April, 1932, his bankers forced the giant utility holding company into bankruptcy.

Interstate had changed its name to Public Service Indiana in 1931, and under Chicago banker Robert Gallagher the company reorganized in 1941 as Public Service Company of Indiana, Inc. (PSI). On September 8 of that year the company's last two interurban cars were involved in a head-on collision near Columbus. Freed of the interurban business and forced to divest itself of its gas business in 1945, PSI concentrated on electric utility service. It built or expanded large coal-fired generating stations near Gibson, Cayuga, Noblesville, New Albany, and Vincennes. The growth of electric power demand during the 1950s and 1960s in the 69–county area served by the company made PSI one of the state's largest utilities during the period.

The late 1970s and 1980s were a difficult period for electric utilities. Caught between skyrocketing interest rates and double-digit inflation, PSI watched as its investment in the proposed Marble Hill Nuclear Station had to be abandoned. In 1990 the company announced the formation of PSI Energy, Inc., a holding company to control the operating utility and other businesses. Still serving 600,000 customers in a 69–county area, two years later the company announced a proposed merger with Cincinnati Gas and Electric Company, which would have created the nation's 13th largest investor-owned electric utility. In April, 1993, however, INDIANAPOLIS POWER AND LIGHT COMPANY, or IPALCO, announced its own $1.5 billion hostile takeover bid. Both plans were withdrawn a few months later after an acrimonious and highly publicized struggle. Ranked the 12th largest public company in Indiana with 1992 operating revenue of $1.08 billion, PSI continues to serve a combination of homes and businesses throughout central and northern Indiana while providing employment to some 4,400 Hoosiers.

BILL BECK
Lakeside Writers' Group

Carroll H. Blanchar, *Indiana and the Electric Age: The Story of Public Service Indiana* (New York: Newcomen Society in North America, 1969); *Indianapolis Business Journal*, Aug. 30–Sept. 5, 1993.

Public Television. See Broadcasting, Educational and Public

Public Transportation. The origins of public transportation in Indianapolis date to October, 1864, when the Citizens' Street Railroad Company put into service on Illinois Street a new streetcar with cushioned seats for 16 passengers, drawn by mules over iron rails laid down the middle of the city's dirt streets. At first this modest innovation luxuriously overcame the discomforts of in-town travel on dusty, muddy, deep-rutted roads; but as the city grew in the decades after the Civil War, both the expectations of the citizens and the potential value of street railway franchises grew rapidly.

The Citizens' Company, whose principal owner, R. B. Catherwood, lived in New York, secured an exclusive 30–year franchise after a struggle with a local and more popular firm headed by Indianapolis railroad developer Thomas A. Morris. In 1866 control of the Citizens' Company passed to WILLIAM H. ENGLISH, and in 1877 the lines were sold to Louisville operators, who immediately fired the conductors and installed automatic fare boxes, to the disgust of local riders. In 1878, a new company sought permission to construct rival lines radiating out from a depot at the CIRCLE and better serving the suburban fringe. The Citizens' managers successfully defended their monopoly, but they found themselves repeatedly challenged to improve and extend service until 1886, when Charles F. Bidwell opened a new era of competition by proposing an electric road.

The promise of electricity—the potential to eliminate mules (and their wastes) and bring clean, quiet, and inexpensive locomotion to urban public transportation—set off a wild round of maneuvering for developmental franchises in Indianapolis as in other booming American cities. The Citizens' Company started to electrify its

Looking east on Washington Street from
Illinois Street in 1891.
[Indiana Historical Society,
Bass Collection, #211646F]

lines in 1889, but with the original franchise due to expire in just a few years, the owners wanted some security before making extensive new investments. Public faith in their service, however, was less than complete: according to local historian JACOB PIATT DUNN, their 1888 request for a new 99–year charter was "hooted out of consideration" by the City Council.

Protracted negotiations, lawsuits, and injunctions followed as rival groups sought exclusive rights to construct and operate public transit lines that were known to yield extraordinary profits if managed (or mismanaged) "advantageously." Seeking to protect the interests of riders and taxpayers, secure good service, and still attract investors competent to the task, in 1899 the Indianapolis Board of Public Works finally hammered out a franchise with a new Indianapolis Street Railway Company, which consolidated the interests of the Citizens' Company with their most potent rivals.

Through the interurban boom of the early 1900s and the 1920s automobile mania, this firm tried to meet the challenges of growth for another generation. By 1912 Indianapolis boasted one of the finest urban transit systems in the country, but labor conflicts, high prices, low fares, and automotive competition gradually undermined profitability. In the 1920s the system's excellent reputation disintegrated before complaints of corruption, profiteering, incivility, and indifference to the public interest.

The Great Depression found public transportation dying in Indianapolis. The old Indianapolis Street Railway Company staggered under an inflated capital burden of $19 million that gobbled up $811,000 annually in interest, leaving nothing for capital improvements, rolling stock, or expansion. While consumers experimented with automotive travel, the city transit system deteriorated: service fell off, employees grew anxious and disgruntled, cars decayed, and patronage declined further. Facing bankruptcy in 1932, the owners tried radical action. Led by Charles W Chase, who recently had rescued Gary's railway system, a reorganized company, Indianapolis Railways, Inc., launched a daring program of revitalization.

By writing down capitalization, the reorganized company reduced its burden of interest by more than half. Then Chase asked equipment suppliers to sell them shiny new rolling stock on credit, which depressed manufacturers proved willing to do. While awaiting the new equipment, Chase spent what little cash he had to renovate overhead wires and tracks, all the while asking riders and workers what was wrong with the existing operations. Soon 25 new STREETCARS (for the main lines), 15 trackless trolleys (electric cars on rubber tires that could swing out to curbs for loading), and 30 gasoline buses (for low-service routes) graced the streets of Indianapolis, and people climbed aboard approvingly.

Encouraged by signs of enthusiasm, Chase plunged ahead, doubling his equipment order in 1933 and pressing the system for speed and efficiency. Revenues went up; expenses went down: by 1935 new operating income had increased 100 percent while fares remained fixed at seven cents. Flush with victory, Chase secured an unprecedented $3 million loan from the federal Public Works Administration to expand further the Indianapolis system and buy even more state-of-the-art cars. In six years (instead of the promised ten), he had delivered a new transit system, boosted patronage more than 25 percent, and apparently reversed a national trend everybody said was inevitable. Wrote Evan Walker in *Nation's Business* in April, 1938: "Motorists began to leave their cars at home and ride the trolleys to work each day, housewives began to prefer the convenience of shopping on the trolleys rather than in their own automobiles, and business men began to see the economy of riding the street cars instead of using taxicabs for their calls."

The 1930s revitalization of the Indianapolis street railway system energized public transportation everywhere for another generation, but the challenge of the automobile had only been delayed, not destroyed. In the 1950s, federal highway development, the explosion in car manufacturing, and steady improvement in middle class purchasing power finally lured all but the poorest (or stubbornest) riders into the driver's seat. Modern highways, paid for entirely with public funds, heavily subsidized the system of automotive transportation, yet cities like Indianapolis continued to expect their bus and trolley systems to operate as profitable enterprises. The competition grew increasingly unfair as suburban sprawl (encouraged by subsidized mortgages through the Veterans Administration and FHA) developed new neighborhoods complete with roads, electricity, water, and sewer systems— but no trolley lines. Indianapolis Railways tried once more in 1952 to dazzle its customers with new rolling stock, enthusiastically supported this time by local banks. But while the banks backed the transit company, most people sought the future in freewheeling highway construction. In January, 1953, electric railway service in the city stopped.

In the mid–1950s a Chicago-based firm acquired what was then called the Indianapolis Transit System, the all-bus remnant of the old street railway operation. Faced with declining patronage, the new owners began raising fares and curbing expenses (especially for service and promotion) in a self-defeating cycle. Meanwhile, city leaders developed a regional transportation plan centered on seven new "interstate" expressways. After a period of ideological self-isolation (for over a decade Indianapolis would not accept federal development funds), reformers led by Mayor Richard G. Lugar determined to reestablish the hub-city concept of railroad days, this time using the federal interstate highway system. Intended (said the 1968 Regional Transportation Study) to give the city "a degree of access to the national highway network that is virtually unsurpassed by any other city," Indianapolis' "spaghetti bowl" of freeways served instead to facilitate thousands of commuters driving to work along lines ideally served by public transportation. Furthermore, while federal money built the expressways, the $35 million of city-county resources spent on street improvements to accommodate this car culture left local government inexorably invested in the highway network. As the marketplace increasingly favored the automobile, public transit simply could not compete, and by 1971 the Indianapolis Transit System reported net operating losses.

The era of subsidized public transportation in Indianapolis began two years later (1973), when the CITY-COUNTY COUNCIL established the INDIANAPOLIS PUBLIC TRANSPORTATION CORPORATION to take over the foundering bus lines. Metro, as the new firm is known, can tap tax revenues to close the gap between farebox receipts and operating costs, an arrangement that barely affirms the inherent public interest of the community in providing transportation for those on the fringes of the private car culture. How long taxpayers and voters will continue to subsidize a network most of them seldom use, time alone will tell. Following the wheel-and-spoke route design imposed on the city 170 years ago by its original planners, Metro perpetuates both the virtues and vices of earlier street railway systems —easy access to the Circle but cumbersome transfers for cross-town trips. Nevertheless, with Metro in operation, one can still "take the bus" in a city that otherwise has traded all for the private automobile.

JOHN LAURITZ LARSON
Purdue University, West Lafayette

Jacob Piatt Dunn, *Greater Indianapolis* (Chicago, 1910); Richard Hebert, *Highways to Nowhere: The Politics of City Transportation* (Indianapolis, 1972); Jerry Marlette, *Electric Railroads of Indiana* (Indianapolis, 1959).

Public Works, Department of. Department of city-county government. Part of the executive branch, the Department of Public Works is the largest of six UNIGOV departments operating under the MAYOR. Originally established in 1909, the Board of Public Works and Sanitation carried out most of the modern department's functions in addition to its responsibility for streets and public parks. The department's current mission is to provide Indianapolis residents with a clean, healthy, and safe environment.

The jurisdiction of the department is defined as the Indianapolis Sanitary District (ISD), which includes an area larger than the "old city" limits but smaller than the consolidated city boundaries. Its territory is not required to be compact or contiguous, a circumstance which has resulted in islands of service surrounded by territory not served by the district. The ISD constitutes a special taxing district. Residents and organizations within the district as well as other users pay taxes and fees that finance waste disposal, sewage treatment, and bond retirement.

The Department of Public Works has gone through several reorganizations since its inception under Unigov; however, its basic responsibilities have remained fairly constant. The department is responsible for sanitation, flood control, drainage, air pollution control, and the management of municipal property. The department did not receive jurisdiction over air pollution until 1974 when state and federal legislation created such regulations for the first time. The department is no longer responsible for municipal properties; the DEPARTMENT OF METROPOLITAN DEVELOPMENT assumed all real estate functions in 1992.

The director is appointed by the mayor with the approval of the CITY-COUNTY COUNCIL and is responsible for policy, personnel, and fiscal matters. This office formerly handled citizen inquiries, but in the early 1990s the Mayor's Action Center assumed this responsibility for all Unigov departments. The Board of Public Works supervises the director. It is made up of four volunteer members, two appointed by the mayor and two by the City-County Council, each of whom serve one-year terms. The board helps make policy for the department, reviews the budget, holds hearings as required by law, approves all contracts, and determines special assessments for local improvements.

The department is responsible for collecting and disposing of the trash within the ISD, including the removal of dead animals and abandoned vehicles from public property. As of the early 1990s, it also supervised 30 recycling drop-off locations throughout the city.

Other Public Works functions include liquid waste disposal, advanced wastewater treatment, sewer maintenance, and drainage and flood control. The department provides liquid waste disposal services through the operation of the Belmont and Southport Advanced Wastewater Treatment Plants. These facilities treat sewage according to EPA and public health standards before it is discharged into the WHITE RIVER, thereby controlling the pollution of local rivers and streams. Public Works also maintains 2,500 miles of sewer systems and operates 213 lift stations in Marion County. Flood control responsibilities include the operation of Eagle Creek Dam and Reservoir, although not the recreational facilities. Overseeing the design and construction of all sewer and drainage capital improvement projects is yet another departmental function, as is the review of designs and issuance of permits for local private and connecting sewer development.

The department monitors and enforces air quality according to EPA and Marion County air pollution standards. Division professionals investigate citizen complaints, inspect pollution sources, conduct smokestack emission tests, certify industrial and commercial plants, and issue violation citations when necessary. The Air Pollution Control Board, a nine-member appointive committee, oversees policy development and implementation in this area. Monitoring surface and groundwater quality, administering the city-county hazardous materials management program, responding to chemical spills and hazardous materials emergencies, and remediation projects and safety and training programs are other departmental functions.

MICHELLE D. HALE

Pulitzer Prizes (Newspapers). Since 1928, newspaper crusades against governmental corruption or social ills have produced two Pulitzer Prizes for the *INDIANAPOLIS STAR* and one each for the *INDIANAPOLIS NEWS* and the former *INDIANAPOLIS TIMES*. Recognized as the highest honor that can come to a newspaper, the awards to the *Times* and the *News* were for "the most disinterested and meritorious public service rendered by an American newspaper during the year." The 1928 award to the *Times* was for exposing Ku Klux Klan–connected political corruption in Indiana, and that to the *News* in 1932 was for a campaign to reduce waste in city and county governmental management and to lower tax levies. The *Star*'s 1975 Pulitzer was given for "local specialized reporting" and honored a three-member investigative team that disclosed local police corruption and lax law enforcement. Recognition of the *Star* in 1991 was for the "investigative reporting" of two reporters on medical malpractice in which repeat offenders escaped discipline by licensing authorities.

Undoubtedly, the foremost Pulitzer accomplishment was that of the *Times*, whose disclosures shook the foundations of city and state government. Its articles revealed the influence of DAVID CURTIS (D. C.) STEPHENSON, Grand Dragon of the Indiana KU KLUX KLAN, over local and state Republican administrations. *Times* editor Boyd Gurley directed investigations conducted primarily by reporter Frank J. Prince. Prince's most notable revelation concerned a $10,000 bribe offered by then Secretary of State Ed Jackson to Governor Warren T. McCray if he would appoint a Klan-connected lawyer as Marion County prosecuting attorney. McCray refused. At the time of the exposure, Jackson was governor of Indiana. He was indicted by a Marion County grand jury but the statute of limitations had expired.

The *Times* also produced evidence under which Indianapolis Mayor JOHN L. DUVALL was indicted and convicted of violation of the Corrupt Practices Act. He resigned as mayor. Six city councilmen were indicted on charges of accepting bribes and later pleaded guilty to lesser charges, paid fines, and resigned their offices.

The *News*' 1930–1931 campaign for better government, based on extensive studies of city and county budgets and tax rates, revealed wasteful management practices. Reporters under city editor Wayne Guthrie disclosed such things as wide variations in the cost of similar services by one unit of government compared with another one. The efforts of the *News* led to budget changes

in 86 counties that saved taxpayers approximately $12 million over two years.

The *Star*'s first Pulitzer Prize came in 1975 after a secret, six-month investigation by reporters William E. Anderson, Harley R. Bierce, and Richard E. Cady. Their story series alleged police corruption in areas of prostitution, bootlegging, narcotics, gambling, and other areas of law enforcement. Results noted by the *Star* included reorganization of the police department and the election defeat of Noble R. Pearcy, the incumbent prosecuting attorney.

The 1991 Pulitzer recognized the investigative reporting of *Star* reporters Susan M. Headden and Joseph T. Hallinan. Their stories documented medical malpractice cases in which a small number of Indiana doctors had lost multiple civil suits against them but suffered no later form of punishment from licensing authorities. Following the awards, the reporters noted that their articles apparently had had no effect on the system.

Two other Pulitzer awards have gone to Indianapolis figures. A dramatic photograph of a crazed Anthony Kiritsis holding realtor Richard Hall hostage at gunpoint won a Pulitzer Prize for spot news photography in 1978 for John H. Blair, a free-lancer for the United Press International at Indianapolis. Charles G. Werner, the *Star*'s editorial cartoonist since 1947, won the Pulitzer Prize for editorial cartooning in 1939 when he worked for the *Daily Oklahoman* of Oklahoma City, Oklahoma. His subject was Hitler's march into the Sudetenland.

JAMES E. FARMER

J. Douglas Bates, *The Pulitzer Prize* (1991); *Indianapolis Times*, May 8, 1928; *Indianapolis News*, May 3, 1932; *Indianapolis Star*, May 6, 1975, Apr. 10, 1991.

Pulliam, Eugene C. (May 3, 1889–June 23, 1975). Newspaper publisher. Born in Ulysses, Kansas, Eugene C. Pulliam wielded an unusual amount of influence over Indianapolis after World War II as the publisher of the state's two largest daily newspapers. His father, Irvin B. Pulliam, had been earning a comfortable living not far from Indianapolis in the 1880s, in Danville, Illinois. Converted to Christianity, he was called to the mission field in western Kansas by the Methodist church. His son, Eugene, came to Indiana to attend the church's school, DePauw University, where he and other students started Sigma Delta Chi. Now the Society of Professional Journalists, it became the largest journalism organization in the nation.

After a year as a reporter at the *Kansas City Star*, Pulliam purchased the *Atchison Champion* in Kansas, married, and returned to Indiana where he purchased the *Franklin Evening Star* and later the *Lebanon Reporter*. From Lebanon he began buying and selling newspapers all over the country, purchasing at least 50 newspapers during his lifetime. The Great Depression slowed his ambitions to own and manage several large newspapers, but the entrepreneurial experience prepared him for opportunities during and after World War II.

Pulliam purchased the INDIANAPOLIS STAR in 1944, along with the *Muncie Star*, then bought the INDIANAPOLIS NEWS in 1948. In 1946 he also purchased the *Arizona Republic* and *Phoenix Gazette* in Phoenix, which was then a small state capital of 65,000 people. He later sold many smaller newspapers to people who had worked for him, leaving his own company, Central Newspapers, Inc., with newspapers in Indianapolis, Phoenix, Muncie, and Vincennes.

While buying his major newspapers he began traveling the globe in an effort to report to readers how the world had changed. His visits to more than 75 countries included several stops in Turkey, where one series he wrote contributed to the 1958 overthrow of the government headed by Prime Minister Adnan Menderes. His travels also convinced him that big government, whether fascist or socialist, was a threat to the freedom that Americans had fought to preserve in World War II.

His conservative political philosophy, concern for community welfare, and a desire for government free of political corruption had a significant impact on Indianapolis and Phoenix. The conservative emphasis of his editorial pages affected Indiana and Indianapolis political races, since the support or opposition of his newspapers could make the difference in close elections. His afternoon *Indianapolis News* began a campaign for countywide government in 1954, along with supporting downtown improvements, airport expansion, and a convention center. For stories detailing police corruption, the *Indianapolis Star* won the PULITZER PRIZE just before his death in 1975.

In 1974 Pulliam started a program for young journalists finishing college. The Pulliam Fellows program, headed by *Indianapolis News* editor Harvey Jacobs, continued after his death, and the alumni include three Pulitzer Prize winners.

Pulliam's philosophy is expressed in a passage from the Bible, II Cor. 3:17, which has remained the motto for his newspapers: "Where the Spirit of the Lord is, there is liberty."

RUSSELL PULLIAM
Indianapolis News

Puryear, John A. (Feb., 1855–Nov. 18, 1930). City councilman. Puryear was born in North Carolina and came to Indianapolis about 1878. In 1891, he was elected city councilman from the fourth ward, one of the first African-Americans to hold a seat on the council. He served from 1892 to 1897, during the administrations of mayors THOMAS L. SULLIVAN, CALEB S. DENNY, and THOMAS TAGGART. During his tenure, in 1894, he started the packing and transfer business of Harris & Puryear, which was succeeded in 1908 by the successful and well-known firm of Puryear & Porter. The latter partnership was in business until 1928. Puryear attended BETHEL AFRICAN METHODIST EPISCOPAL CHURCH and was a member of the Columbia Lodge, Knights of Pythias, and the Lincoln Union, Independent Order of Odd Fellows. Upon his departure from the City Council in 1897, the street on the city's near north side that he had proposed be named Midway was instead voted by the council to be named Puryear.

LEIGH DARBEE
Indiana Historical Society

Indianapolis Star, Nov. 19, 1930; *Indianapolis Recorder*, Nov. 22, 1930.

The Pyramids (3500 DePauw Boulevard). Roche and Dinkeloo of New Haven, Connecticut, designed these concrete and glass buildings for the College Life Insurance Company of America.

A nine-building complex was conceived originally as a vast storage space for insurance records, but advances in computer technology rendered six of the buildings unnecessary. Construction of three buildings began in 1971, with the first occupancy occurring in fall, 1972. Expressing the use of power in form, Roche and Dinkeloo employed massive expanses of concrete on the north and west sides and glass on the south and east sides of each modern structure. Each of the three buildings contains 100,000 square feet of office space, rises eleven stories in a pyramidal shape, and connects to the others by an elevated walkway. Located in an office complex known as College Park, the Pyramids overlook a meadow and a pond—a clever juxtaposition of the severe modernity of glass and concrete with a pastoral setting that recalls the rural roots of the area. Unique in design, the Pyramids have earned a national reputation as an outstanding example of modern architecture.

LINDA B. WEINTRAUT

Leland M. Roth, *A Concise History of American Architecture* (New York, 1980).

Quakers. See Society of Friends

R

Rabb, Kate Milner (Aug. 9, 1866–July 3, 1937). Newspaper columnist and local historian. Born in Rockport, Indiana, Kate Milner attended Rockport High School and received a B.A. and M.A. from Indiana University in 1886 and 1888 respectively. She taught at Rockport High School before marrying in 1891.

Always interested in writing, she submitted articles to the Rockport paper while still in college. She published *National Epics* in 1896, translated *The Boer Boys* in 1900, and edited *The Wit and Humor of America* in 1907. She served as editor of *Indiana Woman*, a weekly Indianapolis newspaper from 1897 to 1898. She also wrote for *Atlantic Monthly, Delineator, St. Nicholas,* and *Youth's Companion.*

Rabb's interest in history began when she wrote the 1916 centennial pageant for Spencer County, Indiana. After her husband's death in 1918, she began a weekly column in the *INDIANAPOLIS STAR* featuring the adventures of John Parsons, a fictional character based on her research. She published the series in 1920 as *A Tour through Indiana in 1840.* She then wrote a thrice-weekly column entitled "The Old Town" that featured the history of Indianapolis. Her most popular column, "The Hoosier Listening Post," ran daily from July 20, 1920, until her death, and featured local, state, and regional history. During this period she co-edited, with WILLIAM HERSCHELL, *An Account of Indianapolis and Marion County* (1924). In 1928 she edited *Indiana Coverlets and Coverlet Weavers.* She was appointed to the Indiana Historical Commission in 1924 and served for one year.

Rabb was a member of the INDIANA HISTORICAL SOCIETY, Phi Beta Kappa, Women's Press Club of Indiana (which she served as president during 1929–1930), the CONTEMPORARY CLUB, and the Players Club, which she and her husband organized.

NORALEEN YOUNG

"Death of Kate Milner Rabb '86," *Indiana University Alumni Quarterly,* 24 (Summer, 1937), 372–377.

Ragtime. This uniquely American musical genre, based upon African-American rhythms and styles rendered initially by black banjoists

Indianapolis native May Aufderheide wrote popular tunes such as the 1908 "Dusty Rag." [Indiana State Library]

and pianists, flourished throughout the United States from the late 1890s to the end of World War I. During this period Indianapolis contributed several distinguished ragtime composers and performers. Many were African-Americans who performed along INDIANA AVENUE, although little of their music was published. Most composers were middle class whites, including numerous young women.

MAY AUFDERHEIDE (1888–1972) composed several popular piano rags between 1908 and 1913: "Dusty Rag," "Thriller Rag," and "The Richmond Rag." Sophus Jergensen lived in Indianapolis in the early 1900s and composed "Hoosier Rag" and "Mingle Your Eye-Brows with Mine." Joseph F. Cohen owned a music publishing company and composed "Dancing at the Georgia Jubilee," "Golden Glow," and "Love Dreams." Pianist Julia Lee Niebergall (1886–1968) composed "Horseshoe Rag" and "Red Rambler Rag," taught music at MANUAL HIGH SCHOOL, and accompanied silent movies and dance classes. Abe Olman came to Indianapolis from Cincinnati in 1908 and managed the L. S. Ayres and Company sheet music department for four years before moving to New York to become a music publisher; while in Indianapolis he composed "Honeymoon Rag," "Candlestick Rag," "Seaweeds Rag," "Halloween Rag," and "Egyptia." Paul Pratt (1890–1948) managed the John H. Aufderheide music publishing firm and composed "Vanity Rag," "Colonial Glide," and "Walhalla." J. Russel Robinson (1892–1963) began playing piano in Indianapolis movie theaters around 1905. After leaving town in 1908, he composed several ragtime pieces including "Sapho Rag" and "Dynamite Rag"; from 1919 to 1921 he toured and recorded with the Original Dixieland Jazz Band and composed several popular and jazz hits including "Margie," "Singin' the Blues," and "Palesteena." African-American pianist Russell Smith (1890–1969) used Indianapolis as a home base beginning in the 1910s and composed "That Demon Rag" and "The Microbe Rag." Cecil Duane Crabb (1890–1953) came to Indianapolis in 1908 and composed "Fluffy Ruffles," "Orinoco," and, with Will B. Morrison, "Trouble Rag" and "Klassicle Rag." Seventeen-year-old black pianist Jesse Crump arrived in Indianapolis from Dallas in 1923 and performed as a pianist at the Golden West Cafe on Indiana Avenue, recording his only known ragtime composition, "Mr. Crump Rag," at Gennett Records later that year; Crump composed many songs for blues singers and recorded with Ida Cox on Paramount Records and Nina Reeves on Gennett.

Indianapolis sheet music publishers specializing in ragtime included Warner C. Williams, John H. Aufderheide, Isadore Seidel, Abby Music Publishing, Carlin & Lennox, and Duane Crabb.

LAWRENCE E. MCCULLOUGH
Indiana University–Purdue University,
Indianapolis

John Edward Hasse and Frank J. Gillis, *Indiana Ragtime: A Documentary Album*, liner notes (Indianapolis: Indiana Historical Society, 1981).

Railroad Strike of 1877. The labor uprisings that affected the nation's railroads were larger and had more serious consequences than other strikes during the economic depression of the 1870s. The strikes were largely a manifestation of frustration and desperation in the face of steadily worsening economic conditions over which workers had no control. Beginning in the East as a result of announced wage cuts, the railroad strike spread west quickly. Freight trains on most lines came to a standstill, including those at Pittsburgh, Cincinnati, St. Louis, Cleveland, Columbus, and Indianapolis.

On Saturday, July 21, 1877, union workers assembled in the courtyard of the Indiana State House to rally in support of their eastern counterparts, causing work stoppages in Fort Wayne, In-

dianapolis, Terre Haute, Evansville, Elkhart, and Vincennes. Passenger trains initially were allowed to run, but later all rail transportation throughout Indiana was paralyzed. Both Mayor JOHN CAVEN and Governor James D. Williams adopted a conciliatory attitude toward the strikers, refusing to use force. Railroad operators, unable to persuade the governor to involve the militia, turned to Federal District Judge WALTER Q. GRESHAM to remedy the situation. The operators were able to pursue this strategy because several of the railroad lines were in receivership of the federal courts. Gresham, who was less sympathetic with the strikers, asked President Rutherford B. Hayes to send troops to Indianapolis to control the strikes, but was informed that none were available.

As a U.S. marshal Gresham possessed the authority to call for whatever assistance was needed to protect life and property, and the unique situation of this strike made it a federal offense. Gresham thereupon declared that the situation in Indianapolis was critical and dangerous and organized a committee of public safety, which included ex-governor Conrad Baker, Senator Joseph E. McDonald, and future president BENJAMIN HARRISON. When President Hayes sent troops in support of Gresham's efforts, it marked the first time that federal troops had been involved in a national labor dispute.

Governor Williams took a similar stand and issued a proclamation declaring that the strikes threatened the peace of Indianapolis and that the strikers' grievances should be remedied in the courts. He asked the strikers to withdraw and formed an arbitration committee to assist in the settlement of the strikes. Judge Gresham ordered the strikers back to work and the strike began to collapse, finally ending on August 1. Most of the workers returned to work without any promise of wage restoration. When the freight trains resumed operations in Indianapolis federal troops were present to prevent any violence or disorder, though their services were not needed.

Fifteen strikers were arrested on July 27 and charged with contempt for interfering with the operation of railroad lines. These men were tried with no jury in federal court by Judge Thomas Drummond. Of the 15 arrested, 13 were found guilty and sentenced from one to six months in jail; one was acquitted, and the other freed with one year good behavior and a $5,000 bond. The strikers regarded these arrests as a betrayal of pledges made by the arbitration committee during the strike. After public denouncements and the threat of impeachment, Drummond released the convicted men on $500 recognizance each, with the stipulation that they refrain for one year from interfering with property in control of the federal courts.

DONNA J. MUNDEN

Emma Lou Thornbrough, *Indiana in the Civil War Era, 1850–1880* (Indianapolis, 1965); Philip S. Foner, *The Great Labor Uprising of 1877* (New York, 1977).

Railroad Track Elevation. The proposal to elevate steam railway lines over city streets in the MILE SQUARE was a significant political issue of the early 20th century. Tracks reaching UNION STATION and running south of the Warehouse District posed two closely related problems—of traffic congestion and traveler safety—on such southward running streets as Virginia, Delaware, Pennsylvania, Meridian, and Illinois. The success of an 1888 street railway tunnel running under the tracks on Illinois Street may have helped to confirm the belief that elevation of the tracks and the creation of underpasses for pedestrians and vehicles was a solution.

The issue enjoyed support from civic boosters, including the leaders of the Indianapolis COMMERCIAL CLUB, political leaders who saw civic and patronage advantages in a public works project, and residents of the southern part of the city. Construction of the overpasses began with the Virginia Avenue viaduct in 1892 and proceeded to include much of the route of the BELT LINE RAILROAD by the 1920s. Mayors of the era, beginning with THOMAS L. SULLIVAN, claimed political credit for parts of the improvements. Later interpreters often place track elevation within the context of professionally managed civic improvements championed during the Progressive era.

MIRIAM K. GEIB

Railroadmen's Federal Savings and Loan Association. Financial institution. Founded in 1887 by William T. Cannon, paymaster of the Indianapolis Union Railroad, the association originally assisted railroad workers to save money and invest in new homes. Through consistently focusing on home mortgages, Railroadmen's grew steadily and claimed to be the largest savings and loan in the world by the 1920s. A dependable business, it grew even larger after World War II by offering mortgages to returning veterans.

For the next 30 years the company remained a solid financial investment, but deregulation of the banking industry, high interest rates, and inflation created financial strain for the firm in the 1980s. In 1984 Railroadmen's posted a net loss of 1.4 percent, but within the next three years returned to profitability with a 2.1 percent growth. The company switched from mutual ownership to stock ownership in 1987. Attesting to its conservative investment practices, the company's stock hit its highest point during the national savings and loan crisis of the late 1980s when bad investments forced many savings and loans to file for bankruptcy.

Continuing to focus on residential mortgages, Railroadmen's purchased or merged with the following institutions: Brown County Federal Savings and Loan (1981), Heritage Federal Savings Bank (1987), and Archer Federal Savings and Loan (1991). This activity, resulting in a total of 15 bank offices and 185 employees, made Railroadmen's one of the largest savings and loans in the state. In 1992 the company posted record earnings of $6.61 million, an increase attributable to mortgage loan production. In November, 1993, Railroadmen's shareholders voted to merge with the Ohio-based Huntington Bancshares, Inc., for a price of $88 million. Railroadmen's $660 million assets raised Huntington's total assets in Indiana to nearly $1.06 billion.

STACEY NICHOLAS

Railroads. In the 1850s, when several new rail lines converged on Indiana's fledgling state capital, there developed a popular view that Indianapolis was the "Railroad City." The sheer number of railroads penetrating the MILE SQUARE helped prompt this conclusion, as did the fact that tracks crowded in on the little town from several directions. The original UNION STATION (1853) located just south of the CIRCLE became almost instantaneously the hub of a large "transportational wheel" whose spokes projected outward to many points of the compass. Other developing urban centers from the Atlantic coast westward were also becoming focal points for rail lines, some of them—Chicago, for example—outstripping Indianapolis in the number of lines penetrating them. Nevertheless, Indianapolis over succeeding decades remained a conspicuous example of this kind of transportation and urban development and deserves its appellation. These numerous rail lines not only helped bring commercial and industrial prosperity to Indianapolis, but also played a prime role in determining the geographic pattern of the developing city by establishing extensive corridors from Union Station outward where businesses could locate. Positive and negative aspects of this spatial process represent a legacy that these early railroads left.

The years from 1830 to 1870 mark the "pioneer" period of Indianapolis' railroad development. Of the eight initial railroad charters issued by the State of Indiana (1832), five of them directly involved Indianapolis. No rail lines were built under these earliest charters but two of the lines so authorized, the Lawrenceburgh & Indianapolis and the Madison, Indianapolis & Lafayette, were to receive financial help from the state under the Mammoth Internal Improvements Act of 1836. An abbreviated version of the latter line (renamed the MADISON AND INDIANAPOLIS, or M&I) became Indiana's first operable steam railroad (1847). As a reaction to the initial success of the M&I and the state's liberalized charter policy under the 1851 Constitution, construction began on several other projected lines. By 1855 seven of the sixteen lines that would ultimately serve the city were in place: the Bellefontaine (to Union City); the Terre Haute & Richmond (to Terre Haute); the Jeffersonville (to Jeffersonville via the M&I tracks down to Columbus); the Peru & Indianapolis (to Noblesville); the Lafayette & Indianapolis; the Lawrenceburgh & Upper Mississippi (to Lawrenceburgh with connections to Cincinnati); and the Indiana Central (to the Ohio state line via Richmond). Twelve years

Irvington train station, ca. 1890.
[Indiana Historical Society, #C5630]

later two additional lines opened: the Indianapolis & Vincennes; and the Cincinnati, Hamilton & Indianapolis (a second line to Cincinnati).

This early group of railroads performed multiple functions that their later counterparts would adopt and expand. They served as a convenient and inexpensive method for moving large commodities into and out of Indianapolis' developing hinterland. They also provided Indianapolis with transportation connections to distant regions—the Atlantic seaboard, the trans-Mississippi West via St. Louis, and the American South via Louisville and Cincinnati. Commodities brought into Indianapolis over these pioneer lines for local consumption, processing, or transshipment typically were surplus Hoosier farm and forest products, along with growing quantities of industrial products identified during the early years simply as "merchandise."

Most Indianapolis rail lines during the Civil War were at least marginally prosperous while helping the city serve as an important logistics center for Union armies in the western campaigns. After some initial managerial confusion the railroads proceeded to do on a larger scale what they had grown accustomed to doing over the preceding decade: haul various kinds of freight and transport people. Their crucial contribution to the war effort paved the way for expansion of peacetime services, but problems and organizational changes quickly followed and continued almost to the close of the century.

A basic postwar issue, reminiscent of the mid–1850s, was the competition among Indiana's rail lines, including those terminating in Indianapolis. A standard "solution" to this problem was to gain an advantage over the competition by improving services. Since such effort led to increased developmental and operational costs, the railroad companies most firmly rooted financially had a clear advantage. Generally this meant the large railroad systems established headquarters in eastern cities. Major eastern rail corporations—among them the PENNSYLVANIA, the NEW YORK CENTRAL, and the BALTIMORE & OHIO—extended their influence to the midwestern states and the city of Indianapolis. Preceding the assimilation of the Indianapolis rail lines into these large systems, most of the lines experienced bankruptcy or operation under receivership. The corporate relationship between the individual rail lines and the systems varied, but localized lines generally lost their earlier titles and became identified popularly as well as officially with their new corporate parents. Indianapolis lines eventually absorbed into the Pennsylvania Railroad system were the Jeffersonville (the Jeffersonville, Madison and Indianapolis), the Indianapolis & Vincennes, the Terre Haute & Richmond, and the Indiana Central. Those coming under control of the "Big Four" portion of the New York Central system were the Indianapolis & Bellefontaine, the Lafayette & Indianapolis, the Lawrenceburgh & Upper Mississippi, the Indianapolis & St. Louis, and both the eastern and western sections of the Indianapolis, Bloomington & Western. The Baltimore & Ohio established an east-west line through Indianapolis by taking over what had been the Cincinnati, Hamilton & Indianapolis and combining it with the Indianapolis, Bloomington & Springfield. Meanwhile other consolidations designed to enhance Indianapolis' rail connections took place. What had once been the Peru & Indianapolis was absorbed by the Lake Erie & Western. The Louisville, New Albany & Chicago Railroad ("MONON RAILROAD"), an in-state rail system, assumed control of the partially narrow-gauged Chicago & Indianapolis Airline, thus establishing an additional link between Indianapolis and the Chicago region.

Because of its involvement with railroads and its developing industrial establishment, Indianapolis experienced serious economic troubles in the 1870s. One notable episode of the decade was Mayor JOHN CAVEN'S effort during the nationwide RAILROAD STRIKE OF 1877 to end a hunger crisis in the city by putting jobless men to work resuming construction of the BELT LINE RAILROAD. Circuiting a major part of the youthful city, the Belt Line gave versatility to the several lines centered at Union Station and added to the commercial and industrial potential of areas of the city it traversed.

Along with the further development of its rail facilities during the postwar decades, the city showed impressive population, territorial, and economic gains. By 1900 its population had risen to 169,164 and its boundaries extended as far as six miles from the Circle. New manufacturing facilities, particularly foundries, machine shops, and other metal working establishments, created an industrial atmosphere in the growing city. By the close of the century the huge stockyard and meatpacking facilities on the White River, served by four rail lines plus the Belt, were processing over a million hogs annually—almost triple the number identified with the city of Cincinnati when it had the coveted nickname of "Porkopolis." By 1900 total assessed value of property in Marion County had grown to over $138 million, about 3 percent of which represented railroad company properties. The latter included locomotives, cars, rights-of way, classification yards, several small depots and freight houses, the new Union Station (1888), and several repair shops. The New York Central installation at BEECH GROVE in the southeastern part of the county was destined to become the largest and most comprehensive railroad repair facility in Indianapolis.

For the eastern half of the United States, the state of Indiana, and the city of Indianapolis, the first two decades of the 20th century mark a high plateau of railroad service and achievement. Two lines were added to the Indianapolis rail network after 1900—chiefly for the hauling of coal mined in the southwestern part of the state. (These were the Illinois Central to Effingham, Illinois, 1903, and the Pennsylvania line linking Indianapolis and Frankfort, 1914.) Most of the earlier lines improved and enlarged their facilities, greatly increased the frequency of freight and passenger runs, and continued to pursue technological advances that led to further convenience and safety. Although by 1920 the enormous steel mills of Indiana's Calumet region had enabled Lake County to surpass Marion County in manufacturing, development of Indianapolis industry continued on a dramatic scale. As in earlier years, manufacturing establishments old and new relied heavily on their proximity to railroad service, with the city's Belt Line continuing to play a prime role in this total transportation complex. During the 1900–1920 period manufacture of automobiles and auto parts emerged as a major industry, with Indianapolis a leading center. Likewise the building of railroad cars became a major Indianapolis enterprise by 1920, surpassing the still growing meat industry. Industries relating to food, clothing, and furniture reached significant levels in the city during the 1900–1910 decade.

World War I prompted an array of transportation problems not unlike those of the Civil War over a half century earlier. Again Indianapolis railroads helped provide the transport services required to support "the boys over there." The American Railway Act (December, 1917) authorized a federal agency to oversee operation of the nation's railroads, which on the whole functioned well. However, by the time of the withdrawal of this wartime jurisdiction (March, 1920), the country's passenger business had dropped 14 percent and its freight business 23 percent. Generally the country recovered from the post–World War I depression rather quickly, but its railroads had a difficult time returning to normal. A major reason for this was the formidable competition resulting from the expanding use of automobile transportation—trucks, buses, and family cars. Indianapolis inevitably shared in this rail service decline. Indiana's elaborate electric INTERURBAN system, centered in the capital city during the 1920s, also contributed to the diminishing volume of passengers to be seen at Union Station.

During the Great Depression of the 1930s railroads serving Indianapolis remained in place despite the "hard times" that threatened bankruptcy and road abandonment. Preparation for war in the late 1930s placed a priority on use of rail resources throughout the country. America's formal entry into World War II accelerated this demand as the nation's railroads for the third time in a century provided much of the transport infrastructure for the military effort. Hustle and bustle at Union Station reached unprecedented levels, and the city's total rail establishment came to life with renewed vigor and dedication. Then, following what might be called their "finest hour," Indianapolis' rail lines in the postwar years returned to the precarious condition that renewed transportation rivalry fostered.

Like other American urban centers, Indianapolis in the decades after World War II continued to undergo the transportation revolution that had been well advanced during the prewar years. Other factors were involved, but it was the extensive use of family autos and large semitrailers that was most responsible for these changes. Indianapolis assimilated these transport alternatives and, simultaneously, phased out what had become viewed as obsolescent. What to retain and what to eliminate became a crucial question.

Initially, federal and state governments of the post–World War II years sought to curb the increasing number of rail abandonments by financially strapped companies. Following precedents established years earlier by rail corporations, government policy encouraged giant railroad consolidations such as the Penn Central (1968) and the later Conrail (1972), NORFOLK SOUTHERN, and CSX. Meanwhile a series of periodically updated "Indiana State Rail Plans," prepared under the auspices of the state's Division of Railroads, called for the subsidized preservation of portions of the surviving rail system on the basis of economic feasibility and the transportation needs of specific regions and communities of the state.

In keeping with this general policy Indianapolis has retained its relative importance as a rail center, but there are several differences in what is shipped into and out of the capital as well as in the volume of transport business in "carload" terms. Since heavy industry does not predominate in the city, raw materials used in much of its manufacturing are relatively light and hence transportable by truck. This applies also to many of the city's finished products. Only a small portion of coal and farm products, the state's two largest commodity shipments, are directed toward Indianapolis. Thus the city's previous role as a central clearing point for distribution of goods by rail in several directions has been significantly altered.

But despite cutbacks, changes in the quantity and variety of commodities entering and exiting from the city, and the acceleration of transport competition—including that from airlines—Indianapolis has retained many of the features that a century ago prompted the title "Railroad City." Eight of the sixteen lines of track that once traversed the city's boundaries remained in use in 1993, and the Belt Line circumventing much of the core of the city is still in operation. With three major rail freight systems (Conrail, CSX, Norfolk Southern) plus Amtrak serving the capital, Indianapolis remains a vital "station" on Indiana's revised rail network.

VICTOR M. BOGLE
Indiana University, Kokomo

Emma Lou Thornbrough, *Indiana in the Civil War Era, 1850–1880* (Indianapolis, 1965); Clifton J. Phillips, *Indiana in Transition, 1880–1920* (Indianapolis, 1968); Indiana Department of Transportation, *Indiana State Rail Plan, 1987 Update* (Bloomington, Ind., 1987).

Ralston, Alexander (1771–Jan. 5, 1827). Surveyor of Indianapolis. Born in Scotland, Ralston worked as surveyor and engineer for Lord Roslin on his estate in Great Britain. After immigrating to America, he assisted in the mapping of Washington, D.C., working on the survey until 1794. He later moved to Louisville, Kentucky, where, in 1806, Aaron Burr hired him to survey western territories. Ralston unknowingly became connected with Burr's conspiracy to invade and conquer the Southwest. Although innocent, Ralston probably remained in the West to escape public charges of being Burr's spy.

Ralston resided in Harrison County, Indiana, around 1814 and later moved to Salem, where he lived from 1818 to 1820. There he met Judge Christopher Harrison, appointed in January, 1821, as commissioner for the survey of Indiana's new capital. Harrison selected Ralston and Englishman ELIAS PYM FORDHAM to survey and plat the city, which they began in April, 1821. Ralston suggested the "MILE SQUARE" plan with most streets crossing at right angles and four diagonal avenues radiating from a central circle, reminiscent of Pierre L'Enfant's plan for the nation's capital. Upon completion of the survey, town lots were sold beginning in October, 1821.

Ralston, a bachelor, must have been pleased with the new capital since he established his residence here in early 1822. He built a brick house west of Capitol (then Tennessee) Avenue on Maryland Street where he lived with his African-American housekeeper Chaney. Ralston served as Marion County surveyor until his death. In February, 1825, the state legislature commissioned him to survey the WHITE RIVER and to estimate the expense for keeping it navigable.

At his death, the *Indiana Journal* eulogized Ralston as an honest gentleman of "extreme sensibilities." Although Indianapolis residents held him in high regard, proposals to honor his memory, including SAMUEL MERRILL's plan to establish a park, went unfulfilled. In 1874, as the city planned to abandon Greenlawn Cemetery, Ralston's remains were reinterred in the "destitute teachers lot" at CROWN HILL CEMETERY. Around 1890, an effort to create a Ralston memorial collected only $325. An attempt in 1907 to convince the city park board to erect a statue in University Square also failed. Finally, on November 9, 1937, the Indianapolis Teachers' Federation erected a marker on Ralston's grave using monies from the 1890s fund drives. The marker bears the 1821 plat of the Mile Square.

In 1971 the chair of the Indianapolis Sesquicentennial Commission suggested naming I–465 the "Ralston Expressway." No action was taken, however, and the city still has no appropriate memorial to its planner.

SHERYL D. VANDERSTEL

Jacob Piatt Dunn, *Greater Indianapolis* (Chicago, 1910); Emmett A. Rice, "A Forgotten Man of Indianapolis," *Indiana Magazine of History*, 34 (Sept., 1938), 283–297.

Ransburg. Developers of painting and automation equipment. In 1938 Harold Ransburg and Harry Green began experiments in Indianapolis attempting to conserve paint, in short supply during the Great Depression, by reducing wasted overspray through an electrical process. Assisted by Emery P. Miller, a physics professor from Purdue University, Ransburg and Green refined their process and were granted a patent on July 1, 1941. Financed and owned by Harold's father, Harper Ransburg, the young company began manufacturing painting machinery. During World War II the U.S. War Department contracted with the Ransburg Company for the production of special machinery for painting ammunition and weapons. Wartime profits financed the development of more efficient painting methods.

In 1957 the company built an 80,000–square-foot facility on West 56th Street. Increased manufacturing capacity enabled Ransburg to virtually monopolize the spray painting market with its patented processes. In 1962 ownership transferred to Harold Ransburg and the company began to diversify. Ransburg Japan Ltd. was formed in 1963.

From the 1960s through the 1980s the Indianapolis-based company diversified its operations adding Ransburg Canada Ltd. (Canada), Ransburg Gmbh (Germany) and Ransburg S.A. (France), Ransburg Systems, Glas-Craft, Electro Painters, Mako Marine, Micro-Poise, Rol-Lift, Roto-Finish, Welltronic, Cybotech, Globe Tool & Engineering, GEMA, Industra Products, Statomat-Globe Maschinenfabrik Gmbh and Acro Automations.

The recession of the 1980s thwarted the growth of Ransburg's many divisions and the company's financial performance declined. A first-time loss of $5 million in 1984 deepened to a $16 million loss by 1987. To reduce financial losses, several divisions were sold. At this point Ransburg had 325 employees in Indianapolis and a total of 1,550 employees worldwide. On April 1, 1989, Ransburg's operations were purchased by Illinois Tool Works (ITW). In 1993 the company operated as ITW Finishing Systems.

MICHAEL WATSON

Beverly K. Bell, *A History of Ransburg* (1990).

Ransom, Freeman Bailey (July 7, 1884–Aug. 6, 1947). Lawyer, businessman, and civic activist. Born in Grenada, Mississippi, Ransom graduated from the law department of Walden University in Nashville, Tennessee, in 1908, and took postgraduate work in the School of Law at Columbia University. Following his move to Indianapolis in 1910, Ransom's future became entwined with that of MADAM C. J. WALKER. He became the attorney and later the general manager for the Madam C. J. Walker Company, which manufactured and distributed hair care products primarily for the black population. Under Ransom's leadership the company set a national standard of entrepreneurship in the African-American business community.

As the Walker Company grew in importance, so did Ransom's influence. He became the attorney for several Indianapolis businesses and civic organizations, including the SENATE AVENUE YMCA, Dr. E. N. Perkins Cream Float Soap Company, and the Frederick Douglass Life Insurance Company. He was a city councilman, alternate delegate to the Democratic national convention, and a trustee of the INDIANA SCHOOL FOR THE BLIND and the BETHEL AFRICAN METHODIST EPISCOPAL CHURCH. He was also heavily involved with FLANNER HOUSE, the Senate Avenue YMCA, and the PHYLLIS WHEATLEY YWCA.

Ransom became acquainted with William Pickens, field secretary of the NAACP and director of its branches, and he was often consulted by national officers when questions arose about racism and segregation in the Midwest in general and Indiana in particular. Pickens and other African-American leaders frequently stayed in the Ransom home when they had occasion to visit Indianapolis.

STANLEY WARREN
DePauw University

Frank L. Mather, ed., *Who's Who of the Colored Race*, Vol. 1 (Chicago, 1915); *Indianapolis Star*, Aug. 7, 1947; *Indianapolis Recorder*, Aug. 9, 1947.

Ransom Place. Historic neighborhood located eight blocks north and five blocks west of Monument Circle. This six-square-block area is an intact remnant of the oldest neighborhood associated with the city's African-American population. The Ransom Place Historic District is bounded by Martin Luther King, Jr., St. Clair, Paca, and 10th streets.

Ransom Place, a combination of lots platted by John Meikel in 1865 and William Y. Wiley in 1871, is a remnant of a larger community comprised of immigrants and free blacks dating from as early as 1836. This area experienced most of its growth between 1880 and 1920. The houses were of modest vernacular styles, mostly one-story frame houses, but including some shotgun and larger-scale houses. By 1925 the neighborhood was a prestigious community of prominent and well-established black residents, including physicians, a city councilman, and several attorneys, most notably neighborhood namesake FREEMAN B. RANSOM.

From 1929 on the neighborhood declined. In 1955 the Indianapolis Redevelopment Commission designated the neighborhood as the city's first rehabilitation area. Nevertheless, during the expansion of IUPUI much of the housing within Ransom Place was demolished. In 1991 the Ransom Place Neighborhood Association was founded to encourage preservation of the housing and to promote the area's history. Ransom Place was named to the National Register of Historic Places in 1992.

DAVID AND MARY FRISBY

———

James Divita, *Ethnic Settlement Patterns in Indianapolis* (Indianapolis, 1988); National Register of Historic Places nomination (copy available at Historic Landmarks Foundation of Indiana).

Rappaport, Philip (Mar., 1845–Dec. 7, 1913). Editor and attorney. Born and educated in Bavaria, Germany, Rappaport came to the United States in 1863. Settling first in Wheeling, West Virginia, he later moved to Pittsburgh and then to Cincinnati where he studied law. In 1873 Rappaport moved to Indianapolis and went into practice with Robert Parker, retiring several years later due to deteriorating hearing.

In 1874 he purchased the *German Daily Tribune*, later known as the *Indiana Tribune*, serving

Philip Rappaport.
[Indiana State Library]

as both editor and publisher until 1900 when he sold the paper to August Tamm. After the marriage of his daughter, Emma, to RICHARD LIEBER in 1893, Rappaport hired Lieber as a reporter for the *Indiana Tribune*. Following the sale of his paper, Rappaport continued to write and lecture on a series of economic and social issues. Considered a prominent freethinker, Rappaport's best known book was *Looking Forward*, described by the *Indianapolis Star* as "a speculative political treatise of a decidedly socialistic tone." Vehemently opposed to William Jennings Bryan's economic theories, he played an active role in the 1896 presidential campaign by making frequent speeches against Bryan and his policies to the German-American community.

JEFFERY A. DUVALL

———

Indianapolis Star, Dec. 8, 1913.

Ravenswood. Northside community roughly bounded by White River on the north and west, Keystone Avenue on the east, and 71st Street to the south. Platted in 1910 by the Marion Trust Company, Ravenswood began as a riverside resort community. The electric STREETCARS brought city dwellers for summer outings on the river, where on some days as many as 10,000 people swam, fished, and rented canoes and boats. At night, diners and dancers favored the Wharf House, a restaurant known for its steaks and entertainment. Affluent families built cottages and even some elaborate homes in the Terrace Beach enclave along Fitch Avenue.

In the mid–1920s, however, the river changed course, the beach eroded, and low-lying areas became swampy. The summer crowd moved out and year-round residents moved in, attracted to low-cost cottages and the town's bohemian atmosphere. By the 1950s and 1960s, the once-posh resort community was a neighborhood in turmoil. Flooding was a continual problem, property values were depressed, and city tax revenues proved inadequate for basic services.

In the 1970s new residents, lured by the location and affordable housing, began to purchase and restore some of the older homes. Property values rose and the county undertook flood control projects to alleviate drainage problems. Ravenswood has suffered setbacks, however, in the last few years. Population declined from a peak of 650 in 1970 to an estimated 460 in 1988. In December, 1988, the town council, citing lack of revenue and citizen apathy, voted to dissolve and asked the City of Indianapolis to assume control. Then in January, 1991, a rain-swollen White River overflowed and caused widespread property damage. Most residents, however, expressed an intention to remain in the neighborhood, though looking to the city and the Army Corps of Engineers for eventual solutions to the flooding problems.

CATHLEEN DONNELLY

Indianapolis Star, Feb. 12, Aug. 27, 1989, Jan. 1–7, 1991.

Ray, James M. (1800–Feb. 22, 1881). Early settler, businessman, and civic leader. Born at Caldwell, New Jersey, Ray studied at Columbia University before migrating in 1818 to Lawrenceburg, Indiana, and later Connersville, serving as deputy clerk in both towns. He moved to Indianapolis to become clerk of the public land auctions in October, 1821. On April 1, 1822, Ray, the "Whitewater faction" candidate, fought a hotly contested race against MORRIS MORRIS of the "Kentucky faction" to become the first Marion County clerk (1822–1834). Ray also served as county recorder (1829–1834), cashier of the State Bank of Indiana (1834–1855), then cashier and subsequently president of the BANK OF THE STATE

OF INDIANA (1857–1865). He served in the Internal Revenue Department in Washington, D.C. (1871–1875) before retiring to Indianapolis.

Ray participated in numerous local business ventures. He was a stockholder in the INDIANAPOLIS STEAM MILL COMPANY (1828), director of the Indiana Mutual Fire Insurance Company (1837–1855), executive committee member of the BOARD OF TRADE (1853), director of the Indianapolis and Cincinnati Railroad (1854), builder of the Trade Palace (1859), and president of the Union Insurance Company (1865-?).

Actively involved in civic benevolence and reform, Ray, a Presbyterian, helped organize the town's first Sabbath school (1822), serving as its first superintendent, and Bible Society (1825). He was secretary of the Temperance Society (1828), Colonization Society (1829), and the Marion County Engine Company (1835), and secretary-treasurer of the INDIANAPOLIS BENEVOLENT SOCIETY (1836–1865?), all which he helped organize. Ray took a leading role in establishing CROWN HILL CEMETERY (1863) and was, at his death, president of the cemetery's trustees.

An advocate of improved education, Ray served on the Board of National Popular Education (1847), an organization devoted to sending qualified eastern teachers to western schools. He helped obtain the charter for the Presbyterian-sponsored INDIANAPOLIS FEMALE INSTITUTE (1836) and became a trustee of the Indianapolis Collegiate Institute (1850), successor to the female institute. A proponent for a blind school, Ray sponsored a visit in 1846 by blind Kentucky educator William H. Churchman, and in 1847 was named trustee for the new blind institute.

SHERYL D. VANDERSTEL

Gayle Thornbrough et al., eds., *The Diary of Calvin Fletcher* (9 vols., Indianapolis, 1972–1983), passim; John H. B. Nowland, *Early Reminiscences of Indianapolis* (Indianapolis, 1870); *Indianapolis Journal*, Feb. 23, 1881.

RCA Dome. See Hoosier Dome.

RCA—Radio Corporation of America. See Thomson Consumer Electronics.

Real Estate Development and Developers. The first real estate sale in Indianapolis took place on October 8, 1821, at Matthias Nowland's tavern near what is now the corner of Washington and Missouri streets. Although this early venture failed (only one lot sold), many Indianapolis citizens and companies have since steered the physical evolution of the city through real estate development.

Antebellum development involved a host of Indianapolis' most prominent men and women. In 1849, taking advantage of the excitement over the 1847 arrival of the MADISON AND INDIANAPOLIS RAILROAD, several residents platted subdivisions within or near Indianapolis' MILE SQUARE. In the 1850s CALVIN FLETCHER, NICHOLAS MCCARTY, HERVEY BATES, OVID BUTLER, and Janet McQuat also became developers. Fletcher Place's 458 lots sold "like hotcakes" after Fletcher and Amasa Stone platted the area in 1853. One hundred homes were built in the subdivision in 1854 alone.

By the 1870s the city had entered a boom period; in 1873 more than 8,700 properties were bought and sold. Judge Elijah B. Martindale's addition along Delaware Street attracted lawyer BENJAMIN HARRISON and other prominent citizens to the near north side. Many of Indianapolis' later suburbs were also platted during this period, including IRVINGTON, WOODRUFF PLACE, and BRIGHTWOOD. However, a real estate collapse that followed the Panic of 1873 temporarily halted development by the late 1870s.

A new boom began in the 1890s aided by an annexation movement, expansion and electrification of streetcar lines, and the discovery of natural gas. When the state fairgrounds were moved to their new Maple Road (now 38th Street) location, Willard W. Hubbard, Edward F. Claypool, and Judge Martindale purchased the former site. They platted 280 residential building lots and named the area Morton Place after its Civil War moniker, CAMP MORTON. Within Indianapolis, population density increased as developers erected duplexes for rental property. On the northwest side the Fairview streetcar line was an impetus for development.

The beginning of the 20th century brought increasing activity. Alfred F. Potts constructed a small community of English Tudor homes, known as "Pottstown," on 15th Street. On the southside, in 1902 William L. Elder donated eight acres to the United Brethren in Christ Church for the erection of Indiana Central University (now the UNIVERSITY OF INDIANAPOLIS). In return for the donation the church furnished many of the buyers for the 446 lots Elder platted in University Heights. In 1906 the Wocher brothers purchased 740 acres south of the city for the NEW YORK CENTRAL RAILROAD. They also took options on an additional 1,600 acres, organizing the Beech Grove Improvement Company to plat and sell them. In 1910 George R. Brown & Co. platted lots in the Northview addition on College Avenue. The next year Warfleigh addition's 618 lots, with "graveled streets, cement walks, five-cent street car fare" and a location "30 minutes from Washington St." went on sale.

Indianapolis real estate developers formed the Indianapolis Real Estate Board with James S. Cruse as president in 1911. That year the Greater Indianapolis Industrial Association developed MARS HILL, an industrial and residential suburb which was to be Indianapolis' answer to Gary, the northern Indiana steel town. Gary flourished but Mars Hill foundered. CARL G. FISHER, JAMES A. ALLISON, ARTHUR NEWBY, FRANK WHEELER, and Lem Trotter were more successful with their industrial-residential suburban town, Speedway City (now SPEEDWAY). In 1912 the men, who had earlier erected the INDIANAPOLIS MOTOR SPEEDWAY, platted the town where lots could be had for "$10.00 down and $10.00 per month." (In 1915 Fisher directed his entrepreneurial skills toward a new development—Miami Beach, Florida—creating a land boom that lasted for 10 years but eventually cost him his fortune.) Predating a national move toward "garden suburbs" by five years or so, in 1915 the Spencer Aughinbaugh Realty Company began offering tracts in GOLDEN HILL for $2,000 to $3,000 each.

Locally, the number of new real estate developments reached record heights in the 1920s, mirroring national trends. High rises, apartment buildings, and suburban communities were all popular. In this decade many of Indianapolis' most prominent citizens moved to the tony "estate developments" of Golden Hill, Woodstock,

CROWS NEST, and WILLIAMS CREEK. Subdivisions such as FOREST MANOR, located at Maple Road and developed by Gates-Kinnear Company realtors, and Highlands Addition, at 52nd Street and Michigan Road, owned by Reliable Realty Company, were directed at the middle-income home buyer. In the 1920s Edgar J. Spink & Co. constructed the city's first one- and two-bedroom apartments with kitchenettes, adding 60 apartment buildings to the Indianapolis skyline. Spink's company followed a national trend of developers who purchased land, constructed, and then managed the completed apartment or office buildings.

The GREAT DEPRESSION nearly halted development in Indianapolis, although in the early 1930s speculators continued to build homes in wealthy areas such as North Meridian Street. In 1935 a new type of development took shape nationally as the federal government sought to boost the economy by financing rental and low-income housing construction. The Public Works Administration helped to fund the "slum clearance" project near downtown Indianapolis that resulted in the demolition of 363 homes and the construction of the 748–unit LOCKEFIELD GARDENS public housing development.

By the end of World War II developers, aided by infrastructure improvements which allowed access to outlying districts, no longer sold building plots only. They also built and sold moderately priced houses in large additions. Indianapolis experienced a huge "suburban land boom" in this period and land values increased at a rate above most other metropolitan areas. By 1957 many large tracts of former farmland had been converted to suburban use. Industry played a part in new development in LAWRENCE where the opening of nearby Chrysler, Ford, and Western Electric plants initiated a 30–year period of growth. In 1955 a National Homes development, EAGLEDALE, opened on the city's westside. These aluminum-sided homes proved as popular in Indianapolis as they were nationally (by 1950 the company was building 12,000 per year in the United States). In Eagledale developers William Jennings and John Lookabill sold 100 homes per week.

As suburban housing increased in the 1950s developers constructed shopping and service ar-

A Herron-Morton Place postcard, ca. 1907, depicts the large homes and wide boulevards that attracted affluent residents to the neighborhood from 1900 to 1930. [Indiana Historical Society, #C5765]

eas nearby, creating self-contained suburban communities. Two such developments, the Triangle Shopping Center on Shadeland Avenue and Meadows Shopping Center on East 38th Street, brought services into the neighborhoods. Concurrent with this suburban boom, downtown properties continued to sell, although often at prices below their assessed values. Indianapolis African-Americans, who had been excluded from membership in the local real estate board, founded a local branch of the National Association of Real Estate Brokers, facilitating the move of middle class blacks into the suburbs.

The opening of I–465 in the 1960s extended the scope of suburban development. Single-family and apartment developments sprang up along the entire circumference of the beltway. Developer Gene B. Glick was among the many who took advantage of the increased access provided by I–465; in the 1950s and 1960s he constructed Glick's Post Road, Mount Vernon, and Glick's 38th Street and 42nd Street developments along the eastern edge of the highway. Industrial developments such as Park Fletcher were also sited along the beltway.

In 1967 College Life Insurance Company began construction of its $85–million commercial-residential development on the city's far northwestside. The development, College Park and North Willow Farms, included three 12–story apartment buildings, a 110–acre office complex, a shopping center, single-family homes, townhouses, and garden apartments, and was the "largest proposed development in the history of

Marion County" to that time. It served as a model for successive projects. In 1970 ROBERT V. WELCH transformed the former STOUGHTON A. FLETCHER, II, estate, Laurel Hall, into 84 acres of condominiums called Windridge; an additional 25 acres became Windridge Center, a shopping area. Indun Realty, Inc., Hunt Development Company, and Northland Shopping Center Company constructed the 200–acre Keystone Crossing Office Center, one of the largest suburban office centers in the state, in the 1970s. It included the Fashion Mall, restaurants, a hotel, and offices; the partners estimated landscaping costs alone at $2 million. At the other end of the spectrum, the federally funded Model Cities program and the Federal Housing Administration (FHA) helped FLANNER HOUSE construct a 294–family, low-rent apartment complex in the inner city.

Following a recession in the early 1980s, by 1986 a new boom had begun. In 1989, 2,500 single-family lots were platted in Pike Township alone. Residential developments included the Shorewood Corporation's expensive, single-family homesites around GEIST RESERVOIR, as well as more moderately priced subdivisions. Some developers began marketing subdivisions for "target audiences"; A.H.M. GRAVES targeted "empty-nesters" for its Lake Kesslerwood development on the northeastside. Others moved outside Marion County to CARMEL or FISHERS for new suburban projects.

Over the years some developers have lamented the conservative attitude of local banks as a brake on Indianapolis' development, believing that "speculative building was never as popular here as in some cities." Local home prices may bear out that assertion. Although it has increased 33 percent since 1981, Indianapolis' median home price in 1992 was $83,700, compared to the national median of $103,700. Still, Indianapolis real estate development has come a long way since that first failed land sale. One measure of success: in 1993 the city ranked twelfth in *U.S. News and World Report*'s list of "most desirable" housing markets.

CONNIE J. ZEIGLER

Real Silk Hosiery Mills. Hosiery, lingerie, and undergarment manufacturer. Real Silk began operations in 1922 under the direction of J. A. and L. L. Goodman. At its peak the company sold more than 12 million pairs of women's hosiery annually.

The company experienced financial difficulties in the early 1930s as a result of the Great Depression, and a bank committee assumed control of the business. Real Silk's financial situation improved shortly thereafter when Gustave Efroymson gained control of the company in 1932. Although confronted with a violent workers' strike in April and May, 1934, which resulted in 16 arrests, Real Silk rebounded during World War II by manufacturing parachute bomb sleeves and hosiery for male and female military personnel. Efroymson successfully rebuilt the company before his death in November, 1946, at which time his son ROBERT A. EFROYMSON became president.

As profits worsened in the early 1950s Efroymson closed the company's manufacturing operations in Indianapolis and Dalton, Georgia, liquidated its manufacturing holdings, and sold the bulk of its machinery and inventory. In the mid–1950s Efroymson registered Real Silk Investments, Inc., with the Securities and Exchange Commission as a closed-end investment company. In 1961 the investment company transferred its hosiery and lingerie business to Realsilk, Inc., converted its 6–acre, 425,000–square foot manufacturing center at 611 North Park into the Printing Arts Center, Inc., which housed a variety of printing-related businesses until the 1970s, and conveyed its remaining real estate to SLK Realty Corp. In 1986 the INDIANAPOLIS HISTORIC PRESERVATION COMMISSION approved converting the vacant Real Silk factory into apartments and condominiums. Today, the company name continues with Real Silk Investments, Inc.

PAUL BROCKMAN
Indiana Historical Society

Real Silk Company Collection, Indiana Historical Society.

Real Silk Hosiery Mills Strike (April-May, 1934). One of the city's most famous and violent labor strikes. In June, 1933, the U.S. Congress passed the National Industrial Recovery Act (NIRA) as part of the New Deal efforts to recover from the Great Depression. Section 7(a) of the act assured workers "the right to organize and bargain collectively through representatives of their own choosing"; the act also established the National Labor Board (NLB) to settle labor disputes. Both the act and the board, however, proved inadequate, and by the time of the Real Silk strike in the spring of 1934 labor nationwide experienced the frustration of securing the enforcement of section 7(a).

The American Federation of Full-Fashioned Hosiery Workers (AFHW), affiliated with the American Federation of Labor (AFL), sought recognition in October, 1933, as the bargaining representative for the skilled knitters and other hosiery workers in the Real Silk plants in Indianapolis. At the time the Employees Mutual Benefit Association (EMBA), a company union, claimed to have represented all workers at Real Silk for the previous 12 years. An election, held under the auspices of the NIRA, allowed all Real Silk employees to select a union, even though nearly 66 percent of the workers were not eligible for membership in the AFHW. Predictably, the EMBA won by a 2–1 margin. The AFHW protested to the NLB, claiming that unskilled workers were allowed to vote in the election. After the labor board upheld the election, the AFHW membership voted on April 6, 1934, to strike. Approximately 800 Real Silk workers participated, seeking union scale wages and the abolition of bonus and penalty systems.

Violence flared in the city within days. Employees were threatened, property was damaged, and "scabs" were beaten. The company launched a harsh publicity campaign against the striking minority. When the AFHW lost its appeal to the NLB, workers continued their strike. This attracted federal attention and made Indianapolis a focal point of the Roosevelt administration's attempts to settle labor problems while keeping recovery efforts from stagnating.

In early May the National Labor Board and Secretary of Labor Frances Perkins sent two mediators to settle the strike. Violence intensified during their negotiations. Street fights, attacks on

buses carrying company workers, and a successful bombing of an employee's home (another effort failed) moved Mayor REGINALD H. SULLIVAN and Chief of Police MICHAEL MORRISSEY, who labor charged with possessing a financial interest in the company, to invoke special police powers and Real Silk management to increase its publicity campaign against the "misguided strikers" utilizing "un-American methods."

After recalling the unsuccessful mediators the NLB asserted its jurisdiction, reopened the matter, and set May 22, 1934, for a hearing at its Washington, D.C., headquarters. The final settlement left no one a clear winner. Real Silk and the Employees Mutual Benefit Association claimed victory since the NLB had upheld the majority vote of the workers, which allowed the EMBA to retain worker representation at the largest of Real Silk's Indianapolis plants. The Hosiery Workers claimed victory because the same ruling secured their representational rights at Real Silk's two smaller Indianapolis plants where the union had obtained a majority of the votes. On May 24 union members voted 512–212 to return to work.

MARK J. KEEFE

Real Silk Company Collection, Indiana Historical Society; *Indianapolis Star* and *Indianapolis News*, April–May, 1934.

Reck, Abraham (1790–1869). Lutheran minister and missionary. Born at Littlestown, Pennsylvania, Reck studied for the ministry and held his first pastorate at Winchester, Virginia (now West Virginia). He also served as a missionary in remote parts of Maryland, Virginia, and Pennsylvania, and as treasurer of the Evangelical Lutheran Synod of Maryland and Virginia. In 1828 he accepted a call to Middletown, Maryland, where he remained until the mid–1830s. Around 1835–1836 Reck joined a group of Maryland farmers who migrated to Marion County. Settling northeast of Indianapolis along Millersville Road, he established Ebenezer Lutheran Church with 40 members on August 6, 1836, and served as pastor until 1840. Reck also helped to organize the Hopewell Evangelical Lutheran

Church (now Salem Lutheran) at John Klingensmith's farm near Augusta Station (now New Augusta) in 1836.

In early 1837 local residents called Reck to organize Mt. Pisgah Lutheran Church, commonly known as First English Lutheran Church and the first Lutheran body in Indianapolis. The congregation purchased a lot on the southeast corner of Meridian and Ohio streets and erected a brick building in 1838 where Reck served until 1841.

During the 1830s Pastor Reck participated in the founding of eight LUTHERAN congregations in the area. He resigned his pastorates in 1841 to organize an English Lutheran Church in the Cincinnati area. Reck also held positions in Germantown, Tarleton, and Lancaster, Ohio, where he later died.

DAVID G. VANDERSTEL
Indiana University–Purdue University,
Indianapolis

Henry Waltmann, ed., *History of the Indiana-Kentucky Synod of the Lutheran Church in America* (Indianapolis, 1971); Abdel Ross Wentz, *History of the Evangelical Lutheran Synod of Maryland* (Harrisburg, 1920).

Red Key Tavern. In 1933 George and R. H. Duke opened the Olde English Tavern in a new building at 52nd Street and College Avenue. Since the Dukes could not afford to decorate their new establishment they asked their mother, a local artist, to paint murals on the walls. The pictures, painted from memories of scenes from her studies in England and Europe, can still be seen in the Red Key.

The Olde English was known as a neighborhood tavern for families, and local residents listened to a three-piece combo that played every Friday and Saturday night. The Dukes sold the tavern in 1935, and the name was changed to the Red Key sometime before it changed ownership in 1959. Hoosier author Dan Wakefield, once a regular patron of the establishment, mentions it in his novel, *GOING ALL THE WAY.*

The Red Key is known locally for its unique method of collecting charitable contributions from patrons. A donated dollar bill, wrapped around several silver dollars and a tack, is thrown upward, attaching it to the ceiling. Several thousand dollars are transferred from the Red Key's ceiling to local charities annually.

WILLIAM D. DALTON

Regional Center Plans (RCP). Series of three reports describing existing conditions and plans for the downtown area. The METROPOLITAN DEVELOPMENT COMMISSION adopts the plans, each a periodic update of the previous one, to guide its policies. Part of a larger body of Indianapolis-area planning studies conducted throughout the 20th century, the regional center district covers a 5.2 square mile area, also called the "inner loop," which is bounded by I–65 and I–70 to the north, east, and south, and by the WHITE RIVER and Harding Street to the west.

The idea of planning specifically for the regional center originated as a special project of the Unified Planning Program (1970–1972), funded by a federal HUD grant awarded to the DEPARTMENT OF METROPOLITAN DEVELOPMENT (DMD) and inspired by UNIGOV. The main purpose of the plan was to combat deterioration of the urban core by providing services and a pleasant environment to attract new development. DMD staff and planning consultants completed the study in 1970. Projects identified by this study included increased recreation and park space, especially along White River; modernization of UNION STATION for use as a transportation center; beautification of MONUMENT CIRCLE; a Washington Street bus and pedestrian transitway; and development of the CITY MARKET area and street corridor. Of these initial goals, only a revamped City Market (1972), Monument Circle (1978), and Market Street (1980) were realized by 1980, although other public projects were also completed during the 1970s, spurred by the increased downtown interest.

In 1978 the GREATER INDIANAPOLIS PROGRESS COMMITTEE (GIPC), the mayor's office, the DMD, and the Commission for Downtown (now INDIANAPOLIS DOWNTOWN, INC.) funded and implemented an update of the earlier RCP. Mayor William H. Hudnut III appointed 150 civic leaders to the GIPC task force, who worked with city planners to provide guidelines, policies, and goals for future downtown planning in a 1981 document, "Indianapolis 1980–2000 Regional Center General Plan."

The second RCP aimed to stimulate downtown business, office space, industry, and retail development. Other subcommittees focused on urban design, transportation, historic preservation, recreation and tourism, downtown housing and neighborhoods, and public facilities. Proposed public projects included expansion of the INDIANA CONVENTION CENTER, rehabilitation of CIRCLE THEATRE and Union Station (this time as a mall and tourist attraction), the creation of IUPUI physical education facilities, WHITE RIVER STATE PARK, a retail mall, Washington Street Mall, and Legion Mall. Many of these projects were realized by 1990.

This rapid progress during the 1980s led to a third RCP, a decade ahead of schedule. The 1990 committee and planning process, organized and supported in the same way as the 1981 RCP, involved over 460 civic leaders and included even more public participation. The focus of "Indianapolis Regional Center Plan, 1990–2010" shifted from buildings and jobs to linking neighborhoods, providing social services, and promoting human relations and the arts to make Indianapolis a more livable city. Other important goals included completion of CIRCLE CENTRE MALL and White River State Park, additional museums and cultural opportunities, expanded government structures, beautification of parks and monuments, continued preservation of historic buildings, and development of more research and technology jobs.

MICHELLE D. HALE

Department of Metropolitan Development, "Indianapolis Regional Center, Core Development and Historic Information" (Indianapolis, 1970); "Indianapolis 1980–2000 Regional Center General Plan" (Indianapolis, 1981); "Indianapolis Regional Center Plan, 1990–2010" (Indianapolis, 1991).

Reilly Tar & Chemical Corporation. Indianapolis-based chemical company. Peter Celestine Reilly (d. 1952) came to Indianapolis in 1895 to run a small tar distilling plant on Miley Avenue in the HAUGHVILLE neighborhood. When the parent company instructed Reilly to close the Indianapolis plant and move to St. Louis, the Providence, Rhode Island, native offered to buy the plant.

In 1905 Reilly incorporated the Republic Creosoting Company. Reilly had already expanded his operations to Mobile, Alabama, and Minneapolis, Minnesota. Republic specialized in creosoting wood poles for utility work, pilings, and railroad crossties. In 1921 the company's Indianapolis plant was moved to a much larger facility on Maywood Avenue; Republic was renamed Reilly Tar & Chemical Company, and it expanded rapidly during the 1920s, adding wood preserving plants and tar refineries at sites from Renton, Washington, to Norfolk, Virginia. The company's major acquisition took place during the depths of the Great Depression. On May 15, 1932, Reilly acquired the property of the International Combustion Tar & Chemical Corporation, which operated six tar refineries, primarily located adjacent to steel mills.

Increasingly over the years Reilly Tar & Chemical's focus turned to chemical pursuits. In 1930 the company opened laboratory facilities on South Tibbs Avenue in Indianapolis. (In recent years this site has come under scrutiny by the Environmental Protection Agency because of serious contamination problems.) During the 1940s Reilly perfected a formula for synthetic pyridine, a coal tar extract that is used in several hundred different commercial applications. Among other things, pyridine is an active ingredient in products like dandruff shampoo and mouthwash.

During the past 20 years Reilly has gradually pulled back from the wood preservation and tar business, concentrating almost entirely on chemical products made at its facilities in Indianapolis and in Belgium. Following the death of P. C. Reilly in 1952, he was succeeded at the helm of the family-owned company by his son, brothers, and nephews.

BILL BECK
Lakeside Writers' Group

George A. Reilly, "The Story of Reilly Tar & Chemical Corporation" (unpublished manuscript in company files, 1969).

Religion and Race. Race was a public issue in Indianapolis from the city's earliest years. Numerous state laws restricted blacks' rights, starting with legislation in the early 1800s that prohibited African-Americans from testifying in court and outlawed marriage between blacks and whites. More severe laws followed, including an 1831 bill requiring that blacks migrating to the state post bond. The Indiana Constitution of 1851 prohibited blacks from migrating to the state altogether and fined anyone caught employing black migrants. Despite these antebellum legal constraints blacks in Indianapolis numbered 498 in 1860, about 3 percent of the total population.

The racial intolerance characteristic of Indianapolis from its earliest days stemmed in part from the city's above-average proportion of white southerners compared to other midwestern areas. It also reflected the city's overwhelmingly Protestant composition. Consequently, racial and religious exclusivity prevailed in Indianapolis with the two dimensions functioning in mutually supportive ways.

Systematically separated from the larger context of Indianapolis, black residents created social and institutional worlds of their own. Black churches, among the first institutions to form, became centers of black social organization. For example, the African Methodist Episcopal congregations responded to the exclusion of blacks from public schools by founding their own schools in the 1850s. The AME church simultaneously played a leading role in organizing challenges to the restrictive legal status of blacks across the state.

The issue of race assumed greater importance for Indianapolis as the North-South confrontation over slavery edged closer to war. Routine partisan strife between Indianapolis Republicans and Democrats increased as they were forced to deal directly with the slavery issue. Republican loyalties were with Lincoln and the Union. Some Democrats, however, sympathized with the South. Indiana Democrats serving in the U.S. Congress, for instance, voted with the South on every issue related to slavery. When war began in 1861, local Democrats briefly pledged their fealty to the Union's war effort but soon resumed their opposi-

tional stance. Through it all, white churches were not noticeably vocal.

With emancipation came a large influx of blacks into Indianapolis, the number reaching close to 16,000 by the end of the century, or 9.4 percent of the population. The new black arrivals, often destitute, received food, clothing, and shelter from black churches. Among whites, the influx of blacks generated mostly a series of new legislative initiatives on race. Some of this legislation attempted to ease restrictions on African-Americans' rights; most of it sought to strengthen restrictions or impose new ones. One piece of postbellum legislation favoring black rights was an 1885 Civil Rights Act passed by the Indiana General Assembly which prohibited discrimination in hotels, restaurants, places of amusement, and public transportation. The law, however, was rarely enforced. Some local black ministers played important roles in the legal battle for black rights in the latter 1800s. For example, the pastor of SECOND BAPTIST CHURCH organized black resistance to discriminatory public policies and actively mobilized blacks into the Republican party.

In the early 1900s Indianapolis' white Protestant homogeneity gradually but discernibly eroded as Roman Catholics, Jews, and blacks arrived in larger numbers. This increasing diversity generated significant white Protestant hostility. The KU KLUX KLAN was formed in Indiana in 1920 and achieved state and local political power by the mid–1920s through a rhetoric hostile to Catholics, Jews, immigrants, and blacks. The Klan's active membership was large but its support from nonmembers was even larger, with many Protestant denominations maintaining silence and numerous individual ministers vocally supporting the Klan. Although the Protestant Episcopal Diocese of Indianapolis denounced the Klan, most formal opposition to the Klan derived from Roman Catholic, black Protestant, and a few other nonchurch sources. Among the more prominent opponents were Catholic and black newspapers such as the INDIANA CATHOLIC AND RECORD and the INDIANAPOLIS FREEMAN, although neither Roman Catholics nor blacks universally opposed the Klan. Some black clergymen collaborated directly with the KKK; many others simply withheld criticism of it. In both cases, identification with the Klan's Protestantism and reliance on Klan-infiltrated public institutions were factors in this black support.

The Klan's emergence was only one indicator of white resistance to the changing demographic composition of Indianapolis. The 1920s witnessed significant formalization of racial segregation in the city. Official school policies separated elementary school students into single-race schools, and the city established a black high school, Crispus Attucks, for all black secondary students. Legal and illegal efforts to prevent blacks from purchasing homes within white neighborhoods strengthened existing patterns of residential segregation. At the same time, numerous public accommodations, including hospitals, hotels, restaurants, and recreation facilities, denied service to blacks, openly flouting the 1885 law prohibiting such discrimination.

By the late 1920s the Klan had lost political strength, though its decline resulted more from internal scandal than from the strength of forces opposing racism. Nevertheless, the beginnings of organized, interracial, religious resistance to discrimination in Indianapolis can be traced to this decade. The CHURCH FEDERATION OF GREATER INDIANAPOLIS, a Protestant council founded in 1912, established an auxiliary committee on race relations in 1920 and mandated it to report back on housing needs and employment discrimination. The five blacks who served on the 35–member committee and the black ministers brought in to address it represented the first serious involvement by blacks in the federation's activities. The primary results of the committee's work during the 1920s were the appointment of blacks to the federation's principal committees and the development of pulpit exchanges between black and white churches, especially on one Sunday each year designated as Race Relations Sunday.

During the 1930s the federation continued serving as a politically moderate clearinghouse on race, urging the end of discrimination in the city. Meanwhile, more aggressive antidiscrimination action was being taken in the black community. With black economic and job security most adversely affected by the Great Depression, black civic leaders launched boycotts against businesses that refused to hire blacks, a strategy supported

within black church circles such as the Baptist Ministerial Alliance.

Interracial and interreligious organizational efforts against discrimination gained momentum throughout the 1940s. The Indianapolis Citizen's Council, formed with Church Federation assistance in 1943, included participation from the Indianapolis Catholic Diocese and the Jewish Federation. The same year a local branch of the National Conference of Christians and Jews was organized.

Interreligious cooperation on race issues was well established by this point, producing additional groups for an antidiscrimination consensus with each decade. By the 1950s, for example, the Roman Catholic Inter-Racial Council and the JEWISH COMMUNITY RELATIONS COUNCIL were working alongside the Church Federation, jointly sponsoring a conference on religion and race. Also, the INDIANA INTERRELIGIOUS COMMISSION ON HUMAN EQUALITY emerged in the 1960s, an organization comprised of Jewish, Catholic, Baha'i, Muslim, Unitarian Universalist, and Protestant supporters. The Indianapolis City Council established a Human Rights Commission in 1952–1953 to advise government officials and educate citizens about race relations and issues.

Despite this activity, discrimination proved stubborn. The General Assembly finally passed a bill ending legal segregation in 1949, although implementation and enforcement proceeded slowly. From the perspective of some black religious leaders, the timidness of white religious leadership contributed to the slow pace of progress. By the 1960s most black Protestants had concluded that the antidiscrimination activities of groups like the Church Federation were insignificant. Blacks therefore invested their energies in their own organizational structures. The Indiana Christian Leadership Conference, formed in 1969, became a prominent black political voice in Indianapolis. Black ministerial groups like the Interdenominational Ministerial Alliance and Concerned Clergy also became outlets for political expression.

The 1960s produced federal antidiscrimination laws but compliance in Indianapolis was halting. It took a federal court order in the early 1970s to force a systematic approach to public

SCHOOL DESEGREGATION in Indianapolis. The goals remained unfulfilled in the 1990s. Desegregation of neighborhoods and public facilities was carried out more successfully, although enduring pockets of resistance have required continued attention. Police-community relations issues became prominent in the 1970s and worsened with each decade and each new police action shooting of blacks.

Throughout Indianapolis' history, racism has been a persistent issue. Although the city's religious community has not been as persistent in responding to it, it has produced leadership important to the racial progress which has been achieved.

R. DREW SMITH
Indiana University, Bloomington

Religion and Social Services. From the earliest churches in Indianapolis religion and social services have lived in a complex and evolving relationship. Not every act of care and compassion in those earliest days came from religious hands or motivations. Nonetheless, as congregations of BAPTISTS, METHODISTS, PRESBYTERIANS, DISCIPLES, QUAKERS, LUTHERANS, CATHOLICS, and JEWS emerged, ecologies of care developed within and around them almost immediately. They did not provide the panoply of specialized help that we now call social services. But as congregations cared for their own members, supported families during crises, and ministered to the strangers who came into their local communities, they acted on the same impulses and responded to the same basic human needs for food, clothing, shelter, medical care, and counseling that people still manifest today.

Religion did not and still does not respond to these needs monolithically. Instead, particular groups, the German Lutherans or the African-American Baptists for example, responded out of their own traditions to the new challenges posed by a changing city. Further, these groups employed a variety of strategies to care for their fellow citizens. At various times they provided direct services, created alliances of groups to respond to larger social problems, motivated people to support secular means of care, invented new institutions which could provide new forms of help, and led in public advocacy for social change. While there are clear historical developments in the unfolding relationship of religion and social services—chief among them the professionalization and specialization of care and the muting of sectarian differences in the face of growing social need—the religious communities of Indianapolis continue to make use of all of these strategies in the 1990s.

The earliest official public pattern of care for the poor and ill was established by the Indiana Constitution of 1816, which provided for several types of public assistance: (1) indoor relief, which placed indigent people on poor farms or in poor houses; (2) a farming out system, which paid private citizens to care for either individuals or groups of the poor; (3) an apprentice system, which placed minor children in the hands of responsible adults; and (4) outdoor relief, which supported individuals and families in their own homes. In addition the jails and county asylums housed the deviant and ill. At first little differentiation occurred between poor, elderly, sick, insane, dependent children, and homeless poor. But as needs and resources grew, public homes for the blind, the deaf and dumb, and the insane appeared in the 1840s.

This minimal public infrastructure was supplemented in countless ways by private acts of religious individuals and their churches and synagogues. Gradually, various private agencies were created to deliver forms of care that exceeded the capacities of individuals and local congregations. Already in 1835 the INDIANAPOLIS BENEVOLENT SOCIETY was organized to provide food, clothing, and grocery store vouchers for the poor. Directed by a coalition of clergy and lay leaders, the society served the needs of a city of less than 3,000 inhabitants. Orphanages like St. Vincent's School and improvement organizations like the YOUNG MEN'S CHRISTIAN ASSOCIATION began to serve the city in 1851 and 1854 respectively.

These early forms of direct care were augmented by other strategies. Methodists, for example, were leading political advocates for causes like temperance and abolition in the 1850s. At that time the largest denomination in the state, Methodists used their pulpits and publications to crusade against two of the largest social problems of the age, alcohol abuse and slavery. Clergy like the Reverend James Havens, presiding elder of the Indianapolis district of the Methodist church, and his fellow clergy crusader, the Reverend Samuel P. Crawford, went so far as to help create a short-lived new political party, the Fusionists, in order to address and change social realities.

Major social dislocations like the Civil War and an economic depression in the 1870s occasioned a wide variety of institutional creativity. Orphaned children were housed in a new General Protestant Orphan Home after 1867. This home served more than 2,000 children between the time of its founding and 1941 when it merged with the Indianapolis Orphans' Home and the Evangelical Lutheran Orphans' Home. By 1971 the orphanage had become the PLEASANT RUN CHILDREN'S HOME, a nonsectarian residential treatment center for victims of child abuse, neglect, and abandonment. This single institutional history illustrates patterns of secularization and shifting social need as its purpose changed along with its institutional identity. That pattern repeated itself numerous times as institutions begun under specific religious auspices became secular in the face of changing funding sources and social circumstances.

Sometimes congregations played distinctive roles in responding to new social needs. PLYMOUTH (CONGREGATIONAL) CHURCH transformed itself under the leadership of Reverend OSCAR CARLETON MCCULLOCH into an institutional church, a new type of congregation that created programs within the church to address social needs. Beginning in 1877, McCulloch challenged Plymouth to respond to the needs of the city in new ways. The established church on the Circle featured clubs that could educate young men and women from impoverished backgrounds, teaching them everything from mathematics to the social graces. McCulloch's preaching began to concern itself with painful social issues such as the relation of capital to labor, exploitation of child labor, and the unsanitary living conditions of the poor. By 1884 Plymouth Church was ministering to such a large variety of needs—educational, recreational, and social—that the church moved to a new building with expanded facilities like a gymnasium, auditorium, and library. The local congregation was on its way toward being a full-service institution.

McCulloch was not content to invent a new type of congregation in the image of the Social Gospel. He went on to head almost every important social agency then in existence in the city. As president of the Indianapolis Benevolent Society he came to see the need for a new way to more effectively organize the charity of the city. In 1879 he took lessons learned by the Sanitary Commission's national reorganization of care for the wounded of the Civil War and created the CHARITY ORGANIZATION SOCIETY, which attempted to coordinate the inefficient and unscientific charity of Indianapolis' many churches and benevolent associations. In addition, McCulloch helped formulate legislation that created the State Board of Charities in 1889. Under his leadership Indianapolis became a national leader of the institutional church and the charity organization movements.

Throughout the 1880s and 1890s various religious groups continued to make their own particular contributions. Two Lutheran congregations created the Evangelische Lutherische Waisenhaus Gesselschaft in 1883, an orphanage which grew in the 20th century to become LUTHERAN CHILD AND FAMILY SERVICES, a denominationally sponsored institution offering a full range of professional counseling services. The SALVATION ARMY began its work in Indianapolis in 1889, providing food, clothing, shelter, and spiritual guidance. Its red kettles and brass bands are still in evidence in the city, but now it serves more than 300,000 meals annually and runs substance abuse programs, homeless shelters, day camps, and senior citizens programs.

Due to the growing complexity of urban life and to professionalization championed by new forms of higher education in the late 19th and early 20th centuries, social work began to lose its specific religious moorings and to take on the coloring of a secular profession. A formal training course begun in 1890 by the Charity Organization Society became a precursor to the establishment of the Indiana University Department of Social Service in Indianapolis in 1911, which in turn became the IU School of Social Work in 1966. New institutions and new types of caregivers (service providers) quickly followed. In 1905 Anna Stover, a faithful member of the Disciples of Christ denomination, and Edith Surbey, a lapsed Catholic, opened CHRISTAMORE HOUSE in response to the urban revivalism they experienced at Chicago's Moody Bible Institute. Christamore was an early settlement house opened to provide a new kind of care for the city's immigrants. These houses resembled college residence halls and offered a wide range of educational and cultural opportunities at the same time that they provided health clinics, baths, and kindergartens. By 1911 Christamore's religious leaders were gone following a dispute with the house's board of directors over how explicit the religious identity of the institution should be. Christamore became a provider of a wide range of social services and finally evolved into a community center which still serves an Indianapolis neighborhood.

The secularization of Christamore House was not a universal pattern in the creation of new social service institutions. Two other Indianapolis settlement houses, the AMERICAN SETTLEMENT and FLANNER HOUSE, both welcomed and depended on support from the Disciples denomination for leadership and financial help until Indianapolis reorganized its charity work under the auspices of the Community Fund (organized in 1923). The American Settlement served as an Americanizing institution for immigrants from southeastern Europe, while Flanner House served the needs of African-American immigrants from the South. Flanner House's separate existence was a sign of the ambiguity present in almost all forms of charity and social service provided in Indianapolis. While expressing genuine compassion and desire to help those in need, these institutions also participated in and perpetuated patterns of racism, nativism, and classism which were part of the civic and national ethos.

During the 1920s and 1930s Indianapolis grew to become a city of more than 300,000. Its reorganization of SOCIAL WORK followed increasingly professional lines and reflected the impact of new federal legislation which created Social Security and a wide variety of public agencies in the 1930s. This new federal presence often seemed to overwhelm religious organizations, leaving them with difficult choices between significant new sources of support and the freedom to maintain their distinct religious identities. Major institutions like METHODIST HOSPITAL and ST. VINCENT HOSPITAL went through exponential experiences of growth and secularization in the post–World War II era even as they struggled to maintain their religious identities.

Religious communities did not simply sit back and let the government and the professionals take over social service provision. As new needs presented themselves they pioneered once again. In 1952 the Reverend Charles Oldham created the Lighthouse Mission to care for indigent men in the inner city. The Episcopalians created the JULIAN CENTER in 1975 to respond to adult female victims of child sexual abuse, rape, and domestic violence. Roman Catholics joined Episcopalians in 1987 to open the DAMIEN CENTER to minister to the AIDS crisis. Two years earlier, Jewish philanthropists Clarence and ROBERT EFROYMSON created the MORIAH FUND to support programs for Jewish people in need.

But religion often played behind the scenes roles in providing social services to the city. GLEANERS FOOD BANK of Indiana, for example, used federal funds, along with private philanthropic dollars, to help build a national food bank network. In Indiana this network supports more than 15,000 charities which provide direct help to hungry people. Many of those who staff and volunteer throughout this complex network are recruited in local congregations, as are many of those who serve throughout the immense secular social service network of the city.

Religion's presence in social service continues to be immense and complex. The 1992 edition of the *Community Resources Handbook*, which lists social service agencies currently serving Indiana, identifies more than 800 distinct agencies. Of those, more than 100 have religious identifiers in their names. They offer a range of services and boast a spectrum of heritages which no one could have predicted in the 1820s when the first religious institutions appeared on the city's young horizon.

JAMES P. WIND
Lilly Endowment

Religious Architecture. Houses of worship have occupied prominent positions on Indianapolis' landscape from the rustic village of the 1820s to the rise of suburbia. Design and ornamentation set these buildings apart as sacred places differing in purpose from surrounding structures. Size, architecture, building materials, and location also reflect the wealth, influence, and tastes of a congregation's members. In surveying the city's rich heritage of religious architecture, only a limited number of extant sacred structures are cited here as outstanding examples of styles or illustrative of trends.

After Indianapolis' founding in 1820, settlers began establishing congregations within the original MILE SQUARE. They erected simple churches of wood or brick that were superseded eventually by more substantial structures. By the 1850s congregations of major religious bodies occupied buildings in the favored architectural styles of antebellum America. Greek Revival was most influential, as its model, the Greek temple, was regarded as the ideal building. Four prominent churches built in Greek or classical styles were located on the CIRCLE by the mid–1850s—First (1843) and SECOND PRESBYTERIAN (1840), Christ Church (1838), and Methodist Church (1829). (The buildings no longer exist.) The style gaining influence by the Civil War was Gothic Revival, with pointed arches in window and door casings of simple and elaborate structures. This trend is reflected in William Tinsley's design of CHRIST CHURCH CATHEDRAL (Episcopal) on the Circle, the city's oldest extant religious building, a pleasing English country Gothic Revival structure completed in 1859 and superseding an earlier Greek Revival building.

After the Civil War, replacing church buildings and forming new congregations stimulated a wave of church construction. In addition to Gothic Revival, Romanesque Revival with its characteristic rounded Roman arches was an influential style. Red brick was a popular building material with a minority of churches built in stone. Solid and massive in appearance, built close to the street, and most having spires directing attention skyward, the new houses of worship conveyed a sense of religion's authority in the community.

Central Avenue United Methodist Church, corner of Central Avenue and 12th Street, is a good example of a Romanesque Revival church in Indianapolis. [Indiana Historical Society, Bass Collection, #838]

German immigrant DIEDRICH A. BOHLEN emerged as the most influential late 19th century designer of churches. His Gothic Revival ST. JOHN CATHOLIC CHURCH (1871) was then the state's largest church. Bohlen's other structures include the Gothic Chapel at CROWN HILL CEMETERY (1875–1877) and St. Paul Lutheran Church (1882). His major Romanesque Revival building is the stately limestone ROBERTS PARK UNITED METHODIST CHURCH (1876) that resembles the City Temple in London. The Bohlen firm under Diedrich's son Oscar designed Lockerbie Square United Methodist Church in Romanesque Revival style (1892) and Zion United Church in Christ, a Gothic Revival structure built in 1913.

Gothic Revival churches of other architects include such southside landmarks as the former Fletcher Place United Methodist Church, designed by Charles Tinsley (1872–1880), and Sacred Heart Catholic Church (1883–1891) built by Adrian Wewers. The former Trinity Danish Evangelical Lutheran Church (1872), now the Church of Jesus Christ of Apostolic Faith, is a small neighborhood church that reflects a builder's interpretation of Gothic Revival of which there were once many examples.

Romanesque Revival buildings of the period include First Lutheran Church (1887), built by Peter P. Cookingham, and Central Christian Church (1892). Central Avenue United Methodist Church (1891), a magnificent red brick monument, was designed by Williams and Otter of Dayton. Another southside landmark, Immanuel United Church of Christ, was completed in 1894. St. Bridget Catholic Church (1879) is a builder's simple version of this style. George Bedell designed several brick Romanesque Revival structures for neighborhood parishes such as the former St. Francis de Sales Catholic Church (1913), now a part of MARTIN UNIVERSITY. Historic BETHEL AFRICAN METHODIST EPISCOPAL CHURCH was remodeled with a Romanesque Revival tower in the 1890s.

By the early 20th century, Classical styles, especially those reflecting Renaissance influences, reemerged in American church architecture. Catholic parishes in particular were drawn to this style, including SS. PETER AND PAUL CATHEDRAL (1906–1907), designed by New York architect William Renwick and with facade designed in 1936 by the Bohlen firm; Holy Cross Catholic Church, an Italian Renaissance structure, Cornelius Curtin, architect, (1922); and Holy Rosary Catholic Church, designed in Neoclassical style by J. Edwin Kopf and Kenneth Wooling (1925). St. Joan of Arc Catholic Church (1928–1929) was built in a triumphant Italian Renaissance style with soaring campanile by noted Chicago architect Henry Schlacks. St. Patrick Catholic Church (1928) was designed by ADOLPH SCHERRER in Spanish Renaissance style. The trend can be found in the Assembly Hall of Jehovah's Witnesses, built in 1912 for Second Church of Christ, Scientist, in a massive Neoclassical style by Solon S. Beman, and Woodruff Place Baptist Church, executed in Italian Renaissance style in 1926.

A new Gothic movement emerged in the early 20th century whose leading national figure was Boston architect Ralph Adams Cram. Its partisans considered Gothic the ideal religious architecture as its arches pointed upward to the heavens. Unlike the Gothic Revival forms, the new version imitated more closely the massive-

ness of medieval French and English Gothic cathedrals with long naves and tall, square towers usually built in stone, not brick. The city's most imposing edifice in this style is the massive SCOTTISH RITE CATHEDRAL, the design of George F. Schreiber, located downtown along North Meridian Street since 1929. Another downtown example, St. Mary's Catholic Church, was begun in 1912 and designed by German architect Herman Gaul to resemble the Cologne Cathedral.

Leading Protestant congregations built outstanding Gothic structures in fashionable neighborhoods during the 1920s: First-Meridian Heights Presbyterian Church (1927); Broadway United Methodist Church, a splendid limestone complex designed by HERBERT FOLTZ (1925); North United Methodist Church (1931), the design of Atlanta architect Charles H. Hopson; Tabernacle Presbyterian Church (1921), the work of ROBERT FROST DAGGETT; and Irvington Presbyterian Church, started in 1928. A variation of the style is the Irvington United Methodist Church, a brick English Gothic gem built by Herbert Foltz (1926).

The Art Deco style with its geometric ornamentation, popular in commercial and apartment buildings of the 1920s, is found in the former Third Church of Christ, Scientist, now Phillips Temple Christian Methodist Episcopal Church, a limestone monument by Robert Frost Daggett completed in 1928.

The Great Depression and World War II limited church building nationally and locally. After 1945 construction boomed as the suburbs attracted residents forming new congregations and drew old congregations relocating from downtown sites. New houses of worship often adapted traditional Gothic and Romanesque styles for large structures designed with ample meeting and class rooms. Their sites allowed space for parking lots and well landscaped lawns. The most distinguished building of this trend is Second Presbyterian Church, relocating in 1959 from downtown to a magnificent limestone French Gothic structure designed by McGuire, Shook, Compton, and Richey. American traditions were affirmed in the new interest in Colonial Revival or Neo-Georgian buildings through the 1950s. A harbinger of this trend is the elegant Fourth Church of Christ, Scientist, in IRVINGTON, begun in 1936. The most imposing example is the Meridian Street United Methodist Church, a red brick Georgian Revival complex completed in 1952 by architects William Russ and Merritt Harrison.

In the late 1950s several congregations showed some daring by breaking away from traditional styles in favor of adapting current trends in modern architecture. A functional approach informed some interior arrangements as architects devised seating to allow worshippers to be closer to the center of religious ceremonies. Some noteworthy buildings reflect this modern trend. The INDIANAPOLIS HEBREW CONGREGATION was completed in 1958 in a striking contemporary design. Holy Trinity Greek Orthodox Church was designed in contemporary style using Romanesque arches by McGuire, Shook, Compton, and Richey (1960). Third Christian Church (1963), designed by James Associates, echoes some elements of modern formalism. St. Luke's United Methodist Church (1960s) by Edward Dart makes imaginative use of skylighting. The steep-pitched, A-frame roof popular in many suburban churches is found in Friedens United Church of Christ (1967), designed by James Associates. St. Thomas Aquinas Catholic Church, a design of Woollen Associates with hexagonal floor plan and lighting from above, was completed in 1970.

The recent era's most distinguished complex of modern religious buildings is the CHRISTIAN THEOLOGICAL SEMINARY, built in stages from the 1960s with the library completed in 1977 and Sweeney Chapel in 1987. World-class architect Edward Larrabee Barnes' design reflects Middle Eastern architecture from the time of Christ.

Through the decades the city's religious buildings have generally followed national trends in architectural styles. The cycle of urban growth and development has affected sacred structures as it has the rest of the built environment. Such change has caused the elimination of Greek Revival and the earliest Gothic Revival styles of buildings that evoke the antebellum past, reduced the concentration of churches once numerous in the central city, and dispersed religious buildings across the metropolitan area. Sacred structures now neither appear as prominent on the landscape, nor do they provide the sense of ubiquity

of sacred places in the built environment that they did in the 19th century.

JOSEPH M. WHITE

Historic Landmarks Foundation of Indiana, *Center Township, Marion County, Interim Report, Indiana Sites and Structures Inventory* (Indianapolis, 1991); Indiana Architectural Foundation, *Indianapolis Architecture* (Indianapolis, 1975).

Religious Broadcasting. Religious programs were part of the broadcast schedules of many of the country's first radio stations. Locally, one of the oldest continuous radio broadcasts was the weekly program from the Wheeler Rescue Mission (now WHEELER MISSION MINISTRIES). The Sunday night program aired on WFBM (predecessor to WNDE) from 1925 to 1989. Another long running broadcast on WFBM was the "Christian Men's Builders' Hour" from the Third Christian Church, which aired from 1926 through 1955. The CADLE TABERNACLE of Indianapolis also was a mainstay on radio; its broadcasts originated through the facilities of WLW, Cincinnati, and were fed to the Mutual radio network.

Religious programs have been part of the local television schedule since the 1950s. While most programs aired on Sunday mornings, WISH-TV Channel 8 featured "Chapel Door" each weekday morning until 1969. Also, paid specials, such as those hosted by evangelist Billy Graham, occasionally replaced network fare on the major commercial stations.

The first local radio station to adopt a religious format was WBRI (1500 AM) in 1964. Two other AM stations—WNTS (1590 AM) and WXLW (950 AM)—abandoned traditional formats in favor of religion in the late 1970s. These smaller AM stations were hampered by increasing costs and decreasing advertising revenues as FM stations became more popular. WBRI brought religious programming to FM in 1980 when it created WXIR from the former WART, Plainfield (98.3 FM). WGRT (107.1 FM in Danville, then 810 AM) tried a gospel music format in the early and mid–1980s. Most other stations have limited religious music and programming to Sundays.

The metropolitan area's first religious television station was WHMB, Channel 40, which broadcasts from nearby Noblesville in Hamilton County. This UHF outlet was bankrupt when purchased by South Bend evangelist Lester Sumrall in 1972; advertising generated by old network reruns and children's shows helped Sumrall support his television ministry. In 1987 California-based Trinity Broadcasting put WCLJ, Channel 42, on the air.

MICHAEL SPILLMAN

Hal Erickson, *Religious Radio and Television in the United States, 1921–1991* (Jefferson, N.C., 1992); *Broadcasting & Cable Yearbook* (1993).

Religious Press. The growth of Indianapolis during the mid–19th century led to the establishment of a thriving newspaper industry in the Hoosier capital. The portability of movable type systems and the increase in literacy among the Indiana population made it possible for religious congregations to publish broadsheet weekly and monthly newspapers after about 1850. Most of the early religious newspapers that called Indianapolis home were originally published in southern Indiana and later moved to the growing capital city.

Perhaps the first such publication to issue from Indianapolis was the *Christian Messenger*, which was moved up the Michigan Road from Madison in Jefferson County to Indianapolis in October, 1846, by the Reverend E. D. Owens. Elder Elijah Goodwin of the Christian Church moved the *Christian Record* from Bloomington in 1850 and published the newspaper monthly until the beginning of the Civil War, when it became a weekly. In 1866 the newspaper moved to Cincinnati and merged with the *Christian Standard*.

Another newspaper that moved from Madison to Indianapolis was the *Gospel Herald*. The Reverend B. F. Foster moved the newspaper to Indianapolis in late 1853, but its stay was rather short. In 1855 it was combined with the *Golden Era* of St. Louis, Missouri. Until the renamed *Herald and Era* was discontinued in the early 1860s, the newspaper was published by Isaac D. Williamson, T. C. Eaton, Thomas Abbott, and Mandeville

G. Lee in both St. Louis and Indianapolis. The *Western Universalist*, published by the Reverend Erasmus Manford from 1855 to 1857, and the *Witness*, started by Dr. M. G. Clarke as a religious and family publication in 1857 and discontinued in 1864, are other examples of early religious publications in Indianapolis.

The advent of the Sunday school movement during the 1860s and 1870s led to the establishment of several weekly and monthly newspapers aimed at Christian youth. Combining sermons with puzzles, games, and instructional serials, the Sunday school newspapers enjoyed a strong measure of popularity during the latter third of the 19th century. The *Little Busy Bee*, of which relatively little is known, was first published in 1860. It was superseded by the *Little Sower*, which was begun in 1865 as a monthly Sunday school newspaper for the Christian Church. The publication's frequency changed to bimonthly in 1866; it appeared as a weekly after 1869. Difficult financial circumstances forced the church to cut the frequency back to monthly in the early 1870s, and in 1884 the publication changed its name to the *Sunday School Evangelist*. The publication went through one more name change, to the *Young Evangelist*, before it was discontinued before the turn of the century.

Reverend W. W. Dowling of the Christian Church published the *Little Watchman* as a Sunday school newspaper in 1870. The newspaper was soon discontinued, but Dowling tried again in 1877 when he started the short-lived *Good Seed*. In 1891 Dowling purchased the *Christian Sunday School Teacher* and renamed it the *Little Watchman*. Like its earlier namesake, the newspaper had a brief existence.

Much of the impetus for 19th-century religious publishing in Indiana originated from the TEMPERANCE movement. Closely identified with progressive Protestantism, the temperance movement spawned a host of religious temperance newspapers in Indianapolis. In mid–1848 B. T. Kavanaugh and John D. DeFrees started the *Family Visitor*, a weekly temperance newspaper that was published until 1850 when it was succeeded by the *Temperance Chart* and then the *Temperance Union* (1853) before it passed from the Indianapolis scene. The *Indiana Christian Advocate*, which espoused temperance and women's suffrage, was begun in April, 1871, by the Reverend Thomas Goodwin and W. H. Ongley. Published by the Methodist Episcopal Church, the newspaper folded in 1872, but Goodwin reestablished the newspaper under the same name in 1886. Published weekly by the Advocate Publishing Company, the second *Indiana Christian Advocate* lasted until 1890.

The temperance issue was of particular importance to quasi-religious organizations like the WOMEN'S CHRISTIAN TEMPERANCE UNION (WCTU). The *Ladies Tribune*, a short-lived temperance weekly unaffiliated with any Indianapolis congregations, was published by Mrs. Sarah E. Underhill in 1857. Lodie E. Reed and Mollie G. Hoy started the *Organizer* to support the temperance movement about 1882; for the last two decades of the 19th century the newspaper was the weekly organ of the Indiana WCTU.

Indianapolis women were also prominent in the founding and operation of the *Missionary Tidings*, founded in 1883. Mrs. S. E. Shortridge served as editor of the newspaper, which was the official organ of the Christian Woman's Board of Missions, from 1883 until 1890. Other editors of the newspaper, which ceased publication after 1910, were Helen E. Moses, Anna R. Atwater, and Effie L. Cunningham.

The *Octographic Review*, an Indianapolis newspaper published for Indiana members of the CHURCH OF JESUS CHRIST OF LATTER-DAY SAINTS, was formed from a merger of the *Octograph* and the *American Christian Review* in the spring of 1887. Daniel Sommer owned and operated the weekly Mormon newspaper until it halted publication in 1918. After 1917, Sommer, his wife, and sons published the *Apostolic Review*, a weekly newspaper for members of the Church of Christ.

Indiana BAPTISTS got their own weekly newspaper in 1880 when the Reverend G. H. Elgin and his brother-in-law, U. M. Choille, began publishing the *Gospel Trumpet* for the Central Baptist Publishing Company. Central Baptist Press had published an earlier newspaper, the *Journal and Messenger*, which appeared periodically and lasted from 1875 until 1879. In 1881 the *Gospel Trumpet* changed its name to the *Indiana Baptist*, and Elgin and Choille operated the newspaper

until Elgin left the venture in the late 1880s. Choille sold the weekly to the Indiana Baptist Publishing Company in 1891, which named C. M. Carter as the new editor. C. E. W. Dobbs became the editor in 1894, and the name of the publication was changed to the *Indiana Baptist Outlook* at the turn of the century. The newspaper ceased publication two years later.

The influx of German and Irish immigrants to Indiana following the Revolution of 1848 and the Irish potato famine in the mid–19th century laid the seeds for a thriving Catholic press in Indianapolis. The earliest Catholic newspapers in the Hoosier capital were printed for ethnic CATHOLICS, rather than for the Catholic community as a whole. Although not strictly a religious newspaper, the *Western Citizen* attempted to reach the city's Irish Catholic community and contained much news of Irish spiritual life, including the activities of Irish priests and reports of baptisms, weddings, and funerals in the Irish community. Started by Joseph Marshall and C. E. McSheehy in 1876, the paper was owned and edited by Thomas McSheehy when it folded in 1883. From 1862 to 1905 the city's German Catholics were served by the German language weekly, *Die Glocke*. Founded in 1882 as a weekly Catholic publication by William Kuhlman, Father Carl Kuhlman, and Arthur Preus, *Die Glocke* moved to Chicago around 1905. Father MARINO PRIORI, a noted pastor among the Italian Catholics living in near southside neighborhoods, published the *Eternal Light*, a weekly—and later a monthly—magazine for Italian Catholics during the First World War.

The roots of the CRITERION, the weekly newspaper of the Indianapolis Catholic Archdiocese, go back to the formation of the *New Record*, a weekly Catholic newspaper, by Richard Outler in 1883. Alexander Chomel started the *Catholic Record* in 1889 as a continuation of the *New Record* and it was merged into the *Catholic Columbian* of Columbus, Ohio, in 1899 to form the *Catholic Columbian-Record*. The newspaper published editions in Columbus and Indianapolis. In 1910 Joseph P. O'Mahony of the Indiana Catholic Printing and Publishing Company, began publication of the *Indiana Catholic*, which absorbed the *Catholic Columbian-Record* in 1915. O'Mahony edited the merged INDIANA CATHOLIC AND RECORD until the 1940s, when he was succeeded as editor by Monsignor Raymond T. Bosler. Bosler remained as editor in 1960 when the Indianapolis Archdiocese bought control of the weekly newspaper and renamed it the *Criterion*.

The rise of fundamentalism during the first decade of the 20th century spawned a number of Indianapolis religious newspapers. The *Pentecost Herald* was started up about 1900 as a religious and temperance weekly for the Pentecost Bands of the World. Mrs. Flora B. Nelson took over editorship of the paper in 1903, when it was renamed the *Herald of Light*. The newspaper continued in circulation until 1913. Other short-lived religious newspapers of the period included the *Ram's Horn* (early 1890s) and the *Informer* (1909). Pilgrim Publishing House started a religious weekly in 1956 called the *Pilgrim Holiness Advocate*. Paul W. Thomas and A. D. Peiskar served as editors of the newspaper, which increased its frequency to twice weekly in 1965 before closing its doors in 1968.

The Indianapolis Jewish community has been served by several publications since the 1920s. Nathan J. Gould began publishing the *Indiana Jewish Chronicle* in July, 1921. Gould was succeeded as editor by Rabbi Jacob Bienefeld (1922–1923) and Morris Strauss (1923–1969). Mary L. Morey replaced Strauss as editor and publisher in 1969 and served in that position until the paper's demise in the early 1970s. A competing newspaper, the *Indiana Jewish Tribune*, had a brief existence under editor Aaron M. Neustadt in the early 1930s. The *Jewish Bulletin* published in the city from 1944 until it closed down about 1958.

The longest-lasting Jewish newspaper in the city is the JEWISH POST AND OPINION. Still in existence, the newspaper was begun in the spring of 1933 by Leonard Rothschild as the *Jewish Post*. Originally a monthly Jewish community newspaper, the *Jewish Post* changed to twice-monthly publication frequency in 1934 and went weekly in March, 1935. Rothschild sold his interest at the end of 1935 to Gabriel M. Cohen of the Spokesman Company, which changed the name of the weekly to the *National Jewish Post* in 1946 and to the *National Jewish Post and Opinion* in 1947. Cohen changed the name again to the *Indiana Jewish Post and Opinion* in 1966. The news-

paper continues to publish in 1994 as the *Jewish Post and Opinion*.

BILL BECK
Lakeside Writers' Group

Remy, William Henderson (Dec. 18, 1892–Sept. 2, 1968). Marion County prosecutor. Born in Columbus, Indiana, Remy attended public schools in Indianapolis, graduating from Manual High School in 1910. Admitted to the bar in 1915 after completing studies at Indiana Law School, Remy practiced law in Indianapolis until he enlisted in the Army during World War I. Briefly returning to private law practice after the war, in 1921 Remy began work at the prosecutor's office as deputy to prosecutor William Evans. When Evans resigned two years later, Remy served out his term. Remy won election to the office in 1924 on an anti-Klan platform.

Dubbed the "boy prosecutor" by the press for his youthful looks, Remy led the state's successful case against KU KLUX KLAN leader DAVID CURTIS (D. C.) STEPHENSON in his 1925 trial for the murder of Madge Oberholtzer. He served as Marion County prosecuting attorney until 1928 before returning to private practice. He later served as president of the city's Board of Public Safety under Mayor ROBERT TYNDALL. Remy left Indianapolis in the early 1950s and died in Marissa, Illinois.

DEBORAH B. MARKISOHN

_____

Indianapolis News, Sept. 2, 1968.

Republican Party. On July 15, 1856, the newly formed Republican party held its first convention in Indianapolis. Delegates and friends began with a parade down Washington Street to the State House, highlighted by a group of young men costumed as the pro-southern "Border Ruffians" who were then terrorizing the Kansas Territory. At each intersection the performers staged tableaux illustrating different abuses undertaken by the actual Ruffians against the free state advocates and settlers of that new territory. Laughter and cheers built the crowd's enthusiasm for the speeches and evening torchlight procession that followed. Although Republicans were narrowly defeated in the following fall election, the rally heralded the arrival of a significant political party.

The Republicans who convened in 1856 were a product of the disorderly realignment of voter allegiance that followed the passage of the 1854 Kansas-Nebraska Act. Using a label earlier employed by the followers of Thomas Jefferson, the new party was a fusion of several followings. Some were former Whigs, who continued to speak a language of economic development that stressed government support for internal improvements and for banking systems that encouraged sound money. Allied with them were free soil elements who sought, as their name suggested, both the elimination of slavery from the western territories and the passage of a homestead act. Present also were a variety of Protestant social reformers, some motivated by abolitionist thinking and others by hostility to the sale and consumption of alcohol. They were joined after 1856 by former members of the short-lived American, or Know-Nothing, party who favored a program of immigration restriction. However diverse and contentious they appeared, all were united by a desire to defeat the DEMOCRATIC PARTY.

By 1860 the new party had succeeded in Marion County, helping to secure the election of Abraham Lincoln while carrying local and state candidates. The party's support for Lincoln carried over into support for the Union cause during the ensuing period of secession and war, and caused some in the Republican ranks to accuse the Democrats of being Copperheads, traitors to the Union cause. Union veterans would play a prominent role in the party for many years after the war that they often called the War of the Southern Rebellion.

Many of the features present in its formative years characterized the rhetorical appeals and programmatic goals of the Republican party for decades to come. These included emphases upon both economic growth and moral reform, respect for the Union, and contempt for the Democratic opposition. Later interpreters have argued that the Republican appeals were particularly successful in attracting ethnic and religious groups whose values and beliefs emphasized personal piety and self-reliance. The diversity of the Republican support base also helps to account for a recurring party tendency to factional division.

The 19th-century party was organized primarily through campaign committees that formed for each election. Members of the committees were generally leading party spokesmen and editors, incumbent officeholders, prospective candidates, and local organizers with proven ability to turn out voters on election day. At a time when Indiana was an intensely competitive two-party state, whose electoral vote might well decide the presidency, the national Republican party often took an active hand in local organization, providing funds, speakers, and advisers. The nomination of BENJAMIN HARRISON of Indianapolis in 1888 and 1892 confirmed this close connection; the creation of the COLUMBIA CLUB as a marching society for Harrison in 1888 illustrates the ad hoc nature of many early campaign activities.

The closeness of voting, particularly after a Democratic surge that began in the 1880s, caused local Republicans to seek a more formal party structure. The result was an organization composed of committeemen representing geographic subdivisions of the county called precincts. Precinct leaders, in turn, often relied heavily upon present and prospective government workers, lending a strong emphasis upon patronage to the formal workings of the local party. The ensuing tension between the voters' interest in issues and candidates, and the party workers' interest in government offices and jobs, continued well into the 20th century.

As Civil War issues began to fade, and voters with no personal memory of that conflict began to enter the electorate, the Republicans (now often styling themselves the Grand Old Party, or GOP) began to seek new appeals. Some were local initiatives, such as John Caven's BELT LINE RAILROAD project in the 1870s. Others were national, such as the attacks upon the perceived radicalism of William Jennings Bryan in 1896. Local and national trends could come together, as they did during the Progressive era, when some Republicans championed the ideas of government efficiency and social justice identified with Theodore Roosevelt, ALBERT J. BEVERIDGE, and other party leaders. Yet because the appeal of Progressivism ran counter to more established issues in the party, it encouraged a new factionalism that culminated in the Bull Moose division of 1912.

The key figure in reorganizing the local party to meet the electoral challenges of this situation was CHARLES W. JEWETT, who became party chairman in 1914 and mayor in 1918. A Harvard-trained lawyer, Jewett built a following among younger voters through an organization called the Republican Union. Legally unable to succeed himself as mayor, Jewett was forced to seek accommodation with the individual he had defeated for the 1917 mayoral nomination, SAMUEL LEWIS SHANK. In 1921 Shank secured his own nomination for mayor, and a year later was able to use the distribution of city jobs to committeemen to assure the selection of his choice, William Freeman, for party chair. Shank, in turn, quickly encountered the rivalry of GEORGE "CAP" COFFIN, county clerk and former county sheriff. Long active in party affairs, and still supported by many sheriff's deputies, Coffin launched his bid for full control of the party in 1924, running for party chairman against Shank's choice, Robert Miller. Their struggle led to a tense county convention marked by attempts to disqualify committeemen by court order, with large numbers of armed police loyal to Shank facing large numbers of armed deputies loyal to Coffin, before a close vote favored Coffin.

Coffin's victory came at a time when the KU KLUX KLAN was bidding for power in Indiana, and Coffin had sought and received the support of the Klan. Unlike some other Klan-backed leaders, who quickly fell from power, Coffin retained his hold on the local party until the early 1930s. The faction he led, with some changes in loyalty over time, would remain a contender for party control until the 1940s. The effects were soon felt. Coffin and his allies sought, with some success, to attract white, working class Democrats to the Republican standard, but saw the GOP lose its traditional support in the African-American community. Coffin, however, never totally controlled local Republican officeholders, and was unable to prevent an anti-Klan Republican prosecutor, William Remy, from securing indictments and convictions of several Coffin allies including mayor JOHN DUVALL.

Factionalism, growing public antipathy to the Klan, the loss of the African-American vote, and the onset of the Great Depression during the Herbert Hoover presidency came together to defeat the Republican ticket in 1929, ushering in a fairly long period of Democratic advantage in local politics. Faced with this challenge, the local Republican party entered a period of factionalism marked by vigorously contested county conventions and shifting personal and group alliances. Between 1930 and 1944 the party chose eight different individuals as chairman. Best remembered were probably JAMES L. BRADFORD and Henry Ostrum, who gained reputations for their emphasis upon door-to-door canvassing (then called "polling") and election day voter turnout efforts. These rebuilding activities began to produce results in the early 1940s as the party started to win significant local offices. ROBERT TYNDALL'S victory for mayor in 1942 marked the return of the GOP as a force in local affairs.

Larger state and national concerns played significant roles in the shape of the party in that era. The Republicans often enjoyed more success in carrying state and national tickets than they did local slates, while the success of the GOP in capturing the State House after 1948 led to a marked interest in state, as opposed to local, patronage. The economic conservatism that flowed from resistance to the taxes and regulation associated with the Democratic New Deal caused many local Republicans to stress a rhetoric of free enterprise and individual initiative. Vigorous champions of the American war effort after Pearl Harbor, the Republicans included a strong patriotic emphasis in their appeals. After 1945 returning veterans were welcomed, and often recruited as candidates, while veterans' groups such as the AMERICAN LEGION were a significant entry path to political participation.

Many of these considerations came together in the 1952 election. The bulk of the GOP organization favored the presidential candidacy of a conservative midwesterner, Ohio Senator Robert Taft. But many voters, and one key party official, H. DALE BROWN, supported the successful candidacy of Dwight Eisenhower. Although unsuccessful in supplying much local support for Eisenhower at the Republican national convention, Brown won favor for his efforts—and a major voice in national patronage and funding for the next eight years. From his public offices, notably as county clerk, and from his party post as national committeeman, Brown became the key power broker in the party. He was able to control the selection of county chairmen, to institute a process of candidate screening that assisted the nomination of his local candidates, and to form alliances with two succeeding Republican governors, George Craig and Harold Handley.

Brown's interests thus often touched upon state and national concerns, and his critics were quick to point out that he was less successful locally. As one example, he was never able to elect a GOP mayor for the old city of Indianapolis. But Brown's influence did not begin to decline seriously until his party lost the White House in the 1960 election. Brown held power for a few more years, actually serving his only terms as county chairman from 1962 to 1966. But his flirtation with the Nelson Rockefeller campaign of 1964 prior to Barry Goldwater's nomination, and a subsequent poor organizational showing in support of Goldwater, combined to attract new allies to Brown's long-standing party opponents. In 1964 these critics formed a Republican Victory Committee to oppose him, and two years later that committee was substantially broadened to become the Republican Action Committee (RAC).

The RAC set in motion a reorganization of the Marion County GOP that shaped the party until the 1990s. Led by such individuals as L. Keith Bulen, Charles Applegate, John Burkhart, and W. W. Hill, the RAC was successful in carrying a slate of primary candidates in opposition to Brown, and then in electing Bulen as county chairman. Victory in the November, 1966, county election was followed by the nomination and election of Richard Lugar as mayor in 1967. Lugar's election set the stage for a sweep of the county's legislative delegation in 1968 and the ensuing passage of the 1969 Unigov law. By combining the old city and the remainder of the county for the election of the mayor and council, UNIGOV enabled the GOP to draw upon its growing suburban base in future elections.

Many of these successes were institutionalized during the lengthy party chairmanship of John Sweezy. An engineer by training, and a former city director of public works, Sweezy suc-ceeded Bulen as party chairman in 1972, winning the first of ten unopposed elections to that position. A skilled planner and manager, Sweezy redirected the party into an emphasis upon volunteer participation, extensive fund raising, and recruitment. Sweezy went on to compile a series of election successes, especially for the less visible offices of local government. He also played an active role in recruiting ticket-leading candidates with strong media appeal, such as the two mayors who succeeded Lugar: William H. Hudnut III and Steven Goldsmith. Yet the emphasis upon candidates and media in campaigns served as a reminder that there was always more to local politics than just organizational efforts. By the 1990s new national issues, a new generation of voters, and growing reliance upon the media all suggested that another party reorganization was likely.

GEORGE W. GEIB
Butler University

Resort Condominiums International.

Travel services firm. Indianapolis-based Resort Condominiums International (RCI) was founded in 1974 by Jon and Christel DeHaan, working from their northside home. RCI's revenues for that first year totaled $16,000. In 1975 RCI confirmed 236 vacation exchanges for 1,000 members who vacationed at 35 U.S.-based resorts. Christel De-Haan purchased her former husband's interest in RCI as part of a 1989 divorce settlement.

RCI succeeded by carving out a market niche that combined two new marketing concepts: resort timesharing and vacation exchange. Timesharing allows vacationers to purchase a limited interest—usually a one week interval—in a resort condominium. Vacation exchange allows owners of timeshare intervals to exchange accommodations for comparable resort facilities worldwide. RCI arranges exchanges for its members through its network of affiliated resorts.

RCI employs over 1,200 people at its Indianapolis headquarters, with a total of more than 2,600 employees worldwide. In 1992 RCI confirmed over 1.1 million vacation exchanges for its more than 1.6 million members. Projected sales for 1992 were expected to exceed $230 million. RCI is affiliated with 2,415 resorts in 76 countries.

In addition to offering travel exchange services, RCI's interests include a travel agency and the travel magazine *Endless Vacation*.

DEBORAH B. MARKISOHN

Retailing. The earliest retail businesses in Indianapolis were general stores, farmers' markets, and workshops. Currency was not widely available in the city until the State Bank branch opened in 1834, so customers bartered home-grown crops and hand-produced products for manufactured goods like nails and calico. Farmers sold their products at a city market first held in June, 1822—in the maple grove on the Governor's Circle. A more permanent market house was built in 1832 on the half square just north of the courthouse on East Market Street. Artisans such as tailors, milliners, and shoemakers also manufactured items in their workshops and sold or bartered them.

The new settlement's first merchant, Daniel Shaffer, opened a little store on the high ground south of POGUE'S RUN in the spring of 1821. He was followed by merchants who built stores in the platted area of the city, especially on Washington Street. A successful early merchant was CHARLES MAYER, a German immigrant who opened a general store at 29 West Washington Street in November, 1840. He sold goods such as candies, beer, groceries, "nerve and bon[e] lineament," china, lumber, and toys. He bought local products from a brewer and an eggwoman and stored them in a rented cellar. He also ordered manufactured goods from Cincinnati and had them transported by Conestoga wagon up the rutted MICHIGAN ROAD.

The first railroad to reach Indianapolis, the MADISON AND INDIANAPOLIS RAILROAD on October 1, 1847, changed the way local businessmen did business. On November 24, 1847, Charles Mayer advertised in the *Indiana State Sentinel* that shipment of freight was 50 percent less expensive by means of the railroad and that he could now sell a wider variety of goods at a lower cost. But within a few years the trend in retail businesses was to specialize and deal in a few lines of goods to lower expenses and prices.

The city's 1857 business directory listed about 240 retailers. There were 60 grocery and produce dealers, 23 saloons, and 18 dry goods stores, as well as 2 agricultural stores, 5 bakeries, 8 booksellers and stationers, 16 boot and shoe dealers, 1 candle manufacturer, 2 carriage makers, 6 tobacco dealers, 3 coal dealers, 2 coopers, 6 confectioneries, 8 druggists, 4 gunsmiths, 1 ice dealer, 10 jewelers, 2 marble dealers, 1 silversmith, 1 straw goods dealer, and 1 wagon manufacturer. Nine women were listed as milliners and dressmakers, and for many years these were the only retail businesses in which women were listed.

During the Civil War the transient population of Federal troops and their dependents temporarily boosted retail business. Illinois Street became lined with small retailers such as restaurants, clothing stores, jewelry stands, saloons, and grocery stores. New businesses began to locate on cross streets away from Washington Street as the city spread out. There was a rise in wages, but the depreciation in the value of currency and the inflationary increase of prices put a damper on the city's business. The retail grocers agreed not to accept credit for goods, there were fewer manufactured goods available to customers, and most residents had to live frugally. In 1865 there were still only about 250 retail businesses listed in Indianapolis directories.

The growth of the city accelerated after the Civil War and the number and variety of retail stores grew with it. The gradual introduction of gas, electricity, telephones, a street railway, and road pavement, as well as provision of a water supply and sewerage to the business district, helped the proliferation of new businesses. There were about 1,280 retailers listed in 1873, 2,090 in 1883, 3,390 in 1894, and 4,250 in 1904. The types of stores ranged from small specialized businesses, such as Frederick W. Simon's neighborhood grocery store at 188 North Noble Street, Craig's Confectionery Store at 6 East Washington Street, or Allison's Perfection Fountain Pen Store at 157 North Illinois Street, to Pettis' "New York Store" at 25–35 East Washington Street, which sold a wide variety of dry goods.

Some of the city's famous retail firms began or expanded during the post–Civil War era. CLEMENS VONNEGUT began selling hardware in 1851 and continued his business at 120–124 East Washington Street. Solomon Strauss began selling clothing in 1853 and L. STRAUSS AND COMPANY emerged as a leading seller of men's clothing. In 1872 LYMAN S. AYRES bought controlling interest in the Trade Palace, a dry goods store at 26–28 West Washington Street, and assumed management two years later. In 1880 Bertermann Brothers Florist Shop was located at 74 East Washington Street. Julius A. Haag ran a drugstore at 87 North Pennsylvania Street in the new DENISON HOTEL, and by 1889 the Haag family had one of the city's first multiple listings with three stores. In 1889 black businessman Henry L. Sanders opened his Gent's Furnishings store at $15^1/_2$ Indiana Avenue and developed a successful uniform-making business that continued for over 50 years. By 1894 H. P. WASSON AND COMPANY was selling dry goods at 12–18 West Washington Street, and Polk's Creamery was in operation at 325 East Seventh Street. In 1904 STOUT'S SHOE STORE was listed at 318 Massachusetts Avenue.

At the beginning of the 20th century retailers did not open on Sundays, the highest volume sales day was Saturday, and the highest volume month was December. The new INTERURBANS provided customers with transportation to and from the downtown area and the retail stores of the new neighborhoods and suburbs of the expanding city. Some retailers took advantage of the new automobile manufacturing business in Indianapolis. National Motor Vehicles, for example, sold electric and gasoline autos at East 22nd Street and the Monon Railroad tracks. By 1904 ten stores were selling electrical supplies and one sold telephone apparatus. There were also 125 restaurants, 590 saloons, 750 grocery stores, several fruit stands run by Italian families in the East Market House, and John A. Hook's drugstore at 1101 South East Street.

One retailing family successfully made the transition from the "horse-and-buggy" days to the automobile age by changing its line of business. A Scottish immigrant named Peter F. Bryce opened Bryce's Steam Bakery at 14–16 East South Street about 1873, which specialized in "homemade" bread and butter crackers. In the 1920s his son, Robert M. Bryce, razed the old bakery and surrounding buildings and opened his own automobile filling station on the block, which he operated successfully for many years.

The Star Store, shown here in 1919, sold dry goods, clothing, and home furnishings at 360–370 West Washington Street. [Indiana Historical Society, Bass Collection, #68108]

There were two separate national trends in retailing at the beginning of the 20th century. The first trend was to sell an increasingly diverse variety of goods in one store. Many dry goods stores, such as Pettis', which generally sold material to make women's clothing, began to employ dressmakers and milliners, as well as to sell shoes, carpets, and furniture. This was the first stage in the development of the department store. L. S. AYRES AND COMPANY opened Indianapolis' first modern department store on October 2, 1905, at 1 West Washington Street. Ayres eventually sold everything from books and flowers to men's and women's clothing and china to baked goods and candies. The store also provided a cafeteria and an elegant Tea Room. Other downtown retailers, such as WILLIAM H. BLOCK AND COMPANY at 26 North Illinois Street, also developed into department stores, but another form of the trend was the "five-and-dime" store that sold all of its goods at a low price. Turpin and Mathews was Indianapolis' first "five-and-dime," listed in 1893, and in 1906 the national chain S. S. Kresge opened a store at 23 West Washington Street.

The second trend in retailing at this time was the abundance of small, family-owned, neighborhood stores. These businesses were easy to start, required little formal training and long hours of work, and provided a living for many families. In 1914 there were about 4,200 retailers listed in Indianapolis, and about 1,000 of these were neighborhood grocery stores.

Automobile retailers were the fastest growing type of modern businessmen in the first two decades of the 20th century. There were electric and gasoline automobile manufacturers who also sold autos and parts retail and automobile dealers who also ran recharging stations and filling stations, as well as used car dealers, auto accessory stores, tire stores, and gasoline filling stations. There was 1 auto retailer in Indianapolis in 1900, 8 in 1904, 55 in 1914, 99 in 1917, and in 1921 about 130 retailers sold autos and auto accessories, not including 20 filling stations. These retailers provided the city with the transportation to expand beyond its old limits.

In 1921 about 5,000 retailers had business listings in the city. Again the food selling business was the largest, with about 1,300 grocers, 570 meat markets, 370 restaurants, 130 confectioneries, and 180 soft drink sellers. Also, Standard Grocery stores had opened 31 units, the national Piggly-Wiggly chain had 12 grocery stores in the city, and HAAG DRUG COMPANY and HOOK'S DRUG STORES had five stores each. Though modern items such as phonographs, film, refrigerators, machinery, electrical supplies, and furnaces were being sold widely, there were still 46 blacksmiths, 11 harness and saddlery shops, and 3 horse and mule dealers listed.

The federal government first took the census of the retail trade in 1929, and it was taken about every five years thereafter. The census counted 4,920 retailers in Indianapolis in 1929. The most dramatic change in retailing since 1921 was the number of chain stores, which increased from about 70 total to 472 units of local chains, 176 units of sectional chains, and 396 units of national chains. These chains included not only grocery stores and drugstores, but also variety stores, shoe stores, and filling stations. The automobile group of retailers increased to 769, including 392 filling stations.

By 1933 the GREAT DEPRESSION had hit Indianapolis hard. The number of retailers dropped to 4,494, the average annual net sales declined from $44,808 to $23,181, and the average number of employees per store declined from five to three. The hardest hit retailer was the small neighborhood grocery store, the number of which dropped to about 800. By 1939 the number of retailers rebounded to 5,208 with average annual net sales of $36,204. There was not a dramatic increase in any one type of retailer, and the population remained stable though residents continued to move away from the center of the city and neighborhood retailers were more predominant.

During World War II a retail census was not taken, but the 1948 retail census showed a sizable increase in retail sales with a general consolidation of business. In 1948 there were 4,650 retailers in Indianapolis with average annual net sales of $126,063. In 1954 there were 4,632 retailers in the city, but their average net sales increased to $166,344 and they employed an average of eight employees each. From 1929 to 1954 the number of grocery stores and other food-selling establishments dropped from 1,757 to 905, but the number of eating and drinking places increased from 584 to 933.

In the early post–World War II era street corner drugstores such as Hook's and Haag's became anchors of a few connected retail outlets at the busiest intersections around the city's neighborhoods. This led to the development of 17 shopping plazas throughout Indianapolis by 1961. Eastgate opened in 1957 at 7150 East Washington Street with 52 outlets, and Glendale in 1958 at 6101 North Keystone Avenue with 54 outlets. The bigger plazas had at least one department store as an anchor for the other business outlets, which included grocery, drug, shoe, variety, hardware, and wearing apparel stores, eating and drinking places, and other specialized retailers.

The total number of retailers in Indianapolis varied between 1958 and 1987. By 1958 the city's increase in population and in business accounts for the 5,159 retailers in the city, but the general exodus of the middle class to the suburbs outside the city's limits probably caused the number to drop to 3,905 in 1963. The expansion of the city's boundaries by Unigov brought the 1972 count of retailers to 5,766. This number fell to 4,760 in 1987 because of the increase in the number of large volume national chain stores that local small retailers could not compete against. The average annual net sales per store climbed steadily from $167,846 in 1958 to $348,835 in 1972, jumped to $610,945 in 1977, and doubled in 1987 to $1,384,904. The average number of employees per store between 1958 and 1982 stayed between 8 and 11, but increased to 16 in 1987. By 1987 the retail census listed 196 building material and garden supply, 110 general merchandise, and 435 food stores, 293 automotive dealers, 334 gasoline service stations, 492 apparel and accessory stores, 394 furniture and home furnishings stores, 1,373 eating and drinking places, 159 drugstores, and 1,017 miscellaneous retail stores within the Unigov boundaries of Indianapolis.

Developers continued to build ever-larger SHOPPING CENTERS around the periphery of Indianapolis in the 1960s and 1970s. Greenwood Shopping Center opened to the south of Indianapolis in May, 1965, and Lafayette Square to the west in August, 1968. After I–465 looped around the city by the early 1970s, Castleton Square opened to the north of the city in September, 1972, and Washington Square to the east in October, 1974. This combination of malls and plazas drained the downtown area of its retail business by 1976. After the huge bicentennial celebration in downtown Indianapolis, the city's leaders conducted a well-planned campaign to revive the retail business downtown, especially in the restored UNION STATION. But the economic slump of the late 1980s affected all the city's retailers. In January, 1992, L. S. Ayres closed its original flagship store, which eventually left downtown Indianapolis without a department store for the first time since 1905.

In the 1980s and early 1990s the city of Indianapolis and a shopping mall developer began to plan and build a shopping center called the CIRCLE CENTRE MALL to be located in the old retail district of downtown. It will be situated on three and one-half blocks bounded by Market, Meridian, Georgia, and Illinois streets. The Circle Centre Mall's main entrance will be on the southwest quadrant of Monument Circle. It will contain about one million square feet with about 180 retail shops, stores, and restaurants, including the historic, renovated L. S. Ayres building.

ROBERT F. GILYEAT

Jacob Piatt Dunn, *Greater Indianapolis* (Chicago, 1910); R. L. Polk & Company, *Indianapolis City Directory* (Indianapolis, 1878- 1989); U.S. Bureau of Census, *Census of Retail Trade: Indiana* (Washington, D.C., 1929–1987).

Revels, Willis R. (1810–Mar. 6, 1879). African-American Methodist minister. Born in Fayetteville, North Carolina, of free parents, Revels first came to Indiana when he attended Union Literary Institute, a Quaker academy. His brother, Hiram Rhodes Revels, also attended this school and later became a United States senator from Mississippi (1870–71).

Early in his career Revels was an itinerant preacher for the African Methodist Episcopal (AME) Church, ministering to churches in New Orleans, St. Louis, Louisville, Chicago, and Terre Haute. In 1845, the Indiana Colonization Society contracted him to be their agent and travel to Liberia to report on conditions there, with the intention of gaining blacks' confidence in the plan. After protest from the national AME Church, he refused to go or to support the colonization effort.

Revels was pastor of BETHEL AFRICAN METHODIST EPISCOPAL CHURCH in Indianapolis' Fourth Ward as early as 1845 and ministered there through the Civil War. During this time, he was heavily involved with the Freedman's Aid Society, which assisted runaway slaves and black migrants. One of the few local black residents to be active in this work, he hosted in his home black refugees passing through Indianapolis and helped others to find work locally. It is believed that opponents of his work set fire to his church in 1864.

In 1862, Revels wrote to Governor OLIVER P. MORTON on behalf of the local African-American community asking for permission to serve in the Home Guard for Indianapolis. The governor rejected the offer, concluding that the guard was large enough and that he had no authority to accept black troops. Instead, Revels served as a recruiting officer for black soldiers who then fought with Massachusetts troops, and he also had the responsibility of caring for these soldiers' families.

Revels was elected to the national AME Church conference and was one of five blacks appointed to attend the white national Methodist conference in 1864. At that time, he reflected the change in AME opinion in favor of colonization efforts in Liberia. In 1865, Revels hosted several national black leaders to mark the anniversary of the Emancipation Proclamation. That same year he joined with a group of Quakers to present a petition to the Indiana General Assembly requesting the expansion of rights for Indiana's black residents.

MICHELLE D. HALE

Revivalism. Revivalism is a method whereby a speaker—an evangelist—attempts to bring people to a conversion experience, an acceptance of God's saving grace. While periods of religious awakening or revivals have occurred throughout the history of Christianity and are common to all religions, the development of a method designed to bring about such an awakening is an American phenomenon, predominantly operating within the Protestant tradition.

The first recorded revival in Indianapolis occurred at Wesley Chapel in 1838 and lasted from March 3 to April 5. At that time Indianapolis had only 6,000 inhabitants and three church buildings—Methodist (Wesley Chapel), Baptist, and Presbyterian. Led by the churches' ministers and supported by regular members, the revival occurred during a period of particularly harsh weather, yet despite the snow and cold hundreds of people attended nightly. The meetings led to 265 conversions and, according to observers, left a feeling of religion and moral uplift that permeated the city for months.

Despite this assessment, in its early days Indianapolis developed a reputation for coolness to evangelists. One major revival took place between December, 1865, and March, 1866, under the leadership of Reverend A. S. Kinnan, resulting in 326 conversions. This event was followed in 1869 by a revival led by a Reverend Hammond that lasted for four weeks, but little else seems to have transpired until the last two decades of the 19th century. Indianapolis then experienced three large revivals led by men who had national reputations. These included J. Wilbur Chapman, a Presbyterian minister, director of the Winona Lake (Indiana) Bible Conference, and a colleague of the noted evangelist Dwight L. Moody, and Charles R. Scoville, a Disciples of Christ minister

who served as president of the Disciples' Evangelistic Association.

This period of evangelistic fervor began in 1881 with a major revival held at ROBERTS PARK METHODIST EPISCOPAL CHURCH. Led by the noted boy evangelist Thomas Harrison, the revival lasted from March 28 through June, 1881. Although it started slowly because of sleet, snow, and cold during the first week, by April 10 the crowds had grown so large that the church building could not contain them and many were sent home or to other churches. The crowds continued at this level through the succeeding months, and other churches held services at the same time as the revival in order to handle the multitudes. Organizers claimed 1,218 conversions, with numerous other people committed to church membership.

The increased ease of transportation, the building of larger churches, and a concern for urban evangelism led to the growth of institutionalized evangelistic and revival work in the late 19th and early 20th centuries. In Indianapolis, from 1921 until 1969, CADLE TABERNACLE, located at the corner of Ohio and New Jersey streets, was the center of revival and evangelistic activity in the city. Built by E. Howard Cadle, a local evangelist and one of the first national radio preachers, Cadle Tabernacle was dedicated by the British evangelist Rodney "Gipsy" Smith on October 9, 1921, as the final act of a 31–day revival that he led.

Cadle Tabernacle represented a kind of permanent revival spirit. Seating 7,000, it was the largest building designed solely for religious services in the country. During its history some of the most important revivalists in America used its facilities. Oral Roberts brought his faith-healing ministry to the city in 1956, and Bob Jones, Jr., preached at the tabernacle's anniversary service in 1948. Cadle also regularly undertook evangelistic work there.

One person who did not appear at Cadle, since even with its size it could not have held the crowds who flocked to hear him, was Billy Graham. His crusade in Indianapolis occurred when he was the most famous evangelist in the United States. Held at the INDIANA STATE FAIRGROUNDS, the revival ran from October 5 to November 1, 1959. This crusade, which required nearly three years of planning, held 25 services and attracted over 350,000 people. Graham was at his 1950s best, declaiming on the dangers of godless communism, the immorality rampant in America, and the need to turn to God. This message fell on receptive ears, and by the end of the crusade over 9,300 people had converted.

With the razing of Cadle Tabernacle in 1969 the city no longer had a permanent structure dedicated solely to evangelistic work, but revivalism did not disappear from Indianapolis. Churches committed to spreading the gospel hold revivals as a part of their normal work, and religious ministries dedicated to that goal are often underway in the city. Gospel sings are held regularly at the Murat Temple. The HOOSIER DOME and MARKET SQUARE ARENA are regular venues for "Praise-Fests" and religious conventions. While these religious activities take place outside the view of most people, they are well known among the theologically conservative Protestants who make up the majority of their audience.

EDWARD L. QUEEN II
Lilly Endowment

Rice, Thurman Brooks (Aug. 17, 1888–Dec. 27, 1952). Physician, public health leader, medical historian, educator, author. Rice, a native Hoosier, moved to Indianapolis in 1917 after having taught at Winona College (1914–1916). He received his medical degree from Indiana University in 1921. While working as a medical student in the Indiana State Board of Health (ISBH), he came under the influence of then-secretary of the board JOHN NEWELL HURTY. In August, 1922, Hurty sent Rice to investigate a serious epidemic of typhoid fever at Winona Lake, Indiana, with instructions "to do anything reasonable and necessary to protect the public health."

From this point on, Rice served the people of Indiana and the ISBH in many capacities, including director of the laboratory of the Indiana State Board of Health (1924–1926), professor of bacteriology and public health at Indiana University (1926–1946), assistant director of the Indiana Division of Public Health (1933–1936), acting state health commissioner during World War II, and

editor of the *ISBH Monthly Bulletin* from 1933 until his death. The auditorium of the ISBH Building was named Rice Auditorium in his honor.

A principal source for students of Indiana medical history, Rice was the author of over 20 books, including *The Hoosier Health Officer: A Biography of Dr. John N. Hurty* (1946), which is virtually a history of the public health movement in Indiana during the late 19th and early 20th centuries, and *History of the Medical Campus, Indianapolis, Indiana* (1949). His unfinished "One Hundred Years of Medicine: Indianapolis, 1820–1920" appeared in the *ISBH Monthly Bulletin*.

LUCRETIA ANN SAUNDERS
Indiana State Board of Health (retired)

Donald E. Thompson, *Indiana Authors and Their Books, 1917–1966* (Crawfordsville, Ind., 1974); *Who Was Who in America.*

Richards, Myra Reynolds (Jan. 31, 1882–Dec. 28, 1934). Sculptor, painter, and teacher. Born in Indianapolis, Richards studied art at the JOHN HERRON ART INSTITUTE under painter J. OTTIS ADAMS and sculptor RUDOLF SCHWARZ. From 1918 to 1929 Richards herself was a teacher at Herron, heading the anatomy and sculpture department.

During her lifetime, Richards' bronze work was widely exhibited in such shows as the HOOSIER SALON in Indianapolis, A Century of Progress (Chicago), and the Pennsylvania Academy of Fine Arts in Philadelphia. In Indiana, permanent installations of her work include a statue of JAMES WHITCOMB RILEY at Court House Square in Greenfield; fountain figures in UNIVERSITY PARK and FOUNTAIN SQUARE in Indianapolis; and a group of figures representing the advancement of women in Turkey Run State Park. Richards also executed bronze busts of such notables as Russian pianist Jan Cherniavsky, writer MEREDITH NICHOLSON, attorney John S. Duncan, *Indianapolis News* founder JOHN H. HOLLIDAY, and judge Napoleon Taylor.

In 1929 Richards left her teaching post at the John Herron Art Institute and traveled to Paris to continue her study of sculpture under G. J. Zolnay. In 1933 she returned to the United States, opening a studio in New York City before her death a year later.

FRANK N. OWINGS, JR.

Mary Q. Burnet, *Art and Artists of Indiana* (New York, 1921); *Indianapolis News*, Dec. 29, 1934.

Richardson, Henry J., Jr. (June 21, 1902–Dec. 5, 1983). Lawyer, jurist, politician, and civil rights leader. Born in Huntsville, Alabama, Richardson came to Indianapolis in his teens to study at SHORTRIDGE HIGH SCHOOL, where he graduated in 1921. He then attended the University of Illinois for two years. In 1925 Richardson was admitted to the Indiana Law School in Indianapolis, where he received an LL.B. degree in 1928.

After law school, Richardson became active in local and state politics. In 1930 he was appointed a temporary judge in the Marion County Superior Court, becoming the first African-American to serve in such a post. Two years later he was elected to the Indiana House of Representatives, making him among the first African-Americans to be elected to the state legislature in the 20th century.

Throughout his long and active career, Richardson was a tireless supporter of civil rights. During his tenure as a state legislator from 1933 to 1935 he co-authored welfare legislation, authored the first fair employment practices law in the country, fought to end segregation in Indiana University's dormitories, and assisted in efforts to change the state constitution's ban on African-Americans in the Indiana National Guard. From 1932 to 1938 he was also director of the Civil Liberties Division of the National Bar Association. In 1938 Richardson helped found the Federation of Associated Clubs, which spearheaded the fight to end racial segregation in local theaters. Nine years later, he chaired a committee that wrote the 1947 Indiana Anti-Hate Law. In 1948, Richardson obtained an injunction to keep the Dixiecrat party off the ballot in Indiana. He also played a pivotal role in ensuring passage of the 1949 Indiana school desegregation law. In 1953 Richardson, as NAACP legal representative, worked closely with Thurgood Marshall and Constance Baker Motley to win a landmark integrated housing discrimination case, *Jessie Woodbridge, et al. v. Housing Authority of Evansville, Indiana.*

Richardson remained active in civil rights throughout the 1950s and 1960s. He served on the board of the Indianapolis CHURCH FEDERATION, the Indiana Board of Public Welfare, the Indiana State Real Estate Commission, and the federal Civil Rights Commission. In 1958 he became the first Indiana life member of the NAACP. In 1965 he not only organized and founded the Indianapolis branch of the URBAN LEAGUE but also served on that organization's national board from 1966 to 1970. For many years Richardson was also active in the United Negro College Fund, serving both as local chairman and a member of the national board.

Richardson's work on behalf of civil rights garnered him many citations and awards. Among these were three appointments as a Sagamore of the Wabash and an honorary Doctor of Laws degree from the University of Indianapolis.

MONROE H. LITTLE, JR.
Indiana University–Purdue University,
Indianapolis

Alan F. January and Justin E. Walsh, *A Century of Achievement: Black Hoosiers in the Indiana General Assembly, 1881–1986* (Indianapolis, 1986); Emma Lou Thornbrough, *Since Emancipation: A Short History of Indiana Negroes, 1863–1963* (Indianapolis, 1963).

Henry J. Richardson, Jr., and his family at home in the Butler-Tarkington neighborhood in the early 1950s. [Indiana Historical Society, #C5610]

Rigg, Mary (1888–June 19, 1971). Social worker. Born in Kansas, Rigg moved to Indiana during her youth. She graduated from Rockville High School, and then received her bachelor's degree in education from Indiana University in 1915. After teaching for a short time she moved to New York City to study social work, her true interest. During World War I, Rigg worked for the Women's Division of the Department of Labor doing educational and social welfare work. Afterward, she directed a social hygiene program. Rigg moved to Indianapolis in 1919 and worked for the CHURCH FEDERATION for four years, helping juvenile delinquents. At the same time, she earned her master's degree at the newly opened Indiana University School of Social Work.

As a result of her thesis work with an immigrant community in Indianapolis, Rigg was hired as director of the AMERICAN SETTLEMENT in 1924. She turned the struggling settlement house into a thriving community center for immigrants and their children. As one of the first professionally trained social workers in Indianapolis, Rigg implemented modern social and educational programming at the settlement.

Moving the settlement house in 1940 to a modern facility on the southwest side of Indianapolis, Rigg directed the renamed Southwest Community Center until her retirement in 1960. Even after her retirement, she volunteered at the center. Never married, Rigg formed close personal ties with the communities in which she worked. The center, at 1917 West Morris, is now named in her honor.

MICHELLE D. HALE

Lotys Benning Stewart, "Miss Mary Rigg . . . Eighteen Years for Others," *Indianapolis Star*, Jan. 25, 1942; Mary Rigg Collection, Indiana State Library.

Riley, James Whitcomb (Oct. 7, 1849–July 22, 1916). The Hoosier Poet. Riley was born in Greenfield, Indiana, third child of Reuben A. and Elizabeth (Marine) Riley. Growing up in small-town Indiana, Riley developed an ear for the character and cadences of rural speech. He is best remembered today for his poetry in dialect.

Riley left school at 16, but not before a teacher inspired in him an interest in literature. Staying in the Greenfield area, he read law at his father's office briefly, then drifted among temporary jobs. His first published poem appeared in 1870. After working at several other newspapers, in 1877 he got a job at the *INDIANAPOLIS JOURNAL* doing routine assignments but versifying on the side. In 1883, he published—under the moniker "Benj. F. Johnson, of Boone"—his first group of poems in book form, *"The Old Swimmin' Hole" and 'Leven More Poems*.

With the appearance of this book, Riley developed a wide readership. The privately printed edition of 1,000 copies sold out quickly, and its success prompted Indianapolis publishers Merrill, Meigs and Company to bring out a second edition. That firm and its successors, Bowen-Merrill and BOBBS-MERRILL, became Riley's primary publisher, a partnership that would be lucrative for both. *The Boss Girl* (1886) began a virtually annual succession of Riley books that continued until about 1908.

With Riley's growing popularity in print, he was increasingly in demand on the lecture circuit. Beginning in the mid–1880s, he followed a heavy schedule of public appearances around the country and abroad.

Riley never married, and in 1893 he established residence in Indianapolis in rented rooms on Lockerbie Street, where he lived until his death. His tenancy in the elegant Italianate house symbolized the outwardly honor-filled course of his life. He was awarded several honorary degrees, elected to the American Academy of Arts and Letters, and in 1912 received the gold medal for poetry from the National Institute of Arts and Letters, the first poet so honored. Riley received many distinguished visitors on Lockerbie Street and was invited everywhere, including the White House. On his birthday in 1911 school children organized a celebration that was held annually for many years thereafter, and that came to be known as Riley Day. Honors continued even after the poet's death. The house on Lockerbie Street opened as a museum in 1922 and became a National Historic Landmark in 1963. The RILEY HOSPITAL FOR CHILDREN opened in Indianapolis in 1924. His birthplace in Greenfield became a museum in 1936, and "Riley

Days" are still celebrated in the town on the October weekend closest to his birthday.

Riley's life may not have been as happy as it appeared, however. There is evidence that he regretted never marrying, and that his poems to and about children were an attempt to counterweigh his bachelor state. It is likely that Riley was an alcoholic, and it has even been suggested that he suffered from syphilis. It may be that Riley's poems were a means of escape as much for him as for his audience.

Riley's poems offered a golden vision of the past, excluding the world's harsher and uglier aspects. Writing at a time of great turmoil in American life, he gave Hoosiers an idealized past to believe in and the nation an image of Indiana as the wellspring of solid heartland values in the midst of change. His socially marginal characters like Orphant Annie and the Raggedy Man appeared not as welfare problems but rather as vessels of goodness, simplicity, and rustic wisdom.

Riley was never a favorite of critics in his own period, and his work is ignored in those circles today. While his current reputation among the general public is a mere shadow of that during his lifetime, his poems are still familiar to and loved by many Hoosiers.

LEIGH DARBEE
Indiana Historical Society

R. E. Banta, *Indiana Authors and Their Books, 1816–1916* (Crawfordsville, Ind., 1949); Jared Carter, "Defrosting the Punkin: Another Look at Riley," *Indiana Writes*, 2 (Fall, 1977), 20–35; Arthur W. Shumaker, *A History of Indiana Literature* (Indianapolis, 1962).

Riley Hospital for Children. Children's hospital. After the death of poet JAMES WHITCOMB RILEY in 1916, local physician Lafayette Page suggested construction of a pediatric hospital to memorialize the man whose poetry reflected his love of children. Eventually established at the INDIANA UNIVERSITY MEDICAL CENTER, the hospital broke ground on July 12, 1922, and opened in October, 1924, rapidly filling its 150 beds. Supported by grants, fees, and contributions, with much of this funding raised by the Riley Memorial Association, Riley provides services not available in the community hospitals throughout the state, especially

Children undergoing physical therapy at Riley Hospital in 1925. [IUPUI Archives]

for complex or difficult cases. Still the only children's hospital in the state, Riley serves as a specialty referral center for infants, children, and adolescents in Indiana and surrounding states and is one of the nation's major centers for children's cardiovascular surgery. Riley also is the major educational facility in Indiana for professions serving children's health needs. Educational programs help parents cope with their child's illness.

Riley has earned a national reputation for quality of care, particularly in cardiovascular surgery. Other specialties include cancer, leukemia, arthritis, gastroenterology, infectious diseases, ophthalmology, and newborn care. In addition to physicians, surgeons, and nurses, Riley employs a large staff of full-time allied health professionals. Social workers, occupational and physical therapists, speech and audiology therapists, psychologists, and nutritionists provide an unequalled resource for children's medical needs.

Much of Riley's expansion has been made possible by charitable donations. In 1930 the Kiwanis District of Indiana established the $167,500 "K" Wing for the treatment of orthopedic patients. In the mid–1950s the $123,000 Kiwanis Diagnostic and Outpatient Center was added. The Rotary Clubs of Indiana provided the $250,000 Rotary Convalescent Center. More recently, the Burn Unit was provided by Kappa Kappa Kappa Sorority. In 1965 the new surgery wing opened, and in 1971 the hospital completed its first of two major expansions. The second expansion phase, completed in 1986, won awards from *Modern Healthcare* and the American Institute of Architects for excellence in planning and design, and increased the facility's inpatient capacity to 268 beds. In 1993 construction began for another addition, the Riley Children's Cancer Center, a facility that will specialize in bone marrow transplants.

KATHY INGELS HELMOND

Ritchey, James O. (Feb. 1, 1891–Dec. 4, 1981). Distinguished physician, teacher, and medical administrator. Born on a farm in Carroll County, Indiana, Ritchey earned B.S. (1916) and M.D. (1918) degrees from Indiana University. He joined the faculty of the INDIANA UNIVERSITY SCHOOL OF MEDICINE in 1919 and remained active until his death, a period of 62 years, serving as chairman of the Department of Medicine from 1931 until 1956. In addition, he served the school in such important positions as chairman of the Medical School Admissions Committee for over 40 years.

Ritchey was a master clinician who served as a role model for beginning medical students and experienced physicians alike. He had a profound influence on thousands of practicing physicians in Indiana and in the nation. He trained many leading internists, medical investigators, chairmen of departments of medicine, and deans of medical schools. Among his many honors was his designation in 1959 as the first Distinguished Professor in the School of Medicine. The James O. Ritchey Professorship in Medicine was created in 1964. He was also a governor of the American College of Physicians and the first from Indiana to become a Master of that organization.

GLENN W. IRWIN, JR., M.D.

Ritter, Joseph Elmer (July 20, 1892–June 10, 1967). First archbishop of the Archdiocese of Indianapolis. Ritter was born in New Albany, Indiana. Upon entering St. Meinrad Seminary in 1906, he began his journey to the priesthood and was ordained in the Abbey Church on May 30, 1917. Father Ritter's first assignment was St. Patrick's Church in Indianapolis, but the young priest soon became second assistant at SS. PETER AND PAUL CATHEDRAL.

On February 3, 1933, Ritter was appointed Titular Bishop of Hippus and Auxiliary to the Bishop of Indianapolis. He later became the vicar general. In an unusual move, Ritter, the auxiliary bishop of Indianapolis, was appointed bishop of the Diocese of Indianapolis on March 24, 1934. On November 17, 1944, the Diocese of Indianapolis was elevated to the rank of an archdiocese and Ritter became the archbishop. He was moved to the archbishopric of St. Louis, Missouri, on July 21, 1946. In both Indianapolis and St. Louis, Archbishop Ritter ordered the end of racial segregation in the Catholic schools and threatened excommunication for anyone who interfered with the execution of the order.

Pope John XXIII elevated Archbishop Ritter to the cardinalate on January 16, 1961. As Cardinal Ritter, he participated in the election of Pope Paul VI and attended the Second Vatican Council. Joseph Ritter died in St. Louis. Ritter High School, established in 1964, is named in his honor.

MARCUS EUGENE WOODS, II

J. W. Baker, *The New Catholic Encyclopedia* (1974 supplement); Francis Beauchesne Thornton, *Our American Princes: The Story of the Seventeen American Cardinals* (New York, 1963), 296–312.

Riverside Amusement Park. Riverside Amusement Park, located on West 30th Street at White River, began as a joint venture of Pittsburgh investor and amusement park developer Frederick Ingersoll and Indianapolis businessmen J. Clyde Power, Albert Lieber, and Bert Feibleman. By 1903 the park contained a "double eight toboggan railway" and numerous concessions. The owners soon added the "Old Mill," a replica of a working flour mill through which passengers

Early attractions at Riverside Amusement Park included a roller coaster and a Ferris wheel.
[Indiana Historical Society, #C5933]

rode in boats and were entertained by electrically lighted scenes. Riverside grew in popularity by capitalizing on the "Coney Island craze" and adding new amusements, including a 350–foot-long "Shoot the Chutes" waterslide, reputed to be one of the steepest and most terrifying in the country.

To increase park attendance, business manager J. Sandy did not charge an admission fee, but relied on revenues generated from individual rides and concession leases. Sandy introduced live entertainment shows and also arranged for additional streetcar service to the park.

In 1919, attorney Lewis A. Coleman organized the Riverside Exhibition Company and gained control of the business. Coleman had provided legal services for Riverside's owners for years and took payment in company stock. The new company issued more stock, which allowed expansion and modernization of the park's amusements. This included two large roller coasters, "The Flash" and "The Thriller," a 2,200–foot-long miniature railroad, and a string of concrete block buildings that housed games and food concessions.

A key attraction at Riverside was the roller skating rink. Erected in the early 1900s, it first served as a dance hall, attracting thousands on the weekends to dance to live orchestras and dance bands. The hall was eventually transformed into a 100–by–200–foot skating rink, which proved to be an inexpensive and safe place for recreational activities into the 1960s.

Riverside experienced many prosperous years under the leadership of John D. Coleman, son of Lewis, who became president in 1939. Throughout World War II Riverside sponsored several wartime relief programs to assist families of servicemen, thereby guaranteeing a steady visitation of patrons who wished to demonstrate their patriotism. Attendance rose into the 1950s as Indianapolis residents became more mobile and acquired more leisure time. In 1952, an estimated 1 million visitors crowded Riverside's midway and skating rink. During the late 1950s Riverside introduced several expensive amusements, including an automobile turnpike ride modeled after Disneyland's popular attraction.

With Lewis Coleman's acquisition of the park Riverside adopted a policy of "whites only patronage," although African-Americans were permitted to visit on designated "Colored Frolic Days." This discriminatory policy angered integrationists who picketed the park during the early 1960s and eventually convinced John Coleman to remove the "whites only" signs.

By this time, however, Riverside was experiencing serious problems. The deteriorating neighborhood deterred people from visiting the park, while reduced revenues affected park maintenance. By the mid–1960s the park was losing over $30,000 annually. At the end of 1970 Riverside finally closed, and its rides were sold off or demolished. Coleman attributed the park's demise to the high cost of new rides, maintenance and insurance fees, and the competition from the nation's major amusement-theme parks.

DAVID G. VANDERSTEL
CONNIE ZEIGLER
Indiana University–Purdue University,
Indianapolis

Riviera Club. Private recreation club. James Makin and a group of northside residents founded the club in 1933 to provide low-cost private recreational facilities for families. Popularly known as "The Rivie," the club is located at 5640 North Illinois Street, on a 26–acre triangle of land between the White River and the Central Canal.

The club's recreational facilities are highlighted by its six swimming pools. The swim program, coached by several nationally acclaimed coaches, including Johnny Galvich and Gene Lee, has brought national exposure to the club. Its swimmers have won hundreds of local, state, and national championships and count among their ranks many All-Americans and a few Olympic team members. Most notable is Kathy Ellis, who won four medals at the 1964 Olympics.

In 1974 the Riviera Club experienced further notoriety when a club member and his African-American friend filed a lawsuit alleging racial discrimination in club admission policies. The club settled out of court in 1982 by agreeing to the plaintiffs' demands to change its membership and guest policies and the selection of directors. As a result of continued legal pressure through the mid–1980s, the Riviera Club had accepted eight minority families into membership by 1985. The club attracts most of its current 4,500 family membership from the BUTLER-TARKINGTON neighborhood and surrounding area.

MICHELLE D. HALE

Roads and Highways. More than most state capitals, Indianapolis has relied on land transportation. Early expectations for navigation on WHITE RIVER quickly proved false, so roads and highways were especially necessary to connect a landlocked Indianapolis to state and nation.

While Indiana was still a territory, the federal government began to establish post roads. That process continued in the 1820s and 1830s, thus influencing the development of roads through central Indiana. As settlements emerged, Congress designated more post roads throughout the region, such as the one between Indianapolis and Fort Wayne (a route followed much later by S.R. 37). In the 1820s the state legislature authorized the designation of several state roads that would link the principal towns of Indiana with one another and with the new state capital. Many of today's highways follow these early routes. Much of the old Lafayette Road, for example, ultimately became U.S. 52. In Marion County several stagecoach stops along this and other roads grew into villages that were later absorbed by the growing city, leaving their names and a few architectural remnants to mark their previous existence. Among these are Flackville, Bootjack, and TRADERS POINT, all on Lafayette Road.

The most ambitious early state road was the MICHIGAN ROAD linking Lake Michigan to the Ohio River via Indianapolis. Completed in the 1830s, its route through Marion County essentially followed what is today Southeastern Avenue and Martin Luther King, Jr. Street. In the same decade the federally administered NATIONAL ROAD extended westward through Ohio and was surveyed across Indiana. It came through Indianapolis on Washington Street, which required the building of an impressive two-lane covered timber bridge over White River in 1834.

As the town took shape, it became obvious that roads needed considerable improvement in

order to accommodate the increasing number of wheeled vehicles. Early attempts at road "improvement" consisted primarily of widening the lanes through the forest and laying a "corduroy" bed of logs across the numerous swampy sections of Marion County. Wooden bridges, often covered, were built where the more important thoroughfares crossed White River and FALL CREEK.

The Mammoth Internal Improvements Act of 1836, in addition to funding canals and railroad connections, authorized new surveys for additional overland routes linking Indianapolis to far-flung settlements throughout the state. Still, little real improvement in the roads took place until the brief fad for plank roads in the late 1840s and early 1850s, which a number of Indianapolis newspapers promoted. Private companies chartered by the Indiana General Assembly laid these roads of eight-foot boards that rested on two parallel rows of wooden stringers. Around 1850 portions of the National Road west out of Indianapolis were improved in this manner. But plank roads held up poorly and enthusiasm quickly waned, especially when RAILROADS began their rapid development in the 1850s.

With the heyday of railroads after the Civil War, there was little new road construction and road maintenance dwindled. Aside from connecting local villages, roads in the 1870s and 1880s functioned largely as feeders to the railroads. A number of private gravel road companies that formed after the Civil War assumed the building and maintenance of roads, using this surface material that was readily available in Indiana. Usually landowners along the route formed such companies. For example, the Indianapolis and Oakland Gravel Road Company was created in 1867 to improve the Pendleton Pike in northeastern Marion County. Similarly, the Augusta Gravel Road Company took on the responsibility to resurface and maintain a portion of the old Michigan Road. As had the plank road companies these enterprises set up toll houses at points along the way as a means of recouping their investment and raising funds for maintenance. In the 1880s the county began to buy up the privately administered improved roads to assure that they would remain public thoroughfares. Within ten years all such roads in the region were free and so designated on contemporary maps (Bluff Free Gravel Road in southern Marion County, for example).

The coming of the railroads led to the development of metal truss BRIDGES to accommodate the heavier loads. In the 1870s this bridge construction began to appear on roads as well, although covered wooden bridges continued to be built in Marion County at least until the turn of the century. No metal truss vehicular bridges from the 19th or early 20th centuries, and only a few from later years, remain in use in the county. An expanding population and increasingly heavy traffic required more and better bridges of reinforced concrete, which first appeared in the early 1900s.

The boom in BICYCLING in the 1880s, along with the simultaneous clamor for rural free delivery of mail (which required roads that were passable year-round), stimulated what became known nationally as the Good Roads Movement. Initially the emphasis was on farm-to-market roads, but the numerous cycling clubs in Marion County by the 1890s added their support for improved rural road surfaces. As the movement expanded, its priorities changed; established in 1910, the Indiana Good Roads Association stressed the need for dependable connecting routes between towns.

It was the development of the automobile during the 1890s that added weight to the Good Roads Movement, and several Indianapolis automotive pioneers were involved. The HOOSIER MOTOR CLUB, begun in 1902, scouted out the best roads, published guides, and offered travel advice to motorists. Perhaps most notable are CARL G. FISHER's contributions to early highway development. A bicycle enthusiast and early automobile promoter, Fisher held a grand vision of a hardsurfaced, coast-to-coast highway. In 1912 he and other automobile manufacturers and dealers began planning what became the Lincoln Highway. To promote the idea of an improved transcontinental highway, the following summer Fisher and several others drove their automobiles on what they touted as the Hoosier Trail Blazers' Tour from Indianapolis to San Francisco. Ironically, the completed Lincoln Highway bypassed Indianapolis by well over a hundred miles to the north.

A plethora of copycat highway associations followed that of the Lincoln. Using existing roads

for the most part, the associations posted distinctive signs and published guidebooks to mark their routes, such as the National Old Trails Road that followed the former National Road. Another such route that passed through Indianapolis was part of Carl Fisher's Dixie Highway, which led from Michigan to his new resort development at Miami Beach, Florida, generally following what ultimately became U.S. 31.

The labyrinth of privately administered highways, most of which were not that much improved, led to considerable confusion and discontent among the growing population of automobile owners. The federal government finally responded, and in 1916 Congress passed a bill appropriating funds for states to build rural post roads and designate "main market highways." The Dixie Highway and the National Old Trails Road became two of Indiana's five main market highways. Federal funds required establishment of a state road department, so the General Assembly created the State Highway Commission in 1917 and reaffirmed it in 1919 after litigation questioned its validity. Immediately the commission took on the task of laying out a system of state highways that would reach all county seats and cities of over 5,000 population and link these routes with improved highways in adjoining states. It drew up a plan in 1920 designating 51 roads with assigned numbers, with the old Dixie Highway and the National Road assigned numbers 1 and 3, respectively. By 1930 state road numbers and their routes more closely resembled those of today; Pendleton Pike, for example, had become S.R. 67, and Bluff Road and the route south to Bloomington, S.R. 37. In the mid–1920s the federal government, too, began its system of numbered highways, and in 1927 the venerable National Road became U.S. 40. With federal routes 31, 36, 40, and 52 meeting in Indianapolis, as well as several major state roads, the city staked a legitimate claim to being the "Crossroads of America."

During the 1920s the highway department began to construct bypasses around the business centers of larger cities and entirely past smaller villages, such as that of S.R. 67 around OAKLANDON. New buildings containing businesses geared toward the highway traveler, such as short order restaurants and filling stations, appeared along these bypasses and approaches to towns. Paradise, now a group of rental properties on the south side of Oaklandon, began as a motley collection of tourist cabins, along with a grocery and gas station, serving the new S.R. 67 bypass in the late 1920s. There still exist scattered examples of this development along the present but especially the former state highway routes in Marion County, which give clues as to the past suburbanization of Indianapolis. Present Bluff Road, the former S.R. 37, is perhaps the county's most intact roadscape from this early period of state highways.

Road improvement continued in the 1930s, slowed at first by the Great Depression but boosted in turn by the New Deal work projects, especially those of the Works Progress Administration (WPA). The farm-to-market roads once favored by the Good Roads Movement at last became a state priority. Scores of miles of Marion County's rural roads were improved with WPA labor that constructed drainage ditches, culverts, crowns, berms, and in many cases, bridges. One program set out to eliminate hump railroad crossings. New Deal projects extended and improved the state and federal highways through the city as well. Probably the most visible of WPA roads in Marion County is Fall Creek Parkway, which was intended to provide a scenic link from Indianapolis to FORT BENJAMIN HARRISON.

As early as 1937 some Indianapolis civic leaders conceived the idea of a beltway around the periphery of the city and took the proposal to the State House with the endorsement of several highway engineers. Soon the idea of the Marion County Belt Parkway, later Road 100, took hold, and by the early 1950s its north side and most of its east side were established on 86th/82nd streets and Shadeland Avenue, respectively. Almost before Road 100's plans were even begun on the west and south sides, however, its proposed routes were absorbed into the grander scheme of Interstate 465, with the beltways being part of the nation's vast plan of interstate highways, several of which would cross at Indianapolis. By the late 1950s the existing Road 100 was too built up to be incorporated into the planned limited-access beltway, and considerable protest arose, especially from the Warren [Township] Civic Association, over the

government's proposed interstate route on the east side. Nonetheless, by late 1970 I–465 was completed as planned, and within a few years so was the network of interstates through Indianapolis, with the exception of the phantom I–69, which enters the county from the northeast and stops near CASTLETON. Two of the interstates, I–70 and I–65, form the Inner Loop around downtown on all but the west side. The superhighways plunged through neighborhoods, splitting them in two and cutting off streets. A secondary result of this neighborhood disintegration was the closing of most of the schools located adjacent to the interstates.

Post–World War II growth of the city and the exponential rise of automobile use required other significant changes in the county's arterial road system, which in turn led to irretrievable alterations in the roadscape. The widening and rerouting of state and federal highways caused the abandonment of older roadside businesses and seemingly uncontrolled strip development farther and farther from the center of the city. The profusion of restaurants, shopping malls, and the like, followed by satellite development of apartment complexes and housing tracts, has served to weaken the cohesiveness and the identity of Indianapolis. Perhaps no road more exemplifies this problem than U.S. 31 leading out of Indianapolis in either direction. Yet vestiges of the spokes that formed the original crossroads that was Indianapolis remain. While Allisonville Road will take one only to the spot on I–465 where once the town stood, with diligence the traveler may still follow Zionsville, Rockville, Mooresville, Brookville, and other such roads to their original destinations. Along the way, even in the dips and curves, are the traces of their earlier character.

GLORY-JUNE GREIFF

Robbins, Lewis Corwin (July 7, 1909–June 14, 1990). Physician and public health pioneer. Robbins, a native of Indianapolis, graduated from INDIANA UNIVERSITY SCHOOL OF MEDICINE in 1935 and received a Master's degree in Public Health from Johns Hopkins University in 1938. Robbins began his career at Methodist Hospital and the Indiana State Board of Health. In 1941, he joined the U.S. Public Health Service where he was one of the initiators of the landmark Framingham Study linking heart disease and smoking. During the 1950s, he served as a health officer in the international health programs of the United States in Indochina, Southeast Asia, the Near East, and Africa.

Robbins served as the first chief of cancer control of the Public Health Service (1957–1965) and in 1964 co-authored the first Surgeon General's "Report on Smoking and Health." He also played a key role in the development of mammography for the control of breast cancer, the flexible proctosigmoidoscope for colon-rectal cancer, and the Pap smear for cervical cancer. Robbins received a commendation medal for his contributions to cancer control in 1963.

Throughout his career, Robbins' primary concern was the prevention of disease and injury. Using data from prospective studies like Framingham, Robbins developed a diagnostic tool, the Health Risk Appraisal (HRA), to identify the health risks linked to various individual lifestyles. By identifying these lifestyle problems through the HRA, Robbins hoped in many cases to avert the onset of disease and to extend useful life expectancy. His book, *How to Practice Prospective Medicine*, was published in 1970. The HRA is now widely used in preventive medicine.

ELIZABETH J. VAN ALLEN

Robert Hanna (aka *General Hanna*). Reputedly the only steamboat ever to ascend the White River to Indianapolis. The vessel was named for General Robert Hanna, who had contracted to build a portion of the National Road. He used the steamer and an accompanying barge to haul timber and stone for the NATIONAL ROAD bridge. The arrival of the steamboat in April, 1831, caused great excitement. A citizens committee drafted a resolution to the General Assembly claiming that the event proved the WHITE RIVER was navigable and that the state should undertake to improve the waterway. Enthusiasm waned when the steamboat ran aground on its return trip and remained stranded for some time. The White River never proved to be navigable, and the city

eventually looked elsewhere for transportation connections.

ROBERT G. BARROWS
Indiana University–Purdue University,
Indianapolis

William R. Holloway, *Indianapolis* (Indianapolis, 1870), 39–40.

The Robert K. Greenleaf Center for Servant-Leadership. An international, not-for-profit organization that advocates a new approach to leadership. Robert K. Greenleaf, retired AT&T executive and author of *Servant-Leadership*, founded the Center for Applied Ethics near Boston in 1964. It was renamed the Greenleaf Center in 1985 and moved to Indianapolis in 1990.

The center's mission is to promote the concept of servant-leadership, which emphasizes increased service to others, a holistic approach to work, a sense of community, and shared decision making. Its goals are to preserve and promote the writings of Robert K. Greenleaf, to produce and publish new resources on servant-leadership, to provide a focal point and opportunities for discussion of servant-leadership, and to connect servant-leaders in a learning network. Its programs include distributing materials and sponsoring lectures, workshops, and an annual conference.

Through its programs and publication sales, it reaches 5,000 persons annually. In the last 20 years combined sales of "The Servant as Leader" and *Servant-Leadership* have totaled more than 400,000 copies. Income for its 1992 budget of $360,000 came from membership, workshop, and conference fees, sale of materials, grants, royalties, and investments.

LARRY SPEARS
The Robert K. Greenleaf Center
for Servant-Leadership

Roberts Dairy. Popular name for William H. Roberts and Sons, a dairy and home delivery business. William H. Roberts (1860–1922) formed a business partnership, Tyner-Roberts, with brother-in-law Silas Tyner in 1877. They sold fresh milk from a mule-drawn vehicle. Roberts bought out Tyner and around 1910 sons Ralph and Guy Roberts joined him in business. The enterprise became a corporation—William H. Roberts and Sons—in 1919 when sons J. Benjamin and W. Henry also joined. During its 110 years of operation Roberts remained a family-run concern.

Early milk customers supplied their own containers; route drivers filled the vessels from a large can. Around 1900, the year in which the company purchased property at 4201 Millersville Road, Roberts became the first area dairy to use glass milk bottles. Besides delivering Roberts products, company drivers carried bread, eggs, orange juice, butter, bacon, sausage, and ice cream. Accounts with stores, schools, and hospitals began in 1935, though home deliveries remained the bigger part of the business. Roberts used horse-drawn vehicles for home delivery until 1946. Motor deliveries continued until March, 1987, when routes had declined from 150 to 10.

Roberts bought Indiana, Wisconsin, Michigan, Minnesota, and Iowa milk to process into various dairy products. Roberts also bought other dairies. Hornaday was a 1963 acquisition. In 1982, Roberts purchased LINDNER'S DAIRY Centers, raising the number of Roberts employees from 350 to 700.

Roberts declared bankruptcy in June, 1987. Changing milk-buying habits were a growing problem, but a local milk price war was the immediate cause of the company's demise. Another local dairy, Maplehurst Farms, acquired the right to use the firm's name and logo and still markets "Roberts" products.

JOANNE KEATON

Roberts Park United Methodist Church.

In 1842, with METHODISTS in Indianapolis numbering over 600, the Indiana Conference divided the Indianapolis station into the Eastern and Western charges. The Eastern charge moved into a building at the northeast corner of Pennsylvania and Market streets and was named Roberts Chapel in honor of Bishop Robert R. Roberts, the first Methodist bishop to reside in Indiana.

In 1847, the women's sewing circle purchased a bell that called the congregation to worship, sounded the hours, and served as the city's

Roberts Park Chapel in its first location on the northeast corner of Pennsylvania and Market Streets, looking north from Washington Street in 1856. This is one of the earliest existing photographs of the city. [Indiana Historical Society, Bass Collection, #17804]

fire bell. The town clock was also installed in the bell tower in 1853. By the 1860s Roberts Chapel had sponsored eight other congregations—a trend that would continue through the 1960s, by which time Roberts Park had sponsored 18 other churches.

The congregation remained at its first location until 1869 when it purchased its present one-acre lot at the corner of Vermont and Delaware streets. Renamed Roberts Park to reflect its park-like setting, the new church building was completed and dedicated by Bishop Matthew Simpson in 1876. Designed by DIEDRICH A. BOHLEN, the Romanesque building was patterned after the City Temple of London and built of Indiana limestone and black walnut from the site.

During the remainder of the 19th century and through the first quarter of the 20th century, the congregation grew in influence. Prominent members included CALVIN FLETCHER, Governor James Brown Ray, and JAMES A. ALLISON. During the 1870s and 1880s the congregation established several missionary groups (one was the forerunner of the YMCA) and sponsored the first public library. Women's groups hosted annual festivals and plays at TOMLINSON HALL in the 1890s. During the 1920s the congregation supported a city missionary and broadcast services on radio station WFBM. In 1927 Roberts Park added classrooms, a dining room, and a gymnasium, and used these facilities in World War II as a servicemen's center, serving over 90,000 meals and providing entertainment.

By the 1940s Roberts Park was one of the largest Methodist congregations in Indiana with approximately 1,700 members. Many suburban members continued to commute to the church, and in the 1950s the congregation decided to remain in the downtown area. Programming for elderly neighborhood residents and the downtown business population became a focus in the 1960s.

In 1982 the church building was placed on the National Register of Historic Places. By the 1990s membership had dropped to 425, most of whom were suburban commuters, but the congregation, now surrounded by a commercial district, has remained active in the downtown area and participates in the Riley-Lockerbie Ministerial Association.

TOMMY L. FARIS

Robinson, J(oseph) Russel (July 8, 1892–Sept. 30, 1963). Ragtime and jazz songwriter and pianist. A native of Indianapolis, Robinson left Shortridge High School to begin his career as a pianist by accompanying silent films in local theaters. Between 1908 and 1912 his family lived in various southern cities where he and his brother John performed in movie houses. Possessing a distinctive playing style since his right arm was crippled by polio, Robinson became popular with piano-roll companies and obtained contracts to record dozens of rolls for Imperial and the United States Music Company in Chicago (1917–1918). Later he moved to New York where he recorded blues songs for the QRS Company (1918–1921). Robinson also served as a pianist for the Original Dixieland Jazz Band (1919–1921) and accompanied numerous jazz and blues singers in the 1930s before moving to California in the 1940s.

Robinson collaborated extensively with African-American musicians, including W. C. Handy, NOBLE SISSLE, and Spencer Williams, who praised Robinson as "the white man with the colored fingers." Although he later developed a reputation for his blues- and jazz-influenced compositions, he made his initial mark by composing rags, all of

which were published in Indianapolis: "Sapho Rag" (1909), "Dynamite Rag," "Minstrel Man," and "Erratic Rag" (1911). His "Eccentric Rag" (1912) became a standard in the jazz repertory. Best known for his popular song "Margie" (1920), Robinson also composed "Singin' the Blues (Til My Daddy Comes Home)" (1920), "Aggravatin' Papa (Don't You Try to Two-Time Me)," and "Beale Street Mama" (1923).

DAVID G. VANDERSTEL
Indiana University–Purdue University,
Indianapolis

John Edward Hasse, "The Creation and Dissemination of Indianapolis Ragtime, 1897–1930" (Ph.D. dissertation, Indiana University, 1981).

Rock Island Refining Corporation. Oil refinery. In 1940 Oklahoma and Kansas businessmen L. E. Kincannon, L. E. Winkler, and L. B. Simmons built Indianapolis' only oil refinery, which began processing crude oil in October, 1941. By the mid–1940s the northwestside facility at 5000 West 86th Street was producing 7,500 barrels of crude oil a day. The refinery increased production over the next several decades and by 1981 sales were $592 million, making it Indiana's largest independent refinery. Besides supplying products for its own United gasoline station chain, Rock Island also sold petroleum products to other independents such as Kocolene and Crystal Flash.

In March, 1989, Houston, Texas-based Marathon Oil Company paid about $140 million to acquire Rock Island, making it one of five Marathon refineries. The principal owners, members of the Winkler and Kincannon families, sold the refinery because they were no longer involved in the management of the company and there were no heirs interested in taking over the operation. Before the Marathon purchase, the refinery employed about 300 people with additional workers at 28 United filling stations. Rock Island also held a 50–percent interest in the Wake-Up gasoline chain.

As of the early 1990s the facility refined 50,000 barrels of oil a day. In 1991 Marathon agreed to pay $3.9 million in fines and environmental improvements for violations of the federal Clean Water Act. In July, 1993, Marathon announced it would close the refinery by the end of the year and lay off the majority of its 260 employees owing to the expense of complying with provisions of the Clean Air Act.

DEBORAH B. MARKISOHN

Indianapolis Business Journal, Nov. 28–Dec. 1, 1988; *Indianapolis Star*, July 1, 1993.

Rocky Ripple. Suburban town bounded by 54th Street, the Central Canal, 51st Street, and White River. Settled in 1910 as a working class resort on WHITE RIVER, Rocky Ripple often experienced floods in its early years. Indeed, in 1921 Indianapolis Mayor SAMUEL (LEW) SHANK proposed turning the area into a lake. Instead Rocky Ripple's citizens incorporated their town in 1927. Isolated from the city around it by the canal and White River, with access provided by only one bridge throughout most of its history, the town grew up as a working-class neighborhood with a 1930 population of 133. In 1937 the federal Works Progress Administration funded the construction of a levee that mitigated the town's flooding problems, and by 1940 the population had more than doubled. In 1956 the town had over 650 residents, 1,000 acres, and the highest tax rate in Marion County.

When Indianapolis and the county merged under UNIGOV, Rocky Ripple retained its status as an incorporated town and continued to fund its own police and fire protection under the auspices of its town council. Since Unigov was enacted the town has lost residents, however, dropping from 1,192 in 1970 to 751 in 1990. In 1993 the lower- to middle-income residents of this town-within-the-city live in homes ranging from turn-of-the-century cottages to ranches and split-levels and now have the lowest tax rate in the county.

CONNIE J. ZEIGLER

Rogers, Bruce (May 14, 1870–May 18, 1957). Book designer, printer, and typographer. Born in Lafayette, Indiana, Rogers showed early talent for drawing and penmanship. He entered Purdue University at 16 and decided to become an illustrator, working on several yearbooks, the university catalog and magazine, and an edition of William Cullen Bryant's *Forest Hymn*. The arrangement of type on paper fascinated Rogers and, after receiving a B.A. degree in 1890, he moved to Indianapolis, working first for the Indiana Illustrating Company, then as an illustrator for the INDIANAPOLIS NEWS.

Newspaper life did not suit him, however, and Rogers returned to Lafayette where he painted landscapes modeled after those of T. C. STEELE. Later he again moved to Indianapolis and in 1893 designed his first published book, *Botany in Pharmacy*, for ELI LILLY AND COMPANY. In the title page, initials, and chapter headings for RICHARD B. GRUELLE's *Notes of the Walter Collection* (1895), Rogers sought to unify the catalog's pages through his decorations, thus setting the direction of his subsequent career.

Rogers met Joseph M. Bowles, founder of the periodical *Modern Art*, one of the first American reflections of the Arts and Crafts movement; Rogers' design work in the form of initials and decorations appeared regularly in that publication. Bowles also showed Rogers several early Kelmscott Press books, which further aroused his interest in the book as an artifact. L. Prang and Company subsidized *Modern Art* and moved it and Bowles to Boston; Rogers went also, bringing to an end his residence in Indiana but signaling the beginning of a career that brought him international fame.

Rogers became typographic advisor to the Riverside Press (1895–1912), and later to the Metropolitan Museum Press; the university presses at Cambridge, Harvard, and Oxford; the Press of William E. Rudge; and Emery Walker, Ltd. in London. Montaigne (1901) was Rogers' first type design, but Centaur (1915) was his most famous.

In 1953 Rogers designed the third edition of Logan Esarey's *The Indiana Home* for Indiana University Press; it features his sketches of pioneer tools, implements, and furnishings. One of Rogers' "devices" carries the words "Bruce Rogers of Indiana," whereby he acknowledges his roots in the soil that set him on his chosen path.

BRUCE L. JOHNSON
Indiana Historical Society

Paul A. Bennett, *Bruce Rogers of Indiana* (Providence, [R.I.?], 1936).

Romanians. Immigrants from Romania began arriving in the United States during the late 19th century. Settling primarily in urban industrial areas, these immigrants were typically young males, sometimes with wives and families, from small rural villages, with few if any trade skills, who intended to become rich and return to Romania. Many found their dreams realized within the growing ethnic community in Indianapolis.

Romanians never constituted a sizable portion of Indianapolis' population. The *Indianapolis News* estimated that 1,000 lived in the city in 1908, although the 1910 census reported only 132 Romanian-born and 29 native-born of foreign parents. By 1930 there were 848 Romanians (477 foreign-born and 371 of foreign parentage). Romanians numbered 768 (including 289 foreign-born) in 1960, and 715 Indianapolis residents (752 in Marion County) reported Romanian ancestry in 1990. Recent additions to the community have resulted in part from upheavals in eastern Europe during the late 1980s.

Upon arriving in Indianapolis, the earliest Romanians settled in two principal locations: the area bounded by New York and West streets, Kentucky Avenue, and White River; and HAUGHVILLE. They found employment primarily in the automobile industry and the meat-processing factories, working for KINGAN AND COMPANY, Armour, and STARK, WETZEL AND COMPANY as cutters, trimmers, slaughterers, and packers.

Although residing among fellow eastern Europeans and within the boundaries of the Slovenian national parish, Romanians established institutions to preserve their faith and national culture in their adopted homeland. In 1908 they organized the Romanian Star Benefit Association, a fraternal mutual aid society, which sponsored a "flag day" parade and celebration at Germania Hall on August 2. They also founded, on October 23, 1909, the Romanian Progressive Club, an ethnic national social club dedicated to encouraging loyalty to the United States through citizenship instruction and developing an understanding between peoples. On November 28, 1929, the club dedicated a new building at 636 West Washington Street (near Blackford Street). The Reunion of Romanian Women, which reported 100 women active in local social service, performed a Romanian operetta at FAIRVIEW PARK in August, 1913. The United Romanian Societies of America held its 19th annual convention in Indianapolis September 1–7, 1925. The Romanians also maintained a national hall on Kentucky Avenue where they staged plays. The AMERICAN SETTLEMENT likewise proved important to Romanians, especially the women, by offering sewing and cooking classes and assorted clinics.

Romanians attempted to organize a church around 1906, but did not succeed until 1910–1911 when a Romanian priest from Indiana Harbor helped establish a Romanian Orthodox congregation in the 600 block of West Market Street at Blackford Street. The original parish priests were also immigrants who conducted a weekly language school to maintain the mother tongue among the second generation. Following the purchase of its property by ACME-EVANS COMPANY in 1947, St. Constantine and Elena Romanian Orthodox Church relocated to 3237 West 16th Street in April, 1949, where it continues as a center of Romanian cultural activity. In 1911 Romanian Baptists residing in MARS HILL established a congregation with the assistance of a local Baptist preacher. They dedicated their first building in 1940 under the leadership of Rev. Vasile Prodan, who came to Indianapolis in 1936 after immigrating to the United States in 1913.

A high point in the history of Indianapolis' Romanian community was the visit by Queen Marie and the Romanian royal family on November 17, 1926. They were honored by a downtown parade and a banquet at the COLUMBIA CLUB, among other activities.

G. LAWRENCE ALBEAN
DAVID G. VANDERSTEL

Indianapolis News, Aug. 3, 1908, Nov. 17, 1939; *Indianapolis Sun*, Aug. 4, 1913; *Indianapolis Star*, Nov. 17, 18, 1926, Aug. 18, 1929.

Rose, Chauncey (Dec. 24, 1794–Aug. 13, 1877). Merchant, railroad builder, and philanthropist. A native of Wethersfield, Connecticut, Rose had no education beyond common school. He moved west in 1817 at age 23 and, after traveling the Ohio and Mississippi river valleys for two years, he settled in Terre Haute, Indiana. He opened a lumber mill, became a retail merchant, and began to buy land in what would become the city's downtown. By the late 1840s Rose was Terre Haute's most prominent citizen.

Although he became a stockholder and director of the Wabash and Erie Canal, Rose soon saw that RAILROADS would make canal transportation obsolete. Thus, with his own money and what he could raise from friends and associates, he undertook to build a railroad. At his urging, the Indiana General Assembly passed an act in 1847 to incorporate the Terre Haute and Richmond Railroad Company. In May, delegates from several Indiana counties gathered in Indianapolis at a convention to discuss the possibility of connecting St. Louis with Cincinnati, an action that would result in "continuous railroad communication with the eastern Atlantic cities." That was precisely what Rose, one of the convention organizers, had in mind. Subsequently he joined with representatives of three other railroads—the MADISON AND INDIANAPOLIS, the Peru and Indianapolis, and the Indianapolis and Bellefontaine—and prominent citizens of the capital city to establish a joint rail track and depot in Indianapolis. The Indianapolis Union Railroad Company organized in 1850 with Rose as president. Its facilities, which opened on September 20, 1853, were the first union tracks and station in the United States. The tracks from Indianapolis to Richmond—now the Indiana Central Railroad Company—were completed in time for the grand opening of the east-west rail connection in 1853. By 1877, the year of his death, Rose's main enterprise, now named the Terre Haute and Indianapolis Railroad Company, had large holdings in western Indiana and eastern Illinois. Thus, while not a resident of Indianapolis, Rose had a significant impact on the development of the capital city's railroad network and facilities during the 19th century.

Rose had no heirs and set out in his later years to distribute his wealth in a way that would bring the most benefit to society. His many philanthropies included the library of the State Normal School, now Indiana State University, and Rose Polytechnic Institute, now Rose-Hulman Institute of Technology.

WILLIAM B. PICKETT
Rose-Hulman Institute of Technology

H. W. Beckwith, *History of Vigo and Parke Counties* (Chicago, 1880); Wylie J. Daniels, *The Village at the End of the Road: A Chapter in Early Indiana Railroad History* (Indianapolis: Indiana Historical Society, 1938); George Irving Reed, ed., *Encyclopedia of Biography of Indiana*, Vol. I (Chicago, 1895).

Rubins, David Kresz (Sept. 5, 1902–Mar. 6, 1985). Sculptor and teacher. A native of Minneapolis, Rubins studied at Dartmouth, the Beaux Arts Institute of Design, New York City, the Ecole des Beaux Arts in Paris, and the Academie Julian. He won the Paris prize in 1924 and the Prix de Rome in 1928. Returning to New York he served for seven years as an assistant in the studio of James Earle Fraser, famed for his equestrian sculptures and the design for the buffalo nickel. He became a member of the John Reed Club, an association of political activists that included left-wing Democrats like Rubins. However, his few lithographs and drawings of social activism are uncharacteristic of his work, which is marked by a quiet introspection and compassion.

Rubins joined the faculty of the HERRON SCHOOL OF ART in 1935, teaching sculpture, drawing, art history, and anatomy during his 35-year tenure. He published *The Human Figure: An Anatomy for Artists* in 1953. He was awarded a Grant in Sculpture from the National Institute of Arts and Letters, 1954, and was made a Sagamore of the Wabash by Governor Matthew Welsh, 1964. Outside the city he exhibited at the Minneapolis Institute of Art, and in New York at the National Academy of Design, Architectural League, and American Sculpture Today, at the Metropolitan Museum (1951).

His method of teaching reflected the shop system; his students could observe his work on commissioned pieces as well as those entered in competition. His best-known public sculptures are the statue of a young Lincoln, State Office Building, Indianapolis (1963), and the cherub (1948) that adorned the L. S. AYRES AND COM-

PANY clock each Christmas season. Other major works are the figure on the steps, National Archives Building, Washington, D.C. (1933); spandrels and keystones over truck entrances, Federal Building, Indianapolis (1936); Lilly Monument, CROWN HILL CEMETERY, (1961); commemorative plaques in RILEY CHILDREN'S HOSPITAL; and *Stumbling Man*, INDIANAPOLIS MUSEUM OF ART (IMA) grounds (1962). There are busts of Governor Henry Schricker, State House (1964); Frederick M. Ayres, formerly at the downtown L. S. Ayres store; Evans Woollen, IMA (1944); Dr. JOHN D. VANNUYS, Riley Hospital; Dr. Albert G. Han, Evansville; and William Henry Harrison, PARK TUDOR SCHOOL. Rubins' work is in the Indianapolis Museum of Art, the Minneapolis Institute of Art, Herron School of Art (IUPUI), National Collection of Fine Arts at the Smithsonian Institution, Washington, D.C., and private collections.

MARY JANE MEEKER

Rubush and Hunter. Premier Indianapolis architectural firm of the early 20th century. Preston C. Rubush and Edgar O. Hunter were the architects most responsible for the changing streetscape of downtown Indianapolis in the early 20th century, including four extant buildings on MONUMENT CIRCLE. Although the wrecking ball

The architectural firm of Rubush and Hunter designed several Indianapolis theaters including the Circle Theatre, seen here in 1955.
[Indiana Historical Society, Bass Collection, #289710-F1]

has removed a large body of their work in Indianapolis, many of their finest buildings remain.

The successful partnership began in 1905. Rubush, born in Fairfield, Indiana, in 1867, was a product of the Builders' Course at the University of Illinois; after working for a time in Peoria, he came to Indianapolis in the 1890s and entered into partnership with J. H. Scharn. Hunter was born in Versailles, Indiana, in 1873 and took his architectural training at the University of Pennsylvania. He came to Indianapolis in 1897 to work for the prominent firm of VONNEGUT AND BOHN. Hunter's younger brother Frank, who was to become a well-known residential architect in his own right, worked for a short time for Preston Rubush after the turn of the century and may well have been the catalyst that brought Rubush and Edgar Hunter together.

Among the most important of the firm's earliest commissions was Castle Hall at 230 East Ohio, designed for the Knights of Pythias in 1905 and completed the following year. For another lodge of the same organization Rubush and Hunter produced a Tudor-influenced structure at 115 East Ohio. Fraternal and social clubs quickly became a mainstay of the firm. Among those that survive are the Masonic Temple (completed 1907) at 535 North Illinois, the Oriental Lodge (1915), and the prestigious COLUMBIA CLUB on the Circle (1925), as well as the 1922 addition to the exotic MURAT TEMPLE.

Rubush and Hunter designed numerous public buildings from the beginning of their partnership; among the most ambitious was the new campus for the INDIANA SCHOOL FOR THE DEAF on East 42nd Street, begun in 1906. Although the original plan called for 22 buildings within a landscaped complex, only half of them—the main structures—were built. In 1908 the city commissioned the young firm to design the new City Hall at 202 North Alabama according to their plans in the Beaux Arts style. Around this time Rubush and Hunter also produced the original Coliseum and Livestock Pavilion on the INDIANA STATE FAIRGROUNDS. The architects designed a number of schools, most of which have been demolished, such as the terra cotta–embellished Nebraska Cropsey School 22 on South Illinois (1920). Probably their finest extant school building is the Henry P. Coburn School 66 on East 38th, built in 1915 and since converted into senior housing.

Besides several substantial single-family residences the firm produced over the years, Rubush and Hunter designed apartment buildings, including the innovative U-shaped Buckingham Apartments on North Meridian in 1910. Their Lincoln Hotel, an impressive 14–story flatiron building of which they were part-owners, was completed in 1921. It stood at Washington and Kentucky until the 1970s.

Rubush and Hunter are noted for their fabulous theater buildings, few of which remain. Two of their finest do survive, however: the CIRCLE THEATRE (1916) and the Spanish Baroque INDIANA THEATRE (1927), both exuberantly clad in glazed cream terra cotta, a material the architects seemed to favor. Indeed, what has been touted as the first terra cotta–faced building in Indianapolis, the 1910 Sommers Building (since demolished) at 143–149 West Washington, was their design. Lost, too, is their much-admired Hume-Mansur Building (1911), also wrapped in glazed white terra cotta.

Although other architectural firms designed buildings in the Art Deco style (then termed "modernistic"), Rubush and Hunter were the city's most prolific practitioners. To demonstrate their skill in this mode and to house their offices, the architects in 1928–1929 remodeled their own three-story building at 333 North Pennsylvania into one of ten stories adorned with Egyptian figures representing Architects and Builders, the name of the structure. This creation was quickly followed by the CIRCLE TOWER (1930), the city's premier Art Deco building. Still in the same style but even more exuberant was the COCA-COLA BOTTLING PLANT on Massachusetts Avenue, completely sheathed in glazed white terra cotta. In 1936 Rubush and Hunter unified three older buildings into one streamlined Deco facade for the H. P. WASSON AND COMPANY department store at Washington and Meridian streets.

The partners retired in 1939; their chief draftsman, Philip Weisenburgh, and Ernest Werner, their superintendent of construction, took over the company in 1940. Rubush and Hunter had designed numerous buildings during Florida's boom in the 1920s, starting with a hotel for Hoosier CARL G. FISHER in Miami Beach. Both partners moved there in the 1940s, where they died, Rubush in 1947 and Hunter in 1949.

GLORY-JUNE GREIFF

Patricia J. Casler, "The Architecture of Rubush and Hunter" (M.S. thesis, School of Architecture and Planning, Columbia University, 1985).

Ruth Lilly Center for Health Education. Organization providing instruction in general health, substance abuse prevention, nutrition, sports fitness, and human growth and development for children and adults of central Indiana. Its programs are designed to enhance the health curriculum of Indiana schools. Using specialized theaters, the center teaches healthy lifestyles and helps young people cope with peer pressure and other stressful conditions.

The center is located at 2055 North Senate Avenue and is run by Life/Leadership Development, Inc., a not-for-profit corporation founded in 1983 by six service clubs (Exchange, Kiwanis, Lions, Optimist, Rotary, and Sertoma). Early support for the center came from ELDON CAMPBELL, president of the Methodist Health Foundation and a leader of the Rotary Club. With land provided by METHODIST HOSPITAL, the assistance of LILLY ENDOWMENT grants, the involvement of all major hospitals in the city, and a lead gift of $1 million from Ruth Lilly, a $4 million capital campaign was begun in 1986 and successfully concluded with completion of the building in spring, 1989. The first programs were offered in November, 1989.

By summer, 1992, over 184,000 students, ages 4 to 94, had attended programs at the center. In 1992 slightly more than half of the operating funds were provided by charitable donations, with the remainder coming from fees for services. Three full-time administrators and one half-time administrator along with eight part-time teachers made up the staff as of spring, 1992.

DWIGHT F. BURLINGAME
Indiana University–Purdue University,
Indianapolis

Ruth Lilly Poetry Prizes. Ruth Lilly, niece of ELI LILLY, established two prestigious poetry prizes to honor master poets and to encourage and identify emerging poets. In 1986, she established the Ruth Lilly Poetry Prize to honor a U.S. poet whose accomplishments warrant extraordinary recognition. The prize, originally $25,000 but raised to $75,000 in 1993, is the largest poetry prize in the country, and is awarded annually to one American master poet. The editor of *Poetry* magazine and two other judges selected annually review the nominations. *Poetry* and its publisher, the Modern Poetry Association, co-sponsor the prize along with the American Council for the Arts. Adrienne Rich (1986), Philip Levine (1987), Anthony Hecht (1988), Mona Van Duyn (1989), Hayden Carruth (1990), David Wagoner (1991), John Ashbery (1992), and Charles Wright (1993), and Donald Hall (1994) are past winners.

In 1989 Lilly created the Ruth Lilly Fellowship, awarded annually to a college undergraduate or graduate for the study and practice of poetry. Young poets are invited to compete at the National Collegiate Poetry Convocation at Indiana University in Bloomington. Lilly also has endowed the Lilly Professorship for instruction in the composition of poetry at Indiana University in Bloomington, and continues to support a number of writing and poetry projects in Indianapolis.

CATHLEEN F. DONNELLY

Indianapolis Star, Apr. 15, 1993, June 6, 1994.

Saengerchor. German-American singing and social society. Founded in 1885 by ten German tradesmen dedicated to the goals of the labor reform movement that swept the nation in the late 19th century, the society initially called itself the "Socialist-Labor Saengerbund." Members gathered in private homes and rented rooms to sing songs of solidarity and justice for the working classes. Over the next 35 years the political focus of the society gradually gave way, replaced by the fosterage of friendship and harmony. By 1920 the members decided to rename the club simply the "Indianapolis Saengerbund." Another name change prior to World War II resulted in the society's present name "Indianapolis Saengerchor" or "singers' chorus." The club underwent a further transformation in 1928 when the previously all-male chorus admitted its first female members.

The Saengerchor purchased its present clubhouse, at 521 East 13th Street, from the Sahara Grotto in 1942. Members remodeled the house, which dates nearly to the Civil War, to include a rathskeller, meeting rooms, and an auditorium that is used for the society's two annual concerts. Traditional German dinners and holiday celebrations also constitute part of the Saengerchor's yearly calendar. The society participates in the choral festivals of the North American Singers Union.

SUZANNE G. SNYDER

St. Elmo Steak House. In October, 1902, nautical buff Joe Stahr opened St. Elmo Steak House at 127 South Illinois Street, naming his restaurant for the patron saint of sailors. Stahr sold the restaurant in 1947 to Burt Condon, a local tavern operator. Condon lasted six months before selling St. Elmo's in 1948 to Harry Roth and his brothers, Sam and Ike. In 1956 Roth's brothers left and Isadore Rosen teamed up with Harry Roth. This arrangement lasted for 30 years until 1986 when Roth and Rosen sold the business to Stephen M. Huse and Jeff Dunaway. (Huse had started the Noble Roman's pizza chain.) The business has expanded into neighboring buildings over the years. Since its founding prominent entertainers, sports figures, and locals have patron-

ized St. Elmo's, which continues to be well known outside Indianapolis.

DEBORAH B. MARKISOHN

St. Francis Hospital. One of the largest Catholic hospitals in Indiana. In 1912, two members of the Poor Sisters of St. Francis Seraph of the Perpetual Adoration traveled from their motherhouse in Lafayette to select a location for a new hospital in Indianapolis. At that time no hospital existed in Indianapolis south of Washington Street or east of Senate Avenue.

Sister Cunegunda, later the hospital's first sister superior, and Sister Laboria met with Rev. Peter J. Killian, who had organized the Holy Name parish in BEECH GROVE in 1906. Killian urged the sisters to choose a location in rapidly growing Beech Grove, and for $1,000 he purchased a five-acre tract of land on the corner of Troy Avenue and Sherman Drive. The hospital began construction in 1912, and admitted its first patient on July 13, 1914. The 75–bed hospital cost $75,000.

For many years, the hospital featured a unique all-nun nursing staff, as the order prohibited lay nurses. Charity and elderly cases accounted for a large proportion of patients. However, an ever-increasing patient population soon necessitated several expansion projects. In 1931 the hospital dedicated a new south wing, doubling the bed capacity. As part of a citywide hospital expansion plan, the hospital added a five-story north wing in 1957, increasing bed capacity to 275. In the early 1970s the hospital constructed the six-story Bonzel Towers and added additional stories in 1983. By 1990 the hospital housed 441 beds and admitted 56,000 patients per year. In early 1994 work was progressing on a new St. Francis facility called South Campus to be located at Emerson Avenue and Stop 11 Road.

St. Francis pioneered several medical advances, including Indiana's first cobalt therapy unit (1957); the first Betatron nuclear accelerator for cancer treatment in an Indiana hospital (1967); the first Coulter Senior Blood Analyzer in an Indianapolis hospital, providing complete blood analysis in 40 seconds (1969); and the first family-centered maternity department in Indianapolis (1973).

HEIDI K. MARTIN

Edward W. Cotton, "They Dedicated Their Lives to Mankind," *Indianapolis Star Magazine*, July 5, 1964; "St. Francis Hospital Center: The Hospital with a Heart," *Indianapolis Star*, special supplement, Mar. 8, 1981; *Indianapolis Star*, Aug. 3, 1993.

St. John Catholic Church. City's oldest Catholic parish. The forerunner of St. John the Evangelist Catholic Church was founded in November, 1837, by Rev. Vincent Bacquelin, an itinerant priest who split his time between Indianapolis and two other central Indiana parishes. After holding services in rented rooms for the first three years, the parish built the Church of the Holy Cross in 1840. This small, 40– by– 24– foot frame structure on the north side of Washington Street between West and California streets served the city's approximately 200 CATHOLICS. Originally, the parish included all of Marion County.

To accommodate the influx of Catholics into the city, a new 40 by 80 foot brick church was built in 1850 on the site of the present structure at 126 West Georgia Street. The church was renamed St. John the Evangelist after the patron saint of the priest then serving the parish. Seven years later the building was enlarged to serve the growing congregation.

The present church building, begun in 1867, was completed in 1871. Designed by architect DIEDRICH A. BOHLEN, it drew from several periods and styles. Due to limited funds, embellishments such as the two spires and the stained glass windows were not added until 1893. The building was placed on the National Register of Historic Places in 1980. Although not officially designated a cathedral, St. John served as the center of the diocese from 1878 to 1892.

At the beginning of the 20th century St. John's congregation numbered about 900 families. Within 15 years the population of the parish began to dwindle as factories and warehouses replaced neighborhood homes, driving many parish residents to other areas of the city. The church began serving primarily transients and people staying in the downtown hotels. By 1940 St. John's membership had dropped to around 500 parishioners. In 1959 city planners discussed demolishing the church to make way for a civic auditorium but soon dropped the idea. The parish continued to shrink during the next decade, declining to 136 parishioners by 1968.

Restoration of St. John to mark its centennial in 1971 spurred renewed interest in the church. The downtown congregation has also benefited from its proximity to the Indiana Convention Center and Hoosier Dome and draws many tourists and conventioneers to services. As of the early 1990s, St. John celebrates mass six days a week and sponsors a Tridentine (Latin) mass every other month. Although few members of the congregation currently live near the church, a loyal core of about 300 financial supporters helps to sustain St. John.

DEBORAH B. MARKISOHN

Sister Rose Angela Horan, *The Story of Old St. John's: A Parish Rooted in Pioneer Indianapolis* (1971).

St. Joseph. Near northside neighborhood roughly bounded by I–65, Fort Wayne and Central avenues, St. Clair and Meridian streets. A mixture of commercial, industrial, and residential structures makes the area now known as St. Joseph a uniquely diverse urban neighborhood. Platted in the 1850s and '60s and developed between 1870 and 1930, St. Joseph prospered because of its proximity to downtown and the Fort Wayne Road (now Fort Wayne Avenue).

Large residential structures were built in the 1870s along the major north-south thoroughfares such as Delaware Street, while cottages were constructed on the east-west streets. Fifteen architectural styles are represented in the neighborhood, including Italianate, Queen Anne, Tudor Revival, and American Foursquare. Multifamily housing was also built in St. Joseph. Four architecturally significant rowhouse complexes still survive in the district, along with a number of duplexes and apartments. While much of the commercial development in the neighborhood was originally small-scale, the Buschmann Block (1870) and the Lewis Meier Building (1915) were large retail and manufacturing properties.

A period of decline that began in 1940 was reversed in the 1980s when new residents and developers recognized the district's architectural significance and renovated numerous single-family homes, apartments, and rowhouses. In 1991 the area was listed on the National Register of Historic Places and named St. Joseph after a local street.

About 800 people lived in the neighborhood in 1990. Residents organized the St. Joseph Historic Neighborhood Association to preserve the area's diverse mix of structures and encourage new development. The group also has taken an active role in addressing displacement issues and the needs of social service agencies in the area.

CATHLEEN F. DONNELLY

National Register of Historic Places registration forms (copy available in Social Sciences Reference Division, Indianapolis-Marion County Public Library).

St. Richard's School. Founded in 1960 by the Reverend G. Ernest Lynch, St. Richard's has a distinctive academic tradition in Indianapolis. The only independent Episcopal day school in Indiana, it was patterned intentionally after the parish day schools of Great Britain and incorporates the best aspects of that educational system. In keeping with the British tradition, St. Richard's introduces skills and concepts to students at an earlier age than its public and private counterparts and the curriculum reflects unusual breadth and depth and high academic expectations. Foreign language is required at every grade level. The original faculty members were British, brought to the United States specifically to teach at St. Richard's. The British influence carries over into the school's architecture. Like adjoining Trinity Episcopal Church, with which it is affiliated, St. Richard's is built in the medieval English Country Gothic style.

The school has long-standing ties to the city's African-American community, welcoming minority students and racial diversity since its inception. Socioeconomic diversity has also been important to the St. Richard's community.

Starting with a kindergarten of 18 students in the autumn of 1960, by the early 1990s St. Richard's encompassed transitional kindergarten through the eighth grade. In addition to honoring St. Richard of Chichester, an English saint and scholar, the name Richard also commemorates the then retiring Episcopal bishop of Indianapolis, The Right Reverend Richard A. Kirchhoffer, who was interested in education and the parish school concept. No other school in the United States has the name of St. Richard's.

JAMES P. FADELY

St. Vincent Hospital. Pioneer health care institution. On April 26, 1881, four Daughters of Charity of St. Vincent de Paul arrived in Indianapolis, bringing a willingness to help the poor, sick, and injured—and $34.77. They came in response to a request by Bishop FRANCIS SILAS CHATARD, who had petitioned them to attend to the health care needs of the community. The sisters moved into an empty seminary in which the bishop had already placed three patients. He added $50 to their assets and the sisters opened St. Vincent Infirmary.

As Indianapolis grew, so did the infirmary. Soon 50 beds were in operation and the infirmary took a new name: St. Vincent Hospital. During the first eight years of operation the hospital treated 1,012 patients, one of whom stayed three years and whose bill was $1,254.33. Total hospital expenses during the same period were $33,695.78. In 1896 the sisters opened the St. Vincent School of Nursing, which trained generations of nurses until it closed in 1970.

A highlight of the early years was the admission, on September 23, 1902, of President Theodore Roosevelt. During a speaking tour the president sustained a slight leg injury that developed into an abscess. Admitted to St. Vincent's men's unit, the president immediately recognized Sister Regina, who had cared for his fever-stricken Rough Riders in Cuba. Roosevelt stayed for a few hours and left under the care of his physician.

In 1918, a visitor of another sort, the "Spanish flu," came to St. Vincent, which was now at its third location. (The hospital moved from its original site near Vermont and East streets to South and Delaware streets in 1889 and, in 1913, to Fall Creek Parkway.) Most of the sisters became ill, and 36 of the 80 medical students working at the institution were down with "la grippe," which killed 445,000 people in the United States in only four months.

Following World War II, the hospital made tremendous strides in its clinical and support programs. In 1952, Dr. Arthur Richter opened St. Vincent's first heart clinic. This presaged numerous advancements in diagnosis and treatment in several specialties. In 1963, the hospital opened the first coronary care and first intensive care units in Indianapolis and in 1973 implemented an open heart surgery program. The St. Vincent Hospital Foundation was organized to promote charitable support of the institution, which moved to a new facility at 2001 West 86th Street on March 31, 1974.

In 1979, St. Vincent opened the first wellness center east of the Mississippi. That same year, the hospital signed a contract with New Hope of Indiana, a residential facility for young adults with developmental disabilities or traumatic brain injuries, to provide management services; a decade later St. Vincent New Hope became an official part of the hospital.

St. Vincent celebrated 100 years of service in 1981. The next year it opened the first of several new facilities, the St. Vincent Stress Center, providing mental health and chemical dependency services and a hospice for the terminally ill and their families. That same year, the main St. Vincent facility expanded to provide improved emergency and outpatient services. In 1984, the St. Vincent Family Life Center began providing family-centered care during childbearing, and in 1985 the St. Vincent Carmel Hospital opened to serve the needs of a growing Hamilton County. In the late 1980s, St. Vincent began or enhanced many programs, including the St. Vincent Laser Center (the largest of its kind in the state), the Indiana Heart Institute, the Institute on Aging, the Breast Care Centers, and the Vascular Center.

By the early 1990s the rechristened St. Vincent Hospitals and Health Services offered programs at more than a dozen locations around the Indianapolis area and, through affiliations with other health care providers, in several cities in the region. The medical staff numbered approximately 1,100. Annual admissions were almost 34,000, while outpatient visits totaled roughly

Early nursing staff of St. Vincent Hospital. [Indiana Historical Society, #C2331]

220,000. Additions begun in 1991 were expected to nearly double the size of the hospital's 86th Street campus. A member of the not-for-profit Daughters of Charity National Health System, St. Vincent's derives its funding principally from patient revenues.

MARTIN R. SPITZ
Manager of Publications
St. Vincent Hospitals and Health Services

Marie D'Andrea Loftus, *St. Vincent Hospital and Health Care Center, Indianapolis, Indiana, 1881–1981* (Indianapolis, 1981); Bain J. Farris, *St. Vincent Hospital and Health Care Center, Inc.: Past, Present and Future* (Indianapolis, 1988).

SS. Peter and Paul Cathedral. Seat of the Catholic archbishop of Indianapolis, built in 1905–1906 in a design inspired by St. John Lateran in Rome. The facade was completed in 1936 and renovated in the mid–1980s.

In 1878 Bishop FRANCIS SILAS CHATARD of Vincennes established residence in Indianapolis, the largest city in his diocese. Twelve years later he purchased the southeast corner of 14th and Meridian streets for an episcopal residence and adjoining chapel, designed by the New York firm of Renwick, Aspinwall & Russell, W. L. Coulter. Because he had lived in Rome for 20 years before becoming bishop, Chatard dedicated the chapel to the great Roman saints Peter and Paul on March 25, 1892. When the Diocese of Vincennes became the Diocese of Indianapolis in 1898, Chatard employed William Whetten Renwick of New York (nephew of the architect of St. Patrick's Cathedral) to design a cathedral for Indianapolis. Although its facade was unfinished, the $200,000 building was dedicated on December 21, 1906.

Chatard loved imported furnishings. He commissioned Roman sculptor Cesare Aureli to carve statues of Mary and Child, Joseph, and Francis de Sales (the bishop's patron saint). He procured a copy of 18th-century sculptor Antonio Montauti's *Pietà*. The Crucifixion scene on the reredos, the episcopal throne, and the grandiose pulpit were made of Carrara marble. The parish chapel became Blessed Sacrament Chapel. Mosaics, stained glass from Munich, and paintings after Fra Angelico, Guido Reni, and Bartolome Murillo created the sacred ambience. Theresa O'Connor, daughter of an Irish-born wholesale grocer, financed its $30,000 cost. The chapel was dedicated on September 7, 1918, the day of the elderly bishop's death.

Bishop JOSEPH CHARTRAND sought to make the cathedral the spiritual center of the diocese. He emphasized devotion to the Eucharist and spent many hours each day hearing confessions. Today a stained glass window bearing his portrait marks the site of his confessional and memorializes his concern for the laity.

In 1936 Bishop JOSEPH E. RITTER employed Indianapolis architect August Bohlen to complete the facade. Bohlen's design required the use of 2,500 tons of Indiana limestone and featured four 56–foot fluted columns with a $5^1/_2$–foot diameter. Harold W. Rambusch of New York designed new lighting and stained glass, the transept windows showing the episcopal arms of Chatard and Chartrand. Rambusch employee Leif Neandross designed the apse mosaic of an enthroned Christ flanked by Saints Peter and Paul.

Almost four decades later, Archbishop GEORGE J. BISKUP decided to renovate the deteriorating building, a decision carried out by Archbishop EDWARD T. O'MEARA (1980–1992). Minnesota architect Edward A. Sovik supervised the controversial modification of the interior to conform to liturgical thinking after the Second Vatican Council. The altar, reredos, and archiepiscopal chair were relocated; moveable chairs replaced fixed pews; an elevator was installed to provide handicapped access; and Chatard's art in marble was moved or replaced. The budgeted cost was $1.7 million.

The cathedral was rededicated on May 14, 1986, and is currently used not only by a small parish congregation, but also for archdiocesan events such as the administration of Confirmation and Holy Orders and the celebration of Mass for special groups.

JAMES J. DIVITA
Marian College

James J. Divita, *Indianapolis Cathedral: A Construction History of Our Three Mother Churches* (Indianapolis, 1986).

Salvation Army. Ministry to the poor and homeless. The Salvation Army began in Indianapolis in March, 1889, at 76–78 East New York Street. Following the pattern set by William and Catherine Booth, founders of the first Salvation Army in 1865 in the East London slums, the local organization provided food, clothing, shelter, and spiritual guidance to the destitute and despairing. As part of an international evangelical movement, the local Salvation Army finds the basis for its beliefs and practices in the Bible.

Since its establishment, services have expanded and now include drug and alcohol treatment, homeless shelters for men and women, domestic violence programs, food pantries, youth

A Salvation Army band helped kick off the group's annual Christmas kettle drive in the early 1960s. The group began operations in Indianapolis in 1889. [Indianapolis Newspapers Inc.]

activities, day camps, and senior citizens' programs. It operates three corps–community centers (Eagle Creek, Fountain Square, Central City), which provide religious services, senior citizens' programs, and social and educational services. It also operates social service programs at the Adult Rehabilitation Center, Ruth Lilly Social Service Center, and Harbor Light Center, which provide drug and alcohol treatment, emergency shelter for women with children and single women, a domestic violence program, a mental health program, emergency material assistance, life skills education, family camping, and the Christmas Bureau.

In 1991, the Salvation Army served 314,000 meals and provided other services (nonreligious) to 226,638 persons. Funds for its $6.5 million budget come from donor contributions (27%), local, state, and federal government (25%), UNITED WAY (9%), and other sources (39%).

LEE ANN VRIESMAN

Fred Sanders Case. Case involving an Indianapolis parochial school teacher's fatal shooting of an Indianapolis police officer. On the evening of August 14, 1988, Indianapolis Patrolman Matt John Faber responded to a complaint from a Forest Manor resident that a dog owned by Fred Sanders, a teacher at St. Luke School, was running loose in the neighborhood. When Faber arrived at Sanders' home, an altercation occurred between the officer and Sanders.

When other officers responded to Faber's call for assistance, they joined Faber in forcing their way into the Sanders home. When the police entered, Sanders fired a shotgun at the officers, striking Faber in the back. The other policemen opened fire at Sanders and three shots hit him. Police beat Sanders after his arrest. Faber died from his wound nine days later.

Although originally charged with murder, Sanders finally pled guilty to involuntary manslaughter through an agreement reached with the Marion County Prosecutor's Office. On March 3, 1989, the Marion County Superior Court sentenced Sanders to seven years in prison. Two police officers were indicted for beating Sanders, although a jury convicted only one. Several offic-

ers were disciplined by the INDIANAPOLIS POLICE DEPARTMENT (IPD) for their roles in the Sanders case.

In May, 1991, Sanders was released from prison when a judge allowed him to withdraw his guilty plea. The Indiana Supreme Court, however, reversed that decision in July, 1992, and Sanders went back to prison in mid–1993 following an unsuccessful appeal to the U.S. Supreme Court and after denial of Sanders' request for an early release.

Sanders' case against the city and 20 police officers for violating his civil rights was decided in November, 1992, when a federal jury awarded him $1.5 million in damages. The U.S. District Court later reduced the amount to $78,000.

The city's media provided extensive coverage of the incident and the subsequent trials, which revealed a public sharply divided over the propriety of police actions. The case led to a reexamination within IPD of policies concerning the investigation of civilian complaints.

RAY BOOMHOWER
Indiana Historical Society

Sanders, Mozel (May 24, 1924–Sept. 1, 1988). Minister and community leader. Sanders was born in East St. Louis, Illinois. Shortly after his father's death, when Sanders was five years old, he and his mother moved to Canton, Mississippi. In 1945 he arrived in Indianapolis, where he worked in a foundry by day, sang with a religious group at night, and preached at church meetings. Sanders became pastor of the Mount Vernon Missionary Baptist Church in 1959 and served there until his death.

He founded and was chairman of the Indianapolis chapter of Opportunities Industrialization Centers, Inc. (OIC), a national job training organization. During his last 16 years, Sanders hosted a radio program called "The Way Out," which aired weekdays from 5–6 A.M. on WTLC-FM. The program was a mixture of gospel music, prayers, Scripture readings, and social commentary. A civil rights activist, Sanders is best known for beginning a traditional Thanksgiving dinner to feed the needy in Indianapolis. He served 20 people that first year, 1974; in 1987, the year before his death, 16,000 people were served Thanksgiving dinners.

After his death, Haughville Park on the west side of Indianapolis was renamed as Rev. Mozel Sanders Park. Posthumously, Sanders was named the *Indianapolis Star's* Man of the Year for 1988.

REBECCA M. MAIER

Indianapolis News, Sept. 2, 1988; *Indianapolis Star*, Jan. 8, 1989.

Sangernebo, Alexander (May 1, 1856– Jan. 22, 1930). Master terra cotta designer and sculptor for numerous Indianapolis buildings. Sangernebo was responsible for most of the architectural terra cotta ornamentation, along with several examples of applied sculpture in stone, in Indianapolis before 1930. Estonian born, Sangernebo came to the United States after an impressive education, most notably from the Ecole des Arts Decoratifs in Paris. He arrived in St. Louis in the mid–1880s, and joined the Indianapolis Terra Cotta Company (located in BRIGHTWOOD) as its chief sculptor in the early 1890s, taking up residence at the English Hotel. Among the earliest examples of his extant work is the terra cotta ornamentation on the ATHENAEUM, of which he was a charter member. In 1898 Sangernebo opened his own studio in Brightwood, where he was living at the time. Later he moved both his residence and his studio to locations in the OLD NORTHSIDE.

In the early 20th century, buildings ornamented with glazed terra cotta were extremely popular, and Indianapolis was undergoing a construction boom before and after World War I. Sangernebo's work graced the massive Traction Terminal downtown, the National Guard Armory (now Tyndall Armory) on North Pennsylvania, the new Columbia Club, and L. S. Ayres department store. Sangernebo applied his terra cotta or fanciful stone creations to virtually every sort of building, from churches such as St. Joan of Arc to railroad stations (his work may be seen on UNION STATION). Theaters in particular lent themselves to fanciful terra cotta ornament, and while most have been torn down, the MURAT TEMPLE and the INDIANA THEATRE survive as testimony to Sangernebo's artistry. His designs also adorned a number of schools, notably Crispus Attucks and Shortridge high schools. Much of Sangernebo's most exuberant work has been demolished, perhaps the most notable example being the terra cotta banding and medallions of Oscar McCulloch School 5. His playful side is evident from the gnome-like monks in full relief above the entrance to the Carnegie library at Washington and Rural streets. His last designs were for the Big Four building at Meridian and Maryland streets, still under construction at his death.

GLORY-JUNE GREIFF

Saturday Evening Post. Indianapolis-based bimonthly journal. Benjamin Franklin started the *Saturday Evening Post* in Philadelphia in 1724. It began as a weekly broadsheet newspaper that published fiction, poetry, and household tips. CURTIS PUBLISHING, a Philadelphia-based company, bought the *Post* in 1897. Under Curtis' direction the journal continued as a weekly publication focusing on fiction, poetry, and anecdotal humor. It became famous for its cover illustrations, particularly those of Norman Rockwell, during the 1950s.

The *Post* experienced financial difficulties in the late 1960s and went out of print in February, 1969. In 1971 local entrepreneur Beurt SerVaas purchased Curtis Publishing and moved its operations to Indianapolis. SerVaas reorganized the *Post* as publisher and editor and named his wife, Cory, executive editor. The first edition of the new *Saturday Evening Post* appeared on October 10, 1971. The new format included fiction, poetry, cartoons, and a medical questionnaire feature edited by Cory SerVaas. The first issue sold all 630,000 copies and print runs had risen to 800,000 by 1972. Cory SerVaas took over her husband's position as publisher and editor in the mid–1970s, and the magazine began to shift its focus toward personal health issues.

In 1982 the Benjamin Franklin Literary and Medical Society, an Indianapolis organization founded by Cory SerVaas in 1977, bought the *Post* from Curtis Publishing. The magazine was rededicated to the society's mission of improving personal health and developing volunteer initiative in the United States. In the early 1990s the bimonthly publication had a circulation of 555,000 and a readership of three million.

WILLIAM D. DALTON

Schaefer, Ferdinand (Dec. 11, 1861–Apr. 18, 1953). Founder of the INDIANAPOLIS SYMPHONY ORCHESTRA (ISO). Born in Dotzheim, Germany, Schaefer attended public schools and received his first violin lesson from his father as punishment for a boyish prank.

Schaefer entered the military at age 17, where he played in an orchestra in the Kaiser's army. He resumed his violin studies and made financial ends meet by tutoring. During his years in Europe, he graduated with honors from the University of Leipzig in Germany, formed and directed many orchestras, taught violin to Crown Prince Gustave of Sweden, and performed under the direction of Johannes Brahms as a member of the Gewandhaus Orchestra.

Schaefer came to Indianapolis in 1903 to become a violin teacher at the Indiana College of Music and Fine Arts. He taught at the old Indianapolis Conservatory of Music, at Lafayette Conservatory, and at Ball State Teachers College. He conducted an orchestra at the Kirschbaum Community Center prior to starting the ISO in November, 1929, undaunted by the beginning of the Great Depression. The symphony musicians were paid by splitting the box office receipts, sometimes making $5 a night. The orchestra's first performance took place in 1930. Schaefer resigned as ISO director in 1937 but continued to perform occasional concerts until his farewell appearances on February 6–7, 1943. He became a U.S. citizen in 1921 and received an honorary degree of doctor of music from Indiana University in 1940. Known affectionately as "Papa" by the city's music-loving community, he remained in Indianapolis following his retirement from the symphony, continued to offer violin instruction into his late eighties, and was feted with a gala celebration at the Athenaeum shortly before his death.

SUSAN GUYETT

Indiana Biography Series, Indiana State Library; "Indiana Musicians" file, Indianapolis–Marion County Public Library.

Scherrer, Adolph (Aug. 30, 1847–Feb. 13, 1925). Architect. Born in St. Gaul, Switzerland, Scherrer studied in Vienna and Budapest before immigrating to New York City in 1870. After a two-year stay in Chicago, he arrived in Indianapolis by 1873. His first position in this city was as draftsman to EDWIN MAY, one of Indianapolis' leading architects. May, who was commissioned to design the new state capitol, died in 1880 before the plan was completed. Scherrer finished the design for the STATE HOUSE, which was completed in 1888.

Scherrer designed many late 19th century public edifices in Indianapolis. Included among them are the Gothic, spired arches at the 34th Street and Boulevard Place entrance to CROWN HILL CEMETERY (1885); the Pathology Department (now the Old Pathology Building, 1896) at CENTRAL STATE HOSPITAL, as well as many additions to the hospital; the Maennerchor Building at 502 North Illinois (since demolished), erected for instruction about and appreciation of the great German composers (1906); and the Independent Turnverein building at 902 North Meridian (1913), now upscale apartments. Scherrer was an innovative architect as well as a prolific one. Some of his later residential designs, including 4375 North Meridian Street (1911), were early examples of the Prairie School style of architecture created by Frank Lloyd Wright.

In 1891, Mayor Thomas Sullivan appointed Scherrer to the first Indianapolis Board of Public Works, which was responsible for hiring the engineer who designed the city's first comprehensive sewage system. Scherrer's sons, Anton and Herman, also became well-known Indianapolis architects, working first in collaboration with their

Architect Adolph Scherrer. [Indiana Historical Society, #C5901]

father and, after his death, on their own under the name Adolph Scherrer and Sons. Scherrer, who was a fellow in the American Institute of Architects, experienced a serious stroke six years before his death, which caused some paralysis and effectively ended his career. Many of his buildings still stand in Indianapolis.

CONNIE J. ZEIGLER

Indiana Biography Series, Indiana State Library; Jacob Piatt Dunn, *Greater Indianapolis* (Chicago, 1910).

School Desegregation. Although Indiana's early school laws made no reference to race, few African-American children attended local township schools, relying instead upon churches and sympathetic Quakers to obtain an education. In 1847 blacks meeting in Indianapolis unsuccessfully petitioned the state legislature to provide school funds for their children: "The white people of this state ought not to reproach us with being ignorant, degraded, and poor . . . while they tax our property . . . to educate their own children, while denying to ours the benefits and blessings conferred by this taxation." An 1855 law exempted black-owned property from taxation for local schools, but by the 1860s there were four private day schools and five Sabbath schools for blacks in Indianapolis, including those sponsored by MOSES BROYLES of Second Baptist Church and by the AME Church, both of which dated from the 1850s.

Following the Civil War, Indiana's legislature faced mounting pressure to fund black schools. Indianapolis School Board Commissioner Dr. Thomas B. Elliott reported in 1866 that "the colored people of the state and city have . . . been deprived of advantages of the school fund, or any privileges of the schools . . . [and] should receive the benefit of our common school system." Superintendent ABRAM C. SHORTRIDGE likewise noted the "very creditable" proportion of black children attending subscription schools, and that their schools were "maintained under great disadvantages—without the generous sympathy of the public generally." The city provided a building in Ward Four for black students with Broyles as principal; ROBERT B. BAGBY and his brothers Ben-

jamin and James also served as principals of other black schools.

During and after the Civil War, public opinion gradually turned in favor of state funding for African-American schools. The Indiana Colored Equal Rights League, the Indiana State Teachers Association, the Indianapolis school board, the state superintendent of public instruction, and Governor OLIVER P. MORTON all recommended educational appropriations for African-American children. In 1869 state representatives approved legislation requiring separate schools for black children when numbers were sufficient and allowing trustees to make alternate arrangements when there were too few black pupils to organize a separate school. The law also placed white- and black-owned property on an equal basis for assessment of school taxes.

Communities without separate schools faced another dilemma. In Lawrence Township, a black parent sought to enroll his children in a white school and was denied. Claiming a violation of both the 14th Amendment and the Indiana Constitution, Carter won his case in Marion County Superior Court. In *Cory et al. v. Carter* (1874), the Indiana Supreme Court reversed the lower court decision and interpreted the 1869 school law to forbid African-American pupils from attending schools with whites under any circumstance. The General Assembly amended the school law in 1877 and allowed black children into white schools when no separate school existed. With some exceptions, however, most African-American children in Indianapolis attended segregated elementary schools.

The influx of southern blacks into Indianapolis after World War I placed additional strains on the community and its school facilities. Increased enrollment forced black elementary children to attend half day sessions. By 1925 1,000 African-Americans attended the city's four high schools. The 1920s crusade mounted by civic leaders, parents' organizations, women's groups, the CHAMBER OF COMMERCE, and the KU KLUX KLAN to require strict segregation in city schools led to the opening of the all-black CRISPUS ATTUCKS HIGH SCHOOL in 1927 and kept education facilities racially separate until passage of the state's 1949 antisegregation law. Ignoring pleas from the black community, school commissioners redrew district lines for the new black schools and required all black high school students to attend Crispus Attucks regardless of where they lived in the city. Under a 1935 state law, however, the Indianapolis school board provided transportation for black pupils attending separate schools.

While segregated schools became a way of life in Indianapolis, developments elsewhere foreshadowed local changes. Labor shortages during the era of World War II brought a reevaluation of the role of African-Americans in the economy. Black, business, and labor leaders helped to establish the Indiana Bi-racial Cooperation Plan (1940) to improve job opportunities for blacks. In June, 1941, President Franklin D. Roosevelt created the Fair Employment Practices Committee, designed to end job discrimination. As wartime labor needs opened employment opportunities for blacks in positions previously reserved for whites, African-Americans championed the idea that their children deserved much better schooling than they were getting in local segregated schools.

The campaign to end school segregation intensified in the 1940s as critics labeled Indianapolis the largest northern city with a segregated school system. The school board fought desegregation because of "current local practices," the anticipated increased capital outlay for buildings, and the potential dismissal of tenured black teachers within the system. To prevent total desegregation, in 1948 the school board transferred 100 black students to all-white schools, which generated protests by white parents. HENRY J. RICHARDSON, JR., a black attorney and former state legislator, appeared before the school board in September, 1948, stating, "We have waited, pleaded and worked on this particular problem for more than ten years; . . . it is high time the school board throw out and abolish its old Klan policy of 1926."

Assisted by civic, church, and labor groups, the local NAACP lobbied to secure passage of the state's 1949 desegregation law which provided "equal, non-segregated, non-discriminatory educational opportunities and facilities for all." The Indianapolis school board announced a plan for compliance and abolished separate elementary school districts based on race. Beginning in 1951

black teachers were assigned to white schools, and by 1953 the process of desegregating the city's high schools was completed. Nevertheless, many white residents resisted attempts to integrate the schools, a resistance that revealed the powerful legacy left by the Ku Klux Klan's domination of Indianapolis politics in the 1920s.

Reinforcement of Indiana's desegregation law came in the 1954 U.S. Supreme Court decision *Brown v. Board of Education of Topeka,* which declared separate schools unconstitutional. Following the ruling Indianapolis blacks attempted to find housing in white neighborhoods and to enroll their children in white schools. Creating single-race residential school districts, however, was one of the most effective means of maintaining segregated schools; therefore, housing quickly became the pivotal issue in the separate school debate, with claims that property owners and real estate agents colluded to exclude blacks from particular neighborhoods. Thus, segregated schools continued in Indianapolis for several years beyond 1954.

By the 1960s critics condemned the INDIANAPOLIS PUBLIC SCHOOLS (IPS) for perpetuating racial segregation. Subsequent investigations by the NAACP and federal attorneys coupled with a parent's complaint led the U.S. Justice Department to file suit against the Indianapolis Board of School Commissioners on May 31, 1968, for violating the Civil Rights Act of 1964 and the equal protection clause of the 14th Amendment. IPS responded that neighborhood schools were a sound concept and that one-race schools resulted solely from residential patterns, not from intentional policies. To assuage its critics, IPS ordered limited teacher reassignments to relieve segregated patterns. Several teachers attempted to block the order, and a local residents organization, Citizens for Quality Schools, fought the suit to protect their neighborhood schools.

On August 18, 1971, U.S. District Court Judge S. Hugh Dillin found that Indianapolis schools had not desegregated after the 1949 state law or the 1954 *Brown* decision and had continued to operate a *de jure* segregated school system. Local officials, he concluded, had actively promoted segregation through the drawing of school districts (90 percent of 360 boundary changes since 1954 supported racial segregation), creation of new "feeder" schools, and placement of low-rent housing. The court enjoined IPS to reassign staff and faculty, revise transfer policies, and negotiate with suburban school corporations for the transfer of minority students. Concluding that UNIGOV had fostered segregation by expanding the city limits to encompass the predominantly white surrounding townships and excluding the increasingly black Indianapolis school district from that expansion, Dillin sought to include the outlying school corporations in the court's proposed solution.

The issue of desegregation dragged through the federal courts for several more years. Attorneys for black students argued for the adoption of an interdistrict or unified school plan. While the state of Indiana denied responsibility for perpetuating segregation in Indianapolis schools, Judge Dillin proved that the state possessed control over local school districts and had approved three new high schools at the outer limits of IPS, all without African-American students. Arguing that a lasting remedy should include the suburban school districts, Dillin ordered the one-way busing of black IPS students to some of Marion County's suburban schools, with IPS absorbing the expenses.

In 1981, ten years after Dillin's decision, the busing of nearly 7,000 African-American students to white schools in Perry, Wayne, Franklin, Decatur, Lawrence, and Warren townships began. Although 19,000 students were bused within the IPS district under the desegregation order, no township students were bused to IPS schools to ensure racial balance.

Most of Marion County felt the impact of the court-ordered desegregation plan. Parents of township school children who opposed the busing order began a campaign to oust Judge Dillin. Others formed the Community Desegregation Advisory Council, a volunteer group to arbitrate complaints and monitor the progress of desegregation; it ceased operations in fall, 1991. Whites continued to display unease about court-ordered busing and moved to predominantly white suburbs, even though many more city neighborhoods were being integrated. As a result, IPS encountered plummeting enrollment (from 108,000 in 1971 to 47,000 in 1993) and a deteriorating infrastructure. Many African-Americans who lamented the loss of neighborhood schools also resented implications that their children learned best in white schools and that their children were singled out for one-way busing. Over time, shifting demographics called the original court order into question and seemed to affirm the court's position that only a metropolitan-wide desegregation plan would work and prevent resegregation.

School desegregation in Indianapolis is an unfinished story. Amidst increased pressure to end forced busing, in 1992 IPS Superintendent Shirl Gilbert II, arguing that the "desegregation plan has simply eroded," requested the district court to review its desegregation order and to accept a proposed "Select Schools" plan. In February, 1993, Judge Dillin, acknowledging the partial failure of the original desegregation order, allowed IPS to begin implementing a limited school-choice program termed SELECT SCHOOLS in fall, 1993.

STANLEY WARREN
DePauw University

DAVID G. VANDERSTEL
Indiana University–Purdue University,
Indianapolis

Emma Lou Thornbrough, *Since Emancipation: A Short History of Indiana Negroes, 1863–1963* (Indianapolis, 1963); Emma Lou Thornbrough, "The Indianapolis School Busing Case," in *We The People: Indiana and the United States Constitution* (Indianapolis, 1987); Frank D. Aquila, *Race Equity in Education: The History of Social Desegregation, 1849–1979* (Bloomington, Ind., 1980).

School Desegregation Case (*U.S. v. Board of School Commissioners*). Indianapolis Public Schools (IPS) desegregation case. In 1968, upon complaints from the NAACP and an IPS parent, the U.S. Justice Department investigated alleged racist practices and policies of the IPS system and subsequently filed suit against IPS for violating the Civil Rights Act of 1964.

Judge S. Hugh Dillin of the Federal District Court for Southern Indiana drew the case, which went to trial in 1971. On August 18, 1971, Dillin found IPS guilty of *de jure* segregation—segregation from deliberate administrative acts—based on racially motivated building and transfer policies, optional attendance zones, and school boundary changes enacted by the IPS board. Dillin ordered the immediate desegregation of CRISPUS ATTUCKS HIGH SCHOOL and all other single-race IPS schools. He also added the State of Indiana and over 20 metropolitan school corporations as defendants in an effort to secure a long-term solution to "white flight" to suburban schools.

IPS, the State of Indiana, and the suburban schools appealed the decision to the U.S. Court of Appeals for the Seventh Circuit, which upheld Dillin's *de jure* ruling and remanded the case to Dillin to decide the responsibility of the state and the suburban schools in IPS segregation. Meanwhile, a group of Indianapolis students were added as plaintiffs, lessening the Justice Department's role.

After a second trial which took four weeks, Dillin ruled on July 20, 1973, that the State of Indiana, due to its extensive authority over local school administration and its lack of leadership over IPS, acted to inhibit IPS desegregation and was thus partially responsible for the remedy. Dillin also found that suburban schools were not guilty of *de jure* segregation, but he concluded that no lasting remedy for IPS desegregation could be achieved without including them. He ordered the General Assembly to enact legislation allowing student transfers across school corporation boundaries and, in the meantime, to begin the immediate busing of a limited number of black IPS students to suburban schools.

Appeals delayed busing to suburban schools, but transfers within IPS began in September, 1973, after two Dillin appointees devised a reassignment plan according to his 1971 order. In 1974 the Court of Appeals upheld Dillin in regard to the state's responsibility for IPS segregation, but disallowed those defendants outside Marion County not included in UNIGOV. The higher court then remanded the case to Dillin to decide whether Unigov's enactment warranted a metropolis-wide remedy.

On August 1, 1975, Dillin ruled that Unigov, because it did not expand the school city along with civic boundaries, was a deliberate attempt to inhibit school desegregation. He thus ordered 15

percent of the black IPS students bused one-way to suburban schools in Marion County. The state and suburban school corporations appealed the decision, with the case going to the Court of Appeals, U.S. Supreme Court, and back again to the Court of Appeals, which in turn remanded the case to Dillin several times. Eventually both higher courts upheld Dillin's decision, even though retreating from busing remedies elsewhere, because Unigov's intent made Indianapolis different from other cities, such as Detroit.

By 1979, after hearing alternate desegregation plans, Dillin finally approved "Plan A," which provided for the transfer of black students to eight township school districts. He reasoned that only the General Assembly had the jurisdiction to create a metropolitan school system and only in that event could suburban students be bused to the inner city. Speedway and Beech Grove schools were exempted from busing because they were not part of Unigov, as were Washington and Pike townships, which had already desegregated.

On October 6, 1980, the Supreme Court refused to hear any further appeals, and the following fall black elementary students and high school freshmen were bused to township schools. In 1983 the case finally closed after fees for the plaintiffs' three attorneys were settled at $1.3 million.

The case has been reopened several times since 1983. In 1984 Dillin ruled in favor of parents of children bused to township schools who asked to be able to vote in and run for township school board elections. In 1988 Dillin denied an IPS petition to receive $67 million in additional state funding for new and continuing desegregation programs. And in 1993 he approved the IPS request to replace the intra-IPS busing plan with the SELECT SCHOOLS program. This program, implemented in fall 1993, allowed limited parental choice within IPS boundaries but maintained federally mandated racial quotas and busing to the townships.

MICHELLE D. HALE

Sharon Pearcy, "Busing, An Historical Overview," *Indianapolis Monthly* (Aug., 1981), 40–49; Emma Lou Thornbrough, "The Indianapolis School Busing Case," in *We the People: Indiana and the United States Constitution* (Indianapolis, 1987).

School Districts. Units of local government that provide public education. Provided for by state law, school districts are legally distinct from the municipal or township governments within whose boundaries they operate. There are 11 school districts in Marion County: INDIANAPOLIS PUBLIC SCHOOLS (IPS), School City of Beech Grove, School Town of Speedway, Franklin Township Community School District, and the Metropolitan School Districts of Decatur, Lawrence, Perry, Pike, Warren, Washington, and Wayne townships. The school district boundaries have not been affected by the school consolidation law of 1958, the creation of UNIGOV, or numerous attempts to consolidate all Marion County schools. The IPS district retains the old city boundaries; SPEEDWAY and BEECH GROVE districts have preserved their municipal boundaries; and the township districts have jurisdiction over the remaining areas within their respective township boundaries.

Voters within most districts elect their own school boards, either by geographic districts or at large, but the town or city council appoints the boards in the Speedway and Beech Grove districts. All boards have five members except IPS, Warren Township, and Wayne Township, which have seven members. According to state guidelines the school boards are responsible for appointing a superintendent, setting an annual budget, financing the budget through property taxes and/or bond issues, furnishing teachers and equipment, constructing and maintaining school facilities, and approving school policy. The boards must present their budgets to the County Board of Tax Adjustment for annual review.

MICHELLE D. HALE

School Finance. Even though school finance in Indianapolis has often hinged upon the limitations of the state constitution or the actions of the General Assembly, Indianapolis citizens early played a major role in the creation of the free school system and have since provided a large percentage of the financial support for local schools. When first presented to the General Assembly in 1847, a proposed new city charter provided for a local property tax levy to support free schools. Previously, state law allowed local governments to collect taxes for schools but payment was optional. Opponents of free public education argued that it would unfairly require all to pay for the education of a few. The charter passed only when legislators required a public referendum to approve the levy. Subsequently, Indianapolis voters overwhelmingly endorsed "free schools" by a vote of 406 to 28. The first property tax, levied in 1847, raised $1,981, which was spent on the purchase of lots and buildings. Teachers' salaries could not be paid from the tax fund, and so parents still had to pay tuition.

The public support of free schools in Indianapolis sparked state legislation in 1851 which, among other things, made newly created local school boards responsible for school finances. It also provided the first state funds for teachers' salaries and for books. The first totally free school session in Indianapolis was held later that year and lasted two months when state tuition funds expired. The Indianapolis school board attempted to raise additional taxes for tuition to extend the school sessions, but the Indiana Supreme Court ruled it unconstitutional for townships to tax themselves to maintain schools after state funds had been exhausted. The following year, 1855, the General Assembly passed a law that created independent local school boards with the full power to levy taxes for the support of public schools. Three years later the state Supreme Court declared this law unconstitutional, arguing that all Indiana children should be provided with equal education. The power to levy local taxes then reverted to the City Council, to which the school board could only recommend the amount needed to fund schools. The school board successfully appealed to citizens to support voluntary scholarships to allow public schools to remain open for the full year. But by the following term public support had waned. For the next several years the length of the free school term each year depended on the meager but slowly growing state tuition funding. For the rest of the year private schools operated, some in the public school buildings.

As the city grew so did the local property tax. In 1857 the city collected $20,239 for the purchase of school buildings and permanent improvements. By 1863 the City Council authorized a fifteen cent tax per $100 of taxable property for schools and the school board soon had purchased property worth $88,500.

ABRAM C. SHORTRIDGE became the Indianapolis school superintendent in 1863 and successfully lobbied the legislature to create independent, locally elected school boards. These boards had full power to levy taxes to support schools, including teachers' salaries. Although almost identical to the unconstitutional 1855 law, this statute was not challenged. With public opinion in favor of free education, a constitutional amendment in 1867 authorized local taxes in support of tuition.

Education reforms in the 1890s dramatically affected school finances on the state and local level. In 1891 the General Assembly authorized an additional five cent property tax for manual education buildings and maintenance. The Indianapolis school board borrowed money in anticipation of this new tax revenue, incurring the board's first debt and starting a trend in local school finance.

As the board's budget grew, stimulated by the enactment of a compulsory school law in 1897, the election of the local school board became increasingly political, with local banks competing for custody of the school funds. As a result of public concern, the Indianapolis COMMERCIAL CLUB studied the issue and proposed legislation to correct political abuses. The General Assembly approved the proposal in 1899. Patterned after the "Cleveland Plan," it greatly limited the local school board's control over school funds. While boards still controlled the distribution of funds, the city auditor and treasurer gained actual custody and supervision of the funds. By 1908 the school budget had reached over $1 million.

Throughout the 20th century schools have been financed through an increasingly complex combination of state and (more recently) federal monies and grants, as well as local taxes, bond issues, and non-tax forms of revenue. The state's contribution to public education mainly supports teacher and administrative salaries, instructional costs, and, in recent years, transportation. Originally funded by a gross income tax, various excise taxes, and other miscellaneous taxes, the state's contribution in the 1990s also derives from sales and corporate taxes and lottery revenues. Each school corporation is allotted state funds on the basis of a complicated formula intended to ensure

that all Indiana children receive equal educational instruction. The formula is based on teacher experience, an adjusted allowance per pupil, average daily attendance, and local property tax wealth. Since 1935 the state has also provided low-interest loans out of the Common Fund for local school construction. Throughout the 20th century the state has taken over more responsibility for local school funding, rising from 17.8 percent of the Indianapolis budget to 47 percent as of 1993.

Prior to the 1960s Indianapolis schools received almost no federal assistance. Since that time Indianapolis schools have received federal monies through the state for special programs and expenditures that the school board could not otherwise afford, but not for general operating costs. The federal share of the Indianapolis budget rose from 0.2 percent in 1960 to 9.93 percent in 1993.

Historically, most local funding comes from property taxes whose maximum amount is limited by state law. By 1993 Indianapolis Public Schools (IPS) derived 43 percent of its revenue from this source. Although this figure represents a decline in the proportion of total income available for public education, the property tax rate has increased steadily throughout the 20th century. In 1909 local property taxes for schools had risen to 58 cents per every $100 of taxable property. Forty-two cents was allocated to the general operating fund; the rest went for buildings and maintenance, manual training, the city library, teachers' pensions, and free kindergartens. By 1919 the property tax rate had risen to 70 cents, and by 1940 to 96 cents, although throughout the Great Depression the school budget actually decreased. In 1959 a countywide school tax of 25 cents was added to the city tax. From that time local property taxes increased so rapidly that by the 1970s local school officials worried about a voter backlash. Despite recurrent complaints that property taxes are inadequate as the foundation for school funding, as of 1993 no significant changes had been made.

Bond issues and lease-rental arrangements are other important sources of local school revenues used largely for the purchase of land, buildings, and permanent improvements. The Indiana constitution limits the amount of general obligation bonds that can be outstanding at any given time. Indianapolis has regularly issued general obligation bonds throughout the 20th century. Temporary loans, called tax anticipation warrants, are used for school operating purposes and must be paid back within a year. Since 1947 the General Assembly has allowed school corporations to create public holding corporations, and since 1957 privates ones as well. These corporations can borrow money, build buildings, and lease these buildings to the school corporation. The lease obligation is paid by the school from property taxes levied for the school's debt service fund, just as general obligation bonds are repaid, but the lease obligation is not limited by the state constitution.

School corporations were not included in the Unigov consolidation implemented in 1970. Since a U.S. District Court judge ruled in 1980 that IPS was guilty of *de facto* segregation, IPS alone must pay its desegregation costs. This decision has put a large strain on the IPS budget in recent years.

As of 1993 there are eleven school corporations in Marion County, but IPS remains by far the largest in terms of distributed revenues, total budget, and student population. IPS also receives the overwhelming majority of the county's federal revenues for schools. The IPS school budget for 1993 was $352,132,757, with an expenditure of $4,993 per pupil plus desegregation costs.

MICHELLE D. HALE

Jacob Piatt Dunn, *Greater Indianapolis* (Chicago, 1910), 268–278; Indianapolis Public Schools, "Superintendent's Report" (1930); State Board of Accounts, "A Study of the Financial and Administrative Needs of the Indianapolis Public Schools" (1919); Department of Metropolitan Development, "Reports of Marion County School Districts" (1971).

Schools, Alternative. Alternative schools provide options within the public educational system to students and parents who prefer nontraditional forms of education. By the early 1990s, there were numerous alternatives to traditionally organized schools in Marion County. Within the INDIANAPOLIS PUBLIC SCHOOLS (IPS) system, for example, School 91 is a Montessori School for grades K–6. The Montessori option is also available at Schools 67 and 56. Magnet schools, another type of alternative, offer an especially strong curriculum in some areas. Arsenal Technical High School's Math and Science Magnet, Shortridge Junior High School's Foreign Language Magnet, and the Broad Ripple High School Center for the Humanities are examples. Learning Unlimited is a school-within-a-school. Established in 1974 at Washington Township's North Central High School, it stresses individualized instructional programs, experiential learning, and the use of community resources. The Wayne Enrichment Center, an off-campus alternative to Ben Davis High School, serves academically disadvantaged youth in Wayne Township. Its students earn high school credit while acquiring occupational skills.

The KEY SCHOOL (IPS School 97), established in 1987, enrolls some 150 students selected by citywide lottery. Founded upon cognitive psychologist Howard Gardner's theory of multiple intelligences, it is designed to give all seven intelligences (for example, kinesthetic and musical) equal emphasis through the use of an interdisciplinary curriculum. Special interest classes, or "pods," foster the development of the various intelligences. In the school's Flow Center, students select their own activities and enjoy them uninterruptedly. Student progress is assessed in nontraditional ways. The school originated from the vision of director Patricia Bolanos and seven other teachers who designed the school themselves, then convinced the district to fund it.

ELIZABETH SPALDING

Schools, Americanization programs in. Americanization programs were aimed at socializing immigrants and their children to the norms of middle-class, native-born Americans. That Americanization was one of the early purposes of free, public education can be seen by Indiana's School Law of 1855, which required that the common schools be taught in the English language, a requirement reiterated in the School Law of 1865. At the time of the first law, the non-native population of Indianapolis was composed primarily of Germans, who numbered close to 4,000; as of 1869, however, only 34 German-born children were enrolled in Indianapolis public schools.

Those who supported the teaching of German in public schools argued that instruction in their native language would hasten the Americanization of German-speaking students and entice more German parents to enroll their children in public schools. By the early 1880s, Indianapolis offered a dual language (German-English) program aimed at both native-English and German-speaking pupils. This unique program was one of the earliest to promote assimilation through bilingual education. But German immigration virtually ended in the 1890s, and by 1917, in response to World War I, the teaching of German in common schools was banned.

In 1915, Indianapolis' immigrant population, largely eastern and southern Europeans, was estimated at 14,000, less than 10 percent of the total population. Manual High School and Public School 5 offered night classes to "foreigners." Courses included beginning English, citizenship preparation, and vocational classes. Enrollment at these two centers totaled 269, but other agencies also conducted Americanization classes for immigrants.

Pre–World War I Americanization programs focused primarily on teaching English, plus social and vocational skills. After the war, Americanization acquired a more nationalistic tone. Teachers were pressured to incorporate into the curriculum Americanization lessons stressing the importance of citizenship, democracy, and patriotism. Indiana University Extension Division offered classes and institutes to train teachers to teach Americanization. The State Board of Education proclaimed October 24, 1919, "Americanization Day" and urged all public schools to celebrate with programs of patriotic songs and readings.

In 1926, the Director of Naturalization for Indianapolis recommended that the public schools organize an evening citizenship class for adults. The first class was held October 16, 1926, at Manual High School. Taught by a history teacher at the high school, the course consisted of 30 two-hour lessons in United States history and government. Ability to speak and write English was a prerequisite. Enrollment in the first three sessions totaled 185. Soon all other agencies dis-

Public school Americanization programs, this one involving a 1932 Haughville kindergarten class, were designed to teach immigrant children middle-class American values. For these events children often dressed in traditional ethnic clothing such as the costumes from Bulgaria, Slovenia, Holland, and Austria seen here.
[Indiana Historical Society, #C5404]

continued their classes and urged attendance at this centralized location.

By the 1930s the number of immigrants in Indianapolis, and their percentage of the city's population, had declined. In 1933, nine out of ten students enrolled in night schools were American-born. Concern with immigrant socialization waned in the face of this demographic reality.

ELIZABETH SPALDING

Crystal Benton Fall, "The Foreigner in Indianapolis" (M.A. thesis, Indiana University, 1916); Bertha Leming, "Work of the Social Services Department of the Indianapolis Schools" (M.A. thesis, Indiana University, 1931).

Schools, Christian. Numerous schools in the Indianapolis area are classified as "Christian" schools. There is no unified administrative structure or common educational philosophy for these schools. Some are a subsidiary to specific denominational congregations and draw both their student body and administrative personnel from the church itself. Others are affiliated with larger organizations, consisting of schools which share similar theological views. Most Christian day schools in Indianapolis are guided by conservative theological precepts and follow a strict interpretation of biblical admonition. There are no boarding facilities in these schools. Some, but not all, provide student transportation.

Four Marion County schools are affiliated with the Indiana Association of Christian Schools (IACS). Baptist Academy and Suburban Baptist Schools, both including kindergarten through grade twelve, as well as Eagledale Christian and Colonial Hill Christian schools, both elementary institutions, are members of IACS. The association includes Independent Baptist Schools in Indiana and serves as liaison to other such institutions throughout the country.

Three schools are members of Associated Christian Schools International (ACSI), another liaison group for Independent Baptist Schools. Colonial Christian, Gray Road Christian, and Heritage Christian schools belong to ACSI.

Many other schools are truly independent. Faithway Christian School is an independent unit connected with the congregation of Faithway Baptist Church. Calvary Christian School, kindergarten through grade twelve, is affiliated with Calvary United Pentecostal Church. Westside Christian School is totally independent, located in facilities provided by a Church of the Nazarene. Indianapolis Baptist High School, opened in 1971, is an educational adjunct to the Baptist Temple congregation and is not affiliated with other schools in the county.

Indianapolis Christian Schools are independent though closely tied to the Church of Christ. The elementary school accepts students in kindergarten through grade six and is accredited by the Indiana Department of Education. The junior-senior high school, grades seven through twelve, is not accredited by the state's Department of Education. Indianapolis Christian Schools hold membership in the National Christian Schools Association with headquarters in York, Nebraska.

HELEN JEAN MCCLELLAND NUGENT
WITH TIMOTHY O'SHEA
AND JOHN D. PROHASKA
Franklin College of Indiana

Schools, Curricula of. The earliest common schools in Indianapolis taught a basic curriculum of penmanship, spelling, reading, arithmetic, grammar, and geography. The spelling book was the most important, and sometimes only, text: students were deemed ready to read only after they had mastered the words in the speller. Spellers were also used to teach geography, grammar, and moral philosophy.

Prior to the establishment of the public high school, public and private seminaries provided secondary education to the few who pursued it. The seminaries offered a college preparatory curriculum—more advanced study of the common school subjects, plus history, natural sciences, and classical languages—or a curriculum considered appropriate to the education of women, emphasizing such subjects as music, drawing, and French.

In 1855, shortly after the establishment of free common schools in Indianapolis, the state legislature enumerated the subjects which formed the "common branches" of the curriculum: spelling, reading, writing, arithmetic, geography, and English grammar. The same law stipulated that the common school was to be taught in English. This point was reiterated by the School Law of 1865, which added "good behavior" to the list of subjects to be taught. In 1869 legislators added two more subjects to the common school curriculum: physiology and United States history. Teachers were required to be examined in these subjects in order to obtain a common school license. And since teachers had to be of good moral character, they were expected to instill such character into their charges.

Just as the common school curriculum reflected older patterns from the Northeast, reinforced by teacher licensing requirements, so the earliest public high school curriculum in Indianapolis was also influenced by university admission requirements. In 1873 admission to the state university required proficiency in spelling, reading, geography, grammar, arithmetic, U.S. history, composition, word analysis, geometry, algebra, and Latin grammar, composition, and literature. From its earliest days Indianapolis High School had offered all these subjects, and by 1873 had added a number of others: German, the United States and Indiana constitutions, morals, natural philosophy, mental science, and the beginnings of a commercial course of study. Most high school students did not go to college, however, so many pupils studied advanced English or modern subjects. At this time the aim of the Indianapolis High School curriculum was, as one writer put it, to give students "the greatest amount of practical and useful knowledge, adapted to their wants in any position in life."

The last decades of the 19th century were devoted to organizing the now firmly established public schools. Large cities such as Boston and Chicago had already provided an organizational model with the eight year graded elementary school. Graded schools required a carefully arranged course of study so that pupils could be classified and promoted accordingly. Therefore, in 1874 Indiana county school superintendents met to devise a "plain, simple, and practical" course of study which would insure uniformity in instruction throughout the state. Walter S. Smith, superintendent of Marion County, drafted the most complete syllabus and it formed the basis of the curriculum submitted to the State Board of Education in 1875. This course of study did not add subjects to or delete them from the common school curriculum; nor did it detail activities or methods of instruction. Rather, it prescribed at what level and in what increments the content was to be taught. In fact, the course of study closely followed the organization of textbooks already widely used in the state. Smith's course of study was not mandated by the state, but in 1877 the use of state-adopted texts was. To bring about even greater uniformity, the state's school superintendents in 1883 appointed a standing committee to prepare questions for the examination of graduates from public schools. The pattern of curriculum derived from textbooks and externally developed examinations was thus established.

By 1915 Indianapolis had three commissioned public high schools: Indianapolis (later SHORTRIDGE HIGH SCHOOL), Indianapolis Manual Training (later MANUAL HIGH SCHOOL), and ARSENAL TECHNICAL HIGH SCHOOL. Together their course offerings reflected three prominent influences on American curriculum at the time: mental discipline, manual training, and vocational-technical education. Popular opinion held that the

mind, like a muscle, could be improved through training and that a disciplined intellect guided the other mental faculties, resulting in the development of good moral character. Subjects such as Greek, Latin, English grammar, algebra, and geometry disciplined the mind through logic and memorization. The sciences too were justified for their disciplinary rather than practical value. Numerous science courses were offered—astronomy, botany, physiology, zoology, geology, chemistry—in which memorization played an important role.

The manual training movement was to some extent a reaction against mental discipline. Proponents of manual training sought to restore the dignity of hand labor and argued that all youth would benefit intellectually and morally by engaging in practical occupations. Art, home economics for girls, and industrial arts for boys were thus added to the secondary curriculum. The demand for vocational-technical training grew as high school enrollments rose dramatically, encompassing an increasingly diverse body of students many of whom were not interested in a college preparatory curriculum. Accordingly, courses in stenography, bookkeeping, machine fitting, and forging were offered (see EDUCATION, VOCATIONAL).

Despite the diversity of course offerings and students' aspirations, requirements for high school graduation remained essentially the requirements for college entrance: three years of classical or modern languages, three years of mathematics, two years of science, four years of English, three years of history, plus electives. In the 1904 course of study, State Superintendent of Public Instruction Fassett A. Cotton allowed terminal students the option of substituting commercial arithmetic or bookkeeping for solid geometry. This course of study, which remained virtually unchanged throughout the first decades of the 20th century, reflected the recommendation of the 1892 Committee on Secondary School Studies (known as the Committee of Ten). Their report recommended that terminal students be given the same program as college-bound students and that fewer subjects be studied over a longer period of time. This report reaffirmed college influence upon the high school curriculum and represented a step toward the development of modern subjects (e.g., Greek and Latin were being supplanted by modern foreign languages).

In 1918 three works were published that became extremely influential nationally and locally. *The Curriculum* by Franklin Bobbitt popularized the scientific study of curriculum. Bobbitt introduced activity analysis, the breaking down of school activities into minute steps, and the now common practice of prescribing differentiated curricula appropriate for students' probable social and occupational roles. Indiana, like many other school systems across the country, invited a team of experts—the General Education Board of New York City along with faculty from colleges and universities around the state—to conduct a thorough, scientific study of public education in Indiana. Their findings reflected the quest for scientific efficiency, calling for the requirement of only such subjects as dealt with the fundamentals of English language and literature, made a direct contribution to citizenship and social efficiency, addressed materials of common need, and contributed to physical well-being. Also in pursuit of efficiency, the courses of study published in the 1920s, 1930s, and 1940s prescribed the number of minutes per day to be allotted to instruction in the various subject areas.

The second influential publication of 1918 was W. H. Kilpatrick's *The Project Method*. A professor at Columbia Teachers College, Kilpatrick, influenced by the work of John Dewey at the University of Chicago Laboratory School, crusaded for a curriculum consisting of activities arising from students' shared and individual interests. The subject areas should be related to and integrated with these interests. In 1929 state Superintendent Roy P. Wisehart announced a major program of curriculum revision in Indiana with all courses of study from kindergarten through high school being worked out on an "activities basis." The new courses of study emphasized group work, application of knowledge, problem solving, and the central role of the teacher in planning experiences for students appropriate to their interests and abilities. The ultimate goal was the integration of the student into society. Junior high schools, established in Indianapolis in 1919, were seen as particularly suited to this goal, and "exploratory" courses in foreign languages and ca-

reers were introduced in grades seven through nine.

Finally, 1918 saw the publication of the report of the Commission on the Reorganization of Secondary Education. The report enumerated seven Cardinal Principles or aims of the high school curriculum: health; command of fundamental processes; worthy home membership; vocational efficiency; civic participation; worthy use of leisure time; and ethical character. These aims, so general and all-inclusive that few could disagree with them, were adopted in Indiana as the aims of secondary, as well as elementary, education.

The Cardinal Principles continued to influence the Indianapolis curriculum throughout the 1930s, 1940s, and 1950s. Guidance programs were instituted in schools. Extracurricular activities—furthering the aims of civic participation and worthy use of leisure time—were promoted and given time during the school day. Courses such as health, safety, and physical education were introduced. Social studies, seen as integrating the seven aims, became increasingly important. At the secondary level the curriculum became more and more differentiated, offering separate courses of study for students seeking college entrance and those specializing in home economics, industrial arts, agriculture, or commercial skills. At the administrative level, curriculum specialists oversaw the steadily growing array of course offerings. In spite of all this curricular activity, however, the Indiana School Study Commission found in 1948 "an over-emphasis on mere rote memorization" in elementary schools and an excessive reliance on textbooks in secondary schools.

By the 1940s a new educational movement had arisen: life adjustment education. Despite public schools' attempts to provide a curriculum that met the needs of every student, nationally the dropout rate stood at 40 percent. While this may have been attributable to such factors as military enlistment and the availability of jobs in industry, life adjustment educators blamed the irrelevance of most school subjects for the mass of students. They urged the development of a curriculum which would prepare the nation's youth for "real life." Courses such as "Family Living," "Boy-Girl Relationships," and "Learning to Work" were introduced. In Indianapolis school and community leaders cooperated to construct a course entitled "Indianapolis at Work" to teach students about business and industry. The Parent-Teacher Association of Manual High School purchased a bus to take students on "interesting and meaningful" tours of museums, stores, factories, parks, and other points of interest.

The launching of Sputnik in 1957, however, put an end to life adjustment education. The mass media blamed "soft" American education for the Soviet technological victory. In 1958 Congress passed the National Defense Education Act calling for the "fullest development of the mental resources and technical skills of the nation's youth." The educational goal of intellectual development was once again in the forefront, with science, mathematics, and foreign languages emphasized and the identification and appropriate education of gifted youth a high priority.

Over the last several decades federal and state legislation has helped shape the curriculum of IN-DIANAPOLIS PUBLIC SCHOOLS. Desegregation led to the development of MAGNET SCHOOLS, which offer specialized curricula in areas like foreign languages, technology, and performing arts. Special education programs, reading improvement programs, and programs for limited English proficient (LEP) students were developed with state and federal funds. The Division of Curriculum of the state Department of Education has sponsored numerous curriculum development projects funded by outside agencies, in such areas as arts education, environmental education, ethnic studies, and Indiana history. During the 1980s, mirroring the national trend, Indiana increased minimum requirements for high school graduation and developed curriculum proficiency guidelines stated in terms of growth learners are expected to achieve rather than in terms of content teachers are expected to teach. In the Indianapolis public school system special emphasis has been placed on integrating technology, especially computers, into the curriculum.

The curriculum now offered in Indianapolis Public Schools is an amalgam of much that has gone before. The "common branches" of learning still form the backbone of the elementary school curriculum. Even the subject of "Scientific Tem-

perance," mandated by the legislature in 1895, remains in place under the name "Substance Abuse Education." High school graduation requirements have changed only slightly since Cotton's superintendency and are still geared toward college admission requirements, reflecting the aspirations of the 49 percent of IPS graduates who now enroll in college. The curriculum, kindergarten through twelfth grade, still attempts to achieve the aims of the Cardinal Principles. The "activities" movement has reemerged in the "Whole Language" teaching method and in innovative settings like the nationally recognized KEY SCHOOL, which draws upon the theory of multiple intelligences or the idea that intelligence exists in numerous forms other than mental. Students engage in activities such as gardening, photography, or musical composition, and study a curriculum centered around schoolwide, interdisciplinary themes. The goals of social and scientific efficiency are apparent in the proliferation of tests, ability tracks, and special programs for special student populations. The courses popularized by the manual training movement remain in place, as do many developed by life adjustment educators.

ELIZABETH SPALDING

Richard G. Boone, *A History of Education in Indiana* (New York, 1892); F. A. Cotton, *Education in Indiana (1793 to 1934)* (Bluffton, Ind., 1934); Harold C. Mason, "Some Aspects of the Development of Educational Theory in Indiana from 1851 to 1920" (Ed.D. dissertation, Indiana University, 1945).

Schools, Foreign language instruction in. The first foreign language taught in Indianapolis public schools was German, primarily because the city's vocal German community demanded instruction in its native language. In 1866, a teacher of German was hired to teach in the Ninth Ward, where three-fourths of the population was German. Ironically, German was taught in English, since the school laws of 1855 and 1865 required that the common schools be taught in English.

In 1869 the school law changed to require all public schools to offer German language instruction if 25 or more parents asked for it. By the following year 1,063 students were enrolled in

German classes with five teachers. Separate classes were organized: children of German-speaking parents studied German in grades two through eight; children of English-speaking parents studied German in grades six through eight. Lessons lasted 20 minutes each day.

In 1873, CHARLES E. EMMERICH became supervisor of German instruction in the public schools. Emmerich, working with Augusta Franck, eventually combined the two separate sets of classes at centralized locations. By the early 1880s, Emmerich and Franck had organized an innovative bilingual education program for grades six through eight. English-speaking teachers taught math, grammar, and reading; German-speaking teachers taught German, geography, history, spelling (in English), drawing, and music. The school system's annual report pronounced the experiment a success: by the end of the first year all students could converse easily in German or English and write examinations in either language with equal facility. Further, the new method of instruction saved the public schools $3,300 per year. From this point on, German language instruction flourished in Indianapolis—by the 1910s over one-fifth of the city's students studied German—until the nativism of the World War I years brought it to a halt.

Both German and Latin were offered at the Indianapolis High School from its founding, and three years of one or the other was required. In the fourth year, students could choose between Latin or French. In 1883, Greek was added to the curriculum. Latin, Greek, and French were valued as college preparatory subjects, whereas German was considered more "practical." Foreign language study was thought to develop mental discipline through deliberate memorization and the problem-solving exercise of translation.

The "grammar-translation" method of instruction reigned in Indianapolis high schools for decades. But as high school enrollments expanded, fewer and fewer students appreciated the mental discipline instilled by foreign language study. In 1919, the State Board of Education made foreign language study optional. Shortly thereafter, the state study courses urged teachers to use the "direct method" of foreign language instruction, which identified speech as the primary form

of language and emphasized the importance of culture. Thus, Latin teachers were advised to use conversational Latin, to stress the connections between Latin and English, and to organize Latin clubs. French, a language more amenable to "direct method" teaching, began to increase in popularity at this time. By 1930, Spanish had been added to the high school curriculum and German reinstated.

Foreign language instruction remained in the high schools exclusively until the development of junior highs in the 1930s. Indianapolis' junior highs offered electives in Latin, French, German, and Spanish, as well as a course called Introductory Language which offered language guidance for students who had "linguistic ability." Students lacking this ability could also be identified and steered toward a more appropriate course of high school study.

Throughout the 1930s Latin continued to be the city's most commonly taught foreign language. But World War II created needs for people who spoke a second language, and the launching of Sputnik in the 1950s spurred new calls for increased foreign language study. Technological developments brought tape recorders into classrooms and foreign language labs to teach via the audiolingual method. This method, growing out of government training efforts in World War II, emphasized speaking and hearing. In Indianapolis and elsewhere, foreign language instruction was increasingly directed toward "academically talented" students.

During the 1960s INDIANAPOLIS PUBLIC SCHOOLS (IPS) initiated a long-range plan to improve and expand foreign language instruction. Continuous in-service training in the audiolingual method was offered to foreign language teachers. Edith Allen, who eventually became Indianapolis' first supervisor of foreign language instruction, developed a pilot program that brought daily 15–minute Spanish lessons into elementary classrooms via television. In 1964, over 4,000 students in 50 schools were enrolled in the TV classes.

Funding cuts and widespread disillusionment with the mechanistic audiolingual method led to declining enrollments throughout the 1970s. Even a successful program that brought Latin to urban elementary students with the goals of improving their English language functioning and stimulating their interest in the humanities was discontinued.

The creation of MAGNET SCHOOLS was the next major development in foreign language instruction in IPS. Shortridge Junior High School and ARSENAL TECHNICAL HIGH SCHOOL were designated foreign language magnets. Currently, students who choose this option can pursue a six-year sequence of Arabic, Chinese, Japanese, or Russian, as well as the more commonly taught languages.

Foreign language instruction in IPS is now based on proficiency guidelines, first developed in the 1980s by the American Council on the Teaching of Foreign Languages. The guidelines consist of rating scales of proficiency in speaking, listening, reading, and writing the target language. The magnet program enrolls some 350 students, with Japanese and Russian the most popular languages. Foreign language electives are available in all IPS junior high schools. Students identified as "academically talented" may follow a twelve-year sequence in Spanish, an option which may be unique to IPS. In fact, Spanish has become the most commonly taught language in IPS and enrollments increased substantially for the 1991–1992 school year. German and Latin have all but disappeared from the curriculum, and soon will be offered only at the magnet centers. As of 1990, about 27 percent of high school students in IPS were studying foreign languages.

ELIZABETH SPALDING

Schools, Private. Educational endeavors in Marion County between 1821 and 1853 were private or religiously supported despite provisions for free public education (which were never implemented) in Indiana's 1816 Constitution. Following the adoption of Indiana's 1851 Constitution and the school law of 1852, improved funding and local township organization made education almost wholly public.

The earliest recorded private nonreligious educational efforts in Indianapolis may have been classes in "architectural draughting and drawing" offered by John E. Baker (1823) and a military school operated by a Major Sullinger in 1824 for

Founded in 1832, the Marion County Seminary later served as the public high school before it was demolished in 1860.
[Indiana Historical Society, #C5774]

the instruction of militia officers and soldiers. When an 1826 local census indicated that 209 of 760 residents were children of school age, many individuals were prompted to establish schools. Ebenezer Sharpe, a Marylander who taught previously at Transylvania University in Lexington, Kentucky, began the Indianapolis Academy with his son Thomas in 1826.

Other short-lived attempts, including special schools for penmanship and bookkeeping, kept the idea of education alive until the founding of the Marion County Seminary in 1832. The seminary, which opened on University Square in September, 1834, under the direction of Ebenezer Dumont and supervised by an elected board of trustees, became well known throughout central Indiana for a curriculum that approached collegiate quality. For years an "old boys" alliance of seminary alumni, including LEW WALLACE, BERRY R. SULGROVE, and CALVIN FLETCHER'S sons, was prominent in civic activities and the early administrations of the public school system. The seminary later became the high school of the public school system (established 1853); the original building was used until 1859 and demolished in 1860.

Other seminaries existed during the period. The Indianapolis High School (later the Franklin Institute), established by community leaders in 1837 and directed briefly by Gilman Marston, a Dartmouth College graduate and later governor of Idaho, offered higher level courses. Mary J. and

Harriet Axtell of Courtlandville, New York, began a female seminary in 1837. The INDIANAPOLIS FEMALE INSTITUTE, a Baptist school established in 1858, opened the next year and enrolled 320 students in 1865–1866. Boarding facilities were available, and two clergymen, the Revs. C. W. Hewes and Lucian Hayden, filled the position of principal; teaching was by female faculty. A German school opened around 1859 and by 1871 reported over 250 students. In the 1860s other private schools began offering specialized courses in business education.

Following the educational reforms of the 1850s, rapid expansion of public schools throughout the state ended most of the private academies. A new type of private educational institution appeared, however: college preparatory and finishing schools. The Indianapolis Classical School, begun in 1879 by Harvard graduate Theodore Lovett Sewall, prepared young men for successful admission to the eastern colleges. Sewall later sold his interest in the school and joined with his wife MAY WRIGHT SEWALL in opening the Classical School for Girls in 1882. The boys' school closed in 1889, but the girls' school existed into the early 20th century.

The classical schools influenced private education in Indianapolis long after they closed their doors. JULIA ETHEL LANDERS, daughter of a former Democratic politician, was a student of and former assistant to Mrs. Sewall at the Classical School for Girls. She served as principal of the Episcopal Knickerbacker Hall (originally St. Mary's Seminary, chartered in 1844) until it closed in 1912, and then conducted Miss Landers' School for Girls.

Two other schools offered college preparatory education. A former faculty member of Sewall's girls' school, Fredonia Allen, established Tudor Hall for girls in 1902. She hired graduates of eastern women's colleges to introduce eastern "culture" and education to the Midwest and established residence quarters for boarding students. To prepare young men for college, Brooks School for Boys opened in 1914. Following its acquisition in 1920 by local businessmen and a relocation to facilities near Thomas Taggart Park, the school became known as Park School. It continued its males-only admissions policy until admit-

ting girls to the lower grades in the mid–1960s. After moving to 7200 North College Avenue in 1966, Park School merged with Tudor Hall in 1970 to become PARK TUDOR SCHOOL, which offers a complete pre-kindergarten through grade twelve curriculum. Other private (or parent-supported) schools include ORCHARD COUNTRY DAY SCHOOL (opened October 2, 1922) and Sycamore School (opened 1985), each with a pre-school through grade eight curriculum.

Some schools faced the necessity of changing their mission due to higher tuition expenses, declining interest in boarding facilities, and lessened doctrinal emphasis on religious education. Two schools which began as Roman Catholic institutions and have remained affiliated with the church, though not with the Archdiocese of Indianapolis, are Brebeuf Preparatory School and Cathedral High School. Both have successfully made the transition to private operation and are more nearly proprietary institutions than parochial in any sense of the word.

Brebeuf, founded as a men's school in 1962 by the Chicago Province of the Society of Jesus, admitted women for the first time in 1976 following the closing of Ladywood–St. Agnes. Unlike the other 47 Jesuit high schools in the nation, Brebeuf is an interfaith school. Roman Catholics comprise almost 49 percent of the student body; 41 percent of the students are Protestant, and 10 percent are Jewish and other faiths. Named for St. Jean de Brebeuf, a Jesuit missionary to the Huron Indians who was martyred in 1649, Brebeuf offers a college preparatory program from which 99 percent of its graduates are admitted to colleges and universities around the nation. For the 1993–1994 year Brebeuf enrolled 668 students in grades nine through twelve; tuition was $5,700.

Cathedral High School passed from administration by the Diocese of Indianapolis to become the property of the Midwest Province of the Holy Cross Brothers in 1964. That affiliation ceased in 1973, and financial problems threatened to close the school. Alumni, parents, and friends of the school rallied to create a not-for-profit corporation, Cathedral Trustees, Inc. The 1973 school year began under the administration of a 24–member lay board of trustees. In 1976 the Sisters of Providence offered to sell the Ladywood–St. Agnes campus on East 56th Street. Although controversy surrounded the decision, Cathedral became coeducational and vacated its downtown location across from SS. PETER AND PAUL CATHEDRAL, which had given the school its name. By 1990 the student body was approximately 53 percent male, 47 percent female; 26 percent of the students were non–Roman Catholic. Increased enrollment brought new faculty positions; 40 percent of the instructors were non–Roman Catholic. Cathedral, which places at least 96 percent of its graduates in colleges and universities, won the 1989 U.S. Department of Education's "Award for Excellence," given for academic excellence among American schools. The alumni rolls contain names of prominent local businessmen, politicians, athletes, and church officials. The school, located on the former Ladywood campus at 5225 East 56th Street, enrolled 876 students in grades nine through twelve in 1993–1994; tuition was $4,100. Cathedral began a $4 million fund-raising effort to mark its 75th anniversary in 1993.

Privately owned preschool facilities also exist in Indianapolis, many of which are affiliated with national organizations. LaPetite Centers, a national chain targeting children aged six weeks through twelve years, have been in the city since the late 1970s. The facilities are expanded in some centers to include kindergarten instruction, curriculum enhancement programs for older children to supplement their regular course of instruction, and summer programs. Montessori schools are part of an international curriculum that began in Italy in 1907 and arrived in Indianapolis in 1966. These schools serve children ages $2^{1}/_{2}$ to 9 years, or through third grade. For the 1992–1993 school year, Montessori enrolled 740 students in seven programs in Indianapolis at $2,800 tuition. INDIANAPOLIS PUBLIC SCHOOLS uses Montessori options in a variant program for grades K–6.

Private educational facilities as an alternative to public or religious schools are available in Indianapolis from preschool through grade twelve. Tuition costs limit enrollment and the number of private schools remains small. All of the schools accept male and female students of any race or religion. Their principal purpose has been to prepare young men and women for college, and their success rate indicates the task is being accomplished.

HELEN JEAN MCCLELLAND NUGENT
WITH JOHN M. GRAY
AND TAMARA D. KING
Franklin College of Indiana

Richard G. Boone, *A History of Education in Indiana* (New York, 1892; reprint, Indianapolis: Indiana Historical Bureau, 1941); Jacob Piatt Dunn, *Greater Indianapolis* (Chicago, 1910), esp. Chapter XIII, "The Early Schools."

Schools, Religious. Early educational opportunities in Indianapolis were religious efforts by Protestant groups. Often those schools were the work of one person and thus short-lived. The rapid growth of public schools throughout the Midwest during the late 19th century ended many of the religious efforts. When free public schools began in Indianapolis in 1853, religious attempts to maintain separate educational facilities gradually declined. The early CATHOLIC schools had lower enrollment percentages in Indianapolis than in Fort Wayne, Madison, Vincennes, and other midwestern cities with larger Roman Catholic populations, but they remain on the Indianapolis scene. Some present-day LUTHERAN schools also trace their beginnings to the mid–19th century.

PRESBYTERIANS, METHODISTS, and BAPTISTS all maintained educational institutions prior to the Civil War, but by the 1870s most Protestant schools and academies throughout the state of Indiana were either closed or absorbed by the rapidly growing public schools. Denominational differences produced some rivalry between the schools in the early years. Historian Jacob Piatt Dunn quoted a Methodist minister who charged that Presbyterians in the Midwest used public funds to create supposedly public schools that were as denominational as if Presbyterians alone had contributed the funds. Following the Civil War denominational differences declined, support for the public schools grew, and most Protestant schools in Marion County disappeared.

EPISCOPALIAN efforts at education began with a Seminary for Young Ladies, opened in November, 1839, by Susan B. (Mrs. James B.) Britton, wife of the Christ Church rector. The school existed for several years and in 1844 was succeeded by St. Mary's Seminary, another girls' school, which was chartered by the state legislature with the vestry of Christ Church as trustees ex officio. Financial difficulties threatened by 1863, and St. Mary's did not survive the Civil War. Some years later the Indianapolis diocese of the Episcopal church operated Knickerbacker Hall, named for Bishop David Buell Knickerbacker, who headed the diocese from 1883 to 1894. The effort was short-lived, ending in 1912. Nearly a half century later, in 1960, Episcopalians opened ST. RICHARD'S SCHOOL for elementary students. Though located adjacent to Trinity Church, the parish exercises no control over the school. St. Richard's is modeled on the traditional English country day school, requiring daily chapel attendance and rigid uniform dress. St. Richard's is accredited by the Independent Schools Association of the Central States and is unclassified by the Indiana Department of Education (DOE).

Lutheran congregations formed schools during the mid–19th century to serve German language areas, and some of them continue to the present time. Zion, Second German, and St. Paul's congregations had affiliated schools, although not all were located in Marion County. Zion, in New Palestine, erected a log school in 1848. That building was replaced in 1873 and a modern building was erected in 1950. A split in the congregation led to the creation of Second German Church, which also established a school near CUMBERLAND. Trinity School originated within the St. Paul's congregation in 1872, although the original St. Paul's School preceded Trinity. St. John's School began in rural surroundings in 1852. German language instruction stopped during WORLD WAR I, and the German heritage is no longer heavily emphasized. The older Lutheran schools are unique for having served several generations of families; in some instances six generations have been educated in the same school. More recent Lutheran efforts have produced Emmaus School, dating from 1904, and Calvary School, which opened in 1944. (These elementary schools are all certified by DOE.) In 1976 Lutherans recognized a need for secondary educational facilities, and Indianapolis Lutheran High School began with 17 pupils. Increased en-

rollment at the high school level resulted in a new building at 5555 South Arlington in September, 1991. Lutheran High School holds a first-class commission from the state Department of Education. All of these Lutheran schools are affiliated with the Missouri Synod of the Lutheran Church and are responsible to education offices located in Fort Wayne, Indiana. Another Lutheran school in Marion County, Divine Savior, is responsible to the Wisconsin Evangelical Lutheran Synod headquartered in Milwaukee. This school, opened in 1978, is unclassified by DOE.

The largest and most complete religious education system in Marion County consists of Roman Catholic schools. Most began as parochial schools, intended to serve the particular ethnic populations of individual parishes. Various religious orders operated separate institutions for boys and girls. Shifting populations and changes within Roman Catholicism have caused many changes to the system, but it remains strong in the 1990s. Roman Catholic parishes were established later than the Protestant congregations, and the first school did not begin until 1859. In order to serve the German Catholic parish, St. John's established St. John's Academy for Girls in that year. The same parish also established a school for boys and a secondary school. Sacred Heart, another largely German parish, began school facilities in 1895. In 1916 the parish opened a coeducational high school under the direction of the Sisters of St. Joseph. The Irish population was served by elementary schools founded in two parishes in the late 19th century; both St. Mary's and St. Patrick's had schools for boys and girls by 1896. In 1893 the Sisters of Providence opened St. Agnes Academy as a secondary school for girls. The school, located in the near downtown area, served girls from any parish. SS. PETER AND PAUL CATHEDRAL parish commemorated the silver jubilee of Bishop JOSEPH CHARTRAND'S ordination by establishing Cathedral High School as a downtown secondary school for boys in 1918. Brothers of the Holy Cross of Notre Dame administered and taught at the school. The Sisters of Providence obtained property from the Stoughton Fletcher estate and began Ladywood School in the northeastern part of the city in 1926. This campus took both day and boarding secondary students. Benedictine

Sisters established another boarding school, Our Lady of Grace, in Beech Grove in 1956.

Dramatic changes took place in parochial schools following World War II. A gradual decline in the number of religious vocations made increased numbers of lay teachers an expensive necessity. Population moved to the suburbs and declining congregations of the older parishes could no longer support parochial schools. Students attending Cathedral and St. Agnes faced time-consuming daily trips. Interest in boarding facilities died. The Sisters of Providence opened Chartrand High School, on the south side of Indianapolis, in 1962. The school was dedicated to the memory of Bishop Joseph Chartrand, a driving force behind Catholic education in Indiana. Shortly after, in 1970, the order merged St. Agnes and Ladywood at the northside campus, eliminating boarding students and the downtown facilities.

Archbishop PAUL SCHULTE championed a plan to provide adequate secondary facilities in each of the city's four deaneries. The East Deanery opened secondary facilities in 1953 with a school named for Father Thomas Scecina of Linton, Indiana, the only priest from the diocese to be killed in action during World War II. "Father Tom" had served St. John's parish before he entered military service in 1940. His courageous record and death is emphasized by the name Scecina Memorial given to the facilities located at 5000 Nowland Avenue. In 1961 Bishop Chatard High School, at 5885 Crittenden Avenue, was opened in the North Deanery. FRANCIS SILAS CHATARD, the first American-born Bishop of Indianapolis, was a strong advocate of Catholic education. During his episcopacy (1898–1918), more than 40 schools were founded in the diocese. In the West Deanery, Cardinal Ritter High School, at 3360 West 30th Street, opened in 1964. JOSEPH E. RITTER, a native of New Albany, served as rector of SS. Peter and Paul Cathedral in Indianapolis before being named the nation's youngest bishop in 1933. He was later Archbishop of St. Louis.

Two schools existed in the South Deanery, and neither was in solid fiscal health. Sacred Heart, renamed Kennedy High School in 1966 to honor the nation's first Roman Catholic president, had years of tradition but poor physical facilities. Chartrand, opened in 1962, had insufficient en-

Jewish children attending Hebrew School, ca. 1950.
[Indiana Historical Society,
Indianapolis Recorder Collection, #C5800]

rollment to justify continued existence. Merger was difficult, but in 1969 students chose Roncalli, the family name of Pope John XXIII, for the consolidation located at 3300 Prague Road.

The Kennedy-Chartrand merger eliminated one high school, but other schools closed and changed. The oldest secondary school, St. John's Academy, closed in 1959, its centennial year. All-female schools were no longer feasible. Our Lady of Grace ended boarding facilities in 1975 and closed entirely in 1977. In 1976 the Sisters of Providence closed Ladywood. All-male schools also disappeared. Cathedral High School, administered as a private rather than parochial institution since 1973, purchased the Ladywood campus on East 56th Street. Cathedral became coeducational and removed the last "downtown" school to the north side. Brebeuf Preparatory School, founded by the Chicago Province of the Society of Jesus as a men's school in 1962, has never been administered by the Diocese of Indianapolis. Like Cathedral, it functions as a private institution rather than under religious direction and is coeducational. In 1992 the Archdiocese of Indianapolis administered schools throughout the southern half of the state: 71 schools in 39 counties. This included four high schools and 29 elementary schools in Marion County. None was administered by religious orders, and only a few priests, brothers, or sisters were among the faculty. The organization of schools in the Indianapolis area parallels the deanery structure of the church.

Nearly 15,000 students attend Roman Catholic schools in Marion County. Non–Roman Catholic students, approximately 12–14 percent of the current enrollment, participate in religion classes and scheduled religious activities. Textbooks and teacher certification are in accordance with Indiana Department of Education requirements. All high schools and most of the elementary schools hold first class commissions. All high schools have music, art, drama, athletic programs, and a wide range of extracurricular activities. Uniforms are not required, but dress codes are enforced. ISTEP testing is administered at all levels, and mean scores for Roman Catholic schools are consistently above the state means.

Twelve consecutive years of declining enrollment in the archdiocesan schools motivated a media blitz in 1989 to increase public awareness of Catholic education. The attempt was renewed in 1991. Newspapers, radio, television, billboards, direct mail campaigns, and videotape presentations were used to emphasize the values of Roman Catholic schools. The campaign resulted in an increase in the archdiocesan enrollment of 0.5 percent during the 1990–1991 school year, growing to 2.54 percent in 1991–1992. The enrollment in Indianapolis schools was up 5.25 percent in 1991–1992.

Although archdiocesan high schools are not intended as strictly college preparatory institutions, 73 percent of the 1991 spring graduates entered a college or university in the fall, compared with 47 percent from INDIANAPOLIS PUBLIC SCHOOLS. More than 90 percent of students who enter the Catholic high schools as freshmen graduate four years later, compared to slightly less than 75 percent for IPS.

Population shifts and court decisions to limit religious activities in public schools encouraged renewed interest in religious education during the late 20th century. Many Protestant congregations, usually conservative in theological interpretation, maintain educational institutions separate from public schools. The Baptists, Methodists, and Presbyterians have not participated in this revitalization, but many individual congregations of those denominations have pre-kindergarten facilities.

A number of institutions in the Indianapolis area are classified as CHRISTIAN SCHOOLS. There is no unified administrative structure or common educational philosophy for such schools. Some are a subsidiary to specific denominational congregations and attract students and administrative personnel from the church itself. Others are affiliated with a larger body. Some affiliations are less binding than others. Most Christian day schools in Indianapolis are guided by conservative theological precepts and follow a strict interpretation of Biblical admonition. Many came into existence following court decisions to remove religious symbolism and celebrations from public schools. No boarding facilities exist in any of the Indianapolis schools, but some provide student transportation. Four Marion County schools are affiliated with the Indiana Association of Christian Schools; three others are members of Associated Christian Schools International. Both of these groups include Independent Baptist Schools in Indiana and serve as liaison to other such institutions throughout the country. Two other schools are members of the National Christian Schools Association, which has headquarters in York, Nebraska. There are currently about a dozen elementary schools and five secondary institutions categorized as Christian day schools.

The Hebrew Academy of Indianapolis has grown steadily since its founding in 1971. Some controversy existed within the Jewish community concerning the school's Orthodox orientation, and the JEWISH FEDERATION OF GREATER INDIANAPOLIS has never fully supported the institution. Nevertheless, the school has grown. In 1971 a primary division opened with eight students. Gradually eight grades and a nursery school were added. High school classes began in 1991 but were discontinued the next year due to insufficient enrollment. The institution, located at 6602 Hoover Road, enrolled 274 in 1992 with tuition of $4,410. The Hebrew Academy, for grades pre-kindergarten through eight, holds continuous commission from the DOE.

SEVENTH-DAY ADVENTIST educational institutions began in Marion County before World War II. There are now two schools in Marion County: Capitol City Church School enrolls students in grades one through eight, and Indianapolis Junior Academy in grades one through ten. Each has a local school board and is responsible to authorities of the Lake Union Region with headquarters in Berrien Springs, Michigan. No Adventist secondary facilities exist in Marion County, but Cicero High School in Hamilton County serves the area. The Adventist schools are not accredited by DOE, but are responsible for national standards set by Seventh-day Adventist administrators.

The Indiana Department of Education considers about 70 Marion County educational institutions, ranging from preschools to secondary schools, as religious schools. Not all religious schools choose to be commissioned by the Department of Education because they prefer more control over choice of textbooks and teacher licensing requirements.

Educational costs are a critical factor in religious schools. Parents play a vital role in fundraising efforts. Faculty salaries are often 20 to 25 percent lower than in public schools. Students may assist with maintenance tasks by emptying wastebaskets, washing chalkboards, clearing lunch tables, or sweeping floors. Economic necessity and emphasis on stewardship mandated recycling and other conservation methods in religious schools long before public awareness encouraged such efforts. All schools make some effort to provide assistance for capable students who cannot afford full tuition costs. Tuition and financial assistance vary widely from system to system.

In August, 1991, Golden Rule Insurance Company introduced a pilot program to test the feasibility of providing parents with a choice between public and private education. The company committed $400,000 per year to the Educational Choice Charitable Trust for a three-year period and promised to seek additional voluntary funding. The goal was to provide financial assistance for 500 students in the Indianapolis area to allow them to attend a private or religious school. Seven hundred students enrolled that year, and another 200 were placed on a waiting list. For 1992–1993 the program obtained a total of $520,000, and provided assistance for 925 students. More than 95 percent of the students enrolled in religious schools, 60 percent in Roman Catholic institutions.

All schools include extracurricular activities appropriate to their religious connection. Enrollment is not always restricted to a particular religious body, but students and parents are required to acknowledge the school's affiliation.

In 1942 the INDIANA HIGH SCHOOL ATHLETIC ASSOCIATION opened full membership to all public, private, parochial, black, and institutional high schools of the state offering and maintaining three or four years of high school work. Religious schools have participated in IHSAA competitions since then. Male and female teams have won championships in volleyball, football, tennis, and golf.

Religion has been an important component of education since the earliest days of settlement in Indianapolis. During the 19th century denominational differences motivated the establishment of many separate schools, most of which closed before the mid–20th century. Court decisions that enforced separation of religious values from school experiences triggered the founding of new schools by conservative Christian bodies. Parochial schools decreased in number and control of Roman Catholic schools shifted from religious orders to administration by the Archdiocese of Indianapolis. Enrollment in Christian and non-Christian institutions has increased over the past quarter century. As Indianapolis enters the 21st century, many residents will pay thousands of dollars in tuition each year because they are committed to education based on religious values.

HELEN JEAN MCCLELLAND NUGENT
WITH SHANE R. FALLIS, ARTHUR D. TERHUNE,
TIMOTHY A. O'SHEA, AND JOHN D. PROHASKA
Franklin College of Indiana

Sister Mary Barromeo Brown, *History of the Sisters of Providence of St. Mary-of-the-Woods*, Vol. I (New York, Boston, Cincinnati, and Chicago: Benzinger Brothers, 1949); Eli Lilly, *History of the Little Church on the Circle: Christ Church Parish, 1837–1955* (Indianapolis, 1957); "Zion Lutheran Church: 125 Years of Growth with the Grace of God" (unpublished congregational history, 1978).

Schools, Social Services in. One of the most dramatic developments in American education during the 20th century has been the steady expansion of a wide array of social services provided for students. All types of services aimed at fostering physical and psychological well-being in students, from health care and hot lunches to career and psychological counseling, now commonplace, are evidence of the ever-increasing responsibility American society has placed on educational institutions. The schools of Indianapolis reflect this national trend.

In 19th-century Indianapolis private charity organizations provided social services for school-age children. Children were the main beneficiaries of the majority of charitable agencies in Indianapolis during the 19th century. These benevolent, voluntary groups raised funds for and administered a number of institutions that filled needs not met by public agencies. In the 1840s both the INDIANA SCHOOL FOR THE BLIND and the INDIANA SCHOOL FOR THE DEAF were established. Other agencies provided food, clothing, and shelter for children in need. By the late 19th century various civic and organizational leaders saw the need for greater coordination of charitable services to avoid duplication of effort and increase financial efficiency. In 1879 a number of the leading benevolent organizations in Indianapolis joined to form the CHARITY ORGANIZATION SOCIETY (COS). The COS provided an umbrella organization for the coordination of charitable services and served as a clearinghouse for information. Charity organizations in Indianapolis and nationwide reflected the business impulse toward efficiency, organization, and rationalization in late 19th-century America.

The quest for organization and centralization also preoccupied professional educators in the first two decades of the 20th century. Like business organizations, school systems were growing rapidly. Reaching as many students as possible was a prime concern of professional educators. In Indianapolis the public school system created the Department of Attendance and Census to monitor the number of school-age children in the population at large as compared to the number of children actually attending schools. The Indianapolis municipal government passed a series of compulsory attendance laws that, by 1920, covered all children between the ages of 5 and 16. The Department of Attendance and Census had the responsibility of investigating failures to conform to the requirements of attendance laws.

The desire for efficiency combined with the new social theories developed under the label "Progressive" education to provide an impetus for schools to widen the scope of their activity. Many reformers believed that American society, being in the throes of massive and bewildering change, needed more guidance from professionals trained in understanding and analyzing community needs. In the early 20th century many Americans also placed a heightened emphasis on the role of education in molding children into citizens able to function wisely and properly in the new organizational world. Administrators and teachers welcomed this enlarged role as confirmation of their professional status. Many educators believed that schools occupied a crucial position in alleviating many of the problems of rapid industrialization, such as truancy, juvenile delinquency, poor health care and habits, and family disintegration.

This shift from pure organizational efficiency toward discovering and eliminating problems that affected student performance and attendance in schools was reflected in the 1921 decision by the Indianapolis public school system to change the name of the Department of Attendance and Census to the Social Service Department. Professionally trained case workers replaced truant officers as representatives of the schools' desire to reach as many children as possible. Failure to attend or poor performance in school was no longer looked upon as a moral shortcoming to be transformed through charity or punished by law enforcement, but as a problem caused by the dislocation and alienation resulting from modern society. By using modern social work techniques, educators could discover, analyze, and remedy these problems.

The early work of the Social Service Department concentrated on a number of areas. Visiting teachers conducted home visits to evaluate children's needs. If necessary, visiting teachers referred families to particular COS agencies. The department was responsible for issuing employment certificates to school-age children after determining family income needs. Child labor laws limited the number of jobs available to school-age children in the 1920s, leading the department to develop a scholarship program that provided carfare, lunch money, and textbooks to students who otherwise could not afford to attend school. Various COS agencies collected money for these scholarships but the Department of Social Services administered its distribution.

During the Progressive era educators in Indianapolis worked with a number of other agencies dedicated to social reform in the growing city. Vocational, remedial, and language classes were sponsored by the school system and taught by public school teachers at the AMERICAN SETTLEMENT for European immigrants and their children and FLANNER HOUSE for the growing African-American population. The YMCA and the YWCA sponsored Hi-Y clubs for high school students. The Public Health Nursing Association provided health services in the schools.

The pattern of providing social services in the schools of Indianapolis has continued to expand throughout the 20th century. School programs aimed at disadvantaged youth and social work methods, such as casework that examines the myriad factors influencing a student's performance and behavior, have proliferated and become integral to the Indianapolis school system. The various dynamic programs developed by the schools aimed at curbing juvenile delinquency, promoting health care, and providing guidance are a measure of how effective Progressive educators were at convincing the public that the schools' role goes far beyond academics. Since the beginning of this century educating students no longer means simply imparting knowledge but also aiding in their socialization. The expansion of social service in the schools is also a measure of the need of institutions in a highly complex, modern, industrial society to provide services that once were the responsibility of the family, community, and charity organizations.

ALEXANDER URBIEL
Indiana University, Bloomington

Schrader, Christian (Jan. 6, 1842–Feb. 20, 1920). Businessman and amateur artist who produced sketches of early Indianapolis. Schrader's German-born father worked on the CENTRAL CANAL and NATIONAL ROAD. From 1843 to 1847, the Schraders lived in a small eastside German neighborhood on Alabama Street facing

Christian Schrader drawing of the East Market House which operated from the 1840s until the 1860s on the site now occupied by the City Market.
[Indiana State Library]

Courthouse Square and from 1849 to 1880 across town in a small frame house half-a-square north of the old STATE HOUSE. In a northwest room of the State House between 1853 and 1860 Schrader received his art education by watching JACOB COX, James Bolivar Dunlap, and Henry Waugh paint temperance panoramas. For practical reasons he decided against an artistic career and went into the china painting and purveying business, opening a shop in 1872 on Washington Street that he ran until his retirement in 1909.

In a 60–year span Schrader had witnessed the total rebuilding of the city. When he retired he decided to record Indianapolis as it had existed in his boyhood up to the building of the Union Depot in 1853, the structure that symbolized the beginning of the boom. Schrader drew semblances of 178 residences, shops, churches, and manufactories within the MILE SQUARE. Since few other visual records existed, Schrader relied on his memory, which the *Indianapolis Star* described as "remarkable." When his recollections were clear, his drawings were detailed and highly finished; when more vague, the drawings were little more than thumbnail sketches. Nevertheless, the 113 drawings and 12 paintings given by Schrader's daughters to the INDIANA STATE LIBRARY a decade after the artist's death in Madison, Indiana, provide an invaluable, if unverifiable, catalogue of antebellum Indianapolis.

MARTIN KRAUSE

Indianapolis Remembered: Christian Schrader's Sketches of Early Indianapolis (Indianapolis: Indiana Historical Bureau, 1987).

Schulte, Paul Clarence (Mar. 18, 1890–
Feb. 17, 1984). Second Catholic Archbishop of
Indianapolis (1946–1970). Born in Frederick-
town, Missouri, Schulte was ordained on June 11,
1915. He ministered at the old St. Louis Cathedral
and wrote its history, and was consecrated bishop
of Leavenworth, Kansas, in 1937. Transferred to
Indianapolis, the tall, lean, and dignified Schulte
was installed archbishop on October 10, 1946. He
held that position longer than any other bishop in
the 20th century.

Schulte organized 18 new parishes in response to the increasing Catholic population in
Marion County after World War II. Strongly committed to Catholic education, he authorized five
new archdiocesan high schools (Scecina, Brute
Latin, Chatard, Chartrand, and Ritter) and the
opening of Our Lady of Grace Academy and
Brebeuf Preparatory High School between 1953
and 1964. Elementary school enrollment increased during his tenure from 13,877 (1946) to
37,920 (1965). Since Indianapolis was one of the
largest cities in the United States without a Catholic college for men, he asked the Sisters of St.
Francis to open their Cold Spring Road campus to
men (1954), making MARIAN COLLEGE the state's
first Catholic coeducational college.

Schulte's episcopate was a time of growth in
an atmosphere of stability and traditional conservatism. Ironically, the archbishop participated in
the Second Vatican Council (1962–1965), which
promoted change in the name of adaptation and
modernization. In his last years Schulte was troubled by questioning of traditional beliefs and practices, liturgical innovation, clerical resignations,
and a general decline in church discipline.

On January 14, 1970, Schulte retired and
was appointed titular archbishop of Elicroca. He
donated to Marian College his materials on the
history of the church in the Midwest and his
working papers as a Vatican Council participant.
Residing in St. Augustine's Home, he died there at
age 94, nearly the oldest bishop in the country,
and was interred in the mausoleum chapel of Calvary Cemetery.

JAMES J. DIVITA
Marian College

Schwarz, Rudolf (1846–Apr. 14, 1912).
Sculptor. Born in Vienna, Austria, Schwarz at-
tended the Vienna Academy of Art for six years.
Upon graduating in 1889, he became a student of
Joseph Kaffsack and later of Geiger and Eberlein,
all prominent sculptors in Berlin.

Schwarz came to Indianapolis in December,
1897, when he was commissioned by architect
Bruno Schmitz to carve the stone "War" and
"Peace" groups at the foot of the SOLDIERS AND
SAILORS MONUMENT on the Circle. Criticized for
making his figures too Germanic in appearance,
Schwarz altered the original design by "shaving"
the soldiers' beards and anglicizing their faces. He
also carved two smaller figures, named "Dying"
and "Return," on the east and west sides of the
monument as well as the soldiers positioned at
each corner.

Other works by Schwarz located in Indianapolis include the statue of Governor OLIVER P.
MORTON at the east entrance to the STATE HOUSE,
a monument for Mrs. Albertina Allen Forrest in
CROWN HILL CEMETERY, as well as many bronze
works for mausoleums at Crown Hill. Schwarz
also continuously taught classes in sculpting at
the JOHN HERRON ART INSTITUTE.

Schwarz is known for at least 30 other works
throughout Indiana, many of them war memorials. He created a few pieces for Wabash College in
Crawfordsville. He also did some out-of-state
commissions, including the statue of Governor
Hazen Pingree at Michigan's State House and a
bronze tablet for the Americans of German Ancestry at Cincinnati's Memorial Hall.

For the statue of Pingree, Schwarz revived
the lost art of wax casting and used this method
to make the first bronze cast ever done in Indiana.
While this process became a trademark of his
bronze pieces, Schwarz lost money on almost all
of his commissions due to imperfections in this
casting method. His Hoosier friends Carl Lieber
and Theodore Stempfel tried to help his career by
building a studio, securing work, and managing
his financial affairs, but Schwarz so consistently
underbid his work that he died in poverty.

MICHELLE D. HALE

Theodore Stempfel, *Ghosts of the Past* (Indianapolis, 1936).

Scott, William Edouard (1884–May 15, 1964). African-American artist. Born in Indianapolis, Scott attended Public School 23 and MANUAL HIGH SCHOOL, where he studied under OTTO STARK. After high school, Scott spent a year working and studying at JOHN HERRON ART INSTITUTE before enrolling at the Art Institute of Chicago. In his fourth and fifth years at the institute he won the Frederick Magnus Brand Prize for pictorial composition.

Scott left for France in 1909 where he studied at the Academie Julian and with black painter Henry Ossawa Tanner. During this time he had three paintings accepted at the Salon des Beaux Arts at Toquet. His painting *La Pauvre Voisine* was accepted at the great spring salon in Paris in 1912 and was purchased by the Argentine Republic for $600. That same year Scott had an exhibit of 26 paintings in Indianapolis at the studio of Otto Stark.

In 1913 he had paintings accepted by the Royal Academy in London and the Salon at La Loque, France, and accepted a commission from INDIANAPOLIS PUBLIC SCHOOLS to paint murals in elementary schools. In 1915 he was the only black among a group of artists (principally Herron alumni) commissioned to create murals for the Indianapolis City Hospital (now WISHARD MEMORIAL HOSPITAL). His 1912 painting, *Rainy Day Etaples*, was purchased in 1913 by a group of black Indianapolis residents and presented to the Herron Art Institute for its collection.

The Harmon Foundation presented Scott in 1927 with a special gold medal for distinctive achievement in fine art. He received a Rosewald fellowship to study in Haiti in 1931 and while there completed over 100 works. The president of Haiti purchased ten of Scott's paintings and in 1936 presented him with a national medal of honor. In 1943 his sketch for his mural, *Frederick Douglass Appealing to President Lincoln*, was selected by the National Anonymous Mural Competition as one of seven murals for the Recorder of Deeds Building in Washington, D.C.

WILLIAM E. TAYLOR
Afro-American Studies
Indiana University–Purdue University
Indianapolis

William E. Taylor, "William Edouard Scott: Indianapolis Painter," *Black History News & Notes*, No. 33 (Aug., 1988), 4–7.

Scottish Rite Cathedral (650 North Meridian Street). Headquarters building for the Scottish Rite Valley of Indianapolis, a Masonic organization. The structure, the largest Scottish Rite cathedral in the world, faces the greenspace on the northern end of the INDIANA WORLD WAR MEMORIAL PLAZA. Designed by architect-member George F. Schreiber in 1926—a time of great membership growth for the organization—the building was completed in 1929 at a cost of $2.5 million. It is of a basic Tudor design with Gothic ornamentation, and is 330 feet long and 120 feet wide. The entire building is laid out in multiples of 33 feet, symbolizing the 33 years of Christ's life. The most spectacular exterior feature is the Gothic tower that rises 212 feet above the sidewalk level on the front of the cathedral and which houses a carillon of 54 bells, one of the largest carillons in the United States.

Upon entering the building one finds the polished marble floor set with a bronze centerpiece depicting the signs of the Zodiac and the emblems of four principal degrees of the Scottish Rite. The chandelier overhead is cast bronze, centered in a room that is a perfect 33–foot cube. The main lobby, 66 feet square, also has a marble floor with walls and beams of white oak. North of the lobby

Completed in 1929 at a cost of $2.5 million, the Scottish Rite Cathedral was placed on the National Register of Historic Places in 1983.
[Scottish Rite Cathedral, Indianapolis]

are the working offices and the Lodge of Perfection room; a lounge, 99 feet long, is to the south. A library adjacent to the lounge is an octagon 33 feet in diameter, walled with white oak bookcases. West of the lobby is a grand staircase, 33 feet wide, leading up to the ballroom and down to the dining hall. The eight art glass windows in the east wall are dedicated to medicine, law, music, painting, sculpture, electricity, engineering, and education, while those on the west wall represent several degrees of the Scottish Rite.

On the second floor is a ballroom, famous for its "floating floor" that is laid on springs and felt for resilience. It is two stories high, with a balcony running around three sides. A central crystal chandelier, suspended on a winch for lowering, has 187 incandescent bulbs and weighs 2,500 pounds. At the north end of the second floor is an auditorium with 1,100 permanent seats and an arena 33 feet square. The walls are paneled with curly Russian white oak, with a vaulted, double hammer beamed ceiling.

The building, which was listed on the National Register of Historic Places in 1983, is open daily for tours by nonmembers.

H. ROLL McLAUGHLIN, F.A.I.A.

Scudder, Caleb (Jan. 18, 1795–Mar. 6, 1866). Mayor of Indianapolis, 1851–1854, Whig. Born in Trenton, New Jersey, where he learned the cabinetmaking trade, Scudder settled with his family in Dayton, Ohio, in 1820, and moved to Indianapolis in 1821. He established a home and cabinet shop on West Washington Street that was the scene of a number of Indianapolis firsts: the first SUNDAY SCHOOL was held there in April, 1823; and the formal organization of First Presbyterian (July, 1823) and Third Presbyterian (September, 1851) churches took place there. He was the first captain of the first fire company, the Marion Fire, Hose and Protective Company, 1835. His other business interests included a cigar factory, a cotton mill, and cotton oil business. Examples of his fine cabinetry still exist and are highly valuable.

In 1838 he was a councilman from the fifth ward, and he served as a justice of the peace for many years. Upon the resignation of Mayor HOR-ATIO C. NEWCOMB in November, 1851, the city council appointed Scudder to the post and he won election as mayor in 1853. Apparently he was a poor administrator; his popularity declined toward the end of his second term and his defeat in 1854 was of landslide proportions.

WILLIAM F. GULDE

Jacob Piatt Dunn, *Greater Indianapolis* (Chicago, 1910).

Sculpture. Public sculpture in Indianapolis, often quite visible but largely unnoticed, through the years has followed trends typical throughout the state. It may be categorized into three broad areas—commemorative, religious, and aesthetic—although some pieces defy classification.

Commemorative sculpture first became popular after the Civil War with a proliferation of monuments to Indiana's soldiers in towns and cemeteries throughout the state. Indianapolis was no exception. Dominating downtown as well as MONUMENT CIRCLE, the gargantuan SOLDIERS AND SAILORS MONUMENT was completed in 1902. Wars preceding the Civil War are included on the monument; later conflicts have their own memorials. World War I is commemorated with an imposing building that includes heroic sculptured figures in a Classical frieze, as well as the bronze giant *Pro Patria* (1929) by Henry Hering. Hering also designed the four bronze relief panels on the Obelisk north of the Indiana World War Memorial and the seated figure of Abraham Lincoln (1934) in UNIVERSITY PARK.

Indianapolis contains numerous heroic bronzes honoring national notables with Indiana connections, with Lincoln the most obvious example. A very different depiction from that of Hering stands outside the INDIANA GOVERNMENT CENTER, the *Young Abe Lincoln* (1963) by David K. Rubins. The STATE HOUSE grounds, the Circle, and University Park have the greatest concentrations of such statues. Among the first Indiana figures to be immortalized in bronze was the unlikely Schuyler Colfax, a piece no doubt more important as a very early work (1887) of the famous sculptor Lorado Taft.

Bronze versions of Civil War governor OLIVER P. MORTON are prominent both at the State House and on the Circle. These works are by noted sculptors RUDOLF SCHWARZ and JOHN H. MAHONEY, respectively. Schwarz was the primary sculptor of the Soldiers and Sailors Monument. Two of the surrounding statues on the Circle are Mahoney's work: George Rogers Clark and William Henry Harrison. Perhaps the most interesting commemorative sculptures honor anonymous figures, such as the *Pioneer Family* (1924) in FOUNTAIN SQUARE by MYRA REYNOLDS RICHARDS, one of a handful of female sculptors working in Indiana in the early 20th century. John Szabo sculpted a detailed statue of a coal miner, erected on the west lawn of the State House in 1969.

CROWN HILL CEMETERY is a sometimes overlooked collection of sculptural art, either commemorative or religious in theme, such as the Forrest monument by Rudolf Schwarz, depicting a woman in repose. Other cemeteries in the area, too, are repositories of sculpture; a fine tribute to the World War II heroes, *The Four Chaplains*, stands in Washington Park Cemetery. Religious sculpture may also be found at churches and religious institutions. Some particularly fine examples include Joseph Quarmby's *St. John Pondering the Scriptures* (1871) on ST. JOHN CATHOLIC CHURCH downtown and Adolph Wolter's *Door of the Reformer* (1959) on SECOND PRESBYTERIAN CHURCH.

Aesthetic sculpture—or sculpture for art's sake—was almost nonexistent in the sense we know it today before World War II. Exceptions include Stirling Calder's Depew Fountain (1919) in University Park. Another example was the collection of ornate ironworks in WOODRUFF PLACE, where lifesize lions guarded every entrance. Once there were nine fountains, three of which, since recast, today grace the intersections at Cross Drive.

Until about 1930 buildings often sported noteworthy decorative sculpture, using Classical or other "artistic" themes. The cornice line of the English Hotel and Theater on the Circle featured medallions sculpted by Henry M. Saunders depicting members of the English family and several Indiana governors. The surviving medallions appear today as individual sculptures in a half dozen county seats in Indiana. The heroic Greek goddesses that once graced the old Marion County courthouse suffered a similar fate. Two stand as part of ELMER TAFLINGER's *Ruins* in HOLLIDAY PARK, a work that features another architectural sculpture, Karl Bitter's *The Races of Man*, from a demolished building in New York.

The 1960s witnessed a movement for public art, much of it abstract, such as David von Schlegell's untitled giant "L"s erected in the late 1970s on the IUPUI campus. An even more controversial and largely unloved work is Mark di Survero's *Snowplow* (1972), first erected at the Indiana Convention Center, later relegated to a remote location on West 30th Street before plans were made to move the piece onto the grounds of the INDIANAPOLIS MUSEUM OF ART (IMA). The IMA, the INDIANAPOLIS ART CENTER, the Eiteljorg Museum, and even THE CHILDREN'S MUSEUM all exhibit collections of modern outdoor sculpture. Glenna Goodacre's *Tug O' War* (1988), an exuberant representational work, is on display at The Children's Museum.

Corporations have commissioned much of the city's public sculpture. Among the most controversial is *Reaching* (1987) by Zeno Frudakis at downtown's Capital Center, a sculpture that consists of a nude male and female. A companion piece, *Flying*, stands on the other side of the building. John Spaulding's joyful *Jazz on the Avenue* (1989) stands at the INDIANA AVENUE entrance to today's LOCKEFIELD GARDENS. Corporate-backed art continues in the 1990s, as represented by Lyle London's abstract *Equipoise 14* in front of the newly constructed Indiana Insurance Company building.

GLORY-JUNE GREIFF

Seals and Flags. The county commissioners adopted the current Seal of Marion County, officially the county's third such emblem, on December 8, 1841. The seal is circular, with the words "Commissioners Seal of Marion County, Indiana" printed around the margin. Inside the circle are representations of a basket of fruit and a Berkshire pig. The basket of fruit symbolizes improvements in agriculture, especially fruit production, during the early 1800s. The Berkshire pig represents the region's prominence in livestock raising and pork production at the time of the seal's adoption.

The Seal of the City of Indianapolis first adopted by the Common Council on June 7, 1847, was readopted under the Charter of 1891. It displays traditional governmental symbols: an American eagle holding a set of balance scales in its beak. The 1847 version of the seal showed the eagle perched atop a globe.

There have been three versions of an official flag for the city of Indianapolis. A commission appointed by Mayor Lew Shank approved the first design in 1911, but the design was not adopted by the Common Council as the city's official flag. The council did approve a revised version of the design in 1915, but no actual flags were made until 1960.

The design for the third and current official flag of the city of Indianapolis was developed by Roger Gohl, then a student at the HERRON SCHOOL OF ART, for a contest held in 1962. Gohl placed a white cross with a circle at its center on a blue field, with a red star in the center of the circle. The new flag first flew from the City-County Building on November 7, 1963.

The star symbolizes Indianapolis' status as Indiana's capital city and center of commerce. The circle represents MONUMENT CIRCLE at the center of downtown. The white cross against the blue field symbolizes the intersection of Meridian and Washington streets, as well as an Indianapolis nickname, "Crossroads of America." The red, white, and blue colors represent the patriotism of the city's residents.

RICHARD S. LOFTIN

Second Baptist Church.

Second Baptist Church. First African-American Baptist congregation in Indianapolis. Organized in 1846 by a Cincinnati missionary, the congregation originally met in a home at what is now West and Ohio streets. In 1850 the church purchased a lot and erected a sanctuary on Missouri between New York and Ohio streets. Church membership grew slowly, hampered by many internal disputes and the lack of strong and stable leadership.

In 1857 MOSES BROYLES joined Second Baptist and was elected pastor. Under Broyles' leader-

ship the church erased its debt, made repairs to the building, and slowly began to attract a larger membership. Since many of the African-Americans migrating to Indianapolis during and after the Civil War were BAPTISTS, the church continued to grow steadily. By 1867 the congregation relocated to West Michigan Street near the Central Canal and built a sanctuary capable of seating 1,200. During this growth, Second Baptist sponsored several other local black Baptist congregations including Mount Zion and New Bethel Baptist churches.

In the decades after Broyles' death in 1882 the church declined to the point that the sanctuary was condemned in the early 1900s. The struggling congregation started building a structure on West Michigan Street in 1912, but it was not completed until 1920. Under Rev. B. J. F. Westbrook, minister between 1919 and 1932, the church experienced some stability.

J. Hall, who succeeded Westbrook and served Second Baptist between 1932 and 1978, helped the church revive, with membership peaking at 2,500. But in Hall's later years city development began to hurt the congregation by forcing members to move from the surrounding neighborhoods. In the late 1980s the congregation decided to sell the church and relocate. Developers purchased the building in 1992 and renovated it into the Westbrook Church Condominiums. The congregation has since moved to a westside location, and as of 1993 membership was growing and programming was expanding.

MICHELLE D. HALE

Second Bapist Church Collection, Indiana Historical Society.

Second Presbyterian Church. One of the city's oldest churches and now one of its largest, Second Presbyterian was officially organized on November 19, 1838, by 15 members who departed the "Old School" First Presbyterian Church. The immediate cause of the split lay in intradenominational disputes between the stricter Calvinism of the "Old School" and the "New School's" emphasis on human initiative in salvation.

HENRY WARD BEECHER was the first pastor, serving 1839–1849. Under his dramatic preaching, the church grew from 32 parishioners to well over 200 and took a prominent part in the frontier civic life of the state capital. Many members of the judiciary attended Beecher's messages on personal faith, slavery, TEMPERANCE, and education. The church's first permanent building, dedicated in 1840, stood on the northwest corner of Market Street and the Circle. Nicknamed the "Pepper-box Church" because of the shape of its steeple, it resembled a New England–style church. The founding years set patterns which have continued down to the present: a prominent role in civic life, liberal theology, and learned and eloquent preaching.

Outstanding leadership helped Second Presbyterian adjust its ministries to post–CIVIL WAR urban conditions. The Reverend Hanford Edson (d. 1920), pastor from 1864 to 1873, brought a vision for the whole city, as was shown by his influential call for a public library in Indianapolis. During his pastorate the church constructed a neo-Gothic edifice with a spire over 160 feet tall on the northeast corner of Vermont and Pennsylvania streets. Starting new churches and missions was characteristic of this period. By the 20th century, Second Presbyterian had been instrumental in planting seven churches or missions. Programs combining evangelism and social services such as the Exposition Sunday School, opened in 1867 and later renamed the Peck Mission, and the Mayer Chapel on the south side, beginning its ministries in 1893, represented responses to new urban problems.

In 1921 the Reverend Jean S. Milner (d. 1964) began a long pastorate that lasted until 1960. In a series of evening lectures he opposed fundamentalism on the issue of evolution, and his book *The Sky Is Red* (1935) represented the modernist position. Under his leadership the congregation grew to 1,816 members by its centennial celebration in 1938. On October 4, 1959, the church began services in its current building at 7700 North Meridian Street. The large French Gothic building has several fine stained glass windows and a powerful pipe organ.

The pastorate from 1964 to 1973 of the Reverend William H. Hudnut III, later mayor of Indianapolis, reflected the moderate but active stance

Second Presbyterian Church in 1994.
[Indiana Historical Society.
Photo by Kim Charles Ferrill]

of the congregation toward the social upheavals of the 1960s. Hudnut helped to guide the church through changes within the Presbyterian denomination and on issues such as race relations and the Vietnam War. Continuity with the congregation's traditional blend of social concern and evangelism was also exemplified by the Reverend Richard S. Armstrong, pastor from 1975–1979, with his Ambassadors visitation program and ideas on service evangelism. As of 1992, the congregation numbered 3,200 members.

WILLIAM L. ISLEY, JR.

George W. Geib, *Lives Touched by Faith: Second Presbyterian Church, 150 Years* (Indianapolis, 1988).

Select Schools. INDIANAPOLIS PUBLIC SCHOOLS (IPS) student assignment system. In trying to combat continuing trends of poor student achievement, lack of parent and community involvement, and segregation in certain schools, IPS officials under Superintendent Shirl E. Gilbert II devised a new student assignment plan. Select Schools was approved by U.S. District Court Judge S. Hugh Dillin in February, 1993, and implemented that fall. Labeled a "limited choice" plan, it allowed parents to identify their preferences for their children's school within the IPS district on the basis of building capacities and federal court-ordered racial guidelines.

The plan divided the IPS district into three regions and converted all junior high schools to middle schools. Parents could choose their school preferences from anywhere in the district, but were required to provide transportation to a school out of their home district. Children living in the immediate neighborhood of a school were guaranteed entrance to that school if they chose to go there. Areas mandated for busing to suburban schools would continue to be so. All schools were to develop a unique focus or feature to their curriculum, with IPS officials monitoring the popularity and success of the various programs and allocating resources accordingly.

The plan was very controversial during its early planning and operation. Some school board members and the teachers' union were against spending over $16 million to implement the plan, which included a large informational campaign, transportation expenses, and the middle school conversions, especially with the school district already millions of dollars in debt. After student assignments were announced in May, 1993, many parents, mostly white, protested their children's assignments, some even removing their children from the school district. Additionally, there was widespread confusion in assignments and bus routes, and IPS officials had to reconfigure the system several times throughout September. As of late 1993 IPS planned to continue the Select Schools program.

MICHELLE D. HALE

Selfridge, Reynolds L. (Sandy) (Sept. 30, 1898–Oct. 16, 1974). Landscape and portrait painter. Reynolds Selfridge was born in Jasonville, Indiana. After graduating from high school, he attended DePauw University in Greencastle, Indiana, and later studied at the JOHN HER-RON ART INSTITUTE with WILLIAM FORSYTH. His art education also took him to Provincetown, Massachusetts, where he was a student of Charles Hawthorne. In February, 1926, Selfridge joined the art teaching faculty of ARSENAL TECHNICAL HIGH SCHOOL; and, in 1928, he became an art instructor at Herron.

Primarily an oil painter, Selfridge's work was well balanced and possessed a keen sense of color. He exhibited in a number of juried shows throughout his career, including the HOOSIER SALON, Indiana State Fair, and Indiana Artists Club art competitions. He produced his most successful work during the 1920s and 1930s. At the annual exhibitions of Indiana artists at Herron, he won the $200 Landon Prize for his painting *Old Mill* in 1926, and in 1929 he received the Holcomb Prize for his work *Dinty's Home*.

Selfridge's work is located in both private and public art collections. Four of his canvases are in the INDIANAPOLIS MUSEUM OF ART: *Street Scene*, *In the Park*, *Monhegan, Maine*, and *East Coast U.S.A.*

FRANK N. OWINGS, JR.

_____

Peter Hastings Falk, ed., *Who Was Who in American Art* (Madison, Conn., 1985); Indianapolis Museum of Art, registrar's office and library vertical file.

Selleck, Roda E. (1847–Nov. 15, 1924). Art teacher and artist. A native of Michigan, Selleck taught 43 years for the Indianapolis public school system, 40 of them at Indianapolis High School (later SHORTRIDGE HIGH SCHOOL). Initially hired as a drawing teacher, Selleck also trained her students in watercolor and charcoal, as well as art history and art appreciation. Dedicated to students and art, Selleck often stayed at the school until the early morning monitoring the pottery kiln. She instructed a generation of Indiana artists and craftsmen, as well as being an accomplished artist herself and serving on the board of directors of the JOHN HERRON ART INSTITUTE. Prior to its conversion to a junior high school, the Shortridge High School building at 34th and Meridian streets housed the Roda Selleck Art Gallery, named in her honor.

STACEY NICHOLAS

Sells, Dallas W., Jr. (Oct. 3, 1919–Mar. 20, 1993). United Auto Workers and AFL-CIO leader. Born in Anderson, Indiana, Sells came of age with the emerging industrial union movement of the 1930s. He attended General Motors Institute and was employed as an industrial electrician at Delco-Remy in Anderson. Following two years' wartime service in the U.S. Navy, Sells became increasingly active in UAW Local 662, serving as president from 1951 to 1953. In 1954 he was elected state president of the Congress of Industrial Organizations (CIO) and, after its merger with the American Federation of Labor, headed the combined Indiana AFL-CIO from 1958 to 1968.

Active in public affairs and in the Democratic party, Sells worked to repeal the state's "right-to-work" statute following its 1957 passage. This law, which prohibited employers and unions from contractually requiring that union-represented workers maintain union membership, was repealed in 1965. Sells also fought, unsuccessfully, enactment of the sales tax in Indiana.

Following the UAW's 1968 break with the national AFL-CIO, a schism brought on by national policy and personality conflicts, Sells resigned as president of the Indiana AFL-CIO. He became legislative representative for UAW Region 3, spanning Indiana and Kentucky, and later moved to Detroit as a Regional Coordinator for the UAW's Community Action Program. In 1971 he was appointed to the unexpired term of Ray Berndt as director of Region 3 and was thereafter elected to that position until his 1984 retirement.

Sells served dozens of community, charitable, governmental, civil rights, and educational organizations, frequently as president or chair. Known for these commitments, for his biting wit, and for his abstinence from alcohol, tobacco, and profanity, Sells was widely considered the premier leader in the post–World War II era of Indiana labor.

JAMES WALLIHAN
Division of Labor Studies
Indiana University–Purdue University,
Indianapolis

Senate Avenue YMCA. African-American branch of the Indianapolis YMCA. Early in

Senate Avenue YMCA, one of the largest and most active African-American Y's in the nation, opened in 1913. Dignitaries attending the dedication included (in front row, from left) George Knox, Madam C. J. Walker, Booker T. Washington, Alex Manning, R. W. Bullock, and Thomas Taylor. Standing in the second row are Freeman B. Ransom and Joseph Ward. [Indiana Historical Society, Madam C. J. Walker Collection, #C2137]

1900 white officials of the Indianapolis YMCA asked the national association for help in establishing a separate branch for the city's black population. Jesse E. Moorland, one of two black officials of the national YMCA, visited Indianapolis and recommended the preliminary organization of a "Young Men's Band." In October, 1900, Henry L. Hummons and Dan H. Brown, two African-American physicians, gathered a small group of black men at the Ninth Presbyterian Church to discuss the lack of "wholesome" recreational facilities. After consulting the secretary of the city's white YMCA, the group established a "Young Men's Prayer Band" in December, 1900. The Indiana YMCA recognized the group in March, 1902, and in 1910 the "Young Men's Prayer Band" became the black YMCA of Indianapolis.

During the first decade of its existence the group met in private homes, various churches, and the Flanner Guild, a deserted neighborhood house. In 1910 Julius Rosenwald, president of Sears, Roebuck & Company, offered to contribute $25,000 to every African-American YMCA able to raise $75,000 for a building. In October, 1911, black and white YMCA members launched a fund-raising campaign in Indianapolis. Within ten days they had received pledges exceeding

$100,000. In October, 1912, the cornerstone of the black YMCA building was laid at Michigan Street and Senate Avenue and in July, 1913, Booker T. Washington dedicated the structure.

The Senate Avenue YMCA offered a variety of cultural, recreational, religious, and physical exercise programs, as well as educational classes and dormitory facilities. YMCA officials assisted school teachers in providing black boys with vocational guidance and negotiated with white employers and black employees to promote better race relations. In 1904 the Senate Avenue YMCA initiated the "Monster Meetings," an annual series of public lectures that brought nationally known speakers such as Paul Robeson, W.E.B. Du Bois, Eleanor Roosevelt, Adam Clayton Powell, and Thurgood Marshall to Indianapolis.

Throughout the first 50 years of its existence the Senate Avenue branch had the largest membership of any African-American YMCA in the country. Membership rose steadily, from 17 in 1904 to nearly 3,000 during World War II. In 1946 the national YMCA ended its policy of segregation and urged local branches to integrate their facilities. In December, 1950, the Indianapolis YMCA dropped the word "Negro" from its bylaws. Although no longer segregated, the Senate Avenue YMCA continued to serve a predominantly black membership even after it moved to a new location at West 10th Street and Fall Creek Parkway in 1959 and changed its name to the Fall Creek YMCA.

NINA MJAGKIJ
Ball State University

"The Indianapolis 'Y'," *The Crisis* (Mar., 1924), 205–208; George C. Mercer, *One Hundred Years of Service, 1854–1954: A History of the YMCA of Indianapolis* (Indianapolis, [1954]); Nina Mjagkij, "History of the Black YMCA in America, 1853–1946" (Ph.D. dissertation, University of Cincinnati, 1990).

Senior Services. Housing and programs provided for those 65 and over. Before Indiana became a state, Congress provided help for elderly people in the Northwest Territory through a system of township trustees. Indiana's Constitution of 1816 provided for one or more poor farms as an "asylum for persons whose age, infirmity, or misfortune have claim." Indianapolis opened its poor farm in 1832. The Marion County Health Care Center survives as one of the few remaining "homes," and trustees are still responsible for paying for indigent care.

Among the earliest voluntary self-help efforts benefiting the elderly were burial payments from mutual benefit societies such as the Odd Fellows (est. 1819, later headquartered in Indianapolis). Taxing for public relief did not occur until 1896, when the General Assembly allowed levies on property for the trustees' relief fund. If the recipients were found likely to become public charges, they were sent to the poor farm. Since "the most deserving of the necessitous [would] not apply to the Trustee," voluntary associations developed. The Indianapolis Home for Friendless Women (now the INDIANAPOLIS RETIREMENT HOME) began in 1867 as a shelter for female relatives of Confederate prisoners of war held in Indianapolis. When it merged with the Katherine Home in 1905, it became a shelter for "elderly women of good character, but limited means."

In the late 19th century, religious and ethnic groups established institutions for the elderly. The ALPHA HOME for African-American retired domestics opened in 1883, Little Sisters of the Poor in 1893, and the Jewish Shelter House and Old Home in 1905 (a precursor to Hooverwood). The Old Folks Home Association (now ALTENHEIM), established in 1910 by the Zion Evangelical Church, perhaps the county's first "retirement home," had a volunteer doctor and nurse available to the residents, who paid $300 upon admission.

By 1933 the Great Depression overwhelmed local relief efforts, forcing the elderly poor to rely on state pensions. Later, old-age pensions were subsumed under the Welfare Act of 1936 when Indiana joined the national system established by the Social Security Act. State participation in old-age assistance ended in 1972; Congress added Title XVI to the Social Security Act and established Supplemental Security Income payments as the only truly national benefits for the elderly poor.

Impetus for community care of the elderly reemerged in 1955 under the leadership of the city's Dr. Morton Leeds, first secretary to the Indiana Commission on Aging and Aged. Commission publications exposed the high number of elderly in state-supported institutions (6,000), more than half of whom were in mental hospitals (3,600), and the era of deinstitutionalization began. A prophetic 1957 report by the precursor of the COMMUNITY SERVICE COUNCIL identified housing and a downtown senior center as major needs. In 1959 Leeds published the first directory of recreation and leisure time activities. In 1960 the Community Service Council reiterated the call for a senior center, and in 1962 the INDIANAPOLIS FOUNDATION and the LILLY ENDOWMENT funded the Indianapolis Senior Citizens Center. As the center opened, the city counted 60,000 people age 65 and older; over 30 years later this population has increased by half; by the 21st century it will have increased by two thirds.

With the Senior Citizens Center, the John Barton Apartments (high-rise public housing for the elderly opened in July, 1968), and senior programs multiplying under the influence of the Model Cities program and Employment Opportunity programs, Mayor Richard Lugar set up a task force on aging in 1971, headed by Indianapolis Senior Center board president Allen H. Warne. Warne established priorities that called for voluntary action and shared responsibility: low interest loans for household repairs, carpools for transportation, and day care and nutritional health centers. Receiving a grant from the Commission on Aging (Older Americans Act funds) to operate luncheon programs, the task force served 1,025 seniors at 16 senior centers and sites in 1973. The following year, under amendments to the act allowing the establishment of area agencies on aging, the task force became the CENTRAL INDIANA COUNCIL ON AGING, with Warne its first president. Twenty years later the lunch program serves 4,000 seniors a year at over 50 sites in 8 central Indiana counties and over 900 people a day with home-delivered meals.

In 1974 the former ST. VINCENT HOSPITAL became subsidized senior housing. Senior Enterprises, an employment program for seniors who needed and wanted to work, opened in 1976. In 1980 Holy Trinity Catholic Church became the site of the first adult day care program in the city; a former convent at St. Andrew Church was converted into congregate housing for the more mobile seniors; and New Life Manor opened as

elderly subsidized housing, managed by a multiservice center with a senior citizens program. In 1991 Public School 66 was converted into Coburn Place, an assisted living community financed by a community development corporation.

As Indianapolis moves toward the 21st century, the needs identified by the Lugar Task Force on Aging and Chairman Warne (housing, transportation, adequate nutrition, and appropriate activities) are as critical as they ever were.

ROBERT ADSIT AND DUEANE J. ETIENNE
Central Indiana Council on Aging

Serbs. The 1910 federal census reported 43 Bulgarians, Serbs, and Montenegrins in the city; in 1993 the Serbian contingent was estimated at around 300 residents.

The first Serb here was bookkeeper John Peterson (Jovan Perich, 1886–1978), who arrived in 1904 from Prizren in Old Serbia. Other men soon followed, found work at KINGAN AND COMPANY meat packers, and formed the largest Old Serbian community abroad. During World War I, however, many heeded King Peter I's appeal to overseas Serbs to return and defend their land; most of them became casualties. After 1920 Serbian men were joined by their families or brides-to-be from their war-ravaged homeland. Many Serbs operated restaurants, taverns, billiards parlors, and barber shops in the 400–600 blocks of West Washington Street. In the 1930s they moved to the area around West 16th Street and Tibbs Avenue and into SPEEDWAY.

Serbs organized St. George Lodge #245 Serbian National Federation and a companion St. George Lodge affiliated with the Jedinstvo Federation. A tamburitza orchestra kept alive Serbian music and kolo dancing. In 1931 these groups dedicated what became the Serbian National Home at 3626 West 16th Street. They also sponsored national observances and provided food and clothing for Serbian prisoners of war during World War II.

At first Serbs had no permanent church or priest. They held discussions in private homes near Kingan's and worshipped in nearby Greek, Romanian, or Bulgarian churches. On March 12, 1950, 30 members organized St. Nicholas Serbian Orthodox Church. Parishioners belong to the Serbian Orthodox Free (anti-Communist) Diocese, headquartered in Grayslake, Illinois. Their dead are usually interred in Floral Park Cemetery.

Conscious of traditional culture, Sam Salatich organized the Yovan Duchich choir in 1957; the St. Nicholas folklore dance group was founded in 1984. Cooperating with their Romanian and Bulgarian coreligionists, the Serbs attracted attention in the broader community by sponsoring the first Balkan Festival in 1992.

JAMES J. DIVITA
Marian College

Seventh-day Adventists. Christian denomination. The Seventh-day Adventist (SDA) church was organized in 1863 by former adherents to the Millerite movement, which predicted (from Bible prophecy) that Jesus would return to earth in 1844. Today, Adventists hold much in common with other conservative Christians, believing in salvation through Jesus Christ, the ultimate revelation of God's character. They also expect an early return of Jesus bringing judgment, emphasize health for the total person, and stress observance of the seventh day (Sabbath).

Adventists place great emphasis on education at all levels and often pursue higher education in SDA schools. Unusual numbers are physicians and other professionals, although occupational diversity is the rule in Indianapolis churches. Women serve many churches as leaders and elders, and women pastors, although they are not currently ordained, may baptize and perform marriages.

The church in Indiana was mainly rural until after the Indiana Conference was organized in 1872. In 1876 Arthur Bartlett formed a Sabbath School in Indianapolis. In 1885 a "city mission" and lecture room were opened on Cherry Street, and a congregation was organized in 1888. Ellen White (regarded as a prophetess by most Adventists) and evangelist Alonzo T. Jones visited Indianapolis in 1889, and several camp meetings were held on the north side of the city.

At the turn of the century there were nearly 200 Adventists in Indianapolis and by 1907 the original congregation had moved to Central Avenue and 23rd Street (the "Octagon Church"). In the 1930s the church purchased the Blaker School property at 23rd and Alabama streets, and in 1962 moved to its present location near Rural and East 62nd streets as the Glendale Church.

The southside congregation, which has spawned four new churches since 1950, began as the Rural Street Church about 1907. In 1923 this group constructed a building at Orange and Laurel streets and in 1973 moved to its present location at 4801 Shelbyville Road.

Most early SDAs were strongly against slavery; African-Americans were accepted into their churches. Adventist work specifically among blacks in Indianapolis began in 1907 when L. W. Browne and William Green won 15 converts through tent meetings. A building was purchased in 1911. Rapid growth in the 1930s under the leadership of J. H. Laurence led to construction of a new building on Capitol Avenue. In 1977 the congregation moved to its present location as the Capitol City Church.

In 1945 separate black conferences were formed for most of the United States to give African-American Adventists more control over their own church affairs and provide more opportunities for talented black pastors. The Capitol Avenue Church joined the new Lake Region Conference (LRC). Relations between black and white Adventists are cordial and members transfer freely among churches regardless of race.

By 1950 Adventist membership in Indianapolis totaled over 700. By 1990 there were 11 churches with nearly 2,500 members in the area, supporting three church schools. In 1990 Indianapolis hosted the General (world) Conference of SDAs, reporting a predominantly third-world church with over 6 million members and an extensive network of schools and medical enterprises.

DONALD RHOADS

Sevitzky, Fabien (Sept. 30, 1893–Feb. 3, 1967). Conductor who led the INDIANAPOLIS SYMPHONY ORCHESTRA (ISO) to national prominence. Born in Russia, Sevitzky took up the double bass when no scholarship was available in piano or vi-

Fabien Sevitzky conducted the Indianapolis Symphony Orchestra from 1937 to 1955. [Indianapolis Symphony Orchestra]

olin at the Conservatory of Music in St. Petersburg. He mastered the instrument in two weeks and won the scholarship for the double bass, graduating with honors in 1911.

Sevitzky arrived in the United States in 1923 when he was 29. He worked for the Philadelphia Orchestra and later formed a string orchestra that embraced his policy of including at least one American composition in concerts. Later, he was musical director and conductor of the People's Symphony Orchestra of Boston.

Sevitzky first visited Indianapolis as a guest conductor in 1936. He returned in 1937 to take over for retiring ISO founder FERDINAND SCHAEFER. He immediately reorganized the orchestra and significantly increased the concert schedule. His other musical contributions include the founding of the INDIANAPOLIS SYMPHONIC CHOIR, which he conducted until 1955, and his founding of the Indianapolis Scottish Rite Symphony Orchestra in 1946. (He was a 33rd degree Mason.)

A colorful figure, Sevitzky was a friend to band leader Fred Waring, and he encouraged Hoosier songwriter Hoagy Carmichael to write for the symphony. But temperamental outbursts and arguments with symphony officials left critics calling him unmanageable and tempestuous. Dismissed from the ISO in 1955, he took a job in Miami. He died of a heart attack in Athens, Greece, while on tour.

SUSAN GUYETT

Indiana Biography Series, Indiana State Library; *Indianapolis Star*, Jan. 3, 1955, Feb. 5, 1967.

Sewall, May (Mary Eliza) Wright (May 27, 1844–July 22, 1920). Educator, suffragist, feminist, peace advocate. Born at Greenfield, Wisconsin, Sewall taught school before entering North Western Female College at Evanston, Illinois, where she received the laureate of science degree (1866) and an honorary master of science degree (1871). She and her first husband, Edwin W. Thompson, moved to Franklin, Indiana, in the early 1870s, where he served as superintendent of schools, and she was named principal of the high school. They came to Indianapolis in 1874 to teach at Indianapolis High School, but Edwin died the following year. In 1880, she married Theodore Lovett Sewall (1852–1895), who had established the Indianapolis Classical School for Boys. The prestigious Classical School for Girls, which they opened in 1882, gained an excellent reputation for academic work and prepared many young women for eastern colleges.

With ZERELDA WALLACE, wife of former Governor David Wallace, Sewall helped found the Equal Suffrage Society of Indianapolis. Because of strong anti-suffrage feeling in the city, suffrage advocates had to meet in secret to form the organization. As a delegate of the local and state societies, Sewall attended her first national suffrage meeting in 1878 in Rochester, New York. There she met Susan B. Anthony, Elizabeth Cady Stanton, and others with whom she began to work at the national level. In Indiana, she participated in the suffragists' efforts in the early 1880s to amend the state constitution, presiding over a mass meeting at the Grand Opera House that appointed delegates to attend the state political conventions to persuade legislators to give women the vote. From 1882 to 1890, she was chair of the executive committee of the National Woman's Suffrage Association.

Sewall's interest in women's rights broadened when the NWSA, in 1888, sponsored a meeting of national and international organizations. From this meeting came "the Council idea," for which Sewall is credited. Stanton suggested the international meeting in 1888, but it was Sewall who envisioned a permanent organization of national councils of women from many nations. She served as president of the National Council of Women of the United States, 1891–1895 and 1897–1899.

From 1899 to 1904, she was president of the International Council of Women. At the World's Columbian Exposition in Chicago in 1893, she developed a special congress for women and brought together outstanding feminists from the United States and abroad. In 1900, President William McKinley appointed her as a Special Representative to the Congress of Women at the *Exposition Universelle* in Paris, representing the organized work of U.S. women.

Sewall contributed significantly to the civic and social life of Indianapolis. In 1876, she was one of the founders of the INDIANAPOLIS WOMAN'S CLUB, and for many years was an officer of the ART ASSOCIATION, the predecessor of the INDIANAPOLIS MUSEUM OF ART. The Indianapolis PROPYLAEUM, built in 1890, resulted from her idea two years earlier for a club building to be owned and managed by women. Sewall also was a founder of the CONTEMPORARY CLUB, the Indiana branch of the Western Association of Collegiate Alumnae (a forerunner of the Association of American University Women), the Local Council of Women, and the Alliance Francaise.

Her interest in peace began as early as 1895. She chaired the International Council of Women's standing committee on peace and international arbitration from 1904 to 1914. In addition to her speeches and writings for international understanding and cooperation, she organized a women's conference at the Panama-Pacific Exposition at San Francisco in 1915. Later that year, she sailed to Europe on the much-ridiculed Henry Ford Peace Ship.

Sewall left Indianapolis in 1907 after the sale of her school, living for the most part in New England, writing and lecturing. In 1919, in ill health, she returned to the city. Shortly before her death, the BOBBS-MERRILL Company published her book on spiritualism, *Neither Dead Nor Sleeping* (1920), which described her conversations with her deceased husband Theodore and other psychic experiences. After her death, a May Wright Sewall Memorial Fund was established to place books in the public library in her memory and two bronze standards were erected to light the entrance to the JOHN HERRON ART INSTITUTE. These have since been moved to the Indianapolis Museum of Art.

HESTER ANNE HALE

Jane Stephens, "May Wright Sewall: An Indiana Reformer," *Indiana Magazine of History*, 78 (Dec., 1982), 273–295.

Shank, Samuel Lewis (Lew) (Jan. 23, 1872–Sept. 24, 1927). Mayor of Indianapolis, 1910–1913, 1922–1926, Republican. Born in Marion County, Shank worked at a variety of jobs before entering politics. In 1902 he successfully ran for county recorder on the Republican ticket. In 1909 he was elected mayor for the first time. During his tenure he gained national fame by auctioning carloads of farmers' vegetables to consumers from the steps of city hall. Thereafter called the "potato mayor," he considered his auctions a means of fighting what he called unfair pricing by wholesalers.

Shank crusaded against Sunday saloon openings, appointed a vice commission, and supported women's suffrage. His last year in office saw a series of disasters in the city including the 1913 flood and the 1913 streetcar and teamster strikes. During the streetcar strike many policemen, sympathetic to the strikers, mutinied, refusing to man the streetcars and protect the strikebreakers who operated them. In turn, Shank refused the governor's request that he order the policemen to assume their stations on the cars. Four weeks before his term ended Shank resigned his office in the midst of threatened impeachment proceedings over his encouragement of the earlier police mutiny. However, one contemporary noted that the chances of impeachment were slim to nonexistent and suggested that Shank may have resigned as a publicity stunt; he had already signed a contract to go on the VAUDEVILLE circuit with a monologue about his time as mayor. Shank performed in vaudeville for 26 weeks after leaving office, opening in Kansas City before performing for 14 weeks in New York City. Although his act featured his monologue, it also included a trained horse.

After his return to Indianapolis Shank ran unsuccessfully for mayor in 1918. In his last campaign, beginning in 1921, his wife Sarah was his campaign manager. Shank's "me and Sarah" speeches were widely known for their colloquial language and common man themes. Shank won the election with the largest majority in the city's history to that time. During his second term in office he led a group of hundreds of marchers to the State House to protest the Public Service Commission's grant of a rate increase to the INDIANAPOLIS WATER COMPANY. In 1921 he made the first local radio speech on Indianapolis' first station, WLK. Near the close of his term he constructed the Shank Fireproof Storage Company, an auction and warehouse on North Illinois Street, sometimes leaving the mayor's office for a few hours to conduct auctions there. In 1924 while still mayor he entered the governor's race; he lost the Republican nomination to Ed Jackson.

After leaving office the second time in January, 1926, Shank appeared for one week at an Indianapolis vaudeville theater before settling into a career as an auctioneer and public speaker. Shank was planning to run in the 1928 election for the 7th district congressional seat when he died.

CONNIE J. ZEIGLER

———

Clipping File, Indiana Division, Indiana State Library; *Indianapolis News*, Sept. 24, 1927.

Shapiro's (1905–present). Delicatessen-cafeteria started as a storefront grocery at 808 South Meridian Street by Louis Shapiro, a Russian immigrant from Odessa. During the early years Shapiro sold kosher meats and groceries to the Jewish community living on the south side. After Prohibition ended, the store sold cold beer for 10 cents a bottle, three bottles for a quarter. Soon customers were asking for "something to eat" with their beer. Shapiro responded to their requests by making and serving deli sandwiches, kosher corned beef, and pastrami.

The grocery business suffered in the 1930s as the city's southside Jewish community dispersed and gradually relocated to the north side, a move that had begun in the 1920s. The shift in population hurt the grocery business, which closed in the late 1930s, but the deli-cafeteria flourished. Over the years the sandwiches and other kosher foods served by Louis Shapiro continued to be the mainstay of the restaurant's menu. Shapiro's has remained a family business and still follows a simple set of rules established by its founder: "Cook

Known today as a deli-cafeteria, Shapiro's began as a small southside grocery in 1905.
[Indiana Historical Society, #C1951]

Good; Serve Generously; Price Modestly; People Will Come."

Today the storefront grocery has expanded into a deli-cafeteria that seats over 200 people. Another Shapiro's Delicatessen-Cafeteria now operates on the north side.

CAROLYN S. BLACKWELL

———

David S. Powell, "Max the Deli Man," *Indianapolis Star*, Oct. 16, 1983.

Shaw, (Warren) Wilbur (Oct. 31, 1902–Oct. 30, 1954). Three-time winner of the INDIANAPOLIS 500–MILE RACE, later president and general manager of the Indianapolis Motor Speedway Corporation. Born near Shelbyville, Indiana, Shaw spent his formative years divided between Shelbyville and Greensburg. He moved to Indianapolis at age 16, found employment in a variety of automotive-related jobs, and soon began constructing his own racing car. After several successful seasons of driving for other car owners on local dirt tracks, Shaw placed fourth in the 1927 Indianapolis 500, his first of 13 starts there.

Half a dozen lean years followed before he embarked on a streak which resulted in finishes of either first or second in the 500 six times in eight years. In addition to winning in 1937, 1939, and 1940—the first to triumph in consecutive years—Shaw also was runnerup in 1933, 1935, and

1938. He almost won again in 1941, only to have a collapsing wire wheel force him to strike the outer retaining wall while leading at 152 of the 200 laps.

With the Speedway shuttered during World War II, Shaw relocated to Akron, Ohio, to work with the aircraft division of Firestone Tire & Rubber Company. Appalled by the dilapidated condition of the track when he returned to test tires near the conclusion of hostilities, Shaw quickly confirmed that the facility was for sale. The result of his celebrated virtual one-man campaign to save the track came in November, 1945, when the ownership was transferred from Eddie Rickenbacker's group to Anton Hulman, Jr., of the Terre Haute grocery concern. Hulman installed Shaw as track president and general manager, posts he still held at the time of his death in a private aircraft crash near Decatur, Indiana.

DONALD DAVIDSON
United States Auto Club

_____

Wilbur Shaw, *Gentlemen, Start Your Engines* (New York, 1955).

Shelby County. County adjacent to Indianapolis–Marion County on the southeast and part of the Indianapolis Metropolitan Statistical Area. The first settlers of the area that is now Shelby County came by Whetzel's Trace after 1818. By the time of the county's organization in 1821 settlements had been made throughout the area. Most of the original settlers were Methodists; there was a class meeting in Shelby County by 1821. Shelbyville was established as the county seat in 1822.

Shelby County had excellent farmland, but the area was poorly served by the state's road system. In an attempt to open the markets at Indianapolis and Madison to Shelby County farmers, Shelbyville businessmen in 1849 financed the construction of the Shelbyville Lateral Branch, a 16–mile railway line that connected Shelbyville to the MADISON AND INDIANAPOLIS RAILROAD at Edinburgh. This and other small Shelby County lines were abandoned soon after the completion of the Cincinnati, Indianapolis and St. Louis Railroad through Shelbyville in 1853. This line

Selected Statistics for Shelby County, 1990

Population	40,307
Population per Square Mile	98
Percent African-American	0.8
Percent 0 to 17 Years	27.3
Percent 65 Years and Over	12.2
Percent 25 Years and Over with a High School Degree or Equivalency	74.1
Percent 25 Years and Over with a College Degree	9.9
Per Capita Income in 1989	$15,509
Unemployment Rate (%)	7.0
Married-Couple Families as a Percent of Total Households	64.0
Median Home Value	$51,300

opened the major midwestern markets to Shelby County crops and pork, and Shelbyville became an agricultural center in its own right. By the 1870s furniture manufactories began to appear in Shelbyville. The city soon became a manufacturing center; by 1909 it boasted a dozen furniture factories and was known as the "Furniture City of the Middle West." At that time it was a growing city of 12,000 connected to the state capital by a railroad and an interurban line.

Shelby County was the home of one of the first Catholic churches in central Indiana. Residents formed a Catholic church in 1836, and in 1839 they built St. Vincent DePaul near Shelbyville. During this time the few Catholic settlers in Indianapolis were under the dependency of the pastor of St. Vincent. Once a month the pastor would travel to Indianapolis, an arrangement that lasted until 1846 when a Catholic church was established in the capital.

In 1902 the Seventh-day Adventists established a school at Boggstown in Shelby County. Originally called the Boggstown Manual Training Academy, the institution moved to a grove near Fairland and the name was changed to Beechwood Manual Training Academy in 1903. The school operated at this site until the 1940s when it moved to Cicero in Hamilton County and became the Indiana Academy of Seventh-day Adventists.

The demise of the railroad and the INTERURBANS after 1930 hurt Shelbyville's industry, and the city has grown very little since 1909 (12,000 in 1909, 15,000 in 1990). Today Shelby County is a rural area with a relatively stable population of 40,307 (1990). Farms cover much of the land in the county, but the main employers are small manufacturers in the Shelbyville and Morristown areas.

WILLIAM D. DALTON

_____

Edward H. Chadwick, *History of Shelby County, Indiana* (Indianapolis, 1909); U.S. Census.

Shelton, Jim (May 23, 1919–Feb. 11, 1993). Professional name of radio broadcaster and host of the "Pick-A-Pocket" show on WIBC. A native of Loveland, Ohio, whose full name was James Shelton Undercoffer, Shelton took his first radio job in 1940 at WCMI in Ashland, Kentucky. In 1941 he moved to WIBC in Indianapolis where he worked for 50 years, interrupted by three years of service in the Army Air Force during World War II.

Responding to FCC regulations regarding game shows, Shelton created "Pick-A-Pocket," a popular 15–minute quiz show, which aired at 12:15 P.M. from the CIRCLE THEATRE marquee November 24, 1947, through October 8, 1968. Donning a 15–pocket apron designed by his wife Dorothy, Shelton asked people to "pick-a-pocket" and answer questions to win money and prizes. During its 21–year run the program aired 6,390 times and was the most listened to program on Indianapolis radio for 19 of those years.

Shelton also was an announcer for the INDIANAPOLIS MOTOR SPEEDWAY RADIO NETWORK from 1948 to 1978. In addition to his work behind the microphone, Shelton served as a sales account executive for WIBC from 1969 until his 1991 retirement. He was the station's top sales person for nine of those years.

A recipient of over 100 awards for his civic contributions, Shelton was named to the Indiana Broadcasters Hall of Fame in 1989 for services to the radio industry. At his retirement he was named a Sagamore of the Wabash.

JACK D. MORROW
WIBC (retired)

_____

Indianapolis News, Sept. 8, 1982, Sept. 17, 1987, Dec. 13, 1990.

Sheridan, Lawrence Vinnedge (July 8, 1887–Jan. 26, 1972). Landscape architect. Born in Frankfort, Indiana, Sheridan earned his B.S. from Purdue University and then studied at Harvard School of Landscape Architecture in 1917. Sheridan worked on the KESSLER BOULEVARD AND PARK SYSTEM in Indianapolis, served on the Indianapolis Board of Park Commissioners (1911–1914), and the City Plan Commission (1921–1923).

In his private practice he designed the Frederic Ayres estate, Walden, on Sunset Lane, for which he was featured in *American Landscape Architect* in 1931. He served for several years as the consulting landscape architect at CROWN HILL CEMETERY. In the 1930s Sheridan was the project landscape architect for LOCKEFIELD GARDENS, a public housing project in Indianapolis. He worked with project developers on placement of the buildings to maximize sunlight in the apartments. The focal point of his Lockefield Gardens design was a central court with a grove of red oak trees.

Sheridan began a private practice in 1937, the same year he became a regional counselor of the National Resources Planning Board (1937–1941). During World War II he served in the Army Corps of Engineers, attaining the rank of colonel. After the war, Sheridan focused his attention on city planning in Indianapolis and elsewhere. In 1957 the American Institute of Planners awarded him their distinguished service award, honoring his work in over 100 communities. In his later years he founded Metropolitan Planners, a planning, landscape architecture, and civil engineering firm.

CONNIE J. ZEIGLER

Shopping Centers/Malls. Multi-enterprise retail store marketplaces. Downtown stores dominated Indianapolis retail shopping until the middle of the 20th century. Neighborhood shopping areas that developed in IRVINGTON, BROAD RIPPLE, FOUNTAIN SQUARE, and elsewhere offered little competition.

In the 1950s, with increased suburbanization, small shopping centers were established close to the customer populations and began to divert the downtown retail business. In the late 1950s, six downtown stores accounted for 90 percent of department store sales in Marion County. By 1972, downtown sales had dropped to 18 percent.

Some of the earlier shopping centers built specifically to hold a collection of retail stores were: Twin-Aire Center, 1956; Eastgate Shopping Center, 1957; Glendale Shopping Center, 1958; Devington Plaza, 1959; Southern Plaza, 1961; and Greenwood Shopping Center, 1968. These were strip centers with lines of stores facing in on a common plaza.

The opening of Lafayette Square at 3919 Lafayette Road in 1968 set a standard for future Indianapolis malls. It was the city's first enclosed mall, with over one million square feet of space, and designed to attract customers from a wide area rather than from a limited neighborhood. It boasted three department stores—WILLIAM H. BLOCK COMPANY, Sears, and J. C. Penney— and later added L. S. AYRES AND COMPANY and Lazarus. It contained nearly 100 smaller stores, predominantly clothing shops, but had a diversity of specialty shops and services such as restaurants, a supermarket, theater, bank, bakery, and florist. This large collection of retail shops was intended to meet every shopping need in one convenient location. Other attractions included the climate-controlled interior, fountains, live tropical plants, a staff of hostesses, security patrols, ample free parking, free promotional entertainment, and easy accessibility from major streets and highways. The success of Lafayette Square prompted its developer, the Edward J. DeBartolo Corporation of Youngstown, Ohio, to build two similar malls: Castleton Square, 6020 East 82nd Street, in 1972, and Washington Square, 10202 East Washington Street, in 1974.

MELVIN SIMON AND ASSOCIATES, a major mall developer headquartered in Indianapolis, purchased the Greenwood and the Eastgate shopping centers, enclosed them under roofs, and remodeled and expanded them to compete in size and appeal with the other major malls in the city. The firm enclosed and remodeled the Glendale shopping center in 1969 and expanded it in 1973. It also opened the Keystone at the Crossing center in 1973, along with two adjacent shopping areas, the Bazaar and the Fashion Mall. The Fashion Mall was expanded in 1980, 1982, 1988 (in conjunction with razing the Bazaar), and again in 1993.

Satellite centers, or strip centers built adjacent to major malls, proliferated across the city in the 1980s, offering tenants low rental and access to the automobile traffic generated by the large malls. Examples of satellite centers include Castleton Shoppes near Castleton Square Mall; Lafayette Shoppes near Lafayette Square Mall; Washington Shoppes near Washington Square Mall; and Greenwood Shoppes near Greenwood Park Mall.

In the late 1980s and early 1990s, in spite of the closing of downtown department stores such as Block's, Ayres, and Lazarus, there was a movement to restore the downtown area to retail shopping prominence. This included the opening of the Claypool Court collection of shops in 1985, the renovation and reopening of UNION STATION as a historic site and retail center in 1986, and plans for the CIRCLE CENTRE MALL, a large shopping complex to encompass several city blocks, including a full quadrant of MONUMENT CIRCLE.

The large malls have had a sociological effect on the community. Praised for their convenience to customers and for the jobs and tax base dollars they bring to the economy, they have also been criticized for their competitive commercialism and environmental pollution. They became popular meeting and gathering places, much as small town public squares were in the past. Teenagers find the malls convenient and congenial locations to meet friends, shop, and socialize, although sometimes in such large numbers as to cause consternation among the retailers and older shoppers. Members of mall walker clubs daily walk the measured distances of mall concourses for exercise. Nursing homes bring busloads of seniors on outings, and school children exhibit their art work.

Malls are often solicited as sites for demonstrations by various organizations that desire exposure to large numbers of persons. While many Indianapolis malls make their facilities available for community and charitable activities, most do not welcome political, religious, or controversial demonstrations. They are upheld in this decision by a U.S. Supreme Court ruling and Indiana law, which decrees that malls are private property and therefore have the right to restrict activities.

RICHARD W. WORTH

Shortridge, Abram Crum (Oct. 23, 1833–Oct. 8, 1919). Public schools superintendent who reopened the high school in Indianapolis (later called SHORTRIDGE HIGH SCHOOL). Born in Henry County, Indiana, Shortridge spent his teen years in farming, learning to be a printer, and attending a country school. After a few months of additional study at Fairview Academy in Rush County, Shortridge taught at schools in Wayne County. His formal education ended with a brief stint as a student at Greenmount College near Richmond. Between 1855 and 1861 he was on the staff of Whitewater College in Centerville, much of this time in the capacity of school manager.

Shortridge moved to Indianapolis in 1861 to teach in the preparatory department of North Western Christian University (later BUTLER UNIVERSITY). Two years later he became superintendent of the Indianapolis public schools, which were coming out of a period of decline. In 1858 the Indiana Supreme Court had ruled against towns collecting taxes to pay for school tuition, which resulted in the severe curtailment of classes and the closing of the high school in Indianapolis. When Shortridge became superintendent in 1863, the school system was beginning to receive increased funds, since the state Supreme Court now allowed additional taxation. Shortridge was thus able to expand educational facilities and offerings substantially and to increase enrollments.

Among his major contributions was the reopening in 1865 of the high school in Indianapolis. Shortridge also introduced a graded system, a reform increasingly common in urban areas, and he lengthened the school year from three and one-half months to nine months. Under his superintendency, school buildings, modeled on the design of a three-story Boston, Massachusetts, school, were constructed in two Indianapolis wards. Shortridge was instrumental in establishing the Indianapolis Public Library and in reopening the Indianapolis public schools to black children. He was, in brief, a major figure in shaping education in early Indianapolis.

Following his suggestion, the school board hired a predominantly female teaching force in Indianapolis. In Shortridge's view, low salaries made it necessary to turn to women to fill the expanding number of teaching positions. In order to train these women, Shortridge organized a teachers' training school in Indianapolis that opened on March 1, 1867. He also named a young woman, NEBRASKA CROPSEY, as supervisor of primary instruction for the city.

Shortridge resigned from the superintendency in 1874 to serve briefly as president of Purdue University, where he helped get the university's first regular classes under way. At odds with the school's benefactor, John Purdue, and suffering from poor health, Shortridge left the university at the end of 1875. Thereafter, he was occupied with farming just south of the Indianapolis suburb of IRVINGTON and in serving as Warren Township justice of the peace. However, a brief note in the *Indiana School Journal* mentioning him as part owner of a private academy in 1882 offers evidence that his interest in education continued.

Throughout the last 20 years of his life Shortridge was completely blind, and in 1906 he was forced to have part of his leg amputated after being hit by an interurban. The degree of hardship that he suffered during his lifetime makes his achievements in the field of education all the more remarkable.

AMY C. SCHUTT
Indiana University, Bloomington
and *History of Education Quarterly*

Laura S. Gaus, *Shortridge High School* (Indianapolis, 1985); Indiana Biography Series, Indiana State Library.

Shortridge High School. Converted in 1981 to a junior high school, Shortridge, originally named Indianapolis High School, was the first public high school in the city. Although Indianapolis was served by several private academies in the first half of the 19th century, public funding for a high school became available only in 1853. School was held in the old County Seminary building in University Square, with approximately 150 students attending. There were slightly more boys than girls—a majority that would not recur until near the end of the century.

Closed in 1858 when the Indiana Supreme Court, in *City of Lafayette v. Jenners*, declared local taxation for schools to be unconstitutional, Indianapolis High School was not reopened for full

terms until ABRAM C. SHORTRIDGE became superintendent of schools in 1863. From that point it
experienced steady growth, moving into the
former Baptist Female Seminary building at Michigan and Pennsylvania streets, later razing and rebuilding at that site, and, in 1928, moving to a
new location at 34th and Meridian streets. In
1897, as a result of the recent construction of a
second high school, MANUAL HIGH SCHOOL on the
south side, Indianapolis High School was renamed in honor of Professor Shortridge.

By the latter part of the century Shortridge
had developed a national reputation for academic
excellence and innovation. It offered many extracurricular activities, including an early version of
student government and the nation's first daily
student newspaper, the Shortridge DAILY ECHO.

While Shortridge had incorporated a manual
training department into its curriculum in the
1880s, vocational education was relegated to other
city high schools, particularly Manual High School
and ARSENAL TECHNICAL HIGH SCHOOL. This determination to remain "academic" was reinforced in
1964 as a part of an attempt to rehabilitate the high
school's status through a reorganization termed the
Shortridge Plan. Although *Newsweek* and *Time* in
1957 ranked Shortridge among 38 high schools of
distinguished merit, by the 1960s shifting demographics had caused some to fear both a continued
erosion of academic standards and the *de facto* creation of another all-black high school. In reaction to
this situation, the Shortridge Plan made the high
school selective based on teacher ratings, mental
ability, and achievement records of the students.
The organizing concept was homogeneous grouping or tracking, with vocational students and those
"eligible" for special classes bused to other sites.
This attempt to emphasize an academic rather than
a more comprehensive curriculum was consistent
with the school's history. The result, however, was
more a partial shifting of nonwhite students to
surrounding high schools than an influx of white
students from other districts. Ultimately, the
Shortridge Plan failed, and Indianapolis' first high
school ceased to exist, except in the memories of its
graduates and in the educational history of
Indianapolis.

TED STAHLY
Indiana University, Bloomington

Laura S. Gaus, *Shortridge High School* (Indianapolis, 1985); Holman Hamilton and Gayle Thornbrough, eds., *Indianapolis in the "Gay Nineties": High
School Diaries of Claude G. Bowers* (Indianapolis,
1964).

Showalter, Grace Montgomery (Mar. 9,
1893–July 23, 1972). Philanthropist and community leader. Born in Shelbyville, Indiana, Grace
Montgomery moved to Indianapolis after graduating from Indiana University in 1913. She married Ralph W. Showalter, later a vice-president
and board member of ELI LILLY AND COMPANY.
Showalter matched the wealth and prominence
that came with her husband's position with her
own considerable energy and passion for community involvement. During World War II she
chaired the local women's division of the war
bond sales drive. An active Republican, she served
as a member of the Indianapolis Park Board during the administrations of mayors ROBERT TYN-
DALL (1943–1947) and ALEX M. CLARK (1952–
1956).

Showalter was best known for her philanthropic activities. Her substantial gifts endowed
IUPUI's Center for Advanced Research and
funded construction of the Showalter Pavilion at
the INDIANAPOLIS MUSEUM OF ART, an auditorium
that houses the CIVIC THEATRE. When she died
she left Indiana University $7.5 million, $5 million of which went to the INDIANA UNIVERSITY
SCHOOL OF MEDICINE in Indianapolis and $1.2
million to the Indiana University Foundation for
a new building. She also left a $2 million trust
fund to METHODIST HOSPITAL for its cardiac care
division.

KEVIN CORN
Indiana University–Purdue University,
Indianapolis

Sigma Gamma Rho. National collegiate
community service sorority for African-American
women, organized by seven teachers, six of whom
were seeking undergraduate degrees at BUTLER
UNIVERSITY. The sorority's original purpose was to
encourage African-American women teachers to
seek higher education. This aim soon broadened

to encompass all black women interested in higher education as well as a community service component.

The founders began meeting in 1920 as the Aurora Club with the intention of eventually becoming a national sorority. During the first three years they established the sorority's organizational structure, goals, and symbols. In 1922 the group was incorporated as the Alpha Chapter of Sigma Gamma Rho and became the only national sorority founded in Indianapolis. The sorority soon became popular in Indianapolis, and a second chapter, Alpha Sigma, was established for alumnae members.

In 1925 the founders hosted the sorority's first convention in Indianapolis and launched a national campaign. The sorority grew steadily, and the founders immediately relinquished sole control over the sorority. Members of the Alpha Sigma chapter, however, have been continuously active in national leadership positions. The Alpha Sigma chapter has also provided local community service by supporting scholarships and sponsoring a children's literature collection at Butler, as well as organizing many community programs focusing mainly on African-American school children and the local African-American community.

MICHELLE D. HALE

Pearl S. White, *Behind These Doors, A Legacy: The History of Sigma Gamma Rho Sorority* (Chicago, 1974).

Sigma Theta Tau International. Nursing honorary. What is now one of the world's largest NURSING associations had its modest genesis at the Indiana University Training School for Nurses (now the Indiana University School of Nursing) in 1922. World War I had recently concluded, and six nursing students founded a society to elevate nursing as a profession, recognize scholarship and leadership, encourage excellence, and supply a social forum for its members. Today, the honor society is comprised of approximately 200,000 nurse leaders affiliated with more than 350 chapters at accredited colleges and universities in the United States, Canada, South Korea, and Taiwan. Membership is conferred only upon nursing students in baccalaureate or graduate programs demonstrating excellence in nursing or upon qualified bachelors, masters, and doctoral graduates exhibiting exceptional achievement in the nursing profession. More than 60 percent of Sigma Theta Tau International's renewing members hold graduate degrees.

The organization's accomplishments include: awarding the first known nursing research grant in 1936 and providing seed money for scientific investigations on an ongoing basis thereafter; publishing *IMAGE: Journal of Nursing Scholarship*, the most widely read scholarly nursing research journal; sponsoring acclaimed local, national, and international educational conferences; recognizing stellar nursing achievements with international awards; successfully conducting the first national capital funds campaign in nursing's history and establishing the $5 million, 32,000–square foot International Center for Nursing Scholarship on the campus of INDIANA UNIVERSITY–PURDUE UNIVERSITY, INDIANAPOLIS; creating the Virginia Henderson International Nursing Library, an electronic, state-of-the-science facility; and hosting the first national cable television program profiling nursing.

LINDA BRIMMER
Sigma Theta Tau

Simons, Henry L. (ca. 1884–Sept. 18, 1954). Local builder and real estate developer. Born in Potter County, Pennsylvania, Simons moved to Indianapolis in 1920. He formed H. L. Simons Designers and Builders, employing architects M. Carlton Smith and Orville Williamson as designers and F. H. Bremerman as construction superintendent. With their help, Simons erected more than 300 houses on Indianapolis' north side. Simons constructed residences in many areas of Indianapolis, and in other cities in the state, but he is best known as the builder of several homes in the North Meridian Street Historic District, constructed primarily on speculation. He was the first local developer to build speculation houses in the $100,000 range.

Simons' firm designed homes in a variety of the architectural styles popular at the time, including Tudor Revival, Colonial Revival, and French Provincial. His houses were known especially for their attractive interior designs. His office was in his own Simons-designed home at 5151 North Meridian Street until the 1940s, when he moved to a location on Broadway Street.

CONNIE J. ZEIGLER

———

Indiana Biography Series, Indiana State Library.

Single Family Residential Architecture.

The single family dwelling occupies a special place in the history and development of Indianapolis. The Hoosier capital called itself "A City of Homes," perhaps rightfully so: it had one of the highest rates of dwellings per capita of any United States city during the late 1800s and early 1900s. The city had few geographic barriers, so neighborhoods of free-standing homes developed on all sides of the original 1821 plat. Since land values were higher north and east of the plat, these areas soon were considered best for residential development. Indianapolis citizens were conservative in artistic matters; new house styles or types were not embraced until they were generally popular.

The first European-descended settlers came from eastern or southern states. They brought with them building traditions that had been handed down for many years. Accordingly, the city's first homes had little pretense to style. Log cabins were the earliest form of housing, usually of the single pen (one room) type. No log cabins have survived in the original MILE SQUARE, but several still stand in Marion County.

Very few examples of early housing exist in the city. Most surviving early residences are the more substantial houses of the era rather than the most typical. Large, extended families often lived in these homes, and rooms had to serve multiple functions. Kitchens often served as dining and work rooms, and bedrooms had to shelter several family members at a time. As circumstances improved, rooms might be added to the original house. The average 1800s homesite included an array of domestic outbuildings, such as a privy, summer kitchen, and carriage house. Indicative of early housing conditions is the Sanders-Childers House (ca. 1823) at 1016 Palmer Street. Believed to be the oldest house in the city, its four-room

plan and formal facade were probably considered pretentious for its day.

Both average and exceptional houses representing a cross section of living conditions exist from the 1850s and 1860s. Gradually, house plans with specialized rooms developed. Heating and cooking stoves improved domestic life. Houses began to appear less functional and incorporated elements of Greek Revival, Gothic Revival, Italianate, and Second Empire styles into their design. Architects who had settled in the city during this period introduced fashionable domestic architectural styles.

A typical house of this era is the Williams House (ca. 1856), 709 Lexington Avenue. Built for a painter, this simple gable-front cottage features a Greek Revival style cornice. Builders' pattern books also began to inspire designs. The house at 1925 North Central Avenue (ca. 1860), for example, likely derives its Gothic Revival style from sources such as A. J. Downing's *Architecture of Country Houses* (1850). Conversely, the Hannah-Oehler-Elder House (ca. 1858), 3801 Madison Avenue, represents a wealthy man's country seat of the pre–Civil War era. Homes of this class often had servants' quarters in the attic of a rear, one-story wing. Architecturally, the blocky massing and bracketed cornice mark the house as an early example of the Italianate style.

A popular middle class house form during the 1860s was the two-story, three-bay, side hall "townhouse." It probably derived from an earlier vernacular prototype. The Wallace-Bosart House (1862), 4704 East Washington Street, is a fine example of this type, which was perpetuated well into the late 1800s.

Indianapolis expanded rapidly in the decade after the Civil War. Houses of the wealthy became increasingly elaborate while middle and working class houses became standardized. Gas lights and central furnaces became common features in Indianapolis homes. During this decade builders introduced the common wood-framed cottage types with L, T, and cruciform plans. Under the guise of various architectural styles, they served as the most common house types until the early 1900s. The Frederick Faut House (1873), 536 East New York Street, is a good example of a vernacular cottage.

For the wealthy, Italianate was the most popular style of the 1870s. The Bals-Wocher House (1870), 951 North Delaware Street, and the Eden-Talbott House (1878), 1336 North Delaware Street, are imposing examples featuring masonry construction.

Exotic architectural styles became popular during the 1870s. The Johnson-Earle-Payne House (1876), 5631 University Avenue, combines elements of the emerging Queen Anne style with Victorian Gothic features in its eclectic design.

The latest architectural style, Queen Anne, dominated the last two decades of the 1800s. Although vernacular house types continued to be erected, their forms were now sheathed in elaborate Queen Anne millwork. Such Queen Anne cottages may be found in nearly every old (pre–1900) neighborhood in the city. Although the inspiration for the style came from the East Coast, local architects embraced the new mode enthusiastically. Resident architect LOUIS HENRY GIBSON, the only local architect known to have authored a nationally distributed pattern book, published several house pattern books featuring Queen Anne and Shingle Style dwellings. The Harry Crossland House (1889), 1468 North Alabama Street, was likely inspired by plate 12 of Gibson's *Convenient Houses* (1889). It is a typical middle class example of Queen Anne. The HERRON-MORTON and WOODRUFF PLACE neighborhoods have the best collections of Queen Anne dwellings.

More pretentious examples featured towers, projecting bays, and turned spindle work. Masonry construction often differentiated mansions from houses. Details from the less common Victorian Gothic, Romanesque Revival, or other sources were applied. The Tate-Willis House (1892, Charles Mueller, architect) at 228 North East Street, for example, has Germanic Renaissance Revival detailing.

Indianapolis homes of the 1880s and 1890s continued the trend toward specialized rooms, but plans gradually became more open and flexible. Indoor plumbing became more common, although the privy was still a fact of life for many. Large porches were standard in house designs.

The early 1900s was a period of unparalleled growth for Indianapolis. Except for a brief lapse during World War I, the pace of home building was dramatic. Speculative construction became big business; it was not uncommon for a developer to purchase, subdivide, and build on an entire block.

Shortly after 1900 a new form of housing, the bungalow, became very popular in Indianapolis. The term was derived from "bangla," a simple native dwelling of India. A bungalow is a one- to one-and-one-half-story house usually having a broad porch and low pitched roof. Radically different from the cottages of the 1800s, the bungalow was conceived and inspired by architects and popular publications. The bungalow craze was a national phenomenon, and by 1910 it had swept across Indiana. The bungalow and other early 1900s dwellings were modern houses. For the first time, indoor plumbing, gas cooking stoves, and electricity were standard in the average house. Plans were open and informal, featuring a living room rather than a parlor. Bungalows and other early 1900s house types were smaller than late 1800s homes, since the average Indianapolis family was smaller (5.27 persons in 1870 compared to 4 persons in 1910) and fewer could afford to hire live-in servants. After 1910, garages to accommodate the family automobile were common.

A typical bungalow is the Joseph Hooser House (1914), 5033 North Broadway Street. The so-named Bungalow Company of Indianapolis erected the Hooser House. In contrast, the Layton Allen House (1911, Layton Allen, architect) at 28 North Audubon Road is a larger, finely detailed bungalow.

Another popular house type of the early 1900s was the American Four-Square, consisting of a two-story, box-like, hip-roofed building with a large porch. Variants of this type can be found in nearly every old neighborhood of the city.

Closely related to the bungalow and Four-Square types was the Prairie Style. Indianapolis was close to the epicenter of the Prairie movement (Chicago), but historians often note that the city has few or no examples of Prairie Style residences. In fact, although Frank Lloyd Wright never had a commission in Indianapolis, several of his more conservative proteges did work here. Howard Van Doren Shaw, for example, planned the CHARLES FAIRBANKS House (1913), 2960 North Meridian Street, and the Louis Huesman

House (1908) at 3148 North Pennsylvania Street. Indianapolis residents, however, mostly relied on local architects to provide conservative, Prairie-influenced homes—just as they had for other architectural styles.

Contrasting with the modern styles of the early 1900s were the academic revival styles. These period revival homes often did not include porches and had more formal plans. Colonial and Tudor Revival were the most popular of these academic styles. Best suited to large homes, Colonial Revival was common in middle to upper class neighborhoods. The Bliss House (1909), 2810 North Meridian Street, is an early example. English-born architect Wilson Parker designed several Colonial Revival homes in Indianapolis, including the stately Joseph Scaf House (1924) at 4101 North Pennsylvania Street. Tudor Revival homes were first built in Indianapolis by 1910. Two early examples are the Forrest-Howe House (1910), 30 North Audubon Road, and the Glossbrenner Mansion (1910, Alfred Grindle, architect), 3202 North Meridian Street.

Designing adequate small houses was an important social issue during the 1920s. To this end, a quasi-public agency, the Architect's Small House Service Bureau, was established, with Indianapolis serving as the headquarters for the "Lake Division" from the program's inception in 1924 until 1942. The agency likely influenced local house designs in the adaptation of Colonial Revival and Tudor Revival styles to the small house. The "Tudor Cottage" assumed the popularity of the bungalow, although the plans are often similar. Many one-story Tudor Revival homes can be found near East 10th Street in IRVINGTON and in the MERIDIAN-KESSLER area.

Home building in Indianapolis was curtailed by the Great Depression of the 1930s. The next major phase of construction came after World War II. New suburbs crept away from the old city limits. Speculative home construction resumed the pace set in the late 1920s. Symbolic of postwar Indianapolis is the ranch house that featured specialized rooms, such as a formal (and seldom used) living room for entertaining and the family room to accommodate burgeoning families. Air conditioning eliminated the need for porches. Scores of ranch houses were built during the 1950s and 1960s. The 1970s and 1980s witnessed periods of great residential growth. Planned unit developments included hundreds of standardized houses. Custom builders have followed the national trend back to traditional house exteriors with Colonial Revival or Tudor Revival facades.

Lack of geographic barriers continues to allow residential growth in all directions in Marion County. It appears that the single family house will remain an important part of the cultural landscape of Indianapolis well into the future.

PAUL C. DIEBOLD
Division of Historic Preservation
and Archaeology,
Indiana Department of Natural Resources

Indianapolis Architecture (Indianapolis, 1975); Wilbur Peat, *Indiana Houses of the Nineteenth Century* (Indianapolis, 1962).

Sissle, Noble Lee (July 10, 1889–Dec. 17, 1975). Musician, playwright, and composer. As a young boy, Noble Sissle, a native of Indianapolis, worked as an office boy for Dr. SUMNER FURNISS, a well-known black physician. Sissle attended SHORTRIDGE HIGH SCHOOL until his family moved to Cleveland, Ohio, in 1906, where he completed high school. The family returned to Indianapolis in 1913 after his father's death. In the fall of 1913, Sissle attended DePauw University in Greencastle, Indiana, for one semester before transferring to BUTLER UNIVERSITY in Indianapolis. Both attempts to earn a college degree failed because of Sissle's involvement in the world of music. While at Butler, he wrote several "yells" for the football team.

Since childhood, Sissle had been interested in singing and writing songs. Though he had very little formal training as a musician, he had gained quite a reputation in high school and college as an entertainer with an excellent tenor singing voice. At the request of the owner of the Severin Hotel, Sissle formed a 12–piece orchestra to play regularly there. After numerous Indianapolis engagements Sissle was fortunate enough, during his first trip to the East Coast, to team with Eubie Blake, a brilliant pianist and composer. This was the beginning of the rise to fame of the team of Sissle

Noble Sissle (left) with Russell Smith in "The Chocolate Dandies," a vaudeville routine. [Indiana Historical Society, Duncan Schiedt Collection, #C2538]

and Blake as entertainers, composers, and theatrical entrepreneurs.

The 1921 musical *Shuffle Along*, written and produced by Sissle, Blake, Flournoy Miller, and Aubrey Lyle, marked the revival of African-American folk humor, jazz dance, and RAGTIME. During its more than 500 performances, many on Broadway, *Shuffle Along* served as a beacon to other talented blacks interested in the theater and introduced such performers as Florence Mills and Josephine Baker. The song, "I'm Just Wild About Harry," usually associated with the Truman-Dewey presidential race of 1948, was written by Sissle and Blake as part of the *Shuffle Along* repertoire. Other memorable songs by Sissle and Blake included "Love Will Find A Way" and "You Were Meant For Me." During the 1930s, Sissle periodically returned to Indianapolis with his orchestra for engagements at the Indiana Roof Ballroom.

STANLEY WARREN
DePauw University

Robert Kimball and William Bolcom, *Reminiscing With Sissle and Blake* (New York, 1973); *New York Times*, Dec. 18, 1975.

Slack, L. Ert (Oct. 8, 1874–Feb. 24, 1952). Mayor of Indianapolis, 1927–1930, Democrat. Born and raised in Johnson County, Indiana, Lemuel Ertus Slack moved to Indianapolis as a young man, reading law and working at CENTRAL STATE HOSPITAL. In 1897, he graduated from Indiana Law School, established a law practice in Johnson County, and was appointed deputy prosecuting attorney. He was county attorney of Johnson County, 1898–1904, state representative, 1901–1905, state senator, 1905–1909, and unsuccessfully sought the Democratic nomination for governor in 1908. He returned to Indianapolis in 1913, served as United State District Attorney under President Woodrow Wilson, 1916–1920, and was a special federal prosecutor, 1920–1923.

On November 8, 1927, after the criminal conviction of Mayor JOHN DUVALL, the City Council elected Slack on the 38th ballot to finish Duvall's term. In April, 1928, the continuing investigation led to resignations from the Council, and Slack and a Council of five newly appointed Republicans, two new Democrats, and two originally elected Democrats governed until January 6, 1930. They consulted frequently with civic organizations, made additions to the City Hospital, and widened many streets. Slack eased many Duvall appointees out of executive jobs, replacing them with Democrats.

After leaving office, Slack resumed his law practice. In 1936, he was appointed by Governor Paul McNutt to finish a term, ending December 31, 1938, on the Superior Court. Slack died in the Masonic Home in Franklin, Indiana, where he had lived in retirement for five years, and was buried in Franklin.

CHARLES JOHNSON TAGGART

Biographical Directory of the Indiana General Assembly, Vol. 2 (Indianapolis, 1984); *Indianapolis News*, Feb. 25, 1952.

Slippery Noodle Inn. Tavern and nationally known blues venue. "The Noodle," located on the corner of South and Meridian streets (372 S. Meridian) is the oldest standing commercial building in the metropolitan area, and claims to be the oldest tavern in Indiana. The HISTORIC LANDMARKS FOUNDATION OF INDIANA cites it as the state's oldest continuously operating bar in the original building on the original site. Its colorful history includes episodes as an Underground Railroad station, hangout for the JOHN DILLINGER gang, and a bordello.

The inn was built in 1850 as a roadhouse called the Tremont House. In the 1860s it became the Concordia House, the first German American club in Indianapolis, and was later called the Germania House. During World War I owner Louis Beck changed the name to Beck's Saloon. Walter Moore ran the saloon before Prohibition as Moore's Beer Tavern, and during Prohibition as Moore's Restaurant, even though alcoholic beverages were made in the basement. The stills were in place when the Yeagy family bought the inn in 1963 and gave it its current name. In 1985 the Noodle became a BLUES venue, and is known nationally for booking local, regional, national, and international artists.

SALLY CARR CHILDS-HELTON
Indiana Historical Society

Slogans and Nicknames. Geographic location, publicity and advertising campaigns, and even rival cities, among other sources, have provided numerous slogans and nicknames for Indiana's capital. These monikers are frequently descriptive ("The Capital City"), associated with a prominent industry ("The Railroad City"), geographical ("Crossroads of America"), sports-related (home of "The Greatest Spectacle in Racing"), religiously inspired ("City of Churches"), derogatory ("Naptown," "India-no-place," "End-of-No-Place "), or abbreviations ("Indy").

When legislators approved the site for a new state capital in 1821 there was a heated debate over its proposed name. State representative Jeremiah Sullivan of Madison suggested combining the state name "Indiana" with "polis," the Greek word for city, or literally, the "City of Indiana." Al-though Indian names like "Suwarrow" and "Tecumseh" had been rejected, not all residents of the state and future city were enthusiastic about "Indianapolis." One newspaper editor called the naming process "one of the most ludicrous acts" and ridiculed Indianapolis "not as a name for man, woman or child; for empire, city, mountain, or morass; for bird, beast, fish nor creeping thing." He later noted mendaciously that reversing the letters of the town's name produced Hindi words meaning "head without brains."

The nickname "Circle City" undoubtedly originated from the distinctive design utilized by ALEXANDER RALSTON and ELIAS PYM FORDHAM in the platting and mapping of the town in the spring of 1821. The CIRCLE served as a center of activity from Indianapolis' earliest years, but especially following the completion of the SOLDIERS AND SAILORS MONUMENT in 1902. The first appearance of the name is uncertain, however.

"City of Railroads," a somewhat boastful and optimistic title, was first used in the Indianapolis *LOCOMOTIVE* of September, 1849, two years following the arrival of the MADISON AND INDIANAPOLIS RAILROAD and four years before the opening of the first UNION STATION. Referring to the city's numerous rail lines and the nation's first Union Station, journalist WILLIAM R. HOLLOWAY called Indianapolis "the Railroad City" in his 1870 city history. *The People's Guide*, a Marion County directory published in 1874, pronounced Indianapolis "the greatest railroad center in the United States and perhaps the greatest in the world."

Late 19th century promotional slogans coined by civic booster organizations and local business leaders emphasized the city's transportation facilities. "The City That Has the Resources to Fit Your Business Needs," "The Opportunity City," and "The Hub of the Nationwide Transportation System" were commonly found in Indianapolis BOARD OF TRADE and CHAMBER OF COMMERCE publications.

Obvious nicknames describing Indianapolis as the state capital include "The Capital City," "The Hoosier Capital," and "The Hoosier City." Although the term "Hoosier" is properly applied to Indiana residents, a resident of Indianapolis, according to *What Do You Call a Person from . . . ? A Dictionary of Resident Names*, is called an "Ini," a term that most inhabitants of the city would not recognize.

Indianapolis earned additional titles during its early 20th century development. Home to over a dozen national and international labor unions in the early 1900s the city was occasionally referred to as the "nation's labor capital." Author MEREDITH NICHOLSON, in an article in the June, 1904, *Atlantic Monthly*, described Indianapolis as a "City of Homes." When the community dedicated its new City Hall in 1909, local leaders summed up their feelings for Indianapolis with a quote inspired by Acts 21:39—"I am myself a citizen of no mean city." The phrase had been used by earlier politicians, including former president BENJAMIN HARRISON in April, 1897.

Indianapolis was the hub for several rail lines and the intersection of several major roads and was casually referred to as "the crossroads of America." Even though the Indiana General Assembly adopted "The Crossroads of America" as the official state motto in 1937, Indianapolis utilized the moniker for its own, even designing a special logo for its 1971 sesquicentennial celebration based on that motto.

Even though Indianapolis developed a rather dubious reputation as the headquarters of the Indiana KU KLUX KLAN during the 1920s, there are no known nicknames or titles attributed to the city for that connection. Recent historical treatments, however, have assigned specific tags to the city. David M. Chalmers, in *Hooded Americanism* (1965), called Indianapolis "the queen city of Northern Klandom." Kenneth T. Jackson's *The Ku Klux Klan in the City, 1915–1930* (1967) labeled Indianapolis the "unrivaled bastion of the Invisible Empire in Mid-America."

Nicknames such as "Naptown" and "Indiano-place," the origins of which are uncertain, refer to the perceived absence of social and cultural activities in the capital. Sobriquets like "brickyard in a cornfield," which implied a dull, small-town image, did little to counter the city's mid–20th century reputation as a sleepy midwestern town. Humorist Will Rogers reportedly described Indianapolis as "the only farm I've ever seen with a monument in the center."

By the 1970s and 1980s city leaders sought to improve the city's image by adopting an initiative that would make Indianapolis a major sports center. After constructing multimillion dollar athletic facilities, attracting numerous sports governing bodies, and hosting several world-class sporting events, Indianapolis quickly earned the nicknames "Sportsville, USA" and "Amateur Sports Capital" from the media.

By the mid–1980s Indianapolis had undergone something of a renaissance and was viewed in an increasingly positive light by much of the American public. The national media described Indianapolis with such accolades as the "Star of the Snowbelt," the "Cinderella of the Rust Belt," a "Corn Belt City with Sun Belt Sizzle," and a "Diamond in the Rust." Such positive assessments have been beneficial for the city's growing tourism and convention industries and have enhanced the city's national reputation for "Hoosier Hospitality."

DEBORAH B. MARKISOHN

Slovenes. Residents of the Habsburg Austrian provinces of Carniola, Styria, Carinthia, and the Littoral, Slovenes arrived in Indianapolis' industrial suburb of HAUGHVILLE in the 1890s and settled in the area bounded by 10th, Holmes, Michigan, and Haugh streets. George Lambert (Juri Lampert), a Slovene from Besnica, recruited fellow countrymen to work for the National Malleable Castings Company, a Cleveland-based firm that operated a foundry on the northwest corner of Michigan Street and Holmes Avenue. They also found employment at KINGAN AND COMPANY meat packers, LINK-BELT, and other local factories. By the 1930s, some Slovenes sought to escape the drudgery of the factory or housing boarders by farming along the Morgan-Brown county line. Others operated their own businesses, such as bakery (Dezelan), dry goods (Koren), hardware (Urbancic), saloon (Gasnik, Turk, Milharcic), tailoring (Urajner), and grocery (Bucar, Fon, Zeunik, Matelko), which sustained the local community.

By World War I, the Slovene community of approximately 1,200 was sufficiently numerous to organize several supporting institutions. Mutual aid societies provided members with income during sickness and their families benefits in case of

Many Slovenian families lived in the Haughville neighborhood between the 1890s and the 1940s. [Indiana Historical Society, #C4952]

a member's death. The first society was St. Aloysius Lodge (1900), followed by St. Joseph Lodge and the socialist-oriented Franc Preseren Lodge (1905). Members' attitudes toward religion distinguished one lodge from another. The popular quip was that St. Aloysius members always prayed, St. Joseph members frequently prayed, but Preseren members never prayed. In 1918, over 400 stockholders organized the SLOVENIAN NATIONAL HOME. The facility, which served as a social center, meeting place, and theater, moved to its present location at 10th Street and Warman Avenue in 1940.

Because of disagreements with the local Irish-American pastor, the St. Aloysius and St. Joseph lodges agitated and raised funds for a separate Slovene parish. The bishop reluctantly agreed to organize Holy Trinity parish in 1906 with Father Joseph Lavric as its first pastor. One year later, Slovenes attended the dedication of the present brick and stone church on the corner of Holmes Avenue and St. Clair Street. Between 1906 and 1919, over 1,000 infants were baptized there. The parish school, founded in 1911, had 434 pupils by 1923. Continued growth led to the construction of a new school–social hall in 1927.

Besides the church, community life featured numerous athletic activities. Slovenes were especially adept at playing "kick the wicket" and team sports. In 1936 the West Side Jugoslav football team was the undefeated city league champion. Three years later, Indianapolis hosted a national Slovene athletic meet.

After World War II, the Slovene neighborhood began to disintegrate. The death of immigrant parents, the pursuit of educational opportunities, and the closing of local factories enabled young Slovene-American families to leave Haughville for SPEEDWAY or the Chapel Hill and Chapel Glen subdivisions along West 10th Street. In 1948 Holy Trinity ceased being a national parish and opened membership to all neighborhood Catholics, producing a peak membership of 2,250 in 1956.

Despite the dispersal of the Slovene-American population, community life continues to center on the lodges, Holy Trinity parish, the Slovenian National Home, and the Slovenian Cultural Society. The lodges are affiliated with three national fraternal organizations; however, members may belong to more than one lodge since earlier religious differences have disappeared. While providing life insurance coverage, the lodges serve primarily as social outlets and sponsors of athletic events. The parish sponsors fund-raising events including the annual sale of potica, a bread containing walnuts, raisins, and honey. Basketball and bowling teams continue to meet teams from other Slovene-American communities, which helps to maintain ethnic solidarity.

The Slovenian Cultural Society, founded in 1987, sponsors quarterly educational and cultural programs. It popularizes Slovene culture in the broader local community and maintains ties with other Slovene communities. The independence of Slovenia proclaimed in 1991 has generated increased ethnic awareness and membership.

JAMES J. DIVITA
Marian College

_____

James J. Divita, *Slaves to No One: A History of the Holy Trinity Catholic Community in Indianapolis on the Diamond Jubilee of the Founding of Holy Trinity Parish* (Indianapolis, 1981).

Slovenian National Home. Private membership club of Americans of Slovene ancestry, founded in 1918 and currently located at 2717 West Tenth Street. Slovene immigrants who were less interested in religion (socialists, freethinkers, anticlericals) organized the *Slovenski Narodni Dom* as a counterweight to nearby Holy Trinity Slovenian Catholic Church. Four hundred stockholders invested $10 each to finance the club at 729 North Holmes Avenue, which opened on May 26, 1918.

The older generation called this club "The Home," while the younger generation called it "The Nash." It was a meeting hall on Sunday mornings for local mutual aid societies, and a place where members could drink and play cards with friends or practice *balina* (bowling with a six-inch wooden ball) in a cement alley constructed in the backyard. Through the 1930s, the Home also hosted dances for young people, glee club singing, and Slovene plays. During the late 1930s, stockholders approved construction of a larger facility at Tenth Street and Warman Avenue. Old passions were declining, for Holy Trinity clergy were invited to participate in the dedication program on October 19, 1940.

The club continues as a center of Slovene community activities. The facility hosts monthly lodge meetings, gatherings of women (Slovene Women's Club) and men (Yaggers), and the annual Grape Arbor dance. The hall is rented for wedding receptions and birthday and anniversary parties. Open house, an occasion for socializing and card playing, occurs on the third Sunday of each month. The Home sponsors Independence Day and Labor Day picnics on grounds it owns in western Marion County.

JAMES J. DIVITA
Marian College

James J. Divita, *Slaves to No One: A History of the Holy Trinity Catholic Community in Indianapolis on the Diamond Jubilee of the Founding of Holy Trinity Parish* (Indianapolis, 1981).

Smith, Asa J. (Jan. 20, 1894–Feb. 12, 1973). Lawyer. Born in Wabash, Indiana, Smith graduated from DePauw University in 1915 and came to Indianapolis to study law at Indiana Law School. He graduated and was admitted to the Indiana bar in 1917. After serving in World War I, he worked as secretary to U.S. Senator Harry S. New from 1919 to 1921. Smith was a state representative in the General Assembly in 1923, lead-

ing a successful battle for a law giving the State Board of Accounts the authority to inspect the completed projects of public contractors. As the Oberholtzer family attorney, Smith was called to the deathbed of Madge Oberholtzer to take her statements which led to the conviction of Ku Klux Klan leader DAVID CURTIS (D. C.) STEPHENSON for her murder in 1925. He represented INDIANAPOLIS WATER COMPANY customers in a successful 1928 petition to the Public Service Commission to require the utility company rather than the customer to pay for the installation of water meters.

Following service as lieutenant colonel in the Marines during World War II, Smith was appointed United States Commissioner of the Federal District Court of Southern Indiana (1947–1950), and later was special master to that court (1950–1954). Appointed in 1954 as chief deputy by the MARION COUNTY PROSECUTOR, Smith conducted the preliminary investigations of the State Highway Department that led to the 1957 scandal and trial in which ten people were convicted of bribery and related charges.

JOAN CUNNINGHAM

Indiana Biography Series, Indiana State Library.

Smith, Caleb Blood (Apr. 16, 1808–Jan. 7, 1864). Politician. Born in Boston, Massachusetts, Smith moved to Ohio with his parents in 1814. He attended Miami University from 1825 to 1826. In 1827, Smith began to study law in Connersville, Indiana, and in 1828 he was admitted to the bar. From 1832 to 1833 Smith edited the *Connersville Sentinel*. A supporter of the Whig party, he utilized the newspaper to expound Whig principles.

In 1833, Smith's own political career was launched when he was elected to the Indiana General Assembly. Representing Fayette County, he served in the House from 1833 to 1837 and from 1840 to 1841. He was twice elected speaker of the House. From 1843 to 1849 Smith served in the U.S. House of Representatives. As a congressman he opposed the war with Mexico and the annexation of Texas. From 1849 to 1851 he served on the Mexican Claims Commission. Returning to private practice, he moved to Cincinnati in 1851 and to Indianapolis in 1858. Nominated as Lincoln's secretary of the interior, Smith became the first Hoosier to serve in the Cabinet of the United States (March 5, 1861–January 1, 1863).

Resigning from the Cabinet, Smith returned to Indianapolis in 1863 as judge of the U.S. District Court. He filled this position until his death.

KATE STAMM

Biographical Directory of the Indiana General Assembly, Vol. 1 (Indianapolis, 1980).

Smith, Delavan (Dec. 28, 1861–Aug. 25, 1922). *Indianapolis News* publisher. Delavan Smith was born in Cincinnati to William Henry and Emeline (Reynolds) Smith. Educated at Lake Forest College in Illinois and the Massachusetts Institute of Technology, Delavan joined his father in the management of the Western Press Association. His 30–year affiliation with the INDIANAPOLIS NEWS began in 1892 when his father became part owner of the paper. Delavan assisted his father with the *News* until 1896 when he inherited his father's interest, and in 1911 he became sole owner. Although he sold three-fourths interest to his cousin CHARLES W. FAIRBANKS in 1917, Delavan continued as owner and publisher until his death in 1922. The paper reflected his views as an "independent Republican," loyal only so long as the party lived up to his publishing motto: "The greatest good for the greatest number."

Smith also had several business interests. He held stock in the Merganthaler Corporation, a linotype system cofounded by his father. He served as vice-president of the Oliver Typewriter Company, and president of the Cox Multi-Mailer Company, which manufactured newspaper bundling machines.

Smith bequeathed several million dollars to charitable organizations including the INDIANAPOLIS FOUNDATION, METHODIST HOSPITAL, the ART ASSOCIATION OF INDIANAPOLIS, and the Indianapolis FLOWER MISSION. His and his father's papers and libraries, along with a sizable endowment, were left to the INDIANA HISTORICAL SOCIETY to establish the William Henry Smith Memorial Library.

JOAN E. HOSTETLER

"Delavan Smith" (editorial), *Indianapolis News*, Aug. 27, 1922; John W. Miller, *Indiana Newspaper Bibliography* (Indianapolis, 1982).

Smith, Gerald L. K. (Feb. 27, 1898–Apr. 15, 1976). Evangelist. Born in Pardeeville, Wisconsin, to a third-generation Disciples of Christ minister, Smith rose from poverty to become, in H. L. Mencken's words, "the greatest rabble-rouser since Saint Paul." While a student of biblical history and rhetoric at Valparaiso University, 1915–1917, he began preaching in Gary and Deep River, Indiana. A mellifluous voice and dramatic gesturing became the hallmarks of his style.

Smith's spectacular sermon at a 1922 St. Louis ministerial convention prompted the call to become pastor of the Seventh Christian Church in Indianapolis, effective January 1, 1924. His energetic evangelism quickly transformed the church, increasing membership by 1,150 in $2\frac{1}{2}$ years. He also became president of the Marion County Sunday School Union. In September, 1926, Smith assumed the pulpit of the University Place Christian Church, quadrupling its membership. Emphasizing work among BUTLER UNIVERSITY students, Smith was the only northside pastor to conduct year-round evening services.

Smith intended to remain in Indianapolis, but his wife contracted tuberculosis, forcing their relocation to the milder climate of Shreveport, Louisiana, in 1929. There he left the ministry for politics, becoming chief organizer for Senator Huey Long's Share Our Wealth movement. Smith's career peaked in 1936 with a series of electrifying speeches at anti–New Deal political conventions. Thereafter he devoted his life to leading nationalist, anti-Semitic movements, including the Christian Nationalist Crusade and America First party.

VAL HOLLEY

Glen Jeansonne, *Gerald L. K. Smith, Minister of Hate* (New Haven, Conn., 1988); David Bennett, *Demagogues in the Depression* (New Brunswick, N.J., 1969).

Smith, Oliver Hampton

Smith, Oliver Hampton (Oct. 23, 1794–Mar. 19, 1859). Pioneer attorney, state legislator, U.S. congressman and senator, railroad entrepreneur. Born in Bucks County, Pennsylvania, of Quaker stock, Smith journeyed first to New York and Pittsburgh before arriving in Indiana in 1817. He lived in Rising Sun before removing to Lawrenceburg in the winter of 1818, where he read law under the tutelage of James Dill, a friend of William Henry Harrison.

Following admission to the bar in 1820, he moved his practice to Connersville, was elected to the Indiana House of Representatives in 1822, and served as chairman of the judiciary committee. In 1824, Governor William Hendricks appointed him prosecuting attorney for the third district, and in 1826, upon the conclusion of his term, Smith was elected as a Jacksonian Democrat to the 20th Congress.

Following his term in the House, Smith returned to the practice of law until 1836 when he was elected as a Whig to the U.S. Senate, defeating Governor Noah Noble and former Governor Hendricks. Smith probably first moved his residence to Indianapolis in 1838, during his service as a senator. After losing his bid for reelection, he entered the full time practice of law, becoming the recognized leader of the Indianapolis bar. He authored the first city CHARTER (1847), and promoted public education in the city.

His travels on horseback over rough trails as a circuit riding lawyer and politician made him a strong advocate for internal improvements. He received a charter for the Indianapolis and Bellefontaine Railroad in 1848 and became its first president. A tireless promoter, Smith established the route, appointed the appraisers, obtained the support and financial backing of counties to be served, and solicited stock subscriptions. The line was to connect Indianapolis with Lake Erie and rail lines to the East. Known as the "Bee Line," it eventually became a part of the NEW YORK CENTRAL system.

Smith was a participant in the St. Louis Convention of 1849, an effort to lay the groundwork for the "Pacific Railroad." That same year he organized and effectively promoted the Union Company, which provided trackage joining all Indianapolis railroads and enabling the construction of the first Union Depot. A less successful enterprise was the Straight Line Railroad projected from Indianapolis to Evansville to connect with Memphis. The effort fell victim to the faltering economy in 1857 and was never completed.

Many of Smith's recollections of frontier life were carried in serial form in the INDIANAPOLIS DAILY JOURNAL beginning in 1857 and expanded in his book, *Early Indiana Trials and Sketches* (1858). He is buried in CROWN HILL CEMETERY.

JULIAN L. RIDLEN

Oliver Hampton Smith, *Early Indiana Trials and Sketches: Reminiscences by Hon. O. H. Smith* (Cincinnati, 1858); William Wesley Woollen, *Biographical and Historical Sketches of Early Indiana* (Indianapolis, 1883); Jacob Piatt Dunn, *Greater Indianapolis* (Chicago, 1910).

Smith, Walter Bedell "Beetle"

Smith, Walter Bedell "Beetle" (Oct. 5, 1895–Aug. 9, 1961). Army general, diplomat, and author. A native of Indianapolis, Smith was one of the most distinguished military figures the city has produced. He attended Public School 10 and MANUAL HIGH SCHOOL, and in 1910 joined the INDIANA NATIONAL GUARD. Following American entry into World War I, Smith attended the officers' training camp at FORT BENJAMIN HARRISON in 1917, and served as a lieutenant in France.

Upon his return from Europe, Smith chose to remain in the service and pursued military studies at the army's Infantry School, the Command and General Staff College, and the Army War College, ascending to the rank of captain. He was assigned to the War Department General Staff in October, 1939, where his dedication and indefatigable work ethic attracted the attention of his superiors. By February, 1942, he held the rank of brigadier general. Chosen as the U.S. Secretary of the Combined Chiefs of Staff, Smith was General Dwight D. Eisenhower's chief of staff in the North African and European campaigns. For his work on the Combined Chiefs of Staff he was awarded the Distinguished Service Medal and subsequently received a Bronze Oak Leaf Cluster for his service in Tunisia. He became a full general in 1951.

During the years 1946–1949, Smith served as ambassador to the Soviet Union. He was in Moscow during the Berlin blockade and the beginning of the Cold War, and his firm demeanor reflected the hardening U.S. policy toward the Kremlin. He believed in American military strength to preempt and contain Soviet aggression and Communist expansion. Smith was the director of the Central Intelligence Agency from 1950 to 1953, and he urged that the agency be freed from the divisiveness of domestic politics. He was subsequently undersecretary of state (1953–1957). Appointed by Eisenhower, Smith was an understudy of John Foster Dulles. He strove to guide the State Department through the complexities of evolving Cold War foreign policy and to cushion its impact on America's allies, particularly in Europe. He also grappled with Communist expansion in Southeast Asia in the 1950s.

Smith authored three works: *Europe as a Bulwark of Peace* (Washington, 1949); *My Three Years in Moscow* (Philadelphia, 1949); and *Eisenhower's Six Great Decisions: Europe, 1944–45* (New York, 1956).

JAMES R. BISHOP

Indiana Biography Series, Indiana State Library; *Who Was Who in America*, Vol. 4 (Chicago, 1968); *New York Times Magazine*, Oct. 10, 1954.

Smoke Abatement. As early as 1898, Indianapolis passed an anti-smoke ordinance in an effort to improve air quality in the city. However, this initial law lacked penalties for violators and failed to provide a means of enforcement. In 1904 the city revised the ordinance and hired a smoke

The problem addressed by the smoke abatement campaign is apparent in this view of downtown Indianapolis looking east from the Haughville neighborhood. [Indianapolis Newspapers Inc.]

inspector, but these actions did little to reduce the pollution level. A 1912 map of soot deposits in the MILE SQUARE indicated that the southeastern section of the city, near UNION STATION, accumulated 58 pounds of soot an acre in a 24–hour period.

RAILROADS, industry, and homeowners alike were responsible for the smoke that resulted when soft coal was burned in inefficient heating systems. The smoke was especially noxious in the downtown area during the winter months. A 1926 report ranked Indianapolis as the sixth smokiest city in the United States, estimating that people in the downtown area inhaled more than a teaspoonful of soot every day. Concerned citizens formed the Indianapolis Smoke Abatement League three years later. The league pushed for tough smoke abatement laws and was critical of CITIZENS GAS & COKE UTILITY for "its failure to provide city residents with smokeless fuel at reasonable prices."

Smoke pollution in the city peaked during the 1930s when the city burned over one million tons of coal annually and the resulting smoke blocked out a third of the city's sunshine during winter months. More alarming was the 63–percent increase in the city's pneumonia death rate from 1932 (370 deaths) to 1936 (604 deaths), which city health officials attributed directly to the smoke. The INDIANA STATE MEDICAL ASSOCIATION characterized the continued breathing of the city's smoke-filled air a "positive harm" to one's health.

A smoke blackout in the city on November 10, 1937, created near-zero visibility. Another serious blackout almost two weeks later filled the hallways of Riley, Long, and Coleman hospitals with smoke, aggravating patient illnesses. Photographs in city newspapers show barely visible street corners obscured by a thick gray haze. A WPA-funded study of soot levels in Indianapolis reported that in January, 1938, 1098.3 tons of soot fell in the city, averaging almost 21 tons of soot per square mile. The city's near southeast side continued to be most affected, with one neighborhood receiving almost 54.5 tons of soot per square mile in just one month. Despite these figures, city administrators argued that smoke abatement measures were adequate if enforced.

Newspapers estimated that the excessive smoke cost city residents $6.5 million annually, including lost work time due to sickness, increased costs of inefficient heating, and extra expenditures for laundry, painting, and lighting. The thick smoke also created a shrinking tax base as people left the center city for the relatively cleaner air of the suburbs.

By 1940 city officials announced that smoke had been reduced 25 percent during the previous year. Gradually the city's smoke problem improved as railroads began using diesel fuel, industries started burning oil, and individual homeowners switched to alternate heating sources. These gradual changes, coupled with the city's tougher stance on smoke abatement, led to an improvement in air quality by the late 1940s.

Industries cooperated more readily with the new smoke abatement laws than did individuals, who continued to account for many of the violations, as many as 700 annually, well into the 1950s. In 1952 the *Indianapolis Times* reported that smoke in the city had been reduced by 50 percent during the past three years. The city's last major smoke blackout occurred December 12, 1955. By the late 1950s Indianapolis' progress had been recognized nationally with the city receiving several clean air awards.

DEBORAH B. MARKISOHN

Indianapolis Newspaper Index, Indiana State Library.

Soap Box Derby. The Indianapolis Soap Box Derby began in 1934, one year after the initial race was held in Dayton, Ohio. From 1934 to 1972 the Chevrolet Division of General Motors served as national sponsor of the annual event; the *Indianapolis Star* provided local sponsorship from 1934 to 1964.

In the early years the Indianapolis event was run on city streets, including a hill on North Meridian and the hilly streets overlooking White River. Boys raced gravity-powered vehicles made from oil drums or wooden crates, fitted with wheels from lawn mowers or baby carriages. As interest grew, so did the craftsmanship; now most vehicles feature sleek fiberglass bodies.

The Soap Box Derby enjoyed its heyday during the 1950s and 1960s, when the event drew several hundred racers. In 1953, the Wilbur Shaw

Memorial Hill was built at 30th Street and Cold Spring Road. The hill, named for the three-time Indianapolis 500 winner, has served as the venue ever since. Girls were accepted as competitors beginning in 1971. Since 1934, local winners have advanced to the national championship in Akron, Ohio, where Indianapolis winner Chris Fulton won the national title in 1980.

Participation has declined since the late 1960s; the event now typically draws 15–20 competitors each year.

JUDY KEENE

"Soap Box Derby" clipping file at the Indiana State Library.

Soccer. Local athletic and social clubs have sponsored youth soccer leagues for years, but the sport was not organized on the state level until the establishment of the Indiana Youth Soccer Association (IYSA) in 1971. The IYSA is headquartered in Indianapolis and sponsors boys and girls soccer leagues in various age groups and competition levels. For the past 22 years the IYSA has held state tournaments in five different age groups, with the winners competing in the United States Soccer Federation Midwest Regional Tournament each summer. Several local clubs have won state championships at various age groups, including Dynamo FC and United FC of Indianapolis and Team Carmel from CARMEL. In June, 1988, Indianapolis Saints SC under–19 boys team became the only local club to win the Midwest Regionals but lost in the national semifinals.

In 1975 the Indiana High School Soccer Association inaugurated a state high school soccer tournament. The finals were held at the IUPUI Track and Field Stadium until 1987 when they moved to the newly built Pan American Soccer Stadium on West 16th Street (now known as Kuntz Stadium). North Central, Carmel, Park Tudor, Pike, Cathedral, and Brebeuf are all local high school teams that have made it to the boys final four at least once in the tournament's 19–year history. North Central defeated Carmel for the boys title in 1982 and 1993 while Carmel was state champion in 1985, 1987, and 1991. In 1993 the INDIANA HIGH SCHOOL ATHLETIC ASSOCIATION announced its decision to sanction boys and girls soccer and assume control of the state tournament beginning in 1994.

Indianapolis was home to the American Soccer League Daredevils for the 1978 and 1979 seasons. A crowd of 6,112 saw the Daredevils win their home opener at the Butler Bowl on April 30, 1978. After two mediocre seasons the Daredevils declared bankruptcy, ending Indianapolis' brief association with professional soccer.

Perhaps the city's most exciting experience with soccer came during the PAN AMERICAN GAMES in August, 1987. Over 12,000 spectators crowded the Pan Am Soccer Stadium to see Argentina eliminate the United States from the tournament. Six days later, 14,000 soccer faithful watched Brazil beat Chile 2–0 for the gold medal. The Pan Am Stadium also hosted the U.S. Olympic soccer team in May, 1988, when 9,500 local soccer fans watched a 4–1 exhibition victory by the United States over El Salvador.

WILLIAM D. DALTON

Social Health Association of Central Indiana. Social service agency focusing on the prevention of sexually transmitted diseases. In 1938 Lydia Woollen Ritchey and Nell Harrington established the Anti-Syphilis Society of Indiana, a local chapter of the American Social Hygiene Association, in response to growing concern over venereal diseases. In 1942 the organization limited its focus to the Indianapolis area in order to receive support from the Community Chest and changed its name to the Indianapolis Social Hygiene Association (ISHA). Located at the Public Health Center at 1140 East Market Street, a city-operated facility to treat noncriminal venereal disease patients, ISHA hired ROBERTA WEST NICHOLSON as executive director in 1943 to coordinate support services and educate community groups. As venereal disease rates declined after the widespread introduction of penicillin in 1945, ISHA turned to the broader field of sex education for long-term solutions to venereal disease control.

When the Public Health Center closed in 1953, ISHA moved to the English Foundation Building and in 1960 changed its name to the Social Health Association of Indianapolis and Mar-

ion County (SHA). After Nicholson retired in 1960 subsequent directors expanded SHA's sex education efforts to include elementary and secondary students, when requested by parents and school officials, through programming and curricular development in central Indiana schools, including the Indianapolis Public Schools. Expansion of the organization's activities beyond Marion County led to the adoption of the current name in 1976.

In 1992 SHA reached over 51,000 people through its educational programs. Its budget of almost $127,000 came largely from the UNITED WAY (80 percent) with additional support from members' fees and fund-raising efforts.

NORALEEN A. YOUNG

Social Work, History of. Before 1890 social work in Indianapolis was a diffuse activity generally identified as charity work and carried out by persons of diverse backgrounds. In that year the Indianapolis CHARITY ORGANIZATION SOCIETY, a predecessor of the Family Service Association (FSA), organized a formal lecture series for the training of its paid and volunteer staff. This effort was one of the first formal training courses in the United States. It produced several of the first executives and supervisors for other social work agencies in Indianapolis. Another early training program was provided by CHRISTAMORE HOUSE, a college settlement house established in 1905 and originally affiliated with Butler University. Organized in 1909 and continuing for more than 50 years, the Indianapolis Social Workers Club was created as a forum to allow staff and board members of social agencies in Indianapolis to present their developing programs and to exchange ideas and discuss problems.

In 1911 the Indiana University (IU) Department of Social Service was established in Indianapolis. It became the IU School of Social Work in 1966, and represents the oldest professional school of social service in the United States begun and continuously functioning as part of a university.

During the first two decades of the 20th century numerous social work organizations established branches in Indianapolis, including Legal

Aid Bureau, CAMP FIRE GIRLS, BOY SCOUTS and GIRL SCOUTS, Tuberculosis Association, Traveler's Aid Society, and Christmas Clearing House. Government services also grew, especially during the Great Depression. A special session of the Indiana General Assembly in 1936 established employment security and public welfare programs. The newly created State Department of Public Welfare (now the Department of Family and Children's Services) coordinated statewide program offices. The increase in services and the advent of a central coordinating agency significantly increased the need for trained social workers and the demands upon the IU social services training program. During the 1936–1937 academic year, the IU program established the two-year master's degree as the only recognized professional degree and in effect discontinued any undergraduate social work program.

Both statewide and in Indianapolis, demand for trained social service staff grew at such a pace during and after World War II that many persons were offered positions even before finishing their course of professional study. The war had taken many trained professionals from social service agencies in Indianapolis, and had reduced enrollment in the IU training program to two full-time and a few part-time students.

In response, the Indianapolis Community Fund and the Indiana Department of Social Services developed a graduate study plan and funded it at $6,000 a year for five years. The plan called for the training of resident students in Marion County on the condition that they remain in the community and accept any offer of employment by the Community Fund. One outcome was that by 1950 Indianapolis was known for its well-developed social services in the city school system.

During the 1960s—stimulated by social change and activism, federal efforts such as the War on Poverty, and amendments to the Social Security Act that increased service delivery in public welfare—the need for social work specialists increased again. The IU school grew and at the end of the decade became part of IUPUI. The school reintroduced a baccalaureate program that developed into an accredited undergraduate program beginning in 1974. The school's most recent development (1993) was approval to establish a Ph.D. program beginning in 1994.

GARY R. LOWE

Helen Cintilda Rogers, *Seventy Years of Social Work Education at Indiana University* (Indianapolis: Indiana University School of Social Work, 1982); Ruth Hutchinson Crocker, "Christamore: An Indiana Settlement House from Private Dream to Public Agency," *Indiana Magazine of History*, 83 (June, 1987), 113–140.

Socialist Parties and Movements. In the summer of 1901, more than 100 men and women met in the Masonic Hall in Indianapolis, sang the "Marseillaise," and founded the Socialist Party of America. Most of the delegates had come to the party from utopian socialism, Populism, or industrial unionism.

The party was the creation of Eugene V. Debs of Terre Haute and other leaders of the Social Democratic party uniting with the Kangaroo faction of the Socialist Labor party which, unlike Daniel DeLeon, head of the SLP, wished to try to convert American Federation of Labor members to socialism. The new party was certain that capitalism could not reform itself. Its founders confidently expected the American people to flock to socialism once it had been explained to them.

The early strength of socialism in Indianapolis owed much to the city's sizable German population. In 1890, German-born and first generation German-Americans numbered about 25 percent of the city's population. Germans who fled after the failed 1848 revolutions in their homeland were much more militant and radical than earlier emigres. Many German-American workers on the south side of Indianapolis became socialists.

Indianapolis was never a center of socialism in the United States or even in Indiana. It was, however, a major center for unionism (nine national unions had their headquarters in the city by 1905) and many union leaders were socialist-minded. But despite the presence of Debs and the prominence of Hoosier-born John Harriman, who had briefly attended BUTLER UNIVERSITY in Indianapolis and was Debs' running mate in 1900, Indianapolis played a minor role in the Socialist party. For example, in the 1904 gubernatorial race in Indiana, only 4 percent of the votes in

Terre Haute, Indiana, native Eugene V. Debs was prominent in founding the Socialist Party of America in Indianapolis in 1901.
[Indiana Historical Society, #C2283]

Marion County were cast for all non-major parties. The Prohibition party often got more votes than the Socialist party. In 1912 the Socialist party in Indianapolis received 5,300 votes, but the Progressive party received 20,200.

The Socialist party nationally reached its zenith just before World War I. And in Indianapolis in 1920 all the non-major parties combined received only 2.8 percent of the votes in the gubernatorial race. The national party collapsed during the Great Depression. It did no better in Indiana. In the whole state of Indiana in 1936 only 4,000 people voted Socialist; in Marion County only 915 (0.4 percent) voted for all non-major parties. The Socialist party as a political force was dead, although the less prominent Socialist Labor party continued to draw votes in Indiana into the 1980s.

After World War II, despite the efforts of Indianapolis socialists like POWERS HAPGOOD, son of an Indianapolis pioneer in employee ownership of plants, the local Socialist party remained electorally ineffectual. While there were committed individuals after 1950, socialism was not an effective force in Indianapolis.

MILTON FARBER
Butler University

David A. Shannon, *The Socialist Party of America* (New York, 1955); George T. Probst, *The Germans in Indianapolis* (Indianapolis, 1989).

Society of Friends (Quakers).

The Quakers are among the few sects with roots in the turmoil of the English Revolution of the 1640s that have survived to the present. Until the late 19th century they were distinctive in many ways: their repudiation of pastoral ministry in their "meetings for worship," their advocacy of the equality of women, their plain style of living, and their belief in the "Inward Light"—that each soul had a certain measure of divine light that, if heeded, would lead to salvation.

In the early 19th century thousands of Quakers moved into Ohio and Indiana, mainly from Virginia and North Carolina. William Townsend was apparently the first in Marion County, arriving in 1820. The main Quaker settlements, however, were in DECATUR TOWNSHIP; Friends founded six different congregations there between 1825 and 1859. Quakers also settled in southwestern Hamilton County during the early 1830s, establishing the towns of Bethlehem (now CARMEL) in 1833 and Westfield in 1834.

A short-lived meeting appeared in Indianapolis in 1834. Friends founded another in 1856, the origin of Indianapolis First Friends. They built a meetinghouse at Delaware and St. Clair streets, with a school adjacent. They were involved in traditional Quaker reform efforts, especially prison reform and human welfare. In 1896 First Friends opened a new meetinghouse at 13th and Alabama streets. In 1891 another meeting, later known as West Indianapolis and Second Friends, was established in the city.

The theological splits into Orthodox and Hicksite bodies in the 19th century had little impact here. Virtually all Indiana Friends were Orthodox, meaning that their beliefs about Christ and Scripture were essentially Protestant. In the 1870s the introduction of revivalism and the end of the plain life led to the separation of a few conservative members. In 1892, 1897, and 1902 First Friends hosted national conferences of Friends, the last of which founded the Five Years Meeting, the first national Quaker organization with legislative powers.

The 20th century brought changes. Friends adopted pastoral worship and became outwardly indistinguishable from most other Protestants. The rural meetings in Decatur Township slowly declined. First Friends grew steadily, coming to be recognized as one of the nation's most important Quaker congregations and attracting leading Friends such as David M. Edwards (1872–1939) and Errol T. Elliott (1894–1992) as pastors. In 1956 it followed a number of other downtown churches to the north side. Other area Friends, such as Edward D. Evans (1862–1944), Alvin T. Coate (1870–1955), and the brothers Sumner A. Mills (1895–1984) and Howard S. Mills, Sr. (1898-), achieved international reputations in Quaker affairs.

Since 1950 Indianapolis Quakers have become more diverse. Some have become fundamentalist in sympathy, others more liberal. In 1959 a small group split from First Friends because of the congregation's refusal to accept a black member and formed Lanthorn Meeting, an unprogrammed group. In 1979 another unprogrammed group, North Meadow, formed. It became a center of controversy in 1988 when it began to celebrate same-sex marriages. There were approximately 1,130 Quakers in Marion County in 1993.

THOMAS D. HAMM
Earlham College

Society of Indiana Pioneers. Hereditary organization founded in Indianapolis in 1916 as part of the state centennial, and still headquartered in the capital. Its purpose is "to honor the memory and the work of the pioneers who opened Indiana to civilization." Members file papers to prove descent from a pioneer ancestor who meets the residence requirements established by the organization. Eligibility dates depend on the area of the state in which the pioneer ancestor originally settled. In its early years the society's membership was heavily weighted toward Marion County (67 percent in 1921); in 1990 the county accounted for 304 of the society's 1,650 members.

Offices of the society are located in the INDIANA STATE LIBRARY AND HISTORICAL BUILDING. The group organized the first Indiana History Conference in 1919, and sponsors two pilgrimages per year for members to historical areas. An annual meeting and dinner are held in November, usually in conjunction with the annual meeting of the INDIANA HISTORICAL SOCIETY. The society also publishes a yearbook that includes an annual report, articles of historical interest, a roster of members and their approved ancestors, and a necrology.

RUTH DORREL
Indiana Historical Society

Murray Holliday, *A History of the Society of Indiana Pioneers* (Greenfield, Ind., [1983]).

Soil and Groundwater Contamination. Marion County is not heavily contaminated, and potable groundwater is readily available. Most contaminated sites should be cleaned up by the year 2000. The origin, location, and extent of soil and groundwater contamination within Marion County is derived from: the soil types and underlying GEOLOGY at the location; the present and past land uses at the location; the lack of, or amount of, pollution prevention practiced at the location.

Similar to other industrialized urban areas, Indianapolis has myriad individual sites and even entire portions of the city which are contaminated to some degree. The origin of the contamination ranges from small gasoline stations to manufacturing sites to large Superfund sites such as Southside Landfill. While contaminated sites occur in all portions of the county, the area south and west of downtown from WHITE RIVER to Washington Street is by far the most heavily contaminated due to the age, types, and concentration of industries, and the high permeability of the saturated outwash deposits.

Nearly every industrial site has had some sort of chemical spill; however, most are typically small. Much industrial (manufacturing) contamination is either older or has been discharged to the White River or the atmosphere and not directly to soil. The Marion County CERCLIS (Comprehensive Environmental Response Compensation and Liability Inventory System) list developed by the U.S. Environmental Protection Agency (EPA) had 97 older industrial sites listed in July, 1992, but most of these require no further action. In 1992 there were at least 755 sites which stored one or more chemicals requiring Community-Right-to-Know reporting (SARA Title III), and at least 195 sites which stored Extremely Hazardous Sub-

stances (EHS). Most storage is within specially designed areas.

Three designated EPA Superfund sites are located on the near south side. These are: Carter-Lee
Lumber Company, Reilly Industries, and Southside Landfill. All three sites have a range of chemical contamination, and all three have some degree
of direct chemical input into migrating groundwater. Perhaps the most serious is the Southside
Landfill, which is built on outwash and is immediately adjacent to White River. A landfill has been in
operation at the site for several decades, and it contains nearly any chemical or waste ever available to
citizens or industries within Marion County. The
landfill is known to have subsurface contamination moving toward the river; this movement has
been retarded by the late–1980s installation of a
subsurface cement grout curtain around the landfill. Both Carter-Lee and Reilly are scheduled to be
cleaned up by the year 2000, with Southside
Landfill contamination a much larger and long-
term issue.

Underground Storage Tanks (USTs) containing petroleum hydrocarbons are the most widespread potential contamination point sources
within Marion County. In December, 1992, there
were 1,762 sites registered with the Indiana Department of Environmental Management with
one or more tanks and 632 tanks were reported to
have leaked some amount. Most USTs which have
leaked have affected only a very small area adjacent to the tanks. These soils are typically either
excavated and disposed of at landfill, or are
cleaned on site through aeration and/or bioreme-
diation methods. Some of the largest known UST
problems involve large bulk storage facilities of refined products and unrefined crude oil.

Numerous landfills exist within Marion
County in addition to Southside Landfill. These
include the older and now closed Julietta, Banta
Road, and Southport Road municipal solid waste
landfills. Many construction-demolition debris
landfills are scattered across the county. These are
mainly located within old sand and gravel pits
near White River, and more recently in borrow
pits along the interstate highways. Many former
WETLANDS along streams and rivers were filled
("reclaimed") with all manner of wastes early in
the city's history.

Several highway and street salt storage piles
have contaminated soil and groundwater around
the facilities. In a few cases this has caused residential water wells to become unfit for human use.
Salt contamination along roadways and ditches
can be a localized problem with vegetation kills
and surface runoff to streams.

Septic systems have long been recognized as
a major localized, yet areally dispersed source of
biologic contamination in the form of fecal
coliforms and E. coli bacteria. While these materials are biodegradable, they can have significant
impacts in the immediate system area, especially
in larger unsewered subdivisions with water wells
or those that discharge into surface water.

Recently, the amount and areal extent of soil
and groundwater contamination caused by "nonpoint sources" has been recognized. These sources
included hydrocarbons and other fluids from motorized vehicles, road salt, random chemical spills,
agricultural chemicals, and contaminants deposited locally by wind and precipitation. The
amount of contamination varies greatly on a site
basis.

KEVIN STRUNK
Wabash Resources and Consulting

Soldiers and Sailors Monument. Indianapolis' "signature" structure, located in the center
of the city's original MILE SQUARE plat. Conceived,
designed, and built as the state's memorial to Indiana's Civil War veterans, the Indiana State Soldiers
and Sailors Monument was built from 1888
to 1901. Governor OLIVER P. MORTON initiated
the first public discussion of a Civil War monument soon after the war ended. Following two decades of lobbying led by George J. Langsdale,
editor of the *Greencastle Banner*, the General Assembly in 1887 designated a commission to plan
and oversee construction of a suitable memorial.

An international design competition was
held in 1887 with the winning entry selected the
following year. The commission was looking for a
design for an original "American Monument" free
of the iconography of antiquity. German architect
Bruno Schmitz, who became Wilhelmine Germany's greatest monument designer, submitted

the winning proposal from among 70 designs. The monument, Schmitz' only work outside Germany and Switzerland, was integrated into the Circle location with terraced steps, fountains, pools, an obelisk shaft, and an abundance of statuary. A comparison of the built monument and the original design reveals variations in some of the statuary.

Construction began with the laying of the foundation in 1888, and the cornerstone was set on August 22, 1889. The shaft was constructed between 1889 and 1892. The first pieces of sculpture added were the date astragal, a sculptured band, in 1892, and the crowning figure of *Victory* (more popularly known as *Miss Indiana*) in 1893. The two bronze pieces are the work of sculptor George T. Brewster, who won the two design competitions. Brewster also sculpted the bronze naval astragal following another design competition. Installed in 1892, it depicts the prow of the USS *Hartford*. The fourth sculptural competition for the monument was won by German sculptor Nicolaus Geiger. His bronze army astragal was cast in Berlin and installed in 1895.

By 1893 the World's Columbian Exhibition in Chicago was attracting design competitors away from the Indianapolis monument, forcing the commissioners to suspend further competitions. Frustration over the delay in the monument's completion led the General Assembly to dissolve the Board of Monument Commissioners in 1895 and replace it with the Board of Monument Regents. The regents turned to Schmitz to expedite the completion of the monument; he supplied designs for the remaining sculptures, lamp standards, and cascade fountains.

Austrian RUDOLF SCHWARZ won the final competition in 1899 and was selected to execute the last elements envisioned in Schmitz's design. Schwarz, a native of Vienna, had worked with Schmitz on his many projects in Germany. Concerned about realism and accuracy, Schwarz originally sculpted the limestone soldiers with beards, but shaved them when told of the youthfulness of the Indiana troops.

After 14 years of construction, the monument was completed in 1901 and formally dedicated on May 15, 1902. The gala event, for which LEW WALLACE was master of ceremonies, in-

Construction of the Soldiers and Sailors Monument began in 1889 and continued until 1901.
[Indiana Historical Society, Bass Collection, #333101]

cluded the recitation of a poem by JAMES WHITCOMB RILEY and the playing of a march by John Philip Sousa, both composed for the occasion. John W. Foster, an Indiana native and secretary of state under BENJAMIN HARRISON, delivered the principal address.

The monument has had a lasting impact on Indianapolis and Indiana. It has been the focus and symbol of the city, dominating the downtown skyline until the arrival of the high-rise office buildings. It redefined the Circle and the local perception of civic and monumental architecture and open spaces, a definition reinforced by the massive INDIANA WORLD WAR MEMORIAL PLAZA of the following generation. The monument also launched the career of Rudolf Schwarz as Indiana's monument sculptor and designer; he later executed several county memorial monuments. The monument continues its role as a civic focal point as Christmas celebrations, festivals, and memorial services are staged on its terraces. The structure has changed little since its completion, but was the object of a much-needed major restoration from 1986 to 1990.

WILLIAM L. SELM

Mary Ellen Gadski, James A. Glass, and William L. Selm, "Indiana State Soldiers' and Sailors' Monument, Indianapolis–Marion County Register of Historic Properties Nomination Form," June 27, 1983, copies in the files of the Indianapolis Historic Preservation Commission.

Solomon, Izler (Jan. 11, 1910–Dec. 12, 1987). Music director and conductor of the INDIA-

NAPOLIS SYMPHONY ORCHESTRA (ISO), 1956–1975. American born and trained, Solomon began his conducting career at age 22 with the Lansing Symphony Orchestra. In the ensuing 25 years he led the Illinois Symphony, the Women's Symphony of Chicago, and orchestras in Columbus (Ohio), Buffalo, and New Orleans. Solomon first appeared with the ISO in 1955 as guest conductor, and on April 14, 1956, was named the orchestra's third conductor.

Solomon was a popular guest conductor throughout his 19 years with the ISO. In addition to guesting with most of the major American orchestras, he appeared in Canada, Israel, Germany, and Mexico. He also served as music director of Wolf Trap Farm Center and headed both the Aspen Music Festival and the Flagstaff Summer Festival. His numerous awards include the National Music Council's Award of Honor, the Alice M. Ditson Award "for distinguished services to American music," and an award from the National Association of American Conductors and Composers. He made more than 40 recordings and received six honorary doctorates.

One June 6–7, 1975, Solomon's last pair of concerts were held to capacity houses at CLOWES MEMORIAL HALL. The program of "All Time Favorites" included Beethoven's Symphony No. 3 in E-flat Major (*Eroica*), the Academic Festival Overture by Brahms, and Elgar's Enigma Variations.

JOAN C. DALTON

Southport. Small city in southern Marion County bounded by Buck Creek, Stop 11 Road, McFarland Road, and Madison Avenue. In 1822 Jacob Smock settled on the land south of Buck Creek, followed soon after by other settlers. The area gained its name from pioneers traveling south from Indianapolis who used the small town as their first stop (or port) outside the capital. Southport was not platted until 1849, following the construction of the MADISON AND INDIANAPOLIS RAILROAD through the settlement. An addition to the original plat occurred in 1850, and in 1853 Southport incorporated.

The town grew slowly through the 19th century; its population in 1880 was only 388. Railroad crossings on the southern edge of India-

napolis made travel to the south side difficult until tracks were elevated in the 1920s. Following this change, and the introduction of the INTERURBAN, residents in Southport could commute to jobs in Indianapolis and the town gained a number of new inhabitants. The enlargement of Madison Avenue in the 1960s further increased accessibility to the south side. In 1960 Southport's population was 892; by 1980 it was 2,266. The implementation of UNIGOV in 1970 encompassed Southport, but it remained an EXCLUDED CITY within the Unigov system. Like Beech Grove, Lawrence, and Speedway, it retained its own mayor, city council, and police department.

Southport is a city of single-family dwellings; the housing stock in the city dates primarily from the 1960s and 1970s, although some historic homes remain. There are few businesses within the city limits and most residents work outside its borders. Southport's 1993 population was approximately 2,300.

CONNIE J. ZEIGLER

Spanish-American War (Apr. 21–Aug. 12, 1898). As the nation called for war against Spain following the February 15, 1898, sinking of the USS *Maine* in Havana harbor, Indianapolis newspapers hesitated to blame Spain for the act. Only the *Indianapolis American Tribune*, a GRAND ARMY OF THE REPUBLIC weekly, expressed any eagerness for military action. The *Catholic Record* (one predecessor to the *Indiana Catholic and Record*) initially opposed American intervention in Cuba, but later encouraged Catholic youth to prove their loyalty by volunteering for military service.

Following the United States' declaration of war against Spain (April 25, 1898, retroactive to April 21) and Governor James A. Mount's mobilization of the INDIANA NATIONAL GUARD, about 5,000 men reported to the State Fairgrounds (designated Camp Mount) at Indianapolis. By mid-May three infantry regiments and two artillery batteries mustered into federal service and transferred to Chickamauga Park, Georgia, for training. Other units followed in the ensuing weeks. In July the 161st Regiment Infantry organized in the city under the command of future governor Winfield T. Durbin. It did not leave the state until mid-August and served as an occupying force in Cuba following the war.

Included among the Indiana volunteers were several companies of Indianapolis men—Companies "A," "D," and "H" of the 158th Regiment Indiana Infantry; and Battery "A," 27th Indiana Light Artillery, which was on the firing line in Puerto Rico when peace was declared. Two local companies of African-Americans under the command of Captains Jacob M. Porter and John J. Buckner of Indianapolis never saw combat and were dismissed in late October. Other local men rounded out the rosters of Indiana units.

Patriotism in the city was strong throughout the war. Parades and military events were frequent, beginning with the departure of the first regiments in May. Memorial Day (May 30) featured the usual parade in downtown Indianapolis along with speeches and the decoration of graves in the national cemetery at Crown Hill. On August 11 a crowd estimated at over 12,000 gathered in Garfield Park to watch a reenactment of the Battle of Santiago. Although inefficient transportation slowed their arrival at the event, those attending witnessed an outstanding military display. Military units returning home later in the year and in 1899 were also greeted by cheering throngs of Indianapolis citizens.

Several of Indianapolis' more notable citizens volunteered for service during the war, including Russell Harrison (son of former President Benjamin Harrison), Harry S. New (son of ex-Consul General and Indianapolis Journal publisher John C. New), and William Eastin English (son of William H. English, candidate for vice-president in 1880). Captain New served on the staff of General Fitzhugh Lee; Captain English was an aide to Major General Joseph Wheeler. Upon returning home, English founded the National Association of United Spanish War Veterans and served as its first commander-in-chief.

At least one member of the black 10th U.S. Cavalry, killed in an advance up San Juan Hill, was an Indianapolis native. Will H. White's sacrifice was highlighted in a local newspaper article published in June, 1898. Other local combatants were occasionally featured in the Indianapolis Star.

The 158th Indiana Volunteers march out of Indianapolis to fight in the Spanish-American War on May 16, 1898.
[Indiana Historical Society, #C5724]

In addition to the military presence at Camp Mount, the United States Arsenal on the city's east side was commissioned to manufacture canvas haversacks for the army and employed over 100 people to accomplish this task. Also, the fairgrounds served as a staging area for volunteers throughout the war. Despite this, the annual State Fair managed to take place as usual in the fall of 1898. The last regiment of volunteers disbanded on May 3, 1899, bringing an end to the city's participation in the Spanish-American War.

Following the war Indianapolis remained somewhat divided over the issue of American expansionism. The Catholic Record claimed "it was a misnomer to call our war with Spain a war for humanity." The Democratic Indianapolis Sentinel opposed annexation of Hawaii, Puerto Rico, or the Philippines, while Republican papers like the Indianapolis News, though unenthusiastic about expansion, eventually accepted annexation as the official party position.

Wayne Sanford

Indianapolis Star, May, 1898–May, 1899; William J. Watt and James R. H. Spears, Indiana's Citizen Soldiers: The Militia and National Guard in Indiana History (Indianapolis, 1980); Record of Indiana Volunteers in the Spanish-American War, 1898–1899 (Indianapolis, 1900).

Special Service Districts. Jurisdictions for Indianapolis city police protection, fire protection, and other services delivery. These districts have artificial legal boundaries that do not correspond with any other currently existing local government unit. The UNIGOV reorganization of local government in Marion County did not extend all previous Indianapolis city services outward to the Marion County boundaries. As a result, "special service districts" were designated inside Marion County for Indianapolis city services that covered less than the territory of the new consolidated city.

The Indianapolis Police Special Service District is the area served by the INDIANAPOLIS POLICE DEPARTMENT and is essentially the same as the pre-Unigov City of Indianapolis. The Indianapolis Fire Special Service District is the area served by the INDIANAPOLIS FIRE DEPARTMENT and is also roughly the same as the pre-Unigov city, although not exactly the same as the Police Special Service District. These two special service districts were created at the time the Unigov reorganization took effect in 1970. The operations of both are administered by the Indianapolis DEPARTMENT OF PUBLIC SAFETY.

In 1976 the Indianapolis Solid Waste Collection Special Service District was created, separating it from the Indianapolis Sanitary District of which it had been a part. It is administered by the DEPARTMENT OF PUBLIC WORKS. Residents within the Solid Waste Collection Special Service District have their trash picked up by Indianapolis city government crews, while private haulers collect the garbage for most Marion County residents living outside the special service district. The creation of this new special service district allowed city garbage collection, and the taxes paying for it, to be separated from the countywide services of sewage collection and disposal and wastewater treatment and discharge.

The CITY-COUNTY COUNCIL retains the authority to extend the territory of special service districts, and minor extensions have occurred for each of the three existing districts, but all three remain confined essentially to the central portion of Marion County corresponding with the pre-Unigov City of Indianapolis. The City-County Council is also authorized by state law to create additional special service districts and define their powers and responsibilities.

The special service districts finance their operations, improvements, and debt services through various combinations of property taxes imposed on residents within the districts and user fees or service charges collected from recipients of their services. Property taxes to fund the special service districts are restricted to property within the districts' boundaries. If a district provides services beyond its boundaries it may collect a service charge from those nonresidents.

Each special service district is governed by a Special Service District Council, which is a subset of the City-County Council. The Special Service District Council for a district consists of the four at-large members of the City-County Council plus the other members whose council districts lie wholly or mostly within that special service district. The Special Service District Council has authority to conduct the initial review and approval of the budget, appropriations, tax rates, and user fees or service charges for its special service district. Because their service areas are so nearly identical, one Special Service District Council governs both the Police Special Service District and the Fire Special Service District.

The inclusion on the Special Service District Councils of the at-large members of the City-County Council, and of other City-County Council members whose districts were only partially included within a special service district, precipitated two lawsuits. The controversy stemmed largely from the fact that including these members created Republican majorities on each of the councils, which otherwise would have had Democratic majorities. Both lawsuits were unsuccessful. The first, *Bryant v. Whitcomb* (1970), concerned the inclusion of the City-County Council members whose districts were only partially within the affected special service districts. The second, *Cantwell v. Hudnut* (1976), concerned the inclusion of the at-large members of the City-County Council; although the challengers prevailed in federal district court, the district judge's decision was reversed by the Seventh Circuit Court of Appeals.

AMY H. SCHUFF

Spectator Sport (1978). Novel based on the INDIANAPOLIS 500–MILE RACE. Written by Gosport, Indiana, native James Alexander Thom, the story focuses on the rain-shortened, crash-marred 1973 race and the deaths of drivers Art Pollard (in qualifications) and Swede Savage. The event is seen through the eyes of a number of spectators who interact with one another. Published in a paperback edition of 250,000 copies (and now out of print), the book received a mixed reaction locally. One reviewer from Indianapolis chided the author for his "outlandish vocabulary," while another called his story "compelling, believable, and, in consonance with the topic, fast moving."

Born on May 28, 1933, Thom is a 1951 graduate of Indianapolis ARSENAL TECHNICAL HIGH SCHOOL. A Korean War veteran, he received a bachelor of arts degree in journalism from BUTLER UNIVERSITY. He worked for the *INDIANAPOLIS STAR* from 1960 to 1967, serving as the business editor and writing a financial column. He later was a senior editor for the *SATURDAY EVENING POST* before becoming a freelance writer.

Thom is the author of several other books including *Long Knife* (1979); *Follow the River* (1981); *From Sea to Shining Sea* (1984); and *Panther in the Sky* (1989).

RAY BOOMHOWER
Indiana Historical Society

Donald E. Thompson, *Indiana Authors and Their Books, 1967–1980* (Crawfordsville, Ind., 1981).

Speech and Dialect. There have been no studies of speech and dialect of only Indianapolis, but studies including Indiana and the Midwest give some indication of the settlement patterns, cultural backgrounds, and social structures that influenced the speech and dialect of Hoosiers living in and around Indianapolis. As early as 1900, scholars divided rural Indiana into two distinct speech areas represented by the northern and southern parts of the state. This division only applied to the rural areas of the state; city speech was considered to be nearly uniform with that of other large cities in the country, for reasons that included greater population mobility, better schools, ready access to books and newspapers, and technological advances in communication. It was not until 1920, however, that the state's urban population reached 50 percent, leaving considerable rural influences in city areas.

Further, various scholars did not agree upon where to draw the line between northern and southern influences. The major study in Indiana was done by Albert H. Marckwardt several years before World War II with elderly informants and was published in 1940 as part of the Linguistic Atlas of America project. Marckwardt found that the southern influence extended well above the middle of the state; Raven I. McDavid, Jr., supported this view in a 1958 study. Marvin D. Carmony's study in 1972 argued for a line running approximately through the middle of the state, while Robert F. Dakin's 1971 study considered the central part of the state to be a transition area. James M. Bergquist's 1981 study also considered the central part of the state as an area distinct from its northern and southern extremes, with mixed language characteristics reflecting an amalgamation of northern and southern cultures.

Marckwardt and his supporters based their conclusions in large part on settlement patterns in the state as reflected by early census data. For example, in 1860 Indiana had only 41,000 citizens who were born in New York and the New England states, while 140,000 were born in Kentucky, Tennessee, Virginia, and North Carolina. These earlier scholars drew fairly clear language use lines based on the northern culture–southern culture dichotomy, and they also felt that the distribution was influenced by people moving west from Pennsylvania along the old NATIONAL ROAD.

Later scholars who view the central part of the state (including Indianapolis) as a transitional area also base their conclusions on settlement patterns, but their reasoning is more complex. Dialectologists believe the strongest influence upon an area's language comes from its first settlers (in Indiana, this excludes Native American societies). Those who come later, even in larger numbers, have a difficult time displacing the earlier patterns.

Central Indiana was settled primarily between the end of the War of 1812 and the Panic of 1837, and many of the settlers who came originally from the South stopped in Ohio before moving into central Indiana. The middle Ohio Valley area around Cincinnati was well developed before the War of 1812, and attracted both northern and upland-southern settlers. The area became the first great meeting place for these two cultures, and after the War of 1812 became a major gateway into central Indiana. With the New Purchase of 1818 and the sale of lands in central Indiana beginning in 1821, the Indiana legislature decided to move the state capital to the center of the New Purchase lands, recognizing that the flood of new settlers would radically change the state's center of population.

The hybrid Ohio Valley culture became the basis for the settlement of central Indiana. Many settlers stopped in Ohio until Indiana opened up, and they became accustomed to this mixture of northern and southern cultures. Children of southern parents born into this mixed culture grew up not knowing pure southern culture. Further, a strong economic cultural connection existed between central Indiana and the Cincinnati area from about 1820 through the Civil War. Early central Indiana farmers, mostly from the upland South, found themselves moving from subsistence to commercial farming, and Cincinnati, already an important source of supplies and materials from the East, became an important outlet for corn and hogs as well. This economic tie formed the basis for the corn-belt culture in central Indiana, and included the culture traits of speech and dialect.

The speech and dialect patterns of the central Indiana culture area, including Indianapolis, were indeed based upon a synthesis of northern and southern patterns; even the large ethnic populations that settled in the area could not change the earlier established pattern except in ethnic neighborhoods. Today Indianapolis is open to the same leavening influences of speech and dialect cited at the beginning of the century— improved education, transportation, and media access. Language is one of humanity's most rapidly changing culture traits, and the speech and dialect of Indianapolis will continue to change as an important part of its history.

SALLY CARR CHILDS-HELTON
Indiana Historical Society

Marvin Carmony, *Indiana Dialects in Their Historical Setting* (Terre Haute, Ind.: Indiana Council of Teachers of English, 1979); Albert H. Marckwardt, "Folk Speech in Indiana and Adjacent States," *Indiana History Bulletin*, 17 (Jan., 1940), 120–140; James M. Bergquist, "Tracing the Origins of a Midwestern Culture: The Case of Central Indiana," *Indiana Magazine of History*, 77 (May, 1981), 1–32.

Speedway. Marion County town located about seven miles northwest of Monument Circle. In 1912 real estate developer Lemon Trotter laid out Speedway City for his clients CARL G. FISHER, JAMES A. ALLISON, ARTHUR C. NEWBY, and FRANK H. WHEELER, founders of the INDIANAPOLIS MOTOR SPEEDWAY. They envisioned an attractive "horseless city" of automotive industries and workers' homes adjacent to the racetrack. Trotter designed an expansive Main Street with a commercial district on the west side and industrial facilities on the east side of the new community.

Speedway's future was secured when industries moved to the area. The PREST-O-LITE COMPANY, owned by Fisher and Allison, opened an acetylene cylinder factory as Speedway City was platted in 1912. Within a few years four additional factories were built: the Electric Steel Company (1913), Allison Engineering Company (1917), American Art Clay (1919), and Esterline Angus (1923). Though some of the company names and products changed over the years, these firms provided residents with secure jobs and a strong tax base.

In 1926 residents of Speedway City petitioned for incorporation as the Town of Speedway. Four years later the town numbered over 1,400 residents. Though the Great Depression slowed residential and commercial expansion, World War II brought lucrative government contracts for local industries and more jobs. By 1950 about 5,500 people lived in Speedway.

The town's most intensive period of growth occurred from 1950 to 1970, when the population nearly tripled. Apartments and single-family limestone and brick ranches were built for new residents. With the influx of families came the need for additional schools. Formed in 1928, the school corporation expanded in the 1950s and 1960s to include four elementary schools, one junior high, and a senior high school. School population peaked in the early 1970s but stabilized in the 1990s at 1,500 students. St. Christopher's Catholic School also serves Speedway students.

Speedway is best known for "The Track" at the edge of town. The Indianapolis Motor Speedway provides jobs for residents and a vital economic boost—as well as some municipal headaches—to the community during the months of May and August.

Residents of this conservative, middle class town have successfully resisted annexation by Indianapolis, preferring to remain one of the EX-CLUDED CITIES under UNIGOV. An elected five-member town council governs Speedway and supervises the school system. The 4.2–square-mile town maintains its own police and fire departments, library, water company, and wastewater treatment plant for the current population of 13,000 citizens.

CATHLEEN F. DONNELLY

History Committee of the Speedway Civic Committee, *The Story of Speedway* (1966); *Indianapolis News*, May 23, 1989.

Spink, Edgar George (Feb. 7, 1867–Mar. 17, 1927). Builder. Born in Washington, Indiana, Spink operated a construction company in Lexington, Kentucky, in the mid–1890s. In 1904 he moved to Indianapolis where he became associated with Home Building and Realty Company in real estate sales and construction. In 1912 he formed E. G. Spink Company.

During World War I, Indianapolis, like many United States cities, suffered from a lack of housing. Spink's company addressed that problem by constructing large apartment and hotel buildings that contained many small apartments. Spink reputedly began the idea of one- or two-bedroom apartments with kitchenettes in Indianapolis. His apartments were designed to appeal especially to the growing number of "bachelor and professional women" as well as to elderly and newly married couples. He erected over 60 apartment buildings in Indianapolis. Some of the largest are the Hotel Spink at 233–235 South McCrea Street, the Spink-Arms Hotel (now the Lionel Artis Cen-

ter) at 410 North Meridian Street, and the MA-ROTT HOTEL (1926) at 2625 North Meridian Street, which was once the largest apartment hotel in the city. The value of buildings erected by the Spink company exceeded $11 million.

After an extended illness, Spink died at the Fletcher Sanitorium where his sister, Mary A. Spink, was president. Following his death, his sister became manager of his business enterprises.

CONNIE J. ZEIGLER

Indiana Biography Series, Indiana State Library.

Spink, Mary Angela (Nov. 18, 1863–Sept. 3, 1937). Neurologist. Born in Washington, Indiana, Spink came to Indianapolis from Cincinnati in 1884 as a nurse for Central Hospital for the Insane (now CENTRAL STATE HOSPITAL), and to attend medical school. She received her M.D. from the Medical College of Indiana in 1887.

Spink served as pathologist at Central State and in 1888, with Dr. WILLIAM B. FLETCHER, opened the Fletcher Sanatorium. In 1907 she became the sanatorium's chief administrator. Spink developed a system for preserving circulation within the skull, that was considered a significant contribution to the field of neurology. She was also a surgeon on the staff of Indianapolis City Hospital (now WISHARD MEMORIAL HOSPITAL) and a member of the State Board of Charities for many years. Following the death of her brother EDGAR GEORGE SPINK in 1927, Mary succeeded him as president and general manager of Spink-Arms Hotel Corporation and General Apartments, Inc., which operated numerous apartment buildings in the city.

NANCY PIPPEN ECKERMAN
Indiana University School of Medicine

Jacob Piatt Dunn, *Indiana and Indianans* (Chicago, 1919).

Sports Broadcasting. Indianapolis broadcasting and sports have been linked since the early 1920s. In 1922 stations WLK and WOH broadcast reports on the Indianapolis 500–Mile Race, while the finals of the IHSAA Boys' Basketball Tourney were first broadcast by an Indianapolis station in 1925. College and professional sports teams became the focus of live coverage in the late 1930s.

In 1946 Mutual radio began exclusive live reports on race day from the Indianapolis Motor Speedway, anchored by the network's Bill Slater. When illness kept Slater off the broadcast in 1951, WIBC personality SID COLLINS became chief announcer. The Speedway and WIBC radio created the INDIANAPOLIS MOTOR SPEEDWAY RADIO NETWORK in 1952; Collins remained as chief announcer, with announcers from other Indianapolis stations reporting from various positions around the track. Collins continued as the "Voice of the 500" until his death in 1977. Paul Page (1977–1987), Lou Palmer (1988–1989), and Bob Jenkins (1990–) have succeeded Collins as chief announcer for the $4^1/_2$–hour broadcast.

WFBM-TV, Channel 6, used the race as the focal point of the station's first day on the air in 1949, televising the race in its entirety. The station also carried the rain-shortened race in 1950, but it was 1964 before the race again was telecast live. That year WFBM produced the closed circuit broadcast made available in theaters throughout the country. Channel 13 provided reports to ABC's "Wide World of Sports" in the early 1960s; in 1965 the network began its own coverage on "Wide World." In 1971 ABC Sports televised an edited version of the race in prime time on Memorial Day. In 1986 the network signed a deal to carry the race live, and in 1988 Paul Page joined ABC Sports and became anchor for the telecast.

The IHSAA Boys' Basketball Tourney began its association with local radio in 1925. Brothers Blythe and Thomas Hendricks broadcast the finals from the State Fairgrounds Exposition Building on WFBM. From the 1940s into the middle 1960s, WFBM, WIRE, and WIBC all carried tourney games from Butler Fieldhouse. The tournament first came to television (Channel 6) in 1951. The telecasts moved to WTTV Channel 4 in 1976 under a new television rights arrangement with the IHSAA.

The city's oldest professional sport is minor league baseball, and Indianapolis Indians games have been broadcast since 1937 when Norm Perry, Jr., son of the team owner, did play-by-play

on WIRE. Indians' broadcasts bounced between WIRE and WIBC over the next ten years before settling at WISH radio in 1948. Announcer LUKE WALTON became a fixture behind the WISH microphone, broadcasting Indians' games until 1956 when he left the station. JIM MCINTYRE succeeded Walton, handling the broadcasts through the 1960 season. In 1963 Walton returned for one season of weekend play-by-play on his own radio station, WIGO. He aired home games live, and used teletype accounts of road games to recreate broadcasts. After two seasons off the air the Indians returned to local radio from 1966 to 1971 on WGEE-FM; in 1973 the broadcasts began on a string of suburban FM stations. Brooklyn native Howard Kellman has done play-by-play since 1974, often assisted by Tom Akins, timpanist for the Indianapolis Symphony Orchestra. When the Indians' broadcasts moved to WNDE in 1993 it marked the first time in 23 years the games had been heard on an Indianapolis radio station. Local television coverage of the Indians has been limited. Channel 6 carried the games in 1949 and the early 1950s, while Channel 4, Channel 6, and Channel 8 telecast games in the early 1960s. Only a few isolated games have been carried by Channel 4 since then.

Professional basketball broadcasts date from the early 1950s. Luke Walton was the play-by-play voice of the Indianapolis Olympians, the city's entry in the National Basketball Association from 1949 to 1953. Pro basketball did not return to the city until 1967 when the Indiana Pacers became charter members of the American Basketball Association. WIRE radio carried Pacers' games from 1967 to 1972 with Jerry Baker, a former air personality on WIFE, doing the broadcasts. WIBC secured radio rights in 1972, with Joe McConnell taking over announcing duties. McConnell broadcast the team's last four seasons in the ABA and first in the NBA (1976–1977) before Bob Lamey became WIBC's play-by-play voice for seven seasons. Jerry Gross replaced Lamey in 1984. WIRE regained broadcast rights in 1985; Greg Papa did the games. When the broadcasts returned to WIBC in 1986, Greg Lucas, then Mike Inglis were announcers. Since 1988 Mark Boyle has been the voice of the Pacers, first on WIBC, and since 1989 on WNDE. Channel 13 was the first station to telecast Indiana Pacers games; Channel 4 and Channel 59 also have handled television coverage, with Channel 4 the team's TV home for most seasons. The Pacers and Channel 4 tried a different approach in 1974 when a former local sportscaster, Larry Atkinson, was teamed with Phyllis Ackerman, an Indianapolis woman with no broadcasting experience. Reaction to a female basketball announcer was mixed, but the station did not renew her one-year contract.

Major league hockey had a short stint in Indianapolis with the Indianapolis Racers of the World Hockey Association. WIBC broadcast their games, with Bob Lamey handling announcing from 1974 through 1977. When Lamey took over Pacers' broadcasts in 1977, Mike Fornes became the station's hockey announcer, a job he handled until the Racers folded early the next season.

When the National Football League's Baltimore Colts moved to Indianapolis in 1984, WIBC obtained local radio rights. Jerry Baker did play-by-play of the team's first preseason game, but Bob Lamey was the principal announcer when the season started and broadcast the team's first eight seasons. In 1992 the Colts turned over their local radio and television to Sports Marketing Corp. of Cleveland. That group selected WFBQ-WNDE as the new radio home of the Colts, marking the first time in Indianapolis that FM was the principal outlet for one of the city's professional sports teams. Joe McConnell returned to the city as play-by-play announcer, assisted by former Colts linebacker Barry Krause.

The national radio and television networks also have broadcast sporting events from Indianapolis. Mutual, NBC, and CBS Radio carried reports from the Indianapolis Motor Speedway in the 1930s; the earliest national telecast from the city was a welterweight championship bout at the Coliseum in 1952. ABC-TV has been a fixture at the Indianapolis 500 since 1965 and also carried the first Brickyard 400 stock car race in 1994. ABC also has aired figure skating, track and field, golf, and bowling from Indianapolis, as well as the city's first NFL "Monday Night Football" game on Halloween, 1988. CBS has televised NFL games from the city, and also telecast the Pan American Games in 1987 and the 1991 PGA Golf Championship.

Sid Collins, known as the "Voice of the 500," was the most famous of Indianapolis sports broadcasters. [Indianapolis Motor Speedway]

The network also carried two basketball leagues' All-Star games from Indianapolis; the ABA game in the Coliseum in 1970 was that league's first national telecast, while the NBA game in 1985 was televised from the Hoosier Dome. CBS also broadcast the NCAA Men's Basketball Final Four from the Dome in 1991. NBC was on hand in 1980 to televise the NCAA Final Four from Market Square Arena, and also has televised tennis from the Sports Center, as well as NFL football.

MICHAEL SPILLMAN

Sports Medicine. Well before the term "sports medicine" had come into common use, a few Indianapolis physicians began concentrating on the treatment of injured high school and college athletes. Their services were offered in a clinic at the INDIANA UNIVERSITY MEDICAL CENTER. This was consistent with developments in other major metropolitan areas, where the sports medicine movement grew out of an academic environment. The state's major colleges and universities offered curricula in athletic development and treatment of related injuries.

A major boost to sports medicine development in Indianapolis came when city leaders began an effort to increase the community's involvement in amateur athletics. As part of that effort, civic and corporate leaders convinced the board of trustees of the American College of Sports Medicine (ACSM) to locate a new headquarters in the city. Mayor William H. Hudnut III and ACSM president William Haskell broke ground on December 15, 1983. The facility, one of the anchor projects of the downtown CENTRAL

CANAL area redevelopment, opened in October, 1984, thanks to contributions from LILLY ENDOWMENT, KRANNERT CHARITABLE TRUST, the City of Indianapolis, William B. Stokely, Jr. Foundation, Eli Lilly and Company Foundation, Quaker Oats Company, Nautilus, and ACSM members.

As the city began attracting national and international sporting events, local physicians and hospitals created additional sports medicine clinics. One of the first facilities in Indianapolis designated solely for athletic injuries was the Thomas A. Brady Sports Medicine Center. In less than ten years the facility, which became affiliated with METHODIST HOSPITAL, was seeing more than 8,000 amateur and professional athletes annually. During the 1980s, other local hospitals such as ST. VINCENT, COMMUNITY, and ST. FRANCIS also began giving greater attention to sports injuries, adding orthopedic specialists, physical therapists, and trainers to their staffs. In addition to those facilities, which operated with varying degrees of success, several independent facilities opened in the latter part of the decade, including Indianapolis Physical Therapy & Sports Medicine and Indiana SporTherapy to name just two. Indeed, by the early 1990s the Indianapolis telephone directories included numerous listings under the "sports medicine" heading.

MATTHEW C. MORRIS

Spring Hill. Northwestside town bounded by 44th Street, White River, 42nd Street, and Cold Spring Road. In 1926 local issues such as the need for fire protection, road improvements, and a new bridge across WHITE RIVER prompted a group of five or six homeowners along Cold Spring Road to incorporate the town of Spring Hill. Several residents, such as J. I. Holcomb and Mrs. Frank Flanner, were prominent in the Indianapolis community. The town featured homes of executives and professionals, built on the bluff overlooking the river. For almost 60 years the town counted about 25 residents. The 1980 census confirmed Spring Hill as the state's smallest town. Then developers purchased the Holcomb estate from BUTLER UNIVERSITY and in 1984 built condominiums for affluent residents. The town's population increased to 112 by 1990. Under UNIGOV, Spring Hill maintains its special status as an INCLUDED TOWN, governed by a council and a mayor. It continues to be a small, quiet enclave of homes for upper-income residents.

CATHLEEN F. DONNELLY

Indianapolis Star Magazine, July 19, 1984.

Spruance, Raymond Ames (July 3, 1886–Dec. 13, 1969). U.S. Navy officer. Born in Baltimore, Maryland, and raised in Indianapolis, Baltimore, and New Jersey, Spruance is best remembered for his victorious tactics against the Japanese Navy in the Battle of Midway, June 4–6, 1942, during World War II.

Spruance was the first child of Annie Ames Hiss, a member of an aristocratic Baltimore family, and Alexander Spruance, an Indianapolis businessman. Annie became an editor for BOBBS-MERRILL in Indianapolis, and sent her son back east to live with her parents and sisters. Upon the bankruptcy of his grandfather years later, Raymond returned to Indianapolis where he graduated from SHORTRIDGE HIGH SCHOOL in 1902 at age 15. Having no money for college, his mother sought and obtained a Naval Academy appointment for him from Indiana. Meanwhile, he had earned an appointment to the academy from New Jersey, but upon the urging of his aunts, Raymond accepted the Indiana appointment. Spruance graduated from the Naval Academy in 1906, 26th in his class, and embarked on a navy career. He returned to Indianapolis in 1914 to marry.

Standing in for the hospitalized Adm. William Halsey in 1942, Spruance, then a rear admiral, was placed in command of Naval Task Force 16. Outnumbered nearly three to one by Japanese ships and personnel, Spruance conserved his resources and successfully surprise-attacked the Japanese fleet, which was headed for Midway Island and its airfield crucial to American military operations in the Pacific.

Soon after Midway Spruance was named chief of staff to Adm. C. W. Nimitz, Pacific fleet commander, and in 1943 he became commander of the Navy's massive Fifth Fleet in the Pacific. He was promoted to the rank of admiral in 1944. Other battles in which he commanded victorious naval forces include the Gilbert Islands, Marshall Islands, Mariana Islands, Iwo Jima, and Okinawa. After the war he became president of the Naval War College, a post he held until his retirement in 1948. His last role in national service was that of ambassador to the Philippines, 1952–1955.

Spruance was posthumously honored by the U.S. Navy when a class of 30 destroyers, named the Spruance Class, was launched in 1973. The first ship in the class was christened USS *Spruance*.

STAN SOLLARS
The Nineteenth State

Thomas B. Buell, *The Quiet Warrior* (Boston, 1974); Gordon W. Prange, *Miracle at Midway* (New York, 1982).

Squirrels, Migrations of (1822, 1845). During the fall of 1822, Indianapolis residents witnessed a massive westward migration of gray squirrels, crossing "the river at several places in almost countless numbers" and swarming through the town. Local attorney CALVIN FLETCHER reported "many people lost whole cornfields" and that the region's corn crop was "literally destroyed," noting that 12 squirrels were capable of as much devastation as one hog. Fletcher cited one local farmer who "killed round one corn field 248 [squirrels] in 3 days." Others who hunted in their fields observed that the "massacre made no impression on their countless numbers." The migration could be attributed to the failure of surrounding woodlands to produce sufficient mast (nuts) to support the squirrel population. Several other migrations occurred over the decades. Even though the 1845 "invasion" was less extensive and destructive than the 1822 occurrence, the squirrels caused thousands of dollars in damage as they swept through town.

DAVID G. VANDERSTEL
Indiana University–Purdue University, Indianapolis

Gayle Thornbrough, ed., *The Diary of Calvin Fletcher*, Vol. I (Indianapolis, 1972), 88; Ignatius Brown, "History of Indianapolis," in *Logan's Indianapolis Directory* (1868), 11; Berry R. Sulgrove, *History of Indianapolis and Marion County* (Philadelphia, 1884), 49; Howard Johnson, *A Home in the Woods: Oliver Johnson's Reminiscences of Early Marion County* (Indianapolis, 1951).

Stanley K. Lacy Executive Leadership Series. Leadership development program that educates and motivates participants for community service. The Stanley K. Lacy (SKL) Series was named in memory of Stanley K. (Lucky) Lacy, banker, emerging community leader, and active participant in numerous civic projects in Indianapolis, who died in an automobile accident in 1973 at the age of 27. The Lacy Foundation, established in December, 1973, by his mother, EDNA BALZ LACY, channels funds through the Indianapolis Chamber of Commerce Foundation to underwrite the series.

An anonymous selection committee, composed of SKL program graduates and community leaders, designates 25 participants annually. From September through June, by means of seminars, study groups, tours, special projects, and interaction with community leaders, participants become acquainted with current issues of local government, education, health care, social services, criminal justice, economic development, the arts, and the future, as well as basic information about the community.

In 1992, of the 400 graduates of the series, 85 percent were members of the SKL Alumni, which provides a mechanism for continuing participation in community affairs. SKL graduates were responsible for initiating Circle Fest, Volunteers for Youth (now Partners for Youth), and the Indianapolis Race Relations History Project.

SUZETTE BROWN
Stanley K. Lacy Alumni

Stark, Otto (Jan. 29, 1859–Apr. 14, 1926). Artist and teacher; one of the HOOSIER GROUP of Indiana painters. Born in Indianapolis, Stark received formal art training at age 16 as an apprentice to a lithographer in Cincinnati. He also enrolled as a night student at the School of Design of the University of Cincinnati. Stark moved to New York City in 1879, and for several years worked as an illustrator while studying at the Art Students' League under the tutelage of WILLIAM

Artist Otto Stark.
[Indiana State
Library]

MERRITT CHASE, Walter Shirlaw, and Carroll Beckwith. Seeking more intensive training, he enrolled in the Academie Julian in Paris during 1885. There he studied with Gustave Clarence Rodolphe Boulanger (1824–1888) and Jules-Joseph Lefebvre (1836–1911) as well as in the atelier of Fernand Cormon (1845–1924). He exhibited paintings in the Paris Salons of 1886 and 1887.

With his French wife, Marie Nitschelm, and their one-year-old daughter, Stark returned to New York City in 1888. He took a job in commercial art, supplementing his earnings with illustration work for *Scribner's Monthly* and *Harper's Weekly*. After the family moved to Philadelphia in 1890, Marie, whose health had been weakened by successive childbirths, died in 1891. Stunned by her death, Stark took his four young children to Indianapolis, leaving them in the care of his father and sister while he pursued lithography in Cincinnati.

Two years later, Stark returned to Indianapolis where he taught classes in oil and watercolor from his studio on East Market Street. In 1899, he became the Supervisor of Art at MANUAL HIGH SCHOOL, and, in 1905, joined the faculty of the JOHN HERRON ART INSTITUTE as an instructor of composition and illustration. As a teacher, Stark was known as much for his soft-spoken ways as for his technical competence in the classroom. Among the artists he influenced were ELMER TAFLINGER, Marie Goth, SIMON BAUS, PAUL HADLEY, and WILLIAM EDOUARD SCOTT.

Despite Stark's busy teaching schedule, he continued to produce exhibition pieces. While outdoor scenes dominated his work, Stark usually included figures in his compositions. Indeed,

his focus was usually on the figure(s), rather than elements of the landscape. Of the Hoosier Group, his work showed most clearly the impact of Impressionism.

Through the years he participated in such exhibitions as the 1894 "Five Hoosier Painters" at Chicago, the 1898 Trans-Mississippi and International Exposition at Omaha, the 1904 Louisiana Purchase Exposition at St. Louis, the 1910 International Exhibition at Buenos Aires and Santiago, and the 1915 Panama-Pacific International Exposition at San Francisco. He also displayed his paintings in numerous regional exhibits.

Stark held his positions at Manual and John Herron until retiring from both in 1919. No longer bound by the academic calendar, he extended his yearly sketching trips with colleague J. OTTIS ADAMS to Leland, Michigan, and New Smyrna, Florida. Stark continued to paint in his Indianapolis studio until the end of his life. His work is represented in the collections of the INDIANAPOLIS MUSEUM OF ART, the INDIANA STATE MUSEUM, and Manual High School.

JUDITH VALE NEWTON

Judith Vale Newton, *The Hoosier Group: Five American Painters* (Indianapolis, 1985); Indianapolis Museum of Art, *Otto Stark: 1859–1926* (Indianapolis, 1977).

Stark, Wetzel and Company. Meat packing firm. Specializing in luncheon meat and sausage, the company, founded in 1936 by George Stark and Erwin Wetzel, served Indianapolis and the surrounding area. Throughout their years of operation the company slaughtered hogs and cattle, operated a rendering facility to produce animal feeds, and eventually moved into the food marketing and distribution business. "Stark & Wetzel," as the firm was popularly known, was the first meat packing company in Indiana to produce skinless wieners. The company also produced patented frozen beef patties that were distributed nationally. The business grew to a $50 million operation by 1958. To reflect the direction the business had grown, the company's name was changed in 1972 to Stark, Wetzel Foods, Inc. North American Laboratory (NAL), a subsidiary of Stark, Wetzel, was established in 1959 to blend spices for the company's products. NAL later began producing seasoning spices for other companies, meat sauces, and soy protein mixes. The company became SW, Inc., in 1974, and later that year was sold to Rath Packing Company.

SHELLY CHENOWETH

Starlight Musicals. Resident, professional musical theatre company. Each summer for almost 50 years the company offered Broadway musicals, both recent shows and revivals, as well as occasional one-night concerts.

A production of Gilbert and Sullivan's *Pirates of Penzance*, staged at GARFIELD PARK in 1944, marked the beginning of Starlight Musicals. The popularity of *Penzance* made the subsequent three-night run of *HMS Pinafore* a sellout. More than 20,000 people attended, sparking interest in a permanent summer theatre. Initially, the company operated under the names "Stars under the Stars" or "Indianapolis Theatre Association," performing at the Butler Bowl and the INDIANA STATE FAIRGROUNDS. However, the board of directors, with the assistance of the Indianapolis Board of Park Commissioners, selected as a permanent home a site at 400 West 49th Street, which was Parks Department property. *South Pacific* opened the 1955 season in the new open-air HILTON U. BROWN Theatre.

In 1962 the board adopted the "star system" of production, engaging nationally acclaimed stars to lead a resident company. Robert Preston, Yul Brenner, Carol Burnett, Ethel Merman, Jack Benny, Liberace, and Liza Minnelli, among many others, performed at Starlight over the years. Responding to increasing demand, a balcony was added in 1979 creating a seating capacity of 4,000 persons. During the 1970s the company also added a roof to the theatre and built a new rehearsal hall, design studios, and box office. By 1980, Starlight had moved away from the resident company concept and booked pre-packaged touring shows. In 1989 the need for renewed direction and greater community involvement prompted a return to the resident company concept. At the same time the board established a development program to cultivate individual and corporate support.

In addition to Broadway musicals and concert artists, Starlight offered college intern and high school apprentice programs. For younger children, several full-day workshops called the "Theatre Crawl" actively engaged area youth in all aspects of theatrical production. A seven-member staff administered the company, which employed over 250 theatre professionals in the summer. An annual budget (in the early 1990s) of $1.6 million came from ticket sales and corporate and individual donations.

In early June, 1993, just days before the first scheduled performance, the Starlight board of directors voted to close the operation. Lagging ticket sales, explained in part by the competition of other summer venues, led the board to believe that the season could not be completed and that ceasing production was the only realistic alternative.

MARGOT L. ECCLES
Board of Directors
Starlight Musicals

_____

Indianapolis Star, June 10, 1993.

State Bank of Indiana. There have been three State Banks of Indiana, which performed with varying success the functions of furnishing a stable currency and providing credit to support commercial and industrial growth. They were chartered at times when there was no national bank to fulfill those functions. Although the first of these banks antedated Indianapolis, the second and third were chartered at the state capital, were directed from Indianapolis, and had branches there.

The first State Bank (1814–1822), chartered by the territorial legislature, had 14 branches. It ran into trouble partly because a steam mill in Vincennes in which it had invested heavily burned, partly because of competition from the Second Bank of the United States (B.U.S.) chartered in 1816, and partly because of a depression in 1818–1819.

The second State Bank (1834–1858) was chartered for 25 years as the Second B.U.S. came to the end of its charter. Half the bank's stock was owned by the state, which was expected to profit from bank dividends. SAMUEL MERRILL was its first president (1834–1844); James F. D. Lanier and Hugh McCulloch were among its officials. It successfully withstood the Panic of 1837, but later failed to keep pace with the state in expanding its resources.

During the early 1850s the state chartered a number of "free banks"; speculative "wildcat" operations led to a run on many of these banks in 1854. By the next year the legislature was ready to charter a third State Bank (1855–1865). Though the charter and its passage were controversial, this bank, led by future Treasury Secretary Hugh McCulloch, pursued a sound, conservative policy until it was superseded by the National Banking Act of 1863, under which many of its 19 branches became national banks.

CHARLES LATHAM, JR.
Indiana Historical Society

Constructed in 1835 for approximately $60,000, the original Indiana State House, built in Greek Revival style, stood on the site of the present structure. [Indiana Historical Society, #C5896]

John D. Barnhart and Donald F. Carmony, *Indiana: From Frontier to Industrial Commonwealth* (New York, 1954), Vol. I, chs. 18, 19, Vol. II, ch. 4; Logan Esarey, *State Banking in Indiana* (Bloomington, Ind., 1912).

State House. The first "State House" in Indianapolis was the original Marion County court house, erected between 1822 and 1825 as a home for state offices, the state legislature, and the fledgling county government. The General Assembly met between 1825 and 1835 in the court house, which stood in the Court House Square of the ALEXANDER RALSTON'S plan, at Washington and Delaware streets.

In 1830 the General Assembly decided that enough funds could be raised to erect a separate State House. An architectural competition was held, and the Assembly selected the plans submitted by the firm of Town and Davis of New York. The winning design called for a Greek Doric temple surmounted by an Italian Renaissance dome. The architects had just completed a similar Greek temple capitol in New Haven, Connecticut, and were becoming widely known for their Greek-inspired public buildings.

Completed in 1835 for the modest cost of about $60,000, the new State House of brick, wood, and stucco stood at Washington and Tennessee (now Capitol) streets, in the State House

Square of the Ralston Plan. The architects modeled the Doric porticos at either end of the rectangular building on those of the Parthenon in Athens, Greece. They styled the flank walls into "antae," or pilasters, to hide the windows required in a modern building. The entire exterior, covered with lath and stucco scored to resemble stone, imparted a more permanent and imposing impression on the observer. Above the center of the State House, Town and Davis placed a wooden dome, which rested on a brick cylinder enclosing a rotunda. The House and Senate chambers flanked the rotunda on the second floor, while legislative committee rooms, the governor's office, state library, and other state offices occupied the first floor.

After only 30 years of use, the 1835 State House had become overcrowded; moreover, it had begun to disintegrate. In 1877 the General Assembly passed an act to erect another, more permanent structure. A Board of State House Commissioners created by the act selected the plans of Indianapolis architect EDWIN MAY. ADOLPH SCHERRER, May's chief draftsman, succeeded his employer as supervising architect when May died in 1880 and completed the new State House in 1888 for a cost within the initial estimate of $2 million.

As constructed, May's and Scherrer's five-part design consisted of a central dome and rotunda, flanked by four-story wings running north and south within an enlarged State House grounds between Washington and Ohio streets. The north-south wings each intersected at their far end with a wing running east and west. The north-south wings contained the governor's office and the offices of other state officials on the main (second) floor, legislative and Supreme Court offices on the third, and legislative committee rooms on the fourth. The northern east-west wing contained the court room of the Indiana Supreme Court, while the southern east-west wing contained the reading room and stacks of the State Library. To the east and west of the rotunda, two abbreviated wings contained the House and Senate chambers.

When the General Assembly and state officials occupied the new Indiana State House in 1887 and 1888, they found a monumental, stately, and fireproof edifice, with exterior walls constructed of brick and covered with an oolitic limestone veneer. The exterior design formula owed much to architect Thomas U. Walter's design for the United States Capitol in Washington, D.C.: on the east elevation projecting end wings faced with Corinthian temple fronts symmetrically balanced a projecting central portico with Corinthian columns. Recessed north-south wings covered with Corinthian pilasters linked the central pavilion and end wings. In the interiors of the two north-south wings, grand courts with skylights provided abundant natural light. The design of the sky-lit courts derived from the architecture of the Italian Renaissance.

During the 20th century, the 1888 State House became overcrowded with offices and was remodeled repeatedly. Permanent alterations between 1946 and 1948 removed the original House and Senate chambers. In 1966 and between 1973 and 1974, the House and Senate chambers respectively were again rebuilt. In 1986 the General Assembly appropriated funds for the removal of the piecemeal alterations that had been made to the public areas of the State House. An $11 million restoration completed in 1988 returned much of the 1888 atmosphere to the interior.

JAMES A. GLASS
Division of Historic Preservation
and Archaeology,
Indiana Department of Natural Resources

James A. Glass, "The Architects Town and Davis and the Second Indiana Statehouse," *Indiana Magazine of History*, 80 (Dec., 1984), 329–347; Berry R. Sulgrove, *History of Indianapolis and Marion County* (Philadelphia, 1884).

Steak n Shake. Nation's second oldest restaurant chain. In 1934, A. H. "Gus" Belt opened a hamburger and milkshake restaurant in Normal, Illinois, where customers could watch their food being cooked. (This led to the firm's slogan, "In sight, it must be right.") The chain expanded, adding restaurants in Illinois and Missouri before coming to Indianapolis in 1954. Belt died that year and his wife, Edith, took over and ran the company until the late 1960s when she sold her interest to the Franklin Corporation, an Indiana company that moved Steak n Shake's headquarters to Indianapolis.

The company continued to grow, but by the late 1970s it was having financial difficulties. In 1980 it sold off 27 unprofitable restaurants and the next year sold controlling interest to Florida-based Kelly & Partners, Ltd. Steak n Shake was reorganized in 1984 and is now a wholly owned subsidiary of an Indianapolis-based holding company, Consolidated Products. In 1985 Consolidated Products lost more than $500,000, but the following year the company recovered and began posting record earnings. As of 1992 Steak n Shake operated 120 restaurants, primarily in the Midwest.

DEBORAH B. MARKISOHN

Indiana Business (Apr., 1990), 37.

Steele, Rembrandt (Brandt) (Nov. 16, 1870–Mar. 20, 1965). Noted designer and potter. Son of the celebrated Hoosier artist T. C. STEELE, Brandt was reared in Indianapolis and attended Indianapolis High School (later SHORTRIDGE HIGH SCHOOL).

Briefly employed by a number of leading architects in Indianapolis, by the summer of 1894 he moved to Paris, studying at the Academie Julian, the Academie Colarossi, and the Aman Jean School. He took classes with designer Eu-

gene Grasset at the Ecole Normale d'Enseigne-
ment du Dessin and created end and headpieces
as well as decorative borders for Joseph Bowles'
journal *Modern Art*. After continuing his study in
Munich in 1895, he returned to Indianapolis in
1897 where he began Brandt Steele Pottery. A year
later, he displayed both ceramics and designs at
the First Exhibition of the Arts & Crafts held at
the high school building. Steele absorbed both Parisian *Art Noveau* and German *Jugendstil* influences but added his own flavor of American and
English Arts and Crafts to form a distinct midwestern style.

During the first decade of the 20th century,
Steele was active as a designer-architect for some
of the leading art patrons in Indianapolis. He designed interiors as well as stained glass and furniture for Herman, Robert, and Carl Lieber. From
1902 to 1909 he taught courses in "design and
modern ornament" at the JOHN HERRON ART IN-
STITUTE. Steele was head of the design department
at H. LIEBER COMPANY from about 1910 to the
1930s. During the last years of his life he was
involved with the Indianapolis Camera Club,
exhibiting photographs nationally and internationally. Around 1945, with Kurt Vonnegut, Sr.,
he again began making pottery. The collections of
the Indianapolis Museum of Art include several
examples of his work.

BARRY L. SHIFMAN
Indianapolis Museum of Art

Steele, T. C.

Steele, T. C. (Sept. 11, 1847–July 24,
1926). Indiana artist and member of the HOOSIER
GROUP of Impressionist painters. Born in Owen
County, Indiana, and educated at the Waveland
Academy, Theodore Clement Steele studied art in
Chicago for a short time before starting a career as
a portrait painter. He opened a studio in Indianapolis and is said to have survived the financial
Panic of 1873 by painting signs for commercial
buildings with poet JAMES WHITCOMB RILEY, who
became a lifelong friend. Steele later moved his
studio to West Washington Street and organized
the Indianapolis Art Association with John W.
Love.

By 1880, Steele's talent had drawn the attention and support of a group of Indianapolis busi-

Artist T. C. Steele
[Indiana State
Library]

nessmen, led by Herman Lieber, who sponsored
Steele's five years at the Royal Academy of Art in
Munich, Germany. After one year of life drawing
under Gyula Benczun, the artist studied portrai-
ture with Ludwig von Loefftz, winning a First
Class Prize his final term.

Steele returned to Indianapolis and leased
the Tinker House (Talbot Place) at 16th Street and
Pennsylvania Avenue. There he painted the portraits of those individuals who had sponsored his
education abroad. For the next decade, Steele supported his family by teaching art and doing commissioned portrait work. Among his portraits are
those of five Indiana governors.

WILLIAM FORSYTH joined Steele in 1891 to incorporate the Indiana School of Art at the northwest corner of Market Street and MONUMENT
CIRCLE. In 1894 a Chicago exhibition of five Indiana painters was dubbed the Hoosier Group.
They were Steele, Forsyth, OTTO STARK, RICHARD
GRUELLE, and J. OTTIS ADAMS. In 1895 Steele
stopped teaching to devote full time to painting
and, in 1896, founded the Society of Western Artists with Adams and Forsyth.

Although commercial success came from
painting portraits in Indianapolis, Steele's overriding passion was creating landscapes. He was
fascinated by the changing light and atmosphere
he discovered in outdoor compositions. With Adams he purchased "the Hermitage" in Brookville,
Indiana, and spent summers painting landscapes.
Steele continued to winter at Talbot Place for three
years after his wife's death in 1899. The site became the JOHN HERRON ART INSTITUTE in 1902.

In his quest for new landscapes, Steele discovered Brown County and purchased 211 acres of
wooded hills in 1907. He built the House of the

Singing Winds and remarried that summer. Students and faculty from Indiana University, neighbors, and friends from Indianapolis all came to visit the famous Hoosier artist in his hilltop retreat.

In 1922 Steele became artist-in-residence and honorary professor at Indiana University. Among the many honors he received the two most notable were his election to the National Academy of Design in 1913 and his presidency of the Society of Western Artists. In recent years the work of Steele and the other Hoosier Group artists has experienced a resurgence in popularity. His acceptance as a significant American Impressionist is evidenced by exhibits such as "The Best Years" at the INDIANA STATE MUSEUM in 1985–1986, publication of *The Hoosier Group* (1985) and *The Passage* (1990), and his inclusion in William Gerdts, *American Impressionism* (New York, 1984).

T. C. Steele died in Brown County at age 78. The House of the Singing Winds and its collections were donated to the State of Indiana by his wife Selma shortly before her death in 1946; the property is now the T. C. Steele State Historic Site.

RACHEL B. PERRY

Judith Vale Newton, *The Hoosier Group* (Indianapolis, 1985); Martin Krause, *The Passage: Return of Indiana Painters from Germany, 1880–1905* (Indianapolis, 1990); Selma N. Steele, Theodore L. Steele, and Wilbur D. Peat, *The House of the Singing Winds* (Indianapolis, 1966, 1989).

Steers, Edwin K. (Jan. 19, 1915–Nov. 30, 1992). Indiana attorney general. Born in Indianapolis, Steers was the son of Edwin M. S. Steers, former treasurer of the state Republican party. Graduating from Indiana University Law School in 1937, he was admitted to the bar and became associated with his father's law firm. He served four years as Marion County deputy prosecutor (1940–1942, 1947–1949) and for two years was in charge of the grand jury.

After serving in the Navy in World War II from 1943 to 1946, Steers returned home to resume his law practice and work with the Marion County Prosecutor's Office, but was recalled to active duty during the Korean conflict. He served from 1951 to 1953 as defense counsel, General Court Martial for the Great Lakes area, during which time he became the Republican candidate for Indiana attorney general.

Elected in 1952 despite his absence, Steers eventually served three consecutive terms as attorney general, being reelected in 1956 and 1960. His administration was uncontroversial except when he opposed the 1963 state sales tax. Governor Matthew Welsh accused Steers of deserting his legal responsibility to the state in favor of politics, but Steers claimed legal reasons.

Steers returned to private practice in 1964, and in 1969 was appointed general counsel for the Shrine of North America in Chicago. Other major clients included the State Automobile Insurance Group and Statesman Insurance Group. At the time of his death he had been a partner of Steers, Sullivan, McNamar, and Rogers for 55 years.

MICHELLE D. HALE

Indianapolis Newspaper Index, Indiana State Library.

Steffen, Elmer Andrew (Jan. 11, 1890–June 3, 1963). Cofounder of the INDIANAPOLIS SYMPHONIC CHOIR, composer, and music director for the Roman Catholic archdiocese. A lifelong resident of Indianapolis, Steffen was active in Indianapolis music circles from an early age. When he was 16 he directed a Catholic Mass service with several choirs and orchestras. He later served as soloist and master director of the Schola Cantorum Choir at SS. PETER AND PAUL CATHEDRAL, and from 1937 to 1955 held the position of archdiocesan director of music.

Steffen was cofounder with FABIEN SEVITZKY of the Indianapolis Symphonic Choir and served as its director for many years. He also cofounded the Mendelssohn Choir, predecessor of the symphonic group, and was its conductor. He was particularly interested in sacred music and the revival of the Gregorian chant. Steffen composed two major works, *Missa Eucharista* and *Ecce Sacerdos*, and numerous motets incorporated into hymnals across the country.

For his service in sacred music Steffen was made a Knight of St. Gregory by Pope Pius XII in 1939. He also served on the advisory board of the

Gregorian Institute of America and was active in a number of local civic and private organizations.

CATHLEEN F. DONNELLY

Indiana Biography Series, Indiana State Library.

Stem, John H. (Oct. 3, 1847–Aug., 1910). Architect. Born in Ohio, Stem came to Indianapolis in 1868 to work with his architect brother, Hartzel Stem. During his residence John Stem designed the Fletcher-Wasson home (1876), the L. Sohl house (1880), the offices for the Cincinnati, Indianapolis, St. Louis, and Chicago Railroad (1880), the freight depot and general offices of the Indianapolis, Peru, and Chicago Railroad (1881), the Henry C. G. Bals residence (1883), and Third Christian Church (1887). He also designed several blocks on South Meridian Street, among them the George W. Stout building (1888) included in the Union Station-WHOLESALE DISTRICT historic area. Other local projects included the residences of HILTON U. BROWN, FRANK FLANNER, DAVID M. PARRY, and CHARLES W. FAIRBANKS, the Newton-Claypool Building, White City Amusement Park, and St. Anthony's Catholic Church. Stem also designed buildings in other Indiana cities.

Stem was a charter member of the Indiana chapter of the American Institute of Architects (1884), and partners with ISAAC HODGSON and Charles A. Wallingford during the 1880s. His son Allen H. Stem also became an architect. Stem closed his office in the city a few years before his death, spent time in New York, opened an office in Houston, Texas, and designed amusement parks in Kansas City, Missouri, and Newark, New Jersey.

JOAN CUNNINGHAM

Indianapolis News, Aug. 31, 1910.

Stephenson, David Curtis (D. C.) (Aug. 21, 1891–June 28, 1966). Grand Dragon of KU KLUX KLAN in Indiana during the 1920s. Born in Houston, Texas, Stephenson moved with his family to Maysville, Oklahoma, in 1901. He was active in the Socialist party in Oklahoma, and served briefly in the U.S. Army during WORLD WAR I. After moving to Evansville, Indiana, in 1920, he

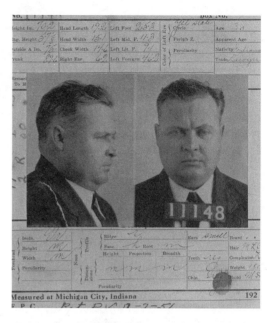

Prison mug shot of notorious Ku Klux Klan leader D. C. Stephenson. Stephenson, like other criminals held at Michigan City from 1897 to 1932, was measured according to the Bertillon system which held that individuals could be identified by certain body measurements. Other information on the card was probably self-reported and is inaccurate. Stephenson apparently gave prison officials false information as to his age—he said 30, he was actually 34—and his profession—he said lawyer, when actually he had an eighth grade education and had previously worked as a typesetter, a grocer, and a traveling salesman. [Indiana State Archives, Commission on Public Records. All rights reserved.]

became involved in Democratic politics. He also joined the Ku Klux Klan, which had begun to seek northern members, and soon became one of the Klan's most successful recruiters.

Stephenson ran unsuccessfully for the U.S. Congress in Evansville in 1922, then moved to Indianapolis. In November, 1922, he helped Hiram Evans unseat the Klan's imperial wizard, William Simmons. Evans became the new imperial wizard and named Stephenson grand dragon of Indiana and 22 other northern states. Under Stephenson's leadership the Klan grew to about 250,000 members in Indiana. He became extremely wealthy as a result of commissions on new memberships and the sale of Klan regalia, and purchased a large home in IRVINGTON.

Stephenson broke with Evans and the national Klan in September, 1923, and named himself grand dragon of a rival Klan group. During the 1924 elections, he supported several political candidates, including former secretary of state Ed Jackson, a Republican, who successfully ran for governor.

In November, 1925, Stephenson received a life sentence for his role in the death of Madge Oberholtzer, whom he had brutally raped. He served 31 years in the Indiana State Prison at Michigan City before his release in 1956. While in prison, Stephenson leaked damaging information to the newspapers about his involvement in state politics. His charges ended the political careers of Governor Jackson, Indianapolis Mayor JOHN DU-VALL, and several other politicians. The INDIANAP-OLIS TIMES won a Pulitzer Prize in 1928 for its investigation of the Klan.

Stephenson disappeared from Indiana in 1962; it was later learned that he moved to Jonesboro, Tennessee, where he died.

M. WILLIAM LUTHOLTZ

M. William Lutholtz, *Grand Dragon: D. C. Stephenson and the Ku Klux Klan in Indiana* (West Lafayette, Ind., 1991).

Sterne, Albert Eugene (Apr. 28, 1866–June 30, 1931). Neurologist and medical educator. Born in Cincinnati, Sterne studied at Harvard (B.A.) and the University of Berlin (M.D.) and continued his education in hospitals in Dublin, London, Strasbourg, and Berlin. In 1893 he came to Indianapolis to practice general medicine.

The Central College of Physicians and Surgeons appointed Sterne the chairman of the department of mental and nervous disorders in 1894. In this capacity, he supported efforts to centralize medical education in Indiana and retained the chairmanship of his department when INDIANA UNIVERSITY SCHOOL OF MEDICINE was formed. His classroom techniques included innovative visual aids of his own design, such as colored slides.

Sterne established Norways Sanatorium in Indianapolis in 1896. Norways specialized in research, diagnosis, and study of nervous and mental disorders and attracted patients from across the country. In addition to teaching and his medical practice, Sterne published extensively and was associate editor of the *Journal of Nervous and Mental Diseases* and editor of *The Medical Monitor*. He was appointed Assistant Surgeon General of Indiana by Governor Winfield Durbin, and he was president of the Ohio Valley (1910) and later the Mississippi Valley medical associations.

NANCY PIPPEN ECKERMAN
Indiana University School of Medicine

Stevens, Thaddeus Merrill (Aug. 24, 1829–Nov. 8, 1885). Father of the public health movement in Indiana. Nephew and namesake of the famous congressman from Pennsylvania, Stevens was a lifelong resident of Indianapolis. After attending private schools he graduated from Indiana Central Medical College in Indianapolis in the early 1850s. In 1870 Stevens was Professor of Toxicology, Medical Jurisprudence, and Chemistry at the Indiana Medical College and in 1874 he held the same chair in the College of Physicians and Surgeons. During this same period he also served briefly as editor of the *Indiana Journal of Medicine*. Beginning in the 1870s, Stevens presented a series of influential papers to the State Medical Society on "State Medicine." He wanted the state to be responsible for the care of the insane, preservation of health, the registration of births and deaths, licensure of physicians, and medical education. As a result, the State Medical Society appointed a commission to make recommendations and named Stevens its chairman.

Ultimately, the work of this commission led to legislation establishing the Indiana State Board of Health in March, 1881. Stevens became the first secretary of that board, but had considerable difficulty getting it underway. He managed, however, to organize local health boards, collect reports on epidemics, and send out forms for the registration of births and deaths. Stevens issued the first annual report of the State Board of Health covering nine months from January 1 to September 30, 1882. The report's 355 pages included tabulated vital statistics—age, sex, occupation, cause of death, as well as births and marriages listed by counties. He was also responsible for making the first sanitary survey of both the state and the city of Indianapolis.

Stevens was dismissed from the board in March, 1883. Thereafter he operated a medical laboratory and devoted the remainder of his life to his plan to erect public hospitals for the poor across the state with the best medical and surgical practice that the times could afford. In this he anticipated the public-owned hospitals which now dot the state.

LUCRETIA ANN SAUNDERS
Indiana State Board of Health (retired)

Thurman B. Rice, *The Hoosier Health Officer* (Indianapolis, 1946); John H. B. Nowland, *Sketches of Prominent Citizens of 1876* (Indianapolis, 1877), 269–270.

Stevenson, Frances (Fanny) Van de Grift (Mar. 10, 1840–Feb. 18, 1914). Author and critic. Fanny Van de Grift Stevenson, an Indianapolis native, attended the Third Ward School and the city's first high school in University Square, where she demonstrated a flair for composition and art. She married Samuel Osbourne in 1857. This marriage produced three children; however, the match proved to be unhappy. To avoid the scandal of divorce, she embarked for Europe in 1875 to study art. While residing at Grez, France, an artists' colony, she met the author Robert Louis Stevenson.

Fanny returned to the United States in 1879 and divorced Osbourne in January, 1880. On May 19, 1880, Fanny and Stevenson married. They began a nomadic life seeking a climate that would benefit Robert's delicate health, eventually settling on Upolu, Samoa. Fanny collaborated with Robert as critic, muse, and nurse until his death in 1894, after which she returned to the United States. Shortly after the completion of her book, *The Cruise of the "Janet Nichol"* (1914), she suffered a fatal cerebral hemorrhage. Fanny's ashes were buried on Mt. Vaea, Samoa, beside Robert Louis Stevenson's grave. Her account of life in the Pacific, *Our Samoan Adventure* (1955), was published posthumously.

GEORGIA A. CRAVEY

Margaret MacKay, *The Violent Friend: The Story of Mrs. Robert Louis Stevenson* (New York, 1968).

Stewart and Bowen. Nineteenth-century booksellers. Stewart and Bowen had its beginnings in 1833 when two Cincinnati men opened a bookstore in Indianapolis (Hubbard and Edmands). The business changed hands ten times before 1853 when it reorganized as West and Stewart. SAMUEL MERRILL also was involved in this partnership but later withdrew. The following year William Stewart and Silas T. Bowen purchased the business, renaming it Stewart and Bowen. Located at 18 West Washington Street, the bookstore was one of the two largest in the city at the time. In addition to a wholesale and retail book trade, it dealt in stationery, paper, and printing supplies. When Stewart died in 1860 the firm was reorganized as Bowen, Stewart and Company.

By 1881 the company had annual sales of over $200,000, carried an inventory worth $70,000, and employed a total of 24 assistants. Three traveling salesmen covered Indiana, Illinois, and Ohio selling books wholesale. In 1885 Bowen, Stewart and Company joined with Merrill, Meigs and Company to incorporate as the Bowen-Merrill Company with Silas T. Bowen as the first president. In addition to selling books and stationery, the firm acted as a publisher. In 1890 Bowen retired; in 1903 the Bowen-Merrill Company became the BOBBS-MERRILL COMPANY. Six years later the retail book business was sold to William Kerfoot Stewart, a descendant of the founder of Stewart and Bowen. After several changes in ownership, the descendent of the retail branch of the Stewart and Bowen business continues today as Stationers, Inc.

DEBORAH B. MARKISOHN

Indianapolis Times, Dec. 4, 1933; *Indianapolis Star*, Dec. 31, 1947, Aug. 18, 1957.

Stewart-Carey. Glass wholesaler and retailer. Stewart-Carey began as a combination glass and drug store in Greensburg, Indiana, in 1840. Founder Daniel Stewart moved his business to Indianapolis in 1863 with the purchase of Wm.

Hannaman & Co., a wholesale and retail drug dealer. By 1875 the firm was known as the Daniel Stewart Company. After Stewart's death in the 1890s, Stewart's sons-in-law, John N. Carey and William Scott, operated the firm until 1908 when the glass and drug divisions separated. Carey purchased the glass division, incorporating it as the Stewart-Carey Glass Company, and Scott continued to operate the drug division, which later became the Kiefer-Stewart Drug Company.

Stewart-Carey continued as a wholesale distributor of flat glass products for the next 30 years, adding a contract glazing department in the late 1930s that provided glass installation for new construction projects. The firm continued to grow during the 1950s and 1960s, adding several new divisions and services. During its zenith around 1980, annual revenues peaked at $10 million and the company employed over 125 workers operating seven Indiana outlets, including four in Indianapolis.

Descendants of the founder sold the company in 1984; the new owners cut employment and shifted the firm's emphasis to commercial remodeling and residential glass and mirror work. Large-scale construction projects were deemphasized and sales of automotive glass, paint, and wallpaper were discontinued. These changes did not save Stewart-Carey from filing for Chapter 11 bankruptcy in June, 1984. The firm ceased operations in September, 1987.

DEBORAH B. MARKISOHN

Indianapolis Star, Dec. 28, 1952, Jan. 11, 1970; *Indianapolis Business Journal*, Sept. 14–20, 1987.

Stewart-Warner. In 1937 Chicago-based Stewart-Warner Corporation purchased the old Nordyke-Marmon plant at 1514 Drover Street on the city's near south side. Early the next year the company moved its refrigerator manufacturing operations from Chicago to Indianapolis. Stewart-Warner expanded production at the local plant during WORLD WAR II, making aircraft heating units, rockets, field stoves, bomb detonating mechanisms, and aircraft engine gear assemblies for the U.S. Army. In 1943 Stewart-Warner moved its heater division, which produced the South

Wind gasoline car heater, to the Indianapolis plant, which then became known as the South Wind Division.

By the late 1950s the plant employed 1,000 people making heating equipment for both commercial and military aircraft. Stewart-Warner closed an out-of-state plant in 1962 and transferred its production to Indianapolis, adding 300 jobs. During the mid–1960s the South Wind Division developed a heat exchanger used by NASA in the Apollo space program.

In September, 1987, Stewart-Warner became a wholly owned subsidiary of the British conglomerate BTR PLC. Company officials announced the closure of the Indianapolis plant the next year, citing facilities that were too large and too expensive to maintain. Critics charged that lower labor costs elsewhere fueled the move. Despite city and state financial incentives, including property tax abatement and job training, 250 union employees lost their jobs as Stewart-Warner moved production facilities to Tell City, Indiana. After the plant's closure the South Wind Division maintained corporate headquarters and laboratory facilities on the city's southwest side, employing about 100 people.

DEBORAH B. MARKISOHN

Stockyards. In 1876 Indianapolis financed the construction of the Union Railroad Transfer and Stock Yards Company, which comprised the first public property in the capital for unloading, watering, and marketing cattle, hogs, sheep, and horses. Before it opened on November 12, 1877, private yards and packers had been the only outlet for the sale of livestock in the city. Located along the BELT LINE RAILROAD at 1501 Kentucky Avenue, the stockyards covered 12 acres. In 1881 the firm's name changed to Indianapolis Belt Railroad and Stockyard Company. Indianapolis boosters claimed the stockyards—under the management of Samuel E. Rauh, president, Julius A. Hanson, vice-president, and JOHN H. HOLLIDAY, secretary—was the most important spot in the country for selling livestock. In this single location, the Indianapolis market provided shippers and owners 20 to 30 commission sales firms and buyers.

In 1904 fire destroyed most of the stockyards complex, but it was soon rebuilt. Between 1877 and 1909 it received over 40 million hogs and 5 million head of cattle. Over the years the stockyards expanded to encompass 147 acres, and gained a reputation as a steady market with low rates for housing and feed.

In 1941 the company invested $150,000 for renovations and facility improvements. Business at the yards had reached $1 million daily by 1954, but labor problems plagued the enterprise and strikes closed it twice during the 1950s. In 1961 the establishment changed its name to the Indianapolis Stockyards Company, Inc.

ELI LILLY AND COMPANY purchased the stockyards and its land for a future expansion site in November, 1967, and leased the property to the United Stockyards Corporation of Chicago. When the pharmaceutical company began construction of its industrial center on the stockyards site in 1972, the yards relocated to new facilities on Kentucky Avenue.

Until January, 1992, the Indianapolis Stockyards contained several commission firms that sold livestock. Animals were sold both at auction and in silent bids at their pens. Since that time, Producers Marketing, a local branch of the Michigan Livestock Corporation, has managed the stockyards for its owner, the Indiana Farm Bureau Cooperative Association and is the only firm selling livestock on commission at the yards.

PAUL BROCKMAN
Indiana Historical Society

Stokely, William Burnett, Jr. (Mar. 9, 1900–Oct. 17, 1966). Canning company executive. Born in Newport, Tennessee, Stokely was two years younger than the canning plant founded by his father and namesake in Tennessee in 1898. A 1918 graduate of the Newport high school, he served in the U.S. Army during World War I prior to receiving an A.B. degree in commerce at the University of Tennessee, Knoxville, in 1922.

Young Stokely joined the family firm, Stokely Brothers and Company, becoming its treasurer. In June, 1929, he moved to Louisville, Kentucky, as president of the company. Four

years later he relocated to Indianapolis where the Stokely firm had purchased the assets of the Van Camp Products Company and Van Camp Packing Company. Stokely served as president and chairman of STOKELY–VAN CAMP, Inc., and its numerous subsidiaries. He also was a director of Merchants National Bank and a member of numerous Indianapolis clubs. In 1963 the Stokely family sold his mansion at 3040 Cold Spring Road to MARIAN COLLEGE.

BILL BECK
Lakeside Writers' Group

Indiana Biography Series, Indiana State Library; *Indianapolis Star*, Oct. 18, 1966.

Stokely–Van Camp. Canning and food packaging company. Stokely–Van Camp is the successor to Van Camp Packing Company, an Indianapolis packer founded in 1861, and Stokely Brothers and Company, a Newport, Tennessee, canning firm founded in 1898.

Gilbert Van Camp began a canning business in the Fruit House Grocery Building on Missouri Street in Indianapolis during 1861. The fledgling company obtained its first major contract when it sold provisions to the Union Army. By 1882 the G. C. Van Camp & Son Packing Company (incorporated 1875) was producing 8 million cans of pork and beans a year from its factory in the 300 block of Kentucky Avenue. In 1890 Van Camp began a series of full-page advertisements in na-

By the 1880s, millions of cans of Indianapolis-based Van Camp's products were sold each year. [Indiana Historical Society, #C5726]

tional magazines, pricing his product at six cents per can. Early in the 20th century Van Camp began production of Worcestershire sauce and canned extra-fine tomatoes.

In 1898 Anna R. Stokely invested $3,000 in a cannery along the banks of the French Broad River in east Tennessee. She and her sons James R., George, John B., and William B. Stokely, Jr., installed a steam engine to cook tomatoes grown on family farms prior to canning. Crates of canned tomatoes were then shipped by barge to market. Around 1908 George traveled to Indianapolis to learn about modern canning procedures from the Van Camp company.

WILLIAM B. STOKELY, JR., moved to Louisville in 1929 to head his family's company, then relocated to new headquarters in Indianapolis in 1933 when the company merged with Van Camp Packing Company. Stokely introduced frozen foods to its product line later in the 1930s and during WORLD WAR II developed the famous Army "C" rations at its Indianapolis facilities. In 1944 Stokely–Van Camp, Inc., became the official corporate name. By the 1960s Stokely–Van Camp owned and operated more than 70 plants in 17 states, Canada, and Venezuela. The company's flagship plant at 2002 South East Street was one of the world's largest tomato packing facilities. In 1967 Stokely–Van Camp acquired the rights to produce and market the now-successful Gatorade line of beverages.

The 1980s brought significant changes to Stokely–Van Camp. The company sold its frozen food section to United Foods in Tennessee in 1982 and signed a licensing agreement for its fruit, vegetable, and tomato products with the Oconomowoc Canning Company of Wisconsin in 1983. The next year food giant Quaker Oats, in a spirited bidding war with Pillsbury, acquired Stokely–Van Camp. In 1985 Quaker Oats sold the Stokely label to the Oconomowoc Canning Company, which changed its name to Stokely USA and markets canned vegetable products under the Stokely label. Although Quaker Oats continues to market Gatorade and Van Camp products, Stokely has ceased operations in the city.

BILL BECK
Lakeside Writers' Group

Van Camp, Inc., *Looking Back and Looking Forward: The Story of 75 Years of Progress and Leadership in the Canned Foods Industry, 1861–1936* (Indianapolis, 1936); Newspaper Clipping File, Indiana State Library.

Stout Field. Headquarters of the INDIANA NATIONAL GUARD. On Indianapolis' southwest side, Stout Field sits west of Holt Road and north and south of Minnesota Street. In 1926 the City of Indianapolis leased 200 acres south of Minnesota Street for its first municipal airport. The site was in turn leased to the State of Indiana, and officers and men of the 113th Observation Squadron of the Indiana National Guard were hired to operate the new airport. It was alternately known as MARS HILL Airport, the National Guard Flying Field, and the Indianapolis National Guard Airport. Informally at first, and later officially, the site became known as Stout Field in honor of Lt. Richard H. Stout, a decorated veteran of World War I and a member of the Indiana National Guard, who died in an airplane crash at FORT BENJAMIN HARRISON.

Curtiss (later Curtiss-Wright) Flying Service leased part of the field for air passenger service operations and a flying school. Curtiss' manager was Captain WEIR COOK, another Indiana National Guardsman for whom the city's second municipal airport would later be named. Stout Field was established as one of 12 stops along a Transcontinental Air Transport (TAT) route from New York to Los Angeles. Passengers traveled by train at night and by air during the day in an almost non-stop trip across the country.

A larger airport was needed, and Stout Field could not be expanded to the necessary size. So the city purchased 1,000 acres on the site of today's INDIANAPOLIS INTERNATIONAL AIRPORT, opened a new municipal airport there in 1931, and the state purchased Stout Field. Both Curtiss and TAT moved to the new site even before it was formally dedicated.

During World War II the U.S. Army Air Corps (later the U.S. Army Air Forces) leased the field for one dollar a year from the state, and it became Stout Field Army Air Base. The new Troop Carrier Command was established at Stout, and conducted training and directed world-wide air transport operations from there throughout the war.

The army purchased 80 acres north of Minnesota Street for a base housing area. Following the war it became a public housing area (known as Tyndall Towne), and was purchased by the state in 1956. A new armory sits there today. The army also purchased 16 acres south of the field for a temporary housing area (known as Tent City). It was deeded to the city in the 1970s. Stout Field Elementary School sits there today.

Following the war the Indiana State Police moved into Stout. In 1948 additional land was purchased to the west for runway extensions, but in 1953 it and much of the former field proper were sold because of the inability to handle military jet aircraft. In 1964, following a State Police relocation, the Indiana National Guard headquarters moved to Stout. In 1971 the National Guard's last air operations were moved away from the field. Stout Field serves today as the headquarters location for the Indiana National Guard and several of its units.

ROBERT T. FISCHER
Colonel, AUS (retired)

Stout's Shoe Store. In 1886 Harry Stout opened a small shoe store at 318 Massachusetts Avenue, which his mother helped run while he finished his engineering degree at Purdue University. Stout incorporated his business in 1901 and began to expand the store. Over the next two decades Stout's opened six additional stores downtown, which were connected by a party line telephone and a bicycle riding delivery boy. During the Great Depression Stout's branch stores began to close, with the last one closing in 1960. Following the expansion of the city, Stout's opened new stores in Carmel (1985) and Greenwood (1991).

Specializing in hard-to-find sizes, the downtown store continues to use an old-fashioned basket and cable system from the turn of the century. Customers pay for their shoes and receive numbered metal tags. The shoes and money are placed in a basket and transported by cable to an elevated office where employees wrap the shoes and make correct change. The transaction is completed when shoes and change are returned by cable to the customer on the sales floor.

DEBORAH B. MARKISOHN

"That's Shoe Biz," *Indianapolis Monthly* (Feb., 1986); *Indianapolis News*, Mar. 7, 1986, Mar. 26, 1992.

Street Paving Exposition. First United States exposition of street paving methods. Forty days after the formation of the COMMERCIAL CLUB (now the CHAMBER OF COMMERCE), its officers, including president COL. ELI LILLY and secretary WILLIAM FORTUNE, hosted the nation's first street paving exposition. Members of the club believed that progress for Indianapolis depended upon improvements to its streets. To that end they invited major street paving contractors and manufacturers of paving materials to present their services and wares and educate Indianapolis citizens in "rational" or scientific paving methods. Up to this time the city had tried many different types of pavements ranging from macadamization to Nicholson block, with most failing the test of time.

The exposition, April 1–5, 1890, marked the beginning of modern street paving in Indianapolis. Held in TOMLINSON HALL, it featured 55 exhibitors and attracted representatives from 40 cities, as well as a host of locals; 12,000 persons attended the event. Vendors explained the merits of paving products including brick, clay, crushed stone, and Indiana limestone blocks. As a result of this display the number of miles of asphalted city streets nearly tripled in 1891. The exposition also established the beginning of a public-private partnership between the Commercial Club and the city.

CONNIE J. ZEIGLER

Jacob Piatt Dunn, *Greater Indianapolis* (Chicago, 1910); George and Miriam Geib, *Indianapolis First* (Indianapolis, 1990).

Street Paving Methods. Indianapolis streets originally consisted of dirt paths hewn from the forest, in which the stumps gradually were removed, "corduroy" logs occasionally were laid in wet places, and sometimes (grudgingly) ditches were cut to drain off water and sewage. In 1836 the city named its first surveyor and engineer to establish proper levels and define the corners of public streets. Except for Washington Street, which in 1837 the federal government paved with broken stone (macadamizing) as part of the NATIONAL ROAD, city streets received no significant improvements before the 1850s. During the last decade before the Civil War, many streets were graded and graveled and a few routes were "boulderized" with cobblestones.

Dramatic growth and prosperity following the Civil War produced new demands for improved paving and the means with which to proceed. Cobblestones provided the most durable, time-tested street surface, but they jarred vehicular traffic and generated irritating noise. Beginning in the 1870s pavers experimented with different kinds of wooden blocks, yielding a smoother, quieter surface, but one that lacked durability and proved very slippery when wet. Brick paving debuted soon after (in the 1890s College Avenue was beautifully paved with bricks), but results depended largely on the condition of underlying foundations. "Asphalt" sheet paving, using natural asphalt or various bituminous residues mixed with sand and crushed limestone, sometimes topped stone or macadam roadbeds. In 1888 the city experimented with a new coal tar material called "vulcanite" (it turned gummy in hot weather). Nothing worked satisfactorily, and as new water, sewer, and gas utilities repeatedly dug up the city's streets, conditions continued to deteriorate.

By the end of the 19th century Indianapolis had become a modern city with distinctly primitive streets. To help promote improvements a new COMMERCIAL CLUB was founded in 1890. That body's first significant act was to sponsor a National STREET PAVING EXPOSITION (April, 1890) at which suppliers exhibited the latest materials and methods. Experts continued to recommend granite blocks laid over a foundation of "hydraulic cement concrete" as the ideal (if expensive) pavement for urban thoroughfares; but as long as property owners paid the assessment (in ten installments thanks to the 1889 "Barrett Law"), the search for cheap, durable substitutes continued.

In the 20th century, vendors of wood blocks, bricks, cobblestones, macadam, and asphalt pavement continued their rivalry until concrete emerged as the street paving material of choice. Long recommended for foundations, scientifically formulated concrete displaced other methods beginning in the 1920s, influenced particularly by research disseminated at Purdue University's new Annual Road School. The majority of Indianapolis streets have been widened and rebuilt several times in this century, but examples of older technologies occasionally can be found in alleys, back streets, and underlying modern pavement at excavation sites.

JOHN LAURITZ LARSON
Purdue University, West Lafayette

Jacob Piatt Dunn, *Greater Indianapolis* (Chicago, 1910); William Fortune, "Street Paving in America," *The Century Illustrated Monthly Magazine*, 46 (Oct. 1983), 894–910.

Street Railway Strikes (1892 and 1913). During the 70–plus years that Indianapolis had operating STREETCARS, it experienced two major strikes by street railway employees. The first raised the issue of the importance of public services versus the protection of private property rights. The second created a state of near anarchy in the city.

On January 1, 1892, the president of the Indianapolis Citizens Street Railway, John P. Frenzel, requested that company employees return the badges which allowed them free streetcar transportation even when not working. This move angered laborers already resentful about their long workday. On January 4, 1892, they struck the company. Eight days later, on January 12, M. M. Dugan, president of the Brotherhood of Car Drivers, Motormen, and Conductors of Indianapolis, offered to end the strike if the company would agree to arbitration on worker grievances. Following nine days of idle streetcars, the company responded favorably, and the men resumed work at 11 P.M., January 14, 1892.

Although the company returned the free-ride badges to workers, it did not address their other grievances about wages and the length of the

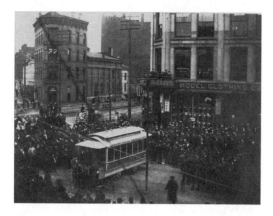

A street railway strike, 1892.
[Indiana Historical Society, Bass Collection, #15314]

workday, so the strike resumed on February 21. Striking workers physically prevented the company from moving the streetcars, even after city policemen were brought on board the cars to disperse strikers. Two days later WILLIAM P. FISHBACK, a prominent Republican attorney, filed a complaint with the Superior Court requesting that the court place the streetcar company in receivership. Fishback claimed that he acted on behalf of himself and "thousands" of Indianapolis citizens who were being harmed by the lack of public transportation. That night Superior Court Judge N. B. Taylor appointed a receiver for the company on the grounds that it had failed to fulfill its contract with Indianapolis citizens to provide regular transportation. After this action the strikers resumed work.

On March 4, 1892, the crisis seemingly over, the court ordered that the reins of the streetcar company be replaced in Frenzel's hands. Although no further gains were made regarding the workers' grievances, the drivers and motormen chose to remain at their jobs, fearing that they would gain nothing by resuming the strike.

In August, 1913, labor organizers from the Amalgamated Association of Street and Electric Railway Employees of America attempted to unionize Indianapolis Traction and Terminal Company trainmen. The organizers found a receptive audience in the employees of the Indianapolis Street Railway Company, since 1899 a division of the Traction and Terminal Company,

whose long hours and low pay made them prime candidates for unionization.

Fearing this union agitation, the railway company hired men to follow the labor organizers. Although the company refuted claims that they had armed their agents, violence occurred between the two groups and resulted in injuries to the union men. On October 31, 1913, prounion employees struck the company.

That night union sympathizers attacked workers who resisted the job action. The striking employees vandalized streetcars and effectively closed down business. The following day 65 crews reported to work, but strikers prevented the movement of the streetcars and demanded that employers recognize the union.

When the company imported strikebreakers from Chicago, one man was murdered and others were beaten in the resulting violence. Although city police were enlisted to control the disorder, some officers refused to ride the streetcars with the strikebreakers. Damaged cars littered the tracks of the city, and citizens had to use bicycles and wagons as conveyances. On November 3 agitators stoned the railway company's president and superintendent. By November 4 Governor Samuel Ralston had ordered 2,200 national guardsmen, the state's entire contingent, to the city to control the violence.

Three days later, meeting separately with union men and company officers, Ralston formulated a plan to end the strike. Counterproposals from both the company and union were melded into a final agreement which called for the return to work of all employees not involved in the violence, including those discharged by the company. Any employee not reinstated could present his case before the Public Service Commission (PSC). The agreement allowed workers to present grievances to the company and, if the grievances were not addressed, to refer them to the PSC, which would hear them within 30 days. The PSC's decisions would be final. The employees voted unanimously in favor of accepting this agreement and the strike ended at 6 P.M., November 7, 1913. The strikebreakers, shielded by National Guard troops, left the city by train.

On November 14 an employee committee presented its 23 grievances to the company. When the company refused to address the list, the employees took their requests to the PSC. The commission's Court of Arbitration heard 153 witnesses, representing both company and employee interests, during the next seven weeks. On February 9, 1914, the court presented an 80–page report. Among its decisions: the company was to increase employee pay; reduce the workday to nine hours; give motormen and conductors one Sunday per month off work; and grant the employees the right to organize in a union. It also required that there should be a three-year period before employees could again strike.

CONNIE J. ZEIGLER

Jacob Piatt Dunn, *Greater Indianapolis* (Chicago, 1910); *Indianapolis News*, Jan. 14, Mar. 4, 1892, Nov. 3, 6, 7, 8, 11, 12, 1913, Feb. 11, 1914; *Indianapolis Star Magazine*, Oct. 27, 1963.

Streetcars. The streets of Indianapolis have known three kinds of externally guided vehicles offering scheduled passenger service. The mule car (1864–1894), pulled by mules along pairs of rails, typically had 14 passenger seats. The electric streetcar (also "street car" or "trolley car"; 1890–1953), pulled along rails by an electric motor or motors drawing power through a trolley from an overhead wire, usually seated 40 passengers. The 40–passenger trackless trolley (or "trolleybus"; 1932–1957) ran on rubber tires powered by an electric motor and two trolleys connected to positive and negative overhead wires. The Public Service Commission of Indiana began regulating operations in 1913; earlier, franchises to operate were granted by local governments.

Six successive for-profit corporations ran the guided-vehicle system for Indianapolis proper and nearby areas. The Citizens' Street Railway Company operated mule cars on Illinois Street in 1864 and expanded the system steadily. Under various franchises, it reached IRVINGTON, HAUGHVILLE, and other suburbs. Founded by New Yorkers, control passed to a group led by WILLIAM H. ENGLISH in 1865 or 1866 and then in 1877 to one led by Tom L. Johnson, a street railway entrepreneur and later reform mayor of Cleveland, Ohio.

A downtown streetcar transfer platform, ca. 1909. [Indiana Historical Society, Bass Collection, #15583]

The Citizens' Street Railroad Company, founded by investors from Chicago, bought the system in 1888 and converted it from animal to electric power (1890–1894) before experiencing financial problems.

The Indianapolis Street Railway Company bought the system in 1899, let INTERURBANS use its lines in 1900, and bought control of the Indianapolis–Broad Ripple line (opened 1894) in 1902. It was founded by HUGH J. McGOWAN, a skillful organizer with wealthy contacts. The Indianapolis Traction and Terminal Company, also founded by McGowan, leased the system in 1903, made extensions, and built the INDIANAPOLIS TRACTION TERMINAL. After McGowan's death in 1911, it too experienced financial problems.

Lessor and lessee merged in 1919 as the Indianapolis Street Railway Company, which began operating buses in 1925, bought a rival bus company in 1927, and went into receivership in 1930 (along with the Terre Haute, Indianapolis & Eastern Traction Company, which had wholly owned it since 1920), although it continued to operate.

In 1932, Indianapolis Railways, Inc. (renamed Indianapolis Transit System in 1953) purchased the system and became the first transit operator anywhere to use the trackless trolley in downtown traffic. Gradually, this vehicle—quiet, fumeless, and using an easily maintained guidance system—replaced the traditional streetcar (last used January 9–10, 1953, on the Broad Ripple line). The trackless trolley ceased to be used in Indianapolis in 1957 when it was replaced by the bus, which was even more maneuverable and had no wires to maintain.

CHARLES JOHNSON TAGGART

Jacob Piatt Dunn, *Greater Indianapolis* (Chicago, 1910); James Farmer, "From Donkeys to Diesels," *Indianapolis Star Magazine*, Oct. 2, 1949; *Indianapolis Star*, July 17, 1938, Sept. 27, 1953.

Streight, Abel (June 17, 1828–May 27, 1892). Colonel and brevet brigadier general, Union Army; prominent businessman and Republican politician. Born in New York, Streight began his career as a building contractor, branching into the lumber business and later into publishing. He soon became active in Republican politics. In 1859 he moved to Indianapolis.

He published a pamphlet in early 1861 advocating preservation of the Union, by force if necessary. Governor OLIVER P. MORTON sent him to Springfield, Illinois, as his personal emissary to Abraham Lincoln and later authorized him to organize the 51st Indiana Regiment. He became its colonel in September, 1861, and served with it in the Army of the Cumberland.

Streight is probably best remembered for his 1863 raid across northern Alabama to break a railroad. The entire force was captured by Confederates under Nathan Bedford Forrest, and Streight was sent to Libby Prison. In February, 1864, he escaped. He returned to his regiment, by then exchanged, served as a brigade commander, and was breveted brigadier general. He left military service March 13, 1865.

Streight returned to publishing and the lumber business, began manufacturing chairs, and resumed participation in Republican politics. He won election as state senator in 1876, but failed to obtain the Republican nomination for governor in 1880. Upon his death, Streight was buried at his residence, and in 1902 was reinterred at CROWN HILL CEMETERY.

RICHARD G. GROOME

John H. B. Nowland, *Sketches of Prominent Citizens of 1876* (Indianapolis, 1877); Berry R. Sulgrove, *History of Indianapolis and Marion County* (Philadelphia, 1884).

Stringtown. Westside neighborhood roughly bounded by Michigan, White River Parkway, Washington and Belmont streets. In 1833 the NATIONAL ROAD and bridge were extended to the west bank of WHITE RIVER. Reportedly, a string of homes sprang up along the road, giving the area its name. Stringtown was an agricultural community until the railroads located shops and rail lines there in the 1870s. Then German and Irish immigrants who worked for the railroads built modest, single-family cottages, most of them in the Carpenter-Builder style, on narrow lots. Indianapolis annexed the working class community in 1897.

The flood of 1913 devastated Stringtown when the levee broke and homes were inundated. In the years following the flood, the ethnic character of the neighborhood changed. As the GERMANS and IRISH moved out, white Protestants from the American South moved in to purchase or rent homes. The Evans Flour Mill, along with other nearby industries, provided employment for these new residents.

By the 1960s, Stringtown declined as industries shut down, unemployment soared, and housing stock deteriorated. Ten years later, about 4,500 residents lived in the area. The expansion of WHITE RIVER STATE PARK and the INDIANAPOLIS ZOO displaced residents and industries in the 1980s. Stringtown continued to struggle with a number of social and economic problems in the early 1990s.

CATHLEEN F. DONNELLY

Albert Hurtado et al., "Stringtown Survey Report" (unpublished manuscript, IUPUI Center for American Studies, 1985).

Stubbs, George W. (Sept., 1837–Mar. 3, 1911). Indianapolis police court judge and creator of the city's juvenile court. Born in Shelby County, Indiana, Stubbs was studying law when the Civil War began. Enlisting as a private in the 16th Indiana Volunteer Regiment, he later served in the Signal Corps. After the war he resumed his law studies and eventually opened a law practice in Shelbyville. In 1871 he moved his practice to Indianapolis.

Stubbs, who lost his left arm in an 1899 hunting accident, was elected Marion County Police Court judge in 1901. He soon became concerned about the large number of children who were tried as adults in the court system. Aided by Indianapolis Police Chief G. A. Taft and Judge James A. Collins, Stubbs prepared a bill in 1903 that gave jurisdiction over juveniles to circuit courts, except in Marion County, where a special juvenile court was established.

Appointed by Governor Winfield Durbin to be the juvenile court's first judge, Stubbs' efforts on behalf of children attracted worldwide attention. European social workers and court officials came to Indianapolis to study the new system, and similar courts were created in Italy and Sweden.

On his way home from working at the juvenile court on the afternoon of March 3, 1911, Stubbs was struck by an Indianapolis & Cincinnati traction car while crossing Delaware Street in front of the Marion County Courthouse. Taken to his home at 2460 Bellefontaine Street, he died later that evening.

RAY BOOMHOWER
Indiana Historical Society

Indianapolis Star, Mar. 4, 1911.

Stutz. Indianapolis-produced automobile. Harry C. Stutz (1876–1935) moved from his native Ohio to Indianapolis in 1903. By 1910 the Stutz Auto Parts Company manufactured rear-axle-mounted transmissions. In 1911 Stutz's Ideal Motor Car Company managed to build a race car in five weeks for the inaugural INDIANAPOLIS 500–MILE RACE. The car placed tenth, and the Stutz became known as the "car that made good in a day." Models offered by this company (221 East 10th Street) included roadsters, tonneau, and touring cars, each costing $2,000; the famous Bearcat first appeared in 1912. Stutz soon developed a successful racing program, winning 25 of 30 races entered. He then organized the Stutz Motor Car Company in May, 1913, through the merger of the Stutz Auto Parts and Ideal Motor Car companies. The number of cars produced increased to 2,207 in 1917. These successes led to

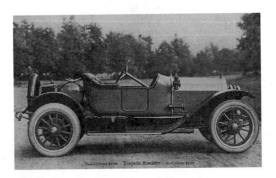

The Stutz Torpedo Roadster.
[Indiana Historical Society, #C5441]

the building of a factory complex (1914–1920) at 1008 North Capitol Avenue.

In 1916 the financier Alan A. Ryan took control of the company after it had gone public. A Bethlehem Steel Corporation director, Charles M. Schwab, subsequently took control in 1922. By 1919 Stutz had withdrawn to form the HCS Motor Company (1402 North Capitol Avenue). Automotive engineer Frederick E. Moskovics helped revive the Stutz line by introducing in 1926, the best year for Stutz, the Vertical Eight, Safety Chassis model. Despite an attempt to survive the depressed 1930s with production of the Pak-Age-Car, the company failed in 1937.

ALAN CONANT

Beverly Rae Kimes and Henry Austin Clark, Jr., *Standard Catalog of American Cars, 1805–1942* (Iola, Wisc., 1985).

Sulgrove, Berry R. (Mar. 16, 1827 or 1828–Feb. 20, 1890). Journalist and writer. Born in Indianapolis, Sulgrove attended several different private schools in the city—public education was then unavailable—and worked in his father's harness and saddle making shop. In 1847 he entered Bethany College in West Virginia where he completed the college's course of study in one year, received honors in all five departments, and gave a graduation speech in Greek.

In 1848 Sulgrove returned to Indianapolis to study and then practice law. He married in 1853. During this time he began writing for the periodical press. Under the nom de plume "Timothy Tugmutton," he wrote sketches in the *LOCOMOTIVE* of the members of the 1850–1851 Indiana Constitutional Convention. He also wrote an Indiana column for the *Cincinnati Gazette* and was a leading writer for the *Hoosier City*. In 1855 he headed the editorial department of the INDIANA STATE JOURNAL, a position he held throughout the CIVIL WAR. Following the war he joined the newly formed INDIANAPOLIS NEWS, continuing his association with that paper until his death in 1890. Sulgrove was active during a transitional era when newspapers were moving from a focus on political editorializing to increasing emphasis on news reporting, and he was credited with being the first editor in Indianapolis to institute timely news reporting.

Though recognized for his contributions to journalism, Sulgrove's legacy resides in his work as a writer. In 1884 he published *A History of Indianapolis and Marion County, Indiana* (Philadelphia: L. H. Everts & Co.). This volume reflects his powers of observation, attention to detail, and gentle wit, combining an anecdotal style with an extraordinary quantity of factual detail on wide-ranging topics. Still frequently consulted by those interested in the city's 19th-century history, it remains Sulgrove's major contribution, yet it went unrecorded in his numerous and laudatory obituaries.

REBECCA THOMPSON

John H. B. Nowland, *Sketches of Prominent Citizens of 1876* (Indianapolis, 1877); Indiana Scrapbook Collection, Indiana State Library; Indiana Biography Series, Indiana State Library.

Sullivan, Reginald H. (Mar. 10, 1876– Jan. 30, 1980). Mayor of Indianapolis, 1930– 1935, 1939–1943, Democrat. Born in Indianapolis, Sullivan came from a long line of Indiana politicians. His great-grandfather, Jeremiah Sullivan, a state legislator and later state Supreme Court justice, served on a commission in 1820 to find a suitable site for a new state capital and suggested the name Indianapolis for the new city. Reginald Sullivan's father, THOMAS L. SULLIVAN, served as Indianapolis mayor from 1890 to 1893.

As a youth Sullivan attended the private Classical Boys School, then Wabash College, graduating in 1897. While at the college he was quarterback and captain of the football team. Sullivan went on to the Indiana University Law School, where he graduated in 1899. Practicing law in Indianapolis, he teamed up with Frank Ross and Edward Knight in the firm Ross, Sullivan & Knight.

Like his ancestors, Sullivan was politically active. He served one term as state senator (1911 to 1913) and was elected Indianapolis comptroller in 1916. He resigned in 1917 to become one of the first Army officers to be trained at FORT BENJAMIN HARRISON but was honorably discharged after an injury.

In 1929, Sullivan was the Democratic nominee for mayor, running against Republican Alfred M. Glossbrenner. Despite being confined to ST. VINCENT HOSPITAL for much of the campaign owing to injuries suffered in a plane crash, Sullivan easily won election, beating Glossbrenner by approximately 33,000 votes—at that time the largest margin of victory any local candidate had ever received.

To help ease the economic hardships caused by the Great Depression, Sullivan instituted the "Made Work Program." Under this program, the mayor urged the unemployed to go door-to-door to solicit work. A more direct method to ease unemployment under Sullivan's administration was the building of Weir Cook Municipal Airport (now INDIANAPOLIS INTERNATIONAL AIRPORT), which was dedicated in September, 1931. In his first term Sullivan also worked to acquire CITIZENS GAS AND COKE UTILITY for the city.

In 1938, Marion County DEMOCRATIC PARTY chairman E. Kirk McKinney presented a petition signed by 50,000 people urging Sullivan to run again for mayor. He accepted the call and in the general election captured his second term in office by defeating GOP challenger Herman C. Wolff. During World War II the Sullivan administration removed approximately 40 miles of STREETCAR tracks and installed a citywide air raid warning system. As Indianapolis Civilian Defense Council chairman, Sullivan often personally handed out diplomas to Indianapolis men and women trained as air raid wardens. Also during his second term, the mayor launched a SMOKE ABATEMENT drive aimed at improving the city's air quality.

Sullivan, who returned to his law practice after his second term in office ended in 1943, was a lifelong city resident. A bachelor, Sullivan lived for a number of years at his family's home on North Capitol Avenue. He was a member of numerous organizations, including the INDIANAPOLIS ATH-LETIC CLUB, ATHENAEUM Turners, the Indiana Democratic Club, and St. Paul's Episcopal Church. In 1974 he was one of the first three persons named to the Indiana Democratic Hall of Fame. Sullivan died in Indianapolis at the age of 103.

RAY BOOMHOWER
Indiana Historical Society

Thomas Lennox Sullivan served as mayor of Indianapolis from 1890 to 1893. [Indiana Historical Society, #C5903]

Indiana Biography Series, Indiana State Library; *Biographical Directory of the Indiana General Assembly*, Vol. 2 (Indianapolis, 1984).

Sullivan, Thomas Lennox (Oct. 6, 1846–July 9, 1936). Mayor of Indianapolis, 1890–1893, Democrat. The first mayor born in the city, Sullivan lived all his life in various residences in the downtown area, the last 54 years at 503 North Capitol, a house built by his maternal grandfather, Judge OLIVER H. SMITH, a United States senator. His connections to the city were extensive: his paternal grandfather, Jeremiah Sullivan of Madison, is credited with naming Indianapolis; one of his sons, REGINALD H. SULLIVAN, also served as mayor (1930–1935, 1939–1943).

Educated in the city's schools, Thomas Sullivan graduated from Racine College in Wisconsin in 1869, read law in a local firm, attended Indiana Law School, and opened a law practice in 1872. In 1888 he was appointed to a vacancy on the Marion-Hendricks County circuit court. He lost election to that post later that year by 45 votes, but carried Marion County by more than a thousand in a year in which BENJAMIN HARRISON headed the Republican presidential ticket. Such demonstrated popularity brought Sullivan the Democratic nomination for mayor the following year.

Sullivan once remarked that as mayor he had found Indianapolis a country town, but that after his term it was becoming a city. His claim has merit. In 1889 he campaigned on a platform of public improvements. As mayor, Sullivan served as one of three city officials on the nine-member, public-private committee organized to draft a new city CHARTER (adopted in March, 1891) that granted unprecedented powers of appointment to the mayor and provided for a board of public works. Even before the charter's adoption, Sullivan had initiated carefully drawn annual department reports (he had inherited a city in debt) and had adopted a systematic approach to the planning and construction of streets and concrete sewers. During his four years electric trolleys and street lights replaced horse cars and gaslights; the Virginia Avenue viaduct was built, removing a barrier which had divided the city; street signs were put up and the streets renumbered; and the city entered into a contract with the water company on terms more favorable to residents. Despite his record of accomplishments, the Panic of 1893 hurt Democrats and Sullivan lost his bid for a third term.

After leaving office, Sullivan successfully lobbied the legislature for a compulsory school attendance law (1897) and a popularly elected school board for the city (1899). He lost for judge of the superior court in 1899. He served for many years as president of the city's sinking fund and as a trustee and then president of the Indianapolis Gas and Coke Company (1907–1936). Sullivan was a 32nd degree Mason and a trustee and vestryman for many years at St. Paul's Episcopal Church.

WILLIAM DOHERTY
Marian College

Jacob P. Dunn, *Greater Indianapolis*, vols. I, II (Chicago, 1910); *Indianapolis Star*, July 10, 1936.

Summer Mission for Sick Children (also known as the Fresh Air Mission). Private charity dedicated to improving the lives of poor children; city's first "fresh air mission" or summer camp. Founded in 1890 by OSCAR C. MCCULLOCH, the mission ministered to sick children and nursing mothers by sending them to summer camp outside the city. The mission was part of a larger national movement to ameliorate the plight of many urban children.

At the camp, mothers received information on nutrition, health, and infant care; children enjoyed a day in the country. Located at FAIRVIEW PARK, the mission expanded its operations throughout the late 19th and early 20th centuries to include permanent dormitories, a hospital, a dispensary, and a camp for tuberculosis patients. The mission also employed a physician and nurse and offered the children free medical care.

As its services expanded, the mission sought innovative ways to raise funds. In 1905, the INDIANAPOLIS STAR formed the Fresh Air Fund and recruited children to raise money for the camp. By the 1910s, a number of other organizations in Indianapolis provided care for poor children, and raising money for the camp became increasingly difficult. No longer able to maintain its facilities properly, the Summer Mission, Cheeryvale (another summer camp located near OAKLANDON), the Children's Aid Association, and Relief for Children consolidated their work on an experimental basis in 1918. The Summer Mission kept its property and endowment funds and continued operating until 1924 as part of the Children's Aid Association. At that time, it closed its camp and later sold the land to BUTLER UNIVERSITY.

The organization operates today as a private foundation that makes grants to organizations with goals similar to those of the Summer Mission. Jameson Camp and Happy Hollow Camp, children's summer camps, are major recipients of these funds.

KATHERINE MANDUSIC MCDONELL

Indianapolis Summer Mission collection, Indiana Historical Society.

Sunday Closing Laws. Laws governing the observance of the Sabbath have existed in Indiana since 1807 when territorial governor William Henry Harrison approved "An Act for the Prevention of Vice and Immorality." When the first state legislature met in 1816–1817, it addressed Sunday observance as part of "An Act to Prevent Certain Immoral Practices," which levied fines for anyone over age 14 found "rioting, hunting, fishing, quarreling, [or] at common labor" on Sunday. Thus, state laws initially governed local community behavior. In 1837, however, Indianapolis town trustees adopted the first local ordinance regarding Sunday activities, imposing a maximum $5 fine on conviction for anyone playing cricket, bandy, or corner ball, pitching quoits or coins, or pursuing any other public game or amusement on Sunday. This law continued in existence until being revised in the early 20th century.

Whether the local law was enforced over the years is questionable. Attorney CALVIN FLETCHER never mentioned any prosecution or conviction of Sabbath breakers in his diaries. Reverend HENRY WARD BEECHER, pastor of Second Presbyterian Church, often alluded to the lax attitude of westerners about keeping the Sabbath holy. In an effort to prevent "the desecration of the Christian Sabbath," delegates attended a statewide Sabbath convention at First Presbyterian Church on December 10, 1845. The next December, Roberts Chapel hosted a second convention attended primarily by ministers. Fletcher also attended and spoke in favor of changing the time of commencing courts to Tuesdays instead of Mondays, thereby removing the need to travel on Sundays. Addressing the convention, Fletcher noted that most northern railroads and canals had stopped operating on Sunday and that "scarcely a post office in the whole land . . . is open on Sunday." He concluded that a request from the convention to the legislature for stronger Sunday laws "would come with great moral force" since "the people are now more disposed to regard the Sabbath, than ever before."

On January 15, 1877, the city council adopted "an ordinance prohibiting (upon the first day of the week commonly called Sunday) any person from conducting any theatrical or Negrominstrel exhibition, or engaging in any such exhibition as actor, doorkeeper, usher, manager, or in other capacity." Violations brought maximum fines of $50.

Statewide Sunday laws were expanded over the years and included with the recodification of criminal laws in 1905. In Indianapolis, although the revised general ordinances of 1904 continued to include the 1837 law, the city faced new challenges from theaters, barbers, and baseball in the early 20th century. Local barber William Armstrong, proprietor of the CLAYPOOL HOTEL shop, challenged the state's 1907 Sunday Barber Law, but a judge found the law to be constitutional.

The issue of Sunday baseball created a major confrontation between legislators from Marion County, who regularly introduced bills to allow the hometown INDIANAPOLIS INDIANS to compete on Sundays, and representatives from the rest of Indiana. In 1907 Thomas W. Brolley, a Catholic Democrat from Jennings County, failed to secure passage of his bill allowing Sunday ball games. Two years later the Brolley bill passed both houses, but was vetoed by Governor Thomas R. Marshall; the General Assembly subsequently overrode the governor's veto. Thus, after an 18–year battle, which included organized protests from the Christian Endeavor Union and the Ministerial Association of Indianapolis, the Indianapolis Indians were finally allowed to play Sunday ball; their first Sunday game, on April 18, 1909, drew nearly 8,000 fans. In May Marion County Superior Court Judge James A. Pritchard declared the bill unconstitutional. Indianapolis Indians manager Charles Carr was subsequently charged with desecrating the Sabbath and arrested. Although tried, convicted, and fined $1 after the season ended, Carr successfully appealed his case to the state Supreme Court. Through the legislative session of 1919 there were numerous unsuccessful efforts to repeal the Brolley bill, including an attempt to outlaw all forms of activity on Sunday.

In October, 1909, local movie theater owners, who had formed the Citizens Charity Organization, sponsored a charity event on Sunday despite the 1877 ordinance which prohibited theatrical productions. Following the arrest of a local theater owner a jury found him not guilty, thus establishing a precedent for theater operations on Sundays. By November, 1910, more than 50 movie picture shows had opened on Sundays, and vaudeville theaters and play houses maintained Sunday hours by showing movies. Nevertheless, for another decade police occasionally arrested theater managers and actors who performed on Sundays.

Although legislators attempted to change the laws, the 1905 statute remained in effect for decades. Local groups such as Respect Sundays, Inc. (1958), which garnered support from over 100 Protestant churches in Marion County, and Citizens for Sunday Freedom (1963) were established. The late 1950s also witnessed an unsuccessful attempt to "encourage" the county's grocery stores and supermarkets to close Sundays.

In May, 1961, the U.S. Supreme Court ruled that similar Sunday closing laws in Pennsylvania, Massachusetts, and Maryland were constitutional. After authorities in Lake County, Fort Wayne, and South Bend began enforcing Sunday closing laws, Marion County officials announced in early October that they would begin enforcement of local laws within two weeks. Two groups of merchants immediately secured an injunction. Stores previously opened on Sundays but closed after the announcement of enforcement began to reopen. Those not traditionally keeping Sunday hours, including downtown stores, also began to open, citing competition as the principal reason. Within a few years the majority of retail shopping areas had Sunday hours and the police announced they would only enforce the law if the public demanded it. A new Sunday Closing Bill, which would have prohibited the operation of most retail businesses on Sunday, died after it failed to pass the Indiana Senate in February, 1976, and after 150 years the controversy finally subsided.

JOAN CUNNINGHAM
DAVID G. VANDERSTEL

Indiana Law Journal, 37 (1962), 397–416; "Proceedings of the Second Annual Sabbath Convention of Indiana: at Indianapolis, December 16, 1846" (Indianapolis, 1846); *Indianapolis Times*, Oct. 22, 1961, Mar. 7, 9, 1965; Justin E. Walsh, *Centennial History of the Indiana General Assembly* (Indianapolis, 1987).

Sunday Schools. Presbyterian physician ISAAC COE started the first Sunday school in Indianapolis in 1823. The Indianapolis Sabbath School met at Caleb Scudder's cabinet shop, and the 30 attendant scholars were asked to bring Bibles, spelling books, and any other books that they might have. This meeting soon became known as the Indianapolis Union Sunday School. As most students could not read or write, the focus of the class was on general rather than religious education. The school library contained all the books the small community could muster. The scholars were taught to read from the Bible and received awards for memorizing verses. The Union school was interdenominational, with its founding committee representing five different churches. By the end of its second year the school had 161 enrolled scholars and an average attendance of 75.

In the late 1820s congregations began establishing their own Sunday schools. By 1843 the Methodists and Presbyterians had two Sunday schools, and the Episcopalian, Baptist, and Christian Reformed churches each had one. These schools followed guidelines established by the Sabbath School Union Society, which was organized in Clark County in 1825. The society produced prescriptive books and pamphlets that addressed the roles of superintendents, teachers, and scholars, dictated which books were read and memorized, and set down library regulations. These well-organized schools drew some of the young city's leading citizens, most notably CALVIN FLETCHER, who served as both a teacher and a superintendent in the Methodist Episcopal Sunday school in the early 1840s. HENRY WARD BEECHER and BENJAMIN HARRISON were two other influential citizens involved in Indianapolis Sunday schools.

After 1867 the public school system blossomed in Indiana and church involvement in general education diminished. The Sunday school movement continued to grow, but its leaders now stressed religious and moral education. Indianapolis' SECOND PRESBYTERIAN CHURCH was the site of the 1872 National Sunday School Convention that marked the establishment of the International Uniform Lesson System. The system offered a seven-year lesson series that covered the entire

Bible. The Indiana Sunday School Association, headquartered in Indianapolis, promoted the new uniform system and aided new Sunday schools. During William H. Levering's two presidencies between 1873 and 1887, Indiana's Sunday schools added 150,000 children.

After a brief decline, Indianapolis publisher Charles D. Meigs revived the Sunday school movement in the 1890s. He started *The Awakener* during his superintendency of the Indiana Sunday School Association in 1893. His journal was an effective promotional instrument, and its profits helped offset the association's debts. Meigs later founded the Meigs Publishing House, which is still a major supplier of Sunday school publications.

The Sunday school movement declined rapidly after World War II. In the late 1940s the annual state convention was cancelled after 85 years due to indifference and lack of funds. Separate denominations began to take control of religious education and the ecumenical focus of the earlier Sunday school movement faded. Today Indianapolis' Sunday schools are organized and conducted independently by the city's many congregations.

WILLIAM D. DALTON

Grover L. Hartman, *A School for God's People: A History of the Sunday School Movement in Indiana* (Indianapolis, 1980).

Sunshine Promotions. Special events and entertainment promotion company. Dave Lucas and Steve Sybesma founded Sunshine Promotions in 1971 to promote local rock concerts. Off to a slow start, Sunshine booked only four shows the first year. That number gradually grew until today the company books an average of 200 or more shows a year in 15 cities in Indiana and surrounding states. Sunshine Promotions also produces fairs and expositions, truck pulls, exhibition basketball, closed circuit boxing, four wheel drive truck racing, and ice skating. The company is reportedly among the top five promoters in the country.

In 1989, Sunshine Promotions overcame residential opposition to build DEER CREEK MUSIC CENTER, a 20,000–capacity amphitheater in nearby rural Hamilton County. The center hosts performing artists representing a variety of musical styles. It is also the site of an annual fair that features concerts and sports events.

Headquartered in Indianapolis, Sunshine Promotions has branched out into a number of related businesses: Karma Records; Tour Design, a company producing radio and television spots for the music touring industry; Global Management, a firm arranging concert and special event sponsorship; and Suntex, a sportswear manufacturing company.

CATHLEEN F. DONNELLY

Swift, Lucius Burrie (July 31, 1844–July 3, 1929). Civil service reformer. Born in Orleans County, New York, Swift attended local schools and worked on the family farm until the outbreak of the CIVIL WAR, in which he served with the 28th New York Infantry. He graduated from the University of Michigan in 1870 and studied law for two years before moving to La Porte, Indiana, in 1872 to accept a teaching position. Later he became superintendent of schools. In 1879 Swift moved to Indianapolis to practice law.

During the 1880s and 1890s, while maintaining a modest practice, Swift became nationally known for his efforts in reforming the civil service system. In 1885, in concert with William Dudley Foulke and LOUIS HOWLAND, Swift helped organize the Indiana Civil Service Reform Association and became chairman of the executive committee. Over the next several years Swift investigated the local post office and the Indiana Hospital for the Insane, finding violations of civil service law and widespread political patronage. In 1889 he founded the monthly *Civil Service Chronicle*, a national journal dealing with reform and patronage that he edited and published until 1896.

During World War I, Swift supported the war effort, spoke out against German aggression, and published a pro-Ally propaganda pamphlet entitled *America's Debt to England* (1917). After the war he served on the Indianapolis Board of Sanitary Commissioners and wrote several booklets about the origins of American liberties, including *How We Got Our Liberty*.

JEFF TENUTH
Indiana State Museum

William Dudley Foulke, *Lucius B. Swift* (Indianapolis, 1930).

T

Taflinger, Elmer E. (Mar. 3, 1891–Aug. 13, 1981). Artist. "Taf," as he was called, was born in Indianapolis and attended Manual High School where he learned art from OTTO STARK and George Bridgeman. He also studied at the New York Art Students' League for six years and worked under prominent New York stage designer David Belasco (1914–1922), who sponsored his studies of the classic figure form in Florence, Italy. Taf eventually returned to Indianapolis in 1928 because of his belief in the art movement toward "regionalism." He worked in the studio of GEORGE JO MESS, a nationally known printmaker, and eventually moved to his own permanent studio in the Carriage House at 158 East 14th Street where he taught popular life-drawing classes. He also taught at the Indianapolis Art League (now INDIANAPOLIS ART CENTER).

Taflinger always enjoyed controversy, addressing such diverse issues as faculty turnover in the 1930s at the JOHN HERRON ART INSTITUTE; contesting a commission for the 1934 Chicago World's Fair given to non–Indiana artist Thomas Hart Benton; entering a sales tax debate during the McNutt administration in the 1930s; and beginning a 20–year-long controversy over the HOLLIDAY PARK project. But Taf continued to teach, both in his studio and at the Indianapolis Art League, until 1965. His most notable achievements were the inclusion of his drawings in a classical anatomy textbook by George Bridgeman; the mural *Apotheosis of Science* (1938, now at MANUAL HIGH SCHOOL), exhibited from Indiana to New York; the fresco *The Triumph of the Ideal* (1940), a wedding gift to his sister Coral; and his most enduring project, *The Ruins* in Holliday Park, dedicated in 1978.

JOYCE A. SOMMERS
Indianapolis Art Center

Taggart, Thomas (Nov. 17, 1856–Mar. 6, 1929). Mayor of Indianapolis, 1895–1901, Democrat; local, state, and national Democratic leader; hotelier. Born in Amyvale, County Monaghan, Ireland, Thomas came to the United States in 1861 with his family, settling in Xenia, Ohio, where the senior Taggart was a railroad station

Thomas Taggart, mayor of Indianapolis from 1895 to 1901. [Indiana Historical Society, #C5749]

agent. He went to work at age 15 as a clerk for the N. and G. Ohmer Company in their railroad restaurant and hotel. Taggart never completed high school and was transferred to the depot restaurant in Garrett, Indiana, in 1875, and to the company's restaurant at UNION STATION in Indianapolis in 1877. In 1887 Taggart became the sole proprietor of the depot restaurant in the new Union Station. He later acquired control of the Grand Hotel and the DENISON HOTEL.

The winning personality that led to success in business made him a natural for politics. In 1886, he was elected auditor of heavily Republican Marion County. He won reelection in 1890. While auditor, Taggart served successively as city, county, and state Democratic chairman. As county chairman in 1888, he carried Marion County for Grover Cleveland over native son BENJAMIN HARRISON, the first time the county had voted Democratic in a presidential election. As state chairman in 1892, Taggart carried Indiana for Cleveland in Harrison's reelection bid. Knowing him to be a master political organizer, Indianapolis Democrats nominated Taggart for mayor in 1895. He won three successive contests, defeating Republicans Preston C. Trusler in 1895, William M. Harding in 1897, and CHARLES A. BOOKWALTER in 1899. Taggart's three city administrations were marked by public improvements and fiscal efficiency. His major achievement was the purchase of over 900 acres along the White River to form the nucleus of an extensive public PARK system, making Taggart a leader in the movement to conserve urban natural resources for public use.

Taggart embarked upon a business venture in 1901 that would shape the rest of his life when he organized a syndicate that purchased the French Lick Springs Hotel in Orange County, Indiana. The hotel soon acquired a reputation as one of the world's most elegant spas, as well as contributing to the French Lick area's national reputation for illegal gambling activity.

Taggart sat on the Democratic National Committee for 16 years, 1900–1916, serving a term as chairman in 1904–1908. Thus, he managed the presidential campaign of Judge Alton B. Parker of New York in 1904. Although Parker lost to incumbent Theodore Roosevelt, the campaign brought Taggart added national prominence. Taggart was, in essence, the Democratic boss of Indiana during the first quarter of the 20th century and exerted power and influence in the national party because of Indiana's political balance and electoral importance. He was instrumental in nominating JOHN WORTH KERN for vice-president in 1908 and Woodrow Wilson for president and Thomas R. Marshall for vice-president in 1912. He had virtually secured the presidential nomination for Senator Samuel Ralston in 1924 when Ralston withdrew because of poor health. When Senator Benjamin Franklin Shively died in 1916, then-Governor Ralston, a Taggart political ally, appointed Taggart to fill the vacancy. During his brief tenure in the Senate, Taggart advocated fiscal efficiency and fought against federal waste. His opponent in the special election of 1916, James Watson of Rushville, rode the Republican sweep of Indiana to victory. Democrats persuaded a reluctant Taggart to again seek the Senate seat against Watson in 1920, but Watson won in the Harding victory.

Taggart resided in Indianapolis, French Lick, and Hyannis Port, Massachusetts. He was chairman of the board of directors of Fletcher American National Bank (1925–1929); a director of the Indianapolis Light, Heat and Power Company; treasurer of the Indiana Lincoln Union; and a member of the George Rogers Clark Memorial Commission.

JAMES P. FADELY

George Irving Reed (ed.), *Encyclopedia of Biography of Indiana* (Chicago, 1899); *Indianapolis Men of Affairs* (Indianapolis, 1923); *Pictorial and Biographical Memoirs of Indianapolis and Marion County, Indiana* (Chicago, 1893); *Biographical Directory of the American Congress*.

Talbot, Ona Bryant (May, 1865–Jan. 17, 1955). Impresario. Talbot was born in Richview, Illinois, while her family was en route from Iowa to Indianapolis. She graduated from SHORTRIDGE HIGH SCHOOL, married Richard L. Talbot, and became involved in early attempts to organize music festivals. When Carl Schneider founded the original Indianapolis Symphony Orchestra in 1905, Talbot served as recording secretary on the board of directors for the few seasons the orchestra survived. As early as 1901 she had begun organizing her own concerts, bringing other orchestras to the city with the financial backing of local businessmen.

In 1903 Talbot engaged Mme. Ernestine Schumann-Heink, an operatic contralto at the height of her career, to sing in the assembly room of the new CLAYPOOL HOTEL. She guaranteed the singer's agent $600 and began selling tickets. For the next 25 years the Ona B. Talbot Fine Arts Association would waver in its financial success, even to the point of bankruptcy in 1913, as it presented internationally known artists to Indianapolis audiences. She directed musical programs at the White House during the Woodrow Wilson administration and, in 1914, made local music history when she filled the Murat Theatre with the largest audience ever assembled in the city for a subscription concert. Mme. Schumann-Heink was again the artist.

Talbot died in Pittsburgh, Pennsylvania; she is buried in CROWN HILL CEMETERY, Indianapolis.

JEROME DONAHUE

Indiana Biography Index, Indiana State Library; *Indianapolis News*, Mar. 20, 1914, June 19, 1926; Crown Hill Cemetery records.

Tally Sheet Forgeries. 1886 voting scandal. The Tally Sheet Forgeries occurred during the 1886 midterm election in Indianapolis. The scandal centered on the alteration of voter tally sheets from several precincts. In city elections two sets of voter records were made from the informal returns. One set went to the county clerk and the other set to the canvassing board. When the canvassing board met to check the tally sheets it became apparent that records from several precincts had been altered. In that election Democrats had won all but two county offices. The altered tally sheets were for those two offices, allowing Democrats to win both. Since the canvassing board was made up of Democratic inspectors, Republicans suspected fraud.

Several grand juries investigated but failed to return indictments. In March, 1887, a witness came forth offering to testify that he had altered tally sheets in the 2nd precinct of the 18th ward at the request of SIMEON COY, then chairman of the Marion County Democratic party and representative from the 18th ward. On May 20, 1887, Coy and 10 others were indicted. The first trial took place in July, 1887, but failed to reach a verdict. A second trial, in January, 1888, convicted Coy and several others. Coy was fined $100 and sentenced to 18 months in prison. After his release in June, 1889, Coy resumed his seat on the City Council and was reelected that same year.

JEFF TENUTH
Indiana State Museum

Simeon Coy, *The Great Conspiracy* (Indianapolis, 1889); Jacob Piatt Dunn, *Greater Indianapolis* (Chicago, 1910), I, 292–298.

Tarkington, (Newton) Booth (July 29, 1869–May 19, 1946). Novelist, playwright, essayist, poet, and illustrator. Pseudonyms include: John Corburton, Cecil Woodford, and Milton Kilgalen.

Tarkington was born in Indianapolis, the son of a circuit court judge. Like his juvenile hero, PENROD, the young Tarkington adored the theater and was drawn to mischief. He starred in his own elaborate melodrama based on the life of Jesse James while still in high school and was sent off to a New England boarding school after playing truant for over nine weeks. Tarkington returned to Indiana to start college at Purdue University, but the pivotal point in his education came at Princeton. He distinguished himself in dramatics, edited three major campus publications, and founded the Princeton Triangle theatrical group. "Tark," as he was called, was as well known for his late hours and his spectacular capacity for liquor as he was for his literary pursuits.

After leaving Princeton, Tarkington returned to Indiana planning for a career in writing, but for the next six years all he earned were rejection slips. Then in 1898 Tarkington's older sister, Haute, staged a sit-in at the offices of publisher S. S. McClure, vowing not to leave until the editor agreed to read her brother's manuscript for *The Gentleman from Indiana* (1899). McClure accepted the novel for publication as a book and serialization in *McClure's Magazine*. It was an instant success, propelling Tarkington into the national limelight. At home the book was less well received; some Hoosiers felt that Tarkington was making fun of them. As his national reputation grew, however, they adopted him as a favorite son. His second book, *Monsieur Beaucaire* (1900), was so successful that in 1902 he was able to win a seat in the Indiana House of Representatives without actively campaigning. His term of office was cut short by typhoid fever.

That same year Tarkington married Laurel Louisa Fletcher, the daughter of a prominent local banker. The marriage was not a happy one. Their only child, Laurel, suffered from an extreme form of schizophrenia, and died of pneumonia at the age of 16. His daughter's illness aggravated Tarkington's alcoholism, causing his wife to sue for divorce in 1911. A year later, Tarkington married Susannah Robinson, following a pledge to give up drinking and devote himself totally to writing.

During this period Tarkington teamed with fellow author and playwright Harry Leon Wilson. Together they penned a string of moderately successful plays, and Tarkington's contribution to the American theater ranks him as an important playwright of the early 20th century. His 1913 novel *The Flirt* marked an important turning point in Tarkington's career. While it was not as successful as some of his earlier works, it foreshadowed the vivid characterization and style of his later young adult novels. When *Penrod* (1914) and *Seventeen* (1916) appeared, they were instant and smashing successes. Critics have acclaimed Tarkington's realistic depictions of childhood experiences, often comparing them to Mark Twain's *Tom Sawyer*.

Tarkington broke new ground with the publication of his *Growth* trilogy. These three novels—*The Turmoil* (1915), THE MAGNIFICENT AMBERSONS (1918), and *The Midlander* (1924)—used a fictionalized version of Indianapolis to describe the transformation of midwestern life by urban industrialization. Of the works that comprise the series, *The Magnificent Ambersons* is best remembered. Tarkington received the Pulitzer Prize for this novel in 1919. He won again for *ALICE ADAMS* (1921), which some critics consider to be an extension of the *Growth* trilogy and Tarkington's masterpiece.

To escape the noise and smoke of the changing urban world which he at times lamented in his work, Tarkington moved in 1923 from his family home at 1100 North Pennsylvania Street to a more suburban site at 4270 North Meridian. This house became a showplace for the works of art he loved to collect; it was here that Tarkington died in 1946.

Best remembered for his wholesome, adventure-filled young adult fiction, Tarkington is also still admired by critics for the well-crafted plots, realistic portrayals of midwestern life during the early years of the 20th century, and sheer entertainment value in his works.

STEVEN J. SCHMIDT
Indiana University–Purdue University,
Indianapolis

James Woodress, *Booth Tarkington: Gentleman from Indiana* (Philadelphia, 1955); Susanah Mayberry, *My Amiable Uncle: Recollections about Booth Tarkington* (West Lafayette, Ind., 1983); Dorothy Ritter Russo and Thelma Lois Sullivan, *A Bibliography of Booth Tarkington* (Indianapolis, 1949).

Tarzian, Sarkes (Oct. 5, 1900–Oct. 7, 1987). Manufacturer, media owner, developer of radio and television. Born in Kharpoot, Armenia, where his father was a businessman, Tarzian moved to the United States with his family in 1907. He grew up in Philadelphia and received B.S. and M.S. degrees in electrical engineering from the University of Pennsylvania in 1924 and 1927, respectively. After working as chief product engineer for the Atwater-Kent Manufacturing Company from 1924 to 1936, he served the next four years as the chief engineer for RCA-Victor in Buenos Aires, Argentina, and spent his summers as a radio consultant to Centrum Radio in Sweden.

RCA assigned Tarzian in 1940 to be chief engineer in organizing a radio receiving manufacturing operation in Bloomington, Indiana. He also managed the production of the RCA proximity fuze, a radio-controlled detonation device used during World War II. In 1944 Tarzian and his wife Mary formed Sarkes Tarzian, Inc., in Bloomington. Beginning with four employees, the company manufactured television tuners and selenium rectifiers and eventually employed 2,000. In the mid–1970s Tarzian moved his manufacturing operations to Mexico and Taiwan, and by 1980 he had sold those concerns.

Tarzian diversified into broadcasting and publishing. His initial television holding was WTTV Channel 4, which first aired from studios in Bloomington on November 11, 1949. The station later moved its tower and boosted its signal to cover Indianapolis and built studios on the south side of Marion County. He sold the station in 1978 to Teleco of Indiana, Inc., a group of Detroit investors, for $26 million, reputed to be the highest price paid to that time for an independent television station. It was the last of the four original stations in Indianapolis to bow to new ownership. Tarzian also owned, at one time or another, WATI-AM (Indianapolis), WTTS-FM and WGTC-AM (Bloomington), WAJI-FM (Fort Wayne), KTVN-TV (Reno, Nevada), and WRCB-TV (Chattanooga, Tennessee). He founded the *Bloomington Tribune* in 1966, which merged with the *Bloomington Star-Courier* in 1968, and continued as its publisher until April, 1972. He also published the *Banner-Graphic* in Greencastle, 1968 through 1980.

Tarzian served on the board of the University of Pennsylvania and created the Tarzian professorship of Armenian history and culture.

JOHN SHERMAN

Indianapolis Star, Sept. 4, 1977, Oct. 8, 1987; "Indianapolis' Six TV Stations," *Indianapolis Magazine* (Feb., 1979).

Taxes. The real property tax—a tax on land and buildings—is the primary source of local tax support for Marion County, the city of Indianapolis and the other municipalities within the county, and the school districts, library district, and townships in the county. In 1992 Marion County contained 63 areas with different combinations of local governments and their associated property tax levies, so there were potentially 63 different total property tax rates in the county.

The MARION COUNTY ASSESSOR and the nine township assessors are responsible for determining the value of real property for purposes of taxation. Under current Indiana law, property is assessed for tax purposes at one-third of its "true tax value." The state provides little guidance concerning how the true tax value of a parcel of real property should be figured, so the role of local assessors is very important.

Property owners who believe that the tax value of their property has been assessed wrongly can appeal the assessment to the Marion County Board of Tax Review. This five-member board includes the Marion County assessor, auditor, and treasurer, plus two residents appointed by the judge of the Marion County Circuit Court. In addition to hearing and voting on assessment appeals, the Board of Tax Review considers and replies to residents' questions about the assessment process.

A property tax rate, or total levy, is applied to the assessed value of the real property to determine the amount of tax owed by the property owner. The MARION COUNTY AUDITOR's office calculates and publishes the property tax rates that will apply to property within the county. Residents pay their property taxes to the MARION COUNTY TREASURER. The treasurer's office then distributes the property tax collections to the appropriate local governments within the county.

The total levy is a combination of individual levies imposed by the state, county, cities, townships, school districts, and special districts in the county. In 1992, for example, a property owner's total levy could represent a sum of up to 45 individual levies, depending on which combination of municipalities, school district, township, and special districts serve that property. The property tax rate, therefore, depends on where a parcel of property is located in the county. Property tax rates in Marion County payable in 1992 ranged from a low of $7.92 per $100 of assessed valuation in four areas (CROWS NEST, North Crows Nest, High Woods, and SPRING HILL) to a high of $13.09 per $100 of assessed valuation in part of Center Township.

Property tax bills facing local residents can rise either because the assessed value of their property has risen, or because the property tax rate has risen, or both. During the period from 1980 to 1989, for example, total property taxes collected by the Marion County treasurer from within the city of Indianapolis rose 80 percent, from $72,075,087 to $129,596,122. During that period the total assessed valuation of property in the city rose 17 percent, from $2,656,031,910 to $3,117,265,270. The remainder of the growth in property tax collections was due to rate increases.

In Indiana real property traditionally has been reassessed once every ten years, but a 1989 law effective in 1993 mandated a reassessment every four years. Because real property values tend to rise, reassessment usually results in a higher assessed valuation for most properties. The total property tax rate is usually adjusted downward after a reassessment to generate the same amount of revenue from the higher-valued property. For example, the property tax rate for the city of Indianapolis rose from $3.95 per $100 assessed valuation in 1970 to $4.25 in 1979, then dropped to $3.50 in 1980 after the 1979 property reassessment. The rate then rose again to $5.178 per $100 assessed valuation in 1989 before dropping to $3.914 in 1990 after the 1989 reassessment.

Increases in property tax rates and the unpopularity of the property tax led state and local government officials in Indiana to search for other sources of revenue. In Marion County, income, sales, and excise taxes have been used to supplement local property taxes in supporting local government projects and operations.

In 1984, under a state law, Marion County adopted the County Option Income Tax (COIT). As of 1993 the COIT rate in Marion County is 0.007, or 7/10 of 1 percent of taxable income. The revenue generated by this local income tax supports several local governments in Marion County. The first $2 million of COIT revenues helps to fund the Metropolitan Emergency Communications Agency (MECA). Another 10 percent of COIT receipts supports the homestead property tax credit, which reduces homeowners' property tax liability. The remaining revenue from the local income tax is distributed to the county, the townships, and the cities within Marion County in proportion to their property tax levies, so local governments with higher property tax levies receive a larger share of COIT dollars.

Under this distribution formula the city of Indianapolis normally receives about one-half of the revenues generated by the local income tax in Marion County. Revenue from this source has risen even more rapidly than from the property tax: since its adoption in 1984 Indianapolis' share of COIT receipts has grown from just below $5 million in 1985 to nearly $40 million in 1991.

Indianapolis, Marion County, and other local governments that provide transportation-related services also receive a distribution of the state of Indiana's motor vehicle excise tax and surtax. In addition, Marion County imposes the state-authorized optional county wheel tax. Revenues from these taxes are dedicated exclusively for transportation and transportation-related projects and operations. Since its adoption in 1982 Indianapolis' share of the county wheel tax has grown from just under $4 million in 1983 to over $9 million in 1991.

Another revenue source designed to offset property tax increases is the state tax on the income of financial institutions such as banks. The state distributes financial institution taxes to local governments in proportion to their property tax levies; again, the higher the property tax levy imposed by a local government the greater its share of revenue from this tax.

Taxes and charges upon the income generated from convention, tourism, and entertainment activity within the county support local capital improvement projects such as the Hoosier Dome and Indiana Convention Center and Market Square Arena. An admissions tax is charged on all paid admissions to the Hoosier Dome or Market Square Arena. An entertainment tax of 1 percent is charged on sales of prepared food and beverages by Indianapolis retailers. A hotel occupancy fee, known as the innkeepers' tax, of up to 5 percent is charged on top of the 5 percent state sales tax imposed on those who buy lodging within the county.

William Blomquist
Indiana University–Purdue University,
Indianapolis

Taxing Districts, Special. Jurisdictions used to raise revenues for particular services from the residents or properties within Marion County that receive the services. When the area of benefit for a service does not conform precisely to the boundaries of the Consolidated City of Indianapolis, or for other reasons, by state law the City-County Council may create a special taxing district within which taxes or service charges can be collected to pay for the delivery of that service.

The special taxing districts that have been created as of 1993 are: the Redevelopment Special Taxing District, which imposes taxes and uses intergovernmental funds to support economic and community development activities; the Sanitary Special Taxing District, which imposes service charges to support wastewater and sewage treatment and disposal; the Flood Control Special Taxing District, which imposes taxes to support flood control and surface drainage services; the Metropolitan Thoroughfare Special Taxing District, which imposes taxes and collects fees and charges to support maintenance and operations for arterial streets, bridges, and highways; the Public Safety Communications Facilities Special Taxing District, which imposes taxes and collects service charges to support the enhanced–911 emergency communications system; and the Park Special Taxing District, which imposes taxes and collects charges to support recreational facilities.

Most of these special taxing districts now cover the entire county. The exceptions are the Redevelopment District, which is limited to the Consolidated City area, and the Sanitary District, which includes the Consolidated City area plus Southport.

William Blomquist
Indiana University–Purdue University,
Indianapolis

Taylor, Charles I. "C. I." (ca. 1872–ca. Feb. 25, 1922). Baseball player, manager, and executive. A transplanted North Carolinian, Taylor was a co-founder of baseball's Negro National League (NNL). Taylor played third base for Atlanta's Clark College and served with the U.S. Army during the Spanish-American War before becoming manager of the Negro League Birmingham Giants in 1904. Taylor moved the renamed Sprudels to West Baden, Indiana, in 1910. In 1914, he shifted the franchise to Indianapolis where it was rechristened the ABCs in honor of the team's sponsor, Indianapolis' American Brewing Company. Taylor's 1916 ABCs, starring the likes of OSCAR CHARLESTON, Bingo DeMoss, and Taylor's brothers Ben, Johnny, and "Candy" Jim, defeated the legendary Rube Foster's Chicago American Giants five games to four in the Negro World Series.

On February 13, 1920, in Kansas City, Missouri, Foster and Taylor met with other Negro baseball owner-managers to form the Negro National League. With Foster as president and Taylor as vice-president, the NNL became the most successful Negro baseball league. The circuit survived until the Great Depression destroyed its economic viability in 1932.

One of Negro baseball's premier field managers, Taylor was a strict but fair disciplinarian. He insisted that all ABC players wear collars, ties, and shined shoes when not in uniform. The ABCs became role models for black youth in Indianapolis, and Taylor was rumored to be worth nearly $10,000 by 1922. His fatal heart attack early that year sent the ABCs into a prolonged decline that culminated in their demise in 1939. Taylor is buried in CROWN HILL CEMETERY.

R. DALE OGDEN
Indiana State Museum

David L. Porter, ed., *Biographical Dictionary of American Sports: Baseball* (New York, 1987); John B. Holway, *Blackball Stars: Negro League Pioneers* (Westport, Conn., 1988); *Indianapolis World*, Mar. 3, 1922.

Taylor, Marshall W. "Major" (Jan. 26, 1878–June 21, 1932). World champion bicycle racer. Born into poverty in rural Marion County, Indiana, Major Taylor became one of his generation's wealthiest and most famous athletes. Marshall Taylor's father, Gilbert, a Civil War veteran, worked as a coachman for the Southard family of Indianapolis. As a companion for young Daniel Southard, Marshall received many benefits not normally accorded a black child of the era. Included were a semiformal education and his own

"Major" Taylor with his wife and daughter, ca. 1907. [Indiana State Museum]

bicycle. In 1892, Taylor's skill on his bike earned him a dollar a day job as a trick rider for the local Hay and Willits bicycle shop, performing stunts as advertising. The military style uniform provided for the position gained him the nickname "Major."

At the age of 14 Taylor defeated a top amateur field in a 10–mile road race. On June 30, 1895, he won a professional 75–mile road race between Indianapolis and Matthews, Indiana. In August of 1896 he set several unofficial records at Indianapolis' Capital City bike track. Such feats resulted in numerous death threats, and Indianapolis tracks were subsequently restricted to whites only.

Seeking greater racing opportunities, Taylor and his mentor, Louis "Birdie" Munger of Indianapolis' Munger Bicycle Company, moved to Worcester, Massachusetts, in 1896. Over the following decade, Major Taylor established world bicycle racing records for seven different distances. He reigned as American Champion in 1898, and as World One-Mile Sprint Champion in 1899. An 1898 race at Indianapolis' Newby Oval drew over 18,000 fans. A 1901 barnstorming tour of Europe produced 42 victories in 57 races against the continental champions.

Racing before admiring throngs throughout Europe and Australia between 1902 and 1909, Taylor earned as much as $35,000 annually. Taylor, his wife, Daisy, and daughter, Sydney traveled first class on great French and German steamships, stayed in elegant continental hotels, and dined at the world's finest restaurants. In an era when baseball, prizefighting, and bicycle racing vied for America's attention, Taylor dominated the world's sports pages.

In the United States, Taylor faced constant harassment. He was often prohibited from racing on American tracks. In cities where he was allowed to race, he had difficulty finding accommodations. Though widely admired for the religious devotion inspired by his mother, Saphronia, Taylor endured racist cycling organizations, his rivals' physical assaults, and self-serving promoters. Extreme exhaustion led to his retirement in 1910.

Little is known of Taylor's later years. He lost $15,000 in the failed manufacture of a patented automobile wheel prior to World War I. Bad investments, the financial failure of his 1928 autobiography, *The Fastest Bicycle Rider in the World*, a 1930 divorce from Daisy, and chronic heart disease left him penniless. Moving from Worcester to Chicago in 1930, he took up residence at the South Wabash Avenue YMCA. In 1932, Taylor died in the charity ward of Cook County Hospital and was buried in an unmarked pauper's grave. In 1948, Frank Schwinn of the Schwinn Bicycle Company provided a private grave and tombstone for the fallen hero. His connection with Indianapolis has been commemorated with the naming of the Major Taylor Velodrome in his honor.

R. DALE OGDEN
Indiana State Museum

Andrew Ritchie, *Major Taylor: The Extraordinary Career of a Champion Bicycle Racer* (San Francisco, 1988); Marshall W. "Major" Taylor, *The Fastest Bicycle Rider in the World* (Worcester, Mass., 1928).

Michael Taylor Case. Police-custody shooting case. When Michael Taylor, Jr., was shot on September 24, 1987, while in police custody, the incident ignited community concern and symbolized the public relations problems between the INDIANAPOLIS POLICE DEPARTMENT (IPD) and the African-American community that had been building since the 1970s, a decade with a high incidence of police shootings involving white officers and black victims.

Sixteen-year-old Taylor had been arrested for attempted car theft and at the time of the shooting was handcuffed and sitting in the back of a police car in front of the Juvenile Detention Center. Police at the scene concluded that Taylor, while his hands were handcuffed behind his back, had shot himself using a gun hidden in his high-topped athletic shoe. The victim's family and African-American community leaders disputed this explanation, believing that a police cover-up was involved.

The police investigation occurred amidst intense media coverage and pressure from African-American community leaders. In an effort to gain public support and build communication with the African-American community, Mayor William H. Hudnut III created a Human Relations Task Force to investigate the causes of the African-American community's mistrust of police.

On October 7 Police Chief Paul A. Annee held an unprecedented broadcast press conference to affirm earlier IPD conclusions that Taylor's death was self-inflicted and that the two arresting officers had been negligent in their searches of Taylor. The following day hundreds of African-Americans demonstrated outside IPD headquarters. Subsequently, a group of African-American ministers hired a private investigator and demanded that both the Marion County Coroner and the U.S. Justice Department conduct further investigations.

All three investigations upheld IPD findings, but segments of the African-American community remained distrustful and pressed for further investigation. Meanwhile, the Human Relations Task Force issued a report calling for changes in police training and arrest procedures. Few changes in the police department resulted; instead police officials emphasized training and community relations programs already in place. A municipal ordinance enacted in 1989 defined procedures to investigate similar future incidents but city officials resisted creation of a meaningful citizen review process of police-action shootings.

MICHELLE D. HALE

Indianapolis Newspaper Index, Indiana State Library.

Teacher Unions. There are two fundamentally different national organizations that serve as advocates for educators' interests. The National Education Association (NEA) is open to all educators, both teachers and administrators alike, and the American Federation of Teachers (AFT) represents primarily the interests of classroom teachers only. The NEA, the older of the two, sees all educators united because of their common interest in student welfare. Conflicts among educators are worked out through professional negotiation. The AFT believes the interests of classroom teachers are at times in conflict with school administrators and school board members. The AFT promotes collective bargaining between classroom teachers and school boards as the primary means of protecting their members' interests. Both the NEA and the AFT have sought to represent Indianapolis school teachers, often with opposite results.

The AFT has never been able to establish and maintain a strong local affiliate in Indianapolis. Unlike teachers in a number of northern Indiana school districts, such as Hammond and Gary, Indianapolis school teachers have not joined the AFT in great numbers. Indianapolis Local 447 was the first AFT affiliate in the city, having an original membership of ten. The local survived from February to August, 1936. A second attempt at organization was made in 1938 with the founding of Indianapolis Local 581, which had an original membership of 40. Local 581 eventually changed its name to Local 500 and had a peak membership of approximately 600 members before its demise in the early 1980s. Currently, Indianapolis teachers who belong to the AFT do not have a local unit of representation but are considered members at large and participate in union activities at the state and national level.

The NEA has been the more successful of the two organizations. The Indianapolis Federation of Public School Teachers, founded in the early 20th century, and its successor, the Indianapolis Education Association (IEA), is the local unit of the Indiana State Teachers Association (ISTA), which, in turn, is the state unit of the NEA. Until the late 1960s the IEA was mainly a professional organization for Indianapolis educators. On May 21, 1969, Indianapolis teachers selected the IEA as their exclusive bargaining agent in collective negotiations with INDIANAPOLIS PUBLIC SCHOOLS (IPS). Since then the IEA's role as a teacher union has been emphasized. The IEA has negotiated contracts every one or two years for all IPS teachers since 1969. Currently, about 75 percent of the teachers in Indianapolis Public Schools are members of the IEA.

ALEXANDER URBIEL
Indiana University, Bloomington

Teamsters Union. Labor union, formally the International Brotherhood of Teamsters, that had its national headquarters in Indianapolis (1903–1953). Founded as the Team Drivers International Union in Detroit in January, 1899, and chartered by the American Federation of Labor, the union initially represented unskilled wagon drivers and haulers. A Chicago-based splinter group, the Teamsters National Union (1902), merged with the Team Drivers in 1903 to become the International Brotherhood of Teamsters. The union, led by president Cornelius P. Shea (1903–1907), selected Indianapolis as its national headquarters because of the city's central location and railroad connections. Maintaining its offices at 147 East Market Street until 1909, the Teamsters then occupied two floors of the Carpenters Union national headquarters at 222 East Michigan Street. Irish-born Daniel J. Tobin, who served as the Teamsters' second president (1907–1952), resided in Indianapolis until his death in 1955.

The first half century of the American labor movement was marked by strikes and violence. Strikes by Teamsters in Chicago, Philadelphia, and elsewhere caused community panic because urban populations relied on team drivers to deliver food, clothing, and other daily necessities. Riots and bloodshed often resulted, with casualties on both sides. As union activity spread, it became common management practice to use organized crime thugs to break strikes. In defense and retaliation, big-city Teamsters, as well as other unions, often made alliances with local gangsters, which spawned continuing involvement of organized crime in labor affairs.

Indianapolis experienced some degree of this violence. Following the STREET RAILWAY STRIKE of October 31–November 7, 1913, Teamsters Local No. 240 voted November 30 to strike over wages. Anticipating public disorder, Mayor HARRY R. WALLACE reorganized the police department and issued proclamations against crowds exceeding three people. He dispatched police car patrols and deputized 250 business and professional men equipped with revolvers to protect the lives and property of citizens. Within a week the special force numbered nearly 1,000. IRVINGTON residents raised $500 to hire officers to patrol their neighborhood after one resident was attacked for breaking the strike. Vehicle owners of Indianapolis established the "Commercial Vehicle Protective Association" to protect their property and combat union activities by offering rewards for the arrest and conviction of the "lawless element." Although union officials urged strikers to avoid violence and criticized special officers for provoking street fighting, the public and the Employers' Association (later the ASSOCIATED EMPLOYERS OF INDIANAPOLIS), disturbed by the shattered peace, held the Teamsters responsible. By 1920 these forces had succeeded in reversing the course of unionization by defeating local labor-supported candidates, securing passage of antiboycott and antipicketing ordinances, and advocating state legislation for mediation and arbitration.

During its years in Indianapolis, the Teamsters grew from a motley group of small union locals to the largest, wealthiest, and most powerful labor union in the country. For years the union expanded gradually, organizing drivers, stablemen, and warehouse workers in major cities. Membership grew from approximately 60,000 nationwide in 1915 to 76,000 by 1924. Growth mushroomed during the 1930s due, in part, to extended rights that labor derived from new federal legislation. But more directly, it was the result of innovative Teamsters activities in Minneapolis, conducted by Teamsters officer Farrell Dobbs and a militant group of Communists.

Dobbs was an avowed Trotskyite in the Socialist Workers party, an American wing of the Communist party that supported Leon Trotsky and opposed Joseph Stalin. Dobbs saw the labor movement as a vehicle for a Communist revolution in America. In 1934 he called a strike of all Teamsters in Minneapolis, seeking increased hourly wages for warehousemen and drivers. The strike was successful, following violent clashes and a declaration of martial law by the governor. Seeking to expand his jurisdiction and power, Dobbs organized long-distance truck drivers, who were just beginning to compete with railroads for long freight hauls, and required that all drivers delivering to his unionized Minneapolis terminals be union members. He also organized freight terminal warehousemen in other cities, making the same requirements of drivers who delivered there. This tactic became a key strategic factor and a turning point in Teamsters' growth. In the far west, Teamsters' leader Dave Beck adopted Dobbs' tactic, as did Jimmy Hoffa who later assumed control of Dobbs' Minneapolis local. By 1939 the union's membership had reached 420,000.

In Indianapolis, Teamsters' president Tobin opposed Dobbs' activities, preferring to concentrate on AFL affairs and Democratic politics rather than centralized Teamsters' activities. But, since this was a time when Communist activity in unions generated intense public pressure and government scrutiny, Tobin resisted Dobbs and his Trotskyites, causing Dobbs to leave the Teamsters in 1940 to work full time on Socialist Workers party activities. Tobin then purged the Trotskyites from the Minneapolis local in 1941.

Californian Dave Beck was elected Teamsters president upon Tobin's retirement in 1952. The next year, when the Teamsters counted nearly 9,000 members locally and over one million nationally, Beck moved the national headquarters to Washington, D.C., to serve better the lobbying and legislative interests of the union.

RICHARD W. WORTH

Alvin Schwartz, *The Unions* (New York, 1972); Steven Brill, *The Teamsters* (New York, 1978); *Indianapolis Star*, Dec. 1, 2, 3, 1913; *Indianapolis Times*, July 30, 1961.

Temperance and Prohibition. Alcohol long has been an accepted part of American life. By the early 19th century many people and physicians believed that alcoholic beverages in moderation were beneficial to one's health. Political candidates even distributed whiskey freely at polling places to win support from voters. During those same years there were growing concerns about the misuse of alcohol and its impact on personal health and family life. Religious revivals preached the evils of "intoxicating drink" and sobered up many converts who joined "the cause." Strong nativist feelings against German and Irish immigrants inspired local efforts to restrict production and sales of liquor. As a result, alcoholic beverages and politics proved to be a volatile mix throughout Indianapolis' history.

Beginning in eastern states during the early 1800s the temperance movement quickly spread nationwide. On October 3, 1828, Indianapolis residents met at the Methodist meetinghouse to organize the Temperance Society of Marion County. They pledged "to discontinue the use of ardent spirits, except as medicine" and agreed that "entire abstinence is the only course which promises success in suppressing intemperance." In December, 1829, representatives from around Indiana met in Indianapolis to organize the Indiana Temperance Society, which considered "the habitual use of ardent spirits [to be] injurious to health, destructive to the mental faculties, and tends to shorten human life."

Even though the words temperance and prohibition were often used interchangeably, they had different meanings and produced different agendas. Temperance suggested voluntary abstinence, whereas prohibition implied legal remedies and restrictions. Temperance came first, with the American Temperance Society, the Washingtonians, and assorted fraternal organizations collecting abstinence pledges, mounting public marches, and working to develop a consensus against alcoholic beverages. In early 1852 Indianapolis hosted a temperance revival during which nearly 900 people formed the Social Order of Temperance and "signed the pledge." Between 1830 and 1850 groups such as these helped secure the passage of more than 125 local laws throughout Indiana that encouraged temperance by regulating prices and quantities of alcohol sold, not by enforcing abstinence.

Voluntary abstinence soon gave way to demands for prohibition. The People's party, a forerunner of the Republican party, won a major statewide victory in 1854 on a platform advocating temperance and opposing the extension of slavery. The General Assembly subsequently enacted a law in 1855 to prohibit the manufacture and sale of alcohol, except for medicinal purposes. Local Germans and Irish opposed the law, although one Indianapolis newspaper proclaimed the law a success since it "diminished crime, reduced drunkenness, saved money, and emptied jails." But the state Supreme Court in the 1855 BEEBE TEMPERANCE CASE, which originated in Marion County, declared the law unconstitutional on grounds that it violated property rights and the guarantee against unreasonable search and seizure.

New temperance groups arose following the Civil War, including the WOMEN'S CHRISTIAN TEMPERANCE UNION (1874). A coalition of groups unsuccessfully promoted various restrictive laws, including one that would make saloonkeepers liable for customer injuries resulting from the use of alcoholic beverages. The first significant temperance law enacted by the General Assembly after the war was the Baxter Act (1873), which required the approval of a majority of voters in a ward, town, or township before a liquor license could be granted. In Indianapolis, however, the Democrats won control of the city council for the first time since 1860; the *Indianapolis Journal* attributed Republican losses to "ill-conceived and misdirected zeal of the so-called temperance people." Later in 1881 the Indiana General Assembly proposed a constitutional amendment to prohibit the manufacture or sale of alcoholic beverages in the state. The amendment became linked with a women's suffrage bill and the following year both were defeated after anti-prohibition Democrats swept the elections.

An important temperance advocate was Governor J. Frank Hanly who in 1908 pushed a county local option law through the General Assembly. In response 70 of 92 counties by November, 1909, had voted to forbid the sale of alcoholic beverages; it appears that Marion County remained "wet." Following his term as governor Hanly founded the Flying Squadron of America in Indianapolis to promote national prohibition and established the National Enquirer, which became a leading temperance newspaper.

Although the Democratic-controlled legislature repealed the county option measure in 1911, the General Assembly enacted a statewide prohibition law in 1917. Two years later Indiana ratified the 18th Amendment to the U.S. Constitution, which prohibited the manufacture, sale, and transportation of intoxicating liquors. Following the adoption of statewide prohibition, Indianapolis immediately witnessed the impact of the legislation. Police reported a 74 percent decline in arrests during the law's first week of implementation; only 26 people were arrested over the first weekend, compared to the usual 100. "The sudden decrease in the number of brawls, shootings and other disturbances, usually common on Saturday nights, was attributed by policemen to the fact that the city's 500 or more saloons closed their doors last Tuesday at midnight," reported the *Indianapolis News*. The first month of the law saw a 35 percent decline in crime in the city. The county workhouse, where criminal offenders paid fines with work, was soon closed because of a lack of business.

Prohibition was never strictly a party issue. But given the socioeconomic characteristics of political parties, Republicans tended to favor prohibition and strict regulation, whereas most Democrats favored less or no regulation. In both state and city politics, a candidate's stance on temperance could truly make the difference on election day.

About this time Methodist minister Edward S. Shumaker came to Indianapolis to head the Indiana Anti-Saloon League. Formerly superintendent of the league's South Bend district, Shumaker secured the passage in 1925 of a "bone dry law" that strengthened prohibition enforcement. Found guilty of contempt for criticizing the Indi-

City policemen conducted unannounced raids during Prohibition, seizing homemade alcohol such as the "white mule" produced by this 1920 still. The still was found on a farm near New Bethel.
[Indiana Historical Society, Bass Collection, #72861]

ana Supreme Court's prohibition law decisions, Shumaker served a 60-day sentence at the State Farm in 1929. Considered a hero for the cause, he died a few months following his release.

Prohibition reduced some crime, but law enforcement officials could not keep up with illegal efforts to make and sell alcoholic beverages. The proposed repeal of prohibition just before the Great Depression began in 1929 failed, but by the 1932 election the voters were ready to end the experiment, and state and national prohibition laws were repealed soon thereafter.

Following the legislature's repeal of the "bone dry law" in 1933, Governor Paul McNutt and the Democratic party established regulations over the newly legal business through the Alcoholic Beverage Commission. Liquor and politics continued to mix, this time through the use of liquor licenses as political patronage. When the Republicans took over state government after World War II, they likewise used liquor regulation to distribute political rewards. In Indianapolis the county government regulation of the industry also provided political patronage, controversy, and scandal.

By the 1980s there was growing awareness of the social impact of drinking. In 1981 the nation recorded 25,000 fatalities attributed to drunken drivers, including 282 deaths in Indiana. Marion County Prosecutor Stephen Goldsmith launched a statewide crusade against the crime as head of the Governor's Task Force on Drunk Driving. Local chapters of Mothers Against Drunk Driving (MADD) and Students Against Drunk Driving (SADD) were organized in 1982. The Indiana General Assembly adopted stricter laws in 1983 to reduce the deaths attributed to this crime. Public health advocates issued warnings about the dangers of alcoholic beverages, especially for babies in mothers' wombs. Elected in 1988, Governor Evan Bayh promptly banned the use of hard liquor at public events in the Governor's Residence and later added beer and wine to the ban.

No matter which way public opinion swings, the subject of alcoholic beverages keeps returning to the political table—through campaigns to crack down on drunk driving, through efforts by neighborhood associations to oppose renewals of local liquor licenses, or through proposals to contain damages that come from their abuse.

RUSSELL PULLIAM
Indianapolis News

Justin E. Walsh, *The Centennial History of the Indiana General Assembly, 1816–1978* (Indianapolis, 1987).

Tennis. Little information has survived concerning tennis in Indianapolis in the 19th century. The earliest recorded tournaments in the city were hosted by the Indianapolis Athletic Club in the summer of 1887. The IAC sponsored three city tournaments that year, but the sport did not take root in Indianapolis until after the first state tournament held at Irwin Field in 1907. Over 100 entrants from all over Indiana competed. The tournament's success prompted tennis enthusiasts from the Indianapolis Country Club, North Illinois Street Country Club, and the Irvington Tennis Club to form the Indianapolis Tennis Association later in 1907. The ITA had its own courts on East 10th Street (where ARSENAL TECHNICAL HIGH SCHOOL now stands), and worked with other clubs to promote tennis throughout the city.

By the 1920s Indianapolis was recognized nationally as a tennis center, ranking just behind New York, San Francisco, and Philadelphia. The Western Open, the oldest amateur tournament in the United States, came here for the first time in 1922, bringing the world's top-ranked tennis players with it. Woodstock Country Club was the host, and the tournament was so successful that the Western Tennis Association decided that Indianapolis would be the host city every other year. In the late 1920s and 1930s Johnny Hennesy, a product of the old Hawthorne Tennis Club located at 34th Street and Central Avenue, brought fame to the city by winning the Western Open and playing for the U.S. Davis Cup team.

Tennis experienced a decline in interest in the 1950s but rebounded in the 1960s. Traditionally known throughout the city as "tennis week," the Western Open was the social event of every other summer. Local families vied for the privilege of billeting players, and many residents postponed their summer vacations until after the tournament. Indianapolis began hosting the tournament every year in 1966. This arrangement was short-lived, however, because of the United States Tennis Association's (USTA) decision to move the U.S. Clay Court Championships to Indianapolis from Milwaukee in 1969 (the Western Open moved to Cincinnati). The Clay Courts enjoyed great initial success in Indianapolis. Woodstock hosted the tournament from 1969 until 1974 when low seating capacity forced its move to the Indianapolis Racquet Club. The U.S. Open's switch from grass to clay in 1975 made the Clay Courts, always the last major tournament before the U.S. Open, a popular event among the world's top-ranked players. Demand for tickets spurred the construction of the 15,000–seat Indianapolis Sports Center downtown in 1978. The Sports Center began hosting the Clay Courts in 1979.

The Clay Courts' fortunes suffered a major reversal after the U.S. Open moved from clay to hard courts in 1978. Top players began entering hard-court tournaments as tune-ups before the Open, and by 1986 the Clay Courts managed to draw only one player ranked among the men's top 20. The following year the Clay Courts lost the women's draw, and in the fall the USTA moved the Clay Courts to Wild Dunes, South Carolina, after Indianapolis announced its intention to pave the Sports Center courts in an effort to draw top-ranked players to the city. In the spring of 1988 the Sports Center's courts were paved over as part of a $13 million improvement plan that included the construction of an indoor tennis complex. The move paid off. In December, 1988, the USTA made the Sports Center one of its regional training centers and the new hard-court tournament, now sponsored annually by RCA, has again become popular among the world's top-ranked men as a tune-up for the U.S. Open.

Indianapolis hosted its first Women's Professional Tennis tournament in 1972 when the Virginia Slims Grand Prix made a stop at the State Fairgrounds Coliseum. Women's pro tennis returned ten years later when Virginia Slims made the Indianapolis Racquet Club a stop on its Ginny circuit, a series of tournaments designed for young women just entering the top ranks of professional tennis. Virginia Slims continued to hold a tournament in Indianapolis until 1987 when the Racquet Club stop became part of the Kraft series of Women's Tennis Association tournaments. In 1993 the Indianapolis tournament was moved to Schenectady, New York.

From 1975 to 1978 Indianapolis was home to the Indiana Loves of the World Team Tennis league. The Loves played their home matches at the INDIANA CONVENTION CENTER for three seasons before moving to MARKET SQUARE ARENA in 1978. The Loves folded after the 1978 season, along with the rest of the WTT franchises.

High school tennis was slow to develop on the state level. In Indianapolis, Shortridge, Tech, Cathedral, and Broad Ripple competed in the first city high school tournament in 1950. By the end of the decade Scecina, Howe, and Attucks had joined the field, but the first INDIANA HIGH SCHOOL ATHLETIC ASSOCIATION state tournament was not played until 1967. The boys finals were moved to North Central High School after the completion of a 27–court complex there in 1971, and the girls had their first finals there in 1974. Both finals are still held at North Central, where the host Panthers have experienced tremendous success. The girls have won the championship 8 times since 1976, while the boys have won 13 times over the same period, including 5 straight titles from 1982 through 1986.

Youth tennis programs have enjoyed great support in Indianapolis over the past 25 years. In 1969 Barbara Wynne began offering public tennis lessons for 100 children in Riverside Park. Her classes developed into the city's two largest youth tennis programs, with the Riverside Park program growing to 500 participants when the National Junior Tennis League took it over in 1973. By 1980 the NJTL was offering free tennis lessons to 2,500 Indianapolis youths at 20 different sites. In 1993 the organization served over 3,000 participants at 24 different sites. In 1973 Wynne moved to North Central and started the Washington Township Schools Community Tennis Program. Over the past 20 years her program, with 1,000 players in 1993, has produced some of the best players in the state and contributed greatly to North Central's success.

WILLIAM D. DALTON

Terrell, William Henry Harrison (Nov. 13, 1827–May 16, 1884). Indiana adjutant general and secretary of the state bureau of finance during the Civil War. Born in Henry County, Kentucky, Terrell moved with his family to Bartholomew County, Indiana, the following year. He held several county offices and was editor of the *Columbus Gazette*, a Whig newspaper. He was admitted to the bar in the early 1850s and in 1857 moved to Vincennes, becoming bookkeeper of a short-lived distillery. In January, 1862, Governor OLIVER P. MORTON selected Terrell as his military secretary.

In 1863 the General Assembly refused to appropriate funds for military affairs, whereupon the governor established a bureau of finance, raised monies privately, and appointed Terrell to administer the fund. In November, 1864, Terrell became Indiana adjutant general with the rank of colonel and by special legislation was made brigadier general in March, 1865. Governor Morton and others praised his excellent administration of war finance.

At the close of the war Terrell authored and supervised the compilation of *Report of the Adjutant General of Indiana* (1869). This monumental eight-volume work is indispensable to an understanding of Indiana's role in the war.

President Grant named Terrell in 1869 as third assistant postmaster in Washington, D.C. He returned to Indianapolis to serve as U.S. pension agent. He is buried in CROWN HILL CEMETERY.

JAMES A. TRULOCK

Theater, Children's. The first children's theater of record, and the main source of theater activity for children in Indianapolis for several decades, was launched by the Little Theatre Society when, in 1927, it initiated "The Children's Hour," a program providing a different theatrical program each month.

In 1929 the Little Theatre Society, now named the CIVIC THEATRE, produced its first play for children, *The Steadfast Tin Soldier.* Two years later, Civic was staging four plays annually for child audiences, using both children and adults as actors. By 1942 the rapidly expanding program included high school age students. Both a mothers' support group and the Junior League provided volunteer leadership as Junior Civic, as it was now called, stretched into the summer months. Gradually professional staff were added and classes both during the school year and in the summer were expanded. In 1979 the Kid Connection, a touring company of semi-professional performers, initiated tours to area schools.

During the 1950s and 1960s, theater for children in Indianapolis expanded as other community theaters added plays for children to their seasons. Also, THE CHILDREN'S MUSEUM provided some productions.

In 1972 INDIANA UNIVERSITY–PURDUE UNIVERSITY AT INDIANAPOLIS launched a summer touring theater company for the Department of Parks and Recreation. Simultaneously, the university began to offer course work for students in areas of children's theater, creative dramatics, and puppetry. The touring company, begun during the summer of 1972, gradually developed into a full "bus and truck" tour bringing fully staged productions to schools and community centers throughout Indiana. Additionally, company members, both students and faculty, led workshops in the schools for teachers and children. In 1983 the University Theatre initiated a biennial national playwriting contest to promote plays of high quality for children. Although the topics addressed at the symposium change, the format remains constant. Winning plays are showcased and national leaders confront current issues critical to creating outstanding scripts. Both Marian College and Butler University also provide productions for young audiences.

The INDIANA REPERTORY THEATRE, a professional theater, originated an outreach program in 1973 and by 1976 was touring to 36 schools in 14 cities. Although the touring company was eventually eliminated, the IRT subsequently launched a season of three productions for elementary age children on its "upper stage." These performances, combined with "main stage" plays for high school students, constitute a wide range of professionally produced theater. In the early 1990s both Civic Theatre and EDYVEAN REPERTORY THEATRE at Christian Theological Seminary expanded their performance schedules to include matinees suitable for high school and junior high school age audiences. The Lilly Theatre at The Children's Museum is the site for small professional touring companies, workshops, and inhouse productions. Professional companies tour to Indianapolis with performances at CLOWES MEMORIAL HALL and the MURAT TEMPLE.

Various individuals and agencies offer workshops and courses in theater for young people. Some of these focus on theater for the general development of the child while others specialize in training for professional careers.

DOROTHY WEBB
Indiana University–Purdue University,
Indianapolis

Theater, Professional. The first professional dramatic performance in Indianapolis was given Wednesday, December 31, 1823, in the dining room of Major Thomas Carter's Rosebush Tavern. Under the direction of a Mr. Smith, the company of actors held several performances. Smith returned a year later, though apparently with less success.

At that time many religious people considered the theater immoral, so it was not until about 1838 that another traveling company, led by a Mr. Lindsay, performed in the city. They came from Cincinnati by wagon, bringing scenery in rolls so it could be used in a variety of rooms. Their theater was Olleman's wagon shop; the seating, two-inch planks without backs. Lindsay's company returned in 1839–1840, performing in the dining room of Browning's Hotel. The following year Lindsay adapted the old *Indiana Democrat* office, a one-story brick building, for use as a theater.

In 1843–1844 the New York Company of Comedians, managed by John Powell, leased the second story of Gaston's carriage factory as a theater. After that there were no important productions until the new Masonic Hall became available in the spring of 1850. Later Morrison's Opera Hall was built, and the better productions were held there.

In 1852 a company directed by F. W. Robinson performed at the first INDIANA STATE FAIR. Robinson later managed a stock company at the just-completed Washington Hall for two seasons, moving to the new Atheneum for the 1854–1855 season. Other managers then leased the Atheneum, but without much success.

Valentine Butsch built the city's first real theater, the 1,500–seat Metropolitan, in 1858. It did not do well until troops arriving in the city during the Civil War created a demand for entertainment. In 1868 Butsch built the Academy of Music, with 2,500 seats; it was destroyed by fire a few years later. The Metropolitan burned in 1877, and again in 1897, after which George Dickson and Henry Talbott rebuilt it as the Park Theater (later known as the Strand and the Capitol).

Adding to the busy theater scene in the city, the Dickson Grand Opera House was built in 1875. In 1880 WILLIAM H. ENGLISH built English's Opera House, later the English Theater, modeled on the New York Grand Opera House. It was dubbed "English's folly" because some people believed there were already enough theaters in the city, but it proved successful. English's featured the largest stage in the city. In 1886 it was leased to Dickson and Talbott, who then controlled all of the top theaters in Indianapolis until 1897. The Majestic Theater, featuring a stock company, was built in 1907. The English Theater was torn down in 1949.

As talking pictures became popular movie palaces began to replace live theater, and the theater presence in Indianapolis diminished. In 1936 Keith's Theater, built in 1908 on the site of the old

Grand, housed the Federal Players, a troupe of the Works Progress Administration's FEDERAL THEATRE PROJECT. The company disbanded in 1937.

Three professional theaters in Indianapolis currently offer full seasons of locally produced plays. The INDIANA REPERTORY THEATRE is an Equity theater using full-time professionals. Productions at the PHOENIX THEATRE use vocational and non-vocational artists. Beef and Boards, also an Equity company, provides dinner theater to Indianapolis patrons.

JOYCE K. JENSEN

Jacob Piatt Dunn, *Greater Indianapolis* (Chicago, 1910); Berry R. Sulgrove, *History of Indianapolis and Marion County* (Philadelphia, 1884).

Theaters. In its earliest years theater was not a high priority in Indianapolis, and a variety of structures welcomed the troupes passing through town. The city's first theatrical production was held in the dining room of Thomas Carter's new tavern on New Year's Eve, 1823. For several years makeshift theaters included places such as Olleman's wagon shop, where two-inch planks served as seats and tallow candles as footlights, the dining room of Browning's Hotel, the upper floor of Gaston's Carriage House, and the former offices of the *INDIANA DEMOCRAT*. Performances were staged in churches, the courthouse, an old foundry building, and occasionally in the House of Representatives. In 1850 the Masonic Hall was built with a hall suitable for public performances. It became the venue of nearly all the city's entertainments until replaced by Morrison's Opera House, the first vaudeville house in Indianapolis. In 1851 the Masonic Hall hosted the state Constitutional Convention during the day and a theatrical troupe in the evening. Finally, in 1858, the city's first real theater, the Metropolitan, opened complete with a gallery, vaulted ceiling, and frescoes. Still, since Hoosiers were not ready to devote an entire building to frivolity, the theater occupied the building's two upper floors while the ground level housed businesses, as did the Atheneum (1844–1858) and the Academy of Music (1868). During the next three decades several theaters destined to become landmarks in Indianapolis were built: the

The Park Theater.
[Indiana Historical Society, Bass Collection, #6451]

Grand Opera House (1875), which became Keith's and was operated by the WPA FEDERAL THEATRE PROJECT in 1936; English's Opera House (1880), modeled on the New York City Opera House; the Empire (1892), which presented both burlesque and sporting events; and the ATHENAEUM (1894), present home of the AMERICAN CABARET THEATRE.

At the turn of the century, with the advent of motion pictures, theaters appeared on the Indianapolis landscape like mushrooms. Between 1900 and 1930 nearly 200 theaters opened. Most of them were small neighborhood nickelodeons but several could be described as "magnificent movie palaces," although most theaters fitting this description were designed to accommodate live entertainment as well. They represented a myriad of architectural styles. The Adams style was seen in Loew's State (1921), Arabian in the Murat (1910), English Guild Hall in the Little (1926), Egyptian in the Zaring Egyptian (1925), Gothic-American in the MAENNERCHOR (1906), Italian in the Fountain Square (1928), and Spanish in the INDIANA THEATRE (1927). Occasionally they combined styles, as in the CIRCLE THEATRE's (1916) use of Grecian and Old English and the Lyric's (1906) incorporation of Italian and French elements in its 1927 renovation.

After 1930 relatively few new theaters were built in Indianapolis. However, during this period the Hilton U. Brown Theatron, home of STARLIGHT MUSICALS outdoor productions, the Black Curtain Dinner Theatre, and CLOWES HALL, the city's first multi-purpose theaters, were introduced. The first drive-in theater, the Pendleton Pike, made its appearance in 1940. By 1974 there were a dozen others; today that number has dwindled to four. During the 1940s and 1950s motion picture theaters were everywhere. By the 1960s they had largely moved to suburban shopping malls and outlying areas. Theaters became smaller, less ornate structures with a single lobby and multiple screens that were undoubtedly more profitable but definitely less individualistic. During the same time, theaters for live performances were also being built as components of other buildings. Some examples of this trend are the INDIANAPOLIS CIVIC THEATRE, DeBoest Hall, and the Outdoor Concert Terraces at the Indianapolis Museum of Art; Sheldon Auditorium at the Christian Theological Seminary; and the Warren Performing Arts Center at Warren Central High School.

Over time many theaters in Indianapolis have seen several incarnations. Two were restaurants at one time, two became churches, several vaudeville, burlesque, and movie houses successively. One began as a private residence, became home to two fraternal organizations, and now is once more a clubhouse. Most of the marvelous old theaters in Indianapolis were destroyed to make space for businesses, office buildings, or parking lots. A few have survived and, as of the early 1990s, were still being used as theaters, notably the Indiana, the Circle, the Hedback (Little), and the Theatre on the Square.

The following list includes some of the more significant theaters from Indianapolis' past.

Arlington (1025 North Arlington Avenue). Opened October 6, 1949. Seating capacity 1,100. Movies; later converted to music hall. Closed early 1990s.

Athenaeum (401 East Michigan Street). Opened February 22, 1894. Former home of Indiana Repertory Theatre (1972–1979) and current home of American Cabaret Theatre.

Bijou (108 East Washington Street). Opened February 10, 1906. Possibly first movie theater in town. Closed December, 1941.

Cadle Tabernacle (Corner Ohio and New Jersey streets). Opened October 9, 1921. Seating capacity over 10,000. Conventions, rallies, concerts, and religious services. Closed November, 1968.

Circle Theatre (Monument Circle). Opened August 30, 1916. Seating capacity 3,100. Concerts and movies. Reputed to be the first local theater to show a sound movie, "The Jazz Singer." Home of the Indianapolis Symphony Orchestra since 1984.

Colonial (240 North Illinois Street). Opened November 22, 1909. Later Empress Theatre (April, 1937) and Fox Theatre (December, 1937). Vaudeville, movie, and later burlesque house. Closed December, 1975.

Emerson (4630 East 10th Street). Opened 1928 as the Eastland. Seating capacity 542. Movie house, now a concert venue.

Empire (138 North Delaware Street). Opened September 5, 1892. Later Columbia Theatre (August, 1913). Seating capacity 2,010. Concert and sports venue. Closed unknown.

English Opera House (Monument Circle). Opened September 27, 1880. Seating capacity 2,000. Theater, opera, movie, and vaudeville house. Closed April 30, 1948.

Fountain Square (1105 Shelby Street). Opened May, 1928. Seating capacity 1,800. Movies. Closed April 2, 1960.

Granada (1045 Virginia Avenue). Opened April 8, 1928. Movies. Closed March 5, 1951.

Grand Opera House (117 North Pennsylvania Street). Opened September 13, 1875. Later B. F. Keith's Theatre (September 5, 1910). Seating capacity 1,608. Reputed to be first U.S. theater to be electrically lighted. "High class" vaudeville and movies. Closed July 30, 1964.

Indiana (136 West Washington Street). Opened June 18, 1927. Seating capacity 3,000. Movies and stage productions. Home of Indiana Repertory Theatre since 1980.

Irving (5509 East Washington Street). Opened 1915. Later Festival Theatre (May, 1970), Zenon (1982). Refurbished in 1987 to show art and foreign films.

Little (1847 North Alabama Street). Opened February 18, 1926. Later Civic Theatre (June 25, 1929), Booth Tarkington Civic Theatre (March 20, 1949). Currently Hedback Community Theatre (May, 1974) and home of Footlite Musicals.

Loews State (35 North Pennsylvania Street). Opened February 14, 1921. Later Loews Palace (March, 1928). Seating capacity 2,600. Movies. Razed July, 1970.

Lyric (121–135 North Illinois Street). Opened February, 1906. Seating capacity 200. Rebuilt 1912 with seating for 1,400. Movies. Closed ca. 1969.

Metropolitan (148 West Washington Street). Opened September 27, 1858. Seating capacity 900. Later Park Theatre (1882), Lyceum (August, 1913), Strand (January, 1916), Park (September, 1916), Capitol (August, 1923). First Indianapolis building constructed as a theater. Closed September 17, 1935.

Morrison's Opera House (Northeast corner of Meridian and Maryland streets). Early vaudeville theater. Destroyed by fire, January 17, 1870.

Murat (502 North New Jersey Street). Opened February 28, 1910. Seating capacity 1,800. Theater productions and movies.

Ohio (40 West Ohio Street). Opened November 15, 1919. Seating capacity 1,500. Movies and band concerts. Closed January, 1970.

Ritz (3422 North Illinois Street). Opened February 22, 1927. Seating capacity 1,400. Movies, burlesque house, and later rock/jazz venue. Closed mid 1970s.

Rivoli (3155 East 10th Street). Opened September 15, 1927. Seating capacity 1,220. Movies, music, art and adult films.

Tomlinson Hall (200 East Market Street). Opened June 2, 1886. Seating capacity 3,800. Concerts and stage productions. Destroyed by fire, October 30, 1958.

Vogue (6257 North College Street). Opened June 18, 1938. Movies. Currently nightclub showcasing assorted musical groups.

Walker (603 Indiana Avenue). Opened December 26, 1927. Seating capacity 1,500. Movies and vaudeville. Closed 1978; reopened 1988.

Zaring Egyptian (2741 Central Avenue). Opened November 2, 1925. Movies. Reputed to be second theater in America with an Egyptian motif. Razed 1968–1969.

RITA W. HARLAN
BILL ELLIOTT

Gene Gladson, *Indianapolis Theaters from A to Z* (Indianapolis, 1976); Indianapolis Newspaper Index, Indiana State Library.

Third Parties and Independent Candidates.

Though many have tried, none have succeeded in dislodging the hold that Republicans and Democrats (or, in the antebellum period, the Whigs and Democrats) have exerted in Marion County politics. One of the first serious challengers to the two dominant parties was the National Independent Greenback party. Formed as the Independent party at a state convention in Indianapolis in 1874, the Greenbacks went national in 1875 after winning five seats in the Indiana House of Representatives. The party's national headquarters was in Indianapolis and the INDIANAPOLIS SUN was its official organ. However, the 1876 elections were disastrous for the Greenback party. Their presidential candidate received fewer than 10,000 votes in Indiana, while their candidates for state offices polled fewer than 13,000 votes.

In 1890 Indiana delegates from the Greenback-Labor party (formerly the National Independent Greenback party), the Grange, the Union Labor party, and the Farmers Alliance met in Indianapolis and formed the People's party. Their candidates polled fewer than 17,000 votes in the 1891 state elections, but their platform appealed to farmers all over the Midwest. At a November, 1891, convention in Indianapolis to announce the merger of the Farmers Alliance and the Farmers Mutual Benefit Association, thousands of delegates from a dozen different states determined to form a national third party. This national People's party, commonly referred to as the Populists, did well in the 1892 elections nationally, but won less than 4 percent of the total vote in Indiana and only 581 of 40,926 presidential votes cast in Marion County. Though both parties were originally organized in the city, neither the Greenbacks nor the Populists ever won an office in Indianapolis.

The Prohibitionist party made its debut in Marion County in 1892. Wilson S. Doan was permanent chairman of the Indianapolis Prohibitionist convention in the early 1900s, and George Hitz was nominated for mayor several times during that period. The party's platform stressed improved enforcement of prohibition laws. While the party never enjoyed wide support, it continued to nominate candidates for city and county offices into the 1960s.

Another third party which arose in the unrest of the late 19th century and had its best successes in its earliest efforts was the Socialist party. Building on the public discontent tapped by the Populists, the March, 1900, national convention of the Socialist party, held in Indianapolis, nominated Hoosiers Eugene V. Debs and Job Harriman for president and vice-president. It was the first of five times that the Socialists would nominate Debs for the nation's highest office. In Indianapolis, George Lehnert was the Socialist candidate for mayor three times between 1904 and 1934. Lehnert also ran for the State Senate in 1906 and the Marion County Board of Commissioners in 1913. SHORTRIDGE HIGH SCHOOL and Harvard University graduate POWERS HAPGOOD, who lived on a farm near SOUTHPORT, was the Socialist candidate for governor in 1932. His wife MARY DONOVAN HAPGOOD, several times the Socialist candidate for vice-president of the United States, was the first woman to run for governor of Indiana. None of the Socialist candidates enjoyed any electoral success in Indianapolis or Marion County.

The 1912 election was the one serious challenge in Indianapolis history to the two party system. In that year the Progressive party mounted the strongest third party ever organized in Marion County. The Progressives won more votes than the Republicans, and almost 60 percent of the number of votes garnered by the Democrats. Its success, like that of most other third parties in Indianapolis, was linked to the history and fortunes of a national cause, in this instance the renegade candidacy of former president Theodore Roosevelt. The discontent that produced the earlier Socialist party was also responsible for several other local third party efforts over the years, although each continued to be tied to a national campaign.

In 1992 the independent presidential candidacy of H. Ross Perot did well in Marion County because it tapped into a national frustration regarding government and politicians. In spite of his withdrawal and later reentry into the race, Perot captured 57,878 Marion County presidential votes, or 17.8 percent of the total votes cast. His support organization continued locally in the mid–1990s at the Indianapolis office of United We Stand, America, Perot's national organization.

ROBERT D. MASSIE
Massie & Associates

Thomson Consumer Electronics. The world's fourth largest home electronics company with headquarters in Paris, France; Indianapolis is the site of corporate headquarters for North and South America. Thomson traces its Indianapolis roots through the Radio Corporation of America (RCA) to a small Westinghouse light bulb factory at the corner of LaSalle and Michigan streets in the early 1920s. Initially formed to market radio equipment produced by General Electric and Westinghouse, RCA cut free from its corporate parents within a decade and acquired the assets and manufacturing capability of the Victor Talking Machine Company of Camden, New Jersey. In 1930 it purchased the inactive Westinghouse factory in Indianapolis, which had been converted to radio tube production. The Great Depression dampened the market for radios and RCA stopped tube production in the city altogether in late 1930. When the company resumed operations in July, 1936, displacing Works Progress Administration offices then housed at the plant site, it manufactured the Photophone Sound System used for motion picture sound. By the end of 1937 radio tube manufacturing had again started in Indianapolis.

Within three years the plant was making sound equipment, public address systems, radio tubes, and recording gear. An ambitious expansion plan announced in early 1939 added 1,000 new jobs to the local RCA payroll. Sound equipment rolled off Indianapolis production lines for both the 1939 New York World's Fair and the San Francisco Exposition. A new business also began in Indianapolis—pressing phonograph records.

International tensions in late 1940 led to the Navy's decision to spend more than $2.7 million to expand RCA's facilities in Camden, New Jersey (the company's research base) and in Indianapolis. After Pearl Harbor the Indianapolis plant shifted to war production, including a land mine detector used effectively during the Normandy invasion.

Conversion to civilian production after the war was swift, and by 1947 the plant was building electronic television components even before Indianapolis citizens had a TV station to watch. In 1950 employment at the city's RCA plant peaked at 8,200. Ten years later RCA moved its consumer electronics headquarters to Indianapolis from New Jersey. Soon Indianapolis was the site of the home electronics division's design, engineering, research, marketing and sales, and administrative functions.

RCA underwent tremendous changes in the 1970s. Operations in Indianapolis continued to focus on consumer electronics, including the development of the ill-fated Videodisc system that lost out to the videocassette recorder as the preferred method of viewing recorded programs. In 1986 General Electric again entered the picture when it acquired RCA in what was (at the time) the largest non-oil merger ever attempted. GE moved its own consumer electronics division (based in Portsmouth, Virginia) to Indianapolis shortly after the purchase. In late 1987 GE announced its intention to sell the unprofitable consumer electronics business to French-owned Thomson. The RCA brand, which introduced commercial television service and color television to U.S. viewers, and the GE consumer electronics line are now branches of the Thomson family. A third brand, ProScan, a premier line of color TVs, VCRs, and laserdisc players, has limited national distribution. Thompson's major manufacturing centers in Indiana include the world's largest color TV assembly plant at Bloomington; the Marion television tube plant, which produces color TV picture tubes up to 35 inches in size (the first to manufacture 35–inch direct-view tubes in America); and the Indianapolis plastic components plant, which manufactures printed circuit boards for color TVs, plastic cabinets, remote control units, and other component parts.

Thomson's Americas headquarters is located just north of I–465 and North Meridian Street in two distinctive buildings designed by renowned architect and Indianapolis native Michael Graves. Product design, engineering, research, marketing and sales, and administrative support to Thomson's employees in the USA, Canada, Mexico, and Brazil are all coordinated from the North Meridian Street complex. More than 1,200 people work in the two Thomson buildings, which include administrative offices and a technical center.

DAVID H. ARLAND
Thomson Consumer Electronics

300 North Meridian. This 27–story structure, begun by Browning Investments in 1987 and designed by Haldeman Miller Bregman Hamann, encompasses 18 floors of office space atop 9 floors of enclosed parking. Floors 18 through 27 are occupied by the law firm of Baker and Daniels. The building's exterior, alternating columns of polished Barrister granite with a lighter-colored base and reflective glass accented by unpolished Barrister granite buckles, has stepped north and south facades. The principal facade faces east, overlooking UNIVERSITY PARK. It is topped by a copper-colored, octagonal dome that rises above the copper and glass shoulder featuring four dormers each on its north and south facades. Directly under the dome is the 27th-floor reception area with its 11–foot ceilings, marble compasses in the floors, and three glass walls looking out over the city. At street level the oversize brass doors open into a two-story Great Hall finished in brass, cherry, and polished granite. To the north is a sitting area with a fireplace and couches. There are high ceilings, wood paneling, polished brass, and light walls throughout.

RITA W. HARLAN

Indianapolis Star, May 28, 1989.

Tinsley, William (Feb. 7, 1804–June 14, 1885). Architect of Christ Church Cathedral. Born in 1804, in Clonmel, County Tipperary, Ireland, Tinsley came from a family of builders and stonemasons. He designed many buildings in his native land, but in 1851 he immigrated to Cincinnati, Ohio. Within two years he submitted plans in a contest to design the building for North Western Christian University (later BUTLER UNIVERSITY) in Indianapolis. After he won the $100 contest prize in 1853, he moved to the Indiana capital.

Tinsley later designed Center Hall at Wabash College in Crawfordsville, Indiana, and Ascension Hall at Kenyon College in Gambier, Ohio, as well as other buildings in Indiana and elsewhere.

Tinsley's most famous Indianapolis edifice is the CHRIST CHURCH CATHEDRAL, constructed in 1860. English Country Gothic in style, this stone church, located at North Meridian Street and MONUMENT CIRCLE, has a cruciform floor plan. Its spire was completed in 1869.

In 1857, after his second wife's death, Tinsley returned to Cincinnati where he continued his career, helping to design that city's open-air Plaza. He went into semiretirement in 1874 at the age of 70. He is buried in CROWN HILL CEMETERY.

CONNIE J. ZEIGLER

Eli Lilly, _History of the Little Church on the Circle_ (Indianapolis, 1957).

Todd, Marie Childs (Apr. 23, 1871–Dec. 17, 1951). Artist and art teacher. Todd graduated from Indianapolis High School and studied at the Pratt Institute in New York, the Art Institute of Chicago, and JOHN HERRON ART INSTITUTE. She taught briefly at Herron around 1915, and then at Shortridge from 1919 to 1937, thus having considerable influence on art education in the city. In addition to her teaching, she drew designs for tiles and greeting cards.

Todd's artistic abilities included woodcarving, oil and watercolor painting, and pastel drawing. In 1933 her work was the opening exhibition in the second annual series of one-artist shows at Herron. She was a charter member of the Indianapolis Artists Club, which she served as both vice-president and director. Several of her paintings are in the collection of the Indianapolis Public Schools.

ELLEN TEVAULT

Tomlinson Hall. Civic building. Local druggist Stephen D. Tomlinson died in November, 1870, leaving his estate to his wife. His will stipulated that upon her death the balance of the estate was to finance the construction of a building at Delaware and Market streets "for the use of

Tomlinson Hall, located on the corner of Market and Delaware streets, in 1903. [Indiana Historical Society, Bass Collection, #1726]

citizens and city authorities." In 1876, the City Council reached an agreement with Mrs. Tomlinson allowing them to proceed with plans for the structure. They sponsored an architectural competition, won by local architect DIEDRICH A. BOHLEN. Work began on the new hall in 1883, and the building was dedicated June 1, 1886.

Built at a cost of $125,000, the massive brick structure possessed large hip roofed towers at each corner and a triple arched main entrance covered by a balcony supported by heavily carved limestone brackets. Above the balcony four stone pilasters supported a pediment with a cornice below incised with "Tomlinson Hall." The facade utilized limestone detailing, creating a monumental exterior. The first floor housed businesses and market activity from the adjoining CITY MARKET. The upper floor was a large performing hall, designed to seat 4,200, with a stage capable of accommodating 650 people. The acoustically impressive auditorium possessed oak paneling, grand chandeliers, and comfortable theater seats.

Throughout its history, Tomlinson Hall was an important public meeting site. Its dedication was part of the Grand Army of the Republic Music Festival, held to raise money for a Civil War memorial (the SOLDIERS AND SAILORS MONUMENT) and attended by General William Tecumseh Sherman and other dignitaries. The COMMERCIAL CLUB sponsored a national STREET PAVING EXPOSITION there in April, 1890. The hall served as a shelter for victims of the 1913 flood and as a site for political, labor, and patriotic rallies.

Tomlinson Hall burned in 1958. A single doorway arch, discovered during the restoration of the City Market in the 1970s, stands in the market's courtyard as a monument to the hall and its benefactor.

SHERYL D. VANDERSTEL

Jacob Piatt Dunn, *Greater Indianapolis* (Chicago, 1910), II, 1072; *Indianapolis Daily Journal*, June 3, 1886.

Topics Suburban Newspapers. Chain of suburban newspapers focusing on community news. The group of 15 papers was purchased in 1992 by Central Newspapers, Inc., which also publishes the INDIANAPOLIS STAR and INDIANAPOLIS NEWS.

The *Noblesville Daily Ledger* (also *Republican Ledger, Hamilton County Ledger,* and *Daily Ledger*) made its weekly debut in 1871 under the direction of William Bodenhamer and Oscar Miles. In 1914, 43 years and 18 owners later, the newspapers were sold by the Ledger Company to the Enterprise Publishing Company, headed by Edward E. and Charles S. Neal, who merged their *Enterprise* into the *Ledger*. A daily edition, the *Daily Ledger*, was started in 1887, changing the name of the weekly edition to *Hamilton County Ledger* in 1888. The Neal brothers changed the name of the corporation to the Noblesville Daily Ledger, Inc. and dropped the weekly *Hamilton County Ledger* around 1916. Three generations later, John R. and James T. Neal continued to operate the *Ledger* through 1985 when it was sold to LeRoy W. Stauffer, a publishing executive from Ohio.

Phoebe E. Hudler started *North Side Topics* in 1922. When she retired in 1969, William Pace, who had been the editor since 1958, became publisher and general manager of the four Topics papers: *North Side Topics* (1922), *Nora News-Dispatch* (formerly *Nora Topics, Washington Patriot*) (1961), *Castleton Banner* (formerly *Northeast Topics*) (1966), and *North Meridian Observer* (1961). When Topics Suburban Newspapers bought the *Sheridan News* (est. 1882) in 1980, Pace had already added five other papers to the chain: *Carmel News-Tribune* (formerly *Carmel Topics*) (1969),

Lawrence Times (formerly *Lawrence Topics*) (1970), *Pike Register* (formerly *Northwest Topics*) (1972), *Westfield Enterprise* (formerly *Westfield Topics*) (1978), and *Fisher Sun-Herald* (1980). The *Heights Herald* was started in 1981.

In 1986 Stauffer bought the Topics newspapers and merged them with the Noblesville Daily Ledger, Inc. He closed the *Noblesville Telegraph* (est. 1980s) and *Southeastern AdNews* (est. 1980s), and added three others: *Geist Gazette* (1988), *Carmel Daily Ledger* (1989), and the *Ledger Leader* (1991). *Zionsville Eagle*, which was started in the 1980s, was discontinued in 1991.

The *Noblesville Daily Ledger* and *Carmel Daily Ledger* are published Monday-Saturday and delivered to approximately 10,000 homes. *Sheridan News*, the only paid weekly of the Topics papers, and the other 12 Topics newspapers have a combined controlled circulation of 87,000. The weekly papers are typically distributed at no subscription cost every Wednesday to approximately 91 percent of all households in Clinton, Tipton, Boone, Hamilton, and Marion counties. A focus on community events, school news, and other important information highlighting the positive aspects of each community has made the Topics papers popular in their respective areas.

CHRISTY M. MCKAY

Topography. The surface of Marion County is part of the physiographic province called the Tipton Till Plain, which is named after Tipton County (two counties north of Marion County) and is underlain by glacial deposits known as "till." In Marion County the surface elevation of the lowest point is about 650 ft. (200 m) above sea level and the surface elevation of the highest point is about 900 ft. (275 m) above sea level. The two points are on opposite sides of the county. The lowest point is on the county line where the southward-flowing WHITE RIVER leaves Marion County. The highest point is on a hill on the northern county line just west of where the southward-flowing Eagle Creek enters Marion County; it is not, as is commonly believed, the hill in CROWN HILL CEMETERY that contains James Whitcomb Riley's remains, which rises to only 840 ft. (256 m). Monument Circle at the center of In-

dianapolis is at an elevation about 715 ft. (218 m) above sea level.

Although the total relief (the difference in elevation between the lowest and highest points on the surface) for the 402 square miles (1,372 square km) of Marion County as a whole is about 267 ft. (80 m), the local relief for any particular part of the county is considerably lower. Thus, the topographic impression one sees from an aerial view is a generally flattish landscape with several narrow incisions caused by the erosion of the main streams. Overall, the surface slopes gently toward White River with a topographic relief at any given section of about 10 to 30 ft. (about 3 to 9 m). Perhaps the most prominent topographic features in this generally flattish landscape are several isolated hills or short ridges that rise about 100 to 130 ft. (about 30 to 40 m) above the surface. These hills are glacial landforms called *kames*, which are deposits of sand and gravel that were entrapped in pockets along the margin of a glacier that once covered this area or in crevasses within the glacier. The best known of these hills is the one mentioned above at Crown Hill Cemetery, but other kame-hills are in the southern half of the county. The relief of the steep valley walls of the major streams looks rugged, but actually is at most only about 100 ft. (about 30 m) or slightly higher.

ARTHUR MIRSKY
Indiana University–Purdue University,
Indianapolis

U.S. Geological Survey, "Topographic Map of Marion County, Indiana, Scale 1:48,000, Contour Interval 5 feet" (1958).

Townsend Recovery Plan Convention (June 22–25, 1939). The convention was the fourth national gathering of an organization founded in 1934 by Francis Townsend, a 67–year-old California physician, in response to the dire economic conditions of the Great Depression. Townsend proposed a $200 monthly pension to everyone over 60 to be financed by a 2 percent transaction tax. By the mid–1930s, millions of elderly persons had joined Townsend Clubs to push for congressional enactment of the Townsend Recovery Plan.

As the hub of the strongest Townsendite territory, Indianapolis was an ideal convention site. Statewide membership was 312,000, and eight of Indiana's 12 congressmen were elected with Townsendite support. Further, because Indiana's gross income tax was similar to the Townsendites' proposed transaction tax, the convention delegates wanted to know more about the Indiana tax's viability.

Packed into CADLE TABERNACLE in stifling summer heat, the delegates heard their staunchest allies in Congress predict that, despite the June 1, 1939, defeat of the Townsend bill in the House of Representatives, Congress would eventually see the wisdom of the plan and adopt it. The convention passed resolutions to work for reelection of representatives who voted for the plan and to purge those who did not.

Tax experts from Hawaii and Indiana, the two jurisdictions imposing the gross income tax, were among the speakers. To a tumultuous ovation, Louis Silva (Hawaii) said business there was burgeoning, and as tax rates rose the selling price of merchandise had gone down. On the other hand, Clarence Jackson of the Indiana State Treasury admitted that while Indiana's gross income tax raised considerable sums, it incited widespread tax evasion and was hard to collect. When Jackson pointed out unfeasible aspects of the Townsend plan, such as the nearly 1.5 million extra Internal Revenue agents necessary to administer it, cries of "throw him out!" erupted in the hall.

Townsend announced a goal to raise $1 million for a radio advertising program. Reverend E. Howard Cadle, proprietor of the tabernacle, initiated a collection with a $100 bill. As the organ thundered "The Battle Hymn of the Republic," over $3,500 was heaped into a large wastebasket on the stage. Despite the enthusiasm and commitment generated at the Indianapolis convention, the Townsend plan never again came to a vote in Congress. Increasing concern with international affairs and improved economic conditions largely eliminated interest in the measure.

VAL HOLLEY

Abraham Holtzman, *The Townsend Movement: A Political Study* (New York, 1963); David Bennett, *Demagogues in the Depression* (New Brunswick, N.J., 1969).

Townships. Units of local government. The Indiana Constitution provides for the existence of townships, and successive state laws have instituted township government and its officers. Within each county the Board of County Commissioners may create or abolish townships and their boundaries upon the petition of a majority of its citizens.

There are nine townships in Marion County: the northern tier consists of Pike, Washington, and Lawrence townships; Wayne, Center, and Warren townships make up the middle tier; and the southern tier includes Decatur, Perry, and Franklin townships. (See separate entries on individual townships.) Center Township, which contains most of the pre-Unigov City of Indianapolis, has the largest population, the lowest income per capita, and the highest total property value in Marion County.

Each Marion County township elects its own trustee, board, assessor, and (except in Franklin Township) a constable and small claims court judge. Officers serve four-year terms, not to exceed eight consecutive years. Residence in the township is the only qualification for any office. Township officers' salaries are based upon a combination of population and geographic size. Elected township officers have the power to appoint and hire deputies and employees to help them fulfill their responsibilities.

Because of their relatively large populations, Marion County townships tend to operate differently from most other townships in Indiana. All Marion County townships employ a full-time trustee and separate assessor, while most townships elsewhere employ only a part-time trustee who acts as both trustee and assessor. Additionally, no other townships in Indiana operate small claims courts, and few others employ a constable.

The trustee, the township's chief administrative officer, is responsible for management and improvement of all township property, such as township cemeteries, parks, buildings, and infrastructure. Trustees also provide direct poor relief, which includes food, clothing, heating fuel, medical help, utilities, transportation for employment, and school lunches. Also, except in Center Township, the trustee provides emergency and fire protection. The trustee can assess taxes or levy bonds for these purposes. Additionally, he/she must prepare the township budget as well as present an annual financial report to the State Board of Accounts for review.

A three-member Township Board advises the trustee in each township. At the board's two annual meetings and any necessary special meetings, it adopts the annual budget, approves township contracts, and sets tax rates and township employee salaries.

Since all the Marion County townships have a population over 5,000 each has an assessor who establishes the value of real and personal property for tax purposes. As of the early 1990s the assessors in Marion County are paid by the county and work under the direct supervision of the county assessor to promote intra-county uniformity.

Marion County townships, except for Franklin, also operate small claims courts. Indiana law created these courts in Marion County in 1975 to replace the former justice of the peace courts, which at that time were abolished in the rest of the state. The Marion County Circuit Court judge supervises these judges. Each township constable serves to enforce the orders of the small claims courts by serving summonses, warrants, and subpoenas.

Since the 1930s critics of township government have repeatedly attempted to abolish such governments statewide by merging them into county or municipal governments. As a result, some township duties have been reallocated, especially in Marion County where the combined Indianapolis–Marion County government provides myriad services. Township trustees statewide have been relieved of responsibility over schools, roads, and bridges, and their welfare functions have been reduced to providing only immediate emergency relief. In Marion County the county assessor now hires professionals to conduct most of the townships' property reassessment. In 1992 the DEPARTMENT OF METRO-POLITAN DEVELOPMENT of Indianapolis assigned each township an administrator to act as liaison between Indianapolis government and residents who have problems with city services. In Center Township the INDIANAPOLIS FIRE DEPARTMENT provides emergency and fire protection.

Throughout the 20th century township officials have been criticized for abuse, nepotism, lack of accountability, and inefficiency. Several Center Township trustees have been charged with overspending and incompetence, although state laws governing poor relief mandate certain services and thus constrain trustees' ability to control their expenditures. Additionally, a 1993 probe by the U.S. district attorney found that Marion County constables often charged unlawful fees for tenant eviction, making several constables the highest paid officials in the state.

MICHELLE D. HALE

Indiana State Library, Newspaper Clipping File, "Townships"; Indianapolis Public Library, Clipping Files, "Pike, Washington, Lawrence, Wayne, Center, Warren, Decatur, Perry, and Franklin Townships"; League of Women Voters, *Unigov Handbook* (Indianapolis: League of Women Voters Education Fund, 1985).

Traders Point. Residential area located on Lafayette Road, north of 71st Street in northwest Marion County. In 1864, John Jennings and Josiah Coughran built a mill at the point where Eagle Creek meets the Lafayette Road. The settlement may have been named for an old Indian trading post or because it was a convenient place for farmers to trade livestock. Later, two groceries, a sawmill, a cooper's shop, stockyards, and a blacksmith shop were built.

The area retained its rural character into the 20th century. In 1940, Traders Point counted only 50 residents. Later, affluent Indianapolis families built large homes and country estates in the area. Business in the community suffered when Lafayette Road (U.S. 52) was widened and improved for motor traffic in 1935. Some of the older firms declined and were replaced by a service station and restaurants. Then in the 1960s, when Eagle Creek Reservoir was constructed, the area was deemed to be in the floodplain and the few remaining commercial structures were leveled.

The Traders Point Hunt Charity Horse Show, an annual event held a few miles away in southern Boone county, benefits the HUMANE SOCIETY OF INDIANAPOLIS and helps to perpetuate the Traders Point name.

CATHLEEN F. DONNELLY

"Traders Point Gives Up the Ghost," *Indianapolis News*, Aug. 1, 1968.

Transportation, Department of. Plans, constructs, maintains, and regulates traffic flow on streets and bridges in Marion County. The department is not responsible for streets located in the cities of BEECH GROVE and LAWRENCE or in the town of SPEEDWAY, or for state and federal highways. Within its service area the department also sees to snow and ice removal; pavement markings and traffic signs and signals; street cleaning; roadside drainage, mowing, and weed control; shoulder, curb, and sidewalk maintenance; parking meter installation, maintenance, and coin collection; permit investigation and issuance; property acquisition and maintenance and contract administration; and community relations services such as offering public presentations and encouraging ridesharing programs.

Administrative responsibility in the department is centered in the director, who is appointed by the MAYOR with the approval of the CITY-COUNTY COUNCIL. The director also chairs the five-member Board of Transportation, which establishes and reviews departmental policies and programs and the department's annual budget. The other members of the Board of Transportation are appointed, two by the City-County Council and two by the mayor. These members serve renewable one-year terms without pay. The board holds regular meetings every other month and reports to the mayor and the City-County Council's transportation committee.

The Department of Transportation is currently organized into four divisions. The Operations Division is responsible for the construction, maintenance, and traffic-flow services of the department. The Development Division focuses on long-term transportation planning, review of private development projects, and the acquisition and maintenance of property. The Finance and Administration Division provides the needed internal management of the department, including purchasing, accounting, payroll administration, and data processing. The Quality Control Division inspects and evaluates the performance of the other divisions for their compliance with fed-eral, state, and local standards and requirements, and reports to the director. This division also arranges public meetings and presentations.

In January, 1994, the agency was renamed the Department of Capital Assets Management.

WILLIAM BLOMQUIST
CHARLES AUDRITSH

Tribe of Ishmael. Nineteenth-century group studied by poor relief agencies. In 1878 the Reverend OSCAR CARLETON MCCULLOCH, pastor of Plymouth Congregational Church, became interested in the poor of Indianapolis and how society could provide relief for them. He encountered a group that he labeled "the Ishmaelites" and described in his diary on January 20, 1878: "They are a wandering lot of beings, marrying, intermarrying, cohabiting, etc. They live mostly out of doors, in the river bottoms, in old houses, etc. They are largely illegitimate, subject to fits. . . . They are hardly human beings." Influenced by his belief in the social applications of Christianity and moved by a study conducted by Richard L. Dugdale for the New York Prison Association in 1878, McCulloch was convinced that eugenics (improving hereditary qualities through selective "breeding") might prevent the group's undesirable social behavior.

Believing that the Ishmaelites possessed defective hereditary traits, McCulloch and his collaborator J. Frank Wright, a local newspaperman, worked for ten years compiling histories on 250 families and 5,000 individuals. At the National Conference of Charities and Correction in 1888 McCulloch reported on their findings, using diagrams of the interrelations of 30 families (1,692 individuals) over six generations. He concluded that heredity contributed to the perpetuation of this "pauper class" and that public relief and benevolence, distributed indiscriminately, contributed to "their idle and wandering life."

The rhetoric of McCulloch's work is enough to raise suspicions about the quality of his research. One family history record on Robert Ross, a man of "low cunning" and "rank smell," noted how he "seduced all his daughters and made them his mistresses" and "taught his boys to steal." A case history of the same man from the FAMILY

SERVICE ASSOCIATION of Indianapolis described him as a "very industrious sober man," an assessment with which Ross' employer and minister agreed.

It appears that McCulloch and Wright saw largely what they wanted to see. Dismissing educational, social, and economic factors, they decided that restricting the poor's ability to reproduce would be advantageous to the larger society. This idea was well received in Indiana where the state government led the nation in passing eugenics legislation and mandating the sterilization of the "unfit."

In 1977 Ph.D. candidate Hugo P. Leaming contributed an alternative assessment of the Tribe, turning McCulloch's thesis on its head. Rather than being immoral degenerates, the Ishmaelites were an admirable, pioneering clan of African, Native American, and Muslim origins, "a lost-found nation in the wilderness of North America." Leaming described the group as possessing arts that were "the wonder of the region" and the home of Tom Ishmael as a "vast log mansion, three-cornered and . . . of a most curious design." The basic problem with Leaming's conclusion was that the only source on the Ishmaelites, the McCulloch-Wright study, mentioned nothing about their Islamic background, little favorable about the individuals themselves, and only that the three-cornered log cabin was "perhaps the queerest structure for shape in the state." Leaming, however, argued that it was "necessary to extrapolate a good deal from little evidence."

Virtually every page of Leaming's article contains distortions, matched only by those of the eugenicists who prepared the original sources. Given that, neither side proves its case and, in the end, there are only two myths, clear to those with faith, opaque to those who look for their historical basis. There was no Tribe of Ishmael; there were only the poor of Indianapolis.

ROBERT HORTON
Indiana State Archives

Oscar C. McCulloch and J. Frank Wright, "The Tribe of Ishmael" (manuscript, 1888), Indiana State Archives; Oscar C. McCulloch, *The Tribe of Ishmael: A Study in Social Degradation* (Indianapolis, 1888); Hugo P. Leaming, "The Ben Ishmael Tribe," in Melvin Holli and Peter d'A. Jones, eds., *The Ethnic Frontier: Essays in the History of Group Survival in Chicago and the Midwest* (Chicago, 1977).

Trustee Leadership Development. A national leadership education program based in Indianapolis that serves not-for-profit organizations, their boards, and staffs. Administered by Trinity Episcopal Church, Indianapolis, and funded by the LILLY ENDOWMENT, Trustee Leadership Development (TLD) seeks to increase the capacity of not-for-profit boards to serve and lead more effectively.

The TLD trustee education process focuses on what has been traditionally missing from board education and training efforts—the development of leadership as practice. Trustee education prepares board members for this responsibility through engaging them in an exploration of four important concepts: the organization's history, mission, publics, and future.

A national network of almost 200 (including 100 from Indiana) trustee educators, trained by TLD, provides consultation, referral services, and continuing education to 250 not-for-profit organizations annually. TLD also provides written educational materials and audiovisual resources to further develop the trusteeship of such groups.

KATHERINE TYLER SCOTT
Trustee Leadership Development

Trustee Renewal Project. Resource development project to assist nonprofit boards of trustees. This four-year (1989–1993) research and resource development project was sponsored by the ROBERT K. GREENLEAF CENTER and funded by the LILLY ENDOWMENT. Its purpose was to develop materials to assist board members and staff members of nonprofit organizations to understand better the responsibilities and roles of trustees.

Three products emerged from the project: *The Dynamics of Trusteeship*, a collection of autobiographical stories that explore personal motivations for serving on boards, the ways boards and trustees exercise power, and the inherent tensions and ambiguities of board and organizational life; "Nominating: Making Decisions for the Future, Nominating Committees as Change Agents," a year-long curriculum and workplan that assists nominating committees to reflect on the history, mission, and vision of their organization; and "A Balcony Perspective, Clarifying the Trustee Role," an essay that explores the role and power of trustees. These materials are available through the Greenleaf Center.

DIANA C. LESLIE

Tuckaway. Residence (3128 N. Pennsylvania) and site of a famed Indianapolis salon. Built in 1906, "tucked away" among mature trees, the affectionately named house represents one of the earliest examples of the bungalow style in the city. Art patrons George Philip Meier and Nellie Simmons Meier acquired the property in 1910, and remodeled the house to accommodate their active social life as well as their collections of art and period furnishings. In addition to their contributions to local arts organizations, the Meiers were also benefactors of individual writers, artists, actors, dancers, and musicians, and sponsored visits of nationally known performers and artists to Indianapolis.

George Meier designed women's apparel, establishing a national reputation with his original creations. He began an affiliation with L. S. AYRES & COMPANY in 1902, and traveled to Europe annually in that capacity. Nellie Meier was a palmist of considerable fame who counted Albert Einstein and Lowell Thomas among her friends. Celebrity guests called frequently at Tuckaway to have their characters assessed. Evening entertainments at the bungalow included such notables as Eleanor Roosevelt, George Gershwin, Sergei Rachmaninoff, Walt Disney, Helen Hayes, Joan Crawford, Mary Pickford, Alfred Lunt, and Lynn Fontanne. Indiana actress Carole Lombard called at Tuckaway the day before her untimely death in an airplane crash.

Nellie Meier's book, *Lions' Paws* (1937), collected the handprints of famous personalities; these included local authors JAMES WHITCOMB RILEY, George Ade, MEREDITH NICHOLSON, and LEW WALLACE, who were frequent guests at the Meiers' home.

In 1941, Meier turned the house over to her niece, Ruth Austin McGinnis Peaslee Cannon.

The present owner, Kenneth E. Keene, Jr., purchased the house in 1972 and has maintained its decor and traditions. Numerous accounts regarding ghostly sightings at Tuckaway add to the romantic charm of the house. Tuckaway is listed on the National Register of Historic Places.

GEORGIA A. CRAVEY

Turner, Roscoe (Sept. 29, 1895–June 23, 1970). Air racing pilot and aviation entrepreneur. America's greatest air racing pilot, Turner was born in a log cabin near Corinth, Mississippi. An early interest in automobiles led to work as a truck driver, mechanic, and enlistment in World War I as an ambulance driver. Transferred to the Army Signal Corps, Turner was commissioned a 2nd lieutenant and sent to Europe as a pilot. After the war, Turner formed a "Flying Circus." This group performed numerous aerial thrill acts throughout the South, along with aerial promotions for several clothing and other stores.

In 1925, Turner bought America's largest air transport, the 14–passenger Sikorsky S–29A. The twin-engined plane, which featured a fully enclosed cabin, quickly became popular as a deluxe charter craft and promotional vehicle for various businesses. In 1929, the plane was sold to Howard Hughes for use as a German Gotha bomber in the World War I air epic, "Hell's Angels." The same year, Turner formed Nevada Air Lines, operating between Los Angeles and Reno. Using a Lockheed Vegas, the line claimed to be the "Fastest in the World." Unfortunately, the Great Depression struck, and the manufacturer

Pilot Roscoe Turner performed daring aerial stunts and competed in speed races. [Indiana State Archives, Commission on Public Records. All rights reserved.]

repossessed the company's planes after only seven months of operation.

Turner made his major air race debut at the 1929 National Air Races, when he scored second and third in two closed circuit races, flying one of the Nevada Air Lines Vegas planes. He then finished first in both the transcontinental dash and a speed dash at the 1933 Nationals, and first in the Thompson speed race in 1934. He won the Thompson again in 1938 and 1939, becoming the first and only three time winner of air racing's premier speed dash.

In 1934, Turner and his crew flew an American Boeing 247D airliner to second place in the transport division of the world's longest race, the MacRobertson Trophy Race from London to Melbourne, Australia. His other flying awards included the Henderson Trophy (for America's No. 1 Speed Pilot) three times, and the Harmon Trophy (for America's Premier Aviator) twice.

Following his 1939 Thompson win, Turner established an air school in Indianapolis. Operating from the Municipal Airport, the school trained pilots, mechanics, and control tower operators for both civil and military positions. In 1947, he formed Turner Air Lines, a local service line, selling his interest in 1950 when the line was renamed LAKE CENTRAL AIRLINES. Turner remained active in his airport operation until his death.

JERRY MARLETTE

Turners/Turnvereins. Members of the historically utopian, nationalistic turnvereins (gymnastic societies), which were among the many cultural associations brought to America by German immigrants during the 19th century, and which still exist today. Turner societies worked initially to promote physical fitness, free thought, liberal politics, German language and culture, and improved working conditions for workers. By 1900, more than 300 turner societies thrived in cities across America. Today, most of the fewer than 100 remaining turnvereins focus on the social and historical aspect of their German heritage.

Turner gymnastics were first introduced in America in the 1820s by German exiles who migrated to Boston and established an outdoor turnplatz at Harvard University. But it was not until after the unsuccessful German revolts of 1848 and 1849, which sent thousands of new refugees to American shores, that revolutionary emigres began to organize turner societies. The first American turner societies were established in Cincinnati and Louisville in 1848. There, leaders sought to combine physical and intellectual training into a rational whole for the turner members, and to campaign for universal physical education in their local communities.

The Indianapolis Turngemeinde opened its doors on July 28, 1851, in a one-story wooden building on West Washington Street opposite the State Capitol. During the same year the Socialist Turnverein was founded by Dr. August Homburg. By 1852 the two societies merged, becoming the politically liberal and actively socialist Turngemeinde. Turners were rarely hesitant to express their opinions, however, and this pattern of split and merger would continue until the end of the century. By 1900 the Indianapolis Athenaeum Turnverein and the South Side Turners were firmly established, and remain today as the two turnvereins in the city.

Before 1900, most turners in older American cities such as Boston and New York were middle class first- and second-generation immigrants who lived and worked in predominantly German subcommunities. Further west, in cities such as Milwaukee and Indianapolis where there were large thriving German communities, a majority of the members were white-collar professionals, skilled artisans, and entrepreneurs. Ultimately, however, German turner groups were less class-based than any other ethnic athletic organization among immigrant groups.

Turnvereins built turnhalles (halls) that served as complete social centers for the group. They usually contained a gymnasium, library, billiard room, bowling alleys, rathskeller (bar and restaurant), women's auxiliary room, and a variety of meeting and lecture rooms. Some, such as the Chicago North Side turnhalle or Das Deutsche Haus in Indianapolis, were so large that they also had dance halls and auditoriums that served as major cultural centers for the entire city. Das Deutsche Haus, located at New Jersey and Michigan streets near the heart of downtown Indianapolis, was built in 1894 to accommodate many German-American cultural organizations. It is an excellent example of the grandeur and extent to which the turners went to ensure that their facilities would indeed provide an environment where members could work to remain true to their motto: "Mens sana in corpore sano" ("A Sound Mind in a Sound Body").

Turnvereins after the Civil War were less radical politically, except for their advocacy for the inclusion of physical education into the American public school system. The North American Turnerbund, the turners' national governing body, helped this process by establishing the first professional training program for physical educators. It also established an annual national turnfest in 1851, which brought together hundreds of men, women, and children for a celebration of German gymnastics, language, and culture. After the Civil War this turnfest occurred every four years, and has continued with few interruptions ever since. The latest such event occurred in June, 1991, when Indianapolis hosted several hundred American and German turners in a week of athletic and cultural competitions for men, women, and children of all ages.

Turnvereins reached their zenith of popularity in America immediately before World War I, by which time the German-American urban community enjoyed general economic prosperity. From 1914 until 1975 American turnvereins dwindled in popularity due to anti-German sentiment and the assimilation of German immigrants and their descendants. Furthermore, as universities and colleges assumed the professional training of physical educators, turnvereins were no longer as necessary for the continuation of the profession. In order to survive, many groups such as the Indianapolis ATHENAEUM turnverein anglicized their programs and facilities, and opened membership to those of non-German heritage.

Today, most turner societies nationwide are comprised of enthusiastic but small numbers of individuals who tend to focus on the social and historic aspects of turner life. Often, as in Indianapolis, the groups are actively involved in the restoration of German-American heritage buildings such as Das Deutsche Haus (Athenaeum). They also encourage the German cultural programs that highlight the contribution of this important ethnic group to the development of many large American cities. The records of the city's Athenaeum Turners and South Side Turners, as well as the archives of the American Turners, have been deposited in the IUPUI Special Collections and Archives.

ALIDA J. MOONEN

Henry Metzner, *A Brief History of the American Turnerbund* (Pittsburgh, 1924); George Theodore Probst, *The Germans in Indianapolis, 1840–1918*, rev. ed. by Eberhard Reichmann (Indianapolis, 1989); Theodore Stempfel, *Fifty Years of Unrelenting German Aspirations in Indianapolis*, ed. Giles R. Hoyt, Claudia Grossman, Elfrieda Lang, and Eberhard Reichmann (Indianapolis, 1991).

Tuteweiler, Henry Wesley (Jan. 8, 1842–Nov. 4, 1917) and **Harry Dunn** (July 19, 1869–June 3, 1945). Undertakers and funeral directors. Henry W. Tuteweiler was the middle son of an early Indianapolis builder and contractor, Henry Tuteweiler, who was also one of the first city councilmen and an organizer of the old Roberts Chapel. When the younger Henry was a student at North Western Christian (later BUTLER UNIVERSITY), he enlisted in Company D, 17th Indiana Volunteer Infantry. At the close of the Civil War, he joined his brothers in a stove and tinware business. Later, he opened a retail shoe firm called "Boot Upside Down." During the 1870s, he served two terms as city treasurer. In 1885, he became a mortician, establishing Tuteweiler & Son on West Market Street.

Like his father, son Harry D. Tuteweiler was a mortician and an active Republican. In 1902 and

Henry Wesley Tuteweiler. [Indiana State Library]

again in 1904 he was elected Marion County coroner, and served on the State Examining Board of Embalmers. His particular contribution to Indianapolis was in the development of recreational facilities. He established the first public bathhouse in 1906 and later donated it to the city. He promoted swimming pools and playgrounds throughout Indianapolis. He also chaired the recreation committee of the Children's Aid Association and served on the city's playground commission, 1909–1914.

HESTER ANNE HALE

Tyndall, Robert (May 2, 1877–July 9, 1947). Mayor of Indianapolis, 1943–1947, Republican. Born in Indianapolis and educated in its public schools, Tyndall enlisted in the 27th Indiana Volunteers in 1897 and fought in the Spanish-American War. He remained in the army until 1941, retiring as a major general in command of the 38th Division of the National Guard. As a civilian following World War I, he was a vice-president of Fletcher American Bank and in 1925 became treasurer of the Carl G. Fisher Company. From 1932 to 1942 he was associated with the Russell B. Moore Company, Inc., a consulting engineer firm.

When elected in 1943 Tyndall was the city's first Republican mayor since 1926. During his administration Tyndall secured passage of legislation to operate City Hospital on a nonpartisan basis, planned for a Veterans Administration hospital, addressed the issue of SMOKE ABATEMENT, and amended the 1925 thoroughfare plan to include widening and resurfacing city streets. His administration created the COMMITTEE ON POST-WAR PLANNING to develop a seven-year plan for city improvement through a public works program that would employ returning World War II veterans. The committee also established the Indianapolis Redevelopment Commission (duties now part of the Department of Metropolitan Development) which, under a 1945 state law, cleared and rezoned blighted areas in the city. In his last official act as mayor Tyndall approved $1.8 million for sewer system improvements.

Before becoming mayor Tyndall served as a director of the Marion County Civilian Defense Council and also as director of the Marion County Red Cross. Military decorations included the Distinguished Service Medal, the Croix de Guerre (French), and the Commander of the Legion of Honor (French). TYNDALL ARMORY was named in his honor in 1967.

JOAN CUNNINGHAM

Indianapolis Star, July 10, 1947.

Tyndall Armory. National Guard armory. In 1921, following service in WORLD WAR I, regiments of the INDIANA NATIONAL GUARD began to organize again throughout the state. For the first time in Indiana, Headquarters 38th Division was organized in Indianapolis in 1923. A new headquarters of this size, along with its immediate supporting units, needed a permanent armory suited for military use. Heretofore commercial buildings had been rented as makeshift armories.

Maj. Gen. ROBERT H. TYNDALL, the division commander, and Col. Robert L. Moorhead, a member of the Indiana State Armory Board (which would build the armory), were instrumental in getting the new armory approved. Out of 21 proposed sites, the one at 711 North Pennsylvania Street was chosen. General Tyndall was also the AMERICAN LEGION's national treasurer, and Colonel Moorhead was instrumental in getting Indianapolis selected as the permanent site of the legion's national headquarters. Because of their dual positions, it was no accident that the armory site was chosen just across the street to the east from the developing INDIANA WORLD WAR MEMORIAL grounds and the legion's new home.

The armory was built by the state for $425,000. Construction began in September, 1925, was completed late in the summer of 1926, and the building has been in constant use since. It is of Florentine design with limestone facing and terra cotta detailing. During the 1930s through the 1970s, with two other armories on the south side of the city, it was frequently called the North Side Armory. In 1967 it was formally named the Tyndall Armory in honor of General Tyndall.

ROBERT T. FISCHER
Colonel, AUS (ret.)

Michael G. Tyson Case. Michael G. Tyson, world heavyweight boxing champion from 1986 to 1990, was prosecuted in Indianapolis in 1992 in one of the most highly publicized trials in the city's history. Tyson, who at 20 years of age was the youngest person ever to win a world heavyweight boxing title, was a guest celebrity at INDIANA BLACK EXPO in Indianapolis in July, 1991. He was invited to visit a rehearsal of the 1991 Miss Black America Pageant, which was being conducted in the city at the same time. Tyson went to the rehearsal on July 18, made a promotional tape with the 23 contestants, and was thereafter charged with raping one of the contestants who met him at the rehearsal and was with him in his hotel room later that night.

The charges were prosecuted by a team led by J. Gregory Garrison, a former Marion County deputy prosecutor who was employed as a special prosecutor for this case. Tyson's defense was led by Vincent L. Fuller, an attorney from Washington, D.C., who had successfully defended John W. Hinckley, Jr., in 1982 with a plea of insanity in Hinckley's trial for the attempted assassination of President Ronald Reagan.

The rape allegations were initially submitted to a Marion County grand jury for consideration on August 16, 1991. During the following two weeks Tyson's accuser and several of the contestants in the beauty pageant testified before the grand jury. On August 30 the defense team then took the unusual step of having Tyson appear voluntarily as a witness in an effort to persuade the grand jury not to return an indictment. The effort failed by one vote, however, and the grand jury indicted Tyson by a 5–1 vote.

On January 27, 1992, the criminal trial began before Judge Patricia J. Gifford, a former Marion County deputy prosecutor who specialized in prosecuting rape charges. Over 100 news organizations from around the world submitted requests to send reporters to cover the trial. Since the courtroom could seat only 50 spectators, Gifford obtained a special order from the Indiana Supreme Court which permitted members of the news media to view the trial by closed circuit television.

Because of the intense publicity concerning the trial Gifford sequestered the jury in the INDIANAPOLIS ATHLETIC CLUB. On February 4, a fire broke out in the Athletic Club during the night, apparently from faulty wiring in a refrigerator. Two firefighters and a guest at the club died in the fire, but all of the jurors were escorted safely from the building. One of the jurors was excused from further service, however, because he indicated that he could not concentrate on the remainder of the trial.

The trial ended on February 10, 1992, after 13 days which included testimony by 16 of the pageant contestants, among them Tyson's accuser, and by Tyson, who testified in his own defense. After nearly ten hours of deliberation the jury returned a verdict of guilty as charged. Tyson was sentenced to serve six years in prison to be followed by four years on probation. Under this sentence he was entitled to be released from prison after three years, conditional upon good behavior. Tyson was denied bail pending his appeal and began serving his sentence on March 26, 1992.

After the trial Tyson employed Alan M. Dershowitz, a noted Harvard law professor, to appeal his conviction. Dershowitz and his brother, Nathan, argued the Tyson appeal before the Indiana Court of Appeals on February 15, 1993. This court, in a 2–1 decision, affirmed the conviction on August 13, 1993. On September 22, 1993, the Indiana Supreme Court, in a 2–2 decision, decided not to review the decision of the Court of Appeals. The 2–2 decision was made possible because the chief justice of the court disqualified himself from participation after his wife and Dershowitz inadvertently discussed the appeal at a Yale Law School alumni reunion. In early 1994 a second appeal was pending before the Indiana Court of Appeals, and Dershowitz had begun the necessary procedures to request the United States Supreme Court to reverse the conviction.

WILLIAM A. KERR
Indiana University–Purdue University,
Indianapolis

Mark Shaw, *Down for the Count* (Champaign, Ill., 1993).

Unigov, Creation of (1967-1971). Indianapolis had an unusual municipal government structure as of 1967. A nine-member city council, known as the COMMON COUNCIL, was elected at four-year intervals by a hybrid district/at-large system that reflected the importance of parties in Indiana politics. The major parties slated six council candidates, with one candidate from each of the city's six council districts. These 12 candidates appeared on an at-large ballot at the general election, with the top nine vote-getters constituting the Common Council. This system guaranteed each party at least three council seats. In addition, slating procedures adopted informally by the parties generally ensured the election of at least one black council member. A separately elected city clerk, with responsibility for maintaining municipal documents and records, doubled as secretary to the Common Council.

Indianapolis also had what municipal government textbooks call a "strong mayor." The MAYOR was separately elected for a four-year term, with appointment and veto powers. However, from 1913 until 1963 Indiana law barred the mayor from seeking reelection, which weakened the position politically. And many, if not most, local government functions were performed by the nine TOWNSHIPS in Marion County or by 16 independent, special-purpose municipal corporations governed by boards over which the mayor had limited appointive powers and even less control.

In the municipal elections of 1967, Democrat John J. Barton became the first mayor in Indianapolis history to seek reelection after seeking a four-year term. Barton had strengthened the office during his term, proposing reforms to enhance its appointive powers and creating the mayor-appointed GREATER INDIANAPOLIS PROGRESS COMMITTEE (GIPC) to help set and mobilize support for the city's agenda. Barton's opponent in the 1967 mayor's race was a GIPC member, Richard G. Lugar, also a prominent figure on the INDIANAPOLIS PUBLIC SCHOOLS board. Lugar defeated Barton to become only the third Republican elected mayor of Indianapolis since 1925. Republicans also captured a majority of the Common Council seats. Thus, Republicans held majorities on the city council and the county council at the same time.

Most previous accounts of the creation of Unigov have emphasized Richard Lugar's role, in light of the high visibility of the mayor's office. As a member of GIPC and the school board, Lugar had taken an interest in reforming local government. GIPC had supported a strengthening and territorial expansion of the Mass Transit Authority, which passed, and a county-wide consolidation of police and fire services, which withered under vigorous local opposition. Lugar had suggested that the 11 public school districts within Marion County be combined, but dropped the idea upon seeing the intensity of public disapproval.

However, a strategy for city-county consolidation was developed primarily by an informal group organized and convened by Marion County Council President Beurt SerVaas. SerVaas had been a founder and treasurer of the Republican Action Committee (RAC), a reform group within the local party. SerVaas gathered other RAC members, including Lugar, RAC chairman John Burkhardt, Indianapolis Common Council President Thomas C. Hasbrook, Marion County Republican party chairman L. Keith Bulen, and John Mutz, and added Indianapolis Chamber of Commerce executive vice-president Carl Dortch. This group met throughout 1968, usually at Burkhardt's home, to discuss the pros and cons of city-county consolidation and strategies for its adoption. SerVaas also raised the funds needed to hire local attorney Lewis C. Bose to compose a memorandum exploring the legal dimensions of metropolitan consolidation. Noting the absence of a local home rule tradition in Indiana and the state's complete legal authority over local government structure and powers, Bose observed that consolidation could be taken through the Indiana General Assembly without either a state constitutional amendment or a local referendum.

Such an approach made favorable outcomes in the 1968 elections for state offices strategically important for the consolidation proponents. Lugar campaigned energetically around the state for Republican legislative candidates. Bulen delivered the Marion County delegation at the 1968 Republican state convention for gubernatorial candidate Ed Whitcomb, who won the Republican nomination for governor over Indiana House Speaker Otis Bowen and Purdue University dean and professor

Earl Butz. As the state elections neared in the fall of 1968, Lugar named a 40–member GIPC Governmental Reorganization Task Force (with a smaller executive committee) to further refine the a consolidation strategy, and formally recognized Bose's role in recruiting the legal talent needed to compose a consolidation statute to be introduced in the Indiana General Assembly's 1969 session. Bose appointed an 11–member Lawyers' Task Force, headed by attorney Charles Whistler.

On November 5, 1968, the morning after election day, Indianapolis Republicans awoke to find their party in charge of the Indianapolis mayor's office, the Indianapolis city council, the Marion County council, the Marion County delegation to the Indiana General Assembly, both houses of the General Assembly, and the governor's office. Whitcomb had been elected governor, and Republicans held 73 of the 100 seats in the State House of Representatives and 35 of the 50 seats in the Senate. All eight state senators and all 15 state representatives from Marion County after the 1968 election were Republicans. Lugar went public with the consolidation plan, and two months of intensive legal and political work ensued.

The Governmental Reorganization Task Force executive committee members built upon the core of the consolidation strategy developed earlier by the informal group. City and county legislative and executive bodies would be combined into a single strong council and a single countywide chief executive. Related municipal functions would be grouped into a minimal number of administrative departments under the chief executive's direction. Special taxing and service districts would be employed to provide municipal services over different areas within the county. The reorganization model devised by the Task Force acquired the name "Unigov," for "unified government."

In reality, the reorganization was considerably less than "unified." The informal group, anticipating public sentiment as well as legal and practical considerations, had excluded several elements of local government from consolidation, and the executive committee followed suit. Opposition to any merger of local public school systems, or of the city's police or fire departments with the county sheriff's department or the town-

Richard Lugar, mayor of Indianapolis between 1968 and 1976, was instrumental in the formation of Unigov. [Courtesy John Walls]

ship fire departments, kept these elements out of the consolidation. The township system was left intact, including the system of providing poor relief through the office of township trustee. The incorporated cities of BEECH GROVE and LAWRENCE and the town of SPEEDWAY would not be absorbed by the new municipal government, although their residents would be allowed to vote for the countywide executive and council. The county offices of assessor, auditor, clerk, coroner, prosecutor, recorder, sheriff, surveyor, and treasurer would be retained, since (save for the assessor) they were provided for in the Indiana Constitution. Merging or eliminating them would require constitutional amendment, a time-consuming process that could delay and potentially derail adoption and implementation of the reorganization. And six of the 16 independent municipal corporations providing local government services within Marion County would remain independent—the CAPITAL IMPROVEMENT BOARD, the CITY-COUNTY BUILDING AUTHORITY, the HEALTH AND HOSPITAL CORPORATION, the INDIANAPOLIS AIRPORT AUTHORITY, the INDIANAPOLIS PUBLIC TRANSPORTATION CORPORATION, and the INDIANAPOLIS-MARION COUNTY PUBLIC LIBRARY.

By mid-December, 1968, the Task Force had produced the outlines of its reorganization plan. Action shifted to the Lawyers' Task Force, with the responsibility for crafting legislation in time for the Indiana General Assembly session beginning in January. Each member of the Lawyers' Task Force took an element of the reorganization, with Whistler and Bose assuming the task of integrating those components into a single bill. Their efforts yielded a 162–page "Act concerning reorganization of government in counties containing a city of the first class," which was introduced in the Indiana State Senate as Senate Bill 199 (Borst) on January 21, 1969. After early Senate committee hearings revealed some of the proposal's technical defects and political opposition, a revised draft of the Unigov bill was introduced on February 4 as Senate Bill 543, with Representatives Lamkin and Mills co-sponsoring the legislation in the House. County Council President SerVaas and Mayor Lugar lobbied the legislators on behalf of the Unigov bill.

There was substantial opposition to the Unigov legislation, on several different grounds. Democrats nicknamed the proposal "Unigrab," objecting to the obvious partisan advantage to be gained by the Republicans in shifting the electoral base of Indianapolis government from the city to the county. Many of Indianapolis' black residents shared a similar concern about the dilution of their community's political influence if the population were expanded to include 250,000 mostly white county residents. Opponents also objected to the absence of a referendum provision in the Unigov legislation, believing that since annexation would have required approval in a referendum, so should consolidation. Others were concerned about the post-Unigov status of the several incorporated and unincorporated communities within Marion County. And public officials and residents of adjacent counties were wary of a "consolidated colossus" in the center of the metropolitan area that might soon cast its eye upon their communities as well, since Indiana law permitted municipalities to annex territory beyond county boundaries.

Supporters addressed some of these objections through refinements of the legislation. A "Minigov" amendment authorized the simultaneous empowerment of neighborhood- and town-level governing boards to preserve some community identity and autonomy within the county. Another provision blocked the new Consolidated City of Indianapolis from annexing territory outside Marion County. These provisions deflected the concerns of suburban Republicans in and around Marion County, and kept them from joining Democrats and blacks to present a unified opposition to the bill.

Supporters were not, however, willing to accept an amendment requiring a referendum on Unigov. A referendum provision could have been added, but was not required under Indiana law. Indiana retained the "Dillon's Rule" legal doctrine with respect to local governments: local governments are creatures of the state and may be created, enlarged, contracted, merged, or destroyed by the legislature without regard to the preferences of the local residents. Unigov's supporters, therefore, technically did not have to place the issue before the voters. Moreover, supporters were concerned about the likely outcome of a referendum. In the candid appraisal of State Representative Robert L. Jones, Jr. (R-Indianapolis), proponents of Unigov opposed a referendum because "at the present time it would be defeated."

After the Unigov bill passed the Senate by a vote of 28 to 16, attention focused on the prospect of a referendum amendment during the bill's consideration in the House of Representatives. Representative Lamkin, the floor manager for the bill in the House, maintained Republican cohesion to defeat Democratic attempts to add a referendum requirement during the second reading of the bill in the House on February 27. A tense week followed as Speaker Bowen, whom Marion County Republicans had denied the gubernatorial nomination in 1968, tantalized opponents and supporters with the possibility that he might refuse to hand the bill down unless he could be assured that a majority of Marion County residents favored it. On March 5, the last day that legislation could pass, Bowen handed the bill down for the third reading, but without his endorsement. The vote, 66 to 29, closely followed party lines in the House. Governor Whitcomb signed the legislation on March 13, 1969, to become effective on January 1, 1970.

On January 1, 1970, the five-member Marion County Council and the nine-member Indianapolis Common Council merged to form an interim City-County Council (composed of nine Republicans and five Democrats), and Richard G. Lugar assumed the post of mayor of the Consolidated City of Indianapolis. This arrangement was maintained until the municipal elections of 1971, in which Marion County voters reelected Lugar and chose the first 29–member

City-County Council. That mayor-council structure provides the core of the political leadership of the Consolidated City to the present.

A friendly "validation suit" was brought in the name of Carl Dortch, the executive vice-president of the Indianapolis CHAMBER OF COMMERCE, to ensure the Unigov legislation against an anticipated future stream of legal challenges. The suit, *Dortch v. Lugar*, 24 Ind. Dec. 357, 266 NE2d 25 (1971), raised numerous possible arguments against the Unigov act. On January 26, 1971, the Indiana Supreme Court unanimously upheld the validity of the consolidation. Thus Unigov became the first major city-county consolidation to occur in the United States without a referendum since the creation of Greater New York in 1897.

WILLIAM A. BLOMQUIST
Indiana University–Purdue University,
Indianapolis

Unigov, Structure of. City-county consolidation in Indianapolis is not a one-community, one-government system. Although the consolidation was named "Unigov" for "unified government," Marion County retains 50 separate local governments (down from 60 in 1967), and the number of separate taxing units has grown since 1970 to approximately 100. In some respects, the Unigov structure is even more complicated than the system it replaced.

The Unigov legislation enacted by the Indiana General Assembly in 1969 provided a new legal status for Indianapolis. Previously designated the state's only First-Class City on the basis of its population, Indianapolis became the state's only Consolidated City, with the Unigov Act specifying the Consolidated City's governmental structure and authority.

The outer boundaries of the Consolidated City of Indianapolis are contiguous with those of Marion County. Unigov reorganization expanded the Consolidated City's territorial jurisdiction from 82 to 402 square miles, increased its population from approximately 480,000 to 740,000 residents, and enlarged its electorate from about 293,000 to 406,000 registered voters.

The legislative body for this new Consolidated City is a 29–member CITY-COUNTY COUN-CIL, which replaced the Indianapolis COMMON COUNCIL and the Marion County Council. Twenty-five of the City-County councillors represent single-member districts; the remaining four are elected at-large. All City-County Council seats are up for election every four years, during the municipal elections held in Indiana the year before presidential election years. There is no limit on the number of terms a City-County councillor may serve.

The City-County Council appoints a clerk, who serves a one-year term and serves at the pleasure of the Council. The previous separately elected position of city clerk was eliminated in the Unigov reorganization.

The executive branch of the Consolidated City is headed by the MAYOR, who is elected county-wide at the same four-year intervals as the City-County Council. Following an amendment to the Unigov legislation in 1983, there is now no limit to the number of terms the mayor may serve. Within the office of mayor are deputy mayors with responsibilities for certain policy or programmatic areas. The mayor appoints all deputy mayors and department directors, as well as the heads of some of the divisions within departments, subject to confirmation by the City-County Council. Once confirmed, appointees serve at the pleasure of the mayor. The mayor may veto legislative actions taken by the City-County Council subject to an override by a vote of two-thirds of the council. The mayor may veto line items within the Consolidated City budget ordinance, but may not veto the budgets or appropriations for certain constitutionally required county offices, the courts, or some independent municipal corporations retained under the Unigov structure.

Below the office of the mayor, the executive branch of the Consolidated City is organized into six administrative departments. The original design for the Unigov reorganization called for eight departments, but political opposition led to the cancellation of plans for a Department of Local Government Organization and for the inclusion of the HEALTH AND HOSPITAL CORPORATION in a Department of Public Health. The six that remained are the departments of ADMINISTRATION, METROPOLITAN DEVELOPMENT, PARKS AND RECREATION, PUBLIC SAFETY, PUBLIC WORKS, and TRANS-

PORTATION. Each of these departments contains divisions, and some of the divisions are further subdivided into sections.

Prior to the Unigov reorganization, 16 independent special-purpose municipal corporations performed local government functions over varying territorial jurisdictions within Marion County. The six Unigov departments within the Consolidated City's executive branch subsumed some of these municipal corporations, making them either departments or divisions within departments. Among these were: the Air Pollution Control Commission, the HUMAN RIGHTS COMMISSION, the Indianapolis Department of Flood Control, the INDIANAPOLIS HOUSING AUTHORITY, the Indianapolis Parks Department, the Indianapolis Redevelopment Commission, the METROPOLITAN DEVELOPMENT COMMISSION, and the Metropolitan Thoroughfare Authority.

Six of the independent municipal corporations remain outside the direct governance of the Consolidated City: the CAPITAL IMPROVEMENT BOARD, the CITY-COUNTY BUILDING AUTHORITY, the Health and Hospital Corporation of Marion County, the INDIANAPOLIS AIRPORT AUTHORITY, the INDIANAPOLIS PUBLIC TRANSPORTATION CORPORATION, and the INDIANAPOLIS–MARION COUNTY PUBLIC LIBRARY. These units remain separate local governments, although they come under the indirect control of the Consolidated City in two ways: their governing boards are appointed according to different formulas by the mayor and Council (or county officials); and their budgets are subject to varying degrees of review by the mayor and Council.

The six independent municipal corporations are by no means the only local governments units left out of the city-county consolidation known as Unigov. Marion County continues to exist as a separate governmental entity. The elected county offices of assessor, auditor, clerk, coroner, prosecutor, recorder, sheriff, surveyor, and treasurer all remain, each elected county-wide in presidential election years. The Marion County Board of Voter Registration, the Marion County Department of Public Welfare, and the Marion County Election Board retain separate existence as well.

The MARION COUNTY COMMISSIONERS, who used to function as a collective executive for the county, are no longer elected separately. The Marion County assessor, auditor, and treasurer now serve ex officio (and without additional pay) as the Marion County Commissioners. Most of the county-wide executive functions that used to reside with the county commissioners have been transferred to the office of the mayor. Indeed, under a 1972 amendment to the Unigov legislation, all powers of the county commissioners now belong to the mayor's office save for those already transferred to the City-County Council, those relating to bonds previously issued, or those given to the commissioners directly by the Indiana Constitution.

The Consolidated City structure also does not include the Marion County court system. The jurisdictions and judicial selection processes of the Marion County Circuit Court, Municipal Courts, Small Claims Courts, and Superior Court were not affected by Unigov, although the budget for the court system is subject to review by the City-County Council.

Marion County's nine TOWNSHIPS continue as separate governments, with independently elected township assessors, constables, and trustees. The nine township trustees still administer poor relief within their respective jurisdictions. The eight townships around the outside of Marion County (i.e., excluding CENTER TOWNSHIP) also are the territorial basis for eight volunteer fire departments, and for eight of the county's 11 separate public school districts (the other three being Indianapolis Public Schools and the school systems in the city of Beech Grove and the town of Speedway).

Indianapolis, of course, was not the only municipality in Marion County at the time of Unigov reorganization. The Unigov law excluded from the Consolidated City any incorporated city other than Indianapolis and any incorporated town with a population over 5,000. This stipulation singled out the cities of Beech Grove and Lawrence and the town of Speedway. Subsequently, by incorporating as a city just before the Unigov law took effect on January 1, 1970, Southport also attained exclusion from the Consolidated City. These four municipalities, known as the "EXCLUDED CITIES," retain their own government structures intact and provide several municipal services directly to their residents. Because they pay taxes to the county and receive county services, voters in the excluded cities also may vote for the Consolidated City mayor and for a district City-County councillor and the four at-large City-County councillors.

The other 17 incorporated municipalities within Marion County at the time of the Unigov reorganization are known as the "INCLUDED TOWNS." Although included within the Consolidated City, the towns may retain their governmental status, levy property taxes, and provide local services. Some of the included towns still have a town board, and some retain a town marshal, but most included towns have not remained actively functioning governments. If an included town has a functioning town board that enacts town ordinances, these must not conflict with ordinances of the Consolidated City. The City-County Council must approve the issuance of general obligation bonds by an included town.

The continued existence of the county, the townships, the SCHOOL DISTRICTS, the excluded cities, the included towns, and six of the special-purpose municipal corporations means that the Consolidated City of Indianapolis is far from being the only provider of municipal services in Marion County. It also means that the territory within Marion County over which the Consolidated City provides services varies from one service to another (see UNIGOV AND SERVICE DELIVERY). Some Consolidated City services extend over the territory of the Consolidated City (i.e., Marion County minus the excluded cities), others extend county-wide, and still others extend over areas that correspond with none of the above.

Key components of the Unigov structure that allow for the provisions of Consolidated City services over different portions of Marion County are SPECIAL SERVICE DISTRICTS and SPECIAL TAXING DISTRICTS. Within the Consolidated City governmental structure are several Special Service Districts and Special Taxing Districts, each performing a local government function over a specified domain, financed by a levy upon the residents within that area. For example, the INDIANAPOLIS POLICE DEPARTMENT (now a division of the city's Department of Public Safety) serves the Police Special Service District, an area somewhat larger than the "old city" but not as extensive as

the Consolidated City. Outside the Police Special Service District, Marion County residents receive police protection from the Marion County Sheriff's Department or from the municipal force of an excluded city. By contrast, the Department of Transportation is a county-wide Special Taxing District. The boundaries of Special Service and Special Taxing Districts may be adjusted by the City-County Council and the mayor, subject to the provisions of the Unigov Act.

The use of the Special Service and Special Taxing District devices, in combination with the remaining local governments in Marion County, adds considerable complexity to the Unigov structure, as well as to public finance within the Consolidated City. A resident in a given location in Marion County may receive services from, and pay taxes for, several of these districts within the Consolidated City, plus county offices, a township, a school district, and special-purpose municipal corporations (see UNIGOV AND PUBLIC FINANCE).

WILLIAM A. BLOMQUIST
Indiana University–Purdue University,
Indianapolis

Unigov and Political Participation. The 1969 reorganization of Indianapolis-Marion County local government known as Unigov had profound effects on patterns of political participation and political influence within the county. Some of those effects clearly were anticipated; others may not have been. The three most distinctive results have been the dominance of the RE-PUBLICAN PARTY in local elections, the loss of the political influence of the black community, and the decline in voter participation rates as measured by registration and election turnout.

Partisanship has governed Indianapolis politics since the Civil War. Accordingly, the most frequently discussed effect of the Unigov reorganization on local politics has been its shift in the balance of power between Republicans and Democrats. Unigov was born of Republican victories in the city, county, and state elections of 1967 and 1968. Its enabling legislation passed both chambers of the Indiana General Assembly on essentially party-line votes. The partisan Republican

**Table 1:
Municipal Election Results
in Indianapolis, 1951–1991**

Year	Winning Mayoral Candidate	Number and Pct. of Votes	Losing Mayoral Candidate	Number and Pct. of Votes	City Council Seats R	D
1951	Clark (R)	68,415 (55.6)	Bayt (D)	54,744 (44.4)	6	3
1955	Bayt (D)	74,682 (56.1)	Birr (R)	58,497 (43.9)	3	6
1959	Boswell (D)	70,031 (57.4)	Sharp (R)	51,994 (42.6)	3	6
1963	Barton (D)	68,316 (48.1)	Drayer (R)	63,091 (44.4)	3	6
1967	Lugar (R)	72,278 (53.3)	Barton (D)	63,284 (46.7)	6	3
1971	Lugar (R)	155,164 (60.5)	Neff (D)	101,367 (39.5)	21	8
1975	Hudnut (R)	124,100 (52.2)	Welch (D)	109,761 (46.1)	19	10
1979	Hudnut (R)	124,515 (73.9)	Cantwell (D)	43,955 (26.1)	22	7
1983	Hudnut (R)	134,550 (67.5)	Sullivan (D)	63,240 (21.7)	23	6
1987	Hudnut (R)	109,107 (66.3)	Senden (D)	38,193 (23.2)	22	7
1991	Goldsmith (R)	110,545 (56.2)	Mahern (D)	79,817 (40.6)	18	11

motivation associated with Unigov could be seen in both the Democrats' nickname for the reorganization—"Unigrab"—and by a comment made at the time by Marion County Republican Party Chairman L. Keith Bulen. Referring to Unigov's expansion of the Indianapolis electorate from 293,371 to 406,155 registered voters, Bulen rejoiced, "It's my greatest coup of all time, moving out there and taking in 85,000 Republicans."

Prior to 1969, elections for municipal and county offices usually were strongly contested and victory margins narrow, but the result fell into a distinctive pattern. Democrats typically won Indianapolis city races, and Republicans prevailed in county and suburban contests. The "normal Democratic vote" in the pre-Unigov city of Indianapolis was estimated to be about 57 percent at the end of the 1960s, so Republican candidates faced uphill battles in elections for MAYOR and the COMMON COUNCIL, which was elected at-large.

Unigov fulfilled Republican hopes for a change in this electoral pattern. In the 20 years before Unigov reorganization took effect on January 1, 1970, Democrats won three of five mayoral contests and elected majorities to the Common Council in four of those five elections. In the first

20 years after Unigov, Republicans won the mayor's office and majorities on the City-County Council in all five municipal elections. Republican victories in some of the mayor's races have been lopsided, and Republican majorities on the CITY-COUNTY COUNCIL have been overwhelming (see Table 1). Through its enlargement of the municipal electorate to include all county voters, Unigov converted a substantial Democratic edge in Indianapolis elections into a decided Republican advantage.

The Marion County DEMOCRATIC PARTY, seriously debilitated through the 1970s and 1980s, found it difficult at times to offer formidable challengers for local offices, including that of mayor. Only a resurgence of Democratic strength at the state level prompted a rebound of Democratic electoral prospects in Marion County in the early 1990s. By contrast, the Marion County Republican party thrived through the 1970s and 1980s, presenting one of the nation's few remaining likenesses to an "urban political machine."

At times, the Republican party's post-Unigov success brought allegations of insensitivity and "arrogance of power." Such charges came into sharpest focus in 1986 when a court order was necessary to halt the practice of City-County Council Republicans taking votes on budgetary and other important matters in closed party caucuses, in clear violation of the state's "Open Door" law. Some observers of local politics have also commented on a lack of public debate and dissent and a rather exclusive character to local government decision-making. On the other hand, the stability of political leadership in Indianapolis under Unigov may account to some degree for the city's success in promoting economic development and attracting investment during two recessionary decades, at least as experienced by other northern and midwestern cities.

In Indiana, political conflict occurs primarily between political parties, and Unigov's effect on the political interests of Indianapolis' black residents must be viewed in terms of its impact on the two major parties. Numerous black residents opposed Unigov because adding predominately white suburban county voters to the city electorate would dilute black voting strength. Approximately 87 percent of all black Marion County residents lived in the CENTER TOWNSHIP core of pre-Unigov Indianapolis. Enlarging the city's boundaries added relatively few blacks but nearly a quarter of a million whites. Some observers saw this as a step backward for the city's African-American constituency. The proportion of black residents had grown from 15 percent of Indianapolis' population in 1950 to 21 percent in 1960 to about 27 percent in 1969. Following the Unigov expansion, the 1970 census showed an African-American population of approximately 18 percent, a figure of pre–1960 proportions.

The more important effect of Unigov on black political influence was the shift in the balance of power between the two major parties. Even at the 1969 proportion of 27 percent, African-Americans were a decided minority of the city population. However, given blacks' overwhelming identification with the Democratic party, that percentage was fast approaching half of the city's "normal Democratic vote" of 57 percent. Thus, heavy Democratic votes in black wards occasionally proved decisive in city elections.

Given the black constituency's high level of voting cohesion, African-Americans in Indianapolis in 1969 were on the verge of becoming the base vote of the city's majority party. After Unigov, Indianapolis blacks had only minority status within a minority party, a party that proved unable to win a mayoral race or a council majority for the next 20 years.

Unigov reorganization arguably had some important beneficial effects for Indianapolis' African-American residents. Changes in the selection of council members provided them a more direct role in electing municipal representatives. Prior to Unigov, the at-large system of electing members of the city's Common Council left blacks dependent on local party organizations to slate enough African-American candidates to ensure the election of at least one. Since Unigov, the 29–member City-County Council has been composed of 25 single-member districts plus four at-large seats. Several of the 25 single-member districts contain enough black majorities, which make the election of African-American council members more probable. Even the most creative efforts to draw 25 City-County Council districts cannot avoid producing several predominantly black districts.

Table 2:
Voting Turnout in Indianapolis, Municipal and Presidential Election Years, 1951–91

	Municipal Elections		Presidential Elections	
		Pct. of Voting–		Pct. of Voting–
	Total	Age		Age
Year	Votes Cast	Population	Year	Population
1951	123,159	42.0%	1952	73.0%
1955	133,179	45.4	1956	61.9
1959	122,025	41.1	1960	68.0
1963	142,116	47.9	1964	65.9
1967	135,562	45.2	1968	61.2
1971	256,531	53.8	1972	59.7
1975	237,848	52.4	1976	61.9
1979	168,470	33.6	1980	54.5
1983	199,436	39.3	1984	54.7
1987	164,523	29.1	1988	54.0
1991	192,543	34.1	1992	54.5

Average turnout of voting-age population in municipal elections:
| 1951–67 | 44.32% |
| 1971–91 | 40.38% |

Unigov supporters argued that Indianapolis blacks would benefit from the broader tax base that accompanied the incorporation of wealthier suburban areas into the city. But Unigov excluded from City-County control two of the services—public education and welfare—upon which lower-income (and disproportionately black) Center Township residents depended. Unigov did not broaden the tax base for either the township poor-relief system or INDIANAPOLIS PUBLIC SCHOOLS. At the same time, other services on which residents of the "old city" depend—police and fire protection, and sanitation—were brought into Unigov departments under the direction of the Republican mayor and council, while their tax bases remained fixed within the limits of their respective SPECIAL SERVICE DISTRICTS.

Apart from Unigov's intended effect on the balance of power between the two major parties is the question of its effect on political participation rates. One of the charges directed toward the pre-Unigov structure of local government was that its excessive complexity and insufficient accountability frustrated and turned off voters—a charge crystalized in the 1959 LEAGUE OF WOMEN VOTERS' pamphlet, *Who's in Charge Here?* By implication, Unigov's consolidation of political leadership in a strong mayor and council was supposed to restore accountability and reawaken the electorate's interest in their local government. Comparison of pre-Unigov and post-Unigov voting turnout percentages in municipal or county election years do not offer much support for either notion. Local government's pre-Unigov complexity did not diminish voter involvement, nor have Unigov's clearer lines of governmental authority encouraged greater voter participation.

As Table 2 illustrates, although voting turnout was somewhat higher in 1971 and 1975—the first two municipal elections after Unigov—it dropped sharply thereafter and has been below pre-Unigov levels in each of the municipal election years. Similarly, voting turnout in county elections (which coincide with presidential, congressional, gubernatorial, and state legislative elections) remained strong through 1976 and then decreased markedly. The sharp drop in both cases is attributable almost entirely to a reduction in Democratic votes.

Whatever Unigov's effects on the service delivery and public finances in the city of Indianapolis, the effects on political participation have been and remain controversial. At a minimum, the comparison of the 20 years prior to Unigov with the 20 years since reveals that there has been a decline in party competition and an associated drop in voting turnout in municipal elections in Marion County.

WILLIAM A. BLOMQUIST
Indiana University–Purdue University,
Indianapolis

Unigov and Public Finance. The UNIGOV reorganization of local government affected public finance—governmental revenues, expenditures, and indebtedness—within Indianapolis and Marion County. As with service delivery, few aspects of public finance were actually consolidated under Unigov. Instead, Unigov increased the reliance of city-county government on SPECIAL SERVICE DISTRICTS and SPECIAL TAXING DISTRICTS covering portions of the county for collecting revenue to support additional or improved governmental services.

Revenues. Primary revenue sources for the city of Indianapolis are local TAXES and fees and federal and state funds. Historically, the local property tax has been Indianapolis' major source of revenue. But voter resistance to rising local property taxes led to the Indiana General Assembly's adoption of a property tax reform program in 1973. The state legislature limited future increases in property tax rates by local governments, substituting a system of property tax replacement funds generated by an increase in the state sales tax. While the property tax continues to be the largest local tax source into the 1990s, its share of city-county government's total revenue has declined. As a result, local officials have searched for and increased their reliance on other sources.

Federal and state funds were one such source, although they have been subject to similar political pressures from the so-called taxpayer revolt of the past two decades. During the 1980s, for example, Congress ended one significant source of local support, the federal general revenue sharing program. Federal block grants—such as the Community Development Block Grants (CDBG) and the Job Training Partnership Act (JTPA)—continue to be used to transfer funds to local government for broad purposes.

To replace the loss of federal revenue sharing funds the Indiana General Assembly in 1982 authorized counties to adopt a County Option Income Tax. Indianapolis–Marion County government adopted this local income tax in 1983. The CITY-COUNTY COUNCIL was also permitted to adopt a 10 percent additional county excise tax on automobiles and wheel tax on trucks to be used for curb, sidewalk, and street resurfacing and repair. In addition, the state of Indiana distributes to local governments some of the revenue it collects from automobile excise taxes and taxes on motor vehicle fuel, alcohol, tobacco, and intangible assets held by financial institutions.

Fees and charges for specific services have also been used to replace reduced federal funds and limits on local property tax rates. These fees have included sewer volume charges, solid waste collection fees, air pollution monitoring charges, zoning petition and building permit fees, and charges to local telephone users for 911 emergency service.

Under the Unigov reorganization, Indianapolis' property tax base is potentially the entire Consolidated City (Marion County minus the EXCLUDED CITIES of Beech Grove, Lawrence, Southport, and Speedway). Unigov's expansion of the territory of the city of Indianapolis increased its total assessed property valuation—its potential property tax base—by 70 percent.

Despite Unigov's effort at city-county consolidation, however, Marion County still contains many different taxing jurisdictions and property tax rates. There are 50 taxing units within the Consolidated City alone. The overlapping territories of taxing units in the county produce an even larger number of total property tax rates faced by Marion County residents depending on where they live. The notice of property tax rates payable in 1992 in Marion County, published by the county auditor and county treasurer, presented a 3,780–cell matrix of property tax rates. There were 60 applicable property tax levies and 63 defined taxing jurisdictions within the county. Total nominal property tax rates varied from a low of $7.92 per $100 assessed valuation in parts of Washington Township to a high of $13.09 per $100 assessed valuation in the pre-Unigov city of Indianapolis inside Center Township.

Center Township includes many large and valuable properties in and around downtown Indianapolis. However, several of them are exempt from property taxation because they belong to government or charitable organizations, or because they have been temporarily exempted under arrangements to encourage redevelopment. At the same time, Center Township residents have the greatest needs for public assistance and other services in the county. Public assistance for Center Township residents is currently supported by property taxes imposed only on Center Township properties.

City-county consolidation has not led to much redistributive use of the city-county government's larger territory and tax base. Most extensions of the tax base since 1970 have supported capital improvements rather than direct public services. Under the public finance structure of local government as a whole in Marion County, the property tax bases for the public services on which poorer residents rely most heavily—public safety, public education, and public assistance—remain confined to the inner city. There have been repeated, unsuccessful efforts to shift the tax base for support of the MARION COUNTY SHERIFF's Department from the whole county to the outer county

areas that are patrolled by the Sheriff's Department. Currently, residents of pre-Unigov Indianapolis pay property taxes for the Sheriff's Department as well as the INDIANAPOLIS POLICE DEPARTMENT, while residents of the outer county areas pay for the Sheriff's Department but not the Indianapolis Police Department.

The property tax base and property tax rates have been used more aggressively to support local economic development policy. Indianapolis promotes economic development by providing tax-related assistance in the form of abatements, enterprise zones, and tax-increment financing districts.

There are two types of property taxes—one on real estate such as land and buildings, the other on personal property such as business equipment and inventories. Property tax abatements, which lower the tax on buildings and machinery, make holding vacant land less attractive and developing property more attractive. On the other hand, because abatements reduce the amount of tax collected from those properties, it may be necessary to raise other tax rates to make up for the forgone revenue.

Enterprise zones provide tax incentives to businesses that locate within them. These incentives include forgoing the personal property tax on inventories.

Tax-increment financing (TIF) uses the expected increase in property revenues from a development project to pay for the project. TIF makes redevelopment self-financing but, like abatement, may force other taxing units to increase rates because they do not share in the growth of the real property tax base.

City-county government has employed each of these economic development incentives, but it is difficult to determine their relative success because several other factors also contributed to Indianapolis' strong economic performance during the 1980s. City-county government can also use its power of eminent domain to assemble parcels of land, and may build a parking garage as part of a private developer's project. The INDIANAPOLIS AIRPORT AUTHORITY, which is responsible for the development and administration of an air transportation system for not only Marion County but the eight-county metropolitan area, also plays a key role in economic development.

Revenues, Expenditures, and Outstanding Debt for the City of Indianapolis, Year Ending December 31, 1991

Revenues by Source	Amount	Per Capita	Pct. of Total
Taxes	$216,675,686	$291.98	53.44%
Property	144,331,750	194.50	
Income	39,438,933	53.15	
Wheel	9,289,023	12.52	
Other	23,615,980	31.82	
Service Charges	81,689,531	110.08	20.15
Intergovernmental Revenue	63,877,130	86.08	5.76
Federal	27,475,900	37.03	
State & Other	36,401,230	49.05	
Licenses/Permits	5,777,695	7.79	1.43
Fines & Court Fees	1,400,876	1.89	0.34
Other	36,008,020	48.52	8.88
TOTAL	$405,428,938	$546.34	100.00%

Expenditures by Category	Amount	Per Capita	Pct. of Total
Protection of People and Property	$115,790,625	$156.04	26.76%
Environmental Service	81,915,260	110.39	18.93
Debt Service	65,233,270	87.91	15.07
Capital Outlay	63,735,874	85.89	14.73
Transportation and Related Services	33,812,146	45.56	7.81
Community Development and Welfare	31,479,140	42.42	7.28
Administrative Services	20,855,038	28.10	4.82
Community Cultural and Recreation	15,475,386	20.85	3.58
Government Operations	4,352,807	5.87	1.01
TOTAL	$432,649,546	$583.03	100.00%

Outstanding Debt	Amount	Per Capita
General Obligation and Special District Bonds	$229,137,000	$308.78
Revenue Bonds	25,742,994	34.69
Tax Increment Revenue Bonds	305,834,464	412.13

Source: City of Indianapolis Component Unit Financial Report, December 31, 1991

Expenditures. Expenditures reflect the functions and financing methods of government. Protection of people and property is the largest expenditure category in the city's budget, accounting for about 27 percent of all city expenditures during 1991. Environmental services (including solid waste collection and disposal, and wastewater and sewage collection, treatment, and disposal) accounted for another 19 percent. Debt service (interest payments and redemption of outstanding bonds) and capital outlays (expenditures for construction and infrastructure) represented the next largest categories at 15 percent each of total expenditures, followed by transportation, community development, and welfare.

During the 10–year period from 1982 to 1991, city government expenditures in Indianapolis rose 88 percent, from $230,510,084 to $432,649,546. This increase exceeded both the rate of population growth and the rate of inflation during the decade. The expenditure categories with the greatest rates of increase from 1982 to 1991 were administrative services, government operations, debt service, capital outlays, and environmental services.

Indebtedness. The city borrows money primarily to fund large-scale projects that are impractical to fund from a single year's budget and that will generate benefits over a long period. The usual method of borrowing is to sell bonds. Buyers of the city's bonds are repaid from either the city government's general revenues or the specific revenues generated by the project for which the money was borrowed.

The Unigov reorganization improved the city's ability to borrow substantial amounts of money at favorable interest rates. The inclusion of outer-county suburban areas raised the city's total property valuation and therefore raised the debt limit available to the city of Indianapolis. This eased borrowing for several large-scale capital projects during the 1980s.

Indianapolis has also maintained beneficial bond ratings that keep interest costs relatively low. Municipal bond rating agencies have shown financial confidence in Indianapolis, giving the city AAA and AA bond ratings for a number of years. These bond ratings attract outside investors to the city's bonds, reducing the interest rate the city must offer in order to find buyers.

To maintain this confidence in the city's financial condition, and to maintain service quality despite restraints on revenues, city officials have given increased attention to measuring the effectiveness of government expenditures. Alternative means of delivering services are being considered. Agencies are being urged to clearly articulate outcome-oriented goals and measurable objectives and to report annually their progress toward them. Continued public confidence in government depends upon effective accounting for where tax dollars go.

ROBERT KIRK
INDIANA UNIVERSITY–PURDUE UNIVERSITY, INDIANAPOLIS

Unigov and Service Delivery. Some local public services in Marion County are provided countywide, others more nearly match the pre-Unigov "old city" of Indianapolis, a few extend over the UNIGOV area (Marion County minus the EXCLUDED CITIES), and still others cover areas that match none of the above. Despite Unigov, the continued presence of county government, nine townships, eleven school districts, four excluded cities, sixteen INCLUDED TOWNS, and six municipal corporations means that the Consolidated City of Indianapolis does not provide all local government services in Marion County. Further, some of the services delivered by the Consolidated City of Indianapolis cover different portions of Marion County through the use of additional jurisdictions known as SPECIAL SERVICE DISTRICTS and SPECIAL TAXING DISTRICTS.

Police protection in Marion County is provided by the INDIANAPOLIS POLICE DEPARTMENT (which serves the Police Special Service District, roughly equivalent to the pre-Unigov area of Indianapolis), by additional municipal police departments in Beech Grove, Lawrence, Southport, and Speedway, and by the Marion County Sheriff's Department (which serves all other areas within the county as well as maintaining countywide corrections facilities). Some of the included towns also supplement the Sheriff's Department protection with their own patrols.

The INDIANAPOLIS FIRE DEPARTMENT offers fire protection within the Fire Special Service District (approximately the pre-Unigov city of Indianapolis). Separate township fire departments in the eight outer townships serve the remainder of the county. All fire protection units within the county are linked by mutual aid agreements.

Emergency communications for public safety agencies are provided over the whole county by the Metropolitan Emergency Communications Agency (MECA). MECA operates an enhanced–911 service that is funded by a charge on local telephone users.

Prior to the Unigov reorganization, the Indianapolis–Marion County Parks and Recreation District was an independent municipal corporation. Today, park and recreation services are provided countywide by the Indianapolis DEPARTMENT OF PARKS AND RECREATION, whose activities are sup-

ported financially by a special taxing district. Some excluded cities operate and maintain their own parks and recreational facilities.

Prior to Unigov, the Mass Transportation Authority was responsible for arterial roads, the city of Indianapolis maintained streets and regulated traffic within its boundaries, some of the smaller municipalities did the same within their boundaries, the county served unincorporated areas, and the park district managed the parkways and the roadways within the parks. Today, the Indianapolis DEPARTMENT OF TRANSPORTATION performs street maintenance and traffic flow regulation throughout the county, with some of the excluded cities still performing additional maintenance on their streets. The Indianapolis Public Transportation Corporation, administered by the Indianapolis Department of Transportation, provides bus service countywide. The INDIANAPOLIS AIRPORT AUTHORITY, an independent municipal corporation created before Unigov, manages airport facilities throughout the county.

In 1943 the Indiana General Assembly passed a bill to place the Indianapolis City Hospital under the supervision of a five-member bipartisan board. In 1951 the state legislature created that board's successor, the HEALTH AND HOSPITAL CORPORATION, a separate municipal corporation that provides public health and hospital services countywide. The original Unigov bill in 1969 proposed replacing this separate government with a Department of Public Health, but legislators deleted that provision in response to strong political support for keeping the Health and Hospital Corporation separate. It retains considerable independence from the rest of the Unigov structure today.

The nine township trustees provide public assistance for the poor, including temporary housing and clothing assistance. The Indiana Family and Social Services Administration and its local agency, the Marion County Department of Public Welfare, administer federal and state public assistance programs, such as AFDC and Medicaid. The INDIANAPOLIS HOUSING AUTHORITY has administered public housing countywide since its creation in 1955. The housing authority is now located within the DEPARTMENT OF METROPOLITAN DEVELOPMENT, and its activities are supported by a property tax over a redevelopment district that corresponds to the area of the Consolidated City—the county minus the four excluded cities.

Public elementary and secondary education is provided by the INDIANAPOLIS PUBLIC SCHOOLS (a separate unit of local government with boundaries roughly coterminous with those of the pre-Unigov city of Indianapolis) and by school districts in the eight outer townships, the city of Southport, and the town of Speedway. A 1964 proposal to consolidate the school districts met with fierce political opposition, and they remain separate units of government.

In 1947 the Indianapolis Public Library District was created as a separate municipal corporation. It has since become the Indianapolis–Marion County Library District and extended its library services (and taxing area) beyond the city limits.

Countywide planning, zoning, and land-use regulation are governed by the METROPOLITAN DEVELOPMENT COMMISSION and administered by the Department of Metropolitan Development. The Metropolitan Development Commission was created in the Unigov legislation and succeeded to the functions of the Metropolitan Planning Commission, which had been created in 1955. The Department of Metropolitan Development consolidated several planning and redevelopment functions and extended their territorial reach to the Consolidated City.

Garbage collection is performed in some portions of the Solid Waste Collection Special Service District (approximately the area of the Consolidated City) by city employees working for the Indianapolis DEPARTMENT OF PUBLIC WORKS, and elsewhere by private haulers under the supervision of the Department of Public Works. Garbage disposal is financed through the Solid Waste Disposal Special Service District, and performed by private operators supervised by the Department of Public Works. One private operator manages a waste-to-energy mass-burn incinerator. Another operator manages a sanitary landfill for items not taken to the incinerator.

The Indianapolis Department of Public Works maintains sanitary sewers and stormwater drains throughout the county. Sewage sludge treatment and disposal and wastewater treatment are performed and financed countywide through special taxing districts. Both services and their special taxing districts are under the administration of the Department of Public Works. Some areas in the county remain without sewers.

WILLIAM BLOMQUIST
Indiana University–Purdue University,
Indianapolis

Union Federal Savings Bank.

Union Federal Savings Bank traces its origins to 1887 when it began as the Indianola Building and Loan Association. The business converted to a federal savings and loan association 50 years later. Union Federal is not to be confused with a separate enterprise, the Union Trust Company, founded in 1893. Union Trust merged with Indiana National Bank in 1950 in a $375 million transaction.

In 1948 Union Federal opened its first branch at 7 East Maple Road (now 38th Street) and expanded again in 1959 through a merger with Colonial Savings and Loan. It continued to grow during the next two decades, opening its first branch bank inside a MARSH supermarket in 1981. Today Union Federal has more than a dozen such branches associated with the grocery chain.

The early 1980s were difficult for savings and loans nationally, and Union Federal was no exception. Rising interest rates on deposits could not be recouped through money earned on low interest, long-term, fixed-rate mortgages. Union Federal's problems were compounded by a series of unwise commercial loans. It had been losing money at an average rate of $4.5 million every six months since 1980, and by early 1982 had a negative net worth.

In September, 1984, Fort Wayne–based Waterfield Mortgage Company paid $6.1 million in cash to acquire Union Federal, with help from the Federal Savings and Loan Insurance Corporation (FSLIC). At the time Union Federal had 11 Indianapolis-area offices and showed a negative net worth of $20 million. Waterfield instituted changes after the buyout, selling off $130 million in mortgages and adding automobile loans, consumer loans, and an expanded variety of mortgage products for Union Federal customers.

In 1986 Union Federal received permission from federal regulators to convert to a savings bank, becoming the Union Federal Savings Bank, and it was named by the *American Banker* magazine as the number one thrift in its class in the country for return on assets. The next year Union Federal acquired the struggling Community Federal Savings and Loan Association of Hamilton, Ohio, near Cincinnati, in another deal arranged by the FSLIC. The merger gave Union Federal assets of $1.2 billion and a total of 33 branch offices. As of the early 1990s Union Federal had 35 Indianapolis-area branch offices. Employing almost 550 people, the bank's total assets exceeded $1.4 billion.

DEBORAH B. MARKISOHN

Union Station (39 Jackson Place). Currently a "festival marketplace," but historically the hub of an extensive passenger rail network. The country's first "union station"—that is, a centralized station for the common use of passengers of many independent rail lines—was constructed south of the present station in 1852–1853. Planned by Captain Thomas A. Morris and designed by architect JOSEPH CURZON, the brick structure with clerestory served five tracks. Despite enlargement in 1866, this depot was outgrown within 30 years and was demolished in 1886.

The current Union Station, designed by architect and engineer Thomas Rodd of Pittsburgh, was built as a replacement in 1887–1888. It is one of the finest examples of the Romanesque Revival style in the Midwest and one of the city's most historically and architecturally significant buildings. The three-story-high, barrel-vaulted, skylit waiting room has been likened to a cathedral and is one of the most outstanding public spaces in Indiana. Major alterations and additions to the station, designed by the local firm of D. A. Bohlen and Son in 1912–1913, resulted in such features as the waiting room's stained-glass wheel windows, a canopy over the Jackson Place entrance, and the immigrant waiting room.

At the turn of the century 200 passenger trains a day passed through the 1880s train shed, which was built of cast iron and wood at grade

View of Union Station's Grand Hall.
[Indiana Historical Society, #C5835]

level. Passengers were forced to walk across tracks to board their trains, and traffic jams occurred when trains blocked vehicles in the streets surrounding the station. An ambitious program of RAILROAD TRACK ELEVATION was begun by 1915. While the 14 elevated tracks and train platform were completed in 1918, the intervention of World War I delayed completion of the train shed and pedestrian concourse until late in 1922. Price and McLanahan of Philadelphia served as architects. Recognized for its major achievements in traffic engineering, the seven-acre train shed complex is among less than a dozen that survive in the United States today.

Union Station went through a slow deterioration during the 20th century. Traffic had almost ceased by 1970 when the Penn Central fell into bankruptcy. Several attempts were made to stabilize the building in the late 1970s following its listing (1974) on the National Register of Historic Places, but it took the comprehensive approach of developer Robert Borns to save the station as a festival marketplace. Preserving the most significant architectural elements, the $30–million restoration completed in 1986 focused on retaining the experience of a station in its conversion to over 100 restaurants and shops. As an example of the extensive work necessary in the two-year project, nearly 90 percent of the ornate plaster in the head house (1880s building) had to be replaced because of water damage. The development of the trackside market retained the open structural supports of the train shed, incorporating skylights above and references to the rails in the new floor. BROWNING DAY MULLINS DIERDORF was architect of the station's renovation and the conversion of the west portion of the shed into a hotel; WOOLLEN, MOLZAN AND PARTNERS was architect of the train shed's transformation.

The renovated facility's early success dimmed in the late 1980s because of low revenues, high turnover among its shops, and inadequate security. New management addressed many of these problems, with mixed success. In 1993 over 4.2 million people visited the station's 34 retail stores, 18 fast food outlets, and 7 restaurants and bars.

MARY ELLEN GADSKI

Thomas M. Slade, *Historic American Buildings Survey in Indiana* (Bloomington, Ind., 1983); *Indianapolis News*, Apr. 18, 1986 (supplement).

Unitarians-Universalists. In 1961 the Unitarian and Universalist churches in the United States and Canada merged to form a new body called the Unitarian Universalist Association of Congregations in North America. Both groups could point to a long organizational history in the United States reaching back to the 18th century. Unitarian Universalists uphold a rational noncreedal faith emphasizing spiritual freedom and the universal love of God.

The formal introduction of Universalism to Indianapolis can be traced to an 1830 debate between Universalist Jonathan Kidwell and Methodist Edwin M. Ray held in the Methodist meetinghouse. Organizationally, the Oaklandon Universalist Church dates its beginnings to 1838 and the formation of the Universalist Society of Lawrence Township. The OAKLANDON body formally organized in 1850 with 25 members. The present church building at 6450 Oaklandon Road arose in 1926 from the ashes of a second devastating fire in that decade. The church claims to be the oldest continuous church in the township.

The Unitarians did not organize in Indianapolis until 1868. The denomination floundered until 1903 and the founding of All Souls Unitarian Church and the 32–year pastorate of Frank Scott Corey Wicks (1905–1937). The congregation selected "All Souls" because it wished to include anyone desiring a liberal fellowship regardless of personal beliefs and previous affiliation. The church's slogan became "A Religious Center with a Civic Circumference," expressive of the congregation's interest in community work and social justice issues that have been hallmarks of Unitarianism-Universalism in the city. In 1911 All Souls built a sanctuary at Alabama and 15th streets and enlarged it in the early 1930s. The church moved to its present location at 5805 East 56th Street in 1959. All Souls, the largest Unitarian Universalist church in the county, serves over 700 adults and children.

Both Oaklandon and All Souls chose to retain their historical names after the consolidation in 1961. Newer bodies elected to identify themselves with the names of both faiths. The Circle Unitarian Universalist Fellowship, composed of former All Souls members, formed in 1971. Its decision to remain a fellowship rather than become a church reflected the congregation's desire to forego formality and professional leadership for self-generating programs and shared leadership responsibilities. The "Circle" in its name defines its structural preference for circular seating, symbolic of participant equality. The fellowship purchased its present building at 37 West Fall Creek Parkway, South Drive, in 1979.

In like manner, 93 persons from All Souls and from throughout the metropolitan area chartered the Unitarian Universalist Church of Indianapolis, which held its first service on January 7, 1979, at Central Avenue United Methodist Church. In the spring of 1981 the congregation took out loans to buy the campus of Noble School for Retarded Children at 615 West 43rd Street. The four-building complex is now home to the 250–member church.

All four Indianapolis-area churches associate in the Ohio Valley Unitarian Universalist District.

ROBERT M. TAYLOR, JR.
Indiana Historical Society

United Airlines Indianapolis Maintenance Center. United Airlines began construction of an $800–million aircraft maintenance facility at the INDIANAPOLIS INTERNATIONAL AIRPORT in August, 1992. However, plans for the Indianapolis maintenance center, which performs heavy maintenance work on the airline's fleet of Boeing 737 and 757 aircraft, actually began at least three years earlier when United Airlines identified the need for a new facility to ease the burden at its already crowded San Francisco maintenance center.

Indianapolis was chosen as the site of the 2.6 million-square-foot facility after intense competition from more than 90 bidders. United officials cited the financial incentives offered by the city and the state of Indiana, as well as the city's available work force, economic stability, school systems, and housing costs, as important elements of their decision. The public partners in the project offered $297.7 million in financial incentives. The city of Indianapolis supplied $111.5 million from a sale of bonds; the state of Indiana, $159 million from bonds and $15.2 million in grants; and Hendricks County, $8 million.

The facility will be built in several phases over a 12–year period. When completed it will feature 11 hangers with 18 aircraft bays, two nose bays, and an array of support facilities. The first phase involved 200 of the 300 acres allocated to the project, and includes eight service bays and one nose bay with associated shop buildings, supply building, central plant, main commons building, roads, and parking, to be completed in 1995. The first hanger—a part of Phase I—was completed in December, 1993, and the first plane arrived for repairs in 1994. Every one of United's Boeing 737s and 757s will come through the Indianapolis Maintenance Center every 13 to 15 months for a two-to-three-day maintenance process. Every four years each aircraft will undergo a heavy maintenance visit, which effectively involves disassembling and reassembling the entire aircraft. The maintenance center projects employment of 6,300 by 2004.

SHERRI MASSA
Sease, Gerig, & Associates

United Auto Workers, Region 3. Labor union. In 1935 the leadership of the American Federation of Labor (AFL) granted a charter to the United Auto Workers (UAW) as an International Union and appointed regional officers. Led by Forrest Wood, Region 3 was headquartered on the third floor of the old KNIGHTS OF PYTHIAS BUILDING in Indianapolis. In 1936 the UAW left the AFL, affiliated itself with the Congress of Industrial Organizations (CIO), and launched a successful organizing campaign against General Motors (GM), the country's largest automobile manufacturer. Following a series of disturbances in nearby Muncie and Anderson—actions that preceded a 42–day "sit-down" strike in Flint, Michigan—GM recognized the union in February, 1937. Chrysler, Packard, Hudson, Briggs, and nearly 400 other companies soon followed GM's lead; in 1941 Ford accepted the UAW as its workers' union.

During the 1950s and early 1960s Region 3 was a leader in the UAW's successful fight to implement the "agency-shop" program throughout the automobile industry, a procedure under which workers need not join a union to hold a job but must pay the union sums equal to the fees and dues paid by union members. The National Labor Relations Board (NLRB) upheld the "agency-shop" concept in 1961 and ordered GM to bargain with the UAW for the 14,000 nonunion workers in Indiana. In the 1990s Region 3 has been in the forefront in the UAW's attempts to organize Japanese-owned automotive plants.

Region 3's membership peaked in the 1950s at 140,000. In 1982 Indiana's membership in Region 3 of the UAW was 100,000 (with 28,000 members in Marion County). By the 1990s, however, membership in Region 3 had fallen to 85,000. From 1936 to 1949 Region 3 included all of Indiana and Kentucky as well as the southern half of Illinois. In 1949 Region 3's territory was reduced to its present boundaries of Indiana and Kentucky. The regional headquarters was moved in 1954 to a new facility located at 1701 West 18th Street; in 1985 the headquarters relocated to its present site in Indianapolis, 5850 Fortune Circle West.

DALLAS SELLS (d. 1993)
JEFFERY A. DUVALL

United Christmas Service (UCS).
United Way of Central Indiana program providing Christmas gifts to needy families. During the Great Depression of the 1930s local newspapers began providing assistance to families asking for help at CHRISTMAS. In 1952, reporters asked UNITED WAY to accept responsibility for these requests. In November and December of each year, UCS staff, 200 volunteers, media, and a policy committee of 25 persons raise and distribute more than $500,000. Some 9,000 families are helped by vouchers or gifts from donor groups. UCS also provides a clearinghouse for community groups, to avoid duplication.

DOROTHEA S. GREEN
United Christmas Service

United Church of Christ (UCC). This church is a young denomination, formed in 1957 as a result of the uniting of four groups, the Congregational Church, the Christian Church, the Reformed Church, and the German Evangelical Church. The merging of these Protestant denominations began in 1926 with talks between the National Council of Congregational Churches (NCCC) and the General Convention of the Christian Church or the Christian Connection.

Congregationalism, though energetically sending missionaries from New England to Indiana, did not have a large following here. The first Indianapolis church, Plymouth, was organized in 1857 and quickly became the center of the denomination in Indiana. The Christian Church, on the other hand, had its origins in more southern "primitivist" movements and therefore exerted a greater influence through immigration to the city. In 1931 these two bodies merged as the Congregational Christian Church.

Three years later, in 1934, in Cleveland, a union took place between the Evangelical Synod and the Reformed Church, thus the Evangelical and Reformed Church. The Reformed Church's strength lay in Ohio and Pennsylvania yet Indiana in 1906 could boast of having the fourth largest number of Reformed churches in the nation. The First Reformed Church in Indianapolis was founded at Ohio and Noble streets in 1852. The Evangelical Synod of North America, formed in

1872, had a background of German piety. Strong in southwestern Indiana, it had two churches in Indianapolis by 1866, including Zion Evangelical, which in 1990 had 1,085 members, the most of any UCC body in Marion County. Zion, founded in 1841, is considered the "mother" church of the denomination.

During the war years of the 1940s, the Congregational Christian Church and the Evangelical and Reformed Church began discussions which resulted in the organization of the United Church of Christ in 1957.

The UCC in Marion County is made up of 14 churches, only six of which survive from the 19th century. Five of the remaining eight churches have been established since 1960, with Ellenberger being the latest (1989). All the churches are members of the Southeast Association of the Indiana-Kentucky Conference (IKC). The IKC was established in 1963 for the purpose of aiding local churches in their congregational and social ministries. In that year Indianapolis hosted the first annual conference of the newly formed IKC and became its headquarters.

The coming together of the four denominations did more than simply link churches administratively. While it highlighted the ecumenical conviction of the bodies, the merger also integrated histories that emphasized pietism, progressive theology, and social consciousness. The concern for the aged, the ill, and orphans is seen in the Evangelicals' founding of Deaconess Hospital in 1895 at South and Delaware streets. The General Protestant Orphans' Home, another Evangelical establishment, came into being in 1867. It is now PLEASANT RUN CHILDREN'S HOMES. Members from Zion Evangelical, concerned about the elderly of their congregation, organized the ALTENHEIM Community in 1909. The United Church home, now located at 3525 East Hanna Street, offers independent living, assisted living, and health care. OSCAR C. MCCULLOCH, minister of PLYMOUTH (CONGREGATIONAL) CHURCH from 1877 until his death in 1891, proved to be a vocal and nationally known advocate of social justice and labor rights.

The churches of the UCC support many social welfare organizations financially and with volunteers. Centers for the homeless, food banks, health organizations, and youth ministries are beneficiaries of the UCC's generosity, as are national organizations such as Habitat for Humanity. Churches host senior citizens groups, the Red Cross, Parents without Partners, Scouts, and pre-schools. The UCC has long supported campus ministries. Dr. Wayne C. Olson, a UCC minister, served as Campus Ministries director in Indianapolis and initiated campus and church programs on AIDS. He also formed the Indiana AIDS Pastoral Care Network. This legacy of broad philanthropic initiatives and siding with the oppressed has helped define the character of the modern UCC.

Despite nearly four decades of organic unity, the constituent members still maintain close ties to their respective heritages. This is particularly true in the older Evangelical and Reform traditions where Lutheran observances can be detected in services and in the old architecture. Zion Evangelical Church's custom of holding two services in German annually is an example of the retentive strength of treasured customs. While the ordination of women in the UCC may seem modern, this practice too is deeply rooted in the Congregationalist tenet of the ministry of all believers. The UCC in Indianapolis has ordained women and has worked to remove sexist language from pulpits and publications.

This uniquely structured denomination therefore has managed to maintain some of the old cultural and theological diversity while it works in harmony to help fill the needs of people in modern Indianapolis.

JEAN R. BUSCHMANN

United Mine Workers of America. Industrial union representing coal miners. Created by a merger of local KNIGHTS OF LABOR assemblies and the National Federation of Miners and Mine Laborers (founded in Indianapolis in September, 1885; later known as the National Progressive Union), the United Mine Workers of America (UMWA) became the official representative of coal miners across the country on January 25, 1890, when it received an industrial charter from the American Federation of Labor.

The UMWA selected Indianapolis for its national headquarters in 1898 because of its central location near the coal-mining regions; it held its annual conventions here until 1934, enabling the city to witness the inner workings of the UMWA firsthand. These conventions were extremely important: delegates decided upon how to best deal with coal operators, engaged in numerous intra- and interorganizational debates, and formulated a unique organizational structure that allowed the UMWA to prosper. Though wage increases were its foremost concern, the UMWA was also instrumental in abolishing the "company store" and prohibiting work for boys under 16. Furthermore, it generated great union experience and loyalty that workers carried to other industries after coal mining began to decline in the 1920s.

Soon after its formation the UMWA gained notoriety and additional members as a result of its successful 1896–1897 prosecution of a strike against operators in the Central Competitive Field, comprised of Indiana, Ohio, Illinois, and western Pennsylvania. The UMWA's efforts resulted in a standard wage rate and an eight-hour day for miners in the Central Field. Indianapolis also witnessed the unfolding of the famous anthracite strike of 1902 in which the UMWA delegates and operators met in Indianapolis several times before President Theodore Roosevelt ordered both sides to a meeting at the White House where operators agreed to higher wages, ending the strike.

The CLAYPOOL HOTEL, the Stevenson Building, and TOMLINSON HALL housed many volatile encounters. At its 1906 convention, the UMWA prepared to strike. It demanded, as it had in 1902, that operators allow the southwestern states (Texas, Arkansas, Missouri, Indian Territory [later Oklahoma], and Kansas) to join the Central Competitive Field, enabling the UMWA to negotiate one contract with a 12.5 percent increase in wages plus seven other demands. Again President Roosevelt intervened and arranged a meeting at the Claypool Hotel. The operators offered to raise wages, the UMWA dropped its other demands, and the strike was averted. In the course of these negotiations, intraorganizational debates raged among miners. The UMWA's rival, Western Federation of Miners, citing the excluded Colorado miners, accused UMWA president John Mitchell of selling out.

It was under Mitchell, however, that the UMWA developed its system of voluntary arbitration. Made up of both miners and operators, a scale committee met in Indianapolis annually to negotiate terms for the following year. By doing so the UMWA avoided confrontations with operators while simultaneously securing better wages and working conditions.

Under the leadership of John L. Lewis (1919–1960), who maintained the union's offices on the 11th floor of the MERCHANTS BANK BUILDING, tension-filled conventions abounded in the 1920s. Lewis' rigid style encouraged factionalism and, combined with a coal surplus and the Great Depression of the 1930s, resulted in a dramatic decline in membership, from a high of 500,000 during World War I to 100,000 by the end of the 1920s. With little fanfare the national headquarters of the UMWA moved from Indianapolis to Washington, D.C., in 1934, thus ending the city's ties to the influential union.

LISA W. PHILLIPS

Harold Aurand, *From the Molly Maguires to the United Mine Workers* (Philadelphia, 1971); Elizabeth Levy and Tad Richards, *Struggle and Lose, Struggle and Win: The United Mine Workers* (New York, 1977); "History of UMWA," *Indianapolis News*, Jan. 17, 1914; *Indianapolis Star*, Jan. 24, 1934.

United Northwest Area. Neighborhood bounded by 38th, Meridian, and 10th streets and White River. The United Northwest Area is located in what was once a large, unincorporated area known as NORTH INDIANAPOLIS. North Indianapolis was platted up to 31st Street in 1873 by several men whose names now appear as street names in the United Northwest neighborhood (Rader, Roache, and Udell). The CENTRAL CANAL and the BELT LINE RAILROAD, which had its western terminus in North Indianapolis, attracted industry to the undeveloped area. The Udell Ladder Works, North Indianapolis Wagon Works, and Henry Ocow Manufacturing Company all moved to the area during 1873. The greatest period of residential development was the decade between 1910 and 1920, and over 75 percent of the area's hous-

ing stock was built before 1939. Most of the neighborhood's commercial development occurred along the Clifton Street electric railway line.

The United Northwest Area Association was formed in 1967 by a group of concerned residents to address increasing poverty and crime, poor city and police services, and below average reading ability among the area's children. Participation in the Community Development Block Grant program since 1975 has resulted in resurfaced streets, new curbs and sidewalks, and over 150 houses rehabilitated. In 1978 United Northwest Area incorporated and added an economic development branch to its neighborhood association. One of the association's initiatives was a tutoring program that began with high school students and eventually extended to the area's elementary school students as well before lack of funds forced its discontinuance in the late 1980s.

United Northwest Area, Inc., is an umbrella organization that covers three separate neighborhoods. The larger area was broken down into the three sub-areas in the mid–1970s—Riverside to the south, United Northwest in the center, and Crown Hill to the north—and each developed its own neighborhood association. Much of the land on the west side of the Riverside area is covered by Riverside Park and Golf Course and South Grove Golf Course. BUSH STADIUM and Kuntz Soccer Stadium are located in the southwest corner. The majority of the Crown Hill area is covered by the 555–acre CROWN HILL CEMETERY, with residential development along the eastern and southern boundaries. ST. VINCENT HOSPITAL was the neighborhood's largest employer during its 61 years (1913–1974) in the area. United Northwest neighborhood is mainly residential, with sporadic commercial development along Clifton Street and Dr. Martin Luther King, Jr. Boulevard.

In 1990 just over 16,000 people lived in the United Northwest Area neighborhoods. All three sub-areas are served by their own neighborhood associations and by United Northwest Area Corporation, an economic development organization, and United Northwest Area, Inc., a social services agency. Both have offices at 1100 West 30th Street.

WILLIAM D. DALTON

U.S. Army Finance Center. Longtime center of Army financial operations and the largest Army building in existence. The principal organization housed in the building has been known by a variety of names: Finance Center, U.S. Army (1953–1972); U.S. Army Finance Support Agency (1972–1974); U.S. Army Finance & Accounting Center (1975–1991); and Defense Finance Accounting Service Indianapolis Center (1991–present).

The original Finance Center, U.S. Army was located in a converted ammunition plant at St. Louis, but it lost its building when the Korean War made manufacture of ammunition a priority. A nationwide search for a new home ended in the selection of Schoen Field, a flying field at FORT BENJAMIN HARRISON. Ground for a new building was broken on August 10, 1951. Eighty-three thousand cubic yards of concrete and 1.3 million pounds of steel were used in construction, producing a building with 1.5 million square feet of office space that cost $19 million. Despite its size, as well as a tornado and a trucking strike during construction, the Finance Center was dedicated on October 9, 1953, ahead of schedule and under cost. The Finance Center's impact on Indianapolis was immediate and has remained significant to this day. In the 1950s it was the third largest employer in the area, with 6,000 to 8,000 workers, 4,000 of whom were hired in Indianapolis.

Throughout its history the Finance Center has been the working hub of Army financial operations. It pays Active Army and Reserve Component soldiers and families; retired soldiers, families, and annuitants; and eligible former soldiers and spouses. The Finance Center also pays transportation bills for the Army, Air Force, Secretary of Defense, Defense Logistics Agency, Job Corps, and some Department of Defense agencies. Finally, the Finance Center ensures accurate monetary payments of many kinds and gathers financial data on many Army programs. These accurate data reflect the increasing role financial management plays in the military.

On May 7, 1987, the Finance Center was renamed the Major General Emmett J. Bean Center in honor of its first commander. General Bean (Ret.) was present for the dedication ceremony,

The U.S. Army Finance Center, dedicated in 1953, occupies 14 acres. [Defense Finance and Accounting Service—Indianapolis Center]

the first time a major U.S. Army building had ever been named for a living soldier.

On January 20, 1991, the Finance Center was transferred from the Army to the Department of Defense in an effort to standardize and consolidate financial and accounting policies. Reduction in the size of the U.S. military during the early 1990s and the planned closure of Fort Harrison led to proposals that the Finance Center's responsibilities be divided and relocated. Civic leaders in Indianapolis and the city of Lawrence (in which the center is located) lobbied strenuously to retain the facility. In the spring of 1994 the Department of Defense announced plans to maintain some of the Finance Center's operations in Indianapolis.

WILLIAM H. CARNES, JR.
Army Finance Corps Museum

U.S. Arsenal (1863–1903). Governor OLIVER P. MORTON established a state arsenal in 1861 to provide Indiana troops with munitions, placing Col. Herman Sturm in charge of operations. Sturm, who had studied ammunition manufacturing in Germany, had a gunpowder factory on the northwest corner of the State House grounds. In 1863, when it was considered too dangerous because of its size, the facility was moved to a tract of farmland on the near east side belonging to Sturm. Ammunition was purchased from the Indiana arsenal until after the fall of Vicksburg and Chattanooga, when the manufacture of ammunition in the West became less necessary. The state arsenal closed April 18, 1864.

On July 11, 1862, Congress passed an act providing for the erection of three permanent federal arsenals, including one at Indianapolis, at a cost of $100,000 each. In March, 1863, 76 acres directly north of the Sturm property on today's East Michigan Street were purchased for $35,000. In August, 1863, Ordnance Captain Thomas J. Treadwell was appointed commander of the federal arsenal. That same month he sent Chief of Ordnance General James W. Ripley a plan for the site of the Indianapolis facility and excavation started that fall. Calvin Fletcher, Jr., Allen R. Benton, and Sturm sold the land needed for a road (now called Arsenal Avenue) to connect the arsenal grounds with the NATIONAL ROAD (Washington Street). According to the keystone of the south archway, the arsenal tower was completed in 1865. Nine other buildings were added by 1893 at an overall cost of $500,000. The grounds were landscaped with trees, roses, lilacs, and a grape arbor.

Between 1865 and the outbreak of the Spanish-American War the arsenal was used primarily as a storage facility for heavy artillery, lighter arms, and a limited amount of ammunition. At one time 100,000 rifles were stored on the second and third floors of the principal building. During the Spanish-American War, the arsenal was upgraded from a third to a first class facility and the shops were used to manufacture knapsacks, haversacks, blanket bags, and harnesses. After the war, the arsenal rapidly declined.

In August, 1902, an act of Congress ordered the arsenal vacated and closed. On March 27, 1903, the grounds were purchased for $154,000 by a committee of Indianapolis citizens with money donated for the purpose of starting a trade school. This school, Winona Technical Institute, began in September, 1904, adding different trades until it had financial difficulties in 1909. Put into receivership in 1910, it gradually discontinued operations. Printing and machine shops were maintained when ARSENAL TECHNICAL HIGH SCHOOL opened on the site in September, 1912. Litigation concerning the property continued until 1916 when the Indiana Supreme Court confirmed an earlier circuit court decision conveying

the arsenal grounds to the city schools to be held in trust by the school board and forever to be kept intact and dedicated to educational uses.

JOHN M. AND MARILYN L. HOFFMAN
Indiana Civil War Round Table

Emma Lou Thornbrough, *Indiana in the Civil War Era, 1850–1880* (Indianapolis, 1965); *The Arsenal Cannon*, June 6, 1916, May 22, 1947; W. H. H. Terrell, *Indiana in the War of the Rebellion* (Indianapolis, 1960).

United States Auto Club. Race sanctioning body. Located at 4910 West 16th Street in Speedway, the United States Auto Club (USAC) operates as a not-for-profit sanctioning organization which annually conducts in excess of 150 automobile racing events, including the INDIANAPOLIS 500–MILE RACE. It is governed by a nine-man board of directors and supplemented by an "advisory" board and various competition commissions. USAC's role is to establish sets of rules and regulations at events for which its services have been retained by race organizers. Operating capital is derived from participant licensing and race organizer sanction fees.

Founded in the fall of 1955, USAC serves as the sanctioning body of land speed record attempts at the Bonneville (Utah) salt flats and other locations for the worldwide governing body, Federation Internationale de l'Automobile. In addition, USAC Properties, Inc., was established in 1970 for the purpose of conducting impartial tests on automotive and non-automotive products. Many national advertising campaigns have utilized USAC's Seal of Approval to assure the public that the claims made for a product are justified.

USAC came into existence out of necessity when the American Automobile Association unexpectedly announced on Wednesday, August 3, 1955, that its Contest Board would be dissolved at the end of the year after having been the nation's leading sanctioning body since 1902. Two days later, before any rival group could react, INDIANAPOLIS MOTOR SPEEDWAY president Anton Hulman, Jr., unveiled a plan to a handful of influential participant friends in a private meeting at the track offices, then located at 729 North Capitol Avenue. While he believed the 500 conceivably could stand on its own merit for years to come, Hulman thought it should continue to be a part of a seasonal national championship. He also endorsed the concept of less expensive forms of racing to serve as a training system for potential 500 drivers and suggested that a new group could be formed to assume AAA's long-established role. Hulman's plan was announced publicly five days later and USAC was officially formed on Friday, September 16. Work began immediately on a new rule book for 1956. USAC headquarters relocated several times in its first eight years before finally settling at the current address in August, 1964.

Completing its 38th season in 1993, USAC had sanctioned over 5,000 events since January 8, 1956, while distributing almost $150 million in prize money. USAC also had long since become internationally known for numerous advancements in safety, not only in the structure of racing cars but in protective participant apparel and racetrack construction requirements as well.

While there is occasionally some confusion between USAC and the United States Auto Club, Motoring Division, Inc., the latter is in fact a multibenefit automobile service organization for the general public. It is licensed by USAC and its logo is similar in appearance.

DONALD DAVIDSON
Statistician and Historian
United States Auto Club

U.S. v. Board of School Commissioners. See School Desegregation Case

United Way of Central Indiana. Not-for-profit association engaged in human service planning, problem solving, fund raising, allocations, and program evaluation. United Way originated in 1920 as the Community Chest, adopting the federated fund-raising model of the World War I War Chest. It was subsequently known as the Community Fund (1923), Indianapolis Community Chest (1950), Indianapolis United Fund (1958), United Fund of Greater Indianapolis (1962), and United Way of Greater Indianapolis (1970–1986). The organization conducted the War Fund during World War II, enlarging its fi-

Soldiers and policemen guard the coffers of the War Chest, a predecessor of the local United Way fund drive, in 1918. [Indiana Historical Society, Bass Collection, #63327F]

nancial support from mostly local services to inclusion of wartime and international services.

Denver, Colorado, laid claim to the first community-wide fund-raising federation in 1887 but did not sustain the program for long. Cleveland, Ohio, followed in 1913 with the form of program that exists today in over 2,300 communities in the United States and in 200 cities in 24 other countries.

When the first local Community Chest campaign in 1921 required an extended campaign to raise $401,000 from 12,000 contributors, those involved in the campaign were discouraged. However, a review at the end of the fifth year showed growth to 38,000 donors supporting 38 previously separate appeals. The review lauded the Community Fund for the economy of combined fund raising and the businesslike management of funds, and for being the "social conscience" of Indianapolis. The Community Fund was key to the creation in 1923 of the Indianapolis Council of Social Agencies (now the United Way–Community Service Council), which consisted of 80 organizations with human services interests.

The Community Fund boosted its campaign receipts in the period of economic turndown, surpassing $1 million in 1931. The bulk of the proceeds (82% in 1932) were allotted to relief programs instead of to services emphasizing character building. Giving stagnated during the Great Depression but revived to new levels with the outbreak of war and the addition once again of special programs to meet national and international crises. Beginning in 1958, national organizations, especially in health, were added to the campaign.

In the early 1960s, the service area grew beyond Marion County to include Boone, Hamilton, Hancock, Hendricks, and Morgan counties. United Way added agencies and new services, but fund-raising efforts could not keep pace with the great growth of the human services field. The concept of "one campaign for all," the dream of United Way founders in 1920, was not realized for several reasons: stringent United Way eligibility and accountability standards; the desire of some agencies—particularly national health groups—to remain independent; the huge presence of government welfare programs (and concomitant taxation); and the sheer size of combined voluntary fund raising.

In 1978, United Way merged operations with the COMMUNITY SERVICE COUNCIL and began to emphasize greater effectiveness in service delivery. It was instrumental in creating systems of service, funding new services as new needs emerged (such as legal assistance for persons with AIDS), and developing close working relationships with state and local government. Collaboration with other funders became essential and took place to some extent through a non-incorporated group known as the Coalition for Human Services Planning, founded in 1978.

In 1980, United Way initiated a donor choice program, which allows givers to designate all or portions of their contributions to non–United Way human service organizations. In 1991, United Way shifted from its traditional stance of deficit funding (the difference between monies agencies receive from other sources—grants, fees, supplemental fund raising—and what they expend on operations) to distribution of funds based on an assessment of human service needs of the community and a priority system created to address such needs. Services devoted to the prevention of problems also became a priority. Funding was opened to non–United Way agencies if they had programs to meet critical problem areas.

United Way operates several central services. Its UNITED CHRISTMAS SERVICE raises funds during the holiday season for families in need and serves as a clearinghouse for holiday charitable efforts. The Volunteer Action Center is a major resource for recruiting, training, and placement of volunteers in service in a broad spectrum of civic organizations. Merger with Youth as Resources, a program involving young people in volunteer service, was initiated in late 1992. Other programs in which United Way plays a strong role include organized labor's Community Services program, the Winter Assistance Fund (financed largely through the Federal Emergency Management Agency), and the Minority Affairs Program, which includes a volunteer recognition program, a leadership training program for young professionals, and an intern program to introduce promising minority youth to human services careers.

A major study of the Community Chest by outside researchers in the early 1950s resulted in the publication of *Community Chest: A Case Study in Philanthropy* (1957). The survey was "to determine why the Community Chest has been a failure in 75 percent of its campaigns in the last 30 years." The book caused a storm with its critique of the "Hoosier Way" and the "independent" manner of the local citizenry. An Indianapolis newspaper columnist reflected the community's objections to the book when he stated that "the authors sneer at the Hoosier antipathy toward Federal control and their desire to go their own way solving their own problems."

From the $401,000 raised in 1920, the annual campaign reached more than $33 million in 1992. Central Indiana's United Way ranks among the top 25 in the United States in the amount of money raised. Through its own programs and its 76 supported agencies, it serves an estimated 400,000–500,000 persons annually. Its income comes from contributions, private and government grants, investment income, and service fees. In the past 20 years United Way has emerged as the largest local citizen-funded organization dealing with human services.

DAN MACDONALD

Unity. The Unity movement is a distinctive, indigenous American Christian religion founded by Myrtle and Charles Fillmore in 1889. Partially a product of the New Thought movement of that era, Unity churches or centers stress individual freedom and fulfillment, the teachings of Jesus, the omnipresence of God, the indwelling Christ in all humankind, and affirmative prayer. It is non-creedal, an attitude and teaching rather than a doctrine. A prayer ministry, called Silent Unity, is a major feature, along with a large publishing program that includes the *Daily Word* magazine and America's oldest children's magazine, *Wee Wisdom*. Unity's headquarters is in Unity Village, Missouri, and is called the Unity School of Christianity Unity churches fellowship in an Association of Unity Churches.

Indianapolis Unity, 907 North Delaware Street, grew out of a study class begun in 1914 on Blake Street and incorporated in 1923. Murle Powell Douglass ministered to the church from 1918 to 1950 in various locations around the city. In 1952 Unity purchased the middle strip of land at its present address and erected a building. In December, 1964, the members dedicated a new 480–seat sanctuary, reported to be the first built in downtown Indianapolis in 25 years. Designed by James Rennard, the outer lobby features a stone waterfall symbolizing the living waters of truth and a terrazzo floor mosaic depicting the gospel account of the two fishes and basket of bread. The old building was used for offices and Sunday School facilities. In 1965 a building to the south was purchased, rented out, and in 1972 joined to the existing facility. The church's Dial-A-Prayer functions 24 hours a day.

The other Unity church in the metropolitan area is the Unity Church of Today located at 845 West Carmel Drive in the Carmel Science and Technology Center. Founded in 1988, the church met originally in the Mohawk Trails Elementary School before moving to the industrial complex. The entrance way bookstore points up the centrality of publishing to Unity. The church provides a Dial-A-Thought phone service.

ROBERT M. TAYLOR, JR.
Indiana Historical Society

Unity, 169 (Apr., 1989); *Indianapolis News*, Dec. 5, 1964; *Noblesville Daily Ledger*, July 7, 1989.

University Heights. Southside community roughly bordered by Hanna Avenue, State and Lawrence streets, and Madison Avenue. University Heights began as a business deal between the Church of the United Brethren in Christ and William Elder, an Indianapolis realtor. In 1902 Elder offered to donate eight acres for a church-affiliated university and to construct a campus building if church members would buy lots in his nearby Marion Heights subdivision. Investors were to recoup their money when homesites located immediately south of the campus were developed. By 1904 the lots were sold and Elder erected the first Indiana Central University building.

Although the college opened the following year, development of the 446–lot subdivision proceeded slowly. In 1907, when the Marion Heights subdivision was incorporated as University Heights, there were seven homes. The 1910 census counted 100 residents and the following year the president of the university reported 70 homes had been constructed. By 1920 the population had grown to nearly 500. Houses were built in a variety of architectural styles reflecting middle class tastes from the early 1900s to the 1950s. Streets were originally named for bishops in the Church of United Brethren—Edwards, Mills, and Bowman, among others. In 1923 the neighborhood successfully sought annexation by Indianapolis.

Over the last 70 years, University Heights has retained its residential character with few commercial intrusions. Most homes were built by the 1960s, when there were an estimated 1,000 residents. Although the community once was closely linked to the school, by the early 1990s it had little direct contact with the UNIVERSITY OF INDIANAPOLIS.

CATHLEEN F. DONNELLY

Jerrold K. Footlick, "University Heights: College and Community Are One," *Indianapolis Times*, Mar. 11, 1962.

University of Indianapolis. Private, residential, comprehensive, southside university. Approximately 3,700 degree-seeking students pursue 65 major fields of study in day and

The University of Indianapolis' original building
housed classrooms, science laboratories,
administrative offices, a library, and an auditorium
when it opened in 1905.
[Indiana Historical Society, Bass Collection, #3861]

evening programs at the University of Indianapolis, which was founded by the Church of the United Brethren in Christ and chartered by the State of Indiana in 1902. As a result of denominational mergers, the university was an Evangelical United Brethren institution from 1946 to 1968 and is now affiliated with the United Methodist Church. Chartered as Indiana Central University, the institution was popularly known as Indiana Central College from 1921 to 1975 when usage reverted to the original name. In 1986 the name was changed to University of Indianapolis.

When the university opened its doors to students in 1905, it had an eight-acre campus and one building. By 1926 it had added 50 acres and built four dormitories and a gymnasium. Since 1956 12 buildings and a stadium have been erected, and the original neoclassical building has been remodeled extensively. A fine arts center, completed in spring, 1994, is the first phase of a new master plan to enhance facilities and beautify the campus.

The University of Indianapolis has had six presidents, three of whom served for a total of 72 years. Irby J. Good, business manager, was elected president in 1915 because the board of trustees found no one else willing to take the responsibility; he accepted the position for the same reason. When Good assumed the presidency, receivership seemed imminent, but he was able to fend off creditors, fund the debt, enlarge the campus, erect five buildings, and restore confidence in the institution's viability. For several years he functioned as

president, business manager, and dean; on at least one occasion he also served as a general contractor for the construction of a dormitory. He was a frugal manager, and despite the Great Depression, the indebtedness was liquidated about six months after he retired in 1944.

Shortly after the arrival of I. LYND ESCH, president from 1945 to 1970, the university attained regional accreditation and balanced its budget for the first time. Under Esch's leadership the institution, heretofore primarily committed to and dependent upon the sponsoring church, broadened its mission. To serve the community more effectively, the university added business and health science programs to the traditional curriculum of liberal arts and teacher education and began scheduling classes in the evenings, on weekends, and off campus to make them more accessible to non-traditional students. When the Evening Division was created in 1958, it was the only place in Indianapolis where one could earn a baccalaureate degree through evening courses alone. After master's degrees became mandatory for most Indiana teachers, an evening graduate program was instituted in 1966. The Center for Continuing Education and Management Development and the Community Music Center also were established during Esch's tenure, and eight buildings were erected to accommodate expanding programs and rising enrollment.

While Gene E. Sease was president, 1970 to 1988, identification with the community was furthered by changing the name to University of Indianapolis and establishing the Office of Community Services. The Executive MBA program, founded in 1978, and the graduate physical therapy and graduate occupational therapy programs, begun in 1980 and 1983 respectively, were the first such programs in Indiana. Restructuring in 1983 organized the university into the College of Arts and Sciences; School of Business; School of Education; School of Nursing; and five graduate programs, one of which is the Krannert Graduate School of Physical Therapy.

Notable additions to the physical plant during Sease's tenure were the Ruth Lilly Center for Health and Fitness and the Krannert Memorial Library. The library's collection includes papers and memorabilia of Senator Richard G. Lugar, Mayor

William H. Hudnut III, and Republican party stalwart L. Keith Bulen.

The university is committed to providing education with an international dimension. Each year students and faculty take advantage of opportunities to study, travel, or work abroad. In a typical year the university enrolls more than 100 students from about 40 countries. It offers an associate degree program in Cyprus, has an articulation agreement with International College in Athens, Greece, and is affiliated with Tunghai University in Taichung, Taiwan. Travel grants, endowed by the late Leon G. Zerfas to foster cross-cultural understanding, are awarded to about a dozen faculty members each year.

In athletics, the university is a member of NCAA Division II and competes in the Great Lakes Valley Conference and the Midwest Intercollegiate Football Conference. It fields teams in 20 intercollegiate sports, as many as any other university in Indiana.

The University of Indianapolis is accredited by the North Central Association of Schools and Colleges. Various programs are accredited by the Department of Education of the State of Indiana, National Council for Accreditation of Teacher Education, National League for Nursing, National Association of Schools of Music, American Physical Therapy Association, American Occupational Therapy Association, and Association of Collegiate Business Schools and Programs.

FREDERICK D. HILL
University of Indianapolis

Marvin L. Henricks, *From Parochialism to Community: A Sociohistorical Interpretation of Indiana Central University, 1902–1977* ([n.p.], 1977); Russell E. Vance, Jr., *Fifty Years of Christian Education: A Short History of Indiana Central College, 1905–1955* ([n.p.], 1955).

University Park. City park bounded by New York, Vermont, Pennsylvania, and Meridian streets. While ALEXANDER RALSTON's original city plan called for this land to be used as a state university, it never realized that purpose. Throughout its history University Square, as it was originally known, served as the location of the Marion County Seminary (1833–1853) and the first city high school (1853–1858). The seminary building was demolished in 1860 and the land then used as a drilling ground for Union troops during the Civil War.

In response to a growing national trend toward the creation of public spaces, University Park opened as a city park in 1876. The park originally consisted of walks, grass, and a bandstand. In 1887 the *Schuyler Colfax* statue, designed by Lorado Taft, became the first piece of statuary placed in the park. Today the park includes several sculptures, the centerpiece of which is the De-Pew Fountain. The fountain was designed by Karl Bitter, executed by Sterling Calder, and dedicated in 1919. Other statues include *Benjamin Harrison* (Charles Niehaus, 1980; plaza and pedestal, Henry Bacon), *Syrinx and Pan* (current sculptures by Roger White ca. 1978 to replace stolen originals), and the *Seated Lincoln* (Henry Herring, 1935).

SUZANNE T. ROLLINS

Upland Southerners. From its beginning Indianapolis possessed a significant population of natives and former residents of the Upland South, a region which includes the Appalachian portions of Maryland, Virginia, and North Carolina, and all of Kentucky, Tennessee, and West Virginia. The capital city's proximity to the region, its linkages via road and rail to the Ohio River, and its economic growth over the decades lured thousands of migrants from that area, giving Indianapolis the unofficial title of "the most southern of northern cities."

In 1850, the first year that the federal census recorded inhabitants' birthplaces, the Upland South accounted for 31.3 percent of people migrating to Indianapolis; this constituted a larger portion than from any other region except the Old Northwest, which supplied 32.4 percent of the city's residents (Ohio alone accounted for 30.8 percent). Natives of Kentucky constituted 15.4 percent; North Carolina, 6 percent; Virginia (then including West Virginia), 5.6 percent; Maryland, 3.1 percent; and Tennessee, 1.3 percent. Perhaps in response to the nation's political and social turmoil following the Civil War, the

Upland South portion of Indianapolis' population declined to 18.5 percent in 1870, though Kentucky remained the largest source of the city's settlers (11.9 percent).

Although the Panic of 1873 temporarily halted postwar activity and growth, the economic resurgence of the late 1870s helped to increase Indianapolis' population to 75,000 by 1880. Upland Southerners, most likely drawn by employment opportunities as well as by existing cultural ties with the Hoosier capital, constituted 22.3 percent of the non-Indiana born population of Indianapolis; Kentucky alone accounted for 14.2 percent. In subsequent years natives of Kentucky and Tennessee came increasingly to dominate the Upland South immigrant stream to Indianapolis.

The 1910 census indicated that 29.4 percent of U.S.-born migrants to Indianapolis were native to the Upland South. Only those from the east north central region (Ohio, Illinois, Michigan, Wisconsin) provided more immigrants (29.5 percent). In the following years out-of-state immigrants became a decreasing portion of the city's population, but the Upland South component continued to expand. By 1920 natives of the region accounted for 42.7 percent of Indianapolis' immigrants; by 1930 they comprised 44.5 percent. Upland Southerners came increasingly from Kentucky and Tennessee, which together provided 25.2 percent in 1910 and 40.8 percent in 1930. Migrations from Maryland, Virginia, and North Carolina, however, decreased. Kentucky became not simply the leading state of origin for Upland Southerners but also the single largest source of out-of-state immigrants to Indianapolis —1910, 21.1 percent; 1920, 30 percent; 1930, 30.9 percent. The percentage of Tennessee natives rose from 4.1 percent in 1910 to 9.9 percent in 1930.

Beginning with the 1940 census, different data regarding population origin were collected. Rather than requesting state of birth for U.S.-born natives, census canvassers asked a sample of the population to identify their place of residence five years previously. Thus, these data were not directly comparable to the simple birthplace data of earlier censuses. In addition, the most recent published censuses do not include detailed information on birthplace or internal migration.

The leading source of native-born (excluding Indiana-born) migrants to Indianapolis in 1940 was the east north central region, where 43.6 percent had lived in 1935. Illinois (19.1 percent) and Ohio (14.4 percent) were the major suppliers. The Upland South sent the next largest group to the city (24.3 percent), with Kentucky providing 16.8 percent of the migrants and Tennessee 4.9 percent.

By 1960 the Upland South's proportion of native-born immigrants to Indianapolis had increased by nearly the same percentage as the east north central region's proportion had decreased. Based upon residences five years previous, 34.4 percent moved from the east north central region (12.9 percent from Illinois, 11.5 percent from Ohio) and 31.8 percent came from the Upland South. Kentucky provided a larger percentage of the immigrants (16.2 percent) than any other state; Tennessee supplied 8.1 percent, Virginia 2.6 percent, and West Virginia 2.3 percent.

The 1970 census published regional birthplace information that revealed 38.8 percent of Indianapolis' native-born in-migrants were born in the east south central region (Kentucky, Tennessee, Alabama, Mississippi), compared to 28.6 percent in 1960. Extrapolating from trends seen in previous censuses, one can safely assume that the vast majority hailed from the Upland South. This steady increase of Upland Southerners in post-World War II Indianapolis illustrated their efforts to escape the poverty and limited economic growth in Appalachian regions by pursuing industrial and service employment opportunities in nearby and strongly growing cities such as Indianapolis.

A connection also exists between Upland Southern natives and African-Americans in Indianapolis. Blacks comprised 6.5 percent of the city's 1850 population, a much larger proportion than the 1.1 percent they formed statewide. Given the proportional distribution of the black population in the United States in 1850, it is not surprising that natives of southeastern states comprised the majority of African-Americans in Indianapolis. Black migrants to the city, however, tended to come primarily from the Upland South portions of those states. The largest group of blacks were born in North Carolina (38.5 percent of the immigrants), which probably reflected the close association between blacks and the North Carolina Quakers. The second largest group was native to Kentucky (22.3 percent). Other sources of black migration were Virginia (then including West Virginia, 13.2 percent), Tennessee (7.2 percent), and Maryland (1.7 percent).

By 1930 African-Americans formed 12.1 percent of the city's population. Mirroring the change in origins for the entire Upland Southern population, Virginia and North Carolina became far less significant sources of black immigrants (less than 3 percent). Kentucky and Tennessee were more significant, providing 42.4 percent and 24.4 percent, respectively, of non-Indiana born residents of Indianapolis. The only state not in the Upland South providing a considerable group of natives to the city was Ohio, from which 4.9 percent of the immigrants hailed.

Using internal migration statistics from the 1940 and 1960 censuses, sources of African-American immigrants can be determined. In 1940 the Upland South provided 49.9 percent of black migrants; 30 percent originated in Kentucky, 17.1 percent in Tennessee, and 1.3 percent in West Virginia. Although the total number of African-American migrants had increased by 1960, the Upland South's proportion declined, accounting for only 20.7 percent of the immigrants (Tennessee, 9.8 percent; Kentucky, 9.0 percent). The major southern source of black migrants to Indianapolis was now the Deep South. In 1940, 9.6 percent had lived in Mississippi and 4.6 percent in Alabama; by 1960, 9.2 percent came from Mississippi (the percentage was less than 1940 but the number was over three times larger) and 2.4 percent from Alabama. Also in 1960, much larger percentages of blacks came to Indianapolis from Georgia, Illinois, and Ohio than had 20 years previously.

Information about region of birth from the 1960 and 1970 censuses provides another perspective on the origin of Indianapolis' African-American population. In 1960, 73.7 percent of black immigrants to the city had been born in the east south central region (Kentucky, Tennessee, Alabama, Mississippi) and 9.3 percent in the south Atlantic region (Delaware, Maryland, District of Columbia, Virginia, North and South Carolina, Georgia, Florida). According to the 1970 census, 68.9 percent had been born in the east south central region and 11.4 percent in the south Atlantic region. African-American southerners were primarily from the Upland South, especially Kentucky and Tennessee, with increasing proportions from the Deep South.

The increased number of Indianapolis immigrants from southern Indiana, which had been settled primarily by Upland Southerners, heightened the southern flavor of the capital city. Many cultural geographers have identified southern Indiana as part of a transitional zone between northern and southern cultural regions. This zone typically extends from the Ohio River to the NATIONAL ROAD (U.S. 40) and includes southern Ohio and southern Illinois where cities, such as Columbus, Ohio, and Indianapolis, display a strong degree of Upland Southern population and cultural influence. The influence of Upland Southerners in Indianapolis has been strong from the city's founding. While their early dominance may have reduced or discouraged the immigration of settlers native to other regions, as principal settlers Upland Southerners set the tone for future developments in the city, including personal anecdotes and jokes, family histories, cultural characteristics (such as SPEECH AND DIALECT), and traditions of the city's past and present inhabitants.

GREGORY S. ROSE
The Ohio State University, Marion

Gregory S. Rose, "Upland Southerners: The County Origins of Southern Migrants to Indiana by 1850," *Indiana Magazine of History*, 82 (Sept., 1986), 242–263; Gregory S. Rose, "Hoosier Origins: The Nativity of Indiana's United States-Born Population in 1850," *Indiana Magazine of History*, 81 (Sept., 1985), 201–232; Gregory S. Rose, "The Distribution of Indiana's Ethnic and Racial Minorities in 1850," *Indiana Magazine of History*, 87 (Sept., 1991), 224–260.

Urban League. See Indianapolis Urban League

USA Group. Holding company specializing in education loans. From its national headquarters in FISHERS, Indiana, USA Group, Inc., serves as a parent company for five affiliates: USA Funds, Inc.; USA Services, Inc.; Education Loan Servicing Center (ELSC); Secondary Market Services, Inc.

(SMS); and USA Enterprises, Inc. USA Funds was the original company established in 1960. It is a nationwide guarantor of federally sponsored education loans. Since USA Funds' first loan in 1961, it has guaranteed $13 billion in education loans to more than 3 million customers. USA Services assists 12 states, including Indiana, in administering education loan programs. ELSC services education loans, totaling over $485 million in 1992. SMS, incorporated in 1986, buys and sells student loan portfolios for a national network of lenders. USA Enterprises, the only for-profit affiliate, markets America's Tuition Plan, a method of budgeting higher education expenses. USA Group affiliates process one in three student loan guarantees in the United States; together they have served more than 6 million students nationwide.

In 1991 USA Group moved from leased office space in Marion County to its newly constructed national headquarters in Fishers. Designed by EVERETT I. BROWN COMPANY, the complex features a 15,000–square-foot day care center that serves 185 children of employees. More than 1,300 of the company's over 2,000 employees are located at the Fishers complex. An additional 500 occupy offices in CASTLETON. USA Group also has offices in 13 other states.

CONNIE J. ZEIGLER

USS *Indianapolis*. Three ships have been named for the city of Indianapolis. The first *Indianapolis*, launched on July 4, 1918, was used by the Navy during World War I to carry supplies to Europe. The ship was decommissioned almost a year after it was first launched.

The second, and most famous, ship to be named for the capital city was the ill-fated heavy cruiser, christened by Lucy Taggart, daughter of former Indianapolis Mayor THOMAS TAGGART, in ceremonies on November 7, 1931, in Camden, New Jersey. In peacetime the ship carried Secretary of the Navy Claude Swanson on an inspection tour of the Pacific in 1933, and took President Franklin D. Roosevelt on a goodwill cruise to South America in 1936.

During World War II the ship, commanded by Capt. Charles B. McVay III, served as the flagship for Adm. RAYMOND A. SPRUANCE, Fifth Fleet commander. The *Indianapolis* and its crew of 1,196 men fought in campaigns at New Guinea, the Aleutian Islands, the Marianas Islands, and at Okinawa, where it was heavily damaged during a kamikaze attack.

On July 17, 1945, the ship left San Francisco for the Pacific island of Tinian carrying vital components for the atomic bomb, nicknamed "Little Boy," that was dropped on Hiroshima. After safely delivering its vital cargo on July 26, the *Indianapolis* stopped at Guam before continuing unescorted to Leyte in the Philippines where it was to undergo training in preparation for the planned invasion of the Japanese home islands. Shortly after midnight on July 30, the ship was hit by three of six torpedoes fired from the Japanese submarine I–58. Without power, the ship was unable to radio for help and sank in just 12 minutes. Due to confusion at Leyte, the *Indianapolis* was not missed for several days. During that time, the 850 men who managed to escape from the sinking ship had to go without water and were attacked repeatedly by sharks. On August 2, a Navy PBY plane finally spotted what were now only 318 survivors.

The ship's sinking, one of the worst disasters in U.S. Navy history, produced years of controversy. Captain McVay was convicted at a December, 1945, court martial for failing to sail a zigzag course to elude enemy submarines. The *Indianapolis* tragedy has been the subject of numerous books, a 1981 play, *Failure to Zigzag*, produced by the INDIANA REPERTORY THEATRE in Indianapolis, and a 1991 TV movie. A granite and limestone memorial to the *Indianapolis* is situated on the east bank of the CENTRAL CANAL (at approximately the 700 block of North Senate Avenue).

To commemorate the cruiser's sinking, the Navy launched a Los Angeles–class nuclear attack submarine named for the city on July 30, 1977, in Groton, Connecticut. The submarine was christened by Mrs. William G. Bray of Indianapolis, wife of the Indiana congressman who had asked the Navy Department to name a ship for the city. Also on hand for the launching were 60 survivors of the World War II cruiser's sinking.

RAY BOOMHOWER
Indiana Historical Society

Dan Kurzman, *Fatal Voyage: The Sinking of the USS Indianapolis* (New York, 1990).

Van Camp Hardware. Largest general hardware firm in the state during the first half of the 20th century. The founder, Courtland Van Camp, came to Indianapolis from Franklin County, Indiana, in the late 1860s. He originally formed a partnership in 1876 with J. A. Hanson and D. C. Bergundthal to sell blacksmith supplies, general store goods, and general hardware. The company was known as Hanson–Van Camp until 1888, when it became Van Camp Hardware & Iron Company; it incorporated in 1893. By that time its line of goods had expanded to include tinners' supplies, woodwork for carriages and wagons, and guns. The downtown location of the company changed several times, but its longest residence was in an eight-story structure it built at 401 West Maryland Street, where it remained until 1961. The final move was to the 5000 block of West 86th Street.

The company expanded greatly in the first half of the 20th century, sending salesman throughout the states of Indiana, Illinois, Michigan, Kentucky, and Ohio, as well as into Iowa and Missouri. Courtland Van Camp was active in the business until his death in 1923. The firm remained in family hands until 1967. By the mid–1950s the company boasted 80,000 items in stock, with 100 sales staff and 200 other employees. The company name changed to Graystone Corporation in 1976, and the principal offices moved to New York City; Graystone dissolved in 1977.

LEIGH DARBEE
Indiana Historical Society

Van Nuys, John D. (Oct. 10, 1907–Feb. 15, 1964). Leader in medical education in Indiana. A native of New Castle, Indiana, the son and grandson of physicians, and a graduate of Wabash College in 1929, Van Nuys received an M.D. degree from Indiana University in 1936 and took an internship and residency in medicine from 1936 to 1940 at the Indiana University Hospital. In 1940 he was appointed medical director of these hospitals, and in 1947 he became dean of the IN-DIANA UNIVERSITY SCHOOL OF MEDICINE, a position he held until his death.

Many advances occurred at the medical school under Van Nuys' leadership. Outside research support, approximately $11,000 when he became dean, increased to about $5 million during his last year. The clinical faculty had been largely part-time or volunteer until the Van Nuys years. He was able to attract nationally recognized chairmen of departments and faculty. In 1958 the medical sciences building that now bears his name was completed, and for the first time first-year medical students were admitted at Indianapolis instead of Bloomington. The medical school's class increased from 130 to 216, making it among the five largest schools in the nation. Much construction at the Medical Center occurred during the Van Nuys years, including the Union Building, Van Nuys Medical Sciences Building, Veterans Administration Hospital, Larue Carter Psychiatric Hospital, and additions to Riley Hospital. During the last year of his life, plans were being developed for a new Indiana University Hospital.

Dean Van Nuys was active in national medical education affairs, holding several important positions in the Association of American Medical Colleges. He received numerous honors from medical organizations and an honorary doctorate from Wabash College.

GLENN W. IRWIN, JR., M.D.

Vaudeville. An American form of variety theater popular from the 1880s through the 1930s. The history of vaudeville in Indianapolis parallels that of other cities. Touring shows (circuses, musical comedy, melodrama, burlesque, variety, minstrel and medicine shows) were performed in theaters, tents, beer halls, and saloons as precursors to vaudeville in the city. Even after vaudeville was well established in the late 1890s it shared the stage with other types of entertainment, especially variety, burlesque, and legitimate theater, and later with silent and talking movies.

Long a popular stopping place for performers (since it was close to a number of other large cities) Indianapolis offered first-class theaters with luxurious accommodations for audiences and performers alike from the 1870s on. Over the years the city's audiences saw vaudeville's best, including Anna Held, Eva Tanguay, Eddie Cantor, Fannie Brice, the Marx Brothers, and Harry Houdini.

In the 1870s Indianapolis' larger THEATERS—the Grand Opera House, Metropolitan, and Academy of Music—provided legitimate theater and the more popular genres. In spite of the elegant settings some variety acts were too risque for local tastes, and in April, 1877, the *Indianapolis News* reported police raids of the Metropolitan. Variety and burlesque also played in smaller halls, saloons, and gardens, such as the Garden Theatre and Gilmore's Zoological Garden. Some businesses continued to openly break the 1864 law prohibiting the serving of alcoholic beverages during performances, and the city especially tried to control these "concert saloons" through licensing.

By the 1880s there were Sunday performances, and the larger theaters began offering more variety and burlesque to bolster sagging profits. This led to complaints about bawdy entertainment and rude audiences, even though theaters reported record attendance in 1887, and caused the editor of the *News* to threaten to publish the names of disruptive patrons if their demeanor did not improve.

"Dime museums," including the Park Museum and the Casino Circus and Museum, provided another venue for variety shows in the 1880s. Along with exhibits of dwarfs and wax figures in historic tableaux, patrons could view shows with acrobats, dancers, and animal acts.

As vaudeville came into its own in the 1890s more touring acts played in the city's new vaudeville theaters (like the Empire), as well as older legitimate venues such as English's Opera House. After the turn of the century "high vaudeville" flourished in Indianapolis, and by 1912 large theaters devoted to vaudeville included the Colonial, the Washington, the Majestic, and the Lyric. The Colonial opened in 1909, and was the first vaudeville theater in the city to schedule intermissions. "Big time" vaudeville was firmly established in 1910 when the Grand Opera House was bought by the B. F. Keith circuit; it remained a vaudeville house until 1928. Houdini performed at Keith's in 1911, escaping from a tank of beer provided by the Indianapolis Brewing Company.

Vaudeville shows, such as the performances by Indianapolis-based G. G. Dawson, featured music and comedy routines. [Indiana Historical Society, #C5784]

The new Lyric, a major vaudeville house also on the Keith circuit, opened on October 14, 1912. Mayor SAMUEL (LEW) SHANK was the first person to speak from the new stage, and a motion picture of patrons entering and exiting the theater was made and shown the following Sunday.

In the 1910s and 1920s many new theaters built as legitimate theater or movie houses also played vaudeville, including the Murat and Circle theaters. Venues for vaudeville in the 1910s included the airdomes—outdoor theaters also known as hippodromes. Between 1909 and 1915 at least 22 of these facilities opened in the city.

The black vaudeville tradition was also present. Beginning in 1916 the Washington offered the best of the Negro vaudeville circuit, and pit band cornetist Frank Clay became known as the "Black Sousa." The Walker Theatre also offered vaudeville and moving pictures.

Some Indianapolis performers became nationally known, including NOBLE SISSLE and ragtime composer Russell Smith of the Chocolate Dandies, and John "Bubbles" Sublett of the popular Buck and Bubbles. The Charlie Davis band of the Circle and Indiana theaters gained national acclaim, and its singer, Dick Powell, went on to Hollywood. Charles Green's all-girl band, the Parisian

Redheads, took top billing over the Marx Brothers at New York's Palace Theater in 1929.

Vaudeville ended in Indianapolis (as it did in the rest of the country) a victim of talking pictures and the Great Depression. In the late 1920s the "vaude-pic" show became common, and large theaters—including Loews Palace, the Circle, and the new Indiana—offered shortened vaudeville reviews with motion pictures. When the Palace Theater closed in New York in 1932 many considered vaudeville dead, but the transitional vaude-pic show continued in Indianapolis into the 1940s. Most theaters became movie venues, but some continued to offer live big-band shows; a few, like the Colonial and the Majestic, retained the live show component as burlesque.

SALLY CARR CHILDS-HELTON
Indiana Historical Society

Gene Gladson, *Indianapolis Theaters from A to Z* (Indianapolis, 1976); Joseph Laurie, *Vaudeville* (New York, 1953).

Vaughan v. Williams (1845).

Fugitive slave lawsuit. Singleton Vaughan, a Missouri slaveholder, purchased Sam, Mariah, and their child from a slave trader in 1836. In 1837, with help from the Underground Railroad, the slave family escaped from Missouri to Hamilton County, Indiana, where they farmed under the name of Rhodes. Vaughan discovered them in 1844 and, after obtaining a warrant for their arrest, went to claim his property. When Vaughan forcibly served the warrant, neighbors came to the Rhodes' aid. Vaughan agreed to take his case to the Noblesville court to adjudicate the dispute, but on the road to Noblesville amid a crowd of over 150 neighbors the Rhodes' wagon escaped.

Vaughan filed a lawsuit in federal court in Indianapolis charging Owen Williams, the Quaker ringleader of the crowd, with obstruction. Meanwhile, the Rhodes' neighbors organized an aid association to pay for the defense. The defense's first tactic was to claim that, since Indiana had not been a state when the U.S. Constitution was ratified (the Fourth Article required that fugitive slaves be returned), a slaveholder could not reclaim his property in Indiana. The judge ruled

against this proposition, arguing that when Indiana accepted statehood it agreed to abide by the Constitution.

Vaughan lost the case against Williams, however, because the jury found the Rhodes entitled to their freedom before Vaughan had even bought them. Their previous master had moved with the slaves to Illinois and, upon learning that they should have gained their freedom after living in a free state for six months, abducted them and sold them to a slave trader in Missouri, who in turn unlawfully sold them to Vaughan.

The case set the precedent for the return of runaway slaves from free states that had entered the Union after 1789, thus ensuring that the local Underground Railroad would remain in operation. The case also affirmed a right to freedom if slaves lived in a free state for more than six months with their master. Finally, it demonstrated the support of a local antislavery community in Hamilton County and Indianapolis that engineered and paid for the Rhodes' defense.

MICHELLE D. HALE

---

28 Federal Cases 1115 (1845); Gayle Thornbrough et al., eds., *The Diary of Calvin Fletcher* (Indianapolis, 1974), III, 94n.

Veterans Administration Hospitals.

Indianapolis has been the location of three Veterans Administration (VA) hospitals, two of which are now consolidated under one management as the Richard L. Roudebush Veterans Administration Medical Center.

Thanks largely to the efforts of Indiana congressman LOUIS L. LUDLOW and local veterans organizations, the first VA hospital in Indianapolis opened in 1932 on Cold Spring Road on a bluff overlooking the White River. This facility was also the first general-medical VA hospital in the state. Between 1932 and 1941, the hospital expanded to more than double its original 150–bed capacity.

The end of World War II produced serious overcrowding problems at the Indianapolis hospital. Since postwar VA policy favored the affiliation of veterans hospitals with university medical schools, the VA decided to establish a new 500–

bed hospital on West 10th Street near the INDIANA UNIVERSITY SCHOOL OF MEDICINE rather than expand the existing facility. From 1946 to 1953, the former Billings U.S. Army General Hospital at FORT BENJAMIN HARRISON served as a temporary VA hospital during construction of the West 10th Street facility. In 1952, the new hospital opened, and the following year the Cold Spring Road hospital was converted into a special tuberculosis treatment center.

Between 1955 and 1958 the VA consolidated these two hospitals as the Indianapolis Veterans Administration Medical Center. In 1982 the VA renamed the medical center in honor of former Indiana congressman and VA administrator Richard L. Roudebush.

BRADLEY KENT DAMON

Bradley Kent Damon, "'To Care for Him Who Shall Have Borne the Battle': A History of the Indianapolis Veterans Administration Hospitals, 1928–1978" (M.A. thesis, Indiana University, 1990).

Victory Corps. National extracurricular organization for high school students during World War II. Organized by the federal government and administered by the United States Office of Education, the Victory Corps prepared students for civilian and military participation in national defense efforts. Membership required participation in a physical fitness program, in war related activities such as scrap drives or USO work, and enrollment in specified academic courses such as mathematics, science, and pre-flight aeronautics.

Several Indianapolis high schools participated in the Victory Corps program beginning in 1942. DeWitt Morgan, superintendent of the Indianapolis Public Schools, appointed Wilbur Barnhart, the vice-principal and a commerce teacher at MANUAL HIGH SCHOOL, as the director of the program in the city. Students involved in the Victory Corps participated in a wide array of local war-related activities, including bond sales, scrap drives, and other volunteer work.

CHARLES TITUS
Eastern Illinois University

Max Parvin Cavnes, *The Hoosier Community at War* (Bloomington, Ind., 1961); Richard M. Ugland, "The Adolescent Experience during World War II: Indianapolis as a Case Study" (Ph.D. dissertation, Indiana University, 1977).

Vietnam War (Feb., 1962–Mar., 1973). The Vietnam War divided Indianapolis as no conflict had since the Civil War. The city experienced its first antiwar demonstrations in 1964 when police arrested 20 marchers on Monument Circle. Despite this early protest Indianapolis remained a relatively calm "hawk" bastion for the first few years of the war. Even the city's colleges and universities remained quiet into the mid–1960s. In December, 1965, the state's university students presented a petition from the Student Committee for the Defense of Vietnam to Governor Roger Branigin at the State House. Led by students at the Indiana University Law School in Indianapolis, the group urged a "policy of strength against the Viet Cong and oppos[ed] Vietnik demonstrators."

If more antiwar sentiment was expressed locally in the early years of the war, Indianapolis newspapers did not report it. When President Lyndon B. Johnson visited the city in 1966 the *Indianapolis News*, in its report on the "thousands of cheering, screaming Hoosiers" who welcomed him, carried only a brief mention of the 30 young antiwar demonstrators who were arrested for disturbing the peace before Johnson arrived. Many of the city's residents and most of its media were clearly pro-war. Although local papers did not report the views of antiwar "doves," they devoted much editorial space to attacks on antiwar sentiment. In November, Alan M. Simons, organizer of "Vietnam Summer: Indianapolis Project (VIP)," an affiliate of a national program to promote peace in Vietnam, condemned the local papers for ignoring news "they disapprove of," such as the VIP project. He claimed there was a "great deal of latent sentiment for peace" in Indianapolis. The *Indianapolis News* and the *Indianapolis Star*, both published by EUGENE C. PULLIAM, one of the city's most vocal hawks, took strong stands in favor of the war. On July 26, 1967, the Student Committee for Victory in Vietnam named JAMESON G. CAMPAIGNE, the *Star*'s editor, honorary chairman of their pro-war movement in respect for his pro-war stand.

A sincere concern for the future of American freedom fueled the anticommunist passion of the hawks. Although South Vietnamese freedom from communism lay at the heart of the struggle, war supporters believed that communism's spread threatened everyone. They condemned antiwar protest as the work of pacifists, leftists, and communists.

Despite media condemnations, doves believed fervently in the cause of peace. They protested the futility of a war that they believed could not be won and emphasized the mounting casualties of the conflict. In May, 1967, the nearby Plainfield Friends Church conducted programs about the draft and offered counseling for conscientious objectors.

Local citizens became involved with the war in a myriad of ways. The Lawrence Lions Club produced a four-page newsletter full of community news for servicemen from that city. On July 7, 1967, the AMERICAN LEGION conducted a pro-war parade in which 12,000 people participated and 30,000 watched. Floats constructed by Naval Avionics and the JOHN BIRCH SOCIETY won the governor's cup and the national commander's cup, respectively. Local radio personality JIM SHELTON took his "Pick-A-Pocket" show to the troops in Vietnam.

After the sixth year of the war, in May, 1968, the United States began peace negotiations with North Vietnam. Sentiment in Indianapolis, even among hawks, welcomed the possibility of an end to the war and the divisions at home, both of which were nightly fare on national news broadcasts. Although the News noted that Marion County's war death toll was lower than elsewhere in the state, standing at 107 men, the erection in 1968 of a mock Vietnam village used to train soldiers at FORT BENJAMIN HARRISON reminded citizens that the war was still raging. In June the Board of County Commissioners ordered the American flag in front of the City-County Building flown at half-staff each Wednesday in commemoration of the men fighting in Vietnam.

By 1969, 34,000 servicemen and women had died in Vietnam. On July 4, 20 members of the antiwar Draft Project, headquartered at 222 East 16th Street, gathered on the steps of the Federal Building and read the name of each U.S. fatality as a testimony to "all the men of many nations who have had their lives taken from them in the Vietnam conflict."

The nation's first "Vietnam War Moratorium Day" took place in October, 1969. Tens of thousands of war protesters marched on Washington, D.C. In Indianapolis, although protest was still unsanctioned by the city's press and many citizens, it received news coverage. A rundown of local moratorium events was included in an article which cited South Bend's University of Notre Dame and Quaker-operated Earlham College in Richmond, Indiana, as the sites of most antiwar activity in the state. Butler University held a candlelight procession and memorial service, and both Butler and Christian Theological Seminary sponsored forum discussions about the war. Indiana Central (now University of Indianapolis) students commenced a 24–hour peace and fasting vigil; their counterparts at Marian College rallied on the lawn in front of the Student Activities Center. The Indiana Mobilization Committee distributed end-the-war leaflets in city high schools from its base of operations at CHRIST CHURCH CATHEDRAL. However, a public opinion poll conducted by the News after the moratorium indicated "overwhelming popular approval of standing by America's commitment" in Vietnam, 45 percent of respondents favoring President Richard Nixon's position of "seeking an honorable end to the war." Another 40 percent wanted to resume bombing in pursuit of a military victory. Only 15 percent favored an immediate end to the conflict. The News editorial staff cited these results in support of the claim of Vice-President Spiro Agnew that demonstrations were not a popular mandate to end the war.

In May, 1970, after National Guardsmen fired on student protesters at Kent State University in Ohio, killing four, Butler students conducted a mock funeral for the victims. Seven hundred and fifty students marched from MILITARY PARK to the Federal Building, some waving the North Vietnamese flag.

In spring, 1971, many Indianapolis area residents protested the conviction of Army Lt. William Calley for the premeditated murder of South

Vietnamese civilians at My Lai by signing petitions and contributing money to the lieutenant's appeal fund. Two Indianapolis women set up a booth on the steps of Christ Church Cathedral and in a jeep parked in a vacant downtown lot and collected 2,500 signatures on pro-Calley petitions and $600 in donations. A local man offered to post $100,000 bond for Calley's release pending appeal and Governor Edgar Whitcomb ordered the flag on the State House to be flown at half-staff.

By summer, 1971, Indianapolis' experience with the war entered a new phase. As the United States withdrew from the conflict, concern over POWs and MIAs emerged. The local Sertoma club collected thousands of letters asking for humane treatment of POWs by the North Vietnamese and in July sent a delegation of 12 central Indiana residents to Paris to present the letters at the Paris peace talks. Two local Jaycees groups sold POW bracelets, each engraved with the name of one POW or MIA. The names of Indianapolis residents Maj. Carl W. Lasiter and Col. James Kasler were among those listed as POWs on bracelets worn by citizens.

In March, 1973, President Nixon ended American military operations in Vietnam. Mayor Richard G. Lugar opened a Veterans Administration Center at 36 South Pennsylvania Street, one of 20 in the nation, designed to help new veterans obtain benefits and services. But veterans locally and nationally resented the country's lack of recognition for and belittlement of their efforts in the controversial war.

In 1975, when the South Vietnamese government fell, Indianapolis quickly joined the effort to offer aid to Vietnamese refugees. Citizens adopted orphans and even entire families in the "tidal wave of concern" which swept the country. But by August, 1975, that sentiment subsided, and although members of Gethsemane Lutheran Church, Holy Spirit Catholic Church, and Irvington Friends Church joined to bring a Vietnamese family to Indianapolis, the community at large donated only $100.

The legacy of the Vietnam War persisted into the 1980s and 1990s. In 1987 the Indiana legislature authorized the construction of a Vietnam War memorial, to be built with private funds, in honor of Indiana citizens who lost their lives in Southeast Asia. The area where the monument will be placed was dedicated in 1993 at the INDIANA WORLD WAR MEMORIAL PLAZA in downtown Indianapolis. The names of 1,533 Hoosiers are to be inscribed on the Indiana limestone memorial, 215 of them, including 13 MIAs, from Marion County. For many families in Marion County the legacy of the Vietnam war remains clear and present.

CONNIE J. ZEIGLER
THOMAS KEISER

Vision Committee. A broad-based citizens' planning committee that devised proposals to guide local civic and governmental groups in the 1990s. Based on other municipal "visioning" projects, the privately funded committee was established in 1992 and sponsored jointly by the Mayor's Office, Indianapolis CHAMBER OF COMMERCE, GREATER INDIANAPOLIS PROGRESS COMMITTEE, and United Way's COMMUNITY SERVICE COUNCIL. The Vision Committee sought to distinguish itself from previous citizen planning efforts by its concern with the Indianapolis metropolitan area and multiple study issues.

The committee began its work in September, 1992, conducting a series of forums and a public survey that together involved over 4,600 Indianapolis residents. Its report in June, 1993, entitled "Vision Indianapolis Tomorrow," recommended a total of 46 changes in education, neighborhoods, race relations, and local government and identified over 200 civic and governmental "partners" to implement each proposal. Many of the proposals paralleled changes planned by the Goldsmith administration, including use of city staff and an independent organization to service neighborhood needs, creating a multicounty regional planning organization, providing government employee training programs, and increasing use of citizen and neighborhood panels in government decision-making.

MICHELLE D. HALE

Voluntarism. Until the mid–1800s, most charitable services in America were provided by private individuals and organizations. Even as government assumed a larger role, Americans remained committed to the voluntary giving of time and services to meet society's needs. This tradition of voluntary service in the nonprofit sector has been a major characteristic of Indianapolis culture.

The Indianapolis Benevolent Society (IBS) was organized in 1835 as a voluntary society to help needy persons. IBS volunteers visited poor families in their assigned service districts, learned about residents' needs, and provided them with food, clothing, and fuel as needed. IBS remained an all-volunteer organization until 1879; its membership roster included a number of leading citizens, among them JAMES BLAKE, CALVIN FLETCHER, and JAMES M. RAY.

Volunteers in the YOUNG MEN'S CHRISTIAN ASSOCIATION, formed in 1854, strove to provide a homelike environment for young men moving to the city. A similar attention to social concerns was exhibited by women's clubs, which shifted their focus in the 1860s and 1870s from being literary and social clubs to dealing with issues such as child welfare and public health. In this spirit, the Indianapolis Flower Mission Society was formed in 1876, following a concept originally developed in Boston. FLOWER MISSION volunteers began by delivering flowers to the poor and sick in City Hospital and then expanded their efforts to provide food and nursing services. Later they were instrumental in setting up a newsboys' home, a tuberculosis sanitarium, and a children's hospital.

The national importance of voluntarism was reflected in the forming of a local chapter of the Volunteers of America in 1896. Members provided services to offenders in correctional facilities, supervised parolees, and provided food and clothing for the needy and homeless.

By the turn of the century the settlement house movement was absorbing many hours of volunteer service. These agencies were organized by educated women with volunteer staff to improve conditions in poor neighborhoods. FLANNER HOUSE was established in 1898 in Indianapolis as an employment, education, and health center for blacks. In 1905, CHRISTAMORE HOUSE began to provide social services to poor residents of the racially mixed Atlas neighborhood.

Health issues were the focus of a range of voluntary organizations begun in the first de-

cades of the 1900s. Those organizations included Indianapolis' first guild, St. Margaret's Hospital Guild, founded in 1907 to provide extra services to hospital patients. Other health-oriented volunteer organizations were focused on specific diseases and included both lay and medical persons. The first such agency in the nation was the Pennsylvania Society for the Prevention of Tuberculosis, founded in 1892; the Marion County Tuberculosis Association was organized in 1914. World War I provided the impetus for establishing the Indianapolis chapter of the American Red Cross in 1916; locally, 15,000 Red Cross volunteers were involved in providing for war needs and local relief.

From the 1930s into the 1950s, concerns about public health led to the development of local chapters of national organizations; they included the National Foundation for Infantile Paralysis in 1938, the American Cancer Society and the LITTLE RED DOOR in 1945, the American Heart Association in 1948, the Marion County Mental Health Association in 1949, the Muscular Dystrophy Association in 1952, United Cerebral Palsy in 1953, and the Multiple Sclerosis Society in 1954.

Early in the 20th century organizations were developed to promote and coordinate volunteer services in the community. The Family Welfare Society (later the Family Service Association) was started in 1922, following a national trend advocating the use of volunteers to supplement the role of social workers. Two years later the Council of Social Agencies, a forerunner to the COMMUNITY SERVICE COUNCIL and Volunteer Action Center, was established to encourage and help coordinate citizen participation in community volunteer service. The present Volunteer Action Center of the UNITED WAY was formed in 1980. It provides a volunteer recruitment and referral program, volunteer recognition programs, a management assistance program for volunteers and staff of nonprofit organizations, the board and committee resource file, and the Ardath Burkhart Board Leadership Development Series.

Voluntarism began to be strenuously promoted by the federal government in the 1960s through agencies such as the Peace Corps, Volunteers in Service to America (VISTA), and ACTION, which focused on senior citizen volunteers. In Indianapolis, senior volunteer programs were provided by the American Association of Retired Persons (AARP), the Foster Grandparents Program, the Retired Senior Volunteer Program (RSVP), and the Senior Companion Program. In 1974, the Society of Retired Executives, the first of its kind in the country, was created to use the talent and skills of retired executives and professionals. Services include management consultation for small businesses, not-for-profits, and government agencies, as well as a mentor program for high school students and job preparation workshops.

Sports events have accounted for many hours of volunteer time in Indianapolis, beginning with the NATIONAL SPORTS FESTIVAL (now the U.S. Olympic Festival), which was held in Indianapolis in 1982. Over 6,000 volunteers supported the INDIANA SPORTS CORPORATION and the U.S. Olympic Committee in the planning, organizing, and promoting of this event, which was attended by 2,600 athletes and tens of thousands of spectators. In 1987, the Tenth PAN AMERICAN GAMES were held in Indianapolis. More than 30,000 volunteers participated in staging this event, attended by several hundred thousand spectators and 4,453 athletes from 38 countries.

A survey of volunteer activity conducted in 1991 by the INDIANA UNIVERSITY CENTER ON PHILANTHROPY revealed that 52 percent of the people in Indiana had volunteered services, which was higher than the national average. Almost half of those surveyed volunteered for religious organizations, about one-third for education, and slightly over one-fourth for both health and human services. In addition, some voluntary activity, especially in minority cultures, goes unrecorded.

Volunteer service in Indianapolis is consistent with the high level of activity in the state as a whole. In 1991, nearly 45,000 volunteers provided services to the 25 largest agencies of United Way; in total, United Way volunteers contributed almost $13 million in services to the Indianapolis economy. More than 3,500 voluntary organizations in Indianapolis, some with a few volunteers and some with thousands, provide services in religion, education, health, human services, the environment, recreation, and the arts.

STEPHEN E. KIRCHHOFF

Indiana Gives, Volunteering and Giving in Indiana: 1991 (Indianapolis, 1992); John R. Seeley, et al., *Community Chest: A Case Study in Philanthropy* (Toronto, 1957; New Brunswick, 1989); Susan J. Ellis and Katherine H. Noyes, *By the People: A History of Americans as Volunteers* (San Francisco, 1990).

Von Tilzer, Harry (July 8, 1872-Jan. 10, 1946) and **Albert** (Mar. 29, 1878 –Oct. 1, 1956). Popular Tin Pan Alley–style songwriters.

Harry Gumm, born in Detroit, moved to Indianapolis as a boy where he was intrigued by local minstrel and VAUDEVILLE shows. He joined a traveling repertory company at age 15, adopted his mother's maiden name of Tilzer, and affixed "von" for theatrical appeal. He arrived in New York City in 1892, working as a comic vaudeville entertainer and aspiring composer. Harry Von Tilzer's first hit, "My Old New Hampshire Home," was co-written with lyricist Andrew B. Sterling in 1898 and later sold two million sheet music cop-

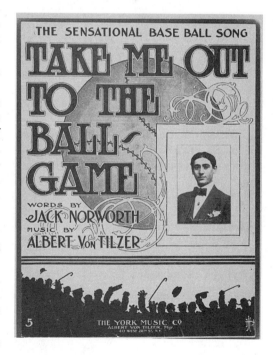

Indianapolis native Albert Von Tilzer wrote the music for the classic baseball song "Take Me Out to the Ball-Game" in 1908.
[Indiana Historical Society, #C5780]

ies. In 1902, he formed his own publishing company and produced such hit songs as "A Bird in a Gilded Cage," "Wait 'Til the Sun Shines, Nellie," "I Want a Girl Just Like the Girl," and "Alexander, Don't You Love Your Baby No More?," believed to be the inspiration for Irving Berlin's "Alexander's Ragtime Band." Harry Von Tilzer reportedly composed 8,000 songs and published 2,000 before his death in New York City.

Albert, born in Indianapolis, followed in his older brother's footsteps, writing music for numerous hit songs: "Take Me Out to the Ball Game," "I'm the Lonesomest Gal in Town," "Where the Swanee River Flows," "Oh, How She Could Yacki Hacki Wicki Wacki Woo," "Dapper Dan, the Sheik of Alabam'," and the World War I ballad, "I May Be Gone for a Long, Long Time." With brothers Will and Jack, he pursued a series of successful music publishing ventures until moving to Hollywood in 1930 to work in film music. He died in Los Angeles.

LAWRENCE E. MCCULLOUGH
Indiana University–Purdue University,
Indianapolis

David Ewen, *Great Men of American Popular Song* (Englewood Cliffs, N.J., 1972); David A. Jasen, *Tin Pan Alley* (New York, 1988).

Vonnegut, Bernard (Aug. 8, 1855–Aug. 7, 1908). Architect. The second son of Indianapolis merchant CLEMENS VONNEGUT and his wife Katrina, Bernard attended various German-American schools and graduated from Indianapolis High School (later SHORTRIDGE HIGH SCHOOL). After a short career as a stone carver, he graduated from the Massachusetts Institute of Technology and completed advanced work in architecture at the Polytechnic Institute in Hanover, Germany.

In 1888, Vonnegut established an architectural partnership in Indianapolis with a fellow German-American, Arthur Bohn. Their firm, VONNEGUT AND BOHN, designed such well-known city structures as the L. S. Ayres Building, Das Deutsche Haus (ATHENAEUM), JOHN HERRON ART INSTITUTE, Shortridge High School, and the Hotel Severin. The firm also designed the Student Union Building at Indiana University, Blooming-

ton, Eliza Fowler Hall at Purdue University, and the Federal Building in Vincennes, Indiana.

Vonnegut was a member of the Architectural League of New York, joined when he worked for noted architect George B. Post, and the American Institute of Architects. In support of their ethnic community, Vonnegut and Bohn taught descriptive geometry classes at the German-American School operated by the Indianapolis TURNVEREIN.

JOHN WARNER

Jacob Piatt Dunn, *Indiana and Indianans*, Vol. 5 (Chicago, 1919); George T. Probst, *The Germans in Indianapolis, 1848–1918* (Indianapolis, 1989).

Vonnegut, Clemens, Sr. (Nov. 20, 1824–Dec. 13, 1906). Merchant and civic leader. Born in Muenster, Westphalia, Germany, Vonnegut became involved in the manufacture of silk ribbon. In 1851 he sailed for America to conduct business for his employer, decided to remain in the United States, and shortly thereafter relocated to Indianapolis. Vonnegut soon formed a general merchandise retail partnership with fellow immigrant Charles Volmer. In 1858 Vonnegut became the sole proprietor and carried only hardware at his East Washington Street store. VONNEGUT HARDWARE COMPANY remained a multigenerational, family-owned Indianapolis institution until the early 1970s.

Vonnegut was dedicated to his family and civic responsibilities. He had four sons—Clemens, Jr., Bernard, Franklin, and George. All but Bernard followed in the hardware business; he formed the architectural firm of VONNEGUT AND BOHN. The civic activities of Clemens Vonnegut, Sr., included 28 years on the Indianapolis school board, and co-founding and leadership of the German-English Independent School, the Indianapolis Turngemeinde, and the city's first gymnastic society, the Athenaeum Turners. He was also an active member of the MAENNERCHOR, the Free-Thinker Society, and the Gewerbeschulverein, which introduced manual training to the local public school curriculum. Vonnegut was the author of *A Proposed Guide for Instruction in Morals from the Standpoint of a Freethinker* (Indianapolis, 1900).

WILLIAM L. SELM

Jacob Piatt Dunn, *Indiana and Indianans* (Chicago, 1919), Vol. 5; *Indianapolis Star Magazine*, May 25, 1952.

Vonnegut and Bohn. Architects. In 1888 BERNARD VONNEGUT and Arthur Bohn formed a partnership that lasted until Vonnegut's death in 1908, and that evolved into an architectural firm which remained active in Indianapolis in the 1990s.

Vonnegut (who was born in Indianapolis) and Bohn (who moved to the city as a child) worked together for the first time in 1884 teaching geometry in an industrial training school backed by the GERMAN-ENGLISH SCHOOL SOCIETY. In 1888 the two men formed an architectural firm, Vonnegut and Bohn. Their first major commission was the design of Das Deutsche Haus (now the ATHENAEUM). A celebration of the architects' German heritage, the building was one of the largest social clubhouses in the United States and included a large auditorium, gymnasium, restaurant, bar, and beer garden. Constructed between 1893 and 1897, the red brick structure featured elaborate limestone ornamentation on its German Renaissance Revival facade. It was placed on the National Register of Historic Places in 1973.

Before Das Deutsche Haus was completed, the firm designed the Pembroke Arcade. Inspired by the architecture of the World's Columbian Exposition in Chicago in 1893, the arcade was a forerunner of the modern shopping mall. Located at 133–137 East Washington Street, the building had gold leaf trim, pressed steel radiators, and glasswork by Louis Millet. It was razed in 1943.

Among Vonnegut and Bohn's buildings still standing in the city is the original HERRON SCHOOL OF ART at 1701 North Pennsylvania Street (1902), designed in the Neoclassical style popularized by the Columbian Exposition. Two years later they were the architects for the French Romanesque Schnull-Rauh residence at 3050 North Meridian Street (now home of the JUNIOR LEAGUE), which featured a prominent tower and red tile roof. In the last years of the 19th century they designed Indianapolis Public Schools 9, 15, 35, and 45. In 1903–1904 Vonnegut and Bohn were architects for the Louis H. Levey home at 2902 North Meridian Street (owned by Indianapolis Life Insurance Company), and in 1905 the firm planned the L. S. AYRES AND COMPANY department store building at 1 West Washington Street. Outside the city, they designed buildings for both Purdue and Indiana universities. Although they employed various building styles, one trademark of their designs was the use of shields as ornamentation in the cornice work.

Bernard Vonnegut died in 1908. By this time his son Kurt, trained at MIT, had joined the firm, which retained the name Vonnegut and Bohn after the loss of its senior member. The partnership between Kurt Vonnegut, Sr., and Arthur Bohn produced the Lyric Theatre, which once stood at 125 North Illinois Street (1910–1919); the Severin Hotel at 40 West Jackson Place (1912–1913, now part of the Omni Severin); the KAHN TAILORING COMPANY building at 800 North Capitol (1912, now Litho Press); the terra cotta–ornamented WILLIAM H. BLOCK COMPANY at 50 North Illinois Street (1912); and the Neoclassical American Fletcher National Bank building at 108 North Pennsylvania (1915, now Fletcher Trust). In the 1920s the firm gained a partner, Otto N. Mueller, and operated under the name Vonnegut, Bohn and Mueller. It designed Treadwell Hall at ARSENAL TECHNICAL HIGH SCHOOL (1920) and the Gothic Revival–inspired Roosevelt Building at 9 North Illinois Street (1923, demolished as part of the CIRCLE CENTRE MALL project). Following a very slow period in the years of the Great Depression, the firm designed the first INDIANA BELL buildings as well as the pre–World War II HOOK'S DRUG STORES throughout the state.

In the 1940s Arthur Bohn retired. By 1945 the firm's name had changed to Vonnegut and Wright with Kurt Vonnegut as president and George C. Wright as secretary-treasurer. Over the next 12 years they added and lost partners, changing names with each new addition. WRIGHT, PORTEUS AND LOWE/Bonar Architects and Engineers is the most current incarnation of the firm that began with the partnership of Bernard Vonnegut and Arthur Bohn over 100 years ago.

CONNIE J. ZEIGLER

Vonnegut Hardware Company. Retail hardware, manufacturing, and industrial supply company. CLEMENS VONNEGUT (1824–1906), a native of Germany, immigrated to America at age 27 and started Vollmer and Vonnegut with Charles Vollmer. Vonnegut became the sole owner after several years and changed the firm's name to Clemens Vonnegut, Hardware. Agricultural equipment, carpenters' tools, dry goods, and groceries were among the early supplies sold.

The first store, a one-room building, was at 8 East Washington Street, and there were later moves to several other addresses along this major thoroughfare. The first branch store opened in 1930 in IRVINGTON, and several other branches were located in shopping centers in the post–World War II years. In 1940 a Vonnegut wholesale and industrial supply building was constructed at 402 West Maryland. Clemens' four sons—Franklin, George, Clemens, Jr., and BERNARD VONNEGUT —as well as other descendants were active in the business. In its heyday it was the largest and most prominent hardware store in Indianapolis.

Vonnegut Hardware sold appliances, machinery, tools, and even silverware, ca. 1908.
[Indiana Historical Society, Bass Collection, #C814]

Incorporated in 1908, Vonnegut Hardware was a privately held company until it was sold to the Schlage Lock Company of San Francisco in 1965. There were 12 stores and 3 operating divisions—retail, industrial, and Von Duprin locks—at the time of the sale. Schlage kept only the Von Duprin lock division and in 1966 sold the retail business, by then Vonnegut's Inc., to local developer William Atkinson. He operated the stores briefly but in the early 1970s closed some and sold others. By the end of the decade, all Vonnegut stores were gone.

JOANNE KEATON

Voshell, Harry E. (1870–Apr. 5, 1947). Fire chief. Voshell joined the INDIANAPOLIS FIRE DEPARTMENT in 1904 and served at Engine House No. 18. In 1928 Mayor L. ERT SLACK appointed him fire chief and he was retained as chief by Mayor REGINALD H. SULLIVAN until 1935.

During his seven years as chief Voshell instituted several changes that increased the department's efficiency. He remodeled all the firehouses and built four new ones, all with modern housing for his fire fighters. He centralized maintenance activities and installed a radio communication system in all the trucks and firehouses. Saving the city thousands of dollars during the GREAT DEPRESSION, he ordered department mechanics to build all new fire trucks and equipment rather than buy them. He also had the department use smaller hoses and fight fires "from inside," a policy that drew nationwide attention for its ability to put out fires quickly and with less water damage to property. During his term as fire chief the department had one of the lowest per capita fire rate losses in the country.

Voshell made equally significant contributions by leading relief efforts during the Great Depression. After the stock market crash in 1929 he established two soup kitchens to feed hungry, jobless men. The firemen voluntarily funded the soup kitchens from their wages; the kitchens were located at the department headquarters and at Fire House No. 1 on Indiana Avenue. The fire department served over 340,000 meals and firemen also delivered coal and food baskets to the needy.

MICHELLE D. HALE

W

WAIV (105.7 FM). The second independent commercial FM station in the city, WAIV went on the air in 1961 from studios in the Dearborn Hotel on East Michigan Street. What made WAIV unique was its classical format and its owners, all Ph.D.s and M.D.s from ELI LILLY AND COMPANY. Microbiologist Carl W. Godzeski was president and program director, while another Ph.D., Norbert Neuss, was in charge of classical music.

With its limited commercial appeal, WAIV never made money for its owners. In 1966 the station solicited donations from its listeners, a forerunner of the fund drives now common on public radio and television stations. WAIV was sold in 1967 to a local group of prominent Democratic politicians, led by Marion County party chairman James Beatty and the president of the Metropolitan Plan Commission, Dr. Frank Lloyd. That group changed the station to WTLC.

Neuss continued his support of classical music by founding the FINE ARTS SOCIETY OF INDIANAPOLIS in 1968. Using the records from the old WAIV library he created the classical "Second Programme," which the Society made available to WIAN. The "Second Programme" was moved to the University of Indianapolis station, WICR, in 1982.

MICHAEL SPILLMAN

WAJC. The city's first nonprofit educational radio station was also its first permanent FM station. WAJC, licensed to the Arthur Jordan Conservatory of Music (which later became part of BUTLER UNIVERSITY), went on the air in September, 1950, from studios on the third floor of the LYMAN S. AYRES home at 1204 North Delaware Street. The station's first manager was Tom Carnegie, then a sportscaster at WIRE. WAJC originally broadcast its mostly classical format on a frequency of 91.9, but because of interference with local TV reception it moved to 104.5 in the vacant commercial section of the FM band in 1956.

Butler drama professor James Phillippe became manager of the station in 1964. Under his direction WAJC expanded its training of university students, offering live news and public affairs shows and play-by-play of Butler sports. The station also broadcast the Metropolitan Opera, and joined National Public Radio in 1982. In the late 1980s the station featured New Age music in the afternoon, classical at night, and alternative rock overnight.

As FM radio became more popular, WAJC's commercial frequency became more valuable. Butler's administration decided to emphasize the university's television station and sold WAJC in 1993 for more than $7 million to Susquehanna Broadcasting, owners of WFMS. The station changed to a "new hit country" format, adopting new call letters WGRL.

MICHAEL SPILLMAN

WBRI (1500 AM) and WXIR (98.3 FM). In October, 1963, Radio One Five Hundred Inc., a subsidiary of New York City–based brokerage firm Edwin Tornberg and Co., chose Indianapolis for its first radio station because it was a typical American market. The station, broadcasting from its studios at 4802 East 62nd Street, first aired as WNDY in January, 1964, with a popular music format. Later in 1964, when local operators became delinquent on their agreement to fund the station, Tornberg and his associates Edward Wetter and Douglas D. Kahle bought and managed the station. The new owners, representing three major faiths, changed the call letters to WBRI, "Wonderful Bible Radio of Indiana," and adopted an all-religious program format.

WBRI offers the oldest all-religious programming in Indiana, featuring nationally known religious leaders. Many programs, such as "Back to the Bible," "Chapel of the Air," "Haven of Rest," and "Heaven and Home Hour," are independently produced and nationally syndicated for the radio audience. Locally produced programs include the "Challenge of Faith Hour," offered by the Faith Assembly of God in Beech Grove, and "Gospel Light" with Rev. Ray Hampton, both of which have aired for 30 years. WBRI, which plays no music, also presents a national call-in program, "Point of View," and a local talk show, "Focus," addressing social and religious issues affecting the evangelical community. WXIR-FM, purchased by WBRI in 1980, broadcasts in stereo 24 hours daily and presents adult contemporary Christian music. The stations' audiences average 75,000 weekly.

CHRISTY MCKAY

WCKN. See WIRE

WFBM. See WNDE (radio); WRTV (television)

WFBQ (94.7 FM). Popular FM radio station. WFBQ went on the air in 1959 as WFBM-FM. Like other radio stations in the United States, WFBM-AM added the new frequency modulation station as a low-budget, automated-programming alternative which played recorded music. For many years WFBM-FM was considered secondary to its AM sister. It was not until the late 1960s and early 1970s, when FM began rock and roll programming aimed at teens and young adults, that WFBM-FM and other FM stations gained a significant audience.

In February, 1978, under new ownership, WFBM-FM changed its call letters to WFBQ; its AM sister station later became WNDE. WFBQ disc jockeys called the station, located at 94.7 on the radio dial, "Q95." In 1983 two new morning personalities, Bob Kevoian and Tom Griswold, moved from Petoskey, Michigan, and joined the staff at WFBQ. Their show was originally known as the "Q-Zoo," but its name was changed to the "Bob and Tom Show" within a few years. The duo quickly gained popularity, and their program became the most listened-to morning show in the city. Their fame brought controversy as well as revenue to WFBQ, however. In the mid–1980s Carmel attorney John Price formed Decency in Broadcasting, a group which charged that the "Bob and Tom Show" used pornographic material. Decency in Broadcasting appealed to the show's sponsors to withdraw their advertising. Although their campaign to reduce WFBQ's revenue had little success, the group continued to monitor the program and on October 12, 1985, filed a complaint against the show with the Federal Communications Commission (FCC). The FCC took no action against the station in this instance, but Decency in Broadcasting continued to

file complaints. In July, 1990, the FCC fined WFBQ $10,000 for broadcasting four "indecent" comedy routines on the "Bob and Tom Show." That same year Price sued the station and two of its on-air personalities, Tom Griswold and Chick McGee, over an election morning broadcast in front of Price's campaign headquarters in Carmel in which the two broadcasters compared Price's attacks against the station to Nazism. The station responded by temporarily suspending Griswold and McGee, but a local court rejected the suit.

Throughout this period the "Bob and Tom Show" and WFBQ's listenership continued to grow. In the 1980s station owners began airing the popular morning show on their AM station as well as at its regular FM slot. The readers of *Rolling Stone* magazine voted WFBQ "1990 Station of the Year" in a medium-sized market.

In 1993, still at its original location at 6161 Fall Creek Road, WFBQ's annual revenue exceeded $10 million and, according to Arbitron Ratings Service, it was the highest rated album-oriented rock station in the country. The station in 1993 was owned by Broadcast Alchemy L.P., a Cincinnati, Ohio, corporation.

CONNIE J. ZEIGLER

_____

Sam Stall, "Bob & Tom—Happy Anniversary, Baby," *Indianapolis Monthly*, 16 (Mar., 1993), 72–79, 155.

WFMS (95.5 FM). Cambridge City native MARTIN R. WILLIAMS, formerly chief engineer for WFBM, began broadcasting Indianapolis' first permanent commercial FM station on March 17, 1957. Choosing the call letters WFMS, Williams broadcast primarily classical and "popular concert" music from the Antlers Hotel at 750 North Meridian Street. The station's motto became "Music in a polite way." In the late 1960s, Williams relocated his transmitter, studio, and offices to 2255 North Hawthorne Lane to escape downtown interference to his signal. After experiencing financial difficulties for several years, Williams sold WFMS to Susquehanna Radio Company of York, Pennsylvania, in July, 1972.

On February 2, 1973, a fire caused by faulty wiring gutted the studio's interior and halted broadcasts for 57 hours. Seeking to capitalize on the fire, station promoters adopted the advertising line, "WFMS is carrying the torch for Indy." Despite the efforts to increase listenership, WFMS, the third "beautiful music" station in Indianapolis, was not doing well financially. In 1976 the station changed to a country music format, which proved successful. The station's Arbitron ratings moved from 1.4 in 1976 to 9.0 in 1980. WFMS moved to its present location at 8120 Knue Road in May, 1981. By 1985 WFMS was the sole country-format station in central Indiana. In spring, 1993, WFMS-FM ranked first in overall listenership in Indianapolis radio with a 15.8 share. That summer Susquehanna Broadcasting acquired WAJC, adopted new call letters WGRL, and changed to a "new hit country" format to complement WFMS programming.

CHRISTY MCKAY

Philip K. Eberly, *Susquehanna Radio: The First 50 Years* (1992).

WFYI (90.1 FM). The first noncommercial, educational radio station in Indianapolis to qualify for federal funds from the Corporation for Public Broadcasting, and the city's first affiliate of National Public Radio. The station first aired as WIAN on November 1, 1954, through the efforts of SHORTRIDGE HIGH SCHOOL and its PTA. Although initially a low power operation broadcasting only to the blocks surrounding Shortridge, the station became an important part of the curriculum of the INDIANAPOLIS PUBLIC SCHOOLS (IPS), which owned and operated it from 1954 to 1986. As part of IPS' Radio and Television Department, WIAN broadcast instructional programs. From its inception through the 1960s Shortridge students operated the studio and served as on-the-air announcers.

In September, 1963, WIAN began a regular schedule of student broadcasts every Friday evening during the school year. These programs featured live coverage of high school football and basketball games and taped broadcasts of concerts by IPS high school music groups. By the mid-1960s the WIAN sports staff included representatives from all IPS high schools. In 1969 the FINE

ARTS SOCIETY OF INDIANAPOLIS began a 13–year association with WIAN by providing additional classical programming.

The Radio and Television Department of IPS moved to a new Center for Instructional Radio and Television at 931 Fletcher Avenue in 1969–1970. The facility housed the studios and broadcasting equipment for the school district's new closed-circuit television system, which reached all IPS schools. This relocation effectively ended student operations and the Shortridge era of WIAN.

After boosting the transmitting power to 11,000 watts to increase the station's listening audience, WIAN qualified for a special grant from the Corporation for Public Broadcasting in spring, 1971. This allowed the station to develop its professional staff and budget to meet the minimum standards necessary to qualify as a public radio station. With this accomplished, WIAN became an affiliate of National Public Radio, the noncommercial network, and began broadcasting NPR programs in July, 1971.

Listenership to WIAN's educational programs gradually declined during the 1970s because of the closed-circuit delivery of instructional television to IPS classrooms. Consequently, in 1979 the station dropped instructional programs from its schedule and adopted a new emphasis on full-service public radio programming. Increased funds from the Corporation for Public Broadcasting allowed further development of the staff and programs emphasizing news and public affairs, classical music, and jazz. Included in the broadcast schedule were folk, blues, concert band, and ethnic music programs.

During the 1980s WIAN had considerable success in gaining financial and volunteer support from its listeners. However, concern about the financial resources of the Indianapolis Public Schools caused the administration and the school board to question the appropriateness of a school system's operation of a professionally staffed public radio station. As a result, IPS sold the station to Indianapolis Public Broadcasting, owners of WFYI-TV, on December 1, 1986. The call letters were subsequently changed to WFYI-FM.

In recent years WFYI has expanded its programming. Besides continuing its offerings from National Public Radio, WFYI also airs locally pro-

duced programs such as rebroadcasts of INDIA-
NAPOLIS SYMPHONY ORCHESTRA and INDIANAPOLIS
OPERA performances, "Nothing But the Blues,"
and other fine arts programming.

WFYI's estimated listenership in mid–1993
was 72,000 per week. The station reported 3,800
"friends" who contributed $186,000 toward a to-
tal budget of $340,000.

JUDY SCHWARTZ

Indianapolis Star, Oct. 31, 1954; *Indianapolis
News*, Nov. 25, 1968; WFYI files.

WFYI (Channel 20). Public broadcasting
station. With a budget of $221,000, three black
and white cameras, and nine employees, WFYI
signed on the air October 4, 1970, at the INDIA-
NAPOLIS MUSEUM OF ART under the direction of
Warren Wright. ARDATH BURKHART had organized
nearly 7,000 women from Indianapolis and vicinity ("Ardath's Army") to conduct a subscription
campaign to fund the station. Today WFYI has a
state-of-the-art facility at 1401 North Meridian
Street, a staff of 70, over 35,000 subscribers, an
annual budget of $3 million, and is viewed on 58
cable systems. Annual on-air fund drives solicit
new members and corporate and individual contributions. Frank Meek served as general manager
of WFYI from 1972 to 1989, when he was succeeded by Lloyd Wright.

In addition to its PBS programming, WFYI is
Indiana's largest producer of television programs
for statewide viewing. Three programs on Indiana
are presented. The magazine style "Across Indiana" travels the state in search of both typical and
atypical Indiana culture. "Indiana Lawmakers" offers reporting on the Indiana General Assembly,
including interviews with legislators and lobbyists. In order to provide more complete coverage
of Indiana politics, WFYI joined with WISH-TV
(CHANNEL 8) to produce "Indiana Week in Review," the first collaboration between WFYI and a
local network affiliate on a weekly series. Reflecting WFYI's concern for the quality of life in the
community, the station organized the "Nitty
Gritty City Group" composed of urban grassroots
problem-solvers who share ideas, struggles, and
successes concerning urban problems.

WFYI's commitment to educational programming is evident by "Learning in Indiana" on
which educators, community leaders, corporate
executives, teachers, and parents are interviewed.
Other projects are "GED on TV" and a series of
"Yes to School, No to Drugs" rallies. Over 30 percent of WFYI's weekly schedule is devoted to children's programming such as "Sesame Street,"
"Mister Roger's Neighborhood," "Reading Rainbow," and "Kid's Club."

JUDY SCHWARTZ

WIAN. See WFYI (90.1 FM)

WIBC (1070 AM). Popular AM radio station. WIBC's official broadcast debut was October 31, 1938. Owned by Glenn Van Auken's
Indiana Broadcasting Company and managed by
C. A. McLaughlin, the station broadcast at 1050
kilocycles. In 1941 the Federal Communications
Commission changed the dial locations of all Indianapolis radio stations; at that time WIBC
moved to 1070 on the AM dial—where it can still
be found today.

In the 1940s WIBC's Easy Gwynn became
the city's first deejay and newsman Frank Edwards broadcast a national news program over
WIBC and the Mutual Network, becoming the
first Indianapolis newsman with a regular network broadcast. The *Indianapolis News* bought
WIBC in 1944, and station general manager
Richard Fairbanks bought it in 1948. Four years
later WIBC and the Indianapolis Motor Speedway formed the INDIANAPOLIS MOTOR SPEEDWAY
RADIO NETWORK, to broadcast the 500–Mile Race
nationally.

In the decade of the 1950s WIBC's Dick
Sumner hosted a nightly popular music program
from atop Merrill's Hi-Decker drive-in and JIM
SHELTON emceed "Pick-A-Pocket," a man-
on-the-street quiz show. In 1956 the Grand Ole'
Opry nominated announcer Jack Morrow "Mr.
Dee Jay U.S.A." for his live-talent country music
program. Morrow also hosted weekly gospel
concerts from the CADLE TABERNACLE in Indianapolis and he ranked second in the nation for
on-air sales.

Fred Heckman joined the station as news director in 1957, retaining that position for 35 years. The station's focus on news kept it among the most listened to in the city even after other AM stations lost the majority of their audiences to FM radio. Breaking coverage of incidents such as the 1963 explosion at the Indiana State Fairgrounds Coliseum and Heckman's at-the-scene arbitration during the 1977 TONY KIRITSIS CASE kept the station at the forefront of radio news coverage even as others were downsizing or eliminating their news teams.

In 1985 WIBC ranked first among area stations in Arbitron ratings. Its popular morning program hosted by Gary Todd battled with the equally popular "Bob and Tom Show" on WFBQ for many years before finally losing the first place position in 1988. In 1989 WIBC's news-and-information format earned the station three-fourths of the $12 million in total AM revenue in the area.

Sconnix Broadcasting Company purchased WIBC in 1987 and by the early 1990s had begun making significant changes to the news format. The station shifted from "police blotter style" to "headlines" news, eliminating four people from its news staff in the process. In 1992 WIBC lost the contract to broadcast INDIANAPOLIS COLTS games to WNDE/WFBQ. The controversial retirements of longtime newsman Joe Pickett in 1991 and news director Heckman in 1993 brought negative publicity and age discrimination complaints.

By the summer of 1993, having adopted a "talk-radio" format, WIBC ranked third in the city's Arbitron ratings with a 10.4 share of the available audience. Although lower than its first place ranking in 1987, this showing was still the highest among area AM stations.

CONNIE J. ZEIGLER

WICR (88.7 FM). An operation of the UNIVERSITY OF INDIANAPOLIS (formerly Indiana Central University), WICR began broadcasting in August, 1962, featuring a variety of musical and educational programs. It initially served a limited audience within a ten-mile radius of the station. During the late 1970s, however, LILLY ENDOWMENT granted $175,000 to upgrade WICR's broadcasting facilities. The station also received

permission from the Federal Communications Commission to boost its power from 10 watts to 2,500 watts and to increase its broadcast tower height, which allowed the use of a 1,000–foot tower owned by WRTV (Channel 6) at 79th Street and Township Line Road. The new facilities expanded WICR's stereo broadcast range from Kokomo to Columbus and from New Castle to Greencastle. Shortly thereafter, the station increased its broadcast day to 24 hours.

Gene Sease, president of the university at the time, and Norbert Neuss, president of the FINE ARTS SOCIETY OF INDIANAPOLIS, led the effort to upgrade WICR's facilities and broadcast power. The improved facilities led to an alliance of interest between the university and the Fine Arts Society; the university is responsible for jazz, news, and public affairs programming, and the Fine Arts Society for all of the classical music programming. In addition, the station acts as a laboratory training facility for students in a Department of Communications practicum. The noncommercial station also presents adult contemporary and big band music and University of Indianapolis sports.

CHRISTY MCKAY

WIFE (1310 AM; 107.9 FM). Former WISH AM-FM, purchased by Omaha radio owner Don Burden's Star Stations in 1963. WIFE changed Indianapolis radio with big-money contests, air personalities known as "WIFE Good Guys," and a rock format aimed at younger listeners. However, the station may be best remembered for its battles with the Federal Communications Commission. The FCC charged WIFE with manipulating ratings, running fraudulent contests, creating false billing, slanting newscasts, and giving free advertising to the campaign of then U.S. Senator Vance Hartke. The station never was granted a full three-year license and, in an unprecedented move, the FCC stripped Burden of all his licenses in 1975. The commission gave the WIFE-AM license to a local group led by Jerry Kunkel; WIFE-FM was ordered off the air the next year.

The AM's new owners struggled as more of WIFE's traditional audience moved to the FM dial. In 1981 the station was sold to Communicom, a group which tried an all news format. Two years later a Denver-based company, Chagrin Valley, took over. That company adopted the "Music of Your Life" nostalgia format and replaced the WIFE call letters with WMLF (later changed to WTUX). In 1984 the station became part of the group which owned WTLC-FM; owners in 1992 dropped the nostalgia format in favor of a format aimed at older African-American listeners, and the station became WTLC-AM.

On the FM side, eight groups applied for the vacant WIFE-FM license, but it was 1984 before the FCC ruled in favor of a group headed by local businessman Dan Cantor. The new station, WTPI, went on the air in October of that year.

MICHAEL SPILLMAN

WIRE (1430 AM). Founded by radio pioneers Carl and NOBLE B. WATSON, WKBF began broadcasting on November 29, 1926, from a Ford automobile showroom on East Washington Street and moved in December to its own studio at the Hoosier Athletic Club, 902 North Meridian Street. WKBF's typical daily program schedule in 1927 included a recipe exchange, market, weather, and farm bulletins, and various music programs, as well as the state basketball tourney finals. To counter WFBM's competition, WKBF joined with the *Indianapolis News* in May, 1927, to broadcast the INDIANAPOLIS 500–MILE RACE. Later in July, WKBF broadcast the Jack Dempsey–Jack Sharkey fight from New York's Yankee Stadium. Since the station was not equipped for live coverage, it presented the fight through re-created wire reports. In September, however, WKBF and WFBM broadcast the Dempsey–Gene Tunney fight live from Chicago, the first network broadcast in the city. The next year, WKBF joined with WFBM in an unsuccessful fund-raising campaign to eliminate static from the airwaves.

Curtis Broadcasting Company, incorporated by Curtis Mushlitz and Henry B. Walker of Evansville and Noble Watson, purchased WKBF in 1929 and incorporated it as Indianapolis Broadcasting Company with D. E. "Plug" Kendrick as general manager. The station became an NBC Radio affiliate in 1933. WKBF aired the popular "The Nation's Family Prayer Period" produced by CADLE TABERNACLE (1931–1935), and other programs like "Fibber McGee and Molly" and "Bachelor's Children." In September, 1934, WKBF broadcast nationwide a program of music and news from the American Central Life Insurance Company auditorium, which was transmitted by shortwave to Rear Admiral Richard Byrd at his Little America post in Antarctica. To avoid confusion with WFBM, the Federal Communications Commission changed the station's call letters to WIRE in November, 1935. The FCC also approved in December, 1936, the sale of WIRE to Central Newspapers, Inc., whose president EUGENE C. PULLIAM relocated the station in 1940 to new studios on the top floor of the CLAYPOOL HOTEL. WIRE, which broadcast over 60 programs daily, received a new frequency assignment (1430 AM) from the FCC in 1941. Eight years later, the station moved to the Star-News Building where it joined forces with the local papers on newsgathering and reporting.

Pulliam's ownership led to an expanded community role for the station. During the 1937 Ohio River flood WIRE and WFBM broadcast news, emergency bulletins from relief agencies, and personal messages, and led local appeals for supplies and money. In the 1940s WIRE was the first station to use a pack transmitter, a portable remote unit that allowed announcers to broadcast within a 1.5 mile radius of the studio. It also presented public service programs such as "Welfare Column of the Air" and "Inside the Indiana State Capitol." Pulliam sold WIRE to Joseph C. Amaturo in July, 1960, who sold the station in 1964 to newspaper publishers Len and Burrell Small of Kankakee, Illinois.

During the 1970s, WIRE received numerous awards. *Billboard Magazine* named WIRE, among seven others, as Station of the Year. The International Radio Programming Forum named it Country Music Station of the Year for 1968, 1970, 1972, 1974, and 1975.

The station, which underwent several format and call letter changes in the late 1980s and became WCKN in 1992, maintains its studios at 4560 Knollton Road.

CHRISTY MCKAY

Burk Friedersdorf, *From Crystal to Color: WFBM* (Indianapolis, 1964).

WISH (1310 AM; 107.9 FM).

In June, 1940, C. BRUCE MCCONNELL founded the Capitol Broadcasting Corporation to establish a new radio station in Indianapolis. The company secured its license in November, which authorized operations at 1310 kilocycles with a power of 5,000 watts daytime and 1,000 watts at night. The station erected two 470–foot towers on a 40–acre site at Post Road and Rawls Avenue, and maintained offices and studios in the Board of Trade Building at Meridian and Ohio streets. WISH-AM began broadcasting at 6:30 P.M. on August 2, 1941, as an affiliate of the NBC "Blue" network, which became the ABC network in 1945. It remained an ABC affiliate until shortly after WISH-TV first aired in 1954, at which time both stations switched affiliations to CBS.

Late in 1947 FRANK E. MCKINNEY, SR., local banker and political leader, created the Universal Broadcasting Corporation and purchased WISH-AM for $554,000. Shortly thereafter in 1948 McConnell regained control of the station by becoming a majority stockholder in Universal. In anticipation of a television license, WISH-AM moved in February, 1950, to larger quarters at 1440 North Meridian Street (the 1994 location of WXIN). Personalities who attended the facility's dedication included Casey Stengel and Joe DiMaggio of the New York Yankees, Al Lopez of the Indianapolis Indians, and Wayne Coy, then chairman of the Federal Communications Commission.

In July, 1956, J. H. "Jock" Whitney of the New York banking house of J. H. Whitney and Company purchased WISH-TV, WISH-AM, WIN-TV in Waterloo, Indiana, and WANE-AM in Fort Wayne for $10 million and assigned the stations to the Corinthian Broadcasting Corporation, a subsidiary of the Whitney firm. Corinthian subsequently put WISH-FM on the air in 1961, which began stereophonic broadcasting on January 15, 1962. The WISH radio and television stations continued operating from the North Meridian Street studios until 1963 when Corinthian sold its radio stations; Star Stations of Indiana, Inc., acquired WISH-AM-FM and changed

the call letters to WIFE-AM-FM to distinguish them from the television station.

DAVID L. SMITH
Ball State University

WISH-TV (Channel 8).

The Universal Broadcasting Company, owner of WISH radio and led by president C. BRUCE MCCONNELL, put Indianapolis' second television station on the air at 5:56 P.M. on July 1, 1954. Shareholders in the venture included FRANK E. MCKINNEY, SR., FRANK MCHALE, LUKE WALTON, P. R. MALLORY AND COMPANY, and Robert B. McConnell, son of the company's president.

Operating out of the expanded WISH radio studios at 1440 North Meridian Street, WISH-TV began broadcasting at a maximum power of 316,000 watts, transmitting from a new 1,000–foot television tower at Post Road and Rawls Avenue. Channel 8 was initially affiliated with the American Broadcasting Company (ABC) because of WISH radio's network affiliation. Since WFBM-TV (now WRTV) was the only other television station in the city, WISH began carrying programs from the CBS, NBC, and Dumont networks. By the end of its first year of operation, however, WISH became an exclusive affiliate of CBS.

At the 1956 National Association of Broadcasters convention in Chicago, C. Bruce McConnell saw a demonstration of the first working model of a videotape recorder produced by Ampex. He ordered one off the floor and had it in-

Luke Walton, seen here ca. 1954, hosted WISH-TV sports. [Indiana State Museum]

stalled in the WISH studios by 1958. It was reputed to be the first videotape machine in the state and one of the first in the nation. The new technology quickly made WISH a leader in local broadcasting.

Also in 1956 Corinthian Broadcasting Corporation, a subsidiary of the New York banking house of J. H. Whitney and Company, paid $10 million for WISH-AM-TV, WIN-TV–Channel 15 in Waterloo, Indiana, and WANE radio in Fort Wayne. Corinthian sold its radio stations in 1963 to concentrate on the developing television industry. WISH-AM and its recently begun FM station were sold to Star Stations of Indiana, Inc. Shortly thereafter the stations became WIFE-AM-FM.

As television grew WISH-TV required more space. The station moved to new offices and studios at 1950 North Meridian Street in May, 1965. Designed by architects Ralph Anderson of Houston and Robert T. Reid of Indianapolis, the building, a two-story glass veneer box inside a formal white sculptured colonnade, was modeled after the then recently completed Lincoln Center in New York City.

In 1971 the firm of Dun and Bradstreet purchased WISH-TV along with four other Corinthian television stations in Houston, Sacramento, Tulsa, and Fort Wayne. They later sold those stations in 1984 with WISH-TV and WANE-TV going to LIN Broadcasting Corporation.

WISH-TV has won numerous broadcasting awards, including a CASPER award for its coverage of the blizzard of 1978. Two former Channel 8 reporters also have attained national reputations—John Stehr, a correspondent for CBS, and Jane Pauley, former co-anchor of NBC's *Today* show. As of 1994 WISH-TV news anchor Mike Ahern had been reporting local news for 27 years, second only to the 35 years of news reporting by WRTV's Howard Caldwell.

DAVID L. SMITH
Ball State University

Indianapolis Times, July 4, 1954; Burk Friedersdorf, *From Crystal to Color: WFBM* (Indianapolis, 1964).

WKBF. See WIRE

WKLR (93.1 FM). Originally WNAP-FM; since 1988, WKLR-FM. WNAP started the movement of young listeners to the FM dial when it went on the air in July, 1968. Indianapolis-based Fairbanks Broadcasting owned WNAP along with WIBC, and WNAP originally was designed to protect WIBC by taking listeners from the then-dominant AM station in the market, WIFE. WNAP offered an alternative to traditional Top–40 stations by playing a wide variety of rock music almost never heard on AM radio. The station's young air staff came from the Indiana University campus radio station in Bloomington. WNAP was particularly popular with college-age students, and one of its first promotional items was a black and white poster featuring a peace sign. The station became particularly visible in the 1970s, sponsoring an annual raft race on the White River north of BROAD RIPPLE, and adopting the nickname "The Buzzard." Each hour the station would identify itself as "The Wrath of the Buzzard—WNAP, Indianapolis."

With increased competition for young adult listeners on the FM dial in the early 1980s, the station declined in the ratings. In 1985 the WNAP call letters were replaced by WEAG, and a station moniker of "The Eagle." The contemporary hits format accompanying the change was not successful, though, and another change came in 1988 when the station adopted an oldies format and the new call letters WKLR. The station has been owned by Sconnix Broadcasting since 1987.

MICHAEL SPILLMAN

WLK. First radio station. On December 31, 1921, local engineer FRANCIS F. HAMILTON's radio station, 9ZJ, signed on with an address from Mayor SAMUEL (LEW) SHANK. Broadcasting from Hamilton's garage at 2011 North Alabama Street, Shank made the city's first radio blooper: "Hamilton, do you mean to tell me that people can actually hear me over that damn' dingus?" In 1922 Hamilton joined forces with the *INDIANAPOLIS NEWS* and moved his broadcasting equipment to the 10th floor of the *News* building. The first program after the merger featured zither solos by J. Fremont Frey.

When in 1922 the U.S. Department of Commerce assigned all stations east of the Mississippi River call letters beginning with "W," Hamilton's 9ZJ became WLK. After a second radio station, WOH, began, WLK broadcast on Tuesday, Thursday, and Sunday evenings; WOH transmitted on Monday, Wednesday, and Saturday evenings. The stations shared air time to decrease expenses and the difficulty of finding local entertainers and topics—the staple of their programming.

In April, 1922, L. S. AYRES AND COMPANY joined Hamilton and the *News* as one of the station's co-owners. Financial difficulties forced WLK off the air in March, 1923.

CONNIE J. ZEIGLER

_____

Burk Friedersdorf, *From Crystal to Color: WFBM* (Indianapolis, 1964).

WNDE (1260 AM). Indianapolis' first commercially successful radio station. On November 4, 1924, Clem Portman, John Tribby, Hobart Ashlock, and Frank Sharp introduced WFBM radio to Indianapolis listeners. The first broadcast featured returns of that year's presidential election.

Owned by Merchants Heat and Light Company (all but Sharp were Merchants employees), the station's programming was primarily local in nature during its first years on the air. State basketball tourneys proved to be an early favorite for listeners. Other early programs included the "Christian Men's Builders Hour," hosted by Merle Sidener from the Third Christian Church; "Wheeler Rescue Mission," an hour-long broadcast of inspirational messages and hymns; and live remotes from such venues as the INDIANA STATE FAIR.

In 1928 WFBM joined Columbia Broadcasting System (CBS), becoming the first network-affiliated station in the city. This affiliation greatly increased program choices, but local broadcasts remained popular as well. In the 1930s local programming included Hoagy Carmichael's orchestra live from the COLUMBIA CLUB and Herron Art Institute director WILBUR D. PEAT's series of lectures on art. By the 1940s, through their CBS affiliation, the station brought Edward R. Murrow, Kate Smith, and Burns and Allen into Indianapolis homes.

WFBM became the only local station to send a correspondent to the war front in 1944 when newsman GILBERT FORBES, one of World War II's six accredited, non-network correspondents, interviewed Hoosier soldiers at Omaha Beach on D-Day and elsewhere in the European theater, broadcasting his reports back to Indiana over WFBM. Following the war, in 1947 over 1 million listeners in Indianapolis and the surrounding area tuned in to "The Best of the 48," a series of dramatizations of Indiana history.

In 1949 the station's owners created the city's first television station, WFBM-TV (now WRTV). Time, Inc. purchased WFBM AM-TV in 1956–1957, and, in 1959, added an FM sister station WFBM-FM (now WFBQ). Within a few years these two additions would eclipse the original AM station in ratings. In step with national trends, Indianapolis radio listeners shifted their attention to television and FM stations in the late 1960s and 1970s. Along with AM stations nationwide, WFBM-AM lost much of its audience during this period.

Following an ownership change in 1978, WFBM-AM became WNDE; its FM sister station became WFBQ. In an attempt to fit a niche which FM radio did not cover, the station shifted to an "Oldies and Fun" format in 1982 and began broadcasting in AM stereo in 1983. However, low advertising revenue brought another change in 1989 when the station began an all-news, talk, and sports format. By 1991 WNDE, with men aged 25 to 54 as its target audience, ranked 10th in ratings among Indianapolis-area radio stations. That year Great American Broadcasting sold WNDE and WFBQ to Cincinnati, Ohio–based Broadcast Alchemy, L.P.

In 1992 the new owners contracted with the INDIANAPOLIS COLTS organization for exclusive rights to broadcast Colts football games. WNDE also broadcast the INDIANA PACERS (professional basketball) and the Indianapolis Ice (professional hockey) games in a revised sports-and-talk format that kept it popular among Indianapolis-area radio stations. In 1993 WNDE-AM and WFBQ-FM operated at 6161 Fall Creek Road.

CONNIE J. ZEIGLER

Burk Friedersdorf, *From Crystal to Color: WFBM* (Indianapolis, 1964).

WOH. NOBLE B. WATSON began WOH—Indianapolis' second radio station—on March 29, 1922. Sponsored by the Hatfield Electronics Company, local dealers in radios and radio components, WOH shared air time with the city's other station, WLK. Shortly after WOH's opening, the station moved its studio to the Hoosier Athletic Club at 920 North Meridian Street (now the Turnverein Apartments) and the *Indianapolis Star* became an additional sponsor. WOH was the first station to broadcast the INDIANAPOLIS 500-MILE RACE, using only one microphone and one announcer. In 1923, WOH and WLK both went off the air due to financial difficulties.

CHRISTY MCKAY

WRTV (Channel 6). Consolidated Television and Radio Broadcasters, Inc., parent of WFBM radio and headed by Harry M. Bitner, Sr., of Pittsburgh, received approval from the Federal Communications Commission (FCC) in early 1948 to establish Indianapolis' first commercial television station. By March, 1949, the company was promoting the advent of the new medium and encouraging the purchase of television receivers through demonstrations at the INDIANA STATE FAIRGROUNDS.

Transmitting from a 228-foot tower atop the MERCHANTS NATIONAL BANK BUILDING, WFBM-TV first aired at 10 A.M. on May 30, 1949, with "Crucible of Speed," a half-hour history of the Indianapolis Motor Speedway. This was followed by a live broadcast of the INDIANAPOLIS 500-MILE RACE. Regular programming began later that evening with "TeleNews," a newsreel compiled by the International News Service, cartoons, "People's Platform" and "Kobb's Korner," and an hour-long CBS variety show, "54th Street Revue."

As the city's premier television station WFBM could claim "firsts" in nearly every local endeavor. During the summer of 1949 WFBM telecast several Indianapolis Indians' baseball games from Victory Field (now BUSH STADIUM). In mid-1950 it hired BILL CRAWFORD as the city's first TV weather-

man. WFBM also broadcast a series of ten Indianapolis Symphony Orchestra concerts beginning in December, 1951. WFBM teamed with WTTV to televise the first coast-to-coast sporting event from Indianapolis on May 28, 1952—a welterweight boxing match pairing Kid Gavilan and Fitzie Pruden at the Fairgrounds Coliseum. That same year WFBM joined with *Life* magazine to broadcast "*Life* Goes to School," a series of reports on Marion County schools. The fall of 1952 brought early efforts at religious broadcasting and the city's first televised election coverage, headed by GILBERT FORBES.

The station, which soon built a new facility at 1330 North Meridian Street, obtained permission in 1953 to erect a new tower and transmitter on the city's far north side, enabling it to broadcast at the maximum power allowed by the FCC. WFBM aired programs that originated from the national networks, were filmed off the television screen, and flown to Indianapolis from New York. The completion of a series of microwave relay towers in the mid-1950s allowed the station to receive direct network broadcasts.

WFBM began its network affiliation in 1950 with the Columbia Broadcasting System (CBS). When WISH-TV Channel 8 dropped its American Broadcasting Company (ABC) affiliation in September, 1954, and switched to CBS, WFBM signed an agreement with the National Broadcasting Company (NBC), a relationship that continued until 1979.

By 1956 Bitner had agreed to sell the WFBM radio and television stations to Crowell-Collier Publishing Company in a $16 million package that would include stations in Minneapolis, Minnesota, and Grand Rapids and Flint, Michigan. After Crowell-Collier withdrew its offer, Bitner began negotiations with Time, Inc. (later Time-Life, Inc.), and concluded a $15.75 million sale in 1957.

WFBM expanded its broadcasting capabilities throughout the 1960s and began color programming in 1967. Its documentary, "The Negro in Indianapolis," broadcast in the fall of 1969, earned the coveted Peabody Award in 1970. McGraw-Hill acquired WFBM in 1972 and changed the call letters to WRTV since FCC regulations prohibited cross-ownership of cable and broadcast television stations in the same market. The sale was part of a $57 million package, which included unprecedented programming, employment, and training for minorities. Viewing ABC's "total commitment to news" as "tremendously important," WRTV severed its ties with NBC in 1979 to become an ABC affiliate.

WRTV won a local CASPER Award for public service in 1989 for its documentary on police and community relations. The station has also produced the award-winning program "At the Zoo," in conjunction with the INDIANAPOLIS ZOO. In 1993 WRTV began a one-half hour newscast at 10 P.M. on WTTV Channel 4 after that station eliminated its own news department. 1994 saw the retirement of news anchor Howard Caldwell. During his 35 years at the station news programming expanded from a 10–minute early evening segment to a 90–minute evening newscast and other news broadcasts throughout the day.

STEPHEN J. FLETCHER
Indiana Historical Society

Burk Friedersdorf, *From Crystal to Color: WFBM* (Indianapolis, 1964).

WTHR (Channel 13). The fourth and last full power VHF television station in Indianapolis, WLW-I Channel 13 first aired on October 30, 1957, emerging from years of licensing battles. The station's owner was Crosley Broadcasting of Cincinnati, which operated WLW radio in Cincinnati and television stations in Cincinnati, Dayton, and Columbus, Ohio, and Atlanta, Georgia. Following the initial license application by WIRE radio (owned at the time by *Indianapolis Star* and *Indianapolis News* publisher EUGENE C. PULLIAM), three other groups vied for the station, including Crosley, WIBC radio (operated by Richard Fairbanks, former owner of the *News*), and Mid-West TV, Inc., a group led by Union Federal Savings president George Sadlier. The Federal Communications Commission (FCC) first awarded the license to the Mid-West group in 1955. Following an appeal by the losing parties, the FCC voted in March, 1957, to issue the license to Crosley instead. The reversal caused controversy since the last local station belonged to a Cincinnati company and since the decision had been leaked during a congressional hearing.

WIBC sued the FCC, but in the interim Crosley put WLW-I on the air. Studios were located in the Wulsin Building at 222 East Ohio Street and offices in the Merchants National Bank Building, but were merged in 1958 in a new facility at 1401 North Meridian Street (the 1994 location of WFYI). That same year the District of Columbia Court of Appeals overturned the FCC decision and ordered a rehearing, although it allowed Crosley to continue broadcasting pending a new decision. In late 1961 the FCC awarded the license to WIBC, concluding that local owners could better serve the local community, and ordered Crosley to shut down its Channel 13 operations. Crosley and WIBC concluded an FCC-approved deal in 1962 which allowed Crosley to keep Channel 13 and Fairbanks-owned WIBC and Fairbanks to acquire Crosley's Atlanta station.

WLW-I Channel 13 was an ABC affiliate, but also carried many of the programs produced by Crosley's stations, including "Ruth Lyons 50–50 Club," "Midwestern Hayride," and Cincinnati Reds baseball. The station also produced its own broadcasts of Butler and Indiana universities' basketball games, and was the first television home of the INDIANA PACERS.

A 1974 study by AVCO, parent company of Crosley, described its Indianapolis station as a "third-rate, lackluster station lacking in a variety of the most fundamental professional credentials." The next year Crosley sold the station to the Wolfe family of Columbus, Ohio, operators of WBNS-AM-FM-TV there. The new owners, incorporated as VideoIndiana, Inc., changed the call letters to WTHR, improved facilities, and made programming changes. Station manager Chris Duffy launched a major promotional campaign, much of it centered around the station's NewsCenter and news anchor Paul Udell, who would do extensive reporting from the field.

In 1979 Channel 13 and Channel 6 switched network affiliations. WTHR joined NBC after ABC moved its affiliation to WRTV. At the signoff on Channel 13's last night with ABC, the station showed a loving cup, awarded by ABC to mark an anniversary of Channel 13's affiliation, being shot by an off-camera rifle.

WTHR moved to new studios and offices at the northwest corner of West 10th and North Meridian streets in 1982. The station received a national Emmy award in 1982 for Tom Cochrun's documentary on the KU KLUX KLAN, and has won numerous other national media awards over the years.

In 1994 WTHR began operating a low power television station, Channel 27, featuring news and public affairs programs.

STEPHEN J. FLETCHER
Indiana Historical Society
MICHAEL SPILLMAN

WTLC (105.7 FM; 1310 AM). Indianapolis' only African-American owned and operated radio station. WTLC made its FM debut in January, 1968, when a biracial group of Marion County Democrats organized the Indianapolis Radio Corporation and took over the FCC license of financially plagued WAIV. WTLC became the first Indianapolis station to provide 24–hour radio programming for African-Americans. It captured a sizable following initially, but the stockholders soon split over the station's management style and level of community service. A group led by Dr. Frank Lloyd formed Community Media in 1973 and bought out the former partners, making WTLC a predominately black-owned station.

During the 1970s WTLC continued to provide a wide range of "black music," including soul, rhythm and blues, gospel, and jazz, but made significant changes in other areas. The station expanded its news staff, instituted full-service news coverage, and began programs such as "Tell It Like It Is" and "Morning with the Mayor" to raise community awareness. The station also sponsored a variety of community service projects.

Broadcast Enterprises National, Inc., a Philadelphia-based African-American radio chain, bought WTLC in 1981 and made few changes in the following decade. By the 1980s the station consistently ranked fourth among local radio stations due to its ability to reach 90 percent of the African-American listening audience. Since 1987 WTLC has been owned by Panache Broadcasting of Philadelphia.

Economics forced WTLC out of the full-service news business in 1992, although the station maintained its strong community service programming. WTLC added sister station 1310 AM in August, 1992, to meet the listening preferences of older African-Americans. As of 1993 WTLC had won more national, state, and local awards for its investigative news and community service programming than any other African-American-owned station in the nation and was ranked seventh overall among local radio stations.

MICHELLE D. HALE

WTTV (Channel 4). SARKES TARZIAN, a former engineer at RCA in Bloomington, Indiana, who started his own company manufacturing television tuners and other electronic components, put WTTV on the air November 11, 1949. WTTV occupied channel 10, which was originally assigned to Indianapolis. Tarzian asked that it be moved to Bloomington since his home and business were there. The FCC granted his request and WTTV went on the air with a transmitter and studio camera made by Tarzian engineers. The

Sarkes Tarzian, ca. 1960, founder of WTTV.
[Indiana State Museum]

first transmitter was 1,000 watts and the tower, located at the studio building (a former drug store), was 275 feet high.

On February 21, 1954, a new tower was put into use in Cloverdale in the hope the station could cover both Terre Haute and Indianapolis. On that same date, WTTV switched from channel 10 to channel 4. In 1957, Tarzian petitioned the FCC to move his tower to its current location at Trafalgar to concentrate on the Indianapolis audience.

At its beginning, WTTV gave Bloomington the distinction of being the smallest city in the world to have a television station. After carrying programs from all networks, WTTV became an independent when WTHR (Channel 13) went on the air in Indianapolis in 1957 as an ABC affiliate.

Tarzian, who initially considered his station as more of an experiment than a commercial operation, sold the station to Teleco in September, 1978. It was sold again in March, 1984, to Tel-Am, which was headed by then general manager Elmer Snow. During Tel-Am's ownership, channel 29 in Kokomo was purchased in an attempt to give WTTV improved coverage in northern Indianapolis and Hamilton County. Heavy debt forced WTTV into bankruptcy in the late 1980s. After a deal with locally-based Emmis Broadcasting fell through, the stations were sold to Capitol Broadcasting in July, 1988, and again in October, 1991, to River City Broadcasting.

WTTV telecasts syndicated programs, reruns, movies, and a variety of Indiana college and high school athletic events.

DAVID L. SMITH
Ball State University

Wilbur James Richter, "The History and Development of Television Station WTTV" (M.A. thesis, Indiana University, 1957).

WXIN (Channel 59). WXIN began broadcasting as WPDS on February 1, 1984, four years after Melvin and Fred Simon and Gerald Kraft, then vice-president of MELVIN SIMON AND ASSOCIATES, applied as Indianapolis Television, Incorporated, for the license for the city's last full-power commercial television station. The company planned to broadcast, in part, programming of local interest, such as INDIANAPOLIS SYMPHONY ORCHESTRA and INDIANA REPERTORY THEATRE performances and sporting events not likely to draw national corporate advertising. It also planned to provide subscription television, requiring viewers to purchase decoder boxes to receive a scrambled signal.

The Federal Communications Commission granted the license in mid–1983, but shortly thereafter the Simons organized a new ownership team with ANACOMP Corporation as the majority shareholder while maintaining a minority interest themselves. Under the name USA Communications, Inc., the station's call letters, WPDS, represented the last names of its principal owners: RONALD D. PALAMARA, president of Anacomp; Christopher Duffy; and Melvin Simon. The station operated from the Riddick Building at 1440 North Meridian Street in studios previously used by WISH-TV.

Although USA Communications' first priority was television broadcasting, it intended to engage in commercial production and equipped its renovated studios with state-of-the-art engineering and production facilities. The company's goal was to become a communications company, using its television station as "leverage" for Anacomp expertise in computer services operations, telecommunications, satellite transmission, graphics, and teletext and videotext. The station initially wanted to use teletext as a way of listing daily programming and Dow Jones reports on the television screen, and later providing interactive videotext to offer home shopping and banking by subscription, presumably calling upon the retail know-how of the Simons.

By the time WPDS debuted, however, CABLE TELEVISION had made significant headway in the city, forcing the station to cancel its plans for subscription television. The station heralded its "59 Headline News," featuring "hard-rock, nonpersonality" news, and local programming such as "Al Hobb's Love Express," a gospel music show simulcast on radio station WTLC, "Video Crackers" featuring local comedians, and original dramas by the Broad Ripple Playhouse. WPDS eventually pared its local programming from 15 to 3 hours a week and discontinued its hour-long daily news program, replacing it with periodic 90–second reports.

After less than nine months of ownership the company accepted an unsolicited bid of $22 million from Outlet Communications of Providence, Rhode Island, a subsidiary of the Rockefeller Group of New York. The price tag was reportedly the most money ever paid for a television station in its first year of broadcasting. In July, 1985, Outlet changed the station's call letters to WXIN because viewers reportedly confused its call letters with those of PBS (Public Broadcasting System) and WTBS (Ted Turner's cable "superstation"). Also in July, WXIN became the first commercial television station locally to broadcast in stereo.

In June, 1986, WXIN became a Fox Network affiliate. Indianapolis-based EMMIS BROADCASTING CORPORATION, a radio broadcasting company owned by Jeff Smulyan, agreed to purchase the station from Outlet in May, 1988, but Outlet rescinded the agreement after concluding the $17.5 million purchase price was insufficient. Outlet later sold the station to Chase Communications of Hartford, Connecticut, in August, 1989. The current owner, Renaissance Communications of Greenwich, Connecticut, agreed to purchase the station in September, 1992, but the owner of Bloomington station WIIB petitioned against the acquisition, delaying the official purchase until March, 1993.

STEPHEN J. FLETCHER
Indiana Historical Society

WXLW (950 AM). On August 18, 1948, Radio Indianapolis Inc., led by Conrad Ruckelshaus and Frederic M. Ayres, Jr., put WXLW on the air, occupying 1590 AM during daylight hours. The station, headquartered at 30th Street and Kessler Boulevard, broadcast music, news, sports events, and important public interest features. Well-known announcers of the time included Mike "Sports Page" Dunn and Bob Bruner, who handled the music shows. WXLW reputedly was the first local station to broadcast remote from "news cars" around the city.

WXLW completed a new 5,000–watt transmitter at 56th Street and Guion Road in January, 1955, and shifted from 1590 AM to 950 AM. The inaugural program at its new frequency, held on March 12, 1955, featured Indiana Senators Homer E. Capehart and William E. Jenner, and Indianapolis Mayor ALEX M. CLARK. In December, 1962, Greater Indianapolis Broadcasting, headed by long-time WXLW manager and partial owner Robert D. Enoch, purchased the station from Radio Indianapolis for $675,000. He later sold the station to Grewe Enterprises of Wheeling, West Virginia, in September, 1970.

Local broadcaster Bill Shirk, who served as manager of WXLW, bought the station in 1974. After continuing traditional AM programming and adding the Mutual Radio Network in 1979, Shirk adopted a religious format, though he included special blues, gospel, and big band programs and a home shopping feature. The station moved in October, 1991, to its present location at 6264 LaPas Trail, where Shirk also broadcasts contemporary urban music on WHHH (96.3 FM) and low power television station WAV-TV Channel 53.

CHRISTY MCKAY

Walker, Madam C. J. (Dec. 23, 1867–May 25, 1919). African-American entrepreneur, philanthropist, and political activist. Born Sarah Breedlove to ex-slaves on a Delta, Louisiana, cotton plantation, she was orphaned by age seven. At 14 she married Moses McWilliams, who died in 1887 when she was 20. That year she and her two-year-old daughter, A'Lelia, moved from Vicksburg, Mississippi, to St. Louis where she worked as a laundress for the next 18 years. In 1905, with $1.50 in savings, she moved to Denver to start her own business after developing a hair care product for African-American women.

Madam C. J. Walker, one of America's first African-American woman millionaires.
[Indiana Historical Society, Madam C. J. Walker Collection, #2140]

In January, 1906, she married Charles Joseph Walker, a newspaper sales agent, who helped design her early advertisements and mail order operation. Following a custom affected by some businesswomen of the era, she adopted her husband's name and added the title "Madam."

While Walker is often credited with popularizing the metal "hot comb"—once widely used by black women to straighten their hair—she stressed grooming, conditioning, and scalp treatments in her Walker System. She advertised extensively in the black press and held annual conventions to promote her products and outdistance her competitors. Her entrepreneurial strategies and organizational skills revolutionized what became a multi–billion dollar ethnic hair care and cosmetics industry by the last decade of the 20th century.

From 1906 to 1918 Walker traveled throughout the United States, Central America, and the West Indies promoting her business. She settled briefly in Pittsburgh, then moved the company to Indianapolis in 1910, building a factory and vastly increasing her annual sales.

With the endorsement and encouragement of INDIANAPOLIS FREEMAN publisher GEORGE L. KNOX, she quickly became a leader of the city's black business community. Her national reputation as a philanthropist was solidified in 1911 when she contributed $1,000 to the building fund of the SENATE AVENUE YMCA. In 1916, she joined her daughter in Harlem, leaving the day-to-day management of her manufacturing operation in Indianapolis to attorney and general manager FREEMAN B. RANSOM, attorney ROBERT L. BROKENBURR, and factory forewoman Alice Kelly.

In her business philosophy Walker stressed economic independence for the 20,000 former maids, farm laborers, housewives, and school teachers she employed in her beauty schools, factory, office, and as sales agents. As her wealth and visibility grew, Walker became increasingly outspoken, using her clout to support legislation to make lynching a federal crime and to demand improved treatment and facilities for black officers and enlisted men during World War I.

When she died at age 51 at Villa Lewaro—her Irvington-on-Hudson, New York, estate—she was widely considered the wealthiest black woman in America and reputed to be the first black American woman millionaire. In April, 1992, her accomplishments were recognized by her induction into the Junior Achievement National Business Hall of Fame. Her will directed thousands of dollars to national and local educational, civic, and social institutions, including the ALPHA HOME for the Aged in Indianapolis. The Walker Building and Walker Theatre, planned by her and completed in 1928, are located on INDIANA AVENUE and listed in the National Register of Historic Places.

A'LELIA PERRY BUNDLES

A'Lelia Perry Bundles, *Madam C. J. Walker—Entrepreneur* (New York, 1991); Madam C. J. Walker Collection, Indiana Historical Society.

Walker Group (formerly Walker Research). Indianapolis-based market research holding company. In 1939 Dorothy "Tommie" Walker began doing part-time market research, working at home from her dining room table. That year she completed four studies with total billings of $500. Some of her early studies focused on radio listening habits, vitamins, greeting cards, and vacuum cleaners.

By 1949 the company's first out-of-home office opened in a converted garage on East 62nd Street. After her husband died in 1952, Walker's previously part-time business venture supported herself and two sons. By 1957 Walker had a staff of 60 part-time interviewers who contacted an average of 10,000 people each month. The next year she built the first independent research consumer test center in the country, housing an ultramodern kitchen and testing areas. Incorporated in 1964, the firm became Walker Research, Inc. In 1968 the company opened its first branch office in a St. Louis shopping mall and annual billings topped the $1 million mark.

During the early 1970s the company conducted surveys on coffee, drive-in restaurants, and cereals, doubling its annual billings in just five years. By the next decade Walker had become an industry leader, with corporate revenues topping $16 million in 1983. By 1986 more than 95 percent of the company's business came from outside Indiana.

In 1992 Walker Research changed its name to Walker Group to reflect the company's increasing diversification. As of 1994 the Walker Group serves as a holding company and provider of administrative and financial support services for a group of six companies—Walker Clinical Evaluations, DataSource, CSM Worldwide, Walker CSM, Walker Direct, and Walker Research & Analysis—and employs over 1,000 people nationwide, including about 700 in the Indianapolis area. It was ranked among the top 15 firms in the industry in 1993.

DEBORAH B. MARKISOHN

"The First 50 Years: A History of Walker Research, Inc., 1939–1989" (copy in the files of Walker Group); *Indianapolis Business Journal*, Jan. 21–27, 1991; *Indianapolis Star*, June 2, 1992.

Wallace, Harry R. (Feb. 16, 1869–Sept. 17, 1915). Mayor of Indianapolis, November 28, 1913–January 5, 1914, Republican. The son of Mayor WILLIAM J. WALLACE, 1856–1858, Harry Wallace was a lifelong resident of the city. Out of economic necessity he left school and worked four years as a teamster for the city and private contractors. He joined the police force and won a reputation in the IRISH HILL district as the "fighting patrolman." A member of the department's first bicycle squad, Wallace rose to sergeant and to detective with the support of Democratic Mayor THOMAS TAGGART, an old friend of his father. He resigned in 1903 to become deputy to county recorder SAMUEL LEWIS SHANK. Elected county recorder in 1906, he served from 1907 to 1910.

Wallace's public life reached its apex during the city's crisis of late 1913. Appointed city controller in the Shank administration, Wallace became mayor, as stipulated in the Charter of 1891, when Shank, having failed to mediate a teamster strike successfully, resigned on November 28. The strike of more than 3,000 teamsters, following the police mutiny during a trolley strike a few weeks earlier, raised fears of widespread disorder. Wallace immediately moved the mayor's office to police headquarters, taking direct control of the police, again as permitted under the charter. He banned groups of more than three men from the

streets, swore in 250 special policemen—prominent business and professional men armed with revolvers—and announced he would enforce the law on all classes impartially. While there was some violence, the strike ended a week later and the city returned to normal.

For many years party chairman of the south side's 10th ward, and a two-term Republican county chairman, Wallace was said to be able to call more men in the city by name than anyone else. He had intended to run for mayor at the next election, but suffered a fatal heart attack at age 46.

WILLIAM DOHERTY
Marian College

Indianapolis Star, Nov. 29–Dec. 8, 1913, Sept. 18, 1915; Jacob Piatt Dunn, *Greater Indianapolis* (Chicago, 1910).

Wallace, Lewis (Lew) (Apr. 10, 1827–Feb. 15, 1905). Lawyer, soldier, diplomat, and author of the classic novel *Ben-Hur*. Originally from Brookville, Indiana, Wallace was one of four boys born to David and Esther (Test) Wallace. Wallace's father served in the legislature and as lieutenant governor. In 1837, following his election as Indiana governor, he moved the family to Indianapolis.

As a youth, Wallace was uninterested in school, even briefly running away from home at one point with thoughts of joining the Texas navy during its struggle for independence from Mexico. Thereafter, he worked for the Marion County clerk's office and reported on the legislature for the *INDIANAPOLIS DAILY JOURNAL*. Although he studied for a career as an attorney in his father's Indianapolis law office, Wallace failed to pass the bar examination in 1846. Instead, he volunteered for service in the army during the Mexican War.

Upon his return, Wallace was admitted to the bar in 1849 and opened a law practice in Covington, where he served two terms as prosecuting attorney. He moved to Crawfordsville in 1853, where he was elected to the state Senate in 1856. Also that year he put together a military group called the Montgomery (County) Guards, which became known as Zouaves because of their colorful uniforms, modeled upon a French army unit.

With the outbreak of the Civil War, Wallace was appointed adjutant general by Governor OLIVER P. MORTON and was responsible for organizing the state's quota of regiments for the Union cause. In eventual command of the Eleventh Indiana (Zouave) Regiment, Wallace, before leaving Indianapolis, had his men march to the State House where they swore to avenge the alleged cowardice of Indiana troops at the battle of Buena Vista in the Mexican War.

Wallace rose through the ranks, reaching the position of major general and seeing action at the battles of Fort Donelson, Shiloh, and Monocacy. Wallace's military career was tarnished at Shiloh, where he was heavily and perhaps unfairly criticized by his superiors for his delay in reaching the field on the battle's first day.

After the war, Wallace returned to Crawfordsville and ran an unsuccessful campaign for Congress. In 1878, President Rutherford B. Hayes appointed him governor of the New Mexico Territory. Three years later, President James Garfield appointed Wallace as U.S. minister to Turkey, a post he held until 1885.

Although engaged in government service, Wallace found time to pursue his avocation—writing. He produced such works as *The Fair God* (1873), the bestselling *Ben-Hur* (1880), and *The Prince of India* (1893). Wallace continued to make his home in Crawfordsville, but spent a considerable amount of time in his old hometown of Indianapolis. In 1893, he began constructing Indianapolis' first major apartment building, known as "Blacherne." Completed in 1896, the seven-story structure was located on the northwest corner of Meridian and Vermont streets. Wallace kept an apartment for himself in the building.

RAY BOOMHOWER
Indiana Historical Society

Irving McKee, *"Ben-Hur" Wallace: The Life of General Lew Wallace* (Berkeley and Los Angeles, 1947).

Wallace, William J. (Mar. 16, 1814–Jan. 9, 1894). First Republican mayor of Indianapolis, 1856–1858. He was born in County Donegal, Ireland, and his family immigrated to the United States when he was four years old. As a young man he moved to Madison, Indiana, and served as a deputy sheriff in Jefferson County. He moved to Switzerland County and then to Indianapolis ca. 1848. He operated a grocery at the corner of Washington and Delaware streets. An active Whig, Wallace embraced the Republicans after the breakup of the Whig party.

Wallace became mayor as the result of a special election upon the death of HENRY F. WEST. He won reelection in May, 1857, resigning the office just days before the end of his term to become sheriff of Marion County. He served two terms as sheriff, 1858–1862. During the Civil War he was a draft commissioner and, as a member of the Indianapolis Sanitary Commission, made several trips to visit Indiana soldiers in Tennessee. He was a member of the City Council, 1863–1865, and county clerk, 1870–1874. Wallace lost a great deal of money in the Panic of 1873 and never recovered financially. He died virtually penniless in Indianapolis in 1894 at the onset of another depression.

WILLIAM F. GULDE

Jacob Piatt Dunn, *Greater Indianapolis* (Chicago, 1910); Ignatius Brown, "History of Indianapolis," in *Logan's Indianapolis Directory* (Indianapolis, 1868).

Wallace, Zerelda Gray Sanders (Aug. 6, 1817–Mar. 19, 1901). Temperance and suffrage activist. Born in Millersburg, Kentucky, she was the eldest of five girls. Her father, Dr. John Sanders, moved the family to Indianapolis in 1830 and established a successful medical practice in the capital. At 19, Zerelda married Lieutenant Governor David Wallace, a widower with three children (one of whom was LEW WALLACE, author of *Ben-Hur*). David Wallace became governor (1837–1840), then congressman (1841–1843); the couple had six more children before he died in 1859.

Although she had to take in boarders for a short time after her husband's death, her first public and independent work came with the Woman's Temperance Crusade of 1873 from which evolved the Indiana branch of the WOMEN'S CHRISTIAN TEMPERANCE UNION (WCTU). She addressed the Indiana legislature in 1875, but her memorial en-

Zerelda Wallace.
[Indiana State
Library]

dorsing temperance was ignored despite signatures of 10,000 women. Thus converted to advocacy of women's suffrage, she prepared a suffrage resolution for the WCTU national convention. Although most members were not pro-ballot, they respected Wallace and her resolution passed without debate.

After organizing the Indiana WCTU, Wallace was its president from 1874 until 1877 and again from 1879 to 1883. She helped found the Equal Suffrage Society of Indianapolis (1878) and was its first president. She headed the national WCTU franchise department (1883–1888) and in 1881 lobbied in the state legislature for WOMEN'S RIGHTS AND SUFFRAGE and prohibition. She was described as an "inspirational" speaker who could give impromptu two-hour lectures. Lew Wallace identified her as the model for Ben-Hur's appealing mother.

Wallace died of a bronchial ailment at the Cataract, Owen County, home of daughter Agnes, and was buried in CROWN HILL CEMETERY in Indianapolis.

ANN COLBERT
Indiana University–Purdue University,
Fort Wayne

Ruth Bordin, *Woman and Temperance: The Quest for Power and Liberty, 1873–1900* (New Brunswick, N.J., 1990); Edward T. James et al., eds., *Notable American Women* (Cambridge, Mass., 1974); Mark Edward Lender, *Dictionary of American Temperance Biography* (Westport, Conn., 1984).

Walther Cancer Institute. A cancer research organization. Dr. Joseph E. Walther (b.

1912) and a group of Indianapolis leaders founded the Walther Cancer Institute in 1985. They sold WINONA MEMORIAL HOSPITAL, which Walther founded in 1966, and used the proceeds for an endowment fund to establish the institute. It relies on endowment interest and fund-raising for its annual budget of ca. $3.7 million. Its mission is to eliminate cancer through basic or laboratory research, clinical research, and research designed to improve the care given to patients and family members.

The institute leveraged its assets through collaborative agreements with various statewide medical and educational institutions. INDIANA UNIVERSITY SCHOOL OF MEDICINE is the primary partner. The Walther Oncology Center, located at the INDIANA UNIVERSITY MEDICAL CENTER, is the main site for basic research. The institute also has laboratory research programs at Purdue University and the University of Michigan.

The Hoosier Oncology Group, a statewide organization of oncology physicians and nurses who conduct clinical trials, operates under the umbrella of the institute. The Mary Margaret Walther Program for cancer care research is based at the Indiana Unversity School of Nursing. Affiliated hospitals include COMMUNITY, METHODIST, RILEY HOSPITAL FOR CHILDREN, and Indiana University hospitals in Indianapolis and St. Elizabeth Hospital in Lafayette.

Institute researchers have contributed to a range of significant research, including helping develop a lifesaving technique using umbilical cord blood cells instead of bone marrow transplants and coordinating Indiana's participation in a large-scale study testing a new drug treatment for the prevention of breast cancer.

CAROLYN G. ROBERSON
Walther Cancer Institute

Walton, Luke (Apr. 4, 1907–June 18, 1990). Known as the dean of Hoosier sportscasters in the 1940s and 1950s. Recognized for his rapid-fire delivery, Walton broadcast high school, college, and professional sports including baseball, basketball, football, hockey, swimming, and auto racing.

A graduate of BUTLER UNIVERSITY, Walton got his first job on radio at WBOW in Terre Haute in 1931. Later he served radio station WIRE before joining WISH, both in Indianapolis. He was instrumental in the late 1940s in organizing the INDIANAPOLIS MOTOR SPEEDWAY RADIO NETWORK that survives today, and was a participant in the annual broadcast until 1988.

Walton was the voice of the INDIANAPOLIS INDIANS baseball play-by-play over WISH radio from 1948 to 1955 and then on WIGO in 1963. He left WISH in 1956 to form the Luke Walton Advertising Agency, which he operated until 1983. However, he continued his broadcast involvement, frequently doing commercials. In 1963 he acquired an AM license and put WIGO on the air, selling it six months later to SARKES TARZIAN, owner of WTTV. Walton is in the Broadcast Hall of Fame.

HOWARD CALDWELL
WRTV Channel 6

Wanamaker. Franklin Township community centered at the intersection of Southeastern Avenue and South Post Road. In the 1820s settlers traveled the Michigan Road to the area now known as Wanamaker. Several cabins were already at the site when John Messinger platted a village, New Bethel, in 1834. New Bethel prospered serving travelers and farmers and in 1884 counted about 150 people. Five years later townspeople renamed the village Wanamaker, after President BENJAMIN HARRISON's postmaster general, John Wanamaker. Local debate on the change, however, continued for 50 years, as road signs and residents used both names.

The interurban arrived in 1902 and some residents commuted to Indianapolis to work. Others found employment at the nearby BEECH GROVE railroad shops that opened in 1906. A local street fair begun in 1931 by the New Bethel Baptist Church grew to become the MARION COUNTY FAIR. In 1954 the fair moved to its present location on Troy Avenue north of Wanamaker.

The popularity of commuting by automobile led to the construction of subdivisions such as Wanamaker Village and Wanamaker Estates in the 1950s. Twenty years later population was estimated at 4,500 when Wanamaker became a part of Indianapolis under UNIGOV. Residential development in the 1980s and 1990s has begun to transform the once rural community into a suburb.

CATHLEEN F. DONNELLY

Berry R. Sulgrove, *History of Indianapolis and Marion County* (Philadelphia, 1884); *Indianapolis Star*, June 6, 1984.

War Manpower Commission. Industries producing war material geared up immediately following Pearl Harbor. To meet the demand for labor, the employment services of each state came under federal control. By November, 1942, the Indianapolis area office was organized as the Indianapolis Area War Manpower Commission (WMC) and included Boone, Hamilton, Hancock, Hendricks, Johnson, Marion, Morgan, Putnam, and Shelby counties. By early 1943 the commission had adopted a statement of objectives and recommended community practices and policies. Duties included stabilizing employment, channeling workers into essential industries, curbing absenteeism, overseeing Production Board certification and apprentice training, and supervising utilization and employment ceiling programs.

Originally classified Group III by the WMC, the Indianapolis area was reclassified to Group II, an area expecting a labor shortage within six months, in June, 1943. In response to figures submitted by the Indianapolis branch of the Employment Office reporting a shortage of workers, Indianapolis was reclassified to Group I, an area with a critical worker shortage, on October 1, 1943. A Group I classification meant no new war contracts for the 421 factories in the area producing war material, 167 of which produced war material exclusively. To return to Group II status Indianapolis had to institute a 48–hour work week by November 15, hire additional workers, and reduce absenteeism and job switching. Businesses protested the reclassification and formed the Indianapolis Man Power Emergency Committee to assist in a quick reclassification. By February, 1944, the Indianapolis area had been returned to its Group II status, but was again reclassified as Group I in April, 1945, where it remained until September when the WMC was dissolved.

JOAN CUNNINGHAM

War Memorial. See Indiana World War Memorial Plaza

Ward, Joseph H. (Aug., 1870–Dec. 12, 1956). African-American physician. Born in Wilson, North Carolina, Ward came to Indianapolis as a young man and worked and lived with Dr. George Hasty of the Physiomedical College of Indiana. A 1900 graduate of that institution, Ward set up a practice in the 400 block of INDIANA AVENUE.

Upon America's entry into World War I, Ward quit his practice and enlisted in the army. Sent to Des Moines for training he was promoted from private to first lieutenant. In France, Ward commanded a base hospital, the first African-American to be given such a responsibility. He was discharged from the army with the rank of colonel.

In 1922, Ward was named superintendent of the Tuskegee Veterans Administration Hospital, the first black ever to hold such a post. He remained at the VA hospital in Alabama for 12 years, then returned to Indianapolis and reestablished his medical practice. Ward was one of the founders of the SENATE AVENUE YMCA and served as chairman of its committee of management. He also was vice-president of the board of trustees for the YMCA Metropolitan Board. A 33rd degree Mason and Grand Chancellor of the Knights of Pythias, Ward was also a member of the American Legion and a congregant of BETHEL AFRICAN METHODIST EPISCOPAL CHURCH.

RAY BOOMHOWER
Indiana Historical Society

Warren Park. Eastside town bordered by 16th Street, Shadeland Avenue, 10th Street, and Perry Drive. Warren Park was a small farming community when platted in 1913. When the town was incorporated 15 years later approximately 50 homes, a grocery store, and an appliance store, Sharper and Gardener, were located there. Town life centered on nearby Pleasant Run, which provided recreational activities for children and adults alike.

Warren Park remained small, quiet, and isolated until the 1950s when Indianapolis expanded and new development surrounded the town. Apartment construction by the Justus Company brought many new residents into the area. Between 1950 and 1970 the town's population increased from 336 to 1,887. In the 1990 census Warren Park counted 1,763 residents. Primarily residential, the town has only a few businesses, including retail stores, restaurants, and the Hilltop Tavern, a fixture for over 30 years. Three churches—Warren Park Wesleyan, Friends Church of Irvington, and Gethesemane Lutheran—continue to serve the community.

Under UNIGOV, Warren Park has the status of an INCLUDED TOWN. The elected four-person town council contracts for fire protection from the Warren Township Volunteer Fire Department and employs a street commissioner and a police chief.

CATHLEEN F. DONNELLY

Kimberly K. Caldwell, *The History of the Town of Warren Park* ([Indianapolis]: Warren Central High School, 1980).

Warren Township. Eastern Marion County township. When township boundaries were defined in 1822, commissioners named the area after Dr. Joseph Warren, a Massachusetts patriot in the Revolutionary War. Early settlement began along roads cut through the district, including the National, Brookville, and Michigan roads. Cumberland Hall, a way station for travelers on the NATIONAL ROAD, opened in 1830 and attracted a cluster of homes that became CUMBERLAND, the township's first community.

Farther south, Julietta was platted in 1870 as an agricultural service center on Brookville Road. In the 1880s the hamlet had a population of 50 and boasted stores, a blacksmith's shop, and a post office. Julietta was later known as the site of the Marion County Hospital for the Insane, which opened about 1900. The facility was plagued by

Selected Statistics for Warren Township, 1990

Population	87,989
Population per Square Mile	1,825
Percent African-American	13.2
Percent 0 to 17 Years	25.7
Percent 65 Years and Over	13.3
Percent 25 Years and Over with a High School Degree or Equivalency	77.6
Percent 25 Years and Over with a College Degree	14.9
Per Capita Income in 1989	$13,224
Unemployment Rate (%)	4.6
Married-Couple Families as a Percent of Total Households	52.3
Median Home Value	$57,300

mismanagement, neglect, and a shortage of funds. When patients were transferred to Central State Hospital in 1938, the buildings housed inmates from the county poor asylum. Today, the MARION COUNTY HEALTHCARE CENTER occupies the site.

About five miles from the Circle, IRVINGTON was laid out in 1870 as a suburban refuge for wealthy families. An attractive curvilinear street plan, spacious homes, and a thriving cultural community made Irvington a unique neighborhood. WARREN PARK was platted in 1913 as an agricultural settlement between 10th and 16th streets. Although now intensively developed with homes and apartments, Warren Park remains a quiet residential community.

Township settlements benefited from three rail lines that were constructed in the area between 1847 and 1855. Interurbans operated in the township from the early 1900s to the 1930s, but it was the automobile that made most of Warren Township easily accessible to downtown. In the 1960s and 1970s construction of I–465, I–70, and I–74 spurred additional development.

Population figures for Warren Township indicate slow growth in the 19th and early 20th centuries, but post–World War II developments brought sudden change. In 1900 the township counted about 4,000 residents; by 1940 that number had increased to 22,000. Between 1950 and 1970 the population increased from 34,000 to 86,000. In 1990 there were nearly 88,000 Warren Township residents.

The township's peak period of growth coincided with the development of Shadeland Avenue in the 1950s and 1960s as an industrial corridor. WESTERN ELECTRIC, FORD MOTOR COMPANY, CHRYSLER, and RCA (now THOMSON CONSUMER ELECTRONICS) opened expansive operations along the avenue and employed thousands of workers, many of whom built homes nearby. By the 1980s, however, several of the plants were idled and growth slowed. Ten years later the township's largest employers included COMMUNITY HOSPITALS, Ford, HOOK'S DRUGS, Washington Square Mall, NAVISTAR INTERNATIONAL, and the NAVAL AIR WARFARE CENTER, Aircraft Division.

Enrollment figures for the Metropolitan School District of Warren Township have stabilized as growth has slowed. In the 1992–1993 school year about 9,300 pupils were enrolled in the ten elementaries, two junior highs, and one senior high school, while one new school was scheduled for completion in 1994. The township also boasts the Warren Performing Arts Center that serves both the senior high school and the local community with concerts and performances by professional artists.

CATHLEEN F. DONNELLY

Berry R. Sulgrove, *History of Indianapolis and Marion County* (Philadelphia, 1884), 613–623; Department of Metropolitan Development, *Warren Township Comprehensive Planning Study* (1990); U.S. Census.

Warvel, John H., Sr. (Nov., 1893–June 19, 1967). Pioneer in treatment of diabetes. A native of Bradford, Ohio, Warvel received his medical degree from Ohio State University in 1916. He moved to Indianapolis in 1919 and became one of the first physicians to use INSULIN in the treatment of diabetes, soon after its discovery in 1922. He became a consultant to ELI LILLY AND COMPANY on the use of insulin for diabetes after the company became the first commercial producer of the drug in 1923. One of the founders of the Indianapolis Diabetes Association, Warvel served as that group's first president. With others, he also organized the Youth Camp for Diabetic Children at Bradford Woods near Martinsville.

KATHY INGELS HELMOND

Washington Township. Northern Marion County township. Settlement began in 1819 when John Allison reportedly brought his family from Kentucky to homestead along the Winchester State Road (now Allisonville Road). Fourteen years later he platted ALLISONVILLE, the area's first town. To the southwest the state's ambitious CENTRAL CANAL project stimulated the platting of two villages, BROAD RIPPLE and Wellington, in 1837. Another water route, FALL CREEK, was the site of grist mills and the village of MILLERSVILLE.

Two rail lines provided a small boost to Washington Township communities. In 1872 Malott Park was platted adjacent to the Wabash, St. Louis, and Pacific Railroad. For a time the town flourished with churches, a school, a blacksmith shop, and a grocery, but it later foundered and was annexed by Indianapolis. Track was laid for the Chicago and Indianapolis Airline (later the Monon line) in 1883, linking Broad Ripple and NORA to the capital.

After 1900 the interurbans and streetcars played an important role in developing residential areas in the southern part of the township, such as Mapleton, BUTLER-TARKINGTON, and MERIDIAN-KESSLER. Streetcar lines ran north on College Avenue to White City Amusement Park in Broad Ripple and north on Illinois Street to FAIRVIEW PARK.

The most important stimulus to growth in Washington Township, however, was the automobile. By 1920 affluent neighborhoods extended north of 38th Street, particularly along North Meridian Street. Residents enjoyed easy access to downtown via newly built roads and bridges over Fall Creek. Farther north and west other commuter suburbs such as CROWS NEST were platted in the 1920s and 1930s, along with MERIDIAN HILLS, WILLIAMS CREEK, SPRING HILL, Shooter's Hill, and WYNNEDALE. Census figures record the township's dramatic growth. In 1910 there were 5,700 residents; by 1920, 12,500; and by 1930 nearly 35,000.

Though growth slowed slightly in the 1930s and 1940s, another housing boom occurred north of White River and east of Fall Creek after World War II. Thousands of middle class families moved to new subdivisions and commuted by car to downtown jobs. Shopping centers, such as Meadows and Glendale, opened to serve nearby

Selected Statistics for Washington Township, 1990

Population	133,969
Population per Square Mile	2,706
Percent African-American	25.3
Percent 0 to 17 Years	21.6
Percent 65 Years and Over	14.1
Percent 25 Years and Over with a High School Degree or Equivalency	89.5
Percent 25 Years and Over with a College Degree	41.9
Per Capita Income in 1989	$20,790
Unemployment Rate (%)	3.5
Married-Couple Families as a Percent of Total Households	45.6
Median Home Value	$87,000

residents. By 1950 the township counted 62,000 people; in 1960, 98,000; in 1970, 126,000. Planned communities extended development northwest to the 96th Street boundary, west to Kessler Boulevard North Drive, and north along Allisonville Road. Residential growth slowed in the 1970s, however, after most land had been developed. In the 1990 census Washington Township numbered nearly 134,000 residents.

Today, Washington Township is predominantly residential, with most commercial growth concentrated along 86th and 82nd streets, Keystone Avenue, College Avenue, and 38th Street. In 1993 the township's major employers include ST. VINCENT HOSPITAL, The Women's Hospital, and BUTLER UNIVERSITY.

The Metropolitan School District of Washington Township is another large employer, with a work force of over 1,200. It has long enjoyed a regional reputation as a well-financed and innovative district. As of 1993 there were nearly 10,000 students enrolled in the eight elementaries, three middle schools, and one high school. Two state educational facilities, the Indiana schools for the deaf and the blind, are also located in the township.

Though growth has slowed with limited availability of land, Washington Township continues to attract homeowners drawn to the area's affluent neighborhoods, stable school system, and proximity to downtown.

CATHLEEN F. DONNELLY

Berry R. Sulgrove, *History of Indianapolis and Marion County* (Philadelphia, 1884), 623–647; U.S. Census.

Waterways. The waterways of Indianapolis are part of the Wabash River Drainage Basin, which covers two thirds of Indiana. Most of Indianapolis lies within the White River Subbasin, except for about 45 square miles along the southeastern edge of the city that drains into Buck Creek, a tributary of the East Fork White River. The major streams in Indianapolis are the WHITE RIVER and its two principal tributaries, FALL CREEK and Eagle Creek. Other large tributaries include Buck, Mud, Indian, Williams, Crooked, Little Eagle, Lick, and East Fork White Lick creeks and Pleasant Run.

The surface-water system of present-day Indianapolis is significantly different from the conditions found by early settlers. In 1821 the area was covered with stands of hardwood, and the poorly drained uplands were dotted with ponds and marshes. The slow release of stored surface water and the seepage of groundwater into stream channels helped maintain streamflows during periods of little or no rainfall. The natural conditions changed drastically as settlers cut the timber, dredged streambeds, and drained the land. The loss of the water storage capacity of forests and marshes contributed to an increase in storm runoff to streams during heavy rains and a decrease in streamflow during dry periods.

Modern urbanization has further modified streamflow characteristics. Roads, buildings, and other structures increase storm runoff by covering the ground with relatively impervious surfaces, thereby decreasing the effectiveness of underlying soils in absorbing and slowly releasing excess water. A complex network of storm drains, ditches, and culverts quickly routes the increased volume of stormwater to the city's waterways. The dredging and straightening of many watercourses further increases drainage efficiency, and levees and floodwalls confine excess water to engineered channels.

Variability in flow is a notable aspect of both natural and artificial waterways. During dry weather many creeks in Indianapolis cease flowing. In contrast, normally placid streams can be transformed into raging torrents after heavy rains. Daily streamflows recorded on several tributaries of White River range from zero to more than 3,000 cubic feet per second. The daily flow on

White River near NORA ranges from 49 to 58,500 cubic feet per second; flow on Fall Creek at MILLERSVILLE ranges from 8 to 22,000 cubic feet per second; and flow on Eagle Creek near Lynhurst Drive ranges from zero to 28,800 cubic feet per second.

Controlled releases of water from three reservoirs constructed between 1943 and 1968 have helped stabilize flow in downstream reaches by reducing flood intensity and increasing dry-weather flow. GEIST RESERVOIR in northeastern Indianapolis releases water to Fall Creek, and Eagle Creek Reservoir on the city's northwestside supplements flow in Eagle Creek. Streamflow in White River in Indianapolis is augmented by releases from Morse Reservoir into Cicero Creek, a major tributary entering White River in Hamilton County. The INDIANAPOLIS WATER COMPANY constructed Geist and Morse reservoirs for water supply purposes, whereas the City of Indianapolis built Eagle Creek Reservoir to alleviate downstream flooding and provide water supply storage.

The diversion of streamflow for public and industrial water supply is a major water management feature of Indianapolis. Of the five public water utilities serving Marion County, SPEEDWAY and Indianapolis are primarily supplied by surface water from streams and reservoirs. Two power generating stations in Indianapolis rely on White River as a source of cooling water. A few businesses and industries also withdraw water from White River or other major streams, although most companies that supply their own water rely on groundwater.

The Indianapolis Water Company (IWC) is the largest water utility serving Indianapolis and has the largest total surface water usage. In 1904 the IWC began to supplement its groundwater pumpage by treating water from White River for public water supply. Surface water pumpage steadily increased, and by 1985 the utility obtained more than 90 percent of its total average daily use of 100 million gallons per day from the city's stream systems. The CENTRAL CANAL diverts water from White River at BROAD RIPPLE and flows southward to IWC's White River Treatment Plant near 16th Street. Excess water in the canal which is not taken into the treatment plant is discharged into Fall Creek south of 21st Street. The IWC's other intakes are located on Fall Creek at Keystone Avenue and on Eagle Creek Reservoir at 56th Street. The town of Speedway pumps water from Eagle Creek in conjunction with its groundwater supply.

The combined effect of the large water supply diversions from White River and Fall Creek can noticeably reduce minimum daily streamflow downstream of the diversions, particularly during dry summer months. Analyses of streamflow records show that minimum daily discharge and statistical low flows on White River at Morris Street (located downstream of the water supply diversions) are lower than comparable flows at the unaffected Nora gauging station, located 18 river miles upstream from the Morris Street gauge. During the drought year of 1941 as much as 83 percent of the water in White River was diverted for water supply; however, most of it was returned downstream as treated wastewater.

Average to low streamflows on White River and Fall Creek can be affected by several instream dams. The Broad Ripple dam in White River ensures sufficient flow into the canal. The pooling of streamflow behind instream dams in White River near Washington Street and near Harding Street ensures adequate channel storage to support water withdrawals at two power plants. Several low dams in other reaches of the White River and along Fall Creek similarly help maintain channel storage.

The water quality of streams in Indianapolis is influenced by the return of unused diversions, the discharge of treated municipal and industrial wastewater, return flow of cooling water from power plants, combined sewer overflows, erosion and sedimentation from construction sites, chemical spills, wastewater bypasses, and nonpoint urban runoff from streets, parking lots, rooftops, and other surfaces. Prior to the 1980s White River through downtown Indianapolis and several segments of Fall Creek, Eagle Creek, POGUE'S RUN, East Fork White Lick Creek, and other tributaries were severely degraded. On White River, poor water quality conditions often existed for more than 50 miles downstream of Indianapolis, and fish kills were frequent. Contaminants commonly found in the city's major waterways included fecal bacteria, dissolved metals, ammonia, organic sub-

Boating was popular on the White River near Broad Ripple, ca. 1908.
[Indiana Historical Society, #C5762]

stances, nutrients, suspended solids, and toxic substances such as chlordane and polychlorinated biphenyls (PCBs).

By the early 1980s the quality of White River and its major tributaries had started to improve. Many industries and all but one of the incorporated communities in Marion County that formerly discharged directly to White River or its tributaries were connected to sewer systems that lead to one of the two Indianapolis wastewater treatment facilities. Both facilities were upgraded to tertiary treatment in 1983, and many sewer defects and problems with the city's wastewater effluent were corrected.

Although White River south of downtown Indianapolis remains of below-average quality by state standards, most segments of the river now support a diverse warmwater fishery, particularly smallmouth bass, largemouth bass, and channel catfish. In 1989 the Indiana State Board of Health lifted the fish consumption advisory for White River throughout Indianapolis that had been in effect for several years because of elevated levels of PCBs and chlordane in sediments and fish tissue.

The improvement in stream quality is expected to continue throughout the 1990s as regulatory agencies enforce strict water quality standards passed in December, 1989, by the Indiana Water Pollution Control Board. The protection of stream corridors is expected to receive more attention, particularly as the popularity of river cleanups and related activities continue to draw participants from conservation groups, universities, neighborhood associations, civic groups, and local agencies.

The improved quality of the city's waterways has been accompanied by an increase in water-based recreation and economic development. Boating and fishing are common along many of the city's major waterways. White River and its tributaries are included within several riverfront parks, and Eagle Creek Reservoir is a popular feature of EAGLE CREEK PARK. Fourteen streams throughout the city will be part of the Indianapolis Metropolitan Greenways Plan, scheduled for implementation beginning in 1993. Plans for the WHITE RIVER STATE PARK, under various stages of development since 1979, would encompass White River and nearby lands in Indianapolis.

CYNTHIA J. CLENDENON
Indiana Department of
Environmental Management

Edwin J. Hartke et al., *Geology for Environmental Planning in Marion County, Indiana* (Indiana Department of Natural Resources, Geological Survey, Special Report 19 [Environmental Study 15], 1980); William Meyer, J. P. Reussow, and D. C. Gillies, *Availability of Groundwater in Marion County, Indiana* (U.S. Geological Survey, Open-File Report 75–312, 1975).

Watson, Noble Butler (Oct. 21, 1895–May 16, 1972). Radio pioneer. Born in Shelbyville, Indiana, Watson received his amateur radio license in 1914. He joined the Marconi Wireless Telegraph Company in 1917 as a ship radio operator and, during World War I, managed radio traffic in New York City harbor for troop transports. In 1925, Watson was listed as "Radio Engineer" in the program of the First Radio Exposition in Indianapolis.

During 1925, Watson began one of the first radio stations in Indianapolis, WBBZ, which he operated from his home on Iowa Street. This station quickly went out of business due to financial problems. On November 29, 1926, he and his brother Carl introduced station WKBF, broadcasting from the Ford Motor Company showroom on East Washington Street. WKBF was one of the first Indianapolis radio stations to join a major network broadcast when it aired the Dempsey-Tunney fight over NBC in 1927. Watson and others incorporated WKBF as Indianapolis Broadcasting Company in 1929; not long afterwards,

the station's call letters were changed to WIRE. In 1936, Indianapolis Broadcasting sold the station to a group headed by EUGENE C. PULLIAM.

During World War II, Watson developed a means of "phone-patching" that provided a radio link to this country's telephone system and allowed servicemen overseas to talk to their families at home. Watson also served as an instructor for the U.S. Navy at Harvard and for the Naval Radio School in New York City. In his later years, he owned and operated a motel in Kokomo, Indiana.

CONNIE J. ZEIGLER

Burk Friedersdorf, *From Crystal to Color: WFBM* (Indianapolis, 1964); *Indianapolis Star Magazine*, Nov. 25, 1951.

Wayne Township. Western Marion County township bounded by 38th Street, Belmont Avenue, Troy Avenue, and Raceway Road. Settlement began in 1821 along Eagle Creek, and in the following year Wayne Township was organized.

Transportation routes determined the location of township communities. BRIDGEPORT was founded in 1830 at the site of a tollhouse along the NATIONAL ROAD (now U.S. 40). Farther east along the road the village of Mount Jackson sprang up where a public house opened in 1837.

Railroad developments from 1850 to 1880 spurred the growth of several hamlets. CLERMONT was platted in 1849 as a stop on the Indiana, Bloomington, and Western Railroad, while BEN DAVIS resulted when residents successfully lobbied a Vandalia Railroad superintendent of that name for a depot in 1877. The BELT LINE RAILROAD on the west side of WHITE RIVER facilitated the location of stockyards and industry, including the foundry of Benjamin Haugh in 1880. Foundry workers, many of them from eastern Europe, settled the town of HAUGHVILLE. On the southern edge of Wayne Township a gristmill operation, originally called Beeler's Station, attracted workers and craftsmen. In 1873 the village was platted as MAYWOOD on the Vincennes Railroad. By 1880 the township and its growing communities counted about 4,800 residents.

Selected Statistics for Wayne Township, 1990

Population	125,699
Population per Square Mile	2,560
Percent African-American	13.5
Percent 0 to 17 Years	24.8
Percent 65 Years and Over	11.4
Percent 25 Years and Over with a High School Degree or Equivalency	74.0
Percent 25 Years and Over with a College Degree	14.4
Per Capita Income in 1989	$12,806
Unemployment Rate (%)	5.0
Married-Couple Families as a Percent of Total Households	46.8
Median Home Value	$49,100

In the 20th century new forms of transportation brought commercial and residential growth. The town of SPEEDWAY, platted in 1912, developed adjacent to the racetrack built to test and race automobiles. During and after World War II communities such as LYNHURST (1941) and EAGLEDALE (1955) emerged as commuter suburbs for working class families. Beginning in the 1960s homes and businesses flanked Interstates 70, 74, and 465.

The aviation industry also played an important role in the development of Wayne Township. In 1931 the Indianapolis Municipal Airport opened, though it was renamed Weir Cook Municipal Airport (after a World War I flying ace) in 1944 and later became INDIANAPOLIS INTERNATIONAL AIRPORT. Nearby acreage has been developed for hotels, the Park Fletcher office park, and industrial facilities. The airport was one of the township's major employers in the 1990s, along with OLIN BRASS, ALLISON DIVISIONS OF GENERAL MOTORS, REILLY TAR AND CHEMICAL, CHRYSLER, and the INDIANAPOLIS MOTOR SPEEDWAY. In 1994 a new UNITED AIRLINES INDIANAPOLIS MAINTENANCE CENTER opened and employed a large work force.

As the township has grown so has the Metropolitan School District of Wayne Township, which in 1992–1993 boasted 12,500 students in ten elementary schools, three junior highs, and Ben Davis High School. Pupils from Indianapolis Public Schools have been bused to the area since 1981 when 1,400 students were reassigned in a court-ordered desegregation plan. The township also counts several private schools and a liberal arts college, MARIAN COLLEGE, located on Cold Spring Road.

About 126,000 residents lived in Wayne Township in 1990. The population has stabilized in the last 20 years after a dramatic increase from 27,500 residents in 1920 to 100,000 in 1960. Housing stock is varied, with a median value of $49,100. Residents cited drainage, surface water control, and the encroachment of industry as problems in Wayne Township in the early 1990s.

CATHLEEN F. DONNELLY

Berry R. Sulgrove, *History of Indianapolis and Marion County* (Philadelphia, 1884), 647–666; Marjie Gates Giffin, *A Walk Through Time: A History of Wayne Township* ([Indianapolis]: Wayne Township Schools, 1991).

Wehr, Paul Adam (May 16, 1914–Oct. 2, 1973). Illustrator and designer. Born in Mount Vernon, Indiana, Wehr graduated from the HERRON SCHOOL OF ART with a B.F.A. in 1937. He then became an instructor in advertising art at the school, later serving as head of the commercial art department until 1944. In that year he became an illustrator with the Stevens-Gross Studios in Chicago, where he remained until his retirement in 1968. Wehr produced paintings for the advertising campaigns of Coca-Cola, Standard Oil, and Ford. His illustrations appeared on the covers of many national magazines. Additionally, he illustrated stories in several magazines of fiction.

Wehr received numerous awards for his paintings and designs and exhibited at the American Water Color Society, Art Institute of Chicago, Philadelphia Water Color Society, Indiana Artists Exhibition, HOOSIER SALON, and the INDIANAPOLIS MUSEUM OF ART. In 1966, he won first prize in the competition for the design of the Indiana Sesquicentennial emblem and also designed the five cent postage stamp that commemorates the Hoosier state's 150th anniversary.

An expert in the field of illustration and advertising, Wehr was particularly admired for his control of watercolor and related media. He was a member of the Indiana Artists and the Portfolio Clubs of Indianapolis, as well as the Hoosier Salon. His works appear in the collections of the

Herron School of Art, the INDIANA STATE MUSEUM, and DePauw University.

MARY JANE MEEKER

Weir Cook Airport. See Indianapolis International Airport

Welch, Robert V. (May 26, 1927–Sept. 11, 1992). Entrepreneur, civic leader. A lifelong Indianapolis resident, Welch graduated from Cathedral High School and the University of Notre Dame. He served in the Navy during World War II and with the Army during the Korean conflict.

Returning to Indianapolis in 1952, Welch joined a construction firm to learn the business and in 1954 cofounded Baker, McHenry, and Welch, mechanical contractors. Later, R. V. Welch Investments, Inc., emerged as a development, construction, and investment business—building over 10,000 homes and apartments, as well as shopping centers, office complexes, and small manufacturing facilities. Welch also founded the Fidelity and Landmark banks, published the *Indianapolis Commercial*, and occasionally operated restaurants.

These business ventures were conducted on an ambitious scale, often in volatile circumstances. Consequently, over four decades Welch made and lost millions of dollars. Nevertheless, he simultaneously plunged into civic life, frequently tackling major projects that common wisdom deemed impossible. When the Holy Cross brothers decided to close Cathedral High School in 1972, Welch formed a lay board that raised funds to keep the school open. He was influential in opening the school to girls and relocating it to a spacious campus. After losing the mayoral election in 1975 to William H. Hudnut III, Welch crusaded to bring the National Football League to Indianapolis. He campaigned to build the HOOSIER DOME and lobbied NFL team owners to grant Indianapolis an expansion team, which he would own. That hope vanished in 1984 when the Baltimore Colts suddenly moved to Indianapolis.

In 1991 Governor Evan Bayh named Welch executive director of the WHITE RIVER STATE PARK

Commission, with a mandate to revitalize its ebbing planning process. Welch involved key community leaders in his vision, persuading three of them (MICHAEL A. CARROLL, FRANK E. MCKINNEY, JR., and JOHN R. WELIEVER) to fly with him to a floral exposition in Ohio for inspiration. All four men died following a midair collision shortly after takeoff.

ANN WAGNER ELY

Indianapolis Star, Sept. 12–15, 1992.

Weliever, John R. (Oct. 23, 1941–Sept. 11, 1992). Indiana government official and businessman. A graduate of Arsenal Technical High School and Butler University, Weliever worked in the restaurant business and operated automobile dealerships in Morgan County. He served as president of the Marion County Sheriff Department's Merit Board and the Indiana Restaurant Association, and was a board member for the Indiana Automobile Association.

A lifelong Democrat, Weliever was appointed by Governor Evan Bayh in January, 1989, as Indiana Department of Administration commissioner. In December of that year, Bayh picked him to take over as Hoosier Lottery director following the resignation of Jack Crawford. Weliever served as Lottery director until October, 1991, when he left the job to become a partner with his son in a Lebanon, Indiana, automobile dealership.

Weliever was one of four Indianapolis civic leaders who died on September 11, 1992, in a southern Marion County plane crash. The four men—MICHAEL A. CARROLL, Lilly Endowment, Inc. vice-president; FRANK E. MCKINNEY, JR., Bank One, Indiana Corp. board of directors chairman; ROBERT V. WELCH, White River State Park Development Commission executive director; and Weliever—were traveling to AmeriFlora '92 in Columbus, Ohio, to investigate possible ideas for the WHITE RIVER STATE PARK in Indianapolis when their plane collided in midair with another aircraft.

RAY BOOMHOWER
Indiana Historical Society

Indianapolis News, Sept. 12–15, 1992.

West, Henry F. (Mar. 14, 1796–Nov. 8, 1856). Mayor of Indianapolis, 1856, Democrat. West was the first of three mayors to die in office. Though his term was very brief, he is noteworthy in the history of Indianapolis and Indiana for his work in educational reform.

Born in Pittsfield, Massachusetts, West moved to Indianapolis in 1845. He immediately became a spokesman for improving Indiana's schools and traveled the state documenting the conditions that existed. In his publication *Common School Advocate* (Oct. 1846–Sept. 1847) he agitated for free schools. West and his brother George established the publishing firm H. F. West & Company, which eventually merged with the Bowen-Merrill Company.

On May 6, 1856, West defeated Republican Sims Colley for mayor, 1,515 votes to 1,183, with his party winning 10 of 14 council seats. When West died in November, CHARLES G. COULON, a lawyer and justice of the peace, was appointed interim mayor by the City Council until a special election could be held.

WILLIAM F. GULDE

West Indianapolis. Industrial suburb. The boundaries of the former West Indianapolis are roughly Washington Street, White River Parkway, Raymond Street, and Belmont Avenue. After the construction of the BELT LINE RAILROAD and the Union Stockyards in the 1870s, West Indianapolis developed as an extension of the STOCKYARDS near the small town of Belmont, and was established along the southern loop of the railway. Located in industrial surroundings, the area was also a residential, blue-collar neighborhood, most of whose citizens worked at the stockyards. The 1,565–acre suburb grew from 421 residents in 1882 to 3,527 in 1890 when it was the most densely populated suburban town in the Indianapolis area. In 1894 West Indianapolis incorporated as a city with three wards and seven precincts. That year its citizens elected their first and only mayor, A. B. Tolin, a senior member of a stockyards livestock commission. In 1897 West Indianapolis became one of six suburbs annexed by Indianapolis during the decade of the 1890s.

Although West Indianapolis no longer exists as a separate city, the area it once encompassed remains an industrial and residential neighborhood. The current housing stock ranges from working class two-story Victorian to post–World War II aluminum-sided tract homes. Although the stockyards left the district in the 1970s, many industrial firms are located in the area. Among them are Crescent Paper Company, Rexnord Corporation, and General Motors Truck and Bus Corporation.

CONNIE J. ZEIGLER

Jacob Piatt Dunn, *Greater Indianapolis* (Chicago, 1910).

West Newton. Small Decatur Township town. West Newton's approximate boundaries are Mendenhall Road on the north, Goose Creek on the east, Milton Street on the south, and Mooresville Road on its southwestern tip. David Klime settled in the area of current West Newton in 1819; in 1823 Henry Hobbs located nearby. Both were Quakers and helped establish the Sanders Creek Friends Meeting in 1827. In 1857 the meeting moved to the town Christopher Furnas had platted as Newton in 1851. Newton's first permanent postmaster, Isaac Hawkins, changed its name to West Newton to distinguish it from another town in Indiana.

Boosted by the construction of the Mooresville Road in 1863–1864, the town replaced the original meetinghouse with a second meetinghouse and school building in 1870. However, the number of residents increased slowly throughout the late 19th century and into the mid–20th. In fact, into the 1980s all of Decatur Township grew slowly, and West Newton merely mirrored the pattern of the township. Today, incorporated into the city of Indianapolis by UNIGOV, West Newton is a bedroom community of fewer than 100 homes. The West Newton Friends Church serves as a reminder of the town's Quaker heritage.

CONNIE J. ZEIGLER

Western Association of Writers. In 1885 Marie L. Andrews of Connersville, Indiana, suggested forming a midwestern writers group to encourage the development of a regional literature. Three contributors to the *Indianapolis Herald* and the *Indianapolis Journal*—J. N. Matthews, H. W. Taylor, and Richard Lew Dawson —joined Andrews in calling for an "association of the literary professions for mutual strength, profit, and acquaintance." On June 30, 1886, 75 individuals convened at Indianapolis' PLYMOUTH CHURCH and selected Maurice Thompson as the first president. During a subsequent meeting on October 5, 1886, the group adopted a constitution and the name "American Association of Writers." The name proved unpopular, however, since it gave a false impression of the organization's scope and composition; members were not all writers by profession and the association emphasized a regional not national literary fraternity. Consequently, at the third convention held at Plymouth Church on June 29–30, 1887, the group adopted the name "Western Association of Writers." From 1889 through 1904, the organization held its annual convention at Spring Fountain Park (later Winona Park), a resort on Eagle Lake near Warsaw, Indiana.

Seeking an identity distinct from eastern literary circles, the association became an outlet for writers from western states, though primarily from Indiana. Meetings included a variety of literary presentations, many of which were compiled in souvenir volumes of proceedings. Notable members included MEREDITH NICHOLSON, Paul Laurence Dunbar, BOOTH TARKINGTON, Charles Major, LEW WALLACE, Mary Hartwell Catherwood, and JACOB PIATT DUNN.

After 1900, attendance at annual conventions declined rapidly. The last recorded meeting, which 25 members attended, occurred on May 4, 1907, at the CLAYPOOL HOTEL in Indianapolis. Initially the group had great potential to become an influential regional association of professional authors. Its demise by 1908, however, could be attributed to its failure to maintain high literary standards, its inability to attract new authors, and its propensity for being, according to its critics, a "mutual back-scratching society."

HAROLD J. SANDER

George S. Cottman, "The Western Association of Writers," *Indiana Magazine of History*, 29 (Mar., 1933),

187–197; James L. Weygand, *Winona Holiday: The Story of the Western Association of Writers* (Nappanee, Ind., 1948).

Western Censor & Emigrants' Guide.

Indianapolis' second newspaper, later retitled the *Indiana Journal*. Established on March 7, 1823, the *Western Censor & Emigrants' Guide* was launched nearly one year after the appearance of the city's first newspaper, the *INDIANAPOLIS GAZETTE*. Begun by two Kentuckians, HARVEY GREGG and DOUGLASS MAGUIRE, the *Western Censor* operated out of a house on Washington Street owned by Gregg.

On October 19, 1824, Gregg sold his interest in the newspaper to JOHN DOUGLASS, who had established the *Western Clarion* in Madison, Indiana, before becoming the state printer in Corydon in 1823. In the fall of 1824 Douglass moved to the new state capital, Indianapolis, and purchased an interest in the *Western Censor*. Douglass and Maguire, who would later serve as a state representative and Indiana auditor, operated the newspaper until January 11, 1825, when it was renamed the *INDIANA JOURNAL*.

The *Western Censor* strongly opposed Democratic candidate Andrew Jackson's campaign for the White House in the 1824 presidential election, which saw Jackson competing for the presidency with John Quincy Adams, Henry Clay, and William Crawford (Maguire and Clay were friends). The newspaper continued its opposition to Jackson and his followers after the election.

RAY BOOMHOWER
Indiana Historical Society

John W. Miller, *Indiana Newspaper Bibliography* (Indianapolis, 1982); Jacob Piatt Dunn, *Greater Indianapolis* (Chicago, 1910).

Western Electric.

Former Bell Telephone manufacturing unit with a huge factory at 2525 North Shadeland Avenue. Other units of the American Telephone and Telegraph Company (AT&T) succeeded to Western Electric's properties following the company's court-ordered divestiture on January 1, 1984.

Women working on the Western Electric assembly line in the mid-1960s.
[Indiana Historical Society, Bass Collection, #316636-4]

Western Electric's predecessor obtained control of the telephone equipment factory managed by Ezra T. Gilliland southeast of State and English avenues in Marion County in 1881 and moved its operations to Chicago the next year. Licensed in 1879 by the Bell company to make switchboards and telephone attachments, the Gilliland factory was noted for improvements in switchboards and for experiments in mass production.

In 1948 Western Electric leased space in SPEEDWAY to train workers and began building the Shadeland factory on what had been farmland. The factory made telephones for issue to the Bell system's subscribers starting in 1950. It was the world's largest telephone factory, covering 40 acres of ground. Trips within it were made on golf carts. During most of its history it had one of the largest payrolls in central Indiana, about 8,000 employees. Hundreds of kinds of telephones were made there, the black dial telephone being the principal product at first. Emphasis shifted later to smaller models in pastels. Specialized telephones, such as for fire boxes and coal mines, were also made there, and the building contained a testing laboratory.

Over time, changes in telephone technology—some of them introduced at the Shadeland factory—greatly reduced the amount of space needed to make telephones and increased the difficulty of defending the Bell system's complete control of the telephone business. In 1983 plans were announced to close the Shadeland factory, where about half of the employees were on layoff. Production ended in 1985. Empty for some years, the factory eventually became an industrial rental property—Western Select—but many areas remained without tenants.

In 1965 Western Electric opened a printing plant at 2855 North Franklin Road to print training manuals for employees of Bell operating companies. After the breakup the plant printed manuals for users of AT&T computers.

CHARLES JOHNSON TAGGART

Westview Hospital. Westside osteopathic hospital. Until the 1970s local medical doctors did not accept osteopathic methods of treatment using muscle and skeletal manipulation and excluded osteopaths from practicing in all area hospitals except Marion County General (now WISHARD MEMORIAL HOSPITAL). In 1960 ten osteopathic doctors organized the Joint Venture Group to establish a hospital in which their dwindling numbers could practice and to provide an alternative to traditional hospital services. The group met with successive roadblocks in zoning, financing, and lack of cooperation from the local medical community. When it was ready to start building the hospital in 1970, the Health Planning Council of Marion County refused to certify the proposal, despite a recognized need for more local hospital services. Only when Mayor Richard G. Lugar, who had previously served as Westview's fund-raising chairperson, asked the council to review its decision was the plan approved, with the stipulation that the hospital include medical doctors on its staff and offer traditional services.

Westview opened in 1975, financed in part by an earlier $200,000 grant from the LILLY ENDOWMENT in 1972. The hospital featured private rooms, individualized care, and cost-effective, holistic services, but it continued to suffer from financial and image problems. To build the hospital's reputation as a professional and stable institution, Westview became a site for osteopathic and nursing intern programs and a leading fund-raiser for the local United Way. In 1978 Westview was accepted into the Alliance of Indianapolis Hospitals, at last assuring its standing in the local hospital community.

During the early 1980s Westview expanded its facilities, equipment, and services. While specializing in foot, back, and leg problems, the hospital currently offers services in all medical areas except obstetrics and trauma cases. As of 1994 Westview treats over 50,000 patients annually. With a significant proportion of its 195–member staff being osteopaths, Westview defies the national trend of osteopathic hospitals closing or merging with traditional hospitals.

MICHELLE D. HALE

Clipping Files, "Indianapolis Hospitals—Westview," Indiana State Library.

Wetlands. Early historians described pioneer Marion County as having an abundance of swamps, bottoms, bayous, and sloughs. Their accounts noted that these areas, now known as wetlands, were viewed as nothing more than wastelands that required draining to become productive farms. Drained wetlands were also deemed healthier for the growing city and its populace. These attitudes were not unique to Indianapolis or to the 19th century. Federal, state, and local governments have long encouraged and engaged in wetland destruction. In Indiana an estimated 87 percent or approximately 4.85 million acres of an original 5.6 million acres of wetlands have been destroyed. One can reasonably assume that the Indianapolis area has lost a similar percentage. Wetland losses continue in the 1990s, due primarily to pressure from land development interests.

Still commonly known as swamps, marshes, bayous, and sloughs, wetlands constitute transitional zones between dry land and deep water. These semiaquatic areas occur along rivers, streams, lakes, and other fresh (and salt) water bodies. They also occur in isolated situations such as natural depressions in the landscape. One can readily observe wetlands along WHITE RIVER, FALL CREEK, Eagle Creek, Buck Creek, and other streams that flow through the city and county. Wetlands can also be observed at some of the city's parks including Eagle Creek, Holliday, and South-

westway parks. Wetland plants such as cattails, waterlilies, and duckweed can be seen easily in Indianapolis.

Like sponges, wetlands temporarily store floodwater and surface runoff that overflow river banks. They also provide shoreline stabilization and protection from erosion. Through various biological and chemical processes, wetlands remove nutrients such as phosphorous and nitrogen from water before it flows into adjacent lakes and streams and process some chemical and organic wastes from water. Thus Indianapolis area wetlands, especially above Eagle Creek, Geist, and Morse reservoirs, contribute to the city's water quality and its ability to control flooding.

Wetlands provide habitat for innumerable fish and wildlife species and constitute the most productive areas for these resources. Remaining wetlands along Indianapolis' creeks, rivers, and reservoirs provide vital nesting, resting, spawning, and feeding areas for both fish and wildlife. A large variety of wetland birds including raptors, songbirds, ducks, geese, and other migratory birds require wetlands for all or part of their habitat requirements. Most of these birds can be observed along White River or Fall Creek at various times of the year; examples include the osprey, great blue heron, and scarlet tanager. Mammals including beaver and muskrat live almost entirely in wetlands while other species such as white-tailed deer use wetlands for food, shelter, and travel ways. Evidence of these animals can easily be observed along Indianapolis' larger streams and reservoirs. In Indiana approximately 180 plant and animal species that occur naturally in wetlands are listed by the state as endangered, threatened, or rare. A few state-listed plants that can be seen in Indianapolis include tufted hairgrass, goldenseal, and brook-pimpernel; examples of state listed animal species include bald eagle, black-crowned night-heron, and spotted turtle. Recent surveys by the United States Fish and Wildlife Service indicate that the federally endangered Indiana bat utilizes Fall Creek at Fort Benjamin Harrison for summer habitat.

Although federal regulations and incentive programs have helped, wetlands continued to be lost in Indianapolis and throughout the nation to various development activities. Attempts to legislate wetland protection in Indiana have met with failure in the General Assembly, although a few cities and towns have local ordinances that regulate the development of wetlands. To date, Indianapolis does not have a wetlands ordinance or a zoning ordinance that directly addresses wetlands.

STEVE JOSE

Wheaton Van Lines. Moving company. Ohio native Earnest S. Wheaton founded Wheaton Van Lines in 1945. He had entered the moving business in 1916 with a job at the Cotter Transfer and Storage Company in Mansfield, Ohio, before buying the firm nine years later and renaming it Pioneer Storage. Pioneer became an agent for Indianapolis-based Aero Mayflower Transit Company in 1931, and two years later Wheaton left Pioneer to become a Mayflower executive. Wheaton stayed with Mayflower until 1945 when he started his own company, Clipper Van Lines.

Clipper began operations that September with four employees in its first office in the Century Building, making its first household move in January, 1946. By 1951 annual revenue topped $1 million. That year Clipper lost a lawsuit to Pan American World Airways over the use of the word "Clipper" and the firm became Wheaton Van Lines. The company began making international moves in 1958. Wheaton moved to its current northeastside office in the mid–1970s. As of 1992 Wheaton was the country's 11th largest carrier with revenues of $42 million.

DEBORAH B. MARKISOHN

Wheeler, Clifton A. (Sept. 4, 1883–May 10, 1953). Fine arts painter, muralist, and teacher. Born in Hadley, Indiana, Wheeler attended the JOHN HERRON ART INSTITUTE, and studied under WILLIAM MERRITT CHASE both in New York City and in Europe. He was also a student of Robert Henri while in New York.

In 1914, he joined the group of Indianapolis area artists to paint the decorative murals for the Indianapolis City Hospital (now WISHARD MEMORIAL HOSPITAL). Wheeler also painted the mural *Garden in Ice and Snow* for the Carnegie Library in Thorntown, Indiana, and, in 1916, he created the classical mural above the marquee of the CIRCLE THEATRE in downtown Indianapolis.

Wheeler was a frequent exhibitor in the HOOSIER SALON, Indiana Artists Club, INDIANA STATE FAIR, John Herron Art Institute, and Richmond Art Association annual shows. He won numerous awards in these competitions, including the Foulke Prize at the Richmond show in 1917, and the Holcomb Prize (1923) and Indianapolis Art Association Award (1924) at the Herron Institute exhibitions of Indiana artists. Residing in the Indianapolis eastside community of Irvington, Wheeler was associated with the IRVINGTON GROUP of artists who held annual exhibitions from 1928 to 1937. He was also a member of the Society of Western Artists, the Indiana Artists Club, the Portfolio Club, and the INDIANAPOLIS LITERARY CLUB.

Wheeler taught classes at the Herron School of Art until 1933, and thereafter was an art instructor at SHORTRIDGE HIGH SCHOOL in Indianapolis. He spent many of his summer vacations sketching and painting the Rocky Mountains and the Smoky Mountains in oil and watercolor. Other favorite subjects for his paintings were Brown County scenes and the common views around Irvington, especially along Pleasant Run Creek.

Besides his public murals, Wheeler's work is located in the permanent collections of the INDIANAPOLIS MUSEUM OF ART, Ball State University, BUTLER UNIVERSITY, Purdue University, Indiana University, the INDIANAPOLIS PUBLIC SCHOOLS, and the Irvington Historical Society. His paintings can also be found in the homes of many Indianapolis area residents.

FRANK N. OWINGS, JR.

Mary Q. Burnet, *Art and Artists of Indiana* (New York, 1921); Irvington Historical Society, *The Irvington Group* (Indianapolis, 1984); Flora Lauter, *Indiana Artists Active 1940* (Spencer, Ind., 1941).

Wheeler, Frank H. (Oct. 24, 1864–May 27, 1921). Founder of carburetor manufacturing business and brass works; and cofounder of the

Indianapolis Motor Speedway. Wheeler was a native of Manchester, Iowa, coming to Indianapolis from California in 1904. He reportedly made and lost two fortunes in business before arriving in Indiana.

Shortly after his arrival Wheeler met George Schebler, the inventor of one of the first successful carburetors for internal combustion engines; the two formed the Wheeler-Schebler Company, which began manufacturing the units in a small room on Alabama Street near Washington Street. Wheeler provided financial backing and office management skills, while Schebler was in charge of production. The firm grew into one of the best companies of its kind in the world, soon expanding its product line to include the manufacture of magnetos and small electric motors used in ignition systems. In 1915, Wheeler purchased his partner's interest in the business for a reported $1 million. Wheeler extended his business involvement beyond automobiles, serving as president of the Langenskamp-Wheeler Brass Works and as a director for the Stutz Fire Engine Company.

Through his involvement in automobile parts manufacturing, Wheeler developed a friendship with CARL G. FISHER, and along with Fisher and JAMES A. ALLISON, became an original investor in the development of the INDIANAPOLIS MOTOR SPEEDWAY. During 1912–1913 Wheeler built a magnificent, buff-colored villa on a 30–acre tract adjacent to Fisher's home on Cold Spring Road. (The two estates, along with that of Allison, now comprise much of the campus of MARIAN COLLEGE.) During this time his involvement in Indianapolis activities grew to include the COLUMBIA CLUB and SCOTTISH RITE. Wheeler was fond of children, and he was known to provide vegetables, fruit, and flowers from his garden to children throughout the city.

MATTHEW C. MORRIS

Wheeler Mission Ministries. Full service mission to the needy in Indianapolis. In 1893, William V. Wheeler, a sales manager for the hardware firm of Layman and Carey, opened an unpretentious mission in a small room on South Street. In 1905, it was incorporated as the Rescue Mission and Home of Indianapolis. Wheeler's

name was not used until after his death in 1908. In 1918, the Wheeler Mission and the City Mission on East Washington Street formed the Wheeler City Rescue Mission and, shortly after, moved to the old Empire Theater on Wabash Street. In 1922, it moved to its present site at 245 North Delaware where its present building, considered one of the best equipped mission buildings in America, was completed in 1929. In 1968, Wheeler City Rescue Mission was renamed and reincorporated as Wheeler Rescue Mission, Inc., and in 1990 it was renamed Wheeler Mission Ministries.

The mission's services include a men's shelter, free meals and medical care, a "dime" store with donated items, programs for youths of all ages, a mothers' club, and discretionary financial assistance. It also operates a 240–acre camp for families and youths, and a home for girls (13–18) with a history of abuse. The mission serves an average of 500 persons a day; annually it provides 20,000 nights of lodging, 25,000 articles of clothing, and 80,000 meals. Of its $1 million budget, 85 percent comes from individuals, the remainder from churches and businesses.

RICK A. ALVIS
Wheeler Mission Ministries

When Store. Men's clothing and furnishings store. Constructed in 1874, the When Building at 36 North Pennsylvania Street got its name in 1875 after owner JOHN T. BRUSH temporarily closed it during remodeling. After twice changing the reopening date on the sign on the front of the building, Brush finally hung a sign that read simply, "WHEN?" Beginning in February, 1875, store advertisements printed in the *Indianapolis News* also carried only the one-word question. At last, on March 20, 1875, the When Store, as it was thereafter called, reopened as a branch store for a New York City wholesale house and became "the largest one price clothing store" in Indianapolis.

The newly remodeled When Store was luxuriously appointed, with a mansard roof, cast-iron balustrades and balconies on the second and third floors, and an interior courtyard. Brush erected a band shell on the second floor, and the When Band became a popular attraction at the clothing

The When Store got its name from a catchy advertising campaign that aroused public curiosity as to "when" the store would open.
[Indiana Historical Society, Bass Collection, #6514]

emporium. Another attraction was a large, natural gas torch that burned in front of the building. Brush, president of a New York National League baseball club and a pioneer in organized professional BASEBALL, owned the building until his death in 1912.

In the 1930s, Stationers began a 60–year occupancy of a portion of the former When Building. The building's owners modernized it in the 1940s, eliminating the balconies and balustrades and renaming it the Ober Building. When Stationers terminated its occupancy in 1993, the building's current owner, the SALVATION ARMY, removed the remaining tenants and placed it for sale.

CONNIE J. ZEIGLER

White, Ryan (Dec. 6, 1971–Apr. 8, 1990). Nationally known AIDS patient and activist. Ryan White, then a middle school student living near Kokomo, Indiana, contracted AIDS (Acquired Immune Deficiency Syndrome) at age 12 through a blood transfusion for hemophilia. After his diagnosis at RILEY HOSPITAL FOR CHILDREN in Indianapolis in late 1984, the local school superintendent banned White from attending classes. Ryan and his mother, Jeanne White, successfully appealed to the Indiana Department of Education, and Ryan's return to school in February, 1986, was a national media event, making him a spokesperson for AIDS victims' rights. Continu-

ing discrimination, however, caused the Whites to move to Cicero, Hamilton County, Indiana, in 1987.

After the move, White attended Hamilton Heights High School and began his crusade to educate the public about AIDS. In September, 1987, he promoted the establishment of the Ryan White National Fund, a fund-raising program for prevention of discrimination against children with AIDS. The following year, Ryan testified before the White House AIDS Commission and gave a cover story interview about life with AIDS to *People* magazine. He was also nominated for an Emmy for an AIDS segment on the public television program "3-2-1 Contact." *The Ryan White Story*, a 1989 television movie, portrayed White's struggles. As he gained recognition as an AIDS activist, he met and became friends with numerous entertainment celebrities. White died at Riley Hospital after a brief hospitalization that attracted national news coverage. His funeral, televised locally, was held at the SECOND PRESBYTERIAN CHURCH in Indianapolis. Mourners included then–First Lady Barbara Bush, pop-rock singers Michael Jackson and Elton John, and TV talk show host Phil Donahue. White was buried at Cicero Cemetery.

Following Ryan's death Jeanne White lobbied successfully for the passage of the federal "Ryan White Comprehensive AIDS Resources Emergency Act" (CARE) to provide emergency clinical care, coordination of AIDS services, and early intervention. But Congress allocated only $110 million of the $875 million requested, a slight increase over extant federal AIDS funding. Jeanne

Ryan White.
[Indianapolis Newspapers Inc.]

White also helped publish the best-selling book, *Ryan White: My Own Story* (1991), based on her son's manuscript. That same year readers of the *Indianapolis Star* posthumously chose Ryan White as the *Star's* Man of the Year.

CONNIE J. ZEIGLER

Indianapolis Star, Apr. 9, 1990.

White River. Principal Marion County waterway. The south-flowing White River enters the county at 96th Street, meandering 31.4 miles through portions of Washington, Wayne, Center, Decatur, and Perry townships. The downtown average discharge is 1,400 cubic feet per second (CFS). Indianapolis was located at the confluence of the river and FALL CREEK in hopes that commercial river traffic would connect the city to the Wabash River. While the White River is legally navigable, no commercial transportation has occurred since the early 1800s due to shallow water. The location proved poor due to the confluence WETLANDS and frequent floods, particularly the disastrous 1913 flood (estimated discharge 70,000 CFS). The river was dredged, widened, leveed, and straightened following the flood. The river has 35 major tributaries within the county. Seven city parks have river frontage, and plans call for the river corridor to become the White River Greenway with additional access sites.

The river has five identifiable segments. The ponded, residential segment north of the BROAD RIPPLE dam is a popular boating area. The dam allows for diversion of 75 million gallons of river water per day to the CENTRAL CANAL, it being the principal source of drinking water for Indianapolis. Downstream of the dam, the scenic, free-flowing river is a popular canoeing and fishing segment to 38th Street. The 16th Street (Emricksville) dam ponds water to 38th Street, and this park-lined segment is called Lake Indy. Downstream of Emricksville Dam the river corridor is more urban, with an artificially wide channel and concrete floodwalls that border WHITE RIVER STATE PARK and IUPUI. The water quality of the river declines greatly south of 16th Street due to combined sewer overflows, industrial discharges, and the Belmont Sewage Treatment

Plant. At Raymond Street the river corridor becomes less urban near the confluences of Pleasant Run and Eagle Creek. South of Interstate 465 the river is more rural, but the water quality reflects the urban inputs. The river passes Southport Sewage Treatment Plant, Southwestway Park, and a large wetland oxbow prior to entering Johnson County.

KEVIN STRUNK
Wabash Resources and Consulting

Friends of the White River (Kevin Strunk), "1991 State of the White River Corridor Report"; Department of Metropolitan Development, City of Indianapolis, "Comprehensive Parks, Recreation and Open Space Plan" (1992).

White River Park State Games. Annual statewide amateur athletic competition. In July, 1983, Indiana held the first annual White River Park State Games, co-sponsored by the WHITE RIVER STATE PARK Development Commission and the Governor's Council on Physical Fitness and Sport, to promote fitness and a healthy lifestyle. Other objectives were to provide Indiana residents of all ages with an opportunity to compete and develop their athletic skills, to nurture Olympic-caliber athletes, and to create grass-roots support for all amateur sports.

The INDIANA SPORTS CORPORATION agreed to organize and coordinate the event, and that first year 5,600 athletes representing 84 of the state's 92 counties entered the competition. More than 3,500 finalists traveled to Indianapolis to compete in the finals in ten sports, with gold, silver, and bronze medals going to the top competitors, just as in the Olympics. Each year, the number of participants and sports increased, and by 1991 there were 24,000 Hoosier athletes competing in 950 events in 20 sports. Competitors were matched according to age, skill, and sport. In 1991, two alumni of the White River Park State Games competed for spots on 1992 Olympic squads.

Indiana was the fourth state to adopt a state games program. Earlier, states had used tryouts to select finalists, but organizers of Indiana's state games wanted every contestant to have the opportunity to compete in actual events. Indiana established a regional-state finals format, and by

1986 preliminary contests were being held in eight regions, with the winners advancing to the finals in Indianapolis. A positive by-product of the arrangement was the influx of new dollars in host cities where thousands of visiting athletes and their families frequent restaurants, hotels, and retail shops.

In the ensuing years, the White River Park State Games became a model for other states that wanted to initiate similar games. In September, 1984, Indianapolis held the first national symposium on state games. The symposium led to the development of the National Congress for State Games, which has been instrumental in helping more than 40 states develop contests.

Indiana's first state games were funded almost entirely by the state. Over time the games became nearly self-supporting, with one-third of the budget coming from the White River State Park Commission and the remainder from corporate sponsorships and entry fees.

DELORES J. WRIGHT

White River State Park. Located along both sides of White River just west of the Mile Square, encompassing 267 acres between Washington and New York streets, this project, on land that had become an industrial slum, was conceived by the same community leaders whose dreams of Indianapolis as an amateur sports and tourist center sparked the city's dramatic growth throughout the 1980s. The park's connection to this trend could be seen in the kinds of facilities initially suggested for the site in the 1981 master plan: a domed stadium, new zoo, world class amateur athletic complex, museums and theaters, botanical gardens, and theme park comparable to Tivoli in Copenhagen or Ontario Place in Toronto. The stadium and athletic complex were ultimately built elsewhere, but the park remained a prime location for everything else on the list.

The park was different from other city projects because it was to be an urban state park. State legislators from central Indiana led a bipartisan effort to gain state support. A promise of $5 million in seed money from the LILLY ENDOWMENT helped their cause. But many legislators from other parts of the state were reluctant supporters at best, and the park became a source of continuing controversy.

Even after completion of the new INDIANAPOLIS ZOO at the site in the mid–1980s, questions persisted about the park's administration, cost, and design objectives. Ironically, these problems occurred within an administrative structure—a quasi-independent commission—that was supposed to insulate the project from normal political pressure. But the commission had to rely on legislative funding amounting to $10 million initially and another $25 million for property acquisition and preparation over the next ten years. And the park was still not completed.

Deciding how to proceed and what to include became matters of some controversy. Many people wanted the park to feature a family entertainment complex that could attract visitors to the water's edge. Others believed this would violate the tranquility and dedication to nature of a traditional park. Still others noted that the legislature never intended the White River State Park to be a traditional park, but rather something that was uniquely urban. They saw the entertainment center as necessary to meet this objective and to generate enough revenue to make the park self-sustaining.

Design experts who were brought together in the commission's first planning exercise issued a report that could be read to support either of these views. Subsequent plans, however, made the entertainment center central to the project's success. The commission accepted the latter proposition and sought private developers to build and manage the complex. Several times they came close— Knotts Berry Farm briefly fronted a proposal in 1991—but in the end the developers withdrew, generally citing uncertainty about public acceptance and the political commitment to see the project through.

These delays tended to overshadow what had been accomplished. By the late 1980s many of the elements of the master plan were in place. These included the new zoo, a state-of-the-art center for fitness and sport with a strong emphasis on research, and the cornerstone of a cultural complex in the EITELJORG MUSEUM OF AMERICAN INDIAN AND WESTERN ART. But not in sight were what planners saw as the park's most important goals: a reclaimed WHITE RIVER that would be the site's visual and recreational showpiece, a restored historic canal to connect the river and the heart of downtown, and finally a tourist attraction on the river's bank. In 1992 the legislature failed to renew the park commission, but Governor Evan Bayh extended the agency by executive order; the following year the commission was renewed by the General Assembly.

In early 1993 the commission shifted its vision to an education, science, and technology theme that could embrace and offer recreation, arts, and culture. The commission is also pursuing the integration of advanced telecommunications as a means of programmatic outreach to connect the state's residents to the park's features and activities.

In 1993 the commission produced a 10–page newspaper, the *White River State Park Review,* relating the park's 14–year history. Among the accomplishments the commission cited are the nationally recognized River Promenade, a half-mile walking and jogging trail adjacent to the zoo's eastern boundary, and the relocation of the Washington Street bridge to allow easier park access. The park is now poised to begin the next phase of its development, which will commence in spring, 1994.

JEROLD KNIGHT

Wholesale District. Bounded by Maryland, Delaware, and South streets and Capitol Avenue, the Wholesale District grew up around UNION STATION. Its proximity to the railroads and Washington Street retailers allowed local, regional, and national distribution of wholesalers' merchandise.

Following the Civil War the district rapidly gained businesses. The variety of commercial concerns peaked in the early 1900s when the area housed enterprises ranging from Hatfield Electric Company, suppliers of electric and power equipment, to Mooney-Mueller Drug Company. In addition to the vast range of products available, the area also featured an array of building styles including Gothic and Romanesque Revival, Neoclassical, and Italianate. Among the area's 47 extant buildings, dating from 1863 to 1930, are

Fahnley & McCrea Millinery Company (1905–1906, 240–242 South Meridian Street), the city's first wholesale millinery house, D. P. Erwin & Company dry goods (1888–1889, 206–214 South Meridian), Holland and Ostermeyer Building (1867–1868, 219 East Maryland Street), which housed the Johnston and [Col. Eli] Lilly pharmaceutical firm, and the Kothe, Wells and Bauer Company wholesale grocers, whose Ko-We-Ba brand canned goods were a household word throughout the state.

The Wholesale District contains the greatest concentration of 19th-century commercial buildings in the city. A Who's Who of Indianapolis firms designed buildings for the area, among them: VONNEGUT AND BOHN (1912–1913, Hotel Severin, 45 West Georgia Street), R. P. Daggett & Co. (1888–1889, McKee Building, 202–204 South Meridian Street), D. A. Bohlen and Son (1894–1895, MAJESTIC BUILDING, 47 South Pennsylvania Street), and JOHN H. STEM (1888, George W. Stout Building, 207–209 South Meridian Street). In 1974 the district was listed on the National Register of Historic Places (boundaries amended 1982). In 1993 it remains a commercial area where retail businesses are interspersed with restaurants, hotels, and office space.

CONNIE J. ZEIGLER

Willard, William (1809–1888). Pioneer in deaf education. Born in Vermont and deafened as the result of a childhood illness, Willard graduated from the American Asylum for the Deaf at Hartford, Connecticut. An exceptional teacher, Willard joined the original faculty at the Ohio School for the Deaf in Columbus where he taught using American Sign Language. In 1843 he moved to Indiana and spent a summer traveling the state on horseback while recruiting pupils for a small private school which he opened at Indianapolis. In January, 1844, the state legislature passed an act transforming Willard's first permanent school into a state-funded institution, the Indiana Asylum for the Education of the Deaf and Dumb. Willard headed this school with 16 pupils, first located at the southeast corner of Illinois and Maryland streets, for one year until he was replaced as superintendent by a hearing man.

Trustees of the institution assumed that deafness disqualified Willard from performing effectively as superintendent. He taught for another 20 years at the school until he brought suit against its trustees for decreasing his salary without cause.

Willard amassed a significant fortune with lucrative investments in banks, insurance and fire stocks, real estate, and as a commissioner of the National Road. The Willard family lived in a ten-room Greek Revival house at WOODRUFF PLACE on 80 acres which he bought in 1847. Willard Park at Washington and State streets, one former site of the INDIANA SCHOOL FOR THE DEAF, is dedicated to his memory.

PHYLLIS KLEIN VALENTINE
Indiana University–Purdue University,
Indianapolis

————

Jacob Piatt Dunn, *Greater Indianapolis* (Chicago, 1910), I, 109–110.

William B. Burford Printing Company.

The Burford Printing Company had its beginnings in the 1860s in a partnership between Miles W. Burford, a banker then living in Independence, Missouri, and his son-in-law, William Braden, a printer in Indianapolis. This partnership of Braden and Burford was involved in both printing and real estate; it ended in 1875 when Burford died and Braden left Indianapolis following financial problems that stemmed from the Panic of 1873.

In 1875 Miles Burford's son, WILLIAM B. BURFORD (1846–1927), who had been a cavalryman in Missouri during the Civil War and had later worked with Braden, took over the printing business. He built it up into what was probably the most successful business of its kind in Indiana. The firm held the printing contract for the state government and for all 92 counties. It did the finest engraving in the state and ran a fully stocked stationery store. The printing offices were at 40 South Meridian Street, the stationery store at 36 West Washington Street. Burford also dealt in real estate and joined many civic enterprises to improve and develop Indianapolis.

After Burford's death, leadership of the firm remained in the family with his son-in-law Henry R. Danner (1870–1950) and Danner's son and grandson. The stationery store, which also carried office furniture, continued until 1964. The printing business moved in 1935 to 603 East Washington Street, in 1964 to 3448 Shelby Street, and in 1993 to Zionsville. At present it specializes in commercial printing and multipart forms.

CHARLES LATHAM, JR.
Indiana Historical Society

————

Burford Printing Company Collection, Indiana Historical Society.

William H. Block Company.

Indianapolis retailer. In 1896 Herman Wilhelm Bloch, who later anglicized his name to William H. Block, opened a small department store at 9 East Washington Street. Block had emigrated to New York from Hungary in 1876, where he had studied to be a rabbi. He changed careers with financial help from an immigrant aid society and began peddling dry goods in Pennsylvania, Ohio, and Indiana. Initially, Block carried goods in a backpack,

The William H. Block Company occupied two adjoining buildings on Washington Street in 1906. [Indiana Historical Society, Bass Collection, #6542[1]]

but he soon began carrying samples and shipping orders to customers. Quitting peddling after a few years, he teamed with Abraham Thalman (ca. 1880) to open the Block and Thalman Wholesale and Retail Department Store in Kokomo, Indiana, with branch stores in Anderson and Columbus. In 1894 Block sold his interest to Thalman and spent the next year in New York manufacturing women's apparel. Two years later he settled in Indianapolis and opened his store on Washington Street.

Initially, Block's store had little frontage. He annexed an adjoining six-story building around the turn of the century, more than doubling the store's size. In 1907 the store was incorporated as the William H. Block Company. Three years later, Block built a large eight-story building at Illinois and Market streets, strategically located across the street from the Traction Terminal. More than 70,000 people turned out for the grand opening of the store, which included a luncheonette, a grocery, and an in-store candy shop. When Block died in 1928, his sons—Meier, Rudolph, and Edward—took over the company.

During the mid–1930s, Block's undertook a two-year remodeling and expansion of its downtown store. During the next three decades the company continued to expand, opening suburban branch stores as well as several appliance stores and tire centers in the 1950s and 1960s. In 1962 the founder's sons sold the business to Allied Stores Corporation, a New York retail conglomerate. Allied was purchased in 1986 by the Canadian Campeau Corporation, which quickly sold Block's to Federated Stores. In January, 1988, all Indiana Block's stores became part of the Lazarus chain, headquartered in Cincinnati. Lazarus, which operates five Indianapolis locations, closed the old Block's downtown store in January, 1993, due to insufficient profits.

DEBORAH B. MARKISOHN

William P. Jungclaus Company. The Jungclaus-Campbell Company is the oldest general contractor in Indianapolis and one of the oldest in the nation. It has built many of the city's historic buildings, including the CIRCLE TOWER, COLUMBIA CLUB, and INDIANA THEATRE.

William P. Jungclaus, the son of a sea captain, ran away from his home in Hanover, Germany, at age 11 to become a seaman. After eight years he came to the United States to visit his uncle, prominent architect DIEDRICH A. BOHLEN, and soon began his own company. The company was incorporated in 1875, two years after Jungclaus and John A. Schumacher founded it from the back of a wagon. The partnership, which lasted 21 years, was dissolved in 1895.

Jungclaus died in 1924, and his son Henry took control of the company. When Henry died in 1935, Fred W. Jungclaus acquired full interest in the company. In 1980 the firm became the Jungclaus-Campbell Company Inc., in recognition of a shift in ownership to the fourth generation of the family.

Jungclaus now specializes in hospital and school construction projects throughout the state. The list of the company's clients includes such corporate giants as IBM, ELI LILLY AND COMPANY, and General Motors Corporation. The company's office has been located at 825 Massachusetts Avenue since 1895 and there is now a branch office in Terre Haute.

GRETA E. SHANKLE

Williams, Martin Risser (1905–Dec. 17, 1986). Broadcast engineer and founder of WFMS-FM. Williams was born in Cambridge City, Indiana, and built an amateur radio station there while still in high school. After completing radio school in Valparaiso, he worked for RCA in Chicago and Cleveland and, in 1929, installed the first two-way radio in a commercial aircraft.

Williams returned to Indiana in 1930 as chief engineer of radio station WFBM. While there he built the city's first two-way radio mobile news and remote units, and did the original engineering for the Indiana State Police communication network. After leaving WFBM in 1940 he became a consulting engineer and helped put a number of Indiana stations on the air.

In March, 1957, Williams founded WFMS (95.5 FM), the first permanent commercial FM station in Indianapolis. In December, 1963, the outlet became the first in Indianapolis to broadcast continuously in stereo. Because Williams disputed repeated claims that WFMS had a small audience, he went on the air in 1971 and asked listeners to send him a dollar to show their support for the station. More than 500 people sent almost $700.

After rejecting a number of earlier offers for WFMS, Williams sold the station in 1972 to a Pennsylvania company, Susquehanna Broadcasting, for $605,000. Two years later he became principal owner and manager of WIUC, Winchester, Indiana. He retired from that station in 1979, but continued consulting work. He was selected to the Indiana chapter of the Broadcast Pioneers' Hall of Fame in 1982.

MICHAEL SPILLMAN

Williams Creek. Northside town bounded by 81st Street, College Avenue, Williams Creek, and Pennsylvania Street. In 1925, Washington Bank and Trust Company advertised Williams Creek Estates as "the Switzerland of Marion County." The bank developed the area as a planned community for affluent families eager to escape city traffic and taxes. Four miles of curving streets were laid out following wooded, hilly terrain alongside the creek. An architectural firm, PIERRE AND WRIGHT, designed and built five model homes in different styles—English Tudor, Spanish, French Chateau, Italian, and Colonial. Construction continued at a steady pace until the Great Depression, when home sales plummeted and Washington Bank and Trust went into receivership. In 1932, residents took control of town services. Since then, Williams Creek has been governed by a three-person council elected to serve four-year terms. Under UNIGOV, the community has the status of an INCLUDED TOWN.

Construction resumed after World War II and most of the lots were sold. Williams Creek became known as a prestigious address as bankers, attorneys, and executives moved to the area. The town has remained exclusively residential and in 1993 counted 147 homes and 580 residents. Williams Creek continues to be a quiet, secluded, upper class community.

CATHLEEN F. DONNELLY

Winona Memorial Hospital. Recognized as the first private, for-profit hospital in Indianapolis. The institution, known then as Memorial Clinic, opened its doors to patients in 1956. The Glossbrenner mansion, 3202 North Meridian Street (a site on the National Register of Historic Places), served as headquarters for the 24–bed clinic established by Joseph E. Walther, a practitioner of general and internal medicine. Walther founded the clinic at his office location because of his frustration with the shortage of hospital beds encountered by his emergency patients. The clinic secured private start-up funding for $1 million with the assistance of *Indianapolis Star* and *Indianapolis News* publisher EUGENE C. PULLIAM, attorney Frank McHale, and banker FRANK E. MCKINNEY, SR.

Memorial Clinic expanded to 42 beds in 1958. In 1965, groundbreaking ceremonies took place for Winona Memorial Hospital at 3232 North Meridian Street, a 278–bed medical-surgical complex built at a cost of $6.8 million. Walther named the hospital in honor of his mother, Winona McCampbell. Opened in December, 1966, the hospital complex later added a professional building and convalescent center, increasing its capacity to 405 beds. In 1983, a $16.6 million wing opened, featuring new emergency and ambulatory care facilities as well as the 24–bed Mary Margaret Walther Critical Care Unit, named after Dr. Walther's wife. Today the complex covers a city block.

Texas-based Republic Health Corp. purchased Winona Hospital for $56 million in 1985. Proceeds from the sale established the WALTHER CANCER INSTITUTE, a project given impetus by the death of Dr. Walther's wife from cancer. Winona Hospital was renamed Midwest Medical Center from July, 1991 to February, 1994. The hospital has over 20 specialized medical departments, including a physical rehabilitation institute, sleep-wake disorders center, and behavioral services program. More than 600 physicians are on staff.

TIM MULHERIN

Lloyd B. Walton, "The Man Who Made Winona Work," *Indianapolis Star Magazine,* Mar. 25, 1984.

Wishard, William Niles, Sr. (Oct. 10, 1851–Jan. 23, 1941). Pioneer in urology, "father" of City Hospital (now WISHARD MEMORIAL HOSPITAL), and medical educator. Born in Greenwood, Indiana, Wishard received M.D. degrees from Indiana Medical College in 1874 and Miami Medical College, Cincinnati, in 1876. He began his practice in Indianapolis, serving as coroner. Appointed superintendent of City Hospital in 1879, he served until January 1, 1887.

As superintendent, Wishard initiated the construction (1882–1885) of a modern general hospital to replace the inadequate facility he inherited. He also helped establish Indiana's first nursing school, Indianapolis Training School for Nurses, and worked for the merger of the Indiana medical schools that formed Indiana Medical College, the predecessor of INDIANA UNIVERSITY SCHOOL OF MEDICINE.

After his resignation as superintendent of City Hospital, Wishard pursued further medical studies in genito-urinary surgery and urology. An early specialist in this field, he left Indianapolis for a brief period to study in New York. Upon returning he practiced exclusively in genito-urinary and venereal diseases and served as chairman of that specialty for 49 years at Indiana Medical College and Indiana University School of Medicine. He is credited with pioneering work in prostate gland surgery.

Wishard was an originator of the Medical Practice Act of 1897, which established the State Board of Medical Registration and Examination. Throughout his life he held many influential positions in state and national organizations: member, Founders' Group of the American Board of Urology; president, Mississippi Valley Medical Association; president, American Urological Association; Surgeon General of Indiana. In 1975, Marion County General Hospital (formerly City Hospital) was renamed William Niles Wishard Memorial Hospital.

NANCY PIPPEN ECKERMAN
Indiana University School of Medicine

William Niles Wishard, Jr., "Wm. Niles Wishard, Sr.: Urologist, Educator, Administrator, Medical Statesman, Church and Family Man," *Urological Survey*, 19 (June, 1969), 113–121.

Wishard Memorial Hospital. Indianapolis' oldest hospital. For most of its history, Wishard Hospital's primary purpose has been to provide health care for the indigent. The idea of establishing a city-run hospital dates to the 1830s when LIVINGSTON DUNLAP, a prominent local physician, stressed the need for a permanent place to care for the sick, especially smallpox and cholera victims. Not until 1854, however, did construction of a hospital building begin, and when the facility was completed three years later the city decided that a hospital was no longer necessary and debated its future. With the outbreak of the Civil War, the city transferred the building to the federal government for use as a hospital for sick and wounded troops. At the war's end, the federal government gave the hospital building back to the city. In August, 1866, the city opened the Indianapolis City Hospital as a 75–bed charity hospital. As with all municipal hospitals, political problems, underfunding, and overcrowding plagued the institution almost from its inception.

During the late 19th century, the basic character of hospitals changed. Initially viewed as places of last resort for the unwanted of society, they became institutions offering advanced diagnosis and specialty services. At City Hospital, many improvements occurred under the administration of WILLIAM NILES WISHARD, SR. (1879–1886). Wishard obtained money to build additional ward space, established antiseptic procedures, and introduced a trained nursing staff. Various MEDICAL SCHOOLS used City Hospital for teaching purposes. By the end of the century, the hospital began offering specialty services such as obstetrics-gynecology, ophthalmology, gastroenterology, neurology, and urology. Despite these improvements, the hospital remained overcrowded and lacked adequate space for tuberculosis patients. Not until 1917, when Sunnyside Sanitarium opened, did the hospital have proper facilities to care for those suffering from tuberculosis.

City Hospital's constant overcrowding was a result of both chronic underfunding and its duty to care for a disproportionate share of the city's sick poor and all of the city's African-American population. In the 1920s and 1930s it was the only hospital in the city to care for blacks (both poor and pay patients). Because the hospital lacked proper funding and because of prevailing prejudices, the care of blacks at the institution was often inferior.

Despite these problems, City Hospital witnessed a number of improvements during the 1920s, including the relocation of the City Dispensary to the hospital, which gave the institution an outpatient department. The hospital also constructed a new surgery unit. In 1929, the hospital received a $50,000 anonymous donation to establish a clinical research laboratory. The laboratory was run by ELI LILLY AND COMPANY and continues in operation today.

The most significant improvements in the hospital's history occurred during the administration of Dr. CHARLES W. MYERS, who served as superintendent from 1931 to 1951. (After his retirement as superintendent, he served on the board of directors until 1968.) Myers was instrumental in securing the appointment of blacks to the hospital staff and the opening of new wards for black patients in 1939. He was also responsible for the purchase of the first iron lung (for use by polio victims), the opening of the first municipal cancer clinic, improved care for tuberculosis patients through the construction of a 100–bed FLOWER MISSION Hospital in 1936, new facilities for psychiatric patients, and the opening of the Krannert Institute of Cardiology in 1963. But increasing costs associated with modern medicine meant that the hospital could no longer rely exclusively on tax money for improvements. From the 1930s onward, the institution looked to philanthropy to fund a number of major improvements.

From 1905 to the late 1940s, the Board of Health and Charities governed the hospital. In 1945 and 1947 laws were passed to create the Department of Public Health and Hospitals. In 1951 Myers was instrumental in creating the HEALTH AND HOSPITAL CORPORATION, the current governing body, to remove the hospital from politics. In 1947 Myers changed the name of the hospital from the Indianapolis City Hospital to Indianapolis General Hospital. In 1959, the name changed to Marion County General Hospital to reflect the broader base of population served by the institution.

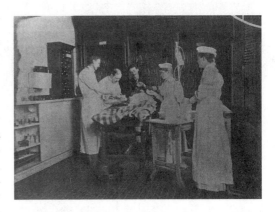

The first operating room in Indianapolis City Hospital (now Wishard Memorial Hospital).
[Indiana Historical Society, #C5614]

Despite the improvements introduced by Myers, his tenure was not without problems. After the construction of new patient wards in 1939, Myers was unable to gain approval for any more construction projects until 1962. Moreover, World War II took its toll on the hospital; approximately 50 percent of the active staff was called for military duty. Conditions became so bad that in 1956 the INDIANAPOLIS MEDICAL SOCIETY appointed a citizens' committee to investigate the situation. They concluded that the nursing board, the executive director, and the superintendent failed to communicate with each other; and the hospital lacked adequate equipment and supplies and suffered from insufficient funding and undue political influence.

Not until the 1960s were major changes undertaken to rectify the hospital's problems. Sunnyside Sanitarium and General Hospital merged in 1961 and the next year the hospital undertook a $16 million expansion. In 1969, the hospital entered into a formal agreement with Indiana University allowing faculty of the school to share joint appointments at Indiana University and at General Hospital.

By the 1970s, the hospital had 726 beds and numerous outpatient clinics. In an attempt to offer better services and consolidate its efforts, the hospital opened in 1975 the new Regenstrief Clinic, which had been substantially funded by the donations of Eli Lilly and Company and the Regenstrief family. Emphasis during these years was on improved service. Psychiatric care was offered both on the wards and at the Midtown Community Mental Health Center.

Delivery of services, however, was hindered by an image problem. Because the hospital was viewed exclusively as a charity hospital, its care was believed to be inferior and it thus had trouble attracting pay patients. To overcome this problem, the hospital in 1975 changed its name to Wishard Memorial Hospital and allowed Indiana University to manage the facility. Although the hospital remained a separate legal entity, it became a functional component of the INDIANA UNIVERSITY SCHOOL OF MEDICINE. The hospital also established a burn unit (1977) and became known for its treatment of trauma cases.

In the 1980s, skyrocketing medical costs and the hospital's obligation to care for the county's indigent and uninsured patients placed severe financial strains on Wishard. In 1988, a report commissioned by the hospital board (known as the Pettinga report) noted that the hospital provides a major service to the community and to the medical school. For those reasons, the commission recommended that the hospital seek more compensation from city and state governments to fulfill its original mission.

Lack of sufficient outpatient clinics to serve the community, an image problem, high black infant mortality, overcrowding, and the lack of funding remain problems in the 1990s. Still, Wishard Memorial Hospital is the county's largest provider of health care services to the indigent and is well known for its treatment of trauma and burn patients.

The fiscal affairs of the hospital have improved with the increase of support from federal programs such as Medicare and Medicaid, as well as private insurance coverage. Tax support of the hospital represents less than 25 percent of its total budget. Many city-county hospitals have closed but Wishard continues as a success story.

KATHERINE MANDUSIC MCDONELL

Wolter, Adolph Gustav (Sept. 7, 1903–Oct. 15, 1980). Sculptor and teacher. Wolter was born in Reutlingen, Germany, and attended the Academy of Fine Arts in Stuttgart before immigrating to Minneapolis in 1922. He moved to In-

dianapolis in 1933 to carve the sculptured figure reliefs for the INDIANA STATE LIBRARY AND HISTORICAL BUILDING. He graduated from HERRON SCHOOL OF ART and taught sculpture at the INDIANAPOLIS ART LEAGUE.

His local achievements include a bust of Crispus Attucks (1943) for CRISPUS ATTUCKS HIGH SCHOOL, a fountain statue in UNIVERSITY PARK (1973), and the Louis Chevrolet memorial at the INDIANAPOLIS MOTOR SPEEDWAY (1975). He carved the exterior stone figures and interior religious carvings that grace SECOND PRESBYTERIAN CHURCH (1958), items for Broadway United Methodist Church, CHRIST CHURCH CATHEDRAL, Meridian Street Methodist Church, and figures at Washington Park Cemetery East. He designed and produced the CASPER award for the COMMUNITY SERVICE COUNCIL. Wolter's Indiana exterior designs adorn buildings at Purdue, DePauw, and Ball State universities. A significant memorial is *The Four Freedoms*, completed at Detroit in 1948.

MARY JANE MEEKER

Woman's Department Club. Women's civic association. LUELLA FRANCES SMITH MCWHIRTER organized the Woman's Department Club in 1912 to stimulate spiritual, ethical, artistic, and educational growth among Indianapolis women through study and community work. The club first met at the roof garden of the Hume-Mansur Building and had six departments—art, drama, music, education, literature, and home, civic, and social welfare. Over time the club organized new departments to accommodate the changing needs of women and the community. For example, a new section for blind women was organized in July, 1920, modeled after a similar club in Fort Wayne.

The Woman's Department Club early began to undertake community projects. In 1913 members aided in flood relief. They began a nutritional emphasis in the Indianapolis Public Schools by furnishing school lunches, primarily for children of immigrants. In 1917 the club purchased a house at 1702 North Meridian Street to remodel for meetings and work. During World War II rooms in the clubhouse were donated to help the Red Cross two days a week. The club sponsored first aid and home nursing. During the 1950s members counseled and provided clothing to women being released from the Indiana Women's Prison. The Art Department provided space for local artists to exhibit their work, and the clubhouse became the first gallery for one-person art shows in Indianapolis. In 1964 meetings were moved to the Krannert Room of Clowes Memorial Hall on the Butler University campus.

ELLEN TEVAULT

Women in Politics. Despite its reputation for political conservatism, Indianapolis produced several women who were among the first in the nation to participate actively in the political process. In 1850 Indiana became the first state in the nation with an organized suffrage group, and in the 1870s the Indianapolis Equal Suffrage Society was founded. Prominent in that society were ZERELDA WALLACE (stepmother of author LEW WALLACE and wife of Governor David Wallace) and MAY WRIGHT SEWALL, who became national figures in the women's suffrage movement. By 1890 Indianapolis was a center for crusading suffragettes: in 1897 Susan B. Anthony, a popular speaker in Indianapolis, addressed the Indiana General Assembly in a joint session recommending that it ask Congress to pass a constitutional amendment enfranchising women; and in 1899 the National Suffrage Association, of which Anthony was president, met in both the PLYMOUTH (CONGREGATIONAL) CHURCH and the old DENISON HOTEL in Indianapolis.

The Indiana Federation of Clubs, founded in the early 20th century, taught women how to organize. Many prominent Indianapolis women participated in a national society of clubwomen called Pioneer Workers. Among its members May Wright Sewall, Mary Evans Woollen, GRACE JULIAN CLARKE, Elizabeth Barnett Hitt, and Susan Hatch Perkins were Indianapolis women active on behalf of women's suffrage.

The Women's Franchise League of Indiana, which had been organized in Terre Haute in the early 1900s, made its headquarters in Indianapolis until 1917. Prominent local members included LUELLA FRANCES SMITH MCWHIRTER (who served as a director of Peoples State Bank, founded by her husband Felix), CHARITY DYE, Belle O'Hair, and Dr. AMELIA R. KELLER. When suffrage came in 1919, the Franchise League was no longer necessary and was replaced by the LEAGUE OF WOMEN VOTERS.

Two of the women's groups most active at the turn of the century—the suffragists and the YOUNG WOMEN'S CHRISTIAN ASSOCIATION—had racially integrated memberships. Rhonda Hanley, who launched a voter registration drive in the early 1920s, was the first in Indianapolis to organize politically in the local black community.

Despite this auspicious beginning, political activity by Indianapolis women as well as women nationally declined dramatically following universal suffrage. Marion County resident Effie M. Blue was defeated in her attempt to become a state senator in 1920, the year women gained the vote. In 1922 Elizabeth Rainey became the first Indianapolis woman elected to the General Assembly, but few women followed her into the political arena. When in the late 1940s Mayor ALBERT G. FEENEY appointed Agnes R. Conner as the first woman to head the Indianapolis Parks Board in its 50-year history, the news made page one. When the *Indianapolis Star* ran an article in November, 1955, saluting "Career Gals," not one was a political activist and most had decidedly stereotypical careers. Reports in local news media following the 1958 local elections showed one woman elected to the City Council and one elected as county recorder; both were identified by their husband's name.

The lack of significant political involvement by Indianapolis women was of sufficient concern to then-Mayor Richard G. Lugar that in August, 1972, he appointed Mary Ann Butters to chair a task force on women, with Frances Dodson Rhome as vice-chair. The early 1970s also saw the establishment of an Indianapolis chapter of the National Women's Political Caucus, formed to encourage women's participation at all levels of elected government. The original members of that group included many women who would later become prominent in Indianapolis politics. Virginia Dill McCarty served as president of the IWPC and also was the first woman candidate for state attorney general. Sheila Suess was an unsuccessful Republican candidate for U.S. Congress in 1980.

Paula Parker (later Paula Parker-Sawyers) was elected to two terms on the City-County Council and later became the city's first black female deputy mayor. One of the most active early members of the caucus was Marge O'Laughlin, at that time the city clerk, who later was one of the top vote getters for the state Republican party, first as clerk of the courts and subsequently as state treasurer. In 1993 Pam Carter became the first African-American woman to serve as Indiana attorney general.

SHEILA SUESS KENNEDY

Women in Religion. As long as there have been churches in Indianapolis, there have been churchwomen involved in religious work. In 1822 an interdenominational group of residents formed the Indianapolis Sabbath School Union; women comprised half the Sabbath School teachers. Although national women's suffrage was still far in the future, at some early churches, including AME Zion, women members could vote on church matters, which gave them a voice in governing their congregation. In 1898 evangelical churchwomen organized a Missionary Social Union of Indianapolis to help direct and coordinate the activities of women's church groups. This group joined a national organization of Federated Church Women (now CHURCH WOMEN UNITED) in the 1930s, linking local women's activities with national missionary society movements. Women's organizations cooked meals for church gatherings and conducted fund raisers. Before 1925 the Ladies Alliance of Corinthian Baptist Church secured enough money through fundraising activity to pay for the construction of a new church building. Countless women also were active in social welfare and social reform initiatives—everything from orphanages to temperance—that were not necessarily sponsored or endorsed by their own congregation but were nonetheless religiously motivated.

These women played an important if unheralded role in the lives of their churches. They provided economic and emotional support for the congregation and its missions, but rarely served in congregation-wide leadership roles. Although Indianapolis churchwomen continue to fill support positions, since the 1970s they have also stepped into the arena of church leadership. Today women are pastors of congregations, professors at theological seminaries, and officers of ministerial associations. In Indianapolis, as elsewhere, positions in religious organizations once held exclusively by men are now open to women.

Women in Religious Professions. The number of Indianapolis congregations with women serving as ministers, priests, or rabbis has visibly increased during the past 20 years, although not all denominations accept the practice. In some cases Indianapolis has had the distinction of being first in the nation in the inclusion of women in non-traditional religious leadership positions.

Rabbi Sandy Eisenberg Sasso was the first woman ordained from the Reconstructionist Rabbinical College. In 1977 she became the first female rabbi in Indianapolis where she and her husband, Rabbi Dennis C. Sasso, served the Beth-El Zedeck congregation. They were the first rabbinical couple in Jewish history. She also was a member of many service organization boards and was cofounder of the Women's Interfaith Table, which brings together for dialogue Jewish, Catholic, and Protestant women.

National attention was also focused on Indianapolis January 1, 1977, when Jackie Means became the first woman in the United States to be ordained an Episcopal priest in accordance with church regulations. She gained a national reputation for her work in prison ministry in the city and state. The following month Tanya Beck Vonnegut became an Episcopal priest. She was honored as the founding mother of the JULIAN CENTER, which ministers to women through classes, counseling, and therapy groups and sponsors the Sojourner Shelter for abused women.

During the past 20 years the employment of women as religious professionals has become more acceptable to many congregations. The enrollment figures at CHRISTIAN THEOLOGICAL SEMINARY (CTS) reflect this trend. Their registrar's report indicates that in 1961 women comprised only 8 percent of the seminary's students. The percentage of women had doubled ten years later (to 16 percent) and more than doubled during the following decade (to 35 percent by 1981). By the early 1990s over 50 percent of students at CTS were women; there were six women on the teaching staff. Sue Cardwell, the first woman professor at CTS (1979), was also the first woman president of the American Association of Pastoral Counselors and the first from the Christian Church (Disciples of Christ) to be a seminary professor.

Interracial dialogue to create more understanding is a major concern of women, as evidenced by Rev. A. H. Byfield, pastor of Robinson Community African Methodist Episcopal (AME) Church. She was the 1991 recipient of the YWCA Phyllis Wheatley Salute Award for working to eliminate racism in Indianapolis, as well as the first black woman to serve as president of the INDIANA INTERRELIGIOUS COMMISSION ON HUMAN EQUALITY (IICHE). In 1991 Byfield became the first woman to be elected a member of and to chair the Indiana delegation to the AME National General Assembly and was the first woman elected president of the AME Ministerial Alliance of Indiana.

Catholic sisters have long worked as teachers or hospital staff. Today, excluding the priesthood, there are few limits to the options open to them. Sister (Sr.) Theresa Mount was the first sister appointed as rector of St. Maur's when it was a seminary for Catholic men. Sr. Jane Bodine, an expert in finance, with support from LILLY ENDOWMENT educated religious communities in Indianapolis and across the nation about development and stewardship. Sr. Nancy Crowder opened and operated the city's first facility for the homeless—the Holy Family Shelter. Sr. Loretta Schafer became the first woman chancellor of the Indianapolis Archdiocese and was among the first women in the United States to serve in that capacity.

Laywomen in Staff or Volunteer Religious Positions. During the past 30 years the leadership positions in most religious bodies have gradually included laywomen in positions traditionally held by laymen.

Valerie Dillon was the first Catholic laywoman to be a director in the Indianapolis Archdiocese, serving as Director of Family Life (1982–1991). She was also the first woman to serve as acting editor of the *Criterion* and as president of the Professional Association of Catholic National Family Life Ministries. Indianapolis Archdiocese Chancellor, Susan Magnant, was the first lay-

woman in this position. Ellen Healey, the first woman president of the Archdiocese, also chaired an historic Women's Consultation to give Catholic women the opportunity to express their feeling, positive and negative, about the church.

Other laywomen have served as volunteer leaders to respond to social concerns. For instance, Birdie Whiteside mobilized women volunteers from inner-city and suburban churches of many denominations to help with the Guiding Light Christian Service, started in 1953 as a project to minister to shut-ins, nursing home residents, and prison inmates. Churchwomen were also instrumental in beginning adult day care centers and in creating food pantries, including the GLEANERS FOOD BANK. Other changes include a new role for the clergy spouse. Formerly always female, she was considered hired without pay to work for the church along with her husband. Now the spouse may be a husband and the majority are employed, sometimes in religious vocations or volunteerism beyond their own congregation. United Methodist Dorothea Green, for example, was the first woman president (1975–1977) of the Indianapolis-based Indiana Council of Churches (ICC) and the first woman director of the IICHE.

Women's religious work in Indianapolis began with service as Sunday School teachers and has progressed through a wide variety of other support activities (meal preparation, fund raising) to full-time ministerial positions. Mirroring and sometimes leading the national experience of churchwomen, Indianapolis has been and continues to be fertile soil for women in religious work.

JANE S. FRIBLEY
Church Women United
and Indiana Women's History Archives

Women in the Professions and Business.
Homemaking and farming were the first occupations for pioneering Indianapolis women, who settled in the city along with men in the early 1820s. As Indianapolis grew, women such as Elizabeth Nowland and poet SARAH T. BOLTON were known to operate taverns and inns for travelers. Widows continued farms and businesses they had begun with their deceased spouses. Other

women made a living as prostitutes during the railroad and canal building booms that hit Indianapolis in the 1830s and 1840s. During this period women generally did not speak in public, and acting was not respectable for women until the 1850s. However, education did become more acceptable for women. Young women with as little as an eighth-grade education found their first professional jobs as teachers because they could be paid less than men.

Women's colleges and coed colleges educated upper class women, although not necessarily for employment outside the home. Numerous college-educated women joined civic organizations using their educations and leadership skills to establish many of Indianapolis' schools, hospitals, cultural centers, and social services agencies and programs. The overwhelming predominance of women in professional social work today is rooted in those early volunteer endeavors.

During the 1860s the Civil War left women in charge of farms and businesses as the men marched off to fight. This war also opened up the field of nursing for Indianapolis women who volunteered in hospitals set up to care for wounded soldiers. Jane Merrill Ketcham, CATHARINE MERRILL, Bettie Bates, Jane Graydon, Caroline Test Coburn, and Adelia Carter New, among others, served as nurses. Some of them, such as C. Annette Buckel, a physician, also handled administrative and supervisory duties. Yet, formal nurses' training was not available in Indianapolis until 1883, and the Indiana State Nurses Association was not founded in the city until 1904.

Women were participating in the business community of Indianapolis in the 1870s, but chroniclers recorded little about them. In *Sketches of Prominent Citizens of 1876*, author John Nowland lists four pages of men's names and only one woman, his mother, Elizabeth Nowland. However, this biographical sketch, which describes her as a devoted mother and friend to all, does not mention that she is the same woman who ran a tavern in the 1830s. The 1893 *Pictorial and Biographical Memoirs of Indianapolis and Marion County, Indiana* listed over a hundred men and only nine women. These nine were educators, librarians, an elocutionist, a writer, a farmer, and a florist.

Women began moving into business as typists and secretaries during the 1880s and 1890s. In 1893 there were three women reporters working on Indianapolis' daily newspapers. Some businesswomen and women attorneys started as secretaries or court reporters; one such was Indiana's first woman attorney, Antoinette Dakin Leach, born in Indianapolis in 1859. Leach was admitted to practice after appealing to the Indiana Supreme Court in 1893 when her application to the Sullivan, Indiana, bar was denied. She later practiced in Indianapolis in the firm of Enslow and Leach until her retirement in 1917. However, it was not until 1931 that eight Indianapolis women helped found the Indiana Women Lawyers Association and later held annual joint meetings with women physicians in efforts to repeal legislative and traditional restrictions on women professionals.

Early in the 20th century, MADAM C. J. WALKER's cosmetics and hair care business made her Indianapolis' and the nation's first black woman millionaire. She trained her door-to-door agents and gave many black women their first start in business. Prejudice kept black women segregated except as domestics until the civil rights movement of the 1960s, but many supported themselves and their families as teachers, doctors, nurses, journalists, social workers, and businesswomen in their own neighborhoods. In 1900, LILLIAN THOMAS FOX was the first black columnist for the *Indianapolis News*. She, Dr. Beulah Wright Porter, Ida Webb Bryant, and members of the Women's Improvement Club later helped establish (1905) and run a tuberculosis camp to care for infected blacks.

During the early 1900s women continued to broaden their professional and business opportunities. Indiana's Federation of Business and Professional Women began in Indianapolis in 1913. Then the "man" shortages on the home front during World Wars I and II allowed women to enter some occupations previously closed to them.

The positions of the women recognized annually by the early Women's Council of the CHAMBER OF COMMERCE changed dramatically from the 1940s to the mid–1970s. The executive secretaries, teachers, and retail personnel gave way to more women owners and presidents of their companies. Ruth Queisser, owner of Ruth's Cozy

Sandwich Shop, was the first woman to earn the Chamber's "Businessman [sic] of the Year" award in 1972.

In recent years the numbers of women significantly increased in many business and professional fields. In 1979 only 9 percent of the Indianapolis police force was female and there were no women firefighters, but lawsuits (or threats of suits) changed that. By the early 1990s, 15 percent of "sworn officers" (and 75 percent of civilian employees) in the INDIANAPOLIS POLICE DEPARTMENT were women, and the INDIANAPOLIS FIRE DEPARTMENT had recruited 21 women (approximately 3 percent) as firefighters. Women continue to be heavily represented in the field of education, comprising almost four-fifths of all teachers in the INDIANAPOLIS PUBLIC SCHOOLS as of 1992. There has been a significant movement of women into the legal profession during the past two decades, a change reflected in the membership of the Indianapolis Bar Association which is now about one-fifth female. In 1957 women made up 32 percent of Marion County's employment force (a reduction from the 1940s war years), but in 1989 women comprised just over half—50.3 percent—of the county's employees.

A rarity, businesswoman ARDATH BURKHART served on the boards of 12 different businesses and organizations in 1972, yet a 1990 survey found that only 9 percent or 25 of 278 officers, senior managers, and directors of the ten largest companies headquartered in Indianapolis were women. In fact, few top businesses and law firms reported more than one woman at the top level, on their boards or as partners. The difficulty of breaking the so-called glass ceiling, cited by a 1990 U.S. Department of Labor report, is one reason why women started their own businesses. It is probable that the glass ceiling will shatter in the 21st century, or women-owned businesses in Indianapolis will boom.

JILL LOUGH CHAMBERS

Women's Christian Temperance Union (WCTU).

National organization founded and comprised entirely of women, with the avowed goal of abolishing the traffic and consumption of liquor. Tired of the abuse and neglect they and their children had received from drunken husbands, these women decided that the only way to defeat the evils of drink was by outlawing alcohol entirely. To accomplish this, the women relied on a combination of prayer, persuasion, witnessing, and propaganda. Intent on demonstrating the purity of freedom from drink, the symbol worn by all members of the WCTU was a bow of white ribbon.

Indiana had known temperance movements before, but the first formal appearance of the WCTU in Indiana was on March 3, 1874, when the Indiana Central WCTU was founded. ZERELDA WALLACE, widow of a former governor of Indiana and stepmother of General LEW WALLACE (the author of Ben-Hur), became the first president (1874–1876). Mrs. Thomas B. Harvey became president of the first Indianapolis chapter of the WCTU. The first WCTU meeting in Indianapolis occurred in ROBERTS PARK METHODIST CHURCH at Vermont and Delaware streets. A mass rally, also in Indianapolis, followed on September 3 and 4, 1874, in the FIRST BAPTIST CHURCH at the corner of Vermont and Meridian streets.

Insisting that liquor traffic would be halted only by means of the ballot, and believing that women were the chief sufferers of the effects of alcohol abuse, Wallace urged women to fight for the right to vote. Women's suffrage thus became one of the issues identified with the WCTU. Wallace returned to serve a second term as president of the Indiana WCTU (1878–1882). Four subsequent presidents (through 1968) were from Indianapolis, and WCTU conventions often were held in the capital city.

For more than a century the WCTU of Indiana sought to end the drinking of liquor and, until women achieved the ballot in 1920, pushed for the right of women to vote. Their activities not only attracted thousands of members to the WCTU, but resulted in changes in Indiana's liquor laws. The Indiana WCTU engaged in numerous social welfare activities; homes for orphans and unwed mothers were established, and contests for the best poems, stories, and slogans about temperance were held. The Indianapolis chapter of the WCTU was equally fervent, holding its own prayer meetings, publishing temperance pamphlets and newspapers, and doing its own share of social work through the WHEELER MISSION MINISTRIES. The WCTU never lost sight of its original goal, which was complete abstinence from alcohol, but in the post–World War II years chose to revive the Christian part of the organization by encouraging ecumenism as well as temperance. The WCTU, with a small chapter in Irvington, remains active in Marion County in the 1990s, though with a lower profile than during its heyday in the late 19th and early 20th centuries.

PATRICIA FOGLEMAN

Frances B. Hendrickson, *Hoosier Heritage, 1874–1974: Women's Christian Temperance Union* (Indianapolis, 1974); Mrs. E. Kemp, *History of the Frances E. Willard WCTU in Indianapolis* (Indianapolis, 1917); Mrs. Burt S. Taylor, *Indianapolis Central Women's Christian Temperance Union Historical Report* (Indianapolis, 1958); *Indianapolis News*, Dec. 30, 1993.

Women's Clubs. The club movement in Indianapolis closely paralleled that in the rest of the country. Possibilities for intellectual and cultural growth for women were limited in 1875, when the first woman's club in the city was founded. The women who came together to organize the INDIANAPOLIS WOMAN'S CLUB were inquisitive and adventurous enough to try to broaden their vision of the world. They were not, however, adventurous enough to try to do it all at once or to embrace women's suffrage, although several of them personally did so. In a day when it was widely regarded as a woman's duty to stay at home and take care of her house and children, the Indianapolis Woman's Club's object, "to form an organized center for the mental and social culture of its members, and for the improvement of domestic life," may well have seemed adventurous to some. The first program, "To be a good housekeeper, is it necessary to devote one's entire time to the work," seems designed to silence or to answer the many critics this venture must have had. Much traditionalism and conservatism had to be overcome or sidestepped in order to advance their considerable interest in disciplined study of a variety of topics.

Once the dam of resistance was broken, however, women's clubs proliferated. Among early clubs were Fortnightly (founded in 1885), Over the Teacups (1890), and the CATHARINE MERRILL Club (1885; named for a famous local educator). By 1888, having outgrown members' front parlors as meeting places, clubwomen founded the PROPYLAEUM so that women's groups could have a place to meet for their study of literature, music, science, fine arts, and fostering civic responsibility. In 1890, Miss Elizabeth Nicholson suggested that the Indianapolis Woman's Club's first meeting of the year be followed by a reception for representatives of other women's literary clubs. Thus began the first state organization of clubs, the Indiana Union of Literary Clubs, which later (1906) consolidated with the Indiana State Federation of Clubs. By 1900 the newspapers thought club programs newsworthy enough that they published the entire annual programs of Clio, InterNos, Philomathean, Irvington Fortnightly Club, Magazine Club, Indianapolis Woman's Club, Research Club, Parlor Club, Fortnightly Literary Club, Irvington Women's Club, Local Council of Women, Conversation Club, Over the Teacups, Sketching Club, Catharine Merrill Club, and MATINEE MUSICALE.

By the beginning of the 20th century, women were also organizing as volunteers to meet the needs of the community as they pertained to schools, health, welfare, education, and libraries, as well as culture. The Indianapolis Woman Suffrage Association and the WOMEN'S CHRISTIAN TEMPERANCE UNION are examples of women's broadening interest and determination to participate fully in the life of the community. The tension between those who wished to stay with the traditional literary role and those who wanted to become involved in civic affairs did not keep women of this generation apart, however. They discussed and resolved their differences, sometimes by agreeing to disagree. And, indeed, the proliferation of clubs allowed women to follow diverse interests. An editorial of the period remarked that it has "not been good enough to belong to one club; the argument has apparently been that if one is good, more is better." The many cross-club memberships allowed women to fulfill their own agendas without altering those of the clubs to which they belonged. By 1909 the 7th District Federation of Clubs directory listed 83 clubs in Marion County alone.

As an increasing number of women began to attend colleges and universities, alumnae associations for women's colleges were formed, as were sorority alumnae clubs. The Vassar Club was the first to be formed, in 1902, followed by clubs for other women's colleges and alumnae of coeducational institutions. These clubs have been important for the social life of their members as well as providing support for their institutions. The AMERICAN ASSOCIATION OF UNIVERSITY WOMEN, formed first in 1909 as the Association of Collegiate Alumni, provided support for education and continued to provide an important forum on education.

An understanding of the breadth of women's interests can be seen in the organization of the WOMAN'S DEPARTMENT CLUB of Indianapolis, founded in 1912. LUELLA FRANCES SMITH MCWHIRTER invited some of her friends and the presidents of all clubs in the 7th district federation to help plan. On February 29, 1912, all clubwomen in Indianapolis were invited to a lunch on the roof garden of the Hume-Mansur Building and nearly 700 responded, 600 of whom became charter members. The constitutional object was "to enable the women of Indianapolis, by study, practical work, and united effort, to do their part in promoting spiritual, ethical, artistic and educational growth of their city and in advancing its general welfare." Meeting at the Propylaeum for its first five years, it bought a club building at 1702 North Meridian in 1917, which it was forced to abandon in 1964. The original departments of the club, which were renamed and expanded over the years, were Civic, Art, Music, Social Welfare, Education, Home Economics, and Literature. Philanthropic clubs flourished too. Kappa Kappa Kappa was founded in 1901, followed by innumerable other Greek letter groups from all segments of society whose aims were to help deserving girls by giving scholarships and awards.

The passage of the 19th Amendment gave further impetus to those women who wanted to devote their energy and expertise to the management of local affairs, at least in a voluntary capacity. The LEAGUE OF WOMEN VOTERS of Indianapolis, organized in 1920 as one of the original city chapters in the nation, presented citizenship schools and studied a host of governmental topics. As soon as it became apparent that the League would not be affiliated with a political party, women organized the Woman's Democratic Club in 1921 and the 7th District Republican Club in 1922. Not directly involved in the political sector, the JUNIOR LEAGUE OF INDIANAPOLIS was organized in 1921 to promote voluntarism and to develop the potential for voluntary participation in community affairs. Latreians, dedicated to social service, followed in 1925

The following decades saw women organizing to pursue interests closer to home. Beginning in 1929 Marion County Extension Homemakers Clubs began meeting in small neighborhood groups. In 1980 there were 96 such clubs with 1,350 members. Garden clubs also proved to be popular. The North End Garden Club was founded in 1928 by Anna Hosea, followed in 1930 by the Indianapolis Garden Club. By 1988 the Central District of the Garden Clubs of Indiana, Inc., could list 35 such organizations in Marion and surrounding counties. Garden clubs have been responsible for beautifying many public areas in the city.

Over the decades women formed clubs based upon mutual interests and upon professional affiliations: Extension Homemakers Club, Indianapolis branches of the National Council of Negro Women and the National Council of Jewish Women, Business and Professional Women's Club, Women in Communications, Newcomers clubs, and hobby clubs for everything from dolls to buttons. Always, however, the object of these organizations was to provide some kind of service either to the community or to their own families. Women have also joined auxiliaries of men's organizations. The first such was the Athenaeum Auxiliary, founded in 1876 to aid the Turners and to provide a scholarship fund. Today auxiliaries still exist for the AMERICAN LEGION, the Jaycees, the Sheriff's Department, the Marion County Medical Society, and the Indianapolis District Dental Society.

In 1959, the *Indianapolis Star* began publishing a directory of women's clubs. The 10th edition of that directory appeared October 15, 1978, headed by this observation: "Volunteer efforts are a necessity if the needs of a million plus population are to be met. In recent years activities have become more professional in nature . . . and many have opened their membership to men." From Altrusa to Zonta, from 25 chapters of American Business Women Association to Women Lions, Women Rotary, Women's Council of the Chamber of Commerce, over 170 organizations are listed. This includes, of course, women's voluntary organizations that assist local hospitals and social service centers and support arts organizations, and women's groups devoted to political action, especially that concerning women's rights. The 1988 *Woman's Guide to Organizations for Women* categorizes these organizations: Support groups, Volunteer, Professional, and Social. Among the social groups listed are Circle City Chapter of Sweet Adelines, Inc., innumerable sororities, hobby groups, and two chapters of the Daughters of the American Revolution.

From 1875 until today, women have formed clubs in order to improve their lives and the lives of their communities. Just as they organized in small groups of like-minded women, they soon saw the need to gain additional support for the projects they were advocating. The INDIANAPOLIS COUNCIL OF WOMEN was founded in 1892 to bring clubs together so that they might communicate and strengthen their efforts. Early women's club organizers seemed to have had the agenda that may yet prevail. In 1990, 135 clubs with 30,000 members were represented on the Council, and today working in coalition with others is an accepted and necessary method for women who want to make a difference in the life of the community. Woman's clubs were, in a sense, precursors of today's support groups. From the early literary clubs, where fellow members were sympathetic and supportive listeners, through the social, service, and educational clubs, where ideas could be tested and strength for reform came from numbers, women in clubs were supporting each other's growth and development as full-fledged members of their community.

Women in Indianapolis, from MAY WRIGHT SEWALL to present day movers and shakers, have always dealt with community problems in a practical way. When, in earlier times, men had all the power to pass laws and to make policy, they formed clubs to inform and to reinforce one another as they persuaded their husbands and sons

to think about issues important to women. They also found niches in which they could perform service to the community. As women gained the vote and an increasing voice in community decisions, they continued to use their club networks to reinforce their volunteer contribution to the well-being of Indianapolis and all its citizens. A hallmark of this city is the prevalence of public-private partnerships, the history of which can be partially traced to the conviction of women and their clubs that local problems have local solutions and that they, as citizens, should become involved in the process. Cultural organizations, hospitals, social service organizations, as well as individual students who receive recognition and scholarships, have prospered in direct relationship to the contributions of women's clubs in Indianapolis.

BARBARA E. ZIMMER

Jane Cunningham Croly, *History of the Woman's Club Movement* (1898); Grace Gates Courtney, *History Indiana Federation of Clubs* [sic] (1939); Mary L. Ely and Eve Chappell, *Women in Two Worlds* (1938).

Women's Movement (1960-Present).

In the years since the passage of the 19th Amendment no decades saw more change in the status of women than those between 1960 and 1990. The national women's movement that began in the 1960s was well represented in Indianapolis, where participants aggressively pursued legal, political, and social changes to improve women's status in the face of local opposition. The consequences of this late 20th century movement continue to have an impact on the city into the 1990s.

In 1963 President John F. Kennedy created a President's Commission on the Status of Women which recommended extensive legal and social changes in women's roles. In Indianapolis and across the nation the commission's report spurred discussion about the status of women. In March, 1968, Governor Roger Branigin sponsored a "Status of Women" conference at the Indiana State Fairgrounds. The conference included sessions on the present and future roles of women in government, business, the professions, and voluntary work.

In the 1970s women created an agenda for their "movement." In Indianapolis, according to the *Indianapolis Star*, "the concept of equal rights [for women] was supported by Indiana lawmakers, educators, housewives and husbands." Although the *Star* may have overstated the case, there were clear indications of change locally as well as nationally. In 1971 the Indiana General Assembly amended the 1961 Indiana Civil Rights Law, making sex discrimination in employment illegal. The amended law passed but was strongly opposed by the only woman state senator, Indianapolis' Joan M. Gubbins, who would later lead the fight against passage of the Equal Rights Amendment (ERA) in Indiana. On October 13, 1971, the same day the U.S. House of Representatives passed the ERA, the Greater Indianapolis Women's Political Caucus formed. Many of its members were also members of the Indianapolis Women's Liberation Organization who had participated in the August, 1971, Women's March for Equality in downtown Indianapolis to celebrate the anniversary of the 19th Amendment and the new movement for "women's equality."

In 1971 Indianapolis made national headlines when one Mari McCloskey obtained a court injunction against the Indianapolis Motor Speedway guaranteeing her the right to enter the pits and garage area, which previously had been off limits to women. The next year the Indianapolis Chapter of the NATIONAL ORGANIZATION FOR WOMEN (NOW) organized and as one of its early objectives worked to expand opportunities for women and blacks in radio and television. Success came when NOW protests led to the hiring of Jane Pauley by WISH-TV Channel 8 in 1972. NOW members also collected statistics about women workers, endorsed women candidates, and lobbied the legislature on issues such as displaced homemakers, equal pay, child support, and credit access.

Following a new federal mandate that no person shall be excluded on the basis of sex from any program receiving federal assistance (Title IX), the INDIANA HIGH SCHOOL ATHLETIC ASSOCIATION, headquartered in Indianapolis, hired the first female member of its executive staff and the following year sanctioned girls' sports. In 1972 the Indianapolis LEAGUE OF WOMEN VOTERS and the YWCA brought together women's groups at a "Question Your Candidate" session with the goal of informing the electorate about women's issues.

All this activity among and for women created a positive atmosphere locally for the ERA in the campaign year of 1972. Lobbying efforts of Indianapolis native and National Women's Political Caucus spokesperson Jill Ruckelshaus helped persuade the national Republican party to support ERA in its platform. The first attempt to ratify the amendment in Indiana was unsuccessful, however, thanks in large part to Senators Joan Gubbins and Angeline P. Alstatt, both of Indianapolis, who led the anti-ERA group in the State Senate. Gubbins and Alstatt championed the traditional role of mother and the nuclear family, which they said was threatened by the amendment. Local pro-ERA groups attempted to rebut this argument: Women in Communication distributed an ERA educational package, the Greater Indianapolis ERA Coalition lobbied for passage. The INDIANAPOLIS PRESS CLUB, the League of Women Voters, and Concerned Women Lawyers also supported the amendment. These groups were finally successful on January 18, 1977, when Indiana ratified the ERA. Although the Stop-ERA movement led nationally by Phyllis Schlafly and aided locally by attorney Evelyn Pitschke began a movement in the late 1970s to rescind the amendment, Indiana's legislature never withdrew its support of the controversial measure.

The struggle over ERA consumed much of the energy of local women's rights groups, but these groups tackled other issues of importance as well. In 1973 Mayor Richard G. Lugar's Task Force on Women released a report on the status of women and girls in Marion County which cited lingering discrepancies in job availabilities and pay levels for women. Also in 1973 the Woman's Anti-Crime Crusade, a volunteer group composed of thousands of Indianapolis women and the Mayor's Task Force, formed Women United Against Rape and initiated the nation's first 24-hour rape crisis centers at nine Indianapolis hospitals. Indianapolis NOW formed its own task forces in 1973 and charged them with three separate goals: to attack stereotyping of women and girls in elementary school textbooks and their absence from both history and science texts; to examine the issues of health and well-being of women with particular focus on abortion and rape; and to battle discriminatory practices against women employees and in the areas of housing and credit. NOW promoted a pro-choice state amendment following the U.S. Supreme Court's decision in *Roe v. Wade*, but the Indiana General Assembly passed a law in 1973 which allowed abortions but placed restrictions both on when and how they could be performed in the state.

The year 1975, the "International Women's Year," proved to be a landmark for women in Indianapolis. The Rt. Reverend John P. Craine of the Episcopal Diocese of Indianapolis vowed to ordain no more priests until the 1976 General Convention of the church allowed the ordination of women. Two years later an Indianapolis woman, Jackie Means, became the denomination's first ordained priest. In 1975 Mayor Richard Lugar named Carlyn Johnson as the first woman to serve on the METROPOLITAN DEVELOPMENT COMMISSION. The INDIANAPOLIS POLICE DEPARTMENT appointed a new team headed by a woman to have sole responsibility for sex-related crimes. The year also marked the foundation of the Julian Mission (now the JULIAN CENTER), a counseling center for women in crisis founded by the woman who would become Indianapolis' second ordained Episcopal priest, Tanya Beck Vonnegut. The Julian Center created the Sojourner Shelter for abused women in 1977. By the end of the 1970s Indianapolis attorney Virginia Dill McCarty became the first woman federal prosecutor in the nation in 1977, and Janet Guthrie made national headlines as the first woman to attempt to qualify for the Indianapolis 500–Mile Race. And inspired by the "consciousness raising" of the women's movement, a group of homemakers in Indianapolis formed a chapter of the Martha Movement with the goal of improving and upgrading the image of homemakers.

Not all area women agreed with the direction of the women's movement, however. Local and statewide right-to-life groups, Stop-ERA, and Indiana Pro-America had gathered a contingent which outnumbered feminists four to one at the local International Women's Year convention in 1977. Thirty-two Indianapolis women joined the thousands who attended the national Women's Rights Convention in Houston later that year. Although the convention would present a feminist women's rights agenda to the nation, Indiana's delegation was overwhelmingly pro-family, pro-life, and anti-ERA.

The 1980s brought new issues to the forefront of the women's movement and saw increasing numbers of women entering traditionally male professions as barriers fell. In 1981 the Womankind Center opened in Indianapolis, offering "womanspace for women's needs," including time-shared office space. *Womankind*, a nationally known feminist newspaper, was published at the center, and a feminist bookstore, Dreams and Swords, located there. In 1983 the Indianapolis League of Women Voters published a 56–page booklet, "Financial Awareness for Women in Indiana," which was a guide to state laws that concerned women. The following year an 18–month study of metropolitan Indianapolis girls and women conducted at IUPUI found the majority of respondents were torn between the traditional roles of wife and mother and the modern roles of careerwomen. In 1984 an unlikely alliance of anti-porn feminists and religious fundamentalists, led by national feminist leaders Andrea Dworkin and Catharine MacKinnon, successfully lobbied the Indianapolis City-County Council for an ordinance that classified pornography as a form of sexual discrimination. In 1985 in *AMERICAN BOOKSELLERS ASSOCIATION, INC. V. HUDNUT* the U.S. Supreme Court upheld a lower court decision that the ordinance was unconstitutional.

In 1985 New York-based *Savvy* magazine declared Indianapolis one of the six worst cities in the nation for working women. Although some women agreed with the assessment, others cited changes that showed women's status was improving but allowed that women often had to work harder to achieve promotions. That year the city saw its first woman promoted to captain in the Indianapolis Police Department (IPD), with the first woman IPD major the following year. Also in 1985 "From a Woman's Point of View," a local conference focusing on women's health, sexuality, family relations, and aging won a CASPER award for "outstanding communication achievements."

In 1986 Jill Andresky Fraser's *The Best U.S. Cities for Working Women* listed Indianapolis among the 70 top cities in the U.S., calling it a "turnaround" city with "as yet unfulfilled" potential for women to advance. Still, a survey of Indianapolis women attorneys in 1989 found a preponderance of males in management positions.

In the 1990s Indianapolis women continued to struggle with issues that were first delineated in the 1960s, although improvements were evident. In 1990 women represented 62 percent of the Indianapolis labor force, comprised 14.7 percent of the IPD force (compared with 9 percent in 1979), and represented 20 percent of the Indianapolis Bar Association (compared with 11.7 percent in 1980). In 1961, 8 percent of students enrolled at the Christian Theological Seminary were women; by the 1990s over half were female. Indianapolis also mirrored national trends which revealed that 51 percent of its new businesses were started by women. In 1990 the city instituted Municipal Court 2 to handle only restraining orders, thus making it easier for women to protect themselves from abusive partners. By 1992 IPD, the Marion County Sheriff's Department, and the Marion County prosecutor all offered victim's assistance in rape cases. In 1993 Indianapolis native Pam Carter became the first black woman to serve as a state attorney general in the U.S.

Not all women's issues have been addressed and equality remained elusive in many areas. By 1990 only 9 percent of the officers, senior managers, and directors of the ten largest companies headquartered in Indianapolis were women. The feminization of poverty, which has been defined as a women's issue since the 1970s, revealed itself in Indianapolis as elsewhere in the number of households headed by single women (20 percent of all families in the city) and increasingly in the number of homeless women and children (60 percent of the city's homeless population).

The women's movement which began in the 1960s continues in the 1990s to address issues of importance to women. Despite strong opposition at times, the movement in Indianapolis can claim much success in raising the status of women in the work place and in society.

CONNIE J. ZEIGLER
FRANCES DODSON RHOME

Jill Andresky Fraser, *The Best U.S. Cities for Working Women* (New York, 1986); Dorothy McBride Stetson, *Women's Rights in the U.S.A.: Policy Debates and Gender Roles* (Pacific Grove, Calif., 1991); Clipping Files, Indiana Division, Indiana State Library: "Women, 1969," "Women, 1970–1979," "Women, 1980 –1989."

Women's Rights and Suffrage. The first Conference on Women's Rights took place in Seneca Falls, New York, in 1848. Its primary issues of women's property rights and female suffrage set the agenda for the battle for women's rights in Indianapolis.

A local woman first entered the public debate on women's rights in 1850 as the male delegates at the state's constitutional convention bickered over whether or not married women should have the right to prevent husbands from selling their wives' personal property. Indianapolis poet SARAH T. BOLTON supported the constitutional changes in newspaper articles published throughout the state, which explained the grievances of women's status under the current law. Although the convention delegates did not include the property rights clause in the revised constitution, Bolton organized a testimonial in honor of its supporter, Robert Dale Owen. The following year when Owen helped pass a law which gave widows the right to bequeath their family property, a right that formerly belonged only to men, he praised Bolton's continuing efforts as instrumental in bringing about the change.

Although the Indiana Woman's Suffrage Association (IWSA) formed in 1851, no Indianapolis women were among its founders. However in November, 1854, when the city hosted the first of many Woman's Rights conventions at the Ma-

Suffragist May Wright Sewall. [Indiana State Library]

sonic Hall, Mrs. Priscilla H. Drake, a longtime Indianapolis resident, was nominated as the group's vice-president. That year nationally known suffragist Lucy Stone gave a series of lectures in the city on women's right to employment, self-support, and suffrage. Attendance was high, but at least some of the participants were more interested in Stone's "Bloomer costume" than in her discourse. The following year Indianapolis heard the famous suffragists Frances Gage, Lucretia Mott, and Ernestine L. Rose at the Woman's Rights Convention. In 1856 local newswoman Sarah Underhill, publisher of the *Ladies Tribune*, a short-lived temperance paper, spoke at the convention about the effects that the legal disabilities of women had on society. That year the IWSA officially declared that the "right of suffrage is [the] cornerstone" to acquiring equal rights, and its members increased their efforts to gain suffrage.

In 1859 three members of the IWSA presented a petition to the General Assembly asking for suffrage and increased property rights. Although the association's minutes called the presentation "a grand success," the local press reported that the gathering turned into a "noisy and foolish meeting." An antisuffrage article in the next day's *Indiana Journal* asserted that women did not need the vote and advised them to go home where their rights would be "safe in the true love of your good man."

During the Civil War even the most ardent suffragists temporarily suspended their pursuit of women's rights to give full attention to their country's needs. However, the war provided ample opportunities for women to demonstrate that they deserved equal legal treatment. Women capably managed property, businesses, and manufactories while their men were away. Indianapolis women manufactured literally tons of blankets, socks, gloves, wool shirts, and "drawers" at the request of Governor Oliver P. Morton, nursed the sick at local hospitals, and in November, 1863, earned $40,000 at the state's first Sanitary Fair, called the "Ladies Soldiers' Aid Festival."

When the war ended most women went back to the domestic sphere but an increasing number began to wonder why few people recognized their contributions. Many women objected to the use of the word "male" in the 14th Amendment, which,

for the first time, placed gender-exclusive language in the U.S. Constitution. When the 15th Amendment guaranteed the vote to African-American males, women grew increasingly bitter over their own exclusion from the polls.

The first Woman's Rights Convention in Indianapolis after the war was held in 1869. That year the IWSA chose ministers Henry Blanchard, E. P. Ingersoll, and J. Cummings Smith, and Mrs. Erie Locke, all from Indianapolis, as delegates to the Western Woman's Suffrage Association to be held in Chicago.

The 1870s marked a significant increase in local participation in the suffrage and women's rights movement. In 1870 the Indianapolis Turnverein, a German organization, split over the issue of women's rights, and the more liberal members withdrew to form the Socialer Turnverein. Susan B. Anthony spoke at the 1870 convention on women's rights, and members outlined a plan that called for a mass meeting of women's rights activists and the presentation of a suffrage petition to the General Assembly.

On January 20, 1871, Amanda M. Way and Emma B. Swank (both listed as Indianapolis residents in the IWSA minutes) presented this petition to a joint session of the General Assembly. Although this legislature rebuffed their efforts, the suffrage association began regularly to send written memorials to the assembly requesting universal suffrage, married women's property control, and equal pay for equal work. They also began to work for the election of candidates favorable to their causes, especially for men who supported female suffrage.

In 1873 the legislature made women eligible to hold any office elected by the General Assembly or appointed by the governor, and granted them the ability to control the real estate of an insane spouse. In 1877 legislators decreed that the managing board of the women's prison should consist only of women. This concession was requested by the state suffrage association, whose vice-president was Mary Haggart, the publisher of the *Woman's Tribune*, an Indianapolis weekly paper devoted to women's rights.

In an effort to appear more amenable to the women's rights movement, after 1875 state representatives allowed suffragists to use their chambers for evening gatherings. Elizabeth Cady Stanton spoke there in the 1870s, as did ZERELDA WALLACE, widow of former governor David Wallace. In 1877 IRVINGTON resident GRACE JULIAN CLARKE, chairwoman of the central committee of the IWSA and daughter of the suffragist U.S. Congressman GEORGE JULIAN, took up her father's cause and spoke at the convention of the National Woman's Suffrage Association in St. Louis.

In 1878 the women of the city formed their own suffrage association, the Indianapolis Equal Suffrage Society. Founding members included MAY WRIGHT SEWALL, founder of the Girls' Classical School, lawyer LAURA DONNAN, and Zerelda Wallace. Both Wallace and Sewall became influential suffragists on a national scale, working with Susan B. Anthony's National Woman's Suffrage Association. Wallace, a member of the WOMEN'S CHRISTIAN TEMPERANCE UNION, was also influential in reversing the antisuffrage policy of that group in the 1870s.

In the 1880s Indiana women gained additional property rights and briefly thought they had won the suffrage battle as well. In 1881 women gained absolute control of their own property as well as the ability to sue alone in actions regarding it. On April 8, 1881, after receiving a memorial in favor of suffrage from Indianapolis and 30 Indiana counties, and a call to action from Governor Albert G. Porter, the General Assembly approved a resolution to give women the franchise through an amendment to the state constitution. But amendments were required to pass two consecutive sessions of the legislature, and in the following session, as the suffrage issue became linked with a temperance amendment, both resolutions failed to pass the now Democratic-controlled legislature. Three years later female suffrage was again considered and rejected in both houses of the General Assembly.

By the turn of the century Indianapolis women, like women in other states, had made significant, although piecemeal, gains in property rights, but suffrage continued to elude them. In 1890 Wyoming entered the Union as the first state to include women's suffrage in its state constitution since New Jersey, which had enfranchised women in 1776 only to repeal that right in 1807. Indianapolis made less significant advances in the 1890s. Indiana suffragist Ida Husted Harper joined the editorial staff of the *Indianapolis News* in 1890. In 1897 Susan B. Anthony asked a joint session of the Indiana General Assembly to request a women's suffrage amendment to the U.S. Constitution. Two years later Anthony was working on the six-volume *History of Woman's Suffrage* when she and other officers of the National Woman's Suffrage Association met in Plymouth Church in Indianapolis.

Over the next 20 years no fewer than 10 women's suffrage bills were proposed in the Indiana legislature, and each time the item was either rejected or not considered. Concurrently the Indianapolis suffragists were finding new leaders and new approaches in their fights to acquire the vote. In the 1900s May Wright Sewall founded the Indiana Federation of Clubs which, although not a suffrage association, increased women's power by teaching them how to organize and by placing their names in the public arena. In 1909 Dr. AMELIA R. KELLER and the Indiana Federation of Clubs led a movement which placed MARY E. NICHOLSON on the Indianapolis Board of School Commissioners. After this success the group attempted to gain for women the right to vote in school board elections throughout the state. While some women, including the wife of Governor Thomas Marshall, opposed female suffrage in federal elections, believing "men are more capable," most generally approved of women's involvement in school board elections. Despite the popularity of the movement, women did not gain even this right.

In 1914 Mrs. LUELLA FRANCES SMITH MCWHIRTER, a director of PEOPLES BANK, helped found the Legislative Council of Indiana Women (later the Woman's Suffrage League). The council's 1,000 members included teacher and author CHARITY DYE and president Dr. Amelia Keller. By 1917 the council had persuaded many prominent Indianapolis citizens to telegraph the five U.S. senators deemed most likely to vote in favor of a constitutional amendment for universal suffrage.

Again in 1917 women briefly celebrated their potential enfranchisement when Congress passed a partial suffrage bill. Locally the Legislative Council offered home study classes to educate women on the voting process and the issues before the electorate and African-American women's clubs formed suffrage groups to study the duties of citizenship.

When the Supreme Court declared the bill unconstitutional, women's groups, locally and across the nation, again took up the suffrage banner. Sara Lauter of Indianapolis, president of the Woman's Suffrage League, spoke from a "suffrage wagon" in New York City and took turns with others in the group speaking locally "whenever we could get two people together to listen."

Finally, in 1919, the years of hard work by two generations of women reached fruition when Congress passed a new suffrage bill. A special session of the Indiana General Assembly ratified the 19th Amendment on January 16, 1920. In Indianapolis the Woman's Suffrage League held a Ratification Opera performing songs such as "Twas the Night 'Fore Election" and "For I've Struggled Long in the Cause, Mother." A special state election in September, 1921, granted women the vote at the state level.

CONNIE J. ZEIGLER

Women's Voluntary Organizations. A reader of any Indianapolis newspaper from the late 19th century to the present would find listings in the women's section of a wide range of recreational, educational, and charitable activities run by women for women on a volunteer basis. These activities were not unlike men's organizations, since both sexes participated in the American obsession to join together for a common interest or cause. What differed for women was that for most of the 19th and 20th centuries their volunteer activities fit socially prescribed gender roles. For many years these roles limited participation to religious and charitable organizations, a respectable way for women to extend their "moral superiority" as nurturing mothers and wives into the larger society.

But what happened in Indianapolis, as well as in other American communities, was that many of these volunteer activities awakened women's intellectual and recreational interests. Through their involvement, women developed skills and abilities which they later transferred to the workplace and to civic affairs, expanding the roles of women in society. Women not only received a personal benefit from their volunteer activities, but they also became an important voice in the cultural and philanthropic life of Indianapolis.

Prior to the Civil War, local women's organizations focused on the care of the less fortunate. An early example was the Widows' and Orphans' Friends Society (1850), which established the Indianapolis Orphans' Asylum in 1866. No public agency existed to take care of destitute women and children, so this organization filled an important need. It did not threaten society's expectations about women's roles: taking care of other women and children fit conveniently within women's "proper sphere." Women also joined auxiliaries of men's fraternal organizations. The 1857 Indianapolis city directory, for example, lists a chapter of the Daughters of Rebekah, the women's counterpart to the Odd Fellows. And many churches in the community had women's groups that focused on supporting the churches' own activities, such as the antebellum Ladies Sewing Society of Second Presbyterian Church, a group that made and sold items to support the congregation.

During the Civil War women in Indianapolis organized to collect funds and items for soldiers at the front. Many women aided the work of both the federal and state sanitary commissions. These experiences exposed women to the advantages of large-scale organized efforts for a common cause.

During the last half of the 19th century many middle class women had more leisure time. With most public sector positions closed to them, they looked to volunteer activities to fulfill their intellectual, recreational, and political interests. Women's volunteer work in Indianapolis continued to reflect a strong religious theme, as seen in the Indianapolis Female Bible Society for Distribution of the Scriptures Among Neglected Classes (ca. 1890) or in charitable causes such as the FLOWER MISSION (1876), first established to bring flowers to the city's hospitals but which quickly moved into the care of sick women and children. These charitable groups often organized along ethnic or religious lines, as evidenced by the Hebrew Ladies Benevolent Society (1859) and the German Ladies Aid Society (1886). However, women of different faiths sometimes worked together; the Ladies Society for the Relief of the Poor

(1869), for example, enlisted both Catholic and Protestant members. Some causes, such as temperance, often derived from strong religious values. The fight against alcohol was a national movement in which Indianapolis women participated, establishing a local chapter of the WOMEN'S CHRISTIAN TEMPERANCE UNION in 1873.

An explosion in volunteer activities occurred when women looked for recreational and self-improvement activities as their educational levels and leisure time increased. At the national level women established study clubs, groups that met regularly to discuss agreed-upon topics ranging from literature to current events. Study clubs provided an opportunity to meet, hear presentations from fellow members, and develop skills in public speaking. The first local study club was the INDI-ANAPOLIS WOMAN'S CLUB (1875), but others soon followed. Sometimes named for the day they met, such as the Monday Conversation Club (1897), and sometimes on a lighter note, like the Over the Teacups Club (1890), they also adopted names descriptive of their purpose, such as the Woman's Research Club (1899). These discussion clubs were often organized by women with the same ethnic or religious background. Catholic women founded the Proctor Club (1898) for instance, and women from the German community founded the Indianapolis Women's Literary Club (1889). These clubs also supported charitable efforts and identified community issues that became a focus for club activity. The INDIANAPOLIS COUNCIL OF WOMEN (1892) coordinated communication between the women's clubs on projects involving civic welfare.

Beyond study clubs, no interest was without its women's voluntary organization. Women established the INDIANAPOLIS MATINEE MUSICALE (1877). The Daughters of the American Revolution founded its first chapter in the Indianapolis area in 1894 with the Caroline Scott Harrison Chapter. Female relatives of Civil War veterans joined the Women's Relief Corps (1884), an auxiliary of the GRAND ARMY OF THE REPUBLIC.

By the late 19th century, as they joined the work force in increasing numbers, women formed organizations associated with their employment, such as the Bookbinders Bindery Girls Union (ca. 1910). The YOUNG WOMEN'S CHRISTIAN ASSOCIA-

TION (1895) provided housing, education, and a noontime lunch and rest area in the downtown area for young working women. The Mutual Aid Association (1903) assisted unfortunate working women by providing housing and financial assistance.

Women's clubs remained active in charitable work. The Southside Hebrew Ladies Sheltering House (1902), the ALPHA HOME Association (1883), and the Mother's Aid Society (1907) reflected the long-standing interest in assisting the less fortunate. But increasingly women looked to the larger causes of poverty and social problems and sought reform by lobbying government bodies. Sometimes referred to as "municipal housekeeping," such activities permitted women to expand traditional roles and become active in the larger community. Lacking the vote, women used volunteer activities to achieve social change, either by assuming the obligation themselves or by persuading the community to assume responsibility for it. Sixteen Indianapolis women's clubs joined an umbrella organization, the 7th District of the Indiana General Federation of Women's Clubs (1909), to promote their common interests to the community.

Many women believed the best way to effect change was through the ballot box. The Indianapolis Equal Suffrage Society (1878), which eventually extended statewide, was an early advocate for women's right to vote. The Indianapolis Woman's Franchise League (1911) took an even more active role in promoting women's suffrage. After ratification of the 19th Amendment in 1920 ensured their right to vote, women established the Indianapolis chapter of the LEAGUE OF WOMEN VOTERS (1920), which incorporated many of the previous suffrage groups and worked to educate the new voters. The Marion County Women's Democratic Club (1921) and the Indianapolis Woman's Republican Club (1922) provided outlets for women's partisan political activities.

During the first part of the 20th century women's voluntary organizations became a national phenomenon. Many communities, including Indianapolis, established local chapters of national groups. To meet the needs of girls and young women, area women established local chapters and troops of the Camp Fire Girls (1913),

GIRL SCOUTS (1917), and the YMCA's Girl Reserves (1920). Women's community and social groups patterned after men's service organizations emerged during the early 20th century and included the ALTRUSA CLUB (1917), the JUNIOR LEAGUE (1922), and Zonta International (1929). African-American women established a chapter of the National Council of Negro Women (1935). Women also organized around topics that reflected their activities within the home. The Indianapolis Housewife's League (1919) sought to lower prices on foodstuffs and discussed the possibility of community kitchens and other chore-sharing options. Organized by wards, the Housewife's League even established local markets to purchase fresh food. Women were increasingly a part of the business community; the Woman's Rotary Club (1919) and the Indianapolis Business and Professional Women's Council (1914) were begun during this period.

Women's groups continued to support charitable interests, and during the 1930s this support often centered on specific institutions within the community. The Methodist Hospital White Cross Guild (1931), The Children's Museum Guild (1933), and the Women's Symphony Committee (1937) for the INDIANAPOLIS SYMPHONY ORCHESTRA provided much needed financial support during the decade of the Great Depression.

Women also organized around shared recreational interests. The Indiana Chapter of the Ninety-Nines (1939), located in Indianapolis, was a group of women airplane pilots who sponsored airplane races locally and throughout the state. Women interested in motorcycles established the Harlyettes (1940), an auxiliary to the local Harley Motorcycle Club.

Women's participation in the work force grew rapidly before and after World War II. While men's organizations provided opportunities for developing business contacts, women usually found themselves left out of these groups. They responded by forming their own professional organizations and associations. The Indianapolis Chapter, American Society of Women Accountants (1938), the Indianapolis Association of Insurance Women (1942), the Indianapolis Credit Women's Breakfast Club (ca. 1954), and the Women's Construction League of Indianapolis (1955) reflected the diversity of working women and their need for professional networks.

Although women had achieved the vote in 1920, opportunities for them to be full partners in community—and especially political—life remained limited. Traditional women's organizations offered some access to political decision making, but younger women and often the community at large discounted these previous efforts. By the 1960s women had established new organizations, focused primarily on political issues related to women. Early groups in Indianapolis included Women for Better Government (1955) and the Women's Civic Club (1962), which worked within the established government and political circles to achieve change. Later, the Woman's Anti-Crime Crusade joined with the Mayor's Task Force on Women to form Women United Against Rape (1973), which was the first group in the country to establish a 24–hour rape crisis center, a program that existed at nine Indianapolis hospitals. Several of the older women's organizations and some newer ones created the Greater Indianapolis Women's Political Caucus (1971) to support candidates and lobby for issues important to women. Women who believed in more fundamental change established local chapters of groups such as the National Organization for Women (NOW) to fight specifically for women's rights. Greater awareness of issues directly related to women's lives led to new organizations: the JULIAN CENTER (1975) assisted women who found themselves unprepared for changes in their lives and for women in abusive situations; and the Martha Movement (1978) sought to improve and upgrade the housewife's image.

The tradition of women's participation in philanthropic activities did not abate during these decades, despite the larger number of women in the work force. The Black Pearls (1969) was a social and civic club for young African-American women concerned with bettering conditions on INDIANA AVENUE. Girls were a focus of volunteer activities with the creation of local chapters of BIG SISTERS (1974) and Girls Clubs (1969). Alliance for Girls Services (1981) brought several local organizations like Planned Parenthood, Girl Scouts, and GIRLS, INC., together to address the needs of girls in the community.

Women's voluntary organizations in Indianapolis have reflected diversity of women in the community and their recreational, educational, and charitable interests. Yet as social expectations of women and their roles changed so did the need for female-only groups. Increasingly, volunteer organizations organized around topical interests regardless of gender. The local chapter of the national organization Mothers Against Drunk Driving, for example, has both male and female members.

Throughout the city's history, women's groups have helped women develop skills that they were able to use in changing the community. These groups have also created self-confidence for individual women to enter the public sphere. But most importantly, women's volunteer organizations in Indianapolis have contributed numerous hours to improve the physical and social life of the community over the years and have expanded society's view about women's participation in the larger community.

NORALEEN YOUNG

Wonderland Amusement Park.

Milwaukee and Indianapolis investors established the Wonderland Construction Company in 1905 to furnish amusements on Indianapolis' east side. On Saturday evening, May 16, 1906, the company opened its Wonderland Amusement Park, located at East Washington and Gray streets, the former site of the Indianapolis baseball team's playing field. Over 8,000 people attended the opening festivities.

The park, led by president E. I. Fisher of Indianapolis, included 24 buildings and amusements surrounding an artificial lake, landscaped gardens, and a 125–foot electric tower. Among the most popular attractions were the half mile scenic railway, the "Johnstown Flood" that employed special lighting effects to describe the disaster, a giant "Shoot the Chutes" waterslide, a funhouse, and other rides. The park also sponsored special attractions such as trick cyclists, acrobats, bands, and an Igorrote tribe from the Philippines. One of the park's most incredible spectacles was "Kann's War Air-Ship," a dirigible the size of two streetcars, which floated over the park.

Entrance to Wonderland Amusement Park, ca. 1906. [The Children's Museum]

In 1909, management sought a beer license for the park's proposed German Village, but neighborhood women protested. The Indianapolis Brewers Exchange, seeking to minimize public opposition to the liquor trade, helped to force the withdrawal of the application. Two years later, the park opened a "Blind Tiger" (a place that sells intoxicants illegally), which the police raided.

On Sunday, August 27, 1911, Wonderland Amusement Park burned to the ground. Fisher estimated losses at $20,000 and decided against rebuilding. The grounds later became the site of P. R. MALLORY AND COMPANY.

DAVID G. VANDERSTEL
CONNIE ZEIGLER
Indiana University–Purdue University,
Indianapolis

Woodburn Sarven Wheel Company.

Largest manufacturer of the patented "Sarven Wheel" in the United States during the late 19th century. In the mid–1860s J. R. Osgood and S. F. Smith established a business producing wagon and carriage materials on South Illinois Street. In 1870, with Jacob Woodburn of St. Louis, they incorporated the Woodburn Sarven Wheel Company. Woodburn held the patent, which was a great improvement in design over the traditional wheel. The spokes and hub were still mortised and tenoned, but the joint was reinforced with two iron flanges riveted through the wood. This technique offered extra strength to the junction of hub and spokes without sacrificing the wood's inherent flexibility.

Osgood and Smith ran the business in Indianapolis, while Woodburn continued manufacturing the wheel in St. Louis. By the 1880s the Indianapolis factory had expanded to cover approximately 7 acres on South Illinois Street, between South Street and POGUE'S RUN, and it had over 500 workers. Both Osgood and Smith died in the 1870s, at which time the firm was taken over by Addison Bybee and J. F. Pratt. Sales of $150,000 in 1870 jumped to $600,000 by 1882. The company was in business until 1890. After that, the plant was taken over by the Parry Manufacturing Company, run by Bybee and Pratt in partnership with Thomas H. and DAVID M. PARRY of Rushville. Parry Manufacturing was in business until 1919. (David M. Parry left the business about 1909, presumably to start the Parry Automobile Company, incorporated in 1910.)

LEIGH DARBEE
Indiana Historical Society

Berry R. Sulgrove, *History of Indianapolis and Marion County* (Philadelphia, 1884); *Manufacturing and Mercantile Resources of Indianapolis* (Indianapolis, 1883).

Woodruff, Hale Aspacio (Aug. 6, 1900–Sept. 6, 1980). African-American artist. Born in Cairo, Illinois, Woodruff attended elementary and high school in Nashville, Tennessee, and moved to Indianapolis in the summer of 1919. He lived at the SENATE AVENUE YMCA where he did odd jobs to earn money for his lodging and art school. In 1920 he enrolled in the JOHN HERRON ART INSTITUTE, studying under WILLIAM FORSYTH. He also worked for the INDIANAPOLIS FREEMAN as a freelance political cartoonist. In 1926, he won second place in the first Harmon Foundation awards for Negro artists. The $100 Harmon money and another $250 from art patrons enabled Woodruff to go to Europe in 1927 where he studied in Paris at the Academie Scandinave and the Academie Moderne. During 1927–1928, as a foreign correspondent for the Sunday edition of the INDIANAPOLIS STAR, he received $10 for each illustrated article about the art scene in Paris.

In 1931 Woodruff returned to the United States and took a job as art director at Atlanta University, introducing the first fine art classes offered there. He also worked as a Works Progress Administration painter. From the late 1920s to the early 1940s, Woodruff entered works in the INDIANA STATE FAIR and almost always won an award. With a WPA grant in 1938–1939, he produced his most famous mural at Talladega College's Savery Library, *The Amistad Mutiny*. This was followed in 1940 by a second mural there, *Founding of Talladega College, 1867*. His painting *Little Boy* was exhibited with the work of three other Atlanta artists at the 1939 New York World's Fair. He established the annual exhibition of art by American Negroes at Atlanta in 1941. He used a two-year Rosenwald Fellowship awarded in 1943 to go to Mississippi and create a series of paintings on *Erosion of the Land.* In 1946 he was appointed Associate Professor of Art Education at New York University. The Golden State Mutual Life Insurance Company, Los Angeles, in 1949 commissioned Woodruff and Charles Alston to paint a mural, *History of California.* The following year, he was commissioned to paint a series of six murals, *The Art of the Negro*, at the Atlanta University Library. He retired from NYU in 1967 and in 1978 received an honorary Doctor of Fine Arts degree from INDIANA UNIVERSITY–PURDUE UNIVERSITY AT INDIANAPOLIS.

WILLIAM E. TAYLOR
Indiana University–Purdue University,
Indianapolis

Jane Allison, "OK, Museum, Why Not a Woodruff?" *Indianapolis News,* Mar. 5, 1977; *Hale Woodruff: 50 Years of His Art* (New York: The Studio Museum in Harlem, 1979).

Woodruff Place. Near eastside subdivision, bounded by East 10th Street, East Drive, East Michigan Street, and West Drive. James O. Woodruff came to Indianapolis in 1869 to start the city's first water company. In 1872 he purchased 80 acres east of Indianapolis and platted Woodruff Place. He laid out three boulevards—West, Middle, and East drives—with one intersecting street, Cross Drive. The three main drives were bisected by esplanades containing cast-iron statuary and multitiered fountains. Concrete fences lined the northern edge of the town, creating a sense of seclusion and separation from the larger city nearby. Walking Woodruff Place's tree-lined streets became a popular entertainment for Indianapolis residents.

The Panic of 1873 bankrupted Woodruff and, within a few years, forced him to move from his Woodruff Place home, but in 1876 he led the initial property owners in a successful petition to incorporate as a town. Because it had neither schools nor police and fire protection, Woodruff Place residents contracted with Indianapolis for these services. In the 1890s the town experienced a building boom. Homes in the area were constructed in a variety of popular architectural styles, including Eastlake-Stick, Edwardian, and Queen Anne. Homeowners were primarily, though not exclusively, affluent. The Amberson Addition in BOOTH TARKINGTON'S novel THE MAGNIFICENT AMBERSONS (1918) was modeled after Woodruff Place.

Following World War I, Woodruff Place began a gradual decline as wealthy families left the town to move to the tony northern suburbs. The Great Depression caused further decline when many of the remaining residents could not afford to maintain their large Woodruff Place homes. Following World War II, many of the larger dwellings were subdivided into apartments.

Attempts by the City of Indianapolis to annex the town began in the 1890s. By the 1920s the town was surrounded on all sides by the metropolis. In 1953 the city began charging Woodruff Place $25,000 for police and fire protection, hoping to force the residents to succumb. The town successfully resisted annexation until 1962, fighting the city to the Indiana Supreme Court and appealing that court's decision to the U.S. Supreme Court, which refused to hear the case. Finally, on March 20, 1962, residents turned over the key to the Woodruff Place town hall to the City of Indianapolis.

Beginning in the 1970s, new residents moved into the neighborhood, renovating the large, old homes. On July 31, 1972, Woodruff Place was added to the National Register of Historic Places. In the 1980s and '90s, the Woodruff Place Civic League worked to preserve a sense of community among the area's 1,100 residents. Many of the community's 300 homes remain divided into apartments, but several have been renovated as single-family residences. The Civic League uses funds from activities such as the annual Woodruff Place yard sale to restore and maintain the neighborhood's statuary and fountains; the Cross Drive fountains are now the oldest in Indianapolis.

CONNIE J. ZEIGLER

Timothy J. Sehr, "Three Gilded Age Suburbs of Indianapolis," *Indiana Magazine of History*, 77 (Dec., 1981), 305–332.

Woollen, Molzan and Partners. Begun in 1955 as the individual practice of architect Evans Woollen, FAIA, Woollen, Molzan and Partners is today one of the city's more prominent architectural firms. Woollen, a native of Indianapolis whose family settled in the area in the 1840s, received both his B.A. and M.A. degrees in architecture at Yale University. After working in the Connecticut offices of Phillip Johnson and John Johansen, he returned to Indianapolis to establish his own practice. The firm's early work centered on the design of local private houses.

By 1968 when the firm was incorporated as Woollen Associates, its work included a full range of building types: commercial structures, notably banks; several innovative churches, including St. Thomas Aquinas Church (1968), 46th and Illinois streets; governmental structures including public housing (Barton Towers, [1967], 555 Massachusetts Avenue) and the Minton-Capehart Federal Building, 575 North Pennsylvania Street; and numerous campus buildings, including dormitories, instructional buildings (Fesler Hall addition at HERRON SCHOOL OF ART, 1962), and perhaps best known, CLOWES MEMORIAL HALL (1963) on the Butler University campus.

The firm's name changed to Woollen, Molzan and Partners in 1982. By the mid–1980s the firm had developed particular strengths in libraries, buildings for the performing arts, and academic structures. Notable buildings from around the state constructed during the 1970s and 1980s include the Indiana University Musical Arts Center in Bloomington (1972); the New Harmony Inn (1975); the Cushwa-Leighton Library at St. Mary's College in Notre Dame (1982); and St. Meinrad Archabbey's new monastery and library (1984). Two major projects involving renovation of Indianapolis' historic landmarks were the INDIANA REPERTORY THEATRE (1982) and Union Station's train shed (1986). The firm also undertook the renovation of the MAJESTIC BUILDING, 47 South Pennsylvania Street, where its office is located.

Recent buildings in Indianapolis that exemplify the firm's work include its addition to THE CHILDREN'S MUSEUM (1989), 3000 North Meridian Street; St. Phillip's Church (1986), 720 Dr. Martin Luther King, Jr. Drive; Holy Cross Lutheran Church (1990), 8115 Oaklandon Road; and St. Monica's Church (1993), 6131 Michigan Road. A considerable part of the firm's practice extends beyond the state and includes such major projects as St. Andrew's Abbey Church in Cleveland, Ohio (1985); the Moody Music Center in Tuscaloosa, Alabama (1987); and Grainger Library on the University of Illinois' Champaign-Urbana campus (1994).

Woollen, Molzan and Partners has received 20 design awards from the American Institute of Architects as well as numerous major national awards. Its work has received considerable attention in the architectural press, having been published in two dozen journals both here and abroad.

MARY ELLEN GADSKI

Mary Ellen Gadski, *Comprehensive Bibliography of the Works of Woollen, Molzan and Partners, 1955–87* (Monticello, Ill.: Vance Bibliographies, Apr., 1988), copy available at the Indiana Historical Society Library.

Woollen's Garden. Park and nature preserve. Woollen's Garden of Birds and Botany, its formal name, is a 55–acre city park that includes a 38–acre state-dedicated nature preserve. Located on the south valley wall of FALL CREEK, the tract was donated to the city by William Watson Woollen in 1909.

Woollen's Garden contains mesic to wet-mesic upland, old growth and second growth forest dominated by beech, sugar maple, hackberry,

red oak, chinquapin oak, black maple, buckeye, tulip, and blue ash. This uncommon mixture is due to calcareous gravelly soils, resulting in a forest with floodplain affinities. The canopy trees are up to 40 inches in diameter. Ground-level plants and spring wildflowers include anemones, trilliums, wild ginger, hepatica, Solomon's Seal, Christmas fern, celandine poppy, and Dutchman's Breeches. A contiguous tract on the north side of Fall Creek (a part of the Fall Creek Corridor Park) consists of an old field, a floodplain forest, and a wetland slough. This area has a mixture of sycamores and pin oaks on the north blending into a beech-maple mixture to the south toward Fall Creek.

To the north of Woollen's Garden and Fall Creek is Skiles Test Nature Park, an 80–acre mixture of old fields and woodlands given to the city in 1981 as a nature study center. The wooded areas along the north valley wall of Fall Creek are similar in composition to Woollen's Garden, but are more disturbed. These tracts form a unique contiguous natural area including both wooded valley walls and the mostly wooded floodplain.

Access to Woollen's Garden has been rendered difficult by the construction of Interstate 465 on the east and an apartment complex on the south. Long-term plans call for access via a footbridge crossing the creek from Fall Creek Corridor Park.

KEVIN STRUNK
Wabash Resources and Consulting

Department of Metropolitan Development, City of Indianapolis, "Fall Creek Parkway–Woollen's Garden–Skiles Test Nature Park Master Plan" (1988); Division of Nature Preserves, Indiana Department of Natural Resources, *Directory of Nature Preserves* (1991).

Wooton Patent Desks. Elaborately crafted desks created by Wooton and Company, an Indianapolis furniture firm established in 1870 with headquarters on East Washington Street.

The Wooton Patent Desk was the creation of William S. Wooton who, along with his furniture expertise, was a longtime Quaker minister. Born in Preble County, Ohio, on May 12, 1835, he was the eighth of 13 children. The family moved often between Ohio and Indiana before finally settling

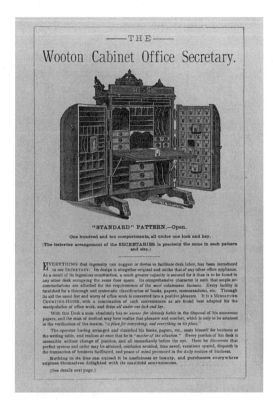

A Wooten Desk advertisement ca. 1880.
[Indiana Historical Society, #C5915]

tary." Resembling an ornate Victorian cabinet when closed, the Wooton Desk, when opened, revealed approximately 100 separate compartments and a writing desk. Wooton's contribution to the furniture trade was critically acclaimed, winning an award at the 1876 Centennial Exhibition in Philadelphia.

The desk was also an instant success with businessmen of the time at home and abroad. Wooton desks were owned by such influential figures as Jay Gould, Ulysses S. Grant, Sidney Lanier, Joseph Pulitzer, John D. Rockefeller, and Charles Scribner. Reportedly, even Queen Victoria owned a Wooton Desk.

By the 1880s, sales of Wooton Desks were on the decline. Wooton himself left the firm in 1880, moving to Danville, Indiana, which possibly contributed to the company's downfall. For the rest of his life, Wooton served as a Quaker minister in a number of cities. He died on August 26, 1907, in Denver, Colorado.

RAY BOOMHOWER
Indiana Historical Society

Betty Lawson Walters, *The King of Desks: Wooton's Patent Secretary* (Washington, D.C., 1969).

in Grant County, Indiana, in 1849. Wooton, who worked as a patternmaker in Richmond, married Theodocia Stratton in 1862.

A partner in George H. Grant and Company, a furniture manufacturing firm that produced office and school furnishings, Wooton moved to Indianapolis in 1870, becoming one of many who made the city a booming marketplace for furniture manufacturing during the 19th century. He established William S. Wooton and Company with offices on East Washington Street. The Wooton firm was soon producing school desks and managed to win a contract to supply city schools with new furniture after another company was unable to meet the contract's requirements.

The Wooton Company, however, would make its mark not with school desks, but with a unique office desk that would become known as "The King of Desks." On October 6, 1874, the United States Patent Office issued Wooton a patent for "Wooton's Patent Cabinet Office Secre-

Work Force. Founded in the first two decades of the 19th century, Indianapolis remained a small town until the late 1840s. Business in the state capital was almost entirely local. In 1847 the city had 6,000 residents and acquired the legal status of a city. The completion of the MADISON AND INDIANAPOLIS RAILROAD in that year began the development of Indianapolis as the commercial and industrial center of the state. In the 1850s the number of manufacturing industries increased and labor was in great demand; by 1860 the city's population had tripled to 18,000. The decade of the Civil War witnessed greater economic development and population increases. The depression of the 1870s halted growth, but even with economic stagnation the population of Indianapolis in 1880 had reached 75,000. The number of manufacturing establishments grew from 100 in 1860 to nearly 700 in 1880; the number of people employed in these places increased from about 700 in 1860 to 10,000 in 1880. Although the city lagged behind Louisville, Detroit, and Cincinnati in the number of manufacturing establishments and amount of capital invested, it had far outdistanced all other Indiana cities as a manufacturing center and had two and one-half times as many people as Evansville.

The labor force in Indianapolis in this period reflected the regional and increasingly national orientation of its ever more diverse economy. Of the nearly 28,000 men and women employed in the city in 1880, one quarter (7,000) worked in trade and transportation, one third (10,000) in professional and personal services, and one third (10,000) in manufacturing industries. The single most important category for men was manufacturing, an indication of the growing importance of this sector of the economy. The nearly 8,800 men employed in manufacturing worked in a variety of industries, but the two most important were meat packing and the metal trades. By 1870 there were two rolling mills in Indianapolis. Small foundries and machine shops also employed a significant number of people. The largest meatpacking company was KINGAN AND COMPANY, an Irish-owned firm that began operations in Indianapolis in 1864. The first meat-packing firm in the state to use refrigeration to allow slaughtering and packing year-round, Kingan employed 300 to 600 people by the mid–1870s and was one of the largest packinghouses in the world. By 1875 Indianapolis ranked fourth among the cities in the nation as a pork-packing center.

Women comprised 18 percent of the labor force in 1880. Two of every three working females were in the professional and personal services category, the vast majority of these as domestic servants. Another 29 percent of working women were in manufacturing, where they constituted 14 percent of all workers. A few women (197) worked in trade and transportation, but the retail sector was still small-scale and clerk jobs had not yet been feminized.

The vast majority of Indianapolis workers in 1880 (77 percent) had been born in the United States. Eleven percent (3,100) were of German origin, and 7 percent (1,900) were Irish. Foreign-born workers tended to cluster in certain occupational categories. Nearly three fifths of the 1,075 Irish-born workers in 1880 were employed in pro-

fessional and personal services—no doubt most of these were domestic servants. Many of the 485 Irish immigrants employed in manufacturing likely worked at Kingan and Company. Reputedly, many Irish came to Indianapolis so confident of finding jobs at Kingan's that they addressed their trunks to the plant. Lending credence to this claim, an ethnic neighborhood called IRISH HILL developed near the plant. The first Germans in Indianapolis were artisans and laborers; by 1880 Germans comprised half of all brewers and maltsters in the city and one third of all bakers, shoemakers, and cabinetmakers. Forty-six percent of all German-born workers in 1880 labored in manufacturing and mechanical trades. But an equal number of German-born workers in 1880 were employed in tertiary sector jobs; in that year, a large part of the businesses in downtown Indianapolis were owned by German families.

Indianapolis changed dramatically between 1880 and 1920. As its economy grew and diversified, so did its work force. The size of the work force increased more than five fold, from 28,000 in 1880 to 146,000 in 1920. The occupational distribution also changed. Most striking were the dominance of manufacturing, which employed 38 percent of all men in the labor force in 1880 but 50 percent of all men working in 1920, and the growth of retail and office clerk jobs.

Until 1919, when Lake County (with Gary and Hammond) overtook it, Marion County held first place in the state in the value of its manufactured products. In 1909, 22 percent of the state's value of manufactured products came from Indianapolis alone. The city was the leader of the state's slaughtering and meat-packing industries, its flour-milling industry, and its auto industry. It was a nationally important city, too: in 1919 it ranked fifth among meat-packing cities in the United States; ELI LILLY AND COMPANY, incorporated in 1881, became one of the three or four largest producers of prescription drugs in the United States. Metal trades continued to be important; in 1890 railroad car construction and repair shops were the fourth largest employer in Indianapolis. In 1920 there were more than 1,000 manufacturing establishments in Indianapolis employing 64,000 people. The places ranged in size from small machine shops employing a handful of people to large plants that employed hundreds of people on several shifts.

The advance of commerce and manufacturing and the growth in population and urban development transformed and increased the number of jobs in the service sector between 1880 and 1920. There were 18,500 clerical workers in Indianapolis in 1920, alone comprising 13 percent of the city's work force. The growth of office and retail clerk jobs contributed to the increased number of women in the Indianapolis labor force. Fully half the clerical labor force in 1920 was female. Women also constituted 16 percent of the 22,000 people employed in trade in that year; most of these were retail salesclerks, a new occupation for women that reflected the emergence of the department stores like L. S. Ayres and Company, which opened in 1872 and became one of the largest employers of women in Indianapolis. Another new service occupation that was regarded as a female job was telephone operator: most of the 1,400 women employed in transportation in 1920 were phone operators. The reorganization of the female labor market shifted the occupational distribution of women in Indianapolis. Most notably, the number of women employed in professional and personal service increased in absolute terms between 1880 and 1920, but their share of the female labor force dropped dramatically from 67 percent to 38 percent.

The Indianapolis labor force in 1920 remained overwhelmingly white and native-born but there were some changes from 1880. The proportion of the foreign-born population in Indianapolis fell from 10 percent in 1900 to 5.4 percent in 1920. And the largest share of foreign immigrants (one third) in 1920 were from Germany; only a small number of immigrants from southern and eastern Europe came to Indianapolis. In contrast, there was a large increase in the black population of the city. By 1920 there were 35,000 African-Americans, comprising 11 percent of the city's population, one of the highest ratios among major cities in the northern United States. Black workers, who greatly outnumbered those of foreign birth, were restricted to the lowest paid and least skilled occupations. More than half of all black men employed in Indianapolis in 1920 were industrial laborers and one fifth were domestic and personal service workers. Black women had even fewer job options. In 1920, 83 percent of all employed black women worked in domestic and personal service; and black women comprised half of all women employed in this occupational category.

The decades after 1920 witnessed both the maturation and the onset of decline in the industrial economy of Indianapolis. In the 1920s new industries opened shop in the city; P. R. MALLORY AND COMPANY, Westinghouse Lamp Works, and a Radio Corporation of American plant (forerunner of the later THOMSON CONSUMER ELECTRONICS complex) all opened during that decade. In the Great Depression the diverse industrial economy of Indianapolis protected it somewhat from the massive unemployment that afflicted cities like Gary, which depended heavily on one or two basic industries. And although Indianapolis led the state in 1929 in the number of companies with more than 500 employees (20), the city's largest manufacturing firms were small compared to those of other cities; prior to World War II Indianapolis had only two large manufacturing enterprises, LINK-BELT and REAL SILK HOSIERY MILLS, each of which employed approximately 3,000 people. The smaller size of firms also moderated somewhat the impact of the depression. But Indianapolis workers did feel the impact of economic collapse. The manufacturing work force fell by half, from 59,000 in 1920 to 30,000 in 1933. In October, 1933, ten thousand families in Marion County were on relief. New Deal work relief projects employed people (mostly white men) primarily on public construction. By the end of the 1930s the economy had begun to recover, especially as the federal government expanded its national defense program.

World War II brought short-term and long-term changes. Rural out-migration, halted during the depression, resumed as people sought higher paying war jobs and armed services jobs. Between October, 1940, and October, 1941, alone, 12,600 people moved into Indianapolis, 53 percent of these from elsewhere in Indiana, almost all from rural areas and small towns. The number of people employed in the Indianapolis area increased by half during the war. Indianapolis did very well by federal defense contracts. Factory employment more than doubled, a rate of increase half again as rapid as the United States as a whole. Plants employed people around the clock to produce war goods. At its peak in 1943 Allison Division of General Motors, for example, employed 23,019 women and men on three shifts, seven days a week. More firms found the city a good location; Bridgeport Brass, the FORD MOTOR COMPANY, the CHRYSLER Corporation, RCA, and WESTERN ELECTRIC all expanded or opened plants during World War II and remained after 1945.

Indianapolis continued to grow industrially after World War II. Industrial production soared from $140 million in 1939 to $940 million in 1954. But like other cities in what eventually would be labeled the Rust Belt, Indianapolis began to suffer the ill effects of a series of recessions, decentralization, and industrial decline. Beginning in the 1960s manufacturing plants moved or closed. The closing in 1966 of Hygrade Food Products, the former Kingan and Company factory and still the largest meat-packing plant in Indianapolis with 2,000 employees, helped focus attention on weaknesses in the industrial sector and the need for job retraining and development. Between 1950 and 1970 the absolute number of people employed in manufacturing in the metropolitan area increased from 104,700 to 138,700, but their number relative to total employment dropped from 32 percent to 29 percent. The economic crisis in durable goods manufacturing in the late 1970s–early 1980s exacted its toll from Indianapolis. By 1987 the number of people employed in manufacturing had fallen to 106,000 and they represented just 17.8 percent of the metropolitan labor force.

The post–World War II expansion of nonmanufacturing industries such as finance, government, retail, and other services compensated for the decline in manufacturing. Between 1950 and 1970 the number of people employed in wholesale and retail jobs rose from 66,900 to 95,000; those in finance increased their numbers from 13,500 to 28,300. The category that experienced the greatest growth relative to total employment between 1950 and 1970 was government, whose share rose from 9.2 percent to 13.9 percent.

The expansion of the service sector created a demand for female labor at the same time as families regardless of class came increasingly to depend on more than one adult income. Women comprised a steadily increasing share of the city's labor force, from 29 percent in 1940 to 44 percent in 1980. They also gained greater access to male-defined occupations. In 1980, for example, there were 5,350 skilled tradeswomen and 337 female lawyers and judges in Indianapolis; each group represented 8 percent and 11.7 percent, respectively, of people so employed. Yet although these proportions were greater than comparable 1940 figures of 3 percent and 1 percent, women's still small share of such jobs indicated that the ever-increasing number of women in the labor force had taken conventional "women's" jobs. In 1980 women comprised 40 percent of those employed in managerial and professional occupations; within this category there were 7,100 nurses and 12,800 elementary and secondary education teachers. The number of women exceeded the number of men employed in technical, sales, and administrative support occupations in 1980. Indeed, this category employed 48.7 percent of all working women in the city that year. But the two most important jobs held by women in this category—and the two most common jobs for all 235,000 women employed in Indianapolis in 1980—were as salesclerks and secretaries.

Although the occupational distribution of women did not change very much over the course of this century, their marital status did. In 1970, 45.5 percent of all women aged 16 and older were in the Indianapolis labor force. Of these 180,000 women, 59 percent were married; in 1940, 39 percent of all working women were married. Increasing numbers of women with children work. Half of all employed women in the city in 1970 had children under the age of 18.

African-Americans experienced some improvement in their labor market status over the course of the 20th century. The demand for labor during World War II offered a measure of upward occupational mobility; some of these gains survived demobilization and reconversion. In 1970, for example, 14.6 percent of all African-American men in the city's work force were lower-paid manufacturing laborers, compared to a figure of 30 percent in 1940. Moreover, 38 percent of all black men in the metropolitan labor force in 1970 were craftsmen and operatives, higher-paid and more highly skilled jobs formerly closed to them. For black women, the picture also has changed. About one fifth of all black women in 1970 worked as service and private household workers, compared to four fifths in 1940. Black women have gained access to clerical and manufacturing jobs; in 1970, 43 percent of all employed black women in the city held these jobs, which they had been almost completely denied in 1940. Continuity, however, is also apparent. The single most important occupational category for African-American women in 1970 still was service; 7,260 women—29 percent of all black working women—worked in food, health, and cleaning service jobs that year. In contrast, black women made up a mere 5 percent of all saleswomen in the city in 1970, demonstrating the persistence of racial as well as gender hierarchies in the labor market.

As Indianapolis approaches the 21st century, assessments of the health of its economy and the prospects of its work force are generally optimistic. The decreasing significance of manufacturing has enabled the city to withstand national economic downturns such as the one in the early 1980s. At the same time, economic development has increased the number of jobs. In 1987 Indianapolis was the 17th fastest growing area for jobs in the United States. The transformation of the urban economic base from manufacturing to service has changed the composition of the city's work force in significant and impressive ways. The implications of these changes are not yet fully understood. But if there is cause to doubt the view that a work force so heavily dependent on service jobs is somehow better off than one with a large share of manufacturing jobs, there also is reason to acknowledge the ability of Indianapolis to avoid the fate of so many other cities undergoing deindustrialization.

NANCY F. GABIN
Purdue University, West Lafayette

Workingmen's Party. Nineteenth-century political party. One of several labor movements that emerged during the industrialization of the late 19th century, Indiana's Workingmen's party organized its first state convention in No-

vember, 1865, in Indianapolis, and two years later the party nominated a full slate of candidates which lost to the Republicans in the city election. The leader of this movement was JOHN FEHRENBATCH, a member of the Machinists and Blacksmiths Union, and its main objective was the establishment of an eight-hour workday. Both major parties were quick to offer eight-hour planks, but little action was taken. At the same time Republican supporters of the eight-hour workday accused the Workingmen's party of Confederate sympathies because of its ties to the DEMOCRATIC PARTY.

During the 1870s several more Workingmen's party conventions were held in Indianapolis, the party's increased popularity due in part to the difficult economic times following the Panic of 1873. The Workingmen's party also allied with the Grangers and the Greenback party to achieve currency reform, better wages, and benefits. In 1876 the Workingmen's platform called for an income tax and the issuing of more Greenbacks instead of bank notes. In the 1877 Indianapolis municipal election an entire ticket of Workingmen's party candidates was submitted to the voters, but it received only 4 percent of the vote. Major party candidates, however, often discussed labor-oriented planks but took little action until after the turn of the century.

JEFF TENUTH
Indiana State Museum

Emma Lou Thornbrough, *Indiana in the Civil War Era, 1850–1880* (Indianapolis, 1965); William G. Carleton, "The Money Question in Indiana Politics, 1865–1890," *Indiana Magazine of History*, 42 (Dec., 1946), 107–150.

Workman's Circle (Arbeiter Ring). A fraternal order of Jewish workingmen sympathetic to the Socialist party. The Workman's Circle was founded in 1892 by a small group of eastern European immigrants in New York City, and by 1908 Indianapolis had organized a branch. The goals of local groups paralleled those of the national organization: support socialism; stress the study of Yiddish culture and language; assist members in the event of illness or death. By 1913 Indianapolis had two branches, both of which met at the Communal Building at 17 West Morris Street. However, Branch 175 was able to purchase a building at 1218 South Meridian Street.

The Indianapolis Circle supported socialism by holding May Day banquets, conducting debates on the American socialist movement, and raising funds for the Socialist party and the defense of incarcerated socialists. The maintenance of Jewish identity and transmission of Yiddish culture was a major part of the Circle as reflected in the support of a Yiddish library, Yiddish afternoon school, and Hebrew Immigrant Aid Society.

In late 1918 a decrease in eastern European immigration and the changing status of many workingmen to shopkeepers and small merchants forced the Circle to admit non-Jews with socialist sympathies. During the years 1921–1930 a conflict between the Left and Right wings of the Socialist party weakened the Circle. By the 1950s membership had decreased drastically and the Workman's Circle closed.

CAROLYN S. BLACKWELL

Judith E. Endelman, *The Jewish Community of Indianapolis* (Bloomington, Ind., 1984); Maximilian Hurwitz, *The Workman's Circle* (New York, 1936).

World War I (Apr. 2, 1917–Nov. 11, 1918). During World War I Indianapolis experienced profound changes. The societal transformation was marked by widespread community service and patriotism, cultural intolerance and discrimination, and an overall spirit of purpose and industriousness.

Prior to the United States' entry into the war, portions of the Indianapolis community participated in the emerging peace movement. The city hosted the Indiana Peace Society in March, 1915, which met to coordinate efforts among other peace organizations. Later in the year Stanford University president David Starr Jordan, a former BUTLER UNIVERSITY professor, lectured for the World Peace Foundation, and MAY WRIGHT SEWALL joined Henry Ford's ill-fated peace mission to Europe in December, 1915.

Isolationist attitudes prevailed in Indianapolis as residents showed little concern over potential threats to American security. Leading the drive for

military preparedness, however, were BOOTH TARKINGTON, JAMES WHITCOMB RILEY, George Ade, William D. Foulke, and MEREDITH NICHOLSON. Local Progressive reformer LUCIUS B. SWIFT also advocated a larger military force, and presented an anti-German polemic at the INDIANAPOLIS LITERARY CLUB in October, 1915.

Although Hoosiers supported the Allied cause by 1916, it was not until 1917 that concerns about German military actions stirred local residents. LOUIS HOWLAND of the *Indianapolis News* wrote that the war was "one between civilization and barbarism, and we should stand for civilization." On March 31, 1917, a mass meeting chaired by Episcopal Bishop Joseph M. Francis at TOMLINSON HALL urged Congress to declare war on Germany.

Following the U.S. declaration of war, most Hoosiers closed ranks behind the war effort. The *Indiana Catholic and Record*, previously an antiwar paper, urged all Americans to support their nation's cause. Local German-Americans threw their support behind the Allies. Columnist WILLIAM HERSCHELL of the *Indianapolis News* wrote "Long Boy," "The Kid Has Gone to the Colors," and "We Are Coming, Little Peoples," poems set to music to rally public sentiment.

The Marion County Council of Defense, reporting to the Indiana State Council of Defense (established May, 1917), served as the city's umbrella organization for war activities. Chaired by John M. Judah, a prominent businessman and lawyer, and secretary Russell B. Harrison, son of former president Benjamin Harrison, the council consisted of seven citizens including JOHN HAMPDEN HOLLIDAY, James Fesler, and Laura (Mrs. William B.) Elder. Though tension occasionally existed between county and state councils, the organization nonetheless succeeded in coordinating widespread support on the homefront.

Indianapolis women contributed enormously to the local effort. They first began a "socks for soldiers" campaign, knitting thousands of socks for Indiana regiments departing for France. The County Council of Defense established a Women's Section, led by Laura Elder, to oversee programs ranging from volunteer registration drives to the local Liberty Kitchen, a successful program to assist women to minimize their use of meat, wheat, sugar, and fat in food preparation. The Patriotic Gardeners Association of Indianapolis made significant contributions to food economy by placing more than 70,000 home and vacant lot gardens under cultivation. The Child Welfare Committee sponsored clinics to raise health care standards, while other women collaborated with organizations ranging from the Red Cross to the YWCA's War Work Council.

Local businesses and industries also geared up to join the cause. The CHAMBER OF COMMERCE opened a war contract bureau to provide information regarding government contracts. PREST-O-LITE manufactured munitions; NORDYKE AND MARMON and Allison Engineering made airplane engines; Indianapolis Gas Company converted some operations to produce explosives; and KAHN TAILORING COMPANY supplied military uniforms.

Indianapolis played an important military role in the war. Though most Indiana conscripts trained elsewhere, FORT BENJAMIN HARRISON hosted Army officers in two training camps in May–August, 1917, and a third camp in August – November, 1917. Specialty camps conducted at the fort attracted approximately 10,000 troops to receive instruction as engineers and railroad specialists; over 6,000 officers and enlisted men were trained in medicine. BASE HOSPITAL NO. 32, mobilized at the fort in September, 1917, and staffed by local doctors and nurses, served in Contrexeville, France. General Hospital No. 25 opened in September, 1918, for treatment of "shell shock" victims.

Vocational camps commanded by military officers were established at the Hotel Metropole and the state schools for the blind and the deaf. Men received training in gunsmithing, engine mechanics, and blacksmithing, and some became known as the "Blue Overalls Detachment" as they hiked to city schools and local shops where they received training. JAMES A. ALLISON tendered a machine shop to the government for the production of aircraft parts, and the INDIANAPOLIS MOTOR SPEEDWAY was converted into an airport to serve as a cross-country refueling station and major repair depot.

As was true elsewhere, Indianapolis subscribed to Liberty Loan campaigns and promoted the sale of War Savings Stamps and Red Cross

Returning World War I soldiers march through a huge victory arch on Monument Circle for Welcome Home Day, May 7, 1919. [Indiana Historical Society, Bass Collection, #66369F]

subscriptions to aid the expensive war effort. Local businesses encouraged employees to buy bonds; the Boy Scouts and churches also joined in various campaigns. By July, 1917, residents had donated over $500,000 to the Red Cross. One loan drive in May, 1918, generated $15 million in contributions. During the fourth Liberty Loan drive in October, 1918, Marion County surpassed its $23.4 million quota by $682,000.

Patriotism also was an important component of the war effort, and local authorities made strong attempts to encourage nationalism and suppress dissent. The war spawned over 35 patriotic organizations, and residents met frequently for rallies, noontime community sings on MONUMENT CIRCLE, and parades. A crowd of 200,000 lined downtown streets in August, 1917, to honor the 150th Artillery Division, commanded by Col. ROBERT TYNDALL, as it departed for Europe. Both the editorials and general reporting of local papers were unequivocal in their support of the Allies. Patriotism could scarcely be described as voluntary, however, as mechanisms were soon imposed to ensure it.

The State Council of Defense requested the creation of local "Protection" committees to communicate directly with federal law enforcement agents regarding disloyal neighbors and questionable activities. Governor James Goodrich established the paramilitary "Liberty Guards" in

December, 1917, to keep order and eliminate subversion at the county level. The Indianapolis Common Council passed Ordinance No. 35 of 1917, outlawing disloyalty to, disrespect for, or defiance of the government, the president, and the armed services; the council also made it unlawful to "incite, urge or advise strikes or disturbances" in war-related factories. In 1918 the council adopted Ordinance No. 11 against "war loafers," those not engaged in lawful employment or who spent time in the streets. Overlooking constitutional protections for the freedom of speech, city officials encouraged citizens to report neighbors who demonstrated any sort of disloyalty or pacifism.

The State Council's Education Section reported that it had taken "particular pains . . . to bring to the public schools lofty and reliable messages of impartial attachment to the principles at stake in the war." Throughout Marion County most schools reportedly spent 10 to 30 minutes daily on "patriotic exercises" or producing articles for soldiers. Over 40,000 school children marched in 65 parades around the city in June, 1918, to sell War Savings Stamps. To discourage dissent, the Indianapolis school board added a loyalty clause to teachers' contracts in 1918–1919.

Indianapolis' German population and its institutions bore a disproportionate share of the suspicion fostered by zealous patriots. Before the United States entered the war many local German-Americans sided with their homeland, called for the United States to cease munitions sales, and even organized to help local residents return to Germany to fight. After the declaration of war most joined in support of the Allied cause. Even so, the local German community was a target for attacks by individuals and groups who associated German heritage with disloyalty to the United States. The *Indianapolis Star* printed names and addresses of 800 unnaturalized Germans; anti-German rhetoric was fierce among local leaders; and many German cultural institutions became targets of vandals. In response these organizations anglicized or changed their German names. (Das Deutsche Haus, for example, became the ATHENAEUM.) Even the German language newspaper *Telegraph und Tribune* ceased publication. Despite serious legal concerns, language instruction in German was banned in elementary schools beginning in January, 1918. Still, the local German-American community raised funds for the Allied effort, passed proclamations declaring their loyalty, and even formed a company of the state militia in hopes of fighting against the Kaiser. RICHARD LIEBER, a local German-born businessman and military secretary to Gov. Goodrich, helped to rally the German-Americans for the American cause.

On November 7, 1918, a United Press bulletin, released by former Indianapolis newspaperman ROY HOWARD, announced an armistice. News of the actual armistice signing reached the city in the early morning of November 11, 1918, beginning days of celebration. A massive homecoming for Hoosier soldiers was held on Monument Circle on May 7, 1919. As the city began to readjust to the liberties and pleasures of peacetime, the newly established AMERICAN LEGION (November, 1919) selected Indianapolis for its national headquarters and plans were made to construct the INDIANA WORLD WAR MEMORIAL PLAZA to honor the nearly 3,400 Hoosier soldiers (approximately 350 from Indianapolis) who did not return home.

The war stimulated internationalist sentiments in many quarters. Local supporters of the movement to create the League of Nations included William D. Foulke, Louis Howland, and Booth Tarkington. Both the *Indianapolis Star* and *Indianapolis News* moderately supported American involvement with the Allies to preserve the peace. Others, including ALBERT J. BEVERIDGE and LUCIUS SWIFT, spoke against the league, fearing the loss of national sovereignty. Meanwhile, the city began to reconvert its industries to peacetime production and Indianapolis residents in general regained their isolationist attitudes.

MARK E. SCHNEIDER

Indiana State Council of Defense Records, Indiana State Archives; Ellis Searles, "History of Marion County, Indiana, in the World War" (Indianapolis, 1924); *Gold Star Honor Roll, 1914–1918* (Indianapolis, 1921); Mark E. Schneider, "Over Here: The Homefront in Indianapolis During World War I" (unpublished manuscript, 1992).

World War Memorial. See Indiana World War Memorial Plaza

World War II. Although one author declared Indianapolis "among the best prepared" cities in America when war came, it is doubtful that it was any more ready for the outbreak of World War II than the rest of America. Despite the alarm bells sounded by many, the city, capital of a decidedly isolationist state and home of national war referendum sponsor LOUIS LUDLOW, could not have fully appreciated the changes the war was to bring to its demographic, social, and physical structure, or to the lives of its citizens.

The most obvious and immediate change was the increased military presence in the city, especially at its major military installation, FORT BENJAMIN HARRISON, a sleepy facility brought to life by rumors of war. The Induction and Reception Center, which was to become the largest in the country before being transferred to Camp Atterbury in 1944, brought many recruits to the city and spurred expansion of the fort with numerous buildings and new acreage. Construction completed during the war included an administration center, warehouses, firehouse, recruit buildings, 20 barracks, and an infirmary. The fort also hosted the U.S. ARMY FINANCE CENTER, a chaplain's school, the Finance Replacement Training Center, and a school for cooks and bakers. Billings General Hospital, which opened in July, 1941, and eventually grew to a 2,000–bed complex, became known for its rehabilitation of patients. In 1944–1945 approximately 550 German and Italian prisoners of war were housed at the fort, mainly to ease an ongoing labor shortage.

Indianapolis greatly benefited from activities at the fort, but one installation caused controversy. The Midwest Branch of the U.S. Army Disciplinary Barracks moved into the abandoned induction center buildings in 1944, eventually bringing with it 2,700 prisoners. Many citizens were unhappy with the facility's location in Indianapolis—especially since it was adjacent to the hospital where many residents visited or worked. An inmate riot that led to the death of a fireman and guard and serious injury to others heightened their concern. Feelings quieted when a section of the disciplinary barracks was moved away from the hospital, but flared anew when a civilian guard was attacked. Also, a crime wave troubling the city was blamed on escapees.

City residents hurried to buy newspapers on V-E Day. [Indiana Historical Society, #C5723]

Fort Harrison was not the only military installation in the city. STOUT FIELD, on the southwest side, was home to a troop carrier command and paratrooper training, while radio operators were taught at the Naval Armory located on White River near Riverside Park. Two ordnance plants and specialized depots for chemical weapons and the Army Air Force also served the war effort.

Indianapolis' central location assured that vast numbers of the military—over six million by one estimate—passed through the city during the war. Like cities everywhere, Indianapolis tried to provide as many comforts as possible; churches, civic groups, local government, and individuals sought to do something "for the boys."

Servicemen's centers were among the most conspicuous efforts to aid morale. The first was the Army, Navy, and Marine Service Men's Club, which opened on May 22, 1941, in an abandoned freight house on West Wabash Street. The facility was not initially as popular as expected, primarily because women were not allowed on the premises. Attendance grew when a new director changed the rules, encouraged females to visit, and organized dances.

After Pearl Harbor the Union Station Canteen addressed needs of transient servicemen. Open 24 hours daily, the canteen eventually served meals to two million military personnel. Other centers opened on Illinois Street and at CHRIST CHURCH CATHEDRAL and ROBERTS PARK METHOD-

IST CHURCH. Although African-Americans were not specifically barred from the clubs, there was a separate facility for black servicemen on Senate Avenue. Fourteen service centers were welcoming members of the armed forces by 1943.

Indianapolis residents did not need the centers to make them aware of the war. Seemingly everything around them was tied to or affected by the conflict. Food and other essential items were rationed. There was the usual "black marketeering" or other under-the-table trade, but Indianapolis appears to have been no different than any other large city. Restaurants removed sugar bowls from tables in response to rationing and "sugar looting" by customers. City clocks were set on "war time" (daylight savings time). Blackouts, fire drills, and air raid alerts were rehearsed. Women volunteers learned how to handle fire bombs and helped roll the city's quota of bandages.

Support for the war effort was nearly universal, even among the more ardent isolationists. Indianapolis was quick to lend its support to many causes. There were numerous drives to collect silk, scrap metal, kitchen fat, rubber, books, and blood; residents volunteered to work in servicemen's clubs, firehouses, and numerous other organizations needing help. They also gave money. Spurred on by publicity campaigns and exhortations by Hollywood celebrities, the people of Indianapolis bought a substantial share of the millions of dollars in bonds sold to Hoosiers during the eight war loan drives. Famed movie actress Carole Lombard died in a plane crash on her return home from a bond drive which concluded in Indianapolis, an event that became part of Hollywood's cultural memory.

The war affected the Indianapolis economy also. Like the rest of Indiana, the city was still living under the shadow of the GREAT DEPRESSION. Personal and manufacturing incomes, down since 1929, were driven up by the war. The most direct impetus was defense spending. By 1941 over 70 local firms accounted for $600 million in contracts, placing Indianapolis among the top ten American cities in war production. Marion County industries had received $2 billion in defense contracts by 1944. Estimates suggested that one third of all Hoosier wages, including Indianapolis, were tied to the war effort, ranking the state fourth in the nation. Contracts awarded to Indianapolis firms ranged from a few hundred dollars to the millions awarded major defense contractors like Allison, which built over 70,000 aircraft engines, and Curtiss-Wright, largest maker of propellers in the nation. Scores of smaller concerns provided gears, chains, or other needed supplies. The downside of economic growth was inflation. A 1945 study of moderate-income families in Indianapolis showed that over 60 percent of their income was budgeted for "essentials," a 39 percent increase over 1935 levels.

The war also changed the composition of the work force: one third of factory workers statewide in 1943 were women. The acceptance of other nontraditional employees into the skilled work force did not progress so smoothly. African-Americans of both sexes were hired reluctantly by many Indianapolis industries. Although RCA hired large numbers of black workers, gains were fewer at other important concerns like Allison, where some white workers struck when blacks were put on the line. African-American women found it even more difficult to move from their traditional roles into skilled jobs.

Racial prejudice remained very evident in the city. Even though everyone supported a "war for democracy," *de facto* segregation existed. Still refused service by many restaurants and taxis, often relegated to the poorest housing, and denied a truly open door to the work place, African-Americans made progress during the war, but there were not many major improvements in their condition.

Prejudice was just one of Indianapolis' societal problems created or worsened by the war. The increase of women in the work force created child care problems resolved with only moderate success. The influx of people drawn to jobs in the city led to a housing shortage and rent controls. Juvenile delinquency made headlines, and citizens noted with concern the rising rates (32–percent increase between 1941–1942) of teen drinking, criminality, and sexual activity. Working mothers and absent fathers, the emotional trauma associated with the war, and overcrowding all received blame for the problem. Solutions included more supervised recreational programs; the city's POLICE ATHLETIC LEAGUE, for example, began in 1943.

Overcrowding was also given as a reason Indianapolis had one of the nation's highest tuberculosis rates (48 per 100,000 for whites, 150 per 100,000 for blacks). The venereal disease rate in the city rose so precipitously that the Army considered making the entire city off-limits to its personnel.

Indianapolis cheered lustily the end of a war that brought good and bad to its environs. Revelers swam in the Monument Circle pool while others turned the road around it into a miniature INDIANAPOLIS MOTOR SPEEDWAY. Stores, city offices, and bars closed to allow celebration and reflection. The war helped make Indianapolis bigger, more modern, more industrial, more diverse, and perhaps, more cosmopolitan and open. It brought the challenge of reconverting factories to peacetime production in order to avoid factory closings and massive unemployment. It also brought problems and promises that would affect the city long into the future.

TIMOTHY CRUMRIN
Conner Prairie

Stephen C. Bower, *A History of Fort Benjamin Harrison, 1903–1982* (Fort Benjamin Harrison, 1984); James H. Madison, *Indiana Through Tradition and Change: A History of the Hoosier State and Its People, 1920–1945* (Indianapolis, 1982).

Wright Porteous and Lowe. Architects. By 1945 the architecture firm of VONNEGUT AND BOHN had evolved into a partnership between Kurt Vonnegut, Sr., George Caleb Wright, and Alfred J. Porteous. In 1959 Vonnegut retired and C. Charles Lowe joined the firm, which then became Wright Porteous and Lowe, Inc.

In 1962 the firm was co-architect for the City-County Building on East Market Street. In 1968 they designed the Indiana University Law School at 735 West New York Street on the Indiana University–Purdue University, Indianapolis campus.

In the decade of the 1970s the firm designed many of Indianapolis' contemporary-style public structures. Among their most important works were the INB BANK TOWER, for many years Indiana's tallest building (1970, with co-architect Thomas E. Stanley); the Fashion Mall at Keystone at the Crossing and the Lawrence City Hall (1973); the Indiana Society of Architects' award-winning Bazaar at the Crossing (1974); the bronze-glass Market Square Center (1975); and THE CHILDREN'S MUSEUM (1976). More recently, following a merger with Bonar Associates in 1989, the firm designed the state-of-the-art Hurco Manufacturing Company headquarters at Park 100 (1991).

CONNIE J. ZEIGLER

Newspaper clipping files ("Architects & Architecture"), Indiana State Library.

Wynn, Frank Barbour (May 28, 1860–July 26, 1922). Physician, educator, and naturalist. Wynn was born and reared on a farm near Brookville, Indiana, a setting that stimulated his interest in nature. Although he chose medicine as a career, he retained an intense interest in preserving areas of natural beauty and historic significance.

After receiving both an A.B. and a Master's degree in chemistry from Indiana Asbury College (now DePauw University), Wynn graduated from the Medical College of Ohio in 1885. His medical training included two years of postgraduate education in Europe. He began his practice of medicine in downtown Indianapolis in the fall of 1893, and the next year was appointed to the faculty of the Medical College of Indiana, developing its pathology museum and a very extensive medical library. He became the first city sanitarian in 1895.

Wynn was instrumental in unifying the state's three principal proprietary medical schools into a state institution and was a guiding clinical influence, along with Dr. WILLIAM N. WISHARD, in revising the medical curriculum and medical faculty during the formative years of the INDIANA UNIVERSITY SCHOOL OF MEDICINE. Wynn's annual teaching exhibits (1896–1899) for the INDIANA STATE MEDICAL ASSOCIATION were the origin of the annual scientific exhibit of the American Medical Association.

Wynn was appointed to the Indiana Centennial Commission in 1911 and, later, was a member and president of the Indiana Historical Commission. He was actively involved with the commission's Park Committee, which inaugurated Indiana's state park system, and was active as well in the movement for national parks. Mt. Wynn in Glacier National Park recognizes his work in this area.

CHARLES A. BONSETT, M.D.
Indiana University School of Medicine

Wynnedale. Northwestside town bordered by 44th Street, Cold Spring Road, 42nd Street, and 2400 West. In 1932, Thomas Wynne, an executive with INDIANAPOLIS POWER AND LIGHT COMPANY, divided his family's farm and platted the town of Wynnedale. Located near the bluffs overlooking WHITE RIVER, Wynnedale was designed to be exclusively residential. Winding tree-lined streets and distinctive streetlights set off the tract from nearby areas.

In an effort to control development, residents met at Wynne's home on 42nd Street in March, 1939, and voted to incorporate. From the beginning, residents built homes in a variety of architectural styles, including Colonial and Tudor Revival, Bungalow, and Spanish. Lot and house sizes were also varied. Homeowners in the 1950s and '60s built ranch houses on undeveloped parcels.

The 38th Street bridge over White River, opened in 1962, provides easy access to the neighborhood, yet the area remains secluded. Residents eager to keep out additional traffic blocked the county's attempt to widen and pave Knollton Road as it cuts through Wynnedale. The town erected a barrier across the road in 1954 and then won a lengthy court battle to retain it. Under Unigov, Wynnedale retained its special status as an included town. In 1993, the town counts 270 residents and an interesting mix of middle class homes.

CATHLEEN F. DONNELLY

Yandes, Daniel (Jan. 28, 1793–June 10, 1878). Pioneer businessman and community leader. Born in Fayette County, Pennsylvania, Yandes served in the War of 1812 under General William Henry Harrison. Following his marriage in 1815, Yandes engaged in coal mining and the operation of a flour mill. In 1818, Yandes and his family moved to Connersville, Indiana, and in 1821 to Indianapolis.

In partnership with his brother-in-law, Yandes erected the first saw and grist mill in the new capital city. In partnership with John Wilkins, he opened the city's first tannery in 1823. In 1825, Yandes and Franklin Merrill, brother of state treasurer SAMUEL MERRILL, opened a general store and in 1831 he opened another store in partnership with Edward T. Porter. In 1833 Yandes went into partnership with Samuel Merrill and built a grist mill, a saw mill, and the first cotton spinning factory in the region. A few years later he built the first paper mill in the county, with William Sheets, on the canal west of the STATE HOUSE grounds. Following several years of financial difficulties, Yandes built 10 miles of the MADISON AND INDIANAPOLIS RAILROAD in 1847. In 1852, he and Alfred Harrison built 30 miles of the eastern end of the Bellefontaine Railroad in Indiana and in partnership with Edward T. Sinker, Yandes opened the Western Machine Works of Indianapolis in 1860. In addition to his business concerns in Marion County, Yandes also owned and operated stores, mills, and factories throughout the state.

Throughout his life, Yandes made substantial contributions to various charities in Indianapolis. The most notable of these gifts was a large donation to aid in the construction of First Presbyterian, one of the first churches in the city. Politically,

Yandes was a supporter of first the Whig and then the Republican parties. Although he did not actively seek office, Yandes served as the first treasurer of Marion County and in 1838 he served on the State Internal Improvements Board at the request of Governor Noah Noble.

MARK WYNN

Jacob Piatt Dunn, *Greater Indianapolis* (Chicago, 1910).

YMCA. See Young Men's Christian Association.

Yohn, Frederick Coffay (Feb. 8, 1875–June 6, 1933). Illustrator, especially of military and frontier subjects. Born in Indianapolis, Yohn was a pupil of WILLIAM FORSYTH. His first commercial assignments were sketches for Ernest P. Bicknell's *Indianapolis Illustrated* (1893), and the *INDIANAPOLIS NEWS*. In 1894 he moved to New York and studied at the Art Students League. Hired by Harper and Brothers, he became popular for his illustrations in Theodore Roosevelt's *Frontier Sketches* and Henry Cabot Lodge's *Story of the American Revolution*. His work appeared regularly in *Harper's*, *Scribner's*, and *Collier's Weekly*. He also provided illustrations for MEREDITH NICHOLSON's *A Hoosier Chronicle*, *The Hero of Vincennes* by Lowell Thomas, and Maurice Thompson's *Alice of Old Vincennes*.

Yohn's forte was accuracy of expression and a preference for much composition and plenty of action. He and his publisher gave his oil painting, *The Fall of Ft. Sackville*, to the INDIANA HISTORICAL BUREAU. This painting became the subject of a U.S. postage stamp issued February 25, 1929, on the 150th anniversary of the surrender of Ft. Sackville, and it was also widely reproduced during the years of the nation's bicentennial celebration.

MARY JANE MEEKER

Peggy and Harold Samuels, *The Illustrated Biographical Encyclopedia of Artists of the American West* (Garden City, N.Y., 1976).

Indianapolis pioneer Daniel Yandes. [Indiana State Library]

Young Audiences of Indiana. Nonprofit community-based arts education program affiliated with Young Audiences, Inc., a national arts education organization. Indianapolis-based Young Audiences of Indiana (YA) was founded in 1961 to educate school-age children about the arts. While YA initially emphasized arts education through classical music, the organization now includes programming by professional artists in the visual arts, storytelling, theater, dance, and language arts.

YA employs over 60 artists who present programs at schools, community centers, parks, libraries, and museums statewide. During the 1992–1993 school year YA reached over 250,000 students in 49 counties, including 150,000 children in Indianapolis, through approximately 900 workshops and 800 performances. Young Audiences of Indiana had a 1992–1993 annual budget of around $435,000, with funding coming from both public and private donations.

DEBORAH B. MARKISOHN

The Brightwood YMCA, southwest corner of Roosevelt Avenue and Station Street, provided leisure activities for many railroad workers.
[Indiana Historical Society, Bass Collection, #4501]

Young Men's Christian Association (YMCA).
Founded in 1854 after a series of organizational meetings at local churches, the Indianapolis YMCA (or Y) was originally led by a small group of evangelical Protestants. Its first offices were in Blake's Commercial Row, across the street from the BATES HOUSE. Despite continual financial problems the YMCA built its own building at 33–37 North Illinois Street in 1871, which was later rebuilt on the same site in 1887. In 1907 it erected a new headquarters building at the corner of Illinois and New York streets, where it remained until 1971.

The first local branch of the YMCA appeared in 1878 and involved railroad men; college men formed another branch at BUTLER UNIVERSITY in the 1890s. African-Americans started a prayer band in 1900, which eventually led to a branch recognized by the state YMCA in 1902 and by the Indianapolis organization in 1910. This branch, known as the SENATE AVENUE YMCA, was one of the largest, most active black branches in the country. During the 1940s the Y established four neighborhood branches on each side of the city. The branches had separate offices but provided services mainly through local churches and schools. When membership soared in the 1950s and 1960s the Y built new facilities for seven, mostly suburban, branches. As of the early 1990s the YMCA of Greater Indianapolis includes six full facility branches, four program offices, a camping facility, and an administrative office.

Originally, YMCA members had to be active church members and the organization was highly religious in nature. Local ministers often accused the YMCA of duplicating their work. Early programming included a reading room, public lectures on Christian themes, daily and weekly interdenominational services, and charity work. By the 1870s the YMCA began to sever its church ties and increasingly focused its work on serving the poor and outcast. Members helped organize the Home for Friendless Women, the Indiana Boys' and Girls' Schools, a Newsboys' and Bootblacks' Home, temperance work, and mission Sunday schools for children and workers. During the late 19th century the YMCA hosted social and recreational activities, charging fees for member attendance and facility use. In order to expand these activities it built a five-acre athletic park, bowling alley, pool, and gym, and started a night school. By the 1890s programming had expanded to include a boys' department. As the organization's emphasis shifted, mission work and lectures became less important and the reading room collection was absorbed into the public library.

Under general secretary Arthur H. Godard in the early 1900s, the association further distanced itself from direct charitable and religious aims. The

YMCA remained Christian in spirit but it became more of an organization that provided moral and healthful options for the use of men's free time. Godard revived the lecture series, renamed "Big Meetings," which met in the ENGLISH OPERA HOUSE, hosted large crowds, and featured more secular topics. Athletics and recreation soon overshadowed the lectures and religious services, as evidenced by the fact that the new central building's facilities included a barber shop, swimming pool, bowling alley, cafe, and residence rooms. Programming expanded throughout the 1920s and 1930s into numerous clubs, athletic leagues, job and training programs, and social activities.

Both World War I and World War II interrupted regular activities, during which time the YMCA adjusted to meet emergency needs by providing special programming for soldiers. Women were highly involved in these activities and after the war became full members. In the postwar years the YMCA also expanded its focus to include a boys' camp at Flat Rock River and neighborhood branches. The eastside branch, with new facilities built in 1959, was the country's first family Y, with other branches soon following. During the 1960s programming reflected this family focus by including activities and clubs for members ranging from senior citizens to infants.

As the suburban branches and other organizations increasingly serviced the recreational needs of Indianapolis, the Central YMCA closed in 1971 in favor of implementing the Central Urban Outreach Program, which included two neighborhood sites and a mobile van program. In 1992, after a 20–year absence, the YMCA resumed downtown programming in permanent facilities at the ATHENAEUM. In the early 1990s the Y continues to provide Christian opportunities for its members through such social and recreational programming as preschool, fitness, sports, camping, and after-school programming. The YMCA of Greater Indianapolis currently serves over 100,000 people annually, almost half of whom are under the age of 18 or are female.

MICHELLE D. HALE

George C. Mercer, *One Hundred Years of Service, 1854–1954* (Indianapolis: YMCA, 1954); Clipping File: "Indianapolis YMCA," Indiana State Library.

Young Women's Christian Association (YWCA). Incorporated in 1892, the YWCA's aim was to promote the physical, intellectual, social, and spiritual advancement of young women, especially young working women. The Indianapolis chapter did not hold its first meeting until May 6, 1895, with Ella McCrea later elected as the first president. Two rented rooms at 139 North Meridian served as the first meeting space until growth forced the YWCA to move into other temporary downtown locations. Finally, in 1909, the organization built a home at 329 North Pennsylvania that included meeting rooms, the first indoor swimming pool in the city, and residence facilities. By 1911 it hosted the Third National Biennial YWCA Convention. Other facilities included safe houses for young women at 247 North Pennsylvania Street and 122 East Michigan Street, the Blue Triangle Residence at 725 North Pennsylvania Street (1924–1971), and branches at 717 South Alabama and 1627 Prospect to serve the south side. A campaign to raise money for a new building failed in 1973, and in 1974 the headquarters temporarily relocated to 822 Fort Wayne Avenue. In 1976, the YWCA moved into the renovated Dolphin Swim Club property at 4460 Guion Road.

African-American members began in 1914 to discuss the need for their own branch. Granted official branch status in 1925, they built a structure in 1929 and operated the PHYLLIS WHEATLEY BRANCH until the organization was integrated in 1959.

The YWCA first directed its educational and recreational programs toward young working women and throughout the years expanded to include women of all ages and their families. The initial focus on working women led the organization to provide a place to get lunch and take a noon hour rest in the downtown area. In 1898 the YWCA developed clubs among local industries, and in 1918 divided the extension clubs into an Industrial Department and a Department Store Department. The Travelers Aid Society, cosponsored by the YWCA, provided 24–hour service at UNION STATION during World War I. During World War II the YWCA provided housing for women in the military and hosted activities at FORT BENJAMIN HARRISON.

As women's roles changed, the YWCA offered programs and courses on topics relevant to the needs of its members and the community. In the 1950s it was child care and home economic courses; in the 1960s, single parents and truants. During the 1970s the YWCA supported the EQUAL RIGHTS AMENDMENT and with the Indianapolis Public Schools began a learning center for unwed pregnant girls. In the 1980s the organization highlighted day care and latchkey programs for children as well as senior citizen activities. In the early 1990s, with a full-time staff of 20 and an annual budget of approximately $1 million, the YWCA continues to provide recreational activities to its roughly 2,000 members and social service programs to the community-at-large.

NORALEEN YOUNG

Madge Dishman, *INDYW Celebrates Ninety Years of Service to Women by Women . . . A History of the Indianapolis YWCA, 1895–1985* (Indianapolis, 1985); Ruth Hamlin Bell, "A History of the Phyllis Wheatley Branch of the Indianapolis YWCA, 1923–1944" (M.A. thesis, Indiana University, 1948).

Z

Zelda Dameron (1904). Novel by MEREDITH NICHOLSON. This book, Nicholson's second novel but his first to be set in Indianapolis, offers a glimpse of life in the state capital as it was lived by the city's upper classes just before the advent of the automobile. Published by BOBBS-MERRILL, and filled with comments about various city landmarks and institutions but not necessarily people, the book was well received locally and nationally. The story, of the type for which Nicholson later became famous, is a light romance with elements of mystery and skullduggery, and a happy ending. Nicholson's characters, however, are well drawn and the book, despite triteness of plot and its focus on a narrow segment of the population, remains a valuable social document. He used the device of having his title character, an engaging young heiress from "Mariona" (Indianapolis), return from an extended trip abroad in order to introduce her, and his readers, to the capital city at century's end. Nicholson incorporates some of the insights he had developed at greater length in his history of *The Hoosiers* (1900), and he is particularly effective at evoking the transportation methods employed in the 1890s and the dramatic change represented by the advent of the electric INTERURBAN. Identifiable settings in the novel include the Morris and Mansur homes, Meridian and Lockerbie streets, and the COLUMBIA CLUB. The book's popularity was soon eclipsed by that of Nicholson's most famous and successful book, *The House of a Thousand Candles*, published the following year and set in northern Indiana.

RALPH D. GRAY
Indiana University–Purdue University,
Indianapolis

Dorothy Ritter Russo and Thelma Lois Sullivan, *Bibliographical Studies of Seven Authors of Crawfordsville, Indiana* (Indianapolis, 1952); *Indianapolis News*, Oct. 15, 1904 (two articles, including one entitled "Local Atmosphere of 'Zelda Dameron' ").

Ziegner, Edward Henry (Aug. 8, 1920–June 22, 1993). Political journalist. An Indianapolis native, Ziegner graduated from SHORTRIDGE HIGH SCHOOL in 1938 and attended Wabash College and Indiana University. He began his journalism career in 1941, but it was soon interrupted by overseas service as an antiaircraft artillery officer in World War II. After the war Ziegner became an assistant State House reporter with the INDIANAPOLIS NEWS. In 1953 he was put in charge of the *News'* legislative bureau and directed it for the next 32 years, covering 27 regular sessions and seven special sessions of the General Assembly. After his retirement in 1985, Ziegner continued to write a weekly political column until 1990.

Eugene S. Pulliam, publisher of the *News* and the *Indianapolis Star*, described Ziegner as "one of the best political reporters I have ever known." National political reporters made a point of checking in with him to find out what was going on in the state. A Democrat, Ziegner believed he was doing his job well "as long as he was getting complaints from both parties."

Ziegner received numerous professional awards, including the American Political Science Association award for distinguished public affairs reporting, the Indianapolis Press Club's Newsman of the Year, and induction into the Indiana Journalism Hall of Fame. Indiana governors twice named Ziegner a Sagamore of the Wabash, the highest civilian honor in the state.

DEBORAH B. MARKISOHN

Indianapolis News, June 23, 1993; *Indianapolis Star*, June 23, July 1, 1993.

Zionsville. Boone County town located northwest of Indianapolis along S.R. 334 (116th Street). Zionsville began as a depot on the Indianapolis, Cincinnati, and Lafayette Railroad. In 1852 William Zion of Lebanon surveyed the Elijah Cross farm adjacent to the tracks. Sixty-four lots were laid out and the name Zionsville selected in honor of the surveyor. The first church was organized in 1854, the first school in 1858. A town newspaper, the *Zionsville Times*, was founded in 1860. It has survived several name changes and was still publishing in the early 1990s.

Zionsville was incorporated in 1866 and grew slowly throughout the 19th and early 20th centuries. In 1880 the town counted 855 residents; by 1930 there were 1,131. Significant growth occurred after 1970, when new residential subdivisions more than doubled the population. By 1990 the town numbered about 5,300 residents. Despite its recent rapid growth, Zionsville has deliberately restricted residential and commercial development. Zoning laws have blocked intrusive construction and new housing units have been limited to 50 per year since 1983.

Zionsville's popularity as a commuter suburb is due to several factors, including easy access to Indianapolis via interstate highways and the village's quaint charm. In the 1950s and '60s, the Chamber of Commerce led a drive to remodel the downtown in an early American theme. Townspeople restored many of the 19th-century cottages and the village became a popular tourist attraction.

Zionsville residents have played an important role in the establishment of the town's cultural organizations. Bequests provided for the founding of the Hussey-Mayfield Memorial Public Library, the Patrick Henry Sullivan Museum, and the Zionsville Munce Art Center. Residents also provided funds and volunteer assistance to establish a local historical society and municipal parks.

CATHLEEN F. DONNELLY

Indianapolis Times, June 8, 1952; *Indianapolis News*, Apr. 22, 1976; *Indianapolis Star*, Mar. 12, 1989.

Zoning. Municipal regulation of land uses. A 1921 state law gave Indiana cities jurisdiction over land planning and zoning for the first time, although by 1905 the Indianapolis COMMON COUNCIL had some authority to regulate against factories in residential areas. Following the 1921 legislation the Common Council created a ten-member volunteer City Plan Commission and passed the city's first zoning ordinance in 1922. This ordinance, which affected only new development, established five types of "use districts," including residential dwelling, apartment, business, and two kinds of industrial districts. The City Plan Commission had broad powers to create the boundaries of use districts as well as hear zoning appeals, and a commissioner of buildings enforced the ordinance. In 1935 state law required the commission to create a master plan for the city as well as subdivisions five miles outside of the city limits.

The intent of the zoning legislation was to protect neighborhoods from "undesirable elements" and to avoid the creation of blighted areas through stabilized use. Generally, the central downtown core was designated for business; the north and east sides were zoned almost exclusively residential; and the west and south sides included a mix of industrial, business, and residential uses. Initially, there were relatively few zoning disputes, except for upper-income northside residents' efforts to keep business out of the Meridian Street corridor. The Common Council could amend zoning ordinances or overturn decisions, but these powers were rarely exercised before World War II.

During and after World War II city planners, concerned by spreading urban blight and decentralization, successfully lobbied for professional staff to conduct postwar planning. After much subsequent tinkering with city zoning ordinances, the state legislature consolidated the Indianapolis and Marion County planning and zoning functions in 1955 when it adopted the Metropolitan Planning Law and created the Metropolitan Planning Commission of Marion County.

As Indianapolis grew, so did public discontent with zoning decisions and enforcement of violations. Northside residents fought continued business encroachment, citizens on the northeast and east sides resisted industrial rezoning in their neighborhoods, and residents throughout the city called for a reevaluation of the zoning ordinances.

Under UNIGOV, effective in 1970, the METROPOLITAN DEVELOPMENT COMMISSION (MDC), a supervisory body of the DEPARTMENT OF METROPOLITAN DEVELOPMENT (DMD), succeeded the Metropolitan Planning Commission. The MDC's zoning functions include adopting and implementing a Comprehensive Plan for Marion County, which like earlier master plans, guides and regulates the county's growth by designating geographic boundaries of land uses. Under state law the following considerations must guide land use decisions: "assuring adequate life, air, convenience of access, and safety from fire, flood, and other dangers; lessening or avoiding congestion of public ways; and promoting public health, safety, comfort, morals, convenience, and general welfare."

The Comprehensive Plan is actually a series of studies corresponding to Marion County townships, Center Township neighborhoods, and the Indianapolis central business district. Originally designed to be revised every 20 years, the plan has required revision approximately every five years because of the rapid pace of development in the Indianapolis metropolitan area since the 1970s. As of the 1990s each component of the plan is the result of a lengthy process of discussion between neighborhood organizations, developers, residents, and DMD planning staff. Planners use the information gained from these discussions to create a map and text that describe current land uses and recommend future uses.

Under the Comprehensive Plan in effect in 1993, property in Marion County is zoned for one of the following types of use: commercial, residential, central business district, industrial, airport, park, hospital, university, and various special uses such as schools and churches. Secondary zoning districts also define restrictions or requirements for property use. These districts include the historic preservation and regional center districts, both of which require a special design review, as well as flood control and gravel pit designations.

Land use for a particular parcel of real estate may be changed either through a rezoning of the site or a variance in zoning. A rezoning makes a permanent and legal change in the approved use of the property in question. A variance is an administrative decision which does not change the zoning of the land but permits the current owner to use the property for another purpose. Landowners must file a petition for a rezoning or variance and notify affected landowners and residents, who are allowed to give testimony at a final hearing. DMD staff prepare recommendations for all rezoning and variance requests based upon site reviews and compliance with Comprehensive Plan provisions and municipal zoning ordinances.

The Metropolitan Development Commission decides rezoning requests, but approved rezoning decisions can be appealed to the CITY-COUNTY COUNCIL. The Metropolitan Board of Zoning Appeals hears requests for zoning variances. The board may allow or deny a variance pertaining to use, height, bulk, area, and on special exceptions to a zoning ordinance. It has countywide jurisdiction except for the municipalities of BEECH GROVE, LAWRENCE, and SPEEDWAY, which operate their own zoning appeals boards with the approval of the larger metropolitan board. Zoning decisions and policies are implemented through a system of permits and inspection conducted by DMD staff. Property owners not in compliance with zoning regulations can be fined.

Soon after the Unigov reorganization of zoning officials, public dissatisfaction with zoning decisions and policy erupted in several investigations into the high percentages of variances and rezoning requests being granted by the MDC, especially to politically well-connected individuals. Concurrently, newly organized and vocal neighborhood associations called for less political and developer dominance and more neighborhood involvement in the zoning process, as well as a greater MDC adherence to the Comprehensive Plan.

Areas without strong neighborhood groups, however, often fell prey to large rezoning and development plans. Some lower-income downtown neighborhoods were rezoned and demolished to accommodate an expanding transportation network and downtown business and cultural districts. Also, previously undeveloped areas on the periphery of the city, like CASTLETON, were sometimes turned from small towns into malls and corporate parks with insufficient attention to development's impact on resources.

Since the 1970s city government has increasingly responded to citizens' zoning concerns. The mayoral ADMINISTRATION OF WILLIAM H. HUDNUT III encouraged more community involvement in planning and zoning by including neighborhood groups in the Comprehensive Plan process. The ADMINISTRATION OF STEPHEN GOLDSMITH also has strengthened citizen access by appointing township administrators who, among other things, act as a conduit between DMD staff and community groups. Zoning staff have also revised resident notifications and created a supplemental review process to increase the level of communication and interaction with residents.

MICHELLE D. HALE

Zwara, John (ca. 1880s-ca. 1940s). Watercolorist and artist. Known as the "mystery artist of Indianapolis," Zwara was born in Austria in the 1880s. Having attended art schools in Prague and Berlin, he left Austria for the United States in 1900. Zwara spoke little English and had trouble communicating with others. Before coming to Indianapolis in the 1930s, he lived as a vagabond wandering across the country.

Zwara had no family and few friends in Indianapolis. Sleeping on the streets and subsisting on a diet of bread and coffee, he earned a living by selling his paintings to Lyman and Brothers and the H. LIEBER COMPANY in Indianapolis. Alexander Vonnegut, who eventually befriended Zwara, recognized his remarkable talent with watercolors, but also realized that he had mental problems and had him committed in 1936 to CENTRAL STATE HOSPITAL. At the hospital, physicians diagnosed Zwara as schizophrenic but allowed him to paint. Zwara stayed only six months at the institution and then left. He died in the 1940s at the Little Sisters of the Poor.

Zwara was a prolific painter, reportedly producing ten paintings a week. He worked mainly in watercolors, painting landscapes, but occasionally produced an oil portrait or landscape. The INDIANA MEDICAL HISTORY MUSEUM has one of the largest collections of his paintings.

KATHERINE MANDUSIC MCDONELL

Charles A. Bonsett, "John Zwara," *Indiana Medical History Quarterly*, 1 (July, 1974), 3–5; Walter Bruetsch, "Case of J.Z.," *Journal of Nervous and Mental Disorders*, 95 (1942), 69; Lloyd B. Walton, "The Mystery Artist of Indianapolis," *Indianapolis Star Magazine* (Mar. 28, 1978), 38.

TIMELINE

1816 U.S. Congress authorizes a state government for Indiana on April 19 and donates four sections of land to locate a seat for state government.

1818 Treaty of St. Mary's (Ohio) signed on October 3. By this treaty, Delaware and Miami tribes agree to leave central Indiana by 1821, thereby opening the land to organized settlement.

1820 John McCormick settles on the east bank of White River, near present-day Washington Street, on February 26. On March 2, blacksmith George Pogue arrives.

State capital selection committee, convening at McCormick's cabin on June 7, locates Indiana's new state capital at the confluence of White River and Fall Creek.

1821 General Assembly approves site selected by the commissioners and adopts the name Indianapolis on January 6. Corydon continues as state capital until 1825.

Joseph C. Reed opens first school at Kentucky and Washington streets.

Samuel G. Mitchell moves from Kentucky in April to become town's first resident doctor. That same month Elias Pym Fordham and Alexander Ralston appointed surveyors of the capital city.

Methodist gathering at Isaac Wilson's house during the summer forms nucleus of town's first church.

City lots go on sale October 8. When sale ends seven days later, 314 lots have been purchased.

Indianapolis' population is between 400 and 500 (est.) by fall.

Marion County created on December 31.

1822 George Smith and Nathaniel Bolton publish the *Indiana Gazette*, Indianapolis' first newspaper, on January 28.

Samuel Henderson appointed postmaster of town's first post office in February.

First Marion County election held on April 1, with 336 voters (224 in Indianapolis) participating.

Elected county officers meet for the first time on April 15 and divide the county into townships for administrative purposes.

First Baptist Church established on October 10.

1823 Nicholas McCarty opens one of town's first general stores, located on southwest corner of Washington and Pennsylvania streets.

On March 7 Douglas Maguire and fellow Kentuckian Harvey Gregg establish town's second newspaper, the *Western Censor & Emigrants' Guide*.

First Presbyterian Church organized on July 5.

Town's first theatrical production opens on December 31 in dining room of Thomas Carter's tavern.

1824 Marion County Courthouse completed. The building serves as first State House in Indianapolis.

On January 20, General Assembly makes Indianapolis the seat of state government effective January 1, 1825.

State Treasurer Samuel Merrill takes 11 days to move state documents, silver from the state treasury, and a printing press from Corydon to Indianapolis in October. Net cost: $65.55.

1825 State legislature convenes in Marion County Courthouse on January 10.

John Douglass and Douglas Maguire begin publishing the *Indiana Journal* on January 11.

1826 Indianapolis Sabbath School Union is established.

First volunteer fire company in Indianapolis organized on June 20.

1827 Indianapolis' population is 1,066 (1008 whites, 58 African-Americans).

U.S. Congress donates ground on which Military Park is located for militia training purposes.

1828 Temperance Society of Marion County organizes on October 3.

1829 Methodists erect a brick church, Roberts Chapel, at southwest corner of the Circle and Meridian Street.

On December 26, finding that a slave woman and her three children passing through Indiana with their owner are free, Marion County circuit court judge Bethuel F. Morris hands down one of the nation's first rulings against a slaveholder's right to transport slaves through a free state.

1830   Indianapolis' population is 1,900 (est.).

Two short-lived female academies open in March, one the Indianapolis Female School.

1831   Arrival of the steamboat *Robert Hanna* on White River in April generates requests for state funds to improve the waterway. Enthusiasm wanes when the steamboat runs aground on its return trip.

1832   Town of Indianapolis incorporated on September 3 and local government placed under the direction of five trustees elected on September 29.

1833   John O'Kane, a Virginia evangelist and "Campbellite," establishes the Church of Christ on June 12. The congregation later becomes known as Central Christian Church.

Asiatic cholera sweeps through Indianapolis during the summer, causing 62 deaths in one month.

1834   Whigs, forerunner of the Republican party, form a local political organization on May 17.

Marion County Seminary, a public academy, opens on September 1 and becomes known as one of the leading schools in central Indiana.

1835   Indianapolis' population is 1,683 (1,602 whites, 81 African-Americans).

Rev. Claude Francis of Logansport offers first Catholic Mass in Indianapolis at Powers Tavern on West Washington Street.

Indianapolis Benevolent Society formed "to give temporary aid to meet the needs of individuals and families on a community wide basis without regard to race or creed."

First annual fair of the Marion County Agricultural Society is held at the Courthouse Square on October 30–31.

New State House, built of brick, wood, and stucco, completed in December (cost: ca. $60,000).

1836   Construction on the Central Canal begins.

First African Methodist Episcopal church in Indianapolis (named Bethel in 1869) organizes and meets in private homes.

1837   General Assembly appoints Calvin Fletcher and Thomas Johnson on February 4 to oversee draining of swamps that surround the Mile Square.

Jacob Coil plats Broad Ripple north of the Central Canal in April.

Thirty persons sign agreement of association to organize the Parish of Christ Church (now Christ Church Cathedral) on July 13, and congregation occupies its first building on the Circle on November 18, 1838.

Fr. Vincent Bacquelin, a French-born priest, organizes first Catholic parish in December.

1838   General Assembly reincorporates Indianapolis on February 17 with a new charter that provides a town council with taxing, licensing, and legislative powers.

During the summer a town ordinance provides for paving gutters and grading and graveling Washington Street.

Second Presbyterian Church officially organized on November 19 by 15 members who depart the "Old School" First Presbyterian Church. Henry Ward Beecher hired as first pastor.

1839   Nine miles of Central Canal open for traffic on June 27, but state's bankruptcy brings work to a sudden halt.

1840   Indianapolis' population is 2,692.

German immigrant Charles Mayer opens a general store on Washington Street.

Holy Cross Catholic Church established.

1841   Jacob P. and George A. Chapman purchase *Indiana Democrat* (1830) in July, renaming it the *Indiana State Sentinel*.

1842   On October 19 the Methodist conference divides Indianapolis into two charges with Meridian Street as divider. Methodists living east of the line establish Roberts Chapel; others remain charges of Wesley Chapel.

1843   Indiana State Asylum for the Deaf and Dumb opens in rented quarters.

Rev. Henry Ward Beecher of Second Presbyterian Church publishes *Seven Lectures to Young Men* which offers practical cautions against Indianapolis vices.

1844   Marion County Library forms a subscription library, housed in the county courthouse.

St. Paul's Evangelical Lutheran Church, considered the "mother church" of Indianapolis' German Lutheran churches, organizes on June 5 in a building at Alabama Street below Washington Street.

1845   Torrential rains in March cut off communications from Indianapolis to the East and temporarily halt mail delivery.

1846   In a popular referendum on April 6 residents of Center Township vote 602 to 211 against granting licenses for retail sale of liquor.

1847   On March 27, by an overwhelming majority of 449 to 19, voters endorse a new charter that takes effect March 30 and makes Indianapolis an incorporated city.

Samuel Henderson elected Indianapolis' first mayor on April 24. Out of 500 votes cast in the city election, 406 favor free schools, 28 oppose them. First tax levy raises $1,981 for schools.

Madison and Indianapolis Railroad, first steam railroad completed in Indiana, arrives at Indianapolis on October 1.

1848   Julius Boetticher begins the *Volksblatt*, the first German language newspaper in the city.

Indianapolis Hospital for the Insane admits its first five patients on November 21 and expands to 300 within ten years. It becomes Central Indiana Hospital in 1889 and in 1929 its name changes to Central State Hospital.

1849   Polish-born merchant Alexander Franco and English-born clerk Moses Woolf are first Jews to arrive in Indianapolis.

Indiana Central Medical College, first proprietary medical school in Indianapolis, is established on

East Washington Street. The college closes in 1852, and another medical school does not appear in Indiana until 1869.

Horatio Cooley Newcomb wins election in April as mayor at age 27, youngest mayor in the city's history.

Smallpox scare in June causes city council to order vaccinations for everyone in town, to establish a board of health, and to erect a hospital. When epidemic does not spread as feared, plans for the hospital are canceled.

Widows and Orphans Friends Society establishes the Indianapolis Orphans Asylum in December.

1850 Indianapolis' population is 8,091.

North Western Christian University (later Butler University) chartered on January 15, with Ovid Butler providing 20 acres at College and Home avenues for the facility.

Local skilled artisans form the Mechanics Mutual Protection in June and call for increased wages, improved educational opportunities, and better health care.

State constitutional convention, meeting in Indianapolis in October, drafts proposal to prevent migration of African-Americans and mulattos into Indiana. Voters statewide overwhelmingly approve the measure; Marion County votes 2,509 to 308 in favor. The measure subsequently becomes Article 13 of 1851 state constitution.

1851 Indianapolis Turngemeinde opens on West Washington Street on July 28 to promote physical fitness, freethought, liberal politics, and German language and culture.

1852 Construction of nation's first "union station," a central station for the common use of passengers of several rail lines.

Through a random drawing in May, Indianapolis local of the National Typographical Union becomes Typographical Union Local No. 1, which still exists.

First Indiana State Fair opens at Military Park on October 20.

1853 City's first free schools, funded by tax revenues, open with two male and twelve female teachers. Average attendance jumps from 340 students in April to 700 in May; still, less than one half of city's children attend school.

Thirty-six of city's leading businessmen and boosters form the first Indianapolis Board of Trade, forerunner of the Commercial Club (established 1890).

Voters approve a new city charter on March 27, establishing a common council of 14 members elected from 7 wards, and a mayor elected citywide.

Indianapolis High School, the city's first public high school, opens on September 1. It closes in 1858 when Indiana Supreme Court declares local taxation for schools to be unconstitutional.

1854 Maennerchor, German-American male singing society and oldest continuously existing men's choir in the U.S., organizes.

The common council passes ordinance establishing a regular, paid police department of 14 officers, two from each of the city's wards.

Small group of evangelical Protestants found Indianapolis YMCA.

1855 First superintendent of public schools is Silas T. Bowen, head of Bowen, Stewart & Co. booksellers-publishers. His annual salary is $400 for one-third time.

North Western Christian University opens its doors on November 1 under sponsorship of the Disciples of Christ. It is one of the first universities in U.S. to admit students without regard to race or gender.

1856 City's two leading newspapers begin receiving news through the Associated Press news service.

Germans capture city offices of clerk, marshal, and assessor in local elections. The city council adopts resolution allowing German students to receive instruction in their own language.

Newly formed Republican party holds its first state convention in Indianapolis on July 15, beginning with parade down Washington Street.

Fourteen Jews meet at Julius Glaser's house on November 2 to organize Indianapolis Hebrew Congregation. They secure funds to buy 3 1/2 acres of land for a Jewish cemetery at South Meridian and Kelly streets.

1857 Indianapolis schools employ 35 teachers (mainly female); school system's average attendance is 1,800 students, or one third of city's children.

Local attorney Ignatius Brown publishes first history of Indianapolis in 1857 city directory.

Moses Broyles comes to Indianapolis to teach at one of the city's first schools for African-Americans. He joins the Second Baptist Church that same year and becomes its minister.

1858 The Metropolitan opens as Indianapolis' first real theater complete with gallery, vaulted ceilings, and frescoes.

After Indiana Supreme Court overturns tax-supported free public education, Indianapolis schools close on April 17.

1859 Sisters of Providence establish city's first Catholic school at St. John's Catholic school.

Christian Frederick Schmidt and Charles Jaeger establish city's first successful brewery, C. F. Schmidt Brewery.

Common council votes in August to establish Indianapolis' first regular paid fire department.

1860 Indianapolis' population is 18,611, a 130–percent increase since 1850. The city ranks 48th among U.S. cities. There are 498 African-Americans, or 2.6 percent of the population.

Street lights illuminate 8.5 miles of city streets.

Indianapolis acquires its first steam-operated fire engine.

1861 Van Camp Packing Company secures its first major contract to supply pork and beans to the

Union Army. In 1933 it merges with Stokely Brothers & Co. to become Stokely–Van Camp.

President-elect Abraham Lincoln visits Indianapolis on February 11 during his trip to Washington, D.C. for his inauguration. Speaking from the balcony of the Bates House, he states that his primary duty is the preservation of the Union.

Private John C. Hollenbeck, killed June 27 near Romney, Virginia, is city's first casualty in the Civil War.

1862   Irishman Samuel Kingan opens meat-packing plant in Indianapolis and employs workers recruited in Ireland.

Camp Morton in Indianapolis is converted in February to a prison for Confederate soldiers. By month's end some 3,700 prisoners-of-war arrive.

U.S. Congress enacts measure on July 11 providing for a permanent arsenal in Indianapolis.

Indianapolis physician and real estate broker Dr. Richard J. Gatling receives U.S. Patent No. 36,836 in November for his Gatling Gun, an early rapid-firing weapon or machine gun.

1863   Abram Shortridge becomes school superintendent and reopens the city's schools. He urges school board to hire female teachers, as they receive smaller salaries.

John Caven becomes mayor of Indianapolis. Elected to office a record five times, the first three unopposed, Caven serves longer than any other mayor until William H. Hudnut III (1976–1991).

As Democrats leave their state convention by train on May 20, armed soldiers stop the train to search for weapons, which are subsequently discarded into Pogue's Run. Incident becomes known as the Battle of Pogue's Run.

1864   Crown Hill Cemetery, city's new burial ground, dedicated on June 1.

Mule–drawn, 12–seat streetcars begin service October 3 on a one-mile line between Union Station and Military Park just in time for the Indiana State Fair. Other lines open along Virginia, Massachusetts, and Fort Wayne avenues with the Illinois line reaching north to Crown Hill Cemetery by 1867.

In a trial by a partisan military commission, Lambdin P. Milligan and four other Democrats are found guilty on December 10 of treason and are sentenced to be hanged. U.S. Supreme Court on December 17, 1866 rules that civilians residing in a state in which the civil courts are functioning cannot be tried before a military commission. Known as *Ex parte Milligan*, it is regarded as a landmark civil liberties case.

1865   Steamboat *Governor Morton* launched at Indianapolis and steamboating reappears on White River, but only briefly as the vessel sinks at its moorings in 1866.

Lincoln's funeral train arrives in a rainy Indianapolis at 7 a.m. on April 30. The coffin is transferred to a hearse drawn by four white horses, and a procession led by Governor Oliver P. Morton and Major

General Joseph Hooker accompanies the president's body to the State House where public viewing lasts from 8 a.m. until 10 p.m.

On May 22 a fire destroys the Kingan and Company plant, the nation's largest pork packing facility. Losses total more than $200,000.

1866   Home for Friendless Women opens "for the aid and improvement of abandoned women."

Grand Army of the Republic (GAR) holds its first national encampment in Indianapolis.

Indianapolis City Hospital (now Wishard Memorial Hospital) opens as a 75–bed charity hospital in August.

1867   Governor's Circle is renamed Circle Park.

The General German Protestant Orphan Home founded to house Civil War orphans at South State Avenue. In 1971 it becomes Pleasant Run Children's Home.

The Maennerchor, a German-American male singing society, hosts North American Saengerbund's Fifteenth National Saengerfest, a four-day event consisting of three concerts, parade, Grand Ball, and picnic. Indianapolis hosts the event again in 1908.

Two amateur baseball clubs from Indianapolis play the first baseball game in the city on July 19.

1868   Danish immigrants who came to assist in construction of St. Paul's Lutheran Church establish what may be the nation's first Danish Lutheran congregation on city's south side.

Rev. Hanford A. Edson preaches a sermon November 26 on the need for a public library that will provide culture and values for residents and commercial growth for the city. Sermon triggers a public library campaign.

1869   Catharine Merrill is appointed professor of English at North Western Christian University, becoming nation's second woman professor.

Earliest appearance of the bicycle in the city is a demonstration of the high-wheeled "ordinary" on the Circle.

Leon Kahn is first Jew elected to Indianapolis Common Council and serves eight years between 1869 and 1881.

Following General Assembly's adoption in the fall of the School Act of May 13, 1869, providing separate schools for African-American children, Indianapolis opens elementary schools for blacks.

On December 7 reporter John Hampden Holliday, age 23, establishes *Indianapolis News*, now the city's oldest newspaper.

1870   Indianapolis' population is 48,244.

City has nine miles of paved streets, 18 miles of paved sidewalks, three miles of streets illuminated by gas lights, and a sewage system.

Wooton and Company, an Indianapolis furniture firm manufacturing elaborately crafted desks that become known as "The King of Desks," establishes headquarters on East Washington Street.

Orthodox Friends (Quakers) establish Indianapolis Asylum for Friendless Colored Children, the sole orphanage in the state to care for African-American children, and one of a handful in the country.

Enos B. Read starts *People*, a Sunday weekly dedicated to politics, literature, society, and news. It is the first Indianapolis newspaper to use woodcut illustrations and becomes known for stories of sensationalized crimes and scandals.

1871 Samuel Elbert of Indianapolis is the first African-American in Indiana to receive a medical degree.

Swedish immigrant Peter Lawson founds town of Nora, originally centered near current Westfield Boulevard and 86th Street.

City begins collecting climate data on April 2 by installing the first weather instruments at Blackford's Block at southeast corner of Washington and Meridian streets.

Water Works Company of Indianapolis, chartered the previous year by the city council and predecessor of Indianapolis Water Company, begins supplying consumers on June 1 from two large wells. Within a year company reports 439 customers.

1872 Local women establish Indianapolis Equal Suffrage Society.

The male singing sections of two German secret fraternal organizations, the Druiden Lodge and the Rothmaenner ("Red Men"), merge on July 4 to form the Indianapolis Liederkranz, meaning "wreath of songs."

1873 Local chapter of Women's Christian Temperance Union forms.

James L. Mitchell becomes first Democratic mayor of the city since mid–1850s.

Sisters of the Good Shepherd open a home on Raymond Street west of Meridian Street for females of "wayward character."

Indianapolis Library, located in one room of the high school building at northeast corner of Pennsylvania and Michigan streets, opens on April 9 with 12,790 volumes ready for 500 registered borrowers.

1874 Lyman S. Ayres purchases controlling interest in the N. R. Smith and Company dry goods store. At his death in 1896 the store is renamed L. S. Ayres and Company.

Entrepreneurs build harness racing park named Southern Riding Park but later sell it to the city. In 1881 it is renamed Garfield Park in memory of assassinated President James A. Garfield.

1875 North Western Christian University moves to Irvington; renamed Butler University in 1877.

Indianapolis Woman's Club is founded on February 18, aiming "to form an organized center for the mental and social culture of its members, and for the improvements of domestic life."

1876 University Park, bounded by New York, Vermont, Pennsylvania, and Meridian streets, opens as a city park.

James O. Woodruff leads successful petition to incorporate Woodruff Place as a town. Residents contract with Indianapolis for police and fire services.

Col. Eli Lilly begins pharmaceutical manufactory on Pearl Street on May 10.

Indianapolis fields its own professional baseball team during the summer. The Indianapolis Blues join the organized International League the next season.

1877 General Assembly passes an act to erect a new State House.

Oscar C. McCulloch assumes the pastorate at Plymouth (Congregational) Church and begins leading congregation toward a social gospel mission.

Indianapolis Literary Club organizes on January 10 to advance social, literary, and aesthetic culture.

Robert B. Bagby becomes first African-American to serve on Indianapolis City Council (1877–1879).

The first telephones are installed in the city during the fall at Wales & Company, a coal supply firm. By December of 1878, the state's first telephone firm, Indiana District Telephone Company, is organized in Indianapolis.

American United Life Insurance founded in November when Knights of Pythias lodge creates an insurance program, called an endowment rank, for its members and to attract new members.

Nine women gather on November 20 to establish Indianapolis Matinee Musicale, now one of the oldest music organizations in the nation, to study and perform music.

1878 *Indiana Tribuene*, a German Republican weekly, begins and counts 800 subscribers by 1880.

The Belt Line Railroad, a 14–mile track partially encircling the city to prevent congestion at Union Station and to promote local industrial development, completed.

1879 The Charity Organization Society, devoted to providing poor relief, forms at the instigation of Rev. Oscar C. McCulloch of Plymouth Church.

Sponsored by a group of Indianapolis dentists, Indiana Dental College organizes.

In August the Bagby brothers—Benjamin, James, and Robert, all educators—establish the *Leader*, the first African-American paper in Indianapolis. This Republican weekly ceases publication in 1890.

E. T. and James Gilliland, local manufacturers of telephone equipment, establish Indiana's first telephone exchange in Indianapolis under the Bell patents.

1880 Indianapolis' population is 75,056. The first Chinese immigrants—10 males, 8 of whom are laundrymen—appear in the city. African-Americans comprise 6,504 (or 8 percent) of the population.

Indianapolis is third largest pork packing city in the world, behind Chicago and Cincinnati.

There are 211 miles of streets in Indianapolis; 45 miles are paved with cobblestone, 5 miles covered with wood, while the remainder is paved with boulders, gravel, or totally unimproved. Nearly 40 miles of streets are illuminated by street lights.

Indianapolis offers a dual language (German-English) program aimed at both native English speakers and German-speaking pupils. It is one of the earliest to promote assimilation through bilingual education.

James Sidney Hinton, Republican from Indianapolis, elected as the first African-American legislator in Indiana House of Representatives and serves one term.

1881   Indianapolis Common Council grants a franchise to private firm to install electric arc lights on five towers in the center of the city.

The Indianapolis Brush Electric and Power Company, formed on June 17, is first company to bring electric service to the city. It is forerunner to Indianapolis Power and Light Company.

1882   May Wright Sewall opens Classical School for Girls, a preparatory school continuing until 1907, at southeast corner of Pennsylvania and St. Joseph streets.

Indianapolis Free Kindergarten Society established with Eliza Blaker, a crusader for early childhood education, as its first director.

1883   Flower Mission Training School for Nurses, Indianapolis' first nurse training program (later Wishard Memorial Hospital School of Nursing) supplies nursing care for Indianapolis City Hospital (now Wishard) and provides nursing care for the community through system of district nursing.

James Whitcomb Riley, writing as "Benj. F. Johnson, of Boone," publishes his first book of poems, *"The Old Swimmin' Hole" and 'Leven More Poems.*

Members of the Bible society from St. Paul and Trinity Lutheran churches establish the "Evangelische Lutherische Waisenhaus Gesellschaft," an asylum for orphans and aged people. It is later known as Lutheran Child and Family Services, Inc.

1884   The first Shortridge High School is constructed at a cost of $56,500.

John Stough Bobbs founds Indianapolis Medical Society.

In the spring Butler and DePauw play Indiana's first intercollegiate football game at the 7th Street Baseball Grounds. Butler wins, four goals to one.

After disbanding its initial pro baseball team, Indianapolis fields an entrant, appropriately labeled the Hoosiers, in the fledgling American Association and plays home games at the Seventh Street grounds during the summer. The team plays Sunday games outside the city limits at the Bruce Grounds to avoid citywide ban on Sabbath sporting events.

Indianapolis native Thomas A. Hendricks is elected vice president under Grover Cleveland on November 4. Nine months into his term, Hendricks dies at his home in Indianapolis.

1885   Ten German tradesmen form Saengerchor, dedicated to the goals of labor reform movement

sweeping the nation in the late 19th century. The society draws members together in private homes to sing songs of solidarity and justice for the working classes.

First Slovenes arrive in Indianapolis as contract workers at Malleable Foundry.

1886   Henry Kahn opens small tailor shop at 14 East Washington Street. Kahn Tailoring becomes a principal manufacturer of uniforms for U.S. military during World Wars I and II.

Alpha Home, established by the African-American community, opens to provide care for its elderly residents.

City Market opens, occupying the lot designated for the location of a market in original 1821 plat of Indianapolis.

Tomlinson Hall, designed by D. A. Bohlen, is dedicated on June 1 as part of the Grand Army of the Republic Music Festival to raise money for a Civil War memorial (the Soldiers and Sailors Monument).

On September 19 Knights of Labor collaborate with independent trade unions to hold city's first Labor Day parade in which an estimated 4,000 persons participate.

In November, following the municipal election, Democratic party chairman Simeon Coy and 11 other party officials are accused of tampering with tally sheets in order to secure the election of the Democratic candidate for judge of the criminal court. Although convicted and sentenced to prison in February, 1888, Coy remains member of city council.

1887   Democrat Thomas Taggart begins his political career as county auditor, serving until 1895. He serves three two-year terms as mayor and is later elected chairman of national Democratic party.

Instructor Laura Donnan founds Indianapolis High School Senate, in which students take names of U.S. senators and debate issues of the day. Institution lasts nearly 100 years and is widely copied by schools around the country.

Current Union Station, designed by Thomas Rodd of Pittsburgh, built.

1888   On June 25 Republican party nominates Indianapolis attorney Benjamin Harrison, grandson of President William Henry Harrison, for president, and Indianapolis becomes focus of the campaign. Harrison defeats Grover Cleveland on November 6 and serves as president from 1889 to 1893.

Supporters of presidential candidate Benjamin Harrison form "Harrison Marching Society." It acquires a clubhouse and formally organizes on February 13, 1889, as the Columbia Club.

Jonathon W. Laughner opens Boston Confectionery at 4 Indiana Avenue. About 1900, confectionery is remodeled and renamed Laughner's Dairy Lunch, becoming one of the first cafeteria-style restaurants in the Midwest.

A monument designed by Bruno Schmitz is selected in January for the Civil War memorial that is placed in Circle Park. Construction begins the following year.

The Propylaeum, meaning "gateway to higher culture," is incorporated on June 6 by a stock company composed of local women interested in a place for club meetings.

1889 In August the Citizens Street Railway Company purchases the 246–acre Adam Scott farm, located along the Central Canal north of Indianapolis, to create a "suburban park." During its first decade, the park serves as a popular rural retreat for bicyclists and streetcar riders.

1890 Indianapolis' population is 105,436. African-Americans number 9,133.

Col. Eli Lilly, William Fortune, and other businessmen found Indianapolis Commercial Club, later the Chamber of Commerce. Lilly serves as first president.

To cope with continued growth, Indianapolis changes its address numbering system to use Meridian and Washington streets as the dividing lines. City also eliminates all duplicate street names and erects street name signs around city.

Guy and Domenico Montani, local Italian musicians, help organize Indianapolis Protective Union, the city's first musicians' union and the third such union in the country.

United Mine Workers of America locate their headquarters in Indianapolis until 1934.

Thomas Lennox Sullivan is first Indianapolis native to be elected mayor.

First electric streetcars in Indianapolis are placed into operation. By 1894, electrification of city's system is complete.

Chamber of Commerce hosts Street Paving Exposition which showcases leading street paving firms and methods from around the nation.

1891 City adopts new Charter of 1891 that serves until 1970.

Charles H. Black, local carriage manufacturer, claims to have built first gasoline-powered automobile in the United States.

Indianapolis Country Club becomes the city's first country club on June 4. It is the parent of the Country Club of Indianapolis and the Woodstock Country Club.

1892 Indiana Department of Statistics reports that Indianapolis women work an average of 56.3 hours per week for an average wage of $5.66 per week.

Salvation Army establishes a base here.

American Nonconformist, Populist party newspaper, moves to Indianapolis under ownership of Vincent Brothers Publishing Company.

1893 William V. Wheeler, sales manager for Layman & Carey Hardware, opens a small mission on South Street. In 1905, it incorporates as the Rescue Mission and Home of Indianapolis. It is renamed Wheeler Mission Ministries in 1990.

Henry Rauh becomes second Jew to serve on Indianapolis Common Council.

Lew Wallace, Hoosier author and statesman, begins constructing the Blacherne, Indianapolis' first major apartment building. Completed in 1896, the seven-story structure is located on northwest corner of Meridian and Vermont streets.

So many bicycles are clogging Indianapolis streets that the city council adopts ordinance requiring a $1 license fee.

1894 Sumner A. Furniss successfully competes for a City Hospital internship, becoming the first African-American professional to serve at the hospital.

American Federation of Labor moves headquarters from New York to Indianapolis as part of a western revolt against organization's eastern leadership. Reelected as president in 1895, Samuel Gompers becomes displeased with federation's main office and moves it to Washington, D.C., in 1896.

First basketball game played in Indianapolis occurs at the Illinois Street YMCA.

First segment of Das Deutsche Haus (now the Athenaeum), built to accommodate German-American cultural organizations, is dedicated on February 22.

1895 Thomas Taggart elected mayor of Indianapolis. His three terms in office (1895–1901) are marked by public improvements and fiscal efficiency.

John Herron bequeaths $250,000 to the art association with stipulation to build a museum and art school bearing his name.

Indianapolis school system opens industrial training school. In 1910 it is named Emmerich Manual Training High School in honor of Charles Emmerich, school's first principal.

Indianapolis chapter of Young Women's Christian Association, holds its first meeting on May 6.

1896 William H. Block opens small department store at 9 East Washington Street, which in 1907 is incorporated as William H. Block Company.

Marshall "Major" Taylor sets several unofficial records in August at Indianapolis' Capital City bike track, which results in numerous death threats. Indianapolis bicycling tracks are subsequently restricted to whites only.

1897 Indianapolis annexes Haughville, Stringtown, and West Indianapolis.

Indianapolis Board of Trade, encouraged by local manufacturer Hugh H. Hanna, invites midwestern commercial organizations to send delegates to a conference, commonly called the Indianapolis Monetary Convention. The conference, on January 12–13, authorizes its executive committee to create a Monetary Commission of experts and to reaffirm the gold standard. Congress disregards commission's proposal, and new discoveries of gold end the crisis.

The city's first nine-hole golf course opens in the spring at 38th Street and Northwestern Avenue.

1898   On January 20, after receiving an industrial charter from the American Federation of Labor, the United Mine Workers becomes official representative of coal miners across the country, selecting centrally located Indianapolis for its national headquarters.

Rev. Thomas N. Nelson makes Indianapolis headquarters of the Pentecost Bands of the World, a missionary-minded society organized a decade earlier from the Free Methodist Church.

The *Daily Echo*, first and longest running student newspaper in the nation, begins its 72–year existence at Shortridge High School on September 27.

1899   *The Gentleman from Indiana* by Booth Tarkington becomes an instant success, propelling Tarkington into national limelight. In Indianapolis, the book is less well received; some residents feel that Tarkington is making fun of them.

1900   Indianapolis' population is 169,164. African-Americans number 15,931, or 9.4 percent of the population.

Introduced to the state during the 1890s, the first interurban car enters downtown Indianapolis from Greenwood on January 1.

John Hook and Edward F. Roesch found first Hook's Drugstore at 1101 S. East Street. Firm eventually grows into largest drugstore chain in state.

Social Democratic party holds its first national convention in Indianapolis on March 6 and nominates Eugene V. Debs for president and Job Harriman for vice-president.

Democrat William Jennings Bryan opens his presidential campaign by making his acceptance speech in Indianapolis in August.

1901   Indianapolis Day Nursery Association begins providing day care to indigent children.

Methodist church members begin four years of fundraising efforts to establish new hospital. They collect over $200,000 for Methodist Hospital, which opens in 1908.

More than 100 men and women meet during the summer in the Indianapolis Masonic Hall to found Socialist Party of America.

1902   Open-shop movement in Indiana gains momentum when Indianapolis carriage and automobile maker David M. Parry, newly elected president of National Association of Manufacturers, initiates nationwide crusade against unionization.

Senate Avenue YMCA founded. It becomes the nation's largest African-American YMCA.

Church of the United Brethren in Christ establishes Indiana Central University (now the University of Indianapolis).

Indianapolis Power and Light Company forms through consolidation of several smaller firms.

Nordyke and Marmon, manufacturer of flour milling machinery, begins building cars in the city. In 1926 the company drops milling equipment production and becomes known as Marmon Motor Car Company.

Herron School of Art opens on January 13 with 10 pupils and 5 teachers.

The Indiana Soldiers and Sailors Monument is dedicated on May 15.

The Indianapolis Traction and Terminal Company incorporates on August 4 to operate the city street railway.

1903   Indiana University begins developing a medical school by incorporating the teaching staff of Indiana Medical College into its program.

During his administration, Mayor John W. Holtzman works to establish first filter beds of the water company, and fights successfully to create city-owned gas company. His police chief experiments with "Paris system" of controlling vice by registering prostitutes and adopting a policy of noninterference with orderly houses.

Flanner Guild incorporates and works for the settlement and education among African-American population. In 1912 it is renamed Flanner House and serves for years as the city's only social service center for black residents.

Bobbs-Merrill Company, a publishing house, incorporates after existing as Bowen-Merrill Co. since the 1885 merger of Merrill Company and Bowen, Stewart, and Co.

Indianapolis Star, founded by Muncie industrialist George McCulloch, debuts as a daily newspaper on June 6.

During the fall the Teamsters Union selects Indianapolis as its national headquarters.

1904   A municipal golf course opens for golfers unable to afford private club memberships.

Indianapolis businessmen establish Associated Employers of Indianapolis to provide advice and assistance to companies involved in strikes or lockouts and urges them to destroy union shops.

Partners Carl G. Fisher, James A. Allison, and P. C. Avery form Concentrated Acetylene Company to assemble and fill acetylene cylinders used to power automobile headlights. In 1906, the company becomes Prest-O-Lite Company.

Former mayor Thomas Taggart serves as chairman of Democratic National Committee, 1904–1908.

Fort Benjamin Harrison is established June 28 on 1,994 acres in Lawrence Township, Marion County.

Republican party nominates Indianapolis resident Charles Warren Fairbanks as Theodore Roosevelt's vice-president.

While covering the presidential election on December 17, Frank McKinney Hubbard begins to draw the country character Abe Martin, a smiling fellow with whiskers, big shoes, a black coat, and hat. The character first appears in Indianapolis newspapers.

1905   Concerned citizens found Indianapolis Humane Society to prevent cruelty to children and animals.

Jewish Federation of Indianapolis begins to support local and national Jewish organizations and to provide educational opportunities. It becomes the Jewish Welfare Federation in the 1940s.

Indianapolis author Meredith Nicholson publishes a national bestseller and his most famous novel, *The House of a Thousand Candles.*

In May Anna C. Stover and Edith D. Surbey begin settlement house at 1718 Arsenal Avenue. Known as Christamore, it attracts teachers and nurses into a community of women reformers.

1906 The New York Central Railroad purchases 640 acres in Beech Grove to construct $5 million locomotive shop and equipment plant, touted as the "largest locomotive hospital in the world."

Vice-President Charles W. Fairbanks hosts a lawn party at his Meridian Street mansion for visiting President Theodore Roosevelt, unaware that alcoholic beverages are served. A strict prohibitionist, Fairbanks is embarrassed by newspaper references to "Cocktail Charley" and fails to win reelection in 1908 partly because of this incident.

The city's first movie theater—the Bijou, a converted vaudeville house—opens on East Washington Street.

Carl Fisher, Arthur Newby, Frank Wheeler, and James Allison form the Indianapolis Motor Speedway Company to construct a 2 1/2 mile track west of the city.

On May 16 over 8,000 people attend opening activities at Wonderland Amusement Park, located at East Washington and Gray streets. White City Amusement Park, located along White River at Broad Ripple, opens May 26.

Catholic Bishop Francis Silas Chatard dedicates SS. Peter and Paul Cathedral on December 21.

1907 William H. Block incorporates his small department store as the William H. Block Company. It operates until January 1988, when it is purchased by the Lazarus chain.

With efforts of local German Turners, Normal College of the North American Gymnastic Union, devoted to training gymnastics instructors, relocates to Indianapolis from Milwaukee.

1908 Cole Carriage Company builds its first motor cars. Formed the following year, the Cole Motor Car Company markets its Cole luxury car to compete with the Cadillac.

Indianapolis ragtime pianist-composer May Aufderheide publishes her first composition, "Dusty Rag," in May.

A fire in the "Mystic Cave" attraction at White City Amusement Park in Broad Ripple on June 26 spreads and destroys the entire park.

Indianapolis resident John W. Kern, Sr. is nominated at the Democratic national convention (July 7–10) as the vice-presidential candidate with presidential nominee William Jennings Bryan.

1909 Landscape architect and urban planner George Kessler completes an ambitious plan for boulevards and parks for Indianapolis.

Flanner and Buchanan Mortuary purchases city's first motorized ambulance.

A national gas balloon race is held on June 5 at the Indianapolis Motor Speedway, attracting 40,000 spectators.

1910 Indianapolis' population is 233,650. African-Americans number 21,816, the sixth largest black population among U.S. cities.

Acme Milling Company and Wilson's Mill merge to form Acme-Evans. Its best known product is E-Z Bake Flour.

Garfield Thomas Haywood founds Christ Temple Apostolic Faith Assembly and becomes a leader in the Pentecostal Assemblies of the World church.

General Assembly establishes Indiana University Medical Center, effectively uniting three proprietary medical schools—Indiana Medical College, Fort Wayne College of Medicine, and Central College of Physicians and Surgeons.

Madam C. J. Walker relocates her hair products and cosmetics company to Indianapolis where it develops an international reputation.

Harry Stutz begins manufacturing a rear-axle mounted transmission and assembling automobiles. In 1914 he opens a factory complex on North Capitol Avenue to produce automobiles.

1911 The first Indianapolis 500–Mile Race is run on May 30. Ray Harroun, driving a locally built Marmon, wins the race in 6 hours and 42 minutes.

Civic leaders establish Immigrants' Aid Association in response to needs of the city's growing foreign-born population. In October the association opens a settlement house at 617 West Pearl to provide social services and Americanize the immigrants.

1912 Meredith Nicholson publishes *A Hoosier Chronicle,* which explores changes in midwestern society at the turn of the century.

Luella (Mrs. Felix) McWhirter begins the Woman's Department Club.

Indianapolis Church Federation is established on June 7 as an outgrowth of the Federal Council of Churches, the "council of 100" of the Indianapolis Ministerial Association, and the "Men and Religion Forward Movement," a socially oriented evangelistic campaign.

Cornerstone of the Senate Avenue YMCA (African-American) is laid in October at Michigan Street and Senate Avenue and in July, 1913, Booker T. Washington dedicates the structure.

In December the Commercial Club joins several other commercial organizations in a new Indianapolis Chamber of Commerce.

1913 Employers' Association of Indianapolis, absorbing the Commercial Vehicle Protective Association (formed to combat the teamsters' strike in 1913), reorganizes as Associated Employers of

Indianapolis, consisting of 500 individuals and firms seeking to destroy unions in the city.

James A. Allison, founding partner of Prest-O-Lite Company and the Indianapolis Motor Speedway, establishes Allison Speedway Team Company, a machine shop which in 1917 is renamed Allison Engineering Company.

Merchants National Bank completes its new 17–story building, which is the city's tallest for 50 years.

On March 22 a ferocious storm buffets the city with 60–mph winds and six inches of rain over a 24–hour period, causing levees to break. The peak flood stage is estimated at 31.5 feet, or 19.5 feet above flood stage.

Some 800 streetcar operators stop work in the city from October 31 to November 7 to gain union recognition, higher wages, and improved working conditions. Mob activity destroys property and leads to three deaths. Gov. Samuel Ralston mobilizes 1,800 National Guard troops to reestablish order.

Following the practice begun by New York City, Indianapolis erects its first municipal Christmas tree in University Park in December.

1914   Chamber of Commerce sponsors survey of recreational conditions and needs, hiring an agent of the National Playground Association of America (NPAA) to conduct the study. As a result of recommendations to expand facilities, the following year there are 7 bathing beaches, 3 swimming pools, 10 school grounds, 12 swimming holes and bathhouses, and 28 playgrounds.

Joseph E. Bell wins mayor's office in election which attracts seven candidates. Election irregularities lead to the indictment of Bell and others on charges of conspiracy to commit a felony, but the mayor is acquitted.

Indianapolis Boy Scout Council organizes on November 17 with a membership of 100 boys.

1915   Church Federation sponsors interdenominational Holy Week services, which remains an agency program until the 1960s.

Former *Indianapolis Star* cartoonist John Barton Gruelle creates and patents his Raggedy Ann doll.

1916   John Holliday, founder of the *Indianapolis News*, and his wife Evaline deed their 80–acre estate to the city for use as a public park.

The Church Federation's "Indianapolis Plan of Evangelism" enlists all congregations to hold their annual evangelistic campaigns at same time and to join in a citywide publicity blitz.

Indianapolis Foundation founded on January 5.

Following a four-year litigation between the school board and former owners of Winona Institute, Arsenal Technical High School, serving as a technical training school since 1912, officially becomes city's third high school on May 22.

Circle Theatre opens on August 30 as Indianapolis' first building constructed specifically for motion pictures.

1917   Carl Fisher and James Allison sell Prest-O-Lite to Union Carbide and Carbon Corporation. Prest-O-Lite continues distributing automotive batteries from the Speedway plant until 1927.

Anna Marie Ridge establishes the first local Girl Scout troop on July 27 in Irvington.

1918   The War Chest is established "to provide for all war and benevolent needs." It dissolves in 1922 and relinquishes its assets to the Community Chest.

The Magnificent Ambersons by Booth Tarkington published. The second part of a trilogy, it describes the industrial transformation of a fictionalized Indianapolis. Tarkington receives the Pulitzer Prize for this novel in 1919.

Frank Shields, local chemical engineer, manufactures a brushless shaving cream called Barbasol.

Board of School Commissioners ends German language instruction in local schools in January.

1919   National headquarters of the American Legion locates in Indianapolis.

Red Ball Transit, nation's first long distance moving service, founded. In 1939 it becomes American Red Ball Transit Company.

The 18–passenger Lawson Airliner, at the time the world's largest passenger plane, arrives at the Motor Speedway on October 24. Crowds brave ten days of continuing rain to inspect the plane.

1920   Indianapolis' population is 314,194. Foreign population numbers 16,968, largest in the state. African-American population reaches 34,678.

Community Chest organizes to unite fund-raising efforts and coordinate activities of 40 different community service organizations. It is precursor to the United Way of Central Indiana.

First formalized black baseball league, the Negro National League, incorporates with teams in six midwestern cities. The Indianapolis ABCs are managed by C. I. Taylor, a famed early black baseball manager.

Duesenberg Automobile and Motors Company, Inc., establishes manufactory on West Washington Street at Harding Street to build passenger cars.

Group of Indianapolis businessmen incorporate Indianapolis Athletic Club. The nine-story structure at Meridian and Vermont streets is completed in January, 1924.

In January a Citizens Planning Committee designates two city blocks (Vermont to North streets between Meridian and Pennsylvania) for the Indiana World War Memorial Plaza.

After the 19th Amendment ensures women's right to vote, the Woman's Franchise League of Indiana, Indianapolis Branch, disbands on April 16 and establishes a League of Women Voters.

Indianapolis celebrates its centennial with a six-day festival, June 5–10.

Indianapolis Aerial Association opens first public landing field in July with plans of offering flying instruction, passenger rides, and regular service to large cities within a 200–mile radius of Indianapolis. Venture quickly fails.

1921 The musical *Shuffle Along*, written and produced by Indianapolis native Noble Sissle with three other musicians, marks revival of black folk humor, jazz dance, and ragtime.

Booth Tarkington wins Pulitzer Prize for *Alice Adams*.

Cadle Tabernacle, a 10,000–seat revival and convention center, opens. During the 1920s it also hosts Ku Klux Klan rallies, dance marathons, and prize fights.

On December 31 Francis F. Hamilton launches city's first radio station, 9ZJ, later WLK.

1922 David Curtis Stephenson moves to Indianapolis and becomes Grand Dragon of the KKK in Indiana and 22 other northern states. Under his leadership, the Klan grows in numbers and gains extensive political influence in state and local governments.

Eli Lilly and Company, working collaboratively with University of Toronto scientists, develops insulin for use in treatment of diabetes. Indianapolis becomes a leading center for insulin manufacturing.

On March 29 Noble B. Watson begins WOH—Indianapolis' second radio station—sponsored by the Hatfield Electronics Company.

First air mail arrives in Indianapolis from Chicago on May 29 on a demonstration flight of the U.S. Air Mail Service. Another 5 1/2 years pass before Indianapolis joins the air mail system.

Offering a progressive curriculum as an alternative to public or religious education, Orchard Country Day School opens on October 2.

In November Indianapolis becomes the first Indiana city to pass zoning legislation.

1923 American Settlement is created after a consolidation of the Foreign House (established by the Immigrants' Aid Association) and the Presbyterian Chapel, which works mainly with Bulgarian and Rumanian immigrants.

The Phyllis Wheatley Branch of the YWCA for African-American women and girls organizes on January 28.

KKK gains control of Marion County Republican organization in May by electing George Coffin as county chair.

1924 Construction for Indiana World War Memorial Plaza begins but is not completed until 1965.

Indianapolis Foundation makes its first grant by funding the Public Health Nursing Association to hire a nurse for crippled children.

The first use of a lie detector occurs in an Indianapolis city court in March.

Broad Ripple Park hosts the Olympic swimming tryouts June 5–7. Johnny Weissmuller, soon-to-be Hollywood Tarzan, wins 100–meter freestyle qualification.

The James Whitcomb Riley Hospital for Children is dedicated in October as Indiana's only children's hospital.

WFBM radio begins broadcasting on November 4 and is first station to broadcast election results in Indianapolis.

1925 Herman C. Krannert moves to Indianapolis and founds Inland Container Corporation. In 1960 he and wife Ellnora establish Krannert Charitable Trust.

State purchases the Indiana Dental College and incorporates it into Indiana University system as the School of Dentistry.

Mary Stewart Carey founds The Children's Museum of Indianapolis.

The first Hoosier Salon, a juried exhibition of Indiana artists, is held March 9–19 in the galleries of Chicago's Marshall Field & Co. After 1941 exhibition relocates to Indianapolis.

Former Marion County treasurer and Klan member John L. Duvall defeats Democrat Walter Myers in November in the race for mayor, marking the triumph of a Klan-sponsored slate of candidates.

David Curtis Stephenson, Grand Dragon of the Ku Klux Klan, receives a life sentence for his role in the death of Madge Oberholtzer, whom he brutally raped. He serves 31 years in Indiana State Prison at Michigan City before his release in 1956.

1926 Philanthropist Arthur Jordan gives Butler University $1 million to build Jordan Hall on its new northside campus.

On Sunday mornings WFBM begins broadcasting "Christian Men's Builders' Hour" from the Third Christian Church. The program continues until 1955.

Chamber of Commerce chooses "The Cross Roads of America" as the city's motto on June 24.

1927 The Walker Building is erected, eight years after the death of Madam C. J. (Sarah Breedlove) Walker.

The Jewish Welfare Fund is established.

First issue of the *Macedonian Tribune* published in Indianapolis on February 10.

Crispus Attucks High School, an all-black school, opens in September.

After being convicted of violating the state's corrupt practices act, sentenced to 30 days in jail, and fined $1,000, Mayor John Duvall resigns on October 27 at the insistence of the city council. Claude Negley is appointed mayor and is later indicted for soliciting bribes from Duvall in exchange for councilors' votes in impeachment proceedings against him the previous August. Negley and other council members plead guilty, are fined, and resign from the council.

1928 *Indianapolis Times* wins Pulitzer Prize for its 1927 series exposing Ku Klux Klan activities in Indiana.

Butler University moves to Fairview Park on the city's north side.

General Motors Corporation purchases the Allison Engineering Company for $592,000.

Butler University constructs a fieldhouse (now Hinkle Fieldhouse) that is considered, alongside Madison Square Garden, the premier basketball venue in the nation.

Transcontinental Air Transport (TAT), the first major airline to serve the city, begins scheduled service on July 7.

1929   New York artist Henry Herring casts sculpture *Pro Patria* for southern steps of Indiana World War Memorial. The 25–foot-tall, seven-ton statue is reputed to be the largest sculptured bronze casting ever made in America.

Indianapolis purchases 320 acres on South High School Road to construct an airport plus another 627 acres for future expansion.

Scottish Rite Cathedral, designed by architect George F. Schreiber, completed in February.

Ferdinand Schaefer starts the Indianapolis Symphony Orchestra in November.

1930   Indianapolis' population is 364,161.

Goodwill Industries program begun in Indianapolis at the Fletcher Place Methodist Church.

In February Indianapolis becomes one of 15 cities nationwide to adopt a police radio system.

1931   The Art Deco–style Coca-Cola Bottling Plant, designed by Rubush and Hunter and built by William P. Jungclaus Construction Company, opens on Massachusetts Avenue. Following subsequent additions in the 1940s the factory is said to be the largest Coca-Cola bottling plant in the world.

At age 32 Michael F. Morrissey becomes the youngest police chief in the city's history on June 16. He serves until January 1, 1943, longer than any previous chief.

Indianapolis Indians play their first game September 5 in the new 14,500–seat Perry Stadium (now Bush Stadium).

Indianapolis Municipal Airport (now Indianapolis International Airport) is officially dedicated on September 25.

1932   Indiana Birth Control League, led by local resident Anna Ray Burns, is founded on February 4. Later known as Planned Parenthood of Central Indiana, Inc., it initially serves only married women with two or more children who are referred by a physician or a social service agency.

Indianapolis News wins a Pulitzer Prize in May for series of stories and editorials on wasteful government spending.

During September unemployed persons establish a shantytown opposite Kingan and Company packing plant.

1933   Claude Bowers, Indianapolis Democrat and journalist, is appointed by Franklin D. Roosevelt the ambassador to Spain and serves until 1939. He later serves as minister to Chile, 1939–1953.

Herman Phillips, Butler University track coach, initiates the Butler Relays, prestigious American track and field competition. The relays end in 1942.

Indianapolis Football Indians begin playing during September in the National Football League, but play only three games (all lopsided losses) before management disbands the team.

1934   1,800 delegates to the United Mine Workers of America convention in Tomlinson Hall vote on January 23 to relocate UMW headquarters from Indianapolis to Washington, D.C.

A major strike occurs at the Real Silk Hosiery Mills during April and May.

Indianapolis experiences its highest recorded temperature (107°F) on July 25.

The Indiana State Library and Historical Building is dedicated on December 7.

1935   In March nearly 19 percent of Marion County residents receive public relief.

1936   Two schools run by the Sisters of Saint Francis in Oldenburg, Indiana, merge under the name of Marian College and relocate to the Allison estate on the west side of Indianapolis.

1937   Lilly Endowment, later one of the nation's major philanthropic institutions, established.

International Harvester consolidates its motor production by building a foundry and an engine plant on 75 acres on city's southeast side. Employing 1,100, plant produces its first engine in 1938.

Allison Engineering Company develops a 1,000–horsepower airplane engine in April.

1938   Lockefield Gardens, a 748–unit public housing complex, opens in February.

WIBC radio begins broadcasting on October 31.

1939   Indianapolis becomes world's largest hog shipping center.

The federal Public Works Administration constructs new coliseum at State Fairgrounds using both federal and local bond money.

Louis Y. Mazzini develops Mazzini Test for syphilis, which the U.S. Armed Forces employs during World War II.

1940   Indianapolis' population is 386,972.

Robert Lee Brokenburr (Republican), an Indianapolis attorney, becomes first African-American elected to Indiana State Senate and serves 20 years.

City's first drive-in theater, the Pendleton Pike, opens.

1941   Indianapolis physician Lewis Corwin Robbins is one of the initiators of the landmark Framingham Study linking heart disease and smoking.

Baseball player and manager Owen J. Bush and local banker Frank E. McKinney, Sr., buy Indianapolis Indians. Bush remains as president or general manager until 1969.

1942   Naval Avionics Center is commissioned and operated under sole contract by the Lukas-Harold Corporation. Known originally as the Naval Ordnance Plant, the center manufactures the famous World War II Norden bombsight.

Local resident Arcada Campbell Stark (Republican) becomes first woman elected to Indiana Senate.

1943 Mayor Robert H. Tyndall appoints 150–member citizens committee to recommend city's postwar agenda.

Geist Reservoir, created by damming Fall Creek and flooding 1,900 acres, begins supplying water to city.

Ensemble Music Society organizes in December to encourage public presentations of chamber music.

1944 Indianapolis Zoological Society incorporates with intent of developing a city zoo.

The Catholic Diocese of Indianapolis is elevated on November 17 to the rank of an archdiocese and Joseph E. Ritter becomes the archbishop.

1945 Little Red Door Cancer Agency begins operations in a World War II barracks with a red front door.

On July 30, after delivering material for the atomic bomb, the USS *Indianapolis* is sunk by three torpedoes from a Japanese submarine. Only 318 crew members survive.

1946 L. Strauss relocates in April from 33 West Washington Street, its home for 41 years, to the Occidental Building at corner of Illinois and Washington streets.

The Indianapolis 500–Mile Race resumes in May after being suspended in 1942 for the duration of World War II.

1947 Indianapolis Public Library District is created as a separate municipal corporation. It becomes the Indianapolis–Marion County Library District and extends its library services (and taxing area) beyond city limits.

Jim Shelton begins the "Pick-A-Pocket Show" in November on WIBC radio, a quiz show that lasts 21 years.

1948 Jewish Federation and Jewish Welfare Fund merge to form the Jewish Welfare Federation.

In August Eugene C. Pulliam, publisher of the *Indianapolis Star*, buys the *Indianapolis News* for $4 million and forms Indianapolis Newspapers, Inc.

1949 House Bill 242 approved on March 8 by the General Assembly outlaws segregation in state schools. Within a few days Indianapolis school board passes resolution to end segregation in IPS, although the system is later found to have perpetuated the practice.

On May 30 WFBM-TV is first commercial television station to sign on in Indianapolis.

Final encampment of the Grand Army of the Republic is held in Indianapolis on August 31 with six Civil War veterans in attendance, all over 100 years of age and including the sole surviving black veteran.

1950 Indianapolis' population is 427,173. African-Americans number 63,867, or 15 percent of the whole.

Indianapolis Hospital Development Association formed by civic, medical, business, and industrial

leaders to raise funds for construction of new hospitals and expansion of existing facilities.

WAJC, licensed to the Arthur Jordan Conservatory of Music, becomes city's first nonprofit educational radio station in September.

1951 Frank E. McKinney, Sr., local banker and Democratic politician, serves as national chairman of the Democratic party, 1951–1952.

Two Army branch service schools, the Adjutant General's School and the Finance School, move to Fort Benjamin Harrison in March to make it the training base for Army personnel and finance specialists.

In May WIBC broadcasts the Indianapolis 500 live for the first time.

Future home run king Hank Aaron makes his Negro League debut during the summer with the Indianapolis Clowns as a teenage shortstop.

Health and Hospital Corporation of Marion County established.

1952 WIBC and 26 radio stations establish the Indianapolis Motor Speedway Radio Network to broadcast the Indianapolis 500–Mile Race live.

Rev. Charles Oldham founds Lighthouse Mission for indigent men.

Gifts from Edith and George H. A. Clowes and their son, Allen Whitehill Clowes, establish the Clowes Fund, a private foundation.

From January 13–20, 75,000 people attend an indoor camp meeting at Cadle Tabernacle, sponsored by 75 fundamentalist churches.

1953 City builds the Wilbur Shaw Memorial Soap Box Derby Hill at 30th Street and Cold Spring Road.

The City-County Building Authority organizes as a municipal corporation to finance, construct, and operate a new office building for joint use of city and county governments.

Marion County Fair moves to its present site on Troy Avenue at Five Points.

Eli Lilly gives $1 million to the Episcopal diocese for support and maintenance of Christ Church, should it be designated as pro-cathedral (which it was in 1954).

The first Noble School (now Noble Centers) opens in September and by 1960 is providing job opportunities to persons with disabilities.

Integration of all city high schools is completed in October. However, 11 elementary schools remain all black and 27 schools are all white because of their geographical location. Approximately 65 percent of the city's students attend integrated schools.

1954 Indiana's first self-park garage, the Denison, opens at corner of Ohio and Pennsylvania streets, site of the old Denison Hotel (demolished in 1926).

WISH-TV Channel 8 goes on the air in July.

Italians who manage produce firms organize the Indianapolis Produce Terminal.

Holcomb Observatory, funded by millionaire James Irving Holcomb, opens at Butler University. The $500,000 observatory and planetarium is largest in the state.

Marian College becomes the first coeducational Catholic college in the state and one of only five in the nation.

Student-operated radio station WIAN (later WFYI) goes on the air in October after Indianapolis Public Schools installs an FM transmitter at Shortridge High School.

1955   Indianapolis Housing Authority is formed.

Crispus Attucks High School wins the Indiana State High School Basketball Championship in March, repeating in 1956 and 1959. It is the first Indianapolis high school to win since the early 1900s.

The first of its kind, a joint police and fire alarm telephone system begins operating in Indianapolis on December 3.

1956   Meadows Shopping Center on 38th Street opens. It is the city's first mall, offering branches of downtown department stores, a supermarket, retail shops, and parking spaces for 2,000 cars.

1957   Failing to sell his automated hamburger grill, Frank P. Thomas opens first Burger Chef at 1300 West 16th Street and establishes chain's national headquarters in Indianapolis.

Martin R. Williams begins broadcasting Indianapolis' first commercial FM station, WFMS, on March 17.

First 500 Festival is held during May.

1958   Christian Theological Seminary, formerly the School of Religion at Butler University, becomes independent ecumenical seminary.

Mercer Mance becomes Marion County Superior Court judge. He is the first African-American in Indiana elected to such a position.

Tomlinson Hall burns. A single doorway arch, discovered during the 1980s restoration of City Market, now stands in the market's courtyard.

The John Birch Society, a national organization dedicated to protecting the U.S. against Communism, is established on December 8–9 on the city's north side.

1959   Jazz guitarist Wes Montgomery, Indianapolis native, releases his first album, *The Wes Montgomery Trio*.

Second Presbyterian Church holds its last service in its Vermont Street church September 27 and moves to its new structure on North Meridian Street.

The Billy Graham Crusade visits Indianapolis in October and 35,000 faithful attend the final service at the Indiana State Fairgrounds.

1960   Indianapolis' population is 476,258. African-Americans number 98,049, or 21 percent. The city ranks 26th in the national population rankings.

A temporary scaffold filled with spectators collapses on May 30 during the pace lap of the Indianapolis 500. Two people are killed and scores of others injured.

Richard Nixon kicks off his presidential campaign in Indianapolis on September 12.

1961   General Assembly creates the Indianapolis Airport Authority to administer air transportation in Marion County and the seven surrounding counties.

L. S. Ayres and Company forms new discount division, Ayr-Way Stores, and opens its first store in the city.

Pope John XXIII elevates Catholic Archbishop Joseph Ritter to the cardinalate on January 16.

On February 17 Indianapolis native Oscar Robertson, a former Crispus Attucks star and NBA Hall-of-Famer, becomes the first basketball player to appear on the cover of *Time* magazine.

The Mayor's Human Rights Commission is established in April with Rev. Jim Jones, pastor of the Peoples Temple, as its first full-time director.

Jet operations begin on April 30 at Weir Cook Municipal Airport when Trans World Airlines inaugurates service to New York City.

Ground breaking ceremonies are held August 18 for Brebeuf Preparatory School, first Jesuit secondary school in Indiana.

1962   The new City-County Building is completed in January.

After lengthy court battles, Woodruff Place accepts annexation by the city on March 20.

Quarterly statements on June 30 show Indiana National Bank tops $1 billion in holdings, a first for any Indiana bank.

The Indianapolis Christmas Committee decorates the Soldiers and Sailors Monument in December with thousands of Christmas lights, making it the "World's Tallest Christmas Tree."

1963   A team of Indiana University Medical Center physicians develops the echocardiograph (EKG).

St. Vincent Hospital opens first coronary care and first intensive care units in Indianapolis.

Indianapolis Symphony Orchestra moves from the Murat Theater to newly completed 2,200–seat Clowes Memorial Hall at Butler University, October 18–20.

An explosion at the Indiana State Fairgrounds Coliseum on October 31 kills 74 and injures an estimated 400.

1964   Local Democrat Daisy Lloyd is the first African-American woman elected as Indiana state representative.

Eli Lilly and Company develops world's first cephalosporin antibiotic, introducing a whole new class of drugs.

After a 20–year effort led by newspaper columnist Lowell Nussbaum, Indianapolis Zoological Society establishes city's first zoo in Washington Park on April 18.

On April 24 Allison Gas Turbine receives a contract to build the propellant tanks for the lunar excursion module of NASA's Apollo spacecraft.

In the fall Democratic Mayor John J. Barton appoints an advisory committee of business and civic leaders that becomes known as the Greater Indianapolis Progress Committee (GIPC).

1965 The Capital Improvement Board is created to finance, construct, and operate an Indianapolis convention and exhibition center.

Indianapolis builds $5 million incinerator plant to help eliminate problems associated with solid waste.

Indianapolis receives a record daily amount of snow, 12.5 inches on February 26.

Indianapolis Times ceases publication on October 11.

Indianapolis Urban League founded on October 26.

1966 Methodist Hospital of Indiana's Department of Medical Research, founded 1956, conducts studies leading to development of an artificial kidney, one of the first of its kind in the country.

The Benjamin Harrison Home becomes a National Historic Landmark.

In January the Defense Information School moves to Fort Benjamin Harrison to train public affairs specialists for all military services.

Christian Theological Seminary relocates from Butler University on January 25 to a nearby, multimillion dollar facility.

1967 Indiana State Museum opens in January in the renovated former Indianapolis City Hall at Alabama and Ohio streets.

During February businessmen purchase a franchise in the proposed American Basketball Association. The Indiana Pacers begin playing in the 1967–1968 season and become the only team to win three ABA championships before joining the National Basketball Association in 1976.

First turbine engine appears during May in the Indianapolis 500, leading the race for 490 miles before a $6 bearing fails.

On June 9 Indiana National Bank (now NBD Indiana) demolishes the Knights of Pythias Building to construct the 37–story INB Tower, the city's first modern skyscraper.

Richard G. Lugar, a 35–year-old businessman and former Rhodes scholar, defeats incumbent mayor John Barton on November 8 to become the first Republican mayor since 1951. Lugar is reelected in 1971 and presides over eventual unification of Indianapolis and Marion County governments.

1968 Lafayette Square Mall opens. It is the city's first enclosed mall with over one million square feet of space.

Indiana Interreligious Commission on Human Equality founded as a joint effort of Indianapolis Jewish, Catholic, and Protestant faiths.

WTLC-FM debuts in January as Indianapolis' only African-American owned and operated radio station.

Democratic presidential candidate Robert F. Kennedy, speaking before a mostly African-American crowd at 17th and Broadway streets on April 4, announces assassination of Dr. Martin Luther King, Jr., and appeals for calm.

U.S. Department of Justice, acting under authority of 1964 federal Civil Rights Law, brings suit against Indianapolis Public Schools (IPS) on May 31, charging it with *de jure* segregation.

1969 United State Tennis Association moves U.S. Clay Court Championships from Milwaukee to Indianapolis.

The trustees of Indiana University and Purdue University merge operations of their Indianapolis extensions on January 28 to create IUPUI.

Indianapolis native Kurt Vonnegut publishes his best-selling book, *Slaughterhouse-Five*, in February.

Governor Edgar Whitcomb signs the Unigov Act on March 13, effectively consolidating city and county government by legislative act and without referendum.

On June 6–7 Indianapolis experiences rioting along two-block section of Indiana Avenue, with sporadic disturbances in other parts of the city. This lone outbreak contrasts sharply with major riots in other American cities.

1970 Indianapolis' population is 744,624, which reflects the Unigov consolidation.

Unigov legislation becomes effective on January 1 as Marion County (except for Lawrence, Southport, Beech Grove, and Speedway) unifies with the city of Indianapolis.

Tudor Hall (1902), preparatory school for girls, and Park School (1914), preparatory school for boys, merge to create Park Tudor School.

Riverside Amusement Park closes after providing residents with leisure-time activities since 1902.

In May, desiring to be more centrally located in the United States, the Amateur Athletic Union (AAU) becomes first national amateur sports governing body to locate its national headquarters in Indianapolis.

WFYI-Channel 20, the city's first non-commercial public station, goes on the air on October 4.

1971 A year-long sesquicentennial celebration of Indianapolis' founding begins in January.

Indiana Black Expo begins.

The Hispano-American Society opens the Hispano-American Center (now El Centro Hispano).

Sunshine Promotions is founded to promote rock concerts locally.

The U.S. District Court finds the Indianapolis Public Schools guilty of *de jure* segregation on August 18 and orders the immediate desegregation of Crispus Attucks High School and all other single-race IPS schools.

1972 The International Center of Indianapolis established.

Indianapolis Star feature writer Tom Keating starts an annual poll of readers to name the paper's Man and Woman of the Year.

Indiana Convention Center opens, increasing the city's capacity to host large meetings and events.

104–acre Castleton Square Mall opens.

The Pyramids, a northwest side office complex at College Park, opens in the fall.

On November 27 fire destroys the Pendleton Pike Drive-in, the fifth oldest drive-in movie screen in the nation.

1973   Indianapolis Public Transportation Corporation (Metro) is created by ordinance of City-County Council and begins service in 1975 after assuming assets of Indianapolis Transit System, Inc., a private corporation.

Keystone at the Crossing center opens with two shopping areas, the Bazaar and the Fashion Mall, which is subsequently expanded in 1980, 1982, 1988 (in conjunction with razing the Bazaar), and again in 1993.

The Indianapolis Ballet Theatre forms as an outgrowth of the Civic Ballet Society of Indianapolis (founded 1959).

On January 27 Indianapolis and Scarborough, Ontario, Canada, agree to conduct an annual amateur athletic competition, Indianapolis/Scarborough Peace Games, named in honor of the Vietnam Peace Treaty which is signed the same day.

In August several Indianapolis businessmen found Ambassadair, a locally based air travel club. They incorporate American Trans Air as its air carrier, which becomes the nation's largest charter airline in the 1990s.

Propane explosions in the Grant Building on East Washington Street on November 5 create a disaster downtown and cause $15 million in damages.

1974   Boehringer Mannheim Corporation begins its Indianapolis operations.

Jon and Christel DeHaan establish Resort Condominiums International, Indianapolis-based resort timeshare and vacation exchange business.

Indianapolis Star begins a series of reports in February on Indianapolis police corruption. The following year, the series receives a Pulitzer Prize.

Market Square Arena, with over 19,000 seats, opens as the nation's fifth largest sports arena on September 15.

1975   U.S. District Court orders transfer of African-American students to surrounding suburban school districts within Marion County.

Marion County General Hospital changes its name to Wishard Memorial Hospital and enters agreement with Indiana University to manage the facility.

Julian Center is founded by Episcopal Diocese of Indianapolis as a human services agency for women.

City holds its first drawing for the urban homestead program on December 25. "Winners" buy homes for one dollar and agree to complete necessary repairs.

1976   William H. Hudnut III becomes mayor on January 1. Reelected three times (1979, 1983, 1987), Hudnut becomes the longest serving mayor in Indianapolis history.

Despite strong opposition the city changes the name of Weir Cook Airport to Indianapolis International Airport to reflect the expanded role of the facility, including the award of Foreign Trade Zone status.

Indianapolis native Oscar Charleston is posthumously inducted into the Baseball Hall of Fame. Known as "The Hoosier Comet," he played for the ABCs of the Negro National League.

International Festival begins as part of the nation's Bicentennial celebration.

Eastside Community Investments, Inc., becomes the first operating community development corporation in the city.

1977   Martin Center, an educational institution, opens under the leadership of Father Boniface Hardin, O.S.B. Reflecting increased enrollment and diversity of degree programs, it becomes Martin University in 1990.

On January 1 Jacqueline Means becomes first female priest ordained in the Episcopal Church of the United States. The service is held at All Saints Episcopal Church.

Pharmaceutical entrepreneur and philanthropist Eli Lilly dies on January 24, leaving a sizable legacy to several state and local institutions.

On June 26 Market Square Arena is the site of Elvis Presley's last concert.

Indianapolis businessmen establish the Corporate Community Council on September 14 to help corporate leaders identify and support significant community needs.

1978   Wes Montgomery Jazz Festival begins.

Indianapolis receives a record amount of snow in two days—15.5 inches on January 25–26. The total January snowfall of 30.6 inches sets new monthly record and adds to the city's greatest seasonal snowfall—57.8 inches.

Four young employees of the Speedway Burger Chef are reported missing on November 18. The next day, searchers discover their bodies in a wooded area of Johnson County. The murders remain unsolved.

1979   U.S. District Court selects a plan for one-way busing of black students to surrounding suburban school districts along with a plan for desegregation of IPS.

The Madame Walker Urban Life Center, Inc., is created as a not-for-profit organization to save the historic Walker Building from deterioration and demolition.

St. Vincent Hospital opens first wellness center east of the Mississippi.

Edward Thomas O'Meara is named Archbishop of the Catholic Archdiocese of Indianapolis on November 28.

In December the Indiana Sports Corporation incorporates as a private, not-for-profit coalition of government and business leaders to implement the city's objective of becoming a national sports capital.

1980   Indianapolis' population is 700,807.

Amateur boxing coach and Indianapolis resident Thomas "Sarge" Johnson and all 21 U.S. National Boxing Team members die March 14 in an airplane crash near Warsaw, Poland.

Gleaners Food Bank incorporates on April 14 to solicit, collect, and redistribute donated food to charities.

The city publishes the Regional Center Plan which guides downtown redevelopment for the next decade.

1981 The IPS School Board votes February 5 to close Shortridge High School.

1982 American United Life completes its AUL Tower, a 38-story building that becomes the state's tallest structure.

Indianapolis Taxpayers Association, first established in the 1940s and disbanded in 1967, resumes activities to monitor appropriation of tax monies for countywide ambulance system. It defeats $46 million bond issue to support construction and renovation for the Pan American Games.

Eli Lilly and Company produces synthetic human insulin, humilin, the world's first pharmaceutical product based on recombinant DNA technology.

Indianapolis debuts the first International Violin Competition, a quadrennial music competition.

During eight days of competition, July 23–31, the National Sports Festival IV draws an unprecedented crowd of 250,000 spectators to watch more than 2,600 U.S. athletes competing in 33 sports. Indianapolis is the first host city in the festival's history to present U.S. Olympic Committee with a profit.

1983 American College of Sports Medicine relocates to Indianapolis.

Broadcasting personalities Bob Kevoian and Tom Griswold move from Petoskey, Michigan, and join the staff at WFBQ. Originally known as the "Q-Zoo," their show later becomes the "Bob and Tom Show," changing the style of morning radio in the city.

In July Indianapolis holds the first annual White River Park State Games, a state amateur sports competition.

1984 The Hudson Institute, a public policy research institute, moves to Indianapolis from Croton-on-Hudson, New York.

In March the Baltimore Colts relocate to Indianapolis and become the Indianapolis Colts.

The Hoosier Dome, part of the Indiana Convention Center, is completed in May.

The IU Natatorium hosts the Olympic diving trials for the first time on July 4–8. Qualifications return in 1988 and 1992.

On November 19, in *American Booksellers Association v. Hudnut*, the U.S. District Court in Indianapolis permanently enjoins enforcement of a June, 1984, ordinance that prohibited "all discriminatory practices of sexual subordination or inequality through pornography," concluding that it violated the First Amendment. The city appeals and the U.S. Supreme Court on February 24, 1986, unanimously affirms lower courts' decisions.

1985 The Prelude Awards, sponsored by the Penrod Society, The Children's Museum, and The Children's Museum Guild, are initiated to identify, encourage, and reward Marion County high school students who show great potential in dance, instrumental music, literature, theater, visual arts, and vocal music.

43,146 fans pack the Hoosier Dome on February 10 for the National Basketball Association's (NBA) 35th All-Star Game, setting professional basketball's one-game attendance record.

1986 Ruth Lilly, niece of Eli Lilly, establishes the Ruth Lilly Poetry Prize ($25,000) to honor a U.S. poet whose accomplishments warrant extraordinary recognition. The nation's largest poetry prize is raised to $75,000 in 1993.

The renovated Union Station opens on April 26 as a historic site and retail center with over 90 percent of the space leased.

Banc One Corporation (Ohio) in May acquires American Fletcher Corporation, which becomes Banc One, Indiana. American Fletcher National Bank becomes Bank One, Indianapolis.

Indianapolis Indians win the first of four consecutive American Association baseball championships.

Indianapolis Public Schools sells its radio station WIAN on December 1 to Indianapolis Public Broadcasting, which changes the call letters to WFYI-FM.

1987 The Indiana/World Skating Academy and Research Center is founded as a not-for-profit foundation in Indianapolis.

The Arts Council of Indianapolis incorporates.

Christ Church Cathedral (Episcopal) and SS. Peter and Paul Cathedral (Roman Catholic) establish the Damien Center in June.

During the Tenth Pan American Games (August 7–23), 4,453 athletes from 38 nations compete in 30 sports. CBS televises 26 hours of events, and 2,100 journalists representing 628 news organizations from 36 nations cover the action. Indianapolis becomes the first Pan American Games host city to break even financially.

An Air Force jet fighter crashes into the Ramada Inn near the airport on October 20, killing nine hotel employees.

1988 In January William H. Block Company, established in 1896, becomes part of the Lazarus department store chain, headquartered in Cincinnati.

The new Indianapolis Zoo, located along the White River as part of the White River State Park, opens on June 11.

The $10.5 million National Institute for Fitness and Sport opens on November 1.

1989 The $12 million Deer Creek Music Center, located near Noblesville and owned by Sunshine Promotions of Indianapolis, is completed.

DowElanco forms as joint venture of Dow Chemical and Elanco division of Eli Lilly and Company.

Indianapolis business and civic leaders form Community Leaders Allied for Superior Schools (CLASS) to work for educational improvement in the city's public school system.

Demolition of numerous historic buildings in the downtown area on March 2 signals the beginning of the much-delayed Circle Centre Mall project.

The Eiteljorg Museum of American Indian and Western Art opens in June at the entrance to White River State Park.

Indianapolis Campaign for Healthy Babies, a public-private partnership, forms in July to reduce the high black infant mortality rate in the city.

1990   Indianapolis' population is 741,952. African-Americans total 190,570, or 21 percent.

Bank One, Indianapolis, completes 51–story office tower, making it the tallest building in Indiana.

Ryan White, AIDS patient and activist, dies April 8 at Riley Hospital for Children. His funeral at Second Presbyterian Church draws thousands of mourners including national media and celebrities.

Indianapolis Star runs a series in June on Indiana doctors who continue to practice despite losing multiple malpractice lawsuits and receiving no punishment. The series receives a Pulitzer Prize the next year.

1991   Dr. Shirl E. Gilbert II is appointed superintendent of IPS, first African-American to hold that position.

In April the U.S. Department of the Army lists Fort Benjamin Harrison as one of several Army installations slated for closure during the 1990s. The closure plan calls for most of the major activities at the post to move to other locations.

City adopts Regional Center Plan II to guide further redevelopment of the downtown and adjacent neighborhoods.

1992   Stephen Goldsmith becomes mayor in January and begins initiatives to recast city government and enhance service delivery.

James D. Toler is appointed chief of the Indianapolis Police Department, the first African-American to hold that position.

L. S. Ayres and Company closes its downtown department store in January.

World heavyweight boxing champion Mike Tyson is found guilty on February 10 of raping a contestant in the Miss Black America Pageant held at the 1991 Indiana Black Expo. Tyson is sentenced to six years in prison.

National City Corporation (Cleveland) acquires Merchants National Bank in May, which becomes National City Bank, Indiana, in October.

United Airlines begins construction in August on an $800 million maintenance facility at Indianapolis International Airport.

A plane crash September 11 on the city's south side claims the lives of civic leaders Michael A. Carroll, John Weliever, Frank E. McKinney, Jr., and Robert V. Welch.

NBD Bancorp, Inc., of Detroit purchases INB Bank on October 15, changing its name to NBD Indiana in October 1993.

1993   Lazarus, which operates five Indianapolis locations, closes its downtown store (the former William H. Block Company main store) in January.

U.S. District Court Judge S. Hugh Dillin on February 10 allows IPS to proceed with its Select Schools program, a plan to allow parents a limited choice in the schools their children attend.

Indianapolis Motor Speedway president Tony George announces on April 14 the August 4–6, 1994, running of the Brickyard 400, the first non–Indy car event at the Speedway since 1916.

Starlight Musicals, begun in 1944, closes June 9 after falling $300,000 short of its budget for the season.

Forty robed Klansmen rally on the steps of the Indiana State House on October 16. Nearly 1,000 people stage counter-demonstrations nearby, resulting in seven injuries.

1994   Indiana Pacers reach "Final Four" of the National Basketball Association Playoffs, the first time the franchise advanced past the first round.

Capitol Improvement Board agrees to a controversial 10-year, $10-million deal with Thompson Consumer Electronics to rename the Hoosier Dome the RCA Dome.

Encyclopedia of Indianapolis published.

STATISTICAL ABSTRACT
OF INDIANAPOLIS AND MARION COUNTY

The information included in this portion of the *Encyclopedia of Indianapolis* has been organized to serve the broad reference needs of both students and professionals. This work is not intended to be an exhaustive collection of information, but it fills an important gap of earlier works—to provide a summary of statistical data that document important changes in the city's cultural, political, and economic development. This information, in many cases dating back to the mid-19th century, is important towards the appraisal of trends that continue to shape the city today. Accordingly, information has been collected from a variety of public and private sources—primarily to characterize Indianapolis and Marion County since the turn of the century. However, many tables include information for the subdivisions of the city, as well as comparative data for Indiana, the Midwest, and the nation as a whole.

This collection of historical statistics is divided into five major sections: Physical Environment, Population, Economy, Government, and Religion and Philanthropy. The table below lists the contents (by table and figure number) of each section.

CONTENTS

Table 1. Average Temperatures (Fahrenheit) in Indianapolis: 1961 to 1990

Month	Daily high	Daily low	Monthly mean
January	33.7	17.2	25.5
February	38.3	20.9	29.6
March	50.9	31.9	41.4
April	63.3	41.5	52.4
May	73.8	51.7	62.8
June	82.7	61.0	71.9
July	85.5	65.2	75.4
August	83.6	62.8	73.2
September	77.6	55.6	66.6
October	65.8	43.5	54.7
November	51.9	34.1	43.0
December	38.5	23.2	30.9
Average	**62.1**	**42.4**	**52.3**

Source: *Statistical Abstract of the United States,* U.S. Census, 1992.

Table 2. Precipitation, Temperature and Physical Features of Indianapolis

Precipitation		Average no. of days
Clear days		88.7
Partly cloudy days		99.5
Cloudy days		177.2
Precipitation over .01"		125.2
Snow/ice over 1.0"		7.7
Thunderstorms		43.2
Fog (visibility under 1/4 mile)		19.8
Temperature		
Daily high was:	90 and above	17.3
	32 and below	35.2
Daily low was:	32 and below	118
	0 and below	8.5

Average wind speed	9.6 MPH
Mean date of :	
last freeze	April 22
first freeze	October 20
Lowest recorded temperature (January 18, 1994)	-27
Highest recorded temperature (August 25, 1934)	107
Physical features	
Latitude	39° 44' N
Longitude	86° 16' W
Minimum elevation	645 ft above sea level
Maximum elevation	910 ft above sea level

Note: Norms based on data from 1950 to 1990
Source: *Local Climatological data: Annual Summary with Comparitive Data*, Indianapolis, Indiana
(National Oceanic and Atmospheric Administration, 1990), *Indinapolis Star (1994).*

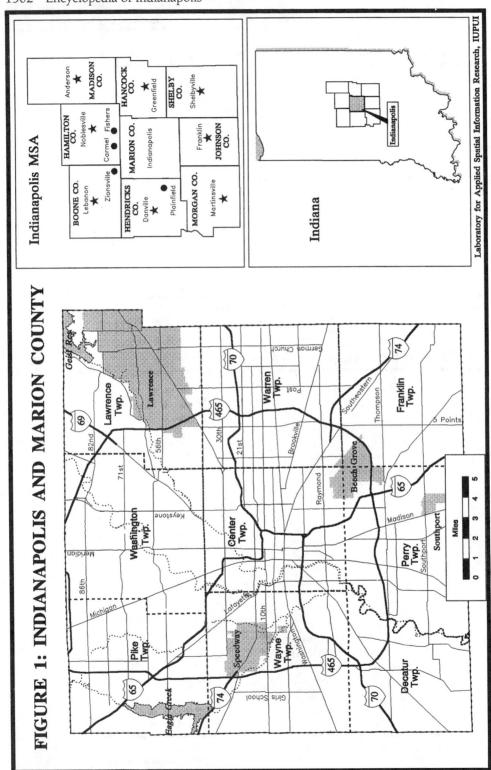

FIGURE 1: INDIANAPOLIS AND MARION COUNTY

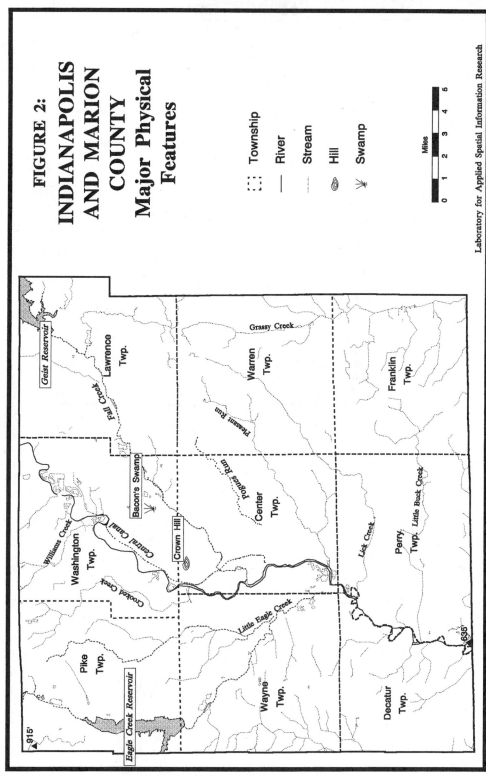

FIGURE 2:
INDIANAPOLIS AND MARION COUNTY Major Physical Features

Township
River
Stream
Hill
Swamp

Miles

Laboratory for Applied Spatial Information Research

Table 3. Population of Indianapolis and Indiana: 1830 to 1990

Year	Indianapolis	Indiana	Percentage
1830	1,900 (est.)	343,031	0.6
1840	2,692	685,866	0.4
1850	8,091	988,416	0.8
1860	18,611	1,850,428	1.0
1870	48,244	1,681,637	2.9
1880	75,056	1,978,301	3.8
1890	105,436	2,192,404	4.8
1900	169,164	2,516,462	6.7
1910	233,650	2,700,876	8.7
1920	314,194	2,930,390	10.7
1930	364,161	3,238,503	11.2
1940	386,972	3,427,796	11.3
1950	427,173	3,934,224	10.9
1960	476,258	4,662,498	10.2
1970	744,624	5,193,669	14.3
1980	700,807	5,490,224	12.8
1990	741,952	5,544,159	13.4

Source: U.S. Census.

Figure 3.   Population of Indianapolis and Marion County: 1840 to 1990

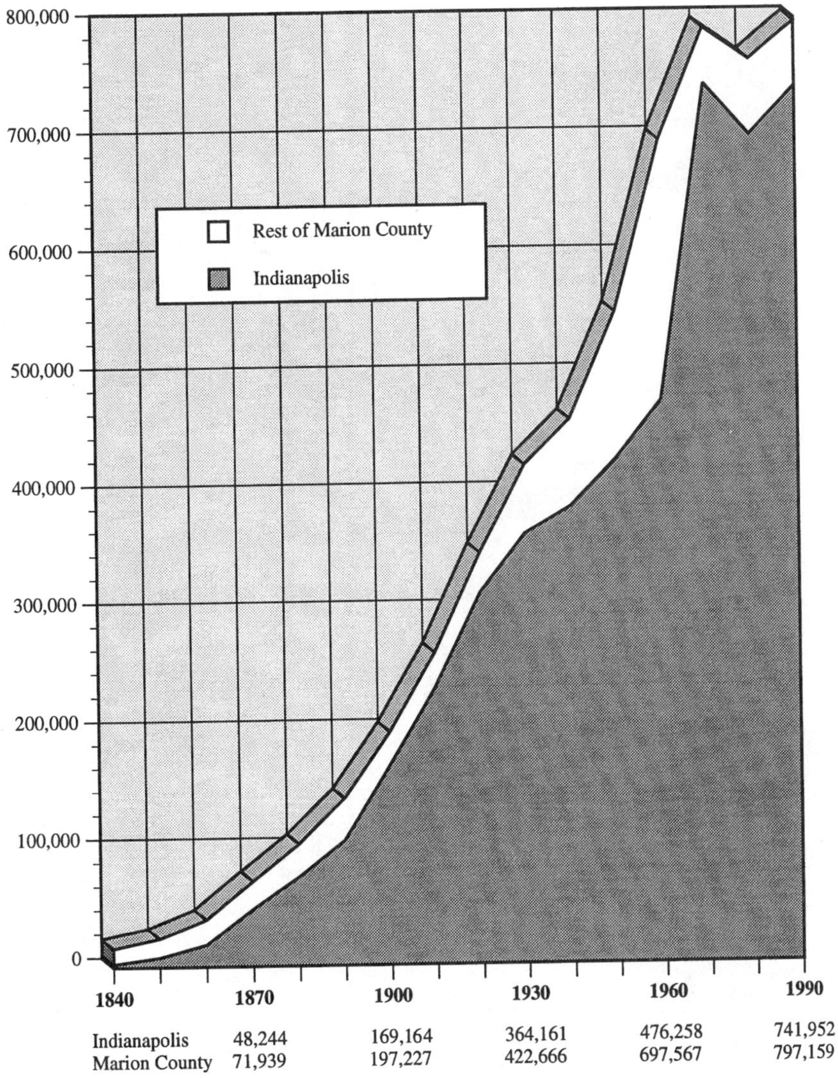

	Indianapolis	Marion County
1840	48,244	71,939
1870	169,164	197,227
1900	364,161	422,666
1930	476,258	697,567
1960	741,952	797,159

Note: Population in Indianapolis from 1970 to 1990 represents consolidation of city and county governments under Unigov.

Source: U.S. Census.

Figure 4. Marion County Population by Township: 1900, 1950, 1990

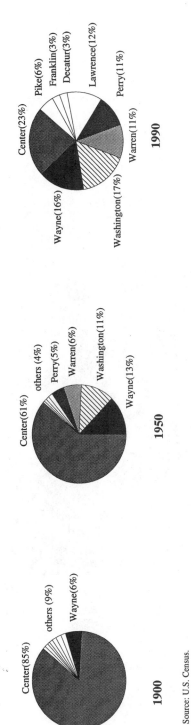

Source: U.S. Census.

Table 4. Marion County Population by Township: 1850 to 1990

	1850	1880	1900	1910	1920	1930	1940	1950	1960	1970	1980	1990
Center	9,774	80,648	167,970	218,497	283,414	300,073	314,505	337,211	333,351	273,598	208,624	182,140
Decatur	1,008	1,647	1,550	1,594	1,636	2,711	3,797	6,237	11,310	15,187	19,426	21,092
Franklin	1,506	2,609	2,178	2,337	2,459	2,918	3,225	4,596	7,357	10,293	16,477	21,458
Lawrence	1,986	2,579	2,372	3,295	3,127	5,747	7,183	8,577	34,405	66,296	75,860	94,548
Perry	1,802	2,598	2,825	4,091	6,228	12,877	15,963	24,947	46,555	73,650	78,485	85,060
Pike	1,928	2,423	2,006	1,944	1,749	2,129	2,404	3,316	6,662	14,962	25,336	45,204
Warren	1,733	3,107	3,942	6,093	9,380	17,899	22,060	33,948	60,344	85,837	89,208	87,989
Washington	2,043	2,399	3,238	5,679	12,517	34,793	42,978	62,147	97,861	126,136	129,008	133,969
Wayne	2,323	4,772	11,146	20,131	27,551	43,519	48,811	70,798	99,722	126,340	122,809	125,699
Indianapolis	8,091	75,056	169,164	233,650	314,194	364,161	386,972	427,173	476,258	744,624	700,807	741,952
Marion County	24,103	102,782	197,227	263,661	348,061	422,666	460,926	551,777	697,567	792,299	765,233	797,159

Note: Population from 1970 reflects Unigov consolidation.
Source: U.S. Census.

Table 5. Population Density Per Square Mile in Marion County Townships: 1900 to 1990

	Sq. miles	1900	1910	1920	1930	1940	1950	1960	1970	1980	1990
Township											
Center	42.6	3,939	5,123	6,646	7,036	7,375	7,907	7,817	6,415	4,892	4,271
Decatur	32.3	48	49	51	84	118	193	351	471	602	654
Franklin	42.1	52	56	58	69	77	109	175	245	392	510
Lawrence	48.4	49	68	65	119	148	177	711	1,369	1,567	1,953
Perry	45.9	62	89	136	281	348	544	1,015	1,605	1,711	1,854
Pike	43.8	46	44	40	49	55	76	152	341	578	1,031
Warren	48.2	82	126	194	371	457	704	1,251	1,779	1,849	1,824
Washington	49.5	65	115	253	702	868	1,254	1,975	2,546	2,604	2,704
Wayne	49.1	227	410	561	887	994	1,442	2,032	2,574	2,502	2,561
Marion County	**402.0**	**497**	**664**	**877**	**1,065**	**1,161**	**1,390**	**1,757**	**1,996**	**1,928**	**2,008**
% of Marion County population in Indianapolis		85.8	88.6	90.3	86.2	84.0	77.4	68.3	94.0	91.6	93.1

Note: Figures beginning in 1970 reflect Unigov consolidation.
Source: U.S. Census.

Table 6. Racial Composition of Marion County: 1900 to 1990

	Total population	White American Population	%	African-American Population	%	Other Non-White Population	%
1900	197,227	179,659	91.1	17,536	8.9	32	0.0
1910	263,661	240,343	91.2	23,256	8.8	62	0.0
1920	348,061	312,317	89.7	35,634	10.2	110	0.0
1930	422,666	377,824	89.4	44,722	10.6	120	0.0
1940	460,926	408,890	88.7	51,949	11.3	87	0.0
1950	551,777	486,502	88.2	65,010	11.8	265	0.0
1960	697,567	596,838	85.6	99,912	14.3	817	0.1
1970	792,299	655,283	82.7	134,486	17.0	2,530	0.3
1980	765,233	601,092	78.6	155,455	20.3	8,686	1.1
1990	797,159	615,039	77.2	169,654	21.3	12,466	1.6

Source: U.S. Census.

Table 7.   Marriage and Divorce in Marion County: 1950 to 1990

Years	Marriages	Divorces	Divorces as a % of marriages
1950	6,896	2,348	34.0
1960	5,809	—	—
1961	5,744	2,864	49.9
1962	6,026	2,502	41.5
1963	6,471	2,531	39.1
1964	6,427	2,409	37.5
1965	6,957	2,691	38.7
1966	7,545	3,029	40.1
1967	7,909	3,423	43.3
1968	8,124	6,442	79.3
1969	8,540	3,493	40.9
1970	8,338	4,024	48.3
1971	8,309	4,355	52.4
1972	8,927	4,464	50.0
1973	9,088	4,897	53.9
1974	8,948	7,701	86.1
1975	8,417	7,815	92.8
1976	8,654	7,590	87.7
1977	8,657	7,264	83.9
1978	8,964	7,686	85.7
1979	9,032	7,852	86.9
1980	9,063	7,482	82.6
1981	8,741	7,679	87.9
1982	9,108	6,906	75.8
1983	8,649	6,639	76.8
1984	8,577	6,693	78.0
1985	8,280	6,792	82.0
1986	8,143	6,337	77.8
1987	8,180	6,784	82.9
1988	8,232	6,583	80.0
1989	8,291	6,890	83.1
1990	8,246	7,102	86.1

Note: Data are counts of marriages performed or divorce permits filed.
Sources: Indiana State Department of Health; *Vital Statistics of the United States,* U.S. Department of Health Education and Welfare, Public Health Services, National Center for Health Statistics, Washington, D.C.; Marion County Clerk's Office.

Table 8.   Marital Status by Race for Persons Over 15 Years of Age in Indianapolis: 1900 to 1990

	1900	1910	1920	1950	1960	1970	1980	1990
Population over 15 years	125,204	179,307	240,864	536,021	339,133	536,021	539,588	624,241
African-American	12,106	17,213	26,968	48,540	65,279	89,758	108,336	123,280
White and other	113,098	162,094	213,896	487,481	273,854	446,263	431,252	500,961
Total married	69,498	104,100	148,313	340,476	223,408	340,476	289,468	313,782
African-American	6,160	9,299	16,542	31,395	41,092	49,639	40,724	41,686
White and other	63,338	94,801	131,771	309,081	182,316	290,837	248,744	272,096
Total percent married	56	58	62	64	66	64	54	50
African-American	51	54	61	65	63	55	38	34
White and other	56	58	62	63	67	65	58	54

* Figures for the White and other population are reported together, since the sum of other racial groups (Asian, American Indian, Eskimo etc.) has always been less than 2% of the city's total population.
Note: Population and population married refer to persons over 15 years of age, except for the years 1950 -1970, which refer to persons over 14 years of age.
Source: U.S. Census.

Figure 5. Births in Marion County: 1900 to 1990

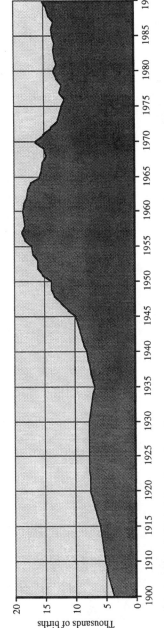

Note: Data prior to 1948 is based on 5-year intervals.
Sources: Department of Health and Human Services, National Center for Health Statistics; Indiana State Department of Health.

Figure 6. Birth Rate for Marion County and the United States: 1900 to 1990

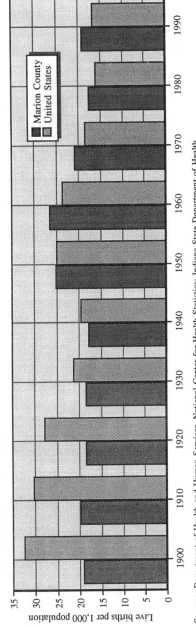

Sources: Department of Health and Human Services, National Center for Health Statistics; Indiana State Department of Health.

Figure 7. Net Migration for Marion County: 1900 to 1990

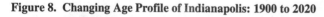

Notes: Net migration is the sum of in-migration and out-migration. Although population growth persists in Marion County, recently this growth has become more attributable to natural increase (e.g. births less deaths) because net out-migration has been prevalent since the 1960s. This out-migration reflects both suburbanization into surrounding counties as well as shifts of population to other states and regions of the country. 1990 figures are projections.
Sources: Indiana State Department of Health, Indiana Business Research Center.

Figure 8. Changing Age Profile of Indianapolis: 1900 to 2020

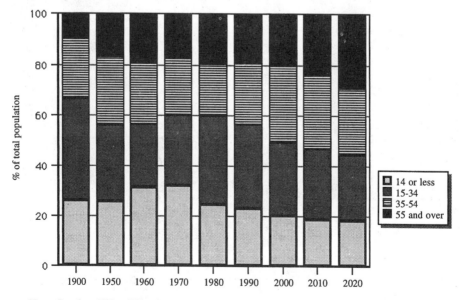

Notes: Data from 1990 to 2020 are projections. Data after 1960 represent Marion County, corresponding to a consolidation of city and county governments.
Sources: U.S. Census; *Indiana County Projections, 1985-2020*, Indiana Business Research Center, Indiana University, 1985.

Table 9: Characteristics of Households in Marion County as a Percentage of all Households: 1970 to 1990

	Year		
Total population	1970	1980	1990
Family households			
Married couple families with children	38.65	26.40	22.47
Married couple families without children	29.49	27.88	24.78
Female headed families with children	5.54	8.30	9.50
Female headed families without children	3.76	4.43	4.34
Male headed families with children	0.67	1.17	1.82
Male headed families without children	1.24	1.43	1.45
Non-family households	20.64	30.39	35.63
Total number of households	**251,522**	**285,092**	**319,471**
African-American population			
Family households			
Married couple families with children	31.94	21.58	17.72
Married couple families without children	22.54	17.27	14.30
Female headed families with children	13.95	19.93	23.34
Female headed families without children	6.23	7.68	6.98
Male headed families with children	1.35	2.01	2.79
Male headed families without children	1.97	2.31	1.87
Non-family households	22.01	29.22	32.99
Total number of households	**38,241**	**50,826**	**61,288**

Source: U.S. Census.

Table 10. Population Distribution by Age and Gender in Indianapolis: 1900 to 1990

	Percentage of the population by decade					
	1900	1950	1960	1970	1980	1990
Males (yrs. of age)						
less than 5	4.4	5.3	6.2	4.6	3.9	4.1
5-14*	8.7	7.8	9.6	11.7	8.8	7.7
15-24*	9.5	5.7	5.2	7.0	8.3	6.3
25-34	9.8	8.2	6.6	6.1	8.4	9.8
35-44	7.3	7.2	6.1	5.6	5.1	7.0
45-54	5.0	6.0	5.4	5.4	4.8	4.4
55-64	2.8	4.4	4.3	4.0	4.4	3.8
65 and up	1.8	3.6	4.1	3.4	3.9	4.3
Females (yrs. of age)						
less than 5	4.3	5.2	6.0	4.4	3.7	3.9
5-14*	8.7	7.7	9.6	11.5	8.5	7.4
15-24*	10.7	6.8	6.4	7.9	9.1	6.8
25-34	10.3	8.9	6.8	6.5	8.9	10.4
35-44	7.3	7.7	6.7	6.0	5.5	7.6
45-54	4.7	6.4	6.1	5.9	5.4	4.9
55-64	2.9	4.6	5.2	4.6	5.1	4.5
65 and up	1.9	4.6	5.8	5.3	6.4	7.1

* From 1950 to 1990, the second and third age cohorts were 5-15 and 16-24 years, respectively.

Note: Data after 1960 represent Marion County, corresponding to a consolidation of city and county governments.

Source: U.S. Census.

Table 11. Death Rates in Indianapolis, Marion County, and the United States: 1900 to 1990

	Deaths per 1,000 inhabitants		
Year	Indianapolis	Marion County	U.S.
1900	17.1	16.2	17.2
1910	16.3	16.1	14.7
1920	14.1	14.7	13.0
1930	13.5	13.7	11.3
1940	12.8	11.7	10.0
1950	12.1	10.6	9.6
1960	11.6	9.6	9.5
1970	—	9.0	9.5
1980	—	9.0	8.8
1990	—	8.9	8.6

Note: Data prior to 1920 for the city (1940 for the county) represent total death rate (e.g. resident and non resident).

Sources: *Indiana Mortality in the 20th Century*, Indiana State Department of Health; U.S. Census, *Vital Statistics of the United States*; *Monthly Vital Statistics Report*, and unpublished data, U.S. National Center for Health Statistics,.

Table 12.   Resident Deaths by Age and Cause of Death in Indianapolis: 1910, 1939/1940, 1980, 1990

1910

Rank	Cause of death	Under 1	1-9	10-19	20-29	30-39	40-49	50+	Total deaths	% of all deaths
1	Tuberculosis of the lungs	6	7	36	147	65	65	94	420	11.0
2	Organic diseases of the heart	4	5	14	10	33	45	264	375	9.8
3	Acute nephritis and Bright's disease	2	5	5	10	23	31	179	255	6.7
4	Diarrhea and enteritis	143	43	0	4	3	4	23	220	5.8
5	Violents deaths (excluding suicide)	5	22	20	38	33	29	58	205	5.4
6	Cerebral hemorrhage and softening	1	0	1	2	14	20	153	191	5.0
7	Pneumonia	18	21	6	20	24	21	81	191	5.0
8	Congenital debility and malformations	180	2	0	0	0	0	0	182	4.8
9	Cancer and other malignant tumors	0	3	0	3	14	52	110	182	4.8
10	Bronchopneumonia	48	41	2	4	3	8	38	144	3.8
11	Typhoid fever		7	9	17	19	7	8	67	1.8
12	Other forms of tuberculosis	3	8	5	16	11	10	13	66	1.7
13	Suicide		0	3	18	11	9	15	56	1.5
14	Influenza	2	4	1	5	4		38	54	1.4
15	Diseases of the stomach	15	3	0	4	5	3	22	52	1.4
	Other causes	130	141	42	64	138	131	518	1,164	30.4
	Total	**557**	**312**	**144**	**362**	**400**	**435**	**1,614**	**3,824**	**100.0**
	Percent of all deaths by age	14.6	8.2	3.8	9.5	10.5	11.4	42.2	100.0	

1939/1940

Rank	Cause of death	Under 1	1-9	10-19	20-29	30-39	40-49	50+	Total deaths	% of all deaths
1	Diseases of heart (other forms)	1	4	8	14	25	55	1,202	1,309	13.3
2	Diseases of coronary arteries, angina pectoris	0	0	0	4	30	89	820	945	9.6
3	Cancer and other malignant tumors	1	3	3	12	41	120	754	934	9.5
4	Nephritis	1	3	5	8	22	50	715	804	8.1
5	Intracranial lesions of vascular origin	1	2	1	8	12	36	702	762	7.7
6	Influenza and pneumonia (all forms)	61	33	9	16	20	34	332	505	5.1
7	Other accidents	4	14	20	16	14	30	250	348	3.5
8	Motor vehicle accidents	0	10	18	43	31	35	89	226	2.3
9	Tuberculosis of respiratory system	3	1	3	40	39	42	96	224	2.3
10	Diabetes mellitus	0	1	2	1	5	12	184	205	2.1
11	Premature birth	161	0	0	0	0	0	0	161	1.6
12	Chronic rheumatic disease of heart	0	2	4	5	10	23	102	146	1.5
13	Suicide	0	0	2	15	24	29	53	123	1.2
14	Syphilis	5	1	1	4	16	23	59	109	1.1
15	Cirrhosis of the liver	0	1	0	0	1	15	52	69	0.7
	All other causes	319	95	89	198	266	409	1,625	3,001	30.4
	Total	**557**	**170**	**165**	**384**	**556**	**1,002**	**7,037**	**9,871**	**100.0**
	Percent of all deaths by age	5.6	1.7	1.7	3.9	5.6	10.2	71.3	100.0	

(continued)

Table 12. (continued)

1980

Rank	Cause of death	Under 1	1-9	10-19	20-29	30-39	40-49	50+	Total deaths	% of all deaths
1	Heart disease	3	4	5	11	23	79	2,301	2,426	37.4
2	Malignant neoplasm	0	7	3	10	40	93	1,342	1,495	23.1
3	Cerebrovascular disease	0	0	1	1	2	14	486	504	7.8
4	Chronic obstructive pulmonary disease	0	0	2	3	1	2	200	208	3.2
5	Accidents, non-motor vehicle	3	12	11	29	8	6	83	152	2.3
6	Diabetes	0	0	0	1	6	3	136	146	2.3
7	Pneumonia/influenza	3	1	0	1	2	2	135	144	2.2
8	Motor vehicle accidents	0	7	23	38	14	10	18	110	1.7
9	Homicide	1	2	12	35	22	13	24	109	1.7
10	Cirrhosis	0	0	0	1	5	13	85	104	1.6
11	Arteriosclerosis	0	0	0	0	0	0	103	103	1.6
12	Perinatal conditions	100	1		0	0	0	0	101	1.6
13	Suicide	0	0	9	13	11	11	37	81	1.3
14	Nephritis/nephrosis	0	0	1	0	1	1	51	54	0.8
15	Congenital anomalies	43	2	3	1	1	0	4	54	0.8
	All other causes	32	10	9	29	21	39	548	688	10.6
	Total	**185**	**46**	**79**	**173**	**157**	**286**	**5,553**	**6,479**	**100.0%**
	Percent of all deaths by age	2.9	0.7	1.2	2.7	2.4	4.4	85.7	100.0	

1990

Rank	Cause of death	Under 1	1-9	10-19	20-29	30-39	40-49	50+	Total deaths	% of all deaths
1	Heart disease	6	0	2	4	14	61	1,898	1,985	29.8
2	Malignant neoplasm	0	5	5	14	37	90	1,604	1,755	26.4
3	Cerebrovascular disease	2	0	0	2	8	13	393	418	6.3
4	Chronic obstructive pulmonary disease	0	0	0	0	2	3	280	285	4.3
5	Pneumonia/influenza	1	1	0	1	12	4	211	230	3.5
6	Diabetes	0	0	0	1	5	13	144	163	2.4
7	Accidents, non-motor vehicle	6	6	11	5	7	4	62	101	1.5
8	Motor vehicle accidents	0	3	15	27	18	12	26	101	1.5
9	Nephritis/nephrosis	3	0	0	1	2		94	100	1.5
10	Suicide	0	0	5	23	22	11	34	95	1.4
11	Arteriosclerosis	0	0	0	0	0	0	85	85	1.3
12	Perinatal conditions	83	2	0	0	0	0	0	85	1.3
13	Homicide	2	5	11	24	20	3	9	74	1.1
14	Septicema	0	1	0	0	3	0	64	68	1.0
15	Cirrhosis	0	0	0	0	7	12	45	64	1.0
	All other causes	78	18	10	30	81	77	753	1,047	15.7
	Total	**181**	**41**	**59**	**132**	**238**	**303**	**5,702**	**6,656**	**100.0**
	Percent of all deaths by age	2.7	0.6	0.9	2.0	3.6	4.6	85.7	100.0	

Note: Data for 1910 are not separated by resident and non-resident deaths. A non-resident death would describe a person who might enter the city prior to death (e.g. for medical care).
Sources: U.S. Census; Marion County Health Department.

Table 13. Infant Mortality in Marion County: 1920 to 1990

| Year | Infant Mortality Rate per 1,000 live births | | |
	Total	White	Non-White
1920	91	84	150
1930	63	55	123
1940	49	48	61
1955	28	25	40
1960	26	23	42
1965	25	21	41
1970	21	20	25
1975	14	12	22
1980	14	11	22
1985	14	11	23
1990	12	10	18

Note: Data prior to 1950 are for Indianapolis, which includes only African-Americans in the non-white population.

Sources: Indiana State Department of Health; U.S. Census; National Center For Health Statistics; and Marion County Health Department.

Table 14. Violent Deaths by Township in Marion County: 1975 to 1992

| Township | Violent deaths | | | Violent deaths as a percent of township deaths | | |
	1975	1985	1992	1975	1985	1992
Center	220	146	156	8.4	6.7	8.0
Decatur	5	7	6	7.4	6.7	4.7
Franklin	6	3	10	9.5	4.1	9.7
Lawrence	35	33	39	13.0	8.9	8.0
Perry	28	21	26	6.1	3.5	4.0
Pike	10	13	17	12.3	7.8	7.2
Warren	37	37	42	5.8	4.7	4.8
Washington	66	66	64	6.4	6.0	5.5
Wayne	68	70	68	8.3	7.5	6.9
Unknown	1	1	1	—	—	—
Marion County	**476**	**397**	**429**	**7.9**	**6.3**	**6.5**

Note: Violent deaths include deaths from suicide, homicide, legal intervention (police action), accidents and adverse effects, and all other external causes.

Source: Marion County Health Department, 1993.

Figure 9. Population of Marion County by Age and Gender: 1850, 1930, 1960, 1990

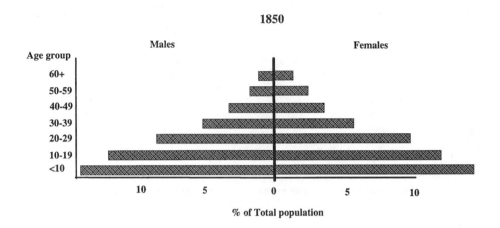

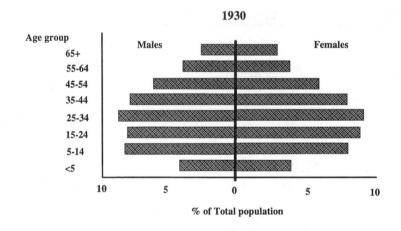

(continued)

Figure 9.   (Continued)

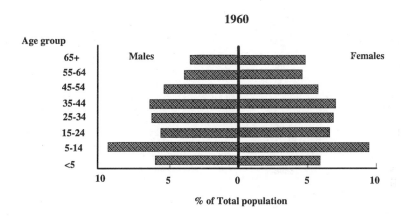

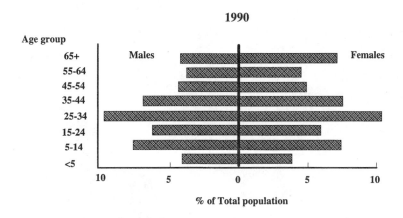

Source: U.S. Census

Table 15. Incidence of AIDS in Indiana and Marion County: 1982 to 1992

Year	Indiana		Marion County	
	Cases	Deaths	Cases	Deaths
1982	6	5	1	0
1983	10	9	1	1
1984	28	27	11	6
1985	55	50	15	7
1986	94	79	31	27
1987	161	146	44	18
1988	232	192	79	34
1989	290	212	125	70
1990	356	239	130	86
1991	447	211	130	95
1992	496	119	165	—
Total reported through 1992	**2,175**	**1,289**	**732**	**344**

Sources: *Indiana Report of Diseases of Public Health Interest, 1990*, Indiana State Board of Health; *Marion County Health Report 1990/1991*, Marion County Health Department and Indiana State Board of Health.

Figure 10. AIDS Cases in Indiana and Marion County: 1982 to 1992

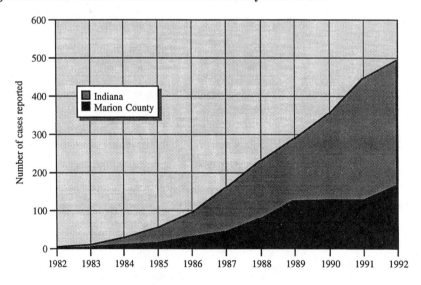

Sources: *Indiana Report of Diseases of Public Health Interest, 1990*, Indiana State Board of Health; *Marion County Health Report 1990/1991*, Marion County Health Department and Indiana State Board of Health.

Table 16. Industry of Employment for Residents of Marion County, Indiana, and the United States: 1880, 1990, 1950, and 1990

	Marion County*		Indiana	
	Employees	%	Employees	%
1880				
Total (all persons 10 and over)	**27,966**	**100.0**	**635,080**	**100.0**
Agriculture	315	1.1	331,240	52.2
Professional and personal services	10,217	36.5	137,281	21.6
Trade and transport	7,166	25.6	56,432	8.9
Manufacturing, mechanical, mining	10,268	36.7	110,127	17.3
1900				
Total (all persons 10 and over)	**72,805**	**100.0**	**898,953**	**100.0**
Agriculture	753	1.0	342,733	38.1
Professional services	4,570	6.3	42,473	4.7
Trade and transport	22,037	30.3	138,545	15.4
Fishing, manufacturing, mining & construction	25,922	35.6	206,611	23.0
Domestic and personal	19,523	26.8	168,591	18.8
1950				
Total (all persons 14 and over)	**233,959**	**100.0**	**1,475,722**	**100.0**
Agriculture, forestry and fisheries	2,593	1.1	176,103	11.9
Mining	177	0.1	15,279	1.0
Construction	12,858	5.5	77,420	5.2
Manufacturing	76,958	32.9	527,836	35.8
Transportation, communications & utilities	22,475	9.6	112,914	7.7
Wholesale and retail trade	50,781	21.7	266,487	18.1
Finance, insurance and real estate	11,670	5.0	39,277	2.7
Business and personal services (not domestic)	14,183	6.1	104,789	7.1
Professional and related services	19,746	8.4	115,029	7.8
Other or not allocated	22,518	9.6	40,588	2.8
1990				
Total (all persons 16 and over)	**401,124**	**108.6**	**2,680,695**	**100.0**
Agriculture, forestry and fisheries	4,085	1.0	67,139	2.5
Mining	366	0.1	8,765	0.3
Construction	21,606	5.4	146,232	5.5
Manufacturing	63,935	15.9	661,641	24.7
Transportation, communications & utilities	31,442	7.8	174,287	6.5
Wholesale and retail trade	91,167	22.7	562,041	21.0
Finance, insurance and real estate	35,412	8.8	149,809	5.6
Business and personal services (not domestic)	34,387	8.6	174,117	6.5
Professional and related services	98,617	24.6	598,683	22.3
Other or not allocated	54,494	13.6	137,981	5.1

* Data for 1900 represent the city of Indianapolis.

Note: No attempt has been made to reconcile changing U.S. Census definitions over time.

Source: U.S. Census.

Table 17: Total Employment in Marion County by Industry as a Percentage of Total Employment: 1948 to 1990

Industry	Year				
	1948	1959	1970	1980	1990
Agriculture	0.07	0.10	0.13	0.17	0.33
Mining	1.04	0.19	0.10	0.24	0.10
Construction	4.88	4.77	5.75	5.38	5.68
Manufacturing	43.44	40.80	36.62	29.31	18.19
Transportation and public utilities	8.51	6.62	6.46	6.37	7.25
Wholesale trade	8.42	8.45	9.46	8.40	7.60
Retail trade	18.66	18.90	17.54	19.45	19.75
Finance, insurance, and real estate	5.16	7.79	8.37	9.21	9.35
Services	9.67	12.01	15.42	21.01	31.49
Other (undefined or not classified)	0.16	0.36	0.16	0.45	0.25
Total Employment	**204,758**	**244,482**	**317,765**	**372,007**	**467,761**

Source: U.S. Census.

Table 18: Occupations of Marion County Residents as a Percentage of the Total Labor Force: 1950 to 1990

Occupation	Year				
	1950	1960	1970	1980	1990
Professional, management, technical, sales, and clerical support	39.50	50.05	52.50	56.73	62.06
Service	7.46	11.22	12.35	13.49	13.52
Precision production, craft and repair	23.03	14.41	13.38	10.82	9.89
Operators, fabricators, and laborers	28.74	23.85	21.48	18.41	13.81
Farming, mining, forestry and fishing	1.27	0.47	0.29	0.54	0.71
Total labor force	**156,823**	**260,146**	**320,849**	**323,462**	**372,602**

Source: U.S. Census.

Table 19. Employment of Indianapolis and Marion County Residents by Race and Gender: 1930 to 1990

	Indianapolis					Marion County		
	1930	1940	1950	1960	1970	1970	1980	1990
Total population								
All males	176,647	185,461	203,244	226,058	356,620	379,655	364,199	378,599
African-American	21,263	24,356	30,571	46,908	63,147	63,224	72,718	78,253
White and other	155,384	161,105	172,673	179,150	293,473	316,431	291,481	300,346
All females	187,514	201,511	223,929	250,200	388,004	412,644	401,034	418,560
African-American	22,704	26,356	35,521	51,776	71,057	71,141	82,737	91,401
White and other	164,810	175,155	188,408	198,424	316,947	341,503	318,297	327,159
Employment								
All males	118,330	102,747	123,180	120,491	180,079	192,968	181,817	203,899
African-American	14,370	10,129	16,276	21,785	25,625	25,669	28,234	32,439
White and other	103,960	92,618	106,904	98,706	154,454	167,299	153,583	171,460
All females	46,103	45,385	63,288	73,214	119,315	127,881	172,421	193,847
African-American	7,687	5,880	10,411	14,778	25,461	25,484	32,006	37,962
White and other	38,416	39,505	52,877	58,436	93,854	102,397	140,415	155,885
Employment as a % of population								
All males	67	55	61	53	50	51	50	54
African-American	68	42	53	46	41	41	39	41
White and other	67	57	62	55	53	53	53	57
All females	25	23	28	29	31	31	43	46
African-American	34	22	29	29	36	36	39	42
White and other	23	23	28	29	30	30	44	48

* Figures for the White and other population are reported together, since the sum of other racial groups (Asian, American Indian, Eskimo etc.) has always been less than 2% of the city's total population.
Note: Figures prior to 1970 are for the pre-Unigov city of Indianapolis.
Source: U.S. Census.

Figure 11. Proportion of Indianapolis Residents Employed by Race and Gender : 1930 to 1990

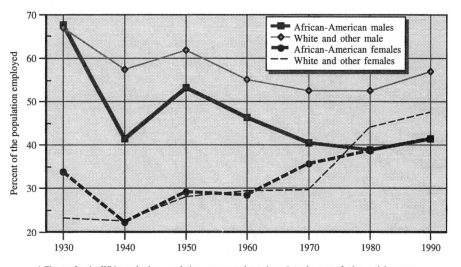

* Figures for the White and other population are reported together, since the sum of other racial groups (Asian, American Indian, Eskimo etc.) has always been less than 2% of the city's total population.
Source: U.S. Census.

Table 20. Earnings[a] by Industry in Marion County: 1929 to 1990

Industry	1929	1940	1950	1959	1970	1980	1990
Farm	2,684	2,315	4,931	4,355	2,989	6,709	10,858
Non-farm	326,314	326,732	1,003,604	1,747,053	3,483,275	8,234,784	15,720,192
Private	303,286	291,128	913,666	1,559,738	3,011,004	7,066,376	13,485,547
Manufacturing	104,228	100,901	375,889	641,633	1,138,928	2,514,648	3,385,374
Mining	3,558	1,928	6,210	4,531	7,645	38,062	41,575
Construction	17,943	12,154	53,712	98,816	225,524	474,207	921,814
Wholesale trade	—	—	—	145,504	284,138	685,513	1,224,332
Retail trade	—	—	—	189,582	363,903	797,216	1,453,820
FIRE (b)	—	—	—	129,362	255,568	596,660	1,302,920
TCPU (c)	42,130	37,678	107,420	149,746	270,297	646,277	1,211,072
Services	39,189	38,244	97,543	199,686	461,496	1,300,379	3,908,190
Agric. serv. (d)	112	113	564	878	3,505	13,414	36,450
Government	23,028	35,604	89,938	187,315	472,271	1,168,408	2,234,645
Federal civilian	3,093	10,175	29,790	72,826	159,955	351,201	659,981
Federal military	1,055	1,986	10,896	15,667	27,430	53,385	104,912
State and local	18,880	23,443	49,252	98,822	284,886	763,822	1,469,752
Total earnings	328,998	329,047	1,008,535	1,751,408	3,486,264	8,241,493	15,731,050

a) Earnings (x $1,000) are collected by county of work, not residence. These earnings have not been adjusted for inflation. They do not include contributions to social insurance, dividends, interest or rental income, yet do include transfer payments.
b) FIRE includes finance, insurance and real estate industries.
c) TCPU includes transportation, communication and public utilities industries.
d) Agricultural services also include forestry and fisheries.
Source: U.S. Bureau of Economic Analysis.

Table 21. Earnings[a] by Industry in Marion County as a Percentage of Indiana Earnings: 1929 to 1990

Industry	1929	1940	1950	1959	1970	1980	1990
Farm	1.3	1.7	1.0	1.3	0.7	1.1	0.9
Non-farm	22.4	22.1	21.5	22.2	21.9	21.8	23.3
Private	22.4	22.3	21.3	22.0	21.6	21.3	23.0
Manufacturing	18.1	16.8	17.7	18.0	17.1	17.1	15.7
Mining	11.9	9.6	9.8	7.3	9.4	9.6	9.2
Construction	22.5	23.3	22.0	21.9	21.3	19.2	22.3
Wholesale trade	—	—	—	37.9	35.9	31.6	32.5
Retail trade	—	—	—	20.4	20.8	21.2	22.7
FIRE (b)	—	—	—	37.8	37.6	35.6	39.1
TCPU (c)	23.9	27.0	26.3	25.6	25.2	24.4	25.7
Services	24.1	25.2	23.4	26.0	25.1	24.6	28.1
Agric. serv. (d)	8.0	8.0	4.7	5.7	8.3	11.4	12.8
Government	22.4	20.4	23.2	24.3	24.8	25.5	25.1
Federal civilian	18.1	15.3	32.8	44.2	39.8	40.3	42.2
Federal military	60.8	63.9	27.8	25.5	32.7	36.0	30.9
State and local	22.5	22.4	19.1	18.2	20.0	21.4	21.0
Total earnings		19.8	20.4	19.5	8.39	20.6	22.6

a) Earnings (x $1,000) are collected by county of work, not residence. These earnings have not been adjusted for inflation. They do not include contributions to social insurance, dividends, interest or rental income, yet do include transfer payments.
b) FIRE includes finance, insurance and real estate industries.
c) TCPU includes transportation, communication and public utilities industries.
d) Agricultural services also include forestry and fisheries.
Source: U.S. Bureau of Economic Analysis.

Figure 12. Unemployment Rate in Marion County and the United States: 1974 to 1992

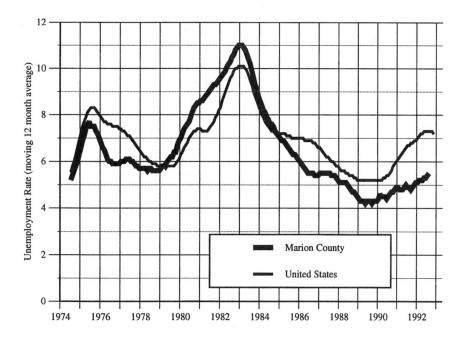

Source: Indiana Business Research Center, Indiana University School of Business.

Figure 13. Females as a Percentage of the Workforce in Indianapolis, Indiana, and the United States: 1880 to 1990

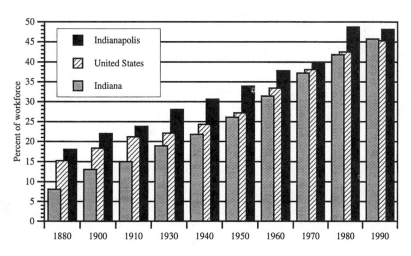

Note: Data from 1970 to 1990 represent Marion County, corresponding to a consolidation of city and county government in 1970.
Source: U.S. Census.

Table 22: Unemployment and Labor Force Participation Rates of Marion County Residents: 1970 to 1990

Total population		Year		
		1970	1980	1990
Male	Labor force participation rate	81.40	78.60	78.00
	Unemployment rate	3.60	7.60	5.70
Female	Labor force participation rate	46.90	55.90	62.30
	Unemployment rate	5.00	5.80	5.30
African-American population				
Male	Labor force participation rate	75.60	72.10	71.70
	Unemployment rate	8.50	16.70	13.20
Female	Labor force participation rate	55.80	61.50	63.70
	Unemployment rate	8.20	10.70	11.00

Source: U.S. Census.
Note: The labor force participation rate is the percent of the total population over the age of 16 that is employed or actively searching for employment. The unemployment rate is the percent of the labor force who that is unemployed.

Figure 14. Sales of Crops and Livestock in Marion County: 1920 to 1990

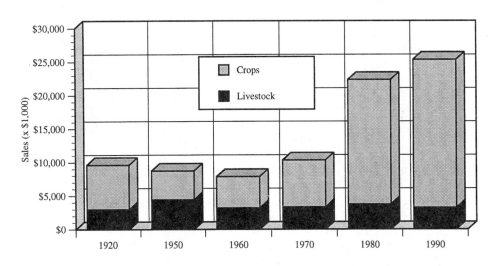

Note: Sales figures are in current dollars (unadjusted for inflation).
    Sources: U.S. Bureau of Economic Analysis, 1970-1990; U.S. Bureau of the Census, *County Business Patterns*, 1952, 1962, 1972; and U.S. Bureau of the Census, Census of Agriculture 1920.

Table 23. Employment by Gender in Indianapolis, Indiana, and the United States: 1880 to 1990

	Indianapolis*		Indiana		United States	
	Employees	Percent of workforce	Employees (x 1000)	Percent of workforce	Employees (x 1000)	Percent of workforce
Total						
1880	27,966	100	635	100	17,392	100
1900	72,836	100	899	100	29,030	100
1910	107,757	100	1,037	100	38,167	100
1930	164,433	100	1,251	100	48,688	100
1940	148,132	100	1,149	100	52,789	100
1950	186,468	100	1,518	100	59,854	100
1960	193,705	100	1,793	100	69,628	100
1970	338,759	100	2,103	100	82,771	100
1980	354,238	100	2,575	100	106,940	100
1990	427,269	100	2,629	100	124,788	100
Male						
1880	22,927	82.0	584	91.9	14,745	84.8
1900	56,826	78.0	782	87.0	23,711	81.7
1910	82,104	76.2	881	85.0	30,092	78.8
1930	118,330	72.0	1,015	81.1	37,933	77.9
1940	102,747	69.4	899	78.2	39,944	75.7
1950	123,180	66.1	1,121	73.9	43,553	72.8
1960	120,491	62.2	1,230	68.6	46,388	66.6
1970	204,116	60.3	1,321	62.8	51,228	61.9
1980	181,817	51.3	1,498	58.2	61,453	57.5
1990	221,858	51.9	1,427	54.3	68,234	54.7
Female						
1880	5,039	18.0	51	8.1	2,647	15.2
1900	16,010	22.0	117	13.0	5,319	18.3
1910	25,653	23.8	156	15.0	8,076	21.2
1930	46,103	28.0	236	18.9	10,755	22.1
1940	45,385	30.6	250	21.8	12,845	24.3
1950	63,288	33.9	397	26.1	16,301	27.2
1960	73,214	37.8	563	31.4	23,240	33.4
1970	134,643	39.7	782	37.2	31,543	38.1
1980	172,421	48.7	1,078	41.8	45,487	42.5
1990	205,411	48.1	1,202	45.7	56,554	45.3

* Data from 1970 to 1990 represent Marion County.

Source: U.S. Census.

Figure 15. Wages, Capital Investment and Value Added in Marion County Compared to Indiana: 1967 to 1987

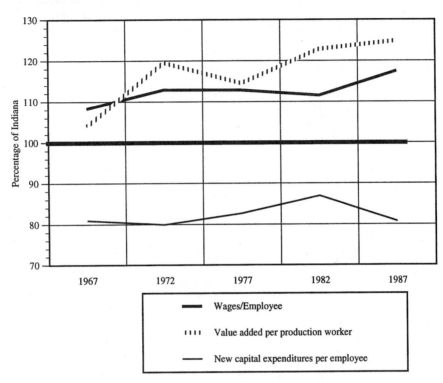

Note: The manufacturing industry in Marion County has become increasingly labor intensive. Rising wages per employee moved further from the statewide average, while new capital expenditures per employee remained below average. Despite the low capital investment, the value added to manufactured products by each worker—a measure of productivity—grew far beyond the statewide average, and faster than wages per production worker.

Source: U.S. Census, *Census of Manufacturing*: 1967, 1972, 1977, 1982, 1987.

Table 24. Manufacturing in Marion County: 1967 to 1987

	1967	1972	1977	1982	1987	Percentage of Indiana				
						1967	1972	1977	1982	1987
Total number of establishments	1,140	1,178	1,226	1,190	1,254	16.5	16.0	15.2	15.0	14.5
20 or more employees	442	422	442	438	466	15.2	13.8	13.7	13.8	12.9
Total number employed (x 1,000)	120	108	106	95	83	16.9	15.3	15.0	16.3	13.7
production workers (x 1,000)	85	72	70	57	51	15.7	13.6	13.4	14.1	11.9
Total payroll *	920	1,187	1,772	2,279	2,544	18.3	17.3	17.0	18.2	16.2
wages/employee	7,657	11,034	16,684	23,939	30,763	108.3	112.9	112.8	111.5	117.5
Value added to manufacture *	1,680	2,298	3,478	4,460	5,814	16.3	16.3	15.3	17.3	14.8
per production worker	19,714	32,046	49,827	77,836	114,891	104.0	119.5	114.5	122.8	124.8
Value of shipments *	3,226	4,149	6,998	9,392	11,358	14.8	14.2	13.4	14.8	13.6
per establishment (x 1,000)	2,830	3,522	5,708	7,892	9,058	89.6	88.8	88.2	99.2	93.4
New capital expenditure *	138	105	259	316	373	13.7	12.2	12.4	14.1	11.1
per establishment *	120,702	89,049	210,848	265,294	297,448	83.2	76.3	81.8	94.6	76.4
per employee	1,145	975	2,434	3,316	4,510	81.0	79.9	82.7	86.9	80.7
Production worker hours (millions)	168	145	139	107	103	15.6	13.9	13.6	14.2	12.0
wages *	577	707	1,051	1,208	1,375	16.7	15.2	14.9	15.5	13.9

* Millions of current dollars (unadjusted for inflation).
Source: U.S. Census, *Census of Manufacturing:* 1967, 1972, 1977, 1982, 1987.

Figure 16. Retail Sales in Marion County: 1948 to 1991

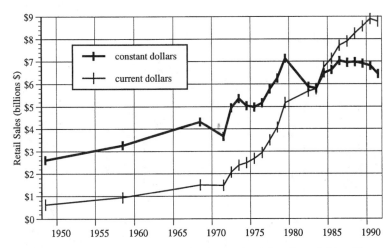

Notes: Data is estimated by interpolation for years between those indicated by vertical bars (|).
Adjustments for inflation (constant dollar retail sales estimates) are based on the consumer price index
(CPI). The CPI includes non-retail items and may actually understate the growth of retail sales because of
rapid increases in non-retail prices.
  Sources: *County Business Patterns,* 1948-68, U.S. Bureau of the Census; *Component Unit Financial
Report,* City of Indianapolis, Indiana, Department of Administration, Division of Finance, 1976, 1981,
1991.

Figure 17. Deposits of Federally Insured Banks in Marion County: 1983 to 1991
[as a percentage of Indiana]

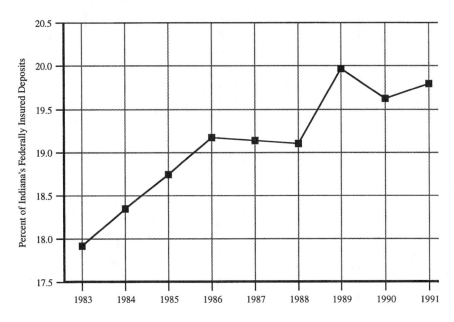

Source: Indiana Business Research Center, Indiana University School of Business.

Table 25. Largest Employers in Indianapolis: 1979 and 1993

Top thirty employers in 1993	Industry	1979 Employees	Rank	1993 Employees	Rank
* City-County Government (1)	government	29,136	1	30,336	1
* State of Indiana (2)	government	17,575	2	24,045	2
Federal Government (3)	government	15,700	3	20,000	3
* Detroit-Diesel Allison Div., General Motors (4)	mfg	15,000	4	10,400	4
* Eli Lilly and Company	mfg	8,650	5	8,750	5
* Methodist Hospital of Indiana Inc.	hospital	4,026	12	6,032	6
* St. Vincent Hospital and Health Care Center	hospital	2,278	21	5,732	7
* Community Hospitals of Indianapolis	hospital	2,660	15	5,150	8
* Marsh Supermarkets Inc/Village Pantry Markets	retail	1,477	33	5,100	9
The Kroger Company, Central Marketing Area	retail	2,302	20	4,800	10
* NBD Indiana Inc.	banking	—	—	3,200	11
* Indiana Bell Telephone Co., Inc	communications	5,685	8	3,134	12
Hardees Food Systems	retail	—	—	3,100	13
Ford Motor Company	mfg	5,100	10	3,030	14
Wal-Mart	retail	—	—	3,000	17
* The Associated Group (Blue Cross)	insurance	2,432	19	3,000	15
* St. Francis Hospital Center	hospital	1,600	27	3,000	16
GM Truck and Bus Operations	mfg	5,500	9	2,700	18
United Parcel Service	transportation	—	—	2,577	19
* Bank One Indianapolis N. A.	banking	—	—	2,500	20
Target Stores and Distribution Center	retail	—	—	2,320	21
* Thomson Consumer Electronics (RCA)	mfg	7,084	7	2,186	22
* National City Bank	banking	—	—	2,100	23
AT&T	communications	—	—	2,037	24
* Indianapolis Power & Light Co.	utility	2,067	23	1,971	25
* U.S.A. Group Inc.	banking	—	—	1,958	26
Navistar International (International Harvester)	mfg	2,650	16	1,816	27
Federal Express	transportation	—	—	1,800	28
* Boehringer Mannheim Corp.	mfg	<250	—	1,793	29
* Brylane, Inc	retail	—	—	1,750	30

Firms that fell from the top thirty largest employers of 1979	Industry	1979 Employees	Rank	1993 Employees	Rank
Western Electric Company, Inc	mfg	8,100	6	—	
Chrysler Corporation - two plants	mfg	4,300	11	1,000	44
FMC Corporation	mfg	3,014	13	—	
L.S. Ayres & Company	retail	2,900	14	1,250	37
Sears, Roebuck & Company	retail	2,500	18	1,215	38
Consolidated Rail Corporation	transportation	2,500	17	850	49
American Fletcher Corporation	banking	2,108	22	—	
Indiana National Corporation	banking	2,051	24	—	
William H. Block Company	retail	2,000	25	—	
* Indianapolis Newspapers, Inc.	printing	1,850	26	1,600	31
K-Mart Discount Stores	retail	1,600	28	1,523	33
* BDP Company, Division Carrier Corporation	mfg.	1,550	29	1,250	37
* American States Insurance Company	insurance	1,549	30	1,200	39

* Indicates home office, regional or divisional headquarters is located in the Indianapolis area.
(1) Includes schools, library, Wishard Hospital and other local government offices but not Citizens Gas and Coke Utility.
(2) Includes IUPUI, IVY Tech and State Government.
(3) Includes Postal Service, Fort Benjamin Harrison, Army Finance Center, VA Hospitals, and other Federal Government.
(4) Allison Gas Turbine Operations (5,700 employees in 1993) and Allison Transmission (4,700 employees in 1993) Divisions of GMC.
Note: American Fletcher Corporation was acquired by Bank One of Columbus, Ohio; Indiana National Corporation was acquired by NBD Bank of Detroit; National City Bank acquired Merchants National Bank; the William H. Block Company became a part of Lazarus in 1988.
Source: Indianapolis Chamber of Commerce 1979, 1993.

Figure 18: Median Household Income in 1989 Dollars by Township in Marion County: 1969, 1979 and 1989

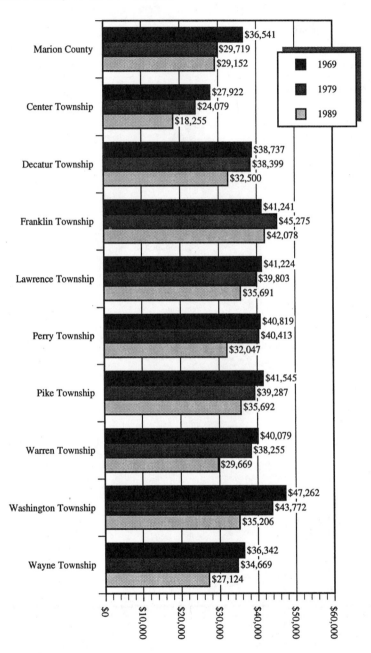

Source: U.S. Bureau of the Census.

Table 26. Cost of Living Index for Indianapolis and Selected Cities: 1977 to 1992

	1977	1982	1987	1988	1989	1990	1991	1992
Atlanta	99.7	103.0	110.8	109.0	107.1	102.0	100.1	98.8
Chicago	111.8	110.0	125.4	123.3	120.1	124.0	124.0	121.9
Columbus, Ohio	97.5	101.8	102.0	103.1	102.4	106.3	107.3	107.6
New York	123.5	130.0	145.8	154.5	—	—	213.3	214.2
Indianapolis	**98.2**	**98.9**	**97.4**	**99.0**	**99.3**	**98.0**	**97.2**	**95.3**

Sources: *Index Report: Intercity Cost of Living Indicators (1977)*, American Chamber of Commerce Researchers Association (ACCRA); and *Intercity Cost of Living Index*, ACCRA.

Table 27: Household, Family, and Per Capita Income of Marion County Residents in 1989 Dollars: 1969 to 1989

		Year	
Total population	1969	1979	1989
Median household income	$30,280	$29,719	$29,152
Median family income	$36,555	$35,559	$35,054
Per capita income	-	$13,112	$14,614
African-American population			
Median household income	$20,678	$22,004	$19,928
Median family income	$26,530	$25,999	$23,266
Per capita income	-	$8,844	$9,196

Source: U.S. Census.

Table 28: Household Income Distribution in Marion County: 1969 to 1989

		Year	
Percent of households in each income range	1969	1979	1989
Top fifth	21.00	18.06	16.98
Fourth fifth	19.82	18.52	18.63
Middle fifth	19.25	20.10	20.34
Second fifth	19.60	21.39	21.42
Bottom fifth	20.32	21.93	22.64

Source: U.S. Census.

Table 29: Marion County Residents and Family Households below Poverty Level: 1969 to 1989

		Year	
Total population	1969	1979	1989
Percentage of all families below poverty level	9.40	11.05	11.81
Percentage of all residents below poverty level	6.81	8.37	9.40
African-American population			
Percentage of all families below poverty level	18.00	19.90	23.40
Percentage of all residents below poverty level	21.80	23.20	25.40

Source: U.S. Census.

Table 30.   Land Use in Indianapolis: 1900

Land use	Acres	% of total
Residential	5,838	25.2
Commercial	274	1.2
Amusement park	474	2.0
Industrial	1,085	4.7
Government	137	0.6
City park	301	1.3
Institution	273	1.2
School	186	0.8
University	47	0.2
Hospital	6	0.0
Church	134	0.6
Cemetery	488	2.1
Road	2,026	8.7
Railroad	380	1.6
Vacant	11,338	48.9
Water	79	0.3
Total acres	**23,177**	**100.0**
Square miles	36.203	100.0

Source: Laboratory for Applied Spatial Information Research (LASIR), Indiana University-Purdue University, Indianapolis.

Table 31. Land Use in Marion County by Township: 1992

Land use	Center*	Decatur	Franklin	Lawrence	Perry	Pike	Warren	Washington	Wayne	Marion County
SF Res.	40.2%	12.6%	12.0%	30.8%	32.0%	16.6%	27.0%	52.8%	32.9%	29.5%
MF Res.	3.2%	1.3%	0.4%	6.2%	2.6%	4.7%	2.0%	7.4%	6.0%	3.9%
Office	3.7%	0.0%	0.1%	0.8%	0.3%	1.3%	0.3%	1.7%	0.5%	1.0%
Retail	8.5%	0.3%	0.5%	2.8%	2.8%	4.1%	3.9%	3.5%	4.4%	3.5%
Lt. Ind.	12.2%	0.7%	0.5%	1.6%	0.6%	5.0%	2.0%	0.7%	3.8%	3.0%
Hvy Ind	15.9%	0.1%	0.9%	0.1%	3.3%	2.2%	4.3%	0.1%	6.3%	3.7%
Public/sem	9.6%	15.8%	5.3%	22.5%	9.3%	25.8%	11.3%	15.8%	26.0%	15.9%
Vacant	6.7%	69.2%	80.3%	35.3%	49.1%	39.6%	49.2%	18.1%	20.3%	39.5%
Total	100.0%	100.0%	100.0%	100.0%	100.0%	100.0%	100.0%	100.0%	100.0%	100.0%
Total acres	**27,367**	**20,695**	**26,987**	**31,064**	**29,420**	**28,140**	**30,986**	**31,795**	**31,227**	**257,681**

Notes: SF Res. = single family residence, MF Res. = multiple family residence, Public/sem = public and semipublic land.
    * Center township land use estimated from 1984 Comprehensive Plan Map of Center Township in 1990. Decatur, Franklin, and Lawrence data derived in 1988. Data for remaining townships were derived in 1985 (Perry township), 1988 (Decatur, Franklin, and Lawrence townships), 1989 (Warren township), 1990 (Washington township), and 1992 (Wayne and Pike townships).
    Sources: Indianapolis Department of Metropolitan Development, Planning Division; and IMAGIS consortium.

Table 32. Residential Real Estate Sales in Indianapolis: 1974 to 1989

Year	Number sold	Total valuation	Average sales price Current dollars	Constant dollars*
1974	—	—	$30,682	$62,214
1975	—	—	$34,067	$63,292
1976	—	—	$36,361	$63,866
1977	12,931	$493,830,433	$38,190	$63,002
1978	14,564	$623,626,707	$42,820	$65,633
1979	15,905	$860,209,394	$54,084	$74,513
1980	9,654	$514,632,250	$53,307	$64,706
1981	8,110	$457,968,781	$56,469	$62,100
1982	6,653	$390,546,687	$58,702	$60,810
1983	9,601	$570,598,364	$59,431	$59,680
1984	10,972	$658,084,174	$59,978	$57,708
1985	12,706	$782,847,853	$61,612	$57,260
1986	15,586	$1,049,007,900	$66,400	$60,533
1987	15,738	$1,106,617,470	$70,315	$61,833
1988	14,698	$1,156,458,976	$75,428	$63,733
1989	15,174	$1,219,868,208	$80,392	$64,806
1990	14,785	$1,294,062,153	$82,530	$63,124
1991	14,391	$1,258,715,980	$92,530	$67,899
1992	16,267	$1,562,883,665	$93,094	$66,302

*In constant dollars, adjusted for inflation with 1982-1984 equal to 100.

Source: Metropolitan Indianapolis Board of Realtors.

Table 33. Owner-Occupied Housing by Date of Construction in Marion County Townships

| | Total housing units in 1990 | Housing units by date of construction | | | | | | |
		1939 or earlier	1940-49	1950-59	1960-69	1970-79	1980-88	1989 to March 1990
Marion County	**349,403**	**67,574**	**34,407**	**56,730**	**71,573**	**61,117**	**52,602**	**5,400**
Center	81,667	40,300	14,493	11,983	8,951	2,989	2,391	560
Decatur	7,636	593	306	1,175	1,769	1,965	1,498	330
Franklin	7,623	619	236	783	1,003	2,560	2,223	199
Lawrence	40,007	937	834	5,600	9,788	10,274	11,517	1,057
Perry	35,634	2,801	2,425	6,116	10,422	8,071	5,201	598
Pike	21,957	323	209	1,129	2,867	6,131	10,276	1,022
Warren	36,888	4,869	3,724	7,710	10,548	6,759	2,999	279
Washington	62,907	9,885	6,375	11,936	13,624	11,506	8,811	770
Wayne	55,084	7,247	5,805	10,298	12,601	10,862	7,686	585

| | Median year constructed | Percentage of housing units by date of construction | | | | | | | |
		1939 or earlier	1940-49	1950-59	1960-69	1970-79	1980-88	1989 to March 1990	Total
Marion County	–	**19.3**	**9.8**	**16.2**	**20.5**	**17.5**	**15.1**	**1.5**	**100.0**
Center	1940	49.3	17.7	14.7	11.0	3.7	2.9	0.7	100.0
Decatur	1970	7.8	4.0	15.4	23.2	25.7	19.6	4.3	100.0
Franklin	1975	8.1	3.1	10.3	13.2	33.6	29.2	2.6	100.0
Lawrence	1973	2.3	2.1	14.0	24.5	25.7	28.8	2.6	100.0
Perry	1966	7.9	6.8	17.2	29.2	22.6	14.6	1.7	100.0
Pike	1980	1.5	1.0	5.1	13.1	27.9	46.8	4.7	100.0
Warren	1962	13.2	10.1	20.9	28.6	18.3	8.1	0.8	100.0
Washington	1962	15.7	10.1	19.0	21.7	18.3	14.0	1.2	100.0
Wayne	1963	13.2	10.5	18.7	22.9	19.7	14.0	1.1	100.0

Source: U.S. Census.

Table 34. Median Value of Owner-Occupied Housing in Marion County by Township, Indiana, the Midwest, and the U.S.: 1980 to 1990

	Median value*		% increase 1980 to 1990	
	1980	1990	Current dollars	Constant dollars**
Marion County	**35,900**	**61,400**	**71.0**	**7.8**
Center	19,500	33,200	70.3	7.3
Decatur	43,300	61,600	42.3	(10.4)
Franklin	56,400	76,200	35.1	(14.9)
Lawrence	45,900	83,500	81.9	14.6
Perry	46,600	69,500	49.1	(6.0)
Pike	56,600	85,000	50.2	(5.4)
Warren	37,700	56,500	49.9	(5.6)
Washington	54,500	86,100	58.0	(0.5)
Wayne	31,300	48,400	54.6	(2.6)
Indiana	37,200	53,900	44.9	(8.7)
Midwest	43,900	62,500	42.4	(10.3)
U.S.	47,300	79,100	67.2	5.4

* Median value in current dollars, not adjusted for inflation.
**Constant dollars are adjusted for inflation.
Sources: U.S. Census.

Table 35. Homeownership in Indianapolis by Race: 1930 to 1990

	1930	1940	1950	1960	1970	1980	1990
Total occupied units	97,081	112,231	131,746	149,904	235,772	260,167	291,946
African-Americans	11,600	14,482	17,334	27,431	38,177	49,956	59,836
Whites and others	85,481	97,749	114,412	122,473	197,595	210,211	232,110
Total owner-occupied	41,067	40,796	69,559	83,005	144,513	153,306	165,584
African-Americans	2,887	2,765	7,593	12,167	18,688	24,084	25,653
Whites and others	38,180	38,031	61,966	70,838	125,825	129,222	139,931
Total renter-occupied	56,014	71,435	62,187	66,899	91,259	106,801	126,362
African-Americans	8,713	11,717	9,741	15,264	19,489	25,872	34,183
Whites and others	47,301	59,718	52,446	51,635	71,770	80,929	92,179
% in owner-occupied units							
Total population	42.3	36.4	52.8	55.4	61.3	58.9	56.7
African-Americans	24.9	19.1	43.8	44.4	49.0	48.2	42.9
Whites and others	44.7	38.9	54.2	57.8	63.7	61.5	60.3

* Figures for the White and other population are reported together, since the sum of other racial groups (Asian, American Indian, Eskimo etc.) has always been less than 2% of the city's total population.
Source: U.S. Census.

Figure 19. Industrial Space by Type in Indianapolis: 1985 and 1992

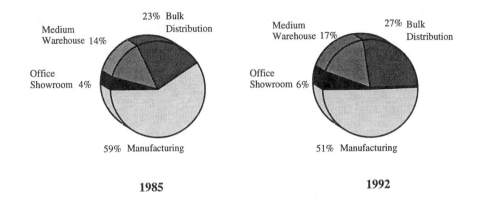

1985   1992

Sources: *Indianapolis Market Report*, CB Real Estate Group; and Coldwell Banker.

Table 36. The Indianapolis Office Market, New Construction and Vacancy Rates: 1983 to 1992

	1983	1984	1985	1986	1987	1988	1989	1990	1991	1992
Occupied office space (mil. sq. ft.)										
Downtown	4.92	5.42	5.97	6.37	6.82	7.21	7.76	8.41	8.31	8.34
Suburban	4.69	5.34	5.84	6.40	7.00	7.85	8.34	8.90	9.09	9.34
New office construction (mil. sq. ft.)										
Downtown	0.00	0.46	0.28	0.34	0.39	1.16	1.13	0.00	0.00	0.38
Suburban	0.84	0.50	0.50	1.10	0.85	0.83	1.16	0.47	0.24	0.09
Office vacancy rate (percent)										
Downtown	11.2	11.2	12.3	10.4	12.6	21.4	19.8	19.2	20.1	20.7
Suburban	—	11.6	17.8	21.2	20.4	22.0	22.5	23.3	23.4	21.3

Sources: Chamber of Commerce; CB Commercial Real Estate Group; and F.C. Tucker Company, Inc.

Table 37. Indianapolis and Marion County Hospitals: 1992

	Year founded	Number of licensed bed	Total admissions	Number of staff physician	Number of staff nurs	Number of employee	Annual billing*
Methodist Hospital of Indiana Inc.	1908	1,120	45,294	1,197	1,950	5,387	340
St. Vincent Hosp./Health Care Ctr. (1)	1881	892	31,704	1,143	1,855	5,094	379
Community Hospital East	1956	804	—	850	890	2,930	314 (2)
Indiana University Medical Center	1914	692 (3)	21,669 (3)	672	300	4,000	327
William N. Wishard Memorial Hospital	1859	618	11,627	737	538	3,184	154
Richard L. Roudebush V.A. Medical Ctr.	1932	553	7,499	80	379	1,559	—
St. Francis Hospital Center	1914	540	40,550	446	850	2,816	186
Midwest Medical Center	1965	405	4,398	415	135	700	76
Community Hospital North	1985	225	—	850	304	900	314 (2)
Humana Women's Hospital-Indpls.	1983	182	4,203	300	271	498	34
Community Hospital South	1963	150	—	363	169	590	314 (2)
Westview Hospital	1961	120	2,020	191	102	260	23
Lifelines of Indianapolis	1987	59	75	3	56	150	10

(1) Includes Indianapolis, Carmel and Stress Center hospitals: statistics are for fiscal year 7/1-6/30.

(2) Numbers are a combination of all Community Hospitals.

(3) Excludes Newborn Treatment

* in millions of dollars

Sources: Individual hospitals and the Indiana State Department of Health.

Table 38. Major Sports Facilities in Marion County: 1993

Facility	Constructed/ rennovated	Seating (est.)	Cost in Millions $
Indianapolis Motor Speedway	1909	450,000	—
Hoosier Dome (football)	1984	60,500	$77.5
Indiana University Track and Field Stadium	1982	19,800	$5.9
Market Square Arena (basketball)	1974	17,000	$23.5
Bush Stadium (baseball)	1930	15,000	n/a
Hinkle Fieldhouse (basketball/volleyball)	1928/1989	10,800	n.a./$1.5
Indianapolis Sports Center (tennis complex)	1979/1988/1990	10,000	$7.0/1.0/2.0
Indiana State Fairgrounds and Pepsi Coliseum (ice hockey)	1939	7,839	—
William Kuntz Soccer Complex	1987	6,500	$1.3
Lake Sullivan BMX Track	1985	5,000	$0.05
Indiana University Natatorium (swimming)	1982	5,000	$21.5
Major Taylor Velodrome (cycling)	1982	5,000	$2.5
Little League Baseball Central Regional Headquarters	1990-1991	2,000	$3.0
Indiana/World Skating Academy and Research Center	1987	1,000	$7.0
Archery Range at Eagle Creek	1987	—	$0.5
National Institute for Fitness and Sport	1988	—	$12.0
Regatta Course at Eagle Creek	1987	—	$0.7

Sources: The Indianapolis Project and the Indianapolis Chamber of Commerce.

Table 39. Lodging Construction and Bookings of Corporate Meetings and Major Special Events in Indianapolis: 1984 to 1992

Year	Number of meetings	Delegates	Number of room nights	New hotels	Rooms added Total	Downtown	North	South	East	West
1984	30	147,150	79,702	4	607	99	480	28	0	0
1985	49	194,997	119,065	6	1,045	360	501	184	0	0
1986	88	329,439	207,277	4	538	276	110	50	0	102
1987	141	450,567	229,522	6	864	359	436	69	0	0
1988	145	479,577	222,765	6	718	0	526	61	0	131
1989	210	578,292	359,430	3	771	572	0	0	124	75
1990	213	573,235	384,524	6	1,104	423	445	0	0	236
1991	222	655,926	411,047	6	523	99	250	174	0	0
1992	263	632,469	401,225	1	126	0	126	0	0	0

Source: The Indianapolis Project, Inc.

Figure 20. Percentage of Marion County Households by Number of Automobiles Owned: 1960 to 1990

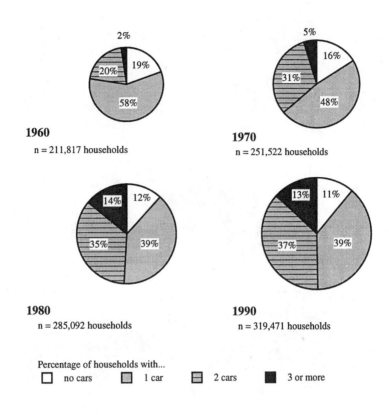

1960
n = 211,817 households

1970
n = 251,522 households

1980
n = 285,092 households

1990
n = 319,471 households

Percentage of households with...
☐ no cars   ▨ 1 car   ▨ 2 cars   ■ 3 or more

Source: U.S. Census.

Table 40. Means of Transportation to Work in Indianapolis: 1970 to 1990

Means of Transportation	1970 Number	1970 Percent	1980 Number	1980 Percent	1990 Number	1990 Percent
Private Vehicle	247,297	83.6	284,398	90.4	331,659	91.4
Driver Only	205,942	69.7	232,168	73.8	282,879	78.0
Passenger	41,355	14.0	52,230	16.6	48,780	13.4
Bus	22,310	7.5	14,983	4.8	11,468	3.2
Taxicab	988	0.3	627	0.2	614	0.2
Walked Only	15,118	5.1	8,965	2.8	8,825	2.4
Other Means	4,732	1.6	2,232	0.7	2,939	0.8
Worked At Home	5,218	1.8	3,487	1.1	7,272	2.0
Total	**295,663**	**100.0**	**314,692**	**100.0**	**362,777**	**100.0**

Note: Total refers to the total population at work during the week of census data collection.
Source: U.S. Census.

Figure 21. Vehicle Registrations and Automobile-Related Deaths in Marion County: 1970 to 1991

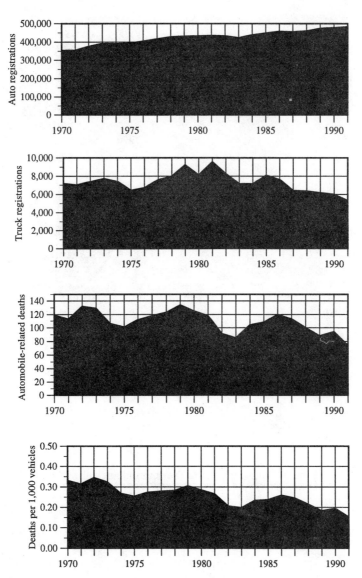

Sources: Indiana State Police; Indiana Bureau of Motor Vehicles

Table 41. Airlines in Indianapolis: 1991

Rank	Airline City/State	Year initiated Local Service	Total No. of Passengers	No. of Full-time employees	1991 Sales* (in millions)
1	USAir	1949	2,265,310	1,061	$6,500
	Arlington, Virginia				
2	Northwest Airlines Inc.	1984	642,040	60	$8,500
	St. Paul, Minnesota				
3	American Airlines	1927	522,301	67	$12,890
	Dallas-Fort Worth, Texas				
4	Delta Air Lines Inc.	1945	496,824	86	$9,000
	Atlanta, Georgia				
5	United Airlines	1983	365,259	42	$11,700
	Chicago, Illinois				
6	American Trans Air	1973	359,802	1,184	$413
	Indianapolis, Indiana				
7	Continental Airlines Inc.	1981	315,075	45	DND
	Houston, Texas				
8	Southwest Airlines	1989	310,283	36	$1,300
	Dallas, Texas				
9	Trans World Airlines Inc.	1929	302,773	45	$3,700
	Kansas City, Missouri				
10	Comair	1981	14,458	0	$217
	Erlanger, Kentucky				
11	Skyway Airlines	1989	11,340	0	$77
	Oak Creek, Wisconsin				
12	Canadian Partner (2)	1991	1,568	0	DND
	Toronto, Ontario, Canada				

Notes: DND = did not disclose.

*All figures are for Indianapolis operations except for sales, which are for the airlines' entire networks.

Source: Information provided by the Indianapolis Airport Authority and the individual airlines.

Figure 22. Air Passenger Traffic in Indianapolis: 1935 to 1992

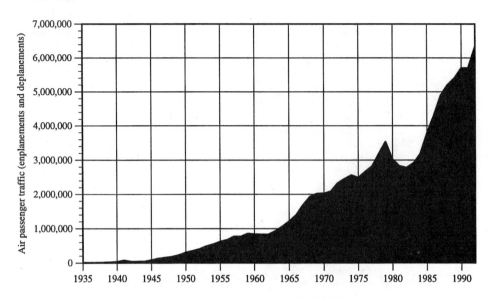

Sources: 1993 *Indianapolis International Passenger Report,* Indianapolis Airport Authority; and the Indianapolis Project Inc.

Table 42. Budget for Indianapolis-Marion County Combined Government: 1976 to 1991

[Figures are in $1,000]

	1976	1981	1986	1989	1991
Total revenue	**273,695**	**466,756**	**613,524**	**815,735**	**907,367**
General revenue	267,447	457,117	592,408	792,980	880,615
Intergovernmental revenue	127,500	240,633	212,775	234,068	253,559
From state	73,269	114,677	141,962	178,391	214,400
From national	54,006	125,116	65,529	53,973	37,374
From other local	225	840	5,284	1,704	1,785
Own-source general	139,947	216,484	379,633	558,912	627,056
Local taxes	86,280	126,403	227,064	354,893	391,870
Property taxes	83,530	120,459	196,077	291,600	299,242
Selective sales taxes	820	2,776	12,632	17,103	19,649
Income taxes	0	0	10,173	36,622	61,328
Other taxes	358	3,168	8,137	9,568	11,651
Current charges	35,229	69,437	118,527	150,122	190,687
Total expenditures	**289,832**	**491,783**	**606,598**	**846,385**	**898,312**
General expenditures	267,392	463,931	538,311	795,104	840,321
Elem & second. schools	1,188	6,672	435	463	432
Public welfare	37,149	45,525	54,811	58,075	65,984
Hospitals	35,560	68,312	86,624	110,995	127,348
Health	12,417	16,721	21,995	22,982	28,769
Highways	36,321	36,611	30,562	43,808	42,131
Air transportation	4,914	12,104	21,768	53,096	65,013
Police protection	25,715	40,956	53,362	73,415	82,014
Fire protection	12,909	18,992	23,109	29,076	34,082
Corrections	5,023	10,392	20,294	22,440	21,019
Sewerage	17,400	101,611	57,423	125,934	70,039
Solid waste	5,773	7,130	10,193	15,434	29,567
Parks & recreation	14,042	11,932	13,920	18,536	22,529
Housing & comm dev.	4,986	11,732	28,845	44,952	26,199
Natural resources	0	2,222	3,981	12,244	12,674
Financial administration	4,223	7,110	14,757	17,715	19,161
Judicial & legal	—	—	—	23,197	25,932
Public buildings	2,385	4,395	5,743	0	4,216
Other administration	—	—	—	12,721	16,262
Total salaries & wages	—	166,690	214,456	249,780	317,750

Notes: Income taxes were instituted in 1984. Judicial and legal costs were separated from the corrections line item following 1985. Total salaries and wages not reported prior to 1979, other administration costs not reported prior to 1987 in this report. Figures are not adjusted for inflation.

Source: U.S. Department of Commerce, Bureau of the Census, *City Government Finances*, Series GF, No 4, annual.

Table 43. Assessed Property Value by Township in Marion County: 1981 and 1991

Township	1981	%	1991	%	% increase/ (decrease)
Center	$912,585,125	25.0	$1,370,628,940	20.1	(4.9)
Decatur	$91,495,820	2.5	$125,938,840	1.8	(0.7)
Franklin	$87,104,230	2.4	$171,787,450	2.5	0.1
Lawrence	$316,880,690	8.7	$819,297,720	12.0	3.3
Perry	$295,179,667	8.1	$523,691,670	7.7	(0.4)
Pike	$232,688,809	6.4	$777,765,140	11.4	5.0
Warren	$532,121,100	14.6	$769,495,510	11.3	(3.3)
Washington	$593,025,680	16.2	$1,222,083,910	17.9	1.7
Wayne	$594,146,593	16.3	$1,043,086,700	15.3	(1.0)
Marion County	$3,655,227,714	100.0%	$6,823,775,880	100.0%	0.0

Sources: *1991 Component Unit Financial Report* (1992); and *1981 Annual Report* (1982), City of Indianapolis.

Figure 23. The Growth of Public Parks in Indianapolis: 1870 to 1991

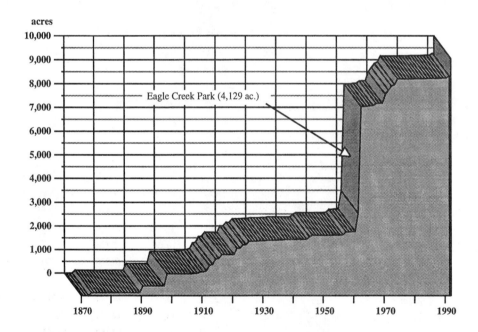

Acreage per capita (thousandths of an acre)

1880	1890	1900	1910	1920	1930	1940	1950	1960	1970	1980	1990
3.9	5.5	4.3	6.4	6.2	6	6.2	6	5.7	11.4	13.1	12.4

Source: Indianapolis Department of Parks and Recreation.

Table 44. The Oldest and Largest Parks in Marion County: 1993

Oldest Parks

Year acquired	Township	Park name	Address	Acreage
1873	Center	Garfield Park	2450 S. Shelby St.	128.5
1890	Center	South Grove Golf Course	1804 Riverside Dr.	130.0
1890	Wayne	Coffin Golf Course	2401 N. Cold Spring Rd.	152.0
1896	Center	Indianola Park	1900 W. Washington St.	1.6
1897	Center	McCarty Triangle Park	1100 W. McCarty St.	1.2
1898	Center	Brookside Park	3500 Brookside Pkwy. S. Dr.	108.4
1898	Center	Pogue's Run	Newman & Commerce sts.	0.3
1898	Center	Riverside Park	2420 N. Riverside E. Dr.	67.2
1898	Center	Spades Park	1800 Nowland Ave.	31.5
1898	Center	Highland Park	1100 E. New York St.	4.0
1898	Center	Riverside Golf Course	3501 Cold Spring Rd.	132.0
1898	Center	Lake Sullivan	3700 Cold Spring Rd.	25.7
1898	Center	Riverside Nursery	3701 White River Pwky. W. Dr.	143.0
1904	Warren	Irvington Circle Park	Audubon Rd. & University Ave.	0.1
1907	Center	Willard Park	1901 E. Washington St.	14.6

Largest Parks

			Park name	Address	Acreage
1.	1962	Pike	Eagle Creek Park	7840 W. 56th St.	4,129.4
2.	1962	Pike	Eagle Creek Golf Course	8802 W. 56th St.	350.0
3.	1961	Decatur	Southwestway Park	8400 S. Mann Rd.	252.0
4.	1912	Center	Pleasant Run Parkway	16th St. Along Pkwy.	229.4
5.	1914	Center	Fall Creek Parkway	Along Pkwy.	222.8
6.	1961	Franklin	Southeastway Park	5624 S E. County Line Rd.	187.8
7.	1970	Perry	Carl Smock Golf Course	3910 S. County Line Rd. E.	160.0
8.	1961	Lawrence	William S. Sahm Golf Course	6800 E. 91st St.	155.8
9.	1890	Wayne	Coffin Golf Course	2401 N. Cold Spring Rd.	152.0
10.	1974	Warren	Whispering Hills Golf Course	Brookville & Senour Rds.	149.3
11.	1898	Center	Riverside Nursery	3701 White River Pwky. W. Dr.	143.0
12.	1898	Center	Riverside Golf Course	3501 Cold Spring Rd.	132.0
13.	1890	Center	South Grove Golf Course	1804 Riverside Dr.	130.0
14.	1923	Center	Washington Park	2801 E. 30th St.	128.7
15.	1873	Center	Garfield Park	2450 S. Shelby St.	128.5
16.	1925	Center	Sarah Shank Golf Course	2901 S. Keystone Ave.	120.5
17.	1957	Pike	Northwestway Park	5300 W. 62nd St.	120.4
18.	1898	Center	Brookside Park	3500 Brookside Pkwy. S. Dr.	108.4
19.	1921	Warren	Pleasant Run Golf Course	601 N. Arlington Ave.	103.6
20.	1972	Decatur	Southwestway Golf Course	8327 S. Mann Rd.	100.0

Total acreage, top 20 largest parks (1991)   7,203.6
Total acreage, all parks (1991)   9,268.7

Source: Indianapolis Department of Parks and Recreation

Table 45. Presidential and Gubernatorial Election Results in Marion County: 1900-1992

			Presidential Elections				Gubernatorial Elections		
	Republican	votes	Democrat	votes	Republican	votes	Democrat	votes
1992	Bush	141,369	Clinton	122,234	Pearson	117,400	Bayh	189,575
1988	Bush	184,519	Dukakis	128,627	Mutz	161,593	Bayh	150,024
1984	Reagan	184,880	Mondale	130,185	Orr	165,048	Townsend	147,049
1980	Reagan	168,680	Carter	126,103	Orr	182,257	Hillenbrand	128,613
1976	Ford	177,767	Carter	145,274	Bowen	180,472	Conrad	141,410
1972	Nixon	206,065	McGovern	102,166	Bowen	173,754	Welsh	132,181
1968	Nixon	162,503	Humphrey	115,715	Whitcomb	166,756	Rock	132,735
1964	Goldwater	143,015	Johnson	152,418	Ristine	135,565	Branigin	159,426
1960	Nixon	166,202	Kennedy	121,336	Parker	150,281	Welsh	136,900
1956	Eisenhower	162,566	Stevenson	99,102	Handley	157,482	Tucker	103,665
1952	Eisenhower	164,466	Stevenson	106,387	Craig	158,630	Watkins	111,757
1948	Dewey	103,603	Truman	97,915	Creighton	90,375	Schricker	111,364
1944	Dewey	116,421	Roosevelt	106,382	Gates	113,722	Jackson	108,735
1940	Wilkie	124,845	Roosevelt	121,907	Hillis	123,617	Schricker	123,270
1936	Landon	87,798	Roosevelt	124,961	Springer	90,639	Townsend	122,295
1932	Hoover	98,256	Roosevelt	106,661	Springer	97,254	McNutt	107,516
1928	Hoover	109,630	Smith	73,309	Leslie	80,258	Dailey	102,055
1924	Coolidge	95,135	Davis	59,498	Jackson	58,654	McCulloch	71,883
1920	Harding	79,957	Cox	61,460	McCray	78,582	McCulloch	62,581
1916	Hughes	40,699	Wilson	35,043	Goodrich	41,278	Adair	34,304
1912	Taft	12,280	Wilson	29,805	Durbin	10,609	Ralston	28,959
1908	Taft	34,351	Bryan	34,078	Watson	31,967	Marshall	36,674
1904	Roosevelt	35,103	Parker	22,336	Hanley	33,768	Kern	23,010
1900	McKinley	29,272	Bryan	23,660	Durbin	28,614	Kern	23,937

Source: Indiana Secretary of State.

Figure 24. Votes Cast for Republican and Democratic Presidential Candidates in Marion County: 1900 to 1992

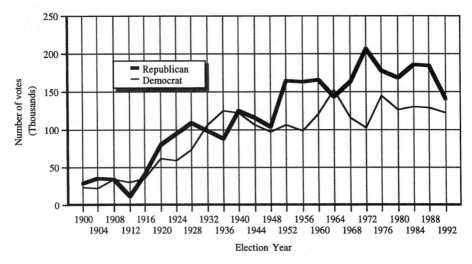

Source: Marion County Clerk.

Figure 25. Votes Cast in Presidential and Municipal Elections as a Percentage of the Total Voting Age Population in Indianapolis: 1951 to 1992

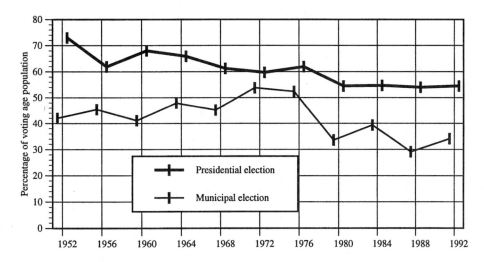

Sources: Indiana Secretary of State; and tabulations based on data from the U.S. Census and the Marion County Clerk.

Table 46. Voter Turnout in Indianapolis during Municipal and Presidential Election Years: 1951 to 1992

	Municipal elections			Presidential elections	
Year	Total votes	% of Voting age	Year	Total votes	% of Voting age
1951	123,159	42.0	1952	—	73.0
1955	133,179	45.4	1956	261,668	61.9
1959	122,025	41.1	1960	288,206	68.0
1963	142,116	47.9	1964	296,381	65.9
1967	135,562	45.2	1968	310,922	61.2
1971	256,531	53.8	1972	309,766	59.7
1975	237,848	52.4	1976	325,576	61.9
1979	168,470	33.6	1980	314,269	54.5
1983	199,436	39.3	1984	317,148	54.7
1987	164,523	29.1	1988	315,095	54.0
1991	192,543	34.1	1992	323,790	54.5

Sources: Indiana Secretary of State; and Marion County Clerk.

Table 47. Municipal Election Results, Indianapolis: 1951 to 1991

Year	Democrati Party	c Number of Votes	(%)	Republica Party	n Number of Votes	(%)	City-Council Seats Dem.	Repub.
1951	Bayt	54,744	44.4	Clark	68,415	55.6	3	6
1955	Bayt	74,682	56.1	Birr	58,497	43.9	6	3
1959	Boswell	70,031	57.4	Sharp	53,994	42.6	6	3
1963	Barton	68,316	48.1	Drayer	63,091	44.4	6	3
1967	Barton	63,284	46.7	Lugar	72,278	53.3	3	6
1971	Neff	101,367	39.5	Lugar	155,164	60.5	8	21
1975	Welch	109,761	46.1	Hudnut	124,100	52.2	10	19
1979	Cantwell	43,955	26.1	Hudnut	124,515	73.9	7	22
1983	Sullivan	63,240	21.7	Hudnut	134,550	67.5	6	23
1987	Senden	38,193	23.2	Hudnut	109,107	66.3	7	22
1991	Mahern	79,817	40.6	Goldsmith	110,545	56.2	11	18

Source: Marion County Clerk.

Table 48. Percentage of Marion County Residents over Age 25 with a High School Education: 1970 to 1990

		Year	
Total population	1970	1980	1990
Male	55.80	68.80	83.30
Female	54.90	66.40	86.04
African-American population			
Male	33.70	51.20	73.19
Female	38.60	54.50	78.40

Source: U.S. Census.

Figure 26. Percentage of High School Graduates for Persons Over 25 in Marion County, Indiana, and the U.S.: 1950 to 1990

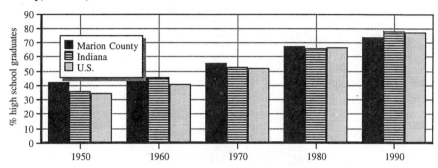

Sources: *City and County Data Book,* 1952, 1962, 1972; U.S. Census.

Figure 27. Percentage of High School Graduates for Persons Over 25 in Marion County Townships: 1970 to 1990

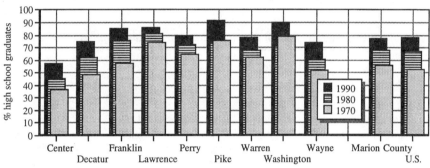

Source: U.S. Census.

Figure 28. Percentage of College Graduates for Persons Over 25 in Marion County Townships: 1970 to 1990

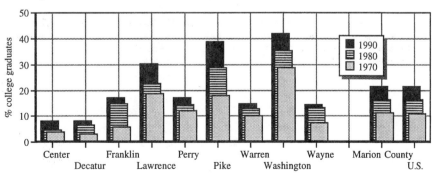

Source: U.S. Census.

Figure 29. Total Public School Enrollment in Marion County : 1965 to 1993

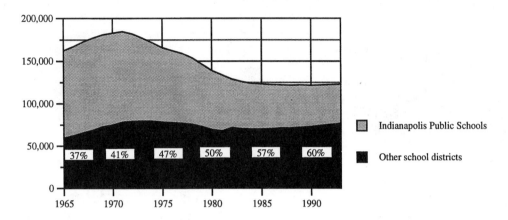

Note: Percentage figures indicate the rising proportion of Marion County students outside Indianapolis Public Schools, from 37% in 1965 to 60% in 1990.
Source: Indiana Department of Education.

Table 49. Enrollment by School District in Marion County: 1965 to 1993

	1965	1970	1975	1980	1985	1990	1993
Indianapolis Public Schools	102,740	107,713	87,642	69,735	53,192	48,805	46,697
Beech Grove City Schools	2,145	2,525	2,755	2,167	1,883	1,974	2,031
Decatur Township MSD	4,066	4,669	4,580	4,460	5,061	5,086	5,084
Franklin Township MSD	2,093	2,542	2,788	3,186	3,892	4,366	4,523
Lawrence Township MSD	6,369	9,405	9,479	8,817	8,800	10,661	12,360
Perry Township MSD	8,799	11,418	13,282	11,147	11,397	11,499	11,454
Pike Township MSD	2,280	2,948	3,583	3,575	3,794	4,886	5,816
Speedway City Schools	2,374	2,439	2,216	1,638	1,357	1,348	1,452
Warren Township MSD	7,437	9,452	10,447	9,266	9,605	9,066	9,320
Washington Township MSD	12,922	15,737	14,591	11,769	10,042	9,753	9,879
Wayne Township MSD	9,236	12,070	12,719	11,341	12,128	12,082	12,387
Total	**162,426**	**182,888**	**166,057**	**139,081**	**123,136**	**121,516**	**122,996**

Note: Metropolitan school districts (MSDs) have different boundaries than townships.
Source: Indiana Department of Education.

Table 50. Appropriations per Student in Marion County: 1981 to 1991

School District	1981	1982	1983	1984	1985	1986	1987	1988	1989	1990	1991
Indianapolis Public Schools	$2,580	$3,036	$3,448	$3,872	$3,999	$4,041	$4,622	$5,205	$5,480	$6,302	$6,299
Beech Grove City Schools	$2,734	$2,630	$3,017	$3,338	$3,380	$3,835	$4,140	$4,167	$4,614	$4,963	$6,505
Decatur Township MSD	$2,324	$2,073	$3,007	$2,760	$2,968	$3,584	$3,768	$4,149	$4,452	$4,664	$5,160
Franklin Township MSD	$2,204	$2,534	$2,857	$2,562	$2,794	$3,038	$3,607	$3,898	$4,889	$5,982	$4,864
Lawrence Township MSD	$2,555	$2,549	$2,865	$3,316	$3,443	$4,026	$4,191	$4,276	$4,584	$5,368	$6,168
Perry Township MSD	$2,381	$2,451	$3,434	$3,202	$3,525	$4,146	$4,193	$5,008	$5,225	$5,322	$5,950
Pike Township MSD	$2,549	$2,552	$3,531	$3,332	$4,006	$3,440	$4,565	$4,850	$4,977	$6,195	$6,540
Speedway City Schools	$2,268	$2,439	$2,622	$3,812	$3,531	$3,827	$4,153	$4,434	$4,809	$5,151	$5,780
Warren Township MSD	$3,119	$3,451	$3,427	$3,381	$3,758	$4,198	$5,159	$5,363	$6,109	$6,545	$6,280
Washington Township MSD	$2,647	$2,973	$2,891	$3,611	$4,208	$4,198	$5,661	$5,925	$5,926	$5,897	$6,748
Wayne Township MSD	$2,666	$2,722	$2,962	$3,101	$3,495	$3,726	$4,225	$4,620	$5,145	$5,494	$5,530
Marion County	**$2,553**	**$2,821**	**$3,209**	**$3,463**	**$3,705**	**$3,900**	**$4,472**	**$4,909**	**$5,239**	**$5,810**	**$6,015**

Notes: Metropolitan school districts (MSDs) have different boundaries than townships. All figures are in current dollars (not adjusted for inflation).
Source: Indiana Department of Education.

Table 51. Graduation Rates (%) by School District in Marion County: 1988 to 1992

School district	1988	1989	1990	1991	1992
Indianapolis Public Schools	43.25	46.10	50.71	55.82	64.73
Beech Grove City Schools	81.26	74.70	79.37	78.71	81.15
Decatur Township MSD	70.72	73.33	64.75	72.60	71.96
Franklin Township MSD	79.62	82.91	75.77	81.59	82.25
Lawrence Township MSD	62.39	74.62	80.64	91.65	91.20
Perry Township MSD	77.59	75.35	78.87	81.57	81.39
Pike Township MSD	91.72	88.97	88.13	88.57	87.60
Speedway City Schools	90.21	89.70	93.44	94.38	97.01
Warren Township MSD	79.87	71.40	76.38	80.74	81.69
Washington Township MSD	81.18	78.17	79.62	75.88	77.27
Wayne Township MSD	78.20	87.19	81.46	84.86	87.66

Note: Metropolitan school districts (MSDs) have different boundaries than townships.
Source: Indiana Department of Education.

Figure 30. SAT Scores for Marion County School Corporations: 1991

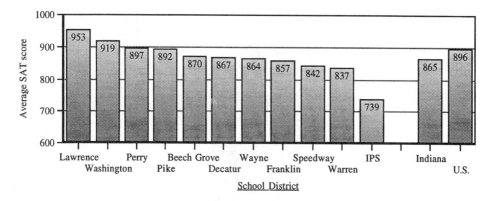

Notes: IPS indicates Indianapolis Public Schools. School districts have different geographical boundaries than the townships for which they are named. U.S. and local SAT scores are not strictly comparable, due to higher Indiana rates of test participation.

Table 52. Religious Accommodations (No. of Seats) in Marion County and Indiana: 1850

	Marion County		Indiana	
Denomination	Total seats	%	Total seats	%
Methodist	11,800	33.6	266,372	37.9
Baptist	8,100	23.1	138,783	19.8
Presbyterian	4,200	12.0	105,582	15.0
Christian	3,125	8.9	65,341	9.3
Lutheran	2,959	8.4	19,050	2.7
Friends	1,850	5.3	44,915	6.4
Moravian	900	2.6	18,250	2.6
Roman Catholic	600	1.7	25,115	3.6
Free	500	1.4	2,750	0.4
Union	500	1.4	1,250	0.2
Episcopal	350	1.0	7,300	1.0
Dutch Reformed	250	0.7	1,275	0.2
German Reformed	—	—	1,150	0.2
Dunker	—	—	5,000	0.7
Unitarian	—	—	250	0.0
Total	**35,134**	**100.0**	**702,383**	**100.0**

Note: U.S. Census in 1850 defined accommodations as number of seats in a church building.
Source: U.S. Census, 1850.

Table 53. Religious Affiliation in Marion County and the United States: 1906

	Marion County		Indiana		U.S.	
Denomination	Total	% of all members	Total	% of all members	Total	% of all members
Roman Catholic	**31,394**	**34.5**	**174,849**	**18.6**	**12,079,142**	**30.2**
Methodist	**16,713**	**18.4**	**228,091**	**24.3**	**5,749,838**	**14.4**
Methodist Episcopal	14,012	15.4	210,593	22.4		
Methodist Protestant	396	0.4	10,408	1.1		
African Methodists	2,305	2.5	7,090	0.8		
Baptist	**10,651**	**11.7**	**88,732**	**9.5**	**5,662,234**	**14.2**
Northern & National Convention	10,526	11.6	73,929	7.9		
General Baptists			6,671	0.7		
Primitive Baptists	125	0.1	8,132	0.9		
Presbyterian	**5,539**	**6.1**	**55,417**	**5.9**	**1,830,555**	**4.6**
Presbyterian Church in the U.S.A.	5,476	6.0	49,041	5.2		
Cumberland Presbyterian	63	0.1	6,376	0.7		
Lutheran	**3,815**	**4.2**	**50,091**	**5.3**	**2,112,494**	**5.3**
Lutheran General Synod	652	0.7	7,753	0.8		
Lutheran Synodical Conference	3,163	3.5	34,028	3.6		
Lutheran, Joint Synod of Ohio, etc.			8,310	0.9		
Others	**22,907**	**25.2**	**341,425**	**36.4**	**12,502,182**	**31.3**
Disciples of Christ	8,511	9.4	108,188	11.5	982,701	2.5
German Evangelical Synod	2,503	2.7	21,624	2.3	293,137	0.7
Protestant Episcopal Church	1,916	2.1	7,653	0.8	886,942	2.2
Friends (Orthodox)	1,431	1.6	29,255	3.1	91,161	0.2
Reformed Church in the U.S.	1,179	1.3	8,289	0.9	449,514	1.1
United Brethren in Christ	562	0.6	48,059	5.1	274,649	0.7
Evangelical Association	443	0.5	8,787	0.9	104,898	0.3
Jewish	395	0.4	1,383	0.1	101,457	0.3
Churches of Christ	199	0.2	10,259	1.1	159,658	0.4
Christians (Christian Convention)	90	0.1	21,397	2.3	110,117	0.3
Brethren (Dunkers)	40	0.0	9,949	1.1	97,144	0.2
Other (predominantly Protestant)	5,638	6.2	66,582	7.1	8,950,804	22.4
Total members	**91,019**	**100.0**	**938,605**	**100.0**	**39,936,445**	**100.0**

Source: U.S. Bureau of the Census, *Census of Religious Bodies*, 1906.

Table 54. Religious Affiliation in Marion County: 1970 to 1990

Denomination	Total adherents 1970	Total adherents 1980	Total adherents 1990	% of total population 1970	% of total population 1980	% of total population 1990
Catholic Church	91,820	84,935	84,033	11.59	11.10	10.54
Christian Churches & Churches of Christ						
Christian Churches and Churches of Christ	25,227	22,789	22,836	3.18	2.98	2.86
Christian Church (Disciples of Christ)	19,563	22,874	20,596	2.47	2.99	2.58
Churches of Christ	—	6,495	8,687	—	0.85	1.09
United Church of Christ	9,204	8,297	7,477	1.16	1.08	0.94
Methodist Bodies						
United Methodist Church	46,124	39,431	37,027	5.82	5.15	4.64
Free Methodist Church of North America	1,484	6,831	1,230	0.19	0.89	0.15
Baptist Bodies						
Black Baptist Est.	—	—	56,403	—	—	7.08
American Baptist U.S.A.	18,354	16,446	11,483	2.32	2.15	1.44
Southern Baptist Convention	6,121	8,300	9,353	0.77	1.08	1.17
Free Will Baptists	—	—	283	—	—	0.04
North American Baptist General Conf.	60	145	83	0.01	0.02	0.01
Presbyterian Bodies						
United Presbyterian Church in the USA	24,348	20,074	17,990	3.07	2.62	2.26
Cumberland Presbyterian Church	155	154	138	0.02	0.02	0.02
Reformed Presbyterian Church	190	130	—	0.02	0.02	—
Lutheran Bodies						
Lutheran Church-Missouri Synod	9,954	7,339	7,474	1.26	0.96	0.94
Lutheran Church in America	6,536	5,984	351	0.82	0.78	0.04
Evangelical Lutheran Christian Assoc.	—	2,052	7,553	—	0.27	0.95
American Lutheran Church	2,176	1,916	—	0.27	0.25	—
Latvian Evangelical Lutheran	—	581	409	—	0.08	0.05
Free Lutheran	—	—	206	—	—	0.03
Church of God						
Church of God (Anderson, Indiana)	3,629	4,692	2,158	0.46	0.61	0.27
Church of God (Cleveland, Tennessee)	813	925	1,263	0.10	0.12	0.16
Other						
AME Zion	—	10,328	10,328	—	1.35	1.30
Assembly of God	—	6,501	10,229	—	0.85	1.28
Church of the Nazarene	7,129	6,148	8,570	0.90	0.80	1.08
Independent Non-Charismatic	—	—	7,147	—	—	0.90
Reformed Judaism	—	2,337	6,379	—	0.31	0.80
Episcopal Church	8,882	5,648	4,630	1.12	0.74	0.58
Seventh-day Adventists	1,960	2,170	2,968	0.25	0.28	0.37
Independent Charismatic	—	—	2,535	—	—	0.32
Church of Jesus Christ of Latter-Day Saints	—	2,462	2,116	—	0.32	0.27
Friends-USA (Quakers)	2,510	1,710	1,581	0.32	0.22	0.20
Unitarian-Universalist Association	1,386	1,073	1,151	0.17	0.14	0.14
Wisconsin Evangelical	108	345	638	0.01	0.05	0.08
Mennonite Church	149	115	317	0.02	0.02	0.04
Salvation Army	1,254	46	315	0.16	0.01	0.04
Moravian Church in America , N. Prov.	470	408	271	0.06	0.05	0.03
Reformed Church in America	297	321	220	0.04	0.04	0.03
Church of the Brethren	289	218	189	0.04	0.03	0.02
Christian Reformed Church	176	221	124	0.02	0.03	0.02
Other denominations	70	11,617	4,451	0.01	1.52	0.56
Total Adherents	**290,438**	**312,058**	**361,192**	**100.00**	**100.00**	**100.00**

Note: The Glenmary data are self reported, and thus omits a substantial number of denominations and independent congregations that did not provide information.

Sources: Douglas W. Johnson, Paul R. Picard and Bernard Quinn, *Churches and Church Membership in the United States: An Enumneration by Region, State and County*, Glenmary Research Center, Atlanta, Ga., 1974; Bernard Quinn, Herman Anderson, Martin Bradley, Paul Goetting, and Peggy Shriver, *Churches and Church Membership in the United States 1980: an Enumeration by Region State and County Based on Data Reported by 111 Church Bodies*, Glenmary Research Center, Atlanta, Ga.. 1982; and Martin B. Bradley, Norman M. Green, Jr., Dale E. Jones, Mac Lynn, Lou McNeil, *Churches and Church Membership in The United States 1990: An Enumeration by Region, State and County Based on Data Reported for 133 Church Groupings*, Glenmary Research Center, Atlanta, Ga., 1992.

Figure 31. Indianapolis United Way Campaign Contributions: 1920 to 1992

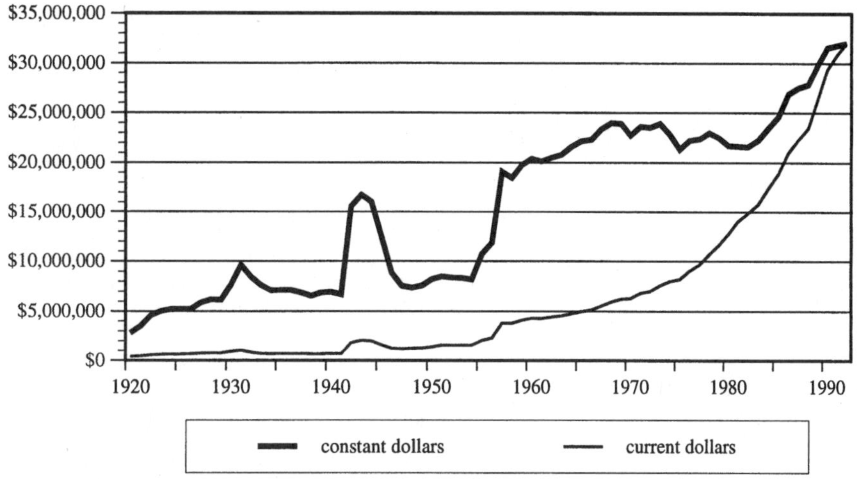

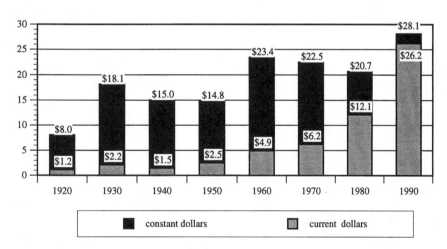

Note: Constant dollars are adjusted for inflation to 1992 dollars.
Source: United Way.

Figure: 32. Charitable Contributions Per Capita to The United Way in Indianapolis: 1920 to 1990

Note: Constant dollars are adjusted for inflation to 1992 dollars. The base population includes Boone, Hamilton, Hancock, Hendricks, Marion and Morgan counties. Prior to 1960, Marion County represented an overwhelming proportion of United Way activity, and was used exclusively in the calculation of per capita giving.
  Source: United Way.

SUBJECT GUIDE

INDEX

Editor: Roberta L. Diehl

Book and Jacket Designer: Sharon L. Sklar

Production Coordinator: Harriet Stafford Curry

Typeface: Berkeley Book/Helvetica

Compositor: Weimer Graphics, Inc.

Printer: Maple Vail Book Manufacturing Co.